CLASSICS
OF
MORAL AND
POLITICAL THEORY

Classics
OF
Moral and
Political Theory

Fourth Edition

Edited by
Michael L. Morgan

Hackett Publishing Company
Indianapolis/Cambridge

13 12 11 10 09   2 3 4 5 6

Cover and interior design by Abigail Coyle
Composition by World Composition Services, Inc., Sterling, VA
Printed at RR Donnelley

For further information, please address:
Hackett Publishing Company, Inc.
P.O. Box 44937
Indianapolis, IN 46244-0937

www.hackettpublishing.com

Library of Congress Cataloging-in-Publication Data
Classics of moral and political theory / edited by Michael L. Morgan—4th ed.
    p. cm.
  Includes bibliographical references.
  ISBN 0-87220-777-3 (cloth)—ISBN 0-87220-776-5 (paper)
  1. Political ethics. 2. Political science. I. Morgan, Michael L., 1944–
JA79.C59   2005
  172—dc22   2005052732

ISBN-13: 978-0-87220-777-6 (cloth)
ISBN-13: 978-0-87220-776-9 (pbk.)

CONTENTS

INTRODUCTION

We have called this anthology *Classics of Moral and Political Theory* in order to suggest by its title some of the volume's important features. First, it contains writings with a certain content. Some of the texts are about moral or ethical theory in the broad sense that includes reflection on the nature of morality and discussion of the content of the moral life, its principles and ideals, its characteristic virtues and vices. Other works deal with political matters, also in a broad way, often treating the relationships among political, legal, religious, philosophical, moral, and psychological issues, discussing the nature of political institutions, political practice, and much else. Some of these works, then, are classic moral texts; some are classic political texts; some are both. All, however, and this is my second point, are classics.

What is a classic? Surely there is no short and simple answer to this question. But perhaps this much will do: A classic text is one that reverberates within one or more traditions. It is a text that articulates powerfully influential views, positions, or conceptions; that exhibits in a paradigmatic way models, motifs, or arguments; and that is recalled, cited, and exhibited in subsequent discussion, inquiry, and debate. A classic, in short, is a work that makes an important difference or at least, from a particular vantage point, is thought to have made and to continue to make such a difference.

Not all texts of course are classics. But while others may be interesting or valuable or helpful, only classic texts are somehow necessary, both for understanding a tradition and for participating in one as well as for calling a tradition into question and seeking to deconstruct or subvert it. To say something significant and important within or against a tradition of discourse, one must, to some degree or other, call upon the resources that constitute that tradition, and classic texts are the chief written repositories of these resources—of the tradition's terms, its alternative views, its examples, formulations, arguments, and indeed all that make up its tools for discussion and debate. In this sense, the writings collected in this anthology are classics, not *the* classics, to be sure—for there are many others, and the very status of being a classic changes in the course of history—but *some of the classics* of the several traditions of reflection about moral and political matters in the West, from Greek antiquity to the late nineteenth century.

These classics, moreover, are of a limited kind. They are all works written by men, largely for men; their conceptions of human nature, the good life, political virtues, and so on exhibit a gender bias. Furthermore, they are Western, European classics that are featured in certain traditions of discussion and debate but should be compared and contrasted with other types—non-Western classics, classics by nonwhites, by women, by Native Americans, by non-Christian authors, and more. For many reasons, excluding such alternative classics is unfortunate, but it has been unavoidable and purposeful. What this volume contains is not a sample of everything; it is, rather, a selection that can serve as a common resource both for those who seek to understand and continue the Western traditions of debate and for those who seek to examine these traditions critically and, in the end, to oppose them.

Each one of these classic texts, moreover, means and has meant many things. Each work meant something, surely many things, when it was written and published and initially read. Each came to mean much else as it was reread, cited, recalled, and reinterpreted in the years and decades thereafter. And each text now means many things to its many current readers, us among them, as it is read again and interpreted in the context of today's debates, issues, and events. Different readers will approach these works for different reasons and with different interests and presuppositions. In a way, then, each of these texts is not one text but many, a vast plurality.

These issues have guided the construction of this anthology. From a much larger list of classic texts of moral and political thought we carved the current table of contents, trying insofar as it was possible to include many of the most influential and significant classics that are currently taught and studied. Moreover, where we could, we chose to include entire works or at least very sizeable chunks. The more we excerpt, the more we limit the reader's perspective and options and hence the more we coopt the reader's role as interpreter and critic. We did not want to do that either to you, the teacher, or to you, the student. Finally, the introductions to each author are not intended as full-scale interpretations of the works; rather they aim to help the student by situating the author and the work historically and by saying some general things about the author's work and thought. In the end, these strategies all serve a single goal: to provide a useful and convenient resource for the critical study of moral and political thinking in the Western historical traditions.

In many ways this work is an empirical enterprise. It does not hope to shape a tradition so much as to respond to and express features of several. For this reason, as years go by and as interests change, it may be advisable, if not necessary, to alter its contents—to add, delete, and replace these classics with others. Your guidance in this process will be invaluable, and we invite it. In such a way, this anthology, which has thus far been a cooperative enterprise, will continue to be one, in a continually useful and significant way.

PREFACE TO THE FOURTH EDITION

For this, the fourth edition of *Classics of Moral and Political Theory*, we have made some important modifications. First, the Grube translations of the *Apology* and *Crito* and the death scene from the *Phaedo* have been replaced with those of C.D.C. Reeve, and the *Euthyphro*, in Reeve's translation, has been added. We have also used Reeve's new, outstanding translation of Plato's *Republic* in the place of his revision of Grube's older translation. Second, we added Mill's *The Subjection of Women* to the selections from his works. Finally, we have chosen to add two new works from two authors not previously included. One is the *Antigone* of Sophocles, an extraordinarily influential tragedy and one that presents in a classic setting the challenges of interpreting the tensions between the individual and the state and much more. We use the excellent translation of the *Antigone* by Paul Woodruff. In addition, we now complete the volume with a fundamental text in twentieth-century social and political philosophy, Max Weber's "Politics as a Vocation," in a superb new translation by Rodney Livingstone.

In this edition, as in all the others, Brian Rak has been as much a collaborator as an editor; I cannot thank him enough for his advice and guidance. As always the staff at Hackett—Abigail Coyle and her colleagues—have been wonderful to work with. Comments from a host of instructors have proven especially helpful; their suggestions have been taken very seriously.

As in previous editions, unbracketed footnotes are an author's own. Bracketed footnotes have been contributed by an editor or a translator. Initialed bracketed footnotes signify the first in a series of notes by a given editor or translator.

PREFACE TO THE FIRST EDITION

In the fall of 1990 Jay Hullett approached me with a proposal for a major anthology of classic texts in the Western traditions of moral and political theory. At every stage, this has been a collegial and cooperative effort. Jay has supervised our work with sensitivity and wisdom; Brian Rak has been a thoughtful and meticulous editor. Dan Kirklin has guided the production process with tremendous attention to detail, constant encouragement, and a great understanding of our goals.

In making my editorial selections I was aided by a number of friends and colleagues—Jeff Isaac, Paul Eisenberg, Milton Fisk—but especially by Brian Rak, with his keen sense for what is used and what is useful in the teaching of ethics and political theory. In preparing the introductions I benefited from a vast amount of biographical, historical, and philosophical work. Jim Tully read all the introductions and made copious recommendations, virtually all of which I accepted and which directed me to avoid infelicities and inaccuracies. Gillian Parker read text and proofs as we tried to make the result as accurate as possible, and Mark Rooks of InteLex provided many texts on disk and scanned others, in order to facilitate the publication process. Audrey, Debbie, Sara, and our two cats, Blaze and Amanda, endured a good deal less attention than they deserved, sympathizing as I worried about deadlines and providing encouragement and distraction as needed.

SOPHOCLES

Poetry, drama, and fiction express the moral and political dimensions of our lives that philosophy attempts to examine and analyze. Indeed, given the character and complexity of moral and political life, literature often is the best avenue we have to its disclosure. Greek tragedy is a classic case of such disclosure. There are features of Greek ethics and Greek thinking in the fifth century B.C.E. that are known to us best from the writings of Aeschylus, Sophocles, and Euripides.

The fifth century was a towering period. The Greek world experienced the Persian Wars, the rise of the Athenian Empire, the war between Sparta and Athens, the flourishing of Periclean Athens as the apex of democracy and its cultural center, and the fall of Athens and the emergence of Sparta as the preeminent Greek *polis*. It experienced too the development of historical writing in the work of Herodotus and Thucydides, the rise of the itinerant teachers called sophists, the epitome of pre-Socratic natural philosophy, and the birth of old comedy. And the fifth century was the century of Socrates and of the tragedians, among them the author of the *Antigone*, Sophocles.

Born in 496 B.C.E., Sophocles died in 406, just prior to the fall of Athens. He composed over 120 plays; it has been calculated that about 96 of them won the first prize at the festival of Dionysus where tragedies and satyr plays were performed. His first victory was in 468; the *Antigone* was first performed in 441. Of this corpus, just seven plays survive.

Sophocles's tragedies are marked by larger-than-life figures who, when confronted with momentous decisions and faced with the forces of fate and *dike* (justice), become victims of the complexity of such forces. In the *Antigone* both Creon and Antigone face such a situation. From antiquity to our own day, readers have puzzled over who the central player is and what Sophocles seeks to show us about how human beings respond to the forces of fate and justice that govern the universe and the affairs of humankind. Readers find within the *Antigone* multiple tensions—between the individual and the state, between familial obligations and duty to the *polis*, between divine command and positive law, between youthful self-sacrifice and adult domination, and more. Whether the drama does in fact display precisely these conflicts or ones like them the reader must make out for herself. What is clear is that Antigone's choice, when faced with her brothers' deaths and the edict of Creon, her uncle, sets in motion a chain of actions that ultimately leave Creon damaged and in despair. From one perspective, while it is Antigone who first confronts the pull of familial devotion and respect under the abiding laws of the gods, on the one hand, and the prohibition uttered by Creon as king, on the other, ultimately it is Creon whose convictions are shown to parent conflict and disaster. There is no easy way to subordinate family loyalty to the allegiance and commitment to the state. There is no escaping fate, no way of cultivating without fault the many modes of *philia* (friendship, mutuality, loyalty).

Modern discussion of the drama falls under the heavy burden of Hegel's famous reading, in which such dichotomies, oppositions, and dialectical reversals take pride of place. But some interpreters suggest that the play is more subtle than that. Every opposition, like those between the family and the state, youth and age, the individual and society, is qualified in the careful speeches that Sophocles creates. It is not as easy as one might initially think to eulogize Antigone for her strength of character and conviction or to denigrate Ismene for her weakness, to demonize Creon or to heroize Haemon. Sophocles' portrayal of the individual is more complex; what we call moral obligations and political responsibilities are less easy to separate than we tend to think. The lives that Socrates, Plato, and Aristotle subject to examination and analysis realize in Sophocles a complexity that we should keep in mind.

1

Recommended Readings

Benardete, Seth. *Sacred Transgressions: A Reading of Sophocles' Antigone*. South Bend, Ind.: St. Augustine Press, 1999.

Bowra, C. M. *Sophoclean Tragedy*. Oxford: Oxford University Press, 1944.

Goldhill, Simon. *Reading Greek Tragedy*. Cambridge: Cambridge University Press, 1986.

Kitto, H.D.G. *Greek Tragedy*. London: Methuen and Company, 1970.

Knox, Bernard. *The Heroic Temper: Studies in Sophoclean Tragedy*. Berkeley: University of Californian Press, 1964.

Lloyd-Jones, H. *The Justice of Zeus*. Berkeley: University of California Press, 1971.

Reinhardt, K. *Sophocles*. Oxford: Oxford University Press, 1979.

Segal, C. P. *Tragedy and Civilization: An Interpretation of Sophocles*. Cambridge: Cambridge University Press, 1981.

Steiner, George. *Antigone*. Oxford: Oxford University Press, 1984.

Winnington-Ingram, R. P. *Sophocles: An Interpretation*. Cambridge: Cambridge University Press, 1980.

ANTIGONE

Cast of Characters

ANTIGONE	daughter and half-sister of Oedipus
ISMENE	Antigone's sister
CHORUS	the council of elders in Thebes
CHORUS LEADER	has lines in conversations
CREON	Antigone's uncle on her mother's side
WATCHMAN	one of those set to guard the corpse
TIRESIAS	prophet of Apollo
HAEMON	Creon's son, Antigone's fiancé
MESSENGER	a servant of Creon's
EURYDICE	Creon's wife, Haemon's mother

Nonspeaking Roles

ATTENDANTS	of Creon
ATTENDANTS	of Antigone (when under arrest)
SERVANTS	of Eurydice
BOY	who guides Tiresias

Scene

The royal house at Thebes, fronting onto a raised platform stage. Wing entrances right and left allow for characters to be seen by the audience and the chorus long before they are seen by the main characters. The great doors of the house stand upstage center.

[Enter Antigone leading Ismene through the great doors that lead from the palace.]

From Sophocles, *Antigone*, translated by Paul Woodruff (Indianapolis: Hackett Publishing Company, 2001). Copyright © 2001. Reprinted by permission of the publisher.

ANTIGONE:
Ismene, dear heart, my true sister:
You and I are left alive to pay
The final penalty to Zeus for Oedipus.
I've never seen such misery and madness—
It's monstrous! Such deep shame and dishonor— 5
As this, which falls upon the pair of us.
And now, a public announcement!
They say the general has plastered it around the city.
Have you heard this terrible news or not?
Our enemies are on the march to hurt our 10
 friends.

ISMENE:
No, Antigone, I have had no news of friends,
Nothing sweet or painful, since the day
We lost our brothers, both of us, on one day,
Both brothers dead by their two hands.
Last night the army that came from Argos 15
Disappeared, and after that I don't know
Anything that could bring me happiness—or
 despair.

ANTIGONE:
I knew it! That's the whole reason
I brought you outside—to hear the news alone.

ISMENE:
Tell me. You're as clear as a fog at sea. 20

ANTIGONE:
It's the burial of our two brothers. Creon
Promotes one of them and shames the other.

[5: Line numbers refer to the Greek text.]
[14–15: The two brothers, Eteoclês and Polyneices, had planned to take turns ruling Thebes; but Eteoclês refused to give Polyneices his time on the throne. An army came from Argos in support of Polyneices' claim and was defeated at the seven gates of the city. The two brothers killed each other. Argos, in the northeast corner of Peloponnesus, was seen as an enemy of Thebes.—P.W.]

Eteoclês—I heard Creon covered him beneath
The earth with proper rites, as law ordains,
25   So he has honor down among the dead.
But Polyneices' miserable corpse—
They say Creon has proclaimed to everyone:
"No Burial of any kind. No wailing, no public
      tears.
Give him to the vultures, unwept, unburied,
30   To be a sweet treasure for their sharp eyes and
      beaks."
That's what they say the good Creon has
      proclaimed
To you. And me. He forbids me, too.
And now he's strutting here to make it plain
To those who haven't heard—he takes
35   This seriously—that if anyone does what he
      forbids
He'll have him publicly stoned to death.
There's your news. Now, show your colors:
Are you true to your birth? Or a coward?

ISMENE:
You take things hard. If we are in this noose,
40   What could I do to loosen or pull tight the knot?

ANTIGONE:
If you share the work and trouble . . .

ISMENE:
In what dangerous adventure?

ANTIGONE:
If you help this hand raise the corpse . . .
      [Indicating her own hand.]

ISMENE:
Do you mean to bury him? Against the city's
      ordinance?

ANTIGONE:
45   But he is mine. And yours. Like it or not, he's
      our brother.
They'll never catch me betraying him.

ISMENE:
How horrible! When Creon forbids it?

ANTIGONE:
He has no right to keep me from my own.

ISMENE:
Oh no! Think carefully, my sister.
Our father died in hatred and disgrace   50
After gouging out his own two eyes
For sins he'd seen in his own self.
Next, his mother and wife—she was both—
Destroyed herself in a knotted rope.
And, third, our two brothers on one day   55
Killed each other in a terrible calamity,
Which they had created for each other.
Now think about the two of us. We are alone.
How horrible it will be to die outside the law,
If we violate a dictator's decree!   60
No. We have to keep this fact in mind:
We are women and we do not fight with men.
We're subject to them because they're stronger,
And we must obey this order, even if it hurts us
      more.
As for me, I will say to those beneath the earth 65
This prayer: "Forgive me, I am held back by
      force."
And I'll obey the men in charge. My mind
Will never aim too high, too far.

ANTIGONE:
I won't press you any further. I wouldn't even let
You help me if you had a change of heart.   70
Go on and *be* the way you choose to be. I
Will bury him. I will have a noble death
And lie with him, a dear sister with a dear
      brother.
Call it a crime of reverence, but I must be good
      to those
Who are below. I will be there longer than with 75
      you.
That's where I will lie. You, keep to your choice:
Go on insulting what the gods hold dear.

ISMENE:
I am not insulting anyone. By my very nature
I cannot possibly take arms against the city.

ANTIGONE:
Go on, make excuses. I am on my way.   80
I'll heap the earth upon my dearest brother's
      grave.

ISMENE:
Oh no! This is horrible for you. I am so worried!

ANTIGONE:
    Don't worry about me. Put your own life straight.

ISMENE:
    Please don't tell a soul what you are doing.
85 Keep it hidden. I'll do the same.

ANTIGONE:
    For god's sake, speak out. You'll be more enemy
        to me
    If you are silent. Proclaim it to the world!

ISMENE:
    Your heart's so hot to do this chilling thing!

ANTIGONE:
    But it pleases those who matter most.

ISMENE:
90 Yes, if you had the power. But you love the
        impossible.

ANTIGONE:
    So? When my strength is gone, I'll stop.

ISMENE:
    But it's the highest wrong to chase after what's
        impossible.

ANTIGONE:
    When you say this, you set yourself against me.
    Your brother will take you to him—as his enemy.
95 So you just let me and my 'bad judgment'
    Go to hell. Nothing could happen to me
    So bad that it would cloud my noble death.

    [*Exit Antigone toward the plain, through the
    stage left wing.*]

ISMENE:
    Then follow your judgment, go. You've lost your
        mind,
    But you are holding to the love of your loved
        ones.

    [*Exit Ismene through the great doors into the
    palace, as the chorus enter from the city, stage
    right wing.*]

CHORUS:

Parodos (Entry-song)

[**Strophe** *a*]

100 Let us praise the Sun:
     These brilliant beams

Shine glory never seen before in Thebes,
Our City of Seven Gates.
O bright eye of golden day!
You came striding over River Dirkê,   105
And the White Shield of Argos ran away.
He has fled,
Man and weapon racing from your light,
On sharpened spur.

He was roused against our land   110
For a fight that Polyneices, haggling, picked.
And, like a screaming eagle,
He dropped on our land:
The shadow of his white-snow wing—
A multitude of armored men,   115
Helmets crested with horsehair.

[**Antistrophe** *a*]

He stooped over our homes,
Mouth gaping wide for the kill,
He engulfed our Seven Gates with spears of
        death;
But he has gone,   120
Gone before plunging his beak in our blood,
Gone before torching our crown of towers
With the flames of Hephaestus.
For behind his back there arose too loud
The clamor of war;   125
His dragon-foe was too strong for him.

Zeus hates an arrogant boast,
With towering hatred.
He saw the river of men attack,
Their golden armor clashing in contempt,   130
And so he struck the man down with a missile of
        fire
As he swooped toward his highest goal,
Eager to shout "Victory!"

[*105: Dirkê is one of the rivers of Thebes.*]
[*126: "Dragon-foe"—The people of Thebes believed
that they were descended from men who grew from the
teeth of a dragon slain by Cadmus.*]
[*131–40: These lines refer to the attacker who boasts
too much; according to the legend, this was an Argive
named Kapaneus.*]

[Strophe *b*]

He crashed to the ground
135 Like a weight slung down in an arc of fire,
This man who had swooped like a dancer in
        ecstasy,
Breathing hurricanes of hatred.
But his threats came to nothing:
The mighty war god, fighting beside us,
140 Swept them aside.

Seven captains at seven gates,
Matched with seven defenders,
All left trophies for Zeus the protector
(They took off their armor and ran).
145 Except for a savage pair, full brothers:
Their two spears stand upright, conquering,
Each in the other's dead breast.

[Antistrophe *b*]

Now Victory is ours,
Great be her name! Now Thebes rejoices.
150 Therefore let us forget our pain.
The war is over: let us dance all night,
Fill all the sacred precincts with joy:
We must now be ruled by Bacchus,
Dance-master of Thebes.

[Enter Creon through the great doors.]

CHORUS:
155 Here is the king of our land
Creon, the son of Menoeceus,
Our new ruler given us by chance and the gods.
What plan has he been churning over on his
        way?
Why has he summoned us—
160 The council of elders—
By public announcement?

CREON:
Gentlemen, the city is safe again, we may thank
        the gods:
After a great upheaval, they have rescued Thebes.
You are here because I chose you from the whole
        crowd
165 And summoned you by escort. You always showed
        respect

For Laius' power when he held the throne,
And the same again for Oedipus, when he
        rescued Thebes.
After he died I know you stood by their sons;
You were always there with good advice.
Now they are dead, both on one day;   170
Each stabbed the other and was stabbed.
Brother struck brother, and the blows were
        cursed.

So now the throne and all the power in Thebes
        are mine,
Because I am closest kin to those who died.

No man has a mind that can be fully known,   175
In character or judgment, till he rules and makes
        law;
Only then can he be tested in the public eye.
I believe that if anyone tries to run a city
On the basis of bad policies and holds his tongue
Because he's afraid to say what is right,   180
That man is terrible. So I have always thought.
But it's even worse when he plays favorites,
Puts family or friends ahead of fatherland.
As for me—I call to witness all-seeing Zeus—
I will never hold my tongue about what I see   185
When ruin is afoot or the city is not safe.
I will never call a man my friend
If he is hostile to this land. I know this well:
The city is our lifeboat: we have no friends at all
Unless we keep her sailing right side up.   190
Such are my laws. By them I'll raise this city
        high.

And I have just announced a twin sister of those
        laws,
To all the citizens, concerning Oedipus' sons:
Eteoclês fought for the city, and for it he died,
After every feat of heroism with his spear.   195
He shall be sanctified by every burial rite
That is given to the most heroic dead below.

As for his blood brother, Polyneices by name,
He broke his exile, he came back hungry for our
        blood,
He wanted to burn his fatherland and family gods 200

Down from the top. He wanted to lead his
   people—
Into slavery. This man will have no grave:
It is forbidden to offer any funeral rites;
No one in Thebes may bury him or mourn for
   him.
205   He must be left unburied. May birds and dogs
Feed on his limbs, a spectacle of utter shame.

Such is the character of my mind: Never, while I
   rule,
Will a criminal be honored higher than a man of
   justice.
But give me a true friend of this city
210   And I will pay him full honor, in death or life.

CHORUS:
   That is your decision, son of Menoeceus,
   As to the one who meant our city well
   And the one who meant it ill. It's up to you:
   Make any law you want—for the dead, or for us
      who live.

CREON:
215   Now, look after my commands. I insist.

CHORUS:
   Ask someone younger to take up the task.

CREON:
   No, no. I have men already watching the corpse.

CHORUS:
   Then what's left for us to do? What are your
      orders?

CREON:
   That you do not side with anyone who disobeys.

CHORUS:
220   No one is foolish enough to ask for death.

CREON:
   Right. That would be their reward. But hope—
   And bribery—often have led men to destruction.

[Enter Watchman from the stage left wing.]

WATCHMAN:
   Sir, I am here. I can't say I am out of breath.
   I have not exactly been "running on light feet."

I halted many times along the road so I could   225
   think,
And I almost turned around and marched right
   back.
My mind kept talking to me. It said, "You poor guy,
Why are you going there? You'll just get your ass
   kicked."
Then it said, "Are you stopping again, you damn
   fool?
If Creon hears this from another man, he'll give   230
   you hell."
Well, I turned this idea up and down like that,
And I hurried along, real slow. Made a short trip
   long.
What got me here in the end was this: My report.
It doesn't amount to much, but I might as well
   give it,
Because I won't let go this handful of hope   235
That things won't be any worse than they have to
   be.

CREON:
   What is it, man—where's your courage?

WATCHMAN:
   First, I want to tell you where I stand:
   I didn't do this thing, and I don't know who did,
   And it wouldn't be fair if I got hurt.   240

CREON:
   All right, your defense perimeter is up.
   Now, let's have your report.

WATCHMAN:
   It's terrible news. I can't come right out with that.

CREON:
   Speak up! And then get lost.

WATCHMAN:
   OK, here it is. The body out there—someone   245
      buried it
   Just now and went away. They spread thirsty dust
   All over the skin and did the ceremony in full.

CREON:
   What? No man would dare! Who did it?

WATCHMAN:
   I don't know. The ground was so hard and dry.
   It showed no marks. No spade scratches,   250

No pickaxe holes, not even chariot ruts.
The perpetrator had not left a single clue.
When the first day-watchman showed it to us,
We were all amazed. It was incredible:
255   The guy had vanished. There was no tomb,
Only fine dust lying over the body, enough to take
The curse away. No sign of wild animals,
No dogs sniffing or tugging at the corpse.

We burst out shouting at each other;
260   Everyone was hurling accusations.
We kept coming to blows, no one to stop us.
Any one of us could have done the thing.
No one caught red-handed, everyone pled ignorance.
We were about to test each other with red-hot iron
265   Or run our hands through fire and swear by all the gods:
"I didn't do it, and I had no part in any plot
To do it, not with anyone else, not by hand or word."
Well, we weren't getting anywhere, and in the end
Someone told us to do a thing we couldn't see how
270   To refuse *or* accept. So we dropped heads, stared at the ground
In fear. There was no way it would turn out good for us.
We simply had to bring word to you,
Because we could not hide a thing like this.
We voted to do it, and I am so damned unlucky
275   I won the lottery to have this lovely job.
I didn't want to come. And you sure didn't want to see me:
No one loves the man who brings bad news.

CHORUS: [*To Creon.*]
You know, sir, as soon as I heard, it came to me:
Somehow the gods are behind this piece of work.

CREON: [*To the chorus leader.*]
280   Stop right there, before I'm gorged with rage!
You want to prove that you're as stupid as you are old?

It's totally unacceptable, what you said about the gods—
That they could have a caring thought for this man's corpse.
You think they buried him for his good deeds?
To give him highest honor? They know he came 285
with fire
To burn down their fine-columned shrines, their land,
Their store of treasure—and to blow their laws away.
Have you ever seen a criminal honored by the *gods*?
Not possible.
        But some *men* here have always champed,
Like surf, against my orders, and obeyed me, if at 290
all,
Without cheer. They shake their heads when I'm not looking,
Pull out of the yoke of justice, and are not content with me.
They are the ones, I'm absolutely sure, who used bribes
To lead our watchmen astray, into this crime.

Money is the nastiest weed ever to sprout 295
In human soil. Money will ravage a city,
Tear men from their homes and send them into exile.
Money teaches good minds to go bad;
It is the source of every shameful human deed.
Money points the way to wickedness, 300
Lets people know the full range of irreverence.
But those who committed this crime for hire
Have set themselves a penalty, which, in time,
they'll pay.

[*To the Watchman.*]

Now listen here. So long as I am reverent to Zeus
I am under oath, and you can be absolutely sure 305
That if you don't find the hand behind this burial
And bring him so I can see him with my own eyes,
Death alone will not be good enough for you—

Not till I've stretched you with ropes and you
   confess
310 To this outrageous crime. That will teach you
Where to look to make a profit. And you will
   learn:
Never accept money from just anyone who comes
   along.
Those who take from a source that is wicked,
   you'll see,
Are ruined far more often than saved.

WATCHMAN:
315 Permission to speak, sir? Or about face and go?

CREON:
Don't you see how badly your report annoyed
   me?

WATCHMAN:
So where's it biting you? On your ears or in your
   mind?

CREON:
What's it to you? Why should you analyze my
   pain?

WATCHMAN:
If it hurts your mind, blame the perpetrator.
If it's only your ears, blame me.

CREON:
320 Damn it, man, will you never stop babbling?

WATCHMAN:
Well, at least I never did the thing.

CREON:
Yes, you did. And for money! You gave up your
   life!

WATCHMAN:
Oh no, no, no.
It's terrible when false judgment guides the judge.

CREON:
All right, play with the word 'judgment.' But
   you'd better catch
325 The man who did this thing or I'll have proof:
You men ruined your miserable lives to make a
   profit!

*[Creon turns and exits through the great doors
to the palace.]*

WATCHMAN:
We'll find him. You'd better believe it.
But if we don't—you know, if he gets lucky—
No way you'll ever see me coming back to you.
As it is, this has gone better than I expected—   330
I'm still alive, thanks be to the gods.

*[Exit Watchman toward the plain, through the
stage left wing.]*

First Stasimon

CHORUS:

[Strophe *a*]

Many wonders, many terrors,
But none more wonderful than the human race
   Or more dangerous.
This creature travels on a winter gale   335
Across the silver sea,
Shadowed by high-surging waves,
While on Earth, grandest of the gods,
He grinds the deathless, tireless land away,
Turning and turning the plow   340
From year to year, behind driven horses.

[Antistrophe *a*]

Light-headed birds he catches
And takes them away in legions. Wild beasts
   Also fall prey to him.
And all that is born to live beneath the sea   345
Is thrashing in his woven nets.
For he is Man, and he is cunning.
He has invented ways to take control
Of beasts that range mountain meadows:
Taken down the shaggy-necked horses,   350
The tireless mountain bulls,
And put them under the yoke.

[Strophe *b*]

Language and a mind swift as the wind
   For making plans—   355
These he has taught himself—

And the character to live in cities under law.
He's learned to take cover from a frost
And escape sharp arrows of sleet.
360 He has the means to handle every need,
Never steps toward the future without the means.
Except for Death: He's got himself no relief from that,
Though he puts every mind to seeking cures
For plagues that are hopeless.

[Antistrophe *b*]

365 He has cunning contrivance,
    Skill surpassing hope,
And so he slithers into wickedness sometimes,
Other times into doing good.
If he honors the law of the land
370 And the oath-bound justice of the gods,
Then his city shall stand high.
But no city for him if he turns shameless out of
    daring.
He will be no guest of mine,
He will never share my thoughts,
375 If he goes wrong.

[*Enter Watchman leading Antigone through the
stage left wing.*]

CHORUS:
Monstrous! What does this mean?
Are gods behind it? I don't know what to think:
Isn't this Antigone? I can't deny it.
You miserable child of misery,
380 Daughter of Oedipus,
What have you done?
Is it you they arrested?
Are you so foolish?
So disloyal to the laws of kings?

WATCHMAN:
Yes, she's the one that did the burial.
385 We caught her in the act. Hey, where's Creon?

[*Enter Creon through the great doors.*]

CHORUS:
Here he is. Coming back from the palace.

CREON:
What's all this? Lucky I turned up now.

WATCHMAN:
Sir, there's no point swearing oaths if you're a
    mortal.
Second thoughts make any plan look bad.
I swore I'd never come to you again   390
Because those threats of yours gave me the
    shakes.
But you know: "Joy beyond hope
Surpasses every other pleasure."
I've come, though I swore on oath I wouldn't.
And I've brought this girl, arrested her at the   395
    grave
When she was tidying it up. No lottery this time.
The windfall's mine and no one else's.
Now it's up to you. Take her, question her,
Make your judgment. As for me,
The right thing is to let me off scot-free.   400

CREON:
Circumstances under which you arrested her?
    Location?

WATCHMAN:
She was burying that man. Now you know it all.

CREON:
Do you honestly know what you are saying?

WATCHMAN:
Well, I saw this girl burying the dead body.
The one you put off-limits. Clear enough for you? 405

CREON:
How did you see this? Caught her in the act?

WATCHMAN:
It was like this. We went back to the body
After all your terrible threats,
And we brushed off the dust that covered it,
So as to make the rotting corpse properly naked.   410
Then we settled down on the hill,
Upwind, so the stink wouldn't hit us.
We kept awake by yelling insults
At each other when a slacker nodded off.
That went on for a long time, till the sun   415
Stood bright in the center of the sky.
And we were really getting cooked. Then,

Suddenly, a tornado struck. It raised dust
All over the plain, grief to high heaven.
420 It thrashed the low-lying woods with terror
And filled the whole wide sky. We shut our eyes
And held out against this plague from the gods.

After a long while it lifted, and then we saw the
     girl.
She gave a shrill cry like a bird when she sees her
     nest
425 Empty, and the bed deserted where her nestlings
     had lain.
That was how she was when she saw the corpse
     uncovered.
She cried out in mourning, and she called down
Curses on whoever had done this thing.
Right away she spread thirsty dust with her hands,
430 Then poured the three libations from a vessel of
     fine bronze.
And so she crowned the corpse with honor.

As soon as we spotted her, we started to run.
She showed no fear; it was easy to catch her.
Then we questioned her about her past and
     present actions.
435 She did not deny a single thing.
For me, that was sweet, and agonizing, too.
It's a great joy to be out of trouble,
But bringing trouble on your friends is agony.
Still I don't mind that so much. It's nature's way
440 For me to put my own survival first.

CREON:
You there! With your head bowed to the
     ground—
Are you guilty? Or do you deny that you did this
     thing?

ANTIGONE:
Of course not. I did it. I won't deny anything.

CREON: *[To the Watchman.]*
You're dismissed. Take yourself where you please;
445 You're a free man, no serious charge against you.

[To Antigone.]

As for you, tell me—in brief, not at length—
Did you know that this had been forbidden?

ANTIGONE:
I knew. I couldn't help knowing. It was
     everywhere.

CREON:
And yet you dared to violate these laws?

ANTIGONE:
What laws? I never heard it was Zeus   450
Who made that announcement.
And it wasn't justice, either. The gods below
Didn't lay down this law for human use.
And I never thought your announcements
Could give you—a mere human being—   455
Power to trample the gods' unfailing,
Unwritten laws. These laws weren't made now
Or yesterday. They live for all time,
And no one knows when they came into the
     light.
No man could frighten me into taking on
The gods' penalty for breaking such a law.   460
I'll die in any case, of course I will,
Whether you announce my execution or not.
But if I die young, all the better:
People who live in misery like mine
Are better dead. So if that's the way   465
My life will end, the pain is nothing.
But if I let the corpse—my mother's son—
Lie dead, unburied, that would be agony.
This way, no agony for me. But you! You think
I've been a fool? It takes a fool to think that.   470

CHORUS:
Now we see the girl's as wild by birth as her
     father.
She has no idea how to bow her head to trouble.

CREON: *[To the chorus.]*
Don't forget: The mind that is most rigid
Stumbles soonest; the hardest iron—
Tempered in fire till it is super-strong—   475
Shatters easily and clatters into shards.
And you can surely break the wildest horse
With a tiny bridle. When the master's watching,
Pride has no place in the life of a slave.
This girl was a complete expert in arrogance   480
Already, when she broke established law.
And now, arrogantly, she adds insult to injury:

She's boasting and sneering about what she's
    done!
Listen, if she's not punished for taking the upper
    hand,
485 Then I am not a man. *She* would be a man!
I don't care if she is my sister's child—
Or closer yet at my household shrine for Zeus—
She and her sister must pay the full price
And die for their crime.

[*The chorus indicate their surprise that both
must die.*]

                          Yes, I say they have equal guilt,
490 Conniving, one with the other, for this burial.

Bring her out. I saw her in there a minute ago;
She was raving mad, totally out of her mind.
Often it's the feelings of a thief that give him
    away
Before the crimes he did in darkness come to
    light.

[*Turning to Antigone.*]

495 But how I hate it when she's caught in the act,
And the criminal still glories in her crime.

ANTIGONE:
You've caught me, you can kill me. What more
    do you want?

CREON:
For me, that's everything. I want no more than
    that.

ANTIGONE:
Then what are you waiting for? More talk?
500 Your words disgust me, I hope they always will.
And I'm sure you are disgusted by what I say.
But yet, speaking of glory, what could be more
Glorious than giving my true brother his burial?
All these men would tell you they're rejoicing
505 Over that, if you hadn't locked their tongues
With fear. But a tyrant says and does
What he pleases. That's his great joy.

CREON:
You are the only one, in all Thebes, who thinks
    that way.

ANTIGONE:
No. They all see it the same. You've silenced
    them.

CREON:
Aren't you ashamed to have a mind apart from   510
    theirs?

ANTIGONE:
There's no shame in having respect for a brother.

CREON:
Wasn't he your brother, too, the one who died on
    the other side?

ANTIGONE:
Yes, my blood brother—same mother, same
    father.

CREON:
When you honor the one, you disgrace the other.
    Why do it?

ANTIGONE:
The dead will never testify against a burial.   515

CREON:
Yes, if they were equal. But one of them deserves
    disgrace.

ANTIGONE:
He wasn't any kind of slave. He was his brother,
    who died.

CREON:
He was killing and plundering. The other one
    defended our land.

ANTIGONE:
Even so, Hades longs to have these laws obeyed.

CREON:
But surely not equal treatment for good and bad?   520

ANTIGONE:
Who knows? Down below that might be blesséd.

CREON:
An enemy is always an enemy, even in death.

[*519: Hades is the god of death; his name is also used
for the underworld, to which the dead belong.*]

ANTIGONE:
I cannot side with hatred. My nature sides with
love.

CREON:
Go to Hades, then, and if you have to love, love
someone dead.
525 As long as I live, I will not be ruled by a woman.

*[Enter Ismene under guard, through the great
doors.)*

CHORUS:
Now Ismene stands before the doors
And sheds tears of sister-love.
From her brows, a blood-dark cloud
Casts a foul shadow
530 And stains her lovely face.

CREON:
Now you. Hiding in my house like a snake,
A coiled bloodsucker in the dark! And I never
realized
I was raising a pair of deadly, crazed
revolutionaries!
Come, tell me: How do you plead? Guilty of this
burial
535 As an accomplice? Or do you swear you knew
nothing?

ISMENE:
I did it, I confess. That is, if we are partners,
anyway.
I am an accomplice, and I bear responsibility
with her.

ANTIGONE:
I will not permit this penalty to fall on you.
No. I never wanted to give you a share.

ISMENE:
540 But these are your troubles! I'm not ashamed;
I'll be your shipmate in suffering.

ANTIGONE:
I have witnesses: the gods below saw who did the
work.
I won't accept a friend who's only friends in
words.

ISMENE:
No, please! You're my sister: Don't despise me!
Let me die with you and sanctify our dead.   545

ANTIGONE:
No, you may not die along with me. Don't say
you did it!
You wouldn't even touch it. Now leave my death
alone!

ISMENE:
Why would I care to live when you are gone?

ANTIGONE:
Creon's the one to ask. He's the one you care for.

ISMENE:
Why are you scolding me? It won't help you.   550

ANTIGONE:
Of course not. It hurts me when my mockery
strikes you.

ISMENE:
But I still want to help you. What can I do?

ANTIGONE:
Escape! Save yourself! I don't begrudge you that.

ISMENE:
O misery! Why am I cut off from your fate?

ANTIGONE:
Because you chose life, and I chose death.   555

ISMENE:
But I gave you reasons not to make that choice.

ANTIGONE: *[Pointing to Creon and the chorus.]*
Oh yes, you are sensible; these men agree.

*[Pointing to the ground, speaking of the dead
or the gods below.]*

                              But *they* agree with me.

ISMENE:
Yes, I know. And now the sin is mine as much as
yours.

ANTIGONE:
Be brave. You are alive. Already my soul is dead.
It has gone to help those who died before me.   560

CREON:
　What a pair of children! One of you lost her
　　mind
　Moments ago; the other was born without hers.

ISMENE:
　That is right, sir. Whenever we commit a crime,
　Our minds, which grew by nature, leave us.

CREON:
565　Yours did, when you deliberately joined a
　　criminal in crime.

ISMENE:
　Without her, why should I live? I'd be alone.

CREON:
　Her? Don't speak of her. She is no more.

ISMENE:
　But will you really kill the bride of your son?

CREON:
　There's other ground for him to plow, you know.

ISMENE:
570　But no one is suited to him as well as she is.

CREON:
　I loathe bad women. She's not for my son.

ANTIGONE (or possibly ISMENE, or possibly
CHORUS):
　O Haemon, dearest, what a disgrace your father
　　does to you!

CREON:
　Shut up! What a pain you are, you and your
　　marriage!

CHORUS (or ISMENE, or ANTIGONE):
　Will you really take away your son's bride?

CREON:
575　Not me. Death will put a stop to this marriage.

CHORUS (or ISMENE):
　So she will die. Has it really been decided?

CREON:
　Yes. By you and me. Now, no more delays.
　Servants! Take them inside. They are women,
　And they must not be free to roam about.
580　Even a brave man flees from Death
　When he sees his life in immediate danger.

[*Servants take Ismene and Antigone through the
great doors.*]

Second Stasimon

CHORUS:

[Strophe *a*]

Happy are they that never taste of crime,
But once a house is shaken by the gods,
Then madness stalks the family without fail,
Disaster for many generations.　　　　　　585
It is like a great salt wave
Kicked up by foul winds from Thrace,
It surges over the hellish depths of the sea,
Roils the bottom,
Churns up black sand,　　　　　　　　　590
And makes the screaming headlands howl
Against the gale.

[Antistrophe *a*]

I see grief falling from old days on Labdacus'
　　family:
New grief heaped on the grief of those who died.
And nothing redeems the generation that is to　595
　　come:
Some god is battering them without relief.
Now I see a saving light
Rising from the sole remaining roots
Of the house of Oedipus. But this, too, falls
In a bloody harvest,　　　　　　　　　600
Claimed by the dust
Of the Underworld gods, doomed by foolish
　　words
And frenzied wits.

[Strophe *b*]

O Zeus! Who could ever curtail thy power?
Not a man, never—　　　　　　　　　605
No matter how far he oversteps his bounds—
Not sleep, that weakens everyone,
Not the untiring months of gods.
No, Zeus, you do not grow weak with time,
You who hold power in the luminous glow of　610
　　Olympus.

And this will be the law,
Now and for time to come, as it was before:
Madness stalks mortals who are great,
Leaves no escape from disaster.

[Antistrophe *b*]

615 Beware of hope! Far-reaching, beguiling, a
        pleasure—
    For a lot of men.
    But a lot are fooled by a light-headed love,
    And deception stalks those who know nothing
    Until they set their feet in fire and burn.
620 Wisdom lies in the famous proverb:
    "Those who judge that crime is good,
    Are in the hands of a driving god
    Who is leading them to madness."
    Time is very short for them,
625 Leaves no escape from disaster.

[Enter Haemon through the stage right wing.]

CHORUS:
    Now, here is Haemon, the last of your children.
    Is he goaded here by anguish for Antigone,
    Who should have been his bride?
    Does he feel injured beyond measure?
630 Cheated out of marriage?

CREON:
    We'll know the answer right away, better than
        prophets:
    Tell me, son, did you hear the final verdict?
    Against your fiancée? Did you come in anger at
        your father?
    Or are we still friends, no matter what I do?

HAEMON:
635 I am yours, Father. You set me straight,
    Give me good advice, and I will follow it.
    No marriage will weigh more with me,
    Than your good opinion.

CREON:
    Splendid, my boy! Keep that always in your heart,
640 And stand behind fatherly advice on all counts.
    Why does a man pray that he'll conceive a child,
    Keep him at home, and have him listen to what
        he's told?

It's so the boy will punish his father's enemies
And reward his friends—as his father would.
But some men beget utterly useless offspring: 645
They have planted nothing but trouble for
    themselves,
And they're nothing but a joke to their enemies.

Now then, my boy, don't let pleasure cloud your
    mind,
Not because of a woman. You know very well:
You'll have a frigid squeeze between the sheets   650
If you shack up with a hostile woman. I'd rather
    have
A bleeding wound than a criminal in the family.
So spit her out. And because the girl's against us,
Send her down to marry somebody in Hades.
You know I caught her in the sight of all,   655
Alone of all our people, in open revolt.
And I will make my word good in Thebes—
By killing her. Who cares if she sings "Zeus!"
And calls him her protector? I must keep my kin
    in line.
Otherwise, folks outside the family will run wild.   660
The public knows that a man is just
Only if he is straight with his relatives.

So, if someone goes too far and breaks the law,
Or tries to tell his masters what to do,
He will have nothing but contempt from me.   665
But when the city takes a leader, you must obey,
Whether his commands are trivial, or right, or
    wrong.
And I have no doubt that such a man will rule
    well,
And, later, he will cheerfully be ruled by
    someone else.
In hard times he will stand firm with his spear   670
Waiting for orders, a good, law-abiding soldier.

But reject one man ruling another, and that's the
    worst.
Anarchy tears up a city, divides a home,
Defeats an alliance of spears.
But when people stay in line and obey,   675
Their lives and everything else are safe.
For this reason, order must be maintained,
And there must be no surrender to a woman.

No! If we fall, better a man should take us down.
680   Never say that a woman bested us!

CHORUS:
Unless old age has stolen my wits away,
Your speech was very wise. That's my belief.

HAEMON:
Father, the gods give good sense to every human
      being,
And that is absolutely the best thing we have.
685   But if what you said is not correct,
I have no idea how I could make the point.
Still, maybe someone else could work it out.

My natural duty's to look out for you, spot any
      risk
That someone might find fault with what you say
      or do.
690   The common man, you see, lives in terror of your
      frown;
690a He'll never dare to speak up in broad daylight
And say anything you would hate to learn.
But I'm the one who hears what's said at night—
How the entire city is grieving over this girl.
No woman has ever had a fate that's so unfair
695   (They say), when what she did deserves honor
      and fame.
She saved her very own brother after he died,
Murderously, from being devoured by flesh-eating
      dogs
And pecked apart by vultures as he lay unburied.
For this, hasn't she earned glory bright as gold?
700   This sort of talk moves against you, quietly, at
      night.

And for me, Father, your continued good fortune
Is the best reward that I could ever have.
No child could win a greater prize than his
      father's fame,
No father could want more than abundant
      success—
From his son.

705   And now, don't always cling to the same anger,
Don't keep saying that this, and nothing else, is
      right.

If a man believes that he alone has a sound
      mind,
And no one else can speak or think as well as he
      does,
Then, when people study him, they'll find an
      empty book.
But a wise man can learn a lot and never be   710
      ashamed;
He knows he does not have to be rigid and close-
      hauled.
You've seen trees tossed by a torrent in a flash
      flood:
If they bend, they're saved, and every twig
      survives,
But if they stiffen up, they're washed out from the
      roots.
It's the same in a boat: if a sailor keeps the   715
      footline taut,
If he doesn't give an inch, he'll capsize, and
      then—
He'll be sailing home with his benches down and
      his hull to the sky.
So ease off, relax, stop being angry, make a
      change.
I know I'm younger, but I may still have good
      ideas;
And I say that the oldest idea, and the best,   720
Is for one man to be born complete, knowing
      everything.
Otherwise—and it usually does turn out
      otherwise—
It's good to learn from anyone who speaks well.

CHORUS:
Sir, you should learn from him, if he is on the
      mark. And you,
Haemon, learn from your father. Both sides spoke   725
      well.

CREON: [To the chorus.]
Do you really think, at our age,
We should be taught by a boy like him?

[715: A footline is the rope that runs from the foot of
the sail, equivalent to what today's sailors call a sheet.
Easing the sheet can save a boat from capsizing in a
sudden gust of wind.]

HAEMON:

No. Not if I am in the wrong. I admit I'm young;
That's why you should look at what I do, not my
age.

CREON:

730   So "what you do" is show respect for breaking
ranks?

HAEMON:

I'd never urge you to show respect for a criminal.

CREON:

So you don't think this girl has been infected
with crime?

HAEMON:

No. The people of Thebes deny it, all of them.

CREON:

So you think the people should tell me what
orders to give?

HAEMON:

735   Now who's talking like he's wet behind the ears?

CREON:

So I should rule this country for someone other
than myself?

HAEMON:

A place for one man alone is not a city.

CREON:

A city belongs to its master. Isn't that the rule?

HAEMON:

Then go be ruler of a desert, all alone. You'd do
it well.

CREON: [*To the chorus.*]

740   It turns out this boy is fighting for the woman's
cause.

HAEMON:

Only if *you* are a woman. All I care about is you!

CREON:

This is intolerable! You are accusing your own
father.

HAEMON:

Because I see you going wrong. Because justice
matters!

CREON:

Is that wrong, showing respect for my job as
leader?

HAEMON:

You have no respect at all if you trample on the   745
rights of gods!

CREON:

What a sick mind you have: You submit to a
woman!

HAEMON:

No. You'll never catch me giving in to what's
shameful.

CREON:

But everything you say, at least, is on her side.

HAEMON:

And on your side! And mine! And the gods'
below!

CREON:

There is no way you'll marry her, not while she's   750
still alive.

HAEMON:

Then she'll die, and her death will destroy
Someone Else.

CREON:

Is that a threat? Are you brash enough to attack
me?

HAEMON:

What threat? All I'm saying is, you haven't
thought this through.

CREON:

I'll make you wish you'd never had a thought in
your empty head!

HAEMON:

If you weren't my father I'd say you were out of   755
your mind.

CREON:

Don't beat around the bush. You're a woman's
toy, a slave.

HAEMON:
  Talk, talk, talk! Why don't you ever want to
    listen?

CREON:
  Really? Listen, you are not going on like this. By
    all the gods,
  One more insult from you, and the fun is over.

    [To attendants.]

760 Bring out that hated thing. I want her to die right
      here,
  Right now, so her bridegroom can watch the
    whole thing.

HAEMON:
  Not me. Never. No matter what you think.
  She is not going to die while I am near her.
  And you will never, ever see my face again. Go
    on,
765 Be crazy! Perhaps some of your friends will stay
      by you.

    [Exit Haemon through the stage left wing.]

CHORUS:
  Sir, the man has gone. He is swift to anger;
  Pain lies heavily on a youthful mind.

CREON:
  Let him go, him and his lofty ambitions! Good
    riddance!
  But those two girls shall not escape their fate.

CHORUS:
770 Are you really planning to kill *both* of them?

CREON:
  Not the one who never touched the crime. You're
    right.

CHORUS:
  By what means will you have the other one
    killed?

CREON:
  I'll take her off the beaten track, where no one's
    around,
  And I'll bury her alive underground, in a grave of
    stone.

I'll leave her only as much food as religious law   775
    prescribes,
So that the city will not be cursed for homicide.

Let her pray to Hades down there; he's the only
    god
That she respects. Maybe she'll arrange for him to
    save her life;
Maybe she'll learn, at last, that she's wasting her
    time
Showing respect for whatever's in Hades.   780

  [Exit Creon through the great doors.]

Third Stasimon

CHORUS:

[Strophe]

In battle the victory goes to Love;
Prizes and properties fall to Love.
Love dallies the night
On a girl's soft cheeks,
Ranges across the sea,   785
Lodges in wild meadows.
O Love, no one can hide from you:
You take gods who live forever,
You take humans who die in a day,
And they take you and go mad.   790

[Antistrophe]

Destroyer Love, you seize a good mind,
And pervert it to wickedness:
This fight is your doing,
This uproar in the family.
And the winner will be desire,   795
Shining in the eyes of a bride,
An invitation to bed,
A power to sweep across the bounds of what is
    Right.
For we are only toys in your hands,
Divine, unbeatable Aphrodite!   800

Kommos

[Enter Antigone under guard through the
great doors.]

CHORUS:
Now I, too, am swept away,
Out of bounds, when I see this.
I cannot contain the surge of tears:
For now I see Antigone, soon to gain
805 The marriage bed where everyone must sleep.

ANTIGONE:
See how I walk the last road,
You who belong to my city,
How I fill my eyes with the last
Shining of the sun.
810 There's no return: I follow death, alive,
To the brink of Acheron,
Where He gives rest to all.
No marriage hymns for me.
No one sounds
815 A wedding march:
I will be the bride of Acheron.

CHORUS:
But won't you have hymns of praise?
So much glory attends you
As you pass into the deep place of the dead.
820 For you are not wasted by disease, not maimed by
     a sword.
But true to your own laws, you are the only one,
Of mortals, who'll go down to Hades while still
     alive.

ANTIGONE:
No. I hear Niobe was lost in utmost misery—
Daughter of Tantalus, visitor in Thebes,
825 Wasted on a Phrygian mountain.
Rock sprouted up around her, firm,
Erect as shoots of ivy,
And it subdued her. So men say.
Rain and snow pelted her
Without a break, and she melted away,
830 Dripping from her mournful brows,
Tears streaming down her flanks.
It's the same for me, exactly:
Something divine lays me to sleep.

[816: Acheron—a river in the underworld.]
[821: "But true to your own laws"—The Greek is *auto-nomos*, rendered by some scholars as "of your own will"; but the word means more than that in ancient Greek, and the root word "law" (*nomos*) is clearly heard.]

CHORUS:
Really! Niobe was a god; she had a god for a
     father.
We are mortal, and our fathers pass away.   835
But you—when you die, you will be great,
You will be equal in memory to the gods,
By the glory of your life and death.

ANTIGONE:
You're laughing at me.
For the gods' sake, why now?   840
You could have waited till I'm gone.
But now you make insults to my face,
You grasping, rich old men! What a city you have!
I call on the rising of rivers in Thebes
And on the great chariot-reaches of the plain. 845
The rivers and the plain are on my side, at least.
They'll testify that no friends wept for me,
That the laws of Thebes sent me to prison
In a rock-hollowed tomb.
They see how unusual and cruel this is.   850
But I have no place with human beings,
Living or dead. No city is home to me.

CHORUS:
You've gone too far! You are extreme, impetuous.
My child, you caught your foot and fell
When you tried to climb against high justice.   855
This is your father's legacy—pain and punishment.

ANTIGONE:
Now you raise the agony that hurts my mind the
     most:
Grief for my father,
Like raw earth plowed three times,
Grief for the whole huge disaster of *us*,   860
Our brilliant family,
Labdacus' descendants.
I weep for the ruin in my mother's bed,
The sexual intercourse and the incest
My father had with our mother.   865
Ill-fated parents make a miserable child.
I am going to them now,
Unholy and unmarried, to lodge with them.
Oh, my brother, you were married once,

[869: "You were married once"—Polyneices married the daughter of the king of Argos, and Argos provided the army that attacked Thebes.]

870   But what a disaster it was:
Your death snuffed out my life.

CHORUS:
You have one kind of reverence.
But a man whose job it is to rule
Will never let you trample on his power.
875   You chose anger, and anger destroyed you.

ANTIGONE:
No tears for me, no friends, no wedding hymns.
They are taking me away
In misery, by the road before me,
Now and forever forbidden to see
880   This blessed eye of light.
No friends cry for me,
No one is mourning.

[*Enter Creon with his attendants through the great doors.*]

CREON:
Singing and wailing? They would never end
Before death, if they made any difference.
885   Take her away immediately. And when she's
     locked up,
In the embrace of her covered tomb—exactly as I
     said—
Leave her alone, deserted. Let her die if she
     wants,
Or else live there in her grave, if she feels at
     home there.
We wash our hands of this girl. But either way,
890   Her permit to reside above the earth is canceled.

ANTIGONE:
My tomb, my marriage, my hollow, scraped in
     dirt,
I'm coming home forever, to be held in
With my own people, most of them dead now,
And gone where Persephone welcomes them.
895   I am the last of them that will go under, and my
     death—
It is the worst by far—so much before my time.
As I leave, even so, I feed this one strong hope:
That I will have a loving welcome from my
     father,
More love from you, my mother, and then, love

From you, dear heart, my brother. When you   900
     died,
I took you up, all three, and laid you out,
And poured libations at your graves.
And, Polyneices, look: This is my reward
For taking care of you. I was right, but wisdom
     knows
I would not do it for a child, were I a mother,   905
Not for a husband either. Let them lie, putrefied,
     dead;
I would not defy the city at such cost for their
     sake.

What law can I claim on my side for this choice?
I may have another husband if the first should die
And get another child from a new man if I'm a   910
     widow.
But my mother and my father lie in the land of
     death,
And there is no ground to grow a brother for me
     now.
That is the law I followed when I made you first
     in honor,
Even though Creon thought I did a terrible thing,
A rash and sinful crime, dear heart, my brother.   915
Now he has taken me by force, he is driving me
     down
Unmarried. I've had no man, no wedding
     celebration,
Shared nothing with a husband, never raised a
     child.
My friends and family have abandoned me in
     misery,
And I am going—alive—to the scraped hollow of   920
     the dead.
What have I ever done against divine justice?
How can I expect a god to help me in my
     misery?
To whom should I pray now? Do you see?
They are counting all my reverence to be
Irreverence. If the gods really agree with this,   925
Then suffering should teach me to repent my sin.
But if the sin belongs to those who condemned me,
I hope they suffer every bit as I do now.

CHORUS:
Still she is tossed by gusts of wind;
They tear through her soul as strongly as before.   930

CREON:
  Listen, it's the guards who will weep
  If they don't get a move on now.

ANTIGONE (or CHORUS): [With a cry of pain.]
  That word —
  It's almost death itself!

CREON:
935   I have no hope to give.
  The death sentence stands.

ANTIGONE:
  City of my fathers, Thebes!
  Gods of my people!
  They are taking me against my will.
940   Look at me, O you lords of Thebes:
  I am the last remnant of kings.
  Look what these wretched men are doing to
      me,
  For my pure reverence!

Fourth Stasimon

CHORUS: [To Antigone.]

[Strophe a]

  Courage! Danaë, too, endured
945   The exchange of heavenly light
  For a bronze-bolted prison.
  And there she was kept down
  Secretly in a bedroom tomb.
  She was of noble birth, too, my daughter, O my
      daughter,
950   And Zeus trusted her to mind his golden-rainfall
      child.
        Fate has a terrible power
        That nothing escapes, not wealth,
        Not warfare, not a fortress tower,
        Not even black ships beating against the
          sea.

[944–50: Danaë's father locked her away from men because of an oracle warning him against any son she
might bear. But Zeus visited her in a shower of gold,
and they conceived a child, Perseus.]

[Antistrophe a]

  Another case: Lycurgus was kept down,   955
  And he was a king in Thrace.
  But because of his angry jeering,
  Dionysus had him jailed in a cell of rock,
  And there the terrible flood-force
  Of his madness trickled away, drop by drop, until 960
      he learned,
  At last, that it was a god he had stung in his
      madness
        With those jeering insults.
        For he tried to quench the holy fire,
        Reined in the god-filled women,
        And drove flute-loving Muses into a rage.   965

[Strophe b]

  At the Black Waters,
  Where a thrust of land divides the Bosporus from
      the Sea,
  Lies a city of Thrace known as Salmydéssus.

[955–65: Lycurgus had tried to suppress the worship
of Dionysus, which involved ecstatic rituals. In some
versions of the story, he went mad and killed his son
before being imprisoned.]
[958: Dionysus was believed by the ancient Greeks to
have brought his worship to Greece from Asia, along
with the practice of making wine.]
[964: "God-filled women" — These women, variously
called Maenads, Bacchae, and bacchants, are women
who worship Dionysus through ecstatic dance and song
in the mountains, away from their homes. "God-filled"
means "inspired."]
[965: "Flute-loving Muses" The aulos, usually translated "flute," was a reed instrument; its music was considered to be the most exciting in ancient Greece.]
[966–87: Phineus, a king in Thrace (northern Greece),
had two sons by his first wife, Cleopatra (no relation to
the famous queen of Egypt). This Cleopatra was the
daughter of an Athenian princess who had been stolen
by Boreas, the North Wind, to be his bride. Cleopatra's
sons were blinded by their stepmother after Phineus had
imprisoned their mother and taken a new wife.]
[966: "Black Waters" — The manuscripts are unclear.
The phrase may refer to the Black Sea or the two Dark
Islands at the mouth of the Bosporus.]

War god Ares was hard by and saw the cursèd
    blows
970 When Phineus' two sons were blinded by the
    beast
        He called a wife. Darkness came
        Over the disks that had been eyes,
        That would have looked for vengeance
        To gashing hands, stained in blood,
975   Shuttles torn from the loom
        And used as knives.

[Antistrophe *b*]

The boys melted away
In misery, mourning their own sad fate
And their mother's, for her marriage was hateful
980 Although she was born to be a queen of the
    ancient line,
    Royal in Athens, and she was raised in distant
    caves
        Where her father's tempests blew.
        For he was North Wind, Boreas,
        And she was a child of gods,
985   Swift as horses on a rocky slope.
        But the eternal Fates kept after her,
        Her too, O my daughter.

[*As the chorus bring their ode to an end, the
attendants lead Antigone out through the stage
left wing. Enter Tiresias, led by a boy, through
the stage right wing.*]

TIRESIAS: [*To the chorus, indicating the boy who
guides him.*]
    Gentlemen of Thebes, we two have come by the
        same path;
    He alone has eyesight, and we both see by this:
990 A blind man takes the way his guide directs.

CREON:
    Why, old Tiresias! What brings you here?

TIRESIAS:
    I will speak: I am the soothsayer, and you will
        learn.

CREON:
    Well, I never have rejected your advice.

TIRESIAS:
    That is how you've been steering the city straight.

CREON:
    Yes, I know firsthand how helpful you are, and I   995
        can testify.

TIRESIAS:
    Then know this: Once again, your fate stands on
        a knife-edge.

CREON:
    What is it? Your voice puts my hair on end!

TIRESIAS:
                                              You'll see.
    Listen to what I have read from the signs of my
        art.
    I took my seat, the ancient seat for seeing
        omens—
    Where all the birds that tell the future come to   1000
        rest—
    And I heard a voice I've never known from a
        bird:
    Wild screeching, enraged, utterly meaningless.
    But the thrashing of their wings told me the
        truth:
    They were clawing each other to death with their
        talons.
    I was frightened. Immediately, I tried burnt   1005
        sacrifice.
    The altar had been blazing high, but not one
        spark
    Caught fire in my offerings. The embers went
        out.
    Juice was oozing and dripping from thighbones,
    Spitting and sputtering in clouds of smoke.
    Bladders were bursting open, spraying bile into   1010
        the sky;
    Wrappings of fat fell away from soggy bones.

    And so the ritual failed; I had no omens to read.
    I learned this from the boy who is my guide,

[*1005*: "Burnt sacrifice"—Ancient Greeks offered thighbones wrapped in fat to the gods, along with other inedible parts of a cow or sheep, by burning these parts on
an altar.]

As I am the guide for others. Now, it was *your* idea

1015 That brought this plague down on our city.
Every single altar, every hearth we have,
Is glutted with dead meat from Oedipus' child,
Who died so badly. Birds and dogs gnawed him to bits
That is why the gods no longer hear our prayers,

1020 Reject our sacrifice of flaming thighbones. And that is why
The birds keep back their shrill message-bearing cries:
Because they have fed on a dead man's glistening blood.

Take thought, my son, on all these things:
It's common knowledge, any human being can go wrong.

1025 But even when he does, a man may still succeed:
He may have his share of luck and good advice
But only if he's willing to bend and find a cure
For the trouble he's caused. It's only being stubborn
Proves you're a fool.

So, now, surrender to the dead man.

1030 Stop stabbing away at his corpse. Will it prove your strength
If you kill him again? Listen, my advice is for your benefit.
Learning from good words is sweet when they bring you gain.

CREON:
I hear you, old man: You people keep shooting arrows at me
Like marksmen at a target. Do you think I don't know?

1035 I have a lot of experience with soothsayers. Your whole tribe
Has made market of me from the start. "Benefit"? "Gain"?
If you want to turn a profit, speculate in gold from India
Or go trade with Sardis for electrum and traffic in that.

You'll never put that man down in a grave,
Not even if eagles snatched morsels of his dead flesh   1040
And carried them up to the very throne of Zeus.
I won't shrink from that. And don't you call it "pollution"
Or tell me I have to bury him to fend off miasma—
Surely no human power could pollute a god.

You're terribly clever, old man, but listen to me: 1045
Clever people tend to stumble into shameful traps
When they make a wicked speech sound good
For their personal gain.

TIRESIAS:
This is very sad:
Does any human being know, or even question . . .

CREON: *[Interrupting.]*
What's this? More of your great "common knowledge"?

TIRESIAS:
How powerful good judgment is, compared to   1050
wealth.

CREON:
Exactly. And no harm compares with heedlessness.

TIRESIAS:
Which runs through you like the plague.

CREON:
I have no desire to trade insults with a soothsayer.

TIRESIAS:
But you're doing it. You implied that I make false prophecies.

CREON:
Prophecies? All your tribe wants to make is   1055
money.

[1038: Electrum is an alloy of gold and silver made in Sardis, the city where Croesus, famous for his wealth, had ruled in the sixth century.]

[1042–4: Pollution, miasma—Either an unburied corpse or an unavenged murder was thought to infect the land with miasma, pollution.]

TIRESIAS:
And what about tyrants? Filthy lucre is all you
    want!

CREON:
Remember, you are speaking about your
    commander-in-chief.

TIRESIAS:
I haven't forgotten. It was by my powers that you
    saved the city.

CREON:
Cunning soothsayer! Yes, but you'd rather do
    what's wrong.

TIRESIAS:
1060   You are provoking me. I have a secret we have
    not touched.

CREON:
Well, touch it then. But do not speak as you've
    been paid to do.

TIRESIAS:
Do you really think that's why I've spoken out?

CREON:
You'll never collect your fee; I'm not changing
    my mind.

TIRESIAS:
So be it. But you must know this and know it
    well:
1065   You'll hardly see the sun race around its course
    Before you'll make a trade with your own boy's
        corpse—
    Your only child, born from your guts, traded for
        corpses.

    You took one who dwells above and tossed her
        below,
    You rejected a living soul and peopled a tomb
        with her.
1070   And you took one who belongs down there and
        kept him here,
    Untouched by gods, unburied, unholy, a corpse
        exposed.

[1067: Haemon is Creon's last surviving child.]

The dead are no business of yours; not even the
    gods above
Own any part of them. You've committed
    violence against them.
For this, an ambush awaits you—slow, crippling
    avengers,
Furies sent by Hades and the gods above.   1075
You will be tangled in the net of your own
    crimes.

Now look carefully: Have I been paid to speak
    out?
No. The passage of a little time will prove the
    point;
Men and women will be wailing over death in
    your family.
And all the cities of our enemies are in a rage   1080
For their dead, whose funeral rites were held by
    dogs
Or wild beasts or vultures, and for the stench of
    bodies
Carried by birds to defile their hearths at home.

These are my arrows. You stung me, and I let fly,
In my anger, like a marksman aiming for your   1085
    heart.
And I never miss. You can't outrun the pain.

    [To his guide.]

Take us home, boy.
Let him vent his anger on younger men;
May he learn to cultivate a gentler tongue
And a mind more cogent than he has shown   1090
    today.

    [Exit Tiresias led by the boy through the stage
    right wing.]

CHORUS:
The man is gone, sir. His prophecies were
    amazing,

[1075: Furies—avenging spirits.]
[1080–3: These lines refer to the tradition, not otherwise
mentioned in this play, that Creon left not just Polyneices but all the enemy troops unburied.]

Terrible. Ever since my hair turned white
I'm quite certain he has never sung a prophecy,
Not once, that turned out to be false for the
city.

CREON:
1095   I know that, too. My mind is shaken.
Giving in would be terrible.
But standing firm invites disaster!

CHORUS:
Good judgment is essential, Creon. Take advice.

CREON:
What should I do? Show me. I'll do what you
say.

CHORUS:
1100   Let the girl go. Free her from underground.
And build a tomb for the boy who lies exposed.

CREON:
Really? You think I should give in?

CHORUS:
As quickly as you can, sir, before you're cut
off.
The gods send Harm racing after wicked fools.

CREON:
1105   It's so painful to pull back; it goes against my
heart.
But I cannot fight against necessity.

CHORUS:
Go and do this *now*. Don't send others in your
place.

CREON:
I'll go immediately. Come on, come on,
everyone,
Wherever you are, grab a pick and shovel,
1110   Hurry up! Get over to the place you see.
It's up to me, now my mind has changed.
I put her away, I must be there to release her.
I'm afraid it is best to obey the laws,
Just as tradition has them, all one's life.

*[Exit Creon, with his attendants, through the
stage left wing.]*

CHORUS:

Fifth Stasimon

[Strophe *a*]

God of many names,   1115
Glorious child of Thebes,
Whose mother was bride
To Zeus' deep thunder!
It is you who guard the fame of Italy,
You who look after the embrace, at Eleusis,   1120
Of Demeter, all-welcoming goddess.
O Bacchus, your home is Thebes,
Thebes, the mother of Maenads,
Where River Ismenus gently flows,
And the fierce dragon-teeth were planted.   1125

[Antistrophe *a*]

Torches flash through smoke,
Catch sight of you at Delphi
High above the twin-peaked crag.
The Castalian Stream has seen you
By nymphs of the cave who dance for Bacchus.   1130
The Nysaean Mountains know you, too,

[1115: "God of many names"—Dionysus is known by
a number of names, including the ones the chorus use
here, "Bacchus" and "Iacchus."]
[1117: The line refers to the mother of Bacchus. Semélê
was a princess of Thebes who became pregnant with
Dionysus, after being visited by Zeus, and gave birth to
the infant god when Zeus struck her with thunder.]
[1119: Italy—Dionysus was evidently honored in the
Greek cities of southern Italy.]
[1124–5: The Ismenus flows through Thebes. According
to legend, Cadmus founded Thebes by killing a dragon
and planting its teeth as seeds; where he planted them,
the warriors of Thebes sprouted from the earth.]
[1127: Delphi—Though sacred mainly to Apollo, Delphi was also a principal site for the worship of Dionysus.]
[1129: The Castalian Stream flows from a sacred spring
at Delphi.]
[1130: Nymphs were minor divinities believed to inhabit
caves and other special places.]
[1131: Nysaean Mountains—probably refers to mountains on the long island of Euboea, separated from Attica
by a narrow strait.]

The ivy-covered shores, the coasts,
The green tangles of grapevines.
They are sending you to Thebes: Watch over us,
1135 Hear our sacred hymns that sound for you.

[Strophe b]

You hold Thebes in honor
Above all cities;
Your mother, too,
Thunderstruck woman.
1140 And now we pray: Watch over us:
The violence of plague
Strikes all our people.
Come, your presence is healing.
Soar above Parnassus
1145 Or cross the howling straits of the sea.

[Antistrophe b]

O Leader in the dance of stars,
That circle across the night,
Breathing fire,
O shepherd of dark voices,
1150 Child of Zeus, let us see you now.
Come, O Lord, with your throng of Maenads
Iacchus, steward of joy,
Grant them ecstasy
To dance all night for you.

[Enter Messenger through the stage left wing.]

MESSENGER:
1155 Listen, all you neighbors of Cadmus' family:
The course of our lives never stops; it runs past
    good
Or ill. I'll never declare success or failure for
    anyone.
It's only chance that keeps your boat upright,
And chance that sinks you—good luck or bad is
    all you have.
1160 Soothsayers give no guarantees for human lives.
This Creon—you know, I used to envy him.
He saved the land of Cadmus from its enemies

[1144: Parnassus is the high mountain dividing Thebes
from Delphi.]

And took command as the only ruler of this
    ground.
He set us straight, and he set his house abloom
With well-born sons. Now all of that is gone.   1165
When every source of joy deserts a man,
I don't call him alive: he's an animated corpse.
For my money, you can get as rich as you want,
You can wear the face of a tyrant,
But if you have no joy in this,   1170
Your life's not worth the shadow of a puff of
    smoke.

CHORUS:
What's this new grief that weighs on the king's
    family?

MESSENGER:
Death. And the living are to blame for it.

CHORUS:
Who's the killer? Who's the victim? Speak up!

MESSENGER:
Haemon is dead, killed by his own flesh and   1175
    blood.

CHORUS:
What! His father? Some other relative?

MESSENGER:
He killed himself, in a rage with his father, for
    her death.

CHORUS:
That soothsayer! He had it right.

MESSENGER:
Those are the facts; the judgment is up to you.

[Enter Eurydice through the great doors.]

CHORUS:
Wait, I see her coming, Creon's wife.   1180
Poor Eurydice, has she heard about her son?
Or did she leave her home by chance?

EURYDICE:
Tell me, men of the city—I caught what you said
As I was about to leave the house
To pray for help to the goddess Athena.   1185
I was just sliding the bolt to unlock the door

When word of disaster in the family struck my
   ears.
I fell back into my servants' arms,
Terrified out of my mind.
1190 Please tell me again. What happened?
Speak freely. I am quite used to hearing bad
   news.

MESSENGER:
I will, beloved queen. I was *there*,
And I'll tell you everything, the whole truth.
No point taking off the rough edges;
1195 You'd soon find out I was lying. Truth's right,
Always.
        Well, I went with your husband as his
   guide
To the upper field where the body was lying,
What was left of Polyneices—Cruel!—torn by
   dogs.
First we prayed to the goddess of passageways,
1200 Pluto also, and we begged that their good will
   attend us.
Then we performed the sacred cleansing of the
   corpse,
Gathered up the pieces we could find,
Burned them over fresh-cut boughs,
And heaped up the earth into a tomb,
A high-crested home for him.
1205   Then we went for the girl,
Toward her deadly marriage bed, blanketed with
   rocks.
There was a voice—you could hear it from far
   off—
It sliced through you, wailing around that
   unsanctified tomb.
One of us got Creon to listen. He crept forward;
   cries of misery
1210 Welled up around him, wordless, without
   meaning.
Suddenly he let out a groan of utter despair—
"Oh no! Now *I* am reading signs: Could this be
   the path?

[1199–1200: Hecate, goddess of passageways (including
the one to the underworld), was honored along roads,
especially at intersections. Pluto, also called Hades, is
god of the underworld.]

The one that that leads me to the worst disaster of
   my life?
My son! My son's voice! Neighbors, be quick,
   please help.
On the tomb, look, that gap in the mound—   1215
Stones ripped out—can you slip in through those
   jaws?
Tell me if I am right, that it *is* Haemon,
Unless the gods have robbed me of my mind."

That was the order our master gave, his courage
   gone.
We looked. In the last depth of the tomb,   1220
She was there, we saw her hanging by the neck
On a noose she'd twisted from her own fine
   clothes.
He was there, too, tumbled around her, hugging
   her waist,
Grieving for his marriage lost, gone under—
His father's doing—as he, in misery, kissed his   1225
   bride.
When Creon saw them, he gave a horrible cry
And came up to them. He was in tears, sobbing:
"Poor soul," he said, "how could you do this?
What were you thinking? Had you lost your
   mind?
O my child, come out, please, I beg you on my   1230
   knees."
The boy did not answer. His eyes were fierce.
He fixed them on his father, then spat in his face
And drew his two-edged sword. The father darted
   back,
Dodged the blow. Thwarted, the angry boy
Turned against himself. He took his blade   1235
And leaned on it, drove it half through his lungs.
Then, still conscious, he pulled the girl into the
   curve
Of his sagging embrace. He gasped and panted,
Spattered blood on her white cheek, a spurt of
   scarlet.
Then he was dead. His body lay with hers;   1240
They'd brought their marriage off at last in the
   house of Death—
Which proves the point: In a human life,
It's deadly for bad judgment to embrace a man.

[*Exit Eurydice through the great doors.*]

CHORUS:
What could it mean? The woman's gone inside.
1245　She did not stay for a word, good or bad.

MESSENGER:
I'm astonished, like you. But I feed on hope. Probably,
When she heard her son was dead, she chose to mourn indoors,
Rather than make a public display of grief.
She'll have her servants join in the lament.
1250　She's always planned ahead, to avoid mistakes.

CHORUS:
I don't know. If you ask me, a silence so extreme
Is as dangerous as a flood of silly tears.

MESSENGER:
We'll know soon enough if she's holding something in,
And hiding it secretly in a seething heart.
1255　I'm going into the house. You may be right:
Silence, when extreme, is dangerous.

[Exit Messenger through the great doors. Creon enters through the stage left wing; assisted by his attendants, he is carrying the body of Haemon.]

CHORUS:
Now here is the king himself. He carries in his arms
A Reminder (I hope I'm right to be blunt)
Pointing clearly to the madness that destroys,
1260　And it's no one else's but his own. The sin was his.

[Strophe *a*]

CREON:
Oh, howl for the sins of a stubborn mind,
Evil-minded, death-dealing! O you who are witnesses,
You saw those who killed and those who died,
All in one family,
1265　Cry out against the sacrilege that I called strategy!
Oh, howl, my son, my young son, for your young death.
Ah! Ah!

You were expelled from life
By my bad judgment, never yours.

CHORUS:
Yes, it is late, but you have seen where justice　　1270
lies.

[Strophe *b*]

CREON:
Oh yes:
I have learned, and it is misery.
Some god leapt full force onto my head
And steered me onto a wild path, shaking my
· reins,
And I have trampled joy with sharp hooves.　　1275
Oh weep, weep for the pain of human pain!

[Enter Messenger through the great doors.]

MESSENGER:
You have so many troubles, master, troubles in hand—
You carry them yourself. And troubles at home—
You'll see them for yourself, soon enough, when　　1280
you arrive.

CREON:
What, after this, could be worse?

·MESSENGER:
Your wife is dead, poor woman.
Fresh-killed, a mother to match this dead boy.

[Antistrophe *a*]

CREON:
Howl, howl! O Death, refuge that cannot be appeased,
Why me? Why me, Destroyer?

[To the Messenger.]

　　　　　　　　　　　　　And you,　　1285
What is this noise you're making? Your horrible message?
It is only grief.
I was a man in ruins, and you crushed me again.
Speak to me, my son, tell me, is there more killing?

1290 Ah! Ah!
Is it a woman's sacrifice,
Her death piled on yours?

*[The great doors open, and Eurydice's body is
brought out or revealed.]*

CHORUS (or MESSENGER):
Look, she is here, brought out from the inner
rooms.

[Antistrophe *b*]

CREON:
Oh yes:
1295 Here's the second disaster for my misery to see.
What could be worse? Does fate have more for
me?
A moment ago, I took my dead son in my arms.
Now I see her face to face—my wife. And she is
dead.
Oh weep, weep for the mother in torment, weep
for the child.

MESSENGER:
1300 She died at the altar.
A sharp sword-thrust brought darkness to her eyes,
But first she grieved over Megareus, dead before
his wedding,
And then over Haemon.
Last of all she called out to you,
1305 "These are your crimes, Childkiller!"

[Strophe *c*]

CREON:
Ah! Ah!
I am on wings of fear.
Take a sharp sword, someone.
Why don't you kill me now?
1310 My misery is so huge,
I am dissolved in misery.

[1302: Megareus—Haemon's only brother, son of Creon
and Eurydice. The audience probably knew that Megareus had been sacrificed earlier to ensure victory over
Argos.]

MESSENGER:
Yes, she brought this charge against you as she
died:
"You're to blame for his death, and the other
boy's, too."

CREON:
Tell me, how was she killed?

MESSENGER:
Stabbed in the guts by her own hand,   1315
As soon as she heard what horrors came over her
boy.

[Strophe *d*]

CREON:
The grief is mine, all mine.
I'll never pin the blame on anyone else that's
human.
I was the one, I killed you, poor child.
I did it. It is all true.   1320
Now, my neighbors,
Please take me away,
Take me quickly.
I must not be underfoot;
I am worth less than a nobody.   1325

CHORUS:
A worthy request—if there's any value in
suffering.
Shortest way is strongest way when trouble's afoot.

[Antistrophe *c*]

CREON:
Let it come! Let it come!
I look for the light
Of my last day.   1330
My ultimate fate
Oh, let it come
I never want to face another day!

CHORUS:
That lies in the future. Our duty is for the
present.
Leave your death to the Ones whose concern it   1335
is.

CREON:
  But that's what I long for. I prayed for that.

CHORUS:
  Then don't pray at all.
  A mortal has no escape from fate.

[Antistrophe d]

CREON: *[Praying.]*
  Please take this useless man,
1340 Put him out of your way. He killed you, my
      child,
  Though that is not what he wished.
  And you, too, my wife.

What a miserable wretch I am!
Never to see them again!
On whom can I lean?   1345
Everything I touch turns against me,
My head bows to the fate that has leapt on it.

CHORUS:
Wisdom is supreme for a blesséd life,
And reverence for the gods
Must never cease.   1350
Great words, sprung from arrogance,
Are punished by great blows.
So it is one learns, in old age, to be wise.

—END—

[1348: "Wisdom is supreme for a blesséd life" — *Phronein* (wisdom, good sense) is essential for *eudaimonia* (flourishing, happiness in a broad sense).]

PLATO

In 399 B.C.E., five years after the conclusion of the Peloponnesian War (431–404 B.C.E.), Socrates (469–399)
was charged with impiety, tried by the Athenian court, and executed. To this day scholars debate the character
and significance of this event. What were the real issues that led to Socrates' trial and execution? What was
Athens like in 399, and why were the majority of dicasts (jurors) convinced of Socrates' guilt? Indeed, of what
was Socrates really guilty? What kind of life did he live? How did he defend himself? Does the event teach
us anything in general about the role of philosophy in society and the relation between philosophy and morality
or philosophy and politics?

By the time this trial took place, Socrates was an old man of seventy. He had been born in Athens and left
it only two, perhaps three times, for military service. We know very little of his life. He was a citizen of modest
means, who had a deep commitment to Athens, who was married with young children at the time of the
trial, and who had been associated, in the popular mind, with the Sophists, those itinerant educators of fifth-
century Greece, teachers of language, rhetoric, oratory, argument, and political skills. There is reason to think
that early in his life, when Athens flourished under Pericles and was the hub of Greek intellectual activity,
Socrates had been interested in the investigations of nature of people like Democritus and Anaxagoras. At
some point, however, probably prior to the outbreak of the Peloponnesian War in 431, he turned to other
matters, to the examination of beliefs about ethical notions. He came to hold the primacy of the soul and its
well-being and became committed to seeking knowledge of the good and the truth about the best human
life. His fellow Athenians found him difficult, annoying, an enigma, and perhaps even a threat. Many of his
associates and students, e.g., Alcibiades and Critias, were pro-Spartan, aristocratic, and antidemocratic, and it
is possible that his characteristic conduct, the *elenchos* or critical interrogation, led many to think that he too
opposed the democracy. At the very least, some took him to be a threat to Athenian values or disdainful of
them. If Plato's *Apology* is an accurate portrayal of his defense, he was not able—or perhaps did not even
try—to persuade them otherwise.

Modern students of Greek philosophy and culture have found Socrates to be a richly rewarding subject.
He wrote nothing, but many of Plato's dialogues are taken to reflect with some fidelity his method of
philosophical interrogation, his moral and religious views, and his political thought. But the picture we get
from Plato, especially when it is supplemented from other ancient sources, e.g., Xenophon, Aristophanes, and
Aristotle, is unclear and hard to fill in consistently. Socrates was committed to the primacy of soul or character
in living the best human life. Knowledge was central to that commitment, and hence philosophy, as the quest
for moral knowledge, was also fundamental. Moreover, Socrates was convinced that the best character and
knowledge were closely tied to right conduct, and that harmful or unjust action was self-destructive. But the
intricacies of these and other of his views are complex and have led to much debate, as has the nature of
Socrates' political thought and his primary political allegiance. One wonders how perspicuous was the average
Athenian's understanding of this man.

While many Athenians may have been satisfied, if not pleased, with the verdict against Socrates and his
execution, some clearly were not. Among this group of Socrates' friends, associates, and disciples was a young
Athenian aristocrat who labored for a lifetime under the shadow of these events. Later in life he reports the
disturbing effects that these events had on him and his thinking:

When I was a young man I had the same ambitions as many others: I thought of entering public life as soon as I came of age. And certain happenings in public affairs favored me. . . . a new government was set up [the Thirty Tyrants]. Some of these men happened to be relatives and acquaintances of mine, and they invited me to join them. . . . I thought that they were going to lead the city out of the unjust life she had been living and establish her in the path of justice.

But this young aristocrat realized he was wrong when this government acted corruptly, on one occasion commanding "Socrates, an older friend of mine whom I should not hesitate to call the wisest and justest man of that time," to participate in the assassination of Leon of Salamis, "planning thereby to make Socrates willy-nilly a party to their actions." He refused, to his credit, but later, after the democracy had been reinstated in 403,

certain powerful persons brought into court this same friend Socrates, . . . charged him with impiety, and the jury condemned and put to death the very man who, at the time when his accusers were themselves in misfortune and exile, had refused to have a part in the unjust arrest of one of their friends.

Here Plato (427–347), in his famous Seventh Letter, reflects on the pivotal role that Socrates' trial had had on his life and on his thinking about justice, human nature, and the state.

Plato was born in 427, probably in Athens. Both his father Ariston and his mother Perictione were of distinguished lineage; indeed, Perictione traced her descent from the great lawgiver Solon. Critias, Perictione's cousin, was one of the most violent and most hated of the Thirty Tyrants of 404, the oligarchic government which Sparta enforced at the conclusion of the war, while Charmides, her brother, was also a member of the Thirty and one of the overseers of the Piraeus, the Athenian port. Plato had two brothers, Glaucon and Adiemantus, who appear as major players in the *Republic*, and one sister, Potone, whose son Speusippus was appointed head of the Academy (see below) upon Plato's death.

We know nothing in detail of Plato's youth. Doubtless he would have had the normal Athenian education in culture and gymnastics that he describes in the *Republic*. Clearly he developed a high degree of literary skill and studied the various subjects taught by the Sophists and natural investigators. He became acquainted with Socrates no later than when he was twenty and, given his status, certainly had military service, probably in the cavalry.

After Socrates' death, Plato and some other disciples left Athens to join Euclides, a close associate of Socrates, in Megara, where he remained until 395 or so, when he would have been called to serve in the Corinthian War. During the next several years, we may surmise, Plato wrote many of the early, short dialogues in which Socrates is the chief character and which aim to clarify and portray the Socratic life. These dialogues include the *Apology, Crito, Laches, Lysis, Charmides, Euthyphro, Ion, Hippias Major*, and *Hippias Minor*.

When he was forty, in 387, Plato made the first of three visits to Italy and Sicily. Later sources claim that his trip was motivated by his desire to meet the Pythagorean philosophers and religious thinkers there, especially the important mathematician, Archytas of Tarentum, who became a lifelong friend and may have influenced Plato's belief in the immortality of the soul and the importance of mathematics to philosophy. While in Sicily, moreover, Plato met Dion, then twenty, the brother-in-law of the powerful tyrant of Syracuse, Dionysus I. With Dion Plato developed a close, indeed intimate relationship. Dion was a brilliant and receptive student who quickly became Plato's disciple and a convinced Socratic, committed to the life of virtue and goodness and opposed to the hedonistic, luxurious style of Italian and Sicilian life.

Once back in Athens, in 387, Plato purchased some buildings and a grove of trees nearly a mile outside the walls of Athens. There he founded a society or religious fellowship (*thiasos*), on the model of an Orphic-Pythagorean religious association, which he called the Academy, after the hero Hecademus, to whom the spot was sacred. Until his death he was its director, organizing and coordinating its activities, from meals held according to fairly strict rules, to lectures, discussions, guided research, and visits by foreign scholars. Among the many subjects studied and examined in the Academy, philosophical inquiry, mathematics, and moral-political thought were probably preeminent. During the 380s, moreover, Plato wrote further dialogues, but these dialogues develop his own thinking, on Socratic foundations, on matters such as moral character, virtue (*arete*), inquiry, knowledge, metaphysics, and more. These writings include the *Protagoras, Gorgias,* and *Meno,* followed by the middle dialogues, in which his own thinking emerges in full form, the *Phaedo, Symposium, Republic, Phaedrus,* and *Cratylus.* In these dialogues, he first displays his famous theory of Forms or Ideas, develops his understanding of philosophical inquiry, its stages and ultimate goal, sketches an account of philosophical education and moral development, identifies various capacities and states of the soul in an increasingly subtle psychology, and works out the features of his moral view and its political implications.

In 368 Dionysus I of Syracuse died and was replaced immediately by his inexperienced and insecure son Dionysus II. To Dion, who was dazzled by the possibilities of Plato's moral and political thinking and all too unrealistic in his expectations, the situation seemed propitious. He persuaded the young ruler to invite Plato to Syracuse, and he himself wrote to Plato suggesting that the young Dionysus might be an ideal subject for Plato's proposals about philosophy and political rule as expressed in the *Republic.* Whatever Plato's hopes or misgivings, he accepted the invitation but, upon arriving in Syracuse, found a situation of jealousy, conflict, and intrigue. Eventually, Dion was expelled from Sicily, and, when war broke out with Carthage, Plato was sent home. By 365 Dion had joined Plato in Athens, where for four years Plato directed research, taught, and wrote, all the while keeping abreast of affairs in Sicily. By this time too Plato's disenchantment with politics had grown deeper; it was directed not only at Dionysus and Sicily but also at Athens and the city's misguided efforts to regain her power, her empire, and her prestige.

By 362 a new invitation had arrived from Dionysus II, who showed signs of the commitment to philosophy that Plato had long sought. Full of doubts, Plato once again sailed to Sicily, and once again his plans came to naught. The young Dionysus refused Plato's directions for philosophical education, began to sell off Dion's property while he was still a virtual exile, and in the end held Plato under house arrest. Only the intervention of Plato's old friend Archytas enabled him to escape and return to Athens.

Amid all this turmoil, Plato had begun a serious deepening of his own thinking about knowledge, inquiry, reality, politics, morality, and law. He wrote or at least began an extraordinarily rich set of dialogues, the *Parmenides, Theaetetus, Politicus,* and *Sophist.* In the remaining thirteen years of his life, he completed these works, began several new ones, and continued to direct the affairs of the Academy. He died in 347, leaving unfinished his last great work, the *Laws.* In it Plato's sense of political realism emerges in full force. He attempts to set out in detail the structure, goals, and character of a *polis* that is both ideal and realistic, a *polis* in which expert rulers play their roles alongside an elaborate legal order that coordinates philosophy, political life, religion, and ethics.

Since the 360s Plato had appreciated the demands on the worldly career of philosophy; already in the *Republic* he had tried to reconcile the philosopher's religious goals, his aspiration to transcendence, with his political responsibilities and the complex psychology of the embodied soul. By the time he begins the *Laws,* Plato is fully aware of the limitations on human hopes and possibilities. The prominence of law and all its accoutrements in his last work expresses that awareness and all that comes with it, the sober recognition that human life is a fragile but difficult blending of this world and beyond and that any genuine understanding of philosophy and the moral-political life must appreciate that blending to the fullest.

Recommended Readings

Allen, R. E. *Socrates and Legal Obligation.* Minneapolis: University of Minnesota Press, 1980.

Annas, Julia. *An Introduction to Plato's Republic.* Oxford: Oxford University Press, 1981.

Brickhouse, Tom, and Nicholas Smith. *Socrates on Trial.* Princeton: Princeton University Press, 1989.

Cross, R. C., and A. D. Woozley. *Plato's Republic. A Philosophical Commentary.* London. Macmillan, 1964.

Dover, K. J. *Greek Popular Morality in the Time of Plato and Aristotle*. Oxford: Blackwell's, 1974.

Gulley, Norman. *The Philosophy of Socrates*. London: Macmillan, 1968.

Guthrie, W.K.C. *A History of Greek Philosophy*. Vols. III–IV. Cambridge: Cambridge University Press, 1969, 1975, 1978.

Irwin, T. H. *Classical Thought*. Oxford: Oxford University Press, 1989.

Irwin, T. H. *Plato's Ethics*. Oxford: Oxford University Press, 1995.

Irwin, T. H. *Plato's Moral Theory*. Oxford: Oxford University Press, 1977.

Kraut, Richard (ed.). *The Cambridge Companion to Plato*. Cambridge: Cambridge University Press, 1992.

Kraut, Richard. *Socrates and the State*. Princeton: Princeton University Press, 1984.

Morgan, Michael L. *Platonic Piety: Philosophy and Ritual in Fourth Century Athens*. New Haven: Yale University Press, 1990.

Murphy, N. R. *The Interpretation of Plato's Republic*. Oxford: Oxford University Press, 1951.

Okin, Susan Moller. *Women in Western Political Thought*. Princeton: Princeton University Press, 1979.

Price, Anthony W. *Love and Friendship in Plato and Aristotle*. Oxford: Oxford University Press, 1989.

Reeve, C.D.C. *Philosopher-Kings*. Princeton: Princeton University Press, 1988.

Reeve, C.D.C. *Socrates in the Apology*. Indianapolis: Hackett, 1989.

Santas, Gerismos. *Socrates*. London: Routledge, 1979.

Vlastos, Gregory (ed.). *The Philosophy of Socrates*. Garden City: Doubleday, 1971.

Vlastos, Gregory (ed.). *Plato*. Vol. II. Garden City: Doubleday, 1970.

Vlastos, Gregory. *Socrates, Ironist and Moral Philosopher*. Ithaca: Cornell, 1991.

White, N. P. *A Companion to Plato's Republic*. Indianapolis: Hackett, 1979.

Woozley, A. D. *Law and Obedience: The Arguments of Plato's Crito*. London: Duckworth, 1970.

EUTHYPHRO

2a EUTHYPHRO:[1] What's new, Socrates, to make you leave the Lyceum,[2] where you usually spend your time, to spend it here today at the court of the King Archon?[3] Surely, *you* don't have some sort of lawsuit before the King, as I do.

SOCRATES: *Athenians* don't call it a lawsuit, Euthyphro, but an indictment.[4]

EUTHYPHRO: What? Someone has indicted you, b apparently, for I'm not going to accuse *you* of indicting someone else!

SOCRATES: No, I certainly haven't.

EUTHYPHRO: But someone else has indicted you?

SOCRATES: Exactly.

EUTHYPHRO: Who is he?

SOCRATES: I hardly know the man myself, Euthyphro. He's young and unknown, it seems. But I believe his name's Meletus. He belongs to the Pitthean deme—if you recall a Meletus from that deme, with straight hair, not much of a beard, and a slightly hooked nose?

EUTHYPHRO: No, I don't recall him, Socrates. But tell me, what indictment has he brought against you? c

SOCRATES: What indictment? Not a trivial one, it seems to me. I mean, it's no small thing for a young man to have come to know such an important matter. You see, according to him, he knows how the young men are being corrupted, and who's corrupting them. He's probably a wise man, who's seen that my own ignorance is corrupting his contemporaries, and is coming to accuse me to their mother the city, so to speak. In fact, he seems to me to be the only one who's starting up in politics correctly. For it is correct to take care of the young first, to make them the best d possible, just as it's reasonable for a good farmer to take care of the young plants first, and all the others afterward. And so Meletus, too, is presumably first weeding out those of us who corrupt the young shoots, 3a as he claims. Then, after that, he'll clearly take care of the older people and bring about the greatest goods, both in number and in quality, for the city. That, at any rate, is the likely outcome of such a start.

EUTHYPHRO: I hope it happens, Socrates, but I'm terribly afraid the opposite may result. You see, by attempting to do an injustice to you, it seems to me he's simply starting out by wronging the city at its very hearth.[5] Tell me, what on earth does he say you're doing that corrupts the young?

SOCRATES: Strange things, my excellent friend, at any rate on first hearing: he says I'm an inventor b of gods. And because I invent new gods, and don't acknowledge the old ones, he's indicted me for the latter's sake, so he says.

From *The Trials of Socrates*, translated and edited by C.D.C. Reeve (Indianapolis: Hackett Publishing Company, 2002). Copyright © 2002. Reprinted by permission of the publishers.

1. [Euthyphro was a *mantis*, or prophet (3b9–c5, 3e3), a self-proclaimed authority on Greek religion (4e4–5a2), who takes very literally the stories embodied in its myths (5c3–6b6). — C.D.C.R.]

2. [The Lyceum was one of three great gymnasia outside the city walls of Athens (the others were the Cynosarges and the Academy).]

3. [The nine archons, chosen annually, were the chief public officials in Athens: one was civilian head of state, one was head of the army (*polemarchos*), and six had judicial roles (*thesmothetai*). The King Archon dealt with important religious matters (such as the indictment against Socrates for impiety) and also with homicide (the subject of Euthyphro's indictment). His court or porch (*stoa*) was in the marketplace (*agora*).]

4. [A lawsuit (*dikē*) was either private (*dikē idia*) or public (*dikē dēmosia*). A public suit was one thought to affect the community as a whole, and so any free adult male citizen could prosecute it. An indictment (*graphē*) was a specific sort of public suit.]

5. [The reference is to the communal hearth in the Prytaneum (*Apology* 36d7 note), which was the symbolic center of Athens.]

EUTHYPHRO: I understand, Socrates. That's no doubt because you say your daimonic sign comes to you on each occasion. So he has written this indictment against you for making innovations in religious matters and comes before the court to slander you, knowing that such things are easy to misrepresent to the majority of people. Why, they even mock *me* as if I were crazy, when I speak in the Assembly on religious

c matters and predict the future for them! And yet not one of my predictions has failed to come true. But all the same, they envy anyone like ourselves. We mustn't give them a thought, though. Just meet them head on.

SOCRATES: Yes, my dear Euthyphro, but being mocked is presumably nothing to worry about. Athenians, it seems to me, aren't much concerned if they think someone's clever, so long as he doesn't teach his own wisdom. But if they think he's making other people wise like himself, they get angry, whether out

d of envy, as you say, or for some other reason.

EUTHYPHRO: As to that, I certainly have no desire to test their attitude toward *me*.

SOCRATES: Don't worry. They probably think you rarely put yourself at other people's disposal, and aren't willing to teach your own wisdom. But I'm afraid they think my love of people makes me tell whatever little I know unreservedly to any man, not only without charging a fee, but even glad to lose money, so long as someone cares to listen to me. So, as I was just saying, if they were going to mock me,

e as you say they do you, there'd be nothing unpleasant about their spending time in the law court playing around and laughing. But if they're going to be serious, the outcome's unclear, except to you prophets.

EUTHYPHRO: Well, it will probably come to nothing, Socrates, and you'll fight your case satisfactorily, as I think I'll fight mine.

SOCRATES: But now, Euthyphro, what *is* this case of yours? Are you defending or prosecuting?

EUTHYPHRO: Prosecuting.

SOCRATES: Whom?

EUTHYPHRO: Someone I'm again thought to be

4a crazy for prosecuting.

SOCRATES: What's that? Is your prosecution a wild goose chase?

EUTHYPHRO: The goose is long past chasing: he's quite old.

SOCRATES: Who is he?

EUTHYPHRO: My father.

SOCRATES: My good man! Your own *father*?

EUTHYPHRO: Yes, indeed.

SOCRATES: But what's the charge? What's the lawsuit about?

EUTHYPHRO: Murder, Socrates.

SOCRATES: In the name of Heracles![6] Well, Euthyphro, I suppose most people don't know how it can be correct to do this. I mean, I can't imagine any ordinary person taking that action correctly, but only someone who's already far advanced in wisdom. b

EUTHYPHRO: Yes, by Zeus,[7] Socrates, far advanced indeed.

SOCRATES: Is the man your father killed one of your relatives then? Of course he must be, mustn't he? You'd hardly be prosecuting him for murder on behalf of a stranger.

EUTHYPHRO: It's ridiculous, Socrates, for you to think it makes any difference whether the dead man's a stranger or a relative. It's ridiculous not to see that the sole consideration should be whether the killer killed justly or not. If he did, let him go, if he didn't, prosecute—if, that is to say, the killer shares your own hearth and table. For the pollution's the same if you c knowingly associate with such a person and don't cleanse yourself and him by bringing him to justice.

In point of fact, though, the victim was a day laborer of mine, and when we were farming on Naxos,[8] he worked the land there for us. Well, he got drunk, became enraged with one of our household slaves, and cut his throat. So my father tied him hand and foot, threw him in a ditch, and sent a man here to find out from the official interpreter[9] what should be done. In the meantime, he ignored and neglected his captive as a murderer, thinking it mattered nothing d

---

6. [Heracles (Hercules) was a hero of legendary strength. His famous labors—twelve extraordinarily difficult tasks—are alluded to at *Apology* 22a6–8.]

7. [The greatest of the Greek gods (5d6–6a1) and king of the Greek pantheon. It was common, and not blasphemous, to swear by him, and by the other gods.]

8. [A large island southeast of Athens.]

9. [The *exēgētai* ("interpreters") were three men chosen—perhaps by the Delphic Oracle (*Apology* 21a4 note)—with advising people on difficult legal cases involving bloodshed and other such religious matters.]

if he did die. And that's just what happened: hunger, cold, and being tied up caused his death before the messenger got back from the interpreter.

That's precisely why my father and my other relatives are angry with me: because I'm prosecuting my father for murder on the murderer's behalf, when my father didn't even kill him, so they claim, and when, even if he definitely did kill him, it's wrong—since the dead man was a murderer—to concern yourself with the victim in that case. You see, it's impious, they say, for a son to prosecute his father for murder.
e Little do they know, Socrates, about the gods' position on the pious and the impious!

SOCRATES: But, in the name of Zeus, Euthyphro, do you think *you* have such exact knowledge about the positions the gods take, and about the pious and the impious, that in the face of these events, you've no fear of acting impiously yourself in bringing your father to trial?

EUTHYPHRO: I'd be no use at all, Socrates, and Euthyphro would be no different from the majority
5a of people, if I didn't have exact knowledge of all such things.

SOCRATES: So, my excellent Euthyphro, the best thing, it seems, is for me to become your student, and to challenge Meletus on this very point before his case comes to trial, telling him that even in the past I always considered it of great importance to know about religious matters, and that now, when he says I've done wrong through improvising and innovating concerning the gods, I've become your student. Shouldn't I say to him, "Meletus, if you agree that Euthyphro is wise
b about the gods, you should also regard me as correctly acknowledging them and drop the charge. But if you don't agree, prosecute this teacher of mine rather than me, for corrupting the old men—myself and his own father, me by his teaching, and his father by admonishment and punishment." If he isn't convinced by me, and doesn't drop the charge or prosecute you instead of me, shouldn't I say the same things in court as in my challenge to him?

EUTHYPHRO: Yes, by Zeus, Socrates, and if he tried bringing an indictment against *me*, I think I'd soon find
c his weak spots, and the question in court would very quickly be about him rather than about me.

SOCRATES: I realize that as well as you do, my dear friend, and that's why I'm eager to become your student. I know that this Meletus, as well as others no doubt, pretends not to notice *you* at all, whereas he has seen *me* so sharply and so easily that he has indicted me for impiety.

Now then, in the name of Zeus, tell me what you were just claiming to know so clearly. What sort of thing would you say the holy and the unholy are, whether in cases of murder or of anything else? Or
d isn't the pious itself the same as itself in every action? And conversely, isn't the impious entirely the opposite of the pious? And whatever's going to count as impious, isn't it itself similar to itself—doesn't it, as regards impiety, possess one single characteristic?

EUTHYPHRO: Absolutely, Socrates.

SOCRATES: Tell me, then, what do you say the pious and the impious are?

EUTHYPHRO: Very well, I say that what's pious is precisely what I'm doing now: prosecuting those who commit an injustice, such as murder or temple robbery, or those who've done some other such wrong, regardless of whether they're one's father or one's mother or anyone else whatever. Not prosecuting
e them, on the other hand, is what's impious.

Why, Socrates, look at the powerful evidence I have that the law requires this—evidence I've already offered to show other people that such actions are right, that one must not let an impious person go, no matter who he may happen to be. You see, those very people acknowledge Zeus as the best and most just of the gods, and yet they agree that he put his own father in fetters
6a because he unjustly swallowed down his children, and that *he*, in his turn, castrated *his* father because of other similar injustices.[10] Yet they're extremely angry with *me*, because I'm prosecuting *my* father for his injustice. And so they contradict themselves in what they say about the gods and about me.

SOCRATES: Could this be the reason, Euthyphro, I face indictment, that when people say such things about the gods, I find them somehow hard to accept? That, it seems, is why some people will say I'm a

10. [Cronus mutilated his father, Uranus (Sky), by cutting off his genitals when he was copulating with Gaea (Earth). He ate the children he had with his sister Rhea. Aided by her, however, their son Zeus escaped, overthrew Cronus, and fettered him. See Hesiod, *Theogony* 137–210, 456–508.]

wrongdoer. But now if you, who know so much about such matters, share these views, it seems that the rest
b of us must assent to them too. I mean, what can we possibly say in reply, when we admit ourselves that we know nothing about them? But tell me, by the god of friendship,[11] do you really believe those stories are true?

EUTHYPHRO: Yes, and still more amazing things, Socrates, that the majority of people don't know.

SOCRATES: And do you believe that there really is war among the gods? And terrible hostilities and battles, and other such things of the sort the poets relate, and that the good painters embroider on our
c sacred objects—I'm thinking particularly of the robe covered with embroideries of such scenes that's carried up to the Acropolis at the Great Panathenaean festival?[12] Are we to say that these are true, Euthyphro?

EUTHYPHRO: Not only those, Socrates, but as I mentioned just now, I will, if you like, tell you lots of other things about religious matters that I'm sure you'll be amazed to hear.

SOCRATES: I wouldn't be surprised. But tell me about them some other time, when we've the leisure. Now, however, try to answer more clearly the very
d question I asked before. You see, my friend, you didn't teach me adequately earlier when I asked what the pious was, but you told me that what you're now doing is pious, prosecuting your father for murder.

EUTHYPHRO: Yes, and what I said was true, Socrates.

SOCRATES: Perhaps. But surely, Euthyphro, there are also many other things you call pious.

EUTHYPHRO: Yes, indeed.

SOCRATES: Do you remember, then, that what I urged you to do wasn't to teach me about one or two of the many pieties, but rather about the form itself,

11. [Namely, Zeus.]

12. [The Acropolis, set on the steep rocky hill that dominates Athens, was the central fortress and principal sanctuary of the goddess Athena. It was the site of the Parthenon, as well as of other temples. The Great Panathenaean festival took place every four years and was a more elaborate version of the yearly festival that marked Athena's birthday. At it, her statue in the Parthenon received a new robe embroidered with scenes from the mythical battle of the gods and the giants.]

by virtue of which all the pieties are pious? You see, you said, I believe, that it was by virtue of one characteristic that the impieties are impious, and the pieties pious. Or don't you remember?   e

EUTHYPHRO: I do indeed.

SOCRATES: Then teach me what that characteristic itself is, in order that by concentrating on it and using it as a model, I may call pious any action of yours or anyone else's that is such as it, and may deny to be pious whatever isn't such as it.

EUTHYPHRO: If that's what you want, Socrates, that's what I'll tell you.

SOCRATES: That *is* what I want.

EUTHYPHRO: In that case: what's loved by the gods is pious, and what's not loved by the gods is impious. 7a

SOCRATES: Excellent, Euthyphro! You've now given the sort of answer I was looking for. Whether it's true, however, that I don't know. But clearly you'll go on to demonstrate fully that what you say *is* true.

EUTHYPHRO: Yes, indeed.

SOCRATES: Come on, then, let's examine what it is we're saying. A god-loved thing or a god-loved person is pious, whereas a god-hated thing or a god-hated person is impious. And the pious isn't the same as the impious, but its exact opposite. Isn't that what we're saying?

EUTHYPHRO: It is indeed.

SOCRATES: And does it seem to be true?

EUTHYPHRO: It does seem so, Socrates.   b

SOCRATES: And haven't we also said that the gods quarrel and differ with one another, and that there's mutual hostility among them?

EUTHYPHRO: Indeed, we did say that.

SOCRATES: But what are the issues, my good friend, on which differences produce hostility and anger? Let's examine it this way. If you and I differed about which of two groups was more numerous, would our differences on this issue make us hostile and angry toward one another? Or would we turn to calculation and quickly resolve our differences?   c

EUTHYPHRO: Of course.

SOCRATES: Again, if we differed about which was larger or smaller, we'd turn to measurement and quickly put a stop to our difference.

EUTHYPHRO: That's right.

SOCRATES: And we'd turn to weighing, I imagine, to settle a dispute about which was heavier or lighter?

EUTHYPHRO: Certainly.

SOCRATES: Then what sorts of issues *would* make us angry and hostile toward one another if we disagreed about them and were unable to reach a settlement? Perhaps you can't say just offhand. But examine, while I'm speaking, whether they're issues about the just and unjust, fine and shameful, good and bad. Whenever we become enemies, aren't these the issues on which disagreement and an inability to reach a settlement make enemies of us—both you and I and all other human beings?

EUTHYPHRO: That is the difference, Socrates, and those are the things it has to do with.

SOCRATES: And what about the *gods*, Euthyphro? If indeed they differ, mustn't it be about those same things?

EUTHYPHRO: Absolutely.

SOCRATES: Then, according to your account, my noble Euthyphro, different sets of gods, too, consider different things to be just, or fine or shameful, or good or bad. For if they didn't differ about these, they wouldn't quarrel, would they?

EUTHYPHRO: That's right.

SOCRATES: Then are the very things that each group of them regards as fine, good, and just also the ones they love, and are the opposites of these the ones they hate?

EUTHYPHRO: Of course.

SOCRATES: But the very same things, so you say, that some gods consider to be just and others unjust are also the ones that lead them to quarrel and war with one another when they have disputes about them. Isn't that right?

EUTHYPHRO: It is.

SOCRATES: Then the same things, it seems, are both hated and loved by the gods, and so the same things would be both god-hated and god-loved.

EUTHYPHRO: It seems that way.

SOCRATES: So, on your account, Euthyphro, the same things would be both pious and impious.

EUTHYPHRO: Apparently.

SOCRATES: So, you haven't answered my question, my excellent friend. You see, I wasn't asking you what the self-same thing is that's both pious and impious. But a thing that's god-loved is, it seems, also god-hated. It follows, Euthyphro, that it wouldn't be at all surprising if what you're now doing in prosecuting your father

was something pleasing to Zeus but displeasing to Cronus and Uranus, or lovable to Hephaestus and displeasing to Hera,[13] and similarly for any other gods who may differ from one another on the matter.

EUTHYPHRO: But, Socrates, I think that on this point, at least, none of the gods do differ—that anyone who has unjustly killed another should be punished.

SOCRATES: Is that so? Well, what about men, Euthyphro? Have you never heard them arguing that someone who has killed unjustly or done anything else unjustly should *not* be punished?

EUTHYPHRO: Why yes, they never stop arguing like that, whether in the law courts or in other places. For people who've committed all sorts of injustices will do or say anything to escape punishment.

SOCRATES: But do they agree, Euthyphro, that they've committed injustice, and, in spite of agreeing, do they still say that they shouldn't be punished?

EUTHYPHRO: No, they certainly don't say that.

SOCRATES: So it isn't just anything that they'll do or say. You see, I don't think they'd dare to say or argue that if they act *unjustly*, they should not be punished. Instead, I think they deny acting unjustly, don't they?

EUTHYPHRO: That's true, they do.

SOCRATES: So they don't argue that someone who acts unjustly should not be punished, though they do, perhaps, argue about *who* acted unjustly, *what* his unjust action consisted of, and *when* he did it.

EUTHYPHRO: That's true.

SOCRATES: Then doesn't the very same thing happen to the gods as well—if indeed they do quarrel about just and unjust actions, as on your account they do, and if one lot says that others have done wrong, and another lot denies it? For surely no one, my excellent friend, whether god or human being, dares to say that one who acts unjustly should not be punished.

13. [Hephaestus, the god of fire and of blacksmithing, was armor maker to the gods. His mother, Hera, the wife and sister of Zeus (4b3 note), threw him off Olympus because he was lame and deformed. This pleased her, not him. In revenge, he made her a throne that held her captive when she sat on it. This pleased him, not her. Similarly, Cronus cannot have been pleased at being fettered by Zeus (see 6a3 note).]

EUTHYPHRO: Yes, what you say is true, Socrates, at least the main point.

SOCRATES: I think that men and gods who argue, Euthyphro, if indeed gods really do argue, argue instead about *actions*. It's about some action that they differ, some of them saying that it was done justly, others unjustly. Isn't that so?

EUTHYPHRO: Of course.

SOCRATES: Come then, my dear Euthyphro, and 9a teach me, too, that I may become wiser. A man committed murder while employed as a day laborer and died as a result of being tied up before the master who tied him up found out from the proper authorities what to do about him. What evidence do you have that all the gods consider this man to have been killed unjustly, and that it's right for a *son* to prosecute and denounce his *father* for murder on behalf of such a b man? Come, try to give me a clear proof that all gods undoubtedly consider this action to be right. If you can give me adequate proof of that, I'll never stop praising your wisdom.

EUTHYPHRO: But presumably that's no small task, Socrates, though I could of course prove it to you very clearly.

SOCRATES: I understand. You think I'm a slower learner than the jury, since it's clear that you'll prove to *them* that those actions of your father's were unjust and that the gods all hate them.

EUTHYPHRO: I'll prove it to them very clearly, Socrates, provided they'll listen to what I say.

SOCRATES: They'll listen all right, provided you c seem to speak well. But a thought occurred to me while you were speaking, and I'm still examining it in my own mind: "Suppose Euthyphro so taught me that I became thoroughly convinced that all the gods do consider a death like that to be unjust. What more would I have learned from Euthyphro about what the pious and the impious are? *That action* would indeed be god-hated, so it seems. Yet it became evident just now that the pious and the impious aren't defined by that fact, since it became evident that what's god-hated is also god-loved. So I'll let you off on that point, Euthyphro. If you like, let's suppose that all the gods consider the action unjust, and that d they all hate it. Is that, then, the correction we're now making in the account, that what *all* the gods hate is impious while what they *all* love is pious, and that

whatever some love and others hate is neither or both? Is that how you'd now like us to define the pious and the impious?

EUTHYPHRO: What's to prevent it, Socrates?

SOCRATES: Nothing on my part, Euthyphro. But you examine your own view, and whether by assuming it you'll most easily teach me what you promised.

EUTHYPHRO: All right, I'd say that the pious is what all the gods love, and its opposite, what all the e gods hate, is the impious.

SOCRATES: Then aren't we going to examine that in turn, Euthyphro, to see whether what we said is true? Or are we going to let it alone and accept it from ourselves and from others just as it stands? And if someone merely asserts that something is so, are we going to concede that it's so? Or are we going to examine what the speaker says?

EUTHYPHRO: We're going to examine it. However, I for my part think that this time what we said *is* true.

SOCRATES: Soon, my good friend, we'll be better able to tell. Consider the following: is the pious loved 10a by the gods because it's pious? Or is it pious because it's loved?

EUTHYPHRO: I don't know what you mean, Socrates.

SOCRATES: All right, I'll try to put it more clearly. We speak of a thing's being carried or carrying, and of its being led or leading, and of being seen or seeing. And you understand that these things are all different from one another and how they differ?

EUTHYPHRO: I think I understand, at any rate.

SOCRATES: Then is there also something that's loved, and is it different from something that's loving?

EUTHYPHRO: Certainly.

SOCRATES: Then tell me whether the carried thing is a carried thing because it's carried or because b of something else.

EUTHYPHRO: No, it's because of that.

SOCRATES: Again, the led thing is so, then, because it's led and the seen thing because it's seen?

EUTHYPHRO: Of course.

SOCRATES: So it's not seen because it's a seen thing; on the contrary, it's a seen thing because it's seen; nor is it because it's a led thing that it's led, rather it's because it's led that it's a led thing; nor is something carried because it's a carried thing, rather it's a carried thing because it's carried. So is what I mean completely clear, Euthyphro? I mean this: if something's changed in some way or affected in some way, it's not changed because it's a changed thing; rather, it's a changed thing because it's changed. Nor is it affected because it's an affected thing; rather, it's an affected thing because it's affected. Or don't you agree with that?

EUTHYPHRO: I do.

SOCRATES: Then isn't a loved thing, too, either a thing changed or a thing affected by something?

EUTHYPHRO: Of course.

SOCRATES: And so the same holds of it as of our earlier examples: it's not because it's a loved thing that it's loved by those who love it; rather it's because it's loved that it's a loved thing?

EUTHYPHRO: Necessarily.

SOCRATES: Now what are we saying about the pious, Euthyphro? On your account, isn't it loved by all the gods?

EUTHYPHRO: Yes.

SOCRATES: So is that because it's pious or because of something else?

EUTHYPHRO: No, it's because it's pious.

SOCRATES: So it's loved because it's pious, not pious because it's loved?

EUTHYPHRO: Apparently.

SOCRATES: On the other hand, what's god-loved is loved—that is to say, god-loved—because the gods love it?

EUTHYPHRO: Certainly.

SOCRATES: Then the god-loved is not what's pious, Euthyphro, nor is the pious what's god-loved, as you claim, but one differs from the other.

EUTHYPHRO: How so, Socrates?

SOCRATES: Because we agreed that the pious is loved because it's pious, not pious because it's loved. Didn't we?

EUTHYPHRO: Yes.

SOCRATES: The god-loved, on the other hand, is so because it is loved by the gods; it's god-loved by the very fact of being loved. But it's not because it's god-loved that it's being loved.

EUTHYPHRO: That's true.

SOCRATES: But if the god-loved and the pious were really the same thing, my dear Euthyphro, then, if the pious were loved because it's pious, what's god-loved would in turn be loved because it's god-loved; and if what's god-loved were god-loved because it was loved by the gods, the pious would in turn be pious because it was loved by them. But, as it is, you can see that the two are related in the opposite way, as things entirely different from one another. For one of them is lovable because it's loved, whereas the other is loved because it's lovable.

And so, Euthyphro, when you're asked what the pious is, it looks as though you don't want to reveal its being to me, but rather to tell me one of its affections—that this happens to the pious, that it's loved by all the gods. What explains it's being loved, however, you still haven't said. So please don't keep it hidden from me, but rather say again from the beginning what it is that explains the pious' being loved by the gods or having some other affection— for we won't disagree about which ones it has. Summon up your enthusiasm, then, and tell me what the pious and the impious are.

EUTHYPHRO: But Socrates, I have no way of telling you what I have in mind. For whatever proposals we put forward keep somehow moving around and won't stay put.

SOCRATES: Your proposals, Euthyphro, seem to be the work of my ancestor, Daedalus! Indeed, if I were to state them and put them forward myself, you might perhaps make a joke of me, and say that it's because of my kinship with him that my works of art in words run away and won't stay put.[14] But, as it is, the proposals are your own. So you need a different joke, since it's for *you* that they won't stay put, as you can see yourself.

EUTHYPHRO: But it seems to me, Socrates, that pretty much the same joke does apply in the case of our definitions. You see, *I'm* not the one who makes them move around and not stay put. Rather, *you* seem to me to be the Daedalus, since as far as I'm concerned they would have stayed put.

---

14. [Daedalus was a legendary sculptor of great skill. His statues were so lifelike that they moved around by themselves just like living things. Socrates' father, Sophroniscus, is alleged to have been a sculptor or stone carver (Diogenes Laertius II.18), and some of the statues on the Acropolis may have been attributed to Socrates himself (Pausanias I.22).]

SOCRATES: Then, my friend, it looks as though I've grown cleverer in my area of expertise than my venerated ancestor, in that he made only his own works not stay put, whereas I do this to my own, it seems, and also to other people's. And the most subtle thing about my area of expertise is that I'm wise in it without wanting to be. You see, I'd prefer to have accounts stay put and be immovably established for me than to acquire the wealth of Tantalus[15] and the

e wisdom of Daedalus combined. But enough of this. Since you seem to me to be getting sated, I'll do my best to help you teach me about the pious—and don't you give up before you do. See whether you don't think that the pious as a whole must be just.

EUTHYPHRO: Yes, I do.

SOCRATES: Then is the just as a whole also pious? Or while the pious as a whole is just, is the just as a

12a whole not pious, but part of it pious and part of it something else?

EUTHYPHRO: I don't follow what you're saying, Socrates.

SOCRATES: And yet you're as much younger as wiser than I. But as I say, your wealth of wisdom has weakened you. Well, pull yourself together, my dear fellow. What I'm saying isn't hard to understand. You see, what I'm saying is just the opposite of what the poet said, who wrote:

> With Zeus the maker, who caused all these
>   things to come about,
> You will not quarrel, since where there's
b   dread there's shame too.[16]

I disagree with this poet. Shall I tell you where?

EUTHYPHRO: Of course.

SOCRATES: It doesn't seem to me that "where there's dread there's shame too." For many people seem to me to dread disease and poverty and many

other things of that sort, but though they dread them, they feel no shame at what they dread. Or don't you agree?

EUTHYPHRO: Of course.

SOCRATES: But where there's shame, there is also dread. For if anyone feels shame at a certain action— if he's ashamed of it—doesn't he fear, doesn't he dread, a reputation for wickedness at the same time? c

EUTHYPHRO: He certainly does dread it.

SOCRATES: Then it isn't right to say that "where there's dread, there's shame too." But where there's shame there's also dread, even though shame isn't found everywhere there's dread. You see, dread is broader than shame, I think. For shame is a part of fear, just as odd is of number. Hence where there's a number, there isn't something odd too, but where there's something odd there is also a number. Do you follow me now at least?

EUTHYPHRO: Of course.

SOCRATES: Well, that's the sort of thing I was asking just now: whenever there's something just, is there also something pious? Or is something just whenever it's pious, but not pious whenever it's just, d because the pious is part of the just? Is that what we're to say, or do you disagree?

EUTHYPHRO: No, let's say that, since it seems to me you're right.

SOCRATES: Then consider the next point. If the pious is a part of what's just, we must, it seems, find out what part of the just the pious is. Now if you asked me about one of the things we just mentioned, for example, which part of number is the even—that is to say, what sort of number it is—I'd say that it's any number not indivisible by two, but divisible by it. Or don't you agree?

EUTHYPHRO: Yes, I do.

SOCRATES: Then you try to teach me in the same fashion what part of the just is pious. Then we can e tell Meletus not to treat us unjustly any longer or indict us for impiety, since I've now been sufficiently instructed by you about what things are holy or pious and what aren't.

EUTHYPHRO: Well then, it seems to me, Socrates, that the part of the just that's holy or pious is the one concerned with tending to the gods, while the remaining part of the just is concerned with tending to human beings.

---

15. [Tantalus, son of Zeus, was a legendary king proverbial for his wealth, who enjoyed the privilege of dining with the gods. He killed and cooked his son, Pelops, and mixed pieces of his flesh in with their food to see if they could detect it. He was punished in Hades by being "tantalized"—any food or water he reached for always eluded his grasp.]

16. [Author unknown.]

SOCRATES: You seem to me to have put that very well, Euthyphro. But I'm still lacking one small piece of information. You see, I don't yet understand this tending you're talking about. You surely don't mean that in just the way that there's tending to other things, there's tending to the gods too. We do speak this way, don't we? We say, for example, that not everyone knows how to tend to horses, but only horse trainers. Isn't that right?

EUTHYPHRO: Of course.

SOCRATES: Because horse training is expertise in tending to horses?

EUTHYPHRO: Yes.

SOCRATES: Nor does everyone know how to tend to dogs, but only dog trainers.

EUTHYPHRO: That's right.

SOCRATES: Because dog training is expertise in tending to dogs.

EUTHYPHRO: Yes.

SOCRATES: And cattle breeding is expertise in tending to cattle.

EUTHYPHRO: Of course.

SOCRATES: Well, but piety or holiness is tending to the gods, Euthyphro? That's what you're saying?

EUTHYPHRO: It is.

SOCRATES: But doesn't all tending accomplish the same end? I mean something like some good or benefit for what's being tended to—as you see that horses tended to by horse trainers are benefited and made better. Or don't you agree that they are?

EUTHYPHRO: Yes, I do.

SOCRATES: And so dogs, of course, are benefited by dog training and cattle by cattle breeding, and similarly for all the others. Or do you think that tending aims to harm what's being tended?

EUTHYPHRO: No, by Zeus, I don't.

SOCRATES: Rather, it aims to benefit it?

EUTHYPHRO: Certainly.

SOCRATES: Then if piety is tending to the gods, does it benefit the gods and make the gods better? Would you concede that whenever you do something pious, you're making some god better?

EUTHYPHRO: No, by Zeus, I wouldn't.

SOCRATES: No, I didn't think that that was what you meant, Euthyphro—far from it. But it is why I asked what you did mean by tending to the gods, because I didn't think you meant that sort of tending.

EUTHYPHRO: And you were right, Socrates, since that's not the sort I meant.

SOCRATES: All right. But then what sort of tending to the gods would the pious be?

EUTHYPHRO: The very sort of tending, Socrates, that slaves provide to their masters.

SOCRATES: I understand. Then it would seem to be some sort of service to the gods.

EUTHYPHRO: It is indeed.

SOCRATES: Now could you tell me about service to doctors? What result does that service—insofar as it is service—aim to produce? Don't you think it aims at health?

EUTHYPHRO: I do.

SOCRATES: What about service to shipbuilders? What result does the service aim to produce?

EUTHYPHRO: Clearly, Socrates, its aim is a ship.

SOCRATES: And in the case of service to builders, I suppose, the aim is a house?

EUTHYPHRO: Yes.

SOCRATES: Then tell me, my good friend, at what result does service to the gods aim? Clearly, you know, since you say you've a finer knowledge of religious matters than any other human being.

EUTHYPHRO: Yes, and what I say is true, Socrates.

SOCRATES: Then tell me, in the name of Zeus, what is that supremely fine result that the gods produce by using our services?

EUTHYPHRO: They produce many fine ones, Socrates.

SOCRATES: So too do generals, my friend. Nonetheless, you could easily tell me the main one, which is to produce victory in war, is it not?

EUTHYPHRO: Certainly.

SOCRATES: And farmers, too, I think, produce many fine results. Nonetheless, the main one is to produce food from the earth.

EUTHYPHRO: Of course.

SOCRATES: What, then, about the many fine results that the gods produce? Which is the main one they produce?

EUTHYPHRO: I told you a moment ago, Socrates, that it's a pretty difficult task to learn the exact truth about all these matters. But to put it simply: if a person knows how to do and say the things that are pleasing to the gods in prayer and sacrifice—those are the ones that are pious. And actions like them preserve both the private welfare of households and the common welfare of the city, whereas those that are the opposite of pleasing are unholy, and they, of course, overturn and destroy everything.

SOCRATES: If you'd wanted to, Euthyphro, you could have put the main point I asked about much more briefly. But you're not eager to teach me—that's c clear. You see, when you were just now on the point of answering you turned away. If you had given the answer, I'd already have been adequately instructed by you about piety. But as it is, the questioner must follow the one being questioned wherever he leads. Once again, then, what are you saying that the pious, or piety, is? Didn't you say that it was some sort of knowledge of sacrificing and praying?

EUTHYPHRO: Yes, I did.

SOCRATES: And sacrificing is giving to the gods, and praying is asking from them?

EUTHYPHRO: Yes, indeed, Socrates.

SOCRATES: So, on that account, piety would be knowing how to ask from the gods and how to give d to them.

EUTHYPHRO: You've grasped my meaning perfectly, Socrates.

SOCRATES: Yes, my friend, that's because I really desire your wisdom and apply my mind to it, so that what you say won't fall on barren ground. But tell me, what is this service to the gods? You say it's asking for things from them and giving things to them?

EUTHYPHRO: I do.

SOCRATES: Well then, wouldn't asking in the right way consist of asking for the things we need from them?

EUTHYPHRO: What else could it be?

SOCRATES: And, conversely, giving in the right e way would consist of giving them, in turn, the things they need from us? For surely giving someone what he didn't at all need isn't something that an expert in the art of giving would do.

EUTHYPHRO: That's true, Socrates.

SOCRATES: Then piety, Euthyphro, would be a sort of expertise in mutual trading between gods and men.

EUTHYPHRO: Yes, trading, if that's what you prefer to call it.

SOCRATES: I don't prefer anything, if it isn't true. But tell me, what benefit do the gods get from the gifts they receive from us? I mean, what they give is clear to everyone, since we possess nothing good that they don't give us. But how are they benefited by 15a what they receive from us? Or do we get so much the better of them in the trade that we receive all our good things from them while they receive nothing from us?

EUTHYPHRO: But Socrates, do you really think gods are benefited by what they receive from us?

SOCRATES: If not, Euthyphro, what could those gifts of ours to gods possibly be?

EUTHYPHRO: What else do you think but honor and reverence and—as I said just now—what's pleasing to them.

SOCRATES: So is the pious pleasing to the gods, Euthyphro, but not beneficial to them or loved by b them?

EUTHYPHRO: No, I think that it's in fact the most loved of all.

SOCRATES: So, once again, it seems, the pious is what's loved by the gods.

EUTHYPHRO: Absolutely.

SOCRATES: Well, if you say that, can you wonder that your accounts seem not to stay put but to move around? And will you accuse me of being the Daedalus who makes them move, when you yourself are far more expert than Daedalus in the art of making them move in a circle? Or don't you see that our account has circled back again to the same place? For surely you remember that earlier we discovered the pious and the god-loved c are not the same, but different from one another. Or don't you remember that?

EUTHYPHRO: Yes, I do.

SOCRATES: Then don't you realize that you're now saying the pious is what the gods love? And that's the same, isn't it, as what's god-loved? Or is that not so?

EUTHYPHRO: Of course, it is.

SOCRATES: Then either we weren't right to agree before, or, if we were right, our present suggestion is wrong.

EUTHYPHRO: So it seems.

SOCRATES: So we must examine again from the beginning what the pious is, since I won't willingly give up until I learn this. Don't scorn me, but apply your mind to the matter in as many ways and as fully d as you can, and then tell me the truth—for you must know it, if indeed any human being does, and, like Proteus,[17] you mustn't be let go until you tell it. For if you didn't know with full clarity what the pious and the impious are, you'd never have ventured to prosecute your old father for murder on behalf of a day laborer. On the contrary, you wouldn't have risked acting wrongly because you'd have been afraid before the gods and ashamed before men. As things stand, however, I well know that you think you have fully clear knowledge of what's pious and what isn't. So tell me what you think it is, my excellent Euthyphro, and don't conceal it.

EUTHYPHRO: Some other time, Socrates. You see, I'm in a hurry to get somewhere, and it's time for me to be off.

SOCRATES: What a way to treat me, my friend! Going off like that and dashing the high hopes I had that I'd learn from you what things are pious and what aren't. Then I'd escape Meletus' indictment by showing him that Euthyphro had now made me wise in religious matters, and ignorance would no longer cause me to improvise and innovate about them. What's more, I'd live a better way for the rest of my life.

17. [Proteus, the Old Man of the Sea, was a god who could change himself into any shape he wished. In this way, he avoided being captured, until his daughter, Eidothea, revealed the secret: keep tight hold of him, no matter what he changes into. See Homer, *Odyssey* IV.351–569.]

APOLOGY

17a I don't know, men of Athens,[1] how you were affected by my accusers. As for me, I was almost carried away by them, they spoke so persuasively. And yet almost nothing they said is true. Among their many falsehoods, however, one especially amazed me: that you must be careful not to be deceived by me, since I'm a dangerously clever speaker.

b That they aren't ashamed at being immediately refuted by the facts, once it becomes apparent that I'm not a clever speaker at all, that seems to me most shameless of them. Unless, of course, the one they call "clever" is the one who tells the truth. If that's what they mean, I'd agree that I'm an orator—although not one of their sort. No, indeed. Rather, just as I claimed, they have said little or nothing true, whereas from me you'll hear the whole truth. But not, by Zeus, men of Athens, expressed in elegant language like theirs, arranged in fine words and

c phrases. Instead, what you hear will be spoken extemporaneously in whatever words come to mind, and let none of you expect me to do otherwise—for I put my trust in the justice of what I say. After all, it wouldn't be appropriate at my age, gentlemen, to come before you speaking in polished, artificial language like a young man.[2]

Indeed, men of Athens, this I positively entreat of you: if you hear me making my defense using the same sort of language[3] that I'm accustomed to use both in the marketplace next to the bankers' tables—where many of you have heard me—and also in other places, please don't be surprised or create an uproar on that account. For the fact is that this is the first

d time I've appeared before a law court, although I'm seventy years old. So the language of this place is totally foreign to me. Now, if I were really a foreigner, you'd certainly forgive me if I spoke in the accents and manner in which I'd been raised. So now, too,

18a I'm asking you, justly it seems to me, to overlook my manner of speaking (maybe it will be less good, maybe it will be better), but consider and apply your mind to this alone, whether I say what's just or not. For that's the virtue or excellence of a juror,[4] just as the orator's lies in telling the truth.

The first thing justice demands, then, men of Athens, is that I defend myself from the first false accusations made against me and from my first accusers, and then from the later accusations and the later accusers. You see, many people have been accusing me in front of you for very many years now—and nothing they say

b is true. And I fear them more than Anytus[5] and the

From *The Trials of Socrates*, translated and edited by C.D.C. Reeve (Indianapolis: Hackett Publishing Company, 2002). Copyright © 2002. Reprinted by permission of the publisher.

1. [Socrates reserves the more common formula "gentlemen of the jury" (ō andres dikastai) for those who, because they vote for his acquittal, merit the name "juror." See 40a2.—C.D.C.R.]

2. [A reference to Socrates' accuser Meletus (19b1), who is characterized as "young and unknown" (*Euthyphro* 2b8–9) and as guilty of "youthful rashness" (26e9 below).]

3. [At 27a10–b2 Socrates makes clear he is referring especially to his characteristic style of argumentative questioning and examining—the so-called elenchus.]

4. [A member of an Athenian jury (a *dikastēs*) combined the responsibilities divided between judge and jury in our legal system. Hence *dikastēs* is sometimes translated as "judge" and sometimes (as in the present translation) as "juror."]

5. [Anytus was a democratic leader who helped restore democracy to Athens in 403 B.C.E. after the overthrow of the Thirty Tyrants (32c4 note), under whom he had lost most of his wealth. As a general in the Athenian army he faced indictment, but allegedly "bribed the jury and was acquitted" (Aristotle, *Constitution of Athens* 27.5). There is evidence that he believed Socrates was responsible for the ruin of his son (Xenophon, *Socrates'*

rest, though the latter are dangerous as well. But the earlier ones, gentlemen, are more dangerous. They got hold of most of you from childhood and persuaded you with their accusations against me—accusations no more true than the current ones. They say there's a man called Socrates, a "wise" man, a thinker about things in the heavens, an investigator of all things below the earth, and someone who makes the weaker

c argument the stronger. Those who've spread this rumor, men of Athens, are my dangerous accusers, since the people who hear them believe that those who investigate such things do not acknowledge the gods either. Moreover, those accusers are numerous and have been accusing me for a long time now. Besides, they also spoke to you at that age when you would most readily believe them, when some of you were children or young boys. Thus they simply won their case by default, as there was no defense. But what's most unreasonable in all this is that I can't discover even their names and tell them to you—unless one

d of them happens to be a comic playwright.[6] In any case, the ones who used malicious slander to persuade you—as well as those who persuaded others after having been persuaded themselves—all of these are impossible to deal with. One cannot bring any of them here to court or cross-examine them. One must literally fight with shadows to defend oneself and cross-examine with no one to respond.

So you too, then, should allow, as I claimed, that there are two groups of accusers: those who accused me just now and the older ones I've been discussing.

e Moreover, you should consider it proper for me to defend myself against the latter first, since you've heard them accusing me earlier, and at much greater length, than these recent ones here.

All right. I must defend myself, then, men of Athens, and try to take away in this brief time prejudices

19a you acquired such a long time ago. Certainly, that's the outcome I'd wish for—if it's in any way better for you and for me—and I'd like to succeed in my defense. But I think it's a difficult task, and I am not at all unaware of its nature. Let it turn out, though, in whatever way pleases the god. I have to obey the law and defend myself.

Let's examine, then, from the beginning, what the charge is from which the slander against me arose—the very one on which Meletus relied when he wrote b the present indictment of me. Well, then, what exactly did the slanderers say to slander me? Just as if they were real accusers their affidavit must be read. It's something like this:

> Socrates commits injustice and is a busybody, in that he investigates the things beneath the earth and in the heavens, makes the weaker argument the stronger, and teaches these things to others.

c

Indeed, you saw these charges expressed yourselves in Aristophanes' comedy.[7] There, some fellow named Socrates swings around claiming he's walking on air and talking a lot of other nonsense on subjects that I know neither a lot nor a little but nothing at all about. Not that I mean to disparage this knowledge, if anyone's wise in such subjects—I don't want to have to defend myself against more of Meletus' lawsuits!—but I, men of Athens, take no part in them. I call on the majority of you as witnesses to this, and d I appeal to you to make it perfectly plain to one another—those of you who've heard me conversing (as many of you have). Tell one another, then, whether any of you has ever heard me discussing such subjects, either briefly or at length, and from this you'll realize that the other things commonly said about me are of the same baseless character.

In any case, none of them is true. And if you've heard from anyone that I undertake to educate people and charge fees, that's not true either. Although, it also seems to me to be a fine thing if anyone's able e to educate people in the way Gorgias of Leontini does, and Prodicus of Ceos, and Hippias of Elis.[8] For

---

Defense 29–31), and that he was passionately opposed to the sophists (Plato, *Meno* 89e6–92c5).]

6. [The great Athenian dramatist Aristophanes (c. 450–385 B.C.E.), whose play *Clouds*, referred to below, presents a hostile portrait of Socrates.]

7. [The version of *Clouds* referred to here, which is earlier than the revised version we possess, was first staged in 423 B.C.E..]

8. [All three, like Evenus of Paros mentioned below, were sophists—itinerant professors who charged sometimes substantial fees for popular lectures and specialized instruction in a wide variety of fields, including natural

each of them, gentlemen, can enter any city and persuade the young—who may associate with any of their own fellow citizens they want to free of charge—to abandon those associations, and associate with them instead, pay them a fee, and be grateful to them besides.

Since we're on that topic, I heard that there's another wise gentleman here at present, from Paros. For I happened to run into a man who has spent more money on sophists than everyone else put together—Callias, the son of Hipponicus.[9] So I questioned him, since he has two sons himself.

"Callias," I said, "if your two sons had been born colts or calves, we could engage and pay a knowledgeable supervisor—one of those expert horse breeders or farmers—who could turn them into fine and good examples of their proper virtue or excellence. But now, seeing that they're human beings, whom do you have in mind to engage as a supervisor? Who is it that has the knowledge of *this* virtue, the virtue of human beings and of citizens? I assume you've investigated the matter, because you have two sons. Is there such a person," I asked, "or not?"

"Certainly," he replied.

"Who is he?" I said.

"His name's Evenus, Socrates," he replied, "from Paros. He charges five minas."[10]

I thought Evenus blessedly happy if he truly did possess that expertise and taught it for so modest a fee. I, at any rate, would pride myself and give myself airs if I had knowledge of those things. But in fact, men of Athens, I don't know them.

Now perhaps one of you will interject: "But Socrates, what, then, is *your* occupation? What has given rise to these slanders against you? Surely if you weren't in fact occupied with something out of the ordinary, if you weren't doing something different from most people, all this rumor and talk wouldn't have arisen. Tell us, then, what it is, so that we don't judge you hastily." These are fair questions, I think, for the speaker to ask, and I'll try to show you just what it is that has brought me this slanderous reputation. Listen, then. Perhaps, some of you will think I'm joking. But you may be sure that I'll be telling you the whole truth.

You see, men of Athens, I've acquired this reputation because of nothing other than a sort of wisdom. What sort of wisdom, you ask, is that? The very sort, perhaps, that is *human* wisdom. For it may just be that I really do have that sort of wisdom, whereas the people I mentioned just now may, perhaps, be wise because they possess *superhuman* wisdom. I don't know what else to call it, since I myself certainly don't possess that knowledge, and whoever says I do is lying and speaking in order to slander me.

Please don't create an uproar, men of Athens, even if you think I'm somehow making grand claims. You see, I'm not the author of the story I'm about to tell, though I'll refer you to a reliable source. In fact, as a witness to the existence of my wisdom—if indeed it is a sort of wisdom—and to its nature, I'll present the god at Delphi to you.[11]

---

science, rhetoric, grammar, ethics, and politics. Sophists did not constitute a single school or movement, however, and were neither doctrinally nor organizationally united. Gorgias of Leontini in Sicily (c. 480–376) was primarily a teacher of rhetoric, noted for his distinctive style. He is the author of the *Defense of Palamedes*, parts of which bear a striking resemblance to the *Apology* and may have either influenced or been influenced by it. Plato named a dialogue critical of rhetoric after him. Prodicus of Ceos, about whom little is known, was also a fifth-century teacher of rhetoric, with an interest in fine distinctions of meaning (*Protagoras* 337a1–c4) and the correctness of names (*Cratylus* 384a8–c2). Hippias of Elis, like Prodicus a contemporary of Socrates, claimed expertise in astronomy, physics, grammar, poetry, and other subjects. Two Platonic dialogues are named after him; he also appears in *Protagoras* (315b9–c7, 337c6–338b1).]

9. [Callias was one of the richest men in Greece and a patron of the sophists. Both Plato's *Protagoras* and Xenophon's *Symposium* are set in his house.]

10. [Evenus is described as a poet (*Phaedo* 60c8–e1) and as an orator (*Phaedrus* 267a1–5). A few fragments of his elegies survive. A drachma was a day's pay for someone engaged in public works; a mina was a hundred silver drachmas.]

11. [Apollo—god of, among other things, healing, prophecy, purification, care for young citizens, music, poetry.]

You remember Chaerephon, no doubt.[12] He was a friend of mine from youth and also a friend of your party, who shared your recent exile and restoration.[13] You remember, then, what sort of man Chaerephon was, how intense he was in whatever he set out to do. Well, on one occasion in particular he went to Delphi and dared to ask the oracle[14]—as I said, please don't create an uproar, gentlemen—he asked, exactly as I'm telling you, whether anyone was wiser than myself. The Pythia[15] drew forth the response that no one is wiser. His brother here will testify to you about it, since Chaerephon himself is dead.[16]

Please consider my purpose in telling you this, since I'm about to explain to you where the slander against me has come from. You see, when I heard these things, I thought to myself as follows: "What can the god be saying? What does his riddle mean?[17] For I'm only too aware that I've no claim to being wise in anything either great or small. What can he mean, then, by saying that I'm wisest? Surely he can't be lying: that isn't lawful[18] for him."

For a long time I was perplexed about what he meant. Then, very reluctantly, I proceeded to examine it in the following sort of way. I approached one of the people thought to be wise, assuming that in his company, if anywhere, I could refute the pronouncement and say to the oracle, "Here's someone wiser than I, yet you said I was wisest."

Then I examined this person—there's no need for me to mention him by name; he was one of our politicians. And when I examined him and talked with him, men of Athens, my experience was something like this: I thought this man seemed wise to many people, and especially to himself, but wasn't. Then I tried to show him that he thought himself wise, but wasn't. As a result, he came to dislike me, and so did many of the people present. For my part, I thought to myself as I left, "I'm wiser than that person. For it's likely that neither of us knows anything fine and good, but he thinks he knows something he doesn't know, whereas I, since I don't in fact know, don't think that I do either. At any rate, it seems that I'm wiser than he in just this one small way: that what I don't know, I don't think I know." Next, I approached another man, one of those thought to be wiser than the first, and it seemed to me that the same thing occurred, and so I came to be disliked by that man too, as well as by many others.

After that, then, I kept approaching one person after another. I realized, with distress and alarm, that I was arousing hostility. Nevertheless, I thought I must attach the greatest importance to what pertained to the god. So, in seeking what the oracle meant, I had to go to all those with any reputation for knowledge. And, by the dog,[19] men of Athens—for I'm obliged to tell the truth before you—I really did experience something like this: in my investigation in response to the god, I found that, where wisdom is concerned, those who had the best reputations were practically

12. [A long-time companion of Socrates.]

13. [Members of the democratic party left Athens when the Thirty Tyrants came to power in 404 B.C.E. They returned to power when the tyrants were overthrown in 403.]

14. [The Delphic Oracle was one of the most famous in antiquity. There were two methods of consulting it. One, involving the sacrifice of sheep and goats, was quite expensive but resulted in a written response. The other— the so-called method of the two beans—was substantially cheaper but resulted only in a response by lot. Since Chaerephon was notoriously poor, it seems probable that he consulted the oracle by the latter method (something also suggested by Socrates' characterization of the priestess as *drawing forth* the response at 21a6–7). The inscriptions on the walls of the temple well convey the spirit the oracle stood for: know thyself; nothing in excess; observe the limit; hate hubris; bow before the divine; glory not in strength.]

15. [The priestess at Delphi who delivered the oracle's pronouncement.]

16. [The brother is Chaerecrates.]

17. [Many of the attested Delphic pronouncements were riddles. Delphi seems to have encouraged care in their interpretation, treating a cavalier acceptance of them at face value as an example of the hubris it condemned.]

18. [What is lawful (*themis*) in the relevant sense accords with the divine law embodied in the universe, in contravention of which nothing can occur.]

19. [Probably the dog-headed Egyptian god Anubis. The oath is an emphatic one, like "my goodness" or "by all that's holy," with no particular religious significance.]

the most deficient, whereas men who were thought to be their inferiors were much better off. Accordingly, I must present all my wanderings to you as if they were labors of some sort that I undertook in order to prove the oracle utterly irrefutable.

b You see, after the politicians, I approached the poets—tragic, dithyrambic,[20] and the rest—thinking that in their company I'd catch myself in the very act of being more ignorant than they. So I examined the poems with which they seemed to me to have taken the most trouble and questioned them about what they meant, in order that I might also learn something from them at the same time.

Well, I'm embarrassed to tell you the truth, gentlemen, but nevertheless it must be told. In a word, almost all the people present could have discussed these poems better than their authors themselves. And so, in the case of the poets as well, I soon realized it wasn't wisdom that enabled them to compose their poems, but some sort of natural inspiration, of just c the sort you find in prophets and soothsayers. For these people, too, say many fine things, but know nothing of what they speak about. The poets also seemed to me to be in this sort of situation. At the same time, I realized that, because of their poetry, they thought themselves to be the wisest of people about the other things as well when they weren't. So I left their company, too, thinking that I had gotten the better of them in the very same way as of the politicians.

Finally, I approached the craftsmen. You see, I was d conscious of knowing practically nothing myself, but I knew I'd discover that they, at least, would know many fine things. And I wasn't wrong about this. On the contrary, they did know things that I didn't know, and in that respect they were wiser than I. But, men of Athens, the good craftsmen also seemed to me to have the very same flaw as the poets: because he performed his own craft well, each of them also thought himself to be wisest about the other things, the most important ones; and this error of theirs seemed to overshadow their wisdom. So I asked myself e on behalf of the oracle whether I'd prefer to be as I am, not in any way wise with their wisdom nor ignorant with their ignorance, or to have both qualities

20. [A dithyramb was a choral song in honor of the god Dionysus.]

as they did. And the answer I gave to myself, and to the oracle, was that it profited me more to be just the way I was.

From this examination, men of Athens, much hostility has arisen against me of a sort that is harshest 23a and most onerous. This has resulted in many slanders, including that reputation I mentioned of being "wise." You see, the people present on each occasion think that I'm wise about the subjects on which I examine others. But in fact, gentlemen, it's pretty certainly the god who is really wise, and by his oracle he meant that human wisdom is worth little or nothing. And it seems that when he refers to the Socrates here before you and uses my name, he makes me an example, as if he were to say, "That one among you b is wisest, mortals, who, like Socrates, has recognized that he's truly worthless where wisdom's concerned."

So even now I continue to investigate these things and to examine, in response to the god, any person, citizen, or foreigner I believe to be wise. Whenever he seems not to be so to me, I come to the assistance of the god and show him that he's not wise. Because of this occupation, I've had no leisure worth talking about for either the city's affairs or my own domestic ones; rather, I live in extreme poverty because of my service to the god.   c

In addition to these factors, the young people who follow me around of their own accord, those who have the most leisure, the sons of the very rich, enjoy listening to people being cross-examined. They often imitate me themselves and in turn attempt to cross-examine others. Next, I imagine they find an abundance of people who think they possess some knowledge, but in fact know little or nothing. The result is that those they question are angry not at themselves, but at me, and say that Socrates is a d thoroughly pestilential fellow who corrupts the young. Then, when they're asked what he's doing or teaching, they've nothing to say, as they don't know. Yet, so as not to appear at a loss, they utter the stock phrases used against all who philosophize: "things in the sky and beneath the earth," and "not acknowledging the gods," and "making the weaker argument the stronger." For they wouldn't be willing to tell the truth, I imagine: that it has become manifest they pretend to know, but know nothing. So, seeing that these people are, I imagine, ambitious, vehement, *e* and numerous, and have been speaking earnestly and persuasively about me, they've long been filling your ears with vehement slanders. On the basis of these slanders, Meletus has brought his charges against me, and Anytus and Lycon[21] along with him: Meletus is aggrieved on behalf of the poets, Anytus on behalf of the artisans and politicians, and Lycon on behalf of *24a* the orators. So, as I began by saying, I'd be amazed if I could rid your minds of this slander in the brief time available, when there's so much of it in them.

There, men of Athens, is the truth for you. I've spoken it without concealing or glossing over anything, whether great or small. And yet I pretty much know that I make enemies by doing these very things. And that's further evidence that I'm right—that this is the prejudice against me and these its causes. Whether you investigate these matters now or later, *b* you'll find it to be so.

Enough, then, for my defense before you against the charges brought by my first accusers. Next, I'll try to defend myself against Meletus—who is, he claims, both good and patriotic—and against my later accusers. Once again, then, just as if they were really a different set of accusers, their affidavit must be examined in turn. It goes something like this:

> Socrates is guilty of corrupting the young, and of not acknowledging the gods the city acknowledges, but new daimonic activities instead.

c Such, then, is the charge. Let us examine each point in this charge.

Meletus says, then, that I commit injustice by corrupting the young. But I, men of Athens, reply that it's Meletus who is guilty of playing around with serious matters, of lightly bringing people to trial, and of professing to be seriously concerned about things he has never cared about at all—and I'll try to prove this.[22]

21. [Otherwise unknown.]

22. [Under Athenian law, any citizen could bring an indictment against another whom he believed to be guilty of wrongdoing. As a result, a citizen who brought such a legal action typically played two roles, which in our system of criminal law are kept separate, that of prosecutor and that of chief witness for the prosecution. Meletus is both charging Socrates with impiety, there-

Step forward, Meletus, and answer me. You regard it as most important, do you not, that our young people be as good as possible?

I certainly do.   *d*

Come, then, and tell these jurors who improves them. Clearly you know, since you care. For having discovered, as you assert, the one who corrupts them—namely, myself—you bring him before these jurors and accuse him. Come, then, speak up, tell the jurors who it is that improves them. Do you see, Meletus, that you remain silent and have nothing to say? Yet don't you think that's shameful and sufficient evidence of exactly what I say, that you care nothing at all? Speak up, my good man. Who improves them?

The laws.

But that's not what I'm asking, my most excellent fellow, but rather which *person*, who knows the laws *e* themselves in the first place, does this?

These gentlemen, Socrates, the jurors.

What are you saying, Meletus? Are they able to educate and improve the young?

Most certainly.

All of them, or some but not others?

All of them.

That's good news, by Hera, and a great abundance of benefactors that you speak of! What, then, about the audience present here? Do they improve the young or not?   *25a*

Yes, they do so too.

And what about the members of the Council?[23]

Yes, the councilors too.

But, if that's so, Meletus, surely those in the Assembly, the assemblymen, won't corrupt the young, will they? Won't they all improve them too?

Yes, they will too.

___

fore, and attesting (together with Anytus and Lycon) that he did specific impious things. Meletus' indictment is both a charge, then, and a sworn affidavit supporting the charge.]

23. [The Council consisted of 500 male citizens over the age of 30, elected annually by lot, 50 from each of the 10 tribes of Athens. The Council met daily (except for some holidays and the like) as a steering committee for the Assembly. Its responsibilities included state finance, public buildings, and the equipment of navy and cavalry.]

But then it seems that all the Athenians except for me make young people fine and good, whereas I alone corrupt them. Is that what you're saying?

Most emphatically, that's what I'm saying.

I find myself, if you're right, in a most unfortunate situation. Now answer me this. Do you think that the same holds of horses? Do people in general improve them, whereas one particular person corrupts them *b* or makes them worse? Or isn't it wholly the opposite: one particular person—or the very few who are horse trainers—is able to improve them, whereas the majority of people, if they have to do with horses and make use of them, make them worse? Isn't that true, Meletus, both of horses and of all other animals? Of course it is, whether you and Anytus say so or not. Indeed, our young people are surely in a very happy situation if only one person corrupts them, whereas all the rest benefit them.

Well then, Meletus, it has been adequately estab-*c* lished that you've never given any thought to young people—you've plainly revealed your indifference— and that you care nothing about the issues on which you bring me to trial.

Next, Meletus, tell us, in the name of Zeus, whether it's better to live among good citizens or bad ones. Answer me, sir. Surely, I'm not asking you anything difficult. Don't bad people do something bad to whoever's closest to them at the given moment, whereas good people do something good?

Certainly.

d Now is there anyone who wishes to be harmed rather than benefited by those around him? Keep answering, my good fellow. For the law requires you to answer. Is there anyone who wishes to be harmed?

Of course not.

Well, then, when you summon me here for corrupting the young and making them worse, do you mean that I do so intentionally or unintentionally?

Intentionally, *I* say.

What's that, Meletus? Are you so much wiser at your age than I at mine, that you know bad people do something bad to whoever's closest to them at the given moment, and good people something good? *e* Am I, by contrast, so very ignorant that I don't know even this: that if I do something bad to an associate, I risk getting back something bad from him in return?

And is the result, as you claim, that I do so very bad a thing intentionally?

I'm not convinced by you of that, Meletus, and neither, I think, is anyone else. No, either I'm not corrupting the young or, if I am corrupting them, it's *un*intentionally, so that in either case what you say is false. But if I'm corrupting them unintentionally, *26a* the law doesn't require that I be brought to court for such mistakes—that is, unintentional ones—but that I be taken aside for private instruction and admonishment. For it's clear that if I'm instructed, I'll stop doing what I do unintentionally. You, however, avoided associating with me and were unwilling to instruct me. Instead, you bring me here, where the law requires you to bring those in need of punishment, not instruction.

Well, men of Athens, what I said before is absolutely clear by this point, namely, that Meletus has never cared about these matters to any extent, great or small. Nevertheless, please tell us now, *b* Meletus, how is it you say I corrupt the young? Or is it absolutely clear, from the indictment you wrote, that it's by teaching them not to acknowledge the gods the city acknowledges, but new daimonic activities instead? Isn't that what you say I corrupt them by teaching?

I most emphatically do say that.

Then, in the name of those very gods we're now discussing, Meletus, speak yet more clearly, both for my sake and for that of these gentlemen. You see, I'm unable to tell what you mean. Is it that I teach *c* people to acknowledge that some gods exist—so that I, then, acknowledge their existence myself and am not an out-and-out atheist and am not guilty of that— yet not, of course, the very ones acknowledged by the city, but different ones? Is that what you're charging me with, that they're different ones? Or are you saying that I myself don't acknowledge any gods at all, and that that's what I teach to others?

That's what I mean, that you don't acknowledge any gods at all.

You're a strange fellow, Meletus! What makes you say that? Do I not even acknowledge that the sun *d* and the moon are gods, then, as other men do?

No, by Zeus, gentlemen of the jury, he doesn't, since he says that the sun's a stone and the moon earth.

My dear Meletus, do you think it's Anaxagoras[24] you're accusing? Are you that contemptuous of the jury? Do you think they're so illiterate that they don't know that the books of Anaxagoras of Clazomenae are full of such arguments? And, in particular, do young people learn these views from me, views they can occasionally acquire in the Orchestra[25] for a

e drachma at most and that they'd ridicule Socrates for pretending were his own—especially as they're so strange? In the name of Zeus, is that really how I seem to you? Do I acknowledge the existence of no god at all?

No indeed, by Zeus, none at all.

You aren't at all convincing, Meletus, not even, it seems to me, to yourself. You see, men of Athens, this fellow seems very arrogant and intemperate to me and to have written this indictment simply out of some sort of arrogance, intemperance, and youthful rashness. Indeed, he seems to have composed a sort

27a of riddle in order to test me: "Will the so-called wise Socrates recognize that I'm playing around and contradicting myself? Or will I fool him along with the other listeners?" You see, he seems to me to be contradicting himself in his indictment, as if he were to say, "Socrates is guilty of not acknowledging gods, but of acknowledging gods." And that's just childish playing around, isn't it?

Please examine with me, gentlemen, why it seems to me that this is what he's saying. And you, Meletus, answer us. But you, gentlemen, please remember what I asked of you at the beginning: don't create an

b uproar if I make my arguments in my accustomed manner.

Is there anyone, Meletus, who acknowledges that human activities exist but doesn't acknowledge human beings? Make him answer, gentlemen, and don't let him make one protest after another. Is there anyone who doesn't acknowledge horses but does acknowledge equine activities? Or who doesn't acknowledge that musicians[26] exist but does acknowledge musical activities? There's no one, best of men—if you don't want to answer, I must answer for you and for the others here. But at least answer my next question. Is there anyone who acknowledges the existence of daimonic activities but doesn't acknowl- *c* edge daimons?

No, there isn't.

How good of you to answer, if reluctantly and when compelled to by these gentlemen. Well then, you say that I acknowledge daimonic activities, whether new or familiar, and teach about them. But then, on your account, I do at any rate acknowledge daimonic activities, and to this you've sworn in your indictment against me. However, if I acknowledge daimonic activities, surely it's absolutely necessary that I acknowledge daimons. Isn't that so? Yes, it is—I assume you agree, since you don't answer. But don't we believe that daimons are either gods or, at any rate, children of gods? Yes or no? *d*

Of course.

Then, if indeed I do believe in daimons, as you're saying, and if daimons are gods of some sort, that's precisely what I meant when I said that you're presenting us with a riddle and playing around: you're saying that I don't believe in gods and, on the contrary, that I do believe in gods, since in fact I do at least believe in daimons. But if, on the other hand, daimons are children of gods, some sort of bastard offspring of a nymph, or of whomever else tradition says each one is the child, what man could possibly believe that children of gods exist, but not gods? That would be just as unreasonable as believing in the children of horses and asses—namely, mules—while not believ- *e* ing in the existence of horses and asses.

Well then, Meletus, you must have written these things to test us or because you were at a loss about what genuine injustice to charge me with. There's no conceivable way you could persuade any man with even the slightest intelligence that the same person believes in both daimonic activities and gods, and,

---

24. [Anaxogoras of Clazomenae (c. 500–428 B.C.E.) settled in Athens (c. 456 B.C.E.) where he remained until he fled to Lampsacus to escape indictment for impiety (c. 436 B.C.E.). He was a friend of the great Athenian statesman Pericles, and the indictment may have been motivated at least in part by political hostility to the latter. Anaxagoras accorded a fundamental cosmological role to (divine) Mind.]

25. [The Orchestra was part of the marketplace (*agora*) in Athens.]

26. [Literally, aulos players. The aulos was a reed instrument rather like an oboe.]

on the contrary, that this same person believes neither
28a in daimons, nor in gods, nor in heroes.[27]

In fact, then, men of Athens, it doesn't seem to
me to require a long defense to show that I'm not
guilty of the charges in Meletus' indictment, but what
I've said is sufficient. But what I was also saying earlier,
that much hostility has arisen against me and among
many people—you may be sure that's true. And *it's*
what will convict me, if I am convicted: not Meletus
or Anytus, but the slander and malice of many people.
It has certainly convicted many other good men as
well, and I imagine it will do so again. There's no
b danger it will stop with me.

But perhaps someone may say, "Aren't you
ashamed, Socrates, to have engaged in the sort of
occupation that has now put you at risk of death?" I,
however, would be right to reply to him, "You're not
thinking straight, sir, if you think that a man who's
any use at all should give any opposing weight to the
risk of living or dying, instead of looking to this alone
whenever he does anything: whether his actions are
just or unjust, the deeds of a good or bad man. You
c see, on your account, all those demigods who died
on the plain of Troy were inferior people, especially
the son of Thetis, who was so contemptuous of danger
when the alternative was something shameful.[28]
When he was eager to kill Hector, his mother, since
she was a goddess, spoke to him, I think, in some
such words as these: 'My child, if you avenge the
death of your friend Patroclus and slay Hector, you
will die yourself immediately,' so the poem goes, 'as
your death is fated to follow next after Hector's.' But
though he heard that, he was contemptuous of death
and danger, for he was far more afraid of living as a
bad man and of failing to avenge his friends: 'Let me
d die immediately, then,' it continues, 'once I've given
the wrongdoer his just deserts,[29] so that I do not
remain here by the curved ships, a laughingstock and

27. [Heroes are demigods (28c2), children of gods and
mortals, whose existence therefore entails the existence
of gods. Hence someone who denies the existence of
gods denies that of heroes too.]

28. [Thetis' son, born of a mortal father, Peleus, and
hence a demigod, is Achilles.]

29. ["Once I've given . . . deserts" is a Socratic addition
to Homer's text.]

a burden upon the earth.' Do you really suppose he
gave a thought to death or danger?"

You see, men of Athens, this is the truth of the matter:
Wherever someone has stationed himself because he
thinks it best, or wherever he's been stationed by his
commander, there, it seems to me, he should remain,
steadfast in danger, taking no account at all of death or
of anything else, in comparison to what's shameful. I'd
therefore have been acting scandalously, men of Athens, if, when I'd been stationed in Potidea, Amphipolis, e
or Delium[30] by the leaders you had elected to lead me,
I had, like many another, remained where they'd stationed me and run the risk of death. But if, when the
god stationed me here, as I became thoroughly convinced he did, to live practicing philosophy, examining
myself and others, I had—for fear of death or anything
else—abandoned my station.   29a

That would have been scandalous, and someone
might have rightly and justly brought me to court for
not acknowledging that gods exist, by disobeying the
oracle, fearing death, and thinking I was wise when
I wasn't. You see, fearing death, gentlemen, is nothing
other than thinking one is wise when one isn't, since
it's thinking one knows what one doesn't know. I
mean, no one knows whether death may not be the
greatest of all goods for people, but they fear it as if
they knew for certain that it's the worst thing of all.
Yet surely this is the most blameworthy ignorance of b
thinking one knows what one doesn't know. But I,
gentlemen, may perhaps differ from most people by
just this much in this matter too. And if I really were
to claim to be wiser than anyone in any way, it would
be in this: that as I don't have adequate knowledge
about things in Hades, so too I don't think that I have
knowledge. To act unjustly, on the other hand, to
disobey someone better than oneself, whether god or
man, that I do know to be bad and shameful. In any
case, I'll never fear or avoid things that may for all I
know be good more than things I know are bad.

Suppose, then, you're prepared to let me go now
and to disobey Anytus, who said I shouldn't have been c
brought to court at all,[31] but that since I had been

30. [Three battles in the Peloponnesian War between
Athens and its allies and Sparta and its allies.]

31. [Anytus presumably thought that Socrates would
exile himself to escape trial, as Anaxagoras had done.]

brought to court, you had no alternative but to put me to death because, as he stated before you, if I were acquitted, soon your sons would all be entirely corrupted by following Socrates' teachings. Suppose, confronted with that claim, you were to say to me, "Socrates, we will not obey Anytus this time. Instead, we are prepared to let you go. But on the following condition: that you spend no more time on this investigation and don't practice philosophy, and if you're caught doing so, you'll die." Well, as I just said, if *d* you were to let me go on these terms, I'd reply to you, "I've the utmost respect and affection for you, men of Athens, but I'll obey the god rather than you, and as long as I draw breath and am able, I won't give up practicing philosophy, exhorting you and also showing the way to any of you I ever happen to meet, saying just the sorts of things I'm accustomed to say:

My excellent man, you're an Athenian, you belong to the greatest city, renowned for its wisdom and strength; are you not ashamed that you take care to acquire as much wealth as possible—and reputation and honor—but that *e* about wisdom and truth, about how your soul may be in the best possible condition, you take neither care nor thought?

Then, if one of you disagrees and says that he *does* care, I won't let him go away immediately, but I'll question, examine, and test him. And if he doesn't seem to me to possess virtue, though he claims he does, I'll reproach him, saying that he treats the most *30a* important things as having the least value, and inferior ones as having more. This I will do for anyone I meet, young or old, alien or fellow citizen—but especially for you, my fellow citizens, since you're closer kin to me. This, you may be sure, is what the god orders me to do. And I believe that no greater good for you has ever come about in the city than my service to the god. You see, I do nothing else except go around trying to persuade you, both young and old alike, not to care about your bodies or your money as intensely *b* as about how your soul may be in the best possible condition. I say,

It's not from wealth that virtue comes, but from virtue comes money, and all the other things

that are good for human beings, both in private and in public life.

Now if by saying this, I'm corrupting the young, *this* is what you'd have to think to be harmful. But if anyone claims I say something other than this, he's talking nonsense."

"It's in that light," I want to say, "men of Athens, that you should obey Anytus or not, and let me go or not—knowing that I wouldn't act in any other way, not even if I were to die many times over." *c*

Don't create an uproar, men of Athens. Instead, please abide by my request not to create an uproar at what I say, but to listen. For I think it will profit you to listen. You see, I'm certainly going to say some further things to you at which you may perhaps exclaim—but by no means do so.

You may be sure that if you put me to death—a man of the sort I said I was just now—you won't harm me more than you harm yourselves. Certainly, Meletus or Anytus couldn't harm me in any way: that's not possible. For I don't think it's lawful for a better man to be harmed by a worse. He may, of *d* course, kill me, or perhaps banish or disenfranchise me. And these *he* believes to be very bad things, and others no doubt agree. But *I* don't believe this. Rather, I believe that doing what he's doing now—attempting to kill a man unjustly—is far worse.

So, men of Athens, I'm far from pleading in my own defense now, as might be supposed. Instead, I'm pleading in yours, so that you don't commit a great wrong against the god's gift to you by condemning me. If you put me to death, you won't easily find *e* another like me. For, even if it seems ridiculous to say so, I've literally been attached to the city, as if to a large thoroughbred horse that was somewhat sluggish because of its size and needed to be awakened by some sort of gadfly. It's as just such a gadfly, it seems to me, that the god has attached me to the city—one that awakens, cajoles, and reproaches each and every one of you and never stops alighting everywhere on you the whole day. You won't easily find another like *31a* that, gentlemen. So if you obey me, you'll spare my life. But perhaps you'll be resentful, like people awakened from a doze, and slap at me. If you obey Anytus, you might easily kill me. Then you might spend the rest of your lives asleep, unless the god, in his compassion for you, were to send you someone else.

That I am indeed the sort of person to be given as a gift to the city by the god, you may recognize from this: it doesn't seem a merely human matter—does it?—for me to have neglected all my own affairs and to have put up with this neglect of my domestic life for so many years now, but always to have minded your business, by visiting each of you in private, like a father or elder brother, to persuade you to care about virtue. Of course, if I were getting anything out of it or if I were being paid for giving this advice, my conduct would be intelligible. But, as it is, you can plainly see for yourselves that my accusers, who so shamelessly accused me of everything else, couldn't bring themselves to be so utterly shameless as to call a witness to say that I ever once accepted or asked for payment. In fact, it's *I* who can call what I think is a sufficient witness that I'm telling the truth—my poverty.

But perhaps it may seem strange that I, of all people, give this advice by going around and minding other people's business in private, yet do not venture to go before your Assembly and give advice to the city in public. The reason for that, however, is one you've heard me give many times and in many places: A divine and daimonic thing comes to me—the very thing Meletus made mocking allusion to in the indictment he wrote. It's something that began happening to me in childhood: a sort of voice comes, which, whenever it does come, always holds me back from what I'm about to do but never urges me forward. *It* is what opposes my engaging in politics—and to me, at least, its opposition seems entirely right. For you may be sure, men of Athens, that if I'd tried to engage in politics I'd have perished long ago and have benefited neither you nor myself.

Please don't resent me if I tell you the truth. The fact is that no man will be spared by you or by any other multitude of people if he genuinely opposes a lot of unjust and unlawful actions and tries to prevent them from happening in the city. On the contrary, anyone who really fights for what's just, if indeed he's going to survive for even a short time, must act privately not publicly.

I'll present substantial evidence of that—not words, but what you value, deeds. Listen, then, to what happened to me, so you may see that fear of death wouldn't lead me to submit to a single person contrary to what's just, not even if I were to perish at once for not submitting. The things I'll tell you are of a vulgar sort commonly heard in the law courts, but they're true nonetheless.

You see, men of Athens, I never held any other public office in the city, but I've served on the Council. And it happened that my own tribe, Antiochis, was presiding[32] when you wanted to try the ten generals—the ones who failed to rescue the survivors of the naval battle—as a group.[33] That was unlawful, as you all came to recognize at a later time. On that occasion, I was the only presiding member opposed to your doing something illegal, and I voted against you. And though the orators[34] were ready to lay information against me and have me summarily arrested, and you were shouting and urging them on, I thought that I should face danger on the side of law and justice, rather than go along with you for fear of imprisonment or death when your proposals were unjust.

This happened when the city was still under democratic rule. But later, when the oligarchy had come to power, it happened once more. The Thirty[35] sum-

32. [A *phulē* is not a tribe in our sense, but an administrative division of the citizen body, most probably of military origin. The presiding committee of the Council consisted of the fifty members of one of the ten tribes, selected by lot to serve for one-tenth of the year. It arranged meetings of the Council and Assembly, received envoys and letters to the state, and conducted other routine business.]

33. [After the naval battle at Arginusae on the Ionian coast of Asia Minor (406 B.C.E.), ten Athenian generals were indicted for failing to rescue survivors and pick up the bodies of the dead. Both Council and Assembly voted to try them as a group, which was against Athenian law.]

34. [The politicians supporting the mass trial.]

35. [After Athens was defeated by Sparta in 404 B.C.E., its democratic government was replaced by a brutal oligarchy, the so-called Thirty Tyrants, which survived barely eight months. During that time it allegedly executed some fifteen hundred people, and many more went into exile to escape. Two members of the Thirty—Critias and Charmides—were relatives of Plato's and appear as Socratic interlocutors in the dialogues named

moned me and four others to the Tholus[36] and ordered us to arrest Leon of Salamis[37] and bring him from Salamis to die. They gave many such orders to many other people too, of course, since they wanted to implicate as many as possible in their crimes. On *that* occasion, however, I showed once again not by
d words but by deeds that I couldn't care less about death—if that isn't putting it too bluntly—but that all I care about is not doing anything unjust or impious. You see, that government, powerful though it was, didn't frighten me into unjust action: when we came out of the Tholus, the other four went to Salamis and arrested Leon, whereas I left and went home. I might have died for that if the government hadn't fallen shortly afterward.

There are many witnesses who will testify before
e you about these events.

Do you imagine, then, that I'd have survived all these years if I'd been regularly active in public affairs, and had come to the aid of justice like a good man, and regarded that as most important, as one should? Far from it, men of Athens, and neither would any
33a other man. But throughout my entire life, in any public activities I may have engaged in, it was evident I was the sort of person—and in private life I was the same—who never agreed to anything with anyone contrary to justice, whether with others or with those who my slanderers say are my students. In fact, I've never been anyone's teacher at any time. But if anyone, whether young or old, wanted to listen to me while I was talking and performing my own task, I never begrudged that to him. Neither do I engage in conversation only when I receive a fee and not when
b I don't. Rather, I offer myself for questioning to rich and poor alike, or, if someone prefers, he may listen to me and answer my questions. And if any one of these turned out well, or did not do so, I can't justly be held responsible, since I never at any time prom-

ised any of them that they'd learn anything from me or that I'd teach them. And if anyone says that he learned something from me or heard something in private that all the others didn't also hear, you may be sure he isn't telling the truth.

Why, then, you may ask, do some people enjoy spending so much time with me? You've heard the answer, men of Athens. I told you the whole truth: *c* it's because they enjoy listening to people being examined who think they're wise but aren't. For it's not unpleasant. In my case, however, it's something, you may take it from me, I've been ordered to do by the god, in both oracles and dreams, and in every other way that divine providence ever ordered any man to do anything at all.

All these things, men of Athens, are both true and easily tested. I mean, if I really do corrupt the young or have corrupted them in the past, surely if any of *d* them had recognized when they became older that I'd given them bad advice at some point in their youth, they'd now have come forward themselves to accuse me and seek redress. Or else, if they weren't willing to come themselves, some of their family members—fathers, brothers, or other relatives—if indeed their kinsmen had suffered any harm from me— would remember it now and seek redress.

In any case, I see many of these people present here: first of all, there's Crito, my contemporary and fellow demesman, the father of Critobulus here;[38] then there's Lysanius of Sphettus, father of Aeschines *e* here;[39] next, there's Epigenes' father, Antiphon of Cephisia here.[40] Then there are others whose brothers

---

after them. Socrates' association with them is often thought to have been one of the things that led to his indictment.]

36. [The Tholus was a dome-shaped building, also called the Skias ("parasol"). The presiding committee of the Council took its meals there.]

37. [Leon is otherwise unknown. The episode, however, is widely reported.]

38. [Crito was a well-off farm owner, able and willing to help his friends financially. His relationship with Socrates is that of an old close friend and neighbor, who is also to some degree a patron or benefactor and adviser on practical matters. Critobulus, his son, was also a member of Socrates' circle and was present at his death.]

39. [Aeschines of Sphettus (fourth-century B.C.E.) was a devoted follower of Socrates, present at his death. He taught oratory and wrote both speeches for the law courts and Socratic dialogues, only fragments of which are extant. His father is otherwise unknown.]

40. [Epigenes was present at Socrates' death and was a member of his circle. Neither he nor his father are otherwise known.]

have spent time in this way: Nicostratus, son of Theozotides,[41] brother of Theodotus—by the way, Theodotus is dead, so that Nicostratus is at any rate not being held back by him; and Paralius here, son of Demodocus, whose brother was Theages;[42] and 34a there's Adeimantus, the son of Ariston, whose brother is Plato here,[43] and Aeantodorus, whose brother here is Apollodorus.[44] And there are many others I could mention, some of whom Meletus most certainly ought to have called as witnesses in the course of his own speech. If he forgot to do so, let him call them now—I yield time to him. Let him tell us if he has any such witness. No, it's entirely the opposite, gentlemen. You'll find that they're all prepared to come to my aid, their corruptor, the one who, Meletus and Anytus claim, is doing harm to their families. Of course, the corrupted ones themselves might indeed b have reason to come to my aid. But the *un*corrupted ones, their relatives, who are older men now, what reason could they possibly have to support me, other than the right and just one: that they know perfectly well that Meletus is lying, whereas I am telling the truth?

Well then, gentlemen, those, and perhaps other similar things, are pretty much all I have to say in my defense. But perhaps one of you might be resentful when he recalls his own behavior. Perhaps when he c was contesting even a lesser charge than this charge, he positively entreated the jurors with copious tears, bringing forward his children and many other relatives and friends as well, in order to arouse as much pity as possible. And then he finds that I'll do none of these things, not even when I'm facing what might

be considered the ultimate danger. Perhaps someone with these thoughts might feel more willful where I'm concerned and, made angry by these very same thoughts, cast his vote in anger. Well, if there's someone like that among you—of course, I don't expect d there to be, but *if* there is—I think it appropriate for me to answer him as follows: "I do indeed have relatives, my excellent man. As Homer puts it,[45] I too 'wasn't born from oak or from rock' but from human parents. And so I do have relatives, sons too, men of Athens, three of them, one already a young man while two are still children. Nonetheless, I won't bring any of them forward here and then entreat you to vote for my acquittal."

Why, you may ask, will I do none of these things? Not because I'm willful, men of Athens, or want to dishonor you—whether I'm boldly facing death or e not is a separate story. The point has to do with reputation—yours and mine and that of the entire city: it doesn't seem noble to me to do these things, especially at my age and with my reputation—for whether truly or falsely, it's firmly believed in any case that Socrates is superior to the majority of people 35a in some way. Therefore, if those of *you* who are believed to be superior—in either wisdom or courage or any other virtue whatever—behave like that, it would be shameful.

I've often seen people of this sort when they're on trial: they're thought to be someone, yet they do astonishing things—as if they imagined they'd suffer something terrible if they died and would be immortal if only you didn't kill them. People like that seem to me to bring such shame to the city that any foreigner might well suppose that those among the Athenians who are superior in virtue—the ones they select from b among themselves for political office and other positions of honor—are no better than women. I say this, men of Athens, because none of us who are in any way whatever thought to be someone should behave like that, nor, if we attempt to do so, should you allow it. On the contrary, you should make it clear you're far more likely to convict someone who makes the city despicable by staging these pathetic scenes than someone who minds his behavior.

41. [Theozotides introduced two important democratic reforms after the fall of the Thirty Tyrants. His sons are otherwise unknown.]

42. [Otherwise largely unknown. Spurious works in the Platonic canon are named after Theages and Demodocus.]

43. [This is one of three places in his dialogues that Plato mentions himself—38b6 and *Phaedo* 59b10 are the others. Adeimantus, with his brother Glaucon, plays an important role in the *Republic*.]

44. [Apollodorus, an enthusiastic follower of Socrates, given to emotion is the narrator in the *Symposium*. His brother is otherwise unknown.]

45. [Penelope is speaking to her husband, Odysseus, whom she hasn't yet recognized.]

Reputation aside, gentlemen, it doesn't seem just to me to entreat the jury—nor to be acquitted by entreating it—but rather to inform it and persuade it. After all, a juror doesn't sit in order to grant justice as a favor, but to decide where justice lies. And he has sworn on oath not that he'll favor whomever he pleases, but that he'll judge according to law.[46] We shouldn't accustom you to breaking your oath, then, nor should you become accustomed to doing so— neither of us would be doing something holy if we did. Hence don't expect me, men of Athens, to act toward you in ways I consider to be neither noble, nor just, nor pious—most especially, by Zeus, when I'm being prosecuted for *impiety* by Meletus here. You see, if I tried to persuade and to force you by entreaties, after you've sworn an oath, I clearly would be teaching you not to believe in the existence of gods, and my defense would literally convict me of not acknowledging gods. But that's far from being the case: I do acknowledge them, men of Athens, as none of my accusers does. I turn it over to you and to the god to judge me in whatever way will be best for me and for yourselves.[47]

• • •

There are many reasons, men of Athens, why I'm not resentful at this outcome—that you voted to convict me—and this outcome wasn't unexpected by me. I'm much more surprised at the number of votes cast on each side: I didn't think that the decision would be by so few votes but by a great many. Yet now, it seems, that if a mere thirty votes had been cast differently,

I'd have been acquitted.[48] Or rather, it seems to me that where Meletus is concerned I've been acquitted even as things stand. And not merely acquitted. On the contrary, one thing at least is clear to everyone: if Anytus had not come forward with Lycon to accuse me, Meletus would have been fined a thousand drachmas, since he wouldn't have received a fifth of the votes.[49]

But be that as it may, the man demands the death penalty for me. Well then, what counterpenalty should I now propose to you, men of Athens? Or is it clear that it's whatever I deserve? What then should it be? What do I deserve to suffer or pay just because I didn't mind my own business throughout my life? Because I didn't care about the things most people care about—making money, managing an estate, or being a general, a popular leader, or holding some other political office, or joining the cabals and factions that come to exist in a city—but thought myself too honest, in truth, to engage in these things and survive? Because I didn't engage in things, if engaging in them was going to benefit neither you nor myself, but instead went to each of you privately and tried to perform what I claim is the greatest benefaction? That was what I did. I tried to persuade each of you to care first not about any of his possessions, but about himself and how he'll become best and wisest; and not primarily about the city's possessions, but about the city itself; and to care about all other things in the same way.

What, then, do I deserve to suffer for being such a man? Something good, men of Athens, if I'm indeed to propose a penalty that I truly deserve. Yes, and the sort of good thing, too, that would be appropriate for me. What, then, is appropriate for a poor man who is a public benefactor and needs to have the leisure to exhort you? Nothing could be more appropriate,

46. [The gist of this oath, which may be pieced together from references such as this one, was as follows: "I will judge according to the laws and decrees of Athens, and I will decide matters about which there are no laws by the most just opinion."]

47. [The jury returns a guilty verdict. Meletus proposes the death penalty. The law permits Socrates to propose an alternative, or counterpenalty, which he proceeds to do in the next part of his defense. Later members of the jury will choose whichever of the penalty and the counterpenalty they deem the more appropriate punishment.]

48. [A jury of 500 (or 501) was usual for an indictment of impiety. It follows that the vote was 280 to 220, since a tied vote resulted in acquittal.]

49. [Socrates is imagining that his accusers received around 90 votes each, or a third of the 280 guilty votes. This is less than the 100 votes that Meletus needed to receive in order to avoid paying the fine to which Socrates refers, which was instituted by law to deter frivolous suits.]

men of Athens, than for such a man to be given free meals in the Prytaneum—much more so for him, at any rate, than for anyone of you who has won a victory at Olympia, whether with a single horse or with a pair or a team of four.[50] You see, he makes you think you're happy, whereas I make you actually happy. Besides, he doesn't need to be sustained in that way, but I do need it. So if, as justice demands, I must propose a penalty I deserve, that's the penalty I propose: free meals in the Prytaneum.

Now perhaps when I say this, you may think I'm speaking in a quite willful manner—just as when I talked about appeals to pity and supplications. That's not so, men of Athens, rather it's something like this: I'm convinced that I never intentionally do injustice to any man—but I can't get you to share my conviction, because we've talked together a short time. I say this, because if you had a law, as other men in fact do, not to try a capital charge in a single day, but over several, I think you'd be convinced.[51] But as things stand, it isn't easy to clear myself of huge slanders in a short time.

Since I'm convinced that I've done injustice to no one, however, I'm certainly not likely to do myself injustice, to announce that I deserve something bad and to propose a penalty of that sort for myself. Why should I do that? In order not to suffer what Meletus proposes as a penalty for me, when I say that I don't know whether it's a good or a bad thing? As an alternative to that, am I then to choose one of the things I know very well to be bad and propose it? Imprisonment, for example? And why should I live in prison, enslaved to the regularly appointed officers, the Eleven?[52] All right, a fine with imprisonment until I pay? But in my case the effect would be precisely the one I just now described, since I haven't the means to pay.

Well then, should I propose exile? Perhaps that's

what you'd propose for me. But I'd certainly have to have an excessive love of life, men of Athens, to be so irrational as to do that. I see that you, my fellow citizens, were unable to tolerate my discourses and discussions but came to find them so burdensome and odious that you're now seeking to get rid of them. Is it likely, then, that I'll infer that others will find them easy to bear? Far from it, men of Athens. It would be a fine life for me, indeed, a man of my age, to go into exile and spend his life exchanging one city for another, because he's always being expelled. You see, I well know that wherever I go, the young will come to hear me speaking, just as they do here. And if I drive them away, they will themselves persuade their elders to expel me; whereas if I don't drive them away, their fathers and relatives will expel me because of these same young people.

Now perhaps someone may say, "But by keeping quiet and minding your own business, Socrates, wouldn't it be possible for you to live in exile for us?" This is the very hardest point on which to convince some of you. You see, if I say that to do *that* would be to disobey the god, and that this is why I can't mind my own business, you won't believe me, since you'll suppose I'm being ironical.[53] But again, if I say it's the greatest good for a man to discuss virtue every day, and the other things you've heard me discussing and examining myself and others about, on the grounds that the unexamined life isn't worth living for a human being, you'll believe me even less when I say that. But in fact, things are just as I claim them to be, men of Athens, though it isn't easy to convince you of them. At the same time, I'm not accustomed to thinking that I deserve anything bad. If I had the means, I'd have proposed a fine of as much as I could afford to pay, since that would have done me no harm at all. But as things stand, I don't have them—unless you want me to propose as much as I'm in fact able to pay. Perhaps I could pay you about a mina of silver. So I propose a fine of that amount.

One moment, men of Athens. Plato here, and Crito, Critobulus, and Apollodorus as well, are urging me to propose thirty minas and saying that they

---

50. [The Prytaneum, a building on the northeast slope of the Acropolis, was the symbolic center of Athens, where the communal hearth was housed. Guests of the city and victors in the Olympic and other games were given free meals there.]

51. [Sparta had a law of this sort.]

52. [Officials appointed by lot to be in charge of prisons and executions.]

53. [Ancient irony (*eirōneia*) involved not simply meaning the contrary of what one said, but saying it with the intention to deceive.]

themselves will guarantee it.[54] I propose a fine of that amount, therefore, and these men will be sufficient guarantors to you of the silver.

• • •

c   For the sake of a little time, men of Athens, you're going to earn from those who wish to denigrate our city both the reputation and the blame for having killed Socrates—that wise man. For those who wish to reproach you will, of course, claim that I'm wise, even if I'm not. In any case, if you'd waited a short time, this would have happened of its own accord. You, of course, see my age, you see that I'm already far along in life and close to death. I'm saying this d not to all of you, but to those who voted for the death penalty. And to those same people I also say this: Perhaps you imagine, gentlemen, that I was convicted for lack of the sort of arguments I could have used to convince you, if I'd thought I should do or say anything to escape the penalty. Far from it. I *have* been convicted for a lack—not of arguments, however, but of boldfaced shamelessness and for being unwilling to say the sorts of things to you you'd have been most pleased to hear, with me weeping and wailing, and doing and saying many other things I claim are unworthy of me, but that are the very sorts e of things you're used to hearing from everyone else. No, I didn't think then that I should do anything servile because of the danger I faced, and so I don't regret now that I defended myself as I did. I'd far rather die after such a defense than live like that.

You see, whether in a trial or in a war, neither I nor anyone else should contrive to escape death at 39a all costs. In battle, too, it often becomes clear that one might escape death by throwing down one's weapons and turning to supplicate one's pursuers. And in each sort of danger there are many other ways one can contrive to escape death, if one is shameless enough to do or say anything. The difficult thing, gentlemen, isn't escaping death; escaping villainy is much more difficult, since it runs faster than death. b And now I, slow and old as I am, have been overtaken

by the slower runner while my accusers, clever and sharp witted as they are, have been overtaken by the faster one—vice. And now I take my leave, convicted by you of a capital crime, whereas they stand forever convicted by the truth of wickedness and injustice. And just as I accept my penalty, so must they. Perhaps, things *had* to turn out this way, and I suppose it's good they have.

Next, I want to make a prophecy to those who con- c victed me. Indeed, I'm now at the point at which men prophesy most—when they're about to die. I say to you men who condemned me to death that as soon as I'm dead vengeance will come upon you, and it will be much harsher, by Zeus, than the vengeance you take in killing me. You did this now in the belief that you'll escape giving an account of your lives. But I say that quite the opposite will happen to you. There will be more people to test you, whom I now restrain, d though you didn't notice my doing so. And they'll be all the harsher on you, since they're younger, and you'll resent it all the more. You see, if you imagine that by killing people you'll prevent anyone from reproaching you for not living in the right way, you're not thinking straight. In fact, to escape is neither possible nor noble. On the contrary, what's best and easiest isn't to put down other people, but to prepare oneself to be the best one can. With that prophecy to those of you who voted to convict me, I take my leave.

However, I'd gladly discuss this result with those who voted for my acquittal while the officers of the court e are busy and I'm not yet on my way to the place where I must die. Please stay with me, gentlemen, just for that short time. After all, there's nothing to prevent us from having a talk with one another while it's still in our power. To you whom I regard as friends I'm willing to show the meaning of what has just now 40a happened to me. You see, gentlemen of the jury— for in calling *you* "jurors" I no doubt use the term correctly—an amazing thing has happened to me. In previous times, the usual prophecies of my daimonic sign were always very frequent, opposing me even on trivial matters, if I was about do something that wasn't right. Now, however, something has happened to me, as you can see for yourselves, that one might think to be, and that's generally regarded as being, the worst

---

54. [Thirty minas (three thousand silver drachmas) was almost ten years' salary for someone engaged in public works.]

of all bad things. Yet the god's sign didn't oppose me
b when I left home this morning, or when I came up
here to the law court, or anywhere in my speech
when I was about to say something, even though in
other discussions it has often stopped me in the middle of what I was saying. Now, however, where this
affair is concerned, it has opposed me in nothing I
either said or did.

What, then, do I suppose is the explanation for
that? I'll tell you. You see, it's likely that what has
happened to me is a good thing and that those of
you who suppose death to be bad make an incorrect
c supposition. I've strong evidence of this, since there's
no way my usual sign would have failed to oppose
me, if I weren't about to achieve something
good.

But let's bear in mind that the following is also a
strong reason to hope that death may be something
good. Being dead is one of two things: either the
dead are nothing, as it were, and have no awareness
whatsoever of anything at all; or else, as we're told,
it's some sort of change, a migration of the soul from
here to another place. Now, if there's in fact no awareness, but it's like sleep—the kind in which the sleeper
has no dream whatsoever—then death would be an
d amazing advantage. For I imagine that if someone
had to pick a night in which he slept so soundly that
he didn't even dream and had to compare all the
other nights and days of his life with that one, and
then, having considered the matter, had to say how
many days or nights of his life he had spent better or
more pleasantly than that night—I imagine that not
just some private individual, but even the great king,[55]
e would find them easy to count compared to the other
days and nights. Well, if death's like that, I say it's
an advantage, since, in that case, the whole of time
would seem no longer than a single night.

On the other hand, if death's a sort of journey from
here to another place, and if what we're told is true,
and all who've died are indeed there, what could be
41a a greater good than that, gentlemen of the jury? If
on arriving in Hades and leaving behind the people
who claim to be jurors here, one's going to find those

who are truly jurors or judges, the very ones who are
said to sit in judgment there too—Minos, Rhadamanthys, Aeachus, Triptolemus,[56] and all the other
demigods who were just in their own lifetimes—
would the journey be a wretched one?

Or again, what would any one of you not give to
talk to Orpheus and Museus, Hesiod and Homer?[57]
I'd be willing to die many times over, if that were
true. You see, for myself, at any rate, spending time
there would be amazing: when I met Palamedes[58] or b
Ajax, the son of Telemon,[59] or anyone else of old who
died because of an unjust verdict, I could compare my
own experience with theirs—as I suppose it wouldn't
be unpleasing to do. And in particular, the most important thing: I could spend time examining and
searching people there, just as I do here, to find
out who among them is wise, and who thinks he is,
but isn't.

55. [The king of Persia, whose wealth and power made
him a popular exemplar of human success and
happiness.]

56. [Minos was a legendary king of Crete. He judges
among the dead in Hades as he did among the living—
though not for wrongs they committed in this life. Rhadamanthys is usually thought to judge not in Hades but
in the Isles of the Blessed. Aeachus is the judge and
lawgiver of Aegina and an arbiter among the gods. Triptolemus, a hero from Eleusis, had a prominent role in
mystery cults.]

57. [Orpheus was a legendary bard and founder of the
mystical religion of Orphism. Museus, usually associated
with Orpheus, was also a legendary bard. Hesiod, an
early Greek poet, is the author of *Theogony* (a work on
the genealogy of the gods) and *Works and Days* (a work of
practical advice and moral suasion). Homer, the greatest
Greek epic poet, is the author of the *Iliad* (which deals
with events in the war between the Greeks and the
Trojans) and the *Odyssey* (which deals with the adventures of Odysseus during his journey home from the
Trojan War).]

58. [Aeschylus, Sophocles, and Euripides all wrote tragedies named after him, and Gorgias wrote a defense of
him. Odysseus hid gold in his tent, forged a letter that
compromised him, accused him of treason, and had him
stoned to death.]

59. [Ajax was cheated of the armor of Achilles in competition with Odysseus. Driven mad, as a result of this
injustice, he committed suicide. Sophocles' *Ajax* deals
with these events.]

What wouldn't one give, gentlemen of the jury, to be able to examine the leader of the great expedition against Troy,[60] or Odysseus,[61] or Sisyphus,[62] or countless other men and women one could mention? To talk to them there, to associate with them and examine them, wouldn't that be inconceivable happiness? In any case, the people there certainly don't kill one for doing it. For if what we're told is true, the people there are both happier in all other respects than the people here and also deathless for the remainder of time.

But you too, gentlemen of the jury, should be of good hope in the face of death, and bear in mind this single truth: nothing bad can happen to a good man, whether in life or in death, nor are the gods unconcerned about his troubles. What has happened to me hasn't happened by chance; rather, it's clear to me that to die now and escape my troubles was a better thing for me. It was for this very reason that my sign never opposed me. And so, for my part, I'm not at all angry with those who voted to condemn me or with my accusers. And yet this wasn't what they had in mind when they were condemning and accusing me. No, they thought to harm me—and for that they deserve to be blamed.

This small favor, however, I ask of them. When my sons come of age, gentlemen, punish them by harassing them in the very same way that I harassed you, if they seem to you to take care of wealth or anything before virtue, if they think they're someone when they're no one. Reproach them, just as I reproached you: tell them that they don't care for the things they should and think they're someone when they're worth nothing. If you will do that, I'll have received my own just deserts from you, as will my sons.

But now it's time to leave, I to die and you to live. Which of us goes to the better thing, however, is unclear to everyone except the god.

60. [Agamemnon, king of Mycenae.]

61. [Odysseus is a legendary hero of the Trojan War, prominent in Homer's *Iliad* and central to his *Odyssey*. He was as famous for his cunning as for his skill in battle.]

62. [Sisyphus is a legendary king and founder of Corinth. A trickster who tried to cheat death, he was punished in Hades by having to roll a boulder to the top of a hill, only to have to do so over and over again, since it always rolled back down.]

CRITO

SOCRATES: Why have you come at this hour, 43a Crito? Isn't it still early?

CRITO: It is indeed.

SOCRATES: About what time?

CRITO: Just before dawn.

SOCRATES: I'm surprised the prison warden was willing to let you in.

CRITO: He knows me by now, Socrates, I come here so often. And besides I've done him a good turn.

SOCRATES: Have you just arrived or have you been here for a while?

CRITO: For quite a while.

SOCRATES: Then why didn't you wake me right b away, instead of sitting there in silence?

CRITO: In the name of Zeus, Socrates, I wouldn't do that! I only wish I weren't so sleepless and distressed myself. I've been amazed all this time to see how peacefully you were sleeping, and I deliberately kept from waking you, so that you could pass the time as pleasantly as possible. In the past—indeed, throughout my entire life—I've often counted you happy in your disposition, but never more so than in this present misfortune. You bear it so easily and calmly.

SOCRATES: Well, Crito, it would be an error for someone of my age to complain when the time has come when he must die.

c CRITO: Other people get overtaken by such misfortunes too, Socrates, but their age doesn't prevent them in the least from complaining about their fate.

SOCRATES: That's right. But tell me, why *have* you come so early?

CRITO: I bring bad news, Socrates. Not bad in your view, it seems to me, but bad and hard in mine and that of all your friends—and hardest of all, I think, for me to bear.

SOCRATES: What news is that? Or has the ship returned from Delos, at whose return I must die?[1] d

CRITO: No, it hasn't returned *yet*, but I think it will arrive today, judging from the reports of people who've come from Sunium,[2] where they left it. It's clear from these reports that it will arrive today. And so tomorrow, Socrates, you must end your life.

SOCRATES: I pray that it may be for the best, Crito. If it pleases the gods, let it be so. All the same, I don't think it will arrive today.

CRITO: What evidence have you for that? 44a

SOCRATES: I'll tell you. I must die on the day after the ship arrives.

CRITO: That's what the authorities say, at least.

SOCRATES: Then I don't think it will arrive today, but tomorrow. My evidence for this comes from a dream I had in the night a short while ago. So it looks as though you chose the right time not to wake me.

CRITO: What was your dream?

SOCRATES: I thought a beautiful, graceful woman came to me, robed in white. She called me and said, "Socrates, you will arrive 'in fertile Phthia' on the b third day."[3]

---

1. [Legend had it that Athens was once obliged to send King Minos of Crete an annual tribute of seven young men and seven maidens to be given to the Minotaur—a monster, half man and half bull, that he kept in a labyrinth. With the help of a thread given to him by Minos' daughter Ariadne, Theseus, a legendary king of Athens, made his way through the labyrinth, killed the Minotaur, and escaped, thus ending the tribute. Each year, Athens commemorated these events by sending a mission of thanks to the sanctuary of Apollo on the sacred island of Delos. No executions could take place in Athens until it returned from its voyage.—C.D.C.R.]

2. [A headland on the southeast coast of Attica, about 30 miles from Athens.]

3. [The quotation is from Homer, *Iliad* IX.363. Agamemnon, leader of the Greek forces, has insulted Achilles by taking back his war prize, Briseis. Achilles

From *The Trials of Socrates*, translated and edited by C.D.C. Reeve (Indianapolis: Hackett Publishing Company, 2002). Copyright © 2002. Reprinted by permission of the publisher.

CRITO: What a strange dream, Socrates.

SOCRATES: Yet its meaning is quite clear, Crito—at least, it seems so to me.

CRITO: All too clear, apparently. But look here, Socrates, it's still not too late to take my advice and save yourself. You see, if you die, I won't just suffer a single misfortune. On the contrary, not only will I lose a friend the like of whom I'll never find again, but, in addition, many people, who don't know you or me well, will think that I didn't care about you, since I could have saved you if I'd been willing to spend the money. And indeed what reputation could be more shameful than being thought to value money more than friends? For the majority of people won't believe that it was you yourself who refused to leave this place, though we were urging you to do so.

SOCRATES: But my dear Crito, why should we care so much about what the majority think? After all, the most decent ones, who are worthier of consideration, will believe that matters were handled in just the way they were in fact handled.

CRITO: But you can surely see, Socrates, that one should care about majority opinion too. Your present situation itself shows clearly that the majority can do not just minor harms but the very worst things to someone who's been slandered in front of them.

SOCRATES: I only wish, Crito, that the majority *could* do the very worst things, then they might also be able to do the very best ones—and everything would be fine. But as it is, they can do neither, since they can't make someone either wise or unwise—the effects *they* produce are really the result of chance.

CRITO: Well, if you say so. But tell me this, Socrates. You're not worried about me and your other friends, are you—fearing that if you escaped, the informers would give us trouble, and that we might be forced to give up all our property, pay heavy fines, or even suffer some further penalty? If you're afraid of anything like that, dismiss it from your mind. After all, we're surely justified in running this risk to save you or an even greater one if need be. Now take my advice, and don't refuse me.

SOCRATES: Yes, those things do worry me, Crito, among many others.

CRITO: Then don't fear them: the sum of money that certain people I know will accept in order to save you and get you out of here isn't that large. Next, don't you see how cheap these informers are and how little money is needed to deal with them? My own wealth's available to you, and it, I think, should be enough. Next, even if your concern for me makes you unwilling to spend my money, there are foreign visitors here who are willing to spend theirs. One of them, Simmias of Thebes, has even brought enough money for this very purpose; and Cebes, too, and a good many others are also willing to contribute.[4] So, as I say, don't let these fears make you hesitate to save yourself. And don't let it trouble you, as you were saying in court, that if you went into exile you wouldn't know what to do with yourself. You see, wherever else you may go, there'll be people to welcome you. If you want to go to Thessaly, I have friends there who'll make much of you and protect you, so that no one in Thessaly will give you any trouble.[5]

Besides, Socrates, I think that what you're doing isn't just: throwing away your life, when you could save it, and hastening the very sort of fate for yourself that your enemies would hasten—and indeed have hastened—in their wish to destroy you. What's more I think you're also betraying those sons of yours by going away and deserting them when you could bring them up and educate them. So far as you're concerned, they must take their chances in life; and the chance they'll get, in all likelihood, is just the one that orphans usually get when they lose their parents. No. Either one shouldn't have children at all, or one ought to see their upbringing and education through

---

withdraws from the battle, so that the Greeks suffer terrible losses. Agamemnon, realizing his mistake, offers enormous recompense but without coming to apologize in person. In response, Achilles threatens to set sail the next morning, so that with good weather he will arrive at his home "in fertile Phthia" on the third day. The dream means that Socrates' soul will find its home on the third day (counting, as usual among the Greeks, both the first and last member of the series).]

4. [Simmias and Cebes (also from Thebes) were followers of Socrates and serve as his chief interlocutors in *Phaedo*.]

5. [Thessaly is a region in the north of Greece.]

to the end. But you seem to me to be choosing the easiest way out, whereas one should choose whatever a good and brave man would choose—particularly when one claims to have cared about virtue throughout one's life.

I feel ashamed on your behalf and on behalf of myself and your friends. I fear that it's going to seem *e* that this whole business of yours has been handled with a certain cowardice on our part. The case was brought to court when it needn't have been brought. Then there was the actual conduct of the trial. And now, to crown it all, this absurd finale to the affair. It's going to seem that we let the opportunity slip because of some vice, such as cowardice, on our part, *46a* since we didn't save you nor did you save yourself, although it was quite possible had we been of even the slightest use.

See to it, then, Socrates, that all this doesn't turn out badly and a shameful thing both for you and for us. Come, deliberate—or rather, at this hour it's not a matter of deliberating but of having deliberated already— and only one decision remains. You see, everything must be done this coming night; and if we delay, it will no longer be possible. For all these reasons, Socrates, please take my advice and don't refuse me.

SOCRATES: My dear Crito, your enthusiasm's *b* most valuable, provided it's of the right sort. But if it isn't, the greater it is, the more difficult it will be to deal with. We must therefore examine whether we should do what you advise or not. You see, I'm not the sort of person who's just now for the first time persuaded by nothing within me except the argument that on rational reflection seems best to me; I've *always* been like that. I can't now reject the arguments I stated before just because this misfortune has befallen me. On the contrary, they seem pretty much the same *c* to me, and I respect and value the same ones as I did before. So if we have no better ones to offer in the present situation, you can be sure I won't agree with you—not even if the power of the majority to threaten us, as if we were children, with the bogeymen of imprisonment, execution, and confiscation of property were far greater than it is now.

What, then, is the most reasonable way to examine these matters? Suppose we first take up the argument you stated about people's opinions. Is it true or not *d* that one should pay attention to some opinions but

not to others? Or was it true before I had to die, whereas it's now clear that it was stated idly, for the sake of argument, and is really just childish nonsense? For my part, I'm eager to join you, Crito, in a joint examination of whether this argument will appear any differently to me, now that I'm here, or the same, and of whether we should dismiss it from our minds or be persuaded by it.

It used to be said, I think, by people who thought they were talking sense, that, as I said a moment ago, one should take some people's opinions seriously but *e* not others. By the gods, Crito, don't you think that was true? You see, in all human probability, *you* are not going to die tomorrow, and so the present situation won't distort your judgment. Consider, then, don't you *47a* think it's a sound argument that one shouldn't value all the opinions people have, but some and not others, and not those of everyone, but those of some people and not of others? What do you say? Isn't that true?

CRITO: It is.

SOCRATES: And we should value good opinions, but not bad ones?

CRITO: Yes.

SOCRATES: And the good ones are those of wise people and the bad ones those of unwise people?

CRITO: Of course.

SOCRATES: Come then, what of such questions as this? When a man's primarily engaged in physical training, does he pay attention to the praise or blame or opinion of every man or only to those of the one *b* man who's a doctor or a trainer?

CRITO: Only to those of the one man.

SOCRATES: Then he should fear the blame and welcome the praise of that one man, but not those of the majority of people.

CRITO: Clearly.

SOCRATES: So his actions and exercises, his eating and drinking, should be guided by the opinion of the one man, the knowledgeable and understanding supervisor, rather than on that of all the rest?

CRITO: That's right.

SOCRATES: Well, then, if he disobeys that one man and sets no value on his opinion or his praises *c* but values those of the majority of people who have no understanding, won't something bad happen to him?

CRITO: Of course.

SOCRATES: And what is this bad effect? Where does it occur? In what part of the one who disobeys?

CRITO: Clearly, it's in his body, since that's what it destroys.

SOCRATES: That's right. And isn't the same true in other cases, Crito? No need to go through them all, but, in particular, in cases of just and unjust things, shameful and fine ones, good and bad ones—in cases of what we're now deliberating about—is it the opinion of the majority we should follow and

d fear? Or is it the opinion of the one man—if there is one who understands these things—we should respect and fear above all others? On the grounds that, if we don't follow it, we shall seriously damage and maim that part of us which, as we used to say, is made better by what's just but is destroyed by what's unjust. Or is there no truth in that?

CRITO: I certainly think there is, Socrates.

SOCRATES: Come then, suppose we destroy the part of us that is made better by what's healthy but is seriously damaged by what causes disease when we don't follow the opinion of people who have understanding. Would our lives be worth living once it has been seriously damaged? And that part, of course, is

e the body, isn't it?

CRITO: Yes.

SOCRATES: Then are our lives worth living with a wretched, seriously damaged body?

CRITO: Certainly not.

SOCRATES: But our lives *are* worth living when the part of us that's maimed by what's unjust and benefited by what's just is seriously damaged? Or do we consider it—whichever part of us it is to which justice and injustice pertain—to be inferior to the

48a body?

CRITO: Certainly not.

SOCRATES: On the contrary, it's more valuable?

CRITO: Far more.

SOCRATES: Then, my very good friend, we should not give so much thought to what the majority of people will say about us, but think instead of what the person who understands just and unjust things will say—the one man and the truth itself. So your first claim—that we should give thought to the opinion of the majority about what's just, fine, good, and their opposites—isn't right.

"But," someone might say, "the majority can put us to death."

CRITO: That's certainly clear too. It would indeed be said, Socrates.

b

SOCRATES: That's right. And yet, my dear friend, the argument we've gone through still seems the same to me, at any rate, as it did before. And now examine this further one to see whether we think it still stands or not: the most important thing isn't living, but living well.

CRITO: Yes, it still stands.

SOCRATES: And the argument that living well, living a fine life, and living justly are the same—does it still stand or not?

CRITO: It still stands.

SOCRATES: Then in the light of these agreements, we should examine whether or not it would be just for me to try to get out of here when the Athenians haven't acquitted me. And if it does seem just, we c should make the attempt, and if it doesn't, we should abandon the effort.

As for those other considerations you raise about loss of money and people's opinions and bringing up children—they, in truth, Crito, are appropriate considerations for people who readily put one to death and would as readily bring one back to life again if they could, without thinking; I mean, the majority of people. For us, however, the argument has made the decision. There's nothing else to be examined besides the very thing we just mentioned: whether we—both the ones who are rescued and also the rescuers themselves—will be acting justly if we pay money to those who would get me out of here and do them favors, or whether we will in truth be acting d unjustly if we do those things. And if it appears that we will be acting unjustly in doing them, we have no need at all to give any opposing weight to our having to die—or suffer in some other way—if we stay here and mind our behavior when the alternative is doing injustice.

CRITO: What you *say* seems true to me, Socrates. But I wish you'd consider what we're to *do*.

SOCRATES: Let's examine that question together, my dear friend, and if you can oppose anything I say, oppose it, and I'll be persuaded by you. But if you can't, be a good fellow and stop telling me the same e thing over and over, that I should leave here against

the will of the Athenians. You see, I think it very important that I act in this matter having persuaded you, rather than against your will. Consider, then, the starting point of our inquiry, to see if you find it adequately formulated, and try to answer my ques-
49a tions as you really think best.

CRITO: I'll certainly try.

SOCRATES: Do we say that one should never do injustice intentionally? Or may injustice be done in some circumstances but not in others? Is doing injustice never good or fine, as we have often agreed in the past? Or have all these former agreements been discarded during these last few days? Can you and I at our age, Crito, have spent so long in serious discussion with one another without realizing that we ourselves were no better than a pair of children? Or is what
b we used to say true above all else: that whether the majority of people agree or not, and whether we must suffer still worse things than at present or ones that are easier to bear, it's true, all the same, that doing injustice in any circumstances is bad and shameful for the one who does it? Is that what we say or not?

CRITO: It is what we say.

SOCRATES: So one should never do injustice.

CRITO: Certainly not.

SOCRATES: So one shouldn't do injustice in return for injustice, as the majority of people think— seeing that one should *never* do injustice.

c   CRITO: Apparently not.

SOCRATES: Well then, should one do wrong or not?

CRITO: Certainly not, Socrates.

SOCRATES: Well, what about when someone does wrong in return for having suffered wrongdoing? Is that just, as the majority of people think, or not just?

CRITO: It's not just at all.

SOCRATES: No, for there's no difference, I take it, between doing wrong and doing injustice?

CRITO: That's right.

SOCRATES: So one must neither do injustice in return nor wrong any man, no matter what one has suffered at his hands. And, Crito, in agreeing to this, watch out that you're not agreeing to anything con-
d trary to what you believe. You see, I know that only a few people do believe or will believe it. And between those who believe it and those who don't, there's no common basis for deliberation, but each necessarily

regards the other with contempt when they see their deliberations. You too, then, should consider very carefully whether you share that belief with me and whether the following is the starting point of our deliberations: that it's never right to do injustice, or to do injustice in return, or to retaliate with bad treatment when one has been treated badly. Or do you disagree and not share this starting point? You see, I've believed this for a long time myself and still believe it now. But if you've come to some other e opinion, say so. Instruct me. If you stand by the former one, however, then listen to my next point.

CRITO: Yes, I do stand by it and share it with you, so go on.

SOCRATES: Then I'll state the next point—or rather, ask a question: should one do the things one has agreed with someone to do, provided they are just, or should one cheat?

CRITO: One should do them.

SOCRATES: Then consider what follows. If we leave this place without having persuaded the city, are we treating some people badly—and those whom 50a we should least of all treat in that way—or not? Are we standing by agreements that are just or not?

CRITO: I can't answer your question, Socrates, since I don't understand it.

SOCRATES: Well, look at it this way. Suppose we were about to run away from here—or whatever what we'd be doing should be called. And suppose the Laws and the city community came and confronted us, and said,

"Tell us, Socrates, what do you intend to do? Do you intend anything else by this act you're attempting than to destroy us Laws, and the city as a whole, to b the extent that you can? Or do you think that a city can continue to exist and not be overthrown if the legal judgments rendered in it have no force, but are deprived of authority and undermined by the actions of private individuals?"

What shall we say in response to that question, Crito, and to others like it? For there's a lot that one might say—particularly, if one were an orator—on behalf of this law we're destroying, the one requiring that legal judgments, once rendered, have authority. Or shall we say to them, "Yes, that's what we intend, for the city treated us unjustly and didn't judge our c lawsuit correctly." Is that what we're to say—or what?

CRITO: Yes, by Zeus, that's what we're to say, Socrates.

SOCRATES: Then what if the Laws replied, "Was that also part of the agreement between you and us, Socrates? Or did you agree to stand by whatever judgments the city rendered?" Then, if we were surprised at the words, perhaps they might say, "Don't be surprised at what we're saying, Socrates, but answer us—since you're so accustomed to using question and answer. Come now, what charge have you to bring against the city and ourselves that you should try to destroy us? In the first place, wasn't it we who gave you birth—wasn't it through us that your father married your mother and produced you? Tell us, do you have some complaint about the correctness of those of us Laws concerned with marriage?"

"No, I have no complaint," I'd reply.

"Well then, what about the Laws dealing with the bringing up and educating of children, under which you were educated yourself? Didn't those of us Laws who regulate that area prescribe correctly when we ordered your father to educate you in the arts and physical training?"

"They prescribed correctly," I'd reply.

"Good. Then since you were born, brought up, and educated, can you deny, first, that you're our offspring and slave, both yourself and your ancestors? And if that's so, do you think that what's just is based on an equality between you and us, that whatever we try to do to you it's just for you to do to us in return? As regards you and your father (or you and your master, if you happened to have one), what's just isn't based on equality, and so you don't return whatever treatment you receive—answering back when you're criticized or striking back when you're struck, or doing many other such things. As regards you and your fatherland and its Laws, then, are these things permitted? If we try to destroy you, believing it to be just, will you try to destroy us Laws and your fatherland, to the extent that you can? And will you claim that you're acting justly in doing so—you the man who really cares about virtue? Or are you so wise that it has escaped your notice that your fatherland is more worthy of honor than your mother and father and all your other ancestors; that it is more to be revered and more sacred and is held in greater esteem both among the gods and among those human beings who have

any sense; that you must treat your fatherland with piety, submitting to it and placating it more than you would your own father when it is angry; that you must either persuade it or else do whatever it commands; that you must mind your behavior and undergo whatever treatment it prescribes for you, whether a beating or imprisonment; that if it leads you to war to be wounded or killed, that's what you must do, and that's what is just—not to give way or retreat or leave where you were stationed, but, on the contrary, in war and law courts, and everywhere else, to do whatever your city or fatherland commands or else persuade it as to what is really just; and that while it is impious to violate the will of your mother or father, it is yet less so than to violate that of your fatherland."

What are we to say to that, Crito? Are the Laws telling the truth or not?

CRITO: Yes, I think they are.

SOCRATES: "Consider, then, Socrates," the Laws might perhaps continue, "whether we're also telling the truth in saying this: that you aren't treating us justly in what you're now trying to do. You see, we gave you birth, upbringing, and education, and have provided you, as well as every other citizen, with a share of all the fine things we could. Nonetheless, if any Athenian—who has been admitted to adult status and has observed both how affairs are handled in the city and ourselves, the Laws—is dissatisfied with us and wishes to leave, we grant him permission to take his property and go wherever he pleases. Not one of us Laws stands in his way or forbids it. If any one of you is dissatisfied with us and the city and wishes to go to a colony or to live as an alien elsewhere,[6] he may go wherever he wishes and hold on to what's his.

"*But* if any of you stays here, after he has observed the way we judge lawsuits and the other ways in which we manage the city, then we say that he has agreed with us by his action to do whatever we command. And we say that whoever does not obey commits a threefold injustice: he disobeys us as his parents; he

---

6. [When the population of a Greek city became too large for its available resources, it often sent some of its citizens out to found a new city elsewhere. This so-called colony (*apoikia*) was politically autonomous but typically retained some significant ties with its mother city.]

disobeys us as those who brought him up; and, after having agreed to obey us, he neither obeys nor persuades us, if we're doing something that isn't right. Yet we offer him a choice and do not harshly command him to do what he's told. On the contrary, we offer two alternatives: he must either persuade us or do what we say. And he does neither. These, then, are the charges, Socrates, to which we say you too will become liable, if you do what you have in mind—and you won't be among the least liable of the Athenians, but among the most."

Then, if I were to say, "Why is that?" perhaps they might justifiably reproach me by saying that I am among the Athenians who have made that agreement with them in the strongest terms.

"Socrates," they would say, "we have the strongest evidence that you were satisfied with us and with the city. After all, you'd never have stayed at home here so much more consistently than all the rest of the Athenians if you weren't also much more consistently satisfied. You never left the city for a festival, except once to go to the Isthmus.[7] You never went anywhere else, except for military service. You never went abroad as other people do. You had no desire to acquaint yourself with other cities or other laws. On the contrary, we and our city sufficed for you. So emphatically did you choose us and agree to live as a citizen under us, that you even produced children here. *That's* how satisfied you were with the city.

"Moreover, even at your very trial, you could have proposed exile as a counterpenalty if you'd wished, and what you're now trying to do against the city's will, you could then have done with its consent. On that occasion, you prided yourself on not feeling resentful that you had to die. You'd choose death before exile—so you said. Now, however, you feel no shame at those words and show no regard for us Laws as you try to destroy us. You're acting exactly the way the most wretched slave would act by trying to run away, contrary to your commitments and your agreements to live as a citizen under us.

"First, then, answer us on this very point: are we telling the truth when we say that you agreed, by

deeds not words, to live as a citizen under us? Or is that untrue?"

What are we to reply to that, Crito? Mustn't we agree?

CRITO: We must, Socrates.

SOCRATES: "Well then," they might say, "surely you're breaking the commitments and agreements you made with us. You weren't coerced or tricked into agreeing or forced to decide in a hurry. On the contrary, you had seventy years in which you could have left if you weren't satisfied with us or if you thought those agreements unjust. You, however, preferred neither Sparta nor Crete—places you often say have good law and order—nor any other Greek or foreign city. On the contrary, you went abroad less often than the lame, the blind, or other handicapped people. Hence it's clear that you, more than any other Athenian, have been consistently satisfied with your city and with us Laws—for who would be satisfied by a city but not by its laws? Won't you, then, stand by your agreements now? Yes, you will, if you're persuaded by us, Socrates, and at least you won't make yourself a laughingstock by leaving the city.

"For consider now: if you break those agreements, if you commit any of these wrongs, what good will you do yourself or your friends? You see, it's pretty clear that your friends will risk being exiled themselves as well as being disenfranchised and having their property confiscated. As for you, if you go to one of the nearest cities, Thebes or Megara—for they both have good laws—you will be arriving there, Socrates, as an enemy of their political systems, and those who care about their own cities will look on you with suspicion, regarding you as one who undermines laws. You will also confirm your jurors in their opinion, so that they will think they judged your lawsuit correctly. For anyone who undermines laws might very well be considered a corruptor of young and ignorant people.

"Will you, then, avoid cities with good law and order, and men of the most respectable kind? And if so, will your life be worth living? Or will you associate with these people and be shameless enough to converse with them? And what will you say, Socrates? The very things that you said here, about how virtue and justice are man's most valuable possessions, along with law and lawful conduct. Don't you think Socrates

7. [The narrow strip of land connecting the Peloponnese to the rest of Greece, where the Isthmian Games were held.]

and everything about him will look unseemly? Surely, you must.

d   "Or will you keep away from those places and go to Crito's friends in Thessaly? After all, there's complete disorder and laxity there, so perhaps they'd enjoy hearing about your absurd escape from prison when you dressed up in disguise, wore a peasant's leather jerkin or some other such escapee's outfit, and altered your appearance. And will no one remark on the fact that you, an old man, with probably only

e   a short time left to live, were so greedy for life that you dared to violate the most important laws? Perhaps not, provided you don't annoy anyone. Otherwise, you'll hear many disparaging things said about you. Will you live by currying favor with every man and acting the slave—and do nothing in Thessaly besides eat, as if you'd gone to live in Thessaly for a good dinner? As for those arguments about justice and the

54a rest of virtue, where, tell us, will they be?

"Is it that you want to live for your children's sake, then, to bring them up and educate them? Really? Will you bring them up and educate them by taking them to Thessaly and making foreigners of them, so they can enjoy that privilege too? If not, will they be better brought up and educated here without you, provided that you're still alive? 'Of course,' you may say, because your friends will take care of them. Then will they take care of them if you go to Thessaly, but not take care of them if you go to Hades? If those who call themselves your friends are worth anything

b   at all, you surely can't believe that.

"No, Socrates, be persuaded by us who reared you. Don't put a higher value on children, on life, or on anything else than on what's just, so that when you reach Hades you may have all this to offer as your defense before the authorities there. For if you do do that, it doesn't seem that it will be better for you *here*, or for any of your friends, or that it will be more just or more pious. And it won't be better for you when you arrive *there* either. As it is, you'll leave here—if you do leave—as one who has been treated unjustly not by us Laws, but by men. But suppose you leave,

c   suppose you return injustice for injustice and bad treatment for bad treatment in that shameful way, breaking your agreements and commitments with us and doing bad things to those whom you should least of all treat in that way—yourself, your friends, your fatherland, and ourselves. Then we'll be angry with you while you're still alive, and our brothers, the Laws of Hades, won't receive you kindly there, knowing that you tried to destroy us to the extent you could. Come, then, don't let Crito persuade you to follow his advice rather than ours."

d

That, Crito, my dear friend, is what I seem to hear them saying, you may be sure. And, just like those Corybantes who think they are still hearing the flutes,[8] the echo of their arguments reverberates in me and makes me incapable of hearing anything else. No, as far as my present thoughts go, at least, you may be sure that if you argue against them, you will speak in vain. All the same, if you think you can do any more, please tell me.

CRITO: No, Socrates, I've nothing to say.

SOCRATES: Then, let it be, Crito, and let's act in that way, since that's the way the god is leading us.

e

8. [The Corybantes dance to the sound of flutes in the orgiastic rites of Dionysus—the god of wine and intoxication. Their music was supposed to induce a state of frenzied exhaustion in hysterical or emotionally disturbed people, from which they awoke relieved of their symptoms.]

PHAEDO DEATH SCENE
(115B1–118A17)

A number of Socrates' friends have come to visit him in prison on the last day of his life. Their conversation focuses on the nature of the soul, arguments for its immortality, and the afterlife. We join it in its final stage. Phaedo—a close friend of Socrates from Elis in the Peloponnese—is the narrator.

115b "Well, Socrates," Crito said, "what are your final instructions for these others or for me concerning your children or anything else? What can we do that would please you most?"

"Just the things I'm always saying, Crito," he said. "Nothing very new. If you take care of your own selves,[1] you'll please both me and mine and yourselves in whatever you do—even if you make no agreements now. But if you don't take care of your own selves and are unwilling to live following the tracks, as it were, of our present and past discussions, then however much you may agree to do at this moment, and however earnestly, you'll accomplish c nothing."

"We'll try hard, then, to do as you say," he said. "But how are we to bury you?"

"Whatever way you like," he said, "provided you can catch me, and I don't elude you." And laughing quietly and looking toward us, he said, "Gentlemen, I can't persuade Crito that I am Socrates here, the one who's talking to you now and setting out in order each of the arguments put forward. He thinks I'm that corpse he'll see in a little while and actually d asks how to bury me! As for the lengthy argument I've been making, that when I drink the poison[2] I'll no longer stay put, but will take my leave of you and depart for certain happy conditions of the blessed—all that, I suppose, he regards as idle talk, intended to console all of you and myself as well. So I want you to give a guarantee to Crito on my behalf," he said, "the opposite guarantee to the one he gave to the jurors. His was that I'd stay put, whereas you must guarantee that I won't stay put when I die, but take my leave of you and depart. In that way, Crito will bear it more easily when he e sees my body being burned or buried, and he won't feel resentful on my behalf, as if I were suffering terrible things, and won't say at the funeral that it's *Socrates* they're laying out, or bearing to the grave, or burying. You see, you may be sure, my dearest Crito," he said, "that false speaking is not only an error in its own terms, but also does something bad to men's souls. No, you should be of good cheer, and say you're burying *my body*, and bury it in any way you like and think most customary." 116a

After saying that, he got up and went into another room to take his bath.[3] Crito followed him, but he told us to stay where we were. So we stayed there, talking among ourselves about what had been said and reexamining it, and sometimes going over again how great a misfortune had befallen us. It was, we thought, simply as if we'd lost a father and would spend the rest of our lives as orphans.

When he had bathed and his children had been brought to him—two of his sons were small while b

From *The Trials of Socrates*, translated and edited by C.D.C. Reeve (Indianapolis: Hackett Publishing Company, 2002). Copyright © 2002. Reprinted by permission of the publisher.

1. [See *Apology* 29d2–30b4.—C.D.C.R.]

2. [Executions in Athens were by poison hemlock.]

3. [Socrates has said that he will bathe before taking the hemlock so as "to save the women the trouble of washing the corpse" (115a8–9).]

one was older—and those women of his household[4] had come, he spoke with them in Crito's presence and gave instructions as to his wishes. He then asked the women and children to leave while he himself returned to us.

It was now almost sunset, since he'd spent a long time inside. He came and sat down, fresh from his bath, and didn't talk much after that. Then the agent of the Eleven came and stood by him: "Socrates," he said, "I won't reproach you, as I reproach others, if you're angry with me and curse me, when, on the orders of the officials, I tell you to drink the poison. During the rest of the time you've spent here, I've known you as the most decent, gentlest, and best man who's ever come to this place. And now, in particular, I'm sure that you won't be angry with me, but with those whom you know to be responsible. Now then, you know the message I've come to bring. Fare you well, and try to bear the inevitable as easily as you can." As he said this, he burst into tears and turned to leave.

Socrates looked up at him: "Fare you well too," he said, "we'll do that." And turning to us, he said, "What a courteous fellow! During the entire time I've been here he's come in and talked to me on occasion, like the excellent man he is. And now how decent of him to weep for me! Come then, Crito, let's do as he asks and have the poison brought if it's ready. If not, have the man prepare it."

"But Socrates," said Crito, "I think the sun's still on the mountains and hasn't yet set. What's more, I know that other people drink the poison long after the order's been given, enjoying themselves with a good dinner and plenty to drink and even, in some cases, by having sex with whomever they happen to desire. Don't be in a hurry: there's still time left."

And Socrates replied, "It's quite reasonable, Crito, for those people to do those things, since they think they gain something by doing them. And it's reasonable too for me not to do them, since I think I'll gain nothing by drinking the poison a little later—apart, that is, from making myself look absurd in my own

eyes by clinging greedily to life and sparing the dregs.[5] Go on, now, do as I ask," he said, "and don't refuse me."

Hearing this, Crito nodded to the slave who was standing nearby. The slave went out and after a time returned with the man who was going to administer the poison and was carrying it already mixed in a cup. When Socrates saw the man, he said, "Well, my friend, you know all about these things: what should I do?"

"Just drink it," he said, "and walk around until your legs feel heavy; then lie down, and it will act of itself." With that, he handed Socrates the cup.

He took it quite calmly, Echecrates,[6] without a tremor or any change of color or countenance; but giving the man his customary mischievous stare, he said, "What do you say about pouring a libation to someone from this drink? Is it permitted or not?"

"We prepare only as much as we think will be the sufficient dose, Socrates," he said.

"I understand," he said. "But one is, I suppose, permitted to utter a prayer to the gods—and one should do so—that one's journey from this world to the next will prove fortunate. That is my prayer; may it be fulfilled." And with these words, he put the cup to his lips and without the least difficulty or distaste drained it. Most of us had been fairly well able to restrain our tears till then. But when we saw him drinking it, and then that he had drunk it, we could do so no longer. In my own case, the tears were pouring down my cheeks despite my efforts, so that I covered my face and wept for myself—not for *him*, certainly not, but for my own misfortune in losing such a man as a friend. Crito had got up and moved away even before I did, when he was unable to hold back his tears. And Apollodorus, who earlier still had been weeping steadily, now burst forth in such a storm of tears and distress that he made everyone present break down—except, that is, for Socrates himself.

4. [Presumably his wife, Xanthippe, and others (60a3–5).]

5. [See Hesiod, *Works and Days* 368–9: "When the cask has just been opened, and when it's almost gone, drink as much as you want; / Be sparing when its half full; but it's useless to spare the dregs."]

6. [Echecrates, an adherent of Pythagorean philosophy, is the person to whom Phaedo is narrating his account.]

"What a way to behave, my friends!" he said. "Why it was for just this reason, you know, that I sent the women away, so they wouldn't commit these sorts of errors. I've heard indeed that one should die in rever-
e ent silence. Come, mind your behavior and control yourselves."

When we heard this we were ashamed and checked our tears. He walked around, and when his legs felt heavy, as he said, he lay down on his back—as the man told him—and then the man, the one who'd given him the poison, took hold of him[7] and after a while examined his feet and legs. He then pinched his foot hard and asked if he could feel it, and Socrates said, "No." After that, he did the same thing in turn
118a to his shins; and moving upward in this way he showed us that he was becoming cold and numb. He himself continued to keep hold of him and said that when the coldness reached his heart, he'd be gone.

Well, by this time the coldness was somewhere in the region of his groin, when, uncovering his head—it had been covered up—he spoke—and these were in fact the last words he uttered. "Crito," he said, "we owe a cock to Asclepius.[8] Please, don't forget to pay the debt."

"It shall be done," said Crito. "Is there anything else you want to say?"

To this question he gave no answer. But shortly afterward he stirred, and when the man uncovered him his eyes were fixed. Seeing this, Crito closed his mouth and his eyes.

Such was the end of our friend, Echecrates, a man who, we would say, was the best of all those we've experienced and, generally speaking, the wisest and the most just.

7. [Probably in order to steady Socrates during the convulsions that usually accompany hemlock poisoning. Plato may have omitted more explicit reference to these in order, among other things, to dramatize Socrates' tranquil acceptance of his fate. See C. Gill, "The Death of Socrates," *Classical Quarterly* 23 (1973): 225–8.]

8. [Asclepius is the god of healing. The significance of Socrates' dying words has been much debated. See Glenn W. Most, "'A Cock for Asclepius,'" *Classical Quarterly* 43 (1993): 96–111.]

REPUBLIC

BOOK I

SOCRATES' NARRATION BEGINS: *I went down to the Piraeus yesterday with Glaucon, the son of Ariston, to say a prayer to the goddess,[1] and also because I wanted to see how they would manage the festival, since they were holding it for the first time. I thought the procession of the local residents was beautiful, but the show put on by the Thracians was no less so, in my view. After we had said our prayer and watched the procession, we started back toward town. Then Polemarchus, the son of Cephalus, saw us from a distance as we were hurrying homeward, and told his slave boy to run and ask us to wait for him. The boy caught hold of my cloak from behind.*

SLAVE: Polemarchus wants you to wait.

I turned around and asked where he was.

SLAVE: He is coming up behind you; please wait for him.
GLAUCON: All right, we will.

Shortly after that, Polemarchus caught up with us. Adeimantus, Glaucon's brother, was with him, and so were Niceratus, the son of Nicias, and some others, all of whom were apparently on their way from the procession.

POLEMARCHUS: It looks to me, Socrates, as if you two are hurrying to get away to town.
SOCRATES: That isn't a bad guess.
POLEMARCHUS: But do you see how many we are?
SOCRATES: Certainly.
POLEMARCHUS: Well, then, either you must prove yourselves stronger than all these people or you will have to stay here.
SOCRATES: Isn't there another alternative still: that we persuade you that you should let us go?
POLEMARCHUS: But could you persuade us, if we won't listen?
GLAUCON: There is no way we could.
POLEMARCHUS: Well, we won't listen; you had better make up your mind to that.
ADEIMANTUS: You mean to say you don't know that there is to be a torch race on horseback for the goddess tonight?
SOCRATES: On horseback? That is something new. Are they going to race on horseback and hand the torches on in relays, or what?
POLEMARCHUS: In relays. And, besides, there will be an all-night celebration that will be worth seeing. We will get up after dinner and go to see the festivities. We will meet lots of young men there and have a discussion. So stay and do as we ask.
GLAUCON: It looks as if we will have to stay.
SOCRATES: If you think so, we must.

So, we went to Polemarchus' house, and there we found Lysias and Euthydemus, the brothers of Polemarchus, and what is more, Thrasymachus of Chalcedon was there too, and Charmantides of Paeania, and Clitophon, the son of Aristonymus. Polemarchus' father, Cephalus, was also inside, and I thought he looked quite old. You see, I hadn't seen him for some time. He was sitting on a sort of chair with cushions and had a wreath on his head, as he had been offering a sacrifice in the courtyard. We sat down

From Plato, *Republic*, translated by C.D.C. Reeve (Indianapolis: Hackett Publishing Company, 2004). Copyright © 2004. Reprinted by permission of the publisher.

1. [*Hê theos*: Most probably—as 354a10–11 implies—the Thracian goddess Bendis, whose cult had recently been introduced in Piraeus. However, for Athenians, Athena is *hê theos*.—C.D.C.R.]

beside him, since some chairs were arranged in a circle there. As soon as he saw me, Cephalus greeted me:

Socrates, you don't often come down to the Piraeus to see us. Yet you should. If it were still easy for me to make the trip to town, you wouldn't have to come here. On the contrary, we would come to you. But
d as it is, you ought to come here more often. I want you to know, you see, that in my case at least, as the other pleasures—the bodily ones—wither away, my appetites for discussions and their pleasures grow stronger. So please do as I ask: have your conversation with these young men, and stay here with us, as you would with your close friends and relatives.

SOCRATES: I certainly will, Cephalus. In fact, I enjoy engaging in discussion with the very old. I
e think we should learn from them—since they are like people who have traveled a road that we too will probably have to follow—what the road is like, whether rough and difficult or smooth and easy. And I would be particularly glad to find out from you what you think about it, since you have reached the point in life the poets call old age's threshold. Is it a difficult time of life? What have you to report about it?

CEPHALUS: By Zeus, Socrates, I will tell you ex-
329a actly what I think. You see, a number of us who are more or less the same age often get together, so as to preserve the old saying.[2] When they meet, the majority of our members lament, longing for the lost pleasures of their youth and reminiscing about sex, drinking parties, feasts, and the other things that go along with them. They get irritated, as if they had been deprived of important things, and had lived well then but are not living now. Some others, too, even moan about the abuse heaped on old people by their
b relatives, and for *that* reason recite a litany of all the evils old age has caused them. But I don't think they blame the real cause, Socrates. After all, if that were the cause, I too would have had the same experiences, at least as far as old age is concerned, and so would everyone else of my age. But as it is, I have met others in the past who don't feel that way—in particular, the poet Sophocles. I was once present when he was

asked by someone, "How are you as far as sex goes, Sophocles? Can you still make love to a woman?" c "Quiet, man," he replied, "I am very glad to have escaped from all that, like a slave who has escaped from a deranged and savage master." I thought at the time what he said was sensible, and I still do. You see, old age brings peace and freedom from all such things. When the appetites cease to stress and impor- tune us, everything Sophocles said comes to pass, and we escape from many insane masters. But in these d matters, and in those concerning one's relatives, the real cause isn't old age, Socrates, but the way people live. If they are orderly and contented, old age, too, is only moderately onerous; if they aren't, both old age, Socrates, *and* youth are hard to bear.

I admired him for saying that, and I wanted him to tell me more, so I urged him on.

I imagine when you say that, Cephalus, the masses e do not accept it. On the contrary, they think you bear old age more easily, not because of the way you live, but because you are wealthy. For the wealthy, they say, have many consolations.

CEPHALUS: That's true, they are not convinced. And there is something in their objection, though not as much as they think. Themistocles' retort is relevant here. When someone from Seriphus insulted him by saying his high reputation was due to his city, not to himself, he replied that, had he been a 330a Seriphian, he would not be famous; but nor would the other, had he been an Athenian. The same account applies to those who are not rich and find old age hard to bear: a good person would not easily bear old age if it were coupled with poverty, but one who wasn't good would not be contented himself even if he were wealthy.

SOCRATES: Did you inherit most of your wealth, Cephalus, or did you make it yourself?

CEPHALUS: What did I make for myself, Socrates, you ask. As a moneymaker I am in between my grand- b father and my father. You see, my grandfather and namesake inherited about the same amount of wealth as I possess and multiplied it many times. However, my father, Lysanias, diminished that amount to even less than I have now. As for me, I am satisfied to

2. ["God ever draws together like to like."]

leave my sons here no less, but a little more, than I inherited.

SOCRATES: The reason I asked is that you do not seem particularly to love money. And those who have not made it themselves are usually like that. But those who have made it themselves love it twice as much as anyone else. For just as poets love their poems and fathers their children, so those who have made money take their money seriously both as something they have made themselves and—just as other people do—because it is useful. This makes them difficult even to be with, since they are unwilling to praise anything except money.

CEPHALUS: That's true.

SOCRATES: Indeed, it is. But tell me something else. What do you think is the greatest good you have enjoyed as a result of being very wealthy?

CEPHALUS: What I have to say probably would not persuade the masses. But you are well aware, Socrates, that when someone thinks his end is near, he becomes frightened and concerned about things he did not fear before. It is then that the stories told about Hades, that a person who has been unjust here must pay the penalty there—stories he used to make fun of—twist his soul this way and that for fear they are true. And whether because of the weakness of old age, or because he is now closer to what happens in Hades and has a clearer view of it, or whatever it is, he is filled with foreboding and fear, and begins to calculate and consider whether he has been unjust to anyone. If he finds many injustices in his life, he often even awakes from sleep in terror, as children do, and lives in anticipation of evils to come. But someone who knows he has not been unjust has sweet good hope as his constant companion—a nurse to his old age, as Pindar says. For he puts it charmingly, Socrates, when he says that when someone lives a just and pious life,

Sweet hope is in his heart
Nurse and companion to his age
Hope, captain of the ever-twisting
Mind of mortal men.

How amazingly well he puts that. It is in this connection I would say the possession of wealth is most valuable, not for every man, but for a good and orderly one. Not cheating someone even unintentionally, not lying to him, not owing a sacrifice to some god or money to a person, and as a result departing for that other place in fear—the possession of wealth makes no small contribution to this. It has many other uses, too, but putting one thing against the other, Socrates, I would say that for a man with any sense, that is how wealth is most useful.

SOCRATES: A fine sentiment, Cephalus. But speaking of that thing itself, justice, are we to say it is simply speaking the truth and paying whatever debts one has incurred? Or is it sometimes just to do these things, sometimes unjust? I mean this sort of thing, for example: everyone would surely agree that if a man borrows weapons from a sane friend, and if he goes mad and asks for them back, the friend should not return them, and would not be just if he did. Nor should anyone be willing to tell the whole truth to someone in such a state.

CEPHALUS: That's true.

SOCRATES: Then the following is not the definition of justice: to speak the truth and repay what one has borrowed.

Polemarchus interrupted:

It certainly is, Socrates, if indeed we are to trust Simonides at all.

CEPHALUS: Well, then, I will hand over the discussion to you, since it is time for me to look after the sacrifices.

POLEMARCHUS: Am I, Polemarchus, not heir of all your possessions?

Cephalus replied with a laugh:

Certainly.

And off he went to the sacrifice.

SOCRATES: Then tell us, heir to the discussion, just what Simonides said about justice that you think is correct.

POLEMARCHUS: He said it is just to give to each what is owed to him. And a fine saying it is, in my view.

SOCRATES: Well, now, it is not easy to disagree

with Simonides, since he is a wise and godlike man. But what exactly does he mean? Perhaps you know, Polemarchus, but I do not understand. Clearly, he does not mean what we said a moment ago—namely, giving back to someone whatever he has lent to you, even if he is out of his mind when he asks for it. And 332a yet what he has lent to you is surely something that is owed to him, isn't it?

POLEMARCHUS: Yes.

SOCRATES: But when he is out of his mind, it is, under no circumstances, to be given to him?

POLEMARCHUS: True.

SOCRATES: Then it seems Simonides must have meant something else when he says that to return what is owed is just.

POLEMARCHUS: Something else indeed, by Zeus! He meant friends owe something good to their friends, never something bad.

SOCRATES: I understand. You mean someone does not give a lender what he is owed by giving him gold, when the giving and taking would be harmful, b and both he and the lender are friends. Isn't that what you say Simonides meant?

POLEMARCHUS: It certainly is.

SOCRATES: Now what about this? Should one also give to one's enemies whatever is owed to them?

POLEMARCHUS: Yes, by all means. What is *in fact* owed to them. And what an enemy owes an enemy, in my view, is also precisely what is appropriate— something bad.

SOCRATES: It seems, then, Simonides was speaking in riddles—just like a poet!—when he said what c justice is. For what he meant, it seems, is that it is just to give to each *what is appropriate to him*, and this is what he called giving him *what he is owed*.

POLEMARCHUS: What else did you think he meant?

SOCRATES: Then what, in the name of Zeus, do you think he would answer if someone asked him: "Simonides, what owed or appropriate things does the craft we call medicine give, and to which things?"

POLEMARCHUS: Clearly, he would say it gives drugs, food, and drink to bodies.

SOCRATES: And what owed or appropriate things does the craft we call cooking give, and to which things?

POLEMARCHUS: It gives pleasant flavors to food. d

SOCRATES: Good. Now what does the craft we would call justice give, and to whom or what does it give it?

POLEMARCHUS: If we are to follow the previous answers, Socrates, it gives benefit to friends and harm to enemies.

SOCRATES: Does Simonides mean, then, that treating friends well and enemies badly is justice?

POLEMARCHUS: I believe so.

SOCRATES: And who is most capable of treating sick friends well and enemies badly in matters of disease and health?

POLEMARCHUS: A doctor.

SOCRATES: And who can do so best in a storm at sea? e

POLEMARCHUS: A ship's captain.

SOCRATES: What about the just person? In what actions and what work is he most capable of benefiting friends and harming enemies?

POLEMARCHUS: In wars and alliances, I imagine.

SOCRATES: All right. Now when people are not sick, Polemarchus, a doctor is useless to them.

POLEMARCHUS: True.

SOCRATES: And so is a ship's captain to those who are not sailing?

POLEMARCHUS: Yes.

SOCRATES: So to people who are not at war, a just man is useless?

POLEMARCHUS: No, I don't think that at all.

SOCRATES: So justice is also useful in peacetime?

POLEMARCHUS: Yes, it is useful. 333a

SOCRATES: And so is farming, isn't it?

POLEMARCHUS: Yes.

SOCRATES: For providing produce?

POLEMARCHUS: Yes.

SOCRATES: And shoemaking as well, of course?

POLEMARCHUS: Yes.

SOCRATES: For the acquisition of shoes, I suppose you would say?

POLEMARCHUS: Of course.

SOCRATES: Tell me, then, what is justice useful for using or acquiring in peacetime?

POLEMARCHUS: Contracts, Socrates.

SOCRATES: And by contracts you mean partnerships, or what?

POLEMARCHUS: Partnerships, of course.

SOCRATES: So is it a just man who is a good and
b useful partner in a game of checkers, or an expert
checkers player?

POLEMARCHUS: An expert checkers player.

SOCRATES: And in laying bricks and stones, is a
just person a better and more useful partner than
a builder?

POLEMARCHUS: Not at all.

SOCRATES: Well, in what kind of partnership,
then, is a just person a better partner than a builder
or a lyre player, in the way a lyre player is better than
a just person at hitting the right notes?

POLEMARCHUS: In money matters, I think.

SOCRATES: Except, I presume, Polemarchus, in
using money. You see, whenever one needs to buy
or sell a horse jointly, I think a horse breeder is a
c more useful partner. Isn't he?

POLEMARCHUS: Apparently.

SOCRATES: And when it is a boat, a boat builder
or a ship's captain?

POLEMARCHUS: It would seem so.

SOCRATES: In what joint use of silver or gold,
then, is a just person a more useful partner than
anyone else?

POLEMARCHUS: When yours must be deposited
for safekeeping, Socrates.

SOCRATES: You mean whenever there is no need
to use it, but only to keep it?

POLEMARCHUS: Of course.

SOCRATES: So when money is not being used,
d that is when justice is useful for it?

POLEMARCHUS: It looks that way.

SOCRATES: And when one needs to keep a pruning knife safe, justice is useful both in partnerships
and for the individual. When you need to use it,
however, it is the craft of vine pruning that is useful?

POLEMARCHUS: Apparently.

SOCRATES: And would you also say that when one
needs to keep a shield and a lyre safe and not use
them, justice is a useful thing, but when you need
to use them it is the soldier's craft or the musician's
that is useful?

POLEMARCHUS: I would have to.

SOCRATES: And so in all other cases, too, justice
is useless when they are in use, but useful when they
are not?

POLEMARCHUS: It looks that way.

SOCRATES: Then justice cannot be something excellent, can it, my friend, if it is only useful for useless e
things. But let's consider the following point. Isn't
the person who is cleverest at landing a blow, whether
in boxing or any other kind of fight, also cleverest at
guarding against it?

POLEMARCHUS: Of course.

SOCRATES: And the one who is clever at guarding
against disease is also cleverest at producing it
unnoticed?

POLEMARCHUS: That is my view, at any rate.

SOCRATES: And the one who is a good guardian
of an army is the very one who can steal the enemy's 334a
plans and dispositions?

POLEMARCHUS: Of course.

SOCRATES: So whenever someone is a clever
guardian of something, he is also clever at stealing it.

POLEMARCHUS: It seems so.

SOCRATES: So if a just person is clever at guarding
money, he must also be clever at stealing it.

POLEMARCHUS: So the argument suggests, at
least.

SOCRATES: It seems, then, that a just person has
turned out to be a kind of thief. You probably got
that idea from Homer. For he loves Autolycus, the
maternal grandfather of Odysseus, whom he describes b
as better than everyone at stealing and swearing false
oaths.[3] According to you, Homer, and Simonides,
then, justice seems to be some sort of craft of stealing—one that benefits friends and harms enemies.
Isn't that what you meant?

POLEMARCHUS: No, by Zeus, it isn't. But I do
not know anymore what I meant. I still believe this,
however, that benefiting one's friends and harming
one's enemies is justice.

SOCRATES: Speaking of friends, do you mean
those a person believes to be good and useful, or c
those who actually are good and useful, even if he
does not believe they are, and similarly with enemies?

POLEMARCHUS: Probably, one loves those one
considers good and useful and hates those one considers bad.

SOCRATES: But don't people make mistakes about
this, so that lots of those who seem to them to be
good and useful aren't, and vice versa?

3. [*Odyssey* 19.392–8.]

POLEMARCHUS: They do.

SOCRATES: So, for them, good people are enemies and bad ones friends?

POLEMARCHUS: Of course.

SOCRATES: All the same, it is then just for them
d to benefit bad people and harm good ones?

POLEMARCHUS: Apparently.

SOCRATES: Yet good people are just and are not the sort to do injustice.

POLEMARCHUS: True.

SOCRATES: According to your account, then, it is just to do bad things to those who do no injustice.

POLEMARCHUS: Not at all, Socrates. It is *my account* that seems to be bad.

SOCRATES: It is just, then, is it, to harm unjust people and benefit just ones?

POLEMARCHUS: That seems better than the other view.

SOCRATES: Then it follows, Polemarchus, that it is just for many people—the ones who are mistaken
e in their judgment—to harm their friends, since they are bad for them, and benefit their enemies, since they are good. And so we will find ourselves claiming the very opposite of what we said Simonides meant.

POLEMARCHUS: Yes, that certainly follows. But let's change our definition. For it looks as though we did not define friends and enemies correctly.

SOCRATES: How did we define them, Polemarchus?

POLEMARCHUS: We said that a friend is someone who is believed to be good.

SOCRATES: And how are we to change that now?

POLEMARCHUS: Someone who is both believed to be good and is good is a friend; someone who is believed to be good, but is not, is believed to be a
335a friend but is not. And the same goes for enemies.

SOCRATES: According to that account, then, a good person will be a friend and a bad one an enemy.

POLEMARCHUS: Yes.

SOCRATES: So you want us to add something to what we said before about the just man. Then we said that it is just to treat friends well and enemies badly. Now you want us to add to this: to treat a friend well, *provided he is good*, and to harm an enemy, *provided he is bad*?

b   POLEMARCHUS: Yes, that seems well put to me.

SOCRATES: Should a just man really harm anyone whatsoever?

POLEMARCHUS: Of course. He should harm those who are both bad and enemies.

SOCRATES: When horses are harmed, do they become better or worse?

POLEMARCHUS: Worse.

SOCRATES: With respect to the virtue that makes dogs good, or to the one that makes horses good?

POLEMARCHUS: With respect to the one that makes horses good.

SOCRATES: And when dogs are harmed, they become worse with respect to the virtue that makes dogs, not horses, good?

POLEMARCHUS: Necessarily.

SOCRATES: And what about human beings, comrade; shouldn't we say that, when they are harmed,   c they become worse with respect to human virtue?

POLEMARCHUS: Of course.

SOCRATES: But isn't justice human virtue?

POLEMARCHUS: Yes, that's necessarily so, too.

SOCRATES: Then, my dear Polemarchus, people who have been harmed are bound to become more unjust.

POLEMARCHUS: So it seems.

SOCRATES: Now, can musicians use music to make people unmusical?

POLEMARCHUS: No, they can't.

SOCRATES: Or can horsemen use horsemanship to make people unhorsemanlike?

POLEMARCHUS: No.

SOCRATES: Well, then, can just people use justice to make people unjust? In a word, can good people use their virtue or goodness to make people bad?   d

POLEMARCHUS: No, they can't.

SOCRATES: For it isn't the function of heat to cool things down, I imagine, but that of its opposite.

POLEMARCHUS: Yes.

SOCRATES: Nor the function of dryness to make things wet, but that of its opposite.

POLEMARCHUS: Of course.

SOCRATES: So the function of a good person isn't to harm, but that of his opposite.

POLEMARCHUS: Apparently.

SOCRATES: And a just person is a good person?

POLEMARCHUS: Of course.

SOCRATES: So it isn't the function of a just person

to harm a friend or anyone else, Polemarchus, but that of his opposite, an unjust person.

POLEMARCHUS: I think you are absolutely right, Socrates.

SOCRATES: So if someone tells us it is just to give *e* to each what he is owed, and understands by this that a just man should harm his enemies and benefit his friends, the one who says it is not wise. I mean, what he says is not true. For it has become clear to us that it is never just to harm anyone.

POLEMARCHUS: I agree.

SOCRATES: You and I will fight as partners, then, against anyone who tells us that Simonides, Bias, Pittacus, or any of our other wise and blessedly happy men said this.

POLEMARCHUS: I, for my part, am willing to be your partner in the battle.

SOCRATES: Do you know whose saying I think it *336a* is, that it is just to benefit friends and harm enemies?

POLEMARCHUS. Whose?

SOCRATES: I think it is a saying of Periander, or Perdiccas, or Xerxes, or Ismenias of Thebes, or some other wealthy man who thought he had great power.

POLEMARCHUS: That's absolutely true.

SOCRATES: All right. Since it has become apparent, then, that neither justice nor the just consists in benefiting friends and harming enemies, what else should one say it is?

Now, while we were speaking, Thrasymachus *b* *had tried many times to take over the discussion but was restrained by those sitting near him, who wanted to hear our argument to the end. When we paused after what I had just said, however, he could not keep quiet any longer: crouched up like a wild beast about to spring, he hurled himself at us as if to tear us to pieces. Polemarchus and I were frightened and flustered as he roared into our midst:*

What nonsense you two have been talking all this *c* time, Socrates! Why do you act like naïve people, giving way to one another? If you really want to know what justice is, don't just ask questions and then indulge your love of honor by refuting the answers. You know very well it is easier to ask questions than to answer them. Give an answer yourself and tell us

what *you* say the just is. And don't tell me it is the right, the beneficial, the profitable, the gainful, or *d* the advantageous, but tell me clearly and exactly what you mean. For I won't accept such nonsense from you.

His words startled me and, looking at him, I was afraid. And I think if I had not seen him before he looked at me, I would have been dumbstruck.[4] But as it was, I happened to look at him just as he began to be exasperated by our argument, so I was able to answer; and trembling a little, *e* *I said:*

Do not be too hard on us, Thrasymachus. If Polemarchus and I made an error in our investigation of the accounts, you may be sure we did so involuntarily. If we were searching for gold, we would never voluntarily give way to each other, if by doing so we would destroy our chance of finding it. So do not think that in searching for justice, a thing more honorable than a large quantity of gold, we would foolishly give way to one another or be less than completely serious about finding it. You surely must not think that, my friend, but rather—as I do—that we are incapable of finding it. Hence it is surely far more appropriate for us to be pitied by you clever people than to be given rough treatment. *337a*

When he heard that, he gave a loud sarcastic laugh:

By Heracles! That is Socrates' usual irony for you! I knew this would happen. I even told these others earlier that you would be unwilling to answer, that you would be ironic and do anything rather than give an answer, if someone questioned *you*.

SOCRATES: That is because you are a wise fellow, Thrasymachus. You knew very well if you ask someone how much twelve is, and in putting the question you warn him, "Don't tell me, man, that twelve is *b* twice six, or three times four, or six times two, or four times three; for I won't accept such nonsense from you"—it was obvious to you, I imagine, that no one

---

4. [In Greek superstition, anyone seen by a wolf before he sees it is struck dumb.]

could respond to a person who inquired in that way. But suppose he said to you: "What do you mean, Thrasymachus; am I not to give any of the answers you mention, not even if twelve happens to be one of those things? You are amazing. Do you want me to say something other than the truth? Or do you mean something c else?" What answer would you give him?

THRASYMACHUS: Well, so you think the two cases are alike?

SOCRATES: Why shouldn't I? But even if they are not alike, yet seem so to the person you asked, do you think he is any less likely to give the answer that seems right to him, whether we forbid him to do so or not?

THRASYMACHUS: Is that what you are going to do, give one of the forbidden answers?

SOCRATES: I would not be surprised—provided it is the one that seems right to me after I have investigated the matter.

THRASYMACHUS: What if I show you another answer about justice, one that is different from all these d and better than any of them? What penalty would you deserve then?

SOCRATES: The very one that is appropriate for someone who does not know—what else? And what is appropriate is to learn from the one who does know. That, therefore, is what I deserve to suffer.

THRASYMACHUS: What a pleasant fellow you are! But in addition to learning, you must pay money.

SOCRATES: I will if I ever have any.

GLAUCON: He has it already. If it is a matter of money, speak, Thrasymachus. We will all contribute for Socrates.

THRASYMACHUS: Oh yes, sure, so that Socrates e can carry on as usual: he gives no answer himself, and if someone else does, he takes up his account and refutes it.

SOCRATES: How can someone give an answer, my excellent man, when, first of all, he does not know and does not claim to know, and then, even if he does have some opinion about the matter, is forbidden by no ordinary man to express any of the things he thinks? No, it is much more appropriate for you to 338a answer, since you say you do know and can tell us. Don't be obstinate. Give your answer as a favor to me and do not begrudge your teaching to Glaucon and the others.

While I was saying this, Glaucon and the others begged him to do as I asked. Thrasymachus clearly wanted to speak in order to win a good reputation, since he thought he had a very good answer. But he pretended to want to win a victory at my expense by having me do the answering. However, he agreed in the end, and then said:

That is Socrates' wisdom for you: he himself isn't b willing to teach but goes around learning from others and isn't even grateful to them.

SOCRATES: When you say I learn from others, you are right, Thrasymachus; but when you say I do not give thanks, you are wrong. I give as much as I can. But I can give only praise, since I have no money. And just how enthusiastically I give it, when someone seems to me to speak well, you will know as soon as you have answered, since I think you will speak well.

THRASYMACHUS: Listen, then. I say justice is nothing other than what is advantageous for the stronger. c Well, why don't you praise me? No, you are unwilling.

SOCRATES: First, I must understand what you mean. For, as things stand, I do not. What is advantageous for the stronger, you say, is just. What on earth do you mean, Thrasymachus? Surely you do not mean something like this: Polydamas, the pancratist, is stronger than we are. Beef is advantageous for his body. So, this food is also both advantageous and just for us who are weaker than he?   d

THRASYMACHUS: You disgust me, Socrates. You interpret my account in the way that does it the most evil.

SOCRATES: That's not it at all, my very good man; I only want you to make your meaning clearer.

THRASYMACHUS: Don't you know, then, that some cities are ruled by a tyranny, some by a democracy, and some by an aristocracy?

SOCRATES: Of course I do.

THRASYMACHUS: And that what is stronger in each city is the ruling element?

SOCRATES: Certainly.

THRASYMACHUS: And each type of rule makes laws that are advantageous for itself: democracy makes e democratic ones, tyranny tyrannical ones, and so on with the others. And by so legislating, each declares that what is just for its subjects is what is advantageous for itself—the ruler—and it punishes anyone who deviates from this as lawless and unjust. That, Socrates, is what I say justice is, the same in all cities: what is advantageous for the established rule. Since 339a the established rule is surely stronger, anyone who does the rational calculation correctly will conclude that the just is the same everywhere—what is advantageous for the stronger.

SOCRATES: Now I see what you mean. Whether it is true or not, I will try to find out. But you yourself have answered that what is just is what is advantageous, Thrasymachus, whereas you forbade me to answer that. True, you have added *for the stronger* to it.

THRASYMACHUS: And I suppose you think that is b an insignificant addition.

SOCRATES: It isn't clear yet whether it is significant. What *is* clear is that we must investigate whether or not it is true. I agree that what is just is something advantageous. But you add *for the stronger*. I do not know about that. We will have to look into it.

THRASYMACHUS: Go ahead and look.

SOCRATES: That is just what I am going to do. Tell me, then, you also claim, don't you, that it is just to obey the rulers?

THRASYMACHUS: I do.

SOCRATES: And are the rulers in each city infalli- c ble, or are they liable to error?

THRASYMACHUS: No doubt, they are liable to error.

SOCRATES: So, when they attempt to make laws, they make some correctly, others incorrectly?

THRASYMACHUS: I suppose so.

SOCRATES: And a law is correct if it prescribes what is advantageous for the rulers themselves, and incorrect if it prescribes what is disadvantageous for them? Is that what you mean?

THRASYMACHUS: It is.

SOCRATES: And whatever laws the rulers make must be obeyed by their subjects, and that is what is just?

THRASYMACHUS: Of course.

SOCRATES: According to your account, then, it d isn't only just to do what is advantageous for the stronger, but also the opposite: what is not advantageous.

THRASYMACHUS: What is that you are saying?

SOCRATES: The same as you, I think. But let's examine it more closely. Haven't we agreed that the rulers are sometimes in error as to what is best for themselves when they give orders to their subjects, and yet that it is just for their subjects to do whatever their rulers order? Wasn't that agreed?

THRASYMACHUS: I suppose so.

SOCRATES: You will also have to suppose, then, that you have agreed that it is just to do what is e disadvantageous for the rulers and those who are stronger, whenever they unintentionally order what is bad for themselves. But you say, too, that it is just for the others to obey the orders the rulers gave. You are very wise, Thrasymachus, but doesn't it necessarily follow that it is just to do the opposite of what you said, since the weaker are then ordered to do what is disadvantageous for the stronger?

POLEMARCHUS: By Zeus, Socrates, that's abso- 340a lutely clear.

And Clitophon interrupted:

Of course it is, if you are to be his witness, at any rate.

POLEMARCHUS: Who needs a witness? Thrasymachus himself agrees that the rulers sometimes issue orders that are bad for them, and that it is just for the others to obey them.

CLITOPHON: That, Polemarchus, is because Thrasymachus maintained that it is just to obey the orders of the rulers.

POLEMARCHUS: Yes, Clitophon, and he also maintained that what is advantageous for the stronger is just. And having maintained both principles, he b went on to agree that the stronger sometimes order the weaker, who are subject to them, to do things that are disadvantageous for the stronger themselves. From these agreements it follows that what is advantageous for the stronger is no more just than what is not advantageous.

CLITOPHON: But what he meant by what is advantageous for the stronger is what the stronger *believes* to be advantageous for him. That is what he maintained the weaker must do, and that is what he maintained is what is just.

POLEMARCHUS: But it is not what he said.

SOCRATES: It makes no difference, Polemarchus. If Thrasymachus wants to put it that way now, let's c accept it. But tell me, Thrasymachus, is that what you intended to say, that what is just is what the stronger believes to be advantageous for him, whether it is in fact advantageous for him or not? Is that what we are to say you mean?

THRASYMACHUS: Not at all. Do you think I would call someone who is in error stronger at the very moment he errs?

SOCRATES: I did think you meant that, when you agreed that the rulers are not infallible but sometimes make errors.

THRASYMACHUS: That is because you are a quibbler in arguments, Socrates. I mean, when someone makes an error in the treatment of patients, do you call him a doctor in virtue of the fact that he made that very error? Or, when someone makes an error in calculating, do you call him an accountant in virtue of the fact that he made that very error in calculation? I think we express ourselves in words that, taken literally, do say that a doctor is in error, or an accountant, or a grammarian. But each of these, to the extent that he is what we call him, never makes errors, so that, according to the precise account (and you are a stickler for precise accounts), no craftsman ever makes errors. It is when his knowledge fails him that he makes an error, and, in virtue of the fact that he made that error, he is no craftsman. No craftsman, wise man, or ruler makes an error at the moment when he is ruling, even though everyone will say that a physician or a ruler makes errors. It is in this loose way that you must also take the answer I gave just now. But the most precise answer is this: a ruler, to the extent that he is a ruler, never makes errors and unerringly decrees what is best for himself, and that is what his subject must do. Thus, as I said from the first, it is just to do what is advantageous for the stronger.

SOCRATES: Well, Thrasymachus, so you think I quibble, do you?

THRASYMACHUS: Yes, I do.

SOCRATES: And you think that I asked the questions I did in a premeditated attempt to do you evil in the argument?

THRASYMACHUS: I am certain of it. But it won't do you any good. You will never be able to do me evil by covert means, and without them, you will never be able to overpower me by argument.

SOCRATES: Bless you, Thrasymachus; I would not so much as try! But to prevent this sort of confusion from happening to us again, would you define whether you mean the ruler and stronger in the ordinary sense or in what you were just now calling the precise sense, when you say that it is just for the weaker to do what is advantageous for him, since he is the stronger?

THRASYMACHUS: I mean the ruler in the most precise sense. Now do *that* evil, if you can, and practice your quibbling on it—I ask no favors. But you will find there is nothing you can do.

SOCRATES: Do you think that I am crazy enough to try to shave a lion[5] and quibble with Thrasymachus?

THRASYMACHUS: Well, you certainly tried just now, although you were a good-for-nothing at it, too!

SOCRATES: That's enough of that! Tell me: is a doctor—in the precise sense, the one you mentioned before—a moneymaker or someone who treats the sick? Tell me about the one who is really a doctor.

THRASYMACHUS: Someone who treats the sick.

SOCRATES: What about a ship's captain? Is the true captain a ruler of sailors, or a sailor?

THRASYMACHUS: A ruler of sailors.

SOCRATES: In other words, we should not take any account of the fact that he sails in a ship, and he should not be called a sailor for that reason. For it is not because he is sailing that he is called a ship's captain, but because of the craft he practices and his rule over sailors?

THRASYMACHUS: True.

SOCRATES: And is there something that is advantageous for each of these?

THRASYMACHUS: Certainly.

SOCRATES: And isn't it also the case that the natural aim of the craft is to consider and provide what is advantageous for each?

THRASYMACHUS: Yes, that is its aim.

SOCRATES: And is anything advantageous for each of the crafts themselves besides being as perfect as possible?

THRASYMACHUS: How do you mean?

SOCRATES: It is like this: suppose you asked me whether it is satisfactory for a body to be a body, or whether it needs something else. I would answer, "Of

5. [Proverbial characterization of an almost impossible task.]

course it needs something. In fact, that is why the craft of medicine has been discovered—because a body is deficient and it is not satisfactory for it to be like that. To provide what is advantageous, that is what the craft was developed for." Do you think I am speaking correctly in saying this, or not?

THRASYMACHUS: Correctly.

SOCRATES: What about medicine itself? Is it defi-
342a cient? Does a craft need some further virtue, as the eyes are in need of sight and the ears of hearing, so that another craft is needed to consider and provide what is advantageous for them? Does a craft have some similar deficiency itself, so that each craft needs another to consider what is advantageous for it? And does the craft that does the considering need still another, and so on without end? Or does each con-sider by itself what is advantageous for it? Does it need
b neither itself nor another craft to consider what—in light of its own deficiency—is advantageous for it? Indeed, is there no deficiency or error in any craft? And is it inappropriate for any craft to consider what is advantageous for anything besides that with which it deals? And since it is itself correct, is it without fault or impurity so long as it is wholly and precisely the craft it is? Consider this with that precision of language you mentioned. Is it so or not?

THRASYMACHUS: It appears to be so.

SOCRATES: Doesn't it follow that medicine does not consider what is advantageous for medicine, but
c for the body?

THRASYMACHUS: Yes.

SOCRATES: And horse breeding does not consider what is advantageous for horse breeding, but for horses? Indeed, no other craft considers what is advan-tageous for itself—since it has no further needs—but what is advantageous for that with which it deals?

THRASYMACHUS: Apparently so.

SOCRATES: Now surely, Thrasymachus, the vari-ous crafts rule over and are stronger than that with which they deal?

He gave in at this point as well, very reluctantly.

SOCRATES: So no kind of knowledge considers or enjoins what is advantageous for itself, but what is
d advantageous for the weaker, which is subject to it.

He finally agreed to this too, although he tried to fight it. When he had agreed, however, I said:

Surely then, no doctor, to the extent that he is a doctor, considers or enjoins what is advantageous for himself, but what is advantageous for his patient? For we agreed that a doctor, in the precise sense, is a ruler of bodies, not a moneymaker. Isn't that what we agreed?

THRASYMACHUS: Yes.

SOCRATES: So a ship's captain, in the precise sense, is a ruler of sailors, not a sailor?

THRASYMACHUS: That is what we agreed.   e

SOCRATES: Doesn't it follow that a ship's captain and ruler won't consider and enjoin what is advanta-geous for a captain, but what is advantageous for a sailor and his subject?

He reluctantly agreed.

SOCRATES: So then, Thrasymachus, no one in any position of rule, to the extent that he is a ruler, considers or enjoins what is advantageous for himself, but what is advantageous for his subject—that on which he practices his craft. It is to his subject and what is advantageous and proper for it that he looks, and everything he says and does, he says and does for it.

When we reached this point in the argument and it was clear to all that his account of justice   343a had turned into its opposite, instead of answer-ing, Thrasymachus said:

Tell me, Socrates, do you still have a wet nurse?

SOCRATES: What is that? Shouldn't you be giving answers rather than asking such things?

THRASYMACHUS: Because she is letting you run around sniveling and doesn't wipe your nose when you need it, since it is her fault that you do not know the difference between sheep and shepherds.

SOCRATES: What exactly is it I do not know?

THRASYMACHUS: You think that shepherds and cowherds consider what is good for their sheep and   b cattle, and fatten them and take care of them with some aim in mind other than what is good for their master and themselves. Moreover, you believe that rulers in cities—true rulers, that is—think about their subjects in a different way than one does about sheep, and that what they consider night and day is something other than what is advantageous for themselves.

c You are so far from understanding justice and what is just, and injustice and what is unjust, that you do not realize that justice is really the good of another, what is advantageous for the stronger and the ruler, and harmful to the one who obeys and serves. Injustice is the opposite, it rules those simpleminded—for that is what they really are—just people, and the ones it rules do what is advantageous for the other who is stronger; and they make the one they serve happy, but they do not make themselves the least bit happy.

d You must consider it as follows, Socrates, or you will be the most naïve of all: a just man must always get less than does an unjust one. First, in their contracts with one another, when a just man is partner to an unjust, you will never find, when the partnership ends, that the just one gets more than the unjust, but less. Second, in matters relating to the city, when taxes are to be paid, a just man pays more on an equal amount of property, an unjust one less; but when the city is giving out refunds, a just man gets nothing while an unjust one makes a large profit.

e Finally, when each of them holds political office, a just person—even if he is not penalized in other ways—finds that his private affairs deteriorate more because he has to neglect them, that he gains no advantage from the public purse because of his justice, and that he is hated by his relatives and acquaintances because he is unwilling to do them an unjust favor. The opposite is true of an unjust man in every respect. I mean, of course, the person I described before: the man of great power who does better than everyone else. He is the one you

344a should consider if you want to figure out how much more advantageous it is for the individual to be unjust than just. You will understand this most easily if you turn your thoughts to injustice of the most complete sort, the sort that makes those who do injustice happiest, and those who suffer it—those who are unwilling to do injustice—most wretched. The sort I mean is tyranny, because it uses both covert means and force to appropriate the property of others—whether it is sacred or secular, public or private—not little by little, but all at once. If someone commits a part of this sort of injustice and gets caught, he is punished and b greatly reproached—temple robbers,[6] kidnappers, housebreakers, robbers, and thieves are what these partly unjust people are called when they commit those harms. When someone appropriates the possessions of the citizens, on the other hand, and then kidnaps and enslaves the possessors as well, instead of these shameful names he is called happy and blessed: not only by the citizens themselves, but even c by all who learn that he has committed the whole of injustice. For it is not the fear of doing injustice, but of suffering it, that elicits the reproaches of those who revile injustice.

So you see, Socrates, injustice, if it is on a large enough scale, is stronger, freer, and more masterful than justice. And, as I said from the beginning, justice is what is advantageous for the stronger, while injustice is profitable and advantageous for oneself.

Having, like a bath attendant, emptied this great flood of words into our ears all at once, Thrasy- d *machus was thinking of leaving. But those present wouldn't let him. They made him stay and give an account of what he had said. And I myself was particularly insistent:*

You are marvelous, Thrasymachus; after hurling such a speech at us, you surely cannot be thinking of leaving before you have adequately instructed us—or learned yourself—whether you are right or not. Or do you think it is a trivial matter you are trying e to determine, and not rather a way of life—the one that would make living life that way most profitable for each of us?

THRASYMACHUS: Do you mean that I do not think it is a serious matter?

SOCRATES: Either that, or you care nothing for us and so are not worried about whether we will live better or worse lives because of our ignorance of what you claim to know. No, be a good fellow and show

6. [The temples served as public treasuries, so that a temple robber is the equivalent of a present-day bank robber.]

some willingness to teach us—you won't do badly for
345a yourself if you help a group as large as ours. For my
own part, I will tell you that I am not persuaded. I
do not believe that injustice is more profitable than
justice, not even if you should give it full scope to
do what it wants. Suppose, my good fellow, that there
is an unjust person, and suppose he *does* have the
power to do injustice, whether by covert means or
open warfare; nonetheless, he does not persuade me
that injustice is more profitable than justice. Perhaps
b someone here besides myself feels the same as I do.
So, blessed though you are, you are going to have to
fully persuade us that we are wrong to value justice
more highly than injustice in deliberating.

THRASYMACHUS: And how am I to persuade you?
If you are not persuaded by what I said just now,
what more can I do? Am I to take my argument and
pour it into your very soul?

SOCRATES: No, by Zeus, do not do that! But first,
stick to what you have said, or, if you change your
position, do it openly and do not try to deceive us.
You see, Thrasymachus, having defined the true
doctor—to continue examining the things you said
c before you did not consider it necessary to maintain the same level of exactness when you later turned
to the true shepherd. You do not think a shepherd—
to the extent that he is a shepherd—fattens sheep
with the aim of doing what is best for them. But you
think that, like a guest about to be entertained at a
feast, his aim is to eat well or to make a future sale—
d as if he were a moneymaker rather than a shepherd.
But of course, the only concern of the craft of
shepherding is to provide what is best for that with
which it deals, since it itself is adequately provided
with all it needs to be at its best, as we know, when
it does not fall short in any way of being the craft of
shepherding. That is why I, at any rate, thought it
necessary for us to agree before that every kind of
rule—to the extent that it is a kind of rule—does not
seek anything other than what is best for the thing it
rules and cares for, and this is true both in political
e and in private rule. But do you think that those who
rule cities—the ones who are truly rulers—rule
willingly?

THRASYMACHUS: I do not think it, by Zeus, I
know it.

SOCRATES: But, Thrasymachus, don't you realize

that in other kinds of rule there is no willing ruler?
On the contrary, they demand to be paid on the
assumption that their ruling will benefit not themselves, but their subjects. For tell me, don't we say
that each craft differs from every other in what it is 346a
capable of doing? Blessed though you are, please
don't answer contrary to your belief, so that we can
come to some definite conclusion.

THRASYMACHUS: Yes, that is what differentiates
them.

SOCRATES: And doesn't each craft provide us with
a particular benefit, different from the others? For
example, medicine provides us with health, captaincy
with safety at sea, and so on with the others?

THRASYMACHUS: Certainly.

SOCRATES: And doesn't wage-earning provide us
with wages, since that is what it is capable of doing? Or b
would you call medicine the same craft as captaincy?
Indeed, if you want to define matters precisely, as
you proposed, even if someone who is a ship's captain
becomes healthy because what is advantageous for
him is sailing on the sea, you would not for that
reason call what he does medicine, would you?

THRASYMACHUS: Of course not.

SOCRATES: Nor would you call wage-earning
medicine, even if someone becomes healthy while
earning wages?

THRASYMACHUS: Of course not.

SOCRATES: Nor would you call medicine wage-
earning, even if someone earns pay while healing?

THRASYMACHUS: No.   c

SOCRATES: We are agreed then, aren't we, that
each craft brings its own special benefit?

THRASYMACHUS: Yes, we are.

SOCRATES: So whatever benefit all craftsmen
jointly receive must clearly derive from their joint
practice of some additional craft that is the same for
each of them.

THRASYMACHUS: It seems so.

SOCRATES: And we say that the additional craft
in question, which benefits the craftsmen by earning
them wages, is the craft of wage-earning?

He reluctantly agreed.

SOCRATES: Then this very benefit, receiving
wages, is not provided to each of them by his own

d craft. On the contrary, if we are to examine the matter precisely, medicine provides health and wage-earning provides a wage; house-building provides a house, and wage-earning, which accompanies it, provides a wage; and so on with the other crafts. Each of them does its own work and benefits that with which it deals. So, wages aside, is there any benefit that craftsmen get from their craft?

THRASYMACHUS: Apparently not.

SOCRATES: But he still provides a benefit, even *e* when he works for nothing?

THRASYMACHUS: Yes, I think he does.

SOCRATES: Then, it is clear now, Thrasymachus, that no type of craft or rule provides what is beneficial for itself; but, as we have been saying for some time, it provides and enjoins what is beneficial for its subject, and aims at what is advantageous for *it*—the weaker, not the stronger. That is why I said just now, my dear Thrasymachus, that no one chooses to rule voluntarily and take other people's troubles in hand and straighten them out, but each asks for wages. You see, anyone who is going to practice his type of craft *347a* well never does or enjoins what is best for himself— at least not when he is acting as his craft prescribes— but what is best for his subject. It is because of this, it seems, that wages must be provided to a person if he is going to be willing to rule, whether they are in the form of money or honor or a penalty if he refuses.

GLAUCON: What do you mean, Socrates? I am familiar with the first two kinds of wages, but I do not understand what penalty you mean, or how you can call it a wage.

SOCRATES: Then you do not understand the sort of wages for which the best people rule, when they are willing to rule. Don't you know that those who *b* love honor and those who love money are despised, and rightly so?

GLAUCON: I do.

SOCRATES: Well, then, that is why good people won't be willing to rule for the sake of money or honor. You see, if they are paid wages openly for ruling, they will be called hirelings, and if they take them covertly as the fruits of their rule, they will be called thieves. On the other hand, they won't rule for the sake of honor either, since they are not ambitious honor-lovers. So, if they are going to be willing to rule, *c* some compulsion or punishment must be brought to

bear on them—that is probably why wanting to rule when one does not have to is thought to be shameful. Now, the greatest punishment for being unwilling to rule is being ruled by someone worse than oneself. And I think it is fear of that that makes good people rule when they do rule. They approach ruling, not as though they were going to do something good or as though they were going to enjoy themselves in it, but as something necessary, since it cannot be entrusted to anyone better than—or even as good as— *d* themselves. In a city of good men, if it came into being, the citizens would fight in order *not to rule*, just as they now do in order to rule. There it would be quite clear that anyone who is really and truly a ruler does not naturally seek what is advantageous for himself, but what is so for his subject. As a result, anyone with any sense would prefer to be benefited by another than to go to the trouble of benefiting him. So I cannot at all agree with Thrasymachus that justice is what is advantageous for the stronger. But *e* we will look further into that another time. What Thrasymachus is now saying—that the life of an unjust person is better than that of a just one—seems to be of far greater importance. Which life would you choose, Glaucon? And which of our views do you think is closer to the truth?

GLAUCON: I think the life of a just person is more profitable.

SOCRATES: Did you hear all the good things Thrasymachus attributed a moment ago to the *348a* unjust man?

GLAUCON: I did, but I am not persuaded.

SOCRATES: Then do you want us to persuade him, if we can find a way, that what he says is not true?

GLAUCON: Of course I do.

SOCRATES: Well, if we oppose him with a speech parallel to his speech enumerating in turn the many good things that come from being just, and he replies, and then we do, we will have to count and measure the good things mentioned on each side, and we will need a jury to decide the case. But if, on the other *b* hand, we investigate the question, as we have been doing, by seeking agreement with each other, we ourselves can be both jury and advocates at once.

GLAUCON: Certainly.

SOCRATES: Then which approach do you prefer?

GLAUCON: The second.

SOCRATES: Come on then, Thrasymachus, answer us from the beginning. You say, don't you, that complete injustice is more profitable than complete justice?

THRASYMACHUS: I certainly have said that. And I
c have told you why.

SOCRATES: Well, then, what do you say about this? Do you call one of the two a virtue and the other a vice?

THRASYMACHUS: Of course.

SOCRATES: That is to say, you call justice a virtue and injustice a vice?

THRASYMACHUS: Is that likely, sweetest one, when I say that injustice is profitable and justice is not?

SOCRATES: Then what exactly do you say?

THRASYMACHUS: The opposite.

SOCRATES: That justice is a vice?

THRASYMACHUS: No, just very noble naiveté.[7]

d SOCRATES: So you call injustice deviousness?

THRASYMACHUS: No, I call it being prudent.

SOCRATES: Do you also consider unjust people to be wise and good, Thrasymachus?

THRASYMACHUS: Yes, if they do complete injustice and can bring cities and whole nations under their power. Perhaps, you thought I meant pickpockets? Not that such crimes aren't also profitable, if they are not found out. But they are not worth discussing by comparison to what I described.

SOCRATES: Yes, I am not unaware of what you
e mean. But this did surprise me: that you include injustice with virtue and wisdom, and justice with their opposites.

THRASYMACHUS: Nevertheless, that is where I put them.

SOCRATES: That is now a harder problem, comrade, and it is not easy to know what to say in response. If you had declared that injustice is more profitable, but agreed that it is a vice or shameful, as some others do, we could be discussing the matter on the basis of conventional views. But now, obviously, you will say that injustice is fine and strong and apply to it all

the attributes we used to apply to justice, since you 349a dare to include it with virtue and wisdom.

THRASYMACHUS: You have guessed my views exactly.

SOCRATES: All the same, we must not shrink from pursuing the argument and looking into this, just as long as I take you to be saying what you really think. You see, I believe that you really are not joking now, Thrasymachus, but saying what you believe to be the truth.

THRASYMACHUS: What difference does it make to you, whether *I* believe it or not? Isn't it *my account* you are supposed to be refuting?

SOCRATES: It makes no difference. But here is a further question I would like you to try to answer: do you think that a just person wants to do better than b another just person?

THRASYMACHUS: Not at all. Otherwise, he would not be the civilized and naïve person he actually is.

SOCRATES: What about than the just action?

THRASYMACHUS: No, not than that, either.

SOCRATES: And does he claim that he deserves to do better than an unjust person and believe that it is just for him to do so, or doesn't he believe that?

THRASYMACHUS: He would want to do better than him, and he would claim to deserve to do so, but he would not be able.

SOCRATES: That is not what I am asking, but whether a just person wants, and claims to deserve, to do better than an unjust person, but not than a c just one?

THRASYMACHUS: He does.

SOCRATES: What about an unjust person? Does he claim that he deserves to do better than a just person or a just action?

THRASYMACHUS: Of course he does, he thinks he deserves to do better than everyone.

SOCRATES: Then will an unjust person also do better than an *unjust* person or an *unjust* action, and will he strive to get the most he can for himself from everyone?

THRASYMACHUS: He will.

SOCRATES: Then let's put it this way: a just person does not do better than someone like himself, but someone unlike himself, whereas an unjust person does better than those who are like *and* those who are unlike him.   d

---

7. [*Euëtheia, kakoëtheia:* Thrasymachus uses *euëtheia* in the bad sense, to mean stupidity. Socrates takes him to mean it in the good sense of being straightforward, and so contrasts it with *kakoëtheia*—deviousness.]

THRASYMACHUS: Very well put.

SOCRATES: Now, an unjust person is wise and good, and a just one is neither?

THRASYMACHUS: That is well put, too.

SOCRATES: So isn't an unjust person also *like* a wise and good person, while the just person is not?

THRASYMACHUS: Of course. How could he fail to be like people who have such qualities, when he has them himself? But the unjust person is not like them.

SOCRATES: Fine. Then each of them has the qualities of the people he is like?

THRASYMACHUS: What else could he have?

SOCRATES: All right, Thrasymachus. Do you call *e* one person musical and another non-musical?

THRASYMACHUS: I do.

SOCRATES: Which of them is wise in music and which is not?

THRASYMACHUS: The musical one is wise, presumably, and the other not wise.

SOCRATES: And in the things in which he is wise, he is good; and in the things in which he is not wise, he is bad?

THRASYMACHUS: Yes.

SOCRATES: Isn't the same true of a doctor?

THRASYMACHUS: It is.

SOCRATES: Do you think, then, Thrasymachus, that a man who is a musician, when he is tuning his lyre and tightening and loosening the strings, wants to do better than another musician, and does he claim that that is what he deserves?

THRASYMACHUS: I do not.

SOCRATES: But he does want to do better than a non-musician?

THRASYMACHUS: Necessarily.

SOCRATES: What about a doctor? When he is pre-
350a scribing food and drink, does he want to do better than another doctor or than medical practice?

THRASYMACHUS: Certainly not.

SOCRATES: But he does want to do better than a non-doctor?

THRASYMACHUS: Yes.

SOCRATES: In any branch of knowledge or ignorance, do you think that a knowledgeable person would intentionally try to take more for himself than another knowledgeable person, or to do or say more, and not rather exactly what the one like himself would do in the same situation?

THRASYMACHUS: No, I imagine it must be as you say.

SOCRATES: And what about an ignorant person? Doesn't he want to do better than both a knowledgeable person and an ignorant one?   *b*

THRASYMACHUS: I suppose so.

SOCRATES: A knowledgeable person is wise?

THRASYMACHUS: I agree.

SOCRATES: And a wise one is good?

THRASYMACHUS: I agree.

SOCRATES: So, a good and wise person does not want to do better than someone like himself, but someone both unlike and opposite to him.

THRASYMACHUS: So it seems.

SOCRATES: But a bad and ignorant person wants to do better than both his like and his opposite.

THRASYMACHUS: Apparently.

SOCRATES: Well, Thrasymachus, we found that an unjust person tries to do better than those like him and those unlike him. Didn't you say that?

THRASYMACHUS: I did.

SOCRATES: And that a just person won't do better than those like him, but those unlike him?   *c*

THRASYMACHUS: Yes.

SOCRATES: Then a just person is like a wise and good person, and an unjust person is like an ignorant and bad one.

THRASYMACHUS: It looks that way.

SOCRATES: Moreover, we agreed that each has the qualities of the one he resembles.

THRASYMACHUS: Yes, we did.

SOCRATES: A just person has turned out to be good and wise, then, and an unjust one ignorant and bad.

Thrasymachus agreed to all this, not easily as I am telling it, but reluctantly, with toil, trouble,   *d* *and—since it was summer—a quantity of sweat that was amazing to behold. And then I saw something I had never seen before—Thrasymachus blushing. But in any case, after we had agreed that justice is virtue and wisdom and that injustice is vice and ignorance, I said:*

All right, let's take that as established. But we also said that injustice is a strong thing, or don't you remember that, Thrasymachus?

THRASYMACHUS: I remember. But I am not satisfied with what you are now saying. I could make a speech about it, but if I did, I know that you would say I was engaging in demagoguery. So, either allow
e me to say as much as I want to say or, if you want to keep on asking questions, go ahead and ask them, and I shall say to you—as one does to old women telling stories—"All right," and nod or shake my head.

SOCRATES: No, don't do that; not contrary to your own belief.

THRASYMACHUS: Then I will answer to please you, since you won't let me make a speech. What else do you want?

SOCRATES: Nothing, by Zeus. But if that is what you are going to do, do it, and I will ask the questions.

THRASYMACHUS: Ask them, then.

SOCRATES: All right, I will ask precisely what I asked before, so that we may proceed in an orderly fashion with our argument about what sort of thing
351a justice is, as opposed to injustice. For it was claimed, I believe, that injustice is stronger and more powerful than justice. But now, if justice is indeed wisdom and virtue, it will be easy to show, I suppose, that it is stronger than injustice, since injustice is ignorance— no one could now be ignorant of that. However, I, at any rate, do not want to consider the matter in such simple terms, Thrasymachus, but to look into it in some such way as this: would you say that a city
b may be unjust and try to enslave other cities unjustly, and succeed at enslaving them, and hold them in subjection which it enslaved in the past?

THRASYMACHUS: Of course. And that is what the best city will especially do, the one that is most completely unjust.

SOCRATES: I understand that that is your argument, but the point I want to examine is this: will the city that becomes stronger than another achieve this power without justice, or will it need the help of justice?

THRASYMACHUS: If what you said a moment ago
c stands, and justice is wisdom, it will need the help of justice; but if things are as I stated, it will need the help of injustice.

SOCRATES: I am impressed, Thrasymachus, that you are not merely nodding or shaking your head, but giving these fine answers.

THRASYMACHUS: That is because I am trying to please you.

SOCRATES: You are doing well at it, too. So please me some more by answering this question: do you think that a city, an army, a band of robbers or thieves, or any other group with a common unjust purpose would be able to achieve it if its members were unjust to each other?

THRASYMACHUS: Of course not.					d

SOCRATES: What if they were not unjust to one another? Would they achieve more?

THRASYMACHUS: Certainly.

SOCRATES: Because, Thrasymachus, injustice causes factions, hatreds, and quarrels among them, while justice brings friendship and a sense of common purpose. Isn't that so?

THRASYMACHUS: I will say it is, in order not to disagree with you.

SOCRATES: You are still doing well on that front, which is very good of you. So tell me this: if the function of injustice is to produce hatred wherever it occurs, then whenever it arises, whether among free men or slaves, won't it make them hate one another, form factions, and be unable to achieve any common purpose?					e

THRASYMACHUS: Of course.

SOCRATES: What if it arises between two people? Won't they be at odds, hate each other, and be enemies both to one another and to just people?

THRASYMACHUS: They will.

SOCRATES: Well, then, my amazing fellow, if injustice arises within a single individual, will it lose its power or will it retain it undiminished?

THRASYMACHUS: Let's say that it retains it undiminished.

SOCRATES: Apparently, then, its power is such that whenever it comes to exist in something— whether in a city, a family, an army, or anything else whatsoever—it makes that thing, first of all, incapable of acting in concert with itself, because of the faction 352a and difference it creates; and, second of all, an enemy to itself, and to what is in every way its opposite: namely, justice. Isn't that so?

THRASYMACHUS: Of course.

SOCRATES: And in a single individual, too, I presume, it will produce the very same effects that it is in its nature to produce. First, it will make him incapable of acting because of inner faction and not being of one mind with himself; second, it will make him his own enemy as well as the enemy of just people. Isn't that right?

THRASYMACHUS: Yes.

SOCRATES: But, my dear fellow, aren't the gods also just?

THRASYMACHUS: Let's say they are.

SOCRATES: Then an unjust person will also be an
b enemy of the gods, Thrasymachus, while a just person will be their friend?

THRASYMACHUS: Feast yourself confidently on the argument! Don't worry, I won't oppose you, so as not to arouse the enmity of our friends here.

SOCRATES: Come on, then, complete the banquet for me by continuing to answer as you have been doing now. We have shown that just people are wiser and better and more capable of acting, while unjust ones are not even able to act together. For
c whenever we speak of men who are unjust acting together to effectively achieve a common goal, what we say is not altogether true. They would never have been able to keep their hands off each other if they were completely unjust. But clearly there must have been some sort of justice in them that at least prevented them from doing injustice among themselves at the same time as they were doing it to others. And it was this that enabled them to achieve what they did. When they started doing unjust things, they were only halfway corrupted by their injustice. For those who are wholly bad and completely unjust are also completely incapable of acting. All this I now see to be the truth, and not what you first maintained.
d However, we must now examine the question, as we proposed to do before,[8] of whether just people also live better and are happier than unjust ones. I think it is clear even now from what we have said that this is so, but we must consider it further. After all, the argument concerns no ordinary topic, but the way we ought to live.

THRASYMACHUS: Go ahead and consider.

SOCRATES: I will. Tell me, do you think there is such a thing as the function of a horse?

THRASYMACHUS: I do.

e SOCRATES: And would you take the function of a horse or of anything else to be that which one can do only with it, or best with it?

[347e.]

THRASYMACHUS: I don't understand.

SOCRATES: Let me put it this way: is it possible for you to see with anything except eyes?

THRASYMACHUS: Certainly not.

SOCRATES: Or for you to hear with anything except ears?

THRASYMACHUS: No.

SOCRATES: Would it be right, then, for us to say that these things are their functions?

THRASYMACHUS: Of course.

SOCRATES: Again, couldn't you use a dagger, a carving knife, or lots of other things in pruning a vine? 353a

THRASYMACHUS: Certainly.

SOCRATES: But nothing would do a better job than a pruning knife designed for the purpose?

THRASYMACHUS: That's true.

SOCRATES: Shall we take pruning to be its function, then?

THRASYMACHUS: Yes.

SOCRATES: Now I think you will understand better what I was asking earlier when I asked whether the function of each thing is what it alone can do or what it can do better than anything else.

THRASYMACHUS: I do understand, and I think that that is the function of anything. b

SOCRATES: All right. Does there seem to you also to be a virtue for each thing to which some function is assigned? Let's go over the same ground again. We say that eyes have some function?

THRASYMACHUS: They do.

SOCRATES: So eyes also have a virtue?

THRASYMACHUS: They do.

SOCRATES: And ears have a function?

THRASYMACHUS: Yes.

SOCRATES: So they also have a virtue?

THRASYMACHUS: They have a virtue too.

SOCRATES: What about everything else? Doesn't the same hold?

THRASYMACHUS: It does.

SOCRATES: Well, then. Could eyes perform their function well if they lacked their proper virtue but c had the vice instead?

THRASYMACHUS: How could they? For don't you mean if they had blindness instead of sight?

SOCRATES: Whatever their virtue is. You see, I am not now asking about that, but about whether it is by means of their own proper virtue that their function performs the things it performs well, and by means of vice badly?

THRASYMACHUS: What you say is true.

SOCRATES: So, if ears are deprived of their own virtue, they too perform their function badly?

THRASYMACHUS: Of course.

SOCRATES: And the same argument applies to d everything else?

THRASYMACHUS: So it seems to me, at least.

SOCRATES: Come on, then, and let's next consider this: does the soul have some function that you could not perform with anything else—for example, taking care of things, ruling, deliberating, and all other such things? Is there anything else besides a soul to which you could rightly assign these and say that they are special to it?

THRASYMACHUS: No, there is nothing else.

SOCRATES: Then what about living? Don't we say that it is a function of a soul?

THRASYMACHUS: Absolutely.

SOCRATES: And don't we also say that a soul has a virtue?

THRASYMACHUS: We do.

SOCRATES: Will a soul ever perform its functions e well, then, Thrasymachus, if it is deprived of its own proper virtue, or is that impossible?

THRASYMACHUS: It is impossible.

SOCRATES: It is necessary, then, that a bad soul rules and takes care of things badly, and that a good soul does all these things well?

THRASYMACHUS: It is necessary.

SOCRATES: Now, didn't we agree that justice is a soul's virtue and injustice its vice?

THRASYMACHUS: Yes, we did agree.

SOCRATES: So a just soul and a just man will live well and an unjust one badly.

THRASYMACHUS: Apparently so, according to your argument.

SOCRATES: And surely anyone who lives well is 354a blessed and happy, and anyone who does not is the opposite.

THRASYMACHUS: Of course.

SOCRATES: Therefore, a just person is happy and an unjust one wretched.

THRASYMACHUS: Let's say so.

SOCRATES: But surely it is profitable, not to be wretched, but to be happy.

THRASYMACHUS: Of course.

SOCRATES: So then, blessed Thrasymachus, injustice is never more profitable than justice.

THRASYMACHUS: Let that be your banquet, Socrates, at the feast of Bendis.

SOCRATES: Given by you, Thrasymachus, after you became gentle with me and ceased to be difficult. Yet I have not had a good banquet. But that is my fault, not yours. I seem to have behaved like those b gluttons who snatch at every dish that passes and taste it before having properly savored the preceding one. Before finding the first thing we inquired about— namely, what justice is—I let that go, and turned to investigate whether it is a kind of vice and ignorance or a kind of wisdom and virtue. Then an argument came up about injustice being more profitable than justice, and I could not refrain from abandoning the previous one and following up on it. Hence the result of the discussion, so far as I am concerned, is that I know nothing. For when I do not know what justice is, I will hardly know whether it is a kind of virtue c or not, or whether a person who has it is happy or unhappy.

BOOK II

SOCRATES' NARRATION CONTINUES: *When I had said this, I thought I had done with the discussion. But it all turned out to be only a prelude,* 357a *as it were. You see, Glaucon, who is always very courageous in everything, refused on this occasion, too, to accept Thrasymachus' capitulation. Instead, he said:*

Do you want to *seem* to have persuaded us, Socrates, that it is better in every way to be just rather than unjust, or do you want to *really* persuade us of this? b

SOCRATES: I want to really persuade you, if I can.

GLAUCON: Well, then, you certainly are not doing what you want. Tell me, do you think there is a sort of good we welcome, not because we desire its consequences, but because we welcome it for its own sake—enjoying, for example, and all the harmless pleasures from which nothing results afterward beyond enjoying having them?

SOCRATES: Certainly, I think there is such a thing.

GLAUCON: And is there a sort of good we love for
c its own sake, and also for the sake of its consequences—
Knowing, for example, and seeing, and being healthy?
For we welcome such things, I imagine, on both
counts.

SOCRATES: Yes.

GLAUCON: And do you also recognize a third kind
of good, such as physical training, medical treatment
when sick, medicine itself, or ways of making money
generally? We would say that these are burdensome
but beneficial to us, and we would not choose them
for their own sake, but for the sake of their rewards
d and other consequences.

SOCRATES: Yes, certainly, there is also this third
kind. But what of it?

GLAUCON: In which of them do you place justice?

358a SOCRATES: I myself put it in the finest one—the
one that anyone who is going to be blessed with
happiness must love both because of itself and because of its consequences.

GLAUCON: That is not what the masses think. On
the contrary, they think it is of the burdensome kind:
the one that must be practiced for the sake of the
rewards and the popularity that are the consequences
of a good reputation, but that is to be avoided as
intrinsically burdensome.

SOCRATES: I know that is the general view. Thrasymachus has been faulting justice and praising injustice on these grounds for some time. But it seems
that I am a slow learner.

GLAUCON: Come on, then, listen to what I have to
b say as well, and see whether you still have that problem.
You see, I think Thrasymachus gave up before he had
to, as if he were a snake you had charmed. Yet, to my
way of thinking, there was still no demonstration on
either side. For I want to hear what justice and injustice
are, and what power each has when it is just by itself in
the soul. I want to leave out of account the rewards and
the consequences of each of them.

So, if you agree, I will renew the argument of
Thrasymachus. First, I will state what sort of thing
c people consider justice to be, and what its origins
are. Second, I will argue that all who practice it do so
unwillingly, as something necessary, not as something
good. Third, I will argue that they have good reason
act as they do. For the life of the unjust person is,
say, much better than that of the just one.

It isn't, Socrates, that I believe any of that myself.
I am perplexed, indeed, and my ears are deafened
listening to Thrasymachus and countless others. But
I have yet to hear anyone defend justice in the way
I want, as being better than injustice. I want to hear d
it praised *on its own*, and I think that I am most likely
to learn this from you. That is why I am going to
speak at length in praise of the unjust life: by doing
so, I will be showing you the way I want to hear you
praising justice and denouncing injustice. But see
whether you want me to do what I am saying or not.

SOCRATES: I want it most of all. Indeed, what
subject could a person with any sense enjoy talking
and hearing about more often?

GLAUCON: Excellent sentiments. Now, listen to
what I said I was going to discuss first—what justice e
is like and what its origins are. People say, you see,
that to do injustice is naturally good and to suffer
injustice bad. But the badness of suffering it far exceeds the goodness of doing it. Hence, those who
have done and suffered injustice and who have tasted
both—the ones who lack the power to do it and avoid
suffering it—decide that it is profitable to come to
an agreement with each other neither to do injustice 359a
nor to suffer it. As a result, they begin to make laws
and covenants; and what the law commands, they
call lawful and just. That, they say, is the origin and
very being of justice. It is in between the best and
the worst. The best is to do injustice without paying
the penalty; the worst is to suffer it without being
able to take revenge. Justice is in the middle between
these two extremes. People love it, not because it is
a good thing, but because they are too weak to do
injustice with impunity. Someone who has the power b
to do it, however—someone who is a real man—
would not make an agreement with anyone, neither
to do injustice nor to suffer it. For him, that would
be insanity. That is the nature of justice, according
to the argument, Socrates, and those are its natural
origins.

We can see most clearly that those who practice
it do so unwillingly, because they lack the power to
do injustice, if we imagine the following thought-
experiment. Suppose we grant to the just and the
unjust person the freedom to do whatever they like. c
We can then follow both of them and see where
their appetites would lead. And we will catch the just

person red-handed, traveling the same road as the unjust one. The reason for this is the desire to do better than others. This is what every natural being naturally pursues as good. But by law and force, it is made to deviate from this path and honor equality.

They would especially have the freedom I am talking about if they had the power that the ancestor of Gyges of Lydia is said to have possessed. The story
d goes that he was a shepherd in the service of the ruler of Lydia. There was a violent thunderstorm, and an earthquake broke open the ground and created a chasm at the place where he was tending his sheep. Seeing this, he was filled with amazement and went down into it. And there, in addition to many other amazing things of which we are told stories, he saw a hollow, bronze horse. There were windowlike openings in it and, peeping in, he saw a corpse, which seemed to be of more than human size, wearing
e nothing but a gold ring on its finger. He took off the ring and came out of the chasm. He wore the ring at the usual monthly meeting of shepherds that reported to the king on the state of the flocks. And as he was sitting among the others, he happened to turn the setting of the ring toward himself, toward the inside of his hand. When he did this, he became
360a invisible to those sitting near him, and they went on talking as if he had gone. He was amazed at this and, fingering the ring, he turned the setting outward again and became visible. So, he experimented with the ring to test whether it indeed had this power—and it did. If he turned the setting inward, he became invisible; if he turned it outward, he became visible again. As soon as he realized this, he arranged to become one of the messengers sent to report to the king. On arriving there, he seduced the king's wife,
b attacked the king with her help, killed him, and in this way took over the kingdom.

Let's suppose, then, that there were two such rings, one worn by the just person, the other by the unjust. Now no one, it seems, would be so incorruptible that he would stay on the path of justice, or bring himself to keep away from other people's possessions and not touch them, when he could take whatever he wanted from the marketplace with impunity, go into people's houses and have sex with anyone he wished, kill or
c release from prison anyone he wished, and do all the other things that would make him like a god among

humans. And in so behaving, he would do no differently than the unjust person, but both would pursue the same course.

This, some would say, is strong evidence that no one is just willingly, but only when compelled. No one believes justice to be a good thing when it is kept private, since whenever either person thinks he can do injustice with impunity, he does it. Indeed, all men believe that injustice is far more profitable to themselves than is justice. And what they believe is
d true, so the exponent of this argument will say. For someone who did not want to do injustice, given this sort of opportunity, and who did not touch other people's property, would be thought most wretched and most foolish by everyone aware of the situation. Though, of course, they would praise him in public, deceiving each other for fear of suffering injustice. So much for my second topic.

As for decision itself about the life of the two we are discussing, if we contrast the extremes of justice
e and injustice, we shall be able to make the decision correctly; but if we don't, we won't. What, then, is the contrast I have in mind? It is this: we will subtract nothing from the injustice of the unjust person, and nothing from the justice of the just one. On the contrary, we will take each to be perfect in his own pursuit. First, then, let the unjust person act like a clever craftsman. An eminent ship's captain or doctor, for example, knows the difference between what his craft can and cannot do. He attempts the first but lets the second go by. And if he happens to slip, he
361a can put things right. In the same way, if he is to be completely unjust, let the unjust person correctly attempt unjust acts and remain undetected. The one who is caught should be thought inept. For the extreme of injustice is to be believed to be just without actually being so. And our completely unjust person must be given complete injustice—nothing must be subtracted from it. We must allow that, while doing the greatest injustice, he has nonetheless provided himself with the greatest reputation for justice. If he does happen to slip up, he must be able to put it
b right, either through his ability to speak persuasively if any of his unjust activities are discovered, or to use force if force is needed, because he is courageous and strong and has provided himself with wealth and friends.

Having hypothesized such a person, let's now put the just man next to him in our argument—someone who is simple and noble and who, as Aeschylus says, does not want to be believed to be good, but to be so.[1] We must take away his reputation. For a reputation for *c* justice would bring him honor and rewards, so that it would not be clear whether he is being just for the sake of justice, or for the sake of those honors and rewards. We must strip him of everything except justice, and make his situation the opposite of the unjust person's. Though he does no injustice, he must have the greatest reputation for it, so that he may be tested with regard to justice by seeing whether or not he can withstand a bad reputation and its consequences. Let him stay like that, unchanged, until he is dead— *d* just, but all his life believed to be unjust. In this way, both will reach the extremes, the one of justice and the other of injustice, and we will be able to judge which of them is happier.

SOCRATES: Whew! My dear Glaucon, how vigorously you have scoured each of the men in our competition, just as you would a pair of statues for an art competition.

GLAUCON: I am doing the best I can. Since the two are as I have described, in any case, it should not be difficult to complete the account of the sort of life that awaits each of them, but it must be done. *e* And if what I say sounds crude, Socrates, remember that it is not *I* who speak, but those who praise injustice at the expense of justice. They will say that the just person in such circumstances will be whipped, stretched on a rack, chained, blinded with a red-hot iron, and, at the end, when he has suffered every sort *362a* of bad thing, he will be impaled, and will realize then that one should not want to be just, but to be believed to be just. Indeed, Aeschylus' words are far more correctly applied to the unjust man. For people will say that it is really the unjust person who does not want to be believed to be unjust, but actually to be so, because he bases his practice on the truth about things and does not allow reputation to regulate his life. He is the one who "harvests a deep furrow in

his mind, where wise counsels propagate." First, he *b* rules his city because of his reputation for justice. Next, he marries into any family he wishes, gives his children in marriage to anyone he wishes, has contracts and partnerships with anyone he wants, and, besides benefiting himself in all these ways, he profits because he has no scruples about doing injustice. In any contest, public or private, he is the winner and does better than his enemies. And by doing better than them, he becomes wealthy, benefits his friends, and harms his enemies. He makes adequate sacrifices *c* to the gods and sets up magnificent offerings to them, and takes much better care of the gods—and, indeed, of the human beings he favors—than the just person. So he may reasonably expect that the gods, in turn, will love him more than the just person. That is why they say, Socrates, that gods and humans provide a better life for the unjust person than for the just one.

When Glaucon had said this, I had it in mind to respond, but his brother Adeimantus intervened: *d*

You surely do not think that the argument has been adequately stated?

SOCRATES: Why shouldn't I?

ADEIMANTUS: The most important point has not been mentioned.

SOCRATES: Well, then, as the saying goes, a man's brother must stand by him.[2] So if Glaucon has omitted something, you must help him. Though, for my part at any rate, what he has already said is quite enough to throw me to the canvas and make me incapable of coming to the aid of justice.

ADEIMANTUS: Nonsense. But listen to what more I have to say, as well. You see, in order to clarify what *e* Glaucon has in mind, we should also fully explore the arguments that are opposed to the ones he gave— those that praise justice and disparage injustice.

As you know, when fathers speak to their sons to give them advice, they say that one must be just, as do all those who have others in their charge. But they do not praise justice itself, only the good reputation *363a* it brings: the inducement they offer is that if we are reputed to be just, then, as a result of our reputation,

1. [In *Seven against Thebes* 592–4, it is said of Amphiaraus that "he did not wish to be believed to be the best but to be it." The passage continues with the words Glaucon quotes below at 362a–b.]

2. [See Homer, *Odyssey* 16.97–8.]

we will get political offices, good marriages, and all the things that Glaucon recently said that the just man would get as a result of having a good reputation.

But these people have even more to say about the consequences of reputation. For by throwing in being well thought of by the gods, they have plenty of good things to talk about—all the ones the gods are said to give to those who are pious. For example, the noble Hesiod and Homer say such things. For Hesiod says
b that the gods make the oak trees "bear acorns at the top, bees in the middle, and fleecy sheep heavy laden with wool" for those who are just, and tells of many other good things akin to these.[3] And Homer says pretty much the same:

> When a good king, in his piety,
> Upholds justice, the black earth bears
> Wheat and barley for him, and his trees are
c>   heavy with fruit,
> His sheep bear lambs unfailingly and the sea
>   yields up its fish.[4]

Musaeus and his son claim that the gods give just people even more exciting goods than these. In their account, they lead the just to Hades, seat them on couches, provide them with a symposium of pious people, crown them with wreaths, and make them spend all their time drinking—as if they thought eter-
d nal drunkenness was the finest wage of virtue. Others stretch even further the wages that virtue receives from the gods. For they say that someone who is pious and keeps his promises leaves his children's children and a whole race behind him.

In these and other similar ways, they praise justice. But the impious and unjust they bury in mud in Hades, and they force them to carry water in a sieve. They bring them into bad repute while they are still alive. And all those penalties that Glaucon gave to
e just people who are thought to be unjust, they give to the unjust ones. But they have nothing else to say.

That, then, is the praise and blame given to each. But in addition, Socrates, there is another kind of argument about justice and injustice for you to consider—one that is used both by private individuals and by poets. With one voice they all chant the hymn 364a that justice and temperance are fine things, but difficult and onerous, while intemperance and injustice are sweet and easy to acquire and are only shameful by repute and convention. They also say that unjust deeds are, for the most part, more profitable than just ones; and whereas they are perfectly willing to bestow public and private honors on bad people—provided they have wealth and other types of power—and to declare them to be happy, they dishonor and disregard those who happen to be in any way weak or poor, even though they admit that they are better than the others.   b

But most amazing of all are the accounts they give of the gods and virtue, and how it is that the gods, too, assign misfortune and a bad life to many good people, and the opposite fate to their opposites. Begging priests and prophets go to the doors of rich people and persuade them that, through sacrifices and incantations, they have acquired a god-given power: if the rich person or any of his ancestors has committed c an injustice, they can fix it with pleasant rituals. And if he wishes to injure an enemy, he will be able to harm a just one or an unjust one alike at little cost, since by means of spells and enchantments they can persuade the gods to do their bidding.

And the poets are brought forward as witnesses to all these accounts. Some harp on the ease of vice, on the grounds that

> Vice in abundance is easy to get,
> The road is smooth and begins beside you,   d
> But the gods have put sweat between us and
>   virtue

and a road that is long, rough, and steep.[5] Others quote Homer to bear witness that the gods can be influenced by humans, since he too said:

> Even the gods themselves can be swayed by
>   prayer.
> And with sacrifices and soothing promises,
> Incense and libation-drinking, human beings
>   turn them from their purpose,   e
> When someone has transgressed and sinned.[6]

---

3. [Hesiod, *Works and Days* 332–3.]
4. [Homer, *Odyssey* 19.109.]

5. [*Works and Days* 287–9, with minor alterations.]
6. [*Iliad* 9.497–501, with minor alterations.]

And they present a noisy throng of books by Musaeus and Orpheus—who are the offspring, they claim, of Selene and the Muses—on which they base their rituals. And they persuade not only private individuals, but whole cities, that there are in fact absolutions and purifications for unjust deeds. For the living, these consist of ritual sacrifices and pleasant games. 365a But there are also special rites for the dead. These initiations, as they call them, free people from evils hereafter, while terrible things await those who have not performed the rituals.

With so many things of this sort, my dear Socrates, being said about virtue and vice, and about how human beings and gods honor them, what effect do we suppose they have on the souls of young people? I mean those who are naturally gifted and able to flit, so to speak, from one of these sayings to another and gather from them an impression of what sort of people they should be, and of how best to travel the road of b life. He would surely ask himself Pindar's question: "Is it by justice or by crooked tricks that I will scale the higher wall," and so live out my life surrounded by secure defenses? And he will answer: "As for what people say, they say that there is no advantage in my being just if I am not also thought just, whereas the troubles and penalties of being just are apparent; but the unjust person, who has secured for himself a reputation for justice, lives the life of a god. Since, then, 'opinion forcibly overcomes truth,' and 'controls c happiness,' as the wise men say, I must surely turn entirely to it.[7] I should create an illusionist painting of virtue around me to deceive those who come near, but keep behind it the wise Archilochus' greedy and cunning fox."

"But surely," someone will object, "it is not easy for evil to remain always hidden." We will reply that nothing great is easy. And, in any case, if we are to d be happy, we must go where the tracks of the arguments lead. To remain undiscovered we will form secret societies and political clubs. And there are teachers of persuasion to make us clever in dealing with assemblies and law courts. Therefore, partly by persuasion, partly by force, we will contrive to do better than other people, without paying the penalty.

7. [The quotation is attributed to Simonides, who is cited by Polemarchus in Book 1.]

"But surely we cannot hide from the gods or overpower them by force!" Well, if the gods do not exist, or do not concern themselves with human affairs, why should we worry at all about hiding from them? On the other hand, if they do exist, and do care about us, we know nothing about them except what we e have learned from the laws and from the poets who give their genealogies. But these are the very people who tell us that the gods can be persuaded and influenced by sacrifices, gentle prayers, and offerings. Hence, we should believe them on both matters, or on neither. If we believe them, we should be unjust and offer sacrifices from the fruits of our injustice. For if we are just, our only gain is not to be punished 366a by the gods, but we will lose the profits of our injustice. But if we are unjust, we will get those profits, and afterward we will entreat the gods and, persuading them, escape with our crimes and transgressions unpunished.

"But in Hades, won't we pay the penalty for crimes committed here, either ourselves or through our children's children?" "My friend," the young man will say as he does his rational calculation, "mystery rites and the gods of absolution have great power. The greatest cities tell us this, as do those children of the gods who have become the gods' poets and prophets b and reveal it to be so."

On the basis of what further argument, then, should we choose justice over the greatest injustice? For if we possess such injustice with a false façade, we will do as we have a mind to among gods and humans, both while we are living and when we are dead, as both the masses and the eminent claim. So given all that has been said, Socrates, what device could get someone with any power—whether of mind, wealth, c body, or family—to be willing to honor justice, and not laugh aloud when he hears it praised?

Indeed, if anyone can show that what we have said is false, and has adequate knowledge that justice is best, what he feels for unjust people won't be anger, but a large measure of forgiveness. After all, he knows that apart from someone of godlike character who is disgusted by doing injustice, or someone who has gained knowledge and avoids injustice for that reason, no one is just willingly. Through cowardice or old d age or some other weakness, people do indeed object to injustice. But it is obvious that they do so only because they lack the power to do injustice. For the first of them to gain that power is the first to do as much injustice as he can.

And all this has no other cause than the one that led to the whole of Glaucon's and my argument with you, Socrates. "Socrates, you amazing man," we said, "of all of you who claim to praise justice, beginning *e* from the earliest heroes of old whose accounts survive up to the men of the present day, not one has ever blamed injustice or praised justice except by mentioning the reputations, honors, and rewards that are their consequences. No one has ever adequately described what each does itself, through its own power, by its presence in the soul of the person who possesses it, even if it remains hidden from gods and humans. No one, whether in poetry or in private discussions, has adequately argued that injustice is the greatest evil a soul can have in it, and justice the greatest good. If all of you had spoken in this way and had tried to persuade us from our earliest youth, we would not *367a* now be guarding against one another's injustice, but each would be his own best guardian, afraid that by doing injustice he would be living on intimate terms with the worst thing possible."

That, Socrates, and probably other things in addition, are what Thrasymachus (or possibly someone else) might say in discussing justice and injustice— crudely inverting their power, in my view. But I— for I have no reason to hide anything from you—want to hear the opposite from you, and that is why I am *b* speaking with all the force I can muster. So do not merely demonstrate to us by argument that justice is stronger than injustice, but tell us what each one itself does, because of itself, to someone who possesses it, that makes the one bad and the other good. Follow Glaucon's advice and do not take reputations into account.[8] For if you do not deprive justice and injustice of their true reputations and attach false ones to them, we will say that it is not justice you are praising, but its reputation; nor injustice you are condemning, *c* but its reputation; and that you are encouraging us to be unjust but keep it secret. In that case, we will say that you agree with Thrasymachus that justice is the good of another, the advantage of the stronger,

8. [At 361b–c.]

while injustice is one's own advantage and profit, though not the advantage of the weaker.

You agree that justice is one of the greatest goods, the ones that are worth having for the sake of their consequences, but much more so for their own sake— such as seeing, hearing, knowing, being healthy, of course, and all the others that are genuine goods by *d* nature and not simply by repute. This is what I want you to praise about justice. How does it—because of its very self—benefit its possessor, and how does injustice harm him? Leave wages and reputations for others to praise.

I can put up with other people praising justice and blaming injustice in that way—extolling the reputations and wages of the one and denigrating those of the other. But I won't put up with that from you (unless you insist on it). For you have spent your whole life investigating this and nothing else. So do not merely demonstrate to us by argument that justice *e* is stronger than injustice, but show what effect each one itself has, because of itself, on the person who has it—the one for good, the other for bad—whether it remains hidden from gods and human beings or not.

Now, I had always admired the natural characters of Glaucon and Adeimantus, but I was especially pleased when I heard what they had to say on this occasion, and I replied:

Sons of that man, Glaucon's lover was not wrong to *368a* begin the elegy he wrote, when you distinguished yourselves at the battle of Megara, by addressing you as "Sons of Ariston, godlike family of a famous man." That, my dear friends, was well said, in my view. For something altogether godlike must have affected you if you are not convinced that injustice is better than justice and yet can speak like that on its behalf. And I do believe that you really are unconvinced by your own words. I infer this from your general character, *b* since if I had only your arguments to go on, I would not trust you. The more I trust you, however, the more I am at a loss as to what to do. I do not see how I can be of help. Indeed, I believe I am incapable of it. And here is my evidence: I thought that what I said to Thrasymachus showed that justice is better than injustice, but you won't accept that from me as a proof. On the other hand, I do not see how I can refue my help. For I fear that it may even be impious to have breath in one's body and the ability to speak, and yet stand idly by and not defend justice when it is being prosecuted. The best thing, then, is to give justice any assistance I can.

Glaucon and the others begged me not to abandon the argument but to help in every way to track down what justice and injustice each is, and the truth about their respective benefits. So I told them what I had in mind:

The investigation we are undertaking is not an easy one, in my view, but requires keen eyesight. So, since we are not clever people, I think we should adopt the method of investigation that we would use if, lacking keen eyesight, we were told to identify small letters from a distance, and then noticed that the same letters existed elsewhere in a larger size and on a larger surface. We would consider it a godsend, I think, to be allowed to identify the larger ones first, and then to examine the smaller ones to see whether they are really the same.

ADEIMANTUS: Of course we would. But how is this case similar to our investigation of justice in your view?

SOCRATES: I will tell you. We say, don't we, that there is a justice that belongs to a single man, and also one that belongs to a whole city?

ADEIMANTUS: Certainly.

SOCRATES: And a city is larger than a single man?

ADEIMANTUS: Yes, it is larger.

SOCRATES: Perhaps, then, there will be more justice in the larger thing, and it will be easier to discern. So, if you are willing, let's first find out what sort of thing justice is in cities, and afterward look for it in the individual, to see if the larger entity is similar in form to the smaller one.

ADEIMANTUS: I think that is a fine idea.

SOCRATES: If, in our discussion, we could look at a city coming to be, wouldn't we also see its justice coming to be, and its injustice as well?

ADEIMANTUS: We probably would.

SOCRATES: And once that process is completed, could we expect to find what we are looking for more easily?

ADEIMANTUS: Yes, much more easily.

SOCRATES: Do you think we should try to carry it out then? It is no small task, in my view. So, think it over.

ADEIMANTUS: It has been thought over. Don't do anything besides try.

SOCRATES: Well, then, a city comes to exist, I believe, because none of us is individually self-sufficient, but each has many needs he cannot satisfy. Or do you think that a city is founded on some other principle?

ADEIMANTUS: No, none.

SOCRATES: Then because we have many needs, and because one of us calls on another out of one need, and on a third out of a different need, we gather many into a single settlement as partners and helpers. And we call such a shared settlement a city. Isn't that so?

ADEIMANTUS: Yes, indeed.

SOCRATES: And if they share things with one another—if they give something to one another, or take something from one another—don't they do so because each believes that this is better for himself?

ADEIMANTUS: Of course.

SOCRATES: Come on, then, let's, in our discussion, create a city from the beginning. But its real creator, it seems, will be our need.

ADEIMANTUS: Certainly.

SOCRATES: Now, the first and greatest of our needs is to provide food in order to sustain existence and life.

ADEIMANTUS: Yes, absolutely.

SOCRATES: The second is for shelter, and the third is for clothes and things of that sort.

ADEIMANTUS: That's right.

SOCRATES: Tell me, then, how will a city be able to provide all this? Won't one person have to be a farmer, another a builder, and another a weaver? And shouldn't we add a shoemaker to them, or someone else to take care of our bodily needs?

ADEIMANTUS: Of course.

SOCRATES: A city with the barest necessities, then, would consist of four or five men?

ADEIMANTUS: Apparently.

SOCRATES: Well, then, should each of them contribute his own work for the common use of all? I mean, should a farmer, although he is only one person, provide food for four people, and spend quadruple the time and labor to provide food to be shared by them all? Or should he not be concerned about everyone else? Should he produce one quarter the food in one quarter the time for himself alone? Should he spend the other three quarters providing a house, a cloak, and shoes? Should he save himself the bother of sharing with other people and mind his own business on his own?

ADEIMANTUS: The first alternative, Socrates, is perhaps easier.

SOCRATES: There is nothing strange in that, by Zeus. You see, it occurred to me while you were speaking that, in the first place, we are not all born alike. On the contrary, each of us differs somewhat in nature from the others, one being suited to one job, another to another. Or don't you think so?

ADEIMANTUS: I do.

SOCRATES: Well, then, would one person do better work if he practiced many crafts or if he practiced one?

ADEIMANTUS: If he practiced one.

SOCRATES: And it is also clear, I take it, that if one misses the opportune moment in any job, the work is spoiled.

ADEIMANTUS: It is clear.

SOCRATES: That, I take it, is because the thing that has to be done won't wait until the doer has the leisure to do it. No, instead the doer must, of necessity, pay close attention to what has to be done and not leave it for his idle moments.

ADEIMANTUS: Yes, he must.

SOCRATES: The result, then, is that more plentiful and better-quality goods are more easily produced, if each person does one thing for which he is naturally suited and does it at the opportune moment, because his time is freed from all the others.

ADEIMANTUS: Absolutely.

SOCRATES: Then, Adeimantus, we are going to need more than four citizens to provide the things we have mentioned. For a farmer won't make his own plow, it seems, if it is going to be a good one, nor his hoe, nor any of his other farm implements. Nor will a carpenter — and he, too, needs lots of tools. And the same is true of a weaver and a shoemaker, isn't it?

ADEIMANTUS: It is.

SOCRATES: So carpenters, metalworkers, and many other craftsmen of that sort will share our little city and make it bigger.

ADEIMANTUS: Yes, indeed.

SOCRATES: Yet it still would not be a very large settlement, even if we added cowherds, shepherds, and other herdsmen, so that the farmers would have cows to do their plowing, the builders oxen to share with the farmers in hauling their materials, and the weavers and shoemakers hides and fleeces to use.

ADEIMANTUS: It would not be a small city either, if it had to hold all that.

SOCRATES: Moreover, it is almost impossible, at any rate, to establish the city itself in the sort of place where it will need no imports.

ADEIMANTUS: Yes, that is impossible.

SOCRATES: Then we will need still other people who will import whatever is needed from another city.

ADEIMANTUS: We will.

SOCRATES: And if our servant goes empty-handed to another city, without any of the things needed by those from whom he is trying to get what his own people need, he will come away empty-handed, won't he?

ADEIMANTUS: I should think so.

SOCRATES: Our citizens, then, must produce not only enough for themselves at home, but also goods of the right quality and quantity to satisfy the needs of others.

ADEIMANTUS: Yes, they must.

SOCRATES: So we will need more farmers and other craftsmen in our city.

ADEIMANTUS: Yes.

SOCRATES: And also other servants, I imagine, who are to take care of imports and exports. These are merchants, aren't they?

ADEIMANTUS: Yes.

SOCRATES: We will need merchants too, then.

ADEIMANTUS: Of course.

SOCRATES: And if the trade is carried on by sea, we will need a great many others who have expert knowledge of the business of the sea.

ADEIMANTUS: A great many, indeed.

SOCRATES: Again, within the city itself, how will people share with one another the things they each produce? It was in order to *share*, after all, that we associated with one another and founded a city.

ADEIMANTUS: Clearly, they must do it by buying and selling.

SOCRATES: Then we will need a marketplace and a currency for such exchange.

ADEIMANTUS: Yes, indeed.

SOCRATES: So if a farmer or any other craftsman
c brings some of his products to the marketplace, and he does not arrive at the same time as those who want to exchange things with him, is he to sit idly in the marketplace, neglecting his own craft?

ADEIMANTUS: Not at all. On the contrary, there will be people who notice this situation and provide the requisite service—in well-organized cities, they are generally those whose bodies are weakest and who are not fit to do any other sort of work. Their job is
d to wait there in the marketplace and exchange money for the goods of those who have something to sell, and then to exchange goods for the money of those who want to buy them.

SOCRATES: This need, then, causes retailers to be present in our city. Those who wait in the marketplace, and provide this service of buying and selling, are called retailers, aren't they, whereas those who travel between cities are merchants?

ADEIMANTUS: Yes, that's right.

SOCRATES: There are also other servants, I think, whose minds would not altogether qualify them for
e membership in our community, but whose bodies are strong enough for hard labor. So they sell the use of their strength for a price called a wage, and that is why they are called wage-earners. Isn't that so?

ADEIMANTUS: Yes.

SOCRATES: So the wage-earners too, it seems, serve to complete our city?

ADEIMANTUS: I think so.

SOCRATES: Well, then, Adeimantus, has our city now grown to completeness?

ADEIMANTUS: Maybe it has.

SOCRATES: Then where are justice and injustice to be found in it? With which of the people we considered did they come in?

ADEIMANTUS: I have no idea, Socrates, unless it
372a is somewhere in some need that these people have of one another.

SOCRATES: Perhaps what you say is right. We must look into it and not back off. First, then, let's see what sort of life people will lead who have been

provided for in this way. They will make food, wine, clothes, and shoes, won't they? And they will build themselves houses. In the summer, they will mostly work naked and barefoot, but in the winter they will wear adequate clothing and shoes. For nourishment, b they will provide themselves with barley meal and wheat flour, which they will knead and bake into noble cakes and loaves and serve up on a reed or on clean leaves. They will recline on couches strewn with yew and myrtles and feast with their children, drink their wine, and, crowned with wreaths, hymn the gods. They will enjoy having sex with one another, but they will produce no more children than their resources allow, lest they fall into either poverty or war.   c

At this point Glaucon interrupted and said:

It seems that you make your people feast without any relishes.

SOCRATES: True enough, I was forgetting that they will also have relishes—salt, of course, and olives and cheese, and they will boil roots and vegetables the way they boil them in the country. We will give them desserts too, I imagine, consisting of figs, chickpeas, and beans. And they will roast myrtles and acorns before the fire and drink in moderation. And so they will live in peace and good health, it seems, d and when they die at a ripe old age, they will pass on a similar sort of life to their children.

GLAUCON: If you were founding a city of pigs, Socrates, isn't that just what you would provide to fatten *them*?

SOCRATES: What, then, would you have me do, Glaucon?

GLAUCON: Just what is conventional. If they are not to suffer hardship, they should recline on proper couches, I suppose, dine at tables, and have the relishes and desserts that people have nowadays.   e

SOCRATES: All right, I understand. It isn't merely the origins of a city that we are considering, it seems, but those of a city that is *luxurious*, too. And that may not be a bad idea. For by examining such a city, we might perhaps see how justice and injustice grow up in cities. Yet the true city, in my view, is the one we have described: the healthy one, as it were. But if you also want to look at a feverish city, so be it. There

373a is nothing to stop us. You see, the things I mentioned earlier, and the way of life I described, won't satisfy some people, it seems; but couches, tables, and other furniture will have to be added to it, and relishes, of course, and incense, perfumes, prostitutes, pastries— and the multifariousness of each of them. In particular, we cannot just provide them with the necessities we mentioned at first, such as houses, clothes, and shoes; no, instead we will have to get painting and embroidery going, and procure gold and ivory and all sorts of everything of that sort. Isn't that so?

b   GLAUCON: Yes.

SOCRATES: Then we will have to enlarge our city again: the healthy one is no longer adequate. On the contrary, we must now increase it in size and population and fill it with a multitude of things that go beyond what is necessary for a city—hunters, for example, and all those imitators. Many of the latter work with shapes and colors; many with music— poets and their assistants, rhapsodes, actors, choral dancers, theatrical producers. And there will have to be craftsmen of multifarious devices, including, among other things, those needed for the adornment of women. In particular, then, we will need more

c   servants—don't you think—such as tutors, wet nurses, nannies, beauticians, barbers, and relish cooks and meat cooks, too? Moreover, we will also need people to farm pigs. This animal did not exist in our earlier city, since there was no need for it, but we will need it in this one. And we will also need large numbers of other meat-producing animals, won't we, if someone is going to eat them?

GLAUCON: We certainly will.

SOCRATES: And if we live like that, won't we have

d   a far greater need for doctors than we did before?

GLAUCON: Yes, far greater.

SOCRATES: And the land, I take it, that used to be adequate to feed the population we had then will now be small and inadequate. Or don't you agree?

GLAUCON: I do.

SOCRATES: Won't we have to seize some of our neighbors' land, then, if we are to have enough for pasture and plowing? And won't our neighbors want to seize part of ours in turn, if they too have abandoned themselves to the endless acquisition of money and overstepped the limit of their necessary desires?

e   GLAUCON: Yes, that is quite inevitable, Socrates.

SOCRATES: And the next step will be war, Glaucon, don't you agree?

GLAUCON: I do.

SOCRATES: Now, let's not say yet whether the effects of war are good or bad, but only that we have now found the origin of war: it comes from those same factors, the occurrence of which is the source of the greatest evils for cities and the individuals in them.

GLAUCON: Indeed, it does.

SOCRATES: The city must be further enlarged, then, my dear Glaucon, and not just a little, but by the size of a whole army. It will do battle with the invaders in defense of the city's wealth, and of all the 374a other things we just described.

GLAUCON: Why so? Aren't the inhabitants themselves adequate for that purpose?

SOCRATES: No, not, at any rate, if the agreement that you and the rest of us made when we were founding the city was a good one. I think we agreed, if you remember, that it is impossible for a single person to practice many crafts well.

GLAUCON: True, we did say that.

SOCRATES: Well, then, don't you think that warfare is a craft?   b

GLAUCON: It is, indeed.

SOCRATES: So, should we be more concerned about the craft of shoemaking than the craft of warfare?

GLAUCON: Not at all.

SOCRATES: Well, now, we prevented a shoemaker from trying to be a farmer, weaver, or builder at the same time, instead of just a shoemaker, in order to ensure that the shoemaker's job was done well. Similarly, we also assigned just the one job for which he had a natural aptitude to each of the other people, and said that he was to work at it his whole life, free from having to do any of the other jobs, so as not to miss the opportune moments for performing it well. c But isn't it of the greatest importance that warfare be carried out well? Or is fighting a war so easy that a farmer, a shoemaker, or any other artisan can be a soldier at the same time, even though no one can become so much as a good checkers player or dice player if he considers it only as a sideline and does not practice it from childhood? Can someone just pick up a shield, or any other weapon or instrument of war and immediately become a competent fighter d in an infantry battle or whatever other sort of battle it may be, even though no other tool makes someone who picks it up a craftsman or an athlete, or is even of any service to him unless he has acquired knowledge of it and has had sufficient practice?

GLAUCON: If tools could do that, they would be valuable indeed.

SOCRATES: Then to the degree that the guardians' *e* job is most important, it requires the most freedom from other things, as well as the greatest craft and practice.

GLAUCON: I should think so.

SOCRATES: And doesn't it also require a person whose nature is suited to that very practice?

GLAUCON: Certainly.

SOCRATES: Then our task, it seems, is to select, if we can, which natures, which sorts of natures, suit people to guard the city.

GLAUCON: Yes, that is our task.

SOCRATES: By Zeus, it is no trivial task that we have taken on, then. All the same, we must not shrink from it, but do the best we can.

375a   GLAUCON: No, we must not.

SOCRATES: Do you think that there is any difference, when it comes to the job of guarding, between the nature of a noble hound and that of a well-bred youth?

GLAUCON: What do you mean?

SOCRATES: I mean that both of them have to be sharp-eyed, quick to catch what they see, and strong, too, in case they have to fight what they capture.

GLAUCON: Yes, they need all these things.

SOCRATES: And they must be courageous, surely, if indeed they are to fight well.

GLAUCON: Of course.

SOCRATES: Now, will a horse, a dog, or any other animal be courageous if it is not spirited? Or haven't you noticed just how invincible and unbeatable spirit *b* is, so that its presence makes the whole soul fearless and unconquerable in any situation?

GLAUCON: I have noticed that.

SOCRATES: Then it is clear what physical qualities the guardians should have.

GLAUCON: Yes.

SOCRATES: And as far as their souls are concerned, they must, at any rate, be spirited.

GLAUCON: That too.

SOCRATES: But with natures like that, Glaucon, how will they avoid behaving like savages to one another and to the other citizens?

GLAUCON: By Zeus, it won't be easy for them.

SOCRATES: But surely they must be gentle to their own people and harsh to their enemies. Otherwise, *c* they will not wait around for others to destroy them, but will do it themselves first.

GLAUCON: That's true.

SOCRATES: What are we to do, then? Where are we to find a character that is both gentle and high-spirited at the same time? For, of course, a gentle nature is the opposite of the spirited kind.

GLAUCON: Apparently.

SOCRATES: But surely if someone lacks either of these qualities, he cannot be a good guardian. Yet the combination of them seems to be impossible. And so it follows, then, that a good guardian is impossible. *d*

GLAUCON: I am afraid so.

I could not see a way out, and on reexamining what had gone before, I said:

We deserve to be stuck, my dear Glaucon. For we have lost track of the analogy we put forward.

GLAUCON: How do you mean?

SOCRATES: We have overlooked the fact that there *are* natures of the sort we thought impossible, ones that include these opposite qualities.

GLAUCON: Where?

SOCRATES: You can see the combination in other animals, too, but especially in the one to which we compared the guardian. For you know, of course, that noble hounds naturally have a character of that *e* sort. They are as gentle as can be to those they are familiar with and know, but the opposite to those they do not know.

GLAUCON: Yes, I do know that.

SOCRATES: So the combination we want *is* possible, after all, and what we are seeking in a good guardian is not contrary to nature.

GLAUCON: No, I suppose not.

SOCRATES: Now, don't you think that our future guardian, besides being spirited, must also be, by nature, philosophical?

GLAUCON: How do you mean? I don't understand.

376a

SOCRATES: It too is something you see in dogs, and it should make us wonder at the merit of the beast.

GLAUCON: In what way?

SOCRATES: In that when a dog sees someone it does not know, it gets angry even before anything bad happens to it. But when it knows someone, it welcomes him, even if it has never received anything good from him. Have you never wondered at that?

GLAUCON: I have never paid it any mind until now. But it is clear that a dog does do that sort of thing.

SOCRATES: Well, that seems to be a naturally re-
b fined quality, and one that is truly philosophical.

GLAUCON: In what way?

SOCRATES: In that it judges anything it sees to be either a friend or an enemy on no other basis than that it knows the one and does not know the other. And how could it be anything besides a lover of learning if it defines what is its own and what is alien to it in terms of knowledge and ignorance?

GLAUCON: It surely could not be anything but.

SOCRATES: But surely the love of learning and philosophy are the same, aren't they?

GLAUCON: Yes, they are the same.

SOCRATES: Then can't we confidently assume that the same holds for a human being too—that if he is going to be gentle to his own and those he
c knows, he must be, by nature, a lover of learning and a philosopher?

GLAUCON: We can.

SOCRATES: Philosophy, then, and spirit, speed, and strength as well, must all be combined in the nature of anyone who is going to be a really fine and good guardian of our city.

GLAUCON: Absolutely.

SOCRATES: Then that is what he would have to be like at the outset. But how are we to bring these people up and educate them? Will inquiring into that topic bring us any closer to the goal of our inquiry, which is to discover the origins of justice and injustice
d in a city? We want our account to be adequate, but we do not want it to be any longer than necessary.

And Glaucon's brother replied:

I for one certainly expect that this inquiry will help us.

SOCRATES: By Zeus, in that case, my dear Adeimantus, we must not abandon it, even if it turns out to be a somewhat lengthy affair.

ADEIMANTUS: No, we must not.

SOCRATES: Come on, then, and like people in a fable telling stories at their leisure, let's in our discussion educate these men.

ADEIMANTUS: Yes, let's.   e

SOCRATES: What, then, will the education be? Or is it difficult to find a better one than the one that has been discovered over a long period of time— physical training for bodies and musical training for the soul?

ADEIMANTUS: Yes, it is.

SOCRATES: Now, won't we start musical training before physical training?

ADEIMANTUS: Of course.

SOCRATES: And you include stories under musical training, don't you?

ADEIMANTUS: I do.

SOCRATES: But aren't there two kinds of stories, one true and the other false?

ADEIMANTUS: Yes.

SOCRATES: And education must make use of both, but first of the false ones?   377a

ADEIMANTUS: I do not understand what you mean.

SOCRATES: Don't you understand that we first begin by telling stories to children? And surely they are false on the whole, though they have some truth in them. And we use stories on children before physical training.

ADEIMANTUS: That's true.

SOCRATES: That, then, is what I meant by saying that musical training should be taken up before physical training.

ADEIMANTUS: And you were right.

SOCRATES: Now, you know, don't you, that the beginning of any job is the most important part, especially when we are dealing with anything young and tender? For that is when it is especially malleable b and best takes on whatever pattern one wishes to impress on it.

ADEIMANTUS: Precisely so.

SOCRATES: Shall we carelessly allow our children to hear any old stories made up by just anyone, then, and to take beliefs into their souls that are, for the most part, the opposite of the ones we think they should hold when they are grown up?

ADEIMANTUS: We certainly won't allow that at all.

SOCRATES: So our first task, it seems, is to supervise the storytellers: if they make up a good story, we
c must accept it; if not, we must reject it. We will
persuade nurses and mothers to tell the acceptable
ones to their children, and to spend far more time
shaping their souls with these stories than they do
shaping their bodies by handling them. Many of the
stories they tell now, however, must be thrown out.

ADEIMANTUS: Which sorts?

SOCRATES: In the more significant stories, we will
see the less significant ones as well. For surely the
more significant ones and the less significant ones
both follow the same pattern and have the same
d effects. Don't you think so?

ADEIMANTUS: Indeed, I do. But I do not understand at all what more significant ones you mean.

SOCRATES: The ones Homer, Hesiod, and other
poets tell us. After all, they surely composed false
stories, which they told and are still telling to people.

ADEIMANTUS: Which stories do you mean? And
what is the fault you find in them?

SOCRATES: The first and most important fault that
one ought to find, especially if the falsehood has no
good features.

ADEIMANTUS: Yes, but what *is* it?

SOCRATES: Using a story to create a bad image
e of what the gods and heroes are like, just as a painter
might paint a picture that is not at all like the things
he is trying to paint.

ADEIMANTUS: Yes, you are right to find fault with
that. But what cases in particular, what sorts of cases,
do you mean?

SOCRATES: First, the biggest falsehood about the
most important things has no good features—I mean
Hesiod telling us about how Uranus behaved, how
Cronus punished him for it, and how he was in turn
378a punished by his own son.[9] But even if these stories

9. [Uranus prevented his wife, Gaia, from giving birth to
his children by blocking them up inside her. Gaia gave a
sickle to one of these children, Cronus, which he used to
castrate his father when the latter next had intercourse
with her. Cronus ate the children he had by his wife,
Rhea, until, by deceiving him with a stone, she was able
to save Zeus from suffering this fate. Zeus then overthrew
his father. See Hesiod, *Theogony* 154–210, 453–506.]

were true, they should be passed over in silence, I
would think, and not told so casually to the foolish
and the young. And if, for some reason, they must
be told, only a very few people should hear them—
people who are pledged to secrecy and have had to
sacrifice not just a pig, but something so large and
scarce that the number of people who hear them is
kept as small as possible.

ADEIMANTUS: Yes, those stories are certainly
troubling.

SOCRATES: And they should not be told in our
city, Adeimantus. No young person should hear it b
said that if he were to commit the worst crimes, he
would be doing nothing amazing, or that if he were
to inflict every sort of punishment on an unjust father,
he would only be doing the same as the first and
greatest of the gods.

ADEIMANTUS: No, by Zeus, I do not think myself
that these stories are fit to be told.

SOCRATES: Indeed, we must not allow *any* stories
about gods warring, fighting, or plotting against one
another if we want the guardians of our city to think
that it is shameful to be easily provoked into mutual
hatred. After all, those stories are not true either. Still c
less should battles between gods and giants, or the
many other multifarious hostilities of gods and heroes
toward their families and friends, occur in the stories
the guardians hear or in the embroidered pictures
they see. On the contrary, if we are somehow going
to persuade our people that no citizen has ever hated
another, and that it is impious to do so, then *those*
are the things their male and female elders should
tell them from childhood on. And the poets they d
listen to as they grow older should be compelled to
tell them the same sort of thing. Stories about Hera
being chained by her son, on the other hand, or about
Hephaestus being hurled from the heavens by his
father when he tried to save his mother from a beating,
or about the battle of the gods in Homer, should not
be admitted into our city, either as allegories or non-
allegories. For the young cannot distinguish what is
allegorical from what is not. And the beliefs they
absorb at that age are difficult to erase and tend to
become unalterable. For these reasons, then, we e
should probably take the utmost care to ensure that
the first stories they hear about virtue are the best
ones for them to hear.

ADEIMANTUS: Yes, that makes sense. But if, at this point too,[10] someone were once again to ask us what stories these are, how should we reply?

SOCRATES: You and I are not poets at present, Adeimantus, but we *are* founding a city. And it is appropriate for the founders to know the patterns on which the poets must base their stories, and from which they must not deviate. But they should not themselves make up any poems.

ADEIMANTUS: That's right. But what precisely are the patterns that stories about the gods must follow?

SOCRATES: Something like this: whether in epic, lyric, or tragedy, a god must always be represented as he is.

ADEIMANTUS: Yes, he must.

SOCRATES: Now, gods, of course, are really good, aren't they, and must be described as such?

ADEIMANTUS: Certainly.

SOCRATES: And surely nothing good is harmful, is it?

ADEIMANTUS: I suppose not.

SOCRATES: Well, can what is not harmful do any harm?

ADEIMANTUS: No, never.

SOCRATES: And can what does no harm do anything bad?

ADEIMANTUS: No, it can't do that either.

SOCRATES: But what does nothing bad could not be the cause of anything bad, could it?

ADEIMANTUS: No, it could not.

SOCRATES: What about what is good? Is it beneficial?

ADEIMANTUS: Yes.

SOCRATES: So, it is the cause of doing well?

ADEIMANTUS: Yes.

SOCRATES: What is good is not the cause of all things, then. Instead, it is the cause of things that are good, while of bad ones it is not the cause.

ADEIMANTUS: Exactly.

SOCRATES: So, since gods are good, they are not— as the masses claim—the cause of everything. Instead, they are a cause of only a few things that happen to human beings, while of most they are not the cause. For good things are fewer than bad ones in our lives.

Of the good things, they alone are the cause, but we must find some other cause for the bad ones, not the gods.

ADEIMANTUS: That's absolutely true in my view.

SOCRATES: Then we won't accept from Homer— or from anyone else—the foolish mistake he makes about the gods when he says: "There are two urns at the threshold of Zeus, one filled with good fates, the other with bad ones," and the person to whom Zeus gives a mixture of these "sometimes meets with a bad fate, sometimes with a good one." But the one who receives his fate entirely from the second urn, "evil famine drives over the divine earth." Nor will we tolerate the saying that "Zeus is the dispenser of both good and bad to mortals." As for the breaking of the oaths and the truce by Pandarus, if anyone tells us that it was brought about by Athena and Zeus, or that Themis and Zeus were responsible for strife and contention among the gods, we won't praise him. Nor will we allow the young to hear the words of Aeschylus: "A god makes mortals guilty, when he wants to destroy a house utterly."[11] And if anyone composes a poem, such as the one those lines are from, about the sufferings of Niobe, or about the house of Pelops, or the tale of Troy, or anything else of that sort, he should be required to say that these things are not the works of a god. Or, if they are the works of a god, then the poet must look for roughly the sort of account of them we are now seeking: he must say that the actions of the gods are good and just, and that the people they punish are benefited by them. We won't allow him to say that those who are punished are made wretched, and that it was a god who made them so; but we will allow him to say that bad people are wretched because they are in need of punishment, and that in paying the penalty they are benefited by that god. But as for saying that a god, who is himself good, is the cause of evils, we will fight that in every way. We won't allow anyone to say it in his own city, if it is to be well governed, or anyone to hear it either—whether young or old,

---

10. [As at 377d10.]

11. [The first three quotations are from *Iliad* 24.527–32. The sources for the fourth, and for the quotation from Aeschylus, are unknown. The story of Athena urging Pandarus to break the truce is told at *Iliad* 4.73–126.]

c whether with meter or without meter. For these stories are impious, disadvantageous to us, and not in concord with one another.

ADEIMANTUS: I like your law, and I will vote with you for it.

SOCRATES: This, then, will be one of the laws or patterns relating to gods that speakers and poets will have to follow: that gods are not the cause of all things, but only of good ones.

ADEIMANTUS: And an entirely satisfactory one it is.

SOCRATES: Now, what about this second law? Do
d you think that gods are sorcerers who deliberately take different forms at different times, sometimes by changing on their own and altering their own form into a large number of shapes, sometimes by deceiving us into thinking they have done so? Or are they simple beings, and least of all likely to abandon their own form?

ADEIMANTUS: I can't say offhand.

SOCRATES: Well, if something abandons its own form, mustn't it either cause the change itself or be
e changed by something else?

ADEIMANTUS: It must.

SOCRATES: Now, the best things are least liable to alteration or change, aren't they? For example, a body is altered by food, drink, and labors, and all plants by sun, winds, and other similar affections—but the healthiest and strongest is least altered, isn't that so?

381a   ADEIMANTUS: Of course.

SOCRATES: And wouldn't a soul that is most courageous and most knowledgeable be least disturbed or altered by any outside influence?

ADEIMANTUS: Yes.

SOCRATES: And the same account surely also applies even to manufactured items, such as implements, houses, and clothes: those that are good and well made are least altered by time or any other influences.

ADEIMANTUS: That's right.

SOCRATES: So whatever is in good condition—
b whether due to nature or craft or both—is least subject to change by something else.

ADEIMANTUS: It seems so.

SOCRATES: But gods, of course, as well as the things belonging to them, are best in every way.

ADEIMANTUS: They certainly are.

SOCRATES: So, on this view, gods would be least likely to have many forms.

ADEIMANTUS: Least likely, indeed.

SOCRATES: Then would they change or alter themselves?

ADEIMANTUS: Clearly so, if indeed they are altered at all.

SOCRATES: Do they change themselves into something better and more beautiful, or into something worse and uglier, than themselves?

ADEIMANTUS: It would have to be into something worse, if indeed they are altered at all. For surely we *c* won't say that gods are deficient in either beauty or virtue.

SOCRATES: You are absolutely right. And do you think, Adeimantus, that anyone, whether god or human, would deliberately make himself worse in any way?

ADEIMANTUS: No, that is impossible.

SOCRATES: It is also impossible, then, for a god to want to alter himself. On the contrary, since each god is, it seems, as beautiful and as good as possible, he must always unqualifiedly retain his own form.

ADEIMANTUS: In my view, at least, that is absolutely necessary.

SOCRATES: None of our poets, then, my very good man, is to say that "The gods, like strangers *d* from foreign lands, assume many disguises when they visit our cities."[12] Nor must they tell lies about Proteus and Thetis, or present Hera, in their tragedies or other poems, disguised as a priestess collecting alms for "the life-giving sons of the Argive river Inachus,"[13] or tell us any of the many other such lies. Nor should mothers, influenced by these *e* stories, which terrify children, tell bad tales about gods who go wandering around at night in the guises of many strange and multifarious beings, lest they blaspheme the gods and, at the same time, make their children too cowardly.

ADEIMANTUS: Indeed, they should not.

---

12. [*Odyssey* 17.485–6.]

13. [Inachus was the father of Io, who was persecuted by Hera because Zeus was in love with her. The source for the part of the story Plato quotes is unknown.]

SOCRATES: But, though the gods themselves are the sorts of things that cannot change, do they make us think that they appear in multifarious guises, deceiving us and using sorcery on us?

ADEIMANTUS: Perhaps they do.

382a SOCRATES: What? Would a god be willing to lie by presenting in word or deed what is only an illusion?

ADEIMANTUS: I don't know.

SOCRATES: Don't you know that all gods and humans hate a *true* lie, if one may call it that?

ADEIMANTUS: What do you mean?

SOCRATES: I mean that no one intentionally wants to lie about the most important things to what is most important in himself. On the contrary, he fears to hold a lie there more than anything.

ADEIMANTUS: I still don't understand.

SOCRATES: That is because you think I am saying
b something deep. I simply mean that to lie and to have lied to the soul about the things that are, and to be ignorant, and to have and hold a lie there, is what everyone would least of all accept; indeed, they especially hate it there.

ADEIMANTUS: They certainly do.

SOCRATES: But surely, as I was saying just now, it would be most correct to say that it is truly speaking a lie—the ignorance in the soul of the one to whom the lie was told. For a lie in words is a sort of imitation of this affection in the soul, an image of it that comes into being after it, and not an altogether pure lie.
c Isn't that so?

ADEIMANTUS: Yes, it is.

SOCRATES: A real lie, then, is hated not only by the gods, but also by human beings.

ADEIMANTUS: I think it is.

SOCRATES: What about a lie in words? Aren't there times when it is useful, and so does not merit hatred? What about when we are dealing with enemies, or with so-called friends who, because of insanity or ignorance, are attempting to do something bad? Isn't it a useful drug for preventing them? And consider the case of those stories we were talking about just now—those we tell because
d we do not know the truth about those ancient events: by making the lies that they contain as much like the truth as possible, don't we make them useful?

ADEIMANTUS: We most certainly do.

SOCRATES: In which of these ways, then, could a lie be useful to a god? Would he lie by making likenesses of the truth about ancient events because of his ignorance of them?

ADEIMANTUS: It would be ridiculous to think that.

SOCRATES: Then there is nothing of the lying poet in a god?

ADEIMANTUS: Not in my view.

SOCRATES: Would he lie, then, through fear of his enemies?

ADEIMANTUS: Hardly.   e

SOCRATES: Because of the foolishness or insanity of his family or friends, then?

ADEIMANTUS: No one who is foolish or mad is a friend of the gods.

SOCRATES: So a god has no reason to lie?

ADEIMANTUS: None.

SOCRATES: So both what is daimonic and what is divine are entirely free of lies.

ADEIMANTUS: Absolutely.

SOCRATES: A god, then, is altogether simple, true in both word and deed. He does not change himself or deceive others by means of images, by words, or by sending signs, whether they are awake or dreaming.

ADEIMANTUS: That is my view—at any rate, now that I have heard what you have to say.   383a

SOCRATES: You agree, then, that this is the second pattern people must follow when speaking or composing poems about the gods: the gods are not sorcerers who change themselves, nor do they mislead us by telling lies in word or deed.

ADEIMANTUS: I agree.

SOCRATES: Even though we praise many things in Homer, then, we won't approve of Zeus' sending the dream to Agamemnon, nor of Aeschylus when he makes Thetis say that Apollo sang, in prophecy at her wedding: b

About the good luck my children would
    have,
Free of disease throughout their long lives,
And of all the blessings the friendship of the
    gods would bring me.
I hoped that Phoebus' divine mouth would
    be free of lies,

Endowed as it is with the craft of prophecy.
But the very god who sang, the one at the
     feast,
The one who said all that, he himself it is
Who killed my son.[14]

c Whenever anyone says such things about a god, we
will be angry with him, refuse him a chorus, and not
allow teachers to use what he says for the education
of the young—not if our guardians are going to be
as god-fearing and godlike as human beings can be.

ADEIMANTUS: I agree completely about these patterns, and I would use them as laws.

BOOK III

SOCRATES' NARRATION CONTINUES:

386a   SOCRATES: Where the gods are concerned, then,
it seems that those are the sorts of stories the future
guardians should and should not hear from childhood
on, if they are to honor the gods and their parents,
and not treat lightly their friendship with one another.

ADEIMANTUS: I am sure we are right about that.

SOCRATES: What about if they are to be courageous? Shouldn't they be told stories that will make
them least likely to fear death? Or do you think that
anyone ever becomes courageous if he has that fear
b in his heart?

ADEIMANTUS: No, by Zeus, I do not.

SOCRATES: What about if someone believes that
Hades exists and is full of terrible things? Can anyone
with that fear be unafraid of death and prefer it to
defeat in battle and slavery?

ADEIMANTUS: Not at all.

SOCRATES: Then we must also supervise those
who try to tell such stories, it seems, and ask them not
to disparage the life in Hades in this undiscriminating
way, but to speak well of it, since what they now tell
c us is neither true nor beneficial to future warriors.

ADEIMANTUS: Yes, we must.

14. [At *Iliad* 2.1–34, Zeus sends a dream to Agamemnon
to promise success if he attacks Troy immediately. The
promise is false. The source for the quotation from
Aeschylus is unknown.]

SOCRATES: We will start with the following lines,
then, and expunge everything like them: "I would
rather labor on earth in another man's service, a man
who is landless, with little to live on, than be king over
all the dead";[1] and this: "He feared that his home d
should be revealed to mortals and immortals as dreadful, dank, and hated even by the gods";[2] and: "Alas,
there survives in the Halls of Hades a soul, a mere phan-
tasm, with its wits completely gone";[3] and this: "He
alone can think others to be flitting shadows";[4] and:
"The soul, leaving his limbs, made its way to Hades,
lamenting its fate, leaving manhood and youth
behind";[5] and this: "His soul went below the earth like 387a
smoke, screeching as it went";[6] and:

As when bats in an awful cave
Fly around screeching if one of them falls
From the cluster on the ceiling, all clinging
     to one another,
So their souls went screeching.[7]

We will beg Homer and the rest of the poets not to b
be angry if we delete these and all similar passages—
not because they are not poetic and pleasing to the
masses when they hear them, but because the more
poetic they are, the more they should be kept away
from the ears of children and men who are to be free
and to fear slavery more than death.

ADEIMANTUS: Absolutely.

SOCRATES: Then, in addition, we must also get
rid of the terrible and frightening names that occur

1. [*Odyssey* 11.489–91. Odysseus is being addressed by
Achilles in Hades.]

2. [*Iliad* 20.64–5. Hades is afraid that the earth will split
open and reveal what his home is like.]

3. [*Iliad* 23.103–4. Achilles speaks these lines as the soul
of the dead Patroclus leaves for Hades.]

4. [*Odyssey* 10.493–5. Circe speaking to Odysseus about
the prophet Tiresias.]

5. [*Iliad* 16.856–7. The words refer to Patroclus, who
has just been mortally wounded by Hector.]

6. [*Iliad* 23.100. The soul referred to is that of Patroclus.]

7. [*Odyssey* 14.6–9. The souls are those of Penelope's
suitors, whom Odysseus has killed.]

c in such passages: Cocytus, Styx,[8] "those below," "the sapless ones," and all the other names of the same pattern that supposedly make everyone who hears them shudder. Perhaps they are useful for other purposes, but our fear is that all that shuddering will make our guardians more emotional and soft than they ought to be.

ADEIMANTUS: And our fear is justified.

SOCRATES: Should we remove them, then?

ADEIMANTUS: Yes.

SOCRATES: And follow the opposite pattern in speech and poetry?

ADEIMANTUS: Clearly.

SOCRATES: Shall we also remove the lamenta-
d tions and pitiful speeches of famous men?

ADEIMANTUS: If what we did before was necessary, so is that.

SOCRATES: Consider, though, whether we will be right to remove them or not. What we claim is that a good man won't think that death is a terrible thing for another good one to suffer—even if the latter happens to be his friend.

ADEIMANTUS: Yes, we do claim that.

SOCRATES: So, he won't mourn for him as if he had suffered a terrible fate.

ADEIMANTUS: Certainly not.

SOCRATES: But we also claim this: a good person is most self-sufficient when it comes to living well, and is distinguished from other people by having the
e least need of anyone or anything else.

ADEIMANTUS: True.

SOCRATES: So it is less terrible for him than for anyone else to be deprived of a son, brother, possessions, or the like.

ADEIMANTUS: Yes, much less.

SOCRATES: So, he will lament it the least and bear it the most calmly when some such misfortune overtakes him.

ADEIMANTUS: Of course.

SOCRATES: We would be right, then, to remove the lamentations of famous men. We would leave them to women (provided they are not excellent
388a women) and cowardly men, so that those we say we

are training to guard our land will be ashamed to do such things.

ADEIMANTUS: That's right.

SOCRATES: In addition, then, we will have to ask Homer and the other poets not to represent Achilles, who was the son of a goddess, as:

Lying now on his side, now on his back, now again
On his belly; then standing up to wander distracted
This way and that on the shore of the unharvested sea;[9]

or to make him pick up ashes with both hands and pour them over his head, weeping and lamenting to b the extent and in the manner Homer describes;[10] or to represent Priam, a close descendant of the gods, as "begging and rolling around in dung, as he calls upon each of his men by name."[11] And yet more insistently than that, we will ask them at least not to make *the gods* lament and say: "Woe is me, unfortunate that I am, wretched mother of a great son."[12] c But, if they do make the gods do such things, at least they must not dare to represent *the greatest of the gods* in so unlikely a fashion as to make him say: "Alas, with my own eyes I see a man who is most dear to me being chased around the city, and my heart laments";[13] or "Woe is me, that Sarpedon, who is most dear to me, should be fated to be killed by Patroclus, the son of Menoetius."[14] You see, my dear d Adeimantus, if our young people listen seriously to these stories without ridiculing them as not worth hearing, none of them is going to consider such things to be unworthy of a mere human being like himself, or rebuke himself if it occurred to him to do or say any of them. On the contrary, without shame

8. ["Cocytus" means river of wailing or lamenting; "Styx," river of hatred.]

9. [*Iliad* 24.3–12.]

10. [*Iliad* 18.23–4.]

11. [*Iliad* 22.414–5.]

12. [*Iliad* 18.54. Thetis, the mother of Achilles, is mourning his fate among the Nereids.]

13. [*Iliad* 22.168–9. Zeus is watching Hector being pursued by Achilles.]

14. [*Iliad* 16.433–4.]

or perseverance, he would chant many dirges and laments at the slightest sufferings.

e   ADEIMANTUS: That's absolutely true.

SOCRATES: But that must not happen, as our argument has shown—and we must remain persuaded by it until someone shows us a better one.

ADEIMANTUS: No, it must not.

SOCRATES: Moreover, they must not be lovers of laughter either. For whenever anyone gives in to violent laughter, a violent reaction pretty much always follows.

ADEIMANTUS: I agree.

SOCRATES: So, if someone represents worthwhile people as overcome by laughter, we must not accept it, and we will accept it even less if they represent 389a the gods in that way.

ADEIMANTUS: Much less.

SOCRATES: Then we must not accept the following sorts of sayings about the gods from Homer: "And unquenchable laughter arose among the blessed gods as they saw Hephaestus limping through the hall."[15] According to your argument, they must be rejected.

ADEIMANTUS: Yes, if you want to attribute it to b me, but they must be rejected in any case.

SOCRATES: Moreover, we have to be concerned about truth as well. For if what we said just now is correct and a lie is really useless to the gods, but useful to human beings as a form of drug, it is clear that it must be assigned to doctors, whereas private individuals must have nothing to do with it.

ADEIMANTUS: It is clear.

SOCRATES: It is appropriate for the rulers, then, if anyone, to lie because of enemies or citizens for the good of the city. But no one else may have anything to do with it. On the contrary, we will say that for a c private individual to lie to such rulers is as bad a mistake as for a sick person not to tell his doctor or an athlete his trainer the truth about his physical condition, or for someone not to tell the captain the things that are true about the ship and the sailors, or about how he himself or one of his fellow sailors is faring—indeed, it is a worse mistake.

ADEIMANTUS: That's absolutely true.

SOCRATES: So, if anyone else is caught telling lies in the city—"any of the craftsmen, whether a prophet, d a doctor who heals the sick, or a carpenter who works in wood"[16]—he will be punished for introducing a practice that is as subversive and destructive of a city as of a ship.

ADEIMANTUS: Indeed it is, at any rate, if what people do is influenced by what he says.

SOCRATES: What about temperance? Won't our young people also need that?

ADEIMANTUS: Of course.

SOCRATES: And aren't the most important aspects of temperance for the majority of people, at any rate, to obey the rulers and to rule over the pleasures of drink, sex, and food for themselves?   e

ADEIMANTUS: That is my view, anyway.

SOCRATES: So we will claim, I imagine, that it is fine to say the sort of thing that Diomedes says in Homer: "Sit down in silence, my friend, and be persuaded by my story";[17] and what follows it: "The Achaeans went in silently, breathing valor, afraid of their commanders";[18] and anything else of that sort.

ADEIMANTUS: Yes, it is fine.

SOCRATES: But what about things like, "You drunkard, with the eyes of a dog and the heart of a deer," and what follows it?[19] Are they, then, fine things to say? And what about all the other headstrong 390a things that private individuals say to their rulers in works of prose or poetry?

ADEIMANTUS: No, they are not fine.

SOCRATES: That, I imagine, is because they are not suitable for inculcating temperance in the young people who hear them. But it would not be surprising if they were found pleasant in some other context. What do you think?

ADEIMANTUS: The same as you.

15. [*Iliad* 1.599–600.]

16. [*Odyssey* 17.384.]

17. [*Iliad* 4.412. Agamemnon has unfairly rebuked Diomedes for cowardice. Diomedes' squire protests, but Diomedes quiets him with these words. By obeying, the squire exhibits the kind of moderation that most people can come to possess.]

18. [A mix of *Iliad* 3.8 and 4.431.]

19. [*Iliad* 1.225. Achilles is insulting his commander, Agamemnon.]

SOCRATES: What about making the wisest man say that the best thing of all, as it seems to him, is when "the tables are well laden with bread and meat, and the wine-bearer draws wine from the mixing bowl, brings it, and pours it in the cups"?[20] Do you think that hearing things like that is suitable for inculcating self-mastery in young people? Or that "death by starvation is the most pitiful fate"?[21] Or about how Zeus stayed awake alone deliberating, when all the other gods and mortals were asleep, and then easily forgot all his plans because of his sexual appetite, and was so overcome by the sight of Hera that he did not even want to go to their bedroom, but to possess her there on the ground, saying that his appetite for her was even greater than it was when they first made love to one another "without their parents' knowledge"?[22] Or what about the chaining together of Ares and Aphrodite by Hephaestus[23] for similar reasons?

ADEIMANTUS: No, by Zeus, that does not seem suitable to me.

SOCRATES: On the other hand, if there are any words or deeds of famous men that express perseverance in the face of everything, surely they must be seen and heard. For example, "He struck his chest and spoke to his heart: 'Bear up, my heart, you have suffered more shameful things than this.'"[24]

ADEIMANTUS: Absolutely.

SOCRATES: And we must not, of course, allow our men to be bribable with gifts or to be money-lovers.

ADEIMANTUS: Certainly not.

SOCRATES: Then they must not sing: "Gifts persuade gods, and gifts persuade revered kings."[25] Nor must we praise Phoenix, the tutor of Achilles, for being moderate, when he advises Achilles to take the gifts and defend the Achaeans, but not to lay aside his anger without gifts.[26] Nor should we agree that Achilles himself was such a money-lover as to accept the gifts of Agamemnon, or to release a corpse when he got paid for it, but otherwise to refuse.[27]

ADEIMANTUS: No, it certainly is not right to praise such things.

SOCRATES: It is only out of respect for Homer, indeed, that I hesitate to say that it is positively impious to accuse Achilles of such things, or to believe them when others say them. Or to believe that he said to Apollo: "You have injured me, Farshooter, most deadly of the gods; And I would punish you, if only I had the power."[28] Or that he disobeyed the river—a god—and was ready to fight it.[29] Or that he consecrated hair to the dead Patroclus, which he had already consecrated to the other river, Sphercheius: "To the hero, Patroclus, I give my hair to take with him."[30] We must not believe that he did that. Nor is it true that he dragged the dead Hector around the tomb of Patroclus[31] or massacred the captives on his pyre.[32] So we will deny these things. Nor will we allow our people to believe that Achilles—the son of a goddess and of Peleus (who was himself the most temperate of men and the grandson of Zeus), and the pupil of the most wise Cheiron—was so full of inner disorder as to have two opposite diseases within him: illiberality accompanied by the love of money on the one hand, and arrogance toward gods and humans on the other.

ADEIMANTUS: That's right.

SOCRATES: Moreover, we will neither believe nor allow it to be said that Theseus, the son of Poseidon, and Peirithous, the son of Zeus, ever attempted those terrible rapes,[33] nor that any other child of a god and hero dared to do any of the terrible and impious deeds that are now falsely attributed to them. We will compel the poets either to deny that they did such

391a

---

20. [*Odyssey* 9.8–10.]

21. [*Odyssey* 12.342. Eurylochus urges the men to slay the cattle of Helios in Odysseus' absence.]

22. [*Iliad* 14.294–341.]

23. [*Odyssey* 8.266ff.]

24. [*Odyssey* 20.17–8. The speaker is Odysseus.]

25. [The source of the passage is unknown. Cf. Euripides, *Medea* 964.]

26. [*Iliad* 9.602–3.]

27. [*Iliad* 19.278ff., 24.594.]

28. [*Iliad* 22.15, 20.]

29. [*Iliad* 21.232ff.]

30. [*Iliad* 23.151–2.]

31. [*Iliad* 14.14–8.]

32. [*Iliad* 23.175.]

33. [According to some legends, Theseus and Peirithous abducted Helen and tried to abduct Persephone from Hades.]

things, or else to deny that they were children of the gods. But they must not say both or attempt to persuade our young people that the gods produce evils, nor that heroes are no better than humans. After all, as we were saying earlier, these things are neither pious nor true. For we demonstrated, I take it, that it is impossible for the gods to produce evils.

ADEIMANTUS: We certainly did.

SOCRATES: And they are also positively harmful to those who hear them. You see, everyone will be ready to excuse himself when he is bad, if he has been persuaded that similar things are done and were done by "close descendants of the gods, near kin of Zeus, whose ancestral altar is in the ether on Ida's peak," and "in whom the blood of daimons has not weakened."[34] That is why we must put a stop to such stories; if we do not, they will produce in our young people a very casual attitude to evil.

ADEIMANTUS: Exactly.

SOCRATES: What kind of stories are still left, then, about which we must determine whether or not they may be told? I mean, we have discussed how gods, heroes, daimons, and things in Hades should be portrayed.

ADEIMANTUS: We have.

SOCRATES: Then wouldn't stories about human beings be left?

ADEIMANTUS: Obviously so.

SOCRATES: But it is not possible, my friend, to discuss them here.

ADEIMANTUS: Why not?

SOCRATES: Because what we are going to say, I imagine, is that poets and prose writers get the most important things about human beings wrong. They say that many unjust people are happy and many just ones wretched, that doing injustice is profitable if it escapes detection, and that justice is another's good but one's own loss. We will forbid them to say such things, I imagine, and order them to sing and tell the opposite. Don't you think so?

ADEIMANTUS: No, I *know* so.

SOCRATES: Well, then, if you agree that what I said is correct, won't I say to you that you have conceded the point we were investigating all along?

ADEIMANTUS: And your claim would be correct.

SOCRATES: Then we won't come to an agreement about what stories should be told about human beings until we have discovered what sort of thing justice is, and how, given its nature, it profits the one who has it, whether he is believed to be just or not.

ADEIMANTUS: That's absolutely right.

SOCRATES: Our discussion of the content of stories is complete, then. Our next task, I take it, is to investigate their style. And then we will have completely investigated both what they should say and how they should say it.

ADEIMANTUS: I don't understand what you mean.

SOCRATES: Well, we must see that you do. Maybe this will help you to grasp it better: isn't everything said by poets and storytellers a narration of past, present, or future events?

ADEIMANTUS: Of course.

SOCRATES: And don't they proceed by narration alone, narration through imitation, or both?

ADEIMANTUS: I need a still clearer understanding of that, too.

SOCRATES: What a ridiculously unclear teacher I seem to be! So, I will do what incompetent speakers do: I won't try to deal with the subject as a whole. Instead, I will take up a particular example and use that to explain what I mean. Tell me, do you know the beginning of the *Iliad* where the poet tells us that Chryses begged Agamemnon to release his daughter, that Agamemnon got angry, and that Chryses, having failed to get what he wanted, prayed to his god[35] to punish the Achaeans?

ADEIMANTUS: I do.

SOCRATES: You know, then, that up to the lines, "He begged all the Achaeans, but especially the commanders of the army, the two sons of Atreus,"[36] the poet himself is speaking and is not trying to make us think that the speaker is anyone but himself. After that, however, he speaks as if he himself were Chryses, and tries as hard as he can to make us think that the speaker is not Homer, but the priest himself, who is an old man. And all the rest of his narration of the events in Ilium and Ithaca, and all of the *Odyssey*, are written in pretty much the same way.

---

34. [Thought to be from Aeschylus' lost play *Niobe*.]

35. [Apollo.]

36. [*Iliad* 1.15ff.]

ADEIMANTUS: Yes, they are.

SOCRATES: Now, each of the speeches, as well as the material between them, is narration, isn't it?

ADEIMANTUS: Of course.

SOCRATES: But when he makes a speech as if he
c were someone else, won't we say that he makes his own style as much like that of the person he tells us is about to speak?

ADEIMANTUS: We certainly will.

SOCRATES: Now, to make oneself like someone else in voice or appearance is to imitate the person one makes oneself like, isn't it?

ADEIMANTUS: Of course.

SOCRATES: Then in a passage of that sort, it seems, he, and the rest of poets as well, produce their narration through imitation.

ADEIMANTUS: Yes, indeed.

SOCRATES: But if the poet never disguised himself, his entire poem would be narration without imi-
d tation. To prevent you from saying that you still do not understand, I will tell you what that would be like. If Homer said that Chryses came with a ransom for his daughter to supplicate the Achaeans, especially the kings, and if after that Homer had gone on speaking, not as if he had become Chryses, but still as Homer, you know that it would not be imitation but narration pure and simple. It would have gone something like this—I will speak without meter since I am not a poet: the priest came and prayed that the
e gods would grant it to the Achaeans to capture Troy and have a safe return home, and he entreated them to accept the ransom and free his daughter, out of reverence for the god.[37] When he had said this, the others approved of it and consented. But Agamemnon was angry and ordered him to leave and never return, or else his priestly wand and the wreaths of the god would not protect him. He said that the priest's daughter would grow old in Argos by his side sooner than be freed. He ordered Chryses to leave and not make him angry if he wanted to get home safely. When
394a the old man heard this, he was frightened and went off in silence. And once he had left the camp, he prayed at length to Apollo, invoking the cult names of the god, reminding him of his past gifts, and asking

to be repaid for any that had found favor with him, whether they were temples he had built or victims he had sacrificed. He prayed that, in return for these things, the arrows of the god would make the Achaeans pay for his tears. That, comrade, is how we get pure narration without any imitation.   b

ADEIMANTUS: I understand.

SOCRATES: Also understand, then, that the opposite occurs when one omits the words between the speeches and leaves the speeches on their own.

ADEIMANTUS: I understand that, too; it is what happens in tragedies, for example.

SOCRATES: You have got it absolutely right. And now I think I can make clear to you what I could not before. One sort of poetry and storytelling employs only imitation—tragedy, as you said, and comedy.   c
Another sort, which you find primarily in dithyrambs, employs only narration by the poet himself. A third sort, which uses both, is what we find in epic poetry and many other places. Do you follow me?

ADEIMANTUS: Yes, now I understand what you meant.

SOCRATES: And before that, as you remember, we said that we had already dealt with *content*, but that we had yet to investigate *style*.

ADEIMANTUS: Yes, I remember.

SOCRATES: What I meant, then, was just this: we need to come to an agreement about whether to allow   d
our poets to narrate as imitators, or as imitators of some things, but not others—and what sorts of things these are; or not to allow them to imitate at all.

ADEIMANTUS: I imagine that you are considering whether we will admit tragedy and comedy into our city or not.

SOCRATES: Perhaps so, but it may be an even wider question than that. I really do not know yet. But wherever the wind of argument blows us, so to speak, that is where we must go.

ADEIMANTUS: Yes, well put.

SOCRATES: What I want you to consider, then, Adeimantus, is whether our guardians should be imitators or not. Or does the answer follow from what   e
we have said already—namely, that whereas each individual can practice one pursuit well, he cannot practice many well, and if he tried to do this and dabbled in many things, he would surely fail to achieve distinction in all of them?

37. [Apollo as at 393a1 and 394a3.]

ADEIMANTUS: Of course. Why wouldn't it?

SOCRATES: Then doesn't the same principle also apply to imitation— namely, that a single individual cannot imitate many things as well as he can imitate one?

ADEIMANTUS: No, he cannot.

SOCRATES: Then he will hardly be able to prac-
395a tice any pursuit worth talking about while at the same time imitating lots of things and being an imitator. For, as you know, even when two sorts of imitation are thought to be closely akin, the same people are not able to practice both of them well simultaneously. The writing of tragedy and comedy is an example. Didn't you just call both of these imitations?

ADEIMANTUS: I did, and you are quite right; the same people cannot do both.

SOCRATES: Nor can they be both rhapsodes and actors simultaneously.

ADEIMANTUS: True.

SOCRATES: Indeed, the same men cannot be used as both tragic and comic actors. And all these are
b imitations, aren't they?

ADEIMANTUS: They are.

SOCRATES: And human nature, Adeimantus, seems to me to be minted in even smaller coins than this, so that an individual can neither imitate many things well nor perform well the actions themselves of which those imitations are likenesses.

ADEIMANTUS: That's absolutely true.

SOCRATES: So, if we are to preserve our first argument, that our guardians must be kept away from all other crafts so as to be the most exact craftsmen of the
c city's freedom, and practice nothing at all except what contributes to this, then they must neither do nor imitate anything else. But if they imitate anything, they must imitate right from childhood what is appropriate for them—that is to say, people who are courageous, temperate, pious, free, and everything of that sort. On the other hand, they must not be clever at doing or imitating illiberal or shameful actions, so that they won't acquire a taste for the real thing from imitating
d it. Or haven't you noticed that imitations, if they are practiced much past youth, get established in the habits and nature of body, tones of voice, and mind?

ADEIMANTUS: I have indeed.

SOCRATES: Since those we claim to care about are *men*, then, and men who must become good, we won't allow them to imitate a *woman*, young or old, as she abuses her husband, quarrels with the gods, brags because she thinks herself happy, or suffers misfortune and is possessed by sorrows and lamentations—and
e still less a woman who is ill, passionately in love, or in labor.

ADEIMANTUS: Absolutely not.

SOCRATES: Nor must they imitate either male or female slaves doing servile actions.

ADEIMANTUS: No, they must not.

SOCRATES: Nor cowardly, bad men, it seems, or those whose actions are the opposite of what we described just now—men who libel and ridicule each other, and use shameful language when drunk or even when sober, or who wrong themselves and others by word or deed in the other ways that are typical of such people. And they must not get into 396a the habit, I take it, of acting or talking like madmen. They must *know*, of course, about mad and evil men and women, but they must not do or imitate anything they do.

ADEIMANTUS: That's absolutely true.

SOCRATES: What about metalworkers or other craftsmen, or those who row in triremes, or their coxswains, or the like—should they imitate them? b

ADEIMANTUS: No, they should not, since they are not allowed even to pay any mind to those pursuits.

SOCRATES: And what about neighing horses, bellowing bulls, roaring rivers, the crashing sea, thunder, or the like—will they imitate them?

ADEIMANTUS: No, they have already been forbidden to be mad or to imitate madmen.

SOCRATES: So you are saying, if I understand you, that there is one kind of style and narration that a really good and fine person would use whenever he had to say something, and another kind, unlike that one, which his opposite by nature and education c would always favor, and in which he would narrate his story.

ADEIMANTUS: What kinds are they?

SOCRATES: In my view, when a moderate man comes upon the words or actions of a good man in the course of a narration, he will be willing to report them as if he were that man himself, and he won't be ashamed of that sort of imitation. He will be most willing to imitate the good man when he is acting in a faultless and intelligent manner, but less willing d and more reluctant to do so when he is upset by disease, passion, drunkenness, or some other misfortune. When he comes upon a character who is beneath him, however, he will be unwilling to make himself resemble this inferior character in any serious way—except perhaps for a brief period in which he is doing something good. On the contrary, he will be ashamed to do something like that, both because he is unpracticed in the imitation of such people, and also because he cannot stand to shape and mold himself on an inferior pattern. In his mind he despises

e that, except when it is for the sake of amusement.

ADEIMANTUS: Probably so.

SOCRATES: Won't he use the sorts of narration, then, that we described in dealing with the Homeric epics a moment ago? And though his style of speaking will involve both imitation and the other sort of narration, won't imitation play a small part even in a long story? Or am I talking nonsense?

ADEIMANTUS: Not at all. That must indeed be the pattern followed by that sort of speaker.

SOCRATES: As for the other sort of speaker, the

397a more inferior he is, the more willing he will be to narrate anything and to consider nothing beneath him. Hence he will undertake to imitate, before a large audience and in a serious way, all the things we just mentioned: thunder and the sounds of winds, hail, axles, and pulleys; trumpets, flutes, pipes, and all the other instruments; and even the cries of dogs, sheep, and birds. And his style will consist entirely of

b imitation in voice and gesture, won't it, with possibly a small bit of plain narration thrown in?

ADEIMANTUS: Yes, that must be so, too.

SOCRATES: Well, then, that is what I meant when I said that there are two kinds of style.

ADEIMANTUS: And you were right; there are.

SOCRATES: Now, one of them involves little variation.[38] Hence if an appropriate harmony and rhythm are provided for this style, won't anyone who speaks in it correctly come close to speaking in a single harmony and, what is more, in a rhythm of pretty much the same sort, since the variations involved in

c it are slight?

ADEIMANTUS: Yes, that's precisely what he will do.

SOCRATES: What about the other kind of style? Won't it need the opposite: namely, every harmony and every rhythm, if it, too, is going to be spoken in properly, since it is multifarious in the forms of its variations?

ADEIMANTUS: Yes, that's very much what it is like.

SOCRATES: Now, doesn't every poet and speaker adopt a style that fits one or the other of these patterns, or a mixture of both?

ADEIMANTUS: Necessarily.

SOCRATES: What are we to do, then? Shall we admit all of these into our city, or one of the pure d sorts, or the mixed one?

ADEIMANTUS: If my view prevails, we will admit only the pure imitator of the good person.

SOCRATES: And yet, Adeimantus, the mixed style *is* pleasing. And the one that is most pleasing to children, their tutors, and the vast majority of people is the opposite of the one you chose.

ADEIMANTUS: Yes, it is the most pleasing.

SOCRATES: But perhaps you would say that it does not harmonize with our constitution, because there is no twofold or manifold man among us, since each e does only one job.

ADEIMANTUS: Indeed, it does not harmonize with it.

SOCRATES: And isn't that the reason that it is only in a city like ours that we will find a shoemaker who is a shoemaker, not a ship's captain who also makes shoes; and a farmer who is a farmer, not a juror who also farms; and a soldier who is a soldier, not a moneymaker who also soldiers, and so on?

ADEIMANTUS: True, it is.

SOCRATES: Suppose, then, that a man whose wisdom enabled him to become multifarious and imitate 398a everything were to arrive in person in our city and want to give a performance of his poems. It seems that we would bow down before him as someone holy, amazing, and pleasing. But we would tell him that there is no man like him in our city, and that it is not in accord with divine law for there to be one. Then we would anoint his head with perfumes, crown him with a woolen wreath,[39] and send him away to

38. [*Metabolê*: variation in general, but also a technical term in music for the transition from one harmony to another.]

39. [As was traditionally done to statues of the gods.]

another city. But, for our own benefit, we would
employ a more austere and less pleasant poet and
b storyteller ourselves—one who would imitate the
speech of a good person and make his stories fit the
patterns we laid down at the beginning, when we
undertook to educate our soldiers.

ADEIMANTUS: Yes, that is certainly what we would
do, if it were up to us.

SOCRATES: And now, my friend, it looks to me
as though we have completed our discussion of the
branch of musical training that deals with speech and
stories. After all, we have discussed both what is to
be said and how it is to be said.

ADEIMANTUS: Yes, it seems that way to me, too.

SOCRATES: Wouldn't what is left for us to discuss
c next, then, be lyric odes and songs?

ADEIMANTUS: Clearly.

SOCRATES: And couldn't anyone discover by now
what to say about what they must be like, if indeed
it is going to be concordant with what has already
been said?

And Glaucon laughed and said:

I am afraid, Socrates, that "anyone" does not include
me. You see, it is not sufficiently clear to me at
the moment what we are to say, though I have my
suspicions.

SOCRATES: Nonetheless, you are sufficiently clear
about this: first, that a song consists of three elements—
d speech, harmony, and rhythm.

GLAUCON: Yes, I do know that, at least.

SOCRATES: Now, as far as speech is concerned,
at any rate, it is no different, is it, from speech that
is not part of a song, in that it must still be spoken
in conformity to the patterns we established just now?

GLAUCON: True.

SOCRATES: Further, the harmony and rhythm
must fit the speech.

GLAUCON: Of course.

SOCRATES: But we said that there is no longer a
need for dirges and lamentations in words.[40]

GLAUCON: No, there is not.

SOCRATES: What are the lamenting harmonies,
e then? You tell me; you are musical.

GLAUCON: The mixo-Lydian, the syntono-
Lydian, and some others of that sort.

SOCRATES: Shouldn't we exclude them, then?
After all, they are even useless for helping women to
be as good as they should be, let alone men.

GLAUCON: We certainly should.

SOCRATES: Now, surely drunkenness is also entirely inappropriate for our guardians, and softness
and idleness as well.

GLAUCON: Of course.

SOCRATES: What, then, are the soft harmonies,
and the ones suitable for drinking parties?

GLAUCON: There are some Ionian ones that are
called "relaxed," and also some Lydian ones.

SOCRATES: Could you use any of them, my friend,
on men who are warriors?   399a

GLAUCON: No, never. So it looks as though you
have got the Dorian and Phrygian left.

SOCRATES: I do not know the harmonies, so just
leave me that harmony that would appropriately imitate the vocal sounds and tones[41] of a courageous
person engaged in battle or in other work that he is
forced to do, and who—even when he fails and faces
wounds or death or some other misfortune—always b
grapples with what chances to occur, in a disciplined
and resolute way. And also leave me another harmony
for when he is engaged in peaceful enterprises, or in
those he is not forced to do but does willingly; or for
when he is trying to persuade someone of something,
or entreating a god though prayer, or a human being
through instruction and advice; or for when he is
doing the opposite—patiently listening to someone
else, who is entreating or instructing him, or trying
to change his mind through persuasion. Leave me
the harmony that will imitate him, when he does not
behave arrogantly when these things turn out as he
intends; but, on the contrary, is temperate and moderate in all these enterprises, and satisfied with their
outcomes. Leave me these two harmonies, then— c
the forced and the willing—that will best imitate the
voices of temperate and courageous men in good
fortune and in bad.

40. [387d–388e.]

41. [*Phthongos, prosôdia: phthongos* is a human voice,
an animal cry, or more generally a sound of some sort;
prosôdia is the tone or accent of a syllable, or a song
accompanied by music.]

GLAUCON: You are asking to be left with the very ones I just mentioned.

SOCRATES: Well, then, we will have no need for multi-stringed or polyharmonic instruments to accompany our odes and songs.

GLAUCON: No, it seems to me we won't.

SOCRATES: Then we won't maintain craftsmen who make triangular lutes, harps, and all other such multi-stringed and polyharmonic instruments.

GLAUCON: Apparently not.

SOCRATES: What about flute-makers and flute players? Will you allow them into the city? Or isn't the flute the most multi-stringed of all? And aren't polyharmonic instruments all imitations of it?

GLAUCON: Clearly, they are.

SOCRATES: You have the lyre and the cithara left, then, as useful in our city; and in the countryside, by contrast, there would be a sort of pipe for the herdsman to play.

GLAUCON: That is what our argument suggests, anyway.

SOCRATES: Well we are certainly not doing anything new, my friend, in preferring Apollo and his instruments to Marsyas and his.[42]

GLAUCON: No, by Zeus, I suppose we aren't.

SOCRATES: And, by the dog,[43] we have certainly been unwittingly re-purifying the city we described as luxurious a while ago.

GLAUCON: That just shows how temperate we are.

SOCRATES: Then let's complete the purification. Now, the next topic after harmonies is the discussion of rhythms. We should not chase after complexity or multifariousness in the basic elements.[44] On the contrary, we should try to discover the rhythms of a life that is ordered and courageous, and then adapt the metrical foot and the melody to the speech characteristic of it, not the speech to them. What rhythms these would be is for you to say, just as you did in the case of the harmonies.

GLAUCON: No, by Zeus, I cannot tell you that. However, I can tell you from observation that there are three kinds of metrical feet[45] out of which the others are constructed, just as there are four, in the case of voices, from which come all the harmonies. But I cannot tell you which sort imitates which sort of life.

SOCRATES: Well, then, we will also have to consult with Damon, on this point, and ask him which metrical feet suit illiberality, arrogance, madness, and the other vices, and which their opposites. I think I have heard him using the unclear terms "warlike," "complex," "fingerlike," and "heroic" to describe one foot, which he arranged, I do not know how, to be equal up and down in the interchange of long and short.[46] And I think he called one foot an iamb and another a trochee, and assigned long and short quantities to them. In the case of some of these, I think he approved or disapproved of the tempo of the foot as much as of the rhythm itself, or of some combination of the two—I cannot tell you which. But, as I said, we will leave these things to Damon, since to decide them would take a long discussion. Or do you think we should try it?

GLAUCON: No, by Zeus, I do not.

SOCRATES: But you are able to decide this, at least, aren't you: that grace goes along with good rhythm and lack of grace with bad rhythm?

GLAUCON: Of course.

SOCRATES: Furthermore, good rhythm goes along with fine speaking and is similar to it, while bad

---

42. [After Athena had invented the flute, she discarded it because playing it distorted her features. It was picked up by the satyr Marsyas, who was foolish enough to challenge Apollo (inventor of the lyre) to a musical contest. He was defeated, and Apollo flayed him alive. Satyrs were bestial in their behavior and desires—especially their sexual desires.]

43. [*Nê ton kuna*: probably the dog-headed Egyptian god Anubis.]

44. [Rhythm is poetic meter, and the elements are the metrical feet.]

45. [Probably those in which the foot is divided in the ratio of: (1) 2:2—e.g., the dactyl ($-\smile\smile$) or the spondee ($--$); (2) 3:2—e.g., the paeon ($\smile\smile\smile\smile$); (3) 1:2 or 2:1—e.g., the iamb ($\smile-$) or the trochee ($-\smile$).]

46. [The foot being described is probably the dactyl ($-\smile\smile$): it is warlike and heroic, because Greek heroic poetry was written in dactylic hexameter; complex, because it consists of a long syllable and two short ones; equal up and down in the interchange of long and short, because a long syllable is equal in length to two short ones; and fingerlike, because the first joint on a finger is roughly equal in length to the other two.]

rhythm goes along with the opposite sort, and the same goes for harmony and disharmony; since, as we said just now, rhythm and harmony must conform to speech, and not vice versa.

GLAUCON: Yes, they certainly must conform to speech.

SOCRATES: And what about the style of speaking and what is said? Don't they go along with the character of the speaker's soul?

GLAUCON: Of course.

SOCRATES: And don't all the rest go along with the style of speaking?

GLAUCON: Yes.

SOCRATES: Fine speech, then, as well as harmony, grace, and rhythm, go along with naiveté. I
e do not mean the stupidity for which naiveté is a euphemism, but the quality a mind has when it is equipped with a truly good and fine character.

GLAUCON: Absolutely.

SOCRATES: And mustn't our young people try to achieve these on every occasion, if they are going to do the job that is really theirs?

GLAUCON: Yes, they must indeed.

SOCRATES: Now, surely painting and all the crafts
401a similar to it are full of these qualities—weaving is full of them, as are embroidery, architecture, and likewise the manufacture of implements generally; and so, furthermore, is the nature of bodies and that of the other things that grow. For in all these there is grace or the lack of it. And lack of grace, bad rhythm, and disharmony are akin to bad speech and bad character, while their opposites are akin to and imitate their opposite—a character that is temperate and good.

GLAUCON: Absolutely.

SOCRATES: Is it only poets we have to supervise,
b then, compelling them either to embody the image of a good character in their poems or else not to practice their craft among us? Or mustn't we also supervise all the other craftsmen, and forbid them to represent a character that is bad, intemperate, illiberal, and graceless, in their images of living beings, in their buildings, or in any of the other products of their craft? And mustn't the one who finds this impossible be prevented from practicing in our city, so that our guardians will not be brought up on images
c of evil as in a meadow of bad grass, where they crop

and graze every day from all that surrounds them until, little by little, they unwittingly accumulate a large amount of evil in their souls? Instead, mustn't we look for craftsmen who are naturally capable of pursuing what is fine and graceful in their work, so that our young people will live in a healthy place and be benefited on all sides as the influence exerted by those fine works affects their eyes and ears like a healthy breeze from wholesome regions, and imperceptibly guides them from earliest childhood into d
being similar to, friendly toward, and concordant with the beauty of reason?

GLAUCON: Yes, that would be by far the best education for them.

SOCRATES: Then aren't these the reasons, Glaucon, that musical training is most important? First, because rhythm and harmony permeate the innermost element of the soul, affect it more powerfully than anything else, and bring it grace, such education makes one graceful if one is properly trained, and the opposite if one is not. Second, because anyone e
who has been properly trained will quickly notice if something has been omitted from a thing, or if that thing has not been well crafted or well grown. And so, since he feels distaste correctly, he will praise fine things, be pleased by them, take them into his soul, and, through being nourished by them, become fine and good. What is ugly or shameful, on the other hand, he will correctly condemn and hate while he 402a
is still young, before he is able to grasp the reason. And, because he has been so trained, he will welcome the reason when it comes and recognize it easily because of its kinship with himself.

GLAUCON: Yes, it seems to me that these are the goals of musical training.

SOCRATES: It is like learning to read, then. We became adequately proficient only when the few letters that there are did not escape us in any of the different words in which they are scattered about; and when we did not disregard them, either in a small word or a big one, as if they were not worth noticing; but tried hard to distinguish them wherever they b
occur, knowing that we would not be competent readers until we knew our letters.

GLAUCON: True.

SOCRATES: And isn't it also true that if there are images of letters reflected in water or mirrors, we won't know them until we know the letters themselves, for both abilities are parts of the same craft and discipline?

GLAUCON: Absolutely.

SOCRATES: Then, by the gods, aren't I right in
c saying that neither we nor the guardians we claim to be educating will be musically trained until we know the different forms of temperance, courage, generosity, high-mindedness, and all their kindred, and their opposites, too, which are carried around all over the place; and see them in the things in which they are, both themselves and their images; and do not disregard them, either in small things or in large, but accept that the knowledge of both belongs to the same craft and discipline?

GLAUCON: Yes, that necessarily follows.

SOCRATES: Then, if the fine habits in someone's
d soul and those in his physical form agree and are in concord with one another, so that both share the same pattern, wouldn't that be the most beautiful sight for anyone capable of seeing it?

GLAUCON: By far.

SOCRATES: And surely the most beautiful is also the most loveable, isn't it?

GLAUCON: Of course.

SOCRATES: A really musical person, then, would passionately love people who are most like that. But a disharmonious person, he would not passionately love.

GLAUCON: No, he would not—at least, not if the defect were in the soul. If it were only in the body, however, he would put up with it and still be willing
e to embrace the boy who had it.

SOCRATES: I understand that you love or have loved such a boy yourself, and I agree with you. But tell me this: does excessive pleasure share anything in common with temperance?

GLAUCON: How can it? It surely drives one no less mad than pain does.

SOCRATES: What about with any other virtue?

403a GLAUCON: Never.

SOCRATES: Then, what about with arrogance and intemperance?

GLAUCON: Yes, with them most of all.

SOCRATES: Can you think of any pleasure that is greater or keener than sexual pleasure?

GLAUCON: No, I cannot—or of a more insane one either.

SOCRATES: But isn't the right sort of passion a naturally moderate and musically educated passion for order and beauty?

GLAUCON: Yes.

SOCRATES: Then nothing insane and nothing akin to dissoluteness can be involved in the right love?

GLAUCON: No, they cannot.

SOCRATES: Then sexual pleasure must not be in-
b volved, must it, and the lover and the boy who passionately love and are loved in the right way must have no share in it?

GLAUCON: No, by Zeus, Socrates, it must not be involved.

SOCRATES: It seems, then, that you will lay it down as a law in the city we are founding that a lover—if he can persuade his boyfriend to let him—may kiss him, be with him, and touch him, as a father would a son, for the sake of beautiful things. But in all other respects, his association with the one he cares about must never seem to go any further than this. Otherwise, he will be reproached as untrained in c
music, and as lacking in appreciation for beautiful things.

GLAUCON: That's right.

SOCRATES: Do you agree, then, that our account of musical training has come to an end? At any rate, it ought to end where it has ended, for surely training in the musical crafts ought to end in a passion for beauty.

GLAUCON: I agree.

SOCRATES: Now, after musical training, our young people must be given physical training.

GLAUCON: Of course.

SOCRATES: And in this, too, they must have a careful training, which starts in childhood and continues throughout life. It would, I believe, be something like this—but you should consider what you think, too. You see, I, for my part, do not believe that a d
healthy body, by means of its own virtue, makes the soul good. On the contrary, I believe that the opposite is true: a good soul, by means of its own virtue, makes the body as good as possible. What do you think?

GLAUCON: I think so, too.

SOCRATES: Then if we give adequate care to the mind, entrust it with the detailed supervision of the body, and content ourselves with indicating the general patterns to be followed rather than going on

at great length, wouldn't we be proceeding in the
e right way?

GLAUCON: Yes, indeed.

SOCRATES: Now, we said that our prospective
guardians must avoid drunkenness.[47] For surely a
guardian is the last person who should get so drunk
that he does not know where on earth he is.

GLAUCON: Yes, it would be ridiculous for a *guardian* to need a guardian himself!

SOCRATES: What about food? These men are athletes in the greatest contest, aren't they?

GLAUCON: Yes.

SOCRATES: Then would the regimen of ordinary,
404a trained athletes be suitable for them?

GLAUCON: Maybe.

SOCRATES: But it seems to be a soporific sort of
regimen and unreliable as regards health. Or haven't
you noticed that these athletes sleep their lives away,
and that if they deviate even a little from their orderly
regimen, they become seriously and violently ill?

GLAUCON: I have noticed that.

SOCRATES: Then we need a more refined sort of
training for our warrior-athletes, since they must be
like sleepless hounds, as it were, who have the keenest
possible sight and hearing, and whose health is not
so precarious that it cannot sustain the frequent
changes of water and diet generally, and the heat
b waves and winter storms typical of war.

GLAUCON: I agree.

SOCRATES: Wouldn't the best physical training,
then, be akin to the simple musical training we described a moment ago?

GLAUCON: How do you mean?

SOCRATES: I mean a simple and good physical
training, and one that is especially adapted to the
conditions of war.

GLAUCON: In what way?

SOCRATES: You could learn *that* even from
Homer. For you know that when his heroes are at
war, he does not portray them banqueting on fish[48] —
even though they are by the sea in the Hellespont —
c or boiled meat, but roasted meat only, which is the
sort most easily available to soldiers. For it is pretty

much always easier to use an open fire than to carry
pots and pans around everywhere.

GLAUCON: Quite right.

SOCRATES: Nor, I believe, does Homer mention
rich sauces anywhere. In fact, isn't everyone else who
is in training also aware that if he is planning to
stay in good physical condition, he must avoid such
things altogether?

GLAUCON: Yes, and they are certainly right to be
aware of it and to avoid them.

SOCRATES: If you think they are right to do that,
my dear Glaucon, you apparently do not approve of
Syracusan cuisine or complex Sicilian relishes.   d

GLAUCON: I suppose not.

SOCRATES: Then you also object to men having
a Corinthian girlfriend, if they are planning to be in
good physical condition.[49]

GLAUCON: Absolutely.

SOCRATES: And also to their enjoying the reputed
delights of Attic pastries?

GLAUCON: I would have to.

SOCRATES: And the reason for that, I take it, is
that we would be right to compare this sort of diet,
and this lifestyle, to the polyharmonic songs and lyric
odes that make use of every sort of rhythm.   e

GLAUCON: Of course.

SOCRATES: There complexity engendered intemperance, didn't it, and here it engenders illness;
whereas simplicity in musical training engenders temperance in the soul, and in physical training health
in the body?

GLAUCON: That's absolutely true.

SOCRATES: And as intemperance and disease
breed in a city, aren't many law courts and surgeries   405a
opened? And don't the legal and medical professions
give themselves airs when even free men in large
numbers take them very seriously?

GLAUCON: How could it be otherwise?

SOCRATES: Could you find better evidence that
a city's education is in a bad and shameful state than
when eminent doctors and lawyers are needed, not
only by inferior people and handicraftsmen, but by
those who claim to have been brought up in the
manner of free men? Indeed, don't you think it is

---

47. [398e6.]

48. [Fish was a luxury item in Plato's Athens.]

49. [Corinthian prostitutes enjoyed an international reputation in the Classical period.]

b shameful and strong evidence of lack of education to be forced to make use of a justice imposed by others, as if they were one's masters and judges, because one lacks such qualities oneself?

GLAUCON: That is the most shameful thing of all.

SOCRATES: Do you really think so? Isn't it even more shameful not just to spend a good part of one's life in court defending oneself and prosecuting someone else, but to be so vulgar that one is persuaded to take pride in this and regard oneself as amazingly clever at doing injustice, and as so accomplished at
c every trick and turn that one can wiggle through any loophole, and avoid punishment—and to do all that for the sake of little worthless things, and because one is ignorant of how much better and finer it is to arrange one's own life so that one won't need to find a judge who is asleep?

GLAUCON: Yes, that is even more shameful.

SOCRATES: What about needing the craft of medicine for something besides wounds or some seasonal illnesses? What about needing it because idleness and
d the regimen we described has filled one full of gasses and phlegm, like a stagnant swamp, so that sophisticated Asclepiad doctors are forced to come up with names like "flatulence" and "catarrh" to describe one's diseases? Don't you think that is shameful?

GLAUCON: Yes, it is; and those truly are strange new names for diseases.

SOCRATES: And of a sort that I do not imagine even existed in the time of Asclepius himself. My
e evidence for this is that his sons at Troy did not criticize the woman who treated the wounded Eurypylus with Pramneian wine that had lots of barley meal and grated cheese sprinkled on it, even though
406a such treatment is now thought to cause inflammation. Moreover, they did not criticize Patroclus, who prescribed the treatment.[50]

GLAUCON: Yet, surely it *was* a strange drink for someone in that condition.

SOCRATES: Not if you recall that the sort of modern medicine that coddles the disease was not used by the Asclepiads before the time of Herodicus. Hero-

dicus was a physical trainer who became ill and, through a combination of physical training and medicine, tormented first and foremost himself, and then
b lots of other people as well.

GLAUCON: How did he do that?

SOCRATES: By making his death a lengthy process. You see, although he was always tending his illness, he was not able to cure it, since it was terminal. And so he spent his life under medical treatment, with no free time for anything else whatsoever. He suffered torments if he departed even a little from his accustomed regimen; but, thanks to his wisdom, he struggled against death and reached old age.

GLAUCON: A fine reward for his craft that was!

SOCRATES: And appropriate for someone who did not know that it was not because of ignorance or inex-
c perience of this kind of medicine that Asclepius failed to teach it to his sons, but because he knew that everyone in a well-regulated city has his own work to do, and that no one has the time to be ill and under treatment all his life. We see how ridiculous this would be in the case of craftsmen, but we do not see it in the case of those who are supposedly happy—the rich.

GLAUCON: What do you mean?

SOCRATES: When a carpenter is ill, he expects to get a drug from his doctor that will make him throw
d up what is making him sick or evacuate it through his bowels; or to get rid of his disease through surgery or cautery. If anyone prescribes a lengthy regimen for him and tells him that he should rest with his head bandaged and so on, he quickly replies that he has no time to be ill, and that it is not profitable for him to live like that, always minding his illness and neglecting the work at hand. After that, he says good-
e bye to his doctor, resumes his usual regimen, lives doing his own job, and recovers his health; alternatively, if his body cannot withstand the illness, he dies and escapes his troubles.

GLAUCON: That does seem to be the correct way for someone like that to use the craft of medicine.

SOCRATES: Isn't that because he had a job to do, and that if he could not do it, it would not profit him
407a to go on living?

GLAUCON: Clearly.

SOCRATES: But a rich person, it is said, has no job assigned to him of the sort that would make his life not worth living if he had to keep away from it.

---

50. [At *Iliad* 11.580ff. Eurypylus is wounded, but not treated in this way (see 11.828–36). However, Machaon, the son of Asclepius, does receive this treatment at 11.624–50.]

GLAUCON: So it is said, at least.

SOCRATES: What, have you not heard the saying of Phocylides that once one has the means of life, one must practice virtue?[51]

GLAUCON: And even earlier, in my view.

SOCRATES: Let's not quarrel with him about that. But let's try to find out for ourselves whether this virtue is something a rich person must practice, and if his life is not worth living if he does not practice
b it; or whether nursing an illness, while an obstacle to putting your mind to carpentry and other crafts, is no obstacle whatever to taking Phocylides' advice.

GLAUCON: But, by Zeus, it is: excessive care of the body that goes beyond simple physical training is pretty much the biggest obstacle of all. For it's a nuisance in household management, in military service, and even in sedentary political office.

SOCRATES: And most important of all, surely, is
c that it makes any sort of learning, thought, or private meditation difficult, by forever causing imaginary headaches or dizziness and accusing philosophy of causing them. Hence, wherever this sort of virtue is practiced and submitted to philosophical scrutiny, excessive care of the body hinders it. For it is constantly making you imagine that you are ill and never lets you stop agonizing about your body.

GLAUCON: Yes, probably so.

SOCRATES: Then won't we say that Asclepius knew this, too, and that he invented the craft of medicine for people whose bodies are healthy in nature
d and habit, but have some specific disease in them? That is the type of person and condition for which he invented it. He rid them of their disease by means of drugs or surgery, and then prescribed their normal regimen, so that affairs of politics would not be harmed. However, he did not attempt to prescribe regimens for those whose bodies were riddled with disease, so that by drawing off a little here and pouring in a little there, he could make their life a prolonged misery and enable them to produce offspring in all probability like themselves. He did not think that he should treat someone who could not live a normal
e life, since such a person would profit neither himself nor his city.

GLAUCON: Asclepius was a true man of politics, in your view.

SOCRATES: Clearly so. And it was because he was like that, don't you see, that his sons, too, turned out to be good men in the war at Troy, and practiced 408a the craft of medicine as I say they did. Don't you remember that they "sucked out the blood and applied gentle drugs" to the wound Pandarus inflicted on Menelaus? But they no more prescribed what he should eat or drink after that than they did for Eurypylus?[52] That was because they assumed that their drugs were sufficient to cure men who were healthy and living an orderly life before being wounded, even if they happened to drink wine mixed with barley and cheese right afterward. But they b thought that the lives of naturally sick and intemperate people were profitable neither to themselves nor to anyone else, that the craft of medicine shouldn't be practiced on them, and that they should not be given treatment, not even if they were richer than Midas.

GLAUCON: The sons of Asclepius were indeed very sophisticated, in your view.

SOCRATES: It is the right view to hold of them. And yet it is on just this point that Pindar and the tragedians are not persuaded by us. They say that Asclepius, even though he was the son of Apollo, was bribed with gold to heal a rich man who was already dying, and that that is why he was struck by lightning. c But, in view of what we said before, we won't accept both claims from them. On the contrary, we will say that if Asclepius was the son of a god, he was not a money-grubber; and that if he was a money-grubber, he was not the son of a god.

GLAUCON: That's absolutely right. But what do you say about the following, Socrates? Won't we need to have good doctors in our city? And the best, I take it, will be those who have treated the greatest number of healthy and diseased people. In the same way, the best judges will be those who have associated with d people with multifarious natures.

SOCRATES: I certainly agree that we need good ones. But do you know which ones I regard as such?

GLAUCON: I will, if you will tell me.

---

51. [Phocylides of Miletus was a mid-sixth–century elegiac and hexameter poet best known for his epigrams.]

52. [*Iliad* 4.218–9. In the extant text, Machaon is acting alone.]

SOCRATES: Well, I will try. However, you ask about things that are not alike in the same question.

GLAUCON: What do you mean?

SOCRATES: Doctors, it is true, would become cleverest if, in addition to learning the craft of medicine, they associated with the greatest possible number of the most diseased bodies right from childhood, had themselves experienced every illness, and were not, by nature, very healthy. After all, they do not treat a body with a body. If they did, we would not allow their bodies to be or become bad. But it is with a soul that a body is treated, and it is not possible for a soul to treat anything well if it is or has become bad itself.

GLAUCON: That's right.

SOCRATES: But a *judge*, my friend, does rule a soul with a soul. And it is not possible for a soul to be nurtured among bad souls from childhood, to have associated with them, and to have itself indulged in every sort of injustice, so as to be able to draw exact inferences from itself about the injustices of others, as in the case of diseases of the body. On the contrary, it itself must have no experience of, and be uncontaminated by, bad characters while it is young, if as a fine and good soul itself, it is going to make judgments about what is just in a healthy way. That is precisely the reason, indeed, that good people are thought to be naïve when they are young and easily deceived by unjust ones: they do not have models within themselves of the behavior of bad ones.

GLAUCON: Yes, indeed, that is precisely what happens to them.

SOCRATES: That is why a good judge must not be young, but old—a late learner of what sort of thing injustice is, who has become aware of it, not as something at home in his own soul, but as an alien thing present in other people's souls. He must have trained himself over many years to discern how naturally bad it is by using his theoretical knowledge, not his own intimate experience of it.

GLAUCON: At any rate, it would seem that *the noblest* judge would be like that.

SOCRATES: And so is the *good* one you asked about, since the one who has a good soul is good. The clever and suspicious person, on the other hand, who has committed many injustices himself and thinks of himself to be unscrupulous and wise, appears clever when he associates with those like himself, because he is on his guard and looks to the models within himself. But when he meets with good people who are older, he is seen to be stupid, distrustful at the wrong time, and ignorant of what a healthy character is, since he has no model of this within himself. But because he meets bad people more often than good ones, he seems more wise than foolish, both to himself and to them as well.

GLAUCON: That's absolutely true.

SOCRATES: Then we must not look for a good judge among people like that, but among the sort we described earlier. For while a bad person could never come to know either vice or virtue, a naturally virtuous person, when educated, will in time acquire knowledge of both virtue and vice. And it is someone like that, and not a bad person, who becomes a wise judge in my view.

GLAUCON: And I share your view.

SOCRATES: Then won't you establish by law in your city both the craft of medicine we mentioned and this craft of judging along with it? And these crafts will care for such of your citizens as have naturally good bodies and souls; but those whose bodies are not like that they will allow to die, while those whose souls are naturally and incurably bad they will themselves put to death.

GLAUCON: Yes, we have seen that that is best both for those who receive such treatment and for the city.

SOCRATES: And so it is clear that *your* young people will be wary of coming to need a judge, since they employ that simple sort of musical training, which we said engenders temperance.

GLAUCON: Of course.

SOCRATES: And won't a person who is musically trained hunt for a type of physical training by following these same tracks, and catch it, if he chooses? And won't the result be that he will have no need of the craft of medicine, except when absolutely necessary?

GLAUCON: That's my view, at any rate.

SOCRATES: And he will undertake even the regimens and exertions of physical training with an eye less to strength than to arousing the spirited part of his nature, unlike all other athletes who use diets and exertions only to gain muscle power.

GLAUCON: That's absolutely right.

SOCRATES: Then, doesn't it follow, Glaucon, that those who established musical training and physical training did not establish them with the aim that some people attribute to them: namely, to treat the body with the former and the soul with the latter?

GLAUCON: What was it then?

SOCRATES: It looks as though they established both chiefly for the sake of the soul.

GLAUCON: How so?

SOCRATES: Have you never noticed the mind-set of those who have a lifelong association with physical training but stay away from musical training? Or, again, that of those who do the opposite?

GLAUCON: What do you mean?

SOCRATES: Savagery and toughness, in the one case; softness and over-cultivation, in the other.

GLAUCON: I have certainly noticed that people who devote themselves exclusively to physical training turn out to be more savage than they should, while those who devote themselves to musical training turn out to be softer than is good for them.

SOCRATES: And surely the savageness derives from the spirited element of their nature, which, if rightly nurtured, becomes courageous, but, if overstrained, is likely to become hard and harsh.

GLAUCON: So it seems.

SOCRATES: What about the cultivation? Wouldn't it derive from the philosophic element of their nature, which, if relaxed too much, becomes softer than it should, but, if well nurtured, is cultivated and orderly?

GLAUCON: That's right.

SOCRATES: Now, we said that our guardians must have both these natures.[53]

GLAUCON: Yes, they must.

SOCRATES: And mustn't the two be harmonized with one another?

GLAUCON: Of course.

SOCRATES: And isn't the soul of the person thus harmonized temperate and courageous?

GLAUCON: Certainly.

SOCRATES: And that of the inharmonious person, cowardly and savage?

GLAUCON: Exactly.

SOCRATES: So when someone gives himself over to musical training and lets the flute pour into his soul through his ears, as through a funnel, those sweet, soft, and plaintive harmonies we mentioned; and when he spends his whole life humming, entranced by song, the first result is that whatever spirit he had, he softens the way he would iron and makes useful, rather than useless and brittle. But when he keeps at it unrelentingly and charms his spirit, the next result is that he melts it and dissolves it completely until he has cut out, so to speak, the very sinews of his soul and makes himself "a feeble warrior."[54]

GLAUCON: Yes, indeed.

SOCRATES: And if he has a spiritless nature to begin with, this happens quickly. But if he has a spirited one, his spirit becomes weak and unstable, quickly inflamed by trivial things and quickly extinguished. As a result, people like that become quick-tempered and prone to anger, instead of spirited, and filled with peevishness.

GLAUCON: Absolutely.

SOCRATES: On the other hand, what about someone who works hard at physical training, eats very well, and never touches musical training or philosophy? At first, because his body is in good strong condition, isn't he full of pride and spirit, and more courageous than he was before?

GLAUCON: He certainly is.

SOCRATES: But what happens if he does nothing but this and never enters into partnership with a Muse? Even if there was some love of learning in his soul, because it never tastes any sort of instruction or investigation, and never participates in any discussion or in any of the rest of musical training, doesn't it become weak, deaf, and blind, because it never receives any stimulation or nourishment, and its senses are never purified?

GLAUCON: Yes, it does.

SOCRATES: Then a person like that, I take it, becomes an unmusical hater of argument[55] who no longer uses argument to persuade people, but force and savagery, behaves like a wild beast, and lives in awkward ignorance without rhythm or grace.

---

53. [375c6–8.]

54. [*Iliad* 17.588.]

55. [*Misologos*: the opposite of a philosopher, who is a *philologos*, a lover of argument.]

GLAUCON: That's exactly how it is.

SOCRATES: So I, for one, would claim that it is to deal with *these* two things, so it seems, that a god has given two crafts to human beings— musical training and physical training—to deal with the philosophical and spirited elements, and not, except as a byproduct, with the soul and the body; but with these two, so that they might be harmonized with one another by being stretched and relaxed to the appropriate degree.

412a

GLAUCON: Yes, it seems so.

SOCRATES: Then it is the person who makes the best blend of musical and physical training, and applies them in the most perfect proportion to his soul, that we would be most correct to describe as completely trained in music and as most in harmony— far more so than the one who merely attunes his strings to one another.

GLAUCON: Probably so, Socrates.

SOCRATES: Then won't we also need this sort of person in our city, Glaucon, as a permanent overseer, if indeed its constitution is to be preserved?

b

GLAUCON: Yes, we will need him most of all.

SOCRATES: Those, then, would be the patterns of their education and upbringing. For why should we enumerate their dances, hunts, chases with hounds, athletic contests, and horse races? After all, it is pretty much clear that they should be consistent with these patterns, and so there should no longer be any difficulty in discovering them.

GLAUCON: No, presumably there should not.

SOCRATES: All right. Now, what is the next question we have to settle? Isn't it which of these same people will rule and which be ruled?

c

GLAUCON: Of course.

SOCRATES: Well, isn't it clear that the older ones must rule, whereas the younger ones must be ruled?

GLAUCON: Yes, it is clear.

SOCRATES: And that the rulers must be the best among them?

GLAUCON: Yes, that's clear, too.

SOCRATES: And aren't the best farmers the ones who are best at farming?

GLAUCON: Yes.

SOCRATES: In the present case, then, since the rulers must be the best of the guardians, mustn't they be the ones who are best at guarding the city?

GLAUCON: Yes.

SOCRATES: Then mustn't they be knowledgeable and capable in this matter, and, in addition, mustn't they care for the city?

GLAUCON: Yes, they must.

d

SOCRATES: But a person would care most for what he loved.

GLAUCON: Necessarily.

SOCRATES: And he would love something most if he thought that the same things were advantageous both for it and for himself, and if he thought that when it did well, he would do well, too; and that if it didn't, the opposite would happen.

GLAUCON: That's right.

SOCRATES: Then we must choose from among our guardians the sort of men who seem on the basis of our observation to be most inclined, throughout their entire lives, to do what they believe to be advantageous for the city, and most unwilling to do the opposite.

e

GLAUCON: Yes, they would be suitable for the job.

SOCRATES: I think, then, that we will have to observe them at every stage of their lives to make sure that they are good guardians of this conviction, and that neither compulsion nor sorcery will cause them to discard or forget their belief that they must do what is best for the city.

GLAUCON: What do you mean by discarding?

SOCRATES: I will tell you. It seems to me that the departure of a belief from someone's mind is either voluntary or involuntary—voluntary when he learns that the belief is false; involuntary in the case of all true beliefs.

413a

GLAUCON: I understand the voluntary sort, but I still need instruction about the involuntary.

SOCRATES: What? Don't you know that people are involuntarily deprived of good things, but voluntarily deprived of bad ones? And isn't being deceived about the truth a bad thing, whereas possessing the truth is a good one? Or don't you think that to believe things that are is to possess the truth?

GLAUCON: No, you are right. And I do think that people are involuntarily deprived of true beliefs.

SOCRATES: Then isn't it through theft, sorcery, and compulsion that this happens?

b

GLAUCON: Now I do not understand again.

SOCRATES: I suppose I am making myself as clear as a tragic poet! By those who have their beliefs stolen from them, I mean those who are over-persuaded, or those who forget; because argument, in the one case, and time, in the other, takes away their beliefs without their noticing. You understand now, don't you?

GLAUCON: Yes.

SOCRATES: Well then, by those who are compelled, I mean those who are made to change their beliefs by some suffering or pain.

GLAUCON: I understand that, too, and you are right.

SOCRATES: And the victims of sorcery, I think c you would agree, are those who change their beliefs because they are charmed by pleasure or terrified by some fear.

GLAUCON: It seems to me that all deception is a form of sorcery.

SOCRATES: Well then, as I was just saying, we must discover which of them are best at safeguarding within themselves the conviction that they must always do what they believe to be best for the city. We must watch them right from childhood, and set them tasks in which a person would be most likely to forget such a conviction or be deceived out of it. And we d must select the ones who remember and are difficult to deceive, and reject the others. Do you agree?

GLAUCON: Yes.

SOCRATES: And we must also subject them to labors, pains, and contests, and watch for the same things there.

GLAUCON: That's right.

SOCRATES: Then we must also set up a third kind of competition for sorcery. Like those who lead colts into noise and tumult to see if they are afraid, we must subject our young people to fears and then plunge them once again into pleasures, so as to test e them much more thoroughly than people test gold in a fire. And if any of them seems to be immune to sorcery, preserves his composure throughout, is a good guardian of himself and of the musical training he has received, and proves himself to be rhythmical and harmonious in all these trials—he is the sort of person who would be most useful, both to himself and to the city. And anyone who is tested as a child, youth, and adult, and always emerges as being without 414a impurities, should be established as a ruler of the city as well as a guardian, and should be honored in life and receive the most prized tombs and memorials

after his death. But those who do not should be rejected. That is the sort of way, Glaucon, that I think rulers and guardians should be selected and established. Though I have provided only a pattern, not the precise details.

GLAUCON: I also think much the same.

SOCRATES: Then wouldn't it really be most correct to call these people complete guardians—the b ones who guard against external enemies and internal friends, so that the former will lack the power, and the latter the desire, to do any evil; but to call the young people to whom we were referring as guardians just now, *auxiliaries* and supporters of the guardians' convictions?

GLAUCON: Yes, I think it would.

SOCRATES: How, then, could we devise one of those useful lies we were talking about a while ago,[56] a single noble lie that would, preferably, persuade c even the rulers themselves; but, failing that, the rest of the city?

GLAUCON: What sort of lie?

SOCRATES: Nothing new, but a sort of Phoenician story[57] about something that happened in lots of places prior to this—at least, that is what the poets say and have persuaded people to believe. It has not happened in our day, and I do not know if it could happen. It would take a lot of persuasion to get people to believe it.

GLAUCON: You seem hesitant to tell the story.

SOCRATES: You will realize that I have every reason to hesitate, when I do tell it.

GLAUCON: Out with it. Do not be afraid.

SOCRATES: All right, I will—though I do not know where I will get the audacity or the words to tell it. d I will first be trying to persuade the rulers and the soldiers, and then the rest of the city, that the upbringing and the education we gave them were like dreams; that they only imagined they were undergoing all the things that were happening to them, while in fact they themselves were at that time down inside the earth being formed and nurtured, and that their weap-

56. [382a4–d3.]

57. [Apparently a reference, first, to the legend of the Phoenician hero, Cadmus, who sowed the earth with dragon's teeth from which giants grew; and, second, to the *Odyssey*, and the tales Odysseus tells to the Phaeacians.]

ons and the rest of their equipment were also manu-
e factured there. When they were entirely completed,
the earth, their mother, sent them up, so that now,
just as if the land in which they live were their mother
and nurse, they must deliberate on its behalf, defend
it if anyone attacks it, and regard the other citizens
as their earthborn brothers.

GLAUCON: It is not for nothing that you were
ashamed to tell your lie earlier.

SOCRATES: No, it was only to be expected. But
all the same, you should listen to the rest of the story.
415a "Although all of you in the city are brothers," we will
say to them in telling our story, "when the god was
forming you, he mixed gold into those of you who
are capable of ruling, which is why they are the most
honorable; silver into the auxiliaries; and iron and
bronze into the farmers and other craftsmen. For the
most part, you will produce children like yourselves;
but, because you are all related, a silver child will
b occasionally be born to a golden parent, a golden
child to a silver parent, and so on. Therefore, the first
and most important command from the god to the
rulers is that there is nothing they must guard better
or watch more carefully than the mixture of metals
in the souls of their offspring. If an offspring of theirs
is born with a mixture of iron or bronze, they must
not pity him in any way, but assign him an honor
c appropriate to his nature and drive him out to join
the craftsmen or the farmers. On the other hand, if
an offspring of the latter is found to have a mixture
of gold or silver, they will honor him and take him
up to join the guardians or the auxiliaries. For there
is an oracle that the city will be ruined if it ever has
an iron or a bronze guardian." So, have you a device
that will make them believe this story?

GLAUCON. No, none that would make this group
d believe it themselves. But I do have one for their
sons, for later generations, and for all other people
who come after them.

SOCRATES: Well, even that would have a good
effect, by making them care more for the city and
for each other. For I think I understand what you
mean—namely, that all this will go where *tradition*
leads. What *we* can do, however, when we have armed
our earthborn people, is lead them forth with their
rulers at their head. They must go and look for the
best place in the city for a military encampment, a

site from which they can most easily control anyone
in the city who is unwilling to obey the laws, or repel e
any outside enemy who, like a wolf, attacks the fold.
And when they have established their camp and sacrificed to the appropriate gods, they must make their
sleeping quarters, mustn't they?

GLAUCON: Yes.

SOCRATES: And mustn't these provide adequate
shelter against the storms of winter and the heat of
summer?

GLAUCON: Yes, of course. After all, I assume you
are talking about their living quarters.

SOCRATES: Yes, but ones for *soldiers*, not moneymakers.

GLAUCON: What difference do you think there is
between the two, again?   416a

SOCRATES: I will try to tell you. You see, it is
surely the most terrible and most shameful thing in
the world for shepherds to rear dogs as auxiliaries to
help them with their flocks in such a way that those
dogs themselves—because of intemperance, hunger,
or some other bad condition—try to do evil to the
sheep, acting not like sheepdogs but like wolves.

GLAUCON: Of course, that is terrible.

SOCRATES: So, mustn't we use every safeguard to
prevent our auxiliaries from treating the citizens like b
that—because they are stronger—and becoming savage masters rather than gentle allies?

GLAUCON: Yes, we must.

SOCRATES: And wouldn't they have been provided with the greatest safeguard possible if they have
been really well educated?

GLAUCON: But surely they have been.

SOCRATES: That is not something that deserves
to be asserted so confidently, my dear Glaucon. But
what does deserve it is what we were saying just now,
that they must have the right education, whatever it
is, if they are going to have what will do most to make c
them gentle to one another and to the ones they
are guarding.

GLAUCON: That's right.

SOCRATES: But anyone with any sense will tell us
that, besides this education, they must be provided
with living quarters and other property of the sort
that will neither prevent them from being the best
guardians nor encourage them to do evil to the
other citizens.   d

GLAUCON: And he would be right.

SOCRATES: Consider, then, whether or not they should live and be housed in some such way as this, if they are going to be the sort of men we described. First, none of them should possess any private property that is not wholly necessary. Second, none should have living quarters or storerooms that are not open for all to enter at will. Such provisions as are required by temperate and courageous men, who are warrior-athletes, they should receive from the other citizens as wages for their guardianship, the amount being fixed so that there is neither a shortfall nor a surplus at the end of the year. They should have common messes to go to, and should live together like soldiers in a camp. We will tell them that they have gold and silver of a divine sort in their souls as a permanent gift from the gods, and have no need of human gold in addition. And we will add that it is impious for them to defile this divine possession by possessing an admixture of mortal gold, because many impious deeds have been done for the sake of the currency of the masses, whereas their sort is pure. No, they alone among the city's population are forbidden by divine law to handle or even touch gold and silver. They must not be under the same roof as these metals, wear them as jewelry, or drink from gold or silver goblets. And by behaving in that way, they would save both themselves and the city. But if they acquire private land, houses, and money themselves, they will be household managers and farmers instead of guardians — hostile masters of the other citizens, instead of their allies. They will spend their whole lives hating and being hated, plotting and being plotted against, much more afraid of internal than of external enemies — already rushing, in fact, to the brink of their own destruction and that of the rest of the city as well. For all these reasons, let's declare that *that* is how the guardians must be provided with housing and the rest, and establish it as a law. Or don't you agree?

GLAUCON: Of course I do.

BOOK IV

SOCRATES' NARRATION CONTINUES: *Adeimantus interrupted:*

How will you defend yourself, Socrates, *he said,* if someone objects that you are not making these men very happy and, furthermore, that it is their own fault that they are not? I mean, the city really belongs to them, yet they derive no good from the city. Others own land, build fine, big houses, acquire furnishings to go along with them, make their own private sacrifices to the gods, entertain guests, and also, of course, possess what you were talking about just now: gold and silver and all the things that those who are going to be blessedly happy are thought to require. Instead of that, he might say, they seem simply to be paid auxiliaries established in the city as a garrison, and nothing else.

SOCRATES: Yes, and what is more, they do it just for upkeep and get no wages in addition to their upkeep, as other men do. So, they won't even be able to take a personal trip out of town if they want to, or give presents to their girlfriends, or spend money in whatever other ways they might wish, as people do who are considered happy. You have omitted these and a host of other similar facts from your list of charges.

ADEIMANTUS: Well, let them too be added to the charges.

SOCRATES: How will we defend ourselves? Is that what you are asking?

ADEIMANTUS: Yes.

SOCRATES: I think we will discover what to say if we follow the same path as before. You see, our reply will be this: it would not be at all surprising if these people were happiest just as they are. However, in establishing our city, we are not looking to make any one group in it outstandingly happy, but to make the whole city so as far as possible. For we thought that we would be most likely to find justice in such a city, and injustice, by contrast, in the one that is governed worst. And we thought that by observing both cities, we would be able to decide the question we have been inquiring into for so long. At the moment, then, we take ourselves to be forming a happy city — not separating off a few happy people and putting them in it, but making the city as a whole happy. (We will look at the opposite city soon.)[1]

1. [This discussion begins at 445c, but is interrupted and does not resume again until Book VIII.]

Suppose, then, that we were painting a statue[2] and someone came up to us and started to criticize us, saying that we had not applied the most beautiful colors to the most beautiful parts of the statue; because the eyes, which are the most beautiful part, had been painted black rather than purple. We would think it reasonable to offer the following defense: "My amaz-
d ing fellow, you must not expect us to paint the eyes so beautifully that they no longer look like eyes at all, nor the other parts either. On the contrary, you must look to see whether, by dealing with each part appropriately, we are making the whole thing beautiful. Similarly, in the present case, you must not force us to give our guardians the sort of happiness that would make them something other than guardians.
e You see, we know how to clothe the farmers in purple robes, festoon them with gold jewelry, and tell them to work the land whenever they please. We know we could have our potters recline on couches from right to left in front of the fire,[3] drinking and feasting with their wheel beside them for whenever they have a desire to make pots. And we can make all the others happy in the same way, so that the whole city is happy. But please do not urge us to do this. For if we are persuaded by you, a farmer won't be a farmer,
421a nor a potter a potter, nor will any of the others from which a city is constituted remain true to type. But for most of the others, it matters less: cobblers who become inferior and corrupt, and claim to be what they are not, do nothing terrible to the city. But if the guardians of our laws and city are not really what they seem to be, you may be sure that they will destroy the city utterly and, on the other hand, that they alone have the opportunity to govern it well and make it happy."

Now, if we are making genuine guardians, the sort
b least likely to do the city evil, and if our critic is making pseudo-farmers—feasters happy at a festival, so to speak, not in a city—he is not talking about a city, but about something else. What we have to consider, then, is whether our aim in establishing the

2. [Ancient Greek statues were painted and gilded.]
3. [At formal drinking parties (*sumposia*), the toastmaster (*sumposiarchos*) sat at the head of the table. The others sat in order of their importance, from his right counterclockwise around the table to his left.]

guardians is the greatest possible happiness for them, or whether—since our aim is to see this happiness develop for the whole city—we should compel or persuade the auxiliaries and guardians to ensure that c they, and all the others as well, are the best possible craftsmen at their own work; and then, with the whole city developing and being governed well, leave it to nature to provide each group with its share of happiness.

ADEIMANTUS: Yes, I think what you say is right.

SOCRATES: Well, then, will you also think me reasonable if I say something closely related?

ADEIMANTUS: What exactly?

SOCRATES: Take the rest of the craftsmen again, and consider whether these things corrupt them to such an extent that they actually become bad. d

ADEIMANTUS: What things?

SOCRATES: Wealth and poverty.

ADEIMANTUS: What do you mean?

SOCRATES: This: do you think that a potter who has become wealthy will still be willing to devote himself to his craft?

ADEIMANTUS: Not at all.

SOCRATES: Won't he become idler and more careless than he was?

ADEIMANTUS: Much more.

SOCRATES: Then won't he become a worse potter?

ADEIMANTUS: Yes, much worse.

SOCRATES: And surely if poverty prevents him from providing himself with tools, or any of the other things he needs for his craft, he will make poorer products himself and worse craftsmen of his sons or anyone else he teaches. e

ADEIMANTUS: Of course.

SOCRATES: So poverty and wealth make the products and the practitioners of the crafts worse.

ADEIMANTUS: Apparently.

SOCRATES: It seems, then, that we have found other things that our guardians must prevent in every way from slipping into the city undetected.

ADEIMANTUS: What things?

SOCRATES: Wealth and poverty. For the former makes for luxury, idleness, and revolution; and the 422a latter for illiberality, bad work, and revolution as well.

ADEIMANTUS: That's right. But consider this, Socrates: how will our city be able to fight a war if it has acquired no wealth — especially if it has to fight a great and wealthy city?

SOCRATES: Obviously, it will be harder to fight b one such city, but easier to fight two.

ADEIMANTUS: How do you mean?

SOCRATES: First of all, if our city has to fight a city of the sort you mention, won't it be a case of warrior-athletes fighting rich men?

ADEIMANTUS: Yes, it will.

SOCRATES: Well, then, Adeimantus, don't you think that a single boxer who has had the best possible training could easily fight two non-boxers who are rich and fat?

ADEIMANTUS: Maybe not at the same time.

SOCRATES: Not even if he could start to run away and then turn and hit the one who caught up with c him first, and could do this often, out in the stifling heat of the sun? Couldn't a man like that overcome even more than two such enemies?

ADEIMANTUS: It certainly would not be surprising if he could.

SOCRATES: Well, don't you think that rich people have more knowledge and experience of boxing than of how to fight a war?

ADEIMANTUS: I do.

SOCRATES: In all likelihood, then, our athletes will easily be able to fight two or three times their number.

ADEIMANTUS: I will have to grant you that, since I think what you say is right.

SOCRATES: Well, then, what if they sent an envoy d to another city with the following true message: "We use no gold or silver. It is against divine law for us to do so, but not for you. So join us in this war and you can have the property of our enemy." Do you think that anyone who heard this message would choose to fight hard, lean hounds, rather than to join the hounds in fighting fat and tender sheep?

ADEIMANTUS: No, I do not. But if the wealth of all other cities were amassed by a single one, don't e you think that would endanger your non-wealthy city?

SOCRATES: You are happily innocent if you think that any city besides the one we are constructing deserves to be called *a* city.

ADEIMANTUS: What should we call them, then?

SOCRATES: We will have to find a "greater" title for the others because each of them is a great many

cities, but not *a* city, as they say in the game.[4] They contain two, at any rate, which are at war with one another: the city of the poor and that of the rich. And within each of these, there are a great many more. 423a So if you treat them as one city, you will be making a big mistake. But if you treat them as many and offer one the money, power, and the very inhabitants of another, you will always find many allies and few enemies. And as long as your own city is temperately governed in the way we just arranged, it will be the greatest one — not in reputation; I do not mean that; but the greatest in fact — even if it has only a thousand soldiers to defend it. For you won't easily find one city so great among either Greeks or barbarians, though you will find many that are reputed to be many times greater. Or do you disagree?   b

ADEIMANTUS: No, by Zeus, I do not.

SOCRATES: This, then, would also provide our rulers with the best limit for determining the proper size of the city, and how much land they should mark off for a city that size, letting the rest go.

ADEIMANTUS: What limit is that?

SOCRATES: I think it is this: as long as it is willing to remain *one* city, it may continue to grow, but not beyond that point.

ADEIMANTUS: And it is a good one.   c

SOCRATES: Then we will also give our guardians this further order, that they are to guard in every possible way against the city's being either small in size or great in reputation, rather than adequate in size and one in number.

ADEIMANTUS: No doubt, *that* will be a trivial instruction for them to follow!

SOCRATES: Here is another that is even more trivial. We mentioned it earlier as well.[5] We said that if an offspring of the guardians is inferior, he must be sent off to join the other citizens, and that if the others have an excellent offspring, he must join the d guardians. This was meant to make clear that every other citizen, too, must be assigned to what naturally

---

4. [The reference is obscure; it may be to a saying or proverb, or to a game like checkers called *poleis*, or cities, in which the set of pieces on each side, or perhaps any subset of them, were called cities, while the individual members of the sets were called dogs.]

5. [415a–c.]

suits him, with one person assigned to one job so that, practicing his own pursuit, each of them will become not many but one, and the entire city thereby naturally grow to be one, not many.

ADEIMANTUS: Oh, yes, that is a more minor one!

SOCRATES: Really, my good Adeimantus, the orders we are giving them are neither as numerous nor as difficult as one would think. Indeed, they are all insignificant provided, as the saying goes, they safeguard
e the one great thing—or rather not great but adequate.

ADEIMANTUS: What's that?

SOCRATES: Their education and upbringing. For if a good education makes them moderate men, they will easily discover all this for themselves—and everything else that we are now omitting, such as the possession of women, marriages, and the procreation of children, and how all these must be governed as
424a far as possible by the old proverb that friends share everything in common.

ADEIMANTUS: Yes, that would be best.

SOCRATES: And surely once our constitution is well started, it will, as it were, go on growing in a circle. For good education and upbringing, if they are kept up, produce good natures; and sound natures, which in turn receive such an education, grow up even better than their predecessors in every respect—but particularly with respect to their offspring, as in
b the case of all the other animals.

ADEIMANTUS: Yes, probably so.

SOCRATES: To put it briefly, then, what the overseers of our city must cling to, not allow to become corrupted without their noticing it, and guard against everything, is this: there must be no innovation in musical or physical training that goes against the established order. On the contrary, they must guard against that as much as they can. And they should dread to hear anyone say that "people think most of the song that floats newest from the singer's lips,"[6] in case someone happens to suppose that the poet
c means not new *songs*, but a new *way of singing*, and praises that. We should not praise such a claim, however, or take it to be what the poet meant. You see, a change to a new kind of musical training is something to beware of as wholly dangerous. For one

6. [*Odyssey* 1.351–2. Our text of Homer is slightly different.]

can never change the ways of training people in music without affecting the greatest political laws. That is what Damon says, and I am convinced he is right.

ADEIMANTUS: You can also count me among those who are convinced.

SOCRATES: It seems, then, that it is in musical training that the guardhouse of our guardians must d surely be built.

ADEIMANTUS: At any rate, this sort of lawlessness easily inserts itself undetected.

SOCRATES: Yes, because it is supposed to be only part of a game that, as such, can do no harm.

ADEIMANTUS: And it does not do any—except, of course, that when it has established itself there, it slowly and silently flows over into people's habits and practices. From these it travels forth with greater vigor into private contracts, and then from private contracts it advances with the utmost insolence into the laws and constitution, Socrates, until in the end it over- e throws everything public and private.

SOCRATES: Well, is that so?

ADEIMANTUS: I think it is.

SOCRATES: Then, as we were saying at the beginning, our children must take part in games that are more law-abiding right from the start, since, if their games become lawless and the children follow suit, isn't it impossible for them to grow up into excellent and law-abiding men?   425a

ADEIMANTUS: Of course.

SOCRATES: So whenever children play in a good way right from the start and absorb lawfulness from musical training, there is the opposite result: lawfulness follows them in everything and fosters their growth, correcting anything in the city that may have been neglected before.

ADEIMANTUS: That's true.

SOCRATES: And so such people rediscover the seemingly insignificant conventional views their predecessors had destroyed.

ADEIMANTUS: Which sort?

SOCRATES: Those dealing with things like this: the silence appropriate for younger people in the presence of their elders; the giving up of seats for b them and standing up in their presence; the care of parents; hairstyles; clothing; shoes; the general appearance of the body; and everything else of that sort. Don't you agree?

ADEIMANTUS: I do.

SOCRATES: To legislate about such things is naïve, in my view, since verbal or written decrees will never make them come about or last.

ADEIMANTUS: How could they?

SOCRATES: At any rate, Adeimantus, it looks as though the start of someone's education determines
c what follows. Or doesn't like always encourage like?

ADEIMANTUS: It does.

SOCRATES: And the final outcome of education, I imagine we would say, is a single, complete, and fresh product that is either good or the opposite.

ADEIMANTUS: Of course.

SOCRATES: That is why I, for my part, would not try to legislate about such things.

ADEIMANTUS: And with good reason.

SOCRATES: Then, by the gods, what about all that marketplace business, the contracts people make with one another in the marketplace, for example, and
d contracts with handicraftsmen, and slanders, injuries, indictments, establishing juries, paying or collecting whatever dues are necessary in marketplace and harbors, and, in a word, the entire regulation of marketplace, city, harbor, or what have you—dare we legislate about any of these?

ADEIMANTUS: No, it would not be appropriate to dictate to men who are fine and good. For they will easily find out for themselves whatever needs to be
e legislated about such things.

SOCRATES: Yes, my friend, provided that a god grants that the laws we have already described are preserved intact.

ADEIMANTUS: If not, they will spend their lives continually enacting and amending such laws in the hope of finding what is best.

SOCRATES: You mean they will live like those sick people who, because they are intemperate, are not willing to abandon their bad way of life.

ADEIMANTUS: That's right.

SOCRATES: Such people really do lead a charm-
426a ing life! Their medical treatment achieves nothing, except to make their illnesses worse and more complex, and they are always hoping that someone will recommend some new drug that will make them healthy.

ADEIMANTUS: Yes, that's exactly what happens to invalids of this sort.

SOCRATES: And isn't it another charming feature of theirs that they think their worst enemy of all is the one who tells them the truth—that until they give up drunkenness, overeating, sexual indulgence, and idleness, then no drug, cautery, or surgery, no charms, b amulets, or anything else of that sort will do them any good?

ADEIMANTUS: It is not charming at all. Being harsh to someone who tells the truth is not charming.

SOCRATES: You do not approve of such men, apparently.

ADEIMANTUS: No, by Zeus, I do not.

SOCRATES: Then nor will you approve of an entire city that behaves in the way we were just describing. Or don't you think that such invalids behave in the very same way as cities where the following occurs? Because they are badly governed politically, the citizens are warned not to change the city's whole political system, and the one who does is threatened with c the death penalty. But the one who serves these cities most pleasantly, while they remain politically governed in that way; who indulges them, flatters them, anticipates their wishes, and is clever at fulfilling them; isn't he, on that account, honored by them as a good man who is wise in the most important matters?

ADEIMANTUS: Yes, I think their behavior is the same and I do not approve of it at all.

SOCRATES: What about those who are willing and eager to provide treatment for such cities? Don't you d approve of their courage and also their lighthearted irresponsibility?

ADEIMANTUS: I do indeed—except for those who are actually deluded and suppose themselves to be true men of politics because they are praised by the masses.

SOCRATES: What do you mean? Have you no sympathy for these men? Or do you think it is possible for a man who does not know how to measure anything not to believe that he is four cubits tall[7] when many others, who are similarly ignorant, tell him that he is? e

ADEIMANTUS: No, I do not think that.

SOCRATES: Then do not be too hard on them. You see, such people are surely the most charming of all. They pass and amend the sorts of laws we have

7. [Roughly seven feet. A cubit is between seventeen and twenty-two inches long.]

just been describing, and are always expecting that they will find a way to put a stop to cheating on contracts, and the other evildoings I mentioned just now, not realizing that they are really just cutting off a Hydra's head.[8]

427a   ADEIMANTUS: Yet that is all they are really doing.

SOCRATES: I would have thought, then, that a true lawgiver should not bother with laws or constitutions of this kind, whether in a politically badly governed or in a politically well-governed city—in the one because it is useless and accomplishes nothing; in the other because some of them are discoverable by anyone, while the others follow automatically from the practices already described.

ADEIMANTUS: What remains for us to legislate,
b then?

SOCRATES: For us, nothing; but for the Delphic Apollo, there remain the greatest, finest, and first of legislations.

ADEIMANTUS: What are they about?

SOCRATES: The establishing of temples and sacrifices, and other forms of service to gods, daimons, and heroes; the burial of the dead, and the services that ensure the favor of those who have gone to the other world. For we, of course, have no knowledge of these things and so, when we are founding a city, we won't take anyone else's advice, if we have any
c sense, or employ any interpreter except our ancestral one. And in fact, this god—as he delivers his interpretations from his seat at the navel of the earth[9]— is the ancestral guide on these matters for the whole human race.

ADEIMANTUS: Well put. That is what we must do.

SOCRATES: So then, son of Ariston, your city
d would now seem to be founded. As the next step, look inside it, having got hold of an adequate light somewhere. Look yourself and invite your brother and Polemarchus and the rest of us to help you, to see where justice and injustice might be in it, how

they differ from one another, and which of the two must be possessed by the person who is going to be happy, whether that fact is hidden from all gods and humans or not.

And Glaucon said:

That's nonsense! You promised you would look for them yourself, because you said it was impious for you not to defend justice in every way you could.[10]   e

SOCRATES: You are right to remind me, and I must do what I promised. But you will have to help.

GLAUCON: We will.

SOCRATES: I expect, then, to find justice in the following way. I think our city, if indeed it has been correctly founded, is completely good.

GLAUCON: Yes, it must be.

SOCRATES: Clearly, then, it is wise, courageous, temperate, and just.

GLAUCON: Clearly.

SOCRATES: Then if we find any of these in it, what remains will be what we have not found?

GLAUCON: Of course.   428a

SOCRATES: Therefore, as in the case of any other four things, if we were looking for one of them in something and recognized it first, that would be enough to satisfy us. But if we recognized the other three first, that itself would enable us to recognize what we were looking for, since clearly it could not be anything other than the one that remains.

GLAUCON: That's right.

SOCRATES: So, since there also happen to be four things we are interested in, mustn't we look for them in the same way?

GLAUCON: Clearly.

SOCRATES: Now, the first thing I think I can see clearly in the city is wisdom. And there seems to be something odd about it.   b

GLAUCON: What?

SOCRATES: I think that the city we described is really wise. And that is because it is prudent,[11] isn't it?

---

8. [The Hydra was a mythical monster. When one of its heads was cut off, two or three new heads grew in its place. Heracles (or Hercules) had to slay the Hydra as one of his labors.]

9. [The oracle of Apollo at Delphi was traditionally consulted by all Greeks on religious and other such matters. A stone there marked the supposed center of the earth.]

10. [368b7–c3.]

11. [*Euboulos:* In Greek cities, the *boulê* was the council that had day-to-day responsibility for public affairs. In kingships it served as an advisory body to the kings; in democratic Athens it served as an advisory body and

GLAUCON: Yes.

SOCRATES: And surely it is clear that this very thing, prudence, is some sort of knowledge. I mean, it certainly is not through *ignorance* that people do the prudent thing, but through knowledge.

GLAUCON: Clearly.

SOCRATES: But there are, of course, many multifarious sorts of knowledge in the city.

GLAUCON: Certainly.

SOCRATES: So, is it because of the knowledge possessed by the carpenters that the city deserves to be described as wise and prudent?

GLAUCON: Not at all. It is called skilled in carpen-
c try because of that.

SOCRATES: So a city shouldn't be called wise because it has the knowledge that deliberates about how wooden things can be best.

GLAUCON: Certainly not.

SOCRATES: What about this, then? What about the knowledge of things made of bronze, or anything else of that sort?

GLAUCON: Not anything of that sort either.

SOCRATES: And not the knowledge of how to produce crops from the soil. On the contrary, it is skilled in farming because of that.

GLAUCON: That's my view.

SOCRATES: Then is there some knowledge in the city we have just founded, which some of its citizens have, that does not deliberate about some particular
d thing in the city, but about the city as a whole, and about how its internal relations and its relations with other cities will be the best possible.

GLAUCON: There is indeed.

SOCRATES: What is it and who has it?

GLAUCON: It is the craft of guardianship. And the ones who possess it are those rulers we just now called complete guardians.[12]

SOCRATES: Because it has this knowledge, then, how do you describe the city?

GLAUCON: As prudent and really wise.

SOCRATES: Now, do you think that there will be more metalworkers in the city, or more of these
e true guardians?

_____

steering committee for the assembly of all the adult male citizens.]

12. [414b1–6.]

GLAUCON: There will be far more metalworkers.

SOCRATES: Of all those who are called by a certain name because they have some sort of knowledge, wouldn't the true guardians be the fewest in number?

GLAUCON: By far.

SOCRATES: So, it is because of the smallest group or part of itself, and the knowledge that is in it— the part that governs and rules—that a city founded according to nature would be wise as a whole. And this class— which seems to be, by nature, the smallest— is the one that inherently possesses a share of the knowledge that alone among all the other sorts of   429a
knowledge should be called wisdom.

GLAUCON: That's absolutely true.

SOCRATES: So we have found—though I do not know how—this one of the four and its place in the city, too.

GLAUCON: It seems to me, at least, that it has been well and truly found.

SOCRATES: But surely courage and the part of the city it is in, and because of which the city is described as courageous, is not very difficult to spot.

GLAUCON: How so?

SOCRATES: Who would describe a city as cowardly or courageous by looking at anything other than   b
that part which defends it and wages war on its behalf?

GLAUCON: No one would look at anything else.

SOCRATES: Because, I take it, whether the others are courageous or cowardly doesn't make it one or the other.

GLAUCON: No, it doesn't.

SOCRATES: So courage, too, belongs to a city because of a part of itself— because it has in that part the power to preserve through everything its belief that the things, and the sorts of things, that should inspire terror are the very things, and sorts of things,   c
that the lawgiver declared to be such in the course of educating it. Or don't you call that courage?

GLAUCON: I do not completely understand what you said. Would you mind repeating it?

SOCRATES: I mean that courage is a sort of preservation.

GLAUCON: What sort of preservation?

SOCRATES: The preservation of the belief, inculcated by the law through education, about what things, and what sorts of things, inspire terror. And by its preservation "through everything," I mean pre-

serving it though pains, pleasures, appetites, and fears
d and not abandoning it. I will compare it to something I think it resembles, if you like.

GLAUCON: I would like that.

SOCRATES: You know, then, that when dyers want to dye wool purple, they first select from wools of many different colors the ones that are naturally white. Then they give them an elaborate preparatory treatment, so that they will accept the color as well as possible. And only at that point do they dip them in the purple dye. When something is dyed in this
e way, it holds the dye fast, and no amount of washing, whether with or without detergent, can remove the color. But you also know what happens when things are not dyed in this way, when one dyes wools of other colors, or even these white ones, without preparatory treatment.

GLAUCON: I know they look washed out and ridiculous.

SOCRATES: You should take it, then, that we too were trying as hard as we could to do something similar when we selected our soldiers and educated them in musical and physical training. It was con-
430a trived, you should suppose, for no purpose other than to ensure that—persuaded by us—they would absorb the laws in the best possible way, just like wool does a dye; that as a result, their beliefs about what things should inspire terror, and about everything else, would hold fast because they had the proper nature and rearing; so fast that the dye could not be washed out even by those detergents that are so terribly effective at scouring—pleasure, which is much more terribly effective at this than any chalestrian[13] or alkali, and pain and fear and appetite, which are worse than
b any detergent. This power, then, to preserve through everything the correct and law-inculcated belief about what should inspire terror and what should not is what I, at any rate, call courage. And I will assume it is this, unless you object.

GLAUCON: No, I have no objection. For I presume that the sort of correct belief about these same matters that you find in animals and slaves, which is not the result of education and has nothing at all to do with law, is called something other than courage.

13. [Carbonate of soda from Chalestra, a town and lake in Macedonia.]

SOCRATES: You are absolutely right.   c

GLAUCON: Well, then, I accept your account of courage.

SOCRATES: Yes, do accept it, at any rate, as my account of *political* courage, and you will be right to accept it. If you like, we will discuss that more fully some other time. You see, at the moment, our inquiry is not about courage but about justice. And for the purpose of that inquiry, I think that what we have said is sufficient.

GLAUCON: You are right.

SOCRATES: Two things, then, remain for us to find in the city: temperance and—the goal of our entire inquiry—justice.   d

GLAUCON: Yes, indeed.

SOCRATES: How could we find justice, then, so we won't have to bother with temperance any further?

GLAUCON: Well I, for my part, do not know of any, nor would I want justice to appear first if that means that we are not going to investigate temperance any further. So if you want to please me, look for it before the other.

SOCRATES: Of course I want to. It would be wrong not to.   e

GLAUCON: Go ahead and look, then.

SOCRATES: I will. And seen from here, it is more like a sort of concord and harmony than the previous ones.

GLAUCON: How so?

SOCRATES: Temperance is surely a sort of order, the mastery of certain sorts of pleasures and appetites. People indicate as much when they use the term "self-mastery"—though I do not know in what way. This and other similar things are like tracks that temperance has left. Isn't that so?

GLAUCON: Absolutely.

SOCRATES: Isn't the term "self-mastery" ridiculous, though? For, of course, the one who is master of himself is also the one who is weaker, and the one who is weaker is also the one who masters. After all, the same person is referred to in all these descriptions.   431a

GLAUCON: Of course.

SOCRATES: It seems to me, however, that what this term is trying to indicate is that within the same person's soul, there is a better thing and a worse one. Whenever the naturally better one masters the worse, this is called being master of oneself. At any rate, it

is praised. But whenever, as a result of bad upbringing or associating with bad people, the smaller and better one is mastered by the inferior majority, this is blamed as a disgraceful thing and is called being weaker than
b oneself, or being intemperate.

GLAUCON: Yes, that seems plausible.

SOCRATES: Now, then, take a look at our new city and you will find one of these conditions present in it. For you will say that it is rightly described as master of itself, if indeed anything in which the better rules the worse is to be described as temperate and master of itself.

GLAUCON: I am looking, and what you say is true.

SOCRATES: Furthermore, pleasures, pains, and appetites that are numerous and multifarious are
c things one would especially find in children, women, household slaves, and in the so-called free members of the masses—that is, the inferior people.

GLAUCON: Yes.

SOCRATES: But the pleasures, pains, and appetites that are simple and moderate, the ones that are led by rational calculation with the aid of understanding and correct belief, you would find in those few people who are born with the best natures and receive the best education.

GLAUCON: That's true.

SOCRATES: Don't you see, then, that this too is present in your city, and that the appetites of the masses—the inferior people—are mastered there by
d the wisdom and appetites of the few—the best people?

GLAUCON: I do.

SOCRATES: So, if any city is said to be master of its pleasures and appetites and of itself, it is this one.

GLAUCON: Absolutely.

SOCRATES: So isn't it also temperate because of all this?

GLAUCON: Yes, indeed.

SOCRATES: And moreover, if there is any city in which rulers and subjects share the same belief about
e who should rule, it is this one. Or don't you agree?

GLAUCON: Yes, I certainly do.

SOCRATES: And in which of them do you say temperance is located when they are in this condition? In the rulers or the subjects?

GLAUCON: In both, I suppose.

SOCRATES: Do you see, then, that the hunch we had just now—that temperance is like a sort of harmony—was quite plausible?

GLAUCON: Why is that?

SOCRATES: Because its operation is unlike that of courage and wisdom, each of which resides in one part and makes the city either courageous or wise. 432a Temperance does not work like that, but has literally been stretched throughout the whole, making the weakest, the strongest, and those in between all sing the same song in unison—whether in wisdom, if you like, or in physical strength, if you prefer; or, for that matter, in numbers, wealth, or anything else. Hence we would be absolutely right to say that this unanimity is temperance—this concord between the naturally worse and the naturally better, about which of the two should rule both in the city and in each individual.

GLAUCON: I agree completely.   b

SOCRATES: All right. We have now spotted three kinds of virtue in our city. What kind remains, then, that would give the city yet another share of virtue? For it is clear that what remains is justice.

GLAUCON: It is clear.

SOCRATES: So then, Glaucon, we must now station ourselves like hunters surrounding a wood and concentrate our minds, so that justice does not escape us and vanish into obscurity. For it is clear that it is around here somewhere. Keep your eyes peeled and do your best to catch sight of it, and if you happen c to see it before I do, show it to me.

GLAUCON: I wish I could help. But it is rather the case that if you use me as a follower who can see only what you point out to him, you will be using me in a more reasonable way.

SOCRATES: Pray for success, then, and follow me.

GLAUCON: I will. You have only to lead.

SOCRATES: And it truly seems to be an impenetrable place and full of shadows. It is dark, at any rate, and difficult to search through. But all the same, we must go on.

GLAUCON: Yes, we must.   d

And then I caught sight of something and shouted:

SOCRATES: Ah ha! Glaucon, it looks as though there is a track here, and I do not think our quarry will altogether escape us.

GLAUCON: That's good news.

SOCRATES: Oh dear, what a stupid condition in which to find ourselves!

GLAUCON: How so?

SOCRATES: It seems, blessed though you are, that the thing has been rolling around at our feet from the very beginning, and yet, like ridiculous fools, we could not see it. For just as people who are holding something in their hands sometimes search for the very thing they are holding, we did not look in the
e right direction but gazed off into the distance, and perhaps that is the very reason we did not notice it.

GLAUCON: What do you mean?

SOCRATES: This: I think we have been talking and hearing about it all this time without understanding ourselves, or realizing that we were, in a way, talking about it.

GLAUCON: That was a long prelude! Now I want to hear what you mean!

SOCRATES: Listen, then, and see whether there is anything in what I say. You see, what we laid down
433a at the beginning when we were founding our city, about what should be done throughout it—that, I think, or some form of that, is justice. And surely what we laid down and often repeated, if you remember, is that each person must practice one of the pursuits in the city, the one for which he is naturally best suited.

GLAUCON: Yes, we did say that.

SOCRATES: Moreover, we have heard many people say, and have often said ourselves, that justice is doing one's own work and not meddling with what
b is not one's own.

GLAUCON: Yes, we have.

SOCRATES: This, then, my friend, provided it is taken in a certain way, would seem to be justice—this doing one's own work. And do you know what I take as evidence of that?

GLAUCON: No, tell me.

SOCRATES: After our consideration of temperance, courage, and wisdom, I think that what remains in the city is the power that makes it possible for all of these to arise in it, and that preserves them when
c they have arisen for as long as it remains there itself. And we did say that justice would be what remained when we had found the other three.[14]

14. [428a2–9.]

GLAUCON: Yes, that must be so.

SOCRATES: Yet, surely, if we had to decide which of these will most contribute to making our city good by being present in it, it would be difficult to decide. Is it the agreement in belief between the rulers and the subjects? The preservation among the soldiers of the law-inculcated belief about what should inspire terror and what should not? The wisdom and guard-
d ianship of the rulers? Or is what most contributes to making it good the fact that every child, woman, slave, free person, craftsman, ruler, and subject each does his own work and does not meddle with what is not?

GLAUCON: Of course it's a difficult decision.

SOCRATES: It seems, then, that this power—which consists in everyone's doing his own work—rivals wisdom, temperance, and courage in its contribution to the city's virtue.

GLAUCON: It certainly does.

SOCRATES: And wouldn't you say that justice is certainly what rivals them in contributing to the city's virtue?
e

GLAUCON: Absolutely.

SOCRATES: Look at it this way, too, if you want to be convinced. Won't you assign to the rulers the job of judging lawsuits in the city?

GLAUCON: Of course.

SOCRATES: And will they have any aim in judging other than this: that no citizen should have what is another's or be deprived of what is his own?

GLAUCON: No, they will have none but that.

SOCRATES: Because that is just?

GLAUCON: Yes.

SOCRATES: So from that point of view, too, having and doing of one's own, of what belongs to one, would be agreed to be justice.
434a

GLAUCON: That's right.

SOCRATES: Now, see whether you agree with me about this: if a carpenter attempts to do the work of a shoemaker, or a shoemaker that of a carpenter, or they exchange their tools or honors with one another, or if the same person tries to do both jobs, and all other such exchanges are made, do you think that does any great harm to the city?

GLAUCON: Not really.

SOCRATES: But I imagine that when someone who is, by nature, a craftsman or some other sort of

moneymaker is puffed up by wealth, or by having a
b majority of votes, or by his own strength, or by some
other such thing, and attempts to enter the class of
soldiers; or when one of the soldiers who is unworthy
to do so tries to enter that of judge and guardian, and
these exchange their tools and honors; or when the
same person tries to do all these things at once, then
I imagine you will agree that these exchanges and
this meddling destroy the city.

GLAUCON: Absolutely.

SOCRATES: So, meddling and exchange among
these three classes is the greatest harm that can hap-
c pen to the city and would rightly be called the worst
evil one could do to it.

GLAUCON: Exactly.

SOCRATES: And wouldn't you say that the worst
evil one could do to one's own city is injustice?

GLAUCON: Of course.

SOCRATES: That, then, is what injustice is. But
let's put it in reverse: the opposite of this—when the
moneymaking, auxiliary, and guardian class each do
their own work in the city—is justice, isn't it, and
makes the city just?

d GLAUCON: That's exactly what I think too.

SOCRATES: Let's not state it as fixedly established
just yet. But if this kind of thing is agreed by us to
be justice in the case of individual human beings as
well, then we can assent to it. For what else will there
be for us to say? But if it is not, we will have to look
for something else. For the moment, however, let's
complete the inquiry in which we supposed that if
we first tried to observe justice in some larger thing
that possessed it, that would make it easier to see what
it is like in an individual human being.[15] We agreed
that this larger thing is a city, and so we founded the
e best city we could, knowing well that justice would
of course be present in one that was good. So, let's
apply what has come to light for us there to an individual, and if it is confirmed, all will be well. But if
something different is found in the case of the individual, we will go back to the city and test it there. And
perhaps by examining them side by side and rubbing
435a them together like fire-sticks, we can make justice
blaze forth and, once it has come to light, confirm
it in our own case.

15. [368c7–369a3.]

GLAUCON: Well, the road you describe is the right
one, and we should follow it.

SOCRATES: Well, then, if you call a bigger thing
and a smaller thing by the same name, are they un-
alike in the respect in which they are called the same,
or alike?

GLAUCON: Alike.

SOCRATES: So a just man won't differ at all from
a just city with respect to the form of justice but will b
be like it.

GLAUCON: Yes, he will be like it.

SOCRATES: But now, the city, at any rate, was
thought to be just because each of the three natural
classes within it did its own job; and to be temperate,
courageous, and wise, in addition, because of certain
other conditions or states of these same classes.

GLAUCON: That's true.

SOCRATES: Then, my friend, we would expect an
individual to have these same kinds of things in his
soul, and to be correctly called by the same names
as the city because the same conditions are present c
in them both.

GLAUCON: Inevitably.

SOCRATES: Well, you amazing fellow, here is another trivial investigation we have stumbled into: does
the soul have these three kinds of things in it or not?

GLAUCON: It does not look at all trivial to me.
Perhaps, Socrates, there is some truth in the old saying
that everything beautiful is difficult.

SOCRATES: Apparently so. In fact, you should be
well aware, Glaucon, that it is my belief we will never
ever grasp this matter precisely by methods of the sort d
we are now using in our discussions. However, there
is in fact another longer and more time-consuming
road that does lead there. But perhaps we can manage
to come up to the standard of our previous statements
and inquiries.

GLAUCON: Shouldn't we be content with that? It
would be enough for me, at least for now.

SOCRATES: Well, then, it will be quite satisfactory
for me, too.

GLAUCON: Then do not weary, but go on with
the inquiry.

SOCRATES: Well, isn't it absolutely necessary for
us to agree to this much: that the very same kinds of e
things and conditions exist in each one of us as exist
in the city? After all, where else would they come

from? You see, it would be ridiculous for anyone to think that spiritedness did not come to be in cities from the private individuals who are reputed to have this quality, such as the Thracians, Scythians, and others who live to the north of us; or that the same is not true of the love of learning, which is mostly 436a associated with our part of the world; or of the love of money, which is said to be found not least among the Phoenicians and Egyptians.

GLAUCON: It certainly would.

SOCRATES: We may take that as being so, then, and it was not at all difficult to discover.

GLAUCON: No, it certainly was not.

SOCRATES: But this, now, *is* difficult. Do we do each of them with the same thing or, since there are three, do we do one with one and another with another: that is to say, do we learn with one, feel anger with another, and with yet a third have an appetite for the pleasures of food, sex, and those closely akin to them? Or do we do each of them with the whole b of our soul, once we feel the impulse? *That* is what is difficult to determine in a way that is up to the standards of our argument.

GLAUCON: I think so, too.

SOCRATES: Well, then, let's try in this way to determine whether they are the same as one another or different.

GLAUCON: What way?

SOCRATES: It is clear that the same thing cannot do or undergo opposite things; not, at any rate, in the same respect, in relation to the same thing, at the same time. So, if we ever find that happening here, we will know that we are not dealing with one c and the same thing, but with many.

GLAUCON: All right.

SOCRATES: Consider, then, what I am about to say.

GLAUCON: Say it.

SOCRATES: Is it possible for the same thing, at the same time, and in the same respect, to be standing still and moving?

GLAUCON: Not at all.

SOCRATES: Let's come to a more precise agreement, in order to avoid disputes later on. You see, if anyone said of a person who is standing still but moving his hands and head, that the same thing is moving and standing still at the same time, we would not consider, I imagine, that he should say that; but

rather that in one respect the person is standing still, while in another he is moving. Isn't that so?   d

GLAUCON: It is.

SOCRATES: Then, if the one who said this became still more charming and made the sophisticated point that spinning tops, at any rate, stand still as a whole at the same time as they are also in motion, when, with the peg fixed in the same place, they revolve, or that the same holds of anything else that moves in a circle on the same spot—we would not agree, on the grounds that in such situations it is not in the same respects that these objects are both moving and standing still. On the contrary, we would say that e these objects have both a straight axis and a circumference in them, and that with respect to the straight axis they stand still—since they do not wobble to either side—whereas with respect to the circumference they move in a circle. But if their straight axis wobbles to the left or right or front or back at the same time as they are spinning, we will say that they are not standing still in any way.

GLAUCON: And we would be right.

SOCRATES: No such objection will disturb us, then, or make us any more likely to believe that the same thing can—at the same time, in the same respect, and in relation to the same thing—undergo, be, or do opposite things.   437a

GLAUCON: They won't have that effect on me at least.

SOCRATES: All the same, in order to avoid going through all these objections one by one and taking a long time to prove them all untrue, let's hypothesize that what we have said is correct and carry on—with the understanding that if it should ever be shown to be incorrect, all the consequences we have drawn from it will be invalidated.

GLAUCON: Yes, that's what we should do.

SOCRATES: Now, wouldn't you consider assent and dissent, wanting to have something and rejecting b it, taking something and pushing it away, as all being pairs of mutual opposites—whether of opposite doings or of opposite undergoings does not matter?

GLAUCON: Yes, they are pairs of opposites.

SOCRATES: What about thirst, hunger, and the appetites as a whole, and also wishing and willing? Would you include all of them somewhere among the kinds of things we just mentioned? For example, c wouldn't you say that the soul of someone who has an appetite wants the thing for which it has an appetite, and draws toward itself what it wishes to have; and, in addition, that insofar as his soul wishes something to be given to it, it nods assent to itself as if in answer to a question, and strives toward its attainment?

GLAUCON: I would.

SOCRATES: What about not-willing, not-wishing, and not-having an appetite? Wouldn't we include them among the very opposites, cases in which the soul pushes and drives things away from itself?

d GLAUCON: Of course.

SOCRATES: Since that is so, won't we say that there is a kind consisting of appetites, and that the most conspicuous examples of them are what we call hunger and thirst?

GLAUCON: We will.

SOCRATES: Isn't the one for food, the other for drink?

GLAUCON: Yes.

SOCRATES: Now, insofar as it is thirst, is it an appetite in the soul for more than what we say it is for? I mean, is thirst a thirst for hot drink or cold, or much drink or little, or—in a word—for drink of a certain sort? Or isn't it rather that if heat is present in addition to thirst, it causes the appetite to be for
e something cold as well, whereas the addition of cold makes it an appetite for something hot? And if there is much thirst, because of the presence of muchness, won't it cause the desire to be for much drink, and where little for little? But thirst itself will never be for anything other than the very thing that it is in its nature to be an appetite for: namely, drink itself; and, similarly, hunger is for food.

GLAUCON: That's the way it is. By itself, at any rate, each appetite is for its natural object only, while an appetite for an object of this or that sort depends on additions.

SOCRATES: No one should catch us unprepared,
438a then, or disturb us by claiming that no one has an appetite for drink but rather for good drink, nor for food but rather for good food, since everyone's appetite is for good things. And so, if thirst is an appetite, it will be an appetite for good drink or good whatever, and similarly for the other appetites.

GLAUCON: Yes, there might seem to be something in that objection.

SOCRATES: But surely, whenever things are related to something, those that are of a particular sort are related to a particular sort of thing, as it seems to me, whereas those that are just themselves are related b only to a thing that is just itself.

GLAUCON: I do not understand.

SOCRATES: Don't you understand that the greater is such as to be greater than something?

GLAUCON: Of course.

SOCRATES: Than the less?

GLAUCON: Yes.

SOCRATES: And the much greater than the much less. Isn't that so?

GLAUCON: Yes.

SOCRATES: And the once greater than the once less? And the going-to-be greater than the going-to-be less?

GLAUCON: Certainly.

SOCRATES: And doesn't the same hold of the more in relation to the fewer, the double to the half, and c everything of that sort; and also of heavier to lighter and faster to slower; and, in addition, of hot to cold, and all other similar things?

GLAUCON: Yes, indeed.

SOCRATES: What about the various kinds of knowledge? Aren't they the same way? Knowledge itself is of what can be learned itself (or of whatever we should take the object of knowledge to be), whereas a particular knowledge of a particular sort is of a particular thing of a particular sort. I mean something like this: when knowledge of building houses was developed, it differed from the other kinds of knowledge, d and so was called knowledge of building. Isn't that so?

GLAUCON: Of course.

SOCRATES: And wasn't that because it was a different sort of knowledge from all the others?

GLAUCON: Yes.

SOCRATES: And wasn't it because it was of a particular sort of thing that it itself became a particular sort of knowledge? And isn't this true of all the crafts and sciences?

GLAUCON: It is.

SOCRATES: Well, then, you should think of that as what I wanted to get across before—if you understand it now—when I said that whenever things are related to something, those that are just themselves are related to things that are just themselves, whereas those of a particular sort are related to things of a particular sort. And I do not at all mean that the sorts in question have to be the same for them both—that the knowledge of health and disease is healthy and diseased, or that that of good and bad things is good and bad. On the contrary, I mean that when knowledge occurred that was not just knowledge of the thing itself that knowledge is of, but of something of a particular sort, which in this case was health and disease, the result was that it itself became a particular sort of knowledge; and this caused it to be no longer called simply knowledge but, with the addition of the particular sort, medical knowledge.

GLAUCON: I understand and I think you are right.

SOCRATES: Returning to thirst, then, wouldn't you include it among the things that are related to something just by being what they are? Surely thirst is related to. . . .

GLAUCON: I would. It is related to drink.

SOCRATES: So a particular sort of thirst is for a particular sort of drink. Thirst itself, however, is not for much or little, good or bad, or, in a word, for drink of a particular sort; rather, thirst itself is, by nature, just for drink itself. Right?

GLAUCON: Absolutely.

SOCRATES: Hence the soul of the thirsty person, insofar as it is simply thirsty, does not want anything else except to drink, and this is what it longs for and is impelled to do.

GLAUCON: Clearly.

SOCRATES: Then if anything in it draws it back when it is thirsty, wouldn't it be something different from what thirsts and, like a beast, drives it to drink? For surely, we say, the same thing, in the same respect of itself, in relation to the same thing, and at the same time, cannot do opposite things.

GLAUCON: No, it cannot.

SOCRATES: In the same way, I imagine, it is not right to say of the archer that his hands at the same time push the bow away and draw it toward him. On the contrary, we should say that one hand pushes it away, while the other draws it toward him.

GLAUCON: Absolutely.

SOCRATES: Now, we would say, wouldn't we, that some people are thirsty sometimes, yet unwilling to drink?

GLAUCON: Many people often are.

SOCRATES: What, then, should one say about them? Isn't it that there is an element in their soul urging them to drink, and also one stopping them—something different that masters the one doing the urging?

GLAUCON: I certainly think so.

SOCRATES: Doesn't the element doing the stopping in such cases arise—when it does arise—from rational calculation, while the things that drive and drag are present because of feelings and diseases?

GLAUCON: Apparently so.

SOCRATES: It would not be unreasonable for us to claim, then, that there are two elements, different from one another; and to call the element in the soul with which it calculates, the rationally calculating element; and the one with which it feels passion, hungers, thirsts, and is stirred by other appetites, the irrational and appetitive element, friend to certain ways of being filled and certain pleasures.

GLAUCON: No, it would not. Indeed, it would be a very natural thing for us to do.

SOCRATES: Let's assume, then, that we have distinguished these two kinds of elements in the soul. Now, is the spirited element—the one with which we feel anger—a third kind of thing, or is it the same in nature as one of these others?

GLAUCON: As the appetitive element, perhaps.

SOCRATES: But I once heard a story and I believe it. Leontius, the son of Aglaeon, was going up from the Piraeus along the outside of the North Wall when he saw some corpses with the public executioner nearby. He had an appetitive desire to look at them, but at the same time he was disgusted and turned himself away. For a while he struggled and put his hand over his eyes, but finally, mastered by his appetite, he opened his eyes wide and rushed toward the corpses, saying: "Look for yourselves, you evil wretches; take your fill of the beautiful sight."[16]

GLAUCON: I have also heard that story myself.

16. [A fragment of the comedy *Kapêlides* by Theopompus (410–370 B.C.E.) tells us that a certain Leontius (emended to Leontius because of Plato's reference here) was known for his love of boys as pale as corpses. So his desire is probably sexual in origin, and for that reason appetitive. The North and South Walls enclosed an area connecting Athens to Piraeus.]

SOCRATES: Yet, surely, the story suggests that anger sometimes makes war against the appetites as one thing against another.

GLAUCON: Yes, it does suggest that.

SOCRATES: And don't we often notice on other occasions that when appetite forces someone contrary to his rational calculation, he reproaches himself and feels anger at the thing in him that is doing the forcing; and just as if there were two warring factions, such a person's spirit becomes the ally of his reason? But spirit partnering the appetites to do what reason has decided should not be done—I do not imagine you would say that you had ever seen that, either in yourself or in anyone else.

GLAUCON: No, by Zeus, I would not.

SOCRATES: And what about when a person thinks he is doing some injustice? Isn't it true that the nobler he is, the less capable he is of feeling angry if he suffers hunger, cold, or the like at the hands of someone whom he believes to be inflicting this on him justly; and won't his spirit, as I say, refuse to be aroused?

GLAUCON: It is true.

SOCRATES: But what about when a person believes he is being unjustly treated? Doesn't his spirit boil then, and grow harsh and fight as an ally of what he holds to be just? And even if it suffers hunger, cold, and every imposition of that sort, doesn't it stand firm and win out over them, not ceasing its noble efforts until it achieves its purpose, or dies, or, like a dog being called to heel by a shepherd, is called back by the reason alongside it and becomes gentle?

GLAUCON: Your simile is perfect. And, in fact, we did put the auxiliaries in our city to be like obedient sheepdogs for the city's shepherdlike rulers.

SOCRATES: You have understood what I was trying to say very well. But have you also noticed something else about it?

GLAUCON: What?

SOCRATES: That it is the opposite of what we recently thought about the kind of thing spirit is. You see, then we thought of it as something appetitive.[17] But now, far from saying that, we say that in the faction that takes place in the soul, it is far more likely to take arms on the side of the rationally calculating element.

GLAUCON: Absolutely.

SOCRATES: Is it also different from this, then, or is it some kind of rationally calculating element, so that there are not three kinds of things in the soul, but two—the rationally calculating element and the appetitive one? Or rather, just as there were three classes in the city that held it together— the money-making, the auxiliary, and the deliberative—is there also this third element in the soul, the spirited kind, which is the natural auxiliary of the rationally calculating element, if it has not been corrupted by bad upbringing?

GLAUCON: There must be a third.

SOCRATES: Yes, provided, at any rate, that it can be shown to be as distinct from the rationally calculating element as it was shown to be from the appetitive one.

GLAUCON: But it is not difficult to show that. After all, one can see it even in small children: they are full of spirit right from birth, but as for rational calculation, some of them seem to me never to possess it, while the masses do so quite late.

SOCRATES: Yes, by Zeus, you put that really well. Besides, one can see in animals that what you say is true. But, in addition to that, our earlier quotation from Homer also bears it out: "He struck his chest and spoke to his heart."[18] You see, in it Homer clearly presents what has calculated about better and worse, rebuking what is irrationally angry as though it were something different.

GLAUCON: That's exactly right.

SOCRATES: Well, we have had a difficult swim through all that, and we are pretty much agreed that the same classes as are in the city are in the soul of each individual, and an equal number of them too.

GLAUCON: That's true.

SOCRATES: Then doesn't it already necessarily follow that the private individual is wise in the same way and because of the same element as is the city?

GLAUCON: Of course.

SOCRATES: And that the city is courageous in the same way and because of the same element as is the

17. [439e5.]   18. [*Odyssey* 20.17. See 390d.]

d private individual? And that in everything else that pertains to virtue, both are alike?

GLAUCON: Necessarily.

SOCRATES: And so, Glaucon, I take it we will also say that a man is just in exactly the same way as is a city.

GLAUCON: That too follows with absolute necessity.

SOCRATES: But we surely have not forgotten that the city was just because each of the three classes in it does its own work.

GLAUCON: I do not think we have.

SOCRATES: We should also bear in mind, then, that in the case of each one of us as well, the one in whom each of the elements does its own job will be *e* just and do his own job.

GLAUCON: Certainly.

SOCRATES: Then isn't it appropriate for the rationally calculating element to rule, since it is really wise and exercises foresight on behalf of the whole soul; and for the spirited kind to obey it and be its ally?

GLAUCON: Of course.

SOCRATES: Now, as we were saying, isn't it a mixture of musical and physical training that makes these elements concordant, tightening and nurturing the *442a* first with fine words and learning, while relaxing, soothing, and making gentle the second by means of harmony and rhythm?

GLAUCON: Yes, exactly.

SOCRATES: And these two elements, having been trained in this way and having truly learned their own jobs and been educated, will be put in charge of the appetitive element—the largest one in each person's soul and, by nature, the most insatiable for money. They will watch over it to see that it does not get so filled with the so-called pleasures of the body that it becomes big and strong, and no longer does its own job but attempts to enslave and rule over the classes *b* it is not fitted to rule, thereby overturning the whole life of anyone in whom it occurs.

GLAUCON: Yes, indeed.

SOCRATES: And wouldn't these two elements also do the finest job of guarding the whole soul and body against external enemies—the one by deliberating, the other by fighting, following the ruler, and using its courage to carry out the things on which the former had decided?

GLAUCON: Yes, they would.

SOCRATES: I imagine, then, that we call each individual courageous because of the latter part—that is, when the part of him that is spirited in kind preserves through pains and pleasures the pronouncements of *c* reason about what should inspire terror and what should not.

GLAUCON: That's right.

SOCRATES: But we call him wise, surely, because of the small part that rules in him, makes those pronouncements, and has within it the knowledge of what is advantageous—both for each part and for the whole, the community composed of all three.

GLAUCON: Yes, indeed.

SOCRATES: What about temperance? Isn't he temperate because of the friendly and concordant relations between these same things: namely, when both the ruler and its two subjects share the belief that the rationally calculating element should rule, and do not engage in faction against it?   *d*

GLAUCON: Temperance in a city and in a private individual is certainly nothing other than that.

SOCRATES: But surely, now, a person will be just because of what we have so often described and in the way we have so often described.

GLAUCON: Necessarily.

SOCRATES: Well, then, has our justice become in any way blurred? Does it look like anything other than the very thing we found in the city?

GLAUCON: It doesn't seem so to me, at least.

SOCRATES: We could make perfectly sure, if there is still anything in our souls that disputes this, by applying everyday tests to it.   *e*

GLAUCON: Which ones?

SOCRATES: For example, if we had to come to an agreement about whether a man similar in nature and training to this city of ours had embezzled gold or silver he had accepted for deposit, who do you think would consider him more likely to have done so rather than men of a different sort?   *443a*

GLAUCON: No one.

SOCRATES: And would he have anything to do with temple robberies, thefts, or betrayals of friends in private life or of cities in public life?

GLAUCON: No, nothing.

SOCRATES: And he would be in no way untrustworthy when it came to promises or other agreements.

GLAUCON: How could he be?

SOCRATES: And surely adultery, disrespect for parents, and neglect of the gods would be more characteristic of any other sort of person than of this one.

GLAUCON: Of any other sort, indeed.

SOCRATES: And isn't the reason for all this, the
b fact that each element within him does its own job where ruling and being ruled are concerned?

GLAUCON: Yes, that and nothing else.

SOCRATES: Are you still looking for justice to be something besides this power that produces men and cities of the sort we have described?

GLAUCON: No, by Zeus, I am not.

SOCRATES: The dream we had has been completely fulfilled, then—I mean the suspicion we expressed that right from the beginning, when we were founding the city, we had, with the help of some god, chanced to hit upon the origin and pattern of
c justice.[19]

GLAUCON: Absolutely.

SOCRATES: So, Glaucon, it really was—which is why it was so helpful—a sort of image of justice, this principle that it is right for someone who is, by nature, a shoemaker to practice shoemaking and nothing else, for a carpenter to practice carpentry, and the same for all the others.

GLAUCON: Apparently so.

SOCRATES: And in truth, justice is, it seems, something of this sort. Yet it is not concerned with someone's doing his own job on the outside. On the contrary, it is concerned with what is inside; with himself,
d really, and the things that are his own. It means that he does not allow the elements in him each to do the job of some other, or the three sorts of elements in his soul to meddle with one another. Instead, he regulates well what is really his own, rules himself, puts himself in order, becomes his own friend, and harmonizes the three elements together, just as if they were literally the three defining notes of an octave— lowest, highest, and middle—as well as any others that may be in between. He binds together all of these and, from having been many, becomes entirely
e one, temperate and harmonious. Then and only then should he turn to action, whether it is to do something concerning the acquisition of wealth or concerning the care of his body, or even something political, or concerning private contracts. In all these areas, he considers and calls just and fine the action that preserves this inner harmony and helps achieve it, and wisdom the *knowledge* that oversees such action; and he considers and calls unjust any action that destroys this harmony, and ignorance the *belief* that oversees it.[20]   444a

GLAUCON: That's absolutely true, Socrates.

SOCRATES: Well, then, if we claim to have found the just man, the just city, and what justice really is in them, we won't, I imagine, be thought to be telling a complete lie.

GLAUCON: No, by Zeus, we certainly won't.

SOCRATES: Shall we claim it, then?

GLAUCON: Yes, let's.

SOCRATES: So be it, then. I take it we must look for injustice next.

GLAUCON: Clearly.

SOCRATES: Mustn't it, in turn, be a kind of faction among those three—their meddling and interfering b with one another's jobs; the rebellion of a part of the soul against the whole in order to rule in it inappropriately, since its nature suits it to be a slave of the ruling class. We will say something like that, I imagine, and that their disorder and wandering is injustice, licentiousness, cowardice, ignorance, and, in a word, the whole of vice.

GLAUCON: That is precisely what they are.

SOCRATES: Doing unjust actions, then, and being unjust; and, the opposite, doing just ones—they all c surely become clear at once, don't they, provided that both injustice and justice are also clear?

GLAUCON: What do you mean?

SOCRATES: That they do not differ in any way from healthy actions and unhealthy ones, that what the latter are in the body, they are in the soul.

GLAUCON: In what respect?

SOCRATES: Surely, healthy actions engender health, unhealthy ones disease.

GLAUCON: Yes.

SOCRATES: Well, doesn't doing just actions also engender justice, unjust ones injustice?   d

---

19. [432d2–433b4.]

20. [The difference between knowledge (*epistêmê*) and belief (*doxa*) is explored at 475d1–480a13.]

GLAUCON: Necessarily.

SOCRATES: But to produce health is to put the elements that are in the body in their natural relations of mastering and being mastered by one another; while to produce disease is to establish a relation of ruling and being ruled by one another that is contrary to nature.

GLAUCON: That's right.

SOCRATES: Doesn't it follow, then, that to produce justice is to establish the elements in the soul in a natural relation of mastering and being mastered by one another, while to produce injustice is to establish a relation of ruling and being ruled by one another that is contrary to nature?

GLAUCON: Absolutely.

SOCRATES: Virtue, then, so it seems, is a sort of health, a fine and good state of the soul; whereas vice
e seems to be a shameful disease and weakness.

GLAUCON: That's right.

SOCRATES: And don't fine practices lead to the possession of virtue, shameful ones to vice?

GLAUCON: Necessarily.

SOCRATES: So it now remains, it seems, for us to
445a consider whether it is more profitable to do just actions, engage in fine practices, and be just, whether one is known to be so or not; or to do injustice and be unjust, provided that one does not have to pay the penalty and become a better person as a result of being punished.

GLAUCON: But, Socrates, that question seems to me, at least, to have become ridiculous, now that the two have been shown to be as we described. Life does not seem worth living when the body's natural constitution is ruined, not even if one has food and drink of every sort, all the money in the world, and every political office imaginable. So how—even if
b one could do whatever one wished, except what would liberate one from vice and injustice and make one acquire justice and virtue—could it be worth living when the natural constitution of the very thing by which we live[21] is ruined and in turmoil?

SOCRATES: Yes, it is ridiculous. All the same, since in fact we have reached a point from which we can see with the utmost clarity, as it were, that these things are so, we must not give up.

GLAUCON: That's absolutely the last thing we should do.

SOCRATES: Come up here, then, so that you can see how many kinds of vice there are—the ones, at c any rate, that are worth seeing.

GLAUCON: I am following. Just tell me.

SOCRATES: Well, from the vantage point, so to speak, that we have reached in our argument, it seems to me that there is one kind of virtue and an unlimited number of kinds of vice, four of which are worth mentioning.

GLAUCON: What do you mean?

SOCRATES: It seems likely that there are as many types of soul as there are types of political constitution of a specific kind.

GLAUCON: How many is that?

SOCRATES: Five types of constitution, and five of soul.   d

GLAUCON: Tell me what they are.

SOCRATES: I will tell you that one type would be the constitution we have been describing. However, there are two ways of referring to it: if one outstanding man emerges among the rulers, it is called a kingship; if more than one, it is called an aristocracy.

GLAUCON: That's true.

SOCRATES: Well, then, that is one of the kinds I had in mind. You see, whether many arise or just one, they won't change any of the laws of the city that are worth mentioning, since they will have been e brought up and educated in the way we described.

GLAUCON: No, they probably won't.

BOOK V

SOCRATES' NARRATION CONTINUES:

SOCRATES: That, then, is the sort of city and constitution—and the sort of man—I call good and 449a correct. And if indeed this one is correct, all the others are bad and mistaken, both as city governments and as ways of organizing the souls of private individuals. The deficient ones fall into four kinds.

GLAUCON: What are they?

I was going to describe them in the order in which I thought they developed out of one another.[1] *But*

21. [I.e., the soul. See 353d9–10.]

1. [This task is taken up in Book VIII.]

b   *Polemarchus, who was sitting not far from Adeimantus, extended his hand, gripped the latter's cloak by the shoulder from above, drew Adeimantus toward him, and, leaning forward himself, said some things in his ear. We overheard nothing of what he said, other than this:*

Shall we let it go, then, or what?

ADEIMANTUS: (*Now speaking aloud.*) Certainly not.

SOCRATES: What is it exactly you won't let go?

ADEIMANTUS: You!

c   SOCRATES: Why exactly?

ADEIMANTUS: We think you are being lazy, that you are robbing us of a whole important section of the argument in order to avoid having to explain it. You thought we would not notice when you said—as though it were something inconsequential—that, as regards women and children, anyone could see that it will be a case of friends sharing everything in common.

SOCRATES: But isn't that correct, Adeimantus?

ADEIMANTUS: Yes, it is. But it is just like all the rest we have discussed; its correctness requires an explanation of how the sharing will be arranged, since there are many ways to bring it about. So, do

d   not omit to tell us about the particular one you have in mind. We have all been waiting for a long time in the expectation that you would surely discuss how procreation will be handled, how the children that are born will be reared, and the whole subject of what you mean by sharing women and children. You see, we think that this makes a considerable difference—indeed, all the difference—to whether a constitution is correct or incorrect. So now that you are beginning to describe another constitution without having analyzed this matter adequately, we are resolved, as you

450a overheard, not to let you go until you explain all this just as you did the rest.

GLAUCON: Include me, too, as having a share in this vote.

And Thrasymachus said:

In fact, you can take it as the resolution of *all* of us, Socrates.

SOCRATES: What a thing to do, attacking me like that. You have started up a huge discussion about the

constitution—it will be like starting from the beginning. I was delighted to think I had already completed its description by this time and was satisfied to have what I had said earlier be accepted as is. You do not realize what a swarm of arguments you are now stirring up by making this demand. It was because I could see it that I left the topic aside, to avoid all the *b* trouble it would cause us.

THRASYMACHUS: What of it? Don't you think these people have come here now to listen to arguments, not to smelt ore?[2]

SOCRATES: Yes—within moderation, at least.

GLAUCON: But surely it is within moderation, Socrates, for people with any sense to listen to such arguments their whole life long. So never mind about *us*. Don't *you* get tired of explaining your views on what we asked about: namely, what the sharing of children and women will amount to for our guardians, *c* and how the children will be brought up while they are still small. After all, the time between birth and the beginning of formal education seems to be the most troublesome period of all. So, try to tell us in what way it should be handled.

SOCRATES: It is not easy to explain, my happy fellow. It raises even more doubts than the topics we have discussed so far. One might, in fact, doubt whether what we proposed is possible, and, even if one granted that it is entirely so, one might still have doubts about whether it would be for the best. That, then, is why I was somewhat hesitant to bring it up: I was afraid, my dear comrade, that our argument might seem to be no more than wishful thinking.   *d*

GLAUCON: Do not hesitate at all. You see, your audience won't be inconsiderate, or incredulous, or hostile.

SOCRATES: My very good fellow, are you saying that because you want to encourage me?

GLAUCON: I am.

SOCRATES: Well, you are having precisely the opposite effect. If I were confident that I was speaking with knowledge, your encouragement would be all very well. When one is among knowledgeable and

---

2. [A proverbial expression applied to those who neglect the task at hand for an uncertain profit. Thrasymachus is reminding Socrates of his own words at 336e4–9.]

beloved friends, and one is speaking what one knows to be the truth about the most important and most beloved things, one can feel both secure and confi-
e   dent. But to produce arguments when one is uncertain and searching, as I am doing, is a frightening
451a thing and makes one feel insecure. I am not afraid of being ridiculed—that would be childish, indeed—but I am afraid that if I fail to secure the truth, just where it is most important to do so, I will not only fall myself but drag my friends down as well. So I bow to Adrasteia, Glaucon, for what I am about to say. You see, I suspect that involuntary homicide is a lesser crime than misleading people about beautiful, good, and just conventions. That is a risk it would be better to run among enemies than among friends.
b   So you have well and truly encouraged me.

   Glaucon laughed and said:

Well, Socrates, if we suffer from any false note you strike in the argument, we will release you, as we would in a homicide case, as guiltless and no deceiver of us. So you may speak with confidence.

SOCRATES: Well, it is true; the one who is acquitted in that situation is guiltless, so the law says. And if it is true there, it is probably true here, too.

GLAUCON: On these grounds, then, tell us.

SOCRATES: I will have to go back again, then, and say now what perhaps I should have said then in the
c   proper place. But maybe it is all right, after having completed a male drama, to perform a female one next[3]—especially when you demand it in this way. For people born and educated as we have described, then, there is, I believe, no correct way to acquire and employ children and women other than to follow the path on which we first set them. Surely, in our argument, we tried to establish the men as guard-dogs of their flock.

GLAUCON: Yes.

SOCRATES: Then let's proceed by giving corres-
d   ponding rules for birth and rearing, and see whether they suit us or not.

GLAUCON: How?

SOCRATES: As follows. Do we think that the females of our guard-dogs should join in guarding precisely what the males guard, hunt with them, and share everything with them? Or do we think that they should stay indoors and look after the house,[4] on the grounds that they are incapable of doing this because they must bear and rear the puppies, while the males should work and have the entire care of the flock?

GLAUCON: They should share everything—except that we employ the females as we would weaker animals, and the males as we would stronger ones.

SOCRATES: Is it possible, then, to employ an animal for the same tasks as another if you do not give it the same upbringing and education?

GLAUCON: No, it is not.

SOCRATES: Then if we employ women for the same tasks as men, they must also be taught the same things.

GLAUCON: Yes.

SOCRATES: Now, we gave the latter musical and physical training.

GLAUCON: Yes.

SOCRATES: So, we must also give these two crafts, as well as military training, to the women, and employ them in the same way.

GLAUCON: That seems reasonable, given what you say.

SOCRATES: But perhaps many of the things we are now saying, because they are contrary to custom, would seem ridiculous if they were put into practice.

GLAUCON: Indeed, they would.

SOCRATES: What do you see as the most ridiculous aspect of them? Isn't it obvious that it is the idea of the women exercising stripped in the palestras alongside the men?[5] And not just the young women, but the older ones too—like the old men we see b

---

3. [This may be an allusion to the mimes of Sophron of Syracuse (c. 470–400 B.C.E.), which were divided into male mimes, in which men were represented, and female ones, in which women were represented.]

4. [Respectable, well-to-do women lived secluded lives in most Greek states: they were confined to the household (see 579b8) and to domestic work and were largely excluded from the public spheres of culture, politics, and warfare.]

5. [The women will be *gumnozomenas*, which can mean stripped naked, but often also means wearing a tunic, or undergarment, without a cloak (see 457a6–7). A palestra was a wrestling school and training ground.]

in gymnasiums who, even though their bodies are wrinkled and not pleasant to look at, still love physical training.

GLAUCON: Yes, by Zeus, that *would* look really ridiculous, at least under present conditions.

SOCRATES: Yet, since we have started to discuss the matter, we must not be afraid of the various jokes that the wits will make both about this sort of change in musical and physical training and—even more c so—about the change in the bearing of arms and the mounting of cavalry horses.[6]

GLAUCON: You are right.

SOCRATES: But since we have started, we must move on to the rougher part of the law, and ask these wits *not* to do their own job, but to be serious. And we will remind them that it is not long since the *Greeks* thought it shameful and ridiculous (as many barbarians still do) for *men* to be seen stripped, and that when first the Cretans and then the Lacedaemonians began the gymnasiums, the wits of the time had the opportunity to make a comedy of it all. Or don't d you think so?

GLAUCON: I certainly do.

SOCRATES: But when it became clear, I take it, to those who employed these practices, that it was better to strip than to cover up all such parts, the laughter in the eyes faded away because of what the arguments had proved to be best. And this showed that it is a fool who finds anything ridiculous except what is bad, or tries to raise a laugh at the sight of anything except what is stupid or bad, or—putting e it the other way around—who takes seriously any standard of what is beautiful other than what is good.

GLAUCON: Absolutely.

SOCRATES: Well, then, shouldn't we first agree about whether our proposals are viable or not? And mustn't we give anyone who wishes to do so—whether it is someone who loves a joke or someone serious— the opportunity to dispute whether the female human 453a does have the natural ability to share in *all* the tasks

6. [A reference, perhaps, to Aristophanes, *Assembly Women*, which makes fun of the idea of women having political power and making laws like these. As in English, the term *hoplon* ("weapon" or "tool") was used to refer to the male genitals, and *ocheuein* ("mounting," "riding") to refer to sexual intercourse (as at 454e1).]

of the male sex, or in none at all, or in some but not others; and, in particular, whether this holds in the case of warfare? By making the best beginning in this way, wouldn't one also be likely to reach the best conclusion?

GLAUCON: Of course.

SOCRATES: So, would you like us to dispute with one another on their behalf, so that their side of the argument won't be attacked without defenders?

GLAUCON: Why not?   b

SOCRATES: Then let's say this on their behalf: "Socrates and Glaucon, you do not need *other people* to dispute you. After all, you yourselves, when you were beginning to found your city, agreed that each one had to do the one job for which he was naturally suited."

GLAUCON: We did agree to that, I think. Of course we did.

SOCRATES: "Can it be, then, that a woman is not by nature very different from a man?"

GLAUCON: Of course she is different.

SOCRATES: "Then isn't it also appropriate to assign a different job to each of them, the one for which they are naturally suited?"

GLAUCON: Certainly.   c

SOCRATES: "How is it, then, that you are not making a mistake now and contradicting yourselves, when you say that men and women must do the same jobs, seeing that they have natures that are most distinct?" Do you have any defense, you amazing fellow, against that attack?

GLAUCON: It is not easy to think of one on the spur of the moment. On the contrary, I shall ask— indeed, I am asking—you to explain the argument on our side as well, whatever it is.

SOCRATES: That, Glaucon, and many other problems of the same sort, which I foresaw long ago, was what I was afraid of when I hesitated to tackle the d law concerning the possession and upbringing of women and children.

GLAUCON: No, by Zeus, it certainly does not seem to be a simple matter.

SOCRATES: No, it is not. But the fact is that whether one falls into a small diving pool or into the middle of the largest sea, one has to swim all the same.

GLAUCON: Of course.

SOCRATES: Then we must swim, too, and try to save ourselves from the sea of argument, hoping for a dolphin to pick us up, or for some other unlikely rescue.[7]

e   GLAUCON: It seems so.

SOCRATES: Come on, then, let's see if we can find a way out. We have agreed, of course, that different natures must have different pursuits, and that the natures of a woman and a man are different. But we now say that those different natures must have the same pursuits. Isn't that the charge against us?

GLAUCON: Yes, exactly.

SOCRATES: What a noble power, Glaucon, the
454a craft of disputation possesses!

GLAUCON: Why is that?

SOCRATES: Because many people seem to me to fall into it even against their wills, and think they are engaging not in eristic, but in discussion. This happens because they are unable to examine what has been said by dividing it up into kinds. Instead, it is on the purely verbal level that they look for the contradiction in what has been said, and employ eristic, not dialectic, on one another.

GLAUCON: Yes, that certainly does happen to many people. But surely it is not pertinent to us at the moment, is it?

SOCRATES: It most certainly is. At any rate, we
b are in danger of unconsciously dealing in disputation.

GLAUCON: How?

SOCRATES: We are trying to establish the principle that different natures should not be assigned the same pursuits in a bold and eristic manner, *on the verbal level*. But we did not at all investigate what kind of natural difference or sameness we had in mind, or in what regard the distinction was pertinent, when we assigned different pursuits to different natures and the same ones to the same.

GLAUCON: No, we did not investigate that.

SOCRATES: And because we did not, it is open to
c us, apparently, to ask ourselves whether the natures of bald and long-haired men are the same or opposite. And, once we agree that they are opposite, it is open to us to forbid the long-haired ones to be shoemakers, if that is what the bald ones are to be, or *vice versa*.

GLAUCON: But that would be ridiculous.

SOCRATES: And is it ridiculous for any other reason than that we did not have in mind *every* kind of difference and sameness in nature, but were keeping our eyes only on the kind of difference and sameness that was pertinent to the pursuits themselves? We meant, for example, that a male and female whose *d* souls are suited for medicine have the same nature. Or don't you think so?

GLAUCON: I do.

SOCRATES: But a male doctor and a male carpenter have different ones?

GLAUCON: Of course, completely different.

SOCRATES: In the case of both the male and the female sex, then, if one of them is shown to be different from the other with regard to a particular craft or pursuit, we will say that is the one who should be assigned to it. But if it is apparent that they differ in this respect alone, that the female bears the offspring while the male mounts the female, we will say it has not yet been demonstrated that a woman is different *e* from a man with regard to what we are talking about, and we will continue to believe our guardians and their women should have the same pursuits.

GLAUCON: And rightly so.

SOCRATES: Next, won't we urge our opponent to tell us the precise craft or pursuit, relevant to the *455a* organization of the city, for which a woman's nature and a man's are not the same but different?

GLAUCON: That would be a fair question, at least.

SOCRATES: Perhaps, then, this other person might say, just as you did a moment ago,[8] that it is not easy to give an adequate answer on the spur of the moment, but that after reflection it would not be at all difficult.

GLAUCON: Yes, he might say that.

SOCRATES: Do you want us to ask the one who disputes things in this way, then, to follow us to see whether we can somehow show him that there is no *b* pursuit relevant to the management of the city that is peculiar to women?

GLAUCON: Of course.

SOCRATES: Come on, then, we will say to him, give us an answer: "Is this what you meant by one person being naturally well suited for something and

---

7. [The story of Arion's rescue by the dolphin is told in Herodotus, *Histories* 1.23–4.]

8. [453c7–9.]

another naturally unsuited: that the one learns it easily, the other with difficulty; that the one, after a little instruction, can discover a lot for himself in the subject being studied, whereas the other, even if he gets a lot of instruction and attention, does not even retain what he was taught; that the bodily capacities of the one adequately serve his mind, while those of the other obstruct his? Are there any other factors

c than these, by which you distinguish a person who is naturally well suited for each pursuit from one who is not?"

GLAUCON: No one will be able to mention any others.

SOCRATES: Do you know of anything practiced by human beings, then, at which the male sex is not superior to the female in all those ways? Or must we make a long story of it by discussing weaving and the preparation of baked and boiled food⁹—the very pursuits in which the female sex is thought to excel, and in which its defeat would expose it to the greatest

d ridicule of all?

GLAUCON: It is true that the one sex shows greater mastery than the other in pretty much every area. Yet there are many women who are better than many men at many things. But on the whole, it is as you say.

SOCRATES: Then, my friend, there is no pursuit relevant to the management of the city that belongs to a woman because she is a woman, or to a man because he is a man; but the various natural capacities are distributed in a similar way between both creatures, and women can share by nature in every pursuit, and men in every one, though for the purposes

e of all of them women are weaker than men.

GLAUCON: Of course.

SOCRATES: So shall we assign all of them to men and none to women?

GLAUCON: How could we?

SOCRATES: We could not. For we will say, I imagine, that one woman is suited for medicine, another not, and that one is naturally musical, another not.

GLAUCON: Of course.

SOCRATES: Won't one be suited for physical train-

ing or war, then, while another is unwarlike and not   456a a lover of physical training?

GLAUCON: I suppose so.

SOCRATES: And one a philosopher (lover of wisdom), another a "misosopher" (hater of wisdom)? And one spirited, another spiritless?

GLAUCON: That too.

SOCRATES: So there is also a woman who is suited to be a guardian, and one who is not. Or wasn't that the sort of nature we selected for our male guardians, too?¹⁰

GLAUCON: It certainly was.

SOCRATES: A woman and a man can have the same nature, then, relevant to guarding the city—except to the extent that she is weaker and he is stronger.

GLAUCON: Apparently so.

SOCRATES: Women of that sort, then, must be selected to live and guard with men of the same sort,   b since they are competent to do so and are akin to the men by nature.

GLAUCON: Of course.

SOCRATES: And mustn't we assign the same pursuits to the same natures?

GLAUCON: Yes, the same ones.

SOCRATES: We have come around, then, to what we said before, and we are agreed that it is not against nature to assign musical and physical training to the female guardians.

GLAUCON: Absolutely.

SOCRATES: So, we are not legislating impossibilities or mere fantasies, at any rate, since the law we were proposing is in accord with nature. Rather, it is the contrary laws that we have now that turn out to   c be more contrary to nature, it seems.

GLAUCON: It does seem that way.

SOCRATES: Now, wasn't our inquiry about whether our proposals were both viable and best?

GLAUCON: Yes, it was.

SOCRATES: And that they are in fact viable has been agreed, hasn't it?

GLAUCON: Yes.

SOCRATES: So, we must next come to an agreement about whether they are for the best?

9. [Men were in charge of roasting meat. See 404b10–c4.]

10. [374e4–376c5.]

GLAUCON: Clearly.

SOCRATES: Now, as regards producing a woman who is equipped for guardianship, we won't have one sort of education that will produce our guardian men, will we, and another our women—especially not when

d it will have the same nature to work on in both cases?

GLAUCON: No, we won't.

SOCRATES: What is your belief about this, then?

GLAUCON: What?

SOCRATES: The notion that one man is better or worse than another—or do you think they are all alike?

GLAUCON: Not at all.

SOCRATES: In the city we are founding, who do you think will turn out to be better men: our guardians, who get the education we have described, or the shoemakers, who are educated in shoemaking?

GLAUCON: What a ridiculous question!

SOCRATES: I realize that. Aren't the guardians the

e best of the citizens?

GLAUCON: By far.

SOCRATES: And what about the female guardians? Won't they be the best of the women?

GLAUCON: Yes, they are by far the best, too.

SOCRATES: Is there anything better for a city than that the best possible men and women should come to exist in it?

GLAUCON: No, there is not.

SOCRATES: And that is what musical and physical training, employed as we have described, will

457a achieve?

GLAUCON: Of course.

SOCRATES: Then the law we were proposing was not only possible, but also best for a city?

GLAUCON: Yes.

SOCRATES: Then the female guardians must strip, clothing themselves in virtue instead of cloaks. They must share in warfare, and whatever else guarding the city involves, and do nothing else. But within these areas, the women must be assigned lighter tasks than the men, because of the weakness of their sex. And the man who laughs at the sight of women stripped for physical training, when their stripping is

b for the best, is "plucking the unripe fruit of laughter's wisdom,"[11] and knows nothing, it seems, about what

he is laughing at or what he is doing. For it is, and always will be, the finest saying that what is beneficial is beautiful; what is harmful ugly.

GLAUCON: Absolutely.

SOCRATES: May we claim, then, that we are avoiding one wave,[12] as it were, in our discussion of the law about women, so that we are not altogether swept away when we declare that our male and female guardians must share all their pursuits, and that our argument is somehow self-consistent when it states c that this is both viable and beneficial?

GLAUCON: It is certainly no small wave that you are avoiding.

SOCRATES: You won't think it is so big when you see the next one.

GLAUCON: I won't see it unless you tell me about it.

SOCRATES: The law that is consistent with that one, and with the others that preceded it, is this, I take it.

GLAUCON: What?

SOCRATES: That all these women should be shared among all the men, that no individual woman and man should live together, and that the children, d too, should be shared, with no parent knowing its own offspring, and no child its parent.

GLAUCON: That wave *is* far bigger and more dubitable than the other, both as regards its viability and its benefit.

SOCRATES: As far as its benefit is concerned, at least, I do not think anyone would argue that the sharing of women and children is not the greatest good, if indeed it is viable. But I imagine there would be a lot of dispute about whether or not it is viable.

GLAUCON: No, *both* could very well be disputed.   e

SOCRATES: You mean I will have to face a coalition of arguments. I thought I had at least escaped one of them—namely, whether you thought the proposal was beneficial—and that I would just be left with the argument about whether it is viable or not.

GLAUCON: Well, you did not escape unnoticed. So you will have to give an argument for both.

11. [Plato is adapting a phrase of Pindar.]

12. [The metaphor begins at 453c10–d7.]

SOCRATES: I must pay the penalty. But do me this favor: let me take a holiday and act like those lazy people who make a banquet for themselves of their own thoughts when they are walking alone. People like that, as you know, do not bother to find out how any of their appetites might actually be fulfilled, so as to avoid the trouble of deliberating about what is possible and what is not. They assume that what they want is available, and then proceed to arrange all the rest, taking pleasure in going through everything they will do when they get it—thus making their already lazy souls even lazier. Well, I, too, am succumbing to this weakness at the moment and want to postpone consideration of the viability of our proposals until later. I will assume now that they are viable, if you will permit me to do so, and examine how the rulers will arrange them when they come to pass. And I will try to show that, if they were put into practice, they would be the most beneficial arrangements of all, both for the city and for its guardians. These are the things I will try to examine with you first, leaving the others for later—if indeed you will permit this.

GLAUCON: You have my permission; so proceed with the examination.

SOCRATES: Well, then, I imagine that if indeed our rulers, and likewise their auxiliaries, are worthy of their names, the latter will be prepared to carry out orders, and the former to give orders, obeying our laws in some cases and imitating them in the others that we leave to their discretion.

GLAUCON: Probably so.

SOCRATES: Now, you are their lawgiver, and in just the way you selected these men, you will select as the women to hand over to them those who have natures as similar to theirs as possible. And because they have shared dwellings and meals, and none of them has any private property of that sort, they will live together; and through mixing together in the gymnasia and in the rest of their daily life, they will be driven by innate necessity, I take it, to have sex with one another. Or don't you think I am talking about necessities here?

GLAUCON: Not *geometric* necessities, certainly, but *erotic* ones; and they probably have a sharper capacity to persuade and attract most people.

SOCRATES: They do, indeed. But the next point, Glaucon, is that for them to have unregulated sexual intercourse with one another, or to do anything else of that sort, would not be a pious thing in a city of happy people, and the rulers won't allow it.

GLAUCON: No, it would not be just.

SOCRATES: It is clear, then, that we will next have to make marriages as sacred as possible. And sacred marriages will be those that are most beneficial.

GLAUCON: Absolutely.

SOCRATES: How, then, will the most beneficial ones come about? Tell me this, Glaucon. I see you have hunting dogs and quite a flock of noble birds at home.[13] Have you, by Zeus, noticed anything in particular about their "marriages" and breeding?

GLAUCON: Like what?

SOCRATES: In the first place, though they are all noble animals, aren't there some that are, or turn out to be, the very best?

GLAUCON: There are.

SOCRATES: Do you breed from them all to the same extent, then, or do you try hard to breed as far as possible from the best ones?

GLAUCON: From the best ones.

SOCRATES: And do you breed from the youngest, the oldest, or as far as possible from those in their prime?

GLAUCON: From those in their prime.

SOCRATES: And if they were not bred in this way, do you think that your race of birds and dogs would get much worse?

GLAUCON: I do.

SOCRATES: And what do you think about horses and other animals? Is the situation any different with them?

GLAUCON: It would be strange if it were.

SOCRATES: Good heavens, my dear comrade! Then our need for eminent rulers is quite desperate, if indeed the same also holds for the human race.

GLAUCON: Well, it does hold of them. But so what?

SOCRATES: It follows that our rulers will then have to employ a great many drugs. You know that when people do not need drugs for their bodies, and they are prepared to follow a regimen, we regard even an inferior doctor as adequate. But when drugs are

13. [Both hunting dogs and aviaries were common in rich Greek households.]

needed, we know that a much bolder doctor is required.

GLAUCON: That's true. But what is your point?

SOCRATES: This: it looks as though our rulers will have to employ a great many lies and deceptions for the benefit of those they rule. And you remember, I
d suppose, we said all such things were useful as a kind of drug.[14]

GLAUCON: And we were correct.

SOCRATES: Well, in the case of marriages and procreation, its correctness is particularly evident.

GLAUCON: How so?

SOCRATES: It follows from our previous agreement that the best men should mate with the best women in as many cases as possible, while the opposite should hold of the worst men and women; and that the offspring of the former should be reared, but not that of the latter, if our flock is going to be an
e eminent one. And all this must occur without anyone knowing except the rulers—if, again, our herd of guardians is to remain as free from faction as possible.

GLAUCON: That's absolutely right.

SOCRATES: So then, we will have to establish by law certain festivals and sacrifices at which we will bring together brides and bridegrooms, and our poets must compose suitable hymns for the marriages that
460a take place. We will leave the number of marriages for the rulers to decide. That will enable them to keep the number of males as constant as possible, taking into account war, disease, and everything of that sort; so that the city will, as far as possible, become neither too big nor too small.

GLAUCON: That's right.

SOCRATES: I imagine that some sophisticated lotteries will have to be created, then, so that an inferior person of that sort will blame chance rather than the rulers at each mating time.

GLAUCON: Yes, indeed.

SOCRATES: And presumably, the young men who
b are good at war or at other things must—among other prizes and awards—be given a greater opportunity to have sex with the women, in order that a pretext may also be created at the same time for having as many children as possible fathered by such men.

14. [382c6–d3.]

GLAUCON: That's right.

SOCRATES: And then, as offspring are born, won't they be taken by the officials appointed for this purpose, whether these are men or women or both— for surely our offices are also open to both women and men.

GLAUCON: Yes.

SOCRATES: And I suppose they will take the offspring of good parents to the rearing pen and hand them over to special nurses who live in a separate c part of the city. But those of inferior parents, or any deformed offspring of the others, they will hide in a secret and unknown place, as is fitting.[15]

GLAUCON: Yes, if indeed the race of guardians is going to remain pure.

SOCRATES: And won't these nurses also take care of the children's feeding by bringing the mothers to the rearing pen when their breasts are full, while devising every device to ensure that no mother will recognize her offspring? And won't they provide other women as wet nurses if the mothers themselves have d insufficient milk—taking care, however, that the mothers breast-feed the children for only a moderate period of time, and assigning sleepless nights and similar burdens to the nurses and wet nurses?

GLAUCON: You are making childbearing a soft job for the guardians' women.

SOCRATES: Yes, properly so. But let's take up the next thing we proposed. We said, as you know, that offspring should be bred from parents who are in their prime.[16]

GLAUCON: True.

SOCRATES: Do you agree that a woman's prime lasts, on average, for a period of twenty years and a e man's for thirty?

GLAUCON: Which years are those?

SOCRATES: A woman should bear children for the city from the age of twenty to that of forty; whereas a man should beget them for the city from the time that he passes his peak as a runner until he reaches fifty-five.[17]

15. [Infanticide by exposure was commonly used in ancient Greece as a method of birth control.]
16. [452b1–3.]
17. [Greek women were often married before they turned twenty.]

GLAUCON: At any rate, that is the physical and
461a mental prime for both.

SOCRATES: Then if any male who is younger or
older than that engages in reproduction for the community, we will say that his offense is neither pious nor
just. For the child he fathers for the city, if it escapes
discovery, will be begotten and born without the benefit of sacrifices, or of the prayers that priestesses, priests,
and the entire city will offer at every marriage festival,
asking that from good and beneficial parents ever
better and more beneficial offspring should be pro-
b duced. On the contrary, it will be born in darkness
through a terrible act of lack of self-control.

GLAUCON: That's right.

SOCRATES: The same law will apply if a man who
is still of breeding age has sex with a woman in her
prime when the rulers have not mated them. We will
say that he is imposing an illegitimate, unauthorized,
and unholy child on the city.

GLAUCON: That's absolutely right.

SOCRATES: But when women and men have
passed breeding age, I imagine we will leave them free
to have sex with whomever they wish—except that a
c man may not have sex with his daughter, mother,
daughters' daughters, or mother's female ancestors, or
a woman with her son and his descendants or her father
and his ancestors. And we will permit all that only after
telling them to be very careful not to let even a single
fetus see the light of day, if one should happen to be
conceived; but if one does force its way out, they must
dispose of it on the understanding that no nurture is
available for such a child.

GLAUCON: All that sounds reasonable. But how
will they recognize one another's fathers, daughters,
d and the others you mentioned?

SOCRATES: They won't. Instead, from the day a
man becomes a bridegroom, he will call all offspring
born in the tenth month afterward (and in the seventh,
of course) his sons,[18] if they are male, and his daughters,
if they are female; and they will call him father. Similarly, he will call their children his grandchildren, and
they, in turn, will call the group to which he belongs
grandfathers and grandmothers. And those who were

born at the same time as their mothers and fathers were
breeding, they will call their brothers and sisters. Thus,
as we were saying just now, they will avoid sexual rela- e
tions with each other. However, the law *will* allow
brothers and sisters to have sex with one another, if the
lottery works out that way and the Pythia approves.[19]

GLAUCON: You are absolutely right.

SOCRATES: That, then, Glaucon, or something
like it, is how the sharing of women and children by
the guardians of your city will be handled. The next
point we need to have confirmed by argument, then,
is that this arrangement is both consistent with the
rest of the constitution and by far the best. Isn't that so?

GLAUCON: Yes, by Zeus, it is.   462a

SOCRATES: As a beginning step toward reaching
agreement, shouldn't we ask ourselves what we think
is the greatest good for the organization of the city—
the one at which the legislator should aim in making
its laws—and what the greatest evil? And then examine whether what we have just described is in harmony with the tracks of the good we have found, and
in disharmony with those of the bad?

GLAUCON: Absolutely.

SOCRATES: Now, do we know of any greater evil
for a city than what tears it apart and makes it many
instead of one? Or any greater good than what binds b
it together and makes it one?

GLAUCON: No, we do not.

SOCRATES: Well, doesn't sharing pleasure and
pain bind it together— when, as far as possible, all
the citizens feel more or less the same joy or pain at
the same gains or losses?

GLAUCON: Absolutely.

SOCRATES: On the other hand, doesn't the privati-
zation of these things dissolve the city—when some
are overwhelmed with distress and others overjoyed
by the same things happening to the city or some of
its inhabitants?   c

GLAUCON: Of course.

SOCRATES: And isn't that what happens when
people do not apply such phrases as "mine" and "not
mine" in unison in the city? And similarly with "someone else's"?

18. [These are lunar months. The period is from roughly
seven to roughly nine calendar months. A fetus of less
than seven months was considered nonviable.]

19. [Greek law did not usually permit marriage between
biological siblings, who will be included in the class
referred to here.]

GLAUCON: Precisely.

SOCRATES: Then isn't the city that is best governed the one in which the vast majority of people apply "mine" and "not mine" to the same things on the basis of the same principle?

GLAUCON: Certainly.

SOCRATES: And isn't it the city whose condition is most like that of a single person? I mean, when one of us somehow hurts his finger, you know the entire partnership—the one that binds body and soul together into a single system under the ruling part within it—is aware of this, and all of it as a whole feels the pain

d in unison with the part that suffers. That is why we say that this person has a pain in his finger. And the same principle applies, doesn't it, to any other part of a person, whether it is suffering pain or relieved by pleasure?

GLAUCON: Yes, the same one. And, to answer your question, the city that manages to come closest to this condition *is* the best-governed one.

SOCRATES: I imagine, then, that whenever one of its citizens has an experience, whether good or bad, such a city will most certainly say that the experi-

e ence is its own, and all of it together will share his pleasure or pain.

GLAUCON: That must be so, since it is well governed.

SOCRATES: It is time for us to return to our own city, then, to look there for the features we have agreed on and to see whether it, or rather some other city, possesses them to the greatest degree.

GLAUCON: Yes, it is.

SOCRATES: Well, now, what about those other cities? Presumably there are rulers and people in them

463a as well as in ours?

GLAUCON: There are.

SOCRATES: And won't all of them call one another "citizens"?

GLAUCON: Of course.

SOCRATES: But besides "citizens," what do the people in those other cities call the rulers?

GLAUCON: In most, they call them "masters," but in democracies they are called just that—"rulers."[20]

SOCRATES: What about the people in our city? Besides "citizens," what do they call the rulers?

GLAUCON: "Preservers" and "auxiliaries."   b

SOCRATES: And what do *they* call the people?

GLAUCON: "Paymasters" and "providers."

SOCRATES: What do the rulers in other cities call the people?

GLAUCON: "Slaves."

SOCRATES: And what do the rulers call each other?

GLAUCON: "Co-rulers."

SOCRATES: And ours?

GLAUCON: "Co-guardians."

SOCRATES: Now, can you tell me whether a ruler in other cities could address one of his co-rulers as his kinsman and another as an outsider?

GLAUCON: Many do, at any rate.

SOCRATES: And doesn't he regard and speak of his kinsman as belonging to him, while he regards the outsider as not doing so?   c

GLAUCON: Yes.

SOCRATES: What about your guardians? Could any of them regard or address a co-guardian as an outsider?

GLAUCON: Certainly not. He will regard everyone he meets as a brother or a sister, a father or a mother, a son or a daughter, or some ancestor or descendant of these.

SOCRATES: Very well put. But tell me this, too: will your laws require them simply to use these terms of kinship, or must they also do all the things that go along with the names? In the case of fathers, for d example, must they show them the customary respect, solicitude, and obedience owed to parents? Will they fare worse at the hands of gods or men, as people whose actions are neither pious nor just, if they do otherwise? Will these be the sayings that are chanted by all the citizens, and that sound in their ears right from their earliest childhood? Or will they hear something else about their fathers—or the ones they are told to regard as their fathers—or about their other relatives?

GLAUCON: They will hear those. It would be ridiculous if they only mouthed the terms of kinship, e without the actions.

SOCRATES: So, in this city more than in any other, when someone is doing well or badly, they will utter

20. [The Athenian democracy had nine rulers (archons) in Plato's time. These included the chief magistrates, the chief military leader, and an important authority in religious matters.]

in concord the words we mentioned a moment ago, and say "*my* such-and-such is doing well" or "*my* so-and-so is doing badly."

GLAUCON: That's absolutely true.

SOCRATES: Well, didn't we say that this conviction and way of talking are accompanied by the having of pleasures and pains in common?[21]

464a

GLAUCON: Yes, and we were right to do so.

SOCRATES: Then won't our citizens share to the fullest, and call "mine," the very same thing? And because they share it, won't they experience to the fullest the sharing of pleasures and pains?

GLAUCON: Of course.

SOCRATES: And—in the context of the rest of the political system—isn't the sharing of women and children by the guardians responsible for it?

GLAUCON: Yes, it is by far the most important cause.

SOCRATES: But we further agreed that this sharing is the greatest good for a city, when we compared a well-governed city to the way a human body relates to pain and pleasure in one of its parts.

b

GLAUCON: And we were right to agree.

SOCRATES: Then we have shown that the cause of the greatest good for our city is the sharing of women and children by the auxiliaries.

GLAUCON: Yes, we certainly have.

SOCRATES: And what is more, it is consistent with what we said before. For we said, as you know, that if these people are going to be real guardians, they should not have private houses, land, or any other possession, but should receive their upkeep from the other citizens as a wage for their guardianship, and should all eat communally.[22]

c

GLAUCON: That's right.

SOCRATES: So, as I say, doesn't what was said earlier, as well as what is being said now, make them into even better guardians and prevent them from tearing the city apart by applying the term "mine" not to the same thing, but to different ones—with one person dragging into his own house whatever he, apart from the others, can get his hands on, and another into a different house to a different wife and

d

children, who create private pleasures and pains at things that are private? Instead of that, don't our guardians share a single conviction about what is their own, aim at the same goal, and, as far as possible, feel pleasure and pain in unison?

GLAUCON: Absolutely.

SOCRATES: What about lawsuits and accusations? Won't they pretty much disappear from among them because they have no private possessions except their own bodies and share all the rest? As a result, won't they be free from faction—at any rate, from the sort of faction that the possession of property, children, and families causes among people?

e

GLAUCON: Yes, they will inevitably be entirely free of it.

SOCRATES: Moreover, neither lawsuits for violence nor for assault should justifiably occur among them. For we will declare, surely, that for people to defend themselves against others of the same age is a fine and just thing, since it will compel them to stay in good physical shape.

GLAUCON: That's right.

SOCRATES: This law is also correct for another reason: if a spirited person vents his anger in this way, he will be less likely to move on to more serious sorts of faction.

465a

GLAUCON: He certainly will.

SOCRATES: As for an older person, he will be authorized to rule and punish all the younger ones.

GLAUCON: Clearly.

SOCRATES: And, unless the rulers command it, it is unlikely that a younger person will ever employ any sort of violence against an older one, or strike him. And I do not imagine he will fail to show him respect in other ways either, since two guardians— fear and shame—are sufficient to prevent it. Shame will prevent him from laying a hand on his parents, as will the fear that the others would come to his victim's aid—some because they are his sons, some because they are his brothers, and some because they are his fathers.

b

GLAUCON: Yes, that is what would happen.

SOCRATES: Then won't the laws induce men to live at peace with one another in all respects?

GLAUCON: Very much so.

SOCRATES: And if there is no faction among the guardians, there is no terrible danger that the rest of

21. [462b4–c9.]
22. [416d3–417b8.]

the city will form factions, either against them or among themselves.

GLAUCON: No, there is not.

SOCRATES: As for the pettiest of the evils the guardians would escape, they are so unseemly, I hesitate even to mention them: the flatteries of the rich by the poor; the perplexities and sufferings involved in bringing up children; the need to make the money necessary to feed the household— the borrowings, the defaults, and all the things people have to do to provide an income to hand over to their wives and slaves to spend on housekeeping. The various troubles men endure in these areas, my dear Glaucon, are obvious, quite demeaning, and not worth discussing.

GLAUCON: They are obvious even to the blind.

SOCRATES: They will escape from all these things, then, and live a more blessedly happy life than the most blessedly happy one—that of the victors in the Olympian games.

GLAUCON: How so?

SOCRATES: Surely, these victors are considered happy on account of only a small part of what the guardians possess, since the latter victory is even finer, and their upkeep from public funds more complete.[23] After all, the victory they gain is the salvation of the whole city, and the crown of victory they and their children receive is their upkeep and all the necessities of life. They receive privileges from their own city during their lifetime and a worthy burial after their death.

GLAUCON: Yes, those are very fine rewards.

SOCRATES: Now, do you remember that earlier in our discussion we were rebuked by an argument—I forget whose—to the effect that we had not made our guardians happy, that though it was possible for them to have everything that belongs to the citizens, they actually had nothing? We said, didn't we, that if this happened to come up at some point, we would look into it then, but that our concern at the time was to make our guardians *guardians*, and to make the *city* the happiest possible, rather than looking to any one group within it and molding it for happiness?[24]

GLAUCON: I remember.

SOCRATES: Well, then, if indeed the life of our auxiliaries has been shown to be much finer and better than that of Olympian victors, is there any need to compare it with the lives of shoemakers or any other craftsmen, or with that of the farmers?

GLAUCON: I do not think there is.

SOCRATES: Nevertheless, it is surely right to repeat here what I also said on that earlier occasion: if a guardian tries to become happy in such a way that he is no longer a guardian at all, and is not satisfied with a life that is moderate, stable, and (we claim) best, but is seized by a foolish, adolescent belief about happiness, which incites him to use his power to take everything in the city for himself—he will come to realize the true wisdom of Hesiod's saying that, in a sense, "the half is worth more than the whole."[25]

GLAUCON: If he takes my advice, he will keep to the former life.

SOCRATES: Do you agree, then, that the women should share with the men, in the way we described, in the areas of education, children, and guarding the other citizens; that whether they remain in the city or go out to war, they must guard together and hunt together, as hounds do, and share everything to the extent possible; and that by behaving in this way, they will be doing what is best, not something contrary to the natural relationship of female to male, and the one they are most naturally fitted to share in with one another?

GLAUCON: I do agree.

SOCRATES: Then doesn't it remain for us to determine whether it is also possible among human beings, as it is among other animals, for this sort of sharing to come about, and if so, how?

GLAUCON: You took the words out of my mouth.

SOCRATES: As far as war is concerned, I think it is clear how they will wage it.

GLAUCON: How?

SOCRATES: They will go to war together. What is more, they will take the children with them to the war, when they are sturdy enough, so that, like the children of other craftsmen, they can see what they will have to do in their own craft when they are grown

---

23. [Men victorious in the Olympic games were often awarded free meals for life by their cities.]

24. [419a1–421c6.]

25. [*Works and Days* 40.]

up. But in addition to observing, they should help
467a and assist in every aspect of war, and take care of
their mothers and fathers. For haven't you noticed
in the other crafts how the children of potters, for
example, assist and watch for a long time before actually putting their hands to the clay?

GLAUCON: I have, indeed.

SOCRATES: Well, should these people take more
care than the guardians in training their children by
appropriate experience and observation?

GLAUCON: Of course not. That would be completely ridiculous.

SOCRATES: Besides, every animal will fight better
b in the presence of its young.

GLAUCON: That's right. But there is a risk, Socrates, and not a small one either, that in the event of a
disaster of the sort that is likely to happen in a war,
they will lose their children's lives as well as their own,
making it impossible for the rest of the city to recover.

SOCRATES: That's true. But, in the first place, do
you think they should arrange for the avoidance of
all risk?

GLAUCON: Not at all.

SOCRATES: Well, then, if they must face some
risk, shouldn't it be one in which they will be improved by success?

GLAUCON: Clearly.

SOCRATES: But you think, do you, that it makes
little difference—and so is not worth the risk—
c whether or not men who are going to be warriors
watch warfare when they are still boys?

GLAUCON: No, it does make a difference to what
you are talking about.

SOCRATES: Starting from the assumption, then,
that we are to make the children observers of war,
we must further devise some way of keeping them
safe. Then everything will be fine, won't it?

GLAUCON: Yes.

SOCRATES: Well, in the first place, their fathers
won't be ignorant, will they, but rather as knowledgeable as people can be, about which military cam-
d paigns are dangerous and which are not?

GLAUCON: Presumably so.

SOCRATES: So, they will take the children on the
latter, but be wary of taking them on the former.

GLAUCON: That's right.

SOCRATES: And they will not put the worst people

in charge of them, I presume, but those whose experience and age qualifies them to be leaders and tutors.

GLAUCON: Yes, that would be proper.

SOCRATES: But we will say that the unexpected
happens to many people and on many occasions.

GLAUCON: Yes, indeed.

SOCRATES: So, with that in mind, my friend, we
must provide the young children with wings at the
outset, so that, if the need arises, they can fly away
and escape.

GLAUCON: What do you mean?   e

SOCRATES: We must mount them on horses when
they are still very young, and when they have been
taught to ride, they must be taken to view the fighting,
not on spirited or aggressive horses, but on the fastest
and most manageable ones. In this way, they will get
the best view of their own future job, and will be
able to make the safest escape, if the need arises, by
following their older leaders.

GLAUCON: I think you are right.

SOCRATES: What about warfare itself? How
should your soldiers behave toward one another and 468a
the enemy? Are my views correct or not?

GLAUCON: Tell me what they are.

SOCRATES: If one of them leaves his post, throws
away his shield, or does anything else of that sort out
of cowardice, shouldn't he be demoted to craftsman
or farmer?

GLAUCON: Certainly.

SOCRATES: And if anyone is captured alive by the
enemy, shouldn't he be presented to his captors as a
catch to use however they wish?

GLAUCON: Absolutely.   b

SOCRATES: But if someone distinguishes himself
and earns high honors, do you or don't you think
that in the first place, while still on campaign, he
should be crowned in turn by each of the adolescents
and children who are with the army?

GLAUCON: I do.

SOCRATES: What about shaking him by the
right hand?

GLAUCON: That too.

SOCRATES: But I do not imagine you would go
so far as this.

GLAUCON: As what?

SOCRATES: That he should kiss, and be kissed by,
each of them.

GLAUCON: By all means. And I would add to the law that while they are still on campaign, no one he wants to kiss shall be allowed to refuse, so that if
c anyone passionately loves another, whether male or female, he will try harder to win the prize for bravery.

SOCRATES: Excellent! For we have already mentioned that more opportunities for marriage will be available for a good man,[26] and that men like him will be selected more often than others for such things, so that as many children as possible may be produced from them.

GLAUCON: Yes, we did mention that.

SOCRATES: Moreover, according to Homer too, it is just to honor in such ways those young people who are good. For Homer says that when Ajax distin-
d guished himself in battle, he "was rewarded with the whole backbone,"[27] since he considered that to be an appropriate honor for a courageous young man because it honored him and built up his strength at the same time.

GLAUCON: That's absolutely right.

SOCRATES: Then we will follow Homer in this matter, at any rate. I mean that at sacrifices and all other such occasions, we too will honor good men— insofar as they have exhibited their goodness—not only with hymns and all the other things we mentioned, but also with "seats of honor, cuts of meats, and well-filled cups of wine,"[28] so that while honoring
e our good men and women, we may train them at the same time.

GLAUCON: That's an excellent idea.

SOCRATES: All right. And if any of those who died while on campaign has had a particularly distinguished death, won't we, in the first place, declare that he belongs to the golden race?

GLAUCON: Absolutely.

SOCRATES: And won't we believe with Hesiod that, whenever any of that race die, they become
469a "unsullied daimons living upon the earth, noble beings, protectors against evil, guardians of articulate mortals?"[29]

GLAUCON: We will certainly believe that.

SOCRATES: Won't we ask the god,[30] then, to tell us how and with what distinction these daimons, these godlike people, should be buried, and perform their burial in whatever way he prescribes?

GLAUCON: Of course.

SOCRATES: And for the remainder of time, won't we regard their graves as those of daimons, and take care of them and worship at them? And won't we follow these same rites whenever anyone who has b been judged outstandingly good throughout his life dies of old age, or in some other way?

GLAUCON: It would be just to do so, at any rate.

SOCRATES: Now, what about enemies? How will our soldiers behave toward them?

GLAUCON: In what respect?

SOCRATES: First, as regards enslavement, do you think it is just for Greek cities to enslave other Greeks, or should they try as hard as possible not even to allow other cities to do so, and make a habit of sparing the Greek race as a precaution against being enslaved by barbarians? c

GLAUCON: Sparing them is by far the best course.

SOCRATES: So, they should not possess any Greek slaves themselves, and should advise the other Greeks to do the same?

GLAUCON: By all means. In that way, at any rate, they would be more likely to turn against the barbarians and keep their hands off one another.

SOCRATES: What about despoiling the dead? Is it a good thing to strip the dead of anything besides their armor after a victory? Doesn't it give cowards a pretext for not facing the enemy, since when they d are greedily bending over corpses, they will be performing an important duty? And haven't many armies been lost because of such plundering?

GLAUCON: Yes, indeed.

SOCRATES: Don't you think it is illiberal and money-loving to strip a corpse? And isn't it small-minded and womanish to regard a dead body as your enemy, when the enemy himself has flitted away leaving behind only the instrument with which he fought? Do you think that people who do this are any different from dogs who get angry with the stones

---

26. [460b1–5.]

27. [*Iliad* 7.321.]

28. [*Iliad* 8.162.]

29. [*Works and Days* 122.]

30. [Apollo.]

e thrown at them but leave the person throwing them alone?

GLAUCON: No different at all.

SOCRATES: So they should not strip corpses, should they, or refuse the enemy permission to pick up their dead?

GLAUCON: No, by Zeus, they certainly should not.

SOCRATES: Moreover, we surely won't take weapons to the temples as offerings, and if we care anything about the goodwill of other Greeks, we especially 470a won't do this with Greek weapons. On the contrary, we would even be afraid of polluting the temples if we brought them such things from our own race, unless, of course, the god ordains otherwise.

GLAUCON: That's absolutely right.

SOCRATES: What about ravaging Greek land and burning Greek houses? How will your soldiers behave toward their enemies?

GLAUCON: I would like to hear what *you* believe about that.

SOCRATES: Well, I believe they should do neither of these things, but destroy only the year's harvest. *b* Do you want me to tell you why?

GLAUCON: Of course.

SOCRATES: It seems to me that just as we have the two names "war" and "faction," so there are also two things, and the names apply to differences between the two. The two I mean are, on the one hand, what is one's own and kin, and, on the other, what is foreign and strange. "Faction" applies to hostility toward one's own, "war" to hostility toward strangers.

GLAUCON: Yes, there is nothing wrong with that claim.

SOCRATES: Consider, then, whether this too is *c* correct. I say that the Greek race, in relation to itself, is its own and kin, but, in relation to barbarians, is strange and foreign.

GLAUCON: That's right.

SOCRATES: When Greeks fight with barbarians, then, or barbarians with Greeks, we will say that that is warfare, that they are natural enemies, and that such hostilities should be called war. But when Greeks engage in such things with Greeks, we will say they are natural friends, that Greece is sick and divided into factions in such a situation, and that *d* such hostilities should be called faction.

GLAUCON: I, for one, agree to think that way.

SOCRATES: Now, notice that whenever something of the sort that is currently called faction occurs and a city is divided, if each side devastates the land and burns the houses of the other, the faction is thought abominable and neither party is thought to love the city—otherwise they would never have dared to ravage their own nurse and mother. But it is thought reasonable for the ones who have proved stronger to carry off the weaker ones' crops, and to have the attitude of mind of people who will one day be recon- *e* ciled and won't always be at war.

GLAUCON: That attitude of mind is far more civilized than the other.

SOCRATES: What about the city you are founding? Won't it be Greek?

GLAUCON: It will have to be.

SOCRATES: So won't its citizens be good and civilized people?

GLAUCON: Indeed, they will.

SOCRATES: Then won't they be lovers of Greeks? Won't they consider Greece as their own and share the same religious festivals as other Greeks?

GLAUCON: Yes, indeed.

SOCRATES: Then won't they regard their conflicts with Greeks—their own people—as faction, and not 471a even use the name "war"?

GLAUCON: No, they won't use it.

SOCRATES: And so, they will quarrel with the aim of being reconciled, won't they?

GLAUCON: Of course.

SOCRATES: They will discipline their foes in a friendly spirit, then, and not punish them with enslavement and destruction, since they are discipliners, not enemies.

GLAUCON: That's right.

SOCRATES: As Greeks, then, they won't devastate Greece or burn its houses, nor will they agree that *all* the inhabitants in any city—men, women, and children—are their enemies, but only those few responsible for the conflict. For all these reasons, they won't be willing to devastate their country, since the *b* majority of the inhabitants are their friends, nor destroy the houses, and they will pursue the conflict only to the point at which those responsible are forced to pay the penalty by the innocent ones who are suffering painfully.

GLAUCON: I agree that this is how our citizens should treat their enemies, but they should treat barbarians the way Greeks currently treat each other.

SOCRATES: Then shall we also establish this law for the guardians, that they should neither ravage
c Greek land nor burn Greek houses?

GLAUCON: Yes, let's establish it. And let's assume that this law and its predecessors are right. But, Socrates, I think that if you are allowed to go on talking about this sort of thing, you will never remember the topic you set aside in order to say all this—namely, whether it is possible for this constitution to come into existence, and how it could ever do so. I agree that *if* it came into existence, everything would be lovely for the city that had it. I will even add some advantages that you have left out: they would fight excellently against their enemies because they would
d be least likely to desert each other. After all, they recognize each other as brothers, fathers, and sons, and call each other by those names. And if the women, too, joined in their campaigns, either stationed in the same ranks or in the rear, either to strike terror in the enemy or to provide support should the need ever arise, I know that this would make them quite unbeatable. And I also see all the good things they would have at home that you have omitted. Take
e it for granted that I agree that all these benefits, as well as innumerable others, would result, *if* this constitution came into existence, and say no more about it. Instead, let's now try to convince ourselves of just this: that it is possible and how it is possible, and let's leave the rest aside.

SOCRATES: All of a sudden, you have practically
472a assaulted my argument and lost all sympathy for my holding back. Perhaps you do not realize that just as I have barely escaped from the first two waves of objections, you are now bringing the biggest and most difficult of the three down upon me.[31] When you see and hear it, you will have complete sympathy and recognize that I had good reason after all for hesitating and for being afraid to state and try to examine so paradoxical an argument.

GLAUCON: The more you talk like that, the less we will let you get away without explaining how this constitution could come into existence. So explain
b it, and do not delay any further.

SOCRATES: The first thing to recall, then, is that it was our inquiry into the nature of justice and injustice that brought us to this point.

GLAUCON: True. But what of it?

SOCRATES: Oh, nothing. However, if we discover the nature of justice, should we also expect the just man not to differ from justice itself in any way, but, on the contrary, to have entirely the same nature it does? Or will we be satisfied if he approximates as closely as possible to it and partakes in it far more c than anyone else?

GLAUCON: Yes, we will be satisfied with that.

SOCRATES: So, it was in order to have a model that we were inquiring into the nature of justice itself and of the completely just man, supposing he could exist, and what he would be like if he did; and similarly with injustice and the most unjust man. We thought that by seeing how they seemed to us to stand with regard to happiness and its opposite, we would also be compelled to agree about ourselves as well: that the one who was most like them would have a fate most like theirs. But d we were not doing this in order to demonstrate that it is possible for these men to exist.

GLAUCON: That's true.

SOCRATES: Do you think, then, that someone would be any less good a painter if he painted a model of what the most beautiful human being would be like, and rendered everything in the picture perfectly well, but could not demonstrate that such a man could actually exist?

GLAUCON: No, by Zeus, I do not.

SOCRATES: What about our own case, then? Weren't we trying, as we put it, to produce a model in our discussion of a good city? e

GLAUCON: Certainly.

SOCRATES: So, do you think that our discussion will be any less satisfactory if we cannot demonstrate that it is possible to found a city that is the same as the one we described in speech?

GLAUCON: Not at all.

SOCRATES: Then that is the truth of the matter. But if, in order to please you, we must do our best to demonstrate how, and under what condition, this would be most possible, you must again grant me the same points for the purposes of that demonstration.

---

31. [The third wave was proverbially the greatest.]

GLAUCON: Which ones?

SOCRATES: Is it possible for anything to be carried
473a out exactly as described in speech, or is it natural for
practice to have less of a grasp of truth than speech
does, even if some people do not think so? Do you
agree with this or not?

GLAUCON: I do.

SOCRATES: Then do not compel me to demonstrate it as coming about in practice exactly as we
have described it in speech. Rather, if we are able to
discover how a city that most closely approximates to
what we have described could be founded, you must
admit that we have discovered how all you have pre-
b scribed could come about. Or wouldn't you be satisfied with that? *I* certainly would.

GLAUCON: Me, too.

SOCRATES: Then next, it seems, we should try to
discover and show what is badly done in cities nowadays that prevents them from being managed our way,
and what the smallest change would be that would
enable a city to arrive at our sort of constitution—
preferably one change; otherwise, two; otherwise, the
fewest in number and the least extensive in effect.

c GLAUCON: Absolutely.

SOCRATES: Well, there is one change we could
point to that I think would accomplish this. It certainly
is not small or easy, but it *is* possible.

GLAUCON: What is it?

SOCRATES: I am now about to confront what we
likened to the greatest wave. Yet, it must be stated,
even if it is going to drown me in a wave of outright
ridicule and contempt, as it were. So listen to what
I am about to say.

GLAUCON: Say it.

SOCRATES: Until philosophers rule as kings in
their cities, or those who are nowadays called kings
and leading men become genuine and adequate
d philosophers so that political power and philosophy
become thoroughly blended together, while the numerous natures that now pursue either one exclusively
are forcibly prevented from doing so, cities will have
no rest from evils, my dear Glaucon, nor, I think,
will the human race. And until that happens, the
same constitution we have now described in our dis-
e cussion will never be born to the extent that it can,
or see the light of the sun. It is this claim that has
made me hesitate to speak for so long. I saw how very

unbelievable it would sound, since it is difficult to
accept that there can be no happiness, either public
or private, in any other way.

GLAUCON: Socrates, what a speech, what an argument you have let burst with! But now that you have
uttered it, you must expect that a great many people—
and not undistinguished ones either—will immediately throw off their cloaks and, stripped for action, 474a
snatch any available weapon and make a headlong
rush at you, determined to do terrible things to you.
So, if you do not defend yourself by argument and
escape, you really will pay the penalty of general
derision.

SOCRATES: But aren't *you* the one who is responsible for this happening to me?

GLAUCON: And I was right to do it. Still, I won't
desert you. On the contrary, I will defend you in any
way I can. And what I can do is provide good will and
encouragement, and maybe give you more careful
answers to your questions than someone else. So, with
the promise of this sort of assistance, try to demon- b
strate to the unbelievers that things are as you claim.

SOCRATES: I will have to, especially when you
agree to be so great an ally! If we are going to escape
from the people you mention, I think we need to
define for them who the philosophers are that we
dare to say should rule; so that once that is clear, one
can defend oneself by showing that some people are
fitted by nature to engage in philosophy *and* to take c
the lead in a city, while there are others who should
not engage in it, but should follow a leader.

GLAUCON: This would be a good time to define them.

SOCRATES: Come on, then, follow me on the path
I am about to take, to see if it somehow leads to an
adequate explanation.

GLAUCON: Lead on.

SOCRATES: Do I have to remind you, or do you
recall, that when we say someone loves something,
if the description is correct, it must be clear not just
that he loves some part of it but not another; but, on
the contrary, that he cherishes the whole of it?

GLAUCON: You will have to remind me, it seems.
I do not recall the point at all. d

SOCRATES: I did not expect you to give that response, Glaucon. A passionate man should not forget
that *all* boys in the bloom of youth somehow manage

to sting and arouse a passionate lover of boys, and seem to merit his attention and passionate devotion. Isn't that the way you people behave to beautiful boys? One, because he is snub-nosed, you will praise as "cute"; another who is hook-nosed you will say is "regal"; while the one in the middle you say is "well proportioned." Dark ones look "manly," and pale ones are "children of the gods." As for the "honey-colored," do you think that this very term is anything but the euphemistic coinage of a lover who found it easy to tolerate a sallow complexion, provided it was accompanied by the bloom of youth? In a word, you people find any excuse, and use any expression, to avoid rejecting anyone whose flower is in full bloom.

GLAUCON: If you insist on taking *me* as your example of what passionate men do, I will go along with you . . . for the sake of argument!

SOCRATES: What about lovers of wine? Don't you observe them behaving in just the same way? Don't they find any excuse to indulge their passionate devotion to wine of any sort?

GLAUCON: They do, indeed.

SOCRATES: And you also observe, I imagine, that if honor-lovers cannot become generals, they serve as lieutenants,[32] and if they cannot be honored by important people and dignitaries, they are satisfied with being honored by insignificant and inferior ones, since it is honor as a whole of which they are desirers.

GLAUCON: Exactly.

SOCRATES: Then do you affirm this or not? When we say that someone has an appetite for something, are we to say that he has an appetite for everything of that kind, or for one part of it but not another?

GLAUCON: Everything.

SOCRATES: Then in the case of the philosopher, too, won't we say that he has an appetite for *wisdom*— not for one part and not another, but for all of it?

GLAUCON: True.

SOCRATES: So, if someone is choosy about what he learns, especially if he is young and does not have a rational grasp of what is useful and what is not, we won't say that he is a lover of learning or a philosopher—any more than we would say that someone who is choosy

about his food is famished, or has an appetite for food, or is a lover of food rather than a picky eater.

GLAUCON: And we would be right not to say it.

SOCRATES: But someone who is ready and willing to taste every kind of learning, who turns gladly to learning and is insatiable for it, *he* is the one we would be justified in calling a philosopher. Isn't that so?

GLAUCON: In that case, many strange people will be philosophers! I mean, all the lovers of seeing are what they are, I imagine, because they take pleasure in learning things. And the lovers of listening are very strange people to include as philosophers: they would never willingly attend a serious discussion or spend their time that way; yet, just as if their ears were under contract to listen to every chorus, they run around to all the Dionysiac festivals, whether in cities or villages, and never miss one. Are we to say that these people— and others who are students of similar things or of petty crafts—are philosophers?

SOCRATES: Not at all, but they are *like* philosophers.

GLAUCON: Who do you think, then, are the true ones?

SOCRATES: The lovers of seeing the truth.

GLAUCON: That, too, is no doubt correct, but what exactly do you mean by it?

SOCRATES: It would not be easy to explain to someone else. But you, I imagine, will agree to the following.

GLAUCON: What?

SOCRATES: That since beautiful is the opposite of ugly, they are two things.

GLAUCON: Of course.

SOCRATES: And since they are two things, each of them is also one?

GLAUCON: That's true too.

SOCRATES: And the same argument applies, then, to just and unjust, good and bad, and all the forms: each of them is itself one thing, but because they appear all over the place in partnership with actions and bodies, and with one another, each of them appears to be many things.

GLAUCON: That's right.

SOCRATES: Well, then, that is the basis of the distinction I draw: on one side are the lovers of seeing, the lovers of crafts, and the practical people you

---

32. [*Trittarchousi*: "command the soldiers in a trittys." A trittys was one third of one of the ten tribes of which Athens consisted.]

mentioned a moment ago; on the other, those we are
b arguing about, the only ones it is correct to call
philosophers.

GLAUCON: How do you mean?

SOCRATES: The lovers of listening and seeing are
passionately devoted to beautiful sounds, colors,
shapes, and everything fashioned out of such things.[33]
But their thought is unable to see the nature of the
beautiful itself or to be passionately devoted to it.

GLAUCON: That's certainly true.

SOCRATES: On the other hand, won't those who
are able to approach the beautiful itself, and see it
by itself, be rare?

c GLAUCON: Very.

SOCRATES: What about someone who believes in
beautiful things but does not believe in the beautiful
itself, and would not be able to follow anyone who
tried to lead him to the knowledge of it? Do you
think he is living in a dream, or is he awake? Just
consider. Isn't it dreaming to think—whether asleep
or awake—that a likeness is not a likeness, but rather
the thing itself that it is like?

GLAUCON: I certainly think that someone who
does that is dreaming.

SOCRATES: But what about someone who, to take
the opposite case, does believe in the beautiful itself,
is able to observe both it and the things that participate
d in it, and does not think that the participants are it,
or that it is the participants—do you think he is living
in a dream or is awake?

GLAUCON: He is very much awake.

SOCRATES: So, because this person knows these
things, we would be right to describe his thought as
knowledge; but the other's we would be right to describe as belief, because he believes what he does?

GLAUCON: Certainly.

SOCRATES: What if the person we describe as believing but not knowing is angry with us and disputes
the truth of what we say? Will we have any way of
e soothing and gently persuading him, while disguising
the fact that he is not in a healthy state of mind?

GLAUCON: We certainly need one, at any rate.

SOCRATES: Come on, then, consider what we will
say to him. Or—once we have told him that nobody

envies him any knowledge he may have—that, on
the contrary, we would be delighted to discover that
he knows something—do you want us to question
him as follows? "Tell us this: does someone who
knows know something or nothing?" You answer
for him.

GLAUCON: I will answer that he knows something.

SOCRATES: Something that is or something that
is not?

GLAUCON: That is. How could something that is
not be known?   477a

SOCRATES: We are adequately assured of this,
then, and would remain so, no matter how many ways
we examined it: what completely is, is completely an
object of knowledge; and what in no way is, is not
an object of knowledge at all?

GLAUCON: Most adequately.

SOCRATES: Good. In that case, then, if anything
is such as to be and also not to be, wouldn't it lie in
between what purely is and what in no way is?

GLAUCON: Yes, in between them.

SOCRATES: Then, since knowledge deals with
what is, ignorance must deal with what is not, while
we must look in between knowledge and ignorance
for what deals with what lies in between, if there *is*
anything of that sort.   b

GLAUCON: Yes.

SOCRATES: So, then, do we think there is such a
thing as belief?

GLAUCON: Of course.

SOCRATES: Is it a different power from knowledge,
or the same?

GLAUCON: A different one.

SOCRATES: So, belief has been assigned to deal
with one thing, then, and knowledge with another,
depending on what power each has.

GLAUCON: Right.

SOCRATES: Now, doesn't knowledge naturally
deal with what is, to know how what is is? But first
I think we had better go through the following.

GLAUCON: What?

SOCRATES: We think powers are a type of thing   c
that enables us—or anything else that has an ability—
to do whatever we are able to do. Sight and hearing
are examples of what I mean by powers, if you understand the kind of thing I am trying to describe.

GLAUCON: Yes, I do.

---

33. [A poem or play is fashioned out of sounds, a painting out of colors and shapes.]

SOCRATES: Listen, then, to what I think about them. A power has no color for me to see, nor a shape, nor any feature of the sort that many other things have, and that I can consider in order to distinguish them for myself as different from one another. In the case of a power, I can consider only what it

d deals with and what it does, and it is on that basis that I come to call each the power it is: those assigned to deal with the same things and do the same, I call the same; those that deal with different things and do different things, I call different. What about you? What do you do?

GLAUCON: The same.

SOCRATES: Going back, then, to where we left off, my very good fellow: do you think knowledge is itself a power? Or to what type would you assign it?

GLAUCON: To that one. It is the most effective power of all.

SOCRATES: What about belief? Shall we include

e it as a power or assign it to a different kind?

GLAUCON: Not at all. Belief is nothing other than the power that enables us to believe.

SOCRATES: But a moment ago you agreed that knowledge and belief are not the same.

GLAUCON: How could anyone with any sense think a fallible thing is the same as an infallible one?

SOCRATES: Fine. Then clearly we agree that be-

478a lief is different from knowledge.

GLAUCON: Yes, it is different.

SOCRATES: Each of them, then, since it has a different power, deals by nature with something different?

GLAUCON: Necessarily.

SOCRATES: Surely knowledge deals with what is, to know what is as it is?

GLAUCON: Yes.

SOCRATES: Whereas belief, we say, believes?

GLAUCON: Yes.

SOCRATES: The very same thing that knowledge knows? Can the object of knowledge and the object of belief be the same? Or is that impossible?

GLAUCON: It is impossible, given what we have agreed. If different powers by nature deal with different things, and both opinion and knowledge are powers but, as we claim, different ones, it follows from

b these that the object of knowledge and the object of belief cannot be the same.

SOCRATES: Then if what is is the object of knowledge, mustn't the object of belief be something other than what is?

GLAUCON: Yes, it must be something different.

SOCRATES: Does belief, then, believe what is not? Or is it impossible even to believe what is not? Consider this: doesn't a believer take his belief to deal with something? Or is it possible to believe, yet to believe nothing?

GLAUCON: No, it is impossible.

SOCRATES: In fact, there is some single thing that a believer believes?

GLAUCON: Yes.

SOCRATES: But surely what is not is most correctly characterized not as a single thing, but as nothing?

GLAUCON: Of course.

SOCRATES: But we had to assign ignorance to what is not and knowledge to what is?

GLAUCON: Correct.

SOCRATES: So belief neither believes what is nor what is not?

GLAUCON: No, it does not.

SOCRATES: Then belief cannot be either ignorance or knowledge?

GLAUCON: Apparently not.

SOCRATES: Well, then, does it lie beyond these two, surpassing knowledge in clarity or ignorance in opacity?

GLAUCON: No, it does neither.

SOCRATES: Then does belief seem to you to be more opaque than knowledge but clearer than ignorance?

GLAUCON: Very much so.

SOCRATES: It lies within the boundaries determined by them?

GLAUCON: Yes.

SOCRATES: So belief will lie in between the two?

GLAUCON: Absolutely.

SOCRATES: Now, didn't we say earlier that if something turned out both to be and not to be at the same time, it would lie in between what purely is and what in every way is not, and that neither knowledge nor ignorance would deal with it; but whatever it was again that turned out to lie in between ignorance and knowledge would?

GLAUCON: Correct.

SOCRATES: And now, what we are calling belief has turned out to lie in between them?

GLAUCON: It has.

SOCRATES: Apparently, then, it remains for us to
e find what partakes in both being and not being, and cannot correctly be called purely one or the other, so that if we find it, we can justifiably call it the object of belief, thereby assigning extremes to extremes and in-betweens to in-betweens. Isn't that so?

GLAUCON: It is.

SOCRATES: Now that all that has been established, I want him to tell me this—the excellent fellow who believes that there is no beautiful itself, no form of
479a beauty itself that remains always the same in all respects, but who does believe that there are many beautiful things—I mean, that lover of seeing who cannot bear to hear anyone say that the beautiful is one thing, or the just, or any of the rest—I want him to answer this question: "My very good fellow," we will say, "of all the many beautiful things, is there one that won't also seem ugly? Or any just one that won't seem unjust? Or any pious one that won't seem impious?"

GLAUCON: There is not. On the contrary, it is inevitable that they would somehow seem both beau-
b tiful and ugly; and the same with the other things you asked about.

SOCRATES: What about the many things that are doubles? Do they seem to be any the less halves than doubles?

GLAUCON: No.

SOCRATES: And again, will things that we say are big, small, light, or heavy be any more what we say they are than they will be the opposite?

GLAUCON: No, each of them is always both.

SOCRATES: Then is each of the many things any more what one says it is than it is not what one says it is?

GLAUCON: No, they are like those puzzles one hears at parties, or the children's riddle about the
c eunuch who threw something at a bat—the one about what he threw at it and what it was in.[34] For these

things, too, are ambiguous, and one cannot understand them as fixedly being or fixedly not being, or as both, or as neither.

SOCRATES: Do you know what to do with them, then, or anywhere better to put them than in between being and not being? Surely they cannot be more opaque than what is not, by not-being more than it; nor clearer than what is, by *being* more than it.   d

GLAUCON: That's absolutely true.

SOCRATES: So, we have now discovered, it seems, that the majority of people's many conventional views about beauty and the rest are somehow rolling around between what is not and what purely is.

GLAUCON: We have.

SOCRATES: And we agreed earlier that if anything turned out to be of that sort, it would have to be called an object of belief, not an object of knowledge—a wandering, in-between object grasped by the in-between power.

GLAUCON: We did.

SOCRATES: As for those, then, who look at many beautiful things but do not see the beautiful itself, e and are incapable of following another who would lead them to it; or many just things but not the just itself, and similarly with all the rest—these people, we will say, have beliefs about all these things, but have no knowledge of what their beliefs are about.

GLAUCON: That is what we would have to say.

SOCRATES: On the other hand, what about those who in each case look at the things themselves that are always the same in every respect? Won't we say that they have knowledge, not mere belief?

GLAUCON: Once again, we would have to.

SOCRATES: Shall we say, then, that these people are passionately devoted to and love the things with which knowledge deals, as the others are devoted to and love the things with which belief deals? We have 480a not forgotten, have we, that the latter love and look at beautiful sounds, colors, and things of that sort,

---

34. [The riddle seems to have been this: a man who is not a man saw and did not see a bird that was not a bird in a tree (*xulon*) that was not a tree; he hit (*ballein*) and did not hit it with a stone that was not a stone. The

answer is that a eunuch with bad eyesight saw a bat on a rafter, threw a pumice stone at it, and missed. For "he saw a bird" is ambiguous between "he saw what was actually a bird" and "he saw what he took to be a bird," *xulon* means both "tree" and "rafter" or "roof tree," and *ballein* means both "to throw" and "to hit." The rest is obvious.]

but cannot even bear the idea that the beautiful itself is a thing that is?

GLAUCON: No, we have not.

SOCRATES: Will we be striking a false note,[35] then, if we call such people "philodoxers" (lovers of belief) rather than "philosophers" (lovers of wisdom or knowledge)? Will they be very angry with us if we call them that?

GLAUCON: Not if they take my advice. It is not in accord with divine law to be angry with the truth.

SOCRATES: So, those who in each case are passionately devoted to the thing itself are the ones we must call, not "philodoxers," but "philosophers"?

GLAUCON: Absolutely.

BOOK VI

SOCRATES' NARRATION CONTINUES.

SOCRATES: Who the philosophers are, then, Glaucon, and who they aren't has, through a somewhat lengthy argument and with much effort, somehow been made clear.

GLAUCON: That's probably because it could not easily have been done through a shorter one.

SOCRATES: I suppose not. Yet I, at least, think that the matter would have been made even clearer if we had had only that topic to discuss, and not the many others that remain for us to explore if we are to discover the difference between the just life and the unjust one.

GLAUCON: What comes after this one, then?

SOCRATES: What else but the one that comes next? Since the philosophers are the ones who are able to grasp what is always the same in all respects, while those who cannot—those who wander among the many things that vary in every sort of way—are not philosophers, which of the two should be the leaders of a city?

GLAUCON: What would be a reasonable answer for us to give?

SOCRATES: Whichever of them seems capable of guarding a city's laws and practices should be established as guardians.

GLAUCON: That's right.

SOCRATES: So, is the answer to the following question clear: should a guardian who is going to keep watch over something be blind or keen-sighted?

GLAUCON: Of course it is.

SOCRATES: Well, do you think there is any difference, then, between the blind and those who are really deprived of the knowledge of each thing that is, and have no clear model of it in their souls—those who cannot look away, like painters, to what is most true, and cannot, by making constant reference to it and by studying it as exactly as possible, establish here on earth conventional views about beautiful, just, or good things when they need to be established, or guard and preserve those that have been established?

GLAUCON: No, by Zeus, there is not much difference between them.

SOCRATES: Shall we appoint these blind people as our guardians, then, or those who know each thing that is, have no less experience than the others, and are not inferior to them in any other part of virtue?

GLAUCON: It would be absurd to choose anyone but philosophers, if indeed they are not inferior in these other things. For the very area in which they are superior is just about the most important one.

SOCRATES: Shouldn't we explain, then, how the same men can have both sets of qualities?

GLAUCON: Certainly.

SOCRATES: Then, as we were saying at the beginning of this discussion, it is first necessary to understand the nature of philosophers. And I think that if we can agree sufficiently about that, we will also agree that the same people *can* have both qualities, and that they alone should be leaders in cities.

GLAUCON: How so?

SOCRATES: Let's agree that philosophic natures always love the sort of learning that makes clear to them some feature of the being that always is and does not wander around between coming-to-be and decaying.

GLAUCON: Yes, let's.

SOCRATES: And further, let's agree that they love all of it and are not willing to give up any part, whether large or small, significant or insignificant, just like the honor-lovers and passionate men we described before.

---

35. [See 451b3.]

GLAUCON: That's right.

SOCRATES: Consider next whether there is a further feature they must have in their nature if they are going to be the way we described.

GLAUCON: What?

SOCRATES: Truthfulness; that is to say they must never willingly tolerate falsehood in any form. On the contrary, they must hate it and have a natural affection for the truth.

GLAUCON: They probably should have that feature.

SOCRATES: But it is not only *probable*, my friend; it is entirely necessary for a naturally passionate man to love everything akin to or related to the boys he loves.

GLAUCON: That's right.

SOCRATES: Well, could you find anything that is more intimately related to wisdom than truth?

GLAUCON: Of course not.

SOCRATES: Then is it possible for the same nature to be a philosopher (lover of wisdom) and a lover of falsehood?

GLAUCON: Certainly not.

SOCRATES: So, right from childhood, a genuine lover of learning must strive above all for truth of every kind.

GLAUCON: Absolutely.

SOCRATES: But in addition, when someone's appetites are strongly inclined in one direction, we surely know that they become more weakly inclined in the others, just like a stream that has been partly diverted into another channel.

GLAUCON: Of course.

SOCRATES: Then when a person's desires flow toward learning and everything of that sort, they will be concerned, I imagine, with the pleasures that the soul experiences just by itself, and will be indifferent to those that come through the body—if indeed the person is not a counterfeit, but rather a true, philosopher.

GLAUCON: That's entirely inevitable.

SOCRATES: A person like that will be temperate, then, and in no way a lover of money. After all, money and the big expenditures that go along with it are sought for the sake of things that other people may take seriously, but that he does not.

GLAUCON: That's right.

SOCRATES: And of course, there is also this to consider when you are going to judge whether a nature is philosophic or not.

GLAUCON: What?

SOCRATES: You should not overlook its sharing in illiberality; for surely petty-mindedness is altogether incompatible with that quality in a soul that is always reaching out to grasp all things as a whole, whether divine or human.

GLAUCON: That's absolutely true.

SOCRATES: And do you imagine that a thinker who is high-minded enough to look at all time and all being will consider human life to be a very important thing?

GLAUCON: He couldn't possibly.

SOCRATES: Then he won't consider death to be a terrible thing either, will he?

GLAUCON: Not in the least.

SOCRATES: Then a cowardly and illiberal nature could not partake, apparently, in true philosophy.

GLAUCON: Not in my opinion.

SOCRATES: Well, then, is there any way that an orderly person, who is not money-loving, illiberal, a lying imposter, or a coward, could come to drive a hard bargain or be unjust?

GLAUCON: There is not.

SOCRATES: Moreover, when you are considering whether someone has a philosophic soul or not, you will consider whether he is just and gentle, right from the time he is young, or unsociable and savage.

GLAUCON: Of course.

SOCRATES: And you won't ignore this either, I imagine.

GLAUCON: What?

SOCRATES: Whether he is a slow learner or a fast one. Or do you expect someone to love something sufficiently well when it pains him to do it and a lot of effort brings only a small return?

GLAUCON: No, it could not happen.

SOCRATES: What if he could retain nothing of what he learned, because he was completely forgetful? Could he fail to be empty of knowledge?

GLAUCON: Of course not.

SOCRATES: Then if he is laboring in vain, don't you think that in the end he is bound to hate himself and what he is doing?

GLAUCON: Of course.

SOCRATES: So let's never include a person with a forgetful soul among those who are sufficiently
d philosophical; the one we look for should be good at remembering.

GLAUCON: Absolutely.

SOCRATES: Moreover, we would deny that an unmusical and graceless nature is drawn to anything besides what is disproportionate.

GLAUCON: Of course.

SOCRATES: And do you think that truth is akin to what is disproportionate or to what is proportionate?

GLAUCON: To what is proportionate.

SOCRATES: Then, in addition to those other things, let's look for a mind that has a natural sense of proportion and grace, one whose innate disposition makes it easy to lead to the form of each thing which is.

GLAUCON: Indeed.

SOCRATES: Well, then, do you think the proper-
e ties we have gone through aren't interconnected, or that any of them is in any way unnecessary to a soul that is going to have a sufficiently complete grasp of what is?

487a GLAUCON: No, they are all absolutely necessary.

SOCRATES: Is there any criticism you can find, then, of a pursuit that a person cannot practice adequately unless he is naturally good at remembering, quick to learn, high-minded, graceful, and a friend and relative of truth, justice, courage, and temperance?

GLAUCON: Not even Momus could criticize a pursuit like that.

SOCRATES: Well, then, when people of this sort are in perfect condition because of their education and their stage of life, wouldn't you entrust the city to them alone?

And Adeimantus replied:

No one, Socrates, would be able to contradict these
b claims of yours. But all the same, here is pretty much the experience people have on any occasion on which they hear the sorts of things you are now saying: they think that because they are inexperienced in asking and answering questions, they are led astray a little bit by the argument at every question, and that when these little bits are added together at the end of the

discussion, a big false step appears that is the opposite of what they said at the outset. Like the unskilled, who are trapped by the clever checkers players in the end and cannot make a move, they too are trapped in the end, and have nothing to say in this different c kind of checkers, which is played not with pieces, but with words. Yet they are not a bit more inclined to think that what you claim is true. I say this in relation to the present case. You see, someone might well say now that he is unable to find the words to oppose you as you ask each of your questions. Yet, when it comes to facts rather than words, he sees that of all those who take up philosophy—not those who merely dabble in it while still young in order to complete their upbringing, and then drop it, but those who continue in it for a longer time—the majority d become cranks, not to say completely bad, while the ones who seem best are rendered useless to the city because of the pursuit you recommend.

When I had heard him out, I said:

Do you think that what these people say is false?

ADEIMANTUS: I do not know. But I would be glad to hear what you think.

SOCRATES: You would hear that they seem to me to be telling the truth.

ADEIMANTUS: How, then, can it be right to say that there will be no end to evils in our cities until e philosophers—people we agree to be useless to cities—rule in them?

SOCRATES: The question you ask needs to be answered by means of an image.[1]

ADEIMANTUS: And you, of course, are not used to speaking in images!

SOCRATES: So! After landing me with a claim that is so difficult to establish, are you mocking me, too? Anyway, listen to my image, and you will appreciate 488a all the more how I have to strain to make up images. What the best philosophers experience in relation to cities is so difficult to bear that there is no other single experience like it. On the contrary, one must construct one's image and one's defense of these philosophers from *many* sources, just as painters paint

---

1. [*Eikos*: also, likeness.]

goat-stags by combining the features of different things.

Imagine, then, that the following sort of thing happens either on one ship or on many. The shipowner is taller and stronger than everyone else on board. But he is hard of hearing, he is a bit shortsighted,

b and his knowledge of seafaring is correspondingly deficient. The sailors are quarreling with one another about captaincy. Each of them thinks that he should captain the ship, even though he has not yet learned the craft and cannot name his teacher or a time when he was learning it. Indeed, they go further and claim that it cannot be taught at all, and are even ready to cut to pieces anyone who says it can. They are always crowding around the shipowner himself, pleading

c with him, and doing everything possible to get him to turn the rudder over to them. And sometimes, if they fail to persuade him and others succeed, they execute those others or throw them overboard. Then, having disabled their noble shipowner with mandragora[2] or drink or in some other way, they rule the ship, use up its cargo drinking and feasting, and make the sort of voyage you would expect of such people. In addition, they praise anyone who is clever at persuading or forcing the shipowner to let them rule,

d calling him a "sailor," a "skilled captain," and "an expert about ships" while dismissing anyone else as a good-for-nothing. They do not understand that a true captain must pay attention to the seasons of the year, the sky, the stars, the winds, and all that pertains to his craft if he is really going to be expert at ruling a ship. As for *how* he is going to become captain of

e the ship, whether people want him to or not, they do not think it possible to acquire the craft or practice of doing this at the same time as the craft of captaincy. When that is what is happening onboard ships, don't you think that a true captain would be sure to be called a "stargazer," a "useless babbler," and a "good-

489a for-nothing" by those who sail in ships so governed?

ADEIMANTUS: I certainly do.

SOCRATES: I do not think you need to examine the image to see the resemblance to cities and how they're disposed toward true philosophers, but you already understand what I mean.

ADEIMANTUS: Indeed, I do.

SOCRATES: First teach this image, then, to the person who is surprised that philosophers are not honored in cities, and try to persuade him that it would be far more surprising if they were honored. *b*

ADEIMANTUS: I will.

SOCRATES: Furthermore, try to persuade him that you are speaking the truth when you say that the best among the philosophers are useless to the masses. But tell him to blame their uselessness on those who do not make use of them, not on those good philosophers. You see, it is not natural for the captain to beg the sailors to be ruled by him, nor for the wise to knock at the doors of the rich. The man who came up with that bit of sophistry was lying.[3] What is truly natural is for the sick person, rich or poor, to go to doctors' doors, and for anyone who needs to be ruled *c* to go to the doors of the one who can rule him. It is not for the ruler—if he is truly any use—to beg the subjects to accept his rule. Tell him he will make no mistake if he likens our present political rulers to the sailors we mentioned a moment ago, and those who are called useless stargazers by them to the true ship's captains.

ADEIMANTUS: That's absolutely right.

SOCRATES: For those reasons, then, and in these circumstances, it is not easy for the best pursuit to be highly honored by those whose pursuits are its very opposites. But by far the greatest and most serious slander is brought on philosophy by those who claim *d* to practice it—the ones about whom the prosecutor of philosophy declares, as you put it, that the majority of those who take it up are completely bad, while the best ones are useless. And I admitted that what you said was true, didn't I?[4]

ADEIMANTUS: Yes.

SOCRATES: Haven't we now explained why the good ones are useless?

ADEIMANTUS: We certainly have.

SOCRATES: Do you next want us to discuss why it is inevitable that the greater number are bad, and

---

2. [An intoxicant.]

3. [Aristotle, *Rhetoric* 1391a7–12, says that when Simonides was asked whether it was better to be rich or wise, he replied: "Rich—because the wise spend their time at the doors of the rich."]

4. [487d10.]

try to show, if we can, that philosophy is not responsi-
e ble for this either?

ADEIMANTUS: Certainly.

SOCRATES: Then let's begin our dialogue by re-
calling the starting point of our description of the
nature that someone must have if he is to become a
fine and good person. First of all, if you remember,
490a he was led by truth,[5] and he had to follow it wholeheartedly and unequivocally, on pain of being a lying
imposter with no share at all in true philosophy.

ADEIMANTUS: That's what we said.

SOCRATES: Well, isn't that fact alone completely
contrary to the belief currently held about him?

ADEIMANTUS: It certainly is.

SOCRATES: So, won't it be reasonable, then, for
us to plead in his defense that a real lover of learning
naturally strives for what is? He does not linger over
each of the many things that are believed to be,
b but keeps on going, without losing or lessening his
passion, until he grasps what the nature of each thing
itself is with the element in his soul that is fitted to
grasp a thing of that sort because of its kinship with
it. Once he has drawn near to it, has intercourse with
what really is, and has begotten understanding and
truth, he knows, truly lives, is nourished, and—at that
point, but not before—is relieved from his labor
pains.

ADEIMANTUS: Nothing could be more reasonable.

SOCRATES: Well, then, will a person of that sort
love falsehood or, in completely opposite fashion, will
he hate it?

c ADEIMANTUS: He will hate it.

SOCRATES: And if truth led the way, we would
never say, I imagine, that a chorus of evils could
follow it.

ADEIMANTUS: Of course not.

SOCRATES: On the contrary, it is followed by a
healthy and just character, and the temperance that
accompanies it.

ADEIMANTUS: That's right.

SOCRATES: What need is there, then, to go back to
the beginning and compel the rest of the philosophic
nature's chorus to line up all over again? You surely
remember that courage, high-mindedness, ease in

learning, and a good memory all belong to philosophers. Then you objected that anyone would be compelled to agree with what we are saying, but that if
he left the arguments aside and looked at the very d
people the argument is about, he would say that some
of those he saw were useless, while the majority of
them were thoroughly bad. Trying to discover the
reason for this slander, we have arrived now at this
question: why are the majority of them bad? And *that*
is why we have again taken up the nature of the true
philosophers and defined what it necessarily has to be.

ADEIMANTUS: That's right.   e

SOCRATES: What we now have to do is look at the
ways this nature gets corrupted; how it gets completely
destroyed in the majority of cases, while a small number escape—the very ones that are called useless, rather
than bad. After that, we must next look at those who
imitate this nature and adopt its pursuit. We must see 491a
what natures the souls have that enter into a pursuit
that is too valuable and too high for them—souls that,
by often striking false notes, give philosophy the reputation that you said it has with everyone everywhere.

ADEIMANTUS: What sorts of corruption do you
mean?

SOCRATES: I will try to explain them to you if I
can. I imagine that everyone would agree with us
about this: the sort of nature that possesses all the
qualities we prescribed just now for the person who
is going to be a complete philosopher, is seldom
found among human beings, and there will be few b
who possess it. Or don't you think so?

ADEIMANTUS: I most certainly do.

SOCRATES: Consider, then, how many great
sources of destruction there are for those few.

ADEIMANTUS: What are they?

SOCRATES: The most surprising thing of all to
hear is that each one of the things we praised in that
nature tends to corrupt the soul that has it and drag
it away from philosophy. I mean courage, temperance, and the other things we mentioned.

ADEIMANTUS: That does sound strange.

SOCRATES: Furthermore, in addition to those, all
so-called good things also corrupt it and drag it away— c
beauty, wealth, physical strength, powerful family
connections in the city, and all that goes along with
these. You understand the general pattern of things
I mean?

5. [485c3.]

ADEIMANTUS: I do, and I would be glad to acquire a more precise understanding of it.

SOCRATES: Grasp the general principle correctly and the matter will become clear to you, and what I said about it before won't seem so strange.

ADEIMANTUS: What are you telling me to grasp?

SOCRATES: In the case of every seed or growing *d* thing, whether plant or animal, we know that if it fails to get the food, climate, or location suitable for it, then the more vigorous it is, the more it is deficient in the qualities proper to it. For surely bad is more opposed to good than to not-good.

ADEIMANTUS: Of course.

SOCRATES: So, I suppose it is reasonable that the best nature comes off worse than an inferior one from unsuitable nurture.

ADEIMANTUS: It is.

SOCRATES: Well, then, Adeimantus, won't we *e* also say that if *souls* with the best natures get a bad education, they become exceptionally bad? Or do you think that great injustices and unalloyed evil originate in an inferior nature, rather than in a vigorous one that has been corrupted by its upbringing? Or that a weak nature is ever responsible for great good things or great bad ones?

ADEIMANTUS: No, you are right.

SOCRATES: Well, then, if the nature we proposed *492a* for the philosopher happens to receive the proper instruction, I imagine it will inevitably grow to attain every virtue. But if it is not sown, planted, and grown in a suitable environment, it will develop in entirely the opposite way, unless some god comes to its aid. Or do you too believe, as the masses do, that some young people are corrupted by sophists—that there are sophists, private individuals, who corrupt them to a significant extent? Isn't it, rather, the very people who say this who are the greatest sophists of all, who *b* educate most effectively and produce young and old men and women of just the sort they want?

ADEIMANTUS: When do they do that?

SOCRATES: When many of them sit together in assemblies, courts, theaters, army camps, or any other gathering of a mass of people in public and, with a loud uproar, object excessively to some of the things that are said or done, then approve excessively of others, shouting and clapping; and when, in addition to these people themselves, the rocks and the sur-

rounding space itself echo and redouble the uproar *c* of their praise or blame. In a situation like that, how do you think—as the saying goes—a young man's heart is affected?[6] How will whatever sort of private education he received hold up for him, and not get swept away by such praise and blame, and go be carried off by the flood wherever it goes, so that he will call the same things beautiful or ugly as these people, practice what they practice, and become like them?

ADEIMANTUS: The compulsion to do so will be enormous, Socrates.   *d*

SOCRATES: And yet we have not mentioned the greatest compulsion of all.

ADEIMANTUS: What is that?

SOCRATES: It is what these educators and sophists impose by their actions if their words fail to persuade. Or don't you know that they punish anyone who is not persuaded, with disenfranchisement, fines, or death?

ADEIMANTUS: They most certainly do.

SOCRATES: What other sophist, then, or what sort of private conversations do you think will oppose these and prove stronger?

ADEIMANTUS: None, I imagine.   *e*

SOCRATES: No, indeed, even to try would be very foolish. You see, there is not now, never has been, nor ever will be, a character whose view of virtue goes contrary to the education these provide. I mean a human character, comrade—the divine, as the saying goes, is an exception to the rule. You may be sure that if anything is saved and turns out well in the political systems that exist now, you won't be mistaken *493a* in saying that divine providence saved it.

ADEIMANTUS: That is what I think, too.

SOCRATES: Well, then, you should also agree to this.

ADEIMANTUS: What?

SOCRATES: None of those private wage-earners— the ones these people call sophists and consider to be their rivals in craft—teaches anything other than the convictions the masses hold when they are assembled together, and this he calls wisdom. It is just as if someone were learning the passions and appetites of a huge, strong beast that he is rearing—how to

---

6. [See Homer, *Iliad* 24.367.]

b approach and handle it, when it is most difficult to deal with or most docile and what makes it so, what sounds it utters in either condition, and what tones of voice soothe or anger it. Having learned all this through associating and spending time with the beast, he calls this wisdom, gathers his information together as if it were a craft, and starts to teach it. Knowing nothing in reality about which of these convictions or appetites is fine or shameful, good or bad, just or

c unjust, he uses all these terms in conformity with the great beast's beliefs—calling the things it enjoys good and the things that anger it bad. He has no other account to give of them, but calls everything he is compelled to do just and fine, never having seen how much the natures of necessity and goodness really differ, and being unable to explain it to anyone. Don't you think, by Zeus, that someone like that would make a strange educator?

ADEIMANTUS: I do, indeed.

SOCRATES: Then does this person seem any different from the one who believes that wisdom is understanding the passions and pleasures of the masses—

d multifarious people—assembled together, whether in regard to painting, music, or politics for that matter? For if a person associates with the masses and exhibits his poetry or some other piece of craftsmanship to them or his service to the city, and gives them mastery over him to any degree beyond what is unavoidable, he will be under Diomedean compulsion,[7] as it is called, to produce the things of which they approve. But that such things are truly good and beautiful— have you ever heard anyone presenting an argument for that conclusion that was not absolutely ridiculous?

ADEIMANTUS.   No, and I do not suppose I ever

e will.

SOCRATES: So then, bearing all that in mind, recall our earlier question: can the majority in any way tolerate or accept that the beautiful itself (as opposed to the many beautiful things), or each thing itself (as

494a opposed to the corresponding many), exists?

ADEIMANTUS: Not in the least.

SOCRATES: It is impossible, then, for the majority to be philosophic.

ADEIMANTUS: It is impossible.

SOCRATES: And so, those who practice philosophy are inevitably disparaged by them?

ADEIMANTUS: Inevitably.

SOCRATES: And also by those private individuals who associate with the majority and want to please them.

ADEIMANTUS: Clearly.

SOCRATES: On the basis of these facts, then, do you see any way to preserve a philosophic nature and ensure that it will continue to practice philosophy and reach the end? Consider the question in light of what we said before. We agreed that ease in learning, a good memory, courage, and high-mindedness be- *b* long to the philosophic nature.

ADEIMANTUS: Yes.

SOCRATES: Right from the start, then, won't someone like that be first among the children in everything, especially if his body's nature matches that of his soul?

ADEIMANTUS: Of course he will.

SOCRATES: So as he gets older, I imagine his family and fellow citizens will want to make use of him in connection with their own affairs.

ADEIMANTUS: Certainly.

SOCRATES: They will get down on their knees, begging favors from him and honoring him, flattering *c* ahead of time the power that is going to be his, so as to secure it for themselves.

ADEIMANTUS: That's usually what happens, at least.

SOCRATES: What do you think someone like that will do in such circumstances—especially if he happens to be from a great city where he is rich and noble, and if he is good-looking and tall as well? Won't he be filled with an impractical expectation and think himself capable of managing the affairs, not only of the Greeks, but of the barbarians, too? And won't he exalt himself to great heights, as a result, and be brimming with pretension and empty, *d* senseless pride?[8]

ADEIMANTUS: He certainly will.

SOCRATES: Now, suppose someone gently approaches a young man in that state of mind and tells him the truth: that he has no sense, although he

---

7. [An inescapable compulsion. The origin of the phrase is uncertain.]

8. [Plato seems to have had Alcibiades in mind here and in what follows. Alcibiades' extraordinary career is described in Thucydides, Books 6–8.]

needs it, and that it cannot be acquired unless he works like a slave to attain it. Do you think it will be easy for him to hear that message through the evils that surround him?

ADEIMANTUS: Far from it.

SOCRATES: And suppose that, because of his noble nature and his natural affinity for such arguments, e he somehow sees the point and is turned around and drawn toward philosophy. What do we suppose those people will do if they believe that they are losing his services and companionship? Is there anything they won't do or say in his regard to prevent him from being persuaded? Or anything they won't do or say in regard to his persuader to prevent him from succeeding, whether it is in private plots or public court cases?[9]

495a ADEIMANTUS: There certainly is not.

SOCRATES: Then is there any chance that such a person will practice philosophy?

ADEIMANTUS: None at all.

SOCRATES: Do you see, then, that we weren't wrong to say that when a philosophic nature is badly brought up, its very components—together with the other so-called goods, such as wealth and every provision of that sort—are somehow the cause of its falling away from the pursuit?

ADEIMANTUS: No, we were not. What we said was right.

SOCRATES: There you are, then, you amazing fellow! That is the extent of the sort of destruction and corruption that the nature best suited for the noblest b pursuit undergoes. And such a nature is a rare occurrence anyway, we claim. Moreover, men who possess it are the ones that do the worst things to cities and individuals, and also—if they happen to be swept that way by the current—the greatest good. For a petty nature never does anything great, either to a private individual or a city.

ADEIMANTUS: That's very true.

SOCRATES: So when these men, for whom philosophy is most appropriate, fall away from her, they leave her desolate and unwed, and themselves lead c a life that is inappropriate and untrue. Then others, who are unworthy of her, come to her as to an orphan

9. [The trial of Socrates in 399 B.C.E. is the obvious case in point.]

bereft of kinsmen, and shame her. They are the ones responsible for the reproaches that you say are cast upon philosophy by her detractors—that some of her consorts are useless, while the majority deserve many evils.

ADEIMANTUS: Yes, that is what they say.

SOCRATES: And it is a reasonable thing to say. For other worthless little men see that this position has become vacant, even though it is brimming with fine accolades and pretensions, and—like prisoners d escaping from jail who take refuge in a temple—leap gladly from their crafts to philosophy. These are the ones who are most sophisticated at their own petty craft. You see, at least in comparison to other crafts, and even in its present state, philosophy still has a grander reputation. And that is what many people are aiming at, people with defective natures, whose souls are as cramped and spoiled by their menial tasks as their bodies are warped by their crafts and occupations. Isn't that inevitably what happens?   e

ADEIMANTUS: It certainly is.

SOCRATES: Do you think that they look any different than a little, bald-headed blacksmith who has come into some money and, newly released from debtor's prison, has taken a bath, put on a new cloak, got himself up as a bridegroom, and is about to marry the master's daughter because she is poor and abandoned?

ADEIMANTUS: They are no different at all.   496a

SOCRATES: What sort of offspring are they likely to beget, then? Won't their children be wretched illegitimates?

ADEIMANTUS: Inevitably.

SOCRATES: What about when men who are unworthy of education approach philosophy and associate with her in a way unworthy of her? What kinds of thoughts and beliefs are we to say they beget? Won't they be what are truly and appropriately called sophisms, since they have nothing genuine or truly wise about them?

ADEIMANTUS: Absolutely.

SOCRATES: Then there remains, Adeimantus, only a very small group who associate with philosophy in a way that is worthy of her: a noble and well b brought-up character, perhaps, kept down by exile, who stays true to his nature and remains with philosophy because there is no one to corrupt him; or a great

soul living in a small city, who disdains the city's affairs and looks beyond them. A very few might perhaps come to philosophy from other crafts that they rightly despise because they have good natures. And some might be held back by the bridle that restrains our friend Theages—you see, he meets all the other
c conditions needed to make him fall away from philosophy, but his physical illness keeps him out of politics and prevents it. Finally, my own case is hardly worth mentioning—my daimonic sign—since I don't suppose it has happened to anyone else or to only a few before. Now, those who have become members of this little group have tasted how sweet and blessed a possession philosophy is. At the same time, they have also seen the insanity of the masses and realized that there is nothing healthy, so to speak, in public affairs, and that there is no ally with whose aid the champion
d of justice can survive; that instead he would perish before he could profit either his city or his friends, and be useless both to himself and to others—like a man who has fallen among wild animals and is neither willing to join them in doing injustice nor sufficiently strong to oppose the general savagery alone. Taking all this into his calculations, he keeps quiet and does his own work, like someone who takes refuge under a little wall from a storm of dust or hail driven by the wind. Seeing others filled with lawlessness, the philosopher is satisfied if he can somehow lead his present life pure of injustice and impious acts, and
e depart from it with good hope, blameless and content.

ADEIMANTUS: Well, that is no small thing for him
497a to have accomplished before departing.

SOCRATES: But no very great one either, since he did not chance upon a suitable constitution. In a suitable one, his own growth will be fuller and he will save the community, as well as himself. Anyway, it seems to me that we have now said enough about the slander brought against philosophy and why it is unjust—unless, of course, you have got something to add.

ADEIMANTUS: I have nothing further to add on that issue. But which of our present constitutions do you think is suitable for philosophy?

SOCRATES: None of them. But that is exactly my
b complaint. There is not one city today with a constitution worthy of the philosophic nature. That is precisely why it is perverted and altered. It is like foreign

seed sown in alien ground: it tends to be overpowered and to fade away into the native species. Similarly, the philosophic species does not maintain its own power at present, but declines into a different character. But if it were to find the best constitution, as it is itself the best, it would be clear that it is really
c divine and that other natures and pursuits are merely human. Obviously, you are going to ask next what that constitution is.

ADEIMANTUS: You are wrong there. You see, I was not going to ask that, but whether it was the constitution we described when we were founding our city or a different one.

SOCRATES: In all other respects, it is that one. But we said even then that there must always be some people in the city who have a rational account of the constitution, the same one that guided you, the lawgiver, when you made the laws.
d

ADEIMANTUS: Yes, we did say that.

SOCRATES: But we did not explain it clearly enough, for fear of what our own objections have made clear: namely, that the demonstration of it would be long and difficult. Indeed, even what remains is not the easiest of all things to discuss.

ADEIMANTUS: What is that?

SOCRATES: How a city can engage in philosophy without being destroyed. You see, all great things are prone to fall and, as the saying goes, beautiful things are really difficult.

ADEIMANTUS: All the same, the demonstration won't be complete until this has been cleared up.
e

SOCRATES: If anything prevents that, it won't be lack of willingness, but lack of ability. At any rate, you will see how passionate I am. Look now, in fact, at how passionately and recklessly I am going to argue that a city should practice philosophy in the opposite way to the present one.

ADEIMANTUS: How?

SOCRATES: At present, those who take it up at all do so as young men, just out of childhood, who have yet to take up household management and money-making. Then, just when they reach the most difficult
498a part they abandon it and are regarded as the most fully trained philosophers. By the most difficult part, I mean the one concerned with arguments.[10] In later

10. [I.e., dialectic.]

life, if others are engaged in it and they are invited and deign to listen to them, they think they have done a lot, since they think this should only be a sideline. And, with a few exceptions, by the time they reach old age they are more thoroughly extinguished than the sun of Heraclitus, since they are never
b rekindled.[11]

ADEIMANTUS: What should they do instead?

SOCRATES: Entirely the opposite. As young men and children, they should occupy themselves with an education and philosophy suitable to the young. Their bodies are blooming and growing into manhood at this time, and they should take very good care of them, so as to acquire a helper for philosophy. But as they grow older and their soul begins to reach maturity, they should make its exercises more rigorous. Then, when their strength begins to fail and they have retired from politics and military service, they
c should graze freely in the pastures of philosophy and do nothing else, except as a sideline—I mean those who are going to live happily and, when the end comes, crown the life they have lived with a fitting providence in that other place.

ADEIMANTUS: You seem to be arguing with real passion, Socrates. But I am sure that most of your hearers will oppose you with even greater passion and won't be convinced in the least—beginning with Thrasymachus.

SOCRATES: Please do not try to raise a quarrel between me and Thrasymachus just as we have become friends—not that we were enemies before. You
d see, we won't relax our efforts until we convince him and the others—or at least do something that may benefit them in a later incarnation when, reborn, they happen upon these arguments again.

ADEIMANTUS: You are talking about the short term, I see!

SOCRATES: It is certainly nothing compared to the whole of time! However, it is no wonder that the masses are not convinced by our arguments. I mean, they have never seen a *man* that matched our *plan*—though they have more often seen words
e purposely chosen to rhyme with one another than

just happening to do so as in the present case.[12] But a man who, as far as possible, matched and rhymed with virtue in word and deed, and wielded dynastic power in a city of the same type—that is something they have never seen even once. Or do 499a you think they have?

ADEIMANTUS: No, definitely not.

SOCRATES: Nor, bless you, have they spent enough time listening to fine and free arguments that vigorously seek the truth in every way, so as to acquire knowledge and keep their distance from all the sophistries and eristic quibbles that—whether in public trials or private gatherings—strive for nothing except reputation and disputation.

ADEIMANTUS: No, they have not.

SOCRATES: It was for these reasons, and because we foresaw these difficulties, that we were afraid. All the same, we were compelled by the truth to say that b no city, no constitution, and no individual man will ever become perfect until some chance event compels those few philosophers who are not vicious (the ones who are now called useless) to take care of a city, whether they are willing to or not, and compels the city to obey them—or until a true passion for true philosophy flows by some divine inspiration into the sons of the men now wielding dynastic power or sovereignty, or into the men themselves. Now, it can- c not be reasonably maintained, in my view, that either or both of these things is impossible. But if they were, we would be justly ridiculed for indulging in wishful thinking. Isn't that so?

ADEIMANTUS: It is.

SOCRATES: Then if, in the limitless past, some necessity forced those who were foremost in philosophy to take charge of a city, or is doing so now in some barbaric place far beyond our ken, or will do so in the future, this is something we are prepared d to fight about—our argument that the constitution we have described has existed, does exist, and will exist, at any rate, whenever it is that the muse of philosophy gains mastery of a city. It is not impossible

11. [Heraclitus' sun was extinguished at night but rekindled the next morning.]

12. [Plato is mocking the rhetoricians who were fond of forced rhyme. His own words *ou gar pôpote eidon genomenon to nun legomenon*—"they've never seen anything come into existence that matches our account"—exhibit the phenomenon he is mocking.]

for this to happen, so we are not speaking of impossibilities—that it is *difficult*, we agree ourselves.

ADEIMANTUS: I certainly think so.

SOCRATES: But the masses do not—is that what you are going to say?

ADEIMANTUS: They probably don't.

SOCRATES: Bless you, you should not make such a wholesale charge against the masses! They will surely come to hold a different belief if, instead of wanting
e to win a victory at their expense, you soothe them and try to remove their slanderous prejudice against the love of learning. You must show them what you mean by philosophers and define their nature and
500a pursuit the way we did just now. Then they will realize you do not mean the same people they do. And if they once see it that way, even you will say that they will have a different opinion from the one you just attributed to them and will answer differently. Or do you think that anyone who is gentle and without malice is harsh to one who is not harsh, or malicious to one who is not malicious? I will anticipate you and say that I think a few people may have such a harsh character, but not the majority.

ADEIMANTUS: And I agree, of course.

SOCRATES: Then don't you also agree that the
b harshness of the masses toward philosophy is caused by those outsiders who do not belong and who have burst in like a band of revelers, abusing one another, indulging their love of quarreling, and always arguing about human beings—something that is least appropriate in philosophy?

ADEIMANTUS: I do, indeed.

SOCRATES: For surely, Adeimantus, someone whose mind is truly directed toward the things that are has not the leisure to look down at human affairs and be filled with malice and hatred as a result of
c entering into their disputes. Instead, as he looks at and contemplates things that are orderly and always the same, that neither do injustice to one another nor suffer it, being all in a rational order, he imitates them and tries to become as like them as he can. Or do you think there is any way to prevent someone from associating with something he admires without imitating it?

ADEIMANTUS: He can't possibly.

SOCRATES: Then the philosopher, by associating with what is orderly and divine, becomes as divine and orderly as a human being can. Though, mind you, there are always plenty of slanders around.   d

ADEIMANTUS: Absolutely.

SOCRATES: And if he should come to be compelled to make a practice—in private and in public—of stamping what he sees there into the people's characters, instead of shaping only his own, do you think he will be a poor craftsman of temperance, justice, and the whole of popular virtue?

ADEIMANTUS: Not at all.

SOCRATES: And when the masses realize that what we are saying about him is true, will they be harsh with philosophers or mistrust us when we say that e there is no way a city can ever find happiness unless its plan is drawn by painters who use the divine model?

ADEIMANTUS: They won't be harsh, if they do realize this. But what sort of drawing do you mean?   501a

SOCRATES: They would take the city and people's characters as their sketching slate, but first they would wipe it clean—which is not at all an easy thing to do. And you should be aware that this is an immediate difference between them and others—that they refuse to take either a private individual or a city in hand, or to write laws, unless they receive a clean slate or are allowed to clean it themselves.

ADEIMANTUS: And rightly so.

SOCRATES: And after that, don't you think they would draw the plan of the constitution?

ADEIMANTUS: Of course.

SOCRATES: And I suppose that, as they work, they would look often in each direction: on the one hand, b toward what is in its nature just, beautiful, temperate, and all the rest; and, on the other, toward what they are trying to put into human beings, mixing and blending pursuits to produce a human likeness, based on the one that Homer too called divine and godly when it appeared among human beings.

ADEIMANTUS: Right.

SOCRATES: They would erase one thing, I suppose, and draw in another, until they had made people's characters as dear to the gods as possible.   c

ADEIMANTUS: At any rate, the drawing would be most beautiful that way.

SOCRATES: Are we at all persuading the people you said were rushing to attack us, then, that the philosopher we were praising to them is really this sort of painter of constitutions? They were angry because we were entrusting cities to him; are they any calmer at hearing it now?

ADEIMANTUS: They will be much calmer, if they have any sense.

SOCRATES: After all, how could they possibly dispute it? Will they deny that philosophers are lovers both of what is and of the truth?

ADEIMANTUS: That would be silly.

SOCRATES: Or that their nature, as we have described it, is akin to the best?

ADEIMANTUS: They cannot deny that either.

SOCRATES: Or that such a nature, when it happens to find appropriate pursuits, will not be as completely good and philosophic as any other? Or are they going to claim that the people we excluded are more so?

ADEIMANTUS: Certainly not.

SOCRATES: Will they still be angry, then, when we say that until the philosopher class gains mastery of a city, there will be no respite from evils for either city or citizens, and the constitution we have been describing in our discussion will never be completed in practice?

ADEIMANTUS: They will probably be less so.

SOCRATES: If it is all right with you, then, let's not say that they will simply be less angry, but that they will become altogether gentle and persuaded; so that out of shame, if nothing else, they will agree.

ADEIMANTUS: All right.

SOCRATES: So let's assume that they have been convinced of this. Will anyone contend, then, that there is no chance that the offspring of kings or men in power could be natural-born philosophers?

ADEIMANTUS: No one could.

SOCRATES: Could anyone claim that if such offspring are born, they must inevitably be corrupted? We agree ourselves that it is difficult for them to be saved. But that in the whole of time not one of them could be saved—could anyone contend that?

ADEIMANTUS: Of course not.

SOCRATES: But surely the occurrence of one such individual is enough, provided his city obeys him, to bring to completion all the things that now seem so incredible.

ADEIMANTUS: Yes, one is enough.

SOCRATES: For I suppose that if a ruler established the laws and practices we have described, it is hardly

impossible that the citizens would be willing to carry them out.

ADEIMANTUS: Not at all.

SOCRATES: Would it be either surprising or impossible, then, that others should think as we do?

ADEIMANTUS: I don't suppose so.

SOCRATES: But I think our earlier discussion was sufficient to show that these arrangements are best, provided they are possible.

ADEIMANTUS: Indeed, it was.

SOCRATES: It seems, then, that the conclusion we have now reached about legislation is that the one we are describing is best, provided it is possible; and that while it is difficult for it to come about, it certainly is not impossible.

ADEIMANTUS: Yes, that is the conclusion we have reached.

SOCRATES: Now that this conclusion has, with much effort, been reached, we must next deal with the remaining issues—in what way, by means of what subjects and pursuits, the saviors of our constitution will come to exist, and at what ages they will take up each of them.

ADEIMANTUS: Yes, we must deal with that.

SOCRATES: I gained nothing by my cleverness, then, in omitting from our earlier discussion the troublesome topic of acquiring women, begetting children, and establishing rulers, because I knew the whole truth would provoke resentment and would be difficult to bring about. As it turned out, the need to discuss them arose anyway. Now, the subject of women and children has already been discussed. But that of the rulers has to be taken up again from the beginning. We said,[13] if you remember, that they must show themselves to be lovers of the city, when tested by pleasures and pains, by not abandoning this conviction through labors, fears, and all other adversities. Anyone who was incapable of doing so was to be rejected, while anyone who always came through pure—like gold tested in a fire—was to be made ruler and receive gifts and prizes, both while he lived and after his death. These were the sorts of things we were saying while our argument veiled its

13. [At 412b–414a. The conviction referred to is identified at 412e6.]

b face and slipped by, for fear of stirring up the very problems that now confront us.

ADEIMANTUS: That's absolutely true. I do remember.

SOCRATES: I was reluctant, my friend, to say the things we have now dared to say anyway. But now, let's also dare to say that we must establish philosophers as guardians in the most exact sense.

ADEIMANTUS: Let's do so.

SOCRATES: Bear in mind, then, that there will probably be only a few of them. You see, they have to have the nature we described, and its parts rarely consent to grow together in one person; rather, its many parts grow split off from one another.

c ADEIMANTUS: How do you mean?

SOCRATES: Ease of learning, good memory, astuteness, and smartness, as you know, and all the other things that go along with them, such as youthful passion and high-mindedness, are rarely willing to grow together simultaneously with a disposition to live an orderly, quiet, and completely stable life. On the contrary, those who possess the former traits are carried by their quick wits wherever chance leads them, and have no stability at all.

ADEIMANTUS: That's true.

SOCRATES: Those with stable characters, on the other hand, who do not change easily, whom one would employ because of their greater reliability, and

d who in battle are not easily moved by fears, act in the same way when it comes to their studies. They are hard to get moving and learn with difficulty, as if they are anesthetized, and are constantly falling asleep and yawning whenever they have to work hard at such things.

ADEIMANTUS: They are.

SOCRATES: Yet we say that someone must have a good and fine share of both characters, or he won't receive the truest education or honor, or be allowed to rule.

ADEIMANTUS: That's right.

SOCRATES: Then don't you think this will rarely occur?

ADEIMANTUS: Of course.

e SOCRATES: He must be tested, then, in the labors, fears, and pleasures we mentioned before. He must also be exercised in many other subjects, however, which we did not mention but are adding now, to

see whether his nature can endure the most important subjects or will shrink from them like the cowards who shrink from the other tests. 504a

ADEIMANTUS: It is certainly important to find that out. But what do you mean by the most important subjects?

SOCRATES: Do you remember when we distinguished three kinds of things in the soul in order to help bring out what justice, temperance, courage, and wisdom each is?[14]

ADEIMANTUS: If I didn't, I would not deserve to hear the rest.

SOCRATES: Do you also remember what preceded it?

ADEIMANTUS: No, what?

SOCRATES: We said, I believe, that in order to get the finest view of these matters, we would need to b take a longer road, which would make them plain to anyone who took it, but that it was possible to give demonstrations that would be up to the standard of the previous discussion.[15] All of you said that was enough. The result was that our subsequent discussion, as it seemed to me, was less than exact. But whether or not it satisfied all of you is for you to say.

ADEIMANTUS: I, at any rate, thought you gave us good measure. And so, apparently, did the others.

SOCRATES: No, my friend, any measure of such things that falls short in any way of what is, is not c good measure at all, since nothing incomplete is a measure of anything. Some people, however, are occasionally of the opinion that an incomplete treatment is already adequate and that there is no need for further inquiry.

ADEIMANTUS: Yes, a lot of people feel like that. Laziness is the cause.

SOCRATES: Well, that is a feeling that is least appropriate in a guardian of a city and its laws.

ADEIMANTUS: No doubt.

SOCRATES: He will have to take the longer road then, comrade, and put no less effort into learning than into physical training. For otherwise, as we were d just saying, he will never pursue the most important and most appropriate subject to the end.

14. [434d–444e.]
15. [435d.]

ADEIMANTUS: Why, aren't these virtues the most important things? Is there something yet more important than justice and the other virtues we discussed?

SOCRATES: Not only is it more important, but, even in the case of the virtues themselves, it is not enough to look at a mere sketch as we are doing now, while neglecting the most finished portrait. I mean, it is ridiculous, isn't it, to strain every nerve to attain the utmost exactness and clarity about other things
e of little value, while not treating the most important things as meriting the most exactness?

ADEIMANTUS: It certainly is. But do you think that anyone is going to let you off without asking you what you mean by this most important subject, and what it is concerned with?

SOCRATES: No, I do not. And you may ask it, too. You have certainly heard the answer often, but now either you are not thinking or you intend to make trouble for me again by interrupting. And I suspect
505a it is more the latter. You see, you have often heard it said that the form of the good is the most important thing to learn about, and that it is by their relation to it that just things and the others become useful and beneficial. And now you must be pretty certain that that is what I am going to say, and, in addition, that we have no adequate knowledge of it. And if we do not know it, you know that even the fullest possible knowledge of other things is of no benefit to us, any more than if we acquire any possession without the good. Or do you think there is any benefit in possess-
b ing everything but the good? Or to know everything without knowing the good, thereby knowing nothing fine or good?

ADEIMANTUS: No, by Zeus, I do not.

SOCRATES: Furthermore, you also know that the masses believe pleasure to be the good, while the more refined believe it to be knowledge.

ADEIMANTUS: Of course.

SOCRATES: And, my friend, that those who believe this cannot show us what sort of knowledge it is, but in the end are forced to say that it is knowledge of the good.

ADEIMANTUS: Which is completely ridiculous.

SOCRATES: How could it not be, when they
c blame us for not knowing the good and then turn around and talk to us as if we did know it? I mean, they say it is knowledge of the good—as if we

understood what they mean when they utter the word "good."

ADEIMANTUS: That's absolutely true.

SOCRATES: What about those who define the good as pleasure? Are they any less full of confusion than the others? Or aren't even they forced to admit that there are bad pleasures?

ADEIMANTUS: Most definitely.

SOCRATES: I suppose it follows, doesn't it, that they have to admit that the same things are both good and bad?

ADEIMANTUS: It certainly does.   d

SOCRATES: Isn't it clear, then, that there are lots of serious disagreements about the good?

ADEIMANTUS: Of course.

SOCRATES: Well, isn't it also clear that many people would choose things that are believed to be just or beautiful, even if they are not, and would act, acquire things, and form beliefs accordingly? Yet no one is satisfied to acquire things that are *believed* to be good. On the contrary, everyone seeks the things that *are* good. In this area, everyone disdains mere reputation.

ADEIMANTUS: Right.

SOCRATES: That, then, is what every soul pursues, and for its sake does everything. The soul has a hunch that the good is something, but it is puzzled and   e cannot adequately grasp just what it is or acquire the sort of stable belief about it that it has about other things, and so it misses the benefit, if any, that even those other things may give. Are we to accept that even the best people in the city, to whom we entrust   506a everything, must remain thus in the dark about something of this kind and importance?

ADEIMANTUS: That's the last thing we would do.

SOCRATES: Anyway, I imagine that just and fine things won't have acquired much of a guardian in someone who does not even know why they are good. And I have a hunch that no one will have adequate knowledge of them until he knows this.

ADEIMANTUS: That's a good hunch.

SOCRATES: But won't our constitution be perfectly ordered if such a guardian, one who knows these things, oversees it?   b

ADEIMANTUS: It is bound to be. But you yourself, Socrates, do you say the good is knowledge or pleasure, or is it something else altogether?

SOCRATES: What a man! You made it good and clear long ago that other people's opinions about these matters would not satisfy you.

ADEIMANTUS: Well, Socrates, it does not seem right to me for you to be willing to state other people's convictions but not your own, when you have spent
c so much time occupied with these matters.

SOCRATES: What? Do you think it is right to speak about things you do not know as if you do know them?

ADEIMANTUS: Not as if you know them, but you ought to be willing to state what you believe as what you believe.

SOCRATES: What? Haven't you noticed that beliefs without knowledge are all shameful and ugly things, since the best of them are blind? Do you think that those who have a true belief without understanding are any different from blind people who happen to travel the right road?

ADEIMANTUS: They are no different.

SOCRATES: Do you want to look at shameful, blind, and crooked things, then, when you might hear
d fine, illuminating ones from other people?

And Glaucon said:

By Zeus, Socrates, do not stop now, with the end in sight, so to speak! We will be satisfied if you discuss the good the way you discussed justice, temperance, and the rest.

SOCRATES: That, comrade, would well satisfy me too, but I am afraid that I won't be up to it and that I will disgrace myself and look ridiculous by trying. No, bless you, let's set aside what the good itself is for the time being. You see, even to arrive at my
e current beliefs about it seems beyond the range of our present discussion. But I am willing to tell you about what seems to be an offspring of the good and most like it, if that is agreeable to you; or otherwise to let the matter drop.

GLAUCON: Tell us, then. The story about the father remains a debt you will pay another time.

507a SOCRATES: I wish I could repay it, and you recover the debt, instead of just the interest. So here, then, is this child and offspring of the good itself. But take care I do not somehow deceive you

unintentionally by giving you an illegitimate account of the child.[16]

GLAUCON: We will take as much care as possible. So speak on.

SOCRATES: I will once I have come to an agreement with you and reminded you of things we have already said here as well as on many other occasions.

GLAUCON: Which things?   b

SOCRATES: We say that there are many beautiful, many good, and many other such things, thereby distinguishing them in words.

GLAUCON: We do.

SOCRATES: We also say there is a beautiful itself and a good itself. And so, in the case of all the things that we then posited as many, we reverse ourselves and posit a single form belonging to each, since we suppose there is a single one, and call it what each is.

GLAUCON: That's true.

SOCRATES: And we say that the one class of things is visible but not intelligible, while the forms are intelligible but not visible.

GLAUCON: Absolutely.

SOCRATES: With what of ours do we see visible things?   c

GLAUCON: With our sight.

SOCRATES: And don't we hear audible things with hearing and perceive all other perceptible things with our other senses?

GLAUCON: Of course.

SOCRATES: Have you ever thought about how lavish the craftsman of our senses was in making the power to see and be seen?

GLAUCON: No, not really.

SOCRATES: Well, think of it this way. Do hearing and sound need another kind of thing in order for the former to hear and the latter to be heard—a third thing in whose absence the one won't hear or the d other be heard?

GLAUCON: No.

SOCRATES: And I think there cannot be many— not to say any—others that need such a thing. Or can you think of one?

GLAUCON: No, I cannot.

16. [Throughout, Socrates is punning on the word *tokos*, which means either a child or the interest on capital.]

SOCRATES: Aren't you aware that sight and the visible realm have such a need?

GLAUCON: In what way?

SOCRATES: Surely sight may be present in the eyes and its possessor may try to use it, and colors may be present in things; but unless a third kind of thing is present, which is naturally adapted for this specific purpose, you know that sight will see nothing and the colors will remain unseen.

GLAUCON: What kind of thing do you mean?

SOCRATES: The kind you call light.

GLAUCON: You are right.

SOCRATES: So it is no insignificant form of yoke, then, that yokes the sense of sight and the power to be seen. In fact, it is more honorable than any that yokes other yoked teams. Provided, of course, that light is not something without honor.

GLAUCON: And it is surely far from being without honor.

SOCRATES: Which of the gods in the heavens would you say is the controller of this—the one whose light makes our sight see best and visible things best seen?

GLAUCON: The very one you and others would name. I mean, it is clear that what you are asking about is the sun.[17]

SOCRATES: And isn't sight naturally related to that god in the following way?

GLAUCON: Which one?

SOCRATES: Neither sight itself nor that in which it comes to be—namely, the eye—is the sun.

GLAUCON: No, it is not.

SOCRATES: But it is, I think, the most sunlike of the sense organs.

GLAUCON: By far the most.

SOCRATES: And doesn't it receive the power it has from the sun, just like an influx from an overflowing treasury?

GLAUCON: Certainly.

SOCRATES: The sun is not sight either; yet as its cause, isn't it seen by sight itself?

GLAUCON: It is.

SOCRATES: Let's say, then, that this is what I called the offspring of the good, which the good begot as

17. [Helios—the sun—was considered a god.]

its analogue. What the latter is in the intelligible realm in relation to understanding and intelligible things, the former is in the visible realm in relation to sight and visible things.

GLAUCON: How? Tell me more.

SOCRATES: You know that when our eyes no longer turn to things whose colors are illuminated by the light of day, but by the lights of night, they are dimmed and seem nearly blind, as if clear sight were no longer in them.

GLAUCON: Of course.

SOCRATES: Yet I suppose that whenever they are turned to things illuminated by the sun, they see clearly and sight is manifest in those very same eyes?

GLAUCON: Indeed.

SOCRATES: Well, think about the soul in the same way. When it focuses on something that is illuminated both by truth and what is, it understands, knows, and manifestly possesses understanding. But when it focuses on what is mixed with obscurity, on what comes to be and passes away, it believes and is dimmed, changes its beliefs this way and that, and seems bereft of understanding.

GLAUCON: Yes, it does seem like that.

SOCRATES: You must say, then, that what gives truth to the things known and the power to know to the knower is the form of the good. And as the cause of knowledge and truth, you must think of it as an object of knowledge. Both knowledge and truth are beautiful things. But if you are to think correctly, you must think of the good as other and more beautiful than they. In the visible realm, light and sight are rightly thought to be sunlike, but wrongly thought to be the sun. So, here it is right to think of knowledge and truth as goodlike, but wrong to think that either of them is the good—for the state of the good is yet more honored.

GLAUCON: It is an incredibly beautiful thing you are talking about, if it provides both knowledge and truth but is itself superior to them in beauty. I mean, you surely do not think that *it* could be pleasure.

SOCRATES: No words of ill omen, please! Instead, examine our analogy in more detail.

GLAUCON: How?

SOCRATES: The sun, I think you would say, not only gives visible things the power to be seen but also provides for their coming-to-be, growth, and nourishment—although it is not itself coming to be.

GLAUCON: I would.

SOCRATES: Therefore, you should also say that not only do the objects of knowledge owe their being known to the good, but their existence and being are also due to it; although the good is not being, but something yet beyond being, superior to it in rank and power.

And Glaucon quite ridiculously replied:

c By Apollo, what daimonic hyperbole![18]

SOCRATES: It is your own fault, you forced me to tell my beliefs about it.

GLAUCON: And don't you stop, either—at least, not until you have finished discussing the good's similarity to the sun, if you are omitting anything.

SOCRATES: I am certainly omitting a lot.

GLAUCON: Well don't, not even the smallest detail.

SOCRATES: I think I will have to omit a fair amount. All the same, as far as is now possible, I won't purposely omit anything.

GLAUCON: Please don't.

SOCRATES: Then you should think, as we said, d that there are these two things, one sovereign of the intelligible kind and place, the other of the visible— I do not say "of the heavens," so as not to seem to you to be playing the sophist with the name.[19] In any case, do you understand these two kinds, visible and intelligible?

GLAUCON: I do.

SOCRATES: Represent them, then, by a line divided into two unequal sections. Then divide each section—that of the visible kind and that of the intelligible—in the same proportion as the line.[20] In

18. [Socrates' claim ends with the words *dunamei huperechontas* ("superior in . . . power"), Glaucon responds with the punning *daimonias huperbolês*. Hence the joke.]

19. [The play seems to be on the similarity of sound between *orano* ("the heavens") and *orato* ("visible").]

20.

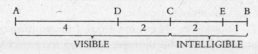

terms now of relative clarity and opacity, you will have as one subsection of the visible, images. By e images I mean, first, shadows, then reflections in bodies of water and in all close-packed, smooth, and 510a shiny materials, and everything of that sort. Do you understand?

GLAUCON: I do understand.

SOCRATES: Then, in the other subsection of the visible, put the originals of these images—that is, the animals around us, every plant, and the whole class of manufactured things.

GLAUCON: I will.

SOCRATES: Would you also be willing to say, then, that, as regards truth and untruth, the division is in this ratio: as what is believed is to what is known, so the likeness is to the thing it is like?

GLAUCON: Certainly.   b

SOCRATES: Next, consider how the section of the intelligible is to be divided.

GLAUCON: How?

SOCRATES: As follows: in one subsection, the soul, using as images the things that were imitated before, is forced to base its inquiry on hypotheses, proceeding not to a first principle, but to a conclusion. In the other subsection, by contrast, it makes its way to an unhypothetical first principle, proceeding from a hypothesis, but without the images used in the previous subsection, using forms themselves and making its investigation through them.

GLAUCON: I do not fully understand what you are saying.

SOCRATES: Let's try again. You see, you will understand it more easily after this explanation. I think c you know that students of geometry, calculation, and the like hypothesize the odd and the even, the various figures, the three kinds of angles, and other things akin to these in each of their investigations, regarding them as known. These they treat as hypotheses and do not think it necessary to give any argument for them, either to themselves or to others, as if they were evident to everyone. And going from these first principles through the remaining steps, they arrive d in full agreement at the point they set out to reach in their investigation.

GLAUCON: I certainly know that much.

SOCRATES: Then don't you also know that they use visible forms and make their arguments about them, although they are not thinking about them, but about those other things that they are like? They make their arguments with a view to the square itself and the diagonal itself, not the diagonal they draw, and similarly with the others. The very things they make and draw, of which shadows and reflections in water are images, they now in turn use as images in seeking to see those other things themselves that one 511a cannot see except by means of thought.

GLAUCON: That's true.

SOCRATES: This, then, is the kind of thing that I said was intelligible. The soul is forced to use hypotheses in the investigation of it, not traveling up to a first principle, since it cannot escape or get above its hypotheses, but using as images those very things of which images were made by the things below them, and which, by comparison to their images, were thought to be clear and to be honored as such.

GLAUCON: I understand that you mean what is b dealt with in geometry and related crafts.

SOCRATES: Also understand, then, that by the other subsection of the intelligible I mean what reason itself grasps by the power of dialectical discussion, treating its hypotheses, not as first principles, but as genuine hypotheses (that is, stepping stones and links in a chain), in order to arrive at what is unhypothetical and the first principle of everything. Having grasped this principle, it reverses itself and, keeping hold of what follows from it, comes down to a conclusion, c making no use of anything visible at all, but only of forms themselves, moving on through forms to forms, and ending in forms.

GLAUCON: I understand, though not adequately—you see, in my opinion you are speaking of an enormous task. You want to distinguish the part of what is and is intelligible, the part looked at by the science of dialectical discussion, as clearer than the part looked at by the so-called sciences—those for which hypotheses are first principles. And although those who look at the latter part are forced to do so by means of thought rather than sense perception, still, because they do not go back to a genuine first principle in considering it, but proceed from hypotheses, you do not think that they have true d understanding of them, even though—given such a first principle—they are intelligible. And you seem to me to call the state of mind of the geometers—

and the others of that sort—thought but not understanding; thought being intermediate between belief and understanding.

SOCRATES: You have grasped my meaning most adequately. Join me, then, in taking these four conditions in the soul as corresponding to the four subsections of the line: understanding dealing with the highest, thought dealing with the second; assign belief to the third, and imagination to the last. Arrange them e in a proportion and consider that each shares in clarity to the degree that the subsection it deals with shares in truth.

GLAUCON: I understand, agree, and arrange them as you say.

BOOK VII

SOCRATES' NARRATION CONTINUES:

SOCRATES: Next, then, compare the effect of education and that of the lack of it on our nature to an 514a experience like this. Imagine human beings living in an underground, cavelike dwelling, with an entrance a long way up that is open to the light and as wide as the cave itself. They have been there since childhood, with their necks and legs fettered, so that they are fixed in the same place, able to see only in front of them, because their fetter prevents them from turning their heads around. Light is provided by a fire burning b far above and behind them. Between the prisoners and the fire, there is an elevated road stretching. Imagine that along this road a low wall has been built—like the screen in front of people that is provided by puppeteers, and above which they show their puppets.

GLAUCON: I am imagining it.

SOCRATES: Also imagine, then, that there are people alongside the wall carrying multifarious artifacts that project above it—statues of people and other c animals, made of stone, wood, and every material. 515a And as you would expect, some of the carriers are talking and some are silent.

GLAUCON: It is a strange image you are describing, and strange prisoners.

SOCRATES: They are like us. I mean, in the first place, do you think these prisoners have ever seen anything of themselves and one another besides the shadows that the fire casts on the wall of the cave in front of them?

GLAUCON: How could they, if they have to keep
b their heads motionless throughout life?

SOCRATES: What about the things carried along the wall? Isn't the same true where they are concerned?

GLAUCON: Of course.

SOCRATES: And if they could engage in discussion with one another, don't you think they would assume that the words they used applied to the things they see passing in front of them?

GLAUCON: They would have to.

SOCRATES: What if their prison also had an echo from the wall facing them? When one of the carriers passing along the wall spoke, do you think they would believe that anything other than the shadow passing in front of them was speaking?

GLAUCON: I do not, by Zeus.

SOCRATES: All in all, then, what the prisoners
c would take for true reality is nothing other than the shadows of those artifacts.

GLAUCON: That's entirely inevitable.

SOCRATES: Consider, then, what being released from their bonds and cured of their foolishness would naturally be like, if something like this should happen to them. When one was freed and suddenly compelled to stand up, turn his neck around, walk, and look up toward the light, he would be pained by doing all these things and be unable to see the things whose shadows he had seen before, because of the
d flashing lights. What do you think he would say if we told him that what he had seen before was silly nonsense, but that now—because he is a bit closer to what is, and is turned toward things that *are* more— he sees more correctly? And in particular, if we pointed to each of the things passing by and compelled him to answer what each of them is, don't you think he would be puzzled and believe that the things he saw earlier were more truly real than the ones he was being shown?

GLAUCON: Much more so.

SOCRATES: And if he were compelled to look at
e the light itself, wouldn't his eyes be pained and wouldn't he turn around and flee toward the things he is able to see, and believe that they are really clearer than the ones he is being shown?

GLAUCON: He would.

SOCRATES: And if someone dragged him by force away from there, along the rough, steep, upward path, and did not let him go until he had dragged him into the light of the sun, wouldn't he be pained and angry at being treated that way? And when he came into the light, wouldn't he have his eyes filled with sunlight 516a and be unable to see a single one of the things now said to be truly real?

GLAUCON: No, he would not be able to—at least not right away.

SOCRATES: He would need time to get adjusted, I suppose, if he is going to see the things in the world above. At first, he would see shadows most easily, then images of men and other things in water, then the things themselves. From these, it would be easier for him to go on to look at the things in the sky and the sky itself at night, gazing at the light of the stars and the moon, than during the day, gazing at the sun and the light of the sun.   b

GLAUCON: Of course.

SOCRATES: Finally, I suppose, he would be able to see the sun—not reflections of it in water or some alien place, but the sun just by itself in its own place— and be able to look at it and see what it is like.

GLAUCON: He would have to.

SOCRATES: After that, he would already be able to conclude about it that it provides the seasons and the years, governs everything in the visible world, and is in some way the cause of all the things that he c and his fellows used to see.

GLAUCON: That would clearly be his next step.

SOCRATES: What about when he reminds himself of his first dwelling place, what passed for wisdom there, and his fellow prisoners? Don't you think he would count himself happy for the change and pity the others?

GLAUCON: Certainly.

SOCRATES: And if there had been honors, praises, or prizes among them for the one who was sharpest at identifying the shadows as they passed by; and was best able to remember which usually came earlier, which later, and which simultaneously; and who was thus best able to prophesize the future, do you think d that our man would desire these rewards or envy those among the prisoners who were honored and held power? Or do you think he would feel with Homer that he would much prefer to "work the earth as a serf for another man, a man without possessions of his own,"[1] and go through any sufferings, rather than share their beliefs and live as they do?

GLAUCON: Yes, I think he would rather suffer
e anything than live like that.

SOCRATES: Consider this too, then. If this man went back down into the cave and sat down in his same seat, wouldn't his eyes be filled with darkness, coming suddenly out of the sun like that?

GLAUCON: Certainly.

SOCRATES: Now, if he had to compete once again with the perpetual prisoners in recognizing the shadows, while his sight was still dim and before his eyes
517a had recovered, and if the time required for readjustment was not short, wouldn't he provoke ridicule? Wouldn't it be said of him that he had returned from his upward journey with his eyes ruined, and that it is not worthwhile even to try to travel upward? And as for anyone who tried to free the prisoners and lead them upward, if they could somehow get their hands on him, wouldn't they kill him?

GLAUCON: They certainly would.

SOCRATES: This image, my dear Glaucon, must
b be fitted together as a whole with what we said before. The realm revealed through sight should be likened to the prison dwelling, and the light of the fire inside it to the sun's power. And if you think of the upward journey and the seeing of things above as the upward journey of the soul to the intelligible realm, you won't mistake my intention—since it is what you wanted to hear about. Only the god knows whether it is true. But this is how these phenomena seem to me: in the knowable realm, the last thing to be seen is the form of the good, and it is seen only with toil and trouble.
c Once one has seen it, however, one must infer that it is the cause of all that is correct and beautiful in anything, that in the visible realm it produces both light and its source, and that in the intelligible realm it controls and provides truth and understanding; and that anyone who is to act sensibly in private or public must see it.

GLAUCON: I agree, so far as I am able.

---

1. [*Odyssey* 11.489–90. The shade of Achilles speaks these words to Odysseus, who is visiting Hades. Plato is likening the cave dwellers to the dead.]

SOCRATES: Come on, then, and join me in this further thought: you should not be surprised that the ones who get to this point are not willing to occupy themselves with human affairs, but that, on the contrary, their souls are always eager to spend their time above. I mean, that is surely what we would expect, if indeed the image I described before is also accurate here.   d

GLAUCON: It is what we would expect.

SOCRATES: What about when someone, coming from looking at divine things, looks to the evils of human life? Do you think it is surprising that he behaves awkwardly and appears completely ridiculous, if—while his sight is still dim and he has not yet become accustomed to the darkness around him—he is compelled, either in the courts or elsewhere, to compete about the shadows of justice, or about the statues of which they are the shadows; and to dispute the way these things are understood by people who have never seen justice itself?   e

GLAUCON: It is not surprising at all.

SOCRATES: On the contrary, anyone with any sense, at any rate, would remember that eyes may be   518a confused in two ways and from two causes: when they change from the light into the darkness, or from the darkness into the light. If he kept in mind that the same applies to the soul, then when he saw a soul disturbed and unable to see something, he would not laugh absurdly. Instead, he would see whether it had come from a brighter life and was dimmed through not having yet become accustomed to the dark, or from greater ignorance into greater light and was dazzled by the increased brilliance. Then he would consider the first soul happy in its experience and   b life, and pity the latter. But even if he wanted to ridicule it, at least his ridiculing it would make him less ridiculous than ridiculing a soul that had come from the light above.

GLAUCON: That's an entirely reasonable claim.

SOCRATES: Then here is how we must think about these matters, if that is true: education is not what some people boastfully declare it to be. They presumably say they can put knowledge into souls that lack it, as if they could put sight into blind eyes.   c

GLAUCON: Yes, they do say that.

SOCRATES: But here is what our present account shows about this power to learn that is present in everyone's soul, and the instrument with which each of us learns: just as an eye cannot be turned around from darkness to light except by turning the whole body, so this instrument must be turned around from what-comes-to-be together with the whole soul, until it is able to bear to look at what is and at the brightest thing that is—the one we call the good. Isn't that

d right?

GLAUCON: Yes.

SOCRATES: Of this very thing, then, there would be a craft—namely, of this turning around—concerned with how this instrument can be most easily and effectively turned around, not of putting sight into it. On the contrary, it takes for granted that sight is there, though not turned in the right way or looking where it should look, and contrives to redirect it appropriately.

GLAUCON: That's probably right.

SOCRATES: Then the other so-called virtues of the soul do seem to be closely akin to those of the body: they really are not present in it initially, but are added

e later by habit and practice. The virtue of wisdom, on the other hand, belongs above all, so it seems, to something more divine, which never loses its power, but is either useful and beneficial or useless and harmful, depending on the way it is turned. Or haven't

519a you ever noticed in people who are said to be bad, but clever, how keen the vision of their little soul is and how sharply it distinguishes the things it is turned toward? This shows that its sight is not inferior, but is forced to serve vice, so that the sharper it sees, the more evils it accomplishes.

GLAUCON: I certainly have.

SOCRATES: However, if this element of this sort of nature had been hammered at right from childhood, and struck free of the leaden weights, as it were, of kinship with becoming, which have been fastened

b to it by eating and other such pleasures and indulgences, which pull its soul's vision downward—if, I say, it got rid of these and turned toward truly real things, then the same element of the same people would see them most sharply, just as it now does the things it is now turned toward.

GLAUCON: That's probably right.

SOCRATES: Isn't it also probable, then—indeed, doesn't it follow necessarily from what was said before—that uneducated people who have no ex-

perience of true reality will never adequately govern a city, and neither will people who have been allowed c to spend their whole lives in education. The former fail because they do not have a single goal in life at which all their actions, public and private, inevitably aim; the latter because they would refuse to act, thinking they had emigrated, while still alive, to the Isles of the Blessed.

GLAUCON: True.

SOCRATES: It is our task as founders, then, to compel the best natures to learn what was said before[2] to be the most important thing: namely, to see the good; to ascend that ascent. And when they have ascended and looked sufficiently, we must not allow them to d do what they are allowed to do now.

GLAUCON: What's that, then?

SOCRATES: To stay there and refuse to go down again to the prisoners in the cave and share their labors and honors, whether the inferior ones or the more excellent ones.

GLAUCON: You mean we are to treat them unjustly, making them live a worse life when they could live a better one?

SOCRATES: You have forgotten again, my friend, that the law is not concerned with making any one e class in the city do outstandingly well, but is contriving to produce this condition in the city as a whole, harmonizing the citizens together through persuasion or compulsion, and making them share with each other the benefit they can confer on the community.[3] 520a It produces such men in the city, not in order to allow them to turn in whatever direction each one wants, but to make use of them to bind the city together.

GLAUCON: That's true. Yes, I had forgotten.

SOCRATES: Observe, then, Glaucon, that we won't be unjustly treating those who have become philosophers in our city, but that what we will say to them, when we compel them to take care of the others and guard them, will be just. We will say: "When people like you come to be in other cities, they are justified in not sharing in the others' labors. b After all, they have grown there spontaneously, against

2. [505a–b.]

3. [420b–421c, 462a–466c.]

the will of the constitution in each of them. And when something grows of its own accord and owes no debt for its upbringing, it has justice on its side when it is not keen to pay anyone for its upbringing. But both for your own sakes and for that of the rest of the city, we have bred you to be leaders and kings in the hive, so to speak. You are better and more completely educated than the others, and better able to share in both types of life.[4] So each of you in turn

c must go down to live in the common dwelling place of the other citizens and grow accustomed to seeing in the dark. For when you are used to it, you will see infinitely better than the people there and know precisely what each image is, and also what it is an image of, because you have seen the truth about fine, just, and good things. So the city will be awake, governed by us and by you; not dreaming like the majority of cities nowadays, governed by men who fight against one another over shadows and form fac-

d tions in order to rule—as if that were a great good. No, the truth of the matter is surely this: a city in which those who are going to rule are least eager to rule is necessarily best and freest from faction, whereas a city with the opposite kind of rulers is governed in the opposite way."

GLAUCON: Yes, indeed.

SOCRATES: Then do you think the people we have nurtured will disobey us when they hear these things, and be unwilling to share the labors of the city, each in turn, while living the greater part of their time with one another in the pure realm?

GLAUCON: No, they couldn't possibly. After all,

e we will be giving just orders to just people. However, each of them will certainly go to rule as to something necessary, which is exactly the opposite of what is done by those who now rule in each city.

SOCRATES: That's right, comrade. If you can find a way of life that is better than ruling for those who

521a are going to rule, your well-governed city will become a possibility. You see, in it alone the truly rich will rule—those who are rich not in gold, but in the wealth the happy must have: namely, a good and rational life. But if beggars—people hungry for private goods of their own—go into public life, thinking that

the good is there for the seizing, then such a city is impossible. For when ruling is something fought over, such civil and domestic war destroys these men and the rest of the city as well.

GLAUCON: That's absolutely true.

SOCRATES: Do you know of any other sort of life that looks down on political offices besides that of b true philosophy?

GLAUCON: No, by Zeus, I do not.

SOCRATES: But surely it is those who are not lovers of ruling who must go do it. Otherwise, the rivaling lovers will fight over it.

GLAUCON: Of course.

SOCRATES: Who else, then, will you compel to go be guardians of the city if not those who know best what results in good government, and have different honors and a better life than the political?

GLAUCON: No one else.

SOCRATES: Do you want us to consider now how such people will come to exist, and how we will lead c them up to the light, like those who are said to have gone up from Hades to the gods?

GLAUCON: Yes, of course that's what I want.

SOCRATES: It seems, then, that this is not a matter of flipping a potsherd,[5] but of turning a soul from a day that is a kind of night in comparison to the true day—that ascent to what is, which we say is true philosophy.

GLAUCON: Yes, indeed.

SOCRATES: Then mustn't we try to discover what subjects have the power to bring this about?   d

GLAUCON: Of course.

SOCRATES: So what subject is it, Glaucon, that draws the soul from what is coming to be to what is? It occurs to me as I am speaking that we said, didn't we, that these people must be athletes of war when they are young?[6]

GLAUCON: Yes, we did say that.

---

4. [I.e., the practical life of ruling and the theoretical life of doing philosophy.]

5. [A proverbial expression, referring to a children's game. The players were divided into two groups. A shell or potsherd—white on one side, black on the other—was thrown into space between them to the cry of "night or day?" (Note the reference to night and day in what follows.) According as the white or black fell uppermost, one group ran away pursued by the other.]

6. [404a, 412b–417b.]

SOCRATES: Then the subject we are looking for must also have this characteristic in addition to the former one.

GLAUCON: Which?

SOCRATES: It must not be useless to warlike men.

GLAUCON: If possible, it must not.

SOCRATES: Now, earlier they were educated by us in musical and physical training.

GLAUCON: They were.

SOCRATES: And surely physical training is concerned with what-comes-to-be and dies, since it oversees the growth and decay of the body.

GLAUCON: Obviously.

SOCRATES: So it could not be the subject we are looking for.

GLAUCON: No, it could not.

SOCRATES: Is it, then, the musical training we described before?

GLAUCON: But it is just the counterpart of physical training, if you remember. It educated the guardians through habits, conveying by harmony a certain harmoniousness of temper, not knowledge; and by rhythm a certain rhythmical quality. Its stories, whether fictional or nearer the truth, cultivated other habits akin to these. But as for a subject that leads to the destination you have in mind, of the sort you are looking for now, there was nothing of that in it.

SOCRATES: Your reminder is exactly to the point. It really does not have anything of that sort. You're a marvelous fellow, Glaucon, but what is there that does? The crafts all seemed to be somehow menial.[7]

GLAUCON: Of course. And yet, what subject is left that is separate from musical and physical training, and from the crafts?

SOCRATES: Well, if we have nothing left beyond these, let's consider one of those that touches all of them.

GLAUCON: Which?

SOCRATES: Why, for example, that common thing, the one that every type of craft, thought, and knowledge uses, and that is among the first things everyone has to learn.

GLAUCON: Which one is that?

SOCRATES: That inconsequential matter of distinguishing the numbers one, two, and three. In short, I mean number and calculation. Or isn't it true that every type of craft and knowledge must share in them?

GLAUCON: Indeed it is.

SOCRATES: Then warfare must too.

GLAUCON: It must.

SOCRATES: In tragedies, at any rate, Palamedes is always showing up Agamemnon as a totally ridiculous general. Haven't you noticed? He says that by inventing numbers he established how many troops there were in the army at Ilium and counted their ships and everything else. The implication is that they had not been counted before, and that Agamemnon apparently did not even know how many feet he had, since he did not know how to count. What kind of general do you think that made him?

GLAUCON: A very strange one, I'd say, if there is any truth in that.

SOCRATES: Won't we posit this subject, then, as one a warrior has to learn so he can count and calculate?

GLAUCON: It is more essential than anything else—if, that is, he is going to know anything at all about marshaling his troops—or if he is even going to be human, for that matter.

SOCRATES: Then do you notice the same thing about this subject as I do?

GLAUCON: What?

SOCRATES: That in all likelihood it is one of the subjects we were looking for that naturally stimulate the understanding. But no one uses it correctly, as something that really is fitted in every way to draw us toward being.

GLAUCON: How do you mean?

SOCRATES: I will try to make what I believe clear, at any rate. I will distinguish for myself the things that lead in the direction we mentioned from those that do not. Then you must look at them along with me, and either agree or disagree, so that we may see more clearly whether the distinction is as I imagine.

GLAUCON: Show me the things you mean.

SOCRATES: All right, I will show you, if you can see that some sense-perceptions do not summon the understanding to look into them, because the judgment of sense-perception is itself adequate; whereas others encourage it in every way to look into them,

7. [495c–e.]

because sense-perception does not produce a sound result.

GLAUCON: You are obviously referring to things appearing in the distance and illusionist paintings.

SOCRATES: No, you are not quite getting what I mean.

GLAUCON: Then what do you mean?

SOCRATES: The ones that do not summon the understanding are all those that do not at the same time result in an opposite sense-perception. But the

c ones that do I call *summoners*. That is when sense-perception does not make one thing any more clear than its opposite, regardless of whether what strikes the senses is close by or far away. What I mean will be clearer if you look at it this way: these, we say, are three fingers—the smallest, the second, and the middle finger.

GLAUCON: Of course.

SOCRATES: Assume that I am talking about them as being seen from close by. Now consider this about them with me.

GLAUCON: What?

SOCRATES: It is obvious, surely, that each of them is equally a finger, and it makes no differ-

d ence whether it is seen to be in the middle or at either end; whether it is dark or pale, thick or thin, or anything else of that sort. You see, in all these cases, the soul of most people is not compelled to ask the understanding what a finger is, since sight does not at any point suggest to it that a finger is at the same time the opposite of a finger.

GLAUCON: No, it does not.

SOCRATES: It is likely, then, that a perception of that sort would not summon or awaken the under-

e standing.

GLAUCON: It is likely.

SOCRATES: Now, what about their bigness and smallness? Does sight perceive them adequately? Does it make no difference to it whether one of them is in the middle or at the end? And is it the same with the sense of touch, as regards thickness and thinness, hardness and softness? What about the other senses, then—do they make such things sufficiently clear? Or doesn't each of them work as follows: in the first place, the sense that deals with

524a hardness must also deal with softness; and it reports

to the soul that it perceives the same thing to be both hard and soft?

GLAUCON: That's right.

SOCRATES: In cases of this sort then, isn't the soul inevitably puzzled as to what this sense-perception means by hardness, if it says that the same thing is also soft; and in the case of the sense-perception of lightness and heaviness, what it means lightness and heaviness are, if what is heavy is light or what is light heavy?

GLAUCON: Yes, indeed, those are strange mes- b sages for the soul to receive and do need to be examined.

SOCRATES: It is likely, then, that it is in cases of this sort that the soul, summoning calculation and understanding, first tries to determine whether each of the things reported to it is one or two.

GLAUCON: Of course.

SOCRATES: If there are obviously two, won't each of them be obviously one and distinct?

GLAUCON: Yes.

SOCRATES: If each of them is one, then, and both together are two, the soul will understand that the two are separate. I mean, it would not understand inseparable things as two, but as one. c

GLAUCON: That's right.

SOCRATES: But sight, we say, saw bigness and smallness, not as separate, but as mixed up together. Right?

GLAUCON: Yes.

SOCRATES: And to get clear about this, understanding was compelled to see bigness and smallness, too, not mixed up together, but distinguished—the opposite way from sight.

GLAUCON: True.

SOCRATES: Isn't it in cases like this that it first occurs to us to ask what bigness is, and smallness, too?

GLAUCON: Absolutely.

SOCRATES: Which is why we called one section the intelligible and the other the visible.

GLAUCON: Right. d

SOCRATES: That, then, is what I was trying to express before when I said that some things summon thought, while others do not. I define summoners as those that strike the relevant sense at the same time as do their opposites. Those that do not do this, I said, do not wake up the understanding.

GLAUCON: I understand now, and I think you are right.

SOCRATES: Well then, to which of them does number, including the number one, belong?

GLAUCON: I do not know.

SOCRATES: Use what has already been said as an analogy. If the number one is adequately *seen* just by itself, or grasped by any of the other senses, then just as we were saying in the case of fingers, it would not draw the soul toward being. But if something opposite to it is always seen at the same time, so that it no more appears to be one than the opposite of one, then there would be a need at that point for someone to decide the matter. And he would compel the soul within him to be puzzled, to inquire, to stir up the understanding within itself, and to ask what the number one itself is. So, learning about the number one will be among the subjects that lead the soul and turn it around to look at what is.

GLAUCON: But surely the visual perception of it has just that feature, since we do see the same thing as one and as an unlimited number at the same time.

SOCRATES: Then if this is true of the number one, won't it also be true of all numbers?

GLAUCON: Of course.

SOCRATES: But now, calculation and arithmetic are wholly concerned with numbers.

GLAUCON: Right.

SOCRATES: Then they obviously lead toward truth.

GLAUCON: To an unnatural degree.

SOCRATES: Then they would belong, it seems, among the subjects we are seeking. I mean, a soldier must learn them in order to marshal his troops; and a philosopher, because it is necessary to be rising up out of becoming so as to grasp being, or he will never become able to calculate.

GLAUCON: That's right.

SOCRATES: And our guardian is, in fact, both a warrior and a philosopher.

GLAUCON: Of course.

SOCRATES: Then it would be appropriate, Glaucon, to prescribe this subject in our legislation and to persuade those who are going to take part in what is most important in the city to go in for calculation and take it up, not as laymen do, but staying with it until they reach the point at which they see the nature

of the numbers by means of understanding itself; not like tradesmen and retailers, caring about it for the sake of buying and selling, but for the sake of war and for ease in turning the soul itself around from becoming to truth and being.

GLAUCON: Very well put.

SOCRATES: Moreover, it occurs to me now that the subject of calculation has been mentioned, how refined it is and in how many ways it is useful for our purposes, provided you practice it for the sake of knowledge rather than trade.

GLAUCON: Which ways?

SOCRATES: Why, in the very one we were talking about just now. It gives the soul a strong lead upward and compels it to discuss the numbers themselves, never permitting anyone to propose for discussion numbers attached to visible or tangible bodies. I mean, you surely know what people who are clever in these matters are like. If, in the course of the argument, someone tries to divide the number one itself, they laugh and won't permit it. If *you* divide it, they multiply it, taking care that the number one never appears to be, not one, but many parts.

GLAUCON: That's very true.

SOCRATES: Then what do you think would happen, Glaucon, if someone were to ask them: "What kind of numbers are you amazing fellows discussing, where the number one is as you assume it to be, wholly equal in each and every case, without the least difference, and having no internal parts?" What do you think they would answer?

GLAUCON: I think they would answer that they are talking about those that are accessible only to thought and can be grasped in no other way.

SOCRATES: Do you see then, my friend, that this subject really does seem to be necessary to us, since it apparently compels the soul to use understanding itself on the truth itself?

GLAUCON: It does so very strongly, in fact.

SOCRATES: Now, have you ever noticed that those who are naturally good at calculation are also naturally quick in all subjects, so to speak, and that those who are slow, if they are educated and exercised in it, even if they are benefited in no other way, nonetheless improve and become generally sharper than they were?

GLAUCON: That's right.

SOCRATES: Moreover, I do not think you will easily find many subjects that are harder to learn or c practice than it.

GLAUCON: No indeed.

SOCRATES: For all these reasons, then, this subject is not to be neglected. On the contrary, the very best natures must be educated in it.

GLAUCON: I agree.

SOCRATES: Well, then, let's require that one. Second, let's consider whether the subject that follows after it is also appropriate for our purposes.

GLAUCON: Which one? Or do you mean geometry?

SOCRATES: That's it exactly.

GLAUCON: Insofar as it pertains to war, it is clearly d appropriate. You see, when it comes to setting up camp, occupying a region, gathering and ordering troops, and all the other maneuvers armies make whether in battle itself or on the march, it makes all the difference whether someone is skilled in geometry or not.

SOCRATES: But still, for things like that, even a little bit of geometry—and of calculation—would suffice. What we need to consider is whether the greater and more advanced part of it tends to make it easier e to see the form of the good. And that tendency, we say, is to be found in anything that compels the soul to turn itself around toward the region in which lies the happiest of the things that are; the one the soul must do everything possible to see.

GLAUCON: You are right.

SOCRATES: Therefore, if geometry compels one to look at being, it is appropriate; but if at becoming, it is inappropriate.

GLAUCON: Yes, that's what we are saying.

SOCRATES: Now, no one with even a little experi-527a ence of geometry will dispute with us that this science is itself entirely the opposite of what is said about it in the accounts of its practitioners.

GLAUCON: How so?

SOCRATES: Well, they say completely ridiculous things about it because they are so hard up. I mean, they talk as if they were practical people who make all their arguments for the sake of action. They talk of squaring, applying, adding, and the like; whereas, in fact, the entire subject is practiced for the sake of b acquiring knowledge.

GLAUCON: Absolutely.

SOCRATES: Mustn't we also agree on a further point?

GLAUCON: What?

SOCRATES: That it is knowledge of what always is, not of something that comes to be and passes away.

GLAUCON: That's easy to agree to, since geometry is knowledge of what always is.

SOCRATES: In that case, my noble fellow, it can draw the soul toward truth and produce philosophical thought by directing upward what we now wrongly direct downward.

GLAUCON: More than anything else.

SOCRATES: More than anything else, then, we must require the inhabitants of your beautiful city c not to neglect geometry in any way, since even its byproducts are not insignificant.

GLAUCON: What are they?

SOCRATES: The ones you mentioned that are concerned with war. And in addition, when it comes to being better able to pick up any subject, we surely know there is a world of difference between someone with a grasp of geometry and someone without one.

GLAUCON: Yes, by Zeus, a world of difference.

SOCRATES: Shall we prescribe it, then, as a second subject for the young?

GLAUCON: Let's.

SOCRATES: What about astronomy? Shall we make it the third? What do you think? d

GLAUCON: That's fine with me, at least. I mean, a better awareness of the seasons, months, and years is no less appropriate for a general than for a farmer or navigator.

SOCRATES: You are funny! You are like someone who is afraid that the masses will think he is prescribing useless subjects. It is no inconsequential task— indeed it is a very difficult one—to become persuaded that in everyone's soul there is an instrument that is purified and rekindled by such subjects when it has been blinded and destroyed by other pursuits—an e instrument that it is more important to preserve than 10,000 eyes, since only with it can the truth be seen. Those who share your belief that this is so will think you are speaking incredibly well, while those who are completely unaware of it will probably think you are talking nonsense, since they can see no other benefit worth mentioning in these subjects. So, decide right now which group you are engaging in discussion. Or is it neither of them, and are you making your arguments mostly for your own sake—though you do not begrudge anyone else whatever profit he can get from them?

GLAUCON: That's what I prefer—to speak, question, and answer mostly for my own sake.

SOCRATES: Let's backtrack a bit. You see, we were wrong just now about the subject that comes after geometry.

GLAUCON: How so?

SOCRATES: After a plain surface, we went immediately to a solid that was revolving, without taking one just by itself. But the right way is to take up the third dimension after the second. And it, I suppose, consists of cubes and of whatever shares in depth.

GLAUCON: Yes, you are right. But Socrates, that subject has not even been investigated yet.

SOCRATES: There are two reasons for that. Because no city values it, it is not vigorously investigated, due to its difficulty. And investigators need a director if they are to discover anything. Now, in the first place, such a director is difficult to find. Second, even if he could be found, as things stand now, those who investigate it are too arrogant to obey him. But if an entire city served as his co-director and took the lead in valuing this subject, then they would obey him, and consistent and vigorous investigation would reveal the facts about it. For even now, when it is not valued by the masses and is hampered by investigators who lack any account of its usefulness—all the same, in spite of all these handicaps, the force of its appeal has caused it to be developed. So it would not be at all surprising if the facts about it were revealed in any case.

GLAUCON: Yes, indeed, it *is* an outstandingly appealing subject. But explain more clearly to me what you were saying just now. You took geometry, presumably, as dealing with plane surface.

SOCRATES: Yes.

GLAUCON: Then at first you put astronomy after it, but later you went back on that.

SOCRATES: Yes, the more I hurried to get through them all, the slower I went! You see, the subject dealing with the dimension of depth was next. But because of the ridiculous state the investigation of it is in, I passed it by and spoke of astronomy—which

deals with the motion of things having depth—after geometry.

GLAUCON: That's right.

SOCRATES: Let's then prescribe astronomy as the fourth subject, on the assumption that solid geometry, which we are now omitting, will be available if a city takes it up.

GLAUCON: That seems reasonable. And since you reproached me just now, Socrates, for praising astronomy in a vulgar manner, I will now praise it your way. You see, I think it is clear to everyone that it compels the soul to look upward and leads it from things here to things there.

SOCRATES: It is clear to everyone except me, then, since that is not how I think of it.

GLAUCON: Then how do you think of it?

SOCRATES: As it is handled today by those who teach philosophy, it makes the soul look very much downward.

GLAUCON: How do you mean?

SOCRATES: In my opinion, your conception of "higher studies" is a good deal too generous! I mean, if someone were looking at something by leaning his head back and studying ornaments on a ceiling, it seems as though you would say that he is looking at them with his understanding, not with his eyes! Maybe you are right and I am foolish. You see, I just cannot conceive of any subject making the soul look upward except the one that is concerned with what is—and that is *invisible*. If anyone tries to learn something about perceptible things, whether by gaping upward or squinting downward, I would say that he never really learns—since there is no knowledge to be had of such things—and that his soul is not looking up but down, whether he does his learning lying on his back on land or on sea!

GLAUCON: A fair judgment! You are right to reproach me. But what did you mean, then, when you said that astronomy must be learned in a different way than people learn it at present, if it is going to be useful with regard to what we are talking about?

SOCRATES: It is like this: these ornaments in the heavens, since they are ornaments in something visible, may certainly be regarded as having the most beautiful and most exact motions that such things can have. But these fall far short of the true ones—those motions in which the things that are really fast or really slow, as measured in true numbers and as forming all the true geometrical figures, are moved relative to one another, and that move the things that are in them. And these, of course, must be grasped by reason and thought, not by sight. Don't you agree?

GLAUCON: Of course.

SOCRATES: Therefore, we should use the ornaments in the heavens as models to help us study these other things. It is just as if someone chanced to find *e* diagrams by Daedalus or some other craftsman or painter, which were very carefully drawn and worked out. I mean, anyone experienced in geometry who saw such things would consider them to be very beautifully executed, I suppose. But he would think it ridiculous to examine them seriously in order to find there the truth about equals, doubles, or any other *530a* ratio.

GLAUCON: How could it be anything but ridiculous?

SOCRATES: Don't you think, then, that a real astronomer will feel the same way when he looks at the motions of the stars? He will believe that the craftsman of the heavens arranged them and all that is in them in the most beautiful way possible for such things. But as for the ratio of night to day, of these to a month, of a month to a year, or of the motions of the stars to them or to each other, don't you think *b* he will consider it strange to believe that they are always the same and never deviate in the least, since they are connected to body and are visible things, or to seek by every means possible to grasp the truth about them?

GLAUCON: That's what I think—anyway, now that I hear it from you!

SOCRATES: Just as in geometry, then, it is by making use of problems that we will pursue astronomy too. We will leave the things in the heavens alone, if we are really going to participate in astronomy and make the naturally wise element in the soul useful *c* instead of useless.

GLAUCON: The task you are prescribing is a lot bigger than anything now attempted in astronomy.

SOCRATES: And I suppose we will prescribe other subjects in the same way, if we are to be of any benefit as lawgivers. But can you in fact suggest any other appropriate subjects?

GLAUCON: Not at the moment, anyway.

SOCRATES: But motion, it seems to me, presents itself, not just in one form, but in several. A wise person could probably list them all, but there are two that are evident even to us.   *d*

GLAUCON: What are they?

SOCRATES: Besides the one we have discussed, there is also its counterpart.

GLAUCON: What's that?

SOCRATES: It is probable that as the eyes fasten on astronomical motions, so the ears fasten on harmonic ones, and that these two sciences are somehow akin, as the Pythagoreans say. And we agree, Glaucon. Don't we?

GLAUCON: We do.

SOCRATES: Then, since the task is so huge, *e* shouldn't we ask them their opinion and whether they have anything to add, all the while guarding our own requirement?

GLAUCON: What's that?

SOCRATES: That those we will be rearing should never attempt to learn anything incomplete,[8] anything that does not always come out at the place all things should reach—the one we mentioned just now in the case of astronomy.[9] Or don't you know that people do something similar with harmony, too? *531a* They measure audible concordances and sounds against one another, and so labor in vain, just like astronomers.

GLAUCON: Yes, by the gods, and pretty ridiculous they are, too. They talk about something they call a "dense interval" or quarter tone[10]—putting their ears to their instruments, like someone trying to overhear what the neighbors are saying. And some say they hear a tone in between, and that *it* is the shortest interval by which they must measure, while others argue that this tone sounds the same as a quarter tone. Both groups put ears before the understanding. *b*

SOCRATES: You mean those excellent fellows who vex their strings, torturing them and stretching them on pegs. I won't draw out the analogy by speaking of blows with the pick, or the charges laid against strings

---

8. [504c.]

9. [528b.]

10. [A dense interval is evidently the smallest difference in pitch that was recognized in ancient music.]

that are too responsive or too unresponsive. Instead, I will drop the analogy and say that I do not mean these people, but the ones we just said we were going to question about harmonics. You see, they do the same as the astronomers do. I mean, it is in these *c* audible concordances that they search for numbers, but they do not ascend to problems or investigate which numbers are in concord and which are not, or what the explanation is in each case.

GLAUCON: But that would be a daimonic task!

SOCRATES: Yet, it is useful in the search for the beautiful and the good! Pursued for any other purpose, though, it is useless.

GLAUCON: I suppose so.

SOCRATES: Moreover, I take it that if the investigation of all the subjects we have mentioned arrives at *d* what they share in common with one another and what their affinities are, and draws conclusions about their kinship, it does contribute something to our goal and is not labor in vain; but that otherwise it is in vain.

GLAUCON: I have the same hunch myself. But you are still talking about a very big task, Socrates.

SOCRATES: Do you mean the prelude, or what? Or don't you know that all these subjects are merely preludes to the theme[11] itself that must be learned? I mean, you surely do not think that people who are *e* clever in these matters are dialecticians.

GLAUCON: No, by Zeus, I do not. Although, I have met a few exceptions.

SOCRATES: But did it ever seem to you that those who can neither give an account nor approve one know what any of the things are that we say they must know?

GLAUCON: Again, the answer is no.

SOCRATES: Then isn't this at last, Glaucon, the *532a* theme itself that dialectical discussion sings? It itself is intelligible. But the power of sight imitates it. We said that sight tries at last to look at the animals themselves, the stars themselves, and, in the end, at the sun itself. In the same way, whenever someone tries, by means of dialectical discussion and without the aid of any sense-perceptions, to arrive through reason at the being of each thing itself, and does not give up until he grasps what good itself is with understanding itself, he

reaches the end of the intelligible realm, just as the *b* other reached the end of the visible one.

GLAUCON: Absolutely.

SOCRATES: Well, then, don't you call this journey[12] dialectic?

GLAUCON: I do.

SOCRATES: Then the release from bonds and the turning around from shadows to statues and the light; and then the ascent out of the cave to the sun; and there the continuing inability to look directly at the animals, the plants, and the light of the sun, but instead at divine reflections in water and shadows of the things that are, and not, as before, merely at shadows of statues thrown by another source of light *c* that, when judged in relation to the sun, is as shadowy as they—all this practice of the crafts we mentioned has the power to lead the best part of the soul upward until it sees the best among the things that are, just as before the clearest thing in the body was led to the brightest thing in the bodily and visible world. *d*

GLAUCON: I accept that this is so. And yet, I think it is very difficult to accept; although—in another way—difficult not to accept! All the same, since the present occasion is not our only opportunity to hear these things, but we will get to return to them often in the future, let's assume that what you said about them just now is true and turn to the theme itself, and discuss it in the same way as we did the prelude. So, tell us then, in what way the power of dialectical discussion works, into what kinds it is divided, and what roads it follows. I mean, it is these, it seems, that would lead us at last to that place which is a rest *e* from the road, so to speak, for the one who reaches it, and an end of his journey.

SOCRATES: You won't be able to follow me any farther, my dear Glaucon—though not because of *533a* any lack of eagerness on my part. You would no longer see an image of what we are describing, but the truth itself as it seems to me, at least. Whether it is really so or not—that's not something on which it is any longer worth insisting. But that there is some such thing to be seen, *that* is something on which we must insist. Isn't that so?

11. [*Nomos*: also, law.]

12. [*Poreia*: An *aporia* (puzzle, problem—literally, a blockage on one's journey forward) is what dialectic attempts to solve.]

GLAUCON: Of course.

SOCRATES: And mustn't we also insist that the power of dialectical discussion could reveal it only to someone experienced in the subjects we described, and cannot do so in any other way?

GLAUCON: Yes, that is worth insisting on, too.

SOCRATES: At the very least, no one will dispute
b our claim by arguing that there is another road of inquiry that tries to acquire a systematic and wholly general grasp of what each thing itself is. By contrast, all the other crafts are concerned with human beliefs and appetites, with growing or construction, or with the care of growing or constructed things. As for the rest, we described them as to some extent grasping what is—I mean, geometry and the subjects that follow it. For we saw that while they do dream about what is, they cannot see it while wide awake as long
c as they make use of hypotheses that they leave undisturbed, and for which they cannot give any argument. After all, when the first principle is unknown, and the conclusion and the steps in between are put together out of what is unknown, what mechanism could possibly turn any agreement reached in such cases into knowledge?

GLAUCON: None.

SOCRATES: Therefore, dialectic is the only investigation that, doing away with hypotheses, journeys to
d the first principle itself in order to be made secure. And when the eye of the soul is really buried in a sort of barbaric bog, dialectic gently pulls it out and leads it upward, using the crafts we described to help it and cooperate with it in turning the soul around. From force of habit, we have often called these branches of knowledge. But they need another name, since they are clearer than belief and darker than knowledge. We distinguished them by the term "thought" somewhere before.[13] But I don't suppose we will dispute about names, with matters as impor-
e tant as those before us to investigate.

GLAUCON: Of course not, just as long as they express the state of clarity the soul possesses.

SOCRATES: It will be satisfactory, then, to do what we did before and call the first section knowledge, the second thought, the third opinion, and the fourth imagination. The last two together we call belief, the 534a other two, understanding.[14] Belief is concerned with becoming; understanding with being. And as being is to becoming, so understanding is to belief; and as understanding is to belief, so knowledge is to belief and thought to imagination. But as for the ratios between the things these deal with, and the division of either the believable or the intelligible section into two, let's pass them by, Glaucon, in case they involve us in discussions many times longer than the ones we have already gone through.

GLAUCON: I agree with you about the rest of them, anyway, insofar as I am able to follow.   b

SOCRATES: So don't you, too, call someone a dialectician when he is able to grasp an account of the being of each thing? And when he cannot do so, won't you, too, say that to the extent that he cannot give an account of something either to himself or to another, to that extent he does not understand it?

GLAUCON: How could I not?

SOCRATES: Then the same applies to the good. Unless someone can give an account of the form of the good, distinguishing it from everything else, and can survive all examination as if in a battle, striving c to examine[15] things not in accordance with belief, but in accordance with being; and can journey through all that with his account still intact, you will say that he does not know the good itself or any other good whatsoever. And if he does manage to grasp some image of it, you will say that it is through belief, not knowledge, that he grasps it; that he is dreaming and asleep throughout his present life; and that, before he wakes up here, he will arrive in Hades and go to sleep forever.   d

GLAUCON: Yes, by Zeus, I will certainly say all that.

---

13. [511d6–511e4.]

14. [The reference is to 511d6–e5, where the first section is called understanding (noêsis), not knowledge (epistêmê). Since thought (dianoia) is not now a kind of knowledge, noêsis and epistêmê have in effect become one and the same. Epistêmê and dianoia are now jointly referred to as noêsis, because that whole section of the line on which they appear consists of intelligible objects (noêton).]

15. [Elengchein: ("to examine," "to refute")—as in the Socratic elenchus.]

SOCRATES: Then as for those children of yours, the ones you are rearing and educating in your discussion, if you ever reared them in fact, I don't suppose that, while they are still as irrational as the proverbial lines,[16] you would allow them to rule in your city or control the most important things.

GLAUCON: No, of course not.

SOCRATES: Won't you prescribe in your legislation, then, that they are to give the most attention to the education that will enable them to ask and answer questions most knowledgeably?

e GLAUCON: I will prescribe it—together with you.

SOCRATES: Doesn't it seem to you, then, that dialectic is just like a capstone we have placed on top of the subjects, and that no other subject can rightly be placed above it, but that our account of the subjects 535a has now come to an end?

GLAUCON: It does.

SOCRATES: Then it remains for you to deal with the distribution of these subjects: to whom we will assign them and in what way.

GLAUCON: Clearly.

SOCRATES: Do you remember what sort of people we chose in our earlier selection of rulers?[17]

GLAUCON: How could I not?

SOCRATES: Well then, as regards the other requirements too, you must suppose that these same natures are to be chosen, since we have to select the most stable, the most courageous, and—as far as possible—the best-looking. In addition, we must b look not only for people who have a noble and valiant character, but for those who also have natural qualities conducive to this education of ours.

GLAUCON: Which ones in particular?

SOCRATES: They must be keen on the subjects, bless you, and learn them without difficulty. For people's souls are much more likely to give up during strenuous studies than during physical training. The pain is more their own, you see, since it is peculiar to them and not shared with the body.

GLAUCON: That's true.

SOCRATES: We must also look for someone who has a good memory, is persistent, and is wholeheartedly in love with hard work. How else do you suppose c he would be willing to carry out such hard physical labors and also complete so much learning and training?

GLAUCON: He would not, not unless his nature were an entirely good one.

SOCRATES: In any case, the mistake made at present—which, as we said before, explains why philosophy has fallen into dishonor—is that unworthy people take it up. For illegitimate people should not have taken it up, but genuine ones.

GLAUCON: How do you mean?

SOCRATES: In the first place, the one who takes it up must not be half-hearted in his love of hard work, with one half of him loving hard work and the other shirking it. That is what happens when someone d is a lover of physical training and a lover of hunting and a lover of all kinds of hard bodily labor; yet is not a lover of learning, a lover of listening, or a keen investigator, but hates the work involved in all such things. And someone whose love of hard work tends in the opposite direction is also defective.

GLAUCON: That's absolutely true.

SOCRATES: Similarly with regard to truth, won't we say that a soul is maimed if it hates a voluntary lie, cannot endure to have one in itself, and is greatly e angered when others lie; but is nonetheless content to accept an involuntary lie, does not get irritated when it is caught being ignorant, and bears its ignorance easily, wallowing in it like a pig?[18]

GLAUCON: Absolutely.   536a

SOCRATES: And with regard to temperance, courage, high-mindedness, and all the other parts of virtue, too, we must be especially on our guard to distinguish the illegitimate from the genuine. You see, when private individuals or cities do not know how to investigate all these things fully, they unwittingly employ defectives and illegitimates as their friends or rulers for whatever services they happen to need.

GLAUCON: Yes, that's just what happens.

SOCRATES: So we must take good care in all these matters, since, if we bring people who are sound of

---

16. [A pun made possible by the fact that *alogon* can mean "irrational" (as applied to people) and "incommensurable" (as applied to lines in geometry).]

17. [412b8–417b9.]

18. [The difference between voluntary and involuntary lies is explained at 382a1–383a7.]

b limb and mind to so important a subject, and train and educate them in it, justice itself will not find fault with us, and we will save both the city and its constitution. But if we bring people of a different sort to it, we will achieve precisely the opposite and let loose an even greater flood of ridicule upon philosophy as well.

GLAUCON: That would be a shame.

SOCRATES: It certainly would. But I seem to have made myself a little ridiculous just now.

GLAUCON: In what way?

c   SOCRATES: I forgot we were playing and spoke too vehemently. You see, while I was speaking I looked upon philosophy, and when I saw it undeservedly showered with abuse, I suppose I got irritated and, as if I were angry with those responsible, I said what I had to say in too serious a manner.

GLAUCON: Not too serious for me, by Zeus, as a member of the audience.

SOCRATES: But too serious for me as the speaker. In any case, let's not forget that in our earlier selection we chose older people, but here that is not permitted.
d You see, we must not believe Solon when he says that as someone grows older, he is able to learn a lot. On the contrary, he is even less able to learn than to run. It is to young people that all large and frequent labors properly belong.

GLAUCON: Necessarily so.

SOCRATES: Well, then, calculation, geometry, and all the preparatory education that serves as preparation for dialectic must be offered to them in childhood—and not in the shape of compulsory instruction, either.

GLAUCON: Why's that?

SOCRATES: Because a free person should learn
e nothing slavishly. For while compulsory physical labors do no harm to the body, no compulsory instruction remains in the soul.

GLAUCON: That's true.

SOCRATES: Well, then, do not use compulsion, my very good man, to train the children in these subjects; use play instead. That way you will also be
537a able to see better what each of them is naturally suited for.

GLAUCON: What you say makes sense.

SOCRATES: Don't you remember that we also said that the children were to be led into war on horseback as observers, and that, wherever it is safe, they should be brought to the front and given a taste of blood, just like young dogs?

GLAUCON: I do remember.

SOCRATES: Those who always show the greatest facility in dealing with all these labors, studies, and fears must be enrolled in a unit.

GLAUCON: At what age?   *b*

SOCRATES: After they are released from compulsory physical training. For during that period, whether it is two or three years, they are incapable of doing anything else, since weariness and sleep are enemies of learning. At the same time, one of the important tests of each of them is how he fares in physical training.

GLAUCON: It certainly is.

SOCRATES: Then, after that period, those selected from among the twenty-year-olds will receive greater honors than the others. Moreover, the subjects they learned in no particular order in their education as children, they must now bring together into a unified *c* vision of their kinship with one another and with the nature of what is.

GLAUCON: That, at any rate, is the only instruction that remains secure in those who receive it.

SOCRATES: It is also the greatest test of which nature is dialectical and which is not. For the person who can achieve a unified vision is dialectical, and the one who cannot isn't.

GLAUCON: I agree.

SOCRATES: Well, then, you will have to look out for those among them who most possess that quality; who are resolute in their studies and also *d* resolute in war and the other things conventionally expected of them. And when they have passed their thirtieth year, you will have to select them in turn from among those selected earlier and assign them yet greater honors, and test them by means of the power of dialectical discussion to see which of them can relinquish his eyes and other senses, and travel on in the company of truth to what itself is. And here, comrade, you have a task that needs a lot of safeguarding.

GLAUCON: How so?

SOCRATES: Don't you realize the harm caused by dialectical discussion as it is currently practiced? *e*

GLAUCON: What harm?

SOCRATES: Its practitioners are filled with law-lessness.

GLAUCON: They certainly are.

SOCRATES: Do you think it is at all surprising that this happens to them? Aren't you sympathetic?

GLAUCON: Why should I be?

SOCRATES: It is like the case of a supposititious child brought up amid great wealth, a large and pow-erful family, and many flatterers, who finds out, when he has become a man, that he is not the child of his professed parents and that he cannot discover his real ones. Do you have any hunch as to what his attitude would be to the flatterers, and to his supposed parents, during the time when he did not know about the exchange, and, on the other hand, when he did know? Or would you rather hear my hunch?

GLAUCON: I would.

SOCRATES: Well, then, my hunch is that he would be more likely to honor his father, his mother, and the rest of his supposed family than the flatterers, less likely to overlook any of their needs, less likely to treat them lawlessly in word or deed, and less likely to disobey them than the flatterers in any matters of importance, in the time when he did not know the truth.

GLAUCON: Probably so.

SOCRATES: But when he became aware of the truth, on the other hand, my hunch is that he would withdraw his honor and devotion from his family and increase them for the flatterers, whom he would obey far more than before, and he would begin to live the way they did, spend time with them openly, and—unless he was thoroughly good by nature—care noth-ing for that father of his or any of the rest of his supposed family.

GLAUCON: All that would probably happen as you say. But how is it like the case of those who take up argument?

SOCRATES: As follows. I take it we hold from child-hood convictions about what things are just and fine; we are brought up with them as with our parents; we obey and honor them.

GLAUCON: Yes, we do.

SOCRATES: And there are also other practices, op-posite to those, which possess pleasures that flatter our soul and attract it to themselves, but which do not persuade people who are at all moderate—who continue to honor and obey the convictions of their fathers.

GLAUCON: That's right.

SOCRATES: What happens, then, when someone of that sort is met by the question, "What is the fine?" and, when he answers what he has heard from the traditional lawgiver, the argument refutes him; and by refuting him often and in many ways, reduces him to the belief that the fine is no more fine than shameful, and the same with the just, the good, and the things he honored most—what do you think he will do after that about honoring and obeying his earlier convictions?

GLAUCON: It is inevitable that he won't honor or obey them in the same way.

SOCRATES: Then when he no longer regards them as honorable or as his own kin the way he did before, and cannot discover the true ones, will he be likely to adopt any other sort of life than the one that flat-ters him?

GLAUCON: No, he won't.

SOCRATES: And so he will be taken, I suppose, to have changed from being law-abiding to being lawless.

GLAUCON: Inevitably.

SOCRATES: Isn't it likely, then, that this is what will happen to people who take up argument in that way, and, as I said just now, don't they deserve a lot of sympathy?

GLAUCON: Yes, and pity too.

SOCRATES: Then if you do not want your thirty-year-olds to be objects of such pity, won't you have to employ every sort of precaution when they take up argument?

GLAUCON: Yes, indeed.

SOCRATES: And isn't one very effective precaution not to let them taste argument while they are young? I mean, I don't suppose it has escaped your notice that when young people get their first taste of argu-ment, they misuse it as if it were playing a game, always using it for disputation. They imitate those who have refuted them by refuting others themselves, and, like puppies, enjoy dragging and tearing with argument anyone within reach.

GLAUCON: Excessively so.

SOCRATES: Then, when they have refuted many themselves and been refuted by many, they quickly

c fall into violently disbelieving everything they believed before. And as a result of this, they themselves
and the whole of philosophy as well are discredited
in the eyes of others.

GLAUCON: That's absolutely true.

SOCRATES: But an older person would not be willing to take part in such madness. He will imitate
someone who is willing to engage in dialectical discussion and look for the truth, rather than someone
who plays at disputation as a game. He will be more
moderate himself and will bring honor, rather than
d discredit, to the practice.

GLAUCON: That's right.

SOCRATES: And wasn't everything we said before
this also said as a precaution—that those with whom
one takes part in arguments are to be orderly and
steady by nature, and not, as now, those, however
unsuitable, who chance to come along?

GLAUCON: Yes, it was.

SOCRATES: Is it enough, then, if someone devotes
himself continuously and strenuously to taking part
in argument, doing nothing else, but training in it
just as he did in the physical training that is its counterpart, but for twice as many years?

e GLAUCON: Do you mean six years or four?

SOCRATES: It does not matter. Make it five. You
see, after that, you must make them go down into
the cave again, and compel them to take command
in matters of war and the other offices suitable for
young people, so that they won't be inferior to the
others in experience. And in these offices, too, they
must be tested to see whether they will remain stead-
540a fast when they are pulled in different directions, or
give way.

GLAUCON: How much time do you assign to that?

SOCRATES: Fifteen years. Then, at the age of fifty,
those who have survived the tests and are entirely
best in every practical task and every science must
be led at last to the end and compelled to lift up the
radiant light of their souls, and to look toward what
itself provides light for everything. And once they
have seen the good itself, they must use it as their
model and put the city, its citizens, and themselves
in order throughout the remainder of their lives, each
b in turn. They will spend the greater part of their time
doing philosophy, but, when his turn comes, each
must labor in politics and rule for the city's sake, not

as something fine, but rather as something that must
be done. In that way, always having educated others
like themselves to take their place as guardians of the
city, they will depart for the Isles of the Blessed and
dwell there. And the city will publicly establish memorials and sacrifices to them as daimons, if the
Pythia agrees; but if not, as happy and divine people. c

GLAUCON: Like a sculptor, Socrates, you have
produced thoroughly beautiful ruling men!

SOCRATES: And ruling women, too, Glaucon.
You see, you must not think that what I have said
applies any more to men than it does to those women
of theirs who are born with the appropriate natures.

GLAUCON: That's right, if indeed they are to share
everything equally with the men, as we said.

SOCRATES: Well, then, do you agree that the
things we have said about the city and its constitution d
are not altogether wishful thinking; that it is difficult
for them to come about, but possible in a way, and
in no way except the one we described: namely, when
one or more true philosophers come to power in
a city—people who think little of present honors,
regarding them as illiberal and worthless, who prize
what is right and the honors that come from it above
everything, and who consider justice as the most im- e
portant and most essential thing, serving it and fostering it as they set their city in order?

GLAUCON: How will they do that?

SOCRATES: Everyone in the city who is over ten
years old they will send into the country. They will 541a
take over the children, and far removed from current
habits, which their parents possess, they will bring
them up in their own ways and laws, which are the
ones we described before. And with the city and constitution we were discussing thus established in the
quickest and easiest way, it will itself be happy and
bring the greatest benefit to the people among whom
it comes to be.

GLAUCON: That's by far the quickest and easiest
way. And in my opinion, Socrates, you have well
described how it would come into existence, if it
ever did.   b

SOCRATES: Haven't we said enough, then, about
this city and the man who is like it? For surely it is
clear what sort of person we will say he has to be.

GLAUCON: Yes, it is clear. And as for your question, I think we have reached the end of this topic.

BOOK VIII

SOCRATES' NARRATION CONTINUES:

SOCRATES: All right. We are agreed, then, Glaucon, that if a city is going to be eminently well governed, women must be shared; children and their entire education must be shared; in both peace and war, pursuits must be shared; and their kings must be those among them who have proved best both in philosophy and where war is concerned.

GLAUCON: We are agreed.

SOCRATES: Moreover, we also granted this: once the rulers are established, they will lead the soldiers and settle them in the kind of dwellings we described earlier, which are in no way private, but wholly shared. And surely we also came to an agreement, if you remember, about what sort of possessions they should have.

GLAUCON: Yes, I do remember. We thought that none of them should acquire any of the things that others now do; but that, as athletes of war and guardians, they should receive their minimum yearly upkeep from the other citizens as a wage for their guardianship, and take care of themselves and the rest of the city.[1]

SOCRATES: That's right. But since we have completed that discussion, let's recall the point at which we began the digression that brought us here, so that we can continue on the same path again.

GLAUCON: That is not difficult. You see, much the same as now, you were talking as if you had completed the description of the city.[2] You were saying that you would class both the city you described and the man who is like it as good, even though, as it seems, you had a still finer city and man to tell us about. But in any case, you were saying that the others were defective, if it was correct. And you said, if I remember, that of the remaining kinds of constitution four were worth discussing, each with defects we should observe; and that we should do the same for the people like them in order to observe them all, come to an agreement about which man is best and

which worst, and then determine whether the best is happiest and the worst most wretched, or whether it is otherwise. I was asking you which four constitutions you had in mind, when Polemarchus and Adeimantus interrupted.[3] And that is when you took up the discussion that led here.

SOCRATES: That's absolutely right.

GLAUCON: Like a wrestler, then, give me the same hold again, and when I ask the same question, try to tell me what you were about to say before.

SOCRATES: If I can.

GLAUCON: In any case, I really want to hear for myself what four constitutions you meant.

SOCRATES: It won't be difficult for you to hear them. You see, the ones I mean are the very ones that already have names: the one that is praised by "the many," your Cretan or Laconian[4] constitution. The second—and second in the praise it receives—is called oligarchy, a constitution filled with a host of evils. Antagonistic to it, and next in order, is democracy. And "noble" tyranny, surpassing all of them, is the fourth and most extreme disease of cities. Can you think of another form of constitution—I mean, another distinct in form from these? For, no doubt, there are dynasties and purchased kingships and other similar constitutions in between these, which one finds no less among barbarians than among Greeks.

GLAUCON: Many strange ones are certainly mentioned, at least.

SOCRATES: Are you aware, then, that there must be as many forms of human character as there are of constitutions? Or do you think constitutions arise from oak or rock[5] and not from the characters of the people in the cities, which tip the scales, so to speak, and drag the rest along with them?

GLAUCON: No, they could not possibly arise from anything other than that.

SOCRATES: So, if there are five of cities, there must also be five ways of arranging private individual souls.

GLAUCON: Of course.

---

1. [415d6–420a7.]
2. [445c1–450c5.]
3. [449b1–2.]
4. [I.e., Spartan.]
5. [Homer, *Odyssey* 19.163.]

SOCRATES: Now, we have already described the one who is like aristocracy, the one we rightly describe as good and just.

545a GLAUCON: Yes, we have described him.

SOCRATES: Mustn't we next describe the inferior ones—the victory-loving and honor-loving, which correspond to the Laconian constitution, followed by the oligarchic, democratic, and tyrannical—so that, having discovered the most unjust of all, we can oppose him to the most just and complete our investigation into how pure justice and pure injustice stand with regard to the happiness or wretchedness of the one who possesses them; and be persuaded either by Thrasymachus to practice injustice or by the argu-
b ment that is now coming to light to practice justice.

GLAUCON: That's exactly what we must do.

SOCRATES: Then just as we began by looking for the virtues of character in constitutions before looking for them in private individuals, thinking they would be clearer in the former, shouldn't we first examine the honor-loving constitution? I do not know another name that is commonly applied to it; it should be called either timocracy or timarchy. Then shouldn't we examine that sort of man by comparing him to
c it, and, after that, oligarchy and the oligarchic man, and democracy and the democratic man? Fourth, having come to a city that is under a tyrant and having examined it, shouldn't we look into a tyrannical soul, and so try to become adequate judges of the topic we proposed for ourselves?[6]

GLAUCON: That, at any rate, would be a reasonable way for us to go about observing and judging.

SOCRATES: Come on, then, let's try to describe how timocracy emerges from aristocracy. Or is it sim-
d ply the case that, in all constitutions, change originates in the ruling element itself when faction breaks out within it; but that if this group remains of one mind, then—however small it is—change is impossible?

GLAUCON: Yes, that's right.

SOCRATES: How, then, Glaucon, will our city be changed? How will faction arise, either between the auxiliaries and the rulers or within either group? Or do you want us to be like Homer and pray to the
e Muses to tell us "how faction first broke out,"[7] and

have them speak in tragic tones, playing and jesting with us, as if we were children and they were speaking in earnest?

GLAUCON: How do you mean?

SOCRATES: Something like this: "It is difficult for a city constituted in this way to change. However, 546a since everything that comes-to-be must decay, not even one so constituted will last forever. On the contrary, it, too, must face dissolution. And this is how it will be dissolved: not only plants that grow in the earth, but also animals that grow upon it, have periods of fertility and infertility of both soul and bodies each time their cycles complete a revolution. These cycles are short for what is short-lived and the opposite for what is the opposite. However, even though they are wise, the people you have educated to be leaders in your city will, by using rational calculation combined b with sense-perception, nonetheless fail to ascertain the periods of good fertility and of infertility for your species. Instead, these will escape them, and so they will sometimes beget children when they should not.

"Now, for the birth of a divine creature there is a cycle comprehended by a perfect number;[8] while for a human being, it is the first number in which are found increases involving both roots and powers, comprehending three intervals and four terms, of factors that cause likeness and unlikeness, cause increase and decrease, and make all things mutually agreeable and rational in their relations to one another. Of these factors, the base ones—four in relation to three, c together with five—give two harmonies when thrice increased. One is a square, so many times a hundred. The other is of equal length one way, but oblong. One of its sides are 100 squares of the rational diameter of five each diminished by one, or alternatively 100 squares of the irrational diameter each diminished by two. The other side are 100 cubes of three. This whole geometrical number controls better and worse births.[9]

6. [Most recently at 544a2–8.]

7. [Apparently an adaptation of Iliad 16.112–3.]

8. [The divine creature seems to be the world or universe. See Timaeus 30b–d, 32d, 34a–b. Plato does not specify what its number is.]

9. [The human geometrical number is the product of 3, 4, and 5 "thrice increased": if $(3 \times 4 \times 5) \times (3 \times 4 \times 5) = (3 \times 4 \times 5)^2$ is one increase, $(3 \times 4 \times 5) \times (3 \times 4 \times 5) (3 \times 4 \times 5) \times (3 \times 4 \times 5) = (3 \times 4 \times 5)^4$ is three.

"And when, through ignorance of these, your
d guardians join brides and grooms at the wrong time,
the children will be neither good-natured nor fortunate. The older generation will choose the best of
these children, even though they do not deserve them.
And when they in turn acquire their fathers' powers,
the first thing they will begin to neglect as guardians
will be us, by paying less attention to musical training
than they should; and the second is physical training.
Hence your young people will become more unmusical. And rulers chosen from among them won't
be able to guard well the testing of Hesiod's and

your own races—gold, silver, bronze, and iron.[10] e
The intermixing of iron with silver and bronze with 547a
gold will engender lack of likeness and unharmonious
inequality, and these always breed war and hostility
wherever they arise. We must declare faction to be
'of this lineage,'[11] wherever and whenever it arises."

GLAUCON: And we will declare that they have
answered correctly.

SOCRATES: They must. They are Muses, after all!

GLAUCON: What do the Muses say next?   b

SOCRATES: When faction arose, each of these two
races, the iron and the bronze, pulled the constitution
toward moneymaking and the acquisition of land,
houses, gold, and silver. The other two, by contrast,
the gold and silver races—since they are not poor,
but naturally rich in their souls—led toward virtue
and the old political system. Striving and struggling
with one another, they compromised on a middle
way: they distributed the land and houses among
themselves as private property; enslaved and held as
serfs and servants those whom they had previously
guarded as free friends and providers of upkeep; and c
took responsibility themselves for making war and for
guarding against the ones they had enslaved.

GLAUCON: I think that is how the transformation begins.

SOCRATES: Wouldn't this constitution, then, be
somehow in the middle between aristocracy and
oligarchy?

GLAUCON: Of course.

SOCRATES: Anyway, that is how the transformation occurs. But once transformed, how will it be
managed? Or isn't it obvious that it will imitate the
first constitution in some respects and oligarchy in d
others, since it is in the middle between them; and
that it will also have some features unique to itself?

GLAUCON: That's right.

SOCRATES: In honoring the rulers, then, and in
the fighting class's abstention from farming, handi-
crafts, and other ways of making money, in providing
communal meals and being devoted to physical training and training for war—in all such ways, won't the
constitution be like the previous one?

This formula included "increases involving both roots
and powers": $(3 \times 4 \times 5)$ is a root; its indices are powers.
It "comprehends" three "intervals," symbolized by ×, and
four "terms"—namely, the roots. The resulting number,
12,960,000, can be represented geometrically as: (1) a
square whose sides are 3,600, or (2) an "oblong" or
rectangle whose sides are 4,800 and 2,700. (1) is "so
many times 100": 36 times. (2) is obtained as follows. The
"rational diameter" of 5 is the nearest rational number to
the real diameter of a square whose sides are 5. This
diameter $= \sqrt{5^2 + 5^2} = \sqrt{50} - 7$. Since the square of 7
is 49, we get the longer side of the rectangle by diminishing 49 by 1 and multiplying the result by 100. This
gives 4,800. The "irrational diameter" of 5 is $\sqrt{50}$. When
squared ($= 50$), diminished by 2 ($= 48$), and multiplied
by 100, this, too, is 4,800. The short side, "100 cubes of
three," $= 2,700$. The significance of the number is more
controversial. The factors "that cause likeness and unlikeness, cause increase and decrease, and make all
things mutually agreeable and rational in their relations
to one another" are probably the numbers, since odd
numbers were thought to cause likeness and even ones
unlikeness (Aristotle, *Physics* 203ª13–5). Of the numbers
significant in human life, one is surely the 100 years of
its maximum span (615a8–b1). Another might be the
number of days in the year (roughly 360), and a third
might be the divisions of those days into smaller units
determined by the sun's place in the sky, since it is the
sun that provides for "the coming-to-be, growth, and
nourishment" of all visible things (509b2–4). Assuming
that those units are the 360 degrees of the sun's path
around the earth (a suggestion due to Robin Waterfield),
the number of moments in a human life that have a
potential effect on its coming-to-be, growth, and nourishment would be $100 \times 360 \times 360$, or 12,960,000—Plato's
human geometrical number.]

---

10. [414d1–415c7; Hesiod, *Works and Days* 109–202.]

11. [Homer, *Iliad* 6.211.]

GLAUCON: Yes.

SOCRATES: But in its fear of appointing wise people as rulers, on the grounds that men of that sort are no longer simple and earnest but mixed; in its inclination toward spirited and simpler people, who are more naturally suited for war than peace; in its honoring the tricks and stratagems of war; and spending all its time making war—in these respects, by contrast, isn't it pretty much unique?

548a

GLAUCON: Yes.

SOCRATES: Such men will have an appetite for money just like those in oligarchies, passionately adoring gold and silver in secret, owning storehouses and private treasuries where they can deposit them and keep them hidden; and they will have walls around their houses, real private nests, where they can spend lavishly on their women or on anyone else they please.

b

GLAUCON: That's absolutely true.

SOCRATES: They will be stingy with money, since they honor it and do not possess it openly, but they will love to spend other people's money because of their appetites. They will enjoy their pleasures in secret, running away from the law like boys from their father, since they have not been educated by persuasion but by force. This is because they have neglected the true Muse, the companion of discussion and philosophy, and honored physical training more than musical training.

c

GLAUCON: The constitution you are describing is a thorough mixture of good and bad.

SOCRATES: Yes, it is mixed. But because of its mastery by the spirited element, only one thing really stands out in it—the love of victories and honors.

GLAUCON: And very noticeable it is.

SOCRATES: That, then, is how this constitution would come to exist, and that is what it would be like. It is just an outline sketch of the constitution in words, not an exact account of it, since even from a sketch we will be able to see the most just man and most unjust one. It would be an incredibly long task to discuss every constitution and every character without omitting any detail.

d

GLAUCON: Yes, that's right.

SOCRATES: Who, then, is the man corresponding to this constitution? How does he come to exist and what sort of man is he?

ADEIMANTUS: I think he would be very like Glaucon here, at least as far as the love of victory is concerned.

SOCRATES: Maybe in that respect, but in the following ones I do not think his nature would be like that.

ADEIMANTUS: Which ones?

e

SOCRATES: He would have to be more stubborn and less well trained in music; a lover of music and of listening, yet not at all skilled in speaking; the sort of person who is harsh to slaves instead of looking down on them, as an adequately educated person does; gentle to free people and very submissive to rulers; a lover of ruling and of honor, who does not base his claim to rule on his ability to speak or anything like that, but on his exploits in war and anything having to do with war; a lover of physical training and of hunting.

549a

ADEIMANTUS: Yes, that is indeed the character belonging to this constitution.

SOCRATES: As regards money, too, wouldn't someone like that look down on it when he is young; but as he grows older, wouldn't he love it more and more because he shares in the money-lover's nature and is not pure in his attitude to virtue, since he lacks the best guardian?

b

ADEIMANTUS: What's that?

SOCRATES: Reason mixed with musical training. You see, only it dwells within the person who possesses it as the lifelong preserver of his virtue.

ADEIMANTUS: Well put.

SOCRATES: That, then, is what a timocratic youth is like; he is like the corresponding city.

ADEIMANTUS: Yes, indeed.

c

SOCRATES: And he comes to exist in some such way as this: sometimes he is the young son of a good father, who lives in a city that is not politically well governed; avoids honors, political office, lawsuits, and all such meddling in other people's affairs; and who is even willing to be put at a disadvantage so as to avoid trouble.

ADEIMANTUS: Yes, but how does he become timocratic?

SOCRATES: It first happens when he listens to his mother complaining that her man is not one of the rulers and that she is at a disadvantage among the other women as a result. Next, she sees that he is not *d* very serious about money, either; does not fight or exchange insults in private lawsuits or in the public assembly, but takes easily everything of that sort; has a mind always absorbed in its own thoughts; and does not overvalue her or undervalue her either. As a result of all those things, she complains and tells her son that his father is unmanly and too easygoing, and makes a litany of the other sorts of things women love *e* to recite on such occasions.

ADEIMANTUS: Yes, indeed, it is just like them to have lots of such complaints.

SOCRATES: You know, then, that the servants of such men—the ones thought to be loyal—also say similar things to the sons in private. If they see someone who owes the father money or has wronged him in some other way, whom he does not prosecute, they urge the son to punish all such people when he becomes a man, and be more of a man than his *550a* father. And when he goes out, the boy hears and sees other similar things: those who do their own work in the city are called fools and held to be of little account, while those who do not are honored and praised. When the young man hears and sees all this, then, and, on the other hand, also listens to what his father says, and sees his practices from close at hand and compares them with those of the others, he is pulled by both—his father nourishing the rational element *b* in his soul and making it grow; the others nourishing the appetitive and spirited elements. And, because he is not a bad man by nature, but has kept bad company, he compromises on a middle way when he is pulled in these two directions, and surrenders the rule within him to the middle element—the victory-loving and spirited one—and becomes a proud and honor-loving man.

ADEIMANTUS: I think you have exactly described how such a man comes to exist.

SOCRATES: So, we now have the second constitu-*c* tion and the second man.

ADEIMANTUS: We have.

SOCRATES: Next then, shall we, like Aeschylus, talk of "another man ordered like another city,"[12] or follow our plan and talk about the city first?

ADEIMANTUS: The latter, of course.

SOCRATES: And I suppose oligarchy would come next after such a constitution.

ADEIMANTUS: And what kind of political system do you mean by oligarchy?

SOCRATES: The constitution based on a property assessment, the one in which the rich rule and the poor man does not participate in ruling. *d*

ADEIMANTUS: I understand.

SOCRATES: So, mustn't we first describe how timarchy is transformed into oligarchy?

ADEIMANTUS: Yes.

SOCRATES: And surely the way it is transformed is clear even to the blind.

ADEIMANTUS: How?

SOCRATES: That storehouse filled with gold we mentioned,[13] which each possesses, destroys such a constitution. First, you see, the timocrats find ways of spending their money, then they alter the laws to allow them to do so, and then they and their women disobey the laws altogether.

ADEIMANTUS: Probably so.

SOCRATES: Next, I suppose, through one person seeing another and envying him, they make the majority behave like themselves. *e*

ADEIMANTUS: Probably so.

SOCRATES: After that then, they become further involved in moneymaking; and the more honorable they consider it, the less honorable they consider virtue. Or isn't virtue so opposed to wealth that if they were set on the scale of a balance, they would always incline in opposite directions?

ADEIMANTUS: It certainly is.

SOCRATES: So, when wealth and the wealthy are honored in a city, virtue and good people are hon-*551a* ored less.

ADEIMANTUS: Clearly.

SOCRATES: And what is honored is always practiced, and what is not honored, neglected.

ADEIMANTUS: Yes.

SOCRATES: So, in the end, victory-loving and honor-loving men become lovers of making money and money-lovers, and they praise and admire the wealthy man and appoint him as ruler, and dishonor the poor one.

12. [The line does not occur in the extant plays, but it may be an adaptation of *Seven against Thebes* 451.]

13. [548a7–8.]

ADEIMANTUS: Of course.

SOCRATES: Isn't it then that they pass a law, which is a defining characteristic of an oligarchic constitution, establishing a wealth qualification—higher

b where it is more oligarchic, lower where it is less so—and proclaim that anyone whose property does not reach the stated assessment cannot participate in ruling? And they either put this through by force of arms, or else, without resorting to that, they use intimidation to establish this sort of constitution. Isn't that so?

ADEIMANTUS: It is.

SOCRATES: That, then, is, generally speaking, how it is established.

ADEIMANTUS: Yes, it is. But what is the constitu-

c tion like? What are the defects we said it had?[14]

SOCRATES: First of all, consider its defining characteristic. I mean, what would happen if ship captains were appointed like that, on the basis of property assessments, and a poor person was turned away even if he were a better captain?

ADEIMANTUS: People would make a very bad voyage!

SOCRATES: And doesn't the same apply to any other sort of rule whatsoever?

ADEIMANTUS: I suppose so.

SOCRATES: Except of a city? Or does it apply to that of a city, too?

ADEIMANTUS: It applies to it most of all, since it is the most difficult and most important kind of rule there is.

SOCRATES: That, then, is one major defect in

d oligarchy.

ADEIMANTUS: So it seems.

SOCRATES: And what about this one? Is it any smaller than the other?

ADEIMANTUS: Which?

SOCRATES: That a city of this sort is not one, but inevitably two—a city of the poor and one of the rich, living in the same place and always plotting against one another.

ADEIMANTUS: By Zeus, that's no smaller a defect.

SOCRATES: And this is hardly a good quality either: the likelihood of being unable to fight a war because of having to arm and use the majority, and so having to fear them more than the enemy; or else,

e because of not using them, and so having to show up as true oligarchs[15] on the battlefield; and because, at the same time, the fact that they are money-lovers makes them unwilling to pay mercenaries.

ADEIMANTUS: That is not good.

SOCRATES: And what about what we condemned long ago[16]—the fact that in this constitution there is the meddling in other people's affairs that occurs when the same people are farmers, moneymakers, and soldiers simultaneously? Or do you think it is 552a right for things to be that way?

ADEIMANTUS: Not at all.

SOCRATES: Now, let's see whether it is the first to admit the greatest of all evils.

ADEIMANTUS: Which is?

SOCRATES: Allowing someone to sell all his possessions and someone else to buy them, and then allowing the seller to continue living in the city while not being any one of its parts—neither moneymaker nor craftsman, nor cavalryman, nor hoplite, but a poor person without means.

ADEIMANTUS: It is the first.   b

SOCRATES: Anyway, this sort of thing certainly is not forbidden in oligarchies. I mean, if it were, some of their citizens would not be super rich and others totally impoverished.

ADEIMANTUS: That's right.

SOCRATES: Now, consider this: when a person like that was rich and spending his money, was he then of any greater use to the city in the ways we have just mentioned? Or did he merely seem to be one of the rulers, while in fact he was neither ruler nor subject of it, but only a squanderer of property?

ADEIMANTUS: That's right. He seemed to be a ruler but was nothing but a squanderer.   c

SOCRATES: Do you want us to say of him, then, that as a drone existing in a cell is an affliction to the hive, so this person existing in a household is a drone and affliction to the city?

ADEIMANTUS: Yes, indeed, Socrates.

---

14. [544c4–5.]

15. [I.e., as being few in number. *Oligos* means few.]
16. [374b6–c2.]

SOCRATES: And hasn't the god, Adeimantus, made all the winged drones stingless, as well as some of the footed ones, while other footed ones have terrible stings? And don't those who end up as beggars in old age come from among the stingless ones, while *d* all those with stings are called evildoers?

ADEIMANTUS: That's absolutely true.

SOCRATES: Clearly then, in any city where you see beggars, somewhere in the neighborhood there are thieves hidden, and pickpockets, temple robbers, and craftsmen of all such sorts of evil.

ADEIMANTUS: Clearly.

SOCRATES: What about oligarchic cities? Don't you see beggars in them?

ADEIMANTUS: Nearly everyone is one, apart from the rulers.

SOCRATES: Mustn't we suppose, then, that there *e* are also many evildoers there with stings, whom the rulers forcibly keep in check by their cautiousness?

ADEIMANTUS: We certainly must suppose it.

SOCRATES: And aren't we saying that the presence of such people is the result of lack of education, bad rearing, and a bad constitutional system?

ADEIMANTUS: We are.

SOCRATES: Well, then, that is roughly what the oligarchic city would be like. It would contain all these evils and probably others as well.

ADEIMANTUS: That's pretty much it.

SOCRATES: Let's take it, then, that we have dis-
553a posed of the constitution they call oligarchy, which gets its rulers on the basis of a property assessment. Next, let's consider how the person who is like it comes to exist, and what sort of person he is when he does.

ADEIMANTUS: Yes, let's.

SOCRATES: Doesn't the transformation from timocrat to oligarch mostly occur in this way?

ADEIMANTUS: Which?

SOCRATES: It happens when a son of his is born who begins by emulating his father and following in *b* his footsteps, and then sees him suddenly crashing against the city as against a reef, and sees him and all his possessions spilling overboard. He had held a generalship or some other high office, was brought to court by sycophants, and was put to death or exiled, or was disenfranchised and had all his property confiscated.

ADEIMANTUS: Probably so.

SOCRATES: Anyway, my friend, after seeing and experiencing all that, and losing his property, the son is afraid, I imagine, and immediately throws the honor-loving and spirited element headlong from the throne in his own soul. And humbled by poverty, *c* he turns greedily to moneymaking and, little by little, saving and working, he amasses property. Don't you think that someone like that will then establish the appetitive and moneymaking element on that throne, and make it a great king within himself, adorned with golden tiaras and collars and Persian swords?[17]

ADEIMANTUS: I do.

SOCRATES: And I suppose he makes the rational and spirited elements sit on the ground beneath it, one on either side, and be slaves. He won't allow the *d* first to calculate or consider anything except how a little money can be made into more; or the second to admire or honor anything except wealth and wealthy people, or to love being honored for anything besides the possession of wealth and whatever contributes to it.

ADEIMANTUS: There is no other way to turn an honor-loving young man into a money-loving one that is as swift and sure as that!

SOCRATES: Isn't this, then, the oligarchic person? *e*

ADEIMANTUS: Well, he certainly developed from the sort of man who resembled the constitution from which oligarchy came.

SOCRATES: Then let's see whether he resembles it.

ADEIMANTUS: Let's.   *554a*

SOCRATES: Wouldn't he resemble it, primarily, by attaching the greatest importance to money?

ADEIMANTUS: Of course.

SOCRATES: And also by being a thrifty worker who satisfies only his necessary appetites and spends nothing on other things but enslaves his other appetites as pointless.

ADEIMANTUS: Yes, indeed.

SOCRATES: A pretty squalid fellow, at any rate, who tries to make a profit from everything: a treasury-builder—the sort the majority admire. Isn't that the sort of man who resembles this sort of constitution? *b*

---

17. [For the Greeks, the king of Persia was emblematic of absolute rule.]

ADEIMANTUS: I certainly think so. At any rate, money is honored more than anything else by both the city and the one who is like it.

SOCRATES: Because I don't suppose someone like that has paid any attention to education.

ADEIMANTUS: I don't think so. I mean, if he had, he would not have chosen a blind leader for his chorus and honored him most.[18]

SOCRATES: Well put! But consider this. Wouldn't we say that though the dronish appetites exist in him because of his lack of education, some of them beggars and others evildoers, they are forcibly kept in check by his general cautiousness?

c

ADEIMANTUS: Certainly.

SOCRATES: Do you know, then, where you should look to see the evils such people do?

ADEIMANTUS: Where?

SOCRATES: Where they are guardians of orphans, or any other situation like that, where they have ample opportunity to do injustice.

ADEIMANTUS: True.

SOCRATES: So, doesn't that make it clear that in other contractual matters, where someone like that has a good reputation and is thought to be just, something good of his is forcibly holding in check the other bad appetites within; not persuading them that they had better not, nor taming them with arguments, but using compulsion and fear, because he is terrified of losing his other possessions?

d

ADEIMANTUS: Exactly.

SOCRATES: Yes, by Zeus, my friend, you will find that most of them, when they have other people's money to spend, have appetites in them akin to those of the drone.

ADEIMANTUS: Indeed, you certainly will!

SOCRATES: So, someone like that would not be entirely free from internal faction, and would not be a single person but somehow a twofold one, although his better appetites would generally master his worse appetites.

e

ADEIMANTUS: That's right.

SOCRATES: Because of this, I suppose someone like that would be more respectable than many other

18. [I.e., Plutus, the god of wealth, who is often represented as being blind.]

people; but the true virtue of a single-minded and harmonious soul would somehow far escape him.

ADEIMANTUS: I suppose so.

SOCRATES: Furthermore, the thrifty man is a worthless individual contestant in the city for any prize of victory or any of the other fine things the love of honor craves. He is unwilling to spend money 555a for the sake of fame or other such results of competition, and, fearing to arouse his appetites for spending by allying them with love of victory, he fights in true oligarchic fashion, with only a few of his resources, and is mostly defeated, but remains rich!

ADEIMANTUS: Exactly.

SOCRATES: Are we still in any doubt, then, that, as regards resemblance, a thrifty moneymaker corresponds to an oligarchic city? b

ADEIMANTUS: Not at all.

SOCRATES: Then democracy, it seems, must be considered next—both the way it comes to exist and what it is like when it does—so that when we know the character of this sort of man, we can present him for judgment in turn.

ADEIMANTUS: At any rate, that would be consistent with what we have been doing.

SOCRATES: Well, then, isn't the change from an oligarchy to a democracy due in some way or other to the insatiable desire for the good set before it—the need to become as rich as possible?

ADEIMANTUS: How so?

SOCRATES: Since the rulers rule in it because they own a lot, I suppose they are not willing to enact laws c to prevent young people who have become intemperate from spending and wasting their wealth, so that by buying and making loans on the property of such people, the rulers themselves can become even richer and more honored.

ADEIMANTUS: That's their primary goal, at any rate.

SOCRATES: So, isn't it clear by now that you cannot honor wealth in a city and maintain temperance in the citizens at the same time, but must inevitably neglect one or the other? d

ADEIMANTUS: That is pretty clear.

SOCRATES: The negligent encouragement of intemperance in oligarchies, then, sometimes reduces people who are not ill born to poverty.

ADEIMANTUS: Indeed, it does.

SOCRATES: And these people sit around in the city, I suppose, armed with stings or weapons, some of them in debt, some disenfranchised, some both—hating and plotting against those who have acquired their property, and all the others as well; passionately
e longing for revolution.

ADEIMANTUS: That's right.

SOCRATES: These moneymakers, with their heads down,[19] pretending not to see them, inject the poison of their money into any of the rest who do not resist, and, carrying away a multitude of offspring in interest from their principal, greatly increase the size of the
556a drone and beggar class in the city.

ADEIMANTUS: They certainly do increase it greatly.

SOCRATES: In any case, they are not willing to quench evil of this sort as it flares up, either by preventing a person from doing whatever he likes with his own property, or alternatively by passing this other law to do away with such abuses.

ADEIMANTUS: What law?

SOCRATES: The one that is next best and that compels the citizens to care about virtue. You see, if someone prescribed that most voluntary contracts be
b entered into at the lender's own risk, money would be less shamelessly pursued in the city and fewer of those evils we were mentioning just now would develop in it.

ADEIMANTUS: Far fewer.

SOCRATES: But as it is, and for all these reasons, the rulers in the city treat their subjects in the way we described. And as for themselves and those belonging to them, don't they bring up the young to be fond of luxury, incapable of effort either mental or physical,
c too soft to endure pleasures or pains, and lazy?

ADEIMANTUS: Of course.

SOCRATES: And haven't they themselves neglected everything except making money and been no more concerned about virtue than poor people are?

ADEIMANTUS: Yes, they have.

SOCRATES: And when rulers and subjects, socialized in this way, meet on journeys or some other shared undertakings, whether in an embassy or a military campaign; or as shipmates or fellow soldiers;

or when they watch one another in dangerous situations—in these circumstances, don't you think d the poor are in no way despised by the rich? On the contrary, don't you think it is often the case that a poor man, lean and suntanned, is stationed in battle next to a rich one, reared in the shade and carrying a lot of excess flesh, and sees him panting and completely at a loss? And don't you think he believes that it is because of the cowardice of the poor that such people are rich and that one poor man says to another when they meet in private: "These men are ours for the taking; they are good for nothing"?
e

ADEIMANTUS: I know very well they do.

SOCRATES: Well, just as a sick body needs only a slight shock from outside to become ill and sometimes, even without external influence, becomes divided into factions, itself against itself, doesn't a city in the same condition need only a small pretext—such as one side bringing in allies from an oligarchy or the other from a democracy—to become ill and fight with itself? And doesn't it sometimes become divided into factions even without any external influence?

ADEIMANTUS: Yes, violently so.   557a

SOCRATES: Then democracy comes about, I suppose, when the poor are victorious, kill or expel the others, and give the rest an equal share in the constitution and the ruling offices, and the majority of offices in it are assigned by lot.

ADEIMANTUS: Yes, that is how a democratic political system gets established, whether it comes to exist by force of arms or because intimidation drives its opponents into exile.

SOCRATES: In what way, then, do these people live? What sort of constitution do they have? For clearly the sort of man who is like it will turn out to b be democratic.

ADEIMANTUS: Clearly.

SOCRATES: Well, in the first place, aren't they free? And isn't the city full of freedom and freedom of speech? And isn't there license in it to do whatever one wants?

ADEIMANTUS: That's what they say, anyway.

SOCRATES: And where there is license, clearly each person would arrange his own life in whatever way pleases him.

ADEIMANTUS: Clearly.

19. [Their heads are down because their appetite for money forces their souls to look downward.]

SOCRATES: I imagine it is in this constitution,
c then, that multifarious people come to exist.

ADEIMANTUS: Of course.

SOCRATES: It looks, then, as though it is the most beautiful of all the constitutions. For just like an embroidered cloak embroidered with every kind of ornament, it is embroidered with every sort of character, and so would appear to be the most beautiful. And presumably, many people would behave like women and children looking at embroidered objects and actually judge it to be the most beautiful.

ADEIMANTUS: They certainly would.

SOCRATES: What is more, bless you, it is also a
d handy place in which to look for a constitution!

ADEIMANTUS: Why is that?

SOCRATES: Because it contains all kinds of constitutions, as a result of its license. So whoever wants to organize a city, as we were doing just now, probably has to go to a democracy and, as if he were in a supermarket of constitutions, pick out whatever pleases him and establish it.

ADEIMANTUS: He probably wouldn't be at a loss
e for examples, anyway!

SOCRATES: There is no compulsion to rule in this city, even if you are qualified to rule, or to be ruled if you do not want to be; or to be at war when the others are at war, or to keep the peace when the others are keeping it, if you do not want peace; or, even if there happens to be a law preventing you from ruling or from serving on a jury, to be any the less free to rule or serve on a jury—isn't that a
558a heavenly and pleasant way to pass the time, while it lasts?

ADEIMANTUS: It probably is—while it lasts.

SOCRATES: And what about the calm of some of their condemned criminals? Isn't that a sophisticated quality? Or have you never seen people who have been condemned to death or exile in a constitution of this sort staying on all the same and living right in the middle of things, without anyone giving them a thought or staring at them, while they stroll around like a hero?[20]

ADEIMANTUS: Yes, I have seen it a lot.

20. [Dead heroes were worshipped as minor deities in Greek religion, particularly in their birthplaces, where their spirits were thought to linger.]

SOCRATES: And what about the city's tolerance, its complete lack of petty-mindedness, and its utter b disregard for the things we took so seriously when we were founding the city—that unless someone had transcendent natural gifts, he would never become a good man if he did not play fine games right from early childhood and engage in practices that are all of that same sort? Isn't it magnificent how it tramples all that underfoot, gives no thought to what sort of practices someone went in for before he entered politics, and honors him if only he tells them he wishes the majority well? c

ADEIMANTUS: That's true nobility!

SOCRATES: These, then, and others akin to them are the characteristics a democracy would possess. And it would, it seems, be a pleasant constitution—lacking rulers but not complexity, and assigning a sort of equality to equals and unequals alike.

ADEIMANTUS: Yes, that's well known!

SOCRATES: Look and see, then, what sort of private individual resembles it. Or should we first consider, as we did in the case of the constitution, how he comes to exist?

ADEIMANTUS: Yes.

SOCRATES: Well, doesn't it happen this way? Mightn't we suppose that our thrifty oligarchic man had a son brought up by his father with his father's d traits of character?

ADEIMANTUS: Of course.

SOCRATES: Then he too would rule by force the pleasures that exist in him—the spendthrift ones that do not make money; the ones that are called unnecessary.

ADEIMANTUS: Clearly.

SOCRATES: In order not to have a discussion in the dark, would you like us first to define which appetites are necessary and which are not?

ADEIMANTUS: I would.

SOCRATES: Well, then, wouldn't those we cannot deny rightly be called necessary? And also those whose satisfaction benefits us? For we are by nature com- e pelled to try to satisfy them both. Isn't that so?

ADEIMANTUS: Of course.

SOCRATES: So, we would be right to apply the term "necessary" to them? 559a

ADEIMANTUS: We would be right.

SOCRATES: What about those someone could get

rid of if he started practicing from childhood, those whose presence does no good but may even do the opposite? If we said that all of them were unnecessary, would we be right?

ADEIMANTUS: We would be right.

SOCRATES: Let's pick an example of each, so that we have a pattern to follow.

ADEIMANTUS: Yes, let's.

SOCRATES: Wouldn't the desire to eat to the point of health and well-being, and the desire for bread

b and relishes be necessary ones?

ADEIMANTUS: I suppose so.

SOCRATES: The desire for bread is surely necessary on both counts, in that it is beneficial and that unless it is satisfied, we die.[21]

ADEIMANTUS: Yes.

SOCRATES: And so is the one for relishes, insofar as it is beneficial and conduces to well-being.

ADEIMANTUS: Indeed.

SOCRATES: What about an appetite that goes beyond these and seeks other sorts of foods; that, if it is restrained from childhood and educated, most people can get rid of; and that is harmful to the body and harmful to the soul's capacity for wisdom and temper-

c ance? Wouldn't it be correct to call it unnecessary?

ADEIMANTUS: Entirely correct.

SOCRATES: Wouldn't we also say that the latter desires are spendthrift, then, whereas the former are moneymaking because they are useful where work is concerned?

ADEIMANTUS: Certainly.

SOCRATES: And won't we say the same about sexual appetites and the rest?

ADEIMANTUS: Yes.

SOCRATES: And didn't we say that the person we just now called a drone is full of such pleasures and appetites and is ruled by the unnecessary ones, while the one who is ruled by his necessary appetites is a

d thrifty oligarch?

ADEIMANTUS: Of course we did.

SOCRATES: Let's go back, then, and say how the democrat develops from the oligarch. It seems to me as if it mostly happens this way.

ADEIMANTUS: What way?

SOCRATES: When a young man who is reared in the uneducated and thrifty manner we described just now tastes the honey of the drones and associates with wild and terrible creatures who can provide multifarious pleasures of every degree of complexity and sort, that probably marks the beginning of his transfor-

e mation from having an oligarchic constitution within him to having a democratic one.

ADEIMANTUS: It most certainly does.

SOCRATES: So, just as the city changed when one party received help from a like-minded alliance outside, doesn't the young man change in turn when external appetites of the same type and quality as it come to the aid of one of the parties within him?

ADEIMANTUS: Absolutely.

SOCRATES: And I suppose if a counter-alliance comes to the aid of the oligarchic party within him — whether from his father or from the rest of his family, who exhort and reproach him — then there is a faction

560a and an opposing faction within him, and he battles against himself.

ADEIMANTUS: Of course.

SOCRATES: And sometimes, I suppose, the democratic party yields to the oligarchic, some of its appetites are overcome while others are expelled, and a kind of shame rises in the young man's soul and order is restored.

ADEIMANTUS: That does sometimes happen.

SOCRATES: Moreover, I suppose, as some appetites are expelled, others akin to them are being nurtured undetected because of the father's ignorance

b of upbringing, and become numerous and strong.

ADEIMANTUS: At any rate, that's what usually happens.

SOCRATES: Then these desires draw him back to his old associates[22] and, in secret intercourse, breed a multitude of others.

ADEIMANTUS: Of course.

SOCRATES: Finally, I suppose, they seize the citadel of the young man's soul, since they realize that it is empty of the fine studies and practices and the true arguments that are the best watchmen and guardians in the minds of men loved by the gods.

c ADEIMANTUS: By far the best.

---

21. [Bread is used here to mean "the staff of life." That is why one dies for want of it.]

22. [Described at 559d7–e2.]

SOCRATES: Then, I suppose, beliefs and arguments that are lying imposters rush up and occupy this same part of him in place of the others.

ADEIMANTUS: They do, indeed.

SOCRATES: Won't he then return to those Lotus-eaters and live with them openly? And if any help should come to the thrifty part of his soul from his relatives, don't those imposter arguments, having barred the gates of the royal wall within him, prevent the allied force itself from entering and even refusing to admit arguments of older, private individuals as *d* ambassadors? Proving stronger in the battle, won't they call reverence foolishness and drive it out as a dishonored fugitive? And calling temperance cowardliness, won't they shower it with abuse and banish it? As for moderate and orderly expenditure, won't they persuade him that it is boorish and illiberal, and join with a multitude of useless appetites to drive it over the border?

ADEIMANTUS: They will indeed.

SOCRATES: And when they have somehow emptied and purged these from the soul of the one they *e* are seizing hold of and initiating with solemn rites, they then immediately proceed to return arrogance, anarchy, extravagance, and shamelessness from exile in a blaze of torchlight, accompanied with a vast chorus of followers and crowned with garlands. They praise them and give them fine names, calling arrogance "good breeding," anarchy "freedom," extravagance "magnificence," and shamelessness "courage." *561a* Isn't it in some such way as this that a young person exchanges an upbringing among necessary appetites for the freeing and release of useless and unnecessary pleasures?

ADEIMANTUS: Yes, that's clearly the way it happens.

SOCRATES: Then in his subsequent life, I suppose, someone like that spends no less money, effort, and time on the necessary pleasures than on the unnecessary pleasures. But if he is lucky and does not go beyond the limits in his bacchic frenzy, and if, as a result of his growing somewhat older, the great tumult within him passes, he welcomes back some of the *b* exiles and ceases to surrender himself completely to the newcomers. Then, putting all his pleasures on an equal footing, he lives, always surrendering rule over himself to whichever desire comes along, as if

it were chosen by lot,[23] until it is satisfied; and after that to another, dishonoring none but satisfying all equally.

ADEIMANTUS: He does, indeed.

SOCRATES: And he does not accept or admit true argument into the guardhouse if someone tells him that some pleasures belong to fine and good appetites and others to bad ones, and that he must practice *c* and honor the former and restrain and enslave the latter. On the contrary, he denies all this and declares that they are all alike and must be honored on an equal basis.

ADEIMANTUS: That's exactly what he feels and does.

SOCRATES: And so he lives from day to day, gratifying the appetite of the moment. Sometimes he drinks heavily while listening to the flute, while at others he drinks only water and is on a diet. Sometimes he goes in for physical training, while there are others when he is idle and neglects everything. Sometimes *d* he spends his time engaged in what he takes to be philosophy. Often, though, he takes part in politics, leaping to his feet and saying and doing whatever happens to come into his mind. If he admires some military men, that is the direction in which he is carried; if some moneymakers, then in that different one. There is neither order nor necessity in his life, yet he calls it pleasant, free, and blessedly happy, and follows it throughout his entire life.

ADEIMANTUS: You have perfectly described the life of a man devoted to legal equality.[24] *e*

SOCRATES: I certainly think he is a multifarious man and full of all sorts of characters, beautiful and complex, like the democratic city. Many men and women would envy his life because of the great number of examples of constitutions and characters it contains within it.

ADEIMANTUS: Yes, that's right.

SOCRATES: Well, then, will we set this man alongside democracy as the one who would rightly be *562a* called democratic?

ADEIMANTUS: We will.

23. [Many public officials in democratic Athens were elected by lot.]

24. [*Isonomia:* an important democratic value.]

SOCRATES: The finest constitution and the finest man remain for us to discuss: tyranny and the tyrant.

ADEIMANTUS: Absolutely.

SOCRATES: Come on, then; tell me, my dear comrade, how does tyranny come to exist? That it evolves from democracy, you see, is fairly clear.

ADEIMANTUS: It is clear.

SOCRATES: So, isn't the way democracy evolves from oligarchy much the same as that in which tyranny evolves from democracy?

ADEIMANTUS: How do you mean?

SOCRATES: The good they proposed for themselves, and because of which oligarchy was established, was wealth, wasn't it?

ADEIMANTUS: Yes.

SOCRATES: And its insatiable desire for wealth and its neglect of other things for the sake of moneymaking was what destroyed it.

ADEIMANTUS: True.

SOCRATES: So, isn't democracy's insatiable desire for what it defines as the good also what destroys it?

ADEIMANTUS: What do you think it does define as the good?

SOCRATES: Freedom. For surely, in a democratic city, that is what you would hear described as its finest possession, and as what makes it the only place worth living in for someone who is naturally free.

ADEIMANTUS: Yes, you often hear that said.

SOCRATES: As I was about to say, then, isn't it the insatiable desire for this good and the neglect of other things that changes this constitution and prepares it to need a dictatorship?

ADEIMANTUS: How does it do that?

SOCRATES: I suppose it is when a democratic city, athirst for freedom, happens to get bad cupbearers for its leaders and gets drunk by drinking more than it should of unmixed wine.[25] Then, if the rulers are not very gentle and do not provide plenty of freedom, it punishes them and accuses them of being filthy oligarchs.

ADEIMANTUS: Yes, that is what it does.

SOCRATES: It showers with abuse those who obey the rulers as voluntary slaves and nonentities, but both in public and private it praises and honors rulers who are like subjects, and subjects who are like rulers. And isn't it inevitable in such a city that freedom should spread everywhere?

ADEIMANTUS: Of course.

SOCRATES: Yes, my friend, and so it is bound to make its way into private households until finally it breeds anarchy among the very animals.

ADEIMANTUS: What do you mean by that?

SOCRATES: For instance, a father gets into the habit of behaving like a child and fearing his son, and the son gets into the habit of behaving like a father, feeling neither shame nor fear in front of his parents—all in order to be *free*. A resident alien feels himself equal to a citizen and a citizen to him, and a foreigner likewise.

ADEIMANTUS: Yes, those sorts of things do happen.

SOCRATES: They do—and so do other little things of the same sort. A teacher in such circumstances is afraid of his students and flatters them, while the students belittle their teachers and do the same to their tutors, too. In general, the young are the spitting images of their elders and compete with them in words and deeds, while the old stoop to the level of the young and are full of wit and indulgence, imitating the young for fear of being thought disagreeable and masterful.

ADEIMANTUS: Absolutely.

SOCRATES: The ultimate freedom for the majority, my friend, comes about in such a city, when males and females bought as slaves are no less free than those who bought them. Then there is the case of women in relation to men, and men to women, and the extent of their legal equality and freedom—we almost forgot to mention that!

ADEIMANTUS: Are we not, with Aeschylus, going to "say whatever it was came to our lips just now?"[26]

SOCRATES: Certainly. At any rate, I *am* going to say it. I mean, no one who had not experienced it would believe how much freer domestic animals are here than in any other city. Bitches follow the proverb exactly and become like their mistresses. Horses and donkeys are in the habit of proceeding with complete freedom and dignity, bumping into anyone they meet

---

25. [The Greeks drank their wine mixed with water.]

26. [At 562e4–5. We no longer possess the play from which this fragment comes.]

on the road who does not get out of their way. And
d everything else is full of freedom, too.

ADEIMANTUS: It is my own dream you are telling
me.[27] That often happens to me when I go to the
country.

SOCRATES: Summing up all these things together, then, do you notice how sensitive they make
the citizens' souls, so that if anyone tries to impose
the least degree of slavery, they get irritated and
cannot bear it? In the end, as I am sure you are
aware, they take no notice of the laws—written or
e unwritten—in order to avoid having any master
at all.

ADEIMANTUS: I certainly am aware.

SOCRATES: This, my friend, is the fine and impetuous beginning from which tyranny seems to me
to grow.

ADEIMANTUS: It is certainly impetuous. But what
comes next?

SOCRATES: The same disease that developed in
oligarchy and destroyed it also develops here—only
more widespread and virulent because of the general
permissiveness—and eventually enslaves democracy.
In fact, excessive action in one direction usually sets
up a great reaction in the opposite direction. This
happens in seasons, in plants, in bodies, and particu-
564a larly in constitutions.

ADEIMANTUS: That's probably right.

SOCRATES: For extreme freedom probably cannot
lead to anything but a change to extreme slavery,
whether in a private individual or a city.

ADEIMANTUS: No, it probably can't.

SOCRATES: Tyranny probably does not evolve
from any constitution other than democracy, then—
the most severe and cruel slavery evolving from what
I suppose is the most eminent degree of freedom.

ADEIMANTUS: Yes, that's reasonable.

SOCRATES: But I think you were asking, not
that, but rather what sort of disease develops both
b in oligarchy and democracy alike, and enslaves the
latter.

ADEIMANTUS: That's true.

SOCRATES: Well, then, I meant that class of idle
and extravagant men, with the bravest as leaders and

the more cowardly as followers. We compared them
to drones: the leaders to drones with stings, the followers to stingless ones.[28]

ADEIMANTUS: Rightly so.

SOCRATES: These two cause problems in any constitution in which they arise, like phlegm and bile in
the body.[29] And it is against them that the good doctor
and lawgiver of a city must take no less advance c
precaution than a wise beekeeper. He should preferably prevent them from arising at all. But if they should
happen to arise, he must cut them out, cells and all,
as quickly as possible.

ADEIMANTUS: Yes, by Zeus, and as thoroughly
as possible.

SOCRATES: Then let's take up the question in this
way, in order to see what we want more distinctly.

ADEIMANTUS: In what way?

SOCRATES: Let's in our discussion divide a democratic city into three parts—which is also how it is
actually divided. One part is surely this class of drones, d
which, because of the general permissiveness, grows
in it no less than in an oligarchy.

ADEIMANTUS: So it does.

SOCRATES: But it is much fiercer in it than in
the other.

ADEIMANTUS: How so?

SOCRATES: There, because it is not honored but
is excluded from the ranks of the rulers, it does not
get any exercise and does not become vigorous. However, in a democracy, with few exceptions, it is surely
the dominant class. Its fiercest part does all the talking
and acting, while the other one settles near the speaker's platform. It buzzes and does not tolerate any
dissent. As a result, this class is in charge of everything
in such a constitution—with a few exceptions.[30] e

ADEIMANTUS: That's right.

SOCRATES: Then, there is a second distinct class
that is constantly emerging from the majority.

27. [I.e., you are telling me what I already know.]

28. [552c2–e3.]

29. [Phlegm and bile were two of the so-called humors
Greek medicine thought responsible for health and
disease.]

30. [The exceptions in question are presumably the various offices—such as the chief military official—to which
in the Athenian democracy were appointed on the basis
of expertise.]

ADEIMANTUS: Which one?

SOCRATES: Surely, when everyone is trying to make money, the ones who are by nature most orderly generally become the wealthiest.

ADEIMANTUS: Probably so.

SOCRATES: Then that is where the most plentiful honey for the drones exists, I take it, and the easiest for them to extract.

ADEIMANTUS: How could anyone extract it from those who have very little?

SOCRATES: I suppose, then, that these rich people, as they are called, are fodder for the drones.

ADEIMANTUS: Pretty much.

565a SOCRATES: The people—those who work their own land, take no part in politics, and own few possessions—would be the third class. This is the largest and most powerful class in a democracy when it meets in assembly.

ADEIMANTUS: Yes, it is. But it is not willing to meet often, if it does not get a share of the honey.

SOCRATES: So, it always does get a share—one that allows the leaders, in taking the wealth of the rich and distributing it to the people, to keep the greatest share for themselves.

b ADEIMANTUS: Yes, that is the sort of share they get.

SOCRATES: Then I suppose that those whose wealth is taken away are compelled to defend themselves by speaking in the popular assembly and doing whatever else they can.

ADEIMANTUS: Of course.

SOCRATES: At which point—even if they have no appetite for revolution at all—they get accused by the others of plotting against the people and of being oligarchs.

ADEIMANTUS: They do.

SOCRATES: Finally, when they see the people—not intentionally, but through misapprehension and being misled by the accusers—trying to do injustice

c to them, then, whether they wish it or not, they really do become oligarchs—not from choice, though, but because the drone, by stinging them, engenders this evil.

ADEIMANTUS: Absolutely.

SOCRATES: Then there are impeachments, judgments, and trials on both sides.

ADEIMANTUS: Right.

SOCRATES: And don't the people always tend to set up one man as their special leader, nurturing him and making him great?

ADEIMANTUS: Yes.

SOCRATES: And it is clear that when a tyrant arises,   d the position of popular leader is the sole root from which he springs.

ADEIMANTUS: It is.

SOCRATES: What is the beginning, then, of the transformation from popular leader to tyrant? Isn't it clear that it happens when the popular leader begins to behave like the character in the story told about the temple of the Lycaean Zeus[31] in Arcadia?

ADEIMANTUS: What story?

SOCRATES: That whoever tastes the one piece of human innards cut up with those of all the other sacrificial victims inevitably becomes a wolf. Haven't you heard that story?   e

ADEIMANTUS: I have.

SOCRATES: Isn't it the same, then, with a popular leader? Once he really takes over a docile mob, he does not restrain himself from shedding a fellow citizen's blood. But by leveling the usual false charges and bringing people into court, he commits murder. And by blotting out a man's life, his impious tongue and lips taste kindred blood. Then he banishes and kills and drops hints about the cancellation of debts and the redistribution of land. And after that, isn't   566a such a man inevitably fated either to be killed by his enemies or to be a tyrant, transformed from a man into a wolf?

ADEIMANTUS: Yes. That is the inevitable outcome.

SOCRATES: He is the one, then, who stirs up faction against the rich.

ADEIMANTUS: He is.

SOCRATES: And if he happens to be exiled but, despite his enemies, manages to return, doesn't he come back as a full-fledged tyrant?[32]

31. [Zeus the wolf-god.]

32. [Plato seems to be alluding to the tyrant Peisistratus. In 560 B.C.E., Peisistratus made himself tyrant with the help of a bodyguard granted to him by the Athenian people. After five years, he was expelled. Eventually he returned to Athens and used mercenaries to establish himself firmly as tyrant. He died in 527. See Herodotus 1.59–64.]

ADEIMANTUS: Obviously.

SOCRATES: And if they are unable to expel him
b or put him to death by accusing him before the city,
they plot a violent death for him by covert means.

ADEIMANTUS: That's what tends to happen,
anyway.

SOCRATES: And everyone who has reached this
stage soon discovers the famous tyrannical request—
to ask the people to give him a bodyguard to keep
their popular leader safe for them.

ADEIMANTUS: Right.

SOCRATES: And the people give it to him, I suppose, fearing for his safety but confident of their own.

c ADEIMANTUS: Right.

SOCRATES: So, when a wealthy man sees this and
is charged with being an enemy of the people because
of his wealth, then, comrade, in the words of the
oracle to Croesus, he "flees without delay to the banks
of the many-pebbled Hermus, and is not ashamed at
all of his cowardice."[33]

ADEIMANTUS: He would certainly never get a second chance to be ashamed!

SOCRATES: If he is caught, I would imagine he
is put to death.

ADEIMANTUS: Inevitably.

SOCRATES: As for this popular leader of ours, he
clearly does not lie on the ground "mighty in his
d might,"[34] but, having brought down all those others,
he stands in the chariot of the city as a complete
tyrant instead of a popular leader.

ADEIMANTUS: That's for sure.

SOCRATES: Shall we next describe the happiness
of this man and of the city in which such a creature arises?

ADEIMANTUS: Yes, let's.

SOCRATES: To start with, in the early days of his
reign, won't he greet everyone he meets with a smile,
deny he is a tyrant, promise all sorts of things in
e private and in public, free the people from debt,
redistribute the land to them and to his followers,
and pretend to be gracious and gentle to all?

ADEIMANTUS: Inevitably.

33. [The story of the Delphic Oracle to Croesus is found
in Herodotus 1.55.]

34. [See *Iliad* 16.776.]

SOCRATES: But once he has dealt with his exiled
enemies by making peace with some and destroying
others, and all is calm on that front, his primary
concern, I imagine, is to be constantly stirring up
some war or other, so that the people will need a
leader.

ADEIMANTUS: Very likely.

SOCRATES: And also, wouldn't you say, so that   567a
impoverished by war taxes, they will be forced to
concentrate on their daily needs and be less likely to
plot against him?

ADEIMANTUS: Clearly.

SOCRATES: And in addition, I suppose, so that if
there are some free-thinking people he suspects of
rejecting his rule, he can find pretexts for putting
them at the mercy of the enemy and destroying them?
For all these reasons, isn't a tyrant bound to be always
stirring up war?

ADEIMANTUS: He is.

SOCRATES: Don't all these actions tend to make
him more hateful to the citizens?   b

ADEIMANTUS: Of course.

SOCRATES: And don't some of those who helped
establish his tyranny and hold positions of power
within it, the ones who are bravest, speak freely to
him and to each other, criticizing what is happening?

ADEIMANTUS: Probably.

SOCRATES: Then the tyrant will have to do away
with all of them if he intends to rule, until he is left
with no friend or enemy who is worth anything at all.

ADEIMANTUS: Obviously.

SOCRATES: He will have to keep a sharp lookout,
then, for anyone who is brave, magnanimous, wise,
or rich. He is so happy, you see, that he is forced,
whether he wants to or not, to be their enemy and   c
plot against all of them until he has purged the city.

ADEIMANTUS: A fine purge that is!

SOCRATES: Yes. The opposite of the one doctors
perform on our bodies. They draw off the worst and
leave the best, whereas he does just the opposite!

ADEIMANTUS: Yet that's what he has to do; it
seems, if he is to rule.

SOCRATES: It is a blessedly happy necessity he is
bound by, then, which requires him to live with infe-   d
rior masses even though hated by them, or not live
at all!

ADEIMANTUS: It is.

SOCRATES: And the more he makes the citizens hate him by doing those things, the larger and more trustworthy a bodyguard he will need, won't he?

ADEIMANTUS: Of course.

SOCRATES: And who will these trustworthy people be? And from where will he get them?

ADEIMANTUS: Lots of them will come swarming of their own accord, if he pays them.

SOCRATES: Drones again, by the dog! That is what I think you are talking about. Foreign, multifarious *e* ones!

ADEIMANTUS: Yes, you are right.

SOCRATES: What about the domestic ones? Wouldn't he be willing to deprive citizens of their slaves somehow, set them free, and enlist them in his bodyguard?

ADEIMANTUS: He certainly would, since they are the ones he can trust the most.

SOCRATES: What a blessedly happy thing this tyrant business is on your view, if these are the sorts of friends and trusted men he must employ after *568a* destroying his former ones!

ADEIMANTUS: Nonetheless, they are the sorts he does employ.

SOCRATES: And these friends and new citizens admire and associate with him, whereas the good ones hate and avoid him?

ADEIMANTUS: Of course.

SOCRATES: It is no wonder, then, that tragedy seems to be something wholly wise, or that Euripides is outstanding in it.

ADEIMANTUS: Why is that?

SOCRATES: Because, among other things, he expressed the following shrewd thought: "tyrants are *b* wise by associating with the wise." He meant evidently that these associates of the tyrant are the wise ones.[35]

ADEIMANTUS: Yes. And he also praises tyranny as godlike, and lots of other things besides—and the other poets do, too.

SOCRATES: Then surely, since the tragic poets are

---

35. [The fragment is from an unknown play. Euripides meant that tyrants gain wisdom from the wise people who, as Simonides said, "knock at the doors of the rich" (489b7–8). Plato twists his words to mean that the drones and slaves, who are the tyrant's last resort, are wise, since they associate with him.]

so wise, they will forgive us and those with constitutions like ours if we do not admit them into our city, since they hymn the praises of tyranny.

ADEIMANTUS: For my part, I think they will forgive us—the more refined of them, anyway. *c*

SOCRATES: They can go around to all the other cities instead, I suppose, drawing large crowds and hiring actors with fine, loud, persuasive voices, and lead their constitutions to become tyrannies and democracies.

ADEIMANTUS: Yes, indeed.

SOCRATES: What's more, they are paid and honored for it, primarily—as one might expect—by tyrants and secondly by democracy. But the higher they go on the ascending scale of constitutions, the more their honor diminishes, as if unable to proceed for *d* lack of breath.

ADEIMANTUS: Absolutely.

SOCRATES: But all that is a digression. Let's return to our tyrant's camp—the one that is beautiful, populous, complex, and never the same—and ask how he is going to maintain it.

ADEIMANTUS: If there are sacred treasuries in the city, he will obviously use them for as long as they last, as well as the property of those he has destroyed, so the taxes he will require from the people will be smaller.

SOCRATES: What about when these resources give out? *e*

ADEIMANTUS: Clearly, his father's estate will have to support him, his drinking companions, and his boyfriends and girlfriends, too.

SOCRATES: I understand. You mean the people who fathered the tyrant will have to support him and his friends.

ADEIMANTUS: They will have no choice.

SOCRATES: What if the people get irritated and say it is not just for a grown-up son to be supported by his father? On the contrary, the father should be supported by his son. They did not father him and establish him in power, they say, so that, when he had become strong, they would be enslaved to their *569a* own slave and have to support him, his slaves, and other assorted rabble as well; but so that, with him as their popular leader, they would get free from the rule of the rich and the so-called fine and good people in the city. At that point, they order him and his friends to leave the city, as a father might drive a son and his troublesome drinking companions from his house. What do you think would happen then?

ADEIMANTUS: Then, by Zeus, the people will soon learn what kind of creature they have fathered, welcomed, and made strong, and that it is a case of b the weaker trying to drive out the stronger.

SOCRATES: What do you mean? Will the tyrant dare to use force against his father or hit him if he does not obey?

ADEIMANTUS: Yes—once he has taken away his weapons.

SOCRATES: A tyrant is a parricide as you describe him, then, and a harsh nurse of old age; and we do now seem to have an acknowledged tyranny. And so the people, by trying to avoid the proverbial frying pan of enslavement to free men, have fallen into the c fire of having slaves as their masters; and, in exchange for the excessive and inappropriate freedom they had before, have put upon themselves the harshest and most bitter slavery to slaves.

ADEIMANTUS: That's exactly what happens.

SOCRATES: Well, then, wouldn't we be justified in saying that we have adequately described how tyranny evolves from democracy, and what it is like once it has come to exist?

ADEIMANTUS: We would. Our description was entirely adequate.

BOOK IX

SOCRATES' NARRATION CONTINUES:

SOCRATES: The tyrannical man himself remains 571a to be investigated: how he evolves from a democratic one, what he is like once he has come to exist, and whether the way he lives is wretched or blessedly happy.

ADEIMANTUS: Yes, he still remains.

SOCRATES: Do you know what else I still miss?

ADEIMANTUS: What?

SOCRATES: I do not think we have adequately distinguished the nature and number of our appetites. And if that subject is not adequately dealt with, our b investigation will lack clarity.

ADEIMANTUS: Well, isn't now as fine a time as any?

SOCRATES: It certainly is. So, consider what I want to look at in them. It is this: among unnecessary pleasures and appetites, there are some that seem to me to be lawless. These are probably present in all of us, but they are held in check by the laws and by our better appetites allied with reason. In a few people they have been eliminated entirely or only a few weak ones remain, while in others they are stronger and more numerous.   c

ADEIMANTUS: Which ones do you mean?

SOCRATES: The ones that wake up when we are asleep, whenever the rest of the soul—the rational, gentle, and ruling element—slumbers. Then the bestial and savage part, full of food or drink, comes alive, casts off sleep, and seeks to go and gratify its own characteristic instincts. You know it will dare to do anything in such a state, released and freed from all shame and wisdom. In fantasy, it does not shrink from trying to have sex with a mother or with anyone else— d man, god, or beast. It will commit any foul murder, and there is no food it refuses to eat. In a word, it does not refrain from anything, no matter how foolish or shameful.

ADEIMANTUS: That's absolutely true.

SOCRATES: On the other hand, I suppose someone who keeps himself healthy and temperate will awaken his rational element before going to sleep and feast it on fine arguments and investigations, which he has brought to an agreed conclusion within himself. As for the appetitive element, he neither starves nor overfeeds it, so it will slumber and not e disturb the best element with its pleasure or pain but will leave it alone, just by itself and pure, to investigate 572a and reach out for the perception of something— whether past, present, or future—that it does not know. He soothes the spirited element in a similar way and does not get angry and fall asleep with his spirit still aroused. And when he has calmed these two elements and stimulated the third, in which wisdom resides, he takes his rest. You know this is the state in which he most readily grasps the truth and in which the visions appearing in his dreams are least lawless. b

ADEIMANTUS: I completely agree.

SOCRATES: Well, we have been led a bit astray and said a bit too much. What we want to pay attention to is this: there are appetites of a terrible, savage, and lawless kind in everyone—even in those of us who seem to be entirely moderate. This surely becomes clear in sleep. Do you think I am talking sense? Do you agree with me?

ADEIMANTUS: Yes, I do agree.

SOCRATES: Now, recall what we said the democratic man is like.[1] He was the result, we presumed, c of a childhood upbringing by a thrifty father who honored only appetites that made money and despised the unnecessary ones whose objects are amusement and showing off. Isn't that right?

ADEIMANTUS: Yes.

SOCRATES: And by associating with more sophisticated men who are full of the appetites we just described, he starts to indulge in every kind of arrogance and adopt their kind of behavior, because of his hatred of his father's thrift. But, since he has a better nature than his corrupters, he is pulled in both directions and settles in the middle between their two ways of life. And enjoying each in what he takes to be d moderation, he lives a life that is neither illiberal nor lawless, transformed now from an oligarch to a democrat.

ADEIMANTUS: Yes, that was—and still is—our belief about someone like that.

SOCRATES: Suppose, then, that this man has now in turn become older and has a son who is also brought up in his father's way of life.

ADEIMANTUS: I will.

SOCRATES: Suppose, too, that the same things happen to him as happened to his father: he is led into all the kinds of lawlessness that those leading e him call total freedom. His father and the rest of his family come to the aid of the appetites that are in the middle, while the others help the opposite ones. And when these terrible enchanters and tyrant-makers have no hope of keeping hold of the young man in any other way, they contrive to implant a powerful passion in him as the popular leader of those idle and 573a profligate appetites—a sort-of great, winged drone. Or do you think passion is ever anything else in such people?

ADEIMANTUS: I certainly do not think it is.

SOCRATES: And when the other appetites come buzzing around—filled with incense, perfumes, wreaths, wine, and all the other pleasures found in such company, they feed the drone, make it grow as large as possible, and plant the sting of longing in it. Then this popular leader of the soul adopts madness as its bodyguard and is stung to frenzy. If it finds any b beliefs or appetites in the man that are regarded as good or are still moved by shame, it destroys them and throws them out, until it has purged him of temperance and filled him with imported madness.

ADEIMANTUS: You have perfectly described how a tyrannical man comes to exist.

SOCRATES: Is that, then, why Passion has long been called a tyrant?

ADEIMANTUS: Probably so.

SOCRATES: And hasn't a drunken man, my friend, something of a tyrannical cast of mind, too?   c

ADEIMANTUS: He has.

SOCRATES: And of course someone who is mad and deranged attempts to rule not only human beings, but gods as well, and expects to be able to rule them.

ADEIMANTUS: Of course.

SOCRATES: A man becomes tyrannical in the precise sense, then, you marvelous fellow, when his nature or his practices or both together lead him to drunkenness, passion, and melancholia.

ADEIMANTUS: Absolutely.

SOCRATES: So, that, it seems, is how a tyrannical man comes to exist. Now, what is his life like?

ADEIMANTUS: Why don't *you* tell *me*, as askers of riddles usually do?   d

SOCRATES: I will tell you. You see, I think someone in whom the tyrant of Passion dwells, and in whom it serves as captain of everything in the soul, next goes in for festivals, revelries, luxuries, girlfriends, and all that sort of thing.

ADEIMANTUS: Inevitably.

SOCRATES: And don't lots of terrible appetites sprout up each day and night beside it, creating needs for all sorts of things?

ADEIMANTUS: Indeed, they do.

SOCRATES: So, any income someone like that has is soon spent.

ADEIMANTUS: Of course.

SOCRATES: And the next thing, surely, is borrowing and expenditure of capital.   e

---

1. [558c–562a2.]

ADEIMANTUS: What else?

SOCRATES: And when everything is gone, won't the violent crowd of appetites that have nested within him inevitably shout in protest? And when people of this sort are driven by the stings of these other appetites, but particularly of Passion itself, which leads all the others as if they were its bodyguard, stung to frenzy, don't they look to see who possesses anything 574a that can be taken from him by deceit or force?

ADEIMANTUS: Certainly.

SOCRATES: He must take it from every source, then, or live in great suffering and pain.

ADEIMANTUS: He must.

SOCRATES: And just as the late-coming pleasures within him do better than the older ones and steal away their satisfactions, won't he himself, young as he is, think he deserves to do better than his father and mother? And if he has spent his own share, won't he try to take some of his father's wealth by converting it to his own use?

ADEIMANTUS: Of course.

SOCRATES: And if his parents resist him, won't he b first try to steal it and deceive them?

ADEIMANTUS: Certainly.

SOCRATES: And if he cannot, won't he next try to seize it by force?

ADEIMANTUS: I suppose so.

SOCRATES: And if, you amazing man, the old man and woman stand their ground and put up a fight, would he take care and be reluctant to act like a tyrant?

ADEIMANTUS: I am not very optimistic about the parents of someone like that!

SOCRATES: But in the name of Zeus, Adeimantus, do you really think that for the sake of his latest love, an unnecessary girlfriend, he would strike his mother, who is his oldest and necessary friend? Or that for c the sake of his latest and unnecessary boyfriend, who is in the bloom of youth, he would strike his aged and necessary father, the oldest of his friends, who is no longer in the bloom of youth? Or that he would enslave his parents to them, if he brought them into the same house?

ADEIMANTUS: Yes, by Zeus, he would.

SOCRATES: It seems to be a great blessing to produce a tyrannical son!

ADEIMANTUS: It certainly does!

SOCRATES: What happens to someone like that when the possessions of his father and mother give out and the swarm of pleasures now inside him has d grown dense? Won't he first try to break into someone's house or snatch the cloak of someone walking late at night? Next, won't he try to clean out some temple? And in the course of all that, his old childhood beliefs about fine or shameful things—beliefs that are accounted just—are mastered by the new ones that have been released from slavery and, as the bodyguard of Passion, hold sway along with it. These are the ones that used to be freed in sleep as a dream, when he himself, since he was still subject to the laws and his father, had a democratic constitution e within him. But under the tyranny of Passion, what he used to become occasionally in his dreams he has now become permanently while awake, and so there is no terrible murder, no food, and no act from which he will refrain. On the contrary, Passion lives like a tyrant within him in complete anarchy and lawless- 575a ness, as his sole ruler, and drives him, as if he were a city, to dare anything that will provide sustenance for itself and the unruly mob around it—some of which have come in from the outside as a result of his bad associates, while others have come from within, freed and let loose by his own bad habits. Isn't this the life such a man leads?

ADEIMANTUS: It is.

SOCRATES: And if there are only a few men like that in a city, and the majority of the others are temperate, they emigrate in order to become the body- b guard of some other tyrant or serve as paid auxiliaries if there happens to be a war somewhere. But if they chance to live in a time of peace and calm, they stay right there in the city and cause lots of little evils.

ADEIMANTUS: What sort of evils do you mean?

SOCRATES: They steal, break into houses, snatch purses, steal clothes, rob temples, and kidnap people. Sometimes, if they are capable speakers, they become sycophants and bear false witness and accept bribes.

ADEIMANTUS: You mean they are small evils— provided there are only a few such people. c

SOCRATES: Yes. After all, small evils are small by comparison to big ones. And when it comes to producing corruption and misery in a city, all these evils together do not—as the saying goes—come within a mile of a tyrant. But when you get a large number of these people and their followers in a city, and they become aware of their numbers, they are the ones who together with the foolishness of the people — create the tyrant out of the one among them who has in his soul *d* the greatest and strongest tyrant of all.

ADEIMANTUS: Naturally, since he would be the most tyrannical.

SOCRATES: That's if they submit willingly. But if the city doesn't put itself in his hands, then just as he once chastised his mother and father, he will now punish his fatherland in the same way, if he can, bringing in new friends and making and keeping his once beloved motherland — as the Cretans call it — or fatherland their slaves. And that is surely the end at which the appetites of a man like that aim.

e ADEIMANTUS: It most certainly is.

SOCRATES: So, isn't this what such men are like in private life, before they start to rule? In the first place, don't they associate with flatterers who are ready to do anything to serve them? Or, if they need something from someone themselves, won't they *576a* grovel and willingly engage in any sort of posturing, the way slaves do? But once they get what they need, isn't it a different story altogether?

ADEIMANTUS: Yes, completely different.

SOCRATES: So, those with a tyrannical nature live their entire lives without ever being friends with anyone, always masters to one man or slaves to another, but never getting a taste of freedom or true friendship.

ADEIMANTUS: Exactly.

SOCRATES: Wouldn't we be right to call people like that untrustworthy?

ADEIMANTUS: Of course.

SOCRATES: And as unjust as anyone can be — assuming we were right in our earlier conclusions *b* about what justice is like.

ADEIMANTUS: And we certainly were right.

SOCRATES: Let's sum up the worst type of man, then. He is surely the one who, when awake, is like the dreaming person we described earlier.

ADEIMANTUS: Exactly.

SOCRATES: And he evolves from someone who, since he is by nature most tyrannical, achieves sole rule. And the longer he lives as tyrant, the more like that he becomes.

"Inevitably," *said Glaucon, taking over the argument.*

SOCRATES: Well, then, won't the one who is plainly worst also be plainly most wretched? And the one who for the longest time is most a tyrant, won't *c* he also be most wretched for the longest time, if truth be told? Though the views of the masses[2] on the subject are naturally also many.

GLAUCON: All that, at any rate, must be true.

SOCRATES: Doesn't a tyrannical man correspond to and most resemble a city ruled by a tyrant, a democratic man a democratically ruled city, and similarly with the others?

GLAUCON: Of course.

SOCRATES: And the comparison between city and city, as regards their virtue and happiness, isn't it the same as the comparison between man and man?

GLAUCON: Certainly. *d*

SOCRATES: As regards virtue, then, how does a city ruled by a tyrant compare to a city of the sort we described first that is ruled by a king?

GLAUCON: They are absolute opposites: one is the best, and the other is the worst.

SOCRATES: I won't ask you which is which, since it is obvious. But as regards happiness and wretchedness, is your judgment the same or different? And let's not become dazzled by looking at the tyrant — since he is just one man — or at the few who surround him. Instead, as is necessary, let's go in and study the city as a whole and, when we have gone down and looked into every corner, only then present what *e* we believe.

GLAUCON: That's a good suggestion. And it is clear to everyone that there is no city more wretched than a tyrannical one and none happier than one ruled by a king.

SOCRATES: Would it also be right, then, to suggest the same thing about the men — that the only fit judge *577a* of them is someone who can, in thought, go down into a man's character and discern it — not someone who sees it from the outside, the way a child does, and is dazzled by the façade that tyrants adopt for the outside world, but someone who discerns it adequately? And what if I were to assume that the person we must all listen to is the one who has this capacity to judge; who has lived in the same house

2. [Literally, the many.]

as a tyrant and witnessed his behavior at home; who has seen how he deals with each member of his household, when he can best be observed stripped *b* of his tragic costume;[3] and who has also seen how he deals with public dangers? Shouldn't we ask the one who has seen all that to tell us how the tyrant compares to the others with respect to happiness and wretchedness?

GLAUCON: That's also a very good suggestion.

SOCRATES: Then, in order to have someone to answer our questions, do you want us to pretend that we are among the ones who can make such a judgment, and that we have met tyrannical people already?[4]

GLAUCON: I certainly do.

SOCRATES: Come on, then, and examine the mat-
c ter like this for me. Bearing in mind the resemblance between the city and the man, examine each in turn and describe its condition.

GLAUCON: What kinds of things do you want me to describe?

SOCRATES: Describe the city first. Would you say that a tyrannical city is free or enslaved?

GLAUCON: As enslaved as it is possible to be.

SOCRATES: Yet you can surely see masters and free people in it.

GLAUCON: I can certainly see a small group of people like that. But pretty much the whole population, and the best part of it, is shamefully and wretchedly enslaved.

SOCRATES: If a man and his city are similar, then,
d mustn't the same structure exist in him, too? Mustn't his soul be full of slavery and illiberality, with those same parts of it enslaved, while a small part, the most wicked and most insane, is master?

GLAUCON: It must.

SOCRATES: Will you describe such a soul as enslaved, then, or as free?

GLAUCON: Enslaved, of course.

SOCRATES: And, to go back, isn't the enslaved, tyrannical city least able to do what it wishes?

GLAUCON: By far the least.

SOCRATES: So, a tyrannical soul will also least do *e* what it wishes—I am talking about the soul as a whole—and will be full of disorder and regret, since it is always forcibly driven by a gadfly.

GLAUCON: Of course.

SOCRATES: Rich or poor? Which must a tyrannical city be?

GLAUCON: Poor.

SOCRATES: So, a tyrannical soul, too, must always be poor and insatiable.   *578a*

GLAUCON: It must.

SOCRATES: What about fear? Mustn't a city of this sort and a man of this sort be filled with it?

GLAUCON: They certainly must.

SOCRATES: And do you think you will find more wailing, groaning, lamenting, or painful suffering in any other city?

GLAUCON: No.

SOCRATES: What about in a man? Do you think such things are more common in anyone than in this tyrannical man, maddened by his appetites and passions?

GLAUCON: How could I?

SOCRATES: I imagine it is in view of all these things, then, as well as others like them, that you *b* judged this city to be the most wretched of cities.

GLAUCON: And wasn't I right?

SOCRATES: Yes, of course. But how, again, do you describe the tyrannical man in view of these same things?

GLAUCON: He is by far the most wretched of them all.

SOCRATES: There your description is no longer right.

GLAUCON: How so?

SOCRATES: This man, I think, is not yet the most wretched.

GLAUCON: Then who is?

SOCRATES: Presumably, you will regard this next one as even more wretched.

GLAUCON: What one?

SOCRATES: The tyrannical man who does not live out his life as a private individual, but is unlucky, in *c* that some misfortune gives him the opportunity of becoming an actual tyrant.

GLAUCON: On the basis of what we have already said, I infer that what you are saying is true.

3. [I.e., the façade referred to earlier. Greek tragedies often had tyrants as characters.]

4. [Plato spent time with Dionysius I, tyrant of Sicily.]

SOCRATES: Yes. But it is not good enough to believe these claims, one must carefully examine someone like that by means of argument. After all, the investigation concerns the most important thing—a good life and a bad one.

GLAUCON: That's absolutely right.

SOCRATES: So, consider, then, whether there is anything in what I say. You see, I think we should *d* investigate him on the basis of the following.

GLAUCON: What?

SOCRATES: On the basis of each and every one of the wealthy private citizens in our cities who own many slaves. For they resemble a tyrant in ruling over many, although the number ruled by the tyrant is different.

GLAUCON: It is different.

SOCRATES: You know, then, that these people feel secure and do not fear their slaves.

GLAUCON: Of what have they to be afraid, after all?

SOCRATES: Nothing. But do you know why?

GLAUCON: Yes. Because the whole city is ready to defend each of its private citizens.

SOCRATES: That's right. But now, suppose some *e* god were to lift one of these men, who has fifty or more slaves, out of the city, and put him down— with his wife, his children, his slaves, and his other property—in a deserted place, where no free men could come to his assistance? Can you imagine the sort and amount of fear he would feel that he and his wife and children would be killed by his slaves?

GLAUCON: It would be huge, if you ask me.

SOCRATES: Wouldn't he at that point be com- *579a* pelled to start fawning on some of his slaves, promising them all sorts of things and setting them free— even though there was nothing he wanted to do less— and wouldn't he turn out to be a flatterer of slaves?

GLAUCON: He would have to be. Otherwise, he would be killed.

SOCRATES: Now, suppose the god were to settle many other neighbors around him who would not tolerate anyone claiming to be master of another, but if they caught such a person, would inflict the most extreme punishments on him?

GLAUCON: I suppose he would be in even worse *b* trouble, since he would be surrounded by nothing but enemies.

SOCRATES: So, isn't this, then, the kind of prison in which the tyrant is held—the one whose nature we have described, filled with multifarious fears and passions? Though his soul is really greedy, he is the only one in the city who cannot go abroad or look at the sights at which other free people yearn to look. Instead, he is mostly stuck in house, living like a woman, envying any other citizen who goes abroad and sees some good thing. *c*

GLAUCON: Absolutely.

SOCRATES: Isn't such a harvest of evils, then, a measure of the difference between a tyrannical man who is badly governed politically on the inside— whom you judged just now to be most wretched— and one who does not live out his life as a private individual, but is compelled by some chance to become an actual tyrant and try to rule others, when he cannot even master himself? It is as if someone with a body that is sick and cannot master itself were compelled, not to spend his life in private pursuits, but to compete and fight with other bodies. *d*

GLAUCON: That's exactly what he is like. Your description is absolutely true, Socrates.

SOCRATES: And so, my dear Glaucon, isn't his condition completely wretched, and isn't the life of a tyrant even harsher than the one you judged to be harshest?

GLAUCON: It certainly is.

SOCRATES: So, in truth, then, and whatever some people may think, a real tyrant is really a slave to the worst sorts of fawning and slavery, and a flatterer of the worst kind of people. He is so far from satisfying his appetites in any way that he is in the greatest need *e* of most things and truly poor—as is apparent if one knows how to look at a whole soul. He is full of fear throughout his life and overflowing with convulsions and pains, if in fact his condition is like that of the city he rules. And it is like it, isn't it?

GLAUCON: Yes, of course.

SOCRATES: And, in addition, shouldn't we also attribute to the man the qualities we mentioned earlier? We said that he is inevitably envious, untrustwor- *580a* thy, unjust, friendless, impious, and a host and nurse to every kind of vice; that ruling makes him even more so than before; and that, as a consequence, he is extremely unfortunate and goes on to make those near him so.

GLAUCON: No one with any sense could possibly contradict that.

SOCRATES: Come on, then, and tell me now at last, like the judge who makes the final decision,[5] who you believe is first in happiness and who second, and judge the others similarly, making five altogether—kingly, timocratic, oligarchic, democratic, tyrannical.

GLAUCON: That's an easy judgment. You see, I rank them in the order of their appearance, just as if they were choruses, both in virtue and vice and in happiness and its opposite.

SOCRATES: Shall we, then, hire a herald, or shall I myself announce that the son of Ariston[6] has given as his verdict that the best and most just is the most happy, and that he is the one who is most kingly and rules like a king over himself; whereas the worst and most unjust is the most wretched, and he, again, is the one who, because he is most tyrannical, is the greatest tyrant over himself and his city?

GLAUCON: You have announced it!

SOCRATES: And shall I add that it holds whether or not their characters remain hidden from all human beings and gods?

GLAUCON: Do add it.

SOCRATES: Well, then, that is one of our demonstrations. But look at this second one and see if you think there is anything in it.

GLAUCON: What is it?

SOCRATES: In just the way a city is divided into three classes, the soul of each person is also divided in three. That is the reason I think there is another demonstration.

GLAUCON: What is it?

SOCRATES: The following. It seems to me that the three also have three kinds of pleasure, one peculiar to each. The same holds of appetites and kinds of rule.

GLAUCON: How do you mean?

SOCRATES: One element, we say, is that with which a person learns; another, that with which he feels anger. As for the third, because it is multiform, we had no one special name for it but named it after the biggest and strongest thing it has in it. I mean we called it the appetitive element because of the intensity of its appetites for food, drink, sex, and all the things that go along with them. We also called it the money-loving element,[7] because such appetites are most easily satisfied by means of money.

GLAUCON: And we were right.

SOCRATES: So, if we said its pleasure and love are for profit, wouldn't that best bring it together under one heading for the purposes of our argument and make clear to us what we mean when we speak of this part of the soul? And would we be right in calling it money-loving and profit-loving?

GLAUCON: I think so, anyway.

SOCRATES: What about the spirited element? Don't we say that its whole aim is always mastery, victory, and high repute?

GLAUCON: Certainly.

SOCRATES: Then wouldn't it strike the right note for us to call it victory-loving and honor-loving?

GLAUCON: The absolutely right one.

SOCRATES: But surely it is clear to everyone that the element we learn with is always wholly straining to know where the truth lies, and that of the three it cares least for money and reputation.

GLAUCON: By far the least.

SOCRATES: Wouldn't it be appropriate, then, for us to call it learning-loving and philosophic?

GLAUCON: Of course.

SOCRATES: And doesn't it rule in some people's souls, while one of the others—whichever it happens to be—rules in other people's?

GLAUCON: Yes.

SOCRATES: And isn't that why we say there are three primary types of people, philosophic, victory-loving, and profit-loving?

GLAUCON: Absolutely.

SOCRATES: And also three kinds of pleasure, one assigned to each of them?

GLAUCON: Exactly.

SOCRATES: You realize, then, that if you chose to ask each of these three types of people in turn to tell you which of their lives is most pleasant, each would give the highest praise to his own? Won't the money-

5. [The reference is to the way plays were judged at dramatic festivals in Athens. A herald announced the results.]

6. [Glaucon, but also, perhaps, his brother Plato.]

7. [At 553c5.]

maker say that, compared to that of making a profit,
d the pleasures of being honored or of learning are
worthless unless there is something in them that
makes money?

GLAUCON: True.

SOCRATES: What about the honor-lover? Doesn't
he think the pleasure of making money is vulgar,
while the pleasure of learning—except to the extent
that learning brings honor—is smoke and nonsense?

GLAUCON: He does.

SOCRATES: As for the philosopher, what do you
suppose he thinks of the other pleasures in compari-
e son to that of knowing where the truth lies and always
enjoying some variety of it while he is learning? Won't
he think they are far behind? And won't he call them
really necessary, since he would have no need for
them if they were not necessary for life?

GLAUCON: He will. We can be sure of that.

SOCRATES: Since the pleasures of each kind and
the lives themselves dispute with one another—not
about which life is finer or more shameful or better
or worse—but about which is more pleasant and less
painful, how are we to know which of them is speaking
582a the absolute truth?

GLAUCON: I have no idea how to answer that.

SOCRATES: Consider the matter this way. How
should we judge things if we want to judge them well?
Isn't it by experience, knowledge, and argument? Or
could someone have better criteria than these?

GLAUCON: No, of course not.

SOCRATES: Consider, then. Of the three types of
men, which has most experience of the pleasures we
mentioned? Do you think the profit-lover learns what
the truth itself is like, or has more experience of the
pleasure of knowing, than the philosopher does of
b making a profit?

GLAUCON: There is a big difference between
them. You see, the latter has to have tasted the other
kinds of pleasure beginning from childhood. But it is
not necessary for the profit-lover to taste or experience
how sweet is the pleasure of learning the nature of
the things that are—and even if he were eager to, he
could not easily do so.

SOCRATES: So, the philosopher is far superior to
the profit-lover in his experience of both kinds of
pleasures.

GLAUCON: Very far superior.   c

SOCRATES: What about compared to the honor-
lover? Is he more inexperienced in the pleasure of
being honored than the latter is in the pleasure of
knowing?

GLAUCON: No. Honor comes to all of them, provided they accomplish their several aims. For the rich
man, too, is honored by many people, as well as
are the courageous and the wise ones. So, all have
experienced what the pleasure of being honored is
like. But the pleasure pertaining to the sight of what
is cannot be tasted by anyone except the philosopher.

SOCRATES: So, as far as experience goes, then, he
is the finest judge among the three types of men.   d

GLAUCON: By far.

SOCRATES: And he alone will have gained his
experience with the help of knowledge.

GLAUCON: Of course.

SOCRATES: Moreover, the tool that should be
used to judge is not the tool of the profit-lover or the
honor-lover, but of the philosopher.

GLAUCON: What one is that?

SOCRATES: Surely we said that judgment should
be made by means of arguments. Didn't we?

GLAUCON: Yes.

SOCRATES: And arguments are, above all, his tool.

GLAUCON: Absolutely.

SOCRATES: If the things being judged were best
judged by means of wealth and profit, the praise
and criticism of the profit-lover would necessarily be e
closest to the truth.

GLAUCON: It would indeed.

SOCRATES: And if by means of honor, victory,
and courage, wouldn't it be those of the honor-lover
and victory-lover?

GLAUCON: Clearly.

SOCRATES: But since it is by means of experience,
knowledge, and argument?

GLAUCON: The praise of the philosopher and ar-
gument-lover must be closest to the truth.

SOCRATES: So, of the three pleasures, then, the
most pleasant would be that of the part of the soul 583a
with which we learn, and the one of us in whom it
rules has the most pleasant life.

GLAUCON: How could it be otherwise? The
knowledgeable person at least praises with authority
when he praises his own life.

SOCRATES: What life and pleasure does the judge say are in second place?

GLAUCON: Clearly, those of the warrior and honor-lover, since they are closer to his own than those of the moneymaker.

SOCRATES: Then those of the profit-lover come last, apparently.

GLAUCON: Of course.

SOCRATES: Well, then, that makes two in a row. And twice the just person has defeated the unjust one. Now comes the third, which is dedicated in Olympic fashion to our savior, Olympian Zeus.[8] Observe, then, that the other pleasures—apart from that of the knowledgeable person—are neither entirely true nor pure. On the contrary, they are like some sort of illusionist painting, as I think I have heard some wise person say. Yet, if that were true, it would be the greatest and most decisive of the overthrows.

GLAUCON: By far the greatest. But what exactly do you mean?

SOCRATES: I will find out, if you answer the questions while I ask them.

GLAUCON: Start asking, then.

SOCRATES: Tell me, then, don't we say that pain is the opposite of pleasure?

GLAUCON: Yes.

SOCRATES: Isn't there also a state of feeling neither enjoyment nor pain?

GLAUCON: There is.

SOCRATES: Isn't it in the middle between these two, a sort of quiet state of the soul where they are concerned? Or wouldn't you describe it that way?

GLAUCON: I would.

SOCRATES: So then do you recall the sorts of things ill people say when they are ill?

GLAUCON: Which ones?

SOCRATES: That nothing is more pleasant than being healthy, but they had not realized it was most pleasant until they fell ill.

GLAUCON: I do remember that.

8. [The first toast at a banquet was to the Olympian Zeus, the third to our savior, Zeus. By combining both in a single form of address, Plato seems to be emphasizing the importance of this final proof.]

SOCRATES: Don't you also hear people who are in great pain saying that nothing is more pleasant than the cessation of one's suffering?

GLAUCON: I do.

SOCRATES: And there are many similar circumstances, I presume, in which you see people in pain praising not enjoyment, but freedom from pain, and respite from that sort of thing, as most pleasant.

GLAUCON: Yes. For at such times, the respite presumably becomes pleasant enough to content them.

SOCRATES: And when someone ceases to enjoy something, this respite from pleasure will be painful.

GLAUCON: Presumably.

SOCRATES: So, the quiet state we just now described as being in between the two will sometimes be both pain and pleasure.

GLAUCON: Apparently.

SOCRATES: And is it possible for what is neither to become both?

GLAUCON: Not in my view.

SOCRATES: Furthermore, when what is pleasant and what is painful arise in the soul, they are both a sort of motion, aren't they?

GLAUCON: Yes.

SOCRATES: And didn't we see just now that what is neither painful nor pleasant is a respite and in the middle between the two?

GLAUCON: Yes, we did.

SOCRATES: How can it be right, then, to think that the absence of pain is pleasant or the absence of enjoyment painful?

GLAUCON: There's no way it can be.

SOCRATES: So, it is not right. But when the quiet state is next to what is painful, it appears pleasant; and when it is next to what is pleasant, it appears painful. And there is nothing sound in these illusions as far as the truth about pleasure is concerned. On the contrary, they are a sort of sorcery.

GLAUCON: That's what the argument suggests, at any rate.

SOCRATES: Well, then, take a look at pleasures that do not derive from pains, so that you won't be likely to think that, *in their case*, it is the nature of pleasure to be just the cessation of pain or of pain to be just the cessation of pleasure.

GLAUCON: Where am I to look? What pleasures do you mean?

SOCRATES: There are lots of others, but you might especially want to think about the pleasures of smell. You see, without being preceded by pain, they suddenly become incredibly intense. And when they cease, they leave no pain behind.

GLAUCON: That's absolutely true.

SOCRATES: So, let's not be persuaded that pure
c pleasure is relief from pain, or pure pain relief from pleasure.

GLAUCON: No, let's not.

SOCRATES: However, of the so-called pleasures that reach the soul through the body, pretty much the greatest number—and the most intense ones, too—are of that kind: they are some sort of relief from pains.

GLAUCON: Yes, they are.

SOCRATES: And aren't those pleasures and pains of anticipation, which arise from the expectation of future pleasures or pains, of the same kind?

GLAUCON: They are.

SOCRATES: Do you know what they are like and
d what they most resemble?

GLAUCON: What?

SOCRATES: Do you think there is such a thing in the natural world as an up, a down, and a middle?

GLAUCON: I do.

SOCRATES: Don't you imagine, then, that if someone were brought from down below to the middle, he would think anything other than that he was moving upward? And if he stood at the middle and saw where he had come from, could he possibly think he was anywhere other than the upper region, since he hadn't seen the one that is truly up above?

GLAUCON: By Zeus, I do not see how he could think anything else.

SOCRATES: But if he were brought back again,
e wouldn't he think he was being brought down? And wouldn't he be thinking the truth?

GLAUCON: Of course.

SOCRATES: And wouldn't all this happen to him because he is inexperienced in what is truly and really up, middle, and down?

GLAUCON: Clearly.

SOCRATES: Would it surprise you, then, if those who are inexperienced in the truth have unsound beliefs about lots of other things as well—that they are so disposed toward pleasure, pain, and the middle state that, whenever they descend to the painful, they think the truth and really are in pain; but that, when 585a they ascend from the painful to the middle state, they firmly think they have reached fulfillment and pleasure? Like people who compare black to gray without having experienced white, don't they compare pain to painlessness while being inexperienced in pleasure, and so get deceived?

GLAUCON: No, by Zeus, it would not surprise me! In fact, I would be very surprised if it were not like that.

SOCRATES: Think of it this way, then: Aren't hunger, thirst, and the like some sort of emptiness related to the state of the body?   b

GLAUCON: They are.

SOCRATES: And isn't foolishness and lack of knowledge, in turn, some sort of emptiness related to the state of the soul?

GLAUCON: It certainly is.

SOCRATES: Aren't people filled when they take in nourishment or gain understanding?

GLAUCON: Of course.

SOCRATES: Does the truer filling belong to what *is* less or to what *is* more?

GLAUCON: Clearly, it belongs to what is more.

SOCRATES: Which of the two types, then, partakes more of pure being? The sorts belonging to bread, drink, relishes, and nourishment in general? Or the kind belonging to true belief, knowledge, understanding, and, in sum, to all of virtue? Judge it this way: c what belongs to what is always the same, immortal, and true, is itself of that sort, and comes to be in something of that sort—it *is* more, don't you think, than what belongs to what is never the same and mortal, is itself of that kind, and comes to be in something of that kind?

GLAUCON: Far more. What belongs to what is always the same is far superior.

SOCRATES: And does the being of what is always the same partake any more of being than of knowledge?

GLAUCON: Not at all.

SOCRATES: What about of truth?

GLAUCON: Not of it, either.

SOCRATES: And if less of truth, less of being, too?

GLAUCON: Necessarily.

SOCRATES: Isn't it generally true that the types concerned with the care of the body partake less in d truth and being than do those concerned with the care of the soul?

GLAUCON: Yes, much less.

SOCRATES: Don't you think the same holds of the body in comparison to the soul?

GLAUCON: I do.

SOCRATES:· Then isn't what is filled with things that are more, and is itself more, more really filled than what is filled with things that are less, and is itself less?

GLAUCON: Of course.

SOCRATES: So, then, if being filled with what is appropriate to our nature is pleasant, what is more filled with things that *are* more is more really and
e truly caused to enjoy a more true pleasure; whereas what partakes of things that *are* less is less truly and surely filled and partakes of a less trustworthy and less true pleasure.

GLAUCON: That's absolutely inevitable.

SOCRATES: So, those who lack experience of
586a knowledge or virtue, but are always occupied with feasts and the like, are brought down, apparently, and then back up to the middle state; and wander in this way throughout their lives, never reaching beyond this to what is truly higher up, never looking up at it or brought up to it, never filled with what really is, and never tasting any stable or pure pleasure. On the contrary, they are always looking downward like cattle and, with their heads bent over the earth or the dinner table, they feed, fatten, and fornicate. And, in order to do better than others
b in these things, they kick and butt with iron horns and hooves, killing each other, because their desires are insatiable. For they aren't using things that *are* to fill the part of themselves that *is* a thing that is, and a leak-proof vessel.[9]

GLAUCON: You have described the life of "the many," Socrates, just like an oracle!

SOCRATES: So, isn't it necessary, then, for these people to live with pleasures that are mixed with pains, mere phantoms and illusionist paintings of true pleasures? And aren't they so colored by their juxtapo-
c sition with one another that they appear intense, beget mad passions for themselves in the foolish, and are

9. [*Stegnon*: contrasted in the *Gorgias* (493a1–b3) with the "leaking jar" in which the appetites are located.]

fought over—as Stesichorus tells us the phantom of Helen was fought over at Troy—through ignorance of the truth?[10]

GLAUCON: Something like that must be what happens.

SOCRATES: Mustn't similar things happen to someone who succeeds in satisfying the spirited element? Mustn't his love of honor be so colored by envy, his love of victory by violence, and his spiritedness by peevishness,[11] that he pursues the satisfactions of honor, victory, and spiritedness without rational cal- d
culation or understanding?

GLAUCON: The same sorts of things must happen with regard to that element, too.

SOCRATES: Can't we confidently assert, then, that, even where the desires of the profit-loving and honor-loving parts are concerned, those that follow knowledge and argument, and pursue with their help the pleasures that wisdom prescribes, will attain— to the degree that they can attain true pleasure at all—the truest pleasures, because they follow truth, and those that are most their own; if, indeed, what e
is the best for each thing is also what is most its own?

GLAUCON: But that, of course, is what is most its own.

SOCRATES: So, when the entire soul follows the philosophic element and does not engage in faction, the result is that each element does its own work and is just; and, in particular, each enjoys its own pleasures, the best pleasures and—to the degree possible—the truest.   587a

GLAUCON: Absolutely.

SOCRATES: So, when one of the other parts gains mastery, the result is that it cannot discover its own pleasure and compels the other parts to pursue an alien, and not a true pleasure.

GLAUCON: Yes.

10. [According to the story, Stesichorus wrote a poem defaming Helen and was punished by being struck with blindness. His sight was restored when he added a verse to the poem in which he claimed that it was a phantom of Helen and not Helen herself who was at Troy.]

11. [Envy, violence, and peevishness are all painful conditions that enhance the honor-lover's pleasures through contrast.]

SOCRATES: And wouldn't what is most distant from philosophy and reason be most likely to produce that result?

GLAUCON: By far.

SOCRATES: And isn't what is most distant from reason the very thing that is most distant from law and order?

GLAUCON: Clearly.

SOCRATES: And wasn't it made evident that the b passionate and tyrannical appetites are most distant?

GLAUCON: By far the most.

SOCRATES: And the kingly and orderly ones least distant?

GLAUCON: Yes.

SOCRATES: Then the tyrant, I suppose, will be most distant from a true pleasure that is his own, while the king will be least distant.

GLAUCON: It is inevitable.

SOCRATES: And so, the tyrant will live most unpleasantly and the king most pleasantly.

GLAUCON: It is absolutely inevitable.

SOCRATES: Do you know, then, how much more unpleasant the tyrant's life is than the king's?

GLAUCON: Not unless you tell me.

SOCRATES: There are, it seems, three pleasures: one genuine and two illegitimate. The tyrant is at c the extreme end of the illegitimate ones, since he flees both law and reason and lives with a bodyguard of slavish pleasures. But it is not at all easy to say just how inferior he is—except perhaps as follows.

GLAUCON: How?

SOCRATES: The tyrant is somehow at a third remove from the oligarch, since the democrat was in the middle between them.[12]

GLAUCON: Yes.

SOCRATES: Won't he also live with a phantom of pleasure, then, that, as regards truth, is at a third remove from that other—if what we said before is true?

GLAUCON: He will.

SOCRATES: But the oligarch, in turn, is at a third remove from the king,[13] if we assume king and aristo-d crat to be the same.

12. [Third because the Greeks always counted the first as well as the last member of a series. The day after tomorrow was the third day.]

13. [Because the timocrat is between them.]

GLAUCON: Yes, third.

SOCRATES: So a tyrant is removed from true pleasure by a numerical value of three times three.

GLAUCON: Apparently.

SOCRATES: So, on the basis of the size of this numerical value, it seems the phantom of the tyrant's pleasure is a plane figure.

GLAUCON: Exactly.

SOCRATES: On the basis of its square and cube, in that case, it becomes clear how far removed it is.

GLAUCON: Clear to someone skilled in calculation, anyway!

SOCRATES: Turning it the other way around, then, if someone wants to say how far the king is removed from the tyrant in terms of true pleasure, e he will find, if he completes the calculation, that he lives 729 times more pleasantly, while the tyrant lives the same number of times more painfully.[14]

GLAUCON: That's an extraordinary calculation of the difference between the two men—the just one and the unjust one—in terms of their pleasure and 588a pain!

SOCRATES: And yet it is a number that is both true and appropriate to human lives—if indeed days, nights, months, and years are appropriate to them.

14. [Socrates' mathematics is difficult to follow. He seems to have something like this in mind: the tyrant's pleasure is a two-dimensional image (a plane figure) of the true, three-dimensional pleasure of the philosopher. Hence, if a one-unit square represents the degree of closeness to true pleasure of an image nine times removed from it, true pleasure should be represented by a nine-unit cube. It follows that the king lives 729 times more pleasantly than the tyrant. However, in order to reach the significant number 729—there are 729 days and nights in a year of 364 twenty-four-hour days and 729 months in the "great year" recognized by the Pythagorean philosopher Philolaus—Socrates has had to make two rather fast moves. First, he illegitimately capitalizes on the Greek manner of counting series in order to count the oligarch twice, once as the last term in his first series (tyrant, democrat, oligarch) and again as the first term in his second series (oligarch, timocrat, king). Second, he multiplies the number of times the tyrant is removed from the oligarch by the number of times the oligarch is removed from the king, when he should have added them. In fact, the tyrant is only five times removed from the king, and so lives only 125 times less pleasantly!]

GLAUCON: And of course they are appropriate.

SOCRATES: If the victory of the good and just person over the bad and unjust one in terms of pleasure is as great as that, won't his victory in terms of its grace, beauty, and virtue be extraordinarily greater?

GLAUCON: Extraordinarily greater, indeed, by Zeus!

SOCRATES: All right, then. Since we have reached
b this point in the argument, let's return to the first things we mentioned that led us here. I think someone said that doing injustice profits a completely unjust person who is believed to be just. Wasn't that the claim?

GLAUCON: Yes, it was.

SOCRATES: Let's discuss it with its proponent, then, since we have now agreed on the respective effects of doing unjust and doing just things.

GLAUCON: How?

SOCRATES: By fashioning an image of the soul in words, so that the one who said that will know what he was saying.

c GLAUCON: What sort of image?

SOCRATES: One of those creatures that ancient legends say used to exist. The Chimera, Scylla, Cerberus, and the numerous other cases where many different kinds are said to have grown together into one.

GLAUCON: Yes, they do describe such things.

SOCRATES: Well, then, fashion a single species of complex, many-headed beast, with a ring of tame and savage animal heads that it can grow and change at will.

GLAUCON: That's a task for a clever fashioner of
d images! Still, since language is easier to fashion than wax and the like, consider the fashioning done.

SOCRATES: Now, fashion another single species— of lion—and a single one of human being. But make the first much the largest and the second, second in size.

GLAUCON: That's easier—the fashioning is done.

SOCRATES: Now, join the three in one, so that they somehow grow together naturally.

GLAUCON: They are joined.

SOCRATES: Then fashion around the outside the image of one of them, that of the human being, so that to anyone who cannot see what is inside, but sees only the outer shell, it will look like a single
e creature, a human being.

GLAUCON: The surrounding shell has been fashioned.

SOCRATES: When someone claims, then, that it profits this human being to do injustice, but that doing what is just brings no advantage, let's tell him that he is saying nothing other than that it profits him to feed well and strengthen the multifarious beast, as well as the lion and everything that pertains to the lion; to starve and weaken the human being, so that
589a he is dragged along wherever either of the other two leads; and not to accustom the two to one another or make them friends, but leave them to bite and fight and devour one another.

GLAUCON: Yes, that's exactly what someone who praises doing injustice is saying.

SOCRATES: On the other hand, wouldn't someone who claims that what is just is profitable be saying we should do and say what will give the inner human being the greatest mastery over the human being, to
b get him to take care of the many-headed beast like a farmer, feeding and domesticating the gentle heads and preventing the savage ones from growing; to make the lion's nature his ally; and to care for all in common, bringing them up in such a way that they will be friends with each other and with himself?

GLAUCON: Yes, that's exactly what someone who praises justice is saying.

SOCRATES: From every point of view, then, the one who praises what is just speaks truly while the one who praises what is unjust speaks falsely. For whether we consider pleasure or good reputation or
c advantage, the one who praises the just tells the truth while the one who condemns it has nothing sound to say and condemns with no knowledge of what he is condemning.

GLAUCON: None at all, in my opinion.

SOCRATES: Then let's persuade him gently—after all, he is not getting it wrong intentionally—by questioning him as follows: "Bless you, but shouldn't we claim that this is also the basis of the conventional views about what is fine and what is shameful: what is fine is what subordinates the beastlike elements in our nature to the human one—or better, perhaps, to the divine, whereas what is shameful is what enslaves
d the tame element to the savage?" Will he agree, or what?

GLAUCON: He will if he takes my advice.

SOCRATES: Is there anyone, then, in light of this argument, who profits by acquiring gold unjustly, if the result is something like this: in taking the gold, he simultaneously enslaves the best element in himself to the most wicked? If he got the gold by enslaving his

e son or daughter to savage and evil men, it would not profit him, no matter how much he got for doing it. So, if he ruthlessly enslaves the most divine element in himself to the most godless and polluted, how could he fail to be wretched, when he accepts golden gifts in return for a far more terrible destruction than

590a that of Eriphyle, who took the necklace in return for her husband's soul?[15]

GLAUCON: A much more terrible one. I will answer for him.

SOCRATES: And don't you think intemperance has long been condemned for reasons of this sort; that it is because of vices like it that that terrible creature, the large and multiform beast, is given more freedom than it should be?

GLAUCON: Clearly.

SOCRATES: And aren't stubbornness and peevishness condemned because they inharmoniously increase and stretch the lionlike and snakelike[16]

b element?

GLAUCON: Certainly.

SOCRATES: And aren't luxury and softness condemned for slackening and loosening this same part, because that produces cowardice in it?

GLAUCON: Of course.

SOCRATES: And aren't flattery and illiberality condemned because they subject this same spirited element to the moblike beast, allow it to be showered

---

15. [Eriphyle was bribed by Polynices to persuade her husband, Amphiaraus, to take part in an attack on Thebes. He was killed, and she was murdered by her son in revenge. See *Odyssey* 11.326–7.]

16. [The snakelike element hasn't been previously mentioned, although it may be included in "all that pertains to" the lion (588e6). It symbolizes some of the meaner components of the spirited part, such as peevishness, which it would be unnatural to attribute to the noble lion. Snakes were thought to guard shrines and other sacred places. Including a snakelike element in the part of the soul dominant in guardians is, therefore, somewhat natural.]

---

with abuse for the sake of money and the latter's insatiability, and habituate it from youth to be an ape instead of a lion?

GLAUCON: Yes, indeed.   *c*

SOCRATES: Why do you think someone is reproached for menial work or handicraft? Or shall we say that it is for no other reason than because the best element is naturally weak in him, so that it cannot rule the beasts within him, but can only serve them and learn what flatters them?

GLAUCON: Apparently.

SOCRATES: In order to ensure, then, that someone like that is also ruled by something similar to what rules the best person, we say that he should be the slave of that best person who has the divine ruler within himself. It is not to harm the slave that we say he should be ruled, as Thrasymachus supposed was *d* true of all subjects, but because it is better for everyone to be ruled by a divine and wise ruler—preferably one that is his own and that he has inside himself; otherwise one imposed on him from outside, so that we may all be as alike and as friendly as possible, because we are all captained by the same thing.

GLAUCON: Yes, that's right.

SOCRATES: This is clearly the aim of the law as well, which is the ally of everyone in the city. It is *e* also our aim in ruling our children. We do not allow them to be free until we establish a constitution in them as in a city. That is to say, we take care of their best part with the similar one in ourselves and equip them with a guardian and ruler similar to our own *591a* to take our place. Only then do we set them free.

GLAUCON: Yes, that's clearly so.

SOCRATES: How, then, will we claim, Glaucon, and on the basis of what argument, that it profits someone to do injustice, or what is intemperate, or some shameful thing that will make him worse, even if it brings more money or power of some other sort?

GLAUCON: There's no way we can.

SOCRATES: Or how can we claim that it profits him to be undetected in his injustice and not pay the penalty? I mean, doesn't the one who remains undetected become even worse, while in the one who *b* is discovered and punished, the bestial element is calmed and tamed and the gentle one freed? Doesn't his entire soul, when it returns to its best nature and acquires temperance and justice along with wisdom, achieve a condition that is as more honorable than that of a body when it acquires strength and beauty along with health, as a soul is more honorable than a body?

GLAUCON: Absolutely.

SOCRATES: Won't anyone with any sense, then, give everything he has to achieve it as long as he lives? First, won't he honor the studies that produce it and not honor the others?

GLAUCON: Clearly.

SOCRATES: Second, as regards the condition and nurture of his body, not only will he not give himself over to bestial and irrational pleasure, and live turned in that direction; but he won't make health his aim nor give precedence to the ways of becoming strong or healthy or beautiful, unless he is also going to become temperate as a result of them. On the contrary, it is clear that he will always be tuning the harmony of his body for the sake of the concord of his soul.

GLAUCON: He certainly will, if indeed he is going to be truly musical.

SOCRATES: Won't he also keep order and concord in his acquisition of money? He won't be dazzled, will he, by what the masses regard as blessed happiness, and—by increasing the size of his wealth without limit—acquire an unlimited number of evils?

GLAUCON: Not in my view.

SOCRATES: On the contrary, he will keep his eye fixed on the constitution within him and guard against disturbing anything there either with too much money or with too little. Captaining himself in that way, he will increase and spend his wealth, as far as possible by reference to it.

GLAUCON: That's exactly what he will do.

SOCRATES: Where honors are concerned, too, he will keep his eye on the same thing. He will willingly share in and taste those he believes will make him better. But those that might overthrow the established condition of his soul, he will avoid, both in private and in public.

GLAUCON: So, he won't be willing to take part in politics, then, if that is what he cares about.

SOCRATES: Yes, by the dog, in his own city, he certainly will. But he may not be willing to do so in his fatherland, unless some divine good luck chances to be his.

GLAUCON: I understand. You mean in the city we have just been founding and describing; the one that exists in words, since I do not think it exists anywhere on earth.

SOCRATES: But there may perhaps be a model of it in the heavens for anyone who wishes to look at it and to found himself on the basis of what he sees. It makes no difference at all whether it exists anywhere or ever will. You see, he would take part in the politics of it alone, and of no other.

GLAUCON: That's probably right.

BOOK X

SOCRATES' NARRATION CONTINUES:

SOCRATES: You know that there are many other things about our city that make me think we were entirely right in founding it as we did, but I am particularly thinking of poetry when I say that.

GLAUCON: What about it?

SOCRATES: Our refusal to admit any of it that is imitative. Indeed, the need not to admit it seems even more evident, in my view, now that we have distinguished the elements in the soul from one another.

GLAUCON: How do you mean?

SOCRATES: Between ourselves—for *you* won't denounce me to the tragic poets or any of the other imitative ones—I think all such poetry is likely to corrupt the mind of those of its hearers who do not have the knowledge of what it is really like as a drug to counteract it.

GLAUCON: What do you have in mind in saying that?

SOCRATES: I will have to tell you, even though a sort of reverential love I have had for Homer since childhood makes me hesitate to speak. You see, he seems to have been the first teacher and leader of all these fine tragedians. All the same, a man should not be honored more than the truth. So, as I say, I will have to tell you.

GLAUCON: Of course.

SOCRATES: Listen, then—or rather, answer my questions.

GLAUCON: Ask away.

SOCRATES: Could you tell me what imitation in general is? You see, I do not entirely understand what it is supposed to be.

GLAUCON: So is it likely that *I* will?

SOCRATES: There would be nothing strange in that, since there are many things the shortsighted see before the sharp-eyed!

596a

GLAUCON: That's right. But with you present, I could not possibly be very eager to speak out even if there were something I saw. So, you will have to do the looking yourself.

SOCRATES: Do you want us to begin our investigation with the following point, then, in accordance with our usual procedure? I mean, as you know, we usually posit some one particular form in connection with each set of many things to which we apply the same name. Or don't you understand?

GLAUCON: I do.

SOCRATES: Then in the present case, too, let's take any set of many things you like. For example, there are, if you like, many couches and tables.

b

GLAUCON: Of course.

SOCRATES: But the forms connected to these manufactured items are surely just two, one of a couch and one of a table.

GLAUCON: Yes.

SOCRATES: Don't we usually say, too, that the craftsman who makes each manufactured item looks toward the form when he makes the couches or the tables we use, and similarly with other things? For surely no craftsman makes the form itself—

GLAUCON: How could he?

SOCRATES: Well, now, see what you would call *this* craftsman?

c

GLAUCON: Which?

SOCRATES: The one who makes everything each individual handicraftsman makes.

GLAUCON: That's an amazingly clever man you are talking about!

SOCRATES: Wait a minute and you will have even more reason to say that! You see, this same handicraftsman is able to make not only every manufactured item, but he also makes all the plants that grow from the earth, and produces all the animals, including himself; and, in addition, he produces earth and sky and gods and everything in the sky, and everything in Hades beneath the earth.

GLAUCON: You are talking about a wholly amazing sophist!

d

SOCRATES: You do not believe me? Tell me, do you think such a craftsman is completely impossible? Or do you think there is a way in which a maker of all these things could exist, and a way in which he could not? Don't you see there is a certain way in which even you yourself could make all of them?

GLAUCON: What way is that?

SOCRATES: It is not difficult. On the contrary, it is a sort of craftsmanship that is widely available and quick—and quickest of all, I suppose, if you are willing to take a mirror and turn it around in all directions. That way you will quickly make the sun and the things in the sky; you will quickly make the earth, yourself and the other animals, manufactured items, plants, and everything else that was mentioned just now.

e

GLAUCON: Yes, their appearances, but certainly not the things themselves as they truly are.

SOCRATES: Right! You attack the argument at just the right place. For I think the painter is also one of these craftsmen, isn't he?

GLAUCON: Of course.

SOCRATES: But you will say, I think, that he does not make the things he makes as they truly are—even though there is a certain way in which the painter also makes a couch. Isn't that right?

GLAUCON: Yes, he also makes the appearance of one.

SOCRATES: What about the couch-maker? Didn't you just say that he does not make the form—which we say is what a couch is—but only a particular couch?

597a

GLAUCON: Yes, I did say that.

SOCRATES: Now, if he does not make what it is, he is not making what is, but something that is like what is, but is not. So, if someone were to say that the product of a couch-maker or any other handicraftsman completely is, he probably would not be speaking the truth?

GLAUCON: That, at any rate, is what those who occupy themselves with such arguments would think.

SOCRATES: So we should not be surprised if it also turns out to be somewhat dim in comparison to the truth.

GLAUCON: No, we should not.

b

SOCRATES: Would you like us, then, to use these same examples to search for that imitator of ours and what he really is?

GLAUCON: I would, if you would.

SOCRATES: Well, then, we have these three sorts of couches. One, that is in nature, which I think we would say a god makes. Or is it someone else?

GLAUCON: No one, I suppose.

SOCRATES: One the carpenter makes.

GLAUCON: Yes.

SOCRATES: And one the painter makes. Isn't that so?

GLAUCON: It is.

SOCRATES: So painter, carpenter, and god—these three oversee three kinds of couches?

GLAUCON: Yes, three.

SOCRATES: Now, the god, either because he did not want to, or because it was somehow necessary for him not to make more than one that is in its nature a couch, made only the one that is what a couch itself is. Two or more of these have not been naturally developed by the god and never will be naturally developed.

GLAUCON: Why is that?

SOCRATES: Because, if he were to make only two, one would again come to light whose form they in turn would both possess, and *it* would be what a couch itself is, not the two.

GLAUCON: That's right.

SOCRATES: The god knew this, I suppose, and, wishing to be the real maker of the real couch and not just some particular maker of some particular couch, naturally developed the one that is in its nature unique.

GLAUCON: Probably so.

SOCRATES: Would you like us to call him its natural maker, then, or something like that?

GLAUCON: It would be right to do so, at any rate, since it is by nature that he has made it and all the others.

SOCRATES: What about the carpenter? Shouldn't we call him the craftsman who makes a couch?

GLAUCON: Yes.

SOCRATES: And should we call a painter, too, a craftsman and maker of such a thing?

GLAUCON: Certainly not.

SOCRATES: In that case, what is it you say he is, of a couch?

GLAUCON: In my view, the most reasonable thing to call him is this: he is an imitator of what the others are craftsmen of.

SOCRATES: All right. So the one whose product is three removed from the natural one, you call an imitator?

GLAUCON: Certainly.

SOCRATES: So the tragedian too, if indeed he is an imitator, will be someone who is by his nature third from king and truth,[1] and so will all the other imitators.

GLAUCON: It looks that way.

SOCRATES: We are agreed about the imitator, then. Now, tell me this about the painter: in each case, do you think it is what each thing itself is in its nature that he is trying to imitate, or the products of the craftsmen?

GLAUCON: Those of the craftsmen.

SOCRATES: As they are, or as they appear to be? You have still to make that distinction.

GLAUCON: How do you mean?

SOCRATES: This: if you look at a couch from the side or the front or from anywhere else, does it differ in any way from itself? Or, while not differing at all, does it appear different? And similarly with the others?

GLAUCON: The latter. It appears different, but is not different at all.

SOCRATES: Then consider this very point: at what does painting aim in each case? To imitate what is as it is? Or what appears as it appears? Is it an imitation of an illusion, or of truth?

GLAUCON: Of an illusion.

SOCRATES: So, imitation is surely far removed from the truth. And the reason that it produces everything, it seems, is that it grasps only a small part of each thing—and that is an illusion. For example, the painter, we say, can paint us a cobbler, a carpenter, or any other craftsman, even though he knows nothing about these crafts. All the same, if he is a good painter, by painting a carpenter and displaying him at a distance, he might deceive children and foolish adults into thinking it truly is a carpenter.

GLAUCON: Of course.

SOCRATES: In fact, my friend, I imagine that what we must bear in mind in all these cases is this: when

---

1. [God is called king at *Laws* 10.904a6.]

someone tells us he has met a human being who knows every craft as well as everything else anyone knows, and that there is nothing of which he does not have a more exact knowledge than anyone else, d we should assume we are talking to a naïve fellow. He has been deceived, it seems, by an encounter with some sort of sorcerer or imitator, whom he therefore considers to be all-wise. But that is because of his own inability to distinguish between knowledge, lack of knowledge, and imitation.

GLAUCON: That's absolutely true.

SOCRATES: Well, then, we must next consider tragedy and its leader, Homer, since we hear from e some that these men know every craft, everything relevant to human virtue and vice, and even all about divine matters. They claim, you see, that if a good poet is to write beautiful poetry about the things he writes about, he must have knowledge of them when he writes, or else he would be unable to. We should consider, then, whether those who tell us this have been deceived by their encounters with these imitators and do not realize, when they see their works, that they are three removes from what is, and are easy 599a to produce without knowledge of the truth. For they produce illusions, not things that are. Or whether there is something in what they say, and good poets really do have knowledge of the things about which the masses think they speak so well.

GLAUCON: We certainly must consider that.

SOCRATES: Do you think, then, that if someone could make both what is imitated and its image, he would allow himself to take making images seriously, and put it at the forefront of his life as the best ability b he had?

GLAUCON: No, I do not.

SOCRATES: But if he truly had knowledge of what he imitates, I suppose he would take deeds much more seriously than their imitations, would try to leave behind many beautiful deeds as his own memorials, and would be much more eager to be the subject of a eulogy than the author of one.

GLAUCON: I suppose so. I mean, these things certainly are not equal either in honor or in benefit.

SOCRATES: Let's not demand an account, then, of the other things from Homer or any other poet. c Let's not ask if any of them is a doctor or only an imitator of what doctors say; or which people any of the poets, old or new, has reportedly made healthy, as Asclepius did; or which students of medicine he left behind, as Asclepius did his sons. And let's not ask them about the other crafts either, but leave them aside. When it comes, however, to the most important and most beautiful things of which Homer undertakes to speak—warfare, generalship, city government, and a person's education—surely, it *is* fair to question him as follows: "My dear Homer, if you are not third removed from the truth about virtue, and are not the d sort of craftsman of an image, which is what we defined an imitator to be, but if you are even in second place and capable of knowing what practices make people better or worse in private or in public life, tell us which cities are better governed because of you, as the Lacedaemonians are because of Lycurgus, and as many others—big and small—are because of many other men. What city gives you credit for having e proved to be a good lawgiver who benefited it? Italy and Sicily give it to Charondas, and we give it to Solon. Who gives it to you?" Will he be able to name one?

GLAUCON: I suppose not. At any rate, none is mentioned even by the Homeridae themselves.[2]

SOCRATES: Then is any war in Homer's time remembered that was well fought because of his leadership or advice?   600a

GLAUCON: None at all.

SOCRATES: Then as you would expect in the case of a man wise in deeds, are we told of his many ingenious inventions in the crafts or other activities, as we are about Thales of Miletus and Anacharsis the Scythian?

GLAUCON: There's nothing of that sort.

SOCRATES: Then if there is nothing of a public nature, is Homer said to have been a leader, during his own lifetime, in the education of people who loved associating with him and passed on a Homeric way of life to those who came later? Is he like Pythago- b ras, who was himself particularly loved for this reason, and whose followers even today still seem to be conspicuous for a way of life they call Pythagorean?

GLAUCON: Again, we are told nothing of this kind. Indeed, Socrates, Creophylus, the companion of

2. [The rhapsodes and poets who recited and expounded Homer throughout the Greek world.]

Homer, would presumably seem even more ridiculous than his name[3] suggests as an example of such education, if the story told about Homer is true. You see, we are told that while he was alive, Creophylus c completely neglected him.

SOCRATES: Yes, we are told that. But, Glaucon, if Homer had really been able to educate people and make them better, if he had been able, not to imitate such matters but to know about them, wouldn't he have had many companions who honored and loved him? Protagoras of Abdera, Prodicus of Ceos, and a great many others are able to convince anyone who associates with them in private that he wouldn't be d able to manage his household or city unless they themselves supervised his education, and they are so intensely loved because of this wisdom of theirs that their disciples do everything except carry them around on their shoulders. Are we to believe, then, that if Homer had been able to help people become virtuous, his companions would have allowed either him or Hesiod to wander around as rhapsodes, and wouldn't have clung far tighter to them than to gold and compelled them to come home and live with e them? And if persuasion failed, wouldn't they have followed them wherever they went until they had received sufficient education?

GLAUCON: I think what you say is entirely true, Socrates.

SOCRATES: Are we to conclude, then, that all poets, beginning with Homer, imitate images of virtue and of all the other things they write about, and have no grasp of the truth? Although, as we were saying just now, a painter will make what seems to be a shoemaker to those who know as little about shoemak- 601a ing as he does himself, but who look at things in terms of their colors and shapes.

GLAUCON: That's right.

SOCRATES: Similarly, I suppose, we will say that the poet uses words and phrases to paint colored pictures of each of the crafts, even though he knows only how to imitate them; so that others like himself, who look at things in terms of words, will think he speaks extremely well about shoemaking or general-

3. [It derives from two words, *kreas* (meat) and *phylon* (race or kind). A modern equivalent might be "meathead."]

ship or anything else, provided he speaks with meter, rhythm, and harmony. That is how great a natural spell these things cast. For if a poet's works are stripped b of their musical colorings and spoken just by themselves, I think you know what they look like. You have surely seen them.

GLAUCON: I certainly have.

SOCRATES: Don't they resemble the faces of those who are young but not really beautiful, after the bloom of youth has left them?

GLAUCON: Absolutely.

SOCRATES: Come on, then, consider this: the maker of an image—the imitator—knows nothing, we say, about what is, but only about what appears. Isn't that so? c

GLAUCON: Yes.

SOCRATES: Then let's not leave the story half-told. Let's look at the whole thing.

GLAUCON: Go on.

SOCRATES: A painter, we say, will paint reins and a bit?

GLAUCON: Yes.

SOCRATES: But it is the saddler and the blacksmith who make them?

GLAUCON: Of course.

SOCRATES: Does the painter know what the reins and bit should be like, then? Or do not even their makers—the saddler and the blacksmith—know this, but only the one who knows how to use them, the horseman?

GLAUCON: That's absolutely true.

SOCRATES: So, won't we say that the same holds for everything?

GLAUCON: What?

SOCRATES: That for each thing there are these three crafts: one that will use, one that will make, d one that will imitate?

GLAUCON: Yes.

SOCRATES: Then aren't the virtue, goodness, and correctness of each manufactured item, living creature, and activity related to nothing but the use for which each is made or naturally developed?

GLAUCON: They are.

SOCRATES: So it is entirely necessary, then, that the user of each thing has the most experience of it, and that he inform the maker about what the good and bad points are in the actual use of the thing he

uses. For example, it is the flute player, I take it, who
informs the flute-maker about which flutes respond
e well in actual playing, and prescribes how they should
be made, while the maker obeys him.

GLAUCON: Of course.

SOCRATES: Doesn't the one who knows give information, then, about good and bad flutes, whereas the
other, by relying on him, makes them?

GLAUCON: Yes.

SOCRATES: So, as regards the same manufactured
item, its maker—through associating with the one
who knows and having to listen to the one who
knows—has correct belief about its good and bad
602a qualities, while its user has knowledge.

GLAUCON: Exactly.

SOCRATES: What about the imitator? Will he, on
the basis of using the things he paints, have knowledge
of whether they are good and correct or not? Or will
he have correct belief through having to associate
with the one who knows and being told how he should
paint them?

GLAUCON: Neither.

SOCRATES: So an imitator has neither knowledge
nor correct belief about whether the things he makes
are good or bad.

GLAUCON: Apparently not.

SOCRATES: How well situated the poetic imitator
is, then, in relation to wisdom about the subjects of
his poems!

GLAUCON: He isn't really.

SOCRATES: And yet he will go on imitating all
the same, even though he does not know in what
b way each thing is good or bad. On the contrary,
whatever appears good to the masses who know
nothing—that, it seems, is what he will imitate.

GLAUCON: What else?

SOCRATES: Apparently, then, we are fairly well
agreed on the following: that the imitator knows nothing worth mentioning about the things he imitates,
but that imitation is a kind of game, not something
to be taken seriously; and that tragic poets, whether
in iambic or epic verse, are as imitative as they could
possibly be.

GLAUCON: Absolutely.

SOCRATES: In the name of Zeus, then, this busi-
c ness of imitation is concerned with what is third removed from the truth. Isn't that right?

GLAUCON: Yes.

SOCRATES: Now, then, on which of the elements
in a human being does it have its effect?

GLAUCON: What sort of element do you mean?

SOCRATES: This sort: the same object, viewed
from nearby, does not appear the same size, I presume, as when viewed from a distance.

GLAUCON: No, it does not.

SOCRATES: And the same things appear bent and
straight when seen in water or out of it, or concave
and convex because sight is misled by colors; and
every other similar sort of confusion is clearly present
in our soul. It is because it exploits this weakness in *d*
our nature that illusionist painting is nothing short
of sorcery, and neither are jugglery or many other
similar sorts of trickery.

GLAUCON: True.

SOCRATES: And haven't measuring, counting,
and weighing proved to be most welcome assistants
in these cases, ensuring that what appears bigger or
smaller or more numerous or heavier does not rule
within us, but rather what has calculated or measured
or even weighed?

GLAUCON: Of course.

SOCRATES: And that is the task of the soul's rational element?

GLAUCON: Yes, of it.   *e*

SOCRATES: But quite often, when it has measured
and indicates that some things are larger or smaller
than others, or the same size, the opposite simultaneously appears to hold of these same things.

GLAUCON: Yes.

SOCRATES: And didn't we say that it is impossible
for the same thing to believe opposites about the same
thing at the same time?[4]

GLAUCON: Yes, and we were right to say it

SOCRATES: So, the element in the soul that believes contrary to the measurements and the one that
believes in accord with the measurements could not
be the same.   *603a*

GLAUCON: No, they could not.

SOCRATES: But the one that puts its trust in measurement and calculation would be the best element
in the soul.

4. [436b8–c1.]

GLAUCON: Of course.

SOCRATES: So the one that opposes it would be one of the inferior parts in us.

GLAUCON: Necessarily.

SOCRATES: That, then, was what I wanted to get agreement about when I said that painting—and imitation as a whole—are far from the truth when they produce their work; and moreover that imitation really consorts with an element in us that is far from wisdom, and that nothing healthy or true can come *b* from their relationship or friendship.

GLAUCON: That's absolutely right.

SOCRATES: So, imitation is an inferior thing that consorts with another inferior thing to produce inferior offspring.

GLAUCON: So it seems.

SOCRATES: Does this apply only to the imitation that is visible, or also to the one that is audible—the one we call poetry?

GLAUCON: It probably applies to that as well.

SOCRATES: Well, let's not rely solely on a probable analogy with painting. Instead, let's also go directly again to the very element in our mind with which *c* poetic imitation consorts and see whether it is inferior or excellent.

GLAUCON: Yes, we should.

SOCRATES: Then let's put it as follows. Imitative poetry, we say, imitates human beings acting under compulsion or voluntarily, who, as a result of these actions, believe they are doing either well or badly, and so experience either pain or enjoyment in all these situations. Does it imitate anything apart from these?

GLAUCON: Not a thing.

SOCRATES: So, is a human being of one mind in all these circumstances then? Or, just as in the case of visible representation, where he was split into factions *d* and had opposite beliefs in him about the same things at the same time, is he also split into factions and at war with himself in matters of action? But I am reminded that there is really no need now for us to reach agreement on this question. You see, in our earlier arguments, we were sufficiently agreed about all that when we said that our soul is filled with myriad opposites of that sort at the same time.[5]

GLAUCON: And rightly so.

SOCRATES: Yes, it *was* right. But we omitted something then that I now think we must discuss.   *e*

GLAUCON: What's that?

SOCRATES: When a good man suffers some stroke of bad luck, such as the loss of a son or something else he values very highly, we also said in our earlier arguments, as you know, that he will bear it more easily than others.[6]

GLAUCON: We certainly did.

SOCRATES: Now, let's consider this: will he not grieve at all? Or, since that is impossible, will he be somehow measured in the face of pain?

GLAUCON: The latter is probably closer to the truth.

SOCRATES: Now, tell me this about him: do you think he will be more likely to fight and resist pain *604a* when he is seen by his equals, or when he is just by himself in a solitary place?

GLAUCON: He's sure to fight it far more when he is being seen.

SOCRATES: But when he is alone, I imagine, he will venture to say many things he would be ashamed if someone else heard, and to do many things he would not want anyone else to see him doing.

GLAUCON: That's right.

SOCRATES: And isn't it reason and law that tell him to resist, while what urges him to give in to the pains is the feeling itself?   *b*

GLAUCON: True.

SOCRATES: And when there are opposite impulses in a human being in relation to the same thing at the same time, we say that there must be two elements in him.

GLAUCON: Of course.

SOCRATES: Isn't one part ready to be persuaded to follow the law, wherever the law leads?

GLAUCON: Can you explain how?

SOCRATES: The law says, as you know, that it is best to keep as quiet as possible in misfortunes and not get irritated, since what is really good or bad in such things is not clear. There is nothing to be gained by taking them hard, nor is any aspect of human affairs worth getting very serious about. And the very

---

5. [439c2–441c7.]

6. [387d4–e4.]

thing whose aid we need as quickly as possible in
c such circumstances is the one our grieving hinders.

GLAUCON: Which do you mean?

SOCRATES: The capacity to deliberate about what
has happened and, as with the fall of the dice, to
arrange our affairs, given what has befallen us, in
whatever way reason determines would be best. Instead of acting like children who have fallen over,
and who hold on to the hurt part and spend their
time wailing, we should always accustom our souls
to turn as quickly as possible to curing and raising
d up the part that has suffered a fall and is sick, so as
to banish lamentation by means of medicine.

GLAUCON: That would be the most correct way
to deal with bad luck, anyway.

SOCRATES: So it is the best element, we say, that
is willing to follow this rational calculation.

GLAUCON: Clearly.

SOCRATES: As for the part that leads us to recollec-
tions of our suffering and to lamentations, and is
insatiable for these things, won't we say that it is the
element that lacks reason, is idle, and is a friend
of cowardice?

GLAUCON: We certainly will.

SOCRATES: Now, this element—the one that gets
irritated—admits of much complex imitation;
e whereas the wise and quiet character, which always
remains pretty much selfsame, is neither easy to imitate nor easy to understand when imitated—especially
not at a festival where multifarious people are gathered together in theaters. For the experience being
imitated is alien to them.

605a   GLAUCON: Absolutely.

SOCRATES: The imitative poet, then, clearly does
not naturally relate to this best element in the soul,
and his wisdom is not directed to pleasing it—not if
he is going to attain a good reputation with the
masses—but to the irritable and complex character,
because it is easy to imitate.

GLAUCON: Clearly.

SOCRATES: So, it would at last be right to take
him and place him beside the painter as his counterpart. For he is like the latter in producing things that
are inferior as regards truth, and is also similar to him
in associating with the other element in souls, not
b with the best one. So, we would also at last be justified
in not admitting him into a city that is to be well

governed. You see, he arouses and nourishes this
element in the soul and, by making it strong, destroys
the rational one—just as someone in a city who makes
wicked people strong, by handing the city over to
them, ruins the better ones. Similarly, we will say an
imitative poet produces a bad constitution in the soul
of each individual by making images that are very far
removed from the truth and by gratifying the element   c
in it that lacks understanding and cannot distinguish
bigger from smaller, but believes the same things to
be now large, now small.

GLAUCON: He does, indeed.

SOCRATES: But we haven't yet brought our chief
charge against imitation. For its power to corrupt all
but a very few *good* people is surely an altogether
terrible one.

GLAUCON: It certainly is, if it really can do that.

SOCRATES: Listen and consider. When even the
best of us hear Homer, or some other tragic poet,
imitating one of the heroes in a state of grief and
making a long speech of lamentation, or even chant-   d
ing and beating his breast, you know we enjoy it and
give ourselves over to it. We suffer along with the
hero and take his sufferings seriously. And we praise
the one who affects us most in this way as a good poet.

GLAUCON: Of course I know.

SOCRATES: But when one of us suffers a personal
loss, you also realize we do the opposite: we pride
ourselves if we are able to keep quiet and endure it,
in the belief that that is what a *man* does, whereas
what we praised before is what a woman does.   e

GLAUCON: I do realize that.

SOCRATES: Is praise of that sort rightly bestowed,
then? Is it right to look at the sort of man we would
be, not honored, but rather ashamed to resemble,
and instead of being disgusted by what we see to
enjoy and praise it?

GLAUCON: No, by Zeus, that does not seem
reasonable.

SOCRATES: Yes, it does. At least, it does if you
look at it in the following way.   606a

GLAUCON: How?

SOCRATES: If you reflect as follows: what is forcibly
kept in check in our personal misfortunes and has
an insatiable hunger for weeping and lamenting—
since that is what it has a natural appetite for—is the
very factor that gets satisfaction and enjoyment from

the poets. Second, our naturally best element, since it has not been adequately educated by reason or habit, relaxes its guard over the lamenting one, since *b* it is watching the sufferings of somebody else and thinks there is no shame involved for it in praising and pitying another purportedly good man who grieves excessively. On the contrary, it thinks that to be a clear profit—I mean the pleasure it gets. And it would not want to be deprived of it by despising the whole poem. You see, I think only a few people are able to calculate that the enjoyment of other people's sufferings is inevitably transferred to one's own, since, when pity is nourished and strengthened by the former, it is not easily suppressed in the case of one's own sufferings.

c   GLAUCON: That's absolutely true.

SOCRATES: Doesn't the same argument also apply to humor? You see, if there are jokes you would be ashamed to tell yourself, but that you very much enjoy when you hear them imitated in a comedy or even in private, and that you don't hate as something bad, aren't you doing the same as with the things you pity? For the element in you that wanted to tell the jokes, but which you held back by means of reason because you were afraid of being reputed a buffoon, you now release; and having made it strong in that way, you have been led unawares into becoming a comedian in your own life.

GLAUCON: Exactly.

SOCRATES: And in the case of sexual desires, *d* anger, and all the appetites, pains, and pleasures in the soul, which we say accompany every action of ours, the effect of poetic imitation on us is the same. I mean, it nurtures and waters them when they should be dried up, and establishes them as rulers in us when—if we are to be become better and happier rather than worse and more wretched—they should be ruled.

GLAUCON: I cannot disagree with you.

SOCRATES: In that case, Glaucon, when you meet *e* admirers of Homer—who tell us that this is the poet who educated Greece, and that for the management of human affairs and education in them, one should take up his works and learn them and live guided by this poet in the arrangement of one's whole life— you should befriend and welcome them, since they *607a* are the best they are capable of being. And you should

agree that Homer is the most poetic of the tragedians and the first among them. Nonetheless, be aware that hymns to the gods and eulogies of good people are the only poetry we can admit into our city. For if you admit the honeyed Muse, whether in lyric or epic poetry, pleasure and pain will be kings in your city instead of law and the thing that has always been generally believed to be best—reason.

GLAUCON: That's absolutely true.

SOCRATES: Let that, then, be our defense for our return to the topic of poetry, which shows that, *b* given her nature, we were right to banish her from the city earlier, since our argument compelled us. But let's also tell her—in case we are charged with some harshness and boorishness—that there is an ancient quarrel between poetry and philosophy. For such expressions as "the bitch yelping at its master" and "howling," and "great in the empty eloquence of fools," and "control by a mob of the omni-wise," and "the subtle thinkers who are beggars all," and *c* countless others are signs of this old opposition.[7] All the same, let it be said that, if the imitative poetry that aims at pleasure has any argument to show it should have a place in a well-governed city, we would gladly welcome it back, since we are well aware of being charmed by it ourselves. Still, it is not pious to betray what one believes to be the truth. What about you, my friend; aren't you also charmed by it, especially when it is through Homer that you look at it?   *d*

GLAUCON: Very.

SOCRATES: Isn't it just, then, for her to reenter in that way, when she has defended herself in lyric or some other meter?

GLAUCON: Yes, indeed.

SOCRATES: Then we will surely allow her defenders—the ones who are not poets themselves, but lovers of poetry—to argue without meter on her behalf, showing that she gives not only pleasure but also benefit both to constitutions and to human life.

7. [Philosophers, such as Xenophanes and Heraclitus, attacked Homer and Hesiod for their immoral tales about the gods. Poets, such as Aristophanes in his *Clouds*, attacked philosophers for subverting traditional ethical and religious values. The sources of these particular quotations, however, are unknown.]

Indeed, we will listen to them graciously, since we would certainly profit if poetry were shown to be not *e* only pleasant but also beneficial.

GLAUCON: How could we fail to profit?

SOCRATES: But if it is not, my dear comrade, we will behave like men who have fallen in love. If they do not believe their passion is beneficial, hard though it is, they nonetheless stay away. And we too, because of the passion for this sort of poetry implanted in us by our upbringing in those fine constitutions, are well *608a* disposed to have her appear in the best and truest light. But as long as she is not able to produce such a defense, then whenever we listen to her, we will chant to ourselves the argument we just now put forward as a counter-charm to prevent us from slipping back into the childish passion that the masses have. For we have come to see that such poetry is not to be taken seriously, as a serious undertaking that grasps truth; but that anyone who listens to it should be careful, if he is concerned about the consti- *b* tution within him, and should believe what we have said about poetry.

GLAUCON: I completely agree.

SOCRATES: It is a great struggle, my dear Glaucon, greater than people think, to become good rather than bad. So, we must not be tempted by honor, money, or any sort of office whatever—not even by poetry!—into thinking that it is worthwhile to neglect justice and the rest of virtue.

GLAUCON: I agree with you on the basis of what we have said. And so, I think, would anyone else.

SOCRATES: And yet the greatest rewards of virtue, *c* and the prizes proposed for it, have not been discussed.

GLAUCON: You must have something incredibly great in mind, if it is greater than those already mentioned!

SOCRATES: In a short period of time, could anything really great come to pass? I mean, the entire period from childhood to old age is surely short when compared to the whole of time.

GLAUCON: It's a mere nothing.

SOCRATES: Well, then, do you think an immortal thing should be seriously concerned with that period *d* rather than the whole of time?

GLAUCON: I suppose not, but what exactly do you have in mind by that?

SOCRATES: Haven't you realized that our souls are immortal and never destroyed?

He looked at me and said in amazement:

No, by Zeus, I have not. But are you really in a position to assert that?

SOCRATES: I certainly ought to be, and I think you are, too. There is nothing difficult about it.

GLAUCON: There is for me. So I would be glad to hear from you about this non-difficult topic!

SOCRATES: Listen then.

GLAUCON: All you have to do is speak!

SOCRATES: Do you think there is a good and a bad?

GLAUCON: I do.

SOCRATES: And do you think about them the same way I do? *e*

GLAUCON: What way?

SOCRATES: What destroys and corrupts coincides entirely with the bad, while what preserves and benefits coincides entirely with the good.

GLAUCON: I do.

SOCRATES: And do you think there is a good and a bad for each thing, such as ophthalmia for the eyes, sickness for the whole body, blight for grain, rot for wood, rust for iron and bronze, and, as I say, a natural *609a* badness and sickness for nearly everything?

GLAUCON: I certainly do.

SOCRATES: And when one of them attaches itself to something, doesn't it make the thing to which it attaches itself deficient? And in the end, doesn't it break it down completely and destroy it?

GLAUCON: Of course.

SOCRATES: So the badness natural to each thing—the deficiency peculiar to each—destroys it, but if that does not destroy it, there is nothing else left to destroy it. For obviously the good will never destroy anything, and again what is neither good nor *b* bad won't either.

GLAUCON: How could it?

SOCRATES: So if we discover something, the badness of which causes it to deteriorate but cannot break it down and destroy it, won't we immediately know that something with such a nature cannot be destroyed after all?

GLAUCON: That seems reasonable.

SOCRATES: Well, then, what about the soul? Isn't there something that makes it bad?

GLAUCON: Certainly. All the things we were discussing earlier: injustice, intemperance, cowardice, and ignorance.

SOCRATES: Do any of these break it down and destroy it? Think about it, so we are not deceived into believing that when an unjust and foolish person is caught, he is destroyed by injustice, which is a deficiency in a soul. Instead, let's proceed this way: just as the body's deficiency, which is disease, wastes and destroys a body, and brings it to the point of not being a body at all, so all the things we mentioned just now reach the point of not being when their own peculiar badness attaches itself to them, is present in them, and destroys them. Isn't that so?

GLAUCON: Yes.

SOCRATES: Come on, then, and look at the soul in the same way. When injustice and the rest of vices are present in it, does their presence in it and attachment to it corrupt and wither it until they bring it to the point of death and separate it from the body?

GLAUCON: No, they never do that.

SOCRATES: But surely it is unreasonable to suppose that a thing is destroyed by something else's deficiency and not by its own?

GLAUCON: It is unreasonable.

SOCRATES: Think about it, Glaucon. We do not even believe that a body would be destroyed by the deficiency belonging to foods, whether it is staleness, rottenness, or anything else. But if the foods' own deficiency induces bodily deterioration, we will say the body was destroyed *through* them *by* its own badness, which is disease. But we will never admit that the body is destroyed *by* the deficiency belonging to foods—since they and the body are different things—except when external badness induces the natural badness.

GLAUCON: That's absolutely right.

SOCRATES: By the same argument, then, if the body's deficiency does not induce a soul's own deficiency in a soul, we will never admit that a soul is destroyed by external badness in the absence of its own peculiar deficiency—one thing by another's badness.

GLAUCON: Yes, that's reasonable.

SOCRATES: Well, then, let's refute these arguments and show that what we said was not right. Or,

so long as they remain unrefuted, let's never say that the soul even comes close to being destroyed by a fever or any other disease, or by killing for that matter—not even if one were to cut the entire body up into the very smallest pieces—until someone demonstrates to us that these conditions of the body make the soul itself more unjust and more impious. But when an external badness is present, while its own particular badness is absent, let's not allow anyone to say that a soul or anything else whatever is destroyed.

GLAUCON: But you may be sure no one will ever prove that the souls of the dying are made more unjust by death!

SOCRATES: But suppose someone dares to come to grips with our argument and—simply in order to avoid having to agree that our souls are immortal—dares to say that a dying man does become worse and more unjust. We are sure to reply that if what he says is true, injustice must be as deadly as a disease to those who have it, and that those who catch it must die because of its own deadly nature—with the worst cases dying quickly and the less serious ones more slowly—and not as now in fact happens, where the unjust are put to death because of their injustice by others who inflict the penalty.

GLAUCON: By Zeus, injustice won't seem so altogether terrible if it will be deadly to the person who contracts it, since then it would be an *escape* from evils! But I am more inclined to think that it will be shown to be entirely the opposite—something that kills others if it can, but makes its possessor very lively indeed—and not just lively, but positively sleepless! That's how far it is, in my view, from being deadly.

SOCRATES: You are right. After all, if its own deficiency—its own badness—is not enough to kill and destroy the soul, an evil designed for the destruction of something else will hardly destroy the soul, or anything else except what it is designed to destroy.

GLAUCON: "Hardly" is right, it seems.

SOCRATES: Then when something is not destroyed by a single bad thing—whether its own or an external one—clearly it must always exist. And if it always exists, it is immortal.

GLAUCON: It must be.

SOCRATES: Well, then, let's assume it to be so. And if it is so, you realize that the same ones will always exist. I mean, they surely could not become fewer in number if none is destroyed, or more numerous either. For if anything immortal is increased, you know that the increase would have to come from the mortal, and then everything would end up being immortal.

GLAUCON: True.

SOCRATES: Then we must not think such a thing—for our argument does not allow it. And we must not think, either, that the soul in its truest nature b is full of multicolored variety and dissimilarity and conflict with itself.

GLAUCON: How do you mean?

SOCRATES: It is not easy for something to be immortal when it is composed of many elements and is not composed in the most beautiful way—which is how the soul now seemed to us.

GLAUCON: It probably isn't.

SOCRATES: Yet both our recent argument and others as well require us to accept that the soul *is* immortal. But what it is like in truth, seen as it should be, not maimed by its partnership with the body and c other bad things, which is how we see it now, what it is like when it has become pure—*that* we can adequately see only by means of rational calculation. And you will find it to be a much more beautiful thing than we thought and get a much clearer view of all the cases of justice and injustice and of all the other things that we have so far discussed. So far, what we have said about the soul is true of it as it appears at present. But the condition we have seen d it in is like that of all the sea god Glaucus,[8] whose original nature cannot easily be made out by those who catch glimpses of him, because some of the original parts of his body have been broken off, others have been worn away and altogether mutilated by the waves, and other things—shells, seaweeds, and rocks—have grown into him, so that he looks more like any wild beast than what he naturally was. Such, too, is the condition of the soul when we see it beset by myriad bad things. But, Glaucon, we should be looking in another direction.

GLAUCON: Where?

SOCRATES: To its love of wisdom.[9] We must keep in mind what it grasps and the kinds of things with which it longs to associate, because it is akin to what e is divine and immortal and what always exists, and what it would become if it followed this longing with its whole being and if that impulse lifted it out of the sea in which it now is, and struck off the rocks and 612a shells that, because it now feasts on earth, have grown around it in a wild, earthy, and stony profusion as a result of those so-called happy feastings. And then you would see its true nature, whether multiform or uniform,[10] or somehow some other way. But we have given a pretty good account now, I think, of what its condition is and what form it takes in human life.

GLAUCON: We certainly have.

SOCRATES: In the course of our discussion, then, did we respond to the other points, without having to invoke the rewards and reputations of justice, as you all said Homer and Hesiod did?[11] Instead, haven't b we found that justice itself is the best thing for the soul itself, and that the soul should do what is just, whether it has Gyges' ring or not, or even the cap of Hades as well.[12]

GLAUCON: That's absolutely true. We have.

SOCRATES: So, Glaucon, isn't it now at last unobjectionable, in addition, also to give back to justice and the rest of virtue both the kind and quantity of wages they bring to the soul, both from human beings c and from gods, both during life and after death?

GLAUCON: Certainly.

SOCRATES: Then will you give *me* back what you borrowed from me in the course of the discussion?

GLAUCON: What in particular?

SOCRATES: I granted you that the just man should seem unjust and the unjust one just. For you thought that even if it would be impossible for these things to remain hidden from both gods and human beings,

---

8. [Ancient paintings may have represented Glaucus in the way Plato describes him here. His name appears in the accusative (*Glaukon*), suggesting a play on Glaucon (*Glaukōn*).]

9. [*Philosophia*.]

10. [*Eite polueidês eite monoeidês*: having many elements or only one.]

11. [The reference is to the challenge posed by Glaucon and Adeimantus at 357a1–367e5. But they, of course, are renewing the challenge posed by Thrasymachus in Book I (see 358b1–c1).]

12. [The ring of Gyges is discussed at 359c6–360c5. The cap of Hades also made its wearer invisible.]

all the same, it had to be granted for the sake of argument, so that justice itself could be judged in

d relation to injustice itself. Don't you remember?

GLAUCON: *I* would be unjust if I didn't!

SOCRATES: Well, then, since they have now been judged, I ask on behalf of justice for a return of the reputation it in fact has among gods and human beings; and that we agree that it does indeed have such a reputation, and so may carry off the prizes it gains for someone by making him seem just; since we have already seen that it does give the good things that come from being just, and does not deceive those who really possess it.

e GLAUCON: That's a just request.

SOCRATES: Then won't you first give this back, that it certainly does not remain hidden from the gods what each of the two is like?

GLAUCON: We will.

SOCRATES: But if it does not remain hidden, one would be loved by the gods and one hated, as we agreed at the beginning.[13]

GLAUCON: That's right.

SOCRATES: And won't we also agree that everything that comes to the one who is loved by gods — insofar as it comes from the gods themselves — is the

613a best possible, unless it is some unavoidable bad thing due to him for an earlier mistake?[14]

GLAUCON: Certainly.

SOCRATES: Similarly, we must suppose that if a just man falls into poverty or disease or some of the other things that seem bad, it will end well for him during his lifetime or even in death. For surely the gods at least will never neglect anyone who eagerly wishes to become just and, by practicing virtue, to make himself as much like a god as a human be-

b ing can.

GLAUCON: It is certainly reasonable to think that a man of that sort won't be neglected by one who is like him.

SOCRATES: And mustn't we think the opposite of the unjust one?

GLAUCON: Definitely.

SOCRATES: Those, then, are the sorts of prizes that come from the gods to the just man.

GLAUCON: That's certainly what I believe.

SOCRATES: What about from human beings? What does a just man get from them? If we are to assert what is really the case, isn't it this? Aren't clever but unjust men precisely like runners who run well on the first leg but not on the return one?[15] They leap away sharply at first, but in the end they become ridiculous and, heads drooping, run off the field un-

c crowned. True runners, on the other hand, make it to the end, collect the prizes, and are crowned as victors. And isn't it also generally what happens to just people? Toward the end of each course of action and association and of life as a whole, don't they enjoy a good reputation and collect the prizes that come from human beings?

GLAUCON: Of course.

SOCRATES: Will you then allow me to say about them what *you* said about the unjust?[16] For I will claim that it is the just who, when they are old enough,

d hold the ruling offices in their city if they choose, marry from whatever family they choose, and give their children in marriage to whomever they please. Indeed, all the things that you said about the others, I now say about these. As for the unjust, the majority of them, even if they remain hidden when they are young, are caught by the end of the race and ridiculed, and, by the time they get old, have become wretched and are showered with abuse by foreigners and citizens, beaten with whips, and made to suffer those punishments you rightly described as crude, such as

e racking and burning. Imagine I have claimed that they suffer all such things. Well, as I say, see if you will stand for it.

GLAUCON: Of course I will. What you say is right.

SOCRATES: Well, then, while the just man is alive, these are the sorts of prizes, wages, and gifts he re-

614a ceives from gods and human beings, in addition to those good things that justice itself provides.

GLAUCON: Fine and secure ones they are, too!

SOCRATES: Well, they are nothing in number or size compared to those that await each man after

---

13. [352a10–b2, 363a5–e4.]
14. [A foreshadowing of the doctrine of reincarnation introduced below.]

15. [The race is a sprint from one end of the stadium to the other and back.]
16. [361d7–362c8.]

death. We must hear about them, too, so that, by hearing them, each of these men may get back in full what he is owed by the argument.

GLAUCON: Please describe them, then, since there are not many things it would be more pleasant b to hear.

SOCRATES: Well, it is not an Alcinous-story I am going to tell you, but that of a brave man called Er, the son of Armenias, by race a Pamphylian.[17] Once upon a time, he was killed in battle. On the tenth day, when the rest of the dead were picked up, they were already putrefying, but he was picked up still quite sound. When he had been taken home and was lying on the pyre before his funeral on the twelfth day, he revived and, after reviving, told what he had seen in the other world.

He said that when his soul had departed, it traveled together with many others and came to a daimonic c place, where there were two adjacent openings in the earth and two in the heavens above and opposite them. Judges were seated between these. And, when they had made their judgments, they told the just to go to the right up through the heavens, with signs of the judgments attached to their fronts. But the unjust they told to travel to the left and down. And they too had on their backs signs of all their deeds. When he d himself came forward, they said that he was to be a messenger to human beings to tell them about the things happening there, and they told him to listen to and look at everything in the place.

Through one of the openings in the heavens and one in the earth, he saw souls departing after judgment had been passed on them. Through the other

17. [Books 9–11 of the *Odyssey* were traditionally referred to as *Alkinou apologoi*, the tales of Alcinous. Included among them is the story in Book 11 of Odysseus' descent into Hades. Since the word translated by "brave" is *alkimou*, which is very similar to *Alkinou*, some sort of pun seems to be involved. The following is one attractive way to interpret it. *Alkinou* might be taken as a compound of *alkê* (strength) + *nous* (understanding) and *alkimou* as a compound of *alkê* + *Mousa* (a Muse). Socrates would then be saying something like: it isn't a tale that shows strength of understanding that I'm going to tell but one that shows the strength of the Muse of storytelling.]

two, they were arriving. From the one in the earth they came up parched and dusty, while from the one in the heavens they came down pure. And the ones that had just arrived seemed to have come from a e long journey, and went off gladly to the meadow, like a crowd going to a festival, and set up camp there. Those that knew one another exchanged greetings and those coming up from the earth asked the others about the things up there, while those from the heavens asked about the others' experiences. They told their stories to one another, the former weeping and lamenting as they recollected all they had suffered 615a and seen on their journey below the earth—which lasted a thousand years—and the ones from the heavens telling, in turn, about their happy experiences and the inconceivably beautiful sights they had seen.

To tell it all, Glaucon, would take a long time. But the gist, he said, was this: for all the unjust things they had done and for all the people they had wronged, they had paid the penalty for every one in turn, ten times over for each. That is to say, they paid for each injustice once in every hundred years of their journey, so that, on the assumption that a hundred years is roughly the length of a human life, they b paid a tenfold penalty for each injustice. For example, if some of them had caused many deaths or had betrayed cities or armies and reduced them to slavery, or had taken part in other evildoing, they would receive ten times the pain for each of them. On the other hand, if they had done good deeds and become just and pious, they received commensurate awards.

He said some other things about the stillborn and those who lived for only a short time, but they are c not worth recounting. And he told of even greater wages for impiety or piety toward gods or parents, and for murder. He said he was there, you see, when someone asked where the great Ardiaius was. This Ardiaius had been a tyrant in a city in Pamphylia just a thousand years before that, and was said to have killed his aged father and older brother and committed many other impious deeds as well. He said the d one who was asked responded: "He has not come here and never will. For in fact this, too, was one of the terrible sights we saw. When we were near the mouth, about to come up after all our sufferings were over, we suddenly saw Ardiaius together with some others, almost all of whom were tyrants—although there were also some private individuals among them who had committed great crimes. They thought that they were about to go up, but the mouth would not let them through. Instead, it roared whenever one of these incurably bad people, or anyone else who had not paid a sufficient penalty, tried to go up. At that location, there were savage men, all fiery to look at, standing by, paying attention to the sound, who grabbed some of these people and led them away. But in the case of Ardiaius and others, they bound their feet, hands, and neck and threw them down and flayed them. They dragged them along the road outside, lacerating them on thorn bushes. They explained to those who were passing by at the time why they were being dragged away, and said that they were to be thrown into Tartarus. He said that of the many and multifarious fears they experienced there, the greatest each of them had was that the sound would be heard as he came up, and that each was very pleased when it was silent as he went up. Such then were the penalties and punishments, and the rewards that were their counterparts.

When each group had spent seven days in the meadow, on the eighth they had to move on from there and continue their journey. In four days, they came to a place where they could see stretching from above, through the whole heavens and earth, a straight beam of light, like a column, very closely resembling a rainbow, but brighter and more pure. They reached the beam after traveling another day's journey. And there, in the middle of the light, they saw stretching from the heavens the ends of its bonds—for this light is what binds the heavens, like the cables underneath a trireme, thus holding the entire revolving thing together. From those ends hangs the spindle of Necessity, by means of which all the revolving things are turned. Its shaft and hook were adamant, while its whorl[18] was adamant mixed with materials of other kinds. The nature of the whorl was as follows. Its shape was like the ones here on Earth, but from Er's description, we must think of it as being like this: in one large whorl, hollow and scooped out, lay another just like it, only smaller, that fitted into it exactly, the way nested bowls fit together; and similarly a third

18. [*Sphondulon*: the circular weight that twirls a spindle in weaving.]

and a fourth, and four others. For there were eight whorls altogether, lying inside one another, with their rims appearing as circles from above, while from the back they formed one continuous whorl around the shaft, which is driven right through the center of the eighth.

Now, the first or outermost whorl had the broadest circular rim, that of the sixth was second, third was that of the fourth, fourth that of the eighth, fifth that of the seventh, sixth that of the fifth, seventh that of the third, and eighth that of the second. That of the largest was spangled; that of the seventh was brightest; that of the eighth took its color from the seventh's shining on it; that of the second and fifth were very similar to one another, being yellower than the rest; the third was the whitest in color; the fourth was reddish; and the sixth was second in whiteness.

The spindle as a whole revolved at the same speed, but within the revolving whole the seven inner circles gently revolved in the opposite direction to the whole. Of these, the eighth moved fastest; second, and at the same speed as one another, were the seventh, sixth, and fifth; third, it seemed to them, in the speed of its counter-revolution, was the fourth; fourth was the third; and fifth the second.[19]

19. [Plato's description of the beam of light and the spindle is difficult. He compares the light to *hypozomata*, or the ropes that bind a trireme together. These ropes seem to have girded the trireme from stem to stern and to have entered it at both places. Within the trireme, they were connected to some sort of twisting device that allowed them to be tightened when the water caused them to stretch and become slack. The spindle of Necessity seems to be just such a twisting device. Hence, the extremities of the light's bonds must enter into the universe just as the *hypozomata* enter the trireme, and the spindle must be attached to these extremities, so that its spinning tightens the light and holds the universe together. The light is thus like two rainbows around the universe (or the whorl of the spindle), whose ends enter the universe and are attached to the spindle. The upper half of the whorl of the spindle consists of concentric hemispheres that fit into one another, with their lips or rims fitting together in a single plane. The outer hemisphere is that of the fixed stars; the second is the orbit of Saturn; the third of Jupiter; the fourth of Mars; the fifth of Mercury; the sixth of Venus; the seventh of the sun; and the eighth of the moon. The earth is in

The spindle revolved on the lap of Necessity. On top of each of its circles stood a Siren, who was carried around by its rotation, emitting a single sound, one single note. And from all eight in concord, a single harmony was produced. And there were three other women seated around it equidistant from one an-
c other, each on a throne. They were the daughters of Necessity, the Fates, dressed in white with garlands on their heads—Lachesis, Clotho, and Atropos—and they sang to the accompaniment of the Sirens' harmony, Lachesis singing of the past, Clotho of the present, and Atropos of the future. Clotho, using her right hand, touched the outer circumference of the spindle and helped it turn, pausing from time to time; Atropos, with her left, did the same to the inner ones;
d and Lachesis used each hand in turn to touch both.

When the souls arrived, they had to go straight to Lachesis. A sort of spokesman[20] first arranged them in ranks; then, taking lots and models of lives from the lap of Lachesis, he mounted a high platform, and said:

"The word of Lachesis, maiden daughter of Necessity! Ephemeral souls. The beginning of another death-bringing cycle for mortal-kind! Your daimon will not be assigned to you by lot; you will choose
e him. The one who has the first lot will be the first to choose a life to which he will be bound by necessity. Virtue has no master: as he honors or dishonors it, so shall each of you have more or less of it. Responsibility lies with the chooser; the god is blameless."

After saying that, the spokesman threw the lots out among them all, and each picked up the one that fell next to him—except for Er, who was not allowed. And to the one who picked it up, it was clear what number he had drawn. After that again the spokesman
618a placed the models of lives on the ground before them—many more of them than those who were present. They were multifarious: all animal lives were there, as well as all human lives. There were tyrannies among them, some life-long, others ending halfway through in poverty, exile, and beggary. There were

lives of famous men—some famous for the beauty of their appearance or for their other strengths or athletic prowess, others for their nobility and the virtues of their ancestors, and also some infamous in these
b respects—and similarly for women. But the structure of the soul was not included, because with the choice of a different life it would inevitably become different. But all the other qualities were mixed with each other and with wealth or poverty, sickness or health, or the states in between.

Here, it seems, my dear Glaucon, a human being faces the greatest danger of all, and because of that each must, to the neglect of all other subjects, take care above all else to be a seeker and student of that
c subject which will enable him to learn and discover who will give him the ability and the knowledge to distinguish a good life from a bad, so that he will always and in any circumstances choose the better one from among those that are possible. He must calculate the effect of all the things we have mentioned just now, both jointly and severally, on the virtue of a life, so as to know what the good and bad effects of beauty are when it is mixed with wealth or poverty and this or that state of the soul; what the
d effects are of high and low birth, private lives and ruling offices, physical strength and weaknesses, ease and difficulties in learning, and all the things that are either naturally part of the soul or can be acquired by it, when they are mixed with one another. On the basis of all that he will be able, by considering the nature of the soul, to reason out which life is better and which worse and choose accordingly, calling worse the one that will lead the soul to become more
e unjust, and better the one that leads it to become more just. Everything else he will ignore. For we have seen that this is the best way to choose, whether in life or death.

Holding this belief with adamantine determination, he must go down to Hades, so that even there 619a he won't be dazzled by wealth and other such evils, and won't rush into tyrannies or other similar practices and so commit irreparable evils, and suffer even greater ones; but instead will know to choose the middle life in such circumstances, and avoid either of the extremes, both in this life, so far as is possible, and in the whole of the life to come. For this is how a human being becomes happiest. b

the center. The hemispheres are transparent and the width of their rims is the distance of the heavenly bodies from one another.]

20. [*Prophêtês*: a prophet. Here in the sense of someone who speaks on behalf of a god.]

At that point our messenger from the other world also reported that the spokesman said this: "Even for the one who comes last, if he chooses wisely and lives earnestly, there is a satisfactory life available, not a bad one. Let not the first to choose be careless, nor the last discouraged."

When the spokesman had told them that, Er said, the one who drew the first lot came up and immediately chose the greatest tyranny. In his foolishness and greed, you see, he chose it without adequately examining everything, and did not notice c that it involved being fated to eat his own children, among other evils. When he examined the life at leisure, however, he beat his breast and bemoaned his choice, ignoring the warning of the spokesman. For he did not blame himself for these evils, but chance, daimons, and everything except himself. He was one of those who had come down from the heavens, having lived his previous life in an orderly constitution, sharing in virtue through habit but without philosophy.

d   Generally speaking, not the least number of the people caught out in this way were souls who came from the heavens, and so were untrained in sufferings. The majority of those from the earth, on the other hand, because they had suffered themselves and had seen others doing so, were in no rush to make their choices. Because of that, and also because of the chance of the lottery, there was an exchange of evils and goods for most of the souls. Yet, if a person, whenever he came to the life that is here, always practiced philosophy in a sound manner, and if the fall of the lot did not e put his choice of life among the last, it is likely, from what was reported by Er about the next world, that not only will he be happy here, but also that his journey from here to there and back again will not be underground and rough, but smooth and through the heavens.

He said it was a sight worth seeing how the 620a various souls chose their lives, since seeing it caused pity, ridicule, and surprise. For the most part, their choice reflected the character of their former life. He saw the soul that had once belonged to Orpheus, he said, choosing a swan's life: he hated the female sex because of his death at their hands, and so was unwilling to be conceived in a woman

and born.[21] He saw the soul of Thamyris choosing a nightingale's life, a swan changing to the choice of a human life, and other musical animals doing the same. The twentieth soul chose the life of a lion. It was that of Ajax, son of Telamon, who b avoided human life because he remembered the judgment about the armor.[22] The next was that of Agamemnon, which also hated the human race on account of what it suffered, and so changed to the life of an eagle. Allotted a place in the middle, the soul of Atalanta, when it saw the great honors of a male athlete, unable to pass them by, chose his life. After her, he saw the soul of Epeius, son of Panopeus, taking on the nature of a craftswoman. c Further on, among the last, he saw the soul of the ridiculous Thersites clothing itself as an ape.

Now it chanced that Odysseus' soul drew the last lot of all, and came to make its choice. Remembering its former sufferings, it rejected love of honor, and went around for a long time looking for the life of a private individual who did his own work, and with difficulty it found one lying off somewhere neglected by the others. When it saw it, it said that it would have done the same even if it had drawn the first- d place lot, and chose it gladly. Similarly, souls went from the other animals into human beings, or into one another; the unjust changing into savage animals, the just into tame ones; and every sort of mixture occurred.

When all the souls had chosen lives, in the same allotted order they went forward to Lachesis. She assigned to each the daimon it had chosen, as guardian of its life and fulfiller of its choices. This daimon e first led the soul under the hand of Clotho as it turned the revolving spindle, thus ratifying the allotted fate it had chosen. After receiving her touch, he led the soul to the spinning of Atropos, to make the spun fate irreversible. Then, without turning around, it

21. [According to one myth, Orpheus was killed and dismembered by Thracian women, or Maenads.]
22. [Ajax thought that he deserved to be awarded the armor of the dead Achilles, but instead it was awarded to Odysseus. Ajax was maddened by this injustice and later killed himself because of the terrible things he had done while mad.]

went under the throne of Necessity. When it had 621a passed through that, and when the others had also passed through, they all traveled to the plain of Lethe, through burning and choking and terrible heat, for it was empty of trees and earthly vegetation. They camped, since evening was coming on, beside the river of forgetfulness, whose water no vessel can hold. All of them had to drink a certain measure of this water. But those not saved by wisdom drank more than the measure. And as each of them drank, he forgot everything. When they were asleep and midnight came, there was a clap of thunder and an earth-b quake, and they were suddenly carried away from there, this way and that, up to their births, like shooting stars. But Er himself was prevented from drinking the water. Yet how or where he had come back to his body, he did not know, but suddenly recovering his sight he now saw himself lying on the pyre at dawn.

And so, Glaucon, his story was saved and not lost; and it would save us, too, if we were persuaded by it, since we would safely cross the river Lethe with c our souls undefiled. But if we are persuaded by me, we will believe that the soul is immortal and able to endure every evil and also every good, and always hold to the upward path, practicing justice with wisdom every way we can, so that we will be friends to ourselves and to the gods, both while we remain here on Earth and when we receive the rewards of justice, and go around like victors in the games collecting prizes; and so both in this life and on the thousand-year journey we have described, we will fare well.

ARISTOTLE

Augustine tells us that, in reading Cicero's dialogue *Hortensius*, he was led to turn to a life of philosophy and ultimately to faith and a sense of utter dependence upon divine grace. For Augustine, then, philosophy was the vehicle to a recognition of human finitude and the unrestricted character of God's power. But the *Hortensius* was itself inspired by Cicero's reading of Aristotle's dialogue, the *Protrepticus or Exhortation to Philosophy*. In this work, of which only fragments remain, the young Aristotle (384–322 B.C.E.) calls the reader to a life of searching for knowledge, a life of inquiry, research, and the investigation of all things.

Aristotle himself lived such a life, as one commentator puts it, "driven throughout his life by a single overmastering desire—the desire for knowledge." Later, in the famous first sentence of his *Metaphysics*, Aristotle would acknowledge that he shared this desire with all people: "all men by nature desire to know." Ultimately, it is a desire that would result in Aristotle's remarkable achievements in the study of biology, psychology, logic, physics, ethics, politics, and much else. It would also find its place at the core of his ethics and politics. The relation between virtuous conduct and intellectual activity is a controversial feature of Aristotle's moral thinking, but one interpretation is that he conceived of the good life, which we all desire above all else, as a self-sufficient life devoted to inquiry and contemplation. For Aristotle, then, philosophy or the search for knowledge and understanding will enable man to become as divine as he can ever be; it involves the human recognition of all that human beings can attain and of the way in which divinity is within human grasp. Ironically, the roots of Augustine's life of grace and dependence upon God lie in Aristotle's humanistic and naturalistic conception of the self-sufficient philosophical quest for divine knowledge and thereby for the good life.

Aristotle was born in 384 B.C.E., in Stagira, a small town in Chalcidice in northern Greece. His father, Nicomachus, was a physician in the court of Amyntas, king of Macedon, and a member of a guild devoted to Asclepius, the god of medicine. Although Nicomachus died when Aristotle was still very young, he had probably begun to teach his son something of Greek medicine and biology. These interests had a long-lasting impact on Aristotle.

In 367, at the age of seventeen, Aristotle made the most important move of his life. He left Stagira for Athens, where he became a member of Plato's intellectual and religious fellowship, the Academy. Plato was probably the most dominant intellectual influence on Aristotle throughout his life. He remained in the Academy—studying, teaching, lecturing, and writing—for twenty years, until Plato's death. It was during these years that Aristotle wrote a number of literary dialogues, in the Platonic style, among them the *Protrepticus* and the *Eudemus or On the Soul*, which deals with the separate existence and immortality of the soul. Only fragments of some of these dialogues exist today. It was in this period too that Aristotle tried out radically anti-Platonic views and strategies in works such as the *Categories*.

In 347 Aristotle left the Academy and Athens. Plato had died; his nephew Speusippus had been appointed to replace him, perhaps to keep the property in the family or perhaps for ideological reasons; and in 348 Philip of Macedon sacked the town of Olynthus, provoking a wave of anti-Macedonian feeling, spurred on by the oratory of Demosthenes and his supporters. Aristotle, with a few fellow philosophers, fled Athens, sailing east to the coast of Asia Minor and arriving at Atarneus, at the invitation of its ruler, Hermeias, who settled them in the town of Assos. After two or three years, Aristotle moved to Mytilene, near Lesbos, where he met Theophrastus, who was to become his most important companion and pupil. Aristotle also married Hermeias' niece, Pythias, who bore him two children, a daughter, Pythia, and a son, Nicomachus, after whom the *Nicomachean Ethics* is named.

Two years later, in 342, Aristotle accepted Philip's invitation to settle in Pella, capital of Macedonia, and later in the royal castle at Mieza, to tutor the king's thirteen-year-old son, Alexander. We know little concerning their relationship or about the content of Alexander's education. Subsequent events make it hard to believe that Aristotle taught Alexander anything about ethics or politics. Alexander was strongly committed to a blending of Greek and foreign cultures and conceived of a vast, disparate empire without the centrality of the *polis* (city-state); Aristotle would have differed on both matters. Aristotle is thought to have composed for Alexander a work on monarchy and one on colonies, but we know nothing of their content or influence on Alexander.

In 340 Alexander was made regent, and Aristotle probably settled in Stagira until Philip's death, in 335, when he returned to Athens. The next dozen years were the richest and most productive of Aristotle's life. First, he sought to establish his own school or fellowship (*thiasos*), the Lyceum, renting some buildings in a grove northeast of the city, a site sacred to Apollo Lyceius and, as tradition has it, a favorite spot of Socrates. Second, Aristotle engaged in a vast array of investigations. These were based on prior and ongoing research and the collection of data, views, and positions, conducted by himself and his associates. He lectured, taught, and cultivated an environment of study that yielded writings on biology, logic, rhetoric, physics, metaphysics, ethics, politics, the arts, and more. Only twenty percent of this output remains, but it is sufficient to establish Aristotle as a giant of Western intellectual culture.

In 323 Alexander died. Once again anti-Macedonian feeling erupted in Athens, and Aristotle saw charges of impiety fabricated against him. He fled to Chalcis, in Euboea, "to save the Athenians," as he put it, "from sinning twice against philosophy." There he died a year later, at the age of sixty-two. Diogenes Laertius, the third-century doxographer, preserves his will, in which he arranges his affairs and those of his family with sensitivity, kindness, and generosity. It is a rare opportunity to glimpse the humanity that existed so delicately alongside an incomparable, unrelenting intellect and an all-consuming desire for knowledge.

It is hard to understand with any depth the concrete person whose life spanned these turbulent years. This much, however, is clear, that Aristotle's life and his thinking were joined in an attempt to live the best life possible for a human being. This is the life that he examines, defends, and endorses in his great ethical and political works, especially the *Nicomachean Ethics* and the *Politics*. There he locates the core of human life in the enrichment of our character; there he associates this goal of *eudaimonia* (human flourishing or well-being) with the functioning of soul at its highest level, the level of reason; and there he explores how reason functions, together with desire, pleasure, deliberation, and decision, in everyday life and in the life of inquiry and contemplation. Moreover, the good life is the object of our most important and strongest desire, and the political is the context of associations and structures best suited to enable its achievement.

Aristotle's account rises out of a tradition of natural philosophy in the fifth and fourth centuries; it attempts to unite religious, scientific, and moral aspiration in such a way that human life in fourth-century Greece is seen to take on meaning and purpose. Later, in the Middle Ages and in the modern world, Aristotle's theory loosed itself from the ancient *polis* and found new adherents who agreed with Aristotle that moral character is a complex interplay of rational judgement, deliberation, desire, decision, community, law, and much else. Whether this conception of moral character and the good life could be freed from Aristotelian science and its teleological order was and is a difficult question. But it does nothing to discredit Aristotle's own attempt to practice philosophy and thereby to articulate and to live the best life possible for human beings.

Recommended Readings

Barker, Ernest. *The Politics of Aristotle*. Oxford: Oxford University Press, 1946.

Barnes, J., M. Schofield, and R. Sorabji (eds.). *Articles on Aristotle*. Vol. 2. *Ethics and Politics*. London: Duckworth, 1977.

Broadie, Sarah. *Ethics with Aristotle*. Oxford: Oxford University Press, 1991.

Cooper, John. *Reason and Human Good in Aristotle*. Cambridge: Harvard University Press, 1975; Hackett, 1986.

Hardie, W.F.R. *Aristotle's Ethical Theory*. 2nd ed. Oxford: Oxford University Press, 1980.

Irwin, T. H. *Aristotle's First Principles*. Oxford: Oxford University Press, 1988.

Keyt, David, and Fred Miller (eds.). *Essays on Aristotle's Politics*. Oxford: Blackwell's, 1991.

Kraut, Richard. *Aristotle on the Human Good*. Princeton: Princeton University Press, 1989.

Miller, Fred D., Jr. *Nature, Justice, and Rights in Aristotle's Politics*. Oxford: Oxford University Press, 1997.

Moravcsik, J. (ed.). *Aristotle*. Garden City: Doubleday, 1967.

Mulgan, R. G. *Aristotle's Political Theory*. Oxford: Oxford University Press, 1977.

Nussbaum, Martha C. *The Fragility of Goodness*. Cambridge: Cambridge University Press, 1986, updated 2001.

Okin, Susan Moller. *Women in Western Political Thought*. Princeton: Princeton University Press, 1979.

Reeve, C.D.C. *Practices of Reason*. Oxford: Oxford University Press, 1992.

Rorty, A. O. (ed.). *Essays on Aristotle's Ethics*. Berkeley: University of California Press, 1980.

Sherman, N. *The Fabric of Character*. Oxford: Oxford University Press, 1988.

NICOMACHEAN ETHICS

BOOK I

1

1094a Every craft and every line of inquiry, and likewise every action and decision, seems to seek some good; that is why some people were right to describe the good as what everything seeks. But the ends [that are
5 sought] appear to differ; some are activities, and others are products apart from the activities. Wherever there are ends apart from the actions, the products are by nature better than the activities.

Since there are many actions, crafts, and sciences, the ends turn out to be many as well; for health is the end of medicine, a boat of boat building, victory of generalship, and wealth of household manage-
10 ment. But some of these pursuits are subordinate to some one capacity; for instance, bridle making and every other science producing equipment for horses are subordinate to horsemanship, while this and every action in warfare are, in turn, subordinate to general-ship, and in the same way other pursuits are subordi-nate to further ones. In all such cases, then, the ends of the ruling sciences are more choiceworthy than
15 of the ruling sciences are more choiceworthy than all the ends subordinate to them, since the lower ends are also pursued for the sake of the higher. Here it does not matter whether the ends of the actions are the activities themselves, or something apart from them, as in the sciences we have mentioned.

2

Suppose, then, that the things achievable by action have some end that we wish for because of itself, and because of which we wish for the other things, and

From Aristotle, *Nicomachean Ethics*, second edition, translated by Terence Irwin (Indianapolis: Hackett Publishing Company, 2000). Copyright © 2000. Reprinted by permission of the publisher.

that we do not choose everything because of some- 20 thing else—for if we do, it will go on without limit, so that desire will prove to be empty and futile. Clearly, this end will be the good, that is to say, the best good.

Then surely knowledge of this good also carries great weight for [determining the best] way of life; if we know it, we are more likely, like archers who have a target to aim at, to hit the right mark. If so, we 25 should try to grasp, in outline at any rate, what the good is, and which is its proper science or capacity.

It seems proper to the most controlling science— the highest ruling science. And this appears character-istic of political science. For it is the one that pre-scribes which of the sciences ought to be studied in cities, and which ones each class in the city should 1094b learn, and how far; indeed we see that even the most honored capacities—generalship, household man-agement, and rhetoric, for instance—are subordinate to it. And since it uses the other sciences concerned 5 with action, and moreover legislates what must be done and what avoided, its end will include the ends of the other sciences, and so this will be the human good. For even if the good is the same for a city as for an individual, still the good of the city is apparently a greater and more complete good to acquire and preserve. For while it is satisfactory to acquire and preserve the good even for an individual, it is finer 10 and more divine to acquire and preserve it for a people and for cities. And so, since our line of inquiry seeks these [goods, for an individual and for a community], it is a sort of political science.

3

Our discussion will be adequate if we make things perspicuous enough to accord with the subject matter; for we would not seek the same degree of exactness in all sorts of arguments alike, any more than in the products of different crafts. Now, fine and just things, 15

which political science examines, differ and vary so
much as to seem to rest on convention only, not on
nature. But [this is not a good reason, since] goods
also vary in the same way, because they result in
harm to many people—for some have been destroyed
because of their wealth, others because of their brav-
20 ery. And so, since this is our subject and these are
our premises, we shall be satisfied to indicate the
truth roughly and in outline; since our subject and
our premises are things that hold good usually [but
not universally], we shall be satisfied to draw conclusions of the same sort.

Each of our claims, then, ought to be accepted in
the same way [as claiming to hold good usually]. For
the educated person seeks exactness in each area to
25 the extent that the nature of the subject allows; for
apparently it is just as mistaken to demand demonstrations from a rhetorician as to accept [merely] persuasive arguments from a mathematician. Further, each
1095a person judges rightly what he knows, and is a good
judge about that; hence the good judge in a given
area is the person educated in that area, and the
unqualifiedly good judge is the person educated in
every area.

This is why a youth is not a suitable student of
political science; for he lacks experience of the actions
in life, which are the subject and premises of our
arguments. Moreover, since he tends to follow his
5 feelings, his study will be futile and useless; for the
end [of political science] is action, not knowledge.
It does not matter whether he is young in years or
immature in character, since the deficiency does not
depend on age, but results from following his feelings
in his life and in a given pursuit; for an immature
person, like an incontinent person, gets no benefit
from his knowledge. But for those who accord with
10 reason in forming their desires and in their actions,
knowledge of political science will be of great benefit.

These are the preliminary points about the student,
about the way our claims are to be accepted, and
about what we propose to do.

4

Let us, then, begin again. Since every sort of knowledge and decision pursues some good, what is the
15 good that we say political science seeks? What, [in

other words,] is the highest of all the goods achievable
in action?

As far as its name goes, most people virtually agree;
for both the many and the cultivated call it happiness,
and they suppose that living well and doing well are
the same as being happy. But they disagree about 20
what happiness is, and the many do not give the same
answer as the wise.

For the many think it is something obvious and
evident—for instance, pleasure, wealth, or honor.
Some take it to be one thing, others another. Indeed,
the same person often changes his mind; for when
he has fallen ill, he thinks happiness is health, and
when he has fallen into poverty, he thinks it is wealth.
And when they are conscious of their own ignorance,
they admire anyone who speaks of something grand 25
and above their heads. [Among the wise,] however,
some used to think that besides these many goods
there is some other good that exists in its own right
and that causes all these goods to be goods.

Presumably, then, it is rather futile to examine all
these beliefs, and it is enough to examine those that
are most current or seem to have some argument 30
for them.

We must notice, however, the difference between
arguments from principles and arguments toward
principles. For indeed Plato was right to be puzzled
about this, when he used to ask if [the argument] set
out from the principles or led toward them—just as 1095b
on a race course the path may go from the starting
line to the far end, or back again. For we should
certainly begin from things known, but things are
known in two ways; for some are known to us, some
known without qualification. Presumably, then, *we*
ought to begin from things known to *us*.

That is why we need to have been brought up in 5
fine habits if we are to be adequate students of fine
and just things, and of political questions generally.
For we begin from the [belief] that [something is
true]; if this is apparent enough to us, we can begin
without also [knowing] why [it is true]. Someone who
is well brought up has the beginnings, or can easily
acquire them. Someone who neither has them nor
can acquire them should listen to Hesiod:[1] 'He who 10

1. [Aristotle frequently quotes ancient sources, from
Hesiod and Homer to Sophocles, Euripides, Epi-

grasps everything himself is best of all; he is noble also who listens to one who has spoken well; but he who neither grasps it himself nor takes to heart what he hears from another is a useless man.'

5

But let us begin again from the point from which we digressed. For, it would seem, people quite reasonably reach their conception of the good, i.e., of happiness, from the lives [they lead]; for there are roughly three most favored lives: the lives of gratification, of political activity, and, third, of study.

The many, the most vulgar, would seem to conceive the good and happiness as pleasure, and hence they also like the life of gratification. In this they appear completely slavish, since the life they decide on is a life for grazing animals. Still, they have some argument in their defense, since many in positions of power feel as Sardanapallus² felt, [and also choose this life].

The cultivated people, those active [in politics], conceive the good as honor, since this is more or less the end [normally pursued] in the political life. This, however, appears to be too superficial to be what we are seeking; for it seems to depend more on those who honor than on the one honored, whereas we intuitively believe that the good is something of our own and hard to take from us. Further, it would seem, they pursue honor to convince themselves that they are good; at any rate, they seek to be honored by prudent people, among people who know them, and for virtue. It is clear, then, that—in their view at any rate—virtue is superior [to honor].

Perhaps, indeed, one might conceive virtue more than honor to be the end of the political life. However, this also is apparently too incomplete [to be the good]. For it seems possible for someone to possess virtue but be asleep or inactive throughout his life, and, moreover, to suffer the worst evils and misfortunes.

If this is the sort of life he leads, no one would count him happy, except to defend a philosopher's paradox. Enough about this, since it has been adequately discussed in the popular works as well.

The third life is the life of study, which we shall examine in what follows.

The moneymaker's life is in a way forced on him [not chosen for itself]; and clearly wealth is not the good we are seeking, since it is [merely] useful, [choiceworthy only] for some other end. Hence one would be more inclined to suppose that [any of] the goods mentioned earlier is the end, since they are liked for themselves. But apparently they are not [the end] either; and many arguments have been presented against them. Let us, then, dismiss them.

6

Presumably, though, we had better examine the universal good, and puzzle out what is meant in speaking of it. This sort of inquiry is, to be sure, unwelcome to us, because those who introduced the Forms were friends of ours; still, it presumably seems better, indeed only right, to destroy even what is close to us if that is the way to preserve truth. We must especially do this as philosophers, [lovers of wisdom]; for though we love both the truth and our friends, reverence is due to the truth first.

Those who introduced this view did not mean to produce an Idea for any [series] in which they spoke of prior and posterior [members]; that was why they did not mean to establish an Idea [of number] for [the series of] numbers. But the good is spoken of both in what-it-is [that is, substance], and in quality and relative; and what exists in its own right, that is, substance, is by nature prior to the relative, since a relative would seem to be an appendage and coincident of being. And so there is no common Idea over these.

Further, good is spoken of in as many ways as being [is spoken of]: in what-it-is, as god and mind; in quality, as the virtues; in quantity, as the measured amount; in relative, as the useful; in time, as the opportune moment; in place, as the [right] situation; and so on. Hence it is clear that the good cannot be some common and single universal; for if it were, it

---

charmus, and Simonides. For a comprehensive list of Aristotle's literary references see Terence Irwin, *Aristotle, Nicomachean Ethics*, first edition (Hackett Publishing Company, 1985), 433–36.—M.L.M.]

2. [An Assyrian king (669–626) who lived in legendary luxury.—T.I.]

would be spoken of in only one [of the types of] predication, not in them all.

30   Further, if a number of things have a single Idea, there is also a single science of them; hence [if there were an Idea of good] there would also be some single science of all goods. But, in fact, there are many sciences even of the goods under one [type of] predication; for the science of the opportune moment, for instance, in war is generalship, in disease medicine. And similarly the science of the measured amount in food is medicine, in exertion gymnastics. [Hence there is no single science of the good, and so no Idea.]

35   One might be puzzled about what [the believers in Ideas] really mean in speaking of the So-and-So 1096b Itself, since Man Itself and man have one and the same account of man; for insofar as each is man, they will not differ at all. If that is so, then [Good Itself and good have the same account of good]; hence they also will not differ at all insofar as each is good, [hence there is no point in appealing to Good Itself].

Moreover, Good Itself will be no more of a good by being eternal; for a white thing is no whiter if it 5 lasts a long time than if it lasts a day.

The Pythagoreans would seem to have a more plausible view about the good, since they place the One in the column of goods. Indeed, Speusippus[3] seems to have followed them. But let us leave this for another discussion.

A dispute emerges, however, about what we have 10 said, because the arguments [in favor of the Idea] are not concerned with every sort of good. Goods pursued and liked in their own right are spoken of as one species of goods, whereas those that in some way tend to produce or preserve these goods, or to prevent their contraries, are spoken of as goods because of these and in a different way. Clearly, then, goods are spoken of in two ways, and some are goods in their own 15 right, and others goods because of these. Let us, then, separate the goods in their own right from the [merely] useful goods, and consider whether goods in their own right correspond to a single Idea.

But what sorts of goods may we take to be goods in their own right? Are they the goods that are pursued even on their own—for instance, prudence, seeing,

some types of pleasures, and honors? For even if we also pursue these because of something else, we may nonetheless take them to be goods in their own right. 20 Alternatively, is nothing except the Idea good in its own right, so that the Form will be futile? But if these other things are also goods in their own right, then, [if there is an Idea of good,] the same account of good will have to turn up in all of them, just as the same account of whiteness turns up in snow and in chalk. In fact, however, honor, prudence, and pleasure have different and dissimilar accounts, precisely 25 insofar as they are goods. Hence the good is not something common corresponding to a single Idea.

But how, then, is good spoken of? For it is not like homonyms resulting from chance. Is it spoken of from the fact that goods derive from one thing or all contribute to one thing? Or is it spoken of more by analogy? For as sight is to body, so understanding is to soul, and so on for other cases.

Presumably, though, we should leave these ques- 30 tions for now, since their exact treatment is more appropriate for another [branch of] philosophy. And the same is true about the Idea. For even if there is some one good predicated in common, or some separable good, itself in its own right, clearly that is not the sort of good a human being can achieve in action or possess; but that is the sort we are looking 35 for now.

Perhaps, however, someone might think it is better to get to know the Idea with a view to the goods that we can possess and achieve in action; for [one might 1097a suppose that] if we have this as a sort of pattern, we shall also know better about the goods that are goods for us, and if we know about them, we shall hit on them. This argument certainly has some plausibility, but it would seem to clash with the sciences. For 5 each of these, though it aims at some good and seeks to supply what is lacking, leaves out knowledge of the Idea; but if the Idea were such an important aid, surely it would not be reasonable for all craftsmen to know nothing about it and not even to look for it.

Moreover, it is a puzzle to know what the weaver or carpenter will gain for his own craft from knowing this Good Itself, or how anyone will be better at 10 medicine or generalship from having gazed on the Idea Itself. For what the doctor appears to consider is not even health [universally, let alone good univer-

---

3. [Plato's nephew; succeeded Plato in 347 as head of the Academy. —M.L.M.]

sally], but human health, and presumably the health of this human being even more, since he treats one particular patient at a time.

So much, then, for these questions.

7

15 But let us return once again to the good we are looking for, and consider just what it could be. For it is apparently one thing in one action or craft, and another thing in another; for it is one thing in medicine, another in generalship, and so on for the rest. What, then, is the good of each action or craft? Surely it is that for the sake of which the other things are done;
20 in medicine this is health, in generalship victory, in house-building a house, in another case something else, but in every action and decision it is the end, since it is for the sake of the end that everyone does the other actions. And so, if there is some end of everything achievable in action, the good achievable in action will be this end; if there are more ends than one, [the good achievable in action] will be these ends.

Our argument, then, has followed a different route to reach the same conclusion. But we must try to
25 make this still more perspicuous. Since there are apparently many ends, and we choose some of them (for instance, wealth, flutes, and, in general, instruments) because of something else, it is clear that not all ends are complete. But the best good is apparently something complete. And so, if only one end is complete, the good we are looking for will be this end; if more ends than one are complete, it will be the
30 most complete end of these.

We say that an end pursued in its own right is more complete than an end pursued because of something else, and that an end that is never choiceworthy because of something else is more complete than ends that are choiceworthy both in their own right and because of this end. Hence an end that is always choiceworthy in its own right, never because of something else, is complete without qualification.

Now happiness, more than anything else, seems
1097b complete without qualification. For we always choose it because of itself, never because of something else. Honor, pleasure, understanding, and every virtue we certainly choose because of themselves, since we would choose each of them even if it had no further

result; but we also choose them for the sake of happiness, supposing that through them we shall be happy. 5 Happiness, by contrast, no one ever chooses for their sake, or for the sake of anything else at all.

The same conclusion [that happiness is complete] also appears to follow from self-sufficiency. For the complete good seems to be self-sufficient. What we count as self-sufficient is not what suffices for a solitary person by himself, living an isolated life, but what 10 suffices also for parents, children, wife, and, in general, for friends and fellow citizens, since a human being is a naturally political [animal]. Here, however, we must impose some limit; for if we extend the good to parents' parents and children's children and to friends of friends, we shall go on without limit; but we must examine this another time. Anyhow, we regard something as self-sufficient when all by itself 15 it makes a life choiceworthy and lacking nothing; and that is what we think happiness does.

Moreover, we think happiness is most choiceworthy of all goods, [since] it is not counted as one good among many. [If it were] counted as one among many, then, clearly, we think it would be more choiceworthy if the smallest of goods were added; for the good that is added becomes an extra quantity of goods, and the larger of two goods is always more choiceworthy. Happiness, then, is apparently some- 20 thing complete and self-sufficient, since it is the end of the things achievable in action.

But presumably the remark that the best good is happiness is apparently something [generally] agreed, and we still need a clearer statement of what the best good is. Perhaps, then, we shall find this if we first grasp the function of a human being. For just as the 25 good, i.e., [doing] well, for a flautist, a sculptor, and every craftsman, and, in general, for whatever has a function and [characteristic] action, seems to depend on its function, the same seems to be true for a human being, if a human being has some function.

Then do the carpenter and the leather worker have 30 their functions and actions, but has a human being no function? Is he by nature idle, without any function? Or, just as eye, hand, foot, and, in general, every [bodily] part apparently has its function, may we likewise ascribe to a human being some function apart from all of these?

What, then, could this be? For living is apparently
1098a shared with plants, but what we are looking for is the
special function of a human being; hence we should
set aside the life of nutrition and growth. The life
next in order is some sort of life of sense perception;
but this too is apparently shared with horse, ox, and
every animal.

The remaining possibility, then, is some sort of life
of action of the [part of the soul] that has reason.
One [part] of it has reason as obeying reason; the
5 other has it as itself having reason and thinking. Moreover, life is also spoken of in two ways [as capacity
and as activity], and we must take [a human being's
special function to be] life as activity, since this seems
to be called life more fully. We have found, then,
that the human function is activity of the soul in
accord with reason or requiring reason.

Now we say that the function of a [kind of thing]—
of a harpist, for instance—is the same in kind as the
function of an excellent individual of the kind—of an
10 excellent harpist, for instance. And the same is true
without qualification in every case, if we add to the
function the superior achievement in accord with the
virtue; for the function of a harpist is to play the harp,
and the function of a good harpist is to play it well.
Moreover, we take the human function to be a certain
kind of life, and take this life to be activity and actions
of the soul that involve reason; hence the function of
15 the excellent man is to do this well and finely.

Now each function is completed well by being
completed in accord with the virtue proper [to that
kind of thing]. And so the human good proves to be
activity of the soul in accord with virtue, and indeed
with the best and most complete virtue, if there are
more virtues than one. Moreover, it must be in a
complete life. For one swallow does not make a
20 spring, nor does one day; nor, similarly, does one day
or a short time make us blessed and happy.

This, then, is a sketch of the good; for, presumably,
we must draw the outline first, and fill it in later. If
the sketch is good, anyone, it seems, can advance and
articulate it, and in such cases time discovers more,
or is a good partner in discovery. That is also how
25 the crafts have improved, since anyone can add what
is lacking [in the outline].

We must also remember our previous remarks, so
that we do not look for the same degree of exactness
in all areas, but the degree that accords with a given
subject matter and is proper to a given line of inquiry.
For the carpenter's and the geometer's inquiries about 30
the right angle are different also; the carpenter restricts himself to what helps his work, but the geometer inquires into what, or what sort of thing, the right
angle is, since he studies the truth. We must do the
same, then, in other areas too, [seeking the proper
degree of exactness], so that digressions do not overwhelm our main task.

Nor should we make the same demand for an 1098b
explanation in all cases. On the contrary, in some
cases it is enough to prove rightly that [something is
true, without also explaining why it is true]. This is
so, for instance, with principles, where the fact that
[something is true] is the first thing, that is to say,
the principle.

Some principles are studied by means of induction,
some by means of perception, some by means of some
sort of habituation, and others by other means. In
each case we should try to find them out by means 5
suited to their nature, and work hard to define them
rightly. For they carry great weight for what follows;
for the principle seems to be more than half the
whole, and makes evident the answer to many of
our questions.

8

We should examine the principle, however, not only
from the conclusion and premises [of a deduction],
but also from what is said about it; for all the facts 10
harmonize with a true account, whereas the truth
soon clashes with a false one.

Goods are divided, then, into three types, some
called external, some goods of the soul, others goods
of the body. We say that the goods of the soul are 15
goods most fully, and more than the others, and we
take actions and activities of the soul to be [goods]
of the soul. And so our account [of the good] is right,
to judge by this belief anyhow—and it is an ancient
belief, and accepted by philosophers.

Our account is also correct in saying that some
sort of actions and activities are the end; for in that
way the end turns out to be a good of the soul, not
an external good. 20

The belief that the happy person lives well and does well also agrees with our account, since we have virtually said that the end is a sort of living well and doing well.

Further, all the features that people look for in happiness appear to be true of the end described in our account. For to some people happiness seems to
25 be virtue; to others prudence; to others some sort of wisdom; to others again it seems to be these, or one of these, involving pleasure or requiring it to be added; others add in external prosperity as well. Some of these views are traditional, held by many, while others are held by a few men who are widely esteemed. It is reasonable for each group not to be completely wrong, but to be correct on one point at least, or even on most points.

30 First, our account agrees with those who say happiness is virtue [in general] or some [particular] virtue; for activity in accord with virtue is proper to virtue. Presumably, though, it matters quite a bit whether we suppose that the best good consists in possessing or in using—that is to say, in a state or in an activity [that actualizes the state]. For someone may be in a
1099a state that achieves no good—if, for instance, he is asleep or inactive in some other way—but this cannot be true of the activity; for it will necessarily act and act well. And just as Olympic prizes are not for the
5 finest and strongest, but for the contestants—since it is only these who win—the same is true in life; among the fine and good people, only those who act correctly win the prize.

Moreover, the life of these active people is also pleasant in itself. For being pleased is a condition of the soul, [and hence is included in the activity of the soul]. Further, each type of person finds pleasure in whatever he is called a lover of; a horse, for instance, pleases the horse-lover, a spectacle the lover of specta-
10 cles. Similarly, what is just pleases the lover of justice, and in general what accords with virtue pleases the lover of virtue.

Now the things that please most people conflict, because they are not pleasant by nature, whereas the things that please lovers of the fine are things pleasant by nature. Actions in accord with virtue are pleasant
15 by nature, so that they both please lovers of the fine and are pleasant in their own right.

Hence these people's life does not need pleasure to be added [to virtuous activity] as some sort of extra decoration; rather, it has its pleasure within itself. For besides the reasons already given, someone who does not enjoy fine actions is not good; for no one would call a person just, for instance, if he did not enjoy doing just actions, or generous if he did not enjoy generous actions, and similarly 20 for the other virtues.

If this is so, actions in accord with the virtues are pleasant in their own right. Moreover, these actions are good and fine as well as pleasant; indeed, they are good, fine, and pleasant more than anything else is, since on this question the excellent person judges rightly, and his judgment agrees with what we have said.

Happiness, then, is best, finest, and most pleasant, 25 and the Delian inscription is wrong to distinguish these things: 'What is most just is finest; being healthy is most beneficial; but it is most pleasant to win our heart's desire.' For all three features are found in the best activities, and we say happiness is these activities, or [rather] one of them, the best one.

Nonetheless, happiness evidently also needs external goods to be added, as we said, since we cannot, or cannot easily, do fine actions if we lack the resources. For, first of all, in many actions we use 1099b friends, wealth, and political power just as we use instruments. Further, deprivation of certain [externals]—for instance, good birth, good children, beauty—mars our blessedness. For we do not altogether have the character of happiness if we look utterly repulsive or are ill-born, solitary, or childless; and we have it even less, presumably, if our children or friends are totally bad, or were good but have died. 5

And so, as we have said, happiness would seem to need this sort of prosperity added also. That is why some people identify happiness with good fortune, and others identify it with virtue.

9

This also leads to a puzzle: Is happiness acquired by learning, or habituation, or by some other form of cultivation? Or is it the result of some divine fate, or 10 even of fortune?

First, then, if the gods give any gift at all to human beings, it is reasonable for them to give us happiness more than any other human good, insofar as it is the best of human goods. Presumably, however, this question is more suitable for a different inquiry.

15 But even if it is not sent by the gods, but instead results from virtue and some sort of learning or cultivation, happiness appears to be one of the most divine things, since the prize and goal of virtue appears to be the best good, something divine and blessed. Moreover [if happiness comes in this way] it will be widely shared; for anyone who is not deformed [in his capacity] for virtue will be able to achieve happiness 20 through some sort of learning and attention.

And since it is better to be happy in this way than because of fortune, it is reasonable for this to be the way [we become] happy. For whatever is natural is naturally in the finest state possible. The same is true of the products of crafts and of every other cause, especially the best cause; and it would be seriously inappropriate to entrust what is greatest and finest to fortune.

25 The answer to our question is also evident from our account. For we have said that happiness is a certain sort of activity of the soul in accord with virtue, [and hence not a result of fortune]. Of the other goods, some are necessary conditions of happiness, while others are naturally useful and cooperative as instruments [but are not parts of it].

Further, this conclusion agrees with our opening 30 remarks. For we took the goal of political science to be the best good; and most of its attention is devoted to the character of the citizens, to make them good people who do fine actions.

It is not surprising, then, that we regard neither ox, 1100a nor horse, nor any other kind of animal as happy; for none of them can share in this sort of activity. For the same reason a child is not happy either, since his age prevents him from doing these sorts of actions. If he is called happy, he is being congratulated [simply] because of anticipated blessedness; for, as we have 5 said, happiness requires both complete virtue and a complete life.

It needs a complete life because life includes many reversals of fortune, good and bad, and the most prosperous person may fall into a terrible disaster in old age, as the Trojan stories tell us about Priam. If someone has suffered these sorts of misfortunes and comes to a miserable end, no one counts him happy.

10

Then should we count no human being happy during 10 his lifetime, but follow Solon's[4] advice to wait to see the end? But if we agree with Solon, can someone really be happy during the time after he has died? Surely that is completely absurd, especially when we say happiness is an activity.

We do not say, then, that someone is happy during 15 the time he is dead, and Solon's point is not this [absurd one], but rather that when a human being has died, we can safely pronounce [that he was] blessed [before he died], on the assumption that he is now finally beyond evils and misfortunes. But this claim is also disputable. For if a living person has good or evil of which he is not aware, a dead person also, it seems, has good or evil, if, for instance, he receives 20 honors or dishonors, and his children, and descendants in general, do well or suffer misfortune.

However, this conclusion also raises a puzzle. For even if someone has lived in blessedness until old age, and has died appropriately, many fluctuations of his descendants' fortunes may still happen to him; for some may be good people and get the life they 25 deserve, while the contrary may be true of others, and clearly they may be as distantly related to their ancestor as you please. Surely, then, it would be an absurd result if the dead person's condition changed along with the fortunes of his descendants, so that at one time he would turn out to have been happy [in his lifetime] and at another time he would turn out to have been miserable. But it would also be absurd 30 if the condition of descendants did not affect their ancestors at all or for any length of time.

But we must return to the previous puzzle, since that will perhaps also show us the answer to our present question. Let us grant that we must wait to see the end, and must then count someone blessed, not as now being blessed [during the time he is dead] but because he previously was blessed. Would it not be absurd, then, if, at the very time when he is happy, we refused to ascribe truly to him the happiness he 35

4. [Important Athenian statesman and sage about 600; when he saw the vast wealth of Croesus, king of Lydia, Solon refused to call him the happiest man until he saw how his life ended. — M.L.M.]

1100b has? Such refusal results from reluctance to call him happy during his lifetime, because of its ups and downs; for we suppose happiness is enduring and definitely not prone to fluctuate, but the same person's
5 fortunes often turn to and fro. For clearly, if we take our cue from his fortunes, we shall often call him happy and then miserable again, thereby representing the happy person as a kind of chameleon, insecurely based.

But surely it is quite wrong to take our cue from someone's fortunes. For his doing well or badly does not rest on them. A human life, as we said, needs these
10 added, but activities in accord with virtue control happiness, and the contrary activities control its contrary. Indeed, the present puzzle is further evidence for our account [of happiness]. For no human achievement has the stability of activities in accord with virtue, since these seem to be more enduring even than our knowledge of the sciences. Indeed, the
15 most honorable among the virtues themselves are more enduring than the other virtues, because blessed people devote their lives to them more fully and more continually than to anything else—for this continual activity would seem to be the reason we do not forget them.

It follows, then, that the happy person has the [stability] we are looking for and keeps the character he has throughout his life. For always, or more than
20 anything else, he will do and study the actions in accord with virtue, and will bear fortunes most finely, in every way and in all conditions appropriately, since he is truly 'good, foursquare, and blameless.'

Many events, however, are subject to fortune; some are minor, some major. Hence, minor strokes of good or ill fortune clearly will not carry any weight for his
25 life. But many major strokes of good fortune will make it more blessed; for in themselves they naturally add adornment to it, and his use of them proves to be fine and excellent. Conversely, if he suffers many major misfortunes, they oppress and spoil his blessed-
30 ness, since they involve pain and impede many activities. And yet, even here what is fine shines through, whenever someone bears many severe misfortunes with good temper, not because he feels no distress, but because he is noble and magnanimous.

And since it is activities that control life, as we said,
35 no blessed person could ever become miserable, since

he will never do hateful and base actions. For a truly good and prudent person, we suppose, will bear 1101a strokes of fortune suitably, and from his resources at any time will do the finest actions, just as a good general will make the best use of his forces in war, and a good shoemaker will make the finest shoe from 5 the hides given to him, and similarly for all other craftsmen.

If this is so, the happy person could never become miserable, but neither will he be blessed if he falls into misfortunes as bad as Priam's. Nor, however, will he be inconstant and prone to fluctuate, since he will neither be easily shaken from his happiness nor 10 shaken by just any misfortunes. He will be shaken from it, though, by many serious misfortunes, and from these a return to happiness will take no short time. At best, it will take a long and complete length of time that includes great and fine successes.

Then why not say that the happy person is the one 15 whose activities accord with complete virtue, with an adequate supply of external goods, not for just any time but for a complete life? Or should we add that he will also go on living this way and will come to an appropriate end, since the future is not apparent to us; and we take happiness to be the end, and altogether complete in every way? Given these facts [about the future and about happiness], we shall say 20 that a living person who has, and will keep, the goods we mentioned is blessed, but blessed as a human being is. So much for a determination of this question.

11

Still, it is apparently rather unfriendly and contrary to the [common] beliefs to claim that the fortunes of our descendants and all our friends contribute nothing. But since they can find themselves in many and various circumstances, some of which affect us 25 more, some less, it is apparently a long—indeed endless—task to differentiate all the particular cases. Perhaps a general outline will be enough of an answer.

Misfortunes, then, even to the person himself, differ, and some have a certain gravity and weight for his life, whereas others would seem to be lighter. The 30 same is true for the misfortunes of his friends; and it matters whether they happen to living or to dead people—much more than it matters whether lawless and terrible crimes are committed before a tragic drama begins or in the course of it.

In our reasoning, then, we should also take account of this difference, but even more account, presum-
35 ably, of the puzzle about whether the dead share in
1101b any good or evil. For if we consider this, anything good or evil penetrating to the dead would seem to be weak and unimportant, either without qualification or for them. Even if the good or evil is not so weak and unimportant, still its importance and character are
5 not enough to make people happy who are not already happy, or to take away the blessedness of those who are happy. And so, when friends do well, and likewise when they do badly, it appears to contribute some-thing to the dead, but of a character and size that neither makes happy people not happy nor anything of this sort.

12

10 Now that we have determined these points, let us consider whether happiness is something praisewor-thy, or instead something honorable; for clearly it is not a capacity [which is neither praiseworthy nor honorable].

Whatever is praiseworthy appears to be praised for its character and its state in relation to something. We praise the just and the brave person, for instance,
15 and in general the good person and virtue, because of their actions and achievements; and we praise the strong person, the good runner, and each of the others because he naturally has a certain character and is in a certain state in relation to something good and excellent. This is clear also from praises of the gods; for these praises appear ridiculous because they are
20 referred to us, but they are referred to us because, as we said, praise depends on such a reference.

If praise is for these sorts of things, then clearly for the best things there is no praise, but something greater and better. And indeed this is how it appears. For the gods and the most godlike of men are [not
25 praised, but] congratulated for their blessedness and happiness. The same is true of goods; for we never praise happiness, as we praise justice, but we count it blessed, as something better and more godlike [than anything that is praised].

Indeed, Eudoxus[5] seems to have used the right sort of argument in defending the supremacy of pleasure. By not praising pleasure, though it is a good, we indicate—so he thought—that it is superior to every- 30 thing praiseworthy; [only] the god and the good have this superiority since the other goods are [praised] by reference to them.

[Here he seems to have argued correctly.] For praise is given to virtue, since it makes us do fine actions; but celebrations are for achievements, either of body or of soul. But an exact treatment of this is presumably more proper for specialists in celebrations. For us, anyhow, 35 it is clear from what has been said that happiness is 1102a something honorable and complete.

A further reason why this would seem to be correct is that happiness is a principle; for [the principle] is what we all aim at in all our other actions; and we take the principle and cause of goods to be something honorable and divine.

13

Since happiness is a certain sort of activity of the soul 5 in accord with complete virtue, we must examine virtue; for that will perhaps also be a way to study happiness better. Moreover, the true politician seems to have put more effort into virtue than into anything else, since he wants to make the citizens good and 10 law-abiding. We find an example of this in the Spartan and Cretan legislators and in any others who share their concerns. Since, then, the examination of virtue is proper for political science, the inquiry clearly suits our decision at the beginning.

It is clear that the virtue we must examine is human virtue, since we are also seeking the human good and 15 human happiness. By human virtue we mean virtue of the soul, not of the body, since we also say that happiness is an activity of the soul. If this is so, it is clear that the politician must in some way know about 20 the soul, just as someone setting out to heal the eyes must know about the whole body as well. This is all the more true to the extent that political science is better and more honorable than medicine; even among doctors, the cultivated ones devote a lot of

5. [Famous mathematician and member of Plato's academy.—M.L.M.]

effort to finding out about the body. Hence the politician as well [as the student of nature] must study the soul. But he must study it for his specific purpose,
25 far enough for his inquiry [into virtue]; for a more exact treatment would presumably take more effort than his purpose requires.

[We] have discussed the soul sufficiently [for our purposes] in [our] popular works as well [as our less popular], and we should use this discussion. We have said, for instance, that one [part] of the soul is nonra-
30 tional, while one has reason. Are these distinguished as parts of a body and everything divisible into parts are? Or are they two [only] in definition, and inseparable by nature, as the convex and the concave are in a surface? It does not matter for present purposes.

Consider the nonrational [part]. One [part] of it, i.e., the cause of nutrition and growth, would seem
1102b to be plantlike and shared [with all living things]; for we can ascribe this capacity of the soul to everything that is nourished, including embryos, and the same capacity to full-grown living things, since this is more reasonable than to ascribe another capacity to them.

Hence the virtue of this capacity is apparently shared, not [specifically] human. For this part and
5 this capacity more than others seem to be active in sleep, and here the good and the bad person are least distinct; hence happy people are said to be no better off than miserable people for half their lives. This lack of distinction is not surprising, since sleep is inactivity of the soul insofar as it is called excellent or base, unless to some small extent some movements
10 penetrate [to our awareness], and in this way the decent person comes to have better images [in dreams] than just any random person has. Enough about this, however, and let us leave aside the nutritive part, since by nature it has no share in human virtue.

Another nature in the soul would also seem to be
15 nonrational, though in a way it shares in reason. For in the continent and the incontinent person we praise their reason, that is to say, the [part] of the soul that has reason, because it exhorts them correctly and toward what is best; but they evidently also have in them some other [part] that is by nature something apart from reason, clashing and struggling with reason. For just as paralyzed parts of a body, when we
20 decide to move them to the right, do the contrary and move off to the left, the same is true of the

soul; for incontinent people have impulses in contrary directions. In bodies, admittedly, we see the part go astray, whereas we do not see it in the soul; nonetheless, presumably, we should suppose that the soul also has something apart from reason, countering and opposing reason. The [precise] way it is different does 25 not matter.

However, this [part] as well [as the rational part] appears, as we said, to share in reason. At any rate, in the continent person it obeys reason; and in the temperate and the brave person it presumably listens still better to reason, since there it agrees with reason in everything.

The nonrational [part], then, as well [as the whole soul] apparently has two parts. For while the plantlike [part] shares in reason not at all, the [part] with appe- 30 tites and in general desires shares in reason in a way, insofar as it both listens to reason and obeys it. This is the way in which we are said to 'listen to reason' from father or friends, as opposed to the way in which [we 'give the reason'] in mathematics. The nonrational part also [obeys and] is persuaded in some way by reason, as is shown by correction, and by every 1103a sort of reproof and exhortation.

If, then, we ought to say that this [part] also has reason, then the [part] that has reason, as well [as the nonrational part], will have two parts. One will have reason fully, by having it within itself; the other will have reason by listening to reason as to a father.

The division between virtues accords with this dif- 5 ference. For some virtues are called virtues of thought, others virtues of character; wisdom, comprehension, and prudence are called virtues of thought, generosity and temperance virtues of character. For when we speak of someone's character we do not say that he is wise or has good comprehension, but that he is gentle or temperate. And yet, we also praise the wise person for his state, and the states that are praiseworthy 10 are the ones we call virtues.

BOOK II

1

Virtue, then, is of two sorts, virtue of thought and 15 virtue of character. Virtue of thought arises and grows mostly from teaching; that is why it needs experience and time. Virtue of character [i.e., of *ēthos*] results from habit [*ethos*]; hence its name 'ethical,' slightly varied from 'ethos.'

Hence it is also clear that none of the virtues of character arises in us naturally. For if something is
20 by nature in one condition, habituation cannot bring it into another condition. A stone, for instance, by nature moves downwards, and habituation could not make it move upwards, not even if you threw it up ten thousand times to habituate it; nor could habituation make fire move downwards, or bring anything that is by nature in one condition into another condition. And so the virtues arise in us neither by nature nor
25 against nature. Rather, we are by nature able to acquire them, and we are completed through habit.

Further, if something arises in us by nature, we first have the capacity for it, and later perform the activity. This is clear in the case of the senses; for we
30 did not acquire them by frequent seeing or hearing, but we already had them when we exercised them, and did not get them by exercising them. Virtues, by contrast, we acquire, just as we acquire crafts, by having first activated them. For we learn a craft by producing the same product that we must produce when we have learned it; we become builders, for instance, by building, and we become harpists by
1103b playing the harp. Similarly, then, we become just by doing just actions, temperate by doing temperate actions, brave by doing brave actions.

What goes on in cities is also evidence for this. For
5 the legislator makes the citizens good by habituating them, and this is the wish of every legislator; if he fails to do it well he misses his goal. Correct habituation distinguishes a good political system from a bad one.

Further, the sources and means that develop each virtue also ruin it, just as they do in a craft. For playing the harp makes both good and bad harpists, and it is
10 analogous in the case of builders and all the rest; for building well makes good builders, and building badly makes bad ones. Otherwise no teacher would be needed, but everyone would be born a good or a bad craftsman.

It is the same, then, with the virtues. For what we do in our dealings with other people makes some of
15 us just, some unjust; what we do in terrifying situations, and the habits of fear or confidence that we acquire, make some of us brave and others cowardly.

The same is true of situations involving appetites and anger; for one or another sort of conduct in these situations makes some temperate and mild, others
20 intemperate and irascible. To sum it up in a single account: a state [of character] results from [the repetition of] similar activities.

That is why we must perform the right activities, since differences in these imply corresponding differences in the states. It is not unimportant, then, to acquire one sort of habit or another, right from our youth. On the contrary, it is very important, indeed
25 all-important.

2

Our present discussion does not aim, as our others do, at study; for the purpose of our examination is not to know what virtue is, but to become good, since otherwise the inquiry would be of no benefit to us.
30 And so we must examine the right ways of acting; for, as we have said, the actions also control the sorts of states we acquire.

First, then, actions should accord with the correct reason. That is a common [belief], and let us assume it. We shall discuss it later, and say what the correct reason is and how it is related to the other virtues.

But let us take it as agreed in advance that every
1104a account of the actions we must do has to be stated in outline, not exactly. As we also said at the beginning, the type of accounts we demand should accord with the subject matter; and questions about actions and expediency, like questions about health, have no fixed answers.

While this is the character of our general account,
5 the account of particular cases is still more inexact. For these fall under no craft or profession; the agents themselves must consider in each case what the opportune action is, as doctors and navigators
10 do. The account we offer, then, in our present inquiry is of this inexact sort; still, we must try to offer help.

First, then, we should observe that these sorts of states naturally tend to be ruined by excess and deficiency. We see this happen with strength and health—for we must use evident cases [such as these] as witnesses to things that are not evident. For both
15 excessive and deficient exercise ruin bodily strength,

and, similarly, too much or too little eating or drinking ruins health, whereas the proportionate amount produces, increases, and preserves it.

20   The same is true, then, of temperance, bravery, and the other virtues. For if, for instance, someone avoids and is afraid of everything, standing firm against nothing, he becomes cowardly; if he is afraid of nothing at all and goes to face everything, he becomes rash. Similarly, if he gratifies himself with every pleasure and abstains from none, he becomes
25 intemperate; if he avoids them all, as boors do, he becomes some sort of insensible person. Temperance and bravery, then, are ruined by excess and deficiency, but preserved by the mean.

But these actions are not only the sources and causes both of the emergence and growth of virtues and of their ruin; the activities of the virtues [once
30 we have acquired them] also consist in these same actions. For this is also true of more evident cases; strength, for instance, arises from eating a lot and from withstanding much hard labor, and it is the strong person who is most capable of these very actions. It is the same with the virtues. For abstaining
35 from pleasures makes us become temperate, and once we have become temperate we are most capable of
1104b abstaining from pleasures. It is similar with bravery; habituation in disdain for frightening situations and in standing firm against them makes us become brave, and once we have become brave we shall be most capable of standing firm.

3

5 But we must take someone's pleasure or pain following on his actions to be a sign of his state. For if someone who abstains from bodily pleasures enjoys the abstinence itself, he is temperate; if he is grieved by it, he is intemperate. Again, if he stands firm against terrifying situations and enjoys it, or at least does not find it painful, he is brave; if he finds it painful, he is cowardly. For virtue of character is about pleasures and pains.

10   For pleasure causes us to do base actions, and pain causes us to abstain from fine ones. That is why we need to have had the appropriate upbringing—right from early youth, as Plato says—to make us find enjoy-

ment or pain in the right things; for this is the correct education.

Further, virtues are concerned with actions and feelings; but every feeling and every action implies pleasure or pain; hence, for this reason too, virtue is 15 about pleasures and pains. Corrective treatments also indicate this, since they use pleasures and pains; for correction is a form of medical treatment, and medical treatment naturally operates through contraries.

Further, as we said earlier, every state of soul is naturally related to and about whatever naturally makes it better or worse; and pleasures and pains 20 make people base, from pursuing and avoiding the wrong ones, at the wrong time, in the wrong ways, or whatever other distinctions of that sort are needed in an account. These [bad effects of pleasure and pain] are the reason why people actually define the virtues as ways of being unaffected and undisturbed [by pleasures and pains]. They are wrong, however, 25 because they speak of being unaffected without qualification, not of being unaffected in the right or wrong way, at the right or wrong time, and the added qualifications.

We assume, then, that virtue is the sort of state that does the best actions concerning pleasures and pains, and that vice is the contrary state.

The following will also make it evident that virtue 30 and vice are about the same things. For there are three objects of choice—fine, expedient, and pleasant—and three objects of avoidance—their contraries, shameful, harmful, and painful. About all these, then, the good person is correct and the bad person is in error, and especially about pleasure. For pleasure 35 is shared with animals, and implied by every object 1105a of choice, since what is fine and what is expedient appear pleasant as well.

Further, pleasure grows up with all of us from infancy on. That is why it is hard to rub out this feeling that is dyed into our lives. We also estimate actions [as well as feelings]—some of us more, some 5 less—by pleasure and pain. For this reason, our whole discussion must be about these; for good or bad enjoyment or pain is very important for our actions.

Further, it is more difficult to fight pleasure than to fight spirit—and Heracleitus tells us [how difficult it is to fight spirit]. Now both craft and virtue are in every case about what is more difficult, since a good 10 result is even better when it is more difficult. Hence, for this reason also, the whole discussion, for virtue and political science alike, must consider pleasures and pains; for if we use these well, we shall be good, and if badly, bad.

15   To sum up: Virtue is about pleasures and pains; the actions that are its sources also increase it or, if they are done badly, ruin it; and its activity is about the same actions as those that are its sources.

4

Someone might be puzzled, however, about what we mean by saying that we become just by doing just actions and become temperate by doing temperate actions. For [one might suppose that] if we do gram-
20   matical or musical actions, we are grammarians or musicians, and, similarly, if we do just or temperate actions, we are thereby just or temperate.

But surely actions are not enough, even in the case of crafts; for it is possible to produce a grammatical result by chance, or by following someone else's instructions. To be grammarians, then, we must both
25   produce a grammatical result and produce it grammatically—that is to say, produce it in accord with the grammatical knowledge in us.

Moreover, in any case, what is true of crafts is not true of virtues. For the products of a craft determine by their own qualities whether they have been produced well; and so it suffices that they have the right qualities when they have been produced. But for actions in
30   accord with the virtues to be done temperately or justly it does not suffice that they themselves have the right qualities. Rather, the agent must also be in the right state when he does them. First, he must know [that he is doing virtuous actions]; second, he must decide on them, and decide on them for themselves; and, third, he must also do them from a firm and unchanging state.

1105b   As conditions for having a craft, these three do not count, except for the bare knowing. As a condition for having a virtue, however, the knowing counts for nothing, or [rather] for only a little, whereas the other two conditions are very important, indeed all-important.
5   And we achieve these other two conditions by the frequent doing of just and temperate actions.

Hence actions are called just or temperate when they are the sort that a just or temperate person would do. But the just and temperate person is not the one who [merely] does these actions, but the one who also does them in the way in which just or temperate people do them.

It is right, then, to say that a person comes to be   10 just from doing just actions and temperate from doing temperate actions; for no one has the least prospect of becoming good from failing to do them.

The many, however, do not do these actions. They take refuge in arguments, thinking that they are doing philosophy, and that this is the way to become excellent people. They are like a sick person who listens   15 attentively to the doctor, but acts on none of his instructions. Such a course of treatment will not improve the state of the sick person's body; nor will the many improve the state of their souls by this attitude to philosophy.

5

Next we must examine what virtue is. Since there   20 are three conditions arising in the soul—feelings, capacities, and states—virtue must be one of these.

By feelings I mean appetite, anger, fear, confidence, envy, joy, love, hate, longing, jealousy, pity, and in general whatever implies pleasure or pain. By capacities I mean what we have when we are said to   25 be capable of these feelings—capable of being angry, for instance, or of being afraid or of feeling pity. By states I mean what we have when we are well or badly off in relation to feelings. If, for instance, our feeling is too intense or slack, we are badly off in relation to anger, but if it is intermediate, we are well off; the same is true in the other cases.

First, then, neither virtues nor vices are feelings.   30 For we are called excellent or base insofar as we have virtues or vices, not insofar as we have feelings. Further, we are neither praised nor blamed insofar as we have feelings; for we do not praise the angry or the frightened person, and do not blame the person who is simply angry, but only the person who is angry   1106a in a particular way. We are praised or blamed, however, insofar as we have virtues or vices. Further, we are angry and afraid without decision; but the virtues are decisions of some kind, or [rather] require decision. Besides, insofar as we have feelings, we are said   5 to be moved; but insofar as we have virtues or vices, we are said to be in some condition rather than moved.

For these reasons the virtues are not capacities either; for we are neither called good nor called bad, nor are we praised or blamed, insofar as we are simply
10 capable of feelings. Further, while we have capacities by nature, we do not become good or bad by nature; we have discussed this before.

If, then, the virtues are neither feelings nor capacities, the remaining possibility is that they are states. And so we have said what the genus of virtue is.

6

15 But we must say not only, as we already have, that it is a state, but also what sort of state it is.

It should be said, then, that every virtue causes its possessors to be in a good state and to perform their functions well. The virtue of eyes, for instance, makes the eyes and their functioning excellent, because it
20 makes us see well; and similarly, the virtue of a horse makes the horse excellent, and thereby good at galloping, at carrying its rider, and at standing steady in the face of the enemy. If this is true in every case, the virtue of a human being will likewise be the state that makes a human being good and makes him perform his function well.

25 We have already said how this will be true, and it will also be evident from our next remarks, if we consider the sort of nature that virtue has.

In everything continuous and divisible we can take more, less, and equal, and each of them either in the object itself or relative to us; and the equal is some
30 intermediate between excess and deficiency. By the intermediate in the object I mean what is equidistant from each extremity; this is one and the same for all. But relative to us the intermediate is what is neither superfluous nor deficient; this is not one, and is not the same for all.

If, for instance, ten are many and two are few, we
35 take six as intermediate in the object, since it exceeds [two] and is exceeded [by ten] by an equal amount, [four]. This is what is intermediate by numerical pro-
1106b portion. But that is not how we must take the intermediate that is relative to us. For if ten pounds [of food], for instance, are a lot for someone to eat, and two pounds a little, it does not follow that the trainer will

prescribe six, since this might also be either a little or a lot for the person who is to take it—for Milo [the athlete] a little, but for the beginner in gymnastics a lot; and the same is true for running and wrestling. 5 In this way every scientific expert avoids excess and deficiency and seeks and chooses what is intermediate—but intermediate relative to us, not in the object.

This, then, is how each science produces its product well, by focusing on what is intermediate and making the product conform to that. This, indeed, 10 is why people regularly comment on well-made products that nothing could be added or subtracted; they assume that excess or deficiency ruins a good [result], whereas the mean preserves it. Good craftsmen also, we say, focus on what is intermediate when they produce their product. And since virtue, like nature, is better and more exact than any craft, it will also 15 aim at what is intermediate.

By virtue I mean virtue of character; for this is about feelings and actions, and these admit of excess, deficiency, and an intermediate condition. We can be afraid, for instance, or be confident, or have appetites, or get angry, or feel pity, and in general have 20 pleasure or pain, both too much and too little, and in both ways not well. But having these feelings at the right times, about the right things, toward the right people, for the right end, and in the right way, is the intermediate and best condition, and this is proper to virtue. Similarly, actions also admit of excess, deficiency, and an intermediate condition.

Now virtue is about feelings and actions, in which 25 excess and deficiency are in error and incur blame, whereas the intermediate condition is correct and wins praise, which are both proper to virtue. Virtue, then, is a mean, insofar as it aims at what is intermediate.

Moreover, there are many ways to be in error— 30 for badness is proper to the indeterminate, as the Pythagoreans pictured it, and good to the determinate. But there is only one way to be correct. That is why error is easy and correctness is difficult, since it is easy to miss the target and difficult to hit it. And so for this reason also excess and deficiency are proper to vice, the mean to virtue; 'for we are noble in only one way, but bad in all sorts of ways.' 35

Virtue, then, is a state that decides, consisting in 1107a a mean, the mean relative to us, which is defined by reference to reason, that is to say, to the reason by reference to which the prudent person would define it. It is a mean between two vices, one of excess and one of deficiency.

It is a mean for this reason also: Some vices miss what is right because they are deficient, others be-5 cause they are excessive, in feelings or in actions, whereas virtue finds and chooses what is intermediate.

That is why virtue, as far as its essence and the account stating what it is are concerned, is a mean, but, as far as the best [condition] and the good [result] are concerned, it is an extremity.

10 Now not every action or feeling admits of the mean. For the names of some automatically include baseness—for instance, spite, shamelessness, envy [among feelings], and adultery, theft, murder, among actions. For all of these and similar things are called by these names because they themselves, not their excesses or 15 deficiencies, are base. Hence in doing these things we can never be correct, but must invariably be in error. We cannot do them well or not well—by committing adultery, for instance, with the right woman at the right time in the right way. On the contrary, it is true without qualification that to do any of them is to be in error.

[To think these admit of a mean], therefore, is like 20 thinking that unjust or cowardly or intemperate action also admits of a mean, an excess and a deficiency. If it did, there would be a mean of excess, a mean of deficiency, an excess of excess and a deficiency of deficiency. On the contrary, just as there is no excess or deficiency of temperance or of bravery (since the intermediate is a sort of extreme), so also there is no mean of these vicious actions either, but whatever way anyone does them, he is in error. For in general 25 there is no mean of excess or of deficiency, and no excess or deficiency of a mean.

7

However, we must not only state this general account but also apply it to the particular cases. For among 30 accounts concerning actions, though the general ones are common to more cases, the specific ones are truer, since actions are about particular cases, and our account must accord with these. Let us, then, find these from the chart.

First, then, in feelings of fear and confidence the 1107b mean is bravery. The excessively fearless person is nameless (indeed many cases are nameless), and the one who is excessively confident is rash. The one who is excessive in fear and deficient in confidence is cowardly.

In pleasures and pains—though not in all types, 5 and in pains less than in pleasures—the mean is temperance and the excess intemperance. People deficient in pleasure are not often found, which is why they also lack even a name; let us call them insensible.

In giving and taking money the mean is generosity, 10 the excess wastefulness and the deficiency ungenerosity. Here the vicious people have contrary excesses and defects; for the wasteful person is excessive in spending and deficient in taking, whereas the ungenerous person is excessive in taking and deficient in spending. At the moment we are speaking in outline and summary, and that is enough; later we shall define 15 these things more exactly.

In questions of money there are also other conditions. Another mean is magnificence; for the magnificent person differs from the generous by being concerned with large matters, while the generous person is concerned with small. The excess is ostenta- 20 tion and vulgarity, and the deficiency is stinginess. These differ from the vices related to generosity in ways we shall describe later.

In honor and dishonor the mean is magnanimity, the excess something called a sort of vanity, and the 25 deficiency pusillanimity. And just as we said that generosity differs from magnificence in its concern with small matters, similarly there is a virtue concerned with small honors, differing in the same way from magnanimity, which is concerned with great honors. For honor can be desired either in the right way or more or less than is right. If someone desires it to excess, he is called an honor-lover, and if his desire is deficient he is called indifferent to honor, 30 but if he is intermediate he has no name. The corresponding conditions have no name either, except the condition of the honor-lover, which is called honor-loving.

This is why people at the extremes lay claim to the intermediate area. Moreover, we also sometimes call the intermediate person an honor-lover, and sometimes call him indifferent to honor; and some-

1108a times we praise the honor-lover, sometimes the person indifferent to honor. We will mention later the reason we do this; for the moment, let us speak of the other cases in the way we have laid down.

5   Anger also admits of an excess, deficiency, and mean. These are all practically nameless; but since we call the intermediate person mild, let us call the mean mildness. Among the extreme people, let the excessive person be irascible, and his vice irascibility, and let the deficient person be a sort of inirascible person, and his deficiency inirascibility.

10   There are also three other means, somewhat similar to one another, but different. For they are all concerned with common dealings in conversations and actions, but differ insofar as one is concerned with truth telling in these areas, the other two with sources of pleasure, some of which are found in amusement, and the others in daily life in general. Hence we 15 should also discuss these states, so that we can better observe that in every case the mean is praiseworthy, whereas the extremes are neither praiseworthy nor correct, but blameworthy. Most of these cases are also nameless, and we must try, as in the other cases also, to supply names ourselves, to make things clear and easy to follow.

20   In truth-telling, then, let us call the intermediate person truthful, and the mean truthfulness; pretense that overstates will be boastfulness, and the person who has it boastful; pretense that understates will be self-deprecation, and the person who has it self-deprecating.

In sources of pleasure in amusements let us call the intermediate person witty, and the condition wit; 25 the excess buffoonery and the person who has it a buffoon; and the deficient person a sort of boor and the state boorishness.

In the other sources of pleasure, those in daily life, let us call the person who is pleasant in the right way friendly, and the mean state friendliness. If someone goes to excess with no [ulterior] aim, he will be ingrati- 30 ating; if he does it for his own advantage, a flatterer. The deficient person, unpleasant in everything, will be a sort of quarrelsome and ill-tempered person.

There are also means in feelings and about feelings. Shame, for instance, is not a virtue, but the person prone to shame as well as [the virtuous people we have described] receives praise. For here also one person is called intermediate, and another—the person excessively prone to shame, who is ashamed about everything—is called excessive; the person who is 35 deficient in shame or never feels shame at all is said to have no sense of disgrace; and the intermediate 1108b one is called prone to shame.

Proper indignation is the mean between envy and spite; these conditions are concerned with pleasure and pain at what happens to our neighbors. For the properly indignant person feels pain when someone does well undeservedly; the envious person exceeds 5 him by feeling pain when anyone does well, while the spiteful person is so deficient in feeling pain that he actually enjoys [other people's misfortunes].

There will also be an opportunity elsewhere to speak of these. We must consider justice after these. Since it is spoken of in more than one way, we shall distinguish its two types and say how each of them is a mean. Similarly, we must also consider the virtues 10 that belong to reason.

8

Among these three conditions, then, two are vices— one of excess, one of deficiency—and one, the mean, is virtue. In a way, each of them is opposed to each of the others, since each extreme is contrary both to the intermediate condition and to the other extreme, while the intermediate is contrary to the extremes. 15

For, just as the equal is greater in comparison to the smaller, and smaller in comparison to the greater, so also the intermediate states are excessive in comparison to the deficiencies and deficient in comparison to the excesses—both in feelings and in actions. For 20 the brave person, for instance, appears rash in comparison to the coward, and cowardly in comparison to the rash person; the temperate person appears intemperate in comparison to the insensible person, and insensible in comparison with the intemperate person; and the generous person appears wasteful in comparison to the ungenerous, and ungenerous in comparison to the wasteful person. That is why each of the extreme people tries to push the intermediate person to the other extreme, so that the coward, for 25 instance, calls the brave person rash, and the rash person calls him a coward, and similarly in the other cases.

Since these conditions of soul are opposed to each other in these ways, the extremes are more contrary to each other than to the intermediate. For they are further from each other than from the intermediate, just as the large is further from the small, and the small from the large, than either is from the equal.

Further, sometimes one extreme—rashness or wastefulness, for instance—appears somewhat like the intermediate state, bravery or generosity. But the extremes are most unlike one another; and the things that are furthest apart from each other are defined as contraries. And so the things that are further apart are more contrary.

In some cases the deficiency, in others the excess, is more opposed to the intermediate condition. For instance, cowardice, the deficiency, not rashness, the excess, is more opposed to bravery, whereas intemperance, the excess, not insensibility, the deficiency, is more opposed to temperance.

This happens for two reasons: One reason is derived from the object itself. Since sometimes one extreme is closer and more similar to the intermediate condition, we oppose the contrary extreme, more than this closer one, to the intermediate condition. Since rashness, for instance, seems to be closer and more similar to bravery, and cowardice less similar, we oppose cowardice, more than rashness, to bravery; for what is further from the intermediate condition seems to be more contrary to it. This, then, is one reason, derived from the object itself.

The other reason is derived from ourselves. For when we ourselves have some natural tendency to one extreme more than to the other, this extreme appears more opposed to the intermediate condition. Since, for instance, we have more of a natural tendency to pleasure, we drift more easily toward intemperance than toward orderliness. Hence we say that an extreme is more contrary if we naturally develop more in that direction; and this is why intemperance is more contrary to temperance, since it is the excess [of pleasure].

9

We have said enough, then, to show that virtue of character is a mean and what sort of mean it is; that it is a mean between two vices, one of excess and

one of deficiency; and that it is a mean because it aims at the intermediate condition in feelings and actions.

That is why it is also hard work to be excellent. For in each case it is hard work to find the intermediate; for instance, not everyone, but only one who knows, finds the midpoint in a circle. So also getting angry, or giving and spending money, is easy and everyone can do it; but doing it to the right person, in the right amount, at the right time, for the right end, and in the right way is no longer easy, nor can everyone do it. Hence doing these things well is rare, praiseworthy, and fine.

That is why anyone who aims at the intermediate condition must first of all steer clear of the more contrary extreme, following the advice that Calypso also gives: 'Hold the ship outside the spray and surge.' For one extreme is more in error, the other less. Since, therefore, it is hard to hit the intermediate extremely accurately, the second-best tack, as they say, is to take the lesser of the evils. We shall succeed best in this by the method we describe.

We must also examine what we ourselves drift into easily. For different people have different natural tendencies toward different goals, and we shall come to know our own tendencies from the pleasure or pain that arises in us. We must drag ourselves off in the contrary direction; for if we pull far away from error, as they do in straightening bent wood, we shall reach the intermediate condition.

And in everything we must beware above all of pleasure and its sources; for we are already biased in its favor when we come to judge it. Hence we must react to it as the elders reacted to Helen, and on each occasion repeat what they said; for if we do this, and send it off, we shall be less in error.

In summary, then, if we do these things we shall best be able to reach the intermediate condition. But presumably this is difficult, especially in particular cases, since it is not easy to define the way we should be angry, with whom, about what, for how long. For sometimes, indeed, we ourselves praise deficient people and call them mild, and sometimes praise quarrelsome people and call them manly.

Still, we are not blamed if we deviate a little in excess or deficiency from doing well, but only if we deviate a long way, since then we are easily noticed. But how great and how serious a deviation receives blame is not easy to define in an account; for nothing else perceptible is easily defined either. Such things are among particulars, and the judgment depends on perception.

25 This is enough, then, to make it clear that in every case the intermediate state is praised, but we must sometimes incline toward the excess, sometimes toward the deficiency; for that is the easiest way to hit the intermediate and good condition.

BOOK III

1

30 Virtue, then, is about feelings and actions. These receive praise or blame if they are voluntary, but pardon, sometimes even pity, if they are involuntary. Hence, presumably, in examining virtue we must define the voluntary and the involuntary. This is also useful to legislators, both for honors and for correc-
35 tive treatments.

1110a Now it seems that things coming about by force or because of ignorance are involuntary.

What is forced has an external principle, the sort of principle in which the agent, or [rather] the victim, contributes nothing—if, for instance, a wind or people who have him in their control were to carry him off.

5 But what about actions done because of fear of greater evils, or because of something fine? Suppose, for instance, a tyrant tells you to do something shameful, when he has control over your parents and children, and if you do it, they will live, but if not, they will die. These cases raise dispute about whether they are voluntary or involuntary.

However, the same sort [of unwelcome choice] is
10 found in throwing cargo overboard in storms. For no one willingly throws cargo overboard, without qualification, but anyone with any sense throws it overboard to save himself and the others.

These sorts of actions, then, are mixed, but they are more like voluntary actions. For at the time they are done they are choiceworthy, and the goal of an action accords with the specific occasion; hence we should also call the action voluntary or involuntary on the occasion when he does it. Now in fact he does
15 it willingly. For in such actions he has within him

the principle of moving the limbs that are the instruments [of the action]; but if the principle of the actions is in him, it is also up to him to do them or not to do them. Hence actions of this sort are voluntary, though presumably the actions without [the appropriate] qualification are involuntary, since no one would choose any such action in its own right.

For such [mixed] actions people are sometimes 20 actually praised, whenever they endure something shameful or painful as the price of great and fine results. If they do the reverse, they are blamed; for it is a base person who endures what is most shameful for nothing fine or for only some moderately fine result. In some cases there is no praise, but there is pardon, whenever someone does a wrong action 25 because of conditions of a sort that overstrain human nature, and that no one would endure.

But presumably there are some things we cannot be compelled to do. Rather than do them we should suffer the most terrible consequences and accept death; for the things that [allegedly] compelled Euripides' Alcmaeon to kill his mother appear ridiculous.

It is sometimes difficult, however, to judge what 30 [goods] should be chosen at the price of what [evils], and what [evils] should be endured as the price of what [goods]. It is even more difficult to abide by our judgment, since the results we expect [when we endure] are usually painful, and the actions we are compelled [to endure, when we choose] are usually shameful. That is why those who have been com- 1110b pelled or not compelled receive praise or blame.

What sorts of things, then, should we say are forced? Perhaps we should say that something is forced without qualification whenever its cause is external and the agent contributes nothing. Other things are involuntary in their own right, but choiceworthy on this occasion and as the price of these [goods], and their 5 principle is in the agent. These are involuntary in their own right, but, on this occasion and as the price of these [goods], voluntary. But they are more like voluntary actions, since the actions are particulars, and [in the case of mixed actions] these particulars are voluntary. But what sort of thing should be chosen as the price of what [good] is not easy to answer, since there are many differences in particular [conditions]. 10

But what if someone says that pleasant things and fine things force us, on the ground that they are outside us and compel us? For him, then, everything must be forced, since everyone in every action aims at something fine or pleasant. Moreover, if we are forced and unwilling to act, we find it painful; but if something pleasant or fine is its cause, we do it with pleasure. It is ridiculous, then, for him to ascribe responsibility to external causes, not to himself as being easily snared by such things; and ridiculous to hold himself responsible for his fine actions, but pleasant things responsible for his shameful actions.

What is forced, then, would seem to be what has its principle outside the person forced, who contributes nothing.

Everything caused by ignorance is nonvoluntary, but what is involuntary also involves pain and regret. For if someone's action was caused by ignorance, but he now has no objection to the action, he has done it neither willingly, since he did not know what it was, nor unwillingly, since he now feels no pain. Hence, among those who act because of ignorance, the agent who now regrets his action seems to be unwilling, but the agent with no regrets may be called nonwilling, since he is another case—for, since he is different, it is better if he has his own special name.

Further, action caused by ignorance would seem to be different from action done in ignorance. For if the agent is drunk or angry, his action seems to be caused by drunkenness or anger, not by ignorance, though it is done in ignorance, not in knowledge. Certainly every vicious person is ignorant of the actions he must do or avoid, and this sort of error makes people unjust, and in general bad.

[This] ignorance of what is beneficial is not taken to make action involuntary. For the cause of involuntary action is not [this] ignorance in the decision, which causes vice; it is not [in other words] ignorance of the universal, since that is a cause for blame. Rather, the cause is ignorance of the particulars which the action consists in and is concerned with, since these allow both pity and pardon. For an agent acts involuntarily if he is ignorant of one of these particulars.

Presumably, then, it is not a bad idea to define these particulars, and say what they are, and how many. They are: who is doing it; what he is doing; about what or to what he is doing it; sometimes also what he is doing it with—with what instrument, for example; for what result, for example, safety; in what way, for example, gently or hard.

Now certainly someone could not be ignorant of *all* of these unless he were mad. Nor, clearly, could he be ignorant of who is doing it, since he could hardly be ignorant of himself. But he might be ignorant of what he is doing, as when someone says that [the secret] slipped out while he was speaking, or, as Aeschylus said about the mysteries, that he did not know it was forbidden to reveal it; or, like the person with the catapult, that he let it go when he [only] wanted to demonstrate it. Again, he might think that his son is an enemy, as Merope did; or that the barbed spear has a button on it, or that the stone is pumice stone. By giving someone a drink to save his life we might kill him; and wanting to touch someone, as they do in sparring, we might wound him.

Since an agent may be ignorant of any of these particular constituents of his action, someone who was ignorant of one of these seems to have acted unwillingly, especially if he was ignorant of the most important; these seem to be what he is doing, and the result for which he does it.

Hence the agent who acts involuntarily is the one who acts in accord with this specific sort of ignorance, who must also feel pain and regret for his action.

Since involuntary action is either forced or caused by ignorance, voluntary action seems to be what has its principle in the agent himself, knowing the particulars that constitute the action.

For, presumably, it is not right to say that action caused by spirit or appetite is involuntary. For, first of all, on this view none of the other animals will ever act voluntarily; nor will children. Next, among all the actions caused by appetite or spirit do we do none of them voluntarily? Or do we do the fine actions voluntarily and the shameful involuntarily? Surely [the second answer] is ridiculous, given that one and the same thing [i.e., appetite or spirit] causes [both fine and shameful actions]. And presumably it is also absurd to say [as the first answer implies] that things we ought to desire are involuntary. Indeed, we ought both to be angry at some things and to have appetite for some things—for health and learning, for instance. Again, what is involuntary seems to be painful, whereas what accords with appetite seems to be pleasant.

Moreover, how are errors in accord with spirit any less voluntary than those in accord with rational calcu-

1111b lation? For both sorts of errors are to be avoided. Besides, nonrational feelings seem to be no less human than rational calculation; and so actions resulting from spirit or appetite are also proper to a human being. It is absurd, then, to regard them as involuntary.

2

5 Now that we have defined the voluntary and the involuntary, the next task is to discuss decision; for decision seems to be most proper to virtue, and to distinguish characters from one another better than actions do.

Decision, then, is apparently voluntary, but not the same as the voluntary, which extends more widely. For children and the other animals share in voluntary action, but not in decision; and the actions we do on

10 the spur of the moment are said to be voluntary, but not to accord with decision.

Those who say decision is appetite or spirit or wish or some sort of belief would seem to be wrong. For decision is not shared with nonrational animals, but appetite and spirit are shared with them. Again, the

15 incontinent person acts on appetite, not on decision, but the continent person does the reverse, by acting on decision, not on appetite. Again, appetite is contrary to decision, but not to appetite. Besides, the object of appetite is what is pleasant or painful, whereas neither of these is the object of decision. And still less is spirit decision; for actions caused by spirit seem least of all to accord with decision.

20 But further, it is not wish either, though it is apparently close to it. For we do not decide on impossible things—anyone claiming to decide on them would seem a fool; but we do wish for impossible things—for immortality, for instance—as well as possible things. Further, we wish [not only for results we can achieve], but also for results that are [possible, but] not achievable through our own agency—victory for some actor

25 or athlete, for instance. But what we decide on is never anything of that sort, but what we think would come about through our own agency. Again, we wish for the end more [than for the things that promote it], but we decide on things that promote the end. We wish, for instance, to be healthy, but we decide

to do things that will make us healthy; and we wish to be happy, and say so, but we could not appropriately

30 say we decide to be happy, since in general the things we decide on would seem to be things that are up to us.

Nor is it belief. For belief seems to be about everything, no less about things that are eternal and things that are impossible [for us] than about things that are up to us. Moreover, beliefs are divided into true and false, not into good and bad, but decisions are divided into good and bad more than into true and false.

1112a Now presumably no one even claims that decision is the same as belief in general. But it is not the same as any kind of belief either. For our decisions to do good or bad actions, not our beliefs, form the characters we have. Again, we decide to take or avoid some-

5 thing good or bad. We believe what it is, whom it benefits or how; but we do not exactly believe to take or avoid. Further, decision is praised more for deciding on what is right, whereas belief is praised for believing rightly. Moreover, we decide on something [even] when we know most completely that it is good; but [what] we believe [is] what we do not quite know. Again, those who make the best decisions do not seem

10 to be the same as those with the best beliefs; on the contrary, some seem to have better beliefs, but to make the wrong decisions because of vice. We may grant that decision follows or implies belief. But that is irrelevant, since it is not the question we are asking; our question is whether decision is the same as some sort of belief.

Then what, or what sort of thing, is decision, since it is none of the things mentioned? Well, apparently

15 it is voluntary, but not everything voluntary is decided. Then perhaps what is decided is what has been previously deliberated. For decision involves reason and thought, and even the name itself would seem to indicate that [what is decided, *prohaireton*] is chosen [*haireton*] before [*pro*] other things.

3

Do we deliberate about everything, and is everything open to deliberation? Or is there no deliberation

20 about some things? By 'open to deliberation,' presumably, we should mean that someone with some sense, not some fool or madman, might deliberate about it.

Now no one deliberates about eternal things—about the universe, for instance, or about the incommensurability of the sides and the diagonal; nor about things that are in movement but always come about the same way, either from necessity or by nature or by some other cause—the solstices, for instance, or the rising of the stars; nor about what happens in different ways at different times—droughts and rains, for instance; nor about what results from fortune—the finding of a treasure, for instance. For none of these results could be achieved through our agency.

We deliberate about what is up to us, that is to say, about the actions we can do; and this is what is left [besides the previous cases]. For causes seem to include nature, necessity, and fortune, but besides them mind and everything [operating] through human agency. But we do not deliberate about all human affairs; no Spartan, for instance, deliberates about how the Scythians might have the best political system. Rather, each group of human beings deliberates about the actions that they themselves can do.

There is no deliberation about the sciences that are exact and self-sufficient, as, for instance, about letters, since we are in no doubt about how to write them [in spelling a word]. Rather, we deliberate about what results through our agency, but in different ways on different occasions—about, for instance, medicine and money making. We deliberate about navigation more than about gymnastics, to the extent that it is less exactly worked out, and similarly with other [crafts]. And we deliberate about beliefs more than about sciences, since we are more in doubt about them.

Deliberation concerns what is usually [one way rather than another], where the outcome is unclear and the right way to act is undefined. And we enlist partners in deliberation on large issues when we distrust our own ability to discern [the right answer].

We deliberate not about ends, but about what promotes ends. A doctor, for instance, does not deliberate about whether he will cure, or an orator about whether he will persuade, or a politician about whether he will produce good order, or any other [expert] about the end [that his science aims at]. Rather, we lay down the end, and then examine the ways and means to achieve it.

If it appears that any of several [possible] means will reach it, we examine which of them will reach it most easily and most finely; and if only one [possible] means reaches it, we examine how that means will reach it, and how the means itself is reached, until we come to the first cause, the last thing to be discovered. For a deliberator would seem to inquire and analyze in the way described, as though analyzing a diagram. [The comparison is apt, since], apparently, all deliberation is inquiry, though not all inquiry—in mathematics, for instance—is deliberation. And the last thing [found] in the analysis would seem to be the first that comes into being.

If we encounter an impossible step—for instance, we need money but cannot raise it—we desist; but if the action appears possible, we undertake it. What is possible is what we could achieve through our agency [including what our friends could achieve for us]; for what our friends achieve is, in a way, achieved through our agency, since the principle is in us. [In crafts] we sometimes look for instruments, sometimes [for the way] to use them; so also in other cases we sometimes look for the means to the end, sometimes for the proper use of the means, or for the means to that proper use.

As we have said, then, a human being would seem to be a principle of action. Deliberation is about the actions he can do, and actions are for the sake of other things; hence we deliberate about things that promote an end, not about the end. Nor do we deliberate about particulars, about whether this is a loaf, for instance, or is cooked the right amount; for these are questions for perception, and if we keep on deliberating at each stage we shall go on without end.

What we deliberate about is the same as what we decide to do, except that by the time we decide to do it, it is definite; for what we decide to do is what we have judged [to be right] as a result of deliberation. For each of us stops inquiring how to act as soon as he traces the principle to himself, and within himself to the guiding part; for this is the part that decides. This is also clear from the ancient political systems described by Homer; there the kings would first decide and then announce their decision to the people.

We have found, then, that what we decide to do is whatever action, among those up to us, we deliberate about and [consequently] desire to do. Hence also decision will be deliberative desire to do an action that is up to us; for when we have judged [that it is right] as a result of deliberation, we desire to do it in accord with our wish.

We have said in outline, then, what sorts of things decision is about, and [specifically] that we decide on things that promote the end.

4

15 Wish, we have said, is for the end. But some think that wish is for the good, others that it is for the apparent good.

For those who say the good is wished, it follows that what someone wishes if he chooses incorrectly is not wished at all. For if it is wished, then [on this view] it is good; but what he wishes is in fact bad, if 20 it turns out that way. [Hence what he wishes is not wished, which is self-contradictory.]

But for those who say the apparent good is wished, it follows that nothing is wished by nature. Rather, for each person what is wished is what seems [good to him]; but different things, and indeed contrary things, if it turns out that way, appear good to different people. [Hence contrary things will be wished and nothing will be wished by nature.]

If, then, these views do not satisfy us, should we say that, without qualification and in reality, what is wished is the good, but for each person what is wished 25 is the apparent good? For the excellent person, then, what is wished will be what is [wished] in reality, while for the base person what is wished is whatever it turns out to be [that appears good to him]. Similarly in the case of bodies, really healthy things are healthy to people in good condition, while other things are healthy to sickly people; and the same is true of what 30 is bitter, sweet, hot, heavy, and so on. For the excellent person judges each sort of thing correctly, and in each case what is true appears to him.

For each state [of character] has its own distinctive [view of] what is fine and pleasant. Presumably, then, the excellent person is far superior because he sees what is true in each case, being himself a sort of standard and measure. In the many, however, pleasure would seem to cause deception, since it appears 1113b good when it is not. Certainly, they choose what is pleasant because they assume it is good, and avoid pain because they assume it is evil.

5

We have found, then, that we wish for the end, and deliberate and decide about things that promote it; hence the actions concerned with things that promote 5 the end are in accord with decision and are voluntary. The activities of the virtues are concerned with these things [that promote the end].

Hence virtue is also up to us, and so also, in the same way, is vice. For when acting is up to us, so is not acting, and when no is up to us, so is yes. And so if acting, when it is fine, is up to us, not acting, when it is shameful, is also up to us; and if not acting, 10 when it is fine, is up to us, then acting, when it is shameful, is also up to us. But if doing, and likewise not doing, fine or shameful actions is up to us, and if, as we saw, [doing or not doing them] is [what it is] to be a good or bad person, being decent or base is up to us.

The claim that 'no one is willingly bad or unwill- 15 ingly blessed' would seem to be partly true but partly false. For while certainly no one is unwillingly blessed, vice is voluntary.

If this is not so, we must dispute what has been said, and we must deny that a human being is a principle, begetting actions as he begets children. But if what we have said appears true, and we cannot 20 refer back to other principles apart from those that are up to us, those things that have their principle in us are themselves up to us and voluntary.

There would seem to be evidence in favor of our view not only in what each of us does as a private citizen, but also in what legislators themselves do. For they impose corrective treatments and penalties on anyone who does vicious actions, unless his action 25 is forced or is caused by ignorance that he is not responsible for; and they honor anyone who does fine actions. In all this they assume that they will encourage the second sort of person, and restrain the first. But no one encourages us to do anything that is not up to us and voluntary; people assume it is pointless to persuade us not to get hot or distressed or hungry or anything else of that sort, since persuasion will not stop it happening to us.

Indeed, legislators also impose corrective treat- 30 ments for the ignorance itself, if the agent seems to be responsible for the ignorance. A drunk, for instance, pays a double penalty; for the principle is in him, since he controls whether he gets drunk, and his getting drunk causes his ignorance. They also impose corrective treatment on someone who [does a vicious action] in ignorance of some provision of law that he is required to know and that is not hard [to know]. And they impose it in other cases likewise for any other ignorance that seems to be caused by the agent's inattention; they assume it is up to him not to be ignorant, since he controls whether he pays attention.

But presumably he is the sort of person who is inattentive. Still, he is himself responsible for becoming this sort of person, because he has lived carelessly. Similarly, an individual is responsible for being unjust, because he has cheated, and for being intemperate, because he has passed his time in drinking and the like; for each type of activity produces the corresponding sort of person. This is clear from those who train for any contest or action, since they continually practice the appropriate activities. [Only] a totally insensible person would not know that a given type of activity is the source of the corresponding state; [Hence] if someone does what he knows will make him unjust, he is willingly unjust.

Further, it is unreasonable for someone doing injustice not to wish to be unjust, or for someone doing intemperate action not to wish to be intemperate. This does not mean, however, that if he is unjust and wishes to stop, he will thereby stop and be just. For neither does a sick person recover his health [simply by wishing]; nonetheless, he is sick willingly, by living incontinently and disobeying the doctors, if that was how it happened. At that time, then, he was free not to be sick, though no longer free once he has let himself go, just as it was up to someone to throw a stone, since the principle was up to him, though he can no longer take it back once he has thrown it. Similarly, then, the person who is [now] unjust or intemperate was originally free not to acquire this character, so that he has it willingly, though once he has acquired the character, he is no longer free not to have it [now].

It is not only vices of the soul that are voluntary; vices of the body are also voluntary for some people, and we actually censure them. For we never censure someone if nature causes his ugliness; but if his lack of training or attention causes it, we do censure him. The same is true for weakness or maiming; for everyone would pity someone, not reproach him, if he were blind by nature or because of a disease or a wound, but would censure him if his heavy drinking or some other form of intemperance made him blind. Hence bodily vices that are up to us are censured, while those not up to us are not censured. If so, then in the other cases also the vices that are censured will be up to us.

But someone may say that everyone aims at the apparent good, and does not control how it appears, but, on the contrary, his character controls how the end appears to him. [We reply that] if each person is in some way responsible for his own state [of character], he is also himself in some way responsible for how [the end] appears.

Suppose, on the other hand, that no one is responsible for acting badly, but one does so because one is ignorant of the end, and thinks this is the way to gain what is best for oneself. In that case, one's aiming at the end is not one's own choice; one needs a sort of natural, inborn sense of sight, to judge finely and to choose what is really good. Whoever by nature has this sense in a fine condition has a good nature; for [, according to this view,] this sense is the greatest and finest thing, given that one cannot acquire it or learn it from another, but its natural character determines [his] later condition, and when it is naturally good and fine, that is true and complete good nature. If all this is true, then, surely virtue will be no more voluntary than vice.

For how the end appears is laid down, by nature or in whatever way, for the good and the bad person alike; they trace all the other things back to the end in doing whatever actions they do. Let us suppose, then, that nature does not make the end appear however it appears to each person, but something also depends on him. Alternatively, let us suppose that [how] the end [appears] is natural, but virtue is voluntary because the virtuous person does the other things voluntarily. In either case, vice will be no less voluntary than virtue; for the bad person, no less than the good, is responsible for his own actions, even if not for [how] the end [appears].

Now the virtues, as we say, are voluntary. For in fact we are ourselves in a way jointly responsible for our states of character, and the sort of character we have determines the sort of end we lay down. Hence the vices 25 will also be voluntary, since the same is true of them.

We have now discussed the virtues in common. We have described their genus in outline; they are means, and they are states. Certain actions produce them, and they cause us to do these same actions in accord with the virtues themselves, in the way that correct reason prescribes. They are up to us and voluntary.

30 Actions and states, however, are not voluntary in the same way. For we are in control of actions from the beginning to the end, when we know the particu-1115a lars. With states, however, we are in control of the beginning, but do not know, any more than with sicknesses, what the cumulative effect of particular actions will be. Nonetheless, since it was up to us to exercise a capacity either this way or another way, states are voluntary.

Let us now take up the virtues again, and discuss 5 them one by one. Let us say what they are, what sorts of thing they are concerned with, and how they are concerned with them. It will also be clear at the same time how many of them there are.

6

First let us discuss bravery. We have already made it apparent that there is a mean about feelings of fear and confidence. What we fear, clearly, is what is frightening, and such things are, speaking without qualification, bad things; hence people define fear as expectation of something bad.

10 Certainly we fear all bad things—for instance, bad reputation, poverty, sickness, friendlessness, death— but they do not all seem to concern the brave person. For fear of some bad things, such as bad reputation, is actually right and fine, and lack of fear is shameful; for if someone fears bad reputation, he is decent and properly prone to shame, and if he has no fear of it, he has no feeling of disgrace. Some, however, call 15 this fearless person brave, by a transference of the name; for he has some similarity to the brave person, since the brave person is also a type of fearless person.

Presumably it is wrong to fear poverty or sickness or, in general, [bad things] that are not the results of vice

or caused by ourselves; still, someone who is fearless about these is not thereby brave. He is also called brave by similarity; for some people who are cowardly in the 20 dangers of war are nonetheless generous, and face with confidence the [danger of] losing money.

Again, if someone is afraid of committing wanton aggression on children or women, or of being envious or anything of that sort, that does not make him cowardly. And if someone is confident when he is going to be whipped for his crimes, that does not make him brave.

Then what sorts of frightening conditions concern 25 the brave person? Surely the most frightening; for no one stands firmer against terrifying conditions. Now death is most frightening of all, since it is a boundary, and when someone is dead nothing beyond it seems either good or bad for him any more. Still, not even death in all conditions—on the sea, for instance, or in sickness—seems to be the brave person's concern.

In what conditions, then, is death his concern? 30 Surely in the finest conditions. Now such deaths are those in war, since they occur in the greatest and finest danger. This judgment is endorsed by the honors given in cities and by monarchs. Hence someone is called fully brave if he is intrepid in facing a fine death and the immediate dangers that bring death. 35 And this is above all true of the dangers of war.

Certainly the brave person is also intrepid on the 1115b sea and in sickness, but not in the same way as seafarers are. For he has given up hope of safety, and objects to this sort of death [with nothing fine in it], but seafarers' experience makes them hopeful. Moreover, we act like brave men on occasions when we can use our strength, or when it is fine to be killed; and neither 5 of these is true when we perish on the sea.

7

Now what is frightening is not the same for everyone. We say, however, that some things are too frightening for a human being to resist; these, then, are frightening for everyone, at least for everyone with any sense. What is frightening, but not irresistible for a human 10 being, varies in its seriousness and degree; and the same is true of what inspires confidence.

The brave person is unperturbed, as far as a human being can be. Hence, though he will fear even the sorts of things that are not irresistible, he will stand firm against them, in the right way, as reason prescribes, for the sake of the fine, since this is the end aimed at by virtue.

It is possible to be more or less afraid of these frightening things, and also possible to be afraid of
15 what is not frightening as though it were frightening. The cause of error may be fear of the wrong thing, or in the wrong way, or at the wrong time, or something of that sort; and the same is true for things that inspire confidence.

Hence whoever stands firm against the right things and fears the right things, for the right end, in the right way, at the right time, and is correspondingly confident, is the brave person; for the brave person's actions and feelings accord with what something is worth, and follow what reason prescribes.

20 Every activity aims at actions in accord with the state of character. Now to the brave person bravery is fine; hence the end it aims at is also fine, since each thing is defined by its end. The brave person, then, aims at the fine when he stands firm and acts in accord with bravery.

25 Among those who go to excess the excessively fearless person has no name—we said earlier that many cases have no names. He would be some sort of madman, or incapable of feeling distress, if he feared nothing, neither earthquake nor waves, as they say about the Celts.

The person who is excessively confident about
30 frightening things is rash. The rash person also seems to be a boaster, and a pretender to bravery. At any rate, the attitude to frightening things that the brave person really has is the attitude that the rash person wants to appear to have; hence he imitates the brave person where he can. That is why most of them are rash cowards; for, rash though they are on these [occasions for imitation], they do not stand firm against anything frightening. Moreover, rash people
1116a7 are impetuous, wishing for dangers before they arrive,
8, 9 but they shrink from them when they come. Brave people, on the contrary, are eager when in action, but keep quiet until then.

1115b34 The person who is excessively afraid is the coward, since he fears the wrong things, and in the wrong
35 way, and so on. Certainly, he is also deficient in
1116a confidence, but his excessive pain distinguishes him

more clearly. Hence, since he is afraid of everything, he is a despairing sort. The brave person, on the contrary, is hopeful, since [he is confident and] confidence is proper to a hopeful person.

5 Hence the coward, the rash person, and the brave person are all concerned with the same things, but have different states related to them; the others are excessive or defective, but the brave person has the
7 intermediate and right state.

10 As we have said, then, bravery is a mean about what inspires confidence and about what is frightening in the conditions we have described; it chooses and stands firm because that is fine or because anything else is shameful. Dying to avoid poverty or erotic passion or something painful is proper to a coward, not to a brave person. For shirking burdens is softness, and such a person stands firm [in the face of death] 15 to avoid an evil, not because standing firm is fine.

8

Bravery, then, is something of this sort. But five other sorts of things are also called bravery.

The bravery of citizens comes first, since it looks most like bravery. For citizens seem to stand firm against dangers with the aim of avoiding reproaches and legal penalties and of winning honors; that is 20 why the bravest seem to be those who hold cowards in dishonor and do honor to brave people. That is how Homer also describes them when he speaks of Diomede and Hector: 'Polydamas will be the first to heap disgrace on me,' and 'For some time Hector 25 speaking among the Trojans will say, "The son of Tydeus fled from me." ' This is most like the [genuine] bravery described above, because it results from a virtue; for it is caused by shame and by desire for something fine, namely honor, and by aversion from reproach, which is shameful.

In this class we might also place those who are 30 compelled by their superiors. However, they are worse to the extent that they act because of fear, not because of shame, and to avoid pain, not disgrace. For their commanders compel them, as Hector does; 'If I notice 35 anyone shrinking back from the battle, nothing will save him from being eaten by the dogs.' Commanders who strike any troops who give ground, or who post 1116b them in front of ditches and suchlike, do the same thing, since they all compel them. The brave person, however, must be moved by the fine, not by compulsion.

5 Experience about a given situation also seems to be bravery; that is why Socrates actually thought that bravery is scientific knowledge. Different people have this sort [of apparent courage] in different conditions. In wartime professional soldiers have it; for there seem to be many groundless alarms in war, and the professionals are the most familiar with these. Hence they appear brave, since others do not know that the alarms are groundless. Moreover, their experience makes them most capable in attack and defense, since they
10 are skilled in the use of their weapons, and have the best weapons for attack and defense. The result is that in fighting nonprofessionals they are like armed troops against unarmed, or trained athletes against ordinary people; for in these contests also the best fighters are the strongest and physically fittest, not
15 the bravest.

Professional soldiers, however, turn out to be cowards whenever the danger overstrains them and they are inferior in numbers and equipment. For they are the first to run, whereas the citizen troops stand firm and get killed; this was what happened at the temple
20 of Hermes.[6] For the citizens find it shameful to run, and find death more choiceworthy than safety at this cost. But the professionals from the start were facing the danger on the assumption of their superiority; once they learn their mistake, they run, since they are more afraid of being killed than of doing something shameful. That is not the brave person's character.

25 Spirit is also counted as bravery; for those who act on spirit also seem to be brave—as beasts seem to be when they attack those who have wounded them— because brave people are also full of spirit. For spirit is most eager to run and face dangers; hence Homer's words, 'put strength in his spirit,' 'aroused strength
30 and spirit,' and 'his blood boiled'. All these would seem to signify the arousal and the impulse of spirit.

Now brave people act because of the fine, and their spirit cooperates with them. But beasts act because of pain; for they attack only because they have been wounded or frightened, (since they keep away from us in a forest). They are not brave, then, since distress and spirit drives them in an impulsive rush to meet 35 danger, foreseeing none of the terrifying prospects. For if they were brave, hungry asses would also be 1117a brave, since they keep on feeding even if they are beaten; and adulterers also do many daring actions because of lust.

Human beings as well as beasts find it painful to 5 be angered, and pleasant to exact a penalty. But those who fight for these reasons are not brave, though they are good fighters; for they fight because of their feelings, not because of the fine nor as reason prescribes. Still, they have something similar [to bravery]. 4 The [bravery] caused by spirit would seem to be the most natural sort, and to be [genuine] bravery once 5 it has also acquired decision and the goal.

Hopeful people are not brave either; for their many 9, 10 victories over many opponents make them confident in dangers. They are somewhat similar to brave people, since both are confident. But whereas brave people are confident for the reason given earlier, the hopeful are confident because they think they are stronger and nothing could happen to them; drunks do the same sort of thing, since they become hopeful. 15 When things turn out differently from how they expected, they run away. The brave person, on the contrary, stands firm against what is and appears frightening to a human being; he does this because it is fine to stand firm and shameful to fail.

Indeed, that is why someone who is unafraid and unperturbed in emergencies seems braver than [someone who is unafraid only] when he is warned in advance; for his action proceeds more from his 20 state of character, because it proceeds less from preparation. For if we are warned in advance, we might decide what to do [not only because of our state of character, but] also by reason and rational calculation; but in emergencies [we must decide] in accord with our state of character.

Those who act in ignorance also appear brave, and indeed they are close to hopeful people, though inferior to them insofar as they lack the self-esteem of hopeful people. That is why the hopeful stand firm 25 for some time, whereas if ignorant people have been deceived and then realize or suspect that things are different, they run. That was what happened to the

---

6. [When, in 353, mercenary soldiers were engaged to help the citizens in Coronea, they ran away. —M.L.M.]

Argives when they stumbled on the Spartans and took them for Sicyonians.[7]

We have described, then, the character of brave people and of those who seem to be brave.

9

30 Bravery is about feelings of confidence and fear—not, however, about both in the same way, but more about frightening things. For someone is brave if he is undisturbed and in the right state about these, more than if he is in this state about things inspiring confidence.

As we said, then, standing firm against what is painful makes us call people brave; that is why bravery is both painful and justly praised, since it is harder 35 to stand firm against something painful than to refrain 1117b from something pleasant. Nonetheless, the end that bravery aims at seems to be pleasant, though obscured by its surroundings. This is what happens in athletic contests. For boxers find that the end they aim at, 5 the crown and the honors, is pleasant, but, being made of flesh and blood, they find it distressing and painful to take the punches and to bear all the hard work; and because there are so many of these painful things, the end, being small, appears to have nothing pleasant in it.

And so, if the same is true for bravery, the brave person will find death and wounds painful, and suffer them unwillingly, but he will endure them because 10 that is fine or because failure is shameful. Indeed, the truer it is that he has every virtue and the happier he is, the more pain he will feel at the prospect of death. For this sort of person, more than anyone, finds it worthwhile to be alive, and knows he is being deprived of the greatest goods, and this is painful. But he is no less brave for all that; presumably, indeed, 15 he is all the braver, because he chooses what is fine in war at the cost of all these goods. It is not true, then, in the case of every virtue that its active exercise is pleasant; it is pleasant only insofar as we attain the end.

But presumably it is quite possible for brave people, given the character we have described, not to be the

best soldiers. Perhaps the best will be those who are less brave, but possess no other good; for they are ready to face dangers, and they sell their lives for small gains. 20

So much for bravery. It is easy to grasp what it is, in outline at least, from what we have said.

10

Let us discuss temperance next; for bravery and temperance seem to be the virtues of the nonrational parts. Temperance, then, is a mean concerned with 25 pleasures, as we have already said; for it is concerned less, and in a different way, with pains. Intemperance appears in this same area too. Let us, then, now distinguish the specific pleasures that concern them.

First, let us distinguish pleasures of the soul from those of the body. Love of honor and of learning, for instance, are among the pleasures of the soul; for though a lover of one of these enjoys it, only his 30 thought, not his body, is at all affected. Those concerned with such pleasures are called neither temperate nor intemperate. The same applies to those concerned with any of the other nonbodily pleasures; for lovers of tales, storytellers, those who waste their 35 days on trivialities, are called babblers, but not intemperate. Nor do we call people intemperate if they feel 1118a pain over money or friends.

Temperance, then, will be about bodily pleasures, but not even about all of these. For those who find enjoyment in objects of sight, such as colors, shapes, a painting, are called neither temperate nor intemper- 5 ate, even though it would also seem possible to enjoy these either rightly or excessively and deficiently. The same is true for hearing; no one is ever called intemperate for excessive enjoyment of songs or playacting, or temperate for the right enjoyment of them.

Nor is this said about someone enjoying smells, 10 except coincidentally. For someone is called intemperate not for enjoying the smell of apples or roses or incense, but rather for enjoying the smell of perfumes or cooked delicacies. For these are the smells an intemperate person enjoys because they remind him of the objects of his appetite. And we can see that others also enjoy the smells of food if they are 15 hungry. It is the enjoyment of the things [that he is reminded of by these smells] that is proper to an

7. [In 392, during battle in Corinth, Spartan cavalry took up Sicyonian shields and were confused for them. —M.L.M.]

intemperate person, since these are the objects of
his appetite.

Nor do other animals find pleasures from these
senses, except coincidentally. What a hound enjoys,
20 for instance, is not the smell of a hare, but eating it;
but the hare's smell made the hound perceive it. And
what a lion enjoys is not the sound of the ox, but
eating it; but since the ox's sound made the lion
perceive that it was near, the lion appears to enjoy
the sound. Similarly, what pleases him is not the sight
of 'a deer or a wild goat,' but the prospect of food.

25 The pleasures that concern temperance and intemperance are those that are shared with the other
animals, and so appear slavish and bestial. These
pleasures are touch and taste.

However, they seem to deal even with taste very
little or not at all. For taste discriminates flavors—
the sort of thing that wine tasters and cooks savoring
30 food do; but people, or intemperate people at any
rate, do not much enjoy this. Rather, they enjoy the
gratification that comes entirely through touch, in
eating and drinking and in what are called the pleasures of sex. That is why a glutton actually prayed for
his throat to become longer than a crane's, showing
1118b that he took pleasure in the touching. And so the
sense that concerns intemperance is the most widely
shared, and seems justifiably open to reproach, since
we have it insofar as we are animals, not insofar as
we are human beings.

To enjoy these things, then, and to like them most
of all, is bestial. For indeed the most civilized of
5 the pleasures coming through touch, such as those
produced by rubbing and warming in gymnasia, are
excluded from intemperance, since the touching that
is proper to the intemperate person concerns only
some parts of the body, not all of it.

11

Some appetites seem to be shared [by everyone],
while others seem to be additions that are distinctive
10 [of different people]. The appetite for nourishment,
for instance, is natural, since everyone who lacks nourishment, dry or liquid, has an appetite for it, sometimes for both; and, as Homer says, the young in their
prime [all] have an appetite for sex. Not everyone,
however, has an appetite for a specific sort of food or

drink or sex, or for the same things. That is why an
appetite of this type seems to be distinctive of [each
of] us. Still, this also includes a natural element, since
different sorts of people find different sorts of things
more pleasant, and there are some things that are
more pleasant for everyone than things chosen at
random would be.

In natural appetites few people are in error, and 15
only in one direction, toward excess. Eating indiscriminately or drinking until we are too full is exceeding the quantity that accords with nature; for [the
object of] natural appetite is the filling of a lack. That
is why these people are called 'gluttons,' showing that
they glut their bellies past what is right; that is how 20
especially slavish people turn out.

With the pleasures that are distinctive of different
people, many make errors and in many ways; for
people are called lovers of something if they enjoy
the wrong things, or if they enjoy something in the
wrong way. And in all these ways intemperate people 25
go to excess. For some of the things they enjoy are
hateful, and hence wrong; distinctive pleasures that
it is right to enjoy they enjoy more than is right, and
more than most people enjoy them.

Clearly, then, with pleasures excess is intemperance, and is blameworthy. With pains, however, we
are not called temperate, as we are called brave, for
standing firm against them, or intemperate for not 30
standing firm. Rather, someone is intemperate because he feels more pain than is right at failing to
get pleasant things; and even this pain is produced
by the pleasure [he takes in them]. And someone is
temperate because he does not feel pain at the absence of what is pleasant, or at refraining from it.

The intemperate person, then, has an appetite for 1119a
all pleasant things, or rather for the most pleasant of
them, and his appetite leads him to choose these at
the cost of the other things. That is why he also feels
pain both when he fails to get something and when
he has an appetite for it, since appetite involves pain.
It would seem absurd, however, to suffer pain because 5
of pleasure.

People who are deficient in pleasures and enjoy
them less than is right are not found very much. For
that sort of insensibility is not human; indeed, even
the other animals discriminate among foods, enjoying

some but not others. If someone finds nothing pleas-
10 ant, or preferable to anything else, he is far from
being human. The reason he has no name is that he
is not found much.

The temperate person has an intermediate state in
relation to these [bodily pleasures]. For he finds no
pleasure in what most pleases the intemperate person,
but finds it disagreeable; he finds no pleasure at all
in the wrong things. He finds no intense pleasure in
any [bodily pleasures], suffers no pain at their absence,
15 and has no appetite for them, or only a moderate appetite, not to the wrong degree or at the wrong time or
anything else at all of that sort. If something is pleasant
and conducive to health or fitness, he will desire this
moderately and in the right way; and he will desire in
the same way anything else that is pleasant, if it is no
obstacle to health and fitness, does not deviate from the
fine, and does not exceed his means. For the opposite
sort of person likes these pleasures more than they are
20 worth; that is not the temperate person's character, but
he likes them as correct reason prescribes.

12

Intemperance is more like a voluntary condition than
cowardice; for it is caused by pleasure, which is
choiceworthy, whereas cowardice is caused by pain,
which is to be avoided. Moreover, pain disturbs and
ruins the nature of the sufferer, while pleasure does
nothing of the sort; intemperance, then, is more vol-
25 untary. That is why it is also more open to reproach.
For it is also easier to acquire the habit of facing
pleasant things, since our life includes many of them
and we can acquire the habit with no danger; but
with frightening things the reverse is true.

However, cowardice seems to be more voluntary
than particular cowardly actions. For cowardice itself
involves no pain, but the particular actions disturb
30 us because of the pain [that causes them], so that
people actually throw away their weapons and do all
the other disgraceful actions. That is why these actions
even seem to be forced [and hence involuntary].

For the intemperate person the reverse is true. The
particular actions are the result of his appetite and
desire, and so they are voluntary; but the whole condition is less voluntary [than the actions], since no one
has an appetite to be intemperate.

We also apply the name of intemperance to the *1119b*
errors of children, since they have some similarity.
Which gets its name from which does not matter for
our present purposes, but clearly the posterior is called
after the prior.

The name would seem to be quite appropriately
transferred. For the things that need to be tempered
are those that desire shameful things and tend to grow *5*
large. Appetites and children are most like this; for
children also live by appetite, and desire for the pleasant is found more in them than in anyone else.

If, then, [the child or the appetitive part] is not
obedient and subordinate to its rulers, it will go far
astray. For when someone lacks understanding, his
desire for the pleasant is insatiable and seeks indiscriminate satisfaction. The [repeated] active exercise
of appetite increases the appetite he already had from
birth, and if the appetites are large and intense, they *10*
actually expel rational calculation. That is why appetites must be moderate and few, and never contrary
to reason. This is the condition we call obedient and
temperate. And just as the child's life must follow the
instructions of his guide, so too the appetitive part *15*
must follow reason.

Hence the temperate person's appetitive part must
agree with reason; for both [his appetitive part and
his reason] aim at the fine, and the temperate person's
appetites are for the right things, in the right ways,
at the right times, which is just what reason also prescribes.

So much, then, for temperance.

BOOK IV

1

Next let us discuss generosity. It seems, then, to be
the mean about wealth; for the generous person is
praised not in conditions of war, nor in those in
which the temperate person is praised, nor in judicial *25*
verdicts, but in the giving and taking of wealth, and
more especially in the giving. By wealth we mean
anything whose worth is measured by money.

Both wastefulness and ungenerosity are excesses
and deficiencies about wealth. Ungenerosity is always
ascribed to those who take wealth more seriously *30*

than is right. But when wastefulness is attributed to someone, several vices are sometimes combined. For incontinent people and those who spend money on intemperance are called wasteful. Since these have many vices at the same time, they make wasteful people seem the basest.

These people, however, are not properly called wasteful. For the wasteful person is meant to have 1120a the single vicious feature of ruining his property; for someone who causes his own destruction ['lays waste' to himself, and so] is wasteful, and ruining one's own property seems to be a sort of self-destruction, on the assumption that our living depends on our property. This, then, is how we understand wastefulness.

5 Whatever has a use can be used either well or badly; riches are something useful; and the best user of something is the person who has the virtue concerned with it. Hence the best user of riches will be the person who has the virtue concerned with wealth; and this is the generous person.

Using wealth seems to consist in spending and 10 giving, whereas taking and keeping seem to be possessing rather than using. That is why it is more proper to the generous person to give to the right people than to take from the right sources and not from the wrong sources.

For it is more proper to virtue to do good than to receive good, and more proper to do fine actions than not to do shameful ones; and clearly [the right sort of] giving implies doing good and doing fine actions, while 15 [the right sort of] taking implies receiving well or not doing something shameful. Moreover, thanks go to the one who gives, not to the one who fails to take, and praise goes more [to the giver]. Besides, not taking is easier than giving, since people part with what is their own less readily than they avoid taking what is anoth- 20 er's. Further, those who are called generous are those who give [rightly]. Those who avoid taking [wrongly] are not praised for generosity, though they are praised nonetheless for justice, while those who take [rightly] are not much praised at all. Besides, generous people are loved more than practically any others who are loved because of their virtue; that is because they are beneficial; and they are beneficial in their giving.

Actions in accord with virtue are fine, and aim at the fine. Hence the generous person will also aim at the fine in his giving, and will give correctly; for he 25 will give to the right people, the right amounts, at the right time, and all the other things that are implied by correct giving. Moreover, he will do this with pleasure, or at any rate without pain; for action in accord with virtue is pleasant or at any rate painless, and least of all is it painful.

If someone gives to the wrong people, or does not aim at the fine, but gives for some other reason, he will not be called generous, but some other sort of person. Nor will he be called generous if he finds it 30 painful to give; for such a person would choose wealth over fine action, and that is not how the generous person chooses.

Nor will the virtuous person take wealth from the wrong sources; since he does not honor wealth, this way of taking it is not for him. Nor will he be ready to ask for favors; since he is the one who benefits others, receiving benefits readily is not for him.

He will, however, acquire wealth from the right 1120b sources—from his own possessions, for instance— regarding taking not as fine, but as necessary to provide something to give. Nor will he neglect his own possessions, since he wants to use them to assist people. And he will avoid giving to just anyone, so that he will have something to give to the right people, at the right time, and where it is fine.

It is also very definitely proper to the generous 5 person to exceed so much in giving that he leaves less for himself, since it is proper to a generous person not to look out for himself. However, ['exceed' must be explained;] in speaking of generosity we refer to what accords with one's means. For what is generous does not depend on the quantity of what is given, but on the state [of character] of the giver, and the generous state gives in accord with one's means. Hence one who gives less than another may still be more generous, if he has less to give. 10

Those who have not acquired their means by their own efforts, but have inherited it, seem to be more generous; for they have had no experience of shortage, and, besides, everyone likes his own work more than [other people's], as parents and poets do.

It is not easy for a generous person to grow rich, 15 since he is ready to spend, not to take or keep, and honors wealth for the sake of giving, not for itself. Indeed, that is why fortune is denounced, because those who most deserve to grow rich actually do so least. This is only to be expected, however, since someone cannot possess wealth, any more than other things, if he pays no attention to possessing it.

20 Still, he does not give to the wrong people, at the wrong time, and so on. For if he did, he would no longer be acting in accord with generosity, and if he spent his resources on the wrong sort of giving, he would have nothing left to spend for the right purposes. For, as we have said, the generous person is the one who spends in accord with his means, and for the right purposes, whereas the one who exceeds his means is wasteful. That is why tyrants are not called wasteful, since it seems they will have difficulty
25 exceeding their possessions in giving and spending.

Since generosity, then, is a mean concerned with the giving and the taking of wealth, the generous person will both give and spend the right amounts
30 for the right purposes, in small and large matters alike, and do this with pleasure. He will also take the right amounts from the right sources. For since the virtue is a mean about both giving and taking, he will do both in the right way; for decent giving implies decent taking, and the other sort of taking is contrary to the decent sort. Hence the states that imply each other are present at the same time in the same subject,
1121a whereas the contrary states clearly are not.

If the generous person finds that his spending deviates from what is fine and right, he will feel pain, but moderately and in the right way; for it is proper to virtue to feel both pleasure and pain in the right things and in the right way.

The generous person is also an easy partner to have
5 common dealings with matters of money; for he can easily be treated unjustly, since he does not honor money, and is more grieved if he has failed to spend what it was right to spend than if he has spent what it was wrong to spend—here he does not please Simonides.

The wasteful person is in error here too, since he feels neither pleasure nor pain at the right things or in the right way; this will be more evident as we go on.

10 We have said, then, that wastefulness and ungenerosity are excesses and deficiencies in two things, in giving and taking—for we also count spending as giving. Now wastefulness is excessive in giving and
15 not taking, but deficient in taking. Ungenerosity is

deficient in giving and excessive in taking, but in small matters.

Now the different aspects of wastefulness are not very often combined; for it is not easy to take from nowhere and give to everyone, since private citizens soon outrun their resources in giving, and private citizens are the ones who seem to be wasteful. However, such a person seems to be quite a lot better than the ungenerous person, since he is easily cured, 20 both by growing older and by poverty, and is capable of reaching the intermediate condition. For he has the features proper to the generous person, since he gives and does not take, though he does neither rightly or well. If, then, he is changed, by habituation or some other means, so that he does them rightly and well, he will be generous; for then he will give to the right people and will not take from the wrong sources. 25 This is why the wasteful person seems not to be base in his character; for excess in giving without taking is proper to a foolish person, not to a vicious or ignoble one. Someone who is wasteful in this way seems to be much better than the ungenerous person, both for the reasons just given and because he benefits many, whereas the ungenerous person benefits no one, not even himself.

Most wasteful people, however, as we have said, 30 [not only give wrongly, but] also take from the wrong sources, and to this extent are ungenerous. They become acquisitive because they wish to spend, but cannot do this readily, since they soon exhaust all they have; hence they are compelled to provide from elsewhere. At the same time they care nothing for 1121b the fine, and so take from any source without scruple; for they have an urge to give, and the way or source does not matter to them.

This is why their ways of giving are not generous either, since they are not fine, do not aim at the fine, 5 and are not done in the right way. Rather, these people sometimes enrich people who ought to be poor, and would give nothing to people with sound characters, but would give much to flatterers or to those providing some other pleasure. That is why most of these people are also intemperate. For since they part with money readily, they also spend it lavishly on intemperance; and because their lives do not 10 aim at the fine, they decline toward pleasures.

If, then, the wasteful person has been left without

a guide, he changes into this; but if he receives attention, he might reach the intermediate and the right
state.

Ungenerosity, however, is incurable, since old age
and every incapacity seem to make people ungenerous. And it comes more naturally to human beings
15 than wastefulness; for the many are money-lovers
rather than givers. Moreover, it extends widely and
has many species, since there seem to be many ways
of being ungenerous. For it consists in two conditions,
deficiency in giving and excess in taking; but it is not
found as a whole in all cases. Sometimes the two
20 conditions are separated, and some people go to excess in taking, whereas others are deficient in giving.

For the people called misers, tightfisted, skinflints
and so on, are all deficient in giving, but they do not
go after other people's goods and do not wish to take
them. With some people the reason for this is some
sort of decency in them, and a concern to avoid what
is shameful. For some people seem—at least, this is
25 what they say—to hold on to their money so that they
will never be compelled to do anything shameful.
These include the cheeseparer, and everyone like
that; he is so called from his excessive refusal to give
anything. Others keep their hands off other people's
30 property because they are afraid, supposing that it is
not easy for them to take other people's property
without other people taking theirs too; hence, they
say, they are content if they neither take from others
nor give to them.

Other people, by contrast, go to excess in taking, by
taking anything from any source—those, for instance,
who work at degrading occupations, pimps and all
1122a such people, and usurers who lend small amounts at
high interest; for all of these take the wrong amounts
from the wrong sources.

Shameful love of gain is apparently their common
feature, since they all put up with reproaches for some
gain—more precisely, for a small gain. For those who
5 take the wrong things from the wrong sources on a
large scale—such as tyrants who sack cities and plunder temples—are called wicked, impious, and unjust,
but not ungenerous. The ungenerous, however, include the gambler and the robber, since these are
shameful lovers of gain. For in pursuit of gain both
go to great efforts and put up with reproaches; the
10 robber faces the greatest dangers to get his haul, while

the gambler takes his gains from his friends, the very
people he ought to be giving to. Both of them, then,
are shameful lovers of gain, because they wish to
acquire gains from the wrong sources; and all these
methods of acquisition are ungenerous.

It is plausibly said that ungenerosity is contrary to 15
generosity. For it is a greater evil than wastefulness;
and error in this direction is more common than the
error of wastefulness, as we have described it. So
much, then, for generosity and the vices opposed to it.

2

Next, it seems appropriate to discuss magnificence
also. For it seems to be, like generosity, a virtue concerned with wealth, but it does not extend, as generos- 20
ity does, to all the actions involving wealth, but only
to those involving heavy expenses, and in them it
exceeds generosity in its large scale. For, just as the
name [*megaloprepeia*] itself suggests, magnificence is
expenditure that is fitting [*prepousa*] in its large scale
[*megethos*]. But large scale is large relative to something; for the expenses of the captain of a warship
and of the leader of a delegation are not the same. 25
Hence what is fitting is also relative to oneself, the
circumstances, and the purpose.

Someone is called magnificent only if he spends
the worthy amount on a large purpose, not on a trivial
or an ordinary purpose like the one who 'gave to
many a wanderer'; for the magnificent person is generous, but generosity does not imply magnificence.

The deficiency falling short of this state is called 30
stinginess. The excess is called vulgarity, poor taste,
and such things. These are excesses not because they
spend an excessively great amount on the right things,
but because they show off in the wrong circumstances
and in the wrong way. We shall discuss these vices
later.

The magnificent person, in contrast to these, is
like a scientific expert, since he is able to observe
what will be the fitting amount, and to spend large 35
amounts in an appropriate way. For, as we said at the 1122b
start, a state is defined by its activities and its objects;
now the magnificent person's expenditures are large
and fitting; so also, then, must the results be, since
that is what makes the expense large and fitting to
the result. Hence the result must be worthy of the 5

expense, and the expense worthy of, or even in excess of, the result.

In this sort of spending the magnificent person will aim at the fine; for that is a common feature of the virtues. Moreover, he will spend gladly and readily, since it is stingy to count every penny. He will think more about the finest and most fitting way to spend 10 than about the cost or about the cheapest way to do it.

Hence the magnificent person must also be generous; for the generous person will also spend what is right in the right way. But it is in this spending that the large scale of the magnificent person, his greatness, is found, since his magnificence is a sort of large scale of generosity in these things; and from an expense that is equal [to a nonmagnificent person's] he will 15 make the result more magnificent. For a possession and a result have different sorts of excellence; the most honored [and hence most excellent] possession is the one worth most—for example, gold—but the most honored result is the one that is great and fine, since that is what is admirable to behold. Now what is magnificent is admirable, and the excellence of the result consists in its large scale.

20   This sort of excellence is found in the sorts of expenses called honorable, such as expenses for the gods—dedications, temples, sacrifices, and so on, for everything divine—and in expenses that provoke a good competition for honor, for the common good, if, for instance, some city thinks a splendid chorus or warship or a feast for the city must be provided.

25   But in all cases, as we have said, we fix the right amount by reference to the agent [as well as the task]—by who he is and what resources he has; for the amounts must be worthy of these, fitting the producer as well as the result.

That is why a poor person could not be magnificent; he lacks the means for large and fitting expenditures. If he tries to be magnificent, he is foolish; for he spends more than what is worthy and right for him, whereas correct spending accords with virtue. 30 Large spending befits those who have the means, acquired through their own efforts or their ancestors or connections, or are well born or reputable, and so on; for each of these conditions includes greatness and reputation for worth.

This, then, above all is the character of the mag-

nificent person, and magnificence is found in these sorts of expenses, as we have said, since these are the 35 largest and most honored.

It is found also in those private expenses that arise 1123a only once, such as a wedding and the like, and in those that concern the whole city, or the people in it with a reputation for worth—the receiving of foreign guests and sending them off, gifts and exchanges of gifts. For the magnificent person spends money on the common good, not on himself, and the gifts have 5 some similarity to dedications.

It is also proper to the magnificent person to build a house befitting his riches, since this is also a suitable adornment. He spends more readily on long-lasting results, since these are the finest. In each case he spends on what is fitting. For what suits gods does 10 not suit human beings, and what suits a temple does not suit a tomb.

And since each great expense is great in relation to a particular kind of object, the most magnificent will be a great expense on a great object, and the [magnificent] in a particular area will be what is great in relation to the particular kind of object. Moreover, greatness in the results is not the same as greatness in an expense, since the finest ball or oil bottle has the magnificence 15 proper to a gift for a child, but its value is small and paltry. That is why it is proper to the magnificent person, whatever kind of thing he produces, to produce it magnificently, since this is not easily exceeded, and to produce something worthy of the expense.

This, then, is the character of the magnificent person.

The vulgar person who exceeds [the mean] exceeds 20 by spending more than is right, as has been said. For in small expenses he spends a lot, and puts on an inappropriate display. He gives his club a dinner party in the style of a wedding banquet, and when he supplies a chorus for a comedy, he brings them onstage dressed in purple, as they do at Megara. In all this he aims not 25 at the fine, but at the display of his wealth and at the admiration he thinks he wins in this way. Where a large expense is right, he spends a little, and he spends a lot where a small expense is right.

The stingy person will be deficient in everything. After spending the largest amounts, he will refuse a small amount, and so destroy a fine result. Whatever

30 he does, while he is doing it he will hesitate and consider how he can spend the smallest possible amount; he will even moan about spending this, and will always think he is doing something on a larger scale than is right.

These states, vulgarity and stinginess, are vices. But they do not bring reproaches, since they do no harm to one's neighbors and are not too disgraceful.

3

35 Magnanimity seems, even if we go simply by the name, to be concerned with great things. Let us see 1123b first the sorts of things it is concerned with. It does not matter whether we consider the state itself or the person who acts in accord with it.

The magnanimous person, then, seems to be the one who thinks himself worthy of great things and is really worthy of them. For if someone is not worthy of them but thinks he is, he is foolish, and no virtuous person is foolish or senseless; hence the magnanimous 5 person is the one we have mentioned. For if someone is worthy of little and thinks so, he is temperate, but not magnanimous; for magnanimity is found in greatness, just as beauty is found in a large body, and small people can be attractive and well proportioned, but not beautiful.

Someone who thinks he is worthy of great things, but is not worthy of them, is vain; but not everyone who thinks he is worthy of greater things than he is worthy of is vain.

10 Someone who thinks he is worthy of less than he is worthy of is pusillanimous, whether he is worthy of great or of moderate things, or of little and thinks himself worthy of still less. The one who seems most pusillanimous is the one who is worthy of great things; for consider how little he would think of himself if he were worthy of less.

The magnanimous person, then, is at the extreme insofar as he makes great claims. But insofar as he makes them rightly, he is intermediate; for what he 15 thinks he is worthy of accords with his real worth, whereas the others are excessive or deficient. The pusillanimous person is deficient both in relation to himself [i.e., his worth] and in relation to the 20 magnanimous person's estimate of his own worth.

The vain person makes claims that are excessive for himself, but not for the magnanimous person.

If, then, he thinks he is worthy of great things, and is worthy of them, especially of the greatest things, he has one concern above all. Worth is said to [make one worthy of] external goods; and we would suppose that the greatest of these is the one we award to the gods, the one above all that is the aim of people with a reputation for worth, the prize for the finest [achievements]. All this is true of honor, since it is the 25 greatest of external goods. Hence the magnanimous person has the right concern with honors and dishonors. And even without argument it appears that magnanimous people are concerned with honor; for the great think themselves worthy of honor most of all, but in accord with their worth.

Since the magnanimous person is worthy of the greatest things, he is the best person. For in every case the better person is worthy of something greater, and the best person is worthy of the greatest things; and hence the truly magnanimous person must be good.

Greatness in each virtue also seems proper to the 30 magnanimous person. Surely it would not at all fit a magnanimous person to run away [from danger when a coward would], swinging his arms [to get away faster], or to do injustice. For what goal will make him do shameful actions, given that none [of their goals] is great to him? And if we examine particular cases, we can see that the magnanimous person appears altogether ridiculous if he is not good. Nor would he be worthy of honor if he were base; for honor 35 is the prize of virtue, and is awarded to good people.

Magnanimity, then, would seem to be a sort of 1124a adornment of the virtues; for it makes them greater, and it does not arise without them. That is why it is difficult to be truly magnanimous, since it is not possible without being fine and good.

The magnanimous person, then, is concerned especially with honors and dishonors. When he receives 5 great honors from excellent people, he will be moderately pleased, thinking he is getting what is proper to him, or even less. For there can be no honor worthy of complete virtue; but still he will accept honors [from excellent people], since they have nothing greater to award him. But if he is honored by just 10 anyone, or for something small, he will altogether disdain it; for that is not what he is worthy of. And similarly he will disdain dishonor; for it will not be justly attached to him.

As we have said, then, the magnanimous person is concerned especially with honors. Still, he will also have a moderate attitude to riches and power and
15 every sort of good and bad fortune, however it turns out. He will be neither excessively pleased by good fortune nor excessively distressed by ill fortune, since he does not even regard honor as the greatest good. For positions of power and riches are choiceworthy for their honor; at any rate their possessors wish to be honored on account of them. Hence the magnanimous person, given that he counts honor for little,
20 will also count these other goods for little; that is why he seems arrogant.

The results of good fortune, however, also seem to contribute to magnanimity. For the wellborn and the powerful or rich are thought worthy of honor, since they are in a superior position, and everything superior in some good is more honored. That is why these things also make people more magnanimous, since some people honor their possessors for these
25 goods. In reality, however, it is only the good person who is honorable. Still, anyone who has both virtue and these goods is more readily thought worthy of honor.

Those who lack virtue but have these other goods are not justified in thinking themselves worthy of great things, and are not correctly called magnanimous; that is impossible without complete virtue.
30 They become arrogant and wantonly aggressive when they have these other goods. For without virtue it is hard to bear the results of good fortune suitably, and
1124b when these people cannot do it, but suppose they are superior to other people, they think less of everyone else, and do whatever they please. They do this because they are imitating the magnanimous person though they are not really like him. They imitate him where they can; hence they do not act in accord with
5 virtue, but they think less of other people. For the magnanimous person is justified when he thinks less of others, since his beliefs are true; but the many think less of others with no good reason.

He does not face dangers in a small cause; he does not face them frequently, since he honors few things; and he is no lover of danger. But he faces dangers

in a great cause, and whenever he faces them he is unsparing of his life, since he does not think life at all costs is worth living.

He is the sort of person who does good but is 10 ashamed when he receives it; for doing good is proper to the superior person, but receiving it is proper to the inferior. He returns more good than he has received; for in this way the original giver will be repaid, and will also have incurred a new debt to him, and will be the beneficiary.

Magnanimous people seem to remember the good they do, but not what they receive, since the recipient is inferior to the giver, and the magnanimous person wishes to be superior. And they seem to find pleasure 15 in hearing of the good they do, and none in hearing of what they receive—that also seems to be why Thetis[8] does not tell Zeus of the good she has done him, and the Spartans do not tell of the good they have done the Athenians, but only of the good received from them.

Again, it is proper to the magnanimous person to ask for nothing, or hardly anything, but to help eagerly.

When he meets people with good fortune or a 20 reputation for worth, he displays his greatness, since superiority over them is difficult and impressive, and there is nothing ignoble in trying to be impressive with them. But when he meets ordinary people he is moderate, since superiority over them is easy, and an attempt to be impressive among inferiors is as vulgar as a display of strength against the weak.

He stays away from what is commonly honored, and from areas where others lead; he is inactive and a delayer, except for some great honor or achieve- 25 ment. His actions are few, but great and renowned.

Moreover, he must be open in his hatreds and his friendships, since concealment is proper to a frightened person. He is concerned for the truth more than for people's opinion. He is open in his speech and actions, since his thinking less of other people makes him 30 speak freely. And he speaks the truth, except [when he speaks less than the truth] to the many, [because he is moderate], not because he is self-deprecating.

8. [Thetis, Zeus' daughter, does not remind him that she intervened when the other gods wanted to put him in chains.—M.L.M.]

1125a He cannot let anyone else, except a friend, determine his life. For that would be slavish; and this is why all flatterers are servile and inferior people are flatterers.

He is not prone to marvel, since he finds nothing great, or to remember evils, since it is proper to a magnanimous person not to nurse memories, espe-
5 cially not of evils, but to overlook them.

He is no gossip. For he will not talk about himself or about another, since he is not concerned to have himself praised or other people blamed. Nor is he given to praising people. Hence he does not speak evil even of his enemies, except [when he responds to their] wanton aggression.

10 He especially avoids laments or entreaties about necessities or small matters, since these attitudes are proper to someone who takes these things seriously.

He is the sort of person whose possessions are fine and unproductive rather than productive and advantageous, since that is more proper to a self-sufficient person.

The magnanimous person seems to have slow movements, a deep voice, and calm speech. For since he takes few things seriously, he is in no hurry, and
15 since he counts nothing great, he is not strident; and these [attitudes he avoids] are the causes of a shrill voice and hasty movements.

This, then, is the character of the magnanimous person. The deficient person is pusillanimous, and the person who goes to excess is vain. [Like the vulgar and the stingy person] these also seem not to be evil people, since they are not evildoers, but to be in error.

20 For the pusillanimous person is worthy of goods, but deprives himself of the goods he is worthy of, and would seem to have something bad in him because he does not think he is worthy of the goods. Indeed he would seem not to know himself; for if he did, he would aim at the things he is worthy of, since they are goods. For all that, such people seem hesitant rather than foolish. But this belief of theirs actually seems to make them worse. For each sort of person
25 seeks what [he thinks] he is worth; and these people hold back from fine actions and practices, and equally from external goods, because they think they are unworthy of them.

Vain people, by contrast, are foolish and do not know themselves, and they make this obvious. For

they undertake commonly honored exploits, but are not worthy of them, and then they are found out. 30 They adorn themselves with clothes and ostentatious style and that sort of thing; and since they want everyone to know how fortunate they are, they talk about it, thinking it will bring them honor.

Pusillanimity is more opposed than vanity to magnanimity; for it arises more often, and is worse.

Magnanimity, then, as has been said, is the virtue 35 concerned with honor, and [specifically] with great honor.

4

But, as we said in the first discussion, [just as there 1125b is a virtue for small-scale giving], there would also seem to be a virtue concerned with honor that seems to be related to magnanimity in the way that generosity is related to magnificence. For it abstains, just as generosity does, from anything great, but forms the right attitude in us on medium and small matters. 5

Just as the taking and giving of money admits of a mean, an excess and a deficiency, so also we can desire honor more or less than is right, and we can desire it from the right sources and in the right way. 10 For we blame the honor-lover for aiming at honor more than is right, and from the wrong sources; and we blame someone indifferent to honor for deciding not to be honored even for fine things. Sometimes, however, we praise the honor-lover for being manly and a lover of the fine; and again we praise the indifferent person for being moderate and temperate, as we said in the first discussion.

Clearly, since we speak in several ways of loving something, what we refer to as love of honor is not 15 the same attitude in every case. When we praise it, we refer to loving honor more than the many do. When we blame it, we refer to loving honor more than is right. Since the mean has no name, the extremes look like the only contestants, as though they had the field to themselves. Still, if there is excess and deficiency, there is also an intermediate condition.

Since people desire honor both more and less than 20 is right, it is also possible to desire it in the right way. This state, therefore, a nameless mean concerned with honor, is praised. In relation to love of honor, it appears as indifference to honor; in relation to

indifference, it appears as love of honor; in relation to both, it appears in a way as both. The same would
25 seem to be true of the other virtues too; but in this particular case the extreme people appear to be opposed [only to each other] because the intermediate person has no name.

5

Mildness is the mean concerned with anger. Since the mean is nameless, and the extremes are practically nameless too, we call the intermediate condition mildness, inclining toward the deficiency, which is
30 also nameless. The excess might be called a kind of irascibility; for the relevant feeling is anger, though its sources are many and varied.

The person who is angry at the right things and toward the right people, and also in the right way, at the right time, and for the right length of time, is praised. This, then, will be the mild person, if mildness is praised. For [if mildness is something to be praised,] being a mild person means being undis-
35 turbed, not led by feeling, but irritated wherever rea-
1126a son prescribes, and for the length of time it prescribes. And he seems to err more in the direction of deficiency, since the mild person is ready to pardon, not eager to exact a penalty.

5   The deficiency—a sort of inirascibility or whatever it is—is blamed. For people who are not angered by the right things, or in the right way, or at the right times, or toward the right people, all seem to be foolish. For such a person seems to be insensible and to feel no pain, and since he is not angered, he does not seem to be the sort to defend himself. Such willingness to accept insults to oneself and to overlook insults to one's family and friends is slavish.

10   The excess arises in all these ways—in anger toward the wrong people, at the wrong times, more than is right, more hastily than is right, and for a longer time—but they are not all found in the same person. For they could not all exist together; for evil destroys itself as well as other things, and if it is present as a whole it becomes unbearable.

Irascible people get angry quickly, toward the wrong people, at the wrong times, and more than is
15 right; but they stop soon, and this is their best feature. They do all this because they do not contain their

anger, but their quick temper makes them pay back the offense without concealment, and then they stop.

Choleric people are quick-tempered to extreme, and irascible about everything and at everything; that is how they get their name.

Bitter people are hard to reconcile, and stay angry 20 for a long time, since they contain their [angry] spirit. It stops when they pay back the offense; for the exaction of the penalty produces pleasure in place of pain, and so puts a stop to the anger. But if this does not happen, they hold their grudge. For no one else persuades them to get over it, since it is not obvious; 25 and digesting anger in oneself takes time. This sort of person is most troublesome to himself and to his closest friends.

The people we call irritable are those who are irritated by the wrong things, more severely and for longer than is right, and are not reconciled until [the offender has suffered] a penalty and corrective treatment.

We regard the excess as more opposed than the 30 deficiency to mildness. For it is more widespread, since it comes more naturally to human beings to exact a penalty from the offender [than to overlook an offense]; and, moreover, irritable people are harder to live with.

These remarks also make clear a previous point of ours. For it is hard to define how, against whom, about what, and how long we should be angry, and up to what point someone is acting correctly or in 35 error. For someone who deviates a little toward either excess or deficiency is not blamed; for sometimes we praise deficient people and say they are mild, but 1126b sometimes we say that people who get irritated are manly because we think they are capable of ruling others. How far, then, and in what way must someone deviate to be open to blame? It is not easy to answer in a [general] account; for the judgment depends on particular cases, and [we make it] by perception.

However, this much at least is clear: The intermedi- 5 ate state is praiseworthy, and in accord with it we are angry toward the right people, about the right things, in the right way, and so on. The excesses and deficiencies are blameworthy, lightly if they go a little way, more if they go further, and strongly if they go far. Clearly, then, we must keep to the intermediate state. So much, then, for the states concerned with anger. 10

6

In meeting people, living together, and common dealings in conversations and actions, some people seem to be ingratiating; these are the ones who praise everything to please us and never cross us, but think they
15 must cause no pain to those they meet. In contrast to these, people who oppose us on every point and do not care in the least about causing pain are called cantankerous and quarrelsome.

Clearly, the states we have mentioned are blameworthy, and the state intermediate between them is praiseworthy; in accord with it one accepts or objects
20 to things when it is right and in the right way. This state has no name, but it would seem to be most like friendship; for the character of the person in the intermediate state is just what we mean in speaking of a decent friend, except that the friend is also fond of us.

It differs from friendship in not requiring any special feeling or any fondness for the people we meet. For this person takes each thing in the right way because that is his character, not because he is a
25 friend or an enemy. For he will behave this way to new and old acquaintances, to familiar companions and strangers without distinction, except that he will also do what is suitable for each; for the proper ways to spare or to hurt the feelings of familiar companions are not the proper ways to treat strangers.

We have said, then, that in general he will treat people in the right way when he meets them. [More exactly], he will aim to avoid causing pain or to share pleasure, but will always refer to the fine and the
30 beneficial. For he would seem to be concerned with the pleasures and pains that arise in meeting people; and if it is not fine, or it is harmful, for him to share one of these pleasures, he will object and will decide to cause pain instead. Further, if the other person will suffer no slight disgrace or harm from doing an action, and only slight pain if he is crossed, the virtuous person will object to the action and not accept it.
35 When he meets people with a reputation for worth, his attitude will be different from his attitude to just
1127a anyone; he will take different attitudes to those he knows better and those he knows less well; and similarly with the other differences, according what is suitable to each sort of person. What he will choose

in itself is to share pleasure and avoid causing pain. But he will be guided by consequences, if they are 5 greater—that is to say, by the fine and the expedient; and to secure great pleasure in the future he will cause slight pain.

This, then, is the character of the intermediate person, though he has no name.

Among those who share pleasure the person who aims to be pleasant with no ulterior purpose is ingratiating; the one who does it for some advantage in money and what money can buy is the flatterer. The 10 one who objects to everything is, as we have said, the cantankerous and quarrelsome person. However, the extremes appear to be opposite [only] to each other, because the intermediate condition has no name.

7

The mean that corresponds to boastfulness is also concerned with practically these same [conditions of social life]; and it too is nameless. It is a good idea 15 to examine the nameless virtues as well as the others. For if we discuss particular aspects of character one at a time, we will acquire a better knowledge of them; and if we survey the virtues and see that in each case the virtue is a mean, we will have more confidence in our belief that the virtues are means. As concerns social life, then, having discussed those who aim at giving pleasure or pain when they meet people, let us now discuss those who are truthful and false, both 20 in words and in actions—that is to say, in their claims [about themselves].

The boaster seems to claim qualities that win reputation, though he either lacks them altogether or has less than he claims. The self-deprecator, by contrast, seems to disavow or to belittle his actual qualities. The intermediate person is straightforward, and therefore truthful in what he says and does, acknowledging the qualities he has without exaggerating or belittling. 25

Each of these things may be done with or without an ulterior purpose; and someone's character determines what he says and does and the way he lives, if he is not acting for an ulterior purpose. Now in itself [when no ulterior purpose is involved], falsehood is base and blameworthy, and truth is fine and praiseworthy; in this way the truthful person, like other

30 intermediate people, is praiseworthy, and both the tellers of falsehoods are blameworthy, the boaster to a higher degree. Let us discuss each type of blameworthy person; but first let us discuss the truthful person.

For we do not mean someone who is truthful in 1127b agreements in matters of justice and injustice, since these concern a different virtue, but someone who is truthful both in what he says and in how he lives, when nothing about justice is at stake, simply because that is his state of character. Someone with this character seems to be a decent person. For a lover of the 5 truth who is truthful even when nothing is at stake will be still keener to tell the truth when something is at stake, since he will avoid falsehood as shameful [when something is at stake], having already avoided it in itself [when nothing was at stake]. This sort of person is praiseworthy. He inclines to tell less, rather than more, than the truth; for this appears more suitable, since excesses are oppressive.

10 If someone claims to have more than he has, with no ulterior purpose, he certainly looks as though he is a base person, since otherwise he would not enjoy telling falsehoods; but apparently he is pointlessly foolish rather than bad. Among those who do it with an ulterior purpose, the one who does it for the reputation or honor is not to be blamed too much as a boaster. But the one who does it for money or for means to making money is more disgraceful.

15 It is not a person's capacity, but his decision, that makes him a boaster; for his state of character makes a person a boaster, just as it makes a person a liar. And [boasters differ in their states of character]; one is a boaster because he enjoys telling falsehoods in itself, another because he pursues reputation or gain.

Boasters who aim at reputation, then, claim the qualities that win praise or win congratulation for happiness. Boasters who aim at profit claim the quali-
20 ties that gratify other people and that allow someone to avoid detection when he claims to be what he is not—a wise diviner or doctor, for instance. That is why most [boasters] claim these sorts of things and boast about them; for they have the features just mentioned.

Self-deprecators underestimate themselves in what they say, and so appear to have more cultivated characters. For they seem to be avoiding bombast, not
25 looking for profit, in what they say. The qualities

that win reputation are the ones that these people especially disavow, as Socrates also used to do.

Those who disavow small qualities that they obviously have are called humbugs, and people more readily think less of them. Sometimes, indeed, this even appears a form of boastfulness, as the Spartans' [austere] dress does; for the extreme deficiency, as 30 well as the excess, is boastful. But those who are moderate in their self-deprecation and confine themselves to qualities that are not too commonplace or obvious appear sophisticated.

It is the boaster [rather than the self-deprecator] who appears to be opposite to the truthful person, since he is the worse [of the two extremes].

8

Since life also includes relaxation, and in this we pass 1128a our time with some form of amusement, here also it seems possible to behave appropriately in meeting people, and to say and listen to the right things and in the right way. The company we are in when we speak or listen also makes a difference. And, clearly, in this case also it is possible to exceed the intermediate condition or to be deficient.

Those who go to excess in raising laughs seem to 5 be vulgar buffoons. They stop at nothing to raise a laugh, and care more about that than about saying what is seemly and avoiding pain to the victims of the joke. Those who would never say anything themselves to raise a laugh, and even object when other people do it, seem to be boorish and stiff. Those who joke in appropriate ways are called witty, or, in other 10 words, agile-witted. For these sorts of jokes seem to be movements of someone's character, and characters are judged, as bodies are, by their movements.

Since there are always opportunities at hand for raising a laugh, and most people enjoy amusements and jokes more than they should, buffoons are also called witty because they are thought cultivated; 15 nonetheless, they differ, and differ considerably, from witty people, as our account has made clear.

Dexterity is also proper to the intermediate state. It is proper to the dexterous person to say and listen to what suits the decent and civilized person. For some things are suitable for this sort of person to say 20 and listen to by way of amusement; and the civilized person's amusement differs from the slavish person's. This can also be seen from old and new comedies; for what people used to find funny was shameful 25 abuse, but what they now find funny instead is innuendo, which is considerably more seemly.

Then should the person who jokes well be defined by his making remarks not unsuitable for a civilized person, or by his avoiding pain and even giving pleasure to the hearer? Perhaps, though, this [avoiding pain and giving pleasure] is indefinable, since different people find different things hateful or pleasant. The remarks he is willing to hear made are of the same sort, since those he is prepared to hear made seem to be those he is prepared to make himself.

30 Hence he will not be indiscriminate in his remarks. For since a joke is a type of abuse, and legislators prohibit some types of abuse, they would presumably be right to prohibit some types of jokes too. Hence the cultivated and civilized person, as a sort of law to himself, will take this [discriminating] attitude. This, then, is the character of the intermediate person, whether he is called dexterous or witty.

35 The buffoon cannot resist raising a laugh, and spares neither himself nor anyone else if he can cause laughter, even by making remarks that the sophisti-1128b cated person would never make, and some that the sophisticated person would not even be willing to hear made.

The boor is useless when he meets people in these circumstances. For he contributes nothing himself, and objects to everything; but relaxation and amusement seem to be necessary in life.

5 We have spoken, then, of three means in life, all concerned with common dealings in certain conversations and actions. They differ insofar as one is concerned with truth, the others with what is pleasant. One of those concerned with pleasure is found in amusements, and the other in our behavior in the other aspects of life when we meet people.

9

10 It is not appropriate to treat shame as a virtue; for it would seem to be more like a feeling than like a state [of character]. It is defined, at any rate, as a sort of fear of disrepute. Its expression is similar to that of fear of something terrifying; for a feeling of disgrace

makes people blush, and fear of death makes them 15 turn pale. Hence both [types of fear] appear to be in some way bodily [reactions], which seem to be more characteristic of feelings than of states.

Further, the feeling of shame is suitable for youth, not for every time of life. For we think it right for young people to be prone to shame, since they live by their feelings, and hence often go astray, but are restrained by shame; and hence we praise young peo-20 ple who are prone to shame. No one, by contrast, would praise an older person for readiness to feel disgrace, since we think it wrong for him to do any action that causes a feeling of disgrace.

For a feeling of disgrace is not proper to the decent person either, if it is caused by base actions; for these should not be done. If some actions are really disgraceful and others are base [only] in [his] belief, that does not matter, since neither should be done, and so he 25 should not feel disgrace. On the contrary; being the sort of person who does any disgraceful action is proper to a vicious person.

If someone's state [of character] would make him feel disgrace if he were to do a disgraceful action, and because of this he thinks he is decent, that is absurd. For shame is concerned with what is voluntary, and the decent person will never willingly do base actions.

Shame might, however, be decent on an assump-30 tion; if one were to do [disgraceful actions], one would feel disgrace; but this does not apply to the virtues. If we grant that it is base to feel no disgrace or shame at disgraceful actions, it still does not follow that to do such actions and then to feel disgrace at them is decent.

Continence is not a virtue either. It is a sort of 35 mixed state. We will explain about it in what we say later. Now let us discuss justice.

BOOK V

1

The questions we must examine about justice and in-1129a justice are these: What sorts of actions are they concerned with? What sort of mean is justice? What are 5 the extremes between which justice is intermediate? Let us investigate them by the same line of inquiry as we used in the topics discussed before.

We see that the state everyone means in speaking of justice is the state that makes us just agents — [that is to say], the state that makes us do justice and wish
10 what is just. In the same way they mean by injustice the state that makes us do injustice and wish what is unjust. That is why we also should first assume these things as an outline.

For what is true of sciences and capacities is not true of states. For while one and the same capacity or science seems to have contrary activities, a state
15 that is a contrary has no contrary activities. Health, for instance, only makes us do healthy actions, not their contraries; for we say we are walking in a healthy way if [and only if] we are walking in the way a healthy person would.

Often one of a pair of contrary states is recognized from the other contrary; and often the states are recognized from their subjects. For if, for instance, the
20 good state is evident, the bad state becomes evident too; and moreover the good state becomes evident from the things that have it, and the things from the state. For if, for instance, the good state is thickness of flesh, the bad state must be thinness of flesh, and the thing that produces the good state must be what produces thickness of flesh.
25 If one of a pair of contraries is spoken of in more ways than one, it follows, usually, that the other is too. If, for instance, the just is spoken of in more ways than one, so is the unjust.

Now it would seem that justice and injustice are both spoken of in more ways than one, but since their homonymy is close, the difference is unnoticed, and
30 is less clear than it is with distant homonyms where the distance in appearance is wide (for instance, the bone below an animal's neck and what we lock doors with are called keys homonymously).

Let us, then, find the number of ways an unjust person is spoken of. Both the lawless person and the overreaching and unfair person seem to be unjust; and so, clearly, both the lawful and the fair person will be just. Hence the just will be both the lawful
1129b and what is fair, and the unjust will be both the lawless and the unfair.

Since the unjust person is an overreacher, he will be concerned with goods — not with all goods, but only with those involved in good and bad fortune,

goods which are, [considered] without qualification, always good, but for this or that person not always good. Though human beings pray for these and pursue them, they are wrong; the right thing is to pray 5 that what is good without qualification will also be good for us, but to choose [only] what is good for us.

Now the unjust person [who chooses these goods] does not choose more in every case; in the case of what is bad without qualification he actually chooses less. But since what is less bad also seems to be good 10 in a way, and overreaching aims at more of what is good, he seems to be an overreacher. In fact he is unfair; for unfairness includes [all these actions], and is a common feature [of his choice of the greater good and of the lesser evil].

Since, as we saw, the lawless person is unjust and the lawful person is just, it clearly follows that whatever is lawful is in some way just; for the provisions of legislative science are lawful, and we say that each of them is just. In every matter that they deal with, the laws aim 15 either at the common benefit of all, or at the benefit of those in control, whose control rests on virtue or on some other such basis. And so in one way what we call just is whatever produces and maintains happiness and its parts for a political community.

Now the law instructs us to do the actions of a brave 20 person — for instance, not to leave the battle-line, or to flee, or to throw away our weapons; of a temperate person — not to commit adultery or wanton aggression; of a mild person — not to strike or revile another; and similarly requires actions in accord with the other virtues, and prohibits actions in accord with the vices. The 25 correctly established law does this correctly, and the less carefully framed one does this worse.

This type of justice, then, is complete virtue, not complete virtue without qualification, but complete virtue in relation to another. And that is why justice often seems to be supreme among the virtues, and 'neither the evening star nor the morning star is so marvellous,' and the proverb says, 'And in justice all virtue is summed up.'   30

Moreover, justice is complete virtue to the highest degree because it is the complete exercise of complete virtue. And it is the complete exercise because the person who has justice is able to exercise virtue in relation to another, not only in what concerns himself;

for many are able to exercise virtue in their own concerns, but unable in what relates to another.

1130a   That is why Bias seems to have been correct in saying that ruling will reveal the man; for a ruler is automatically related to another, and in a community. That is also why justice is the only virtue that seems
5 to be another person's good, because it is related to another; for it does what benefits another, either the ruler or the fellow member of the community.

The worst person, therefore, is the one who exercises his vice toward himself and his friends as well [as toward others]. And the best person is not the one who exercises virtue [only] toward himself, but the one who [also] exercises it in relation to another, since this is a difficult task.

10   This type of justice, then, is the whole, not a part, of virtue, and the injustice contrary to it is the whole, not a part, of vice.

Our discussion makes clear the difference between virtue and this type of justice. For virtue is the same as justice, but what it is to be virtue is not the same as what it is to be justice. Rather, insofar as virtue is related to another, it is justice, and insofar as it is a certain sort of state without qualification, it is virtue.

2

15 But we are looking for the type of justice, since we say there is one, that consists in a part of virtue, and correspondingly for the type of injustice that is a part of vice.

A sign that there is this type of justice and injustice is this: If someone's activities accord with the other vices—if, for instance, cowardice made him throw away his shield, or irritability made him revile someone, or ungenerosity made him fail to help someone with money—what he does is unjust, but not over-
20 reaching. But when someone acts from overreaching, in many cases his action accords with none of these vices—certainly not all of them; but it still accords with some type of wickedness, since we blame him, and [in particular] it accords with injustice. Hence there is another type of injustice that is a part of the whole, and a way of being unjust that is a part of the whole that is contrary to law.

25   Further, if A commits adultery for profit and makes a profit, but B commits adultery because of his appetite, and spends money on it to his own loss, B seems

intemperate rather than overreaching, but A seems unjust, not intemperate. Clearly, then, this is because A acts to make a profit.

Further, we can refer every other unjust action to 30 some vice—to intemperance if someone committed adultery, to cowardice if he deserted his comrade in the battle-line, to anger if he struck someone. But if he made an [unjust] profit, we can refer it to no other vice except injustice.

It is evident, then, that there is another type of injustice, special injustice, apart from injustice as a whole, and that it is synonymous with injustice as a whole, since the definition is in the same genus. For 1130b both have their area of competence in relation to another, but special injustice is concerned with honor or wealth or safety (or whatever single name will include all these), and aims at the pleasure that results from making a profit, whereas the concern of injustice as a whole is whatever concerns the excellent person. 5

Clearly, then, there is more than one type of justice, and there is another type besides [the type that is] the whole of virtue; but we must still grasp what it is, and what sort of thing it is.

The unjust is divided into the lawless and the unfair, and the just into the lawful and the fair. The injustice previously described, then, is concerned 10 with the lawless. But the unfair is not the same as the lawless; it is related to it as part to whole, since whatever is unfair is lawless, but not everything lawless is unfair. Hence also the unfair type of injustice and the unfair way of being unjust are not the same as the lawless type, but differ as parts from wholes. For 15 unfair injustice is a part of the whole of injustice, and, similarly, fair justice is a part of the whole of justice. Hence we must describe special as well as general justice and injustice, and equally this way of being just or unjust.

Let us, then, set aside the type of justice and injus- 20 tice that accords with the whole of virtue, justice being the exercise of the whole of virtue, and injustice of the whole of vice, in relation to another. And it is evident how we must distinguish the way of being just or unjust that accords with this type of justice and injustice. For most lawful actions, we might say, are those produced by virtue as a whole; for the law prescribes living in accord with each virtue, and

forbids living in accord with each vice. Moreover,
25 the actions producing the whole of virtue are the
lawful actions that the laws prescribe for education
promoting the common good. We must wait till later,
however, to determine whether the education that
makes an individual an unqualifiedly good man is a
task for political science or for another science; for,
presumably, being a good man is not the same as
being every sort of good citizen.

30   Special justice, however, and the corresponding
way of being just have one species that is found in
the distribution of honors or wealth or anything else
that can be divided among members of a community
who share in a political system; for here it is possible
for one member to have a share equal or unequal
1131a to another's. A second species concerns rectification
in transactions.

This second species has two parts, since one sort
of transaction is voluntary, and one involuntary. Voluntary transactions (for instance, selling, buying,
5 lending, pledging, renting, depositing, hiring out) are
so called because their principle is voluntary. Among
involuntary transactions some are secret (for instance,
theft, adultery, poisoning, pimping, slave-deception,
murder by treachery, false witness), whereas others
involve force (for instance, imprisonment, murder,
plunder, mutilation, slander, insult).

3 – Distributive Justice.

10 Since the unjust person is unfair, and what is unjust
is unfair, there is clearly an intermediate between the
unfair [extremes]. This is the fair; for in any action
where too much and too little are possible, the fair
[amount] is also possible. And so, if the unjust is
unfair, the just is fair (*ison*), as seems true to everyone
even without argument. And since the equal (*ison*)
[and fair] is intermediate, the just is some sort of intermediate.

15   Since the equal involves at least two things [equal
to each other], it follows that the just must be intermediate and equal, and related to something, and for
some people. Insofar as it is intermediate, it must be
between too much and too little; insofar as it is equal,
it involves two things; and insofar as it is just, it is
just for some people. Hence the just requires four

things at least; the people for whom it is just are two,
and the [equal] things involved are two.   20

Equality for the people involved will be the same as
for the things involved, since [in a just arrangement]
the relation between the people will be the same as the
relation between the things involved. For if the people
involved are not equal, they will not [justly] receive
equal shares; indeed, whenever equals receive unequal shares, or unequals equal shares, in a distribution, that is the source of quarrels and accusations.

This is also clear from considering what accords   25
with worth. For all agree that the just in distributions
must accord with some sort of worth, but what they
call worth is not the same; supporters of democracy
say it is free citizenship, some supporters of oligarchy
say it is wealth, others good birth, while supporters
of aristocracy say it is virtue.

Hence the just [since it requires equal shares for   30
equal people] is in some way proportionate. For proportion is special to number as a whole, not only
to numbers consisting of [abstract] units, since it is
equality of ratios and requires at least four terms. Now
divided proportion clearly requires four terms. But so
does continuous proportion, since here we use one
term as two, and mention it twice. If, for instance,   1131b
line A is to line B as B is to C, B is mentioned twice;
and so if B is introduced twice, the terms in the
proportion will be four.

The just also requires at least four terms, with the   5
same ratio [between the pairs], since the people [A
and B] and the items [C and D] involved are divided
in the same way. Term C, then, is to term D as A is
to B, and, taking them alternately, B is to D as A is
to C. Hence there will also be the same relation of
whole [A and C] to whole [B and D]; this is the
relation in which the distribution pairs them, and it
pairs them justly if this is how they are combined.

Hence the combination of term A with C and of   10
B with D is the just in distribution, and this way
of being just is intermediate, whereas the unjust is
contrary to the proportionate. For the proportionate
is intermediate, and the just is proportionate.

This is the sort of proportion that mathematicians
call geometrical, since in geometrical proportion the
relation of whole to whole is the same as the relation
of each [part] to each [part]. But this proportion [in-   15

volved in justice] is not continuous, since there is no single term for both the person and the item. The just, then, is the proportionate, and the unjust is the counterproportionate. Hence [in an unjust action] one term becomes more and the other less; and this is indeed how it turns out in practice, since the one doing injustice has more of the good, and the victim 20 has less.

With an evil the ratio is reversed, since the lesser evil, compared to the greater, counts as a good; for the lesser evil is more choiceworthy than the greater, what is choiceworthy is good, and what is more choiceworthy is a greater good.

This, then, is the first species of the just.

4 — Commutative Justice.

25 The other species is rectificatory, found in transactions both voluntary and involuntary. This way of being just belongs to a different species from the first.

For the just in distribution of common assets will always accord with the proportion mentioned above; 30 for [just] distribution from common funds will also accord with the ratio to one another of different people's deposits. Similarly, the way of being unjust that is opposed to this way of being just is what is counterproportionate.

1132a The just in transactions, by contrast, though it is a sort of equality (and the unjust a sort of inequality), accords with numerical proportion, not with the [geometrical] proportion of the other species. For here it does not matter if a decent person has taken from a base person, or a base person from a decent person, or if a decent or a base person has committed adultery. Rather, the law looks only at differences in the harm [inflicted], and treats the people involved as equals, 5 if one does injustice while the other suffers it, and one has done the harm while the other has suffered it.

And so the judge tries to restore this unjust situation to equality, since it is unequal. For [not only when one steals from another but] also when one is wounded and the other wounds him, or one kills and the other is killed, the action and the suffering are unequally divided [with profit for the offender and 10 loss for the victim]; and the judge tries to restore the [profit and] loss to a position of equality, by subtraction from [the offender's] profit.

For in such cases, stating it without qualification, we speak of profit for the attacker who wounded his victim, for instance, even if that is not the proper word for some cases; and we speak of loss for the victim who suffers the wound. At any rate, when what was suffered has been measured, one part is called the [victim's] loss, and the other the [offender's] profit. Hence the equal is intermediate between more and 15 less. Profit and loss are more and less in contrary ways, since more good and less evil is profit, and the contrary is loss. The intermediate area between [profit and loss], we have found, is the equal, which we say is just. Hence the just in rectification is the intermediate between loss and profit.

That is why parties to a dispute resort to a judge, 20 and an appeal to a judge is an appeal to the just; for the judge is intended to be a sort of living embodiment of the just. Moreover, they seek the judge as an intermediary, and in some cities they actually call a judge a 'mediator,' assuming that if they are awarded an intermediate amount, the award will be just. If, then, the judge is an intermediary, the just is in some way intermediate.

The judge restores equality, as though a line [AB] 25 had been cut into unequal parts [AC and CB], and he removed from the larger part [AC] the amount [DC] by which it exceeds the half [AD] of the line [AB], and added this amount [DC] to the smaller part [CB]. And when the whole [AB] has been halved [into AD and DB], then they say that each person has what is properly his own, when he has got an equal share.

The equal [in this case] is intermediate, by numeri- 30 cal proportion, between the larger [AC] and the smaller line [CB]. This is also why it is called just (*dikaion*), because it is a bisection (*dicha*), as though we said bisected (*dichaion*), and the judge (*dikastes*) is a bisector (*dichastes*). For when [the same amount] is subtracted from one of two equal things and added to the other, then the one part exceeds the other by the two parts; for if a part had been subtracted from the one, but not added to the other, the larger part 1132b would have exceeded the smaller by just one part. Hence the larger part exceeds the intermediate by one part, and the intermediate from which [a part] was subtracted [exceeds the smaller] by one part.

In this way, then, we will recognize what we must

subtract from the one who has more and add to the one who has less [to restore equality]; for to the one who has less we must add the amount by which the intermediate exceeds what he has, and from the greatest amount [held by the one who has more] we must subtract the amount by which it exceeds the intermediate. Let lines AA,' BB', and CC' be equal; let AE be subtracted from AA' and CD be added to CC', so that the whole line DCC' will exceed the line EA' by the parts CD and CF [where CF equals AE]; it follows that DCC' exceeds BB' by CD.

These names 'loss' and 'profit' are derived from voluntary exchange. For having more than one's own share is called making a profit, and having less than what one had at the beginning is called suffering a loss, in buying and selling, for instance, and in other transactions permitted by law. And when people get neither more nor less, but precisely what belongs to them, they say they have their own share and make neither a loss nor a profit. Hence the just is intermediate between a certain kind of loss and profit, since it is having the equal amount both before and after [the transaction].

5

Some people, however, think reciprocity is also just without qualification. This was the Pythagoreans' view, since their definition stated without qualification that what is just is reciprocity with another.

The truth is that reciprocity suits neither distributive nor rectificatory justice, though people take even Rhadamanthys' [primitive] conception of justice to describe rectificatory justice: 'If he suffered what he did, upright justice would be done.'[9] For in many cases reciprocity conflicts [with rectificatory justice]. If, for instance, a ruling official [exercising his office] wounded someone else, he must not be wounded in retaliation, but if someone wounded a ruling official, he must not only be wounded but also receive corrective treatment. Moreover, the voluntary or involuntary character of the action makes a great difference.

In communities for exchange, however, this way of being just, reciprocity that is proportionate rather than equal, holds people together; for a city is maintained by proportionate reciprocity. For people seek to return either evil for evil, since otherwise [their condition] seems to be slavery, or good for good, since otherwise there is no exchange; and they are maintained [in a community] by exchange. Indeed, that is why they make a temple of the Graces prominent, so that there will be a return of benefits received. For this is what is special to grace; when someone has been gracious to us, we must do a service for him in return, and also ourselves take the lead in being gracious again.

It is diagonal combination that produces proportionate exchange. Let A be a builder, B a shoemaker, C a house, D a shoe. The builder must receive the shoemaker's product from him, and give him the builder's own product in return. If, then, first of all, proportionate equality is found, and, next, reciprocity is also achieved, the proportionate return will be reached. Otherwise it is not equal, and the exchange will not be maintained, since the product of one may well be superior to the product of the other. These products, then, must be equalized.

This is true of the other crafts also; for they would have been destroyed unless the producer produced the same thing, of the same quantity and quality as the thing affected underwent. For no community [for exchange] is formed from two doctors. It is formed from a doctor and a farmer, and, in general, from people who are different and unequal and who must be equalized.

This is why all items for exchange must be comparable in some way. Currency came along to do exactly this, and in a way it becomes an intermediate, since it measures everything, and so measures excess and deficiency — [for instance,] how many shoes are equal to a house. Hence, as builder is to shoemaker, so must the number of shoes be to a house; for if this does not happen, there will be no exchange and no community. But proportionate equality will not be reached unless they are equal in some way. Everything, then, must be measured by some one measure, as we said before.

In reality, this measure is need, which holds everything together; for if people needed nothing, or needed things to different extents, there would be either no exchange or not the same exchange. And

9. [In mythology a judge in the underworld. — T.I.]

currency has become a sort of pledge of need, by convention; in fact it has its name (*nomisma*) because it is not by nature, but by the current law (*nomos*), and it is within our power to alter it and to make it useless.

Reciprocity will be secured, then, when things are equalized, so that the shoemaker's product is to the 1133b farmer's as the farmer is to the shoemaker. However, they must be introduced into the figure of proportion not when they have already exchanged and one extreme has both excesses, but when they still have their own; in that way they will be equals and members of a community, because this sort of equality can be 5 produced in them. Let A be a farmer, C food, B a shoemaker, and D his product that has been equalized; if this sort of reciprocity were not possible, there would be no community.

Now clearly need holds [a community] together as a single unit, since people with no need of each other, both of them or either one, do not exchange, as they exchange whenever another requires what one has oneself, such as wine, when they allow the 10 export of corn. This, then, must be equalized.

If an item is not required at the moment, currency serves to guarantee us a future exchange, guaranteeing that the item will be there for us if we need it; for it must be there for us to take if we pay. Now the same thing happens to currency [as other goods], and it does not always count for the same; still, it tends 15 to be more stable. Hence everything must have a price; for in that way there will always be exchange, and then there will be community.

Currency, then, by making things commensurate as a measure does, equalizes them; for there would be no community without exchange, no exchange without equality, no equality without commensuration. And so, though things so different cannot become commensurate in reality, they can become 20 commensurate enough in relation to our needs.

Hence there must be some single unit fixed [as current] by a stipulation. This is why it is called currency; for this makes everything commensurate, since everything is measured by currency. Let A, for instance, be a house, B ten minae, C a bed. A is half of B if a house is worth five minae or equal to them; 25 and C, the bed, is a tenth of B. It is clear, then, how many beds are equal to one house — five. This is clearly how exchange was before there was currency;

for it does not matter whether a house is exchanged for five beds or for the currency for which five beds are exchanged.

We have now said what it is that is unjust and just. 30 And now that we have defined them, it is clear that doing justice is intermediate between doing injustice and suffering injustice, since doing injustice is having too much and suffering injustice is having too little.

Justice is a mean, not as the other virtues are, 1134a but because it is about an intermediate condition, whereas injustice is about the extremes. Justice is the virtue in accord with which the just person is said to do what is just in accord with his decision, distributing good things and bad, both between himself and others and between others. He does not award too much of what is choiceworthy to himself and too little to his 5 neighbor (and the reverse with what is harmful), but awards what is proportionately equal; and he does the same in distributing between others.

Injustice, on the other hand, is related [in the same way] to the unjust. What is unjust is disproportionate excess and deficiency in what is beneficial or harmful; hence injustice is excess and deficiency because it concerns excess and deficiency. The unjust person 10 awards himself an excess of what is beneficial, [considered] without qualification, and a deficiency of what is harmful, and, speaking as a whole, he acts similarly [in distributions between] others, but deviates from proportion in either direction. In an unjust action getting too little good is suffering injustice, and getting too much is doing injustice.

So much, then, for the nature of justice and the 15 nature of injustice, and similarly for just and unjust in general.

6

Since it is possible to do injustice without thereby being unjust, what sort of injustice must someone do to be unjust by having one of the different types of injustice, by being a thief or adulterer or brigand, for instance?

Perhaps it is not the type of action that makes the difference [between merely doing injustice and being unjust]. For someone might lie with a woman and 20 know who she is, but the principle might be feelings rather than decision. In that case he is not unjust, though he does injustice—not a thief, for instance, though he stole, not an adulterer though he committed adultery, and so on in the other cases.

25   Now we have previously described the relation of reciprocity to the just. But we must recognize that we are inquiring not only into the just without qualification, but also into the politically just. This belongs to those who share in common a life aiming at self-sufficiency, who are free and either proportionately or numerically equal. Hence those who lack these features have nothing politically just in their relations, though they have something just insofar as it is similar to the politically just.

30   For the just belongs to those who have law in their relations. Law belongs to those among whom injustice is [possible]; for the judicial process is judgment that distinguishes the just from the unjust. Where there is injustice there is also doing injustice, though where there is doing injustice there need not also be injustice. And doing injustice is awarding to oneself too many of the things that, [considered] without qualification, are good, and too few of the things that, [considered] without qualification, are bad.

35   That is why we allow only reason, not a human being, to be ruler. For a human being awards himself

1134b   too many goods and becomes a tyrant; a ruler, however, is a guardian of the just, and hence of the equal [and so must not award himself too many goods].

If a ruler is just, he seems to profit nothing by it. For since he does not award himself more of what, [considered] without qualification, is good if it is not

5   proportionate to him, he seems to labor for another's benefit. That is why justice is said, as we also remarked before, to be another person's good. Hence some payment [for ruling] should be given; this is honor and privilege. The people who are not satisfied with these rewards are the ones who become tyrants.

10   The just for a master and a father is similar to this, not the same. For there is no unqualified injustice in relation to what is one's own; one's own possession, or one's child until it is old enough and separated, is as though it were a part of oneself. Now no one decides to harm himself. Hence there is no injustice in relation to them, and so nothing politically unjust or just either. For we found that the politically just must accord with law, and belong to those who are

naturally suited for law, and hence to those who have   15 equality in ruling and being ruled. [Approximation to this equality] explains why relations with a wife more than with children or possessions allow something to count as just; for that is the just in households. Still, this too is different from the politically just.

7

One part of the politically just is natural, and the other part legal. The natural has the same validity everywhere alike, independent of its seeming so or   20 not. The legal originally makes no difference [whether it is done] one way or another, but makes a difference whenever people have laid down the rule—that a mina is the price of a ransom, for instance, or that a goat rather than two sheep should be sacrificed. The legal also includes laws passed for particular cases (for instance, that sacrifices should be offered to Brasidas)[10] and enactments by decree.

Now some people think everything just is merely   25 legal. For the natural is unchangeable and equally valid everywhere—fire, for instance, burns both here and in Persia—whereas they see that the just changes [from city to city].

This is not so, though in a way it is so. With us, though presumably not at all with the gods, there is such a thing as the natural, but still all is changeable;   30 despite the change there is such a thing as what is natural and what is not.

Then what sort of thing, among those that [are changeable and hence] admit of being otherwise, is natural, and what sort is not natural, but legal and conventional, if both natural and legal are changeable? It is clear in other cases also, and the same distinction [between the natural and the unchangeable] will apply; for the right hand, for instance, is naturally superior, even though it is possible for every-   35 one to become ambidextrous.

The sorts of things that are just by convention and   1135a expediency are like measures. For measures for wine and for corn are not of equal size everywhere, but in

10. [Brasidas was a Spartan general who after his death received sacrifices in Amphipolis as a liberator; his cult is introduced as an example of a strictly local observance initiated by decree.—T.I.]

wholesale markets they are bigger, and in retail smaller. Similarly, the things that are just by human [enactment] and not by nature differ from place to place, since political systems also differ. Still, only one system is by nature the best everywhere.

Each [type of] just and lawful [action] is related as a universal to the corresponding particulars; for the [particular] actions that are done are many, but each [type] is one, since it is universal.

An act of injustice is different from the unjust, and an act of justice from the just. For the unjust is unjust by nature or enactment; when this has been done, it is an act of injustice, but before it is done it is only unjust. The same applies to an act of justice [in contrast to the just]. Here, however, the general [type of action contrary to an act of injustice] is more usually called a just act, and what is called an act of justice is the [specific type of just act] that rectifies an act of injustice.

Later we must examine each of these actions, to see what sorts of species, and how many, they have, and what they are concerned with.

8

Given this account of just and unjust actions, one does injustice or does justice whenever one does them willingly. Whenever one does them unwillingly, one neither does justice nor does injustice, except coincidentally, since the actions one does are coincidentally just or unjust.

An act of injustice and a just act are defined by the voluntary and the involuntary. For when the action is voluntary, the agent is blamed, and thereby also it is an act of injustice. And so something will be unjust without thereby being an act of injustice, if it is not also voluntary.

As I said before, I say that an action is voluntary just in case it is up to the agent, who does it in knowledge, and [hence] not in ignorance of the person, instrument, and goal (for instance, whom he is striking, with what, and for what goal), and [does] each of these neither coincidentally nor by force (if, for instance, someone seized your hand and struck another [with it], you would not have done it willingly, since it was not up to you). But [a further distinction must be drawn about knowledge. For] it is possible

that the victim is your father, and you know he is a human being or a bystander, but do not know he is your father. The same distinction must be made for the goal and for the action as a whole.

Actions are involuntary, then, if they are done in ignorance; or they are not done in ignorance, but they are not up to the agent; or they are done by force. For we also do or undergo many of our natural [actions and processes], such as growing old and dying, in knowledge, but none of them is either voluntary or involuntary.

Both unjust and just actions may also be coincidental in the same way. For if someone returned a deposit unwillingly and because of fear, we ought to say that he neither does anything just nor does justice, except coincidentally. Similarly, if someone is under compulsion and unwilling when he fails to return the deposit, we should say that he coincidentally does injustice and does something unjust.

In some of our voluntary actions we act on a previous decision, and in some we act without previous decision. We act on a previous decision when we act on previous deliberation, and we act without previous decision when we act without previous deliberation.

Among the three ways of inflicting harms in a community, actions done with ignorance are errors if someone does neither the action he supposed, nor to the person, nor with the instrument, nor for the result he supposed. For he thought, for instance, that he was not hitting, or not hitting this person, or not for this result; but coincidentally the result that was achieved was not what he thought (for instance, [he hit him] to graze, not to wound), or the victim or the instrument was not the one he thought.

If, then, the infliction of harm violates reasonable expectation, the action is a misfortune. If it does not violate reasonable expectation, but is done without vice, it is an error. For someone is in error if the principle of the cause is in him, and unfortunate when it is outside.

If he does it in knowledge, but without previous deliberation, it is an act of injustice; this is true, for instance, of actions caused by spirit and other feelings that are natural or necessary for human beings. For when someone inflicts these harms and commits these errors, he does injustice and these are acts of injustice; but he is not thereby unjust or wicked, since

25 it is not vice that causes him to inflict the harm.
But whenever his decision is the cause, he is unjust
and vicious.

That is why it is right to judge that actions caused
by spirit do not result from forethought [and hence
do not result from decision], since the principle is
not the agent who acted on spirit, but the person who
provoked him to anger. Moreover the dispute is not
about whether [the action caused by anger] happened
or not, but about whether it was just, since anger is
30 a response to apparent injustice. For they do not
dispute about whether it happened or not, as they do
in commercial transactions, where one party or the
other must be vicious, unless forgetfulness is the cause
of the dispute. Rather [in cases of anger] they agree
about the fact and dispute about which action was
just; but [in commercial transactions] the [cheater]
who has plotted against his victim knows very well
1136a [that what he is doing is unjust]. Hence [in cases of
anger the agent] thinks he is suffering injustice, while
[in transactions the cheater] does not think so.

If [the cheater's] decision causes him to inflict the
harm, he does injustice, and this is the sort of act of
injustice that makes an agent unjust, if it violates
proportion or equality. In the same way, a person is
just if his decision causes him to do justice; one
[merely] does justice if one merely does it voluntarily.

5 Some involuntary actions are to be pardoned, and
some are not. For if someone's error is not only committed in ignorance, but also caused by ignorance,
it is to be pardoned. But if, though committed in
ignorance, it is caused not by ignorance but by some
feeling that is neither natural nor human, it is not to
be pardoned.

9

10 If we have adequately defined suffering injustice and
doing injustice, some puzzles might be raised.

First of all, are those bizarre words of Euripides
correct, where he says: ' "I killed my mother—a short
15 tale to tell." "Were both of you willing or both
unwilling?" '? Is it really possible to suffer injustice
willingly, or is it always involuntary, as doing injustice
is always voluntary? And is it always one way or the
other, or is it sometimes voluntary and sometimes involuntary?

The same question arises about receiving justice.
Since doing justice is always voluntary [as doing injustice is], it is reasonable for the same opposition to 20
apply in both cases, so that both receiving justice and
suffering injustice will be either alike voluntary or
alike involuntary. But it seems absurd in the case of
receiving justice as well [as in the case of suffering
injustice] for it to be always voluntary, since some
people receive justice, but not willingly.

We might also raise the following puzzle: Does
everyone who has received something unjust suffer
injustice, or is it the same with receiving as it is with 25
doing? For certainly it is possible, in the case both
of doing and of receiving, to have a share in just
things coincidentally; and clearly the same is true of
unjust things, since doing something unjust is not
the same as doing injustice, and suffering something
unjust is not the same as suffering injustice. The
same is true of doing justice and receiving it; for it 30
is impossible to suffer injustice if no one does injustice
and impossible to receive justice if no one does
justice.

Now if doing injustice is simply harming someone
willingly (and doing something willingly is doing it
with knowledge of the victim, the instrument, and
the way), and the incontinent person harms himself
willingly, he suffers injustice willingly. Hence someone can do injustice to himself; and one of our puzzles
was just this, whether someone can do injustice to 1136b
himself. Further, someone's incontinence might
cause him to be willingly harmed by another who is
willing, so that it would be possible to suffer injustice willingly.

Perhaps, however, our definition [of doing injus-
tice] was incorrect, and we should add to 'harming
with knowledge of the victim, the instrument, and
the way,' the further condition 'against the wish of 5
the victim.' If so, someone is harmed and suffers
something unjust willingly, but no one suffers injustice willingly. For no one wishes it, not even the
incontinent, but he acts against his wish; for no one
wishes for what he does not think is excellent, and
what the incontinent does is not what he thinks it is
right [and hence excellent] to do.

And if someone gives away what is his own, as 10
Homer says Glaucus gave to Diomede 'gold for
bronze, a hundred cows' worth for nine cows'

worth,' he does not suffer injustice. For it is up to him to give them, whereas suffering injustice is not up to him, but requires someone to do him injustice.

Clearly, then, suffering injustice is not voluntary.

15 Two further questions that we decided to discuss still remain: If A distributes to B more than B deserves, is it A, the distributor, or B, who has more, who does injustice? And is it possible to do injustice to oneself?

For if the first alternative is possible, and A rather than B does injustice, it follows that if A knowingly 20 and willingly distributes more to B than to himself, A does injustice to himself. And indeed this is what a moderate person seems to do; for the decent person tends to take less than his share.

Perhaps, however, it is not true without qualification that he takes less. For perhaps he overreaches for some other good, such as reputation or the unqualifiedly fine. Moreover, our definition of doing injustice allows us to solve the puzzle. For since he suffers nothing against his own wish, he does not suffer injus-25 tice, at least not from his distribution, but, at most, is merely harmed.

But it is evidently the distributor who does injustice, and the one who has more does not always do it. For the one who does injustice is not the one who has an unjust share, but the one who willingly does what is unjust, that is to say, the one who has the principle 30 of the action; this is the distributor, not the recipient. Besides, doing is spoken of in many ways, and there is a way in which inanimate things, or hands, or servants at someone else's order, kill; the recipient, then, does not do injustice, but does something that is unjust.

Further, if the distributor judged in ignorance, he does not do injustice in violation of what is legally just, and his judgment is not unjust; in a way, though, it is unjust, since what is legally just is different from what is primarily just. If, however, he judged unjustly, and did it knowingly, he himself as well [as the recipi-1137a ent] is overreaching—for gratitude or to exact a penalty.

And so someone who has judged unjustly for these reasons has also got more, exactly as though he got a share of the [profits of] the act of injustice. For he gave judgment about some land, for instance, on this condition [that he would share the profits], and what he got was not land, but money.

People think doing injustice is up to them; that is 5 why they think that being just is also easy. But it is not. For lying with a neighbor's wife, wounding a neighbor, bribing, are all easy and up to us, but being in a certain state when we do them is not easy, and not up to us.

Similarly, people think it takes no wisdom to know 10 the things that are just and unjust, because it is not difficult to comprehend what the laws speak of. But these are not the things that are just, except coincidentally. Knowing how actions must be done, and how distributions must be made, if they are to be just, takes more work than it takes to know about healthy things. And even in the case of healthy things, know-15 ing about honey, wine, hellebore, burning, and cutting is easy, but knowing how these must be distributed to produce health, and to whom and when, takes all the work that it takes to be a doctor.

For the same reason they think doing injustice is no less proper to the just than to the unjust person, because the just person is no less, and even more, able to do each of the actions. For he is able to lie 20 with a woman, and to wound someone; and the brave person, similarly, is able to throw away his shield, and to turn and run this way or that. But doing acts of cowardice or injustice is not doing these actions, except coincidentally; it is being in a certain state when we do them. Similarly, practicing medicine or healing is not cutting or not cutting, giving drugs or not giving them, but doing all these things in a 25 certain way.

Just things belong to those who have a share in things that, [considered] without qualification, are good, who can have an excess or a deficiency of them. Some (as, presumably, the gods) can have no excess of them; others, the incurably evil, benefit from none of them, but are harmed by them all; others again benefit from these goods up to a point; and this is 30 why the just is something human.

10

The next task is to discuss how decency is related to justice and how the decent is related to the just. For on examination they appear as neither the same

without qualification nor as states of different kinds.
35 Sometimes we praise what is decent and the decent
person, so that even when we praise someone for
1137b other things we transfer the term 'decent' and use it
instead of 'good,' making it clear that what is more
decent is better. But sometimes, when we reason
about the matter, it appears absurd for what is decent
to be something apart from what is just, and still
praiseworthy. For [apparently] either what is just is
not excellent or what is decent is not excellent, if it
5 is something other than what is just; or else, if they
are both excellent, they are the same.

These, then, are roughly the claims that raise the
puzzle about the decent; but they are all correct in
a way, and none is contrary to any other. For the
decent is better than one way of being just, but it is
still just, and not better than the just by being a
10 different kind of thing. Hence the same thing is just
and decent; while both are excellent, what is decent
is superior.

The puzzle arises because the decent is just, but
is not the legally just, but a rectification of it. This
is because all law is universal, but in some areas no
15 universal rule can be correct; and so where a universal
rule has to be made, but cannot be correct, the law
chooses the [universal rule] that is usually [correct],
well aware of the error being made. And the law is
no less correct on this account; for the source of the
error is not the law or the legislator, but the nature
of the object itself, since that is what the subject
matter of actions is bound to be like.

20 And so, whenever the law makes a universal rule,
but in this particular case what happens violates the
[intended scope of] the universal rule, on this point
the legislator falls short, and has made an error by
making an unqualified rule. Then it is correct to
rectify the deficiency; this is what the legislator would
have said himself if he had been present there, and
what he would have prescribed, had he known, in
his legislation.

25 That is why the decent is just, and better than a
certain way of being just—not better than the unqualifiedly just, but better than the error that results from
the omission of any qualification [in the rule]. And
this is the nature of the decent—rectification of law
insofar as the universality of law makes it deficient.

This is also the reason why not everything is guided
by law. For on some matters legislation is impossible,
and so a decree is needed. For the standard applied
to the indefinite is itself indefinite, as the lead standard 30
is in Lesbian building, where it is not fixed, but adapts
itself to the shape of the stone; similarly, a decree is
adapted to fit its objects.

It is clear from this what is decent, and clear that
it is just, and better than a certain way of being just.
It is also evident from this who the decent person is; 35
for he is the one who decides on and does such 1138a
actions, not an exact stickler for justice in the bad
way, but taking less than he might even though he
has the law on his side. This is the decent person,
and his state is decency; it is a sort of justice, and not
some state different from it.

11

Is it possible to do injustice to oneself or not? The
answer is evident from what has been said.

First of all, some just actions are the legal prescrip- 5
tions in accord with each virtue; we are legally forbidden, for instance, to kill ourselves. Moreover, if someone illegally and willingly inflicts harm on another,
not returning harm for harm, he does injustice (a
person acting willingly is one who knows the victim
and the instrument). Now if someone murders him- 10
self because of anger, he does this willingly, in violation of correct reason, when the law forbids it; hence
he does injustice. But injustice to whom? Surely to
the city, not to himself, since he suffers it willingly,
and no one willingly suffers injustice. That is why
the city both penalizes him and inflicts further dishonor on him for destroying himself, on the ground
that he does injustice to the city.

Now consider the type of injustice that belongs 15
to an agent who is only unjust, not base generally.
Clearly the corresponding type of unjust action is
different from the first type. For this second type
of unjust person is wicked in the same [special]
way as the coward is, not by having total wickedness;
hence his acts of injustice do not accord with total
wickedness either. In this case also one cannot do
injustice to oneself. For if one could, the same
person could lose and get the same thing at the 20
same time. But this is impossible; on the contrary,

what is just or unjust must always involve more than one person.

Moreover, doing injustice is voluntary, and results from a decision, and strikes first; for a victim who retaliates does not seem to do injustice. But if someone does injustice to himself, he does and suffers the same thing at the same time. Further, on this view, it would be possible to suffer injustice willingly.

25　Besides, no one does injustice without doing one of the particular acts of injustice. But no one commits adultery with his own wife, or burgles his own house, or steals his own possessions.

And in general the puzzle about doing injustice to oneself is also solved by the distinction about voluntarily suffering injustice.

30　It is also evident that both doing and suffering injustice are bad, since one is having more, one having less, than the intermediate amount, just as in the case of health in medicine and fitness in gymnastics [both more and less than the intermediate amount are bad]. But doing injustice is worse; for it is blameworthy, involving vice that is either complete and unqualified or close to it (since not all voluntary doing of injustice is combined with [the state of] injustice). Suffering injustice, however, involves no vice or in-
35　justice.

1138b　In its own right, then, suffering injustice is less bad; and though it might still be coincidentally a greater evil, that is no concern of a craft. Rather, the craft says that pleurisy is a worse illness than a stumble, even though a stumble might sometimes coincidentally turn out worse—if, for instance, someone stum-
5　bled and by coincidence was captured by the enemy or killed because he fell.

It is possible for there to be a sort of justice, by similarity and transference, not of a person to himself, but of certain parts of a person—not every kind of justice, but the kind that belongs to masters or households. For in these discussions the part of the soul that has reason is distinguished from the nonrational part. People look at these and it seems to them that there is injustice to oneself, because in these parts it is possible to suffer something against one's own desires. Hence it is possible for those parts to be just to each other, as it is for ruler and ruled.

10　So much, then, for our definitions of justice and the other virtues of character.

BOOK VI

1

Since we have said previously that we must choose the intermediate condition, not the excess or the deficiency, and that the intermediate condition is as the 20 correct reason says, let us now determine what it says. For in all the states of character we have mentioned, as well as in the others, there is a target that the person who has reason focuses on and so tightens or relaxes; and there is a definition of the means, which we say are between excess and deficiency because they accord with the correct reason.　25

To say this is admittedly true, but it is not at all clear. For in other pursuits directed by a science, it is equally true that we must labor and be idle neither too much nor too little, but the intermediate amount prescribed by correct reason. But knowing only this, we would be 30 none the wiser about, for instance, the medicines to be applied to the body, if we were told we must apply the ones that medical science prescribes and in the way that the medical scientist applies them.

That is why our account of the states of the soul, in the same way, must not only be true as far as it has gone, but we must also determine what the correct reason is, that is to say, what its definition is.

After we divided the virtues of the soul, we said 35 that some are virtues of character and some of thought. And so, having finished our discussion of 1139a the virtues of character, let us now discuss the others as follows, after speaking first about the soul.

Previously, then, we said there are two parts of the 5 soul, one that has reason, and one nonrational. Now we should divide in the same way the part that has reason. Let us assume there are two parts that have reason: with one we study beings whose principles do not admit of being otherwise than they are, and with the other we study beings whose principles admit of being otherwise. For when the beings are of different kinds, the parts of the soul naturally suited to 10 each of them are also of different kinds, since the parts possess knowledge by being somehow similar and appropriate [to their objects].

Let us call one of these the scientific part, and the other the rationally calculating part; for deliberating

is the same as rationally calculating, and no one deliberates about what cannot be otherwise. Hence the
15 rationally calculating part is one part of the part of
the soul that has reason.

Hence we should find the best state of the scientific
part and the best state of the rationally calculating
part; for this state is the virtue of each of them. Now
a thing's virtue is relative to its own proper function,
[and so we must consider the function of each part].

2

There are three [capacities] in the soul—sense perception, understanding, desire—that control action
and truth. Of these three, sense perception is clearly
20 not the principle of any action, since beasts have
perception, but no share in action.

As assertion and denial are to thought, so pursuit
and avoidance are to desire. Now virtue of character
is a state that decides; and decision is a deliberative
desire. If, then, the decision is excellent, the reason
must be true and the desire correct, so that what
25 reason asserts is what desire pursues. This, then, is
thought and truth concerned with action. The
thought concerned with study, not with action or
production, has its good or bad state in being true or
false; for truth is the function of whatever thinks.
30 But the function of what thinks about action is truth
agreeing with correct desire.

The principle of an action—the source of motion,
not the goal—is decision; the principle of decision is
desire and goal-directed reason. That is why decision
35 requires understanding and thought, and also a state
of character; for acting well or badly requires both
thought and character.

Thought by itself moves nothing; what moves us
is goal-directed thought concerned with action. For
1139b this thought is also the principle of productive
thought; for every producer in his production aims
at some [further] goal, and the unqualified goal is
not the product, which is only the [qualified] goal of
some [production], and aims at some [further] goal.
[An unqualified goal is] what we achieve in *action*,
since acting well is the goal, and desire is for the
goal. That is why decision is either understanding
5 combined with desire or desire combined with

thought; and this is the sort of principle that a human
being is.

We do not decide to do what is already past; no
one decides, for instance, to have sacked Troy. For
neither do we deliberate about what is past, but only
about what will be and admits of being or not being;
and what is past does not admit of not having happened. That is why Agathon[11] is correct to say 'Of
this alone even a god is deprived—to make what is 10
all done to have never happened.'

The function of each of the understanding parts,
then, is truth. And so the virtues of each part will be
the states that best direct it toward the truth.

3

Then let us begin again, and discuss these states of 15
the soul. Let us say, then, that there are five states in
which the soul grasps the truth in its affirmation or
denials. These are craft, scientific knowledge, prudence, wisdom, and understanding; for belief and
supposition admit of being false.

What science is, is evident from the following, if
we must speak exactly and not be guided by [mere]
similarities. For we all suppose that what we know 20
scientifically does not even admit of being otherwise;
and whenever what admits of being otherwise escapes
observation, we do not notice whether it is or is not,
[and hence we do not know about it]. Hence what
is known scientifically is by necessity. Hence it is
everlasting; for the things that are by unqualified necessity are all everlasting, and everlasting things are
ingenerable and indestructible.

Further, every science seems to be teachable, and 25
what is scientifically knowable is learnable. But all
teaching is from what is already known, as we also
say in the *Analytics*; for some teaching is through
induction, some by deduction, [which both require
previous knowledge]. Induction [leads to] the principle, i.e., the universal, whereas deduction proceeds
from the universal. Hence deduction has principles 30
from which it proceeds and which are not themselves
[reached] by deduction. Hence they are [reached]
by induction.

11. [A fifth-century dramatist; his victory is being celebrated in Plato's *Symposium*. —M.L.M.]

Scientific knowledge, then, is a demonstrative state, and has all the other features that in the *Analytics* we add to the definition. For one has scientific knowledge whenever one has the appropriate sort of confidence, and knows the principles; for if one does not know them better than the conclusion, one will have scientific knowledge [only] coincidentally.

So much for a definition of scientific knowledge.

4

1140a What admits of being otherwise includes what is produced and what is achieved in action. Production and action are different; about them we rely also on [our] popular discussions. And so the state involving reason and concerned with action is different from the state involving reason and concerned with production. Nor is one included in the other; for action is not production, and production is not action.

Now building, for instance, is a craft, and is essentially a certain state involving reason concerned with production; there is no craft that is not a state involving reason concerned with production, and no such state that is not a craft. Hence a craft is the same as a state involving true reason concerned with production.

Every craft is concerned with coming to be, and the exercise of the craft is the study of how something that admits of being and not being comes to be, something whose principle is in the producer and not in the product. For a craft is not concerned with things that are or come to be by necessity; nor with things that are by nature, since these have their principle in themselves.

Since production and action are different, craft must be concerned with production, not with action. In a way craft and fortune are concerned with the same things, as Agathon says: 'Craft was fond of fortune, and fortune of craft.'

A craft, then, as we have said, is a state involving true reason concerned with production. Lack of craft is the contrary state involving false reason and concerned with production. Both are concerned with what admits of being otherwise.

5

25 To grasp what prudence is, we should first study the sort of people we call prudent. It seems proper to a prudent person to be able to deliberate finely about things that are good and beneficial for himself, not about some restricted area—about what sorts of things promote health or strength, for instance—but about what sorts of things promote living well in general.

A sign of this is the fact that we call people prudent about some [restricted area] whenever they calculate well to promote some excellent end, in an area where there is no craft. Hence where [living well] as a whole is concerned, the deliberative person will also be prudent.

Now no one deliberates about things that cannot be otherwise or about things that cannot be achieved in his action. Hence, if science involves demonstration, but there is no demonstration of anything whose principles admit of being otherwise (since every such thing itself admits of being otherwise); and if we cannot deliberate about things that are by necessity; it follows that prudence is not science nor yet craft knowledge. It is not science, because what is achievable in action admits of being otherwise; and it is not craft knowledge, because action and production belong to different kinds.

The remaining possibility, then, is that prudence is a state grasping the truth, involving reason, concerned with action about things that are good or bad for a human being. For production has its end in something other than itself, but action does not, since its end is acting well itself.

That is why Pericles and such people are the ones whom we regard as prudent, because they are able to study what is good for themselves and for human beings; we think that household managers and politicians are such people.

This is also how we come to give temperance (*sōphrosunē*) its name, because we think that it preserves prudence, (*sōzousan tēn phronēsin*). It preserves the [right] sort of supposition. For the sort of supposition that is corrupted and perverted by the pleasant or painful is not every sort—not, for instance, the supposition that the triangle does or does not have two right angles—but suppositions about what is achievable in action. For the principles of things achievable in action are their goal, but if someone is corrupted because of pleasure or pain, no [appropriate] principle can appear to him, and it cannot appear that this is the right goal and cause of all his choice and action;

for vice corrupts the principle. And so prudence must be a state grasping the truth, involving reason, and concerned with action about human goods.

Moreover, there is virtue [or vice in the use] of craft, but not [in the use] of prudence. Further, in a craft, someone who makes errors voluntarily is more choiceworthy; but with prudence, as with the virtues, the reverse is true. Clearly, then, prudence is a virtue, 25 not craft knowledge.

There are two parts of the soul that have reason. Prudence is a virtue of one of them, of the part that has belief; for belief is concerned, as prudence is, with what admits of being otherwise.

Moreover, it is not only a state involving reason. A sign of this is the fact that such a state can be forgotten, but prudence cannot.

6

30 Scientific knowledge is supposition about universals, things that are by necessity. Further, everything demonstrable and every science have principles, since scientific knowledge involves reason. Hence there can be neither scientific knowledge nor craft knowledge nor prudence about the principles of what is 35 scientifically known. For what is scientifically known is demonstrable, [but the principles are not]; and 1141a craft and prudence are about what admits of being otherwise. Nor is wisdom [exclusively] about principles; for it is proper to the wise person to have a demonstration of some things.

[The states of the soul] by which we always grasp the truth and never make mistakes, about what can 5 or cannot be otherwise, are scientific knowledge, prudence, wisdom, and understanding. But none of the first three—prudence, scientific knowledge, wisdom—is possible about principles. The remaining possibility, then, is that we have understanding about principles.

7

10 We ascribe wisdom in crafts to the people who have the most exact expertise in the crafts. For instance, we call Pheidias a wise stoneworker and Polycleitus a wise bronze worker; and by wisdom we signify precisely virtue in a craft. But we also think some people

are wise in general, not wise in some [restricted] area, or in some other [specific] way (as Homer says in the 15 *Margites*: 'The gods did not make him a digger or a ploughman or wise in anything else'). Clearly, then, wisdom is the most exact [form] of scientific knowledge.

Hence the wise person must not only know what is derived from the principles of a science, but also grasp the truth about the principles. Therefore wisdom is understanding plus scientific knowledge; it is scientific knowledge of the most honorable things that has received [understanding as] its coping stone.

For it would be absurd for someone to think that 20 political science or prudence is the most excellent science; for the best thing in the universe is not a human being [and the most excellent science must be of the best things].

Moreover, if what is good and healthy for human beings and for fish is not the same, whereas what is white or straight is always the same, everyone would also say that the content of wisdom is the same in 25 every case, but the content of prudence is not. For the agent they would call prudent is the one who studies well each question about his own [good], and he is the one to whom they would entrust such questions. That is why prudence is also ascribed to some of the beasts, the ones that are evidently capable of forethought about their own life.

It is also evident that wisdom is not the same as political science. For if people are to say that science about 30 what is beneficial to themselves [as human beings] counts as wisdom, there will be many types of wisdom [corresponding to the different species of animals]. For if there is no one medical science about all beings, there is no one science about the good of all animals, but a different science about each specific good. [Hence there will be many types of wisdom, contrary to our assumption that it has always the same content]. It does not matter if human beings are the best among the animals; for there are other beings of a far more 1141b divine nature than human beings—most evidently, for instance, the beings composing the universe.

What we have said makes it clear that wisdom is both scientific knowledge and understanding about the things that are by nature most honorable. That is why people say that Anaxagoras or Thales or that 5 sort of person is wise, but not prudent, whenever they see that he is ignorant of what benefits himself. And so they say that what he knows is extraordinary, amazing, difficult, and divine, but useless, because it is not human goods that he looks for.

10   Prudence, by contrast, is about human concerns, about things open to deliberation. For we say that deliberating well is the function of the prudent person more than anyone else; but no one deliberates about things that cannot be otherwise, or about things lacking any goal that is a good achievable in action. The unqualifiedly good deliberator is the one whose aim accords with rational calculation in pursuit of the best good for a human being that is achievable in action.

15   Nor is prudence about universals only. It must also acquire knowledge of particulars, since it is concerned with action and action is about particulars. That is why in other areas also some people who lack knowledge but have experience are better in action than others who have knowledge. For someone who knows that light meats are digestible and [hence] healthy, but

20 not which sorts of meats are light, will not produce health; the one who knows that bird meats are light and healthy will be better at producing health. And since prudence is concerned with action, it must possess both [the universal and the particular knowledge] or the [particular] more [than the universal]. Here too, however, [as in medicine] there is a ruling [science].

8

Political science and prudence are the same state, but their being is not the same.

25   One type of prudence about the city is the ruling part; this is legislative science. The type concerned with particulars [often] monopolizes the name 'political science' that [properly] applies to both types in common. This type is concerned with action and deliberation, since [it is concerned with decrees and] the decree is to be acted on as the last thing [reached in deliberation]. Hence these people are the only ones who are said to be politically active; for these are the only ones who put [political science] into practice, as hand-craftsmen put [a craft] into practice.

30   Similarly, prudence concerned with the individual himself seems most of all to be counted as prudence; and this [type of prudence often] monopolizes the name 'prudence' that [properly] applies [to all types] in common. Of the other types, one is household science, another legislative, another political, one type of which is deliberative and another judicial.

In fact knowledge of what is [good] for oneself is one species [of prudence]. But there is much difference [in opinions] about it. The one who knows about $1142a$ himself, and spends his time on his own concerns, seems to be prudent, while politicians seem to be too active. Hence Euripides says, 'Surely I cannot be prudent, since I could have been inactive, numbered among all the many in the army, and have had an 5 equal share . . . For those who go too far and are too active. . . .' For people seek what is good for themselves, and suppose that this [inactivity] is the right action [to achieve their good]. Hence this belief has led to the view that these are the prudent people. Presumably, however, one's own welfare requires household management and a political system. Fur- 10 ther, [another reason for the difference of opinion is that] it is unclear, and should be examined, how one must manage one's own affairs.

A sign of what has been said [about the unclarity of what prudence requires] is the fact that whereas young people become accomplished in geometry and mathematics, and wise within these limits, prudent young people do not seem to be found. The reason is that prudence is concerned with particulars as well as universals, and particulars become known from experience, but a young person lacks experience, 15 since some length of time is needed to produce it.

Indeed [to understand the difficulty and importance of experience] we might consider why a child can become accomplished in mathematics, but not in wisdom or natural science. Surely it is because mathematical objects are reached through abstraction, whereas in these other cases the principles are reached from experience. Young people, then, [lacking experience], have no real conviction in these 20 other sciences, but only say the words, whereas the nature of mathematical objects is clear to them.

Further, [prudence is difficult because it is deliberative and] deliberation may be in error about either the universal or the particular. For [we may wrongly suppose] either that all sorts of heavy water are bad or that this water is heavy.

25 It is apparent that prudence is not scientific knowledge; for, as we said, it concerns the last thing [i.e., the particular], since this is what is achievable in action. Hence it is opposite to understanding. For understanding is about the [first] terms, [those] that have no account of them; but prudence is about the last thing, an object of perception, not of scientific knowledge. This is not the perception of special objects, but the sort by which we perceive that the last among mathematical objects is a triangle; for it will

30 stop there too. This is another species [of perception than perception of special objects]; but it is still perception more than prudence is.

9

Inquiry and deliberation are different, since deliberation is a type of inquiry. We must also grasp what good deliberation is, and see whether it is some sort of scientific knowledge, or belief, or good guessing, or some other kind of thing.

1142b First of all, then, it is not scientific knowledge. For we do not inquire for what we already know; but good deliberation is a type of deliberation, and a deliberator inquires and rationally calculates.

Moreover, it is not good guessing either. For good guessing involves no reasoning, and is done quickly; but we deliberate a long time, and it is said that we

5 must act quickly on the result of our deliberation, but deliberate slowly. Further, quick thinking is different from good deliberation, and quick thinking is a kind of good guessing.

Nor is good deliberation just any sort of belief. Rather, since the bad deliberator is in error, and the good deliberator deliberates correctly, good deliberation is clearly some sort of correctness.

10 But it is not correctness in scientific knowledge or in belief. For there is no correctness in scientific knowledge, since there is no error in it either; and correctness in belief consists in truth, [but correctness in deliberation does not]. Further, everything about which one has belief is already determined, [but what is deliberated about is not yet determined].

However, good deliberation requires reason; hence the remaining possibility is that it belongs to thought. For thought is not yet assertion; [and this is why it is not belief]. For belief is not inquiry, but already an assertion; but in deliberating, either well or badly, 15 we inquire for something and rationally calculate about it.

But good deliberation is a certain sort of correctness in deliberation. That is why we must first inquire what [this correctness] is and what it is [correctness] about. Since there are several types of correctness, clearly good deliberation will not be every type. For the incontinent or base person will use rational calculation to reach what he proposes to see, and so will have deliberated correctly [if that is all it takes], but 20 will have got himself a great evil. Having deliberated well seems, on the contrary, to be some sort of good; for the sort of correctness in deliberation that makes it good deliberation is the sort that reaches a good.

However, we can reach a good by a false inference, as well [as by correct deliberation], so that we reach the right thing to do, but by the wrong steps, when the middle term is false. Hence this type of deliberation, 25 leading us by the wrong steps to the right thing to do, is not enough for good deliberation either.

Further, one person may deliberate a long time before reaching the right thing to do, while another reaches it quickly. Nor, then, is the first condition enough for good deliberation; good deliberation is correctness that accords with what is beneficial, about the right thing, in the right way, and at the right time.

Further, our deliberation may be either good without qualification or good only to the extent that it promotes some [limited] end. Hence unqualifiedly 30 good deliberation is the sort that correctly promotes the unqualified end [i.e., the highest good], while the [limited] sort is the sort that correctly promotes some [limited] end. If, then, having deliberated well is proper to a prudent person, good deliberation will be the type of correctness that accords with what is expedient for promoting the end about which prudence is true supposition.

10

Comprehension, i.e. good comprehension, makes 1143a people, as we say, comprehend and comprehend well. It is not the same as scientific knowledge in general. Nor is it the same as belief, since, if it were, everyone would have comprehension. Nor is it any one of the specific sciences [with its own specific area], in the

way that medicine is about what is healthy or geometry is about magnitudes. For comprehension is neither
5 about what always is and is unchanging nor about just anything that comes to be. It is about what we might be puzzled about and might deliberate about. That is why it is about the same things as prudence, but not the same as prudence.

For prudence is prescriptive, since its end is what action we must or must not do, whereas comprehen-
10 sion only judges. (For comprehension and good comprehension are the same; and so are people with comprehension and with good comprehension.) Comprehension is neither having prudence nor acquiring it.

Rather, it is similar to the way learning is called comprehending when someone applies scientific knowledge. In the same way comprehension consists in the application of belief to judge someone else's
15 remarks on a question that concerns prudence, and moreover it must judge them finely since judging well is the same as judging finely. That is how the name 'comprehension' was attached to the comprehension that makes people have good comprehension. It is derived from the comprehension found in learning; for we often call learning comprehending.

11

20 The [state] called consideration makes people, as we say, considerate and makes them have consideration; it is the correct judgment of the decent person. A sign of this is our saying that the decent person more than others is considerate, and that it is decent to be considerate about some things. Considerateness is the correct consideration that judges what is decent; and correct consideration judges what is true.

25 It is reasonable that all these states tend in the same direction. For we ascribe consideration, comprehension, prudence, and understanding to the same people, and say that these have consideration, and thereby understanding, and that they are prudent and comprehending. For all these capacities are about the last things, i.e., particulars. Moreover, someone has comprehension and good consideration, or has consider-
30 ateness, in being able to judge about the matters that concern the prudent person; for the decent is the

common concern of all good people in relations with other people.

[These states are all concerned with particulars because] all the things achievable in action are particular and last things. For the prudent person also must recognize [things achievable in action], while comprehension and consideration are concerned with
35 things achievable in action, and these are last things.

Understanding is also concerned with the last things, and in both directions. For there is understanding, not a rational account, both about the first terms and about the last. In demonstrations under-
1143b standing is about the unchanging terms that are first. In [premises] about action understanding is about the last term, the one that admits of being otherwise, and [hence] about the minor premise. For these last terms are beginnings of the [end] to be aimed at, since
5 universals are reached from particulars.

We must, therefore, have perception of these particulars, and this perception is understanding. That is
9, 10 why understanding is both beginning and end; for demonstrations [begin] from these things and are about them.

That is why these states actually seem to grow
6 naturally, so that, whereas no one seems to have natural wisdom, people seem to have natural consideration, comprehension, and judgment. A sign [of their apparent natural character] is our thinking that they also correspond to someone's age, and the fact that understanding and consideration belong to a certain age, as though nature were the cause. And so we must attend to the undemonstrated remarks and beliefs of experienced and older people or of prudent people, no less than to demonstrations. For these people see correctly because experience has given them their eye.

We have said, then, what prudence and wisdom
15 are; what each is about; and that each is the virtue of a different part of the soul.

12

One might, however, go through some puzzles about what use they are. For wisdom is not concerned with any sort of coming into being, and hence will not study
20 any source of human happiness. Admittedly, prudence will study this; but what do we need it for? For
25, 26

knowledge of what is healthy or fit (i.e., of what results from the state of health, not of what produces it) makes
27 us no readier to act appropriately if we are already healthy; for having the science of medicine or gymnas-
21 tics makes us no readier to act appropriately. Similarly, prudence is the science of what is just and what is fine, and what is good for a human being; but this is how
25 the good man acts; and if we are already good, knowledge of them makes us no readier to act appropriately, since virtues are states [activated in actions].

28   If we concede that prudence is not useful for this, should we say it is useful for becoming good? In that
30 case it will be no use to those who are already excellent. Nor, however, will it be any use to those who are not. For it will not matter to them whether they have it themselves or take the advice of others who have it. The advice of others will be quite adequate for us, just as it is with health: we wish to be healthy, but still do not learn medical science.

35   Besides, it would seem absurd for prudence, inferior as it is to wisdom, to control it [as a superior. But this will be the result], since the science that produces also rules and prescribes about its product.

We must discuss these questions; for so far we have only raised the puzzles about them.

1144a   First of all, let us state that both prudence and wisdom must be choiceworthy in themselves, even if neither produces anything at all; for each is the virtue of one of the two [rational] parts [of the soul].

Secondly, they do produce something. Wisdom
5 produces happiness, not in the way that medical science produces health, but in the way that health produces [health]. For since wisdom is a part of virtue as a whole, it makes us happy because it is a state that we possess and activate.

Further, we fulfill our function insofar as we have prudence and virtue of character; for virtue makes the goal correct, and prudence makes the things pro-
10 moting the goal [correct]. The fourth part of the soul, the nutritive part, has no such virtue [related to our function], since no action is up to it to do or not to do.

To answer the claim that prudence will make us no better at achieving fine and just actions, we must begin from a little further back [in our discussion].
15 We begin here: we say that some people who do just actions are not yet thereby just, if, for instance, they do the actions prescribed by the laws either unwill-

ingly or because of ignorance or because of some other end, not because of the actions themselves, even though they do the right actions, those that the excellent person ought to do. Equally, however, it would seem to be possible for someone to do each type of action in the state that makes him a good person, that is to say, because of decision and for the 20 sake of the actions themselves.

Now virtue makes the decision correct; but the actions that are naturally to be done to fulfill the decision are the concern not of virtue, but of another capacity. We must grasp them more perspicuously before continuing our discussion.

There is a capacity, called cleverness, which is such 25 as to be able to do the actions that tend to promote whatever goal is assumed and to attain them. If, then, the goal is fine, cleverness is praiseworthy, and if the goal is base, cleverness is unscrupulousness. That is why both prudent and unscrupulous people are called clever.

Prudence is not cleverness, though it requires this capacity. [Prudence,] this eye of the soul, requires virtue in order to reach its fully developed state, as 30 we have said and as is clear. For inferences about actions have a principle, 'Since the end and the best good is this sort of thing' (whatever it actually is— let it be any old thing for the sake of argument). And this [best good] is apparent only to the good person; 35 for vice perverts us and produces false views about the principles of actions. Evidently, then, we cannot be prudent without being good.   1144b

13

We must, then, also examine virtue over again. For virtue is similar [in this way] to prudence; as prudence is related to cleverness, not the same but similar, so natural virtue is related to full virtue. For each of us seems to possess his type of character to some extent 5 by nature; for in fact we are just, brave, prone to temperance, or have another feature, immediately from birth. But still we look for some further condition to be full goodness, and we expect to possess these features in another way. For these natural states belong to children and to beasts as well [as to adults], but without understanding they are evidently harmful. At 10 any rate, this much would seem to be clear: Just as a heavy body moving around unable to see suffers a heavy fall because it has no sight, so it is with virtue. [A naturally well-endowed person without understanding will harm himself.]

But if someone acquires understanding, he improves in his actions; and the state he now has, though still similar [to the natural one], will be fully virtue. And so, just as there are two sorts of conditions, clever-
15 ness and prudence, in the part of the soul that has belief, so also there are two in the part that has character, natural virtue and full virtue. And of these full virtue cannot be acquired without prudence.

That is why some say that all the virtues are [instances of] prudence, and why the inquiries Socrates used to undertake were in one way correct, and in
20 another way in error. For insofar as he thought all the virtues are [instances of] prudence, he was in error; but insofar as he thought they all require prudence, what he used to say was right.

Here is a sign of this. Whenever people now define virtue, they all say what state it is and what it is related to, and then add that it is the state in accord with the correct reason. Now the correct reason is the
25 reason in accord with prudence; it would seem, then, that they all in a way intuitively believe that the state in accord with prudence is virtue.

But we must make a slight change. For it is not merely the state in accord with the correct reason, but the state involving the correct reason, that is virtue. And it is prudence that is the correct reason in this area. Socrates, then, used to think the virtues are [instances of] reason because he thought they are
30 all [instances of] knowledge, whereas we think they involve reason.

What we have said, then, makes it clear that we cannot be fully good without prudence, or prudent without virtue of character. And in this way we can also solve the dialectical argument that someone might use to show that the virtues are separated from one another. For, [it is argued], since the same person
35 is not naturally best suited for all the virtues, someone will already have one virtue before he gets another. This is indeed possible in the case of the natural virtues. It is not possible, however, in the case of the
1145a [full] virtues that someone must have to be called good without qualification; for one has all the virtues if and only if one has prudence, which is a single state.

And it is clear that, even if prudence were useless in action, we would need it because it is the virtue of this part of the soul, and because the decision will not be correct without prudence or without virtue—   5
for [virtue] makes us achieve the end, whereas [prudence] makes us achieve the things that promote the end.

Moreover, prudence does not control wisdom or the better part of the soul, just as medical science does not control health. For medical science does not use health, but only aims to bring health into being; hence it prescribes for the sake of health, but does not prescribe to health. Besides, [saying that 10
prudence controls wisdom] would be like saying that political science rules the gods because it prescribes about everything in the city.

BOOK VII

1

Let us now make a new start, and say that there are 15
three conditions of character to be avoided—vice, incontinence, and bestiality. The contraries of two of these are clear; we call one virtue and the other continence.

The contrary to bestiality is most suitably called 20
virtue superior to us, a heroic, indeed divine, sort of virtue. Thus Homer made Priam say that Hector was remarkably good; 'nor did he look as though he were the child of a mortal man, but of a god.' And so, if, as they say, human beings become gods because of exceedingly great virtue, this is clearly the sort of state that would be opposite to the bestial state. For indeed, 25
just as a beast has neither virtue nor vice, so neither does a god, but the god's state is more honorable than virtue, and the beast's belongs to some kind different from vice.

Now it is rare that a divine man exists. (This is what the Spartans habitually call him; whenever they very much admire someone, they say he is a divine man.) Similarly, the bestial person is also rare among 30
human beings. He is most often found in foreigners; but some bestial features also result from diseases and deformities. We also use 'bestial' as a term of reproach for people whose vice exceeds the human level.

35   We must make some remarks about this condition later. We have discussed vice earlier. We must now discuss incontinence, softness, and self-indulgence,

1145b and also continence and resistance; for we must not suppose that continence and incontinence are concerned with the same states as virtue and vice, or that they belong to a different kind.

    As in the other cases, we must set out the appearances, and first of all go through the puzzles. In this

5 way we must prove the common beliefs about these ways of being affected—ideally, all the common beliefs, but if not all, most of them, and the most important. For if the objections are solved, and the common beliefs are left, it will be an adequate proof.

    Continence and resistance seem to be good and

10 praiseworthy conditions, whereas incontinence and softness seem to be base and blameworthy conditions. The continent person seems to be the same as one who abides by his rational calculation; and the incontinent person seems to be the same as one who abandons it. The incontinent person knows that his actions are base, but does them because of his feelings, whereas the continent person knows that his appetites are base, but because of reason does not follow them.

15   People think the temperate person is continent and resistant. Some think that every continent and resistant person is temperate, while others do not. Some people say the incontinent person is intemperate and the intemperate incontinent, with no distinction; others say they are different.

    Sometimes it is said that a prudent person cannot be incontinent; but sometimes it is said that some people are prudent and clever, but still incontinent.

20   Further, people are called incontinent about spirit, honor, and gain.

    These, then, are the things that are said.

2

We might be puzzled about what sort of correct supposition someone has when he acts incontinently.

    First of all, some say he cannot have knowledge [at the time he acts]. For it would be terrible, Socrates used to think, for knowledge to be in someone, but

25 mastered by something else, and dragged around like a slave. For Socrates used to oppose the account [of

incontinence] in general, in the belief that there is no incontinence; for no one, in Socrates' view, supposes while he acts that his action conflicts with what is best; our action conflicts with what is best only because we are ignorant [of the conflict].

    This argument, then, contradicts things that appear manifestly. If ignorance causes the incontinent person to be affected as he is, we must look for the type of ignorance that it turns out to be; for it is evident, at 30 any rate, that before he is affected the person who acts incontinently does not think [he should do the action he eventually does].

    Some people concede some of [Socrates' points], but reject some of them. For they agree that nothing is superior to knowledge, but they deny the claim that no one's action conflicts with what has seemed better to him. That is why they say that when the incontinent person is overcome by pleasure he has only belief, not knowledge. 35

    If, however, he has belief, not knowledge, and the 1146a supposition that resists is not strong, but only a weak one, such as people have when they are in doubt, we will pardon failure to abide by these beliefs against strong appetites. In fact, however, we do not pardon vice, or any other blameworthy condition [and incontinence is one of these].

    Then is it prudence that resists, since it is the 5 strongest? This is absurd. For on this view the same person will be both prudent and incontinent; but no one would say that the prudent person is the sort to do the worst actions willingly. Besides, we have shown earlier that the prudent person acts [on his knowledge], since he is concerned with the last things, [i.e., particulars] and that he has the other virtues.

    Further, if the continent person must have strong 10 and base appetites, the temperate person will not be continent nor the continent person temperate. For the temperate person is not the sort to have either excessive or base appetites; but [the continent person] must have both. For if his appetites are good, the state that prevents him from following them must be base, so that not all continence is excellent. If, how- 15 ever, the appetites are weak and not base, continence is nothing impressive; and if they are base and weak, it is nothing great.

    Further, if continence makes someone prone to abide by every belief, it is bad, if, for instance, it

makes him abide by a false as well [as true] belief.
And if incontinence makes someone prone to abandon every belief, there will be an excellent type of
20 incontinence. Take, for instance, Neoptolemus in
Sophocles' *Philoctetes*. For he is praiseworthy for his
failure to abide by [his promise to tell the lies] that
Odysseus had persuaded him [to tell]; [he breaks his
promise] because he feels pain at lying.

Further, the sophistical argument is a puzzle. For
[the sophists] wish to refute an [opponent, by show-
ing] that his views have paradoxical results, so that
they will be clever in encounters. Hence the inference
25 that results is a puzzle; for thought is tied up, whenever it does not want to stand still, because the conclusion is displeasing, but it cannot advance, because it
cannot solve the argument. A certain argument, then,
concludes that foolishness combined with incontinence is virtue. For incontinence makes someone act
contrary to what he supposes [is right]; but since he
30 supposes that good things are bad and that it is wrong
to do them, he will do the good actions, not the bad.

Further, someone who acts to pursue what is pleasant because this is what he is persuaded and decides
to do seems to be better than someone who acts
not because of rational calculation, but because of
incontinence. For the first person is the easier to cure,
because he might be persuaded to act otherwise; but
35 the incontinent person illustrates the proverb 'If water
1146b chokes us, what must we drink to wash it down?' For
if he had been persuaded to do the action he does,
he would have stopped when he was persuaded to
act otherwise; but in fact, though already persuaded
to act otherwise, he still acts [wrongly].

Further, is there incontinence and continence
about everything? If so, who is simply incontinent?
For no one has all the types of incontinence, but we
5 say that some people are simply incontinent.

These, then, are the sorts of puzzles that arise. We
must undermine some of these claims, and leave
others intact; for the solution of the puzzle is the
discovery [of what we are seeking].

3

First, then, we must examine whether the incontinent
has knowledge or not, and in what way he has it.
10 Second, what should we take to be the range of incon-

tinence and continence — every pleasure and pain, or
some definite subclass? Are the continent and the
resistant person the same or different? Similarly we
must deal with the other questions that are relevant
to this study.

We begin by examining whether continence and 15
incontinence differ from other things by their range
or by their attitudes. In other words, is the incontinent
person incontinent because of a specific range of
actions, or because of a specific attitude, or because
of both? Next, is there incontinence and continence
about everything, or not?

For the simply incontinent person is not incontinent about everything, but he has the same range as
the intemperate person. Nor is he incontinent simply 20
by being inclined toward these things — that would
make incontinence the same as intemperance.
Rather, he is incontinent by being inclined toward
them in this way. For the intemperate person acts on
decision when he is led on, since he thinks it is right
in every case to pursue the pleasant thing at hand;
the incontinent person, however, thinks it is wrong
to pursue this pleasant thing, yet still pursues it.

It is claimed that the incontinent person's action 25
conflicts with the true belief, not with knowledge.
But whether it is knowledge or belief that he has does
not matter for this argument. For some people with
belief are in no doubt, but think they have exact
knowledge.

If, then, it is the weakness of their conviction that
makes people with belief, not people with knowledge,
act in conflict with their supposition, it follows that
knowledge will [for these purposes] be no different
from belief; for, as Heracleitus makes clear, some peo- 30
ple's convictions about what they believe are no weaker
than other people's convictions about what they know.

But we speak of knowing in two ways; we ascribe it
both to someone who has it without using it and to
someone who is using it. Hence it will matter whether
someone has the knowledge that his action is wrong,
without attending to his knowledge, or he both has it 35
and attends to it. For this second case seems extraordinary, but wrong action when he does not attend to his
knowledge does not seem extraordinary.

Further, since there are two types of premises, 1147a
someone's action may well conflict with his knowl-

edge if he has both types of premises, but uses only the universal premise and not the particular premise. For it is particulars that are achievable in action. There are also different types of universal, one type referring to the agent himself, and the other referring to the object. Perhaps, for instance, someone knows that dry things benefit every human being, and that he himself is a human being, or that this sort of thing is dry; but he either does not have or does not activate the knowledge that this particular thing is of this sort. These ways [of knowing and not knowing], then, make such a remarkable difference that it seems quite intelligible [for someone acting against his knowledge] to have the one sort of knowledge, but astounding if he has the other sort.

Further, human beings may have knowledge in a way different from those we have described. For we see that having without using includes different types of having; hence some people, such as those asleep or mad or drunk, both have knowledge in a way and do not have it. Moreover, this is the condition of those affected by strong feelings. For spirited reactions, sexual appetites, and some conditions of this sort clearly [both disturb knowledge and] disturb the body as well, and even produce fits of madness in some people. Clearly, then [since incontinents are also affected by strong feelings], we should say that they have knowledge in a way similar to these people.

Saying the words that come from knowledge is no sign [of fully having it]. For people affected in these ways even recite demonstrations and verses of Empedocles. And those who have just learned something do not yet know it, though they string the words together; for it must grow into them, and this takes time. And so we must suppose that those who are acting incontinently also say the words in the way that actors do.

Further, we may also look at the cause in the following way, referring to [human] nature. For one belief is universal; the other is about particulars, and because they are particulars, perception controls them. And in the cases where these two beliefs result in one belief, it is necessary, in one case, for the soul to affirm what has been concluded, but, in the case of beliefs about production, to act at once on what has been concluded. If, for instance, everything sweet must be tasted, and this, some one particular thing, is sweet, it is necessary for someone who is able and unhindered also to act on this at the same time.

Suppose, then, that someone has the universal belief hindering him from tasting; he has the second belief, that everything sweet is pleasant and this is sweet, and this belief is active; but it turns out that appetite is present in him. The belief, then, [that is formed from the previous two beliefs] tells him to avoid this, but appetite leads him on, since it is capable of moving each of the [bodily] parts.

The result, then, is that in a way reason and belief make him act incontinently. The [second] belief is contrary to the correct reason, but only coincidentally, not in its own right. For the appetite, not the belief, is contrary [in its own right to the correct reason]. That is also why beasts are not incontinent, because they have no universal supposition, but [only] appearance and memory of particulars.

How is the ignorance resolved, so that the incontinent person recovers his knowledge? The same account that applies to someone drunk or asleep applies here too, and is not special to this way of being affected. We must hear it from the natural scientists.

Since the last premise is a belief about something perceptible, and controls action, this is what the incontinent person does not have when he is being affected. Or [rather] the way he has it is not knowledge of it, but, as we saw, [merely] saying the words, as the drunk says the words of Empedocles.

And since the last term does not seem to be universal, or expressive of knowledge in the same way as the universal term, even the result Socrates was looking for would seem to come about. For the knowledge that is present when someone is affected by incontinence, and that is dragged about because he is affected, is not the sort that seems to be fully knowledge, but it is only perceptual knowledge.

So much, then, for knowing and not knowing, and for how it is possible to know and still to act incontinently.

4

Next we must say whether anyone is simply incontinent, or all incontinents are incontinent in some particular way; and if someone is simply incontinent, we must say what sorts of things he is incontinent about.

First of all, both continence and resistance and incontinence and softness are evidently about pleasures and pains.

25   Some sources of pleasure are necessary; others are choiceworthy in their own right, but can be taken to excess. The necessary ones are the bodily conditions, i.e., those that concern food, sexual intercourse, and the sorts of bodily conditions that we took temperance and intemperance to be about. Other sources of pleasure are not necessary, but are choiceworthy in them-
30   selves, such as victory, honor, wealth, and similar good and pleasant things.

When people go to excess, against the correct reason in them, in the pursuit of these sources of pleasure, we do not call them simply incontinent, but add the qualification that they are incontinent about wealth, gain, honor, or spirit, and not simply incontinent. For we assume that they are different, and called
35   incontinent [only] because of a similarity, just as the
1148a   Olympic victor named Human[12] was different, since for him the common account [of human being] was only a little different from his special one, but it was different nonetheless.

A sign in favor of what we say is the fact that incontinence is blamed not only as an error but as a vice, either unqualified or partial, while none of these conditions is blamed as a vice.
5   Now consider the people concerned with the bodily gratifications, those that we take temperance and intemperance to be about. Some of these people go to excess in pursuing these pleasant things and avoiding painful things—hunger, thirst, heat, cold, and all the objects of touch and taste—not, however, because they have decided on it, but against their decision and thought. These are the people called
10   simply incontinent, not with the added condition that they are incontinent about, for instance, anger.

A sign of this is the fact that people are also called soft about these [bodily] pleasures, but not about any of the non-necessary ones.

This is also why we include the incontinent and the intemperate person, and the continent and the temperate person, in the same class, but do not include any of those who are incontinent in some partic-   15
ular way. It is because incontinence and intemperance are, in a way, about the same pleasures and pains. In fact they are about the same things, but not in the same way; the intemperate person decides on them, but the incontinent person does not. That is why, if someone has no appetites, or slight ones, for excesses, but still pursues them and avoids moderate pains, we will take him to be more intemperate than the person who does it because he has intense appe-   20
tites. For think of the lengths he would go to if he also acquired vigorous appetites and felt severe pains at the lack of necessities.

Some pleasant things are naturally choiceworthy, some naturally the contrary, some in between, as we divided them earlier. Hence some appetites and pleasures are for fine and excellent kinds of things,   25
such as wealth, profit, victory, and honor. About all these and about the things in between people are blamed not for feeling an appetite and love for them, but for doing so in a particular way, namely to excess.

Some people are overcome by, or pursue, some of   30
these naturally fine and good things to a degree that goes against reason; they take honor, or children, or parents (for instance) more seriously than is right. For though these are certainly good and people are praised for taking them seriously, still excess about them is also possible. It is excessive if one fights, as Niobe[13] did [for her children], even with the gods,   1148b
or if one regards his father as Satyrus,[14] nicknamed the Fatherlover, did—for he seemed to be excessively silly about it. There is no vice here, for the reason we have given, since each of these things is naturally choiceworthy for itself, though excess about them is bad and to be avoided.

Similarly, there is no incontinence here either,   5
since incontinence is not merely to be avoided, but also blameworthy [and these conditions are not]. But because this way of being affected is similar to incontinence, people call it incontinence, adding the qualification that it is incontinence about this or that. Just

12. [The winning boxer in the Olympics of 456 was called Anthropos.—T.I.]

13. [Claimed that her children were more beautiful than those of Leto.—M.L.M.]

14. [Stories are told of Satyrus that he committed suicide in grief when his father died.—M.L.M.]

so they call someone a bad doctor or a bad actor,
10 though they would never call him simply bad, since
each of these conditions is not vice, but only similar
to it by analogy. It is clear, likewise, that the only
condition we should take to be continence or incontinence is the one concerned with what concerns
temperance and intemperance. We speak of incontinence about spirit because of the similarity [to simple
incontinence], and hence add the qualification that
someone is incontinent about spirit, as we do in the
case of honor or gain.

5

15 Some things are naturally pleasant, and some of these
are pleasant without qualification, whereas others correspond to differences between kinds of animals and
of human beings. Other things are not naturally pleasant, but deformities or habits or base natures make
them pleasant; and we can see states that are about
each of these that are similar to [states that are about
naturally pleasant things].

20   By bestial states I mean, for instance, the female
human being who is said to tear pregnant women
apart and devour the children; or the pleasures of
some of the savage people around the Black Sea who
are reputed to enjoy raw meat and human flesh, while
some trade their children to each other to feast on;
or what is said about Phalaris.

25   These states are bestial. Other states result from
attacks of disease, and in some cases from fits of
madness—for instance, the person who sacrificed his
mother and ate her, and the one who ate the liver
of his fellow slave. Others result from diseased conditions or from habit—for instance, plucking hairs,
chewing nails, even coal and earth, and besides these
sexual intercourse between males. For in some people
30 these result from [a diseased] nature, in others from
habit, as, for instance, in those who have suffered
wanton [sexual] assault since their childhood.

If nature is the cause, no one would call these
people incontinent, any more than women would be
called incontinent for being mounted rather than
mounting. The same applies to those who are in a
diseased state because of habit.

1149a   Each of these states, then, is outside the limits of
vice, just as bestiality is. If someone who has them

overcomes them or is overcome by them, that is not
simple [continence or] incontinence, but the type so
called from similarity, just as someone who is overcome by spirit should be called incontinent in relation
to his feeling, but not [simply] incontinent. For 5
among all the excesses of foolishness, cowardice, intemperance, and irritability some are bestial, some
diseased.

If, for instance, someone's natural character makes
him afraid of everything, even the noise of a mouse, he
is a coward with a bestial sort of cowardice. Another
person was afraid of a weasel because of an attack of
disease. Among foolish people also, those who natu- 10
rally lack reason and live only by sense perception, as
some races of distant foreigners do, are bestial. Those
who are foolish because of attacks of disease, such as
epilepsy, or because of fits of madness, are diseased.

Sometimes it is possible to have some of these
conditions without being overcome—if, for instance,
Phalaris had an appetite to eat a child or for some 15
bizarre sexual pleasure, but restrained it. It is also
possible to be overcome by these conditions and not
merely to have them.

One sort of vice is human, and this is called simple
vice; another sort is called vice with an added condition, and is said to be bestial or diseased vice, but
not simple vice. Similarly, then, it is also clear that
one sort of incontinence is bestial, another diseased,
but only the incontinence corresponding to human
intemperance is simple incontinence.   20

It is clear, then, that incontinence and continence
apply only within the range of intemperance and
temperance, and that for other things there is another
form of incontinence, so called by transference of the
name, and not simply.

6

Moreover, let us observe that incontinence about 25
spirit is less shameful than incontinence about appetites. For spirit would seem to hear reason a bit, but
to mishear it. It is like overhasty servants who run out
before they have heard all their instructions, and then
carry them out wrongly, or dogs who bark at any noise
at all, before looking to see if it is a friend. In the
same way, since spirit is naturally hot and hasty, it 30

hears, but does not hear the instruction, and rushes off to exact a penalty. For reason or appearance has shown that we are being slighted or wantonly insulted; and spirit, as though it had inferred that it is right to
35 fight this sort of thing, is irritated at once. Appetite, however, only needs reason or perception to say that this is pleasant, and it rushes off for gratification.

1149b   And so spirit follows reason in a way, but appetite does not. Therefore [incontinence about appetite] is more shameful. For if someone is incontinent about spirit, he is overcome by reason in a way; but if he is incontinent about appetite, he is overcome by appetite, not by reason.

5   Further, it is more pardonable to follow natural desires, since it is also more pardonable to follow those natural appetites that are common to everyone and to the extent that they are common. Now spirit and irritability are more natural than the excessive and unnecessary appetites. It is just as the son said in his defense for beating his father: 'Yes, and he beat his
10 father, and his father beat *his* father before that'; and pointing to his young son, he said, 'And he will beat me when he becomes a man; it runs in our family.' Similarly, the father being dragged by his son kept urging him to stop at the front door, since that was as far as he had dragged his own father.

     Further, those who plot more are more unjust. Now the spirited person does not plot, and neither does spirit; it is open. Appetite, however, is like what
15 they say about Aphrodite, 'trick weaving Cypris,' and what Homer says about her embroidered girdle: 'Blandishment, which steals the wits even of the very prudent.' If, then, incontinence about appetite is more unjust and more shameful than incontinence about
20 spirit, it is simple incontinence, and vice in a way.

     Further, no one feels pain when he commits wanton aggression; but whatever someone does from anger, he feels pain when he does it, whereas the wanton aggressor does what he does with pleasure. Now if whatever more justly provokes anger is more unjust, incontinence caused by appetite is more unjust, since spirit involves no wanton aggression.

25   It is clear, then, how incontinence about appetites is more shameful than incontinence about spirit, and that continence and incontinence are about bodily appetites and pleasures.

     Now we must grasp the varieties of these appetites and pleasures. As we said at the beginning, some appetites are human and natural in kind and degree, some bestial, some caused by deformities and dis-
30 eases. Temperance and intemperance are concerned only with the first of these. This is also why we do not call beasts either temperate or intemperate, except by transference of the name, if one kind of animal exceeds another altogether in wanton aggression, destructiveness, and ravenousness. For beasts have nei-
35 ther decision nor rational calculation, but are outside
1150a [rational] nature, as the madmen among human beings are.

     Bestiality is less grave than vice, but more frightening; for the best part is not corrupted, as it is in a human being, but absent altogether. Hence a comparison between the two is like a comparison between
5 an inanimate and an animate being to see which is worse. For in each case the badness of something that lacks an internal principle of its badness is less destructive than the badness of something that has such an internal principle; and understanding is such an internal principle. It is similar, then, to a comparison between the injustice [of a beast] and an unjust human being; for in a way each [of these] is worse, since a bad human being can do innumerably more bad things than a beast.

7

Let us now consider the pleasures and pains arising
10 through touch and taste, the appetites for these pleasures, and the aversions from these pains. Earlier we defined temperance and intemperance as being about these. Now it is possible for someone to be in the state in which he is overcome, even by [pleasure and pains] which most people overcome; and it is possible to overcome even those that overcome most people. The person who is prone to be overcome by pleasures is incontinent; the one who overcomes is continent; the one overcome by pains is soft; and the one who overcomes them is resistant. The state of most people
15 is in between, though indeed they may lean more toward the worse states.

     Now some pleasures are necessary and some are not. [The necessary ones are necessary] to a certain extent, but their excesses and deficiencies are not. The same is true for appetites and pains. One person

20 pursues excesses of pleasant things because they are excesses and because he decides on it, for themselves and not for some further result. He is intemperate; for he is bound to have no regrets, and so is incurable, since someone without regrets is incurable. The one who is deficient is his opposite, while the intermediate one is temperate. The same is true of the one who avoids bodily pains not because he is overcome, but because he decides on it.

25 One of those who do not [act on] decision is led on because of pleasure; the other is led on because he is avoiding the pain that comes from appetite; hence these two differ from each other.

Now it would seem to everyone that someone who does a shameful action from no appetite or a weak one is worse than if he does it from an intense appetite; and, similarly, that if he strikes another not from 30 anger, he is worse than if he strikes from anger. For [if he can do such evil when he is unaffected by feeling], what would he have done if he had been strongly affected? That is why the intemperate person is worse than the incontinent.

One of the states mentioned [i.e., the decision to avoid pain] is more a species of softness, whereas the other person is intemperate.

The continent person is opposite to the incontinent, and the resistant to the soft. For resistance con- 35 sists in holding out, and continence in overcoming, but holding out is different from overcoming, just as not being defeated differs from winning; hence continence is more choiceworthy than resistance.

1150b Someone who is deficient in withstanding what most people withstand, and are capable of withstanding, is soft and self-indulgent; for self-indulgence is a kind of softness. This person trails his cloak to avoid 5 the labor and pain of lifting it, and imitates an invalid, though he does not think he is miserable—he is [merely] similar to a miserable person.

It is similar with continence and incontinence also. For it is not surprising if someone is overcome by strong and excessive pleasures or pains; indeed, this is pardonable, provided he struggles against them— 10 like Theodectes' Philoctetes bitten by the snake, or Carcinus' Cercyon in the *Alope*, and like those who are trying to restrain their laughter and burst out laughing all at once, as happened to Xenophantus. But it is surprising if someone is overcome by what most people can resist, and is incapable of withstanding it, not because of his hereditary nature or because of disease (as, for instance, the Scythian kings' softness 15 is hereditary, and as the female is distinguished [by softness] from the male).

The lover of amusements also seems to be intemperate, but in fact he is soft. For amusement is a relaxation, since it is a release, and the lover of amusement is one of those who go to excess here.

One type of incontinence is impetuosity, while 20 another is weakness. For the weak person deliberates, but then his feeling makes him abandon the result of his deliberation; but the impetuous person is led on by his feelings because he has not deliberated. For some people are like those who do not get tickled themselves if they tickle someone else first; if they see and notice something in advance, and rouse themselves and their rational calculation, they are not overcome by feelings, no matter whether something is 25 pleasant or painful. Quick-tempered and volatile people are most prone to be impetuous incontinents. For in quick-tempered people the appetite is so fast, and in volatile people so intense, that they do not wait for reason, because they tend to follow appearance.

8

The intemperate person, as we said, is not prone to 30 regret, since he abides by his decision [when he acts]. But every incontinent is prone to regret. That is why the truth is not what we said in raising the puzzles, but in fact the intemperate person is incurable, and the incontinent curable. For vice resembles diseases such as dropsy or consumption, while incontinence is more like epilepsy; vice is a continuous bad condition, but incontinence is not. For the incontinent is similar to those who get drunk quickly from a little 1151a3 wine, and from less than it takes for most people. 4, 5 And in general incontinence and vice are of different 1150b35 kinds. For the vicious person does not recognize that he is vicious, whereas the incontinent person recognizes that he is incontinent.

Among the incontinent people themselves, those 1151a who abandon themselves [to desire, i.e., the impetuous] are better than those [i.e., the weak] who have reason but do not abide by it. For the second type are overcome by a less strong feeling, and do not act without having deliberated, as the first type do.

5   Evidently, then, incontinence is not a vice, though presumably it is one in a way. For incontinence is against one's decision, but vice accords with decision. All the same, incontinence is similar to vice in its actions. Thus Demodocus attacks the Milesians: 'The Milesians are not stupid, but they do what stupid 10 people would do'; in the same way incontinents are not unjust, but will do injustice.

Moreover, the incontinent person is the sort to pursue excessive bodily pleasures against correct reason, but not because he is persuaded [it is best]. The intemperate person, however, is persuaded, because he is the sort of person to pursue them. Hence the incontinent person is easily persuaded out of it, while the intemperate person is not.

15   For virtue preserves the principle, whereas vice corrupts it; and in actions the end we act for is the principle, as the assumptions are the principles in mathematics. Reason does not teach the principles either in mathematics or in actions; [with actions] it is virtue, either natural or habituated, that teaches correct belief about the principle. The sort of person 20 [with this virtue] is temperate, and the contrary sort intemperate.

But there is also someone who because of his feelings abandons himself against correct reason. They overcome him far enough so that his actions do not accord with correct reason, but not so far as to make him the sort of person to be persuaded that it is right to pursue such pleasures without restraint. This, then, is the incontinent person. He is better than the intem- 25 perate person, and is not bad without qualification, since the best thing, the principle, is preserved in him. Another sort of person is contrary to him. [This is the continent person,] who abides [by reason] and does not abandon himself, not because of his feelings at least. It is evident from this that the continent person's state is excellent, and the incontinent person's state is base.

9

30 Then is someone continent if he abides by just any sort of reason and any sort of decision, or must he abide by the correct decision? And is someone incon-

tinent if he fails to abide by just any decision and any reason, or must it be reason that is not false, and the correct decision? This was the puzzle raised earlier.

Perhaps in fact the continent person abides, and the incontinent fails to abide, by just any decision coincidentally, but abides by the true reason and the correct decision in itself. For if someone chooses or 35 pursues one thing because of a second, he pursues 1151b and chooses the second in itself and the first coincidentally. Now when we speak of something without qualification, we speak of it in itself. Hence in one way [i.e., coincidentally] the continent person abides by just any belief, and the incontinent abandons it; but, [speaking] without qualification, the continent person abides by the true belief and the incontinent person abandons it.

Now there are some other people who tend to 5 abide by their belief. These are the people called stubborn, who are hard to persuade into something and not easy to persuade out of it. These have some similarity to continent people, just as the wasteful person has to the generous, and the rash to the confident. But they are different on many points. For the continent person is not swayed because of feeling and appetite; [but he is not inflexible about everything] 10 since he will be easily persuaded whenever it is appropriate. But stubborn people are not swayed by reason; for they acquire appetites, and many of them are led on by pleasures.

The stubborn include the opinionated, the ignorant, and the boorish. The opinionated are as they are because of pleasure and pain. For they find enjoyment in winning [the argument] if they are not per- 15 suaded to change their views, and they feel pain if their opinions are voided, like decrees [in the Assembly]. Hence they are more like incontinent than like continent people.

There are also some people who do not abide by their resolutions, but not because they are incontinent—Neoptolemus, for instance, in Sophocles' *Philoctetes*. Though certainly it was pleasure that made him abandon his resolution, it was a fine pleasure; 20 for telling the truth was pleasant to him, but Odysseus had persuaded him to lie. [He is not incontinent;] for not everyone who does something because of pleasure is either intemperate or base or incontinent, but only someone who does it because of a shameful pleasure.

There is also the sort of person who enjoys bodily things less than is right, and does not abide by reason; hence the continent person is intermediate between this person and the incontinent. For the incontinent fails to abide by reason because of too much [enjoyment]; the other person fails because of too little; but the continent person abides and is not swayed because of too much or too little. If continence is excellent, then both of these contrary states must be base, as indeed they appear. However, the other state is evident in only a few people on a few occasions; and hence continence seems to be contrary only to incontinence, just as temperance seems to be contrary only to intemperance.

Now many things are called by some name because of similarity [to genuine cases]; this has happened also to the continence of the temperate person, because of similarity. For the continent and the temperate person are both the sort to do nothing against reason because of bodily pleasures, but the continent person has base appetites, whereas the temperate person lacks them. The temperate person is the sort to find nothing pleasant against reason, but the continent is the sort to find such things pleasant but not to be led by them.

The incontinent and the intemperate person are similar too; though they are different, they both pursue bodily sources of pleasure. But the intemperate person [pursues them because he] also thinks it is right, while the incontinent person does not think so.

10

Nor can the same person be at once both prudent and incontinent. For we have shown that a prudent person must also at the same time be excellent in character, [and the incontinent person is not]. However, a clever person may well be incontinent. Indeed, the reason people sometimes seem to be prudent but incontinent is that [really they are only clever and] cleverness differs from prudence in the way we described in our first discussion; though they are closely related in definition, they differ in [so far as prudence requires the correct] decision.

Moreover, someone is not prudent simply by knowing; he must also act on his knowledge. But the incon-

tinent person does not. He is not in the condition of someone who knows and is attending [to his knowledge, as he would have to be if he were prudent], but in the condition of one asleep or drunk.

He acts willingly; for in a way he acts in knowledge both of what he is doing and of the end he is doing it for. But he is not base, since his decision is decent; hence he is half base. Nor is he unjust, since he is not a plotter. For one type of incontinent person [i.e., the weak] does not abide by the result of his deliberation, while the volatile [i.e., impetuous] person is not even prone to deliberate at all.

In fact the incontinent person is like a city that votes for all the right decrees and has excellent laws, but does not apply them, as in Anaxandrides' taunt, 'The city willed it, that cares nothing for laws.' The base person, by contrast, is like a city that applies its laws, but applies bad ones.

Incontinence and continence are about what exceeds the state of most people; the continent person abides [by reason] more than most people are capable of doing, the incontinent person less.

The [impetuous] type of incontinence found in volatile people is more easily cured than the [weak] type of incontinence found in those who deliberate but do not abide by it. And incontinents through habituation are more easily cured than the natural incontinents; for habit is easier than nature to change. Indeed the reason why habit is also difficult to change is that it is like nature; as Eunenus says, 'Habit, I say, is longtime training, my friend, and in the end training is nature for human beings.'

We have said, then, what continence and incontinence, resistance and softness are, and how these states are related to each other.

11

Pleasure and pain are proper subjects of study for the political philosopher, since he is the ruling craftsman of the end that we refer to in calling something bad or good without qualification. Further, we must also examine them because we have laid it down that virtue and vice of character are about pains and pleasures, and because most people think happiness involves pleasure —that is why they also call the blessed person by that name (*makarios*) from enjoyment (*chairein*).

Now it seems to some people that no pleasure is a good, either in its own right or coincidentally, on the ground that the good is not the same as pleasure. To others it seems that some pleasures are good, but most are bad. A third view is that even if every pleasure is a good, the best good still cannot be pleasure.

The reasons for thinking it is not a good at all are these: Every pleasure is a perceived becoming toward [the fulfillment of something's] nature; but no becoming is of the same kind as its end—for instance, no [process of] building is of the same kind as a house. Further, the temperate person avoids pleasures. Further, the prudent person pursues what is painless, not what is pleasant. Further, pleasures impede prudent thinking, and impede it more the more we enjoy them; no one, for instance, can think about anything during sexual intercourse. Further, every good is the product of a craft, but there is no craft of pleasure. Further, children and animals pursue pleasure.

To show that not all pleasures are excellent things, people say that some are shameful and reproached, and that some are harmful, since some pleasant things cause disease.

To show that the best good is not pleasure, people say that pleasure is not an end, but a becoming.

These, then, are roughly the things said about it.

12

These arguments, however, do not show that pleasure is not a good, or even that it is not the best good. This will be clear as follows.

First of all, since what is good may be good in either of two ways, as good without qualification or as good for some particular thing or person, this will also be true of natures and states, and hence also of processes and becomings. And so, among the [processes and becomings] that seem bad, some are bad without qualification but for some person not bad, and for this person actually choiceworthy. Some are not choiceworthy for him either, except sometimes and for a short time, not on each occasion. Some are not even pleasures, but appear to be; these are the [processes], for instance, in sick people that involve pain and are means to medical treatment.

Further, since one sort of good is an activity and another sort is a state, the processes that restore us to our natural state are pleasant coincidentally. Here the activity in the appetites belongs to the rest of our state and nature. For there are also pleasures without pain and appetite, such as the pleasures of studying, those in which our nature lacks nothing.

A sign [that supports our distinction between pleasures] is the fact that we do not enjoy the same thing when our nature is being refilled as we enjoy when it is eventually fully restored. When it is fully restored, we enjoy things that are pleasant without qualification, but when it is being refilled, we enjoy even the contrary things. For we even enjoy sharp or bitter things, though none of these is pleasant by nature or pleasant without qualification. Hence [these pleasures] are not pleasures [without qualification] either; for as pleasant things differ from one another, so the pleasures arising from them differ too.

Further, it is not necessary for something else to be better than pleasure, as the end, some say, is better than the becoming. For pleasures are not becomings, nor do they all even involve a becoming. They are activities, and an end [in themselves], and arise when we exercise [a capacity], not when we are coming to be [in some state]. And not all pleasures have something else as their end, but only those in people who are being led toward the completion of their nature.

That is why it is also a mistake to call pleasure a perceived becoming. It should instead be called an activity of the natural state, and should be called not perceived, but unimpeded. The reason it seems to some people to be a becoming is that it is fully good [and hence an activity]; for they think activities are becomings, though in fact these are different things.

To say that pleasures are bad because some pleasant things cause disease is the same as saying that some healthy things are bad for money-making. To this extent both are bad; but that is not enough to make them bad, since even study is sometimes harmful to health.

Neither prudence nor any state is impeded by the pleasures arising from it, but only by alien pleasures. For the pleasures arising from study and learning will make us study and learn all the more.

The fact that pleasure is not the product of a craft is quite reasonable; for a craft does not belong to any other activity either, but to a capacity. And yet, the crafts of perfumery and cooking do seem to be crafts of pleasure.

The claim that the temperate person avoids pleasure, that the prudent person pursues the painless life, and that children and beasts pursue pleasure — all these are solved by the same reply. For we have explained in what ways pleasures are good, and in 30 what ways not all are good without qualification; and it is these pleasures [that are not good without qualification] that beasts and children pursue, whereas the prudent person pursues painlessness in relation to these. These are the pleasures that involve appetite and pain and the bodily pleasures (since these involve appetite and pain) and their excesses, whose pursuit makes the intemperate person intemperate. That is why the temperate person avoids these pleasures [but 35 not all pleasures], since there are pleasures of the temperate person too.

13

1153b Moreover, it is also agreed that pain is an evil, and is to be avoided; for one kind of pain is bad without qualification, and another is bad in a particular way, by impeding [activities]. But the contrary to what is to be avoided, insofar as it is bad and to be avoided, is a good; hence pleasure must be a good. For Speusip-5 pus' solution — [that pleasure is opposite both to pain and to the good] as the greater is contrary both to the lesser and to the equal — does not succeed. For he would not say [as his solution requires] that pleasure is essentially an evil.

Besides, just as one science might well be the best good, even though some sciences are bad, some pleasure might well be the best good, even though most pleasures are bad. Indeed, presumably, if each state 10 has its unimpeded activities, and happiness is the activity — if the activity is unimpeded — of all states or of some one of them, it follows that some unimpeded activity is most choiceworthy. But pleasure is this, [namely, an unimpeded activity]; and so some type of pleasure might be the best good even if most pleasures turn out to be bad without qualification.

15 That is why all think the happy life is pleasant and weave pleasure into happiness, quite reasonably. For no activity is complete if it is impeded, and happiness is something complete. That is why the happy person needs to have goods of the body and external goods added [to good activities], and needs fortune also, so that he will not be impeded in these ways.

Some maintain, on the contrary, that we are happy when we are broken on the wheel, or fall into terrible misfortunes, provided that we are good. Whether they 20 mean to or not, these people are talking nonsense.

And because happiness needs fortune added, some believe good fortune is the same as happiness. But it is not. For when it is excessive, it actually impedes happiness; and then, presumably, it is no longer rightly called *good* fortune, since the limit [up to which it is good] is defined in relation to happiness.

The fact that all, both beasts and human beings, 25 pursue pleasure is some sign of its being in some way the best good: 'No rumor is altogether lost which many peoples [spread]. . . . ' But since the best nature and state neither is nor seems to be the same for all, 30 they also do not all pursue the same pleasure, though they all pursue pleasure. Presumably in fact they do pursue the same pleasure, and not the one they think or would say they pursue; for all things by nature have something divine [in them].

However, the bodily pleasures have taken over the 35 name because people most often aim at them, and all share in them; and so, since these are the only pleasures they know, people suppose that they are 1154a the only pleasures.

It is also apparent that if pleasure is not a good and an activity, it will not be true that the happy person lives pleasantly. For what will he need pleasure for if it is not a good? Indeed, it will even be possible for him to live painfully; for pain is neither an evil 5 nor a good if pleasure is not, and why then would he avoid it? Nor indeed will the life of the excellent person be more pleasant if his activities are not also more pleasant.

14

Those who maintain that some pleasures, such as the 10 fine ones, are highly choiceworthy, but the bodily pleasures that concern the intemperate person are not, should examine bodily pleasures.

If what they say is true, why are the pains contrary to these pleasures deplorable? For it is a good that is contrary to an evil. Then are the necessary [bodily pleasures] good only in the way that what is not bad is good? Or are they good up to a point? [Surely they are good up to a point.] For though some states and processes allow no excess of the better, and hence no excess of pleasure [in them] either, others do allow excess of the better, and hence also allow excess of the pleasure in them. Now the bodily goods allow excess. The base person is base because he pursues the excess, but not because he pursues the necessary pleasures; for all enjoy delicacies and wines and sexual relations in some way, though not all in the right way.

The contrary is true of pain. For the base person avoids pain in general, not [only] an excess of it. For not [all] pain is contrary to excess [of pleasure], except to someone who pursues the excess [of pleasure].

We must, however, not only state the true view, but also explain the false view; for an explanation of that promotes confidence. For when we have an apparently reasonable explanation of why a false view appears true, that makes us more confident of the true view. Hence we should say why bodily pleasures appear more choiceworthy.

First, then, it is because bodily pleasure pushes out pain. Excesses of pain make people seek a cure in the pursuit of excessive pleasure and of bodily pleasure in general. And these cures become intense — that is why they are pursued — because they appear next to their contraries.

Indeed these are the two reasons why pleasure seems to be no excellent thing, as we have said. First, some pleasures are the actions of a base nature — either base from birth, as in a beast, or base because of habit, such as the actions of base human beings. Secondly, others are cures of something deficient, and it is better to be in a good state than to be coming into it. In fact these pleasures coincide with our restoration to complete health, and so are excellent coincidentally.

Further, bodily pleasures are pursued because they are intense, by people who are incapable of enjoying other pleasures. Certainly, these people induce some kinds of thirst in themselves. What they do is not a matter for reproach, whenever [the pleasures] are harmless, but it is base whenever they are harmful. These people do this because they enjoy nothing else,

and many people's natural constitution makes the neutral condition painful to them.

For an animal is always suffering, as the natural scientists also testify, since they maintain that seeing and hearing are painful. However, we are used [to seeing and hearing] by now, so they say, [and so feel no intense pain]. Indeed, the [process of] growth makes young people's condition similar to an intoxicated person's and [hence] youth is pleasant. Naturally volatile people, by contrast, are always requiring a cure, since their constitution causes their body continual turmoil, and they are always having intense desires. A pain is driven out by its contrary pleasure, indeed by any pleasure at all that is strong enough; and this is why such people become intemperate and base.

Pleasures without pains, however, have no excess. These are pleasant by nature and not coincidentally. By coincidentally pleasant things I mean pleasant things that are curative; for the [process of] being cured coincides with some action of the part of us that remains healthy, and hence undergoing a cure seems to be pleasant. Things are pleasant by nature, however, when they produce action of a healthy nature.

The reason why no one thing is always pleasant is that our nature is not simple, but has more than one constituent, insofar as we are perishable; hence the action of one part is against nature for the other nature in us, and when they are equally balanced, the action seems neither pleasant nor painful. For if something has a simple nature the same action will always be the most pleasant.

That is why the god always enjoys one simple pleasure [without change]. For activity belongs not only to change but also to unchangingness, and indeed there is pleasure in rest more than in change. 'Variation in everything is sweet' (as the poet says) because of some inferiority; for just as it is the inferior human being who is prone to variation, so also the nature that needs variation is inferior, since it is not simple or decent.

So much, then, for continence and incontinence and for pleasure and pain, what each of them is, and in what ways some [aspects] of them are good and others bad. It remains for us to discuss friendship as well.

BOOK VIII

1

1155a After that, the next topic is friendship; for it is a virtue, or involves virtue.

5 Further, it is most necessary for our life. For no one would choose to live without friends even if he had all the other goods. Indeed rich people and holders of powerful positions, even more than other people, seem to need friends. For how would one benefit from such prosperity if one had no opportunity for beneficence, which is most often displayed, and most 10 highly praised, in relation to friends? And how would one guard and protect prosperity without friends, when it is all the more precarious the greater it is?

But in poverty also, and in the other misfortunes, people think friends are the only refuge. Moreover, the young need friends to keep them from error. The old need friends to care for them and support the actions that fail because of weakness. And those in their prime need friends to do fine actions; for 'when 15 two go together . . . ,' they are more capable of understanding and acting.

Further, a parent would seem to have a natural friendship for a child, and a child for a parent, not only among human beings but also among birds and 20 most kinds of animals. Members of the same species, and human beings most of all, have a natural friendship for each other; that is why we praise friends of humanity. And in our travels we can see how every human being is akin and beloved to a human being.

Moreover, friendship would seem to hold cities together, and legislators would seem to be more con- 25 cerned about it than about justice. For concord would seem to be similar to friendship, and they aim at concord among all, while they try above all to expel civil conflict, which is enmity. Further, if people are friends, they have no need of justice, but if they are just they need friendship in addition; and the justice that is most just seems to belong to friendship.

30 But friendship is not only necessary, but also fine. For we praise lovers of friends, and having many friends seems to be a fine thing. Moreover, people think that the same people are good and also friends.

Still, there are quite a few disputed points about friendship.

For some hold it is a sort of similarity and that similar people are friends. Hence the sayings, 'similar to similar,' and 'birds of a feather,' and so on. On the 35 other side, it is said that similar people are all like the proverbial potters, quarreling with each other.

On these questions some people inquire at a higher 1155b level, more proper to natural science. Euripides says that when earth gets dry it longs passionately for rain, and the holy heaven when filled with rain longs passionately to fall into the earth; and Heracleitus says 5 that the opponent cooperates, the finest harmony arises from discordant elements, and all things come to be in struggle. Others, such as Empedocles, oppose this view, and say that similar aims for similar.

Let us, then, leave aside the puzzles proper to natural science, since they are not proper to the present examination, and let us examine the puzzles that concern human [nature], and bear on characters and 10 feelings. For instance, does friendship arise among all sorts of people, or can people not be friends if they are vicious? And is there one species of friendship, or are there more? Some people think there is only one species because friendship allows more and less. But here their confidence rests on an inadequate sign; for things of different species also allow more and 15 less. We have spoken about these earlier.

2

Perhaps these questions will become clear once we find out what it is that is lovable. For, it seems, not everything is loved, but [only] the lovable, and this is either good or pleasant or useful. However, it seems that the useful is the source of some good or some pleasure; hence the good and the pleasant are lovable 20 as ends.

Now do people love the good, or the good for themselves? For sometimes these conflict; and the same is true of the pleasant. Each one, it seems, loves the good for himself; and while the good is lovable without qualification, the lovable for each one is the 25 good for himself. In fact, each one loves not what *is* good for him, but what *appears* good for him; but this will not matter, since [what appears good for him] will be what appears lovable.

There are these three causes, then, of love. Now love for an inanimate thing is not called friendship,

since there is no mutual loving, and no wishing of good to it. For it would presumably be ridiculous to
30 wish good things to wine; the most you wish is its preservation so that you can have it. To a friend, however, it is said, you must wish goods for his own sake. If you wish good things in this way, but the same wish is not returned by the other, you would be said to have [only] goodwill for the other. For friendship is said to be *reciprocated* goodwill.

35 But perhaps we should add that friends are aware of the reciprocated goodwill. For many a one has
1156a goodwill to people whom he has not seen but supposes to be decent or useful, and one of these might have the same goodwill toward him. These people, then, apparently have goodwill to each other, but how could we call them friends, given that they are unaware of their attitude to each other? [If they are to be friends], then, they must have goodwill to each
5 other, wish goods and be aware of it, from one of the causes mentioned above.

3

Since these causes differ in species, so do the types of loving and types of friendship. Hence friendship has three species, corresponding to the three objects of love. For each object of love has a corresponding type of mutual loving, combined with awareness of it.

But those who love each other wish goods to each other [only] insofar as they love each other. Those
10 who love each other for utility love the other not in his own right, but insofar as they gain some good for themselves from him. The same is true of those who love for pleasure; for they like a witty person not because of his character, but because he is pleasant to them.

15 Those who love for utility or pleasure, then, are fond of a friend because of what is good or pleasant for themselves, not insofar as the beloved is who he is, but insofar as he is useful or pleasant. Hence these friendships as well [as the friends] are coincidental, since the beloved is loved not insofar as he is who he is, but insofar as he provides some good or pleasure.

20 And so these sorts of friendships are easily dissolved, when the friends do not remain similar [to what they were]; for if someone is no longer pleasant or useful, the other stops loving him.

What is useful does not remain the same, but is different at different times. Hence, when the cause of their being friends is removed, the friendship is dissolved too, on the assumption that the friendship aims at these [useful results]. This sort of friendship seems to arise especially among older people, since
25 at that age they pursue the advantageous, not the pleasant, and also among those in their prime or youth who pursue the expedient.

Nor do such people live together very much. For sometimes they do not even find each other pleasant. Hence they have no further need to meet in this way if they are not advantageous [to each other]; for each finds the other pleasant [only] to the extent that he
30 expects some good from him. The friendship of hosts and guests is taken to be of this type too.

The cause of friendship between young people seems to be pleasure. For their lives are guided by their feelings, and they pursue above all what is pleasant for themselves and what is at hand. But as they grow up [what they find] pleasant changes too. Hence they are
35 quick to become friends, and quick to stop; for their friendship shifts with [what they find] pleasant, and the change in such pleasure is quick. Young people are
1156b prone to erotic passion, since this mostly accords with feelings, and is caused by pleasure; that is why they love and quickly stop, often changing in a single day.

These people wish to spend their days together and
5 to live together; for this is how they gain [the good things] corresponding to their friendship.

But complete friendship is the friendship of good people similar in virtue; for they wish goods in the same way to each other insofar as they are good, and they are good in their own right. [Hence they wish goods to each other for each other's own sake.] Now
10 those who wish goods to their friend for the friend's own sake are friends most of all; for they have this attitude because of the friend himself, not coincidentally. Hence these people's friendship lasts as long as they are good; and virtue is enduring.

Each of them is both good without qualification and good for his friend, since good people are both good without qualification and advantageous for each other. They are pleasant in the same ways too, since
15 good people are pleasant both without qualification and for each other. [They are pleasant for each other]

because each person finds his own actions and actions of that kind pleasant, and the actions of good people are the same or similar.

It is reasonable that this sort of friendship is enduring, since it embraces in itself all the features that
20 friends must have. For the cause of every friendship is good or pleasure, either unqualified or for the lover; and every friendship accords with some similarity. And all the features we have mentioned are found in this friendship because of [the nature of] the friends themselves. For they are similar in this way [i.e., in being good]. Moreover, their friendship also has the other things—what is good without qualification and what is pleasant without qualification; and these are lovable most of all. Hence loving and friendship are found most of all and at their best in these friends.

25 These kinds of friendships are likely to be rare, since such people are few. Further, they need time as well, to grow accustomed to each other; for, as the proverb says, they cannot know each other before they have shared their salt as often as it says, and they cannot accept each other or be friends until each appears lovable to the other and gains the other's confidence. Those
30 who are quick to treat each other in friendly ways wish to be friends, but are not friends, unless they are also lovable, and know this. For though the wish for friendship comes quickly, friendship does not.

4

This sort of friendship, then, is complete both in time and in the other ways. In every way each friend gets
35 the same things and similar things from each, and
1157a this is what must be true of friends. Friendship for pleasure bears some resemblance to this complete sort, since good people are also pleasant to each other. And friendship for utility also resembles it, since good people are also useful to each other.

With these [incomplete friends] also, the friendships are most enduring whenever they get the same
5 thing—pleasure, for instance—from each other, and, moreover, get it from the same source, as witty people do, in contrast to the erotic lover and the boy he loves.

For the erotic lover and his beloved do not take pleasure in the same things; the lover takes pleasure in seeing his beloved, but the beloved takes pleasure in being courted by his lover. When the beloved's

bloom is fading, sometimes the friendship fades too; for the lover no longer finds pleasure in seeing his beloved, and the beloved is no longer courted by the 10 lover. Many, however, remain friends if they have similar characters and come to be fond of each other's characters from being accustomed to them. Those who exchange utility rather than pleasure in their erotic relations are friends to a lesser extent and less enduring friends.

Those who are friends for utility dissolve the friend- 15 ship as soon as the advantage is removed; for they were never friends of each other, but of what was expedient for them.

Now it is possible for bad people as well [as good] to be friends to each other for pleasure or utility, for decent people to be friends to base people, and for someone with neither character to be a friend to someone with any character. Clearly, however, only good people can be friends to each other because of the other person himself; for bad people find no 20 enjoyment in one another if they get no benefit.

Moreover, the friendship of good people is the only one that is immune to slander. For it is not easy to trust anyone speaking against someone whom we ourselves have found reliable for a long time; and among good people there is trust, the belief that he would never do injustice, and all the other things expected in a true friendship. But in the other types of friendship [distrust] may easily arise.   25

[These must be counted as types of friendship.] For people include among friends [not only the best type, but] also those who are friends for utility, as cities are—since alliances between cities seem to aim at expediency—and those who are fond of each other, as children are, for pleasure. Hence we must presumably also say that such people are friends, but say that 30 there are more species of friendship than one.

On this view, the friendship of good people insofar as they are good is friendship primarily and fully, but the other friendships are friendships by similarity. For insofar as there is something good, and [hence] something similar to [what one finds in the best kind], people [in the incomplete friendships] are friends; for what is pleasant is good to lovers of pleasure. But these [incomplete] types of friendship are not very regularly combined, and the same people do not become friends for both utility and pleasure. For

35 things that [merely] coincide with each other are not very regularly combined.

1157b   Friendship has been assigned, then, to these species. Base people will be friends for pleasure or utility, since they are similar in that way. But good people will be friends because of themselves, since they are friends insofar as they are good. These, then, are friends without qualification; the others are friends 5 coincidentally and by being similar to these.

5

Just as, in the case of the virtues, some people are called good in their state of character, others good in their activity, the same is true of friendship. For some people find enjoyment in each other by living together, and provide each other with good things. Others, however, are asleep or separated by distance, and so are not active in these ways, but are in the state 10 that would result in the friendly activities; for distance does not dissolve the friendship without qualification, but only its activity. But if the absence is long, it also seems to cause the friendship to be forgotten; hence the saying, 'Lack of conversation has dissolved many a friendship.'

15   Older people and sour people do not appear to be prone to friendship. For there is little pleasure to be found in them, and no one can spend his days with what is painful or not pleasant, since nature appears to avoid above all what is painful and to aim at what is pleasant.

Those who welcome each other but do not live together would seem to have goodwill rather than friend-
20 ship. For nothing is as proper to friends as living together; for while those who are in want desire benefit, blessedly happy people [who want for nothing], no less than the others, desire to spend their days together, since a solitary life fits them least of all. But people cannot spend their time with each other if they are not pleasant and do not enjoy the same things, as they seem to in the friendship of companions.

25   Now the friendship of good people is friendship most of all, as we have often said. For what is lovable and choiceworthy seems to be what is good or pleasant without qualification, and what is lovable and choiceworthy to each person seems to be what is good or pleasant to himself; and both of these make one good person lovable and choiceworthy to another good person.

Loving would seem to be a feeling, but friendship 30 a state. For loving is directed no less toward inanimate things, but reciprocal loving requires decision, and decision comes from a state; and [good people] wish good to the beloved for his own sake in accord with their state, not their feeling.

Moreover, in loving their friend they love what is good for themselves; for when a good person becomes a friend he becomes a good for his friend. Each of 35 them loves what is good for himself, and repays in equal measure the wish and the pleasantness of his friend; for friendship is said to be equality. And this is true above all in the friendship of good people.   1158a

6

Among sour people and older people, friendship is found less often, since they are worse-tempered and find less enjoyment in meeting people, so that they lack the features that seem most typical and most 5 productive of friendship. That is why young people become friends quickly, but older people do not, since they do not become friends with people in whom they find no enjoyment—nor do sour people. These people have goodwill to each other, since they wish goods and give help in time of need; but they scarcely count as friends, since they do not spend their days together or find enjoyment in each other, and these things seem to be above all typical of 10 friendship.

No one can have complete friendship for many people, just as no one can have an erotic passion for many at the same time; for [complete friendship, like erotic passion,] is like an excess, and an excess is naturally directed at a single individual. And just as it is difficult for many people to please the same person intensely at the same time, it is also difficult, presumably, for many to be good. [To find out whether someone is really good], one must both have experience of him and be on familiar terms with 15 him, which is extremely difficult. If, however, the friendship is for utility or pleasure, it is possible for many people to please; for there are many people of the right sort, and the services take little time.

Of these other two types of friendship, the friendship for pleasure is more like [real] friendship; for they get the same thing from each other, and they 20 find enjoyment in each other, or [rather] in the same things. This is what friendships are like among young people; for a generous [attitude] is found here more [than among older people], whereas it is mercenary people who form friendships for utility.

Moreover, blessedly happy people have no need of anything useful, but do need sources of pleasure. For they want to spend their lives with companions, and though what is painful is borne for a short time, 25 no one could continuously endure even the Good Itself if it were painful to him. That is why they seek friends who are pleasant. But, presumably, they must also seek friends who are good as well [as pleasant], and good for them too; for then they will have everything that friends must have.

Someone in a position of power appears to have separate groups of friends; for some are useful to him, 30 others pleasant, but the same ones are not often both. For he does not seek friends who are both pleasant and virtuous, or useful for fine actions, but seeks one group to be witty, when he pursues pleasure, and the other group to be clever in carrying out instructions; and the same person rarely has both features.

Though admittedly, as we have said, an excellent person is both pleasant and useful, he does not be- 35 come a friend to a superior [in power and position] unless the superior is also superior in virtue; otherwise he does not reach [proportionate] equality by having a proportionate superior. And this superiority both in power and in virtue is not often found.

1158b   The friendships we have mentioned involve equality, since both friends get the same and wish the same to each other, or exchange one thing for another—for instance, pleasure for benefit. But, as we have said, they 5 are friendships to a lesser extent, and less enduring.

They seem both to be and not to be friendships, because of their similarity and dissimilarity to the same thing. For, on the one hand, insofar as they are similar to the friendship of virtue, they are apparently friendships; for that type of friendship includes both utility and pleasure, and one of these types includes

utility, the other pleasure. On the other hand, the friendship of virtue is enduring and immune to slan- 10 der, whereas these change quickly, and differ from it in many other ways as well; to that extent they are apparently not friendships, because of their dissimilarity to that best type.

7

A different species of friendship is the one that rests on superiority—of a father toward his son, for instance, and in general of an older person toward a younger, of a man toward a woman, and of any sort of ruler toward the one he rules. These friendships also differ from each other. For friendship of parents to children is not the same as that of rulers to ruled; 15 nor is friendship of father to son the same as that of son to father, or of man to woman as that of woman to man. For each of these friends has a different virtue and a different function, and there are different causes of love. Hence the ways of loving are different, and so are the friendships.

Now each does not get the same thing from the 20 other, and must not seek it; but whenever children accord to their parents what they must accord to those who gave them birth, and parents accord what they must do to their children, their friendship is enduring and decent.

In all the friendships that rest on superiority, the 25 loving must also be proportional; for instance, the better person, and the more beneficial, and each of the others likewise, must be loved more than he loves; for when the loving accords with the comparative worth of the friends, equality is achieved in a way, and this seems to be proper to friendship.

Equality, however, does not appear to be the same 30 in friendship as in justice. For in justice equality is equality primarily in worth and secondarily in quantity; but in friendship it is equality primarily in quantity and secondarily in worth.

This is clear if friends come to be separated by some wide gap in virtue, vice, wealth, or something else; for then they are friends no more, and do not 35 even expect to be. This is most evident with gods, since they have the greatest superiority in all goods. But it is also clear with kings, since far inferior people 1159a do not expect to be their friends; nor do worthless people expect to be friends to the best or wisest.

Now in these cases there is no exact definition of how long people are friends. For even if one of them
5 loses a lot, the friendship still endures; but if one is widely separated [from the other], as a god is [from a human being], it no longer endures.

This raises a puzzle: Do friends really wish their friend to have the greatest good, to be a god, for instance? For [if he becomes a god], *he* will no longer have friends, and hence no longer have goods, since
10 friends are goods. If, then, we have been right to say that one friend wishes good things to the other for the sake of the other *himself*, the other must remain whatever sort of being he is. Hence it is to the other as a human being that a friend will wish the greatest goods—though presumably not all of them, since each person wishes goods most of all to himself.

8

15 Because the many love honor they seem to prefer being loved to loving. That is why they love flatterers. For the flatterer is a friend in an inferior position, or [rather] pretends to be one, and pretends to love more than he is loved; and being loved seems close to being honored, which the many certainly pursue.

It would seem, however, that they choose honor coincidentally, not in its own right. For the many
20 enjoy being honored by powerful people because they expect to get whatever they need from them, and so enjoy the honor as a sign of this good treatment. Those who want honor from decent people with knowledge are seeking to confirm their own view of themselves, and so they are pleased because the judgment of those who say they are good makes them
25 confident that they are good. Being loved, on the contrary, they enjoy in its own right. That is why it seems to be better than being honored, and friendship seems choiceworthy in its own right.

But friendship seems to consist more in loving than in being loved. A sign of this is the enjoyment a mother finds in loving. For sometimes she gives her child away
30 to be brought up, and loves him as long as she knows about him; but she does not seek the child's love, if she cannot both [love and be loved]. She would seem to be satisfied if she sees the child doing well, and she

loves the child even if ignorance prevents him from returning to her what is due to a mother.

Friendship, then, consists more in loving; and peo- 35 ple who love their friends are praised; hence, it would seem, loving is the virtue of friends. And so friends whose love accords with the worth of their friends 1159b are enduring friends and have an enduring friendship. This above all is how unequals as well as equals can be friends, since this is how they can be equalized.

Equality and similarity, and above all the similarity of those who are similar in being virtuous, is friendship. For virtuous people are enduringly [virtuous] in their own right, and enduring [friends] to each 5 other. They neither request nor provide assistance that requires base actions, but, you might even say, prevent this. For it is proper to good people to avoid error themselves and not to permit it in their friends.

Vicious people, by contrast, have no firmness, since they do not even remain similar to what they were. They become friends for a short time, enjoying each 10 other's vice. Useful or pleasant friends, however, last longer, for as long as they supply each other with pleasures or benefits.

The friendship that seems to arise most from contraries is friendship for utility, of poor to rich, for instance, or ignorant to knowledgeable; for we aim at whatever we find we lack, and give something else 15 in return. Here we might also include the erotic lover and his beloved, and the beautiful and the ugly. That is why an erotic lover also sometimes appears ridiculous, when he expects to be loved in the same way as he loves; that would presumably be a proper expectation if he were lovable in the same way, but it is ridiculous when he is not.

Presumably, however, contrary seeks contrary coin- 20 cidentally, not in its own right, and desire is for the intermediate. For what is good for the dry, for instance, is to reach the intermediate, not to become wet, and the same is true for the hot, and so on. Let us, then, dismiss these questions, since they are rather extraneous to our concern.

9

As we said at the beginning, friendship and justice 25 would seem to be about the same things and to be found in the same people. For in every community

there seems to be some sort of justice, and some type of friendship also. At any rate, fellow voyagers and fellow soldiers are called friends, and so are members of other communities. And the extent of their commu-
30 nity is the extent of their friendship, since it is also the extent of the justice found there. The proverb 'What friends have is common' is correct, since friendship involves community.

But, whereas brothers and companions have everything in common, what people have in common in other types of community is limited, more in some communities and less in others, since some friend-
35 ships are also closer than others, some less close.
1160a What is just is also different, since it is not the same for parents toward children as for one brother toward another, and not the same for companions as for fellow citizens, and similarly with the other types of friendship. Similarly, what is unjust toward each of these is also different, and becomes more unjust as it is practiced on closer friends. It is more shocking,
5 for instance, to rob a companion of money than to rob a fellow citizen, to fail to help a brother than a stranger, and to strike one's father than anyone else. Justice also naturally increases with friendship, since it involves the same people and extends over an equal area.

All the communities [mentioned], however, would seem to be parts of the political community. For
10 people keep company for some advantage and to supply something contributing to their life. And the political community as well [as the others] seems both to have been originally formed and to endure for advantage; for legislators also aim at advantage, and the common advantage is said to be just.
15   Now the other types of community aim at partial advantage. Sea travellers, for instance, seek the advantage proper to a journey, in making money or something like that, while fellow soldiers seek the advantage proper to war, desiring either money or victory or a city; and the same is true of fellow members of a tribe or deme. Some communities—reli-
20 gious societies and dining clubs—seem to arise for pleasure, since these are, respectively, for religious sacrifices and for companionship.

But all these communities would seem to be subordinate to the political community, since it aims not at some advantage close at hand, but at advantage

for the whole of life.... [We can see this in the arrangements that cities make for religious festivals. For] in performing sacrifices and arranging gatherings for these, people both accord honors to the gods and 25 provide themselves with pleasant relaxations. For the long-established sacrifices and gatherings appear to take place after the harvesting of the crops, as a sort of first-fruits, since this was the time when people used to be most at leisure [and the time when relaxation would be most advantageous for the whole of life].

All the types of community, then, appear to be 30 parts of the political community, and these sorts of communities imply the appropriate sorts of friendships.

10

There are three species of political system (*politeia*), and an equal number of deviations, which are a sort of corruption of them. The first political system is kingship; the second aristocracy; and since the third rests on property (*timēma*), it appears proper to call it a timocratic system, though most people usually call it a polity. The best of these is kingship and the 35 worst timocracy.

The deviation from kingship is tyranny. For, 1160b though both are monarchies, they show the widest difference, since the tyrant considers his own advantage, but the king considers the advantage of his subjects. For someone is a king only if he is self-sufficient 5 and superior in all goods; and since such a person needs nothing more, he will consider the subjects' benefit, not his own. For a king who is not like this would be only some sort of titular king. Tyranny is contrary to this; for the tyrant pursues his own good. It is more evident that [tyranny] is the worst [deviation than that timocracy is the worst political system]; but the worst is contrary to the best; [hence kingship is the best].

The transition from kingship is to tyranny. For 10 tyranny is the degenerate condition of monarchy, and the vicious king becomes a tyrant.

The transition from aristocracy [rule of the best people] is to oligarchy [rule of the few], resulting from the badness of the rulers. They distribute the city's goods contrary to people's worth, so that they

distribute all or most of the goods to themselves,
15 and always assign ruling offices to the same people,
counting wealth for most. Hence the rulers are few,
and they are vicious people instead of the most decent.

The transition from timocracy is to democracy [rule
by the people], since these border on each other. For
timocracy is also meant to be rule by the majority,
and all those with the property-qualification are equal;
[and majority rule and equality are the marks of de-
mocracy]. Democracy is the least vicious [of the devia-
20 tions]; for it deviates only slightly from the form of a
[genuine] political system.

These, then, are the most frequent transitions from
one political system to another, since they are the
smallest and easiest.

Resemblances to these—indeed, a sort of pattern
of them—can also be found in households. For the
25 community of a father and his sons has the structure
of kingship, since the father is concerned for his children. Indeed that is why Homer also calls Zeus father,
since kingship is meant to be paternal rule.

Among the Persians, however, the father's rule is
tyrannical, since he treats his sons as slaves. The rule
30 of a master over his slaves is also tyrannical, since it
is the master's advantage that is achieved in it. This,
then, appears a correct form of rule, whereas the
Persian form appears erroneous, since the different
types of rule suit different subjects.

The community of man and woman appears aristocratic. For the man's rule in the area where it is right
accords with the worth [of each], and he commits to
35 the woman what is fitting for her. If, however, the
man controls everything, he changes it into an oligarchy; for then his action does not accord with the
1161a worth [of each], or with the respect in which [each]
is better. Sometimes, indeed, women rule because
they are heiresses; these cases of rule do not accord
with virtue, but result from wealth and power, as is
true in oligarchies.

5 The community of brothers is like a timocratic
[system], since they are equal except insofar as they
differ in age. That is why, if they differ very much in
age, the friendship is no longer brotherly.

Democracy is found most of all in dwellings without a master, since everyone there is on equal terms;
and also in those where the ruler is weak and everyone
is free [to do what he likes].

11

Friendship appears in each of the political systems, 10
to the extent that justice appears also. A king's friendship to his subjects involves superior beneficence.
For he benefits his subjects, since he is good and
attends to them to ensure that they do well, as a
shepherd attends to his sheep; hence Homer also
called Agamemnon shepherd of the peoples. 15

A father's friendship resembles this, but differs in
conferring a greater benefit, since the father is the
cause of his children's being, which seems to be the
greatest benefit, and of their nurture and education.
These benefits are also ascribed to ancestors; and
by nature a father is ruler over sons, ancestors over
descendants, and a king over subjects.

All these are friendships of superiority. That is why 20
parents are also honored. And what is just is not the
same in each of these friendships, but it accords with
worth; for so does the friendship.

The friendship of man to woman is the same as in
an aristocracy. For it accords with virtue, in assigning 25
more good to the better, and assigning what is fitting
to each. The same is true of what is just here.

The friendship of brothers is similar to that of companions, since they are equal and of an age, and such
people usually have the same feelings and characters.
Friendship in a timocracy is similar to this. For there
the citizens are meant to be equal and decent, and
so rule in turn and on equal terms. The same is true,
then, of their friendship. 30

In the deviations, however, justice is found only
to a slight degree; and hence the same is true of
friendship. There is least of it in the worst deviation;
for in a tyranny there is little or no friendship.

For where ruler and ruled have nothing in common, they have no friendship, since they have no 35
justice either. This is true for a craftsman in relation
to his tool, and for the soul in relation to the body. 1161b
For in all these cases the user benefits what he uses,
but there is neither friendship nor justice toward inanimate things. Nor is there any toward a horse or cow,
or toward a slave, insofar as he is a slave. For master
and slave have nothing in common, since a slave is 5
a tool with a soul, while a tool is a slave without a soul.

Insofar as he is a slave, then, there is no friendship
with him. But there is friendship with him insofar as

he is a human being. For every human being seems to have some relation of justice with everyone who is capable of community in law and agreement; hence [every human being seems] also [to have] friendship [with every human being], to the extent that [every human being] is a human being.

Hence there are friendships and justice to only a
10 slight degree in tyrannies also, but to a much larger degree in democracies; for there people are equal, and so have much in common.

12

As we have said, then, every friendship is found in a community. But we should set apart the friendship of families and that of companions. The friendship of citizens, tribesmen, voyagers, and suchlike are
15 more like friendships in a community, since they appear to reflect some sort of agreement; and among these we may include the friendship of host and guest.

Friendship in families also seems to have many species, but they all seem to depend on paternal friendship. For a parent is fond of his children because he regards them as something of himself; and children are fond of a parent because they regard themselves as coming from him.
20 A parent knows better what has come from him than the children know that they are from the parent; and the parent regards his children as his own more than the product regards the maker as its own. For a person regards what comes from him as his own, as the owner regards his tooth or hair or anything; but what has come from him regards its owner as its
25 own not at all, or to a lesser degree. The length of time also matters. For a parent becomes fond of his children as soon as they are born, but children become fond of the parent when time has passed and they have acquired some comprehension or [at least] perception. And this also makes it clear why mothers love their children more [than fathers do].

A parent, then, loves his children as [he loves] himself. For what has come from him is a sort of other himself; [it is other because] it is separate. Children love a parent because they regard themselves as
30 having come from him. Brothers love each other because they have come from the same [parents]. For the same relation to the parents makes the same thing

for both of them; hence we speak of the same blood, the same stock, and so on. Hence they are the same thing in a way, in different [subjects].

Being brought up together and being of an age contributes largely to friendship; for 'two of an age' [get on well], and those with the same character are 35 companions. That is why the friendship of brothers 1162a and that of companions are similar. Cousins and other relatives are akin by being related to brothers, since that makes them descendants of the same parents [i.e., the parents of these brothers]. Some are more akin, others less, by the ancestor's being near to or far from them.

The friendship of children to a parent, like the 5 friendship of human beings to a god, is friendship toward what is good and superior. For the parent conferred the greatest benefits on his children, since he is the cause of their being and nurture and of their education once they have been born. This sort of friendship also includes pleasure and utility, more than the friendship of unrelated people does, to the extent that [parents and children] have more of a life in common.

Friendship between brothers has the features of 10 friendship between companions, especially when [the companions] are decent, or in general similar. For brothers are that much more akin to each other [than ordinary companions], and are fond of each other from birth; they are that much more similar in character when they are from the same parents, nurtured together and educated similarly; and the proof of their reliability over time is fullest and firmest. Among other relatives too the features of friendship are pro- 15 portional [to the relation].

The friendship of man and woman also seems to be natural. For human beings form couples more naturally than they form cities, to the extent that the household is prior to the city, and more necessary, and childbearing is shared more widely among the 20 animals. For the other animals, the community goes only as far as childbearing. Human beings, however, share a household not only for childbearing, but also for the benefits in their life. For the difference between them implies that their functions are divided, with different ones for the man and the woman; hence each supplies the other's needs by contributing a special function to the common good. For this reason their friendship seems to include both utility and pleasure.

25   And it may also be friendship for virtue, if they are decent. For each has a proper virtue, and this will be a source of enjoyment for them. Children seem to be another bond, and that is why childless unions are more quickly dissolved; for children are a common good for both, and what is common holds them together.

30   How should a man conduct his life toward his wife, or, in general, toward a friend? That appears to be the same as asking how they are to conduct their lives justly. For what is just is not the same for a friend toward a friend as toward a stranger, or the same toward a companion as toward a classmate.

13

35   There are three types of friendship, as we said at the beginning, and within each type some friendships rest on equality, while others are in accord with supe-
1162b   riority. For equally good people can be friends, but also a better and a worse person; and the same is true of friends for pleasure or utility, since they may be either equal or unequal in their benefits. Hence equals must equalize in loving and in the other things, because of their equality; and unequals must make the return that is proportionate to the types of superiority.

5   Accusations and reproaches arise only or most often in friendship for utility. And this is reasonable. For friends for virtue are eager to benefit each other, since this is proper to virtue and to friendship; and if this is what they strain to achieve, there are no accusations or fights. For no one objects if the other loves and
10   benefits him; if he is gracious, he retaliates by benefiting the other. And if the superior gets what he aims at, he will not accuse his friend of anything, since each of them desires what is good.

Nor are there many accusations among friends for
15   pleasure. For both of them get what they want at the same time if they enjoy spending their time together; and someone who accused his friend of not pleasing him would appear ridiculous, since he is free to spend his days without the friend's company.

Friendship for utility, however, is liable to accusations. For these friends deal with each other in the expectation of gaining benefits. Hence they always require more, thinking they have got less than is fitting; and they reproach the other because they get less than they require and deserve. And those who confer benefits cannot supply as much as the recipi- 20
ents require.

There are two ways of being just, one unwritten, and one governed by rules of law. And similarly one type of friendship of utility would seem to depend on character, and the other on rules. Accusations arise most readily if it is not the same sort of friendship 25
when they dissolve it as it was when they formed it.

Friendship dependent on rules is the type that is on explicit conditions. One type of this is entirely mercenary and requires immediate payment. The other is more generous and postpones the time [of repayment], but in accordance with an agreement [requiring] one thing in return for another. In this sort of friendship it is clear and unambiguous what is owed, but the postponement is a friendly aspect of it. That is why some cities do not allow legal actions in these cases, but think that people who have formed 30
an arrangement on the basis of trust must put up with the outcome.

Friendship [for utility] that depends on character is not on explicit conditions. Someone makes a present or whatever it is, as to a friend, but expects to get back as much or more, since he assumes that it is not a free gift, but a loan.

If one party does not dissolve the friendship on the terms on which he formed it, he will accuse the other. This happens because all or most people wish for 35
what is fine, but decide to do what is beneficial; and while it is fine to do someone a good turn without 1163a
aiming to receive one in return, it is beneficial to receive a good turn.

We should, if we can, make a return worthy of what we have received, [if the other has undertaken the friendship] willingly. For we should never make a friend of someone who is unwilling, but must suppose that we were in error at the beginning, and received a benefit from the wrong person; for since it was not from a friend, and this was not why he was doing it, 5
we must dissolve the arrangement as though we had received a good turn on explicit conditions. And we will agree to repay if we can. If we cannot repay, the giver would not even expect it. Hence we should

repay if we can. We should consider at the beginning who is doing us a good turn, and on what conditions, so that we can put up with it on these conditions, or else decline it.

It is disputable whether we must measure [the return] by the benefit accruing to the recipient, and make the return proportional to that, or instead by the good turn done by the benefactor. For a recipient says that what he got was a small matter for the benefactor, and that he could have gotten it from someone else instead, and so he belittles it. But the benefactor says it was the biggest thing he had, that it could not be gotten from anyone else, and that he gave it when he was in danger or similar need.

Since the friendship is for utility, surely the benefit to the recipient must be the measure [of the return]. For he was the one who required it, and the benefactor supplies him on the assumption that he will get an equal return. Hence the aid has been as great as the benefit received, and the recipient should return as much as he gained, or still more, since that is finer.

But in friendships in accord with virtue, there are no accusations. Rather, the decision of the benefactor would seem to be the measure, since the controlling element in virtue and character lies in decision.

14

There are also disputes in friendships in accord with superiority, since each friend expects to have more than the other, but whenever this happens the friendship is dissolved.

For the better person thinks it is fitting for him to have more, on the ground that more is fittingly allotted to the good person. And the more beneficial person thinks the same. For it is wrong, they say, for someone to have an equal share if he is useless; the result is a public service, not a friendship, if the benefits from the friendship do not accord with the worth of the actions. [The superior party says this] because he notices that in a financial community the larger contributors gain more, and he thinks the same thing is right in a friendship.

But the needy person, the inferior party in the friendship, takes the opposite view, saying it is proper to a virtuous friend to supply his needy [friends]. For what use is it, as they say, to be an excellent or powerful person's friend if you are not going to gain anything by it?

Well, each of them would seem to be correct in what he expects, and it is right for each of them to get more from the friendship—but not more of the same thing. Rather, the superior person should get more honor, and the needy person more profit, since honor is the reward of virtue and beneficence, while profit is what supplies need.

This also appears to be true in political systems. For someone who provides nothing for the community receives no honor, since what is common is given to someone who benefits the community, and honor is something common. For it is impossible both to make money off the community and to receive honor from it at the same time; for no one endures the smaller share of everything. Hence someone who suffers a monetary loss [by holding office] receives honor in return, while someone who accepts gifts [in office] receives money [but not honor]; for distribution that accords with worth equalizes and preserves the friendship, as we have said.

This, then, is how we should treat unequals. If we benefit from them in money or virtue, we should return honor, and thereby make what return we can. For friendship seeks what is possible, not what accords with worth, since that is impossible in some cases, as it is with honor to gods and parents. For no one could ever make a return in accord with their worth, but someone who attends to them as far as he is able seems to be a decent person.

That is why it might seem that a son is not free to disown his father, but a father is free to disown his son. For a debtor should return what he owes, and since, no matter what a son has done, he has not made a worthy return for what his father has done for him, he is always the debtor. But the creditor is free to remit the debt, and hence the father is free to remit.

At the same time, however, it presumably seems that no one would ever withdraw from a son, except from one who was far gone in vice. For, quite apart from their natural friendship, it is human not to repel aid. The son, however, if he is vicious, will want to avoid helping his father, or will not be keen on it. For the many wish to receive benefits, but they avoid doing them because they suppose it is unprofitable. So much, then, for these things.

BOOK IX

1

In all friendships of friends with dissimilar aims, proportion equalizes and preserves the friendship, as we said; in political friendship, for instance, the cobbler receives a worthy exchange for his shoes, and so do the weaver and the others. Here money is supplied as a common measure; everything is related to this and measured by it.

In erotic friendships, however, sometimes the lover charges that he loves the beloved deeply and is not loved in return; and in fact perhaps he has nothing lovable in him. The beloved, however, often charges that previously the lover was promising him everything, and now fulfills none of his promises.

These sorts of charges arise whenever the lover loves his beloved for pleasure while the beloved loves his lover for utility, and they do not both provide these. For if the friendship has these causes, it is dissolved whenever they do not get what they were friends for; for each was not fond of the other himself, but only of what the other had, which was unstable. That is why the friendships are also unstable. Friendship of character, however, is friendship in itself, and endures, as we have said.

Friends quarrel when they get results different from those they want; for when someone does not get what he aims at, it is like getting nothing. It is like the person who promised the lyre player a reward, and a greater reward the better he played; in the morning, when the player asked him to deliver on his promise, the other said he had paid pleasure in return for pleasure. Now if this was what each of them had wished, it would be quite enough. But if one wished for delight and the other for profit, and one has got his delight and the other has not made his profit, things are not right in their common dealings. For each person sets his mind on what he finds he requires, and this will be his aim when he gives what he gives.

Who should fix the worth [of a benefit], the giver or the one who has already received it? [Surely the latter.] For the giver would seem to entrust [the judgment] to the one who has received. This is what Protagoras is said to have done; for whenever he taught anything at all, he used to tell the pupil to estimate how much the knowledge was worth, and that was the amount he used to collect. In such cases, however, some prefer the rule 'Payment to a man. . . .'

But those who take the money first, and then do nothing that they said they would do, because their promises were excessive, are reasonably accused, since they do not carry out what they agreed to. And presumably the sophists are compelled to make excessive promises. For no one would pay them money for the knowledge they really have; hence they take the payment, and then do not do what they were paid to do, and reasonably are accused.

But where no agreement about services is made, friends who give services because of the friend himself are not open to accusation, as we have said, since this is the character of the friendship that accords with virtue. And the return should accord with the decision [of the original giver], since decision is proper to a friend and to virtue.

And it would seem that the same sort of return should also be made to those who have shared philosophy in common with us. For its worth is not measured by money, and no equivalent honor can be paid; but it is enough, presumably, to do what we can, as we do toward gods and parents.

If the giving is not of this sort, but on some specified condition, presumably the repayment must be, ideally, what each of them thinks accords with the worth of the gift. But if they do not agree on this, then it would seem not merely necessary, but also just, for the party who benefits first to fix the repayment. For if the other receives in return as much benefit as the first received, or as much as he would have paid for the pleasure, he will have got the worthy return from him.

Indeed this is also how it appears in buying and selling. And in some cities there are actually laws prohibiting legal actions in voluntary bargains, on the assumption that if we have trusted someone we must dissolve the community with him on the same terms on which we formed it. The law does this because it supposes that it is more just for the recipient to fix repayment than for the giver to fix it. For usually those who have something and those who want it do not put the same price on it, since, to the giver, what he owns and what he is giving appears to be worth a

lot. But nonetheless the return is made in the amount
20 fixed by the initial recipient. Presumably, however, the price must be not what it appears to be worth when he has got it, but the price he put on it before he got it.

2

Here are some other questions that raise a puzzle. Must you accord [authority in] everything to your father, and obey him in everything? Or must you trust the doctor when he is sick, and should you vote for
25 a military expert to be general? Similarly, should you do a service for your friend rather than for an excellent person, and return a favor to a benefactor rather than do a favor for a companion, if you cannot do both?

Surely it is not easy to define all these matters exactly. For they include many differences of all sorts—in importance and unimportance, and in the
30 fine and the necessary. Still, it is clear that not everything should be rendered to the same person, and usually we should return favors rather than do favors for our companions, just as we should return a loan to a creditor rather than lend to a companion.

But presumably this is not always true. If, for instance, someone has ransomed you from pirates,
35 should you ransom him in return, no matter who he
1165a is? Or if he does not need to be ransomed, but asks for his money back, should you return it, or should you ransom your father instead? Here it seems that you should ransom your father, rather than even yourself.

As we have said, then, we should, generally speaking, return what we owe. But if making a gift [to B] outweighs [returning the money to A] by being finer or more necessary, we should incline to [making the
5 gift to B] instead. For sometimes even a return of a previous favor is not fair [but an excessive demand], whenever [the original giver] knows he is benefiting an excellent person, but [the recipient] would be returning the benefit to someone he thinks is vicious. For sometimes you should not even lend in return to someone who has lent to you. For he expected repayment when he lent to a decent person, whereas you have no hope of it from a bad person. If that is
10 really so, then, the demand [for reciprocity] is not

fair; and even if it is not so, but you think it is so, your refusal of the demand seems not at all absurd.

As we have often said, then, arguments about acting and being affected are no more definite than their subject matter. Clearly, then, we should not render the same things to everyone, and we should not render 15 everything to our fathers, just as we should not make all our sacrifices to Zeus.

And since different things should be rendered to parents, brothers, companions, and benefactors, we should accord to each what is proper and suitable. This is what actually appears to be done; for instance, kinsfolk are the people invited to a wedding, since 20 they share the same family, and hence share in actions that concern it; and for the same reason it is thought that kinsfolk more than anyone must come to funerals.

It seems that we must supply means of support to parents more than anyone. For we suppose that we owe them this, and that it is finer to supply those who are the causes of our being than to supply ourselves in this way. And we should accord honor to our parents, just as we should to the gods, but not every sort of honor; for we should not accord the same honor to 25 a father as to a mother, nor accord to them the honor due to a wise person or a general. We should accord a father's honor to a father, and likewise a mother's to a mother.

We should accord to every older person the honor befitting his age, by standing up, giving up seats, and so on. With companions and brothers we should speak freely, and have everything in common. To kinsfolk, 30 fellow tribesmen, fellow citizens, and all the rest we should always try to accord what is proper, and should compare what belongs to each, as befits closeness of relation, virtue, or usefulness.

Admittedly, this comparison is easier with people of the same kind, and more difficult with people of different kinds. But such difficulty is no reason for giving up the comparison; rather, we should define 35 as far as we can.

3

There is also a puzzle about dissolving or not dissolv- 1165b ing friendships with friends who do not remain the same. With friends for utility or pleasure perhaps there is nothing absurd in dissolving the friendship whenever they are no longer pleasant or useful. For they were friends of pleasure or utility; and if these 5 give out, it is reasonable not to love. We might, however, accuse a friend if he really liked us for utility or pleasure, and pretended to like us for our character. For, as we said at the beginning, friends are most at odds when they are not friends in the way they think they are.

And so, if we mistakenly suppose we are loved for our character, when our friend is doing nothing to 10 suggest this, we must hold ourselves responsible. But if we are deceived by his pretense, we are justified in accusing him—even more justified than in accusing debasers of the currency, to the extent that his evil-doing debases something more precious.

But if we accept a friend as a good person, and then he becomes vicious, and seems so, should we still love him? Surely we cannot, if not everything, 15 but only the good, is lovable. The bad is not lovable, and must not be loved; for we ought neither to love the bad nor to become similar to a base person, and we have said that similar is friend to similar.

Then should the friendship be dissolved at once [as soon as the friend becomes bad]? Surely not with every sort of person, but only with an incurably vicious person. If someone can be set right, we should try 20 harder to rescue his character than his property, insofar as character is both better and more proper to friendship. Still, the friend who dissolves the friendship seems to be doing nothing absurd. For he was not the friend of a person of this sort; hence, if the friend has altered, and he cannot save him, he leaves him.

But if one friend stayed the same and the other became more decent and far excelled his friend in virtue, should the better person still treat the other 25 as a friend? Surely he cannot. This becomes clear in a wide separation, such as we find in friendships beginning in childhood. For if one friend still thinks as a child, while the other becomes a man of the best sort, how could they still be friends, if they neither approve of the same things nor find the same things enjoyable or painful? For they do not even find it so 30 in their life together, and without that they cannot be friends, since they cannot live together—we have discussed this.

Then should the better person regard the other as though he had never become his friend? Surely he must keep some memory of the familiarity they had. Just as we think we must do kindnesses for friends more than for strangers, so also we should accord something to past friends because of the former friend- 35 ship, whenever it is not excessive vice that causes the dissolution.

4

The defining features of friendship that are found 1166a in friendships to one's neighbors would seem to be derived from features of friendship toward oneself. For a friend is taken to be someone who wishes and does goods or apparent goods to his friend for the friend's own sake; or one who wishes the friend to be and to live for the friend's own sake—this is how 5 mothers feel toward their children, and how friends who have been in conflict feel [toward each other]. Others take a friend to be one who spends his time with his friend, and makes the same choices; or one who shares his friend's distress and enjoyment—and this also is especially true of mothers. And people define friendship by one of these features.

Each of these features is found in the decent per- 10 son's relation to himself, and it is found in other people, insofar as they suppose they are decent. As we have said, virtue and the excellent person would seem to be the standard in each case.

For the excellent person is of one mind with himself, and desires the same things in his whole soul. Hence he wishes goods and apparent goods to himself, 15 and achieves them in his actions, since it is proper to the good person to reach the good by his efforts. He wishes and does them for his own sake, since he does them for the sake of his thinking part, and that is what each person seems to be. Moreover, he wishes himself to live and to be preserved. And he wishes this for his rational part more than for any other part.

For being is a good for the good person, and each 20 person wishes for goods for himself. And no one chooses to become another person even if that other will have every good when he has come into being; for, as it is, the god has the good [but no one chooses to be replaced by a god]. Rather [each of us chooses goods] on condition that he remains whatever he is;

and each person would seem to be the understanding part, or that most of all. [Hence the good person wishes for goods for the understanding part.]

Further, such a person finds it pleasant to spend time with himself, and so wishes to do it. For his memories 25 of what he has done are agreeable, and his expectations for the future are good, and hence both are pleasant. And besides, his thought is well supplied with topics for study. Moreover, he shares his own distresses and pleasures, more than other people share theirs. For it is always the same thing that is painful or pleasant, not different things at different times. This is because he practically never regrets [what he has done].

30   The decent person, then, has each of these features in relation to himself, and is related to his friend as he is to himself, since the friend is another himself. Hence friendship seems to be one of these features, and people with these features seem to be friends.

But is there friendship toward oneself, or not? Let us dismiss that question for the present. However, 35 there seems to be friendship insofar as someone is two or more parts. This seems to be true from what we have said, and because an extreme degree of 1166b friendship resembles one's friendship to oneself.

The many, base though they are, also appear to have these features. But perhaps they share in them only insofar as they approve of themselves and sup- 5 pose they are decent. For no one who is utterly base and unscrupulous either has these features or appears to have them.

Indeed, even base people hardly have them. For they are at odds with themselves, and have an appetite for one thing and a wish for another, as incontinent people do. For they do not choose things that seem to be good for them, but instead choose pleasant things that are actually harmful; and cowardice or 10 laziness causes others to shrink from doing what they think best for themselves. And those who have done many terrible actions hate and shun life because of their vice, and destroy themselves.

15   Besides, vicious people seek others to pass their days with, and shun themselves. For when they are by themselves they remember many disagreeable actions, and anticipate others in the future; but they manage to forget these in other people's company. These people have nothing lovable about them, and so have no friendly feelings for themselves.

Hence such a person does not share his own enjoy- 20 ments and distresses. For his soul is in conflict, and because he is vicious one part is distressed at being restrained, and another is pleased [by the intended action]; and so each part pulls in a different direction, as though they were tearing him apart. Even if he cannot be distressed and pleased at the same time, still he is soon distressed because he was pleased, and wishes these things had not become pleasant to him; 25 for base people are full of regret.

Hence the base person appears not to have a friendly attitude even toward himself, because he has nothing lovable about him.

If this state is utterly miserable, everyone should earnestly shun vice and try to be decent; for that is how someone will have a friendly relation to himself and will become a friend to another.

5

Goodwill would seem to be a feature of friendship, 30 but still it is not friendship. For it arises even toward people we do not know, and without their noticing it, whereas friendship does not. We have also said this before.

Nor is it loving, since it lacks intensity and desire, which are implied by loving. Moreover, loving requires familiarity, but goodwill can also arise in a 35 moment, as it arises, for instance, [in a spectator] for 1167a contestants. For [the spectator] acquires goodwill for them, and wants what they want, but would not cooperate with them in any action; for, as we said, his goodwill arises in a moment and his fondness is superficial.

Goodwill, then, would seem to be a beginning of friendship, just as pleasure coming through sight is a beginning of erotic passion. For no one has erotic 5 passion for another without previous pleasure in his appearance. But still enjoyment of his appearance does not imply erotic passion for him; passion consists also in longing for him in his absence and in an appetite for his presence. Similarly, though people cannot be friends without previous goodwill, goodwill does not imply friendship; for when they have goodwill, people only wish goods to the other, and will not cooperate with him in any action, or go to any 10 trouble for him. Hence we might transfer [the name 'friendship'], and say that goodwill is inactive friendship, and that when it lasts some time and they grow accustomed to each other, it becomes friendship.

It does not, however, become friendship for utility or pleasure; for these aims do not produce goodwill
15 either. For a recipient of a benefit does what is just when he returns goodwill for what he has received. But those who wish for another's welfare because they hope to enrich themselves through him would seem to have goodwill to themselves, rather than to him. Likewise, they would seem to be friends to themselves rather than to him, if they attend to him because he is of some use to them.

But in general goodwill results from some sort of virtue and decency, whenever one person finds an-
20 other to be apparently fine or brave or something similar. As we said, this also arises in the case of contestants.

6

Concord also appears to be a feature of friendship. That is why it is not merely sharing a belief, since this might happen among people who do not know
25 each other. Nor are people said to be in concord when they agree on just anything, on astronomical questions, for instance, since concord on these questions is not a feature of friendship. Rather, a city is said to be in concord when [its citizens] agree on what is advantageous, make the same decision, and act on their common resolution.
30 Hence concord concerns questions for action, and, more exactly, large questions where both or all can get what they want. A city, for instance, is in concord whenever all the citizens resolve to make offices elective, or to make an alliance with the Spartans, or to make Pittacus[15] ruler, when he himself is also willing.

But whenever each person wants the same thing all to himself, as the people in the *Phoenissae*[16] do,

15. [After serving as dictator of Mitylene for fourteen years in the early sixth century, he gave up his office, although the citizens unanimously wanted him to continue. — M.L.M.]
16. [Euripides' *Phoenissae* is about the bitter and unscrupulous struggle between Eteocles and Polyneices for absolute power in Thebes. — T.I.]

they are in conflict. For it is not concord when each merely has the same thing in mind, whatever it is. 35 Rather, each must also have the same thing in mind for the same person; this is true, for instance, whenever both the common people and the decent party 1167b want the best people to rule, since when that is so both sides get what they seek.

Concord, then, is apparently political friendship, as indeed it is said to be; for it is concerned with advantage and with what affects life [as a whole].

This sort of concord is found in decent people. 5 For they are in concord with themselves and with each other, since they are practically of the same mind; for their wishes are stable, not flowing back and forth like a tidal strait. They wish for what is just and advantageous, and also seek it in common.

Base people, however, cannot be in concord, ex- 10 cept to a slight degree, just as they can be friends only to a slight degree; for they seek to overreach in benefits [to themselves], and shirk labors and public services. And since each wishes this for himself, he interrogates and obstructs his neighbor; for when people do not look out for the common good, it is ruined. The result is that they are in conflict, trying to compel 15 one another to do what is just, but not wishing to do it themselves.

7

Benefactors seem to love their beneficiaries more than the beneficiaries love them [in return], and this is discussed as though it were an unreasonable thing to happen. In most people's view, this is because the 20 beneficiaries are debtors and the benefactors creditors: The debtor in a loan wishes the creditor did not exist, while the creditor even attends to the safety of the debtor. So also, then, a benefactor wants the beneficiary to exist because he expects gratitude in return, whereas the beneficiary is not attentive about 25 making the return.

Now Epicharmus might say that most people say this because they 'take a bad person's point of view.' Still, it would seem to be a human point of view, since the many are indeed forgetful, and seek to receive benefits more than to give them.

However, it seems that the cause is more proper to [human] nature, and the case of creditors is not

30 even similar. For they do not love their debtors, but in wishing for their safety simply seek repayment. Benefactors, however, love and like their beneficiaries even if they are of no present or future use to them. The same is true of craftsmen; for each likes his own

35 product more than it would like him if it acquired a soul. Presumably this is true of poets most of all, since

1168a they dearly like their own poems, and are fond of them as though they were their children.

This, then, is what the case of the benefactor resem-
5 bles; here the beneficiary is his product, and hence he likes him more than the product likes its producer. The reason for this is that being is choiceworthy and lovable for all, and we are insofar as we are actualized, since we are insofar as we live and act. Now the product is, in a way, the producer in his actualization; hence the producer is fond of the product, because he loves his own being. This is natural, since what he is potentially is what the product indicates in actualization.

10 At the same time, the benefactor's action is fine for him, so that he finds enjoyment in the person he acts on; but the person acted on finds nothing fine in the agent, but only, at most, some advantage, which is less pleasant and lovable.

What is pleasant is actualization in the present, expectation for the future, and memory of the past;
15 but what is most pleasant is the [action we do] insofar as we are actualized, and this is also most lovable. For the benefactor, then, his product endures, since the fine is long-lasting; but for the person acted on, the useful passes away.

Besides, memory of fine things is pleasant, while memory of [receiving] useful things is not altogether pleasant, or is less pleasant—though the reverse would seem to be true for expectation.

20 Moreover, loving is like production, while being loved is like being acted on; and [the benefactor's] love and friendliness are the result of his greater activity.

Further, everyone is fond of whatever has taken effort to produce; for instance, people who have made money themselves are fonder of it than people who have inherited it. And while receiving a benefit seems
25 to take no effort, giving one is hard work. This is also why mothers love their children more [than fathers do], since giving birth is more effort for them, and

they know better that the children are theirs. And this also would seem to be proper to benefactors.

8

There is also a puzzle about whether one ought to love oneself or someone else most of all; for those who like themselves most are criticized and denounced as
30 self-lovers, as though this were something shameful. Indeed, the base person seems to go to every length for his own sake, and all the more the more vicious he is; hence he is accused, for instance, of doing nothing [for any end apart] from himself. The decent person, on the contrary, acts for what is fine, all the more the better he is, and for his friend's sake, disregarding his own [interest].
35

The facts, however, conflict with these claims, and
1168b that is not unreasonable. For it is said that we must love most the friend who is most a friend; and one person is a friend to another most of all if he wishes goods to the other for the other's sake, even if no one will know about it. But these are features most of all of one's relation to oneself; and so too are all the other defining features of a friend, since we have said
5 that all the features of friendship extend from oneself to others.

All the proverbs agree with this too, speaking, for instance, of 'one soul,' 'what friends have is common,' 'equality is friendship,' and 'the knee is closer than the shin.' For all these are true most of all in someone's relations with himself, since one is a friend to himself most of all. Hence he should also love himself most
10 of all.

It is not surprising, then, that there is a puzzle about which view we ought to follow, since both inspire some confidence. Presumably, then, we must divide these sorts of arguments, and distinguish how far and in what ways those on each side are true.
15 Perhaps, then, it will become clear, if we grasp how those on each side understand self-love.

Those who make self-love a matter for reproach ascribe it to those who award the biggest share in money, honors, and bodily pleasures to themselves. For these are the goods desired and eagerly pursued by the many on the assumption that they are best. That is why they are also contested. Those who overreach for these goods gratify their appetites and in
20

general their feelings and the nonrational part of the soul; and this is the character of the many. That is why the application of the term ['self-love'] is derived from the most frequent [kind of self-love], which is base. This type of self-lover, then, is justifiably reproached.

And plainly it is the person who awards himself these goods whom the many habitually call a self-
25 lover. For if someone is always eager above all to do just or temperate actions or any other actions in accord with the virtues, and in general always gains for himself what is fine, no one will call him a self-lover or blame him for it.

This sort of person, however, more than the other sort, seems to be a self-lover. At any rate he awards
30 himself what is finest and best of all, and gratifies the most controlling part of himself, obeying it in everything. And just as a city and every other composite system seems to be above all its most controlling part, the same is true of a human being; hence someone loves himself most if he likes and gratifies this part.

35 Similarly, someone is called continent or incontinent because his understanding is or is not the master,
1169a on the assumption that this is what each person is. Moreover, his own voluntary actions seem above all to be those involving reason. Clearly, then, this, or this above all, is what each person is, and the decent person likes this most of all.

That is why he most of all is a self-lover, but a different kind from the self-lover who is reproached.
5 He differs from him as much as the life guided by reason differs from the life guided by feelings, and as much as the desire for what is fine differs from the desire for what seems advantageous.

Those who are unusually eager to do fine actions are welcomed and praised by everyone. And when everyone strains to achieve what is fine and concen-
10 trates on the finest actions, everything that is right will be done for the common good, and each person individually will receive the greatest of goods, since that is the character of virtue. And so the good person must be a self-lover, since he will both help himself and benefit others by doing fine actions. But the vicious person must not love himself, since he will harm both himself and his neighbors by following his base feelings.

For the vicious person, then, the right actions con- 15 flict with those he does. The decent person, however, does the right actions, since every understanding chooses what is best for itself and the decent person obeys his understanding.

It is quite true that, as they say, the excellent person labors for his friends and for his native country, and will die for them if he must; he will sacrifice money, 20 honors, and contested goods in general, in achieving the fine for himself. For he will choose intense pleasure for a short time over slight pleasure for a long time; a year of living finely over many years of undistinguished life; and a single fine and great action over 25 many small actions. This is presumably true of one who dies for others; he does indeed choose something great and fine for himself. He is also ready to sacrifice money as long as his friends profit; for the friends gain money, while he gains the fine, and so he awards himself the greater good.

He treats honors and offices in the same way; for 30 he will sacrifice them all for his friends, since this is fine and praiseworthy for himself. It is not surprising, then, that he seems to be excellent, since he chooses the fine at the cost of everything. It is also possible, however, to sacrifice actions to his friend, since it may be finer to be responsible for his friend's doing the action than to do it himself.

In everything praiseworthy, then, the excellent per- 35 son awards himself the fine. In this way, then, we must be self-lovers, as we have said. But in the way 1169b the many are, we ought not to be.

9

There is also a dispute about whether the happy person will need friends or not. For it is said that blessedly happy and self-sufficient people have no need of friends. For they already have [all] the goods, and 5 hence, being self-sufficient, need nothing added. But your friend, since he is another yourself, supplies what your own efforts cannot supply. Hence it is said, 'When the god gives well, what need is there of friends?'

It would seem absurd, however, to award the happy person all the goods, without giving him friends; for 10 having friends seems to be the greatest external good. And if it is more proper to a friend to confer benefits than to receive them, and it is proper to the good person and to virtue to do good, and it is finer to benefit friends than to benefit strangers, the excellent person will need people for him to benefit. Indeed, that is why there is a question about whether friends are needed more in good fortune than in ill fortune; for it is assumed that in ill fortune we need people to benefit us, and in good fortune we need others for us to benefit.

Presumably it is also absurd to make the blessed person solitary. For no one would choose to have all [other] goods and yet be alone, since a human being is a political [animal], tending by nature to live together with others. This will also be true, then, of the happy person; for he has the natural goods, and clearly it is better to spend his days with decent friends than with strangers of just any character. Hence the happy person needs friends.

Then what are those on the other side saying, and on what point are they correct? Perhaps they say what they say because the many think that it is the useful people who are friends. Certainly the blessedly happy person will have no need of these, since he has [all] goods. Similarly, he will have no need, or very little, of friends for pleasure; for since his life is pleasant, it has no need of imported pleasures. Since he does not need these sorts of friends, he does not seem to need friends at all.

This conclusion, however, is presumably not true. For we said at the beginning that happiness is a kind of activity; and clearly activity comes into being, and does not belong [to someone all the time], as a possession does. Now if being happy consists in living and being active; the activity of the good person is excellent, and [hence] pleasant in itself, as we said at the beginning; what is our own is pleasant; and we are able to observe our neighbors more than ourselves, and to observe their actions more than our own; it follows that a good person finds pleasure in the actions of excellent people who are his friends, since these actions have both the naturally pleasant [features—they are good, and they are his own]. The blessed person, therefore, will need virtuous friends, given that he decides to observe virtuous actions that are his own, and the actions of a virtuous friend are of this sort.

Further, it is thought that the happy person must live pleasantly. But the solitary person's life is hard, since it is not easy for him to be continuously active all by himself; but in relation to others and in their company it is easier. Hence his activity will be more continuous. It is also pleasant in itself, as it must be in the blessedly happy person's case. For the excellent person, insofar as he is excellent, enjoys actions in accord with virtue, and objects to actions caused by vice, just as the musician enjoys fine melodies and is pained by bad ones.

Further, good people's life together allows the cultivation of virtue, as Theognis says.

If we examine the question more from the point of view of [human] nature, an excellent friend would seem to be choiceworthy by nature for an excellent person. For, as we have said, what is good by nature is good and pleasant in itself for an excellent person.

For animals, life is defined by the capacity for perception, but for human beings, it is defined by the capacity for perception or understanding; moreover, every capacity refers to an activity, and a thing is present fully in its activity; hence living fully would seem to be perceiving or understanding.

Now life is good and pleasant in itself; for it has definite order, which is proper to the nature of what is good. What is good by nature is also good for the decent person; that is why life would seem to be pleasant for everyone. But we must not consider a life that is vicious and corrupted, or filled with pains; for such a life lacks definite order, just as its proper features do. (The truth about pain will be more evident in what follows.)

Life itself, then, is good and pleasant, as it would seem, at any rate, from the fact that everyone desires it, and decent and blessed people desire it more than others do—for their life is most choiceworthy for them, and their living is most blessed.

Now someone who sees perceives that he sees; one who hears perceives that he hears; one who walks perceives that he walks; and similarly in the other cases also there is some [element] that perceives that we are active; so that if we are perceiving, we perceive that we are perceiving, and if we are understanding, we perceive that we are understanding. Now perceiving that we are perceiving or understanding is the same as perceiving that we are, since we agreed that being is perceiving or understanding.

1170b   Perceiving that we are alive is pleasant in itself. For life is by nature a good, and it is pleasant to perceive that something good is present in us. Living is also choiceworthy, for a good person most of all, since being is good and pleasant for him; for he is
5   pleased to perceive something good in itself together [with his own being].

The excellent person is related to his friend in the same way as he is related to himself, since a friend is another himself. Therefore, just as his own being is choiceworthy for him, his friend's being is choiceworthy for him in the same or a similar way. We agreed that someone's own being is choiceworthy because he perceives that he is good, and this sort of
10   perception is pleasant in itself. He must, then, perceive his friend's being together [with his own], and he will do this when they live together and share conversation and thought. For in the case of human beings what seems to count as living together is this sharing of conversation and thought, not sharing the same pasture, as in the case of grazing animals.
15   If, then, for the blessedly happy person, being is choiceworthy, since it is naturally good and pleasant, and if the being of his friend is closely similar to his own, his friend will also be choiceworthy. What is choiceworthy for him he must possess, since otherwise he will in this respect lack something. Anyone who is to be happy, then, must have excellent friends.

10

20   Then should we have as many friends as possible? Or is it the same as with the friendship of host and guest, where it seems to be good advice to 'have neither many nor none'? Is this also good advice in friendship, to have neither no friends nor excessively many?
25   With friends for utility the advice seems very apt, since it is hard work to return many people's services, and life is too short for it. Indeed, more [such] friends than are adequate for one's own life are superfluous, and a hindrance to living finely; hence we have no need of them. A few friends for pleasure are enough also, just as a little seasoning on food is enough.
30   Of excellent people, however, should we have as many as possible as friends, or is there some proper measure of their number, as of the number in a city?

For a city could not be formed from ten people, but it would be a city no longer if it had a hundred thousand. Presumably, though, the right quantity is not just one number, but anything between certain defined limits. Hence there is also some limit defining   1171a
the number of friends. Presumably, this is the largest number with whom you could live together, since we found that living together seems to be most characteristic of friendship.

Clearly you cannot live with many people and distribute yourself among them. Further these many people must also be friends to one another, if they are all to spend their days together; and this is hard   5
work for many people to manage. It also becomes difficult for many to share one another's enjoyments and distresses as their own, since you are quite likely to find yourself sharing one friend's pleasure and another friend's grief at the same time.

Presumably, then, it is good not to seek as many friends as possible, and good to have no more than enough for living together; indeed it even seems impossible   10
to be an extremely close friend to many people. That is why it also seems impossible to be passionately in love with many people, since passionate erotic love tends to be an excess of friendship, and one has this for one person; hence also one has extremely close friendship for a few people.

This would seem to be borne out in what people actually do. For the friendship of companions is not found in groups of many people, and the friendships   15
celebrated in song are always between two people. By contrast, those who have many friends and treat everyone as close to them seem to be friends to no one, except in the way fellow citizens are friends; these people are regarded as ingratiating. Certainly it is possible to have a fellow citizen's friendship for many people, and still to be a truly decent person, not ingratiating; but it is impossible to be many people's friend for their virtue and for themselves. We have reason to be satisfied if we can find even a few   20
such friends.

11

Have we more need of friends in good fortune or in ill fortune? For in fact we seek them in both; for in ill fortune we need assistance, and in good fortune we need friends to live with and to benefit, since then we wish to do good. Certainly it is more necessary to have friends in ill fortune; that is why useful friends are needed here. But it is finer to have them in good fortune. That is why we also seek decent friends; for it is more choiceworthy to do good to them and spend our time with them.

The very presence of friends is also pleasant, in ill fortune as well as good fortune; for we have our pain lightened when our friends share our distress. Indeed, that is why one might be puzzled about whether they take a part of it from us, as though helping us to lift a weight, or, alternatively, their presence is pleasant and our awareness that they share our distress makes the pain smaller. Well, we need not discuss whether it is this or something else that lightens our pain; at any rate, what we have mentioned does appear to occur.

However, the presence of friends would seem to be a mixture [of pleasure and pain]. For certainly the sight of our friends in itself is pleasant, especially when we are in ill fortune, and it gives us some assistance in removing our pain. For a friend consoles us by the sight of him and by conversation, if he is dexterous, since he knows our character and what gives us pleasure and pain.

Nonetheless, awareness of his pain at our ill fortune is painful to us; for everyone tries to avoid causing pain to his friends. That is why someone with a manly nature tries to prevent his friend from sharing his pain. Unless he is unusually immune to pain, he cannot endure pain coming to his friends; and he does not allow others to share his mourning at all, since he is not prone to mourn himself either. Females, however, and effeminate men enjoy having people to wail with them; they love them as friends who share their distress. But in everything we clearly must imitate the better person.

In good fortune, by contrast, the presence of friends makes it pleasant to pass our time and to notice that they take pleasure in our own goods. That is why it seems that we must eagerly call our friends to share our good fortune, since it is fine to do good. But we must hesitate to call them to share our ill fortune, since we must share bad things with them as little as possible; hence the saying 'My misfortune is enough.' We should invite them most of all whenever they will benefit us greatly, with little trouble to themselves.

Conversely, it is presumably appropriate to go eagerly, without having to be called, to friends in misfortune. For it is proper to a friend to benefit, especially to benefit a friend in need who has not demanded it, since this is finer and pleasanter for both friends. In good fortune he should come eagerly to help him, since friends are needed for this also; but he should be slow to come to receive benefits, since eagerness to be benefited is not fine. Presumably, though, one should avoid getting a reputation for being a killjoy, as sometimes happens, by refusing benefits.

Hence the presence of friends is apparently choiceworthy in all conditions.

12

What the erotic lover likes most is the sight of his beloved, and this is the sort of perception he chooses over the others, supposing that this above all is what makes him fall in love and remain in love. In the same way, surely, what friends find most choiceworthy is living together. For friendship is community, and we are related to our friend as we are related to ourselves. Hence, since the perception of our own being is choiceworthy, so is the perception of our friend's being. Perception is active when we live with him; hence, not surprisingly, this is what we seek.

Whatever someone [regards as] his being, or the end for which he chooses to be alive, that is the activity he wishes to pursue in his friend's company. Hence some friends drink together, others play dice, while others do gymnastics and go hunting, or do philosophy. They spend their days together on whichever pursuit in life they like most; for since they want to live with their friends, they share the actions in which they find their common life.

Hence the friendship of base people turns out to be vicious. For they are unstable, and share base pursuits; and by becoming similar to each other, they grow vicious. But the friendship of decent people is decent, and increases the more often they meet. And they seem to become still better from their activities and their mutual correction. For each molds the other in what they approve of, so that '[you will learn] what is noble from noble people.'

15   So much, then, for friendship. The next task will be to discuss pleasure.

BOOK X

1

20   The next task, presumably, is to discuss pleasure. For it seems to be especially proper to our [animal] kind; that is why, when we educate children, we steer them by pleasure and pain. Besides, enjoying and hating the right things seems to be most important for virtue of character. For pleasure and pain extend through the whole of our lives, and are of great importance 25 for virtue and the happy life, since people decide on pleasant things, and avoid painful things.

Least of all, then, it seems, should these topics be neglected, especially since they arouse much dispute. For some say pleasure is the good, while others, on the contrary, say it is altogether base. Presumably, some [who say it is base] say so because they are persuaded that it is so. Others, however, say it because 30 they think it is better for the conduct of our lives to present pleasure as base even if it is not. For, they say, the many lean toward pleasure and are slaves to pleasures, and that is why we must lead them in the contrary direction, because that is the way to reach the intermediate condition.

35   Surely, however, this is wrong. For arguments about actions and feelings are less credible than the facts; hence any conflict between arguments and per-1172b ceptible [facts] arouses contempt for the arguments, and moreover undermines the truth as well [as the arguments]. For if someone blames pleasure, but then has been seen to seek it on *some* occasions, the reason for his lapse seems to be that he regards *every* type of pleasure as something to seek; for the many are not the sort to make distinctions.

5   True arguments, then, would seem to be the most useful, not only for knowledge but also for the conduct of life. For since they harmonize with the facts, they are credible, and so encourage those who comprehend them to live by them.

Enough of this, then; let us now consider what has been said about pleasure.

2

Eudoxus thought that pleasure is the good, because 10 he saw that all [animals], both rational and nonrational, seek it, and in everything, he says, what is choiceworthy is good, and what is most choiceworthy is supreme. The fact that all are drawn to the same thing [i.e., pleasure], indicates, in his view, that it is best for all, since each [kind of animal] finds its own 15 good, just as it finds its own nourishment; and what is good for all, what all aim at, is the good. These arguments of his were found credible because of his virtuous character, rather than on their own [merits]. For since he seemed to be outstandingly temperate, he did not seem to be saying this because he was a friend of pleasure; rather, it seemed that what he said was how it really was.

He thought it was no less evident from consideration of the contrary. For pain in itself, he said, is something to be avoided for all, so that, similarly, its 20 contrary is choiceworthy for all. Now what is most choiceworthy is what we choose not because of, or for the sake of, anything else; and it is agreed that this is the character of pleasure, since we never ask anyone what his end is in being pleased, because we assume that pleasure is choiceworthy in itself.

Moreover, [he argued], when pleasure is added to any other good, to just or temperate action, for instance, it makes that good more choiceworthy; and 25 good is increased by the addition of itself.

This [last] argument, at least, would seem to present pleasure as one good among others, no more a good than any other. For the addition of any other good makes a good more choiceworthy than it is all by itself. Indeed Plato uses this sort of argument to undermine the claim of pleasure to be the good. For, he argues, the pleasant life is more choiceworthy when 30 combined with prudence than it is without it; and if the mixed [good] is better, pleasure is not the good, since nothing can be added to the good to make it more choiceworthy. Nor, clearly, could anything else be the good if it is made more choiceworthy by the addition of anything that is good in itself. Then what is the good that meets this condition, and that we 35 share in also? That is what we are looking for.

But when some object that what everything aims 1173a at is not good, surely there is nothing in what they say. For if things seem [good] to all, we say they are [good]; and if someone undermines confidence in these, what he says will hardly inspire more confidence in other things. For if [only animals] without understanding desired these things, there would be something in the objection; but if prudent [animals] also desire them, how can there be anything in it? And presumably even in inferior [animals] there is something superior to themselves that seeks their own proper good.

The argument [against Eudoxus] about the contrary would also seem to be incorrect. For they argue that if pain is an evil, it does not follow that pleasure is a good, since evil is also opposed to evil, and both are opposed to the neutral condition [without pleasure or pain]. The objectors' general point here is right, but what they say in the case mentioned is false. For if both pleasure and pain were evils, we would also have to avoid both, and if both were neutral, we would have to avoid neither, or else avoid both equally. Evidently, however, we avoid pain as an evil and choose pleasure as a good; hence this must also be the opposition between them.

3

Again, if [as the objectors argue] pleasure is not a quality, it does not follow [as they suppose] that it is not a good. For virtuous activities and happiness are not qualities either.

They say that the good is definite, whereas pleasure is indefinite because it admits of more and less. If their judgment rests on the actual condition of being pleased, it must also hold for justice and the other virtues, where evidently we are said to have a certain character more and less, and to act more and less in accord with the virtues; for we may be more [and less] just or brave, and may do just or temperate actions more and less. If, on the other hand, their judgment rests on the [variety of] pleasures, then surely they fail to state the reason [why pleasures admit of more and less], namely that some are unmixed [with pain] and others are mixed.

Moreover, just as health admits of more and less, though it is definite, why should pleasure not be the same? For not every [healthy person] has the same proportion [of bodily elements], nor does the same

person always have the same, but it may be relaxed and still remain up to a certain limit, and may differ in more and less. The same is quite possible, then, for pleasure also.

They hold that what is good is complete, whereas processes and becomings are incomplete, and they try to show that pleasure is a process and a becoming. It would seem, however, that they are wrong, and pleasure is not even a process. For quickness or slowness seems to be proper to every process—if not in itself (as, for instance, with the universe), then in relation to something else. But neither of these is true of pleasure. For though certainly it is possible to become pleased quickly, as it is possible to become angry quickly, it is not possible to be pleased quickly, even in relation to something else, whereas this is possible for walking and growing and all such things [i.e., for processes]. It is possible, then, to pass quickly or slowly into pleasure, but not possible to be [quickly or slowly] in the corresponding activity, i.e., to be pleased quickly [or slowly].

And how could pleasure be a becoming? For one random thing, it seems, does not come to be from any other; what something comes to be from is what it is dissolved into. Hence whatever pleasure is the becoming of, pain should be the perishing of it.

They do indeed say that pain is the emptying of the natural [condition, and hence the perishing], and that pleasure is its refilling [and hence the becoming]. Emptying and filling happen to the body; if, then, pleasure is the refilling of something natural, what has the refilling will also have the pleasure. Hence it will be the body that has pleasure. This does not seem to be true, however. The refilling, then, is not pleasure, though someone might be pleased while a refilling is going on, and pained when he is becoming empty.

This belief [that pleasure is refilling] seems to have arisen from pains and pleasures in connection with food; for first we are empty and suffer pain, and then take pleasure in the refilling. The same is not true, however, of all pleasures; for pleasures in mathematics, and among pleasures in perception those through the sense of smell, and many sounds, sights, memories, and expectations as well, all arise without [previous] pain. In that case what will they be comings-to-be of? For since no emptiness of anything has come to be, there is nothing whose refilling might come to be.

To those who cite the disgraceful pleasures [to show that pleasure is not a good], we might reply that these [sources of disgraceful pleasures] are not pleasant. For if things are healthy or sweet or bitter to sick people, we should not suppose that they are also healthy, or sweet, or bitter, except to them, or that things appearing white to people with eye disease are white, except to them. Similarly, if things are pleasant to people in bad condition, we should not suppose that they are also pleasant, except to these people.

25 Or else we might say that pleasures are choiceworthy, but not if they come from these sources; just as wealth is desirable, but not if you have to betray someone to get it, and health is desirable, but not if it requires you to eat anything and everything.

Or perhaps pleasures differ in species. For those from fine sources are different from those from shame- 30 ful sources; and we cannot have the just person's pleasure without being just, any more than we can have the musician's without being musicians, and similarly in the other cases.

The difference between a friend and a flatterer seems to indicate that pleasure is not good, or else that pleasures differ in species. For in dealings with us the friend seems to aim at what is good, but the 1174a flatterer at pleasure; and the flatterer is reproached, whereas the friend is praised, on the assumption that in their dealings they have different aims.

And no one would choose to live with a child's [level of] thought for his whole life, taking as much pleasure as possible in what pleases children, or to enjoy himself while doing some utterly shameful action, even if he would never suffer pain for it.

5 Moreover, there are many things that we would be eager for even if they brought no pleasure—for instance, seeing, remembering, knowing, having the virtues. Even if pleasures necessarily follow on them, that does not matter; for we would choose them even if no pleasure resulted from them.

10 It would seem to be clear, then, that pleasure is not the good, that not every pleasure is choiceworthy, and that some are choiceworthy in themselves, differing in species or in their sources [from those that are not].

Let this suffice, then, for discussion of the things said about pleasure and pain.

4

What, then, or what kind of thing, is pleasure? This will become clearer if we take it up again from the beginning. For seeing seems to be complete at any time, since it has no need for anything else to com- 15 plete its form by coming to be at a later time. And pleasure is also like this, since it is some sort of whole, and no pleasure is to be found at any time that will have its form completed by coming to be for a longer time.

That is why pleasure is not a process either. For every process, such as constructing a building, takes 20 time, and aims at some end, and is complete when it produces the product it seeks, or, [in other words, is complete] in this whole time [that it takes]. Moreover, each process is incomplete during the processes that are its parts, i.e., during the time it goes on; and it consists of processes that are different in form from the whole process and from one another.

For laying stones together and fluting a column are different processes; and both are different from the [whole] production of the temple. For the produc- 25 tion of the temple is a complete production, since it needs nothing further [when it is finished] to achieve the proposed goal; but the production of the foundation or the triglyph is an incomplete production, since [when it is finished] it is [the production] of a part. Hence [processes that are parts of larger processes] differ in form; and we cannot find a process complete in form at any time [while it is going on], but [only], if at all, in the whole time [that it takes].

The same is true of walking and the other [pro- 30 cesses]. For if locomotion is a process from one place to another, it includes locomotions differing in form—flying, walking, jumping, and so on. And besides these differences, there are differences in walking itself. For the place from which and the place to which are not the same in the whole racecourse as they are in a part of it, or the same in one part as in another; nor is travelling along one line the same as travelling along another, since what we cover is not 1174b just a line, but a line in a [particular] place, and this line and that line are in different places.

Now we have discussed process exactly elsewhere. But, at any rate, a process, it would seem, is not complete at every time; and the many [constituent] processes are incomplete, and differ in form, since the place from which and the place to which make the form of a process [and different processes begin and end in different places].

The form of pleasure, by contrast, is complete at any time. Clearly, then, it is different from a process, and is something whole and complete. This also seems true because a process must take time, but being pleased need not; for what is present in an instant is a whole. This also makes it clear that it is wrong to say that pleasure is a process or a becoming. For this is not said of everything, but only of what is divisible and not a whole; for seeing, or a point, or a unit, has no coming to be, and none of these is either a process or a becoming. But pleasure is a whole; hence it too has no coming to be.

Every perceptual capacity is active in relation to its perceptible object, and completely active when it is in good condition in relation to the finest of its perceptible objects. For this above all seems to be the character of complete activity, whether it is ascribed to the capacity or to the subject that has it. Hence for each capacity the best activity is the activity of the subject in the best condition in relation to the best object of the capacity.

This activity will also be the most complete and the most pleasant. For every perceptual capacity and every sort of thought and study has its pleasure; the most pleasant activity is the most complete; and the most complete is the activity of the subject in good condition in relation to the most excellent object of the capacity. Pleasure completes the activity.

But the way in which pleasure completes the activity is not the way in which the perceptible object and the perceptual capacity complete it when they are both excellent—just as health and the doctor are not the cause of being healthy in the same way.

Clearly a pleasure arises that corresponds to each perceptual capacity, since we say that sights and sounds are pleasant; and clearly it arises most of all whenever the perceptual capacity is best, and is active in relation to the best sort of object. When this is the condition of the perceptible object and of the perceiving subject, there will always be pleasure, when the producer and the subject to be affected are both present.

Pleasure completes the activity—not, however, as the state does, by being present [in the activity], but as a sort of consequent end, like the bloom on youths. Hence as long as the objects of understanding or perception and the subject that judges or attends are in the right condition, there will be pleasure in the activity. For as long as the subject affected and the productive [cause] remain similar and in the same relation to each other, the same thing naturally arises.

Then how is it that no one is continuously pleased? Is it not because we get tired? For nothing human is capable of continuous activity, and hence no continuous pleasure arises either, since pleasure is a consequence of the activity. Some things delight us when they are new to us, but later delight us less, for the same reason. For at first our thought is stimulated and intensely active toward them, as our sense of sight is when we look closely at something; but later the activity becomes lax and careless, so that the pleasure fades also.

Why does everyone desire pleasure? We might think it is because everyone also aims at being alive. Living is a type of activity, and each of us is active toward the objects he likes most and in the ways he likes most. The musician, for instance, activates his hearing in hearing melodies; the lover of learning activates his thought in thinking about objects of study; and so on for each of the others. Pleasure completes their activities, and hence completes life, which they desire. It is reasonable, then, that they also aim at pleasure, since it completes each person's life for him, and life is choiceworthy.

But do we choose life because of pleasure, or pleasure because of life? Let us set aside this question for now, since the two appear to be combined and to allow no separation; for pleasure never arises without activity, and, equally, it completes every activity.

5

Hence pleasures also seem to differ in species. For we suppose that things of different species are completed by different things. That is how it appears, both with natural things and with artifacts—for

25 instance, with animals, trees, a painting, a statue, a house, or an implement. Similarly, activities that differ in species are also completed by things that differ in species. Now activities of thought differ in species from activities of the capacities for perception, and so do these from each other; so also, then, do the pleasures that complete them.

30   This is also apparent from the way each pleasure is proper to the activity that it completes. For the proper pleasure increases the activity; for we judge each thing better and more exactly when our activity involves pleasure. If, for instance, we enjoy doing geometry, we become better geometers, and understand each question better; and similarly lovers of
35 music, building, and so on improve at their proper function when they enjoy it. Each pleasure increases
1175b the activity; what increases it is proper to it; and since the activities are different in species, what is proper to them is also different in species.

     This is even more apparent from the way some activities are impeded by pleasures from others. For lovers of flutes, for instance, cannot pay attention to a conversation if they catch the sound of someone play-
5 ing the flute, because they enjoy flute playing more than their present activity; and so the pleasure proper to flute playing destroys the activity of conversation.

     The same is true in other cases also, whenever we are engaged in two activities at once. For the more pleasant activity pushes out the other one, all the
10 more if it is much more pleasant, so that we no longer even engage in the other activity. Hence if we are enjoying one thing intensely, we do not do another very much. It is when we are only mildly pleased that we do something else; for instance, people who eat nuts in theatres do this most when the actors are bad.
15   Since, then, the proper pleasure makes an activity more exact, longer, and better, whereas an alien pleasure damages it, clearly the two pleasures differ widely. For an alien pleasure does virtually what a proper pain does. The proper pain destroys activity, so that if, for instance, writing or rational calculation has no pleasure and is in fact painful for us, we do
20 not write or calculate, since the activity is painful. Hence the proper pleasures and pains have contrary effects on an activity; and the proper ones are those that arise from the activity in itself. And as we have said, the effect of alien pleasures is similar to the

effect of pain, since they ruin the activity, though not in the same way as pain.

     Since activities differ in degrees of decency and   25
badness, and some are choiceworthy, some to be avoided, some neither, the same is true of pleasures; for each activity has its own proper pleasure. Hence the pleasure proper to an excellent activity is decent, and the one proper to a base activity is vicious; for, similarly, appetites for fine things are praiseworthy, and appetites for shameful things are blameworthy.   30
And in fact the pleasure in an activity is more proper to it than the desire for it. For the desire is distinguished from it in time and in nature; but the pleasure is close to the activity, and so little distinguished from it that disputes arise about whether the activity is the same as the pleasure.

     Still, pleasure would seem to be neither thought nor perception, since that would be absurd. Rather, it is because [pleasure and activity] are not separated   35
that to some people they appear the same. Hence,   1176a
just as activities differ, so do the pleasures. Sight differs from touch in purity, as hearing and smell do from taste; hence the pleasures also differ in the same way. So also do the pleasures of thought differ from these [pleasures of sense]; and both sorts have different kinds within them.

     Each kind of animal seems to have its own proper pleasure, just as it has its own proper function; for the proper pleasure will be the one that corresponds to its activity. This is apparent if we also study each   5
kind; for a horse, a dog, and a human being have different pleasures, and, as Heracleitus says, an ass would choose chaff over gold, since asses find food more pleasant than gold. Hence animals that differ in species also have pleasures that differ in species; and it would be reasonable for animals of the same species to have the same pleasures also.

     In fact, however, the pleasures differ quite a lot,   10
in human beings at any rate. For the same things delight some people, and cause pain to others; and while some find them painful and hateful, others find them pleasant and lovable. The same is true of sweet things. For the same things do not seem sweet to a feverish and to a healthy person, or hot to an enfeebled and to a vigorous person; and the same is true of   15
other things.

     But in all such cases it seems that what is really

so is what appears so to the excellent person. If this is right, as it seems to be, and virtue, i.e., the good person insofar as he is good, is the measure of each thing, then what appear pleasures to him will also really be pleasures, and what is pleasant will be what he enjoys.

20 And if what he finds objectionable appears pleasant to someone, that is not at all surprising; for human beings suffer many sorts of corruption and damage. It is not pleasant, however, except to these people in these conditions. Clearly, then, we should say that the pleasures agreed to be shameful are not pleasures at all, except to corrupted people.

25 But what about those pleasures that seem to be decent? Of these, which kind, or which particular pleasure, should we take to be the pleasure of a human being? Surely it will be clear from the activities, since the pleasures are consequences of these. Hence the pleasures that complete the activities of the complete and blessedly happy man, whether he has one activity or more than one, will be called the fully human pleasures to the fullest extent. The other pleasures will be human in secondary, or even more remote ways, corresponding to the character of the activities.

6

30 We have now finished our discussion of the types of virtue; of friendship; and of pleasure. It remains for us to discuss happiness in outline, since we take this to be the end of human [aims]. Our discussion will be shorter if we first take up again what we said before.

We said, then, that happiness is not a state. For if it were, someone might have it and yet be asleep for 35 his whole life, living the life of a plant, or suffer the 1176b greatest misfortunes. If we do not approve of this, we count happiness as an activity rather than a state, as we said before.

Some activities are necessary, i.e., choiceworthy for some other end, while others are choiceworthy in their own right. Clearly, then, we should count 5 happiness as one of those activities that are choiceworthy in their own right, not as one of those choiceworthy for some other end. For happiness lacks nothing, but is self-sufficient.

An activity is choiceworthy in its own right if nothing further apart from it is sought from it. This seems to be the character of actions in accord with virtue; for doing fine and excellent actions is choiceworthy for itself. But pleasant amusements also [seem to be 10 choiceworthy in their own right]; for they are not chosen for other ends, since they actually cause more harm than benefit, by causing neglect of our bodies and possessions. Moreover, most of those people congratulated for their happiness resort to these sorts of pastimes. That is why people who are witty participants in them have a good reputation with tyrants, 15 since they offer themselves as pleasant [partners] in the tyrant's aims, and these are the sort of people the tyrant requires. And so these amusements seem to have the character of happiness because people in supreme power spend their leisure in them.

These sorts of people, however, are presumably no evidence. For virtue and understanding, the sources of excellent activities, do not depend on holding supreme power. Further, these powerful people have 20 had no taste of pure and civilized pleasure, and so they resort to bodily pleasures. But that is no reason to think these pleasures are most choiceworthy, since boys also think that the things they honor are best. Hence, just as different things appear honorable to boys and to men, it is reasonable that in the same way different things appear honorable to base and to decent people.

As we have often said, then, what is honorable and 25 pleasant is what is so to the excellent person. To each type of person the activity that accords with his own proper state is most choiceworthy; hence the activity in accord with virtue is most choiceworthy to the excellent person [and hence is most honorable and pleasant].

Happiness, then, is not found in amusement; for it would be absurd if the end were amusement, and our lifelong efforts and sufferings aimed at amusing 30 ourselves. For we choose practically everything for some other end—except for happiness, since it is [the] end; but serious work and toil aimed [only] at amusement appears stupid and excessively childish. Rather, it seems correct to amuse ourselves so that we can do something serious, as Anacharsis says; for amusement would seem to be relaxation, and it is because we cannot toil continuously that we require 35 relaxation. Relaxation, then, is not [the] end; for we pursue it [to prepare] for activity. But the happy life

1177a seems to be a life in accord with virtue, which is a life involving serious actions, and not consisting in amusement.

Besides, we say that things to be taken seriously are better than funny things that provide amusement, 5 and that in each case the activity of the better part and the better person is more serious and excellent; and the activity of what is better is superior, and thereby has more the character of happiness.

Besides, anyone at all, even a slave, no less than the best person, might enjoy bodily pleasures; but no one would allow that a slave shares in happiness, if one does not [also allow that the slave shares in the sort of] life [needed for happiness]. Happiness, then, is found not in these pastimes, but in the activities 10 in accord with virtue, as we also said previously.

7

If happiness is activity in accord with virtue, it is reasonable for it to accord with the supreme virtue, which will be the virtue of the best thing. The best 15 is understanding, or whatever else seems to be the natural ruler and leader, and to understand what is fine and divine, by being itself either divine or the most divine element in us. Hence complete happiness will be its activity in accord with its proper virtue; and we have said that this activity is the activity of study.

This seems to agree with what has been said before, and also with the truth. For this activity is supreme, 20 since understanding is the supreme element in us, and the objects of understanding are the supreme objects of knowledge.

Further, it is the most continuous activity, since we are more capable of continuous study than any continuous action.

Besides, we think pleasure must be mixed into happiness; and it is agreed that the activity in accord 25 with wisdom is the most pleasant of the activities in accord with virtue. Certainly, philosophy seems to have remarkably pure and firm pleasures, and it is reasonable for those who have knowledge to spend their lives more pleasantly than those who seek it.

Moreover, the self-sufficiency we spoke of will be found in study more than in anything else. For admittedly the wise person, the just person, and the other virtuous people all need the good things necessary

for life. Still, when these are adequately supplied, the 30 just person needs other people as partners and recipients of his just actions; and the same is true of the temperate person, the brave person, and each of the others. But the wise person is able, and more able the wiser he is, to study even by himself; and though he presumably does it better with colleagues, even 1177b so he is more self-sufficient than any other [virtuous person].

Besides, study seems to be liked because of itself alone, since it has no result beyond having studied. But from the virtues concerned with action we try to a greater or lesser extent to gain something beyond the action itself.

Besides, happiness seems to be found in leisure; 5 for we deny ourselves leisure so that we can be at leisure, and fight wars so that we can be at peace. Now the virtues concerned with action have their activities in politics or war, and actions here seem to require trouble. This seems completely true for actions in war, since no one chooses to fight a war, and no one continues it, for the sake of fighting a war; 10 for someone would have to be a complete murderer if he made his friends his enemies so that there could be battles and killings. But the actions of the politician also deny us leisure; apart from political activities themselves, those actions seek positions of power and honors, or at least they seek happiness for the politician himself and for his fellow citizens, which is 15 something different from political science itself, and clearly is sought on the assumption that it is different.

Hence among actions in accord with the virtues those in politics and war are preeminently fine and great; but they require trouble, aim at some [further] end, and are choiceworthy for something other than themselves. But the activity of understanding, it 20 seems, is superior in excellence because it is the activity of study, aims at no end apart from itself, and has its own proper pleasure, which increases the activity. Further, self-sufficiency, leisure, unwearied activity (as far as is possible for a human being), and any other features ascribed to the blessed person, are evidently features of this activity. Hence a human 25 being's complete happiness will be this activity, if it receives a complete span of life, since nothing incomplete is proper to happiness.

Such a life would be superior to the human level.

For someone will live it not insofar as he is a human being, but insofar as he has some divine element in him. And the activity of this divine element is as much superior to the activity in accord with the rest of virtue as this element is superior to the compound. Hence if understanding is something divine in comparison with a human being, so also will the life in accord with understanding be divine in comparison with human life. We ought not to follow the makers of proverbs and 'Think human, since you are human,' or 'Think mortal, since you are mortal.' Rather, as far as we can, we ought to be pro-immortal, and go to all lengths to live a life in accord with our supreme element; for however much this element may lack in bulk, by much more it surpasses everything in power and value.

Moreover, each person seems to be his understanding, if he is his controlling and better element. It would be absurd, then, if he were to choose not his own life, but something else's. And what we have said previously will also apply now. For what is proper to each thing's nature is supremely best and most pleasant for it; and hence for a human being the life in accord with understanding will be supremely best and most pleasant, if understanding, more than anything else, is the human being. This life, then, will also be happiest.

8

The life in accord with the other kind of virtue [i.e., the kind concerned with action] is [happiest] in a secondary way, because the activities in accord with this virtue are human. For we do just and brave actions, and the other actions in accord with the virtues, in relation to other people, by abiding by what fits each person in contracts, services, all types of actions, and also in feelings; and all these appear to be human conditions. Indeed, some feelings actually seem to arise from the body; and in many ways virtue of character seems to be proper to feelings.

Besides, prudence is inseparable from virtue of character, and virtue of character from prudence. For the principles of prudence accord with the virtues of character; and correctness in virtues of character accords with prudence. And since these virtues are also connected to feelings, they are concerned with

the compound. Since the virtues of the compound are human virtues, the life and the happiness in accord with these virtues is also human. The virtue of understanding, however, is separated [from the compound]. Let us say no more about it, since an exact account would be too large a task for our present project.

Moreover, it seems to need external supplies very little, or [at any rate] less than virtue of character needs them. For let us grant that they both need necessary goods, and to the same extent; for there will be only a very small difference, even though the politician labors more about the body and suchlike. Still, there will be a large difference in [what is needed] for the [proper] activities [of each type of virtue]. For the generous person will need money for generous actions; and the just person will need it for paying debts, since wishes are not clear, and people who are not just pretend to wish to do justice. Similarly, the brave person will need enough power, and the temperate person will need freedom [to do intemperate actions], if they are to achieve anything that the virtue requires. For how else will they, or any other virtuous people, make their virtue clear?

Moreover, it is disputed whether decision or action is more in control of virtue, on the assumption that virtue depends on both. Well, certainly it is clear that the complete [good] depends on both; but for actions many external goods are needed, and the greater and finer the actions the more numerous are the external goods needed.

But someone who is studying needs none of these goods, for that activity at least; indeed, for study at least, we might say they are even hindrances. Insofar as he is a human being, however, and [hence] lives together with a number of other human beings, he chooses to do the actions that accord with virtue. Hence he will need the sorts of external goods [that are needed for the virtues], for living a human life.

In another way also it appears that complete happiness is some activity of study. For we traditionally suppose that the gods more than anyone are blessed and happy; but what sorts of actions ought we to ascribe to them? Just actions? Surely they will appear ridiculous making contracts, returning deposits, and so on. Brave actions? Do they endure what [they find] frightening and endure dangers because it is fine? Generous actions? Whom will they give to? And

surely it would be absurd for them to have currency
15 or anything like that. What would their temperate
actions be? Surely it is vulgar praise to say that they
do not have base appetites. When we go through them
all, anything that concerns actions appears trivial and
unworthy of the gods. Nonetheless, we all traditionally
20 suppose that they are alive and active, since surely
they are not asleep like Endymion. Then if someone
is alive, and action is excluded, and production even
more, what is left but study? Hence the gods' activity
that is superior in blessedness will be an activity of
study. And so the human activity that is most akin to
the gods' activity will, more than any others, have the
character of happiness.

25   A sign of this is the fact that other animals have no
share in happiness, being completely deprived of this
activity of study. For the whole life of the gods is blessed,
and human life is blessed to the extent that it has something resembling this sort of activity; but none of the
other animals is happy, because none of them shares
in study at all. Hence happiness extends just as far as
30 study extends, and the more someone studies, the happier he is, not coincidentally but insofar as he studies,
since study is valuable in itself. And so [on this argu-
ment] happiness will be some kind of study.

But happiness will need external prosperity also,
35 since we are human beings; for our nature is not self-
sufficient for study, but we need a healthy body, and
need to have food and the other services provided.
1179a Still, even though no one can be blessedly happy
without external goods, we must not think that to
be happy we will need many large goods. For self-
sufficiency and action do not depend on excess.

Moreover, we can do fine actions even if we do
not rule earth and sea; for even from moderate re-
5 sources we can do the actions that accord with virtue.
This is evident to see, since many private citizens
seem to do decent actions no less than people in
power do—even more, in fact. It is enough if moderate resources are provided; for the life of someone
whose activity accords with virtue will be happy.
10   Solon[17] surely described happy people well, when

17. [According to Solon, Tellus of Athens was the happiest man he knew; he was wealthy, lived to see his grandchildren, and died honorably in battle.—M.L.M.]

he said they had been moderately supplied with external goods, had done what he regarded as the finest
actions, and had lived their lives temperately. For it
is possible to have moderate possessions and still to
do the right actions. And Anaxagoras would seem to
have supposed that the happy person was neither rich
nor powerful, since he said he would not be surprised 15
if the happy person appeared an absurd sort of person
to the many. For the many judge by externals, since
these are all they perceive. Hence the beliefs of the
wise would seem to accord with our arguments.

These considerations, then, produce some confidence. But the truth in questions about action is
judged from what we do and how we live, since these 20
are what control [the answers to such questions].
Hence we ought to examine what has been said by
applying it to what we do and how we live; and if it
harmonizes with what we do, we should accept it,
but if it conflicts we should count it [mere] words.

The person whose activity accords with understanding and who takes care of understanding would seem
to be in the best condition, and most loved by the
gods. For if the gods pay some attention to human 25
beings, as they seem to, it would be reasonable for
them to take pleasure in what is best and most akin
to them, namely understanding; and reasonable for
them to benefit in return those who most of all like
and honor understanding, on the assumption that
these people attend to what is beloved by the gods,
and act correctly and finely. Clearly, all this is true 30
of the wise person more than anyone else; hence he
is most loved by the gods. And it is likely that this
same person will be happiest; hence, by this argument
also, the wise person, more than anyone else, will
be happy.

9

We have now said enough in outlines about happiness
and the virtues, and about friendship and pleasure
also. Should we, then, think that our decision [to 35
study these] has achieved its end? On the contrary, 1179b
the aim of studies about action, as we say, is surely
not to study and know about a given thing, but rather
to act on our knowledge. Hence knowing about virtue
is not enough, but we must also try to possess and
exercise virtue, or become good in any other way.

5 Now if arguments were sufficient by themselves to make people decent, the rewards they would command would justifiably have been many and large, as Theognis says, and rightly bestowed. In fact, however, arguments seem to have enough influence to stimulate and encourage the civilized ones among the young people, and perhaps to make virtue take possession of a well-born character that truly loves what is 10 fine; but they seem unable to turn the many toward being fine and good.

For the many naturally obey fear, not shame; they avoid what is base because of the penalties, not because it is disgraceful. For since they live by their feelings, they pursue their proper pleasures and the 15 sources of them, and avoid the opposed pains, and have not even a notion of what is fine and [hence] truly pleasant, since they have had no taste of it.

What argument, then, could reform people like these? For it is impossible, or not easy, to alter by argument what has long been absorbed as a result of one's habits. But, presumably, we should be satisfied to achieve some share in virtue if we already have what we seem to need to become decent.

20 Now some think it is nature that makes people good; some think it is habit; some that it is teaching. The [contribution] of nature clearly is not up to us, but results from some divine cause in those who have it, who are the truly fortunate ones. Arguments and teaching surely do not prevail on everyone, but the 25 soul of the student needs to have been prepared by habits for enjoying and hating finely, like ground that is to nourish seed. For someone who lives in accord with his feelings would not even listen to an argument turning him away, or comprehend it [if he did listen]; and in that state how could he be persuaded to change? And in general feelings seem to yield to 30 force, not to argument. Hence we must already in some way have a character suitable for virtue, fond of what is fine and objecting to what is shameful.

It is difficult, however, for someone to be trained correctly for virtue from his youth if he has not been brought up under correct laws; for the many, especially the young, do not find it pleasant to live in a 35 temperate and resistant way. That is why laws must prescribe their upbringing and practices; for they will not find these things painful when they get used to them.

Presumably, however, it is not enough if they get 1180a the correct upbringing and attention when they are young; rather, they must continue the same practices and be habituated to them when they become men. Hence we need laws concerned with these things also, and in general with all of life. For the many yield to compulsion more than to argument, and to 5 sanctions more than to the fine.

That is why legislators must, in some people's view, urge people toward virtue and exhort them to aim at the fine—on the assumption that anyone whose good habits have prepared him decently will listen to them—but must impose corrective treatments and penalties on anyone who disobeys or lacks the right 10 nature, and must completely expel an incurable. For the decent person, it is assumed, will attend to reason because his life aims at the fine, whereas the base person, since he desires pleasure, has to receive corrective treatment by pain, like a beast of burden. That is why it is said that the pains imposed must be those most contrary to the pleasures he likes.

As we have said, then, someone who is to be good 15 must be finely brought up and habituated, and then must live in decent practices, doing base actions neither willingly nor unwillingly. And this will be true if his life follows some sort of understanding and correct order that prevails on him.

Now a father's instructions lack this power to prevail and compel; and so in general do the instructions of an individual man, unless he is a king or someone 20 like that. Law, however, has the power that compels; and law is reason that proceeds from a sort of prudence and understanding. Besides, people become hostile to an individual human being who opposes their impulses, even if he is correct in opposing them, whereas a law's prescription of what is decent is not burdensome.

And yet, it is only in Sparta, or in a few other cities 25 as well, that the legislator seems to have attended to upbringing and practices. In most other cities they are neglected, and an individual lives as he wishes, 'laying down the rules for his children and wife,' like a Cyclops.

It is best, then, if the community attends to upbring- 30 ing, and attends correctly. But if the community neglects it, it seems fitting for each individual to promote the virtue of his children and his friends—to be able

to do it, or at least to decide to do it. From what we have said, however, it seems he will be better able to do it if he acquires legislative science. For, clearly,
35 attention by the community works through laws, and
1180b decent attention works through excellent laws; and whether the laws are written or unwritten, for the education of one or of many, seems unimportant, as it is in music, gymnastics, and other practices. For just as in a city the provisions of law and the types of character [found in that city] have influence, simi-
5 larly a father's words and habits have influence, and all the more because of kinship and because of the benefits he does; for his children are already fond of him and naturally ready to obey.

Further, education adapted to an individual is actually better than a common education for everyone, just as individualized medical treatment is better. For though generally a feverish patient benefits from rest
10 and starvation, presumably some patient does not; nor does the boxing instructor impose the same way of fighting on everyone. Hence it seems that treatment in particular cases is more exactly right when each person gets special attention, since he then more often gets the suitable treatment.

Nonetheless a doctor, a gymnastics trainer, and everyone else will give the best individual attention
15 if they also know universally what is good for all, or for these sorts. For sciences are said to be, and are, of what is common [to many particular cases]. Admittedly someone without scientific knowledge may well attend properly to a single person, if his experience has allowed him to take exact note of what happens in a given case, just as some people seem to be their own best doctors, though unable to help anyone else
20 at all. Nonetheless, presumably, it seems that someone who wants to be an expert in a craft and a branch of study should progress to the universal, and come to know that, as far as possible; for that, as we have said, is what the sciences are about.

Then perhaps also someone who wishes to make people better by his attention, many people or few,
25 should try to acquire legislative science, if laws are a means to make us good. For not just anyone can improve the condition of just anyone, or the person presented to him; but if someone can, it is the person with knowledge, just as in medical science and the others that require attention and prudence.

Next, then, should we examine whence and how 30 someone might acquire legislative science? Just as in other cases [we go to the practitioner], should we go to the politicians, since, as we saw, legislative science seems to be a part of political science? Or does the case of political science appear different from the other sciences and capacities? For evidently, in the other cases, the same people, such as doctors or painters, who transmit the capacity to others actively prac- 35 tice it themselves. By contrast, it is the sophists who advertise that they teach politics but none of them 1181a practices it. Instead, those who practice it are the political activists, and they seem to act on some sort of capacity and experience rather than thought.

For evidently they neither write nor speak on such questions, though presumably it would be finer to do this than to compose speeches for the law courts or 5 the Assembly; nor have they made politicians out of their own sons or any other friends of theirs. But it would be reasonable for them to do this if they were able; for there is nothing better than the political capacity that they could leave to their cities, and nothing better that they could decide to produce in themselves, or, therefore, in their closest friends.

Nonetheless, experience would seem to contribute 10 quite a lot; otherwise people would not have become better politicians by familiarity with politics. That is why those who aim to know about political science would seem to need experience as well.

By contrast, those of the sophists who advertise [that they teach political science] appear to be a long way from teaching; for they are altogether ignorant about the sort of thing political science is, and the sorts of things it is about. For if they had known what 15 it is, they would not have taken it to be the same as rhetoric, or something inferior to it, or thought it an easy task to assemble the laws with good reputations and then legislate. For they think they can select the best laws, as though the selection itself did not require comprehension, and as though correct judgment were not the most important thing, as it is in music.

[They are wrong;] for those with experience in 20 each area judge the products correctly and comprehend the ways and means of completing them, and what fits with what; for if we lack experience, we must be satisfied with noticing that the product is well or badly made, as with painting. Now laws would

1181b seem to be the products of political science; how, then, could someone acquire legislative science, or judge which laws are best, from laws alone? For neither do we appear to become experts in medicine by reading textbooks.

And yet doctors not only try to describe the [recognized] treatments, but also distinguish different [bodily] states, and try to say how each type of patient 5 might be cured and must be treated. And what they say seems to be useful to the experienced, though useless to the ignorant. Similarly, then, collections of laws and political systems might also, presumably, be most useful if we are capable of studying them and of judging what is done finely or in the contrary way, and what sorts of [elements] fit with what. Those 10 who lack the [proper] state [of experience] when they go through these collections will not manage to judge finely, unless they can do it all by themselves [without training], though they might come to comprehend them better by going through them.

Since, then, our predecessors have left the area of legislation uncharted, it is presumably better to examine it ourselves instead, and indeed to examine political systems in general, and so to complete the 15 philosophy of human affairs, as far as we are able.

First, then, let us try to review any sound remarks our predecessors have made on particular topics. Then let us study the collected political systems, to see from them what sorts of things preserve and destroy cities, and political systems of different types; 20 and what causes some cities to conduct politics well, and some badly. For when we have studied these questions, we will perhaps grasp better what sort of political system is best; how each political system should be organized so as to be best; and what habits and laws it should follow.

Let us discuss this, then, starting from the beginning.

POLITICS

BOOK I

Chapter 1

1252a We see that every city-state is a community of some sort, and that every community is established for the sake of some good (for everyone performs every action for the sake of what he takes to be good). Clearly, then, while every community aims at some good, the community that has the most authority of all and 5 encompasses all the others aims highest, that is to say, at the good that has the most authority of all. This community is the one called a city-state, the community that is political.

Those, then, who think that the positions of statesman, king, household manager, and master of slaves are the same, are not correct. For they hold that each of these differs not in kind, but only in whether the subjects ruled are few or many: that if, for example, someone rules few people, he is a master; if more, a household manager; if still more, he has the position 10 of statesman or king—the assumption being that there is no difference between a large household and a small city-state. As for the positions of statesman and king, they say that someone who is in charge by himself has the position of king, whereas someone 15 who follows the principles of the appropriate science, ruling and being ruled in turn, has the position of statesman. But these claims are not true. What I am saying will be clear, if we examine the matter according to the method of investigation that has guided us elsewhere. For as in other cases, a composite has to be analyzed until we reach things that are incomposite, since these are the smallest parts of the whole, so if 20 we also examine the parts that make up a city-state,

we shall see better both how these differ from each other, and whether or not it is possible to gain some expertise in connection with each of the things we have mentioned.

Chapter 2

If one were to see how these things develop naturally from the beginning, one would, in this case as in 25 others, get the best view of them. First, then, those who cannot exist without each other necessarily form a couple, as [1] female and male do for the sake of procreation (they do not do so from deliberate choice, but, like other animals and plants, because the urge to leave behind something of the same kind as themselves is natural), and [2] as a natural ruler and what 30 is naturally ruled do for the sake of survival. For if something is capable of rational foresight, it is a natural ruler and master, whereas whatever can use its body to labor is ruled and is a natural slave. That is why the same thing is beneficial for both master and slave.

There is a natural distinction, of course, between what is female and what is servile. For, unlike the blacksmiths who make the Delphian knife, nature 1252b produces nothing skimpily, but instead makes a single thing for a single task, because every tool will be made best if it serves to perform one task rather than many. Among non-Greeks, however, a woman and a slave occupy the same position. The reason is that 5 they do not have anything that naturally rules; rather their community consists of a male and a female slave. That is why our poets say "it is proper for Greeks to rule non-Greeks,"[1] implying that non-Greek and slave are in nature the same.

1. [For a comprehensive listing of Aristotle's literary references in the *Politics*, see Aristotle, *Politics*, translated by C.D.C. Reeve (Indianapolis: Hackett Publishing Company, 1998).]

From Aristotle, *Politics*, translated by C.D.C. Reeve (Indianapolis: Hackett Publishing Company, 1998). Copyright © 1998. Reprinted by permission of the publisher.

The first thing to emerge from these two communities is a household, so that Hesiod is right when he said in his poem, "First and foremost: a house, a wife, and an ox for the plow." For an ox is a poor man's servant. The community naturally constituted to satisfy everyday needs, then, is the household; its members are called "meal-sharers" by Charondas and "manger-sharers" by Epimenides the Cretan. But the first community constituted out of several households for the sake of satisfying needs other than everyday ones is a village.

As a colony or offshoot from a household, a village seems to be particularly natural, consisting of what some have called "sharers of the same milk," sons and the sons of sons. That is why city-states were originally ruled by kings, as nations still are. For they were constituted out of people who were under kingships; for in every household the eldest rules as a king. And so the same holds in the offshoots, because the villagers are blood relatives. This is what Homer is describing when he says: "Each one lays down the law for his own wives and children." For they were scattered about, and that is how people dwelt in the distant past. The reason all people say that the gods too are ruled by a king is that they themselves were ruled by kings in the distant past, and some still are. Human beings model the shapes of the gods on their own, and do the same to their way of life as well.

A complete community constituted out of several villages, once it reaches the limit of total self-sufficiency, practically speaking, is a city-state. It comes to be for the sake of living, but it remains in existence for the sake of living well. That is why every city-state exists by nature, since the first communities do. For the city-state is their end, and nature is an end; for we say that each thing's nature—for example, that of a human being, a horse, or a household—is the character it has when its coming-into-being has been completed. Moreover, that for the sake of which something exists, that is to say, its end, is best, and self-sufficiency is both end and best.

It is evident from these considerations, then, that a city-state is among the things that exist by nature, that a human being is by nature a political animal, and that anyone who is without a city-state, not by luck but by nature, is either a poor specimen or else superhuman. Like the one Homer condemns, he too is "clanless, lawless, and homeless." For someone with such a nature is at the same time eager for war, like an isolated piece in a board game.

It is also clear why a human being is more of a political animal than a bee or any other gregarious animal. Nature makes nothing pointlessly, as we say, and no animal has speech except a human being. A voice is a signifier of what is pleasant or painful, which is why it is also possessed by the other animals (for their nature goes this far: they not only perceive what is pleasant or painful but signify it to each other). But speech is for making clear what is beneficial or harmful, and hence also what is just or unjust. For it is peculiar to human beings, in comparison to the other animals, that they alone have perception of what is good or bad, just or unjust, and the rest. And it is community in these that makes a household and a city-state.

The city-state is also prior in nature to the household and to each of us individually, since a whole is necessarily prior to its parts. For if the whole body is dead, there will no longer be a foot or a hand, except homonymously, as one might speak of a stone "hand" (for a dead hand will be like that); but everything is defined by its task and by its capacity; so that in such condition they should not be said to be the same things but homonymous ones. Hence that the city-state is natural and prior in nature to the individual is clear. For if an individual is not self-sufficient when separated, he will be like all other parts in relation to the whole. Anyone who cannot form a community with others, or who does not need to because he is self-sufficient, is no part of a city-state—he is either a beast or a god. Hence, though an impulse toward this sort of community exists by nature in everyone, whoever first established one was responsible for the greatest of goods. For as a human being is the best of the animals when perfected, so when separated from law and justice he is worst of all. For injustice is harshest when it has weapons, and a human being grows up with weapons for virtue and practical wisdom to use, which are particularly open to being used for opposite purposes. Hence he is the most unrestrained and most savage of animals when he lacks virtue, as well as the worst where food and sex are concerned. But justice is a political matter; for justice is the organization of a political community, and justice decides what is just.

Chapter 3

1253b Since it is evident from what parts a city-state is constituted, we must first discuss household management,
for every city-state is constituted from households.
The parts of household management correspond in
turn to the parts from which the household is constituted, and a complete household consists of slaves
and free. But we must first examine each thing in

5 terms of its smallest parts, and the primary and smallest parts of a household are master and slave, husband
and wife, father and children. So we shall have to
examine these three things to see what each of them
is and what features it should have. The three in
question are [1] mastership, [2] "marital" science (for
we have no word to describe the union of woman

10 and man), and [3] "procreative" science (this also
lacks a name of its own). But there is also a part
which some believe to be identical to household management, and others believe to be its largest part. We
shall have to study its nature too. I am speaking of
what is called wealth acquisition.

15 But let us first discuss master and slave, partly to
see how they stand in relation to our need for necessities, but at the same time with an eye to knowledge
about this topic, to see whether we can acquire some
better ideas than those currently entertained. For, as
we said at the beginning, some people believe that
mastership is a sort of science, and that mastership,
household management, statesmanship, and the science of kingship are all the same. But others believe
that it is contrary to nature to be a master (for it is

20 by law that one person is a slave and another free,
whereas by nature there is no difference between
them), which is why it is not just either; for it involves force.

Chapter 4

Since property is part of the household, the science
of property acquisition is also a part of household
management (for we can neither live nor live well
without the necessities). Hence, just as the specialized

25 crafts must have their proper tools if they are going
to perform their tasks, so too does the household
manager. Some tools are inanimate, however, and
some are animate. The ship captain's rudder, for example, is an inanimate tool, but his lookout is an
animate one; for where crafts are concerned every
assistant is classed as a tool. So a piece of property is   30
a tool for maintaining life; property in general is the
sum of such tools; a slave is a piece of animate property
of a sort; and all assistants are like tools for using tools.
For, if each tool could perform its task on command or
by anticipating instructions, and if like the statues of
Daedalus or the tripods of Hephaestus—which the   35
poet describes as having "entered the assembly of the
gods of their own accord"—shuttles wove cloth by
themselves, and picks played the lyre, a master craftsman would not need assistants, and masters would
not need slaves.

What are commonly called tools are tools for pro-   1254a
duction. A piece of property, on the other hand, is
for action. For something comes from a shuttle beyond the use of it, but from a piece of clothing or a
bed we get only the use. Besides, since action and   5
production differ in kind, and both need tools, their
tools must differ in the same way as they do. Life
consists in action, not production. Therefore, slaves
too are assistants in the class of things having to do
with action. Pieces of property are spoken of in the
same way as parts. A part is not just a part of another
thing, but is *entirely* that thing's. The same is also   10
true of a piece of property. That is why a master is
just his slave's *master*, not his simply, while a slave
is not just his master's *slave*, he is entirely his.

It is clear from these considerations what the nature
and capacity of a slave are. For anyone who, despite
being human, is by nature not his own but someone
else's is a natural slave. And he is someone else's   15
when, despite being human, he is a piece of property;
and a piece of property is a tool for action that is
separate from its owner.

Chapter 5

But whether anyone is really like that by nature or
not, and whether it is better or just for anyone to be
a slave or not (all slavery being against nature)—these
are the things we must investigate next. And it is not
difficult either to determine the answer by argument
or to learn it from actual events. For ruling and being
ruled are not only necessary, they are also beneficial,   20
and some things are distinguished right from birth,

some suited to rule and others to being ruled. There are many kinds of rulers and ruled, and the better the ruled are, the better the rule over them always 25 is; for example, rule over humans is better than rule over beasts. For a task performed by something better is a better task, and where one thing rules and another is ruled, they have a certain task. For whenever a number of constituents, whether continuous with one another or discontinuous, are combined into one 30 common thing, a ruling element and a subject element appear. These are present in living things, because this is how nature as a whole works. (Some rule also exists in lifeless things: for example, that of a harmony. But an examination of that would perhaps take us too far afield.)

Soul and body are the basic constituents of an 35 animal: the soul is the natural ruler; the body the natural subject. But of course one should examine what is natural in things whose condition is natural, not corrupted. One should therefore study the human being too whose soul and body are in the best possible condition; one in whom this is clear. For in depraved people, and those in a depraved condition, the body will often seem to rule the soul, because their condi- 1254b tion is bad and unnatural.

At any rate, it is, as I say, in an animal that we can first observe both rule of a master and rule of a statesman. For the soul rules the body with the rule 5 of a master, whereas understanding rules desire with the rule of a statesman or with the rule of a king. In these cases it is evident that it is natural and beneficial for the body to be ruled by the soul, and for the affective part to be ruled by understanding (the part that has reason), and that it would be harmful to everything if the reverse held, or if these elements were equal. The same applies in the case of human 10 beings with respect to the other animals. For domestic animals are by nature better than wild ones, and it is better for all of them to be ruled by human beings, since this will secure their safety. Moreover, the relation of male to female is that of natural superior to natural inferior, and that of ruler to ruled. But, in 15 fact, the same holds true of all human beings.

Therefore those people who are as different from others as body is from soul or beast from human, and people whose task, that is to say, the best thing to come from them, is to use their bodies are in this condition—those people are natural slaves. And it is better for them to be subject to this rule, since it is also better for the other things we mentioned. For 20 he who can belong to someone else (and that is why he actually does belong to someone else), and he who shares in reason to the extent of understanding it, but does not have it himself (for the other animals obey not reason but feelings), is a natural slave. The difference in the use made of them is small, since both slaves and domestic animals help provide the necessities with their bodies. 25

Nature tends, then, to make the bodies of slaves and free people different too, the former strong enough to be used for necessities, the latter useless for that sort of work, but upright in posture and possessing all the other qualities needed for political life—qualities 30 divided into those needed for war and those for peace. But the opposite often happens as well: some have the bodies of free men; others, the souls. This, at any rate, is evident: if people were born whose bodies alone were as excellent as those found in the statues of the gods, everyone would say that those who were 35 substandard deserved to be their slaves. And if this is true of the body, it is even more justifiable to make such a distinction with regard to the soul; but the soul's beauty is not so easy to see as the body's. 1255a

It is evident, then, that there are some people, some of whom are naturally free, others naturally slaves, for whom slavery is both just and beneficial.

Chapter 6

But it is not difficult to see that those who make the opposite claim are also right, up to a point. For slaves and slavery are spoken of in two ways: for there are also slaves—that is to say, people who are in a state of slavery—by *law*. The law is a sort of agreement by 5 which what is conquered in war is said to belong to the victors. But many of those conversant with the law challenge the justice of this. They bring a writ of illegality against it, analogous to that brought against a speaker in the assembly. Their supposition is that it is monstrous if someone is going to be the subject and slave to whatever has superior power and is able to subdue him by force. Some hold the latter view, 10 others the former; and this is true even among the wise.

The reason for this dispute, and for the overlap in the arguments, is this: virtue, when it is equipped with resources, is in a way particularly adept in the use of force; and anything that conquers always does so because it is outstanding in *some* good quality. This makes it seem that force is not without virtue, and that only the justice of the matter is in dispute. For one side believes that justice is benevolence, whereas the other believes that it is precisely the rule of the more powerful that is just. At any event, when these accounts are disentangled, the other arguments have neither force nor anything else to persuade us that the one who is more virtuous should not rule or be master.

Then there are those who cleave exclusively, as they think, to justice of a sort (for law is justice of a sort), and maintain that enslavement in war is just. But at the same time they imply that it is not just. For it is possible for wars to be started unjustly, and no one would say that someone is a slave if he did not deserve to be one; otherwise, those regarded as the best born would be slaves or the children of slaves, if any of them were taken captive and sold. That is why indeed they are not willing to describe *them*, but only non-Greeks, as slaves. Yet, in saying this, they are seeking precisely the natural slave we talked about in the beginning. For they have to say that some people are slaves everywhere, whereas others are slaves nowhere.

The same holds of noble birth. Nobles regard themselves as well born wherever they are, not only when they are among their own people, but they regard non-Greeks as well born only when they are at home. They imply a distinction between a good birth and freedom that is unqualified and one that is not unqualified. As Theodectes' *Helen* says: "Sprung from divine roots on both sides, who would think that I deserve to be called a slave?" But when people say this, they are in fact distinguishing slavery from freedom, well born from low born, in terms of virtue and vice alone. For they think that good people come from good people in just the way that human comes from human, and beast from beast. But often, though nature does have a tendency to bring this about, it is nevertheless unable to do so.

It is clear, then, that the objection with which we began has something to be said for it, and that the one lot are not always natural slaves, nor the other naturally free. But it is also clear that in some cases there is such a distinction—cases where it is beneficial and just for the one to be master and the other to be slave, and where the one ought to be ruled and the other ought to exercise the rule that is natural for him (so that he is in fact a master), and where misrule harms them both. For the same thing is beneficial for both part and whole, body and soul; and a slave is a sort of part of his master—a sort of living but separate part of his body. Hence, there is a certain mutual benefit and mutual friendship for such masters and slaves as deserve to be by nature so related. When their relationship is not that way, however, but is based on law, and they have been subjected to force, the opposite holds.

Chapter 7

It is also evident from the foregoing that the rule of a master is not the same as rule of a statesman and that the other kinds of rule are not all the same as one another, though some people say they are. For rule of a statesman is rule over people who are naturally free, whereas that of a master is rule over slaves; rule by a household manager is a monarchy, since every household has one ruler; rule of a statesman is rule over people who are free and equal.

A master is so called not because he possesses a science but because he is a certain sort of person. The same is true of slave and free. None the less, there could be such a thing as mastership or slavecraft; for example, the sort that was taught by the man in Syracuse who for a fee used to train slave boys in their routine services. Lessons in such things might well be extended to include cookery and other services of that type. For different slaves have different tasks, some of which are more esteemed, others more concerned with providing the necessities: "slave is superior to slave, master to master," as the proverb says. All such sciences, then, are the business of slaves.

Mastership, on the other hand, is the science of using slaves; for it is not in acquiring slaves but in using them that someone is a master. But there is nothing grand or impressive about this science. The master needs to know how to command the things that the slave needs to know how to do. Hence for

35 those who have the resources not to bother with such things, a steward takes on this office, while they themselves engage in politics or philosophy. As for the science of acquiring slaves (the just variety of it), it is different from both of these, and is a kind of warfare or hunting.

These, then, are the distinctions to be made regarding slave and master.

Chapter 8

Since a slave has turned out to be part of property,
1256a let us now study property and wealth acquisition generally, in accordance with our guiding method. The first problem one might raise is this: Is wealth acquisition the same as household management, or a part of it, or an assistant to it? If it is an assistant, is it in
5 the way that shuttle making is assistant to weaving, or in the way that bronze smelting is assistant to statue making? For these do not assist in the same way: the first provides tools, whereas the second provides the matter. (By the matter I mean the substrate, that out of which the product is made—for example, wool for
10 the weaver and copper for the bronze smelter.)

It is clear that household management is not the same as wealth acquisition, since the former uses resources, while the latter provides them; for what science besides household management uses what is in the household? But whether wealth acquisition is a part of household management or a science of a different kind is a matter of dispute. For if someone engaged in wealth acquisition has to study the various sources
15 of wealth and property, and property and wealth have many different parts, we shall first have to investigate whether farming is a part of household management or some different type of thing, and likewise the supervision and acquisition of food generally.

But there are many kinds of food too. Hence the
20 lives of both animals and human beings are also of many kinds. For it is impossible to live without food, so that differences in diet have produced different ways of life among the animals. For some beasts live in herds and others live scattered about, whichever is of benefit for getting their food, because some of
25 them are carnivorous, some herbivorous, and some omnivorous. So, in order to make it easier for them to get hold of these foods, nature has made their ways

of life different. And since the same things are not naturally pleasant to each, but rather different things to different ones, among the carnivores and herbivores themselves the ways of life are different.

Similarly, among human beings too; for their ways of life differ a great deal. The idlest are nomads; for 30 they live a leisurely life, because they get their food effortlessly from their domestic animals. But when their herds have to change pasture, they too have to move around with them, as if they were farming a living farm. Others hunt for a living, differing from one another in the sort of hunting they do. Some live 35 by raiding; some—those who live near lakes, marshes, rivers, or a sea containing fish—live from fishing; and some from birds or wild beasts. But the most numerous type lives off the land and off cultivated 40 crops. Hence the ways of life, at any rate those whose fruits are natural and do not provide food through exchange or commerce, are roughly speaking these: nomadic, raiding, fishing, hunting, farming. But 1256b some people contrive a pleasant life by combining several of these, supplementing their way of life where it has proven less than self-sufficient; for example, some live both a nomadic and a raiding life, others, both a farming and a hunting one, and so on, each spending their lives as their needs jointly compel. 5

It is evident that nature itself gives such property to all living things, both right from the beginning, when they are first conceived, and similarly when they have reached complete maturity. Animals that produce larvae or eggs produce their offspring to- 10 gether with enough food to last them until they can provide for themselves. Animals that give birth to live offspring carry food for their offspring in their own bodies for a certain period, namely, the natural substance we call milk. Clearly, then, we must suppose in the case of fully developed things too that plants 15 are for the sake of animals, and that the other animals are for the sake of human beings, domestic ones both for using and eating, and most but not all wild ones for food and other kinds of support, so that clothes and the other tools may be got from them. If then 20 nature makes nothing incomplete or pointless, it must have made all of them for the sake of human beings. That is why even the science of warfare, since hunting is a part of it, will in a way be a natural part of property acquisition. For this science ought to be used not

only against wild beasts but also against those human
25 beings who are unwilling to be ruled, but naturally
suited for it, as this sort of warfare is naturally just.

One kind of property acquisition is a natural part of
household management, then, in that a store of the
goods that are necessary for life and useful to the community of city-state or household either must be available to start with, or household management must
arrange to make it available. At any rate, true wealth
30 seems to consist in such goods. For the amount of this
sort of property that one needs for the self-sufficiency
that promotes the good life is not unlimited, though
Solon in his poetry says it is: "No boundary to wealth
has been established for human beings." But such a
limit or boundary has been established, just as in the
35 other crafts. For none has any tool unlimited in size or
number, and wealth is a collection of tools belonging
to statesmen and household managers.

It is clear, then, that there is a natural kind of
property acquisition for household managers and
statesmen, and it is also clear why this is so.

Chapter 9

But there is another type of property acquisition
40 which is especially called wealth acquisition, and
justifiably so. It is the reason wealth and property are
1257a thought to have no limit. For many people believe
that wealth acquisition is one and the same thing
as the kind of property acquisition we have been
discussing, because the two are close neighbors. But
it is neither the same as the one we discussed nor all
that far from it: one of them is natural, whereas the
other is not natural, but comes from a sort of experience and craft.
5 Let us begin our discussion of the latter as follows.
Every piece of property has two uses. Both of these
are uses of it as such, but they are not the same uses
of it as such: one is proper to the thing and the other
is not. Take the wearing of a shoe, for example, and
its use in exchange. Both are uses to which shoes can
be put. For someone who exchanges a shoe, for
10 money or food, with someone else who needs a shoe,
is using the shoe as a shoe. But this is not its proper
use because it does not come to exist for the sake of
exchange. The same is true of other pieces of property
as well, since the science of exchange embraces all

of them. It first arises out of the natural circumstance 15
of some people having more than enough and others
less. This also makes it clear that the part of wealth
acquisition which is commerce does not exist by nature: for people needed to engage in exchange only
up to the point at which they had enough. It is evident,
then, that exchange has no task to perform in the first
community (that is to say, the household), but only 20
when the community has become larger. For the
members of the household used to share all the same
things, whereas those in separate households shared
many different things, which they had to exchange with one another through barter when the
need arose, as many non-Greek peoples still do even
to this day. For they exchange useful things for other 25
useful things, but nothing beyond that — for example,
wine is exchanged for wheat, and so on with everything else of this kind.

This kind of exchange is not contrary to nature,
nor is it any kind of wealth acquisition; for its purpose
was to fill a lack in a natural self-sufficiency. None
the less, wealth acquisition arose out of it, and in an 30
intelligible manner. Through importing what they
needed and exporting their surplus, people increasingly got their supplies from more distant foreign
sources. Since not all the natural necessities are easily
transportable, the use of money had of necessity to 35
be devised. So for the purposes of exchange people
agreed to give to and take from each other something
that was a useful thing in its own right and that was
convenient for acquiring the necessities of life: iron
or silver or anything else of that sort. At first, its value
was determined simply by size and weight, but finally
people also put a stamp on it, so as to save themselves 40
the trouble of having to measure it. For the stamp
was put on to indicate the amount.

After money was devised, necessary exchange gave 1257b
rise to the second of the two kinds of wealth acquisition, commerce. At first, commerce was probably a
simple affair, but then it became more of a craft as
experience taught people how and from what sources
the greatest profit could be made through exchange.
That is why it is held that wealth acquisition is concerned primarily with money, and that its task is to 5
be able to find sources from which a pile of wealth
will come. For it is productive of wealth and money,
and wealth is often assumed to be a pile of money,

on the grounds that this is what wealth acquisition and commerce are concerned to provide.

10   On the other hand, it is also held that money itself is nonsense and wholly conventional, not natural at all. For if those who use money alter it, it has no value and is useless for acquiring necessities; and often someone who has lots of money is unable to get the food he needs. Yet it is absurd for something to be wealth if someone who has lots of it will die of
15   starvation, like Midas in the fable, when everything set before him turned to gold in answer to his own greedy prayer. That is why people look for a different kind of wealth and wealth acquisition, and rightly so; for natural wealth and wealth acquisition *are* different. Natural wealth acquisition is a part of household
20   management, whereas commerce has to do with the production of goods, not in the full sense, but *through their exchange*. It is held to be concerned with money, on the grounds that money is the unit and limit of exchange.

The wealth that derives from this kind of wealth acquisition *is* without limit. For medicine aims at
25   unlimited health, and each of the crafts aims to achieve its end in an unlimited way, since each tries to achieve it as fully as possible. (But none of the things that promote the end is unlimited, since the end itself constitutes a limit for all crafts.) Similarly, there is no limit to the end of this kind of wealth acquisition, for its end is wealth in that form, that is to say, the possession of money. The kind of wealth acquisition that is a part of household management,
30   on the other hand, does have a limit, since this is not the task of household management.

In one way, then, it seems that every sort of wealth has to have a limit. Yet, if we look at what actually happens, the opposite seems true, for all wealth acquirers go on increasing their money without limit.
35   The explanation of this is that the two are closely connected. Each of the two kinds of wealth acquisition makes use of the same thing, so their uses overlap, since they are uses of the same property. But they do not use it in accordance with the same principle. For one aims to increase it, whereas the other aims at a different end. So some people believe that this is the task of household management, and go on thinking that they should maintain their store of money or
40   increase it without limit.

The reason they are so disposed, however, is that they are preoccupied with living, not with living well. And since their appetite for life is unlimited, they also want an unlimited amount of what sustains it. 1258a And those who do aim at living well seek what promotes physical gratification. So, since this too seems to depend on having property, they spend all their time acquiring wealth. And the second kind of wealth 5 acquisition arose because of this. For since their gratification lies in excess, they seek the craft that produces the excess needed for gratification. If they cannot get it through wealth acquisition, they try to do so by means of something else that causes it, using each of their powers in an unnatural way. For the end of courage is not to produce wealth but to produce 10 confidence in the face of danger; nor is it the end of generalship or medicine to do so, but rather victory and health. None the less, these people make all of these into forms of wealth acquisition in the belief that acquiring wealth is the end, and that everything ought to promote the end.

We have now said what unnecessary wealth acquisi- 15 tion is and why we need it. We have also said that the necessary kind is different, that it is a natural part of household management concerned with the means of life, and that it is not limitless like this one, but has a limit.

Chapter 10

Clearly, we have also found the solution to our original problem about whether the craft of wealth acquisition is that of a household manager or a statesman, or not—this having rather to be available. For just as 20 statesmanship does not make human beings, but takes them from nature and uses them, so too nature must provide land or sea or something else as a source of food, and a household manager must manage what comes from these sources in the way required. For the task of weaving is not to make wool but to use 25 it, and to know which sorts are useful and suitable or worthless and unsuitable. For one might be puzzled as to why wealth acquisition is a part of household management but medicine is not, even though the members of a household need health, just as they need life and every other necessity. And in fact there 30 is a way in which it is the task of a household manager or ruler to see to health, but in another way it is not his task but a doctor's. So too with wealth: there is a way in which a household manager has to see to it, and another in which he does not, and an assistant craft does. But above all, as we said, nature must 35 ensure that wealth is there to start with. For it is the task of nature to provide food for what is born, since the surplus of that from which they come serves as food for every one of them. That is why the craft of acquiring wealth from crops and animals is natural for all people.

But, as we said, there are two kinds of wealth acquisition. One has to do with commerce, the other with household management. The latter is necessary and commendable, but the kind that has to do with exchange is justly disparaged, since it is not natural but 1258b is from one another. Hence usury is very justifiably detested, since it gets wealth from money itself, rather than from the very thing money was devised to facilitate. For money was introduced to facilitate exchange, but interest makes money itself grow bigger. (That is 5 how it gets its name; for offspring resemble their parents, and interest is money that comes from money.) Hence of all the kinds of wealth acquisition this one is the most unnatural.

Chapter 11

Now that we have adequately determined matters bearing on knowledge, we should go through those bearing on practice. A free person has theoretical 10 knowledge of all of these, but he will gain practical experience of them to meet necessary needs. The practical parts of [1] wealth acquisition are experience of: [1.1] livestock, for example, what sorts of horses, cattle, sheep, and similarly other animals yield the most profit in different places and conditions; for one needs practical experience of which breeds are by 15 comparison with one another the most profitable, and which breeds yield the most profit in which places, as different ones thrive in different places. [1.2] Farming, which is now divided into land planted with fruit and land planted with cereals. [1.3] Bee keeping and the rearing of the other creatures, whether fish or fowl, that can be of some use. These, then, are the 20 parts of the primary and most appropriate kind of wealth acquisition.

[2] Exchange's most important part, on the other hand, is [2.1] trading, which has three parts: [2.1.1] ship owning, [2.1.2] transport, and [2.1.3] marketing. These differ from one another in that some are safer, others more profitable. The second part of exchange is [2.2] money lending; the third is [2.3] wage earning. As for wage earning, some wage earners are [2.3.1] 25 vulgar craftsmen, whereas [2.3.2] others are unskilled, useful for manual labor only.

[3] A third kind of wealth acquisition comes between this kind and the primary or natural kind, since it contains elements both of the natural kind and of exchange. It deals with inedible but useful things from the earth or extracted from the earth. Logging and mining are examples. Mining too is of many 30 types, since many kinds of things are mined from the earth.

A general account has now been given of each of them. A detailed and precise account might be useful for practical purposes, but it would be vulgar to spend one's time developing it. (The operations 35 that are most craftlike depend least on luck; the more they damage the body, the more vulgar they are; the most slavish are those in which the body is used the most; the most ignoble are those least in need of virtue.) Besides, some people have written books on these matters which may be studied by those interested. For example, Chares of Paros and Apollodorus of Lemnos have written on how to 1259a farm both fruit and cereals, and others have written on similar topics.

Moreover, the scattered stories about how people have succeeded in acquiring wealth should be collected, since all of them are useful to those who value wealth acquisition. For instance, there is the scheme 5 of Thales of Miletus. This is a scheme for getting wealthy which, though credited to him on account of his wisdom, is in fact quite generally applicable. People were reproaching Thales for being poor, claiming that it showed his philosophy was useless. 10 The story goes that he realized through his knowledge of the stars that a good olive harvest was coming. So, while it was still winter, he raised a little money and put a deposit on all the olive presses in Miletus and Chios for future lease. He hired them at a low rate, because no one was bidding against him. When the olive season came and many people suddenly sought

olive presses at the same time, he hired them out
15 at whatever rate he chose. He collected a lot
of money, showing that philosophers could easily
become wealthy if they wished, but that this is not
their concern. Thales is said to have demonstrated
his own wisdom in this way. But, as I said, his
20 scheme involves a generally applicable principle of
wealth acquisition: to secure a monopoly if one
can. Hence some city-states also adopt this scheme
when they are in need of money: they secure a
monopoly in goods for sale.

There was a man in Sicily who used some money
that had been lent to him to buy up all the iron
25 from the foundries, and later, when the merchants
came from their warehouses to buy iron, he was
the only seller. He did not increase his prices
exorbitantly and yet he turned his fifty silver talents
into one hundred and fifty. When Dionysius heard
about this, he told the man to take his wealth out,
but to remain in Syracuse no longer, as he had
30 discovered ways of making money that were harmful
to Dionysius' own affairs. Yet this man's insight was
the same as Thales': each contrived to secure a
monopoly for himself.

It is also useful for statesmen to know about these
things, since many city-states have an even greater
need for wealth acquisition and the associated reve-
35 nues than a private household does. That is why
indeed some statesmen restrict their political activities
entirely to finance.

Chapter 12

Household management has proved to have three
parts: [1] one is mastership (which we discussed earlier), [2] another that of a father, and [3] a third,
marital. For a man rules his wife and children both
40 as free people, but not in the same way: instead, he
rules his wife the way a statesman does, and his chil-
1259b dren the way a king does. For a male, unless he is
somehow constituted contrary to nature, is naturally
more fitted to lead than a female, and someone older
and completely developed is naturally more fitted to
lead than someone younger and incompletely developed.

In most cases of rule of a statesman, it is true,
people take turns at ruling and being ruled, because

they tend by nature to be on an equal footing and 5
to differ in nothing. Nevertheless, whenever one
person is ruling and another being ruled, the one
ruling tries to distinguish himself in demeanor, title,
or rank from the ruled; witness what Amasis said
about his footbath. Male is permanently related to
female in this way.

The rule of a father over his children, on the other 10
hand, is that of a king, since a parent rules on the
basis of both age and affection, and this is a type of
kingly rule. Hence Homer did well to address Zeus,
who is the king of them all, as "Father of gods and
men." For a king should have a natural superiority,
but be the same in stock as his subjects; and this is 15
the condition of older in relation to younger and
father in relation to child.

Chapter 13

It is evident, then, that household management is
more seriously concerned with human beings than
with inanimate property, with their virtue more than 20
with its (which we call wealth), and with the virtue
of free people more than with that of slaves.

The first problem to raise about slaves, then, is this:
Has the slave some other virtue more estimable than
those he has as a tool or servant, such as temperance,
courage, justice, and other such states of character?
Or has he none besides those having to do with the 25
physical assistance he provides? Whichever answer
one gives, there are problems. If slaves have temperance and the rest, in what respect will they differ
from the free? If they do not, absurdity seems to result,
since slaves are human and have a share in reason.
Roughly the same problem arises about women and
children. Do they too have virtues? Should women 30
be temperate, courageous, and just, or a child be
temperate or intemperate? Or not?

The problem of natural rulers and natural subjects,
and whether their virtue is the same or different,
needs to be investigated in general terms. If both of
them should share in what is noble-and-good, why
should one of them rule once and for all and the 35
other be ruled once and for all? (It cannot be that
the difference between them is one of degree. Ruling
and being ruled differ in kind, but things that differ
in degree do not differ in that way.) On the other

hand, if the one shares in what is noble-and-good, and not the other, that would be astonishing. For if the ruler is not going to be temperate and just, how will he rule well? And if the subject is not going to 40 be, how will he be ruled well? For if he is intemperate 1260a and cowardly, he will not perform any of his duties. It is evident, therefore, that both must share in virtue, but that there are differences in their virtue (as there are among those who are naturally ruled).

Consideration of the soul leads immediately to this view. The soul by nature contains a part that rules 5 and a part that is ruled, and we say that each of them has a different virtue, that is to say, one belongs to the part that has reason and one to the nonrational part. It is clear, then, that the same holds in the other cases as well, so that most instances of ruling and being ruled are natural. For free rules slaves, male rules female, and man rules child in different ways, 10 because, while the parts of the soul are present in all these people, they are present in different ways. The deliberative part of the soul is entirely missing from a slave; a woman has it but it lacks authority; a child has it but it is incompletely developed. We must suppose, therefore, that the same necessarily holds of 15 the virtues of character too: all must share in them, but not in the same way; rather, each must have a share sufficient to enable him to perform his own task. Hence a ruler must have virtue of character complete, since his task is unqualifiedly that of a master craftsman, and reason is a master craftsman, but each of the others must have as much as pertains to him. It is evident, then, that all those mentioned have virtue of character, and that temperance, cour-20 age, and justice of a man are not the same as those of a woman, as Socrates supposed: the one courage is that of a ruler, the other that of an assistant, and similarly in the case of the other virtues too.

If we investigate this matter in greater detail, it will become clear. For people who talk in generalities, 25 saying that virtue is a good condition of the soul, or correct action, or something of that sort, are deceiving themselves. It is far better to enumerate the virtues, as Gorgias does, than to define them in this general way. Consequently, we must take what the poet says about a woman as our guide in every case: "To a woman silence is a crowning glory"—whereas this 30 does not apply to a man. Since a child is incompletely developed, it is clear that his virtue too does not belong to him in relation to himself but in relation to his end and his leader. The same holds of a slave in relation to his master. But we said that a slave is useful for providing the necessities, so he clearly needs only a small amount of virtue—just so much as will 35 prevent him from inadequately performing his tasks through intemperance or cowardice.

If what we have now said is true, one might raise the problem of whether vulgar craftsmen too need to have virtue; for they often fail to perform their tasks through intemperance. Or are the two cases actually very different? For a slave shares his master's life, whereas a vulgar craftsman is at a greater remove, 40 and virtue pertains to him to just the extent that slavery does; for a vulgar craftsman has a kind of delimited slavery. Moreover, a slave is among the 1260b things that exist by nature, whereas no shoemaker is, nor any other sort of craftsman. It is evident, then, that the cause of such virtue in a slave must be the master, not the one who possesses the science of teaching him his tasks. Hence those who deny reason to slaves, but tell us to give them orders only, are 5 mistaken; for slaves should be admonished more than children.

But we may take these matters to be determined in this way. As for man and woman, father and children, the virtue relevant to each of them, what is good in their relationship with one another and 10 what is not good, and how to achieve the good and avoid the bad—it will be necessary to go through all these in connection with the constitutions. For every household is part of a city-state, these are parts of a household, and the virtue of a part must be determined by looking to the virtue of the whole. Hence both women and children must be educated 15 with an eye to the constitution, if indeed it makes any difference to the virtue of a city-state that its children be virtuous, and its women too. And it must make a difference, since half the free population are women, and from children come those who participate in the constitution.

So, since we have determined some matters, and 20 must discuss the rest elsewhere, let us regard the present discussion as complete, and make a new beginning. And let us first investigate those who have expressed views about the best constitution.

BOOK II

Chapter 1

Since we propose to study which political community is best of all for people who are able to live as ideally as possible, we must investigate other constitutions too, both some of those used in city-states that are
30 said to be well governed, and any others described by anyone that are held to be good, in order to see what is correct or useful in them, but also to avoid giving the impression that our search for something different from them results from a desire to be clever. Let it be held, instead, that we have undertaken this inquiry because the currently available constitutions
35 are not in good condition.

We must begin, however, at the natural starting point of this investigation. For all citizens must share everything, or nothing, or some things but not others. It is evidently impossible for them to share nothing.
40 For a constitution is a sort of community, and so they must, in the first instance, share their location; for one city-state occupies one location, and citizens
1261a share that one city-state. But is it better for a city-state that is to be well managed to share everything possible? Or is it better to share some things but not others? For the citizens could share children, women,
5 and property with one another, as in Plato's *Republic*. For Socrates claims there that children, women, and property should be communal. So is what we have now better, or what accords with the law described in the *Republic*?

Chapter 2

10 That women should be common to all raises many difficulties. In particular, it is not evident from Socrates' arguments why he thinks this legislation is needed. Besides, the end he says his city-state should have is impossible, as in fact described, yet nothing has been settled about how one ought to delimit it. I am talking about the assumption that it is best for a city-state to be as far as possible all one unit; for that is the assumption
15 Socrates adopts. And yet it is evident that the more of a unity a city-state becomes, the less of a city-state it will be. For a city-state naturally consists of a certain multitude; and as it becomes more of a unity, it will

turn from a city-state into a household, and from a household into a human being. For we would surely say that a household is more of a unity than a city-state 20 and an individual human being than a household. Hence, even if someone could achieve this, it should not be done, since it will destroy the city-state.

A city-state consists not only of a number of people, but of people of different kinds, since a city-state does not come from people who are alike. For a city-state is different from a military alliance. An alliance is useful because of the weight of numbers, even if they 25 are all of the same kind, since the natural aim of a military alliance is the sort of mutual assistance that a heavier weight provides if placed on a scales. A nation will also differ from a city-state in this sort of way, provided the multitude is not separated into villages, but is like the Arcadians. But things from which a unity must come differ in kind. That is why reciprocal equality preserves city-states, as we said earlier in the *Ethics*, since this must exist even among 30 people who are free and equal. For they cannot all rule at the same time, but each can rule for a year or some other period. As a result they all rule, just as all would be shoemakers and carpenters if they changed places, instead of the same people always 35 being shoemakers and the others always carpenters. But since it is better to have the latter also where a political community is concerned, it is clearly better, where possible, for the same people always to rule. But among those where it is not possible, because all are naturally equal, and where it is at the same time just for all to share the benefits or burdens of ruling, 1261b it is at least possible to approximate to this if those who are equal take turns and are similar when out of office. For they rule and are ruled in turn, just as if they had become other people. It is the same way 5 among those who are ruling; some hold one office, some another.

It is evident from these considerations that a city-state is not a natural unity in the way some people say it is, and that what has been alleged to be the greatest good for city-states destroys them, whereas what is good for a thing preserves it. It is also evident 10 on other grounds that to try to make a city-state too much a unity is not a better policy. For a household is more self-sufficient than a single person, and a city-state than a household; and a city-state tends to come about as soon as a community's population is large enough to be fully self-sufficient. So, since what is more self-sufficient is more choiceworthy, what is less 15 a unity is more choiceworthy than what is more so.

Chapter 3

But even if it is best for a community to be as much a unity as possible, this does not seem to have been established by the argument that everyone says "mine" and "not mine" at the same time (for Socrates takes this as an indication that his city-state is completely one). For "all" is ambiguous. If it means each individ- 20 ually, perhaps more of what Socrates wants will come about, since each will then call the same woman his wife, the same person his son, the same things his property, and so on for each thing that befalls him. But this is not in fact how those who have women 25 and children in common will speak. They will *all* speak, but not *each*. And the same goes for property: all, not each. It is evident, then, that there is an equivocation involved in "all say." (For "all," "both," "odd," and "even," are ambiguous, and give rise to 30 contentious arguments even in discussion.) Hence in one sense it would be good if all said the same, but not possible, whereas in the other sense it is in no way conducive to concord.

But the phrase is also harmful in another way, since what is held in common by the largest number of people receives the least care. For people give most attention to their own property, less to what is communal, or only as much as falls to them to give. For apart from anything else, the thought that someone 35 else is attending to it makes them neglect it the more (just as a large number of household servants sometimes give worse service than a few). Each of the citizens acquires a thousand sons, but they do not belong to him as an individual: any of them is equally 40 the son of any citizen, and so will be equally neglected 1262a by them all. Besides, each says "mine" of whoever among the citizens is doing well or badly in this sense, that he is whatever fraction he happens to be of a certain number. What he really means is "mine or so-and-so's," referring in this way to each of the thousand or however many who constitute the city-state. And even then he is uncertain, since it is not clear who has had a child born to him, or one who once

born survived. Yet is this way of calling the same 5 thing "mine" as practiced by each of two or ten thousand people really better than the way they in fact use "mine" in city-states? For the same person is called "my son" by one person, "my brother" by another, "my cousin" by a third, or something else in virtue of some 10 other connection of kinship or marriage, one's own marriage, in the first instance, or that of one's relatives. Still others call him "my fellow clansman" or "my fellow tribesman." For it is better to have a cousin of one's own than a son in the way Socrates describes.

Moreover, it is impossible to prevent people from having suspicions about who their own brothers, sons, fathers, and mothers are. For the resemblances that 15 occur between parents and children will inevitably be taken as evidence of this. And this is what actually happens, according to the reports of some of those who write accounts of their world travels. They say that some of the inhabitants of upper Libya have their women in common, and yet distinguish the children 20 on the basis of their resemblance to their fathers. And there are some women, as well as some females of other species such as mares and cows, that have a strong natural tendency to produce offspring resembling their sires, like the mare in Pharsalus called "Just."

Chapter 4

Moreover, there are other difficulties that it is not easy for the establishers of this sort of community to 25 avoid, such as voluntary or involuntary homicides, assaults, or slanders. None of these is pious when committed against fathers, mothers, or not too distant relatives (just as none is even against outsiders). Yet they are bound to occur even more frequently among those who do not know their relatives than among 30 those who do. And when they do occur, the latter can perform the customary expiation, whereas the former cannot.

It is also strange that while making sons communal, he forbids sexual intercourse only between lovers, but does not prohibit sexual love itself or the other practices which, between father and son or a pair of brothers, are most indecent, since even the love alone 35 is. It is strange, too, that Socrates forbids such sexual intercourse solely because the pleasure that comes

from it is so intense, but regards the fact that the lovers are father and son or brother and brother as
40 making no difference.

It would seem more useful to have the farmers rather than the guardians share their women and children. For there will be less friendship where
1262b women and children are held in common. But it is the *ruled* who should be like that, in order to promote obedience and prevent rebellion.

In general, the results of such a law are necessarily the opposite of those of a good law, and the opposite
5 of those that Socrates aims to achieve by organizing the affairs of children and women in this way. For we regard friendship as the greatest of goods for city-states, since in this condition people are least likely to factionalize. And Socrates himself particularly praises unity in a city-state, something that is held to be,
10 and that he himself says is, the result of friendship. (Similarly, in the erotic dialogues, we know that Aristophanes says that lovers, because of their excessive friendship, want to grow together and become one instead of two. The result in such circumstances, however, is that one or both has necessarily perished.) But in a city-state this sort of community inevitably
15 makes friendship watery, in that father hardly ever says "mine" of son, or son of father. For just as adding a lot of water to a drop of sweet wine makes the mixture undetectable, so it is with the kinship connections expressed in these names, since in a constitution of this sort a father has least reason to cherish his
20 sons as sons, or a son his father as a father, or brothers each other as brothers. For there are two things in particular that cause human beings to love and cherish something: their own and their favorite. And neither can exist among those governed in this way.

But there is also a lot of confusion about the way in which the children, once born, will be transferred
25 from the farmers and craftsmen to the guardians, and vice versa. Those who do the transferring and receiving are sure to know who has been transferred to whom. Besides, in these cases the results we mentioned earlier must of necessity happen even more
30 often—I mean assaults, love affairs, and murders. For those who have been transferred to the other citizens will no longer call the guardians "brothers," "children," "fathers," or "mothers," nor will those who have been transferred to the guardians use these terms

of the other citizens, so as to avoid committing, through kinship, any such offenses.

So much for our conclusions about community of 35 women and children.

Chapter 5

The next topic to investigate is property, and how those in the best constitution should arrange it. Should it be owned in common, or not? One could investigate these questions even in isolation from the legislation dealing with women and children. I mean even if women and children belong to separate individuals, which is in fact the practice everywhere, it 1263a still might be best for property either to be owned or used communally. For example, [1] the land might be owned separately, while the crops grown on it are communally stored and consumed (as happens in some nations). [2] Or it might be the other way around: the land might be owned and farmed communally, while the crops grown on it are divided up 5 among individuals for their private use (some non-Greeks are also said to share things in this way). [3] Or both the land and the crops might be communal.

If the land is worked by others, the constitution is different and easier. But if the citizens do the work for themselves, property arrangements will give rise to a lot of discontent. For if the citizens happen to 10 be unequal rather than equal in the work they do and the profits they enjoy, accusations will inevitably be made against those who enjoy or take a lot but do little work by those who take less but do more. It is generally difficult to live together and to share in any human enterprise, particularly in enterprises such as 15 these. Travelers away from home who share a journey together show this clearly. For most of them start quarreling because they annoy one another over humdrum matters and little things. Moreover, we get especially irritated with those servants we employ most regularly for everyday services. 20

These, then, and others are the difficulties involved in the common ownership of property. The present practice, provided it was enhanced by virtuous character and a system of correct laws, would be much superior. For it would have the good of both—by "of both" I mean of the common ownership of property and of private ownership. For while property should 25

be in some way communal, in general it should be private. For when care for property is divided up, it leads not to those mutual accusations, but rather to greater care being given, as each will be attending to what is his own. But where use is concerned, virtue will ensure that it is governed by the proverb "friends
30 share everything in common."

Such a practice is already present in outline form in some city-states, which implies that it is not impracticable. In well-managed city-states, in particular, some elements exist, whereas others could come to be. For although each citizen does own private property, he makes part of it available for his friends to use and keeps part for his own use. For example, in Sparta they pretty much have common use of each
35 other's slaves, and dogs and horses also; and when on a journey in the countryside, they may take what provisions they need from the fields. Evidently, then, it is better for property to be private and its use communal. It is the legislator's special task to see that people are so disposed.

40 Besides, to regard a thing as one's own makes an enormous difference to one's pleasure. For the love each person feels for himself is no accident, but is
1263b something natural. Selfishness is rightly criticized. But it is not just loving oneself, it is loving oneself more than one should, just as in the case of the love of money (since practically everyone does love each
5 of these things). Moreover, it is very pleasant to help one's friends, guests, or companions, and do them favors, as one can if one has property of one's own. But those who make the city-state too much a unity by abolishing private property exclude these pleasures. They also openly take away the tasks of two of the virtues: of temperance in regard to women (for it is a fine thing to stay away from another man's woman
10 out of temperance), and generosity with one's property, since one cannot show oneself to be generous, nor perform any generous action (for it is in the use made of property that generosity's task lies).

15 Such legislation may seem attractive, and humane. For anyone who hears it accepts it gladly, thinking that all will have an amazing friendship for all, particularly when someone blames the evils now existing in constitutions on property's not being communal (I mean lawsuits brought against one another over
20 contracts, perjury trials, and flattery of the rich). Yet

none of these evils is caused by property not being communal but by vice. For we see that those who own and share communal property have far more disagreements than those whose property is separate. But we consider those disagreeing over what they own 25 in common to be few, because we compare them with the many whose property is private. Furthermore, it would be fair to mention not only how many evils people will lose through sharing, but also how many good things. The life they would lead seems to be totally impossible.

One has to think that the reason Socrates goes astray is that his assumption is incorrect. For a house- 30 hold and a city-state must indeed be a unity up to a point, but not totally so. For there is a point at which it will, as it goes on, not be a city-state, and another at which, by being nearly not a city-state, it will be a worse one. It is as if one were to reduce a harmony to a unison, or a rhythm to a single beat. But a city- 35 state consists of a multitude, as we said before, and should be unified and made into a community by means of education. It is strange, at any rate, that the one who aimed to bring in education, and who believed that through it the city-state would be excellent, should think to set it straight by measures of this sort, and not by habits, philosophy, and laws—as in Sparta and Crete, where the legislator aimed to make property communal by means of the messes. 40

And we must not overlook this point, that we should 1264a consider the immense period of time and the many years during which it would not have gone unnoticed if these measures were any good. For practically speaking all things have been discovered, although some have not been collected, and others are known about but not used. The matter would become particularly evident, however, if one could see such a constitution 5 actually being instituted. For it is impossible to construct his city-state without separating the parts and dividing it up into common messes or into clans and tribes. Consequently, nothing else will be legislated except that the guardians should not do any farming, which is the very thing the Spartans are trying to enforce even now. 10

But the fact is that Socrates has not said, nor is it easy to say, what the arrangement of the constitution as a whole is for those who participate in it. The multitude of the other citizens constitute pretty well the entire multitude of his city-state, yet nothing has been determined about them, whether the farmers too should have communal property or each his own private property, or whether their women and children should be private or communal. If all is to be common to all in the same way, how will they differ from the guardians? And how will they benefit from submitting to their rule? Or what on earth will prompt them to submit to it—unless the guardians adopt some clever stratagem like that of the Cretans? For the Cretans allow their slaves to have the same other things as themselves, and forbid them only the gymnasia and the possession of weapons. On the other hand, if they too are to have such things, as they do in other city-states, what sort of community will it be? For it will inevitably be two city-states in one, and those opposed to one another. For he makes the guardians into a sort of garrison, and the farmers, craftsmen, and the others into the citizens. Hence the indictments, lawsuits, and such other bad things as he says exist in other city-states will all exist among them. And yet Socrates claims that because of their education they will not need many regulations, such as town or market ordinances and others of that sort. Yet he gives this education only to the guardians. Besides, he gives the farmers authority over their property, although he requires them to pay a tax. But this is likely to make them much more difficult and presumptuous than the helots, serfs, and slaves that some people have today.

But be that as it may, whether these matters are similarly essential or not, nothing at any rate has been determined about them; neither are the related questions of what constitution, education, and laws they will have. The character of these people is not easy to discover, and the difference it makes to the preservation of the community of the guardians is not small. But if Socrates is going to make their women communal and their property private, who will manage the household in the way the men manage things in the fields? Who will manage it, indeed, if the farmers' women and property are communal? It is futile to draw a comparison with wild beasts in order to show that women should have the same way of life as men: wild beasts do not go in for household management.

The way Socrates selects his rulers is also risky.

He makes the same people rule all the time, which becomes a cause of conflict even among people with no merit, and all the more so among spirited and warlike men. But it is evident that he has to make the same people rulers, since the gold from the god has not been mixed into the souls of one lot of people at one time and another at another, but always into the same ones. He says that the god, immediately at their birth, mixed gold into the souls of some, silver into others, and bronze and iron into those who are going to be craftsmen and farmers.

Moreover, even though Socrates deprives the guardians of their happiness, he says that the legislator should make the whole city-state happy. But it is impossible for the whole to be happy unless all, most, or some of its parts are happy. For happiness is not made up of the same things as evenness, since the latter can be present in the whole without being present in either of the parts, whereas happiness cannot. But if the guardians are not happy, who is? Surely not the skilled craftsmen or the multitude of vulgar craftsmen.

These, then, are the problems raised by the constitution Socrates describes, and there are others that are no less great.

Chapter 9

There are two things to investigate about the constitution of Sparta, of Crete, and, in effect, about the other constitutions also. First, is there anything legislated in it that is good or bad as compared with the best organization? Second, is there anything legislated in it that is contrary to the fundamental principle or character of the intended constitution?

It is generally agreed that to be well-governed a constitution should have leisure from necessary tasks. But the way to achieve this is not easy to discover. For the Thessalian serfs often attacked the Thessalians, just as the helots—always lying in wait, as it were, for their masters' misfortunes—attacked the Spartans. Nothing like this has so far happened in the case of the Cretans. Perhaps the reason is that, though they war with one another, the neighboring city-states never ally themselves with the rebels: it benefits them to do so, since they also possess subject peoples themselves. Sparta's neighbors, on the other hand, the

Argives, Messenians, and Arcadians, were all hostile.
5 The Thessalians, too, first experienced revolts because
they were still at war with their neighbors, the
Achaeans, Perrhaebeans, and Magnesians. If nothing
else, it certainly seems that the management of serfs,
the proper way to live together with them, is a troublesome matter. For if they are given license, they become arrogant and claim to merit equality with those
10 in authority, but if they live miserably, they hate and
conspire. It is clear, then, that those whose system of
helotry leads to these results still have not found the
best way.

Furthermore, the license where their women are
concerned is also detrimental both to the deliberately
chosen aims of the constitution and to the happiness
of the city-state as well. For just as a household has
15 a man and a woman as parts, a city-state, too, is
clearly to be regarded as being divided almost equally
between men and women. So in all constitutions in
which the position of women is bad, half the city-
state should be regarded as having no laws. And this
is exactly what has happened in Sparta. For the legislator, wishing the whole city-state to have endurance,
20 makes his wish evident where the men are concerned,
but has been negligent in the case of the women.
For being free of all constraint, they live in total
intemperance and luxury. The inevitable result, in a
constitution of this sort, is that wealth is esteemed.
This is particularly so if the citizens are dominated
by their women, like most military and warlike races
25 (except for the Celts and some others who openly
esteemed male homosexuality). So it is understandable why the original author of the myth of Ares and
Aphrodite paired the two; for all warlike men seem
obsessed with sexual relations with either men or
30 women. That is why the same happened to the Spartans, and why in the days of their hegemony, many
things were managed by women. And yet what difference is there between women rulers and rulers ruled
by women? The result is the same. Audacity is not
useful in everyday matters, but only, if at all, in war.
35 Yet Spartan women were very harmful even here.
They showed this quite clearly during the Theban
invasion; for they were of no use at all, like women
in other city-states, but caused more confusion than
the enemy.

So it seems that license with regard to women

initially occurred in Sparta for explicable reasons. For
Spartan men spent a great deal of time away from
home during their wars with the Argives, and again 40
with the Arcadians and Messenians. So when leisure 1270a
returned, they placed themselves in the hands of their
legislator, already prepared thanks to military life,
which includes many parts of virtue. But we are told 5
that when he attempted to bring the women under
his laws, they resisted and he retreated. These, then,
are the causes of what happened, and so, clearly, of
the present error as well. But of course we are not
investigating the question of whom we should excuse
and whom not, but what is correct and what is not. 10

The fact that the position of women is not well
handled seems not only to create a certain unseemli-
ness in the constitution, as we said before, but also
to contribute something to the love of money. For
what one might criticize next, after the foregoing, is
the uneven distribution of property. For because some
of the Spartans came to own too much wealth and 15
others very little, the land passed into the hands of a
few. This is poorly organized by the laws as well. For
the legislator quite rightly made it improper to buy
or sell an existing land holding, but he left owners 20
free to give or bequeath their land if they wished,
even though this inevitably leads to the same results
as the other. Indeed, nearly two fifths of all the land
belongs to the women, both because many become
heiresses and because large dowries are given. It
would have been better if it had been organized so 25
that there was no dowry or only a small or moderate
one. But, as it is, one may marry an heiress daughter
to whomever one wishes, and if a man dies intestate,
the person he leaves as his heir gives her to whom
he likes. As a result, in a land capable of supporting
fifteen hundred cavalry and thirty thousand hoplites,
there were fewer than a thousand. The very facts have 30
clearly shown that the organization of these matters
served them badly. For their city-state did not withstand one single blow, but was ruined because of its
shortage of men.

It is said that at the time of their early kings, they
used to give a share in the constitution to others, so
that there was no shortage of men, despite lengthy 35
wars. Indeed, they say that there were once ten thousand Spartiates. Whether this is true or not, a better
way to keep high the number of men in a city-state

is by leveling property. But the law dealing with the procreation of children militates against this reform. For the legislator, intending there to be as many Spartiates as possible, encourages people to have as many children as possible, since there is a law exempting a father of three sons from military service, and a father of four from all taxes. But it is evident that if many children are born, and the land is correspondingly divided, many people will inevitably become poor.

Matters relating to the board of overseers are also badly organized. For this office has sole authority over the most important matters; but the overseers are drawn from among the entire people, so that often very poor men enter it who, because of their poverty, are open to bribery. (This has been shown on many occasions in the past too, and recently among the Andrians; for some, corrupted by bribes, did everything in their power to destroy the entire city-state.) Moreover, because the office is too powerful—in fact, equal in power to a tyranny—even the kings were forced to curry favor with the overseers. And this too has harmed the constitution, for from an aristocracy a democracy was emerging.

Admittedly, the board of overseers does hold the constitution together; for the people remain contented because they participate in the most important office. So, whether it came about because of the legislator or by luck, it benefits Spartan affairs. For if a constitution is to survive, every part of the city-state must want it to exist and to remain as it is. And the kings want this because of the honor given to them; the noble-and-good, because of the senate (since this office is a reward of virtue); and the people, because of the board of overseers (since selections for it are made from all). Still, though the overseers should be chosen from all, it should not be by the present method, which is exceedingly childish.

Furthermore, the overseers have authority over the most important judicial decisions, though they are ordinary people. Hence it would be better if they decided cases not according to their own opinion, but in accordance with what is written, that is to say, laws. Again, the overseers' lifestyle is not in keeping with the aim of the constitution. For it involves too much license, whereas in other respects it is too austere, so that they cannot endure it, but secretly escape from the law and enjoy the pleasures of the body.

Matters relating to the senate also do not serve the Spartans well. If the senators were decent people, with an adequate general education in manly virtue, one might well say that this office benefits the city-state. Although, one might dispute about whether they ought to have lifelong authority in important matters, since the mind has its old age as well as the body. But when they are educated in such a way that even the legislator himself doubts that they are good men, it is not safe. And in fact in many matters of public concern, those who have participated in this office have been conspicuous in taking bribes and showing favoritism. This is precisely why it is better that the senators not be exempt from inspection, as they are at present. It might seem that the overseers should inspect every office, but this would give too much to the board of overseers, and is not the way we say inspections should be carried out.

The method of electing senators is also defective. Not only is the selection made in a childish way, but it is wrong for someone worthy of the office to ask for it: a man worthy of the office should hold it whether he wants to or not. But the fact is that the legislator is evidently doing the same thing here as in the rest of the constitution. He makes the citizens love honor and then takes advantage of this fact in the election of the senators; for no one would ask for office who did not love honor. Yet the love of honor and of money are *the* causes of most voluntary wrongdoings among human beings.

The question of whether or not it is better for city-states to have a kingship must be discussed later; but it is better to choose each new king, not as now, but on the basis of his own life. (It is clear that even the Spartan legislator himself did not think it possible to make the kings noble-and-good. At any rate he distrusts them, on the grounds that they are not sufficiently good men. That is precisely why they used to send out a king's opponents as fellow ambassadors, and why they regard faction between the kings as a safeguard for the city-state.)

Nor were matters relating to the messes (or so-called *phiditia*) well legislated by the person who first established them. For they ought to be publicly supported, as they are in Crete. But among the Spartans each individual has to contribute, even though some are extremely poor and unable to afford the

30 expense. The result is thus the opposite of the legislator's deliberately chosen aim. He intended the institution of messes to be democratic, but, legislated as
they are now, they are scarcely democratic at all,
since the very poor cannot easily participate in them.
35 Yet their traditional way of delimiting the Spartan
constitution is to exclude from it those who cannot
pay this contribution.

The law dealing with the admirals has been criticized by others, and rightly so, since it becomes a
cause of faction. For the office of admiral is established against the kings, who are permanent generals,
40 as pretty much another kingship.

One might also criticize the fundamental principle
1271b of the legislator as Plato criticized it in the *Laws*. For
the entire system of their laws aims at a part of virtue,
military virtue, since this is useful for conquest. So,
as long as they were at war, they remained safe. But
once they ruled supreme, they started to decline,
because they did not know how to be at leisure, and
5 had never undertaken any kind of training with more
authority than military training. Another error, no less
serious, is that although they think (rightly) that the
good things that people compete for are won by virtue
rather than by vice, they also suppose (not rightly)
that these goods are better than virtue itself.

10 Matters relating to public funds are also badly organized by the Spartiates. For they are compelled to
fight major wars, yet the public treasury is empty, and
taxes are not properly paid; for, as most of the land
belongs to the Spartiates, they do not scrutinize one
another's tax payments. Thus the result the legislator
15 has produced is the opposite of beneficial: he has
made his city-state poor and the private individuals
into lovers of money.

So much for the Spartan constitution. For these
are the things one might particularly criticize in it.

BOOK III

Chapter 1

When investigating constitutions, and what each is
and is like, pretty well the first subject of investigation
concerns a city-state, to see what the city-state is. For
as things stand now, there are disputes about this.

Some people say, for example, that a city-state performed a certain action, whereas others say that it
was not the city-state that performed the action, but
rather the oligarchy or the tyrant did. We see, too, 35
that the entire occupation of statesmen and legislators
concerns city-states. Moreover, a constitution is itself
a certain organization of the inhabitants of a city-
state. But since a city-state is a composite, one that
is a whole and, like any other whole, constituted out
of many parts, it is clear that we must first inquire 40
into citizens. For a city-state is some sort of multitude
of citizens. Hence we must investigate who should
be called a citizen, and who the citizen is. For there
is often dispute about the citizen as well, since not 1275a
everyone agrees that the same person is a citizen. For
the sort of person who is a citizen in a democracy is
often not one in an oligarchy.

We should leave aside those who acquire the title
of citizen in some exceptional way; for example, those
who are made citizens. Nor is a citizen a citizen 5
through residing in a place, for resident aliens and
slaves share the dwelling place with him. Again, those
who participate in the justice system, to the extent
of prosecuting others in the courts or being judged
there themselves, are not citizens: parties to treaties
can also do that (though in fact in many places the
participation of resident aliens in the justice system 10
is not even complete, but they need a sponsor, so
that their participation in this sort of communal relationship is in a way incomplete). Like minors who
are too young to be enrolled in the citizen lists or
old people who have been excused from their civic
duties, they must be said to be citizens *of a sort*, but 15
not unqualified citizens. Instead, a qualification must
be added, such as "incomplete" or "superannuated"
or something else like that (it does not matter what,
since what we are saying is clear). For we are looking
for the unqualified citizen, the one whose claim to
citizenship has no defect of this sort that needs to be
rectified (for one can raise and solve similar problems 20
about those who have been disenfranchised or exiled).

The unqualified citizen is defined by nothing else
so much as by his participation in judgment and
office. But some offices are of limited tenure, so they
cannot be held twice by the same person at all, or
can be held again only after a definite period. Another 25
person, however, holds office indefinitely, such as the

juror or assemblyman. Now someone might say that the latter sort are not officials at all, and do not, because of this, participate in any office as such. Yet surely it would be absurd to deprive of office those who have the most authority. But let this make no difference, since the argument is only about a word. For what a juror and an assemblyman have in com-
30 mon lacks a name that one should call them both. For the sake of definition, let it be indefinite office. We take it, then, that those who participate in office in this way are citizens. And this is pretty much the definition that would best fit all those called citizens.

We must not forget, however, that in case of things
35 in which what underlies differs in kind (one coming first, another second, and so on), a common element either is not present at all, insofar as these things are such, or only in some attenuated way. But we see that constitutions differ in kind from one another, and that some are posterior and others prior; for mistaken or deviant constitutions are necessarily posterior
1275b to those that are not mistaken. (What we mean by "deviant" will be apparent later.) Consequently, the citizen in each constitution must also be different.

That is precisely why the citizen that we defined is above all a citizen in a democracy, and may possibly be one in other constitutions, but not necessarily. For
5 some constitutions have no "the people" or assemblies they legally recognize, but only specially summoned councils and judicial cases decided by different bodies. In Sparta, for example, some cases concerning contracts are tried by one overseer, others by another,
10 whereas cases of homicide are judged by the senate, and other cases by perhaps some other official. It is the same way in Carthage, since there certain officials decide all cases. None the less, our definition of a citizen admits of correction. For in the other constitutions, it is not the holder of indefinite office who is assemblyman and juror, but someone whose office is definite. For it is either to some or to all of the latter
15 that deliberation and judgment either about some or about all matters is assigned.

It is evident from this who the citizen is. For we can now say that someone who is eligible to participate in deliberative and judicial office is a citizen in this city-state, and that a city-state, simply speaking, is a
20 multitude of such people, adequate for life's self-sufficiency.

Chapter 2

But the definition that gets used in practice is that a citizen is someone who comes from citizens on both sides, and not on one only—for example, that of father or of mother. Some people look for more here too, going back, for example, two or three or more generations of ancestors. But quick political definitions of this sort lead some people to raise the problem of how these third- or fourth-generation ancestors will 25 be citizens. So Gorgias of Leontini, half perhaps to raise a real problem and half ironically, said that just as mortars are made by mortar makers, so Lariseans too are made by craftsmen, since some of them are Larisean makers. But this is easy: if the ancestors 30 participated in the constitution in the way that accords with the definition just given, they were citizens. For "what comes from a citizen father and mother" cannot be applied to even the first inhabitants or founders.

But perhaps a bigger problem is raised by the next case: those who come to participate in a constitution after a revolution, such as the citizens created in Athens by Cleisthenes after the expulsion of the ty- 35 rants (for he enrolled many foreigners and alien slaves in the tribes). But the dispute in relation to these people is not which of them is a citizen, but whether they are rightly or wrongly so. And yet a further question might be raised as to whether one who is not rightly a citizen is a citizen at all, as "wrong" and 1276a "false" seem to have the same force. But since we see that there are also some people holding office wrongly, whom we say *are* holding it though not rightly, and since a citizen is defined as someone who holds a sort of office (for someone who participates in such office is a citizen, as we said), it is clear that 5 these people too must be admitted to be citizens.

Chapter 3

The problem of rightly and not rightly is connected to the dispute we mentioned earlier. For some people raise a problem about how to determine whether a city-state has or has not performed an action, for example, when an oligarchy or a tyranny is replaced by a democracy. At these times, some do not want to honor treaties, since it was not the city-state but 10 its tyrant who entered into them, nor to do many

other things of the same sort, on the grounds that some constitutions exist by force and not for the common benefit. Accordingly, if indeed some democrats also rule in that way, it must be conceded that the acts of their constitution are the city-state's in just the
15 same way as are those of the oligarchy or the tyranny.

There seems to be a close relation between this argument and the problem of when we ought to say that a city-state is the same, or not the same but a different one. The most superficial way to investigate
20 this problem is by looking to location and people. For a city-state's location and people can be split, and some can live in one place and some in another. Hence the problem must be regarded as a rather tame one. For the fact that a thing is said to be a city-state in many different ways makes the investigation of such problems pretty easy.

Things are similar if one asks when people inhabiting the same location should be considered a single
25 city-state. Certainly not because it is enclosed by walls, since a single wall could be built around the Peloponnese. Perhaps Babylon is like that, or anywhere else that has the dimensions of a nation rather than a city-state. At any rate, they say that when Babylon was captured, a part of the city-state was unaware of it for
30 three days. But it will be useful to investigate this problem in another context. For the size of the city-state, both as regards numbers and as regards whether it is beneficial for it to be one or several, should not be overlooked by the statesman.

But when the same people are inhabiting the same place, is the city-state to be called the same as long as the inhabitants remain of the same stock, even
35 though all the time some are dying and others being born (just as we are accustomed to say that rivers and springs remain the same, even though all the time some water is flowing out and some flowing in)? Or are we to say that human beings can remain the same
40 for this sort of reason, but the city-state is different? For if indeed a city-state is a sort of community, a
1276b community of citizens sharing a constitution, then, when the constitution changes its form and becomes different, it would seem that the city-state too cannot remain the same. At any rate, a chorus that is at one time in a comedy and at another in a tragedy is said
5 to be two different choruses, even though the human beings in it are often the same. Similarly, with any

other community or composite: we say it is different if the form of the composite is different. For example, we call a melody composed of the same notes a different melody when it is played in the Dorian harmony than when it is played in the Phrygian. But if this is so, it is evident that we must look to the constitution 10 above all when saying that the city-state is the same. But the name to call it may be different or the same one whether its inhabitants are the same or completely different people.

But whether it is just to honor or not to honor agreements when a city-state changes to a different 15 constitution requires another argument.

Chapter 4

The next thing to investigate after what we have just discussed is whether the virtue of a good man and of a good citizen should be regarded as the same, or not the same. But surely if we should indeed investigate this, the virtue of a citizen must first be grasped in some sort of outline.

Just as a sailor is one of a number of members of a community, so, we say, is a citizen. And though sailors differ in their capacities (for one is an oarsman, 20 another a captain, another a lookout, and others have other sorts of titles), it is clear both that the most exact account of the virtue of each sort of sailor will be peculiar to him, and similarly that there will also be some common account that fits them all. For the 25 safety of the voyage is a task of all of them, since this is what each of the sailors strives for. In the same way, then, the citizens too, even though they are dissimilar, have the safety of the community as their task. But the community is the constitution. Hence the virtue of a citizen must be suited to his constitution. Consequently, if indeed there are several kinds 30 of constitution, it is clear that there cannot be a single virtue that is the virtue—the complete virtue—of a good citizen. But the good man, we say, does express a single virtue: the complete one. Evidently, then, it is possible for someone to be a good citizen without having acquired the virtue expressed by a good man. 35

By going through problems in a different way, the same argument can be made about the best constitution. If it is impossible for a city-state to consist entirely of good people, and if each must at least perform his own task well, and this requires virtue, and if it is impossible for all the citizens to be similar, then the 40 virtue of a citizen and that of a good man cannot be 1277a a single virtue. For that of the good citizen must be had by all (since this is necessary if the city-state is to be best), but the virtue of a good man cannot be had by all, unless all the citizens of a good city-state are necessarily good men. Again, since a city-state consists of dissimilar elements (I mean that just as 5 an animal consists in the first instance of soul and body, a soul of reason and desire, a household of man and woman, and property of master and slave, so a city-state, too, consists of all these, and of other dissimilar kinds in addition), then the citizens cannot all 10 have one virtue, any more than can the leader of a chorus and one of its ordinary members.

It is evident from these things, therefore, that the virtue of a man and of a citizen cannot be unqualifiedly the same.

But will there, then, be anyone whose virtue is the same both as a good citizen and as a good man? We say, indeed, that an excellent ruler is good and 15 possesses practical wisdom, but that a citizen need not possess practical wisdom. Some say, too, that the education of a ruler is different right from the beginning, as is evident, indeed, from the sons of kings being educated in horsemanship and warfare, and from Euripides saying "No subtleties for me . . . but what the city-state needs," (since this implies that rulers should get a special sort of education). But if 20 the virtue of a good ruler is the same as that of a good man, and if the man who is ruled is also a citizen, then the virtue of a citizen would not be unqualifiedly the same as the virtue of a man (though that of a certain sort of citizen would be), since the virtue of a ruler and that of a citizen would not be the same. Perhaps this is why Jason said that he went hungry except when he was a tyrant. He meant that he did not know how to be a private individual.

25 Yet the capacity to rule and be ruled is at any rate praised, and being able to do both well is held to be the virtue of a citizen. So if we take a good man's virtue to be that of a ruler, but a citizen's to consist in both, then the two virtues would not be equally praiseworthy.

Since, then, both these views are sometimes accepted, that ruler and ruled should learn different things and not the same ones, and that a citizen 30 should know and share in both, we may see what follows from that. For there is rule by a master, by which we mean the kind concerned with the necessities. The ruler does not need to know how to produce these, but rather how to make use of those who do. In fact, the former is servile. (By "the former" I mean 35 actually knowing how to perform the actions of a servant.) But there are several kinds of slaves, we say, since their tasks vary. One part consists of those tasks performed by manual laborers. As their very name implies, these are people who work with their hands. Vulgar craftsmen are included among them. That is 1277b why among some peoples in the distant past craftsmen did not participate in office until extreme democracy arose. Accordingly, the tasks performed by people ruled in this way should not be learned by a good person, nor by a statesman, nor by a good citizen, except perhaps to satisfy some personal need of his own (for then it is no longer a case of one person 5 becoming master and the other slave).

But there is also a kind of rule exercised over those who are similar in birth and free. This we call "political" rule. A ruler must learn it by being ruled, just as one learns to be a cavalry commander by serving under a cavalry commander, or to be a general by 10 serving under a general, or under a major or a company commander to learn to occupy the office. Hence this too is rightly said, that one cannot rule well without having been ruled. And whereas the virtues of these *are* different, a good citizen must have the knowledge and ability both to be ruled and to rule, and this is the virtue of a citizen, to know the rule 15 of free people from both sides.

In fact, a good man too possesses both, even if a ruler does have a different kind of justice and temperance. For if a good person is ruled, but is a free citizen, his virtue (justice, for example) will clearly not be of one kind, but includes one kind for ruling and another for being ruled, just as a man's and a woman's courage and temperance differ. For a man 20 would seem a coward if he had the courage of a woman, and a woman would seem garrulous if she had the temperance of a good man, since even household management differs for the two of them (for his task is to acquire property and hers to preserve it). Practical wisdom is the only virtue peculiar to a ruler; 25

for the others, it would seem, must be common to both rulers and ruled. At any rate, practical wisdom is not the virtue of one who is ruled, but true opinion is. For those ruled are like makers of flutes, whereas rulers are like the flute players who use them.

30   So then, whether the virtue of a good man is the same as that of an excellent citizen or different, and how they are the same and how different, is evident from the preceding.

Chapter 5

But one of the problems about the citizen still remains. For is the citizen really someone who is permitted to participate in office, or should vulgar
35 craftsmen also be regarded as citizens? If, indeed, those who do not share in office should be regarded as citizens, then this sort of virtue cannot belong to every citizen (for these will then be citizens). On the other hand, if none of this sort is a citizen, in what category should they each be put?—for they are neither resident aliens nor foreigners.

      Or shall we say that from *this* argument, at least,
1278a nothing absurd follows, since neither slaves nor freed slaves are in the aforementioned classes either? For the truth is that not everyone without whom there would not be a city-state is to be regarded as a citizen. For children are not citizens in the way men are. The latter are unqualified citizens, whereas the former are only citizens given certain assumptions: they are
5   citizens, but incomplete ones. Vulgar craftsmen were slaves or foreigners in some places long ago, which is why most of them still are even today. The best city-state will not confer citizenship on vulgar craftsmen, however; but if they too are citizens, then what we have characterized as a citizen's virtue cannot be ascribed to everyone, or even to all free people, but
10 only to those who are freed from necessary tasks. Those who perform necessary tasks for an individual are slaves; those who perform them for the community are vulgar craftsmen and hired laborers.

      If we carry our investigation a bit further, it will be evident how things stand in these cases. In fact, it is clear from what we have already said. For since there are several constitutions, there must also be
15 several kinds of citizens, particularly of citizens who are being ruled. Hence in some constitutions vulgar craftsmen and hired laborers must be citizens, whereas in others it is impossible—for example, in any so-called aristocracy in which offices are awarded on the basis of virtue and merit. For it is impossible to engage in virtuous pursuits while living the life of 20 a vulgar craftsman or a hired laborer.

      In oligarchies, however, while hired laborers could not be citizens (since participation in office is based on high property assessments), vulgar craftsmen could be, since in fact most craftsmen become rich (though in Thebes there used to be a law that anyone who had not kept away from the market for ten years could 25 not participate in office).

      In many constitutions, however, the law even goes so far as to admit some foreigners as citizens; for in some democracies the descendant of a citizen mother is a citizen, and in many places the same holds of bastards too. Nevertheless, since it is because of a shortage of legitimate citizens that they make such people citizens (for it is because of underpopulation 30 that they employ laws in this way), when they are well supplied with a crowd of them, they gradually disqualify, first, those who have a slave as father or mother, then those with citizen mothers, until finally they make citizens only of those who come from citizens on both sides.

      It is evident from these considerations, therefore, that there are several kinds of citizens, and that the one who participates in the offices is particularly said 35 to be a citizen, as Homer too implied when he wrote: "like some disenfranchised alien."[2] For people who do not participate in the offices *are* like resident aliens. When this is concealed, it is for the sake of deceiving coinhabitants.

      As to whether the virtue expressed by a good man 40 is to be regarded as the same as that of an excellent citizen or as different, it is clear from what has been 1278b said that in one sort of city-state both are the same person, while in another they are different. And that person is not just anyone, but the statesman, who has authority or is capable of exercising authority in the supervision of communal matters, either by himself or with others.   5

---

2. *Iliad* IX.648, XVI.59. Achilles is complaining that this is how Agamemnon is treating him.—C.D.C.R.]

Chapter 6

Since these issues have been determined, the next thing to investigate is whether we should suppose that there is just one kind of constitution or several, and, if there are several, what they are, how many they are, and how they differ.

A constitution is an organization of a city-state's various offices but, particularly, of the one that has authority over everything. For the governing class has
10 authority in every city-state, and the governing class is the constitution. I mean, for example, that in democratic city-states the people have authority, whereas in oligarchic ones, by contrast, the few have it, and we also say the constitutions of these are different. And we shall give the same account of the other constitutions as well.

15 First, then, we must set down what it is that a city-state is constituted for, and how many kinds of rule deal with human beings and communal life. In our first discussions, indeed, where conclusions were reached about household management and rule by a master, it was also said that a human being is by nature a political animal. That is why, even when
20 they do not need one another's help, people no less desire to live together, although it is also true that the common benefit brings them together, to the extent that it contributes some part of living well to each. This above all is the end, then, whether of everyone in common or of each separately. But human beings also join together and maintain political communities for the sake of life by itself. For there
25 is perhaps some share of what is noble in life alone, as long as it is not too overburdened with the hardships of life. In any case, it is clear that most human beings are willing to endure much hardship in order to cling to life, as if it had a sort of joy inherent in it and a natural sweetness.

But surely it is also easy to distinguish at least the kinds of rule people talk about, since we too often
30 discuss them in our own external works. For rule by a master, although in truth the same thing is beneficial for both natural masters and natural slaves, is nevertheless rule exercised for the sake of the master's
35 own benefit, and only coincidentally for that of the slave. For rule by a master cannot be preserved if the slave is destroyed. But rule over children, wife, and

the household generally, which we call household management, is either for the sake of the ruled or for the sake of something common to both. Essentially, it is for the sake of the ruled, as we see medicine, physical training, and the other crafts to be, but coin-
40
cidentally it might be for the sake of the rulers as
1279a
well. For nothing prevents the trainer from sometimes being one of the athletes he is training, just as the captain of a ship is always one of the sailors. Thus a trainer or a captain looks to the good of those he
5
rules, but when he becomes one of them himself, he shares coincidentally in the benefit. For the captain is a sailor, and the trainer, though still a trainer, becomes one of the trained.

Hence, in the case of political office too, where it has been established on the basis of equality and similarity among the citizens, they think it right to take turns at ruling. In the past, as is natural, they
10
thought it right to perform public service when their turn came, and then to have someone look to *their* good, just as they had earlier looked to his benefit when they were in office. Nowadays, however, because of the profits to be had from public funds and from office, people want to be in office continuously, as if they were sick and would be cured by being always in office. At any rate, perhaps the latter would pursue office in that way.
15

It is evident, then, that those constitutions that look to the common benefit turn out, according to what is unqualifiedly just, to be correct, whereas those which look only to the benefit of the rulers are mistaken and are deviations from the correct constitu-
20
tions. For they are like rule by a master, whereas a city-state is a community of free people.

Chapter 7

Now that these matters have been determined, we must next investigate how many kinds of constitutions there are and what they are, starting first with the correct constitutions. For once they have been defined, the deviant ones will also be made evident.

Since "constitution" and "governing class" signify
25
the same thing, and the governing class is the authoritative element in any city-state, and the authoritative element must be either one person, or few, or many, then whenever the one, the few, or the many rule

for the common benefit, these constitutions must be correct. But if they aim at the private benefit, whether
30 of the one or the few or the multitude, they are deviations (for either the participants should not be called citizens, or they should share in the benefits).

A monarchy that looks to the common benefit we customarily call a kingship; and rule by a few but more than one, an aristocracy (either because the
35 best people rule, or because they rule with a view to what is best for the city-state and those who share in it). But when the multitude governs for the common benefit, it is called by the name common to all constitutions, namely, *politeia*. Moreover, this happens reasonably. For while it is possible for one or a few to be outstandingly virtuous, it is difficult for a larger
40 number to be accomplished in every virtue, but it
1279b can be so in military virtue in particular. That is precisely why the class of defensive soldiers, the ones who possess the weapons, has the most authority in this constitution.

Deviations from these are tyranny from kingship, oligarchy from aristocracy, and democracy from pol-
5 ity. For tyranny is rule by one person for the benefit of the monarch, oligarchy is for the benefit of the rich, and democracy is for the benefit of the poor. But none is for their common profit.

Chapter 8

10 We should say a little more about what each of these constitutions is. For certain problems arise, and when one is carrying out any investigation in a philosophical manner, and not merely with a practical purpose in view, it is appropriate not to overlook or omit any-
15 thing, but to make the truth about each clear.

A tyranny, as we said, exists when a monarchy rules the political community like a master; in an oligarchy those in authority in the constitution are the ones who have property. A democracy is the opposite; those who do not possess much property, and are poor, are in authority. The first problem concerns this defini-
20 tion. Suppose that the majority were rich and had authority in the city-state; yet there is a democracy whenever the majority has authority. Similarly, to take the opposite case, suppose the poor were fewer in number than the rich, but were stronger and had authority in the constitution; yet when a small group

has authority it is said to be an oligarchy. It would seem, then, that these constitutions have not been well defined. But even if one combines being few 25 with being rich in one case, and being a majority with being poor in the other, and describes the constitutions accordingly (oligarchy as that in which the rich are few in number and hold the offices, and democracy as that in which the poor are many and hold them), another problem arises. For what are we 30 to call the constitutions we just described, those where the rich are a majority and the poor a minority, but each has authority in its own constitution—if indeed there is no other constitution besides those just mentioned?

What this argument seems to make clear is that it is a coincidence that the few have authority in oligarchies and the many in democracies, a result of 35 the fact that everywhere the rich are few and the poor many. That is why, indeed, the reasons just mentioned are not the reasons for the differences. What does distinguish democracy and oligarchy from one another is poverty and wealth: whenever some, 40 whether a minority or a majority, rule because of their wealth, the constitution is necessarily an oligar- 1280a chy, and whenever the poor rule, it is necessarily a democracy. But it turns out, as we said, that the former are in fact few and the latter many. For only a few people are rich, but all share in freedom; and these are 5 the reasons they both dispute over the constitution.

Chapter 9

The first thing one must grasp, however, is what people say the defining marks of oligarchy and democracy are, and what oligarchic and democratic justice are. For [1] they all grasp justice of a sort, but they go only to a certain point and do not discuss the whole of what is just in the most authoritative sense. For example, justice seems to be equality, and it is, but 10 not for everyone, only *for equals*. Justice also seems to be inequality, since indeed it is, but not for everyone, only *for unequals*. They disregard the "for whom," however, and judge badly. The reason is that the judgment concerns themselves, and most people are pretty poor judges about what is their own. 15

So since what is just is just *for certain people*, and consists in dividing things and people in the same

way (as we said earlier in the *Ethics*), they agree about what constitutes equality in the thing but disagree about it in the people. This is largely because of what was just mentioned, that they judge badly about what
20 concerns themselves, but also because, since they are both speaking up to a point about justice of a sort, they think they are speaking about what is unqualifiedly just. For one lot thinks that if they are unequal in one respect (wealth, say) they are wholly unequal, whereas the other lot thinks that if they are equal in one respect (freedom, say) they are wholly equal. But about the most authoritative considerations they do not speak.

For suppose people constituted a community and came together for the sake of property; then their
25 participation in a city-state would be proportional to their property, and the oligarchic argument would as a result seem to be a powerful one. (For it is not just that someone who has contributed only one mina to a sum of one hundred minas should have equal shares in that sum, whether of the principal or of the interest,
30 with the one who has contributed all the rest.) But suppose [2] they do not do so only for the sake of life, but rather for the sake of living well, since otherwise there could be a city-state of slaves or animals, whereas in fact there is not, because these share neither in happiness nor in a life guided by deliberative choice.

And suppose [3] they do not do so for the sake of an alliance to safeguard themselves from being wronged by anyone, nor [4] to facilitate exchange
35 and mutual assistance, since otherwise the Etruscans and the Carthaginians, and all those who have treaties with one another would virtually be citizens of one city-state. To be sure, they have import agreements, treaties about refraining from injustice, and formal
40 documents of alliance, but no offices common to all of them have been established to deal with these matters; instead each city-state has different ones. Nor
1280b are those in one city-state concerned with what sort of people the others should be, or that none of those covered by the agreements should be unjust or vicious in any way, but only that neither city-state acts unjustly toward the other. But those who are concerned with
5 good government give careful attention to political virtue and vice. Hence it is quite evident that the city-state (at any rate, the one truly so called and not

just for the sake of argument) must be concerned with virtue. For otherwise the community becomes an alliance that differs only in location from other alliances in which the allies live far apart, and law becomes an agreement, "a guarantor of just behavior 10 toward one another," as the sophist Lycophron said, but not such as to make the citizens good and just.

It is evident that this is right. For even if [5] one were to bring their territories together into one, so that the city-state of the Megarians was attached to that of the Corinthians by walls, it still would not be a single city-state. Nor would it be so if their citizens 15 intermarried, even though this is one of the forms of community characteristic of city-states. Similarly, if there were some who lived separately, yet not so separately as to share nothing in common, and had laws against wronging one another in their business transactions (for example, if one were a carpenter, another a farmer, another a cobbler, another something else 20 of that sort, and their number were ten thousand), yet they shared nothing else in common besides such things as exchange and alliance—not even in this case would there be a city-state.

What, then, is the reason for this? Surely, it is not because of the nonproximate nature of their community. For suppose they joined together while continuing to share in that way, but each nevertheless treated 25 his own household like a city-state, and the others like a defensive alliance formed to provide aid against wrongdoers only. Even then this still would not be thought a city-state by those who make a precise study of such things, if indeed they continued to associate with one another in the same manner when together as when separated.

Evidently, then, a city-state is not [5] a sharing of a common location, and does not exist for the purpose of [4] preventing mutual wrongdoing and [3] ex- 30 changing goods. Rather, while these must be present if indeed there is to be a city-state, when all of them *are* present there is still not yet a city-state, but [2] only when households and families live well as a community whose end is a complete and self-sufficient life. But this will not be possible unless they do inhabit one and the same location and practice 35 intermarriage. That is why marriage connections arose in city-states, as well as brotherhoods, religious sacrifices, and the leisured pursuits of living together.

For things of this sort are the result of friendship, since the deliberative choice of living together constitutes friendship. The end of the city-state is living well, then, but these other things are for the sake of the end. And a city-state is the community of families 40 and villages in a complete and self-sufficient life, 1281a which we say is living happily and nobly.

So political communities must be taken to exist for the sake of noble actions, and not for the sake of living together. Hence those who contribute the most to *this* sort of community have a larger share in the 5 city-state than those who are equal or superior in freedom or family but inferior in political virtue, and those who surpass in wealth but are surpassed in virtue.

It is evident from what has been said, then, that [1] those who dispute about constitutions all speak 10 about a *part* of justice.

Chapter 10

There is a problem as to what part of the state is to have authority, since surely it is either the multitude, or the rich, or decent people, or the one who is best of all, or a tyrant. But all of these apparently involve difficulties. How so? If the poor, because they are the greater number, divide up the property of the rich, 15 isn't that unjust? "No, by Zeus, it isn't, since it seemed just to those in authority." What, then, should we call extreme injustice? Again, if the majority, having seized everything, should divide up the property of the minority, they are evidently destroying the city-state. But virtue certainly does not ruin what has it, nor is justice something capable of destroying a city-20 state. So it is clear, then, that this law cannot be just. Besides, everything done by a tyrant must be just as well; for he, being stronger, uses force, just as the multitude do against the rich.

25 But is it just, then, for the rich minority to rule? If they too act in the same way, plundering and confiscating the property of the multitude, and this is just, then the other case is as well. It is evident, therefore, that all these things are bad and unjust.

But should decent people rule and have authority over everything? In that case, everyone else must be deprived of honors by being excluded from political 30 office. For offices are positions of honor, we say, and when the same people always rule, the rest must necessarily be deprived of honors.

But is it better that the one who is best should rule? But this is even more oligarchic, since those deprived of honors are more numerous.

Perhaps, however, someone might say that it is a bad thing in general for a human being to have authority and not the law, since he at any rate has 35 the passions that beset the soul. But if law may be oligarchic or democratic, what difference will that make to our problems? For the things we have just described will happen just the same.

Chapter 11

As for the other cases, we may let them be the topic of a different discussion. But the view that the multitude rather than the few best people should be in authority 40 would seem to be held, and while it involves a problem, it perhaps also involves some truth. For the many, who are not as individuals excellent men, nevertheless can, when they have come together, be better than the few best people, not individually but 1281b collectively, just as feasts to which many contribute are better than feasts provided at one person's expense. For being many, each of them can have some part of virtue and practical wisdom, and when they come together, the multitude is just like a single human 5 being, with many feet, hands, and senses, and so too for their character traits and wisdom. That is why the many are better judges of works of music and of the poets. For one of them judges one part, another another, and all of them the whole thing.

It is in this way that excellent men differ from each 10 of the many, just as beautiful people are said to differ from those who are not beautiful, and as things painted by craft are superior to real things: they bring together what is scattered and separate into one—although, at least if taken separately, this person's eye and some other feature of someone else will be more beautiful than the painted ones.

Whether this superiority of the many to the few 15 excellent people can exist in the case of every people and every multitude is not clear. Though presumably, by Zeus, it is clear that in some of them it cannot possibly do so, since the same argument would apply to beasts. For what difference is there, practically

speaking, between some people and beasts? But nothing prevents what has been said from being true of
20 *some* multitude.

By means of these considerations, too, one might solve the problem mentioned earlier and also the related one of what the free should have authority over, that is to say, the multitude of the citizens who
25 are not rich and have no claim whatsoever arising from virtue. For it would not be safe to have them participate in the most important offices, since, because of their lack of justice and practical wisdom, they would inevitably act unjustly in some instances and make mistakes in others. On the other hand, to give them no share and not to allow them to participate at all would be cause for alarm. For a state in which a large number of people are excluded from office and are poor must of necessity be full of ene-
30 mies. The remaining alternative, then, is to have them participate in deliberation and judgment, which is precisely why Solon and some other legislators arrange to have them elect and inspect officials, but prevent them from holding office alone. For when they all come together their perception is adequate,
35 and, when mixed with their betters, they benefit their states, just as a mixture of roughage and pure food-concentrate is more useful than a little of the latter by itself. Taken individually, however, each of them is an imperfect judge.

But this organization of the constitution raises problems itself. In the first place, it might be held that the same person is able to judge whether or not
40 someone has treated a patient correctly, and to treat patients and cure them of disease when it is present— namely, the doctor. The same would also seem to hold in other areas of experience and other crafts.
1282a Therefore, just as a doctor should be inspected by doctors, so others should also be inspected by their peers. But "doctor" applies to the ordinary practitioner of the craft, to a master craftsman, and thirdly, to someone with a general education in the craft. For
5 there are people of this third sort in (practically speaking) all the crafts. And we assign the task of judging to generally educated people no less than to experts.

Moreover, it might be held that election is the same way, since choosing correctly is also a task for experts: choosing a geometer is a task for expert geometers, for example, and choosing a ship's captain is a

task for expert captains. For even if some laymen are 10
also involved in the choice of candidates in the case of some tasks and crafts, at least they do not play a larger role than the experts. According to this argument, then, the multitude should not be given authority over the election or inspection of officials.

But perhaps not all of these things are correctly stated, both because according to the earlier argument the multitude may not be too servile, since each may 15 be a worse judge than those who know, but a better or no worse one when they all come together; and because there are some crafts in which the maker might not be either the only or the best judge— the ones where those who do not possess the craft nevertheless have knowledge of its products. For example, the maker of a house is not the only one who has some knowledge about it; the one who uses it is 20 an even better judge (and the one who uses is the household manager). A captain, too, judges a rudder better than a carpenter, and a guest, rather than the cook, a feast.

This problem might be held to be adequately solved in such a way. But there is another connected with it. For it is held to be absurd for inferior people to have authority over more important matters than 25 decent people do. But inspections and elections of officials are very important things. And in some constitutions, as we said, these are assigned to the people, since the assembly has authority over all such matters. And yet those with low property assessments and of whatever age participate in the assembly, and in deliberation and decision, whereas those with high prop- 30 erty assessment are the treasurers and generals and hold the most important offices.

But one can, in fact, also solve this problem in the same way. For perhaps these things are also correctly organized. For it is neither the individual juror, nor the individual councilor, nor the individual assembly- man who is ruling, but the court, the council, and the 35 people, whereas each of the individuals mentioned is only a part of these. (By "part" I mean the councilor, the assemblyman, and the juror.) Hence it is just for the multitude to have authority over the more important matters. For the people, the council, and the court consist of many individuals, and their collec- tive property assessment is greater than the assessment of those who, whether individually or in small groups, 40 hold the important offices. So much for how these matters should be determined.

As to the first problem we mentioned, it makes nothing else so evident as that the laws, when correctly 1282b established, should be in authority, and that the ruler, whether one or many, should have authority over only those matters on which the laws cannot pronounce with precision, because it is not easy to make 5 universal declarations about everything.

It is not yet clear, however, what correctly established laws should be like, and the problem stated earlier remains to be solved. For the laws must necessarily be bad or good, and just or unjust, at the same time and in the same way as the constitutions. Still, 10 at least it is evident that the laws must be established to suit the constitution. But if this is so, it is clear that laws that accord with the correct constitutions must be just, and those that accord with the deviant constitutions not just.

Chapter 12

Since in every science and craft the end is a good, the greatest and best good is the end of the science or craft 15 that has the most authority of all of them, and this is the science of statesmanship. But the political good is justice, and justice is the common benefit. Now everyone holds that what is just is some sort of equality, and up to a point, at least, all agree with what has been determined in those philosophical works of ours deal- 20 ing with ethical issues. For justice is something to someone, and they say it should be something equal to those who are equal. But equality in what and inequality in what, should not be overlooked. For this involves a problem and political philosophy.

Someone might say, perhaps, that offices should be unequally distributed on the basis of superiority in any good whatsoever, provided the people did not differ in their remaining qualities but were exactly 25 similar, since where people differ, so does what is just and what accords with merit. But if this is true, then those who are superior in complexion, or height, or any other good whatsoever will get more of the things with which political justice is concerned. And isn't that plainly false? The matter is evident in the various 30 sciences and capacities. For among flute players equally proficient in the craft, those who are of better

birth do not get more or better flutes, since they will not play the flute any better if they do. It is the superior performers who should also get the superior instruments. If what has been said is somehow not 35 clear, it will become so if we take it still further. Suppose someone is superior in flute playing, but is very inferior in birth or beauty; then, even if each of these (I mean birth and beauty) is a greater good than flute playing, and is proportionately more superior to flute playing than he is superior in flute playing, 40 he should still get the outstanding flutes. For the superiority in wealth and birth would have to contribute to the performance, but in fact they contribute 1283a nothing to it.

Besides, according to this argument every good would have to be commensurable with every other. For if being a certain height counted more, height in general would be in competition with both wealth and 5 freedom. So if one person is more outstanding in height than another is in virtue, and if height in general is of more weight than virtue, then all goods would be commensurable. For if a certain amount of size is better than a certain amount of virtue, it is clear that some amount of the one is equal to some amount of the other. Since this is impossible, it is clear that in political mat- 10 ters, too, it is reasonable not to dispute over political office on the basis of just any sort of inequality. For if some are slow runners and others fast, this is no reason for the latter to have more and the former less: it is in athletic competitions that such a difference wins honor. The dispute must be based on the things from which a city-state is constituted. Hence the well-born, 15 the free, and the rich reasonably lay claim to office. For there must be both free people and those with assessed property, since a city-state cannot consist entirely of poor people, any more than of slaves. But if these things are needed in a city-state, so too, it is clear, are justice and political virtue, since a city-state cannot be managed without these. Rather, without the former a city- 20 state cannot exist, and without the latter it cannot be well managed.

Chapter 13

As regards the existence of a city-state, all, or at any rate some, of these would seem to have a correct claim in the dispute. But as regards the good life,

education and virtue would seem to have the most
25 just claim of all in the dispute, as was also said earlier.
But since those equal in one thing only should not
have equality in everything, nor inequality if they are
unequal in only one thing, all constitutions of this
sort must be deviant.

30   We said before that all dispute somewhat justly,
but that not all do so in an unqualifiedly just way.
The rich have a claim due to the fact that they own
a larger share of the land, and the land is something
common, and that, in addition, they are usually more
trustworthy where treaties are concerned. The free
and the well-born have closely related claims, for
those who are better born are more properly citizens
than those of ignoble birth, and good birth is honored
35 at home by everyone. Besides, they have a claim
because better people are likely to come from better
people, since good birth is virtue of family. Similarly,
then, we shall say that virtue has a just claim in the
dispute, since justice, we say, is a communal virtue,
which all the other virtues necessarily accompany.
40 But the majority too have a just claim against the
minority, since they are stronger, richer, and better,
when taken as the majority in relation to the minority.

If they were all present in a single city-state, therefore (I mean, for example, the good, the rich, the
1283b well-born, and a political multitude in addition), will
there be a dispute as to who should rule or not?
Within each of the constitutions we have mentioned,
to be sure, the decision as to who should rule is
5 indisputable, since these differ from one another because of what is in authority; for example, because
in one the rich are in authority, in another the excellent men, and each of the others differs the same
way. But be that as it may, we are investigating how
the matter is to be determined when all these are
present simultaneously. Suppose, for example, that
10 those who possess virtue are extremely few in number,
how should the matter be settled? Should their few-
ness be considered in relation to the task? To whether
they are able to manage the city-state? Or to whether
there are enough of them to constitute a city-state
by themselves?

But there is a problem that faces all who dispute
over political office. Those who claim that they de-
15 serve to rule because of their wealth could be held
to have no justice to their claim at all, and similarly

those claiming to do so because of their family. For
it is clear that if someone is richer again than everyone
else, then, on the basis of the same justice, this one
person will have to rule them all. Similarly, it is clear
that someone who is outstanding when it comes to
good birth should rule those who dispute on the basis
of freedom. Perhaps the same thing will also occur
in the case of virtue where aristocracies are con- 20
cerned. For if one man were better than the others in
the governing class, even though they were excellent
men, then, on the basis of the same justice, this man
should be in authority. So if the majority too should
be in authority because they are superior to the few,
then, if one person, or more than one but fewer than
the many, were superior to the others, these should 25
be in authority rather than the multitude. All this
seems to make it evident, then, that none of the
definitions on the basis of which people claim that
they themselves deserve to rule, whereas everyone
else deserves to be ruled by them, is correct. For the
multitude would have an argument of some justice
even against those who claim that they deserve to
have authority over the governing class because of 30
their virtue, and similarly against those who base their
claim on wealth. For nothing prevents the multitude
from being sometimes better and richer than the few,
not as individuals but collectively.

Hence the problem that some people raise and 35
investigate can also be dealt with in this way. For
they raise the problem of whether a legislator who
wishes to establish the most correct laws should legislate for the benefit of the better citizens or that of
the majority, when the case just mentioned occurs.
But what is correct must be taken to mean what is
equitable; and what is equitable in relation to the 40
benefit of the entire city-state, and the common benefit of the citizens. And a citizen generally speaking
is someone who participates in ruling and in being
ruled, although in each constitution he is someone 1284a
different. It is in the best one, however, that he is the
one who has the power and who deliberately chooses
to be ruled and to rule with an eye to the virtuous
life. But if there is one person or more than one
(though not enough to make up a complete city-state)
who is so outstanding by reason of his superior virtue 5
that neither the virtue nor the political power of all
the others is commensurable with his (if there is only

one) or theirs (if there are a number of them), then such men can no longer be regarded as part of the city-state. For they would be treated unjustly if they were thought to merit equal shares, when they are so unequal in virtue and political power. For anyone
10 of that sort would reasonably be regarded as a god among human beings. Hence it is clear that legislation too must be concerned with those who are equals both in birth and in power, and that for the other sort there is no law, since they themselves are law. For, indeed, anyone who attempted to legislate for them would be ridiculous, since they would presum-
15 ably respond in the way Antisthenes tells us the lions did when the hares acted like popular leaders and demanded equality for everyone.

That is why, indeed, democratically governed city-states introduce ostracism. For of all city-states these are held to pursue equality most, and so they ostracize those held to be outstandingly powerful (whether be-
20 cause of their wealth, their many friends, or any other source of political power), banishing them from the city-state for fixed periods of time. The story goes, too, that the Argonauts left Heracles behind for this sort of reason: the Argo refused to carry him with the other sailors on the grounds that his weight greatly
25 exceeded theirs. That is also why those who criticize tyranny or the advice that Periander gave Thrasybulus should not be considered to be unqualifiedly correct in their censure. For they say that Periander said nothing to the messenger who had been sent to him for advice, but leveled a cornfield by cutting off the
30 outstandingly tall ears. When the messenger, who did not know why Periander did this, reported what had happened, Thrasybulus understood that he was to get rid of the outstanding men.

This advice is not beneficial only to tyrants, however, nor are tyrants the only ones who follow it. The same situation holds too in oligarchies and democra-
35 cies. For ostracism has the same sort of effect as cutting down the outstanding people or sending them into exile. But those in control of power treat city-states and nations in the same way. For example, as soon as Athens had a firm grip on its imperial rule,
40 it humbled Samos, Chios, and Lesbos, in violation of the treaties it had with them; and the king of the Persians often cut the Medes and Babylonians down
1284b to size, as well as any others who had grown presump-

tuous because they had once ruled empires of their own.

The problem is a general one that concerns all constitutions, even the correct ones. For though the deviant constitutions use such methods with an eye to the private benefit, the position is the same 5 with those that aim at the common good. But this is also clear in the case of the other crafts and sciences. For no painter would allow an animal to have a disproportionately large foot, not even if it were an outstandingly beautiful one, nor would a shipbuilder allow this in the case of the stern or any of the other parts of the ship, nor will a chorus 10 master tolerate a member of the chorus who has a louder and more beautiful voice than the entire chorus. So, from this point of view, there is nothing to prevent monarchs from being in harmony with the city-state they rule when they resort to this sort of practice, provided their rule benefits their city-states. Where acknowledged sorts of superiority are 15 concerned, then, there is some political justice to the argument in favor of ostracism.

It would be better, certainly, if the legislator established the constitution in the beginning so that it had no need for such a remedy. But the next best thing is to try to fix the constitution, should the need arise, with a corrective of this sort. This is not what actually tended to happen in city-states, however. For they did not look to the benefit 20 of their own constitutions, but used ostracism for purposes of faction. It is evident, then, that in each of the deviant constitutions ostracism is privately advantageous and just, but it is perhaps also evident that it is not unqualifiedly just.

In the case of the best constitution, however, there 25 is a considerable problem, not about superiority in other goods, such as power or wealth or having many friends, but when there happens to be someone who is superior in virtue. For surely people would not say that such a person should be expelled or banished, but neither would they say that they should rule over him. For that would be like claiming that they de- 30 served to rule over Zeus, dividing the offices. The remaining possibility—and it seems to be the natural one—is for everyone to obey such a person gladly, so that those like him will be permanent kings in their city-states.

Chapter 14

35 After the matters just discussed, it may perhaps be well to change to an investigation of kingship, since we say that it is one of the correct constitutions. What we have to investigate is whether or not it is beneficial for a city-state or territory which is to be well managed to be under a kingship, or under some other constitution instead, or whether it is beneficial for some but
40 not for others. But first it must be determined whether there is one single type of kingship or several different varieties.

1285a   In fact this is easy to see—that kingship includes several types, and that the manner of rule is not the same in all of them. For kingship in the Spartan constitution, which is held to be the clearest example of kingships based on law, does not have authority over everything, but when the king leaves the country,
5 he does have leadership in military affairs. Moreover, matters relating to the gods are assigned to the kings. [1] This type of kingship, then, is a sort of permanent autocratic generalship. For the king does not have the power of life and death, except when exercising a certain sort of kingship, similar to that exercised in ancient times on military expeditions, on the basis of the law of force. Homer provides a clear example.
10 Agamemnon put up with being abused in the assemblies, but when they went out to fight he had the power even of life and death. At any rate, he says: "Anyone I find far from the battle. . . shall have no hope of escaping dogs and vultures, for I myself shall put him to death."[3] This, then, is one kind of kingship—a generalship for life. Some of these are based
15 on lineage, others elective.

[2] But there is another kind of monarchy besides this, which is like kingships that exist among some non-Greeks. The powers all these have are very like those tyrants have, but they are based on law and are hereditary. Because non-Greeks are by nature more slavish in their character than Greeks, those in Asia being more so than those in Europe, they tolerate
20 rule by a master without any complaint. So for this sort of reason these kingships are tyrannical, but they are stable because hereditary and based on law. Their

bodyguards are kingly and not tyrannical for the same reason. For the citizens guard their kings with their 25 weapons, whereas a foreign contingent guards tyrants. For kings rule willing subjects on the basis of law, whereas the latter rule unwilling ones. Thus the former have bodyguards drawn from the citizens, whereas the latter have their bodyguards to protect them against the citizens.

These, then, are two kinds of monarchy. [3] But there is another, which existed among the ancient Greeks, those they call dictators. Put simply, this is 30 an elected tyranny, which differs from non-Greek kingship not because it is not based on law but only because it is not hereditary. Some hold this office for life, others for a fixed time or purpose. For example, the Mytileneans once elected Pittacus to defend them 35 against the exiles led by Antimenides and the poet Alcaeus. Indeed, it is Alcaeus who makes it clear in one of his drinking songs that they did elect Pittacus tyrant. He complains that "They set up base-born Pittacus as tyrant of that gutless and ill-omened city-state, with great praise from the assembled throng." 1285b These are and were tyrannical because like the rule of a master, but kingly because elective and voluntary.

[4] A fourth kind of kingly monarchy, which existed in the heroic period, was voluntary, elective, and 5 established on the basis of law. For because the first of the line were benefactors of the multitude in the crafts or war, or through bringing them together or providing them with land, they became kings over willing subjects, and their descendants took over from them. They had authority in regard to leadership in war, and religious sacrifices not requiring priests. 10 They also decided legal cases, some doing so under oath, and others not (the oath consisted in lifting up the scepter). In ancient times, they ruled continuously over the affairs of the city-state, both domestic and foreign. But later, when the kings themselves relinquished some of these prerogatives, and others 15 were taken away by the crowd in various city-states, only the sacrifices were left to the kings, and even where there was a kingship worthy of the name, it was only leadership in military affairs conducted beyond the frontiers that the king held on to.

There are, then, these four kinds of kingship. One 20 belongs to the heroic age: this was over willing subjects and served certain fixed purposes; the king was

3. [*Iliad* II.391–393. The last line Aristotle quotes is not in our text.]

general and judge and had authority over matters to
do with the gods. The second is the non-Greek kind,
which is rule by a master based on lineage and law.
25 The third is so-called dictatorship, which is elective
tyranny. Fourth among them is Spartan kingship,
which, simply put, is permanent generalship based
on lineage. These, then, differ from one another in
this way.

[5] But there is a fifth kind of kingship, when one
person controls everything in just the way that each
30 nation and each city-state controls the affairs of the
community. It is organized along the lines of household management. For just as household management is a sort of kingship over a household, so this
kingship is household management of one or more
city-states or nations.

Chapter 15

Practically speaking, then, there are just two kinds of
kingship to be examined, namely, the last one and
the Spartan. For most of the others lie in between
35 them, since they control less than absolute kingship
but more than Spartan kingship. So our investigation
is pretty much about two questions: First, whether or
not it is beneficial for a city-state to have a permanent
general (whether chosen on the basis of family or by
turns). Second, whether or not it is beneficial for one
person to control everything. In fact, however, the
1286a investigation of this sort of generalship has the look
of an investigation of laws rather than of constitutions,
since this is something that can come to exist in any
constitution. So the first question may be set aside. But
5 the remaining sort of kingship *is* a kind of constitution.
Hence we must study it and go through the problems
it involves.

The starting point of the investigation is this:
whether it is more beneficial to be ruled by the best
man or by the best laws. Those who think it beneficial
to be ruled by a king hold that laws speak only of the
10 universal, and do not prescribe with a view to actual
circumstances. Consequently, it is foolish to rule in
accordance with written prescriptions in any craft,
and doctors in Egypt are rightly allowed to change
the treatment after the fourth day (although, if they
do so earlier, it is at their own risk). It is evident, for
the same reason, therefore, that the best constitution

is not one that follows written laws. All the same, the 15
rulers should possess the universal reason as well. And
something to which the passionate element is entirely
unattached is better than something in which it is
innate. This element is not present in the law, whereas
every human soul necessarily possesses it.   20

But perhaps it ought to be said, to oppose this, that
a human being will deliberate better about particulars. In that case, it is clear that the ruler must be a
legislator, and that laws must be established, but they
must not have authority insofar as they deviate from
what is best, though they should certainly have authority everywhere else. As to what the law cannot decide
either at all or well, should the one best person rule,
or everyone? For as things stand now, people come 25
together to hear cases, deliberate, and decide, and the
decisions themselves all concern particulars. Taken
individually, any one of these people is perhaps inferior to the best person. But a city-state consists of many
people, just like a feast to which many contribute, and
is better than one that is a unity and simple. That is
why a crowd can also judge many things better than 30
any single individual. Besides, a large quantity is more
incorruptible, so the multitude, like a larger quantity
of water, are more incorruptible than the few. The
judgment of an individual is inevitably corrupted
when he is overcome by anger or some other passion
of this sort, whereas in the same situation it is a task
to get all the citizens to become angry and make
mistakes at the same time.   35

Let the multitude in question be the free, however,
who do nothing outside the law, except about matters
the law cannot cover—not an easy thing to arrange
where numbers are large. But suppose there were a
number who were both good men and good citizens,
which would be more incorruptible—one ruler, or
a larger number all of whom are good? Isn't it clear
that it would be the larger number? "But such a group
will split into factions, whereas the single person is 1286b
free of faction." One should no doubt oppose this
objection by pointing out that they may be excellent
in soul just like the single person.

So then, if the rule of a number of people, all of
whom are good men, is to be considered an aristocracy, and the rule of a single person a kingship, aristocracy would be more choiceworthy for city-states than 5
kingship (whether the rule is supported by force or

not), provided that it is possible to find a number of people who are similar. Perhaps this too is the reason people were formerly under kingships—because it was rare to find men who were very outstanding in virtue, particularly as the city-states they lived in at that time were small. Besides, men were made kings
10 because of benefactions, which it is precisely the task of good men to confer. When there began to be many people who were similar in virtue, however, they no longer put up with kingship, but looked for something communal and established a polity. But when they began to acquire wealth from the common funds, they became less good, and it was from some such source, so one might reasonably suppose, that oligar-
15 chies arose; for they made wealth a thing of honor. Then from oligarchies they changed first into tyrannies, and from tyrannies to democracy. For by concentrating power into ever fewer hands, because of a shameful desire for profit, they made the multitude stronger, with the result that it revolted and democracies arose. Now that city-states have become even
20 larger, it is perhaps no longer easy for any other constitution to arise besides democracy.

But now if one does posit kingship as the best thing for a city-state, how is one to handle the matter of children? Are the descendants to rule as kings too? If they turn out as some have, it would be harmful.
25 "But perhaps, because he is in control, he will not give it to his children." But this is hardly credible. For it is a difficult thing to do, and demands greater virtue than human nature allows.

There is also a problem concerning force, and whether anyone who is going to rule as king should have some force in attendance with which he can compel anyone who does not wish to obey his rule.
30 If not, how can he possibly manage his office? For even if he were a king exercising authority in accord with the law, and never acted in accordance with his own wishes contrary to the law, it would still be necessary for him to have some power with which to protect the laws. In the case of this sort of king, it is perhaps not difficult to determine the solution. He
35 *should* have a force, but a force of such a kind as to be stronger than an individual, whether by himself or together with many, but weaker than the multitude. This is the way the ancients gave bodyguards when they selected someone from the city-state to be what

they called a dictator or tyrant; and when Dionysius asked for bodyguards, someone advised the Syracusans to give him bodyguards of this sort.   40

Chapter 16

Now that we have reached this point the next topic must be that of the king who does everything according to his own wish, so we must investigate this. For   1287a the so-called king according to law does not, as we said, amount to a kind of constitution, since a permanent generalship can exist in any constitution (for example, in a democracy and an aristocracy), and   5 many places put one person in control of managing affairs. There is an office of this sort in Epidamnus, indeed, and to a lesser extent in Opus as well.

But as regards so-called absolute kingship (which is where the king rules everything in accord with his own wish), some hold that it is not even in accordance with nature for one person, from among all the citi-   10 zens, to be in control, when the city-state consists of similar people. For justice and merit must be by nature the same for those who are by nature similar. Hence, if indeed it is harmful to their bodies for equal people to have unequal food or clothing, the same holds, too, where offices are concerned. The same also holds, therefore, when equal people have what   15 is unequal. Which is precisely why it is just for them to rule no more than they are ruled, and, therefore, to do so in turn. But this is already law; for the organization *is* law. Thus it is more choiceworthy to have law rule than any one of the citizens. And, by this same argument, even if it is better to have certain people rule, they should be selected as guardians of   20 and assistants to the laws. For there do have to be some rulers; although it is not just, they say, for there to be only one; at any rate, not when all are similar. Moreover, the sort of things at least that the law seems unable to decide could not be discovered by a human being either. But the law, having educated the rulers for this special purpose, hands over the rest to be decided and managed in accordance with the most   25 just opinion of the rulers. Moreover, it allows them to make any corrections by introducing anything found by experience to be an improvement on the existing laws. Anyone who instructs law to rule would seem to be asking God and the understanding alone

30 to rule; whereas someone who asks a human being asks a wild beast as well. For appetite is like a wild beast, and passion perverts rulers even when they are the best men. That is precisely why law is understanding without desire.

The comparison with the crafts, that it is bad to give medical treatment in accordance with written prescriptions and more choiceworthy to rely on those who possess the craft instead, would seem to be false.
35 For doctors never do things contrary to reason because of friendship, but earn their pay by healing the sick. Those who hold political office, on the other hand, do many things out of spite or in order to win favor. And indeed if people suspected their doctors of having been bribed by their enemies to do away with them, they would prefer to seek treatment derived from
40 books. Moreover, doctors themselves call in other
1287b doctors to treat them when they are sick, and trainers call in other trainers when they are exercising, their assumption being that they are unable to judge truly because they are judging about their own cases, and while in pain. So it is clear that in seeking what is just they are seeking the mean; for the law is the mean. Again, laws based on custom are more authoritative and deal with matters that have more authority
5 than do written laws, so that even if a human ruler is more reliable than written laws, he is not more so than those based on custom.

Yet, it is certainly not easy for a single ruler to oversee many things; hence there will have to be numerous officials appointed under him. Consequently, what difference is there between having them there from the beginning and having one person
10 appoint them in this way? Besides, as we said earlier, if it really is just for the excellent man to rule because he is better, well, two good ones are better than one. Hence the saying "When two go together . . . ," and Agamemnon's prayer, "May ten such counselors be mine."
15 Even nowadays, however, officials, such as jurors, have the authority to decide some things the law cannot determine. For, as regards those matters the law can determine, certainly no one disputes that the law itself would rule and decide best. But because some matters can be covered by the laws, while others cannot, the latter lead people to raise and investigate
20 the problem whether it is more choiceworthy for the best law to rule or the best man (since to legislate about matters that call for deliberation is impossible). The counterargument, therefore, is not that it is not necessary for a human being to decide such matters, but that there should be many judges, not one only.
25 For each official judges well if he has been educated by the law. And it would perhaps be accounted strange if someone, when judging with one pair of eyes and one pair of ears, and acting with one pair of feet and hands, could see better than many people with many pairs, since, as things stand, monarchs provide themselves with many eyes, ears, hands, and feet. For they
30 appoint those who are friendly to their rule and to themselves as co-rulers. Now if they are not friendly in this way, they will not do as the monarch chooses. But suppose they are friendly to him and his rule— well, a friend is someone similar and equal, so if he thinks they should rule, he must think that those who are equal and similar to him should rule in a similar fashion.

These, then, are pretty much the arguments of those who dispute against kingship.
35

Chapter 17

But perhaps these arguments hold in some cases and not in others. For what is by nature both just and beneficial is one thing in the case of rule by a master, another in the case of kingship, and another in the case of rule by a statesman (nothing is by nature both
40 just and beneficial in the case of a tyranny, however, nor in that of the other deviant constitutions, since they come about contrary to nature). But it is surely evident from what has been said that in a case where people are similar and equal, it is neither beneficial
1288a nor just for one person to control everything. This holds whether there are no laws except the king himself, or whether there are laws; whether he is a good person ruling good people, or a not good one ruling not good ones; and even whether he is their superior in virtue—except in one set of circumstances. What these circumstances are must now be stated—although we have in a way already stated it.
5

First, we must determine what kind of people are suited to kingship, what to aristocracy, and what to polity. A multitude should be under kingship when it naturally produces a family that is superior in the virtue appropriate to political leadership. A multitude is suited to aristocracy when it naturally produces 10 a multitude capable of being ruled with the rule appropriate to free people by those who are qualified to lead by their possession of the virtue required for the rule of a statesman. And a multitude is suited to polity when there naturally arises in it a warrior multitude capable of ruling and being ruled, under a law which distributes offices to the rich on the basis of merit. Whenever it happens, then, that there is a 15 whole family, or even some one individual among the rest, whose virtue is so superior as to exceed that of all the others, it is just for this family to be the kingly family and to control everything, and for this one individual to be king. For, as was said earlier, this not only accords with the kind of justice custom- 20 arily put forward by those who establish constitutions, whether aristocratic, oligarchic, or even democratic (for they all claim to merit rule on the basis of superiority in something, though not superiority in the same kind of thing), but also with what was said earlier. For it is surely not proper to kill or to exile or to 25 ostracize an individual of this sort, nor to claim that he deserves to be ruled in turn. For it is not natural for the part to be greater than the whole, but this is what happens in the case of someone who has this degree of superiority. So the only remaining option is for such a person to be obeyed and to be in control not by turns but unqualifiedly.

30 Kingship, then, and what its varieties are, and whether it is beneficial for city-states or not, and if so, for which and how, may be determined in this way.

Chapter 18

We say that there are three correct constitutions, and that the best of them must of necessity be the one managed by the best people. This is the sort of constitution in which there happens to be either one particular person or a whole family or a number of people 35 whose virtue is superior to that of all the rest, and where the latter are capable of being ruled and the former of ruling with a view to the most choiceworthy life. Furthermore, as we showed in our first discussions, the virtue of a man must of necessity be identical to that of a citizen of the best city-state. Hence it is evident that the ways and means by which a man

becomes excellent are the same as those by which 40 one might establish a city-state ruled by an aristocracy or a king, and that the education and habits that make a man excellent are pretty much the same as those 1288b that make him statesmanlike or kingly.

Now that these matters have been determined, we must attempt to discuss the best constitution, the way it naturally arises and how it is established. Anyone, then, who intends to do this must conduct the investigation in the appropriate way. 5

BOOK IV

Chapter 1

Among all the crafts and sciences that are concerned 10 not only with a part but that deal completely with some one type of thing, it belongs to a single one to study what is appropriate for each type. For example: what sort of physical training is beneficial for what sort of body, that is to say, what sort is best (for the sort that is appropriate for the sort of body that is naturally best and best equipped is necessarily best), and what single sort of training is appropriate for most bodies (since this too is a task for physical training). 15 Further, if someone wants neither the condition nor the knowledge required of those involved in competition, it belongs no less to coaches and physical trainers to provide this capacity too. We see a similar thing in medicine, ship building, clothing manufacture, and every other craft. 20

Consequently, it is clear that it belongs to the same science to study: [1] What the best constitution is, that is to say, what it must be like if it is to be most ideal, and if there were no external obstacles. Also [2] which constitution is appropriate for which city-states. For achieving the best constitution is 25 perhaps impossible for many; and so neither the unqualifiedly best constitution nor the one that is best in the circumstances should be neglected by the good legislator and true statesman. Further, [3] which constitution is best given certain assumptions. For a statesman must be able to study how any given constitution might initially come into existence, and how, once in existence, it might be preserved for the longest time. I mean, for example, when some 30 city-state happens to be governed neither by the best constitution (not even having the necessary resources) nor by the best one possible in the existing circumstances, but by a worse one. Besides all these things, a statesman should know [4] which constitution is most appropriate for all city-states. Consequently, 35 those who have expressed views about constitutions, even if what they say is good in other respects, certainly fail when it comes to what is useful. For one should not study only what is best, but also what is possible, and similarly what is easier and more attainable by all. As it is, however, some seek only the constitution that is highest and requires a lot of 40 resources, while others, though they discuss a more attainable sort, do away with the constitutions actually in place, and praise the Spartan or some other. But what should be done is to introduce the sort of organi-1289a zation that people will be easily persuaded to accept and be able to participate in, given what they already have, as it is no less a task to reform a constitution than to establish one initially, just as it is no less a task to correct what we have learned than to learn it in the first place. That is why, in addition to what 5 has just been mentioned, a statesman should also be able to help existing constitutions, as was also said earlier. But this is impossible if he does not know [5] how many kinds of constitutions there are. As things stand, however, some people think that there is just one kind of democracy and one of oligarchy. But this is not true. So one must not overlook the varieties of 10 each of the constitutions, how many they are and how many ways they can be combined. And [6] it is with this same practical wisdom that one should try to see both which laws are best and which are appropriate for each of the constitutions. For laws should be established, and all do establish them, to suit the constitution and not the constitution to suit the laws. 15 For a constitution is the organization of offices in city-states, the way they are distributed, what element is in authority in the constitution, and what the end is of each of the communities. Laws, apart from those that reveal what the constitution is, are those by which the officials must rule, and must guard against those 20 who transgress them. Clearly, then, a knowledge of the varieties of each constitution and of their number is also necessary for establishing laws. For the same laws cannot be beneficial for all oligarchies or for all

democracies—if indeed there are several kinds, and not one kind of democracy nor one kind of oligar- 25 chy only.

Chapter 2

Since our initial inquiry concerning constitutions, we distinguished three correct constitutions (kingship, aristocracy, polity) and three deviations from them (tyranny from kingship, oligarchy from aristocracy, and democracy from polity), and since we have already discussed aristocracy and kingship, for studying the best constitution is the same as discussing these 30 names, since each of them tends to be established on the basis of virtue furnished with resources; and since further, we have determined how aristocracy and kingship differ from one another, and when a constitution should be considered a kingship, it re- 35 mains to deal with the constitution that is called by the name common to all constitutions, and also with the others—oligarchy, democracy, and tyranny.

It is also evident which of these deviations is worst and which second worst. For the deviation from the first and most divine constitution must of necessity be the worst. But kingship either must be in name 40 only and not in fact or must be based on the great superiority of the person ruling as king. Hence tyranny, being the worst, is furthest removed from being 1289b a constitution; oligarchy is second worst (since aristocracy is very far removed from this constitution); and democracy the most moderate. An earlier thinker has already expressed this same view, though he did not 5 look to the same thing we do. For he judged that when all these constitutions are good (for example, when an oligarchy is good, and also the others), democracy is the worst of them, but that when they are bad, it is the best. But we say that these constitutions are all of them mistaken, and that it is not right to speak of one kind of oligarchy as better than another, but as less bad. 10

But let us leave aside the judgment of this matter for the present. Instead, we must determine: [1] First, how many varieties of the constitutions there are (if indeed there are several kinds of democracy and oligarchy). Next, [2] which kind is most attainable, and which most choiceworthy after the best constitution 15 (if indeed there is some other constitution which,

though aristocratic and well constituted, is at the same time appropriate for most city-states), and also which of the other constitutions is more choiceworthy for which people (for democracy is perhaps more necessary than oligarchy for some, whereas for others the
20 reverse holds). After these things, [3] how someone who wishes to do so should establish these constitutions (I mean, each kind of democracy or oligarchy). Finally, when we have gone as far as we can to give a succinct account of each of these topics, [4] we must try to go through the ways in which constitutions are destroyed and those in which they are preserved,
25 both in general and in the case of each one separately, and through what causes these most naturally come about.

Chapter 3

The reason why there are several constitutions is that every city-state has several parts. For in the first place, we see that all city-states are composed of households; and, next, that within this multitude there have to be
30 some who are rich, some who are poor, and some who are in the middle; and that of the rich and of the poor, the one possessing weapons and the other without weapons. We also see that the people comprise a farming part, a trading part, and a vulgar craftsman part. And among the notables there are differences in wealth and in extent of their property— as, for example, in the breeding of horses, since this
35 is not easy for those without wealth to do. (That is why, indeed, there were oligarchies among those city-states in ancient times whose power lay in their cavalry, and who used horses in wars with their neighbors—as, for example, the Eretrians did, and the Chalcidians, the Magnesians on the river Menander,
40 and many of the others in Asia.) There are also differences based on birth, on virtue, and on everything else of the sort that we characterized as part of a city-
1290a state in our discussion of aristocracy, since there we distinguished the number of parts that are necessary to any city-state. For sometimes all of these parts participate in the constitution, sometimes fewer of them, sometimes more.
5 It is evident, therefore, that there must be several constitutions that differ in kind from one another, since these parts themselves also differ in kind. For

a constitution is the organization of offices, and all consitutions distribute these either on the basis of the power of the participants, or on the basis of some sort of equality common to them (I mean, for example, of the poor or of the rich, or some equality common 10 to both). Therefore, there must be as many constitutions as there are ways of organizing offices on the basis of the superiority and varieties of the parts.

But there are held to be mainly two constitutions: just as the winds are called north or south, and the others deviations from these, so there are also said to be two constitutions, democracy and oligarchy. For 15 aristocracy is regarded as a sort of oligarchy, on the grounds that it is a sort of rule by the few, whereas a so-called polity is regarded as a sort of democracy, just as the west wind is regarded as northerly, and the east as southerly. According to some people, the same thing also happens in the case of harmonies, which are regarded as being of two kinds, the Dorian 20 and the Phrygian, and the other arrangements are called either Phrygian types or Dorian types. People are generally accustomed, then, to think of constitutions in this way. But it is truer and better to distinguish them, as we have, and say that two constitutions (or one) are well formed, and that the others are deviations from them, some from the well-mixed "harmony," and others from the best constitution, the 25 more tightly controlled ones and those that are more like the rule of a master being more oligarchic, and the unrestrained and soft ones democratic.

Chapter 4

One should not assert (as some are accustomed to 30 do now) that democracy is simply where the multitude are in authority (for both in oligarchies and everywhere else, the larger part is in authority). Nor should an oligarchy be regarded as being where the few are in authority over the constitution. For if there were a total of thirteen hundred people, out of which a thousand were rich people who give no share in office to three hundred poor ones, no one would say 35 that the latter were democratically governed even if they were free and otherwise similar to the rich. Similarly, if the poor were few, but stronger than the rich, who were a majority, no one would call such a constitution an oligarchy if the others, though rich,

did not participate in office. Thus it is better to say
40 that a democracy exists when the free are in authority
and an oligarchy exists when the rich are; but it
1290b happens that the former are many and the latter few,
since many are free but few are rich. Otherwise there
would be an oligarchy if offices were distributed on
5 the basis of height (as is said to happen in Ethiopia)
or on the basis of beauty, since beautiful people and
tall ones are both few in number.

Yet these are not sufficient to distinguish these
constitutions. Rather, since both democracy and oligarchy have a number of parts, we must further grasp
that it is not a democracy if a few free people rule
10 over a majority who are not free, as, for example, in
Apollonia on the Ionian Gulf and in Thera. For in
each of these city-states the offices were held by the
well born, the descendants of the first colonists, although they were few among many. Nor is it an
oligarchy if the rich rule because they are the multi-
15 tude, as was formerly the case in Colophon, where
the majority possessed large properties before the war
against the Lydians. Rather, it is a democracy when
the free and the poor who are a majority have the
authority to rule, and an oligarchy when the rich and
20 well born, who are few, do.

It has been stated, then, that there are a number
of constitutions and why this is so. But let us now say
why there are more than the ones mentioned, what
they are, and how they arise, taking as our starting
point what was agreed to earlier. For we are agreed
that every city-state has not only one part but several.

25 If we wanted to grasp the kinds of animals, we
would first determine what it is necessary for every
animal to have: for example, certain of the sense
organs; something with which to work on and absorb
food (such as a mouth and a stomach); and also parts
by which it moves. If these were the only parts, but
they had varieties (I mean, for example, if there were
30 several types of mouths, stomachs, and sense organs,
and also of locomotive parts), then the number of
ways of combining these would necessarily produce
a number of types of animals. For the same animal
cannot have mouths or ears of many different varieties. Hence, when these have been grasped, all the
possible ways of pairing them together will produce
35 kinds of animals, that is to say, as many kinds of
animals as there are combinations of the necessary

parts. It is the same way with the constitutions we
have mentioned. For city-states are constituted not
out of one but many parts, as we have often said.

One of these parts is [1] the multitude concerned
with food, the ones called farmers. A second is [2]
those called vulgar craftsman. They are concerned 40
with the crafts without which a city-state cannot be 1291a
managed (of these some are necessary, whereas others
contribute to luxury or fine living). A third is [3] the
traders (by which I mean those engaged in selling
and buying, retail trade, and commerce). A fourth is 5
[4] the hired laborers. A fifth is [5] the defensive
warriors, which are no less necessary than the others,
if the inhabitants are not to become the slaves of any
aggressor. For no city-state that is naturally slavish
can possibly deserve to be called a city-state at all;
for a city-state is self-sufficient, whereas something
that is slavish is not self-sufficient. 10

That is why what is said in the *Republic*, though
sophisticated, is not adequate. For Socrates says that a
city-state is constituted out of four absolutely necessary
classes, and these, he says, are weavers, farmers, shoemakers, and house builders. Then, on the grounds
that these are not self-sufficient, he adds blacksmiths,
people to look after the necessary livestock, and those 15
engaged in retail trade and commerce. All these become the full complement of his first city-state—as
if every city-state were constituted for the sake of
providing the necessities, not for the sake of what is
noble, and had equal need of both shoemakers and
farmers. Nor does he assign it defensive warriors until,
with the expansion of its territory, it encroaches on 20
that of its neighbors, and gets involved in a war. Yet
even in these communities of four (or however many)
classes, there must be someone to assign and decide
what is just. So if indeed one should regard the soul
as a more important part of an animal than the body,
then, in the case of city-states too, one should regard
things of the following sort to be parts, rather than 25
those dealing with our necessary needs: the warriors;
those who participate in administering judicial justice; and also those who deliberate, since deliberation
is a task for political understanding. It does not matter
to the argument whether these tasks belong to separate
people or the same ones, since in fact it often happens
that the same people both possess weapons and engage in farming. Consequently, if both the former 30

and the latter are to be regarded as parts of a city-state, it is evident that those who possess weapons, at any rate, must be a part of a city-state.

[7] Seventh are those who perform public service by means of their property. This is the class we call the rich. [8] Eighth are the civil servants, those who
35 serve in connection with the various offices, since a city-state cannot exist without officials. There must, therefore, be some who are able to rule and perform this public service for the city-state either continuously or in turn. There remain those we happened to distinguish just now, those who deliberate and decide the claims of people involved in disputes.
40 Therefore, if these things must indeed take place in city-states, and do so in a way that is noble and just, there must also be some who share in the virtue
1291b of statesmen.

As for the other capacities, many hold that they can belong to the same people; for example, that it is possible for the same people to be warriors, farmers, and craftsmen, and both deliberators and judges be-
5 sides. And everyone claims to possess the virtue too, and thinks he is capable of ruling in most offices. But for the same people to be both rich and poor is impossible. Hence these in particular, the rich and the poor, are held to be parts of a city-state. Besides, the fact that the former are usually few in number and the latter many makes it seem that among the
10 parts of the city-state these two are opposites. Consequently, constitutions are established on the basis of the superiority of these, and there are held to be two constitutions, democracy and oligarchy.

That there are a number of constitutions, then, and why this is so has been stated earlier. But we may now say that there are also several kinds of democ-
15 racy and oligarchy. This is in fact evident from what has been said. For there are several kinds both of the people and of the so-called notables. For example, of the people, one is the farmers; another, those concerned with the crafts; the kind involved in trading, which is engaged in buying and selling; and the kind
20 concerned with the sea—of which part is the navy, part is engaged in wealth acquisition, part in ferrying passengers, and part in fishing. (In many places, a particular one of these amounts to a large crowd; for example, fishermen in Tarentum and Byzantium, navy men in Athens, traders in Aegina and Chios,

and ferrymen in Tenedos.) In addition to these, there 25 are the manual laborers, those who have too little property to enable them to be at leisure; the free people who are not of citizen parentage on both sides; and whatever other kind of multitude there may be. The notables are distinguished by wealth, good birth, virtue, education, and the other characteristics that are ascribed on the basis of the same sort of difference.

[1] The first democracy, then, is the one that is 30 said to be most of all based on equality. For the law in this democracy says that there is equality when the poor enjoy no more superiority than the rich and neither is in authority but the two are similar. For if indeed freedom and equality are most of all present in a democracy, as some people suppose, this would be most true in the constitution in which everyone 35 participates in the most similar way. But since the people are the majority, and majority opinion has authority, this constitution is necessarily a democracy. This, then, is one kind of democracy.

[2] Another is where offices are filled on the basis of property assessments, although these are low, and where anyone who acquires the requisite amount may participate, whereas anyone who loses it may not. [3] 40 Another kind of democracy is where all uncontested citizens participate, and the law rules. [4] Another kind of democracy is where everyone can participate 1292a in office merely by being a citizen, and the law rules.

[5] Another kind of democracy is the same in other respects, but the multitude has authority, not the law. This arises when decrees have authority instead of 5 laws; and this happens because of popular leaders. For in city-states that are under a democracy based on law, popular leaders do not arise. Instead, the best citizens preside. Where the laws are not in authority, however, popular leaders arise. For the people be- 10 come a monarch, one person composed of many, since the many are in authority not as individuals, but all together. When Homer says that "manyheaded rule is not good,"[4] it is not clear whether he means this kind of rule, or the kind where there are a number of individual rulers. In any case, a people of this kind, since it is a monarchy, seeks to exercise monarchic 15 rule through not being ruled by the law, and becomes

4. [*Iliad* II.204.]

a master. The result is that flatterers are held in esteem, and that a democracy of this kind is the analog
of tyranny among the monarchies. That is also why
their characters are the same: both act like masters
toward the better people; the decrees of the one are
like the edicts of the other; a popular leader is either
20 the same as a flatterer or analogous. Each of these
has special power in his own sphere, flatterers with
tyrants, popular leaders with a people of this kind.
They are responsible for decrees being in authority
rather than laws because they bring everything before
25 the people. This results in their becoming powerful
because the people have authority over everything,
and popular leaders have it over the people's opinion,
since the multitude are persuaded by them. Besides,
those who make accusations against officials say that
the people should decide them. The suggestion is
gladly accepted, with the result that all offices are destroyed.
30   One might hold, however, that it is reasonable to
object that this kind of democracy is not a constitution
at all, on the grounds that there is no constitution
where the laws do not rule. For the law should rule
universally over everything, while offices and the constitution should decide particular cases. So, since de-
35 mocracy is one of the constitutions, it is evident that
this sort of arrangement, in which everything is managed by decree, is not even a democracy in the most
authoritative sense, since no decree can possibly be
universal.
     The kinds of democracy, then, should be distin-
guished in this way.

Chapter 5

Of the kinds of oligarchy, [1] one has offices filled
on the basis of such a high property assessment that
40 the poor, even though they are the majority, do not
participate, but anyone who does acquire the requisite
amount may participate in the constitution. [2] In
another the offices are filled on the basis of a high
1292b assessment and they themselves elect someone to fill
any vacancy. If they elect from among all of these,
it is held to be more aristocratic; if from some specified
people, oligarchic. [3] In another kind of oligarchy
5 a son succeeds his father. [4] In a fourth what was
just mentioned occurs, and not the law but the offi-

cials rule. This is to oligarchies what tyranny is to
monarchies, and to the democracy we spoke of last
among democracies. Such an oligarchy is called a dy- 10
nasty.
     These, then, are the kinds of oligarchy and democ-
racy. But one must not overlook the fact that it has
happened in many places that constitutions which
are not democratic according to their laws are none
the less governed democratically because of custom
and training. Similarly, in other places, the reverse
has happened: the constitution is more democratic 15
in its laws, but is governed in a more oligarchic way
as a result of custom and training. This happens especially after there has been a change of constitution.
For the change is not immediate, but people are
content at first to take from others in smaller ways.
Hence the pre-existing laws remain in effect, although
those who have changed the constitution are dom- 20
inant.

Chapter 6

It is evident from what has been said that there are
this many kinds of democracy and oligarchy. For
either all of the aforementioned parts of the people
must participate in the constitution, or some must
and others not. [1] So when the part that farms and 25
that owns a moderate amount of property has authority over the constitution, it is governed in accordance
with the laws. For they have enough to live on as
long as they keep working, but they cannot afford any
leisure time. So they put the law in charge and hold
only such assemblies as are necessary. And the others
may participate when they have acquired the property
assessment defined by the laws. Hence all those who 30
have acquired it may participate. For, generally speaking, it is oligarchic when not all of these may participate, though not if what makes being at leisure
impossible is the absence of revenues. This, then, is
one kind of democracy and these are the reasons for it.
     [2] Another kind arises through the following dis-
tinction. For it is possible for everyone of uncontested 35
birth to participate, but for only those who have leisure actually to do so. Hence in this kind of democracy
the laws rule because there is no revenue. [3] A third
kind is when all who are free may participate in the
constitution, but, for the reason just mentioned, they

40 do not participate, so that law necessarily rules in this
kind also. [4] A fourth kind of democracy was the
1293a last to arise in city-states. For because city-states have
become much larger than the original ones and possess abundant sources of revenue, everyone shares in
the constitution, and so the multitude preponderates.
And they all do participate and govern, because even
5 the poor are able to be at leisure, since they get paid.
A multitude of this sort is particularly leisured, indeed,
since care for their own property does not impede
them. But it does impede the rich, who often fail to
take part in the assembly or serve on juries as a result.
Hence the multitude of poor citizens come to have
10 authority over the constitution and not the laws. The
kinds of democracy, then, are such and so many
because of these necessities.

As for the kinds of oligarchy; [1] when a number
of people own property, but a smaller amount—not
too much—this is the first kind of oligarchy. For
anyone who acquires the amount may participate.
15 And because of the multitude participating in the
governing class, law is necessarily in authority, not
human beings. For it is necessary for them to consent
to having the law rule and not themselves, the more
removed they are from exercising monarchy, and the
more they have neither so much property that they
can be at leisure without worrying nor so little that
20 they need to be supported by the city-state.

[2] But if the property owners are fewer and their
properties greater than those mentioned before, the
second kind of oligarchy arises. For, being more powerful, the property owners expect to get more. Hence
they themselves elect from among the rest of the
citizens those who are to enter the governing class.
But as they are not yet powerful enough to rule with-
25 out law, they pass a law of this sort.

[3] But if they tighten this process by becoming
fewer and owning larger properties, the third stage of
oligarchy is reached, where they keep the offices in
their own hands, but do so in accordance with a law
requiring deceased members to be succeeded by their
sons. [4] But when they now tighten it excessively
through their property holdings and the number of
30 their friends, a dynasty of this sort approximates a
monarchy, and human beings are in authority, not
law. This is the fourth kind of oligarchy, corresponding to the final kind of democracy.

Chapter 7

There are also two constitutions besides democracy 35
and oligarchy, one of which is mentioned by everyone
and which we said was one of the four kinds of constitutions. The four they mention are monarchy, oligarchy, democracy, and, fourth, so-called aristocracy.
There is a fifth, however, which is referred to by the
name shared by all constitutions: the one called a
politeia (polity). But because it does not occur often, 40
it gets overlooked by those who try to enumerate the
kinds of constitutions, and, like Plato, list only the
four in their discussion of constitutions.   1293b

It is well to call the constitution we treated in our
first discussions an aristocracy. For the only constitution that is rightly called an aristocracy is the one
that consists of those who are unqualifiedly best as
regards virtue, and not of those who are good men
only given a certain assumption. For only here is it
unqualifiedly the case that the same person is a good 5
man and a good citizen. But those who are good in
other constitutions are so relative to their constitutions. Nevertheless, there are some constitutions that
differ both from constitutions that are oligarchically
governed and from so-called polity, and are called
aristocracies. For a constitution where officials are
elected not only on the basis of wealth but also on
the basis of merit differs from both of these and is 10
called aristocratic. For even in those constitutions
where virtue is not a concern of the community, there
are still some who are of good repute and held to
be decent. Hence wherever a constitution looks to
wealth, virtue, and the people (as it does in Carthage), 15
it is aristocratic, as also are those, like the constitution
of the Spartans, which look to only two, virtue and
the people, and where there is a mixture of these two
things, democracy and virtue. There are, then, these
two kinds of aristocracy besides the first, which is the
best constitution; and there is also a third, namely,
[4] those kinds of so-called polity that lean more 20
toward oligarchy.

Chapter 8

It remains for us to speak about so-called polity and
about tyranny. We have adopted this arrangement,
even though neither polity nor the aristocracies just

mentioned are deviant, because in truth they all fall short of the most correct constitution, and so are counted among the deviations, and these deviations are deviations from them, as we mentioned in the beginning. On the other hand, it is reasonable to treat tyranny last, since it is least of all a constitution, and our inquiry is about constitutions. So much for the reason for organizing things in this way.

But we must now set forth our views on polity. Its nature should be more evident now that we have determined the facts about oligarchy and democracy. For polity, to put it simply, is a mixture of oligarchy and democracy. It is customary, however, to call those mixtures that lean toward democracy polities, and those that lean more toward oligarchy aristocracies, because education and good birth more commonly accompany those who are richer. Besides, the rich are held to possess already what unjust people commit injustice to get, which is why the rich are referred to as noble-and-good men, and as notables. So since aristocracies strive to give superiority to the best citizens, oligarchies too are said to consist primarily of noble-and-good men. And it is held to be impossible for a city-state to be well governed if it is not governed aristocratically, but by bad people, and equally impossible for a city-state that is not well governed to be governed aristocratically. But good government does not exist if the laws, though well established, are not obeyed. Hence we must take good government to exist in one way when the established laws are obeyed, and in another when the laws that are in fact obeyed are well established (for even badly established laws can be obeyed). The second situation can come about in two ways: people may obey either the best laws possible for them, or the unqualifiedly best ones.

Aristocracy is held most of all to exist when offices are distributed on the basis of virtue. For virtue is the defining mark of aristocracy, wealth of oligarchy, and freedom of democracy. But majority opinion is found in all of them. For in oligarchy and aristocracy and in democracies, the opinion of the major part of those who participate in the constitution has authority. Now in most city-states the kind of constitution is wrongly named, since the mixture aims only at the rich and the poor, at wealth and freedom. For among pretty much most people the rich are taken to occupy the place of noble-and-good men. But there are in fact *three* grounds for claiming equal participation in the constitution: freedom, wealth, and virtue. (The fourth, which they call good birth, is a consequence of two of the others, since good birth is a combination of old money and virtue.) Hence it is evident that the mixture of the two, the rich and the poor, ought to be called polity, whereas a mixture of the three most of all the others (except for the true and first kind) deserves to be called an aristocracy.

We have said, then, that there are other kinds of constitutions besides monarchy, democracy, and oligarchy. And it is evident what they are, how aristocracies differ among themselves, and polities from aristocracy; and that they are not far apart from one another.

Chapter 9

After what has been said, let us next discuss how, in addition to democracy and oligarchy, so-called polity arises, and how it should be established. At the same time, however, the defining principles of democracy and oligarchy will also become clear. For what we must do is get hold of the division of these, and then take as it were a token from each to put together.

There are three defining principles of the combination and mixture: [1] One is to take legislation from both constitutions. For example, in the case of deciding court cases, oligarchies impose a fine on the rich if they do not take part in deciding court cases, but provide no payment for the poor, whereas democracies pay the poor but do not fine the rich. But what is common to both constitutions and a mean between them is doing both. And hence this is characteristic of a polity, which is a mixture formed from both. This, then, is one way to conjoin them. [2] Another is to take the mean between the organizations of each. In democracies, for example, membership in the assembly is either not based on a property assessment at all or on a very small one, whereas in oligarchies it is based on a large property assessment. The common position here is to require neither of these assessments but the one that is in a mean between the two of them. [3] A third is to take elements from both organizations, some from oligarchic law and others from democratic law. I mean, for example, it is

held to be democratic for officials to be chosen by lot, and oligarchic by election; democratic not on the basis of a property assessment, oligarchic on
10 such a basis. It is aristocratic, therefore, and characteristic of a polity to take one element from one and another from the other, by making officials elected, as in an oligarchy, but not on the basis of a property assessment, as in a democracy.

This, then, is the way to mix them. But the defining principle of a good mixture of democracy and oligarchy is when it is possible to speak of the same constitu-
15 tion both as an oligarchy and as a democracy. For it is clear that speakers speak of it in this way because the mixture is a good one. The mean too is like this, since each of the extremes is visible in it. This is precisely how it is with the Spartan constitution. For many people attempt to speak of it as if it were a democracy, because it has many democratic elements
20 in its organization. First, for example, there is the way sons are brought up. Those of the rich are brought up like those of the poor, and are educated in a way that the sons of the poor could be. Similarly, at the next age, when they have become men, it is the same
25 way. For nothing distinguishes a rich person from a poor one: the food at the messes is the same for everyone, and the rich wear clothes that any poor person could also provide for himself. A further democratic element is that of the two most important offices, the people elect candidates to one and partici-
30 pate in the other; for they elect the senators and participate in the overseership. But other people call the Spartan constitution an oligarchy on account of its having many oligarchic elements. For example, all the officials are chosen by vote and none by lot; a few have authority to impose death and exile; and there are also many other such elements. In a constitution that is well mixed, however, both elements
35 should be held to be present—and neither; and it should survive because of itself and not because of external factors, and because of itself, not because a majority wishes it (since that could happen in a bad constitution too), but because none of the parts of the city-state as a whole would even want another constitution.

We have now described how a polity should be
40 established and likewise those constitutions that are termed aristocracies.

Chapter 10

It remained for us to speak about tyranny, not because 1295a there is much to say about it, but so that it can take its place in our inquiry, since we assign it too a place among the constitutions. Now we dealt with kingship in our first discussions (when we investigated whether the kind of kingship that is most particularly so called 5 is beneficial for city-states or not beneficial, who and from what source should be established in it, and in what manner). And we distinguished two kinds of tyranny while we were investigating kingship, because their power somehow also overlaps with kingship, owing to the fact that both are based on law. For 10 some non-Greeks choose [1] autocratic monarchs, and in former times among the ancient Greeks there were [2] people called dictators who became monarchs in this way. There are, however, certain differences between these; but both were kingly in as much 15 as they were based on law, and involved monarchical rule over willing subjects; but both were tyrannical, in as much as the monarchs ruled like masters in accordance with their own judgment. But [3] there is also a third kind of tyranny, which is held to be tyranny in the highest degree, being a counterpart to absolute kingship. Any monarchy is necessarily a tyranny of this kind if the monarch rules in an unaccountable fashion over people who are similar to him or better than him, with an eye to his own 20 benefit, not that of the ruled. It is therefore rule over unwilling people, since no free person willingly endures such rule.

The kinds of tyranny are these and this many, then, for the aforementioned reasons.

Chapter 11

What is the best constitution, and what is the best life 25 for most city-states and most human beings, judging neither by a virtue that is beyond the reach of ordinary people, nor by a kind of education that requires natural gifts and resources that depend on luck, nor by the ideal constitution, but by a life that most people can share and a constitution in which most city-states can participate? For the constitutions called aristocra- 30 cies, which we discussed just now, either fall outside the reach of most city-states or border on so-called polities (that is why the two have to spoken about as one).

35   Decision about all these matters depends on the same elements. For if what is said in the *Ethics* is right, and a happy life is the one that expresses virtue and is without impediment, and virtue is a mean, then the middle life, the mean that each sort of person can actually achieve, must be best. These same defining principles must also hold of the virtue and vice

40   of a city-state or a constitution, since a constitution is a sort of life of city-state.

1295b   In all city-states, there are three parts of the city-state: the very rich, the very poor; and, third, those in between these. So, since it is agreed that what is moderate and in a mean is best, it is evident that

5   possessing a middle amount of the goods of luck is also best. For it most readily obeys reason, whereas whatever is exceedingly beautiful, strong, well born, or wealthy, or conversely whatever is exceedingly poor, weak, or lacking in honor, has a hard time obeying reason. For the former sort tend more toward arrogance and major vice, whereas the latter tend too

10   much toward malice and petty vice; and wrongdoing is caused in the one case by arrogance and in the other by malice. Besides, the middle classes are least inclined either to avoid ruling or to pursue it, both of which are harmful to city-states.

Furthermore, those who are superior in the goods of luck (strength, wealth, friends, and other such

15   things) neither wish to be ruled nor know how to be ruled (and this is a characteristic they acquire right from the start at home while they are still children; for because of their luxurious lifestyle they are not accustomed to being ruled, even in school). Those, on the other hand, who are exceedingly deprived of such goods are too humble. Hence the latter do not

20   know how to rule, but only how to be ruled in the way slaves are ruled, whereas the former do not know how to be ruled in any way, but only how to rule as masters rule. The result is a city-state consisting not of free people but of slaves and masters, the one group full of envy and the other full of arrogance. Nothing is further removed from a friendship and a community that is political. For community involves friendship, since enemies do not wish to share even a journey in common. But a city-state, at least, tends to consist

25   as much as possible of people who are equal and

similar, and this condition belongs particularly to those in the middle. Consequently, this city-state, the one constituted out of those from which we say the city-state is naturally constituted, must of necessity be best governed. Moreover, of all citizens, those in the middle survive best in city-states. For neither do they

30   desire other people's property as the poor do, nor do other people desire theirs, as the poor desire that of the rich. And because they are neither plotted against nor engage in plotting, they live out their lives free from danger. That is why Phocylides did well to pray: "Many things are best for those in the middle. I want to be in the middle in a city-state."

It is clear, therefore, that the political community that depends on those in the middle is best too,

35   and that city-states can be well governed where those in the middle are numerous and stronger, preferably than both of the others, or, failing that, than one of them. For it will tip the balance when added to either and prevent the opposing extremes from arising. That is precisely why it is the height of good luck if those who are governing own a

40   middle or adequate amount of property, because when some people own an excessive amount and

1296a   the rest own nothing, either extreme democracy arises or unmixed oligarchy or, as a result of both excesses, tyranny. For tyranny arises from the most vigorous kind of democracy and oligarchy, but much less often from middle constitutions or those close

5   to them. We will give the reason for this later when we discuss changes in constitutions.

That the middle constitution is best is evident, since it alone is free from faction. For conflicts and dissensions seldom occur among the citizens where there are many in the middle. Large city-states are also freer from faction for the same reason,

10   namely, that more are many in the middle. In small city-states, on the other hand, it is easy to divide all the citizens into two, so that no middle is left and pretty well everyone is either poor or rich. Democracies are also more stable and longer lasting than oligarchies because of those in the middle (for they are more numerous in democracies

15   than in oligarchies and participate in office more), since when the poor predominate without these, failure sets in and they are quickly ruined. The fact that the best legislators have come from the

middle citizens should be regarded as evidence of this. For Solon was one of these, as is clear from his poems, as were Lycurgus (for he was not a
20 king), Charondas, and pretty well most of the others.

It is also evident from these considerations why most constitutions are either democratic or oligarchic. For because the middle class in them is often small, whichever of the others preponderates (whether the
25 property owners or the people), those who overstep the middle way conduct the constitution to suit themselves, so that it becomes either a democracy or an oligarchy. In addition to this, because of the conflicts and fights that occur between the people and the rich, whenever one side or the other happens to gain more power than its opponents, they establish neither
30 a common constitution nor an equal one, but take their superiority in the constitution as a reward of their victory and make in the one case a democracy and in the other an oligarchy. Then too each of those who achieved leadership in Greece has looked to their own constitutions and established either democracies or oligarchies in city-states, aiming not at the
35 benefit of these city-states but at their own. As a consequence of all this, the middle constitution either never comes into existence or does so rarely and in few places. For among those who have previously held positions of leadership, only one man has ever been persuaded to introduce this kind of organization, and it has now become customary for those in city-
40 states not even to wish for equality, but either to seek
1296b rule or to put up with being dominated.

What the best constitution is, then, and why it is so is evident from these considerations. As for the other constitutions (for there are, as we say, several kinds of democracies and of oligarchies), which of them is to be put first, which second, and so on in
5 the same way, according to whether it is better or worse, is not hard to see now that the best has been determined. For the one nearest to this must of necessity always be better and one further from the middle worse—provided one is not judging on the basis of certain assumptions. I say "on the basis of certain assumptions," because it often happens that, while one constitution is more choiceworthy, nothing pre-
10 vents a different one from being more beneficial for some.

Chapter 12

The next thing to go through after what has been said is which constitution and which kind of it is beneficial for which and which kind of people. First, though, a general point must be grasped about all of them, namely, that the part of a city-state that wishes the constitution to continue must be stronger than any part that does not. Every city- 15 state is made up of both quality and quantity. By "quality," I mean freedom, wealth, education, and good birth; by "quantity," I mean the superiority of size. But it is possible that the quality belongs to one of the parts of which a city-state is constituted, whereas the quantity belongs to another. For exam- 20 ple, the low-born may be more numerous than the well-born or the poor more numerous than the rich, but yet the one may not be as superior in quantity as it is inferior in quality. Hence these have to be judged in relation to one another. Where the multitude of poor people is superior in the proportion mentioned, there it is natural for a 25 democracy to exist, with each particular kind of democracy corresponding to the superiority of each particular kind of the people. For example, if the multitude of farmers is predominant, it will be the first kind of democracy; if the vulgar craftsmen and wage earners are, the last kind; and similarly for the others in between these. But where the multitude of 30 those who are rich and notable is more superior in quality than it is inferior in quantity, there an oligarchy is natural, with each particular kind of oligarchy corresponding to the superiority of the multitude of oligarchs, in the same way as before.

But the legislator should always include the middle in his constitution: if he is establishing oligarchic laws, he should aim at those in the middle, and if 35 democratic ones, he must bring them in by these laws. And where the multitude of those in the middle outweighs either both of the extremes together, or even only one of them, it is possible to have a stable constitution. For there is no fear that the rich and 40 the poor will conspire together against these, since neither will ever want to serve as slaves to the other; 1297a and if they look for a constitution that is more common than this, they will find none. For they would not put up with ruling in turn, because they distrust

one another; and an arbitrator is most trusted every-
5 where, and the middle person is an arbitrator. The
better mixed a constitution is, the more stable it is.
But many of those who wish to establish aristocratic
constitutions make the mistake not only of granting
more to the rich, but also of deceiving the people.
10 For sooner or later, false goods inevitably give rise to
a true evil; for the acquisitive behavior of the rich
does more to destroy the constitution than that of
the poor.

Chapter 13

The devices used in constitutions to deceive the
people are five in number, and concern the assem-
15 bly, offices, the courts, weapons, and physical training. [1] As regards the assembly: allowing all citizens
to attend assemblies, but either imposing a fine
only on the rich for not attending, or a much
heavier one on them. [2] As regards offices: not
allowing those with an assessed amount of property
20 to swear off, but allowing the poor to do so. [3]
As regards the courts: fining the rich for not serving
on juries, but not the poor, or else imposing a
large fine on the former and a small one on the
latter, as in the laws of Charondas. In some places,
everyone who has enrolled may attend the assembly
and serve on juries, but once they have enrolled,
25 if they do not attend or serve, they are heavily
fined. The aim is to get people to avoid enrolling
because of the fine, and not to serve or to attend
because of not being enrolled. They legislate in
the same way where possessing hoplite arms and
30 physical training are concerned. [4] For the poor
are permitted not to possess weapons, but the rich
are fined if they do not; [5] and if they do not
train, there is no fine for the former, but the latter
are fined. That way the rich will participate because
of the fine, whereas the poor, not being in danger
of it, will not participate.
35 These legislative devices are oligarchic; in democracies there are opposite devices. For the poor are
paid to attend the assembly and serve on juries, and
the rich are not fined for failing to. If one wants to
mix justly, then, it is evident that one must combine
elements from either side, and pay the poor while
40 fining the rich. For in this way everyone would partici-

pate, whereas in the other way the constitution comes
to belong to one side alone. The constitution should   1297b
consist only of those who possess weapons; but it is
impossible unqualifiedly to define the size of the
relevant property assessment, and say that it must be
so much. One should instead look for what amount
is the highest that would let those who participate in
the constitution outnumber those who do not, and   5
fix on that. For the poor are willing to keep quiet
even when they do not participate in office, provided
no one treats them arrogantly or takes away any of
their property (not an easy thing, however, since those
who do participate in the governing class are not   10
always cultivated people). People are also in the habit
of shirking in time of war if they are poor and do
not receive provisions; but if food is provided, they
will fight.

In some places, the constitution consists not only
of those who are serving as hoplites but also of those
who have served as hoplites in the past. In Malea,
the constitution consisted of both, although the officials were elected from among the active soldiers.   15
Also the first constitution that arose among the Greeks
after kingships also consisted of the defensive warriors.
Initially, it consisted of the cavalrymen, since strength
and superiority in war lay in them. For a hoplite
force is useless without organized formations, and
experience in such things and organizations did not   20
exist among the ancients. Hence their strength lay in
their cavalry. But as city-states grew larger and those
with hoplite weapons became a stronger force, more
people came to participate in the constitution. That
is precisely why what we now call polities used to
be called democracies. But the ancient constitutions   25
were oligarchic and kingly, and quite understandably
so. For because of their small population they did
not have much of a middle class, so that, being small
in number and poor in organization, the people put
up with being ruled.

We have said, then, [1] why there are several constitutions — [1.1] why there are others besides those spoken of (for democracy is not one in number, and   30
similarly with the others), [1.2] what their varieties
are, and [1.3] why they arise. In addition, [2] we have
said which constitution is best, for the majority of
cases, and [3] among the other constitutions which
suits which sort of people.

Chapter 14

As regards what comes next, let us once again discuss
35 constitutions generally and each one separately, taking the starting point that is appropriate to the subject.
All constitutions have three parts by reference to
which an excellent legislator must study what is beneficial for each of them. When these parts are in good
condition, the constitution is necessarily in good condition, and constitutions necessarily differ from one
another as a result of differing in each of these parts.
40 One of the three parts [1] deliberates about public
affairs; the second [2] concerns the offices, that is to
1298a say, which offices there should be, with authority
over what things, and in what way officials should be
chosen; and the third [3] is what decides lawsuits.
[1] The deliberative part has authority in relation to
war and peace, the making and breaking of alliances,
5 and laws; and in relation to death, exile, and the
confiscation of property; and in relation to the selection and inspection of officials. It is necessary that
these matters for decision [1.1] be assigned either all
to all citizens, or [1.2] all to some (to some single
office, for example, or to several, or some to some
and others to others), or [1.3] some to all and some
to some.

[1.1] For all to deliberate about all issues is characteristic of a democracy, since this is the equality the
10 people seek. But there are several ways of having all
deliberate. [1.1.1] One way is in turn rather than all
together, as in the constitution of Telecles of Miletus.
There are other constitutions too in which deliberation is carried out by boards of officials meeting
15 jointly, and all enter office in turn from the tribes
and from the smallest parts of the city-state, until
all have been gone through. In these cases all meet
together only to consider legislation and matters pertaining to the constitution, and to listen to official
20 announcements. [1.1.2] Another way is where they
all meet, but only for choosing officials, for legislation,
matters of war and peace, and for inspections; and
other matters are deliberated on by the officials chosen to deal with the particular area in question, these
being chosen from all the citizens either by election
or by lot. [1.1.3] Another way is for the citizens to
25 meet together about offices and inspections, and to
deliberate about war and alliance, and for other mat-

ters to be dealt with by offices of which as few as
possible are filled by election, these being the ones
where it is necessary to have knowledgeable people
holding office. [1.1.4] A fourth way is for all to meet
and deliberate about all matters, while the office decides nothing, but prepares issues for decision only. 30
This is the way in which the final kind of democracy
is actually managed, the one we say is analogous to
a dynastic oligarchy or a tyrannical monarchy.

All these ways, then, are democratic. But [1.2] for
some people to deliberate about all matters is oligarchic. And here too there are several varieties. [1.2.1]
For when they are chosen on the basis of more moder- 35
ate property assessments, and there are more of them
because of the moderateness of the assessments, and
where they follow the law and do not attempt to make
changes that it forbids, and where everyone who has
the assessed amount may participate — such a constitution is certainly an oligarchy, but, on account of
its moderateness, one with the character of a polity.
[1.2.2] When not everyone participates in delibera- 40
tion but only those elected, and when, as before, they 1298b
rule in accordance with law, it is oligarchic. [1.2.3]
When those who have authority over deliberation
elect themselves, and when son succeeds father, and
they have authority over the laws, this organization
is necessarily most oligarchic. [1.3] But, when some
have authority over some matters — for example, when 5
all have it over war and peace and inspections,
whereas officials who are elected, not chosen by lot,
have it in the other areas, it is an aristocracy or a
polity. But if it happens that elected officials have
authority in some areas, whereas officials chosen by
lot, either simply or from a preselected group, have
it in others, or if elected officials and officials chosen
by lot share authority, some of these are features of
an aristocratic constitution and others of polity itself. 10

This is the way, then, that the deliberative part is
distinguished in relation to the various constitutions,
and each constitution administers matters in accord
with the determinations mentioned.

In the kind of democracy that is most particularly
held to be a democracy nowadays (I mean the kind
in which the people have authority over even the
laws), it is beneficial from the point of view of improv- 15
ing deliberation to do precisely the same thing as is
done in oligarchies in regard to the courts. For they

establish a fine for those people they want to have on juries to ensure that they serve (whereas democrats pay the poor). The same should be done in the case of assemblies too, for they will deliberate better if they all deliberate together, the people with the notables, and the latter with the multitude. It is beneficial too if those who do the deliberating are elected, or chosen by lot, in equal numbers from these parts. And even if the democrats among the citizens are greatly superior in numbers, it is beneficial not to provide pay for all of them, but only for a number to balance the number of notables, or to exclude the excess by lot.

In oligarchies, however, it is beneficial either to select some additional people from the multitude of citizens to serve as officials or to establish a board of officials like the so-called preliminary councilors or law-guardians that exist in some constitutions, and then have the assembly deal only with issues that have been considered by this board. In this way, the people will share in deliberation, but will not be able to abolish anything connected to the constitution. It is also beneficial to have the people vote only on decrees brought before them that have already undergone preliminary deliberation, or on nothing contrary to them, or else to let all advise and have only officials deliberate. One should in fact do the opposite of what happens in polities. For the multitude should have authority when vetoing measures but not when approving them; in the latter case, they should be referred back to the officials instead. For in polities, they do the contrary, since the few have authority when vetoing decrees but not when passing them; decrees of the latter sort are always referred to the majority instead.

This, then, is the way the deliberative part, the part that has authority over the constitution, should be determined.

Chapter 15

[2] Next after these things comes the division of the offices. For this part of a constitution too has many varieties: how many offices there are; with authority over what things; with regard to time: how long each office is to last (some make it six months, some less, some make it a year, some a longer period); and

whether they are to be held permanently or for a long time, or neither of these, but instead to be held by the same person several times, or not even twice but only once; and further, as regards the selection of officials: from whom they should come, by whom, and how. For one should be able to determine how many ways all these can be handled, and then fit the kinds of offices to the kinds of constitutions for which they are beneficial.

But even to determine what should be called an office is not easy. For a political community needs many sorts of supervisors, so that not everyone who is selected by vote or by lot can be regarded as an official. In the first place, for example, there are the priests: for a priesthood must be regarded as something other than and apart from the political offices. Besides, patrons of the theater and heralds are elected, ambassadors too. But some sorts of supervision *are* political, either concerned with all the citizens involved in a certain activity (as a general supervises those who are serving as soldiers) or some part of them (for example, the supervisors of women or children). Some are related to household management (for corn rationers are often elected), while others are subordinate, and are of the sort that, when there are the resources, are assigned to slaves.

Simply speaking, however, the offices most properly so called are those to which are assigned deliberation, decision, and issuing orders about certain matters, especially the latter, since issuing orders is most characteristic of office. This problem makes scarcely any difference in practice, but since terminological disputes have not been resolved, there is some theoretical work yet to be done.

One might rather raise a problem with regard to any constitution about what sorts of offices and how many of them are necessary for the existence of a city-state, and which sorts, though not necessary, are yet useful with a view to an excellent constitution, but one might particularly raise it with regard to constitutions in small city-states. For in large city-states one can and should assign a single office to a single task. For because there are many citizens, there are many people to take up office, so that some offices are held again only after a long interval and others are held only once. Also every task is better performed when its supervision is handled as a single

matter rather than as one matter among many. In
small city-states, however, many offices have to be
co-assigned to a few people, since underpopulation
makes it hard to have a lot of people in office; for
who will succeed them in their turn? But sometimes
small city-states need the same offices and laws as
large ones, except that the latter need the same ones
often, whereas the former need them only at long
intervals. That is why, indeed, nothing prevents their
assigning many types of supervision at the same time
(for they will not impede one another), and why,
because of underpopulation, they must make their
boards of officials like spit-lamps.

If, then, we can say how many offices every city-
state must have, and how many it need not but should
have, it will be easier, in the light of this, to determine
which offices it is appropriate to combine into a single
office. It is also appropriate not to overlook the question of which matters should be supervised by many
boards of officials on a local basis, and which a single
office should everywhere have authority over. For
example, good order: should a market supervisor have
authority over this in the marketplace, and another
official in another place, or the same one everywhere?
Should the offices be distinguished by their tasks or
by the people they deal with? I mean, for example,
whether there should be a single office for good order,
or one for children and another for women. And with
regard to the constitutions too, whether the types of
offices also differ in each, or not at all. For example,
whether in a democracy, an oligarchy, an aristocracy,
and a monarchy, the same offices have authority, even
though they are not composed of equal or similar
people, but from different sorts in different constitutions (the generally educated in aristocracies, the rich
in oligarchies, and the free in democracies), or
whether certain offices exist precisely because constitutions differ, with sometimes the same offices and
sometimes different ones being beneficial (since it is
appropriate for the same office to be large in some
places and small in others).

Some offices are indeed peculiar to particular constitutions, for example, that of the preliminary councilors. For it is undemocratic, whereas a council is
democratic, since there must be some body of this
sort to take care of preliminary deliberation on behalf
of the people, so that they can do their work. This is

oligarchic if the councilors are few in number; but the
preliminary councilors are necessarily few in number,
and so this arrangement is oligarchic. Where both
these offices exist, however, the preliminary councilors are established as a check on the councilors; for
a councilor is democratic, a preliminary councilor,
oligarchic. But the power of the council is also destroyed in those kinds of democracies in which the
people themselves come together and transact all
business. This is the usual result when those who
attend the assembly either are rich or receive pay,
since they then have the leisure to meet often and
decide everything themselves. The supervisor of children, the supervisor of women, and any other office
that has authority over this sort of supervision, is an
aristocratic feature, not democratic (for how can one
prevent the women of the poor from going outdoors?)
or oligarchic (since the women of oligarchs live luxu-
riously).

So much about these matters for now, but as regards
the selection of officials, we must try to go through
things from the beginning. Differences here lie in
three defining principles, the combination of which
necessarily yields all the different ways. Of these three,
the first is [2.1] who selects the officials, second, [2.2]
from whom, and, lastly, [2.3] in what way. Of each
of these there are three different varieties. Either
[2.1.1] all the citizens select or [2.1.2] some do; and
they select either [2.2.1] from all or [2.2.2] from
certain specified people (determined by a property
assessment, for example, or by birth, virtue, or some
other such feature, as in Megara where they selected
from those who had returned from exile together and
fought in alliance against the people); and they select
either [2.3.1] by election or [2.3.2] by lot; and, again,
these may be paired—I mean that [2.1.3] all may
select for some offices and some for others, [2.2.3]
some offices may be selected for from all and others
from some, and [2.3.3] some may be selected for by
lot and others by election.

In the case of each of these varieties, there are four
different ways to proceed. Either all select from all
by election or all select from all by lot (and from all
either by sections—by tribe, for example, or by deme
or clan, until all the citizens have been gone
through—or from all on every occasion); or from
some by election or from some by lot; or partly in

the first way and partly in the second. Again, if only some do the selecting, they may do so either from all by election or from all by lot; or from some by election or from some by lot; or partly in the first way and partly in the second—that is to say, for some
30 from all by election and for some by lot. This gives rise to twelve ways, setting aside two of the combinations. Three of these ways of selecting are democratic, namely, when all select from all by election, by lot, or by both (that is, for some offices by election and for some by lot). But when not all select at the same time, but do so for all from all or from some, whether
35 by election, lot, or both, or from all for some offices and from some for others, whether by election, lot, or both (by "both," I mean some by lot and others by election)—it is characteristic of a polity. When some appoint from all, whether by election, lot, or both (for some offices by lot for others by vote), it is oligarchic—although it is more oligarchic to do so
40 by both. But when some offices are selected for from all and others from some or when some are selected for by election and some by vote, this is characteristic
1300b of an aristocratic polity. When some select from some by election, it is oligarchic; also when some select from some by lot (even though this does not happen), and when some select from some in both ways. But when some select from all, and when all select from some by election, it is aristocratic.
5   These, then, are the number of ways of selecting for offices, and this is how they are distinguished in relation to the constitutions. It will become evident which ways are beneficial for which constitutions, and how selections are to be made, when we determine the powers of the offices, and which these are. By the "power of an office" I mean, for example,
10 having authority over revenues or authority over defense. For the kind of power of a generalship, for example, is different from that of authority over marketplace contracts.

Chapter 16

Of the three parts, it remains to speak about [3] the judicial. And we must grasp the ways that it can be organized by following the same supposition as before. The differences between courts are found in
15 three defining principles: from whom; about what; and how. From whom: I mean whether they are selected from all or from some. About what: how many kinds of courts are there. How: whether by lot or by election.

First, then, let us distinguish how many kinds of courts there are. They are eight in number. One is [i] concerned with inspection. Another [ii] deals with anyone who wrongs the community. Another [iii] 20 with matters that affect the constitution. A fourth [iv] deals with officials and private individuals in disputes about fines. A fifth [v] deals with private transactions of some magnitude. Besides these there is [vi] a court that deals with homicide and [vii] one that deals with aliens. The kinds of homicide court, whether having the same juries or not, are: [vi.1] that concerned with premeditated homicide, [vi.2] that concerned with in- 25 voluntary homicide, [vi.3] that concerned with cases where there is agreement on the fact of homicide but the justice of it disputed, and a fourth [vi.4] concerned with charges brought against those who have been exiled for homicide after their return (the court of Phreatto in Athens is said to be an example), but such cases are rare at any time even in large city-states. The aliens' court has [vii.1] a part for aliens disputing with 30 aliens and [vii.2] a part for aliens disputing with citizens. Besides all these, there is [viii] a court that deals with petty transactions: those involving one drachma, five drachmas, or a little more (for judgment must be given in these cases too, but it should not fall to a multitude of jurors to give it). 35

But let us set aside these courts as well as the homicide and aliens' courts and talk about the political ones, which, when not well managed, give rise to factions and constitutional changes. Of necessity, there are just the following possibilities: [3.1] All decide all the cases just distinguished, and are selected either [3.1.1] by lot or [3.1.2] by election; or [3.1] all decide all of them, and [3.1.3] some are selected by 40 lot and some by election; or, [3.1.4] although dealing with the same case, some jurors may be selected by lot and some by election. Thus these ways are four in number. [3.2] There are as many again when 1301a selection is from only some of the citizens. For here again either [3.2.1] the juries are selected from some by election and decide all cases; or [3.2.2] they are selected from some by lot and decide all cases; or [3.2.3] some may be selected by lot and some by

election; or [3.2.4] some courts dealing with the same
5 cases may be composed of both members selected
by lot and elected members. These ways, as we said,
are the counterparts of the ones we mentioned earlier.
[3.3] Furthermore, these same ones may be conjoined—I mean, for example, some may be selected
from all, others from some, and others from both (as
for example if the same court had juries selected partly
from all and partly from some); and the selection may
be either by lot or by election or by both.
10   We have now listed the possible ways the courts
can be organized. Of these the first, [3.1] those which
are selected from all and decide all cases, are democratic. The second [3.2], those which are selected
from some and decide all cases, are oligarchic. The
third [3.3], those which are partly selected from all
and partly from some, are aristocratic or characteristic
15 of a polity.

BOOK VII

Chapter 1

Anyone who intends to investigate the best constitution in the proper way must first determine which
15 life is most choiceworthy, since if this remains unclear, what the best constitution is must also remain
unclear. For it is appropriate for those to fare best
who live in the best constitution their circumstances
allow—provided nothing contrary to reasonable expectation occurs. That is why we should first come
to some agreement about what the most choiceworthy
life is for practically speaking everyone, and then
20 determine whether it is the same for an individual
as for a community, or different.

Since, then, I consider that I have already expressed
much that is adequate about the best life in the "external" works, I propose to make use of them here as
well. For since, in the case of one division at least,
25 there are three groups—external goods, goods of the
body, and goods of the soul—surely no one would
raise a dispute and say that not all of them need be
possessed by those who are blessedly happy. For no
one would call a person blessedly happy who has no
shred of courage, temperance, justice, or practical
wisdom, but is afraid of the flies buzzing around him,

stops at nothing to gratify his appetite for food or 30
drink, betrays his dearest friends for a pittance, and
has a mind as foolish and prone to error as a child's
or a madman's. But while almost all accept these
claims, they disagree about quantity and relative supe- 35
riority. For they consider any amount of virtue, however small, to be sufficient, but seek an unlimitedly
excessive amount of wealth, possessions, power, reputation, and the like.

We, however, will say to them that it is easy to
reach a reliable conclusion on these matters even
from the facts themselves. For we see that the virtues
are not acquired and preserved by means of external 40
goods, but the other way around, and we see that a
happy life for human beings, whether it consists in
pleasure or virtue or both, is possessed more often by 1323b
those who have cultivated their characters and minds
to an excessive degree, but have been moderate in
their acquisition of external goods, than by those who
have acquired more of the latter than they can possibly
use, but are deficient in the former. Moreover, if we 5
investigate the matter on the basis of argument, it is
plain to see. For external goods have a limit, as does
any tool, and all useful things are useful for something; so excessive amounts of them must harm or
bring no benefit to their possessors. In the case of
each of the goods of the soul, however, the more
excessive it is, the more useful it is (if these goods 10
too should be thought of as useful, and not simply
as noble).

It is generally clear too, we shall say, that the relation of superiority holding between the best condition
of each thing and that of others corresponds to that
holding between the things whose conditions we say
they are. So since the soul is unqualifiedly more 15
valuable, and also more valuable to us, than possessions or the body, its best states must be proportionally
better than theirs. Besides, it is for the sake of the
soul that these things are naturally choiceworthy, and
every sensible person should choose them for its sake,
not the soul for theirs. 20

We may take it as agreed, then, that each person
has just as much happiness as he has virtue, practical
wisdom, and the action that expresses them. We may
use God as evidence of this. For he is blessedly happy,
not because of any external goods but because of
himself and a certain quality in his nature. This is

25 also the reason that good luck and happiness are necessarily different. For chance or luck produces goods external to the soul, but no one is just or temperate as a result of luck or because of luck.

30   The next point depends on the same arguments. The happy city-state is the one that is best and acts nobly. It is impossible for those who do not do noble deeds to act nobly; and no action, whether a man's or a city-state's, is noble when separate from virtue and practical wisdom. But the courage, justice, and practical wisdom of a city-state have the same capacity 35 and are of the same kind as those possessed by each human being who is said to be just, practically wise, and temperate.

So much, then, for the preface to our discussion. For we cannot avoid talking about these issues altogether, but neither can we go through all the arguments pertaining to them, since that is a task for another type of study. But for now, let us assume this 40 much, that the best life, both for individuals separately and for city-states collectively, is a life of virtue sufficiently equipped with the resources needed to take part in virtuous actions. With regard to those who 1324a dispute this, if any happen not to be persuaded by what has been said, we must ignore them in our present study, but investigate them later.

Chapter 2

5 It remains to say whether the happiness of each individual human being is the same as that of a city-state or not. But here too the answer is evident, since everyone would agree that they are the same. For those who suppose that living well for an individual consists in wealth will also call a whole city-state blessedly happy if it happens to be wealthy. And those 10 who honor the tyrannical life above all would claim that the city-state that rules the greatest number is happiest. And if someone approves of an individual because of his virtue, he will also say that the more excellent city-state is happier.

Two questions need to be investigated, however. First, which life is more choiceworthy, the one that involves taking part in politics with other people and 15 participating in a city-state, or the life of an alien cut off from the political community? Second, and regardless of whether participating in a city-state is more choiceworthy for everyone or for most but not for all, which constitution, which condition of the city-state, is best? This second question, and not the 20 one about what is choiceworthy for the individual, is a task for political thought or theory. And since that is the investigation we are now engaged in, whereas the former is a further task, our task is the second question.

It is evident that the best constitution must be that organization in which anyone might do best and live a blessedly happy life. But the very people who agree 25 that the most choiceworthy life is the life of virtue are the ones who dispute about whether it is the political life of action that is worthy of choice or rather the one released from external concerns—a contemplative life, for example, which some say is the only life for a philosopher. For it is evident that almost all of those, past or present, with the greatest love for the honor accorded to virtue have chosen between these two lives (I mean the political life 30 and the philosophic one). And it makes no small difference on which side the truth lies, since anyone with sound practical wisdom at least must organize his affairs by looking to the better target—and this applies to human beings individually and to the constitution communally.

Some people think that ruling over one's neighbors 35 like a master involves one of the greatest injustices, and that rule of a statesman, though it involves no injustice, does involve an impediment to one's own well-being. Others think almost the opposite, they say that an active, political life is the only one for a man, since the actions expressing each of the virtues are 40 no more available to private individuals than to those engaged in communal affairs and politics. Some give 1324b this reply, then, but others claim that only a constitution that involves being a master or tyrant is happy.

For some people, indeed, the fundamental aim of the constitution and the laws just is to rule their neighbors like a master. That is why, even though most customs have been established pretty much at 5 random in most cases, anywhere the laws have to some extent a single aim, it is always domination. So in Sparta and Crete the educational system and most of the laws are set up for war. Besides, all the nations that have the power to be acquisitive honor mili- 10 tary power—for example, the Scythians, Persians,

Thracians, and Celts. Indeed, some of them even have laws designed to foster military virtue. It is said that in Carthage, for example, they receive armlets as decorations for each campaign in which they take
15 part. There was once a law in Macedonia too that any man who had not killed an enemy must wear a halter for a belt. Among the Scythians, when the cup passes around at a feast, those who have not killed an enemy are not permitted to drink from it. And among the Iberians, a warlike race, they place small obelisks in the earth around a man's tomb to show
20 the number of enemies he has killed. And there are many other similar practices among other peoples, some prescribed by law, others by custom.

Yet to anyone willing to investigate the matter, it would perhaps seem quite absurd if the task of a statesman involved being able to study ways to rule
25 or master his neighbors, whether they are willing or not. For how could this be a political or legislative task, when it is not even lawful? But to rule not only justly but also unjustly is unlawful, whereas it is quite possible to dominate unjustly. Certainly, this is not what we see in the other sciences; for it is not the
30 doctor's or captain's task to use force on his patients or passengers if he cannot persuade them. Yet many seem to think that statesmanship is the same as mastership, and what they all say is unjust or nonbeneficial when it is done to them, they are not ashamed to do to others. For they seek just rule for themselves, but
35 pay no attention to justice in their dealings with others. It is absurd to deny, however, that one thing is fit to be a master and another not fit to be a master. So, if indeed one is that way, one should not try to rule as a master over everyone, but only over those who are fit to be ruled by a master. Similarly, one should not hunt human beings for a feast or sacrifice,
40 but only animals that are fit to be hunted for these purposes: and that is any wild animal that is edible.

Furthermore, it is possible for even a single city-state to be happy all by itself, provided it is well
1325a governed, since it is possible for a city-state to be settled somewhere by itself and to employ excellent laws. And *its* constitution will not be organized for the purposes of war or of dominating its enemies (for we are assuming that it has none).
5 It is clear, therefore, that all military practices are to be regarded as noble, not when they are pursued

as the highest end of all, but only when they are pursued for the sake of the highest end. The task of an excellent legislator, then, is to study how a city-state, a race of men, or any other community can come to have a share in a good life and in the hap-piness that is possible for them. There will be dif- 10 ferences, of course, in some of the laws that are instituted, and if there are neighboring peoples, it belongs to legislative science to consider what sorts of military training are needed in relation to which sorts of people and which measures are to be used in relation to each.

But the question of which end the best constitution should aim at will receive a proper investigation later. 15

Chapter 3

We must now reply to the two sides who agree that the virtuous life is most choiceworthy, but disagree about how to practice it. For some rule out the hold-ing of political office and consider that the life of a free person is both different from that of a statesman and the most choiceworthy one of all. But others consider that the political life is best, since it is impos- 20 sible for someone inactive to do or act well, and that doing well and happiness are the same. We must reply that they are both partly right and partly wrong. On the one hand, it is true to say that the life of a free person is better than that of a master. For there is certainly nothing grand about using a slave as a slave, since ordering people to do necessary tasks is 25 in no way noble. None the less, it is wrong to consider that every kind of rule is rule by a master. For the difference between rule over free people and over slaves is no smaller than the difference between being naturally free and being a natural slave. We have adequately distinguished them in our first discussions. 30 On the other hand, to praise inaction more than action is not correct either. For happiness is action, and many noble things reach their end in the actions of those who are just and temperate.

Perhaps someone will take these conclusions to imply, however, that having authority over everyone is what is best. For in that way one would have author- 35 ity over the greatest number of the very noblest ac-tions. It would follow that someone who has the power to rule should not surrender it to his neighbor but take it away from him, and that a father should disregard his children, a child his father, a friend his friend, and pay no attention to anything except ruling. For 40 what is best is most choiceworthy, and doing well is best.

What they say is perhaps true, if indeed those who 1325b use force and commit robbery will come to possess the most choiceworthy thing there is. But perhaps they cannot come to possess it, and the underlying assumption here is false. For someone cannot do noble actions if he is not as superior to those he rules as a husband is to his wife, a father to his children, 5 or a master to his slaves. Therefore, a transgressor could never make up later for his deviation from virtue. For among those who are similar, ruling and being ruled in turn is just and noble, since this is equal or similar treatment. But unequal shares for equals or dissimilar ones for similars is contrary to nature; and nothing contrary to nature is noble. 10 Hence when someone else has superior virtue and his power to do the best things is also superior, it is noble to follow and just to obey him. But he should possess not virtue alone, but also the power he needs to do these things.

If these claims are correct, and we should assume that happiness is doing well, then the best life, whether for a whole city-state collectively or for an 15 individual, would be a life of action. Yet it is not necessary, as some suppose, for a life of action to involve relations with other people, nor are those thoughts alone active which we engage in for the sake of action's consequences; the study and thought that are their own ends and are engaged in for their 20 own sake are much more so. For to do or act well is the end, so that action of a sort is the end too. And even in the case of actions involving external objects, the one who does them most fully is, strictly speaking, the master craftsman who directs them by means of his thought.

Moreover, city-states situated by themselves, which have deliberately chosen to live that way, do not necessarily have to be inactive, since activity can take 25 place even among their parts. For the parts of a city-state have many sorts of communal relationships with one another. Similarly, this holds for any human being taken singly. For otherwise God and the entire universe could hardly be in a fine condition; for they have no external actions, only the internal ones proper to them.

It is evident, then, that the same life is necessarily 30 best both for each human being and for city-states and human beings collectively.

Chapter 13

But we must now discuss the constitution itself, and from which and what sorts of people a city-state should be constituted if it is to be blessedly happy and well governed. In all cases, well-being consists in two 25 things: setting up the aim and end of action correctly and discovering the actions that bear on it. These factors can be in harmony with one another or in disharmony. For people sometimes set up the end 30 well but fail to achieve it in action; and sometimes they achieve everything that promotes the end, but the end they set up is a bad one. Sometimes they make both mistakes. For example, in medicine it sometimes happens that doctors are neither correct in their judgment about what condition a healthy body should be in, nor successful in producing the 35 condition they have set up as their end. In the crafts and sciences both of these have to be under control, the end and the actions directed toward it. It is evident that everyone aims at living well and at happiness. But while some can achieve these ends, others, whether 40 because of luck or because of something in their nature, cannot. For we also need resources in order to live a good life, although we need fewer of them 1332a if we are in a better condition, more if we are in a worse one. Others, though they could achieve happiness, search for it in the wrong place from the outset. But since we are proposing to look at the best constitution, and this is the one under which a city-state will be best governed, and since a city-state is best governed under a constitution that would above all 5 make it possible for the city-state to be happy, it is clear that we should not overlook the question of what happiness actually is.

We say, and we have given this definition in our ethical works (if anything in those discussions is of service), that happiness is a complete activation or use of virtue, and not a qualified use but an unqualified one. By "qualified uses" I mean those that are 10 necessary; by "unqualified" I mean those that are noble. For example, in the case of just actions, just retributions and punishments spring from virtue, but are necessary uses of it, and are noble only in a necessary way, since it would be more choiceworthy if no individual or city-state needed such things. On 15 the other hand, just actions that aim at honors and prosperity are unqualifiedly noblest. The former involve choosing something that is somehow bad, whereas the latter are the opposite: they construct and generate goods. To be sure, an excellent man will deal with poverty, disease, and other sorts of bad 20 luck in a noble way. But blessed happiness requires their opposites. For according to the definition established in our ethical works, an excellent man is the sort whose virtue makes *unqualifiedly* good things good *for him*. Clearly, then, his use of them must also be unqualifiedly good and noble. That is why people think that external goods are the causes of 25 happiness. Yet we might as well hold that a lyre is the cause of fine and brilliant lyre playing, and not the performer's craft. It follows, then, from what has been said, that some goods must be there to start with, whereas others must be provided by the legislator. That is why we pray that our city-state will be ideally equipped with the goods that luck controls 30 (for we assume that luck does control them). When we come to making the city-state excellent, however, that is no longer a task for luck but one for scientific knowledge and deliberate choice. A city-state is excellent, however, because the citizens who participate in the constitution are excellent; and in our city-state

all the citizens participate in the constitution. The matter we have to investigate, therefore, is how a man becomes excellent. For even if it is possible for all 35 the citizens to be collectively excellent without being so individually, the latter is still more choiceworthy, since if each is excellent, all are.

But surely people become excellent because of three things. The three are nature, habit, and reason. For first [1] one must possess a certain nature from 40 birth, namely, that of a human, and not that of some other animal. Similarly, one's body and soul must be of a certain sort. But in the case of some of these qualities, there is no benefit in just being born with them, because they are altered by our habits. [2] 1332b For some qualities are naturally capable of being developed by habit either in a better direction or in a worse one. The other animals mostly live under the guidance of nature alone, although some are guided a little by habit. [3] But human beings live under the guidance of reason as well, since they alone have reason. Consequently, all three of these factors need 5 to be harmonized with one another. For people often act contrary to their habits and their nature because of reason, if they happen to be persuaded that some other course of action is better.

We have already determined the sorts of natures people should have if it is to be easy for the legislator to take them in hand. Everything thereafter is a task for education. For some things are learned by habituation, others by instruction. 10

EPICURUS

Often, in the course of Western culture, morality and politics overlap. In the thought of Epicurus (341–271 B.C.E.), they do not, and this fact alone makes him an especially interesting figure, for in the ancient Greek world ethics and the good life were generally conceived in political terms. Hence, it would be surprising if Epicurus' rejection of political involvement were not in part a reaction to the thought of Plato and Aristotle and a return, in a sense, to Socratic thinking and an intense type of psychological therapy. Moreover, it would also be surprising if Epicurus' denial of the political, the avoidance of turbulence and fear, and the striving for psychological equilibrium were not in part a reaction to the pressures of the times—the achievements of Alexander, his death, the fragmentation of the empire, the increased familiarity among diverse cultures, and political crisis.

Epicurus was born on the island of Samos, off the coast of Asia Minor. His father was an Athenian citizen, and Epicurus at eighteen traveled to Athens to perform his military service. At about that time Alexander died, Aristotle left Athens and died a year later, and the Lyceum, Aristotle's school, came under new leadership. Epicurus seems to have returned to live with his family in Colophon and then to have organized his own philosophical circle first in Lesbos and then in Lampsacus, before moving to Athens in 307/306 B.C.E. He remained in Athens until his death in 271.

Upon his return to Athens, Epicurus purchased a house outside the city gates and founded a school, the "Garden," a kind of religious fellowship or society of friends. Apparently Epicurus had followers throughout the Greek world, and he kept in touch with many of them by means of letters, of which some fragments have survived. Epicurus wrote a great deal; Diogenes Laertius, the third-century doxographer, records forty-one of Epicurus' 'best books' and notes that no previous writer had greater productivity. Of this massive corpus, however, only a small portion remains, principally three letters quoted by Diogenes (*To Herodotus*, *To Pythocles*, and *To Menoeceus*), a collection of forty maxims or "principal doctrines" also quoted in Diogenes, and the quantity of Epicurean teaching cited and employed in Lucretius' *De rerum natura* (*On the Nature of Things*).

As A. A. Long has put it, "Epicurus' philosophy is a strange mixture of hard-headed empiricism, speculative metaphysics, and rules for the attainment of a tranquil life." That is, he develops a theory of knowledge that is grounded in sensation and sensory evidence. On this basis, Epicurus accounts for concepts, statements, truth, and rules of logic. He then proceeds to draw on the pre-Socratic atomists, Leucippus and Democritus, to develop his own theory of atoms and the void. From this theory he gives an account of the gods, fate, free will, and such matters. Finally, Epicurus uses these accounts to show how one should live in order to reduce pain and anxiety and thereby to maximize psychic tranquility (*ataraxia*) and pleasure. For example, he argues, tranquility occurs when the knowledge of nature removes our fear of the gods and of death itself. Human beings, Epicurus claims, can dissolve illusion and prejudice and thereby achieve the freedom from pain and the peace of mind that characterize the best life. There is no voluptuary hedonism in this; Epicurus does not fit the later parody of his thought. Rather there is dignity, moderation, and detachment, born of strife and worry but seeking nobility in a world riddled with turbulence, conflict, and superstition.

Recommended Readings

Annas, Julia. *The Morality of Happiness*. Oxford: Oxford University Press, 1993.
Gerson, L., and B. Inwood (trans.). *Hellenistic Philosophy*. Indianapolis: Hackett, 1988.
Irwin, T. H. *Classical Thought*. Oxford: Oxford University Press, 1989.

Long, A. A. *Hellenistic Philosophy*. London: Duckworth, 1974.

Long, A. A., and David Sedley (trans. and commentary). *The Hellenistic Philosophers*. Vols. I and II. Cambridge: Cambridge University Press, 1987.

Mitsis, P. *Epicurus' Ethical Theory*. Ithaca: Cornell University Press, 1988.

Nussbaum, Martha. *The Therapy of Desire*. Princeton: Princeton University Press, 1994.

Prior, William. *Virtue and Knowledge: An Introduction to Ancient Greek Ethics*. London: Routledge, 1991.

Rist, John. *Epicurus*. Cambridge: Cambridge University Press, 1972.

Sharples, R. W. *Stoics, Epicureans and Sceptics*. London: Routledge, 1996.

LETTER TO MENOECEUS

Epicurus to Menoeceus, greetings:

Let no one delay the study of philosophy while young nor weary of it when old. For no one is either too young or too old for the health of the soul. He who says either that the time for philosophy has not yet come or that it has passed is like someone who says that the time for happiness has not yet come or that it has passed. Therefore, both young and old must philosophize, the latter so that although old he may stay young in good things owing to gratitude for what has occurred, the former so that although young he too may be like an old man owing to his lack of fear of what is to come. Therefore, one must practise the things which produce happiness, since if that is present we have everything and if it is absent we do everything in order to have it.

Do and practise what I constantly told you to do, believing these to be the elements of living well. First, believe that god is an indestructible and blessed animal, in accordance with the general conception of god commonly held, and do not ascribe to god anything foreign to his indestructibility or repugnant to his blessedness. Believe of him everything which is able to preserve his blessedness and indestructibility. For gods do exist, since we have clear knowledge of them. But they are not such as the many believe them to be. For they do not adhere to their own views about the gods. The man who denies the gods of the many is not impious, but rather he who ascribes to the gods the opinions of the many. For the pronouncements of the many about the gods are not basic grasps but false suppositions. Hence come the greatest harm from the gods to bad men and the greatest benefits [to the good]. For the gods always welcome men who are like themselves, being congenial to their own virtues and considering that whatever is not such is uncongenial.

Get used to believing that death is nothing to us. For all good and bad consists in sense-experience, and death is the privation of sense-experience. Hence, a correct knowledge of the fact that death is nothing to us makes the mortality of life a matter for contentment, not by adding a limitless time [to life] but by removing the longing for immortality. For there is nothing fearful in life for one who has grasped that there is nothing fearful in the absence of life. Thus, he is a fool who says that he fears death not because it will be painful when present but because it is painful when it is still to come. For that which while present causes no distress causes unnecessary pain when merely anticipated. So death, the most frightening of bad things, is nothing to us; since when we exist, death is not yet present, and when death is present, then we do not exist. Therefore, it is relevant neither to the living nor to the dead, since it does not affect the former, and the latter do not exist. But the many sometimes flee death as the greatest of bad things and sometimes choose it as a relief from the bad things of life. But the wise man neither rejects life nor fears death. For living does not offend him, nor does he believe not living to be something bad. And just as he does not unconditionally choose the largest amount of food but the most pleasant food, so he savours not the longest time but the most pleasant. He who advises the young man to live well and the old man to die well is simple-minded, not just because of the pleasing aspects of life but because the same kind of practice produces a good life and a good death. Much worse is he who says that it is good not to be born, "but when born to pass through the gates of Hades as quickly as possible."[1] For if he really

From *Hellenistic Philosophy*, translated and edited by Brad Inwood and L. P. Gerson (Indianapolis: Hackett Publishing Company, 1988). Reprinted by permission of the publisher.

1. [Theognis 425, 427.—B.I. and L.P.G.]

believes what he says, why doesn't he leave life? For it is easy for him to do, if he has firmly decided on it. But if he is joking, he is wasting his time among men who don't welcome it. We must remember that what will happen is neither unconditionally within our power nor unconditionally outside our power, so that we will not unconditionally expect that it will occur nor despair of it as unconditionally not going to occur.

One must reckon that of desires some are natural, some groundless; and of the natural desires some are necessary and some merely natural; and of the necessary, some are necessary for happiness and some for freeing the body from troubles and some for life itself. The unwavering contemplation of these enables one to refer every choice and avoidance to the health of the body and the freedom of the soul from disturbance, since this is the goal of a blessed life. For we do everything for the sake of being neither in pain nor in terror. As soon as we achieve this state every storm in the soul is dispelled, since the animal is not in a passion to go after some need nor to seek something else to complete the good of the body and the soul. For we are in need of pleasure only when we are in pain because of the absence of pleasure, and when we are not in pain, then we no longer need pleasure.

And this is why we say that pleasure is the starting-point and goal of living blessedly. For we recognized this as our first innate good, and this is our starting point for every choice and avoidance and we come to this by judging every good by the criterion of feeling. And it is just because this is the first innate good, that we do not choose every pleasure; but sometimes we pass up many pleasures when we get a larger amount of what is uncongenial from them. And we believe many pains to be better than pleasures when a greater pleasure follows for a long while if we endure the pains. So every pleasure is a good thing, since it has a nature congenial [to us], but not every one is to be chosen. Just as every pain too is a bad thing, but not every one is such as to be always avoided. It is, however, appropriate to make all these decisions by comparative measurement and an examination of the advantages and disadvantages. For at some times we treat the good things as bad and conversely, the bad things as good.

And we believe that self-sufficiency is a great good, not in order that we might make do with few things under all circumstances, but so that if we do not have a lot we can make do with few, being genuinely convinced that those who least need extravagance enjoy it most; and that everything natural is easy to obtain and whatever is groundless is hard to obtain; and that simple flavours provide a pleasure equal to that of an extravagant life-style when all pain from want is removed, and barley cakes and water provide the highest pleasure when someone in want takes them. Therefore, becoming accustomed to simple, not extravagant, ways of life makes one completely healthy, makes man unhesitant in the face of life's necessary duties, puts us in a better condition for the times of extravagance which occasionally come along, and makes us fearless in the face of chance. So when we say that pleasure is the goal we do not mean the pleasures of the profligate or the pleasures of consumption, as some believe, either from ignorance and disagreement or from deliberate misinterpretation, but rather the lack of pain in the body and disturbance in the soul. For it is not drinking bouts and continuous partying and enjoying boys and women, or consuming fish and the other dainties of an extravagant table, which produce the pleasant life, but sober calculation which searches out the reasons for every choice and avoidance and drives out the opinions which are the source of the greatest turmoil for men's souls.

Prudence is the principle of all these things and is the greatest good. That is why prudence is a more valuable thing than philosophy. For prudence is the source of all the other virtues, teaching that it is impossible to live pleasantly without living prudently, honourably, and justly, and impossible to live prudently, honourably, and justly without living pleasantly. For the virtues are natural adjuncts of the pleasant life and the pleasant life is inseparable from them.

For who do you believe is better than a man who has pious opinions about the gods, is always fearless about death, has reasoned out the natural goal of life and understands that the limit of good things is easy to achieve completely and easy to provide, and that the limit of bad things either has a short duration or causes little trouble?

As to [Fate], introduced by some as the mistress of

all, ⟨he is scornful, saying rather that some things happen of necessity,⟩ others by chance and others by our own agency, and that he sees that necessity is not answerable [to anyone], that chance is unstable, while what occurs by our own agency is autonomous, and that it is to this that praise and blame are attached. For it would be better to follow the stories told about the gods than to be a slave to the fate of the natural philosophers. For the former suggests a hope of escaping bad things by honouring the gods, but the latter involves an inescapable and merciless necessity. And he [the wise man] believes that chance is not a god, as the many think, for nothing is done in a disorderly way by god; nor that it is an uncertain cause. For he does not think that anything good or bad with respect to living blessedly is given by chance to men, although it does provide the starting points of great good and bad things. And he thinks it better to be unlucky in a rational way than lucky in a senseless way; for it is better for a good decision not to turn out right in action than for a bad decision to turn out right because of chance.

Practise these and the related precepts day and night, by yourself and with a like-minded friend, and you will never be disturbed either when awake or in sleep, and you will live as a god among men. For a man who lives among immortal goods is in no respect like a mere mortal animal.

Principal Doctrines

I. What is blessed and indestructible has no troubles itself, nor does it give trouble to anyone else, so that it is not affected by feelings of anger or gratitude. For all such things are a sign of weakness.[1]

II. Death is nothing to us. For what has been dissolved has no sense-experience, and what has no sense-experience is nothing to us.

III. The removal of all feeling of pain is the limit of the magnitude of pleasures. Wherever a pleasurable feeling is present, for as long as it is present, there is neither a feeling of pain nor a feeling of distress, nor both together.

IV. The feeling of pain does not linger continuously in the flesh; rather, the sharpest is present for the shortest time, while what merely exceeds the feeling of pleasure in the flesh lasts only a few days. And diseases which last a long time involve feelings of pleasure which exceed feelings of pain.

V. It is impossible to live pleasantly without living prudently, honourably, and justly and impossible to live prudently, honourably, and justly without living pleasantly. And whoever lacks this cannot live pleasantly.

VI. The natural good of public office and kingship is for the sake of getting confidence from [other] men, [at least] from those from whom one *is* able to provide this.

VII. Some men want to become famous and respected, believing that this is the way to acquire security against [other] men. Thus if the life of such men is secure, they acquire the natural good; but if it is not secure, they do not have that for the sake of which they strove from the beginning according to what is naturally congenial.

VIII. No pleasure is a bad thing in itself. But the things which produce certain pleasures bring troubles many times greater than the pleasures.

IX. If every pleasure were condensed and were present, both in time and in the whole compound [body and soul] or in the most important parts of our nature, then pleasures would never differ from one another.

X. If the things which produce the pleasures of profligate men dissolved the intellect's fears about the phenomena of the heavens and about death and pains and, moreover, if they taught us the limit of our desires, then we would not have reason to criticize them, since they would be filled with pleasures from every source and would contain no feeling of pain or distress from any source—and that is what is bad.

XI. If our suspicions about heavenly phenomena and about death did not trouble us at all and were never anything to us, and, moreover, if not knowing the limits of pains and desires did not trouble us, then we would have no need of natural science.

XII. It was impossible for someone ignorant about the nature of the universe but still suspicious about the subjects of the myths to dissolve his feelings of fear about the most important matters. So it was impossible to receive unmixed pleasures without knowing natural science.

XIII. It was useless to obtain security from men while the things above and below the earth and, generally, the things in the unbounded remained as objects of suspicion.

XIV. The purest security is that which comes from a quiet life and withdrawal from the many, although a certain degree of security from other men does come by means of the power to repel [attacks] and by means of prosperity.

XV. Natural wealth is both limited and easy to acquire. But wealth [as defined by] groundless opinions extends without limit.

---

1. [Scholiast: "Elsewhere he says that the gods are contemplated by reason, and that some exist 'numerically' [i.e., are numerically distinct, each being unique in kind] while others are similar in form, because of a continuous flow of similar images to the same place; and that they are anthropomorphic."—B.I. and L.P.G.]

. XVI. Chance has a small impact on the wise man, while reasoning has arranged for, is arranging for, and will arrange for the greatest and most important matters throughout the whole of his life.

XVII. The just life is most free from disturbance, but the unjust life is full of the greatest disturbance.

XVIII. As soon as the feeling of pain produced by want is removed, pleasure in the flesh will not increase but is only varied. But the limit of mental pleasures is produced by a reasoning out of these very pleasures [of the flesh] and of the things related to these, which used to cause the greatest fears in the intellect.

XIX. Unlimited time and limited time contain equal [amounts of] pleasure, if one measures its limits by reasoning.

XX. The flesh took the limits of pleasure to be unlimited, and [only] an unlimited time would have provided it. But the intellect, reasoning out the goal and limit of the flesh and dissolving the fears of eternity, provided us with the perfect way of life and had no further need of unlimited time. But it [the intellect] did not flee pleasure, and even when circumstances caused an exit from life it did not die as though it were lacking any aspect of the best life.

XXI. He who has learned the limits of life knows that it is easy to provide that which removes the feeling of pain owing to want and makes one's whole life perfect. So there is no need for things which involve struggle.

XXII. One must reason about the real goal and every clear fact, to which we refer mere opinions. If not, everything will be full of indecision and disturbance.

XXIII. If you quarrel with all your sense-perceptions you will have nothing to refer to in judging even those sense-perceptions which you claim are false.

XXIV. If you reject unqualifiedly any sense-perception and do not distinguish the opinion about what awaits confirmation, and what is already present in the sense-perception, and the feelings, and every application of the intellect to presentations, you will also disturb the rest of your sense-perceptions with your pointless opinions; as a result you will reject every criterion. If, on the other hand, in your conceptions formed by opinion, you affirm everything that awaits confirmation as well as what does not, you will not avoid falsehood, so that you will be in the position

of maintaining every disputable point in every decision about what is and is not correct.

XXV. If you do not, on every occasion, refer each of your actions to the goal of nature, but instead turn prematurely to some other [criterion] in avoiding or pursuing [things], your actions will not be consistent with your reasoning.

XXVI. The desires which do not bring a feeling of pain when not fulfilled are not necessary, but the desire for them is easy to dispel when they seem to be hard to achieve or to produce harm.

XXVII. Of the things which wisdom provides for the blessedness of one's whole life, by far the greatest is the possession of friendship.

XXVIII. The same understanding produces confidence about there being nothing terrible which is eternal or [even] long-lasting and has also realized that security amid even these limited [bad things] is most easily achieved through friendship.

XXIX. Of desires, some are natural and necessary, some natural and not necessary, and some neither natural nor necessary but occurring as a result of a groundless opinion.[2]

XXX. Among natural desires, those which do not lead to a feeling of pain if not fulfilled and about which there is an intense effort, these are produced by a groundless opinion and they fail to be dissolved not because of their own nature but because of the groundless opinions of mankind.

XXXI. The justice of nature is a pledge of reciprocal usefulness, [i.e.,] neither to harm one another nor be harmed.

XXXII. There was no justice or injustice with respect to all those animals which were unable to make pacts about neither harming one another nor being harmed. Similarly, [there was no justice or injustice] for all those nations which were unable or unwilling to make pacts about neither harming one another nor being harmed.

---

2. [Scholiast: "Epicurus thinks that those which liberate us from pains are natural and necessary, for example drinking in the case of thirst; natural and not necessary are those which merely provide variations of pleasure but do not remove the feeling of pain, for example expensive foods; neither natural nor necessary are, for example, crowns and the erection of statues."]

XXXIII. Justice was not a thing in its own right, but [exists] in mutual dealings in whatever places there [is] a pact about neither harming one another nor being harmed.

XXXIV. Injustice is not a bad thing in its own right, but [only] because of the fear produced by the suspicion that one will not escape the notice of those assigned to punish such actions.

XXXV. It is impossible for someone who secretly does something which men agreed [not to do] in order to avoid harming one another or being harmed to be confident that he will escape detection, even if in current circumstances he escapes detection ten thousand times. For until his death it will be uncertain whether he will continue to escape detection.

XXXVI. In general outline justice is the same for everyone; for it was something useful in mutual associations. But with respect to the peculiarities of a region or of other [relevant] causes, it does not follow that the same thing is just for everyone.

XXXVII. Of actions believed to be just, that whose usefulness in circumstances of mutual associations is supported by the testimony [of experience] has the attribute of serving as just whether it is the same for everyone or not. And if someone passes a law and it does not turn out to be in accord with what is useful in mutual associations, this no longer possesses the nature of justice. And if what is useful in the sense of being just changes, but for a while fits our basic grasp [of justice], nevertheless it was just for that length of time, [at least] for those who do not disturb themselves with empty words but simply look to the facts.

XXXVIII. If objective circumstances have not changed and things believed to be just have been shown in actual practice not to be in accord with our basic grasp [of justice], then those things were not just. And if objective circumstances do change and the same things which had been just turn out to be no longer useful, then those things were just as long as they were useful for the mutual associations of fellow citizens; but later, when they were not useful, they were no longer just.

XXXIX. The man who has made the best arrangements for confidence about external threats is he who has made the manageable things akin to himself, and has at least made the unmanageable things not alien to himself. But he avoided all contact with things for which not even this could be managed and he drove out of his life everything which it profited him to drive out.

XL. All those who had the power to acquire the greatest confidence from [the threats posed by] their neighbours also thereby lived together most pleasantly with the surest guarantee; and since they enjoyed the fullest sense of belonging they did not grieve the early death of the departed, as though it called for pity.

EPICTETUS

Around 300 B.C.E., two short decades after the death of Alexander the Great and the breakup of the vast Alexandrian empire, there emerged in Athens a philosophical school that became the most influential in the Graeco-Roman world. Stoicism, named after the "porch" or *Stoa poikile* on the Athenian acropolis, where its earliest members convened, was at once a system of logic, a theory of knowledge, a natural philosophy or physics, and an ethics. But most of all it was a way of life, an attempt to confront and deal with the turbulent times and the deep anxiety that arose with the demise of the *polis* as the fixed parameter of moral and political life, and with the limitless horizons of worldwide diversity, competing cultures, and forms of knowledge.

Moreover, Stoic philosophy and the Stoic way of life are not only ancient phenomena. Chiefly through the works of Cicero, Diogenes Laertius, Seneca, Epictetus, and Marcus Aurelius, Stoicism permeated the writings of the Church Fathers and the literature of the Middle Ages. It influenced as well Renaissance thought and modern thinkers as diverse as John Calvin, Richard Hooker, Michel de Montaigne, Descartes, Spinoza, and Kant. Often stoicism was revived in situations as riddled with strain and anxiety as those which first gave rise to it, such as the remarkable neo-stoicism initiated by Justus Lipsius at the end of the sixteenth century.

Epictetus (ca. 55–135 C.E.) is one of three moral philosophers who comprise the Stoic movement known as late or Roman Stoicism. The other two representatives of this movement are Lucius Annaeus Seneca, a wealthy Roman orator, statesman, and author of the first century, and Marcus Aurelius, Emperor of Rome from 161 to 180 C.E. Although the earlier stages of Stoicism—developed by its founder, Zeno of Citium, and the major figures, Chrysippus, Panaetius, and Posidonius—involved sophisticated thinking about language, concepts, reasoning, physics, and much else, Roman Stoicism is primarily a moral doctrine and even a set of moral directives. It clearly relies on the philosophical developments of the Stoic tradition, but it was not itself engaged in serious argumentation and critical analysis. As we indicated above, this moral attractiveness is not surprising. There are doubtless social and political reasons why, in periods of crisis, many turned to Stoicism for solace and guidance. In troubled times its eulogy to philosophical rationality and devotion to self-control provided compelling vehicles for personal tranquility and salvation.

It is not true, however, that Stoicism began as a philosophical inquiry into logic, science, and such things, only later to become a moral doctrine. Indeed, from the beginning, in the hands of Zeno and his disciples, the aim of Stoicism was to determine how best to live. All along, the Stoic interest in technical subjects like logic was propaedeutic to this moral goal. Its materialism, its empiricism, its understanding of nature and fate, all these were intended to lead the Stoic to principles about what human agents can and should do in order to control their lives, reduce anxiety, practice virtue, free themselves from passion, and ultimately gain peace for themselves. For the Stoic, natural philosophy is so coherent that it provides the foundation for a life of harmony with nature, which the Stoic conceived as divine. In this way, the Stoic ideal was a life lived in harmony with the divine. This was an old goal, newly interpreted. Seeking the same freedom from anxiety that Epicurus sought, the Stoics found it in virtue and political participation and ultimately in kinship with rather than in rejection of the divine.

Epictetus was a Phrygian slave from Asia Minor. His master, Epaphroditus, who was Nero's freedman, let Epictetus study with Musonius Rufus, an important Stoic teacher. In 92 the Emperor Domitian banished the philosophers from Rome, and Epictetus settled in Nicopolis, in northwestern Greece, where he taught until his death. He wrote nothing, but one of his students, the future historian Arrian, took notes on his lectures in 115 C.E. and later published them as eight volumes of *Discourses*. These *Discourses*, rhetorical and sermonic, give the best sense of Epictetus' style. Of them four are extant, together with the *Encheiridion* (the *Manual*), which includes 53 extracts, often modified, from the larger work. It is this manual that was so influential in the sixteenth and seventeenth centuries and which Frederick the Great, emperor of Prussia in the eighteenth century, carried wherever he went.

Recommended Readings

Annas, Julia. *The Morality of Happiness*. Oxford: Oxford University Press, 1993.

Gerson, L., and B. Inwood (eds. & trans.). *Hellenistic Philosophy*. Indianapolis: Hackett, 1988.

Inwood, B. *Ethics and Human Action in Early Stoicism*. Oxford: Oxford University Press, 1985.

Long. A. A. *Hellenistic Philosophy*. London: Duckworth, 1974.

Long. A. A. (ed.). *Problems of Stoicism*. London: The Athlone Press, 1971.

Long, A. A. *Stoic Studies*. Cambridge: Cambridge University Press, 1996.

Long, A. A., and David Sedley (trans. and commentary). *The Hellenistic Philosophers*. Vols. I and II. Cambridge: Cambridge University Press, 1987.

Nussbaum, Martha. *The Therapy of Desire*. Princeton: Princeton University Press, 1994.

Rist, John. *Stoic Philosophy*. Cambridge: Cambridge University Press, 1969.

Rist, John (ed.). *The Stoics*. Berkeley: University of California Press, 1978.

Sandbach, F. H. *The Stoics*. London: Chatto and Windus, 1975.

Sharples, R. W. *Stoics, Epicureans and Sceptics*. London: Routledge, 1996.

White, N. (trans.). *The Handbook of Epictetus*. Indianapolis: Hackett, 1983.

ENCHEIRIDION

1

Some things are up to us and some are not up to us. Our opinions are up to us, and our impulses, desires, aversions—in short, whatever is our own doing. Our bodies are not up to us, nor are our possessions, our reputations, or our public offices, or, that is, whatever is not our own doing. The things that are up to us are by nature free, unhindered, and unimpeded; the things that are not up to us are weak, enslaved, hindered, not our own. So remember, if you think that things naturally enslaved are free or that things not your own are your own, you will be thwarted, miserable, and upset, and will blame both gods and men. But if you think that only what is yours is yours, and that what is not your own is, just as it is, not your own, then no one will ever coerce you, no one will hinder you, you will blame no one, you will not accuse anyone, you will not do a single thing unwillingly, you will have no enemies, and no one will harm you, because you will not be harmed at all.

As you aim for such great goals, remember that you must not undertake them by acting moderately,[1] but must let some things go completely and postpone others for the time being. But if you want both those great goals and also to hold public office and to be rich then you may perhaps not get even the latter just because you aim at the former too; and you certainly will fail to get the former, which are the only things that yield freedom and happiness.[2]

From the start, then, work on saying to each harsh appearance,[3] "You are an appearance, and not at all the thing that has the appearance." Then examine it and assess it by these yardsticks that you have, and first and foremost by whether it concerns the things that are up to us or the things that are not up to us. And if it is about one of the things that is not up to us, be ready to say, "You are nothing in relation to me."

2

Remember, what a desire proposes is that you gain what you desire, and what an aversion proposes is that you not fall into what you are averse to. Someone who fails to get what he desires is *un*fortunate, while someone who falls into what he is averse to has met *mis*fortune. So if you are averse only to what is against nature among the things that are up to you, then you will never fall into anything that you are averse to; but if you are averse to illness or death or poverty, you will meet misfortune. So detach your aversion from everything not up to us, and transfer it to what

From *The Handbook of Epictetus*, translated, with introduction and annotation, by Nicholas White (Indianapolis: Hackett Publishing Company, 1983). Reprinted by permission of the publisher.

1. [This may mean simply that the proposed undertaking is difficult. (Oldfather's translation suggests this), or it may mean (as I believe) that the aim cannot be achieved by the Aristotelian policy of pursuing a mean or middle course between extremes.—N.W.]

2. [Epictetus recommends aiming to have one's state of mind in accord with nature, in the sense explained in the previous paragraph and in c. 8. His point here is that if you aim for that and also simultaneously for certain "externals" like wealth, you will probably have neither and clearly will not have the former.]

3. [The word "appearance" translates *phantasia*, which some translators render by "impression" or "presentation." An appearance is roughly the immediate experience of sense or feeling, which may or may not represent an external state of affairs. (The Stoics held, against the Sceptics, that some appearances self-evidently do represent external states of affairs correctly.)]

is against nature among the things that are up to us. And for the time being eliminate desire completely, since if you desire something that is not up to us, you are bound to be unfortunate, and at the same time none of the things that are up to us, which it would be good to desire, will be available to you. Make use only of impulse and its contrary, rejection,[4] though with reservation, lightly, and without straining.

3

In the case of everything attractive or useful or that you are fond of, remember to say just what sort of thing it is, beginning with the least little things. If you are fond of a jug, say "I am fond of a jug!" For then when it is broken you will not be upset. If you kiss your child or your wife, say that you are kissing a human being; for when it dies you will not be upset.

4

When you are about to undertake some action, remind yourself what sort of action it is. If you are going out for a bath, put before your mind what happens at baths—there are people who splash, people who jostle, people who are insulting, people who steal. And you will undertake the action more securely if from the start you say of it, "I want to take a bath and to keep my choices in accord with nature;" and likewise for each action. For that way if something happens to interfere with your bathing you will be ready to say, "Oh, well, I wanted not only this but also to keep my choices in accord with nature, and I cannot do that if I am annoyed with things that happen."

5

What upsets people is not things themselves but their judgments about the things. For example, death is nothing dreadful (or else it would have appeared

dreadful to Socrates), but instead the judgment about death that it is dreadful—*that* is what is dreadful. So when we are thwarted or upset or distressed, let us never blame someone else but rather ourselves, that is, our own judgments. An uneducated person accuses others when he is doing badly; a partly educated person accuses himself, an educated person accuses neither someone else nor himself.

6

Do not be joyful about any superiority that is not your own. If the horse were to say joyfully, "I am beautiful," one could put up with it. But certainly you, when you say joyfully, "I have a beautiful horse," are joyful about the good of the horse. What, then, is your own? Your way of dealing with appearances. So whenever you are in accord with nature in your way of dealing with appearances, then be joyful, since then you are joyful about a good of your own.

7

On a voyage when your boat has anchored, if you want to get fresh water you may pick up a small shellfish and a vegetable by the way, but you must keep your mind fixed on the boat and look around frequently in case the captain calls. If he calls you must let all those other things go so that you will not be tied up and thrown on the ship like livestock. That is how it is in life too: if you are given a wife and a child instead of a vegetable and a small shellfish, that will not hinder you; but if the captain calls, let all those things go and run to the boat without turning back; and if you are old, do not even go very far from the boat, so that when the call comes you are not left behind.

8

Do not seek to have events happen as you want them to, but instead want them to happen as they do happen, and your life will go well.

---

4. [Impulse and rejection (*hormē* and *aphormē*) are, in Stoic terms, natural and non-rational psychological movements, so to speak, that are respectively toward or away from external objects.]

9

Illness interferes with the body, not with one's faculty of choice,[5] unless that faculty of choice wishes it to. Lameness interferes with the limb, not with one's faculty of choice. Say this at each thing that happens to you, since you will find that it interferes with something else, not with you.

10

At each thing that happens to you, remember to turn to yourself and ask what capacity you have for dealing with it. If you see a beautiful boy or woman, you will find the capacity of self-control for that. If hardship comes to you, you will find endurance. If it is abuse, you will find patience. And if you become used to this, you will not be carried away by appearances.

11

Never say about anything, "I have lost it," but instead, "I have given it back." Did your child die? It was given back. Did your wife die? She was given back. "My land was taken." So this too was given back. "But the person who took it was bad!" How does the way the giver[6] asked for it back concern you? As long as he gives it, take care of it as something that is not your own, just as travelers treat an inn.

12

If you want to make progress,[7] give up all considerations like these: "If I neglect my property I will have nothing to live on," "If I do not punish my slave boy

5. ["Faculty of choice" translates "*proairesis*," which designates a rational faculty of the soul (cf. n. 4).]

6. [The "giver" can be taken to be nature, or the natural order of the cosmos, or god, which the Stoics identified with each other.]

7. ["Making progress" (*prokoptein*) is the Stoic expression for movement in the direction of the ideal condition for a human being, embodied by the Stoic "sage" (cf. c. 15, n.).]

he will be bad." It is better to die of hunger with distress and fear gone than to live upset in the midst of plenty. It is better for the slave boy to be bad than for you to be in a bad state. Begin therefore with little things. A little oil is spilled, a little wine is stolen: say, "This is the price of tranquillity; this is the price of not being upset." Nothing comes for free. When you call the slave boy, keep in mind that he is capable of not paying attention, and even if he does pay attention he is capable of not doing any of the things that you want him to. But he is not in such a good position that your being upset or not depends on him.

13

If you want to make progress, let people think you are a mindless fool about externals, and do not desire a reputation for knowing about them. If people think you amount to something, distrust yourself. Certainly it is not easy to be on guard both for one's choices to be in accord with nature and also for externals, and a person who concerns himself with the one will be bound to neglect the other.

14

You are foolish if you want your children and your wife and your friends to live forever, since you are wanting things to be up to you that are not up to you, and things to be yours that are not yours. You are stupid in the same way if you want your slave boy to be faultless, since you are wanting badness not to be badness but something else. But wanting not to fail to get what you desire—this you are capable of. A person's master is someone who has power over what he wants or does not want, either to obtain it or take it away. Whoever wants to be free, therefore, let him not want or avoid anything that is up to others. Otherwise he will necessarily be a slave.

15

Remember, you must behave as you do at a banquet. Something is passed around and comes to you: reach out your hand politely and take some. It goes by: do not hold it back. It has not arrived yet: do not stretch your desire out toward it, but wait until it comes to you. In the same way toward your children, in the same way toward your wife, in the same way toward public office, in the same way toward wealth, and you will be fit to share a banquet with the gods. But if when things are set in front of you, you do not take them but despise them, then you will not only share a banquet with the gods but also be a ruler along with them. For by acting in this way Diogenes and Heraclitus[8] and people like them were deservedly gods and were deservedly called gods.

16

When you see someone weeping in grief at the departure of his child or the loss of his property, take care not to be carried away by the appearance that the externals he is involved in are bad, and be ready to say immediately, "What weighs down on this man is not what has happened (since it does not weigh down on someone else), but his judgment about it." Do not hesitate, however, to sympathise with him verbally, and even to moan with him if the occasion arises; but be careful not to moan inwardly.

17

Remember that you are an actor in a play, which is as the playwright wants it to be: short if he wants it short, long if he wants it long. If he wants you to play a beggar, play even this part skillfully, or a cripple, or a public official, or a private citizen. What is yours is to play the assigned part well. But to choose it belongs to someone else.

8. [Diogenes the Cynic (the one who with his lantern looked for an honest man) and Heraclitus of Ephesus, the presocratic philosopher, were along with Socrates and Zeno people whom the Stoics said might possibly have reached the perfect condition of being sages, which the Stoics took to be conceptually no different from the perfect condition of a god.]

18

When a raven gives an unfavorable sign by croaking,[9] do not be carried away by the appearance, but immediately draw a distinction to yourself and say, "None of these signs is for me, but only for my petty body or my petty property or my petty judgments or children or wife. For all signs are favorable if I wish, since it is up to me to be benefited by whichever of them turns out correct.

19

You can be invincible if you do not enter any contest in which victory is not up to you. See that you are not carried away by the appearance, in thinking that someone is happy when you see him honored ahead of you or very powerful or otherwise having a good reputation. For if the really good things are up to us, neither envy nor jealousy has a place, and you yourself will want neither to be a general or a magistrate or a consul, but to be free. And there is one road to this: despising what is not up to us.

20

Remember that what is insulting is not the person who abuses you or hits you, but the judgment about them that they *are* insulting. So when someone irritates you be aware that what irritates you is your own belief. Most importantly, therefore, try not to be carried away by appearance, since if you once gain time and delay you will control yourself more easily.

9. [Most people in antiquity believed in fortune-telling of various kinds, involving bird-calls, the flight of birds, inspection of entrails, stars, and whatnot. Many Stoics, notably Chrysippus, believed in such things, not least because they saw in them manifestations of the order of the cosmos and the tight and intricate interconnections within it, and thus saw them as scientific rather than superstitious.]

21

Let death and exile and everything that is terrible appear before your eyes every day, especially death; and you will never have anything contemptible in your thoughts or crave anything excessively.

22

If you crave philosophy prepare yourself on the spot to be ridiculed, to be jeered at by many people who will say, "Here he is again, all of a sudden turned philosopher on us!" and "Where did he get that high brow?" But don't *you* put on a high brow, but hold fast to the things that appear best to you, as someone assigned by god to this place. And remember that if you hold to these views, those who previously ridiculed you will later be impressed with you, but if you are defeated by them you will be doubly ridiculed.

23

If it ever happens that you turn outward to want to please another person, certainly you have lost your plan of life. Be content therefore in everything to be a philosopher, and if you want to seem to be one, make yourself appear so to yourself, and you will be capable of it.

24

Do not be weighed down by the consideration, "I shall live without any honor, everywhere a nobody!" For if lack of honors is something bad, I cannot be in a bad state because of another person any more than I can be in a shameful one. It is not your task[10] to gain political office, or be invited to a banquet, is it? Not at all. How then is that a lack of honor? And how will you be a nobody everywhere, if you need to be a somebody only in things that are up to you—

10. [The word translated "task" here and below is *ergon*, which might also be translated by "function."]

in which it is open to you to be of the greatest worth? "But your friends will be without help!" What do you mean, "without help?" Well, they will be without a little cash from you, and you will not make them Roman citizens. Who told you, then, that these things are up to you and not the business of someone else? Who can give to someone else what he does not have himself? "Get money," someone says, "so that we may have some." If I can get it while keeping self-respect and trustworthiness and high-mindedness, show me the way and I will get it. But if you demand that I lose the good things that are mine so that you may acquire things that are not good, see for yourselves how unfair and inconsiderate you are. Which do you want more, money or a self-respecting and trustworthy friend? Then help me more toward this, and do not expect me to do things that will make me lose these qualities. "But my country," he says, "will be without help, in so far as it depends on me!" Again, what sort of "help" is this? So it will not have porticos and baths by your efforts. What does that amount to? For it does not have shoes because of the blacksmith or weapons because of the cobbler, but it is enough if each person fulfills his own task. And if you furnished for it another citizen who was trustworthy and self-respecting, would you in no way be helpful to it? "Yes, I would be." Then neither would you yourself be unhelpful to it. "Then what place," he says "will I have in the city?" The one you can have by preserving your trustworthiness and self-respect. And if while wanting to help it you throw away these things, what use will you be to it if you turn out shameless and untrustworthy?

25

Has someone been given greater honor than you at a banquet or in a greeting or by being brought in to give advice? If these things are good, you should be glad that he has got them. If they are bad, do not be angry that you did not get them. And remember, you cannot demand an equal share if you did not do the same things, with a view to getting things that are not up to us. For how can someone who does not hang around a person's door have an equal share with someone who does, or someone who does not escort him with someone who does, or someone who does not praise him with someone who does? You will be unjust and greedy, then, if you want to obtain these things for free when you have not paid the price for which they are bought. Well, what is the price of heads of lettuce? An obol, say. So if someone who has paid an obol takes the heads of lettuce, and you who do not pay do not take them, do not think that you are worse off than the one who did. For just as he has the lettuce, you have the obol that you did not pay. It is the same way in this case. You were not invited to someone's banquet? You did not give the host the price of the meal. He sells it for praise; he sells it for attention. Then give him the balance for which it is sold, if that is to your advantage. But you are greedy and stupid if you want both not to pay and also to take. Have you got nothing, then, in place of the meal? Indeed you do have something; you did not praise someone you did not wish to praise, and you did not have to put up with the people around his door.

26

It is possible to learn the will of nature from the things in which we do not differ from each other. For example, when someone else's little slave boy breaks his cup we are ready to say, "It's one of those things that just happen." Certainly, then, when your own cup is broken you should be just the way you were when the other person's was broken. Transfer the same idea to larger matters. Someone else's child is dead, or his wife. There is no one would not say, "It's the lot of a human being." But when one's own dies, immediately it is, "Alas! Poor me!" But we should have remembered how we feel when we hear of the same thing about others.

27

Just as a target is not set up to be missed, in the same way nothing bad by nature happens in the world.[11]

11. [According to the Stoic view, the universe as a whole is perfect and everything in it has a place in its overall

28

If someone turned your body over to just any person who happened to meet you, you would be angry. But are you not ashamed that you turn over your own faculty of judgment to whoever happens along, so that if he abuses you it is upset and confused?

29

For each action, consider what leads up to it and what follows it, and approach it in the light of that. Otherwise you will come to it enthusiastically at first, since you have not borne in mind any of what will happen next, but later when difficulties turn up you will give up disgracefully. You want to win an Olympic victory? I do too, by the gods, since that is a fine thing. But consider what leads up to it and what follows it, and undertake the action in the light of that. You must be disciplined, keep a strict diet, stay away from cakes, train according to strict routine at a fixed time in heat and in cold, not drink cold water, not drink wine when you feel like it, and in general you must have turned yourself over to your trainer as to a doctor, and then in the contest "dig in,"[12] sometimes dislocate your hand, twist your ankle, swallow a lot of sand, sometimes be whipped, and, after all that, lose. Think about that and then undertake training, if you want to. Otherwise you will be behaving the way children do, who play wrestlers one time, gladiators another time, blow trumpets another time, then act a play. In this way you too are now an athlete, now a gladiator, then an orator, then a philosopher, yet you are nothing wholeheartedly, but like a monkey you mimic each sight that you see, and one thing after another is to your taste, since you do not undertake a thing after considering it from every side, but only randomly and half-heartedly.

In the same way when some people watch a philos-

design, so that nothing can exist or occur that is bad in its relation to that overall design.]

12. [Nobody knows just what this expression means in this context.]

opher and hear one speaking like Euphrates[13] (though after all who can speak like him?), they want to be philosophers themselves. Just you consider, as a human being, what sort of thing it is; then inspect your own nature and whether you can bear it. You want to do the pentathlon, or to wrestle? Look at your arms, your thighs, inspect your loins. Different people are naturally suited for different things. Do you think that if you do those things you can eat as you now do, drink as you now do, have the same likes and dislikes? You must go without sleep, put up with hardship, be away from your own people, be looked down on by a little slave boy, be laughed at by people who meet you, get the worse of it in everything, honor, public office, law course, every little thing. Think about whether you want to exchange these things for tranquillity, freedom, calm. If not, do not embrace philosophy, and do not like children be a philosopher at one time, later a tax-collector, than an orator, then a procurator of the emperor. These things do not go together. You must be one person, either good or bad. You must either work on your ruling principle,[14] or work on externals, practise the art either of what is inside or of what is outside, that is, play the role either of a philosopher or of a non-philosopher.

30

Appropriate actions[15] are in general measured by relationships. He is a father: that entails taking care of him, yielding to him in everything, putting up with him when he abuses you or strikes you. "But he is a bad father." Does nature then determine that you have a good father? No, only that you have a father.[16] My brother has done me wrong." Then keep your place in relation to him; do not consider his action, but instead consider what you can do to bring your own faculty of choice[17] into accord with nature. Another person will not do you harm unless you wish it; you will be harmed at just that time at which you take yourself to be harmed. In this way, then, you will discover the appropriate actions to expect from a neighbor, from a citizen, from a general, if you are in the habit of looking at relationships.

31

The most important aspect of piety toward the gods is certainly both to have correct beliefs about them, as beings that arrange the universe well and justly, and to set yourself to obey them and acquiesce in everything that happens and to follow it willingly, as something brought to completion by the best judgment. For in this way you will never blame the gods or accuse them of neglecting you. And this piety is impossible unless you detach the good and the bad from what is not up to us and attach it exclusively to what is up to us, because if you think that any of what is not up to us is good or bad, then when you fail to get what you want and fall into what you do not want, you will be bound to blame and hate those who cause this. For every animal by nature flees and turns away from things that are harmful and from what causes them, and pursues and admires things that are beneficial and what causes them. There is therefore no way for a person who thinks he is being harmed to enjoy what he thinks is harming him, just as it is impossible to enjoy the harm itself. Hence a son even abuses his father when the father does not give him a share of things that he thinks are good; and thinking that being a tyrant was a good thing is

13. [Euphrates was a Stoic lecturer noted for his eloquence.]

14. [The "ruling principle" (or "governing principle"), the *hēgemonikon*, in the rather complicated psychological theory adopted by the Stoics, is that central part of the soul that can understand what is good and decide to act on that understanding. Cf. c. 38, n.]

15. ["Appropriate actions" are *kathēkonta*, which Cicero called *officia*, and are in English translations often called "duties," though the notion is actually somewhat different from that of duty. They are the actions that are of a type generally in accord with nature, or with a particular sort of person's place in it.]

16. [The idea here is, roughly, that there are certain relationships of affinity established by the natural order, and that having a father represents one of them, but that having a good father is not entailed by it.]

17. [Cf. c. 9, n., and c. 29, n.]

what made enemies of Polyneices and Eteocles.[18] This is why the farmer too abuses the gods, and the sailor, and the merchant, and those who have lost their wives and children. For wherever someone's advantage lies, there he also shows piety. So whoever takes care to have desires and aversions as one should also in the same instance takes care about being pious. And it is always appropriate to make libations and sacrifices and give firstfruits according to the custom of one's forefathers, in a manner that is pure and neither slovenly nor careless, nor indeed cheaply nor beyond one's means.

32

When you make use of fortune-telling, remember that you do not know what will turn out and have gone to the fortune-teller to find out, but that if you really are a philosopher you have gone already knowing what sort of thing it is. For if it is one of the things that is not up to us, it is bound to be neither good nor bad. Therefore do not bring desire or aversion to the fortune-teller and do not approach him trembling but instead realizing that everything that turns out is indifferent[19] and nothing in relation to you, and that whatever sort of thing it may be, you will be able to deal with it well and no one will hinder that. So go confidently to the gods as advisers, and thereafter when some particular advice has been given to you remember who your advisers are and whom you will be disregarding if you disobey. Approach fortune-telling as Socrates thought a person should, in cases where the whole consideration has reference to the outcome, and no resource is available from reason or any other technique to find out about the matter. So, when it is necessary to share a danger with a friend or with your country, do not use fortune-telling about whether you should share the danger. For if the fortune-teller says that the omens are unfa-

vorable, clearly death is signified or the injury of a part of your body or exile. But reason chooses to stand by your friend and to share danger with your country even under these conditions. For this reason pay attention to the greater fortune-teller, Pythian Apollo, who threw out of the temple the man who did not help his brother when he was being murdered.[20]

33

Set up right now a certain character and pattern for yourself which you will preserve when you are by yourself and when you are with people. Be silent for the most part, or say what you have to in a few words. Speak rarely, when the occasion requires speaking, but not about just any topic that comes up, not about gladiators, horse-races, athletes, eating or drinking—the things that always come up; and especially if it is about people, talk without blaming or praising or comparing. Divert by your own talk, if you can, the talk of those with you to something appropriate. If you happen to be stranded among strangers, do not talk. Do not laugh a great deal or at a great many things or unrestrainedly. Refuse to swear oaths, altogether if possible, or otherwise as circumstances allow. Avoid banquets given by those outside philosophy. But if the appropriate occasion arises, take great care not to slide into their ways, since certainly if a person's companion is dirty the person who spends time with him, even if he happens to be clean, is bound to become dirty too. Take what has to do with the body to the point of bare need, such as food, drink, clothing, house, household slaves, and cut out everything that is for reputation or luxury. As for sex stay pure as far as possible before marriage, and if you have it do only what is allowable. But do not be angry or censorious toward those who do engage in it, and do not always be making an exhibition of the fact that you do not.

If someone reports back to you that so-and-so is saying bad things about you, do not reply to them

18. [The story of the conflict between the brothers Polyneices and Eteocles is best known to modern readers from Sophocles' tragedy, *Antigone*.]

19. [Things that are "indifferent" in the Stoic view are all things that are external and not up to oneself (cf. c. 1, e.g.).]

20. [The idea is that one does not need a fortune-teller to tell one whether one should defend one's country or one's friends, and that this fact was recognized by the oracle of Apollo at Delphi.]

but answer, "Obviously he didn't know my other bad characteristics, since otherwise he wouldn't just have mentioned these."

For the most part there is no need to go to public shows, but if ever the right occasion comes do not show your concern to be for anything but yourself; that is to say, wish to have happen only what does happen, and for the person to win who actually does win, since that way you will not be thwarted. But refrain completely from shouting or laughing at anyone or being very much caught up in it. After you leave, do not talk very much about what has happened, except what contributes to your own improvement, since that would show that the spectacle had impressed you.

Do not go indiscriminately or readily to people's public lectures, but when you do be on guard to be dignified and steady and at the same time try not to be disagreeable.

When you are about to meet someone, especially someone who seems to be distinguished, put to yourself the question, "What would Socrates or Zeno have done in these circumstances?" and you will not be at a loss as to how to deal with the occasion. When you go to see someone who is important, put to yourself the thought that you will not find him at home, that you will be shut out, that the door will be slammed, that he will pay no attention to you. If it is appropriate to go even under these conditions, go and put up with what happens, and never say to yourself, "It wasn't worth all that!" For that is the way of a non-philosopher, someone who is misled by externals.

In your conversations stay away from making frequent and longwinded mention of what you have done and the dangers that you have been in, since it is not as pleasant for others to hear about what has happened to you as it is for you to remember your own dangers.

Stay away from raising a laugh, since this manner slips easily into vulgarity and at the same time is liable to lessen your neighbors' respect for you. It is also risky to fall into foul language. So when anything like that occurs, if a good opportunity arises, go so far as to criticize the person who has done it, and otherwise by staying silent and blushing and frowning you will show that you are displeased by what has been said.

34

Whenever you encounter some kind of apparent pleasure, be on guard, as in the case of other appearances, not to be carried away by it, but let the thing wait for you and allow yourself to delay. Then bring before your mind two times, both the time when you enjoy the pleasure and the time when after enjoying it you later regret it and berate yourself; and set against these the way you will be pleased and will praise yourself if you refrain from it. But if the right occasion appears for you to undertake the action, pay attention so that you will not be overcome by its attractiveness and pleasantness and seductiveness, and set against it how much better it is to be conscious of having won this victory against it.

35

When you do something that you determine is to be done, never try not to be seen doing it, even if most people are likely to think something bad about it. If you are not doing it rightly, avoid the act itself; if you are doing it rightly, why do you fear those who will criticize you wrongly?

36

Just as the propositions "It is day" and "It is night" have their full value when disjoined [*sc.*, in "It is day *or* it is night"] but have negative value when conjoined [*sc.*, in "It is day *and* it is night"], in the same way, granted that taking the larger portion has value for one's body, it has negative value for preserving the fellowship of a banquet in the way one should.[21] So when you eat with another, remember not merely to see the value for your body of what lies in front of you, but also to preserve your respect for your host.

.21. [Very roughly, the idea is that the value of an action has to be judged from all features of the context. The parallel is that allegedly the meaningfulness of a sentence depends in a way on its context.]

37

If you undertake some role beyond your capacity, you both disgrace yourself by taking it and also thereby neglect the role that you were unable to take.

38

Just as in walking about you pay attention so as not to step on a nail or twist your foot, pay attention in the same way so as not to harm your ruling principle.[22] And if we are on guard about this in every action, we shall set about it more securely.

39

The measure of possessions for each person is the body, as the foot is of the shoe. So if you hold to this principle you will preserve the measure; but if you step beyond it, you will in the end be carried as if over a cliff; just as in the case of the shoe, if you go beyond the foot, you get a gilded shoe, and then a purple embroidered one. For there is no limit to a thing once it is beyond its measure.

40

Women are called ladies by men right after they are fourteen. And so when they see that they have nothing else except to go to bed with men, they begin to make themselves up and place all their hopes in that. It is therefore worthwhile to pay attention so that they are aware that they are honored for nothing other than appearing modest and self-respecting.

41

It shows lack of natural talent to spend time on what concerns the body, as in exercising a great deal, eating a great deal, drinking a great deal, moving one's bow-

els or copulating a great deal. Instead you must do these things in passing, but turn your whole attention toward your faculty of judgment.[23]

42

When someone acts badly toward you or speaks badly of you, remember that he does or says it in the belief that it is appropriate for him to do so. Accordingly he cannot follow what appears to you but only what appears to him, so that if things appear badly to him, he is harmed in as much as he has been deceived. For if someone thinks that a true conjunctive proposition[24] is false, the conjunction is not harmed but rather the one who is deceived. Starting from these considerations you will be gentle with the person who abuses you. For you must say on each occasion, "That's how it seemed to him."

43

Everything has two handles, one by which it may be carried and the other not. If your brother acts unjustly toward you, do not take hold of it by this side, that he has acted unjustly (since this is the handle by which it may not be carried), but instead by this side, that he is your brother and was brought up with you, and you will be taking hold of it in the way that it can be carried.

44

These statements are not valid inferences: "I am richer than you; therefore I am superior to you," or "I am more eloquent than you; therefore I am superior

22. [Cf. c. 29, n. 14.]

23. [Cf. c. 29, n. 14. The claim is in effect that one should be concerned wholly with the state of the ruling part of one's soul, and not with external states of affairs or with those aspects of the soul, such as one's affective feelings or desires, that are directly dependent on external states of affairs. One can see here the Stoic view, which seems paradoxical to many, that one's feelings and nonrational desires are in a crucial sense external to one's true self (cf. c. 6 and Introd.).]

24. [Cf. c. 36. A proposition of this sort consists of two component propositions conjoined by "and."]

to you." But rather these are valid: "I am richer than you; therefore my property is superior to yours," or "I am more eloquent than you; therefore my speaking is superior to yours." But you are identical neither with your property nor with your speaking.

45

Someone takes a bath quickly; do not say that he does it badly but that he does it quickly. Someone drinks a great deal of wine; do not say that he does it badly but that he does a great deal of it. For until you have discerned what his judgment was, how do you know whether he did it badly? In this way it will not turn out that you receive convincing appearances of some things but give assent to quite different ones.[25]

46

Never call yourself a philosopher and do not talk a great deal among non-philosophers about philosophical propositions, but do what follows from them. For example, at a banquet do not say how a person ought to eat, but eat as a person ought to. Remember that Socrates had so completely put aside ostentation that people actually went to him when they wanted to be introduced to philosophers, and he took them.[26] He was that tolerant of being overlooked. And if talk about philosophical propositions arises among non-philosophers, for the most part be silent, since there is a great danger of your spewing out what you have not digested. And when someone says to you that you know nothing and you are not hurt by it, then you know that you are making a start at your task. Sheep

do not show how much they have eaten by bringing the feed to the shepherds, but they digest the food inside themselves, and outside themselves they bear wool and milk. So in your case likewise do not display propositions to non-philosophers but instead the actions that come from the propositions when they are digested.

47

When you have become adapted to living cheaply as far as your body is concerned, do not make a show of it, and if you drink water do not say at every opening that you drink water. If you wish to train yourself to hardship, do it for yourself and not for those outside. Do not throw your arms around statues.[27] Instead, when you are terribly thirsty, take cold water into your mouth, and spit it out, and do not tell anyone about it.

48

The position and character of a non-philosopher: he never looks for benefit or harm to come from himself but from things outside. The position and character of a philosopher: he looks for all benefit and harm to come from himself.

Signs of someone's making progress: he censures no one; he praises no one; he blames no one; he never talks about himself as a person who amounts to something or knows something. When he is thwarted or prevented in something, he accuses himself. And if someone praises him he laughs to himself at the person who has praised him; and if someone censures him he does not respond. He goes around like an invalid, careful not to move any of his parts that are healing before they have become firm. He has kept off all desire from himself, and he has transferred all aversion onto what is against nature among the things that are up to us. His impulses toward

25. [A "convincing appearance" is a *kataleptikē phantasia*, the sort of appearance that according to the Stoics is a self-evidently correct representation of the way things actually are (cf. n. 3). "Assent" is *synkatathesis*. Correct assent would of course be assent to self-evidently correct appearances. The line of thought here is, however, quite compressed, and the student will find it a difficult exercise to explain it.]

26. [The allusion is perhaps to the events in the early part of Plato's *Protagoras*.]

27. [According to a story in Diog. Laert. 6.23, Diogenes, the Cynic did this nude in cold weather, to toughen himself. But the statues were outdoors, and Diogenes was a bit of a show-off (but cf. n. 8!).]

everything are diminished. If he seems foolish or ignorant, he does not care. In a single phrase, he is on guard against himself as an enemy lying in wait.

49

When someone acts grand because he understands and can expound the works of Chrysippus,[28] say to yourself, "If Chrysippus had not written unclearly, this man would have nothing to be proud of."

But what do *I* want? To learn to understand nature and follow it. So I try to find out who explains it. And I hear that Chrysippus does, and I go to him. But I do not understand the things that he has written, so I try to find the person who explains them. Up to this point there is nothing grand. But when I do find someone who explains them, what remains is to carry out what has been conveyed to me. This alone is grand. But if I am impressed by the explaining itself, what have I done but ended up a grammarian instead of a philosopher—except that I am explaining Chrysippus instead of Homer. Instead, when someone says to me, "Read me some Chrysippus," I turn red when I cannot exhibit actions that are similar to his words and in harmony with them.

50

Abide by whatever task is set before you as if it were a law, and as if you would be committing sacrilege if you went against it. But pay no attention to whatever anyone says about you, since that falls outside what is yours.

51

How long do you put off thinking yourself worthy of the best things, and never going against the definitive capacity of reason?[29] You have received the philosophical propositions that you ought to agree to and you

28. [On Chrysippus, see the Introduction.]
29. [In brief, the capacity of reason here is that of distinguishing different things from each other and defining them.]

have agreed to them. Then what sort of teacher are you still waiting for, that you put off improving yourself until he comes? You are not a boy any more, but already a full-grown man. If you now neglect things and are lazy and are always making delay after delay and set one day after another as the day for paying attention to yourself, then without realizing it you will make no progress but will end up a non-philosopher all through life and death. So decide now that you are worthy of living as a full-grown man who is making progress, and make everything that seems best be a law that you cannot go against. And if you meet with any hardship or anything pleasant or reputable or disreputable, then remember that the contest is *now* and the Olympic games are *now* and you cannot put things off any more and that your progress is made or destroyed by a single day and a single action. Socrates became fully perfect in this way, by not paying attention to anything but his reason in everything that he met with. You, even if you are not yet Socrates, ought to live as someone wanting to be Socrates.

52

The first and most necessary aspect of philosophy is that of dealing with philosophical propositions, such as "not to hold to falsehood." The second is that of demonstrations, for example, "How come one must not hold to falsehood?" The third is that of the confirmation and articulation of these, for example. "How come this is a demonstration? What is demonstration? What is entailment? What is conflict? What is truth? What is falsity?" Therefore the third is necessary because of the second, and the second because of the first; but the most necessary, and the one where one must rest, is the first. We, however, do it backwards, since we spend time in the third and all of our effort goes into it, and we neglect the first completely. Therefore we hold to falsehood, but we are ready to explain how it is demonstrated that one must not hold to falsehood.

53

On every occasion you must have these thoughts ready:

Lead me, Zeus, and you too, Destiny,
Wherever I am assigned by you;
I'll follow and not hesitate,
But even if I do not wish to,
Because I'm bad, I'll follow anyway.

Whoever has complied well with necessity
Is counted wise by us, and understands
   divine affairs.

Well, Crito, if it is pleasing to the gods this
   way, then let it happen this way.

Anytus and Meletus can kill me, but they
   can't harm me.[30]

---

30. [These four bits of poetry have the following origins. The first is by Cleanthes, who was head of the Stoic school at Athens between Zeno and Chrysippus. The second is a fragment of Euripides (tr. 965 Nauck). The third is Plato, *Crito* 43d, and the fourth is Plato, *Apology* 30c–d (slightly modified as compared with our manuscript texts), both purporting to be quotations from Socrates (cf. n. 8).]

AUGUSTINE

Like the Thirty Years' War (1618–1648) and the French Revolution (1789–1795), the sack of Rome by the Visigoths in 410 C.E. and the destruction of the Roman Empire was an event of momentous significance. At the time many Romans saw their world in ruins and sought to understand the event and to explain it, in part to assign blame and thereby to indict those responsible. Among these were pagan thinkers who ascribed Rome's downfall to Christianity. In 312 Rome had become Christian, under Constantine; the results, these pagans claimed, were the weakened loyalty of its citizens, an otherworldly abandonment of civic responsibility, and desertion of the gods of the city. All this led to Rome's weakness and her destruction and provided an historical refutation of the Church. By 413, Augustine (354–430), the Bishop of Hippo in North Africa, had written the first three books of his reply to these charges, his sweeping panorama of history and eschatology, of the goal of history and the role of the state in it, of the nature of society and the two cities—the City of God and the earthly city—that constitute it, and of the two types of love that ground these two cities. *De Civitate Dei* (*The City of God*), begun in 413 and completed in 426, speaks out of the dramatic encounter between Augustine and the critics of Christianity in the early fifth century, but it is a work that transcends this situation and addresses all subsequent attempts to understand the complex relations among politics, religion, history, and the moral ends of human life. In it, moreover, Augustine not only responds to the critics of Christianity; he also incorporates into his own conception of the "city of man" many central political values of his republican, stoic, and Roman law opponents, thereby providing a vehicle for transmitting these values to medieval Europe.

Augustine was born in 354 in Thagaste, in North Africa. His father was pagan, his mother, Monica, a Christian. As a youngster Augustine studied Latin and the Latin classics. By 370 he was in Carthage, mastering the works of classical rhetoric and becoming increasingly estranged from his mother's Christianity. In 374 he moved back to Thagaste to teach rhetoric, and then returned to Carthage, where he established a school of rhetoric.

During this period Augustine read Cicero's dialogue *Hortensius* (a work now lost) and was stimulated by it to pursue wisdom and truth through philosophy, in place of the irrational Christian doctrines he had rejected. He found an alternative in Manichaeism, a doctrine of two principles, the forces of light and darkness, of good and evil, that are eternally engaged in battle over the soul of each person and over the world itself. Augustine was especially drawn to this dualistic theory as a solution to the problem of the existence of evil, which the theory ascribed to the force of evil and not to God, and the problem of base human desires and passions.

In 383 Augustine moved to Rome, once again to teach rhetoric, and in 384 took the position of municipal professor of rhetoric in Milan. There Augustine was introduced to a neo-Platonic interpretation of Christianity in the sermons of Ambrose, the Bishop of Milan, and through acquaintance with other Christian intellectuals in Ambrose's circle. Here, finally, was the true philosophy which he had been seeking. By 386 Augustine was converted, and in 387 Ambrose baptized him into the Church.

Augustine returned to Thagaste in 388, where he established with friends a small monastic community. Within a few years and against his wishes, he was ordained a priest and called upon to aid the pastoral affairs of the aged Bishop of Hippo, a seaport town one hundred fifty miles west of Carthage. When the Bishop died in 396, Augustine replaced him, a position which he held until his death. During the years of his episcopacy, Augustine wrote extensively—Scriptural commentaries, theological treatises, letters, and much else. He engaged in polemics and controversies, with the Donatists and Pelagians, among others, delivered sermons, and conducted the affairs of his diocese. In 410 he completed his most important doctrinal work, *De Trinitate*

(*On the Trinity*), and in 400 he published his greatest work, the *Confessions*, in which he recounts the spiritual journey of his first thirty-three years.

In 430, twenty years after the Visigoths had sacked Rome, the Vandals, under Genseric, flooded into Northern Africa from Spain and besieged Hippo. In the midst of the crisis, on August 28, 430, Augustine died, in time to avoid seeing the invaders burn his city.

Recommended Readings

Brown, Peter. *Augustine of Hippo*. Berkeley: University of California Press, 1967.

Burns, James (ed.). *Cambridge History of Medieval Political Thought, 350–1450*. Cambridge: Cambridge University Press, 1989.

Gilson, Etienne. *The Christian Philosophy of St. Augustine*. New York: Random House, 1968.

Kirwan, Christopher. *Augustine*. London: Routledge, 1979.

Markus, R. A. (ed.). *Augustine*. Garden City: Doubleday, 1972.

CITY OF GOD

BOOK XIX

Chapter 1

Because I see that I must next discuss the proper ends of the two cities—namely, the earthy and the heavenly—I must first explain, insofar as the limits imposed by the plan of this work allow, the arguments by which mortals have struggled to make themselves happy in the misery of this life. This is necessary in order to clarify the difference between their futilities and our hope, which God has given us, and its object, namely true happiness, which God will give us. This will be done not only through divine authority, but also, for the sake of unbelievers, through reason.

Concerning the ends of goods and evils, philosophers have engaged in many and varied disputes among themselves; but the question they have pursued with the greatest effort, turning it over in their minds, is, What makes man happy? our final good is that for the sake of which other things are desired, but which is itself desired for its own sake; and the final evil is that on account of which other things are avoided, but which is avoided on its own account. Hence, we now call the "final good" not that through which good is destroyed, and so ceases to exist, but that through which it is perfected, and so exists fully; and we call the "final evil" not that through which evil ceases to be, but that through which it produces its greatest harm. Thus, these ends are the supreme good and the supreme evil.

As I said, many who have professed the study of wisdom in the futility of this age have worked hard to discover these ends, as well as to obtain the supreme

From Augustine, *Political Writings*, translated by Douglas Kries and Michael Tkacz, edited by Ernest Fortin and Douglas Kries (Indianapolis: Hackett Publishing Company, 1994). Copyright © 1994 Hackett Publishing Co. Reprinted by permission of the publisher.

good and to avoid the supreme evil in this life. Although they wandered off in different directions, nevertheless the limit of nature did not permit them to deviate from the path of truth so far that they failed to place the final good and final evil in the soul, in the body, or in both. To this tripartite division of schools Marcus Varro, in his book *On Philosophy*, directed his attention, diligently and subtly scrutinizing a large number of different teachings. By applying certain distinctions he easily arrived at 288 possible—though not necessarily actual—schools. . . .

Chapter 2

Then there are those three kinds of life: the first is the leisurely—but not slothful—life, devoted to contemplating or seeking the truth; the second is the busy life devoted to conducting human affairs; and the third is the life which mixes both of these kinds. When it is asked which of these three ought to be chosen, the final good is not being disputed. What is considered by that question is which of these three brings difficulty or assistance for seeking or preserving the final good. When anyone attains the final good, he is forthwith made happy. However, the life devoted to learned leisure, to public business, or to performing both alternately does not necessarily make one happy. Certainly, many are able to live in one or another of these three ways, but err with respect to desiring the final good by which man is made happy.

Therefore, it is one thing to ask about the final good and the final evil, and the answer to that question distinguishes every single one of the philosophical schools. It is quite another thing to ask questions about the social life, the hesitation of the Academics, the dress and diet of the Cynics, and the three kinds of life—the leisurely, the active, and the combined. The final good and evil are not disputed in any of these questions.

By using these four distinctions—that is, the distinctions derived from the social life, the new Academics, the Cynics, and the three kinds of life—Marcus Varro reaches 288 schools. If there are other distinctions, they could be added in the same way. By removing all of those four distinctions, because they do not bear upon the question of pursuing the supreme good and thus do not give rise to what can properly be called "schools," he returns to those twelve in which it is added, What is the good of man, the pursuit of which makes man happy? From these twelve, he shows that one is true and the rest false. . . .

To Varro, it seemed proper that these three schools be treated carefully. He asked, What ought to be chosen? True reason does not permit more than one to be true, whether it is among these three or—as we will see later on—somewhere else. In the meantime, we will examine, as briefly and clearly as we can, how Varro chooses one of these three. Certainly, these three schools arise as follows: either the primary goods of nature are chosen for the sake of virtue, or virtue is chosen for the sake of the primary goods of nature, or both—that is, both virtue and the primary goods of nature—are chosen for their own sakes.

Chapter 4

If, then, we are asked what the city of God would reply to each of these questions, and, most importantly, what it thinks about the final good and final evil, it will reply that eternal life is the supreme good and eternal death the supreme evil, and that in order to attain the one and avoid the other, we must live rightly. That is why it is written, "The just man lives by faith" (Gal 3:11), for we do not at present see our good and thus must seek it through believing, nor does our living rightly derive from ourselves, except insofar as he, who gave the very faith through which we believe ourselves to be in need of help from him, helps us in our believing and praying.

Those, however, who have held that the final good and evil are in this life, whether they place the supreme good in the body, in the soul, or in both—and indeed, to express it more explicitly, whether they place it in pleasure or in virtue or both; whether in rest or virtue or in both; whether in pleasure and rest simultaneously or in virtue or in all these; whether in the primary things of nature or in virtue or in all

these—they wanted to be happy here and now and, through an astonishing vanity, they wanted to be made happy by their own actions. The Truth ridiculed them through the prophet, saying, "The Lord knows the thoughts of men" (Ps 94:11), or as the apostle Paul puts this testimony, "The Lord knows the thoughts of the wise, that they are vain" (1 Cor 3:20).

Indeed, who is able, however great the flood of his eloquence, to expound the miseries of this life? Cicero lamented them, as well as he was able, in the *Consolation* on the death of his daughter, but how much was he able to do? In truth, when, where, and in what way can those things called the primary goods of nature be so well possessed in this life that they are not tossed about under the sway of unforeseen accidents? What pain contrary to pleasure, what restlessness contrary to rest, could not befall the body of a wise man? Certainly, the amputation or the debility of a man's limbs destroys his soundness, deformity his beauty, feebleness his health, exhaustion his strength, numbness or slowness his mobility. Which of these is it that cannot overcome the flesh of a wise person? The postures and movements of the body, when they are fitting and harmonious, are likewise numbered among the primary goods of nature. Yet what if some state of ill health causes the limbs to shake and tremble? What if the spine is so curved that the hands are forced to touch the ground, making the man a sort of quadruped? Is not every type of posture and movement of the body distorted?

What about the primary things of the mind itself, which are called goods? Sense and intellect are placed first since on account of them perception and comprehension of the truth are possible. Yet what sort of and how much sensation remains if, to say nothing of other things, a man becomes deaf and blind? Indeed, if reason and intelligence recede from someone rendered insane by some illness, where would those faculties slumber? The mad, when they speak or act, do many absurd things, for the most part unrelated—indeed, even opposed—to their own good intentions and inclinations. When we either reflect on or observe what they say and do, if we consider them properly, we are barely—if at all—able to contain our tears. What shall I say of those who suffer the assault of demons? Where is their own intelligence hidden or buried when an evil spirit uses both their soul and their body according to its own will? Who is confident that this evil cannot befall a wise man in this life? Next, how well and to what extent do we perceive truth in this flesh, when, as we read in the true book of Wisdom, "The corruptible body weighs down the soul and the earthly dwelling oppresses the intelligence as it considers many things" (Wis 9:15)? An "impulse" or "appetite for action," if in this way Latin rightly names that which the Greeks call *hormé*, is counted as one of the primary goods of nature. Yet is it not precisely this which also produces those miserable motions and deeds of the insane which horrify us when sense is distorted and reason is put to sleep?

Further, virtue itself, which is not among the primary goods of nature because it is added afterward through education, claims to be the highest of human goods; and yet what does it do except conduct perpetual wars with vices, not external but internal ones, not those of others but our very own? It this not the particular struggle of that virtue which in Greek is named *sóphrosyné*, in Latin "temperance," by which the carnal passions are curbed so that they do not drag the mind into consenting to every sort of shameful action? Vice is never absent when, in the words of the apostle, "The flesh desires in opposition to the spirit." To this vice there is a contrary virtue, when, as the same apostle says: "The spirit desires in opposition to the flesh. For these," he says, "are at war with each other, so that what you will is not what you do" (Gal 5:17). What, however, do we will to do when we will to be perfected by the supreme good? It can only be that the flesh not desire in opposition to the spirit and that this vice opposed to what the spirit desires not be in us. We are not strong enough to do this in this life, however much we will, but with the help of God, let us at least not surrender the spirit and so yield to the flesh warring against the spirit, and be dragged into sinning by our own consent. Therefore, let us not believe that, as long as we are in this internal war, we have already attained our happiness, which we will to attain by conquering the flesh. And who is so utterly wise as to have no conflict at all with his lusts?

What about the virtue called prudence? Does not its total vigilance consist in distinguishing goods from evils, so that in seeking the former and avoiding the latter no error sneaks in? Yet in this way does not prudence itself give evidence that we are among evils or that evils are within us? Prudence teaches that evil is consenting to the desire to sin and that good is withholding consent to that desire. Nevertheless, that evil, to which prudence teaches us not to consent, and to which temperance enables us not to consent, is not removed from this life by either prudence or temperance.

What about justice, whose function is to render to each his due, thereby establishing in man a certain just order of nature, so that the soul is subordinated to God, and the flesh to the soul, and consequently the flesh and the soul to God? Does it not demonstrate in performing this function that it is still laboring at its task instead of resting in the completion of its goal? Surely, the less the soul keeps God in its own thoughts, the less it is subordinated to him; and the more the flesh desires in opposition to the spirit, the less is it subordinated to the soul. Therefore, as long as there is in us this weakness, this plague, this weariness, how shall we dare to say that we are already made well? If we are not yet made well, how shall we dare to say that we are already happy in the attainment of final happiness?

As for the virtue called courage, no matter how wise one may be, it bears the clearest witness to human evils, which it is forced to endure patiently. I am astonished to see with what boldness the Stoic philosophers contend that such evils are not evils, yet they allow that if evils become so great that a wise man cannot or ought not endure them, he may be driven to bring about his own death and leave this life. So great is the stupid pride of these men that, while holding that the final good is found in this life and that they are made happy by their own efforts, their wise man (that is, the man whom they describe with an amazing inanity) is one who—even if he is made blind, deaf, dumb, and lame, even if he is tormented by pain and assailed by any other such evils that could be spoken or thought, so that he is driven to bring about his own death—is still not ashamed to call this life so composed of evils "happy"!

O happy life, which seeks the help of death in order to be ended! If it is happy, he should remain in it. In what way are those things not evils? They conquer the good of courage and not only compel the same courage to yield to themselves, but also to rave, so that it both calls the same life happy and persuades one to flee it! Who is so blind that he does not see that if it is happy, one ought not flee it? In saying that such a life must be fled, they openly admit the weakness of their position. The neck of their pride having been broken, why they do not also admit that such a life is miserable? I ask, did Cato kill himself because of endurance or lack of endurance? He would not have done it, except that he could not bear to endure the victory of Caesar.[1] Where is the courage here? Truly, it yielded; truly, it surrendered; truly, it was so completely overcome that it abandoned, deserted, and fled the happy life. Or was it not then happy? Clearly, it was miserable. In what sense, then, were there no evils which made life miserable and something necessary to flee? . . .

If virtues are true — and true virtues cannot exist except in those who possess true piety — they do not profess to be able to protect the men who have them from suffering miseries. True virtues are not such liars as to profess this. They do, however, profess that human life, which is compelled by the great number and magnitude of evils in this world to be miserable, is happy through hope in a future world, and in the same way made well. Indeed, how can it be happy until it is made well? And thus the apostle Paul, speaking not of imprudent, impatient, intemperate, and unjust men, but of men living according to true piety and thereby having true virtues, says: "By hope we are made well. However, hope that is seen is not hope, for how can one hope for what one sees? However, if we hope for what we do not see, we look forward to it with patience" (Rom 8:24–25).

Therefore, as we are made well by hope, so we are made happy by hope; and as we do not presently possess well-being, but look forward to it in the future "with patience," so it is with happiness. This is because we are now among evils, which we must endure patiently, until we arrive at those goods in which we will find only indescribable delight and none of the things which we must now endure. Such well-being, which we will find in the future world, will itself be final happiness. Because they do not see this happiness, the philosophers refuse to believe in it, but struggle to fabricate for themselves in this life an utterly false happiness through a virtue as dishonest as it is proud.

Chapter 6

What about the legal judgments of men concerning other men? No matter how much peace abides in cities, they cannot be eliminated. How wretched, how sad we think they are! Those judging are unable to discern the consciences of those whom they judge. Consequently, they are frequently compelled to investigate the truth by torturing innocent witnesses concerning a case that is not even their own. What about when someone whose own case is at stake is tortured? He is asked whether he is guilty while he is being tortured. Even an innocent person, then, pays a most certain penalty for an uncertain crime, and not because it is discovered that he committed it, but because it is not known that he did not commit it. Thus, the ignorance of the judge is frequently the calamity of the innocent.

What is much more intolerable, what must be lamented and washed, if it were possible, by fountains of tears, is this: a judge, on account of ignorance, tortures an accused in order not to execute an innocent person mistakenly, yet it happens that the judge does execute, through wretched ignorance, one who is both innocent and tortured, one whom the judge had tortured in order that he might not execute an innocent person. If, following the "wise," the accused has chosen to flee this life rather than endure the tortures any longer, he says he has committed what he did not commit. Though he is condemned and executed, the judge still does not know whether the person he tortured in order that he might not mistakenly execute an innocent person was innocent or not. Thus, he both tortures an innocent man in order to know and kills him though he does not know.

In this darkness of the social life, will a judge who is "wise" sit in judgment or not? Certainly he will, for human society, which he considers it a crime to desert, binds him and drags him to this duty. These things he does not consider to be crimes: that innocent witnesses are tortured in the cases of others; that the innocent who are accused are frequently

---

1. [Rather than endure what he considered to be the tyranny of Caesar, Cato of Utica killed himself in 46 B.C. The Stoics considered Cato to be a hero for this. — E.F./D.K.]

overcome by the power of pain when they are tortured, and are then punished on account of falsely confessing; that, although not punished by death, they frequently die while being tortured or as a result of being tortured; or that sometimes the accusers, perhaps desiring to be beneficial to human society by seeing to it that no crimes go unpunished, are unable to prove the charges even though they are true, since the witnesses lie and the defendant himself fiercely endures the torture without confession, and are themselves mistakenly condemned by a judge. This great number and magnitude of evils he does not consider to be sins, for a wise judge does not do them because of a will to harm, but because of the necessity imposed by not knowing, and also because of the necessity of judging imposed by human society.

Accordingly, even if they are not the malice of the wise, these evils are certainly what we call the misery of man. If indeed it is through the necessity of not knowing and of judging that he tortures and punishes the guiltless, is it not enough for him that we do not hold him to be guilty? Must we call him "happy" besides? How much more thoughtful and appropriate it is for man to recognize misery in this necessity, and to hate himself because of it, and if he is wise in the manner of the pious, to cry out to God, "Deliver me from my necessities!" (Ps 25:17)

Chapter 7

After the city or municipality comes the world, which they regard as the third level of human society. Beginning with the household, they progress to the city and then to the world. Like converging waters, as the world is larger, so is it more dangerous. In the first place, the diversity of languages in the world alienates one man from another. Imagine that two people meet and are compelled by some necessity not to pass by but to remain together. If neither knows the language of the other, although they are both human beings, speechless animals—even if they are of different species—will associate with each other more easily. When human beings realize that they cannot communicate between themselves solely because of the difference of language, nothing promotes their association despite their similarity of nature. A man would rather be with his own dog than a foreigner.

Yet it might be said that, by taming peoples through the peace of society, the imperial city attempts to impose not only its yoke but also its language, so that there is no lack of interpreters, but indeed a great abundance. This is true. Yet how does it compensate for the numerous and immense wars, the great slaughter of men, the tremendous effusion of human blood? Even though those evils are now settled, the misery of them is not yet finished. Although bordering, hostile nations have never been and are not presently lacking, and although wars always have been and continue to be waged against them, nevertheless the very size of the empire has given rise to wars of a worse kind; namely, social and civil wars. The human race is shaken by these more miserable wars, either when they are waged so that there might eventually be calm, or when a fresh outbreak of them is feared. If I wanted to speak appropriately of these evils, great and immense destructions, and hard and dire necessities, even though I could by no means do so as the subject demands, where would this lengthy discussion end?

They say, however, that the wise man will wage only just wars—as if, mindful that he is human, he would not much rather lament that he is subject to the necessity of waging just wars. If they were not just, he would not be required to wage them, and thus he would be free of the necessity of war. It is the iniquity on the part of the adversary that forces a just war upon the wise man. Even if it did not give rise to the necessity of war, such iniquity must certainly be lamented by a human being since it belongs to human beings. Therefore, let anyone who reflects with sorrow upon these evils so great, so horrid, and so savage, confess that he is miserable. Anyone, however, who either permits or considers these things without sorrow in mind is certainly much more miserable, since he thinks himself happy because he has lost human feeling.

Chapter 11

Because the name "peace" is also frequently used with respect to things which are subject to death, where there certainly is no eternal life, we prefer to call the end of this city, where its highest good will be, "eternal life" rather than "peace." Of this end the apostle says, "Now, indeed, having been liberated from sin and having become servants of God, you will have your reward in sanctification, your true end in eternal life" (Rom 6:22):

On the other hand, "eternal life" could be taken by those who are not familiar with the Sacred Scriptures to include also the life of the wicked. One might think this either because certain philosophers profess the immortality of the soul, or also because our faith professes the unending punishment of the impious, who certainly could not be eternally tormented unless they also lived eternally.

So that it can be understood more easily by all, it must be said that the end of this city, in which it will have its highest good, is either "peace in eternal life" or "eternal life in peace." Peace is such a great good that even with respect to earthly and mortal things, nothing is heard with greater pleasure, nothing desired more longingly, and in the end, nothing better can be found. If I wish to speak of it somewhat longer I will not, I think, be burdensome to readers, both because my subject is the end of this city and because of the very sweetness of peace, which is dear to all.

Chapter 12

Anyone who pays any attention to human affairs and our common human nature, recognizes as I do that just as there is no one who does not wish to be joyful, so there is no one who does not wish to have peace. Indeed, even those who want war want nothing other than to achieve victory; by warring, therefore, they desire to attain a glorious peace. What else is victory, unless triumphing over the opposition? When this has happened, there will be peace. Therefore, even those who are eager to exercise the military virtues by commanding or fighting wage war with the intention of peace. Consequently, the desired end of war is peace, for everyone seeks peace, even by waging war, but no one seeks war by making peace.

Even those who want the peace they now have to be disturbed do not hate peace, but they desire to change the peace according to their own wishes. Thus, they are not unwilling that there be peace, but they want it on their own terms. Furthermore, even if they have separated themselves from others through sedition, when they conspire or plot amongst themselves they do not achieve what they intend unless they have some sort of peace. Likewise, robbers themselves want to have peace with their partners, so that they might more violently and safely attack to the peace of others. Perhaps one person is so strong and so wary of conspiring with others that he does not ally himself to any partners. Waiting in ambush and prevailing alone, he gains plunder by crushing and annihilating whom he can. Still, with those whom he cannot kill and from whom he wants to hide what he does, he certainly has some sort of a shadow of peace.

In his home, with his wife and children and anyone else who might be there, he surely strives to be at peace. Their complying with his command is no doubt pleasing. If they do not do so, he is enraged; he rebukes and punishes them. He establishes peace in his own home, if it is necessary, even by brutality. He thinks that peace is not possible unless the rest of the household is subject to a ruler, and in his own home he himself is that ruler. That is why, if the service of a great multitude, or of cities, or peoples is offered to him, so that they would serve him in the same manner as he wanted to be served in his own household, then he would no longer conceal himself like a bandit in a hideout, but raise himself up like a visible king, although the same desire and malice would abide in him. Thus, all desire to have peace with their own associates, whom they want to live according to their own decree. Indeed, they want, if they are able, to make even those against whom they wage war into their own associates, and to impose on them, when conquered, the laws of their own peace.

Let us imagine someone of the sort sung about in poetry and myth, someone whom, perhaps because of his unsociability and savageness, they have preferred to call "semihuman" rather than "human." His kingdom was the solitude of his horrible cave. So extraordinary was his malice that a name was invented from it, for in the Greek language evil is called *kakos*, which is what he was named.[2] He had no wife with whom to carry on endearing conversation, no little children to play with, no older children to give orders to, no friends with whom to enjoy speaking. He did

---

2. [The story of Cacus is related by Virgil in *Aeneid* VIII. 184–305.]

not even enjoy the society of his father Vulcan, compared to whom he was happier simply because he had not generated such a monster as himself. He gave nothing to anyone, but took from whomever he could whatever and whenever he wanted.

Nevertheless, in the very solitude of his own cave, in which, as is said, "the ground was always reeking with fresh carnage,"[3] he wanted nothing other than peace—a peace in which no one would molest him, in which the quiet was not disturbed by the violence of anyone or the fear of it. Further, he desired to be at peace with his body, and to the extent that he was at peace with it, all was well with him. When he commanded, the limbs of his body submitted. Yet, his own mortality rebelled against him out of need and stirred up sedition through hunger, aiming to dissociate and exclude the soul from the body. In order to make peace with that mortality as quickly as possible, he plundered, he killed, and he devoured. Though monstrous and savage, he was nevertheless monstrously and savagely providing for the peace of his own life and well-being. Moreover, if he had been willing to make peace with others while he was striving to make peace in his cave and in himself, he would not have been called evil or a monster or semihuman. Also, if the appearance of his body and his breathing horrible fire frightened human society, possibly he was not so much savage because of a desire for harming but because of the necessity of his staying alive.

He might not, however, have even existed, or, what is more believable, he might not have been the same as the description given by the vanity of poetry, for if Cacus were not blamed too much, Hercules would be praised too little.[4] Therefore, it is better, as I have said, to believe that a human or semihuman of that sort never existed, as is the case with many of the imaginings of the poets.

Even the most savage wild animals, from whom Cacus got part of his wildness (for he was even said to be half-wild), care for their own species by means of a certain peace. They do this by associating, begetting, bearing, cherishing, and nourishing the offspring, even though they are for the most part insociable and solitary. I do not mean those animals such as sheep, deer, doves, starlings, and bees, but those such as lions, wolves, foxes, eagles, and owls. Indeed, what tigress, pacifying her wildness, does not gently purr and caress her young? What kite, however much it circles its prey alone, does not unite with a mate, put together a nest, warm the eggs, nourish the young birds, and, as if with the mother of his family, keep peace in his domestic society as much as he can? How much more is man brought by the laws of his nature, as it were, to enter into society and keep peace with all men to the extent that he is able?

After all, even the evil wage war for the sake of the peace of their own associates, and they would want to make everyone their own, if they could, so that everyone and everything would be enslaved to one individual. How would that happen if they did not consent to his peace, either through love or fear? In this manner, pride imitates God in a distorted way. It hates equality with partners under God, but wants to impose its own domination upon its partners in place of God. Consequently, it hates the just peace of God and loves its own iniquitous peace. Nevertheless, it is not able not to love some sort of peace. Truly, there is no defect so contrary to nature that it wipes away even the last vestiges of nature. Accordingly, he who knows to prefer the upright to the deformed, and the ordered to the distorted, sees that the peace of the iniquitous, in comparison to the peace of the just, should not be called "peace" at all. However, it is necessary that even what is distorted be at peace in some way with a part of the things in which it exists or from which it is established. Otherwise, it would not exist at all.

This is just like if someone were to hang with his head downward. The position of the body and the order of the limbs would certainly be distorted, because what nature demands to be above is below, and what it wants to be below is above. This distortion disturbs the peace of the flesh and for that reason is painful. It is nevertheless true that the soul is at peace with the body and is busy struggling for its wellbeing, and thus there is someone suffering. If the soul departs, having been driven out by the pain, as long as the structure of the limbs remains, so does a certain amount of peace, and thus there is still something

---

3. [*Aeneid* VIII. 195.]

4. [Cacus was eventually slain by Hercules.]

hanging there. Because the earthly body tends toward the earth and is resisted by the chain by which it is suspended, it tends to the order of its own peace and requests in a weighty voice, as it were, a place where it might rest. Now lifeless and without any sense, nevertheless it does not depart from the peace of its own natural order, either when it has it or when it reaches toward it.

If embalming potions and treatments are applied, which do not allow the form of the cadaver to break up and dissolve, a sort of peace still unites certain parts to other parts and connects the whole mass in its suitable and therefore peaceful place in the earth. If no one applies the treatment for burying, however, then the cadaver disintegrates in the course of nature. It is in a state of disturbance due to dissenting vapors which are disagreeable to our senses (for this is what is smelled in putrefaction), until it is assimilated to the elements of the world and gradually, little by little, separates into their peace. Nevertheless, in no way is anything withdrawn from the laws of the supreme creator and governor by whom the peace of the universe is administered, for even if tiny animals are born from the cadaver of a greater animal, by the same law of the creator each little body serves its own little soul in the well-being of peace. Even if the flesh of the dead is devoured by other animals, wherever it is carried, whatever the things to which it is joined, whatever the things into which it is changed and altered, it finds those same laws diffused throughout all things for the well-being of every mortal species, making peace by harmonizing suitable elements.

Chapter 13

Thus, the peace of the body is the ordered proportion of its parts. The peace of the irrational soul is the ordered repose of the appetites. The peace of the rational soul is the ordered agreement of knowledge and action. The peace of the body and the soul is the ordered life and well-being of a living thing. The peace between a mortal man and God is an ordered obedience, in faith, under the eternal law.

The peace among human beings is ordered concord. The peace of the household is an ordered concord concerning commanding and obeying among those who dwell together. The peace of the city is an ordered concord concerning commanding and obeying among the citizens. The peace of the heavenly city is a fellowship perfectly ordered and harmonious, enjoying God and each other in God. The peace of all things is the tranquility of order.

Order is the arrangement of things equal and unequal, alloting to each its own position. Hence, the miserable indeed lack the tranquility of order in which there is no disturbance, since insofar as they are miserable, they certainly are not at peace. Nevertheless, since they are deservedly and justly miserable, they are not, in their very own misery, able to be outside that order. They are surely not united to the happy, but, by the law of order, are separated from them. When they are free from disturbance, they are adjusted to the circumstances in which they find themselves by a harmony of some degree. Thus, some tranquility of order belongs to them, and so some peace. Therefore, the reason they are miserable is because, even if they have some freedom from concern and are not suffering, they are still not in a position where they ought to be exempt from concern and suffering. They are more miserable, however, if they are not at peace with the very law by which the order of nature is administered.

Moreover, when they suffer, they suffer in that part in which a disturbance of peace occurs, but there is still peace in that part not disturbed by suffering and in the structure itself, which is not dissolved. As, therefore, there is a kind of life without suffering, but suffering cannot exist without some life, so there is a kind of peace without any war, but war cannot exist without some peace. This does not follow because of what war itself is, but because it is waged by those or in those who are natural beings in some way. They would not exist at all, unless they remained in a peace of some sort.

Accordingly, there is a nature in which there is no evil, or even in which there can be no evil, but there cannot be a nature in which there is no good. Thus, not even the nature of the devil himself, insofar as it is a nature, is evil. Rather, it is the distortion of that nature that makes it evil. Hence, he did not stand firm in the truth, but he did not escape the judgment of the truth. He did not remain in the tranquility of order, but he nevertheless did not avoid the power of the one who orders. The goodness of God, which is in the devil's nature, does not remove him from the justice of God, which orders by punishing him. God did not then reproach the good that he created, but the evil that the devil has committed. Neither does God take away all that he gave to the devil's nature, but some he takes and some he leaves, so that there might be something to suffer the loss of what was taken away. That very suffering is a witness to the good taken away and the good left behind, for unless good were left behind, the devil could not suffer because of the good lost. . . .

Therefore, God, who founded all natures most wisely and ordered them most justly, who established the mortal human race as the greatest embellishment of the earth, gave to mankind certain goods suitable for this life. These goods include a temporal peace proportional to the short span of a mortal life, a peace involving health, preservation, and the society of one's own kind. They also include the things necessary for guarding or recovering this peace (such as what is appropriately and fittingly present to the senses: light, sound, breathable air, drinkable water, and whatever is suitable for feeding, covering, healing, and adorning the body). All this was given through the most equitable stipulation, that he who uses such mortal goods rightly, adapting them to the peace of mortals, would receive more and better goods; namely, the peace of immortality and the glory and honor suitable to it, in an eternal life which is for enjoying God and one's neighbor in God. He, however, who uses mortal goods wrongly, would lose them and would not receive eternal ones.

Chapter 15

God said, "Let him have dominion over the fish of the sea and the winged things of the heavens and all the crawling things which crawl upon the earth" (Gn 1:26). He did not will that the rational being, having been made according to his own image, dominate any except the irrational beings; he did not will that man dominate man, but that man dominate the beasts. Therefore, the first just men were established as shepherds of beasts rather than as kings of men, so that even in this way God might suggest what the order of creatures requires and what the reward of sinners drives away. Surely it is understood that the

condition of slavery is rightly imposed on the sinner. Accordingly, nowhere in the scripture do we read the word "slave" before the just Noah punished the sin of his son with this word. Thus, he earned the name through fault, not through nature. . . .

The first cause of slavery, then, is sin, with the result that man is placed under man by the bondage of this condition. This does not happen except through the judgment of God, in whom there is no iniquity, and who knows how to distribute the various punishments according to the merits of the delinquent. Yet, as the Lord above says, "Anyone who sins is a slave of sin" (Jn 8:34), and thus indeed many religious people enslaved to iniquitous masters are nevertheless not enslaved to the free: "For by whatever one has been conquered, to that one has also been made a slave" (2 Pt 2:19). And it is certainly a happier condition to be enslaved to a man than to a lust, since the very lust for dominating—not to mention others—ravishes the hearts of mortals by a most savage mastery. In that order of peace by which some are subordinated to others, humility is as beneficial to the enslaved as pride is harmful to the dominating.

Nevertheless, by the nature in which God first established man, no one is a slave of man or of sin. It is also true that penal slavery is ordained by that law which commands the preservation and prohibits the disturbance of the natural order, because if nothing had been done contrary to that law, there would have been nothing requiring the restraint of penal slavery. That is why the apostle also warns slaves to be subject to their masters and to serve with good will and from the heart (Eph 6:5), so that if they are not able to be freed by their masters, they might make their slavery in a certain sense free, by serving not with the cunning of fear, but with the faithfulness of affection, until iniquity is transformed and all human rule and power are made void, and God is all in all (1 Cor 15:24, 28).

Chapter 16

. . . Those who are true "fathers of their families" are concerned that all in their family—the slaves as well as the children—should worship and be reconciled to God. Such fathers desire and long to come to the heavenly household, where the duty of ruling mortals is not necessary because the duty of being concerned for the welfare of those already happy in that immortality will no longer be necessary. Until that home is reached, fathers ought to endure more because they rule than slaves do because they serve.

If, however, anyone in the household opposes the domestic peace through disobedience, he is disciplined by word or by whip or by any other kind of just and legitimate punishment, to the extent that human society allows. Such discipline is for the profit of the one being disciplined, so that he is readjusted to the peace from which he had departed. After all, just as it is not kindness to help someone when it would cause him to lose a greater good, so it is not innocent to spare punishment and permit someone to fall more grievously into wickedness. Therefore, in order to be innocent, duty demands not only that one not bring evil to anyone, but also that one restrain another from sin or punish his sin, so that either the person who is punished might be set straight by the experience or others frightened by his example.

Hence, because the human household ought to be the beginning or the building block of the city, and because every beginning is directed to some end of its own kind and every part to the integrity of the whole whose part it is, the consequence is clearly that domestic peace is directed to civic peace. That is to say, the ordered concord concerning commanding and obeying of those dwelling together is directed to the ordered concord concerning commanding and obeying of the citizens. Accordingly, the father of the family should obtain the precepts by which he rules his household from the laws of the city, so that his household might be adapted to the peace of the city.

Chapter 17

The household of those who do not live by faith chases an earthly peace consisting of the affairs and advantages of this temporal life. The household of human beings living by faith, on the other hand, looks forward to the future, to those things which are promised as eternal, and makes use of temporal and earthly things like a traveller. Those things do not seize such a person and turn him away from the path to God. They do not increase the burdens of "the corruptible body which weighs down the soul" (Wis

9:15), but sustain him for more easily enduring them. Consequently, both sorts of men and both sorts of households use the things necessary for this mortal life, but the end of such use is unique to each and varies greatly. So also the earthly city, which does not live by faith, desires earthly peace and it secures the concord concerning commanding and obeying of the citizens, so that there might be a certain orderly arrangement of human wills concerning the things pertaining to mortal life. The heavenly city, however, or rather the part of it which journeys in this mortal life and lives by faith, necessarily uses this peace, too, until the very mortality which makes such a peace necessary might pass away.

Because of this, so long as it leads the life of a captive, as it were, journeying within the earthly city, already having received a promise of redemption and a spiritual gift as a pledge of it, the heavenly city has no doubts about conforming to the laws of the earthly city which administer the things required for the sustainance of the mortal life. Because mortality itself is common to both of the cities, concord between them is preserved with respect to those things pertaining to the mortal life. . . .

So long as this heavenly city journeys on the earth, it calls forth citizens from all peoples and gathers a society of foreigners speaking all languages. It is not troubled at all about differences in customs, laws, and institutions by which the earthly peace is either sought or maintained. So long as they do not impede the religion which teaches the worship of the one, supreme, and true God, the heavenly city abrogates or destroys none of them, but indeed observes and follows them, for whatever the diversities of different nations, they nevertheless strive toward the one and the same end of earthly peace.

Hence, even the heavenly city uses the earthly peace on its journey, and it is concerned about and desires the orderly arrangement of human wills concerning the things pertaining to mortal human nature, insofar as it is agreeable to sound piety and religion. It directs the earthly peace to the heavenly peace, which is so truly peace that it must be held and said that the only peace, at least of rational creatures, is the most ordered and most harmonious society enjoying God and each other in God. When that peace comes, there will not be mortal life, but a whole and certain life; not the ensouled body weighing down the soul in its corruption (Wis 9:15), but a spiritual body with no wants and with every part subordinated to the will. While it journeys, the heavenly city possesses this peace in faith, and out of this faith it lives justly when it directs to the attainment of that peace whatever good actions it performs toward God, and also those performed toward the neighbor, since the life of this city is certainly social.

Chapter 19

The style of dress or manner of living in which anyone follows the faith that leads to God does not matter to the heavenly city, so long as these are not in contradiction with the divine precepts. Thus, even philosophers, when they become Christians, are not required to change their style of dress or eating customs, which do not impede religion, though they are required to change their false teachings. Accordingly, that city does not care at all about the distinction that Varro made concerning the Cynics, so long as nothing is done basely or intemperately.

With respect to those three kinds of life, the leisurely, the active, and the combination of the two, although every one, through sound faith, can lead his life according to any one of them and attain the everlasting reward, what one holds through the love of truth and what one expends through the duty of charity are nevertheless important. Thus, no one ought to be so leisurely that he does not, in his leisure, consider the advantage of his neighbor; neither should anyone be so active that he does not consider the contemplation of God to be necessary.

In leisure, one ought not delight in slothful idleness, but in either the investigation or discovery of truth, so that everyone advances in it and does not withhold his discoveries from others. In action, no one ought to love honor or power in this life, because all is vanity under the sun (Eccl 1:2–3). Rather, the work itself that is done through the same honor or power should be loved, if it is done rightly and profitably. That is to say, it should be loved if it advances the well-being of the subjects, which is according to God, as we have argued earlier.

Because of this the apostle said, "He who desires the episcopacy desires a good work" (1 Tm 3:1). He wanted to explain that the name "episcopacy" is the name of a work not of an honor. Indeed, the word is Greek, and it comes from the fact that he who is set over others "superintends" them; that is, he exercises care for them. Indeed, the Greek word *skopos* means intention; therefore, for *episkopein* we can say, if we want, "superintend." Consequently, he who desires to be over others rather than to benefit others should understand that he is not a bishop.

Thus, no one is prohibited from zealousness for knowledge of the truth, because the life of learned leisure pertains to what is praiseworthy. On the other hand, to desire high position, without which a people cannot be ruled, is indecent, even if the position is held and administered in a decent manner. Because of this, charity for truth seeks holy leisure, while the requirements of charity accept just activity. If this latter burden is not imposed, one is free to grasp for and to contemplate truth. If, however, the burden is imposed, accepting it is on account of the requirements of charity. Even in this instance, however, delight in the truth is not abandoned completely, otherwise that sweetness might be lost and these requirements crush us.

Chapter 21

It is at this place that I will explain, as briefly and clearly as I can, what in the second book of this work I promised that I would demonstrate; namely, that, according to the definition that Scipio uses in the *Republic* of Cicero, there never was a Roman republic. He succinctly defines a "republic" as "the affair of a people." If this definition is true, there never was a Roman republic, because Rome never was the affair of a people, which is Scipio's definition of a republic.

The reason for this is that he defined "a people" as "a fellowship of a multitude united through a consensus concerning right and a sharing of advantage." What he calls "a consensus concerning right" he explains in the dialogue by making it clear that it is not possible for a republic to be managed without justice. Therefore, where there is no true justice, there can be no right. What is done by right is indeed done justly; what is done unjustly, however, cannot be done by right. The iniquitous institutions of human beings must not be said or thought to exist by right, because even those institutions say that right flows from the fountain of justice, and that what is customarily said by those who do not understand right correctly—i.e. that right is the advantage of the strongest—is false.

Accordingly, where there is no true justice, there can be no fellowship of men united through a consensus concerning right, and therefore there can be no people according to the definition of Scipio or Cicero. Moreover, if there is no people, neither can there be an affair of a people, but only of some sort of a multitude which is not worthy of the name of "a people." Consequently, if a republic is "the affair of a people," and there is no people which is not "united by means of a consensus concerning right," and there is no right where there is no justice, without doubt it must be concluded that where there is no justice, there is no republic.

Furthermore, justice is that virtue which distributes to everyone his due. What sort of justice is it, then, that takes a man away from the true God and subjects him to unclean demons? Is *this* to distribute to each his due? Or, is he who takes the ground purchased by someone and gives it to another who has no right to it unjust, but he who takes himself away from the dominion of the God who made him and enslaves himself to malicious spirits just?

Certainly, the cause of justice against injustice is argued very energetically and forcefully in that very same book, *The Republic*. Earlier, the case of injustice against justice was considered and it was said that the republic could not stand firm or be managed except through injustice. It was set down as the most powerful part of the argument that it was unjust for men to serve other men as their masters, but that unless the imperial city to whom the great republic belongs follows such injustice it is not able to rule its provinces. The response from the side of justice was that this rule over the inhabitants of the provinces is just because servitude is advantageous for such men and is done for their benefit when it is done correctly—that is, when the license for wrongdoing is taken away from the wicked. Also, it was argued that they will be in a better condition as a result of having been subdued, because they were in a worse condition before being subdued.

In order to strengthen this reasoning, a famous example was stated as though it was borrowed from nature: "Why, then, does God rule man, the soul rule the body, the reason rule lust and the rest of the corrupt parts of the soul?"[5] Plainly, this example teaches well that servitude is advantageous to some and that serving God is indeed advantageous to all. In serving God, the soul correctly rules the body, and the reason in the soul subordinated to the Lord God correctly rules lust and the rest of the corrupt parts of the soul. Thus, when a man does not serve God, what in him can be reckoned to belong to justice? Indeed, when not serving God, the soul can in no way justly rule the body, or human reason the vices. Furthermore, if there is not any justice in such a man, without doubt neither is there any in a fellowship of human beings which consists of such men. Therefore, this is not that "consensus concerning right" which makes a multitude of human beings a "people," whose affair is called a "republic."

What shall I say concerning that "advantage," the sharing of which also unites a fellowship of men so that it is named "a people," as stipulated by the definition? If you carefully direct your attention, you will see that there is no advantage to any who live impiously, as do all who do not serve God but serve the demons who, the more impious they are, the more they want to receive sacrifice as gods, even though they are the most unclean spirits of all. Yet, what we have said about the consensus concerning right I think is sufficient to make it apparent that, according to this definition, there is no people which might be said to be a republic in which there is no justice.

If our enemies say that the Romans have not served unclean spirits but good and holy gods in their republic, must what we have already said sufficiently, indeed more than sufficiently, be repeated yet again? Who, except the excessively stupid or the shamelessly contentious, having arrived at this point after reading the earlier books of this work, finds it possible to doubt but that the Romans have up to this point served evil and impure demons? Nevertheless, in order to say no more about the sort of gods they are worshipping with sacrifices, I instead cite what is written in the law of the true God: "Anyone sacrificing to the

5. [*Republic* III. 25.]

gods, except only to the Lord, will be eradicated" (Ex 22:20). Thus, he who admonishes with such a threat did not want either good gods or evil ones to receive sacrifice.

Chapter 23

. . . We ourselves—his city—are the best and most radiant sacrifice. We celebrate this mystery through our offerings, which are known to the faithful, as we have argued in the preceding books. Indeed, through the Hebrew prophets the divine oracles thundered that the offering of sacrificial victims by the Jews, a foreshadowing of the future, would cease, and that peoples from the rising of the sun to its setting would offer one sacrifice, as we see happening now. From these oracles we have taken as much as seemed sufficient and have already sprinkled them throughout this work.

Thus, justice exists when the one and supreme God rules his obedient city according to his grace, so that it does not sacrifice to any whatsoever except Him alone. As a result, in everyone belonging to that same city and obeying God, the soul faithfully commands the body, and reason the corrupt parts of the soul, in accord with the lawful order. Consequently, just like a single just man, a fellowship and a people of just men lives by faith, which works through love, by which man loves God as God ought to be loved, and his neighbor as himself. Where that justice does not exist, truly there is no "fellowship of men united through a consensus concerning right and a sharing of advantage." If this justice does not exist, then a people does not exist, if this is the true definition of a people. Therefore, neither does a republic exist, for there is no affair of a people where there is no people.

Chapter 24

If, however, a people is not defined in that way, but in another—if, for example, it is said that a people is "a fellowship of a multitude of rational beings united through sharing in an agreement about what it loves"—then truly, in order to see the character of a people, what it loves must be considered. If it is not a fellowship of a multitude of beasts, but of rational creatures, and is united through sharing in an agreement about what it loves, then, no matter what it loves, it is not unreasonable to call it "a people." It is a better people if it agrees in loving better things; a worse one if it agrees in loving worse things. According to this definition, the Roman people is a people, and its affair is without doubt a republic. However, history gives witness to what that people loved originally and subsequently, and by what morals it arrived at the bloodiest revolutions and then at social and civil wars, utterly shattering and annihilating concord itself, which is, in a certain sense, the well-being of a people. Of this we have said much in the preceding books. . . .

THOMAS AQUINAS

In 1277, three years after the death of Thomas Aquinas (1224–1274), Pope John XXI asked Stephen Tempier, the bishop of Paris, to investigate the dispute between philosophy and theology that had flourished during the thirteenth century, after the rediscovery of Aristotle's works. The result was a set of 219 propositions that were held by the philosophers and that opposed the Christian faith, including, for example, that the world is eternal and that there is no freedom of choice. On March 7, 1277, the bishop condemned these propositions, which included some of Aquinas's attempts to harmonize Aristotelianism and Christian faith. With this act of condemnation the great task of uniting faith and reason, theology and philosophy, reached a turning point. What Aquinas had tried to achieve, both philosophers and theologians began to reject in their different ways, and his grand synthesis, later to be canonized as official Catholic doctrine, came to generate diverse criticisms.

Aquinas was born at the castle of Roccasecca, near Naples, Italy, the youngest son of Landalfo, the count of Aquino. At the age of five, he began his education under the Benedictine monks at nearby Monte Cassino, where he remained until 1239. He then went to the University of Naples and soon became acquainted with a vigorous young group of Dominicans, students of philosophy and theology. By 1244 Aquinas had joined this local convent of Dominican friars, against his family's wishes. When the Dominicans arranged for him to accompany them on a trip to Cologne, with the plan to send him on to study for a Dominican novitiate at the University of Paris, Aquinas's brothers kidnapped him and held him prisoner at Aquino for a year.

In 1245 Aquinas escaped and made his way to Paris, where he remained until 1248. From 1248 to 1252 he was a member of a Dominican house of studies in Cologne and became the student of the famous German Dominican Aristotelian, Albert the Great. In 1252 Aquinas returned to Paris, where he taught until 1259. He then moved to Italy, where, until 1268, he taught in and around Rome. Once again, he returned to Paris and engaged in controversy with the Latin Averroists and followers of Siger of Brabant, who argued for a pure Aristotelianism, and, on the other side, with the followers of Saint Bonaventure, who sought to establish an ultra-Augustinian (or voluntaristic) Christianity and ban Aristotelianism altogether. In 1272 he was sent to Naples to establish a Dominican house of study. By this time, his health was not good; indeed, some conjecture that he had suffered a stroke. When he was called to Lyons by Pope Gregory X to participate in a council, he struck his head and died of complications on the way, on March 7, 1274, at a monastery between Naples and Rome.

Aquinas's life was intellectually rich, filled with study, teaching, and writing. He left an enormous corpus of work. While teaching in Paris from 1252 to 1259, he wrote his commentary on the *Sentences* of Peter Lombard and his treatises *On the Principles of Nature*, *On Being and Essence*, and *On Truth*. The *Summa Contra Gentiles*, a work intended to help Dominican missionaries in Spain and North Africa, was completed while he was in Italy between 1259 and 1268, and the great *Summa Theologica* was written between 1265 and 1273. During his relatively brief lifetime, he also published a variety of other treatises and commentaries on no less than twelve Aristotelian treatises.

Aquinas was both a theologian and a philosopher. As a theologian, he wrote about God and the world based on rational inquiry and the evidence of faith. As a philosopher, he was an Aristotelian who employed the data of the senses, examined and understood in the light of first principles. He sought to understand God in terms of an inquiry into nature and then to return to understand nature with new thoughts based on his grasp of the divine. The twofold character of his thought, moreover, influenced his ethics; in his understanding of man, the soul, human will, appetite, and moral purpose, he used the teleological notions of capacities, potentialities, and purposes. For Aquinas, man's ultimate goal is happiness, which he takes to be the joyful knowledge of God and a life which attempts to realize the nature which God has given to man. It is a goal that can be achieved in a variety of ways; his moral theory focuses on these ways. On the one hand, Aquinas is concerned with virtue and the cultivation of character, as these facilitate human happiness; on the other, he is concerned with law as it directs our conduct from the outside but toward the same goal.

In a way, this dichotomy between internal and external control is also reflected in Aquinas's political theory. His family had imperial connections in southern Italy, and hence he grew up with monarchist sensibilities. But he cast his lot with the democratic-style practices of the Dominican order. The result, in Aquinas's thought, is a commitment to a kind of mixed form of government, a constitutional monarchy. Such a society, he argued, is the most conducive to the best human life, and that means to the life of virtue. The best government is government by law for the common good, the community's well-being. It governs a society that best enables people to achieve happiness, which is a society both political in character and religious in purpose. Moreover, the mixed constitution does this through law, which helps people to prevent evil and to seek the good. For Aquinas, then, the state arises out of religious and moral purposes, and morality emerges from human nature and its tendencies, the object of God's beneficent purposes.

Aquinas's life coincides with a period when Christian faith and Aristotelian philosophy confronted each other and achieved as comfortable a synthesis as they would ever attain. His remarkable collection of works exemplifies that synthesis in a uniquely powerful way. Within two decades Aquinas crystallized the deep mood of an epoch, but his success was short-lived. By 1277, with the Condemnation of Paris, the unity was shattered and the main lines of response already plotted; the nominalist and conciliarist responses of Duns Scotus and William of Ockham were developed in the following generation in opposition to Aquinas's synthesis. Aquinas was, in short, a monumental figure, whose life, works, and intellect blend together as a decisive turning point in medieval thought.

Recommended Readings

Burns, James (ed.). *Cambridge History of Medieval Political Thought, 350–1450*. Cambridge: Cambridge University Press, 1989.

Copleston, Frederick. *Aquinas*. London: Penguin, 1955.

Finnis, John. *Aquinas: Moral, Political, and Legal Theory*. Oxford: Oxford University Press, 1998.

Finnis, John. *Natural Law and Natural Rights*. Oxford: Oxford University Press, 1982.

Gilson, Etienne. *The Christian Philosophy of St. Thomas Aquinas*. New York: Random House, 1956.

Kenny, Antony (ed.). *Aquinas*. Notre Dame: Notre Dame Press, 1976.

Kretzmann, Norman (ed.). *The Cambridge Companion to Aquinas*. Cambridge: Cambridge University Press, 1993.

Maritain, J. *Man and the State*. Chicago: University of Chicago Press, 1951.

Sigmund, Paul (ed.). *St. Thomas Aquinas on Politics and Ethics*. New York: W. W. Norton, 1988.

On Kingship, to the King of Cyprus

BOOK I

Chapter 1

What the Name *King* Signifies

We need, at the outset of our work, to explain what one should understand by the word *king*. And regarding all things ordained for an end, in which there may be this or that way of proceeding, something needs to give the direction whereby they arrive straightaway to the requisite end. For example, ships, which the force of various winds may toss in different directions, would not arrive at their destination unless the efforts of pilots were to guide the ships to port. And human beings have an end for the attainment of which their whole lives and actions are ordained, since those who act intelligently evidently act for the sake of an end. But human beings may advance in different ways toward their intended end, which the very diversity of human endeavors and activities makes clear. Therefore, human beings need something that directs them to their end.

And nature implants in each human being the light of reason, which directs them in their activities toward their end. And if it were appropriate for human beings to live solitarily, like many animals, they would indeed need no other direction to their end. Rather, each would be king unto self under God, the supreme king, since the light of reason divinely bestowed on each would direct individual human beings themselves in their actions. But human beings are, by their nature, social and political, living in community more than every other animal. And natural necessity indeed

makes this evident. For nature has, in the case of other animals, provided food, fur covering, or means of defense (for example, teeth, horns, claws, or at least fleetness for flight). But human beings have been constituted with none of these things provided by nature. Rather, human beings have instead been provided with reason, which enables them to provide all these things for themselves by the work of their hands. And a single human being does not suffice to provide all these things, since single human beings by themselves could not adequately make their way through life. Therefore, it is natural for human beings to live in community with many.

Moreover, nature has implanted in other animals indigenous structures regarding everything useful or harmful for them. For example, sheep, by nature, esteem wolves as enemies. Some animals by their naturally indigenous structure even recognize the medicinal plants and other things necessary to sustain their life. But human beings by nature know only in a general way the things necessary to sustain their life, so that they can arrive at knowledge of particular necessary things for human life by their power to reason from the first principles of nature. And individual human beings cannot attain all such things by their own reason. Therefore, human beings need to live in community, so that they can assist one another, with different human beings engaged in discovering different things by reason (for example, one in medicine, others in this or that).

This is made most clearly evident by the fact that human beings have the characteristic ability to use speech, whereby human beings can completely express their ideas to one another. Other animals indeed communicate their emotions in a general way (for example, dogs express their anger by barking, and other animals their emotions in different ways). Therefore, human beings can communicate with one another more than any other animals can that we see living communally, such as cranes and ants and bees.

Reprinted by permission of the publisher, from Aquinas, *On Law, Morality, and Politics*, second edition, translated by Richard J. Regan, edited by William P. Baumgarth and Richard J. Regan (Indianapolis: Hackett Publishing Company, 2002).

Therefore, Solomon, contemplating this, says in Eccl. 4:9: "Two human beings are better than one, since they have the enrichment of mutual association."

Therefore, if human beings by nature live in association with many others, all of them need to have some power to govern them. For if there are many human beings, and they provide for their own individual interests, the people would split into different factions unless there were also to exist a power to provide for what belongs to the common good. Just so, even the body of a human being or any animal would disintegrate unless there were to exist a general regulative power in the body to strive for the common good of all the body's members. And Solomon, contemplating this, said in Prov. 11:14: "The people will be destroyed if there is no ruler."

And this happens in accord with reason. For what belongs to individuals, and what is common to all, are not the same. Human beings indeed differ by what is proper to each one, and are united by what is common to all. But there are different causes of different things. Therefore, besides what causes individual human beings to act for their own good, there needs to be a power that causes them to act for the common good of the community. And so also regarding all things ordained for one thing, we find a power that governs other things. For example, in the universe of material substances, a primary material substance, namely, the heavenly body, governs other material substances by an ordination of God's providence, and rational creatures by his ordination govern the use of all material substances. Also, in each human being, the soul governs the body, and reason governs the irascible and concupiscible parts of the soul. And likewise, one chief bodily member, whether the heart or the head, moves all the others. Therefore, every people needs to have a power that rules.

And regarding some things ordained for an end, there may be a right or wrong way of proceeding. And so also a people may be governed rightly or wrongly. And a people is governed rightly when it is guided to a suitable end, and wrongly when it is guided to an unsuitable end. And the end suitable to a community of free persons is different from the end suitable for a community of slaves, since free persons are their own agents, and slaves belong to others. Therefore, if a ruler should direct a community of free persons for the common good of the people, there will be a right and just regime, as befits free persons. And if the governance of a ruler be ordained for the private good of the ruler and not for the common good of the people, there will be an unjust and wicked regime. And so also the Lord, speaking through Ezechiel, threatens such rulers in Ez. 34:2: "Woe to the shepherds of Israel who have fed themselves" so as to gain their own advantage. "Are not shepherds to feed their flock?" Shepherds of the flock should indeed seek the good of their flock, and every ruler, the good of the people subject to him.

Therefore, if there be an unjust regime in the hands of only one person who seeks from the regime his own advantage, not the good of the people subject to him, we call such a ruler a tyrant, a name derived from strength, namely, in that he crushes by his power and does not rule justly. And so also the ancients called all powerful persons tyrants. And if there be an unjust regime in the hands of several persons, not one, we call it oligarchy (that is, rule by the few) if it is indeed in the hands of a few persons. This is a case where a few persons crush the people for the sake of riches, and differs from tyranny only by the plurality of rulers. And if a wicked regime is in the hands of many, we call it democracy (that is, rule of the people). This is a case where the mass of common citizens crush the rich by the power of their number. For then even the whole people will be as if a single tyrant.

And likewise, we also need to distinguish just regimes. For if a just regime is in the hands of many people, we call it by the general name *polity* (for example, when a large number of warriors rule in a city or province). And if a just regime is in the hands of a few persons, who are also virtuous, we call it aristocracy (that is, the best rule or rule by the best, whom we call aristocrats for that reason). And if a just regime is in the hands of only one person, we properly call that person king. And so the Lord says through Ezechiel in Ez. 37:24: "My servant David will be king over them, and there will be one shepherd of all of them." And this evidently shows that it belongs to the nature of kingship that there is one person who rules, and that he is a shepherd who seeks the common good of the people and not his own individual good.

And because it belongs to human beings to live in a community, since they are insufficient to secure the necessities of life for themselves if they should remain solitary, the unity of the people is necessarily more complete the more intrinsically self-sufficient it will be to provide the necessities of life. There is indeed a sufficiency of life in one family comprising one household, namely, regarding natural acts of nutrition and procreation and such like. And there is a sufficiency of life in a district, namely, regarding things proper to one occupation. And there is a sufficiency of life in a city, that is, a perfect community, namely, regarding all the necessities of life, but still more in a province because of the need to wage war and afford mutual assistance against enemies. And so we refer to those who rule perfect communities, that is, cities or provinces, as *the* kings. And we call those who rule households fathers of families, not kings, although fathers are analogous to kings, and for that reason we sometimes call kings fathers of their peoples.

Therefore, it is clear from what I have said that a king is a single person who governs the people of a city or province for the common good. And so Solomon says in Eccl. 5:8: "The king rules all the territory subject to him."

SUMMA THEOLOGICA

LAW

ST I–II

QUESTION 90

On the Essence of Law

FIRST ARTICLE
Does Law Belong to Reason?

We thus proceed to the first inquiry. It seems that law does not belong to reason, for the following reasons:

Objection 1. The Apostle in Rom. 7:23 says: "I perceive another law in my bodily members," etc. But nothing belonging to reason belongs to bodily members, since reason does not use bodily organs. Therefore, law does not belong to reason.

Obj. 2. Only power, habits, and acts belong to reason. But law is not the very power of reason. Likewise, law is not a habit of reason, since habits of reason are intellectual virtues, about which I have spoken before. Nor is law an act of reason, since law would cease when the lawmaker ceased to reason (e.g., when he is sleeping). Therefore, law does not belong to reason.

Obj. 3. Law induces those subject to the law to act rightly. But inducing to act rightly belongs in the strict sense to the will, as is evident from what I have said before. Therefore, law belongs to the will rather than to reason, as the Jurist also says: "The pleasure of the ruler has the force of law."

On the contrary, it belongs to law to command and forbid. But to command belongs to reason, as I have maintained before. Therefore, law belongs to reason.

I answer that law is a rule and measure of acts that induces persons to act or refrain from acting. For *law* [Lat.: *lex*] is derived from *binding* [Lat.: *ligare*] because law obliges persons to act. And the rule and measure of human acts is reason, which is the primary source of human acts, as is evident from what I have

said before. For it belongs to reason to order us to our end, which is the primary source regarding our prospective action, as the Philosopher says. And the source in any kind of thing is the measure and rule of that kind of thing (e.g., units in numbers and first movements in movements). And so we conclude that law belongs to reason.

Reply Obj. 1. We say that law, since it is a rule or measure, belongs to something in two ways. It belongs in one way as to what measures and rules. And law in this way belongs only to reason, since measuring and ruling belong to reason. Law belongs to something in a second way as to what is ruled and measured. And then law applies to everything that a law induces to something, so that we can call every inclination resulting from a law, law by participation, as it were, not essentially. And we in this way call the very inclination of bodily members to concupiscence the law of the bodily members.

Reply Obj. 2. Regarding external acts, we can consider the activity and the product of the activity (e.g., building and the building constructed). Just so, regarding acts of reason, we can consider the very acts of reason (i.e., acts of understanding and reasoning) and the things produced by such acts. And regarding theoretical reason, definitions are indeed the first product. Propositions are the second product. And syllogisms and arguments the third product. And practical reason also uses a kind of syllogism regarding prospective actions, as I have maintained before, and as the Philosopher teaches in the *Ethics*. Therefore, there are things in practical reason that are related to actions as propositions in theoretical reason are related to conclusions. And such universal propositions of practical reason related to actions have the nature of law. And reason indeed sometimes actually contemplates and sometimes only habitually retains these propositions.

Reply Obj. 3. Reason has from the will the power to induce activity, as I have said before, since reason commands means because one wills ends. But an act of reason needs to rule the will regarding the means commanded in order that the willing have the nature of law. And we in this way understand that the will of a ruler has the force of law. Otherwise, the willing of the ruler would be injustice rather than law.

Second Article
Is Law Always Ordained for the Common Good?

We thus proceed to the second inquiry. It seems that law is not ordained for the common good as its end, for the following reasons:

Objection 1. It belongs to law to command and forbid. But precepts are ordained for particular goods. Therefore, the end of law is not always the common good.

Obj. 2. Law directs the actions of human beings. But human acts regard particulars. Therefore, law is likewise ordained for particular goods.

Obj. 3. Isidore says in his *Etymologies:* "If law is based on reason, everything founded on reason will be law." But both things ordained for the common good and things ordained for private good are based on reason. Therefore, law is ordained both for the common good and for the private good of individuals.

On the contrary, Isidore says in his *Etymologies* that laws are "enacted for no private convenience but for the common benefit of citizens."

I answer that as I have said, law belongs to the source of human acts, since law is their rule and measure. And as reason is the source of human acts, so also is there in reason itself something that is the source of all other kinds of acts. And so law needs chiefly and especially to belong to this source.

And the first source in practical matters, with which practical reason is concerned, is the ultimate end. But the ultimate end of human life is happiness or blessedness, as I have maintained before. And so law especially needs to regard the ordination to blessedness.

Moreover, law in the strict sense needs to concern ordination to happiness in general, since every part is related to a whole as something imperfect to something perfect. And so also the Philosopher, regarding the cited definition of laws, speaks of both happiness

and political community. For he says in the *Ethics* that "we call those laws just that constitute and preserve happiness and its particulars by citizens' sharing in a political community." For the political community is the perfect community, as he says in the *Politics*.

And regarding any kind of thing, the one most such is the source of the others, and we call the others such by their relation to that one. For example, fire, which is hottest, causes heat in composite material substances, which we call hot insofar as they share in fire. And so, since we speak of law in the first place because of its ordination to the common good, every other precept regarding particular acts has the nature of law only because of its ordination to the common good. And so every law is ordained for the common good.

Reply Obj. 1. Precepts signify the application of laws to things regulated by the laws. And the ordination to the common good, which belongs to law, can be applied to particular ends. And so there can be precepts even regarding particular matters.

Reply Obj. 2. Actions indeed concern particular matters, but such particulars can be related to the common good by sharing in the final cause, insofar as we call the common good the final cause, not by sharing in a genus or species.

Reply Obj. 3. As theoretical reason firmly establishes nothing except by tracing things back to first indemonstrable principles, so practical reason firmly establishes nothing except by ordering things to our ultimate end, that is, our common good. And what reason so establishes has the nature of law.

Third Article
Is Any Person's Reason Competent to Make Law?

We thus proceed to the third inquiry. It seems that any person's reason is competent to make law, for the following reasons:

Objection 1. The Apostle says in Rom. 2:14 that "when the Gentiles, who do not have the law, by nature do the things the law prescribes, they make law for themselves." But we say the same about everybody. Therefore, anyone can make law for oneself.

Obj. 2. As the Philosopher says in the *Ethics*, "law-makers aim to induce human beings to virtue." But any human being can lead others to virtue. Therefore, the reason of any human being is competent to make law.

Obj. 3. As the ruler of a political community governs that community, so the head of a household governs his household. But the ruler of a political community can make laws regarding the political community. Therefore, any head of a household can make laws regarding his household.

On the contrary, Isidore says in his *Etymologies*, and the *Decretum* maintains: "Laws are ordinances of the people whereby elders and commoners together prescribe things." Therefore, not every person's reason is competent to make law.

I answer that law in the strict sense primarily and chiefly regards ordaining things for the common good. But ordaining things for the common good belongs either to the whole people or to persons acting in the name of the whole people. And so lawmaking belongs either to the whole people or to a public personage who has the care of the whole people. For also in all other matters, ordaining things for ends belongs to those to whom the ends belong.

Reply Obj. 1. As I have said before law belongs both to those who rule, and by participation to those who are ruled. And it is in the latter way that everyone makes law for oneself, as one participates in the ordinations of the ruler. And so also the Apostle adds in v. 15: "And they manifest the law's operation written in their hearts."

Reply Obj. 2. Private persons cannot effectively induce others to virtue. For private persons can only offer advice and have no coercive power if their advice should not be accepted. And law should have coercive power in order to induce others effectively to virtue, as the Philosopher says in the *Ethics*. But the people or a public personage has such coercive power and the right to inflict punishment, as I shall explain later. And so it belongs only to the people or a public personage to make law.

Reply Obj. 3. As human beings are parts of a household, so households are parts of a political community, as the *Politics* says. And so, as the good of a human being is not the ultimate end of that individual but is ordained for the common good, so also the

good of a household is ordained for the good of a political community, which is a perfect community. And so those who govern households can indeed make precepts and rules, but such precepts and rules do not have the nature of law in the strict sense.

FOURTH ARTICLE
Is Promulgation an Essential Component of Law?

We thus proceed to the fourth inquiry. It seems that promulgation is not an essential component of law, for the following reasons:

Objection 1. The natural law most has the nature of law. But the natural law does not need to be promulgated. Therefore, promulgation is not an essential component of law.

Obj. 2. Obligation to do or not to do things belongs in the strict sense to law. But both those to whom laws have been promulgated and those to whom laws have not, are obliged to obey laws. Therefore, promulgation is not an essential component of law.

Obj. 3. The obligation to obey laws also extends to the future, since "laws impose obligation regarding future affairs," as the *Code* says. But laws are promulgated to those present at their promulgation. Therefore, promulgation is not an essential component of law.

On the contrary, the *Decretum* says that "laws are established when they are promulgated."

I answer that laws are imposed on others as rules and measures, as I have said. But rules and measures are imposed by being applied to those ruled and measured. And so laws, in order to oblige persons, as is proper to law, need to be applied to those who are to be ruled by the laws. But the promulgation leading them to knowledge achieves such application. And so promulgation is necessary for laws to be in force.

And so we can compose the definition of law from the four characteristics I have mentioned: law is an ordination of reason for the common good by one who has the care of the community, and promulgated.

Reply Obj. 1. The natural law is promulgated by God when he implants it in the minds of human beings so that they know it by nature.

Reply Obj. 2. Those to whom a law is not promulgated are obliged to observe it insofar as others make it known to them, or it can become known to them after it has been promulgated.

Reply Obj. 3. The present promulgation of a law reaches into the future through the durability of written words, which in a way are always promulgating it. And so Isidore says in his *Etymologies* that "we derive *law* [Lat.: *lex*] from *reading* [Lat.: *legere*], since law is written."

QUESTION 91

On Different Kinds of Law

FIRST ARTICLE
Is There an Eternal Law?

We thus proceed to the first inquiry. It seems that there is no eternal law, for the following reasons:

Objection 1. Every law is imposed on particular persons. But there was no one from eternity on whom law could be imposed, since only God was from eternity. Therefore, no law is eternal.

Obj. 2. Promulgation is an essential component of law. But there could be no promulgation from eternity, since there was no one from eternity to whom a law would be be promulgated. Therefore, no law can be eternal.

Obj. 3. Law signifies the direction to an end. But nothing ordained to an end is eternal, since only the ultimate end is eternal. Therefore, no law is eternal.

On the contrary, Augustine says in his work *On Free Choice*: "No one with intelligence can perceive the law called supreme reason not to be immutable and eternal."

I answer that as I have said before, law is simply a dictate of practical reason by a ruler who governs a perfect community. But supposing that God's providence rules the world, as I maintained in the First Part, his reason evidently governs the entire community of the universe. And so the plan of governance of the world existing in God as the ruler of the universe has the nature of law. And since God's reason conceives eternally, as Prov. 8:23 says, not temporally, we need to say that such law is eternal.

Reply Obj. 1. Things that do not exist in themselves exist with God insofar as he foreknows and foreordains them, as Rom. 4:17 says: "And he calls nonexisting things into existence." Therefore, the eternal conception of God's law has the nature of an eternal law insofar as he ordains that law for governance of the world he foreknows.

Reply Obj. 2. Word and inscription promulgate law. And God promulgates his eternal law in both ways, since the Word of God and the inscription of the predestined in the Book of Life are eternal. But as regards the creatures who hear or read God's law, the promulgation cannot be eternal.

Reply Obj. 3. Law signifies actively ordaining things for an end, namely, that law ordain things for an end. And law does not signify being ordained for an end, that is, that law itself be ordained for another end, except incidentally in the case of human rulers, whose end is extrinsic to themselves. And then the rulers' laws also need to be ordained for that extrinsic end. But the end of God's governance is God himself, and his law is indistinguishable from himself. And so the eternal law is not ordained for another end.

SECOND ARTICLE
Is There a Natural Law in Us?

We thus proceed to the second inquiry. It seems that there is no natural law in us, for the following reasons:

Objection 1. The eternal law sufficiently governs human beings. For Augustine says in his work *On Free Choice* that "the eternal law is that whereby it is right that all things be most orderly." But nature does not abound in superfluities, nor is it wanting in necessities. Therefore, there is no natural law for human beings.

Obj. 2. Law ordains human beings to their end regarding their actions, as I have maintained before. But nature does not ordain human actions to their end, as happens in the case of irrational creatures, which act for their ends only by natural appetites. Rather, human beings act for their end by the use of their reason and will. Therefore, there is no natural law for human beings.

Obj. 3. The freer one is, the less one is subject to law. But human beings are freer than all other animals because human beings, unlike other animals, have free choice. Therefore, since other animals are not subject to a natural law, neither are human beings.

On the contrary, a gloss on Rom. 2:14, "When the Gentiles, who do not have the law, do by nature things prescribed by the law," etc., says: "Although they do not have the written law, they have a natural law, whereby each of them understands and is conscious of good and evil."

I answer that as I have said before, law, since it is a rule or measure, can belong to things in two ways: in one way to those who rule and measure; in a second way to those ruled and measured, since things are ruled or measured insofar as they partake of the rule or measure. But the eternal law rules and measures everything subject to God's providence, as is evident from what I have said before. And so everything evidently shares in some way in the eternal law, namely, insofar as all things have inclinations to their own acts and ends from its imprint on them. But the rational creature is subject to God's providence in a more excellent way than other things, since such a creature also shares in God's providence in providing for itself and others. And so it shares in the eternal plan whereby it has its natural inclination to its requisite activity and end. And we call such participation in the eternal law by rational creatures the natural law. And so Ps. 4:6, after saying, "Offer just sacrifices," asks: "Who shows us just things?" and replies: "The light of your countenance, O Lord, has been inscribed on us." The Psalmist thus signifies that the light of natural reason whereby we discern good and evil is simply the imprint of God's light in us. And so it is clear that the natural law is simply rational creatures' participation in the eternal law.

Reply Obj. 1. The argument of this objection would be valid if the natural law were to be something different from the eternal law. But the natural law shares in the eternal law, as I have said.

Reply Obj. 2. Every activity of reason and the will in us is derived from what exists by nature, as I have maintained before, since every process of reasoning is derived from first principles known by nature, and every desire of means is derived from the natural desire of our ultimate end. And so also the natural law needs first to direct our acts to their end.

Reply Obj. 3. Even irrational animals, like rational creatures, share in the eternal law in their own way. But because rational creatures share in the eternal law by using their intellect and reason, we call their participation in the eternal law law in the strict sense, since law belongs to reason, as I

have said before. And irrational creatures do not share in the eternal law by the use of reason. And so we can call the latter participation law only by analogy.

THIRD ARTICLE
Are There Human Laws?

We thus proceed to the third inquiry. It seems that there are no human laws, for the following reasons:

Objection. 1. The natural law shares in the eternal law, as I have said. But the eternal law "renders all things most orderly," as Augustine says in his work *On Free Choice.* Therefore, the natural law suffices for ordering all human affairs. Therefore, there is no need for human laws.

Obj. 2. Law has the nature of a measure, as I have said. But human reason is not the measure of things. Rather, the converse is true, as the *Metaphysics* says. Therefore, human reason can produce no law.

Obj. 3. A measure should be most certain, as the *Metaphysics* says. But dictates of human reason about things to be done are uncertain, as Wis. 9:14 says: "The thoughts of mortal human beings are fraught with fear, and our foresight uncertain." Therefore, human reason cannot produce laws.

On the contrary, Augustine in his work *On Free Choice* posits two kinds of law, one kind eternal, and the other temporal, which he calls human.

I answer that law is a dictate of practical reason, as I have said before. But there are similar processes of practical and theoretical reason, since both proceed from principles to conclusions, as I have maintained before. Therefore, we should say that we advance in theoretical reason from indemonstrable first principles, naturally known, to the conclusions of different sciences, conclusions not implanted in us by nature but discovered by exercising reason. Just so, human reason needs to advance from the precepts of the natural law, as general and indemonstrable first principles, to matters that are to be more particularly regulated. And we call such regulations devised by human reason human laws, provided that the other conditions belonging to the nature of law are observed, as I have said before. And so also Cicero says in his *Rhetoric:* "Human law originally sprang from nature. Then things became customs because of their rational benefit. Then fear and reverence for law validated things that both sprang from nature and were approved by custom."

Reply Obj. 1. Human reason cannot partake of the complete dictates of God's reason but partakes of them in its own way and incompletely. And so regarding theoretical reason, we by our natural participation in God's wisdom know general principles but do not specifically know every truth, as God's wisdom does. Just so regarding practical reason, human beings by nature partake of the eternal law as to general principles but not as to particular specifications of particular matters, although such specifications belong to the eternal law. And so human reason needs to proceed further to determine the particular prescriptions of human law.

Reply Obj. 2. Human reason as such is not the rule of things, but the first principles implanted by nature in human reason are the general rules or measures of everything related to human conduct. And natural reason is the rule and measure of such things, although not of things from nature.

Reply Obj. 3. Practical reason regards practical matters, which are particular and contingent, and does not regard necessary things, as theoretical reason does. And so human laws cannot have the absolute certainty of demonstrated scientific conclusions. Nor need every measure be unerring and certain in every respect. Rather, every measure needs to be such only to the extent possible in its kind of thing.

FOURTH ARTICLE
Did Human Beings Need a Divine Law?

We thus proceed to the fourth inquiry. It seems that human beings did not need any divine law, for the following reasons:

Objection 1. The natural law is our participation in the eternal law, as I have said. But eternal law is divine law, as I have said. Therefore, we do not need another divine law besides the natural law and the human laws derived from natural law.

Obj. 2. Sir. 15:14 says that "God left human beings in the hands of their own deliberation." But deliberation is an act of reason, as I have maintained before. Therefore, God left human beings to the governance of their own reason. But the dictates of human reason

are human laws, as I have said. Therefore, human beings do not need to be governed by another divine law.

Obj. 3. Human nature is more self-sufficient than irrational creatures. But irrational creatures have no divine law besides the inclinations that nature implants in them. Therefore, much less should rational creatures have a divine law besides the natural law.

On the contrary, David petitioned God to lay out the law before him, saying in Ps. 119:33: "Teach me the law, O Lord, in the way of your statutes."

I answer that in addition to the natural law and human laws, divine law was necessary to give direction to human life. And there are four reasons for this.

First, indeed, law directs our acts in relation to our ultimate end. And human beings, if they were indeed ordained only for an end that did not surpass the proportion of their natural ability, would not, regarding reason, need to have any direction superior to the natural law and human laws derived from the natural law. But because human beings are ordained for the end of eternal blessedness, which surpasses their proportional natural human capacity, as I have maintained before, God needed to lay down a law superior to the natural law and human laws to direct human beings to their end.

Second, because of the uncertainty of human judgment, especially regarding contingent and particular matters, different persons may judge differently about various human actions, and so even different and contrary laws result. Therefore, in order that human beings can know beyond any doubt what they should do or should not do, a divinely revealed law, regarding which error is impossible, was needed to direct human beings in their actions.

Third, human beings can make laws regarding things they are able to judge. But human beings can judge only sensibly perceptible external acts, not hidden internal movements. And yet human beings need to live righteously regarding both kinds of acts in order to attain complete virtue. And so human laws could not prohibit or adequately ordain internal acts, and divine law needed to supplement human laws.

Fourth, human laws cannot punish or prohibit all evil deeds, as Augustine says in his work *On Free Choice.* This is because in seeking to eliminate all evils, one would thereby also take away many goods and not benefit the common good necessary for human companionship. Therefore, in order that no evil remain unforbidden or unpunished, there needed to be a divine law forbidding all sins.

And Ps. 19:7 touches on these four reasons when it says: "The law of the Lord is pure," that is, permitting no sinful wickedness; "converting souls," since it directs both external and internal acts; "the Lord's faithful witness" because of its certain truth and rectitude; "offering wisdom to the little ones," since it ordains human beings for a supernatural and divine end.

Reply Obj. 1. The natural law partakes of the eternal law in proportion to the capacity of human nature. But human beings need to be directed in a higher way to their ultimate supernatural end. And so God gives an additional law that partakes of the eternal law in a higher way.

Reply Obj. 2. Deliberation is an inquiry, and so deliberation needs to advance from some principles. And it does not suffice that it advance from first principles implanted by nature, that is, precepts of the natural law, for the aforementioned reasons. Rather, other principles, namely, precepts of divine law, need to be supplied.

Reply Obj. 3. Irrational creatures are not ordained for higher ends than those proportioned to their natural powers. And so the argument of the objection is inapplicable.

QUESTION 94

On the Natural Law

FIRST ARTICLE
Is the Natural Law a Habit?

We thus proceed to the first inquiry. It seems that the natural law is a habit, for the following reasons:

Objection 1. "Three things belong to the soul: powers, habits, and emotions," as the Philosopher says in the *Ethics*. But the natural law is neither a power of the soul nor an emotion. Therefore, the natural law is a habit.

Obj. 2. Basil says that conscience, that is, *synderesis*, is "the law of our intellect," and we can only understand such regarding the natural law. But *synde-*

resis is a habit, as I maintained in the First Part. Therefore, the natural law is a habit.

Obj. 3. The natural law always abides in human beings, as I shall make clear later. But human beings' reason, to which that law belongs, is not always thinking about the natural law. Therefore, the natural law is a habit, not an act.

On the contrary, Augustine says in his work *On the Marital Good* that "habits are the means whereby we do things when we need to." But the natural law is not such, since that law belongs to infants and the damned, who cannot act by reason of its presence. Therefore, the natural law is not a habit.

I answer that we can speak about habits in two ways. We speak of them in one way in the strict sense and essentially, and then the natural law is not a habit. For I have said before that the natural law is constituted by reason, just as propositions are works of reason. And what one does, and the means whereby one does it, are not the same. For example, one makes a fitting speech by means of the habit of grammar. Therefore, since habits are the means whereby one does things, the natural law cannot be a habit in the strict sense and essentially.

We can speak of habits in a second way as what we possess by reason of habits. For example, we call faith what we have by reason of the habit of faith. And so, as reason sometimes actually considers precepts of the natural law and sometimes only habitually possesses them, we can in the latter way say that the natural law is a habit. Just so, the indemonstrable first principles in theoretical matters are principles belonging to the habit of first principles, not the very habit.

Reply Obj. 1. The Philosopher in the cited text is attempting to discover the genus of virtues. And since virtues are evidently sources of activity, he posits only things that are sources of human activity, namely, powers, habits, and emotions. But other things belong to the soul besides the latter three. For example, certain acts belong to the soul: willing to those willing, and things known to those knowing. And the natural properties of the soul, such as immortality and the like, belong to the soul.

Reply Obj. 2. Basil calls *synderesis* the law of our intellect insofar as it is the habit that contains the precepts of the natural law, that is, the first principles of human actions.

Reply Obj. 3. The argument of this objection reaches the conclusion that we possess the natural law in a habitual way, and we concede this.

Qualification to the argument in the section On the contrary. Sometimes, due to an impediment, one cannot make use of what one possesses habitually. For example, human beings cannot make use of habitual knowledge when they are asleep. And likewise, children cannot make use of habitual understanding of first principles, or even of the natural law, which they possess habitually, due to their immature age.

SECOND ARTICLE
Does the Natural Law Include Several Precepts or Only One?

We thus proceed to the second inquiry. It seems that that the natural law includes only one precept, not several, for the following reasons:

Objection 1. Law belongs to the genus of precept, as I have maintained before. Therefore, if there were to be many precepts of the natural law, it would follow logically that there would also be many natural laws.

Obj. 2. The natural law results from the nature of human beings. But human nature as a whole is one, although multiple regarding its parts. Therefore, either there is only one precept of the natural law because of the unity of the whole, or there are many precepts because of the many parts of human nature. And so even things that regard inclinations of concupiscible power will need to belong to the natural law.

Obj. 3. Law belongs to reason, as I have said before. But there is only one power of reason in human beings. Therefore, there is only one precept of the natural law.

On the contrary, the precepts of the natural law in human beings are related to action as the first principles in scientific matters are related to theoretical knowledge. But there are several indemonstrable first principles of theoretical knowledge. Therefore, there are also several precepts of the natural law.

I answer that as I have said before, the precepts of the natural law are related to practical reason as the first principles of scientific demonstrations are related to theoretical reason. For both the precepts of the natural law and the first principles of scientific demonstrations are self-evident principles. And we speak of things being self-evident in two ways: in one way as such; in a second way in relation to ourselves. We indeed speak of self-evident propositions as such when their predicates belong to the nature of their subjects, although such propositions may not be self-evident to those who do not know the definition of the subjects. For example, the proposition "Human beings are rational" is by its nature self-evident, since to speak of something human is to speak of something rational, although the proposition is not self-evident to one who does not know what a human being is. And so, as Boethius says in his work *On Groups of Seven*, there are axioms or universally self-evident propositions, and propositions whose terms all persons know (e.g., "Every whole is greater than one of its parts" and "Things equal to the same thing are themselves equal") are such. But some propositions are self-evident only to the wise, who understand what the proposition's terms signify. For example, for those who understand that angels are not material substances, it is self-evident that angels are not circumscriptively in a place, something not evident to the uneducated, who do not understand the nature of angels.

And there is a priority regarding the things that fall within the understanding of all persons. For what first falls within our understanding is being, the understanding of which is included in everything that one understands. And so the first indemonstrable principle is that one cannot at the same time affirm and deny the same thing. And this principle is based on the nature of being and nonbeing, and all other principles are based on it, as the *Metaphysics* says. And as being is the first thing that without qualification falls within our understanding, so good is the first thing that falls within the understanding of practical reason. And practical reason is ordered to action, since every efficient cause acts for the sake of an end, which has the nature of good. And so the first principle in practical reason is one based on the nature of good, namely, that good is what all things seek. Therefore, the first precept of the natural law is that we should do and seek good, and shun evil. And all the other precepts of the natural law are based on that precept, namely, that all the things that practical reason by nature understands to be human goods or evils belong to precepts of the natural law as things to be done or shunned.

And since good has the nature of end, and evil the nature of the contrary, reason by nature understands to be good all the things for which human beings have a natural inclination, and so to be things to be actively sought, and understands contrary things as evil and to be shunned. Therefore, the ordination of our natural inclinations ordains the precepts of the natural law.

First, for example, human beings have an inclination for good by the nature they share with all substances, namely, as every substance by nature seeks to preserve itself. And regarding this inclination, means that preserve our human life and prevent the contrary belong to the natural law.

Second, human beings have more particular inclinations by the nature they share with other animals. And so the *Digest* says that things "that nature has taught all animals," such as the sexual union of male and female, and the upbringing of children, and the like, belong to the natural law.

Third, human beings have inclinations for good by their rational nature, which is proper to them. For example, human beings by nature have inclinations to know truths about God and to live in society with other human beings. And so things that relate to such inclinations belong to the natural law (e.g., that human beings shun ignorance, that they not offend those with whom they ought to live sociably, and other such things regarding those inclinations).

Reply Obj. 1. All the precepts of the natural law, insofar as they relate to one first precept, have the nature of one natural law.

Reply Obj. 2. All the inclinations of any part of human nature (e.g., the concupiscible and irascible powers), insofar as reason rules them, belong to the natural law and are traced to one first precept, as I have said. And so there are many precepts of the natural law as such, but they share a common foundation.

Reply Obj. 3. Reason, although as such one power, ordains everything that concerns human beings. And so the law of reason includes everything that reason can rule.

THIRD ARTICLE
Do All Virtuous Acts Belong to the Natural Law?

We proceed thus to the third inquiry. It seems that not all virtuous acts belong to the natural law, for the following reasons:

Objection 1. It belongs to the nature of law that law be ordained for the common good, as I have said before. But some virtuous acts are ordained for the private good of an individual, as is particularly evident in the case of acts of the virtue of moderation. Therefore, not all virtuous acts are subject to the natural law.

Obj. 2. All sins are contrary to certain virtuous acts. Therefore, if all virtuous acts belong to the natural law, it seems that all sins are consequently contrary to nature. And yet we say this in a special way about some sins.

Obj. 3. Everybody agrees about things that are in accord with nature. But not everybody agrees about virtuous acts, for things that are virtuous for some are vicious for others. Therefore, not all virtuous acts belong to the natural law.

On the contrary, Damascene says in his work *On Orthodox Faith* that "virtues are natural." Therefore, virtuous acts are subject to the natural law.

I answer that we can speak about virtuous acts in two ways: in one way as virtuous; in a second way as we consider such acts in their own species. Therefore, if we are speaking about virtuous acts as virtuous, then all virtuous acts belong to the natural law. For I have said that everything to which human beings are inclined by their nature belongs to the natural law. But everything is by its nature inclined to the activity that its form renders fitting. For example, fire is inclined to heat things. And so, since the rational soul is the specific form of human beings, everyone has an inclination from one's nature to act in accord with reason. And this is to act virtuously. And so in this regard, all virtuous acts belong to the natural law, since one's own reason by nature dictates that one act virtuously.

But if we should be speaking about virtuous acts as such and such, namely, as we consider them in their own species, then not all virtuous acts belong to the natural law. For we do many things virtuously to which nature does not at first incline us, but which human beings by the inquiry of reason have discovered to be useful for living righteously.

Reply Obj. 1. Moderation concerns the natural desires for food and drink and sex, which desires are indeed ordained for the natural common good, just as other prescriptions of the natural law are ordained for the common moral good.

Reply Obj. 2. We can call the nature proper to human beings the nature of human beings. And so all sins, insofar as they are contrary to reason, are also contrary to nature, as Damascene makes clear in his work *On Orthodox Faith*. Or else we can call the nature common to human beings and other animals the nature of human beings. And so we speak of certain particular sins being contrary to nature. For example, the sexual intercourse of males, which we specifically call the sin contrary to nature, is contrary to the sexual union of male and female, and such sexual union is natural for all animals.

Reply Obj. 3. The argument of this objection is valid regarding virtuous acts as such and such. For then, because of the different conditions of human beings, some acts may be virtuous for some persons, as proportionate and suitable for them, which are nonetheless wicked for other persons, as disproportionate for them.

FOURTH ARTICLE
Is the Natural Law the Same for All Human Beings?

We thus proceed to the fourth inquiry. It seems that the natural law is not the same for all human beings, for the following reasons:

Objection 1. The *Decretum* says that "the natural law is contained in the [Old] Law and the Gospel." But what is contained in the Law and the Gospel is not in the common possession of all, since Rom. 10:16 says: "Some do not heed the Gospel." Therefore, the natural law is not the same for all human beings.

Obj. 2. "We call things in accord with law just," as the *Ethics* says. But the same work says that nothing is so universally just that it is not otherwise for some. Therefore, even the natural law is not the same for all human beings.

Obj. 3. Things to which human beings' nature inclines them belong to the natural law, as I have said before. But nature inclines different human beings to different things. For example, nature inclines some to desire pleasures, others to desire honors, others to desire other things. Therefore, the natural law is not the same for all human beings.

On the contrary, Isidore says in his *Etymologies*: "The natural law is common to all nations."

I answer that things to which nature inclines human beings belong to the natural law, as I have said before, and one of the things proper to human beings is that their nature inclines them to act in accord with reason. And it belongs to reason to advance from the general to the particular, as the *Physics* makes clear. And regarding that process, theoretical reason proceeds in one way, and practical reason in another way. For inasmuch as theoretical reason is especially concerned about necessary things, which cannot be otherwise disposed, its particular conclusions, just like its general principles, are true without exception. But practical reason is concerned about contingent things, which include human actions. And so the more reason goes from the general to the particular, the more exceptions we find, although there is some necessity in the general principles. Therefore, truth in theoretical matters, both first principles and conclusions, is the same for all human beings, although some know only the truth of the principles, which we call universal propositions, and not the truth of the conclusions. But truth in practical matters, or practical rectitude, is the same for all human beings only regarding the general principles, not regarding the particular conclusions. And not all of those with practical rectitude regarding particulars know the truth in equal measure.

Therefore, the truth or rectitude regarding the general principles of both theoretical and practical reason is the same for all persons and known in equal measure by all of them. And the truth regarding the particular conclusions of theoretical reason is the same for all persons, but some know such truth less than others. For example, it is true for all persons that triangles have three angles equal to two right angles, although not everybody knows this.

But the truth or rectitude regarding particular conclusions of practical reason is neither the same for all persons nor known in equal measure even by those for whom it is the same. For example, it is correct and true for all persons that they should act in accord with reason. And it follows as a particular conclusion from this principle that those holding goods in trust should return the goods to the goods' owners. And this is indeed true for the most part, but it might in particular cases be injurious, and so contrary to reason, to return the goods (e.g., if the owner should be seeking to attack one's country). And the more the particular conclusion goes into particulars, the more exceptions there are (e.g., if one should declare that entrusted goods should be returned to their owners with such and such safeguards or in such and such ways). For the more particular conditions are added to the particular conclusion, the more ways there may be exceptions, so that the conclusion about returning or not returning entrusted goods is erroneous.

Therefore, we should say that the natural law regarding general first principles is the same for all persons both as to their rectitude and as to knowledge of them. And the natural law regarding particulars, which are, as it were, conclusions from the general principles, is for the most part the same for all persons both as to its rectitude and as to knowledge of it. Nonetheless, it can be wanting in rather few cases both as to its rectitude and as to knowledge of it. As to rectitude, the natural law can be wanting because of particular obstacles, just as natures that come to be and pass away are wanting in rather few cases because of obstacles. And also as to knowledge of the natural law, the law can be wanting because emotions or evil habituation or evil natural disposition has perverted the reason of some. For example, the Germans of old did not consider robbery wicked, as Caesar's *Gallic Wars* relates, although robbery is expressly contrary to the natural law.

Reply Obj. 1. We should not understand the cited statement to mean that all the matters included in the Law and the Gospel belong to the natural law, since the Law and the Gospel transmit to us many things above nature. Rather, we should understand the statement to mean that the Law and the Gospel completely transmit to us the things that belong to the natural law. And so Gratian, after saying that "the natural law is contained in the Law and the Gospel," immediately adds by way of example: "And everyone is thereby commanded to do unto others what one wishes to be done to oneself."

Reply Obj. 2. We should understand the cited statement of the Philosopher regarding things just by nature as conclusions derived from general principles, not as the general principles. And such conclusions are correct for the most part and are wanting in rather few cases.

Reply Obj. 3. As the power of reason in human beings rules and commands other powers, so reason needs to direct all the natural inclinations belonging to other powers. And so it is universally correct for all persons to direct all their inclinations by reason.

FIFTH ARTICLE
Can the Natural Law Vary?

We thus proceed to the fifth inquiry. It seems that the natural law can vary, for the following reasons:

Objection 1. A gloss on Sir. 17:9, "He [God] supplied them with instruction and the law of life," says: "He wanted the [Old] Law to be written in order to correct the natural law." But what is corrected is changed. Therefore, the natural law can vary.

Obj. 2. The killing of innocent human beings as well as adultery and theft are contrary to the natural law. But God altered these precepts. For example, God on one occasion commanded Abraham to slay his innocent son, as Gen. 22:2 relates. And God on another occasion commanded the Jews to steal vessels the Egyptians had lent them, as Ex. 12:35–36 relates. And God on another occasion commanded Hosea to take a fornicating wife, as Hos. 1:2 relates. Therefore, the natural law can vary.

Obj. 3. Isidore says in his *Etymologies* that "the common possession of all property and the same freedom for all persons belong to the natural law." But we perceive that human laws have altered these prescriptions. Therefore, it seems that the natural law can vary.

On the contrary, the *Decretum* says: "The natural law originates with rational creatures. It does not vary over time and abides without change."

I answer that we can understand the mutability of the natural law in two ways. We can understand it in one way by things being added to it. And then nothing prevents the natural law changing, since both divine law and human laws add to natural law many things beneficial to human life.

We can understand the mutability of the natural law in a second way by way of substraction, namely, that things previously subject to the law cease to be so. And then the natural law is altogether immutable as to its first principles. And as to its secondary precepts, which we said are proper proximate conclusions, as it were, from the first principles, the natural law is not so changed that what it prescribes is not for the most part completely correct. But it can be changed regarding particulars and in rather few cases, due to special causes that prevent observance of such precepts, as I have said before.

Reply Obj. 1. We say that written law has been given to correct the natural law either because the written law supplements what the natural law lacked, or because the natural law in the hearts of some regarding particulars had been corrupted insofar as they thought that things by nature evil were good. And such corruption needed correction.

Reply Obj. 2. All human beings, without exception, both the innocent and the guilty, die when natural death comes. And God's power indeed inflicts such natural death on human beings because of original sin, as 1 Sam. 2:6 says: "The Lord causes death and life." And so, at the command of God, death can without any injustice be inflicted on any human being, whether guilty or innocent.

Likewise, adultery is sexual intercourse with another man's wife, whom the law handed down by God has allotted to him. And so there is no adultery or fornication in having intercourse with any woman at the command of God.

And the argument is the same regarding theft, which consists of taking another's property. One does not take without the consent of the owner (i.e., steal) anything that one takes at the command of God, who is the owner of all property.

Nor is it only regarding human affairs that everything God commands is owed to him. Rather, regarding things of nature, everything God does is also in one respect natural, as I said in the First Part.

Reply Obj. 3. We speak of things belonging to the natural law in two ways. We speak of them belonging in one way because nature inclines us to them. For example, one should not cause injury to another. We speak of them belonging in a second way because nature did not introduce the contrary. For example,

we could say that it belongs to the natural law that human beings are naked, since nature did not endow them with clothes, which human skill created. And it is in the latter way that we say that "the common possession of all property and the same freedom for all persons" belong to the natural law, namely, that the reason of human beings, not nature, introduced private property and compulsory servitude. And so the natural law in this respect varies only by way of addition.

Sixth Article
Can the Natural Law Be Excised from the Hearts of Human Beings?

We thus proceed to the sixth inquiry. It seems that the natural law can be excised from the hearts of human beings, for the following reasons:

Objection 1. A gloss on Rom. 2:14, "When the Gentiles, who do not have the law," etc., says: "The law of righteousness, which sin had wiped out, is inscribed on the inner human being renewed by grace." But the law of righteousness is the natural law. Therefore, the natural law can be wiped out.

Obj. 2. The law of grace is more efficacious than the law of nature. But sin destroys the law of grace. Therefore, much more can the natural law be wiped out.

Obj. 3. What law establishes is rendered just, as it were. But human beings have established many things contrary to the natural law. Therefore, the natural law can be excised from the hearts of human beings.

On the contrary, Augustine says in his *Confessions:* "Your law is inscribed on the hearts of human beings, and indeed no wickedness wipes it out." But the law inscribed on the hearts of human beings is the natural law. Therefore, the natural law cannot be wiped out.

I answer that as I have said before, there belong to the natural law, indeed primarily, very general precepts, precepts that everyone knows, and more particular, secondary precepts, which are like proximate conclusions from first principles. Therefore, regarding the general principles, the natural law in general can in no way be excised from the hearts of human beings. But the natural law is wiped out regarding particular actions insofar as desires or other emotions prevent reason from applying the general principles to particular actions, as I have said before.

And the natural law can be excised from the hearts of human beings regarding the other, secondary precepts, either because of wicked opinions, just as errors in theoretical matters happen regarding necessary conclusions, or because of evil customs or corrupt habits. For example, some did not think robbery a sin, or even sins against nature to be sinful, as the Apostle also says in Rom. 1:24–28.

Reply Obj. 1. Sin wipes out the natural law regarding particulars but not in general, except perhaps regarding secondary precepts of the natural law, in the way I mentioned.

Reply Obj. 2. Although grace is more efficacious than nature, nature is nonetheless more essential to human beings and so more abiding.

Reply Obj. 3. The argument of this objection is valid regarding the secondary precepts of the natural law, contrary to which some lawmakers have passed wicked statutes.

WAR AND KILLING

ST II–II

QUESTION 40

On War

[This question is divided into four articles, one of which is translated here.]

FIRST ARTICLE
Is It Always Sinful to Wage War?

We thus proceed to the first inquiry. It seems that it is always sinful to wage war, for the following reasons:

Objection 1. Punishment is inflicted only for sin. But the Lord declares that those who wage war will be punished, as Mt. 26:52 says: "Those who take to the sword will perish by the sword." Therefore, all wars are unlawful.

Obj. 2. Everything contrary to a divine precept is a sin. But waging war is contrary to a divine precept, since Mt. 5:39 says: "I tell you not to resist evil," and

Rom. 12:19 says: "Do not defend yourselves, dearly beloved, but leave it to [God's] wrath." Therefore, it is always sinful to wage war.

Obj. 3. Only sin is contrary to a virtuous act. But war is contrary to peace. Therefore, war is always a sin.

Obj. 4. Every exercise regarding something lawful is lawful, as is evidently the case with scientific exercises. But the church prohibits the warlike exercises in tournaments, since the church denies those who die in such contests Christian burial. Therefore, war seems to be absolutely sinful.

On the contrary, Augustine says in a sermon on the centurion's servant: "If Christian teaching were altogether to condemn war, the soldiers in the Gospel who sought salutary advice [Lk. 3:14] would be told to cast aside their arms and abandon military service altogether. But Christ told them: 'Do violence to no one, and be content with your pay.' And if Christ commanded them to be satisfied with their pay, he did not forbid military service."

I answer that three things are required for a war to be just. The first requirement is indeed that the ruler at whose command the war is to be waged have the lawful authority to do so. For it belongs to no private citizen to initiate war, since private persons can pursue vindication of their rights through the decisions of their superiors. Likewise, it belongs to no private citizen to initiate war because no private citizen can call on the people to wage war, which has to be done in wars. Rather, since the care of the common weal has been entrusted to rulers, it belongs to them to protect the common weal of the city or kingdom or province subject to them. And they lawfully use physical weapons to defend the common weal against domestic rebels when they punish malefactors, as the Apostle says in Rom. 13:4: "He [the ruler] does not carry a sword without cause, since he is God's servant, an avenger to execute wrath on the evildoer." Just so, it also belongs to rulers to use weapons of war to protect the common weal against foreign enemies. And Ps. 82:4 tells rulers: "Rescue the poor and free the needy from the hands of sinners." And so Augustine says in his work *Against Faustus*: "The natural order conducive to peace among mortals requires that the legitimate authority to undertake war, and deliberation regarding war, be in the hands of rulers."

Second, there needs to be a just cause to wage war, namely, that the enemy deserves to have war waged against it because of some wrong the enemy has inflicted. And so Augustine says in his *Questions on the Heptateuch*: "We usually define just wars as those that avenge wrongs, when peoples or political communities need to be punished either because they have failed to rectify wrongs committed by their subjects, or because they have failed to restore property unjustly seized."

Third, those waging war need to have a right intention, namely, an intention to promote good or avoid evil. And so Augustine says: "For true worshipers of God, wars waged with zeal for peace and not out of desire for gain or out of cruelty, to restrain the wicked and assist the good, are also conducive of peace." But even if legitimate authority declares war, and the cause is just, wars may be unlawful because they are waged with a wicked intention. For Augustine says in his work *Against Faustus*: "Desire to harm, vengeful cruelty, unsatiated and implacable animus, savagery in renewing combat, lust for dominance, and the like are justly condemned in the matter of waging war."

Reply Obj. 1. Augustine says in his work *Against Faustus*: "They take to the sword who take up arms against the life of another without any superior or legitimate authority either commanding or allowing it." But they who use the sword by the authority of a ruler or judge, if they be private citizens, or out of zeal for justice, by the authority of God, as it were, if they be public officials, do not themselves "take to" the sword. Rather, they "use" the sword committed to them by another. And so they do not deserve punishment.

Still, even those who use the sword sinfully are not always slain by the sword, although they always perish by their own sword, since they are eternally punished for their sinful use of the sword unless they repent.

Reply Obj. 2. As Augustine says in his work *On the Lord's Sermon on the Mount*, human beings should always observe such precepts in readiness of spirit, namely, that they be ready, if necessary, not to resist and not to defend themselves. But sometimes one should act otherwise for the sake of the common good, and also for the good of those against whom one is fighting. And so Augustine says in a letter to Marcellinus: "We need to do many things against those whom we punish with a kindly severity against their will. For they are beneficially vanquished who are snatched from the licentiousness of sin, since nothing is more miserable than the happiness of sinners, which feeds a punishable licentiousness and, like an internal enemy, strengthens an evil will."

Reply Obj. 3. Even those who wage just war strive for peace. And so they are only contrary to the evil peace that the Lord "did not come to send upon the earth," as Mt. 10:34 says. And so Augustine says in a letter to Boniface: "We do not seek peace in order to wage war. Rather, we wage war in order to achieve peace. Therefore, be peacemakers in waging war, so that you may, in winning, bring to those against whom you war the benefit of peace."

Reply Obj. 4. Not all military exercises by human beings are forbidden. Rather, only disordered and dangerous military exercises that give rise to slayings and plunderings are forbidden. And the ancients took part in military exercises without such risks. And so the ancients called them "military exercises" or "bloodless wars," as Jerome makes clear in one of his letters.

OBEDIENCE AND SEDITION

QUESTION 42

On Rebellion

[This question is divided into two articles, one of which is translated here.]

SECOND ARTICLE
Is Rebellion Always a Mortal Sin?

We thus proceed to the second inquiry. It seems that rebellion is not always a mortal sin, for the following reasons:

Objection 1. Rebellion signifies "a military insurrection," as a gloss on 2 Cor. 12:20 makes clear. But war is not always a mortal sin and sometimes just and lawful, as I have maintained before. Therefore, much more can there be rebellion without mortal sin.

Obj. 2. Rebellion is a form of discord, as I have said. But there can be discord without mortal sin, and sometimes without any sin. Therefore, there can also be rebellion with mortal sin or any sin.

Obj. 3. We praise those who deliver a people from the power of a tyrant. But this cannot be easily done without a popular insurrection if some of the people strive to maintain the tyrant, and others strive to unseat him. Therefore, there can be rebellion without sin.

On the contrary, the Apostle in 2 Cor. 12:20 prohibits rebellion along with other sins that are mortal. Therefore, rebellion is a mortal sin.

I answer that as I have said, rebellion is contrary to the unity of citizens (that is, the people) of a political community or kingdom. But Augustine says in *The City of God* that wise persons define the people as "a popular assembly legally constituted and bound by common interest, not any popular assembly." And so the unity contrary to rebellion is evidently one of law and common interest. Therefore, rebellion is obviously contrary to both justice and the common good. And so rebellion is, by its nature, a mortal sin and more serious insofar as the common good, which rebellion subverts, surpasses private goods, which private disputes subvert.

And the leaders of rebellions indeed first and chiefly incur the sin of rebellion, and they sin most seriously. Second, supporters of rebellion who disturb the common good also incur the sin of rebellion. But we should not call those resisting the rebels and defending the common good seditious, just as we do not call those defending themselves brawlers, as I have said before.

Reply Obj. 1. Lawful war is waged for the benefit of the community, as I have said before. But rebellion is waged against the common good of the people. And so rebellion is always a mortal sin.

Reply Obj. 2. Discord from what is not clearly good can occur without sin. But discord from what is clearly good cannot happen without sin. And rebellion, which is contrary to the unity of the people, something clearly good, is the latter kind of discord.

Reply Obj. 3. Tyrannical governance is unjust, since it is ordained for the private good of the ruler, not for the common good, as the Philosopher makes clear in the *Politics* and the *Ethics.* And so disturbance of such governance does not have the character of rebellion, except, perhaps, in cases where the tyrant's governance is so inordinately disturbed that the subject people suffer greater harm from the resulting disturbance than from the tyrant's governance. Rather, tyrants, who by seeking greater domination incite discontent and rebellion in the people subject to them, are the rebels. For governance is tyrannical when ordained for the ruler's own good to the detriment of the people.

PROPERTY

QUESTION 66

On Theft and Robbery

FIRST ARTICLE
Is the Possession of External Goods Natural to Human Beings?

We thus proceed to the first inquiry. It seems that the possession of external goods is not natural, for the following reasons:

Objection 1. No one should ascribe to self what belongs to God. But dominion over all creatures belongs uniquely to God, as Ps. 24:1 says: "The Lord's is the earth," etc. Therefore, the possession of goods is not natural to human beings.

Obj. 2. Basil, explaining the words of the rich man who in Lk. 12:18 said, "I shall gather all my harvest and my possessions," says: "Tell me, which goods are yours? Whence did you get them and bring them into existence?" But human beings can appropriately claim that things they possess by nature are their own. Therefore, human beings do not by nature possess external goods.

Obj. 3. Ambrose says in his work *On the Trinity*: "Dominion denotes power." But human beings have no power over external things, since they cannot alter the nature of such things. Therefore, the possession of external goods is not natural to human beings.

On the contrary, Ps. 8:6 says: "You [God] have put all things under their feet," that is, the feet of human beings.

I answer that we can consider external things in two ways. We can consider them in one way regarding their nature, which is subject only to God's power, which all things obey at his whim, not to the power of human beings. We can consider external things in a second way regarding their use. And then human beings have dominion over external things from nature, since human beings can, by their powers of reason and will, make use of external things for personal benefit, as the things were made for human beings' sake. For less perfect things exist for the sake of more perfect things, as I have maintained before. And the Philosopher by the latter argument proves in the *Politics* that the possession of external goods is natural to human beings. And the natural dominion over the other creatures, which according to reason (in which the image of God consists) belongs to human beings, is evident in the very creation of human beings, as Gen. 1:26 says: "Let us make human beings in our likeness and image, and let them have dominion over the fish of the sea," etc.

Reply Obj. 1. God has the chief dominion over all things. And he in his providence has ordained some things for the material sustenance of human beings. And so human beings have dominion from nature regarding the power to use such things.

Reply Obj. 2. The rich man is criticized because he thought external goods belonged chiefly to him, as if he had not received them from another, namely, God.

Reply Obj. 3. The argument of this objection is valid regarding dominion over external goods regarding their nature, which indeed belongs only to God, as I have said.

SECOND ARTICLE
Are Individuals Permitted to Possess Property as Their Own?

We thus proceed to the second inquiry. It seems that individuals are not, for the following reasons:

Objection 1. Everything contrary to the natural law is illicit. But all things are by the natural law common possessions, and individual ownership of possessions is indeed contrary to possession by the community. Therefore, no human being is permitted to appropriate external goods for self.

Obj. 2. Basil, explaining the words of the rich man in Lk. 12:18, says: "As those who come to public events ahead of time would prevent those coming later from attending, by appropriating for selves what is ordained for common use, so the rich think that common goods they seize first, belong to them." But it is illicit to prevent others from possessing common goods. Therefore, it is illicit to appropriate common goods for self.

Obj. 3. Ambrose says, and the *Decretum* holds: "Let no one call one's own what is common property." But he calls external goods common property, as his prior remarks make clear. Therefore, it seems that no one is permitted to appropriate external goods for self.

On the contrary, Augustine says in his work *On Heresies*: "The 'Apostolics' have most arrogantly so designated themselves because they do not receive into their fellowship the married or those possessing their own property. (The Catholic Church likewise has very many monks and celibate clerics.)" But these heretics hold this view because, cut off from the church, they think that the married and possessors of property, which they themselves are not, have no hope of salvation. Therefore, it is false to say that human beings are not permitted to possess their own property.

I answer that two things belong to human beings regarding external goods. One is the power to manage and disperse external goods. And human beings are permitted to possess them as their own in that regard. And this is necessary for human life for three reasons. First, indeed, the power to manage and dispense external goods is necessary for human life because individuals are more careful in managing goods that belong to them alone than goods that are common to all or many. This is so because individuals, shunning work, leave common property to the care of others, as happens when there are many servants.

Second, the power of individuals to manage and dispense external goods is necessary for human life because human affairs are conducted in a more orderly fashion if the requisite care in managing external goods be entrusted to individuals. On the other hand, there would be confusion if unspecified individuals were to manage everything.

Third, the power of individuals to manage and dispense external goods is necessary for human life because human beings content with their own property live in a condition of peace. And so we observe that quarrels arise rather frequently among those who possess goods in common and not individually.

And the use of external goods is the second thing that belongs to human beings regarding the goods. And human beings in that regard should not possess external goods as their own but as common possessions, namely, in such a way that they readily share the goods when others are in need. And so the Apostle says in 1 Tim. 6:17–18: "Teach the rich of this world to distribute and share readily."

Reply Obj. 1. We do not ascribe the common character of external goods to the natural law because the natural law dictates that all such goods should be possessed in common, and nothing possessed as one's own. Rather, we ascribe the common character of external goods to the natural law because there is a division of possessions by human agreement which belongs to positive law, as I have said before, and not

by the natural law. And so the individual ownership of possessions is not contrary to the natural law, although the intervention of human reason adds this to the natural law.

Reply Obj. 2. Those who come early to public events and were to open the way for others to attend, would not act improperly. And likewise, the rich do not act improperly if they before others take possession of property that was in the beginning common, and share the property with others. But the rich sin if they indiscriminately prevent others from using the property. And so Basil says in the same place: "Why are you rich and others beggars, except that you gain the merit of dispensing your wealth well, and that others are rewarded for their patience?"

Reply Obj. 3. When Ambrose says: "Let no one call common property one's own," he is speaking about individual ownership in regard to the use of external goods. And so he adds: "Those who spend too much are guilty of robbery."

NICCOLÒ MACHIAVELLI

Niccolò Machiavelli (1469–1527) was born, lived, and died in Renaissance Florence, but his thought was immersed in antiquity, in the Sparta of Lycurgus, the Athens of Solon and Pericles, and most of all in Republican Rome. And it is this immersion that establishes Machiavelli as the central political thinker in the tradition of Renaissance humanism. Its results are reflections about political ideals and political practice, about Fortune and *virtù* (ingenuity, skill, excellence), about honor, reputation, and power. But Machiavelli's thoughts are not mere fantasies; they are meant to be effective, to order political life, and to renew the past for the present. Writing to his friend Francesco Vettori in Rome, Machiavelli describes himself as a student of just this kind:

> When evening comes, I return to my home, and I go into my study; and on the threshold, I take off my everyday clothes, which are covered with mud and mire, and I put on regal and curial robes; and dressed in a more appropriate manner I enter into the ancient courts of ancient men and am welcomed by them kindly, and there I taste the food that alone is mine, and for which I was born. . . . I have noted down what I have learned from their conversation, and I composed a little work, *De principatibus* [*The Prince*]. . . .

Machiavelli was born on May 3, 1469, into a respectable middle-class family. His father had a deep commitment to the Latin classics, a devotion which he obviously conveyed to his son. In 1498, shortly after the execution of the Dominican prophetic prior Girolamo Savonarola, the unknown and inexperienced Machiavelli was installed as chancellor of the Second Chancery of the city, a position which he held for fourteen years. It was not a prestigious or powerful role but one that involved him with the nitty-gritty of domestic and especially foreign affairs. In the course of those years, he served as secretary to the board assigned to establish a citizens' militia, assisted Piero Soderini, his mentor and the city's chief executive after 1502, and participated in a number of foreign diplomatic missions. On many occasions, Machiavelli was able to observe major political figures, who subsequently in his writings became models for types of political conduct and leadership. These include Cesare Borgia, whom he observed three times between 1502 and 1503, Pope Julius II, and the Emperor Maximilian.

When Soderini was forced to leave Florence and the republic dissolved, Machiavelli was arrested, tortured, and exiled to his country estate. These political events, as one commentator puts it, were "a personal misfortune" but also a "catalyst for his political imagination." Forced into retirement, Machiavelli turned to study and writing. He joined a circle of Florentine intellectuals who met for conversation about literary and political matters at the Oricellari Gardens, owned by Cosimo Rucellai. It was here that he presented ideas that eventually became part of his extensive defense of republican liberty or self-government, the causes and nature of political corruption, the need for a civil religion, and the benefits of mixed constitution, the *Discourses on the First Ten Books of Titius Livius*.

The Prince, Machiavelli's most famous work, was written in this historical setting and for precise purposes. The son of Lorenzo de Medici had been elected Pope Leo X in 1513. With the republic under Soderini in ruins, the Medicis were destined to return to control Florence. The times were propitious for a union of Italian leadership under the Medicis, which would rule both Rome and Florence. In July to December of 1513, Machiavelli interrupted work on his commentary on Livy's *Histories* and set out in *The Prince* his conception of daring political rule, a form of leadership that would exploit the prince's skill (*virtù*) to take advantage of what Fortune provided in order to gain power, glory, and security. It was a conception of instrumental morality, ancient in design, that directly conflicted with Christian morality, but that at the same time was tailored to appeal to the Medicis' needs and aspirations. It was a conception of human excellence appreciating and coping with the changing contingencies of circumstance in such a way that the prince's ultimate goals could be achieved.

The Prince, then, was Machiavelli's handbook for the strategies required to capitalize on the rare opportunity the Medicis faced. It was also his way of showing fidelity to that goal and of advancing himself as a candidate for a political role in the Medician government. He hoped that his friend Vettori, the Florentine ambassador to Rome, would intercede with the Medicis on his behalf, and so he wrote to Vettori about his work. But Vettori never did so, and the plan to seek Medician patronage and political office failed.

For the remainder of his life, Machiavelli lived in exile and neglect. He wrote extensively on war, language, and history. But he was never invited to return to public life. In 1527 he died, living long enough to see the Medici driven out of Florence and the republic reestablished. Four years later, in 1531, the *Discourses* were published, and then in 1532 *The Prince*, the works on which his fame rests to this day. To some, *The Prince* is a work of realism and practical sensitivity; to many, a cynical, immoral treatise that borders on the diabolical; to others, however, *The Prince* exemplifies a return to an early ethic, a morality, born in antiquity, that acknowledges the changes of Fortune, the variety of abilities and skills required to cope with contingencies, and the role of power, boldness, and even violence in political life.

Recommended Readings

Berlin, Isaiah. "The Originality of Machiavelli," in *Against the Current*. ed. H. Hardy. London, 1979, 25–79.

Bock, G., Q. Skinner, M. Viroli (eds.). *Machiavelli and Republicanism*. Cambridge: Cambridge University Press, 1990.

Burns, James (ed.) *Cambridge History of Political Thought, 1450–1700*. Cambridge: Cambridge University Press, 1991.

De Grazia, S. *Machiavelli in Hell*. Princeton: Princeton University Press, 1989.

Gilbert, Felix. *Machiavelli and Guicciardini*. Princeton: Princeton University Press, 1965.

Pocock, J.G.A. *The Machiavellian Moment*. Princeton: Princeton University Press, 1975.

Skinner, Quentin. *The Foundations of Modern Political Thought*. Vol. II. Cambridge: Cambridge University Press, 1978.

Skinner, Quentin. *Machiavelli*. Oxford: Oxford University Press, 1981.

Viroli, Maurizio. *From Politics to Reason of State*. Cambridge: Cambridge University Press, 1992.

Wolin, Sheldon. *Politics and Vision*. New York: Little, Brown and Co., 1960.

LETTER TO
FRANCESCO VETTORI

To His Excellency the Florentine Ambassador to his Holiness the Pope, and my benefactor, Francesco Vettori, in Rome.

Your Excellency. "Favors from on high are always timely, never late."[1] I say this because I had begun to think I had, if not lost, then mislaid your goodwill, for you had allowed so long to go by without writing to me, and I was in some uncertainty as to what the reason could be. All the explanations I could think of seemed to me worthless, except for the possibility that occurred to me, that you might have stopped writing to me because someone had written to tell you I was not taking proper care of your letters to me; but I knew that I had not been responsible for their being shown to anyone else, with the exception of Filippo and Paolo.[2]

Anyway, I have now received your most recent letter of the 23rd of last month. I was delighted to learn you are fulfilling your official responsibilities without fussing and flapping. I encourage you to carry on like this, for anyone who sacrifices his own convenience in order to make others happy is bound to inconvenience himself, but can't be sure of receiving any thanks for it. And since fortune wants to control everything, she evidently wants to be left a free hand; meanwhile we should keep our own counsel and not get in her way, and wait until she allows human beings to have a say in the course of events. That will be the time for you to work harder, and keep a closer eye on events, and for me to leave my country house and say: "Here I am!"

Since I want to repay your kind gesture, I have no alternative but to describe to you in this letter of mine how I live my life. If you decide you'd like to swap my life for yours, I'll be happy to make a deal.

I am still in my country house: Since my recent difficulties began I have not been, adding them all together, more than twenty days in Florence. Until recently I have been setting bird snares with my own hands. I've been getting up before dawn, making the bird-lime, and setting out with a bundle of cages on my back, so I look like Geta when he comes back from the harbor laden down with Amphitryo's books. I always caught at least two thrushes, but never more than six. This is how I spent September;[3] since then I am sorry to say I have had to give up my rather nasty and peculiar hobby, so I will describe the life I lead now.

I get up in the morning at daybreak and go to a wood of mine where I am having some timber felled. I stay there two hours to check on the work done during the preceding day and to chat to the woodcutters, who are always involved in some conflict, either among themselves or with the neighbors. I could tell you a thousand fine stories about my dealings over this wood, both with Frosino da Panzano and with others who wanted some of the timber. Frosino in particular had them supply some cords without mentioning it to me, and when I asked for payment he wanted to knock off ten lire he said I had owed him for four years, ever since he beat me at cards at Antonio Guicciardini's. I began to cut up rough; I threatened to charge with theft the wagon driver who had fetched

From Machiavelli, *Selected Political Writings*, edited and translated by David Wootton (Indianapolis: Hackett Publishing Company, 1994). Copyright © 1994. Reprinted by permission of the publisher.

1. [Petrarch, *Trionfo della Divinità*, 13. — D.W.]

2. [Paolo is Francesco Vettori's brother; Filippo Casavecchia was a close mutual friend.]

3. [Ridolfi points out that Machiavelli must have meant to write November, since this is the month for thrush hunting.]

the wood. However, Giovanni Machiavelli intervened, and got us to settle our differences. Batista
Guicciardini, Filippo Ginori, Tommaso del Bene,
and a number of other citizens each bought a cord
from me when the cold winds were blowing. I made
promises to all of them, and supplied one to Tommaso. But in Florence it turned out to be only half
a cord, because there were he, his wife, his servants,
and his sons to stack it: They looked like Gabburra
on a Thursday when, assisted by his workmen, he
slaughters an ox.[4] Then, realizing I wasn't the one
who was getting a good deal, I told the others I had run
out of wood. They've all complained bitterly about it;
especially Battista, who thinks this is as bad as anything else that has happened as a result of the battle
of Prato.[5]

When I leave the wood I go to a spring, and from
there to check my bird-nets. I carry a book with me:
Dante, or Petrarch, or one of the minor poets, perhaps
Tibullus, Ovid, or someone like that. I read about
their infatuations and their love affairs, reminisce
about my own, and enjoy my reveries for a while.
Then I set out on the road to the inn. I chat to those
who pass by, asking them for news about the places
they come from. I pick up bits and pieces of information, and study the differing tastes and various preoccupations of mankind. It's lunchtime before I know
it. I sit down with my family to eat such food as I
can grow on my wretched farm or pay for with the
income from my tiny inheritance. Once I have eaten
I go back to the inn. The landlord will be there, and,
usually, the butcher, the miller, and a couple of kiln
owners. With them I muck about all day, playing
card games. We get into endless arguments and are
constantly calling each other names. Usually we only
wager a quarter, and yet you could hear us shouting
if you were in San Casciano. So, in the company of
these bumpkins, I keep my brain from turning moldy,
and put up with the hostility fate has shown me. I

am happy for fate to see to what depths I have sunk,
for I want to know if she will be ashamed of herself
for what she has done.

When evening comes, I go back home, and go to
my study. On the threshold I take off my work clothes,
covered in mud and filth, and put on the clothes an
ambassador would wear. Decently dressed, I enter
the ancient courts of rulers who have long since died.
There I am warmly welcomed, and I feed on the only
food I find nourishing, and was born to savor. I am
not ashamed to talk to them, and to ask them to
explain their actions. And they, out of kindness, answer me. Four hours go by without my feeling any
anxiety. I forget every worry. I am no longer afraid
of poverty, or frightened of death. I live entirely
through them.

And because Dante says there is no point in studying unless you remember what you have learned, I
have made notes of what seem to me the most important things I have learned in my dialogue with the
dead, and written a little book On princedoms[6] in
which I go as deeply as I can into the questions
relevant to my subject. I discuss what a principality
is, how many types of principality there are, how one
acquires them, how one holds onto them, why one
loses them. And if any of my little productions have
ever pleased you, then this one ought not to displease
you; and a ruler, especially a new ruler, ought to be
delighted by it. Consequently, I have addressed it to
His Highness Giuliano.[7] Filippo Casavecchia has
seen it; he can give you a preliminary report, both
on the text, and on the discussions I have had with
him: though I am still adding to the text and polish-
ing it.

You may well wish, Your Excellency, that I should
give up this life, and come and enjoy yours with you.
I will do so if I can; what holds me back at the
moment is some business that won't take me more
than six weeks to finish. Though I am a bit concerned
the Soderini family is there,[8] and I will be obliged,

---

4. [In other words, just as the butcher turns a large ox
into a small pile of steaks, so Tommaso and his family
turned a large pile of wood into a small, neat, and
cheap stack.]

5. [The Battle of Prato (1512) had led to the downfall
of Soderini, the return of the Medici, and Machiavelli's
own dismissal from office.]

6. [*De principatibus*, Machiavelli calls it.]

7. [Giuliano de' Medici, the senior member of the
Medici family after his brother, Pope Leo X.]

8. [Piero and his brother Cardinal Francesco were
in Rome.]

if I come, to visit them and socialize with them. My concern is that I might intend my return journey to end at my own house, but find myself instead dismounting at the prison gates. For although this government is well established and solidly based, still it is new, and consequently suspicious, nor is there a shortage of clever fellows who, in order to get a reputation like Pagolo Bertini's, would put me in prison, and leave me to worry about how to get out. I beg you to persuade me this fear is irrational, and then I will make every effort to come and visit you before six weeks are up.

I have discussed my little book with Filippo, asking him whether it was a good idea to present it or not; and if I ought to present it, then whether I should deliver it in person, or whether I should send it through you. My concern is that if I do not deliver it in person Giuliano may not read it; even worse, that chap Ardinghelli[9] may claim the credit for my latest effort. In favor of presenting it is the fact that the wolf is at the door, for my funds are running down, and I cannot continue like this much longer without becoming so poor I lose face. In any case, I would like their lordships, the Medici, to start putting me to use, even if they only assign me some menial task, for if, once I was in their employment, I did not win their favor, I would have only myself to blame. As for my book, if they were to read it, they would see the fifteen years I have spent studying statecraft have not been wasted: I haven't been asleep at my desk or playing cards. Anyone should be keen to employ someone who has had plenty of experience and has learned from the mistakes he made at his previous employers' expense. As for my integrity, nobody should question it: For I have always kept my word, and I am not going to start breaking it now. Someone who has been honest and true for forty-three years, as I have been, isn't going to be able to change character. And that I am honest and true is evident from my poverty.

So: I would like you to write to me again and let me have your opinion on this matter. I give you my regards. Best wishes.

Niccolò Machiavegli in Florence
10 December 1513.

---

9. [Secretary to Pope Leo X.]

THE PRINCE

Niccolò Machiavelli to His Magnificence Lorenzo de' Medici[1]

Those who wish to acquire favor with a ruler most often approach him with those among their possessions that are most valuable in their eyes, or that they are confident will give him pleasure. So rulers are often given horses, armor, cloth of gold, precious stones, and similar ornaments that are thought worthy of their social eminence. Since I want to offer myself to your Magnificence, along with something that will symbolize my desire to give you obedient service, I have found nothing among my possessions I value more, or would put a higher price upon, than an understanding of the deeds of great men, acquired through a lengthy experience of contemporary politics and through an uninterrupted study of the classics. Since I have long thought about and studied the question of what makes for greatness, and have now summarized my conclusions on the subject in a little book, it is this I send your Magnificence.

And although I recognize this book is unworthy to be given to Yourself, yet I trust that out of kindness you will accept it, taking account of the fact there is no greater gift I can present to you than the opportunity to understand, after a few hours of reading, everything I have learned over the course of so many years, and

have undergone so many discomforts and dangers to discover. I have not ornamented this book with rhetorical turns of phrase, or stuffed it with pretentious and magnificent words, or made use of allurements and embellishments that are irrelevant to my purpose, as many authors do. For my intention has been that my book should be without pretensions, and should rely entirely on the variety of the examples and the importance of the subject to win approval.

I hope it will not be thought presumptuous for someone of humble and lowly status to dare to discuss the behavior of rulers and to make recommendations regarding policy. Just as those who paint landscapes set up their easels down in the valley in order to portray the nature of the mountains and the peaks, and climb up into the mountains in order to draw the valleys, similarly in order to properly understand the behavior of the lower classes one needs to be a ruler, and in order to properly understand the behavior of rulers one needs to be a member of the lower classes.

I therefore beg your Magnificence to accept this little gift in the spirit in which it is sent. If you read it carefully and think over what it contains, you will recognize it is an expression of my dearest wish, which is that you achieve the greatness your good fortune and your other fine qualities seem to hold out to you. And if your Magnificence, high up at the summit as you are, should occasionally glance down into these deep valleys, you will see I have to put up with the unrelenting malevolence of undeserved ill fortune.

From Machiavelli, *Selected Political Writings*, edited and translated by David Wootton (Indianapolis: Hackett Publishing Company, 1994). Copyright © 1994. Reprinted by permission of the publisher.

1. [Lorenzo (1492–1519) was the grandson of Lorenzo the Magnificent (1449–92), son of Piero de' Medici (1471–1503, ruler of Florence, 1492–94), and nephew of Giovanni de' Medici (1475–1521), who became Pope Leo X in 1513. Lorenzo became Duke of Urbino in 1516. We know Machiavelli originally intended to give *The Prince* to Lorenzo's uncle and Leo's brother, Giuliano de' Medici (1479–1516). —D.W.]

CHAPTER 1

How many types of principality are there? And how are they acquired?

All states, all forms of government that have had and continue to have authority over men, have been and are either republics or principalities. And principalities are either hereditary, when their rulers' ancestors have long been their rulers, or they are new. And if they are new, they are either entirely new, as was Milan for Francesco Sforza,[2] or they are like limbs added on to the hereditary state of the ruler who acquires them, as the kingdom of Naples has been added on to the kingdom of Spain.[3] Those dominions that are acquired by a ruler are either used to living under the rule of one man, or accustomed to being free; and they are either acquired with soldiers belonging to others, or with one's own; either through fortune or through strength [*virtù*].

CHAPTER 2

On hereditary principalities.

I will leave behind me the discussion of republics, for I have discussed them at length elsewhere. I will concern myself only with principalities. The different types of principality I have mentioned will be the threads from which I will weave my account. I will debate how these different types of principality should be governed and defended.

I maintain, then, it is much easier to hold on to hereditary states, which are accustomed to being governed by the family that now rules them, than it is to hold on to new acquisitions. All one has to do is preserve the structures established by one's forebears, and play for time if things go badly. For, indeed, an hereditary ruler, if he is of no more than normal resourcefulness, will never lose his state unless some extraordinary and overwhelming force appears that can take it away from him; and even then, the occupier has only to have a minor setback, and the original ruler will get back to power.

Let us take a contemporary Italian example: The Duke of Ferrara was able to resist the assaults of the Venetians in '84, and of Pope Julius in 1510, only because his family was long established as rulers of that state. For a ruler who inherits power has few

reasons and less cause to give offense; as a consequence he is more popular; and, as long as he does not have exceptional vices that make him hateful, it is to be expected he will naturally have the goodwill of his people. Because the state has belonged to his family from one generation to another, memories of how they came to power, and motives to overthrow them, have worn away. For every change in government creates grievances that those who wish to bring about further change can exploit.

CHAPTER 3

On mixed principalities.

New principalities are the ones that present problems. And first of all, if the whole of the principality is not new, but rather a new part has been added on to the old, creating a whole one may term "mixed," instability derives first of all from a natural difficulty that is to be found in all new principalities. The problem is that people willingly change their ruler, believing the change will be for the better; and this belief leads them to take up arms against him. But they are mistaken, and they soon find out in practice they have only made things worse. The reason for this, too, is natural and typical: You always have to give offense to those over whom you acquire power when you become a new ruler, both by imposing troops upon them, and by countless other injuries that follow as necessary consequences of the acquisition of power. Thus, you make enemies of all those to whom you have given offense in acquiring power, and in addition you cannot keep the goodwill of those who have put you in power, for you cannot satisfy their aspirations as they thought you would. At the same time you cannot use heavy-handed methods against them, for you are obliged to them. Even if you have an overwhelmingly powerful army, you will have needed the support of the locals to take control of the province. This is why Louis XII of France lost Milan as quickly as he gained it.[4] All that was needed to take

2. [Sforza acquired Milan in 1450. See below, chapter twelve.]

3. [Ferdinand the Catholic (1452–1516) acquired Naples in 1504. See below, chapters three and twenty-one.]

4. [Louis XII (1462–1515) became King of France in 1498 and invaded Italy in 1499. He gained Milan in February 1500 and lost it in April.]

it from him the first time were Ludovico's own troops. For those who had opened the gates to him, finding themselves mistaken in their expectations and disappointed in their hopes of future benefit, could not put up with the burdensome rule of a new sovereign.

Of course it is true that, after a ruler has regained power in rebel territories, he is much more likely to hang on to it. For the rebellion gives him an excuse, and he is able to take firmer measures to secure his position, punishing delinquents, checking up on suspects, and taking precautions where needed. So, if the first time the King of France lost Milan all that was needed to throw him out was Duke Ludovico growling on his borders, to throw him out a second time it took the whole world united against him, and the destruction or expulsion from Italy of his armies.[5] We have seen why this was so.

Nevertheless, he lost Milan both times. We have discussed why he was almost bound to lose it the first time; now we must discuss why he managed to lose it the second. What remedies should he have adopted? What can someone in the King of France's position do to hold on to an acquisition more effectively than he did?

Let me start by saying these territories that are newly added on to a state that is already securely in the possession of a ruler are either in the same geographical region as his existing possessions and speak the same language, or they are not. When they are, it is quite straightforward to hold on to them, especially if they are not used to governing themselves. In order to get a secure hold on them one need merely eliminate the surviving members of the family of their previous rulers. In other respects one should keep things as they were, respecting established traditions. If the old territories and the new have similar customs, the new subjects will live quietly. Thus, Burgundy, Brittany, Gascony, and Normandy have for long quietly submitted to France. Although they do not all speak exactly the same language, nevertheless their customs are similar, and they can easily put up with each other. He who acquires neighboring territories in this way, intending to hold on to them, needs to see to two things: First, he must ensure their previous ruler has no heirs; and second, he must not alter their old laws or impose new taxes. If he follows these principles they will quickly become inseparable from his hereditary domains.

But when you acquire territories in a region that has a different language, different customs, and different institutions, then you really have problems, and you need to have great good fortune and great resourcefulness if you are going to hold on to them. One of the best policies, and one of the most effective, is for the new ruler to go and live in his new territories. This will make his grasp on them more secure and more lasting. This is what the Sultan of Turkey has done in Greece.[6] All the other measures he has taken to hold on to that territory would have been worthless if he had not settled there. For if you are on the spot, you can identify difficulties as they arise, and can quickly take appropriate action. If you are at a distance, you only learn of them when they have become serious, and when it is too late to put matters right. Moreover, if you are there in person, the territory will not be plundered by your officials. The subjects can appeal against their exactions to you, their ruler. As a consequence they have more reason to love you, if they behave themselves, and, if they do not, more reason to fear you. Anyone who wants to attack the territory from without will have to think twice, so that, if you live there, you will be unlucky indeed to lose it.

The second excellent policy is to send colonies to settle in one or two places; they will serve to tie your new subjects down. For it is necessary either to do this, or to garrison your new territory with a substantial army. Colonies do not cost much to run. You will have to lay out little or nothing to establish and maintain them. You will only offend those from whom you seize fields and houses to give to your settlers, and they will be only a tiny minority within the territory. Those whom you offend will be scattered and become poor, so they will be unable to do you any harm. All the rest will remain uninjured, and so ought

5. [Louis regained Milan after the battle of Novara (April 1500), and lost it again after the Battle of Ravenna (April 1512), Ludovico Sforza (1451–1510), younger son of Francesco Sforza, ruled Milan from 1494 to 1500.]

6. [Constantinople became capital of the Turkish empire in 1453.]

to remain quiet; at the same time they will be afraid to make a false move, for they will have before them the fate of their neighbors as an example of what may happen to them. I conclude such colonies are economical, reliable, and do not give excessive grounds for resistance; those who suffer by their establishment are in no position to resist, being poor and scattered, as I have said. There is a general rule to be noted here: People should either be caressed or crushed. If you do them minor damage they will get their revenge; but if you cripple them there is nothing they can do. If you need to injure someone, do it in such a way that you do not have to fear their vengeance.

But if, instead of establishing colonies, you rely on an occupying army, it costs a good deal more, for your army will eat up all your revenues from your new territory. As a result, your acquisition will be a loss, not a gain. Moreover, your army will make more enemies than colonies would, for the whole territory will suffer from it, the burden moving from one place to another as the troops are billeted first here, then there. Everybody suffers as a result, and everyone becomes your enemy. And these are enemies who can hurt you, for they remain, even if beaten, in their own homes. In every respect, then, an occupying army is a liability, while colonies are an asset.

In addition, anyone who finds himself with territory in a region with different customs from those of his hereditary possessions should make himself the leader and protector of neighboring powers who are weaker than he is, and should set out to weaken his powerful neighbors. He should also take care no outsider as powerful as himself has any occasion to intervene. Outside powers will always be urged to intervene by those in the region who are discontented, either because their ambitions are unsatisfied, or because they are afraid of the dominant powers. So, long ago, the Aetolians invited the Romans into Greece;[7] and, indeed, in every other region the Romans occupied they were invited by local people. It is in the nature of things that, as soon as a foreign power enters into a region, all the local states that are weak rally to it, for they are driven by the envy they have felt for the state that has exercised predominance over them. As a result, the invader does not have to make any effort at all to win over these lesser states, because they all immediately ally themselves to the territory he has acquired there. He only has to take care they do not become too strong and exercise too much influence. He can easily, with his own troops and his new allies' support, strike down the powerful states, and make himself the arbiter of all the affairs of the region. Anyone who does not see how to play this role successfully will quickly lose what he has gained, and, while he holds it, will have innumerable difficulties and vexations.

The Romans, in the regions they seized, obeyed these principles admirably. They settled colonies; were friendly towards the weaker rulers, without building up their strength; broke the powerful; and did not allow foreign powers to build up support. Let me take just the region of Greece as an example.[8] The Romans favored the Acheans and the Aetolians; they crushed the Kingdom of Macedon; they expelled Antiochus[9] from the region. Despite the credit the Acheans and the Aetolians had earned with them, they never allowed them to build up any independent power; nor did the blandishments of Philip[10] ever persuade them to treat him as a friend before they had destroyed his power; nor did Antiochus's strength intimidate them into permitting him to retain any territory in that region.

The Romans did in such matters what all wise rulers ought to do. It is necessary not only to pay attention to immediate crises, but to foresee those that will come, and to make every effort to prevent them. For if you see them coming well in advance, then you can easily take the appropriate action to remedy them, but if you wait until they are right on top of you, then the prescription will no longer take effect, because the disease is too far advanced. In this matter it is as doctors say of consumption: In the beginning the disease is easy to cure, difficult to diagnose; but, after a while, if it has not been diagnosed

---

7. [211 B.C. See Livy, bk. 26, ch. 24.]

8. [The events to which Machiavelli refers occurred in 192 B.C. to 189 B.C. See Livy, bk. 37.]

9. [Antiochus III, King of Syria.]

10. [Philip V of Macedon.]

and treated early, it becomes easy to diagnose and hard to cure. So, too, in politics, for if you foresee problems while they are far off (which only a prudent man is able to do) they can easily be dealt with; but when, because you have failed to see them coming, you allow them to grow to the point that anyone can recognize them, then it is too late to do anything.

The Romans always looked ahead and took action to remedy problems before they developed. They never postponed action in order to avoid a war, for they understood you cannot escape wars, and when you put them off only your opponents benefit. Thus, they wanted to have a war with Philip and Antiochus in Greece, so as not to have one with them in Italy. At the time they could have avoided having a war at all, but this they did not want. They never approved the saying that nowadays is repeated *ad nauseam* by the wise: "Take advantage of the passage of time." Rather they relied on their strength [*virtù*] and prudence, for in time anything can happen, and the passage of time brings good mixed with evil, and evil mixed with good.

But let us return to the kings of France, and let us see whether they followed any of the principles I have outlined. I will discuss Louis, not Charles, for, since Louis held territory in Italy for a longer time, we can have a better understanding of the policies he was following.[11] We will see he did the opposite of what one ought to do in order to hold on to territory in a region unlike one's hereditary lands.

King Louis was brought into Italy by the ambition of the Venetians, who hoped to gain half of the territory of Lombardy as a result of his invasion. I do not want to criticize the king's decision to ally with the Venetians. Since he wanted to get a foothold in Italy, and since he had no friends in that region (rather the opposite, for all the gateways to Italy were closed against him as a result of the actions of King Charles), he was obliged to take what allies he could get. His decision would have been a good one, if he had done everything else right. Now when the king had

conquered Lombardy, he at once recovered the reputation Charles had lost for him. Genoa gave itself up and the Florentines became his friends. Everybody came forward to meet him as he advanced and sought his friendship: the Marquis of Mantua, the Duke of Ferrara, Bentivoglio, the Countess of Forlì, the rulers of Faenza, Pesaro, Rimini, Camerino, Piombino, the citizens of Lucca, Pisa, and Siena. Then the Venetians were able to see the risk they had chosen to run; in order to acquire a couple of fortresses in Lombardy, they had made the King of France master of two-thirds of Italy.

Now consider how easy it would have been for the king to preserve his authority in Italy if he had followed the principles I have laid out, and if he had protected and defended all his new friends. They were numerous, weak, and fearful, some afraid of the Church, some of the Venetians, and so had no choice but to remain loyal to him; and with their help he could easily have overwhelmed the surviving great powers. But he had no sooner got to Milan than he did the opposite, coming to the assistance of Pope Alexander so he could occupy the Romagna.[12] He did not realize that by this decision he weakened himself, alienating his friends and those who had flung themselves into his arms; and at the same time strengthened the Church, adding to its already extensive spiritual authority an increased temporal power. And having made one error he was forced to make another, for, in order to put a stop to Alexander's ambitions, and to prevent his gaining control of Tuscany, he was obliged to march into Italy once more. Nor was he satisfied with having strengthened the Church and thrown away his alliances, but in addition, because he wanted the Kingdom of Naples, he agreed to divide it with the King of Spain.[13] Where he had been all-powerful in Italy, he now shared his power with another, giving ambitious rulers in the region and those who were discontented with him someone to whom they could turn. Where he could have left in the Kingdom of Naples a king who was on his payroll, he threw him out, and replaced him

11. [Charles VIII (1470–98) ruled France from 1492 and invaded Italy in 1494. He was crowned King of Naples in 1494, but was forced out of Italy in 1495. Louis invaded Italy in 1499. His forces were decisively defeated as the Second Battle of Novara, 1512.]

12. [See below, chapter seven.]

13. [Louis agreed to divide the Kingdom of Naples with Ferdinand the Catholic in 1500, but lost the whole state to him in 1504.]

with someone who might aspire to kick out the French.

It is perfectly natural and normal to want to acquire new territory; and whenever men do what will succeed towards this end, they will be praised, or at least not condemned. But when they are not in a position to make gains, and try nevertheless, then they are making a mistake, and deserve condemnation. If the King of France had the military capacity to attack Naples, he should have done so; if he did not have it, he should not have proposed to partition the territory. The division of Lombardy between France and Venice was justified because it gave the French a foothold in Italy; the division of Naples was blameworthy, for it was not justifiable on the same grounds.

Thus, Louis had made the following five mistakes: He wasted his alliance with the lesser states; he increased the strength of one of the more powerful Italian states; he invited an extremely powerful foreign state to intervene in Italy; he did not go and live in Italy; he did not establish settlements there. Even these mistakes might have had no evil consequences while he lived, had he not made a sixth, attacking the Venetians. Had he not strengthened the Church and brought the Spanish into Italy, then it would have been reasonable and appropriate to attack them; but having done what he had done, he should never have given his consent to a policy aimed at their destruction. For as long as they remained powerful, the others would never have been prepared to undertake an attack upon Lombardy. For the Venetians would not have consented to Lombardy's falling into the hands of others, and not themselves; while the others would not have wanted to take Lombardy from the King of France only to give it to the Venetians, and would not have had the courage to try to take it away from both of them.

And if someone were to reply that King Louis allowed Alexander to take the Romagna, and the King of Spain to have the Kingdom of Naples, in order to avoid a war, I would answer as I did above: One should never allow a problem to develop in order to avoid a war, for you end up not avoiding the war, but deferring it to a time that will be less favorable. And if others were to appeal to the promise the king had given to the pope, to help him seize the Romagna in return for the pope's giving him a divorce and

making the Bishop of Rouen a cardinal, I would reply with what I will say later on the subject of whether and to what extent rulers should keep their word.

Thus, King Louis lost Lombardy because he did not follow any of the policies others have adopted when they have established predominance within a region and have wanted to hold on to it. There is nothing remarkable about what happened: It is entirely natural and predictable. I spoke about these matters with the Cardinal of Rouen in Nantes, when Valentino (as Cesare Borgia, son of Pope Alexander, was commonly called) was taking possession of the Romagna. The cardinal said to me that the Italians did not understand war; so I told him that the French did not understand politics, for if they did, they would not allow the church to acquire so much power. And in practice we have seen that the strength of the papacy and of the King of Spain within Italy has been brought about by the King of France, and they in turn have been the cause of his own ruin. From this one can draw a general conclusion that will never (or hardly ever) be proved wrong: He who is the cause of someone else's becoming powerful is the agent of his own destruction; for he makes his protegé powerful either through his own skill or through his own strength, and either of these must provoke his protegé's mistrust once he has become powerful.

CHAPTER 4

Why the kingdom of Darius, which Alexander occupied, did not rebel against his successors after Alexander's death.

When you think of the difficulties associated with trying to hold on to a newly acquired state, you might well be puzzled: Since Alexander the Great had conquered Asia in the space of a few years, and then died when he had scarcely had time to take possession of it, at that point you would expect the whole state to rebel.[14] Nevertheless, Alexander's successors

14. [Alexander conquered Asia between 334 and 327 B.C., and died in 323 B.C.]

maintained possession of it and had no difficulty in keeping hold of it, beyond the conflicts that sprung up between themselves as a result of their own ambitions. My explanation is that the principalities recorded in history have been governed in two different ways: either by a single individual, and everyone else has been his servant, and they have helped to govern his kingdom as ministers, appointed by his grace and benevolence; or by a monarch together with barons, who, not by concession of the ruler, but by virtue of their noble lineage, hold that rank. Such barons have their own territories and their own subjects: subjects who recognize them as their lords and feel a natural affection for them. In those states that are governed by a single individual and his servants, the sovereign has more authority in his own hands; for in all his territories there is no one recognized as having a right to rule except him alone; and if his subjects obey anyone else, they do so because he is the ruler's minister and representative, and they do not feel any particular loyalty to these subordinate authorities.

In our own day the obvious examples of these two types of ruler are the Sultan of Turkey and the King of France. All the kingdom of Turkey is ruled by a single monarch, and everyone else is his servant. He divides his kingdom into sanjaks,[15] sending administrators, whom he replaces and transfers as he thinks best, to rule them. But the King of France is placed among a multitude of long-established nobles, whose rights are recognized by their subjects and who are loved by them. They have their own inherited privileges, and the king cannot take them away without endangering himself. If you compare these two states, you will realize it would be difficult to seize the sultan's kingdom, but, once you had got control of it, it would be very easy to hold on to it.

It would be difficult to occupy the lands of the sultan for two reasons: The local authorities of that kingdom will not invite you to invade, nor can you hope those around the ruler will rebel, making your task easier. And this for the reasons I have explained. For, since they are all his slaves, and indebted to him, it is harder to corrupt them; and even if you can corrupt them, they are not going to be much use to

you, for they cannot command the obedience of the people, as I have explained. Consequently, anyone attacking the sultan must expect to find the Turks united in his defense and must rely more on his own strength than on the disorder of his opponents. But once he has defeated them and has destroyed their forces on the field of battle so completely they cannot muster an army, then he has no one to worry about except the sultan's close relatives. Once he has got rid of them, then there is no one left for him to fear, for there is no one else with influence over the people. Just as the invader, before his victory, had no reason to hope for support, so, after his victory, he has no reason to fear opposition.

The opposite is true in kingdoms governed like that of France. For it is easy to invade them, once one has gained the support of some local noble. For in such kingdoms one can always find malcontents who hope to benefit from innovation. These, as we have seen, can ease your entrance into the state and help you win victory. But then, when you try to hold on to power, you will find the nobility, both those who have been your allies and those you have defeated, present you with an infinity of problems. It simply is not sufficient to kill the ruler and his close relatives, for the rest of the nobility will survive to provide leadership for new insurrections. You cannot win their loyalty or wipe them out, so you will always be in danger of losing your kingdom should anything go wrong.

Now if you ask yourself what sort of state it was Darius ruled, you will see it was similar to that of the sultan. So it was necessary for Alexander, first to take on his forces and seize control of the territory. Once he was victorious, and Darius was dead, Alexander had a firm grip on his new lands, for the reasons I have given. And his successors, if they had stayed united, could have enjoyed them at their leisure; nor was there any resistance to them in that kingdom, apart from their own conflicts with one another. But states that are organized after the French model cannot be held onto, once seized, with such ease. This is why there were frequent rebellions in Spain, France,[16] and Greece against the Romans. For there

---

15. [An administrative region.]

16. [Machiavelli uses "France" to refer both to modern France and the ancient province of Gaul. Because one

were many rulers in those territories, and as long as people remembered them, the Romans were always unsure of their grip. Once the memory of these rulers had faded completely away, thanks to the long duration of Roman rule, they became secure in their possession. Even after that, each faction among the Romans, when they fought among themselves, could call on the support of a section of those provinces, depending on the influence they had built up within them. The subjects of these territories, because their former rulers had no heirs, had no loyalties except to Roman leaders. Once you have considered all these matters, you will not be at all surprised at the ease with which Alexander held on to Asia or at the difficulties other conquerors (one might take Pyrrhus as one example among many) have had in keeping control of their acquisitions. The crucial factor in these differing outcomes is not the strength [*virtù*] or weakness of the conqueror but the contrasting character of the societies that have been conquered.

CHAPTER 5

How you should govern cities or kingdoms that, before you acquired them, lived under their own laws.

When the states one acquires by conquest are accustomed to living under their own laws and in freedom, there are three policies one can follow in order to hold on to them: The first is to lay them waste; the second is to go and live there in person; the third is to let them continue to live under their own laws, make them pay you, and create there an administrative and political elite who will remain loyal to you. For since the elite are the creation of the head of state, its members know they cannot survive without both his friendship and his power, and they know it is in their interest to do everything to sustain it. It is easier to rule a city that is used to being self-governing

by employing its own citizens than by other means, assuming you do not wish to destroy it.

Examples are provided by the Spartans and the Romans. The Spartans took Athens and Thebes, establishing oligarchies there. However, they lost them again.[17] The Romans, in order to hold on to Capua, Carthage, and Numantia razed them and never lost them.[18] They sought to govern Greece according to more or less the same policies as those used by Sparta, letting the Greek cities rule themselves and enforce their own laws, but the policy failed, so in the end they were obliged to demolish many cities in that territory in order to hold on to them. The simple truth is there is no reliable way of holding on to a city and the territory around it, short of demolishing the city itself. He who becomes the ruler of a city that is used to living under its own laws and does not knock it down, must expect to be knocked down by it. Whenever it rebels, it will find strength in the language of liberty and will seek to restore its ancient constitution. Neither the passage of time nor good treatment will make its citizens forget their previous liberty. No matter what one does, and what precautions one takes, if one does not scatter and drive away the original inhabitants, one will not destroy the memory of liberty or the attraction of the old institutions. As soon as there is a crisis, they will seek to restore them. This is what happened in Pisa after it had been enslaved by the Florentines for a hundred years.[19]

But when cities or provinces are used to being ruled by a monarch, and one has wiped out his relatives and descendants, then matters are very different. They are used to being obedient. Their old ruler is gone, and they cannot agree among themselves as to who should replace him. They do not know how to rule themselves. The result is that they are slower to take up arms, and it is easier for a new ruler to win them over and establish himself securely in power. But in

---

of his beliefs is that the French have not changed, I have kept his terminology as a reminder of his conviction that there is a real continuity between the ancient world and the present.]

17. [The Spartan-sponsored oligarchies controlled Athens from 404 to 403 B.C. and Thebes from 382 to 379 B.C.]

18. [Capua in 211 B.C., Carthage in 146 B.C., Numantia in 133 B.C.]

19. [Pisa was controlled by Florence from 1406 to 1494, and recaptured in 1509.]

former republics there is more vitality, more hatred, more desire for revenge. The memory of their former freedom gives them no rest, no peace. So the best thing to do is to demolish them or to go and live there oneself.

CHAPTER 6

About new kingdoms acquired with one's own armies and one's own skill [*virtù*].

No one should be surprised if, in talking about completely new kingdoms (that is, states that are governed by someone who was not a ruler before, and were themselves not previously principalities), I point to the greatest of men as examples to follow. For men almost always walk along the beaten path, and what they do is almost always an imitation of what others have done before. But you cannot walk exactly in the footsteps of those who have gone before, nor is it easy to match the skill [*virtù*] of those you have chosen to imitate. Consequently, a prudent man will always try to follow in the footsteps of great men and imitate those who have been truly outstanding, so that, if he is not quite as skillful [*virtù*] as they, at least some of their ability may rub off on him. One should be like an experienced archer, who, trying to hit someone at a distance and knowing the range [*virtù*] of his bow, aims at a point above his target, not so his arrow will strike the point he is aiming at, but so, by aiming high, he can reach his objective.

I maintain that, in completely new kingdoms, the new ruler has more or less difficulty in keeping hold of power depending on whether he is more or less skillful [*virtuoso*]. Now you only find yourself in this situation, a private individual only becomes a ruler, if you are either lucky, or skillful [*virtù*]. Both luck and skill enable you to overcome difficulties. Nevertheless, he who relies least on luck has the best prospect of success. One advantage is common to any completely new sovereign: Because he has no other territories, he has no choice but to come in person and live in his new kingdom. Let us look at those who through their own skill [*virtù*], and not merely through chance, have become rulers. In my view, the greatest have been Moses, Cyrus, Romulus, Theseus, and others like them.[20]

Obviously, we should not discuss Moses' skill, for he was a mere agent, following the instructions given him by God. So he should be admired, not for his own skill, but for that grace that made him worthy to talk with God. But let us discuss Cyrus and the others who have acquired existing kingdoms or founded new ones. You will find them all admirable. And if you look at the actions and strategies of each one of them, you will find they do not significantly differ from those of Moses, who could not have had a better teacher. If you look at their deeds and their lives, you will find they were dependent on chance only for their first opportunity. They seized their chance to make of it what they wanted. Without that first opportunity their strength [*virtù*] of purpose would never have been revealed. Without their strength [*virtù*] of purpose, the opportunity they were offered would not have amounted to anything.

Thus, it was necessary for Moses to find the people of Israel in Egypt, enslaved and oppressed by the Egyptians, so they, in order to escape from slavery, would be prepared to follow him. It was essential for Romulus to have no future in Alba, it was appropriate he should have been exposed at birth, otherwise he would not have formed the ambition of becoming King of Rome and succeeded in founding that nation. It was necessary that Cyrus should find the Persians hostile to the rule of the Medes, and the Medes weak and effeminate from too much peace. Theseus could not have demonstrated his strength of purpose [*virtù*] if he had not found the Athenians scattered. These opportunities made these men lucky; but it was their remarkable political skill [*virtù*] that enabled them to recognize these opportunities for what they were. Thanks to them their nations were ennobled and blessed with good fortune.

Those who become rulers through strength of purpose [*vie virtuose*], as they did, acquire their kingdoms with difficulty, but they hold on to them with ease.

---

20. [Cyrus overcame the Medes around 550 B.C. and founded the Persian Empire. Romulus is the mythical founder of Rome, and Theseus the slayer of the Minotaur and founder of Athens (1234 B.C.): Machiavelli took them to be genuine historical persons.]

And much of the difficulty they have in getting to power derives from the new institutions and customs they are obliged to establish in order to found their governments and make them secure. One ought to pause and consider the fact that there is nothing harder to undertake, nothing more likely of failure, nothing more risky to pull off, than to set oneself up as a leader who plans to found a new system of government. For the founder makes enemies of all those who are doing well under the old system, and has only lukewarm support from those who hope to do well under the new one. The weakness of their support springs partly from their fear of their adversaries, who have the law on their side, partly from their own want of faith. For men do not truly believe in new things until they have had practical experience of them. So it is that, whenever those who are enemies of the new order have a chance to attack it, they do so ferociously, while the others defend it half-heartedly. So the new ruler is in danger, along with his supporters.

It is necessary, however, if we are going to make sense of his situation, to find out if our innovator stands on his own feet, or depends on others to prop him up. That is, we need to know if he is obliged to try to obtain his objectives by pleading, or whether he can resort to force. In the first case, he is bound to come to a bad end, and won't achieve anything. But when he can stand on his own feet, and can resort to force, then he can usually overcome the dangers he faces. Thus it is that all armed prophets are victorious, and disarmed ones are crushed. For there is another problem: People are by nature inconstant. It is easy to persuade them of something, but it is difficult to stop them from changing their minds. So you have to be prepared for the moment when they no longer believe: Then you have to force them to believe. Moses, Cyrus, Theseus, and Romulus would not have been able to make their peoples obey their new structures of authority for long if they had been unarmed. This is what happened, in our own day, to Friar Girolamo Savonarola.[21] He and his new

constitution were destroyed as soon as the multitude began to stop believing in him. He had no way of stiffening the resolution of those who had been believers or of forcing disbelievers to obey.

Thus the founders of new states have immense difficulties to overcome, and dangers beset their path, dangers they must overcome by skill and strength of purpose [*virtù*]. But, once they have overcome them, and they have begun to be idolized, having got rid of those who were jealous of their superior qualities, they are established, they are powerful, secure, honored, happy.

We have looked at some noble examples, and to them I want to add one less remarkable. Nevertheless, it has some points of similarity to them, and I want it to stand for all the other lesser examples I could have chosen. My example is Hiero of Syracuse.[22] He was a private individual who became ruler of Syracuse. He, too, did not depend on luck once he had been given his opportunity. The people of Syracuse were oppressed and elected him as their military commander; so he deserved to be made their ruler. He was so remarkable [*di tanta virtù*], even before he became a ruler, history records "that he had everything one would look for in a king, except a kingdom." He disbanded the old militia and instituted a new one. Dropped his old friends and chose new ones. Since both his friends and his soldiers were his creatures, he had laid the foundations for constructing any political system he chose. He, too, had difficulties enough to overcome in acquiring power, and few in holding on to it.

CHAPTER 7

About new principalities that are acquired with the forces of others and with good luck.

Those who, having started as private individuals, become rulers merely out of good luck, acquire power with little trouble but have a hard time holding on

21. [Girolamo Savonarola (b. 1452) was a Dominican friar and prophetic preacher. He dominated Florentine politics from the expulsion of the Medici in 1494 until 1498, when he was executed as a heretic.]

22. [Hiero II became King of Syracuse in 269 B.C. Machiavelli's sources are Polybius, bk. 7, ch. 8, and Justin, bk. 23, ch. 4.]

to it. They have no problems on the road to power, because they leap over all the obstacles; but dangers crowd around them once they are in power. I am talking about people who are given a state, either in return for money, or out of the goodwill of him who hands it over to them. This happened to many individuals in Greece, in the cities of Ionia and the Hellespont, who were made rulers by Darius, who wanted them to hold their cities for his own greater safety and glory.[23] So, too, with those who, having been private citizens, were made emperors of Rome because they had corrupted the soldiers.[24] Such rulers are entirely dependent on the goodwill and good fortune of whoever has given them power. Good will and good fortune are totally unreliable and capricious. Such rulers do not know how to hold on to their position and cannot do so. They do not know how, because they have always been private citizens, and only a brilliant and immensely skillful [di grande virtù] man is likely to know how to command without having had training and experience. They cannot because they have no troops of their own on whose loyalty and commitment they can count.

Moreover, states that spring up overnight, like all other things in nature that are born and grow in a hurry, cannot have their roots deep in the soil, so they shrivel up in the first drought, blow over in the first storm. Unless, as I have said, those who are suddenly made into rulers are of such extraordinary capacity [virtù] they can work out on the spot how to hold on to the gift fortune has unexpectedly handed them; and those preparations the others made before they became rulers, they must find a way of making after the event.

I want to add to the one and the other of these two ways of becoming a ruler, by skill [virtù] or by luck, two examples drawn from the events that have occurred in our own lifetimes: the examples of Francesco Sforza and Cesare Borgia. Francesco, by using the right methods and consummate skill [virtù], started out as a private citizen and ended up as Duke of Milan. And what he had acquired with painstaking

effort, he held on to without trouble.[25] On the other hand Cesare Borgia, who was called Duke Valentino by the common people, acquired his state thanks to the good fortune of his father, and when that came to an end he lost it.[26] This despite the fact he used every technique and did all the things a prudent and skillful [virtuoso] man ought to do, to entrench himself in those territories that the arms and fortune of others had acquired for him. For, as I said above, he who does not prepare the foundations first can (in principle), if he is immensely skillful [virtù], make up for it later, although the architect will find catching up a painful process, and there is a real danger the building will collapse. So, if we look at all the things Borgia did, we will see he had laid solid foundations for future power. I do not think it irrelevant to discuss his policies, because I cannot think of any better example I could offer a new ruler than that of his actions. And if his strategy did not lead to success, this was not his fault; his failure was due to extraordinary and exceptional hostility on the part of fortune.

Pope Alexander VI, in setting out to make his son the duke into a ruler, was faced with considerable immediate and long-term difficulties. In the first place, he could find no way of making him the lord of any territory, except territory that belonged to the church. And he knew if he took land from the church to give to Cesare, he would have to overcome the opposition of the Duke of Milan, and also of the Venetians, for both Faenza and Rimini were already under Venetian protection. Secondly, he saw the armed forces of Italy, and particularly those he could hope to employ, were under the control of individuals who had reason to fear any increase in papal power. Consequently, he could not regard them as reliable. He could not trust the Orsini, the Colonna, or their associates, but there was no one else to whom he could turn.[27] So it was necessary to break out of this framework, and to bring disorder to the territories of

23. [Machiavelli is refering to Greek-speaking cities in Asia and the Hellespont in the sixth century B.C.]

24. [See below, chapter nineteen.]

25. [See below, chapter twelve.]

26. [Cesare Borgia (1475–1507) was the natural son of Rodrigo Borgia (1431–1503), who became Pope Alexander VI in 1492. He began the conquest of the Romagna in 1499.]

27. [On the Orsini and the Colonna, see below, chapter eleven.]

his opponents, so he could safely seize a part of them. This proved easy, for he found the Venetians, for reasons of their own, had decided to invite the French to invade Italy. He not only did not oppose this, but he facilitated it by dissolving the previous marriage of King Louis. So the king marched into Italy, with the help of the Venetians and the consent of Alexander. No sooner was he in Milan than the pope had borrowed forces from him for the attack on the Romagna, which was ceded to him out of fear of the King of France.

So, once Cesare had been made Duke of the Romagna, and the Colonnesi had been beaten, wanting to hang on to his new territories and make further conquests, he was faced with two obstacles. In the first place, his military forces did not appear reliable. In the second, the King of France might oppose him. He had made use of the troops of the Orsini, but they were likely to abandon him, and not only prevent him from making further acquisitions, but take from him what he had already acquired. And the same was true of the king. He had an indication of how far he could trust the Orsini when, after Faenza had been taken by storm, he attacked Bologna, for he discovered they had no appetite for that battle.[28] And as for the king, he discovered his attitude when, having seized the Duchy of Urbino, he attacked Tuscany, for Louis made him abandon that enterprise.[29] So the duke decided he must no longer depend on the troops and the good fortune of others.

The first thing he did was to weaken the factions of the Orsini and the Colonna in Rome. All the nobles who were allied to these families he won over to himself, making them members of his court, and giving them substantial pensions. He favored them with civil and military appointments appropriate to their standing. Thus, in the course of a few months, their attachment to their factions was dissolved, and they became committed to the duke. Next, he looked for a chance to crush the Orsini, having already defeated the forces of the Colonna family. He soon had his chance and he made the most of it. For the Orsini, having realized late in the day that the growing strength of the duke and the pope would be their ruin, called a meeting at Magione, near Perugia. From that meeting sprang the rebellion of Urbino and the uprisings in the Romagna that almost destroyed the duke; but he overcame all resistance with the help of the French.[30] And, having got back his authority and realizing he could trust neither the French nor other external forces, he decided that, in order to prevent their allying against him, he must deceive them. He so successfully concealed his intentions that the Orsini, represented by Signor Paolo, made peace with him. The duke took every opportunity to ingratiate himself with Paolo, giving him money, clothes, and horses. So the leaders of the Orsini were brought, unsuspecting, to Sinigallia, where they were at his mercy.[31] Having got rid of the leaders and won the allegiance of their followers, the duke could feel he had laid decent foundations for his future power. He had control of all the Romagna and the Duchy of Urbino, and it looked as though he had won over the Romagna and acquired the support of its population, who were beginning to enjoy a new prosperity.

Now, since it is worth paying attention to this question, and since it would be sensible to imitate Cesare's actions, I want to amplify what I have just said. Once the duke had subdued the Romagna, he found it had been under the control of weak nobles, who had rather exploited than governed their subjects and had rather been the source of conflict than of order, with the result the whole province was full of robbers, bandits, and every other type of criminal. So he decided it was necessary, if he was going to make the province peaceful and obedient to his commands, to give it good government. He put Mr. Remiro d'Orco, a man both cruel and efficient, in charge, and gave him absolute power. D'Orco in short order established peace and unity, and acquired immense authority. At that point, the duke decided such unchecked power was no longer necessary, for he feared people might come to hate it. So he established a civil court in the center of the province, placing an

28. [In the spring of 1501.]
29. [In the summer of 1502.]

30. [October 1502.]
31. [They were captured on 31 December 1502. Some were killed at once; others a few weeks later.]

excellent judge in charge of it, and requiring every city to appoint a lawyer to represent it before the court. Since he knew the harsh measures of the past had given rise to some enmity towards him, in order to purge the ill-will of the people and win them completely over to him, he wanted to make clear that, if there had been any cruelty, he was not responsible for it, and that his hard-hearted minister should be blamed. He saw his opportunity and exploited it. One morning, in the town square of Cesena, he had Remiro d'Orco's corpse laid out in two pieces, with a chopping board and a bloody knife beside it.[32] This ferocious sight made the people of the Romagna simultaneously happy and dumbfounded.

But let us get back to where we were. I was saying the duke found himself rather powerful and had taken precautions against immediate dangers, for he had built up a military force that he had planned himself and had in large part destroyed neighboring forces that could be a threat to him. So what remained, if he wanted to make further acquisitions, was the problem of the King of France; for he knew the king had, late in the day, realized his policy towards Borgia had been misconceived and would not allow him to make further conquests. So Borgia began to look for new alliances and to prevaricate with the French when they dispatched a force towards the Kingdom of Naples to attack the Spanish who were laying siege to Gaeta.[33] His intention was to protect himself against them, which he would soon have succeeded in doing, if Alexander had gone on living.

These were the policies he pursued with regard to his immediate concerns. But there were future problems he also had to consider. In the first place, he had to worry that a new pope would be hostile to him and would try to take from him what Alexander had given him. He had four ways of trying to deal with this threat. In the first place, he set out to eliminate all the relatives of those rulers whose lands he had seized, to make it difficult for the pope to restore their previous rulers. Second, he sought to acquire the allegiance of the nobility of Rome, as I have explained, so he could use them to restrict the pope's freedom of action. Third, to make as many as possible of the members of the College of Cardinals his allies. Fourth, to acquire so much power, before the pope died, that he would be able on his own to resist a first attack. Of these four policies he had successfully carried out three by the time Alexander died; the fourth he had almost accomplished. Of the rulers he had dispossessed, he murdered as many as he could get his hands on, and only a very few survived. The Roman nobility were his supporters, and he had built up a very large faction in the College of Cardinals. As far as new acquisitions were concerned, he had plans for conquering Tuscany; he already held Perugia and Piombino; and he had taken Pisa under his protection. And, as soon as he would no longer have to worry about the King of France (which was already the case, for the French had already lost the Kingdom of Naples to the Spanish, with the result that both France and Spain were now obliged to try to buy his friendship), he would be free to seize Pisa. After which, Lucca and Siena would quickly give in, partly because they hated the Florentines, and partly because they would have been terrified. The Florentines could have done nothing.

If he had succeeded in all this (and he was on the point of succeeding in the very year Alexander died) he would have acquired so much strength and so much authority he would have become his own master. He would no longer have depended on events outside his control and on the policies of others, but would have been able to rely on his own power and strength [*virtù*]. But Alexander died only five years after Cesare Borgia had unsheathed his sword.[34] He found himself with only his control over the Romagna firmly established, with everything else up in the air, caught between two powerful hostile armies, and dangerously ill. But the duke was so pugnacious and so strong [*virtù*], he so well understood what determines whether one wins or loses, and he had laid such sound foundations within such a short time, that, if he had not had these enemy armies breathing down his neck, or if he had been in good health, he could have overcome every difficulty.

I am justified in claiming he had laid sound founda-

---

32. [26 December 1502.]
33. [1503.]

34. [18 August 1503.]

tions, for the Romagna remained loyal to him in his absence for more than a month; in Rome, although he was half dead, he was quite safe, and although the Ballioni, the Vitelli, and the Orsini congregated in Rome, they could not muster a following to attack him; and, if he was not in a position to choose who should be pope, he could at least veto anyone he did not trust. So, if he had been well when Alexander died he would have been able to deal with his problems without difficulty. He told me himself, on the day Julius II was elected,[35] that he had asked himself what he would do if his father died and had been confident he could handle the situation, but that it had never occurred to him that when his father died he himself would be at death's door.

So, now I have surveyed all the actions of the duke, I still cannot find anything to criticize. It seems to me I have been right to present him as an example to be imitated by all those who come to power through good luck and thanks to someone else's military might. For, since he was great-hearted and ambitious, he had no choice as to what to do; and he only failed to achieve his goals because Alexander died too soon, and he himself fell ill. So anyone who decides that the policy to follow when one has newly acquired power is to destroy one's enemies, to secure some allies, to win wars, whether by force or by fraud, to make oneself both loved and feared by one's subjects, to make one's soldiers loyal and respectful, to wipe out those who can or would want to hurt one, to innovate, replacing old institutions with new practices, to be both harsh and generous, magnanimous and open-handed, to disband disloyal troops and form new armies, to build alliances with other powers, so kings and princes either have to win your favor or else think twice before going against your wishes— anyone who thinks in these terms cannot hope to find, in the recent past, a better model to imitate than Cesare Borgia.

His only mistake was to allow Julius to be elected pope, for there he made a bad choice. The choice

was his to make, for as I have said, if he could not choose who should be pope, he could veto anyone he did not like, and he should never have agreed to any cardinal's being elected with whom he had been in conflict in the past, or who, once he had been elected, would have been likely to be afraid of him. For men attack either out of fear or out of hatred. Those who had scores to settle with him included San Piero ad Vincula, Colonna, San Giorgio, Ascanio; all the others, if elected pope, would have had good reason to fear him, with the exception of Rouen and of the Spanish cardinals. The Spanish were his relatives and allies; Rouen was powerful, having the support of the King of France. So the duke's first objective should have been to ensure a Spaniard was elected pope; failing that, he should have agreed to the election of Rouen and vetoed that of San Piero ad Vincula. If he imagined recent gestures of goodwill make the powerful forget old injuries, he was much mistaken. So the duke made a mistake during the election of the pope, and this mistake was, in the end, the cause of his destruction.

CHAPTER 8

Of those who come to power through wicked actions.

But since there are two other ways a private citizen can become a ruler, two ways that do not simply involve the acquisition of power either through fortune or strength [*virtù*], I feel I cannot omit discussion of them, although one of them can be more fully treated elsewhere, where I discuss republics. These are, first, when one acquires power through some wicked or nefarious action, and second when a private citizen becomes ruler of his own country because he has the support of his fellow citizens. Here I will talk about the first of these two routes to power, and will use two examples, one ancient, one modern, to show how it is done. These will be sufficient, I trust, to provide a model for anyone who has no alternative options. I do not intend to discuss in detail the rights and wrongs of such a policy.

Agathocles of Sicily became King of Syracuse, although he was not merely a private citizen, but of

---

35. [28 October 1503. Giuliano della Rovere (1443–1513) had been appointed Cardinal of San Piero ad Vincula in 1471, when his uncle became Pope Sixtus IV. For Machiavelli's assessment of his papacy, see below, chapters eleven and twenty-five.]

humble and poverty-stricken origins.[36] He was the son of a potter, and from start to finish lived a wicked life; nevertheless, his wicked behavior testified to so much strength [virtù] of mind and of body that, when he joined the army, he was promoted through the ranks to the supreme command. Having risen so high, he decided to become the sole ruler and to hold on to power, which he had originally been granted by the consent of his fellow citizens, by violence and without being dependent on anyone else. Having entered into a conspiracy with a Carthaginian called Hamilcar, who was commander of a hostile army serving in Sicily, one morning he called together the people and the senate of Syracuse, as if he wanted to discuss matters of government policy, and, at a prearranged signal, had his soldiers kill all the senators and the richest citizens. With them out of the way, he made himself ruler of the city and held power without any resistance. Although the Carthaginians twice defeated his armies and even advanced to the walls of the city, he was not only able to defend his city, but, leaving part of his army behind to withstand the siege, he was able to attack the Carthaginians in Africa with the remainder of his forces. Within a short time he had forced them to lift the siege and was threatening to conquer Carthage. In the end they were obliged to come to terms with him, leaving Sicily to Agathocles in return for security in Africa.

If you consider Agathocles' bold achievements [azioni e virtù], you will not find much that can be attributed to luck; for, as I have said, he did not come to power because he had help from above, but because he worked his way up from below, climbing from rank to rank by undergoing infinite dangers and discomforts until in the end he obtained a monopoly of power, and then holding on to his position by bold and risky tactics.

One ought not, of course, to call it virtù [virtue or manliness] to massacre one's fellow citizens, to betray one's friends, to break one's word, to be without mercy and without religion. By such means one can acquire power but not glory. If one considers the manly qualities [virtù] Agathocles demonstrated in braving and facing down danger, and the strength of character he

showed in surviving and overcoming adversity, then there seems to be no reason why he should be judged less admirable than any of the finest generals. But on the other hand, his inhuman cruelty and brutality, and his innumerable wicked actions, mean it would be wrong to praise him as one of the finest of men. It is clear, at any rate, that one can attribute neither to luck nor to virtue [virtù] his accomplishments, which owed nothing to either.

In our own day, when Alexander VI was pope, Oliverotto of Fermo, whose father had died a few years before, was raised by his maternal uncle, Giovanni Fogliani.[37] As soon as he was old enough he joined the forces of Paolo Vitelli, so that, with a good military training, he could pursue a career in the army.[38] When Paolo died, he signed up with his brother, Vitellozzo. In a very short time, because he was bright and had both a strong body and a lively spirit, he became Vitellozzo's second-in-command. Soon he thought it to be beneath his dignity to serve under another, and so he conspired to occupy Fermo, relying on the help of some citizens of that city who preferred to see their fatherland enslaved than free, and on the support of Vitellozzo. He wrote to his uncle, saying that, since he had been away from home for many years, he wanted to come to visit him and to see his city, and so, in a manner of speaking, reacquaint himself with his inheritance. He said he had only gone to war in order to acquire honor. So his fellow citizens would be able to see he had not been wasting his time, he wanted to arrive in state, accompanied by a hundred men on horseback, some of them his friends, and others his servants. He asked his uncle to ensure that the inhabitants of Fermo received him with respect: This would not only enhance his own reputation, but that of his uncle, who had raised him.

Giovanni did everything he could for his nephew. He ensured he was greeted by the people of Fermo with every honor, and he put him up in his own

36. [Agathocles (361–289 B.C) seized control of Syracuse in 317 B.C. Machiavelli's source is Justin, bk. 22.]

37. [Oliverotto Euffreducci (b. ca. 1475) seized Fermo in 1501. Borgia had him killed at Senigallia in December 1502.]

38. [The Florentines made Vitelli commander of their forces in 1498 and executed him in 1499. See below, chapter twelve.]

house. After a few days had gone by, and he had had time to make the arrangements necessary for the carrying out of his wicked plans, he held a lavish banquet at his uncle's, to which he invited his uncle and the most powerful citizens of Fermo. After the food had been eaten, and the guests had been entertained in all the ways that are customary upon such occasions, Oliverotto deliberately began discussing serious questions, talking about the greatness of Pope Alexander and his son Cesare, and about their undertakings. When his uncle Giovanni and the others picked up the subject, he sprang to his feet, saying such matters should be discussed in a more private place. He withdrew into another room, where Giovanni and all the other leading citizens followed. No sooner had they sat down than soldiers emerged from their hiding places and killed Giovanni along with all the rest. Once the killing was over, Oliverotto got on his horse and took possession of the city, laying siege to the government building. Those in authority were so terrified they agreed to obey him and to establish a new regime of which he was the head. With all those who had something to lose and would have been able to resist him dead, he was able to entrench himself by establishing new civilian and military institutions. Within a year of coming to power, he was not only securely in control of Fermo, but had become a threat to all the cities round about. It would soon have been as difficult to get rid of him as to get rid of Agathocles, had he not allowed himself to be taken in by Cesare Borgia, when, as I have already explained, he got rid of the Orsini and the Vitelli at Sinigallia. Oliverotto was seized at the same time, and, a year after he had killed his uncle, he was strangled along with Vitellozzo from whom he had learned how to be bold [*virtù*] and how to be wicked.

Perhaps you are wondering how Agathocles and others like him, despite their habitual faithlessness and cruelty, have been able to live safely in their homelands year after year, and to defend themselves against their enemies abroad. Why did their fellow subjects not conspire against them? After all, mere cruelty has not been enough to enable many other rulers to hang on to power even in time of peace, let alone during the turmoil of war. I think here we have to distinguish between cruelty well used and cruelty

abused. Well-used cruelty (if one can speak well of evil) one may call those atrocities that are committed at a stroke, in order to secure one's power, and are then not repeated, rather every effort is made to ensure one's subjects benefit in the long run. An abuse of cruelty one may call those policies that, even if in the beginning they involve little bloodshed, lead to more rather than less as time goes by. Those who use cruelty well may indeed find both God and their subjects are prepared to let bygones be bygones, as was the case with Agathocles. Those who abuse it cannot hope to retain power indefinitely.

So the conclusion is: If you take control of a state, you should make a list of all the crimes you have to commit and do them all at once. That way you will not have to commit new atrocities every day, and you will be able, by not repeating your evil deeds, to reassure your subjects and to win their support by treating them well. He who acts otherwise, either out of squeamishness or out of bad judgment, has to hold a bloody knife in his hand all the time. He can never rely on his subjects, for they can never trust him, for he is always making new attacks upon them. Do all the harm you must at one and the same time, that way the full extent of it will not be noticed, and it will give least offense. One should do good, on the other hand, little by little, so people can fully appreciate it.

A ruler should, above all, behave towards his subjects in such a way that, whatever happens, whether for good or ill, he has no need to change his policies. For if you fall on evil times and are obliged to change course, you will not have time to benefit from the harm you do, and the good you do will do you no good, because people will think you have been forced to do it, and they will not be in the slightest bit grateful to you.

CHAPTER 9

Of the citizen-ruler.

But, coming to the alternative possibility, when a private citizen becomes the ruler of his homeland, not through wickedness or some act of atrocity, but through the support of his fellow citizens, so that we may call him a citizen-ruler (remember we are discussing power acquired neither by pure strength [*virtù*] nor mere luck—in this case one needs a lucky cunning), I would point out there are two ways to such power: the support of the populace or the favor of the elite. For in every city one finds these two opposed classes. They are at odds because the populace do not want to be ordered about or oppressed by the elite; and the elite want to order about and oppress the populace. The conflict between these two irreconcilable ambitions has in each city one of three possible consequences: rule by one man, liberty, or anarchy.

Rule by one man can be brought about either by the populace or the elite, depending on whether one or the other of these factions hopes to benefit from it. For if the elite fear they will be unable to control the populace, they begin to build up the reputation of one of their own, and they make him sole ruler in order to be able, under his protection, to achieve their objectives. The populace on the other hand, if they fear they are going to be crushed by the elite, build up the reputation of one of their number and make him sole ruler, in order that his authority may be employed in their defense. He who comes to power with the help of the elite has more difficulty in holding on to power than he who comes to power with the help of the populace, for in the former case he is surrounded by many who think of themselves as his equals, and whom he consequently cannot order about or manipulate as he might wish. He who comes to power with the support of the populace, on the other hand, has it all to himself: There is no one, or hardly anyone, around him who is not prepared to obey. In addition, one cannot honorably give the elite what they want, and one cannot do it without harming others; but this is not true with the populace, for the objectives of the populace are less immoral than those of the elite, for the latter want to oppress, and the former not to be oppressed. Thirdly, if the masses are opposed to you, you can never be secure, for there are too many of them; but the elite, since there are few of them, can be neutralized.

The worst a ruler who is opposed by the populace has to fear is that they will give him no support; but from the elite he has to fear not only lack of support, but worse, that they will attack him. For the elite have more foresight and more cunning; they act in time to protect themselves, and seek to ingratiate themselves with rivals for power. Finally, the ruler cannot get rid of the populace but must live with them; he can, however, get by perfectly well without the members of the elite, being able to make and unmake them each day, and being in a position to give them status or take it away, as he chooses.

In order to clarify the issues, let me point out there are two principal points of view from which one should consider the elite. Either they behave in a way that ties their fortunes to yours, or they do not. Those who tie themselves to you and are not rapacious, you should honor and love; those who do not tie themselves to you are to be divided into two categories. If they retain their independence through pusillanimity and because they are lacking in courage, then you should employ them, especially if they have good judgment, for you can be sure they will help you achieve success so long as things are going well for you, and you can also be confident you have nothing to fear from them if things go badly. But if they retain their independence from you out of calculation and ambition, then you can tell they are more interested in their own welfare than yours. A ruler must protect himself against such people and fear them as much as if they were publicly declared enemies, for you can be sure that, in adversity, they will help to overthrow you.

Anyone who becomes a ruler with the support of the populace ought to ensure he keeps their support; which will not be difficult, for all they ask is not to be oppressed. But anyone who becomes a ruler with the support of the elite and against the wishes of the populace must above all else seek to win the populace over to his side, which will be easy to do if he protects their interests. And since people, when they are well-treated by someone whom they expected to treat them badly, feel all the more obliged to their benefactor, he will find that the populace will quickly become better inclined towards him than if he had come to power with their support. There are numerous ways the ruler can win the support of the populace. They vary so much depending on the circumstances they cannot be reduced to a formula, and, consequently, I will not go into them here. I will simply conclude by saying a ruler needs to have the support of the populace, for otherwise he has nothing to fall back on in times of adversity.

Nabis, ruler of the Spartans, survived an attack by the confederate forces of all Greece, together with an almost invincible Roman army, and successfully defended both his homeland and his own hold on power. All he needed to do, when faced with danger, was neutralize a few; but if he had had the populace opposed to him, this would have been insufficient.[39] Do not think you can rebut my argument by citing the well-worn proverb, "Relying on the people is like building on the sand." This is quite true when a private citizen depends upon them and gives the impression he expects the populace to free him if he is seized by his enemies or by the magistrates. In such a case one can easily find oneself disappointed, as happened to the Gracchi in Rome and to Mr. Giorgio Scali in Florence.[40] But if you are a ruler and you put your trust in the populace, if you can give commands and are capable of bold action, if you are not nonplused by adversity, if you take other necessary precautions, and if through your own courage and your policies you keep up the morale of the populace, then you will never be let down by them, and you will discover you have built on a sound foundation.

The type of one-man rule we are discussing tends to be at risk at the moment of transition from constitutional to dictatorial government. Such rulers either give commands in their own name, or act through the officers of state. In the second case, their situation is more dangerous and less secure. For they are entirely dependent on the cooperation of those citizens who have been appointed to the offices of state, who can, particularly at times of crisis, easily deprive them of their power, either by directly opposing them or by simply failing to carry out their instructions. It is too late for the ruler once a crisis is upon him to seize dictatorial authority, for the citizens and the subjects, who are used to obeying the constituted authorities, will not, in such circumstances, obey him, and he will always have, in difficult circumstances, a shortage of people on whom he can rely. For such a ruler cannot expect things to continue as they were when there were no difficulties, when all the citizens are conscious of what the government can do for them. Then everyone flocked round, everyone promised support, everyone was willing to die for him, when there was no prospect of having to do so. But when times are tough, when the government is dependent on its citizens, then there will be few who are prepared to stand by it. One does not learn the danger of such an erosion of support from experience, as the first experience proves fatal. So a wise ruler will seek to ensure that his citizens always, no matter what the circumstances, have an interest in preserving both him and his authority. If he can do this, they will always be faithful to him.

CHAPTER 10

How one should measure the strength of a ruler.

There is another factor one should take into account when categorizing rulers: One should ask if a ruler has enough resources to be able, if necessary, to look after himself, or whether he will always be dependent on having alliances with other rulers. In order to clarify this question, I would maintain those rulers can look after themselves who have sufficient reserves, whether of troops or of money, to be able to put together a sound army and face battle against any opponent. On the other hand, I judge those rulers to be dependent on the support of others who could not take the field against any potential enemy, but would be obliged to take shelter behind the walls of their cities and castles, and stay there. We have talked already about those who can look after themselves, and we will have more to say in due course; to those who are in

39. [Nabis (ca. 240–192 B.C.) became ruler of Sparta in 207 B.C. Livy (bk. 34) puts the number assassinated at eighty.]

40. [The Gracchi brothers (Tiberius Sempronius [163–133 B.C.] and Gaius Sempronius [153–121 B.C.]) were advocates of agrarian reform who both died in riots. Scali was a populist leader in Florence during the Ciompi rising of 1378 but was executed for an attack on the authorities in 1382.]

the second situation, all one can do is advise them to build defenseworks and stockpile arms, and to give up all thought of holding the open ground. He who has well fortified his city and who has followed the policies towards his own subjects that I have outlined above and will describe below, can be sure his enemies will think twice before they attack him, for people are always reluctant to undertake enterprises that look as if they will be difficult, and no one thinks it will be easy to attack someone who is well-fortified and has the support of the populace.

The cities of Germany are free to do as they please. They have little surrounding territory, and obey the emperor only when they want. They fear neither him nor any other ruler in their region, for they are so well-fortified everyone thinks it will be tedious and difficult to take them. They all have appropriate moats and ramparts, and more than enough artillery. They always keep in the public stores enough food and drink, and enough firewood, to be able to hold out for a year. Moreover, in order to be able to keep the populace quiet and to guarantee tax revenues, they always keep in stock enough supplies to keep their subjects occupied for a year in those crafts that are the basis of the city's prosperity and provide employment for the bulk of the people. They also emphasize military preparedness and have numerous ordinances designed to ensure this.

A ruler, therefore, who has a well-fortified city, and who does not set out to make enemies, is not going to be attacked; and, suppose someone does attack him, his adversary will have to give up in disgrace. For political circumstances change so fast it is impossible for anyone to keep an army in the field for a year doing nothing but maintaining a siege. And if you are tempted to reply that if the people have property outside the city walls and see it burning, then they will not be able patiently to withstand a siege, and that as time goes by, and their own interests are damaged, they will forget their loyalty to their ruler; then I reply that a ruler who is strong and bold will always be able to overcome such difficulties, sometimes encouraging his subjects to think relief is at hand, sometimes terrifying them with stories of what the enemy will do to them if they concede defeat, sometimes taking appropriate action to neutralize those who

seem to him to be agitators. Moreover, it is in the nature of things that the enemy will burn and pillage the countryside when they first arrive, at which time the subjects will still be feeling brave and prepared to undertake their own defense. So the ruler has little to fear, for after a few days, when the subjects are feeling less courageous, the damage will already have been done, and it will be too late to prevent it. Then they will be all the more ready to rally to their ruler, believing him to be in their debt, since they have had their houses burnt and their possessions looted for defending him. It is in men's nature to feel as obliged by the good they do to others, as by the good others do to them. So if you consider all the factors, you will see it is not difficult for a wise ruler to keep his subjects loyal during a siege, both at the beginning and as it continues, providing they are not short of food and of arms.

CHAPTER 11

About ecclesiastical states.

All that remains for us to discuss, at this point, is the ecclesiastical states. As far as they are concerned, all the problems are encountered before one gets possession of them. One acquires them either through strength [*virtù*] or through luck, but one can hold on to them without either. For they are maintained by their long-established institutions that are rooted in religion. These have developed to such a pitch of strength they can support their rulers in power no matter how they live and behave. Only ecclesiastical rulers have states, but no need to defend them; subjects, but no need to govern them. Their states, though they do not defend them, are not taken from them; their subjects, though they do not govern them, do not resent them, and they neither think of replacing their rulers nor are they in a position to do so. So these are the only rulers who are secure and happy. But because they are ruled by a higher power, which human intelligence cannot grasp, I will say no more about them; for, since they have been built up and maintained by God, only a presumptuous and rash person would debate about them. Nevertheless, if someone were to ask me how it comes about that the church has acquired so much temporal power, given that, until the papacy of Alexander [VI], the rulers of Italy, and indeed not only those who called themselves rulers, but every baron and lord, no matter how small, regarded the papacy's temporal power as of little significance, while now a King of France trembles at its power, for a pope has kicked him out of Italy and been the ruin of the Venetians: Though the answer to this question is well known, I think it will not be a waste of time to remind you of the main principles.

Before Charles, King of France, invaded Italy, control over this geographical region was divided between the pope, the Republic of Venice, the King of Naples, the Duke of Milan, and the Republic of Florence.[41] These rulers were obliged to have two principal preoccupations: In the first place, they had to make sure no foreign power brought an army into Italy; in the second, they had to make sure none of the Italian powers increased its territory. The powers they were most concerned about were the pope and the Venetians. In order to prevent the Venetians from expanding all the rest had to cooperate, as happened when the Venetians tried to take Ferrara.[42] In order to keep the pope in his place they relied on the nobles of Rome. These were divided into two factions, the Orsini and the Colonna, and so there was always occasion for friction between them. Because both factions were constantly in arms within sight of the pope, their strength kept the pope weak and sickly. Although there was occasionally a pope who had ambitions, Sixtus [IV] for example, yet neither luck nor skill enabled him to free himself of that handicap.

The real cause was the shortness of the popes' lives. On average, a pope lived ten years, which was scarcely enough time to crush one of the factions. Suppose a pope had almost destroyed the Colonna; his successor would prove to be an enemy of the Orsini, would rebuild the power of the Colonna, and would not have time to crush the Orsini. The result was the temporal power of the pope was not thought by the Italians to be of much importance. Then along came Alexander VI, who, more than all the other popes

there have been, demonstrated how much a pope, using both money and arms, could get his own way. It was Alexander who, by making use of Duke Valentino and by taking advantage of the invasion of Italy by the French, brought about all those things I have mentioned above, when discussing the achievements of the duke.[43] Although his objective was not to make the church, but rather the duke, powerful, nevertheless, he did make the church a power to be reckoned with. It was the church that, after he had died and the duke had been destroyed, inherited the results of his labors.

After him came Julius [II]. The church was already powerful, for it had control of the whole of the Romagna, and the barons of Rome had been crushed, and the two factions of Orsini and Colonna had, as a result of the hiding given them by Alexander, been eliminated. Moreover, Julius had opportunities to accumulate money of a sort that had not existed before Alexander. Julius not only took over where Alexander had left off, but made further advances. He planned to acquire Bologna, to destroy the power of the Venetians, and to throw the French out of Italy. He not only laid plans, but he succeeded in everything he undertook. His achievements were all the more admirable in that his goal was to build up the power of the Church, not of any private individual. He kept the factions of the Orsini and the Colonna in the feeble condition in which he had found them. Although they made some efforts to rise again, two things kept them down: in the first place, the new power of the church, which intimidated them; and in the second, the fact none of their number were cardinals, for it is the cardinals who have been at the origin of the conflicts between the factions. These two factions have never behaved themselves at times when they have had cardinals, for the cardinals, both in Rome and outside Rome, foster the factions, and the barons are obliged to come to their support. Thus the ambition of the prelates is the cause of the conflicts and tumults among the nobility.

Now His Holiness Pope Leo [X] has acquired the papacy, along with all its immense temporal power. We may hope, if his predecessors made it a military

---

41. [Charles VIII invaded Italy in 1494.]

42. [In 1482–84.]

43. [See chapter seven.]

power to be reckoned with, he, who is so good and has so many virtues [*virtù*], will not only increase its power, but also make it worthy of respect.

CHAPTER 12

How many types of army are there, and what opinion should one have of mercenary soldiers?

So far I have discussed one by one the various types of one-man rule I listed at the beginning, and I have to some extent described the policies that make each type succeed or fail. I have shown the various techniques employed by numerous individuals who have sought to acquire and to hold on to power. Now my task is to outline the various strategies for offense and defense that are common to all these principalities. I said above it was necessary for a ruler to lay good foundations; otherwise, he is likely to be destroyed. The principal foundations on which the power of all governments is based (whether they be new, long-established, or mixed) are good laws and good armies. And, since there cannot be good laws where there are not good armies, and since where there are good armies, there must be good laws, I will omit any discussion of laws, and will talk about armies.

Let me begin by saying, then, that a ruler defends his state with armies that are made up of his own subjects, or of mercenaries, or of auxiliary forces, or of some combination of these three types. Mercenaries and auxiliaries are both useless and dangerous. Anyone who relies on mercenary troops to keep himself in power will never be safe or secure, for they are factious, ambitious, ill-disciplined, treacherous. They show off to your allies and run away from your enemies. They do not fear God and do not keep faith with mankind. A mercenary army puts off defeat for only so long as it postpones going into battle. In peacetime they pillage you, in wartime they let the enemy do it. This is why: They have no motive or principle for joining up beyond the desire to collect their pay. And what you pay them is not enough to make them want to die for you. They are delighted to be your soldiers when you are not at war; when you are at war, they walk away when they do not run.

It should not be difficult to convince you of this, because the sole cause of the present ruin of Italy has been the fact that for many years now the Italians have been willing to rely on mercenaries. It is true that occasionally a ruler seems to benefit from their use, and they boast of their own prowess, but as soon as they face foreign troops their true worth becomes apparent. This is why Charles, King of France, was able to conquer Italy with a piece of chalk; and the person who said we were being punished for our sins spoke the truth.[44] But our sins were not the ones of which he was thinking, but those I have been discussing. Because these were the sins of our rulers, our rulers as well as the common people had to pay the price for them.

I want now to make crystal clear the worthlessness of mercenary armies. Mercenary commanders are either excellent or not. If they are excellent, you cannot trust them, for they will always be looking for ways of increasing their own power, either by turning on you, their employer, or by turning on others whom you want them to leave alone. On the other hand, if they are not first rate [*virtuoso*], then they will be the ruin of you in the normal course of events. And if you want to reply the same problems will arise whoever makes up the army, whether they are mercenaries or not, I will argue it depends on whether they take their orders from a sovereign or from a republic. A sovereign ought to go to war himself, and be his own general. A republic has to send one of its citizens. If it chooses someone who turns out not to be a successful soldier, it must replace him; if it chooses someone who is successful, it must tie his hands with laws, to ensure he keeps within the limits assigned to him. Experience shows individual sovereigns and republics that arm the masses are capable of making vast conquests; but mercenary troops are always a liability. Moreover, it is harder for a treacherous citizen to suborn an army consisting of his own fellow subjects than one made up of foreigners.

Rome and Sparta were armed and free for many centuries. The Swiss are armed to the teeth and do not have to take orders from anyone. In ancient history,

44. [The chalk was used by Charles's quartermasters to mark the soldiers' billets. Savonarola attributed Charles's victory to sins such as fornication and usury.]

we can take the Carthaginians as an example of the consequences of relying on mercenaries. They were in danger of being oppressed by their mercenary soldiers when the first war with Rome was over,[45] despite the fact they employed their own citizens as commanders. Philip of Macedon was made general of the Theban armies after the death of Epaminondas; and, after he had won the war, he enslaved the Thebans.[46] In modern times, Milan, after Duke Filippo died, employed Francesco Sforza to fight the Venetians. Once he had defeated the enemy at Caravaggio, he joined forces with them to attack the Milanese, his employers.[47] Sforza his father, who was employed by Queen Giovanna of Naples, abandoned her without warning and without defenses.[48] As a consequence, she was obliged to throw herself into the embrace of the King of Aragon in order to hold on to her kingdom. If the Venetians and the Florentines have in the past succeeded in acquiring new territory with mercenary armies, and if their commanders have not seized the conquests for themselves, but have held onto them for their employers, this, I would argue, is because the Florentines have had more than their share of luck. For of the first-rate [*virtuosi*] commanders, whom they would have had reason to fear, some have not been victorious, some have not been in sole command, and some have turned their ambitions elsewhere. It was John Hawkwood who did not win: We cannot know if he would have proved reliable had he been victorious, but no one can deny that if he had won Florence would have been his for the taking.[49] Sforza always had to share command with the Braccheschi, and neither could act for fear of the other. Francesco turned his ambitions to Lombardy; Braccio[50] turned his against the church and the Kingdom of Naples.

But let us look at what happened only a short time ago. The Florentines made Paolo Vitelli their commander.[51] He was a very astute man, and, despite being of modest origin, he had acquired a tremendous reputation. If he had succeeded in taking Pisa, no one can deny the Florentines would have needed his goodwill, for, if he had transferred his support to their enemies, they would have been without defenses; and if they had managed to keep his support, they would have had no choice but to do as he told them.

Consider next the conquests made by the Venetians. You will see they ran no risks and won magnificent victories as long as they relied on their own troops, which was until they tried to conquer territory on the mainland. When they armed both the nobility and the populace they had a magnificent fighting force [*operorono virtuosissimamente*], but when they began to fight on the mainland they abandoned this sound policy [*questa virtù*], and began to copy the other Italian states. When they began their conquests on the mainland, because they had little territory there, and because their own reputation was fearsome, they had little to fear from their mercenary commanders. But as their conquests extended, as they did under Carmagnola, they began to discover their mistake.[52] They recognized he was a first-rate [*virtuosissimo*] general, and that they had, under his command, defeated the Duke of Milan, but they realized he had lost his taste for war, and concluded they could no longer win with him, because he no longer wanted victory; but they could not dismiss him, or the land they had acquired would go with him. So, in order to neutralize him, they had to kill him. Since then they have employed as commanders of their forces Bartolemeo of Bergamo, Roberto of San Severino, the Count of Pitigliano, and others like them. With such commanders they had reason to fear defeat, not the consequences of victory. And indeed they were defeated at Vailà, where, in one day, they lost all they had acquired with so much effort in eight hundred years.[53] For with mercenary troops one acquires new territory slowly, feebly, after many attempts; but one loses so much so quickly that it seems an act of God.

45. [In 346 B.C.]

46. [In 338 B.C.]

47. [In 1448.]

48. [In 1420.]

49. [Hawkwood (ca. 1320–94) began to be employed by Florence in 1380.]

50. [Andrea Fortebraccio (1368–1424).]

51. [In 1498.]

52. [Francesco Bussone, Count of Carmagnola (b. ca. 1390), hired by the Venetians in 1425, executed in 1432.]

53. [The Battle of Vailà, generally known as Agnadello, 4 May 1509.]

And, since these examples have been drawn from recent Italian experience, and since Italy has been entirely dependent on mercenary forces for many years, I want to trace the present state of affairs back to its source, so that, having seen the origin and development of the problem, it will be easier to see how to correct it. You need to understand, then, that in modern times, as soon as the authority of the Holy Roman Empire began to be rejected in Italy, and the pope began to acquire greater authority in temporal affairs, Italy began to be divided into a number of different states. Many of the larger cities went to war against the nobility of the surrounding countryside, who had been oppressing them, and who were, at first, supported by the emperor. The Church, on the other hand, favored the cities in order to build up its temporal authority. In many other cities individual citizens established princedoms. So Italy came to be more or less divided up between those who owed allegiance to the papacy and a number of independent republican city states. Since neither the priests nor the citizens of the republics were accustomed to fighting wars, they began to employ foreigners in their armies.

The first to win a reputation for these mercenary troops was Alberigo of Conio in the Romagna.[54] Among those who were trained by him were Braccio and Sforza, who were, at the height of their powers, the arbiters of Italian affairs. After them came all the others who have commanded mercenary forces down to the present time. The outcome of all their prowess [*virtù*] has been that Italy has, in quick succession, been overrun by Charles, plundered by Louis, raped by Ferdinand, and humiliated by the Swiss.

The first objective these mercenary commanders have pursued has been to destroy the reputation of the infantry in order to build up that of their own forces. They did this because they have had no resources of their own, but have been dependent on their contracts. A few infantry would have done little for their reputation, while they could not afford to feed a large number. So they specialized in cavalry, for they could feed a reasonably large number, and

with them win respect. It came to the point that in an army of twenty thousand soldiers there would not even be two thousand infantry. In addition, they have done everything they could to free themselves and their troops from trouble and from danger. During skirmishes between opposing forces they did not kill each other: Indeed, they not only took prisoners, but released them without demanding a ransom. They were in no hurry to assault fortifications under cover of darkness, while the defending troops were far from eager to mount sorties against their assailants. When they made camp they did not protect themselves with trenches or palisades. They passed the winters in barracks. And all these practices were permitted by their standing orders and were invented, as I said, so they could avoid effort and risk: so much so that they have reduced Italy to a despicable slavery.

CHAPTER 13

About auxiliary troops, native troops, and composite armies.

Auxiliaries are the other sort of useless troops. You rely on auxiliaries when you appeal to another ruler to come with his own armies to assist or defend you. This is what Pope Julius did in recent times, when, having discovered the incompetence of his mercenary troops during the siege of Ferrara, he decided to rely on auxiliaries, and reached an agreement with King Ferdinand of Spain that he would come to his assistance with his men and arms.[55] Auxiliary troops can be useful and good when fighting on their own behalf, but they are almost always a liability for anyone relying on their assistance. For if they lose, it is you who are defeated; if they win, you are their prisoner. There are plenty of examples of this in ancient history, but I do not want to stray from the contemporary case of Pope Julius II; he can have had no idea what he was doing when, in the hope of acquiring Ferrara, he placed himself entirely into the hands of a foreigner. But he was lucky: The outcome was neither defeat nor imprisonment, so he did not have to pay the price for his foolish decision. His auxiliaries were routed

---

54. [Really the first Italian: He had been preceded, for example, by Hawkwood. He was victor at Marino (1379) and died in 1409.]

55. [In 1510.]

at Ravenna,[56] but then the Swiss came along and drove out the victors, so that, contrary to everyone's expectation, including his own, he did not end up either a prisoner of his enemies, who had fled, or of his auxiliaries, for it was not they who had been victorious. Another example: The Florentines, having no troops of their own, brought ten thousand French soldiers to take Pisa.[57] This decision placed them in more danger than at any other time during their troubles. Again, the Emperor of Constantinople, in order to attack his neighbors, brought ten thousand Turks into Greece. They, when the war was over, had no intention of leaving: This was the beginning of Greece's enslavement to the infidels.[58]

He, then, who has no desire to be the victor should use these troops, for they are much more dangerous than mercenaries. If your auxiliaries win you are ruined, for they are united in their obedience to someone else. If your mercenaries win it takes them more time and more favorable circumstances to turn against you, for they are not united among themselves, and it is you who recruited and paid them. If you appoint an outsider to command them, it takes him time to establish sufficient authority to be able to attack you. In short, where mercenaries are concerned the main risk is cowardice; with auxiliaries it is valor [*virtù*].

A wise ruler, therefore, will always avoid using mercenary and auxiliary troops, and will rely on his own forces. He would rather lose with his own troops than win with someone else's, for he will not regard it a true victory if it is won with troops that do not belong to him. I never hesitate to cite Cesare Borgia as a model to be imitated. This duke entered the Romagna with an auxiliary army, for his troops were all Frenchmen, and he used it to take Imola and Forlì.[59] But since he did not feel such troops were reliable, he then switched over to mercenaries, believing that using them involved fewer risks, and so he hired the Orsini and the Vitelli. But in practice he found them unreliable, treacherous, and dangerous,

and so he got rid of them and formed his own army. And it is easy to see the differences among these three types of army, for you only have to consider how the duke's reputation changed, depending on whether he was relying on the French alone, on the Orsini and the Vitelli, or on his own troops and his own resources. With each change of policy it increased, but he was only taken seriously when everyone could see he was in complete command of his own forces.

I wanted to stick to examples that are both recent and Italian, but I cannot resist mentioning Hiero of Syracuse, since I have already discussed him above. He, when he was made commander-in-chief by the Syracusans, as I have described, quickly realized their mercenary army was worthless, for it was made up of condottieri like our own Italian armies. He decided he could not risk either keeping them on, or letting them go, so he had them massacred. Thereafter, he went to war with troops of his own, not with other people's soldiers. I also want to remind you of an Old Testament story that is relevant. When David proposed to Saul that he should go and fight with Goliath, the Philistine champion, Saul, in order to give him confidence, dressed him in his own armor. David, having tried it on, rejected it, saying he could not give a good account of himself if he relied on Saul's weapons. He wanted to confront the enemy armed with his sling and his knife.[60]

In short, someone else's armor either falls off, or it weighs you down, or it trips you up. Charles VII, father of King Louis XI, having through good luck and valor [*virtù*] driven the English out of France,[61] recognized that it was essential to have one's own weapons and, so, issued instructions for the establishment of a standing army of cavalry and infantry. Later, his son King Louis abolished the infantry[62] and began to recruit Swiss troops. It was this mistake, imitated by his successors, that was, as we can see from recent events, the cause of the dangers faced by that kingdom.[63] For he built up the reputation of the Swiss

---

56. [11 April 1512.]

57. [In 1500.]

58. [The war lasted from 1341 to 1347; Constantinople did not finally fall to the Turks until 1453.]

59. [In the winter of 1499–1500.]

60. [I Kings 17.]

61. [In 1453.]

62. [In 1474.]

63. [Machiavelli is thinking of the defeats of 1512, which had virtually forced the French out of Italy.]

while undermining his own military capacity, for he destroyed his own infantry and made his own cavalry dependent on the support of foreign troops, for they, having become accustomed to fighting alongside the Swiss, no longer think they can win without them. The result is the French dare not fight against the Swiss, and without the Swiss they are ineffective against anyone else. So the French armies have been mixed, partly mercenary and partly native. Such a mixed army is much preferable to one made up only of auxiliaries or only of mercenaries, but it is much inferior to one made up entirely of one's own troops. The French example is sufficient to make the point, for the Kingdom of France would be able to overcome any enemy if the foundations laid by Charles VII had been built upon, or even if his instructions had merely been kept in force. But men are foolish, and they embark on something that is attractive in its outward appearance, without recognizing the evil consequences that will follow from it: a point I have already made when talking about consumption.

A ruler who cannot foresee evil consequences before they have time to develop is not truly wise; but few have such wisdom. And if one studies the first destruction of the Roman Empire one discovers it came about as a result of the first recruitment of Gothic soldiers,[64] for from that moment the armies of the Roman Empire began to grow feeble. And all the strength [virtù] that ebbed from the Romans accrued to the Goths. I conclude, therefore, that no ruler is secure unless he has his own troops. Without them he is entirely dependent on fortune, having no strength [virtù] with which to defend himself in adversity. Wise men have always believed and said that, "Nothing is so fragile as a reputation for strength that does not correspond to one's real capacities." Now one's own troops can be made up out of one's subjects, or one's citizens, or one's dependents: All others are either mercenaries or auxiliaries. And the correct way of organizing one's own troops is easy to find out by looking over the instructions given by the four rulers whose conduct I have approved, or by finding out how Philip, the father of Alexander the Great, and how many other republics and sovereigns

levied and trained troops: I have complete confidence in their methods.

CHAPTER 14

What a ruler should do as regards the militia.

A ruler, then, should have no other concern, no other thought, should pay attention to nothing aside from war, military institutions, and the training of his soldiers. For this is the only field in which a ruler has to excel. It is of such importance [virtù] that military prowess not only keeps those who have been born rulers in power, but also often enables men who have been born private citizens to come to power. On the other hand, one sees that when rulers think more about luxuries than about weapons, they fall from power. The prime reason for losing power is neglect of military matters; while being an expert soldier opens the way to the acquisition of power.

Francesco Sforza, because he had troops, became Duke of Milan,[65] having begun life as a private citizen. His descendants, who had no taste for the sweat and dust of a soldier's life, started out as dukes and ended up as private citizens. For, among the other deleterious consequences of not having one's own troops, one comes to be regarded with contempt. There are several types of disgrace a ruler should avoid, as I will explain below. This is one of them. For there is no comparison between a ruler who has his own troops and one who has not. It is not to be expected that someone who is armed should cheerfully obey someone who is defenseless, or that someone who has no weapon should be safe when his employees are armed. For the armed man has contempt for the man without weapons; the defenseless man does not trust someone who can overpower him. The two cannot get on together. So, too, a ruler who does not know how to organize a militia, beyond the other dangers he faces, which I have already described, must recognize that he will not be respected by his troops, and that he cannot trust them.

64. [In 376.]

65. [In 1450.]

So a ruler must think only of military matters, and in time of peace he should be even more occupied with them than in time of war. There are two ways he can prepare for war: by thinking and by doing. As far as actions are concerned, he should not only keep his troops in good order and see they are well-trained; he should be always out hunting, thereby accustoming his body to fatigue. He should take the opportunity to study the lie of the land, climbing the mountains, descending into the valleys, crossing the plains, fording rivers, and wading through marshes. He should spare no effort to become acquainted with his own land, and this for two reasons. First, the knowledge will stand him in good stead if he has to defend his state against invasion; second, his knowledge and experience on his own terrain will make it easy for him to understand any other landscape with which he has to become acquainted from scratch. The hills, the valleys, the plains, the rivers, the marshes of, for example, Tuscany have a good deal in common with those of the other regions of Italy. A knowledge of the terrain in one region will make it easy for him to learn about the others. A ruler who lacks this sort of skill does not satisfy the first requirement in a military commander, for it is knowledge of the terrain that enables you to locate the enemy and to get the edge over him when deciding where to camp, in what order to march, how to draw up the troops on the field of battle, and where to build fortifications.

Philopoemon,[66] ruler of the Achaeans, is much praised by the historians,[67] but in particular he is admired because during peacetime he thought about nothing but warfare. When he was out riding in the countryside with his friends, he would often halt and ask: "If the enemy were up on those hills, and we were down here with our army, who would have the better position? How should we advance, following the rule book, to attack him? If we wanted to retreat, how would we set about it? If they were retreating, how would we pursue them?" And so he would invite them to discuss, as they rode along, all the possible eventualities an army may have to face. He listened to their views, he explained his own and backed them up with arguments. Thanks to this continual theorizing he ensured that, if he was at the head of an army, he would be perfectly prepared for anything that might happen.

Such theorizing is not enough. Every ruler should read history books, and in them he should study the actions of admirable men. He should see how they conducted themselves when at war, study why they won some battles and lost others, so he will know what to imitate and what to avoid. Above all he should set himself to imitate the actions of some admirable historical character, as great men have always imitated their glorious predecessors, constantly bearing in mind their actions and their ways of behaving. So, it is said, Alexander the Great took Achilles as his model; Caesar took Alexander; Scipio took Cyrus. If you read the life of Cyrus that was written by Xenophon and then study the life of Scipio you will realize to what extent those qualities that are admired in Scipio derive from Cyrus: His chastity, his affability, his kindness, his generosity, all are modelled upon Cyrus as Xenophon portrays him. A wise ruler will follow these examples. He will never relax during peacetime, but will always be working to take advantage of the opportunities peace presents, so he will be fully prepared when adversity comes. When his luck changes, he must be ready to fight back.

CHAPTER 15

About those factors that cause men, and especially rulers, to be praised or censured.

Our next task is to consider the policies and principles a ruler ought to follow in dealing with his subjects or with his friends. Since I know many people have written on this subject, I am concerned it may be thought presumptuous for me to write on it as well, especially since what I have to say, as regards this question in particular, will differ greatly from the recommendations of others.[68] But my hope is to write

---

66. [253–184 B.C.]

67. [Livy, bk. 25, ch. 28. Machiavelli would also have known the accounts in Plutarch and Polybius.]

68. [Machiavelli is thinking in particular of Cicero, *De officiis*, and Seneca, *De clementia*.]

a book that will be useful, at least to those who read it intelligently, and so I thought it sensible to go straight to a discussion of how things are in real life and not waste time with a discussion of an imaginary world. For many authors have constructed imaginary republics and principalities that have never existed in practice and never could; for the gap between how people actually behave and how they ought to behave is so great that anyone who ignores everyday reality in order to live up to an ideal will soon discover he has been taught how to destroy himself, not how to preserve himself. For anyone who wants to act the part of a good man in all circumstances will bring about his own ruin, for those he has to deal with will not all be good. So it is necessary for a ruler, if he wants to hold on to power, to learn how not to be good, and to know when it is and when it is not necessary to use this knowledge.

Let us leave to one side, then, all discussion of imaginary rulers and talk about practical realities. I maintain that all men, when people talk about them, and especially rulers, because they hold positions of authority, are described in terms of qualities that are inextricably linked to censure or to praise. So one man is described as generous, another as a miser [*misero*] (to use the Tuscan term; for "avaricious," in our language, is used of someone who has a rapacious desire to acquire wealth, while we call someone a "miser" when he is unduly reluctant to spend the money he has); one is called open-handed, another tight-fisted; one man is cruel, another gentle; one untrustworthy, another reliable; one effeminate and cowardly, another bold and violent; one sympathetic, another self-important; one promiscuous, another monogamous; one straightforward, another duplicitous; one tough, another easy-going; one serious, another cheerful; one religious, another atheistical; and so on. Now I know everyone will agree that if a ruler could have all the good qualities I have listed and none of the bad ones, then this would be an excellent state of affairs. But one cannot have all the good qualities, nor always act in a praiseworthy fashion, for we do not live in an ideal world. You have to be astute enough to avoid being thought to have those evil qualities that would make it impossible for you to retain power; as for those that are compatible with holding on to power, you should avoid them if you

can; but if you cannot, then you should not worry too much if people say you have them. Above all, do not be upset if you are supposed to have those vices a ruler needs if he is going to stay securely in power, for, if you think about it, you will realize there are some ways of behaving that are supposed to be virtuous [*che parrà virtù*], but would lead to your downfall, and others that are supposed to be wicked, but will lead to your welfare and peace of mind.

CHAPTER 16

On generosity and parsimony.

Let me begin, then, with the qualities I mentioned first. I argue it would be good to be thought generous; nevertheless, if you act in the way that will get you a reputation for generosity, you will do yourself damage. For generosity used skillfully [*virtuosamente*] and practiced as it ought to be, is hidden from sight, and being truly generous will not protect you from acquiring a reputation for parsimony. So, if you want to have a reputation for generosity, you must throw yourself into lavish and ostentatious expenditure. Consequently, a ruler who pursues a reputation for generosity will always end up wasting all his resources; and he will be obliged in the end, if he wants to preserve his reputation, to impose crushing taxes upon the people, to pursue every possible source of income, and to be preoccupied with maximizing his revenues. This will begin to make him hateful to his subjects, and will ensure no one thinks well of him, for no one admires poverty. The result is his supposed generosity will have caused him to offend the vast majority and to have won favor with few. Anything that goes wrong will destabilize him, and the slightest danger will imperil him. Recognizing the problem, and trying to economize, he will quickly find he has acquired a reputation as a miser.

So we see a ruler cannot seek to benefit from a reputation as generous [*questa virtù del liberale*] without harming himself. Recognizing this, he ought, if he is wise, not to mind being called miserly. For, as time goes by, he will be thought of as growing ever more generous, for people will recognize that as a result of his parsimony he is able to live on his income, maintain an adequate army, and undertake new initiatives without imposing new taxes. The result is he will be thought to be generous towards all those whose income he does not tax, which is almost everybody, and stingy towards those who miss out on handouts, who are only a few. In modern times nobody has succeeded on a large scale except those who have been thought miserly; the others came to nothing. Pope Julius II took advantage of a reputation for generosity in order to win election, but once elected he made no effort to keep his reputation, for he wanted to go to war. The present King of France[69] has fought many wars without having to impose additional taxes on his people, because his occasional additional expenditures are offset by his long-term parsimony. The present King of Spain[70] could not have aspired to, or achieved, so many conquests if he had had a reputation for generosity.

So a ruler should not care about being thought miserly, for it means he will be able to avoid robbing his subjects; he will be able to defend himself; he will not become poor and despicable, and he will not be forced to become rapacious. This is one of those vices that make successful government possible. And if you say: But Caesar rose to power thanks to his generosity, and many others have made their way to the highest positions of authority because they have both been and have been thought to be generous. I reply, either you are already a ruler, or you are on your way to becoming one. If you are already a ruler, generosity is a mistake; if you are trying to become one then you do, indeed, need to be thought of as generous. Caesar was one of those competing to become the ruler of Rome; but if, having acquired power, he had lived longer and had not learned to reduce his expenditures, he would have destroyed his own position. You may be tempted to reply: Many established rulers who have been thought to be immensely generous have been successful in war. But my answer is: Rulers either spend their own wealth and that of their subjects, or that of other people. Those who spend their own and their subjects' wealth should be abstemious; those who spend the wealth of others should seize every opportunity to be generous. Rulers who march with their armies, living off plunder, pillage, and confiscations are spending other people's money, and it is essential they should seem generous, for otherwise their soldiers will not follow them. With goods that belong neither to you nor to your subjects, you can afford to be generous, as Cyrus, Caesar, and Alexander were. Squandering other people's money does not do your reputation any harm, quite the reverse. The problem is with squandering your own. There is nothing so self-defeating as generosity, for the more generous you are, the less you are able to be generous. Generosity leads to poverty and disgrace, or, if you try to escape that, to rapacity and hostility. Among all the things a ruler should try to avoid, he must avoid above all being hated and despised. Generosity leads to your being both. So it is wiser to accept a reputation as miserly, which people despise but do not hate, than to aspire to a reputation as generous, and as a consequence, be obliged to face criticism for rapacity, which people both despise and hate.

CHAPTER 17

About cruelty and compassion; and about whether it is better to be loved than feared, or the reverse.

Going further down our list of qualities, I recognize every ruler should want to be thought of as compassionate and not cruel. Nevertheless, I have to warn you to be careful about being compassionate. Cesare Borgia was thought of as cruel; but this supposed cruelty of his restored order to the Romagna, united it, rendered it peaceful and law-abiding. If you think about it, you will realize he was, in fact, much more compassionate than the people of Florence, who, in order to avoid being thought cruel, allowed Pistoia to tear itself apart.[71] So a ruler ought not to mind the disgrace of being called cruel, if he keeps his subjects peaceful and law-abiding, for it is more compassionate to impose harsh punishments on a few than, out of excessive compassion, to allow disorder to spread,

69. [Louis XII.]
70. [Ferdinand the Catholic.]

71. [In 1501.]

which leads to murders or looting. The whole community suffers if there are riots, while to maintain order the ruler only has to execute one or two individuals. Of all rulers, he who is new to power cannot escape a reputation for cruelty, for he is surrounded by dangers. Virgil has Dido say:

> Harsh necessity, and the fact my kingdom is
>   new, oblige me to do these things,
> And to mass my armies on the frontiers.[72]

Nevertheless, you should be careful how you assess the situation and should think twice before you act. Do not be afraid of your own shadow. Employ policies that are moderated by prudence and sympathy. Avoid excessive self-confidence, which leads to carelessness, and avoid excessive timidity, which will make you insupportable.

This leads us to a question that is in dispute: Is it better to be loved than feared, or vice versa?[73] My reply is one ought to be both loved and feared; but, since it is difficult to accomplish both at the same time, I maintain it is much safer to be feared than loved, if you have to do without one of the two. For of men one can, in general, say this: They are ungrateful, fickle, deceptive and deceiving, avoiders of danger, eager to gain. As long as you serve their interests, they are devoted to you. They promise you their blood, their possessions, their lives, and their children, as I said before, so long as you seem to have no need of them. But as soon as you need help, they turn against you. Any ruler who relies simply on their promises and makes no other preparations, will be destroyed. For you will find that those whose support you buy, who do not rally to you because they admire your strength of character and nobility of soul, these are people you pay for, but they are never yours, and in the end you cannot get the benefit of your investment. Men are less nervous of offending someone who makes himself lovable, than someone who makes himself frightening. For love attaches men by ties of obligation, which, since men are wicked, they break whenever their interests are at stake. But fear

restrains men because they are afraid of punishment, and this fear never leaves them. Still, a ruler should make himself feared in such a way that, if he does not inspire love, at least he does not provoke hatred. For it is perfectly possible to be feared and not hated. You will only be hated if you seize the property or the women of your subjects and citizens. Whenever you have to kill someone, make sure you have a suitable excuse and an obvious reason; but, above all else, keep your hands off other people's property; for men are quicker to forget the death of their father than the loss of their inheritance. Moreover, there are always reasons why you might want to seize people's property; and he who begins to live by plundering others will always find an excuse for seizing other people's possessions; but there are fewer reasons for killing people, and one killing need not lead to another.

When a ruler is at the head of his army and has a vast number of soldiers under his command, then it is absolutely essential to be prepared to be thought cruel; for it is impossible to keep an army united and ready for action without acquiring a reputation for cruelty. Among the extraordinary accomplishments of Hannibal, we may note one in particular: He commanded a vast army, made up of men of many different nations, who were fighting far from home, yet they never mutinied and they never fell out with one another, either when things were going badly, or when things were going well.[74] The only possible explanation for this is that he was known to be harsh and cruel. This, together with his numerous virtues [virtù], meant his soldiers always regarded him with admiration and fear. Without cruelty, his other virtues [virtù] would not have done the job. Those who write about Hannibal without thinking things through both admire the loyalty of his troops and criticize the cruelty that was its principal cause. If you doubt my claim that his other virtues [virtù] would have been insufficient, take the case of Scipio.[75] He was not only unique in his own day, but history does not

72. [Virgil, *Aeneid*, I, 563–4.]

73. [Cicero, *De officiis*, bk. 2, ch. 7, § 23–24.]

74. [Hannibal (247–ca. 183 B.C.) campaigned in Italy from 218 to 203 B.C. Machiavelli's source is Polybius, bk. 11, ch. 19.]

75. [Scipio (ca. 236–183 B.C.) defeated Hannibal at Zama in North Africa (202 B.C.).]

record anyone his equal. But his army rebelled against him in Spain.[76] The sole cause of this was his excessive leniency, which meant his soldiers had more freedom than is compatible with good military discipline. Fabius Maximus criticized him for this in the senate and accused him of corrupting the Roman armies. When Locri was destroyed by one of his commanders,[77] he did not avenge the deaths of the inhabitants, and he did not punish his officer's insubordination. He was too easygoing. This was so apparent that one of his supporters in the senate was obliged to excuse him by saying he was no different from many other men, who were better at doing their own jobs than at making other people do theirs. In course of time, had he remained in command without learning from his mistakes, this aspect of Scipio's character would have destroyed his glorious reputation. But, because his authority was subordinate to that of the senate, not only were the consequences of this defect mitigated, but it even enhanced his reputation.

I conclude, then, that, as far as being feared and loved is concerned, since men decide for themselves whom they love, and rulers decide whom they fear, a wise ruler should rely on the emotion he can control, not on the one he cannot. But he must take care to avoid being hated, as I have said.

CHAPTER 18

How far rulers are to keep their word.

Everybody recognizes how praiseworthy it is for a ruler to keep his word and to live a life of integrity, without relying on craftiness. Nevertheless, we see that in practice, in these days, those rulers who have not thought it important to keep their word have achieved great things, and have known how to employ cunning to confuse and disorientate other men. In the end, they have been able to overcome those who have placed store in integrity.

You should therefore know there are two ways to fight: one while respecting the rules, the other with no holds barred. Men alone fight in the first fashion, and animals fight in the second.[78] But because you cannot always win if you respect the rules, you must be prepared to break them. A ruler, in particular, needs to know how to be both an animal and a man. The classical writers, without saying it explicitly, taught rulers to behave like this. They described how Achilles, and many other rulers in ancient times, were given to Chiron the centaur to be raised, so he could bring them up as he thought best. What they intended to convey, with this story of rulers' being educated by someone who was half beast and half man, was that it is necessary for a ruler to know when to act like an animal and when like a man; and if he relies on just one or the other mode of behavior he cannot hope to survive.

Since a ruler, then, needs to know how to make good use of beastly qualities, he should take as his models among the animals both the fox and the lion, for the lion does not know how to avoid traps, and the fox is easily overpowered by wolves.[79] So you must be a fox when it comes to suspecting a trap, and a lion when it comes to making the wolves turn tail. Those who simply act like a lion all the time do not understand their business. So you see a wise ruler cannot, and should not, keep his word when doing so is to his disadvantage, and when the reasons that led him to promise to do so no longer apply. Of course, if all men were good, this advice would be bad; but since men are wicked and will not keep faith with you, you need not keep faith with them. Nor is a ruler ever short of legitimate reasons to justify breaking his word. I could give an infinite number of contemporary examples to support my argument and to show how treaties and promises have been rendered null and void by the dishonesty of rulers; and he who has known best how to act the fox has come out of it the best. But it is essential to know how to conceal how crafty one is, to know how to be a clever counterfeit and hypocrite. You will find people are so simpleminded and so preoccupied with their immediate concerns, that if you set out to deceive them, you will always find plenty of them who will let themselves be deceived.

76. [In 206 B.C. Livy, bk. 28, chs. 24–29.]
77. [In 205 B.C.]

78. [Cicero, *De officiis*, bk. 1, ch. 11, § 34.]
79. [The fox and the lion are from Cicero, *De officiis*, bk. 1, ch. 13, § 41.]

Among the numerous recent cases one could mention, there is one of particular interest. Alexander VI had only one purpose, only one thought, which was to take people in, and he always found people who were willing victims. There never has been anyone who was more convincing when he swore an oath, nor has there been anybody who has ever formulated more eloquent oaths and has at the same time been quicker to break them. Nevertheless, he was able to find gulls one after another, whenever he wanted them, for he was a master of this particular skill.

So a ruler need not have all the positive qualities I listed earlier, but he must seem to have them. Indeed, I would go so far as to say that if you have them and never make any exceptions, then you will suffer for it; while if you merely appear to have them, they will benefit you. So you should seem to be compassionate, trustworthy, sympathetic, honest, religious, and, indeed, be all these things; but at the same time you should be constantly prepared, so that, if these become liabilities, you are trained and ready to become their opposites. You need to understand this: A ruler, and particularly a ruler who is new to power, cannot conform to all those rules that men who are thought good are expected to respect, for he is often obliged, in order to hold on to power, to break his word, to be uncharitable, inhumane, and irreligious. So he must be mentally prepared to act as circumstances and changes in fortune require. As I have said, he should do what is right if he can; but he must be prepared to do wrong if necessary.

A ruler must, therefore, take great care that he never carelessly says anything that is not imbued with the five qualities I listed above. He must seem, to those who listen to him and watch him, entirely pious, truthful, reliable, sympathetic, and religious. There is no quality that it is more important he should seem to have than this last one. In general, men judge more by sight than by touch. Everyone sees what is happening, but not everyone feels the consequences. Everyone sees what you seem to be; few have direct experience of who you really are. Those few will not dare speak out in the face of public opinion when that opinion is reinforced by the authority of the state. In the behavior of all men, and particularly of rulers, against whom there is no recourse at law, people judge by the outcome. So if a ruler wins wars and holds on to power, the means he has employed will always be judged honorable, and everyone will praise them. The common man accepts external appearances and judges by the outcome; and when it comes down to it only the masses count; for the elite are powerless if the masses have someone to provide them with leadership. One contemporary ruler,[80] whom it would be unwise to name, is always preaching peace and good faith, and he has not a shred of respect for either; if he had respected either one or the other, he would have lost either his state or his reputation several times by now.

CHAPTER 19

How one should avoid hatred and contempt.

Because I have spoken of the more important of the qualities I mentioned earlier, I want now to discuss the rest of them briefly under this general heading, that a ruler must take care (I have already referred to this in passing) to avoid those things that will make him an object of hatred or contempt. As long as he avoids these he will have done what is required of him, and he will find having a reputation for any of the other vices will do him no harm at all. You become hateful, above all, as I have said, if you prey on the possessions and the women of your subjects. You should leave both alone. The vast majority of men, so long as their goods and their honor are not taken from them, will live contentedly, so you will only have to contend with the small minority who are ambitious, and there are lots of straightforward ways of keeping them under control. You become contemptible if you are thought to be erratic, capricious, effeminate, pusillanimous, irresolute. You should avoid acquiring such a reputation as a pilot steers clear of the rocks. Make every effort to ensure your actions suggest greatness and endurance, strength of character and of purpose. When it comes to the private business of your subjects, you should aim to ensure you never have to change your decisions once they have been taken, and that you acquire

80. [Ferdinand the Catholic.]

a reputation that will discourage people from even considering tricking or deceiving you.

A ruler who is thought of in these terms has the sort of reputation he needs; and it is difficult to conspire against someone who is respected in this way, difficult to attack him, because people realize he is on top of his job and has the loyalty of his employees. For rulers ought to be afraid of two things: Within the state, they should fear their subjects; abroad, they should fear other rulers. Against foreign powers, a good army and reliable allies are the only defense; and, if you have a good army, you will always find your allies reliable. And you will find it easy to maintain order at home if you are secure from external threats, provided, that is, conspiracies against you have not undermined your authority. Even if foreign powers do attack, if you have followed my advice and lived according to the principles I have outlined, then, as long as you keep a grip on yourself, you will be able to resist any attack, just as I said Nabis of Sparta was able to. But where your subjects are concerned, when you are not being attacked by foreign powers, you have to be wary of secret conspiracies.[81] The best protection against these is to ensure you are not hated or despised, and the people are satisfied with your rule. It is essential to accomplish this, as I have already explained at length.

Indeed, one of the most effective defenses a ruler has against conspiracies is to make sure he is not generally hated. For conspirators always believe the assassination of the ruler will be approved by the people. If they believe the people will be angered, then they cannot screw up the courage to embark on such an enterprise, for conspirators have to overcome endless difficulties to achieve success. Experience shows the vast majority of conspiracies fail. For a conspirator cannot act alone, and he can only find associates among those whom he believes are discontented. As soon as you tell someone who is discontented what you are planning, you give him the means to satisfy his ambitions, because it is obvious he can expect to be richly rewarded if he betrays you. If he betrays you, his reward is certain; if he keeps faith with you, he faces danger, with little prospect of reward. So,

you see, he needs either to be an exceptionally loyal friend or to be a completely intransigent enemy of the ruler, if he is to keep faith with you. So we can sum up as follows: The conspirators face nothing but fear, mutual distrust, and the prospect of punishment, so they lose heart; while the ruler is supported by the authority of his office and by the laws, and protected both by his supporters and by the forces of government. So, if you add to this inbuilt advantage the goodwill of the populace, then it is impossible to find anyone who is so foolhardy as to conspire against you. For in most situations a conspirator has to fear capture before he does the deed; but if the ruler has the goodwill of the people, he has to fear it afterwards as well, for the people will turn on him when the deed is done, and he will have nowhere to hide.

I could give an infinite number of examples to illustrate this, but I will confine myself to one only, a conspiracy that took place during the lifetime of our parents. Mr. Annibale Bentivoglio, grandfather of the present Mr. Annibale, was at the time ruler of Bologna. The Canneschi conspired against him and assassinated him.[82] His only surviving relative was Mr. Giovanni, who was still in the cradle. But as soon as he was killed the people rose up and killed all the Canneschi. This happened because the family of Bentivoglio had, in those days, the goodwill of the people. Their loyalty was such that, there being no surviving member of the family in Bologna who could, now Annibale was dead, take over the government, and they having heard that in Florence there was a member of the family, someone who so far had been nothing more than the son of a blacksmith, the citizens of Bologna came to Florence to fetch him and made him the ruler of their city. He ruled it until Mr. Giovanni was old enough to take office.

I conclude, then, that a ruler need not worry much about conspiracies as long as the people wish him well; but if the people are hostile to him and hate him, then he should fear everything and everyone. States that are well-governed and rulers who are wise make every effort to ensure the elite are not driven to despair, and to satisfy the masses and keep them content; for this is one of the most important tasks a ruler must set himself.

---

81 [Influential in Machiavelli's discussion of conspiracies is Aristotle, *Politics*, bk. 8.]

82. [In 1445.]

Among the states that are well-ordered and well-ruled at the present time is France. There you will find innumerable good institutions that ensure the freedom of action and security of the king. First among them is the *parlement* and its authority.[83] For whoever set up the government of that country understood the powerful are ambitious and insolent, and judged it necessary they should be bridled so they could be controlled, but on the other hand he recognized the hatred most people have for the powerful, whom they have reason to fear, and the consequent need to reassure and protect the great. So he did not want this to be the responsibility of the king, in order to avoid his alienating the powerful by favoring the people or alienating the people by favoring the powerful, and he established an independent tribunal, whose task it is, without incurring blame for the king, to crush the powerful and defend the weak. This arrangement is as intelligent and prudent as could be, and makes a substantial contribution to the security of the king and the stability of the kingdom. This institution enables us to recognize a significant general principle: Rulers should delegate responsibility for unpopular actions, while taking personal responsibility for those that will win favor. And once again I conclude a ruler should treat the powerful with respect, but at all costs he should avoid being hated by the people.

Many perhaps will think, if they consider the lives and deaths of some of the Roman emperors, that these provide examples contrary to the opinion I have expressed. For it would seem some of them lived exemplary lives and demonstrated great strength [*virtù*] of character, yet they fell from power, or rather they were killed by their retainers, who had conspired against them. Since I want to reply to this objection, I will discuss the characters of some of the emperors, explaining the reasons why they were destroyed, and show they do not tell against my argument. This will primarily involve pointing out factors that would seem significant to anyone who read the history of those times. I will confine myself to discussing all those emperors who came after Marcus Aurelius, up to and including Maximilian:[84] that is, Marcus, his son Commodus, Pertinax, Julian, Severus, his son Antoninus Caracalla, Macrinus, Heliogabulus, Alexander, and Maximilian.

The first thing to be remarked is that, where in most states one only has to contend with the ambition of the great and the effrontery of the populace, the emperors of Rome had to face a third problem: They had to put up with the cruelty and greed of their soldiers. This was so difficult to do that it caused the downfall of many of the emperors, for it was almost impossible to satisfy both the soldiers and the populace. The people loved peace and quiet and, for this reason, liked their rulers to be unassuming; but the soldiers wanted the emperor to be a man of war and liked him to be arrogant, cruel, and rapacious. They wanted him to direct his aggression against the populace, so they could double their income and give free rein to their greed and cruelty. The result was those emperors who did not have a sufficiently intimidating reputation to keep both populace and soldiers in check (either because they did not think such a reputation desirable, or because they were incapable of acquiring it) were always destroyed. Most of them, especially those who acquired power without inheriting it, recognizing the difficulty of pleasing both soldiers and people, concentrated on pleasing the soldiers, thinking it could do little harm to alienate the populace. They had no choice, for, since rulers are bound to be hated by someone, their first concern must be to ensure they are not hated by any significant group; and, if they cannot achieve this, then they must make every possible effort to avoid the hatred of those groups that are most powerful. And so those emperors who had not inherited power and, thus, were in need of particularly strong support, attached themselves to the soldiers rather than to the people; a policy that proved successful or not, depending on whether the particular ruler in question knew how to establish his reputation with the army. For these reasons, then, Marcus, Pertinax, and Alexander, all of whom were unassuming, lovers of justice, haters

---

83. [The *parlement* was the highest court of appeal. Its members belonged to a distinct social caste, the *noblesse de robe*.]

84. [In other words, the period from 161 to 238. Machiavelli follows Herodian closely, probably relying on Poliziano's Latin translation.]

of cruelty, sympathetic and kind, all came, apart from Marcus, to a tragic end. Marcus alone lived honorably and died peaceably, for he inherited power, and did not have to repay a debt to either the soldiers or the populace. Moreover, since he had many virtues [*virtù*] that made him widely respected, he was able, during his own lifetime, to keep both groups in their place, and he was never hated or despised. But Pertinax was made emperor against the wishes of the soldiers, who, being accustomed to an unbridled life under Commodus, were unable to tolerate the disciplined way of life Pertinax wanted to impose on them. So he made himself hated, and to this hatred was added contempt, for he was an old man, and so his rule had scarcely begun before he fell from power.

Here we should note one can become hated for the good things one does, as much as for the bad. That is why, as I said above, a ruler who wants to hold on to power is often obliged not to be good, for when some powerful group—whether the populace, the soldiers, or the elite—whose support you feel it is essential to have if you are to survive, is corrupt, then you have to adapt to its tastes in order to satisfy it, in which case doing good will do you harm. But let us turn to Alexander. He was so good that among the other things for which he is praised is the fact that during the fourteen years he retained power, nobody was ever executed at his orders without due trial. Nevertheless, he was thought effeminate, and blamed for being under the influence of his mother, and so he came to be despised, the army conspired against him and killed him.

By contrast, let us consider the qualities of Commodus, of Severus, Antoninus Caracalla, and Maximinus. They were, you will find, in the highest degree bloodthirsty and rapacious. In order to satisfy the soldiery, they did not fail to commit every possible type of crime against the populace; and all of them, with the exception of Severus, came to a bad end. For Severus was such a strong ruler [*in Severo fu tanta virtù*] that, with the support of the army, even though the populace were oppressed by him, he could always rule successfully; for his strength [*virtù*] inspired awe in the minds of both soldiers and people: The people were always to a considerable degree stupefied and astonished by him, while the soldiers were admiring and satisfied. Because his deeds were commendable

in a new ruler, I want to pause to point out how well he understood how to play the part both of the fox and of the lion: These are the two styles of action I have maintained a ruler must know how to imitate. Severus, because he knew what a coward Julian the new emperor was, persuaded the army he had under his command in Slavonia that it was a good idea to march on Rome to revenge the death of Pertinax, who had been killed by his praetorian guard. With this excuse, and without displaying any ambition to seize the throne, he set out for Rome; and his army was in Italy before anyone knew it had left its station. When he reached Rome, the senate, out of fear, elected him emperor and had Julian put to death. Severus, having begun like this, faced two problems if he wanted to gain effective control of the whole empire: In Asia there was Niger, commander of the Asiatic armies, who had had himself proclaimed emperor; in the West there was Albinus, who also aspired to power. Because he thought it would be dangerous to take on both of them at once, he decided to attack Niger and deceive Albinus. So he wrote to Albinus saying now that he had been elected emperor by the senate, he wanted to share his authority with him. He offered him the title of Caesar and had the senate appoint him co-ruler. Albinus accepted these proposals at face value. But as soon as Severus had defeated and killed Niger and pacified the eastern empire, he returned to Rome and attacked Albinus in the senate, complaining that he, far from being grateful for the generosity he had been shown, had wickedly sought to assassinate him. Severus claimed to have no choice but to go and punish this ingrate. So he attacked him in France and deprived him of his offices and of his life.

Anyone who examines Severus's actions with care will find he was both a ferocious lion and a cunning fox. He will find he was feared and respected by all, and he was not hated by the armies. So it is no surprise Severus, who had not inherited power, was able to hold on to a vast empire, for his immense reputation was a constant defense against the hatred the populace might otherwise have felt for his exactions. Antoninus his son was also a man whose remarkable abilities inspired awe in the populace and gratitude in the soldiers. For he was a man of war, able to make light of the most arduous task and contemptuous of delicate food and all other luxuries. This made all his soldiers love him. Nevertheless, his ferocity and cruelty were without parallel. He did not only kill vast numbers of individuals, but, on one occasion, a large part of the population of Rome, and, on another, the whole of Alexandria. So he came to be loathed by everyone, and even his close associates began to fear him, with the result he was killed by a centurion while he was surrounded by his own troops. One should note rulers have no protection against an assassination like this, carried out by a truly determined individual, for anyone who is prepared to die can attack them. But, nevertheless, rulers should not worry unduly about such assassins because they are extremely rare. You should try merely to avoid giving grave injury to anyone you employ who comes close to you in the course of business. Antoninus had done just this, for he had outrageously put to death a brother of the centurion who killed him, and had repeatedly threatened the centurion's own life; yet he employed him as a bodyguard. This was foolhardy, and the disastrous outcome could have been predicted.

Now we come to Commodus, who had no difficulty in holding on to power, because he had inherited it, being the son of Marcus. All he had to do was follow in his father's footsteps, and he would have been satisfactory to both soldiers and populace. But, because he was by nature cruel and brutal, he began to ingratiate himself with the soldiers and to encourage them to be undisciplined, so he would be able to give his own rapacity free rein against the people. On the other hand, he did not maintain his own dignity. Often, when he went to the amphitheater, he came down and fought with the gladiators, and he did other things that were despicable and incompatible with imperial majesty. So he became contemptible in the eyes of his soldiers. He was hated by the people and despised by the soldiers, so there was soon a conspiracy against him and he was killed.

There remains for us to discuss the character of Maximinus. He was a most warlike individual. The armies had been irritated by the feebleness of Alexander, whom I have already discussed, and so, with him out of the way, they elected Maximinus emperor. But he did not hold on to power for long, for there were two things that made him hateful and contemptible.

In the first place, he was of the lowest social status, having once been a shepherd in Thrace (a fact known to everyone, and one that made them all regard him with disdain); in the second, when he was elected emperor he had delayed going to Rome and taking possession of the throne, but had acquired a reputation for terrible cruelty because his representatives, in Rome and throughout the empire, had acted with great ferocity. So everybody was worked up with disdain for his humble origins and agitated with hatred arising from their fear of his ferocity. First Africa rebelled, and then the senate and the whole population of Rome; soon all Italy was conspiring against him. His own army turned against him. They were laying siege to Aquileia, but were finding it hard to take the city, to which was added their distaste for his cruelty. Seeing so many united against him, they lost their fear of him and killed him.

I do not want to discuss Heliogabulus, Macrinus, and Julian, for they were entirely contemptible and fell from power quickly. We can now come to the end of this discussion. I would have you note the rulers of our own day do not face in such an acute form the problem of having to adopt policies that involve breaking the law in order to satisfy their soldiers' appetites; for, although you cannot afford entirely to ignore contemporary soldiers, you can handle them easily. Modern rulers do not face standing armies with long experience of ruling and administering provinces, such as the Roman armies had. But if in those days it was more important to give satisfaction to the soldiers than to the populace, that was because the soldiers were more to be feared than the populace. Now all rulers, with the exception of the sultans of Turkey and of Egypt, need to be more concerned to satisfy the populace than the soldiers, for the populace are the greater threat. I make an exception of the ruler of Turkey, for at all times he is surrounded by twelve thousand infantry and fifteen thousand cavalry, on whom depends the security and strength of his government. It is essential for him, more than anything else, to retain their loyalty. Similarly, the Sultan of Egypt is entirely at the mercy of his soldiers, so that he, too, must keep their loyalty, no matter what the consequences for the populace may be. And one should note the Sultan of Egypt is in a different position from all other rulers; for he is comparable to the Christian pope, who also cannot be described as either a hereditary or a new ruler. For the sons of the old ruler do not inherit his office and remain in power, but the new ruler is elected by a group who have the authority to appoint him. Since this arrangement has long been in existence, you cannot call the sultan a new ruler, for he faces none of the difficulties faced by those who are new to power. Even though he himself is new to power, the principle of succession is long-established, and ensures his authority is acknowledged as unquestioningly as would be the case if he were an hereditary ruler.

Let us return to our subject. I believe everyone should agree in the light of this discussion that hatred and contempt caused the fall of the emperors we have been considering, and will also understand how it comes about that, with one group of them following one line of policy and the other its opposite, in both groups one ruler was successful and the rest were killed. For it was pointless and dangerous for Pertinax and Alexander, who were new rulers, to try to imitate Marcus, who had inherited power; similarly it was a bad mistake for Caracalla, Commodus, and Maximinus to imitate Severus, for they lacked the strength [*virtù*] that would have been necessary for anyone following in his footsteps. Thus, a new ruler, who has not inherited power, should not follow the example of Marcus, but need not follow that of Severus. He ought to imitate in Severus those features that are essential for him to establish himself securely in power, and in Marcus those features that are effective and win glory for someone who is seeking to preserve a government that has already entrenched itself.

CHAPTER 20

Whether the building of fortresses (and many other things rulers regularly do) is useful or not.

Some rulers, in order to ensure they have a firm grip on power, have disarmed their subjects. Others have divided up the territories over which they rule. Some have positively encouraged opposition to their own authority. Others have set out to win over those who were hostile to them when they first came to power.

Some have built fortresses. Others have destroyed them. It is impossible to pass definitive judgment on any of these policies until one considers the particular circumstances that existed in the state where the policy was adopted. Nevertheless, I will talk in general terms in so far as the subject itself permits.

No new ruler, let me point out, has ever disarmed his subjects; on the contrary, when he has found them disarmed, he has always armed them. For, when you arm them, their arms become yours, those who have been hostile to you become loyal, while those who have been loyal remain so, and progress from being your obedient subjects to being your active supporters. Because not every subject can be armed, provided you ensure those who receive arms stand to benefit, you will be more secure in your dealings with the others. When they recognize this diversity of treatment, it will make them all the more obliged to you; while the unarmed will forgive you, for they will recognize it is necessary that those who face more dangers and have more onerous obligations should be better rewarded. But if you take their arms away from those who have been armed, you begin to alienate them. You make it clear you do not trust them, either because you think they are poor soldiers or disloyal. Whichever view they attribute to you, they will begin to hate you. And, since you cannot remain undefended, you will be obliged to rely on mercenary troops, with the consequences we have already discussed. No matter how good they are, they will be unable to defend you against a combination of powerful foreign powers and hostile subjects. So, as I have said, a new ruler who has not inherited power has always formed his own army. There are innumerable examples in history. But when a ruler acquires a new state, which is simply added on to his existing territories, then it is essential to disarm the people, with the sole exception of those who have actively supported you in taking power. And they too, over time, and as opportunity occurs, should be encouraged to become weak and effeminate. You should arrange things so that all the weapons in your new state are in the hands of those of your own troops who were closely associated with you in your old territories.

Our ancestors, particularly those who were thought wise, used to say it was necessary to hold Pistoia by encouraging factional divisions, and Pisa by building fortresses. So, in some of the territory they occupied, they encouraged divisions in order to have better control. This was a sound policy in the days when Italy experienced a balance of power;[85] but I do not think it can be recommended now. For I do not believe any good ever comes of internal conflicts. It is certain that when enemy forces approach you run the risk that divided cities will go over to the other side, for the weaker of the two internal factions will attach itself to the invaders, and the stronger will not be able to retain power against enemies within and without the walls.

The Venetians, following, I believe, the same line of thought as our ancestors, encouraged the division of the cities under their control into the two factions of Guelfs and Ghibellines.[86] Although they never allowed the conflicts between them to go so far as bloodshed, they encouraged these tensions so the inhabitants of these cities would be fully occupied with their own internal disagreements and would not unite against their masters. But history shows this policy did not pay off. For, when they were defeated at Vailà,[87] one of the factions quickly plucked up courage and deprived them of all their territories. Such policies, indeed, imply the ruler is weak, for a robust government would never allow such divisions, since you only benefit from them in time of peace, when they enable you to manage your subjects more easily; when war comes, such a policy proves to be misconceived.

There is no doubt rulers become powerful as they overcome the difficulties they face and the opposition they encounter. So fortune, especially when she wants to make a new ruler powerful (for new rulers have more need of acquiring a reputation than ones who have inherited power), makes him start out surrounded by enemies and endangered by threats, so he can overcome these obstacles and can climb higher on a ladder supplied by his enemies. Therefore, many conclude a wise ruler will, when he has the opportunity, secretly foster opposition to his rule,

so that, when he has put down his opponents, he will be in a more powerful position.

Rulers, and especially those who are new to power, have sometimes found there is more loyalty and support to be had from those who were initially believed to be opposed to their rule, than from those whom from the start they could count on. Pandolfo Petrucci, ruler of Siena, governed his state by relying more on those who were supposed to be hostile to him than on his supporters.[88] But we cannot discuss this policy in general terms, because its success depends upon circumstances. I will only say those men who have been hostile when a ruler first acquires power, but who belong to those social groups that need to rely on government support in order to maintain their position, can always be won over by the new ruler with the greatest of ease. And they are all the more obliged to serve him faithfully because they know it is essential for them to undo by their actions the negative assessment that was initially made of them. Thus, the ruler can always get more out of them than out of those who, being all too confident of his goodwill, pay little attention to his interests.

And, since it is relevant to our subject, I do not want to fail to point out to rulers who have recently acquired a state through the support of people living within it, that they should give careful consideration to the motives of those who supported them. If they did not give their support out of natural affection for you, but gave it only because they were not happy with their previous government, you will find you can only retain their loyalty with much trouble and effort, for there is no way in which you will be able to keep them happy. If you think about it and consider the record of ancient and modern history, you will realize it will be much easier for you to win the loyalty of those men who were happy with the previous government and were therefore opposed to your seizure of power, than of those who, because they were unhappy with it, became your allies and encouraged you to take power from it.

Rulers have been accustomed, in order to have a more secure grip on their territories, to build fortresses. They are intended to be a bridle and bit for those who plan to rebel against you, and to provide

---

85. [From 1454 to 1494.]

86. [These factions were present in many Italian cities. The Guelfs supported the papacy (and later the French), the Ghibellines the Holy Roman Emperor.]

87. [In 1509.]

88. [Petrucci (1450–1512) was effective ruler of Siena from 1487 until his death.]

you with a secure refuge in the event of an unexpected attack. I approve of this policy, for it was used by the Romans. Nevertheless, Mr. Niccolò Vitelli, in our own day, had two fortresses in Città di Castello destroyed so he could hold on to that state.[89] Guido Ubaldo, the Duke of Urbino, when he returned to power, having previously been driven into exile by Cesare Borgia, completely destroyed all the fortresses in his territory.[90] He believed that without them it would be harder to deprive him once again of power. The Bentivogli, when they recovered power in Bologna, adopted the same policy.[91]

We must conclude that fortresses are useful or not, depending on circumstances, and that, if they are useful at one time, they may also do you harm at another. We can identify the relevant factors as follows: A ruler who is more afraid of his subjects than of foreign powers should build fortresses; but a ruler who is more afraid of foreign powers than of his subjects should do without them. The castle of Milan, which was built by Francesco Sforza,[92] has done and will do more damage to the house of Sforza than any other defect in that state. For the best fortress one can have is not being hated by one's subjects; for if you have fortresses, but your subjects hate you, they will not save you, for your subjects, once they have risen in arms, will never be short of foreign allies who will come to their support.

In recent times, there is no evidence that fortresses have been useful to any ruler, except for the Contessa of Forlì, when her husband Count Girolamo died:[93] Because she could take refuge in one she was able to escape the popular uprising, hold out until assistance came from Milan, and retake her state. Circumstances at the time were such that the populace could not get assistance from abroad; but later, even she gained little benefit from her fortresses when Cesare Borgia attacked her, and the populace, still hostile to her, joined forces with the invaders.[94] So, both at first

and later, it would have been safer for her not to have been hated by her people than to have fortresses. Consequently, having considered all these factors, I would praise both those who build fortresses and those who do not, but I would criticize anyone who, relying on his fortresses, thought it unimportant that his people hated him.

CHAPTER 21

What a ruler should do in order to acquire a reputation.

Nothing does more to give a ruler a reputation than embarking on great undertakings and doing remarkable things. In our own day, there is Ferdinand of Aragon, the present King of Spain. He may be called, more or less, a new ruler, because having started out as a weak ruler he has become the most famous and most glorious of all the kings of Christendom. If you think about his deeds, you will find them all noble, and some of them extraordinary. At the beginning of his reign he attacked Granada, and this undertaking was the basis of his increased power.[95] In the first place, he undertook the reconquest when he had no other problems to face, so he could concentrate upon it. He used it to channel the ambitions of his Castilian barons, who, because they were thinking of the war, were no threat to him at home. Meanwhile, he acquired influence and authority over them without their even being aware of it. He was able to raise money from the church and from his subjects to build up his armies. Thus, this lengthy war enabled him to build up his military strength, which has paid off since. Next, in order to be able to engage in more ambitious undertakings, still exploiting religion, he practiced a pious cruelty, expropriating and expelling from his kingdom the Marranos: an act without parallel and truly despicable. He used religion once more as an excuse to justify an attack on Africa.[96] He then attacked Italy and has recently[97] invaded France. He

89. [In 1482.]

90. [In 1503.]

91. [In 1511.]

92. [In 1450.]

93. [In 1488.]

94. [In December 1499.]

95. [The Muslim state of Granada was conquered between 1480 and 1492.]

96. [In 1509.]

97. [In 1512.]

is always plotting and carrying out great enterprises, which have always kept his subjects bewildered and astonished, waiting to see what their outcome would be. And his deeds have followed one another so closely that he has never left space between one and the next for people to plot uninterruptedly against him.

It is also of considerable help to a ruler if he does remarkable things when it comes to domestic policy, such as those that are reported of Mr. Bernabò of Milan.[98] It is a good idea to be widely talked about, as he was, because, whenever anyone happened to do anything extraordinary, whether good or bad, in civil life, he found an imaginative way to reward or to punish them. Above all a ruler should make every effort to ensure that whatever he does it gains him a reputation as a great man, a person who excels.

Rulers are also admired when they know how to be true allies and genuine enemies: That is, when, without any reservations, they demonstrate themselves to be loyal supporters or opponents of others. Such a policy is always better than one of neutrality. For if two rulers who are your neighbors are at war with each other, they are either so powerful that, if one of them wins, you will have to fear the victor, or they are not. Either way, it will be better for you to take sides and fight a good fight; for, if they are powerful, and you do not take sides, you will still be preyed on by the victor, much to the pleasure and satisfaction of his defeated opponent. You will have no excuse, no defense, no refuge. For whoever wins will not want allies who are unreliable and who do not stand by him in adversity; while he who loses will not offer you refuge, since you were not willing, sword in hand, to share his fate.

The Aetolians invited Antiochus to Greece to drive out the Romans.[99] Antiochus sent an ambassador to the Achaeans, who were allies of the Romans, to encourage them to remain neutral; while the Romans urged them to fight on their side. The ruling council of the Achaeans met to decide what to do, and Antiochus's ambassador spoke in favor of neutrality. The Roman ambassador replied: "As for what they say to you, that it would be sensible to keep out of the war, there is nothing further from your true interests. If you are without credit, without dignity, the victor will claim you as his prize."

It will always happen that he who is not your ally will urge neutrality upon you, while he who is your ally will urge you to take sides. Rulers who are unsure what to do, but want to avoid immediate dangers, generally end up staying neutral and usually destroy themselves by doing so. But when a ruler boldly takes sides, if your ally wins, even if he is powerful, and has the ability to overpower you, he is in your debt and fond of you. Nobody is so shameless as to turn on you in so ungrateful a fashion. Moreover, victories are never so overwhelming that the victor can act without any constraint: Above all, victors still need to appear just. But if, on the other hand, your ally is defeated, he will offer you refuge, will help you as long as he is able, and will share your ill-fortune, in the hope of one day sharing good fortune with you. In the second case, when those at war with each other are insufficiently powerful to give you grounds to fear the outcome, there is all the more reason to take sides, for you will be able to destroy one of them with the help of the other, when, if they were wise, they would be helping each other. The one who wins is at your mercy; and victory is certain for him whom you support.

Here it is worth noting a ruler should never take the side of someone who is more powerful than himself against other rulers, unless necessity compels him to, as I have already implied. For if you win, you are your ally's prisoner; and rulers should do everything they can to avoid being at the mercy of others. The Venetians allied with the King of France against the Duke of Milan, when they could have avoided taking sides; they brought about their own destruction.[100] But when you cannot help but take sides (which is the situation the Florentines found themselves in when the pope and the King of Spain were advancing with their armies to attack Lombardy)[101] then you should take sides decisively, as I have explained. Do not for a moment think any state can always take safe decisions, but rather think every decision you take

98. [Bernabò Visconti ruled Milan from 1354 to 1385.]
99. [192 B.C. The source is Livy, bk. 35, chs. 48, 49.]
100. [In 1499.]
101. [In 1512.]

involves risks, for it is in the nature of things that you cannot take precautions against one danger without opening yourself to another. Prudence consists in knowing how to assess risks and in accepting the lesser evil as a good.

A ruler should also show himself to be an admirer of skill [*virtù*] and should honor those who are excellent in any type of work. He should encourage his citizens by making it possible for them to pursue their occupations peacefully, whether they are businessmen, farmers, or are engaged in any other activity, making sure they do not hesitate to improve what they own for fear it may be confiscated from them, and they are not discouraged from investing in business for fear of losing their profits in taxes; instead, he should ensure that those who improve and invest are rewarded, as should be anyone whose actions will benefit his city or his government. He should, in addition, at appropriate times of the year, amuse the populace with festivals and public spectacles. Since every city is divided into guilds or neighborhoods, he ought to take account of these collectivities, meeting with them on occasion, showing himself to be generous and understanding in his dealings with them, but at the same time always retaining his authority and dignity, for this he should never let slip in any circumstances.

CHAPTER 22

About those whom rulers employ as advisers.

A ruler's choice as to whom to employ as his advisers is of foremost importance. Rulers get the advisers they deserve, for good rulers choose good ones, bad rulers choose bad. The easiest way of assessing a ruler's ability is to look at those who are members of his inner circle. If they are competent and reliable, then you can be sure he is wise, for he has known both how to recognize their ability and to keep them faithful. But if they are not, you can always make a negative assessment of the ruler; for he has already proved his inadequacy by making a poor choice of adviser.

Nobody who knew Mr. Antonio of Venafro[102] when

102. [Machiavelli did, indeed, know Antonio Giordani of Venafro.]

he was adviser to Pandolfo Petrucci, ruler of Siena, could fail to conclude that Pandolfo was a brilliant man, for how else would he come by such an adviser? For there are three types of brains: One understands matters for itself, one follows the explanations of others, and one neither understands nor follows. The first is best, the second excellent, the third useless. It followed logically that if Pandolfo was not in the first rank, then he was at least in the second. For anyone who can judge the good or evil someone says and does, even if he does not have an original mind, will recognize what his adviser does well and what he does ill, and will encourage the first and correct the second. An adviser cannot hope to deceive such an employer, and will do his best.

But there is one infallible way for a ruler to judge his adviser. When you see your adviser give more thought to his own interests than yours, and recognize everything he does is aimed at his own benefit, then you can be sure such a person will never be a good adviser. You will never be able to trust him, for he who runs a government should never think of his own interests, but always of his ruler's, and should never suggest anything to his ruler that is not in the ruler's interests. On the other hand the ruler, in order to get the best out of his adviser, should consider his adviser's interests, heaping honors on him, enriching him, placing him in his debt, ensuring he receives public recognition, so that he sees that he cannot do better without him, that he has so many honors he desires no more, so much wealth he desires no more, so much status he fears the consequences of political upheaval. When a ruler has good advisers and knows how to treat them, then they can rely on each other; when it is otherwise, either ruler or adviser will suffer.

CHAPTER 23

How sycophants are to be avoided.

I do not want to omit an important subject that concerns a mistake it is difficult for rulers to avoid making, unless they are very wise and good judges of men. My subject is sycophants, who pullulate at court. For men are so easily flattered and are so easily taken in by praise, that it is difficult for them to defend themselves against this plague, and in defending themselves they run the risk of making themselves despicable. For there is no way of protecting oneself against flattery other than by making it clear you do not mind being told the truth; but, when anyone can tell you the truth, then you are not treated with sufficient respect. So a wise ruler ought to find an alternative to flattery and excessive frankness. He ought to choose wise men from among his subjects, and give to them alone freedom to tell him the truth, but only in reply to specific questions he puts to them, not on any subject of their choice. But he ought to ask them about everything, and listen to their replies; then think matters over on his own, in his own way. His response to each of his advisers and their advice should make it apparent that the more freely they talk, the happier he will be. But he should listen to no one who has not been designated as an adviser, he should act resolutely once he has made up his mind, and he should cling stubbornly to his decisions once they have been taken. He who acts otherwise either is rushed into decisions by flatterers or changes his mind often in response to differing advice. Either way, people will form a poor opinion of him.

I want, on this subject, to refer to an example from recent history. The cleric Luca,[103] an adviser to Maximilian, the present emperor, speaking of his sovereign, said that he did not ask for anyone's advice, and that he never did anything the way he wanted to: which was because he did not follow the principles I have just outlined. For the emperor is a secretive man, he keeps things to himself and never asks anyone's advice. But, when his decisions begin to be discovered, which is when they begin to be put into effect, he begins to be criticized by those who are close to him, and, as one might expect, he is persuaded to change his mind. The result is that he undoes each day what he did the day before; that nobody ever knows what he really wants or intends to do; and that one cannot rely upon his decisions.

A ruler, therefore, should always take advice, but only when he wants to, not when others want him to; he should discourage everybody from giving him advice without being asked; but he should be always asking,

and, moreover, he should listen patiently to the answers, provided they are truthful. But if he becomes persuaded someone, for whatever reason, is not telling him the truth, he should lose his temper. There are many who think some rulers who have a reputation for being prudent do not really deserve to be thought so, claiming that the rulers themselves are not wise, but that they merely receive good advice. But without doubt they are mistaken. For this is a general rule without exceptions: A ruler who is not himself wise cannot be given good advice. Unless, I should say, he hands over all decisions to one other person and has the good luck to pick someone quite exceptionally prudent. But such an exceptional arrangement will not last long, for the man who takes all the decisions will soon take power. But a ruler who is not wise, if he takes advice from more than one person, will never get the same advice from everyone, nor will he be able to combine the different proposals into a coherent policy unless he has help. His advisers will each think about his own interests, and he will not be able to recognize their bias or correct it. This is how it has to be, for you will find men are always wicked, unless you give them no alternative but to be good. So we may conclude that good advice, no matter who it comes from, really comes from the ruler's own good judgment, and that the ruler's good judgment never comes from good advice.

CHAPTER 24

Why the rulers of Italy have lost their states.

The policies I have described, if prudently followed, will make a new ruler seem long-established and will rapidly make his power better entrenched than it would be if he had long held office. For the actions of a new ruler are much more closely scrutinized than those of an hereditary ruler; and new rulers, when they are seen to be strong [*virtuose*], attract much more support and make men more indebted to them than do hereditary rulers. For men are much more impressed by what goes on in the present than by what happened in the past; and when they are satisfied with what is happening now, they are delighted and ask for nothing more. So they will spring

103. [Also known to Machiavelli.]

to a new ruler's defense, provided he plays his part properly. Thus, he will be doubly glorious: He will have begun a new tradition of government, underpinned and ornamented with good laws, good arms, good allies, and good examples; just as he is doubly shamed who, being born a ruler, has lost power through lack of skill in ruling.

And if you consider those Italian rulers who have lost power in recent years, such as the King of Naples, the Duke of Milan, and others, you will find: First, they all had in common an inadequate military preparation, for the reasons I have discussed above at length; second, you will see that some of them either were at odds with their own populace or, if they had the support of the populace, did not know how to protect themselves from the elite; for without these defects they would not have lost states that were strong enough to put an army in the field. Philip of Macedon (not the father of Alexander, but the Philip who was defeated by Titus Quintius)[104] did not have a large state in comparison with the territory controlled by the Romans and the Greeks who attacked him; nevertheless, because he was a military man and a ruler who knew how to treat his populace and how to protect himself from the elite, he was able to sustain a war against superior forces for several years; and if, at the end, he lost control of several cities, he nevertheless retained his kingdom.

So our own rulers, each of whom had been in power for many years and then lost it, should not blame fortune but their own indolence. For when times were quiet they never once considered the possibility that they might change (it is a common human failing not to plan ahead for stormy weather while the sun shines). When difficult times did come, they thought of flight not of self-defense. They hoped the populace, irritated by the insolence of their conquerors, would recall them to power. This plan is a good one if there is no alternative policy available; but it is stupid to adopt it when there are alternatives. No one would be happy to trip and fall merely because he thought someone would help him back to his feet. Either no one comes to your assistance; or if someone does, you are the weaker for it, for your strategy for self-defense has been ignominious, and your fate has not been in your own hands. No method of defense is good, certain, and lasting that does not depend on your own decisions and your own strength [*virtù*].

CHAPTER 25

How much fortune can achieve in human affairs, and how it is to be resisted.

I am not unaware of the fact that many have held and still hold the view that the affairs of this world are so completely governed by fortune and by God that human prudence is incapable of correcting them, with the consequence that there is no way in which what is wrong can be put right. So one may conclude that there is no point in trying too hard; one should simply let chance have its way. This view has come to be more widely accepted in our own day because of the extraordinary variation in circumstances that has been seen and is still seen every day. Nobody could predict such events. Sometimes, thinking this matter over, I have been inclined to adopt a version of this view myself. Nevertheless, since our free will must not be eliminated, I think it may be true that fortune determines one half of our actions, but that, even so, she leaves us to control the other half, or thereabouts. And I compare her to one of those torrential rivers that, when they get angry, break their banks, knock down trees and buildings, strip the soil from one place and deposit it somewhere else. Everyone flees before them, everyone gives way in face of their onrush, nobody can resist them at any point. But although they are so powerful, this does not mean men, when the waters recede, cannot make repairs and build banks and barriers so that, if the waters rise again, either they will be safely kept within the sluices or at least their onrush will not be so unregulated and destructive. The same thing happens with fortune: She demonstrates her power where precautions have not been taken to resist her [*dove non è ordinata virtù a resisterle*]; she directs her attacks where she knows banks and barriers have not been built to hold her. If you think about Italy, which is the location of all these changes in circumstance, and the origin of

---

104. [Philip V, defeated in 197 B.C.]

the forces making for change, you will realize she is a landscape without banks and without any barriers. If proper precautions had been taken [*s'ella fussi reparata da conveniente virtù*], as they were in Germany, Spain, and France, either the flood would not have had the consequences it had, or the banks would not even have been overwhelmed. And what I have said is enough, I believe, to answer the general question of how far one can resist fortune.

But, turning rather to individuals, note we see rulers who flourish one day and are destroyed the next without our being able to see any respect in which they have changed their nature or their attributes. I think the cause of this is, in the first place, the one we have already discussed at length: A ruler who depends entirely on his good fortune will be destroyed when his luck changes. I also think a ruler will flourish if he adjusts his policies as the character of the times changes; and similarly, a ruler will fail if he follows policies that do not correspond to the needs of the times. For we see men, in those activities that carry them towards the goal they all share, which is the acquisition of glory and riches, proceed differently. One acts with caution, while another is headstrong; one is violent, while another relies on skill; one is patient, while another is the opposite: And any one of them, despite the differences in their methods, may achieve his objective. One also sees that of two cautious men, one will succeed, and the other not; and similarly we see that two men can be equally successful though quite different in their behavior, one of them being cautious and the other headstrong. This happens solely because of the character of the times, which either suits or is at odds with their way of proceeding. This is the cause of what I have described: that two men, behaving differently, achieve the same result, and of two other men, who behave in the same way, one will attain his objective and the other will not. This is also the cause of the fact that the sort of behavior that is successful changes from one time to another. Take someone who acts cautiously and patiently. If the times and circumstances develop in such a way that his behavior is appropriate, he will flourish; but if the times and circumstances change, he will be destroyed for he will continue to behave in the same way. One cannot find a man so prudent he knows how to adapt himself to changing circumstances, for he will either be unable to deviate from that style of behavior to which his character inclines him, or, alternatively, having always been successful by adopting one particular style, he will be unable to persuade himself that it is time to change. And so, the cautious man, when it is time to be headstrong, does not know how to act and is destroyed. But, if one knew how to change one's character as times and circumstances change, one's luck would never change.

Pope Julius II always acted impetuously; the style of action was so appropriate to the times and circumstances in which he found himself that the outcome was always successful. Consider his first attack on Bologna, when Mr. Giovanni Bentivoglio was still alive.[105] The Venetians were not happy about it; nor was the King of Spain; he had discussed such an action with the French, who had reached no decision. Nevertheless, because he was ferocious and impetuous, he placed himself personally at the head of his troops. This gesture made the Spanish and the Venetians hesitate and do nothing: the Venetians out of fear, and the Spanish because they wanted to recover the territories they had lost from the Kingdom of Naples. On the other hand, he dragged the King of France along behind him. For the king saw it was too late to turn back, and he wanted an alliance with him in order to weaken the Venetians, so he concluded he could not deny him the support of French troops without giving him obvious grounds for resentment. So Julius, by acting impetuously, achieved something no other pope, no matter how skillful and prudent, had been able to achieve. For, if he had delayed his departure from Rome until everything had been arranged and the necessary alliances had been cemented, as any other pope would have done, he would never have succeeded. The King of France would have found a thousand excuses, and his other allies would have pointed out a thousand dangers. I want to leave aside his other actions, for they were all similar, and they were all successful. He did not live long enough to experience failure. But, if the times had changed so that it was necessary to proceed with caution, he would have been destroyed. He would never have been able to change the style of behavior to which his character inclined him.

105. [In 1506.]

I conclude, then, that since fortune changes, and men stubbornly continue to behave in the same way, men flourish when their behavior suits the times and fail when they are out of step. I do think, however, that it is better to be headstrong than cautious, for fortune is a lady. It is necessary, if you want to master her, to beat and strike her. And one sees she more often submits to those who act boldly than to those who proceed in a calculating fashion. Moreover, since she is a lady, she smiles on the young, for they are less cautious, more ruthless, and overcome her with their boldness.

CHAPTER 26

Exhortation to seize Italy and free her from the barbarians.

Having considered all the matters we have discussed, I ask myself whether, in Italy now, we are living through times suitable for the triumph of a new ruler, and if there is an opportunity for a prudent and bold [*virtuoso*] man to take control of events and win honor for himself while benefiting everyone who lives here. It seems to me so many factors come together at the moment to help out a new ruler that I am not sure if there has ever been a more propitious time for such a man. If, as I said, Moses could only demonstrate his greatness [*virtù*] because the people of Israel were slaves in Egypt; if we would never have known what a great man Cyrus was if the Persians had not been oppressed by the Medes; if the remarkable qualities of Theseus only became apparent because the Athenians were scattered abroad; so now, the opportunity is there for some bold Italian to demonstrate his greatness [*virtù*]. For see the conditions to which Italy has been reduced. She is more enslaved than the Jews, more oppressed than the Persians, more defenseless than the Athenians. She has no leader, no organization. She is beaten, robbed, wounded, put to flight: She has experienced every sort of injury. Although so far there has been the occasional hint of exceptional qualities in someone, so that one might think he had been ordained by God to redeem Italy, yet later events have shown, as his career progressed, that he was rejected by fortune. So Italy has remained at death's door, waiting for someone who could bind her wounds and put an end to the sack of

Lombardy, to the extortion of Tuscany and of the Kingdom of Naples, someone who could heal her sores which long ago became infected. One can see how she prays to God that he will send her someone who will redeem her from this ill treatment and from the insults of the barbarians. One can see every Italian is ready, everyone is eager to rally to the colors, if only someone will raise them high.

At the moment, there is nowhere Italy can turn in her search for someone to redeem her with more chance of success than to your own illustrious family, which is fortunate and resourceful [*virtù*], is favored by God and by the church (indeed the church is now at its command). The undertaking is straightforward, if you keep in mind the lives and the deeds of the leaders I have mentioned. Of course those men were exceptional and marvelous; but, nevertheless, they were only men, and none of them had as good an opportunity as you have at the moment. For their undertakings were not more just than this one, or easier, nor was God more their ally than he is yours. This is truly just: "A war is just if there is no alternative, and the resort to arms is legitimate if they represent your only hope."[106] These circumstances are ideal; and when circumstances are ideal there can be no great difficulty in achieving success, provided your family copies the policies of those I have recommended as your models. Beyond that, we have already seen extraordinary and unparalleled events. God has already shown his hand: The sea has been divided; a cloud has escorted you on your journey; water has flowed out of the rock; manna has fallen from on high. Everything has conspired to make you great. The rest you must do for yourselves. God does not want to have to do the whole thing, for he likes to leave us our free will so we can lay claim to part of the glory by earning it.

There is no need to be surprised that none of the Italian rulers I have discussed has been able to accomplish what I believe your family can achieve, or to be disheartened if during all the wars that have been fought, all the political upheavals that have taken place, it has seemed as if the Italians have completely lost their capacity to fight and win [*la virtù militare*]. This is simply because the traditional

---

106. [Livy, bk. 9, ch. 1.]

way of doing things in Italy is mistaken, and no one has appeared who has known how to bring about change. Nothing does more to establish the reputation of someone who comes new to power than do the new laws and the new institutions he establishes. These, when they are well thought out and noble in spirit, make a ruler revered and admired. In Italy we have the raw materials: You can do anything you wish with them. Here we have people capable of anything [*virtù grande*], all they need are leaders who know what to do. When it comes to fighting one-on-one the Italians prove themselves to be stronger, quicker, cleverer. But when it comes to the clash of armies, the Italians are hopeless. The cause lies in the inadequacy of the leaders. Those who know what to do are not obeyed, and everyone thinks he knows what to do. So far there has been no one who has known how to establish an authority, based on fortune and ability [*virtù*], such that the others will obey him. This is the reason why, through the whole of the last twenty years, during all the wars that have taken place in that time, not a single army consisting solely of Italians has done well. Twenty years ago the Italians were defeated at Taro; since then at Alexandria, Capua, Genoa, Vailà, Bologna, Mestre.

So, if your illustrious family wants to follow in the footsteps of those excellent men who liberated the nations to which they belonged, you must, before you do anything else, do the one thing that is the precondition for success in any enterprise: Acquire your own troops. You cannot hope to have more faithful, more reliable, or more skillful soldiers. And if each soldier will be good, the army as a whole will be better still, once they see their ruler place himself at their head and discover he treats them with respect and sympathy. It is necessary, though, to get such an army ready, if we are to be able to defend Italy from the foreigners with Italian strength and skill [*con la virtù italica*].

It is true that the Swiss and Spanish infantries are thought to be intimidating; nevertheless, they both have their defects, so a third force could not only stand up to them, but could be confident of beating them. For the Spanish cannot withstand a cavalry charge; and the Swiss have reason to be afraid of infantry, should they come up against any as determined to win as they are. Thus, we have seen that the Spanish cannot withstand an attack by the French

cavalry, and we will see in practice that the Swiss can be destroyed by the Spanish infantry. It is true that we have yet to see the Spanish properly defeat the Swiss, but we have seen an indication of what will happen at the Battle of Ravenna,[107] when the Spanish infantry clashed against the German battalions, for the Germans rely on the same formation as the Swiss. There the Spanish, thanks to their agility and with the help of their bucklers, were able to get underneath the pikes of the Germans and were able to attack them in safety, without the Germans' having any defense. If the cavalry had not driven them off, they would have wiped them out. So, since we know the weakness of each of these infantries, we ought to be able to train a new force that will be able to withstand cavalry and will not be afraid of infantry. To accomplish this we need specially designed weapons and new battle formations. This is the sort of new undertaking that establishes the reputation and importance of a new ruler.

So you should not let this opportunity slip by. Italy, so long enslaved, awaits her redeemer. There are no words to describe with what devotion he would be received in all those regions that have suffered from foreign invasions which have flooded across the land. No words can describe the appetite for revenge, the resolute determination, the spirit of self-sacrifice, the tears of emotion that would greet him. What gates would be closed to him? What community would refuse to obey him? Who would dare be jealous of his success? What Italian would refuse to pledge him allegiance? Everyone is sick of being pushed around by the barbarians. Your family must commit itself to this enterprise. Do it with the confidence and hope with which people embark on a just cause so that, marching behind your banner, the whole nation is ennobled. Under your patronage, may we prove Petrarch right:

Virtue [*virtù*] will take up arms against
   savagery,
And the battle will be short.
For the courage of old is not yet dead
In Italian hearts.[108]

---

107. [11 April 1512.]

108. [Petrarch, *Italia mia* (*Ai Signori d'Italia*), ll. 93–6.]

DISCOURSES

Niccolò Machiavelli to Zanobi Buondelmonti and Cosimo Rucellai,[1] Greetings

I send you a present which, if it does not measure up to the obligations I have to you, is unquestionably the most valuable thing Niccolò Machiavelli could send you. For in it I have put in words all that I know and all I have learned from an extensive experience of the affairs of the world and endless reading about them. Neither you nor anybody else could ask more of me, so you have no reason to complain if this is all I have given you. Of course you may regret my inadequate intelligence when you find my discussions inadequate, and my poor judgment when, as I often do, I present a mistaken argument. In the circumstances, I am not sure which of us has least reason to be obliged to the other: I to you, who forced me to write a work which I, left to myself, would never have written, or you to me, if, in writing, I have not given you satisfaction. So accept this gift as we accept all gifts from friends, for then we always give more weight to the intention that lies behind the gift than to the quality of the gift itself.

And please believe that my manuscript gives me only one satisfaction, which is when I think that,

even if I have been mistaken in many particular matters I discuss, I know that I have not made a mistake in at least one thing: in having chosen you, to whom above all others my *Discourses* are addressed. I feel that in so doing I have expressed some gratitude for the benefits I have received from you. Moreover, I have avoided adopting the normal practice of authors, for they nearly always dedicate their books to some ruler, and, blinded by ambition and avarice, they praise him as if he had all possible virtuous [*virtuose*] qualities, when they ought to criticize him for having every despicable characteristic. So I, in order to avoid falling into this mistake, have chosen, not princes, but people whose innumerable fine qualities make them worthy to be princes. I have chosen, not rulers who can reward me with titles, honors, and wealth, but private citizens who would reward me if they could. If you want to make sound judgments, you should admire those who are generous in spirit, not those who have the resources to be generous, respect those who know how to rule, not those who have no idea of how to rule, but are in power. Writers praise Hiero of Syracuse more when they describe him while he was still a private citizen than Perseus of Macedon while he was king, for Hiero was fit to be king, even if he had no kingdom, while Perseus had none of the attributes of a true ruler other than a kingdom.[2]

So enjoy this book if you can. You are responsible for what is good in it, and for what is bad. If your judgment is so poor that you continue to enjoy reading me, then I will not fail to complete my commentary on Livy, as I originally promised you I would. Farewell.

From Machiavelli, *Selected Political Writings*, edited and translated by David Wootton (Indianapolis: Hackett Publishing Company, 1994). Copyright © 1994. Reprinted by permission of the publisher.

1. [Buondelmonti and Rucellai were close friends who took part in discussions of politics with Machiavelli in the Oricellari gardens. They were both of distinguished families. Rucellai died in 1519; Buondelmonti in exile in 1527. In the editions of 1531 this letter appears at the end, not the beginning of the *Discourses*. It is possible that Machiavelli intended to substitute it for the preface to book one, or, alternatively, that it survives from an early draft and was intended to be deleted. — D.W.]

2. [For Hiero, see *The Prince*, chapter six. Perseus, King of Macedon from 179 to 168 B.C., lost his kingdom on the battlefield.]

BOOK I

Preface

Men are by nature envious. It has always been as dangerous to propose new ways of thinking and new institutions as it is to seek unknown oceans and undiscovered continents.[3] People are much quicker to criticize than to praise what others have done. Nevertheless, spurred on by an instinctive desire I have always had to do those things that I believe will further the common good and benefit everybody, I have refused to be intimidated. I have resolved to set out on a road no one has travelled before me. My journey may be tiresome and difficult, but I can hope it will prove rewarding, at least if people are willing to judge sympathetically the purpose of my labors. If my limited intelligence, my lack of experience of contemporary politics, and my inadequate knowledge of classical history will make my efforts defective and of very limited use to others, I will at least be pointing out the way to someone with greater ability [*virtù*], more analytical skill, and better judgment, someone who will be capable of achieving what I have aimed at. Perhaps no one will praise my efforts; in any event, I do not deserve to be reproached.

Think of the respect in which we hold antiquity. Often, to take just one example, a single fragment of an antique statue will be purchased at enormous expense by someone who wants to look at it every day. He will give it a place of honor in his house and allow those who aspire to be sculptors to copy it. The sculptors then make every effort to do work comparable to it. Think, on the other hand, of the immensely skillful [*virtuosissime*] deeds the history books record for us, deeds done by ancient kingdoms and classical republics, by kings, generals, citizens, legislators, and others who have worn themselves out for their homelands. These deeds may be admired, but they are scarcely imitated. Indeed, everybody goes to great lengths to avoid copying them, even if it only concerns an insignificant detail. The result is not a trace of the classical military and political skills [*quella antiqua virtù*] survives. I cannot help but be both astonished

and dismayed by this. Especially when I notice that when citizens find themselves caught up in legal disagreements, or when they fall ill, they always appeal to the legal decisions of the ancients, they always follow the medical remedies prescribed by them. For the civil laws are nothing other than decisions handed down by classical jurists, decisions that have been codified, and are now taught to lawyers by our own jurists. Similarly, medicine is simply the experience of classical doctors, on the basis of which contemporary doctors make their decisions. Nevertheless, in organizing republics, in administering states, in ruling kingdoms, in training armies and fighting wars, in passing judgment on subjects, and in planning new conquests, when it comes to all these activities, one does not find a single ruler or republic who tries to learn from the ancients.

I do not believe the cause of this is the feebleness contemporary religion has instilled in the world, nor the evil consequences that a supercilious indolence has had for many Christian countries and cities. The real problem is people do not properly understand the history books. When they read them they do not get out of them the meaning that is in them. They chew on them but do not taste them. The result is countless people read them and enjoy discovering in them the great variety of events they record, but never think of imitating them, presuming it would not be just difficult but would be simply impossible to do as the ancients did. As if the heavens, the sun, the elements, human beings had changed in their movement, organization, and capacities, and were quite different from what they were in days gone by. My intent has been to rescue men from this mistake, so I have decided I must write about all the books of Livy's history that have survived the ravages of time, explaining whatever I think is important if one is to understand them. In doing so, I will draw on my knowledge of ancient and modern affairs. My hope is that those who read my comments will be able without difficulty to draw from them those practical benefits one ought to expect to gain from the study of history. Although my undertaking is a difficult one, nevertheless, helped by those who have encouraged me to embark on this enterprise, I believe I will have so much success that anyone coming after me will only have a little to do before he completes my task.

3. [Machiavelli presumably had the discoveries of Columbus in mind.]

Chapter 1

On the universal origins of any city whatever, and on how Rome began.

Those who read how the city of Rome began, who established its laws, and how it was organized will not marvel that so much excellence [*virtù*] was preserved in that city for so many centuries; and that later it gave birth to the vast empire the Roman republic eventually controlled. Since I want to talk first about its birth, I will start by saying all cities are constructed either by men born in the place where the city is built or by foreigners. In the first case, the inhabitants decide to build a city because they have been spread out in many tiny settlements in which they have not felt secure, for each settlement on its own, because of its location and because of the small number of its inhabitants, is incapable of resisting the assaults of an attacker. Nor are they in a position to assemble in joint defense when they see the enemy coming, either because it takes too long, or because, even if they could assemble in time, they would be obliged to abandon many of their settlements and would soon see them plundered by their enemies. So, to avoid these dangers, urged on either by their own individual judgments or by some one member of their group who has greater influence among them, they gather together to live in a single place they have chosen, one that will be more convenient to live in, and that will be easier to defend.

Athens and Venice are among the many cities that originated in this way. Athens, under the leadership of Theseus, was constructed by scattered inhabitants for the sort of reasons I have outlined.[4] Venice was established by numerous little groups who had taken refuge on certain tiny islands at the end of the Adriatic sea.[5] They were trying to escape the wars that continually broke out in Italy in the period following the collapse of the Roman empire as a result of the arrival of new groups of barbarians. They organized them-selves, without there being any one individual in overall control, to live according to those laws that were, in their view, most conducive to their preservation. Their enterprise was a success because of the lengthy period of peace the site they had chosen ensured for them, for their lagoon was impenetrable, and the tribes who were invading Italy had no ships with which to attack them. So, from the most humble beginnings, they were able to rise to the eminent position they now occupy.

The second case, when foreigners come and build a city, takes two forms, depending on whether the immigrants are free men or men who owe allegiance to others. In the latter case a republic or a ruler may send out colonists in order to reduce the pressure of population in their existing settlements; or because they have recently conquered new territory and want to defend it effectively and inexpensively (the Romans built many such cities throughout their empire); or such a city may be built by a ruler who does not intend to live there, but to immortalize himself through it, as Alexander did by building Alexandria. Because such cities do not start out free, it rarely happens that they make great strides and come to be regarded as the capital cities of their own countries. It is in this category that we should place the construction of Florence, for (no matter whether it was built by Sulla's soldiers or by the inhabitants of the hilltops of Fiesole, who, given confidence by the long peace that the whole world benefited from under Augustus, came down to live in the plain of the Arno) it was built under Roman rule, nor could it, at the beginning, control any territory beyond what was assigned it at the pleasure of the emperor.

Cities are built by free men when a group of people, either under the command of a ruler or acting on their own, are forced to abandon the land of their birth and to seek new territory because of disease, or hunger, or war. They may occupy the cities that already exist in the territory they conquer, as Moses did, or they may build from scratch, as Aeneas did. It is in this latter case that one can fully appreciate the skill [*virtù*] of the architect as it is reflected in the fate of his city, for the history of the city will be more or less marvelous depending on whether its first founder is more or less skillful [*virtuoso*]. The skill [*virtù*] of the founder can be judged by two things:

---

4. [According to legend, Theseus founded Athens in 1234 B.C.]

5. [Settlement of Venice is supposed to have begun in 451.]

firstly, by his choice of a site for the construction of the new city; secondly, by the laws he draws up for it.

Men act either out of necessity or free choice. Since it seems that men are the most admirable [*maggior virtù*] where they have the least freedom of choice, one must consider whether it might not be better to choose an infertile region for the construction of a city so that its inhabitants will be forced to be industrious and prevented from being self-indulgent, and so that they will be more united, having less occasion for conflict because of the poverty of their land. We can see this happened at Ragusa, and in many other cities built in similar locations. Such a choice of location would be without doubt wiser and would lead to the best outcome, if men were content to live off their own possessions and did not want to try to get control of the property of others. But since men can only secure themselves by building up power, one must avoid building a city in a barren location, but rather settle the most fertile land, whose fecundity will make possible growth, so one will be able both to defend oneself against attackers and to defeat anyone who stands in the way of one's own power. In order to ensure the location does not lead to self-indulgence, one must design the laws to force people to do what the location does not force them to do. Thus, one should imitate those wise men who have lived in countries that have been delightful and fertile, countries apt to produce lazy men who are incapable of any manly [*virtuoso*] work. In order to avoid the disadvantages that would result from the delightfulness of the land if it caused self-indulgence, they required all those who were liable to military service to drill, so that by means of such regulations their inhabitants became better soldiers than those living in territory that is naturally harsh and infertile. The Kingdom of Egypt is an example of this: Despite the fact that the country is exceptionally fertile, the artificial necessity imposed by the laws was so effective that Egypt produced the finest men; and if their names had not been lost in antiquity, we would be able to see they deserved more praise than Alexander the Great and many others whose deeds remain fresh in our memory. And if you had examined the state of the sultan, with its regiments of Mamelukes and its Turkish militia, before they were abolished by

the Sultan Selim,[6] you would have seen there much drilling of soldiers and would have learned how much the Turks feared the self-indulgence the generosity of their country might induce in them, had they not introduced strict legal penalties to prevent it.

So I conclude it is wiser to choose to settle in a fertile place, provided the consequences of that fertility are kept within due limits by legislation. Deinocrates the architect came to Alexander the Great when Alexander wanted to build a city to magnify his own reputation.[7] He showed him how he could build on Mount Athos: The site, apart from being easily defended, could be cut away so the new city would have the shape of a human body, which would be a remarkable and extraordinary thing and worthy of Alexander's greatness. But when Alexander asked him what the inhabitants of the city would live on he replied he had not given the matter any thought. Alexander laughed, and, leaving Mount Athos intact, built Alexandria in a place where people would want to settle because of the fecundity of the countryside and the ease of access to the sea and to the Nile.

Let us now consider the construction of Rome. If you take it that Aeneas was its first founder, you will think of it as one of the cities built by foreigners.[8] If you believe it was founded by Romulus, you will think of it as founded by men born in the vicinity.[9] Either way you will agree it was founded in freedom and was not under any outsider's authority. You will also recognize—we will return to this subject later—the extent to which the laws established by Romulus, Numa, and the other early legislators imposed an artificial necessity upon the inhabitants, so the fertility of the site, the ease of access to the sea, the frequent victories of their armies, and the extensive territory that fell under Roman control could not corrupt them even over the course of many centuries. Their laws ensured they had more admirable qualities [*virtù*]

6. [The Mamelukes ruled Egypt from 1252 to 1516, when they were defeated by the Ottoman Turks.]

7. [Deinocrates designed Alexandria in 322 B.C.]

8. [Aeneas's flight from the defeat of Troy to Italy is recounted by Livy.]

9. [Livy prefers the story of Romulus and Remus, sons of Mars and wolf-children, but, unlike Machiavelli, he treats it as myth, not history.]

than any other city or republic has ever been able to boast of in its citizens.

The deeds of the Romans that are celebrated in Livy's history occurred either as a result of public or of private decisions and either inside or outside the city. I will begin by discussing those things that happened inside the city and as a result of public decision-making, that I take to be worthy of more detailed discussion, and we will need to explore all the consequences that flowed from them. This first book, or at least this first part, will be taken up with a discussion of these matters.

Chapter 2

On the different types of republic that exist, and on how to categorize the Roman republic.

I want to leave aside any discussion of those cities that were under the authority of outsiders from the beginning, and to discuss only those that began completely free of external domination and were ruled by their own wills from the beginning, whether as republics or as princedoms. These cities, since they began in a variety of ways, have had a variety of constitutions and legal systems. In some, either at the very beginning or soon after their foundation, a single individual wrote all the laws at once—Lycurgus, for example, gave the Spartans their laws[10]—while others acquired their laws by chance, little by little, according to the circumstances, as happened in Rome. We can call fortunate any republic in which there appears a leader so prudent he is able to give them a code of law they have no need to revise, but under which they can live securely. We know the Spartans obeyed the laws of Lycurgus for eight hundred years without corrupting them and without any serious internal conflict. On the other hand, we can call in some degree unfortunate any city that does not chance upon a prudent lawmaker, and is obliged to revise its laws for itself. And among these cities, moreover, those are most unfortunate that are furthest from hav-

ing the right laws; and those are furthest astray whose constitution is quite unlike the one that would lead them to their true and ideal goal. For it is almost impossible for a city that finds itself in this situation to have enough good luck to be able to sort itself out. Those others that, if they do not have a perfect constitution, yet have started out in the right direction and are in a position to improve, can, as opportunity presents itself, become perfect. But this is certainly true: One never establishes a constitution without encountering danger. For enough men will never agree to a new law that changes the constitution of the city unless they are persuaded it is essential to pass it, and they will only be persuaded of this if they see themselves to be in danger, so it can easily happen that the republic is destroyed before she arrives at a perfect constitution. The republic of Florence is a good example of this: Defeat in the Battle of Arezzo led to her reorganization;[11] defeat in the Battle of Prato in 1512 led to her dissolution.[12]

I want now to discuss the constitution of Rome and the events that made it possible for her to achieve perfection. Some who have written about constitutions say they are of three types, which they call "monarchy," "aristocracy," and "democracy."[13] They say anyone drawing up the constitution of a city must choose from these the one he thinks most appropriate. Others, who are widely thought to be wiser, say there are six types of constitution, of which three are inherently bad and three are inherently good, although even the good ones are so easily corrupted they, too, can quickly become pernicious. The good ones are the three I have already mentioned; the bad ones are three others that derive from these three, and each of which is so like the good constitution it most resembles that it is easy for one to turn into the other. Thus, monarchies easily become tyrannies, aristocracies become oligarchies, and democracies slide into anarchy. The result is that if a lawmaker establishes a constitution for a city that corresponds to one of the three

---

10. [Lycurgus is supposed to have drawn up his laws ca. 884 B.C.]

11. [Defeat in 1502, and pressure from Cesare Borgia, led to Piero Soderini being made gonfaloniere for life.]

12. [I.e., the restoration of the Medici.]

13. [The rest of this chapter is profoundly influenced by Polybius, *Histories*, bk. 6.]

good forms of government it will not last long, for no precaution is sufficient to ensure it will not slip into its opposite, for the good [*la virtute*] and the bad are, when it comes to constitutions, closely related.

These different types of government developed among men by accident. When the world began, it had few inhabitants, and they lived for a while apart from one another as the animals do. As their numbers multiplied they gathered together, and in order to be better able to defend themselves, they began to defer to one among their number who was stronger and braver than the rest. They made him, as it were, their leader and obeyed him. This was the origin of knowledge of those things that are good and honest as opposed to those that are pernicious and evil. For men saw that, if someone harmed his benefactor, his associates despised him and felt compassion for his victim. They learned to think ill of the ungrateful and to approve of those who were grateful. They came to realize the injuries that were done to someone else could equally be done to themselves. In order to avoid such evils, they gathered together to make laws and to lay down punishments for those who broke them: This was the invention of justice. Thereafter, when they had to choose a ruler, they no longer obeyed the strongest, but he who was most prudent and most just.

Later, however, they began to appoint their ruler by hereditary succession, not by election, with the immediate result that power was inherited by men who were inferior to their ancestors. They no longer acted virtuously [*lasciando l'opere virtuose*], but thought rulers were simply there to outdo other men in extravagance, lasciviousness, and in every other type of vice. The result was that rulers began to be hated, and, because they were hated, to be afraid. Because they were afraid, they went on the attack, and before long kings had become tyrants. These rulers faced the possibility of being destroyed. The conspiracies and plots hatched against them were not begun by those who were fearful or weak, but by those who surpassed their fellows in generosity, spiritedness, wealth, and nobility, for such men could no longer tolerate the dishonorable lives of their rulers. The masses then followed the lead provided by the elite and armed themselves against their ruler, and, when they had got rid of him, obeyed the elite as their liberators. The new rulers hated the idea of one-man rule and, so, established themselves collectively in power.

At first, remembering the evils of tyranny, they governed according to the laws they had established, putting their own interests second and the public good first. They directed and protected both public and private matters with great care. In due course, this government was inherited by their sons, who had never seen power change hands, had never suffered under evil government, and who were unwilling to continue treating their fellow subjects as their equals. They gave themselves over to avarice, to ambition, to chasing other men's wives. So aristocracy degenerated into an oligarchy in which the norms of civilized life were flouted. In a short time, the oligarchs suffered the same fate as the tyrants, for the masses became fed up with their government and gave their support to anyone who was planning any sort of resistance to their rule. Soon someone, with the assistance of the masses, was able to destroy them. Since they could still clearly remember one-man rule, and the harm it had done them, when they destroyed oligarchy they had no desire to restore monarchy, but instead established popular rule. This they organized in such a manner that neither the elite nor a powerful individual could have any influence whatsoever.

In the beginning, all states can command a certain amount of respect, so popular government survived for a while, but not for long, especially once the generation that had established it had passed away. It quickly degenerated into anarchy, in which neither private individuals nor public officials could command any respect. Each person did as he chose, with the result that every day innumerable crimes were committed. So, compelled by necessity, or advised by some good man, or desperate to escape from anarchy, they established once more the rule of one man. And from monarchy, step by step, they degenerated once again into anarchy, repeating the sequence I have already described.

This is the cycle through which all states revolve, and power is still passed, as it always has been, from hand to hand. But it rarely happens that the same people return to power, for scarcely a single state has survived long enough to travel several times through this cycle without being destroyed. Usually, while a state is torn apart by internal dissent, and as a result is weakened and deprived of good leadership, it is conquered by a neighboring state better organized than it is. But if this did not happen, then a state could repeat this cycle of constitutions over and over again.

I conclude all these forms of government are pestilential: The three good ones do not last long, and the three bad ones are evil. Those who know how to construct constitutions wisely have identified this problem and have avoided each one of these types of constitution in its pure form, constructing a constitution with elements of each. They have been convinced such a constitution would be more solid and stable, would be preserved by checks and balances, there being present in the one city a monarch, an aristocracy, and a democracy.

Lycurgus is the most admirable of those who have established constitutions of this sort. He constructed the constitution of Sparta so that it gave distinct roles to king, aristocracy, and people, with the result the state survived for eight hundred years, throughout which time his name was revered and the city lived in harmony. Matters turned out differently for Solon, who drew up the constitution of Athens.[14] Because he constructed a democracy, it survived such a short time that before Solon died he saw Athens under the tyranny of Pisistratus. Although forty years later Pisistratus's heirs were driven into exile and freedom was restored, because the Athenians re-established the democratic constitution drawn up by Solon, their freedom lasted no more than a century, despite the fact that in order to preserve it they introduced numerous reforms Solon had not considered. They did their best to control the insolence of the powerful and the license of the masses. Nevertheless, because they did not allow a proper role for one-man rule and for aristocracy, Athens survived, by comparison with Sparta, a very short time.

Let us turn to Rome. Even though Rome did not have a Lycurgus to establish from the beginning a constitution that would enable her to live free for centuries, nevertheless, she underwent so many political crises, because of the conflicts between the people and the senate, that chance eventually brought about something no legislator had been able to accomplish. For if Rome did not have the first type of good fortune,

she had the second, and although her first constitution was defective, nevertheless, it did not cause her to turn off the right path that could lead her to perfection.

Romulus and all the other kings of Rome made many excellent laws, ones appropriate for a free state. But their goal was the establishment of a kingdom, not a republic, so when Rome became free she lacked many of the laws free government required, for these they had omitted to decree. And although the kings of Rome lost their power for the reasons and in the way I have outlined, nevertheless, those who threw them out quickly established two consuls who played the same role as the kings, so that they expelled from Rome the name of king but not the authority of kingship. The new republic was ruled by the consuls and the senate, so it was a mixture of only two of the three types of power I have described: of monarchy and aristocracy. It failed to give any authority to the populace.

When the Roman nobility became overbearing, for reasons I will explain later, the people rose up against them, with the result that, in order not to lose all power, the nobles were obliged to concede a share of power to the people. On the other hand, the consuls and the senate retained enough authority to be able to hold on to a share of power in the republic. So the tribunes of the people came to be established, after which the constitution of the republic became more stable, for now all three types of authority had a fair share in power. And fortune was so favorable to Rome that, although she passed from monarchy, to aristocracy, to democracy, going through each of the stages I have described for the reasons I have outlined, nevertheless, the aristocracy never seized all power from the monarchical element; nor did the people ever seize all power from the aristocracy; instead, power was added to power, and the mixture that resulted made for a perfect republic. Rome achieved this perfection because of the conflict between senate and people, as I will show at length in the next two chapters.

BOOK II

Preface

Men always praise the olden days and criticize the present, but they do not always have good reason for doing so. They are so biased in favor of the past that

14. [Solon's reforms began in 595 B.C.]

they do not celebrate only those periods they know about because of the surviving descriptions of them written by men alive at the time; they also, once they have become old, praise the way they remember things having been in their youth. When their praise of the past is mistaken, as it usually is, there are, I think, several reasons why history plays tricks on them.

I believe the first is that we are not told the whole truth about the past. For the most part, people keep quiet about those events it would be shameful to record, while those deeds that will make them seem glorious in the eyes of posterity they portray in the most favorable light possible. Most writers place themselves in the service of victory. In order to make fortune's victories glorious they not only exaggerate the skillful [*virtuosamente*] things the victors did, they even improve on the actions of their enemies, with the result anyone who is born in future ages in either of the territories, either that of the victors or that of the vanquished, has good reason to be amazed at the actions of those men and the character of those times, and has no choice but to praise them to the skies and to love them.

Secondly, men hate things either out of fear or jealousy. But these two powerful motives for hatred cease to apply as time passes, for what is past can no longer hurt you, and you no longer have reason to be jealous of it. The opposite is true of those things you can still touch and see for yourself. Because you know them through and through, and nothing is hidden from you, you recognize their good features, but at the same time there are many aspects of them that displease you. So you conclude things were much better in the past, even when in reality actions in the present are much more deserving of fame and of glory. I am not talking about scientific and artistic activities, for their qualities are so transparent there is little time can do to take away or add to the reputation that they properly deserve. I am talking, rather, about the manners and morals of men, reports of which are much harder to assess.

I ought to admit that although the habit of praising the past and condemning the present is as widespread as I have said, nevertheless, people are not always mistaken when they think the past superior to the present. Sometimes their judgment is bound to be justified. Human affairs are always changing, and

when they change it must be either for better or worse. One sees a city or a territory organized for a constitutional government by some one excellent individual; for a while, thanks to the skill [*virtù*] of this founder, the political system will get steadily better and better. Someone who is born in such a state, if he praises the olden times more than his own day, makes a mistake; and he makes this mistake for the reasons I have explained above. But later generations in this same city or territory, born when things have gone into decline, are not mistaken. Thinking about how these things work, I reached the conclusion that the world is always in the same overall condition. There has always been in it as much good as bad, but both the good and the bad are redistributed from territory to territory.

One can see this from what we know about the ancient monarchies. Good and bad were redistributed among them as manners and morals changed, but the overall condition of the world remained the same. There was only this one difference: Where virtue [*virtù*] had at first been resident in Assyria, it later moved to the Kingdom of the Medes, and then to Persia, until eventually it came to Italy, and to Rome. Since the Roman empire, it is true, there has been no lasting empire, and virtue [*virtù*] has not remained concentrated in one place; nevertheless, you can see it was scattered among many nations, each of whom came to live virtuously [*virtuosamente*]: the Kingdoms of France and Turkey; the Sultanate of Egypt; and now the peoples of Germany. Above all, virtue was to be found among the sect of the Saracens, who accomplished so much, occupied so much territory, and were indeed responsible for the destruction of the Roman empire in the east.

In all these territories, then, and in all such sects, virtue [*virtù*] was to be found after the Romans had gone into decline, and still is to be found in some parts of them that still aspire to greatness; there she is deservedly praised. If you are born in one of these virtuous places and praise the olden days more than the present, you may be making a mistake. But if you are born in Italy or in Greece, and if you have not become (if you are Italian) an admirer of the northerners, or (if you are Greek) a supporter of the Turks, then you are right to criticize your own times and praise the past. For in the past, there were plenty of things that deserved admiration; in the present, there is nothing at all to mitigate unalloyed misery, disgrace, and contempt. Now there is no respect for religion, for the law, or for military service; everything is splattered with filth. These vices are all the more detestable because they are most prevalent among those who hold government office, who order everyone else around, and want to be treated like gods.

But let us get back to our subject. I meant to point out that if men's judgment is unreliable when it comes to judging the relative merits of the present and the distant past in matters where one cannot have such detailed knowledge of the past as one can of the present, this does not explain why old men are poor judges of the relative merits of the times of their youth and their old age, for they have had an equal knowledge and experience of the one and the other. Or at least they would have if men throughout their lives had the same capacity to make judgments and were governed by the same appetites. But men change as they grow older, even if their circumstances do not; so things look different to them, even if they have in fact stayed the same, for men have different appetites, different pleasures, different preoccupations in old age from the ones they had when young. For men, as they grow older, become weaker, but at the same time more prudent and astute in their judgment. So those things that seemed to them tolerable, even excellent, when they were young, as they grow old seem to them intolerable and wretched. Where they ought to blame their own changing judgment, they blame the changing times.

Moreover, there is another reason: Human appetites are insatiable. It is in man's nature to be able to and to want to desire all things; it is in the nature of circumstances that he can only realize a few of his desires. The result is that men are always finding themselves discontented and discovering themselves to be dissatisfied with what they possess. This makes them have a low opinion of the present, praise the past, and put their hope in the future, even though they have no good reason for thinking things were better or will improve.

I do not know, however, if I deserve to be included among those whose judgment is flawed, though I might be thought to praise the ancient Romans too much and criticize our own times too severely in

these discourses. Indeed, if the excellence [*virtù*] that was the norm then, and the inadequacy that is to be found everywhere today, were not as plain as day, then I would express myself more cautiously, for fear I might slip into this error for which I criticize others. But the matter is so obvious anyone can recognize the truth, so that I am entitled to speak frankly and express myself bluntly on the differences between our own times and those of the ancient Romans, in the hope any young men who read what I write will be encouraged to reject the world they live in and will want to try to imitate the ancients, should fortune ever give them the opportunity to do so. For it is a worthy undertaking to teach others how to do those admirable things that you, because of corrupt circumstances and hostile fortune, have been unable to perform. If many acquire the ability to do what is needed, then one, if fortune smiles upon him, may be successful.

Having, in the previous book, talked about the decisions the Romans took in matters relating to the internal affairs of the city, in this book we will discuss those things the Roman populace did in order to expand the territory under their control.

Chapter 1

On whether skill [*virtù*] or good fortune was a more significant factor in the Romans' acquisition of an empire.

Many have been of the opinion—among them Plutarch who is an author whose judgment is always to be respected[15]—that the Roman people, in acquiring an empire, benefited more from good fortune than from skill [*virtù*]. One of the various reasons they put forward to support this view is that it is evident, they say, from the actions of the Romans themselves that they attributed all their victories to good luck, for they erected more temples to the goddess Fortune than to any other god. It would seem Livy was more or less of this opinion, for it is rare for him, whenever

15. [Plutarch, *Opera moralia*, 44; *De fortuna Romanorum*.]

he has a Roman speak about skill [*virtù*], not to couple skill with luck.

But I do not want to admit the truth of this opinion under any circumstances, and I do not believe there are good arguments to support it. For if there has never been a republic that has made as extensive gains as Rome did, it is also evident there has never been a republic better organized to make gains than Rome was. It was the skill [*virtù*] of their armies that enabled them to conquer an empire, and it was their way of going about things, which dates back to their first legislator, that enabled them to hold on to what they had conquered, as I will explain at length below, over the course of a number of chapters. Some people say it was good fortune and not skill [*virtù*] that ensured the Roman people never had to face war against two powerful enemies at the same time. Thus, they only found themselves at war with the Latins, when, if they had not really defeated the Samnites, they were at least able to call on their support, for in fighting the Latins they were helping the Samnites. They did not campaign against the Tuscans until they had first conquered the Latins and had almost completely crippled the Samnites. They did not campaign against the Tuscans until they had first conquered the Latins and had almost completely crippled the Samnites by defeating them again and again. If two of these powers had allied when they were fresh and undefeated, then without doubt one could reasonably have predicted they would destroy the Roman republic.

But, however it came about, it is true they never had to fight two extremely powerful enemies at one time. It seems the rise of one always caused the decline of another, or the decline of one made possible the rise of another. This is apparent from the chronology of the wars they fought, for, leaving aside those that took place before Rome was seized by the French, one can see that while they were at war with the Aequi and the Volsci,[16] and so long as those tribes remained powerful, nobody else attacked them. Only after they had been subdued did the war with the Samnites begin,[17] and although the Latin tribes rebelled against the Romans before that war was over,[18] nevertheless, when that rebellion took place the Samnites entered into a league with the Romans and sent their troops to help the Romans punish the Latins for their insolence. Once they were subdued, the war against the Samnites began again.[19] When the Samnites had been beaten in battle after battle, the war with the Tuscans began;[20] and when that had been settled, the Samnites rebelled again as a result of the invasion of Italy by Pyrrhus.[21] When he had been forced to retreat into Greece, they began the first war with the Carthaginians;[22] no sooner was this war over, but all the French, on both sides of the Alps, allied against the Romans, until they were defeated and butchered in large numbers between Popolonia and Pisa, where now stands the tower of St. Vincent.[23]

After this war, there was a period of about twenty years when they were not involved in any major conflicts, for they only fought against the Ligurians[24] and against those remnants of the French who held out in Lombardy. This relative peace lasted until the beginning of the Second Carthaginian War in which Italy was embroiled for sixteen years.[25] Having brought this to a glorious conclusion, they found themselves at war with Macedon,[26] and, after that was over, with Antiochus and with Asia.[27] And after they had been victorious in that war there was not a ruler or a republic in the whole world who, either alone or in alliance with others, could hope to defy the Roman armies.

But anyone who considers the chronology of the wars before this final victory and who studies the policies of the Romans will realize they did not simply rely on fortune. They also employed a quite remark-

16. [493–380 B.C.]
17. [343 B.C.]

18. [340–338 B.C.]
19. [327–314 B.C.]
20. [310–300 B.C.]
21. [281–275 B.C.]
22. [264–241 B.C.]
23. [In 225 B.C.]
24. [223–222 B.C.]
25. [218–201 B.C.]
26. [200–196 B.C.]
27. [193–188 B.C.]

able prudence and skill [*virtù*]. For if you ask youself why they were so fortunate the answer will be obvious. It is evident that when a ruler or a people acquire a reputation such that every neighboring prince and people is spontaneously afraid of attacking them and fearful of being attacked by them, then it will always be the case that no state will ever attack them unless it has no alternative.

The result is that the dominant state will have almost a free choice when it comes to deciding with which of its neighbors it wants to fight a war, and will be able, with a little effort, to pacify the others. They, partly out of fear of the dominant power and partly taken in by the techniques it will employ to give them a false sense of security, will be easy to pacify. The other powers who are not immediate neighbors and who do not have dealings with the victim, will regard the whole business as taking place a long way away and think it no concern of theirs. They will keep making this mistake until they are next in line. By which time they have no defense available except to rely on their own troops. But by then their own troops will be inadequate, for the dominant power will have become overwhelmingly strong.

I will not delay to discuss how the Samnites stood by and watched while the Romans defeated the Volsci and the Aequi, and, in order to be brief, I will confine myself to the case of the Carthaginians. They were very powerful and widely respected at the time the Romans were fighting against the Samnites and the Tuscans, for they already controlled the whole of Africa along with Sardinia, and Sicily, and part of Spain. Because they were so powerful, and because their territory was some distance from that of the Romans, it never occurred to them to attack them, or to come to the assistance of the Samnites and the Tuscans. Thus, they behaved as one does if one thinks time is on one's side, allying with the Romans, and trying to win their good will. They did not recognize their mistake until the Romans had conquered all the peoples between themselves and the Carthaginians, and had begun to challenge them for control of Sicily and Spain.

The same thing happened to the French as to the Carthaginians, and the same thing again to Philip, King of Macedon, and to Antiochus. Each one of them believed, while the people of Rome were occupied with one of the others, that Rome's enemies would win, and that there was plenty of time to defend themselves, either through diplomacy or war, against Rome's advancing power. So I am of the view that the good fortune the Romans had in never having to fight against two enemies at the same time is available to any ruler who acts as the Romans did and is as skillful [*virtù*] as they were.

It would be relevant here for us to explain the policies pursued by the Roman people when occupying newly acquired territory if we had not discussed this question at length in our treatise on Princedoms. You will find an extensive discussion of this question there. I will only say this much in passing: The Romans always tried hard when they were acquiring new territory to have the support of an ally who could serve as a ladder over the defenses, or as a gate through the walls, or as an assistant in retaining control once it was acquired. So they used the Capuans to get entry to Samnium,[28] the Camertini to get into Tuscany,[29] the Mamertini helped them in Sicily,[30] the Saguntines in Spain,[31] the Masinissa in Africa,[32] the Aetolians in Greece,[33] the Eumenes and other rulers in Asia,[34] the Massilians and the Aedui in France.[35] They were never short of such allies to assist them in their undertakings and to help them acquire and hold new territories. Governments that systematically follow this policy will find they have less need of good fortune than those who do not.

So that everyone can clearly recognize how much more important skill [*virtù*] was than good fortune in the acquisition of the Roman empire we will discuss in the next chapter the character of the peoples they had to fight against, and will see just how determined they were to defend their liberty.

28. [340 B.C.]
29. [310 B.C.]
30. [264 B.C.]
31. [218 B.C.]
32. [205 B.C.]
33. [211 B.C.]
34. [193 B.C.]
35. [154 and 122 B.C.]

Chapter 2

On the peoples the Romans had to fight against, and on their determination in defending their liberty.

Nothing made it harder for the Romans to overcome the peoples immediately around them and, indeed, some in more distant territories, than the love many societies in those times had for liberty. They defended their liberty so stubbornly that they could never have been conquered except by a people of quite exceptional strength [virtù]. For there are many examples that show the dangers these societies were willing to endure in order to defend or recover their liberty; and show, too, the revenge they sought to exact on those who had taken their freedom from them.

One learns, too, from the study of history the losses both peoples and cities suffered as a result of their enslavement. While at the present time there is only one geographical region where one can say there are free cities to be found,[36] in classical times there were numerous peoples in every region who lived in complete liberty. One sees how, in the times we are discussing at the moment in Italy there were nothing but free peoples from the Appennines, which now mark the boundary between Tuscany and Lombardy, right down to the southern tip: the Tuscans, the Romans, the Samnites, and many other societies which lived in that section of the peninsula. Nor is there any report of there being any kings other than those who ruled in Rome, plus Porsenna, King of Tuscany—history does not record how many successors he had. But it is evident that when the Romans went to war with Veii, Tuscany was free. Indeed, the Tuscans were so enamored of liberty and so hated the title of king, that, when the inhabitants of Veii, who had appointed a king to take charge of their defense, asked them for help in resisting the Romans, they decided, after much debate, not to come to their assistance. They argued that, so long as they obeyed a king, there was no point in defending the freedom of people who had already given their freedom away.

It is easy to understand how a people acquires such a love of political freedom, for we see by experience that city-states have never been successful, either in expanding their territory or in accumulating wealth, except when they have been free. And really one is bound to be astonished if one considers the extraordinary accumulation of power and wealth in the hands of Athens in the hundred years that followed her freeing herself from the tyranny of Pisistratus.[37] But it is even more breathtaking to consider the astonishing success of Rome once she had freed herself from her kings. It is easy to work out why, for cities become great by pursuing, not the interests of private individuals, but the interests of the community as a whole. And there is no doubt the public interest is never a guiding principle except in republics. There, everything that furthers the common good is carried out, even if one or two private individuals suffer by it. The vast majority have interests that coincide with the public interest, and so they are able to pursue it, even in face of the resistance of the small minority who suffer by it. But the opposite occurs when a city is under the rule of one man, for usually what serves his interests hurts the city, and what would benefit the city is contrary to his interests.

The result is that as soon as a tyranny is established in a city where once there has been political freedom, the least bad outcome for the inhabitants is that their city ceases to make progress and stops accumulating either power or wealth; but usually, indeed nearly always, they begin to lose what they have won. If by chance it were a competent [virtuoso] tyrant who took power, who had the courage and military strength [virtù] to extend the territory under his control, still his society would not benefit at all from his achievements. He would be the only beneficiary. For he would not be able to reward any of his citizens who are strong and good. He must keep such men in servitude for fear they might be a threat to him. Nor can he make the cities he conquers subordinate to his home city or have them pay tribute to it, for if he makes his own city strong he endangers himself. It is in his interest to keep his state divided into distinct territories and to ensure each city and each province

---

36. [Germany.]

37. [510 B.C.]

answers to him directly. So, naturally, he is the only one who benefits from his conquests, while his homeland is no better off. If you want to see my opinion confirmed and to read numerous arguments in support of it, read the treatise Xenophon wrote *On Tyranny.*

Thus, it is not at all surprising that in classical times peoples hunted down tyrants with such bitterness and were so enamored of political freedom, and that the very idea of liberty was held in such respect among them. See, for example, what happened when Hieronymus, the nephew of Hiero of Syracuse, was killed in the city of Syracuse.[38] News of his death reached his army, which was not far away. At first they began to form a mob, seizing weapons to go to kill his murderers; but, when they heard that in Syracuse people were crying out "Liberty!," the word itself was enough to mesmerize them, and at once they quieted down, put aside their anger against the tyrannicides, and began to ask themselves how one could institutionalize political freedom in their city.

Again, it is not at all surprising that peoples pursued extraordinary vendettas against individuals who had taken their liberty from them. There are plenty of examples of this. I intend to refer only to one case that happened in Corcyra, a Greek city, at the time of the Peloponnesian War.[39] Greece was divided between two alliances, one of which was led by the Athenians, the other by the Spartans. The result was that in many cities where there were already internal divisions one faction allied itself with the Spartans, the other with the Athenians. In Corcyra the nobles got the upper hand and deprived the populace of their liberty. The popular party, thanks to Athenian assistance, took back control and seized all the nobles, locking them up in a prison big enough to hold them all. From there they took them out in groups of eight or ten at a time, pretending they had been sentenced to exile in different places, and tortured them to death in the public view. When those who were still alive realized what was happening, they decided to do their best to escape such an ignominious death. Arming

themselves with whatever they could find, they fought with those who wanted to enter the prison, defending the gateway against them. The populace, hearing the noise of the struggle, came running; they wrecked the upper floors of the building and buried their captives under the rubble. Many other similar events, both horrible and remarkable, took place in Greece. They show people go to greater lengths to take revenge on those who have taken their liberty from them than on those who have merely tried to do so.

You may wonder why, in those classical times, peoples were more in love with liberty than they are now. I think the reason is the same as why men in our day are less strong. In my view, both result from the difference between our upbringing and that of classical times, which is rooted in the difference between our religion and theirs. Because our religion has taught us the truth and the right way to salvation, it makes us less concerned with our reputation in this world. The pagans, on the other hand, were much more concerned with reputation and regarded it as the highest good, with the result their deeds were more savage. There are lots of their institutions that could serve as indications of this—one might begin with a comparison between the magnificence of their religious ceremonies and the simplicity of ours. Ours make a show of refinement rather than magnificence and include no actions that require savagery or courage. Their rituals were full of pomp and ceremony, but in addition they sacrificed numerous animals in ceremonies full of blood and savagery. These were cruel rites, and from them the worshipers learned to be cruel men.

Moreover, classical religion only deified men who had already been heaped with worldly glories, men such as generals of armies and rulers of states. Our religion, by contrast, glorifies men who are humble and contemplative, rather than those who do great deeds. In fact, it regards humility, self-abasement, and contempt for worldly goods as the supreme virtues, while classical religion valorized boldness of spirit, strength of body, and all the other qualities that make men redoubtable. It is true our religion requires that you be strong, but it wants you to demonstrate your strength by undergoing suffering without complaint, rather than by overcoming resistance. This set of values, it would seem, has turned the men of our own

38. [Hieronymus was murdered in 215 B.C. after being in power for a year.]

39. [In 427 B.C. Machiavelli's source is Thucydides, bk. 4, chs. 46–48.]

day into weaklings and left them unable to defend themselves against the ravages of the wicked. The wicked have no difficulty in handling their fellow men, for they know the average individual wants rather to endure their blows than to strike back, for he hopes to go to heaven.

Although it seems we have all been made effeminate, and God himself allows injustice to flourish, it is of course the fault of the sinful nature of mankind, which has caused them to interpret the teachings of our religion as suits their lazy temperament and not as brave men would have done [*non secondo la virtù*]. For if they had taken into account the fact that our religion allows us to praise and defend our homeland, they would have realized that if we are religious we ought to love and honor our country and to prepare ourselves to be the sort of people who will be capable of defending it. The upbringing we get, and these false interpretations of our religion, have the consequence that there are not so many republics to be found in the world as there were in classical times; nor, it follows, does one find in the peoples of our day as much love of liberty as there was then.

Another, and perhaps better, explanation is that the strength and military might of the Roman empire destroyed all the republics and all the free cities. And although that empire later collapsed, the cities within it were not able to reconstruct political freedom or rebuild institutions that would foster liberty, except in a very few places. Whatever the real cause, the Romans, no matter where they went, found republics allied together, armed to the teeth, and determined to defend their freedom to the end. Which shows that the Roman people, had they not been of exceptional and extreme strength [*virtù*], would never have been able to defeat them.

I want to give one example among them all and will confine myself to the case of the Samnites. It seems astonishing, but they were so powerful and so effective on the battlefield, that they could, as Livy admits, resist the Romans right down to the time of the consul Papirius Cursor,[40] son of the first Papirius, that is, for a period of forty-six years, despite having been defeated on the battlefield again and again,

having had their crops destroyed repeatedly, and having had their people massacred in their homes. Especially when one sees that their territory, where there were once so many cities and such a dense population, is now almost uninhabited, while in those days the people were so strong and so well organized it would have been impossible to overcome them, had they not been attacked by troops with the strength [*virtù*] of the Romans.

It is easy to establish where the organization they had then came from, and why we are now disorganized. For it is all the result of the fact that in those days they lived as free men, while now we live as slaves. For all the lands and territories, wherever they may be, that live in freedom experience, as I have already said, immense benefits. There you see denser populations, for men are freer to enter into marriage and keener to do so. People are happy to engender children if they think they will be able to feed them and do not fear their family wealth will be confiscated from them. They are happier if they know they will not only be born free, not slaves, but, if they have the right qualities [*virtù*], they will be able to grow up to share in government. There, people see wealth steadily accumulate, both wealth from agriculture and wealth from industry and commerce. For each person tries hard to build up savings and pile up goods if he believes he will have a chance to enjoy what he has acquired. As a result, men are eager to pursue both private and public benefits, and both types of interest are advanced extraordinarily quickly.

The opposite of all this happens in those countries where the people are enslaved. Then their traditional standard of living diminishes in proportion to the severity of their enslavement. Of all harsh enslavements, the harshest is to be enslaved to a republic: in the first place, because republics are more durable, and you have less hope of escaping from their control; in the second, because the objective of a republic is to weaken and consume all other communities in order to strengthen its own. This is not the objective of an individual ruler who forces you to submit to him, unless he is a barbarian, someone who lays waste the countryside and destroys civilized urban life. Oriental rulers act like this. But if he has normal human sentiments, then in most cases he loves all the cities subjected to him equally and leaves them

40. [298 B.C.]

with their commerce intact and with by far the greater part of their ancient institutions, so that if they cannot advance as they could while they were free, they are not ruined because they are enslaved. Here I am talking about the enslavement cities enter into when they are subjected to a foreign ruler, for I have already discussed above the case of cities subjected to one of their own citizens.

If you think about everything I have said, you will not be astonished at the power the Samnites had when they were free, or at the feeble state they were reduced to when they were enslaved. Livy testifies to this at several points, and particularly in his account of the invasion of Hannibal, where he reports the Samnites were being oppressed by a Roman legion based in Nola. They sent ambassadors to Hannibal to ask him to come to their assistance.[41] During their speech they said they had fought against the Romans for a hundred years, relying on their own soldiers and their own commanders. Many times they had stood firm against two consular armies commanded by both consuls; but now they were reduced to such a low condition they could scarcely defend themselves, even against the insignificant Roman legion that was in Nola.

Chapter 20

On the risks a ruler or a republic runs by using auxiliary or mercenary troops.

If I had not discussed at length in another book of mine how useless mercenary and auxiliary troops are, and how necessary it is to have an army of one's own subjects,[42] I would discuss the matter in more detail in this chapter than I will do. But since I have talked in detail about it elsewhere I will be brief here. I did not think, however, I could completely omit the question, having found so many instances of the use of auxiliary troops in Livy. Let me explain that auxiliary troops are those another ruler or republic lends to you, while he provides their commanding officers and their pay. Turning to the text of Livy, I note

that the Romans, on two separate occasions, defeated Samnite armies with their own, which they had sent to help the Capuans.[43] By this assistance they put an end to Samnite aggression against the Capuans. They wanted to withdraw their troops and bring them back to Rome, and were concerned that the Capuans, without an army to defend them, would once again be attacked and defeated by the Samnites. So they left two legions behind in the territory of Capua to defend them. These legions, with time on their hands, began to enjoy living a life of obedience to the senate. It occurred to them that they could take up their arms and seize control of the territory they had already, through their courage and skill [*virtù*], defended. They felt the inhabitants were not worthy to own the property they had been incapable of protecting. Realizing what was happening, Rome took the necessary steps, and in the chapter on conspiracies I will discuss what happened in detail.

For now I want to repeat that, of all the types of soldier, auxiliaries are the greatest liability. For the ruler or the republic who uses them to fight on his side has no control over them. Only the authorities in their homeland can control them. For auxiliary soldiers, as I said, are troops sent to you by another ruler. He supplies their commanders and pays their wages, and it is his standard they fight under. An example is the army we have been discussing that the Romans sent to Capua. Such soldiers, if they win the war, usually plunder impartially those they were fighting for and those they were fighting against; they do so, sometimes because the ruler who has sent them has evil intentions, sometimes because they have their own plans. The Romans had no intention of breaking the alliance and the agreements they had made with the Capuans; nevertheless, the Roman troops thought it would be so easy to crush them they began to think of seizing their land from them and establishing their own government.

One could give plenty of other examples like this; but I want to make do with this one, and with the example of the inhabitants of Rhegium.[44] They had

41. [215 B.C. Livy, bk. 23, ch. 42.]

42. [*The Prince*, ch. twelve.]

43. [Livy, bk. 7, chs. 32–41. The battles were in 443–42 B.C.]

44. [Polybius, bk. 1, ch. 7, in 279 B.C.]

their lives and their land taken from them by a Roman legion that had been sent to protect them. So a ruler (or a republic) ought to do anything rather than resort to bringing auxiliary troops onto his territory to fight in his defense in circumstances where he will be completely dependent on them. Any agreement, any treaty, no matter how harsh, that you can reach with the enemy will be more favorable to you than such a policy. If you study history carefully and analyze contemporary events, you will find that for every occasion on which such a policy has paid off there have been innumerable occasions when it has failed. A monarchy or a republic that is keen to expand cannot hope for a better opportunity to occupy a city or a region than to receive a request to send one of its armies to defend it. While someone who is so keen to acquire new territory that he calls on such assistance, not merely to defend himself, but to attack someone else, is trying to acquire territory he cannot hope to hold, that can easily be taken from him by the ally that acquires it for him.

Yet men are so eaten up with ambition that in their eagerness to get something they want here and now, they do not pause to think about the evil consequences they are storing up for themselves in the not-too-distant future. Neither do they pay attention to the examples provided by ancient history on this subject and on the others discussed in this book; for if they paid attention they would see that the more generous a state appears to be towards its neighbors, and the more it seems to have no interest at all in gobbling them up, the more likely it is to be successful in taking them over, as I will point out below in discussing the case of the Capuans.

Chapter 29

On how fortune blinds men's minds when she does not want them to thwart her plans.

If you will think sensibly about how people's lives are shaped, you will see that often events and accidents occur against which the heavens were determined we should have no protection. Seeing this sort of thing happened to the Romans, who were so skillful

[virtù], pious, and well-organized, it is not surprising that it happens much more often to cities or regions who lack these advantages. Because this subject is a rather good one if one wants to show the influence of the heavens in human affairs, Livy discusses it at length and most eloquently.[45]

He says that, because the heavens had some reason for wanting the Romans to recognize their power, they first made those Fabii who had been sent as ambassadors to the French make mistakes, with the result that their efforts served to incite the French to make war against the Romans, and then they ensured the Romans fell way below their normal standards when it came to making preparations for war. Fate had ensured that Camillus, who would have been able to handle such a difficult situation single-handedly, but for whose abilities there was no substitute, had been banished to Ardea. When the French began to march on Rome, the Romans, who had often appointed a dictator when faced with attacks by the Volsci and other hostile neighbors, failed to appoint one to deal with the French. Moreover, when it came to choosing soldiers, they chose poorly and without making any real effort. They were so slow to muster that they were only just in time to block the French advance where it had to cross the river Allia, a mere ten miles from Rome. There the tribunes pitched camp without taking any of the normal precautions. They did not reconnoiter the site, nor did they surround the camp with a ditch and palisade. In fact, they did not employ any precautions, either natural or supernatural. When it came to drawing up the battle lines they spread the ranks out so they were thin and weak. Neither soldiers nor officers lived up to the standards of the Roman army. The battle itself was bloodless, for the Romans fled before they were attacked, the bulk of the army making for Veii, while the rest withdrew to Rome.[46] When they arrived in Rome they did not even stop by their houses but made straight for the Capitol, with the result the senate did not give any thought to defending the city, did not even bother to close the gates, but some of them fled, and others went with the rest into the

45. [Livy, bk. 5, chs. 37–38.]
46. [390 B.C.]

Capitol. However, when it came to defending the Capitol, they finally began to get organized. They did not hamper the defense by admitting people who would be useless, while they stockpiled all the grain they could collect so they could withstand a siege. Of the vast numbers of those who were useless—the old, women, and children—the majority fled into the surrounding countryside, while the rest remained in Rome at the mercy of the French.

Anyone who read about all the Romans had achieved over the preceding years and then came to read about these events, would be quite incapable of believing these were the same people. When Livy has described this whole series of errors, he concludes with the remark: "So one can see the extent to which fortune will blind men's minds when she does not want them to deflect her onward momentum."[47] This conclusion is as true as could be. It follows that men who regularly encounter extreme adversity or have the habit of success deserve less praise or less blame than one might think. For usually you will find they have been led to either tragedy or triumph because the heavens have pushed them decisively either one way or the other, either making it easy or virtually impossible for them to be able to act effectively [*virtuosamente*].

One thing fortune does is select someone, when she wants him to accomplish great things, who will be sufficiently bold and skillful [*virtù*] to recognize the opportunites she makes for him. In the same way, when she wants to bring about someone's destruction, she chooses a man who will help bring about his own undoing. If there is someone around who might get in her way, then she kills him, or deprives him of all the resources he would need to do any good. You can see this clearly in Livy's account. Fortune, in order to make Rome all the greater and build her up to the power she eventually attained, judged it necessary to give her a nasty shock (I will describe all that happened at length at the beginning of the next book), but did not want, at this point, to destroy her completely. That is why she had Camillus banished, but not killed; had Rome seized by the enemy, but not the Capitol; determined that the Romans did

nothing right when it came to defending Rome, but did everything right when it came to defending the Capitol. So that Rome would fall to the enemy, she ensured the bulk of the forces that had been defeated at the Allia would make for Veii, thus destroying any opportunity of defending the city. But in bringing this about she also laid the ground for Rome's liberation. A complete Roman army stood ready at Veii, and Camillus was nearby at Ardea. So they were able to make a determined effort to liberate their homeland under the command of a general whose reputation was not tarnished by defeat but was unblemished.

Perhaps I should add, in support of what I have said, an example from modern history; but I do not think it necessary, for this one example should be sufficient to satisfy anyone, and so I will move on. But I want to repeat that this is absolutely true, and all history testifies to it. Men can help fortune along, but they cannot resist it; they can swim with the tide, but they can never make headway against it. Of course, they should never give up, for they can never know what fortune has in mind. Her path is often crooked, her route obscure. So there is always reason to hope, and if one has hope one will never give up, no matter how hostile fortune may be, no matter how dreadful the situation in which one finds oneself.

BOOK III

Chapter 1[48]

On how, if you want a [political or religious] movement or a state to survive for long you must repeatedly bring it back to its founding principles.

It is certainly true that everything in the world has a natural life expectancy. But usually creatures live out the full cycle the heavens have determined for them only if they do not abuse their bodies, but keep them in such good shape they either remain unchanged, or if they change it is to get healthier, not weaker. Now my subject is collective bodies, such as republics,

---

47. [Livy, bk. 5, ch. 37.]

political parties, and religious sects, and my claim is that those changes are healthy that bring them back to their founding principles. Consequently, the best constructed organizations, those that will live longest, are those that are organized in such a way they can be frequently reformed; it amounts to the same thing if, for some external reason independent of their structure, reform is thrust upon them. It is clearer than daylight that if organizations are not reformed they cannot survive.

The way to reform an organization is, as I just said, to bring it back to its founding principles. For all political and religious movements, all republics and monarchies must have some good in them at the start. Otherwise, they would not be able to start out with a favorable reputation, nor would they be able to make progress in the early days. But as time goes by, that original goodness becomes corrupted, and, unless something happens that brings them back to first principles, corruption inevitably destroys the organization. Medical doctors say, speaking of the human body, "Everyday it takes in something that, in the end, requires treatment."

This return to founding principles, in the case of states, occurs either through some external accident or through domestic wisdom. As for the first, you can see it was necessary for Rome to fall to the French[49] if she was to have a hope of being reborn; being reborn, she acquired new strength and new skill [virtù], committing herself once again to respect for religion and justice, which, in the old Rome, had begun to be corrupted. This is very evident in Livy's history, when he points out that when they marched out with an army against the French and when they created tribunes with consular authority they did not perform any religious ceremonies. Even more strikingly, not only did they not punish the three Fabii who, contrary to the law of nations, had attacked the French, but they appointed them tribunes. One can reasonably presume the other sound laws that had been introduced by Romulus and by Rome's other wise rulers were increasingly treated with less respect than was reasonable and, indeed, necessary if Rome was to preserve political freedom.

Then this shock came from the outside so that all the institutions of the city could be renewed. It was made evident to the people that it was not only necessary to uphold religion and justice, but also to have respect for good citizens and to place more value on their judgment [virtù] than on the interests they felt they would have to sacrifice if they adopted their policies. And this is, indeed, exactly what happened, for as soon as Rome recovered, they renewed all her old religious ordinances; punished the Fabii for beginning a conflict contrary to the law of nations; and moreover held the judgment [virtù] and goodness of Camillus in such esteem the senate and everyone else put their jealousy to one side and entrusted to him the leadership of the republic.

So it is necessary, as I have said, that men who live together in any sort of institution regularly take stock of themselves, either as a result of external shocks or of internal factors. As far as this second type of reform is concerned, it best arises either as a result of a legal requirement that the members of an institution frequently take stock, or because one good man appears among them and, by his own example and his skillful [virtuose] policies, has the same effect as such a law. So this improvement takes place in a state, either because of the skill [virtù] of a man, or because of the effect [virtù] of a law.

As far as legal authorities are concerned, the institutions that drew the Roman republic back to its first principles were the tribunes of the people, the censors, together with all those laws that were a barrier to the ambition and the insolence of men. Such laws and institutions have to be given life through the will power [virtù] of an individual citizen who determinedly sets out to enforce the laws despite the powerful opposition of those who seek to ignore them. Among such cases of the laws' being enforced, prior to the sack of Rome by the French, one may note the death of the sons of Brutus, the death of the ten citizens, and that of Maelius the corn dealer.[50] After the sack of Rome, there is the death of Manlius Capitolinus, the death of the son of Manlius Torquatus, the prosecution brought by Papirius Cursor against Fabius, his commander of cavalry, and the charges

49. [In 390 B.C.]

50. [Respectively 509 B.C.; 449 B.C. (in fact the Ten were only exiled); 440 B.C.]

brought against the Scipios.[51] These cases involved going to extremes and caught people's attention. Whenever such a case occurred, it made men take stock; and as they became less common there was more opportunity for men to become corrupt, and reform became accompanied by ever greater danger and ever increasing conflict. For between two such dramatic legal decisions no more than ten years ought to go by. If the gap is longer men begin to develop bad habits and to break the laws; and if nothing happens to remind them of the penalties and to reawaken their sense of fear, there are soon so many lawbreakers springing up all over the place that it is no longer possible to punish them without endangering stability.

Those who were in charge of the Florentine state from 1434 to 1494[52] used to say, when discussing this subject, that it was necessary to retake power every five years, otherwise power would slip away from them. What they meant by "retaking power" was inspiring the same fear and terror in their subjects they had inspired when they first came to power, when they had set out to crush those who had acted badly by the standards of the new system of government. But as the memory of that clampdown faded, people began to be emboldened to attempt innovations and to speak ill of their rulers. So it was necessary to provide a remedy by bringing matters back to first principles.

This reform of governments according to their first principles is sometimes the result of the simple virtue [*virtù*] of one man, without being based on any law that inspires him to act rigorously; such men are so respected and admired that good men want to imitate them, and bad men are ashamed to live according to principles at odds with theirs. The individuals in Roman history who are notable for having had such good effects are Horatius Cocles, Scaevola, Fabricius, the two Decii, Regulus Attilius, along with a few others. By their remarkable and virtuous [*virtuosi*] examples they had almost the same effects on their fellow citizens as good laws and good institutions had.

If the individual instances of law enforcement I have mentioned, together with the examples provided by admirable individuals, had occurred at least every ten years in Rome, then it would certainly have been the case that Rome would never have become corrupt. But as both punishments and role models became less frequent, corruption began to spread. After Marcus Regulus there is not a single exemplary individual to be found. It is true the two Catos came along later, but there was such a long gap between Regulus and the first Cato, and then between the first and the second, and they were such isolated instances, that they could not by their own good example have any good effects.[53] This is particularly true of the second Cato, who found the city very generally corrupted and could not by his own example improve the behavior of his fellow citizens. This is all I need to say about republics.

But we should consider movements. We can see similar reforms are necessary if we take the example of our own religion. If this had not been brought back to first principles by St. Francis and St. Dominic it would have completely died away.[54] They, by living lives of poverty and imitating the life of Christ, renewed religion in the minds of men at a time when they had lost all commitment to it. The new orders they founded were so effective that it is only because of them that the dishonesty of the prelates and of the hierarchy does not destroy the church, for the friars continue to live in poverty and have such influence with the people as a result of hearing confession and preaching that they persuade them it is wrong to criticize evil, and it is right quietly to obey the church authorities, and, if they make mistakes, to leave their punishment to God. And so the clergy do as much harm as they can, for they do not fear a punishment they do not see and in which they do not believe. Thus, this reform movement preserved, and continues to preserve, the Christian religion.

Kingdoms, too, need to renew themselves and to reform their laws so they accord with their original principles. One can see what a good effect this policy has in the Kingdom of France. That kingdom lives

51. [Respectively 384 B.C.; 340 B.C.; 326 B.C.; and 189 B.C., the two being Scipio Africanus and his brother Lucius.]

52. [The Medici.]

53. [Regulus died in 250 B.C., Cato the Elder in 149 B.C., Cato the Younger in 46 B.C.]

54. [St. Francis founded the Franciscans in 1210; St. Dominic the Dominicans in 1216.]

according to its laws and respects its institutions more than any other kingdom. These laws and institutions are upheld by the *parlements*, and especially the *Parlement* of Paris. They give them new life every time they enforce them against a prince of the kingdom or condemn the king in one of their judgments. So far, the *parlements* have maintained their role by being determined enforcers of the laws whenever the nobility break them; but should they ever leave first one and then more and more noblemen unpunished, the result would certainly be that they would either have to put things right by provoking a major crisis, or the whole system of government would break down.

One can therefore conclude that there is nothing more essential in any form of communal life, whether of a movement, a kingdom, or a republic, than to restore to it the reputation it had when it was first founded, and to strive to ensure there are either good institutions or good men who can bring this about, so that one is not dependent on having some external intervention before reform can occur. For although an external intervention is sometimes the best remedy, as it proved for Rome, it is so dangerous there are no circumstances in which one should hope for it.

In order to show you how the deeds of individuals made Rome great and had numerous good consequences for that city, I will turn to an account of individual leaders and a commentary on their actions. This third and final section of my commentary on the first ten books of Livy will deal with this subject. And although the kings of Rome did great and remarkable things, nevertheless, since history discusses them at length, I will leave them to one side and will say nothing more about them, except for mentioning one or two things they did in pursuit of their own private interests. I will begin, instead, by talking about Brutus, the father of Roman liberty.

Chapter 9

On how you have to change with the times, if you want always to have good fortune.

I have pointed out several times that whether men have good or bad fortune depends on whether they adjust their style of behavior to suit the times. It is evident that some men set about doing what they want impetuously, while others act cautiously and carefully. Both styles are mistaken, for in both one behaves inappropriately, and deviates from the best path. But, as I have said, the mistake is less important and you will still encounter good fortune if the times are suited to your style and if you always act as nature urges you.

Everyone knows how Fabius Maximus proceeded cautiously and carefully, keeping his army out of battle and avoiding any display of Roman audacity.[55] It was his good fortune that his style corresponded well to the needs of the time. For Hannibal was a young man when he marched into Italy, things were going his way, and he had already defeated the Roman armies twice. Since Rome had lost most of her best soldiers and was demoralized, she was extremely lucky to acquire a general whose delay and caution slowed the enemy down. Nor could Fabius have found himself in circumstances better suited to his style, with the result that he was covered in glory. It is evident Fabius acted in this way because it came naturally to him, not because he had made a conscious choice. For when Scipio wanted to invade Africa with the Roman armies in order to bring the war to an end, Fabius was strongly opposed to his plan.[56] He could not break with his past habits and adopt a different style. If it had been left to him, Hannibal would still be in Italy, for he could not recognize that circumstances had changed, and he needed to change his style of warfare. If Fabius had been King of Rome he might well have lost the war, for he would not have known to change his style of behavior as the times changed. But he was born in a republic, where numerous citizens, all with different temperaments, had a say. So, just as they had Fabius to lead them when he was the best man to avoid defeat, so they had Scipio when he was the best man to ensure victory.

One can see a republic should survive longer and should more frequently have fortune on its side, than a monarchy, for a republic can adapt itself more easily to changing circumstances because it can call on citizens of differing characters. Someone who is used

---

55. [After the defeat at Lake Trasimene in 217 B.C.]
56. [In 205 B.C.]

to proceeding in a particular way will never change, as I have already pointed out, so it is inevitable that when the times change and become unsuitable for his particular style, he will be ruined.

Piero Soderini, as I have already mentioned on several occasions, always proceeded with kindness and patience. Both he and his country did well while the times favored his style of behavior; but when the circumstances were such that he needed to stop being patient and kind, he did not know how to do it; and he and his country were destroyed. Julius II, during the whole time he was pope, proceeded impatiently and always acted in the heat of the moment; and, since the times suited such behavior, he succeeded in all his undertakings. But in other circumstances, when different policies were needed, he would inevitably have brought about his own downfall, for he would not have changed his style of behavior or pursued different policies.

There are two reasons why we are unable to change when we need to: In the first place, we cannot help being what nature has made us; in the second, if one style of behavior has worked well for us in the past, we cannot be persuaded we would be better off acting differently. The consequence is that one's fortune changes, for the times change, and one's behavior does not. Another consequence is that cities are destroyed, for the institutions of a republic are never modified to suit changing circumstances, as I have pointed out at length already. Change comes too late because it is too difficult to accomplish. In order to bring it about the whole society must feel endangered; it is not enough for just one individual to change his methods.

Since I have mentioned Fabius Maximus, who kept Hannibal at bay, I think I will discuss in the next chapter whether a general who is determined to engage the enemy in battle can be prevented from doing so by his opposite number.

THOMAS HOBBES

Thomas Hobbes (1588–1679) was born in Malmesbury on April 5, 1588, the son of a poor minor clergyman who abandoned his family when Hobbes was sixteen. According to Hobbes, his mother went into labor when she heard that the Spanish Armada was approaching, so that, as he put it, "fear and I were born twins together." This familiar tale indicates how Hobbes himself appreciated the central conjunction of mortal fear and human nature in his own thinking and in his life as well.

After excelling in classical languages and poetry as a youngster and studying at Oxford, Hobbes took a position in the household of William Lord Cavendish, the Earl of Devonshire. There and in similar positions throughout his life he served as secretary, tutor, and advisor. This was a common vocation for intellectuals in seventeenth-century England; John Locke was to play a similar role later in the century. From 1610 to 1615, Hobbes accompanied the Lord's son on the Grand Tour of Europe; he returned to the Continent in 1634–36 with Cavendish's grandson. On the early tour, Hobbes visited Venice and became acquainted with the tradition of classical rhetoric; later he would draw on this background as he considered the role of rhetoric in political argument. On the latter tour, he met the leading philosophers of the day, from Galileo to Pierre Gassendi and Marin Mersenne, who put him in touch with René Descartes, then in the Netherlands. By then Hobbes had already been captivated by the rigor of geometry, to which he added a fascination with the new science. During this period, then, Hobbes's interests turned from classical literature to contemporary science and its applications, especially optics and ballistics. In 1629 he had produced his first publication, a translation of Thucydides, whom he revered for his sense of prudence and his sensitivity to the dangers of democracy. By the end of 1640 his scientific thinking had matured and joined with his political interests, resulting in a draft of a large, systematic work which he called the *Elements of Law, Natural and Political*. Among other things, the *Elements* is a work that grounded politics in a conception of natural law derived in part from the Dutch political theorist Hugo Grotius, whose great work *The Laws of War and Peace* had been published in 1625.

In 1640 Charles I was forced to call two Parliaments, and events occurred that eventually would lead to the English Civil War. Hobbes's associations were with the King and his ministers, and hence, as tensions escalated, he feared for his life. In November he fled to France and remained there until 1651–52. In 1642 Hobbes published in Latin a reworked version of the political section of the *Elements* under the title *De Cive* (*Of the Citizen*), a work that was issued in England in an unauthorized translation in 1651, at about the same time that his first English and most famous work, *Leviathan*, appeared. The earlier sections of the *Elements*, *De Corpore* (*Of Matter*) and *De Homine* (*Of Man*), were not published until 1655 and 1658, respectively.

Leviathan has been influential far beyond the historical context of its writing and publication. In its first two parts Hobbes sketches his physics and psychology, outlines his famous account of the state of nature and its laws, develops his version of the social contract, and argues for an undivided sovereignty with all its functions, agencies, and prerogatives. These parts constitute one of the founding texts of modern moral and political theory.

But *Leviathan* does not end here. In parts three and four, Hobbes turns to issues of immediate historical concern. He attacks Roman Catholicism, Aristotelianism in the universities and in general intellectual culture, and the Anglican Church, while defending Erastianism, the doctrine of the political control of religion, and religious Independency, the movement that advocated the independence and control of individual congregations against the claims of a strong, central episcopacy. At the same time, Hobbes's materialism, exhibited especially in part four, seemed to many to imply atheism. It is no wonder that, with the publication of

Leviathan, Hobbes gained the reputation of a materialist and atheist and came to be known as the "beast of Malmesbury."

With *Leviathan*'s publication in 1651, Hobbes returned to England and once again to the service of the Earl of Devonshire. For the remainder of his long life he played the role of a prominent intellectual and controversialist. In the 1650s he confronted John Wallis, an important Presbyterian and mathematician, on a variety of religious and scientific matters, and in the 1660s he debated Robert Boyle on issues of physics and experimentation. During the Restoration, moreover, Hobbes was the subject of severe criticism for his defense of Independency and his abandonment of the Anglicanism renewed under Charles II. His final years, the decades of the 1660s and 1670s, were years of threat and fear, as his religious opponents massed against him. But before they could overtake him, illness did; Hobbes died on December 3, 1679, having found, as he said, a hole whereby to leave the world.

Recommended Readings

Baumgold, Deborah. *Hobbes's Political Theory.* Cambridge: Cambridge University Press, 1988.

Brown, K. C. (ed.). *Hobbes Studies.* Oxford: Oxford University Press, 1965.

Burns, James (ed.). *Cambridge History of Political Thought, 1450–1700.* Cambridge: Cambridge University Press, 1991.

Cranston, M., and R. S. Peters (eds.). *Hobbes and Rousseau.* Garden City: Doubleday, 1972.

Dietz, Mary G. (ed.). *Thomas Hobbes and Political Theory.* Lawrence: University of Kansas Press, 1990.

Gauthier, David. *The Logic of Leviathan.* Oxford: Oxford University Press, 1969.

Goldsmith, M. M. *Hobbes's Science of Politics.* New York: Columbia University Press, 1966.

Hampton, Jean. *Hobbes and the Social Contract Tradition.* Cambridge: Cambridge University Press, 1986.

Hood, F. C. *The Divine Politics of Thomas Hobbes.* Oxford: Oxford University Press, 1964.

Johnston, David. *The Rhetoric of Leviathan.* Princeton: Princeton University Press, 1986.

Kavka, Gregory. *Hobbesian Moral and Political Theory.* Princeton: Princeton University Press, 1986.

McNeilly, F. S. *The Anatomy of Leviathan.* London: Macmillan, 1968.

Macpherson, C. B. *The Political Theory of Possessive Individualism.* Oxford: Oxford University Press, 1962.

Martinich, A. P. *The Two Gods of Leviathan.* Cambridge: Cambridge University Press, 1992.

Martinich, A. P. *Thomas Hobbes.* New York: St. Martin's Press, 1997.

Martinich, A. P. *Hobbes: A Biography.* Cambridge: Cambridge University Press, 1999.

Oakeshott, Michael. *Hobbes on Civil Association.* Oxford: Blackwell's, 1975.

Pocock, J.G.A. "Time, History, and Eschatology in the Thought of Thomas Hobbes," in *Politics, Language, and Time.* New York: Atheneum, 1973.

Rogers, G.A.J., and Alan Ryan (eds.). *Perspectives on Thomas Hobbes.* Oxford: Oxford University Press, 1988.

Skinner, Quentin. "Conquest and Consent: Thomas Hobbes and the Engagement Controversy," in *The Interregnum: the Quest for Settlement.* ed. G. E. Aylmer. London: Macmillan, 1974, 79–98.

Skinner, Quentin. "The Ideological Context of Hobbes's Political Thought," *Historical Journal* 9 (1966), 286–317.

Skinner, Quentin. *Reason and Rhetoric in the Philosophy of Hobbes.* Cambridge: Cambridge University Press, 1996.

Sommerville, Johann P. *Thomas Hobbes: Political Ideas in Historical Context.* London: The Macmillan Press, 1992.

Sorell, T. *Hobbes.* London: Routledge, 1986.

Sorell, Tom (ed.). *The Cambridge Companion to Hobbes*. Cambridge: Cambridge University Press, 1996.

Strauss, Leo. *Natural Right and History*. Chicago: University of Chicago Press, 1953.

Strauss, Leo. *The Political Philosophy of Hobbes*. Oxford: Oxford University Press, 1936.

Tuck, Richard. *Hobbes*. Oxford: Oxford University Press, 1989.

Tuck, Richard. *Philosophy and Government 1572–1651*. Cambridge: Cambridge University Press, 1993.

Warrender, Richard. *The Political Philosophy of Hobbes*. Oxford: Oxford University Press, 1957.

Wolin, Sheldon. *Politics and Vision*. New York: Little, Brown and Co., 1960.

LEVIATHAN

THE CONTENTS OF THE CHAPTERS.

To My Most Honor'd Friend Mr. Francis Godolphin, Of Godolphin

Honor'd Sir,

The text of *Leviathan* reprinted here features modernized spelling and punctuation. Reprinted by arrangement with InteLex, Inc.

Your most worthy brother, Mr. *Sidney Godolphin,* when he lived, was pleased to think my studies something, and otherwise to oblige me, as you know, with real testimonies of his good opinion, great in themselves, and the greater for the worthiness of his person. For there is not any virtue that disposeth a man, either to the service of God or to the service of his country, to civil society or private friendship, that did not manifestly appear in his conversation, not as acquired by necessity or affected upon occasion, but inherent, and shining in a generous constitution of his nature. Therefore, in honour and gratitude to him, and with devotion to yourself, I humbly dedicate unto you this my discourse of Commonwealth.

I know not how the world will receive it, nor how it may reflect on those that shall seem to favour it. For in a way beset with those that contend, on one side for too great liberty, and on the other side for too much authority, 'tis hard to pass between the points of both unwounded. But yet, methinks, the endeavour to advance the civil power, should not be by the civil power condemned; nor private men, by reprehending it, declare they think that power too great. Besides, I speak not of the men, but (in the abstract) of the seat of power (like to those simple and unpartial creatures in the Roman Capitol, that with their noise defended those within it, not because they were they, but there), offending none, I think, but those without, or such within (if there be any such) as favour them.

That which perhaps may most offend are certain texts of Holy Scripture, alleged by me to other purpose than ordinarily they use to be by others. But I have done it with due submission, and also (in order to my subject) necessarily; for they are the outworks of the enemy, from whence they impugn the civil power. If notwithstanding this, you find my labour generally decried, you may be pleased to excuse yourself, and say, I am a man that love my own opinions, and think all true I say, that I honoured your brother, and honour you, and have presumed on that, to assume the title (without your knowledge) of being, as I am,

SIR,
Your most humble, and most obedient Servant,
THOMAS HOBBES.
Paris, April ¹⁵/₂₅, 1651.

THE INTRODUCTION

Nature (the art whereby God hath made and governs the world) is by the *art* of man, as in many other things, so in this also imitated, that it can make an artificial animal. For seeing life is but a motion of limbs, the beginning whereof is in some principal part within; why may we not say, that all *automata* (engines that move themselves by springs and wheels as doth a watch) have an artificial life? For what is the *heart*, but a *spring*; and the *nerves*, but so many *strings*; and the *joints*, but so many *wheels*, giving motion to the whole body, such as was intended by the artificer? *Art* goes yet further, imitating that rational and most excellent work of nature, *man*. For by art is created that great LEVIATHAN called a COMMONWEALTH, or STATE, (in Latin CIVITAS) which is but an artificial man; though of greater stature and strength than the natural, for whose protection and defence it was intended; and in which, the *sovereignty* is an artificial *soul*, as giving life and motion to the whole body; the *magistrates*, and other *officers* of judicature and execution, artificial *joints*; *reward* and *punishment* (by which fastened to the seat of the sovereignty every joint and member is moved to perform his duty) are the *nerves*, that do the same in the body natural; the *wealth* and *riches* of all the particular members, are the *strength*; *salus populi* (the *people's safety*) its *business*; *counsellors*, by whom all things needful for it to know are suggested unto it, are the *memory*; *equity*, and *laws*, an artificial *reason* and *will*; *concord*, *health*; *sedition*, *sickness*; and *civil war*, *death*. Lastly, the *pacts* and *covenants*, by which the parts of this body politic were at first made, set together, and united, resemble that *fiat*, or the *let us make man*, pronounced by God in the creation.

To describe the nature of this artificial man, I will consider

First, the *matter* thereof, and the *artificer*; both which is *man*.

Secondly, *how*, and by what *covenants* it is made; what are the *rights* and just *power* or *authority* of a sovereign; and what it is that *preserveth* and *dissolveth* it.

Thirdly, what is a *Christian commonwealth*.

Lastly, what is the *kingdom of darkness*.

Concerning the first, there is a saying much usurped of late, that *wisdom* is acquired, not by reading of *books*, but of *men*. Consequently whereunto, those persons, that for the most part can give no other proof of being wise, take great delight to show what they think they have read in men, by uncharitable censures of one another behind their backs. But there is another saying not of late understood, by which they might learn truly to read one another, if they would take the pains; and that is, *nosce teipsum, read thyself*: which was not meant, as it is now used, to countenance, either the barbarous state of men in power, towards their inferiors; or to encourage men of low degree, to a saucy behaviour towards their betters; but to teach us, that for the similitude of the thoughts and passions of one man, to the thoughts and passions of another, whosoever looketh into himself, and considereth what he doth, when he does *think, opine, reason, hope, fear,* &c. and upon what grounds; he shall thereby read and know, what are the thoughts and passions of all other men upon the like occasions. I say the similitude of passions, which are the same in all men, *desire, fear, hope,* &c; not the similitude of the objects of the passions, which are the things *desired, feared, hoped,* &c: for these the constitution individual, and particular education, do so vary, and they are so easy to be kept from our knowledge, that the characters of man's heart, blotted and confounded as they are with dissembling, lying, counterfeiting, and erroneous doctrines, are legible only to him that searcheth hearts. And though by men's actions we do discover their design sometimes; yet to do it without comparing them with our own, and distinguishing all circumstances, by which the case may come to be altered, is to decypher without a key, and be for the most part deceived, by too much trust, or by too much diffidence; as he that reads, is himself a good or evil man.

But let one man read another by his actions never so perfectly, it serves him only with his acquaintance, which are but few. He that is to govern a whole nation, must read in himself, not this or that particular man; but mankind: which though it be hard to do, harder than to learn any language or science; yet when I shall have set down my own reading orderly, and perspicuously, the pains left another, will be only to consider, if he also find not the same in himself.

For this kind of doctrine admitteth no other demonstration.

PART 1
OF MAN

Chapter 1

Of Sense

Concerning the thoughts of man, I will consider them first *singly*, and afterwards in *train*, or dependence upon one another. *Singly*, they are every one a *representation* or *appearance*, of some quality, or other accident of a body without us; which is commonly called an *object*. Which object worketh on the eyes, ears, and other parts of a man's body; and by diversity of working, produceth diversity of appearances.

The original of them all, is that which we call SENSE; (For there is no conception in a man's mind, which hath not at first, totally, or by parts, been begotten upon the organs of sense.) The rest are derived from that original.

To know the natural cause of sense, is not very necessary to the business now in hand; and I have elsewhere written of the same at large. Nevertheless, to fill each part of my present method, I will briefly deliver the same in this place.

The cause of sense, is the external body, or object, which presseth the organ proper to each sense, either immediately, as in the taste and touch; or mediately, as in seeing, hearing, and smelling: which pressure, by the mediation of nerves, and other strings and membranes of the body, continued inwards to the brain and heart, causeth there a resistance, or counter-pressure, or endeavour of the heart, to deliver it self: which endeavour, because *outward*, seemeth to be some matter without. And this *seeming*, or, *fancy*, is that which men call *sense*; and consisteth, as to the eye, in a *light*, or *colour figured*; to the ear, in a *sound*; to the nostril, in an *odour*; to the tongue and palate, in a *savour*; and to the rest of the body, in *heat, cold, hardness, softness,* and such other qualities as we discern by *feeling*. All which qualities called *sensible*, are in the object, that causeth them, but so many several motions of the matter, by which it presseth our organs diversely. Neither in us that are pressed, are they any thing else, but divers motions; (for motion produceth nothing but motion.) But their appearance to us is fancy, the same waking, that dreaming. And as pressing, rubbing, or striking the eye, makes us fancy a light; and pressing the ear, produceth a din; so do the bodies also we see, or hear, produce the same by their strong, though unobserved action. For if those colours and sounds were in the bodies, or objects that cause them, they could not be severed from them, as by glasses, and in echoes by reflection, we see they are; where we know the thing we see, is in one place; the appearance in another. And though at some certain distance, the real and very object seem invested with the fancy it begets in us; yet still the object is one thing, the image or fancy is another. So that sense in all cases, is nothing else but original fancy, caused (as I have said) by the pressure, that is, by the motion, of external things upon our eyes, ears, and other organs thereunto ordained.

But the philosophy-schools, through all the universities of Christendom, grounded upon certain texts of *Aristotle*, teach another doctrine; and say, for the cause of *vision*, that the thing seen, sendeth forth on every side a *visible species* (in English) a *visible show*, *apparition*, or *aspect*, or *a being seen*; the receiving whereof into the eye, is *seeing*. And for the cause of *hearing*, that the thing heard, sendeth forth an *audible species*, that is, an *audible aspect*, or *audible being seen*; which entering at the ear, maketh *hearing*. Nay for the cause of *understanding* also, they say the thing understood, sendeth forth *intelligible species*, that is, an *intelligible being seen*; which coming into the understanding, makes us understand. I say not this, as disapproving the use of universities: but because I am to speak hereafter of their office in a commonwealth, I must let you see on all occasions by the way, what things would be amended in them; amongst which the frequency of insignificant speech is one.

Chapter 2

Of Imagination

That when a thing lies still, unless somewhat else stir it, it will lie still for ever, is a truth that no man doubts of. But that when a thing is in motion, it will eternally be in motion, unless somewhat else stay it, though the reason be the same, (namely, that nothing can change it self,) is not so easily assented to. For men measure, not only other men, but all other things, by themselves: and because they find themselves subject after motion to pain, and lassitude, think every thing else grows weary of motion, and seeks repose of its own accord; little considering, whether it be not some other motion, wherein that desire of rest they find in themselves, consisteth. From hence it is, that the schools say, heavy bodies fall downwards, out of an appetite to rest, and to conserve their nature in that place which is most proper for them; ascribing appetite and knowledge of what is good for their conservation, (which is more than man has) to things inanimate, absurdly.

When a body is once in motion, it moveth (unless something else hinder it) eternally; and whatsoever hindreth it, cannot in an instant, but in time, and by degrees quite extinguish it: And as we see in the water, though the wind cease, the waves give not over rolling for a long time after; so also it happeneth in that motion, which is made in the internal parts of a man, then, when he sees, dreams, &c. For after the object is removed, or the eye shut, we still retain an image of the thing seen, though more obscure than when we see it. And this is it, the Latins call *imagination*, from the image made in seeing; and apply the same, though improperly, to all the other senses. But the Greeks call it *fancy*; which signifies *appearance*, and is as proper to one sense, as to another. IMAGINATION therefore is nothing but *decaying sense*; and is found in men, and many other living creatures, as well sleeping, as waking.

The decay of sense in men waking, is not the decay of the motion made in sense; but an obscuring of it, in such manner as the light of the sun obscureth the light of the stars; which stars do no less exercise their virtue, by which they are visible, in the day, than in the night. But because amongst many strokes, which our eyes, ears, and other organs receive from external bodies, the predominant only is sensible; therefore the light of the sun being predominant, we are not affected with the action of the stars. And any object being removed from our eyes, though the impression it made in us remain; yet other objects more present succeeding, and working on us, the imagination of

object → sense → imagination/memory → understanding
↳ train of thought → remembrance → foresight/wisdom
↳ speech → definitions

Leviathan, Pt. 1, Ch. 2   555

the past is obscured, and made weak, as the voice of a man is in the noise of the day. From whence it followeth, that the longer the time is, after the sight or sense of any object, the weaker is the imagination. For the continual change of man's body destroys in time the parts which in sense were moved: so that distance of time, and of place, hath one and the same effect in us. For as at a great distance of place, that which we look at appears dim, and without distinction of the smaller parts; and as voices grow weak, and inarticulate: so also, after great distance of time, our imagination of the past is weak; and we lose (for example) of cities we have seen, many particular streets, and of actions, many particular circumstances. This *decaying sense*, when we would express the thing it self, (I mean *fancy* itself,) we call *imagination*, as I said before: but when we would express the *decay*, and signify that the sense is fading, old, and past, it is called *memory*. So that *imagination* and *memory* are but one thing, which for divers considerations hath divers names.

Much memory, or memory of many things, is called *experience*. Again, imagination being only of those things which have been formerly perceived by sense, either all at once, or by parts at several times; the former, (which is the imagining the whole object, as it was presented to the sense) is *simple imagination*; as when one imagineth a man, or horse, which he hath seen before. The other is *compounded*; as when from the sight of a man at one time, and of a horse at another, we conceive in our mind a Centaur. So when a man compoundeth the image of his own person, with the image of the actions of another man; as when a man imagines himself a *Hercules* or an *Alexander*, (which happeneth often to them that are much taken with reading of romances) it is a compound imagination, and properly but a fiction of the mind. There be also other imaginations that rise in men, (though waking) from the great impression made in sense: as from gazing upon the sun, the impression leaves an image of the sun before our eyes a long time after; and from being long and vehemently attent upon geometrical figures, a man shall in the dark, (though awake) have the images of lines and angles before his eyes: which kind of fancy hath no particular name; as being a thing that doth not commonly fall into men's discourse.

The imaginations of them that sleep are those we call *dreams*. And these also (as all other imaginations) have been before, either totally or by parcels in the sense. And because in sense, the brain and nerves, which are the necessary organs of sense, are so benumbed in sleep, as not easily to be moved by the action of external objects, there can happen in sleep no imagination; and therefore no dream, but what proceeds from the agitation of the inward parts of man's body; which inward parts, for the connexion they have with the brain, and other organs, when they be distempered, do keep the same in motion; whereby the imaginations there formerly made, appear as if a man were waking; saving that the organs of sense being now benumbed, so as there is no new object, which can master and obscure them with a more vigorous impression, a dream must needs be more clear, in this silence of sense, than are our waking thoughts. And hence it cometh to pass, that it is a hard matter, and by many thought impossible to distinguish exactly between sense and dreaming. For my part, when I consider that in dreams, I do not often, nor constantly think of the same persons, places, objects, and actions that I do waking; nor remember so long a train of coherent thoughts, dreaming, as at other times; and because waking I often observe the absurdity of dreams, but never dream of the absurdities of my waking thoughts; I am well satisfied, that being awake, I know I dream not; though when I dream I think myself awake.

And seeing dreams are caused by the distemper of some of the inward parts of the body; divers distempers must needs cause different dreams. And hence it is, that lying cold breedeth dreams of fear, and raiseth the thought and image of some fearful object (the motion from the brain to the inner parts, and from the inner parts to the brain being reciprocal;) and that as anger causeth heat in some parts of the body, when we are awake; so when we sleep the over heating of the same parts causeth anger, and raiseth up in the brain the imagination of an enemy. In the same manner, as natural kindness, when we are awake, causeth desire; and desire makes heat in certain other parts of the body; so also, too much heat in those parts, while we sleep, raiseth in the brain an imagination of some kindness shown. In sum, our dreams are the reverse of our waking imaginations; the motion when we are awake, beginning at one end; and when we dream, at another.

The most difficult discerning of a man's dream, from his waking thoughts, is then, when by some accident we observe not that we have slept: which is easy to happen to a man full of fearful thoughts; and whose conscience is much troubled; and that sleepeth, without the circumstances, of going to bed, or putting off his clothes, as one that noddeth in a chair. For he that taketh pains, and industriously lays himself to sleep, in case any uncouth and exorbitant fancy come unto him, cannot easily think it other than a dream. We read of *Marcus Brutus*, (one that had his life given him by *Julius Caesar*, and was also his favourite, and notwithstanding murdered him), how at *Philippi*, the night before he gave battle to *Augustus Caesar*, he saw a fearful apparition, which is commonly related by historians as a vision; but considering the circumstances, one may easily judge to have been but a short dream. For sitting in his tent, pensive and troubled with the horror of his rash act, it was not hard for him, slumbering in the cold, to dream of that which most affrighted him; which fear, as by degrees it made him wake; so also it must needs make the apparition by degrees to vanish; and having no assurance that he slept, he could have no cause to think it a dream, or any thing but a vision. And this is no very rare accident; for even they that be perfectly awake, if they be timorous, and superstitious, possessed with fearful tales, and alone in the dark, are subject to the like fancies; and believe they see spirits and dead men's ghosts walking in churchyards; whereas it is either their fancy only, or else the knavery of such persons, as make use of such superstitious fear, to pass disguised in the night, to places they would not be known to haunt.

From this ignorance of how to distinguish dreams, and other strong fancies, from vision and sense, did arise the greatest part of the religion of the Gentiles in time past, that worshipped satyrs, fawns, nymphs, and the like; and now-a-days the opinion that rude people have of fairies, ghosts, and goblins, and of the power of witches. For as for witches, I think not that their witchcraft is any real power; but yet that they are justly punished, for the false belief they have, that they can do such mischief, joined with their purpose to do it if they can: their trade being nearer to a new religion than to a craft or science. And for fairies, and walking ghosts, the opinion of them has I think been on purpose, either taught, or not confuted, to keep in credit the use of exorcism, of crosses, of holy water, and other such inventions of ghostly men. Nevertheless, there is no doubt, but God can make unnatural apparitions: But that he does it so often, as men need to fear such things, more than they fear the stay, or change, of the course of nature, which he also can stay, and change, is no point of Christian faith. But evil men under pretext that God can do any thing, are so bold as to say any thing when it serves their turn, though they think it untrue; it is the part of a wise man, to believe them no further, than right reason makes that which they say, appear credible. If this superstitious fear of spirits were taken away, and with it, prognostics from dreams, false prophecies, and many other things depending thereon, by which, crafty ambitious persons abuse the simple people, men would be much more fitted than they are for civil obedience.

And this ought to be the work of the schools: but they rather nourish such doctrine. For (not knowing what imagination, or the senses are), what they receive, they teach: some saying, that imaginations rise of themselves, and have no cause; others, that they rise most commonly from the will; and that good thoughts are blown (inspired) into a man by God, and evil thoughts by the Devil; or that good thoughts are poured (infused) into a man by God, and evil ones by the Devil. Some say the senses receive the species of things, and deliver them to the common sense; and the common sense delivers them over to the fancy, and the fancy to the memory, and the memory to the judgment, like handing of things from one to another, with many words making nothing understood.

The imagination that is raised in man (or any other creature indued with the faculty of imagining) by words, or other voluntary signs, is that we generally call *understanding*; and is common to man and beast. For a dog by custom will understand the call, or the rating of his master; and so will many other beasts. That understanding which is peculiar to man, is the understanding not only his will, but his conceptions and thoughts, by the sequel and contexture of the names of things into affirmations, negations, and other forms of speech; and of this kind of understanding I shall speak hereafter.

Chapter 3

Of the Consequence or Train of Imaginations

By *Consequence*, or TRAIN of thoughts, I understand that succession of one thought to another, which is called (to distinguish it from discourse in words) *mental discourse*.

When a man thinketh on any thing whatsoever, his next thought after, is not altogether so casual as it seems to be. Not every thought to every thought succeeds indifferently. But as we have no imagination, whereof we have not formerly had sense, in whole, or in parts; so we have no transition from one imagination to another, whereof we never had the like before in our senses. The reason whereof is this. All fancies are motions within us, relics of those made in the sense: and those motions that immediately succeeded one another in the sense, continue also together after sense: insomuch as the former coming again to take place, and be predominant, the latter followeth, by coherence of the matter moved, in such manner, as water upon a plain table is drawn which way any one part of it is guided by the finger. But because in sense, to one and the same thing perceived, sometimes one thing, sometimes another succeedeth, it comes to pass in time, that in the imagining of any thing, there is no certainty what we shall imagine next; only this is certain, it shall be something that succeeded the same before, at one time or another.

This train of thoughts, or mental discourse, is of two sorts. The first is *unguided, without design*, and inconstant; wherein there is no passionate thought, to govern and direct those that follow, to it self, as the end and scope of some desire, or other passion: in which case the thoughts are said to wander, and seem impertinent one to another, as in a dream. Such are commonly the thoughts of men, that are not only without company, but also without care of any thing; though even then their thoughts are as busy as at other times, but without harmony; as the sound which a lute out of tune would yield to any man; or in tune, to one that could not play. And yet in this wild ranging of the mind, a man may oft-times perceive the way of it, and the dependance of one thought upon another. For in a discourse of our present civil war, what could seem more impertinent, than to ask (as one did) what was the value of a Roman penny? Yet the coherence to me was manifest enough. For the thought of the war, introduced the thought of the delivering up the king to his enemies; the thought of that, brought in the thought of the delivering up of Christ; and that again the thought of the 30 pence, which was the price of that treason; and thence easily followed that malicious question, and all this in a moment of time; for thought is quick.

The second is more constant; as being *regulated* by some desire, and design. For the impression made by such things as we desire, or fear, is strong, and permanent, or, (if it cease for a time,) of quick return: so strong it is sometimes, as to hinder and break our sleep. From desire, ariseth the thought of some means we have seen produce the like of that which we aim at; and from the thought of that, the thought of means to that mean; and so continually, till we come to some beginning within our own power. And because the end, by the greatness of the impression, comes often to mind, in case our thoughts begin to wander, they are quickly again reduced into the way: which observed by one of the seven wise men, made him give men this precept, which is now worn out, *Respice finem*; that is to say, in all your actions, look often upon what you would have, as the thing that directs all your thoughts in the way to attain it.

The train of regulated thoughts is of two kinds; one, when of an effect imagined, we seek the causes, or means that produce it: and this is common to man and beast. The other is, when imagining any thing whatsoever, we seek all the possible effects, that can by it be produced; that is to say, we imagine what we can do with it, when we have it. Of which I have not at any time seen any sign, but in man only; for this is a curiosity hardly incident to the nature of any living creature that has no other passion but sensual, such as are hunger, thirst, lust, and anger. In sum, the discourse of the mind, when it is governed by design, is nothing but *seeking*, or the faculty of invention, which the Latins called *sagacitas*, and *solertia*; a hunting out of the causes, of some effect, present or past; or of the effects, of some present or past cause. Sometimes a man seeks what he hath lost; and from that place, and time, wherein he misses it, his mind runs back, from place to place, and time to time, to find where, and when he had it; that is to say, to find some certain, and limited time and place, in which to begin a method of seeking. Again, from thence, his thoughts run over the same places and times, to find what action, or other occasion might make him lose it. This we call *remembrance*, or calling to mind: the Latins call it *reminiscentia*, as it were a *re-conning* of our former actions.

Sometimes a man knows a place determinate, within the compass whereof he is to seek; and then his thoughts run over all the parts thereof, in the same manner as one would sweep a room, to find a jewel; or as a spaniel ranges the field, till he find a scent; or as a man should run over the alphabet, to start a rhyme.

Sometime a man desires to know the event of an action; and then he thinketh of some like action past, and the events thereof one after another; supposing like events will follow like actions. As he that foresees what will become of a criminal, recons what he has seen follow on the like crime before; having this order of thoughts, the crime, the officer, the prison, the judge, and the gallows. Which kind of thoughts, is called *foresight*, and *prudence*, or *providence*; and sometimes *wisdom*; though such conjecture, through the difficulty of observing all circumstances, be very fallacious. But this is certain; by how much one man has more experience of things past, than another; by so much also he is more prudent, and his expectations the seldomer fail him. The *present* only has a being in nature; things *past* have a being in the memory only, but things *to come* have no being at all; the *future* being but a fiction of the mind, applying the sequels of actions past, to the actions that are present; which with most certainty is done by him that has most experience; but not with certainty enough. And though it be called prudence, when the event answereth our expectation; yet in its own nature, it is but presumption. For the foresight of things to come, which is providence, belongs only to him by whose will they are to come. From him only, and supernaturally, proceeds prophecy. The best prophet naturally is the best guesser; and the best guesser, he that is

most versed and studied in the matters he guesses at: for he hath most *signs* to guess by.

A *sign* is the event antecedent of the consequent; and contrarily, the consequent of the antecedent, when the like consequences have been observed, before: and the oftener they have been observed, the less uncertain is the sign. And therefore he that has most experience in any kind of business, has most signs, whereby to guess at the future time; and consequently is the most prudent: and so much more prudent than he that is new in that kind of business, as not to be equalled by any advantage of natural and extemporary wit: though perhaps many young men think the contrary.

Nevertheless it is not prudence that distinguisheth man from beast. There be beasts, that at a year old observe more, and pursue that which is for their good, more prudently, than a child can do at ten.

As prudence is a *presumption* of the *future*, contracted from the *experience* of time *past*: so there is a presumption of things past taken from other things (not future but) past also. For he that hath seen by what courses and degrees, a flourishing state hath first come into civil war, and then to ruin; upon the sight of the ruins of any other state, will guess, the like war, and the like courses have been there also. But this conjecture, has the same uncertainty almost with the conjecture of the future; both being grounded only upon experience.

There is no other act of man's mind, that I can remember, naturally planted in him, so as to need no other thing, to the exercise of it, but to be born a man, and live with the use of his five senses. Those other faculties, of which I shall speak by and by, and which seem proper to man only, are acquired, and increased by study and industry; and of most men learned by instruction, and discipline; and proceed all from the invention of words, and speech. For besides sense, and thoughts, and the train of thoughts, the mind of man has no other motion; though by the help of speech, and method, the same faculties may be improved to such a height, as to distinguish men from all other living creatures.

Whatsoever we imagine is *finite*. Therefore there is no idea, or conception of any thing we call *infinite*. No man can have in his mind an image of infinite magnitude; nor conceive infinite swiftness, infinite time, or infinite force, or infinite power. When we say any thing is infinite, we signify only, that we are not able to conceive the ends, and bounds of the things named; having no conception of the thing, but of our own inability. And therefore the name of God is used, not to make us conceive him; (for he is *incomprehensible*; and his greatness, and power are unconceivable;) but that we may honour him. Also because whatsoever (as I said before,) we conceive, has been perceived first by sense, either all at once, or by parts; a man can have no thought, representing any thing, not subject to sense. No man therefore can conceive any thing, but he must conceive it in some place; and indued with some determinate magnitude; and which may be divided into parts; nor that any thing is all in this place, and all in another place at the same time; nor that two, or more things can be in one, and the same place at once: for none of these things ever have, or can be incident to sense; but are absurd speeches, taken upon credit (without any signification at all,) from deceived philosophers, and deceived, or deceiving schoolmen.

Chapter 4

Of Speech

The invention of *printing*, though ingenious, compared with the invention of *letters*, is no great matter. But who was the first that found the use of letters, is not known. He that first brought them into *Greece*, men say was *Cadmus*, the son of *Agenor*, king of Phoenicia. A profitable invention for continuing the memory of time past, and the conjunction of mankind, dispersed into so many, and distant regions of the earth; and withal difficult, as proceeding from a watchful observation of the divers motions of the tongue, palate, lips, and other organs of speech; whereby to make as many differences of characters, to remember them. But the most noble and profitable invention of all other, was that of SPEECH, consisting of *names* or *appellations*, and their connexion; whereby men register their thoughts; recall them when they are past; and also declare them one to another for mutual utility and conversation; without which, there had been amongst men, neither com-

monwealth, nor society, nor contract, nor peace, no more than amongst lions, bears, and wolves. The first author of speech was God himself, that instructed Adam how to name such creatures as he presented to his sight; for the Scripture goeth no further in this matter. But this was sufficient to direct him to add more names, as the experience and use of the creatures should give him occasion; and to join them in such manner by degrees, as to make himself understood; and so by succession of time, so much language might be gotten, as he had found use for; though not so copious, as an orator or philosopher has need of. For I do not find any thing in the Scripture, out of which, directly or by consequence can be gathered, that *Adam* was taught the names of all figures, numbers, measures, colours, sounds, fancies, relations; much less the names of words and speech, as *general, special, affirmative, negative, interrogative, optative, infinitive*, all which are useful; and least of all, of *entity, intentionality, quiddity*, and other insignificant words of the school.

But all this language gotten, and augmented by *Adam* and his posterity, was again lost at the tower of *Babel*, when, by the hand of God, every man was stricken, for his rebellion, with an oblivion of his former language. And being hereby forced to disperse themselves into several parts of the world, it must needs be, that the diversity of tongues that now is, proceeded by degrees from them, in such manner as need (the mother of all inventions) taught them; and in tract of time grew every where more copious.

The general use of speech, is to transfer our mental discourse, into verbal; or the train of our thoughts, into a train of words; and that for two commodities, whereof one is the registering of the consequences of our thoughts; which being apt to slip out of our memory, and put us to a new labour, may again be recalled, by such words as they were marked by. So that the first use of names is to serve for *marks*, or *notes* of remembrance. Another is, when many use the same words, to signify (by their connexion and order,) one to another, what they conceive, or think of each matter; and also what they desire, fear, or have any other passion for. And for this use they are called *signs*. Special uses of speech are these; first, to register, what by cogitation, we find to be the cause of any thing, present or past; and what we find things

Four Uses of Speech
(1) record knowledge, arts
560   (2) to communicate, counsel, teach   HOBBES
        (3) to communicate desires, request help
        (4) to entertain ourselves

present or past may produce, or effect: which in sum, is acquiring of arts. Secondly, to show to others that knowledge which we have attained; which is, to counsel and teach one another. Thirdly, to make known to others our wills, and purposes, that we may have the mutual help of one another. Fourthly, to please and delight ourselves and others, by playing with our words, for pleasure or ornament, innocently.

To these uses, there are also four correspondent abuses. First, when men register their thoughts wrong, by the inconstancy of the signification of their words; by which they register for their conceptions, that which they never conceived, and so deceive themselves. Secondly, when they use words metaphorically; that is, in other sense than that they are ordained for; and thereby deceive others. Thirdly, when by words they declare that to be their will, which is not. Fourthly, when they use them to grieve one another: for seeing nature hath armed living creatures, some with teeth, some with horns, and some with hands, to grieve an enemy, it is but an abuse of speech, to grieve him with the tongue, unless it be one whom we are obliged to govern; and then it is not to grieve, but to correct and amend.

The manner how speech serveth to the remembrance of the consequence of causes and effects, consisteth in the imposing of *names*, and the *connexion* of them.

Of names, some are *proper*, and singular to one only thing, as *Peter, John, this man, this tree*: and some are *common* to many things, as *man, horse, tree*; every of which though but one name, is nevertheless the name of divers particular things; in respect of all which together, it is called an *universal*; there being nothing in the world universal but names; for the things named, are every one of them individual and singular.

One universal name is imposed on many things, for their similitude in some quality, or other accident; and whereas a proper name bringeth to mind one thing only, universals recall any one of those many.

And of names universal, some are of more, and some of less extent; the larger comprehending the less large: and some again of equal extent, comprehending each other reciprocally. As for example, the name *body* is of larger signification than the word *man*, and comprehendeth it; and the names *man* and *rational*, are of equal extent, comprehending mutually one another. But here we must take notice, that by a name is not always understood, as in grammar, one only word; but sometimes by circumlocution many words together. For all these words, *he that in his actions observeth the laws of his country*, make but one name, equivalent to this one word, *just*.

By this imposition of names, some of larger, some of stricter signification, we turn the reckoning of the consequences of things imagined in the mind, into a reckoning of the consequences of appellations. For example, a man that hath no use of speech at all, (such as is born and remains perfectly deaf and dumb,) if he set before his eyes a triangle, and by it two right angles, (such as are the corners of a square figure,) he may by meditation compare and find, that the three angles of that triangle, are equal to those two right angles that stand by it. But if another triangle be shown him, different in shape from the former, he cannot know without a new labour, whether the three angles of that also be equal to the same. But he that hath the use of words, when he observes, that such equality was consequent, not to the length of the sides, nor to any other particular thing in his triangle; but only to this, that the sides were straight, and the angles three; and that that was all, for which he named it a triangle; will boldly conclude universally, that such equality of angles is in all triangles whatsoever; and register his invention in these general terms, *every triangle hath its three angles equal to two right angles*. And thus the consequence found in one particular, comes to be registered and remembered, as an universal rule, and discharges our mental reckoning, of time and place, and delivers us from all labour of the mind, saving the first, and makes that which was found true *here*, and *now*, to be true in *all times* and *places*.

But the use of words in registering our thoughts is in nothing so evident as in numbering. A natural fool that could never learn by heart the order of numeral words, as *one, two*, and *three*, may observe every stroke of the clock, and nod to it, or say *one, one, one*, but can never know what hour it strikes. And it seems, there was a time when those names of number were not in use; and men were fain to apply their fingers of one or both hands, to those things they desired to keep account of; and that thence it proceeded, that

Four Abuses of Speech
(1) inconsistant, shifting word meaning
(2) deceptive metaphorical language
(3) lies
(4) language designed to injure

Leviathan, Pt. 1, Ch. 4   561

now our numeral words are but ten, in any nation, and in some but five, and then they begin again. And he that can tell ten, if he recite them out of order, will lose himself, and not know when he has done. Much less will he be able to add, and subtract, and perform all other operations of arithmetic. So that without words there is no possibility of reckoning of numbers; much less of magnitudes, of swiftness, of force, and other things, the reckonings whereof are necessary to the being, or well-being of mankind.

When two names are joined together into a consequence, or affirmation, as thus, *a man is a living creature*; or thus, *if he be a man, he is a living creature*, if the latter name *living creature*, signify all that the former name *man* signifieth, then the affirmation, or consequence is *true*; otherwise *false*. For *true* and *false* are attributes of speech, not of things. And where speech is not, there is neither *truth* nor *falsehood*. *Error* there may be, as when we expect that which shall not be, or suspect what has not been: but in neither case can a man be charged with untruth.

Seeing then that *truth* consisteth in the right ordering of names in our affirmations, a man that seeketh precise *truth* had need to remember what every name he uses stands for, and to place it accordingly; or else he will find himself entangled in words, as a bird in lime twigs, the more he struggles the more belimed. And therefore in geometry, (which is the only science that it hath pleased God hitherto to bestow on mankind,) men begin at settling the significations of their words; which settling of significations they call *definitions*, and place them in the beginning of their reckoning.

By this it appears how necessary it is for any man that aspires to true knowledge, to examine the definitions of former authors; and either to correct them, where they are negligently set down, or to make them himself. For the errors of definitions multiply themselves according as the reckoning proceeds, and lead men into absurdities, which at last they see, but cannot avoid, without reckoning anew from the beginning, in which lies the foundation of their errors. From whence it happens, that they which trust to books do as they that cast up many little sums into a greater, without considering whether those little sums were rightly cast up or not; and at last finding the error visible, and not mistrusting their first

grounds, know not which way to clear themselves, but spend time in fluttering over their books; as birds that entering by the chimney, and finding themselves enclosed in a chamber, flutter at the false light of a glass window, for want of wit to consider which way they came in. So that in the right definition of names lies the first use of speech; which is the acquisition of science: and in wrong, or no definitions, lies the first abuse; from which proceed all false and senseless tenets; which make those men that take their instruction from the authority of books, and not from their own meditation, to be as much below the condition of ignorant men, as men endued with true science are above it. For between true science and erroneous doctrines, ignorance is in the middle. Natural sense and imagination are not subject to absurdity. Nature itself cannot err; and as men abound in copiousness of language, so they become more wise, or more mad than ordinary. Nor is it possible without letters for any man to become either excellently wise, or (unless his memory be hurt by disease or ill constitution of organs) excellently foolish. For words are wise men's counters, they do but reckon by them; but they are the money of fools, that value them by the authority of an *Aristotle*, a *Cicero*, or a *Thomas*, or any other doctor whatsoever, if but a man.

Subject to names, is whatsoever can enter into or be considered in an account, and be added one to another to make a sum, or subtracted one from another and leave a remainder. The Latins called accounts of money *rationes*, and accounting *ratiocinatio*; and that which we in bills or books of account call *items*, they call *nomina*, that is *names*; and thence it seems to proceed, that they extended the word *ratio* to the faculty of reckoning in all other things. The Greeks have but one word, λόγος, for both *speech* and *reason*; not that they thought there was no speech without reason, but no reasoning without speech: and the act of reasoning they called *syllogism*, which signifieth summing up of the consequences of one saying to another. And because the same things may enter into account for divers accidents, their names are (to show that diversity) diversly wrested and diversified. This diversity of names may be reduced to four general heads.

First, a thing may enter into account for *matter* or *body*; as *living, sensible, rational, hot, cold, moved,*

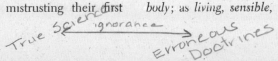
True Science → ignorance → Erroneous Doctrines

quiet; with all which names the word *matter*, or *body*, is understood; all such being names of matter.

Secondly, it may enter into account, or be considered, for some accident or quality, which we conceive to be in it; as for *being moved*, for *being so long*, for *being hot*, &c.; and then, of the name of the thing it self, by a little change or wresting, we make a name for that accident, which we consider; and for *living* put into the account *life*; for *moved*, *motion*; for *hot, heat*; for *long, length*, and the like: and all such names are the names of the accidents and properties by which one matter and body is distinguished from another. These are called *names abstract*, because severed (not from matter, but) from the account of matter.

Thirdly, we bring into account the properties of our own bodies, whereby we make such distinction; as when any thing is *seen* by us, we reckon not the thing it self, but the *sight*, the *colour*, the *idea* of it in the fancy: and when any thing is *heard*, we reckon it not, but the *hearing* or *sound* only, which is our fancy or conception of it by the ear; and such are names of fancies.

Fourthly, we bring into account, consider, and give names, to *names* themselves, and to *speeches*: For *general, universal, special, equivocal*, are names of names. And *affirmation, interrogation, commandment, narration, syllogism, sermon, oration*, and many other such, are names of speeches. And this is all the variety of names *positive*; which are put to mark somewhat which is in nature, or may be feigned by the mind of man, as bodies that are, or may be conceived to be; or of bodies, the properties that are, or may be feigned to be; or words and speech.

There be also other names, called *negative*, which are notes to signify that a word is not the name of the thing in question; as these words *nothing, no man, infinite, indocible, three want four*, and the like; which are nevertheless of use in reckoning, or in correcting of reckoning, and call to mind our past cogitations, though they be not names of any thing, because they make us refuse to admit of names not rightly used.

All other names are but insignificant sounds; and those of two sorts. One when they are new, and yet their meaning not explained by definition; whereof there have been abundance coined by schoolmen, and puzzled philosophers.

Another, when men make a name of two names, whose significations are contradictory and inconsistent; as this name, an *incorporeal body*, or (which is all one) an *incorporeal substance*, and a great number more. For whensoever any affirmation is false, the two names of which it is composed, put together and made one, signify nothing at all. For example, if it be a false affirmation to say *a quadrangle is round*, the word *round quadrangle* signifies nothing, but is a mere sound. So likewise, if it be false to say that virtue can be poured, or blown up and down, the words *in-poured virtue, in-blown virtue*, are as absurd and insignificant as a *round quadrangle*. And therefore you shall hardly meet with a senseless and insignificant word, that is not made up of some Latin or Greek names. A Frenchman seldom hears our Saviour called by the name of *parole*, but by the name of *verbe* often; yet *verbe* and *parole* differ no more, but that one is Latin, the other French.

When a man, upon the hearing of any speech, hath those thoughts which the words of that speech, and their connexion, were ordained and constituted to signify, then he is said to understand it; *understanding* being nothing else but conception caused by speech. And therefore if speech be peculiar to man (as for aught I know it is,) then is understanding peculiar to him also. And therefore of absurd and false affirmations, in case they be universal, there can be no understanding; though many think they understand then, when they do but repeat the words softly, or con them in their mind.

What kinds of speeches signify the appetites, aversions, and passions of man's mind; and of their use and abuse, I shall speak when I have spoken of the passions.

The names of such things as affect us, that is, which please and displease us, because all men be not alike affected with the same thing, nor the same man at all times, are in the common discourses of men of *inconstant* signification. For seeing all names are imposed to signify our conceptions, and all our affections are but conceptions, when we conceive the same things differently, we can hardly avoid different naming of them. For though the nature of that we conceive, be the same; yet the diversity of our reception of it, in respect of different constitutions of body, and prejudices of opinion, gives every thing a tincture of our different passions. And therefore in reasoning a man must take heed of words; which besides the signification of what we imagine of their nature, have a signification also of the nature, disposition, and interest of the speaker; such as are the names of virtues and vices; for one man calleth *wisdom*, what another calleth *fear*; and one *cruelty*, what another *justice*; one *prodigality*, what another *magnanimity*; and one *gravity*, what another *stupidity*, &c. And therefore such names can never be true grounds of any ratiocination. No more can metaphors, and tropes of speech; but these are less dangerous, because they profess their inconstancy; which the other do not.

Chapter 5

Of Reason and Science

When a man *reasoneth*, he does nothing else but conceive a sum total, from *addition* of parcels; or conceive a remainder, from *subtraction* of one sum from another; which (if it be done by words,) is conceiving of the consequence of the names of all the parts, to the name of the whole; or from the names of the whole and one part, to the name of the other part. And though in some things, (as in numbers,) besides *adding* and *subtracting*, men name other operations, as *multiplying* and *dividing*, yet they are the same; for multiplication, is but adding together of things equal; and division, but subtracting of one thing, as often as we can. These operations are not incident to numbers only, but to all manner of things that can be added together, and taken one out of another. For as arithmeticians teach to add and subtract in *numbers*; so the geometricians teach the same in *lines, figures* (solid and superficial,) *angles, proportions, times, degrees of swiftness, force, power*, and the like; the logicians teach the same in *consequences of words*; adding together *two names* to make an *affirmation*, and *two affirmations* to make a *syllogism*; and *many syllogisms* to make a *demonstration*; and from the *sum*, or *conclusion* of a *syllogism*, they subtract one *proposition* to find the other. Writers of politics add together *pactions* to find men's *duties*; and lawyers, *laws* and *facts*, to find what is *right* and *wrong* in

the actions of private men. In sum, in what matter soever there is place for *addition* and *subtraction*, there also is place for *reason*; and where these have no place, there *reason* has nothing at all to do.

Out of all which we may define, (that is to say determine,) what that is, which is meant by this word *reason*, when we reckon it amongst the faculties of the mind. For REASON, in this sense, is nothing but *reckoning* (that is, adding and subtracting) of the consequences of general names agreed upon for the *marking* and *signifying* of our thoughts; I say *marking* them when we reckon by ourselves, and *signifying*, when we demonstrate or approve our reckonings to other men.

And as in arithmetic, unpractised men must, and professors themselves may often err, and cast up false; so also in any other subject of reasoning, the ablest, most attentive, and most practised men may deceive themselves, and infer false conclusions; not but that reason itself is always right reason, as well as arithmetic is a certain and infallible art: but no one man's reason, nor the reason of any one number of men, makes the certainty; no more than an account is therefore well cast up, because a great many men have unanimously approved it. And therefore, as when there is a controversy in an account, the parties must by their own accord, set up for right reason, the reason of some arbitrator, or judge, to whose sentence they will both stand, or their controversy must either come to blows, or be undecided, for want of a right reason constituted by nature; so is it also in all debates of what kind soever. And when men that think themselves wiser than all others, clamour and demand right reason for judge, yet seek no more, but that things should be determined, by no other men's reason but their own, it is as intolerable in the society of men, as it is in play after trump is turned, to use for trump on every occasion, that suite whereof they have most in their hand. For they do nothing else, that will have every of their passions, as it comes to bear sway in them, to be taken for right reason, and that in their own controversies: bewraying their want of right reason, by the claim they lay to it.

The use and end of reason, is not the finding of the sum and truth of one, or a few consequences, remote from the first definitions, and settled significations of names, but to begin at these, and proceed

from one consequence to another. For there can be
no certainty of the last conclusion, without a certainty
of all those affirmations and negations, on which it
was grounded and inferred. As when a master of a
family, in taking an account, casteth up the sums of
all the bills of expense into one sum, and not regarding how each bill is summed up, by those that give
them in account; nor what it is he pays for; he advantages himself no more, than if he allowed the account
in gross, trusting to every of the accountants' skill and
honesty: so also in reasoning of all other things, he
that takes up conclusions on the trust of authors, and
doth not fetch them from the first items in every
reckoning, (which are the significations of names
settled by definitions,) loses his labour; and does not
know any thing, but only believeth.

When a man reckons without the use of words,
which may be done in particular things, (as when
upon the sight of any one thing, we conjecture what
was likely to have preceded, or is likely to follow upon
it;) if that which he thought likely to follow, follows
not, or that which he thought likely to have preceded
it, hath not preceded it, this is called *error*; to which
even the most prudent men are subject. But when
we reason in words of general signification, and fall
upon a general inference which is false, though it be
commonly called error, it is indeed an *absurdity*, or
senseless speech. For error is but a deception, in
presuming that somewhat is past, or to come; of
which, though it were not past, or not to come, yet
there was no impossibility discoverable. But when we
make a general assertion, unless it be a true one, the
possibility of it is inconceivable. And words whereby
we conceive nothing but the sound, are those we call
absurd, *insignificant*, and *nonsense*. And therefore if
a man should talk to me of a *round quadrangle*; or,
accidents of bread in cheese; or *immaterial substances*;
or of *a free subject*; *a free will*; or any *free*, but free
from being hindered by opposition, I should not say
he were in an error, but that his words were without
meaning, that is to say, absurd.

I have said before, (in the second chapter,) that a
man did excel all other animals in this faculty, that
when he conceived any thing whatsoever, he was apt
to inquire the consequences of it, and what effects
he could do with it. And now I add this other degree
of the same excellence, that he can by words reduce

the consequences he finds to general rules, called
theorems, or *aphorisms*; that is, he can reason, or
reckon, not only in number, but in all other things,
whereof one may be added unto, or subtracted
from another.

But this privilege is allayed by another; and that
is, by the privilege of absurdity; to which no living
creature is subject, but man only. And of men, those
are of all most subject to it, that profess philosophy.
For it is most true that Cicero saith of them somewhere; that there can be nothing so absurd, but may
be found in the books of philosophers. And the reason
is manifest. For there is not one of them that begins
his ratiocination from the definitions, or explications
of the names they are to use; which is a method that
hath been used only in geometry; whose conclusions
have thereby been made indisputable.

I. The first cause of absurd conclusions I ascribe
to the want of method; in that they begin not their
ratiocination from definitions; that is, from settled
significations of their words: as if they could cast
account, without knowing the value of the numeral
words, *one*, *two*, and *three*.

And whereas all bodies enter into account upon
divers considerations, (which I have mentioned in
the precedent chapter,) these considerations being
diversely named, divers absurdities proceed from the
confusion, and unfit connexion of their names into
assertions. And therefore,

II. The second cause of absurd assertions, I ascribe
to the giving of names of *bodies* to *accidents*; or of
accidents to *bodies*; as they do, that say, *faith is infused*,
or *inspired*; when nothing can be *poured*, or *breathed*
into any thing, but body; and that, *extension is body*;
that *phantasms* are *spirits*, &c.

III. The third I ascribe to the giving of the names
of the *accidents* of *bodies without us*, to the *accidents*
of our *own bodies*; as they do that say, the *colour is
in the body*; *the sound is in the air*, &c.

IV. The fourth, to the giving of the names of *bodies*
to *names*, or *speeches*; as they do that say, that *there
be things universal*; that *a living creature is genus*, or
a general thing, &c.

V. The fifth, to the giving of the names of *accidents*
to *names* and *speeches*; as they do that say, *the nature
of a thing is its definition*; *a man's command is his
will*; and the like.

VI. The sixth, to the use of metaphors, tropes, and other rhetorical figures, instead of words proper. For though it be lawful to say, (for example) in common speech, *the way goeth, or leadeth hither, or thither; the proverb says this or that* (whereas ways cannot go, nor proverbs speak;) yet in reckoning, and seeking of truth, such speeches are not to be admitted.

VII. The seventh, to names that signify nothing; but are taken up, and learned by rote from the schools, as *hypostatical, transubstantiate, consubstantiate, eternal-now,* and the like canting of schoolmen.

To him that can avoid these things it is not easy to fall into any absurdity, unless it be by the length of an account; wherein he may perhaps forget what went before. For all men by nature reason alike, and well, when they have good principles. For who is so stupid, as both to mistake in geometry, and also to persist in it, when another detects his error to him?

By this it appears that reason is not, as sense and memory, born with us; nor gotten by experience only, as prudence is; but attained by industry; first in apt imposing of names; and secondly by getting a good and orderly method in proceeding from the elements, which are names, to assertions made by connexion of one of them to another; and so to syllogisms, which are the connexions of one assertion to another, till we come to a knowledge of all the consequences of names appertaining to the subject in hand; and that is it, men call SCIENCE. And whereas sense and memory are but knowledge of fact, which is a thing past, and irrevocable; *Science* is the knowledge of consequences, and dependance of one fact upon another: by which, out of that we can presently do, we know how to do something else when we will, or the like, another time; because when we see how any thing comes about, upon what causes, and by what manner; when the like causes come into our power, we see how to make it produce the like effects.

Children therefore are not endued with reason at all, till they have attained the use of speech; but are called reasonable creatures, for the possibility apparent of having the use of reason in time to come. And the most part of men, though they have the use of reasoning a little way, as in numbering to some degree; yet it serves them to little use in common life; in which they govern themselves, some better, some worse, according to their differences of experience, quickness of memory, and inclinations to several ends; but specially according to good or evil fortune, and the errors of one another. For as for *science*, or certain rules of their actions, they are so far from it, that they know not what it is. Geometry they have thought conjuring: but for other sciences, they who have not been taught the beginnings and some progress in them, that they may see how they be acquired and generated, are in this point like children, that having no thought of generation, are made believe by the women that their brothers and sisters are not born, but found in the garden.

But yet they that have no *science*, are in better, and nobler condition, with their natural prudence; than men, that by mis-reasoning, or by trusting them that reason wrong, fall upon false and absurd general rules. For ignorance of causes, and of rules, does not set men so far out of their way, as relying on false rules, and taking for causes of what they aspire to, those that are not so, but rather causes of the contrary.

To conclude, the light of human minds is perspicuous words, but by exact definitions first snuffed, and purged from ambiguity; *reason* is the *pace*; increase of *science*, the *way*; and the benefit of mankind, the *end*. And on the contrary, metaphors, and senseless and ambiguous words, are like *ignes fatui*; and reasoning upon them is wandering amongst innumerable absurdities; and their end, contention and sedition, or contempt.

As much experience, is *prudence*; so, is much science *sapience*. For though we usually have one name of wisdom for them both, yet the Latins did always distinguish between *prudentia* and *sapientia*; ascribing the former to experience, the latter to science. But to make their difference appear more clearly, let us suppose one man endued with an excellent natural use and dexterity in handling his arms; and another to have added to that dexterity, an acquired science, of where he can offend, or be offended by his adversary, in every possible posture or guard: the ability of the former, would be to the ability of the latter, as prudence to sapience; both useful; but the latter infallible. But they that trusting only to the authority of books, follow the blind blindly, are like him that, trusting to the false rules of a master of fence, ventures presumptuously upon an adversary, that either kills or disgraces him.

The signs of science are some, certain and infallible; some, uncertain. Certain, when he that pretendeth the science of any thing, can teach the same, that is to say, demonstrate the truth thereof perspicuously to another; uncertain, when only some particular events answer to his pretence, and upon many occasions prove so as he says they must. Signs of prudence are all uncertain; because to observe by experience, and remember all circumstances that may alter the success, is impossible. But in any business, whereof a man has not infallible science to proceed by; to forsake his own natural judgment, and be guided by general sentences read in authors, and subject to many exceptions, is a sign of folly, and generally scorned by the name of pedantry. And even of those men themselves, that in councils of the commonwealth love to show their reading of politics and history, very few do it in their domestic affairs, where their particular interest is concerned; having prudence enough for their private affairs: but in public they study more the reputation of their own wit, than the success of another's business.

Chapter 6

Of the Interior Beginnings of Voluntary Motions; Commonly Called the Passions; and the Speeches by Which They Are Expressed

There be in animals, two sorts of *motions* peculiar to them: one called *vital*; begun in generation, and continued without interruption through their whole life; such as are the *course* of the *blood*, the *pulse*, the *breathing*, the *concoction, nutrition, excretion*, &c; to which motions there needs no help of imagination: the other is *animal motion*, otherwise called *voluntary motion*; as to *go*, to *speak*, to *move* any of our limbs, in such manner as is first fancied in our minds. That sense is motion in the organs and interior parts of man's body, caused by the action of the things we see, hear, &c.; and that fancy is but the relics of the same motion, remaining after sense, has been already said in the first and second chapters. And because *going, speaking*, and the like voluntary motions, depend always upon a precedent thought of *whither,*

which way, and *what*; it is evident, that the imagination is the first internal beginning of all voluntary motion. And although unstudied men do not conceive any motion at all to be there, where the thing moved is invisible; or the space it is moved in, is (for the shortness of it) insensible; yet that doth not hinder, but that such motions are. For let a space be never so little, that which is moved over a greater space, whereof that little one is part, must first be moved over that. These small beginnings of motion, within the body of man, before they appear in walking, speaking, striking, and other visible actions, are commonly called ENDEAVOUR.

This endeavour, when it is toward something which causes it, is called APPETITE, or DESIRE; the latter, being the general name; and the other, oftentimes restrained to signify the desire of food, namely *hunger* and *thirst*. And when the endeavour is fromward something, it is generally called AVERSION. These words, *appetite* and *aversion*, we have from the *Latins*; and they both of them signify the motions, one of approaching, the other of retiring. So also do the Greek words for the same, which are ὁρμὴ and ἀφορμὴ. For nature itself does often press upon men those truths, which afterwards, when they look for somewhat beyond nature, they stumble at. For the Schools find in mere appetite to go, or move, no actual motion at all: but because some motion they must acknowledge, they call it metaphorical motion; which is but an absurd speech: for though words may be called metaphorical; bodies and motions cannot.

That which men desire, they are also said to LOVE: and to HATE those things for which they have aversion. So that desire and love are the same thing; save that by desire, we always signify the absence of the object; by love, most commonly the presence of the same. So also by aversion, we signify the absence; and by hate, the presence of the object.

Of appetites and aversions, some are born with men; as appetite of food, appetite of excretion, and exoneration, (which may also and more properly be called aversions, from somewhat they feel in their bodies;) and some other appetites, not many. The rest, which are appetites of particular things, proceed from experience, and trial of their effects upon themselves or other men. For of things we know not at all, or believe not to be, we can have no further desire, than to taste and try. But aversion we have for things, not only which we know have hurt us, but also that we do not know whether they will hurt us, or not.

Those things which we neither desire, nor hate, we are said to *contemn*; CONTEMPT being nothing else but an immobility, or contumacy of the heart, in resisting the action of certain things; and proceeding from that the heart is already moved otherwise, by other more potent objects; or from want of experience of them.

And because the constitution of a man's body is in continual mutation, it is impossible that all the same things should always cause in him the same appetites, and aversions: much less can all men consent, in the desire of almost any one and the same object.

But whatsoever is the object of any man's appetite or desire, that is it which he for his part calleth *good*: and the object of his hate and aversion, *evil*; and of his contempt, *vile* and *inconsiderable*. For these words of good, evil, and contemptible, are ever used with relation to the person that useth them: there being nothing simply and absolutely so; nor any common rule of good and evil, to be taken from the nature of the objects themselves; but from the person of the man (where there is no commonwealth;) or, (in a commonwealth,) from the person that representeth it; or from an arbitrator or judge, whom men disagreeing shall by consent set up, and make his sentence the rule thereof.

The Latin tongue has two words, whose significations approach to those of good and evil; but are not precisely the same; and those are *pulchrum* and *turpe*. Whereof the former signifies that, which by some apparent signs promiseth good; and the latter, that which promiseth evil. But in our tongue we have not so general names to express them by. But for *pulchrum* we say in some things, *fair*; in others, *beautiful*, or *handsome*, or *gallant*, or *honourable*, or *comely*, or *amiable*; and for *turpe*, *foul*, *deformed*, *ugly*, *base*, *nauseous*, and the like, as the subject shall require; all which words, in their proper places, signify nothing else but the *mine*, or countenance, that promiseth good and evil. So that of good there be three kinds; good in the promise, that is *pulchrum*; good in effect, as the end desired, which is called *jucundum*, *delight-ful*; and good as the means, which is called *utile*,

profitable; and as many of evil: for *evil* in promise, is that they call *turpe*; evil in effect, and end, is *molestum*, *unpleasant*, *troublesome*; and evil in the means, *inutile*, *unprofitable*, *hurtful*.

As, in sense, that which is really within us, is, (as I have said before,) only motion, caused by the action of external objects, but in apparence; to the sight, light and colour; to the ear, sound; to the nostril, odour, &c.: so, when the action of the same object is continued from the eyes, ears, and other organs to the heart, the real effect there is nothing but motion, or endeavour; which consisteth in appetite, or aversion, to or from the object moving. But the apparence, or sense of that motion, is that we either call *delight*, or *trouble of mind*.

This motion, which is called appetite, and for the apparence of it *delight*, and *pleasure*, seemeth to be a corroboration of vital motion, and a help thereunto; and therefore such things as caused delight, were not improperly called *jucunda*, *(a juvando,)* from helping or fortifying; and the contrary, *molesta*, *offensive*, from hindering, and troubling the motion vital.

Pleasure therefore, (or *delight*,) is the apparence, or sense of good; and *molestation* or *displeasure*, the apparence, or sense of evil. And consequently all appetite, desire, and love, is accompanied with some delight more or less; and all hatred and aversion, with more or less displeasure and offence.

Of pleasures or delights, some arise from the sense of an object present; and those may be called *pleasures of sense*, (the word *sensual*, as it is used by those only that condemn them, having no place till there be laws.) Of this kind are all onerations and exonerations of the body; as also all that is pleasant, in the *sight*, *hearing*, *smell*, *taste*, *or touch*. Others arise from the expectation, that proceeds from foresight of the end, or consequence of things; whether those things in the sense please or displease. And these are *pleasures of the mind* of him that draweth those consequences, and are generally called JOY. In the like manner, displeasures are some in the sense, and called PAIN; others in the expectation of consequences, and are called GRIEF.

These simple passions called *appetite*, *desire*, *love*, *aversion*, *hate*, *joy*, and *grief*, have their names for divers considerations diversified. As first, when they one succeed another, they are diversely called from the opinion men have of the likelihood of attaining what they desire. Secondly, from the object loved or hated. Thirdly, from the consideration of many of them together. Fourthly, from the alteration or succession itself.

For *appetite*, with an opinion of attaining, is called HOPE.

The same, without such opinion, DESPAIR.

Aversion, with opinion of *hurt* from the object, FEAR.

The same, with hope of avoiding that hurt by resistance, COURAGE.

Sudden *courage*, ANGER.

Constant *hope*, CONFIDENCE of ourselves.

Constant *despair*, DIFFIDENCE of ourselves.

Anger for great hurt done to another, when we conceive the same to be done by injury, INDIGNATION.

Desire of good to another, BENEVOLENCE, GOOD WILL, CHARITY. If to man generally, GOOD NATURE.

Desire of riches, COVETOUSNESS: a name used always in signification of blame; because men contending for them, are displeased with one another's attaining them; though the desire in itself, be to be blamed, or allowed, according to the means by which those riches are sought.

Desire of office, or precedence, AMBITION: a name used also in the worse sense, for the reason before mentioned.

Desire of things that conduce but a little to our ends, and fear of things that are but of little hindrance, PUSILLANIMITY.

Contempt of little helps and hindrances, MAGNANIMITY.

Magnanimity, in danger of death or wounds, VALOUR, FORTITUDE.

Magnanimity, in the use of riches, LIBERALITY.

Pusillanimity, in the same, WRETCHEDNESS, MISERABLENESS, or PARSIMONY; as it is liked or disliked.

Love of persons for society, KINDNESS.

Love of persons for pleasing the sense only, NATURAL LUST.

Love of the same, acquired from rumination, that is, imagination of pleasure past, LUXURY.

Love of one singularly, with desire to be singularly beloved, THE PASSION OF LOVE. The same, with fear that the love is not mutual, JEALOUSY.

Desire, by doing hurt to another, to make him condemn some fact of his own, REVENGEFULNESS.

Desire to know why, and how, CURIOSITY; such as is in no living creature but *man*: so that man is distinguished, not only by his reason, but also by this singular passion from other *animals*; in whom the appetite of food, and other pleasures of sense, by predominance, take away the care of knowing causes; which is a lust of the mind, that by a perseverance of delight in the continual and indefatigable generation of knowledge, exceedeth the short vehemence of any carnal pleasure.

Fear of power invisible, feigned by the mind, or imagined from tales publicly allowed, RELIGION; not allowed, SUPERSTITION. And when the power imagined, is truly such as we imagine, TRUE RELIGION.

Fear, without the apprehension of why, or what, PANIC TERROR, called so from the fables, that make *Pan* the author of them; whereas in truth, there is always in him that so feareth, first, some apprehension of the cause, though the rest run away by example, every one supposing his fellow to know why. And therefore this passion happens to none but in a throng, or multitude of people.

Joy, from apprehension of novelty, ADMIRATION; proper to man, because it excites the appetite of knowing the cause.

Joy, arising from imagination of a man's own power and ability, is that exultation of the mind which is called GLORYING: which if grounded upon the experience of his own former actions, is the same with *confidence*: but if grounded on the flattery of others; or only supposed by himself, for delight in the consequences of it, is called VAINGLORY: which name is properly given; because a well grounded *confidence* begetteth attempt; whereas the supposing of power does not, and is therefore rightly called *vain*.

Grief, from opinion of want of power, is called DEJECTION of mind.

The *vain-glory* which consisteth in the feigning or supposing of abilities in ourselves, which we know are not, is most incident to young men, and nourished by the histories, or fictions of gallant persons; and is corrected oftentimes by age, and employment.

Sudden glory, is the passion which maketh those *grimaces* called LAUGHTER; and is caused either by some sudden act of their own, that pleaseth them; or by the apprehension of some deformed thing in another, by comparison whereof they suddenly applaud themselves. And it is incident most to them, that are conscious of the fewest abilities in themselves; who are forced to keep themselves in their own favour, by observing the imperfections of other men. And therefore much laughter at the defects of others, is a sign of pusillanimity. For of great minds, one of the proper works is, to help and free others from scorn; and compare themselves only with the most able.

On the contrary, *sudden dejection*, is the passion that causeth WEEPING; and is caused by such accidents, as suddenly take away some vehement hope, or some prop of their power: and they are most subject to it, that rely principally on helps external, such as are women, and children. Therefore some weep for the loss of friends; others for their unkindness; others for the sudden stop made to their thoughts of revenge, by reconciliation. But in all cases, both laughter, and weeping, are sudden motions; custom taking them both away. For no man laughs at old jests; or weeps for an old calamity.

Grief, for the discovery of some defect of ability, is SHAME, or the passion that discovereth itself in BLUSHING; and consisteth in the apprehension of some thing dishonourable; and in young men, is a sign of the love of good reputation, and commendable: in old men it is a sign of the same; but because it comes too late, not commendable.

The *contempt* of good reputation is called IMPUDENCE.

Grief, for the calamity of another, is PITY; and ariseth from the imagination that the like calamity may befall himself; and therefore is called also COMPASSION, and in the phrase of this present time a FELLOW-FEELING: and therefore for calamity arriving from great wickedness, the best men have the least pity; and for the same calamity, those have least pity, that think themselves least obnoxious to the same.

Contempt, or little sense of the calamity of others, is that which men call CRUELTY; proceeding from security of their own fortune. For, that any man should take pleasure in other men's great harms, without other end of his own, I do not conceive it possible.

Grief, for the success of a competitor in wealth, honour, or other good, if it be joined with endeavour to enforce our own abilities to equal or exceed him, is called EMULATION: but joined with endeavour to supplant, or hinder a competitor, ENVY.

When in the mind of man, appetites, and aversions, hopes, and fears, concerning one and the same thing, arise alternately; and divers good and evil consequences of the doing, or omitting the thing propounded, come successively into our thoughts; so that sometimes we have an appetite to it; sometimes an aversion from it; sometimes hope to be able to do it; sometimes despair, or fear to attempt it; the whole sum of desires, aversions, hopes and fears continued till the thing be either done, or thought impossible, is that we call DELIBERATION.

Therefore of things past, there is no *deliberation*; because manifestly impossible to be changed: nor of things known to be impossible, or thought so; because men know, or think such deliberation vain. But of things impossible, which we think possible, we may deliberate; not knowing it is in vain. And it is called *deliberation*; because it is a putting an end to the *liberty* we had of doing, or omitting, according to our own appetite, or aversion.

This alternate succession of appetites, aversions, hopes and fears, is no less in other living creatures than in man: and therefore beasts also deliberate.

Every *deliberation* is then said to *end*, when that whereof they deliberate, is either done, or thought impossible; because till then we retain the liberty of doing, or omitting, according to our appetite, or aversion.

In *deliberation*, the last appetite, or aversion, immediately adhering to the action, or to the omission thereof, is that we call the WILL; the act, (not the faculty,) of *willing*. And beasts that have *deliberation*, must necessarily also have *will*. The definition of the *will*, given commonly by the Schools, that it is a *rational appetite*, is not good. For if it were, then could there be no voluntary act against reason. For a *voluntary act* is that, which proceedeth from the *will*, and no other. But if instead of a rational appetite, we shall say an appetite resulting from a precedent deliberation, then the definition is the same that I have given here. *Will* therefore *is the last appetite in deliberating*. And though we say in common discourse, a man had a will once to do a thing, that nevertheless he forbore to do; yet that is properly but an inclination, which makes no action voluntary; because the action depends not of it, but of the last inclination, or appetite. For if the intervenient appetites, make any action voluntary; then by the same reason all intervenient aversions, should make the same action involuntary; and so one and the same action, should be both voluntary and involuntary.

By this it is manifest, that not only actions that have their beginning from covetousness, ambition, lust, or other appetites to the thing propounded; but also those that have their beginning from aversion, or fear of those consequences that follow the omission, are *voluntary actions*.

The forms of speech by which the passions are expressed, are partly the same, and partly different from those, by which we express our thoughts. And first, generally all passions may be expressed *indicatively*; as *I love, I fear, I joy, I deliberate, I will, I command*: but some of them have particular expressions by themselves, which nevertheless are not affirmations, unless it be when they serve to make other inferences, besides that of the passion they proceed from. Deliberation is expressed *subjunctively*; which is a speech proper to signify suppositions, with their consequences; as, *if this be done, then this will follow*; and differs not from the language of reasoning, save that reasoning is in general words; but deliberation for the most part is of particulars. The language of desire, and aversion, is *imperative*; as *do this, forbear that*; which when the party is obliged to do, or forbear, is *command*; otherwise *prayer*; or else *counsel*. The language of vain-glory, of indignation, pity and revengefulness, *optative*: but of the desire to know, there is a peculiar expression, called *interrogative*; as, *what is it, when shall it, how is it done*, and *why so?* other language of the passions I find none: for cursing, swearing, reviling, and the like, do not signify as speech; but as the actions of a tongue accustomed.

These forms of speech, I say, are expressions, or voluntary significations of our passions: but certain signs they be not; because they may be used arbitrarily, whether they that use them, have such passions or not. The best signs of passions present, are either in the countenance, motions of the body, actions, and ends, or aims, which we otherwise know the man to have.

And because in deliberation, the appetites, and aversions, are raised by foresight of the good and evil consequences, and sequels of the action whereof we deliberate; the good or evil effect thereof dependeth on the foresight of a long chain of consequences, of which very seldom any man is able to see to the end. But for so far as a man seeth, if the good in those consequences be greater than the evil, the whole chain is that which writers call *apparent*, or *seeming good*. And contrarily, when the evil exceedeth the good, the whole is *apparent*, or *seeming evil*: so that he who hath by experience, or reason, the greatest and surest prospect of consequences, deliberates best himself; and is able when he will, to give the best counsel unto others.

Continual success in obtaining those things which a man from time to time desireth, that is to say, continual prospering, is that men call FELICITY; I mean the felicity of this life. For there is no such thing as perpetual tranquillity of mind, while we live here; because life itself is but motion, and can never be without desire, nor without fear, no more than without sense. What kind of felicity God hath ordained to them that devoutly honour Him, a man shall no sooner know, than enjoy; being joys, that now are as incomprehensible, as the word of schoolmen *beatifical vision* is unintelligible.

The form of speech whereby men signify their opinion of the goodness of any thing, is PRAISE. That whereby they signify the power and greatness of any thing, is MAGNIFYING. And that whereby they signify the opinion they have of a man's felicity, is by the Greeks called μακαρισμός, for which we have no name in our tongue. And thus much is sufficient for the present purpose, to have been said of the PASSIONS.

Chapter 7

Of the Ends, or Resolutions of Discourse

Of all *discourse*, governed by desire of knowledge, there is at last an *end*, either by attaining, or by giving over. And in the chain of discourse, wheresoever it be interrupted, there is an end for that time.

If the discourse be merely mental, it consisteth of thoughts that the thing will be, and will not be, or that it has been, and has not been, alternately. So that wheresoever you break off the chain of a man's discourse, you leave him in a presumption of *it will be*, or, *it will not be*; or *it has been*, or, *has not been*. All which is *opinion*. And that which is alternate appetite, in deliberating concerning good and evil; the same is alternate opinion, in the enquiry of the truth of *past*, and *future*. And as the last appetite in deliberation, is called the *will*; so the last opinion in search of the truth of past, and future, is called the JUDGMENT, or *resolute* and *final sentence* of him that *discourseth*. And as the whole chain of appetites alternate, in the question of good, or bad, is called *deliberation*; so the whole chain of opinions alternate, in the question of true, or false, is called DOUBT.

No discourse whatsoever, can end in absolute knowledge of fact, past, or to come. For, as for the knowledge of fact, it is originally, sense; and ever after, memory. And for the knowledge of consequence, which I have said before is called science, it is not absolute, but conditional. No man can know by discourse, that this, or that, is, has been, or will be; which is to know absolutely: but only, that if this be, that is; if this has been, that has been; if this shall be, that shall be: which is to know conditionally; and that not the consequence of one thing to another; but of one name of a thing, to another name of the same thing.

And therefore, when the discourse is put into speech, and begins with the definitions of words, and proceeds by connexion of the same into general affirmations, and of these again into syllogisms; the end or last sum is called the conclusion; and the thought of the mind by it signified, is that conditional knowledge, or knowledge of the consequence of words, which is commonly called SCIENCE. But if the first ground of such discourse, be not definitions; or if the definitions be not rightly joined together into syllogisms, then the end or conclusion, is again OPINION, namely of the truth of somewhat said, though sometimes in absurd and senseless words, without possibility of being understood. When two, or more men, know of one and the same fact, they are said to be CONSCIOUS of it one to another; which is as much as to know it together. And because such are fittest witnesses of the facts of one another, or of a third; it was, and ever will be reputed a very evil act, for any man to speak against his *conscience*: or to corrupt or force another so to do: insomuch that the plea of conscience, has been always hearkened unto very diligently in all times. Afterwards, men made use of the same word metaphorically, for the knowledge of their own secret facts, and secret thoughts; and therefore it is rhetorically said, that the conscience is a thousand witnesses. And last of all, men, vehemently in love with their own new opinions, (though never so absurd,) and obstinately bent to maintain them, gave those their opinions also that reverenced name of conscience, as if they would have it seem unlawful, to change or speak against them; and so pretend to know they are true, when they know at most, but that they think so.

When a man's discourse beginneth not at definitions, it beginneth either at some other contemplation of his own, and then it is still called opinion; or it beginneth at some saying of another, of whose ability to know the truth, and of whose honesty in not deceiving, he doubteth not; and then the discourse is not so much concerning the thing, as the person; and the resolution is called BELIEF, and FAITH: *faith*, in the man; *belief*, both *of* the man, and *of* the truth of what he says. So that in belief are two opinions; one of the saying of the man; the other of his virtue. To *have faith in*, or *trust to*, or *believe a man*, signify the same thing; namely, an opinion of the veracity of the man: but to *believe what is said*, signifieth only an opinion of the truth of the saying. But we are to observe that this phrase, *I believe in*; as also the Latin, *credo in*; and the Greek, πιστεύω εἰς, are never used but in the writings of divines. Instead of them, in other writings are put, *I believe him*; *I trust him*; *I have faith in him*; *I rely on him*; and in Latin, *credo illi: fido illi*: and in Greek, πιστεύω αὐτῷ: and that this singularity of the ecclesiastic use of the word hath raised many disputes about the right object of the Christian faith.

But by *believing in*, as it is in the creed, is meant, not trust in the person; but confession and acknowledgment of the doctrine. For not only Christians, but all manner of men do so believe in God, as to hold all for truth they hear him say, whether they understand it, or not; which is all the faith and trust can possibly be had in any person whatsoever: but they do not all believe the doctrine of the creed.

From whence we may infer, that when we believe any saying whatsoever it be, to be true, from arguments taken, not from the thing it self, or from the principles of natural reason, but from the authority, and good opinion we have, of him that hath said it; then is the speaker, or person we believe in, or trust in, and whose word we take, the object of our faith; and the honour done in believing, is done to him only. And consequently, when we believe that the Scriptures are the word of God, having no immediate revelation from God himself, our belief, faith, and trust is in the church; whose word we take, and acquiesce therein. And they that believe that which a prophet relates unto them in the name of God, take the word of the prophet, do honour to him, and in him trust, and believe, touching the truth of what he relateth, whether he be a true, or a false prophet. And so it is also with all other history. For if I should not believe all that is written by historians, of the glorious acts of *Alexander*, or *Caesar*; I do not think the ghost of *Alexander*, or *Caesar*, had any just cause to be offended; or any body else, but the historian. If *Livy* say the Gods made once a cow speak, and we believe it not; we distrust not God therein, but *Livy*. So that it is evident, that whatsoever we believe, upon no other reason, than what is drawn from authority of men only, and their writings; whether they be sent from God or not, is faith in men only.

Chapter 8

Of the Virtues Commonly Called Intellectual; and Their Contrary Defects

Virtue generally, in all sorts of subjects, is somewhat that is valued for eminence; and consisteth in comparison. For if all things were equally in all men, nothing would be prized. And by *virtues* INTELLECTUAL, are always understood such abilities of the mind, as men praise, value, and desire should be in themselves; and go commonly under the name of a *good wit*;

though the same word *wit*, be used also, to distinguish one certain ability from the rest.

These *virtues* are of two sorts; *natural*, and *acquired*. By natural, I mean not, that which a man hath from his birth: for that is nothing else but sense; wherein men differ so little one from another, and from brute beasts, as it is not to be reckoned amongst virtues. But I mean, that *wit*, which is gotten by use only, and experience; without method, culture, or instruction. This NATURAL WIT, consisteth principally in two things; *celerity of imagining*, (that is, swift succession of one thought to another;) and *steady direction* to some approved end. On the contrary a slow imagination, maketh that defect, or fault of the mind, which is commonly called DULLNESS, *stupidity*, and sometimes by other names that signify slowness of motion, or difficulty to be moved.

And this difference of quickness, is caused by the difference of men's passions; that love and dislike, some one thing, some another: and therefore some men's thoughts run one way, some another; and are held to, and observe differently the things that pass through their imagination. And whereas in this succession of men's thoughts, there is nothing to observe in the things they think on, but either in what they be *like one another*, or in what they be *unlike*, or *what they serve for*, or *how they serve to such a purpose*; those that observe their similitudes, in case they be such as are but rarely observed by others, are said to have a *good wit*; by which, in this occasion, is meant a *good fancy*. But they that observe their differences, and dissimilitudes; which is called *distinguishing*, and *discerning*, and *judging* between thing and thing; in case, such discerning be not easy, are said to have a *good judgment*: and particularly in matter of conversation and business; wherein, times, places, and persons are to be discerned, this virtue is called DISCRETION. The former, that is, fancy, without the help of judgment, is not commended as a virtue: but the latter which is judgment, and discretion, is commended for it self, without the help of fancy. Besides the discretion of times, places, and persons, necessary to a good fancy, there is required also an often application of his thoughts to their end; that is to say, to some use to be made of them. This done; he that hath this virtue, will be easily fitted with similitudes, that will please, not only by illustration of his discourse, and adorning it with new and apt metaphors; but also, by the rarity of their invention. But without steadiness, and direction to some end, a great fancy is one kind of madness; such as they have, that entering into any discourse, are snatched from their purpose, by every thing that comes in their thought, into so many, and so long digressions, and parentheses, that they utterly lose themselves: which kind of folly, I know no particular name for: but the cause of it is, sometimes want of experience; whereby that seemeth to a man new and rare, which doth not so to others: sometimes pusillanimity; by which that seems great to him, which other men think a trifle: and whatsoever is new, or great, and therefore thought fit to be told, withdraws a man by degrees from the intended way of his discourse.

In a good poem, whether it be *epic*, or *dramatic*; as also in *sonnets, epigrams*, and other pieces, both judgment and fancy are required: but the fancy must be more eminent; because they please for the extravagancy; but ought not to displease by indiscretion.

In a good history, the judgment must be eminent; because the goodness consisteth, in the method, in the truth, and in the choice of the actions that are most profitable to be known. Fancy has no place, but only in adorning the style.

In orations of praise, and in invectives, the fancy is predominant; because the design is not truth, but to honour or dishonour; which is done by noble, or by vile comparisons. The judgment does but suggest what circumstances make an action laudable, or culpable.

In hortatives, and pleadings, as truth, or disguise serveth best to the design in hand; so is the judgment, or the fancy most required.

In demonstration, in counsel, and all rigorous search of truth, judgment does all; except sometimes the understanding have need to be opened by some apt similitude; and then there is so much use of fancy. But for metaphors, they are in this case utterly excluded. For seeing they openly profess deceit; to admit them into counsel, or reasoning, were manifest folly.

And in any discourse whatsoever, if the defect of discretion be apparent, how extravagant soever the fancy be, the whole discourse will be taken for a sign of want of wit; and so will it never when the discretion is manifest, though the fancy be never so ordinary.

The secret thoughts of a man run over all things, holy, profane, clean, obscene, grave, and light, without shame, or blame; which verbal discourse cannot do, farther than the judgment shall approve of the time, place, and persons. An anatomist, or a physician may speak, or write his judgment of unclean things; because it is not to please, but profit: but for another man to write his extravagant, and pleasant fancies of the same, is as if a man, from being tumbled into the dirt, should come and present himself before good company. And it is the want of discretion that makes the difference. Again, in professed remissness of mind, and familiar company, a man may play with the sounds, and equivocal significations of words; and that many times with encounters of extraordinary fancy: but in a sermon, or in public, or before persons unknown, or whom we ought to reverence; there is no gingling of words that will not be accounted folly: and the difference is only in the want of discretion. So that where wit is wanting, it is not fancy that is wanting, but discretion. Judgment therefore without fancy is wit, but fancy without judgment, not.

When the thoughts of a man, that has a design in hand, running over a multitude of things, observes how they conduce to that design; or what design they may conduce unto; if his observations be such as are not easy, or usual, this wit of his is called PRUDENCE; and dependeth on much experience, and memory of the like things, and their consequences heretofore. In which there is not so much difference of men, as there is in their fancies and judgments; because the experience of men equal in age, is not much unequal, as to the quantity; but lies in different occasions; every one having his private designs. To govern well a family, and a kingdom, are not different degrees of prudence; but different sorts of business; no more than to draw a picture in little, or as great, or greater than the life, are different degrees of art. A plain husbandman is more prudent in affairs of his own house, than a privy councillor in the affairs of another man.

To prudence, if you add the use of unjust, or dishonest means, such as usually are prompted to men by fear, or want; you have that crooked wisdom, which is called CRAFT; which is a sign of pusillanimity.

For magnanimity is contempt of unjust, or dishonest helps. And that which the Latins call *versutia*, (translated into English, *shifting*,) and is a putting off of a present danger or incommodity, by engaging into a greater, as when a man robs one to pay another, is but a shorter sighted craft, called *versutia*, from *versura*, which signifies taking money at usury for the present payment of interest.

As for *acquired wit*, (I mean acquired by method and instruction,) there is none but reason; which is grounded on the right use of speech, and produceth the sciences. But of reason and science, I have already spoken in the fifth and sixth chapters.

The causes of this difference of wits, are in the passions; and the difference of passions proceedeth, partly from the different constitution of the body, and partly from different education. For if the difference proceeded from the temper of the brain, and the organs of sense, either exterior or interior, there would be no less difference of men in their sight, hearing, or other senses, than in their fancies and discretions. It proceeds therefore from the passions; which are different, not only from the difference of mens' complexions; but also from their difference of customs, and education.

The passions that most of all cause the differences of wit, are principally, the more or less desire of power, of riches, of knowledge, and of honour. All which may be reduced to the first, that is, desire of power. For riches, knowledge, and honour are but several sorts of power.

And therefore, a man who has no great passion for any of these things; but is as men term it indifferent; though he may be so far a good man, as to be free from giving offence; yet he cannot possibly have either a great fancy, or much judgment. For the thoughts are to the desires, as scouts, and spies, to range abroad, and find the way to the things desired: all steadiness of the mind's motion and all quickness of the same, proceeding from thence: for as to have no desire, is to be dead: so to have weak passions, is dullness; and to have passions indifferently for every thing, GIDDINESS, and *distraction*; and to have stronger and more vehement passions for any thing, than is ordinarily seen in others, is that which men call MADNESS.

Whereof there be almost as many kinds, as of the passions themselves. Sometimes the extraordinary and extravagant passion, proceedeth from the evil constitution of the organs of the body, or harm done them; and sometimes the hurt, and indisposition of the organs, is caused by the vehemence, or long continuance of the passion. But in both cases the madness is of one and the same nature.

The passion, whose violence, or continuance, maketh madness, is either great *vain-glory*; which is commonly called *pride*, and *self-conceit*; or great *dejection* of mind.

Pride, subjecteth a man to anger, the excess whereof, is the madness called RAGE and FURY. And thus it comes to pass that excessive desire of revenge, when it becomes habitual, hurteth the organs, and becomes rage: that excessive love, with jealousy, becomes also rage: excessive opinion of a man's own self, for divine inspiration, for wisdom, learning, form and the like, becomes distraction and giddiness: the same, joined with envy, rage: vehement opinion of the truth of any thing, contradicted by others, rage.

Dejection subjects a man to causeless fears; which is a madness commonly called MELANCHOLY, apparent also in divers manners; as in haunting of solitudes and graves; in superstitious behaviour; and in fearing some one, some another particular thing. In sum, all passions that produce strange and unusual behaviour, are called by the general name of madness. But of the several kinds of madness, he that would take the pains, might enrol a legion. And if the excesses be madness, there is no doubt but the passions themselves, when they tend to evil, are degrees of the same.

(For example,) though the effect of folly, in them that are possessed of an opinion of being inspired, be not visible always in one man, by any very extravagant action, that proceedeth from such passion; yet when many of them conspire together, the rage of the whole multitude is visible enough. For what argument of madness can there be greater, than to clamour, strike, and throw stones at our best friends? Yet this is somewhat less than such a multitude will do. For they will clamour, fight against, and destroy those, by whom all their lifetime before, they have been protected, and secured from injury. And if this be madness in the multitude, it is the same in every particular man. For as in the midst of the sea, though a man perceive no sound of that part of the water next him; yet he is well assured, that part contributes as much to the roaring of the sea, as any other part of the same quantity; so also, though we perceive no great unquietness in one or two men, yet we may be well assured, that their singular passions, are parts of the seditious roaring of a troubled nation. And if there were nothing else that bewrayed their madness; yet that very arrogating such inspiration to themselves, is argument enough. If some man in Bedlam should entertain you with sober discourse; and you desire in taking leave, to know what he were, that you might another time requite his civility; and he should tell you, he were God the Father; I think you need expect no extravagant action for argument of his madness.

This opinion of inspiration, called commonly, private spirit, begins very often, from some lucky finding of an error generally held by others; and not knowing, or not remembering, by what conduct of reason, they came to so singular a truth, (as they think it, though it be many times an untruth they light on,) they presently admire themselves, as being in the special grace of God Almighty, who hath revealed the same to them supernaturally, by his Spirit.

Again, that madness is nothing else, but too much appearing passion, may be gathered out of the effects of wine, which are the same with those of the evil disposition of the organs. For the variety of behaviour in men that have drunk too much, is the same with that of madmen: some of them raging, others loving, others laughing, all extravagantly, but according to their several domineering passions: for the effect of the wine, does but remove dissimulation, and take from them the sight of the deformity of their passions. For, (I believe) the most sober men, when they walk alone without care and employment of the mind, would be unwilling the vanity and extravagance of their thoughts at that time should be publicly seen; which is a confession, that passions unguided, are for the most part mere madness.

The opinions of the world, both in ancient and later ages, concerning the cause of madness, have been two. Some deriving them from the passions; some, from demons, or spirits, either good or bad, which they thought might enter into a man, possess him, and move his organs in such strange and uncouth manner, as madmen use to do. The former sort therefore, called such men, madmen: but the latter, called them sometimes *demoniacs*, (that is, possessed with spirits;) sometimes *enurgumeni*, (that is, agitated or moved with spirits;) and now in *Italy* they are called not only *pazzi*, madmen; but also *spiritati*, men possessed.

There was once a great conflux of people in *Abdera*, a city of the Greeks, at the acting of the tragedy of *Andromeda*, upon an extreme hot day; whereupon, a great many of the spectators falling into fevers, had this accident from the heat, and from the tragedy together, that they did nothing but pronounce iambics, with the names of *Perseus* and *Andromeda*; which, together with the fever, was cured by the coming on of winter; and this madness was thought to proceed from the passion imprinted by the tragedy. Likewise there reigned a fit of madness in another Grecian city, which seized only the young maidens; and caused many of them to hang themselves. This was by most then thought an act of the Devil. But one that suspected, that contempt of life in them, might proceed from some passion of the mind, and supposing they did not contemn also their honour, gave counsel to the magistrates, to strip such as so hanged themselves, and let them hang out naked. This, the story says, cured that madness. But on the other side, the same Grecians, did often ascribe madness to the operation of the Eumenides, or Furies; and sometimes of *Ceres*, *Phoebus*, and other gods; so much did men attribute to phantasms, as to think them aereal living bodies; and generally to call them spirits. And as the Romans in this, held the same opinion with the Greeks, so also did the Jews; for they called madmen prophets, or (according as they thought the spirits good or bad) demoniacs; and some of them called both prophets and demoniacs, madmen; and some called the same man both demoniac, and madman. But for the Gentiles it is no wonder, because diseases and health, vices and virtues, and many natural accidents, were with them termed, and worshipped as demons. So that a man was to understand by demon, as well, (sometimes) an ague, as a devil. But for the Jews to have such opinion, is somewhat strange. For neither *Moses* nor *Abraham* pretended to prophecy by possession of a spirit; but from the voice of God; or by a vision or dream: nor is there any thing in his law, moral or ceremonial, by which they were taught, there was any such enthusiasm, or any possession. When God is said, *Numb.* 11. 25. to take from the spirit that was in *Moses,* and give to the 70 elders, the Spirit of God (taking it for the substance of God) is not divided. The Scriptures, by the Spirit of God in man, mean a man's spirit, inclined to godliness. And where it is said, *Exod.* 28. 3. *whom I have filled with the spirit of wisdom to make garments for Aaron,* is not meant a spirit put into them, that can make garments; but the wisdom of their own spirits in that kind of work. In the like sense, the spirit of man, when it produceth unclean actions, is ordinarily called an unclean spirit, and so other spirits, though not always, yet as often as the virtue or vice so styled, is extraordinary, and eminent. Neither did the other prophets of the old Testament pretend enthusiasm; or, that God spake in them; but to them, by voice, vision, or dream; and the *burthen of the Lord* was not possession, but command. How then could the Jews fall into this opinion of possession? I can imagine no reason, but that which is common to all men; namely, the want of curiosity to search natural causes; and their placing felicity in the acquisition of the gross pleasures of the senses, and the things that most immediately conduce thereto. For they that see any strange, and unusual ability, or defect in a man's mind; unless they see withal, from what cause it may probably proceed, can hardly think it natural; and if not natural, they must needs think it supernatural, and then what can it be, but that either God or the Devil is in him? And hence it came to pass, when our Saviour (*Mark* 3. 21.) was compassed about with the multitude, those of the house doubted he was mad, and went out to hold him: but the Scribes said he had *Beelzebub,* and that was it, by which he cast out devils; as if the greater madman had awed the lesser. And that (*John* 10. 20.) some said, *he hath a devil, and is mad*; whereas others holding him for a prophet, said, *these are not the words of one that hath a devil.* So in the old Testament he that came to anoint *Jehu,* 2 *Kings* 9. 11. was a prophet; but some of the company asked *Jehu, what came that madman for?* So that in sum, it is manifest, that whosoever behaved himself in extraordinary manner, was thought by the Jews to be possessed either with a good, or evil spirit; except by the Sadducees, who erred so far on the other hand, as not to

believe there were at all any spirits, (which is very near to direct atheism;) and thereby perhaps the more provoked others, to term such men demoniacs, rather than madmen.

But why then does our Saviour proceed in the curing of them, as if they were possessed; and not as if they were mad? To which I can give no other kind of answer, but that which is given to those that urge the Scripture in like manner against the opinion of the motion of the earth. The Scripture was written to shew unto men the kingdom of God, and to prepare their minds to become his obedient subjects; leaving the world, and the philosophy thereof, to the disputation of men, for the exercising of their natural reason. Whether the earth's, or sun's motion make the day, and night; or whether the exorbitant actions of men, proceed from passion, or from the devil, (so we worship him not) it is all one, as to our obedience, and subjection to God Almighty; which is the thing for which the Scripture was written. As for that our Saviour speaketh to the disease, as to a person; it is the usual phrase of all that cure by words only, as Christ did, (and enchanters pretend to do, whether they speak to a devil or not.) For is not Christ also said (*Matt.* 8. 26.) to have rebuked the winds? Is not he said also (*Luke* 4. 39.) to rebuke a fever? Yet this does not argue that a fever is a devil. And whereas many of those devils are said to confess Christ; it is not necessary to interpret those places otherwise, than that those madmen confessed him. And whereas our Saviour (*Matt.* 12. 43.) speaketh of an unclean spirit, that having gone out of a man, wandereth through dry places, seeking rest, and finding none, and returning into the same man, with seven other spirits worse than himself; it is manifestly a parable, alluding to a man, that after a little endeavour to quit his lusts, is vanquished by the strength of them; and becomes seven times worse than he was. So that I see nothing at all in the Scripture, that requireth a belief, that demoniacs were any other thing but madmen.

There is yet another fault in the discourses of some men; which may also be numbered amongst the sorts of madness; namely, that abuse of words, whereof I have spoken before in the fifth chapter, by the name of absurdity. And that is, when men speak such words, as put together, have in them no signification at all; but are fallen upon by some, through misunderstanding of the words they have received, and repeat by rote; by others from intention to deceive by obscurity. And this is incident to none but those, that converse in questions of matters incomprehensible, as the School-men; or in questions of abstruse philosophy. The common sort of men seldom speak insignificantly, and are therefore, by those other egregious persons counted idiots. But to be assured their words are without any thing correspondent to them in the mind, there would need some examples; which if any man require, let him take a School-man into his hands and see if he can translate any one chapter concerning any difficult point, as the Trinity; the Deity; the nature of Christ; transubstantiation; free-will, &c. into any of the modern tongues, so as to make the same intelligible; or into any tolerable Latin, such as they were acquainted withal, that lived when the Latin tongue was vulgar. What is the meaning of these words. *The first cause does not necessarily inflow any thing into the second, by force of the essential subordination of the second causes, by which it may help it to work?* They are the translation of the title of the sixth chapter of *Suarez'* first book, *Of the Concourse, Motion, and Help of God.* When men write whole volumes of such stuff, are they not mad, or intend to make others so? And particularly, in the question of transubstantiation; where after certain words spoken, they that say, the white*ness*, round*ness*, magni*tude*, quali*ty*, corruptibili*ty*, all which are incorporeal, &c. go out of the wafer, into the body of our blessed Saviour, do they not make those *nesses*, *tudes*, and *ties*, to be so many spirits possessing his body? For by spirits, they mean always things, that being incorporeal, are nevertheless moveable from one place to another. So that this kind of absurdity, may rightly be numbered amongst the many sorts of madness, and all the time that guided by clear thoughts of their worldly lust, they forbear disputing, or writing thus, but lucid intervals. And thus much of the virtues and defects intellectual.

Chapter 9

Of the Several Subjects of Knowledge

There are of KNOWLEDGE two kinds; whereof one is *knowledge of fact*: the other *knowledge of the consequence of one affirmation to another.* The former is nothing else, but sense and memory, and is *absolute knowledge*; as when we see a fact doing, or remember it done: and this is the knowledge required in a witness. The latter is called *science*; and is *conditional*; as when we know, that, *if the figure shown be a circle, then any straight line through the center shall divide it into two equal parts.* And this is the knowledge required in a philosopher; that is to say, of him that pretends to reasoning.

The register of *knowledge of fact* is called *history.* Whereof there be two sorts: one called *natural history*; which is the history of such facts, or effects of nature, as have no dependence on man's *will*; such as are the histories of *metals, plants, animals, regions,* and the like. The other, is *civil history*; which is the history of the voluntary actions of men in commonwealths.

The registers of science, are such *books* as contain the *demonstrations* of consequences of one affirmation, to another; and are commonly called *books of philosophy*; whereof the sorts are many, according to the diversity of the matter; and may be divided in such manner as I have divided them in the following table.

Chapter 10

Of Power, Worth, Dignity, Honour, and Worthiness

The power *of a man*, (to take it universally,) is his present means, to obtain some future apparent good; and is either *original* or *instrumental*.

Natural power, is the eminence of the faculties of body, or mind: as extraordinary strength, form, prudence, arts, eloquence, liberality, nobility. *Instrumental* are those powers, which acquired by these, or by fortune, are means and instruments to acquire more: as riches, reputation, friends, and the secret working of God, which men call good luck. For the nature of power, is in this point, like to fame, increasing as it proceeds; or like the motion of heavy bodies, which the further they go, make still the more haste.

The greatest of human powers, is that which is compounded of the powers of most men, united by consent, in one person, natural, or civil, that has the use of all their powers depending on his will; such as is the power of a common-wealth: or depending

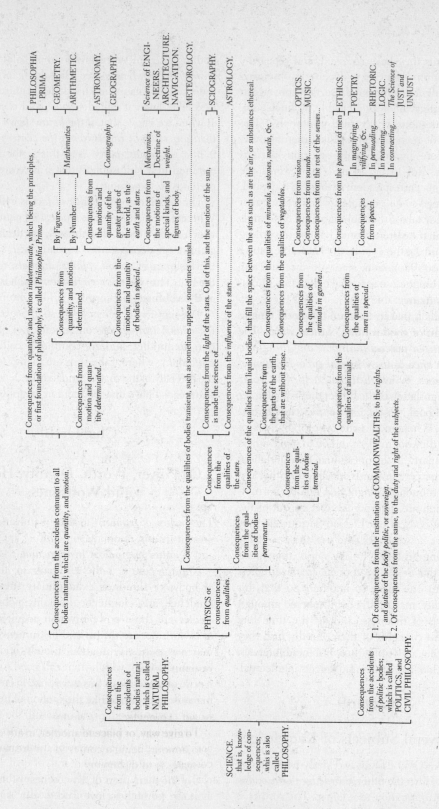

SCIENCE, that is, knowledge of consequences; which is also called PHILOSOPHY.

Consequences from the accidents of bodies natural; which is called NATURAL PHILOSOPHY.

Consequences from the accidents common to all bodies natural; which are *quantity*, and *motion*.

Consequences from quantity, and motion *indeterminate*, which being the principles, or first foundation of philosophy, is called *Philosophia Prima*. — PHILOSOPHIA PRIMA

Consequences from quantity, and motion determined.

Consequences from motion and quantity *determinated*.

By Figure. — GEOMETRY.
By Number. — ARITHMETIC.
Mathematics

Consequences from the motion and quantity of the greater parts of the world, as the *earth* and *stars*.

Consequences from the motion, and quantity of bodies in *special*.

Consequences from the motions of special kinds, and figures of body.
Cosmography

ASTRONOMY.
GEOGRAPHY.

Mechanics, Doctrine of *weight*.

Science of ENGINEERS.
ARCHITECTURE.
NAVIGATION.

PHYSICS or consequences from *qualities*.

Consequences from the qualities of bodies transient, such as sometime appear, sometime vanish. — METEOROLOGY.

Consequences from the qualities of bodies *permanent*.

Consequences from the qualities of the *stars*.

Consequences from the *light* of the stars. Out of this, and the motion of the sun, is made the science of. — SCIOGRAPHY.

Consequences from the *influence* of the stars. — ASTROLOGY.

Consequences of the qualities from liquid bodies, that fill the space between the stars such as are the *air*, or substances ethereal.

Consequences from the qualities of *bodies terrestrial*.

Consequences from the parts of the earth, that are without sense.

Consequences from the qualities of *minerals*, as *stones*, *metals*, &c.

Consequences from the qualities of *vegetables*.

Consequences from the qualities of *animals*.

Consequences from the qualities of *animals in general*.

Consequences from *vision*. — OPTICS.
Consequences from *sounds*. — MUSIC.
Consequences from the rest of the senses.

Consequences from the qualities of *men in special*.

Consequences from the *passions of men*. — ETHICS.

Consequences from *speech*.

In *magnifying*, *vilifying*, &c. — POETRY.
In *persuading*. — RHETORIC.
In *reasoning*. — LOGIC.
In *contracting*. — *The Science of* JUST *and* UNJUST.

Consequences from the accidents of *politic bodies*; which is called POLITICS, and CIVIL PHILOSOPHY.

1. Of consequences from the institution of COMMONWEALTHS, to the *rights*, and *duties* of the *body politic*, or sovereign.

2. Of consequences from the same, to the *duty* and *right of the subjects*.

on the wills of each particular; such as is the power of a faction or of divers factions leagued. Therefore to have servants, is power; to have friends, is power: for they are strengths united.

Also riches joined with liberality, is power; because it procureth friends, and servants: without liberality, not so; because in this case they defend not; but expose men to envy, as a prey.

Reputation of power, is power; because it draweth with it the adherence of those that need protection.

So is reputation of love of a man's country, (called popularity,) for the same reason.

Also, what quality soever maketh a man beloved, or feared of many; or the reputation of such quality, is power; because it is a means to have the assistance, and service of many.

Good success is power; because it maketh reputation of wisdom, or good fortune; which makes men either fear him, or rely on him.

Affability of men already in power, is increase of power; because it gaineth love.

Reputation of prudence in the conduct of peace or war, is power; because to prudent men, we commit the government of ourselves, more willingly than to others.

Nobility is power, not in all places, but only in those commonwealths, where it has privileges: for in such privileges consisteth their power.

Eloquence is power, because it is seeming prudence.

Form is power; because being a promise of good, it recommendeth men to the favour of women and strangers.

The sciences, are small power; because not eminent; and therefore, not acknowledged in any man; nor are at all, but in a few, and in them, but of a few things. For science is of that nature, as none can understand it to be, but such as in a good measure have attained it.

Arts of public use, as fortification, making of engines, and other instruments of war; because they confer to defence, and victory, are power: and though the true mother of them, be science, namely the mathematics; yet, because they are brought into the light, by the hand of the artificer, they be esteemed (the midwife passing with the vulgar for the mother,) as his issue.

The *value*, or WORTH of a man, is as of all other things, his price; that is to say, so much as would be given for the use of his power: and therefore is not absolute; but a thing dependant on the need and judgment of another. An able conductor of soldiers, is of great price in time of war present, or imminent; but in peace not so. A learned and uncorrupt judge, is much worth in time of peace; but not so much in war. And as in other things, so in men, not the seller, but the buyer determines the price. For let a man (as most men do,) rate themselves at the highest value they can; yet their true value is no more than it is esteemed by others.

The manifestation of the value we set on one another, is that which is commonly called honouring, and dishonouring. To value a man at a high rate, is to *honour* him; at a low rate, is to *dishonour* him. But high, and low, in this case, is to be understood by comparison to the rate that each man setteth on himself.

The public worth of a man, which is the value set on him by the commonwealth, is that which men commonly call DIGNITY. And this value of him by the commonwealth, is understood, by offices of command, judicature, public employment; or by names and titles, introduced for distinction of such value.

To pray to another, for aid of any kind, is to HONOUR; because a sign we have an opinion he has power to help; and the more difficult the aid is, the more is the honour.

To obey, is to honour, because no man obeys them, whom they think have no power to help, or hurt them. And consequently to disobey, is to *dishonour*.

To give great gifts to a man, is to honour him; because it is buying of protection, and acknowledging of power. To give little gifts, is to dishonour; because it is but alms, and signifies an opinion of the need of small helps.

To be sedulous in promoting another's good; also to flatter, is to honour; as a sign we seek his protection or aid. To neglect, is to dishonour.

To give way, or place to another, in any commodity, is to honour; being a confession of greater power. To arrogate, is to dishonour.

To show any sign of love, or fear of another, is to honour; for both to love, and to fear, is to value. To contemn, or less to love or fear, than he expects, is to dishonour; for it is undervaluing.

To praise, magnify, or call happy, is to honour; because nothing but goodness, power, and felicity is valued. To revile, mock, or pity, is to dishonour.

To speak to another with consideration, to appear before him with decency, and humility, is to honour him; as signs of fear to offend. To speak to him rashly, to do any thing before him obscenely, slovenly, impudently, is to dishonour.

To believe, to trust, to rely on another, is to honour him; sign of opinion of his virtue and power. To distrust, or not believe, is to dishonour.

To hearken to a man's counsel, or discourse of what kind soever, is to honour; as a sign we think him wise, or eloquent, or witty. To sleep, or go forth, or talk the while, is to dishonour.

To do those things to another, which he takes for signs of honour, or which the law or custom makes so, is to honour; because in approving the honour done by others, he acknowledgeth the power which others acknowledge. To refuse to do them, is to dishonour.

To agree with in opinion, is to honour; as being a sign of approving his judgment, and wisdom. To dissent, is dishonour, and an upbraiding of error; and (if the dissent be in many things) of folly.

To imitate, is to honour; for it is vehemently to approve. To imitate one's enemy, is to dishonour.

To honour those another honours, is to honour him; as a sign of approbation of his judgment. To honour his enemies, is to dishonour him.

To employ in counsel, or in actions of difficulty, is to honour; as a sign of opinion of his wisdom, or other power. To deny employment in the same cases, to those that seek it, is to dishonour.

All these ways of honouring, are natural; and as well within, as without commonwealths. But in commonwealths, where he, or they that have the supreme authority, can make whatsoever they please, to stand for signs of honour, there be other honours.

A sovereign doth honour a subject, with whatsoever title, or office, or employment, or action, that he himself will have taken for a sign of his will to honour him.

The king of *Persia*, honoured *Mordecai*, when he appointed he should be conducted through the streets in the king's garment, upon one of the king's horses, with a crown on his head, and a prince before him, proclaiming, *thus shall it be done to him that the king will honour*. And yet another king of *Persia*, or the same another time, to one that demanded for some great service, to wear one of the king's robes, gave him leave so to do; but with this addition, that he should wear it as the king's fool; and then it was dishonour. So that of civil honour, the fountain is in the person of the commonwealth, and dependeth on the will of the sovereign; and is therefore temporary, and called *civil honour*; such as are magistracy, offices, titles; and in some places coats and scutcheons painted: and men honour such as have them, as having so many signs of favour in the commonwealth; which favour is power.

Honourable is whatsoever possession, action, or quality, is an argument and sign of power.

And therefore to be honoured, loved, or feared of many, is honourable; as arguments of power. To be honoured of few or none, *dishonourable*.

Dominion, and victory is honourable; because acquired by power; and servitude, for need, or fear, is dishonourable.

Good fortune (if lasting,) honourable, as a sign of the favour of God. Ill fortune, and losses, dishonourable. Riches, are honourable; for they are power. Poverty, dishonourable. Magnanimity, liberality, hope, courage, confidence, are honourable; for they proceed from the conscience of power. Pusillanimity, parsimony, fear, diffidence, are dishonourable.

Timely resolution, or determination of what a man is to do, is honourable; as being the contempt of small difficulties, and dangers. And irresolution, dishonourable; as a sign of too much valuing of little impediments, and little advantages: for when a man has weighed things as long as the time permits, and resolves not, the difference of weight is but little; and therefore if he resolve not, he overvalues little things, which is pusillanimity.

All actions, and speeches, that proceed, or seem to proceed from much experience, science, discretion, or wit, are honourable; for all these are powers. Actions, or words that proceed from error, ignorance, or folly, dishonourable.

Gravity, as far forth as it seems to proceed from a mind employed on something else, is honourable; because employment is a sign of power. But if it seem to proceed from a purpose to appear grave, it is dishonourable. For the gravity of the former, is like the steadiness of a ship laden with merchandise; but of the latter, like the steadiness of a ship ballasted with sand, and other trash.

To be conspicuous, that is to say, to be known, for wealth, office, great actions, or any eminent good, is honourable; as a sign of the power for which he is conspicuous. On the contrary, obscurity, is dishonourable.

To be descended from conspicuous parents, is honourable; because they the more easily attain the aids, and friends of their ancestors. On the contrary, to be descended from obscure parentage, is dishonourable.

Actions proceeding from equity, joined with loss, are honourable; as signs of magnanimity: for magnanimity is a sign of power. On the contrary, craft, shifting, neglect of equity, is dishonourable.

Covetousness of great riches, and ambition of great honours, are honourable; as signs of power to obtain them. Covetousness, and ambition, of little gains, or preferments, is dishonourable.

Nor does it alter the case of honour, whether an action (so it be great and difficult, and consequently a sign of much power,) be just or unjust: for honour consisteth only in the opinion of power. Therefore the ancient heathen did not think they dishonoured, but greatly honoured the Gods, when they introduced them in their poems, committing rapes, thefts, and other great, but unjust, or unclean acts: insomuch as nothing is so much celebrated in *Jupiter*, as his adulteries; nor in *Mercury*, as his frauds, and thefts: of whose praises, in a hymn of *Homer*, the greatest is this, that being born in the morning, he had invented music at noon, and before night, stolen away the cattle of *Apollo*, from his herdsmen.

Also amongst men, till there were constituted great commonwealths, it was thought no dishonour to be a pirate, or a highway thief; but rather a lawful trade, not only amongst the Greeks, but also amongst all other nations; as is manifest by the histories of ancient time. And at this day, in this part of the world, private duels are, and always will be honourable, though unlawful, till such time as there shall be honour ordained for them that refuse, and ignominy for them that make the challenge. For duels also are many times effects of courage; and the ground of courage is always strength or skill, which are power; though

for the most part they be effects of rash speaking, and of the fear of dishonour, in one, or both the combatants; who engaged by rashness, are driven into the lists to avoid disgrace.

Scutcheons, and coats of arms hereditary, where they have any eminent privileges, are honourable; otherwise not: for their power consisteth either in such privileges, or in riches, or some such thing as is equally honoured in other men. This kind of honour, commonly called gentry, has been derived from the ancient Germans. For there never was any such thing known, where the German customs were unknown. Nor is it now any where in use where the Germans have not inhabited. The ancient Greek commanders, when they went to war, had their shields painted with such devices as they pleased; insomuch as an unpainted buckler was a sign of poverty, and of a common soldier; but they transmitted not the inheritance of them. The Romans transmitted the marks of their families: but they were the images, not the devices of their ancestors. Amongst the people of *Asia*, *Africa*, and *America*, there is not, nor was ever, any such thing. The Germans only had that custom; from whom it has been derived into *England*, *France*, *Spain*, and *Italy*, when in great numbers they either aided the Romans, or made their own conquests in these western parts of the world.

For *Germany*, being anciently, as all other countries, in their beginnings, divided amongst an infinite number of little lords, or masters of families, that continually had wars one with another; those masters, or lords, principally to the end they might, when they were covered with arms, be known by their followers; and partly for ornament, both painted their armour, or their scutcheon, or coat, with the picture of some beast, or other thing; and also put some eminent and visible mark upon the crest of their helmets. And this ornament both of the arms, and crest, descended by inheritance to their children; to the eldest pure, and to the rest with some note of diversity, such as the old master, that is to say in Dutch, the *Here-alt* thought fit. But when many such families, joined together, made a greater monarchy, this duty of the Herealt, to distinguish scutcheons, was made a private office apart. And the issue of these lords, is the great and ancient gentry; which for the most part bear living creatures, noted for courage, and rapine; or castles, battlements, belts, weapons, bars, palisadoes, and other notes of war; nothing being then in honour, but virtue military. Afterwards, not only kings, but popular commonwealths, gave divers manners of scutcheons, to such as went forth to the war, or returned from it, for encouragement, or recompense to their service. All which, by an observing reader, may be found in such ancient histories, Greek and Latin, as make mention of the German nation and manners, in their times.

Titles of *honour*, such as are duke, count, marquis, and baron, are honourable; as signifying the value set upon them by the sovereign power of the commonwealth: which titles, were in old time titles of office, and command, derived some from the Romans, some from the Germans and French. Dukes, in Latin *duces*, being generals in war: counts, *comites*, such as bare the general company out of friendship, and were left to govern and defend places conquered, and pacified: marquises, *marchiones*, were counts that governed the marches, or bounds of the empire. Which titles of duke, count, and marquis, came into the empire, about the time of *Constantine* the Great, from the customs of the German *militia*. But baron, seems to have been a title of the Gauls, and signifies a great man; such as were the king's, or prince's men, whom they employed in war about their persons; and seems to be derived from *vir*, to *ber*, and *bar*, that signified the same in the language of the Gauls, that *vir* in Latin; and thence to *bero*, and *baro*: so that such men were called *berones*, and after barones; and (in Spanish) *varones*. But he that would know more particularly the original of titles of honour, may find it, as I have done this, in Mr. Selden's most excellent treatise of that subject. In process of time these offices of honour, by occasion of trouble, and for reasons of good and peaceable government, were turned into mere titles; serving for the most part, to distinguish the precedence, place, and order of subjects in the commonwealth: and men were made dukes, counts, marquises, and barons of places, wherein they had neither possession, nor command: and other titles also, were devised to the same end.

WORTHINESS, is a thing different from the worth, or value of a man; and also from his merit, or desert; and consisteth in a particular power, or ability for that, whereof he is said to be worthy: which particular ability, is usually named FITNESS, or *aptitude*.

For he is worthiest to be a commander, to be a judge, or to have any other charge, that is best fitted, with the qualities required to the well discharging of it; and worthiest of riches, that has the qualities most requisite for the well using of them: any of which qualities being absent, one may nevertheless be a worthy man, and valuable for something else. Again, a man may be worthy of riches, office, and employment, that nevertheless, can plead no right to have it before another; and therefore cannot be said to merit or deserve it. For merit presupposeth a right, and that the thing deserved is due by promise: of which I shall say more hereafter, when I shall speak of contracts.

Chapter 11

Of the Difference of Manners

By manners, I mean not here, decency of behaviour; as how one man should salute another, or how a man should wash his mouth, or pick his teeth before company, and such other points of the *small morals*; but those qualities of mankind, that concern their living together in peace, and unity. To which end we are to consider, that the felicity of this life, consisteth not in the repose of a mind satisfied. For there is no such *finis ultimus*, (utmost aim,) nor *summum bonum*, (greatest good,) as is spoken of in the books of the old moral philosophers. Nor can a man any more live, whose desires are at an end, than he, whose senses and imaginations are at a stand. Felicity is a continual progress of the desire, from one object to another; the attaining of the former, being still but the way to the latter. The cause whereof is, that the object of man's desire, is not to enjoy once only, and for one instant of time; but to assure for ever, the way of his future desire. And therefore the voluntary actions, and inclinations of all men, tend, not only to the procuring, but also to the assuring of a contented life; and differ only in the way: which ariseth partly from the diversity of passions, in divers men;

and partly from the difference of the knowledge, or opinion each one has of the causes, which produce the effect desired.

So that in the first place, I put for a general inclination of all mankind, a perpetual and restless desire of power after power, that ceaseth only in death. And the cause of this, is not always that a man hopes for a more intensive delight, than he has already attained to; or that he cannot be content with a moderate power: but because he cannot assure the power and means to live well, which he hath present, without the acquisition of more. And from hence it is, that kings, whose power is greatest, turn their endeavours to the assuring it at home by laws, or abroad by wars: and when that is done, there succeedeth a new desire; in some, of fame from new conquest; in others, of ease and sensual pleasure; in others, of admiration, or being flattered for excellence in some art, or other ability of the mind.

Competition of riches, honour, command, or other power, inclineth to contention, enmity, and war: because the way of one competitor, to the attaining of his desire, is to kill, subdue, supplant, or repel the other. Particularly, competition of praise, inclineth to a reverence of antiquity. For men contend with the living, not with the dead; to these ascribing more than due, that they may obscure the glory of the other.

Desire of ease, and sensual delight, disposeth men to obey a common power: because by such desires, a man doth abandon the protection might be hoped for from his own industry, and labour. Fear of death, and wounds, disposeth to the same; and for the same reason. On the contrary, needy men, and hardy, not contented with their present condition; as also, all men that are ambitious of military command, are inclined to continue the causes of war; and to stir up trouble and sedition: for there is no honour military but by war; nor any such hope to mend an ill game, as by causing a new shuffle.

Desire of knowledge, and arts of peace, inclineth men to obey a common power: For such desire, containeth a desire of leisure; and consequently protection from some other power than their own.

Desire of praise, disposeth to laudable actions, such as please them whose judgment they value; for of those men whom we contemn, we contemn also the praises. Desire of fame after death does the same.

And though after death, there be no sense of the praise given us on earth, as being joys, that are either swallowed up in the unspeakable joys of Heaven, or extinguished in the extreme torments of hell: yet is not such fame vain; because men have a present delight therein, from the foresight of it, and of the benefit that may redound thereby to their posterity: which though they now see not, yet they imagine; and any thing that is pleasure in the sense, the same also is pleasure in the imagination.

To have received from one, to whom we think ourselves equal, greater benefits than there is hope to requite, disposeth to counterfeit love; but really secret hatred; and puts a man into the estate of a desperate debtor, that in declining the sight of his creditor, tacitly wishes him there, where he might never see him more. For benefits oblige, and obligation is thraldom; and unrequitable obligation, perpetual thraldom; which is to one's equal, hateful. But to have received benefits from one, whom we acknowledge for superior, inclines to love; because the obligation is no new depression: and cheerful acceptation, (which men call *gratitude*,) is such an honour done to the obliger, as is taken generally for retribution. Also to receive benefits, though from an equal, or inferior, as long as there is hope of requital, disposeth to love: for in the intention of the receiver, the obligation is of aid, and service mutual; from whence proceedeth an emulation of who shall exceed in benefiting; the most noble and profitable contention possible; wherein the victor is pleased with his victory, and the other revenged by confessing it.

To have done more hurt to a man, than he can, or is willing to expiate, inclineth the doer to hate the sufferer. For he must expect revenge, or forgiveness; both which are hateful.

Fear of oppression, disposeth a man to anticipate, or to seek aid by society: for there is no other way by which a man can secure his life and liberty.

Men that distrust their own subtlety, are in tumult and sedition, better disposed for victory, than they that suppose themselves wise, or crafty. For these love to consult, the other (fearing to be circumvented,) to strike first. And in sedition, men being always in the precincts of battle, to hold together, and use all advantages of force, is a better stratagem, than any that can proceed from subtlety of wit.

Vain-glorious men, such as without being conscious to themselves of great sufficiency, delight in supposing themselves gallant men, are inclined only to ostentation; but not to attempt: because when danger or difficulty appears, they look for nothing but to have their insufficiency discovered.

Vain-glorious men, such as estimate their sufficiency by the flattery of other men, or the fortune of some precedent action, without assured ground of hope from the true knowledge of themselves, are inclined to rash engaging; and in the approach of danger, or difficulty, to retire if they can: because not seeing the way of safety, they will rather hazard their honour, which may be salved with an excuse; than their lives, for which no salve is sufficient.

Men that have a strong opinion of their own wisdom in matter of government, are disposed to ambition. Because without public employment in council or magistracy, the honour of their wisdom is lost. And therefore eloquent speakers are inclined to ambition; for eloquence seemeth wisdom, both to themselves and others.

Pusillanimity disposeth men to irresolution, and consequently to lose the occasions, and fittest opportunities of action. For after men have been in deliberation till the time of action approach, if it be not then manifest what is best to be done, it is a sign, the difference of motives, the one way and the other, are not great: therefore not to resolve then, is to lose the occasion by weighing of trifles; which is pusillanimity.

Frugality, (though in poor men a virtue,) maketh a man unapt to achieve such actions, as require the strength of many men at once: for it weakeneth their endeavour, which is to be nourished and kept in vigour by reward.

Eloquence, with flattery, disposeth men to confide in them that have it; because the former is seeming wisdom, the latter seeming kindness. Add to them military reputation, and it disposeth men to adhere, and subject themselves to those men that have them. The two former, having given them caution against danger from him; the latter gives them caution against danger from others.

Want of science, that is, ignorance of causes, disposeth, or rather constraineth a man to rely on the advice, and authority of others. For all men whom the truth concerns, if they rely not on their own, must rely on the opinion of some other, whom they think wiser than themselves, and see not why he should deceive them.

Ignorance of the signification of words, which is want of understanding, disposeth men to take on trust, not only the truth they know not; but also the errors; and which is more, the non-sense of them they trust: for neither error nor non-sense, can without a perfect understanding of words, be detected.

From the same it proceedeth, that men give different names, to one and the same thing, from the difference of their own passions: as they that approve a private opinion, call it opinion; but they that mislike it, heresy: and yet heresy signifies no more than private opinion; but has only a greater tincture of choler.

From the same also it proceedeth, that men cannot distinguish, without study and great understanding, between the one action of many men, and many actions of one multitude; as for example, between one action of all the senators of *Rome* in killing *Cataline*, and the many actions of a number of senators in killing *Caesar*; and therefore are disposed to take for the action of the people, that which is a multitude of actions done by a multitude of men, led perhaps by the persuasion of one.

Ignorance of the causes, and original constitution of right, equity, law, and justice, disposeth a man to make custom and example the rule of his actions; in such manner, as to think that unjust which it hath been the custom to punish; and that just, of the impunity and approbation whereof they can produce an example, or (as the lawyers which only use this false measure of justice barbarously call it) a precedent; like little children, that have no other rule of good and evil manners, but the correction they receive from their parents and masters; save that children are constant to their rule, whereas, men are not so; because grown strong, and stubborn, they appeal from custom to reason, and from reason to custom, as it serves their turn; receding from custom when their interest requires it, and setting themselves against reason, as oft as reason is against them: which is the cause, that the doctrine of right and wrong, is perpetually disputed, both by the pen and the sword: whereas the doctrine of lines, and figures, is not so; because men care not, in that subject, what be truth, as a thing that crosses no man's ambition, profit or lust. For I doubt not, but if it had been a thing contrary to any man's right of dominion, or to the interest of men that have dominion, *that the three angles of a triangle, should be equal to two angles of a square;* that doctrine should have been, if not disputed, yet by the burning of all books of geometry, suppressed, as far as he whom it concerned was able.

Ignorance of remote causes, disposeth men to attribute all events, to the causes immediate, and instrumental: for these are all the causes they perceive. And hence it comes to pass, that in all places, men that are grieved with payments to the public, discharge their anger upon the publicans, that is to say, farmers, collectors, and other officers of the public revenue; and adhere to such as find fault with the public government; and thereby, when they have engaged themselves beyond hope of justification, fall also upon the supreme authority, for fear of punishment, or shame of receiving pardon.

Ignorance of natural causes disposeth a man to credulity, so as to believe many times impossibilities: for such know nothing to the contrary, but that they may be true; being unable to detect the impossibility. And credulity, because men love to be hearkened unto in company, disposeth them to lying: so that ignorance it self without malice, is able to make a man both to believe lies, and tell them, and sometimes also to invent them.

Anxiety for the future time, disposeth men to inquire into the causes of things: because the knowledge of them, maketh men the better able to order the present to their best advantage.

Curiosity, or love of the knowledge of causes, draws a man from consideration of the effect, to seek the cause; and again, the cause of that cause; till of necessity he must come to this thought at last, that there is some cause, whereof there is no former cause, but is eternal; which is it men call God. So that it is impossible to make any profound inquiry into natural causes, without being inclined thereby to believe there is one God eternal; though they cannot have any idea of him in their mind, answerable to his nature. For as a man that is born blind, hearing men talk of warming themselves by the fire, and being brought to warm himself by the same, may easily conceive, and assure himself, there is somewhat there, which men call *fire*, and is the cause of the heat he

feels; but cannot imagine what it is like; nor have an idea of it in his mind, such as they have that see it: so also, by the visible things of this world, and their admirable order, a man may conceive there is a cause of them, which men call God; and yet not have an idea, or image of him in his mind.

And they that make little, or no inquiry into the natural causes of things, yet from the fear that proceeds from the ignorance it self, of what it is that hath the power to do them much good or harm, are inclined to suppose, and feign unto themselves, several kinds of powers invisible; and to stand in awe of their own imaginations; and in time of distress to invoke them; as also in the time of an expected good success, to give them thanks; making the creatures of their own fancy, their gods. By which means it hath come to pass, that from the innumerable variety of fancy, men have created in the world innumerable sorts of gods. And this fear of things invisible, is the natural seed of that, which every one in himself calleth religion; and in them that worship, or fear that power otherwise than they do, superstition.

And this seed of religion, having been observed by many; some of those that have observed it, have been inclined thereby to nourish, dress, and form it into laws; and to add to it of their own invention, any opinion of the causes of future events, by which they thought they should be best able to govern others, and make unto themselves the greatest use of their powers.

Chapter 12

Of Religion

Seeing there are no signs, nor fruit of *religion*, but in man only; there is no cause to doubt, but that the seed of *religion*, is also only in man; and consisteth in some peculiar quality, or at least in some eminent degree thereof, not to be found in other living creatures.

And first, it is peculiar to the nature of man, to be inquisitive into the causes of the events they see, some more, some less; but all men so much, as to be curious in the search of the causes of their own good and evil fortune.

Secondly, upon the sight of any thing that hath a beginning, to think also it had a cause, which determined the same to begin, then when it did, rather than sooner or later.

Thirdly, whereas there is no other felicity of beasts, but the enjoying of their quotidian food, ease, and lusts; as having little or no foresight of the time to come, for want of observation, and memory of the order, consequence, and dependence of the things they see; man observeth how one event hath been produced by another; and remembereth in them antecedence and consequence; and when he cannot assure himself of the true causes of things, (for the causes of good and evil fortune for the most part are invisible,) he supposes causes of them, either such as his own fancy suggesteth; or trusteth to the authority of other men, such as he thinks to be his friends, and wiser than himself.

The two first, make anxiety. For being assured that there be causes of all things that have arrived hitherto, or shall arrive hereafter; it is impossible for a man, who continually endeavoureth to secure himself against the evil he fears, and procure the good he desireth, not to be in a perpetual solicitude of the time to come; so that every man, especially those that are over provident, are in an estate like to that of *Prometheus*. For as *Prometheus*, (which interpreted, is, *the prudent man*,) was bound to the hill *Caucasus*, a place of large prospect, where, an eagle feeding on his liver, devoured in the day, as much as was repaired in the night: so that man, which looks too far before him, in the care of future time, hath his heart all the day long, gnawed on by fear of death, poverty, or other calamity; and has no repose, nor pause of his anxiety, but in sleep.

This perpetual fear, always accompanying mankind in the ignorance of causes, as it were in the dark, must needs have for object something. And therefore when there is nothing to be seen, there is nothing to accuse, either of their good, or evil fortune, but some *power*, or agent *invisible*: in which sense perhaps it was, that some of the old poets said, that the gods were at first created by human fear: which spoken of the gods, (that is to say, of the many gods of the Gentiles) is very true. But the acknowledging of one God, eternal, infinite, and omnipotent, may more easily be derived, from the desire men have to know the causes of natural bodies, and their several virtues, and operations; than from the fear of what was to befall them in time to come. For he that from any effect he seeth come to pass, should reason to the next and immediate cause thereof, and from thence to the cause of that cause, and plunge himself profoundly in the pursuit of causes; shall at last come to this, that there must be (as even the heathen philosophers confessed) one first mover; that is, a first, and an eternal cause of all things; which is that which men mean by the name of God: and all this without thought of their fortune; the solicitude whereof, both inclines to fear, and hinders them from the search of the causes of other things; and thereby gives occasion of feigning of as many gods, as there be men that feign them.

And for the matter, or substance of the invisible agents, so fancied; they could not by natural cogitation, fall upon any other conceit, but that it was the same with that of the soul of man; and that the soul of man, was of the same substance, with that which appeareth in a dream, to one that sleepeth; or in a looking-glass, to one that is awake; which, men not knowing that such apparitions are nothing else but creatures of the fancy, think to be real, and external substances; and therefore call them ghosts; as the Latins called them *imagines*, and *umbrae*, and thought them spirits, that is, thin aerial bodies; and those invisible agents, which they feared, to be like them; save that they appear, and vanish when they please. But the opinion that such spirits were incorporeal, or immaterial, could never enter into the mind of any man by nature; because, though men may put together words of contradictory signification, as *spirit*, and *incorporeal*; yet they can never have the imagination of any thing answering to them: and therefore, men that by their own meditation, arrive to the acknowledgment of one infinite, omnipotent, and eternal God, choose rather to confess he is incomprehensible, and above their understanding, than to define his nature by *spirit incorporeal*, and then confess their definition to be unintelligible: or if they give him such a title, it is not *dogmatically*, with intention to make the divine nature understood; but *piously*, to honour him with attributes, of significations, as remote as they can from the grossness of bodies visible.

Then, for the way by which they think these invisible agents wrought their effects; that is to say, what immediate causes they used, in bringing things to pass, men that know not what it is that we call *causing*, (that is, almost all men) have no other rule to guess by, but by observing, and remembering what they have seen to precede the like effect at some other time, or times before, without seeing between the antecedent and subsequent event, any dependence or connexion at all: and therefore from the like things past, they expect the like things to come; and hope for good or evil luck, superstitiously, from things that have no part at all in the causing of it: as the Athenians did for their war at *Lepanto*, demand another *Phormio*; the Pompeian faction for their war in *Africa*, another *Scipio*; and others have done in divers other occasions since. In like manner they attribute their fortune to a stander by, to a lucky or unlucky place, to words spoken, especially if the name of God be amongst them; as charming and conjuring (the liturgy of witches;) insomuch as to believe, they have power to turn a stone into bread, bread into a man, or any thing into any thing.

Thirdly, for the worship which naturally men exhibit to powers invisible, it can be no other, but such expressions of their reverence, as they would use towards men; gifts, petitions, thanks, submission of body, considerate addresses, sober behaviour, premeditated words, swearing (that is, assuring one another of their promises,) by invoking them. Beyond that reason suggesteth nothing; but leaves them either to rest there; or for further ceremonies, to rely on those they believe to be wiser than themselves.

Lastly, concerning how these invisible powers declare to men the things which shall hereafter come to pass, especially concerning their good or evil fortune in general, or good or ill success in any particular undertaking, men are naturally at a stand; save that using to conjecture of the time to come, by the time past, they are very apt, not only to take casual things, after one or two encounters, for prognostics of the like encounter ever after, but also to believe the like prognostics from other men, of whom they have once conceived a good opinion.

And in these four things, opinion of ghosts, ignorance of second causes, devotion towards what men fear, and taking of things casual for prognostics, consisteth the natural seed of *religion*; which by reason of the different fancies, judgments, and passions of several men, hath grown up into ceremonies so different, that those which are used by one man, are for the most part ridiculous to another.

For these seeds have received culture from two sorts of men. One sort have been they, that have nourished, and ordered them, according to their own invention. The other have done it, by God's commandment, and direction: but both sorts have done it, with a purpose to make those men that relied on them, the more apt to obedience, laws, peace, charity, and civil society. So that the religion of the former sort, is a part of human politics; and teacheth part of the duty which earthly kings require of their subjects. And the religion of the latter sort is divine politics; and containeth precepts to those that have yielded themselves subjects in the kingdom of God. Of the former sort, were all the founders of commonwealths, and the lawgivers of the Gentiles: of the latter sort, were *Abraham, Moses,* and our *blessed Saviour*; by whom have been derived unto us the laws of the kingdom of God.

And for that part of religion, which consisteth in opinions concerning the nature of powers invisible, there is almost nothing that has a name, that has not been esteemed amongst the Gentiles, in one place or another, a god, or devil; or by their poets feigned to be inanimated, inhabited, or possessed by some spirit or other.

The unformed matter of the world, was a god, by the name of *Chaos*.

The heaven, the ocean, the planets, the fire, the earth, the winds, were so many gods.

Men, women, a bird, a crocodile, a calf, a dog, a snake, an onion, a leek, deified. Besides that, they filled almost all places, with spirits called *demons*: the plains, with *Pan*, and *Panises*, or Satyrs; the woods, with Fawns, and Nymphs; the sea, with Tritons, and other Nymphs; every river, and fountain, with a ghost of his name, and with Nymphs; every house with its *Lares*, or familiars; every man with his *Genius*; hell with ghosts, and spiritual officers, as *Charon, Cerberus*, and the *Furies*; and in the night time, all places with *larvae, lemures*, ghosts of men deceased, and a whole kingdom of fairies and bugbears. They have also ascribed divinity, and built temples to meer accidents, and qualities, such as are time, night, day, peace, concord, love, contention, virtue, honour, health, rust, fever, and the like; which when they prayed for, or against, they prayed to, as if there were ghosts of those names hanging over their heads, and letting fall, or withholding that good, or evil, for, or against which they prayed. They invoked also their own wit, by the name of *Muses*; their own ignorance, by the name of *Fortune*; their own lust, by the name of *Cupid*; their own rage, by the name *Furies*; their own privy members, by the name of *Priapus*, and attributed their pollutions, to *Incubi*, and *Succubae:* insomuch as there was nothing, which a poet could introduce as a person in his poem, which they did not make either a *god*, or a *devil*.

The same authors of the religion of the Gentiles, observing the second ground for religion, which is men's ignorance of causes; and thereby their aptness to attribute their fortune to causes, on which there was no dependence at all apparent, took occasion to obtrude on their ignorance, instead of second causes, a kind of second and ministerial gods; ascribing the cause of fecundity, to *Venus*; the cause of arts, to *Apollo*; of subtlety and craft, to *Mercury*; of tempests and storms, to *Aeolus*; and of other effects, to other gods; insomuch as there was amongst the heathen almost as great variety of gods, as of business.

And to the worship, which naturally men conceived fit to be used towards their gods, namely, oblations, prayers, thanks, and the rest formerly named; the same legislators of the Gentiles have added their images, both in picture, and sculpture; that the more ignorant sort (that is to say, the most part or generality of the people,) thinking the gods for whose representation they were made, were really included, and as it were housed within them, might so much the more stand in fear of them: and endowed them with lands, and houses, and officers, and revenues, set apart from all other human uses; that is, consecrated, and made holy to those their idols; as caverns, groves, woods, mountains, and whole islands; and have attributed to them, not only the shapes, some of men, some of beasts, some of monsters; but also the faculties, and passions of men and beasts; as sense, speech, sex, lust, generation, (and this not only by mixing one with another, to propagate the kind of gods; but also by mixing with men, and women, to beget mongrel gods, and but inmates of heaven, as *Bacchus*, *Hercules*, and

others;) besides anger, revenge, and other passions of living creatures, and the actions proceeding from them, as fraud, theft, adultery, sodomy, and any vice that may be taken for an effect of power, or a cause of pleasure; and all such vices, as amongst men are taken to be against law, rather than against honour.

Lastly, to the prognostics of time to come; which are naturally, but conjectures upon the experience of time past; and supernaturally, divine revelation; the same authors of the religion of the Gentiles, partly upon pretended experience, partly upon pretended revelation, have added innumerable other superstitious ways of divination; and made men believe they should find their fortunes, sometimes in the ambiguous or senseless answers of the priests at *Delphi, Delos, Ammon*, and other famous oracles; which answers, were made ambiguous by design, to own the event both ways; or absurd, by the intoxicating vapour of the place, which is very frequent in sulphurous caverns: sometimes in the leaves of the Sybils; of whose prophecies (like those perhaps of *Nostradamus*; for the fragments now extant seem to be the invention of later times) there were some books in reputation in the time of the Roman republic: sometimes in the insignificant speeches of madmen, supposed to be possessed with a divine spirit, which possession they called enthusiasm; and these kinds of foretelling events, were accounted theomancy, or prophecy: sometimes in the aspect of the stars at their nativity; which was called horoscopy, and esteemed a part of judiciary astrology: sometimes in their own hopes and fears, called thumomancy, or presage: sometimes in the prediction of witches, that pretended conference with the dead; which is called necromancy, conjuring, and witchcraft; and is but juggling and confederate knavery: sometimes in the casual flight, or feeding of birds; called augury: sometimes in the entrails of a sacrificed beast; which was *aruspicina:* sometimes in dreams: sometimes in croaking of ravens, or chattering of birds: sometimes in the lineaments of the face; which was called metoposcopy; or by palmistry in the lines of the hand; in casual words, called *omina:* sometimes in monsters, or unusual accidents; as eclipses, comets, rare meteors, earthquakes, inundations, uncouth births, and the like, which they called *portenta*, and *ostenta*, because they thought them to portend, or foreshow some great calamity to come;

sometimes, in mere lottery, as cross and pile; counting holes in a sieve; dipping of verses in *Homer*, and *Virgil*; and innumerable other such vain conceits. So easy are men to be drawn to believe any thing, from such men as have gotten credit with them; and can with gentleness, and dexterity, take hold of their fear, and ignorance.

And therefore the first founders, and legislators of commonwealths among the Gentiles, whose ends were only to keep the people in obedience, and peace, have in all places taken care; first, to imprint in their minds a belief, that those precepts which they gave concerning religion, might not be thought to proceed from their own device, but from the dictates of some god, or other spirit; or else that they themselves were of a higher nature than mere mortals, that their laws might the more easily be received: so *Numa Pompilius* pretended to receive the ceremonies he instituted amongst the Romans, from the nymph *Egeria*: and the first king and founder of the kingdom of *Peru*, pretended himself and his wife to be the children of the Sun: and *Mahomet*, to set up his new religion, pretended to have conferences with the Holy Ghost, in form of a dove. Secondly, they have had a care, to make it believed, that the same things were displeasing to the gods, which were forbidden by the laws. Thirdly, to prescribe ceremonies, supplications, sacrifices, and festivals, by which they were to believe, the anger of the gods might be appeased; and that ill success in war, great contagions of sickness, earthquakes, and each man's private misery, came from the anger of the gods, and their anger from the neglect of their worship, or the forgetting, or mistaking some point of the ceremonies required. And though amongst the ancient Romans, men were not forbidden to deny, that which in the poets is written of the pains, and pleasures after this life; which divers of great authority, and gravity in that state have in their *harangues* openly derided; yet that belief was always more cherished, than the contrary.

And by these, and such other institutions, they obtained in order to their end, (which was the peace of the commonwealth,) that the common people in their misfortunes, laying the fault on neglect, or error in their ceremonies, or on their own disobedience to the laws, were the less apt to mutiny against their governors. And being entertained with the pomp, and pastime of festivals, and public games, made in honour of the gods, needed nothing else but bread to keep them from discontent, murmuring, and commotion against the state. And therefore the Romans, that had conquered the greatest part of the then known world, made no scruple of tolerating any religion whatsoever in the city of *Rome* itself, unless it had something in it, that could not consist with their civil government; nor do we read, that any religion was there forbidden, but that of the Jews; who (being the peculiar kingdom of God) thought it unlawful to acknowledge subjection to any mortal king or state whatsoever. And thus you see how the religion of the Gentiles was a part of their policy.

But where God himself, by supernatural revelation, planted religion; there he also made to himself a peculiar kingdom; and gave laws, not only of behaviour towards himself, but also towards one another; and thereby in the kingdom of God, the policy, and laws civil, are a part of religion; and therefore the distinction of temporal, and spiritual domination, hath there no place. It is true, that God is king of all the earth: yet may he be king of a peculiar, and chosen nation. For there is no more incongruity therein, than that he that hath the general command of the whole army, should have withal a peculiar regiment, or company of his own. God is king of all the earth by his power: but of his chosen people, he is king by covenant. But to speak more largely of the kingdom of God, both by nature, and covenant, I have in the following discourse assigned another place.

From the propagation of religion, it is not hard to understand the causes of the resolution of the same into its first seeds, or principles; which are only an opinion of a deity, and powers invisible, and supernatural; that can never be so abolished out of human nature, but that new religions may again be made to spring out of them, by the culture of such men, as for such purpose are in reputation.

For seeing all formed religion, is founded at first, upon the faith which a multitude hath in some one person, whom they believe not only to be a wise man, and to labour to procure their happiness, but also to be a holy man, to whom God himself vouchsafeth to declare his will supernaturally; it followeth necessarily, when they that have the government of religion, shall come to have either the wisdom of those men, their sincerity, or their love suspected; or that they shall be unable to show any probable token of divine revelation; that the religion which they desire to uphold, must be suspected likewise; and (without the fear of the civil sword) contradicted and rejected.

That which taketh away the reputation of wisdom, in him that formeth a religion, or addeth to it when it is already formed, is the enjoining of a belief of contradictories: for both parts of a contradiction cannot possibly be true: and therefore to enjoin the belief of them, is an argument of ignorance; which detects the author in that; and discredits him in all things else he shall propound as from revelation supernatural: which revelation a man may indeed have of many things above, but of nothing against natural reason.

That which taketh away the reputation of sincerity, is the doing or saying of such things, as appear to be signs, that what they require other men to believe, is not believed by themselves; all which doings, or sayings are therefore called scandalous, because they be stumbling blocks, that make men to fall in the way of religion: as injustice, cruelty, profaneness, avarice, and luxury. For who can believe, that he that doth ordinarily such actions as proceed from any of these roots, believeth there is any such invisible power to be feared, as he affrighteth other men withal, for lesser faults?

That which taketh away the reputation of love, is the being detected of private ends: as when the belief they require of others, conduceth or seemeth to conduce to the acquiring of dominion, riches, dignity, or secure pleasure, to themselves only, or specially. For that which men reap benefit by to themselves, they are thought to do for their own sakes, and not for love of others.

Lastly, the testimony that men can render of divine calling, can be no other, than the operation of miracles; or true prophecy, (which also is a miracle;) or extraordinary felicity. And therefore, to those points of religion, which have been received from them that did such miracles; those that are added by such, as approve not their calling by some miracle, obtain no greater belief, than what the custom and laws of the places, in which they be educated, have wrought into them. For as in natural things, men of judgment require natural signs, and arguments; so in supernatural things, they require signs supernatural, (which are

miracles,) before they consent inwardly, and from their hearts.

All which causes of the weakening of men's faith, do manifestly appear in the examples following. First, we have the example of the children of Israel; who when *Moses*, that had approved his calling to them by miracles, and by the happy conduct of them out of *Egypt*, was absent but 40 days, revolted from the worship of the true God, recommended to them by him; and setting up (*Exod.* 32. 1, 2.) a golden calf for their god, relapsed into the idolatry of the Egyptians; from whom they had been so lately delivered. And again, after *Moses*, *Aaron*, *Joshua*, and that generation which had seen the great works of God in Israel, (*Judges* 2. 11.) were dead; another generation arose, and served *Baal.* So that miracles failing, faith also failed.

Again, when the sons of *Samuel*, (1 *Sam.* 8. 3.) being constituted by their father judges in *Bersabee*, received bribes, and judged unjustly, the people of Israel refused any more to have God to be their king, in other manner than he was king of other people; and therefore cried out to Samuel, to choose them a king after the manner of the nations. So that justice failing, faith also failed: insomuch, as they deposed their God, from reigning over them.

And whereas in the planting of Christian religion, the oracles ceased in all parts of the Roman empire, and the number of Christians increased wonderfully every day, and in every place, by the preaching of the Apostles, and Evangelists; a great part of that success, may reasonably be attributed, to the contempt, into which the priests of the Gentiles of that time, had brought themselves, by their uncleanness, avarice, and juggling between princes. Also the religion of the church of *Rome*, was partly, for the same cause abolished in *England*, and many other parts of Christendom; insomuch, as the failing of virtue in the pastors, maketh faith fail in the people: and partly from bringing of the philosophy, and doctrine of *Aristotle* into religion, by the Schoolmen; from whence there arose so many contradictions, and absurdities, as brought the clergy into a reputation both of ignorance, and of fraudulent intention; and inclined people to revolt from them, either against the will of their own princes, as in *France* and *Holland*; or with their will, as in *England*.

Lastly, amongst the points by the church of *Rome* declared necessary for salvation, there be so many, manifestly to the advantage of the Pope, and of his spiritual subjects, residing in the territories of other Christian princes, that were it not for the mutual emulation of those princes, they might without war, or trouble, exclude all foreign authority, as easily as it has been excluded in *England*. For who is there that does not see, to whose benefit it conduceth, to have it believed, that a king hath not his authority from Christ, unless a bishop crown him? That a king, if he be a priest, cannot marry? That whether a prince be born in lawful marriage, or not, must be judged by authority from *Rome*? That subjects may be freed from their allegiance, if by the court of *Rome*, the king be judged an heretic? That a king (as *Chilperic* of *France*) may be deposed by a pope (as Pope *Zachary*) for no cause; and his kingdom given to one of his subjects? That the clergy and regulars, in what country soever, shall be exempt from the jurisdiction of their king, in cases criminal? Or who does not see, to whose profit redound the fees of private masses, and vales of purgatory; with other signs of private interest, enough to mortify the most lively faith, if (as I said) the civil magistrate, and custom did not more sustain it, than any opinion they have of the sanctity, wisdom, or probity of their teachers? So that I may attribute all the changes of religion in the world, to one and the same cause; and that is, unpleasing priests; and those not only amongst Catholics, but even in that church that hath presumed most of reformation.

Chapter 13

Of the Natural Condition of Mankind as Concerning Their Felicity, and Misery

Nature hath made men so equal, in the faculties of body, and mind; as that though there be found one man sometimes manifestly stronger in body, or of quicker mind than another; yet when all is reckoned together, the difference between man, and man, is not so considerable, as that one man can thereupon claim to himself any benefit, to which another may not pretend, as well as he. For as to the strength of body, the weakest has strength enough to kill the strongest, either by secret machination, or by confederacy with others, that are in the same danger with himself.

And as to the faculties of the mind, (setting aside the arts grounded upon words, and especially that skill of proceeding upon general, and infallible rules, called science; which very few have, and but in few things; as being not a native faculty, born with us; nor attained, (as prudence,) while we look after somewhat else,) I find yet a greater equality amongst men, than that of strength. For prudence, is but experience; which equal time, equally bestows on all men, in those things they equally apply themselves unto. That which may perhaps make such equality incredible, is but a vain conceit of one's own wisdom, which almost all men think they have in a greater degree, than the vulgar; that is, than all men but themselves, and a few others, whom by fame, or for concurring with themselves, they approve. For such is the nature of men, that howsoever they may acknowledge many others to be more witty, or more eloquent, or more learned; yet they will hardly believe there be many so wise as themselves: For they see their own wit at hand, and other men's at a distance. But this proveth rather that men are in that point equal, than unequal. For there is not ordinarily a greater sign of the equal distribution of any thing, than that every man is contented with his share.

From this equality of ability, ariseth equality of hope in the attaining of our ends. And therefore if any two men desire the same thing, which nevertheless they cannot both enjoy, they become enemies; and in the way to their end, (which is principally their own conservation, and sometimes their delectation only,) endeavour to destroy, or subdue one another. And from hence it comes to pass, that where an invader hath no more to fear, than another man's single power; if one plant, sow, build, or possess a convenient seat, others may probably be expected to come prepared with forces united, to dispossess, and deprive him, not only of the fruit of his labour, but also of his life, or liberty. And the invader again is in the like danger of another.

And from this diffidence of one another, there is no way for any man to secure himself, so reasonable, as anticipation; that is, by force, or wiles, to master the persons of all men he can, so long, till he see no other power great enough to endanger him: and this is no more than his own conservation requireth, and is generally allowed. Also because there be some, that taking pleasure in contemplating their own power in the acts of conquest, which they pursue farther than their security requires; if others, that otherwise would be glad to be at ease within modest bounds, should not by invasion increase their power, they would not be able, long time, by standing only on their defence, to subsist. And by consequence, such augmentation of dominion over men, being necessary to a man's conservation, it ought to be allowed him.

Again, men have no pleasure, (but on the contrary a great deal of grief) in keeping company, where there is no power able to over-awe them all. For every man looketh that his companion should value him, at the same rate he sets upon himself: and upon all signs of contempt, or undervaluing, naturally endeavours, as far as he dares (which amongst them that have no common power to keep them in quiet, is far enough to make them destroy each other), to extort a greater value from his contemners, by damage; and from others, by the example.

So that in the nature of man, we find three principal causes of quarrel. First, competition; secondly, diffidence; thirdly, glory.

The first, maketh men invade for gain; the second, for safety; and the third, for reputation. The first use violence, to make themselves masters of other men's persons, wives, children, and cattle; the second, to defend them; the third, for trifles, as a word, a smile, a different opinion, and any other sign of undervalue, either direct in their persons, or by reflection in their kindred, their friends, their nation, their profession, or their name.

Hereby it is manifest, that during the time men live without a common power to keep them all in awe, they are in that condition which is called war; and such a war, as is of every man, against every man. For WAR, consisteth not in battle only, or the act of fighting; but in a tract of time, wherein the will to contend by battle is sufficiently known: and therefore the notion of *time*, is to be considered in the nature of war; as it is in the nature of weather. For as the nature of foul weather, lieth not in a shower or two

of rain; but in an inclination thereto of many days together: so the nature of war, consisteth not in actual fighting; but in the known disposition thereto, during all the time there is no assurance to the contrary. All other time is PEACE.

Whatsoever therefore is consequent to a time of war, where every man is enemy to every man; the same is consequent to the time, wherein men live without other security, than what their own strength, and their own invention shall furnish them withal. In such condition, there is no place for industry; because the fruit thereof is uncertain: and consequently no culture of the earth; no navigation, nor use of the commodities that may be imported by sea; no commodious building; no instruments of moving, and removing such things as require much force; no knowledge of the face of the earth; no account of time; no arts; no letters; no society; and which is worst of all, continual fear, and danger of violent death; and the life of man, solitary, poor, nasty, brutish, and short.

It may seem strange to some man, that has not well weighed these things; that nature should thus dissociate, and render men apt to invade, and destroy one another: and he may therefore, not trusting to this inference, made from the passions, desire perhaps to have the same confirmed by experience. Let him therefore consider with himself, when taking a journey, he arms himself, and seeks to go well accompanied; when going to sleep, he locks his doors; when even in his house he locks his chests; and this when he knows there be laws, and public officers, armed, to revenge all injuries shall be done him; what opinion he has of his fellow subjects, when he rides armed; of his fellow citizens, when he locks his doors; and of his children, and servants, when he locks his chests. Does he not there as much accuse mankind by his actions, as I do by my words? But neither of us accuse man's nature in it. The desires, and other passions of man, are in themselves no sin. No more are the actions, that proceed from those passions, till they know a law that forbids them: which till laws be made they cannot know: nor can any law be made, till they have agreed upon the person that shall make it.

It may peradventure be thought, there was never

such a time, nor condition of war as this; and I believe it was never generally so, over all the world: but there are many places, where they live so now. For the savage people in many places of *America*, except the government of small families, the concord whereof dependeth on natural lust, have no government at all; and live at this day in that brutish manner, as I said before. Howsoever, it may be perceived what manner of life there would be, where there were no common power to fear; by the manner of life, which men that have formerly lived under a peacefull government, use to degenerate into, in a civil war.

But though there had never been any time, wherein particular men were in a condition of war one against another; yet in all times, kings, and persons of sovereign authority, because of their independency, are in continual jealousies, and in the state and posture of gladiators; having their weapons pointing, and their eyes fixed on one another; that is, their forts, garrisons, and guns upon the frontiers of their kingdoms; and continual spies upon their neighbours; which is a posture of war. But because they uphold thereby, the industry of their subjects; there does not follow from it, that misery, which accompanies the liberty of particular men.

To this war of every man against every man, this also is consequent; that nothing can be unjust. The notions of right and wrong, justice and injustice have there no place. Where there is no common power, there is no law: where no law, no injustice. Force, and fraud, are in war the two cardinal virtues. Justice, and injustice are none of the faculties neither of the body, nor mind. If they were, they might be in a man that were alone in the world, as well as his senses, and passions. They are qualities, that relate to men in society, not in solitude. It is consequent also to the same condition, that there be no propriety, no dominion, no *mine* and *thine* distinct; but only that to be every man's, that he can get; and for so long, as he can keep it. And thus much for the ill condition, which man by mere nature is actually placed in; though with a possibility to come out of it, consisting partly in the passions, partly in his reason.

The passions that incline men to peace, are fear of death; desire of such things as are necessary to commodious living; and a hope by their industry to obtain them. And reason suggesteth convenient articles of peace, upon which men may be drawn to agreement. These articles, are they, which otherwise are called the Laws of Nature: whereof I shall speak more particularly, in the two following chapters.

Chapter 14

Of the First and Second Natural Laws, and of Contracts

The RIGHT OF NATURE, which writers commonly call *jus naturale*, is the liberty each man hath, to use his own power, as he will himself, for the preservation of his own nature; that is to say, of his own life; and consequently, of doing any thing, which in his own judgment, and reason, he shall conceive to be the aptest means thereunto.

By LIBERTY, is understood, according to the proper signification of the word, the absence of external impediments: which impediments, may oft take away part of a man's power to do what he would; but cannot hinder him from using the power left him, according as his judgment, and reason shall dictate to him.

A LAW OF NATURE, (*lex naturalis*,) is a precept, or general rule, found out by reason, by which a man is forbidden to do that, which is destructive of his life, or taketh away the means of preserving the same; and to omit that, by which he thinketh it may be best preserved. For though they that speak of this subject, use to confound *jus*, and *lex*, *right* and *law*; yet they ought to be distinguished; because RIGHT, consisteth in liberty to do, or to forbear; whereas LAW, determineth, and bindeth to one of them: so that law, and right, differ as much, as obligation, and liberty; which in one and the same matter are inconsistent.

And because the condition of man, (as hath been declared in the precedent chapter) is a condition of war of every one against every one; in which case every one is governed by his own reason; and there is nothing he can make use of, that may not be a help unto him, in preserving his life against his enemies; it followeth, that in such a condition, every man has a right to every thing; even to one another's body. And therefore, as long as this natural right of every man to every thing endureth, there can be no security to any man, (how strong or wise soever he be,) of living out the time, which nature ordinarily alloweth men to live. And consequently it is a precept, or general rule of reason, *that every man, ought to endeavour peace, as far as he has hope of obtaining it; and when he cannot obtain it, that he may seek, and use, all helps, and advantages of war.* The first branch of which rule, containeth the first, and fundamental law of nature; which is, *to seek peace, and follow it.* The second, the sum of the right of nature; which is, *by all means we can, to defend ourselves.*

From this fundamental law of nature, by which men are commanded to endeavour peace, is derived this second law; *that a man be willing, when others are so too, as far-forth, as for peace, and defence of himself he shall think it necessary, to lay down this right to all things; and be contented with so much liberty against other men, as he would allow other men against himself.* For as long as every man holdeth this right, of doing any thing he liketh; so long are all men in the condition of war. But if other men will not lay down their right, as well as he; then there is no reason for any one, to divest himself of his: for that were to expose himself to prey, (which no man is bound to) rather than to dispose himself to peace. This is that law of the Gospel; *whatsoever you require that others should do to you, that do ye to them.* And that law of all men, *quod tibi fieri non vis, alteri ne feceris.*

To *lay down* a man's *right* to any thing, is to *divest* himself of the *liberty*, of hindering another of the benefit of his own right to the same. For he that renounceth, or passeth away his right, giveth not to any other man a right which he had not before; because there is nothing to which every man had not right by nature: but only standeth out of his way, that he may enjoy his own original right, without hindrance from him; not without hindrance from another. So that the effect which redoundeth to one man, by another man's defect of right, is but so much diminution of impediments to the use of his own right original.

Right is laid aside, either by simply renouncing it; or by transferring it to another. By *simply* RENOUNCING; when he cares not to whom the benefit thereof redoundeth. By TRANSFERRING; when he intendeth the benefit thereof to some certain person, or persons. And when a man hath in either manner abandoned, or granted away his right; then is he said to be OBLIGED, or BOUND, not to hinder those, to whom such right is granted, or abandoned, from the benefit of it: and that he *ought*, and it is his DUTY, not to make void that voluntary act of his own: and that such hindrance is INJUSTICE, and INJURY, as being *sine jure*; the right being before renounced, or transferred. So that *injury*, or *injustice*, in the controversies of the world, is somewhat like to that, which in the disputations of scholars is called *absurdity*. For as it is there called an absurdity, to contradict what one maintained in the beginning: so in the world, it is called injustice, and injury, voluntarily to undo that, which from the beginning he had voluntarily done. The way by which a man either simply renounceth, or transferreth his right, is a declaration, or signification, by some voluntary and sufficient sign, or signs, that he doth so renounce, or transfer; or hath so renounced, or transferred the same, to him that accepteth it. And these signs are either words only, or actions only; or (as it happeneth most often) both words, and actions. And the same are the BONDS, by which men are bound, and obliged: bonds, that have their strength, not from their own nature, (for nothing is more easily broken than a man's word,) but from fear of some evil consequence upon the rupture.

Whensoever a man transferreth his right, or renounceth it; it is either in consideration of some right reciprocally transferred to himself; or for some other good he hopeth for thereby. For it is a voluntary act: and of the voluntary acts of every man, the object is some *good to himself.* And therefore there be some rights, which no man can be understood by any words, or other signs, to have abandoned, or transferred. As first a man cannot lay down the right of resisting them, that assault him by force, to take away his life; because he cannot be understood to aim thereby, at any good to himself. The same may be said of wounds, and chains, and imprisonment; both because there is no benefit consequent to such patience; as there is to the patience of suffering another to be wounded, or imprisoned; as also because a man cannot tell, when he seeth men proceed against him by violence, whether they intend his death or not. And lastly the motive, and end for which this renouncing, and transferring of right is introduced, is nothing else but the security of a man's person, in his life, and in the means of so preserving life, as not to be weary of it. And therefore if a man by words, or other signs, seem to despoil himself of the end, for which those signs were intended; he is not to be understood as if he meant it, or that it was his will; but that he was ignorant of how such words and actions were to be interpreted.

The mutual transferring of right, is that which men call CONTRACT.

There is difference between transferring of right to the thing; and transferring, or tradition, that is, delivery of the thing it self. For the thing may be delivered together with the translation of the right; as in buying and selling with ready money; or exchange of goods, or lands: and it may be delivered some time after.

Again, one of the contractors, may deliver the thing contracted for on his part, and leave the other to perform his part at some determinate time after, and in the mean time be trusted; and then the contract on his part, is called PACT, or COVENANT: or both parts may contract now, to perform hereafter: in which cases, he that is to perform in time to come, being trusted, his performance is called *keeping of promise*, or faith; and the failing of performance (if it be voluntary) *violation of faith*.

When the transferring of right, is not mutual; but one of the parties transferreth, in hope to gain thereby friendship, or service from another, or from his friends; or in hope to gain the reputation of charity, or magnanimity; or to deliver his mind from the pain of compassion; or in hope of reward in heaven; this is not contract, but GIFT, FREE-GIFT, GRACE: which words signify one and the same thing.

Signs of contract, are either *express*, or *by inference*. Express, are words spoken with understanding of what they signify: and such words are either of the time *present*, or *past*; as, *I give, I grant, I have given, I have granted, I will that this be yours*: or of the future; as, *I will give, I will grant*: which words of the future are called PROMISE.

Signs by inference, are sometimes the consequence of words; sometimes the consequence of silence; sometimes the consequence of actions; sometimes the

consequence of forbearing an action: and generally a sign by inference, of any contract, is whatsoever sufficiently argues the will of the contractor.

Words alone, if they be of the time to come, and contain a bare promise, are an insufficient sign of a free-gift and therefore not obligatory. For if they be of the time to come, as, *tomorrow I will give*, they are a sign I have not given yet, and consequently that my right is not transferred, but remaineth till I transfer it by some other act. But if the words be of the time present, or past, as, *I have given, or do give to be delivered tomorrow*, then is my tomorrow's right given away to day; and that by the virtue of the words, though there were no other argument of my will. And there is a great difference in the signification of these words, *volo hoc tuum esse cras*, and *cras dabo*; that is, between *I will that this be thine tomorrow*, and, *I will give it thee tomorrow*: for the word *I will*, in the former manner of speech, signifies an act of the will present; but in the latter, it signifies a promise of an act of the will to come: and therefore the former words, being of the present, transfer a future right; the latter, that be of the future, transfer nothing. But if there be other signs of the will to transfer a right, besides words; then, though the gift be free, yet may the right be understood to pass by words of the future: as if a man propound a prize to him that comes first to the end of a race, the gift is free; and though the words be of the future, yet the right passeth: for if he would not have his words so be understood, he should not have let them run.

In contracts, the right passeth, not only where the words are of the time present, or past, but also where they are of the future: because all contract is mutual translation, or change of right; and therefore he that promiseth only, because he hath already received the benefit for which he promiseth, is to be understood as if he intended the right should pass: for unless he had been content to have his words so understood, the other would not have performed his part first. And for that cause, in buying, and selling, and other acts of contract, a promise is equivalent to a covenant; and therefore obligatory.

He that performeth first in the case of a contract, is said to MERIT that which he is to receive by the performance of the other; and he hath it as *due*. Also when a prize is propounded to many, which is to be given to him only that winneth; or money is thrown amongst many, to be enjoyed by them that catch it; though this be a free gift; yet so to win, or so to catch, is to *merit*, and to have it as DUE. For the right is transferred in the propounding of the prize, and in throwing down the money; though it be not determined to whom, but by the event of the contention. But there is between these two sorts of merit, this difference, that in contract, I merit by virtue of my own power, and the contractor's need; but in this case of free gift, I am enabled to merit only by the benignity of the giver: in contract, I merit at the contractor's hand that he should depart with his right; in this case of gift, I merit not that the giver should part with his right; but that when he has parted with it, it should be mine, rather than another's. And this I think to be the meaning of that distinction of the Schools, between *meritum congrui*, and *meritum condigni*. For God Almighty, having promised Paradise to those men (hoodwinked with carnal desires,) that can walk through this world according to the precepts, and limits prescribed by him; they say, he that shall so walk, shall merit Paradise *ex congruo*. But because no man can demand a right to it, by his own righteousness, or any other power in himself, but by the free grace of God only; they say, no man can merit Paradise *ex condigno*. This I say, I think is the meaning of that distinction; but because disputers do not agree upon the signification of their own terms of art, longer than it serves their turn; I will not affirm any thing of their meaning: only this I say; when a gift is given indefinitely, as a prize to be contended for, he that winneth meriteth, and may claim the prize as due.

If a covenant be made, wherein neither of the parties perform presently, but trust one another; in the condition of mere nature, (which is a condition of war of every man against every man,) upon any reasonable suspicion, it is void: but if there be a common power set over them both, with right and force sufficient to compel performance, it is not void. For he that performeth first, has no assurance the other will perform after; because the bonds of words are too weak to bridle men's ambition, avarice, anger, and other passions, without the fear of some coercive power; which in the condition of mere nature, where all men are equal, and judges of the justness of their own fears, cannot possibly be supposed. And therefore he which performeth first, does but betray himself to his enemy; contrary to the right (he can never abandon) of defending his life, and means of living.

But in a civil estate, where there is a power set up to constrain those that would otherwise violate their faith, that fear is no more reasonable; and for that cause, he which by the covenant is to perform first, is obliged so to do.

The cause of fear, which maketh such a covenant invalid, must be always something arising after the covenant made; as some new fact, or other sign of the will not to perform: else it cannot make the covenant void. For that which could not hinder a man from promising, ought not to be admitted as a hindrance of performing.

He that transferreth any right, transferreth the means of enjoying it, as far as lieth in his power. As he that selleth land, is understood to transfer the herbage, and whatsoever grows upon it; nor can he that sells a mill turn away the stream that drives it. And they that give to a man the right of government in sovereignty, are understood to give him the right of levying money to maintain soldiers; and of appointing magistrates for the administration of justice.

To make covenants with brute beasts, is impossible; because not understanding our speech, they understand not, nor accept of any translation of right; nor can translate any right to another: and without mutual acceptation, there is no covenant.

To make covenant with God, is impossible, but by mediation of such as God speaketh to, either by revelation supernatural, or by his lieutenants that govern under him, and in his name: for otherwise we know not whether our covenants be accepted, or not. And therefore they that vow any thing contrary to any law of nature, vow in vain; as being a thing unjust to pay such vow. And if it be a thing commanded by the law of nature, it is not the vow, but the law that binds them.

The matter, or subject of a covenant, is always something that falleth under deliberation; (for to covenant, is an act of the will; that is to say an act, and the last act, of deliberation;) and is therefore always understood to be something to come; and which is judged possible for him that covenanteth, to perform.

And therefore, to promise that which is known to be impossible, is no covenant. But if that prove impossible afterwards, which before was thought possible, the covenant is valid, and bindeth, (though not to the thing it self,) yet to the value; or, if that also be impossible, to the unfeigned endeavour of performing as much as is possible: for to more no man can be obliged.

Men are freed of their covenants two ways; by performing; or by being forgiven. For performance, is the natural end of obligation; and forgiveness, the restitution of liberty; as being a retransferring of that right, in which the obligation consisted.

Covenants entered into by fear, in the condition of mere nature, are obligatory. For example, if I covenant to pay a ransom, or service for my life, to an enemy; I am bound by it. For it is a contract, wherein one receiveth the benefit of life; the other is to receive money, or service for it; and consequently, where no other law (as in the condition, of mere nature) forbiddeth the performance, the covenant is valid. Therefore prisoners of war, if trusted with the payment of their ransom, are obliged to pay it: and if a weaker prince, make a disadvantageous peace with a stronger, for fear; he is bound to keep it; unless (as hath been said before) there ariseth some new, and just cause of fear, to renew the war. And even in commonwealths, if I be forced to redeem myself from a thief by promising him money, I am bound to pay it, till the civil law discharge me. For whatsoever I may lawfully do without obligation, the same I may lawfully covenant to do through fear: and what I lawfully covenant, I cannot lawfully break.

A former covenant, makes void a later. For a man that hath passed away his right to one man today, hath it not to pass tomorrow to another: and therefore the later promise passeth no right, but is null.

A covenant not to defend myself from force, by force, is always void. For (as I have showed before) no man can transfer, or lay down his right to save himself from death, wounds, and imprisonment, (the avoiding whereof is the only end of laying down any right, and therefore the promise of not resisting force, in no covenant transferreth any right; nor is obliging. For though a man may covenant thus, *unless I do so, or so, kill me*; he cannot covenant thus, *unless I do so, or so, I will not resist you, when you come to kill me*. For man by nature chooseth the lesser evil, which is danger of death in resisting; rather than the greater, which is certain and present death in not resisting.

And this is granted to be true by all men, in that they lead criminals to execution, and prison, with armed men, notwithstanding that such criminals have consented to the law, by which they are condemned.

A covenant to accuse one self, without assurance of pardon, is likewise invalid. For in the condition of nature, where every man is judge, there is no place for accusation: and in the civil state, the accusation is followed with punishment; which being force, a man is not obliged not to resist. The same is also true, of the accusation of those, by whose condemnation a man falls into misery; as of a father, wife, or benefactor. For the testimony of such an accuser, if it be not willingly given, is presumed to be corrupted by nature; and therefore not to be received: and where a man's testimony is not to be credited, he is not bound to give it. Also accusations upon torture, are not to be reputed as testimonies. For torture is to be used but as means of conjecture, and light, in the further examination, and search of truth: and what is in that case confessed, tendeth to the ease of him that is tortured, not to the informing of the torturers: and therefore ought not to have the credit of a sufficient testimony: for whether he deliver himself by true, or false accusation, he does it by the right of preserving his own life.

The force of words, being (as I have formerly noted) too weak to hold men to the performance of their covenants; there are in man's nature, but two imaginable helps to strengthen it. And those are either a fear of the consequence of breaking their word; or a glory, or pride in appearing not to need to break it. This latter is a generosity too rarely found to be presumed on, especially in the pursuers of wealth, command, or sensual pleasure; which are the greatest part of mankind. The passion to be reckoned upon, is fear; whereof there be two very general objects: one, the power of spirits invisible; the other, the power of those men they shall therein offend. Of these two, though the former be the greater power, yet the fear of the latter is commonly the greater fear. The fear of the former is in every man, his own religion: which hath place in the nature of man before civil society. The latter hath not so; at least not place enough, to keep men to their promises; because in the condition of mere nature, the inequality of power is not discerned, but by the event of battle. So that before the time of civil society, or in the interruption thereof by war, there is nothing can strengthen a covenant of peace agreed on, against the temptations of avarice, ambition, lust, or other strong desire, but the fear of that invisible power, which they every one worship as God; and fear as a revenger of their perfidy. All therefore that can be done between two men not subject to civil power, is to put one another to swear by the God he feareth: which *swearing*, or OATH, is a *form of speech, added to a promise; by which he that promiseth, signifieth, that unless he perform, he renounceth the mercy of his God, or calleth to him for vengeance on himself.* Such was the heathen form, *Let* Jupiter *kill me else, as I kill this beast.* So is our form, *I shall do thus, and thus, so help me God.* And this, with the rites and ceremonies, which every one useth in his own religion, that the fear of breaking faith might be the greater.

By this it appears, that an oath taken according to any other form, or rite, than his, that sweareth, is in vain; and no oath: and that there is no swearing by any thing which the swearer thinks not God. For though men have sometimes used to swear by their kings, for fear, or flattery; yet they would have it thereby understood, they attributed to them divine honour. And that swearing unnecessarily by God, is but prophaning of his name: and swearing by other things, as men do in common discourse, is not swearing, but an impious custom, gotten by too much vehemence of talking.

It appears also, that the oath adds nothing to the obligation. For a covenant, if lawful, binds in the sight of God, without the oath, as much as with it: if unlawful, bindeth not at all; though it be confirmed with an oath.

Chapter 15

Of Other Laws of Nature

From that law of nature, by which we are obliged to transfer to another, such rights, as being retained, hinder the peace of mankind, there followeth a third; which is this, *that men perform their covenants made:* without which, covenants are in vain, and but empty words; and the right of all men to all things remaining, we are still in the condition of war.

And in this law of nature, consisteth the fountain and original of JUSTICE. For where no covenant hath preceded, there hath no right been transferred, and every man has right to every thing; and consequently, no action can be unjust. But when a covenant is made, then to break it is *unjust:* and the definition of INJUSTICE, is no other than *the not performance of covenant.* And whatsoever is not unjust, is *just.*

But because covenants of mutual trust, where there is a fear of not performance on either part, (as hath been said in the former chapter,) are invalid; though the original of justice be the making of covenants; yet injustice actually there can be none, till the cause of such fear be taken away; which while men are in the natural condition of war, cannot be done. Therefore before the names of just, and unjust can have place, there must be some coercive power, to compel men equally to the performance of their covenants, by the terror of some punishment, greater than the benefit they expect by the breach of their covenant; and to make good that propriety, which by mutual contract men acquire, in recompense of the universal right they abandon: and such power there is none before the erection of a commonwealth. And this is also to be gathered out of the ordinary definition of justice in the Schools: for they say, that *justice is the constant will of giving to every man his own.* And therefore where there is no *own,* that is, no propriety, there is no injustice; and where there is no coercive power erected, that is, where there is no commonwealth, there is no propriety; all men having right to all things: therefore where there is no commonwealth, there nothing is unjust. So that the nature of justice, consisteth in keeping of valid covenants: but the validity of covenants begins not but with the constitution of a civil power, sufficient to compel men to keep them: and then it is also that propriety begins.

The fool hath said in his heart, there is no such thing as justice; and sometimes also with his tongue; seriously alleging, that every man's conservation, and contentment, being committed to his own care, there could be no reason, why every man might not do what he thought conduced thereunto: and therefore also to make, or not make; keep, or not keep covenants, was not against reason, when it conduced to one's benefit. He does not therein deny, that there

justice ?
injustice

be covenants; and that they are sometimes broken, sometimes kept; and that such breach of them may be called injustice, and the observance of them justice: but he questioneth, whether injustice, taking away the fear of God, (for the same fool hath said in his heart there is no God,) may not sometimes stand with that reason, which dictateth to every man his own good; and particularly then, when it conduceth to such a benefit, as shall put a man in a condition, to neglect not only the dispraise, and revilings, but also the power of other men. The kingdom of God is gotten by violence: but what if it could be gotten by unjust violence? were it against reason so to get it, when it is impossible to receive hurt by it? and if it be not against reason, it is not against justice; or else justice is not to be approved for good. From such reasoning as this, successful wickedness hath obtained the name of virtue: and some that in all other things have disallowed the violation of faith; yet have allowed it, when it is for the getting of a kingdom. And the heathen that believed, that *Saturn* was deposed by his son *Jupiter,* believed nevertheless the same *Jupiter* to be the avenger of injustice: somewhat like to a piece of law in *Coke's Commentaries on Littleton;* where he says, if the right heir of the crown be attainted of treason; yet the crown shall descend to him, and *eo instante* the attainder be void. from which instances a man will be very prone to infer; that when the heir apparent of a kingdom, shall kill him that is in possession, though his father; you may call it injustice, or by what other name you will; yet it can never be against reason, seeing all the voluntary actions of men tend to the benefit of themselves; and those actions are most reasonable, that conduce most to their ends. This specious reasoning is nevertheless false.

For the question is not of promises mutual, where there is no security of performance on either side; as when there is no civil power erected over the parties promising; for such promises are no covenants: but either where one of the parties has performed already; or where there is a power to make him perform; there is the question whether it be against reason, that is, against the benefit of the other to perform, or not. And I say it is not against reason. For the manifestation whereof, we are to consider; first, that when a man doth a thing, which notwithstanding any thing can

be foreseen, and reckoned on, tendeth to his own destruction, howsoever some accident which he could not expect, arriving may turn it to his benefit; yet such events do not make it reasonably or wisely done. Secondly, that in a condition of war, wherein every man to every man, for want of a common power to keep them all in awe, is an enemy, there is no man can hope by his own strength, or wit, to defend himself from destruction, without the help of confederates; where every one expects the same defence by the confederation, that any one else does: and therefore he which declares he thinks it reason to deceive those that help him, can in reason expect no other means of safety, than what can be had from his own single power. He therefore that breaketh his covenant, and consequently declareth that he thinks he may with reason do so, cannot be received into any society, that unite themselves for peace and defence, but by the error of them that receive him; nor when he is received, be retained in it, without seeing the danger of their error; which errors a man cannot reasonably reckon upon as the means of his security: and therefore if he be left, or cast out of society, he perisheth; and if he live in society, it is by the errors of other men, which he could not foresee, nor reckon upon; and consequently against the reason of his preservation; and so, as all men that contribute not to his destruction, forbear him only out of ignorance of what is good for themselves.

As for the instance of gaining the secure and perpetual felicity of heaven, by any way; it is frivolous: there being but one way imaginable; and that is not breaking, but keeping of covenant.

And for the other instance of attaining sovereignty by rebellion; it is manifest, that though the event follow, yet because it cannot reasonably be expected, but rather the contrary; and because by gaining it so, others are taught to gain the same in like manner, the attempt thereof is against reason. Justice therefore, that is to say, keeping of covenant, is a rule of reason, by which we are forbidden to do any thing destructive to our life; and consequently a law of nature.

There be some that proceed further; and will not have the law of nature, to be those rules which conduce to the preservation of man's life on earth; but to the attaining of an eternal felicity after death, to

which they think the breach of covenant may conduce; and consequently be just and reasonable; (such
are they that think it a work of merit to kill, or depose,
or rebel against, the sovereign power constituted over
them by their own consent.) But because there is no
natural knowledge of man's estate after death; much
less of the reward that is then to be given to breach
of faith; but only a belief grounded upon other men's
saying, that they know it supernaturally, or that they
know those, that knew them, that knew others, that
knew it supernaturally; breach of faith cannot be
called a precept of reason, or nature.

Others, that allow for a law of nature, the keeping
of faith, do nevertheless make exception of certain
persons; as heretics, and such as use not to perform
their covenant to others: and this also is against reason.
For if any fault of a man, be sufficient to discharge
our covenant made; the same ought in reason to have
been sufficient to have hindered the making of it.

The names of just, and injust, when they are attributed to men, signify one thing; and when they are
attributed to actions, another. When they are attributed to men, they signify conformity, or inconformity
of manners, to reason. But when they are attributed
to actions, they signify the conformity, or inconformity to reason, not of manners, or manner of life,
but of particular actions. A just man therefore, is he
that taketh all the care he can, that his actions may
be all just: and an unjust man, is he that neglecteth
it. And such men are more often in our language
styled by the names of righteous, and unrighteous;
than just, and unjust; though the meaning be the
same. Therefore a righteous man, does not lose that
title, by one, or a few unjust actions, that proceed
from sudden passion, or mistake of things, or persons:
nor does an unrighteous man, lose his character, for
such actions, as he does, or forbears to do, for fear:
because his will is not framed by the justice, but by
the apparent benefit of what he is to do. That which
gives to human actions the relish of justice, is a certain
nobleness or gallantness of courage, (rarely found,)
by which a man scorns to be beholding for the contentment of his life, to fraud, or breach of promise.
This justice of the manners, is that which is meant,
where justice is called a virtue; and injustice a vice.

But the justice of actions denominates men, not
just, but *guiltless:* and the injustice of the same,

(which is also called injury,) gives them but the name
of *guilty.*

Again, the injustice of manners, is the disposition,
or aptitude to do injury; and is injustice before it
proceed to act; and without supposing any individual
person injured. But the injustice of an action, (that is
to say injury,) supposeth an individual person injured;
namely him, to whom the covenant was made: and
therefore many times the injury is received by one
man, when the damage redoundeth to another. As
when the master commandeth his servant to give
money to a stranger; if it be not done, the injury is
done to the master, whom he had before covenanted
to obey; but the damage redoundeth to the stranger,
to whom he had no obligation; and therefore could
not injure him. And so also in commonwealths, private men may remit to one another their debts; but
not robberies or other violences, whereby they are
endamaged; because the detaining of debt, is an injury to themselves; but robbery and violence, are
injuries to the person of the commonwealth.

Whatsoever is done to a man, conformable to his
own will signified to the doer, is no injury to him.
For if he that doeth it, hath not passed away his
original right to do what he please, by some antecedent covenant, there is no breach of covenant; and
therefore no injury done him. And if he have; then
his will to have it done being signified, is a release
of that covenant: and so again there is no injury
done him.

Justice of actions, is by writers divided into *commutative,* and *distributive:* and the former they say
consisteth in proportion arithmetical; the latter in proportion geometrical. Commutative therefore, they
place in the equality of value of the things contracted
for; and distributive, in the distribution of equal benefit, to men of equal merit. As if it were injustice to sell
dearer than we buy; or to give more to a man than
he merits. The value of all things contracted for,
is measured by the appetite of the contractors: and
therefore the just value, is that which they be contented to give. And merit, (besides that which is by
covenant, where the performance on one part, meriteth the performance of the other part, and falls
under justice commutative, not distributive,) is not
due by justice; but is rewarded of grace only. And
therefore this distinction, in the sense wherein it useth

to be expounded, is not right. To speak properly, commutative justice, is the justice of a contractor; that is, a performance of covenant, in buying, and selling; hiring, and letting to hire; lending, and borrowing; exchanging, bartering, and other acts of contract.

And distributive justice, the justice of an arbitrator; that is to say, the act of defining what is just. Wherein, (being trusted by them that make him arbitrator,) if he perform his trust, he is said to distribute to every man his own: and this is indeed just distribution, and may be called, (though improperly,) distributive justice; but more properly equity; which also is a law of nature, as shall be shown in due place.

As justice dependeth on antecedent covenant; so does GRATITUDE depend on antecedent grace; that is to say, antecedent free-gift: and is the fourth law of nature; which may be conceived in this form, *that a man which receiveth benefit from another of mere grace, endeavour that he which giveth it, have no reasonable cause to repent him of his good will.* For no man giveth, but with intention of good to himself; because gift is voluntary; and of all voluntary acts, the object is to every man his own good; of which if men see they shall be frustrated, there will be no beginning of benevolence, or trust; nor consequently of mutual help; nor of reconciliation of one man to another; and therefore they are to remain still in the condition of *war*; which is contrary to the first and fundamental law of nature, which commandeth men to *seek peace*. The breach of this law, is called *ingratitude*; and hath the same relation to grace, that injustice hath to obligation by covenant.

A fifth law of nature, is COMPLAISANCE; that is to say, *that every man strive to accommodate himself to the rest.* For the understanding whereof, we may consider, that there is in men's aptness to society, a diversity of nature, rising from their diversity of affections; not unlike to that we see in stones brought together for building of an edifice. For as that stone which by the asperity, and irregularity of figure, takes more room from others, than itself fills; and for the hardness, cannot be easily made plain, and thereby hindereth the building, is by the builders cast away as unprofitable, and troublesome: so also, a man that by asperity of nature, will strive to retain those things which to himself are superfluous, and to others necessary; and for the stubbornness of his passions, cannot

be corrected, is to be left, or cast out of society, as cumbersome thereunto. For seeing every man, not only by right, but also by necessity of nature, is supposed to endeavour all he can, to obtain that which is necessary for his conservation; he that shall oppose himself against it, for things superfluous, is guilty of the war that thereupon is to follow; and therefore doth that, which is contrary to the fundamental law of nature, which commandeth *to seek peace*. The observers of this law, may be called SOCIABLE, (the Latins call them *commodi*;) the contrary, *stubborn, insociable, froward, intractable*.

A sixth law of nature, is this, *that upon caution of the future time, a man ought to pardon the offences past of them that repenting, desire it.* For PARDON, is nothing but granting of peace; which though granted to them that persevere in their hostility, be not peace, but fear; yet not granted to them that give caution of the future time, is sign of an aversion to peace; and therefore contrary to the law of nature.

A seventh is, *that in revenges*, (that is, retribution of evil for evil,) *men look not at the greatness of the evil past, but the greatness of the good to follow.* Whereby we are forbidden to inflict punishment with any other design, than for correction of the offender, or direction of others. For this law is consequent to the next before it, that commandeth pardon, upon security of the future time. Besides, revenge without respect to the example, and profit to come, is a triumph, or glorying in the hurt of another, tending to no end; (for the end is always somewhat to come;) and glorying to no end, is vain-glory, and contrary to reason; and to hurt without reason, tendeth to the introduction of war; which is against the law of nature; and is commonly styled by the name of *cruelty*.

And because all signs of hatred, or contempt, provoke to fight; insomuch as most men choose rather to hazard their life, than not to be revenged; we may in the eighth place, for a law of nature, set down this precept, *that no man by deed, word, countenance, or gesture, declare hatred, or contempt of another.* The breach of which law, is commonly called *contumely*.

The question who is the better man, has no place in the condition of mere nature; where, (as has been shewn before,) all men are equal. The inequality that now is, has been introduced by the laws civil. I know that *Aristotle* in the first book of his *Politics*, for a foundation of his doctrine, maketh men by nature, some more worthy to command, meaning the wiser sort, (such as he thought himself to be for his philosophy;) others to serve, (meaning those that had strong bodies, but were not philosophers as he;) as if master and servant were not introduced by consent of men, but by difference of wit: which is not only against reason; but also against experience. For there are very few so foolish, that had not rather govern themselves, than be governed by others: nor when the wise in their own conceit, contend by force, with them who distrust their own wisdom, do they always, or often, or almost at any time, get the victory. If nature therefore have made men equal, that equality is to be acknowledged: or if nature have made men unequal; yet because men that think themselves equal, will not enter into conditions of peace, but upon equal terms, such equality must be admitted. And therefore for the ninth law of nature, I put this, *that every man acknowledge other for his equal by nature.* The breach of this precept is *pride.*

On this law, dependeth another, *that at the entrance into conditions of peace, no man require to reserve to himself any right, which he is not content should be reserved to every one of the rest.* As it is necessary for all men that seek peace, to lay down certain rights of nature; that is to say, not to have liberty to do all they list: so is it necessary for man's life, to retain some; as right to govern their own bodies; enjoy air, water, motion, ways to go from place to place; and all things else without which a man cannot live, or not live well. If in this case, at the making of peace, men require for themselves, that which they would not have to be granted to others, they do contrary to the precedent law, that commandeth the acknowledgment of natural equality, and therefore also against the law of nature. The observers of this law, are those we call *modest,* and the breakers *arrogant* men. The Greeks call the violation of this law πλεονεξια; that is, a desire of more than their share.

Also if *a man be trusted to judge between man and man,* it is a precept of the law of nature, *that he deal equally between them.* For without that, the controversies of men cannot be determined but by war. He therefore that is partial in judgment, doth what in him lies, to deter men from the use of judges, and arbitrators; and consequently, (against the fundamental law of nature,) is the cause of war.

The observance of this law, from the equal distribution to each man, of that which in reason belongeth to him, is called EQUITY, and (as I have said before) distributive justice: the violation, *acception of persons,* προσωποληψία.

And from this followeth another law, *that such things as cannot be divided, be enjoyed in common, if it can be; and if the quantity of the thing permit, without stint; otherwise proportionably to the number of them that have right.* For otherwise the distribution is unequal, and contrary to equity.

But some things there be, that can neither be divided, nor enjoyed in common. Then, the law of nature, which prescribeth equity, requireth, *that the entire right; or else, (making the use alternate,) the first possession, be determined by lot.* For equal distribution, is of the law of nature; and other means of equal distribution cannot be imagined.

Of *lots* there be two sorts, *arbitrary,* and *natural.* Arbitrary, is that which is agreed on by the competitors: natural, is either *primogeniture,* (which the Greek calls κληρονομία, which signifies, *given by lot;*) or *first seizure.*

And therefore those things which cannot be enjoyed in common, nor divided, ought to be adjudged to the first possessor; and in some cases to the first-born, as acquired by lot.

It is also a law of nature, *that all men that mediate peace, be allowed safe conduct.* For the law that commandeth peace, as the *end,* commandeth intercession, as the *means;* and to intercession the means is safe conduct.

And because, though men be never so willing to observe these laws, there may nevertheless arise questions concerning a man's action; first, whether it were done, or not done; secondly, (if done,) whether against the law, or not against the law; the former whereof, is called a question *of fact;* the latter a question *of right;* therefore unless the parties to the question, covenant mutually to stand to the sentence of another, they are as far from peace as ever. This other, to whose sentence they submit, is called an ARBITRATOR. And therefore it is of the law of nature, *that they that are at controversy, submit their right to the judgment of an arbitrator.*

And seeing every man is presumed to do all things in order to his own benefit, no man is a fit arbitrator in his own cause: and if he were never so fit, yet equity allowing to each party equal benefit, if one be admitted to be judge, the other is to be admitted also; and so the controversy, that is, the cause of war, remains, against the law of nature.

For the same reason no man in any cause ought to be received for arbitrator, to whom greater profit, or honour, or pleasure apparently ariseth out of the victory of one party, than of the other: for he hath taken (though an unavoidable bribe, yet) a bribe; and no man can be obliged to trust him. And thus also the controversy, and the condition of war remaineth, contrary to the law of nature.

And in a controversy of *fact*, the judge being to give no more credit to one, than to the other, (if there be no other arguments,) must give credit to a third; or to a third and fourth; or more: for else the question is undecided, and left to force, contrary to the law of nature.

These are the laws of nature, dictating peace, for a means of the conservation of men in multitudes; and which only concern the doctrine of civil society. There be other things tending to the destruction of particular men; as drunkenness, and all other parts of intemperance; which may therefore also be reckoned amongst those things which the law of nature hath forbidden; but are not necessary to be mentioned, nor are pertinent enough to this place.

And though this may seem too subtle a deduction of the laws of nature, to be taken notice of by all men; whereof the most part are too busy in getting food, and the rest too negligent to understand; yet to leave all men inexcusable, they have been contracted into one easy sum, intelligible, even to the meanest capacity; and that is, *Do not that to another, which thou wouldest not have done to thyself*; which sheweth him, that he has no more to do in learning the laws of nature, but, when weighing the actions of other men with his own, they seem too heavy, to put them into the other part of the balance, and his own into their place, that his own passions, and self-love, may add nothing to the weight; and then there is none of these laws of nature that will not appear unto him very reasonable.

The laws of nature oblige *in foro interno*; that is to say, they bind to a desire they should take place: but *in foro externo*; that is, to the putting them in act, not always. For he that should be modest, and tractable, and perform all he promises, in such time, and place, where no man else should do so, should but make himself a prey to others, and procure his own certain ruin, contrary to the ground of all laws of nature, which tend to nature's preservation. And again, he that having sufficient security, that others shall observe the same laws towards him, observes them not himself, seeketh not peace, but war; and consequently the destruction of his nature by violence.

And whatsoever laws bind *in foro interno*, may be broken, not only by a fact contrary to the law, but also by a fact according to it, in case a man think it contrary. For though his action in this case, be according to the law; yet his purpose was against the law; which, where the obligation is *in foro interno*, is a breach.

The laws of nature are immutable and eternal; for injustice, ingratitude, arrogance, pride, iniquity, acception of persons, and the rest, can never be made lawful. For it can never be that war shall preserve life, and peace destroy it.

The same laws, because they oblige only to a desire, and endeavour, I mean an unfeigned and constant endeavour, are easy to be observed. For in that they require nothing but endeavour; he that endeavoureth their performance, fulfilleth them; and he that fulfilleth the law, is just.

And the science of them, is the true and only moral philosophy. For moral philosophy is nothing else but the science of what is *good*, and *evil*, in the conversation, and society of mankind. *Good*, and *evil*, are names that signify our appetites, and aversions; which in different tempers, customs, and doctrines of men, are different: and divers men, differ not only in their judgment, on the senses of what is pleasant, and unpleasant to the taste, smell, hearing, touch, and sight; but also of what is conformable, or disagreeable to reason, in the actions of common life. Nay, the same man, in divers times, differs from himself; and one time praiseth, that is, calleth good, what another time he dispraiseth, and calleth evil: from whence arise disputes, controversies, and at last war. And therefore so long a man is in the condition of mere nature, (which is a condition of war,) as private appetite is the measure of good, and evil: and consequently all men agree on this, that peace is good, and therefore also the way, or means of peace, which, (as I have shewed before) are *justice, gratitude, modesty, equity, mercy,* and the rest of the laws of nature, are good; that is to say, *moral virtues*; and their contrary *vices,* evil. Now the science of virtue and vice, is moral philosophy; and therefore the true doctrine of the laws of nature, is the true moral philosophy. But the writers of moral philosophy, though they acknowledge the same virtues and vices; yet not seeing wherein consisted their goodness; nor that they come to be praised, as the means of peaceable, sociable, and comfortable living; place them in a mediocrity of passions: as if not the cause, but the degree of daring, made fortitude; or not the cause, but the quantity of a gift, made liberality.

These dictates of reason, men use to call by the name of laws; but improperly: for they are but conclusions, or theorems concerning what conduceth to the conservation and defence of themselves; whereas law, properly, is the word of him, that by right hath command over others. But yet if we consider the same theorems, as delivered in the word of God, that by right commandeth all things; then are they properly called laws.

Chapter 16

Of Persons, Authors, and Things Personated

A person, is he, *whose words or actions are considered, either as his own, or as representing the words or actions of another man, or of any other thing to whom they are attributed, whether truly or by fiction.*

When they are considered as his own, then is he called a *natural person*: and when they are considered as representing the words and actions of another, then is he a *feigned* or *artificial person.*

The word person is Latin: instead whereof the Greeks have πρόσωπον, which signifies the *face,* as *persona* in Latin signifies the *disguise,* or *outward appearance* of a man, counterfeited on the stage; and sometimes more particularly that part of it, which

disguiseth the face, as a mask or vizard: and from the stage, hath been translated to any representer of speech and action, as well in tribunals, as theatres. So that a *person,* is the same that an *actor* is, both on the stage and in common conversation; and to *personate,* is to *act,* or *represent* himself, or another; and he that acteth another, is said to bear his person, or act in his name; (in which sense Cicero useth it where he says, *Unus sustineo tres personas; mei, adversarii, et judicis,* I bear three persons; my own, my adversary's, and the judge's;) and is called in divers occasions, diversly; as a *representer,* or *representative,* a *lieutenant,* a *vicar,* an *attorney,* a *deputy,* a *procurator,* an *actor,* and the like.

Of persons artificial, some have their words and actions *owned* by those whom they represent. And then the person is the *actor*; and he that owneth his words and actions, is the AUTHOR: in which case the actor acteth by authority. For that which in speaking of goods and possessions, is called an *owner,* and in Latin *dominus,* in Greek κύριος; speaking of actions, is called author. And as the right of possession, is called dominion; so the right of doing any action, is called AUTHORITY. So that by authority, is always understood a right of doing any act: and *done by authority,* done by commission, or licence from him whose right it is.

From hence it followeth, that when the actor maketh a covenant by authority, he bindeth thereby the author, no less than if he had made it himself; and no less subjecteth him to all the consequences of the same. And therefore all that hath been said formerly, (*chap.* 14) of the nature of covenants between man and man in their natural capacity, is true also when they are made by their actors, representers, or procurators, that have authority from them, so far forth as is in their commission, but no farther.

And therefore he that maketh a covenant with the actor, or representer, not knowing the authority he hath, doth it at his own peril. For no man is obliged by a covenant, whereof he is not author; nor consequently by a covenant made against, or beside the authority he gave.

When the actor doth any thing against the law of nature by command of the author, if he be obliged by former covenant to obey him, not he, but the author breaketh the law of nature: for though the action be against the law of nature; yet it is not his: but contrarily, to refuse to do it, is against the law of nature, that forbiddeth breach of covenant.

And he that maketh a covenant with the author, by mediation of the actor, not knowing what authority he hath, but only takes his word; in case such authority be not made manifest unto him upon demand, is no longer obliged: for the covenant made with the author, is not valid, without his counter-assurance. But if he that so covenanteth, knew beforehand he was to expect no other assurance, than the actor's word; then is the covenant valid; because the actor in this case maketh himself the author. And therefore, as when the authority is evident, the covenant obligeth the author, not the actor; so when the authority is feigned, it obligeth the actor only; there being no author but himself.

There are few things, that are incapable of being represented by fiction. Inanimate things, as a church, an hospital, a bridge, may be personated by a rector, master, or overseer. But things inanimate, cannot be authors, nor therefore give authority to their actors: yet the actors may have authority to procure their maintenance, given them by those that are owners, or governors of those things. And therefore, such things cannot be personated, before there be some state of civil government.

Likewise children, fools, and madmen that have no use of reason, may be personated by guardians, or curators; but can be no authors, (during that time) of any action done by them, longer than (when they shall recover the use of reason) they shall judge the same reasonable. Yet during the folly, he that hath right of governing them, may give authority to the guardian. But this again has no place but in a state civil, because before such estate, there is no dominion of persons.

An idol, or mere figment of the brain, may be personated; as were the gods of the heathen; which by such officers as the state appointed, were personated, and held possessions, and other goods, and rights, which men from time to time dedicated, and consecrated unto them. But idols cannot be authors: for an idol is nothing. The authority proceeded from the state: and therefore before introduction of civil government, the gods of the heathen could not be personated.

The true God may be personated. As he was; first, by Moses; who governed the Israelites, (that were not his, but God's people,) not in his own name, with *hoc dicit Moses*; but in God's name, with *hoc dicit Dominus*. Secondly, by the Son of man, his own Son, our blessed Saviour Jesus Christ, that came to reduce the Jews, and induce all nations into the kingdom of his father; not as of himself, but as sent from his father. And thirdly, by the Holy Ghost, or Comforter, speaking, and working in the Apostles: which Holy Ghost, was a Comforter that came not of himself; but was sent, and proceeded from them both.

A multitude of men, are made *one* person, when they are by one man, or one person, represented; so that it be done with the consent of every one of that multitude in particular. For it is the *unity* of the representer, not the *unity* of the represented, that maketh the person *one*. And it is the representer that beareth the person, and but one person: and *unity*, cannot otherwise be understood in multitude.

And because the multitude naturally is not *one*, but *many*; they cannot be understood for one; but many authors, of every thing their representative saith, or doth in their name; every man giving their common representer, authority from himself in particular; and owning all the actions the representer doth, in case they give him authority without stint: otherwise, when they limit him in what, and how far he shall represent them, none of them owneth more, than they gave him commission to act.

And if the representative consist of many men, the voice of the greater number, must be considered as the voice of them all. For if the lesser number pronounce (for example) in the affirmative, and the greater in the negative, there will be negatives more than enough to destroy the affirmatives; and thereby the excess of negatives, standing uncontradicted, are the only voice the representative hath.

And a representative of even number, especially when the number is not great, whereby the contradictory voices are oftentimes equal, is therefore oftentimes mute, and incapable of action. Yet in some cases contradictory voices equal in number, may determine a question; as in condemning, or absolving, equality of votes, even in that they condemn not, do absolve; but not on the contrary condemn, in that they absolve not. For when a cause is heard; not to condemn, is to absolve: but on the contrary, to say that not absolving, is condemning, is not true. The like it is in a deliberation of executing presently, or deferring till another time: for when the voices are equal, the not decreeing execution, is a decree of dilation.

Or if the number be odd, as three, or more, (men, or assemblies;) whereof every one has by a negative voice, authority to take away the effect of all the affirmative voices of the rest, this number is no representative; because by the diversity of opinions, and interests of men, it becomes oftentimes, and in cases of the greatest consequence, a mute person, and unapt, as for many things else, so for the government of a multitude, especially in time of war.

Of authors there be two sorts. The first simply so called; which I have before defined to be him, that owneth the action of another simply. The second is he, that owneth an action, or covenant of another conditionally; that is to say, he undertaketh to do it, if the other doth it not, at, or before a certain time. And these authors conditional, are generally called SURETIES, in Latin *fidejussores*, and *sponsores*; and particularly for debt, *praedes*; and for appearance before a judge, or magistrate, *vades*.

PART 2
OF COMMONWEALTH

Chapter 17

Of the Causes, Generation, and Definition of a Commonwealth

The final cause, end, or design of men, (who naturally love liberty, and dominion over others,) in the introduction of that restraint upon themselves, (in which we see them live in commonwealths,) is the foresight of their own preservation, and of a more contented life thereby; that is to say, of getting themselves out from that miserable condition of war, which is necessarily consequent (as hath been shown), to, the natural passions of men, when there is no visible power to keep them in awe, and tie them by fear of punishment to the performance of their covenants, and observa-

tion of those laws of nature set down in the fourteenth and fifteenth chapters.

For the laws of nature (as *justice, equity, modesty, mercy*, and (in sum) *doing to others, as we would be done to,*) of themselves, without the terror of some power, to cause them to be observed, are contrary to our natural passions; that carry us to partiality, pride, revenge, and the like. And covenants, without the sword, are but words, and of no strength to secure a man at all. Therefore notwithstanding the laws of nature, (which every one hath then kept, when he has the will to keep them, when he can do it safely,) if there be no power erected, or not great enough for our security; every man will, and may lawfully rely on his own strength and art, for caution against all other men. And in all places, where men have lived by small families, to rob and spoil one another, has been a trade, and so far from being reputed against the law of nature, that the greater spoils they gained, the greater was their honour; and men observed no other laws therein, but the laws of honour; that is, to abstain from cruelty, leaving to men their lives, and instruments of husbandry. And as small families did then; so now do cities and kingdoms which are but greater families (for their own security) enlarge their dominions, upon all pretences of danger, and fear of invasion, or assistance that may be given to invaders, endeavour as much as they can, to subdue, or weaken their neighbours, by open force, and secret arts, for want of other caution, justly; and are remembered for it in after ages with honour.

Nor is it the joining together of a small number of men, that gives them this security; because in small numbers, small additions on the one side or the other, make the advantage of strength so great, as is sufficient to carry the victory; and therefore gives encouragement to an invasion. The multitude sufficient to confide in for our security, is not determined by any certain number, but by comparison with the enemy we fear; and is then sufficient, when the odds of the enemy is not of so visible and conspicuous moment, to determine the event of war, as to move him to attempt.

And be there never so great a multitude; yet if their actions be directed according to their particular judgments, and particular appetites, they can expect thereby no defence, nor protection, neither against a common enemy, nor against the injuries of one another. For being distracted in opinions concerning the best use and application of their strength, they do not help, but hinder one another; and reduce their strength by mutual opposition to nothing: whereby they are easily, not only subdued by a very few that agree together; but also when there is no common enemy, they make war upon each other, for their particular interests. For if we could suppose a great multitude of men to consent in the observation of justice, and other laws of nature, without a common power to keep them all in awe; we might as well suppose all mankind to do the same; and then there neither would be, nor need to be any civil government, or commonwealth at all; because there would be peace without subjection.

Nor is it enough for the security, which men desire should last all the time of their life, that they be governed, and directed by one judgment, for a limited time; as in one battle, or one war. For though they obtain a victory by their unanimous endeavour against a foreign enemy; yet afterwards, when either they have no common enemy, or he that by one part is held for an enemy, is by another part held for a friend, they must needs by the difference of their interests dissolve, and fall again into a war amongst themselves.

It is true, that certain living creatures, as bees, and ants, live sociably one with another, (which are therefore by *Aristotle* numbered amongst political creatures;) and yet have no other direction, than their particular judgments and appetites; nor speech, whereby one of them can signify to another, what he thinks expedient for the common benefit: and therefore some man may perhaps desire to know, why mankind cannot do the same. To which I answer,

First, that men are continually in competition for honour and dignity, which these creatures are not; and consequently amongst men there ariseth on that ground, envy and hatred, and finally war; but amongst these not so.

Secondly, that amongst these creatures, the common good differeth not from the private; and being by nature inclined to their private, they procure thereby the common benefit. But man, whose joy consisteth in comparing himself with other men, can relish nothing but what is eminent.

Thirdly, that these creatures, having not, (as man) the use of reason, do not see, nor think they see any fault, in the administration of their common business; whereas amongst men, there are very many, that think themselves wiser, and abler to govern the public, better than the rest; and these strive to reform and innovate, one this way, another that way; and thereby bring it into distraction and civil war.

Fourthly, that these creatures, though they have some use of voice, in making known to one another their desires, and other affections; yet they want that art of words, by which some men can represent to others, that which is good, in the likeness of evil; and evil, in the likeness of good; and augment, or diminish the apparent greatness of good and evil; discontenting men, and troubling their peace at their pleasure.

Fifthly, irrational creatures cannot distinguish between *injury*, and *damage*; and therefore as long as they be at ease, they are not offended with their fellows: whereas man is then most troublesome, when he is most at ease: for then it is that he loves to shew his wisdom, and control the actions of them that govern the commonwealth.

Lastly, the agreement of these creatures is natural; that of men, is by covenant only, which is artificial: and therefore it is no wonder if there be somewhat else required (besides covenant) to make their agreement constant and lasting; which is a common power, to keep them in awe, and to direct their actions to the common benefit.

The only way to erect such a common power, as may be able to defend them from the invasion of foreigners, and the injuries of one another, and thereby to secure them in such sort, as that by their own industry, and by the fruits of the earth, they may nourish themselves and live contentedly; is, to confer all their power and strength upon one man, or upon one assembly of men, that may reduce all their wills, by plurality of voices, unto one will: which is as much as to say, to appoint one man, or assembly of men, to bear their person; and every one to own, and acknowledge himself to be author of whatsoever he that so beareth their person, shall act, or cause to be acted, in those things which concern the common peace and safety; and therein to submit their wills, every one to his will, and their judgments, to his judgment. This is more than consent, or concord; it is a real unity of them all, in one and the same person, made by covenant of every man with every man, in such manner, as if every man should say to every man, *I authorise and give up my right of governing myself, to this man, or to this assembly of men, on this condition, that thou give up thy right to him, and authorize all his actions in like manner.* This done, the multitude so united in one person, is called a COMMONWEALTH, in Latin CIVITAS. This is the generation of that great LEVIATHAN, or rather (to speak more reverently) of that *mortal god,* to which we owe under the *immortal God,* our peace and defence. For by this authority, given him by every particular man in the commonwealth, he hath the use of so much power and strength conferred on him, that by terror thereof, he is enabled to form the wills of them all, to peace at home, and mutual aid against their enemies abroad. And in him consisteth the essence of the commonwealth; which (to define it,) is *one person, of whose acts a great multitude, by mutual covenants one with another, have made themselves every one the author, to the end he may use the strength and means of them all, as he shall think expedient, for their peace and common defence.*

And he that carrieth this person, is called SOVEREIGN, and said to have sovereign power; and every one besides, his SUBJECT.

The attaining to this sovereign power, is by two ways. One, by natural force; as when a man maketh his children, to submit themselves, and their children to his government, as being able to destroy them if they refuse; or by war subdueth his enemies to his will, giving them their lives on that condition. The other, is when men agree amongst themselves, to submit to some man, or assembly of men, voluntarily, on confidence to be protected by him against all others. This latter, may be called a political commonwealth, or commonwealth by *institution*; and the former, a commonwealth by *acquisition*. And first, I shall speak of a commonwealth by institution.

Chapter 18

Of the Rights of Sovereigns by Institution

A *commonwealth* is said to be *instituted*, when a *multitude* of men do agree, and *covenant*, every one, with *every one*, that to whatsoever *man*, or *assembly of men*, shall be given by the major part, the *right* to *present* the person of them all, (that is to say, to be their *representative*;) every one, as well he that *voted for it*, as he that *voted against it*, shall *authorize* all the actions and judgments, of that man, or assembly of men, in the same manner, as if they were his own, to the end, to live peaceably amongst themselves, and be protected against other men.

From this institution of a commonwealth are derived all the *rights*, and *faculties* of him, or them, on whom the sovereign power is conferred by the consent of the people assembled.

First, because they covenant, it is to be understood, they are not obliged by former covenant to any thing repugnant hereunto. And consequently they that have already instituted a commonwealth, being thereby bound by covenant, to own the actions, and judgments of one, cannot lawfully make a new covenant, amongst themselves, to be obedient to any other, in any thing whatsoever, without his permission. And therefore, they that are subjects to a monarch, cannot without his leave cast off monarchy, and return to the confusion of a disunited multitude; nor transfer their person from him that beareth it, to another man, or other assembly of men: for they are bound, every man to every man, to own, and be reputed author of all, that he that already is their sovereign, shall do, and judge fit to be done: so that any one man dissenting, all the rest should break their covenant made to that man, which is injustice: and they have also every man given the sovereignty to him that beareth their person; and therefore if they depose him, they take from him that which is his own, and so again it is injustice. Besides, if he that attempteth to depose his sovereign, be killed, or punished by him for such attempt, he is author of his own punishment, as being by the institution, author of all his sovereign shall do: and because it is injustice for a man to do any thing, for which he may be punished by his own authority, he is also upon that title, unjust. And whereas some men have pretended for their disobedience to their sovereign, a new covenant, made, not with men, but with God; this also is unjust: for there is no covenant with God, but by mediation of somebody that representeth God's person; which none doth but God's lieutenant, who hath the sovereignty under God. But this pretence of covenant with God, is so evident a lie, even in the pretenders' own consciences, that it is not only an act of an unjust, but also of a vile, and unmanly disposition.

Secondly, because the right of bearing the person of them all, is given to him they make sovereign, by covenant only of one to another, and not of him to any of them; there can happen no breach of covenant on the part of the sovereign; and consequently none of his subjects, by any pretence of forfeiture, can be freed from his subjection. That he which is made sovereign maketh no covenant with his subjects beforehand, is manifest; because either he must make it with the whole multitude, as one party to the covenant; or he must make a several covenant with every man. With the whole, as one party, it is impossible; because as yet they are not one person: and if he make so many several covenants as there be men, those covenants after he hath the sovereignty are void, because what act soever can be pretended by any one of them for breach thereof, is the act both of himself, and of all the rest, because done in the person, and by the right of every one of them in particular. Besides, if any one, or more of them, pretend a breach of the covenant made by the sovereign at his institution; and others, or one other of his subjects, or himself alone, pretend there was no such breach, there is in this case, no judge to decide the controversy; it returns therefore to the sword again; and every man recovereth the right of protecting himself by his own strength, contrary to the design they had in the institution. It is therefore in vain to grant sovereignty by way of precedent covenant. The opinion that any monarch receiveth his power by covenant, that is to say, on condition, proceedeth from want of understanding this easy truth, that covenants being but words and breath, have no force to oblige, contain, constrain, or protect any man, but what it has from the public sword; that is, from the untied hands of that man, or assembly of men that hath the sovereignty, and whose actions are avouched by them all, and performed by the strength of them all, in him united. But when an assembly of men is made sovereign; then no man imagineth any such covenant to have passed in the institution; for no man is so dull as to say, for example, the people of Rome made a covenant with the Romans, to hold the sovereignty on such or such conditions; which not performed, the Romans might lawfully depose the Roman people. That men see not the reason to be alike in a monarchy, and in a popular government, proceedeth from the ambition of some, that are kinder to the government of an assembly, whereof they may hope to participate, than of monarchy, which they despair to enjoy.

Thirdly, because the major part hath by consenting voices declared a sovereign; he that dissented must now consent with the rest; that is, be contented to avow all the actions he shall do, or else justly be destroyed by the rest. For if he voluntarily entered into the congregation of them that were assembled, he sufficiently declared thereby his will, (and therefore tacitly covenanted) to stand to what the major part should ordain: and therefore if he refuse to stand thereto, or make protestation against any of their decrees, he does contrary to his covenant, and therefore unjustly. And whether he be of the congregation, or not; and whether his consent be asked, or not, he must either submit to their decrees, or be left in the condition of war he was in before; wherein he might without injustice be destroyed by any man whatsoever.

Fourthly, because every subject is by this institution author of all the actions, and judgments of the sovereign instituted; it follows, that whatsoever he doth, it can be no injury to any of his subjects; nor ought he to be by any of them accused of injustice. For he that doth any thing by authority from another, doth therein no injury to him by whose authority he acteth: but by this institution of a commonwealth, every particular man is author of all the sovereign doth; and consequently he that complaineth of injury from his sovereign, complaineth of that whereof he himself is author; and therefore ought not to accuse any man but himself; no nor himself of injury; because to do injury to one's self, is impossible. It is true that they that have sovereign power, may commit iniquity, but not injustice, or injury in the proper signification.

Fifthly, and consequently to that which was said last, no man that hath sovereign power can justly be put to death, or otherwise in any manner by his subjects punished. For seeing every subject is author of the actions of his sovereign; he punisheth another, for the actions committed by himself.

And because the end of this institution, is the peace and defence of them all; and whosoever has right to the end, has right to the means; it belongeth of right, to whatsoever man, or assembly that hath the sovereignty, to be judge both of the means of peace and defence; and also of the hindrances, and disturbances of the same; and to do whatsoever he shall think necessary to be done, both beforehand, for the preserving of peace and security, by prevention of discord at home, and hostility from abroad; and, when peace and security are lost, for the recovery of the same. And therefore,

Sixthly, it is annexed to the sovereignty, to be judge of what opinions and doctrines are averse, and what conducing to peace; and consequently, on what occasions, how far, and what, men are to be trusted withal, in speaking to multitudes of people; and who shall examine the doctrines of all books before they be published. For the actions of men proceed from their opinions; and in the well-governing of opinions, consisteth the well-governing of men's actions, in order to their peace, and concord. And though in matter of doctrine, nothing ought to be regarded but the truth; yet this is not repugnant to regulating of the same by peace. For doctrine repugnant to peace, can no more be true, than peace and concord can be against the law of nature. It is true, that in a commonwealth, where by the negligence, or unskilfulness of governors, and teachers, false doctrines are by time generally received; the contrary truths may be generally offensive: Yet the most sudden, and rough busling in of a new truth, that can be, does never break the peace, but only sometimes awake the war. For those men that are so remissly governed, that they dare take up arms, to defend, or introduce an opinion, are still in war; and their condition not peace, but only a cessation of arms for fear of one another; and they live as it were, in the precincts of battle continually. It belongeth therefore to him that hath the sovereign power, to be judge, or constitute all judges of opinions and doctrines, as a thing necessary to peace; thereby to prevent discord and civil war.

Seventhly, is annexed to the sovereignty, the whole power of prescribing the rules, whereby every man may know, what goods he may enjoy, and what actions he may do, without being molested by any of his fellow-subjects; and this is it men call *propriety*. For before constitution of sovereign power (as hath already been shown) all men had right to all things; which necessarily causeth war: and therefore this propriety, being necessary to peace, and depending on sovereign power, is the act of that power, in order to the public peace. These rules of propriety (or *meum* and *tuum*) and of *good*, *evil*, *lawful*, and *unlawful* in the actions of subjects, are the civil laws; that is to say, the laws of each commonwealth in particular; though the name of civil law be now restrained to the ancient civil laws of the city of *Rome*; which being the head of a great part of the world, her laws at that time were in these parts the civil law.

Eighthly, is annexed to the sovereignty, the right of judicature; that is to say, of hearing and deciding all controversies, which may arise concerning law, either civil, or natural; or concerning fact. For without the decision of controversies, there is no protection of one subject, against the injuries of another; the laws concerning *meum* and *tuum* are in vain; and to every man remaineth, from the natural and necessary appetite of his own conservation, the right of protecting himself by his private strength, which is the condition of war; and contrary to the end for which every commonwealth is instituted.

Ninthly, is annexed to the sovereignty, the right of making war and peace with other nations, and commonwealths; that is to say, of judging when it is for the public good, and how great forces are to be assembled, armed, and paid for that end; and to levy money upon the subjects, to defray the expenses thereof. For the power by which the people are to be defended, consisteth in their armies; and the strength of an army, in the union of their strength under one command; which command the sovereign instituted, therefore hath; because the command of the *militia*, without other institution, maketh him that hath it sovereign. And therefore whosoever is made general of an army, he that hath the sovereign power is always generalissimo.

Tenthly, is annexed to the sovereignty, the choosing of all counsellors, ministers, magistrates, and officers, both in peace, and war. For seeing the sovereign is charged with the end, which is the common peace and defence, he is understood to have power to use such means, as he shall think most fit for his discharge.

Eleventhly, to the sovereign is committed the power of rewarding with riches, or honour; and of punishing with corporal, or pecuniary punishment, or with ignominy every subject according to the law he hath formerly made; or if there be no law made, according as he shall judge most to conduce to the encouraging of men to serve the commonwealth, or deterring of them from doing disservice to the same.

Lastly, considering what values men are naturally apt to set upon themselves; what respect they look for from others; and how little they value other men; from whence continually arise amongst them, emulation, quarrels, factions, and at last war, to the destroying of one another, and diminution of their strength against a common enemy; it is necessary that there be laws of honour, and a public rate of the worth of such men as have deserved, or are able to deserve well of the commonwealth; and that there be force in the hands of some or other, to put those laws in execution. But it hath already been shown, that not only the whole *militia*, or forces of the commonwealth; but also the judicature of all controversies, is annexed to the sovereignty. To the sovereign therefore it belongeth also to give titles of honour; and to appoint what order of place, and dignity, each man shall hold; and what signs of respect, in public or private meetings, they shall give to one another.

These are the rights, which make the essence of sovereignty; and which are the marks, whereby a man may discern in what man, or assembly of men, the sovereign power is placed, and resideth. For these are incommunicable, and inseparable. The power to coin money; to dispose of the estate and persons of infant heirs; to have praeemption in markets; and all other statute prerogatives, may be transferred by the sovereign; and yet the power to protect his subjects be retained. But if he transfer the *militia*, he retains the judicature in vain, for want of execution of the laws: or if he grant away the power of raising money; the *militia* is in vain: or if he give away the government of doctrines, men will be frighted into rebellion with the fear of spirits. And so if we consider any one of the said rights, we shall presently see, that the holding of all the rest will produce no effect, in the conservation of peace and justice, the end for which all commonwealths are instituted. And this division is it, whereof it is said, *a kingdom divided in itself cannot stand*: for unless this division precede, division into opposite armies can never happen. If there had not first been an opinion received of the greatest part of England, that these powers were divided between the King, and the Lords, and the House of Commons, the people had never been divided and fallen into this civil war; first between those that disagreed in politics; and after between the dissenters about the liberty of religion; which have so instructed men in this point of sovereign right, that there be few now (in *England*,) that do not see, that these rights are inseparable, and will be so generally acknowledged at the next return of peace; and so continue, till their miseries are forgotten; and no longer, except the vulgar be better taught than they have hitherto been.

And because they are essential and inseparable rights, it follows necessarily, that in whatsoever words any of them seem to be granted away, yet if the sovereign power itself be not in direct terms renounced, and the name of sovereign no more given by the grantees to him that grants them, the grant is void: for when he has granted all he can, if we grant back the sovereignty, all is restored, as inseparably annexed thereunto.

This great authority being indivisible, and inseparably annexed to the sovereignty, there is little ground for the opinion of them, that say of sovereign kings, though they be *singulis majores*, of greater power than every one of their subjects, yet they be *universis minores*, of less power than them all together. For if by *all together*, they mean not the collective body as one person, then *all together*, and *every one*, signify the same; and the speech is absurd. But if by *all together*, they understand them as one person, (which person the sovereign bears,) then the power of all together, is the same with the sovereign's power; and so again the speech is absurd: which absurdity they see well enough, when the sovereignty is in an assembly of the people; but in a monarch they see it not; and yet the power of sovereignty is the same in whomsoever it be placed.

And as the power, so also the honour of the sovereign, ought to be greater, than that of any, or all the subjects. For in the sovereignty is the fountain of honour. The dignities of lord, earl, duke, and prince are his creatures. As in the presence of the master, the servants are equal, and without any honour at all; so are the subjects, in the presence of the sovereign. And though they shine some more, some less, when they are out of his sight; yet in his presence, they shine no more than the stars in presence of the sun.

But a man may here object, that the condition of subjects is very miserable; as being obnoxious to the lusts, and other irregular passions of him, or them that have so unlimited a power in their hands. And commonly they that live under a monarch, think it the fault of monarchy; and they that live under the government of democracy, or other sovereign assembly, attribute all the inconvenience to that form of commonwealth; whereas the power in all forms, if they be perfect enough to protect them, is the same; not considering that the estate of man can never be without some incommodity or other; and that the greatest, that in any form of government can possibly happen to the people in general, is scarce sensible, in respect of the miseries, and horrible calamities, that accompany a civil war, or that dissolute condition of masterless men, without subjection to laws, and a coercive power to tie their hands from rapine and revenge: nor considering that the greatest pressure of sovereign governors, proceedeth not from any delight, or profit they can expect in the damage or weakening of their subjects, in whose vigour, consisteth their own strength and glory; but in the restiveness of themselves, that unwillingly contributing to their own defence, make it necessary for their governors to draw from them what they can in time of peace, that they may have means on any emergent occasion, or sudden need, to resist, or take advantage on their enemies. For all men are by nature provided of notable multiplying glasses, (that is their passions and self-love,) through which, every little payment appeareth a great grievance; but are destitute of those prospective glasses, (namely moral and civil science,) to see afar off the miseries that hang over them, and cannot without such payments be avoided.

Chapter 19

Of the Several Kinds of Commonwealth by Institution, and of Succession to the Sovereign Power

The difference of commonwealths, consisteth in the difference of the sovereign, or the person representative of all and every one of the multitude. And because the sovereignty is either in one man, or in an assembly of more than one; and into that assembly either every man hath right to enter, or not every one, but certain men distinguished from the rest; it is manifest, there can be but three kinds of commonwealth. For the representative must needs be one man, or more: and if more, then it is the assembly of all, or but of a part. When the representative is one man, then is the commonwealth a MONARCHY: when an assembly of all that will come together, then it is a DEMOCRACY, or popular commonwealth: when an assembly of a part only, then it is called an ARISTOCRACY. Other kind of commonwealth there can be none: for either one, or more, or all, must have the sovereign power (which I have shown to be indivisible) entire.

There be other names of government, in the histories, and books of policy; as *tyranny*, and *oligarchy*: But they are not the names of other forms of government, but of the same forms misliked. For they that are discontented under *monarchy*, call it *tyranny*; and they that are displeased with *aristocracy*, call it *oligarchy*: so also, they which find themselves grieved under a *democracy*, call it *anarchy*, (which signifies want of government;) and yet I think no man believes, that want of government, is any new kind of government: nor by the same reason ought they to believe, that the government is of one kind, when they like it, and another, when they mislike it, or are oppressed by the governors.

It is manifest, that men who are in absolute liberty, may, if they please, give authority to one man, to represent them every one; as well as give such authority to any assembly of men whatsoever; and consequently may subject themselves, if they think good, to a monarch, as absolutely, as to any other representative. Therefore, where there is already erected a sovereign power, there can be no other representative of the same people, but only to certain particular ends, by the sovereign limited. For that were to erect two sovereigns; and every man to have his person represented by two actors, that by opposing one another, must needs divide that power, which (if men will live in peace) is indivisible; and thereby reduce the multitude into the condition of war, contrary to the end for which all sovereignty is instituted. And therefore as it is absurd, to think that a sovereign assembly, inviting the people of their dominion, to send up their deputies, with power to make known their advice, or desires, should therefore hold such deputies, rather than themselves, for the absolute representative of the people: so it is absurd also, to think the same in a monarchy. And I know not how this so manifest a truth, should of late be so little observed; that in a monarchy, he that had the sovereignty from a descent of 600 years, was alone called sovereign, had the title of Majesty from every one of his subjects, and was unquestionably taken by them for their king, was notwithstanding never considered as their representative; that name without contradiction passing for the title of those men, which at his command were sent up by the people to carry their petitions, and give him (if he permitted it) their advice. Which may serve as an admonition, for those that are the true, and absolute representative of a people, to instruct men in the nature of that office, and to take heed how they admit of any other general representation upon any occasion whatsoever, if they mean to discharge the trust committed to them.

The difference between these three kinds of commonwealth, consisteth not in the difference of power; but in the difference of convenience, or aptitude to produce the peace, and security of the people; for which end they were instituted. And to compare monarchy with the other two, we may observe; first, that whosoever beareth the person of the people, or is one of that assembly that bears it, beareth also his own natural person. And though he be careful in his politic person to procure the common interest; yet he is more, or no less careful to procure the private good of himself, his family, kindred and friends; and for the most part, if the public interest chance to cross the private, he prefers the private: for the passions of men, are commonly more potent than their reason. From whence it follows, that where the public and private interest are most closely united, there is the public most advanced. Now in monarchy, the private interest is the same with the public. The riches, power, and honour of a monarch arise only from the riches, strength and reputation of his subjects. For no king can be rich, nor glorious, nor secure, whose subjects are either poor, or contemptible, or too weak through want, or dissention, to maintain a war against their enemies: whereas in a democracy, or aristocracy, the public prosperity confers not so much to the private fortune of one that is corrupt, or ambitious, as doth many times a perfidious advice, a treacherous action, or a civil war.

Secondly, that a monarch receiveth counsel of whom, when, and where he pleaseth; and consequently may hear the opinion of men versed in the matter about which he deliberates, of what rank or quality soever, and as long before the time of action, and with as much secrecy, as he will. But when a sovereign assembly has need of counsel, none are admitted but such as have a right thereto from the beginning; which for the most part are of those who have been versed more in the acquisition of wealth than of knowledge; and are to give their advice in long discourses, which may, and do commonly excite men to action, but not govern them in it. For the *understanding* is by the flame of the passions, never enlightened, but dazzled: Nor is there any place, or time, wherein an assembly can receive counsel with secrecy, because of their own multitude.

Thirdly, that the resolutions of a monarch, are subject to no other inconstancy, than that of human nature; but in assemblies, besides that of nature, there ariseth an inconstancy from the number. For the absence of a few, that would have the resolution once taken, continue firm, (which may happen by security, negligence, or private impediments,) or the diligent appearance of a few of the contrary opinion, undoes to day, all that was concluded yesterday.

Fourthly, that a monarch cannot disagree with himself, out of envy, or interest, but an assembly may; and that to such a height, as may produce a civil war.

Fifthly, that in monarchy there is this inconvenience; that any subject, by the power of one man, for the enriching of a favourite or flatterer, may be deprived of all he possesseth; which I confess is a great and inevitable inconvenience. But the same may as well happen, where the sovereign power is in an assembly: for their power is the same; and they are as subject to evil counsel, and to be seduced by orators, as a monarch by flatterers; and becoming one another's flatterers, serve one another's covetousness and ambition by turns. And whereas the favourites of monarchs, are few, and they have none else to advance but their own kindred; the favourites of an assembly, are many; and the kindred much more numerous, than of any monarch. Besides, there is no favourite of a monarch, which cannot as well succour his friends, as hurt his enemies: but orators, that is to say, favourites of sovereign assemblies, though they have great power to hurt, have little to save. For to accuse, requires less eloquence (such is man's nature) than to excuse; and condemnation, than absolution more resembles justice.

Sixthly, that it is an inconvenience in monarchy, that the sovereignty may descend upon an infant, or one that cannot discern between good and evil: and consisteth in this, that the use of his power, must be in the hand of another man, or of some assembly of men, which are to govern by his right, and in his name; as curators, and protectors of his person, and authority. But to say there is inconvenience, in putting the use of the sovereign power, into the hand of a man, or an assembly of men; is to say that all government is more inconvenient, than confusion, and civil war. And therefore all the danger that can be pretended, must arise from the contention of those, that for an office of so great honour, and profit, may become competitors. To make it appear, that this inconvenience, proceedeth not from that form of government we call monarchy, we are to consider, that the precedent monarch, hath appointed who shall have the tuition of his infant successor, either expressly by testament, or tacitly, by not controlling the custom in that case received: and then such inconvenience, (if it happen) is to be attributed, not to the monarchy, but to the ambition, and injustice of the subjects; which in all kinds of government, where the people are not well instructed in their duty, and the rights of sovereignty, is the same. Or else the precedent monarch hath not at all taken order for such tuition;

and then the law of nature hath provided this sufficient rule, that the tuition shall be in him, that hath by nature most interest in the preservation of the authority of the infant, and to whom least benefit can accrue by his death, or diminution. For seeing every man by nature seeketh his own benefit, and promotion; to put an infant into the power of those, that can promote themselves by his destruction, or damage, is not tuition, but treachery. So that sufficient provision being taken, against all just quarrel, about the government under a child, if any contention arise to the disturbance of the public peace, it is not to be attributed to the form of monarchy, but to the ambition of subjects, and ignorance of their duty. On the other side, there is no great commonwealth, the sovereignty whereof is in a great assembly, which is not, as to consultations of peace, and war, and making of laws, in the same condition, as if the government were in a child. For as a child wants the judgment to dissent from counsel given him, and is thereby necessitated to take the advice of them, or him, to whom he is committed: so an assembly wanteth the liberty, to dissent from the counsel of the major part, be it good, or bad. And as a child has need of a tutor, or protector, to preserve his person and authority: so also (in great commonwealths,) the sovereign assembly, in all great dangers and troubles, have need of *custodes libertatis*; that is of dictators, or protectors of their authority; which are as much as temporary monarchs; to whom for a time, they may commit the entire exercise of their power; and have (at the end of that time) been oftener deprived thereof, than infant kings, by their protectors, regents, or any other tutors.

Though the kinds of sovereignty be, as I have now shown, but three; that is to say, monarchy, where one man has it; or democracy, where the general assembly of subjects hath it; or aristocracy, where it is in an assembly of certain persons nominated, or otherwise distinguished from the rest: yet he that shall consider the particular commonwealths that have been, and are in the world, will not perhaps easily reduce them to three, and may thereby be inclined to think there be other forms, arising from these mingled together. As for example, elective kingdoms; where kings have the sovereign power put into their hands for a time; or kingdoms, wherein the king hath a power limited: which governments, are nevertheless by most writers called monarchy. Likewise if a popular, or aristocratical commonwealth, subdue an enemy's country, and govern the same, by a president, procurator, or other magistrate; this may seem perhaps at first sight, to be a democratical, or aristocratical government. But it is not so. For elective kings, are not sovereigns, but ministers of the sovereign; nor limited kings sovereigns, but ministers of them that have the sovereign power: nor are those provinces which are in subjection to a democracy, or aristocracy of another commonwealth, democratically, or aristocratically governed, but monarchically.

And first, concerning an elective king, whose power is limited to his life, as it is in many places of Christendom at this day; or to certain years or months, as the dictator's power amongst the Romans; if he have right to appoint his successor, he is no more elective but hereditary. But if he have no power to elect his successor, then there is some other man, or assembly known, which after his decease may elect anew, or else the commonwealth dieth, and dissolveth with him, and returneth to the condition of war. If it be known who have the power to give the sovereignty after his death, it is known also that the sovereignty was in them before: for none have right to give that which they have not right to possess, and keep to themselves, if they think good. But if there be none that can give the sovereignty, after the decease of him that was first elected; then has he power, nay he is obliged by the law of nature, to provide, by establishing his successor, to keep those that had trusted him with the government, from relapsing into the miserable condition of civil war. And consequently he was, when elected, a sovereign absolute.

Secondly, that king whose power is limited, is not superior to him, or them that have the power to limit it; and he that is not superior, is not supreme; that is to say not sovereign. The sovereignty therefore was always in that assembly which had the right to limit him; and by consequence the government not monarchy, but either democracy, or aristocracy; as of old time in *Sparta*; where the kings had a privilege to lead their armies; but the sovereignty was in the *Ephori*.

Thirdly, whereas heretofore the Roman people governed the land of *Judea* (for example) by a president; yet was not *Judea* therefore a democracy; because they were not governed by any assembly, into the which, any of them, had right to enter; nor by an aristocracy; because they were not governed by any assembly, into which, any man could enter by their election: but they were governed by one person, which though as to the people of *Rome* was an assembly of the people, or democracy; yet as to people of *Judea*, which had no right at all of participating in the government, was a monarch. For though where the people are governed by an assembly, chosen by themselves out of their own number, the government is called a democracy, or aristocracy; yet when they are governed by an assembly, not of their own choosing, it is a monarchy; not of *one* man, over another man; but of one people, over another people.

Of all these forms of government, the matter being mortal, so that not only monarchs, but also whole assemblies die, it is necessary for the conservation of the peace of men, that as there was order taken for an artificial man, so there be order also taken, for an artificial eternity of life; without which, men that are governed by an assembly, should return into the condition of war in every age; and they that are governed by one man, as soon as their governor dieth. This artificial eternity, is that which men call the right of *succession*.

There is no perfect form of government, where the disposing of the succession is not in the present sovereign. For if it be in any other particular man, or private assembly, it is in a person subject, and may be assumed by the sovereign at his pleasure; and consequently the right is in himself. And if it be in no particular man, but left to a new choice; then is the commonwealth dissolved; and the right is in him that can get it; contrary to the intention of them that did institute the commonwealth, for their perpetual, and not temporary security

In a democracy, the whole assembly cannot fail, unless the multitude that are to be governed fail. And therefore questions of the right of succession, have in that form of government no place at all.

In an aristocracy, when any of the assembly dieth, the election of another into his room belongeth to the assembly, as the sovereign, to whom belongeth the choosing of all counsellors and officers. For that which the representative doth, as actor, every one of the subjects doth, as author. And though the sovereign assembly may give power to others, to elect new men, for supply of their court; yet it is still by their authority, that the election is made; and by the same it may (when the public shall require it) be recalled.

The greatest difficulty about the right of succession, is in monarchy: and the difficulty ariseth from this, that at first sight, it is not manifest who is to appoint the successor; nor many times, who it is whom he hath appointed. For in both these cases, there is required a more exact ratiocination, than every man is accustomed to use. As to the question, who shall appoint the successor, of a monarch that hath the sovereign authority; that is to say, who shall determine of the right of inheritance, (for elective kings and princes have not the sovereign power in propriety, but in use only,) we are to consider, that either he that is in possession, has right to dispose of the succession, or else that right is again in the dissolved multitude. For the death of him that hath the sovereign power in propriety, leaves the multitude without any sovereign at all; that is, without any representative in whom they should be united, and be capable of doing any one action at all: and therefore they are incapable of election of any new monarch; every man having equal right to submit himself to such as he thinks best able to protect him; or if he can, protect himself by his own sword, which is a return to confusion, and to the condition of a war of every man against every man, contrary to the end for which monarchy had its first institution. Therefore it is manifest, that by the institution of monarchy, the disposing of the successor, is always left to the judgment and will of the present possessor.

And for the question (which may arise sometimes) who it is that the monarch in possession, hath designed to the succession and inheritance of his power; it is determined by his express words, and testament; or by other tacit signs sufficient.

By express words, or testament, when it is declared by him in his lifetime, *viva voce*, or by writing; as the first emperors of *Rome* declared who should be their heirs. For the word heir does not of itself imply the children, or nearest kindred of a man; but whomsoever a man shall any way declare, he would have to succeed him in his estate. If therefore a monarch declare expressly, that such a man shall be his heir, either by word or writing, then is that man immedi-

ately after the decease of his predecessor, invested in the right of being monarch.

But where testament, and express words are wanting, other natural signs of the will are to be followed: whereof the one is custom. And therefore where the custom is, that the next of kindred absolutely succeedeth, there also the next of kindred hath right to the succession; for that, if the will of him that was in possession had been otherwise, he might easily have declared the same in his life time. And likewise where the custom is, that the next of the male kindred succeedeth, there also the right of succession is in the next of the kindred male, for the same reason. And so it is if the custom were to advance the female. For whatsoever custom a man may by a word control, and does not, it is a natural sign he would have that custom stand.

But where neither custom, nor testament hath preceded, there it is to be understood, first, that a monarch's will is, that the government remain monarchical; because he hath approved that government in himself. Secondly, that a child of his own, male, or female, be preferred before any other; because men are presumed to be more inclined by nature, to advance their own children, than the children of other men; and of their own, rather a male than a female; because men, are naturally fitter than women, for actions of labour and danger. Thirdly, where his own issue faileth, rather a brother than a stranger; and so still the nearer in blood, rather than the more remote; because it is always presumed that the nearer of kin, is the nearer in affection; and it is evident that a man receives always, by reflection, the most honour from the greatness of his nearest kindred.

But if it be lawful for a monarch to dispose of the succession by words of contract, or testament, men may perhaps object a great inconvenience: for he may sell, or give his right of governing to a stranger; which, because strangers (that is, men not used to live under the same government, nor speaking the same language) do commonly undervalue one another, may turn to the oppression of his subjects; which is indeed a great inconvenience: but it proceedeth not necessarily from the subjection to a stranger's government, but from the unskilfulness of the governors, ignorant of the true rules of politics. And therefore the Romans when they had subdued many nations, to make their government digestible, were wont to take away that grievance, as much as they thought necessary, by giving sometimes to whole nations, and sometimes to principal men of every nation they conquered, not only the privileges, but also the name of Romans; and took many of them into the senate, and offices of charge, even in the Roman city. And this was it our most wise king, king *James,* aimed at, in endeavouring the union of his two realms of *England* and *Scotland.* Which if he could have obtained, had in all likelihood prevented the civil wars, which make both those kingdoms, at this present, miserable. It is not therefore any injury to the people, for a monarch to dispose of the succession by will; though by the fault of many princes, it hath been sometimes found inconvenient. Of the lawfulness of it, this also is an argument, that whatsoever inconvenience can arrive by giving a kingdom to a stranger, may arrive also by so marrying with strangers, as the right of succession may descend upon them: yet this by all men is accounted lawful.

Chapter 20

Of Dominion Paternal, and Despotical

A *commonwealth by acquisition,* is that, where the sovereign power is acquired by force; and it is acquired by force, when men singly, or many together by plurality of voices, for fear of death, or bonds, do authorize all the actions of that man, or assembly, that hath their lives and liberty in his power.

And this kind of dominion, or sovereignty, differeth from sovereignty by institution, only in this, that men who choose their sovereign, do it for fear of one another, and not of him whom they institute: but in this case, they subject themselves, to him they are afraid of. In both cases they do it for fear: which is to be noted by them, that hold all such covenants, as proceed from fear of death, or violence, void: which if it were true, no man, in any kind of commonwealth, could be obliged to obedience. It is true, that in a commonwealth once instituted, or acquired, promises proceeding from fear of death or violence, are no covenants, nor obliging, when the thing promised is contrary to the laws; but the reason is not, because

it was made upon fear, but because he that promiseth, hath no right in the thing promised. Also, when he may lawfully perform, and doth not, it is not the invalidity of the covenant, that absolveth him, but the sentence of the sovereign. Otherwise, whensoever a man lawfully promiseth, he unlawfully breaketh: but when the sovereign, who is the actor, acquitteth him, then he is acquitted by him that extorted the promise, as by the author of such absolution.

But the rights, and consequences of sovereignty, are the same in both. His power cannot, without his consent, be transferred to another: he cannot forfeit it: he cannot be accused by any of his subjects, of injury: he cannot be punished by them: he is judge of what is necessary for peace; and judge of doctrines: he is sole legislator; and supreme judge of controversies; and of the times, and occasions of war, and peace: to him it belongeth to choose magistrates, counsellors, commanders, and all other officers, and ministers; and to determine of rewards, and punishments, honour, and order. The reasons whereof, are the same which are alleged in the precedent chapter, for the same rights, and consequences of sovereignty by institution.

Dominion is acquired two ways; by generation, and by conquest. The right of dominion by generation, is that, which the parent hath over his children; and is called PATERNAL. And is not so derived from the generation, as if therefore the parent had dominion over his child because he begat him; but from the child's consent, either express, or by other sufficient arguments declared. For as to the generation, God hath ordained to man a helper; and there be always two that are equally parents: the dominion therefore over the child, should belong equally to both; and he be equally subject to both, which is impossible; for no man can obey two masters. And whereas some have attributed the dominion to the man only, as being of the more excellent sex; they misreckon in it. For there is not always that difference of strength, or prudence between the man and the woman, as that the right can be determined without war. In commonwealths, this controversy is decided by the civil law: and for the most part, (but not always) the sentence is in favour of the father; because for the most part commonwealths have been erected by the fathers, not by the mothers of families. But the question lieth now in the state of mere nature; where there are supposed no laws of matrimony; no laws for the education of children; but the law of nature, and the natural inclination of the sexes, one to another, and to their children. In this condition of mere nature, either the parents between themselves dispose of the dominion over the child by contract; or do not dispose thereof at all. If they dispose thereof, the right passeth according to the contract. We find in history that the *Amazons* contracted with the men of the neighbouring countries, to whom they had recourse for issue, that the issue male should be sent back, but the female remain with themselves: so that the dominion of the females was in the mother.

If there be no contract, the dominion is in the mother. For in the condition of mere nature, where there are no matrimonial laws, it cannot be known who is the father, unless it be declared by the mother: and therefore the right of dominion over the child dependeth on her will, and is consequently hers. Again, seeing the infant is first in the power of the mother, so as she may either nourish, or expose it; if she nourish it, it oweth its life to the mother; and is therefore obliged to obey her, rather than any other; and by consequence the dominion over it is hers. But if she expose it, and another find and nourish it, the dominion is in him that nourisheth it. For it ought to obey him by whom it is preserved; because preservation of life being the end, for which one man becomes subject to another, every man is supposed to promise obedience, to him, in whose power it is to save, or destroy him.

If the mother be the father's subject, the child, is in the father's power: and if the father be the mother's subject, (as when a sovereign queen marrieth one of her subjects,) the child is subject to the mother; because the father also is her subject.

If a man and woman, monarchs of two several kingdoms, have a child, and contract concerning who shall have the dominion of him, the right of the dominion passeth by the contract. If they contract not, the dominion followeth the dominion of the place of his residence. For the sovereign of each country hath dominion over all that reside therein.

He that hath the dominion over the child, hath dominion also over the children of the child; and over their children's children. For he that hath dominion over the person of a man, hath dominion over all that is his; without which, dominion were but a title, without the effect.

The right of succession to paternal dominion, proceedeth in the same manner, as doth the right of succession to monarchy; of which I have already sufficiently spoken in the precedent chapter.

Dominion acquired by conquest, or victory in war, is that which some writers call DESPOTICAL, from Δεσπότηθ, which signifieth a *lord*, or *master*; and is the dominion of the master over his servant. And this dominion is then acquired to the victor, when the vanquished, to avoid the present stroke of death, covenanteth either in express words, or by other sufficient signs of the will, that so long as his life, and the liberty of his body is allowed him, the victor shall have the use thereof, at his pleasure. And after such covenant made, the vanquished is a SERVANT, and not before: for by the word *servant*, (whether it be derived from *servire*, to serve, or from *servare*, to save, which I leave to grammarians to dispute) is not meant a captive, which is kept in prison, or bonds, till the owner of him that took him, or bought him of one that did, shall consider what to do with him: (for such men, (commonly called slaves,) have no obligation at all; but may break their bonds, or the prison; and kill, or carry away captive their master, justly:) but one, that being taken, hath corporal liberty allowed him; and upon promise not to run away, nor to do violence to his master, is trusted by him.

It is not therefore the victory, that giveth the right of dominion over the vanquished, but his own covenant. Nor is he obliged because he is conquered; that is to say, beaten, and taken, or put to flight; but because he cometh in, and submitteth to the victor; nor is the victor obliged by an enemy's rendering himself, (without promise of life,) to spare him for this his yielding to discretion; which obliges not the victor longer, than in his own discretion he shall think fit.

And that which men do, when they demand (as it is now called) *quarter*, (which the Greeks called Ζωγρία, *taking alive*,) is to evade the present fury of the victor, by submission, and to compound for their life, with ransom, or service: and therefore he that hath quarter, hath not his life given, but deferred till farther deliberation; for it is not an yielding on condition of life, but to discretion. And then only is his life in security, and his service due, when the victor hath trusted him with his corporal liberty. For slaves that work in prisons, or fetters, do it not of duty, but to avoid the cruelty of their task-masters.

The master of the servant, is master also of all he hath; and may exact the use thereof; that is to say, of his goods, of his labour, of his servants, and of his children, as often as he shall think fit. For he holdeth his life of his master, by the covenant of obedience; that is, of owning, and authorizing whatsoever the master shall do. And in case the master, if he refuse, kill him, or cast him into bonds, or otherwise punish him for his disobedience, he is himself the author of the same; and cannot accuse him of injury.

In sum, the rights and consequences of both *paternal* and *despotical* dominion, are the very same with those of a sovereign by institution; and for the same reasons: which reasons are set down in the precedent chapter. So that for a man that is monarch of divers nations, whereof he hath, in one the sovereignty by institution of the people assembled, and in another by conquest, that is by the submission of each particular, to avoid death or bonds; to demand of one nation more than of the other, from the title of conquest, as being a conquered nation, is an act of ignorance of the rights of sovereignty. For the sovereign is absolute over both alike; or else there is no sovereignty at all; and so every man may lawfully protect himself, if he can, with his own sword, which is the condition of war.

By this it appears; that a great family if it be not part of some commonwealth, is of itself, as to the rights of sovereignty, a little monarchy; whether that family consist of a man and his children; or of a man and his servants; or of a man, and his children, and servants together: wherein the father or master is the sovereign. But yet a family is not properly a commonwealth; unless it be of that power by its own number, or by other opportunities, as not to be subdued without the hazard of war. For where a number of men are manifestly too weak to defend themselves united, every one may use his own reason in time of danger, to save his own life, either by flight, or by submission to the enemy, as he shall think best; in the same manner as a very small company of soldiers, surprised by an army, may cast down their arms, and demand quarter, or run away, rather than be put to the sword.

And thus much shall suffice; concerning what I find by speculation, and deduction, of sovereign rights, from the nature, need, and designs of men, in erecting of commonwealths, and putting themselves under monarchs, or assemblies, entrusted with power enough for their protection.

Let us now consider what the Scripture teacheth in the same point. To Moses, the children of *Israel* say thus: *Speak thou to us, and we will hear thee; but let not God speak to us, lest we die.* (*Exod.* 20. 19.) This is absolute obedience to Moses. Concerning the right of kings, God himself by the mouth of Samuel, saith, (1 *Sam.* 8. 11, 12, &c.) *This shall be the right of the king you will have to reign over you. He shall take your sons, and set them to drive his chariots, and to be his horsemen, and to run before his chariots; and gather in his harvest; and to make his engines of war, and instruments of his chariots; and shall take your daughters to make perfumes, to be his cooks, and bakers. He shall take your fields, your vine-yards, and your olive-yards, and give them to his servants. He shall take the tithe of your corn and wine, and give it to the men of his chamber, and to his other servants. He shall take your man-servants, and your maid-servants, and the choice of your youth, and employ them in his business. He shall take the tithe of your flocks; and you shall be his servants.* This is absolute power, and summed up in the last words, *you shall be his servants.* Again, when the people heard what power their king was to have, yet they consented thereto, and say thus, (*verse* 19) *we will be as all other nations, and our king shall judge our causes, and go before us, to conduct our wars.* Here is confirmed the right that sovereigns have, both to the *militia,* and to all *judicature;* in which is contained as absolute power, as one man can possibly transfer to another. Again, the prayer of king Solomon to God, was this (1 *Kings,* 3. 9): *Give to thy servant understanding, to judge thy people, and to discern between good and evil.* It belongeth therefore to the sovereign to be judge, and to prescribe the rules of *discerning good* and *evil:* which rules are laws; and therefore in him is the legislative power. Saul sought the life of *David;* yet when it was in his power to slay *Saul,* and his servants would have done it, *David* forbad them, saying, (1 *Sam.* 24. 9) *God forbid I should do such an act against my Lord, the anointed of God.* For obedience of servants St. *Paul* saith; (*Col.*

3. 20) *Servants obey your masters in all things*; and, (*Verse* 22) *children obey your parents in all things*. There is simple obedience in those that are subject to paternal, or despotical dominion. Again, (*Matt.* 23. 2, 3) *The Scribes and Pharisees sit in Moses' chair, and therefore all that they shall bid you observe, that observe and do.* There again is simple obedience. And St. *Paul*, (*Titus* 3. 2) *Warn them that they subject themselves to princes, and to those that are in authority, and obey them.* This obedience is also simple. Lastly, our Saviour himself acknowledges, that men ought to pay such taxes as are by kings imposed, where he says, *Give to Caesar that which is Caesar's*; and paid such taxes himself. And that the king's word, is sufficient to take any thing from any subject, when there is need; and that the king is judge of that need: for he himself, as king of the Jews, commanded his disciples to take the ass, and ass's colt to carry him into Jerusalem, saying, (*Matth.* 21. 2, 3) *Go into the village over against you, and you shall find a she ass tied, and her colt with her, untie them, and bring them to me. And if any man ask you, what you mean by it, say the Lord hath need of them: and they will let them go.* They will not ask whether his necessity be a sufficient title; nor whether he be judge of that necessity; but acquiesce in the will of the Lord.

To these places may be added also that of *Genesis*, (*Genesis* 3. 5) *Ye shall be as gods, knowing good and evil.* And *verse* 11. *Who told thee that thou wast naked? hast thou eaten of the tree, of which I commanded thee thou shouldest not eat?* For the cognizance or judicature of good and evil, being forbidden by the name of the fruit of the tree of knowledge, as a trial of *Adam's* obedience; the devil to inflame the ambition of the woman, to whom that fruit already seemed beautiful, told her that by tasting it, they should be as gods, knowing *good* and *evil*. Whereupon having both eaten, they did indeed take upon them God's office, which is judicature of good and evil; but acquired no new ability to distinguish between them aright. And whereas it is said, that having eaten, they saw they were naked; no man hath so interpreted that place, as if they had been formerly blind, and saw not their own skins: the meaning is plain, that it was then they first judged their nakedness (wherein it was God's will to create them) to be uncomely;

and by being ashamed, did tacitly censure God himself. And thereupon God saith, *Hast thou eaten, &c.* as if he should say, doest thou that owest me obedience, take upon thee to judge of my commandments? Whereby it is clearly, (though allegorically,) signified, that the commands of them that have the right to command, are not by their subjects to be censured, nor disputed.

So that it appeareth plainly, to my understanding, both from reason, and Scripture, that the sovereign power, whether placed in one man, as in monarchy, or in one assembly of men, as in popular, and aristocratical commonwealths, is as great, as possibly men can be imagined to make it. And though of so unlimited a power, men may fancy many evil consequences, yet the consequences of the want of it, which is perpetual war of every man against his neighbour, are much worse. The condition of man in this life shall never be without inconveniences; but there happeneth in no commonwealth any great inconvenience, but what proceeds from the subject's disobedience, and breach of those covenants, from which the commonwealth hath its being. And whosoever thinking sovereign power too great, will seek to make it less, must subject himself, to the power, that can limit it; that is to say, to a greater.

The greatest objection is, that of the practice; when men ask, where, and when, such power has by subjects been acknowledged. But one may ask them again, when, or where has there been a kingdom long free from sedition and civil war. In those nations, whose commonwealths have been long-lived, and not been destroyed but by foreign war, the subjects never did dispute of the sovereign power. But howsoever, an argument from the practice of men, that have not sifted to the bottom, and with exact reason weighed the causes, and nature of commonwealths, and suffer daily those miseries, that proceed from the ignorance thereof, is invalid. For though in all places of the world, men should lay the foundation of their houses on the sand, it could not thence be inferred, that so it ought to be. The skill of making, and maintaining commonwealths, consisteth in certain rules, as doth arithmetic and geometry; not (as tennis-play) on practice only: which rules, neither poor men have the leisure, nor men that have had the leisure, have hitherto had the curiosity, or the method to find out.

Chapter 21

Of the Liberty of Subjects

LIBERTY, or FREEDOM, signifieth (properly) the absence of opposition; (by opposition, I mean external impediments of motion;) and may be applied no less to irrational, and inanimate creatures, than to rational. For whatsoever is so tied, or environed, as it cannot move, but within a certain space, which space is determined by the opposition of some external body, we say it hath not liberty to go further. And so of all living creatures, whilst they are imprisoned, or restrained, with walls, or chains; and of the water whilst it is kept in by banks, or vessels, that otherwise would spread itself into a larger space, we use to say, they are not at liberty, to move in such manner, as without those external impediments they would. But when the impediment of motion, is in the constitution of the thing itself, we use not to say, it wants the liberty; but the power to move; as when a stone lieth still, or a man is fastened to his bed by sickness.

And according to this proper, and generally received meaning of the word, *a* FREEMAN, *is he, that in those things, which by his strength and wit he is able to do, is not hindered to do what he has a will to.* But when the words *free*, and *liberty*, are applied to any thing but *bodies*, they are abused; for that which is not subject to motion, is not subject to impediment: and therefore, when it is said (for example) the way is free, no liberty of the way is signified, but of those that walk in it without stop. And when we say a gift is free, there is not meant any liberty of the gift, but of the giver, that was not bound by any law, or covenant to give it. So when we *speak freely*, it is not the liberty of voice, or pronunciation, but of the man, whom no law hath obliged to speak otherwise than he did. Lastly, from the use of the word *free-will*, no liberty can be inferred of the will, desire, or inclination, but the liberty of the man; which consisteth in this, that he finds no stop, in doing what he has the will, desire, or inclination to do.

Fear, and liberty are consistent; as when a man throweth his goods into the sea for *fear* the ship should sink, he doth it nevertheless very willingly, and may refuse to do it if he will: it is therefore the action of one that was *free*: so a man sometimes pays his debt, only for *fear* of imprisonment, which because nobody hindered him from detaining, was the action of a man at *liberty*. And generally all actions which men do in commonwealths, for *fear* of the law, are actions, which the doers had *liberty* to omit.

Liberty, and *necessity* are consistent: as in the water, that hath not only *liberty*, but a *necessity* of descending by the channel; so likewise in the actions which men voluntarily do: which, because they proceed from their will, proceed from *liberty*; and yet, because every act of man's will, and every desire, and inclination proceedeth from some cause, and that from another cause, in a continual chain, (whose first link is in the hand of God the first of all causes,) they proceed from *necessity*. So that to him that could see the connexion of those causes, the *necessity* of all men's voluntary actions, would appear manifest. And therefore God, that seeth, and disposeth all things, seeth also that the *liberty* of man in doing what he will, is accompanied with the *necessity* of doing that which God will, and no more, nor less. For though men may do many things, which God does not command, nor is therefore author of them; yet they can have no passion, nor appetite to any thing, of which appetite God's will is not the cause. And did not his will assure the *necessity* of man's will, and consequently of all that on man's will dependeth, the *liberty* of men would be a contradiction, and impediment to the omnipotence and *liberty* of God. And this shall suffice, (as to the matter in hand) of that natural *liberty*, which only is properly called *liberty*.

But as men, for the attaining of peace, and conservation of themselves thereby, have made an artificial man, which we call a commonwealth; so also have they made artificial chains, called *civil laws*, which they themselves, by mutual covenants, have fastened at one end, to the lips of that man, or assembly, to whom they have given the sovereign power; and at the other end to their own ears. These bonds in their own nature but weak, may nevertheless be made to hold, by the danger, though not by the difficulty of breaking them.

In relation to these bonds only it is, that I am to speak now, of the *liberty* of *subjects*. For seeing there is no commonwealth in the world, wherein there be rules enough set down, for the regulating of all the actions, and words of men, (as being a thing impossible:) it followeth necessarily, that in all kinds of actions, by the laws praetermitted, men have the liberty, of doing what their own reasons shall suggest, for the most profitable to themselves. For if we take liberty in the proper sense, for corporal liberty; that is to say, freedom from chains, and prison, it were very absurd for men to clamour as they do, for the liberty they so manifestly enjoy. Again, if we take liberty, for an exemption from laws, it is no less absurd, for men to demand as they do, that liberty, by which all other men may be masters of their lives. And yet as absurd as it is, this is it they demand; not knowing that the laws are of no power to protect them, without a sword in the hands of a man, or men, to cause those laws to be put in execution. The liberty of a subject, lieth therefore only in those things, which in regulating their actions, the sovereign hath praetermitted: such as is the liberty to buy, and sell, and otherwise contract with one another; to choose their own abode, their own diet, their own trade of life, and institute their children as they themselves think fit; and the like.

Nevertheless we are not to understand, that by such liberty, the sovereign power of life and death, is either abolished, or limited. For it has been already shown, that nothing the sovereign representative can do to a subject, on what pretence soever, can properly be called injustice, or injury; because every subject is author of every act the sovereign doth; so that he never wanteth right to any thing, otherwise, than as he himself is the subject of God, and bound thereby to observe the laws of nature. And therefore it may, and doth often happen in commonwealths, that a subject may be put to death, by the command of the sovereign power; and yet neither do the other wrong: as when *Jephtha* caused his daughter to be sacrificed: in which, and the like cases, he that so dieth, had liberty to do the action, for which he is nevertheless, without injury put to death. And the same holdeth also in a sovereign prince, that putteth to death an innocent subject. For though the action be against the law of nature, as being contrary to equity, (as was the killing of *Uriah*, by *David*;) yet it was not an injury to *Uriah*; but to *God*. Not to *Uriah*, because the right to do what he pleased, was given him by *Uriah* himself: and yet to *God*, because *David* was *God's* subject; and prohibited all iniquity by the law of nature. Which distinction, *David* himself, when he repented the fact, evidently confirmed, saying, *To thee only have I sinned*. In the same manner, the people of *Athens*, when they banished the most potent of their commonwealth for ten years, thought they committed no injustice; and yet they never questioned what crime he had done; but what hurt he would do: nay they commanded the banishment of they knew not whom; and every citizen bringing his oystershell into the market place, written with the name of him he desired should be banished, without actual accusing him, sometimes banished an *Aristides*, for his reputation of justice; and sometimes a scurrilous jester, as *Hyperbolus*, to make a jest of it. And yet a man cannot say, the sovereign people of *Athens* wanted right to banish them; or an *Athenian* the liberty to jest, or to be just.

The liberty, whereof there is so frequent and honourable mention, in the histories, and philosophy of the ancient Greeks, and Romans, and in the writings, and discourse of those that from them have received all their learning in the politics, is not the liberty of particular men; but the liberty of the commonwealth: which is the same with that, which every man then should have, if there were no civil laws, nor commonwealth at all. And the effects of it also be the same. For as amongst masterless men, there is perpetual war, of every man against his neighbour; no inheritance, to transmit to the son, nor to expect from the father; no propriety of goods, or lands; no security; but a full and absolute liberty in every particular man: so in states, and commonwealths not dependent on one another, every commonwealth, (not every man) has an absolute liberty, to do what it shall judge (that is to say, what that man, or assembly that representeth it, shall judge) most conducing to their benefit. But withal, they live in the condition of a perpetual war, and upon the confines of battle, with their frontiers armed, and cannons planted against their neighbours round about. The *Athenians*, and *Romans* were free; that is, free commonwealths: not that any particular men had the liberty to resist their own representative; but that their representative had the liberty to resist, or invade other people. There is written on the turrets of the city of *Lucca* in great characters at this day, the word *LIBERTAS*; yet no man can thence infer, that a particular man has more liberty, or immunity from the service of the commonwealth there, than in *Constantinople*. Whether a commonwealth be monarchical, or popular, the freedom is still the same.

But it is an easy thing, for men to be deceived, by the specious name of *liberty*, and for want of judgment to distinguish, mistake that for their private inheritance, and birth right, which is the right of the public only. And when the same error is confirmed by the authority of men in reputation for their writings in this subject, it is no wonder if it produce sedition, and change of government. In these western parts of the world, we are made to receive our opinions concerning the institution, and rights of commonwealths, from *Aristotle, Cicero*, and other men, Greeks and Romans, that living under popular states, derived those rights, not from the principles of nature, but transcribed them into their books, out of the practice of their own commonwealths, which were popular; as the grammarians describe the rules of language, out of the practice of the time; or the rules of poetry, out of the poems of *Homer* and *Virgil*. And because the Athenians were taught, (to keep them from desire of changing their government,) that they were freemen, and all that lived under monarchy were slaves; therefore Aristotle puts it down in his *Politics, (lib. 6. cap. 2.) In democracy, Liberty is to be supposed: for it is commonly held, that no man is Free in any other government.* And as Aristotle; so Cicero, and other writers have grounded their civil doctrine, on the opinions of the Romans, who were taught to hate monarchy, at first, by them that having deposed their sovereign, shared amongst them the sovereignty of *Rome*; and afterwards by their successors. And by reading of these Greek, and Latin authors, men from their childhood have gotten a habit (under a false show of liberty,) of favouring tumults, and of licentious controlling the actions of their sovereigns; and again of controlling those controllers, with the effusion of so much blood; as I think I may truly say, there was never any thing so dearly bought, as these western parts have bought the learning of the Greek and Latin tongues.

To come now to the particulars of the true liberty of a subject; that is to say, what are the things, which though commanded by the sovereign, he may nevertheless, without injustice, refuse to do; we are to consider, what rights we pass away, when we make a commonwealth; or (which is all one,) what liberty we deny ourselves, by owning all the actions (without exception) of the man, or assembly we make our sovereign. For in the act of our *submission*, consisteth both our *obligation*, and our *liberty*; which must therefore be inferred by arguments taken from thence; there being no obligation on any man, which ariseth not from some act of his own; for all men equally, are by nature free. And because such arguments, must either be drawn from the express words, *I authorise all his actions*, or from the intention of him that submitteth himself to his power, (which intention is to be understood by the end for which he so submitteth;) the obligation, and liberty of the subject, is to be derived, either from those words, (or others equivalent;) or else from the end of the institution of sovereignty, namely, the peace of the subjects within themselves, and their defence against a common enemy.

First therefore, seeing sovereignty by institution, is by covenant of every one to every one; and sovereignty by acquisition, by covenants of the vanquished to the victor, or child to the parent; it is manifest, that every subject has liberty in all those things, the right whereof cannot by covenant be transferred. I have shewn before in the 14th chapter, that covenants, not to defend a man's own body, are void. Therefore,

If the sovereign command a man (though justly condemned,) to kill, wound, or maim himself; or not to resist those that assault him; or to abstain from the use of food, air, medicine, or any other thing, without which he cannot live; yet hath that man the liberty to disobey.

If a man be interrogated by the sovereign, or his authority, concerning a crime done by himself, he is not bound (without assurance of pardon) to confess it; because no man (as I have shown in the same chapter) can be obliged by covenant to accuse himself.

Again, the consent of a subject to sovereign power, is contained in these words, *I authorize, or take upon me, all his actions*; in which there is no restriction at all, of his own former natural liberty: for by allowing, him to *kill me*, I am not bound to kill myself when he commands me. It is one thing to say, *kill me, or my fellow, if you please*; another thing to say, *I will kill myself, or my fellow*. It followeth therefore, that

No man is bound by the words themselves, either to kill himself, or any other man; and consequently, that the obligation a man may sometimes have, upon the command of the sovereign to execute any dangerous, or dishonourable office, dependeth not on the words of our submission; but on the intention, which is to be understood by the end thereof. When therefore our refusal to obey, frustrates the end for which the sovereignty was ordained; then there is no liberty to refuse: otherwise there is.

Upon this ground, a man that is commanded as a soldier to fight against the enemy, though his sovereign have right enough to punish his refusal with death, may nevertheless in many cases refuse, without injustice; as when he substituteth a sufficient soldier in his place: for in this case he deserteth not the service of the commonwealth. And there is allowance to be made for natural timorousness; not only to women, (of whom no such dangerous duty is expected,) but also to men of feminine courage. When armies fight, there is on one side, or both, a running away; yet when they do it not out of treachery, but fear, they are not esteemed to do it unjustly, but dishonourably. For the same reason, to avoid battle, is not injustice, but cowardice. But he that inrolleth himself a soldier, or taketh imprest money, taketh away the excuse of a timorous nature; and is obliged, not only to go to the battle, but also not to run from it, without his captain's leave. And when the defence of the commonwealth, requireth at once the help of all that are able to bear arms, every one is obliged; because otherwise the institution of the commonwealth, which they have not the purpose, or courage to preserve, was in vain.

To resist the sword of the commonwealth, in defence of another man, guilty, or innocent, no man hath liberty; because such liberty, takes away from the sovereign, the means of protecting us; and is therefore destructive of the very essence of government. But in case a great many men together, have already resisted the sovereign power unjustly, or committed some capital crime, for which every one of them expecteth death, whether have they not the liberty then to join together, and assist, and defend one another? Certainly they have: for they but defend their lives, which the guilty man may as well do, as the innocent. There was indeed injustice in the first breach of their duty; their bearing of arms subsequent to it, though it be to maintain what they have done, is no new unjust act. And if it be only to defend their persons, it is not unjust at all. But the offer of pardon taketh from them, to whom it is offered, the plea of self-defence, and maketh their perseverance in assisting, or defending the rest, unlawful.

As for other liberties, they depend on the silence of the law. In cases where the sovereign has prescribed no rule, there the subject hath the liberty to do, or forbear, according to his own discretion. And therefore such liberty is in some places more, and in some less; and in some times more, in other times less, according as they that have the sovereignty shall think most convenient. As for example, there was a time, when in *England* a man might enter into his own land, (and dispossess such as wrongfully possessed it,) by force. But in aftertimes, that liberty of forcible entry, was taken away by a statute made (by the king,) in parliament. And in some places of the world, men have the liberty of many wives: in other places, such liberty is not allowed.

If a subject have a controversy with his sovereign, of debt, or of right of possession of lands or goods, or concerning any service required at his hands, or concerning any penalty, corporal, or pecuniary, grounded on a precedent law; he hath the same liberty to sue for his right, as if it were against a subject; and before such judges, as are appointed by the sovereign. For seeing the sovereign demandeth by force of a former law, and not by virtue of his power; he declareth thereby, that he requireth no more, than shall appear to be due by that law. The suit therefore is not contrary to the will of the sovereign; and consequently the subject hath the liberty to demand the hearing of his cause; and sentence, according to that law. But if he demand, or take any thing by pretence of his power; there lieth, in that case, no action of law: for all that is done by him in virtue of his power, is done by the authority of every subject, and consequently, he that brings an action against the sovereign, brings it against himself.

If a monarch, or sovereign assembly, grant a liberty

to all, or any of his subjects, which grant standing, he is disabled to provide for their safety, the grant is void; unless he directly renounce, or transfer the sovereignty to another. For in that he might openly, (if it had been his will,) and in plain terms, have renounced, or transferred it, and did not; it is to be understood it was not his will; but that the grant proceeded from ignorance of the repugnancy between such a liberty and the sovereign power: and therefore the sovereignty is still retained; and consequently all those powers, which are necessary to the exercising thereof; such as are the power of war, and peace, of judicature, of appointing officers, and councillors, of levying money, and the rest named in the 18th chapter.

The obligation of subjects to the sovereign, is understood to last as long, and no longer, than the power lasteth, by which he is able to protect them. For the right men have by nature to protect themselves, when none else can protect them, can by no covenant be relinquished. The sovereignty is the soul of the commonwealth; which once departed from the body, the members do no more receive their motion from it. The end of obedience is protection; which, wheresoever a man seeth it, either in his own, or in another's sword, nature applieth his obedience to it, and his endeavour to maintain it. And though sovereignty, in the intention of them that make it, be immortal; yet is it in its own nature, not only subject to violent death, by foreign war; but also through the ignorance, and passions of men, it hath in it, from the very institution, many seeds of a natural mortality, by intestine discord.

If a subject be taken prisoner in war; or his person, or his means of life be within the guards of the enemy, and hath his life and corporal liberty given him, on condition to be subject to the victor, he hath liberty to accept the condition; and having accepted it, is the subject of him that took him; because he had no other way to preserve himself. The case is the same, if he be detained on the same terms, in a foreign country. But if a man be held in prison, or bonds, or is not trusted with the liberty of his body; he cannot be understood to be bound by covenant to subjection; and therefore may, if he can, make his escape by any means whatsoever.

If a monarch shall relinquish the sovereignty, both for himself, and his heirs; his subjects return to the absolute liberty of nature; because, though nature may declare who are his sons, and who are the nearest of his kin; yet it dependeth on his own will, (as hath been said in the precedent chapter,) who shall be his heir. If therefore he will have no heir, there is no sovereignty, nor subjection. The case is the same, if he die without known kindred, and without declaration of his heir. For then there can no heir be known, and consequently no subjection be due.

If the sovereign banish his subject; during the banishment, he is not subject. But he that is sent on a message, or hath leave to travel, is still subject; but it is, by contract between sovereigns, not by virtue of the covenant of subjection. For whosoever entereth into another's dominion, is subject to all the laws thereof; unless he have a privilege by the amity of the sovereigns, or by special licence.

If a monarch subdued by war, render himself subject to the victor; his subjects are delivered from their former obligation, and become obliged to the victor. But if he be held prisoner, or have not the liberty of his own body; he is not understood to have given away the right of sovereignty; and therefore his subjects are obliged to yield obedience to the magistrates formerly placed, governing not in their own name, but in his. For, his right remaining, the question is only of the administration; that is to say, of the magistrates and officers; which, if he have not means to name, he is supposed to approve those, which he himself had formerly appointed.

Chapter 22

Of Systems Subject, Political, and Private

Having spoken of the generation, form, and power of a commonwealth, I am in order to speak next of the parts thereof. And first of systems, which resemble the similar parts, or muscles of a body natural. By SYSTEMS, I understand any numbers of men joined in one interest, or one business. Of which, some are *regular*, and some *irregular*. *Regular* are those, where one man, or assembly of men, is constituted representative of the whole number. All other are *irregular*.

Of regular, some are *absolute*, and *independent*, subject to none but their own representative: such are only commonwealths; of which I have spoken already in the 5 last precedent chapters. Others are dependent; that is to say, subordinate to some sovereign power, to which every one, as also their representative is *subject*.

Of systems subordinate, some are *political*, and some *private*. *Political*, (otherwise called *bodies politic*, and *persons in law*,) are those, which are made by authority from the sovereign power of the commonwealth. *Private*, are those, which are constituted by subjects amongst themselves, or by authority from a stranger. For no authority derived from foreign power, within the dominion of another, is public there, but private.

And of private systems, some are *lawful*; some *unlawful*. *Lawful*, are those which are allowed by the commonwealth: all other are *unlawful*. Irregular systems, are those which having no representative, consist only in concourse of people; which if not forbidden by the commonwealth, nor made on evil design, (such as are conflux of people to markets, or shows, or any other harmless end,) are lawful. But when the intention is evil, or (if the number be considerable), unknown, they are unlawful.

In bodies politic, the power of the representative is always limited: and that which prescribeth the limits thereof, is the power sovereign. For power unlimited, is absolute sovereignty. And the sovereign, in every commonwealth, is the absolute representative of all the subjects; and therefore no other, can be representative of any part of them, but so far forth, as he shall give leave. And to give leave to a body politic of subjects, to have an absolute representative to all intents and purposes, were to abandon the government of so much of the commonwealth, and to divide the dominion, contrary to their peace and defence, which the sovereign cannot be understood to do, by any grant, that does not plainly, and directly discharge them of their subjection. For consequences of words, are not the signs of his will, when other consequences are signs of the contrary; but rather signs of error, and misreckoning; to which all mankind is too prone.

The bounds of that power, which is given to the representative of a body politic, are to be taken notice of, from two things. One is their writ, or letters from the sovereign: the other is the law of the commonwealth.

For though in the institution or acquisition of a commonwealth, which is independent, there needs no writing, because the power of the representative has there no other bounds, but such as are set out by the unwritten law of nature; yet in subordinate bodies, there are such diversities of limitation necessary, concerning their businesses, times, and places, as can neither be remembered without letters, nor taken notice of, unless such letters be patent, that they may be read to them, and withal sealed, or testified, with the seals, or other permanent signs of the authority sovereign.

And because such limitation is not always easy, or perhaps possible to be described in writing; the ordinary laws, common to all subjects, must determine, what the representative may lawfully do, in all cases, where the letters themselves are silent. And therefore

In a body politic, if the representative be one man, whatsoever he does in the person of the body, which is not warranted in his letters, nor by the laws, is his own act, and not the act of the body, nor of any other member thereof besides himself: because further than his letters, or the laws limit, he representeth no man's person, but his own. But what he does according to these, is the act of every one: for of the act of the sovereign every one is author, because he is their representative unlimited; and the act of him that recedes not from the letters of the sovereign, is the act of the sovereign, and therefore every member of the body is author of it.

But if the representative be an assembly; whatsoever that assembly shall decree, not warranted by their letters, or the laws, is the act of the assembly, or body politic, and the act of every one by whose vote the decree was made; but not the act of any man that being present voted to the contrary; nor of any man absent, unless he voted it by procuration. It is the act of the assembly, because voted by the major part; and if it be a crime, the assembly may be punished, as far forth as it is capable, as by dissolution, or forfeiture of their letters (which is to such artificial, and fictitious bodies, capital) or (if the assembly have a common stock, wherein none of the innocent members have propriety,) by pecuniary mulct. For from corporal penalties nature hath exempted all bodies politic. But they that gave not their vote, are therefore innocent, because the assembly cannot represent any man in things unwarranted by their letters, and consequently are not involved in their votes.

If the person of the body politic being in one man, borrow money of a stranger, that is, of one that is not of the same body, (for no letters need limit borrowing, seeing it is left to men's own inclinations to limit lending), the debt is the representative's. For if he should have authority from his letters, to make the members pay what he borroweth, he should have by consequence the sovereignty of them; and therefore the grant were either void, as proceeding from error, commonly incident to human nature, and an insufficient sign of the will of the granter; or if it be avowed by him, then is the representer sovereign, and falleth not under the present question, which is only of bodies subordinate. No member therefore is obliged to pay the debt so borrowed, but the representative himself: because he that lendeth it, being a stranger to the letters, and to the qualification of the body, understandeth those only for his debtors, that are engaged: and seeing the representer can engage himself, and none else, has him only for debtor; who must therefore pay him, out of the common stock (if there be any), or (if there be none) out of his own estate.

If he come into debt by contract, or mulct, the case is the same.

But when the representative is an assembly, and the debt to a stranger; all they, and only they are responsible for the debt, that gave their votes to the borrowing of it, or to the contract that made it due, or to the fact for which the mulct was imposed, because every one of those in voting did engage himself for the payment: for he that is author of the borrowing, is obliged to the payment, even of the whole debt, though when paid by any one, he be discharged.

But if the debt be to one of the assembly, the assembly only is obliged to the payment, out of their common stock (if they have any:) for having liberty of vote, if he vote the money, shall be borrowed, he votes it shall be paid; if he vote it shall not be borrowed, or be absent, yet because in lending, he voteth the borrowing, he contradicteth his former vote, and is obliged by the latter, and becomes both borrower and lender, and consequently cannot demand pay-

ment from any particular man, but from the common treasure only; which failing he hath no remedy, nor complaint, but against himself, that being privy to the acts of the assembly, and to their means to pay, and not being enforced, did nevertheless through his own folly lend his money.

It is manifest by this, that in bodies politic subordinate, and subject to a sovereign power, it is sometimes not only lawful, but expedient, for a particular man to make open protestation against the decrees of the representative assembly, and cause their dissent to be registered, or to take witness of it; because otherwise they may be obliged to pay debts contracted, and be responsible for crimes committed by other men. But in a sovereign assembly, that liberty is taken away, both because he that protesteth there, denies their sovereignty; and also because whatsoever is commanded by the sovereign power, is as to the subject (though not so always in the sight of God) justified by the command; for of such command every subject is the author.

The variety of bodies politic, is almost infinite: for they are not only distinguished by the several affairs, for which they are constituted, wherein there is an unspeakable diversity; but also by the times, places, and numbers, subject to many limitations. And as to their affairs, some are ordained for government; as first, the government of a province may be committed to an assembly of men, wherein all resolutions shall depend on the votes of the major part; and then this assembly is a body politic, and their power limited by commission. This word province signifies a charge, or care of business, which he whose business it is, committeth to another man, to be administered for, and under him; and therefore when in one commonwealth there be divers countries, that have their laws distinct one from another, or are far distant in place, the administration of the government being committed to divers persons, those countries where the sovereign is not resident, but governs by commission, are called provinces. But of the government of a province, by an assembly residing in the province itself, there be few examples. The Romans who had the sovereignty of many provinces, yet governed them always by presidents, and praetors; and not by assemblies, as they governed the city of *Rome*, and territories adjacent. In like manner, when there were colonies sent from *England*, to plant *Virginia*, and *Sommer-islands*; though the government of them here, were committed to assemblies in *London*, yet did those assemblies never commit the government under them to any assembly there; but did to each plantation send one governor. For though every man, where he can be present by nature, desires to participate of government; yet where they cannot be present, they are by nature also inclined, to commit the government of their common interest rather to a monarchical, than a popular form of government: which is also evident in those men that have great private estates; who when they are unwilling to take the pains of administering the business that belongs to them, choose rather to trust one servant, than an assembly either of their friends or servants. But howsoever it be in fact, yet we may suppose the government of a province, or colony committed to an assembly: and when it is, that which in this place I have to say, is this; that whatsoever debt is by that assembly contracted; or whatsoever unlawful act is decreed, is the act only of those that assented, and not of any that dissented, or were absent, for the reasons before alleged. Also that an assembly residing out of the bounds of that colony whereof they have the government, cannot execute any power over the persons, or goods of any of the colony, to seize on them for debt, or other duty, in any place without the colony itself, as having no jurisdiction, nor authority elsewhere, but are left to the remedy, which the law of the place alloweth them. And though the assembly have right, to impose a mulct upon any of their members, that shall break the laws they make; yet out of the colony itself, they have no right to execute the same. And that which is said here, of the rights of an assembly, for the government of a province, or a colony, is appliable also to an assembly for the government of a town, an university, or a college, or a church, or for any other government over the persons of men.

And generally, in all bodies politic, if any particular member conceive himself injured by the body itself, the cognizance of his cause belongeth to the sovereign, and those the sovereign hath ordained for judges in such causes, or shall ordain for that particular cause; and not to the body itself. For the whole body is in this case his fellow subject, which in a sovereign assembly, is otherwise: for there, if the sovereign be not judge, though in his own cause, there can be no judge at all.

In a body politic, for the well ordering of foreign traffic, the most commodious representative is an assembly of all the members; that is to say, such a one, as every one that adventureth his money, may be present at all the deliberations, and resolutions of the body, if they will themselves. For proof whereof, we are to consider the end, for which men that are merchants, and may buy and sell, export, and import their merchandise according to their own discretions, do nevertheless bind themselves up in one corporation. It is true, there be few merchants, that with the merchandise they buy at home, can freight a ship, to export it; or with that they buy abroad, to bring it home; and have therefore need to join together in one society; where every man may either participate of the gain, according to the proportion of his adventure; or take his own, and sell what he transports, or imports, at such prices as he thinks fit. But this is no body politic, there being no common representative to oblige them to any other law, than that which is common to all other subjects. The end of their incorporating, is to make their gain the greater; which is done two ways; by sole buying, and sole selling, both at home, and abroad. So that to grant to a company of merchants to be a corporation, or body politic, is to grant them a double monopoly, whereof one is to be sole buyers; another to be sole sellers. For when there is a company incorporate for any particular foreign country, they only export the commodities vendible in that country; which is sole buying at home, and sole selling abroad. For at home there is but one buyer, and abroad but one that selleth: both which is gainful to the merchant, because thereby they buy at home at lower, and sell abroad at higher rates: and abroad there is but one buyer of foreign merchandise, and but one that sells them at home; both which again are gainful to the adventurers.

Of this double monopoly one part is disadvantageous to the people at home, the other to foreigners. For at home by their sole exportation they set what price they please on the husbandry, and handy-works of the people; and by the sole importation, what price they please on all foreign commodities the people have need of; both which are ill for the people. On the contrary, by the sole selling of the native commodities abroad, and sole buying the foreign commodities upon the place, they raise the price of those, and abate the price of these, to the disadvantage of the foreigner: for where but one selleth, the merchandise is the dearer; and where but one buyeth the cheaper. Such corporations therefore are no other than monopolies; though they would be very profitable for a commonwealth, if being bound up into one body in foreign markets they were at liberty at home, every man to buy, and sell at what price he could.

The end then of these bodies of merchants, being not a common benefit to the whole body, (which have in this case no common stock, but what is deducted out of the particular adventures, for building, buying, victualling and manning of ships,) but the particular gain of every adventurer, it is reason that every one be acquainted with the employment of his own; that is, that every one be of the assembly, that shall have the power to order the same; and be acquainted with their accounts. And therefore the representative of such a body must be an assembly, where every member of the body may be present at the consultations, if he will.

If a body politic of merchants, contract a debt to a stranger by the act of their representative assembly, every member is liable by himself for the whole. For a stranger can take no notice of their private laws, but considereth them as so many particular men, obliged every one to the whole payment, till payment made by one dischargeth all the rest: but if the debt be to one of the company, the creditor is debtor for the whole to himself, and cannot therefore demand his debt, but only from the common stock, if there be any.

If the commonwealth impose a tax upon the body, it is understood to be laid upon every member proportionably to his particular adventure in the company. For there is in this case no other common stock, but what is made of their particular adventures.

If a mulct be laid upon the body for some unlawful act, they only are liable by whose votes the act was decreed, or by whose assistance it was executed; for in none of the rest is there any other crime but being of the body; which if a crime, (because the body was ordained by the authority of the commonwealth,) is not his.

If one of the members be indebted to the body, he may be sued by the body; but his goods cannot be taken, nor his person imprisoned by the authority of the body; but only by authority of the commonwealth: for if they can do it by their own authority, they can by their own authority give judgment that the debt is due; which is as much as to be judge in their own cause.

These bodies made for the government of men, or of traffic, be either perpetual, or for a time prescribed by writing. But there be bodies also whose times are limited, and that only by the nature of their business. For example, if a sovereign monarch, or a sovereign assembly, shall think fit to give command to the towns, and other several parts of their territory, to send to him their deputies, to inform him of the condition, and necessities of the subjects, or to advise with him for the making of good laws, or for any other cause, as with one person representing the whole country, such deputies, having a place and time of meeting assigned them, are there, and at that time, a body politic, representing every subject of that dominion; but it is only for such matters as shall be propounded unto them by that man, or assembly, that by the sovereign authority sent for them; and when it shall be declared that nothing more shall be propounded, nor debated by them, the body is dissolved. For if they were the absolute representative of the people, then were it the sovereign assembly; and so there would be two sovereign assemblies, or two sovereigns, over the same people; which cannot consist with their peace. And therefore where there is once a sovereignty, there can be no absolute representation of the people, but by it. And for the limits of how far such a body shall represent the whole people, they are set forth in the writing by which they were sent for. For the people cannot choose their deputies to other intent, than is in the writing directed to them from their sovereign expressed.

Private bodies regular, and lawful, are those that are constituted without letters, or other written authority, saving the laws common to all other subjects. And because they be united in one person representative, they are held for regular; such as are all families, in which the father, or master ordereth the whole family. For he obligeth his children, and servants, as far as the law permitteth, though not further, because none of them are bound to obedience in those actions, which the law hath forbidden to be done. In all other actions, during the time they are under domestic government, they are subject to their fathers, and masters, as to their immediate sovereigns. For the father, and master, being before the institution of commonwealth, absolute sovereigns in their own families, they lose afterward no more of their authority, than the law of the commonwealth taketh from them.

Private bodies regular, but unlawful, are those that unite themselves into one person representative, without any public authority at all; such as are the corporations of beggars, thieves and gipsies, the better to order their trade of begging, and stealing; and the corporations of men, that by authority from any foreign person, unite themselves in another's dominion, for the easier propagation of doctrines, and for making a party, against the power of the commonwealth.

Irregular systems, in their nature, but leagues, or sometimes mere concourse of people, without union to any particular design, not by obligation of one to another, but proceeding only from a similitude of wills and inclinations, become lawful, or unlawful, according to the lawfulness, or unlawfulness of every particular man's design therein: and his design is to be understood by the occasion.

The leagues of subjects, (because leagues are commonly made for mutual defence,) are in a commonwealth (which is no more than a league of all the subjects together) for the most part unnecessary, and savour of unlawful design; and are for that cause unlawful, and go commonly by the name of factions, or conspiracies. For a league being a connexion of men by covenants, if there be no power given to any one man, or assembly (as in the condition of mere nature) to compel them to performance, is so long only valid, as there ariseth no just cause of distrust: and therefore leagues between commonwealths, over whom there is no human power established, to keep them all in awe, are not only lawful, but also profitable for the time they last. But leagues of the subjects of one and the same commonwealth, where every one may obtain his right by means of the sovereign power, are unnecessary to the maintaining of peace and justice, and (in case the design of them be evil, or unknown to the commonwealth) unlawful. For all

uniting of strength by private men, is, if for evil intent, unjust; if for intent unknown, dangerous to the public, and unjustly concealed.

If the sovereign power be in a great assembly, and a number of men, part of the assembly, without authority, consult apart, to contrive the guidance of the rest; this is a faction, or conspiracy unlawful, as being a fraudulent seducing of the assembly for their particular interest. But if he, whose private interest is to be debated and judged in the assembly, make as many friends as he can; in him it is no injustice; because in this case he is no part of the assembly. And though he hire such friends with money, (unless there be an express law against it,) yet it is not injustice. For sometimes, (as men's manners are,) justice cannot be had without money; and every man may think his own cause just, till it be heard, and judged.

In all commonwealths, if a private man entertain more servants, than the government of his estate, and lawful employment he has for them requires, it is faction, and unlawful. For having the protection of the commonwealth, he needeth not the defence of private force. And whereas in nations not thoroughly civilized, several numerous families have lived in continual hostility, and invaded one another with private force; yet it is evident enough, that they have done unjustly; or else that they had no commonwealth.

And as factions for kindred, so also factions for government of religion, as of Papists, Protestants, &c. or of state, as patricians, and plebeians of old time in *Rome*, and of aristocraticals and democraticals of old time in *Greece*, are unjust, as being contrary to the peace and safety of the people, and a taking of the sword out of the hand of the sovereign.

Concourse of people, is an irregular system, the lawfulness, or unlawfulness, whereof dependeth on the occasion, and on the number of them that are assembled. If the occasion be lawful, and manifest, the concourse is lawful; as the usual meeting of men at church, or at a public show, in usual numbers: for if the numbers be extraordinarily great, the occasion is not evident; and consequently he that cannot render a particular and good account of his being amongst them, is to be judged conscious of an unlawful, and tumultuous design. It may be lawful for a thousand men, to join in a petition to be delivered to a judge, or magistrate; yet if a thousand men come to present it, it is a tumultuous assembly; because there needs but one or two for that purpose. But in such cases as these, it is not a set number that makes the assembly unlawful, but such a number, as the present officers are not able to suppress, and bring to justice.

When an unusual number of men, assemble against a man whom they accuse; the assembly is an unlawful tumult; because they may deliver their accusation to the magistrate by a few, or by one man. Such was the case of St. *Paul* at *Ephesus*; where *Demetrius*, and a great number of other men, brought two of *Paul's* companions before the magistrate, saying with one voice, *Great is Diana of the Ephesians*; which was their way of demanding justice against them for teaching the people such doctrine, as was against their religion, and trade. The occasion here, considering the laws of that people, was just; yet was their assembly judged unlawful, and the magistrate reprehended them for it, in these words (*Acts* 19. 40.) *If Demetrius and the other workmen can accuse any man, of any thing, there be pleas, and deputies, let them accuse one another. And if you have any other thing to demand, your case may be judged in an assembly lawfully called. For we are in danger to be accused for this day's sedition; because, there is no cause by which any man can render any reason of this concourse of people.* Where he calleth an assembly, whereof men can give no just account, a sedition, and such as they could not answer for. And this is all I shall say concerning *systems*, and assemblies of people, which may be compared (as I said,) to the similar parts of man's body; such as be lawful, to the muscles; such as are unlawful, to wens, biles, and apostems, engendered by the unnatural conflux of evil humours.

Chapter 23

Of the Public Ministers of Sovereign Power

In the last chapter I have spoken of the similar parts of a commonwealth: in this I shall speak of the parts organical, which are public ministers.

A PUBLIC MINISTER, is he, that by the sovereign, (whether a monarch, or an assembly,) is employed in any affairs, with authority to represent in that employment, the person of the commonwealth. And whereas every man, or assembly that hath sovereignty, representeth two persons, or (as the more common phrase is) has two capacities, one natural, and another politic, (as a monarch, hath the person not only of the commonwealth, but also of a man; and a sovereign assembly hath the person not only of the commonwealth, but also of the assembly); they that be servants to them in their natural capacity, are not public ministers; but those only that serve them in the administration of the public business. And therefore neither ushers, nor sergeants, nor other officers that wait on the assembly, for no other purpose, but for the commodity of the men assembled, in an aristocracy, or democracy; nor stewards, chamberlains, cofferers, or any other officers of the household of a monarch, are public ministers in a monarchy.

Of public ministers, some have charge committed to them of a general administration, either of the whole dominion, or of a part thereof. Of the whole, as to a protector, or regent, may be committed by the predecessor of an infant king, during his minority, the whole administration of his kingdom. In which case, every subject is so far obliged to obedience, as the ordinances he shall make, and the commands he shall give be in the king's name, and not inconsistent with his sovereign power. Of a part, or province; as when either a monarch, or a sovereign assembly, shall give the general charge thereof to a governor, lieutenant, praefect or viceroy: and in this case also, every one of that province, is obliged to all he shall do in the name of the sovereign, and that not incompatible with the sovereign's right. For such protectors, viceroys, and governors, have no other right, but what depends on the sovereign's will; and no commission that can be given them, can be interpreted for a declaration of the will to transfer the sovereignty, without express and perspicuous words to that purpose. And this kind of public ministers resembleth the nerves, and tendons that move the several limbs of a body natural.

Others have special administration; that is to say, charges of some special business, either at home, or abroad: as at home; first, for the economy of a commonwealth, they that have authority concerning the *treasure*, as tributes, impositions, rents, fines, or whatsoever public revenue, to collect, receive, issue, or take the accounts thereof, are public ministers: ministers, because they serve the person representative, and can do nothing against his command, nor without his authority: public, because they serve him in his political capacity.

Secondly, they that have authority concerning the *militia*; to have the custody of arms, forts, ports; to levy, pay, or conduct soldiers; or to provide for any necessary thing for the use of war, either by land or sea, are public ministers. But a soldier without command, though he fight for the commonwealth, does not therefore represent the person of it; because there is none to represent it to. For every one that hath command, represents it to them only whom he commandeth.

They also that have authority to teach, or to enable others to teach the people their duty to the sovereign power, and instruct them in the knowledge of what is just, and unjust, thereby to render them more apt to live in godliness, and in peace amongst themselves, and resist the public enemy, are public ministers: ministers, in that they do it not by their own authority, but by another's; and public, because they do it (or should do it) by no authority, but that of the sovereign. The monarch, or the sovereign assembly only hath immediate authority from God, to teach and instruct the people; and no man but the sovereign, receiveth his power *Dei gratia* simply; that is to say, from the favour of none but God: all other, receive theirs from the favour and providence of God, and their sovereigns; as in a monarchy *Dei gratia et regis*; or *Dei providentia et voluntate regis*.

They also to whom jurisdiction is given, are public ministers. For in their seats of justice they represent the person of the sovereign; and their sentence, is his sentence; for, (as hath been before declared) all judicature is essentially annexed to the sovereignty; and therefore all other judges are but ministers of him, or them that have the sovereign power. And as controversies are of two sorts, namely of *fact* and of *law*; so are judgments, some of fact, some of law: and consequently in the same controversy, there may be two judges, one of fact, another of law.

And in both these controversies, there may arise a controversy between the party judged, and the judge; which because they be both subjects to the sovereign, ought in equity to be judged by men agreed on by consent of both; for no man can be judge in his own cause. But the sovereign is already agreed on for judge by them both, and is therefore either to hear the cause, and determine it himself, or appoint for judge such as they shall both agree on. And this agreement is then understood to be made between them divers ways; as first, if the defendant be allowed to except against such of his judges, whose interest maketh him suspect them, (for as to the complainant he hath already chosen his own judge), those which he excepteth not against, are judges he himself agrees on. Secondly, if he appeal to any other judge, he can appeal no further; for his appeal is his choice. Thirdly, if he appeal to the sovereign himself, and he by himself, or by delegates which the parties shall agree on, give sentence; that sentence is final: for the defendant is judged by his own judges, that is to say, by himself.

These properties of just and rational judicature considered, I cannot forbear to observe the excellent constitution of the courts of justice, established both for Common, and also for Public Pleas in England. By Common Pleas, I mean those, where both the complainant and defendant are subjects: and by public, (which are also called Pleas of the Crown) those, where the complainant is the sovereign. For whereas there were two orders of men, whereof one was Lords, the other Commons; the Lords had this privilege, to have for judges in all capital crimes, none but Lords; and of them, as many as would be present; which being ever acknowledged as a privilege of favour, their judges were none but such as they had themselves desired. And in all controversies, every subject (as also in civil controversies the Lords) had for judges, men of the country where the matter in controversy lay; against which he might make his exceptions, till at last twelve men without exception being agreed on, they were judged by those twelve. So that having his own judges, there could be nothing alleged by the party, why the sentence should not be final. These public persons, with authority from the sovereign power, either to instruct, or judge the people, are such members of the commonwealth, as may fitly be compared to the organs of voice in a body natural.

Public ministers are also all those, that have authority from the sovereign, to procure the execution of judgments given; to publish the sovereign's commands; to suppress tumults; to apprehend, and imprison malefactors; and other acts tending to the conservation of the peace. For every act they do by such authority, is the act of the commonwealth; and their service, answerable to that of the hands, in a body natural.

Public ministers abroad, are those that represent the person of their own sovereign, to foreign states. Such are ambassadors, messengers, agents, and heralds, sent by public authority, and on public business.

But such as are sent by authority only of some private party of a troubled state, though they be received, are neither public, nor private ministers of the commonwealth; because none of their actions have the commonwealth for author. Likewise, an ambassador sent from a prince, to congratulate, condole, or to assist at a solemnity, though the authority be public; yet because the business is private, and belonging to him in his natural capacity; is a private person. Also if a man be sent into another country, secretly to explore their counsels, and strength; though both the authority, and the business be public; yet because there is none to take notice of any person in him, but his own; he is but a private minister; but yet a minister of the commonwealth; and may be compared to an eye in the body natural. And those that are appointed to receive the petitions or other informations of the people, and are as it were the public ear, are public ministers, and represent their sovereign in that office.

Neither a councillor, nor a council of state, if we consider it with no authority of judicature or command, but only of giving advice to the sovereign when it is required, or of offering it when it is not required, is a public person. For the advice is addressed to the sovereign only, whose person cannot in his own presence, be represented to him, by another. But a body of councillors, are never without some other authority, either of judicature, or of immediate administration: as in a monarchy, they represent the monarch, in delivering his commands to the public ministers: in a democracy, the council, or senate propounds the result of their deliberations to the people, as a council; but when they appoint judges, or hear causes, or give audience to ambassadors, it is in the quality of a minister of the people: and in an aristocracy, the council of state is the sovereign assembly itself; and gives counsel to none but themselves.

Chapter 24

Of the Nutrition, and Procreation of a Commonwealth

The Nutrition of a commonwealth consisteth, in the *plenty*, and *distribution* of *materials* conducing to life: in *concoction*, or *preparation*; and, (when concocted) in the *conveyance* of it, by convenient conduits, to the public use.

As for the plenty of matter, it is a thing limited by nature, to those commodities, which from (the two breasts of our common mother) land, and sea, God usually either freely giveth, or for labour selleth to mankind.

For the matter of this nutriment, consisting in animals, vegetals, and minerals, God hath freely laid them before us, in or near to the face of the earth; so as there needeth no more but the labour, and industry of receiving them. Insomuch as plenty dependeth (next to God's favour) merely on the labour and industry of men.

This matter, commonly called commodities, is partly *native*, and partly *foreign*: *native*, that which is to be had within the territory of the commonwealth: *foreign*, that which is imported from without. And because there is no territory under the dominion of one commonwealth, (except it be of very vast extent,) that produceth all things needful for the maintenance, and motion of the whole body; and few that produce not something more than necessary; the superfluous commodities to be had within, become no more superfluous, but supply these wants at home, by importation of that which may be had abroad, either by exchange, or by just war, or by labour: for a man's labour also, is a commodity exchangeable for benefit, as well as any other thing: and there have been commonwealths that having no more territory, than hath served them for habitation, have nevertheless, not only maintained, but also increased their power, partly by the labour of trading from one place to another, and partly by selling the manufactures, whereof the materials were brought in from other places.

The distribution of the materials of this nourishment, is the constitution of *mine*, and *thine*, and *his*;

that is to say, in one word *propriety*; and belongeth in all kinds of commonwealth to the sovereign power. For where there is no commonwealth, there is (as hath been already shown) a perpetual war of every man against his neighbour; and therefore every thing is his that getteth it, and keepeth it by force; which is neither *propriety*, nor *community*; but *uncertainty*. Which is so evident, that even *Cicero*, (a passionate defender of liberty,) in a public pleading, attributeth all propriety to the law civil. *Let the civil law,* saith he, *be once abandoned, or but negligently guarded, (not to say oppressed,) and there is nothing, that any man can be sure to receive from his ancestor, or leave to his children.* And again; *Take away the civil law, and no man knows what is his own, and what another man's.* Seeing therefore the introduction of *propriety* is an effect of commonwealth; which can do nothing but by the person that represents it, it is the act only of the sovereign; and consisteth in the laws, which none can make that have not the sovereign power. And this they well knew of old, who called that Νόμος, (that is to say, *distribution*,) which we call law; and defined justice, by *distributing* to every man *his own*.

In this distribution, the first law, is for division of the land itself: wherein the sovereign assigneth to every man a portion, according as he, and not according as any subject, or any number of them, shall judge agreeable to equity, and the common good. The children of Israel, were a commonwealth in the wilderness; but wanted the commodities of the earth, till they were masters of the Land of Promise; which afterward was divided amongst them, not by their own discretion, but by the discretion of *Eleazar* the Priest, and *Joshua* their General, who, when there were twelve tribes, making them thirteen by subdivision of the tribe of *Joseph;* made nevertheless but twelve portions of the land; and ordained for the tribe of *Levi* no land; but assigned them the tenth part of the whole fruits; which division was therefore arbitrary. And though a people coming into possession of a land by war, do not always exterminate the ancient inhabitants, (as did the Jews,) but leave to many, or most, or all of them their estates; yet it is manifest they hold them afterwards, as of the victors' distribution; as the people of *England* held all theirs of *William* the *Conqueror*.

From whence we may collect, that the propriety which a subject hath in his lands, consisteth in a right to exclude all other subjects from the use of them; and not to exclude their sovereign, be it an assembly, or a monarch. For seeing the sovereign, that is to say, the commonwealth (whose person he representeth,) is understood to do nothing but in order to the common peace and security, this distribution of lands, is to be understood as done in order to the same: and consequently, whatsoever distribution he shall make in prejudice thereof, is contrary to the will of every subject, that committed his peace, and safety to his discretion, and conscience; and therefore by the will of every one of them, is to be reputed void. It is true, that a sovereign monarch, or the greater part of a sovereign assembly, may ordain the doing of many things in pursuit of their passions, contrary to their own consciences, which is a breach of trust, and of the law of nature; but this is not enough to authorize any subject, either to make war upon, or so much as to accuse of injustice, or any way to speak evil of their sovereign; because they have authorized all his actions, and in bestowing the sovereign power, made them their own. But in what cases the commands of sovereigns are contrary to equity, and the law of nature, is to be considered hereafter in another place.

In the distribution of land, the commonwealth itself, may be conceived to have a portion, and possess, and improve the same by their representative; and that such portion may be made sufficient, to sustain the whole expense to the common peace, and defence necessarily required: Which were very true, if there could be any representative conceived free from human passions, and infirmities. But the nature of men being as it is, the setting forth of public land, or of any certain revenue for the commonwealth, is in vain; and tendeth to the dissolution of government, and to the condition of mere nature, and war, as soon as ever the sovereign power falleth into the hands of a monarch, or of an assembly, that are either too negligent of money, or too hazardous in engaging the public stock, into a long or costly war. Commonwealths can endure no diet: for seeing their expense is not limited by their own appetite, but by external accidents, and the appetites of their neighbours, the public riches cannot be limited by other limits, than those which the emergent occasions shall require. And whereas in *England*, there were by the Conqueror, divers lands reserved to his own use, (besides forests, and chases, either for his recreation, or for preservation of woods,) and divers services reserved on the land he gave his subjects; yet it seems they were not reserved for his maintenance in his public, but in his natural capacity. For he, and his successors did for all that, lay arbitrary taxes on all subjects' land, when they judged it necessary. Or if those public lands, and services, were ordained as a sufficient maintenance of the commonwealth, it was contrary to the scope of the institution; being (as it appeared by those ensuing taxes) insufficient, and (as it appears by the late small revenue of the crown) subject to alienation and diminution. It is therefore in vain, to assign a portion to the commonwealth; which may sell, or give it away; and does sell and give it away when it is done by their representative.

As the distribution of lands at home; so also to assign in what places, and for what commodities, the subject shall traffic abroad, belongeth to the sovereign. For if it did belong to private persons to use their own discretion therein, some of them would be drawn for gain, both to furnish the enemy with means to hurt the commonwealth, and hurt it themselves, by importing such things, as pleasing men's appetites, be nevertheless noxious, or at least unprofitable to them. And therefore it belongeth to the commonwealth, (that is, to the sovereign only,) to approve, or disapprove both of the places, and matter of foreign traffic.

Further, seeing it is not enough to the sustentation of a commonwealth, that every man have a propriety in a portion of land, or in some few commodities, or a natural property in some useful art, and there is no art in the world, but is necessary either for the being, or well being almost of every particular man; it is necessary, that men distribute that which they can spare, and transfer their propriety therein, mutually one to another, by exchange, and mutual contract. And therefore it belongeth to the commonwealth, (that is to say, to the sovereign,) to appoint in what manner, all kinds of contract between subjects, (as buying, selling, exchanging, borrowing, lending, letting, and taking to hire,) are to be made; and by what words and signs they shall be understood for valid.

And for the matter, and distribution of the nourishment, to the several members of the commonwealth, thus much (considering the model of the whole work) is sufficient.

By concoction, I understand the reducing of all commodities, which are not presently consumed, but reserved for nourishment in time to come, to some thing of equal value, and withal so portable, as not to hinder the motion of men from place to place; to the end a man may have in what place soever, such nourishment as the place affordeth. And this is nothing else but gold, and silver, and money. For gold and silver, being (as it happens) almost in all countries of the world highly valued, is a commodious measure of the value of all things else between nations; and money (of what matter soever coined by the sovereign of a commonwealth,) is a sufficient measure of the value of all things else, between the subjects of that commonwealth. By the means of which measures, all commodities, moveable, and immoveable, are made to accompany a man, to all places of his resort, within and without the place of his ordinary residence; and the same passeth from man to man, within the commonwealth; and goes round about, nourishing (as it passeth) every part thereof; in so much as this concoction, is as it were the sanguification of the commonwealth: for natural blood is in like manner made of the fruits of the earth; and circulating, nourisheth by the way, every member of the body of man.

And because silver and gold, have their value from the matter itself; they have first this privilege, that the value of them cannot be altered by the power of one, nor of a few commonwealths; as being a common measure of the commodities of all places. But base money, may easily be enhanced, or abased. Secondly, they have the privilege to make commonwealths move, and stretch out their arms, when need is, into foreign countries; and supply, not only private subjects that travel, but also whole armies with provision. But that coin, which is not considerable for the matter, but for the stamp of the place, being unable to endure change of air, hath its effect at home only; where also it is subject to the change of laws, and thereby to have the value diminished, to the prejudice many times of those that have it.

The conduits, and ways by which it is conveyed to the public use, are of two sorts; one, that conveyeth it to the public coffers; the other, that issueth the same out again for public payments. Of the first sort, are collectors, receivers, and treasurers; of the second are the treasurers again, and the officers appointed for payment of several public or private ministers. And in this also, the artificial man maintains his resemblance with the natural; whose veins receiving the blood from the several parts of the body, carry it to the heart; where being made vital, the heart by the arteries sends it out again, to enliven, and enable for motion all the members of the same.

The procreation, or children of a commonwealth, are those we call *plantations*, or *colonies*; which are numbers of men sent out from the commonwealth, under a conductor, or governor, to inhabit a foreign country, either formerly void of inhabitants, or made void then, by war. And when a colony is settled, they are either a commonwealth of themselves, discharged of their subjection to their sovereign that sent them, (as hath been done by many commonwealths of ancient time,) in which case the commonwealth from which they went, was called their metropolis, or mother, and requires no more of them, than fathers require of the children, whom they emancipate and make free from their domestic government, which is honour, and friendship; or else they remain united to their metropolis, as were the colonies of the people of *Rome*; and then they are no commonwealths themselves, but provinces, and parts of the commonwealth that sent them. So that the right of colonies (saving honour, and league with their metropolis,) dependeth wholly on their licence, or letters, by which their sovereign authorized them to plant.

Chapter 25

Of Counsel

How fallacious it is to judge of the nature of things, by the ordinary and inconstant use of words, appeareth in nothing more, than in the confusion of counsels, and commands, arising from the imperative manner of speaking in them both, and in many other occasions besides. For the words *do this*, are the words not only of him that commandeth; but also of him that giveth counsel; and of him that exhorteth; and yet there are but few, that see not, that these are very different things; or that cannot distinguish between them, when they perceive who it is that speaketh, and to whom the speech is directed, and upon what occasion. But finding those phrases in men's writings, and being not able, or not willing to enter into a consideration of the circumstances, they mistake sometimes the precepts of counsellors, for the precepts of them that command; and sometimes the contrary; according as it best agreeth with the conclusions they would infer, or the actions they approve. To avoid which mistakes, and render to those terms of commanding, counselling, and exhorting, their proper and distinct significations, I define them thus.

COMMAND is where a man saith, *do this*, or *do not this*, without expecting other reason than the will of him that says it. From this it followeth manifestly, that he that commandeth, pretendeth thereby his own benefit: for the reason of his command is his own will only, and the proper object of every man's will, is some good to himself.

COUNSEL, is where a man saith, *do*, or *do not this*, and deduceth his reasons from the benefit that arriveth by it to him to whom he saith it. And from this it is evident, that he that giveth counsel, pretendeth only (whatsoever he intendeth) the good of him, to whom he giveth it.

Therefore between counsel and command, one great difference is, that command is directed to a man's own benefit; and counsel to the benefit of another man. And from this ariseth another difference, that a man may be obliged to do what he is commanded; as when he hath covenanted to obey: but he cannot be obliged to do as he is counselled, because the hurt of not following it, is his own; or if he should covenant to follow it, then is the counsel turned into the nature of a command. A third difference between them is, that no man can pretend a right to be of another man's counsel; because he is not to pretend benefit by it to himself: but to demand right to counsel another, argues a will to know his designs, or to gain some other good to himself; which (as I said before) is of every man's will the proper object.

This also is incident to the nature of counsel; that whatsoever it be, he that asketh it, cannot in equity accuse, or punish it: for to ask counsel of another, is *what about shooting the messenger?*

to permit him to give such counsel as he shall think best; and consequently, he that giveth counsel to his sovereign, (whether a monarch, or an assembly) when he asketh it, cannot in equity be punished for it, whether the same be conformable to the opinion of the most, or not, so it be to the proposition in debate. For if the sense of the assembly can be taken notice of, before the debate be ended, they should neither ask, nor take any further counsel; for the sense of the assembly, is the resolution of the debate, and end of all deliberation. And generally he that demandeth counsel, is author of it; and therefore cannot punish it; and what the sovereign cannot, no man else can. But if one subject giveth counsel to another, to do any thing contrary to the laws, whether that counsel proceed from evil intention, or from ignorance only, it is punishable by the commonwealth; because ignorance of the law, is no good excuse, where every man is bound to take notice of the laws to which he is subject.

EXHORTATION, and DEHORTATION, is counsel, accompanied with signs in him that giveth it, of vehement desire to have it followed; or to say it more briefly, *counsel vehemently pressed*. For he that exhorteth, doth not deduce the consequences of what he adviseth to be done, and tie himself therein to the rigour of true reasoning; but encourages him he counselleth, to action: as he that dehorteth, deterreth him from it. And therefore they have in their speeches, a regard to the common passions, and opinions of men, in deducing their reasons; and make use of similitudes, metaphors, examples, and other tools of oratory, to persuade their hearers of the utility, honour, or justice of following their advice.

From whence may be inferred, first, that exhortation and dehortation, is directed to the good of him that giveth the counsel, not of him that asketh it, which is contrary to the duty of a counsellor; who (by the definition of counsel) ought to regard, not his own benefit, but his whom he adviseth. And that he directeth his counsel to his own benefit, is manifest enough, by the long and vehement urging, or by the artificial giving thereof; which being not required of him, and consequently proceeding from his own occasions, is directed principally to his own benefit, and but accidentally to the good of him that is counselled, or not at all.

Secondly, that the use of exhortation and dehortation lieth only where a man is to speak to a multitude; because when the speech is addressed to one, he may interrupt him, and examine his reasons more rigorously, than can be done in a multitude; which are too many to enter into dispute, and dialogue with him that speaketh indifferently to them all at once.

Thirdly, that they that exhort and dehort, where they are required to give counsel, are corrupt counsellors, and as it were bribed by their own interest. For though the counsel they give be never so good; yet he that gives it, is no more a good counsellor, than he that giveth a just sentence for a reward, is a just judge. But where a man may lawfully command, as a father in his family, or a leader in an army, his exhortations and dehortations, are not only lawful, but also necessary, and laudable: But then they are no more counsels, but commands; which when they are for execution of sour labour; sometimes necessity, and always humanity requireth to be sweetened in the delivery, by encouragement, and in the tune and phrase of counsel, rather than in harsher language of command.

Examples of the difference between command and counsel, we may take from the forms of speech that express them in Holy Scripture. *Have no other Gods but me; make to thyself no graven image; take not God's name in vain; sanctify the sabbath; honour thy parents; kill not; steal not, &c.* are commands; because the reason for which we are to obey them, is drawn from the will of God our king, whom we are obliged to obey. But these words, *Sell all thou hast; give it to the poor; and follow me*, are counsel; because the reason for which we are to do so, is drawn from our own benefit; which is this, that we shall have *treasure in Heaven*. These words, *Go into the village over against you, and you shall find an ass tied, and her colt; loose her, and bring her to me*, are a command: for the reason of their fact is drawn from the will of their Master: but these words, *Repent and be baptized in the name of Jesus*, are counsel; because the reason why we should so do, tendeth not to any benefit of God Almighty, who shall still be king in what manner soever we rebel; but of ourselves, who have no other means of avoiding the punishment hanging over us for our sins.

As the difference of counsel from command, hath been now deduced from the nature of counsel, consisting in a deducing of the benefit, or hurt that may arise to him that is to be counselled, by the necessary or probable consequences of the action he propoundeth; so may also the differences between *apt*, and *inept* counsellors be derived from the same. For experience, being but memory of the consequences of like actions formerly observed, and counsel but the speech whereby that experience is made known to another; the virtues, and defects of counsel, are the same with the virtues, and defects intellectual: and to the person of a commonwealth, his counsellors serve him in the place of memory, and mental discourse. But with this resemblance of the commonwealth, to a natural man, there is one dissimilitude joined, of great importance; which is, that a natural man receiveth his experience, from the natural objects of sense, which work upon him without passion, or interest of their own; whereas they that give counsel to the representative person of a commonwealth, may have, and have often their particular ends, and passions, that render their counsels always suspected, and many times unfaithful. And therefore we may set down for the first condition of a good counsellor, *that his ends, and interest, be not inconsistent with the ends and interest of him he counselleth.*

Secondly, because the office of a counsellor, when an action comes into deliberation, is to make manifest the consequences of it, in such manner, as he that is counselled may be truly and evidently informed; he ought to propound his advice, in such form of speech, as may make the truth most evidently appear; that is to say, with as firm ratiocination, as significant and proper language, and as briefly, as the evidence will permit. And therefore *rash, and unevident inferences*; (such as are fetched only from examples, or authority of books, and are not arguments of what is good, or evil, but witnesses of fact, or of opinion,) *obscure, confused, and ambiguous expressions, also all metaphorical speeches, tending to the stirring up of passion,* (because such reasoning, and such expressions, are useful only to deceive, or to lead him we counsel towards other ends than his own) *are repugnant to the office of a counsellor.*

Thirdly, because the ability of counselling proceedeth from experience, and long study; and no man

is presumed to have experience in all those things that to the administration of a great commonwealth are necessary to be known, *no man is presumed to be a good counsellor, but in such business, as he hath not only been much versed in, but hath also much meditated on, and considered.* For seeing the business of a commonwealth is this, to preserve the people in peace at home, and defend them against foreign invasion, we shall find, it requires great knowledge of the disposition of mankind, of the rights of government, and of the nature of equity, law, justice, and honour, not to be attained without study; and of the strength, commodities, places, both of their own country, and their neighbours; as also of the inclinations, and designs of all nations that may any way annoy them. And this is not attained to, without much experience. Of which things, not only the whole sum, but every one of the particulars requires the age, and observation of a man in years, and of more than ordinary study. The wit required for counsel, as I have said before (chap. 8.) is judgment. And the differences of men in that point come from different education, of some to one kind of study, or business, and of others to another. When for the doing of any thing, there be infallible rules, (as in engines and edifices, the rules of geometry,) all the experience of the world cannot equal his counsel, that has learnt, or found out the rule. And when there is no such rule, he that hath most experience in that particular kind of business, has therein the best judgment, and is the best counsellor.

Fourthly, to be able to give counsel to a commonwealth, in a business that hath reference to another commonwealth, *it is necessary to be acquainted with the intelligences, and letters* that come from thence, *and with all the records of treaties, and other transactions of state* between them; which none can do, but such as the representative shall think fit. By which we may see, that they who are not called to counsel, can have no good counsel in such cases to obtrude.

Fifthly, supposing the number of counsellors equal, a man is better counselled by hearing them apart, than in an assembly; and that for many causes. First, in hearing them apart, you have the advice of every man; but in an assembly many of them deliver their advice with *aye,* or *no,* or with their hands, or feet, not moved by their own sense, but by the eloquence of another, or for fear of displeasing some that have spoken, or the whole assembly, by contradiction; or for fear of appearing duller in apprehension, than those that have applauded the contrary opinion. Secondly, in an assembly of many, there cannot choose but be some whose interests are contrary to that of the public; and these their interests make passionate, and passion eloquent, and eloquence draws others into the same advice. For the passions of men, which asunder are moderate, as the heat of one brand; in assembly are like many brands, that inflame one another, (especially when they blow one another with orations) to the setting of the commonwealth on fire, under pretence of counselling it. Thirdly, in hearing every man apart, one may examine (when there is need) the truth, or probability of his reasons, and of the grounds of the advice he gives, by frequent interruptions, and objections; which cannot be done in an assembly, where (in every difficult question) a man is rather astonied, and dazzled with the variety of discourse upon it, than informed of the course he ought to take. Besides, there cannot be an assembly of many, called together for advice, wherein there be not some, that have the ambition to be thought eloquent, and also learned in the politics; and give not their advice with care of the business propounded, but of the applause of their motley orations, made of the divers coloured threds, or shreads of authors; which is an impertinence at least, that takes away the time of serious consultation, and in the secret way of counselling apart, is easily avoided. Fourthly, in deliberations that ought to be kept secret, (whereof there be many occasions in public business,) the counsels of many, and especially in assemblies, are dangerous; and therefore great assemblies are necessitated to commit such affairs to lesser numbers, and of such persons as are most versed, and in whose fidelity they have most confidence.

To conclude, who is there that so far approves the taking of counsel from a great assembly of counsellors, that wisheth for, or would accept of their pains, when there is a question of marrying his children, disposing of his lands, governing his household, or managing his private estate, especially if there be amongst them such as wish not his prosperity? A man that doth his business by the help of many and prudent counsellors, with every one consulting apart in his proper element,

does it best, as he that useth able seconds at tennis play, placed in their proper stations. He does next best, that useth his own judgment only; as he that has no second at all. But he that is carried up and down to his business in a framed counsel, which cannot move but by the plurality of consenting opinions, the execution whereof is commonly (out of envy, or interest) retarded by the part dissenting, does it worst of all, and like one that is carried to the ball, though by good players, yet in a wheel-barrow, or other frame, heavy of itself, and retarded also by the inconcurrent judgments, and endeavours of them that drive it; and so much the more, as they be more that set their hands to it; and most of all, when there is one, or more amongst them, that desire to have him lose. And though it be true, that many eyes see more than one; yet it is not to be understood of many counsellors; but then only, when the final resolution is in one man. Otherwise, because many eyes see the same thing in divers lines, and are apt to look asquint towards their private benefit, they that desire not to miss their mark, though they look about with two eyes, yet they never aim but with one; and therefore no great popular commonwealth was ever kept up; but either by a foreign enemy that united them; or by the reputation of some one eminent man amongst them; or by the secret counsel of a few; or by the mutual fear of equal factions; and not by the open consultations of the assembly. And as for very little commonwealths, be they popular, or monarchical, there is no human wisdom can uphold them, longer than the jealousy lasteth of their potent neighbours.

Chapter 26

Of Civil Laws

By CIVIL LAWS, I understand the laws, that men are therefore bound to observe, because they are members, not of this, or that commonwealth in particular, but of a commonwealth. For the knowledge of particular laws belongeth to them, that profess the study of the laws of their several countries; but the knowledge of civil law in general, to any man. The ancient law of *Rome* was called their *civil law*, from the word *civitas*, which signifies a commonwealth:

and those countries, which having been under the Roman empire, and governed by that law, retain still such part thereof as they think fit, call that part the civil law, to distinguish it from the rest of their own civil laws. But that is not it I intend to speak of here; my design being not to show what is law here, and there; but what is law; as *Plato, Aristotle, Cicero,* and divers others have done, without taking upon them the profession of the study of the law.

And first it is manifest, that law in general, is not counsel, but command; nor a command of any man to any man; but only of him, whose command is addressed to one formerly obliged to obey him. And as for civil law, it addeth only the name of the person commanding, which is *persona civitatis,* the person of the commonwealth.

Which considered, I define civil law in this manner. CIVIL LAW, *is to every subject, those rules, which the commonwealth hath commanded him, by word, writing, or other sufficient sign of the will, to make use of, for the distinction of right, and wrong; that is to say, of what is contrary, and what is not contrary to the rule.*

In which definition, there is nothing that is not at first sight evident. For every man seeth, that some laws are addressed to all the subjects in general; some to particular provinces; some to particular vocations; and some to particular men; and are therefore laws, to every of those to whom the command is directed; and to none else. As also, that laws are the rules of just, and unjust; nothing being reputed unjust, that is not contrary to some law. Likewise, that none can make laws but the commonwealth; because our subjection is to the commonwealth only: and that commands, are to be signified by sufficient signs; because a man knows not otherwise how to obey them. And therefore, whatsoever can from this definition by necessary consequence be deduced, ought to be acknowledged for truth. Now I deduce from it this that followeth.

1. The legislator in all commonwealths, is only the sovereign, be he one man, as in a monarchy, or one assembly of men, as in a democracy, or aristocracy. For the legislator is he that maketh the law. And the commonwealth only, prescribes, and commandeth the observation of those rules, which we call law: therefore the commonwealth is the legislator. But the commonwealth is no person, nor has capacity to do any thing, but by the representative, (that is, the sovereign;) and therefore the sovereign is the sole legislator. For the same reason, none can abrogate a law made, but the sovereign; because a law is not abrogated, but by another law, that forbiddeth it to be put in execution.

2. The sovereign of a commonwealth, be it an assembly, or one man, is not subject to the civil laws. For having power to make, and repeal laws, he may when he pleaseth, free himself from that subjection, by repealing those laws that trouble him, and making of new; and consequently he was free before. For he is free, that can be free when he will: nor is it possible for any person to be bound to himself; because he that can bind, can release; and therefore he that is bound to himself only, is not bound.

3. When long use obtaineth the authority of a law, it is not the length of time that maketh the authority, but the will of the sovereign signified by his silence, (for silence is sometimes an argument of consent;) and it is no longer law, than the sovereign shall be silent therein. And therefore if the sovereign shall have a question of right grounded, not upon his present will, but upon the laws formerly made; the length of time shall bring no prejudice to his right; but the question shall be judged by equity. For many unjust actions, and unjust sentences, go uncontrolled a longer time, than any man can remember. And our lawyers account no customs law, but such as are reasonable, and that evil customs are to be abolished: But the judgment of what is reasonable, and of what is to be abolished, belongeth to him that maketh the law, which is the sovereign assembly, or monarch.

4. The law of nature, and the civil law, contain each other, and are of equal extent. For the laws of nature, which consist in equity, justice, gratitude, and other moral virtues on these depending, in the condition of mere nature (as I have said before in the end of the 15th chapter,) are not properly laws, but qualities that dispose men to peace and to obedience. When a commonwealth is once settled, then are they actually laws, and not before; as being then the commands of the commonwealth; and therefore also civil laws: for it is the sovereign power that obliges men to obey them. For in the differences of private men, to declare, what is equity, what is justice, and what is moral virtue, and to make them binding, there

is need of the ordinances of sovereign power, and punishments to be ordained for such as shall break them; which ordinances are therefore part of the civil law. The law of nature therefore is a part of the civil law in all commonwealths of the world. Reciprocally also, the civil law is a part of the dictates of nature. For justice, that is to say, performance of covenant, and giving to every man his own, is a dictate of the law of nature. But every subject in a commonwealth, hath covenanted to obey the civil law, (either one with another, as when they assemble to make a common representative, or with the representative it self one by one, when subdued by the sword they promise obedience, that they may receive life;) and therefore obedience to the civil law is part also of the law of nature. Civil, and natural law are not different kinds, but different parts of law; whereof one part being written, is called civil, the other unwritten, natural. But the right of nature, that is, the natural liberty of man, may by the civil law be abridged, and restrained: nay, the end of making laws, is no other, but such restraint; without the which there cannot possibly be any peace. And law was brought into the world for nothing else, but to limit the natural liberty of particular men, in such manner, as they might not hurt, but assist one another, and join together against a common enemy.

5. If the sovereign of one commonwealth, subdue a people that have lived under other written laws, and afterwards govern them by the same laws, by which they were governed before; yet those laws are the civil laws of the victor, and not of the vanquished commonwealth. For the legislator is he, not by whose authority the laws were first made, but by whose authority they now continue to be laws. And therefore where there be divers provinces, within the dominion of a commonwealth, and in those provinces diversity of laws, which commonly are called the customs of each several province, we are not to understand that such customs have their force, only from length of time; but that they were anciently laws written, or otherwise made known, for the constitutions, and statutes of their sovereigns; and are now laws, not by virtue of the prescription of time, but by the constitutions of their present sovereigns. But if an unwritten law, in all the provinces of a dominion, shall be generally observed, and no iniquity appear in the use

thereof; that law can be no other but a law of nature, equally obliging all mankind.

6. Seeing then all laws, written and unwritten, have their authority, and force, from the will of the commonwealth; that is to say, from the will of the representative; which in a monarchy is the monarch, and in other commonwealths the sovereign assembly; a man may wonder from whence proceed such opinions, as are found in the books of lawyers of eminence in several commonwealths, directly, or by consequence making the legislative power depend on private men, or subordinate judges. As for example, *that the common law, hath no controller but the parliament;* which is true only where a parliament has the sovereign power, and cannot be assembled, nor dissolved, but by their own discretion. For if there be a right in any else to dissolve them, there is a right also to control them, and consequently to control their controllings. And if there be no such right, then the controller of laws is not *parliamentum*, but *rex in parliamento*. And where a parliament is sovereign, if it should assemble never so many, or so wise men, from the countries subject to them, for whatsoever cause; yet there is no man will believe, that such an assembly hath thereby acquired to themselves a legislative power. *Item*, that the two arms of a commonwealth, are *force, and justice; the first whereof is in the king; the other deposited in the hands of the parliament.* As if a commonwealth could consist, where the force were in any hand, which justice had not the authority to command and govern.

7. That law can never be against reason, our lawyers are agreed; and that not the letter, (that is, every construction of it,) but that which is according to the intention of the legislator, is the law. And it is true: but the doubt is of whose reason it is, that shall be received for law. It is not meant of any private reason; for then there would be as much contradiction in the laws, as there is in the Schools; nor yet, (as Sir *Edward Coke* makes it,) an *artificial perfection of reason, gotten by long study, observation, and experience,* (as his was.) For it is possible long study may increase, and confirm erroneous sentences: and where men build on false grounds, the more they build, the greater is the ruin: and of those that study, and observe with equal time, and diligence, the reasons and resolutions are, and must remain discordant: and therefore

it is not that *juris prudentia*, or wisdom of subordinate judges; but the reason of this our artificial man the commonwealth, and his command, that maketh law: and the commonwealth being in their representative but one person, there cannot easily arise any contradiction in the laws; and when there doth, the same reason is able, by interpretation, or alteration, to take it away. In all courts of justice, the sovereign (which is the person of the commonwealth,) is he that judgeth: the subordinate judge, ought to have regard to the reason, which moved his sovereign to make such law, that his sentence may be according thereunto; which then is his sovereign's sentence; otherwise it is his own, and an unjust one.

8. From this, that the law is a command, and a command consisteth in declaration, or manifestation of the will of him that commandeth, by voice, writing, or some other sufficient argument of the same, we may understand, that the command of the commonwealth is law only to those, that have means to take notice of it. Over natural fools, children, or madmen there is no law, no more than over brute beasts; nor are they capable of the title of just, or unjust; because they had never power to make any covenant, or to understand the consequences thereof; and consequently never took upon them to authorize the actions of any sovereign, as they must do that make to themselves a commonwealth. And as those from whom nature, or accident hath taken away the notice of all laws in general; so also every man, from whom any accident, not proceeding from his own default, hath taken away the means to take notice of any particular law, is excused, if he observe it not; and to speak properly, that law is no law to him. It is therefore necessary, to consider in this place, what arguments, and signs be sufficient for the knowledge of what is the law; that is to say, what is the will of the sovereign, as well in monarchies, as in other forms of government.

And first, if it be a law that obliges all the subjects without exception, and is not written, nor otherwise published in such places as they may take notice thereof, it is a law of nature. For whatsoever men are to take knowledge of for law, not upon other men's words, but every one from his own reason, must be such as is agreeable to the reason of all men; which no law can be, but the law of nature. The laws of nature therefore need not any publishing, nor proclamation; as being contained in this one sentence, approved by all the world, *Do not that to another, which thou thinkest unreasonable to be done by another to thyself.*

Secondly, if it be a law that obliges only some condition of men, or one particular man, and be not written, nor published by word, then also it is a law of nature; and known by the same arguments, and signs, that distinguish those in such a condition, from other subjects. For whatsoever law is not written, or some way published by him that makes it law, can be known no way, but by the reason of him that is to obey it; and is therefore also a law not only civil, but natural. For example, if the sovereign employ a public minister, without written instructions what to do; he is obliged to take for instructions the dictates of reason; as if he make a judge, the judge is to take notice, that his sentence ought to be according to the reason of his sovereign, which being always understood to be equity, he is bound to it by the law of nature: or if an ambassador, he is (in all things not contained in his written instructions) to take for instruction that which reason dictates to be most conducing to his sovereign's interest; and so of all other ministers of the sovereignty, public and private. All which instructions of natural reason may be comprehended under one name of *fidelity*; which is a branch of natural justice.

The law of nature excepted, it belongeth to the essence of all other laws, to be made known, to every man that shall be obliged to obey them, either by word, or writing, or some other act, known to proceed from the sovereign authority. For the will of another, cannot be understood, but by his own word, or act, or by conjecture taken from his scope and purpose; which in the person of the commonwealth, is to be supposed always consonant to equity and reason. And in ancient time, before letters were in common use, the laws were many times put into verse; that the rude people taking pleasure in singing, or reciting them, might the more easily retain them in memory. And for the same reason *Solomon* adviseth a man, to bind the ten commandments upon his ten fingers. And for the law which *Moses* gave to the people of Israel at the renewing of the covenant, he biddeth them to teach it their children, by discoursing of it both at home, and upon the way; at going to bed, and at rising from bed, and to write it upon the posts, and doors of their houses; and (*Deut.* 31. 12) to assemble the people, man, woman, and child, to hear it read.

Nor is it enough the law be written, and published; but also that there be manifest signs, that it proceedeth from the will of the sovereign. For private men, when they have, or think they have force enough to secure their unjust designs, and convoy them safely to their ambitious ends, may publish for laws what they please, without, or against the legislative authority. There is therefore requisite, not only a declaration of the law, but also sufficient signs of the author, and authority. The author, or legislator is supposed in every commonwealth to be evident, because he is the sovereign, who having been constituted by the consent of every one, is supposed by every one to be sufficiently known. And though the ignorance, and security of men be such, for the most part, as that when the memory of the first constitution of their commonwealth is worn out, they do not consider, by whose power they use to be defended against their enemies, and to have their industry protected, and to be righted when injury is done them; yet because no man that considers, can make question of it, no excuse can be derived from the ignorance of where the sovereignty is placed. And it is a dictate of natural reason, and consequently an evident law of nature, that no man ought to weaken that power, the protection whereof he hath himself demanded, or wittingly received against others. Therefore of who is sovereign, no man, but by his own fault, (whatsoever evil men suggest,) can make any doubt. The difficulty consisteth in the evidence of the authority derived from him; the removing whereof, dependeth on the knowledge of the public registers, public counsels, public ministers, and public seals; by which all laws are sufficiently verified; verified, I say, not authorized: for the verification, is but the testimony and record; not the authority of the law; which consisteth in the command of the sovereign only.

If therefore a man have a question of injury, depending on the law of nature; that is to say, on common equity; the sentence of the judge, that by commission hath authority to take cognizance of such causes, is a sufficient verification of the law of nature in that individual case. For though the advice of one that professeth the study of the law, be useful for the avoiding of contention; yet it is but advice: it is the judge must tell men what is law, upon the hearing of the controversy.

But when the question is of injury, or crime, upon a written law; every man by recourse to the registers, by himself or others, may (if he will) be sufficiently informed, before he do such injury, or commit the crime, whether it be an injury, or not: nay he ought to do so: for when a man doubts whether the act he goeth about, be just, or unjust; and may inform himself, if he will; the doing is unlawful. In like manner, he that supposeth himself injured, in a case determined by the written law, which he may by himself, or others see and consider; if he complain before he consults with the law, he does unjustly, and bewrayeth a disposition rather to vex other men, than to demand his own right.

If the question be of obedience to a public officer; to have seen his commission, with the public seal, and heard it read; or to have had the means to be informed of it, if a man would, is a sufficient verification of his authority. For every man is obliged to do his best endeavour, to inform himself of all written laws, that may concern his own future actions.

The legislator known; and the laws, either by writing, or by the light of nature, sufficiently published; there wanteth yet another very material circumstance to make them obligatory. For it is not the letter, but the intendment, or meaning; that is to say, the authentic interpretation of the law (which is the sense of the legislator,) in which the nature of the law consisteth; and therefore the interpretation of all laws dependeth on the authority sovereign; and the interpreters can be none but those, which the sovereign, (to whom only the subject oweth obedience) shall appoint. For else, by the craft of an interpreter, the law may be made to bear a sense, contrary to that of the sovereign; by which means the interpreter becomes the legislator.

All laws, written, and unwritten, have need of interpretation. The unwritten law of nature, though it be easy to such, as without partiality, and passion, make use of their natural reason, and therefore leaves the violators thereof without excuse; yet considering there be very few, perhaps none, that in some cases are not blinded by self love, or some other passion; it is now become of all laws the most obscure; and has consequently the greatest need of able interpreters. The written laws, if they be short, are easily misinterpreted, from the divers significations of a word, or two: if long they be more obscure by the divers significations of many words: insomuch as no written law, delivered in few, or many words, can be well understood, without a perfect understanding of the final causes, for which the law was made; the knowledge of which final causes is in the legislator. To him therefore there cannot be any knot in the law, insoluble; either by finding out the ends, to undo it by; or else by making what ends he will, (as *Alexander* did with his sword in the Gordian knot,) by the legislative power; which no other interpreter can do.

The interpretation of the laws of nature, in a commonwealth, dependeth not on the books of moral philosophy. The authority of writers, without the authority of the commonwealth, maketh not their opinions law, be they never so true. That which I have written in this treatise, concerning the moral virtues, and of their necessity, for the procuring, and maintaining peace, though it be evident truth, is not therefore presently law; but because in all commonwealths in the world, it is part of the civil law: For though it be naturally reasonable; yet it is by the sovereign power that it is law: otherwise, it were a great error, to call the laws of nature unwritten law; whereof we see so many volumes published, and in them so many contradictions of one another, and of themselves.

The interpretation of the law of nature, is the sentence of the judge constituted by the sovereign authority, to hear and determine such controversies, as depend thereon; and consisteth in the application of the law to the present case. For in the act of judicature, the judge doth no more but consider, whether the demand of the party, be consonant to natural reason, and equity; and the sentence he giveth, is therefore the interpretation of the law of nature; which interpretation is authentic; not because it is his private sentence; but because he giveth it by authority of the sovereign, whereby it becomes the sovereign's sentence; which is law for that time, to the parties pleading.

But because there is no judge subordinate, nor sovereign, but may err in a judgment of equity; if afterward in another like case he find it more consonant to equity to give a contrary sentence, he is obliged to do it. No man's error becomes his own law; nor obliges him to persist in it. Neither (for the same reason) becomes it a law to other judges, though sworn to follow it. For though a wrong sentence given by authority of the sovereign, if he know and allow it, in such laws as are mutable, be a constitution of a new law, in cases, in which every little circumstance is the same; yet in laws immutable, such as are the laws of nature, they are no laws to the same, or other judges, in the like cases for ever after. Princes succeed one another; and one judge passeth, another cometh; nay, heaven and earth shall pass; but not one title of the law of nature shall pass; for it is the eternal law of God. Therefore all the sentences of precedent judges that have ever been, cannot all together make a law contrary to natural equity: nor any examples of former judges, can warrant an unreasonable sentence, or discharge the present judge of the trouble of studying what is equity (in the case he is to judge,) from the principles of his own natural reason. For example sake, it is against the law of nature, *to punish the innocent*; and innocent is he that acquitteth himself judicially, and is acknowledged for innocent by the judge. Put the case now, that a man is accused of a capital crime, and seeing the power and malice of some enemy, and the frequent corruption and partiality of judges, runneth away for fear of the event, and afterwards is taken, and brought to a legal trial, and maketh it sufficiently appear, he was not guilty of the crime, and being thereof acquitted, is nevertheless condemned to lose his goods; this is a manifest condemnation of the innocent. I say therefore, that there is no place in the world, where this can be an interpretation of a law of nature, or be made a law by the sentences of precedent judges, that had done the same. For he that judged it first, judged unjustly; and no injustice can be a pattern of judgment to succeeding judges. A written law may forbid innocent men to fly, and they may be punished for flying: but that flying for fear of injury, should be taken for presumption of guilt, after a man is already absolved of the crime judicially, is contrary to the nature of a presumption, which hath no place after judgment given. Yet this is set down by a great lawyer for the common law of *England. If a man,* (saith he) *that is innocent, be accused of felony, and for fear flyeth for the same; albeit he judicially acquitteth himself of the felony; yet if it be found that he fled for the felony; he shall notwithstanding his innocency, forfeit all his goods, chattels, debts, and duties. For as to the forfeiture of them, the law will admit no proof against the presumption in law, grounded upon his flight.* Here you see, *an innocent man judicially acquitted, notwithstanding his innocency,* (when no written law forbad him to fly) after his acquittal, *upon a presumption in law,* condemned to lose all the goods he hath. If the law ground upon his flight a presumption of the fact, (which was capital,) the sentence ought to have been capital: if the presumption were not of the fact, for what then ought he to lose his goods? This therefore is no law of *England*; nor is the condemnation grounded upon a presumption of law, but upon the presumption of the judges. It is also against law, to say that no proof shall be admitted against a presumption of law. For all judges, sovereign and subordinate, if they refuse to hear proof, refuse to do justice: for though the sentence be just, yet the judges that condemn without hearing the proofs offered, are unjust judges; and their presumption is but prejudice; which no man ought to bring with him to the seat of justice, whatsoever precedent judgments, or examples he shall pretend to follow. There be other things of this nature, wherein men's judgments have been perverted, by trusting to precedents: but this is enough to show, that though the sentence of the judge, be a law to the party pleading, yet it is no law to any judge, that shall succeed him in that office.

In like manner, when question is of the meaning of written laws, he is not the interpreter of them, that writeth a commentary upon them. For commentaries are commonly more subject to cavil, than the text; and therefore need other commentaries; and so there will be no end of such interpretation. And therefore unless there be an interpreter authorized by the sovereign, from which the subordinate judges are not to recede, the interpreter can be no other than the ordinary judges, in the same manner, as they are in cases of the unwritten law; and their sentences are to be taken by them that plead, for laws in that particular case; but not to bind other judges, in like cases to give like judgments. For a judge may err in the interpretation even of written laws; but no error of a subor-

dinate judge, can change the law, which is the general sentence of the sovereign.

In written laws, men use to make a difference between the letter, and the sentence of the law: and when by the letter, is meant whatsoever can be gathered from the bare words, it is well distinguished. For the significations of almost all words, are either in themselves, or in the metaphorical use of them, ambiguous; and may be drawn in argument, to make many senses; but there is only one sense of the law. But if by the letter, be meant the literal sense, then the letter, and the sentence or intention of the law, is all one. For the literal sense is that, which the legislator intended, should by the letter of the law be signified. Now the intention of the legislator is always supposed to be equity: for it were a great contumely for a judge to think otherwise of the sovereign. He ought therefore, if the word of the law do not fully authorize a reasonable sentence, to supply it with the law of nature; or if the case be difficult, to respite judgment till he have received more ample authority. For example, a written law ordaineth, that he which is thrust out of his house by force, shall be restored by force: it happens that a man by negligence leaves his house empty, and returning is kept out by force, in which case there is no special law ordained. It is evident, that this case is contained in the same law: for else there is no remedy for him at all; which is to be supposed against the intention of the legislator. Again, the word of the law, commandeth to judge according to the evidence: a man is accused falsely of a fact, which the judge saw himself done by another; and not by him that is accused. In this case neither shall the letter of the law be followed to the condemnation of the innocent, nor shall the judge give sentence against the evidence of the witnesses; because the letter of the law is to the contrary: but procure of the sovereign that another be made judge, and himself witness. So that the incommodity that follows the bare words of a written law, may lead him to the intention of the law, whereby to interpret the same the better; though no incommodity can warrant a sentence against the law. For every judge of right, and wrong, is not judge of what is commodious, or incommodious to the commonwealth.

The abilities required in a good interpreter of the law, that is to say, in a good judge, are not the same with those of an advocate; namely the study of the laws. For a judge, as he ought to take notice of the fact, from none but the witnesses; so also he ought to take notice of the law, from nothing but the statutes, and constitutions of the sovereign, alleged in the pleading, or declared to him by some that have authority from the sovereign power to declare them; and need not take care beforehand, what he shall judge; for it shall be given him what he shall say concerning the fact, by witnesses; and what he shall say in point of law, from those that shall in their pleadings show it, and by authority interpret it upon the place. The Lords of parliament in *England* were judges, and most difficult causes have been heard and determined by them; yet few of them were much versed in the study of the laws, and fewer had made profession of them: and though they consulted with lawyers, that were appointed to be present there for that purpose; yet they alone had the authority of giving sentence. In like manner, in the ordinary trials of right, twelve men of the common people, are the judges, and give sentence, not only of the fact, but of the right; and pronounce simply for the complainant, or for the defendant; that is to say, are judges not only of the fact, but also of the right: and in a question of crime, not only determine whether done, or not done; but also whether it be *murder, homicide, felony, assault*, and the like, which are determinations of law: but because they are not supposed to know the law of themselves, there is one that hath authority to inform them of it, in the particular case they are to judge of. But yet if they judge not according to that he tells them, they are not subject thereby to any penalty; unless it be made appear, they did it against their consciences, or had been corrupted by reward.

The things that make a good judge, or good interpreter of the laws, are, first, *a right understanding* of that principal law of nature called *equity*; which depending not on the reading of other men's writings, but on the goodness of a man's own natural reason, and meditation, is presumed to be in those most, that have had most leisure, and had the most inclination to meditate thereon. Secondly, *contempt of unnecessary riches, and preferments*. Thirdly, *to be able in judgment to divest himself of all fear, anger, hatred, love, and compassion*. Fourthly, and lastly, *patience to hear;*

diligent attention in hearing; and memory to retain, digest and apply what he hath heard.

The difference and division of the laws, has been made in divers manners, according to the different methods, of those men that have written of them. For it is a thing that dependeth not on nature, but on the scope of the writer; and is subservient to every man's proper method. In the Institutions of *Justinian*, we find seven sorts of civil laws.

1. The *edicts, constitutions,* and *epistles of the prince,* that is, of the emperor; because the whole power of the people was in him. Like these, are the proclamations of the kings of *England.*

2. *The decrees of the whole people of Rome,* (comprehending the senate,) when they were put to the question by the *senate.* These were laws, at first, by the virtue of the sovereign power residing in the people; and such of them as by the emperors were not abrogated, remained laws, by the authority imperial. For all laws that bind, are understood to be laws by his authority that has power to repeal them. Somewhat like to these laws, are the acts of parliament in England.

3. *The decrees of the common people,* (excluding the senate,) when they were put to the question by the *tribune* of the people. For such of them as were not abrogated by the emperors, remained laws by the authority imperial. Like to these, were the orders of the House of Commons in *England.*

4. *Senatus consulta,* the *orders of the senate*; because when the people of *Rome* grew so numerous, as it was inconvenient to assemble them; it was thought fit by the emperor, that men should consult the senate, instead of the people: and these have some resemblance with the acts of council.

5. *The edicts of praetors,* and (in some cases) of the *aediles*: such as are the chief justices in the courts of *England.*

6. *Responsa prudentum*; which were the sentences, and opinions of those lawyers, to whom the emperor gave authority to interpret the law, and to give answer to such as in matter of law demanded their advice; which answers, the judges in giving judgment were obliged by the constitutions of the emperor to observe: and should be like the reports of cases judged, if other judges be by the law of *England* bound to observe them. For the judges of the common law of *England,*

are not properly judges, but *juris consulti*; of whom the judges, who are either the lords, or twelve men of the country, are in point of law to ask advice.

7. Also, *unwritten customs*, (which in their own nature are an imitation of law,) by the tacit consent of the emperor, in case they be not contrary to the law of nature, are very laws.

Another division of laws, is into *natural* and *positive*. *Natural* are those which have been laws from all eternity; and are called not only *natural*, but also *moral* laws; consisting in the moral virtues, as justice, equity, and all habits of the mind that conduce to peace, and charity; of which I have already spoken in the fourteenth and fifteenth chapters.

Positive, are those which have not been from eternity; but have been made laws by the will of those that have had the sovereign power over others; and are either written, or made known to men, by some other argument of the will of their legislator.

Again, of positive laws, some are *human*, some *divine*; and of human positive laws, some are *distributive*, some *penal*. *Distributive* are those that determine the rights of the subjects, declaring to every man what it is, by which he acquireth and holdeth a propriety in lands, or goods, and a right or liberty of action: and these speak to all the subjects. *Penal* are those, which declare, what penalty shall be inflicted on those that violate the law; and speak to the ministers and officers ordained for execution. For though every one ought to be informed of the punishments ordained beforehand for their transgression; nevertheless the command is not addressed to the delinquent, (who cannot be supposed will faithfully punish himself,) but to public ministers appointed to see the penalty executed. And these penal laws are for the most part written together with the laws distributive; and are sometimes called judgments. For all laws are general judgments, or sentences of the legislator; as also every particular judgment, is a law to him, whose case is judged.

Divine positive laws (for natural laws being eternal, and universal, are all divine,) are those, which being the commandments of God, (not from all eternity, nor universally addressed to all men, but only to a certain people, or to certain persons,) are declared for such, by those whom God hath authorized to declare them. But this authority of man to declare

what be these positive laws of God, how can it be known? God may command a man by a supernatural way, to deliver laws to other men. But because it is of the essence of law, that he who is to be obliged, be assured of the authority of him that declareth it, which we cannot naturally take notice to be from God, *how can a man without supernatural revelation be assured of the revelation received by the declarer?* and *how can he be bound to obey them?* For the first question, how a man can be assured of the revelation of another, without a revelation particularly to himself, it is evidently impossible. For though a man may be induced to believe such revelation, from the miracles they see him do, or from seeing the extraordinary sanctity of his life, or from seeing the extraordinary wisdom, or extraordinary felicity of his actions, all which are marks of God's extraordinary favour; yet they are not assured evidences of special revelation. Miracles are marvellous works: but that which is marvellous to one, may not be so to another. Sanctity may be feigned; and the visible felicities of this world, are most often the work of God by natural, and ordinary causes. And therefore no man can infallibly know by natural reason, that another has had a supernatural revelation of God's will; but only a belief; every one (as the signs thereof shall appear greater, or lesser) a firmer, or a weaker belief.

But for the second, how he can be bound to obey them; it is not so hard. For if the law declared, be not against the law of nature (which is undoubtedly God's law) and he undertake to obey it, he is bound by his own act; bound I say to obey it, but not bound to believe it: for men's belief, and interior cogitations, are not subject to the commands, but only to the operation of God, ordinary, or extraordinary. Faith of supernatural law, is not a fulfilling, but only an assenting to the same; and not a duty that we exhibit to God, but a gift which God freely giveth to whom he pleaseth; as also unbelief is not a breach of any of his laws; but a rejection of them all, except the laws natural. But this that I say, will be made yet clearer, by the examples and testimonies concerning this point in holy Scripture. The covenant God made with *Abraham* (in a supernatural manner) was thus, (*Gen.* 17. 10) *This is the covenant which thou shalt observe between me and thee and thy seed after thee. Abraham's* seed had not this revelation, nor were yet in being; yet they are a party to the covenant, and bound to obey what *Abraham* should declare to them for God's law; which they could not be, but in virtue of the obedience they owed to their parents; who (if they be subject to no other earthly power, as here in the case of *Abraham*) have sovereign power over their children and servants. Again, where God saith to *Abraham, In thee shall all nations of the earth be blessed; for I know thou wilt command thy children, and thy house after thee to keep the way of the Lord, and to observe righteousness and judgment,* it is manifest, the obedience of his family, who had no revelation, depended on their former obligation to obey their sovereign. At Mount *Sinai Moses* only went up to God; the people were forbidden to approach on pain of death; yet were they bound to obey all that Moses declared to them for God's law. Upon what ground, but on this submission of their own, *Speak thou to us, and we will hear thee; but let not God speak to us, lest we die?* By which two places it sufficiently appeareth, that in a commonwealth, a subject that has no certain and assured revelation particularly to himself concerning the will of God, is to obey for such, the command of the commonwealth: for if men were at liberty, to take for God's commandments, their own dreams, and fancies, or the dreams and fancies of private men; scarce two men would agree upon what is God's commandment; and yet in respect of them, every man would despise the commandments of the commonwealth. I conclude therefore, that in all things not contrary to the moral law, (that is to say, to the law of nature,) all subjects are bound to obey that for divine law, which is declared to be so, by the laws of the commonwealth. Which also is evident to any man's reason; for whatsoever is not against the law of nature, may be made law in the name of them that have the sovereign power; and there is no reason men should be the less obliged by it, when it is propounded in the name of God. Besides, there is no place in the world where men are permitted to pretend other commandments of God, than are declared for such by the commonwealth. Christian states punish those that revolt from Christian religion, and all other states, those that set up any religion by them forbidden. For in whatsoever is not regulated by the commonwealth, it is equity, (which is the law of nature, and therefore

an eternal law of God) that every man equally enjoy his liberty.

There is also another distinction of laws, into *fundamental* and *not fundamental*, but I could never see in any author, what a fundamental law signifieth. Nevertheless one may very reasonably distinguish laws in that manner.

For a fundamental law in every commonwealth is that, which being taken away, the commonwealth faileth, and is utterly dissolved; as a building whose foundation is destroyed. And therefore a fundamental law is that, by which subjects are bound to uphold whatsoever power is given to the sovereign, whether a monarch, or a sovereign assembly, without which the commonwealth cannot stand; such as is the power of war and peace, of judicature, of election of officers, and of doing whatsoever he shall think necessary for the public good. Not fundamental is that, the abrogating whereof, draweth not with it the dissolution of the commonwealth; such as are the laws concerning controversies between subject and subject. Thus much of the division of laws.

I find the words *lex civilis*, and *jus civile*, that is to say, *law* and *right civil*, promiscuously used for the same thing, even in the most learned authors; which nevertheless ought not to be so. For *right* is *liberty*, namely that liberty which the civil law leaves us: but *civil law* is an *obligation*; and takes from us the liberty which the law of nature gave us. Nature gave a right to every man to secure himself by his own strength, and to invade a suspected neighbour, by way of prevention: but the civil law takes away that liberty, in all cases where the protection of the law may be safely stayed for. Insomuch as *lex* and *jus*, are as different as *obligation* and *liberty*.

Likewise *laws* and *charters* are taken promiscuously for the same thing. Yet charters are donations of the sovereign; and not laws, but exemptions from law. The phrase of a law is, *jubeo, injungo, I command,* and *enjoin*: the phrase of a charter is, *dedi, concessi, I have given, I have granted*: but what is given or granted, to a man, is not forced upon him, by a law. A law may be made to bind all the subjects of a commonwealth: a liberty, or charter is only to one man, or some one part of the people. For to say all the people of a commonwealth, have liberty in any case whatsoever; is to say, that in such case, there hath been no law made; or else having been made, is now abrogated.

Chapter 27

Of Crimes, Excuses, and Extenuations

A *sin*, is not only a transgression of a law, but also any contempt of the legislator. For such contempt, is a breach of all his laws at once. And therefore may consist, not only in the *commission* of a fact, or in the speaking of words by the laws forbidden, or in the *omission* of what the law commandeth, but also in the *intention*, or purpose to transgress. For the purpose to break the law, is some degree of contempt of him, to whom it belongeth to see it executed. To be delighted in the imagination only, of being possessed of another man's goods, servants, or wife, without any intention to take them from him by force or fraud, is no breach of the law, that saith, *Thou shalt not covet*: nor is the pleasure a man may have in imagining, or dreaming of the death of him, from whose life he expecteth nothing but damage, and displeasure, a sin; but the resolving to put some act in execution, that tendeth thereto. For to be pleased in the fiction of that, which would please a man if it were real, is a passion so adherent to the nature both of man, and every other living creature, as to make it a sin, were to make sin of being a man. The consideration of this, has made me think them too severe, both to themselves, and others, that maintain, that the first motions of the mind, (though checked with the fear of God) be sins. But I confess it is safer to err on that hand, than on the other.

A CRIME, is a sin, consisting in the committing (by deed, or word) of that which the law forbiddeth, or the omission of what it hath commanded. So that every crime is a sin; but not every sin a crime. To intend to steal, or kill, is a sin, though it never appear in word, or fact: for God that seeth the thoughts of man, can lay it to his charge: but till it appear by something done, or said, by which the intention may be argued by a human judge, it hath not the name of crime: which distinction the Greeks observed, in the word ἁμάρτημα, and ἔγκλημα, or αἰτία; whereof the former, (which is translated *sin*,) signifieth any

swerving from the law whatsoever; but the two latter, (which are translated *crime*,) signify that sin only, whereof one man may accuse another. But of intentions, which never appear by any outward act, there is no place for human accusation. In like manner the Latins by *peccatum*, which is *sin*, signify all manner of deviation from the law; but by *crimen*, (which word they derive from *cerno*, which signifies to perceive,) they mean only such sins, as may be made appear before a judge; and therefore are not mere intentions.

From this relation of sin to the law, and of crime to the civil law, may be inferred, first, that where law ceaseth, sin ceaseth. But because the law of nature is eternal, violation of covenants, ingratitude, arrogance, and all facts contrary to any moral virtue, can never cease to be sin. Secondly, that the civil law ceasing, crimes cease: for there being no other law remaining, but that of nature, there is no place for accusation; every man being his own judge, and accused only by his own conscience, and cleared by the uprightness of his own intention. When therefore his intention is right, his fact is no sin: if otherwise, his fact is sin; but not crime. Thirdly, that when the sovereign power ceaseth, crime also ceaseth: for where there is no such power, there is no protection to be had from the law; and therefore every one may protect himself by his own power: for no man in the institution of sovereign power can be supposed to give away the right of preserving his own body; for the safety whereof all sovereignty was ordained. But this is to be understood only of those, that have not themselves contributed to the taking away of the power that protected them: for that was a crime from the beginning.

The source of every crime, is some defect of the understanding; or some error in reasoning; or some sudden force of the passions. Defect in the understanding, is *ignorance*; in reasoning, *erroneous opinion*. Again, ignorance is of three sorts; of the *law*, and of the *sovereign*, and of the *penalty*. Ignorance of the law of nature excuseth no man; because every man that hath attained to the use of reason, is supposed to know, he ought not to do to another, what he would not have done to himself. Therefore into what place soever a man shall come, if he do any thing contrary to that law, it is a crime. If a man come from the *Indies* hither, and persuade men here to receive a new religion, or teach them any thing that tendeth to disobedience of the laws of this country, though he be never so well persuaded of the truth of what he teacheth, he commits a crime, and may be justly punished for the same, not only because his doctrine is false, but also because he does that which he would not approve in another, namely, that coming from hence, he should endeavour to alter the religion there. But ignorance of the civil law, shall excuse a man in a strange country, till it be declared to him; because, till then no civil law is binding.

In the like manner, if the civil law of a man's own country, be not so sufficiently declared, as he may know it if he will; nor the action against the law of nature; the ignorance is a good excuse: in other cases ignorance of the civil law, excuseth not.

Ignorance of the sovereign power, in the place of a man's ordinary residence, excuseth him not; because he ought to take notice of the power, by which he hath been protected there.

Ignorance of the penalty, where the law is declared, excuseth no man: for in breaking the law, which without a fear of penalty to follow, were not a law, but vain words, he undergoeth the penalty, though he know not what it is; because, whosoever voluntarily doth any action, accepteth all the known consequences of it; but punishment is a known consequence of the violation of the laws, in every commonwealth; which punishment, if it be determined already by the law, he is subject to that; if not, then is he subject to arbitrary punishment. For it is reason, that he which does injury, without other limitation than that of his own will, should suffer punishment without other limitation, than that of his will whose law is thereby violated.

But when a penalty, is either annexed to the crime in the law itself, or hath been usually inflicted in the like cases; there the delinquent is excused from a greater penalty. For the punishment foreknown, if not great enough to deter men from the action, is an invitement to it: because when men compare the benefit of their injustice, with the harm of their punishment, by necessity of nature they choose that which appeareth best for themselves: and therefore when they are punished more than the law had formerly determined, or more than others were punished for the same crime; it is the law that tempted, and deceiveth them.

No law, made after a fact done, can make it a crime: because if the fact be against the law of nature, the law was before the fact; and a positive law cannot be taken notice of, before it be made; and therefore cannot be obligatory. But when the law that forbiddeth a fact, is made before the fact be done; yet he that doth the fact, is liable to the penalty ordained after, in case no lesser penalty were made known before, neither by writing, nor by example, for the reason immediately before alleged.

From defect in reasoning, (that is to say, from error,) men are prone to violate the laws, three ways. First, by presumption of false principles: as when men from having observed how in all places, and in all ages, unjust actions have been authorized by the force, and victories of those who have committed them; and that potent men, breaking through the cobweb laws of their country, the weaker sort, and those that have failed in their enterprises, have been esteemed the only criminals; have thereupon taken for principles, and grounds of their reasoning, *that justice is but a vain word: that whatsoever a man can get by his own industry, and hazard, is his own: that the practice of all nations cannot be unjust: that examples of former times are good arguments of doing the like again*; and many more of that kind: which being granted, no act in itself can be a crime, but must be made so (not by the law, but) by the success of them that commit it; and the same fact be virtuous, or vicious, as fortune pleaseth; so that what *Marius* makes a crime, *Sylla* shall make meritorious, and *Caesar*, (the same laws standing) turn again into a crime, to the perpetual disturbance of the peace of the commonwealth.

Secondly, by false teachers, that either misinterpret the law of nature, making it thereby repugnant to the law civil; or by teaching for laws, such doctrines of their own, or traditions of former times, as are inconsistent with the duty of a subject.

Thirdly, by erroneous inferences from true principles; which happens commonly to men that are hasty, and precipitate in concluding, and resolving what to do; such as are they, that have both a great opinion of their own understanding, and believe that things of this nature require not time and study, but only common experience, and a good natural wit; whereof no man thinks himself unprovided: whereas the

knowledge, of right and wrong, which is no less difficult, there is no man will pretend to, without great
and long study. And of those defects in reasoning,
there is none that can excuse (though some of them
may extenuate) a crime, in any man, that pretendeth
to the administration of his own private business;
much less in them that undertake a public charge;
because they pretend to the reason, upon the want
whereof they would ground their excuse.

Of the passions that most frequently are the causes
of crime, one, is vain glory, or a foolish overrating of
their own worth; as if difference of worth, were an
effect of their wit, or riches, or blood, or some other
natural quality, not depending on the will of those
that have the sovereign authority. From whence proceedeth a presumption that the punishments
ordained by the laws, and extended generally to all
subjects, ought not to be inflicted on them, with the
same rigour they are inflicted on poor, obscure, and
simple men, comprehended under the name of the
vulgar.

Therefore it happeneth commonly, that such as
value themselves by the greatness of their wealth,
adventure on crimes, upon hope of escaping punishment, by corrupting public justice, or obtaining pardon by money, or other rewards.

And that such as have multitude of potent kindred;
and popular men, that have gained reputation
amongst the multitude, take courage to violate the
laws, from a hope of oppressing the power, to whom
it belongeth to put them in execution.

And that such as have a great, and false opinion
of their own wisdom, take upon them to reprehend
the actions, and call in question the authority of them
that govern, and so to unsettle the laws with their
public discourse, as that nothing shall be a crime,
but what their own designs require should be so. It
happeneth also to the same men, to be prone to all
such crimes, as consist in craft, and in deceiving of
their neighbours; because they think their designs are
too subtle to be perceived. These I say are effects of
a false presumption of their own wisdom. For of them
that are the first movers in the disturbance of commonwealth, (which can never happen without a civil
war,) very few are left alive long enough, to see their
new designs established: so that the benefit of their
crimes, redoundeth to posterity, and such as would

least have wished it: which argues they were not so
wise, as they thought they were. And those that deceive upon hope of not being observed, do commonly
deceive themselves, (the darkness in which they believe they lie hidden, being nothing else but their
own blindness;) and are no wiser than children, that
think all hid, by hiding their own eyes.

And generally all vain-glorious men, (unless they
be withal timorous,) are subject to anger; as being
more prone than others to interpret for contempt, the
ordinary liberty of conversation: and there are few
crimes that may not be produced by anger.

As for the passions, of hate, lust, ambition, and
covetousness, what crimes they are apt to produce,
is so obvious to every man's experience and understanding, as there needeth nothing to be said of them,
saving that they are infirmities, so annexed to the
nature, both of man, and all other living creatures,
as that their effects cannot be hindered, but by extraordinary use of reason, or a constant severity in punishing them. For in those things men hate, they find
a continual, and unavoidable molestation; whereby
either a man's patience must be everlasting, or he
must be eased by removing the power of that which
molesteth him. The former is difficult; the latter is
many times impossible, without some violation of the
law. Ambition, and covetousness are passions also
that are perpetually incumbent, and pressing; whereas
reason is not perpetually present, to resist them: and
therefore whensoever the hope of impunity appears,
their effects proceed. And for lust, what it wants in
the lasting, it hath in the vehemence, which sufficeth
to weigh down the apprehension of all easy, or uncertain punishments.

Of all passions, that which inclineth men least to
break the laws, is fear. Nay, (excepting some generous
natures,) it is the only thing, (when there is apparence
of profit or pleasure by breaking the laws,) that makes
men keep them. And yet in many cases a crime may
be committed through fear.

For not every fear justifies the action it produceth,
but the fear only of corporeal hurt, which we call
bodily fear, and from which a man cannot see how
to be delivered, but by the action. A man is assaulted,
fears present death, from which he sees not how to
escape, but by wounding him that assaulteth him; if
he wound him to death, this is no crime; because no

we use justification to express the same idea

man is supposed at the making of a commonwealth, to have abandoned the defence of his life, or limbs, where the law cannot arrive time enough to his assistance. But to kill a man, because from his actions, or his threatenings, I may argue he will kill me when he can, (seeing I have time, and means to demand protection, from the sovereign power,) is a crime. Again, a man receives words of disgrace, or some little injuries, (for which they that made the laws, had assigned no punishment, nor thought it worthy of a man that hath the use of reason, to take notice of,) and is afraid, unless he revenge it, he shall fall into contempt, and consequently be obnoxious to the like injuries from others; and to avoid this, breaks the law, and protects himself for the future, by the terror of his private revenge. This is a crime: for the hurt is not corporeal, but phantastical, and (though in this corner of the world, made sensible by a custom not many years since begun, amongst young and vain men,) so light, as a gallant man, and one that is assured of his own courage, cannot take notice of. Also a man may stand in fear of spirits, either through his own superstition, or through too much credit given to other men, that tell him of strange dreams and visions; and thereby be made believe they will hurt him, for doing, or omitting divers things, which nevertheless, to do, or omit, is contrary to the laws; and that which is so done, or omitted, is not to be excused by this fear; but is a crime. For (as I have shown before in the second chapter) dreams be naturally but the fancies remaining in sleep, after the impressions our senses had formerly received waking; and when men are by any accident unassured they have slept, seem to be real visions; and therefore he that presumes to break the law upon his own, or another's dream, or pretended vision, or upon other fancy of the power of invisible spirits, than is permitted by the commonwealth, leaveth the law of nature, which is a certain offence, and followeth the imagery of his own, or another private man's brain, which he can never know whether it signifieth any thing, or nothing, nor whether he that tells his dream, say true, or lie; which if every private man should have leave to do, (as they must by the law of nature, if any one have it) there could no law be made to hold, and so all commonwealth would be dissolved.

From these different sources of crimes, it appears already, that all crimes are not (as the Stoics of old time maintained) of the same allay. There is place, not only for EXCUSE, by which that which seemed a crime, is proved to be none at all; but also for EXTENUATION, by which the crime, that seemed great, is made less. For though all crimes do equally deserve the name of injustice, as all deviation from a straight line is equally crookedness, which the Stoics rightly observed; yet it does not follow that all crimes are equally unjust, no more than that all crooked lines are equally crooked; which the Stoics not observing, held it as great a crime, to kill a hen, against the law, as to kill one's father.

That which totally excuseth a fact, and takes away from it the nature of a crime, can be none but that, which at the same time, taketh away the obligation of the law. For the fact committed once against the law, if he that committed it be obliged to the law, can be no other than a crime.

The want of means to know the law, totally excuseth: For the law whereof a man has no means to inform himself, is not obligatory. But the want of diligence to inquire, shall not be considered as a want of means; nor shall any man, that pretendeth to reason enough for the government of his own affairs, be supposed to want means to know the laws of nature; because they are known by the reason he pretends to: only children, and madmen are excused from offences against the law natural.

Where a man is captive, or in the power of the enemy (and he is then in the power of the enemy, when his person, or his means of living, is so,) if it be without his own fault, the obligation of the law ceaseth; because he must obey the enemy, or die; and consequently such obedience is no crime: for no man is obliged (when the protection of the law faileth,) not to protect himself, by the best means he can.

If a man, by the terror of present death, be compelled to do a fact against the law, he is totally excused; because no law can oblige a man to abandon his own preservation. And supposing such a law were obligatory; yet a man would reason thus, *If I do it not, I die presently; if I do it, I die afterwards; therefore by doing it, there is time of life gained*; nature therefore compels him to the fact.

When a man is destitute of food, or other thing

necessary for his life, and cannot preserve himself any other way, but by some fact against the law; as if in a great famine he take the food by force, or stealth, which he cannot obtain for money, nor charity; or in defence of his life, snatch away another man's sword, he is totally excused, for the reason next before alleged.

Again, facts done against the law, by the authority of another, are by that authority excused against the author; because no man ought to accuse his own fact in another, that is but his instrument: but it is not excused against a third person thereby injured; because in the violation of the law, both the author and actor are criminals. From hence it followeth that when that man, or assembly, that hath the sovereign power, commandeth a man to do that which is contrary to a former law, the doing of it is totally excused: for he ought not to condemn it himself, because he is the author; and what cannot justly be condemned by the sovereign, cannot justly be punished by any other. Besides, when the sovereign commandeth any thing to be done against his own former law, the command, as to that particular fact, is an abrogation of the law.

If that man, or assembly, that hath the sovereign power, disclaim any right essential to the sovereignty, whereby there accrueth to the subject, any liberty inconsistent with the sovereign power, that is to say, with the very being of a commonwealth, if the subject shall refuse to obey the command in any thing, contrary to the liberty granted, this is nevertheless a sin, and contrary to the duty of the subject: for he ought to take notice of what is inconsistent with the sovereignty, because it was erected by his own consent, and for his own defence; and that such liberty as is inconsistent with it, was granted through ignorance of the evil consequence thereof. But if he not only disobey, but also resist a public minister in the execution of it, then it is a crime; because he might have been righted, (without any breach of the peace,) upon complaint.

The degrees of crime are taken on divers scales, and measured, first, by the malignity of the source, or cause: secondly, by the contagion of the example: thirdly, by the mischief of the effect: and fourthly, by the concurrence of times, places, and persons.

The same fact done against the law, if it proceed from presumption of strength, riches, or friends to resist those that are to execute the law, is a greater crime than if it proceed from hope of not being discovered, or of escape by flight: for presumption of impunity by force, is a root, from whence springeth, at all times, and upon all temptations, a contempt of all laws; whereas in the latter case, the apprehension of danger, that makes a man fly, renders him more obedient for the future. A crime which we know to be so, is greater than the same crime proceeding from a false persuasion that it is lawful: for he that committeth it against his own conscience, presumeth on his force, or other power, which encourages him to commit the same again: but he that doth it by error, after the error shewn him, is conformable to the law.

He, whose error proceeds from the authority of a teacher, or an interpreter of the law publicly authorized, is not so faulty, as he whose error proceedeth from a peremptory pursuit of his own principles, and reasoning: for what is taught by one that teacheth by public authority, the commonwealth teacheth, and hath a resemblance of law, till the same authority controlleth it; and in all crimes that contain not in them a denial of the sovereign power, nor are against an evident law, excuseth totally: whereas he that groundeth his actions on his private judgment, ought according to the rectitude, or error thereof, to stand, or fall.

The same fact, if it have been constantly punished in other men, is a greater crime, than if there have been many precedent examples of impunity. For those examples are so many hopes of impunity, given by the sovereign himself: and because he which furnishes a man with such a hope, and presumption of mercy, as encourageth him to offend, hath his part in the offence; he cannot reasonably charge the offender with the whole.

A crime arising from a sudden passion, is not so great, as when the same ariseth from long meditation: for in the former case there is a place for extenuation, in the common infirmity of human nature: but he that doth it with premeditation, has used circumspection, and cast his eye, on the law, on the punishment, and on the consequence thereof to human society; all which in committing the crime, he hath contemned, and postposed to his own appetite. But there is no suddenness of passion sufficient for a total excuse: for all the time between the first knowing of the law, and the commission of the fact, shall be taken for a time of deliberation; because he ought by meditation of the law, to rectify the irregularity of his passions.

Where the law is publicly, and with assiduity, before all the people read and interpreted; a fact done against it, is a greater crime, than where men are left without such instruction, to enquire of it with difficulty, uncertainty, and interruption of their callings, and be informed by private men: for in this case, part of the fault is discharged upon common infirmity; but in the former, there is apparent negligence, which is not without some contempt of the sovereign power.

Those facts which the law expressly condemneth, but the law-maker by other manifest signs of his will tacitly approveth, are less crimes, than the same facts, condemned both by the law and lawmaker. For seeing the will of the law-maker is a law, there appear in this case two contradictory laws; which would totally excuse, if men were bound to take notice of the sovereign's approbation, by other arguments, than are expressed by his command. But because there are punishments consequent, not only to the transgression of his law, but also to the observing of it, he is in part a cause of the transgression, and therefore cannot reasonably impute the whole crime to the delinquent. For example, the law condemneth duels; the punishment is made capital: on the contrary part, he that refuseth duel, is subject to contempt and scorn, without remedy; and sometimes by the sovereign himself thought unworthy to have any charge, or preferment in war. If thereupon he accept duel, considering all men lawfully endeavour to obtain the good opinion of them that have the sovereign power, he ought not in reason to be rigorously punished; seeing part of the fault may be discharged on the punisher: which I say, not as wishing liberty of private revenges, or any other kind of disobedience; but a care in governors, not to countenance any thing obliquely, which directly they forbid. The examples of princes, to those that see them, are, and ever have been, more potent to govern their actions, than the laws themselves. And though it be our duty to do, not what they do, but what they say; yet will that duty never be performed, till it please God to give men an extraordinary, and supernatural grace to follow that precept.

Again, if we compare crimes by the mischief of their effects, first, the same fact, when it redounds to the damage of many, is greater, than when it redounds to the hurt of few. And therefore, when a fact hurteth, not only in the present, but also, (by example) in the future, it is a greater crime, than if it hurt only in the present: for the former, is a fertile crime, and multiplies to the hurt of many; the latter is barren. To maintain doctrines contrary to the religion established in the commonwealth, is a greater fault, in an authorized preacher, than in a private person: so also is it, to live profanely, incontinently, or do any irreligious act whatsoever. Likewise in a professor of the law, to maintain any point, or do any act, that tendeth to the weakening of the sovereign power, is a greater crime, than in another man: also in a man that hath such reputation for wisdom, as that his counsels are followed, or his actions imitated by many, his fact against the law, is a greater crime, than the same fact in another: for such men not only commit crime, but teach it for law to all other men. And generally all crimes are the greater, by the scandal they give; that is to say, by becoming stumbling-blocks to the weak, that look not so much upon the way they go in, as upon the light that other men carry before them.

Also facts of hostility against the present state of the commonwealth, are greater crimes, than the same acts done to private men: for the damage extends itself to all: such are the betraying of the strengths, or revealing of the secrets of the commonwealth to an enemy; also all attempts upon the representative of the commonwealth, be it a monarch, or an assembly; and all endeavours by word, or deed to diminish the authority of the same, either in the present time, or in succession: which crimes the Latins understand by *crimina laesae majestatis*, and consist in design, or act, contrary to a fundamental law.

Likewise those crimes, which render judgments of no effect, are greater crimes, than injuries done to one, or a few persons; as to receive money to give false judgment, or testimony, is a greater crime, than otherwise to deceive a man of the like, or a greater sum; because not only he has wrong, that falls by such judgments; but all judgments are rendered useless, and occasion ministered to force, and private revenges.

Also robbery, and depeculation of the public treasure, or revenues, is a greater crime, than the robbing, or defrauding of a private man; because to rob the public, is to rob many at once.

Also the counterfeit usurpation of public ministry, the counterfeiting of public seals, or public coin, than counterfeiting of a private man's person, or his seal; because the fraud thereof, extendeth to the damage of many.

Of facts against the law, done to private men, the greater crime, is that, where the damage in the common opinion of men, is most sensible. And therefore

To kill against the law, is a greater crime, than any other injury, life preserved.

And to kill with torment, greater, than simply to kill.

And mutilation of a limb, greater, than the spoiling a man of his goods.

And the spoiling a man of his goods, by terror of death, or wounds, than by clandestine surreption.

And by clandestine surreption, than by consent fraudulently obtained.

And the violation of chastity by force, greater, than by flattery.

And of a woman married, than of a woman not married.

For all these things are commonly so valued; though some men are more, and some less sensible of the same offence. But the law regardeth not the particular, but the general inclination of mankind.

And therefore the offence men take, from contumely, in words, or gesture, when they produce no other harm, than the present grief of him that is reproached, hath been neglected in the laws of the Greeks, Romans, and other both ancient, and modern commonwealths; supposing the true cause of such grief to consist, not in the contumely, (which takes no hold upon men conscious of their own virtue,) but in the pusillanimity of him that is offended by it.

Also a crime against a private man, is much aggravated by the person, time, and place. For to kill one's parent, is a greater crime, than to kill another: for the parent ought to have the honour of a sovereign, (though he have surrendered his power to the civil law,) because he had it originally by nature. And to rob a poor man, is a greater crime, than to rob a rich man; because it is to the poor a more sensible damage.

And a crime committed in the time or place appointed for devotion, is greater, than if committed at another time or place: for it proceeds from a greater contempt of the law.

Many other cases of aggravation, and extenuation might be added: but by these I have set down, it is obvious to every man, to take the altitude of any other crime proposed.

Lastly, because in almost all crimes there is an injury done, not only to some private men, but also to the commonwealth; the same crime, when the accusation is in the name of the commonwealth, is called public crime: and when in the name of a private man, a private crime; and the pleas according thereunto called public, *judicia publica*, Pleas of the Crown; or Private Pleas. As in an accusation of murder, if the accuser be a private man, the plea is a Private Plea; if the accuser be the sovereign, the plea is a Public Plea.

Chapter 28

Of Punishments, and Rewards

A PUNISHMENT, *is an evil inflicted by public authority, on him that hath done, or omitted that which is judged by the same authority to be a transgression of the law; to the end that the will of men may thereby the better be disposed to obedience.*

Before I infer any thing from this definition, there is a question to be answered, of much importance; which is, by what door the right, or authority of punishing in any case, came in. For by that which has been said before, no man is supposed bound by covenant, not to resist violence; and consequently it cannot be intended, that he gave any right to another to lay violent hands upon his person. In the making of a commonwealth, every man giveth away the right of defending another; but not of defending himself. Also he obligeth himself, to assist him that hath the sovereignty, in the punishing of another; but of himself not. But to covenant to assist the sovereign, in doing hurt to another, unless he that so covenanteth have a right to do it himself, is not to give him a right to punish. It is manifest therefore that the right which the commonwealth (that is, he, or they that represent it) hath to punish, is not grounded on any concession, or gift of the subjects. But I have also showed formerly, that before the institution of commonwealth, every man had a right to every thing, and to do whatsoever he thought necessary to his own preservation; subduing, hurting, or killing any man in order thereunto. And this is the foundation of that right of punishing, which is exercised in every commonwealth. For the subjects did not give the sovereign that right; but only in laying down theirs, strengthened him to use his own, as he should think fit, for the preservation of them all: so that it was not given, but left to him, and to him only; and (excepting the limits set him by natural law) as entire, as in the condition of mere nature, and of war of every one against his neighbour.

From the definition of punishment, I infer, first, that neither private revenges, nor injuries of private men, can properly be styled punishment; because they proceed not from public authority.

Secondly, that to be neglected, and unpreferred by the public favour, is not a punishment; because no new evil is thereby on any man inflicted; he is only left in the estate he was in before.

Thirdly, that the evil inflicted by public authority, without precedent public condemnation, is not to be styled by the name of punishment; but of an hostile act; because the fact for which a man is punished, ought first to be judged by public authority, to be a transgression of the law.

Fourthly, that the evil inflicted by usurped power, and judges without authority from the sovereign, is not punishment; but an act of hostility; because the acts of power usurped, have not for author, the person condemned; and therefore are not acts of public authority.

Fifthly, that all evil which is inflicted without intention, or possibility of disposing the delinquent, or (by his example) other men, to obey the laws, is not punishment; but an act of hostility; because without such an end, no hurt done is contained under that name.

Sixthly, whereas to certain actions, there be annexed by nature, divers hurtful consequences; as when a man in assaulting another, is himself slain, or wounded; or when he falleth into sickness by the doing of some unlawful act; such hurt, though in respect of God, who is the author of nature, it may be said to be inflicted, and therefore a punishment divine; yet it is not contained in the name of punishment in respect of men, because it is not inflicted by the authority of man.

Seventhly, if the harm inflicted be less than the benefit, or contentment that naturally followeth the crime committed, that harm is not within the definition; and is rather the price, or redemption, than the punishment of a crime: because it is of the nature of punishment, to have for end, the disposing of men to obey the law; which end (if it be less than the benefit of the transgression) it attaineth not, but worketh a contrary effect.

Eighthly, if a punishment be determined and prescribed in the law itself, and after the crime committed, there be a greater punishment inflicted, the excess is not punishment, but an act of hostility. For seeing the aim of punishment is not a revenge, but terror; and the terror of a great punishment unknown, is taken away by the declaration of a less, the unexpected addition is no part of the punishment. But where there is no punishment at all determined by the law, there whatsoever is inflicted, hath the nature of punishment. For he that goes about the violation of a law, wherein no penalty is determined, expecteth an indeterminate, that is to say, an arbitrary punishment.

Ninthly, harm inflicted for a fact done before there was a law that forbade it, is not punishment, but an act of hostility: for before the law, there is no transgression of the law: but punishment supposeth a fact judged, to have been a transgression of the law; therefore harm inflicted before the law made, is not punishment, but an act of hostility.

Tenthly, hurt inflicted on the representative of the commonwealth, is not punishment, but an act of hostility: because it is of the nature of punishment, to be inflicted by public authority, which is the authority only of the representative itself.

Lastly, harm inflicted upon one that is a declared enemy, falls not under the name of punishment: because seeing they were either never subject to the law, and therefore cannot transgress it; or having been subject to it, and professing to be no longer so, by consequence deny they can transgress it, all the harms that can be done them, must be taken as acts of hostility. But in declared hostility, all infliction of evil is lawful. From whence it followeth, that if a subject shall by fact, or word, wittingly, and deliberately deny the authority of the representative of the commonwealth (whatsoever penalty hath been formerly ordained for treason,) he may lawfully be made to suffer whatsoever the representative will. For in denying subjection, he denies such punishment as by the law hath been ordained; and therefore suffers as an enemy of the commonwealth; that is, according to the will of the representative. For the punishments set down in the law, are to subjects, not to enemies; such as are they, that having been by their own act subjects, deliberately revolting, deny the sovereign power.

The first, and most general distribution of punishments, is into *divine*, and *human*. Of the former I shall have occasion to speak, in a more convenient place hereafter.

Human, are those punishments that be inflicted by the commandment of man; and are either *corporal*, or *pecuniary*, or *ignominy*, or *imprisonment*, or *exile*, or mixed of these.

Corporal punishment is that, which is inflicted on the body directly, and according to the intention of him that inflicteth it: such as are stripes, or wounds, or deprivation of such pleasures of the body, as were before lawfully enjoyed.

And of these, some be *capital*, some *less* than *capital*. Capital, is the infliction of death; and that either simply, or with torment. Less than capital, are stripes, wounds, chains, and any other corporal pain, not in its own nature mortal. For if upon the infliction of a punishment death follow not in the intention of the inflictor, the punishment is not to be esteemed capital, though the harm prove mortal by an accident not to be foreseen; in which case death is not inflicted, but hastened.

Pecuniary punishment, is that which consisteth not only in the deprivation of a sum of money, but also of lands, or any other goods which are usually bought and sold for money. And in case the law, that ordaineth such a punishment, be made with design to gather money, from such as shall transgress the same, it is not properly a punishment, but the price of privilege and exemption from the law, which doth not absolutely forbid the fact, but only to those that are not able to pay the money: except where the law is natural, or part of religion; for in that case it is not an exemption from the law, but a transgression of it. As where a law exacteth a pecuniary mulct, of them that take the name of God in vain, the payment of

the mulct, is not the price of a dispensation to swear, but the punishment of the transgression of a law indispensable. In like manner if the law impose a sum of money to be paid, to him that has been injured; this is but a satisfaction for the hurt done him; and extinguisheth the accusation of the party injured, not the crime of the offender.

Ignominy, is the infliction of such evil, as is made dishonourable; or the deprivation of such good, as is made honourable by the commonwealth. For there be some things honourable by nature; as the effects of courage, magnanimity, strength, wisdom, and other abilities of body and mind: others made honourable by the commonwealth; as badges, titles, offices, or any other singular mark of the sovereign's favour. The former, (though they may fail by nature, or accident,) cannot be taken away by a law; and therefore the loss of them is not punishment. But the latter, may be taken away by the public authority that made them honourable, and are properly punishments: such are degrading men condemned, of their badges, titles, and offices; or declaring them incapable of the like in time to come.

Imprisonment, is when a man is by public authority deprived of liberty; and may happen from two divers ends; whereof one is the safe custody of a man accused; the other is the inflicting of pain on a man condemned. The former is not punishment; because no man is supposed to be punished, before he be judicially heard, and declared guilty. And therefore whatsoever hurt a man is made to suffer by bonds, or restraint, before his cause be heard, over and above that which is necessary to assure his custody, is against the law of nature. But the latter is punishment, because evil, and inflicted by public authority, for somewhat that has by the same authority been judged a transgression of the law. Under this word imprisonment, I comprehend all restraint of motion, caused by an external obstacle, be it a house, which is called by the general name of a prison; or an island, as when men are said to be confined to it; or a place where men are set to work, as in old time men have been condemned to quarries, and in these times to galleys; or be it a chain, or any other such impediment.

Exile (banishment) is when a man is for a crime, condemned to depart out of the dominion of the commonwealth, or out of a certain part thereof; and during a prefixed time, or for ever, not to return into it: and seemeth not in its own nature, without other circumstances, to be a punishment; but rather an escape, or a public commandment to avoid punishment by flight. And *Cicero* says, there was never any such punishment ordained in the city of *Rome*; but calls it a refuge of men in danger. For if a man banished, be nevertheless permitted to enjoy his goods, and the revenue of his lands, the mere change of air is no punishment; nor does it tend to that benefit of the commonwealth, for which all punishments are ordained, (that is to say, to the forming of men's wills to the observation of the law;) but many times to the damage of the commonwealth. For a banished man, is a lawful enemy of the commonwealth that banished him; as being no more a member of the same. But if he be withal deprived of his lands, or goods, then the punishment lieth not in the exile, but is to be reckoned amongst punishments pecuniary.

All punishments of innocent subjects, be they great or little, are against the law of nature: For punishment is only for transgression of the law, and therefore there can be no punishment of the innocent. It is therefore a violation, first, of that law of nature, which forbiddeth all men, in their revenges, to look at any thing but some future good: For there can arrive no good to the commonwealth, by punishing the innocent. Secondly, of that, which forbiddeth ingratitude: For seeing all sovereign power, is originally given by the consent of every one of the subjects, to the end they should as long as they are obedient, be protected thereby; the punishment of the innocent, is a rendering of evil for good. And thirdly, of the law that commandeth equity; that is to say, an equal distribution of justice; which in punishing the innocent is not observed.

But the infliction of what evil soever, on an innocent man, that is not a subject, if it be for the benefit of the commonwealth, and without violation of any former covenant, is no breach of the law of nature. For all men that are not subjects, are either enemies, or else they have ceased from being so by some precedent covenants. But against enemies, whom the commonwealth judgeth capable to do them hurt, it is lawful by the original right of nature to make war; wherein the sword judgeth not, nor doth the victor make distinction of nocent, and innocent, as to the

time past; nor has other respect of mercy, than as it conduceth to the good of his own people. And upon this ground it is, that also in subjects, who deliberately deny the authority of the commonwealth established, the vengeance is lawfully extended, not only to the fathers, but also to the third and fourth generation not yet in being, and consequently innocent of the fact, for which they are afflicted: because the nature of this offence, consisteth in the renouncing of subjection; which is a relapse into the condition of war, commonly called rebellion; and they that so offend, suffer not as subjects, but as enemies. For *rebellion*, is but war renewed.

Reward, is either of *gift*, or by *contract*. When by contract, it is called *salary*, and *wages*; which is benefit due for service performed, or promised. When of gift, it is benefit proceeding from the *grace* of them that bestow it, to encourage, or enable men to do them service. And therefore when the sovereign of a commonwealth appointeth a salary to any public office, he that receiveth it, is bound in justice to perform his office; otherwise, he is bound only in honour, to acknowledgment, and an endeavour of requital. For though men have no lawful remedy, when they be commanded to quit their private business, to serve the public, without reward or salary; yet they are not bound thereto, by the law of nature, nor by the institution of the commonwealth, unless the service cannot otherwise be done; because it is supposed the sovereign may make use of all their means, insomuch as the most common soldier, may demand the wages of his warfare, as a debt.

The benefits which a sovereign bestoweth on a subject, for fear of some power, and ability he hath to do hurt to the commonwealth, are not properly rewards; for they are not salaries; because there is in this case no contract supposed, every man being obliged already not to do the commonwealth disservice: nor are they graces; because they be extorted by fear, which ought not to be incident to the sovereign power: but are rather sacrifices, which the sovereign (considered in his natural person, and not in the person of the commonwealth) makes, for the appeasing the discontent of him he thinks more potent than himself; and encourage not to obedience, but on the contrary, to the continuance, and increasing of further extortion.

And whereas some salaries are certain, and proceed from the public treasure; and others uncertain, and casual, proceeding from the execution of the office for which the salary is ordained; the latter is in some cases hurtful to the commonwealth; as in the case of judicature. For where the benefit of the judges, and ministers of a court of justice, ariseth for the multitude of causes that are brought to their cognizance, there must needs follow two inconveniences: one, is the nourishing of suits; for the more suits, the greater benefit: and another that depends on that, which is contention about jurisdiction; each court drawing to itself, as many causes as it can. But in offices of execution there are not those inconveniences; because their employment cannot be increased by any endeavour of their own. And thus much shall suffice for the nature of punishment and reward; which are, as it were, the nerves and tendons, that move the limbs and joints of a commonwealth.

Hitherto I have set forth the nature of man, (whose pride and other passions have compelled him to submit himself to government;) together with the great power of his governor, whom I compared to *Leviathan*, taking that comparison out of the two last verses of the one and fortieth of *Job*; where God having set forth the great power of *Leviathan*, calleth him king of the proud. *There is nothing*, saith he, *on earth, to be compared with him. He is made so as not to be afraid. He seeth every high thing below him; and is king of all the children of pride.* But because he is mortal, and subject to decay, as all other earthly creatures are; and because there is that in heaven, (though not on earth) that he should stand in fear of, and whose laws he ought to obey; I shall in the next following chapters speak of his diseases, and the causes of his mortality; and of what laws of nature he is bound to obey.

Chapter 29

Of Those Things That Weaken, or Tend to the Dissolution of a Commonwealth

Though nothing can be immortal, which mortals make; yet, if men had the use of reason they pretend to, their commonwealths might be secured, at least,

from perishing by internal diseases. For by the nature of their institution, they are designed to live, as long as mankind, or as the laws of nature, or as justice itself, which gives them life. Therefore when they come to be dissolved, not by external violence, but intestine disorder, the fault is not in men, as they are the *matter*; but as they are the *makers*, and orderers of them. For men, as they become at last weary of irregular jostling, and hewing one another, and desire with all their hearts, to conform themselves into one firm and lasting edifice; so for want, both of the art of making fit laws, to square their actions by, and also of humility, and patience, to suffer the rude and cumbersome points of their present greatness to be taken off, they cannot without the help of a very able architect, be compiled, into any other than a crazy building, such as hardly lasting out their own time, must assuredly fall upon the heads of their posterity.

Amongst the *infirmities* therefore of a commonwealth, I will reckon in the first place, those that arise from an imperfect institution, and resemble the diseases of a natural body, which proceed from a defectuous procreation.

Of which, this is one, *that a man to obtain a kingdom, is sometimes content with less power, than to the peace, and defence of the commonwealth is necessarily required.* From whence it cometh to pass, that when the exercise of the power laid by, is for the public safety to be resumed, it hath the resemblance of an unjust act; which disposeth great numbers of men (when occasion is presented) to rebel; in the same manner as the bodies of children, gotten by diseased parents, are subject either to untimely death, or to purge the ill quality, derived from their vicious conception, by breaking out into biles and scabs. And when kings deny themselves some such necessary power, it is not always (though sometimes), out of ignorance of what is necessary to the office they undertake; but many times out of a hope to recover the same again at their pleasure: Wherein they reason not well; because such as will hold them to their promises, shall be maintained against them by foreign commonwealths; who in order to the good of their own subjects let slip few occasions to *weaken* the estate of their neighbours. So was *Thomas Becket*, archbishop of *Canterbury*, supported against *Henry* the Second, by the Pope; the subjection of ecclesiastics to the commonwealth, having been dispensed with by *William the Conqueror* at his reception, when he took an oath, not to infringe the liberty of the church. And so were the *barons*, whose power was by *William Rufus* (to have their help in transferring the succession from his elder brother, to himself,) increased to a degree, inconsistent with the sovereign power, maintained in their rebellion against *King John*, by the French.

Nor does this happen in monarchy only. For whereas the style of the ancient Roman commonwealth, was, *the senate, and people of Rome*; neither senate, nor people pretended to the whole power; which first caused the seditions, of *Tiberius Gracchus, Caius Gracchus, Lucius Saturninus*, and others; and afterwards the wars between the senate and the people, under *Marius* and *Sylla*; and again under *Pompey* and *Caesar*, to the extinction of their democracy, and the setting up of monarchy.

The people of *Athens* bound themselves but from one only action; which was, that no man on pain of death should propound the renewing of the war for the island of *Salamis*; and yet thereby, if *Solon* had not caused to be given out he was mad, and afterwards in gesture and habit of a madman, and in verse, propounded it to the people that flocked about him, they had had an enemy perpetually in readiness, even at the gates of their city; such damage, or shifts, are all commonwealths forced to, that have their power never so little limited.

In the second place, I observe the *diseases* of a commonwealth, that proceed from the poison of seditious doctrines, whereof one is, *That every private man is judge of good and evil actions*. This is true in the condition of mere nature, where there are no civil laws; and also under civil government, in such cases as are not determined by the law. But otherwise, it is manifest, that the measure of good and evil actions, is the civil law; and the judge the legislator, who is always representative of the commonwealth. From this false doctrine, men are disposed to debate with themselves, and dispute the commands of the commonwealth; and afterwards to obey, or disobey them, as in their private judgments they shall think fit. Whereby the commonwealth is distracted and *weakened*.

Another doctrine repugnant to civil society, is, that

whatsoever a man does against his conscience, is sin; and it dependeth on the presumption of making himself judge of good and evil. For a man's conscience, and his judgment is the same thing; and as the judgment, so also the conscience may be erroneous. Therefore, though he that is subject to no civil law, sinneth in all he does against his conscience, because he has no other rule to follow but his own reason; yet it is not so with him that lives in a commonwealth; because the law is the public conscience, by which he hath already undertaken to be guided. Otherwise in such diversity, as there is of private consciences, which are but private opinions, the commonwealth must needs be distracted, and no man dare to obey the sovereign power, farther than it shall seem good in his own eyes.

It hath been also commonly taught, *that faith and sanctity, are not to be attained by study and reason, but by supernatural inspiration, or infusion*, which granted, I see not why any man should render a reason of his faith; or why every Christian should not be also a prophet; or why any man should take the law of his country, rather than his own inspiration, for the rule of his action. And thus we fall again into the fault of taking upon us to judge of good and evil; or to make judges of it, such private men as pretend to be supernaturally inspired, to the dissolution of all civil government. Faith comes by hearing, and hearing by those accidents, which guide us into the presence of them that speak to us; which accidents are all contrived by God Almighty; and yet are not supernatural, but only, for the great number of them that concur to every effect, unobservable. Faith and sanctity, are indeed not very frequent; but yet they are not miracles, but brought to pass by education, discipline, correction, and other natural ways, by which God worketh them in his elect, at such time as he thinketh fit. And these three opinions, pernicious to peace and government, have in this part of the world, proceeded chiefly from the tongues, and pens of unlearned divines; who joining the words of Holy Scripture together, otherwise than is agreeable to reason, do what they can, to make men think, that sanctity and natural reason, cannot stand together.

A fourth opinion, repugnant to the nature of a commonwealth, is this, *that he that hath the sovereign power, is subject to the civil laws*. It is true, that sovereigns are all subject to the laws of nature; because such laws be divine, and cannot by any man, or commonwealth be abrogated. But to those laws which the sovereign himself, that is, which the commonwealth maketh, he is not subject. For to be subject to laws, is to be subject to the commonwealth, that is to the sovereign representative, that is to himself; which is not subjection, but freedom from the laws. Which error, because it setteth the laws above the sovereign, setteth also a judge above him, and a power to punish him; which is to make a new sovereign; and again for the same reason a third, to punish the second; and so continually without end, to the confusion, and dissolution of the commonwealth.

A fifth doctrine, that tendeth to the dissolution of a commonwealth, is, *that every private man has an absolute propriety in his goods; such, as excludeth the right of the sovereign.* Every man has indeed a propriety that excludes the right of every other subject: and he has it only from the sovereign power; without the protection whereof, every other man should have equal right to the same. But if the right of the sovereign also be excluded, he cannot perform the office they have put him into; which is, to defend them both from foreign enemies, and from the injuries of one another; and consequently there is no longer a commonwealth.

And if the propriety of subjects, exclude not the right of the sovereign representative to their goods; much less to their offices of judicature, or execution, in which they represent the sovereign himself.

There is a sixth doctrine, plainly, and directly against the essence of a commonwealth; and it is this, *that the sovereign power may be divided.* For what is it to divide the power of a commonwealth, but to dissolve it, for powers divided mutually destroy each other. And for these doctrines, men are chiefly beholding to some of those, that making profession of the laws, endeavour to make them depend upon their own learning, and not upon the legislative power.

And as false doctrine, so also oftentimes the example of different government in a neighbouring nation, disposeth men to alteration of the form already settled. So the people of the Jews were stirred up to reject God, and to call upon the prophet *Samuel,* for a king after the manner of the nations: so also the lesser cities of *Greece,* were continually disturbed, with sedi-

tions of the aristocratical, and democratical factions; one part of almost every commonwealth, desiring to imitate the Lacedemonians; the other, the Athenians. And I doubt not, but many men, have been contented to see the late troubles in *England,* out of an imitation of the Low Countries; supposing there needed no more to grow rich, than to change, as they had done, the form of their government. For the constitution of man's nature, is of itself subject to desire novelty: When therefore they are provoked to the same, by the neighbourhood also of those that have been enriched by it, it is almost impossible for them, not to be content with those that solicit them to change; and love the first beginnings, though they be grieved with the continuance of disorder; like hot bloods, that having gotten the itch, tear themselves with their own nails, till they can endure the smart no longer.

And as to rebellion in particular against monarchy; one of the most frequent causes of it, is the reading of the books of policy, and histories of the ancient Greeks, and Romans; from which, young men, and all others that are unprovided of the antidote of solid reason, receiving a strong, and delightful impression, of the great exploits of war, achieved by the conductors of their armies, receive withal a pleasing idea, of all they have done besides; and imagine their great prosperity, not to have proceeded from the emulation of particular men, but from the virtue of their popular form of government: not considering the frequent seditions, and civil wars, produced by the imperfection of their policy. From the reading, I say, of such books, men have undertaken to kill their kings, because the Greek and Latin writers, in their books and discourses of policy, make it lawful, and laudable, for any man so to do; provided, before he do it, he call him tyrant. For they say not *regicide,* that is, killing of a king, but *tyrannicide,* that is, killing of a tyrant is lawful. From the same books, they that live under a monarch conceive an opinion, that the subjects in a popular commonwealth enjoy liberty; but that in a monarchy they are all slaves. I say, they that live under a monarchy conceive such an opinion; not they that live under a popular government: for they find no such matter. In sum, I cannot imagine, how any thing can be more prejudicial to a monarchy, than the allowing of such books to be publicly read, without present applying such correctives of discreet masters, as are fit to take away their venom: which venom I will not doubt to compare to the biting of a mad dog, which is a disease the physicians call *hydrophobia*, or *fear of water*. For as he that is so bitten, has a continual torment of thirst, and yet abhorreth water; and is in such an estate, as if the poison endeavoured to convert him into a dog: so when a monarchy is once bitten to the quick, by those democratical writers, that continually snarl at that estate; it wanteth nothing more than a strong monarch, which nevertheless out of a certain *tyrannophobia*, or fear of being strongly governed, when they have him, they abhor.

As there have been doctors, that hold there be three souls in a man; so there be also that think there may be more souls, (that is, more sovereigns,) than one, in a commonwealth; and set up a *supremacy* against the *sovereignty*; *canons* against *laws*; and a *ghostly authority* against the *civil*; working on men's minds, with words and distinctions, that of themselves signify nothing, but bewray (by their obscurity) that there walketh (as some think invisibly) another kingdom, as it were a kingdom of fairies, in the dark. Now seeing it is manifest, that the civil power, and the power of the commonwealth is the same thing; and that supremacy, and the power of making canons, and granting faculties, implieth a commonwealth; it followeth, that where one is sovereign, another supreme; where one can make laws, and another make canons; there must needs be two commonwealths, of one and the same subjects; which is a kingdom divided in itself, and cannot stand. For notwithstanding the insignificant distinction of *temporal*, and *ghostly*, they are still two kingdoms, and every subject is subject to two masters. For seeing the *ghostly* power challengeth the right to declare what is sin it challengeth by consequence to declare what is law, (sin being nothing but the transgression of the law;) and again, the civil power challenging to declare what is law, every subject must obey two masters, who both will have their commands be observed as law; which is impossible. Or, if it be but one kingdom, either the *civil*, which is the power of the commonwealth, must be subordinate to the *ghostly*, and then there is no sovereignty but the *ghostly*; or the *ghostly* must be subordinate to the *temporal*, and then there is no *supremacy* but the *temporal*. When therefore

these two powers oppose one another, the commonwealth cannot but be in great danger of civil war, and dissolution. For the *civil* authority being more visible, and standing in the clearer light of natural reason, cannot choose but draw to it in all times a very considerable part of the people: and the *spiritual*, though it stand in the darkness of School distinctions, and hard words; yet because the fear of darkness, and ghosts, is greater than other fears, cannot want a party sufficient to trouble, and sometimes to destroy a commonwealth, and this is a disease which not unfitly may be compared to the epilepsy, or falling sickness (which the Jews took to be one kind of possession by spirits) in the body natural. For as in this disease, there is an unnatural spirit, or wind in the head that obstructeth the roots of the nerves, and moving them violently, taketh away the motion which naturally they should have from the power of the soul in the brain, and thereby causeth violent, and irregular motions (which men call convulsions) in the parts; insomuch as he that is seized therewith, falleth down sometimes into the water, and sometimes into the fire, as a man deprived of his senses; so also in the body politic, when the spiritual power, moveth the members of a commonwealth, by the terror of punishments, and hope of rewards (which are the nerves of it,) otherwise than by the civil power (which is the soul of the commonwealth), they ought to be moved; and by strange, and hard words suffocates their understanding, it must needs thereby distract the people, and either overwhelm the commonwealth with oppression, or cast it into the fire of a civil war.

Sometimes also in the merely civil government, there be more than one soul: as when the power of levying money, (which is the nutritive faculty,) has depended on a general assembly; the power of conduct and command, (which is the motive faculty,) on one man; and the power of making laws, (which is the rational faculty,) on the accidental consent, not only of those two, but also of a third; this endangereth the commonwealth, sometimes for want of consent to good laws; but most often for want of such nourishment, as is necessary to life, and motion. For although few perceive, that such government, is not government, but division of the commonwealth into three factions, and call it mixed monarchy; yet the truth is, that it is not one independent commonwealth, but three independent factions; nor one representative person, but three. In the kingdom of God, there may be three persons independent, without breach of unity in God that reigneth; but where men reign, that be subject to diversity of opinions, it cannot be so. And therefore if the king bear the person of the people, and the general assembly bear also the person of the people, and another assembly bear the person of a part of the people, they are not one person, nor one sovereign, but three persons, and three sovereigns.

To what disease in the natural body of man I may exactly compare this irregularity of a commonwealth, I know not. But I have seen a man, that had another man growing out of his side, with an head, arms, breast, and stomach, of his own: if he had had another man growing out of his other side, the comparison might then have been exact.

Hitherto I have named such diseases of a commonwealth, as are of the greatest, and most present danger. There be other, not so great; which nevertheless are not unfit to be observed. As first, the difficulty of raising money, for the necessary uses of the commonwealth; especially in the approach of war. This difficulty ariseth from the opinion, that every subject hath of a propriety in his lands and goods, exclusive of the sovereign's right to the use of the same. From whence it cometh to pass, that the sovereign power, which foreseeth the necessities and dangers of the commonwealth, (finding the passage of money to the public treasure obstructed, by the tenacity of the people,) whereas it ought to extend itself, to encounter, and prevent such dangers in their beginnings, contracteth itself as long as it can, and when it cannot longer, struggles with the people by stratagems of law, to obtain little sums, which not sufficing, he is fain at last violently to open the way for present supply, or perish; and being put often to these extremities, at last reduceth the people to their due temper; or else the commonwealth must perish. Insomuch as we may compare this distemper very aptly to an ague; wherein, the fleshy parts being congealed, or by venomous matter obstructed; the veins which by their natural course empty themselves into the heart, are not (as they ought to be) supplied from the arteries, whereby there succeedeth at first a cold contraction, and trembling of the limbs; and afterwards a hot, and strong endeavour of the heart, to force a passage for the blood; and before it can do that, contenteth itself with the small refreshments of such things as cool for a time, till (if nature be strong enough), it break at last the contumacy of the parts obstructed, and dissipateth the venom into sweat; or (if nature be too weak) the patient dieth.

Again, there is sometimes in a commonwealth, a disease, which resembleth the pleurisy; and that is, when the treasure of the commonwealth, flowing out of its due course, is gathered together in too much abundance in one, or a few private men, by monopolies, or by farms of the public revenues; in the same manner as the blood in a pleurisy, getting into the membrane of the breast, breedeth there an inflammation, accompanied with a fever, and painful stitches.

Also the popularity of a potent subject, (unless the commonwealth have very good caution of his fidelity,) is a dangerous disease; because the people (which should receive their motion from the authority of the sovereign,) by the flattery, and by the reputation of an ambitious man, are drawn away from their obedience to the laws, to follow a man, of whose virtues, and designs they have no knowledge. And this is commonly of more danger in a popular government, than in a monarchy; because an army is of so great force, and multitude, as it may easily be made believe, they are the people. By this means it was, that *Julius Caesar*, who was set up by the people against the senate, having won to himself the affections of his army, made himself master, both of senate and people. And this proceeding of popular, and ambitious men, is plain rebellion; and may be resembled to the effects of witchcraft.

Another infirmity of a commonwealth, is the immoderate greatness of a town, when it is able to furnish out of its own circuit, the number, and expense of a great army: as also the great number of corporations; which are as it were many lesser commonwealths in the bowels of a greater, like worms in the entrails of a natural man. To which may be added, the liberty of disputing against absolute power, by pretenders to political prudence; which though bred for the most part in the lees of the people; yet animated by false doctrines, are perpetually meddling with the fundamental laws, to the molestation of the commonwealth; like the little worms, which physicians call *ascarides*.

We may further add, the insatiable appetite, or Bulimia, of enlarging dominion; with the incurable *wounds* thereby many times received from the enemy; and the *wens*, of ununited conquests, which are many times a burthen, and with less danger lost, than kept; as also the *lethargy* of ease, and *consumption* of riot and vain expense.

Lastly, when in a war (foreign or intestine,) the enemies get a final victory; so as (the forces of the commonwealth keeping the field no longer), there is no farther protection of subjects in their loyalty; then is the commonwealth DISSOLVED, and every man at liberty to protect himself by such courses as his own discretion shall suggest unto him. For the sovereign, is the public soul, giving life and motion to the commonwealth; which expiring, the members are governed by it no more, than the carcase of a man, by his departed (though immortal) soul. For though the right of a sovereign monarch cannot be extinguished by the act of another; yet the obligation of the members may. For he that wants protection, may seek it any where; and when he hath it, is obliged (without fraudulent pretence of having submitted himself out of fear,) to protect his protection as long as he is able. But when the power of an assembly is once suppressed, the right of the same perisheth utterly; because the assembly itself is extinct; and consequently, there is no possibility for the sovereignty to reenter.

Chapter 30

Of the Office of the Sovereign Representative

The office of the sovereign, (be it a monarch, or an assembly,) consisteth in the end, for which he was trusted with the sovereign power, namely the procuration of *the safety of the people*; to which he is obliged by the law of nature, and to render an account thereof to God, the author of that law, and to none but him. But by safety here, is not meant a bare preservation, but also all other contentments of life, which every man by lawful industry, without danger, or hurt to the commonwealth, shall acquire to himself.

And this is intended should be done, not by care applied to individuals, further than their protection from injuries, when they shall complain; but by a general providence, contained in public instruction, both of doctrine, and example; and in the making, and executing of good laws, to which individual persons may apply their own cases.

And because, if the essential rights of sovereignty (specified before in the eighteenth chapter) be taken away, the commonwealth is thereby dissolved, and every man returneth into the condition, and calamity of a war with every other man, (which is the greatest evil that can happen in this life;) it is the office of the sovereign, to maintain those rights entire; and consequently against his duty, first, to transfer to another, or to lay from himself any of them. For he that deserteth the means, deserteth the ends; and he deserteth the means, that being the sovereign, acknowledgeth himself subject to the civil laws; and renounceth the power of supreme judicature; or of making war, or peace by his own authority; or of judging of the necessities of the commonwealth; or of levying money, and soldiers, when, and as much as in his own conscience he shall judge necessary; or of making officers, and ministers both of war and peace; or of appointing teachers, and examining what doctrines are conformable, or contrary to the defence, peace, and good of the people. Secondly, it is against his duty, to let the people be ignorant, or misinformed of the grounds, and reasons of those his essential rights; because thereby men are easy to be seduced, and drawn to resist him, when the commonwealth shall require their use and exercise.

And the grounds of these rights, have the rather need to be diligently, and truly taught; because they cannot be maintained by any civil law, or terror of legal punishment. For a civil law, that shall forbid rebellion (and such is all resistance to the essential rights of sovereignty), is not (as a civil law) any obligation, but by virtue only of the law of nature, that forbiddeth the violation of faith; which natural obligation if men know not, they cannot know the right of any law the sovereign maketh. And for the punishment, they take it but for an act of hostility; which when they think they have strength enough, they will endeavour by acts of hostility, to avoid.

As I have heard some say, that justice is but a word, without substance; and that whatsoever a man can by force, or art, acquire to himself (not only in the condition of war, but also in a commonwealth,) is his own, which I have already showed to be false: so there be also that maintain, that there are no grounds, nor principles of reason, to sustain those essential rights, which make sovereignty absolute. For if there were, they would have been found out in some place, or other; whereas we see, there has not hitherto been any commonwealth, where those rights have been acknowledged, or challenged. Wherein they argue as ill, as if the savage people of America, should deny there were any grounds, or principles of reason, so to build a house, as to last as long as the materials, because they never yet saw any so well built. Time, and industry, produce every day new knowledge. And as the art of well building, is derived from principles of reason, observed by industrious men, that had long studied the nature of materials, and the divers effects of figure, and proportion, long after mankind began (though poorly) to build: so, long time after men have begun to constitute commonwealths, imperfect, and apt to relapse into disorder, there may principles of reason be found out, by industrious meditation, to make their constitution (excepting by external violence) everlasting. And such are those which I have in this discourse set forth: which whether they come not into the sight of those that have power to make use of them, or be neglected by them, or not, concerneth my particular interest, at this day, very little. But supposing that these of mine are not such principles of reason; yet I am sure they are principles from authority of Scripture; as I shall make it appear, when I shall come to speak of the kingdom of God, (administered by *Moses*,) over the Jews, his peculiar people by covenant.

But they say again, that though the principles be right, yet common people are not of capacity enough to be made to understand them. I should be glad, that the rich, and potent subjects of a kingdom, or those that are accounted the most learned, were no less incapable than they. But all men know, that the obstructions to this kind of doctrine, proceed not so much from the difficulty of the matter, as from the interest of them that are to learn. Potent men, digest hardly any thing that setteth up a power to bridle their affections; and learned men, any thing that discovereth their errors, and thereby lesseneth their authority: whereas the common people's minds, unless they be tainted with dependance on the potent, or scribbled over with the opinions of their doctors, are like clean paper, fit to receive whatsoever by public authority shall be imprinted in them. Shall whole nations be brought to *acquiesce* in the great mysteries of Christian religion, which are above reason; and millions of men be made believe, that the same body may be in innumerable places, at one and the same time, which is against reason; and shall not men be able, by their teaching, and preaching, protected by the law, to make that received, which is so consonant to reason, that any unprejudicated man, needs no more to learn it, than to hear it? I conclude therefore, that in the instruction of the people in the essential rights (which are the natural, and fundamental laws) of sovereignty, there is no difficulty, (whilst a sovereign has his power entire,) but what proceeds from his own fault, or the fault of those whom he trusteth in the administration of the commonwealth; and consequently, it is his duty, to cause them so to be instructed; and not only his duty, but his benefit also, and security, against the danger that may arrive to himself in his natural person, from rebellion.

And (to descend to particulars) the people are to be taught, first, that they ought not to be in love with any form of government they see in their neighbour nations, more than with their own, nor, (whatsoever present prosperity they behold in nations that are otherwise governed than they,) to desire change. For the prosperity of a people ruled by an aristocratical, or democratical assembly, cometh not from aristocracy, nor from democracy, but from the obedience, and concord of the subjects: nor do the people flourish in a monarchy, because one man has the right to rule them, but because they obey him. Take away in any kind of state, the obedience, (and consequently the concord of the people,) and they shall not only not flourish, but in short time be dissolved. And they that go about by disobedience, to do no more than reform the commonwealth, shall find they do thereby destroy it; like the foolish daughters of *Peleus*, (in the fable;) which desiring to renew the youth of their decrepid father, did by the counsel of *Medea*, cut him in pieces, and boil him, together with strange herbs, but made not of him a new man. This desire of change, is like the breach of the first of God's commandments: for there God says, *Non habebis*

Deos alienos; Thou shalt not have the Gods of other nations; and in another place concerning *kings*, that they are *Gods*.

Secondly, they are to be taught, that they ought not to be led with admiration of the virtue of any of their fellow subjects, how high soever he stand, nor how conspicuously soever he shine in the commonwealth; nor of any assembly, (except the sovereign assembly,) so as to defer to them any obedience, or honour, appropriate to the sovereign only, whom (in their particular stations) they represent; nor to receive any influence from them, but such as is conveyed by them from the sovereign authority. For that sovereign, cannot be imagined to love his people as he ought, that is not jealous of them, but suffers them by the flattery of popular men, to be seduced from their loyalty, as they have often been, not only secretly, but openly, so as to proclaim marriage with them *in facie ecclesiciae* by preachers; and by publishing the same in the open streets: which may fitly be compared to the violation of the second of the ten commandments.

Thirdly, in consequence to this, they ought to be informed, how great a fault it is, to speak evil of the sovereign representative, (whether one man, or an assembly of men;) or to argue and dispute his power; or any way to use his name irreverently, whereby he may be brought into contempt with his people, and their obedience (in which the safety of the commonwealth consisteth) slackened. Which doctrine the third commandment by resemblance pointeth to.

Fourthly, seeing people cannot be taught this, nor when it is taught, remember it, nor after one generation past, so much as know in whom the sovereign power is placed, without setting apart from their ordinary labour, some certain times, in which they may attend those that are appointed to instruct them; it is necessary that some such times be determined, wherein they may assemble together, and (after prayers and praises given to God, the sovereign of sovereigns) hear those their duties told them, and the positive laws, such as generally concern them all, read and expounded, and be put in mind of the authority that maketh them laws. To this end had the *Jews* every seventh day, a *sabbath*, in which the law was read and expounded; and in the solemnity whereof they were put in mind, that their king was God; that having created the world in six days, he

rested the seventh day; and by their resting on it from their labour, that that God was their king, which redeemed them from their servile, and painful labour in *Egypt*, and gave them a time, after they had rejoiced in God, to take joy also in themselves, by lawful recreation. So that the first table of the commandments, is spent all in setting down the sum of God's absolute power; not only as God, but as king by pact, (in peculiar) of the Jews; and may therefore give light, to those that have sovereign power conferred on them by the consent of men, to see what doctrine they ought to teach their subjects.

And because the first instruction of children, dependeth on the care of their parents; it is necessary that they should be obedient to them, whilst they are under their tuition; and not only so, but that also afterwards (as gratitude requireth,) they acknowledge the benefit of their education, by external signs of honour. To which end they are to be taught, that originally the father of every man was also his sovereign lord, with power over him of life and death; and that the fathers of families, when by instituting a commonwealth, they resigned that absolute power, yet it was never intended, they should lose the honour due unto them for their education. For to relinquish such right, was not necessary to the institution of sovereign power; nor would there be any reason, why any man should desire to have children, or take the care to nourish, and instruct them, if they were afterwards to have no other benefit from them, than from other men. And this accordeth with the fifth commandment.

Again, every sovereign ought to cause justice to be taught, which (consisting in taking from no man what is his,) is as much as to say, to cause men to be taught not to deprive their neighbours, by violence, or fraud, of any thing which by the sovereign authority is theirs. Of things held in propriety, those that are dearest to a man are his own life, and limbs; and in the next degree (in most men,) those that concern conjugal affection; and after them riches and means of living. Therefore the people are to be taught, to abstain from violence to one another's person, by private revenges; from violation of conjugal honour; and from forcible rapine, and fraudulent surreption of one another's goods. For which purpose also it is necessary they be showed the evil consequences of false judgment, by corruption either of judges or witnesses, whereby the distinction of propriety is taken away, and justice becomes of no effect: all which things are intimated in the sixth, seventh, eighth, and ninth commandments.

Lastly, they are to be taught, that not only the unjust facts, but the designs and intentions to do them, (though by accident hindered,) are injustice; which consisteth in the pravity of the will, as well as in the irregularity of the act. And this is the intention of the tenth commandment, and the sum of the second table; which is reduced all to this one commandment of mutual charity, *thou shalt love thy neighbour as thyself:* as the sum of the first table is reduced to *the love of God;* whom they had then newly received as their king.

As for the means, and conduits, by which the people may receive this instruction, we are to search, by what means so many opinions, contrary to the peace of mankind, upon weak and false principles, have nevertheless been so deeply rooted in them. I mean those, which I have in the precedent chapter specified: as that men shall judge of what is lawful and unlawful, not by the law itself, but by their own consciences; that is to say, by their own private judgments: that subjects sin in obeying the commands of the commonwealth, unless they themselves have first judged them to be lawful: that their propriety in their riches is such, as to exclude the dominion, which the commonwealth hath over the same: that it is lawful for subjects to kill such, as they call tyrants: that the sovereign power may be divided, and the like; which come to be instilled into the people by this means. They whom necessity, or covetousness keepeth attent on their trades, and labour; and they, on the other side, whom superfluity, or sloth carrieth after their sensual pleasures, (which two sorts of men take up the greatest part of mankind,) being diverted from the deep meditation, which the learning of truth, not only in the matter of natural justice, but also of all other sciences necessarily requireth, receive the notions of their duty, chiefly from divines in the pulpit, and partly from such of their neighbours, or familiar acquaintance, as having the faculty of discoursing readily, and plausibly, seem wiser and better learned in cases of law, and conscience, than themselves. And the divines, and such others as make show of learning, derive their knowledge from the universities, and from the schools of law, or from the books, which by men eminent in those schools, and universities have been published. It is therefore manifest, that the instruction of the people, dependeth wholly, on the right teaching of youth in the universities. But are not (may some man say) the universities of *England* learned enough already to do that? or is it you will undertake to teach the universities? Hard questions. Yet to the first, I doubt not to answer; that till towards the latter end of *Henry the Eighth*, the power of the Pope, was always upheld against the power of the commonwealth, principally by the universities; and that the doctrines maintained by so many preachers, against the sovereign power of the king, and by so many lawyers, and others, that had their education there, is a sufficient argument, that though the universities were not authors of those false doctrines, yet they knew not how to plant the true. For in such a contradiction of opinions, it is most certain, that they have not been sufficiently instructed; and it is no wonder, if they yet retain a relish of that subtle liquor, wherewith they were first seasoned, against the civil authority. But to the latter question, it is not fit, nor needful for me to say either aye, or no: for any man that sees what I am doing, may easily perceive what I think.

The safety of the people, requireth further, from him, or them that have the sovereign power, that justice be equally administered to all degrees of people; that is, that as well the rich and mighty, as poor and obscure persons, may be righted of the injuries done them; so as the great, may have no greater hope of impunity, when they do violence, dishonour, or any injury to the meaner sort, than when one of these, does the like to one of them: For in this consisteth equity; to which, as being a precept of the law of nature, a sovereign is as much subject, as any of the meanest of his people. All breaches of the law, are offences against the commonwealth: but there be some, that are also against private persons. Those that concern the commonwealth only, may without breach of equity be pardoned; for every man may pardon what is done against himself, according to his own discretion. But an offence against a private man, cannot in equity be pardoned, without the consent of him that is injured; or reasonable satisfaction.

The inequality of subjects, proceedeth from the acts of sovereign power; and therefore has no more place in the presence of the sovereign; that is to say, in a court of justice, than the inequality between kings, and their subjects, in the presence of the King of kings. The honour of great persons, is to be valued for their beneficence and the aids they give to men of inferior rank, or not at all. And the violences, oppressions, and injuries they do, are not extenuated, but aggravated by the greatness of their persons; because they have least need to commit them. The consequences of this partiality towards the great, proceed in this manner. Impunity maketh insolence; insolence hatred; and hatred, an endeavour to pull down all oppressing and contumelious greatness, though with the ruin of the commonwealth.

To equal justice, appertaineth also the equal imposition of taxes; the equality whereof dependeth not on the equality of riches, but on the equality of the debt, that every man oweth to the commonwealth for his defence. It is not enough, for a man to labour for the maintenance of his life; but also to fight, (if need be,) for the securing of his labour. They must either do as the Jews did after their return from captivity, in re-edifying the temple, build with one hand, and hold the sword in the other; or else they must hire others to fight for them. For the impositions, that are laid on the people by the sovereign power, are nothing else but the wages, due to them that hold the public sword, to defend private men in the exercise of several trades, and callings. Seeing then the benefit that every one receiveth thereby, is the enjoyment of life, which is equally dear to poor and rich; the debt which a poor man oweth them that defend his life, is the same which a rich man oweth for the defence of his; saving that the rich, who have the service of the poor, may be debtors not only for their own persons, but for many more. Which considered, the equality of imposition, consisteth rather in the equality of that which is consumed, than of the riches of the persons that consume the same. For what reason is there, that he which laboureth much, and sparing the fruits of his labour, consumeth little, should be more charged, than he that living idly, getteth little, and spendeth all he gets; seeing the one hath no more protection from the commonwealth, than the other? But when the impositions, are laid upon those things which men consume, every man payeth equally for what he useth: nor

is the commonwealth defrauded by the luxurious waste of private men.

And whereas many men, by accident inevitable, become unable to maintain themselves by their labour; they ought not to be left to the charity of private persons; but to be provided for, (as far-forth as the necessities of nature require,) by the laws of the commonwealth. For as it is uncharitableness in any man, to neglect the impotent; so it is in the sovereign of a commonwealth, to expose them to the hazard of such uncertain charity.

But for such as have strong bodies, the case is otherwise: they are to be forced to work; and to avoid the excuse of not finding employment, there ought to be such laws, as may encourage all manner of arts; as navigation, agriculture, fishing, and all manner of manufacture that requires labour. The multitude of poor, and yet strong people still increasing, they are to be transplanted into countries not sufficiently inhabited: where nevertheless, they are not to exterminate those they find there; but constrain them to inhabit closer together, and not range a great deal of ground, to snatch what they find; but to court each little plot with art and labour, to give them their sustenance in due season. And when all the world is overcharged with inhabitants, then the last remedy of all is war; which provideth for every man, by victory, or death.

To the care of the sovereign, belongeth the making of good laws. But what is a good law? By a good law, I mean not a just law: for no law can be unjust. The law is made by the sovereign power, and all that is done by such power, is warranted, and owned by every one of the people; and that which every man will have so, no man can say is unjust. It is in the laws of a commonwealth, as in the laws of gaming: whatsoever the gamesters all agree on, is injustice to none of them. A good law is that, which is *needful*, for the *good of the people*, and withal *perspicuous*.

For the use of laws, (which are but rules authorized) is not to bind the people from all voluntary actions; but to direct and keep them in such a motion, as not to hurt themselves by their own impetuous desires, rashness, or indiscretion; as hedges are set, not to stop travellers, but to keep them in the way. And therefore a law that is not needful, having not the true end of a law, is not good. A law may be conceived to be good, when it is for the benefit of the sovereign; though it be not necessary for the people; but it is not so. For the good of the sovereign and people, cannot be separated. It is a weak sovereign, that has weak subjects; and a weak people, whose sovereign wanteth power to rule them at his will. Unnecessary laws are not good laws; but traps for money: which where the right of sovereign power is acknowledged, are superfluous; and where it is not acknowledged, insufficient to defend the people.

The perspicuity, consisteth not so much in the words of the law itself, as in a declaration of the causes, and motives, for which it was made. That is it, that shows us the meaning of the legislator; and the meaning of the legislator known, the law is more easily understood by few, than many words. For all words, are subject to ambiguity; and therefore multiplication of words in the body of the law, is multiplication of ambiguity: besides it seems to imply, (by too much diligence,) that whosoever can evade the words, is without the compass of the law. And this is a cause of many unnecessary processes. For when I consider how short were the laws of ancient times; and how they grew by degrees still longer; methinks I see a contention between the penners, and pleaders of the law; the former seeking to circumscribe the latter, and the latter to evade their circumscriptions; and that the pleaders have got the victory. It belongeth therefore to the office of a legislator, (such as is in all commonwealths the supreme representative, be it one man, or an assembly,) to make the reason perspicuous, why the law was made; and the body of the law itself, as short, but in as proper, and significant terms, as may be.

It belongeth also to the office of the sovereign, to make a right application of punishments, and rewards. And seeing the end of punishing is not revenge, and discharge of choler; but correction, either of the offender, or of others by his example; the severest punishments are to be inflicted for those crimes, that are of most danger to the public; such as are those which proceed from malice to the government established; those that spring from contempt of justice; those that provoke indignation in the multitude; and those, which unpunished seem authorized, as when they are committed by sons, servants, or favourites of men in authority: For indignation carrieth men, not only against the actors, and authors of injustice; but against all power that is likely to protect them; as in the case of *Tarquin*; when for the insolent act of one of his sons, he was driven out of *Rome*, and the monarchy itself dissolved. But crimes of infirmity; such as are those which proceed from great provocation, from great fear, great need, or from ignorance whether the fact be a great crime, or not, there is place many times for lenity, without prejudice to the commonwealth; and lenity when there is such place for it, is required by the law of nature. The punishment of the leaders, and teachers in a commotion; not the poor seduced people, when they are punished, can profit the commonwealth by their example. To be severe to the people, is to punish that ignorance, which may in great part be imputed to the sovereign, whose fault it was, they were no better instructed.

In like manner it belongeth to the office, and duty of the sovereign, to apply his rewards always so, as there may arise from them benefit to the commonwealth: wherein consisteth their use, and end; and is then done, when they that have well served the commonwealth, are with as little expense of the common treasure, as is possible, so well recompensed, as others thereby may be encouraged, both to serve the same as faithfully as they can, and to study the arts by which they may be enabled to do it better. To buy with money, or preferment, from a popular ambitious subject, to be quiet, and desist from making ill impressions in the minds of the people, has nothing of the nature of reward; (which is ordained not for disservice, but for service past;) nor a sign of gratitude, but of fear: nor does it tend to the benefit, but to the damage of the public. It is a contention with ambition, like that of *Hercules* with the monster *Hydra*, which having many heads, for every one that was vanquished, there grew up three. For in like manner, when the stubbornness of one popular man, is overcome with reward, there arise many more (by the example) that do the same mischief, in hope of like benefit: and as all sorts of manufacture, so also malice increaseth by being vendible. And though sometimes a civil war, may be deferred, by such ways as that, yet the danger grows still the greater, and the public ruin more assured. It is therefore against the duty of the sovereign, to whom the public safety is committed, to reward those that aspire to greatness by disturbing the peace of their country, and not rather to oppose the beginnings of such men, with a little danger, than after a longer time with greater.

Another business of the sovereign, is to choose good counsellors; I mean such, whose advice he is to take in the government of the commonwealth. For this word counsel, *consilium*, corrupted from *considium*, is of a large signification, and comprehendeth all assemblies of men that sit together, not only to deliberate what is to be done hereafter, but also to judge of facts past, and of law for the present. I take it here in the first sense only: and in this sense, there is no choice of counsel, neither in a democracy, nor aristocracy; because the persons counselling are members of the person counselled. The choice of counsellors therefore is proper to monarchy; in which, the sovereign that endeavoureth not to make choice of those, that in every kind are the most able, dischargeth not his office as he ought to do. The most able counsellors, are they that have least hope of benefit by giving evil counsel, and most knowledge of those things that conduce to the peace, and defence of the commonwealth. It is a hard matter to know who expecteth benefit from public troubles; but the signs that guide to a just suspicion, is the soothing of the people in their unreasonable, or irremediable grievances, by men whose estates are not sufficient to discharge their accustomed expenses and may easily be observed by any one whom it concerns to know it. But to know, who has most knowledge of the public affairs, is yet harder; and they that know them, need them a great deal the less. For to know, who knows the rules almost of any art, is a great degree of the knowledge of the same art; because no man can be assured of the truth of another's rules, but he that is first taught to understand them. But the best signs of knowledge of any art, are, much conversing in it, and constant good effects of it. Good counsel comes not by lot, nor by inheritance; and therefore there is no more reason to expect good advice from the rich, or noble, in matter of state, than in delineating the dimensions of a fortress; unless we shall think there needs no method in the study of the politics, (as there does in the study of geometry,) but only to be lookers on; which is not so. For the politics is the harder

study of the two. Whereas in these parts of *Europe*, it hath been taken for a right of certain persons, to have place in the highest council of state by inheritance; it is derived from the conquests of the ancient Germans; wherein many absolute lords joining together to conquer other nations, would not enter into the confederacy, without such privileges, as might be marks of difference in time following, between their posterity, and the posterity of their subjects; which privileges being inconsistent with the sovereign power, by the favour of the sovereign, they may seem to keep; but contending for them as their right, they must needs by degrees let them go, and have at last no further honour, than adhereth naturally to their abilities.

And how able soever be the counsellors in any affair, the benefit of their counsel is greater, when they give every one his advice, and the reasons of it apart, than when they do it in an assembly, by way of orations; and when they have premeditated, than when they speak on the sudden; both because they have more time, to survey the consequences of action; and are less subject to be carried away to contradiction, through envy, emulation, or other passions arising from the difference of opinion.

The best counsel, in those things that concern not other nations, but only the ease, and benefit the subjects may enjoy, by laws that look only inward, is to be taken from the general informations, and complaints of the people of each province, who are best acquainted with their own wants, and ought therefore, when they demand nothing in derogation of the essential rights of sovereignty, to be diligently taken notice of. For without those essential rights, (as I have often before said,) the commonwealth cannot at all subsist.

A commander of an army in chief, if he be not popular, shall not be beloved, nor feared as he ought to be by his army; and consequently cannot perform that office with good success. He must therefore be industrious, valiant, affable, liberal and fortunate, that he may gain an opinion both of sufficiency, and of loving his soldiers. This is popularity, and breeds in the soldiers both desire, and courage, to recommend themselves to his favour; and protects the severity of the general, in punishing (when need is) the mutinous, or negligent soldiers. But this love of soldiers, (if caution be not given of the commander's fidelity,) is a dangerous thing to sovereign power; especially when it is in the hands of an assembly not popular. It belongeth therefore to the safety of the people, both that they be good conductors, and faithful subjects, to whom the sovereign commits his armies.

But when the sovereign himself is popular; that is, reverenced and beloved of his people, there is no danger at all from the popularity of a subject. For soldiers are never so generally unjust, as to side with their captain; though they love him, against their sovereign, when they love not only his person, but also his cause. And therefore those, who by violence have at any time suppressed the power of their lawful sovereign, before they could settle themselves in his place, have been always put to the trouble of contriving their titles, to save the people from the shame of receiving them. To have a known right to sovereign power, is so popular a quality, as he that has it needs no more, for his own part, to turn the hearts of his subjects to him, but that they see him able absolutely to govern his own family: nor, on the part of his enemies, but a disbanding of their armies. For the greatest and most active part of mankind, has never hitherto been well contented with the present.

Concerning the offices of one sovereign to another, which are comprehended in that law, which is commonly called the *law of nations*, I need not say any thing in this place; because the law of nations, and the law of nature, is the same thing. And every sovereign hath the same right, in procuring the safety of his people, that any particular man can have, in procuring the safety of his own body. And the same law, that dictateth to men that have no civil government, what they ought to do, and what to avoid in regard of one another, dictateth the same to commonwealths, that is, to the consciences of sovereign princes, and sovereign assemblies; there being no court of natural justice, but in the conscience only; where not man, but God reigneth; whose laws, (such of them as oblige all mankind,) in respect of God, as he is the author of nature, are *natural*; and in respect of the same God, as he is King of kings, are *laws*. But of the kingdom of God, as King of kings, and as King also of a peculiar people, I shall speak in the rest of this discourse.

Chapter 31

Of the Kingdom of God by Nature

That the condition of mere nature, that is to say, of absolute liberty, such as is theirs, that neither are sovereigns, nor subjects, is anarchy, and the condition of war: that the precepts, by which men are guided to avoid that condition, are the laws of nature: that a commonwealth, without sovereign power, is but a word, without substance, and cannot stand: that subjects owe to sovereigns, simple obedience, in all things, wherein their obedience is not repugnant to the laws of God, I have sufficiently proved, in that which I have already written. There wants only, for the entire knowledge of civil duty, to know what are those laws of God. For without that, a man knows not, when he is commanded any thing by the civil power, whether it be contrary to the law of God, or not: and so, either by too much civil obedience, offends the Divine Majesty, or through fear of offending God, transgresses the commandments of the commonwealth. To avoid both these rocks, it is necessary to know what are the laws divine. And seeing the knowledge of all law, dependeth on the knowledge of the sovereign power; I shall say something in that which followeth, of the KINGDOM OF GOD.

God is king, let the earth rejoice, saith the psalmist. (*Psalm* 96. 1). And again, (*Psalm* 98. 1) *God is king though the nations be angry; and he that sitteth on the cherubims, though the earth be moved.* Whether men will or not, they must be subject always to the divine power. By denying the existence, or providence of God, men may shake off their ease, but not their yoke. But to call this power of God, which extendeth itself not only to man, but also to beasts, and plants, and bodies inanimate, by the name of kingdom, is but a metaphorical use of the word. For he only is properly said to reign, that governs his subjects by his word, and by promise of rewards to those that obey it, and by threatening them with punishment that obey it not. Subjects therefore in the kingdom of God, are not bodies inanimate, nor creatures irrational; because they understand no precepts as his: nor atheists; nor they that believe not that God has any care of the actions of mankind; because they acknowledge no word for his, nor have hope of his rewards, or fear of his threatenings. They therefore that believe there is a God that governeth the world, and hath given precepts, and propounded rewards, and punishments to mankind, are God's subjects; all the rest, are to be understood as enemies.

To rule by words, requires that such words be manifestly made known; for else they are no laws: for to the nature of laws belongeth a sufficient, and clear promulgation, such as may take away the excuse of ignorance; which in the laws of men is but of one only kind, and that is, proclamation, or promulgation by the voice of man. But God declareth his laws three ways; by the dictates of *natural reason*, by *revelation*, and by the *voice* of some *man*, to whom by the operation of miracles, he procureth credit with the rest. From hence there ariseth a triple word of God, *rational*, *sensible*, and *prophetic*: to which correspondeth a triple hearing; *right reason*, *sense supernatural*, and *faith*. As for sense supernatural, which consisteth in revelation, or inspiration, there have not been any universal laws so given, because God speaketh not in that manner, but to particular persons, and to divers men divers things.

From the difference between the other two kinds of God's word, *rational*, and *prophetic*, there may be attributed to God, a twofold kingdom, *natural*, and *prophetic*: natural, wherein he governeth as many of mankind as acknowledge his providence, by the natural dictates of right reason; and prophetic, wherein having chosen out one peculiar nation (the Jews) for his subjects, he governed them, and none but them, not only by natural reason, but by positive laws, which he gave them by the mouths of his holy prophets. Of the natural kingdom of God I intend to speak in this chapter.

The right of nature, whereby God reigneth over men, and punisheth those that break his laws, is to be derived, not from his creating them, as if he required obedience, as of gratitude for his benefits; but from his *irresistible power*. I have formerly shown, how the sovereign right ariseth from pact: to show how the same right may arise from nature, requires no more, but to show in what case it is never taken away. Seeing all men by nature had right to all things, they had right every one to reign over all the rest. But because this right could not be obtained by force, it concerned

the safety of every one, laying by that right, to set up men (with sovereign authority) by common consent, to rule and defend them: whereas if there had been any man of power irresistible; there had been no reason, why he should not by that power have ruled, and defended both himself, and them, according to his own discretion. To those therefore whose power is irresistible, the dominion of all men adhereth naturally by their excellence of power; and consequently it is from that power, that the kingdom over men, and the right of afflicting men at his pleasure, belongeth naturally to God Almighty; not as Creator, and gracious; but as omnipotent. And though punishment be due for sin only, because by that word is understood affliction for sin; yet the right of afflicting, is not always derived from men's sin, but from God's power.

This question, *why evil men often prosper, and good men suffer adversity*, has been much disputed by the ancient, and is the same with this of ours, *by what right God dispenseth the prosperities and adversities of this life*; and is of that difficulty, as it hath shaken the faith, not only of the vulgar, but of philosophers, and which is more, of the Saints, concerning the Divine Providence. *How good*, (saith *David*) (*Psalm 72. 1, 2, 3*) *is the God of Israel to those that are upright in heart; and yet my feet were almost gone, my treadings had well-nigh slipt; for I was grieved at the wicked, when I saw the ungodly in such prosperity.* And *Job*, how earnestly does he expostulate with God, for the many afflictions he suffered, notwithstanding his righteousness? This question in the case of *Job*, is decided by God himself, not by arguments derived from *Job's* sin, but his own power. For whereas the friends of *Job* drew their arguments from his affliction to his sin, and he defended himself by the conscience of his innocence, God himself taketh up the matter, and having justified the affliction by arguments drawn from his power, such as this, (*Job* 38. 4) *Where wast thou, when I laid the foundations of the earth*, and the like, both approved Job's innocence, and reproved the erroneous doctrine of his friends. Conformable to this doctrine is the sentence of our Saviour, concerning the man that was born blind, in these words, *Neither hath this man sinned, nor his fathers; but that the works of God might be made manifest in him.* And though it be said, *that death entered into the world by sin*, (by which is meant that if *Adam* had never sinned, he had never died, that is, never suffered any separation of his soul from his body,) it follows not thence, that God could not justly have afflicted him, though he had not sinned, as well as he afflicteth other living creatures, that cannot sin.

Having spoken of the right of God's sovereignty, as grounded only on nature; we are to consider next, what are the Divine laws, or dictates of natural reason; which laws concern either the natural duties of one man to another, or the honour naturally due to our Divine Sovereign. The first are the same laws of nature, of which I have spoken already in the 14th and 15th chapters of this treatise; namely, equity, justice, mercy, humility, and the rest of the moral virtues. It remaineth therefore that we consider, what precepts are dictated to men, by their natural reason only, without other word of God, touching the honour and worship of the Divine Majesty.

Honour consisteth in the inward thought, and opinion of the power, and goodness of another: and therefore to honour God, is to think as highly of his power and goodness, as is possible. And of that opinion, the external signs appearing in the words, and actions of men, are called *worship*; which is one part of that which the Latins understand by the word *cultus*: For *cultus* signifieth properly, and constantly, that labour which a man bestows on any thing, with a purpose to make benefit by it. Now those things whereof we make benefit, are either subject to us, and the profit they yield, followeth the labour we bestow upon them, as a natural effect; or they are not subject to us, but answer our labour, according to their own wills. In the first sense the labour bestowed on the earth, is called *culture*; and the education of children, a *culture* of their minds. In the second sense, where men's wills are to be wrought to our purpose, not by force, but by complaisance, it signifieth as much as courting, that is, a winning of favour by good offices; as by praises, by acknowledging their power, and by whatsoever is pleasing to them from whom we look for any benefit. And this is properly *worship*: in which sense *Publicola*, is understood for a worshipper of the people; and *cultus Dei*, for the worship of God.

From internal honour, consisting in the opinion of power and goodness, arise three passions; *love*, which hath reference to goodness; and *hope*, and *fear*, that relate to power: and three parts of external

worship; *praise*, *magnifying*, and *blessing*: the subject of praise, being goodness; the subject of magnifying and blessing, being power, and the effect thereof felicity. Praise, and magnifying are signified both by words, and actions: by words, when we say a man is good, or great: by actions, when we thank him for his bounty, and obey his power. The opinion of the happiness of another, can only be expressed by words.

There be some signs of honour, (both in attributes and actions,) that be naturally so; as amongst attributes, *good*, *just*, *liberal*, and the like; and amongst actions, *prayers*, *thanks*, and *obedience*. Others are so by institution, or custom of men; and in some times and places are honourable; in others, dishonourable; in others indifferent: such as are the gestures in salutation, prayer, and thanksgiving, in different times and places, differently used. The former is *natural*; the latter *arbitrary* worship.

And of arbitrary worship, there be two differences: for sometimes it is a *commanded*, sometimes *voluntary* worship: commanded, when it is such as he requireth, who is worshipped: free, when it is such as the worshipper thinks fit. When it is commanded, not the words, or gesture, but the obedience is the worship. But when free, the worship consists in the opinion of the beholders: for if to them the words, or actions by which we intend honour, seem ridiculous, and tending to contumely; they are no worship; because no signs of honour; and no signs of honour; because a sign is not a sign to him that giveth it, but to him to whom it is made; that is, to the spectator.

Again, there is a *public*, and a *private* worship. Public, is the worship that a commonwealth performeth, as one person. Private, is that which a private person exhibiteth. Public, in respect of the whole commonwealth, is free; but in respect of particular men it is not so. Private, is in secret free; but in the sight of the multitude, it is never without some restraint, either from the laws, or from the opinion of men; which is contrary to the nature of liberty.

The end of worship amongst men, is power. For where a man seeth another worshipped, he supposeth him powerful, and is the readier to obey him; which makes his power greater. But God has no ends: the worship we do him, proceeds from our duty, and is directed according to our capacity, by those rules of honour, that reason dictateth to be done by the weak to the more potent men, in hope of benefit, for fear of damage, or in thankfulness for good already received from them.

That we may know what worship of God is taught us by the light of nature, I will begin with his attributes. Where, first, it is manifest, we ought to attribute to him *existence*. For no man can have the will to honour that, which he thinks not to have any being.

Secondly, that those philosophers, who said the world, or the soul of the world was God, spake unworthily of him; and denied his existence. For by God, is understood the cause of the world; and to say the world is God, is to say there is no cause of it, that is, no God.

Thirdly, to say the world was not created, but eternal, (seeing that which is eternal has no cause,) is to deny there is a God.

Fourthly, that they who attributing (as they think) ease to God, take from him the care of mankind; take from him his honour: for it takes away men's love, and fear of him; which is the root of honour.

Fifthly, in those things that signify greatness, and power; to say he is *finite*, is not to honour him: for it is not a sign of the will to honour God, to attribute to him less than we can; and finite, is less than we can; because to finite, it is easy to add more.

Therefore to attribute *figure* to him, is not honour; for all figure is finite:

Nor to say we conceive, and imagine, or have an *idea* of him, in our mind: for whatsoever we conceive is finite:

Nor to attribute to him *parts*, or *totality*; which are the attributes only of things finite:

Nor to say he is in this, or that *place*: for whatsoever is in place, is bounded, and finite:

Nor that he is *moved*, or *resteth*: for both these attributes ascribe to him place:

Nor that there be more Gods than one; because it implies them all finite: for there cannot be more than one infinite:

Nor to ascribe to him (unless metaphorically, meaning not the passion but the effect) passions that partake of grief; as *repentance*, *anger*, *mercy*: or of want; as *appetite*, *hope*, *desire*; or of any passive faculty: for passion, is power limited by somewhat else.

And therefore when we ascribe to God a *will*, it is not to be understood, as that of man, for a *rational*

appetite; but as the power, by which he effecteth every thing.

Likewise when we attribute to him *sight*, and other acts of sense; as also *knowledge*, and *understanding*; which in us is nothing else, but a tumult of the mind, raised by external things that press the organical parts of man's body: for there is no such thing in God; and being things that depend on natural causes, cannot be attributed to him.

He that will attribute to God, nothing but what is warranted by natural reason, must either use such negative attributes, as *infinite*, *eternal*, *incomprehensible*; or superlatives, as *most high*, *most great*, and the like; or indefinite, as *good*, *just*, *holy*, *creator*; and in such sense, as if he meant not to declare what he is, (for that were to circumscribe him within the limits of our fancy,) but how much we admire him, and how ready we would be to obey him; which is a sign of humility, and of a will to honour him as much as we can: For there is but one name to signify our conception of his nature, and that is, I AM: and but one name of his relation to us, and that is *God*; in which is contained Father, King, and Lord.

Concerning the actions of divine worship, it is a most general precept of reason, that they be signs of the intention to honour God; such as are, first, *prayers*: For not the carvers, when they made images, were thought to make them gods; but the people that *prayed* to them.

Secondly, *thanksgiving*; which differeth from prayer in divine worship, no otherwise, than that prayers precede, and thanks succeed the benefit; the end both of the one, and the other, being to acknowledge God, for author of all benefits, as well past, as future.

Thirdly, *gifts*; that is to say, *sacrifices*, and *oblations*, (if they be of the best,) are signs of honour: for they are thanksgivings.

Fourthly, *not to swear by any but God*, is naturally a sign of honour: for it is a confession that God only knoweth the heart; and that no man's wit, or strength can protect a man against God's vengeance on the perjured.

Fifthly, it is a part of rational worship, to speak considerately of God; for it argues a fear of him, and fear, is a confession of his power. Hence followeth, that the name of God is not to be used rashly, and to no purpose; for that is as much, as in vain: and it is to no purpose unless it be by way of oath, and by order of the commonwealth, to make judgments certain; or between commonwealths, to avoid war. And that disputing of God's nature is contrary to his honour: for it is supposed, that in this natural kingdom of God, there is no other way to know any thing, but by natural reason; that is, from the principles of natural science; which are so far from teaching us any thing of God's nature, as they cannot teach us our own nature, nor the nature of the smallest creature living. And therefore, when men out of the principles of natural reason, dispute of the attributes of God, they but dishonour him: for in the attributes which we give to God, we are not to consider the signification of philosophical truth; but the signification of pious intention, to do him the greatest honour we are able. From the want of which consideration, have proceeded the volumes of disputation about the nature of God, that tend not to his honour, but to the honour of our own wits, and learning; and are nothing else but inconsiderate, and vain abuses of his sacred name.

Sixthly, in *prayers, thanksgivings, offerings* and *sacrifices,* it is a dictate of natural reason, that they be every one in his kind the best, and most significant of honour. As for example, that prayers and thanksgiving, be made in words and phrases, not sudden, nor light, nor plebeian; but beautiful, and well composed; For else we do not God as much honour as we can. And therefore the heathens did absurdly, to worship images for gods: but their doing it in verse, and with music, both of voice, and instruments, was reasonable. Also that the beasts they offered in sacrifice, and the gifts they offered, and their actions in worshipping, were full of submission, and commemorative of benefits received, was according to reason, as proceeding from an intention to honour him.

Seventhly, reason directeth not only to worship God in secret; but also, and especially, in public, and in the sight of men: For without that, (that which in honour is most acceptable) the procuring others to honour him, is lost.

Lastly, obedience to his laws (that is, in this case to the laws of nature,) is the greatest worship of all. For as obedience is more acceptable to God than sacrifice; so also to set light by his commandments, is the greatest of all contumelies. And these are the laws of that divine worship, which natural reason dictateth to private men

But seeing a commonwealth is but one person, it ought also to exhibit to God but one worship; which then it doth, when it commandeth it to be exhibited by private men, publicly. And this is public worship; the property whereof, is to be *uniform:* for those actions that are done differently, by different men, cannot be said to be a public worship. And therefore, where many sorts of worship be allowed, proceeding from the different religions of private men, it cannot be said there is any public worship, nor that the commonwealth is of any religion at all.

And because words (and consequently the attributes of God) have their signification by agreement, and constitution of men; those attributes are to be held significative of honour, that men intend shall so be; and whatsoever may be done by the wills of particular men, where there is no law but reason, may be done by the will of the commonwealth, by laws civil. And because a commonwealth hath no will, nor makes no laws, but those that are made by the will of him, or them that have the sovereign power; it followeth, that those attributes which the sovereign ordaineth, in the worship of God, for signs of honour, ought to be taken and used for such, by private men in their public worship.

But because not all actions are signs by constitution, but some are naturally signs of honour, others of contumely, these latter (which are those that men are ashamed to do in the sight of them they reverence) cannot be made by human power a part of Divine worship; nor the former (such as are decent, modest, humble behaviour) ever be separated from it. But whereas there be an infinite number of actions, and gestures, of an indifferent nature; such of them as the commonwealth shall ordain to be publicly and universally in use, as signs of honour, and part of God's worship, are to be taken and used for such by the subjects. And that which is said in the Scripture, *It is better to obey God than men,* hath place in the kingdom of God by pact, and not by nature.

Having thus briefly spoken of the natural kingdom of God, and his natural laws, I will add only to this chapter a short declaration of his natural punishments. There is no action of man in this life, that is not the beginning of so long a chain of consequences, as no human providence, is high enough, to give a man a prospect to the end. And in this chain, there are linked together both pleasing and unpleasing events; in such manner, as he that will do any thing for his pleasure, must engage himself to suffer all the pains annexed to it; and these pains, are the natural punishments of those actions, which are the beginning of more harm than good. And hereby it comes to pass, that intemperance is naturally punished with diseases; rashness, with mischances; injustice, with the violence of enemies; pride, with ruin; cowardice, with oppression: negligent government of princes, with rebellion; and rebellion, with slaughter. For seeing punishments are consequent to the breach of laws; natural punishments must be naturally consequent to the breach of the laws of nature; and therefore follow them as their natural, not arbitrary effects.

And thus far concerning the constitution, nature, and right of sovereigns; and concerning the duty of subjects, derived from the principles of natural reason. And now, considering how different this doctrine is, from the practice of the greatest part of the world, especially of these western parts, that have received their moral learning from *Rome*, and *Athens*; and how much depth of moral philosophy is required, in them that have the administration of the sovereign power; I am at the point of believing this my labour, as useless, as the commonwealth of *Plato*; For he also is of opinion that it is impossible for the disorders of state, and change of governments by civil war, ever to be taken away, till sovereigns be philosophers. But when I consider again, that the science of natural justice, is the only science necessary for sovereigns, and their principal ministers; and that they need not be charged with the sciences mathematical, (as by *Plato* they are,) further, than by good laws to encourage men to the study of them; and that neither *Plato*, nor any other philosopher hitherto, hath put into order, and sufficiently or probably proved all the theorems of moral doctrine, that men may learn thereby, both how to govern, and how to obey; I recover some hope, that one time or other, this writing of mine, may fall into the hands of a sovereign, who will consider it himself, (for it is short, and I think clear,) without the help of any interested, or envious interpreter; and by the exercise of entire sovereignty, in protecting the public teaching of it, convert this truth of speculation, into the utility of practice.

A REVIEW AND CONCLUSION

From the contrariety of some of the natural faculties of the mind, one to another, as also of one passion to another, and from their reference to conversation, there has been an argument taken, to infer an impossibility that any one man should be sufficiently disposed to all sorts of civil duty. The severity of judgment, they say, makes men censorious, and unapt to pardon the errors and infirmities of other men: and on the other side, celerity of fancy, makes the thoughts less steady than is necessary, to discern exactly between right and wrong. Again, in all deliberations, and in all pleadings, the faculty of solid reasoning, is necessary: for without it, the resolutions of men are rash, and their sentences unjust: and yet if there be not powerful eloquence, which procureth attention and consent, the effect of reason will be little. But these are contrary faculties; the former being grounded upon principles of truth; the other upon opinions already received, true, or false; and upon the passions and interests of men, which are different, and mutable.

And amongst the passions, *courage*, (by which I mean the contempt of wounds, and violent death) inclineth men to private revenges, and sometimes to endeavour the unsettling of the public peace: and *timorousness*, many times disposeth to the desertion of the public defence. Both these they say cannot stand together in the same person.

And to consider the contrariety of men's opinions, and manners in general, it is, they say, impossible to entertain a constant civil amity with all those, with whom the business of the world constrains us to converse: which business, consisteth almost in nothing else but a perpetual contention for honour, riches, and authority.

To which I answer, that these are indeed great difficulties, but not impossibilities: for by education, and discipline, they may be, and are sometimes reconciled. Judgment and fancy may have place in the same man; but by turns; as the end which he aimeth at requireth. As the Israelites in Egypt, were sometimes fastened to their labour of making bricks, and other times were ranging abroad to gather straw: so also may the judgment sometimes be fixed upon one certain consideration, and the fancy at another time wandering about the world. So also reason, and eloquence, (though not perhaps in the natural sciences, yet in the moral) may stand very well together. For wheresoever there is place for adorning and preferring of error, there is much more place for adorning and preferring of truth, if they have it to adorn. Nor is there any repugnancy between fearing the laws, and not fearing a public enemy; nor between abstaining from injury, and pardoning it in others. There is therefore no such inconsistence of human nature, with civil duties, as some think. I have known clearness of judgment, and largeness of fancy; strength of reason, and graceful elocution; a courage for the war, and a fear for the laws, and all eminently in one man; and that was my most noble and honoured friend, Mr. Sidney Godolphin; who hating no man, nor hated of any, was unfortunately slain in the beginning of the late civil war, in the public quarrel, by an undiscerned, and an undiscerning hand.

To the Laws of Nature, declared in Chapter 15, I would have this added, *that every man is bound by nature, as much as in him lieth, to protect in war, the authority, by which he is himself protected in time of peace.* For he that pretendeth a right of nature to preserve his own body, cannot pretend a right of nature to destroy him, by whose strength he is preserved: it is a manifest contradiction of himself. And though this law may be drawn by consequence, from some of those that are there already mentioned; yet the times require to have it inculcated, and remembered.

And because I find by divers English books lately printed, that the civil wars have not yet sufficiently taught men in what point of time it is, that a subject becomes obliged to the conqueror; nor what is conquest; nor how it comes about, that it obliges men to obey his laws: therefore for further satisfaction of men therein, I say, the point of time, wherein a man becomes subject to a conqueror, is that point, wherein having liberty to submit to him, he consenteth, either by express words, or by other sufficient sign, to be his subject. When it is that a man hath the liberty to submit, I have showed before in the end of Chapter 21; namely, that for him that hath no obligation to his former sovereign but that of an ordinary subject, it is then, when the means of his life is within the guards and garrisons of the enemy; for it is then, that he hath no longer protection from him, but is protected by the adverse party for his contribution. Seeing therefore such contribution is every where, as a thing inevitable, (notwithstanding it be an assistance to the enemy,) esteemed lawful; a total submission, which is but an assistance to the enemy, cannot be esteemed unlawful. Besides, if a man consider that they who submit, assist the enemy but with part of their estates, whereas they that refuse, assist him with the whole, there is no reason to call their submission, or composition an assistance; but rather a detriment to the enemy. But if a man, besides the obligation of a subject, hath taken upon him a new obligation of a soldier, then he hath not the liberty to submit to a new power, as long as the old one keeps the field, and giveth him means of subsistence, either in his armies, or garrisons: for in this case, he cannot complain of want of protection, and means to live as a soldier. But when that also fails, a soldier also may seek his protection wheresoever he has most hope to have it; and may lawfully submit himself to his new master. And so much for the time when he may do it lawfully, if he will. If therefore he do it, he is undoubtedly bound to be a true subject: for a contract lawfully made, cannot lawfully be broken.

By this also a man may understand, when it is, that men may be said to be conquered; and in what the nature of conquest, and the right of a conqueror consisteth: for this submission is it implieth them all. Conquest, is not the victory itself; but the acquisition by victory, of a right, over the persons of men. He therefore that is slain, is overcome, but not conquered: he that is taken, and put into prison, or chains, is not conquered, though overcome; for he is still an enemy, and may save himself if he can: but he that upon promise of obedience, hath his life and liberty allowed him, is then conquered, and a subject; and not before. The Romans used to say, that their general had *pacified* such a *province*, that is to say, in English, *conquered* it; and that the country was *pacified* by victory, when the people of it had promised *imperata facere*, that is, *to do what the Roman people commanded them*: this was to be conquered. But this promise may be either express, or tacit: express, by promise: tacit, by other signs. As for example, a man that hath not been called to make such an express promise, (because he is one whose power perhaps is not considerable;) yet if he live under their protection openly, he is understood to submit himself to the government: but if he live there secretly, he is liable to any thing that may be done to a spy, and enemy of the state. I say not, he does any injustice, (for acts of open hostility bear not that name); but that he may be justly put to death. Likewise, if a man, when his country is conquered, be out of it, he is not conquered, nor subject: but if at his return, he submit to the government, he is bound to obey it. So that *conquest* (to define it) is the acquiring of the right of sovereignty by victory. Which right, is acquired, in the people's submission, by which they contract with the victor, promising obedience, for life and liberty.

In Chapter 29, I have set down for one of the causes of the dissolutions of commonwealths, their imperfect generation, consisting in the want of an absolute and arbitrary legislative power; for want whereof, the civil sovereign is fain to handle the sword of justice unconstantly, and as if it were too hot for him to hold. One reason whereof (which I have not there mentioned) is this, that they will all of them justify the war, by which their power was at first gotten, and whereon (as they think) their right dependeth, and not on the possession. As if, for example, the right of the kings of England did depend on the goodness of the cause of William the Conqueror, and upon their lineal, and directest descent from him; by which means, there would perhaps be no tie of the subjects' obedience to their sovereign at this day in all the world: wherein whilst they needlessly think to justify themselves, they justify all the successful rebellions that ambition shall at any time raise against them, and their successors. Therefore I put down for one of the most effectual seeds of the death of any state, that the conquerors require not only a submission of men's actions to them for the future, but also an approbation of all their actions past; when there is scarce a commonwealth in the world, whose beginnings can in conscience be justified.

And because the name of tyranny, signifieth nothing more, nor less, than the name of sovereignty, be

it in one, or many men, saving that they that use the former word, are understood to be angry with them they call tyrants; I think the toleration of a professed hatred of tyranny, is a toleration of hatred to commonwealth in general, and another evil seed, not differing much from the former. For to the justification of the cause of a conqueror, the reproach of the cause of the conquered, is for the most part necessary: but neither of them necessary for the obligation of the conquered. And thus much I have thought fit to say upon the review of the first and second part of this discourse.

In Chapter 35, I have sufficiently declared out of the Scripture, that in the commonwealth of the Jews, God himself was made the sovereign, by pact with the people; who were therefore called his *peculiar people*, to distinguish them from the rest of the world, over whom God reigned not by their consent, but by his own power: and that in this kingdom Moses was God's lieutenant on earth; and that it was he that told them what laws God appointed them to be ruled by. But I have omitted to set down who were the officers appointed to do execution; especially in capital punishments; not then thinking it a matter of so necessary consideration, as I find it since. We know that generally in all commonwealths, the execution of corporal punishments, was either put upon the guards, or other soldiers of the sovereign power; or given to those, in whom want of means, contempt of honour, and hardness of heart, concurred, to make them sue for such an office. But amongst the Israelites it was a positive law of God their sovereign, that he that was convicted of a capital crime, should be stoned to death by the people; and that the witnesses should cast the first stone, and after the witnesses, then the rest of the people. This was a law that designed who were to be the executioners; but not that any one should throw a stone at him before conviction and sentence, where the congregation was judge. The witnesses were nevertheless to be heard before they proceeded to execution, unless the fact were committed in the presence of the congregation itself, or in sight of the lawful judges; for then there needed no other witnesses but the judges themselves. Nevertheless, this manner of proceeding being not thoroughly understood, hath given occasion to a dangerous opinion, that any man may kill another, in some cases, by a right of zeal; as if the executions done upon offenders in the kingdom of God in old time, proceeded not from the sovereign command, but from the authority of private zeal: which, if we consider the texts that seem to favour it, is quite contrary.

First, where the Levites fell upon the people, that had made and worshipped the Golden Calf, and slew three thousand of them; it was by the commandment of Moses, from the mouth of God; as is manifest, *Exod.* 32. 27. And when the son of a woman of Israel had blasphemed God, they that heard it, did not kill him, but brought him before Moses, who put him under custody, till God should give sentence against him; as appears, *Levit.* 25. 11, 12. Again, (*Numb.* 25. 6, 7) when Phinehas killed Zimri and Cosbi, it was not by right of private zeal: their crime was committed in the sight of the assembly; there needed no witness; the law was known, and he the heir apparent to the sovereignty; and which is the principal point, the lawfulness of his act depended wholly upon a subsequent ratification by Moses, whereof he had no cause to doubt. And this presumption of a future ratification, is sometimes necessary to the safety [of] a commonwealth; as in a sudden rebellion, any man that can suppress it by his own power in the country where it begins, without express law or commission, may lawfully do it, and provide to have it ratified, or pardoned, whilst it is in doing, or after it is done. Also *Numb.* 35. 30, it is expressly said, *Whosoever shall kill the murderer, shall kill him upon the word of witnesses:* but witnesses suppose a formal judicature, and consequently condemn that pretence of *jus zelotarum.* The law of Moses concerning him that enticeth to idolatry, that is to say, in the kingdom of God to a renouncing of his allegiance, (*Deut.* 13. 8) forbids to conceal him, and commands the accuser to cause him to be put to death, and to cast the first stone at him; but not to kill him before he be condemned. And (*Deut.* 17. 4, 5, 6) the process against idolatry is exactly set down: for God there speaketh to the people, as judge, and commandeth them, when a man is accused of idolatry, to enquire diligently of the fact, and finding it true, then to stone him; but still the hand of the witness throweth the first stone. This is not private zeal, but public condemnation. In like manner when a father hath a rebellious son, the law is (*Deut.* 21. 18) that he shall bring him

before the judges of the town, and all the people of the town shall stone him. Lastly, by pretence of these laws it was, that St. Stephen was stoned, and not by pretence of private zeal: for before he was carried away to execution, he had pleaded his cause before the high priest. There is nothing in all this, nor in any other part of the Bible, to countenance executions by private zeal; which being oftentimes but a conjunction of ignorance and passion, is against both the justice and peace of a commonwealth.

In chapter 36, I have said, that it is not declared in what manner God spake supernaturally to Moses: not that he spake not to him sometimes by dreams and visions, and by a supernatural voice, as to other prophets: for the manner how he spake unto him from the mercy-seat, is expressly set down *Numbers* 7. 89, in these words, *From that time forward, when Moses entered into the Tabernacle of the congregation to speak with God, he heard a voice which spake unto him from over the mercy-seat, which is over the Ark of the testimony, from between the cherubims he spake unto him.* But it is not declared in what consisted the preeminence of the manner of God's speaking to Moses, above that of his speaking to other prophets, as to Samuel, and to Abraham, to whom he also spake by a voice, (that is, by vision) unless the difference consist in the clearness of the vision. For *face to face*, and *mouth to mouth*, cannot be literally understood of the infiniteness, and incomprehensibility of the Divine nature.

And as to the whole doctrine, I see not yet, but the principles of it are true and proper; and the ratiocination solid. For I ground the civil right of sovereigns, and both the duty and liberty of subjects, upon the known natural inclinations of mankind, and upon the articles of the law of nature; of which no man, that pretends but reason enough to govern his private family, ought to be ignorant. And for the power ecclesiastical of the same sovereigns, I ground it on such texts, as are both evident in themselves, and consonant to the scope of the whole Scripture. And therefore am persuaded, that he that shall read it with a purpose only to be informed, shall be informed by it. But for those that by writing, or public discourse, or by their eminent actions, have already engaged themselves to the maintaining of contrary opinions, they will not be so easily satisfied. For in such cases, it is natural for men, at one and the same time, both to proceed in reading, and to lose their attention, in the search of objections to that they had read before: Of which in a time wherein the interests of men are changed (seeing much of that doctrine, which serveth to the establishing of a new government, must needs be contrary to that which conduced to the dissolution of the old,) there cannot choose but be very many.

In that part which treateth of a Christian commonwealth, there are some new doctrines, which, it may be, in a state where the contrary were already fully determined, were a fault for a subject without leave to divulge, as being an usurpation of the place of a teacher. But in this time, that men call not only for peace, but also for truth, to offer such doctrines as I think true, and that manifestly tend to peace and loyalty, to the consideration of those that are yet in deliberation, is no more, but to offer new wine, to be put into new cask, that both may be preserved together. And I suppose, that then, when novelty can breed no trouble, nor disorder in a state, men are not generally so much inclined to the reverence of antiquity, as to prefer ancient errors, before new and well proved truth.

There is nothing I distrust more than my elocution, which nevertheless I am confident (excepting the mischances of the press) is not obscure. That I have neglected the ornament of quoting ancient poets, orators, and philosophers, contrary to the custom of late time, (whether I have done well or ill in it,) proceedeth from my judgment, grounded on many reasons. For first, all truth of doctrine dependeth either upon *reason*, or upon *Scripture*; both which give credit to many, but never receive it from any writer. Secondly, the matters in question are not of *fact*, but of *right*, wherein there is no place for *witnesses*. There is scarce any of those old writers, that contradicteth not sometimes both himself and others; which makes their testimonies insufficient. Fourthly, such opinions as are taken only upon credit of antiquity, are not intrinsically the judgment of those that cite them, but words that pass (like gaping) from mouth to mouth. Fifthly, it is many times with a fraudulent design that men stick their corrupt doctrine with the cloves of other men's wit. Sixthly, I find not that the ancients they cite, took it for an ornament, to do the like with those that wrote before them. Seventhly, it is

an argument of indigestion, when Greek and Latin sentences unchewed come up again, as they use to do, unchanged. Lastly, though I reverence those men of ancient time, that either have written truth perspicuously, or set us in a better way to find it out ourselves; yet to the antiquity itself I think nothing due: For if we will reverence the age, the present is the oldest. If the antiquity of the writer, I am not sure, that generally they to whom such honour is given, were more ancient when they wrote, than I am that am writing: But if it be well considered, the praise of ancient authors, proceeds not from the reverence of the dead, but from the competition, and mutual envy of the living.

To conclude, there is nothing in this whole discourse, nor in that I writ before of the same subject in Latin, as far as I can perceive, contrary either to the Word of God, or to good manners; or to the disturbance of the public tranquillity. Therefore I think it may be profitably printed, and more profitably taught in the Universities, in case they also think so, to whom the judgment of the same belongeth. For seeing the Universities are the fountains of civil, and moral doctrine, from whence the preachers, and the gentry, drawing such water as they find, use to sprinkle the same (both from the pulpit, and in their conversation) upon the people, there ought certainly to be great care taken, to have it pure, both from the venom of heathen politicians, and from the incantation of deceiving spirits. And by that means the most men, knowing their duties, will be the less subject to serve the ambition of a few discontented persons, in their purposes against the state; and be the less grieved with the contributions necessary for their peace, and defence; and the governors themselves have the less cause, to maintain at the common charge any greater army, than is necessary to make good the public liberty, against the invasions and encroachments of foreign enemies.

And thus I have brought to an end my Discourse of Civil and Ecclesiastical Government, occasioned by the disorders of the present time, without partiality, without application, and without other design, than to set before men's eyes the mutual relation between protection and obedience; of which the condition of human nature, and the laws divine, (both natural and positive) require an inviolable observation. And though in the revolution of states, there can be no very good constellation for truths of this nature to be born under, (as having an angry aspect from the dissolvers of an old government, and seeing but the backs of them that erect a new,) yet I cannot think it will be condemned at this time, either by the public judge of doctrine, or by any that desires the continuance of public peace. And in this hope I return to my interrupted speculation of bodies natural; wherein, (if God give me health to finish it,) I hope the novelty will as much please, as in the doctrine of this artificial body it useth to offend. For such truth, as opposeth no man's profit, nor pleasure, is to all men welcome.

JOHN LOCKE

A number of recent interpretations of the political writings of John Locke (1632–1704) situate them in the context of the Exclusion Controversy of 1679–1683 and the Glorious Revolution of 1688–1689. This portrait of Locke as a radical activist reminds us that his political and religious writings, like those of Hobbes before him, are intimately associated with the turbulent events of seventeenth-century England. His discussions of toleration, property, civil authority, rebellion, and much else are not detached reflections on perennial themes; rather, they are engaged contributions to real political debate and concrete events. Yet, while these events occasioned many arguments in the *Two Treatises*, it is equally true that Locke was dealing with problems of the origin, extent, and limits to government that were central to political thought in England and Europe since the 1620s and remain central today. Moreover, as with his predecessors, his thinking reverberated well beyond these boundaries, especially in the next century in America, where his account of property, his argument for political obligation, and his justification for the right of a people to rebel against an oppressive government were widely cited in the years preceding the American Revolution. Locke, then, was both a living and a posthumous revolutionary, a defender of liberal government in his own world and in years and places far from his own. There is nothing belated about Locke's importance to the tradition of Western political theory and philosophy.

Locke was born in Somerset in 1632, went to Westminster, an excellent school near London, and matriculated at Christ Church, Oxford, where, as Peter Laslett tells us, he was "urbane, idle, unhappy, and unremarkable." Locke took a medical degree, in order to avoid the clergy, and studied philosophy. His interest in the science of his day continued throughout his life; in 1668 he was elected to the Royal Society, and he was a friend of Robert Boyle, Isaac Newton, Thomas Sydenham, and other figures central to the development of the new science. Like Hobbes, shortly after his graduation Locke became associated with a wealthy, powerful patron. Anthony Ashley Cooper, the first Earl of Shaftesbury, played a major role in Restoration politics and religious life. He strongly advocated toleration, vigorously opposed the threat of Catholic influence in England, and was a leader in the movement to exclude Charles II's brother, James, a Catholic, from the line of succession to the throne. Locke became, first, Shaftesbury's physician, then his research associate, coauthor, and political advisor. In the years of the Exclusion Controversy, Locke was active in Shaftesbury's revolutionary group, and even during Shaftesbury's imprisonment in 1680 and after his death in 1683, Locke continued his participation in this radical political movement.

In 1683, after the failure of the famous Rye House Plot to assassinate Charles II, Locke fled to Holland. There he played an active role in the community of exiled revolutionaries, negotiating transfers of funds, writing, and working in behalf of the aborted attempt to place the Duke of Monmouth on the throne. Prior to his flight to the Continent, Locke deposited with his old friend James Tyrrell a manuscript on political matters. Most likely it was the first of the *Two Treatises*, a detailed critique of the patriarchalism and doctrine of the Adamite right of kings presented in the recently republished work of Robert Filmer. During these years of the Exclusion Controversy and the debate over the rights of government, Locke, like Algernon Sydney (regicide and author of *Discourses Concerning Government*), Tyrrell (author of *Patriarcha Non Monarcha*), and Shaftesbury himself, was absorbed with the notion of political power and the rights of the people. This fragment, the *First Treatise*, was the initial product of these early reflections. But it was not the last. In the 1680s Locke added to his earlier work and by the decade's end had completed a second treatise to accompany the first. In it he developed his famous account of the state of nature in terms of his conception of property and labor, his argument for the role and authority of government, and his defense of the right of resistance and the rights of the people against an oppressive government. The two treatises were published anonymously in 1689, one year after the installation of William and Mary and in the same year as Locke's *Letter on Toleration*.

After his return to England in 1689, Locke became a celebrity. By the end of the year appeared his most famous and influential work, the result of twenty years' labor and the foundation of his intellectual prominence, *An Essay Concerning Human Understanding*. Here Locke registers his important critique of Descartes's doctrine of innate ideas, argues for the empirical foundation of all of our concepts, beliefs, and judgments, and clarifies the nature and extent of our knowledge. Along the way, he discusses those ideas which ground the notion of natural law, which is so fundamental for his account of government in the *Second Treatise*. For his remaining years, Locke was revered as the author of the *Essay*. He produced a stream of works, on education, money, religion, and much else, engaged in public controversies over his work, and served as a public official. In 1696 he became a member of the Board of Trade; later he was to arrange for his friend, Isaac Newton, to be appointed Warden of the Mint.

In 1702 Locke suffered an attack that left him largely deaf, and then, on October 29, 1704, in Essex, in the home of his closest friend, the wife of Francis Masham, Damaris Cudworth, who had cared for him during his final dozen years, he died quietly. Locke the radical had made peace with his notoriety. He had become an intellectual giant and a respected political participant in a world that knew only part of him. For virtually all of his life, it was unknown by most that the great philosopher was also the author of the *Two Treatises of Government*.

Recommended Readings

Ashcraft, Richard. *Locke's Two Treatises of Government*. London: Unwin, 1987.

Ashcraft, Richard. *Revolutionary Politics and Locke's Two Treatises of Government*. Princeton: Princeton University Press, 1986.

Burns, James (ed.). *Cambridge History of Political Thought, 1450–1700*. Cambridge: Cambridge University Press, 1991.

Chappell, Vere (ed.). *The Cambridge Companion to Locke*. Cambridge: Cambridge University Press, 1994.

Cranston, Maurice. *John Locke*. Oxford: Oxford University Press, 1957, 1985.

Dunn, John. *John Locke*. Oxford: Oxford University Press, 1983.

Dunn, John. *The Political Thought of John Locke*. Cambridge: Cambridge University Press, 1969.

Locke, John. *A Letter Concerning Toleration*, James Tully (ed.). Indianapolis: Hackett, 1983.

Macpherson, C. B. *The Political Theory of Possessive Individualism*. Oxford: Oxford University Press, 1962.

Marshall, John. *John Locke: Resistance, Religion and Responsibility*. Cambridge: Cambridge University Press, 1994.

Simmons, A. John. *The Lockean Theory of Rights*. Princeton: Princeton University Press, 1992.

Simmons, A. John. *On the Edge of Anarchy: Locke, Consent and the Limits of Society*. Princeton: Princeton University Press, 1993.

Strauss, Leo. *Natural Right and History*. Chicago: University of Chicago Press, 1953.

Tuck, Richard. *Natural Rights Theories*. Cambridge: Cambridge University Press, 1979.

Tully, James. *An Approach to Political Philosophy: Locke in Contexts*. Cambridge: Cambridge University Press, 1993.

Tully, James. *A Defense of Property*. Cambridge. Cambridge University Press, 1980

Two Treatises of
Civil Government

PREFACE

READER,

Thou hast here the beginning and end of a discourse
concerning government; what fate has otherwise disposed of the papers that should have filled up the
middle, and were more than all the rest, it is not
worth while to tell thee. These, which remain, I hope
are sufficient to establish the throne of our great re-
storer, our present King William; to make good his
title in the consent of the people; which being the
only one of all lawful governments, he has more fully
and clearly than any prince in Christendom; and to
justify to the world the people of England, whose love
of their just and natural rights, with their resolution to
preserve them, saved the nation when it was on the
very brink of slavery and ruin. If these papers have
that evidence I flatter myself is to be found in them,
there will be no great miss of those which are lost,
and my reader may be satisfied without them. For I
imagine, I shall have neither the time nor inclination
to repeat my pains, and fill up the wanting part of
my answer, by tracing Sir Robert again, through all
the windings and obscurities which are to be met
with in the several branches of his wonderful system.
The king, and body of the nation, have since so
thoroughly confuted his hypothesis, that I suppose
no body hereafter will have either the confidence to
appear against our common safety, and be again an
advocate for slavery; or the weakness to be deceived
with contradictions dressed up in a popular style, and
well turned periods. For if any one will be at the pains
himself, in those parts which are here untouched, to
strip Sir Robert's discourses of the flourish of doubtful
expressions, and endeavour to reduce his words to
direct, positive, intelligible propositions, and then
compare them one with another, he will quickly be

satisfied there was never so much glib nonsense put
together in well sounding English. If he think it not
worth while to examine his works all through, let him
make an experiment in that part where he treats of
usurpation; and let him try whether he can, with all
his skill, make Sir Robert intelligible, and consistent
with himself, or common sense. I should not speak
so plainly of a gentleman, long since past answering,
had not the pulpit, of late years, publicly owned his
doctrine, and made it the current divinity of the times.
It is necessary those men, who, taking on them to be
teachers, have so dangerously misled others, should
be openly shewed of what authority this their patriarch
is, whom they have so blindly followed; that so they
may either retract what upon so ill grounds they have
vented, and cannot be maintained; or else justify those
principles which they preached up for gospel, though
they had no better an author than an English courtier.
For I should not have writ against Sir Robert, or taken
the pains to shew his mistakes, inconsistencies, and
want of (what he so much boasts of, and pretends
wholly to build on) scripture-proofs, were there not
men amongst us, who, by crying up his books, and
espousing his doctrine, save me from the reproach
of writing against a dead adversary. They have been
so zealous in this point, that, if I have done him any
wrong, I cannot hope they should spare me. I wish,
where they have done the truth and the public wrong,
they would be as ready to redress it, and allow its just
weight to this reflection, viz. that there cannot be
done a greater mischief to prince and people, than the
propagating wrong notions concerning government;
that so at last all times might not have reason to
complain of the *drum ecclesiastic*. If any one, really
concerned for truth, undertake the confutation of my
hypothesis, I promise him either to recant my mistake,
upon fair conviction; or to answer his difficulties. But
he must remember two things,

First, That cavilling here and there, at some expression, or little incident of my discourse, is not an answer to my book.

Secondly, That I shall not take railing for arguments, nor think either of these worth my notice. Though I shall always look on myself as bound to give satisfaction to any one, who shall appear to be conscientiously scrupulous in the point, and shall shew any just grounds for his scruples.

I have nothing more, but to advertise the reader that A. stands for our author. O. for his Observations on Hobbes, Milton, &c. And that a bare quotation of pages always means pages of his *Patriarcha*, edit. 1680.

SECOND TREATISE OF GOVERNMENT

Chap.

OF CIVIL GOVERNMENT

Chapter 1

1. It having been shewn in the foregoing discourse,

1. That Adam had not, either by natural right of fatherhood, or by positive donation from God, any such authority over his children, or dominion over the world, as is pretended:
2. That if he had, his heirs, yet, had no right to it:
3. That if his heirs had, there being no law of nature, nor positive law of God, that determines, which is the right heir in all cases that may arise, the right of succession, and consequently of bearing rule, could not have been certainly determined:
4. That if even that had been determined, yet the knowledge of which is the eldest line of Adam's posterity, being so long since utterly lost, that in the races of mankind and families of the world, there remains not to one above another the least pretence to be the eldest house, and to have the right of inheritance:

All these premises having, as I think, been clearly made out, it is impossible that the rulers now on earth, should make any benefit, or derive any the least shadow of authority from that, which is held to be the fountain of all power, *Adam's private dominion and paternal jurisdiction;* so that he that will not give just occasion to think that all government in the world is the product only of force and violence, and that men live together by no other rules but that of beasts, where the strongest carries it, and so lay a foundation for perpetual disorder and mischief, tumult, sedition, and rebellion (things that the followers of that hypothesis so loudly cry out against) must of necessity find out another rise of government, another original of political power, and another way of designing and knowing the persons that have it, than what Sir Robert Filmer hath taught us.

2. To this purpose, I think it may not be amiss, to set down what I take to be political power; that the

power of a *magistrate* over a subject may be distinguished from that of a *father* over his children, a *master* over his servant, a *husband* over his *wife*, and a *lord* over his slave. All which distinct powers happening sometimes together in the same man, if he be considered under these different relations, it may help us to distinguish these powers one from another, and shew the difference betwixt a ruler of a commonwealth, a father of a family, and a captain of a galley.

3. *Political power*, then, I take to be a *right* of making laws and penalties of death, and consequently all less penalties for the regulating and preserving of property, and of employing the force of the community, in the execution of such laws, and in the defence of the commonwealth from foreign injury; and all this only for the public good.

Chapter 2

Of the State of Nature

4. To understand political power, right, and derive it from its original, we must consider what state all men are naturally in, and that is, a *state of perfect freedom* to order their actions, and dispose of their possessions and persons, as they think fit, within the bounds of the law of nature; without asking leave, or depending upon the will of any other man.

A *state* also of *equality*, wherein all the power and jurisdiction is reciprocal, no one having more than another; there being nothing more evident, than that creatures of the same species and rank, promiscuously born to all the same advantages of nature, and the use of the same faculties, should also be equal one amongst another without subordination or subjection; unless the lord and master of them all should, by any manifest declaration of his will, set one above another, and confer on him, by an evident and clear appointment, an undoubted right to dominion and sovereignty.

5. This *equality* of men by nature, the judicious Hooker looks upon as so evident in itself, and beyond all question, that he makes it the foundation of that obligation to mutual love amongst men, on which he builds the duties we owe one another, and from whence he derives the great maxims of *justice* and *charity*. His words are, "The like natural inducement hath brought men to know, that it is no less their duty to love others than themselves; for seeing those things which are equal, must needs all have one measure; if I cannot but wish to receive good, even as much at every man's hands, as any man can wish unto his own soul, how should I look to have any part of my desire herein satisfied, unless myself be careful to satisfy the like desire, which is undoubtedly in other men, being of one and the same nature? To have any thing offered them repugnant to this desire, must needs in all respects grieve them as much as me; so that if I do harm, I must look to suffer, there being no reason that others should shew greater measure of love to me, than they have by me shewed unto them: my desire therefore to be loved of my equals in nature, as much as possibly may be, imposeth upon me a natural duty of bearing to themward fully the like affection: From which relation of equality between ourselves and them that are as ourselves, what several rules and canons natural reason hath drawn, for direction of life, no man is ignorant." Eccl. Pol. L. I.

6. But though this be *a state of liberty*, yet *it is not a state of licence*: though man in that state have an uncontrolable liberty to dispose of his person or possessions, yet he has not liberty to destroy himself, or so much as any creature in his possession, but where some nobler use than its bare preservation calls for it. The *state of nature* has a law of nature to govern it, which obliges every one: And reason, which is that law, teaches all mankind, who will but consult it, that being all *equal and independent*, no one ought to harm another in his life, health, liberty, or possessions. For men being all the workmanship of one omnipotent and infinitely wise Maker; all the servants of one sovereign master, sent into the world by his order, and about his business; they are his property, whose workmanship they are, made to last during his, not another's pleasure. And being furnished with like faculties, sharing all in one community of nature, there cannot be supposed any such subordination among us, that may authorize us to destroy another, as if we were made for one another's uses, as the inferior ranks of creatures are for ours. Every one, as he is *bound to preserve himself*, and not to quit his station wilfully, so by the like reason, when his own preservation

comes not in competition, ought he, as much as he can, *to preserve the rest of mankind*, and may not, unless it be to do justice to an offender, take away or impair the life, or what tends to the preservation of life, the liberty, health, limb, or goods of another.

7. And that all men may be restrained from invading others rights, and from doing hurt to one another, and the law of nature be observed, which willeth the peace and *preservation of all mankind*, the *execution* of the law of nature is, in that state, put into every man's hands, whereby every one has a right to punish the transgressors of that law to such a degree as may hinder its violation. For the *law of nature* would, as all other laws that concern men in this world, be in vain, if there were no body that in the state of nature had a *power to execute* that law, and thereby preserve the innocent and restrain offenders. And if any one in the state of nature may punish another for any evil he has done, every one may do so. For in that *state of perfect equality*, where naturally there is no superiority or jurisdiction of one over another, what any may do in prosecution of that law, every one must needs have a right to do.

8. And thus, in the state of nature, *one man comes by a power over another*; but yet no absolute or arbitrary power, to use a criminal, when he has got him in his hands, according to the passionate heats, or boundless extravagancy of his own will; but only to retribute to him, so far as calm reason and conscience dictate, what is proportionate to his *transgression*; which is so much as may serve for *reparation* and *restraint*. For these two are the only reasons, why one man may lawfully do harm to another, which is that we call *punishment*. In transgressing the law of nature, the offender declares himself to live by another rule than that of reason and common equity, which is that measure God has set to the actions of men, for their mutual security; and so he becomes dangerous to mankind, the tye, which is to secure them from injury and violence, being slighted and broken by him. Which being a trespass against the whole species, and the peace and safety of it, provided for by the law of nature; every man upon this score, by the right he hath to preserve mankind in general, may restrain, or, where it is necessary, destroy things noxious to them, and so may bring such evil on any one, who hath transgressed that law, as may make him repent

the doing of it, and thereby deter him, and by his example others, from doing the like mischief. And in this case, and upon this ground, *every man hath a right to punish the offender, and be executioner of the law of nature*.

9. I doubt not but this will seem a very strange doctrine to some men: but before they condemn it, I desire them to resolve me, by what right any prince or state can put to death, or *punish an alien*, for any crime he commits in their country. It is certain their laws, by virtue of any sanction they receive from the promulgated will of the legislative, reach not a stranger. They speak not to him, nor, if they did, is he bound to hearken to them. The legislative authority, by which they are in force over the subjects of that commonwealth, hath no power over him. Those who have the supreme power of making laws in England, France, or Holland, are to an Indian but like the rest of the world, men without authority: And therefore, if by the law of nature every man hath not a power to punish offences against it, as he soberly judges the case to require, I see not how the magistrates of any community can *punish an alien* of another country; since in reference to him, they can have no more power, than what every man naturally may have over another.

10. Besides the crime which consists in violating the law, and varying from the right rule of reason, whereby a man so far becomes degenerate, and declares himself to quit the principles of human nature, and to be a noxious creature, there is commonly injury done to some person or other, and some other man receives damage by his transgression, in which case he who hath received any damage, has besides the right of punishment common to him with other men, a particular right to seek *reparation* from him that has done it. And any other person who finds it just, may also join with him that is injured, and assist him in recovering from the offender so much as may make satisfaction for the harm he has suffered.

11. From these *two distinct rights*, the one of *punishing* the *crime for restraint*, and preventing the like offence, which right of punishing is in every body; the other of taking *reparation*, which belongs only to the injured party; comes it to pass that the magistrate, who by being magistrate, hath the common right of punishing put into his hands, can often, where the

public good demands not the execution of the law, *remit* the punishment of criminal offences by his own authority, but yet cannot *remit* the satisfaction due to any private man, for the damage he has received. That, he who has suffered the damage has a right to demand in his own name, and he alone can remit: The damnified person has this power of appropriating to himself the goods or service of the offender, *by right of self-preservation*, as every man has a power to punish the crime, to prevent its being committed again, *by the right he has of preserving all mankind*; and doing all reasonable things he can in order to that end: And thus it is, that every man, in the state of nature, has a power to kill a murderer, both to deter others from doing the like injury, which no reparation can compensate, by the example of the punishment that attends it from every body, and also *to secure* men from the attempts of a criminal, who having renounced reason, the common rule and measure, God hath given to mankind, hath by the unjust violence and slaughter he hath committed upon one, declared war against all mankind; and therefore may be destroyed as a *lion* or a *tiger*, one of those wild savage beasts, with whom men can have no society nor security: And upon this is grounded the great law of nature, "Whoso sheddeth mans blood, by man shall his blood be shed." And Cain was so fully convinced, that every one had a right to destroy such a criminal, that after the murder of his brother, he cries out, "Every one that findeth me, shall slay me;" so plain was it writ in the hearts of all mankind.

12. By the same reason may a man in the state of nature *punish the lesser breaches* of that law. It will perhaps be demanded, with death? I answer, each transgression may be *punished* to that *degree*, and with so much *severity*, as will suffice to make it an ill bargain to the offender, give him cause to repent, and terrify others from doing the like. Every offence that can be committed in the state of nature, may in the state of nature be also punished equally, and as far forth as it may, in a commonwealth: for though it would be besides my present purpose, to enter here into the particulars of the law of nature, or its *measures of punishment*; yet it is certain there is such a law, and that too, as intelligible and plain to a rational creature, and a studier of that law, as the positive laws of commonwealths, nay possibly plainer; as much as

reason is easier to be understood, than the fancies and intricate contrivances of men, following contrary and hidden interests put into words; for so truly are a great part of the *municipal laws* of countries, which are only so far right, as they are founded on the law of nature, by which they are to be regulated and interpreted.

13. To this strange doctrine, viz. That *in the state of nature every one has the executive power* of the law of nature, I doubt not but it will be objected, that it is unreasonable for men to be judges in their own cases, that self-love will make men partial to themselves and their friends: And on the other side, that ill nature, passion and revenge will carry them too far in punishing others; and hence nothing but confusion and disorder will follow, and that therefore God hath certainly appointed government to restrain the partiality and violence of men. I easily grant, that civil government is the proper remedy for the inconveniencies of the state of nature, which must certainly be great, where men may be judges in their own case, since it is easy to be imagined, that he who was so unjust as to do his brother an injury, will scarce be so just as to condemn himself for it: But I shall desire those who make this objection, to remember, that *absolute monarchs* are but men, and if government is to be the remedy of those evils, which necessarily follow from men's being judges in their own cases, and the state of nature is therefore not to be endured, I desire to know what kind of government that is, and how much better it is than the state of nature, where one man commanding a multitude, has the liberty to be judge in his own case, and may do to all his subjects whatever he pleases, without the least liberty to any one to question or control those who execute his pleasure? and in whatsoever he doth, whether led by reason, mistake or passion, must be submitted to? Much better it is in the state of nature, wherein men are not bound to submit to the unjust will of another: And if he that judges, judges amiss in his own, or any other case, he is answerable for it to the rest of mankind.

14. It is often asked as a mighty objection, *where are*, or ever were, there any *men in such a state of nature?* To which it may suffice as an answer at present: That since all princes and rulers of independent governments, all through the world, are in a state of

nature, it is plain the world never was, nor ever will be, without numbers of men in that state. I have named all governors of independent communities, whether they are, or are not, in league with others. For it is not every compact that puts an end to the state of nature between men, but only this one of agreeing together mutually to enter into one community, and make one body politic; other promises and compacts men may make one with another, and yet still be in the state of nature. The promises and bargains for truck, &c. between the two men in the desert island, mentioned by Garcilasso de la Vega, in his history of Peru; or between a Swiss and an Indian, in the woods of America, are binding to them, though they are perfectly in a state of nature, in reference to one another. For truth and keeping of faith belongs to men as men, and not as members of society.

15. To those that say, there were never any men in the state of nature, I will not only oppose the authority of the judicious Hooker, *Eccl. Pol. lib. I. sect. 10*, where he says, "The laws which have been hitherto mentioned," i.e. the laws of nature, "do bind men absolutely, even as they are men, although they have never any settled fellowship, never any solemn agreement amongst themselves what to do or not to do, but for as much as we are not by our selves sufficient to furnish ourselves with competent store of things, needful for such a life, as our nature doth desire, a life fit for the dignity of man; therefore to supply those defects and imperfections which are in us, as living singly and solely by ourselves, we are naturally induced to seek communion and fellowship with others. This was the cause of men's uniting themselves at first in politic societies." But I moreover affirm, that all men are naturally in that state, and remain so, till by their own consents they make themselves members of some politic society; and I doubt not in the sequel of this discourse to make it very clear.

Chapter 3

Of the State of War

16. The *state of war* is a state of *enmity* and *destruction*: And therefore declaring by word or action, not a passionate and hasty, but a sedate settled design upon another man's life, *puts him in a state of war* with him against whom he has declared such an intention, and so has exposed his life to the other's power to be taken away by him, or any one that joins with him in his defence, and espouses his quarrel: it being reasonable and just I should have a right to destroy that which threatens me with destruction. For *by the fundamental law of nature, man being to be preserved* as much as possible, when all cannot be preserved, the safety of the innocent is to be preferred: And one may destroy a man who makes war upon him, or has discovered an enmity to his being, for the same reason that he may kill a *wolf* or a *lion*; because such men are not under the ties of the common law of reason, have no other rule, but that of force and violence, and so may be treated as beasts of prey, those dangerous and noxious creatures, that will be sure to destroy him whenever he falls into their power.

17. And hence it is, that he who attempts to get another man into his absolute power, does thereby *put himself into a state of war* with him; it being to be understood as a declaration of a design upon his life. For I have reason to conclude, that he who would get me into his power without my consent, would use me as he pleased when he got me there, and destroy me too when he had a fancy to it; for no body can desire to *have me in his absolute power* unless it be to compel me by force to that which is against the right of my freedom, i.e. make me a slave. To be free from such force is the only security of my preservation; and reason bids me look on him, as an enemy to my preservation, who would take away that freedom which is the fence to it; so that he who makes an *attempt to enslave* me, thereby puts himself into a state of war with me. He that, in the state of nature, *would take away the freedom* that belongs to any one in that state, must necessarily be supposed to have a design to take away every thing else, that *freedom* being the foundation of all the rest: As he that, in the state of society, would take away the freedom belonging to those of that society or commonwealth, must be supposed to design to take away from them every thing else, and so be looked on as *in a state of war*.

18. This makes it lawful for a man to *kill a thief*, who has not in the least hurt him, nor declared any design upon his life, any farther, than by the use of

force, so to get him in his power, as to take away his money, or what he pleases, from him; because using force, where he has no right, to get me into his power, let his pretence be what it will, I have no reason to suppose, that he, who would *take away my liberty*, would not, when he had me in his power, take away every thing else. And therefore it is lawful for me to treat him as one who has put *himself into a state of war* with me, i.e. kill him if I can; for to that hazard does he justly expose himself, whoever introduces a state of war, and is aggressor in it.

19. And here we have the plain *difference between the state of nature and the state of war*; which however some men have confounded, are as far distant, as a state of peace, good will, mutual assistance and preservation, and a state of enmity, malice, violence and mutual destruction, are one from another. Men living together according to reason, without a common superior on earth, with authority to judge between them, is *properly the state of nature*. But force, or a declared design of force, upon the person of another, where there is no common superior on earth to appeal to for relief, *is the state of war*: And it is the want of such an appeal gives a man the right of war even against an aggressor, though he be in society and a fellow subject. Thus a *thief*, whom I cannot harm, but by appeal to the law, for having stolen all that I am worth, I may kill, when he sets on me to rob me but of my horse or coat; because the law, which was made for my preservation, where it cannot interpose to secure my life from present force, which, if lost, is capable of no reparation, permits me my own defence, and the right of war, a liberty to kill the aggressor, because the aggressor allows not time to appeal to our common judge, nor the decision of the law, for remedy in a case where the mischief may be irreparable. *Want of a common judge with authority, puts all men in a state of nature: Force without right, upon a man's person, makes a state of war*, both where there is, and is not, a common judge.

20. But when the actual force is over, the *state of war ceases* between those that are in society, and are equally on both sides subjected to the fair determination of the law; because then there lies open the remedy of appeal for the past injury, and to prevent future harm: but where no such appeal is, as in the state of nature, for want of positive laws, and judges with authority to appeal to, *the state of war once begun, continues* with a right to the innocent party to destroy the other whenever he can, until the aggressor offers peace, and desires reconciliation on such terms as may repair any wrongs he has already done, and secure the innocent for the future: nay, where an appeal to the law, and constituted judges, lies open, but the remedy is denied by a manifest perverting of justice, and a barefaced wresting of the laws to protect or indemnify the violence or injuries of some men, or party of men, *there* it *is* hard to imagine any thing but *a state of war*. For wherever violence is used, and injury done, though by hands appointed to administer justice, it is still violence and injury, however coloured with the name, pretences, or forms of law, the end whereof being to protect and redress the innocent, by an unbiassed application of it, to all who are under it; wherever that is not *bona fide* done, *war is made* upon the sufferers, who having no appeal on earth to right them, they are left to the only remedy in such cases, an appeal to heaven.

21. To avoid this *state of war* (wherein there is no appeal but to heaven, and wherein every the least difference is apt to end, where there is no authority to decide between the contenders) is one great *reason of men's putting themselves into society*, and quitting the state of nature. For where there is an authority, a power on earth, from which relief can be had by *appeal*, there the continuance of the *state of war* is excluded, and the controversy is decided by that power. Had there been any such court, any superior jurisdiction on earth, to determine the right between Jephthah and the Ammonites, they had never come to a *state of war*: But we see he was forced to appeal to heaven. "The Lord the Judge," says he, "be judge this day, between the children of Israel and the children of Ammon," *Judg.* xi. 27, and then prosecuting, and relying on his appeal, he leads out his army to battle: and therefore in such controversies, where the question is put, *who shall be judge?* it cannot be meant, who shall decide the controversy; every one knows what Jephthah here tells us, that "the Lord the Judge" shall judge. Where there is no judge on earth, the appeal lies to God in heaven. That question then cannot mean, who shall judge? whether another hath put himself in a *state of war* with me, and whether I may, as Jephthah did, *appeal to heaven* in it? of that

I myself can only be judge in my own conscience, as I will answer it, at the great day, to the supreme judge of all men.

Chapter 4

Of Slavery

22. The *natural liberty* of man is to be free from any superior power on earth, and not to be under the will or legislative authority of man, but to have only the law of nature for his rule. The *liberty of man*, in society, is to be under no other legislative power, but that established, by consent, in the commonwealth; nor under the dominion of any will, or restraint of any law, but what that legislative shall enact, according to the trust put in it. Freedom then is not what Sir Robert Filmer tells us, O, A. 55. "a liberty for every one to do what he lists, to live as he pleases, and not to be tied by any laws:" But *freedom of men under government*, is, to have a standing rule to live by, common to every one of that society, and made by the legislative power erected in it; a liberty to follow my own will in all things, where the rule prescribes not; and not to be subject to the inconstant, uncertain, unknown, arbitrary will of another man: As *freedom of nature* is, to be under no other restraint but the law of nature.

23. This freedom from absolute, arbitrary power, is so necessary to, and closely joined with a man's preservation, that he cannot part with it, but by what forfeits his preservation and life together. For a man, not having the power of his own life, cannot, by compact, or his own consent, enslave himself to any one, nor put himself under the absolute, arbitrary power of another, to take away his life, when he pleases. No body can give more power than he has himself; and he that cannot take away his own life, cannot give another power over it. Indeed, having by his fault forfeited his own life, by some act that deserves death; he, to whom he has forfeited it, may (when he has him in his power) delay to take it, and make use of him to his own service, and he does him no injury by it. For, whenever he finds the hardship of his slavery outweigh the value of his life, it is in

his power, by resisting the will of his master, to draw on himself the death he desires.

24. This is the perfect condition of *slavery*, which is nothing else, but *the state of war continued, between a lawful conqueror and a captive*. For, if once compact enter between them, and make an agreement for a limited power on the one side, and obedience on the other, the state of war and slavery ceases, as long as the compact endures. For, as has been said, no man can, by agreement, pass over to another that which he hath not in himself, a power over his own life.

I confess, we find among the Jews, as well as other nations, that men did sell themselves; but, it is plain, this was only to *drudgery, not to slavery*. For it is evident, the person sold was not under an absolute, arbitrary, despotical power. For the master could not have power to kill him, at any time, whom, at a certain time, he was obliged to let go free out of his service: and the master of such a servant was so far from having an arbitrary power over his life, that he could not, at pleasure, so much as maim him, but the loss of an eye, or tooth, set him free, *Exod.* xxi.

Chapter 5

Of Property

25. Whether we consider natural *reason*, which tells us, that men, being once born, have a right to their preservation, and consequently to meat and drink, and such other things as nature affords for their subsistence: or *revelation*, which gives us an account of those grants God made of the world to Adam, and to Noah, and his sons, it is very clear, that God, as King David says, *Psal.* cxv. 16, "has given the earth to the children of men," given it to mankind in common. But this being supposed, it seems to some a very great difficulty how any one should ever come to have a *property* in any thing: I will not content myself to answer, that if it be difficult to make out *property*, upon a supposition, that God gave the world to Adam, and his posterity in common; it is impossible that any man, but one universal monarch, should have any property upon a supposition, that God gave the world to Adam, and his heirs in succession, exclusive of all the rest of his posterity. But I shall endeavour

to shew, how men might come to have a *property* in several parts of that which God gave to mankind in common, and that without any express compact of all the commoners.

26. God, who hath given the world to men in common, hath also given them reason to make use of it to the best advantage of life, and convenience. The earth, and all that is therein, is given to men for the support and comfort of their being. And though all the fruits it naturally produces, and beasts it feeds, belong to mankind in common, as they are produced by the spontaneous hand of nature; and no body has originally a private dominion, exclusive of the rest of mankind, in any of them, as they are thus in their natural state: yet being given for the use of men, there must of necessity be *a means to appropriate* them some way or other, before they can be of any use, or at all beneficial to any particular man. The fruit, or venison, which nourishes the wild Indian, who knows no enclosure, and is still a tenant in common, must be his, and so his, i.e. a part of him, that another can no longer have any right to it, before it can do him any good for the support of his life.

27. Though the earth, and all inferior creatures, be common to all men, yet every man has a property in his own person: this no body has any right to but himself. The labour of his body, and the work of his hands, we may say, are properly his. Whatsoever then he removes out of the state that nature hath provided, and left it in, he hath mixed his labour with, and joined to it something that is his own, and thereby makes it his property. It being by him removed from the common state nature hath placed it in, it hath by this labour something annexed to it, that excludes the common right of other men. For this labour being the unquestionable property of the labourer, no man but he can have a right to what that is once joined to, at least where there is enough, and as good, left in common for others.

28. He that is nourished by the acorns he picked up under an oak, or the apples he gathered from the trees in the wood, has certainly appropriated them to himself. No body can deny but the nourishment is his. I ask then, when did they begin to be his? When he digested? Or when he eat? Or when he boiled? Or when he brought them home? Or when he picked them up? And it is plain, if the first gathering made

them not his, nothing else could. That *labour* put a distinction between them and common: that added something to them more than nature, the common mother of all, had done; and so they became his private right. And will any one say he had no right to those acorns or apples he thus appropriated, because he had not the consent of all mankind to make them his? Was it a robbery thus to assume to himself what belonged to all in common? If such a consent as that was necessary, man had starved, notwithstanding the plenty God had given him. We see in *commons*, which remain so by compact, that it is the taking any part of what is common, and removing it out of the state nature leaves it in, which *begins the property*; without which the common is of no use. And the taking of this or that part does not depend on the express consent of all the commoners. Thus the grass my horse has bit; the turfs my servant has cut; and the ore I have digged in any place, where I have a right to them in common with others, become my *property*, without the assignation or consent of any body. The *labour* that was mine, removing them out of that common state they were in, hath *fixed* my *property* in them.

29. By making an explicit consent of every commoner necessary to any one's appropriating to himself any part of what is given in common, children or servants could not cut the meat, which their father or master had provided for them in common, without assigning to every one his peculiar part. Though the water running in the fountain be every one's, yet who can doubt, but that in the pitcher is his only who drew it out? His *labour* hath taken it out of the hands of nature, where it was common, and belonged equally to all her children, and *hath* thereby *appropriated* it to himself.

30. Thus this law of reason makes the deer that Indian's who hath killed it; it is allowed to be his goods, who hath bestowed his labour upon it, though before it was the common right of every one. And amongst those who are counted the civilized part of mankind, who have made and multiplied positive laws to determine *property*, this original law of nature, for the *beginning of property*, in what was before common, still takes place; and by virtue thereof, what fish any one catches in the ocean, that great and still remaining common of mankind; or what ambergreise

any one takes up here, is *by* the *labour* that removes it out of that common state nature left it in, *made* his *property*, who takes that pains about it. And even amongst us, the hare that any one is hunting, is thought his who pursues her during the chase. For being a beast that is still looked upon as common, and no man's private possession; whoever has employed so much *labour* about any of that kind, as to find and pursue her, has thereby removed her from the state of nature, wherein she was common, and hath *begun a property.*

31. It will perhaps be objected to this, that *if gathering the acorns, or other fruits of the earth, &c.* makes a right to them, then any one may engross as much as he will. To which I answer, Not so. The same law of nature, that does by this means give us property, does also *bound* that *property* too. "God has given us all things richly," 1 *Tim; vi.* 17, is the voice of reason confirmed by inspiration. But how far has he given it us? *To enjoy.* As much as any one can make use of to any advantage of life before it spoils, so much he may by his labour fix a property in: whatever is beyond this, is more than his share, and belongs to others. Nothing was made by God for man to spoil or destroy. And thus, considering the plenty of natural provisions there was a long time in the world, and the few spenders; and to how small a part of that provision the industry of one man could extend itself, and engross it to the prejudice of others; especially keeping within the *bounds,* set by reason, *of* what might serve for his *use;* there could be then little room for quarrels or contentions about property so established.

32. But the *chief matter of property* being now not the fruits of the earth, and the beasts that subsist on it, but the *earth it self;* as that which takes in, and carries with it all the rest: I think it is plain, that *property* in that too is acquired as the former. *As much land* as a man tills, plants, improves, cultivates, and can use the product of, so much is his *property.* He by his labour does, as it were, enclose it from the common. Nor will it invalidate his right, to say every body else has an equal title to it; and therefore he cannot appropriate, he cannot enclose, without the consent of all his fellow commoners, all mankind. God, when he gave the world in common to all mankind, commanded man also to labour, and the

penury of his condition required it of him. God and his reason commanded him to subdue the earth, i.e. improve it for the benefit of life, and therein lay out something upon it that was his own, his labour. He that, in obedience to this command of God, subdued, tilled, and sowed any part of it, thereby annexed to it something that was his *property,* which another had no title to, nor could without injury take from him.

33. Nor was this *appropriation* of any parcel of *land,* by improving it, any prejudice to any other man, since there was still enough, and as good left; and more than the yet unprovided could use. So that, in effect, there was never the less left for others because of his enclosure for himself. For he that leaves as much as another can make use of, does as good as take nothing at all. No body could think himself injured by the drinking of another man, though he took a good draught, who had a whole river of the same water left him to quench his thirst: And the case of land and water, where there is enough of both, is perfectly the same.

34. God gave the world to men in common; but since he gave it them for their benefit, and the greatest conveniences of life they were capable to draw from it, it cannot be supposed he meant it should always remain common and uncultivated. He gave it to the use of the industrious and rational, (and *labour* was to be *his* title to it) not to the fancy or covetousness of the quarrelsome and contentious. He that had as good left for his improvement, as was already taken up, needed not complain, ought not to meddle with what was already improved by another's labour: If he did, it is plain he desired the benefit of another's pains, which he had no right to, and not the ground which God had given him in common with others to labour on, and whereof there was as good left, as that already possessed, and more than he knew what to do with, or his industry could reach to.

35. It is true, in *land* that is *common* in England, or any other country, where there is plenty of people under government, who have money and commerce, no one can enclose or appropriate any part, without the consent of all his fellow-commoners: Because this is left common by compact, i.e. by the law of the land, which is not to be violated. And though it be common, in respect of some men, it is not so to all mankind, but is the joint property of this country, or

this parish. Besides, the remainder, after such enclosure, would not be as good to the rest of the commoners, as the whole was when they could all make use of the whole: whereas in the beginning and first peopling of the great common of the world, it was quite otherwise. The law man was under, was rather for appropriating. God commanded, and his wants forced him to *labour*. That was his *property* which could not be taken from him wherever he had fixed it. And hence subduing or cultivating the earth, and having dominion, we see are joined together. The one gave title to the other. So that God, by commanding to subdue, gave authority so far to *appropriate:* And the condition of human life, which requires labour and materials to work on, necessarily introduces private possessions.

36. The *measure of property* nature has well set by the extent of men's *labour, and the conveniences of life*: No man's labour could subdue or appropriate all; nor could his enjoyment consume more than a small part; so that it was impossible for any man, this way, to intrench upon the right of another, or acquire to himself a property, to the prejudice of his neighbour, who would still have room for as good, and as large a possession (after the other had taken out his) as before it was appropriated. This *measure* did confine every man's *possession* to a very moderate proportion, and such as he might appropriate to himself, without injury to any body, in the first ages of the world, when men were more in danger to be lost, by wandering from their company, in the then vast wilderness of the earth, than to be straitened for want of room to plant in. And the same measure may be allowed still without prejudice to any body, as full as the world seems. For supposing a man, or family, in the state they were at first peopling of the world by the children of Adam, or Noah; let him plant in some inland, vacant places of America, we shall find that the *possessions* he could make himself, upon the *measures* we have given, would not be very large, nor, even to this day, prejudice the rest of mankind, or give them reason to complain, or think themselves injured by this man's encroachment, though the race of men have now spread themselves to all the corners of the world, and do infinitely exceed the small number was at the beginning. Nay, the extent of *ground* is of so little value, *without labour*, that I have heard it af-

firmed, that in Spain itself a man may be permitted to plough, sow, and reap, without being disturbed, upon land he has no other title to, but only his making use of it. But, on the contrary, the inhabitants think themselves beholden to him, who by his industry on neglected and consequently waste land, has increased the stock of corn, which they wanted. But be this as it will, which I lay no stress on; this I dare boldly affirm, that the same *rule of propriety*, (*viz.*) that every man should have as much as he could make use of, would hold still in the world, without straitening any body, since there is land enough in the world to suffice double the inhabitants, had not the *invention of money*, and the tacit agreement of men to put a value on it, introduced (by consent) larger possessions, and a right to them; which, how it has done, I shall by and by shew more at large.

37. This is certain, that in the beginning, before the desire of having more than man needed had altered the intrinsic value of things, which depends only on their usefulness to the life of man; or had *agreed, that a little piece of yellow metal*, which would keep without wasting or decay, should be worth a great piece of flesh, or a whole heap of corn; though men had a right to appropriate, by their labour, each one to himself as much of the things of nature as he could use: yet this could not be much, nor to the prejudice of others, where the same plenty was still left to those who would use the same industry. To which let me add, that he who appropriates land to himself by his labour, does not lessen, but increase the common stock of mankind. For the provisions serving to the support of human life, produced by one acre of enclosed and cultivated land, are (to speak much within compass) ten times more than those which are yielded by an acre of land of an equal richness lying waste in common. And therefore he that encloses land, and has a greater plenty of the conveniencies of life from ten acres, than he could have from an hundred left to nature, may truly be said to give ninety acres to mankind. For his labour now supplies him with provisions out of ten acres, which were by the product of an hundred lying in common. I have here rated the improved land very low, in making its product but as ten to one, when it is much nearer an hundred to one. For I ask, whether in the wild woods and uncultivated waste of

America, left to nature, without any improvement, tillage, or husbandry, a thousand acres yield the needy and wretched inhabitants as many conveniencies of life, as ten acres equally fertile land do in Devonshire, where they are well cultivated?

Before the appropriation of land, he who gathered as much of the wild fruit, killed, caught, or tamed, as many of the beasts as he could; he that so employed his pains about any of the spontaneous products of nature, as any way to alter them from the state which nature put them in, *by* placing any of his *labour* on them, did thereby *acquire a propriety in them*: but if they perished, in his possession, without their due use; if the fruits rotted, or the venison putrified, before he could spend it, he offended against the common law of nature, and was liable to be punished; he invaded his neighbour's share, for he had *no right, farther than his use* called for any of them, and they might serve to afford him conveniencies of life.

38. The same *measures* governed the *possession of land* too: whatsoever he tilled and reaped, laid up and made use of, before it spoiled, that was his peculiar right; whatsoever he enclosed, and could feed, and make use of, the cattle and product was also his. But if either the grass of his inclosure rotted on the ground, or the fruit of his planting perished without gathering, and laying up, this part of the earth, notwithstanding his inclosure, was still to be looked on as waste, and might be the possession of any other. Thus at the beginning, Cain might take as much ground as he could till, and make it his own land, and yet leave enough to Abel's sheep to feed on; a few acres would serve for both their possessions. But as families increased, and industry enlarged their stocks, their *possessions enlarged* with the need of them; but yet it was commonly *without any fixed property in the ground* they made use of, till they incorporated, settled themselves together, and built cities, and then, by consent, they came in time to set out the *bounds of their distinct territories*, and agree on limits between them and their neighbours; and by laws within themselves settled the *properties* of those of the same society. For we see, that in that part of the world which was first inhabited, and therefore like to be best peopled, even as low down as Abraham's time, they wandered with their flocks, and their herds, which was their substance, freely up and down; and this Abra-

ham did, in a country where he was a stranger. Whence it is plain, that at least a great part of the *land lay in common*; that the inhabitants valued it not, nor claimed property in any more than they made use of. But when there was not room enough in the same place, for their herds to feed together, they by consent, as Abraham and Lot did, *Gen.* xiii. 5. separated and enlarged their pasture, where it best liked them. And for the same reason Esau went from his father, and his brother, and planted in Mount Seir, *Gen.* xxxvi. 6.

39. And thus, without supposing any private dominion, and property in Adam, over all the *world*, exclusive of all other men, which can no way be proved, nor any one's property be made out from it; but supposing the *world* given, as it was, to the children of men *in common*, we see how *labour* could make men distinct titles to several parcels of it, for their private uses; wherein there could be no doubt of right, no room for quarrel.

40. Nor is it so strange, as perhaps before consideration it may appear, that the *property of labour* should be able to over-balance the community of land. For it is *labour* indeed that *puts the difference of value* on every thing; and let any one consider what the difference is between an acre of land planted with tobacco or sugar, sown with wheat or barley, and an acre of the same land lying in common, without any husbandry upon it, and he will find, that the improvement of *labour makes* the far greater part of the value. I think it will be but a very modest computation to say, that of the *products* of the earth useful to the life of man, nine tenths are the *effects of labour*: nay, if we will rightly estimate things as they come to our use, and cast up the several expences about them, what in them is purely owing to *nature*, and what to *labour*, we shall find, that in most of them ninety-nine hundredths are wholly to be put on the account of *labour*.

41. There cannot be a clearer demonstration of any thing, than several nations of the Americans are of this, who are rich in land, and poor in all the comforts of life; whom nature having furnished as liberally as any other people, with the materials of plenty, i.e. a fruitful soil, apt to produce in abundance what might serve for food, raiment, and delight; yet *for want of improving it by labour,* have not one

hundredth part of the conveniencies we enjoy: and a king of a large and fruitful territory there feeds, lodges, and is clad worse than a day labourer in England.

42. To make this a little clearer, let us but trace some of the ordinary provisions of life, through their several progresses, before they come to our use, and see how much they receive of their *value from human industry*. Bread, wine, and cloth, are things of daily use, and great plenty, yet notwithstanding, acorns, water, and leaves, or skins, must be our bread, drink, and cloathing, did not labour furnish us with these more useful commodities. For whatever bread is more worth than acorns, wine than water, and *cloth or silk*, than leaves, skins, or moss, that is *wholly owing to labour* and *industry*. The one of these being the food and raiment which unassisted nature furnishes us with; the other, provisions which our industry and pains prepare for us, which how much they exceed the other in value, when any one hath computed, he will then see how much *labour makes the far greatest part of the value* of things we enjoy in this world: and the ground which produces the materials, is scarce to be reckoned in, as any, or, at most, but a very small part of it: so little, that even amongst us, land that is left wholly to nature, that hath no improvement of pasturage, tillage, or planting, is called, as indeed it is, *waste*; and we shall find the benefit of it amount to little more than nothing.

This shews how much numbers of men are to be preferred to largeness of dominions; and that the increase of lands, and the right of employing of them, is the great art of government: and that prince, who shall be so wise and godlike, as by established laws of liberty to secure protection and encouragement to the honest industry of mankind, against the oppression of power and narrowness of party, will quickly be too hard for his neighbours; but this by the by. To return to the argument in hand.

43. An acre of land, that bears here twenty bushels of wheat, and another in America, which, with the same husbandry, would do the like, are, without doubt, of the same natural intrinsic value: but yet the benefit mankind receives from the one in a year, is worth 5 l. and from the other possibly not worth a penny, if all the profit an Indian received from it were to be valued, and sold here; at least, I may truly say, not one thousandth. It is *labour* then which *puts the greatest part of the value upon land*, without which it would scarcely be worth any thing: it is to that we owe the greatest part of all its useful products; for all that the straw, bran, bread, of that acre of wheat, is more worth than the product of an acre of as good land, which lies waste, is all the effect of labour. For it is not barely the ploughman's pains, the reaper's and thresher's toil, and the baker's sweat is to be counted into the *bread* we eat; the labour of those who broke the oxen, who digged and wrought the iron and stones, who felled and framed the timber employed about the plough, mill, oven, or any other utensils, which are a vast number requisite to this corn, from its being seed to be sown, to its being made bread, must all be *charged on* the account of *labour*, and received as an effect of that: nature and the earth furnished only the almost worthless materials, as in themselves. It would be a strange *catalogue of things, that industry provided and made use of, about every loaf of bread*, before it came to our use, if we could trace them; iron, wood, leather, bark, timber, stone, bricks, coals, lime, cloth, dying drugs, pitch, tar, masts, ropes, and all the materials made use of in the ship, that brought any of the commodities made use of by any of the workmen, to any part of the work, all which it would be almost impossible, at least too long, to reckon up.

44. From all which it is evident, that though the things of nature are given in common, yet man, by being master of himself, and *proprietor of his own person, and the actions or labour of it, had still in himself the great foundation of property*; and that, which made up the great part of what he applied to the support or comfort of his being, when invention and arts had improved the conveniencies of life, was perfectly his own, and did not belong in common to others.

45. Thus *labour*, in the beginning, *gave a right of property*, wherever any one was pleased to employ it upon what was common, which remained a long while the far greater part, and is yet more than mankind makes use of. Men, at first, for the most part, contented themselves with what unassisted nature offered to their necessities: and though afterwards, in some parts of the world, (where the increase of people and stock, with the *use of money*, had made land scarce, and so of some value) the several *communities*

settled the bounds of their distinct territories, and by laws within themselves regulated the properties of the private men of their society, and so, by *compact* and agreement, *settled the property* which labour and industry began; and the leagues that have been made between several states and kingdoms, either expressly or tacitly disowning all claim and right to the land in the others possession, have, by common consent, given up their pretences to their natural common right, which originally they had to those countries, and so have, by *positive agreement, settled a property* amongst themselves, in distinct parts and parcels of the earth; yet there are still *great tracts of ground* to be found, which (the inhabitants thereof not having joined with the rest of mankind, in the consent of the use of their common money) *lie waste*, and are more than the people who dwell on it do, or can make use of, and so still lie in common. Though this can scarce happen amongst that part of mankind that have consented to the use of money.

46. The greatest part of *things really useful* to the life of man, and such as the necessity of subsisting made the first commoners of the world look after, as it doth the Americans now, *are* generally things of *short duration*; such as, if they are not consumed by use, will decay and perish of themselves: gold, silver, and diamonds, are things that fancy or agreement hath put the value on, more than real use, and the necessary support of life. Now of those good things which nature hath provided in common, every one had a right, (as hath been said) to as much as he could use, and property in all that he could affect with his labour; all that his *industry* could extend to, to alter from the state nature had put it in, was his. He that *gathered* a hundred bushels of acorns or apples, had thereby a *property* in them, they were his goods as soon as gathered. He was only to look, that he used them before they spoiled, else he took more than his share, and robbed others. And indeed it was a foolish thing, as well as dishonest, to hoard up more than he could make use of. If he gave away a part to any body else, so that it perished not uselessly in his possession, these he also made use of. And if he also bartered away plums, that would have rotted in a week, for nuts that would last good for his eating a whole year, he did no injury; he wasted not the common stock; destroyed no part of the portion of goods

that belonged to others, so long as nothing perished uselessly in his hands. Again, if he would give his nuts for a piece of metal, pleased with its colour; or exchange his sheep for shells, or wool for a sparkling pebble or a diamond, and keep those by him all his life, he invaded not the right of others, he might heap up as much of these durable things as he pleased; the *exceeding of the bounds of* his *just property* not lying in the largeness of his possession, but the perishing of any thing uselessly in it.

47. And thus *came in the use of money*, some lasting thing that men might keep without spoiling, and that by mutual consent men would take in exchange for the truly useful, but perishable supports of life.

48. And as different degrees of industry were apt to give men possessions in different proportions, so this *invention of money* gave them the opportunity to continue and enlarge them. For supposing an island, separate from all possible commerce with the rest of the world, wherein there were but an hundred families, but there were sheep, horses, and cows, with other useful animals, wholesome fruits, and land enough for corn for a hundred thousand times as many, but nothing in the island, either because of its commonness, or perishableness, fit to supply the place of *money*: What reason could any one have there to enlarge his possessions beyond the use of his family and a plentiful supply to its *consumption*, either in what their own industry produced, or they could barter for like perishable, useful commodities with others? Where there is not something, both lasting and scarce, and so valuable to be hoarded up, there men will not be apt to enlarge their *possessions of land*, were it never so rich, never so free for them to take. For I ask, what would a man value ten thousand, or an hundred thousand acres of excellent *land*, ready cultivated and well stocked too with cattle, in the middle of the inland parts of America, where he had no hopes of commerce with other parts of the world, to draw *money* to him by the sale of the product? It would not be worth the enclosing, and we should see him give up again to the wild common of nature, whatever was more than would supply the conveniencies of life to be had there for him and his family.

49. Thus in the beginning all the world was America, and more so than that is now; for no such thing as *money* was any where known. Find out something

that hath the *use and value of money* amongst his neighbours, you shall see the same man will begin presently to *enlarge* his possessions.

50. But since gold and silver, being little useful to the life of man in proportion to food, raiment, and carriage, has its *value* only from the consent of men, whereof *labour* yet *makes*, in great part, the *measure*, it is plain, that men have agreed to a disproportionate and unequal *possession of the earth*, they having, by a tacit and voluntary consent, found out a way how a man may fairly possess more land than he himself can use the product of, by receiving in exchange for the overplus, gold and silver, which may be hoarded up without injury to any one; these metals not spoiling or decaying in the hands of the possessor. This partage of things in an inequality of private possessions, men have made practicable out of the bounds of society, and without compact, only by putting a value on gold and silver, and tacitly agreeing in the use of money. For in governments, the laws regulate the right of property, and the possession of land is determined by positive constitutions.

51. And thus, I think, it is very easy to conceive, without any difficulty *how labour could at first begin a title of property* in the common things of nature, and how the spending it upon our uses bounded it. So that there could then be no reason of quarrelling about title, nor any doubt about the largeness of possession it gave. Right and conveniency went together; for as a man had a right to all he could employ his labour upon, so he had no temptation to labour for more than he could make use of. This left no room for controversy about the title, nor for encroachment on the right of others; what portion a man carved to himself, was easily seen; and it was useless, as well as dishonest, to carve himself too much, or take more than he needed.

Chapter 6

Of Paternal Power

52. It may perhaps be censured as an impertinent criticism, in a discourse of this nature, to find fault with words and names, that have obtained in the world: and yet possibly it may not be amiss to offer new ones, when the old are apt to lead men into mistakes, as this of *paternal power* probably has done, which seems so to place the power of parents over their children wholly in the *father*, as if the *mother* had no share in it, whereas, if we consult reason or revelation, we shall find she hath an equal title. This may give one reason to ask, whether this might not be more properly called *parental power*. For whatever obligation nature and the right of generation lays on children, it must certainly bind them equally to both concurrent causes of it. And accordingly we see the positive law of God every where joins them together without distinction, when it commands the obedience of children: "Honour thy father and thy mother," *Exod*. xx. 12. "Whosoever curseth his father or his mother," *Lev*. xx. 9. "Ye shall fear every man his mother and his father," *Lev*. xix. 5. "Children, obey your parents," &c. *Eph*. vi. 1, is the style of the Old and New Testament.

53. Had but this one thing been well considered, without looking any deeper into the matter, it might perhaps have kept men from running into those gross mistakes they have made, about this power of parents; which, however it might, without any great harshness, bear the name of absolute dominion, and regal authority, when under the title of *paternal power* it seemed appropriated to the father, would yet have sounded but oddly, and in the very name shewn the absurdity, if this supposed absolute power over children had been called *parental*; and thereby have discovered, that it belonged to the *mother* too. For it will but very ill serve the turn of those men, who contend so much for the absolute power and authority of the fatherhood, as they call it, that the mother should have any share in it. And it would have but ill supported the monarchy they contend for, when by the very name it appeared that that fundamental authority, from whence they would derive their government of a single person only, was not placed in one, but two persons jointly. But to let this of names pass.

54. Though I have said above, chap. ii. "That all men by nature are equal," I cannot be supposed to understand all sorts of *equality*: *age* or *virtue* may give men a just precedency: *excellency of parts* and *merit* may place others above the common level: *birth* may subject some, and *alliance* or *benefits* others, to pay

an observance to those whom nature, gratitude, or other respects, may have made it due, and yet all this consists with the *equality*, which all men are in, in respect of jurisdiction or dominion one over another; which was the *equality* I there spoke of, as proper to the business in hand, being that *equal right*, that every man hath, *to his natural freedom*, without being subjected to the will or authority of any other man.

55. *Children*, I confess, are not born in this state of *equality*, though they are born to it. Their parents have a sort of rule and jurisdiction over them, when they come into the world, and for some time after, but it is but a temporary one. The bonds of this subjection are like the swaddling clothes they are wrapt up in, and supported by, in the weakness of their infancy: Age and reason, as they grow up, loosen them, till at length they drop quite off, and leave a man at his own free disposal.

56. Adam was created a perfect man, his body and mind in full possession of their strength and reason, and so was capable from the first instant of his being to provide for his own support and preservation; and govern his actions according to the dictates of the law of reason which God had implanted in him. From him the world is peopled with his descendants, who are all born infants, weak and helpless, without knowledge or understanding: But to supply the defects of this imperfect state, till the improvement of growth and age hath removed them, Adam and Eve, and after them all *parents* were, by the law of nature, *under an obligation to preserve, nourish, and educate the children*, they had begotten; not as their own workmanship, but the workmanship of their own maker, the Almighty, to whom they were to be accountable for them.

57. The law, that was to govern Adam, was the same that was to govern all his posterity, the *law of reason*. But his offspring having another way of entrance into the world, different from him, by a natural birth, that produced them ignorant and without the use of *reason*, they were not presently *under that law*; for no body can be under a law, which is not promulgated to him: and this law being promulgated or made known by *reason* only, he that is not come to the use of his *reason*, cannot be said to be *under this law*; and Adam's children, being not presently as soon as born, *under this law of reason*, were not pres-

ently free. For law, in its true notion, *is not so much the limitation, as the direction of a free and intelligent agent* to his proper interest, and prescribes no farther than is for the general good of those under that law. Could they be happier without it, the law, as an useless thing, would of it self vanish: and that ill deserves the name of confinement which hedges us in only from bogs and precipices. So that, however it may be mistaken, *the end of law* is not to abolish or restrain, but *to preserve and enlarge freedom*. For in all the states of created beings capable of laws, *where there is no law, there is no freedom.* For liberty is to be free from restraint and violence from others which cannot be where there is no law: but freedom is not, as we are told, "a liberty for every man to do what he lists:" (for who could be free, when every other man's humour might domineer over him?) but a liberty to dispose, and order as he lists, his person, actions, possessions, and his whole property, within the allowance of those laws under which he is, and therein not to be subject to the arbitrary will of another, but freely follow his own.

58. The *power*, then, *that parents have* over their children, arises from that duty which is incumbent on them, to take care of their offspring during the imperfect state of childhood. To inform the mind, and govern the actions of their yet ignorant nonage, till reason shall take its place, and ease them of that trouble, is what the children want, and the parents are bound to. For God having given man an understanding to direct his actions, has allowed him a freedom of will, and liberty of acting, as properly belonging thereunto, within the bounds of that law he is under. But whilst he is in an estate, wherein he has not understanding of his own to direct his will, he is not to have any will of his own to follow: he that understands for him, must will for him too; he must prescribe to his will, and regulate his actions: but when he comes to the estate that made his *father a freeman*, the *son is a freeman* too.

59. This holds in all the laws a man is under, whether natural or civil. Is a man under the law of nature? *What made him free* of that law? What gave him a free disposing of his property according to his own will, within the compass of that law? I answer, a state of maturity, wherein he might be supposed capable to know that law, that so he might keep his

actions within the bounds of it. When he has acquired that state, he is presumed to know how far that law is to be his guide, and how far he may make use of his *freedom*, and so comes to have it; till then, some body else must guide him, who is presumed to know how far the law allows a liberty. If such a state of reason, such an age of discretion *made him free*, the same shall make his son free too. Is a man under the law of England? *What made him free* of that law? That is, to have the liberty to dispose of his actions and possessions according to his own will within the permission of that law? A capacity of knowing that law. Which is supposed by that law, at the age of one and twenty years, and in some cases sooner. If this made the father free, it shall make the son free too. Till then we see the law allows the son to have no will, but he is to be guided by the will of his father or guardian, who is to understand for him. And if the father die, and fail to substitute a deputy in his trust; if he hath not provided a tutor to govern his son, during his minority, during his want of understanding; the law takes care to do it; some other must govern him, and be a will to him, till he hath *attained to a state of freedom*, and his understanding be fit to take the government of his will. But after that, the father and son are equally free as much as tutor and pupil after nonage: equally subjects of the same law together, without any dominion left in the father over the life, liberty, or estate of his son, whether they be only in the state and under the law of nature, or under the positive laws of an established government.

60. But if, through defects that may happen out of the ordinary course of nature, any one comes not to such a degree of reason, wherein he might be supposed capable of knowing the law, and so living within the rules of it; he is *never capable of being a free man*, he is never let loose to the disposure of his own will (because he knows no bounds to it, has not understanding, its proper guide) but is continued under the tuition and government of others, all the time his own understanding is incapable of that charge. And so *lunatics* and *idiots* are never set free from the government of their parents. "Children, who are not as yet come into those years whereat they may have; and innocents which are excluded by a natural defect from ever having; thirdly, madmen, which for the present cannot possibly have the use of right reason

to guide themselves; have for their guide the reason that guideth other men, which are tutors over them, to seek and procure their good for them," says Hooker, Eccl. Pol. Lib. I. Sect. 7. All which seems no more than that duty which God and nature has laid on man, as well as other creatures, to preserve their offspring, till they can be able to shift for themselves, and will scarce amount to an instance or proof of parents regal authority.

61. Thus we are *born free*, as we are born rational; not that we have actually the exercise of either: age, that brings one, brings with it the other too. And thus we see how *natural freedom and subjection to parents* may consist together, and are both founded on the same principle. A *child* is *free* by his father's title, by his father's understanding, which is to govern him till he hath it of his own. The *freedom of a man at years of discretion*, and the *subjection* of a child *to* his parents, whilst yet short of that age, are so consistent, and so distinguishable, that the most blinded contenders for monarchy, *by right of fatherhood*, cannot miss this difference; the most obstinate cannot but allow their consistency. For were their doctrine all true, were the right heir of Adam now known, and by that title settled a monarch in his throne, invested with all the absolute unlimited power, Sir Robert Filmer talks of; if he should die as soon as his heir were born, must not the child, notwithstanding he were never so free, never so much sovereign, be in subjection to his mother and nurse, to tutors and governors, till age and education brought him reason and ability to govern himself and others? The necessities of his life, the health of his body, and the information of his mind, would require him to be directed by the will of others, and not his own; and yet will any one think, that this restraint and subjection were inconsistent with, or spoiled him of, that liberty or sovereignty he had a right to, or gave away his empire to those who had the government of his nonage? This government over him only prepared him the better and sooner for it. If any body should ask me when my son is of *age to be free?* I shall answer, just when his monarch is of age to govern. "But at what time," says the judicious Hooker, Eccl. Pol. Lib. I. Sect. 6 "a man may be said to have attained so far forth the use of reason, as sufficeth to make him capable of those laws whereby he is then bound to guide his actions: this is a great

deal more easy for sense to discern, than for any one by skill and learning to determine."

62. Commonwealths themselves take notice of, and allow, that there is *a time when men* are to *begin to act like free men*, and therefore till that time require not oaths of fealty, or allegiance, or other public owning of, or submission to, the government of their countries.

63. The *freedom* then of man, and liberty of acting according to his own will, is *grounded* on his having *reason,* which is able to instruct him in that law he is to govern himself by, and make him know how far he is left to the freedom of his own will. To turn him loose to an unrestrained liberty, before he has reason to guide him, is not the allowing him the privilege of his nature to be free; but to thrust him out amongst brutes, and abandon him to a state as wretched, and as much beneath that of a man, as theirs. This is that which puts the *authority* into the *parents* hands to govern the *minority* of their children. God hath made it their business to employ this care on their offspring, and hath placed in them suitable inclinations of tenderness and concern to temper this power, to apply it, as his wisdom designed it, to the children's good as long as they should need to be under it.

64. But what reason can hence advance this care of the *parents* due to their offspring into an *absolute arbitrary dominion* of the father, whose power reaches no farther than, by such a discipline as he finds most effectual, to give such strength and health to their bodies, such vigour and rectitude to their minds, as may best fit his children to be most useful to themselves and others; and, if it be necessary to his condition, to make them work, when they are able, for their own subsistence. But in this power the *mother* too has her share with the *father.*

65. Nay, *this* power so little belongs to the father by any peculiar right of nature, but only as he is guardian of his children, that when he quits his care of them, he loses his power over them, which goes along with their nourishment and education, to which it is inseparably annexed; and it belongs as much to the foster-father of an exposed child, as to the natural father of another. So little power does the bare *act of begetting* give a man over his issue; if all his care ends there, and this be all the title he hath to the name and authority of a father. And what will become

of this *paternal power* in that part of the world, where one woman hath more than one husband at a time? or in those parts of America, where, when the husband and wife part, which happens frequently, the children are all left to the mother, follow her, and are wholly under her care and provision? If the father die whilst the children are young, do they not naturally every where owe the same obedience to their mother, during their minority, as to their father were he alive? And will any one say, that the mother hath a legislative power over her children? that she can make standing rules, which shall be of perpetual obligation, by which they ought to regulate all the concerns of their property, and bound their liberty all the course of their lives? or can she enforce the observation of them with capital punishments? For this is the proper *power of the magistrate,* of which the father hath not so much as the shadow. His command over his children is but temporary, and reaches not their life or property: it is but a help to the weakness and imperfection of their nonage, a discipline necessary to their education: and though a father may dispose of his own possessions as he pleases, when his children are out of danger of perishing for want, yet his power extends not to the lives or goods, which either their own industry, or another's bounty has made theirs; nor to their liberty neither, when they are once arrived to the infranchisement of the years of discretion. The *father's empire* then ceases, and can from thence forwards no more dispose of the liberty of his son, than that of any other man: and it must be far from an absolute or perpetual jurisdiction, from which a man may withdraw himself, having licence from divine authority to *leave father and mother, and cleave to his wife.*

66. But though there be a time when a child comes to be as free from subjection to the will and command of his father, as the father himself is free from subjection to the will of any body else, and they are each under no other restraint but that which is common to them both, whether it be the law of nature, or municipal law of their country; yet this freedom exempts not a son from that honour which he ought, by the law of God and nature, to pay his parents. God having made the parents instruments in his great design of continuing the race of mankind, and the occasions of life to their children; as he hath laid on them an obligation to nourish, preserve, and bring

up their offspring; so he has laid on the children a perpetual obligation of *honouring their parents*, which containing in it an inward esteem and reverence to be shewn by all outward expressions, ties up the child from any thing that may ever injure or affront, disturb or endanger, the happiness or life of those from whom he received his; and engages him in all actions of defence, relief, assistance, and comfort of those, by whose means he entered into being, and has been made capable of any enjoyments of life. From this obligation no state, no freedom can absolve children. But this is very far from giving parents a power of command over their children, or an authority to make laws and dispose as they please of their lives and liberties. It is one thing to owe honour, respect, gratitude, and assistance; another to require an absolute obedience and submission. The *honour due to parents*, a monarch in his throne owes his mother, and yet this lessens not his authority, nor subjects him to her government.

67. The subjection of a minor places in the father a temporary government, which terminates with the minority of the child: and the *honour due from a child*, places in the parents a perpetual right to respect, reverence, support and compliance too, more or less, as the father's care, cost, and kindness in his education, have been more or less. This ends not with minority, but holds in all parts and conditions of a man's life. The want of distinguishing these two powers, viz. that which the father hath in the right of *tuition*, during minority, and the right of honour all his life, may perhaps have caused a great part of the mistakes about this matter. For to speak properly of them, the first of these is rather the privilege of children, and duty of parents, than any prerogative of paternal power. The nourishment and education of their children is a charge so incumbent on parents for their children's good, that nothing can absolve them from taking care of it. And though the *power of commanding and chastising* them go along with it, yet God hath woven into the principles of human nature such a tenderness for their offspring, that there is little fear that parents should use their power with too much rigour; the excess is seldom on the severe side, the strong bias of nature drawing the other way. And therefore God Almighty, when he would express his gentle dealing with the Israelites, he tells them,

that though he chastened them, "he chastened them as a man chastens his son," *Deut.* viii. 5. i.e. with tenderness and affection, and kept them under no severer discipline than what was absolutely best for them, and had been less kindness to have slackened. This is that power to which children are commanded obedience, that the pains and care of their parents may not be increased, or ill rewarded.

68. On the other side, *honour* and *support*, all that which gratitude requires to return for the benefits received by and from them, is the indispensable duty of the child, and the proper privilege of the parents. This is intended for the parents advantage, as the other is for the child's; though education, the parents duty, seems to have most power, because the ignorance and infirmities of childhood stand in need of restraint and correction; which is a visible exercise of rule, and a kind of dominion. And that duty which is comprehended in the word *honour*, requires less obedience, though the obligation be stronger on grown than younger children. For who can think the command, "Children, obey your parents," requires in a man that has children of his own the same submission to his father, as it does in his yet young children to him; and that by this precept he were bound to obey all his father's commands, if, out of a conceit of authority, he should have the indiscretion to treat him still as a boy?

69. The first part then of *paternal power*, or rather duty, which is *education*, belongs so to the father, that it terminates at a certain season; when the business of education is over, it ceases of itself, and is also alienable before. For a man may put the tuition of his son in other hands; and he that has made his son an *apprentice* to another, has discharged him, during that time, of a great part of his obedience both to himself and to his mother. But all the *duty of honour*, the other part, remains nevertheless entire to them; nothing can cancel that: It is so inseparable from them both, that the father's authority cannot dispossess the mother of this right, nor can any man discharge his son from *honouring* her that bore him. But both these are very far from a power to make laws, and enforcing them with penalties that may reach estate, liberty, limbs, and life. The power of commanding ends with nonage; and though after that, *honour* and respect, support and defence, and whatsoever gratitude can

oblige a man to, for the highest benefits he is naturally capable of, be always due from a son to his parents; yet all this puts no sceptre into the father's hand, no sovereign power of commanding. He has no dominion over his son's property, or actions; nor any right that his will should prescribe to his son's in all things; however it may become his son in many things not very inconvenient to him and his family, to pay a deference to it.

70. A man may owe *honour* and respect to an ancient, or wise man; defence to his child or friend; relief and support to the distressed; and gratitude to a benefactor, to such a degree, that all he has, all he can do, cannot sufficiently pay it: but all these give no authority, no right to any one, of making laws over him from whom they are owing. And it is plain, all this is due not only to the bare title of father; not only because, as has been said, it is owing to the mother too, but because these obligations to parents, and the degrees of what is required of children, may be varied by the different care and kindness, trouble and expense, which is often employed upon one child more than another.

71. This shews the reason how it comes to pass, that *parents in societies*, where they themselves are subjects, retain a *power over their children*, and have as much right to their subjection as those who are in the state of nature. Which could not possibly be, if all political power were only paternal, and that in truth they were one and the same thing. For then, all paternal power being in the prince, the subject could naturally have none of it. But these two *powers*, *political* and *paternal*, are so perfectly distinct and separate, are built upon so different foundations, and given to so different ends, that every subject that is a father, has as much a paternal power over his children, as the prince has over his: and every prince, that has parents, owes them as much filial duty and obedience, as the meanest of his subjects do to theirs; and cannot therefore contain any part or degree of that kind of dominion which a prince or magistrate has over his subject.

72. Though the obligation on the parents to bring up their children, and the obligation on children to honour their parents, contain all the power on the one hand, and submission on the other, which are proper to this relation, yet there is *another power*

ordinary *in the father*, whereby he has a tie on the obedience of his children; which though it be common to him with other men, yet the occasions of shewing it almost constantly happening to fathers in their private families, and the instances of it elsewhere being rare, and less taken notice of, it passes in the world for a part of paternal jurisdiction. And this is the power men generally have to *bestow their estates* on those who please them best. The possession of the father being the expectation and inheritance of the children, ordinarily in certain proportions, according to the law and custom of each country; yet it is commonly in the father's power to bestow it with a more sparing or liberal hand, according as the behaviour of this or that child hath comported with his will and humour.

73. This is no small tie on the obedience of children: and there being always annexed to the enjoyment of land a submission to the government of the country, of which that land is a part; it has been commonly supposed, that a father could *oblige his posterity to that government*, of which he himself was a subject, and that his compact held them; whereas it being only a necessary condition annexed to the land, and the inheritance of an estate which is under that government, reaches only those who will take it on that condition, and so is no natural tie or engagement, but a voluntary submission. For *every man's children* being by nature as free as himself, or any of his ancestors ever were, may, whilst they are in that freedom, choose what society they will join themselves to, what commonwealth they will put themselves under. But if they will enjoy the inheritance of their ancestors, they must take it on the same terms their ancestors had it, and submit to all the conditions annexed to such a possession. By this power indeed fathers oblige their children to obedience to themselves, even when they are past minority, and most commonly too subject them to this or that political power. But neither of these by any peculiar right of fatherhood, but by the reward they have in their hands to enforce and recompence such a compliance; and is no more power than what a Frenchman has over an Englishman, who, by the hopes of an estate he will leave him, will certainly have a strong tie on his obedience: and if, when it is left him, he will enjoy it, he must certainly take it upon the conditions

annexed to the *possession of land* in that country where it lies, whether it be France or England.

74. To conclude then, though the father's power of commanding extends no farther than the minority of his children, and to a degree only fit for the discipline and government of that age; and though that honour and respect, and all that which the Latins called piety, which they indispensably owe to their parents all their life-time, and in all estates, with all that support and defence which is due to them, gives the father no power of governing, i.e. making laws and enacting penalties on his children; though by all this he has no dominion over the property or actions of his son; yet it is obvious to conceive how easy it was, in the first ages of the world, and in places still, where the thinness of people gives families leave to separate into unpossessed quarters, and they have room to remove or plant themselves in yet vacant habitations, for the *father of the family* to become the prince[1] of it; he had been a ruler from the beginning of the infancy of his children: and since without some government it would be hard for them to live together, it was likeliest it should, by the express or tacit consent of the children when they were grown up, be in the father, where it seemed without any change barely to continue; when indeed nothing more was required to it, than the permitting the father to exercise alone,

1. It is no improbable opinion therefore, which the arch-philosopher was of, "That the chief person in every household was always, as it were, a king: so when numbers of households joined themselves in civil societies together, kings were the first kind of governors amongst them, which is also, as it seemeth, the reason why the name of fathers continued still in them, who, of fathers, were made rulers; as also the ancient custom of governors to do as Melchizedeck, and being kings, to exercise the office of priests, which fathers did, at the first grew perhaps by the same occasion. Howbeit, this is not the only kind of regiment that has been received in the world. The inconveniences of one kind have caused sundry others to be devised; so that in a word, all public regiment of what kind soever, seemeth evidently to have risen from the deliberate advice, consultation and composition between men, judging it convenient and behoveful; there being no impossibility in nature considered by itself, but that man might have lived without any public regiment." Hooker's Eccl. P. L. I. Sect. 10.

in his family, that executive power of the law of nature, which every free man naturally hath, and by that permission resigning up to him a monarchical power, whilst they remained in it. But that this was not by any *paternal right*, but only by the consent of his children, is evident from hence, that no body doubts, but if a stranger, whom chance or business had brought to his family, had there killed any of his children, or committed any other fact, he might condemn and put him to death, or otherwise punish him, as well as any of his children: which it was impossible he should do by virtue of any paternal authority over one who was not his child, but by virtue of that executive power of the law of nature, which, as a man, he had a right to: and he alone could punish him in his family, where the respect of his children had laid by the exercise of such a power, to give way to the dignity and authority they were willing should remain in him, above the rest of his family.

75. Thus it was easy, and almost natural for children, by a tacit, and scarce avoidable consent, to make way for the *father's authority and government*. They had been accustomed in their childhood to follow his direction, and to refer their little differences to him; and when they were men, who fitter to rule them? Their little properties, and less covetousness, seldom afforded greater controversies; and when any should arise, where could they have a fitter umpire than he, by whose care they had every one been sustained and brought up, and who had a tenderness for them all? It is no wonder that they made no distinction betwixt minority and full age; nor looked after one and twenty, or any other age that might make them the free disposers of themselves and fortunes, when they could have no desire to be out of their pupilage. The government they had been under during it, continued still to be more their protection than restraint: and they could no where find a greater security to their peace, liberties, and fortunes, than in the *rule of a father*.

76. Thus the natural *fathers of families* by an insensible change became the *politic monarchs* of them too: and as they chanced to live long, and leave able and worthy heirs, for several successions, or otherwise; so they laid the foundations of hereditary, or elective kingdoms, under several constitutions and manners, according as chance, contrivance, or occasions hap-

pened to mould them. But if princes have their titles in their fathers right, and it be a sufficient proof of the natural *right of fathers* to political authority, because they commonly were those in whose hands we find, *de facto*, the exercise of government: I say, if this argument be good, it will as strongly prove, that all princes, nay princes only, ought to be priests, since it is as certain, that in the beginning, *the father of the family was priest, as that he was ruler in his own household.*

Chapter 7

Of Political or Civil Society

77. God having made man such a creature, that in his own judgment, it was not good for him to be alone, put him under strong obligations of necessity, convenience, and inclination, to drive him into society, as well as fitted him with understanding and language to continue and enjoy it. The first society was between man and wife, which gave beginning to that between parents and children; to which, in time, that between master and servant came to be added; and though all these might, and commonly did meet together, and make up but one family, wherein the master or mistress of it had some sort of rule proper to a family; each of these, or all together, came short of *political society*, as we shall see, if we consider the different ends, ties, and bounds of each of these.

78. *Conjugal society* is made by a voluntary compact between man and woman; and though it consist chiefly in such a communion and right in one another's bodies as is necessary to its chief end, procreation; yet it draws with it mutual support and assistance, and a communion of interests too, as necessary not only to unite their care and affection, but also necessary to their common offspring, who have a right to be nourished and maintained by them, till they are able to provide for themselves.

79. For the end of *conjunction between male and female* being not barely procreation, but the continuation of the species; this conjunction betwixt male and female ought to last, even after procreation, so long as is necessary to the nourishment and support of the young ones, who are to be sustained by those that

got them, till they are able to shift and provide for themselves. This rule, which the infinite wise Maker hath set to the works of his hands, we find the inferior creatures steadily obey. In those viviparous animals which feed on grass, the *conjunction between male and female* lasts no longer than the very act of copulation; because the teat of the dam being sufficient to nourish the young, till it be able to feed on grass, the male only begets, but concerns not himself for the female or young, to whose sustenance he can contribute nothing. But in beasts of prey the conjunction lasts longer: because the dam not being able well to subsist herself, and nourish her numerous offspring by her own prey alone, a more laborious, as well as more dangerous way of living, than by feeding on grass; the assistance of the male is necessary to the maintenance of their common family, which cannot subsist till they are able to prey for themselves, but by the joint care of male and female. The same is to be observed in all birds (except some domestic ones, where plenty of food excuses the cock from feeding, and taking care of the young brood), whose young needing food in the nest, the cock and hen continue mates, till the young are able to use their wing, and provide for themselves.

80. And herein I think lies the chief, if not the only reason, *why the male and female in mankind are tied to a longer conjunction* than other creatures, viz. because the female is capable of conceiving, and *de facto* is commonly with child again, and brings forth too a new birth, long before the former is out of a dependency for support on his parents help, and able to shift for himself, and has all the assistance that is due to him from his parents: whereby the father, who is bound to take care for those he hath begot, is under an obligation to continue in conjugal society with the same woman longer than other creatures, whose young being able to subsist of themselves before the time of procreation returns again, the conjugal bond dissolves of itself, and they are at liberty, till Hymen at his usual anniversary season summons them again to choose new mates. Wherein one cannot but admire the wisdom of the great Creator, who having given to man foresight, and an ability to lay up for the future, as well as to supply the present necessity, hath made it necessary, that *society of man and wife should be more lasting*, than of male and female amongst

other creatures; that so their industry might be encouraged, and their interest better united, to make provision and lay up goods for their common issue, which uncertain mixture, or easy and frequent solutions of conjugal society, would mightily disturb.

81. But though these are ties upon *mankind*, which make the *conjugal bonds* more firm and lasting in man, than the other species of animals; yet it would give one reason to inquire, why this compact, where procreation and education are secured, and inheritance taken care for, may not be made determinable, either by consent, or at a certain time, or upon certain conditions, as well as any other voluntary compacts, there being no necessity in the nature of the thing, nor to the ends of it, that it should always be for life; I mean, to such as are under no restraint of any positive law, which ordains all such contracts to be perpetual.

82. But the husband and wife, though they have but one common concern, yet having different understandings, will unavoidably sometimes have different wills too; it therefore being necessary that the last determination, i.e. the rule, should be placed somewhere; it naturally falls to the man's share, as the abler and the stronger. But this reaching but to the things of their common interest and property, leaves the wife in the full and free possession of what by contract is her peculiar right, and gives the husband no more power over her life than she has over his. The *power of the husband* being so far from that of an absolute monarch, that the *wife* has in many cases a liberty to separate from him, where natural right or their contract allows it; whether that contract be made by themselves in the state of nature, or by the customs or laws of the country they live in; and the children upon such separation fall to the father's or mother's lot, as such contract does determine.

83. For all the ends of *marriage* being to be obtained under politic government, as well as in the state of nature, the civil magistrate doth not abridge the right or power of either naturally necessary to those ends, viz. procreation and mutual support and assistance whilst they are together; but only decides any controversy that may arise between man and wife about them. If it were otherwise, and that absolute sovereignty and power of life and death naturally belonged to the husband, and were *necessary to the society*

between man and wife, there could be no matrimony in any of those countries where the husband is allowed no such absolute authority. But the ends of matrimony requiring no such power in the husband, the condition of conjugal society put it not in him, it being not at all necessary to that state. Conjugal society could subsist and attain its ends without it; nay, community of goods, and the power over them, mutual assistance and maintenance, and other things belonging to conjugal society, might be varied and regulated by that contract which unites man and wife in that society, as far as may consist with procreation and the bringing up of children till they could shift for themselves; nothing being necessary to any society, that is not necessary to the ends for which it is made.

84. The *society betwixt parents and children*, and the distinct rights and powers belonging respectively to them, I have treated of so largely, in the foregoing chapter, that I shall not here need to say any thing of it. And I think it is plain, that it is far different from a politic society.

85. *Master* and *servant* are names as old as history, but given to those of far different condition; for a free man makes himself a servant to another, by selling him, for a certain time, the service he undertakes to do, in exchange for wages he is to receive: and though this commonly puts him into the family of his master, and under the ordinary discipline thereof: yet it gives the master but a temporary power over him, and no greater than what is contained in the *contract* between them. But there is another sort of servants, which by a peculiar name we call *slaves*, who being captives taken in a just war, are by the right of nature subjected to the absolute dominion and arbitrary power of their masters. These men having, as I say, forfeited their lives, and with it their liberties, and lost their estates; and being in the *state of slavery*, not capable of any property, cannot in that state be considered as any part of *civil society*; the chief end whereof is the preservation of property.

86. Let us therefore consider a *master of a family* with all these subordinate relations of *wife*, *children*, *servants*, and *slaves*, united under the domestic rule of a family; which, what resemblance soever it may have in its order, offices, and number too, with a little commonwealth, yet is very far from it, both in its constitution, power, and end: or if it must be thought

a monarchy, and the *paterfamilias* the absolute monarch in it, absolute monarchy will have but a very shattered and short power, when it is plain by what has been said before, that the *master of the family* has a very distinct and differently limited power, both as to time and extent, over those several persons that are in it. For excepting the slave (and the family is as much a family, and his power as *paterfamilias* as great, whether there be any slaves in his family or no) he has no legislative power of life and death over any of them, and none too but what a *mistress of a family* may have as well as he. And he certainly can have no absolute power over the whole family, who has but a very limited one over every individual in it. But how a family, or any other society of men, differ from that which is properly political society, we shall best see by considering wherein political society itself consists.

87. Man being born, as has been proved, with a title to perfect freedom, and an uncontrolled enjoyment of all the rights and privileges of the law of nature, equally with any other man, or number of men in the world, hath by nature a power, not only to preserve his property, that is, his life, liberty, and estate, against the injuries and attempts of other men; but to judge of and punish the breaches of that law in others, as he is persuaded the offence deserves, even with death itself, in crimes where the heinousness of the fact, in his opinion, requires it. But because no *political* society can be, nor subsist, without having in itself the power to preserve the property, and, in order thereunto, punish the offences of all those of that society; there and there only is *political society,* where every one of the members hath quitted his natural power, resigned it up into the hands of the community in all cases that excludes him not from appealing for protection to the law established by it. And thus all private judgment of every particular member being excluded, the community comes to be umpire by settled standing rules, indifferent, and the same to all parties; and by men having authority from the community, for the execution of those rules, decides all the differences that may happen between any members of that society concerning any matter of right; and punishes those offences which any member hath committed against the society, with such penalties as the law has established, whereby it is easy to discern, who are, and who are not, in *political society* together. Those who are united into one body, and have a common established law and judicature to appeal to, with authority to decide controversies between them, and punish offenders, *are in civil society* one with another: but those who have no such common appeal, I mean on earth, are still in the state of nature, each being, where there is no other, judge for himself, and executioner: which is, as I have before shewed, the perfect *state of nature.*

88. And thus the commonwealth comes by a power to set down what punishment shall belong to the several transgressions which they think worthy of it, committed amongst the members of that society, (which is the *power of making laws*) as well as it has the power to punish any injury done unto any of its members, by any one that is not of it, (which is the power of war and peace,) and all this for the preservation of the property of all the members of that society, as far as is possible. But though every man who has entered into civil society, and is become a member of any commonwealth, has thereby quitted his power to punish offences against the law of nature, in prosecution of his own private judgment; yet with the judgment of offences, which he has given up to the legislative in all cases, where he can appeal to the magistrate, he has given a right to the commonwealth to employ his force, for the execution of the judgments of the commonwealth whenever he shall be called to it; which indeed are his own judgments, they being made by himself, or his representative. And herein we have the original of the legislative and executive power of civil society, which is to judge by standing laws, how far offences are to be punished, when committed within the commonwealth; and also to determine, by occasional judgments founded on the present circumstances of the fact, how far injuries from without are to be vindicated; and in both these to employ all the force of all the members, when there shall be need.

89. Whenever therefore any number of men are so united into one society, as to quit every one his executive power of the law of nature, and to resign it to the public, there and there only is a political, or civil society. And this is done, wherever any number of men, in the state of nature, enter into society to make one people, one body politic, under one supreme

government; or else when any one joins himself to, and incorporates with any government already made. For hereby he authorizes the society, or, which is all one, the legislative thereof, to make laws for him, as the public good of the society shall require; to the execution whereof, his own assistance (as to his own degrees) is due. And this puts men out of a state of nature into that of a commonwealth, by setting up a judge on earth, with authority to determine all the controversies, and redress the injuries that may happen to any member of the commonwealth: which judge is the legislative, or magistrate appointed by it. And wherever there are any number of men, however associated, that have no such decisive power to appeal to, there they are still in the state of nature.

90. Hence it is evident, that absolute monarchy, which by some men is counted the only government in the world, is indeed inconsistent with civil society, and so can be no form of civil government at all; for the end of civil society being to avoid and remedy these inconveniencies of the state of nature, which necessarily follow from every man's being judge in his own case, by setting up a known authority, to which every one of that society may appeal upon any injury received, or controversy that may arise, and which every one of the[2] society ought to obey; wherever any persons are, who have not such an authority to appeal to for the decision of any difference between them, there those persons are still *in the state of nature*. And so is every *absolute prince*, in respect of those who are under his dominion.

91. For he being supposed to have all, both legislative and executive power in himself alone, there is no judge to be found, no appeal lies open to any one, who may fairly, and indifferently, and with authority decide, and from whose decision relief and redress may be expected of any injury or inconveniency that may be suffered from the prince, or by his order: so that such a man, however intitled, *czar*, or *grand*

seignior, or how you please, is as much *in the state of nature*, with all under his dominion, as he is with the rest of mankind. For wherever any two men are, who have no standing rule, and common judge to appeal to on earth, for the determination of controversies of right betwixt them, there they are still *in the state of*[3] *nature*, and under all the inconveniencies of it, with only this woful difference to the subject, or rather slave of an absolute prince; that whereas in the ordinary state of nature he has a liberty to judge of his right, and, according to the best of his power, to maintain it; now, whenever his property is invaded by the will and order of his monarch, he has not only no appeal, as those in society ought to have, but, as if he were degraded from the common state of rational creatures, is denied a liberty to judge of, or to defend his right; and so is exposed to all the misery and inconveniencies that a man can fear from one, who being in the unrestrained state of nature, is yet corrupted with flattery, and armed with power.

92. For he that thinks *absolute power purifies men's blood*, and corrects the baseness of human nature, need read but the history of this or any other age, to

---

2. The public power of all society is above every soul contained in "the same society; and the principal use of that power is, to give laws unto all that are under it, which laws in such cases we must obey," unless there be reason shewed which may necessarily inforce, that the law of reason, or of God, doth enjoin the contrary." Hook. Eccl. Pol. L. I. Sect. 16.

3. "To take away all such mutual grievances, injuries and wrongs," i.e. such as attend men in the state of nature, "there was no way but only by growing into composition and agreement amongst themselves, by ordaining some kind of government public, and by yielding themselves subject thereunto, that unto whom they granted authority to rule and govern, by them the peace, tranquillity, and happy state of the rest might be procured. Men always knew that where force and injury was offered, they might be defenders of themselves; they knew that however men may seek their own commodity, yet if this were done with injury unto others, it was not to be suffered, but by all men, and all good means to be withstood. Finally, they knew that no man might in reason take upon him to determine his own right, and according to his own determination proceed in maintenance thereof, in as much as every man is towards himself, and them whom he greatly affects, partial; and therefore that strifes and troubles would be endless, except they gave their common consent, all to be ordered by some, whom they should agree upon, without which consent there would be no reason that one man should take upon him to be lord or judge over another." Hooker's Eccl. Pol. L. I. Sect. 10.

be convinced of the contrary. He that would have been so insolent and injurious in the woods of America, would not probably be much better in a throne; where perhaps learning and religion shall be found out to justify all that he shall do to his subjects, and the sword presently silence all those that dare question it. For what the *protection of absolute monarchy* is, what kind of fathers of their countries it makes princes to be, and to what a degree of happiness and security it carries civil society, where this sort of government is grown to perfection; he that will look into the late relation of Ceylon, may easily see.

93. *In absolute monarchies*, indeed, as well as other governments of the world, the subjects have an appeal to the law, and judges to decide any controversies, and restrain any violence that may happen betwixt the subjects themselves, one amongst another. This every one thinks necessary, and believes he deserves to be thought a declared enemy to society and mankind, who should go about to take it away. But whether this be from a true love of mankind and society, and such a charity as we all owe one to another, there is reason to doubt. For this is no more than what every man, who loves his own power, profit, or greatness, may and naturally must do, keep those animals from hurting, or destroying one another, who labour and drudge only for his pleasure and advantage; and so are taken care of, not out of any love the master has for them, but love of himself, and the profit they bring him. For if it be asked, what security, what fence is there, in such a state, *against the violence and oppression of this absolute ruler?* the very question can scarce be borne. They are ready to tell you, that it deserves death only to ask after safety. Betwixt subject and subject, they will grant, there must be measures, laws, and judges, for their mutual peace and security: but as for the ruler he ought to be *absolute*, and is above all such circumstances; because he has power to do more hurt and wrong, it is right when he does it. To ask how you may be guarded from harm, or injury, on that side where the strongest hand is to do it, is presently the voice of faction and rebellion: as if when men quitting the state of nature entered into society, they agreed that all of them but one should be under the restraint of laws, but that he should still retain all the liberty of the state of nature, increased with power, and made licentious

by impunity. This is to think, that men are so foolish, that they take care to avoid what mischiefs may be done them by *pole cats*, or *foxes*; but are content, nay think it safety, to be devoured by *lions*.

94. But whatever flatterers may talk to amuse people's understandings, it hinders not men from feeling; and when they perceive, that any man, in what station soever, is out of the bounds of the civil society which they are of, and that they have no appeal on earth against any harm they may receive from him, they are apt to think themselves in the state of nature, in respect of him whom they find to be so: and to take care, as soon as they can, to have that *safety and security in civil society*, for which it was instituted, and for which only they entered into it. And therefore, though perhaps at first, (as shall be shewed more at large hereafter in the following part of this discourse) some one good and excellent man having got a pre-eminency amongst the rest, had this deference paid to his goodness and virtue, as to a kind of natural authority, that the chief rule, with arbitration of their differences, by a tacit consent devolved into his hands, without any other caution, but the assurance they had of his uprightness and wisdom; yet when time, giving authority, and (as some men would persuade us) sacredness to customs, which the negligent and unforeseen innocence of the first ages began, had brought in successors of another stamp, the people finding their properties not secure under the government, as then it was, (whereas government has no other end but the preservation of [4] property) could never be safe nor at rest, *nor think themselves in civil society*, till the legislature was placed in collective bodies of men, call them senate, parliament, or what

---

4. "At the first, when some certain kind of regiment was once appointed, it may be that nothing was then farther thought upon for the manner of governing, but all permitted unto their wisdom and discretion, which were to rule, till by experience they found this for all parts very inconvenient, so as the thing which they had devised for a remedy, did indeed but increase the sore, which it should have cured. They saw, that to live by one man's will, became the cause of all men's misery. This constrained them to come into laws, wherein all men might see their duty beforehand, and know the penalties of transgressing them." Hooker's Eccl. Pol. I. I. Sect. 10.

you please. By which means every single person became subject, equally with other the meanest men, to those laws, which he himself, as part of the legislative, had established; nor could any one, by his own authority, avoid the force of the law, when once made; nor by any pretence of superiority plead exemption, thereby to license his own, or the miscarriages of any of his dependents.[5] *No man in civil society can be exempted from the laws of it.* For if any man may do what he thinks fit, and there be no appeal on earth, for redress or security against any harm he shall do; I ask, whether he be not perfectly still in the state of nature, and so can be *no part or member of that civil society:* unless any one will say, the state of nature and civil society are one and the same thing, which I have never yet found any one so great a patron of anarchy as to affirm.

Chapter 8

Of the Beginning of Political Societies

95. Men being, as has been said, by nature, all free, equal, and independent, no one can be put out of this estate, and subjected to the political power of another, without his own consent. The only way, whereby any one divests himself of his natural liberty, and puts on the *bonds of civil society*, is by agreeing with other men to join and unite into a community, for their comfortable, safe, and peaceable living one amongst another, in a secure enjoyment of their properties, and a greater security against any, that are not of it. This any number of men may do, because it injures not the freedom of the rest; they are left as they were in the liberty of the state of nature. When any number of men have so *consented to make one community or government*, they are thereby presently incorporated, and make *one body politic*, wherein the *majority* have a right to act and conclude the rest.

96. For when any number of men have, by the consent of every individual, made a *community*, they have thereby made that *community* one body, with a

5. "Civil law, being the act of the whole body politic, doth therefore over-rule each several part of the same body." Hooker, ibid.

power to act as one body, which is only by the will and determination of the majority. For that which acts any community, being only the *consent* of the individuals of it, and it being necessary to that which is one body to move one way; it is necessary the body should move that way whither the greater force carries it, which is the *consent of the majority:* or else it is impossible it should act or continue one body, one community, which the consent of every individual that united into it, agreed that it should; and so every one is bound by that consent to be concluded by the majority. And therefore we see, that in assemblies, impowered to act by positive laws, where no number is set by that positive law which impowers them, the *act of the majority* passes for the act of the whole, and of course determines, as having, by the law of nature and reason, the power of the whole.

97. And thus every man, by consenting with others to make one body politic under one government, puts himself under an obligation, to every one of that society, to submit to the determination of the majority, and to be concluded by it; or else this *original compact*, whereby he with others incorporate into one society, would signify nothing, and be no compact, if he be left free, and under no other ties than he was in before in the state of nature. For what appearance would there be of any compact? What new engagement if he were no farther tied by any decrees of the society, than he himself thought fit, and did actually consent to? This would be still as great a liberty, as he himself had before his compact, or any one else in the state of nature hath, who may submit himself, and consent to any acts of it if he thinks fit.

98. For if *the consent of the majority* shall not, in reason, be received as *the act of the whole*, and conclude every individual; nothing but the consent of every individual can make any thing to be the act of the whole: But such a consent is next to impossible ever to be had, if we consider the infirmities of health, and avocations of business, which in a number, though much less than that of a commonwealth, will necessarily keep many away from the public assembly. To which if we add the variety of opinions, and contrariety of interests, which unavoidably happen in all collections of men, the coming into society upon such terms would be only like Cato's coming into the theatre, only to go out again. Such a constitution

as this would make the mighty *leviathan* of a shorter duration, than the feeblest creatures, and not let it outlast the day it was born in: which cannot be supposed, till we can think, that rational creatures should desire and constitute societies only to be dissolved. For where the majority cannot conclude the rest, there they cannot act as one body, and consequently will be immediately dissolved again.

99. Whosoever therefore out of a state of nature unite into a community, must be understood to give up all the power, necessary to the ends for which they unite into society, to the majority of the community, unless they expressly agreed in any number greater than the majority. And this is done by barely agreeing to *unite into one political society,* which is *all the compact* that is, or needs be, between the individuals, that enter into, or make up a commonwealth. And thus that, which begins and actually *constitutes any political society,* is nothing, but the consent of any number of freemen capable of a majority, to unite and incorporate into such a society. And this is that, and that only, which did, or could give beginning to any lawful government in the world.

100. To this I find two objections made.

First, *That there are no instances to be found in story, of a company of men independent and equal one amongst another, that met together, and in this way began and set up a government.*

Secondly, *It is impossible of right, that men should do so, because all men being born under government, they are to submit to that, and are not at liberty to begin a new one.*

101. To the first there is this to answer, That it is not at all to be wondered, that *history* gives us but a very little account of *men, that lived together in the state of nature.* The inconveniencies of that condition and the love and want of society, no sooner brought any number of them together, but they presently united and incorporated, if they designed to continue together. And if we may not suppose men ever to have been *in the state of nature,* because we hear not much of them in such a state, we may as well suppose the armies of Salmanasser or Xerxes were never children, because we hear little of them, till they were men, and embodied in armies. Government is every where antecedent to records, and letters seldom come in amongst a people till a long continuation of civil

society has, by other more necessary arts, provided for their safety, ease, and plenty. And then they begin to look after the history of their founders, and search into their original, when they have outlived the memory of it. For it is with commonwealths, as with particular persons, they are commonly *ignorant of their own births and infancies:* and if they know any thing of their original, they are beholden for it to the accidental records that others have kept of it. And those that we have of the beginning of any politics in the world, excepting that of the Jews, where God himself immediately interposed, and which favours not at all paternal dominion, are all either plain instances of such a beginning as I have mentioned, or at least have manifest footsteps of it.

102. He must shew a strange inclination to deny evident matter of fact, when it agrees not with his hypothesis, who will not allow, that the *beginning* of Rome and Venice were by the uniting together of several men free and independent one of another, amongst whom there was no natural superiority or subjection. And if Josephus Acosta's word may be taken, he tells us, that in many parts of America there was no government at all. "There are great and apparent conjectures," says he, "that these men, speaking of those of Peru, for a long time had neither kings nor commonwealths, but lived in troops, as they do this day in Florida, the Cheriquanas, those of Brasil, and many other nations, which have no certain kings, but as occasion is offered, in peace or war, they choose their captains as they please," l. I. c. 25. If it be said, that every man there was born subject to his father, or the head of his family. That the subjection due from a child to a father took not away his freedom of uniting into what political society he thought fit, has been already proved. But be that as it will, these men, it is evident, were actually free; and whatever superiority some politicians now would place in any of them, they themselves claimed it not, but by consent were all equal, till by the same consent they set rulers over themselves. So that their politic societies all began from a voluntary union, and the mutual agreement of men freely acting in the choice of their governors, and forms of government.

103. And I hope those who went away from Sparta with Palantus, mentioned by Justin, l. iii. c. 4, will be allowed to have been freemen, *independent* one

of another, and to have set up a government over themselves, by their own consent. Thus I have given several examples out of history, of *people free and in the state of nature*, that being met together, incorporated and *began a commonwealth*. And if the want of such instances be an argument to prove that governments were not, nor could not be so begun, I suppose the contenders for paternal empire were better let it alone, than urge it against natural liberty. For if they can give so many instances out of history, of governments begun upon paternal right, I think (though at best an argument from what has been, to what should of right be, has no great force) one might, without any great danger, yield them the cause. But if I might advise them in the case, they would do well not to search too much into the *original of governments*, as they have begun *de facto*; lest they should find, at the foundation of most of them, something very little favourable to the design they promote, and such a power as they contend for.

104. But to conclude, reason being plain on our side, that men are naturally free, and the examples of history shewing, that the governments of the world, that were begun in peace, had their beginning laid on that foundation, and were *made by the consent of the people*; there can be little room for doubt, either where the right is, or what has been the opinion, or practice of mankind, about the *first erecting of governments*.

105. I will not deny, that if we look back as far as history will direct us, towards the *original of commonwealths*, we shall generally find them under the government and administration of one man. And I am also apt to believe, that where a family was numerous enough to subsist by itself, and continued entire together, without mixing with others, as it often happens, where there is much land, and few people, the government commonly began *in the father*. For the father having, by the law of nature, the same power with every man else to punish, as he thought fit, any offences against that law, might thereby punish his transgressing children, even when they were men, and out of their pupilage; and they were very likely to submit to his punishment, and all join with him against the offender, in their turns, giving him thereby power to execute his sentence against any transgression, and so in effect make him the law maker, and

governour over all that remained in conjunction with his family. He was fittest to be trusted; paternal affection secured their property and interest under his care; and the custom of obeying him, in their childhood, made it easier to submit to him, rather than to any other. If, therefore, they must have one to rule them, as government is hardly to be avoided amongst men that live together; who so likely to be the man as he that was their common father; unless negligence, cruelty, or any other defect of mind or body made him unfit for it? But when either the father died, and left his next heir, for want of age, wisdom, courage, or any other qualities, less fit for rule; or where several families met, and consented to continue together; there, it is not to be doubted, but they used their natural freedom to set up him whom they judged the ablest, and most likely to rule well over them. Conformable hereunto we find the people of America, who (living out of the reach of the conquering swords, and spreading domination of the two great empires of Peru and Mexico) enjoyed their own natural freedom, though, *caeteris paribus*, they commonly prefer the heir of their deceased king; yet, if they find him any way weak, or incapable, they pass him by, and set up the stoutest and bravest man for their ruler.

106. Thus, though looking back as far as records give us any account of peopling the world, and the history of nations, we commonly find the government to be in one hand; yet it destroys not that which I affirm, viz. that the *beginning of politic society* depends upon the consent of the individuals, to join into, and make one society; who, when they are thus incorporated, might set up what form of government they thought fit. But this having given occasion to men to mistake, and think, that by nature government was monarchical, and belonged to the father; it may not be amiss here to consider, why people in the beginning generally pitched upon this form; which though perhaps the father's pre-eminency might, in the first institution of some commonwealth give rise to, and place in the beginning the power in one hand; yet it is plain that the reason, that continued the form of *government in a single person*, was not any regard or respect to paternal authority; since all petty monarchies, that is, almost all monarchies, near their original, have been commonly, at least upon occasion, *elective*.

107. First then, in the beginning of things, the father's government of the childhood of those sprung from him, having accustomed them to the *rule of one man*, and taught them that where it was exercised with care and skill, with affection and love to those under it, it was sufficient to procure and preserve to men all the political happiness they sought for in society. It was no wonder that they should pitch upon, and naturally run into that form of government, which from their infancy they had been all accustomed to; and which, by experience, they had found both easy and safe. To which, if we add, that monarchy being simple, and most obvious to men, whom neither experience had instructed in forms of government, nor the ambition or insolence of empire had taught to beware of the encroachments of prerogative, or the inconveniencies of absolute power, which monarchy in succession was apt to lay claim to, and bring upon them; it was not at all strange, that they should not much trouble themselves to think of methods of restraining any exorbitancies of those to whom they had given the authority over them, and of balancing the power of government, by placing several parts of it in different hands. They had neither felt the oppression of tyrannical dominion, nor did the fashion of the age, nor their possessions, or way of living, (which afforded little matter for covetousness or ambition) give them any reason to apprehend or provide against it; and therefore it is no wonder they put themselves into such a *frame of government*, as was not only, as I said, most obvious and simple, but also best suited to their present state and condition; which stood more in need of defence against foreign invasions and injuries, than of multiplicity of laws. The equality of a simple poor way of living, confining their desires within the narrow bounds of each man's small property, made few controversies, and so no need of many laws to decide them, or variety of officers to superintend the process, or look after the execution of justice, where there were but few trespasses, and few offenders. Since then those, who liked one another so well as to join into society, cannot but be supposed to have some acquaintance and friendship together, and some trust in another; they could not but have greater apprehensions of others, than of one another: and therefore their first care and thought cannot but be supposed to be, how to secure themselves against

foreign force. It was natural for them to put themselves under a *frame of government* which might best serve to that end, and choose the wisest and bravest man to conduct them in their wars, and lead them out against their enemies, and in this chiefly be their *ruler*.

108. Thus we see, that the *kings* of the Indians in America, which is still a pattern of the first ages in Asia and Europe, whilst the inhabitants were too few for the country, and want of people and money gave men no temptation to enlarge their possessions of land, or contest for wider extent of ground, are little more than *generals of their armies*; and though they command absolutely in war, yet at home and in time of peace they exercise very little dominion, and have but a very moderate sovereignty; the resolutions of peace and war being ordinarily either in the people, or in a council. Though the war itself, which admits not of plurality of governors, naturally devolves the command into the *king's sole authority*.

109. And thus, in Israel itself, the *chief business of their judges, and first kings*, seems to have been *to be captains in war*, and leaders of their armies; which (besides what is signified by *going out and in before the people*, which was to march forth to war, and home again at the heads of their forces) appears plainly in the story of Jephthah. The Ammonites making war upon Israel, the Gileadites in fear sent to Jephthah, a bastard of their family whom they had cast off, and article with him, if he will assist them against the Ammonites, to make him their ruler; which they do in these words, "And the people made him head and captain over them," *Judg*. xi. 11. which was, as it seems, all one as to be judge. "And he judged Israel," *Judg*. xii. 7. that is, was their captain-general, *six years*. So when Jotham upbraids the Shechemites with the obligation they had to Gideon, who had been their judge and ruler, he tells them, "He fought for you, and adventured his life far, and delivered you out of the hands of Midian," *Judg*. ix. 17. Nothing is mentioned of him, but what he did as a *general*: and indeed that is all is found in his history, or in any of the rest of the judges. And Abimelech particularly is called *king*, though at most he was but their *general*. And when, being weary of the ill conduct of Samuel's sons, the children of Israel desired a king, "like all the nations, to judge them, and to go out before them, and to fight their battles," *1 Sam*. viii. 20. God

granting their desire, says to Samuel. "I will send thee a man, and thou shalt anoint him to be captain over my people Israel, that he may save my people out of the hands of the Philistines," c. ix. 16. As if the only *business of a king* had been to lead out their armies, and fight in their defence; and accordingly at his inauguration, pouring a vial of oil upon him, declares to Saul, that "the Lord had anointed him to be captain over his inheritance," c. x. 1. And therefore those who, after Saul's being solemnly chosen and saluted *king* by the *tribes* of Mispah, were unwilling to have him their king, made no other objection but this, "How shall this man save us?" v. 27. as if they should have said, this man is unfit to be our *king*, not having skill and conduct enough in war to be able to defend us. And when God resolved to transfer the government to David, it is in these words, "But now thy kingdom shall not continue: the Lord hath sought him a man after his own heart, and the Lord hath commanded him to be captain over his people," c. xiii. 14. As if the whole kingly authority were nothing else but to be their general: and therefore the tribes who had stuck to Saul's family, and opposed David's reign, when they came to Hebron with terms of submission to him, they tell him, amongst other arguments, they had to submit to him as their king, that he was in effect their king in Saul's time, and therefore they had no reason but to receive him as their king now. "Also" (say they,) "in time past, when Saul was king over us, thou wast he that leddest out, and broughtest in Israel, and the Lord said unto thee, Thou shalt feed my people Israel, and thou shalt be a captain over Israel."

110. Thus, whether a family by degrees *grew up into a commonwealth*, and the fatherly authority being continued on to the elder son, every one in his turn growing up under it, tacitly submitted to it; and the easiness and equality of it not offending any one, every one acquiesced, till time seemed to have confirmed it, and settled a right of succession by prescription: or whether several families, or the descendants of several families, whom chance, neighbourhood, or business brought together, *uniting into society*, the need of a general, whose conduct might defend them against their enemies in war, and the great confidence the innocence and sincerity of that poor but virtuous age (such as are almost all those which begin govern-

ments, that ever come to last in the world), gave men of one another, made the first beginners of commonwealths generally put the rule into one man's hand, without any other express limitation or restraint, but what the nature of the thing and the end of government required: Whichever of those it was that at first put the rule into the hands of a single person, certain it is that no body was entrusted with it but for the public good and safety, and to those ends, in the infancies of commonwealths, those who had it, commonly used it. And unless they had done so, young societies could not have subsisted; without such nursing fathers tender and careful of the public weal, all governments would have sunk under the weakness and infirmities of their infancy, and the prince and the people had soon perished together.

111. But though the *golden age* (before vain ambition, and *amor sceleratus habendi*, evil concupiscence, had corrupted men's minds into a mistake of true power and honour) had more virtue, and consequently better governors, as well as less vicious subjects; and there was then *no stretching prerogative* on the one side, to oppress the people; nor consequently on the other, any *dispute about privilege*, to lessen or restrain the power of the magistrate; and so no contest betwixt rulers and people about governors or government: yet when ambition and luxury in future ages[6] would retain and increase the power, without doing the business for which it was given; and, aided by flattery, taught princes to have distinct and separate interests from their people; men found it necessary to examine more carefully the original and rights of government, and to find out ways to *restrain the exorbitancies*, and prevent the abuses of

---

6. "At first, when some certain kind of regiment was once approved, it may be nothing was then farther thought upon for the manner of governing, but all permitted unto their wisdom and discretion which were to rule, till by experience they found this for all parts very inconvenient, so as the thing which they had devised for a remedy, did indeed but increase the sore which it should have cured. They saw, that to live by one man's will, became the cause of all men's misery. This constrained them to come unto laws wherein all men might see their duty beforehand, and know the penalties of transgressing them." Hooker's Eccl. Pol. L. I. Sect. 10.

that power, which they having entrusted in another's hands only for their own good, they found was made use of to hurt them.

112. Thus we may see how probable it is, that people that were naturally free, and by their own consent either submitted to the government of their father, or united together out of different families to make a government, should generally put the *rule into one man's hands*, and choose to be under the conduct of a single person, without so much as by express conditions limiting or regulating his power, which they thought safe enough in his honesty and prudence. Though they never dreamed of monarchy being *jure divino*, which we never heard of among mankind, till it was revealed to us by the divinity of this last age; nor ever allowed paternal power to have a right to dominion, or to be the foundation of all government. And thus much may suffice to shew, that, as far as we have any light from history, we have reason to conclude, that all peaceful beginnings of government have been *laid in the consent of the people*. I say peaceful, because I shall have occasion in another place to speak of conquest, which some esteem a way of beginning of governments.

The other objection I find urged against the beginning of polities, in the way I have mentioned, is this, viz.

113. *That all men being born under government, some or other, it is impossible any of them should ever be free, and at liberty to unite together, and begin a new one, or ever be able to erect a lawful government.*

If this argument be good, I ask, how came so many lawful monarchies into the world? for if any body, upon this supposition, can shew me any one man in any age of the world free to begin a lawful monarchy, I will be bound to shew him ten other *free men* at liberty at the same time to unite and begin a new government under a regal or any other form. It being demonstration, that if any one, *born under the dominion* of another, may be so free as to have a right to command others in a new and distinct empire, every one that is *born under the dominion* of another may be so free too, and may become a ruler, or subject of a distinct separate government. And so by this their own principle, either all men, however born, are free, or else there is but one lawful prince, one lawful government in the world. And then they have nothing to do, but barely to shew us which that is; which

when they have done, I doubt not but all mankind will easily agree to pay obedience to him.

114. Though it be a sufficient answer to their objection, to shew that it involves them in the same difficulties that it doth those they use it against; yet I shall endeavour to discover the weakness of this argument a little farther.

"All men," say they, "are born under government, and therefore they cannot be at liberty to begin a new one. Every one is born a subject to his father, or his prince, and is therefore under the perpetual tie of subjection and allegiance." It is plain mankind never owned nor considered any such natural *subjection that they were born in*, to one or to the other, that tied them, without their own consents, to a subjection to them and their heirs.

115. For there are no examples so frequent in history, both sacred and profane, as those of men withdrawing themselves, and their obedience from the jurisdiction they were born under, and the family or community they were bred up in, and *setting up new governments* in other places, from whence sprang all that number of petty commonwealths in the beginning of ages, and which always multiplied as long as there was room enough, till the stronger, or more fortunate, swallowed the weaker; and those great ones again breaking to pieces, dissolved into lesser dominions. All which are so many testimonies against paternal sovereignty, and plainly prove, that it was not the natural right of the father descending to his heirs, that made governments in the beginning, since it was impossible, upon that ground, there should have been so many little kingdoms; all must have been but only one universal monarchy, if men had not been *at liberty to separate themselves* from their families, and the government, be it what it will, that was set up in it, and go and make distinct commonwealths and other governments, as they thought fit.

116. This has been the practice of the world from its first beginning to this day; nor is it now any more hindrance to the freedom of mankind, that they are *born under constituted and ancient polities*, that have established laws, and set forms of government, than if they were born in the woods, amongst the unconfined inhabitants, that run loose in them. For those who would persuade us, that, *by being born under any government, we are naturally subjects to it*, and have

no more any title or pretence to the freedom of the state of nature; have no other reason (bating that of paternal power, which we have already answered) to produce for it, but only, because our fathers or progenitors passed away their natural liberty, and thereby bound up themselves and their posterity to a perpetual subjection to the government which they themselves submitted to. It is true, that whatever engagements or promises any one has made for himself, he is under the obligation of them, but cannot, by any compact whatsoever, bind his children or posterity. For his son, when a man, being altogether as free as the father, any *act of the father can no more give away the liberty of the son*, than it can of any body else: he may indeed annex such conditions to the land he enjoyed as a subject of any commonwealth, as may oblige his son to be of that community, if he will enjoy those possessions which were his father's; because that estate being his father's property, he may dispose, or settle it, as he pleases.

117. And this has generally given the occasion to mistake in this matter; because commonwealths not permitting any part of their dominions to be dismembered, nor to be enjoyed by any but those of their community, the son cannot ordinarily enjoy the possessions of his father, but under the same terms his father did, by becoming a member of the society; whereby he puts himself presently under the government he finds there established, as much as any other subject of that commonwealth. And thus *the consent of freemen, born under government, which only makes them members of it*, being given separately in their turns, as each comes to be of age, and not in a multitude together; people take no notice of it, and thinking it not done at all, or not necessary, conclude they are naturally subjects as they are men.

118. But, it is plain, governments themselves understand it otherwise; they claim *no power over the son, because of that they had over the father*; nor look on children as being their subjects, by their fathers being so. If a subject of England have a child, by an English woman in France, whose subject is he? Not the king of England's; for he must have leave to be admitted to the privileges of it. Nor the king of France's: for how then has his father a liberty to bring him away, and breed him as he pleases? And who ever was judged as a traitor or deserter, if he left, or warred

against a country, for being barely born in it of parents that were aliens there? It is plain then, by the practice of governments themselves, as well as by the law of right reasons, that *a child is born a subject of no country or government*. He is under his father's tuition and authority, till he comes to age of discretion; and then he is a freeman, at liberty what government he will put himself under, what body politic he will unite himself to. For if an Englishman's son, born in France, be at liberty, and may do so, it is evident there is no tie upon him by his father's being a subject of this kingdom; nor is he bound up by any compact of his ancestors. And why then hath not his son, by the same reason, the same liberty, though he be born any where else? Since the power that a father hath naturally over his children is the same, wherever they be born, and the ties of natural obligations are not bounded by the positive limits of kingdoms and commonwealths.

119. Every man being, as has been shewed, naturally free, and nothing being able to put him into subjection to any earthly power, but only his own consent; it is to be considered, what shall be understood to be a *sufficient declaration of* a man's *consent, to make him subject* to the laws of any government. There is a common distinction of an express and a tacit consent, which will concern our present case. No body doubts but an express consent, of any man entering into any society, makes him a perfect member of that society, a subject of that government. The difficulty is, what ought to be looked upon as a *tacit consent*, and how far it binds, i.e. how far any one shall be looked on to have consented, and thereby submitted to any government, where he has made no expressions of it at all. And to this I say, that every man, that hath any possessions, or enjoyment of any part of the dominions of any government, doth thereby give his *tacit consent*, and is as far forth obliged to obedience to the laws of that government, during such enjoyment, as any one under it; whether this his possession be of land, to him and his heirs for ever, or a lodging only for a week; or whether it be barely travelling freely on the highway: and, in effect, it reaches as far as the very being of any one within the territories of that government.

120. To understand this the better, it is fit to consider, that every man, when he at first incorporates

himself into any commonwealth, he, by his uniting himself thereunto, annexed also, and submits to the community, those possessions which he has, or shall acquire, that do not already belong to any other government. For it would be a direct contradiction, for any one to enter into society with others for the securing and regulating of property, and yet to suppose, his land, whose property is to be regulated by the laws of the society, should be exempt from the jurisdiction of that government, to which he himself, the proprietor of the land, is a subject. By the same act therefore, whereby any one unites his person, which was before free, to any commonwealth; by the same he unites his possessions, which were before free, to it also: and they become, both of them, person and possession, subject to the government and dominion of that commonwealth, as long as it hath a being. Whoever therefore, from thenceforth, by inheritance, purchase, permission, or otherways, *enjoys any part of the land* so annexed to, and under the government *of that commonwealth, must take it with the condition* it is under; that is, *of submitting to the government of the commonwealth*, under whose jurisdiction it is, as far forth as any subject of it.

121. But since the government has a direct jurisdiction only over the land, and reaches the possessor of it, (before he has actually incorporated himself in the society) only as he dwells upon, and enjoys that; the obligation any one is under, by virtue of such enjoyment, to *submit to the government, begins and ends with the enjoyment:* so that whenever the owner, who has given nothing but such a tacit consent to the government, will, by donation, sale, or otherwise, quit the said possession, he is at liberty to go and incorporate himself into any other commonwealth; or to agree with others to begin a new one, *in vacuis locis*, in any part of the world they can find free and unpossessed: whereas he, that has once, by actual agreement, and any express declaration, given his *consent* to be of any commonwealth, is perpetually and indispensably obliged to be, and remain unalterably a subject to it, and can never be again in the liberty of the state of nature; unless, by any calamity, the government he was under comes to be dissolved, or else by some public act cuts him off from being any longer a member of it.

122. But submitting to the laws of any country,

living quietly, and enjoying privileges and protection under them, *makes not a man a member of that society*: this is only a local protection and homage due to and from all those, who, not being in a state of war, come within the territories belonging to any government, to all parts whereof the force of its laws extends. But this no more *makes a man a member of that society*, a perpetual subject of that commonwealth, than it would make a man a subject to another, in whose family he found it convenient to abide for some time, though, whilst he continued in it, he were obliged to comply with the laws, and submit to the government he found there. And thus we see, that foreigners, by living all their lives under another government, and enjoying the privileges and protection of it, though they are bound, even in conscience, to submit to its administration, as far forth as any denison; yet do not thereby come to be *subjects or members of that commonwealth*. Nothing can make any man so, but his actually entering into it by positive engagement, and express promise and compact. This is that, which I think, concerning the beginning of political societies, and that *consent which makes any one a member of any commonwealth.*

Chapter 9

Of the Ends of Political Society and Government

123. If man in the state of nature be so free, as has been said; if he be absolute lord of his own person and possessions, equal to the greatest, and subject to no body, why will he part with his freedom? why will he give up this empire, and subject himself to the dominion and control of any other power? To which it is obvious to answer, that though in the state of nature he hath such a right, yet the enjoyment of it is very uncertain, and constantly exposed to the invasion of others. For all being kings as much as he, every man his equal, and the greater part no strict observers of equity and justice, the enjoyment of the property he has in this state is very unsafe, very unsecure. This makes him willing to quit this condition, which, however free, is full of fears and continual dangers: and it is not without reason, that he seeks

out, and is willing to join in society with others, who are already united, or have a mind to unite, for the mutual preservation of their lives, liberties, and estates, which I call by the general name, property.

124. The great and *chief end*, therefore, of men's uniting into commonwealths, and putting themselves under government, *is the preservation of their property*. To which in the state of nature there are many things wanting.

First, There wants an established, settled, known law, received and allowed by common consent to be the standard of right and wrong, and the common measure to decide all controversies between them. For though the law of nature be plain and intelligible to all rational creatures; yet men being biassed by their interest, as well as ignorant for want of studying it, are not apt to allow of it as a law binding to them in the application of it to their particular cases.

125. Secondly, In the state of nature there wants *a known and indifferent judge*, with authority to determine all differences according to the established law. For every one in that state being both judge and executioner of the law of nature, men being partial to themselves, passion and revenge is very apt to carry them too far, and with too much heat, in their own cases; as well as negligence, and unconcernedness, to make them too remiss in other men's.

126. Thirdly, In the state of nature, there often wants power to back and support the sentence when right, and to give it due execution. They who by any injustice offended, will seldom fail, where they are able, by force to make good their injustice; such resistance many times makes the punishment dangerous, and frequently destructive, to those who attempt it.

127. Thus mankind, notwithstanding all the privileges of the state of nature, being but in an ill condition, while they remain in it, are quickly driven into society. Hence it comes to pass that we seldom find any number of men live any time together in this state. The inconveniencies that they are therein exposed to, by the irregular and uncertain exercise of the power every man has of punishing the transgressions of others, make them take sanctuary under the established laws of government, and therein seek *the preservation of their property*. It is this makes them so willingly give up every one his single power of punishing, to

be exercised by such alone, as shall be appointed to it amongst them; and by such rules as the community, or those authorized by them to that purpose, shall agree on. And in this we have the original *right and rise of both the legislative and executive power*, as well as of the governments and societies themselves.

128. For in the state of nature, to omit the liberty he has of innocent delights, a man has two powers.

The first is to do whatsoever he thinks fit for the preservation of himself and others within the permission of the *law of nature:* by which law, common to them all, he and all the rest of *mankind are one community*, make up one society, distinct from all other creatures. And, were it not for the corruption and viciousness of degenerate men, there would be no need of any other; no necessity that men should separate from this great and natural community, and by positive agreements combine into smaller and divided associations.

The other power a man has in the state of nature, is the *power to punish the crimes* committed against that law. Both these he gives up, when he joins in a private, if I may so call it, or particular politic society, and incorporates into any commonwealth, separate from the rest of mankind.

129. The first *power, viz. of doing whatsoever he thought fit for the preservation of himself*, and the rest of mankind, *he gives up* to be regulated by laws made by the society, so far forth as the preservation of himself and the rest of that society shall require; which laws of the society in many things confine the liberty he had by the law of nature.

130. *Secondly,* The *power of punishing he wholly gives up*, and engages his natural force, (which he might before employ in the execution of the law of nature, by his own single authority, as he thought fit) to assist the executive power of the society, as the law thereof shall require. For being now in a new state, wherein he is to enjoy many conveniencies, from the labour, assistance, and society of others in the same community, as well as protection from its whole strength; he is to part also, with as much of his natural liberty, in providing for himself, as the good, prosperity, and safety of the society shall require; which is not only necessary, but just, since the other members of the society do the like.

131. But though men, when they enter into society,

give up the equality, liberty, and executive power they had in the state of nature, into the hands of the society, to be so far disposed of by the legislative, as the good of the society shall require; yet it being only with an intention in every one the better to preserve himself, his liberty and property; (for no rational creature can be supposed to change his condition with an intention to be worse) the power of the society, or legislative constituted by them, *can never be supposed to extend farther, than the common good*; but is obliged to secure every one's property, by providing against those three defects above mentioned, that made the state of nature so unsafe and uneasy. And so whoever has the legislative or supreme power of any commonwealth, is bound to govern by established standing laws, promulgated and known to the people, and not by extemporary decrees; by indifferent and upright judges, who are to decide controversies by those laws; and to employ the force of the community at home, *only in the execution of such laws*; or abroad to prevent or redress foreign injuries, and secure the community from inroads and invasion. And all this to be directed to no other *end*, but the *peace, safety*, and *public good* of the people.

Chapter 10

Of the Forms of a Commonwealth

132. The majority having, as has been shewed, upon men's first uniting into society, the whole power of the community naturally in them, may employ all that power in making laws for the community from time to time, and executing those laws by officers of their own appointing; and then the *form of the* government is a perfect *democracy*: or else may put the power of making laws into the hands of a few select men, and their heirs or successors; and then it is an *oligarchy*: or else into the hands of one man, and then it is a *monarchy*: if to him and his heirs, it is an *hereditary monarchy*: if to him only for life, but upon his death the power only of nominating a successor to return to them; an *elective monarchy*. And so accordingly of these the community may make compounded and mixed forms of government, as they think good. And if the legislative power be at first

given by the majority to one or more persons only for their lives, or any limited time, and then the supreme power to revert to them again; when it is so reverted, the community may dispose of it again anew into what hands they please, and so constitute a new form of government. For the *form of government depending upon the placing* the supreme power, which is the *legislative* (it being impossible to conceive that an inferiour power should prescribe to a superiour, or any but the supreme make laws), according as the power of making laws is placed, such is the *form of the commonwealth*.

133. By commonwealth, I must be understood all along to mean, not a democracy, or any form of government, but *any independent community*, which the Latines signified by the word *civitas*; to which the word which best answers in our language, is *commonwealth*, and most properly expresses such a society of men, which community or city in English does not. For there may be subordinate communities in government; and city amongst us has quite a different notion from commonwealth: and therefore, to avoid ambiguity, I crave leave to use the word *commonwealth* in that sense, in which I find it used by King *James the first*: and I take it to be its genuine signification; which if any body dislike, I consent with him to change it for a better.

Chapter 11

Of the Extent of the Legislative Power

134. The great end of men's entering into society being the enjoyment of their properties in peace and safety, and the great instrument and means of that being the laws established in that society; the *first and fundamental positive law* of all commonwealths is *the establishing of the legislative* power; as the *first and fundamental natural law*, which is to govern even the legislative itself, *is the preservation of the society*, and (as far as will consist with the public good) of every person in it. This *legislative* is not only *the supreme power* of the commonwealth, but sacred and unalterable in the hands where the community have once placed it; nor can any edict of any body else, in what form soever conceived, or by what power

soever backed, have the force and obligation of a law, which has not its *sanction from* that *legislative* which the public has chosen and appointed; for without this the law could not have that, which is absolutely necessary to its being a *law,*[7] *the consent of the society;* over whom no body can have a power to make laws, but by their own consent, and by authority received from them; and therefore all the obedience, which by the most solemn ties any one can be obliged to pay, ultimately terminates in this supreme power, and is directed by those laws which it enacts; nor can any oaths to any foreign power whatsoever, or any domestic subordinate power, discharge any member of the society from his *obedience to the legislative,* acting pursuant to their trust; nor oblige him to any obedience contrary to the laws so enacted, or farther than they do allow; it being ridiculous to imagine one can be tied ultimately to obey any power in the society, which is not the supreme.

135. Though the legislative, whether placed in one or more, whether it be always in being, or only by intervals, though it be the supreme power in every commonwealth; yet,

First, It is *not,* nor can possibly be absolutely *arbitrary* over the lives and fortunes of the people. For it being but the joint power of every member of the society given up to that person, or assembly, which is legislator, it can be no more than those persons had in a state of nature before they entered into society, and gave up to the community. For no body can transfer to another more power than he has in himself; and no body has an absolute arbitrary power over himself, or over any other, to destroy his own life, or take away the life or property of another. A man, as has been proved, cannot subject himself to the arbitrary power of another; and having in the state of nature no arbitrary power over the life, liberty, or possession of another, but only so much as the law of nature gave him for the preservation of himself and the rest of mankind; this is all he doth, or can give up to the commonwealth, and by it to the legislative power, so that the legislative can have no more than this. Their power, in the utmost bounds of it, is *limited to the public good* of the society. It is a power, that hath no other end but preservation, and therefore can never[8] have a right to destroy, enslave, or designedly to impoverish the subjects. The obligations of the law of nature cease not in society, but only in many cases are drawn closer, and have by human laws known penalties annexed to them, to enforce their observation. Thus the law of nature stands as an eternal rule to all men, legislators as well as others. The rules that they make for other men's actions, must, as well as their own and other men's actions, be conformable to the law of nature, i.e. to the will of God, of which

7. "The lawful power of making laws to command whole politic societies of men, belonging so properly unto the same entire societies, that for any prince or potentate of what kind soever upon earth, to exercise the same of himself, and not by express commission immediately and personally received from God, or else by authority derived at the first from their consent, upon whose persons they impose laws, it is no better than mere tyranny. Laws they are not therefore which public approbation hath not made so." Hooker's Eccl. Pol. L. I. Sect. 10. "Of this point therefore we are to note, that sith men naturally have no full and perfect power to command whole politic multitudes of men, therefore utterly without our consent, we could in such sort be at no man's commandment living. And to be commanded we do consent when that society, whereof we be a part, hath at any time before consented, without revoking the same after by the like universal agreement. Laws therefore human, of what kind so ever, are available by consent." Ibid.

8. "Two foundations there are which bear up public societies, the one a natural inclination, whereby all men desire sociable life and fellowship; the other an order, expressly or secretly agreed upon, touching the manner of their union in living together: the latter is that which we call the law of a commonweal, the very soul of a politic body, the parts whereof are by law animated, held together, and set on work in such actions as the common good requireth. Laws politic, ordained for external order and regiment amongst men, are never framed as they should be, unless presuming the will of man to be inwardly obstinate, rebellious, and averse from all obedience to the sacred laws of his nature; in a word, unless presuming man to be, in regard of his depraved mind, little better than a wild beast, they do accordingly provide notwithstanding, so to frame his outward actions, that they be no hindrance unto the common good, for which societies are instituted. Unless they do this, they are not perfect." Hooker's Eccl. Pol. L. I. Sect. 10.

that is a declaration; and the *fundamental law of nature being the preservation of mankind*, no human sanction can be good or valid against it.

136. Secondly,[9] The legislative or supreme authority cannot assume to itself a power to rule, by extemporary, arbitrary decrees, but *is bound to dispense justice, and decide the rights of the subject, by promulgated, standing laws, and known authorised judges*. For the law of nature being unwritten, and so no-where to be found, but in the minds of men; they who through passion, or interest, shall miscite, or misapply it, cannot so easily be convinced of their mistake, where there is no established judge: and so it serves not, as it ought, to determine the rights, and fence the properties of those that live under it; especially where every one is judge, interpreter, and executioner of it too, and that in his own case: and he that has right on his side, having ordinarily but his own single strength, hath not force enough to defend himself from injuries, or to punish delinquents. To avoid these inconveniencies, which disorder men's properties in the state of nature, men unite into societies, that they may have the united strength of the whole society to secure and defend their properties, and may have standing rules to bound it, by which every one may know what is his. To this end it is that men give up all their natural power to the society which they enter into, and the community put the legislative power into such hands as they think fit: with this trust, that they shall be governed by *declared laws*, or else their peace, quiet, and property will still be at the same uncertainty, as it was in the state of nature.

137. Absolute arbitrary power, or governing without *settled standing laws*, can neither of them consist with the ends of society and government, which men would not quit the freedom of the state of nature for,

and tie themselves up under, were it not to preserve their lives, liberties, and fortunes, and by *stated rules* of right and property to secure their peace and quiet. It cannot be supposed that they should intend, had they a power so to do, to give to any one, or more, an *absolute arbitrary power* over their persons and estates, and put a force into the magistrate's hand to execute his unlimited will arbitrarily upon them. This were to put themselves into a worse condition than the state of nature, wherein they had a liberty to defend their right against the injuries of others, and were upon equal terms of force to maintain it, whether invaded by a single man, or many in combination. Whereas by supposing they have given up themselves to the absolute arbitrary power and will of a legislator, they have disarmed themselves, and armed him, to make a prey of them when he pleases. He being in a much worse condition, who is exposed to the arbitrary power of one man, who has the command of 100,000, than he that is exposed to the arbitrary power of 100,000 single men; no body being secure, that his will, who has such a command, is better than that of other men, though his force be 100,000 times stronger. And therefore, whatever form the commonwealth is under, the ruling power ought to govern by declared and received laws, and not by extemporary dictates and undetermined resolutions. For then mankind will be in a far worse condition than in the state of nature, if they shall have armed one or a few men with the joint power of a multitude, to force them to obey at pleasure the exorbitant and unlimited decrees of their sudden thoughts, or unrestrained, and till that moment unknown wills, without having any measures set down which may guide and justify their actions; for all the power the government has, being only for the good of the society, as it ought not to be arbitrary and at pleasure, so it ought to be exercised by *established and promulgated laws*; that both the people may know their duty, and be safe and secure within the limits of the law, and the rulers too kept within their bounds, and not to be tempted, by the power they have in their hands, to employ it to such purposes, and by such measures, as they would not have known, and own not willingly.

138. *Thirdly*, The *supreme power cannot take* from any man part of his property without his own consent. For the preservation of property being the end of

9. "Human laws are measures in respect of men whose actions they must direct, howbeit such measures they are as have also their higher rules to be measured by, which rules are two, the law of God, and the law of nature; so that laws human must be made according to the general laws of nature, and without contradiction to any positive law of scripture, otherwise they are ill made." Hooker's Eccl. Pol. L. 3. Sect. 9.

"To constrain men to any thing inconvenient doth seem unreasonable." Ibid. L. I. Sect. 10.

government, and that for which men enter into society, it necessarily supposes and requires, that the people should *have property*, without which they must be supposed to lose that, by entering into society, which was the end for which they entered into it; too gross an absurdity for any man to own. *Men* therefore *in society having property*, they have such right to the goods, which by the law of the community are theirs, that no body hath a right to take their substance or any part of it from them, without their own consent; without this they have no property at all. For I have truly no property in that, which another can by right take from me, when he pleases, against my consent. Hence it is a mistake to think, that the *supreme or legislative power* of any commonwealth can do what it will, and dispose of the estates of the subject arbitrarily, or take any part of them at pleasure. This is not much to be feared in governments where the legislative consists, wholly or in part, in assemblies which are variable, whose members, upon the dissolution of the assembly, are subjects under the common laws of their country, equally with the rest. But in governments, where the legislative is in one lasting assembly always in being, or in one man, as in absolute monarchies, there is danger still, that they will think themselves to have a distinct interest from the rest of the community; and so will be apt to increase their own riches and power by taking what they think fit from the people. For a man's property is not at all secure, though there be good and equitable laws to set the bounds of it between him and his fellow subjects, if he who commands those subjects, have power to take from any private man, what part he pleases of his property, and use and dispose of it as he thinks good.

139. But government, into whatsoever hands it is put, being, as I have before shewed, intrusted with this condition, and *for this end,* that men might have and secure their properties; the prince, or senate, however it may have power to make laws, for the regulating of property between the subjects one amongst another, yet can never have a power to take to themselves the whole, or any part of the subject's property, without their own consent. For this would be in effect to leave them no property at all. And to let us see, that even absolute power where it is necessary, is not arbitrary by being absolute, but is still

limited by that reason, and confined to those ends, which required it in some cases to be absolute, we need look no farther than the common practice of martial discipline. For the preservation of the army, and in it of the whole commonwealth, requires an absolute obedience to the command of every superiour officer, and it is justly death to disobey or dispute the most dangerous or unreasonable of them; but yet we see, that neither the serjeant, that could command a soldier to march up to the mouth of a cannon, or stand in a breach, where he is almost sure to perish, can command that soldier to give him one penny of his money; nor the general, that can condemn him to death for deserting his post, or for not obeying the most desperate orders, can yet, with all his absolute power of life and death, dispose of one farthing of that soldier's estate, or seize one jot of his goods; whom yet he can command any thing, and hang for the least disobedience: because such a blind obedience is necessary to that end, for which the commander has his power, viz. the preservation of the rest; but the disposing of his goods has nothing to do with it.

140. It is true, governments cannot be supported without great charge, and it is fit every one who enjoys his share of the protection, should pay out of his estate his proportion for the maintenance of it. But still it must be with his own consent, i.e. the consent of the majority, giving it either by themselves, or their representatives chosen by them. For if any one shall claim a *power to lay* and levy *taxes* on the people, by his own authority, and without such consent of the people, he thereby invades the *fundamental law of property*, and subverts the end of government. For what property have I in that, which another may by right take when he pleases, to himself?

141. *Fourthly,* The *legislative cannot transfer the power of making laws* to any other hands. For it being but a delegated power from the people, they who have it cannot pass it over to others. The people alone can appoint the form of the commonwealth, which is by constituting the legislative, and appointing in whose hands that shall be. And when the people have said, we will submit to rules, and be governed by laws made by such men, and in such forms, no body else can say other men shall make laws for them; nor can the people be bound by any laws, but such as are

enacted by those whom they have chosen, and authorized to make laws for them. The power of the legislative being derived from the people by a positive voluntary grant and institution, can be no other than what that positive grant conveyed, which being only to make laws, and not to make legislators, the legislative can have no power to transfer their authority of making laws and place it in other hands.

142. These are the bounds which the trust, that is put in them by the society and the law of God and nature, have *set to the legislative* power of every commonwealth, in all forms of government.

First, They are to govern by *promulgated established laws*, not to be varied in particular cases, but to have one rule for rich and poor, for the favourite at court, and the countryman at plough.

Secondly, These laws also ought to be designed for no other end ultimately, but *the good of the people*.

Thirdly, They must *not raise taxes* on the *property of the people*, *without the consent of the people*, given by themselves or their deputies. And this properly concerns only such governments where the legislative is always in being, or at least where the people have not reserved any part of the legislative to deputies, to be from time to time chosen by themselves.

Fourthly, The legislative neither must *nor can transfer the power of making laws* to any body else, or place it any where, but where the people have.

Chapter 12

Of the Legislative, Executive, and Federative Power of the Commonwealth

143. The legislative power is that, which has a right *to direct how the force of the commonwealth* shall be employed for preserving the community and the members of it. But because those laws which are constantly to be executed, and whose force is always to continue, may be made in a little time; therefore there is no need, that the legislative should be always in being, not having always business to do. And because it may be too great a temptation to human frailty, apt to grasp at power, for the same persons, who have the power of making laws, to have also in

their hands the power to execute them, whereby they may exempt themselves from obedience to the laws they make, and suit the law, both in its making and execution, to their own private advantage, and thereby come to have a distinct interest from the rest of the community, contrary to the end of society and government: therefore in well ordered commonwealths, where the good of the whole is so considered, as it ought, the legislative power is put into the hands of divers persons, who, duly assembled, have by themselves, or jointly with others, a power to make laws; which when they have done, being separated again, they are themselves subject to the laws they have made; which is a new and near tie upon them, to take care that they make them for the public good.

144. But because the laws, that are at once, and in a short time made, have a constant and lasting force, and need a *perpetual execution*, or an attendance thereunto: therefore it is necessary there should be a *power always in being*, which should see to the execution of the laws that are made, and remain in force. And thus the legislative and executive power come often to be separated.

145. There is another power in every commonwealth, which one may call *natural*, because it is that which answers to the power every man naturally had before he entered into society. For though in a commonwealth, the members of it are distinct persons still in reference to one another, and as such are governed by the laws of the society; yet in reference to the rest of mankind, they make one body, which is, as every member of it before was, still in the state of nature with the rest of mankind. Hence it is, that the controversies that happen between any man of the society with those that are out of it, are managed by the public; and an injury done to a member of their body engages the whole in the reparation of it. So that, under this consideration, the whole community is one body in the state of nature, in respect of all other states or persons out of its community.

146. This therefore contains the power of war and peace, leagues and alliances, and all the transactions, with all persons and communities without the commonwealth; and may be called *federative*, if any one pleases. So the thing be understood, I am indifferent as to the name.

147. These two powers, executive and federative,

though they be really distinct in themselves, yet one comprehending the execution of the municipal laws of the society within itself, upon all that are parts of it; the other the management of the *security and interest of the public without*, with all those that it may receive benefit or damage from; yet they are always almost united. And though this *federative power* in the well or ill management of it be of great moment to the commonwealth, yet it is much less capable to be directed by antecedent, standing, positive laws, than the executive; and so must necessarily be left to the prudence and wisdom of those whose hands it is in, to be managed for the public good. For the laws that concern subjects one amongst another, being to direct their actions, may well enough precede them. But what is to be done in reference to foreigners, depending much upon their actions, and the variation of designs, and interests, must be left in great part to the prudence of those who have this power committed to them, to be managed by the best of their skill, for the advantage of the commonwealth.

148. Though, as I said, the executive and federative power of every community be really distinct in themselves, yet they are hardly to be separated, and placed at the same time in the hands of distinct persons. For both of them requiring the force of the society for their exercise, it is almost impracticable to place the force of the commonwealth in distinct, and not subordinate hands; or that the executive and federative power should be placed in persons that might act separately, whereby the force of the public would be under different commands: which would be apt some time or other to cause disorder and ruin.

Chapter 13

Of the Subordination of the Powers of the Commonwealth

149. Though in a constituted commonwealth, standing upon its own basis, and acting according to its own nature, that is, acting for the preservation of the community, there can be but *one supreme power*, which is the *legislative*, to which all the rest are and must be subordinate; yet the legislative being only a fiduciary power to act for certain ends, there remains still *in the people a supreme power to remove or alter the legislative*, when they find the legislative act contrary to the trust reposed in them. For all *power given with trust* for the attaining an end, being limited by that end; whenever that end is manifestly neglected or opposed, the trust must necessarily be forfeited, and the power devolve into the hands of those that gave it, who may place it anew where they shall think best for their safety and security. And thus the *community* perpetually *retains a supreme power* of saving themselves from the attempts and designs of any body, even of their legislators, whenever they shall be so foolish, or so wicked, as to lay and carry on designs against the liberties and properties of the subject. For no man, or society of men, having a power to deliver up their preservation, or consequently the means of it, to the absolute will and arbitrary dominion of another; whenever any one shall go about to bring them into such a slavish condition, they will always have a right to preserve what they have not a power to part with; and to rid themselves of those who invade this fundamental, sacred, and unalterable law of self-preservation, for which they entered into society. And thus the community may be said in this respect to be *always the supreme power*, but not as considered under any form of government, because this power of the people can never take place till the government be dissolved.

150. In all cases, whilst the government subsists, the *legislative is the supreme power*. For what can give laws to another, must needs be superiour to him; and since the legislative is no otherwise legislative of the society, but by the right it has to make laws for all the parts, and for every member of the society, prescribing rules to their actions, and giving power of execution, where they are transgressed; the legislative must needs be the supreme, and all other powers, in any members or parts of the society, derived from and subordinate to it.

151. In some commonwealths, where the legislative is not always in being, and the executive is vested in a single person, who has also a share in the legislative; there that single person in a very tolerable sense may also be called supreme; not that he has in himself all the supreme power, which is that of law-making; but because he has in him the supreme execution, from whom all inferiour magistrates derive all their several subordinate powers, or at least the greatest

part of them: having also no legislative superiour to him, there being no law to be made without his consent, which cannot be expected should ever subject him to the other part of the legislative, he is properly enough in this sense *supreme*. But yet it is to be observed, that though *oaths of allegiance* and fealty are taken to him, it is not to him as supreme legislator, but as *supreme executor* of the law, made by a joint power of him with others: allegiance being nothing but an *obedience according to law*, which when he violates, he has no right to obedience, nor can claim it otherwise, than as the public person invested with the power of the law; and so is to be considered as the image, phantom, or representative of the commonwealth, acted by the will of the society, declared in its laws; and thus he has no will, no power, but that of the law. But when he quits this representation, this public will, and acts by his own private will, he degrades himself, and is but a single private person without power, and without will, that has no right to obedience; the members owing no obedience but to the public will of the society.

152. The *executive power*, placed any where but in a person that has also a share in the legislative, is visibly subordinate and accountable to it, and may be at pleasure changed and displaced; so that it is not the *supreme executive power* that is exempt from subordination, but the *supreme executive power* vested in one, who having a share in the legislative, has no distinct superiour legislative to be subordinate and accountable to, farther than he himself shall join and consent; so that he is no more subordinate than he himself shall think fit, which one may certainly conclude will be but very little. Of other ministerial and subordinate powers in a commonwealth, we need not speak, they being so multiplied with infinite variety in the different customs and constitutions of distinct commonwealths, that it is impossible to give a particular account of them all. Only thus much, which is necessary to our present purpose, we may take notice of concerning them, that they have no manner of authority, any of them, beyond what is by positive grant and commission delegated to them, and are all of them accountable to some other power in the commonwealth.

153. It is not necessary, no, nor so much as convenient, that the *legislative* should be *always in being*.

But absolutely necessary that the executive power should; because there is not always need of new laws to be made, but always need of execution of the laws that are made. When the legislative hath put the execution of the laws they make into other hands, they have a power still to resume it out of those hands, when they find cause, and to punish for any maladministration against the laws. The same holds also in regard of the federative power, that and the executive being both *ministerial and subordinate to the legislative*, which, as has been shewed, in a constituted commonwealth is the supreme. The legislative also in this case being supposed to consist of several persons, (for if it be a single person, it cannot but be always in being, and so will, as supreme, naturally have the supreme executive power, together with the legislative) may *assemble, and exercise their legislature*, at the times that either their original constitution, or their own adjournment, appoints, or when they please; if neither of these hath appointed any time, or there be no other way prescribed to convoke them. For the supreme power being placed in them by the people, it is always in them, and they may exercise it when they please, unless by their original constitution they are limited to certain seasons, or by an act of their supreme power they have adjourned to a certain time; and when that time comes, they have a right to assemble and act again.

154. If the legislative, or any part of it, be made up of representatives chosen for that time by the people, which afterwards return into the ordinary state of subjects, and have no share in the legislature but upon a new choice, this power of choosing must also be exercised by the people, either at certain appointed seasons, or else when they are summoned to it; and in this latter case the power of convoking the legislative is ordinarily placed in the executive, and has one of these two limitations in respect of time: that either the original constitution requires their assembling and acting at certain intervals, and then the executive power does nothing but ministerially issue directions for their electing and assembling according to due forms; or else it is left to his prudence to call them by new elections, when the occasions, or exigencies of the public require the amendment of old, or making of new laws, or the redress or prevention of any inconveniencies, that lie on, or threaten the people.

155. It may be demanded here, What if the executive power, being possessed of the force of the commonwealth, shall make use of that force to hinder the *meeting* and *acting of the legislative*; when the original constitution, or the public exigencies require it? I say, using force upon the people without authority, and contrary to the trust put in him that does so, is a state of war with the people, who have a right to *reinstate* their *legislative in the exercise* of their power. For having erected a legislative, with an intent they should exercise the power of making laws, either at certain set times, or when there is need of it; when they are hindered by any force from what is so necessary to the society, and wherein the safety and preservation of the people consists, the people have a right to remove it by force. In all states and conditions, the true remedy of force without authority, is to oppose force to it. The use of force without authority, always puts him that uses it into a *state of war*, as the aggressor; and renders him liable to be treated accordingly.

156. The *power of assembling and dismissing the legislative*, placed in the executive, gives not the executive a superiority over it, but is a fiduciary trust placed in him for the safety of the people, in a case where the uncertainty and variableness of human affairs could not bear a steady fixed rule. For it not being possible that the first framers of the government should, by any foresight, be so much masters of future events as to be able to prefix so just periods of return and duration to the *assemblies of the legislative*, in all times to come, that might exactly answer all the exigencies of the commonwealth; the best remedy could be found for this defect was to trust this to the prudence of one who was always to be present, and whose business it was to watch over the public good. Constant *frequent meetings of the legislative*, and long continuations of their assemblies, without necessary occasion, could not but be burdensome to the people, and must necessarily in time produce more dangerous inconveniencies, and yet the quick turn of affairs might be sometimes such as to need their present help: any delay of their convening might endanger the public; and sometimes too their business might be so great, that the limited time of their sitting might be too short for their work, and rob the public of that benefit which could be had only from their mature deliberation. What then could be done in this case

to prevent the community from being exposed some time or other to eminent hazard, on one side or the other, by fixed intervals and periods, set to the *meeting and acting of the legislative*; but to intrust it to the prudence of some, who being present, and acquainted with the state of public affairs, might make use of this prerogative for the public good? And where else could this be so well placed as in his hands, who was intrusted with the execution of the laws for the same end? Thus supposing the regulation of times for the *assembling and sitting of the legislative* not settled by the original constitution, it naturally fell into the hands of the executive, not as an arbitrary power depending on his good pleasure, but with this trust always to have it exercised only for the public weal, as the occurrences of times and change of affairs might require. Whether *settled periods of their convening*, or *a liberty* left to the prince for *convoking the legislative*, or perhaps a mixture of both, hath the least inconvenience attending it, it is not my business here to inquire; but only to shew, that though the executive power may have the prerogative of *convoking* and *dissolving* such *conventions of the legislative*, yet it is not thereby superiour to it.

157. Things of this world are in so constant a flux, that nothing remains long in the same state. Thus people, riches, trade, power, change their stations, flourishing mighty cities come to ruin, and prove in time neglected desolate corners, whilst other unfrequented places grow into populous countries, filled with wealth and inhabitants. But things not always changing equally, and private interest often keeping up customs and privileges, when the reasons of them are ceased; it often comes to pass, that in governments, where part of the legislative consists of representatives chosen by the people, that in tract of time this representation becomes very unequal and disproportionate to the reasons it was at first established upon. To what gross absurdities the following of custom, when reason has left it, may lead, we may be satisfied, when we see the bare name of a town, of which there remains not so much as the ruins, where scarce so much housing as a sheepcote, or more inhabitants than a shepherd is to be found, sends *as many representatives* to the grand assembly of law-makers, as a whole county numerous in people, and powerful in riches. This strangers stand amazed at, and every one must

confess needs a remedy. Though most think it hard to find one; because the constitution of the legislative being the original and supreme act of the society, antecedent to all positive laws in it, and depending wholly on the people, no inferiour power can alter it. And therefore the people, when the legislative is once constituted, having, in such a government as we have been speaking of, no power to act as long as the government stands; this inconvenience is thought incapable of a remedy.

158. *Salus populi suprema lex*, is certainly so just and fundamental a rule, that he, who sincerely follows it, cannot dangerously err. If therefore the executive, who has the power of convoking the legislative, observing rather the true proportion than fashion of representation, regulates not by old custom, but true reason, the *number of members* in all places that have a right to be distinctly represented, which no part of the people, however incorporated, can pretend to, but in proportion to the assistance which it affords to the public; it cannot be judged to have set up a new legislative, but to have restored the old and true one, and to have rectified the disorders which succession of time had insensibly, as well as inevitably introduced. For it being the interest as well as intention of the people, to have a fair and equal representative; whoever brings it nearest to that, is an undoubted friend to, and establisher of the government, and cannot miss the consent and approbation of the community. Prerogative being nothing but a power in the hands of the prince to provide for the public good, in such cases, which depending upon unforeseen and uncertain occurrences, certain and unalterable laws could not safely direct; whatsoever shall be done manifestly for the good of the people, and the establishing the government upon its true foundations, is, and always will be, just *prerogative*. The power of erecting new corporations, and therewith *new representatives*, carries with it a supposition that in time the *measures of representation* might vary, and those places have a just right to be represented which before had none; and by the same reason, those cease to have a right, and be too inconsiderable for such a privilege, which before had it. It is not a change from the present state, which perhaps corruption or decay has introduced, that makes an inroad upon the government; but the tendency of it to injure or oppress the people,

and to set up one part or party, with a distinction from, and an unequal subjection of the rest. Whatsoever cannot but be acknowledged to be of advantage to the society, and people in general, upon just and lasting measures, will always, when done, justify itself; and whenever the people shall choose their *representatives upon* just and undeniably *equal measures*, suitable to the original frame of the government, it cannot be doubted to be the will and act of the society, whoever permitted or caused them so to do.

Chapter 14

Of Prerogative

159. Where the legislative and executive power are in distinct hands, (as they are in all moderated monarchies and well-framed governments) there the good of the society requires, that several things should be left to the discretion of him that has the executive power. For the legislators not being able to foresee, and provide by laws, for all that may be useful to the community, the executor of the laws having the power in his hands, has by the common law of nature a right to make use of it for the good of the society, in many cases, where the municipal law has given no direction, till the legislative can conveniently be assembled to provide for it. Many things there are, which the law can by no means provide for; and those must necessarily be left to the discretion of him that has the executive power in his hands, to be ordered by him as the public good and advantage shall require: nay, it is fit that the laws themselves should in some cases give way to the executive power, or rather to this fundamental law of nature and government, viz. That, as much as may be, all the members of the society are to be preserved. For since many accidents may happen, wherein a strict and rigid observation of the laws may do harm; (as not to pull down an innocent man's house to stop the fire, when the next to it is burning) and a man may come sometimes within the reach of the law, which makes no distinction of persons, by an action that may deserve reward and pardon; it is fit the ruler should have a power, in many cases, to mitigate the severity of the law, and pardon some offenders. For the *end of government*

being the *preservation of all*, as much as may be, even the guilty are to be spared, where it can prove no prejudice to the innocent.

160. This power to act according to discretion, for the public good, without the prescription of the law, and sometimes even against it, is that which is called *prerogative*. For since in some governments the lawmaking power is not always in being, and is usually too numerous, and so too slow for the dispatch requisite to execution; and because also it is impossible to foresee, and so by laws to provide for all accidents and necessities that may concern the public, or to make such laws as will do no harm, if they are executed with an inflexible rigour on all occasions, and upon all persons that may come in their way; therefore there is a latitude left to the executive power, to do many things of choice which the laws do not prescribe.

161. This power, whilst employed for the benefit of the community, and suitably to the trust and ends of the government, *is undoubted prerogative*, and never is questioned. For the people are very seldom or never scrupulous or nice in the point; they are far from examining prerogative, whilst it is in any tolerable degree employed for the use it was meant; that is, for the good of the people, and not manifestly against it. But if there comes to be a *question* between the executive power and the people, about a thing claimed as a *prerogative*, the tendency of the exercise of such prerogative to the good or hurt of the people will easily decide that question.

162. It is easy to conceive, that in the infancy of governments, when commonwealths differed little from families in number of people, they differed from them too but little in number of laws: and the governors being as the fathers of them, watching over them, for their good, the government was almost all prerogative. A few established laws served the turn, and the discretion and care of the ruler supplied the rest. But when mistake or flattery prevailed with weak princes to make use of this power for private ends of their own, and not for the public good, the people were fain by express laws to get prerogative determined in those points wherein they found disadvantage from it: and thus declared *limitations of prerogative* were by the people found necessary in cases which they and their ancestors had left, in the utmost latitude,

to the wisdom of those princes who made no other but a right use of it; that is, for the good of their people.

163. And therefore they have a very wrong notion of government, who say, that the people have *encroached upon the prerogative*, when they have got any part of it to be defined by positive laws. For in so doing they have not pulled from the prince any thing that of right belonged to him, but only declared, that that power which they indefinitely left in his or his ancestors hands, to be exercised for their good, was not a thing which they intended him when he used it otherwise. For the end of government being the good of the community, whatsoever alterations are made in it, tending to that end, cannot be an encroachment upon any body, since no body in government can have a right tending to any other end: and those only are encroachments which prejudice or hinder the public good. Those who say otherwise, speak as if the prince had a distinct and separate interest from the good of the community, and was not made for it; the root and source from which spring almost all those evils and disorders which happen in kingly governments. And indeed, if that be so, the people under his government are not a society of rational creatures, entered into a community for their mutual good; they are not such as have set rulers over themselves, to guard and promote that good; but are to be looked on as an herd of inferior creatures under the dominion of a master, who keeps them and works them for his own pleasure or profit. If men were so void of reason, and brutish, as to enter into society upon such terms, prerogative might indeed be, what some men would have it, an arbitrary power to do things hurtful to the people.

164. But since a rational creature cannot be supposed, when free, to put himself into subjection to another, for his own harm; (though, where he finds a good and wise ruler, he may not perhaps think it either necessary or useful to set precise bounds to his power in all things) prerogative can be nothing but the people's permitting their rulers to do several things, of their own free choice, where the law was silent, and sometimes too against the direct letter of the law, for the public good; and their acquiescing in it when so done. For as a good prince, who is mindful of the trust put into his hands, and careful of the good of his people, cannot have too much prerogative, that

is, power to do good; so a weak and ill prince, who would claim that power which his predecessors exercised without the direction of the law, as a prerogative belonging to him by right of his office, which he may exercise at his pleasure, to make or promote an interest distinct from that of the public, gives the people an occasion to claim their right, and limit that power, which, whilst it was exercised for their good, they were content should be tacitly allowed.

165. And therefore he that will look into the *history of England*, will find, that prerogative was always *largest* in the hands of our wisest and best princes; because the people, observing the whole tendency of their actions to be the public good, contested not what was done without law to that end: or, if any human frailty or mistake (for princes are but men, made as others) appeared in some small declinations from that end; yet it was visible, the main of their conduct tended to nothing but the care of the public. The people therefore, finding reason to be satisfied with these princes, whenever they acted without, or contrary to the letter of the law, acquiesced in what they did, and without the least complaint, let them enlarge their prerogative as they pleased; judging rightly, that they did nothing herein to the prejudice of their laws, since they acted conformably to the foundation and end of all laws, the public good.

166. Such God-like princes indeed had some title to arbitrary power by that argument, that would prove absolute monarchy the best government, as that which God himself governs the universe by; because such kings partook of his wisdom and goodness. Upon this is founded that saying, That the reigns of good princes have been always most dangerous to the liberties of their people. For when their successors, managing the government with different thoughts, would draw the actions of those good rulers into precedent, and make them the standard of their prerogative, as if what had been done only for the good of the people was a right in them to do, for the harm of the people, if they so pleased; it has often occasioned contest, and sometimes public disorders, before the people could recover their original right, and get that to be declared not to be prerogative, which truly was never so: since it is impossible that any body in the society should ever have a right to do the people harm; though it be very possible, and reasonable, that the people should not go about to set any bounds to the prerogative of those kings, or rulers, who themselves transgressed not the bounds of the public good. For *prerogative is nothing but the power of doing public good without a rule.*

167. The power of calling parliaments in England, as to precise time, place, and duration, is certainly a prerogative of the king, but still with this trust, that it shall be made use of for the good of the nation, as the exigencies of the times, and variety of occasions, shall require. For it being impossible to foresee which should always be the fittest place for them to assemble in, and what the best season, the choice of these was left with the executive power, as might be most subservient to the public good, and best suit the ends of parliaments.

168. The old question will be asked in this matter of prerogative, "But who shall be judge when this power is made a right use of?" I answer: between an executive power in being, with such a prerogative, and a legislative that depends upon his will for their convening, there can be no *judge on earth*; as there can be none between the legislative and the people, should either the executive or the legislative, when they have got the power in their hands, design, or go about to enslave or destroy them. The people have no other remedy in this, as in all other cases where they have no judge on earth, but to *appeal to heaven.* For the rulers, in such attempts, exercising a power the people never put into their hands, (who can never be supposed to consent that any body should rule over them for their harm) do that which they have not a right to do. And where the body of the people, or any single man, is deprived of their right, or is under the exercise of a power without right, and have no appeal on earth, then they have a liberty to appeal to heaven, whenever they judge the cause of sufficient moment. And therefore, *though the people cannot* be *judge,* so as to have, by the constitution of that society, any superior power to determine and give effective sentence in the case; yet they have, by a law antecedent and paramount to all positive laws of men, reserved that ultimate determination to themselves which belongs to all mankind, where there lies no appeal on earth, viz. to judge, whether they have just cause to make their appeal to heaven. And this judgment they cannot part with, it being out of a

man's power so to submit himself to another, as to give him a liberty to destroy him; God and nature never allowing a man so to abandon himself, as to neglect his own preservation: and since he cannot take away his own life, neither can he give another power to take it. Nor let any one think, this lays a perpetual foundation for disorder; for this operates not, till the inconveniency is so great, that the majority feel it, and are weary of it, and find a necessity to have it amended. But this the executive power, or wise princes, never need come in the danger of: and it is the thing, of all others, they have most need to avoid, as of all others the most perilous.

Chapter 15

Of Paternal, Political, and Despotical Power, Considered Together

169. Though I have had occasion to speak of these separately before, yet the great mistakes of late about government having, as I suppose, arisen from confounding these distinct powers one with another, it may not, perhaps, be amiss to consider them here together.

170. *First*, then, *Paternal* or *parental power* is nothing but that which parents have over their children, to govern them for the children's good, till they come to the use of reason, or a state of knowledge, wherein they may be supposed capable to understand that rule, whether it be the law of nature, or the municipal law of their country, they are to govern themselves by: capable, I say, to know it, as well as several others, who live as freemen under that law. The affection and tenderness which God hath planted in the breast of parents towards their children, makes it evident that this is not intended to be a severe arbitrary government, but only for the help, instruction, and preservation of their offspring. But happen it as it will, there is, as I have proved, no reason why it should be thought to extend to life and death, at any time, over their children, more than over any body else; neither can there be any pretence why this *parental power* should keep the child, when grown to a man, in subjection to the will of his parents, any farther than having received life and education from his parents,

obliges him to respect, honour, gratitude, assistance and support, all his life, to both father and mother. And thus, it is true, the paternal is a natural government, but not at all extending itself to the ends and jurisdictions of that which is political. The *power of the father doth not reach* at all to the *property* of the child, which is only in his own disposing.

171. *Secondly, Political power* is that power which every man having in the state of nature, has given up into the hands of the society, and therein to the governors, whom the society hath set over itself, with this express or tacit trust, that it shall be employed for their good, and the preservation of their property: now this *power*, which every man has *in the state of nature*, and which he parts with to the society in all such cases where the society can secure him, is to use such means for the preserving of his own property, as he thinks good, and nature allows him; and to punish the breach of the law of nature in others, so as (according to the best of his reason) may most conduce to the preservation of himself, and the rest of mankind. So that the *end and measure of this power*, when in every man's hands in the state of nature, being the preservation of all of his society, that is, all mankind in general; it can have no other *end or measure*, when in the hands of the magistrate, but to preserve the members of that society in their lives, liberties, and possessions; and so cannot be an absolute arbitrary power, over their lives and fortunes, which are as much as possible to be preserved; but a *power to make laws*, and annex such penalties to them, as may tend to the preservation of the whole, by cutting off those parts, and those only, which are so corrupt, that they threaten the sound and healthy, without which no severity is lawful. And this *power has its original only from compact* and agreement, and the mutual consent of those who make up the community.

172. Thirdly, Despotical power is an absolute, arbitrary power; one man has over another, to take away his life, whenever he pleases. This is a power, which neither nature gives, for it has made no such distinction between one man and another; nor compact can convey. For man not having such an arbitrary power over his own life, cannot give another man such a power over it; but it is *the effect only of forfeiture* which the aggressor makes of his own life, when he

puts himself into the state of war with another. For having quitted reason, which God hath given to be the rule betwixt man and man, and the common bond whereby human kind is united into one fellowship and society; and having renounced the way of peace which that teaches, and made use of the force of war, to compass his unjust ends upon another, where he has no right; and so revolting from his own kind to that of beasts, by making force, which is theirs, to be his rule of right; he renders himself liable to be destroyed by the injured person, and the rest of mankind, that will join with him in the execution of justice, as any other wild beast, or noxious brute, with whom mankind can have neither society nor security.[10] And thus *captives, taken in a just and lawful war, and such only, are subject to a despotical power; which, as it arises not from compact, so neither is it capable of any, but is the state of war continued.* For what compact can be made with a man that is not master of his own life? What condition can he perform? And if he be once allowed to be master of his own life, the *despotical arbitrary power* of his master ceases. He that is master of himself; and his own life, has a right too to the means of preserving it; so that, *as soon as compact enters, slavery ceases,* and he so far quits his absolute power, and puts an end to the state of war, who enters into conditions with his captive.

173. Nature gives the first of these, viz. *paternal power, to parents* for the benefit of their children during their minority, to supply their want of ability and understanding how to manage their property. (By property I must be understood here, as in other places, to mean that property which men have in their persons as well as goods.) *Voluntary agreement gives* the second, viz. *political power to governors* for the benefit of their subjects, to secure them in the possession and use of their properties. And *forfeiture gives* the third *despotical power to lords,* for their own benefit, over those who are stripped of all property.

174. He, that shall consider the distinct rise and extent, and the different ends of these several powers, will plainly see, that *paternal power* comes as far short of that of the *magistrate,* as *despotical* exceeds it; and

that *absolute dominion,* however placed, is so far from being one kind of civil society, that it is as inconsistent with it, as slavery is with property. *Paternal power* is only where minority makes the child incapable to manage his property; *political,* where men have property in their own disposal; and *despotical,* over such as have no property at all.

Chapter 16

Of Conquest

175. Though governments can originally have no other rise than that before-mentioned, nor *polities* be *founded* on any thing but *the consent of the people;* yet such have been the disorders ambition has filled the world with, that in the noise of war, which makes so great a part of the history of mankind, *this consent* is little taken notice of: and therefore many have mistaken the force of arms for the consent of the people, and reckon conquest as one of the originals of government. But conquest is as far from setting up any government, as demolishing an house is from building a new one in the place. Indeed, it often makes way for a new frame of a commonwealth, by destroying the former; but, without the consent of the people, can never erect a new one.

176. That the *aggressor,* who puts himself into the state of war with another, and *unjustly invades* another man's right, can, by such an unjust war, *never* come to *have a right over the conquered,* will be easily agreed by all men, who will not think, that robbers and pirates have a right of empire over whomsoever they have force enough to master; or that men are bound by promises, which unlawful force extorts from them. Should a robber break into my house, and with a dagger at my throat, make me seal deeds to convey my estate to him, would this give him any title? Just such a title, by his sword, has an *unjust conqueror,* who forces me into submission. The injury and the crime are equal, whether committed by the wearer of the crown, or some petty villain. The title of the offender, and the number of his followers, make no difference in the offence, unless it be to aggravate it. The only difference is, great robbers punish little ones, to keep them in their obedience, but the great

---

10. Another copy, corrected by Mr. Locke, has it thus, "Noxious brute that is destructive to their being."

ones are rewarded with laurels and triumphs; because they are too big for the weak hands of justice in this world, and have the power in their own possession, which should punish offenders. What is my remedy against a robber, that so broke into my house? Appeal to the law for justice. But perhaps justice is denied, or I am crippled and cannot stir, robbed and have not the means to do it. If God has taken away all means of seeking remedy, there is nothing left but patience. But my son, when able, may seek the relief of the law, which I am denied: he or his son may renew his appeal, till he recover his right. But the conquered, or their children, have no court, no arbitrator on earth to appeal to. Then they may appeal, as Jephthah did, to heaven, and repeat their appeal till they have recovered the native right of their ancestors, which was, to have such a legislative over them, as the majority should approve, and freely acquiesce in. If it be objected, this would cause endless trouble; I answer, no more than justice does, where she lies open to all that appeal to her. He that troubles his neighbour without a cause, is punished for it by the justice of the court he appeals to. And he that *appeals to heaven* must be sure he has right on his side; and a right too that is worth the trouble and cost of the appeal, as he will answer at a tribunal that cannot be deceived, and will be sure to retribute to every one according to the mischiefs he hath created to his fellow-subjects; that is, any part of mankind: from whence it is plain, that he that *conquers in an unjust war, can thereby have no title to the subjection and obedience of the conquered.*

177. But supposing victory favours the right side, let us consider *a conqueror in a lawful war,* and see what power he gets, and over *whom.*

First, it is plain, *he gets no power by his conquest over those that conquered with him.* They that fought on his side cannot suffer by the conquest, but must at least be as much freemen as they were before. And most commonly they serve upon terms, and on conditions to share with their leader, and enjoy a part of the spoil, and other advantages that attended the conquering sword; or at least have a part of the subdued country bestowed upon them. And *the conquering people are not, I hope, to be slaves by conquest,* and wear their laurels only to shew they are sacrifices to their leader's triumph. They that found absolute

monarchy upon the title of the sword, make their heroes, who are the founders of such monarchies, arrant Drawcansirs, and forget they had any officers and soldiers that fought on their side in the battles they won, or assisted them in the subduing, or shared in possessing, the countries they mastered. We are told by some, that the English monarchy is founded in the Norman conquest, and that our princes have thereby a title to absolute dominion: which if it were true, (as by the history it appears otherwise) and that William had a right to make war on this island; yet his dominion by conquest could reach no farther than to the Saxons and Britons, that were then inhabitants of this country. The Normans that came with him, and helped to conquer, and all descended from them, are freemen, and no subjects by conquest, let that give what dominion it will. And if I, or any body else, shall claim freedom, as derived from them, it will be very hard to prove the contrary; and it is plain, the law, that has made no distinction between the one and the other, intends not there should be any difference in their freedom or privileges.

178. But supposing, which seldom happens, that the conquerors and conquered never incorporate into one people, under the same laws and freedom. Let us see next *what power a lawful conqueror has over the subdued;* and that I say is purely despotical. He has an absolute power over the lives of those who by an unjust war have forfeited them; but not over the lives or fortunes of those who engaged not in the war, nor over the possessions even of those who were actually engaged in it.

179. Secondly, I say then the conqueror gets no power but only over those who have actually assisted, concurred, or consented to that unjust force that is used against him. For the people having given to their governors no power to do an unjust thing, such as is to make an unjust war, (for they never had such a power in themselves) they ought not to be charged as guilty of the violence and injustice that is committed in an unjust war, any farther than they actually abet it; no more than they are to be thought guilty of any violence or oppression their governors should use upon the people themselves, or any part of their fellow-subjects, they having impowered them no more to the one than to the other. Conquerors, it is true, seldom trouble themselves to make the distinc-

tion, but they willingly permit the confusion of war to sweep all together: but yet this alters not the right; for the conqueror's power over the lives of the conquered being only because they have used force to do, or maintain an injustice, he can have that power only over those who have concurred in that force; all the rest are innocent; and he has no more title over the people of that country, who have done him no injury, and so have made no forfeiture of their lives, than he has over any other, who without any injuries or provocations, have lived upon fair terms with him.

180. *Thirdly*, The *power a conqueror gets* over those he overcomes *in a just war, is perfectly despotical:* he has an absolute power over the lives of those, who, by putting themselves in a state of war, have forfeited them; but he has not thereby a right and title to their possessions. This I doubt not but at first sight will seem a strange doctrine, it being so quite contrary to the practice of the world; there being nothing more familiar in speaking of the dominion of countries, than to say such an one conquered it. As if conquest, without any more ado, conveyed a right of possession. But when we consider, that the practice of the strong and powerful, how universal soever it may be, is seldom the rule of right, however it be one part of the subjection of the conquered, not to argue against the conditions cut out to them by the conquering sword.

181. Though in all war there be usually a complication of force and damage, and the aggressor seldom fails to harm the estate, when he uses force against the persons of those he makes war upon; yet it is the use of force only that puts a man into the state of war. For whether by force he begins the injury, or else, having quietly, and by fraud, done the injury, he refuses to make reparation, and by force maintains it, (which is the same thing, as at first to have done it by force) it is the unjust use of force that makes the war. For he that breaks open my house, and violently turns me out of doors; or, having peaceably got in, by force keeps me out; does in effect the same thing; supposing we are in such a state, that we have no common judge on earth, whom I may appeal to, and to whom we are both obliged to submit. For of such I am now speaking. It is the *unjust use of force then, that puts a man into the state of war* with another; and thereby he that is guilty of it makes a forfeiture of his life. For quitting reason, which is the

rule given between man and man, and using force, the way of beasts, he becomes liable to be destroyed by him he uses force against as any savage ravenous beast, that is dangerous to his being.

182. But because the miscarriages of the father are no faults of the children, and they may be rational and peaceable, notwithstanding the brutishness and injustice of the father; the father, by his miscarriages and violence, can forfeit but his own life, but involves not his children in his guilt or destruction. His goods, which nature, that willeth the preservation of all mankind as much as is possible, hath made to belong to the children, to keep them from perishing, do still continue to belong to his children. For supposing them not to have joined in the war, either through infancy, absence, or choice, they have done nothing to forfeit them: *nor has the conqueror any right* to take them away, by the bare title of having subdued him that by force attempted his destruction; though perhaps he may have some right to them, to repair the damages he has sustained by the war, and the defence of his own right; which how far it reaches to the possessions of the conquered, we shall see by and by. So that he that *by conquest has a right over a man's person* to destroy him if he pleases, has not thereby a right *over his estate* to possess and enjoy it. For it is the brutal force the aggressor has used, that gives his adversary a right to take away his life, and destroy him if he pleases as a noxious creature; but it is damage sustained that alone gives him title to another man's goods. For, though I may kill a thief that sets on me in the highway, yet I may not (which seems less) take away his money and let him go: this would be robbery on my side. His force, and the state of war he put himself in, made him forfeit his life, but gave me no title to his goods. The *right* then *of conquest extends only to the lives* of those who joined in the war, *not to their estates*, but only in order to make reparation for the damages received, and the charges of the war; and that too with reservation of the right of the innocent wife and children.

183. Let the conqueror have as much justice on his side as could be supposed, he has no right to seize more than the vanquished could forfeit: his life is at the victor's mercy; and his service and goods he may appropriate, to make himself reparation; but he cannot take the goods of his wife and children: they too

had a title to the goods he enjoyed, and their shares in the estate he possessed. For example, I in the state of nature (and all commonwealths are in the state of nature one with another) have injured another man, and refusing to give satisfaction it comes to a state of war, wherein my defending by force what I had gotten unjustly makes me the aggressor. I am conquered: my life, it is true, as forfeit, is at mercy, but not my wife's and children's. They made not the war, nor assisted in it. I could not forfeit their lives; they were not mine to forfeit. My wife had a share in my estate; that neither could I forfeit. And my children also, being born of me, had a right to be maintained out of my labour or substance. Here then is the case: the conqueror has a title to reparation for damages received, and the children have a title to their father's estate for their subsistence. For as to the wife's share, whether her own labour, or compact, gave her a title to it, it is plain, her husband could not forfeit what was hers. What must be done in the case? I answer; the fundamental law of nature being, that all, as much as may be, should be preserved, it follows, that if there be not enough fully to satisfy both, viz. for the conqueror's losses, and children's maintenance, he that hath, and to spare, must remit something of his full satisfaction, and give way to the pressing and preferable title of those who are in danger to perish without it.

184. But supposing the *charge* and *damages of the war* are to be made up to the conqueror, to the utmost farthing; and that the children of the vanquished, spoiled of all their father's goods, are to be left to starve and perish; yet the satisfying of what shall, on this score, be due to the conqueror, will scarce give him a *title to any country he shall conquer.* For the damages of war can scarce amount to the value of any considerable tract of land, in any part of the world, where all the land is possessed, and none lies waste. And if I have not taken away the conqueror's land, which, being vanquished, it is impossible I should; scarce any other spoil I have done him can amount to the value of mine, supposing it equally cultivated, and of an extent any way coming near what I had over-run of his. The destruction of a year's product or two (for it seldom reaches four or five) is the utmost spoil that usually can be done. For as to money, and such riches and treasure taken away, these are none of nature's goods, they have but a

fantastical imaginary value: nature has put no such upon them: they are of no more account by her standard, than the wampompeke of the Americans to an European prince, or the silver money of Europe would have been formerly to an American. And five years product is not worth the perpetual inheritance of land, where all is possessed, and none remains waste, to be taken up by him that is disseized: which will be easily granted, if one do but take away the imaginary value of money, the disproportion being more than between five and five hundred; though, at the same time, half a year's product is more worth than the inheritance, where there being more land than the inhabitants possess and make use of, any one has liberty to make use of the waste: but there conquerors take little care to possess themselves of the *lands of the vanquished.* No damage therefore, that men in the state of nature (as all princes and governments are in reference to one another) suffer from one another, can give a conqueror power to dispossess the posterity of the vanquished, and turn them out of that inheritance which ought to be the possession of them and their descendants to all generations. The conqueror indeed will be apt to think himself master: and it is the very condition of the subdued not to be able to dispute their right. But if that be all, it gives no other title than what bare force gives to the stronger over the weaker. And, by this reason, he that is strongest will have a right to whatever he pleases to seize on.

185. Over those then that joined with him in the war, and over those of the subdued country that opposed him not, and the posterity even of those that did, the conqueror, even in a just war, hath, by his conquest, no *right of dominion:* they are free from any subjection to him, and if their former government be dissolved, they are at liberty to begin and erect another to themselves.

186. The conqueror, it is true, usually, by the force he has over them, compels them, with a sword at their breasts, to stoop to his conditions, and submit to such a government as he pleases to afford them; but the inquiry is, what right he has to do so? If it be said, they submit by their own consent, then this allows their own *consent* to be *necessary to give the conqueror a title to rule* over them. It remains only to be considered, whether *promises extorted by force,*

without right, can be thought consent, and *how far they bind*. To which I shall say, they *bind not at all;* because whatsoever another gets from me by force, I still retain the right of, and he is obliged presently to restore. He that forces my horse from me, ought presently to restore him, and I have still a right to retake him. By the same reason, he that *forced a promise* from me, ought presently to restore it, i.e. quit me of the obligation of it: or I may resume it myself, i.e. choose whether I will perform it. For the law of nature laying an obligation on me only by the rules she prescribes, cannot oblige me by the violation of her rules: such is the extorting any thing from me by force. Nor does it at all alter the case to say, "I gave my promise," no more than it excuses the force, and passes the right, when I put my hand in my pocket and deliver my purse myself to a thief, who demands it with a pistol at my breast.

187. From all which it follows, that the *government of a conqueror,* imposed by force, on the subdued, against whom he had no right of war, or who joined not in the war against him, where he had right, *has no obligation* upon them.

188. But let us suppose that all the men of that community, being all members of the same body politic, may be taken to have joined in that unjust war, wherein they are subdued, and so their lives are at the mercy of the conqueror.

189. I say this concerns not their children who are in their minority. For since a father hath not, in himself, a power over the life or liberty of his child, no act of his can possibly forfeit it. So that the children, whatever may have happened to the fathers, are free-men, and the absolute power of the conqueror reaches no farther than the persons of the men that were subdued by him, and dies with them: and should he govern them as slaves subjected to his absolute arbitrary power, he *has* no *such right of dominion over their children*. He can have no power over them but by their own consent, whatever he may drive them to say or do; and he has no lawful authority, whilst force, and not choice, compels them to submission.

190. Every man is born with a double right: *first, a right of freedom to his person,* which no other man has a power over, but the free disposal of it lies in himself. *Secondly, a right*, before any other man, *to inherit with* his brethren his *father's goods*.

191. By the first of these, a man is *naturally free* from subjection to any government, though he be born in a place under its jurisdiction. But if he disclaim the lawful government of the country he was born in, he must also quit the right that belonged to him by the laws of it, and the possessions there descending to him from his ancestors, if it were a government made by their consent.

192. By the second, the inhabitants of any country, who are descended, and derive a title to their estates from those who are subdued, and had a government forced upon them against their free consents, *retain a right to the possession of their ancestors*, though they consent not freely to the government, whose hard conditions were by force imposed on the possessors of that country. For, the first *conqueror never having had a title to the land* of that country, the people who are the descendants of, or claim under those who were forced to submit to the yoke of a government by constraint, have always a right to shake it off, and free themselves from the usurpation or tyranny which the sword hath brought in upon them, till their rulers put them under such a frame of government as they willingly and of choice consent to. Who doubts but the Grecian christians, descendants of the ancient possessors of that country, may justly cast off the Turkish yoke, which they have so long groaned under, whenever they have an opportunity to do it? For no government can have a right to obedience from a people who have not freely consented to it; which they can never be supposed to do, till either they are put in a full state of liberty to choose their government and governors, or at least till they have such standing laws, to which they have by themselves or their representatives given their free consent; and also till they are allowed their due property, which is, so to be proprietors of what they have, that no body can take away any part of it without their own consent, without which, men under any government are not in the state of freemen, but are direct slaves under the force of war.

193. But granting that the *conqueror* in a just war has a right to the estates, as well as power over the persons of the conquered; which, it is plain, he *hath* not: nothing of absolute power will follow from hence, in the continuance of the government. Because the descendants of these being all freemen, if he grants

them estates and possessions to inhabit his country (without which it would be worth nothing) whatsoever he grants them, they have, so far as it is granted, property in. The nature whereof is, that *without a man's own consent, it cannot be taken from him.*

194. Their *persons* are *free* by a native right, and their properties, be they more or less, are *their own, and at their own dispose,* and not at his; or else it is no property. Supposing the conqueror gives to one man a thousand acres, to him and his heirs for ever; to another he lets a thousand acres for his life, under the rent of 50*l.* or 500*l.* per annum, has not the one of these a right to his thousand acres for ever, and the other during his life, paying the said rent? and hath not the tenant for life a property in all that he gets over and above his rent, by his labour and industry during the said term, supposing it to be double the rent? Can any one say, the king, or conqueror, after his grant, may, by his power of conqueror, take away all, or part of the land from the heirs of one, or from the other during his life, he paying the rent? Or can he take away from either the goods or money they have got upon the said land, at his pleasure? If he can, then all free and voluntary contracts cease, and are void in the world; there needs nothing to dissolve them at any time but power enough: and all the grants and *promises* of *men in power* are but mockery and collusion. For can there be any thing more ridiculous than to say, I give you and yours this for ever, and that in the surest and most solemn way of conveyance can be devised; and yet it is to be understood, that I have a right, if I please, to take it away from you again to-morrow?

195. I will not dispute now, whether princes are exempt from the laws of their country; but this I am sure, they owe subjection to the laws of God and nature. No body, no power, can exempt them from the obligations of that eternal law. Those are so great, and so strong, in the case of *promises,* that omnipotency itself can be tied by them. *Grants, promises,* and *oaths,* are *bonds* that *hold the Almighty:* whatever some flatterers say to princes of the world, who all together, with all their people joined to them, are in comparison of the great God, but as a drop of the bucket, or a dust on the balance, inconsiderable, nothing!

196. The short of the *case in conquest* is this. The conqueror, if he have a just cause, has a despotical right over the persons of all that actually aided, and concurred in the war against him, and a right to make up his damage and cost out of their labour and estates, so he injure not the right of any other. Over the rest of the people, if there were any that consented not to the war, and over the children of the captives themselves, or the possessions of either, he has no power and so can have, *by virtue of conquest, no lawful title* himself *to dominion* over them, or derive it to his posterity; but is an aggressor, if he attempts upon their properties, and thereby puts himself in a state of war against them: and has no better a right of principality, he, nor any of his successors, than Hingar, or Hubba, the Danes, had here in England; or Spartacus had he conquered Italy, would have had; which is to have their yoke cast off, as soon as God shall give those under their subjection courage and opportunity to do it. Thus, notwithstanding whatever title the kings of Assyria had over Judah, by the sword, God assisted Hezekiah to throw off the dominion of that conquering empire. "And the Lord was with Hezekiah, and he prospered; wherefore he went forth, and he rebelled against the king of Assyria, and served him not," 2 *Kings,* xviii. 7. Whence it is plain, that shaking off a power, which force, and not right, hath set over any one, though it hath the name of *rebellion,* yet is no offence before God, but is that which he allows and countenances, though even promises and covenants, when obtained by force, have intervened. For it is very probable, to any one that reads the story of Ahaz and Hezekiah attentively, that the Assyrians subdued Ahaz, and deposed him, and made Hezekiah king in his father's life-time; and that Hezekiah by agreement had done him homage, and paid him tribute all this time.

Chapter 17

Of Usurpation

197. As conquest may be called a foreign usurpation, so usurpation is a kind of domestic conquest; with this difference, that an usurper can never have right on his side, it being no *usurpation* but where one is got into the *possession of what another has right to.* This, so far as it is *usurpation,* is a change only of

persons, but not of the forms and rules of the government; for if the usurper extend his power beyond what of right belonged to the lawful princes, or governors of the commonwealth, it is *tyranny* added to *usurpation*.

198. In all lawful governments, the designation of the persons, who are to bear rule, is as natural and necessary a part, as the form of the government itself, and is that which had its establishment originally from the people; the anarchy being much alike to have no form of government at all, or to agree, that it shall be monarchical, but to appoint no way to design the person that shall have the power, and be the monarch. Hence all commonwealths, with the form of government established, have rules also of appointing those who are to have any share in the public authority, and settled methods of conveying the right to them. For the anarchy is much alike to have no form of government at all, or to agree that it shall be monarchical, but to appoint no way to know or design the person that shall have the power and be the monarch. Whoever gets into the exercise of any part of the power, by other ways than what the laws of the community have prescribed, hath no right to be obeyed, though the form of the commonwealth be still preserved; since he is not the person the laws have appointed, and consequently not the person the people have consented to. Nor can such an *usurper*, or any deriving from him, ever have a title, till the people are both at liberty to consent, and have actually consented to allow, and confirm in him the power he hath till then usurped.

Chapter 18

Of Tyranny

199. As usurpation is the exercise of power, which another hath a right to, so *tyranny is the exercise of power beyond right*, which no body can have a right to. And this is making use of the power any one has in his hands, not for the good of those who are under it, but for his own private separate advantage. — When the governor, however intitled, makes not the law, but his will, the rule; and his commands and actions are not directed to the preservation of the properties

of his people, but the satisfaction of his own ambition, revenge, covetousness, or any other irregular passion.

200. If one can doubt this to be truth, or reason, because it comes from the obscure hand of a subject, I hope the authority of a king will make it pass with him. King James the first, in his speech to the parliament, 1603, tells them thus: "I will ever prefer the weal of the public, and of the whole commonwealth, in making of good laws and constitutions, to any particular and private ends of mine. Thinking ever the wealth and weal of the commonwealth to be my greatest weal and worldly felicity; a point wherein a lawful king doth directly differ from a tyrant. For I do acknowledge, that the special and greatest point of difference that is between a rightful king and an usurping tyrant, is this, that whereas the proud and ambitious tyrant doth think his kingdom and people are only ordained for satisfaction of his desires and unreasonable appetites, the righteous and just king doth by the contrary acknowledge himself to be ordained for the procuring of the wealth and property of his people." And again, in his speech to the parliament, 1609, he hath these words: "The king binds himself by a double oath to the observation of the fundamental laws of his kingdom; tacitly, as by being a king, and so bound to protect as well the people, as the laws of his kingdom; and expressly, by his oath at his coronation; so as every just king, in a settled kingdom, is bound to observe that paction made to his people by his laws, in framing his government agreeable thereunto, according to that paction which God made with Noah after the deluge: Hereafter, seed-time and harvest, and cold and heat, and summer and winter, and day and night, shall not cease while the earth remaineth. And therefore a king governing in a settled kingdom, leaves to be a king, and degenerates into a tyrant, as soon as he leaves off to rule according to his laws." And a little after, "Therefore all kings that are not tyrants, or perjured, will be glad to bound themselves within the limits of their laws; and they that persuade them the contrary, are vipers, and pests, both against them and the commonwealth." Thus that learned king, who well understood the notions of things, makes the difference betwixt a *king* and a *tyrant* to consist only in this, that one makes the laws the bounds of his power, and the good of the public

the end of his government; the other makes all give way to his own will and appetite.

201. It is a mistake to think this fault is proper only to monarchies; other forms of government are liable to it, as well as that. For wherever the power, that is put in any hands for the government of the people, and the preservation of their properties, is applied to other ends, and made use of to impoverish, harass, or subdue them to the arbitrary and irregular commands of those that have it; there it presently becomes tyranny, whether those that thus use it are one or many. Thus we read of the thirty tyrants at Athens, as well as one at Syracuse; and the intolerable dominion of the decemviri at Rome was nothing better.

202. *Wherever law ends, tyranny begins,* if the law be transgressed to another's harm; and whosoever in authority exceeds the power given him by the law, and makes use of the force he has under his command, to compass that upon the subject, which the law allows not, ceases in that to be a magistrate; and, acting without authority, may be opposed as any other man, who by force invades the right of another. This is acknowledged in subordinate magistrates. He that hath authority to seize my person in the street, may be opposed as a thief and a robber if he endeavours to break into my house to execute a writ, notwithstanding that I know he has such a warrant, and such a legal authority, as will impower him to arrest me abroad. And why this should not hold in the highest, as well as in the most inferiour magistrate, I would gladly be informed. Is it reasonable that the eldest brother, because he has the greatest part of his father's estate, should thereby have a right to take away any of his younger brother's portions? Or, that a rich man, who possessed a whole country, should from thence have a right to seize, when he pleased, the cottage and garden of his poor neighbour? The being rightfully possessed of great power and riches, exceedingly beyond the greatest part of the sons of Adam, is so far from being an excuse, much less a reason for rapine and oppression, which the endamaging another without authority is, that it is a great aggravation of it. For the exceeding the bounds of authority is no more a right in a great, than in a petty officer; no more justifiable in a king than a constable; but is so much the worse in him, in that he has more trust put in him, has already a much greater share than the rest

of his brethren, and is supposed, from the advantages of his education, employment, and counsellors, to be more knowing in the measures of right or wrong.

203. May the *commands* then *of a prince be opposed?* may he be resisted as often as any one shall find himself aggrieved, and but imagine he has not right done him? This will unhinge and overturn all polities, and, instead of government and order, leave nothing but anarchy and confusion.

204. To this I answer, that *force* is to be *opposed* to nothing but to unjust and unlawful *force*; whoever makes any opposition in any other case, draws on himself a just condemnation both from God and man; and so no such danger or confusion will follow, as is often suggested. For,

205. *First,* As, in some countries, the person of the prince by the law is sacred; and so, whatever he commands or does, his person is still free from all question or violence, not liable to force, or any judicial censure or condemnation. But yet opposition may be made to the illegal acts of any inferiour officer, or other commissioned by him; unless he will, by actually putting himself into a state of war with his people, dissolve the government, and leave them to that defence which belongs to every one in the state of nature. For of such things who can tell what the end will be? And a neighbour kingdom has shewed the world an odd example. In all other cases the *sacredness* of the *person exempts him from all inconveniencies,* whereby he is secure, whilst the government stands, from all violence and harm whatsoever; than which there cannot be a wiser constitution. For the harm he can do in his own person not being likely to happen often, nor to extend itself far; nor being able by his single strength to subvert the laws, nor oppress the body of the people, should any prince have so much weakness and ill-nature as to be willing to do it, the inconveniency of some particular mischiefs that may happen sometimes, when a heady prince comes to the throne, are well recompensed by the peace of the public, and security of the government, in the person of the chief magistrate, thus set out of the reach of danger: it being safer for the body that some few private men should be sometimes in danger to suffer, than that the head of the republic should be easily, and upon slight occasions, exposed.

206. *Secondly,* But this privilege belonging only

to the king's person, hinders not, but they may be questioned, opposed, and resisted, who use unjust force, though they pretend a commission from him, which the law authorizes not. As is plain in the case of him that has the king's writ to arrest a man, which is a full commission from the king; and yet he that has it cannot break open a man's house to do it, nor execute this command of the king upon certain days, nor in certain places, though this commission have no such exception in it, but they are the limitations of the law, which if any one transgress, the king's commission excuses him not. For the king's authority being given him only by the law, he cannot impower any one to act against the law, or justify him, by his commission, in so doing. The *commission* or *command of any magistrate, where he has no authority,* being as void and insignificant, as that of any private man. The difference between the one and the other being that the magistrate has some authority so far, and to such ends, and the private man has none at all. For it is not the commission, but the authority, that gives the right of acting; and *against the laws there can be no authority.* But notwithstanding such resistance, the king's person and authority are still both secured, and so *no danger to governor or government.*

207. *Thirdly,* supposing a government wherein the person of the chief magistrate is not thus sacred; yet this *doctrine* of the lawfulness of *resisting* all unlawful exercises of his power, *will not* upon every slight occasion endanger him, or *embroil the government.* For where the injured party may be relieved, and his damages repaired by appeal to the law, there can be no pretence for force, which is only to be used where a man is intercepted from appealing to the law. For nothing is to be accounted hostile force, but where it leaves not the remedy of such an appeal. And it is such force alone, that puts him that uses it *into a state of war,* and makes it lawful to resist him. A man with a sword in his hand, demands my purse in the highway, when perhaps I have not twelve-pence in my pocket: this man I may lawfully kill. To another I deliver £100 to hold only whilst I alight, which he refuses to restore me, when I am got up again, but draws his sword to defend the possession of it by force, if I endeavour to retake it. The mischief this man does me is an hundred, or possibly a thousand times

more than the other perhaps intended me (whom I killed before he really did me any;) and yet I might lawfully kill the one, and cannot so much as hurt the other lawfully. The reason whereof is plain; because the one using force, which threatened my life, I could not have *time to appeal* to the law to secure it: and when it was gone, it was too late to appeal. The law could not restore life to my dead carcass, the loss was irreparable: which to prevent, the law of nature gave me a right to destroy him, who had put himself into a state of war with me, and threatened my destruction. But in the other case, my life not being in danger, I may have the *benefit of appealing* to the law, and have reparation for my £100 that way.

208. *Fourthly,* But if the unlawful acts done by the magistrate be maintained (by the power he has got) and the remedy which is due by law, be by the same power obstructed: yet the *right of resisting,* even in such manifest acts of tyranny, will not suddenly, or on slight occasions, disturb the government. For if it reach no farther than some private men's cases, though they have a right to defend themselves, and to recover by force what by unlawful force is taken from them; yet the right to do so will not easily engage them in a contest, wherein they are sure to perish; it being as impossible for one, or a few oppressed men to *disturb the government,* where the body of the people do not think themselves concerned in it, as for a raving madman, or heady malecontent, to overturn a well-settled state, the people being as little apt to follow the one, as the other.

209. But if either these illegal acts have extended to the majority of the people; or if the mischief and oppression has lighted only on some few, but in such cases, as the precedent and consequences seem to threaten all; and they are persuaded in their consciences, that their laws, and with them their estates, liberties, and lives are in danger, and perhaps their religion too: how they will be hindered from resisting illegal force, used against them, I cannot tell. This is an *inconvenience,* I confess, that *attends all governments* whatsoever, when the governors have brought it to this pass, to be generally suspected of their people; the most dangerous state which they can possibly put themselves in; wherein they are the less to be pitied, because it is so easy to be avoided; it being as impossible for a governor, if he really means the good of his

people, and the preservation of them, and their laws together, not to make them see and feel it, as it is for the father of a family, not to let his children see he loves and takes care of them.

210. But if all the world shall observe pretences of one kind, and actions of another; arts used to elude the law, and the trust of prerogative, (which is an arbitrary power in some things left in the prince's hand to do good, not harm, to the people) employed contrary to the end for which it was given: if the people shall find the ministers and subordinate magistrates chosen suitable to such ends, and favoured, or laid by, proportionably as they promote or oppose them: if they see several experiments made of arbitrary power, and that religion underhand favoured (though publicly proclaimed against) which is readiest to introduce it; and the operators in it supported, as much as may be; and when that cannot be done, yet approved still, and liked the better: if a *long train of actions shew the councils* all tending that way; how can a man any more hinder himself from being persuaded in his own mind, which way things are going; or from casting about how to save himself, than he could from believing the captain of the ship he was in, was carrying him, and the rest of the company, to Algiers, when he found him always steering that course, though cross winds, leaks in his ship, and want of men and provisions did often force him to turn his course another way for some time, which he steadily returned to again, as soon as the wind, weather, and other circumstances would let him?

Chapter 19

Of the Dissolution of Government

211. He that will with any clearness speak of the *dissolution of government,* ought in the first place to distinguish between the *dissolution of the society* and the *dissolution of the government.* That which makes the community, and brings men out of the loose state of nature into *one politic society,* is the agreement which every one has with the rest to incorporate, and act as one body, and so be one distinct commonwealth. The usual, and almost only way whereby *this union is dissolved,* is the inroad of foreign force mak-

ing a conquest upon them. For in that case, (not being able to maintain and support themselves, as *one entire* and *independent body*) the union belonging to that body which consisted therein, must necessarily cease, and so every one return to the state he was in before, with a liberty to shift for himself, and provide for his own safety, as he thinks fit, in some other society. Whenever the *society is dissolved,* it is certain the government of that society cannot remain. Thus conquerors swords often cut up governments by the roots, and mangle societies to pieces, separating the subdued or scattered multitude from the protection of, and dependence on, that society which ought to have preserved them from violence. The world is too well instructed in, and too forward to allow of, this way of dissolving of governments, to need any more to be said of it; and there wants not much argument to prove, that where the *society is dissolved,* the government cannot remain; that being as impossible, as for the frame of a house to subsist when the materials of it are scattered and dissipated by a whirlwind, or jumbled into a confused heap by an earthquake.

212. Besides this overturning from without, *governments are dissolved from within.*

First, When the *legislative* is *altered.* Civil society being a state of peace, amongst those who are of it, from whom the state of war is excluded by the umpirage, which they have provided in their legislative, for the ending all differences that may arise amongst any of them; it is in their legislative, that the members of a commonwealth are united, and combined together into one coherent living body. This *is the soul that gives form, life, and unity* to the commonwealth: from hence the several members have their mutual influence, sympathy, and connexion; and therefore, when the legislative is broken, or dissolved, dissolution and death follows. For, *the essence and union of the society* consisting in having one will, the legislative, when once established by the majority, has the declaring, and as it were keeping of that will. The *constitution of the legislative* is the first and fundamental act of society, whereby provision is made for the *continuation of their union,* under the direction of persons, and bonds of laws, made by persons authorized thereunto, by the consent and appointment of the people; without which no one man, or number of men, amongst them, can have authority of making laws that shall be binding to the rest. When any one, or more, shall take upon them to make laws, whom the people have not appointed so to do, they make laws without authority, which the people are not therefore bound to obey; by which means they come again to be out of subjection, and may constitute to themselves a new legislative, as they think best, being in full liberty to resist the force of those, who without authority would impose any thing upon them. Every one is at the disposure of his own will, when those who had, by the delegation of the society, the declaring of the public will, are excluded from it, and others usurp the place, who have no such authority or delegation.

213. This being usually brought about by such in the commonwealth who misuse the power they have, it is hard to consider it aright, and know at whose door to lay it, without knowing the form of government in which it happens. Let us suppose then the legislative placed in the concurrence of three distinct persons.

1. A single hereditary person, having the constant, supreme, executive power, and with it the power of convoking and dissolving the other two, within certain periods of time.
2. An assembly of hereditary nobility.
3. An assembly of representatives chosen *pro tempore*, by the people. Such a form of government supposed, it is evident,

214. First, That when such a single person, or prince, sets up his own arbitrary will in place of the laws, which are the will of the society, declared by the legislative, then the *legislative is changed*. For that being in effect the legislative, whose rules and laws are put in execution, and required to be obeyed; when other laws are set up, and other rules pretended, and enforced, than what the legislative, constituted by the society, have enacted, it is plain that the *legislative is changed*. Whoever introduces new laws, not being thereunto authorized, by the fundamental appointment of the society, or subverts the old, disowns and overturns the power by which they were made, and so sets up a *new legislative*.

215. Secondly, When the prince hinders the legislative from assembling in its due time, or from acting freely, pursuant to those ends for which it was constituted, the *legislative is altered*: for it is not a certain

balance of powers

number of men, no, nor their meeting, unless they have also freedom of debating, and leisure of perfecting, what is for the good of the society, wherein the legislative consists: when these are taken away or altered, so as to deprive the society of the due exercise of their power, the legislative is truly altered. For it is not names that constitute governments, but the use and exercise of those powers that were intended to accompany them; so that he, who takes away the freedom, or hinders the acting of the legislative in its due seasons, in effect *takes away the legislative*, and *puts an end to the government*.

216. Thirdly, When, by the arbitrary power of the prince, the electors, or ways of election, are altered, without the consent, and contrary to the common interest of the people, there also the *legislative is altered*. For, if others than those whom the society hath authorized thereunto, do choose, or in another way than what the society hath prescribed, those chosen are not the legislative appointed by the people.

217. Fourthly, The delivery also of the people into the subjection of a foreign power, either by the prince, or by the legislative, is certainly a *change of the legislative*, and so a *dissolution of the government*. For the end why people entered into society being to be preserved one intire, free, independent society, to be governed by its own laws; this is lost, whenever they are given up into the power of another.

218. Why, in such a constitution as this, the *dissolution of the government* in these cases is to be imputed to the prince, is evident; because he, having the force, treasure, and offices of the state to employ, and often persuading himself, or being flattered by others, that as supreme magistrate, he is uncapable of control; he alone is in a condition to make great advances toward such changes, under pretence of lawful authority, and has it in his hands to terrify or suppress opposers, as factious, seditious, and enemies to the government: whereas no other part of the legislative, or people, is capable by themselves to attempt any alteration of the legislative, without open and visible rebellion, apt enough to be taken notice of; which, when, it prevails, produces effects very little different from foreign conquest. Besides, the prince in such a form of government having the power of dissolving the other parts of the legislative, and thereby rendering them private persons, they can never in opposition

to him, or without his concurrence, alter the legislative by a law, his consent being necessary to give any of their decrees that sanction. But yet, so far as the other parts of the legislative any way contribute to any attempt upon the government, and do either promote, or not, what lies in them, hinder such designs; they are guilty, and partake in this, which is certainly the greatest crime men can be guilty of one towards another.

219. There is one way more whereby such a government may be dissolved, and that is, when he who has the supreme executive power neglects and abandons that charge, so that the laws already made can no longer be put in execution. This is demonstratively to reduce all to anarchy, and so effectually to *dissolve the government*. For laws not being made for themselves, but to be, by their execution, the bonds of the society, to keep every part of the body politic in its due place and function; when that totally ceases, the *government* visibly *ceases*, and the people become a confused multitude, without order or connexion. Where there is no longer the administration of justice, for the securing of men's rights, nor any remaining power within the community to direct the force, or provide for the necessities of the public; there certainly is *no government left*. Where the laws cannot be executed, it is all one as if there were no laws; and a government without laws is, I suppose, a mystery in politics, inconceivable to human capacity, and inconsistent with human society.

220. In these and the like cases, *when the government is dissolved*, the people are at liberty to provide for themselves, by erecting a new legislative, differing from the other, by the change of persons, or form, or both, as they shall find it most for their safety and good. For the *society* can never, by the fault of another, lose the native and original right it has to preserve itself; which can only be done by a settled legislative, and a fair and impartial execution of the laws made by it. But the state of mankind is not so miserable that they are not capable of using this remedy, till it be too late to look for any. To tell *people* they *may provide for themselves*, by erecting a new legislative, when by oppression, artifice, or being delivered over to a foreign power, their old one is gone, is only to tell them, they may expect relief when it is too late, and the evil is past cure. This is in effect no more,

than to bid them first be slaves, and then to take care of their liberty; and when their chains are on, tell them, they may act like freemen. This, if barely so, is rather mockery than relief; and men can never be secure from tyranny, if there be no means to escape it, till they are perfectly under it: And therefore it is, that they have not only a right to get out of it, but to prevent it.

221. There is, therefore, secondly, another way whereby *governments are dissolved*, and that is, when the legislative, or the prince either of them, act contrary to their trust.

First, The *legislative acts against the trust* reposed in them, when they endeavour to invade the property of the subject, and to make themselves, or any part of the community, masters, or arbitrary disposers of the lives, liberties, or fortunes of the people.

222. The reason why men enter into society, is the preservation of their property; and the end why they choose and authorize a legislative, is, that there may be laws made, and rules set, as guards and fences to the properties of all the members of the society: to limit the power, and moderate the dominion, of every part and member of the society. For since it can never be supposed to be the will of the society, that the legislative should have a power to destroy that, which every one designs to secure, by entering into society, and for which the people submitted themselves to legislators of their own making, whenever the *legislators endeavour to take away and destroy the property of the people*, or to reduce them to slavery under arbitrary power, they put themselves into a state of war with the people, who are thereupon absolved from any farther obedience, and are left to the common refuge, which God hath provided for all men, against force and violence. Whensoever therefore the *legislative* shall transgress this fundamental rule of society; and either by ambition, fear, folly or corruption, *endeavour to grasp* themselves, *or put into the hands of any other an absolute power* over the lives, liberties, and estates of the people; by this breach of trust they *forfeit the power*, the people had put into their hands, for quite contrary ends, and it devolves to the people, who have a right to resume their original liberty, and, by the establishment of a new legislative, (such as they shall think fit) provide for their own safety and security, which is the end for which they

are in society. What I have said here, concerning the legislative in general, holds true also concerning the supreme executor, who having a double trust put in him, both to have a part in the legislative, and the supreme execution of the law, acts against both, when he goes about to set up his own arbitrary will, as the law of the society. He *acts* also *contrary to his trust*, when he either employs the force, treasure, and offices of the society to corrupt the *representatives*, and gain them to his purposes; or openly pre-engages the *electors*, and prescribes to their choice, such, whom he has by solicitations, threats, promises, or otherwise, won to his designs: and employs them to bring in such, who have promised before-hand, what to vote, and what to enact. Thus to regulate candidates and electors, and new model the ways of election, what is it but to cut up the government by the roots, and poison the very fountain of public security? for the people having reserved to themselves the choice of their *representatives,* as the fence to their properties, could do it for no other end, but that they might always be freely chosen, and so chosen, freely act, and advise, as the necessity of the commonwealth, and the public good should, upon examination and mature debate, be judged to require. This, those who give their votes before they hear the debate, and have weighed the reasons on all sides, are not capable of doing. To prepare such an assembly as this, and endeavour to set up the declared abettors of his own will, for the true representatives of the people, and the law-makers of the society, is certainly as great a *breach of trust*, and as perfect a declaration of a design to subvert the government, as is possible to be met with. To which if one shall add rewards and punishments visibly employed to the same end, and all the arts of perverted law made use of, to take off and destroy all that stand in the way of such a design, and will not comply and consent to betray the liberties of their country, it will be past doubt what is doing. What power they ought to have in the society, who thus employ it contrary to the trust that went along with it in its first institution, is easy to determine; and one cannot but see, that he, who has once attempted any such thing as this, cannot any longer be trusted.

223. To this perhaps it will be said, that the people being ignorant, and always discontented, to lay the foundation of government in the unsteady opinion and uncertain humour of the people, is to expose it to certain ruin; and *no government will be able long to subsist*, if the people may set up a new legislative, whenever they take offence at the old one. To this I answer, quite the contrary. People are not so easily got out of their old forms as some are apt to suggest. They are hardly to be prevailed with to amend the acknowledged faults in the frame they have been accustomed to. And if there be any original defects, or adventitious ones introduced by time, or corruption: it is not an easy thing to get them changed, even when all the world sees there is an opportunity for it. This slowness and aversion in the people to quit their old constitutions, has in the many revolutions which have been seen in this kingdom, in this and former ages, still kept us to, or, after some interval of fruitless attempts, still brought us back again to, our old legislative of king, lords, and commons: and whatever provocations have made the crown be taken from some of our princes heads, they never carried the people so far as to place it in another line.

224. But it will be said, this *hypothesis* lays a *ferment* for frequent *rebellion*. To which I *answer*,

First, no more than any other *hypothesis*: for when the people are made miserable, and find themselves *exposed to the ill usage of arbitrary power*, cry up their governors as much as you will, for *sons of Jupiter*; let them be sacred or divine, descended, or authorized from heaven; give them out for whom or what you please, the same will happen. *The people generally ill treated*, and contrary to right, will be ready upon any occasion to ease themselves of a burden that sits heavy upon them. They will wish, and seek for the opportunity, which in the change, weakness, and accidents of human affairs, seldom delays long to offer itself. He must have lived but a little while in the world, who has not seen examples of this in his time; and he must have read very little, who cannot produce examples of it in all sorts of governments in the world.

225. *Secondly*, I answer, such *revolutions happen* not upon every little mismanagement in public affairs. *Great mistakes* in the ruling part, many wrong and inconvenient laws, and all the slips of human frailty, will be borne by the people without mutiny or murmur. But if a long train of abuses, prevarications and artifices, all tending the same way, make the design visible to the people, and they cannot but feel what

they lie under, and see whither they are going; it is not to be wondered, that they should then rouse themselves, and endeavour to put the rule into such hands which may secure to them the ends for which government was at first erected; and without which, ancient names, and specious forms, are so far from being better, that they are much worse, than the state of nature, or pure anarchy; the inconveniencies being all as great and as near, but the remedy farther off and more difficult.

226. *Thirdly*, I answer, that *this doctrine* of a power in the people of providing for their safety anew, by a new legislative, when their legislators have acted contrary to their trust, by invading their property, is the *best fence against rebellion*, and the probablest means to hinder it. For *rebellion* being an opposition, not to persons, but authority, which is founded only in the constitutions and laws of the government; those, whoever they be, who by force break through, and by force justify their violation of them, are truly and properly *rebels*. For when men, by entering into society and civil government, have excluded force, and introduced laws for the preservation of property, peace, and unity amongst themselves; those who set up force again in opposition to the laws, do *rebellare*, that is, bring back again the state of war, and are properly rebels: Which they who are in power, (by the pretence they have to authority, the temptation of force they have in their hands, and the flattery of those about them) being likeliest to do; the properest way to prevent the evil, is to shew them the danger and injustice of it, who are under the greatest temptation to run into it.

227. In both the forementioned cases, when either the legislative is changed, or the legislators act contrary to the end for which they were constituted, those who are guilty are *guilty of rebellion*; for if any one by force takes away the established legislative of any society, and the laws by them made pursuant to their trust, he thereby takes away the umpirage, which every one had consented to, for a peaceable decision of all their controversies, and a bar to the state of war amongst them. They who remove, or change the legislative, take away this decisive power, which no body can have but by the appointment and consent of the people; and so destroying the authority which the people did, and no body else can set up, and

introducing a power which the people hath not authorized, they actually *introduce a state of war*, which is that of force without authority; and thus by removing the legislative established by the society, (in whose decisions the people acquiesced and united, as to that of their own will) they untie the knot, and *expose the people anew to the state of war*. And if those, who by force take away the legislative, are *rebels*, the *legislators* themselves, as has been shewn, can be no less esteemed so; when they, who were set up for the protection and preservation of the people, their liberties and properties, shall by force invade and endeavour to take them away; and so they putting themselves into a state of war with those who made them the protectors and guardians of their peace, are properly, and with the greatest aggravation, *rebellantes*, rebels.

228. But if they, who say, "it lays a foundation for rebellion," mean that it may occasion civil wars, or intestine broils, to tell the people they are absolved from obedience when, illegal attempts are made upon their liberties or properties, and may oppose the unlawful violence of those who were their magistrates, when they invade their properties contrary to the trust put in them; and that therefore this doctrine is not to be allowed, being so destructive to the peace of the world: they may as well say, upon the same ground, that honest men may not oppose robbers or pirates, because this may occasion disorder or bloodshed. If any *mischief* come in such cases, it is not to be charged upon him who defends his own right, but *on him that invades* his neighbour's. If the innocent honest man must quietly quit all he has, for peace sake, to him who will lay violent hands upon it, I desire it may be considered, what a kind of peace there will be in the world, which consists only in violence and rapine; and which is to be maintained only for the benefit of robbers and oppressors. Who would not think it an admirable peace betwixt the mighty and the mean, when the lamb, without resistance, yielded his throat to be torn by the imperious wolf? Polyphemus's den gives us a perfect pattern of such a peace, and such a government, wherein Ulysses and his companions had nothing to do, but quietly to suffer themselves to be devoured. And no doubt Ulysses, who was a prudent man, preached up *passive obedience*, and exhorted them to a quiet submission,

by representing to them of what concernment peace was to mankind; and by shewing the inconveniencies might happen, if they should offer to resist Polyphemus, who had now the power over them.

229. The end of government is the good of mankind: and which is *best for mankind*, that the people should be always exposed to the boundless will of tyranny; or that the rulers should be sometimes liable to be opposed, when they grow exorbitant in the use of their power, and employ it for the destruction, and not the preservation of the properties of their people?

230. Nor let any one say, that mischief can arise from hence, as often as it shall please a busy head, or turbulent spirit, to desire the alteration of the government. It is true, such men may stir, whenever they please; but it will be only to their own just ruin and perdition. For till the mischief be grown general, and the ill designs of the rulers become visible, or their attempts sensible to the greater part, the people, who are more disposed to suffer than right themselves by resistance, are not apt to stir. The examples of particular injustice or oppression, of here and there an unfortunate man, moves them not. But if they universally have a persuasion, grounded upon manifest evidence, that designs are carrying on against their liberties, and the general course and tendency of things cannot but give them strong suspicions of the evil intention of their governors, who is to be blamed for it? Who can help it, if they, who might avoid it, bring themselves into this suspicion? Are the people to be blamed, if they have the sense of rational creatures, and can think of things no otherwise than as they find and feel them? And is it not rather *their fault*, who put things into such a posture, that they would not have them thought to be as they are? I grant, that the pride, ambition, and turbulency of private men, have sometimes caused great disorders in commonwealths, and factions have been fatal to states and kingdoms. But whether *the mischief* hath *oftener* begun *in the peoples wantonness*, and a desire to cast off the lawful authority of their rulers, or in *the rulers insolence*, and endeavours to get and exercise an arbitrary power over their people; whether oppression, or disobedience, gave the first rise to the disorder, I leave it to impartial history to determine. This I am sure, whoever, either ruler or subject, by force goes about to invade the rights of either prince or people, and

lays the foundation for *overturning* the constitution and frame of *any just government*; is highly guilty of the greatest crime, I think, a man is capable of; being to answer for all those mischiefs of blood, rapine, and desolation, which the breaking to pieces of governments bring on a country. And he who does it, is justly to be esteemed the common enemy and pest of mankind, and is to be treated accordingly.

231. That *subjects* or *foreigners*, attempting by force on the properties of any people, may be resisted with force, is agreed on all hands. But that *magistrates*, doing the same thing, may be *resisted*, hath of late been denied: as if those who had the greatest privileges and advantages by the law, had thereby a power to break those laws, by which alone they were set in a better place than their brethren: whereas their offence is thereby the greater, both as being ungrateful for the greater share they have by the law, and breaking also that trust which is put into their hands by their brethren.

232. Whosoever uses *force without right*, as every one does in society, who does it without law, puts himself into a *state of war* with those against whom he so uses it; and in that state all former ties are cancelled, all other rights cease, and every one has a right to defend himself, and to *resist the aggressor*. This is so evident, that Barclay himself, that great assertor of the power and sacredness of kings, is forced to confess, that it is lawful for the people, in some cases, to resist their king; and that too in a chapter, wherein he pretends to shew, that the divine law shuts up the people from all manner of rebellion. Whereby it is evident, even by his own doctrine, that, since they may in some cases resist, all resisting of *princes* is not rebellion. His words are these. "Quod siquis dicat, Ergone populus tyrannicae crudelitati & furori jugulum semper praebebit? Ergone multitudo civitates suas fame, ferro, & flamma vastari, seque, conjuges, & liberos fortunae ludibrio & tyranni libidini exponi, inque omnia vitae pericula omnesque miserias & molestias a rege de luci patientur? Num illis quod omni animantium generi est a natura tributum, denegari debet, ut sc. vim vi repellant, seseq; ab injuria tucantur? Huic brevitur responsum sit, Populo universo negari defensionem, quae juris naturalis est, neque ultionem quae praeter naturam est adversus regem concedi debere. Quapropter si rex non in

singulares tantum personas aliquot privatum odium
exerceat, sed corpus etiam reipublicae, cujus ipse ca-
put est, i.e. totum populum, vel insignem aliquam ejus
partem immani & intoleranda saevitia seu tyrannide
divexet; populo quidem hoc casu resistendi ac tuendi
se ab injuria potestas competit; sed tuendi se tantum,
non enim in principem invadendi: & restituendae injuriae illatae, non recedendi a debita reverentia propter
acceptam injuriam. Praesentem denique impetum
propulsandi non vim praeteritam ulciscendi jus habet.
Horum enim alterum a natura est, ut vitam scilicet
corpusque tueamur. Alterum vero contra naturam, ut
inferior de superiori supplicium sumat. Quod itaque
populus malum, antequam factum sit, impedire
potest, ne fiat; id postquam factum est, in regem auth-
orem sceleris vindicare non potest: populus igitur hoc
amplius quam privatus quispiam habet: quod huic, vel
ipsis adversariis judicibus, excepto Buchanano, nul-
lum nisi in patientia remedium superest. Cum ille si
intolerabilis tyrannus est (modicum enim ferre
omnino debet) resistere cum reverentia possit." Barclay *contra Monarchom.* l. iii. c. 8.

In English thus:

233. "But if any one should ask, Must the people
then always lay themselves open to, the cruelty and
rage of tyranny? Must they see their cities pillaged
and laid in ashes, their wives and children exposed to
the tyrant's lust and fury, and themselves and families
reduced by their king to ruin, and all the miseries of
want and oppression; and yet sit still? Must men alone
be debarred the common privilege of opposing force
with force, which nature allows so freely to all other
creatures for their preservation from injury? I answer:
Self-defence is a part of the law of nature; nor can
it be denied the community, even against the king
himself: but to revenge themselves upon him, must
by no means be allowed them; it being not agreeable
to that law. Wherefore if the king should shew an
hatred, not only to some particular persons, but sets
himself against the body of the commonwealth,
whereof he is the head, and shall, with intolerable
ill-usage, cruelly tyrannize over the whole, or a considerable part of the people, in this case the people have
a right to resist and defend themselves from injury:
but it must be with this caution, that they only defend
themselves, but do not attack their prince: they may
repair the damages received, but must not for any

provocation exceed the bounds of due reverence and
respect. They may repulse the present attempt, but
must not revenge past violences. For it is natural for
us to defend life and limb, but that an inferiour should
punish a superiour, is against nature. The mischief
which is designed them the people may prevent before it be done; but when it is done, they must not
revenge it on the king, though author of the villainy.
This therefore is the privilege of the people in general,
above what any private person hath; that particular
men are allowed by our adversaries themselves (Bu-
chanan only excepted) to have no other remedy but
patience; but the body of the people may with reverence resist intolerable tyranny; for, when it is but
moderate, they ought to endure it."

234. Thus far that great advocate of monarchical
power allows of *resistance*.

235. It is true, he has annexed two limitations to
it, to no *purpose*:

First, He says, it must be with reverence.

Secondly, It must be without retribution, or punishment; and the reason he gives is, "Because an inferiour cannot punish a superiour."

First, *How to resist force without striking again*, or
how to *strike with reverence*, will need some skill to
make intelligible. He that shall oppose an assault only
with a shield to receive the blows, or in any more
respectful posture, without a sword in his hand, to
abate the confidence and force of the assailant, will
quickly be at an end of his *resistance*, and will find
such a defence serve only to draw on himself the
worse usage. This is as ridiculous a way of resisting,
as Juvenal thought it of fighting; "ubi tu pulsas, ego
vapulo tantum." And the success of the combat will
be unavoidably the same he there describes it:

Libertas pauperis haec est:
Pulsatus rogat, & pugnis concisus, adorat,
Ut liceat paucis cum dentibus inde reverti.

This will always be the event of such an imaginary
resistance, where men may not strike again. He therefore *who may resist, must be allowed to strike*. And
then let our author, or any body else, join a knock
on the head, or a cut on the face, with as much
reverence and *respect* as he thinks fit. He that can
reconcile blows and reverence, may, for aught I know,

deserve for his pains a civil, respectful cudgelling, wherever he can meet with it.

Secondly, as to his second, "An inferiour cannot punish a superiour;" that is true, generally speaking, whilst he is his superiour. But to resist force with force, being the *state of war* that *levels the parties*, cancels all former relation of reverence, respect, and *superiority*: And then the odds that remains, is, that he, who opposes the unjust aggressor, has this *superiority* over him, that he has a right when he prevails, to punish the offender, both for the breach of the peace, and all the evils that followed upon it. Barclay therefore, in another place, more coherently to himself, denies it to be lawful to *resist* a king in any case. But he there assigns two cases, whereby a king may unking himself. His words are,

"Quid ergo, nulline casus incidere possunt quibus populo sese erigere atque in regem impotentius dominantem arma capere & invadere jure suo suaque authoritate liceat? Nulli certe quamdiu rex manet. Semper enim ex divinis id obstat, Regem honorificato; & qui potestati resistit, Dei ordinationi resistit: non alias igitur in eum populo potestas est quam si id committat propter quod ipso jure rex esse desinat. Tunc enim se ipse principatu exuit atque in privatis constituit liber: hoc modo populus & superior efficitur, reverso ad eum sc. jure illo quod ante regem inauguratum in interregno habuit. At sunt paucorum generum commissa ejusmodi quae hunc effectum pariunt. At ego cum plurima animo perlustrem, duo tantam invenio, duos, inquam, casus quibus rex ipso facto ex rege non regem se facit & omni honore & dignitate regali atque in subditos potestate destituit; quorum etiam meminit Winzerus. Horum unus est, Si regnum disperdat, quemadmodum de Nerone fertur, quod is nempe senatum populumque Romanum, atque adeo urbem ipsam ferro flammaque vastare, ac novas sibi sedes quaerere, decrevisset. Et de Caligula, quod palam denunciarit se neque civem neque principem senatui amplius fore, inque animo habuerit interempto utriusque ordinis electissimo quoque Alexandriam commigrare, ac ut populum uno ictu interimeret, unam ei cervicem optavit. Talia cum rex aliquis meditatur & molitur serio, omnem regnandi curam & animum ilico abjicit, ac proinde imperium in subditos amittit, ut dominus servi pro derelicto habiti dominium."

236. "Alter casus est, Si rex in alicujus clientelam se contulit, ac regnum quod liberum a majoribus & populo traditum accepit, alienae ditioni mancipavit. Nam tunc quamvis forte non ea mente id agit populo plane ut incommodet: tamen quia quod praecipuum est regiae dignitatis amisit, ut summus scilicet in regno secundum Deum sit, & solo Deo inferior, atque populum etiam totum ignorantem vel invitum, cujus libertatem sartam & tectam conservare debuit in alterius gentis ditionem & potestatem dedidit, hac velut quadam regni ab alienatione efficit, ut nec quod ipse in regno imperium habuit retineat, nec in eum cui collatum voluit, juris quicquam transferat; atque ita eo facto liberum jam & suae potestatis populum relinquit, cujus rei exemplum unum annales Scotici suppeditant." Barclay *contra Monarchom.* l. iii. c. 16.

Which in English runs thus:

237. "What then, can there no case happen wherein the people may of right, and by their own authority, help themselves, take arms, and set upon their king imperiously domineering over them? None at all, whilst he remains a king. Honour the king, and he that resists the power, resists the ordinance of God; are divine oracles that will never permit it. The people therefore can never come by a power over him, unless he does something that makes him cease to be a king. For then he divests himself of his crown and dignity, and returns to the state of a private man, and the people become free and superiour, the power which they had in the interregnum, before they crowned him king, devolving to them again. But there are but few miscarriages which bring the matter to this state. After considering it well on all sides, I can find but two. Two cases there are, I say, whereby a king, ipso facto, becomes no king, and loses all power and regal authority over his people; which are also taken notice of by Winzerus.

The first is, If he endeavour to overturn the government, that is, if he have a purpose and design to ruin the kingdom and commonwealth; as it is recorded of Nero, that he resolved to cut off the senate and people of Rome, lay the city waste with fire and sword, and then remove to some other place. And of Caligula, that he openly declared, that he would be no longer a head to the people or senate, and that he had it in his thoughts to cut off the worthiest men of both ranks, and then retire to Alexandria. and he wished that the people had but one neck, that he might dispatch them all at a blow. Such designs as these, when any king harbours in his thoughts, and seriously promotes, he immediately gives up all care and thought of the commonwealth; and consequently forfeits the power of governing his subjects, as a master does the dominion over his slaves whom he hath abandoned."

238: "The other case is, When a king makes himself the dependent of another, and subjects his kingdom which his ancestors left him, and the people put free into his hands, to the dominion of another. For however perhaps it may not be his intention to prejudice the people, yet because he has hereby lost the principal part of regal dignity, viz. to be next and immediately under God supreme in his kingdom; and also because he betrayed or forced his people, whose liberty he ought to have carefully preserved, into the power and dominion of a foreign nation. By this, as it were, alienation of his kingdom, he himself loses the power he had in it before, without transferring any the least right to those on whom he would have bestowed it; and so by this act sets the people free, and leaves them at their own disposal. One example of this is to be found in the Scotch Annals."

239. In these cases Barclay, the great champion of absolute monarchy, is forced to allow, that a king may be *resisted*, and *ceases to be a king*. That is, in short, not to multiply cases, in whatsoever he has no authority, there he is no king, and may be resisted. For wheresoever the *authority ceases, the king ceases too*, and becomes like other men who have no *authority*. And these two cases the instances differ little from those above-mentioned, to be destructive to governments, only that he has omitted the principle from which his doctrine flows; and that is, the breach of trust, in not preserving the form of government agreed on, and in not intending the end of government itself, which is the public good and preservation of property. When a king has dethroned himself, and put himself in a state of war with his people, what shall hinder them from prosecuting him who is no king, as they would any other man, who has put himself into a state of war with them; Barclay and those of his opinion would do well to tell us. This farther I desire may be taken notice of out of Barclay, that he says, "The mischief that is designed them, the people may prevent before it be done"; whereby he allows "resis-

tance" when tyranny is but in design. "Such designs as these" (says he) "when any king harbours in his thoughts and seriously promotes, he immediately gives up all care and thought of the commonwealth;" so that, according to him, the neglect of the public good is to be taken as an evidence of such "design," or at least for a sufficient cause of "resistance." And the reason of all, he gives in these words, "Because he betrayed or forced his people, whose liberty he ought carefully to have preserved." What he adds, "into the power and dominion of a foreign nation," signifies nothing, the fault and forfeiture lying in the loss of their "liberty," which he "ought to have preserved," and not in any distinction of the persons to whose dominion they were subjected. The people's right is equally invaded, and their liberty lost, whether they are made slaves to any of their own, or a foreign nation; and in this lies the injury, and against this only have they the right of defence. And there are instances to be found in all countries, which shew, that it is not the change of nations in the persons of their governors, but the change of government, that gives the offence. Bilson, a bishop of our church, and a great stickler for the power and prerogative of princes, does, if I mistake not, in his treatise of christian subjection, acknowledge, *that princes may forfeit their power*, and their title to the obedience of their subjects; and if there needed authority in a case where reason is so plain, I could send my reader to Bractan, Fortescue, and the author of the Mirrour, and others, writers that cannot be suspected to be ignorant of our government, or enemies to it. But I thought Hooker alone might be enough to satisfy those men, who relying on him for their ecclesiastical polity, are by a strange fate carried to deny those principles upon which he builds it. Whether they are herein made the tools of cunninger workmen, to pull down their own fabric, they were best look. This I am sure, their civil policy is so new, so dangerous, and so destructive to both rulers and people, that as former ages never could bear the broaching of it; so it may be hoped, those to come, redeemed from the impositions of these Egyptian under taskmasters, will abhor the memory of such servile flatterers, who, whilst it seemed to serve their turn, resolved all government into absolute tyranny, and would have all men born to, what their mean souls fitted them for, slavery.

240. Here, it is like, the common question will be made, *Who shall be judge*, whether the prince or legislative act contrary to their trust? This, perhaps, ill-affected and factious men may spread amongst the people, when the prince only makes use of his due prerogative. To this I reply, "The people shall be judge;" for who shall be *judge* whether his trustee or deputy acts well, and according to the trust reposed in him, but he who deputes him, and must by having deputed him, have still a power to discard him, when he fails in his trust? If this be reasonable in particular cases of private men, why should it be otherwise in that of the greatest moment, where the welfare of millions is concerned, and also where the evil, if not prevented, is greater, and the redress very difficult, dear, and dangerous?

241. But farther, this question, ("Who shall be judge?") cannot mean that there is no judge at all. For where there is no judicature on earth, to decide controversies amongst men, God in heaven is judge. He alone, it is true, is judge of the right. But *every man* is *judge* for himself, as in all other cases, so in this, whether another hath put himself into a state of war with him, and whether he should appeal to the supreme judge, as Jephthah did.

242. If a controversy arise betwixt a prince and some of the people, in a matter where the law is silent, or doubtful, and the thing be of great consequence, I should think the proper *umpire*, in such a case, should be the body of the *people:* for in cases where the prince hath a trust reposed in him, and is dispensed from the common ordinary rules of the law; there, if any men find themselves aggrieved, and think the prince acts contrary to, or beyond that trust, who so proper to *judge* as the body of the *people*, (who, at first, lodged that trust in him) how far they meant it should extend? But if the prince, or whoever they be in the administration, decline that way of determination, the appeal then lies no where but to heaven; force between either persons, who have no known superior on earth, or which permits no appeal to a judge on earth, being properly a state of war, wherein the appeal lies only to heaven; and in that state the *injured party must judge* for himself, when he will think fit to make use of that appeal, and put himself upon it.

243. To conclude, The *power that every individual gave the society*, when he entered into it, can never revert to the individuals again, as long as the society lasts, but will always remain in the community; because without this there can be no community, no commonwealth, which is contrary to the original agreement: so also when the society hath placed the legislative in any assembly of men, to continue in them and their successors, with direction and authority for providing such successors, the *legislative can never revert to the people* whilst that government lasts: Because, having provided a legislative with power to continue for ever, they have given up their political power to the legislative, and cannot resume it. But if they have set limits to the duration of their legislative, and made this supreme power in any person, or assembly, only temporary; or else, when by the miscarriages of those in authority, it is forfeited; upon the forfeiture, or at the determination of the time set, *it reverts to the society*, and the people have a right to act as supreme, and continue the legislative in themselves; or erect a new form, or under the old form place it in new hands, as they think good.

DAVID HUME

The philosophical writings of David Hume (1711–1776) reflect the confluence of a number of important traditions and controversies of the early modern period. Hume was widely read and a powerful intellect; this combination placed him at a critical juncture in eighteenth-century philosophy.

Hume was attracted, for example, to the scientific method exemplified in the work of Isaac Newton, and at the same time he was passionately committed to the humanistic study of Cicero, Seneca, and Virgil, among other classical authors. Furthermore, Hume's greatest insight was that Thomas Hobbes, René Descartes, Baruch Spinoza, and others had trusted too much in reason and its powers, and, in order to show their error, he embraced the modes of skeptical attack found in the writings of Sextus Empiricus and employed by Pierre Bayle, one of his favorite authors. Among other doubts that Hume had about the role and authority of reason, one concerned morality. He admired the moral philosophy of the First Earl of Shaftesbury, Francis Hutcheson, and Bishop Butler, with its focus on the sentiments and on benevolence; he saw in this tradition a response to the pessimism and otherworldliness of Scottish Calvinism and other modes of Christian thought. Hume was also a vigorous opponent of religion but a devoted friend of the good life as lived in this world. In his own day, he sought "literary fame" but achieved it only in measured degree and then only for his historical and political writings. His philosophy influenced but a few until after his death, when its powerful impact on diverse schools of thought established Hume as a member of the pantheon of early modern philosophers.

Hume was born on April 26, 1711, in Edinburgh, Scotland, near the family estate of Ninewells. In 1722 he entered the University of Edinburgh ostensibly to pursue a law degree. After spending four years at the university but refusing to prepare for a law career, he returned home in 1726 for a period of intense reading and studying. In 1734 Hume took a position in Bristol, which was not a success, and in the same year travelled to France, where, from 1734 to 1737, he completed the composition of his great systematic work, *A Treatise of Human Nature*. The first two books were published anonymously in London in 1739, the third book in 1740.

Although the book received some critical notice, it was, in Hume's eyes, largely ignored. He always treated it as a failure. It stimulated no debate and did nothing to cultivate its author's fame. Hume thought that the *Treatise*'s problems stemmed from his literary style. He chose to rewrite the first and third parts and to publish them separately. The *Philosophical Essays* (later *An Inquiry*) *Concerning the Human Understanding* appeared in 1748 and then in a revised version in 1758. *An Enquiry Concerning the Principles of Morals* was published in 1751.

During the decades following the publication of the *Treatise*, Hume held a number of minor positions, private and public, and wrote extensively. Twice he was passed over for academic positions, in 1745 at Edinburgh and again in 1751 in Glasgow. His *Essays Moral and Political*, published in 1741–42, were very well received, and his six-volume history of England, which appeared from 1754 to 1762, made Hume a celebrity in France and at home. His most famous critique of religion, *Dialogues Concerning Natural Religion*, was begun in 1751 but published only three years after his death in 1776. He died in Scotland, where he had lived since 1769. By that time, Hume's secular treatment of morality, his attack on rational religion and deism, and his criticism of Calvinism had made him so notorious that his friend Adam Smith, to whom he had entrusted the manuscript of the *Dialogues*, feared arranging for its publication. When it appeared in 1779, it did so without a publisher's imprint.

Hume's great contribution to moral theory rests on his attack on the primacy and self-sufficiency of reason and on his development of the moral sense tradition of Shaftesbury and Hutcheson. Morality rests not on reason, as Spinoza and Locke had argued, and not on the commands of God, as religious thinkers claimed. Rather, morality is based on our feelings of approval and disapproval and on the benevolence that such feeling positively endorses. Reason does of course play important roles in such a moral view, ordering the sentiments and elsewhere, but ultimately, for Hume, morality is grounded in our sentiments or feelings and not in faith or reason, and its goal is not divine reward or an otherworldly salvation but rather the best and most enjoyable life here on earth. Unlike Hobbes, then, Hume saw human nature as fundamentally good and human life as desirable.

Moreover, Hume's moral thinking is not simply an attempt to understand morality. It is also a vehicle for moral conduct and practice. In his own words: "Be a philosopher; but, amidst all your philosophy, be still a man."

Recommended Readings

Broad, C. D. *Five Types of Ethical Theory*. London: Routledge, 1930.

Chappell, V. (ed.). *Hume*. Garden City: Doubleday, 1966.

Livingston, Donald. *Hume's Philosophy of Common Life*. Chicago: University of Chicago Press, 1984.

MacIntyre, Alasdair. *Whose Justice? Which Rationality?* Notre Dame: University of Notre Dame Press, 1988.

Norton, David Fate. *The Cambridge Companion to Hume*. Cambridge: Cambridge University Press, 1993.

Norton, David Fate. *David Hume: Common Sense Moralist, Sceptical Metaphysician*. Princeton: Princeton University Press, 1982.

Smith, Norman Kemp. *The Philosophy of David Hume*. London: Macmillan, 1941, 1964.

Stroud, Barry. *Hume*. London: Routledge, 1978.

SELECTIONS FROM THE
TREATISE OF
HUMAN NATURE

BOOK II: OF THE PASSIONS

BOOK III: OF MORALS

BOOK II
OF THE PASSIONS

PART III
OF THE WILL AND DIRECT PASSIONS
Section III

Of the Influencing Motives of the Will

Nothing is more usual in philosophy, and even in common life, than to talk of the combat of passion and reason, to give the preference to reason, and assert that men are only so far virtuous as they conform themselves to its dictates. Every rational creature, it is said, is obliged to regulate his actions by reason; and if any other motive or principle challenge the direction of his conduct, he ought to oppose it, till it be entirely subdued, or at least brought to a conformity with that superior principle. On this method of thinking the greatest part of moral philosophy, ancient and modern, seems to be founded; nor is there an ampler field, as well for metaphysical arguments, as popular declarations, than this supposed preëminence of reason above passion. The eternity, invariableness, and divine origin of the former, have been displayed to the best advantage: the blindness, inconstancy, and deceitfulness of the latter, have been as strongly insisted on. In order to show the fallacy of all this philosophy, I shall endeavour to prove *first*, that reason alone can never be a motive to any action of the will; and *secondly*, that it can never oppose passion in the direction of the will.

The understanding exerts itself after two different ways, as it judges from demonstration or probability; as it regards the abstract relations of our ideas, or those relations of objects of which experience only gives us information. I believe it scarce will be asserted, that the first species of reasoning alone is ever the cause of any action. As its proper province is the world of ideas, and as the will always places us in that of realities, demonstration and volition seem upon that account to be totally removed from each

From the *Hume* database in the PAST MASTERS series. Copyright © 1990 by InteLex Corporation. The text of A *Treatise of Human Nature* was drawn from the Everyman's Library edition, edited by Ernest Rhys, E. P. Dutton, 1911. Corrections were introduced from *Essays Moral, Political, and Literary*, edited by T. H. Green and T. H. Grose, Longmans, Green, and Co., 1898.

other. Mathematics, indeed, are useful in all mechanical operations, and arithmetic in almost every art and profession: but it is not of themselves they have any influence. Mechanics are the art of regulating the motions of bodies *to some designed end or purpose*; and the reason why we employ arithmetic in fixing the proportions of numbers, is only that we may discover the proportions of their influence and operation. A merchant is desirous of knowing the sum total of his accounts with any person: why? but that he may learn what sum will have the same *effects* in paying his debt, and going to market, as all the particular articles taken together. Abstract or demonstrative reasoning, therefore, never influences any of our actions, but only as it directs our judgment concerning causes and effects; which leads us to the second operation of the understanding.

It is obvious, that when we have the prospect of pain or pleasure from any object, we feel a consequent emotion of aversion or propensity, and are carried to avoid or embrace what will give us this uneasiness or satisfaction. It is also obvious, that this emotion rests not here, but, making us cast our view on every side, comprehends whatever objects are connected with its original one by the relation of cause and effect. Here then reasoning takes place to discover this relation; and according as our reasoning varies, our actions receive a subsequent variation. But it is evident, in this case, that the impulse arises not from reason, but is only directed by it. It is from the prospect of pain or pleasure that the aversion or propensity arises towards any object: and these emotions extend themselves to the causes and effects of that object, as they are pointed out to us by reason and experience. It can never in the least concern us to know, that such objects are causes, and such others effects, if both the causes and effects be indifferent to us. Where the objects themselves do not affect us, their connection can never give them any influence; and it is plain that, as reason is nothing but the discovery of this connection, it cannot be by its means that the objects are able to affect us.

Since reason alone can never produce any action, or give rise to volition, I infer, that the same faculty is as incapable of preventing volition, or of disputing the preference with any passion or emotion. This consequence is necessary. It is impossible reason could have the latter effect of preventing volition, but by giving an impulse in a contrary direction to our passions; and that impulse, had it operated alone, would have been ample to produce volition. Nothing can oppose or retard the impulse of passion, but a contrary impulse; and if this contrary impulse ever arises from reason, that latter faculty must have an original influence on the will, and must be able to cause, as well as hinder, any act of volition. But if reason has no original influence, it is impossible it can withstand any principle which has such an efficacy, or ever keep the mind in suspense a moment. Thus, it appears, that the principle which opposes our passion cannot be the same with reason, and is only called so in an improper sense. We speak not strictly and philosophically, when we talk of the combat of passion and of reason. Reason is, and ought only to be, the slave of the passions, and can never pretend to any other office than to serve and obey them. As this opinion may appear somewhat extraordinary, it may not be improper to confirm it by some other considerations.

A passion is an original existence, or, if you will, modification of existence, and contains not any representative quality, which renders it a copy of any other existence or modification. When I am angry, I am actually possessed with the passion, and in that emotion have no more a reference to any other object, than when I am thirsty, or sick, or more than five feet high. It is impossible, therefore, that this passion can be opposed by, or be contradictory to truth and reason; since this contradiction consists in the disagreement of ideas, considered as copies, with those objects which they represent.

What may at first occur on this head is, that as nothing can be contrary to truth or reason, except what has a reference to it, and as the judgments of our understanding only have this reference, it must follow that passions can be contrary to reason only, so far as they are *accompanied* with some judgment or opinion. According to this principle, which is so obvious and natural, it is only in two senses that any affection can be called unreasonable. First, When a passion, such as hope or fear, grief or joy, despair or security, is founded on the supposition of the existence of objects, which really do not exist. Secondly, When in exerting any passion in action, we choose means insufficient for the designed end, and deceive ourselves in our judgment of causes and effects. Where a passion is neither founded on false suppositions, nor chooses means insufficient for the end, the understanding can neither justify nor condemn it. It is not contrary to reason to prefer the destruction of the whole world to the scratching of my finger. It is not contrary to reason for me to choose my total ruin, to prevent the least uneasiness of an Indian, or person wholly unknown to me. It is as little contrary to reason to prefer even my own acknowledged lesser good to my greater, and have a more ardent affection for the former than the latter. A trivial good may, from certain circumstances, produce a desire superior to what arises from the greatest and most valuable enjoyment; nor is there anything more extraordinary in this, than in mechanics to see one pound weight raise up a hundred by the advantage of its situation. In short, a passion must be accompanied with some false judgment, in order to its being unreasonable; and even then it is not the passion, properly speaking, which is unreasonable, but the judgment.

The consequences are evident. Since a passion can never, in any sense, be called unreasonable, but when founded on a false supposition, or when it chooses means insufficient for the designed end, it is impossible that reason and passion can ever oppose each other, or dispute for the government of the will and actions. The moment we perceive the falsehood of any supposition, or the insufficiency of any means, our passions yield to our reason without any opposition. I may desire any fruit as of an excellent relish; but whenever you convince me of my mistake, my longing ceases. I may will the performance of certain actions as means of obtaining any desired good; but as my willing of these actions is only secondary, and founded on the supposition that they are causes of the proposed effect; as soon as I discover the falsehood of that supposition, they must become indifferent to me.

It is natural for one, that does not examine objects with a strict philosophic eye, to imagine, that those actions of the mind are entirely the same, which produce not a different sensation, and are not immediately distinguishable to the feeling and perception. Reason, for instance, exerts itself without producing any sensible emotions; and except in the more sub-

lime disquisitions of philosophy, or in the frivolous subtilties of the schools, scarce ever conveys any pleasure or uneasiness. Hence it proceeds, that every action of the mind which operates with the same calmness and tranquillity, is confounded with reason by all those who judge of things from the first view and appearance. Now it is certain there are certain calm desires and tendencies, which, though they be real passions, produce little emotion in the mind, and are more known by their effects than by the immediate feeling or sensation. These desires are of two kinds; either certain instincts originally implanted in our natures, such as benevolence and resentment, the love of life, and kindness to children; or the general appetite to good, and aversion to evil, considered merely as such. When any of these passions are calm, and cause no disorder in the soul, they are very readily taken for the determinations of reason, and are supposed to proceed from the same faculty with that which judges of truth and falsehood. Their nature and principles have been supposed the same, because their sensations are not evidently different.

Beside these calm passions, which often determine the will, there are certain violent emotions of the same kind, which have likewise a great influence on that faculty. When I receive any injury from another, I often feel a violent passion of resentment, which makes me desire his evil and punishment, independent of all considerations of pleasure and advantage to myself. When I am immediately threatened with any grievous ill, my fears, apprehensions, and aversions rise to a great height, and produce a sensible emotion.

The common error of metaphysicians has lain in ascribing the direction of the will entirely to one of these principles, and supposing the other to have no influence. Men often act knowingly against their interest; for which reason, the view of the greatest possible good does not always influence them. Men often counteract a violent passion in prosecution of their interest and designs; it is not, therefore, the present uneasiness alone which determines them. In general we may observe that both these principles operate on the will; and where they are contrary, that either of them prevails, according to the *general* character or *present* disposition of the person. What we call strength of mind, implies the prevalence of the calm passions above the violent; though we may easily observe, there is no man so constantly possessed of this virtue as never on any occasion to yield to the solicitations of passion and desire. From these variations of temper proceeds the great difficulty of deciding concerning the actions and resolutions of men, where there is any contrariety of motives and passions.

BOOK III
OF MORALS

PART I
OF VIRTUE AND VICE IN GENERAL

Section I

Moral Distinctions Not Derived from Reason

There is an inconvenience which attends all abstruse reasoning, that it may silence, without convincing an antagonist, and requires the same intense study to make us sensible of its force, that was at first requisite for its invention. When we leave our closet, and engage in the common affairs of life, its conclusions seem to vanish like the phantoms of the night on the appearance of the morning; and it is difficult for us to retain even that conviction which we had attained with difficulty. This is still more conspicuous in a long chain of reasoning, where we must preserve to the end the evidence of the first propositions, and where we often lose sight of all the most received maxims, either of philosophy or common life. I am not, however, without hopes, that the present system of philosophy will acquire new force as it advances; and that our reasonings concerning *morals* will corroborate whatever has been said concerning the *understanding* and the *passions*. Morality is a subject that interests us above all others; we fancy the peace of society to be at stake in every decision concerning it; and it is evident that this concern must make our speculations appear more real and solid, than where the subject is in a great measure indifferent to us. What affects us, we conclude, can never be a chimera; and, as our passion is engaged on the one side or the other, we naturally think that the question lies within human comprehension; which, in other cases of this nature, we are apt to entertain some doubt of. Without this advantage, I never should have ventured upon a third volume of such abstruse philosophy, in an age wherein the greatest part of men seem agreed to convert reading into an amusement, and to reject every thing that requires any considerable degree of attention to be comprehended.

It has been observed, that nothing is ever present to the mind but its perceptions; and that all the actions of seeing, hearing, judging, loving, hating, and thinking, fall under this denomination. The mind can never exert itself in any action which we may not comprehend under the term of *perception*; and consequently that term is no less applicable to those judgments by which we distinguish moral good and evil, than to every other operation of the mind. To approve of one character, to condemn another, are only so many different perceptions.

Now, as perceptions resolve themselves into two kinds, viz. *impressions* and *ideas*, this distinction gives rise to a question, with which we shall open up our present enquiry concerning morals, *whether it is by means of our* ideas *or* impressions *we distinguish betwixt vice and virtue, and pronounce an action blamable or praiseworthy?* This will immediately cut off all loose discourses and declamations, and reduce us to something precise and exact on the present subject.

Those who affirm that virtue is nothing but a conformity to reason; that there are eternal fitnesses and unfitnesses of things, which are the same to every rational being that considers them; that the immutable measures of right and wrong impose an obligation, not only on human creatures, but also on the Deity himself: all these systems concur in the opinion, that morality, like truth, is discerned merely by ideas, and by their juxtaposition and comparison. In order, therefore, to judge of these systems, we need only consider whether it be possible from reason alone, to distinguish betwixt moral good and evil, or whether there must concur some other principles to enable us to make that distinction.

If morality had naturally no influence on human passions and actions, it were in vain to take such pains to inculcate it; and nothing would be more fruitless than that multitude of rules and precepts with which all moralists abound. Philosophy is commonly divided into *speculative* and *practical*; and as morality is always comprehended under the latter division, it is supposed to influence our passions and actions, and to go beyond the calm and indolent judgments of the understanding. And this is confirmed by common experience, which informs us that men are often governed by their duties, and are deterred from some actions by the opinion of injustice, and impelled to others by that of obligation.

Since morals, therefore, have an influence on the actions and affections, it follows that they cannot be derived from reason; and that because reason alone, as we have already proved, can never have any such influence. Morals excite passions, and produce or prevent actions. Reason of itself is utterly impotent in this particular. The rules of morality, therefore, are not conclusions of our reason.

No one, I believe, will deny the justness of this inference; nor is there any other means of evading it, than by denying that principle on which it is founded. As long as it is allowed, that reason has no influence on our passions and actions, it is in vain to pretend that morality is discovered only by a deduction of reason. An active principle can never be founded on an inactive; and if reason be inactive in itself, it must remain so in all its shapes and appearances, whether it exerts itself in natural or moral subjects, whether it considers the powers of external bodies, or the actions of rational beings.

It would be tedious to repeat all the arguments by which I have proved[1] that reason is perfectly inert, and can never either prevent or produce any action or affection. It will be easy to recollect what has been said upon that subject. I shall only recall on this occasion one of these arguments, which I shall endeavour to render still more conclusive, and more applicable to the present subject.

Reason is the discovery of truth or falsehood. Truth or falsehood consists in an agreement or disagreement either to the *real* relations of ideas, or to *real* existence and matter of fact. Whatever therefore is not susceptible of this agreement or disagreement, is incapable of being true or false, and can never be an object of

our reason. Now, it is evident our passions, volitions, and actions, are not susceptible of any such agreement or disagreement; being original facts and realities, complete in themselves, and implying no reference to other passions, volitions, and actions. It is impossible, therefore, they can be pronounced either true or false, and be either contrary or conformable to reason.

This argument is of double advantage to our present purpose. For it proves *directly*, that actions do not derive their merit from a conformity to reason, nor their blame from a contrariety to it; and it proves the same truth more *indirectly*, by shewing us, that as reason can never immediately prevent or produce any action by contradicting or approving of it, it cannot be the source of moral good and evil, which are found to have that influence. Actions may be laudable or blamable; but they cannot be reasonable or unreasonable: laudable or blamable, therefore, are not the same with reasonable or unreasonable. The merit and demerit of actions frequently contradict, and sometimes control our natural propensities. But reason has no such influence. Moral distinctions, therefore, are not the offspring of reason. Reason is wholly inactive, and can never be the source of so active a principle as conscience, or a sense of morals.

But perhaps it may be said, that though no will or action can be immediately contradictory to reason, yet we may find such a contradiction in some of the attendants of the action, that is, in its causes or effects. The action may cause a judgment, or may be *obliquely* caused by one, when the judgment concurs with a passion; and by an abusive way of speaking, which philosophy will scarce allow of, the same contrariety may, upon that account, be ascribed to the action. How far this truth or falsehood may be the source of morals, it will now be proper to consider.

It has been observed that reason, in a strict and philosophical sense, can have an influence on our conduct only after two ways: either when it excites a passion, by informing us of the existence of something which is a proper object of it; or when it discovers the connexion of causes and effects, so as to afford us means of exerting any passion. These are the only kinds of judgment which can accompany our actions, or can be said to produce them in any manner; and it must be allowed, that these judgments may often be false and erroneous. A person may be affected with

1. Book II. Part III. Sec. III.

passion, by supposing a pain or pleasure to lie in an object which has no tendency to produce either of these sensations, or which produces the contrary to what is imagined. A person may also take false measures for the attaining his end, and may retard, by his foolish conduct, instead of forwarding the execution of any project. These false judgments may be thought to affect the passions and actions, which are connected with them, and may be said to render them unreasonable, in a figurative and improper way of speaking. But though this be acknowledged, it is easy to observe, that these errors are so far from being the source of all immorality, that they are commonly very innocent, and draw no manner of guilt upon the person who is so unfortunate as to fall into them. They extend not beyond a mistake of *fact*, which moralists have not generally supposed criminal, as being perfectly involuntary. I am more to be lamented than blamed, if I am mistaken with regard to the influence of objects in producing pain or pleasure, or if I know not the proper means of satisfying my desires. No one can ever regard such errors as a defect in my moral character. A fruit, for instance, that is really disagreeable, appears to me at a distance, and, through mistake, I fancy it to be pleasant and delicious. Here is one error. I choose certain means of reaching this fruit, which are not proper for my end. Here is a second error; nor is there any third one, which can ever possibly enter into our reasonings concerning actions. I ask, therefore, if a man in this situation, and guilty of these two errors, is to be regarded as vicious and criminal, however unavoidable they might have been? Or if it be possible to imagine that such errors are the sources of all immorality?

And here it may be proper to observe, that if moral distinctions be derived from the truth or falsehood of those judgments, they must take place wherever we form the judgments; nor will there be any difference, whether the question be concerning an apple or a kingdom, or whether the error be avoidable or unavoidable.

For as the very essence of morality is supposed to consist in an agreement or disagreement to reason, the other circumstances are entirely arbitrary, and can never either bestow on any action the character of virtuous or vicious, or deprive it of that character. To which we may add, that this agreement or disagreement, not admitting of degrees, all virtues and vices would of course be equal.

Should it be pretended, that though a mistake of *fact* be not criminal, yet a mistake of *right* often is; and that this may be the source of immorality: I would answer, that it is impossible such a mistake can ever be the original source of immorality, since it supposes a real right and wrong; that is, a real distinction in morals, independent of these judgments. A mistake, therefore, of right, may become a species of immorality; but it is only a secondary one, and is founded on some other antecedent to it.

As to those judgments which are the *effects* of our actions, and which, when false, give occasion to pronounce the actions contrary to truth and reason; we may observe, that our actions never cause any judgment, either true or false, in ourselves, and that it is only on others they have such an influence. It is certain that an action, on many occasions, may give rise to false conclusions in others; and that a person, who, through a window, sees any lewd behaviour of mine with my neighbour's wife, may be so simple as to imagine she is certainly my own. In this respect my action resembles somewhat a lie or falsehood; only with this difference, which is material, that I perform not the action with any intention of giving rise to a false judgment in another, but merely to satisfy my lust and passion. It causes, however, a mistake and false judgment by accident; and the falsehood of its effects may be ascribed, by some odd figurative way of speaking, to the action itself. But still I can see no pretext of reason for asserting, that the tendency to cause such an error is the first spring or original source of all immorality.[2]

---

2. One might think it were entirely superfluous to prove this, if a late author, who has had the good fortune to obtain some reputation, had not seriously affirmed, that such a falsehood is the foundation of all guilt and moral deformity. That we may discover the fallacy of his hypothesis, we need only consider, that a false conclusion is drawn from an action, only by means of an obscurity of natural principles, which makes a cause be secretly interrupted in its operation, by contrary causes, and renders the connexion betwixt two objects uncertain and variable. Now, as a like uncertainty and variety of causes take place, even in natural objects, and produce a like error in our judgment, if that tendency to produce error

Thus, upon the whole, it is impossible that the distinction betwixt moral good and evil can be made by reason; since that distinction has an influence upon our actions, of which reason alone is incapable.

---

were the very essence of vice and immorality, it should follow, that even inanimate objects might be vicious and immoral.

It is in vain to urge, that inanimate objects act without liberty and choice. For as liberty and choice are not necessary to make an action produce in us an erroneous conclusion, they can be, in no respect essential to morality; and I do not readily perceive, upon this system how they can ever come to be regarded by it. If the tendency to cause error be the origin of immorality, that tendency and immorality would in every case be inseparable.

Add to this, that if I had used the precaution of shutting the window while I indulged myself in those liberties with my neighbour's wife, I should have been guilty of no immorality; and that because my action, being perfectly concealed, would have had no tendency to produce any false conclusion.

For the same reason, a thief, who steals in by a ladder at a window, and takes all imaginable care to cause no disturbance, is in no respect criminal. For either he will not be perceived, or if he be it is impossible he can produce any error, nor will any one, from these circumstances, take him to be other than what he really is.

It is well known, that those who are squint-sighted do very readily cause mistakes in others, and that we imagine they salute or are talking to one person, while they address themselves to another. Are they, therefore, upon that account, immoral?

Besides, we may easily observe, that in all those arguments there is an evident reasoning in a circle. A person who takes possession of *another's* goods, and uses them as his *own*, in a manner declares them to be his own; and this falsehood is the source of the immorality of injustice. But is property, or right, or obligation, intelligible without an antecedent morality?

A man that is ungrateful to his benefactor, in a manner affirms that he never received any favours from him. But in what manner? Is it because it is his duty to be grateful? But this supposes that there is some antecedent rule of duty and morals. Is it because human nature is generally grateful, and makes us conclude that a man who does any harm, never receives any favour from the person he harmed? But human nature is not so generally grateful as to justify such a conclusion; or, if it were, is an exception to a general rule in every case criminal, for no other reason than because it is an exception?

Reason and judgment may, indeed, be the mediate cause of an action, by prompting or by directing a passion; but it is not pretended that a judgment of this kind, either in its truth or falsehood, is attended with virtue or vice. And as to the judgments, which are caused by our judgments, they can still less bestow those moral qualities on the actions which are their causes.

But, to be more particular, and to shew that those eternal immutable fitnesses and unfitnesses of things cannot be defended by sound philosophy, we may weigh the following considerations.

If the thought and understanding were alone capable of fixing the boundaries of right and wrong, the character of virtuous and vicious either must lie in some relations of objects, or must be a matter of fact which is discovered by our reasoning. This consequence is evident. As the operations of human understanding divide themselves into two kinds, the comparing of ideas, and the inferring of matter of fact, were virtue discovered by the understanding, it must be an object of one of these operations; nor is there any third operation of the understanding which can discover it. There has been an opinion very industriously propagated by certain philosophers, that morality is susceptible of demonstration; and though no one has ever been able to advance a single step in those demonstrations, yet it is taken for granted that this science may be brought to an equal certainty with geometry or algebra. Upon this supposition, vice

---

But what may suffice entirely to destroy this whimsical system is, that it leaves us under the same difficulty to give a reason why truth is virtuous and falsehood vicious, as to account for the merit or turpitude of any other action. I shall allow, if you please, that all immorality is derived from this supposed falsehood in action, provided you can give me any plausible reason why such a falsehood is immoral. If you consider rightly of the matter, you will find yourself in the same difficulty as at the beginning.

This last argument is very conclusive; because, if there be not an evident merit or turpitude annexed to this species of truth or falsehood, it can never have any influence upon our actions. For who ever thought of forbearing any action, because others might possibly draw false conclusions from it? Or who ever performed any, that he might give rise to true conclusions?

and virtue must consist in some relations; since it is
allowed on all hands, that no matter of fact is capable
of being demonstrated. Let us therefore begin with
examining this hypothesis, and endeavour, if possible,
to fix those moral qualities which have been so long
the objects of our fruitless researches; point out distinctly the relations which constitute morality or obligation, that we may know wherein they consist, and
after what manner we must judge of them.

If you assert that vice and virtue consist in relations
susceptible of certainty and demonstration, you must
confine yourself to those *four* relations which alone
admit of that degree of evidence; and in that case
you run into absurdities from which you will never
be able to extricate yourself. For as you make the
very essence of morality to lie in the relations, and
as there is no one of these relations but what is applicable, not only to an irrational but also to an inanimate
object, it follows that even such objects must be susceptible of merit or demerit. *Resemblance, contrariety,
degrees in quality, and proportions in quantity and
number;* all these relations belong as properly to matter as to our actions, passions, and volitions. It is
unquestionable, therefore, that morality lies not in
any of these relations, nor the sense of it in their discovery.[3]

3. As a proof how confused our way of thinking on
this subject commonly is, we may observe, that those
who assert that morality is demonstrable, do not say that
morality lies in the relations, and that the relations are
distinguishable by reason. They only say, that reason can
discover such an action, in such relations, to be virtuous,
and such another vicious. It seems they thought it sufficient if they could bring the word Relation into the
proposition, without troubling themselves whether it was
to the purpose or not. But here, I think, is plain argument.
Demonstrative reason discovers only relations. But that
reason, according to this hypothesis, discovers also vice
and virtue. These moral qualities, therefore, must be
relations. When we blame any action, in any situation,
the whole complicated object of action and situation
must form certain relations, wherein the essence of vice
consists. This hypothesis is not otherwise intelligible.
For what does reason discover, when it pronounces any
action vicious? Does it discover a relation or a matter
of fact? These questions are decisive, and must not be
eluded.

Should it be asserted, that the sense of morality
consists in the discovery of some relation distinct from
these, and that our enumeration was not complete
when we comprehended all demonstrable relations
under four general heads; to this I know not what to
reply, till some one be so good as to point out to me
this new relation. It is impossible to refute a system
which has never yet been explained. In such a manner
of fighting in the dark, a man loses his blows in
the air, and often places them where the enemy is
not present.

I must therefore, on this occasion, rest contented
with requiring the two following conditions of any
one that would undertake to clear up this system.
First, as moral good and evil belong only to the actions
of the mind, and are derived from our situation with
regard to external objects, the relations from which
these moral distinctions arise must lie only betwixt
internal actions and external objects, and must not
be applicable either to internal actions, compared
among themselves, or to external objects, when
placed in opposition to other external objects. For as
morality is supposed to attend certain relations, if
these relations could belong to internal actions considered singly, it would follow, that we might be guilty
of crimes in ourselves, and independent of our situation with respect to the universe; and in like manner,
if these moral relations could be applied to external
objects, it would follow that even inanimate beings
would be susceptible of moral beauty and deformity.
Now, it seems difficult to imagine that any relation
can be discovered betwixt our passions, volitions, and
actions, compared to external objects, which relation
might not belong either to these passions and volitions, or to these external objects, compared among
themselves.

But it will be still more difficult to fulfil the *second*
condition, requisite to justify this system. According
to the principles of those who maintain an abstract
rational difference betwixt moral good and evil, and
a natural fitness and unfitness of things, it is not
only supposed, that these relations, being eternal and
immutable, are the same, when considered by every
rational creature, but their *effects* are also supposed
to be necessarily the same; and it is concluded they
have no less, or rather a greater, influence in directing
the will of the Deity, than in governing the rational

and virtuous of our own species. These two particulars are evidently distinct. It is one thing to know virtue, and another to conform the will to it. In order, therefore, to prove that the measures of right and wrong are eternal laws, *obligatory* on every rational mind, it is not sufficient to shew the relations upon which they are founded: we must also point out the connexion betwixt the relation and the will; and must prove that this connexion is so necessary, that in every well-disposed mind, it must take place and have its influence; though the difference betwixt these minds be in other respects immense and infinite. Now, besides what I have already proved, that even in human nature no relation can ever alone produce any action; besides this, I say, it has been shewn, in treating of the understanding, that there is no connexion of cause and effect, such as this is supposed to be, which is discoverable otherwise than by experience, and of which we can pretend to have any security by the simple consideration of the objects. All beings in the universe, considered in themselves, appear entirely loose and independent of each other. It is only by experience we learn their influence and connexion; and this influence we ought never to extend beyond experience.

Thus it will be impossible to fulfil the *first* condition required to the system of eternal rational measures of right and wrong; because it is impossible to shew those relations, upon which such a distinction may be founded: and it is as impossible to fulfil the *second* condition; because we cannot prove *a priori*, that these relations, if they really existed and were perceived, would be universally forcible and obligatory.

But to make these general reflections more clear and convincing, we may illustrate them by some particular instances, wherein this character of moral good or evil is the most universally acknowledged. Of all crimes that human creatures are capable of committing, the most horrid and unnatural is ingratitude, especially when it is committed against parents, and appears in the more flagrant instances of wounds and death. This is acknowledged by all mankind, philosophers as well as the people: the question only arises among philosophers, whether the guilt or moral deformity of this action be discovered by demonstrative reasoning, or be felt by an internal sense, and by means of some sentiment, which the reflecting on

such an action naturally occasions. This question will soon be decided against the former opinion, if we can shew the same relations in other objects, without the notion of any guilt or iniquity attending them. Reason or science is nothing but the comparing of ideas, and the discovery of their relations; and if the same relations have different characters, it must evidently follow, that those characters are not discovered merely by reason. To put the affair, therefore, to this trial, let us choose any inanimate object, such as an oak or elm; and let us suppose, that, by the dropping of its seed, it produces a sapling below it, which, springing up by degrees, at last overtops and destroys the parent tree: I ask, if, in this instance, there be wanting any relation which is discoverable in parricide or ingratitude? Is not the one tree the cause of the other's existence, and the latter the cause of the destruction of the former, in the same manner as when a child murders his parent? It is not sufficient to reply, that a choice or will is wanting. For in the case of parricide, a will does not give rise to any *different* relations, but is only the cause from which the action is derived; and consequently produces the *same* relations, that in the oak or elm arise from some other principles. It is a will or choice that determines a man to kill his parent: and they are the laws of matter and motion that determine a sapling to destroy the oak from which it sprung. Here then the same relations have different causes; but still the relations are the same: and as their discovery is not in both cases attended with a notion of immorality, it follows, that that notion does not arise from such a discovery.

But to choose an instance still more resembling; I would fain ask any one, why incest in the human species is criminal, and why the very same action, and the same relations in animals, have not the smallest moral turpitude and deformity? If it be answered, that this action is innocent in animals, because they have not reason sufficient to discover its turpitude; but that man, being endowed with that faculty, which *ought* to restrain him to his duty, the same action instantly becomes criminal to him. Should this be said, I would reply, that this is evidently arguing in a circle. For, before reason can perceive this turpitude, the turpitude must exist; and consequently is independent of the decisions of our reason, and is their object more properly than their effect. According to this system, then, every animal that has sense and appetite and will, that is, every animal must be susceptible of all the same virtues and vices, for which we ascribe praise and blame to human creatures. All the difference is, that our superior reason may serve to discover the vice or virtue, and by that means may augment the blame or praise: but still this discovery supposes a separate being in these moral distinctions, and a being which depends only on the will and appetite, and which, both in thought and reality, may be distinguished from the reason. Animals are susceptible of the same relations with respect to each other as the human species, and therefore would also be susceptible of the same morality, if the essence of morality consisted in these relations. Their want of a sufficient degree of reason may hinder them from perceiving the duties and obligations of morality, but can never hinder these duties from existing; since they must antecedently exist, in order to their being perceived. Reason must find them, and can never produce them. This argument deserves to be weighed, as being, in my opinion, entirely decisive.

Nor does this reasoning only prove, that morality consists not in any relations that are the objects of science; but if examined, will prove with equal certainty, that it consists not in any *matter of fact*, which can be discovered by the understanding. This is the *second* part of our argument; and if it can be made evident, we may conclude that morality is not an object of reason. But can there be any difficulty in proving that vice and virtue are not matters of fact, whose existence we can infer by reason? Take any action allowed to be vicious; wilful murder, for instance. Examine it in all lights, and see if you can find that matter of fact, or real existence, which you call *vice*. In whichever way you take it, you find only certain passions, motives, volitions, and thoughts. There is no other matter of fact in the case. The vice entirely escapes you, as long as you consider the object. You never can find it, till you turn your reflection into your own breast, and find a sentiment of disapprobation, which arises in you, towards this action. Here is a matter of fact; but it is the object of feeling, not of reason. It lies in yourself, not in the object. So that when you pronounce any action or character to be vicious, you mean nothing, but that from the constitution of your nature you have a feeling

or sentiment of blame from the contemplation of it. Vice and virtue, therefore, may be compared to sounds, colours, heat, and cold, which, according to modern philosophy, are not qualities in objects, but perceptions in the mind: and this discovery in morals, like that other in physics, is to be regarded as a considerable advancement of the speculative sciences; though, like that too, it has little or no influence on practice. Nothing can be more real, or concern us more, than our own sentiments of pleasure and uneasiness; and if these be favourable to virtue, and unfavourable to vice, no more can be requisite to the regulation of our conduct and behaviour.

I cannot forbear adding to these reasonings an observation, which may, perhaps, be found of some importance. In every system of morality which I have hitherto met with, I have always remarked, that the author proceeds for some time in the ordinary way of reasoning, and establishes the being of a God, or makes observations concerning human affairs; when of a sudden I am surprized to find, that instead of the usual copulations of propositions, *is*, and *is not*, I meet with no proposition that is not connected with an *ought*, or an *ought not*. This change is imperceptible; but is, however, of the last consequence. For as this *ought*, or *ought not*, expresses some new relation or affirmation, it is necessary that it should be observed and explained; and at the same time that a reason should be given, for what seems altogether inconceivable, how this new relation can be a deduction from others, which are entirely different from it. But as authors do not commonly use this precaution, I shall presume to recommend it to the readers; and am persuaded, that this small attention would subvert all the vulgar systems of morality, and let us see that the distinction of vice and virtue is not founded merely on the relations of objects, nor is perceived by reason.

Section II

Moral Distinctions Derived from a Moral Sense

Thus the course of the argument leads us to conclude, that since vice and virtue are not discoverable merely by reason, or the comparison of ideas, it must be by means of some impression or sentiment they occasion, that we are able to mark the difference betwixt them. Our decisions concerning moral rectitude and depravity are evidently perceptions; and as all perceptions are either impressions or ideas, the exclusion of the one is a convincing argument for the other. Morality therefore, is more properly felt than judged of; though this feeling or sentiment is commonly so soft and gentle that we are apt to confound it with an idea, according to our common custom of taking all things for the same which have any near resemblance to each other.

The next question is, of what nature are these impressions, and after what manner do they operate upon us? Here we cannot remain long in suspense, but must pronounce the impression arising from virtue to be agreeable, and that proceeding from vice to be uneasy. Every moment's experience must convince us of this. There is no spectacle so fair and beautiful as a noble and generous action; nor any which gives us more abhorrence than one that is cruel and treacherous. No enjoyment equals the satisfaction we receive from the company of those we love and esteem; as the greatest of all punishments is to be obliged to pass our lives with those we hate or contemn. A very play or romance may afford us instances of this pleasure which virtue conveys to us; and pain, which arises from vice.

Now, since the distinguishing impressions by which moral good or evil is known, are nothing but *particular* pains or pleasures, it follows, that in all enquiries concerning these moral distinctions, it will be sufficient to shew the principles which make us feel a satisfaction or uneasiness from the survey of any character, in order to satisfy us why the character is laudable or blamable. An action, or sentiment, or character, is virtuous or vicious; why? because its view causes a pleasure or uneasiness of a particular kind. In giving a reason, therefore, for the pleasure or uneasiness, we sufficiently explain the vice or virtue. To have the sense of virtue, is nothing but to *feel* a satisfaction of a particular kind from the contemplation of a character. The very *feeling* constitutes our praise or admiration. We go no further; nor do we enquire into the cause of the satisfaction. We do not infer a character to be virtuous, because it pleases; but in feeling that it pleases after such a particular manner, we in effect feel that it is virtuous. The case

is the same as in our judgments concerning all kinds of beauty, and tastes, and sensations. Our approbation is implied in the immediate pleasure they convey to us.

I have objected to the system which establishes eternal rational measures of right and wrong, that it is impossible to shew, in the actions of reasonable creatures, any relations which are not found in external objects; and therefore, if morality always attended these relations, it were possible for inanimate matter to become virtuous or vicious. Now it may, in like manner, be objected to the present system, that if virtue and vice be determined by pleasure and pain, these qualities must, in every case, arise from the sensations; and consequently any object, whether animate or inanimate, rational or irrational, might become morally good or evil, provided it can excite a satisfaction or uneasiness. But though this objection seems to be the very same, it has by no means the same force in the one case as in the other. For, *first*, it is evident that, under the term *pleasure*, we comprehend sensations, which are very different from each other, and which have only such a distant resemblance as is requisite to make them be expressed by the same abstract term. A good composition of music and a bottle of good wine equally produce pleasure; and, what is more, their goodness is determined merely by the pleasure. But shall we say, upon that account, that the wine is harmonious, or the music of a good flavour? In like manner, an inanimate object, and the character or sentiments of any person, may, both of them, give satisfaction; but, as the satisfaction is different, this keeps our sentiments concerning them from being confounded, and makes us ascribe virtue to the one and not to the other. Nor is every sentiment of pleasure or pain, which arises from characters and actions, of that *peculiar* kind which makes us praise or condemn. The good qualities of an enemy are hurtful to us, but may still command our esteem and respect. It is only when a character is considered in general, without reference to our particular interest, that it causes such a feeling or sentiment as denominates it morally good or evil. It is true, those sentiments from interest and morals are apt to be confounded, and naturally run into one another. It seldom happens that we do not think an enemy vicious, and can distinguish betwixt his opposition to our interest and real villainy or baseness.

But this hinders not but that the sentiments are in themselves distinct; and a man of temper and judgment may preserve himself from these illusions. In like manner, though it is certain a musical voice is nothing but one that naturally gives a *particular* kind of pleasure; yet it is difficult for a man to be sensible that the voice of an enemy is agreeable, or to allow it to be musical. But a person of a fine ear, who has the command of himself, can separate these feelings, and give praise to what deserves it.

Secondly, we may call to remembrance the preceding system of the passions, in order to remark a still more considerable difference among our pains and pleasures. Pride and humility, love and hatred, are excited, when there is any thing presented to us that both bears a relation to the object of the passion, and produces a separate sensation, related to the sensation of the passion. Now, virtue and vice are attended with these circumstances. They must necessarily be placed either in ourselves or others, and excite either pleasure or uneasiness; and therefore must give rise to one of these four passions, which clearly distinguishes them from the pleasure and pain arising from inanimate objects, that often bear no relation to us; and this is, perhaps, the most considerable effect that virtue and vice have upon the human mind.

It may now be asked, *in general*, concerning this pain or pleasure that distinguishes moral good and evil, *From what principles is it derived, and whence does it arise in the human mind?* To this I reply, *first*, that it is absurd to imagine that, in every particular instance, these sentiments are produced by an *original* quality and *primary* constitution. For as the number of our duties is in a manner infinite, it is impossible that our original instincts should extend to each of them, and from our very first infancy impress on the human mind all that multitude of precepts which are contained in the completest system of ethics. Such a method of proceeding is not conformable to the usual maxims by which nature is conducted, where a few principles produce all that variety we observe in the universe, and every thing is carried on in the easiest and most simple manner. It is necessary, therefore, to abridge these primary impulses, and find some more general principles upon which all our notions of morals are founded.

But, in the *second* place, should it be asked, whether we ought to search for these principles in *nature*, or whether we must look for them in some other origin? I would reply, that our answer to this question depends upon the definition of the word Nature, than which there is none more ambiguous and equivocal. If *nature* be opposed to miracles, not only the distinction betwixt vice and virtue is natural, but also every event which has ever happened in the world, *excepting those miracles on which our religion is founded.* In saying, then, that the sentiments of vice and virtue are natural in this sense, we make no very extraordinary discovery.

But *nature* may also be opposed to rare and unusual; and in this sense of the word, which is the common one, there may often arise disputes concerning what is natural or unnatural; and one may in general affirm, that we are not possessed of any very precise standard by which these disputes can be decided. Frequent and rare depend upon the number of examples we have observed; and as this number may gradually encrease or diminish, it will be impossible to fix any exact boundaries betwixt them. We may only affirm on this head, that if ever there was any thing which could be called natural in this sense, the sentiments of morality certainly may; since there never was any nation of the world, nor any single person in any nation, who was utterly deprived of them, and who never, in any instance, showed the least approbation or dislike of manners. These sentiments are so rooted in our constitution and temper, that, without entirely confounding the human mind by disease or madness, it is impossible to extirpate and destroy them.

But *nature* may also be opposed to artifice, as well as to what is rare and unusual; and in this sense it may be disputed, whether the notions of virtue be natural or not. We readily forget that the designs, and projects, and views of men are principles as necessary in their operation as heat and cold, moist and dry; but, taking them to be free and entirely our own, it is usual for us to set them in opposition to the other principles of nature. Should it therefore be demanded, whether the sense of virtue be natural or artificial, I am of opinion that it is impossible for me at present to give any precise answer to this question. Perhaps it will appear afterwards that our sense of some virtues is artificial, and that of others natural.

The discussion of this question will be more proper, when we enter upon an exact detail of each particular vice and virtue.[4]

Mean while, it may not be amiss to observe, from these definitions of *natural* and *unnatural*, that nothing can be more unphilosophical than those systems which assert that virtue is the same with what is natural, and vice with what is unnatural. For, in the first sense of the word, nature, as opposed to miracles, both vice and virtue are equally natural; and, in the second sense, as opposed to what is unusual, perhaps virtue will be found to be the most unnatural. At least it must be owned, that heroic virtue, being as unusual, is as little natural as the most brutal barbarity. As to the third sense of the word, it is certain that both vice and virtue are equally artificial and out of nature. For, however it may be disputed, whether the notion of a merit or demerit in certain actions, be natural or artificial, it is evident that the actions themselves are artificial, and are performed with a certain design and intention; otherwise they could never be ranked under any of these denominations. It is impossible, therefore, that the character of natural and unnatural can ever, in any sense, mark the boundaries of vice and virtue.

Thus we are still brought back to our first position, that virtue is distinguished by the pleasure, and vice by the pain, that any action, sentiment, or character, gives us by the mere view and contemplation. This decision is very commodious; because it reduces us to this simple question, *Why any action or sentiment, upon the general view or survey, gives a certain satisfaction or uneasiness,* in order to shew the origin of its moral rectitude or depravity, without looking for any incomprehensible relations and qualities, which never did exist in nature, nor even in our imagination, by any clear and distinct conception. I flatter myself I have executed a great part of my present design by a state of the question, which appears to me so free from ambiguity and obscurity.

4. In the following discourse, *natural* is also opposed sometimes to *civil*, sometimes to *moral*. The opposition will always discover the sense in which it is taken.

PART II
OF JUSTICE AND INJUSTICE

Section I

Justice, Whether a Natural or Artificial Virtue?

I have already hinted, that our sense of every kind of virtue is not natural; but that there are some virtues that produce pleasure and approbation by means of an artifice or contrivance, which arises from the circumstances and necessity of mankind. Of this kind I assert *justice* to be; and shall endeavour to defend this opinion by a short, and, I hope, convincing argument, before I examine the nature of the artifice, from which the sense of that virtue is derived.

It is evident that, when we praise any actions, we regard only the motives that produced them, and consider the actions as signs or indications of certain principles in the mind and temper. The external performance has no merit. We must look within to find the moral quality. This we cannot do directly; and therefore fix our attention on actions, as on external signs. But these actions are still considered as signs; and the ultimate object of our praise and approbation is the motive that produced them.

After the same manner, when we require any action, or blame a person for not performing it, we always suppose that one in that situation should be influenced by the proper motive of that action, and we esteem it vicious in him to be regardless of it. If we find, upon enquiry, that the virtuous motive was still powerful over his breast, though checked in its operation by some circumstances unknown to us, we retract our blame, and have the same esteem for him, as if he had actually performed the action which we require of him.

It appears, therefore, that all virtuous actions derive their merit only from virtuous motives, and are considered merely as signs of those motives. From this principle I conclude, that the first virtuous motive which bestows a merit on any action, can never be a regard to the virtue of that action, but must be some other natural motive or principle. To suppose that the mere regard to the virtue of the action, may be the first motive which produced the action, and rendered it virtuous, is to reason in a circle. Before we can have such a regard, the action must be really virtuous; and this virtue must be derived from some virtuous motive: and, consequently, the virtuous motive must be different from the regard to the virtue of the action. A virtuous motive is requisite to render an action virtuous. An action must be virtuous before we can have a regard to its virtue. Some virtuous motive, therefore, must be antecedent to that regard.

Nor is this merely a metaphysical subtilty; but enters into all our reasonings in common life, though perhaps we may not be able to place it in such distinct philosophical terms. We blame a father for neglecting his child. Why? because it shews a want of natural affection, which is the duty of every parent. Were not natural affection a duty, the care of children could not be a duty; and it were impossible we could have the duty in our eye in the attention we give to our offspring. In this case, therefore, all men suppose a motive to the action distinct from a sense of duty.

Here is a man that does many benevolent actions; relieves the distressed, comforts the afflicted, and extends his bounty even to the greatest strangers. No character can be more amiable and virtuous. We regard these actions as proofs of the greatest humanity. This humanity bestows a merit on the actions. A regard to this merit is, therefore, a secondary consideration, and derived from the antecedent principle of humanity, which is meritorious and laudable.

In short, it may be established as an undoubted maxim, *that no action can be virtuous, or morally good, unless there be in human nature some motive to produce it distinct from the sense of its morality.*

But may not the sense of morality or duty produce an action, without any other motive? I answer, it may: but this is no objection to the present doctrine. When any virtuous motive or principle is common in human nature, a person who feels his heart devoid of that motive, may hate himself upon that account, and may perform the action without the motive, from a certain sense of duty, in order to acquire, by practice, that virtuous principle, or at least to disguise to himself, as much as possible, his want of it. A man that really feels no gratitude in his temper, is still pleased to perform grateful actions, and thinks he has, by that means, fulfilled his duty. Actions are at first only considered as signs of motives: but it is usual, in this case, as in all others, to fix our attention on the signs, and neglect, in some measure, the thing signified. But

though, on some occasions, a person may perform an action merely out of regard to its moral obligation, yet still this supposes in human nature some distinct principles, which are capable of producing the action, and whose moral beauty renders the action meritorious.

Now, to apply all this to the present case; I suppose a person to have lent me a sum of money, on condition that it be restored in a few days; and also suppose, that after the expiration of the term agreed on, he demands the sum: I ask, *What reason or motive have I to restore the money?* It will perhaps be said, that my regard to justice, and abhorrence of villainy and knavery, are sufficient reasons for me, if I have the least grain of honesty, or sense of duty and obligation. And this answer, no doubt, is just and satisfactory to man in his civilized state, and when trained up according to a certain discipline and education. But in his rude and more natural condition, if you are pleased to call such a condition natural, this answer would be rejected as perfectly unintelligible and sophistical. For one in that situation would immediately ask you, *Wherein consists this honesty and justice, which you find in restoring a loan, and abstaining from the property of others?* It does not surely lie in the external action. It must, therefore, be placed in the motive from which the external action is derived. This motive can never be a regard to the honesty of the action. For it is a plain fallacy to say, that a virtuous motive is requisite to render an action honest, and, at the same time, that a regard to the honesty is the motive of the action. We can never have a regard to the virtue of an action, unless the action be antecedently virtuous. No action can be virtuous, but so far as it proceeds from a virtuous motive. A virtuous motive, therefore, must precede the regard to the virtue; and it is impossible that the virtuous motive and the regard to the virtue can be the same.

It is requisite, then, to find some motive to acts of justice and honesty, distinct from our regard to the honesty; and in this lies the great difficulty. For should we say, that a concern for our private interest or reputation, is the legitimate motive to all honest actions: it would follow that wherever that concern ceases, honesty can no longer have place. But it is certain that self-love, when it acts at its liberty, instead of engaging us to honest actions, is the source of all injustice and violence; nor can a man ever correct those vices, without correcting and restraining the *natural* movements of that appetite.

But should it be affirmed that the reason or motive of such actions is the *regard to public interest*, to which nothing is more contrary than examples of injustice and dishonesty; should this be said, I would propose the three following considerations as worthy of our attention. *First*, Public interest is not naturally attached to the observation of the rules of justice; but is only connected with it, after an artificial convention for the establishment of these rules, as shall be shewn more at large hereafter. *Secondly*, If we suppose that the loan was secret, and that it is necessary for the interest of the person, that the money be restored in the same manner (as when the lender would conceal his riches), in that case the example ceases, and the public is no longer interested in the actions of the borrower; though I suppose there is no moralist who will affirm that the duty and obligation ceases. *Thirdly*, Experience sufficiently proves that men, in the ordinary conduct of life, look not so far as the public interest, when they pay their creditors, perform their promises, and abstain from theft, and robbery, and injustice of every kind. That is a motive too remote and too sublime to affect the generality of mankind, and operate with any force in actions so contrary to private interest as are frequently those of justice and common honesty.

In general, it may be affirmed, that there is no such passion in human minds as the love of mankind, merely as such, independent of personal qualities, of services, or of relation to ourself. It is true, there is no human, and indeed no sensible creature, whose happiness or misery does not, in some measure, affect us, when brought near to us, and represented in lively colours: but this proceeds merely from sympathy, and is no proof of such an universal affection to mankind, since this concern extends itself beyond our own species. An affection betwixt the sexes is a passion evidently implanted in human nature; and this passion not only appears in its peculiar symptoms, but also in inflaming every other principle of affection, and raising a stronger love from beauty, wit, kindness, than what would otherwise flow from them. Were there an universal love among all human creatures, it would appear after the same manner. Any degree of a good quality would cause a stronger affection than the same degree of a bad quality would cause hatred; contrary to what we find by experience. Men's tempers are different, and some have a propensity to the tender, and others to the rougher affections: but in the main, we may affirm, that man in general, or human nature, is nothing but the object both of love and hatred, and requires some other cause, which, by a double relation of impressions and ideas, may excite these passions. In vain would we endeavour to elude this hypothesis. There are no phenomena that point out any such kind affection to men, independent of their merit, and every other circumstance. We love company in general; but it is as we love any other amusement. An Englishman in Italy is a friend; a European in China; and perhaps a man would be beloved as such, were we to meet him in the moon. But this proceeds only from the relation to ourselves; which in these cases gathers force by being confined to a few persons.

If public benevolence, therefore, or a regard to the interests of mankind, cannot be the original motive to justice, much less can *private benevolence, or a regard to the interests of the party concerned*, be this motive. For what if he be my enemy, and has given me just cause to hate him? What if he be a vicious man, and deserves the hatred of all mankind? What if he be a miser, and can make no use of what I would deprive him of? What if he be a profligate debauchee, and would rather receive harm than benefit from large possessions? What if I be in necessity, and have urgent motives to acquire something to my family? In all these cases, the original motive to justice would fail; and consequently the justice itself, and along with it all property, right, and obligation.

A rich man lies under a moral obligation to communicate to those in necessity a share of his superfluities. Were private benevolence the original motive to justice a man would not be obliged to leave others in the possession of more than he is obliged to give them. At least, the difference would be very inconsiderable. Men generally fix their affections more on what they are possessed of, than on what they never enjoyed: for this reason, it would be greater cruelty to dispossess a man of any thing, than not to give it him. But who will assert that this is the only foundation of justice?

Besides, we must consider, that the chief reason why men attach themselves so much to their possessions, is, that they consider them as their property, and as secured to them inviolably by the laws of society. But this is a secondary consideration, and dependent on the preceding notions of justice and property.

A man's property is supposed to be fenced against every mortal, in every possible case. But private benevolence is, and ought to be, weaker in some persons than in others: and in many, or indeed in most persons, must absolutely fail. Private benevolence, therefore, is not the original motive of justice.

From all this it follows, that we have no real or universal motive for observing the laws of equity, but the very equity and merit of that observance; and as no action can be equitable or meritorious, where it cannot arise from some separate motive, there is here an evident sophistry and reasoning in a circle. Unless, therefore, we will allow that nature has established a sophistry, and rendered it necessary and unavoidable, we must allow, that the sense of justice and injustice is not derived from nature, but arises artificially, though necessarily, from education and human conventions.

I shall add, as a corollary to this reasoning, that since no action can be laudable or blamable, without some motives or impelling passions, distinct from the sense of morals, these distinct passions must have a great influence on that sense. It is according to their general force in human nature that we blame or praise. In judging of the beauty of animal bodies, we always carry in our eye the economy of a certain species; and where the limbs and features observe that proportion which is common to the species, we pronounce them handsome and beautiful. In like manner, we always consider the *natural* and *usual* force of the passions, when we determine concerning vice and virtue; and if the passions depart very much from the common measures on either side, they are always disapproved as vicious. A man naturally loves his children better than his nephews, his nephews better than his cousins, his cousins better than strangers, where every thing else is equal. Hence arise our common measures of duty, in preferring the one to the other. Our sense of duty always follows the common and natural course of our passions.

To avoid giving offence, I must here observe, that when I deny justice to be a natural virtue, I make use of the word *natural*, only as opposed to *artificial*. In another sense of the word, as no principle of the human mind is more natural than a sense of virtue, so no virtue is more natural than justice. Mankind is an inventive species; and where an invention is obvious and absolutely necessary, it may as properly be said to be natural as any thing that proceeds immediately from original principles, without the intervention of thought or reflection. Though the rules of justice be *artificial*, they are not *arbitrary*. Nor is the expression improper to call them *Laws of Nature*; if by natural we understand what is common to any species, or even if we confine it to mean what is inseparable from the species.

Section II

Of the Origin of Justice and Property

We now proceed to examine two questions, viz. *concerning the manner in which the rules of justice are established by the artifice of men*; and *concerning the reasons which determine us to attribute to the observance or neglect of these rules a moral beauty and deformity*. These questions will appear afterwards to be distinct. We shall begin with the former.

Of all the animals with which this globe is peopled, there is none towards whom nature seems, at first sight, to have exercised more cruelty than towards man, in the numberless wants and necessities with which she has loaded him, and in the slender means which she affords to the relieving these necessities. In other creatures, these two particulars generally compensate each other. If we consider the lion as a voracious and carnivorous animal, we shall easily discover him to be very necessitous; but if we turn our eye to his make and temper, his agility, his courage, his arms, and his force, we shall find that his advantages hold proportion with his wants. The sheep and ox are deprived of all these advantages; but their appetites are moderate, and their food is of easy purchase. In man alone this unnatural conjunction of infirmity and of necessity may be observed in its greatest perfection. Not only the food which is required for his sustenance flies his search and approach, or at least requires his labour to be produced, but he must be possessed of cloaths and lodging to defend him against the injuries of the weather; though, to consider him only in himself, he is provided neither with arms, nor force, nor other natural abilities which are in any degree answerable to so many necessities.

It is by society alone he is able to supply his defects, and raise himself up to an equality with his fellow-creatures, and even acquire a superiority above them. By society all his infirmities are compensated; and though in that situation his wants multiply every moment upon him, yet his abilities are still more augmented, and leave him in every respect more satisfied and happy than it is possible for him, in his savage and solitary condition, ever to become. When every individual person labours apart, and only for himself, his force is too small to execute any considerable work; his labour being employed in supplying all his different necessities, he never attains a perfection in any particular art; and as his force and success are not at all times equal, the least failure in either of these particulars must be attended with inevitable ruin and misery. Society provides a remedy for these three inconveniences. By the conjunction of forces, our power is augmented; by the partition of employments, our ability encreases; and by mutual succour, we are less exposed to fortune and accidents. It is by this additional *force, ability,* and *security,* that society becomes advantageous.

But, in order to form society, it is requisite not only that it be advantageous, but also that men be sensible of these advantages; and it is impossible, in their wild uncultivated state, that by study and reflection alone they should ever be able to attain this knowledge. Most fortunately, therefore, there is conjoined to those necessities, whose remedies are remote and obscure, another necessity, which, having a present and more obvious remedy, may justly be regarded as the first and original principle of human society. This necessity is no other than that natural appetite betwixt the sexes, which unites them together, and preserves their union, till a new tie takes place in their concern for their common offspring. This new concern becomes also a principle of union betwixt the parents and offspring, and forms a more numerous society, where the parents govern by the advantage of their superior strength and wisdom, and at the same time are restrained in the exercise of their authority by that natural affection which they bear their children. In a little time, custom and habit, operating on the tender minds of the children, makes them sensible of the advantages which they may reap from society, as well as fashions them by degrees for it, by rubbing off those rough corners and untoward affections which prevent their coalition.

For it must be confessed, that however the circumstances of human nature may render a union necessary, and however those passions of lust and natural affection may seem to render it unavoidable, yet there are other particulars in our *natural temper,* and in our *outward circumstances,* which are very incommodious, and are even contrary to the requisite conjunction. Among the former we may justly esteem our *selfishness* to be the most considerable. I am sensible that, generally speaking, the representations of this quality have been carried much too far; and that the descriptions which certain philosophers delight so much to form of mankind in this particular, are as wide of nature as any accounts of monsters which we meet with in fables and romances. So far from thinking that men have no affection for any thing beyond themselves, I am of opinion that, though it be rare to meet with one who loves any single person better than himself, yet it is as rare to meet with one in whom all the kind affections, taken together, do not overbalance all the selfish. Consult common experience; do you not see, that though the whole expence of the family be generally under the direction of the master of it, yet there are few that do not bestow the largest part of their fortunes on the pleasures of their wives and the education of their children, reserving the smallest portion for their own proper use and entertainment. This is what we may observe concerning such as have those endearing ties; and may presume, that the case would be the same with others, were they placed in a like situation.

But though this generosity must be acknowledged to the honour of human nature, we may at the same time remark, that so noble an affection, instead of fitting men for large societies, is almost as contrary to them as the most narrow selfishness. For while each person loves himself better than any other single person, and in his love to others bears the greatest affection to his relations and acquaintance, this must necessarily produce an opposition of passions, and a consequent opposition of actions, which cannot but be dangerous to the new-established union.

It is, however, worth while to remark, that this

contrariety of passions would be attended with but small danger, did it not concur with a peculiarity in our *outward circumstances,* which affords it an opportunity of exerting itself. There are three different species of goods which we are possessed of; the internal satisfaction of our minds; the external advantages of our body; and the enjoyment of such possessions as we have acquired by our industry and good fortune. We are perfectly secure in the enjoyment of the first. The second may be ravished from us, but can be of no advantage to him who deprives us of them. The last only are both exposed to the violence of others, and may be transferred without suffering any loss or alteration; while at the same time there is not a sufficient quantity of them to supply every one's desires and necessities. As the improvement, therefore, of these goods is the chief advantage of society, so the *instability* of their possession, along with their *scarcity,* is the chief impediment.

In vain should we expect to find, in *uncultivated nature,* a remedy to this inconvenience; or hope for any inartificial principle of the human mind which might control those partial affections, and make us overcome the temptations arising from our circumstances. The idea of justice can never serve to this purpose, or be taken for a natural principle, capable of inspiring men with an equitable conduct towards each other. That virtue, as it is now understood, would never have been dreamed of among rude and savage men. For the notion of injury or injustice implies an immorality or vice committed against some other person: And as every immorality is derived from some defect or unsoundness of the passions, and as this defect must be judged of, in a great measure, from the ordinary course of nature in the constitution of the mind, it will be easy to know whether we be guilty of any immorality with regard to others, by considering the natural and usual force of those several affections which are directed towards them. Now, it appears that, in the original frame of our mind, our strongest attention is confined to ourselves; our next is extended to our relations and acquaintance; and it is only the weakest which reaches to strangers and indifferent persons. This partiality, then, and unequal affection, must not only have an influence on our behaviour and conduct in society, but even on our ideas of vice and virtue; so as to make us regard any

remarkable transgression of such a degree of partiality, either by too great an enlargement or contraction of the affections, as vicious and immoral. This we may observe in our common judgments concerning actions, where we blame a person who either centers all his affections in his family, or is so regardless of them as, in any opposition of interest, to give the preference to a stranger or mere chance acquaintance. From all which it follows, that our natural uncultivated ideas of morality, instead of providing a remedy for the partiality of our affections, do rather conform themselves to that partiality, and give it an additional force and influence.

The remedy, then, is not derived from nature, but from *artifice;* or, more properly speaking, nature provides a remedy, in the judgment and understanding, for what is irregular and incommodious in the affections. For when men, from their early education in society, have become sensible of the infinite advantages that result from it, and have besides acquired a new affection to company and conversation, and when they have observed that the principal disturbance in society arises from those goods, which we call external, and from their looseness and easy transition from one person to another, they must seek for a remedy, by putting these goods, as far as possible, on the same footing with the fixed and constant advantages of the mind and body. This can be done after no other manner, than by a convention entered into by all the members of the society to bestow stability on the possession of those external goods, and leave every one in the peaceable enjoyment of what he may acquire by his fortune and industry. By this means every one knows what he may safely possess; and the passions are restrained in their partial and contradictory motions. Nor is such a restraint contrary to these passions; for, if so, it could never be entered into nor maintained; but it is only contrary to their heedless and impetuous movement. Instead of departing from our own interest, or from that of our nearest friends, by abstaining from the possessions of others, we cannot better consult both these interests than by such a convention; because it is by that means we maintain society, which is so necessary to their well-being and subsistence, as well as to our own.

This convention is not of the nature of a *promise;* for even promises themselves, as we shall see afterwards, arise from human conventions. It is only a general sense of common interest; which sense all the members of the society express to one another, and which induces them to regulate their conduct by certain rules. I observe, that it will be for my interest to leave another in the possession of his goods, *provided* he will act in the same manner with regard to me. He is sensible of a like interest in the regulation of his conduct. When this common sense of interest is mutually expressed, and is known to both, it produces a suitable resolution and behaviour. And this may properly enough be called a convention or agreement betwixt us, though without the interposition of a promise; since the actions of each of us have a reference to those of the other, and are performed upon the supposition that something is to be performed on the other part. Two men who pull the oars of a boat, do it by an agreement or convention, though they have never given promises to each other. Nor is the rule concerning the stability of possession the less derived from human conventions, that it arises gradually, and acquires force by a slow progression, and by our repeated experience of the inconveniences of transgressing it. On the contrary, this experience assures us still more, that the sense of interest has become common to all our fellows, and gives us a confidence of the future regularity of their conduct; and it is only on the expectation of this, that our moderation and abstinence are founded. In like manner are languages gradually established by human conventions, without any promise. In like manner do gold and silver become the common measures of exchange, and are esteemed sufficient payment for what is of a hundred times their value.

After this convention, concerning abstinence from the possessions of others, is entered into, and every one has acquired a stability in his possessions, there immediately arise the ideas of justice and injustice; as also those of *property*, *right*, and *obligation*. The latter are altogether unintelligible, without first understanding the former. Our property is nothing but those goods, whose constant possession is established by the laws of society; that is, by the laws of justice. Those, therefore, who make use of the words *property*, or *right*, or *obligation*, before they have explained the origin of justice, or even make use of them in that explication, are guilty of a very gross fallacy, and can

never reason upon any solid foundation. A man's property is some object related to him. This relation is not natural, but moral, and founded on justice. It is very preposterous, therefore, to imagine that we can have any idea of property, without fully comprehending the nature of justice, and shewing its origin in the artifice and contrivance of men. The origin of justice explains that of property. The same artifice gives rise to both. As our first and most natural sentiment of morals is founded on the nature of our passions, and gives the preference to ourselves and friends above strangers, it is impossible there can be naturally any such thing as a fixed right or property, while the opposite passions of men impel them in contrary directions, and are not restrained by any convention or agreement.

No one can doubt that the convention for the distinction of property, and for the stability of possession, is of all circumstances the most necessary to the establishment of human society, and that, after the agreement for the fixing and observing of this rule, there remains little or nothing to be done towards settling a perfect harmony and concord. All the other passions, beside this of interest, are either easily restrained, or are not of such pernicious consequence when indulged. *Vanity* is rather to be esteemed a social passion, and a bond of union among men. *Pity* and *love* are to be considered in the same light. And as to *envy* and *revenge*, though pernicious, they operate only by intervals, and are directed against particular persons, whom we consider as our superiors or enemies. This avidity alone, of acquiring goods and possessions for ourselves and our nearest friends, is insatiable, perpetual, universal, and directly destructive of society. There scarce is any one who is not actuated by it; and there is no one who has not reason to fear from it, when it acts without any restraint, and gives way to its first and most natural movements. So that, upon the whole, we are to esteem the difficulties in the establishment of society to be greater or less, according to those we encounter in regulating and restraining this passion.

It is certain, that no affection of the human mind has both a sufficient force and a proper direction to counterbalance the love of gain, and render men fit members of society, by making them abstain from the possessions of others. Benevolence to strangers is too weak for this purpose; and as to the other passions, they rather inflame this avidity, when we observe, that the larger our possessions are, the more ability we have of gratifying all our appetites. There is no passion, therefore, capable of controlling the interested affection, but the very affection itself, by an alteration of its direction. Now, this alteration must necessarily take place upon the least reflection, since it is evident that the passion is much better satisfied by its restraint than by its liberty, and that, in preserving society, we make much greater advances in the acquiring possessions, than in the solitary and forlorn condition which must follow upon violence and an universal licence. The question, therefore, concerning the wickedness or goodness of human nature, enters not in the least into that other question concerning the origin of society; nor is there any thing to be considered but the degrees of men's sagacity or folly. For whether the passion of self-interest be esteemed vicious or virtuous, it is all a case, since itself alone restrains it; so that if it be virtuous, men become social by their virtue; if vicious, their vice has the same effect.

Now, as it is by establishing the rule for the stability of possession that this passion restrains itself, if that rule be very abstruse and of difficult invention, society must be esteemed in a manner accidental, and the effect of many ages. But if it be found that nothing can be more simple and obvious than that rule; that every parent, in order to preserve peace among his children, must establish it; and that these first rudiments of justice must every day be improved, as the society enlarges: if all this appear evident, as it certainly must, we may conclude that it is utterly impossible for men to remain any considerable time in that savage condition which precedes society, but that his very first state and situation may justly be esteemed social. This, however, hinders not but that philosophers may, if they please, extend their reasoning to the supposed *state of nature*; provided they allow it to be a mere philosophical fiction, which never had, and never could have, any reality. Human nature being composed of two principal parts, which are requisite in all its actions, the affections and understanding, it is certain that the blind motions of the former, without the direction of the latter, incapacitate men for society; and it may be allowed us to consider separately the effects that result from the separate operations of these two component parts of the mind. The same liberty may be permitted to moral, which is allowed to natural philosophers; and it is very usual with the latter to consider any motion as compounded and consisting of two parts separate from each other, though at the same time they acknowledge it to be in itself uncompounded and inseparable.

This *state of nature*, therefore, is to be regarded as a mere fiction, not unlike that of the *golden age* which poets have invented; only with this difference, that the former is described as full of war, violence, and injustice; whereas the latter is painted out to us as the most charming and most peaceable condition that can possibly be imagined. The seasons, in that first age of nature, were so temperate, if we may believe the poets, that there was no necessity for men to provide themselves with cloaths and houses as a security against the violence of heat and cold. The rivers flowed with wine and milk; the oaks yielded honey; and nature spontaneously produced her greatest delicacies. Nor were these the chief advantages of that happy age. The storms and tempests were not alone removed from nature; but those more furious tempests were unknown to human breasts, which now cause such uproar, and engender such confusion. Avarice, ambition, cruelty, selfishness, were never heard of: cordial affection, compassion, sympathy, were the only movements with which the human mind was yet acquainted. Even the distinction of *mine* and *thine* was banished from that happy race of mortals, and carried with them the very notions of property, and obligation, justice and injustice.

This, no doubt, is to be regarded as an idle fiction; but yet deserves our attention, because nothing can more evidently shew the origin of those virtues, which are the subjects of our present enquiry. I have already observed, that justice takes its rise from human conventions; and that these are intended as a remedy to some inconveniences, which proceed from the concurrence of certain *qualities* of the human mind with the *situation* of external objects. The qualities of the mind are *selfishness* and *limited generosity*: and the situation of external objects is their *easy change*, joined to their *scarcity* in comparison of the wants and desires of men. But however philosophers may have been bewildered in those speculations, poets have been guided more infallibly, by a certain taste or common instinct, which, in most kinds of reasoning, goes further than any of that art and philosophy with which we have been yet acquainted. They easily perceived, if every man had a tender regard for another, or if nature supplied abundantly all our wants and desires, that the jealousy of interest, which justice supposes, could no longer have place; nor would there be any occasion for those distinctions and limits of property and possession, which at present are in use among mankind. Encrease to a sufficient degree the benevolence of men, or the bounty of nature, and you render justice useless, by supplying its place with much nobler virtues, and more valuable blessings. The selfishness of men is animated by the few possessions we have, in proportion to our wants; and it is to restrain this selfishness, that men have been obliged to separate themselves from the community, and to distinguish betwixt their own goods and those of others.

Nor need we have recourse to the fictions of poets to learn this; but, beside the reason of the thing, may discover the same truth by common experience and observation. It is easy to remark, that a cordial affection renders all things common among friends; and that married people, in particular, mutually lose their property, and are unacquainted with the mine and thine, which are so necessary, and yet cause such disturbance in human society. The same effect arises from any alteration in the circumstances of mankind; as when there is such a plenty of any thing as satisfies all the desires of men: in which case the distinction of property is entirely lost, and every thing remains in common. This we may observe with regard to air and water, though the most valuable of all external objects; and may easily conclude, that if men were supplied with every thing in the same abundance, or if *every one* had the same affection and tender regard for *every one* as for himself, justice and injustice would be equally unknown among mankind.

Here then is a proposition, which, I think, may be regarded as certain, *that it is only from the selfishness and confined generosity of men, along with the scanty provision nature has made for his wants, that justice derives its origin.* If we look backward we shall find, that this proposition bestows an additional force on some of those observations which we have already made on this subject.

First, We may conclude from it, that a regard to public interest, or a strong extensive benevolence, is not our first and original motive for the observation of the rules of justice; since it is allowed, that if men were endowed with such a benevolence, these rules would never have been dreamed of.

Secondly, We may conclude from the same principle, that the sense of justice is not founded on reason, or on the discovery of certain connexions and relations of ideas, which are eternal, immutable, and universally obligatory. For since it is confessed, that such an alteration as that above mentioned, in the temper and circumstances of mankind, would entirely alter our duties and obligations, it is necessary upon the common system, *that the sense of virtue is derived from reason,* to shew the change which this must produce in the relations and ideas. But it is evident, that the only cause why the extensive generosity of man, and the perfect abundance of every thing, would destroy the very idea of justice, is, because they render it useless; and that, on the other hand, his confined benevolence, and his necessitous condition, give rise to that virtue, only by making it requisite to the public interest, and to that of every individual. It was therefore a concern for our own and the public interest which made us establish the laws of justice; and nothing can be more certain, than that it is not any relation of ideas which gives us this concern, but our impressions and sentiments, without which every thing in nature is perfectly indifferent to us, and can never in the least affect us. The sense of justice, therefore, is not founded on our ideas, but on our impressions.

Thirdly, We may further confirm the foregoing proposition, *that those impressions, which give rise to this sense of justice, are not natural to the mind of man, but arise from artifice and human conventions.* For, since any considerable alteration of temper and circumstances destroys equally justice and injustice; and since such an alteration has an effect only by changing our own and the public interest, it follows that the first establishment of the rules of justice depends on these different interests. But if men pursued the public interest naturally, and with a hearty affection, they would have never dreamed of restraining each other by these rules; and if they pursued their own interest, without any precaution, they would run headlong into every kind of injustice and violence. These rules, therefore, are artificial, and seek their end in an oblique and indirect manner; nor is the interest which gives rise to them of a kind that could be pursued by the natural and inartificial passions of men.

To make this more evident, consider, that, though the rules of justice are established merely by interest, their connexion with interest is somewhat singular, and is different from what may be observed on other occasions. A single act of justice is frequently contrary to *public interest*; and were it to stand alone, without being followed by other acts, may, in itself, be very prejudicial to society. When a man of merit, of a beneficent disposition, restores a great fortune to a miser, or a seditious bigot, he has acted justly and laudably; but the public is a real sufferer. Nor is every single act of justice, considered apart, more conducive to private interest than to public; and it is easily conceived how a man may impoverish himself by a signal instance of integrity, and have reason to wish, that, with regard to that single act, the laws of justice were for a moment suspended in the universe. But, however single acts of justice may be contrary, either to public or private interest, it is certain that the whole plan or scheme is highly conducive, or indeed absolutely requisite, both to the support of society, and the well-being of every individual. It is impossible to separate the good from the ill. Property must be stable, and must be fixed by general rules. Though in one instance the public be a sufferer, this momentary ill is amply compensated by the steady prosecution of the rule, and by the peace and order which it establishes in society. And even every individual person must find himself a gainer on balancing the account; since, without justice, society must immediately dissolve, and every one must fall into that savage and solitary condition, which is infinitely worse than the worst situation that can possibly be supposed in society. When, therefore, men have had experience enough to observe, that, whatever may be the consequence of any single act of justice, performed by a single person, yet the whole system of actions concurred in by the whole society, is infinitely advantageous to the whole, and to every part, it is not long before justice and property take place. Every member of society is sensible of this interest: every one expresses this sense to his fellows, along with the resolution he has taken of squaring his actions by it, on condition that others will do the same. No more is requisite to induce any one of them to perform an act of justice, who has the first opportunity. This becomes an example to others; and thus justice establishes itself by a kind of convention or agreement, that is, by a sense of interest, supposed to be common to all, and where every single act is performed in expectation that others are to perform the like. Without such a convention, no one would ever have dreamed that there was such a virtue as justice, or have been induced to conform his actions to it. Taking any single act, my justice may be pernicious in every respect; and it is only upon the supposition that others are to imitate my example, that I can be induced to embrace that virtue; since nothing but this combination can render justice advantageous, or afford me any motives to conform myself to its rules.

We come now to the *second* question we proposed, viz. *Why we annex the idea of virtue to justice, and of vice to injustice.* This question will not detain us long after the principles which we have already established. All we can say of it at present will be despatched in a few words: and for further satisfaction, the reader must wait till we come to the third part of this book. The *natural* obligation to justice, viz. interest, has been fully explained; but as to the *moral* obligation, or the sentiment of right and wrong, it will first be requisite to examine the natural virtues, before we can give a full and satisfactory account of it.

After men have found by experience, that their selfishness and confined generosity, acting at their liberty, totally incapacitate them for society; and at the same time have observed that society is necessary to the satisfaction of those very passions, they are naturally induced to lay themselves under the restraint of such rules, as may render their commerce more safe and commodious. To the imposition, then, and observance of these rules, both in general, and in every particular instance, they are at first induced only by a regard to interest; and this motive, on the first formation of society, is sufficiently strong and forcible. But when society has become numerous, and has encreased to a tribe or nation, this interest is more remote; nor do men so readily perceive that disorder and confusion follow upon every breach of these rules, as in a more narrow and contracted society. But though, in our own actions, we may frequently lose sight of that interest which we have in maintaining order, and may follow a lesser and more present interest, we never fail to observe the prejudice we receive, either mediately or immediately, from the injustice of others; as not being in that case either blinded by passion, or biassed by any contrary temptation. Nay, when the injustice is so distant from us as no way to affect our interest, it still displeases us; because we consider it as prejudicial to human society, and pernicious to every one that approaches the person guilty of it. We partake of their uneasiness by *sympathy*; and as every thing which gives uneasiness in human actions, upon the general survey, is called Vice, and whatever produces satisfaction, in the same manner, is denominated Virtue, this is the reason why the sense of moral good and evil follows upon justice and injustice. And though this sense, in the present case, be derived only from contemplating the actions of others, yet we fail not to extend it even to our own actions. The *general rule* reaches beyond those instances from which it arose; while, at the same time, we naturally *sympathize* with others in the sentiments they entertain of us. *Thus self-interest is the original motive to the* establishment *of justice: but a sympathy with public interest is the source of the* moral approbation, *which attends that virtue.*

Though this progress of the sentiments be *natural*, and even necessary, it is certain that it is here forwarded by the artifice of politicians, who, in order to govern men more easily, and preserve peace in human society, have endeavoured to produce an esteem for justice, and an abhorrence of injustice. This, no doubt, must have its effect; but nothing can be more evident than that the matter has been carried too far by certain writers on morals, who seem to have employed their utmost efforts to extirpate all sense of virtue from among mankind. Any artifice of politicians may assist nature in the producing of those sentiments, which she suggests to us, and may even, on some occasions, produce alone an approbation or esteem for any particular action; but it is impossible it should be the sole cause of the distinction we make betwixt vice and virtue. For if nature did not aid us in this particular, it would be in vain for politicians to talk of *honourable* or *dishonourable, praiseworthy* or *blamable*. These words would be perfectly unintelligible, and would no more have any idea annexed to them, than if they were of a tongue perfectly unknown to us. The utmost politicians can perform, is

to extend the natural sentiments beyond their original bounds; but still nature must furnish the materials, and give us some notion of moral distinctions.

As public praise and blame encrease our esteem for justice, so private education and instruction contribute to the same effect. For as parents easily observe, that a man is the more useful, both to himself and others, the greater degree of probity and honour he is endowed with, and that those principles have greater force when custom and education assist interest and reflection: for these reasons they are induced to inculcate on their children, from their earliest infancy, the principles of probity, and teach them to regard the observance of those rules by which society is maintained, as worthy and honourable, and their violation as base and infamous. By this means the sentiments of honour may take root in their tender minds, and acquire such firmness and solidity, that they may fall little short of those principles which are the most essential to our natures, and the most deeply radicated in our internal constitution.

What further contributes to encrease their solidity, is the interest of our reputation, after the opinion, *that a merit or demerit attends justice or injustice,* is once firmly established among mankind. There is nothing which touches us more nearly than our reputation, and nothing on which our reputation more depends than our conduct with relation to the property of others. For this reason, every one who has any regard to his character, or who intends to live on good terms with mankind, must fix an inviolable law to himself, never, by any temptation, to be induced to violate those principles which are essential to a man of probity and honour.

I shall make only one observation before I leave this subject, viz. that, though I assert that, in the *state of nature,* or that imaginary state which preceded society, there be neither justice nor injustice, yet I assert not that it was allowable, in such a state, to violate the property of others. I only maintain, that there was no such thing as property; and consequently could be no such thing as justice or injustice. I shall have occasion to make a similar reflection with regard to *promises,* when I come to treat of them; and I hope this reflection, when duly weighed, will suffice to remove all odium from the foregoing opinions, with regard to justice and injustice.

JEAN-JACQUES ROUSSEAU

Writing in 1764, Immanuel Kant acknowledged his debt to Jean-Jacques Rousseau (1712–1778), whose "noble sweep of genius" had uncovered for Kant "the deeply hidden nature of man." This debt is not surprising. Kant was only one among many who benefitted from Rousseau's critique of culture, his commitment to freedom and the natural character of human goodness, and his respect for the new science. Flamboyant, controversial, unorthodox, complex, and brilliant, Rousseau employed his self-taught intelligence in diverse ways and for diverse purposes, from musical theory, drama, and operatic composition, to cultural criticism and political analysis. His mind wandered as he himself did, and while his heart remained bound to Geneva, his birthplace, it was as ambivalent a fidelity as that which characterized many other relationships of his life.

Born in Geneva in 1712, Rousseau had an unhappy childhood. His mother died a week after his birth, and his father, ambitious but irresponsible, was eventually forced to leave Geneva. His younger son, whom his father had educated at home, was at thirteen apprenticed to a harsh, insensitive engraver. In 1728, returning late from a country walk, Rousseau found the city gates locked and, rather than face the man's anger, fled Geneva.

By 1742 Rousseau had become richly educated, encouraged by Madame de Warens, with whom he lived as a guest and then as a lover. In that year he moved to Paris and became secretary to the Comte de Montaigu, the French ambassador to Venice. After a bitter dispute with the ambassador in Venice, Rousseau returned to Paris and was befriended by Denis Diderot, Jean Le Rond d'Alembert, and other *philosophes* of the French Enlightenment. They recognized in Rousseau a rare intellect, with range and fascinating depth. He had already written a play, developed a new system of musical notation, and begun a major work on political institutions.

In 1750, ironically at the urging of Diderot, Rousseau submitted an essay for the prize of the Academy of Dijon on the question: "Has the progress of the sciences and arts contributed to the purification of morals?" In his *Discourse on the Sciences and the Arts*, which won the competition, Rousseau extolled those in antiquity who, like the Spartans, were strong as a result of military discipline, and he assailed moderns who were weak and effeminate because of their lack of such discipline. Furthermore, Rousseau praised the modern scientists, like Francis Bacon and Isaac Newton, who remained independent of court intrigue and corruption and were capable of employing modern science for public benefit. He developed similar themes in a political context and by means of a *scientific* examination of people living in primitive, natural societies in his *Discourse on the Origin of Inequality*, published in 1755.

This second Discourse failed to win the Dijon prize, but it did win Rousseau international fame and recognition. But not by all. By the mid-1750s Rousseau had become estranged from many of his intellectual friends, in part as a result of his vigorous attack on modern culture and the scientific spirit that supported it. At about this time, he converted back to Protestantism and returned to Geneva, only to be compelled to return to France by a dispute with Voltaire and fears of repression in Geneva. It is ironic that for all his devotion to the ideal of Geneva as a small participatory democracy, he never enjoyed life in his birthplace. In 1755 he had dedicated his *Discourse on the Origin of Inequality* to the sovereign citizens of Geneva, but by the 1760s he was to indict the city as an "odious and lawless despotism."

In 1762 Rousseau published *Émile*, his famous account of a mode of education consonant with natural growth and conducted with respect for the child's kinship with nature. In the same year, drawing on his long-term project on political institutions, Rousseau published *On The Social Contract*. In this short work, he grounded sovereignty in the freedom of the citizen and the general will that expresses the common well-being of the people. Both works generated great debate until, on June 9, 1762, the Parlement of Paris authorized

Rousseau's arrest, and, a short time later, both books were condemned. Simultaneously, the two books were burned in Geneva and his arrest was decreed. From then until his death in 1778, Rousseau lived a fitful life, in ill health, constantly moving, and forever defending his views on the corrupting influence of culture, the purity of nature, and the centrality of freedom and equality. It was during this period that Rousseau wrote his famous autobiographical *Confessions*, a work which was completed by 1775 but which remained unpublished until after his death.

Recommended Readings

Cassirer, Ernst. *The Question of Jean-Jacques Rousseau*. Bloomington: Indiana University Press, 1963.

Chavet, John. *The Social Problem in the Philosophy of Rousseau*. Cambridge: Cambridge University Press, 1974.

Cranston, Maurice, and R. Peters (eds.). *Hobbes and Rousseau*. Garden City: Doubleday, 1972.

Gildin, Hilail. *Rousseau's Social Contract*. Chicago: University of Chicago Press, 1982.

Hendel, Charles. *Jean-Jacques Rousseau: Moralist*. Oxford: Oxford University Press, 1936.

Masters, Roger D. *The Political Philosophy of Rousseau*. Princeton: Princeton University Press, 1968.

Okin, Susan Moller. *Women in Western Political Thought*. Princeton: Princeton University Press, 1979.

Shklar, Judith. *Men and Citizens: A Study of Rousseau's Social Theory*. Cambridge: Cambridge University Press, 1969.

DISCOURSE ON THE ORIGIN AND FOUNDATIONS OF INEQUALITY AMONG MEN

by
JEAN-JACQUES ROUSSEAU,
Citizen of Geneva

"Not in depraved things but in those well oriented according to nature, are we to consider what is natural."
—Aristotle, *Politics*, II.

To
The Republic
of Geneva

Magnificent, Most Honored and Sovereign Lords:

Convinced that only a virtuous man may bestow on his homeland those honors which it can acknowledge, I have labored for thirty years to earn the right to offer you public homage. And since this happy occasion supplements to some extent what my efforts have been unable to accomplish, I believed I might be allowed here to give heed to the zeal that urges me on, instead of the right that ought to have given me authorization. Having had the good fortune to be born among you, how could I meditate on the equality which nature has established among men and upon the inequality they have instituted without thinking of the profound wisdom with which both, felicitously combined in this state, cooperate in the manner that most closely approximates the natural law and that is most favorable to society, to the maintenance of public order and to the happiness of private individuals? In searching for the best maxims that good sense

Reprinted from *The Basic Political Writings*, translated by Donald A. Cress (Indianapolis: Hackett Publishing Company, 1987), by permission of the publisher.

could dictate concerning the constitution of a government, I have been so struck on seeing them all in operation in your own, that even if I had not been born within your walls, I would have believed myself incapable of dispensing with offering this picture of human society to that people which, of all peoples, seems to me to be in possession of the greatest advantages, and to have best prevented its abuses.

If I had had to choose my birthplace, I would have chosen a society of a size limited by the extent of human faculties, that is to say, limited by the possibility of being well governed, and where, with each being sufficient to his task, no one would have been forced to relegate to others the functions with which he was charged; a state where, with all private individuals being known to one another, neither the obscure maneuvers of vice nor the modesty of virtue could be hidden from the notice and the judgment of the public, and where that pleasant habit of seeing and knowing one another turned love of homeland into love of the citizens rather than into love of the land.

I would have wanted to be born in a country where the sovereign and the people could have but one and the same interest, so that all the movements of the machine always tended only to the common happiness. Since this could not have taken place unless the people and the sovereign were one and the same person, it follows that I would have wished to be born under a democratic government, wisely tempered.

I would have wanted to live and die free, that is

to say, subject to the laws in such wise that neither I nor anyone else could shake off their honorable yoke: that pleasant and salutary yoke, which the most arrogant heads bear with all the greater docility, since they are made to bear no other.

I would therefore have wanted it to be impossible for anyone in the state to say that he was above the law and for anyone outside to demand that the state was obliged to give him recognition. For whatever the constitution of a government may be, if a single man is found who is not subject to the law, all the others are necessarily at his discretion.[1] And if there is a national leader and a foreign leader as well, whatever the division of authority they may make, it is impossible for both of them to be strictly obeyed and for the state to be well governed.

I would not have wanted to dwell in a newly constituted republic, however good its laws may be, out of fear that, with the government perhaps constituted otherwise than would be required for the moment and being unsuited to the new citizens or the citizens to the new government, the state would be subject to being overthrown and destroyed almost from its inception. For liberty is like those solid and tasty foods or those full-bodied wines which are appropriate for nourishing and strengthening robust constitutions that are used to them, but which overpower, ruin and intoxicate the weak and delicate who are not suited for them. Once peoples are accustomed to masters, they are no longer in a position to get along without them. If they try to shake off the yoke, they put all the more distance between themselves and liberty, because, in mistaking for liberty an unbridled license which is its opposite, their revolutions nearly always deliver them over to seducers who simply make their chains heavier. The Roman people itself—that model of all free peoples—was in no position to govern itself when it emerged from the oppression of the Tarquins. Debased by slavery and the ignominious labors the Tarquins had imposed on it, at first it was but a stupid rabble that needed to be managed and governed with the greatest wisdom, so that, as it gradually became accustomed to breathe the salutary air of liberty, these souls, enervated or rather brutalized under tyranny, acquired by degrees that severity of mores and that high-spirited courage which eventually made them, of all the peoples, most worthy of respect. I would

therefore have sought for my homeland a happy and tranquil republic, whose antiquity was somehow lost in the dark recesses of time, which had experienced only such attacks as served to manifest and strengthen in its inhabitants courage and love of homeland, and where the citizens, long accustomed to a wise independence, were not only free but worthy of being so.

I would have wanted to choose for myself a homeland diverted by a fortunate impotence from the fierce love of conquest, and protected by an even more fortunate position from the fear of becoming itself the conquest of another state; a free city, situated among several peoples none of whom had any interest in invading it, while each had an interest in preventing the others from invading it themselves; in a word, a republic that did not tempt the ambition of its neighbors and that could reasonably count on their assistance in time of need. It follows that in so fortunate a position, it would have had nothing to fear except from itself; and that, if its citizens were trained in the use of arms, it would have been more to maintain in them that martial fervor and that high-spirited courage that suit liberty so well and whet the appetite for it, than out of the necessity to provide for their defense.

I would have searched for a country where the right of legislation was common to all citizens, for who can know better than they the conditions under which it suits them to live together in a single society? But I would not have approved of plebiscites like those of the Romans where the state's leaders and those most interested in its preservation were excluded from the deliberations on which its safety often depended, and where, by an absurd inconsistency, the magistrates were deprived of the rights enjoyed by ordinary citizens.

On the contrary, I would have desired that, in order to stop the self-centered and ill-conceived projects and the dangerous innovations that finally ruined Athens, no one would have the power to propose new laws according to his fancy; that this right belonged exclusively to the magistrates; that even they used it with such caution that the populace, for its part, was so hesitant about giving its consent to these laws, and that their promulgation could only be done with such solemnity that before the constitution was overturned one had time to be convinced that it is above all the great antiquity of the laws that makes them holy and venerable; that the populace soon holds in contempt those laws that it sees change daily; and that in becoming accustomed to neglect old usages on the pretext of making improvements, great evils are often introduced in order to correct the lesser ones.

Above all, I would have fled, as necessarily ill-governed, a republic where the people, believing it could get along without its magistrates or permit them but a precarious authority, would imprudently have held on to the administration of civil affairs and the execution of its own laws. Such must have been the rude constitution of the first governments immediately emerging from the state of nature, and such too was one of the vices which ruined the republic of Athens.

But I would have chosen that republic where private individuals, being content to give sanction to the laws and to decide as a body and upon the recommendation of their leaders the most important public affairs, would establish respected tribunals, distinguish with care their various departments, annually elect the most capable and most upright of their fellow citizens to administer justice and to govern the state; and where, with the virtue of the magistrates thus bearing witness to the wisdom of the people, they would mutually honor one another. Thus if some fatal misunderstandings were ever to disturb public concord, even those periods of blindness and errors were marked by indications of moderation, reciprocal esteem, and a common respect for the laws: presages and guarantees of a sincere and perpetual reconciliation.

Such, MAGNIFICENT, MOST HONORED, AND SOVEREIGN LORDS, are the advantages that I would have sought in the homeland that I would have chosen for myself. And if in addition providence had joined to it a charming location, a temperate climate, a fertile country and the most delightful appearance there is under the heavens, to complete my happiness I would have desired only to enjoy all these goods in the bosom of that happy homeland, living peacefully in sweet society with my fellow citizens, and practicing toward them (following their own example), humanity, friendship, and all the virtues; and leaving behind me the honorable memory of a good man and a decent and virtuous patriot.

If, less happy or too late grown wise, I had seen myself reduced to end an infirm and languishing career in other climates, pointlessly regretting the repose and peace of which an imprudent youth deprived me, I would at least have nourished in my soul those same sentiments I could not have used in my native country; and penetrated by a tender and disinterested affection for my distant fellow citizens, I would have addressed them from the bottom of my heart more or less along the following lines:

My dear fellow citizens, or rather my brothers, since the bonds of blood as well as the laws unite almost all of us, it gives me pleasure to be incapable of thinking of you without at the same time thinking of all the good things you enjoy, and of which perhaps none of you appreciates the value more deeply than I who have lost them. The more I reflect upon your political and civil situation, the less I am capable of imagining that the nature of human affairs could admit of a better one. In all other governments, when it is a question of assuring the greatest good of the state, everything is always limited to imaginary projects, and at most to simple possibilities. As for you, your happiness is complete; it remains merely to enjoy it. And to become perfectly happy you are in need of nothing more than to know how to be satisfied with being so. Your sovereignty, acquired or recovered at the point of a sword, and preserved for two centuries by dint of valor and wisdom, is at last fully and universally recognized. Honorable treaties fix your boundaries, secure your rights and strengthen your repose. Your constitution is excellent, since it is dictated by the most sublime reason and is guaranteed by friendly powers deserving of respect. Your state is tranquil; you have neither wars nor conquerors to fear. You have no other masters but the wise laws you have made, administered by upright magistrates of your own choosing. You are neither rich enough to enervate yourself with softness and to lose in vain delights the taste for true happiness and solid virtues, nor poor enough to need more foreign assistance than your industry procures for you. And this precious liberty, which in large nations is maintained only by exorbitant taxes, costs you almost nothing to pursue.

For the happiness of its citizens and the examples of the peoples, may a republic so wisely and so happily constituted last forever! This is the only wish left for you to make, and the only precaution left for you to take. From here on, it is for you alone, not to bring about your own happiness, your ancestors having saved you the trouble, but to render it lasting by the wisdom of using it well. It is upon your perpetual union, your obedience to the laws, your respect for their ministers that your preservation depends. If there remains among you the slightest germ of bitterness or distrust, hasten to destroy it as a ruinous leaven that sooner or later results in your misfortunes and the ruin of the state. I beg you all to look deep inside your hearts and to heed the secret voice of your conscience. Is there anyone among you who knows of a body that is more upright, more enlightened, more worthy of respect than that of your magistracy? Do not all its members give you the example of moderation, of simplicity of mores, of respect for the laws, and of the most sincere reconciliation? Then freely give such wise chiefs that salutary confidence that reason owes to virtue. Bear in mind that they are of your choice, that they justify it, and that the honors due to those whom you have established in dignity necessarily reflect back upon yourselves. None of you is so unenlightened as to be ignorant of the fact that where the vigor of laws and the authority of their defenders cease, there can be neither security nor freedom for anyone. What then is the point at issue among you except to do wholeheartedly and with just confidence what you should always be obliged to do by a true self-interest, by duty and for the sake of reason? May a sinful and ruinous indifference to the maintenance of the constitution never make you neglect in time of need the wise teachings of the most enlightened and most zealous among you. But may equity, moderation, and the most respectful firmness continue to regulate all your activities and display in you, to the entire universe, the example of a proud and modest people, as jealous of its glory as of its liberty. Above all, beware (and this will be my last counsel) of ever listening to sinister interpretations and venomous speeches, whose secret motives are often more dangerous than the actions that are their object. An entire household awakens and takes warning at the first cries of a good and faithful watchdog who never barks except at the approach of burglars. But people hate the nuisance caused by those noisy animals that continually disturb the public repose

and whose continual and ill-timed warnings are not heeded even at the moment when they are necessary.

And you, MAGNIFICENT AND MOST HONORED LORDS, you upright and worthy magistrates of a free people, permit me to offer you in particular my compliments and my respects. If there is a rank in the world suited to conferring honor on those who hold it, it is without doubt the one that is given by talents and virtue, that of which you have made yourselves worthy, and to which your fellow citizens have raised you. Their own merit adds still a new luster to yours. And I that find you, who were chosen by men capable of governing others in order that they themselves may be governed, are as much above other magistrates as a free people; and above all that the one which you have the honor of leading, is, by its enlightenment and reason, above the populace of the other states.

May I be permitted to cite an example of which better records ought to remain, and which will always be near to my heart. I never call to mind without the sweetest emotion the memory of the virtuous citizen to whom I owe my being, and who often spoke to me in my childhood of the respect that was owed you. I still see him living from the work of his hands, and nourishing his soul on the most sublime truths. I see Tacitus, Plutarch and Grotius mingled with the instruments of his craft before him. I see at his side a beloved son receiving with too little profit the tender instruction of the best of fathers. But if the aberrations of foolish youth made me forget such wise lessons for a time, I have the happiness to sense at last that whatever the inclination one may have toward vice, it is difficult for an education in which the heart is involved to remain forever lost.

Such, MAGNIFICENT AND MOST HONORED LORDS, are the citizens and even the simple inhabitants born in the state you govern. Such are those educated and sensible men concerning whom, under the name of workers and people, such base and false ideas are entertained in other nations. My father, I gladly acknowledge, was in no way distinguished among his fellow citizens; he was only what they all are; and such as he was, there was no country where his company would not have been sought after, cultivated, and profitably too, by the most upright men. It does not behoove me, nor, thank heaven, is it necessary to speak to you of the regard which men of that stamp can expect from you: your equals by education as well as by the rights of nature and of birth; your inferiors by their will and by the preference they owe your merit, which they have granted to it, and for which you in turn owe them some sort of gratitude. It is with intense satisfaction that I learn how much, in your dealings with them, you temper with gentleness and cooperativeness the gravity suited to the ministers of the law; how much you repay them in esteem and attention for the obedience and respect they owe you; conduct full of justice and wisdom, suited to putting at a greater and greater distance the memory of unhappy events which must be forgotten so as never to see them again; conduct all the more judicious because this equitable and generous people makes a pleasure out of its duty, because it naturally loves to honor you, and because those who are most zealous in upholding their rights are the ones who are most inclined to respect yours.

It should not be surprising that the leaders of a civil society love its glory and happiness; but, unfortunately for the tranquility of men, that those who consider themselves as the magistrates, or rather as the masters, of a more holy and more sublime homeland manifest some love for the earthly homeland which nourishes them. How sweet it is for me to be able to make such a rare exception in our favor, and to place in the rank of our best citizens those zealous trustees of the sacred dogmas authorized by the laws, those venerable pastors of souls, whose lively and sweet eloquence the better instills the maxims of the Gospel into people's hearts as they themselves always begin by practicing them. Everyone knows the success with which the great art of preaching is cultivated in Geneva. But since people are too accustomed to seeing things said in one way and done in another, few of them know the extent to which the spirit of Christianity, the saintliness of mores, severity to oneself and gentleness to others reign in the body of our ministers. Perhaps it behooves only the city of Geneva to provide the edifying example of such a perfect union between a society of theologians and of men of letters. It is in large part upon their wisdom and their acknowledged moderation and upon their zeal for the prosperity of the state that I base my hopes for its eternal tranquility. And I note, with a pleasure mixed with amazement

and respect, how much they abhor the atrocious maxims of those sacred and barbarous men of whom history provides more than one example, and who, in order to uphold the alleged rights of God—that is to say, their own interests—were all the less sparing of human blood because they hoped their own would always be respected.

Could I forget that precious half of the republic which produces the happiness of the other and whose gentleness and wisdom maintain peace and good mores? Amiable and virtuous women citizens, it will always be the fate of your sex to govern ours. Happy it is when your chaste power, exercised only within the conjugal union, makes itself felt only for the glory of the state and the public happiness! Thus it was that in Sparta women were in command, and thus it is that you deserve to be in command in Geneva. What barbarous man could resist the voice of honor and reason in the mouth of an affectionate wife? And who would not despise vain luxury on seeing your simple and modest attire, which, from the luster it derives from you, seems the most favorable to beauty? It is for you to maintain always, by your amiable and innocent dominion and by your insinuating wit, the love of laws in the state and concord among the citizens; to reunite, by happy marriages, divided families; and above all, to correct, by the persuasive sweetness of your lessons and by the modest graces of your conversation, those extravagances which our young people come to acquire in other countries, whence, instead of the many useful things they could profit from, they bring back, with a childish manner and ridiculous airs adopted among fallen women, nothing more than an admiration for who knows what pretended grandeurs, frivolous compensations for servitude, which will never be worth as much as august liberty. Therefore always be what you are, the chaste guardians of mores and the gentle bonds of peace; and continue to assert on every occasion the rights of the heart and of nature for the benefit of duty and virtue.

I flatter myself that events will not prove me wrong in basing upon such guarantees hope for the general happiness of the citizens and for the glory of the republic. I admit that with all these advantages it will not shine with that brilliance which dazzles most eyes; and the childish and fatal taste for this is the deadliest enemy of happiness and liberty. Let a dissolute youth go elsewhere in search of easy pleasures and lengthy repentances. Let the alleged men of taste admire someplace else the grandeur of palaces, the beauty of carriages, the sumptuous furnishings, the pomp of spectacles, and all the refinements of softness and luxury. In Geneva we will find only men; but such a sight has a value of its own, and those who seek it are well worth the admirers of the rest.

May you all, MAGNIFICENT, MOST HONORED AND SOVEREIGN LORDS, deign to receive with the same goodness the respectful testimonies of the interest I take in your common prosperity. If I were unfortunate enough to be guilty of some indiscreet rapture in this lively effusion of my heart, I beg you to pardon it as the tender affection of a true patriot, and to the ardent and legitimate zeal of a man who envisages no greater happiness for himself than that of seeing all of you happy.

With the most profound respect, I am, MAGNIFICENT, MOST HONORED AND SOVEREIGN LORDS, your most humble and most obedient servant and fellow citizen.

Jean-Jacques Rousseau
Chambéry
12 June 1754

PREFACE

Of all the branches of human knowledge, the most useful and the least advanced seems to me to be that of man;[2] and I dare say that the inscription on the temple at Delphi alone contained a precept more important and more difficult than all the huge tomes of the moralists. Thus I regard the subject of this discourse as one of the most interesting questions that philosophy is capable of proposing, and unhappily for us, one of the thorniest that philosophers can attempt to resolve. For how can the source of the inequality among men be known unless one begins by knowing men themselves? And how will man be successful in seeing himself as nature formed him, through all the changes that the succession of time and things must have produced in his original consti-

tution, and in separating what he derives from his own wherewithal from what circumstances and his progress have added to or changed in his primitive state? Like the statue of Glaucus, which time, sea and storms had disfigured to such an extent that it looked less like a god than a wild beast, the human soul, altered in the midst of society by a thousand constantly recurring causes, by the acquisition of a multitude of bits of knowledge and of errors, by changes that took place in the constitution of bodies, by the constant impact of the passions, has, as it were, changed its appearance to the point of being nearly unrecognizable. And instead of a being active always by certain and invariable principles, instead of that heavenly and majestic simplicity whose mark its author had left on it, one no longer finds anything but the grotesque contrast of passion which thinks it reasons and an understanding in a state of delirium.

What is even more cruel is that, since all the progress of the human species continually moves away from its primitive state, the more we accumulate new knowledge, the more we deprive ourselves of the means of acquiring the most important knowledge of all. Thus, in a sense, it is by dint of studying man that we have rendered ourselves incapable of knowing him.

It is easy to see that it is in these successive changes of the human constitution that we must seek the first origin of the differences that distinguish men, who, by common consensus, are naturally as equal among themselves as were the animals of each species before various physical causes had introduced into certain species the varieties we now observe among some of them. In effect, it is inconceivable that these first changes, by whatever means they took place, should have altered all at once and in the same manner all the individuals of the species. But while some improved or declined and acquired various good or bad qualities which were not inherent in their nature, the others remained longer in their original state. And such was the first source of inequality among men, which it is easier to demonstrate thus in general than to assign with precision its true causes.

Let my readers not imagine, then, that I dare flatter myself with having seen what appears to me so difficult to see. I have begun some lines of reasoning; I have hazarded some guesses, less in the hope of resolving the question than with the intention of clarifying it and of reducing it to its true state. Others will easily be able to go farther on this same route, though it will not be easy for anyone to reach the end of it. For it is no light undertaking to separate what is original from what is artificial in the present nature of man, and to have a proper understanding of a state which no longer exists, which perhaps never existed, which probably never will exist, and yet about which it is necessary to have accurate notions in order to judge properly our own present state. He who would attempt to determine precisely which precautions to take in order to make solid observations on this subject would need even more philosophy than is generally supposed; and a good solution of the following problem would not seem to me unworthy of the Aristotles and Plinys of our century: *What experiments would be necessary to achieve knowledge of natural man? And what are the means of carrying out these experiments in the midst of society?* Far from undertaking to resolve this problem, I believe I have meditated sufficiently on the subject to dare respond in advance that the greatest philosophers will not be too good to direct these experiments, nor the most powerful sovereigns to carry them out. It is hardly reasonable to expect such a combination, especially with the perseverance or rather the succession of understanding and good will needed on both sides in order to achieve success.

These investigations, so difficult to carry out and so little thought about until now, are nevertheless the only means we have left of removing a multitude of difficulties that conceal from us the knowledge of the real foundations of human society. It is this ignorance of the nature of man which throws so much uncertainty and obscurity on the true definition of natural right. For the idea of right, says M. Burlamaqui, and even more that of natural right, are manifestly ideas relative to the nature of man. Therefore, he continues, the principles of this science must be deduced from this very nature of man, from man's constitution and state.

It is not without surprise and a sense of outrage that one observes the paucity of agreement that prevails among the various authors who have treated it. Among the most serious writers one can hardly find two who are of the same opinion on this point. The Roman jurists — not to mention the ancient philosophers who seem to have done their best to contradict each other

on the most fundamental principles — subject man and all other animals indifferently to the same natural law, because they take this expression to refer to the law that nature imposes on itself rather than the law she prescribes, or rather because of the particular sense in which those jurists understood the word "law," which on this occasion they seem to have taken only for the expression of the general relations established by nature among all animate beings for their common preservation. The moderns, in acknowledging under the word "law" merely a rule prescribed to a moral being, that is to say, intelligent, free and considered in his relations with other beings, consequently limit the competence of the natural law to the only animal endowed with reason, that is, to man. But with each one defining this law in his own fashion, they all establish it on such metaphysical principles that even among us there are very few people in a position to grasp these principles, far from being able to find them by themselves. So that all the definitions of these wise men, otherwise in perpetual contradiction with one another, agree on this alone, that it is impossible to understand the law of nature and consequently to obey it without being a great reasoner and a profound metaphysician, which means precisely that for the establishment of society, men must have used enlightenment which develops only with great difficulty and by a very small number of people within the society itself.

Knowing nature so little and agreeing so poorly on the meaning of the word "law," it would be quite difficult to come to some common understanding regarding a good definition of natural law. Thus all those definitions that are found in books have, over and above a lack of uniformity, the added fault of being drawn from several branches of knowledge which men do not naturally have, and from advantages the idea of which they cannot conceive until after having left the state of nature. Writers begin by seeking the rules on which, for the common utility, it would be appropriate for men to agree among themselves; and then they give the name *natural law* to the collection of these rules, with no other proof than the good which presumably would result from their universal observance. Surely this is a very convenient way to compose definitions and to explain the nature of things by virtually arbitrary views of what is seemly.

But as long as we are ignorant of natural man, it is futile for us to attempt to determine the law he has received or which is best suited to his constitution. All that we can see very clearly regarding this law is that, for it to be law, not only must the will of him who is obliged by it be capable of knowing submission to it, but also, for it to be natural, it must speak directly by the voice of nature.

Leaving aside therefore all the scientific books which teach us only to see men as they have made themselves, and meditating on the first and most simple operations of the human soul, I believe I perceive in it two principles that are prior to reason, of which one makes us ardently interested in our well-being and our self-preservation, and the other inspires in us a natural repugnance to seeing any sentient being, especially our fellow man, perish or suffer. It is from the conjunction and combination that our mind is in a position to make regarding these two principles, without the need for introducing that of sociability, that all the rules of natural right appear to me to flow; rules which reason is later forced to reestablish on other foundations, when, by its successive developments, it has succeeded in smothering nature.

In this way one is not obliged to make a man a philosopher before making him a man. His duties toward others are not uniquely dictated to him by the belated lessons of wisdom; and as long as he does not resist the inner impulse of compassion, he will never harm another man or even another sentient being, except in the legitimate instance where, if his preservation were involved, he is obliged to give preference to himself. By this means, an end can also be made to the ancient disputes regarding the participation of animals in the natural law. For it is clear that, lacking intelligence and liberty, they cannot recognize this law; but since they share to some extent in our nature by virtue of the sentient quality with which they are endowed, one will judge that they should also participate in natural right, and that man is subject to some sort of duties toward them. It seems, in effect, that if I am obliged not to do any harm to my fellow man, it is less because he is a rational being than because he is a sentient being: a quality that, since it is common to both animals and men, should at least give the former the right not to be needlessly mistreated by the latter.

This same study of original man, of his true needs and the fundamental principles of his duties, is also the only good means that can be used to remove those multitudes of difficulties which present themselves regarding the origin of moral inequality, the true foundations of the body politic, the reciprocal rights of its members, and a thousand other similar questions that are as important as they are poorly explained.

In considering human society from a tranquil and disinterested point of view it seems at first to manifest merely the violence of powerful men and the oppression of the weak. The mind revolts against the harshness of the former; one is inclined to deplore the blindness of the latter. And since nothing is less stable among men than those external relationships which chance brings about more often than wisdom, and which are called weakness or power, wealth or poverty, human establishments appear at first glance to be based on piles of shifting sand. It is only in examining them closely, only after having cleared away the dust and sand that surround the edifice, that one perceives the unshakeable base on which it is raised and one learns to respect its foundations. Now without a serious study of man, of his natural faculties and their successive developments, one will never succeed in making these distinctions and in separating, in the present constitution of things, what the divine will has done from what human art has pretended to do. The political and moral investigations occasioned by the important question I am examining are therefore useful in every way; and the hypothetical history of governments is an instructive lesson for man in every respect. In considering what we would have become, left to ourselves, we ought to learn to bless him whose beneficent hand, in correcting our institutions and giving them an unshakeable foundation, has prevented the disorders that must otherwise result from them, and has brought about our happiness from the means that seemed likely to add to our misery.

Learn whom God has ordered you to be, and in what part of human affairs you have been placed.

Notice on the Notes

I have added some notes to this work, following my indolent custom of working in fits and starts. Occasionally these notes wander so far from the subject that they are not good to read with the text. I therefore have consigned them to the end of the Discourse, in which I have tried my best to follow the straightest path. Those who have the courage to begin again will be able to amuse themselves the second time as they beat the bushes and try to run through the notes. There will be little harm done if others do not read them at·all.

[Translator's note: These notes are presented on p. 755. Additions to the text, made by Rousseau in the 1782 edition, are translated here and enclosed by brackets.]

QUESTION

Proposed by the Academy of Dijon
What is the Origin of Inequality Among Men, and is it Authorized by the Natural Law?

DISCOURSE ON THE ORIGIN AND FOUNDATIONS OF INEQUALITY AMONG MEN

It is of man that I have to speak, and the question I am examining indicates to me that I am going to be speaking to men, for such questions are not proposed by those who are afraid to honor the truth. I will therefore confidently defend the cause of humanity before the wise men who invite me to do so, and I will not be displeased with myself if I make myself worthy of my subject and my judges.

I conceive of two kinds of inequality in the human species: one which I call natural or physical, because it is established by nature and consists in the difference of age, health, bodily strength, and qualities of mind or soul. The other may be called moral or political inequality, because it depends on a kind of convention and is established, or at least authorized, by the consent of men. This latter type of inequality consists in the different privileges enjoyed by some at the expense of others, such as being richer, more

honored, more powerful than they, or even causing themselves to be obeyed by them.

There is no point in asking what the source of natural inequality is, because the answer would be found enunciated in the simple definition of the word. There is still less of a point in asking whether there would not be some essential connection between the two inequalities, for that would amount to asking whether those who command are necessarily better than those who obey, and whether strength of body or mind, wisdom or virtue are always found in the same individuals in proportion to power or wealth. Perhaps this is a good question for slaves to discuss within earshot of their masters, but it is not suitable for reasonable and free men who seek the truth.

Precisely what, then, is the subject of this discourse? To mark, in the progress of things, the moment when, right taking the place of violence, nature was subjected to the law. To explain the sequence of wonders by which the strong could resolve to serve the weak, and the people to buy imaginary repose at the price of real felicity.

The philosophers who have examined the foundations of society have all felt the necessity of returning to the state of nature, but none of them has reached it. Some have not hesitated to ascribe to man in that state the notion of just and unjust, without bothering to show that he had to have that notion, or even that it was useful to him. Others have spoken of the natural right that everyone has to preserve what belongs to him, without explaining what they mean by "belonging." Others started out by giving authority to the stronger over the weaker, and immediately brought about government, without giving any thought to the time that had to pass before the meaning of the words "authority" and "government" could exist among men. Finally, all of them, speaking continually of need, avarice, oppression, desires, and pride, have transferred to the state of nature the ideas they acquired in society. They spoke about savage man, and it was civil man they depicted. It did not even occur to most of our philosophers to doubt that the state of nature had existed, even though it is evident from reading the Holy Scriptures that the first man, having received enlightenment and precepts immediately from God, was not himself in that state; and if we give the writings of Moses the credence that every

Christian owes them, we must deny that, even before the flood, men were ever in the pure state of nature, unless they had fallen back into it because of some extraordinary event: a paradox that is quite awkward to defend and utterly impossible to prove.

Let us therefore begin by putting aside all the facts, for they have no bearing on the question. The investigations that may be undertaken concerning this subject should not be taken for historical truths, but only for hypothetical and conditional reasonings, better suited to shedding light on the nature of things than on pointing out their true origin, like those our physicists make everyday with regard to the formation of the world. Religion commands us to believe that since God himself drew men out of the state of nature, they are unequal because he wanted them to be so; but it does not forbid us to form conjectures, drawn solely from the nature of man and the beings that surround him, concerning what the human race could have become, if it had been left to itself. That is what I am asked, and what I propose to examine in this discourse. Since my subject concerns man in general, I will attempt to speak in terms that suit all nations, or rather, forgetting times and places in order to think only of the men to whom I am speaking, I will imagine I am in the Lyceum in Athens, reciting the lessons of my masters, having men like Plato and Xenocrates for my judges, and the human race for my audience.

O man, whatever country you may be from, whatever your opinions may be, listen: here is your history, as I have thought to read it, not in the books of your fellowmen, who are liars, but in nature, who never lies. Everything that comes from nature will be true; there will be nothing false except what I have unintentionally added. The times about which I am going to speak are quite remote: how much you have changed from what you were! It is, as it were, the life of your species that I am about to describe to you according to the qualities you have received, which your education and your habits have been able to corrupt but have been unable to destroy. There is, I feel, an age at which an individual man would want to stop. You will seek the age at which you would want your species to have stopped. Dissatisfied with your present state for reasons that portend even greater grounds for dissatisfaction for your unhappy posterity, perhaps you

would like to be able to go backwards in time. This feeling should be a hymn in praise of your first ancestors, the criticism of your contemporaries, and the dread of those who have the unhappiness of living after you.

Part One

However important it may be, in order to render sound judgments regarding the natural state of man, to consider him from his origin and to examine him, so to speak, in the first embryo of the species, I will not follow his nature through its successive developments. I will not stop to investigate in the animal kingdom what he might have been at the beginning so as eventually to become what he is. I will not examine whether, as Aristotle thinks, man's elongated nails were not at first hooked claws, whether man was not furry like a bear, and whether, if man walked on all fours,[3] his gaze, directed toward the ground and limited to a horizon of a few steps—did not provide an indication of both the character and the limits of his ideas. On this subject I could form only vague and almost imaginary conjectures. Comparative anatomy has as yet made too little progress; the observations of naturalists are as yet too uncertain for one to be able to establish the basis of solid reasoning on such foundations. Thus, without having recourse to the supernatural knowledge we have on this point, and without taking note of the changes that must have occurred in the internal as well as the external conformation of man, as he applied his limbs to new purposes and nourished himself on new foods, I will suppose him to have been formed from all time as I see him today: walking on two feet, using his hands as we use ours, directing his gaze over all of nature, and measuring with his eyes the vast expanse of the heavens.

When I strip that being, thus constituted, of all the supernatural gifts he could have received and of all the artificial faculties he could have acquired only through long progress; when I consider him, in a word, as he must have left the hands of nature, I see an animal less strong than some, less agile than others, but all in all, the most advantageously organized of all. I see him satisfying his hunger under an oak tree, quenching his thirst at the first stream, finding his bed at the foot of the same tree that supplied his meal; and thus all his needs are satisfied.

When the earth is left to its natural fertility[4] and covered with immense forests that were never mutilated by the axe, it offers storehouses and shelters at every step to animals of every species. Men, dispersed among the animals, observe and imitate their industry, and thereby raise themselves to the level of animal instinct, with the advantage that, whereas each species has only its own instincts, man, who may perhaps have none that belongs to him, appropriates all of them to himself, feeds himself equally well on most of the various foods[5] which the other animals divide among themselves, and consequently finds his sustenance more easily than any of the rest can.

Accustomed from childhood to inclement weather and the rigors of the seasons, acclimated to fatigue, and forced, naked and without arms, to defend their lives and their prey against other ferocious beasts, or to escape them by taking flight, men develop a robust and nearly unalterable temperament. Children enter the world with the excellent constitution of their parents and strengthen it with the same exercises that produced it, thus acquiring all the vigor that the human race is capable of having. Nature treats them precisely the way the law of Sparta treated the children of its citizens: it renders strong and robust those who are well constituted and makes all the rest perish, thereby differing from our present-day societies, where the state, by making children burdensome to their parents, kills them indiscriminately before their birth.

Since the savage man's body is the only instrument he knows, he employs it for a variety of purposes that, for lack of practice, ours are incapable of serving. And our industry deprives us of the force and agility that necessity obliges him to acquire. If he had had an axe, would his wrists break such strong branches? If he had had a sling, would he throw a stone with so much force? If he had had a ladder, would he climb a tree so nimbly? If he had had a horse, would he run so fast? Give a civilized man time to gather all his machines around him, and undoubtedly he will easily overcome a savage man. But if you want to see an even more unequal fight, pit them against each other naked and disarmed, and you will soon realize the advantage of constantly having all of one's

forces at one's disposal, of always being ready for any event, and of always carrying one's entire self, as it were, with one.[6]

Hobbes maintains that man is naturally intrepid and seeks only to attack and to fight. On the other hand, an illustrious philosopher thinks, and Cumberland and Pufendorf also affirm, that nothing is as timid as man in the state of nature, and that he is always trembling and ready to take flight at the slightest sound he hears or at the slightest movement he perceives. That may be the case with regard to objects with which he is not acquainted. And I do not doubt that he is frightened by all the new sights that present themselves to him every time he can neither discern the physical good and evil he may expect from them nor compare his forces with the dangers he must run: rare circumstances in the state of nature, where everything takes place in such a uniform manner and where the face of the earth is not subject to those sudden and continual changes caused by the passions and inconstancy of peoples living together. But since a savage man lives dispersed among the animals and, finding himself early on in a position to measure himself against them, he soon makes the comparison; and, aware that he surpasses them in skillfulness more than they surpass him in strength, he learns not to fear them any more. Pit a bear or a wolf against a savage who is robust, agile, and courageous, as they all are, armed with stones and a hefty cudgel, and you will see that the danger will be at least equal on both sides, and that after several such experiences, ferocious beasts, which do not like to attack one another, will be quite reluctant to attack a man, having found him to be as ferocious as themselves. With regard to animals that actually have more strength than man has skillfulness, he is in the same position as other weaker species, which nevertheless subsist. Man has the advantage that, since he is no less adept than they at running and at finding almost certain refuge in trees, he always has the alternative of accepting or leaving the encounter and the choice of taking flight or entering into combat. Moreover, it appears that no animal naturally attacks man, except in the case of self-defense or extreme hunger, or shows evidence of those violent antipathies toward him that seem to indicate that one species is destined by nature to serve as food for another.

[No doubt these are the reasons why negroes and savages bother themselves so little about the ferocious beasts they may encounter in the woods. In this respect, the Caribs of Venezuela, among others, live in the most profound security and without the slightest inconvenience. Although they are practically naked, says Francisco Coreal, they boldly expose themselves in the forest, armed only with bow and arrow, but no one has ever heard of one of them being devoured by animals.]

There are other, more formidable enemies, against which man does not have the same means of self-defense: natural infirmities, childhood, old age, and illnesses of all kinds—sad signs of our weakness, of which the first two are common to all animals, with the last belonging principally to man living in society. On the subject of childhood, I even observe that a mother, by carrying her child everywhere with her, can feed it much more easily than females of several animal species, which are forced to be continually coming and going, with great fatigue, to seek their food and to suckle or feed their young. It is true that if a woman were to perish, the child runs a considerable risk of perishing with her. But this danger is common to a hundred other species, whose young are for quite some time incapable of going off to seek their nourishment for themselves. And although childhood is longer among us, our lifespan is also longer; thus things are more or less equal in this respect,[7] although there are other rules, not relevant to my subject, which are concerned with the duration of infancy and the number of young.[8] Among the elderly, who are less active and perspire little, the need for food diminishes with the faculty of providing for it. And since savage life shields them from gout and rheumatism, and since old age is, of all ills, the one that human assistance can least alleviate, they eventually die without anyone being aware that they are ceasing to exist, and almost without being aware of it themselves.

With regard to illnesses, I will not repeat the vain and false pronouncements made against medicine by the majority of people in good health. Rather, I will ask whether there is any solid observation on the basis of which one can conclude that the average lifespan is shorter in those countries where the art of medicine is most neglected than in those where it is cultivated most assiduously. And how could that be the case, if we give ourselves more ills than medicine can furnish us remedies? The extreme inequality in our lifestyle: excessive idleness among some, excessive labor among others; the ease with which we arouse and satisfy our appetites and our sensuality; the overly refined foods of the wealthy, which nourish them with irritating juices and overwhelm them with indigestion; the bad food of the poor, who most of the time do not have even that, and who, for want of food, are inclined to stuff their stomachs greedily whenever possible; staying up until all hours, excesses of all kinds, immoderate outbursts of every passion, bouts of fatigue and mental exhaustion; countless sorrows and afflictions which are felt in all levels of society and which perpetually gnaw away at souls: these are the fatal proofs that most of our ills are of our own making, and that we could have avoided nearly all of them by preserving the simple, regular and solitary lifestyle prescribed to us by nature. If nature has destined us to be healthy, I almost dare to affirm that the state of reflection is a state contrary to nature and that the man who meditates is a depraved animal. When one thinks about the stout constitutions of the savages, at least of those whom we have not ruined with our strong liquors; when one becomes aware of the fact that they know almost no illnesses but wounds and old age, one is strongly inclined to believe that someone could easily write the history of human maladies by following the history of civil societies. This at least was the opinion of Plato, who believed that, from certain remedies used or approved by Podalirius and Machaon at the siege of Troy, various illnesses which these remedies should exacerbate were as yet unknown among men. [And Celsus reports that diet, so necessary today, was only an invention of Hippocrates.]

With so few sources of ills, man in the state of nature hardly has any need therefore of remedies, much less of physicians. The human race is in no worse condition than all the others in this respect; and it is easy to learn from hunters whether in their chases they find many sick animals. They find quite a few that have received serious wounds that healed quite nicely, that have had bones or even limbs broken and reset with no other surgeon than time, no other regimen than their everyday life, and that are no less perfectly cured for not having been tormented with incisions, poisoned with drugs, or exhausted with fasting. Finally, however correctly administered medicine may be among us, it is still certain that although a sick savage, abandoned to himself, has nothing to hope for except from nature, on the other hand, he has nothing to fear except his illness. This frequently makes his situation preferable to ours.

Therefore we must take care not to confuse savage man with the men we have before our eyes. Nature treats all animals left to their own devices with a partiality that seems to show how jealous she is of that right. The horse, the cat, the bull, even the ass, are usually taller, and all of them have a more robust constitution, more vigor, more strength, and more courage in the forests than in our homes. They lose half of these advantages in becoming domesticated; it might be said that all our efforts at feeding them and treating them well only end in their degeneration. It is the same for man himself. In becoming habituated to the ways of society and a slave, he becomes weak, fearful, and servile; his soft and effeminate lifestyle completes the enervation of both his strength and his courage. Let us add that the difference between the savage man and the domesticated man should be still greater than that between the savage animal and the domesticated animal; for while animal and man have been treated equally by nature, man gives more comforts to himself than to the animals he tames, and all of these comforts are so many specific causes that make him degenerate more noticeably.

It is therefore no great misfortune for those first men, nor, above all, such a great obstacle to their preservation, that they are naked, that they have no dwelling, and that they lack all those useful things we take to be so necessary. If they do not have furry skin, they have no need for it in warm countries, and in cold countries they soon learn to help themselves to the skins of animals they have vanquished. If they have but two feet to run with, they have two arms to provide for their defense and for their needs. Perhaps their children learn to walk late and with difficulty, but mothers carry them easily: an advantage that is lacking in other species, where the mother, on being pursued, finds herself forced to abandon her young or to conform her pace to theirs. [It is possible there are some exceptions to this. For example, the animal

from the province of Nicaragua which resembles a fox and which has feet like a man's hands, and, according to Coreal, has a pouch under its belly in which the mother places her young when she is forced to take flight. No doubt this is the same animal that is called *tlaquatzin* in Mexico; the female of the species Laët describes as having a similar pouch for the same purpose.] Finally, unless we suppose those singular and fortuitous combinations of circumstances of which I will speak later, and which might very well have never taken place, at any rate it is clear that the first man who made clothing or a dwelling for himself was giving himself things that were hardly necessary, since he had done without them until then and since it is not clear why, as a grown man, he could not endure the kind of life he had endured ever since he was a child.

Alone, idle, and always near danger, savage man must like to sleep and be a light sleeper like animals which do little thinking and, as it were, sleep the entire time they are not thinking. Since his self-preservation was practically his sole concern, his best trained faculties ought to be those that have attack and defense as their principal object, either to subjugate his prey or to prevent his becoming the prey of another animal. On the other hand, the organs that are perfected only by softness and sensuality must remain in a state of crudeness that excludes any kind of refinement in him. And with his senses being divided in this respect, he will have extremely crude senses of touch and taste; those of sight, hearing and smell will have the greatest subtlety. Such is the state of animals in general, and, according to the reports of travellers, such also is that of the majority of savage peoples. Thus we should not be surprised that the Hottentots of the Cape of Good Hope can sight ships with the naked eye as far out at sea as the Dutch can with telescopes; or that the savages of America were as capable of trailing Spaniards by smell as the best dogs could have done; or that all these barbarous nations endure their nakedness with no discomfort, whet their appetites with hot peppers, and drink European liquors like water.

So far I have considered only physical man. Let us now try to look at him from a metaphysical and moral point of view.

In any animal I see nothing but an ingenious

machine to which nature has given senses in order for it to renew its strength and to protect itself, to a certain point, from all that tends to destroy or disturb it. I am aware of precisely the same things in the human machine, with the difference that nature alone does everything in the operations of an animal, whereas man contributes, as a free agent, to his own operations. The former chooses or rejects by instinct and the later by an act of freedom. Hence an animal cannot deviate from the rule that is prescribed to it, even when it would be advantageous to do so, while man deviates from it, often to his own detriment. Thus a pigeon would die of hunger near a bowl filled with choice meats, and so would a cat perched atop a pile of fruit or grain, even though both could nourish themselves quite well with the food they disdain, if they were of a mind to try some. And thus dissolute men abandon themselves to excesses which cause them fever and death, because the mind perverts the senses and because the will still speaks when nature is silent.

Every animal has ideas, since it has senses; up to a certain point it even combines its ideas, and in this regard man differs from an animal only in degree. Some philosophers have even suggested that there is a greater difference between two given men than between a given man and an animal. Therefore it is not so much understanding which causes the specific distinction of man from all other animals as it is his being a free agent. Nature commands every animal, and beasts obey. Man feels the same impetus, but he knows he is free to go along or to resist; and it is above all in the awareness of this freedom that the spirituality of his soul is made manifest. For physics explains in some way the mechanism of the senses and the formation of ideas; but in the power of willing, or rather of choosing, and in the feeling of this power, we find only purely spiritual acts, about which the laws of mechanics explain nothing.

But if the difficulties surrounding all these questions should leave some room for dispute on this difference between man and animal, there is another very specific quality which distinguishes them and about which there can be no argument: the faculty of self-perfection, a faculty which, with the aid of circumstances, successively develops all the others, and resides among us as much in the species as in the individual. On the other hand, an animal, at the end of a few months, is what it will be all its life; and its species, at the end of a thousand years, is what it was in the first of those thousand years. Why is man alone subject to becoming an imbecile? Is it not that he thereby returns to his primitive state, and that, while the animal which has acquired nothing and which also has nothing to lose, always retains its instinct, man, in losing through old age or other accidents all that his *perfectibility* has enabled him to acquire, thus falls even lower than the animal itself? It would be sad for us to be forced to agree that this distinctive and almost unlimited faculty is the source of all man's misfortunes; that this is what, by dint of time, draws him out of that original condition in which he would pass tranquil and innocent days; that this is what, through centuries of giving rise to his enlightenment and his errors, his vices and his virtues, eventually makes him a tyrant over himself and nature.[9] It would be dreadful to be obliged to praise as a beneficent being the one who first suggested to the inhabitant on the banks of the Orinoco the use of boards which he binds to his children's temples, and which assure them of at least part of their imbecility and their original happiness.

Savage man, left by nature to instinct alone, or rather compensated for the instinct he is perhaps lacking by faculties capable of first replacing them and then of raising him to the level of instinct, will therefore begin with purely animal functions.[10] Perceiving and feeling will be his first state, which he will have in common with all animals. Willing and not willing, desiring, and fearing will be the first and nearly the only operations of his soul until new circumstances bring about new developments in it.

Whatever the moralists may say about it, human understanding owes much to the passions, which, by common consensus, also owe a great deal to it. It is by their activity that our reason is perfected. We seek to know only because we desire to find enjoyment; and it is impossible to conceive why someone who had neither desires nor fears would go to the bother of reasoning. The passions in turn take their origin from our needs, and their progress from our knowledge. For one can desire or fear things only by virtue of the ideas one can have of them, or from the simple impulse of nature; and savage man, deprived of every sort of enlightenment, feels only the passion of this latter sort. His desires do not go beyond his physical needs.[11] The only goods he knows in the universe are nourishment, a woman and rest; the only evils he fears are pain and hunger. I say pain and not death because an animal will never know what it is to die; and knowledge of death and its terrors is one of the first acquisitions that man has made in withdrawing from the animal condition.

Were it necessary, it would be easy for me to support this view with facts and to demonstrate that, among all the nations of the world, the progress of the mind has been precisely proportionate to the needs received by peoples from nature or to those needs to which circumstances have subjected them, and consequently to the passions which inclined them to provide for those needs. I would show the arts coming into being in Egypt and spreading with the flooding of the Nile. I would follow their progress among the Greeks, where they were seen to germinate, grow and rise to the heavens among the sands and rocks of Attica, though never being able to take root on the fertile banks of the Eurotas. I would point out that in general the peoples of the north are more industrious than those of the south, because they cannot get along as well without being so, as if nature thereby wanted to equalize things by giving to their minds the fertility it refuses their soil.

But without having recourse to the uncertain testimony of history, does anyone fail to see that everything seems to remove savage man from the temptation and the means of ceasing to be savage? His imagination depicts nothing to him; his heart asks nothing of him. His modest needs are so easily found at hand, and he is so far from the degree of knowledge necessary to make him desire to acquire greater knowledge, that he can have neither foresight nor curiosity. The spectacle of nature becomes a matter of indifference to him by dint of its becoming familiar to him. It is always the same order, always the same succession of changes. He does not have a mind for marveling at the greatest wonders; and we must not seek in him the philosophy that a man needs in order to know how to observe once what he has seen everyday. His soul, agitated by nothing, is given over to the single feeling of his own present existence, without any idea of the future, however, near it may be, and his proj-

ects, as limited as his views, hardly extend to the end of the day. Such is, even today, the extent of the Carib's foresight. In the morning he sells his bed of cotton and in the evening he returns in tears to buy it back, for want of having foreseen that he would need it that night.

The more one meditates on this subject, the more the distance from pure sensations to the simplest knowledge increases before our eyes; and it is impossible to conceive how a man could have crossed such a wide gap by his forces alone, without the aid of communication and without the provocation of necessity. How many centuries have perhaps gone by before men were in a position to see any fire other than that from the heavens? How many different risks did they have to run before they learned the most common uses of that element? How many times did they let it go out before they had acquired the art of reproducing it? And how many times perhaps did each of these secrets die with the one who had discovered it? What will we say about agriculture, an art that requires so much labor and foresight, that depends on so many other arts, that quite obviously is practicable only in a society which is at least in its beginning stages, and that serves us not so much to derive from the earth food it would readily provide without agriculture, as to force from it those preferences that are most to our taste? But let us suppose that men multiplied to the point where the natural productions were no longer sufficient to nourish them: a supposition which, it may be said in passing, would show a great advantage for the human species in that way of life. Let us suppose that, without forges or workshops, farm implements had fallen from the heavens into the hands of the savages; that these men had conquered the mortal hatred they all have for continuous work; that they had learned to foresee their needs far enough in advance; that they had guessed how the soil is to be cultivated, grains sown, and trees planted; that they had discovered the arts of grinding wheat and fermenting grapes: all things they would need to have been taught by the gods, for it is inconceivable how they could have picked these things up on their own. Yet, after all this, what man would be so foolish as to tire himself out cultivating a field that will be plundered by the first comer, be it man or beast, who takes a fancy to the crop? And how could each man resolve to spend his life in hard labor, when, the more necessary to him the fruits of his labor may be, the surer he is of not realizing them? In a word, how could this situation lead men to cultivate the soil as long as it is not divided among them, that is to say, as long as the state of nature is not wiped out?

Were we to want to suppose a savage man as skilled in the art of thinking as our philosophers make him out to be; were we, following their example, to make him a full-fledged philosopher, discovering by himself the most sublime truths, and, by chains of terribly abstract reasoning, forming for himself maxims of justice and reason drawn from the love of order in general or from the known will of his creator; in a word, were we to suppose there was in his mind as much intelligence and enlightenment as he needs, and is in fact found to have dullness and stupidity, what use would the species have for all that metaphysics, which could not be communicated and which would perish with the individual who would have invented it? What progress could the human race make, scattered in the woods among the animals? And to what extent could men mutually perfect and enlighten one another, when, with neither a fixed dwelling nor any need for one another, they would hardly encounter one another twice in their lives, without knowing or talking to one another.

Let us consider how many ideas we owe to the use of speech; how much grammar trains and facilitates the operations of the mind. And let us think of the inconceivable difficulties and the infinite amount of time that the first invention of languages must have cost. Let us join their reflections to the preceding ones, and we will be in a position to judge how many thousands of centuries would have been necessary to develop successively in the human mind the operations of which it was capable.

May I be permitted to consider for a moment the obstacles to the origin of languages. I could be content here to cite or repeat the investigations that the Abbé de Condillac has made on this matter, all of which completely confirm my view, and may perhaps have given me the idea in the first place. But since the way in which this philosopher resolves the difficulties he himself raises concerning the origin of conventional signs shows that he assumed what I question (namely, a kind of society already established among the inventors of language), I believe that, in referring to his reflections, I must add to them my own, in order to present the same difficulties from a standpoint that is pertinent to my subject. The first that presents itself is to imagine how languages could have become necessary; for since men had no communication among themselves nor any need for it, I fail to see either the necessity of this invention or its possibility, if it were not indispensable. I might well say, as do many others, that languages were born in the domestic intercourse among fathers, mothers, and children. But aside from the fact that this would not resolve the difficulties, it would make the mistake of those who, reasoning about the state of nature, intrude into it ideas taken from society. They always see the family gathered in one and the same dwelling, with its members maintaining among themselves a union as intimate and permanent as exists among us, where so many common interests unite them. But the fact of the matter is that in that primitive state, since nobody had houses or huts or property of any kind, each one bedded down in some random spot and often for only one night. Males and females came together fortuitously as a result of chance encounters, occasion, and desire, without there being any great need for words to express what they had to say to one another. They left one another with the same nonchalance.[12] The mother at first nursed her children for her own need; then, with habit having endeared them to her, she later nourished them for their own need. Once they had the strength to look for their food, they did not hesitate to leave the mother herself. And since there was practically no other way of finding one another than not to lose sight of one another, they were soon at the point of not even recognizing one another. It should also be noted that, since the child had all his needs to explain and consequently more things to say to the mother than the mother to the child, it is the child who must make the greatest effort toward inventing a language, and that the language he uses should in large part be of his own making, which multiplies languages as many times as there are individuals to speak them. This tendency was abetted by a nomadic and vagabond life, which does not give any idiom time to gain a foothold. For claiming that the mother teaches her child the words he ought to use in asking her for this or that is a good way of showing how already formed languages are taught, but it does not tell us how languages are formed.

Let us suppose this first difficulty has been overcome. Let us disregard for a moment the immense space that there must have been between the pure state of nature and the need for languages. And, on the supposition that they are necessary,[13] let us inquire how they might have begun to be established. Here we come to a new difficulty, worse still than the preceding one. For if men needed speech in order to learn to think, they had a still greater need for knowing how to think in order to discover the art of speaking. And even if it were understood how vocal sounds had been taken for the conventional expressions of our ideas, it would still remain for us to determine what could have been the conventional expressions for ideas that, not having a sensible object, could not be indicated either by gesture or by voice. Thus we are scarcely able to form tenable conjectures regarding the birth of this art of communicating thoughts and establishing intercourse between minds, a sublime art which is already quite far from its origin, but which the philosopher still sees at so prodigious a distance from its perfection that there is no man so foolhardy as to claim that it will ever achieve it, even if the sequences of change that time necessarily brings were suspended in its favor, even if prejudices were to be barred from the academies or be silent before them, and even if they were able to occupy themselves with that thorny problem for whole centuries without interruption.

Man's first language, the most universal, the most energetic and the only language he needed before it was necessary to persuade men assembled together, is the cry of nature. Since this cry was elicited only by a kind of instinct in pressing circumstances, to beg for help in great dangers, or for relief of violent ills, it was not used very much in the ordinary course of life, where more moderate feelings prevail. When the ideas of men begin to spread and multiply, and closer communication was established among them, they sought more numerous signs and a more extensive language. They multiplied vocal inflections and combined them with gestures, which, by their nature, are more expressive, and whose meaning is less dependent on a prior determination. They therefore signi-

fied visible and mobile objects by means of gestures, and audible ones by imitative sounds. But since a gesture indicates hardly anything more than present or easily described objects and visible actions; since its use is not universal, because darkness or the interposition of a body renders it useless; and since it requires rather than stimulates attention, men finally thought of replacing them with vocal articulations, which, while not having the same relationship to certain ideas, were better suited to represent all ideas as conventional signs. Such a substitution could only be made by a common consent and in a way rather difficult to practice for men whose crude organs had as yet no exercise, and still more difficult to conceive in itself, since that unanimous agreement had to have had a motive, and speech appears to have been necessary in order to establish the use of speech.

We must infer that the first words men used had a much broader meaning in their mind than do those used in languages that are already formed; and that, being ignorant of the division of discourse into its constitutive parts, at first they gave each word the meaning of a whole sentence. When they began to distinguish subject from attribute and verb from noun, which was no mean effort of genius, substantives were at first only so many proper nouns; the [present] infinitive was the only verb tense; and the notion of adjectives must have developed only with considerable difficulty, since every adjective is an abstract word, and abstractions are difficult and not particularly natural operations.

At first each object was given a particular name, without regard to genus and species which those first founders were not in a position to distinguish; and all individual things presented themselves to their minds in isolation, as they are in the spectacle of nature. If one oak tree was called A, another was called B. [For the first idea one draws from two things is that they are not the same; and it often requires quite some time to observe what they have in common.] Thus the more limited the knowledge, the more extensive becomes the dictionary. The difficulty inherent in all this nomenclature could not easily be alleviated, for in order to group beings under various common and generic denominations, it was necessary to know their properties and their differences. Observations and definitions were necessary, that is to say, natural history and metaphysics, and far more than men of those times could have had.

Moreover, general ideas can be introduced into the mind only with the aid of words, and the understanding grasps them only through sentences. That is one reason why animals cannot form such ideas or even acquire the perfectibility that depends on them. When a monkey moves unhesitatingly from one nut to another, does anyone think the monkey has the general idea of that type of fruit and that he compares its archetype with these two individuals? Undoubtedly not; but the sight of one of these nuts recalls to his memory the sensations he received of the other; and his eyes, modified in a certain way, announce to his sense of taste the modification it is about to receive. Every general idea is purely intellectual. The least involvement of the imagination thereupon makes the idea particular. Try to draw for yourself the image of a tree in general; you will never succeed in doing it. In spite of yourself, it must be seen as small or large, barren or leafy, light or dark; and if you were in a position to see in it nothing but what you see in every tree, this image would no longer resemble a tree. Purely abstract beings are perceived in the same way, or are conceived only through discourse. The definition of a triangle alone gives you the true idea of it. As soon as you behold one in your mind, it is a particular triangle and not some other one, and you cannot avoid making its lines to be perceptible or its plane to have color. It is therefore necessary to utter sentences, and thus to speak, in order to have general ideas. For as soon as the imagination stops, the mind proceeds no further without the aid of discourse. If, then, the first inventors of language could give names only to ideas they already had, it follows that the first substantives could not have been anything but proper nouns.

But when, by means I am unable to conceive, our new grammarians began to extend their ideas and to generalize their words, the ignorance of the inventors must have subjected this method to very strict limitations. And just as they had at first unduly multiplied the names of individual things, owing to their failure to know the genera and species, they later made too few species and genera, owing to their failure to have considered beings in all their differences. Pushing these divisions far enough would have required more experience and enlightenment than they could have had, and more investigations and work than they were willing to put into it. Now if even today new species are discovered everyday that until now had escaped all our observations, just imagine how many species must have escaped the attention of men who judged things only on first appearance! As for primary classes and the most general notions, it is superfluous to add that they too must have escaped them. How, for example, would they have imagined or understood the words "matter," "mind," "substance," "mode," "figure," and "movement," when our philosophers, who for so long have been making use of them, have a great deal of difficulty understanding them themselves; and when, since the ideas attached to these words are purely metaphysical, they found no model of them in nature?

I stop with these first steps, and I implore my judges to suspend their reading here to consider, concerning the invention of physical substantives alone, that is to say, concerning the easiest part of the language to discover, how far language still had to go in order to express all the thoughts of men, assume a durable form, be capable of being spoken in public, and influence society. I implore them to reflect upon how much time and knowledge were needed to discover numbers,[14] abstract words, aorists, and all the tenses of verbs, particles, syntax, the connecting of sentences, reasoning, and the forming of all the logic of discourse. As for myself, being shocked by the unending difficulties and convinced of the almost demonstrable impossibility that languages could have arisen and been established by merely human means, I leave to anyone who would undertake it the discussion of the following difficult problem: which was the more necessary: an already formed society for the invention of languages, or an already invented language for the establishment of society?

Whatever these origins may be, it is clear, from the little care taken by nature to bring men together through mutual needs and to facilitate their use of speech, how little she prepared them for becoming habituated to the ways of society, and how little she contributed to all that men have done to establish the bonds of society. In fact, it is impossible to imagine why, in that primitive state, one man would have a greater need for another man than a monkey or a wolf has for another of its respective species; or, assuming this need, what motive could induce the other man to satisfy it; or even, in this latter instance, how they could be in mutual agreement regarding the conditions. I know that we are repeatedly told that nothing would have been so miserable as man in that state; and if it is true, as I believe I have proved, that it is only after many centuries that men could have had the desire and the opportunity to leave that state, that would be a charge to bring against nature, not against him whom nature has thus constituted. But if we understand the word *miserable* properly, it is a word which is without meaning or which signifies merely a painful privation and suffering of the body or the soul. Now I would very much like someone to explain to me what kind of misery can there be for a free being whose heart is at peace and whose body is in good health? I ask which of the two, civil or natural life, is more likely to become insufferable to those who live it? We see about us practically no people who do not complain about their existence; many even deprive themselves of it to the extent they are able, and the combination of divine and human laws is hardly enough to stop this disorder. I ask if anyone has ever heard tell of a savage who was living in liberty ever dreaming of complaining about his life and of killing himself. Let the judgment therefore be made with less pride on which side real misery lies. On the other hand, nothing would have been so miserable as savage man, dazzled by enlightenment, tormented by passions, and reasoning about a state different from his own. It was by a very wise providence that the latent faculties he possessed should develop only as the occasion to exercise them presents itself, so that they would be neither superfluous nor troublesome to him beforehand, nor underdeveloped and useless in time of need. In instinct alone, man had everything he needed in order to live in the state of nature; in a cultivated reason, he has only what he needs to live in society.

At first it would seem that men in that state, having among themselves no type of moral relations or acknowledged duties, could be neither good nor evil, and had neither vices nor virtues, unless, if we take these words in a physical sense, we call those qualities that can harm an individual's preservation "vices" in him, and those that can contribute to it "virtues." In

that case it would be necessary to call the one who least resists the simple impulses of nature the most virtuous. But without departing from the standard meaning of these words, it is appropriate to suspend the judgment we could make regarding such a situation and to be on our guard against our prejudices, until we have examined with scale in hand whether there are more virtues than vices among civilized men; or whether their virtues are more advantageous than their vices are lethal; or whether the progress of their knowledge is sufficient compensation for ills they inflict on one another as they learn of the good they ought to do; or whether, all things considered, they would not be in a happier set of circumstances if they had neither evil to fear nor good to hope for from anyone, rather than subjecting themselves to a universal dependence and obliging themselves to receive everything from those who do not oblige themselves to give them anything.

Above all, let us not conclude with Hobbes that because man has no idea of goodness he is naturally evil; that he is vicious because he does not know virtue; that he always refuses to perform services for his fellow men he does not believe he owes them; or that, by virtue of the right, which he reasonably attributes to himself, to those things he needs, he foolishly imagines himself to be the sole proprietor of the entire universe. Hobbes has very clearly seen the defect of all modern definitions of natural right, but the consequences he draws from his own definition show that he takes it in a sense that is no less false. Were he to have reasoned on the basis of the principles he establishes, this author should have said that since the state of nature is the state in which the concern for our self-preservation is the least prejudicial to that of others, that state was consequently the most appropriate for peace and the best suited for the human race. He says precisely the opposite, because he had wrongly injected into the savage man's concern for self-preservation the need to satisfy a multitude of passions which are the product of society and which have made laws necessary. The evil man, he says, is a robust child. It remains to be seen whether savage man is a robust child. Were we to grant him this, what would we conclude from it? That if this man were as dependent on others when he is robust as he is when he is weak, there is no type of excess

to which he would not tend: he would beat his mother
if she were too slow in offering him her breast; he
would strangle one of his younger brothers, should
he find him annoying; he would bite someone's leg,
should he be assaulted or aggravated by him. But
being robust and being dependent are two contradictory suppositions in the state of nature. Man is weak
when he is dependent, and he is emancipated from
that dependence before he is robust. Hobbes did not
see that the same cause preventing savages from using
their reason, as our jurists claim, is what prevents
them at the same time from abusing their faculties,
as he himself maintains. Hence we could say that
savages are not evil precisely because they do not
know what it is to be good; for it is neither the development of enlightenment nor the restraint imposed by
the law, but the calm of the passions and the ignorance of vice which prevents them from doing evil.
*So much more profitable to these is the ignorance of
vice than the knowledge of virtue is to those.* Moreover,
there is another principle that Hobbes failed to notice,
and which, having been given to man in order to
mitigate, in certain circumstances, the ferocity of his
egocentrism or the desire for self-preservation before
this egocentrism of his came into being,[15] tempers
the ardor he has for his own well-being by an innate
repugnance to seeing his fellow men suffer. I do not
believe I have any contradiction to fear in granting the
only natural virtue that the most excessive detractor of
human virtues was forced to recognize. I am referring
to pity, a disposition that is fitting for beings that are
as weak and as subject to ills as we are; a virtue all
the more universal and all the more useful to man
in that it precedes in him any kind of reflection,
and so natural that even animals sometimes show
noticeable signs of it. Without speaking of the tenderness of mothers for their young and of the perils they
have to brave in order to protect them, one daily
observes the repugnance that horses have for trampling a living body with their hooves. An animal does
not go undisturbed past a dead animal of its own
species. There are even some animals that give them
a kind of sepulchre; and the mournful lowing of cattle
entering a slaughterhouse voices the impression they
receive of the horrible spectacle that strikes them.
One notes with pleasure the author of *The Fable of
the Bees*, having been forced to acknowledge man as

a compassionate and sensitive being, departing from
his cold and subtle style in the example he gives, to
offer us the pathetic image of an imprisoned man
who sees outside his cell a ferocious animal tearing
a child from its mother's breast, mashing its frail limbs
with its murderous teeth, and ripping with its claws
the child's quivering entrails. What horrible agitation
must be felt by this witness of an event in which he
has no personal interest! What anguish must he suffer
at this sight, being unable to be of any help to the
fainting mother or to the dying child?

Such is the pure movement of nature prior to all
reflection. Such is the force of natural pity, which the
most depraved mores still have difficulty destroying,
since everyday one sees in our theaters someone affected and weeping at the ills of some unfortunate
person, and who, were he in the tyrant's place, would
intensify the torments of his enemy still more; [like
the bloodthirsty Sulla, so sensitive to ills he had not
caused, or like Alexander of Pherae, who did not dare
attend the performance of any tragedy, for fear of
being seen weeping with Andromache and Priam,
and yet who listened impassively to the cries of so
many citizens who were killed everyday on his orders.
*Nature, in giving men tears, bears witness that she
gave the human race the softest hearts.*] Mandeville
has a clear awareness that, with all their mores, men
would never have been anything but monsters, if
nature had not given them pity to aid their reason;
but he has not seen that from this quality alone flow
all the social virtues that he wants to deny in men.
In fact, what are generosity, mercy, and humanity, if
not pity applied to the weak, to the guilty, or to the
human species in general. Benevolence and even
friendship are, properly understood, the products of
a constant pity fixed on a particular object; for is
desiring that someone not suffer anything but desiring
that he be happy? Were it true that commiseration
were merely a sentiment that puts us in the position
of the one who suffers, a sentiment that is obscure
and powerful in savage man, developed but weak in
man dwelling in civil society, what importance would
this idea have to the truth of what I say, except to
give it more force? In fact, commiseration will be all
the more energetic as the witnessing animal identifies
itself more intimately with the suffering animal. Now
it is evident that this identification must have been

infinitely closer in the state of nature than in the state of reasoning. Reason is what engenders egocentrism, and reflection strengthens it. Reason is what turns man in upon himself. Reason is what separates him from all that troubles him and afflicts him. Philosophy is what isolates him and what moves him to say in secret, at the sight of a suffering man, "Perish if you will; I am safe and sound." No longer can anything but danger to the entire society trouble the tranquil slumber of the philosopher and yank him from his bed. His fellow man can be killed with impunity underneath his window. He has merely to place his hands over his ears and argue with himself a little in order to prevent nature, which rebels within him, from identifying him with the man being assassinated. Savage man does not have this admirable talent, and for lack of wisdom and reason he is always seen thoughtlessly giving in to the first sentiment of humanity. When there is a riot or a street brawl, the populace gathers together; the prudent man withdraws from the scene. It is the rabble, the women of the marketplace, who separate the combatants and prevent decent people from killing one another.

It is therefore quite certain that pity is a natural sentiment, which, by moderating in each individual the activity of the love of oneself, contributes to the mutual preservation of the entire species. Pity is what carries us without reflection to the aid of those we see suffering. Pity is what, in the state of nature, takes the place of laws, mores, and virtue, with the advantage that no one is tempted to disobey its sweet voice. Pity is what will prevent every robust savage from robbing a weak child or an infirm old man of his hard-earned subsistence, if he himself expects to be able to find his own someplace else. Instead of the sublime maxim of reasoned justice, *Do unto others as you would have them do unto you,* pity inspires all men with another maxim of natural goodness, much less perfect but perhaps more useful than the preceding one: *Do what is good for you with as little harm as possible to others.* In a word, it is in this natural sentiment, rather than in subtle arguments, that one must search for the cause of the repugnance at doing evil that every man would experience, even independently of the maxims of education. Although it might be appropriate for Socrates and minds of his stature to acquire virtue through reason, the human race

would long ago have ceased to exist, if its preservation had depended solely on the reasonings of its members.

With passions so minimally active and such a salutary restraint, being more wild than evil, and more attentive to protecting themselves from the harm they could receive than tempted to do harm to others, men were not subject to very dangerous conflicts. Since they had no sort of intercourse among themselves; since, as a consequence, they knew neither vanity, nor deference, nor esteem, nor contempt; since they had not the slightest notion of mine and thine, nor any true idea of justice; since they regarded the acts of violence that could befall them as an easily redressed evil and not as an offense that must be punished; and since they did not even dream of vengeance except perhaps as a knee-jerk response right then and there, like the dog that bites the stone that is thrown at him, their disputes would rarely have had bloody consequences, if their subject had been no more sensitive than food. But I see a more dangerous matter that remains for me to discuss.

Among the passions that agitate the heart of man, there is an ardent, impetuous one that renders one sex necessary to the other; a terrible passion which braves all dangers, overcomes all obstacles, and which, in its fury, seems fitted to destroy the human race it is destined to preserve. What would become of men, victimized by this unrestrained and brutal rage, without modesty and self-control, fighting every day over the object of their passion at the price of their blood?

There must first be agreement that the more violent the passions are, the more necessary the laws are to contain them. But over and above the fact that the disorders and the crimes these passions cause daily in our midst show quite well the insufficiency of the laws in this regard, it would still be good to examine whether these disorders did not come into being with the laws themselves; for then, even if they were capable of repressing them, the least one should expect of them would be that they call a halt to an evil that would not exist without them.

Let us begin by distinguishing between the moral and the physical aspects of the sentiment of love. The physical aspect is that general desire which inclines one sex to unite with another. The moral aspect is what determines this desire and fixes it exclusively on one single object, or which at least gives it a greater degree of energy for this preferred object. Now it is easy to see that the moral aspect of love is an artificial sentiment born of social custom, and extolled by women with so much skill and care in order to establish their hegemony and make dominant the sex that ought to obey. Since this feeling is founded on certain notions of merit or beauty that a savage is not in a position to have, and on comparisons he is incapable of making, it must be almost non-existent for him. For since his mind could not form abstract ideas of regularity and proportion, his heart is not susceptible to sentiments of admiration and love, which, even without its being observed come into being from the application of these ideas. He pays exclusive attention to the temperament he has received from nature, and not the taste [aversion] he has been unable to acquire; any woman suits his purpose.

Limited merely to the physical aspect of love, and fortunate enough to be ignorant of those preferences which stir up the feeling and increase the difficulties in satisfying it, men must feel the ardors of their temperament less frequently and less vividly, and consequently have fewer and less cruel conflicts among themselves. Imagination, which wreaks so much havoc among us, does not speak to savage hearts; each man peacefully awaits the impetus of nature, gives himself over to it without choice, and with more pleasure than frenzy; and once the need is satisfied, all desire is snuffed out.

Hence it is incontestable that love itself, like all other passions, had acquired only in society that impetuous ardor which so often makes it lethal to men. And it is all the more ridiculous to represent savages as continually slaughtering each other in order to satisfy their brutality, since this opinion is directly contrary to experience; and since the Caribs, of all existing peoples, are the people that until now has wandered least from the state of nature, they are the people least subject to jealousy, even though they live in a hot climate which always seems to occasion greater activity in these passions.

As to any inferences that could be drawn, in the case of several species of animals, from the clashes between males that bloody our poultry yards throughout the year, and which make our forests resound in the spring with their cries as they quarrel over a female, it is necessary to begin by excluding all species in which nature has manifestly established, in the relative power of the sexes, relations other than those that exist among us. Hence cockfights do not form the basis for an inference regarding the human species. In species where the proportion is more closely observed, these fights can have for their cause only the scarcity of females in relation to the number of males, or the exclusive intervals during which the female continually rejects the advances of the male, which adds up to the cause just cited. For if each female receives the male for only two months a year, in this respect it is as if the number of females were reduced by five-sixths. Now neither of these two cases is applicable to the human species where the number of females generally surpasses the number of males, and where human females, unlike those of other species, have never been observed to have periods of heat and exclusion, even among savages. Moreover, among several of these animal species, where the entire species goes into heat simultaneously, there comes a terrible moment of common ardor, tumult, disorder and combat: a moment that does not happen in the human species where love is never periodic. Therefore one cannot conclude from the combats of certain animals for the possession of females that the same thing would happen to man in the state of nature. And even if one could draw that conclusion, given that these conflicts do not destroy the other species, one should conclude that they would not be any more lethal for ours. And it is quite apparent that they would wreak less havoc in the state of nature than in society, especially in countries where mores still count for something and where the jealousy of lovers and the vengeance of husbands every day give rise to duels, murders and still worse things; where the duty of eternal fidelity serves merely to create adulterers; and where even the laws of continence and honor necessarily spread debauchery and multiply the number of abortions.

Let us conclude that, wandering in the forests, without industry, without speech, without dwelling, without war, without relationships, with no need for his fellow men, and correspondingly with no desire to do them harm, perhaps never even recognizing any of them individually, savage man, subject to few passions and self-sufficient, had only the sentiments and enlightenment appropriate to that state; he felt only his true needs, took notice of only what he believed he had an interest in seeing; and that his intelligence made no more progress than his vanity. If by chance he made some discovery, he was all the less able to communicate it to others because he did not even know his own children. Art perished with its inventor. There was neither education nor progress; generations were multiplied to no purpose. Since each one always began from the same point, centuries went by with all the crudeness of the first ages; the species was already old, and man remained ever a child.

If I have gone on at such length about the supposition of that primitive condition, it is because, having ancient errors and inveterate prejudices to destroy, I felt I should dig down to the root and show, in the depiction of the true state of nature, how far even natural inequality is from having as much reality and influence in that state as our writers claim.

In fact, it is easy to see that, among the differences that distinguish men, several of them pass for natural ones which are exclusively the work of habit and of the various sorts of life that men adopt in society. Thus a robust or delicate temperament, and the strength or weakness that depend on it, frequently derive more from the harsh or effeminate way in which one has been raised than from the primitive constitution of bodies. The same holds for mental powers; and not only does education make a difference between cultivated minds and those that are not, it also augments the difference among the former in proportion to their culture; for were a giant and a dwarf walking on the same road, each step they both take would give a fresh advantage to the giant. Now if one compares the prodigious diversity of educations and lifestyles in the different orders of the civil state with the simplicity and uniformity of animal and savage life, where all nourish themselves from the same foods live in the same manner, and do exactly the same things, it will be understood how much less the difference between one man and another must be in the state of nature than in that of society, and how much natural inequality must increase in the human species through inequality occasioned by social institutions.

But even if nature were to affect, in the distribution of her gifts, as many preferences as is claimed, what advantage would the most favored men derive from them, to the detriment of others, in a state of things that allowed practically no sort of relationships among them? Where there is no love, what use is beauty? What use is wit for people who do not speak, and ruse to those who have no dealing with others? I always hear it repeated that the stronger will oppress the weaker. But let me have an explanation of the meaning of the word "oppression." Some will dominate with violence; others will groan, enslaved to all their caprices. That is precisely what I observe among us; but I do not see how this could be said of savage men, to whom it would be difficult even to explain what servitude and domination are. A man could well lay hold of the fruit another has gathered, the game he has killed, the cave that served as his shelter. But how will he ever succeed in making himself be obeyed? And what can be the chains of dependence among men who possess nothing? If someone chases me from one tree, I am free to go to another; if someone torments me in one place, who will prevent me from going elsewhere? Is there a man with strength sufficiently superior to mine and who is, moreover, sufficiently depraved, sufficiently lazy and sufficiently ferocious to force me to provide for his subsistence while he remains idle? He must resolve not to take his eyes off me for a single instant, to keep me carefully tied down while he sleeps, for fear that I may escape or that I would kill him. In other words, he is obliged to expose himself voluntarily to a much greater hardship than the one he wants to avoid and gives me. After all that, were his vigilance to relax for an instant, were an unforeseen noise to make him turn his head, I take twenty steps into the forest; my chains are broken, and he never sees me again for the rest of his life.

Without needlessly prolonging these details, anyone should see that, since the bonds of servitude are formed merely from the mutual dependence of men and the reciprocal needs that unite them, it is impossible to enslave a man without having first put him in the position of being incapable of doing without another. This being a situation that did not exist in the state of nature, it leaves each person free of the yoke, and renders pointless the law of the strongest.

After having proved that inequality is hardly observable in the state of nature, and that its influence there is almost nonexistent, it remains for me to show its origin and progress in the successive developments of the human mind. After having shown that *perfectibility*, social virtues, and the other faculties that natural man had received in a state of potentiality could never develop by themselves, that to achieve this development they required the chance coming together of several unconnected causes that might never have come into being and without which he would have remained eternally in his primitive constitution, it remains for me to consider and to bring together the various chance happenings that were able to perfect human reason while deteriorating the species, make a being evil while rendering it habituated to the ways of society, and, from so distant a beginning, finally bring man and the world to the point where we see them now.

I admit that, since the events I have to describe could have taken place in several ways, I cannot make a determination among them except on the basis of conjecture. But over and above the fact that these conjectures become reasons when they are the most probable ones that a person can draw from the nature of things and the sole means that a person can have of discovering the truth, the consequences I wish to deduce from mine will not thereby be conjectural, since, on the basis of the principles I have just established, no other system is conceivable that would not furnish me with the same results, and from which I could not draw the same conclusions.

This will excuse me from expanding my reflections on the way in which the lapse of time compensates for the slight probability of events; concerning the surprising power that quite negligible causes may have when they act without interruption; concerning the impossibility, on the one hand, of a person's destroying certain hypotheses, even though, on the other hand, one is not in a position to accord them the level of factual certitude; concerning a situation in which two facts given as real are to be connected by a series of intermediate facts that are unknown or regarded as such, it belongs to history, when it exists, to provide the facts that connect them; it belongs to philosophy, when history is unavailable, to determine similar facts that can connect them; finally, concerning how, with respect to events, similarity reduces the facts to a much smaller number of different classes

than one might imagine. It is enough for me to offer these objects to the consideration of my judges; it is enough for me to have seen to it that ordinary readers would have no need to consider them.

Part Two

The first person who, having enclosed a plot of land, took it into his head to say *this is mine* and found people simple enough to believe him, was the true founder of civil society. What crimes, wars, murders, what miseries and horrors would the human race have been spared, had someone pulled up the stakes or filled in the ditch and cried out to his fellow men: "Do not listen to this impostor. You are lost if you forget that the fruits of the earth belong to all and the earth to no one!" But it is quite likely that by then things had already reached the point where they could no longer continue as they were. For this idea of property, depending on many prior ideas which could only have arisen successively, was not formed all at once in the human mind. It was necessary to make great progress, to acquire much industry and enlightenment, and to transmit and augment them from one age to another, before arriving at this final stage in the state of nature. Let us therefore take things farther back and try to piece together under a single viewpoint that slow succession of events and advances in knowledge in their most natural order.

Man's first sentiment was that of his own existence; his first concern was that of his preservation. The products of the earth provided him with all the help he needed; instinct led him to make use of them. With hunger and other appetites making him experience by turns various ways of existing, there was one appetite that invited him to perpetuate his species; and this blind inclination, devoid of any sentiment of the heart, produced a purely animal act. Once this need had been satisfied, the two sexes no longer took cognizance of one another, and even the child no longer meant anything to the mother once it could do without her.

Such was the condition of man in his nascent stage; such was the life of an animal limited at first to pure sensations, and scarcely profiting from the gifts nature offered him, far from dreaming of extracting anything from her. But difficulties soon presented themselves to him; it was necessary to learn to overcome them. The height of trees, which kept him from reaching their fruits, the competition of animals that sought to feed themselves on these same fruits, the ferocity of those animals that wanted to take his own life: everything obliged him to apply himself to bodily exercises. It was necessary to become agile, fleet-footed and vigorous in combat. Natural arms, which are tree branches and stones, were soon found ready at hand. He learned to surmount nature's obstacles, combat other animals when necessary, fight for his subsistence even with men, or compensate for what he had to yield to those stronger than himself.

In proportion as the human race spread, difficulties multiplied with the men. Differences in soils, climates and seasons could force them to inculcate these differences in their lifestyles. Barren years, long and hard winters, hot summers that consume everything required new resourcefulness from them. Along the seashore and the riverbanks they invented the fishing line and hook, and became fishermen and fish-eaters. In the forests they made bows and arrows, and became hunters and warriors. In cold countries they covered themselves with the skins of animals they had killed. Lightning, a volcano, or some fortuitous chance happening acquainted them with fire: a new resource against the rigors of winter. They learned to preserve this element, then to reproduce it, and finally to use it to prepare meats that previously they devoured raw.

This repeated appropriation of various beings to himself, and of some beings to others, must naturally have engendered in man's mind the perceptions of certain relations. These relationships which we express by the words "large," "small," "strong," "weak," "fast," "slow," "timorous," "bold," and other similar ideas, compared when needed and almost without thinking about it, finally produced in him a kind of reflection, or rather a mechanical prudence which pointed out to him the precautions that were most necessary for his safety.

The new enlightenment which resulted from this development increased his superiority over the other animals by making him aware of it. He trained himself to set traps for them; he tricked them in a thousand different ways. And although several surpassed him in fighting strength or in swiftness in running, of those that could serve him or hurt him, he became in time

the master of the former and the scourge of the latter. Thus the first glance he directed upon himself produced within him the first stirring of pride; thus, as yet hardly knowing how to distinguish the ranks, and contemplating himself in the first rank by virtue of his species, he prepared himself from afar to lay claim to it in virtue of his individuality.

Although his fellowmen were not for him what they are for us, and although he had hardly anything more to do with them than with other animals, they were not forgotten in his observations. The conformities that time could make him perceive among them, his female, and himself, made him judge those he did not perceive. And seeing that they all acted as he would have done under similar circumstances, he concluded that their way of thinking and feeling was in complete conformity with his own. And this important truth, well established in his mind, made him follow, by a presentiment as sure as dialectic and more prompt, the best rules of conduct that it was appropriate to observe toward them for his advantage and safety.

Taught by experience that love of well-being is the sole motive of human actions, he found himself in a position to distinguish the rare occasions when common interest should make him count on the assistance of his fellowmen, and those even rarer occasions when competition ought to make him distrust them. In the first case, he united with them in a herd, or at most in some sort of free association, that obligated no one and that lasted only as long as the passing need that had formed it. In the second case, everyone sought to obtain his own advantage, either by overt force, if he believed he could, or by cleverness and cunning, if he felt himself to be the weaker.

This is how men could imperceptibly acquire some crude idea of mutual commitments and of the advantages to be had in fulfilling them, but only insofar as present and perceptible interests could require it, since foresight meant nothing to them, and far from concerning themselves about a distant future, they did not even give a thought to the next day. Were it a matter of catching a deer, everyone was quite aware that he must faithfully keep to his post in order to achieve this purpose; but if a hare happened to pass within reach of one of them, no doubt he would have pursued it without giving it a second thought, and that, having obtained his prey, he cared very little about causing his companions to miss theirs.

It is easy to understand that such intercourse did not require a language much more refined than that of crows or monkeys, which flock together in practically the same way. Inarticulate cries, many gestures, and some imitative noises must for a long time have made up the universal language. By joining to this in each country a few articulate and conventional sounds, whose institution, as I have already said, is not too easy to explain, there were individual languages, but crude and imperfect ones, quite similar to those still spoken by various savage nations today. Constrained by the passing of time, the abundance of things I have to say, and the practically imperceptible progress of the beginnings, I am flying like an arrow over the multitudes of centuries. For the slower events were in succeeding one another, the quicker they can be described.

These first advances enabled man to make more rapid ones. The more the mind was enlightened, the more industry was perfected. Soon they ceased to fall asleep under the first tree or to retreat into caves, and found various types of hatchets made of hard, sharp stones, which served to cut wood, dig up the soil, and make huts from branches they later found it useful to cover with clay and mud. This was the period of a first revolution which formed the establishment of the distinction among families and which introduced a kind of property, whence perhaps there already arose many quarrels and fights. However, since the strongest were probably the first to make themselves lodgings they felt capable of defending, presumably the weak found it quicker and safer to imitate them than to try to dislodge them; and as for those who already had huts, each of them must have rarely sought to appropriate that of his neighbor, less because it did not belong to him than because it was of no use to him, and because he could not seize it without exposing himself to a fierce battle with the family that occupied it.

The first developments of the heart were the effect of a new situation that united the husbands and wives, fathers and children in one common habitation. The habit of living together gave rise to the sweetest sentiments known to men: conjugal love and paternal love. Each family became a little society all the better

united because mutual attachment and liberty were its only bonds; and it was then that the first difference was established in the lifestyle of the two sexes, which until then had had only one. Women became more sedentary and grew accustomed to watch over the hut and the children, while the man went to seek their common subsistence. With their slightly softer life the two sexes also began to lose something of their ferocity and vigor. But while each one separately became less suited to combat savage beasts, on the other hand it was easier to assemble in order jointly to resist them.

In this new state, with a simple and solitary life, very limited needs, and the tools they had invented to provide for them, since men enjoyed a great deal of leisure time, they used it to procure for themselves many types of conveniences unknown to their fathers; and that was the first yoke they imposed on themselves without realizing it, and the first source of evils they prepared for their descendants. For in addition to their continuing thus to soften body and mind (those conveniences having through habit lost almost all their pleasure, and being at the same time degenerated into true needs), being deprived of them became much more cruel than possessing them was sweet; and they were unhappy about losing them without being happy about possessing them.

At this point we can see a little better how the use of speech was established or imperceptibly perfected itself in the bosom of each family; and one can further conjecture how various particular causes could have extended the language and accelerated its progress by making it more necessary. Great floods or earthquakes surrounded the inhabited areas with water or precipices. Upheavals of the globe detached parts of the mainland and broke them up into islands. Clearly among men thus brought together and forced to live together, a common idiom must have been formed sooner than among those who wandered freely about the forests of the mainland. Thus it is quite possible that after their first attempts at navigation, the islanders brought the use of speech to us; and it is at least quite probable that society and languages came into being on islands and were perfected there before they were known on the mainland.

Everything begins to take on a new appearance. Having previously wandered about the forests and having assumed a more fixed situation, men slowly came together and united into different bands, eventually forming in each country a particular nation, united by mores and characteristic features, not by regulations and laws, but by the same kind of life and foods and by the common influence of the climate. Eventually a permanent proximity cannot fail to engender some intercourse among different families. Young people of different sexes live in neighboring huts; the passing intercourse demanded by nature soon leads to another, through frequent contact with one another, no less sweet and more permanent. People become accustomed to consider different objects and to make comparisons. Imperceptibly they acquire the ideas of merit and beauty which produce feelings of preference. By dint of seeing one another, they can no longer get along without seeing one another again. A sweet and tender feeling insinuates itself into the soul and at the least opposition becomes an impetuous fury. Jealousy awakens with love; discord triumphs, and the sweetest passion receives sacrifices of human blood.

In proportion as ideas and sentiments succeed one another and as the mind and heart are trained, the human race continues to be tamed, relationships spread and bonds are tightened. People grew accustomed to gather in front of their huts or around a large tree; song and dance, true children of love and leisure, became the amusement or rather the occupation of idle men and women who had flocked together. Each one began to look at the others and to want to be looked at himself, and public esteem had a value. The one who sang or danced the best, the handsomest, the strongest, the most adroit or the most eloquent became the most highly regarded. And this was the first step toward inequality and, at the same time, toward vice. From these first preferences were born vanity and contempt on the one hand, and shame and envy on the other. And the fermentation caused by these new leavens eventually produced compounds fatal to happiness and innocence.

As soon as men had begun mutually to value one another, and the idea of esteem was formed in their minds, each one claimed to have a right to it, and it was no longer possible for anyone to be lacking it with impunity. From this came the first duties of civility, even among savages; and from this every voluntary wrong became an outrage, because along with the harm that resulted from the injury, the offended party saw in it contempt for his person, which often was more insufferable than the harm itself. Hence each man punished the contempt shown him in a manner proportionate to the esteem in which he held himself; acts of revenge became terrible, and men became bloodthirsty and cruel. This is precisely the stage reached by most of the savage people known to us; and it is for want of having made adequate distinctions among their ideas or of having noticed how far these peoples already were from the original state of nature that many have hastened to conclude that man is naturally cruel, and that he needs civilization in order to soften him. On the contrary, nothing is so gentle as man in his primitive state, when, placed by nature at an equal distance from the stupidity of brutes and the fatal enlightenment of civil man, and limited equally by instinct and reason to protecting himself from the harm that threatens him, he is restrained by natural pity from needlessly harming anyone himself, even if he has been harmed. For according to the axiom of the wise Locke, *where there is no property, there is no injury.*

But it must be noted that society in its beginning stages and the relations already established among men required in them qualities different from those they derived from their primitive constitution; that, with morality beginning to be introduced into human actions, and everyone, prior to the existence of laws, being sole judge and avenger of the offenses he had received, the goodness appropriate to the pure state of nature was no longer what was appropriate to an emerging society; that it was necessary for punishments to become more severe in proportion as the occasions for giving offense became more frequent; and it remained for the fear of vengeance to take the place of the deterrent character of laws. Hence although men had become less forebearing, and although natural pity had already undergone some alteration, this period of the development of human faculties, maintaining a middle position between the indolence of our primitive state and the petulant activity of our egocentrism, must have been the happiest and most durable epoch. The more one reflects on it, the more one finds that this state was the least subject to upheavals and the best for man,[16] and that he must have left it only by virtue of some fatal chance happening that, for the common good, ought never have happened. The example of savages, almost all of whom have been found in this state, seems to confirm that the human race had been made to remain in it always; that this state is the veritable youth of the world; and that all the subsequent progress has been in appearance so many steps toward the perfection of the individual, and in fact toward the decay of the species.

As long as men were content with the rustic huts, as long as they were limited to making their clothing out of skins sewn together with thorns or fish bones, adorning themselves with feathers and shells, painting their bodies with various colors, perfecting or embellishing their bows and arrows, using sharp-edged stones to make some fishing canoes or some crude musical instruments; in a word, as long as they applied themselves exclusively to tasks that a single individual could do and to the arts that did not require the cooperation of several hands, they lived as free, healthy, good and happy as they could in accordance with their nature; and they continued to enjoy among themselves the sweet rewards of independent intercourse. But as soon as one man needed the help of another, as soon as one man realized that it was useful for a single individual to have provisions for two, equality disappeared, property came into existence, labor became necessary. Vast forests were transformed into smiling fields which had to be watered with men's sweat, and in which slavery and misery were soon seen to germinate and grow with the crops.

Metallurgy and agriculture were the two arts whose invention produced this great revolution. For the poet, it is gold and silver; but for the philosopher, it is iron and wheat that have civilized men and ruined the human race. Thus they were both unknown to the savages of America, who for that reason have always remained savages. Other peoples even appear to have remained barbarous, as long as they practiced one of those arts without the other. And perhaps one of the best reasons why Europe has been, if not sooner, at least more constantly and better governed than the other parts of the world, is that it is at the same time the most abundant in iron and the most fertile in wheat.

It is very difficult to guess how men came to know

and use iron, for it is incredible that by themselves they thought of drawing the ore from the mine and performing the necessary preparations on it for smelting it before they knew what would result. From another point of view, it is even less plausible to attribute this discovery to some accidental fire, because mines are set up exclusively in arid places devoid of trees and plants, so that one would say that nature had taken precautions to conceal this deadly secret from us. Thus there remains only the extraordinary circumstance of some volcano that, in casting forth molten metal, would have given observers the idea of imitating this operation of nature. Even still we must suppose them to have had a great deal of courage and foresight to undertake such a difficult task and to have envisaged so far in advance the advantages they could derive from it. This is hardly suitable for minds already better trained than theirs must have been.

As for agriculture, its principle was known long before its practice was established, and it is hardly possible that men, constantly preoccupied with deriving their subsistence from trees and plants, did not rather quickly get the idea of the methods used by nature to grow plant life. But their industry probably did not turn in that direction until very late either because trees, which, along with hunting and fishing, provided their nourishment, had no need of their care; or for want of knowing how to use wheat; or for want of tools with which to cultivate it; or for want of foresight regarding future needs; or, finally, for want of the means of preventing others from appropriating the fruits of their labors. Having become more industrious, it is believable that, with sharp stones and pointed sticks, they began by cultivating some vegetables or roots around their huts long before they knew how to prepare wheat and had the tools necessary for large-scale cultivation. Moreover, to devote oneself to that occupation and to sow the lands, one must be resolved to lose something at first in order to gain a great deal later: a precaution quite far removed from the mind of the savage man, who, as I have said, finds it quite difficult to give thought in the morning to what he will need at night.

The invention of the other arts was therefore necessary to force the human race to apply itself to that of agriculture. Once men were needed in order to smelt and forge the iron, other men were needed in order to feed them. The more the number of workers increased, the fewer hands there were to obtain food for the common subsistence, without there being fewer mouths to consume it; and since some needed foodstuffs in exchange for their iron, the others finally found the secret of using iron to multiply foodstuffs. From this there arose farming and agriculture, on the one hand, and the art of working metals and multiplying their uses, on the other.

From the cultivation of land, there necessarily followed the division of land; and from property once recognized, the first rules of justice. For in order to render everyone what is his, it is necessary that everyone can have something. Moreover, as men began to look toward the future and as they saw that they all had goods to lose, there was not one of them who did not have to fear reprisals against himself for wrongs he might do to another. This origin is all the more natural as it is impossible to conceive of the idea of property arising from anything but manual labor, for it is not clear what man can add, beyond his own labor, in order to appropriate things he has not made. It is labor alone that, in giving the cultivator a right to the product of the soil he has tilled, consequently gives him this right, at least until the harvest, and thus from year to year. With this possession continuing uninterrupted, it is easily transformed into property. When the ancients, says Grotius, gave Ceres the epithet of legislatrix, gave the name Thesmophories to a festival celebrated in her honor, they thereby made it apparent that the division of lands has produced a new kind of right: namely, the right of property, different from that which results from the natural law.

Things in this state could have remained equal, if talents had been equal, and if the use of iron and the consumption of foodstuffs had always been in precise balance. But this proportion, which was not maintained by anything, was soon broken. The strongest did the most work; the most adroit turned theirs to better advantage: the most ingenious found ways to shorten their labor. The farmer had a greater need for iron, or the blacksmith had a greater need for wheat; and in laboring equally, the one earned a great deal while the other barely had enough to live. Thus it is that natural inequality imperceptibly manifests itself together with inequality occasioned by the so-

cialization process. Thus it is that the differences among men, developed by those of circumstances, make themselves more noticeable, more permanent in their effects, and begin to influence the fate of private individuals in the same proportion.

With things having reached this point, it is easy to imagine the rest. I will not stop to describe the successive invention of the arts, the progress of languages, the testing and use of talents, the inequality of fortunes, the use or abuse of wealth, nor all the details that follow these and that everyone can easily supply. I will limit myself exclusively to taking a look at the human race placed in this new order of things.

Thus we find here all our faculties developed, memory and imagination in play, egocentrism looking out for its interests, reason rendered active, and the mind having nearly reached the limit of the perfection of which it is capable. We find here all the natural qualities put into action, the rank and fate of each man established not only on the basis of the quantity of goods and the power to serve or harm, but also on the basis of mind, beauty, strength or skill, on the basis of merit or talents. And since these qualities were the only ones that could attract consideration, he was soon forced to have them or affect them. It was necessary, for his advantage, to show himself to be something other than what he in fact was. Being something and appearing to be something became two completely different things; and from this distinction there arose grand ostentation, deceptive cunning, and all the vices that follow in their wake. On the other hand, although man had previously been free and independent, we find him, so to speak, subject, by virtue of a multitude of fresh needs, to all of nature and particularly to his fellowmen, whose slave in a sense he becomes even in becoming their master; rich, he needs their services; poor, he needs their help; and being midway between wealth and poverty does not put him in a position to get along without them. It is therefore necessary for him to seek incessantly to interest them in his fate and to make them find their own profit, in fact or in appearance, in working for his. This makes him two-faced and crooked with some, imperious and harsh with others, and puts him in the position of having to abuse everyone he needs when he cannot make them fear them and does not find it in his interests to be of useful service to them. Finally, consuming ambition, the zeal for raising the relative level of his fortune, less out of real need than in order to put himself above others, inspires in all men a wicked tendency to harm one another, a secret jealousy all the more dangerous because, in order to strike its blow in greater safety, it often wears the mask of benevolence; in short, competition and rivalry on the one hand, opposition of interest[s] on the other, and always the hidden desire to profit at the expense of someone else. All these ills are the first effect of property and the inseparable offshoot of incipient inequality.

Before representative signs of wealth had been invented, it could hardly have consisted of anything but lands and livestock, the only real goods men can possess. Now when inheritances had grown in number and size to the point of covering the entire landscape and of all bordering on one another, some could no longer be enlarged except at the expense of others; and the supernumeraries, whom weakness or indolence had prevented from acquiring an inheritance in their turn, became poor without having lost anything, because while everything changed around them, they alone had not changed at all. Thus they were forced to receive or steal their subsistence from the hands of the rich. And from that there began to arise, according to the diverse characters of the rich and the poor, domination and servitude, or violence and thefts. For their part, the wealthy had no sooner known the pleasure of domination, than before long they disdained all others, and using their old slaves to subdue new ones, they thought of nothing but the subjugation and enslavement of their neighbors, like those ravenous wolves which, on having once tasted human flesh, reject all other food and desire to devour only men.

Thus, when both the most powerful or the most miserable made of their strength or their needs a sort of right to another's goods, equivalent, according to them, to the right of property, the destruction of equality was followed by the most frightful disorder. Thus the usurpations of the rich, the acts of brigandage by the poor, the unbridled passions of all, stifling natural pity and the still weak voice of justice, made men greedy, ambitious and wicked. There arose between the right of the strongest and the right of the first occupant a perpetual conflict that ended only in fights and murders.[17] Emerging society gave way to the most horrible state of war; since the human race, vilified and desolated, was no longer able to retrace its steps or give up the unfortunate acquisitions it had made, and since it labored only toward its shame by abusing the faculties that honor it, it brought itself to the brink of its ruin. *Horrified by the newness of the ill, both the poor man and the rich man hope to flee from wealth, hating what they once had prayed for.*

It is not possible that men should not have eventually reflected upon so miserable a situation and upon the calamities that overwhelm them. The rich in particular must have soon felt how disadvantageous to them it was to have a perpetual war in which they alone paid all the costs, and in which the risk of losing one's life was common to all and the risk of losing one's goods was personal. Moreover, regardless of the light in which they tried to place their usurpations, they knew full well that they were established on nothing but a precarious and abusive right, and that having been acquired merely by force, force might take them away from them without their having any reason to complain. Even those enriched exclusively by industry could hardly base their property on better claims. They could very well say: "I am the one who built that wall; I have earned this land with my labor." In response to them it could be said: "Who gave you the boundary lines? By what right do you claim to exact payment at our expense for labor we did not impose upon you? Are you unaware that a multitude of your brothers perish or suffer from need of what you have in excess, and that you needed explicit and unanimous consent from the human race for you to help yourself to anything from the common subsistence that went beyond your own?" Bereft of valid reasons to justify himself and sufficient forces to defend himself; easily crushing a private individual, but himself crushed by troops of bandits; alone against all and unable on account of mutual jealousies to unite with his equals against enemies united by the common hope of plunder, the rich, pressed by necessity, finally conceived the most thought-out project that ever entered the human mind. It was to use in his favor the very strength of those who attacked him, to turn his adversaries into his defenders, to instill in them other maxims, and to give them other institutions which were as favorable to him as natural right was unfavorable to him.

With this end in mind, after having shown his neighbors the horror of a situation which armed them all against each other and made their possessions as burdensome as their needs, and in which no one could find safety in either poverty or wealth, he easily invented specious reasons to lead them to his goal. "Let us unite," he says to them, "in order to protect the weak from oppression, restrain the ambitious, and assure everyone of possessing what belongs to him. Let us institute rules of justice and peace to which all will be obliged to conform, which will make special exceptions for no one, and which will in some way compensate for the caprices of fortune by subjecting the strong and the weak to mutual obligations. In short, instead of turning our forces against ourselves, let us gather them into one supreme power that governs us according to wise laws, that protects and defends all the members of the association, repulses common enemies, and maintains us in an eternal concord."

Considerably less than the equivalent of this discourse was needed to convince crude, easily seduced men who also had too many disputes to settle among themselves to be able to get along without arbiters, and too much greed and ambition to be able to get along without masters for long. They all ran to chain themselves, in the belief that they secured their liberty, for although they had enough sense to realize the advantages of a political establishment, they did not have enough experience to foresee its dangers. Those most capable of anticipating the abuses were precisely those who counted on profiting from them; and even the wise saw the need to be resolved to sacrifice one part of their liberty to preserve the other, just as a wounded man has his arm amputated to save the rest of his body.

Such was, or should have been, the origin of society and laws, which gave new fetters to the weak and new forces to the rich,[18] irretrievably destroyed natural liberty, established forever the law of property and of inequality, changed adroit usurpation into an irrevocable right, and for the profit of a few ambitious men henceforth subjected the entire human race to labor, servitude and misery. It is readily apparent how the establishment of a single society rendered indispensable that of all the others, and how, to stand head to head against the united forces, it was necessary to unite in turn. Societies, multiplying or spreading rapidly, soon covered the entire surface of the earth; and it was no longer possible to find a single corner in the universe where someone could free himself from the yoke and withdraw his head from the often ill-guided sword which everyone saw perpetually hanging over his own head. With civil right thus having become the common rule of citizens, the law of nature no longer was operative except between the various societies, when, under the name of the law of nations, it was tempered by some tacit conventions in order to make intercourse possible and to serve as a substitute for natural compassion which, losing between one society and another nearly all the force it had between one man and another, no longer resides anywhere but in a few great cosmopolitan souls, who overcome the imaginary barriers that separate peoples, and who, following the example of the sovereign being who has created them, embrace the entire human race in their benevolence.

Remaining thus among themselves in the state of nature, the bodies politic soon experienced the inconveniences that had forced private individuals to leave it; and that state became even more deadly among these great bodies than that state had been among the private individuals of whom they were composed. Whence came the national wars, battles, murders, and reprisals that make nature tremble and offend reason, and all those horrible prejudices that rank the honor of shedding human blood among the virtues. The most decent people learned to consider it one of their duties to kill their fellow men. Finally, men were seen massacring one another by the thousands without knowing why. More murders were committed in a single day of combat and more horrors in the capture of a single city than were committed in the state of nature during entire centuries over the entire face of the earth. Such are the first effects one glimpses of the division of mankind into different societies. Let us return to the founding of these societies.

I know that many have ascribed other origins to political societies, such as conquests by the most powerful, or the union of the weak; and the choice among these causes is indifferent to what I want to establish. Nevertheless, the one I have just described seems to me the most natural, for the following reasons. 1. In the first case, the right of conquest, since it is not a right, could not have founded any other, because the conqueror and conquered peoples always remain in a state of war with one another, unless the nation, returned to full liberty, were to choose voluntarily its conqueror as its leader. Until then, whatever the capitulations that may have been made, since they have been founded on violence alone and are consequently null by this very fact, on this hypothesis there can be neither true society nor body politic, nor any other law than that of the strongest. 2. These words *strong* and *weak* are equivocal in the second case, because in the interval between the establishment of the right of property or of the first occupant and that of political governments, the meaning of these terms is better rendered by the words *poor* and *rich*, because, before the laws, man did not in fact have any other means of placing his equals in subjection except by attacking their goods or by giving them part of his. 3. Since the poor had nothing to lose but their liberty, it would have been utter folly for them to have voluntarily surrendered the only good remaining to them, gaining nothing in return. On the contrary, since the rich men were, so to speak, sensitive in all parts of their goods, it was much easier to do them harm, and consequently they had to take greater precautions to protect themselves. And finally it is reasonable to believe that a thing was invented by those to whom it is useful rather than by those to whom it is harmful.

Incipient government did not have a constant and regular form. The lack of philosophy and experience permitted only present inconveniences to be perceived, and there was thought of remedying the others only as they presented themselves. Despite all the labors of the wisest legislators, the political state always remained imperfect, because it was practically the work of chance; and, because it had been badly begun, time, in discovering faults and suggesting remedies, could never repair the vices of the constitution. People were continually patching it up, whereas they should have begun by clearing the air and putting aside all the old materials, as Lycurgus did in Sparta, in order to raise a good edifice later on. At first, society consisted merely of some general conventions that all private individuals promised to observe, and concerning which the community became the guarantor for each of them. Experience had to demonstrate how weak such a constitution was, and how easy it was for lawbreakers to escape conviction or punishment for faults of which the public alone was to be witness and judge. The law had to be evaded in a thousand ways; inconveniences and disorders had to multiply continually in order to make them finally give some thought to confiding to private individuals the dangerous trust of public authority, and to make them entrust to magistrates the care of enforcing the observance of the deliberations of the people. For to say that the leaders were chosen before the confederation was brought about and that the ministers of the laws existed before the laws themselves is a supposition that does not allow of serious debate.

It would be no more reasonable to believe that initially the peoples threw themselves unconditionally and for all time into the arms of an absolute master, and that the first means of providing for the common security dreamed up by proud and unruly men was to rush headlong into slavery. In fact, why did they give themselves over to superiors, if not to defend themselves against oppression and to protect their goods, their liberties and their lives, which are, as it were, the constitutive elements of their being? Now, since, in relations between men, the worst that can happen to someone is for him to see himself at the discretion of someone else, would it not have been contrary to good sense to begin by surrendering into the hands of a leader the only things for whose preservation they needed his help? What equivalent could he have offered them for the concession of so fine a right? And if he had dared to demand it on the pretext of defending them, would he not have immediately received the reply given in the fable: "what more will the enemy do to us?" It is therefore incontestable, and it is a fundamental maxim of all political right, that peoples have given themselves leaders in order to defend their liberty and not to enslave themselves. *If we have a prince,* Pliny said to Trajan, *it is so that he may preserve us from having a master.*

[Our] political theorists produce the same sophisms about the love of liberty that [our] philosophers have made about the state of nature. By the things they see they render judgments about very different things they have not seen; and they attribute to men a natural inclination to servitude owing to the patience with which those who are before their eyes endure their servitude, without giving a thought to the fact that it is the same for liberty as it is for innocence and virtue: their value is felt only as long as one has them oneself, and the taste for them is lost as soon as one has lost them. "I know the delights of your country," said Brasidas to a satrap who compared the life of Sparta to that of Persepolis, "but you cannot know the pleasures of mine."

As an unbroken steed bristles his mane, paws the ground with his hoof, and struggles violently at the mere approach of the bit, while a trained horse patiently endures the whip and the spur, barbarous man does not bow his head for the yoke that civilized man wears without a murmur, and he prefers the most stormy liberty to tranquil subjection. Thus it is not by the degradation of enslaved peoples that man's natural dispositions for or against servitude are to be judged, but by the wonders that all free peoples have accomplished to safeguard themselves from oppression. I know that enslaved peoples do nothing but boast of the peace and tranquillity they enjoy in their chains and that *they give the name 'peace' to the most miserable slavery.* But when I see free peoples sacrificing pleasures, tranquillity, wealth, power, and life itself for the preservation of this sole good which is regarded so disdainfully by those who have lost it; when I see animals born free and abhorring captivity break their heads against the bars of their prison; when I see multitudes of utterly naked savages scorn European pleasures and brave hunger, fire, sword and death, simply to preserve their independence, I sense that it is inappropriate for slaves to reason about liberty.

As for paternal authority, from which several have derived absolute government and all society, it is enough, without having recourse to the contrary proofs of Locke and Sidney, to note that nothing in the world is farther from the ferocious spirit of despotism than the gentleness of that authority which looks more to the advantage of the one who obeys than to the utility of the one who commands; that by the law of nature, the father is master of the child as long as his help is necessary for him; that beyond this point they become equals, and the son, completely independent of the father, then owes him merely respect and not obedience; for gratitude is

clearly a duty that must be rendered, but not a right that can be demanded. Instead of saying that civil society derives from paternal power, on the contrary it must be said that it is from civil society that this power draws its principal force. An individual was not recognized as the father of several children until the children remained gathered about him. The goods of the father, of which he is truly the master, are the goods that keep his children in a state of dependence toward him, and he can cause their receiving a share in his estate to be consequent upon the extent to which they will have well merited it from him by continuous deference to his wishes. Now, far from having some similar favor to expect from their despot (since they belong to him as personal possessions—they and all they possess—or at least he claims this to be the case), subjects are reduced to receiving as a favor what he leaves them of their goods. He does what is just when he despoils them; he does them a favor when he allows them to live.

In continuing thus to examine facts from the viewpoint of right, no more solidity than truth would be found in the belief that the establishment of tyranny was voluntary; and it would be difficult to show the validity of a contract that would obligate only one of the parties, where all the commitments would be placed on one side with none on the other, and that would turn exclusively to the disadvantage of the one making the commitments. This odious system is quite far removed from being, even today, that of wise and good monarchs, and especially of the kings of France, as may be seen in various places in their edicts, and particularly in the following passage of a famous writing published in 1667 in the name of and by order of Louis XIV: *Let it not be said therefore that the sovereign is not subject to the laws of his state, for the contrary statement is a truth of the law of nations, which flattery has on occasion attacked, but which good princes have always defended as a tutelary divinity of their states. How much more legitimate is it to say, with the wise Plato, that the perfect felicity of a kingdom is that a prince be obeyed by his subjects, that the prince obey the law, and that the law be right and always directed to the public good.* I will not stop to investigate whether, with liberty being the most noble of man's faculties, he degrades his nature, places himself on the level of animals enslaved by instinct, offends even his maker, when he unreservedly renounces the most precious of all his gifts, and allows himself to commit all the crimes he forbids us to commit, in order to please a ferocious or crazed master; nor whether this sublime workman should be more irritated at seeing his finest work destroyed rather than at seeing it dishonored. [I will disregard, if you will, the authority of Barbeyrac, who flatly declares, following Locke, that no one can sell his liberty to the point of submitting himself to an arbitrary power that treats him according to its fancy. *For,* he adds, *this would be selling his own life, of which he is not the master.*] I will merely ask by what right those who have not been afraid of debasing themselves to this degree have been able to subject their posterity to the same ignominy and to renounce for it goods that do not depend on their liberality, and without which life itself is burdensome to all who are worthy of it.

Pufendorf says that just as one transfers his goods to another by conventions and contracts, one can also divest himself of his liberty in favor of someone. That, it seems to me, is very bad reasoning; for, in the first place, the goods I give away become something utterly foreign to me, and it is a matter of indifference to me whether or not these goods are abused; but it is important to me that my liberty is not abused, and I cannot expose myself to becoming the instrument of crime without making myself guilty of the evil I will be forced to commit. Moreover, since the right of property is merely the result of convention and human institution, every man can dispose of what he possesses as he sees fit. But it is not the same for the essential gifts of nature such as life and liberty, which everyone is allowed to enjoy, and of which it is at least doubtful that one has the right to divest himself. In giving up the one he degrades his being; in giving up the other he annihilates that being insofar as he can. And because no temporal goods can compensate for the one or the other, it would offend at the same time both nature and reason to renounce them, regardless of the price. But even if one could give away his liberty as he does his goods, the difference would be very great for the children who enjoy the father's goods only by virtue of a transmission of his right; whereas, since liberty is a gift they receive from nature

in virtue of being men, their parents had no right to divest them of it. Thus, just as violence had to be done to nature in order to establish slavery, nature had to be changed in order to perpetuate this right. And the jurists, who have gravely pronounced that the child of a slave woman is born a slave, have decided, in other words, that a man is not born a man.

Thus it appears certain to me not only that governments did not begin with arbitrary power, which is but their corruption and extreme limit, and which finally brings them back simply to the law of the strongest, for which they were initially to have been the remedy; but also that even if they had begun thus, this power, being illegitimate by its nature, could not have served as a foundation for the rights of society, nor, as a consequence, for the inequality occasioned by social institutions.

Without entering at present into the investigations that are yet to be made into the nature of the fundamental compact of all government, I restrict myself, in following common opinion, to considering here the establishment of the body politic as a true contract between the populace and the leaders it chooses for itself: a contract by which the two parties obligate themselves to observe the laws that are stipulated in it and that form the bonds of their union. Since, with respect to social relations, the populace has united all its wills into a single one, all the articles on which this will is explicated become so many fundamental laws obligating all the members of the state without exception, and one of these regulates the choice and power of the magistrates charged with watching over the execution of the others. This power extends to everything that can maintain the constitution, without going so far as to change it. To it are joined honors that make the laws and their ministers worthy of respect, and, for the ministers personally, prerogatives that compensate them for the troublesome labors that a good administration requires. The magistrate, for his part, obligates himself to use the power entrusted to him only in accordance with the intention of the constituents, to maintain each one in the peaceful enjoyment of what belongs to him, and to prefer on every occasion the public utility to his own interest.

Before experience had shown or knowledge of the human heart had made men foresee the inevitable abuses of such a constitution, it must have seemed all the better because those who were charged with watching over its preservation were themselves the ones who had the greatest interest in it. For since the magistracy and its rights were established exclusively on fundamental laws, were they to be destroyed, the magistracy would immediately cease to be legitimate; the people would no longer be bound to obey them. And since it was not the magistrate but the law that had constituted the essence of the state, everyone would rightfully return to his natural liberty.

The slightest attentive reflection on this point would confirm this by new reasons, and by the nature of the contract it would be seen that it could not be irrevocable. For were there no superior power that could guarantee the fidelity of the contracting parties or force them to fulfill their reciprocal commitments, the parties would remain sole judges in their own case, and each of them would always have the right to renounce the contract as soon as he should find that the other party violated the conditions of the contract, or as soon as the conditions should cease to suit him. It is on this principle that it appears the right to abdicate can be founded. Now to consider, as we are doing, only what is of human institution, if the magistrate, who has all the power in his hands and who appropriates to himself all the advantages of the contract, nevertheless had the right to renounce the authority, a fortiori the populace, which pays for all the faults of the leaders, should have the right to renounce their dependence. But the horrible dissensions, the infinite disorders that this dangerous power would necessarily bring in its wake, demonstrate more than anything else how much need human governments had for a basis more solid than reason alone, and how necessary it was for public tranquillity that the divine will intervened to give to sovereign authority a sacred and inviolable character which took from the subjects the fatal right to dispose of it. If religion had brought about this good for men, it would be enough to oblige them to cherish and adopt it, even with its abuses, since it spares even more blood than fanaticism causes to be shed. But let us follow the thread of our hypothesis.

The various forms of government take their origin from the greater or lesser differences that were found among private individuals at the moment of institution. If a man were eminent in power, virtue, wealth or prestige, he alone was elected magistrate, and the state became monarchical. If several men, more or less equal among themselves, stood out over all the others, they were elected jointly, and there was an aristocracy. Those whose fortune or talents were less disproportionate, and who least departed from the state of nature, kept the supreme administration and formed a democracy. Time made evident which of these forms was the most advantageous to men. Some remained in subjection only to the laws; the others soon obeyed masters. Citizens wanted to keep their liberty; the subjects thought only of taking it away from their neighbors, since they could not endure others enjoying a good they themselves no longer enjoyed. In a word, on the one hand were riches and conquests, and on the other were happiness and virtue.

In these various forms of government all the magistratures were at first elective; and when wealth did not prevail, preference was given to merit, which gives a natural ascendancy, and to age, which gives experience in conducting business and cool-headedness in deliberation. The elders of the Hebrews, the gerontes of Sparta, the senate of Rome, and even the etymology of our word *seigneur* show how much age was respected in former times. The more elections fell upon men of advanced age, the more frequent elections became, and the more their difficulties were made to be felt. Intrigues were introduced; factions were formed; parties became embittered; civil wars flared up. Finally, the blood of citizens was sacrificed to the alleged happiness of the state, and people were on the verge of falling back into the anarchy of earlier times. The ambition of the leaders profited from these circumstances to perpetuate their offices within their families. The people, already accustomed to dependence, tranquillity and the conveniences of life, and already incapable of breaking their chains, consented to let their servitude increase in order to secure their tranquillity. Thus it was that the leaders, having become hereditary, grew accustomed to regard their magistratures as family property, to regard themselves as the proprietors of the state (of which at first they were but the officers), to call their fellow citizens their slaves, to count them like cattle in the number of things that belonged to them, and to call themselves equals of the gods and kings of kings.

If we follow the progress of inequality in these various revolutions, we will find that the first stage was the establishment of the law and of the right of property, the second stage was the institution of the magistracy, and the third and final stage was the transformation of legitimate power into arbitrary power. Thus the class of rich and poor was authorized by the first epoch, that of the strong and the weak by the second, and that of master and slave by the third: the ultimate degree of inequality and the limit to which all the others finally lead, until new revolutions completely dissolve the government or bring it nearer to its legitimate institution.

To grasp the necessity of this progress, we must consider less the motives for the establishment of the body politic than the form it takes in its execution and the disadvantages that follow in its wake. For the vices that make social institutions necessary are the same ones that make their abuses inevitable. And with the sole exception of Sparta, where the law kept watch chiefly over the education of children, and where Lycurgus established mores that nearly dispensed with having to add laws to them, since laws are generally less strong than passions and restrain men without changing them, it would be easy to prove that any government that always moved forward in conformity with the purpose for which it was founded without being corrupted or altered, would have been needlessly instituted, and that a country where no one eluded the laws and abused the magistrature would need neither magistracy nor laws.

Political distinctions necessarily lend themselves to civil distinctions. The growing inequality between the people and its leaders soon makes itself felt among private individuals, and is modified by them in a thousand ways according to passions, talents and events. The magistrate cannot usurp illegitimate power without producing protégés for himself to whom he is forced to yield some part of it. Moreover, citizens allow themselves to be oppressed only insofar as they are driven by blind ambition; and looking more below than above them, domination becomes more dear to them than independence, and they consent to wear chains in order to be able to give them in turn to others. It is very difficult to reduce to obedience someone who does not seek to command; and the most adroit politician would never

succeed in subjecting men who wanted merely to be free. But inequality spreads easily among ambitious and cowardly souls always ready to run the risks of fortune and, almost indifferently, to dominate or serve, according to whether it becomes favorable or unfavorable to them. Thus it is that there must have come a time when the eyes of people were beguiled to such an extent that its leaders merely had to say to the humblest of men, "Be great, you and all your progeny," and he immediately appeared great to everyone as well as in his own eyes, and his descendants were elevated even more in proportion as they were at some remove from him. The more remote and uncertain the cause, the more the effect increased; the more loafers one could count in a family, the more illustrious it became.

If this were the place to go into detail, I would easily explain how [even without government involvement] the inequality of prestige and authority becomes inevitable among private individuals,[19] as soon as they are united in one single society and are forced to make comparisons among themselves and to take into account the differences they discover in the continual use they have to make of one another. These differences are of several sorts, but in general, since wealth, nobility or rank, power and personal merit are the principal distinctions by which someone is measured in society, I would prove that the agreement or conflict of these various forces is the surest indication of a well- or ill-constituted state. I would make it apparent that among these four types of inequality, since personal qualities are the origin of all the others, wealth is the last to which they are ultimately reduced, because it readily serves to buy all the rest, since it is the most immediately useful to well-being and the easiest to communicate. This observation enables one to judge rather precisely the extent to which each people is removed from its primitive institution, and of the progress it has made toward the final stage of corruption. I would note how much that universal desire for reputation, honors, and preferences, which devours us all, trains and compares our talents and strengths; how much it excites and multiplies the passions; and, by making all men competitors, rivals, or rather enemies, how many setbacks, successes and catastrophes of every sort it causes every day, by making so many contenders run the same course. I would show that it is to this ardor for making oneself the topic of conversation, to this furor to distinguish oneself which nearly always keeps us outside ourselves, that we owe what is best and worst among men, our virtues and vices, our sciences and our errors, our conquerors and our philosophers, that is to say, a multitude of bad things against a small number of good ones. Finally, I would prove that if one sees a handful of powerful and rich men at the height of greatness and fortune while the mob grovels in obscurity and misery, it is because the former prize the things they enjoy only to the extent that the others are deprived of them; and because, without changing their position, they would cease to be happy, if the people ceased to be miserable.

But these details alone would be the subject of a large work in which one would weigh the advantages and the disadvantages of every government relative to the rights of the state of nature, and where one would examine all the different faces under which inequality has appeared until now and may appear in [future] ages, according to the nature of these governments and the upheavals that time will necessarily bring in its wake. We would see the multitude oppressed from within as a consequence of the very precautions it had taken against what menaced it from without. We would see oppression continually increase, without the oppressed ever being able to know where it would end or what legitimate means would be left for them to stop it. We would see the rights of citizens and national liberties gradually die out, and the protests of the weak treated like seditious murmurs. We would see politics restrict the honor of defending the common cause to a mercenary portion of the people. We would see arising from this the necessity for taxes, the discouraged farmer leaving his field, even during peacetime, and leaving his plow in order to gird himself with a sword. We would see the rise of fatal and bizarre rules in the code of honor. We would see the defenders of the homeland sooner or later become its enemies, constantly holding a dagger over their fellow citizens, and there would come a time when we would hear them say to the oppressor of their country: *"If you order me to plunge my sword into my brother's breast or my father's throat, and into my pregnant wife's entrails, I will do so, even though my right hand is unwilling."*

From the extreme inequality of conditions and fortunes, from the diversity of passions and talents, from useless arts, from pernicious arts, from frivolous sciences there would come a pack of prejudices equally contrary to reason, happiness and virtue. One would see the leaders fomenting whatever can weaken men united together by disuniting them; whatever can give society an air of apparent concord while sowing the seeds of real division; whatever can inspire defiance and hatred in the various classes through the opposition of their rights and interests, and can as a consequence strengthen the power that contains them all.

It is from the bosom of this disorder and these upheavals that despotism, by gradually raising its hideous head and devouring everything it had seen to be good and healthy in every part of the state, would eventually succeed in trampling underfoot the laws and the people, and in establishing itself on the ruins of the republic. The times that would precede this last transformation would be times of troubles and calamities; but in the end everything would be swallowed up by the monster, and the peoples would no longer have leader or laws, but only tyrants. Also, from that moment on, there would no longer be any question of mores and virtue, for wherever despotism, *in which decency affords no hope*, reigns, it tolerates no other master. As soon as it speaks, there is neither probity nor duty to consult, and the blindest obedience is the only virtue remaining for slaves.

Here is the final stage of inequality, and the extreme point that closes the circle and touches the point from which we started. Here all private individuals become equals again, because they are nothing. And since subjects no longer have any law other than the master's will, nor the master any rule other than his passions, the notions of good and the principles of justice again vanish. Here everything is returned solely to the law of the strongest, and consequently to a new state of nature different from the one with which we began, in that the one was the state of nature in its purity, and this last one is the fruit of an excess of corruption. Moreover, there is so little difference between these two states, and the governmental contract is so utterly dissolved by despotism, that the despot is master only as long as he is the strongest; and as soon as he can be ousted, he has no cause to protest against violence. The uprising that ends in the strangulation or the dethronement of a sultan is as lawful an act as those by which he disposed of the lives and goods of his subjects the day before. Force alone maintained him; force alone brings him down. Thus everything happens in accordance with the natural order, and whatever the outcome of these brief and frequent upheavals may be, no one can complain about someone else's injustice, but only of his own imprudence or his misfortune.

In discovering and following thus the forgotten and lost routes that must have led man from the natural state to the civil state; in reestablishing, with the intermediate positions I have just taken note of, those that time constraints on me have made me suppress or that the imagination has not suggested to me, no attentive reader can fail to be struck by the immense space that separates these two states. It is in this slow succession of things that he will see the solution to an infinity of moral and political problems which the philosophers are unable to resolve. He will realize that, since the human race of one age is not the human race of another age, the reason why Diogenes did not find his man is because he searched among his contemporaries for a man who no longer existed. Cato, he will say, perished with Rome and liberty because he was out of place in his age; and this greatest of men merely astonished the world, which five hundred years earlier he would have governed. In short, he will explain how the soul and human passions are imperceptibly altered and, as it were, change their nature; why, in the long run, our needs and our pleasures change their objects; why, with original man gradually disappearing, society no longer offers to the eyes of the wise man anything but an assemblage of artificial men and factitious passions which are the work of all these new relations and have no true foundation in nature. What reflection teaches us on this subject is perfectly confirmed by observation: savage man and civilized man differ so greatly in the depths of their hearts and in their inclinations, that what constitutes the supreme happiness of the one would reduce the other to despair. Savage man breathes only tranquillity and liberty; he wants simply to live and rest easy; and not even the unperturbed tranquillity of the Stoic approaches his profound indifference for any other objects. On the

other hand, the citizen is always active and in a sweat, always agitated, and unceasingly tormenting himself in order to seek still more laborious occupations. He works until he dies; he even runs to his death in order to be in a position to live, or renounces life in order to acquire immortality. He pays court to the great whom he hates and to the rich whom he scorns. He stops at nothing to obtain the honor of serving them. He proudly crows about his own baseness and their protection; and proud of his slavery, he speaks with disdain about those who do not have the honor of taking part in it. What a spectacle for the Carib are the difficult and envied labors of the European minister! How many cruel deaths would that indolent savage not prefer to the horror of such a life, which often is not mollified even by the pleasure of doing good. But in order to see the purpose of so many cares, the words *power* and *reputation* would have to have a meaning in his mind; he would have to learn that there is a type of men who place some value on the regard the rest of the world has for them, and who know how to be happy and content with themselves on the testimony of others rather than on their own. Such, in fact, is the true cause of all these differences; the savage lives in himself; the man accustomed to the ways of society is always outside himself and knows how to live only in the opinion of others. And it is, as it were, from their judgment alone that he draws the sentiment of his own existence. It is not pertinent to my subject to show how, from such a disposition, so much indifference for good and evil arises, along with such fine discourse on morality; how, with everything reduced to appearances, everything becomes factitious and bogus: honor, friendship, virtue, and often even our vices, about which we eventually find the secret of boasting; how, in a word, always asking others what we are and never daring to question ourselves on this matter, in the midst of so much philosophy, humanity, politeness, and sublime maxims, we have merely a deceitful and frivolous exterior: honor without virtue, reason without wisdom, and pleasure without happiness. It is enough for me to have proved that this is not the original state of man, and that this is only the spirit of society, and the inequality that society engenders, which thus change and alter all our natural inclinations.

I have tried to set forth the origin and progress of

inequality, the establishment and abuse of political societies, to the extent that these things can be deduced from the nature of man by the light of reason alone, and independently of the sacred dogmas that give to sovereign authority the sanction of divine right. It follows from this presentation that, since inequality is practically non-existent in the state of nature, it derives its force and growth from the development of our faculties and the progress of the human mind, and eventually becomes stable and legitimate through the establishment of property and laws. Moreover, it follows that moral inequality, authorized by positive right alone, is contrary to natural right whenever it is not combined in the same proportion with physical inequality: a distinction that is sufficient to determine what one should think in this regard about the sort of inequality that reigns among all civilized people, for it is obviously contrary to the law of nature, however it may be defined, for a child to command an old man, for an imbecile to lead a wise man, and for a handful of people to gorge themselves on superfluities while the starving multitude lacks necessities.

Rousseau's Notes to *Discourse on the Origin of Inequality*

1. Herodotus relates that after the murder of the false Smerdis, the seven liberators of Persia being assembled to deliberate on the form of government they would give the state, Otanes was fervently in support of a republic: an opinion all the more extraordinary in the mouth of a satrap, since, over and above the claim he could have to the empire, a grandee fears more than death a type of government that forces him to respect men. Otanes, as may readily be believed, was not listened to; and seeing that things were progressing toward the election of a monarch, he, who wanted neither to obey nor command, voluntarily yielded to the other rivals his right to the crown, asking as his sole compensation that he and his descendants be free and independent. This was granted him. If Herodotus did not inform us of the restriction that was placed on this privilege, it would be necessary to suppose it, otherwise Otanes, not acknowledging any sort of law and not being accountable to anyone, would have been all powerful in the state and more powerful than the king himself. But there was hardly any likelihood that a man capable of contenting himself, in similar circumstances, with such a privilege, was capable of abusing it. In fact, there is no evidence

that this right ever caused the least trouble in the kingdom, either from wise Otanes or from any of his descendants.

2. From the start I rely with confidence on one of those authorities that are respectable for philosophers, because they come from a solid and sublime reason, which they alone know how to find and perceive.

"Whatever interest we may have in knowing ourselves, I do not know whether we do not have a better knowledge of everything that is not us. Provided by nature with organs uniquely destined for our preservation, we use them merely to receive impressions of external things; we seek merely to extend ourselves outward and to exist outside ourselves. Too much taken with multiplying the functions of our senses and with increasing the external range of our being, we rarely make use of that internal sense which reduces us to our true dimensions, and which separates us from all that is not us. Nevertheless, this is the sense we must use if we wish to know ourselves. It is the only one by which we can judge ourselves. But how can this sense be activated and given its full range? How can our soul, in which it resides, be rid of all the illusions of our mind? We have lost the habit of using it; it has remained unexercised in the midst of the tumult of our bodily sensations; it has been dried out by the fire of our passions; the heart, the mind, the senses, everything has worked against it." *Hist. Nat.,* Vol. IV: *de la Nat. de l'homme,* p. 151.

3. The changes that a long-established habit of walking on two feet could have brought about in the conformation of man, the relations that are still observed between his arms and the forelegs of quadrupeds, and the induction drawn from their manner of walking, could have given rise to doubts about the manner that must have been the most natural to us. All children begin by walking on all fours, and need our example and our lessons to learn to stand upright. There are even savage nations, such as the Hottentots, who, greatly neglecting their children, allow them to walk on their hands for so long that they then have a great deal of trouble getting them to straighten up. The children of the Caribs of the Antilles do the same thing. There are various examples of quadruped men, and I could cite among others that of the child who was found in 1344 near Hesse, where he had been raised by wolves, and who said afterward at the court of Prince Henry that, had the decision been left exclusively to him, he would have preferred to return to the wolves than to live among men. He had embraced to such an extent the habit of walking like those animals, that wooden boards had to be attached to him to force him to stand upright and maintain his balance on two feet.

It was the same with the child who was found in 1694, in the forests of Lithuania, and who lived among bears. He did not give, says M. de Condillac, any sign of reason, walked on his hands and feet, had no language, and formed sounds that bore no resemblance whatever to those of a man. The little savage of Hanover, who was brought to the court of England several years ago, had all sorts of trouble getting himself to walk on two feet. And in 1719, two other savages, who were found in the Pyrenees, ran about the mountains in the manner of quadrupeds. As for the objection one might make that this deprives one of the use of one's hands from which we derive so many advantages, over and above the fact that the example of monkeys shows that the hand can be used quite well in both ways, this would prove only that man can give his limbs a destination more congenial than that of nature, and not that nature has destined man to walk otherwise than it teaches him.

But there are, it seems to me, much better reasons to state in support of the claim that man is a biped. First, if it were shown that he could have originally been formed otherwise than we see him and yet finally become what he is, this would not suffice to conclude that this is how it happened; for, after having shown the possibility of these changes, it would still be necessary, prior to granting them, to demonstrate at least their probability. Moreover, if man's arms seem as if they could have served as legs when needed, it is the sole observation favorable to that system, out of a great number of others which are contrary to it. The chief ones are that the manner in which man's head is attached to his body, instead of directing his view horizontally (as is the case for all other animals and for man himself when he walks upright), would have kept him, while walking on all fours, with his eyes fixed directly on the ground, a situation hardly conducive to the preservation of the individual; that the tail he is lacking, and for which he has no use when walking on two feet, is useful to quadrupeds, and none of them is deprived of one; that the breast of a woman, very well located for a biped who holds her child in her arms, is so poorly located for a quadruped that none has it located in that way; that, since the hind part is of an excessive height in proportion to the forelegs (which causes us to crawl on our knees when walking on all fours), the whole would have made an animal that was poorly proportioned and that walked uncomfortably; that if he had placed his foot as well as his hand down flat, he would have had one less articulation in the hind leg than do other animals, namely the one that joins canon to the tibia; and that by setting down only the tip of the foot, as doubtlessly he would have been forced to

do, the tarsus (not to mention the plurality of bones that make it up) appears too large to take the place of the canon, and its articulations with the metatarsus and the tibia too close together to give the human leg in this situation the same flexibility as those of quadrupeds. Since the example of children is taken from an age when natural forces are not yet developed nor the members strengthened, it proves nothing whatever. I might just as well say that dogs are not destined to walk because several weeks after their birth they merely crawl. Particular facts also have little force against the universal practice of all men; even nations that have had no communication with others could not have imitated anything about them. A child abandoned in a forest before he is able to walk, and nourished by some beast, will have followed the example of his nurse in training himself to walk like her. Habit could have given him capabilities he did not have from nature, and just as one-armed men are successful, by dint of exercise, at doing with their feet whatever we do with our hands, he will finally have succeeded in using his hands as feet.

4. Should there be found among my readers a scientist nasty enough to cause me difficulties regarding the supposition of this natural fertility of the earth, I am going to answer him with the following passage:

"As plants derive much more substance from air and water for their sustenance than they do from the earth, it happens that when they rot they return to the earth more than they have derived from it. Moreover, a forest determines the amount of rainwater by stopping vapors. Thus, in a wooded area that was preserved for a long time without being touched, the bed of earth that serves for vegetation would increase considerably. But since animals return to the soil less than they derive from it, and since men take in huge quantities of wood and plants for fire and other uses, it follows that the bed of vegetative earth of an inhabited country must always diminish and finally become like the terrain of Arabia Petraea, and like that of so many other provinces of the Orient (which in fact is the region that has been inhabited from the most ancient times), where only salt and sand are found. For the fixed salt of plants and animals remains, while all the other parts are volatized." M. de Buffon, Hist. Nat.

To this can be added the factual proof based on the quantity of trees and plants of every sort, which filled almost all the uninhabited islands that have been discovered in the last few centuries, and on what history teaches us about the immense forests all over the earth that had to be cut down to the degree that it was populated or civilized. On this I will also make the following three remarks. First, if there is a kind of vegetation that can make up for the loss of vegetative matter which was occasioned by animals, according to M. de Buffon's reasoning, it is above all the wooded areas, where the treetops and the leaves gather and appropriate more water and vapors than do other plants. Second, the destruction of the soil, that is, the loss of the substance that is appropriate for vegetation, should accelerate in proportion as the earth is more cultivated and as the more industrious inhabitants consume in greater abundance its products of every sort. My third and most important remark is that the fruits of trees supply animals with more abundant nourishment than is possible for other forms of vegetation: an experiment I made myself, by comparing the products of two land masses of equal size and quality, the one covered with chestnut trees and the other sown with wheat.

5. Among the quadrupeds, the two most universal distinguishing traits of voracious species are derived, on the one hand, from the shape of the teeth, and, on the other, from the conformation of the intestines. Animals that live solely on vegetation have all flat teeth, like the horse, ox, sheep and hare, but voracious animals have pointed teeth, like the cat, dog, wolf and fox. And as for the intestines, the frugivorous ones have some, such as the colon, which are not found in voracious animals. It appears therefore that man, having teeth and intestines like frugivorous animals, should naturally be placed in that class. And not only do anatomical observations confirm this opinion, but the monuments of antiquity are also very favorable to it. "Dicaearchus," says St. Jerome, "relates in his books on Greek antiquities that under the reign of Saturn, when the earth was still fertile by itself, no man ate flesh, but that all lived on fruits and vegetables that grew naturally." (*Adv. Jovinian.*, Bk. II) [This opinion can also be supported by the reports of several modern travelers. François Corréal, among others, testifies that the majority of inhabitants of the Lucayes, whom the Spaniards transported to the islands of Cuba, Santo Domingo, and elsewhere, died from having eaten flesh.] From this one can see that I am neglecting several advantageous considerations that I could turn to account. For since prey is nearly the exclusive subject of fighting among carnivorous animals, and since frugivorous animals live among themselves in continual peace, if the human species were of this latter genus, it is clear that it would have had a much easier time subsisting in the state of nature, and much less need and occasion to leave it.

6. All the kinds of knowledge that demand reflection, all those acquired only by the concatenation of ideas and perfected only successively, appear to be utterly beyond the grasp of savage man, owing to the lack of communication with his fellow-men, that is to say, owing to the lack of the instrument which is used for that communication, and to the lack of the needs that make it necessary. His understanding and his industry are limited to jumping, running, fighting, throwing a stone, climbing a tree. But if he knows only those things, in return he knows them much better than we, who do not have the same need for them as he. And since they depend exclusively on bodily exercise and are not capable of any communication or progress from one individual to another, the first man could have been just as adept at them as his last descendants.

The reports of travelers are full of examples of the force and vigor of men of barbarous and savage nations. They praise scarcely less their adroitness and nimbleness. And since eyes alone are needed to observe these things, nothing hinders us from giving credence to what eyewitnesses certify on the matter. I draw some random examples from the first books that fall into my hands.

"The Hottentots," says Kolben, "understand fishing better than the Europeans at the Cape. Their skill is equal when it comes to the net, the hook and the spear, in coves as well as in rivers. They catch fish by hand no less skillfully. They are incomparably good at swimming. Their style of swimming has something surprising about it, something entirely unique to them. They swim with their body upright and their hands stretched out of the water, so that they appear to be walking on land. In the greatest agitation of the sea, when the waves form so many mountains, they somehow dance on the top of the waves, rising and falling like a piece of cork.

"The Hottentots," says the same author further, "are surprisingly good at hunting, and the nimbleness of their running surpasses the imagination." He is amazed that they did not put their agility to ill use more often, which, however, sometimes happens, as can be judged from the example he gives. "A Dutch sailor," he says, "on disembarking at the Cape, charged a Hottentot to follow him to the city with a roll of tobacco that weighed about twenty pounds. When they were both some distance from the crew, the Hottentot asked the sailor if he knew how to run. Run! answered the Dutchman; yes, very well. Let us see, answered the African. And fleeing with the tobacco, he disappeared almost immediately. The sailor, confounded by such marvelous quickness, did not think of following him, and he never again saw either his tobacco or his porter.

"They have such quick sight and such a sure hand that Europeans cannot go near them. At a hundred paces they will hit with a stone a mark the size of a halfpenny. And what is more amazing, instead of fixing their eyes on the target as we do, they make continuous movements and contortions. It appears that their stone is carried by an invisible hand."

Father du Tertre says about the savages of the Antilles nearly the same things that have just been read about the Hottentots of the Cape of Good Hope. He praises, above all, their accuracy in shooting with their arrows birds in flight and swimming fish, which they then catch by diving for them. The savages of North America are no less famous for their strength and adroitness, and here is an example that will lead us to form a judgment about those qualities in the Indians of South America.

In the year 1746, an Indian from Buenos Aires, having been condemned to the galleys of Cadiz, proposed to the governor that he buy back his liberty by risking his life at a public festival. He promised that by himself he would attack the fiercest bull with no other weapon in his hand but a rope; that he would bring him to the ground, seize him with his rope by whatever part they would indicate, saddle him, bridle him, mount him, and so mounted he would fight two other of the fiercest bulls to be released from the Torillo, and that he would put all of them to death, one after the other, the moment they would command him to do so, and without anyone's help. This was granted him. The Indian kept his word and succeeded in everything he had promised. On the way in which he did it and on the details of the fight, one can consult M. Gautier, *Observations sur l'Histoire Naturelle*, Vol. I (in-12°), p. 262, whence this fact is taken.

7. "The lifespan of horses," says M. de Buffon, "is, as in all other species of animals, proportionate to the length of their growth period. Man, who takes fourteen years to grow, can live six or seven times as long, that is to say, ninety or a hundred years. The horse, whose growth period is four years, can live six or seven times as long, that is to say, twenty-five or thirty years. The examples that could be contrary to this rule are so rare, that they should not even be regarded as an exception from which conclusions can be drawn. And just as large horses achieve their growth in less time than slender horses, they also have a shorter lifespan and are old from the age of fifteen."

8. I believe I see another difference between carnivorous and frugivorous animals still more general than the one I have remarked upon in Note 5, since this one extends to birds. This difference consists in the number of young, which never exceeds two in each litter for the species that lives exclusively on plant life, and which ordinarily exceeds this number for voracious animals. It is easy to know nature's plan in this regard by the number of teats, which is only two in each female of the first species, like the mare, the cow, the goat, the doe, the ewe, etc., and which is always six or eight in the other females, such as the dog, the cat, the wolf, the tigress, etc. The hen, the goose, the duck, which are all voracious birds (as are the eagle, the sparrow hawk, the screech owl), also lay and hatch a large number of eggs, which never happens to the pigeon, the turtle-dove, or to birds that eat nothing but grain, which lay and hatch scarcely more than two eggs at a time. The reason that can be given for this difference is that the animals that live exclusively on grass and plants, remaining nearly the entire day grazing and being forced to spend considerable time feeding themselves, could not be up to the task of nursing several young; whereas the voracious animals, taking their meal almost in an instant, can more easily and more often return to their young and to their hunting, and can compensate for the loss of so large a quantity of milk. There would be many particular observations and reflections to make on all this, but this is not the place to make them, and it is enough for me to have shown in this part the most general system of nature, a system which furnishes a new reason to remove man from the class of carnivorous animals and to place him among the frugivorous species.

9. A famous author, on calculating the goods and evils of human life and comparing the two sums, has found that the latter greatly exceeded the former, and that, all things considered, life was a pretty poor present for man. I am not surprised by his conclusion; he has drawn all of his arguments from the constitution of civil man. Had he gone back as far as natural man, the judgment can be made that he would have found very different results, that he would have realized that man has scarcely any evils other than those he has given himself, and that nature would have been justified. It is not without trouble that we have managed to make ourselves so unhappy. When, on the one hand, one considers the immense labors of men, so many sciences searched into, so many arts invented, and so many forces employed, abysses filled up, mountains razed, rocks broken, rivers made navigable, lands cleared, lakes dug, marshes drained, enormous buildings raised upon the earth, the sea covered with ships and sailors; and when, on the other hand, one searches with a little meditation for the true advantages that have resulted from all this for the happiness of the human species, one cannot help being struck by the astonishing disproportion that obtains between these things, and to deplore man's

blindness, which, to feed his foolish pride and who knows what vain sense of self-importance, makes him run ardently after all the miseries to which he is susceptible, and which beneficent nature has taken pains to keep from him.

Men are wicked; a sad and continual experience dispenses us from having to prove it. Nevertheless, man is naturally good; I believe I have demonstrated it. What therefore can have depraved him to this degree, if not the changes that have befallen his constitution, the progress he has made, and the sorts of knowledge he has acquired? Let human society be admired as much as one wants; it will be no less true for it that it necessarily brings men to hate one another to the extent that their interests are at cross-purposes with one another, to render mutually to one another apparent services and in fact do every evil imaginable to one another. What is one to think of an interaction where the reason of each private individual dictates to him maxims directly contrary to those that public reason preaches to the body of society, and where each finds his profit in the misfortune of another? Perhaps there is not a wealthy man whose death is not secretly hoped for by greedy heirs and often by his own children; not a ship at sea whose wreck would not be good news to some merchant; not a firm that a debtor of bad faith would not wish to see burn with all the papers it contains; not a people that does not rejoice at the disasters of its neighbors. Thus it is that we find our advantage in the setbacks of our fellow-men, and that one person's loss almost always brings about another's prosperity. But what is even more dangerous is that public calamities are anticipated and hoped for by a multitude of private individuals. Some want diseases, others death, others war, others famine. I have seen ghastly men weep with the sadness at the likely prospects of a fertile year. And the great and deadly fire of London, which cost the life or the goods of so many unfortunate people, made the fortunes of perhaps more than ten thousand people. I know that Montaigne blames the Athenian Demades for having had a worker punished, who, by selling coffins at a high price, made a great deal from the death of the citizens. But since the reason Montaigne proposes is that everyone would have to be punished, it is evident that it confirms my own. Let us therefore penetrate, through our frivolous demonstration of good will, to what happens at the bottom of our hearts; and let us reflect on what the state of things must be where all men are forced to caress and destroy one another, and where they are born enemies by duty and crooks by interest. If someone answers me by claiming that society is constituted in such a manner that each

man gains by serving others, I will reply that this would be very well and good, provided he did not gain still more by harming them. There is no profit, however legitimate, that is not surpassed by one that can be made illegitimately, and wrong done to a neighbor is always more lucrative than services. It is therefore no longer a question of anything but finding the means of being assured of impunity. And this is what the powerful spend all their forces on, and the weak all their ruses.

Savage man, when he has eaten, is at peace with all nature, and the friend of all his fellow-men. Is it sometimes a question of his disputing over his meal? He never comes to blows without having first compared the difficulty of winning with that of finding his sustenance elsewhere. And since pride is not involved in the fight, it is ended by a few swings of the fist. The victor eats; the vanquished is on his way to seek his fortune, and everything is pacified. But for man in society, these are quite different affairs. It is first of all a question of providing for the necessary and then for the superfluous; next come delights, and then immense riches, and then subjects, and then slaves. He has not a moment's respite. What is most singular is that the less natural and pressing the needs, the more the passions increase and, what is worse, the power to satisfy them; so that after long periods of prosperity, after having swallowed up many treasures and ruined many men, my hero will end by butchering everything until he is the sole master of the universe. Such in brief is the moral portrait, if not of human life, then at least of the secret pretensions of the heart of every civilized man.

Compare, without prejudices, the state of civil man with that of savage man and seek, if you can, how many new doors to suffering and death (other than his wickedness, his needs and his miseries) the former has opened. If you consider the emotional turmoil that consumes us, the violent passions that exhaust and desolate us, the excessive labors with which the poor are overburdened, the still more dangerous softness to which the rich abandon themselves, and which cause the former to die of their needs and the latter of their excesses; if you call to mind the monstrous combinations of foods, their pernicious seasonings, the corrupted foodstuffs, tainted drugs, the knavery of those who sell them, the errors of those who administer them, the poison of the vessels in which they are prepared; if you pay attention to the epidemic diseases engendered by the bad air among the multitudes of men gathered together, to the illnesses occasioned by the effeminacy of our lifestyle, by the coming and going from the inside of our houses to the open air, the use of garments put on or taken off with too little precaution, and all the cares that our excessive sensuality has turned into necessary habits, the neglect or privation of which then costs us our life or our health; if you take into account fires and earthquakes, which, in consuming or turning upside down whole cities, cause their inhabitants to die by the thousands; in a word, if you unite the dangers that all these causes continually gather over our heads, you will realize how dearly nature makes us pay for the scorn we have shown for its lessons.

I will not repeat here what I have said elsewhere about war, but I wish that informed men would, for once, want or dare to give the public the detail of the horrors that are committed in armies by provisions and hospital suppliers. One would see that their not too secret maneuvers, on account of which the most brilliant armies dissolve into less than nothing, cause more soldiers to perish than are cut down by enemy swords. Moreover, no less surprising is the calculation of the number of men swallowed up by the sea every year, either by hunger, or scurvy, or pirates, or fire, or shipwrecks. It is clear that we must also put to the account of established property, and consequently to that of society, the assassinations, the poisonings, the highway robberies, and even the punishments of these crimes, punishments necessary to prevent greater ills, but which, costing the lives of two or more for the murder of one man, do not fail really to double the loss to the human species. How many are the shameful ways to prevent the birth of men or to fool nature: either by those brutal and depraved tastes which insult its most charming work, tastes that neither savages nor animals ever knew, and that have arisen in civilized countries only as the result of a corrupt imagination; or by those secret abortions, worthy fruits of debauchery and vicious honor; or by the exposure or the murder of a multitude of infants, victims of the misery of their parents or of the barbarous shame of their mothers; or, finally by the mutilation of those unfortunates, part of whose existence and all of whose posterity are sacrificed to vain songs, or what is worse still, to the brutal jealousy of a few men: a mutilation which, in this last case, doubly outrages nature, both by the treatment received by those who suffer it and by the use to which they are destined.

[But are there not a thousand more frequent and even more dangerous cases where paternal rights overtly offend humanity? How many talents are buried and inclinations are forced by the imprudent constraint of fathers! How many men would have distinguished themselves in a suitable station who die unhappy and dishonored in another station for which they have no taste! How many happy but unequal marriages have been broken or disturbed, and how many chaste wives dishon-ored by this order of conditions always in contradiction with that of nature! How many other bizarre unions formed by interests and disavowed by love and by reason! How many even honest and virtuous couples cause themselves torment because they were ill-matched! How many young and unhappy victims of their parent's greed plunge into vice or pass their sorrowful days in tears, and moan in indissoluble chains which the heart rejects and which gold alone has formed! Happy sometimes are those whose courage and even virtue tear them from life before a barbarous violence forces them into crime or despair. Forgive me, father and mother forever deplorable. I regrettably worsen your sorrows; but may they serve as an eternal and terrible example to whoever dares, in the name of nature, to violate the most sacred of its rights!

If I have spoken only of those ill-formed relationships that are the result of our civil order, is one to think that those where love and sympathy have presided are themselves exempt from drawbacks?]

What would happen if I were to undertake to show the human species attacked in its very source, and even in the most holy of all bonds, where one no longer dares to listen to nature until after having consulted fortune, and where, with civil disorder confounding virtues and vices, continence becomes a criminal precaution, and the refusal to give life to one's fellow-man an act of humanity? But without tearing away the veil that covers so many horrors, let us content ourselves with pointing out the evil, for which others must supply the remedy.

Let us add to all this that quantity of unwholesome trades which shorten lives or destroy one's health, such as work in mines, various jobs involving the processing of metals, minerals, and especially lead, copper, mercury, cobalt, arsenic, realgar; those other perilous trades which everyday cost the lives of a number of workers, some of them roofers, others carpenters, others masons, others working in quarries; let us bring all of these objects together, I say, and we will be able to see in the establishment and the perfection of societies the reasons for the diminution of the species, observed by more than one philosopher.

Luxury, impossible to prevent among men who are greedy for their own conveniences and for the esteem of others, soon completes the evil that societies have begun; and on the pretext of keeping the poor alive (which it was not necessary to do), luxury impoverishes everyone else, and sooner or later depopulates the state.

Luxury is a remedy far worse than the evil it means to cure; or rather it is itself the worst of all evils in any state, however large or small it may be, and which, in order to feed the hordes of lackeys and wretches it has produced, crushes and ruins the laborer and the citizen—like those scorching south winds that, by covering grass and greenery with devouring insects, take sustenance away from useful animals, and bring scarcity and death to all the places where they make themselves felt.

From society and the luxury it engenders, arise the liberal and mechanical arts, commerce, letters, and all those useless things that make industry flourish, enriching and ruining states. The reason for this decay is quite simple. It is easy to see that agriculture, by its nature, must be the least lucrative of all the arts, because, with its product being of the most indispensable use to all men, its price must be proportionate to the abilities of the poorest. From the same principle can be drawn this rule: that, in general, the arts are lucrative in inverse proportion to their usefulness, and that the most necessary must finally become the most neglected. From this it is clear what must be thought of the true advantages of industry and of the real effect that results from its progress.

Such are the discernible causes of all the miseries into which opulence finally brings down the most admired nations. To the degree that industry and the arts expand and flourish, the scorned farmer, burdened with taxes necessary to maintain luxury and condemned to spend his life between toil and hunger, abandons his fields to go to the cities in search of the bread he ought to be carrying there. The more the capital cities strike the stupid eyes of the people as wonderful, the more it will be necessary to groan at the sight of countrysides abandoned, fields fallow, and main roads jammed with unhappy citizens who have become beggars or thieves, destined to end their misery one day on the rack or on a dung-heap. Thus it is that the state, enriching itself on the one hand, weakens and depopulates itself on the other; and that the most powerful monarchies, after much labor to become opulent and deserted, end by becoming the prey of poor nations which succumb to the deadly temptation to invade them, and which enrich and enfeeble themselves in their turn, until they are themselves invaded and destroyed by others.

Let someone deign to explain to us for once what could have produced those hordes of barbarians which for so many centuries have overrun Europe, Asia and Africa. Was it to the industry of their arts, the wisdom of their laws, the excellence of their civil order that they owed that prodigious population? Would our learned ones be so kind as to tell us why, far from multiplying to that degree, those ferocious and brutal men, without enlightenment, without restraint, without education, did

not all kill one another at every moment to argue with one another over their food or game? Let them explain to us how these wretches even had the gall to look right in the eye such capable people as we were, with such fine military discipline, such fine codes, and such wise laws, and why, finally, after society was perfected in the countries of the north, and so many pains were taken there to teach men their mutual duties and the art of living together agreeably and peaceably, nothing more is seen to come from them like those multitudes of men it produced formerly. I am very much afraid that someone might finally get it into his head to reply to me that all these great things, namely the arts, sciences, and laws, have been very wisely invented by men as a salutary plague to prevent the excessive multiplication of the species, out of fear that this world, which is destined for us, might finally become too small for its inhabitants.

What then! Must we destroy societies, annihilate thine and mine, and return to live in the forests with bears?— a conclusion in the style of my adversaries, which I prefer to anticipate, rather than leave to them the shame of drawing it. Oh you, to whom the heavenly voice has not made itself heard, and who recognize for your species no other destination except to end this brief life in peace; you who can leave in the midst of the cities your deadly acquisitions, your troubled minds, your corrupt hearts and your unbridled desires. Since it depends on you, retake your ancient and first innocence; go into the woods to lose sight and memory of the crimes of your contemporaries, and have no fear of cheapening your species in renouncing its enlightenment in order to renounce its vices. As for men like me, whose passions have forever destroyed their original simplicity, who can no longer feed on grass and acorn[s], nor get by without laws and chiefs; those who were honored in their first father with supernatural lessons; those who will see, in the intention of giving human actions from the beginning a morality they would not have acquired for a long time, the reason for a precept indifferent in itself and inexplicable in any other system; those, in a word, who are convinced that the divine voice called the entire human race to the enlightenment and the happiness of the celestial intelligences; all those latter ones will attempt, through the exercise of virtues they oblige themselves to practice while learning to know them, to merit the eternal reward that they ought to expect for them. They will respect the sacred bonds of the societies of which they are members; they will love their fellowmen and will serve them with all their power; they will scrupulously obey the laws and the men who are their authors and their ministers; they will honor above all the good and wise princes who will know how to prevent, cure or palliate that pack of abuses and evils always ready to overpower us; they will animate the zeal of these worthy chiefs by showing them without fear or flattery the greatness of their task and the rigor of their duty. But they will despise no less for it a constitution that can be maintained only with the help of so many respectable people, who are desired more often than they are obtained, and from which, despite all their care, always arise more real calamities than apparent advantages.

10. Among the men we know, whether by ourselves, or from historians, or from travelers, some are black, others white, others red. Some wear their hair long; others have merely curly wool. Some are almost entirely covered with hair; others do not even have a beard. There have been and perhaps there still are nations of men of gigantic size; and apart from the fable of the Pygmies (which may well be merely an exaggeration), we know that the Laplanders and above all the Greenlanders are considerably below the average size of man. It is even maintained that there are entire peoples who have tails like quadrupeds. And without putting blind faith in the accounts of Herodotus and Ctesias, we can at least draw from them the very likely opinion that had one been able to make good observations in those ancient times when various peoples followed lifestyles differing more greatly among themselves than do those of today, one would have also noted in the shape and posture of the body, much more striking varieties. All these facts, for which it is easy to furnish incontestable proofs, are capable of surprising only those who are accustomed to look solely at the objects that surround them and who are ignorant of the powerful effects of the diversity of climates, air, foods, lifestyle, habits in general, and especially the astonishing force of the same causes when they act continually for long successions of generations. Today, when commerce, voyages and conquests reunite various peoples further, and their lifestyles are constantly approximating one another through frequent communication, it is evident that certain national differences have diminished; and, for example, everyone can take note of the fact that today's Frenchmen are no longer those large, colorless and blond-haired bodies described by Latin historians, although time, together with the mixture of the Franks and the Normans, themselves colorless and blond-haired, should have reestablished what commerce with the Romans could have removed from the influence of the climate in the natural constitution and complexion of the inhabitants. All of these observations on the varieties that a thousand causes can produce and

have in fact produced in the human species cause me to wonder whether the various animals similar to men, taken without much scrutiny by travelers for beasts, either because of some differences they noticed in their outward structure or simply because these animals did not speak, would not in fact be veritable savage men, whose race, dispersed in the woods during olden times, had not had an occasion to develop any of its virtual faculties, had not acquired any degree of perfection, and was still found in the primitive state of nature. Let us give an example of what I mean.

"There are found in the kingdom of the Congo," says the translator of the *Histoire des Voyages*, "many of those large animals called *orangutans* in the East Indies, which occupy a middle ground between the human species and the baboons. Battel relates that in the forests of Mayomba, in the kingdom of Loango, one sees two kinds of monsters, the larger of which are called *pongos* and the others *enjocos*. The former bear an exact resemblance to man, except they are much larger and very tall. With a human face, they have very deep-set eyes. Their hands, cheeks and ears are without hair, except for their eyebrows, which are very long. Although the rest of their body is quite hairy, the hair is not very thick; the color of the hair is brown. Finally, the only part that distinguishes them from men is their leg, which has no calf. They walk upright, grasping the hair of their neck with their hand. Their retreat is in the woods. They sleep in the trees, and there they make a kind of roof which offers them shelter from the rain. Their foods are fruits or wild nuts; they never eat flesh. The custom of the Negroes who cross the forests is to light fires during the night. They note that in the morning, at their departure, the pongos take their place around the fire, and do not withdraw until it is out; because, for all their cleverness, they do not have enough sense to lay wood on the fire to keep it going.

"They occasionally walk in groups and kill the Negroes who cross the forests. They even fall upon elephants who come to graze in the places they inhabit, and they irritate the elephants so much with punches or with whacks of a stick that they force them howling to take flight. Pongos are never taken alive, because they are so strong that ten men would not be enough to stop them. But the Negroes take a good many young ones after having killed the mother, to whose body the young stick very closely. When one of these animals dies, the others cover its body with a pile of branches or leaves. Purchass adds that, in the conversations he has had with Battel, he had learned from him also that a pongo abducted a little Negro who passed an entire month in the society of these animals, for they do not harm men they take by surprise, at least when these men do not pay any attention to them, as the little Negro had observed. Battel had not described the second species of monster.

"Dapper confirms that the kingdom of the Congo is filled with those animals which in the Indies bear the name orangutans, that is to say, inhabitants of the woods, and which the Africans call *quojas-morros.* This beast, he says, is so similar to man, that it has occurred to some travelers that it could have issued from a woman and a monkey: a myth which even the Negroes reject. One of these animals was transported from the Congo to Holland and presented to the Prince of Orange, Frederick Henry. It was the height of a three-year old child, moderately stocky, but square and well-proportioned, very agile and lively; its legs fleshy and robust; the entire front of the body naked, but the rear covered with black hairs. At first sight, its face resembled that of a man, but it had a flat and turned up nose; its ears were also those of the human species; its breast (for it was a female), was plump, its navel sunken, its shoulders very well joined, its hands divided into fingers and thumbs, its calves and heels fat and fleshy. It often walked upright on its legs; it was capable of lifting and carrying heavy burdens. When it wanted to drink, it took the cover of the pot in one hand, and held the base with the other; afterward it graciously wiped its lips. It lay down to sleep with its head on a cushion, covering itself with such skill that it would have been taken for a man in bed. The Negroes tell strange stories about this animal. They assert not only that it takes women and girls by force, but that it dares to attack armed men. In a word, there is great likelihood that it is the satyr of the ancients. Perhaps Merolla is speaking only of these animals whom he relates that Negroes sometimes lay hold of savage men and women in their hunts."

These species of anthropomorphic animals are again discussed in the third volume of the same *Histoire des Voyages* under the name of *beggos* and *mandrills.* But sticking to the preceding accounts, we find in the description of these alleged monsters striking points of conformity with the human species and lesser differences than those that would be assigned between one man and another. From these pages it is not clear what the reasons are that the authors have for refusing to give the animals in question the name "savage men"; but it is easy to conjecture that it is on account of their stupidity and also because they did not speak — feeble reasons for those who know that although the organ of speech is natural to man, nevertheless speech itself is not natural to him, and who knows to what point his perfectibility can have elevated civil man above his original state. The small

number of lines these descriptions contain can cause us to judge how badly these animals have been observed and with what prejudices they have been viewed. For example, they are categorized as monsters, and yet there is agreement that they reproduce. In one place, Battel says that the pongos kill the Negroes who cross the forests; in another place, Purchass adds that they do not do any harm, even when they surprise them, at least when the Negroes do not fix their gaze upon them. The pongos gather around fires lit by the Negroes upon the Negroes' withdrawal, and withdraw in their turn when the fire is out. There is the fact. Here now is the commentary of the observer: *because, for all their cleverness, they do not have enough sense to lay wood on the fire to keep it going.* I would like to hazard a guess how Battel, or Purchass, his compiler, could have known that the withdrawal of the pongos was an effect of their stupidity rather than their will. In a climate such as Loango, fire is not something particularly necessary for the animals; and if the Negroes light a fire, it is less against the cold than to frighten ferocious beasts. It is therefore a very simple matter that, after having been for some time delighted with the flame or being well warmed, the pongos grow tired of always remaining in the same place and go off to graze, which requires more time than if they ate flesh. Moreover, we know that most animals, man not excluded, are naturally lazy, and that they refuse all sorts of cares which are not absolutely necessary. Finally, it seems very strange that pongos, whose adroitness and strength are praised, the pongos who know how to bury their dead and to make themselves roofs out of branches, should not know how to push fagots into the fire. I recall having seen a monkey perform the same maneuver that people deny the pongos can do. It is true that since my ideas were not oriented in this direction, I myself committed the mistake for which I reproach our travelers; I neglected to examine whether the intention of the monkey was actually to sustain the fire or simply, as I believe is the case, to imitate the actions of a man. Whatever the case may be, it is well demonstrated that the monkey is not a variety of man: not only because he is deprived of the faculty of speech, but above all because it is certain that his species does not have the faculty of perfecting itself, which is the specific characteristic of the human species: experiments that do not seem to have been made on the pongos and the orangutan with sufficient care to enable one to draw the same conclusion in their case. However, there would be a means by which, if the orangutan or others were of the human species, even the least sophisticated observers could assure themselves of it by means of demonstration.

But beyond the fact that a single generation would not be sufficient for this experiment, it should pass as unworkable, since it would be necessary that what is merely a supposition be demonstrated to be true, before the test that should establish the fact could be innocently tried.

Precipitous judgments, which are not the fruit of an enlightened reason, are prone to be excessive. Without any fanfare, our travelers made into beasts, under the names *pongos, mandrills, orangutans,* the same beings that the ancients, under the names *satyrs, fauns, sylvans,* made into divinities. Perhaps, after more precise investigations it will be found that they are [neither beasts nor gods but] men. Meanwhile, it would seem to me that there is as much reason to defer on this point to Merolla, an educated monk, an eyewitness, and one who, with all his naïveté, did not fail to be a man of wit, as to the merchant Battel, Dapper, Purchass, and the other compilers.

What judgment do we think such observers would have made regarding the child found in 1694, of whom I have spoken before, who gave no indication of reason, walked on his feet and hands, had no language, and made sounds that bore no resemblance whatever to those of a man? It took a long time, continues the same philosopher who provided me with this fact, before he could utter a few words, and then he did it in a barbarous manner. Once he could speak, he was questioned about his first state, but he did not recall it any more than we recall what happened to us in the cradle. If, unhappily* for him, this child had fallen into the hands of our travelers, there can be no doubt that after having observed his silence and stupidity, they would have resolved to send him back to the woods or lock him up in a menagerie; after which they would have spoken eruditely about him in their fine accounts as a very curious beast who looked rather like a man.

For the three or four hundred years since the inhabitants of Europe inundated the other parts of the world and continually published new collections of travels and stories, I am convinced that we know no other men but the Europeans alone. Moreover, it would appear, from the ridiculous prejudices that have not been extinguished even among men of letters, that everybody does hardly anything under the pompous name of "the study of man" except study the men of his country. Individuals may well come and go; it seems that philosophy travels nowhere; moreover, the philosophy of one people is little suited to another. The reason for this is manifest, at least

for distant countries. There are hardly more than four sorts of men who make long voyages: sailors, merchants, soldiers, and missionaries. Now we can hardly expect the first three classes to provide good observers; and as for those in the fourth, occupied by the sublime vocation that calls them, even if they were not subject to the prejudices of social position as are all the rest, we must believe that they would not voluntarily commit themselves to investigations that would appear to be sheer curiosity, and which would sidetrack them from the more important works to which they are destined. Besides, to preach the Gospel in a useful manner, zeal alone is needed, and God gives the rest. But to study men, talents are needed which God is not required to give anyone, and which are not always the portion of saints. One does not open a book of voyages where one does not find descriptions of characters and mores. But one is utterly astonished to see that these people who have described so many things have said merely what everyone already knew, that, at the end of the world, they knew how to understand only what it was for them to notice without leaving their street; and that those true qualities which characterize nations and strike eyes made to see have almost always escaped theirs. Whence this fine moral slogan, so bandied about by the philosophizing rabble: that men are everywhere the same; that, since everywhere they have the same passions and the same vices, it is rather pointless to seek to characterize different peoples—which is about as well reasoned as it would be for someone to say that Peter and James cannot be distinguished from one another, because they both have a nose, a mouth and eyes.

Will we never see those happy days reborn when the people did not dabble in philosophizing, but when a Plato, a Thales, a Pythagoras, taken with an ardent desire to know, undertook the greatest voyages merely to inform themselves, and went far away to shake off the yoke of national prejudices, in order to learn to know men by their similarities and their differences, and to acquire those sorts of universal knowledge that are exclusively those of a single century or country, but which, since they are of all times and all places, are, as it were, the common science of the wise?

We admire the splendor of some curious men who, at great expense, made or caused to be made voyages to the Orient with learned men and painters, in order to sketch hovels and to decipher or copy inscriptions. But I have trouble conceiving how, in a century where people take pride in fine sorts of knowledge, there are not to be found two closely united men—rich, one in money, the other in genius, both loving glory and aspiring for

---

[*In the copy of the Discourse *sent to Richard Davenport,* Rousseau inserts here: *or perhaps happily.*]

immortality—one of whom sacrifices twenty thousand crowns of his goods and the other ten years of his life for a famous voyage around the world, in order to study, not always rocks and plants, but, for once, men and mores, and who, after so many centuries used to measure and examine the house, would finally be of a mind to want to know its inhabitants.

The academicians who have traveled through the northern parts of Europe and the southern parts of America had for their object to visit them more as geometers than as philosophers. Nevertheless, since they were both simultaneously, we cannot regard as utterly unknown the regions that have been seen and described by La Condamine and Maupertuis. The jeweler Chardin, who has traveled like Plato, has left nothing to be said about Persia. China appeared to have been well observed by the Jesuits. Kempfer gives a passable idea of what little he has seen in Japan. Except for these reports, we know nothing about the peoples of the East Indies, who have been visited exclusively by Europeans interested more in filling their purses than their heads. All of Africa and its numerous inhabitants, as unique in character as in color, are yet to be examined. The entire earth is covered with nations of which we know only the names, and we dabble in judging the human race! Let us suppose a Montesquieu, a Buffon, a Diderot, a Duclos, a d'Alembert, a Condillac, or men of that ilk traveling in order to inform their compatriots, observing and describing as they know how to do, Turkey, Egypt, Barbary, the empire of Morocco, Guinea, the land of the Bantus, the interior of Africa and its eastern coastlines, the Malabars, Mogul, the banks of the Ganges, the kingdoms of Siam, Pegu, and Ava, China, Tartary, and especially Japan; then in the other hemisphere, Mexico, Peru, Chile, the straits of Magellan, not to forget the Patagonias true or false, Tucuman, Paraguay (if possible), Brazil; finally the Caribbean Islands, Florida, and all the savage countries—the most important voyage of all and the one that should be embarked upon with the greatest care. Let us suppose that these new Hercules, back from these memorable treks, then wrote at leisure the natural, moral, and political history of what they would have seen; we ourselves would see a new world sally forth from their pen, and we would thus learn to know our own. I say that when such observers will affirm of an animal that it is a man and of another that it is a beast, we will have to believe them. But it would be terribly simpleminded to defer in this to unsophisticated travelers, concerning whom we will sometimes be tempted to put the same question that they dabble at resolving concerning other animals.

11. That appears utterly evident to me and I am unable to conceive whence our philosophers can derive all the passions they ascribe to natural man. With the single exception of the physically necessary which nature itself demands, all our other needs are such merely out of habit (previous to which they were not needs), or by our own desires; and we do not desire what we are not in a position to know. Whence it follows that since savage man desires only the things he knows and knows only those things whose possession is in his power or easily acquired, nothing should be so tranquil as his soul and nothing so limited as his mind.

12. I find in Locke's *Civil Government* an objection which seems to me too specious for me to be permitted to hide it. "Since the purpose of the society between male and female," says this philosopher, "is not merely to procreate, but to continue the species, this society should last, even after procreation, at least as long as it is necessary for the nurture and support of the procreated, that is to say, until they are capable of seeing to their needs on their own. This rule, which the infinite wisdom of the creator has established upon the works of his hands, we see creatures inferior to man observing constantly and strictly. In those animals which live on grass, the society between male and female lasts no longer than each act of copulation, because, the teats of the mother being sufficient to feed the young until they are able to feed on grass, the male is content to beget and no longer mingles with the female or the young, to whose sustenance he has nothing to contribute. But as far as beasts of prey are concerned, the society lasts longer, because, with the mother being unable to see to her own sustenance and at the same time feed her young by means of her prey alone (which is a more laborious and more dangerous way of taking in nourishment than by feeding on grass), the assistance of the male is utterly necessary for the maintenance of their common family (if one may use that term), which is able to subsist to the point where it can go hunt for prey only through the efforts of the male and the female. We note the same thing in all the birds (with the exception of some domestic birds which are found in places where the continual abundance of nourishment exempts the male from the effort of feeding the young). It is clear that when the young in their nest need food, the male and female bring it to them until the young there are capable of flying and seeing to their own sustenance.

"And, in my opinion, herein lies the principal, if not the only reason why the male and the female in mankind are bound to a longer period of society than is undertaken by other creatures: namely, that the female is capable of conceiving and is ordinarily pregnant again and has a new child long before the previous child is in a position to do without the help of its parents and can take care of itself. Thus, since the father is bound to take care of those he has produced, and to take that care for a long time, he is also under an obligation to continue in conjugal society with the same woman by whom he has had them, and to remain in that society much longer than other creatures, whose young being capable of subsisting by themselves before the time comes for a new procreation, the bond of the male and female breaks of its own accord, and they are both at complete liberty, until such time as that season, which usually solicits the animals to join with one another, obliges them to choose new mates. And here we cannot help admiring the wisdom of the creator, who, having given to man the qualities needed to provide for the future as well as for the present, has willed and has brought it about that the society of man should last longer than that of the male and female among other creatures, so that thereby the industry of man and woman might be stimulated more, and that their interests might be better united, with a view to making provisions for their children and to leaving them their goods—nothing being more to the detriment of the children than an uncertain and vague conjunction, or an easy and frequent dissolution of the conjugal society."*

The same love of truth which has made me to set forth sincerely this objection, moves me to accompany it with some remarks, if not to resolve it, at least to clarify it.

1. I will observe first that moral proofs do not have great force in matters of physics, and that they serve more to explain existing facts than to establish the real existence of those facts. Now such is the type of proof that M. Locke employs in the passage I have just quoted; for although it may be advantageous to the human species for the union between man and woman to be permanent, it does not follow that it has been thus established by nature; otherwise it would be necessary to say that it also instituted civil society, the arts, commerce, and all that is asserted to be useful to men.

2. I do not know where M. Locke has found that among animals of prey, the society of the male and female lasts longer than does the society of those that live on grass, and that the former assists the latter to feed the young; for it is not manifest that the dog, the cat, the bear, or the wolf recognize their female better than the horse, the ram, the bull, the stag, or all the other quadruped animals do theirs. On the contrary, it seems that if the assistance of the male were necessary to the female to preserve her young, it would be particularly in the species that live only on grass, because a long period of time is needed by the mother to graze, and during that entire interval she is forced to neglect her brood, whereas the prey of a female bear or wolf is devoured in an instant, and, without suffering hunger, she has more time to nurse her young. This line of reasoning is confirmed by an observation upon the relative number of teats and young which distinguishes carnivorous from frugivorous species, and of which I have spoken in Note 8. If this observation is accurate and general, since a woman has only two teats and rarely has more than one child at a time, this is one more strong reason for doubting that the human species is naturally carnivorous. Thus it seems that, in order to draw Locke's conclusion, it would be necessary to reverse completely his reasoning. There is no more solidity in the same distinction when it is applied to birds. For who could be persuaded that the union of the male and the female is more durable among vultures and crows than among turtle-doves? We have two species of domestic birds, the duck and the pigeon, which furnish us with examples directly contrary to the system of this author. The pigeon, which lives solely on grain, remains united to its female, and they feed their young in common. The duck, whose voraciousness is known, recognizes neither his female nor his young, and provides no help in their sustenance. And among hens, a species hardly less carnivorous, we do not observe that the rooster bothers himself in the least with the brood. And if in the other species the male shares with the female the care of feeding the young, it is because birds, which at first are unable to fly and which the mother cannot nurse, are much less in a position to get along without the help of the father than are quadrupeds, for which the mother's teat is sufficient, at least for a time.

3. There is much uncertainty about the principal fact that serves as a basis for all of M. Locke's reasoning; for in order to know whether, as he asserts, in the pure state of nature the female ordinarily is pregnant again and has a new child long before the preceding one could see to its needs for itself, it would be necessary to perform experiments that M. Locke surely did not perform and that no one is in a position to perform.

[*Translator's note: This is a translation of the French rendering of Locke's text.]

The continual cohabitation of husband and wife is so near an occasion for being exposed to a new pregnancy that it is very difficult to believe that the chance encounter or the mere impulsion of temperament produced such frequent effects in the pure state of nature as in that of conjugal society: a slowness that would contribute perhaps toward making the children more robust, and that, moreover, might be compensated by the power to conceive, prolonged to a greater age in the women who would have abused it less in their youth. As to children, there are several reasons for believing that their forces and their organs develop much later among us than they did in the primitive state of which I am speaking. The original weakness which they derive from the constitution of the parents, the cares taken to envelop and constrain all of their members, the softness in which they are raised, perhaps the use of milk other than that of their mother, everything contradicts and slows down in them the initial progress of nature. The heed they are forced to pay to a thousand things on which their attention is continually fixed, while no exercise is given to their bodily forces, can also bring about considerable deflection from their growth. Thus, if, instead of first overworking and exhausting their minds in a thousand ways, their bodies were allowed to be exercised by the continual movements that nature seems to demand of them, it is to be believed that they would be in a much better position to walk and to provide for their needs by themselves.

4. Finally, M. Locke at most proves that there could well be in a man a motive for remaining attached to a woman when she has a child but in no way does he prove that the man must have been attached to her before the childbirth and during the nine months of pregnancy. If a given woman is indifferent to the man during those nine months, if she even becomes unknown to him, why will he help her after childbirth? Why will he help her to raise a child that he does not know belongs to him alone, and whose birth he has neither decided upon nor foreseen? Evidently M. Locke presumes what is in question, for it is not a matter of knowing why the man will remain attached to the woman after childbirth, but why he will be attached to her after conception. Once his appetite is satisfied, the man has no further need for a given woman, nor the woman for a given man. The man does not have the least care or perhaps the least idea of the consequences of his action. The one goes off in one direction, the other in another, and there is no likelihood that at the end of nine months they

have the memory of having known one another. For this type of memory, by which one individual gives preference to another for the act of generation, requires, as I prove in the text, more progress or corruption in human understanding than may be supposed in man in the state of animality we are dealing with here. Another woman can therefore satisfy the new desires of the man as congenially as the one he has already known, and another man in the same manner satisfy the woman, supposing she is impelled by the same appetite during the time of pregnancy, about which one can reasonably be in doubt. And if in the state of nature the woman no longer feels the passion of love after the conception of the child, the obstacle to her society with the man thus becomes much greater still, since she then has no further need either for the man who has made her pregnant or for anyone else. There is not, therefore, in the man any reason to seek the same woman, or in the woman any reason to seek the same man. Thus Locke's reasoning falls in ruin, and all the dialectic of this philosopher has not shielded him from the mistake committed by Hobbes and others. They had to explain a fact of the state of nature, that is to say, of a state where men lived in isolation and where a given man did not have any motive for living in proximity to another given man, nor perhaps did a given group of men have a motive for living in proximity to another given group of men, which is much worse. And they gave no thought to transporting themselves beyond the centuries of society, that is to say, of those times when men always have a reason for living in proximity to one another, and when a given man often has a reason for living in proximity to a given man or woman.

13. I will hold back from embarking on the philosophical reflections that there would be to engage in concerning the advantages and disadvantages of this institution of languages. It is not for me to be permitted to attack vulgar errors; and educated people respect their prejudices too much to abide patiently my alleged paradoxes. Let us therefore allow men to speak, to whom it has not been made a crime to risk sometimes taking the part of reason against the opinion of the multitude. *Nor would anything disappear from the happiness of the human race, if, when the disaster and confusion of so many languages has been cast out, mortals should cultivate one art, and if it should be allowed to explain anything by means of signs, movements and gestures. But now it has been so established that the condition of animals commonly believed to be brutes is considerably better than ours in this respect, inasmuch as they articulate their*

feelings and their thoughts without an interpreter more readily and perhaps more felicitously than any mortals can, especially if they use a foreign language. *Is. Vossius de Poëmat. Cant. et Viribus Rythmi, p. 66.

14. In showing how ideas of discrete quantity and its relationships are necessary in the humblest of the arts, Plato mocks with good reason the authors of his time who alleged that Palamedes had invented numbers at the siege of Troy, as if, says this philosopher, Agamemnon could have been ignorant until then of how many legs he had. In fact, one senses the impossibility that society and the arts should have arrived at the point where they already were at the time of the siege of Troy, unless men had the use of numbers and arithmetic. But the necessity for knowing numbers, before acquiring other types of knowledge, does not make their invention easier to imagine. Once the names of the numbers are known, it is easy to explain their meaning and to elicit the ideas which these names represent; but in order to invent them, it was necessary, prior to conceiving of these same ideas, to be, as it were, on familiar terms with philosophical meditations, to be trained to consider beings by their essence alone and independently of all other perception—a very difficult, very metaphysical, hardly natural abstraction, and yet one without which these ideas could never have been transported from one species or genus to another, nor could numbers have become universal. A savage could consider separately his right leg and his left leg, or look at them together under the indivisible idea of a pair without ever thinking that he had two of them; for the representative idea that portrays for us an object is one thing, and the numerical idea which determines it is another. Even less was he able to count to five. And although, by placing his hands one on top of the other, he could have noticed that the fingers corresponded exactly, he was far from thinking of their numerical equality. He did not know the sum of his fingers any more than that of his hairs. And if, after having made him understand what numbers are, someone had said to him that he had as many fingers as toes, he perhaps would have been quite surprised, in comparing them, to find that this was true.

15. We must not confuse egocentrism with love of oneself, two passions very different by virtue of both their nature and their effects. Love of oneself is a natural sentiment which moves every animal to be vigilant in its own preservation and which, directed in man by reason and modified by pity, produces humanity and

[*Translator's note: Rousseau here quotes the Latin text.]

virtue. Egocentrism is merely a sentiment that is relative, artificial and born in society, which moves each individual to value himself more than anyone else, which inspires in men all the evils they cause one another, and which is the true source of honor.

With this well understood, I say that in our primitive state, in the veritable state of nature, egocentrism does not exist; for since each particular man regards himself as the only spectator who observes him, as the only being in the universe that takes an interest in him, as the only judge of his own merit, it is impossible that a sentiment which has its source in comparisons that he is not in a position to make could germinate in his soul. For the same reason, this man could not have either hatred or desire for revenge, passions which can arise only from the belief that offense has been received. And since what constitutes the offense is scorn or the intention to harm and not the harm, men who know neither how to appraise nor to compare themselves can do considerable violence to one another when it returns them some advantage for doing it, without ever offending one another. In a word, on seeing his fellow-men hardly otherwise than he would see animals of another species, each man can carry away the prey of the weaker or yield his own to the stronger, viewing these lootings as merely natural events, without the least stirring of insolence or resentment, and without any other passion but the sadness or the joy of a good or bad venture.

16. It is something extremely remarkable that, for the many years that the Europeans torment themselves in order to acclimate the savages of various countries to their lifestyle, they have not yet been able to win over a single one of them, not even by means of Christianity; for our missionaries sometimes turn them into Christians, but never into civilized men. Nothing can overcome the invincible repugnance they have against appropriating our mores and living in our way. If these poor savages are as unhappy as is alleged, by what inconceivable depravity of judgment do they constantly refuse to civilize themselves in imitation of us, or to learn to live happily among us; whereas one reads in a thousand places that the French and other Europeans have voluntarily taken refuge among those nations, and have spent their entire lives there, no longer able to leave so strange a lifestyle; and whereas we even see level-headed missionaries regret with tenderness the calm and innocent days they have spent among those much scorned peoples? If one replies that they do not have enough enlightenment to make a sound judgment about their state and ours, I will reply that the reckoning of happiness is less an affair of reason than of sentiment. Moreover, this reply can be turned against us with still greater force; for there is

a greater distance between our ideas and the frame of mind one needed to be in in order to conceive the taste which the savages find in their lifestyle, than between the ideas of savages and those that can make them conceive our lifestyle. In fact, after a few observations it is easy for them to see that all our labors are directed toward but two objects: namely, the conveniences of life for oneself and esteem among others. But what are the means by which we are to imagine the sort of pleasure a savage takes in spending his life alone amidst the woods, or fishing, or blowing into a sorry-looking flute, without ever knowing how to derive a single tone from it and without bothering himself to learn?

Savages have frequently been brought to Paris, London and other cities; people have been eager to display our luxury, our wealth, and all our most useful and curious arts. None of this has ever excited in them anything but a stupid admiration, without the least stirring of covetousness. I recall, among others, the story of a chief of some North Americans who was brought to the court of England about thirty years ago. A thousand things were made to pass before his eye in an attempt to give him some present that could please him, but nothing was found about which he seemed to care. Our weapons seemed heavy and cumbersome to him, our shoes hurt his feet, our clothes restricted him; he rejected everything. Finally, it was noticed that, having taken a wool blanket, he seemed to take some pleasure in wrapping it around his shoulders. You will agree at least, someone immediately said to him, on the usefulness of this furnishing? Yes, he replies, this seems to me to be nearly as good as an animal skin. However, he would not have said that, had he worn them both in the rain.

Perhaps someone will say to me that it is habit which, in attaching everyone to his lifestyle, prevents savages from realizing what is good in ours. And at that rate, it must at least appear quite extraordinary that habit has more force in maintaining the savages in the taste for their misery than the Europeans in the enjoyment of their felicity. But to give to this last objection a reply to which there is not a word to make in reply, without adducing all the young savages that people have tried in vain to civilize, without speaking of the Greenlanders and the inhabitants of Iceland, whom people have tried to raise and feed in Denmark, and all of whom sadness and despair caused to perish, whether from languor or in the sea when they attempted to regain their homeland by swimming back to it, I will be content to cite a single, well-documented example, which I give to the admirers of European civilization to examine.

"All the efforts of the Dutch missionaries at the Cape of Good Hope have never been able to convert a single Hottentot. Van der Stel, Governor of the Cape, having taken one from infancy, had raised him in the principles of the Christian religion and in the practice of the customs of Europe. He was richly clothed; he was taught several languages and his progress corresponded very closely to the care that was taken for his education. Having great hopes for his wit, the Governor sent him to the Indies with a commissioner general who employed him usefully in the affairs of the company. He returned to the Cape after the death of the commissioner. A few days after his return, on a visit he made to some of his Hottentot relatives, he made the decision to strip himself of his European dress in order to clothe himself with a sheepskin. He returned to the fort in this new outfit, carrying a bundle containing his old clothes, and, on presenting them to the Governor, he made the following speech to him: *Please, sir, be so kind as to pay heed to the fact that I forever renounce this clothing. I also renounce the Christian religion for the rest of my life. My resolution is to live and die in the religion, ways and customs of my ancestors. The only favor I ask of you is that you let me keep the necklace and cutlass I am wearing. I will keep them for love of you.* Thereupon, without waiting for Van der Stel's reply, he escaped by taking flight and was never seen again at the Cape." *Histoire des Voyages*, Vol. V, p. 175.

17. One could raise against me the objection that, in such a disorder, men, instead of willfully murdering one another, would have dispersed, had there been no limits to their dispersion. But first, these limits would at least have been those of the world. And if one thinks about the excessive population that results from the state of nature, one will judge that the earth in that state would not have taken long to be covered with men thus forced to keep together. Besides, they would have dispersed, had the evil been rapid, and had it been an overnight change. But they were born under the yoke; they were in the habit of carrying it when they felt its weight, and they were content to wait for the opportunity to shake it off. Finally, since they were already accustomed to a thousand conveniences which forced them to keep together, dispersion was no longer so easy as in the first ages, when, since no one had need for anyone but himself, everyone made his decision without waiting for someone else's consent.

18. Marshal de V*** related that, on one of his campaigns, when the excessive knavery of a provisions supplier had made the army suffer and complain, he gave him a severe dressing down and threatened to have him hanged. "This threat has no effect on me," the knave

boldly replied to him, "and I am quite pleased to tell you that nobody hangs a man with a hundred thousand crowns at his disposal." I do not know how it happened, the Marshal added naïvely, but in fact he was not hanged, even though he deserved to be a hundred times over.

19. Distributive justice would still be opposed to this rigorous equality of the state of nature, if it were workable in civil society. And since all the members of the state owe it services proportionate to their talents and forces, the citizens for their part should be distinguished and favored in proportion to their services. It is in this sense that one must understand a passage of Isocrates, in which he praises the first Athenians for having known well how to distinguish which of the two sorts of equality was the more advantageous, one of which consists in portioning out indifferently to all citizens the same advantages, and the other in distributing them according to each one's merit. These able politicians, adds the orator, in banishing that unjust equality that makes no differentiation between wicked and good men, adhered inviolably to that equality which rewards and punishes each according to one's merit. But first, no society has ever existed, regardless of the degree of corruption they could have achieved, in which no differentiation between wicked and good men was made. And in the matter of mores, where the law cannot set a sufficiently precise measurement to serve as a rule for the magistrate, the law very wisely prohibits him from the judgment of persons, leaving him merely the judgment of actions, in order not to leave the fate or the rank of citizens to his discretion. Only mores as pure as those of the ancient Romans could withstand censors; such tribunals would soon have overturned everything among us. It is for public esteem to differentiate between wicked and good men. The magistrate is judge only of strict law [*droit*]; but the populace is the true judge of mores—an upright and even enlightened judge on this point, occasionally deceived but never corrupted. The ranks of citizens ought therefore to be regulated not on the basis of their personal merit, which would be to leave to the magistrate the means of making an almost arbitrary application of the law, but upon the real services which they render to the state and which lend themselves to a more precise reckoning.

On the
Social Contract,
or
Principles of
Political Right

by J.-J. Rousseau,
Citizen of Geneva

—foederis aequas
Dicamus leges
—*Aeneid*, XI

FOREWORD

This little treatise is part of a longer work I undertook some time ago without taking stock of my abilities, and have long since abandoned. Of the various selections that could have been drawn from what had been completed, this is the most considerable, and, it appears to me, the one least unworthy of being offered to the public. The rest no longer exists.

On the Social Contract

BOOK I

I want to inquire whether there can be some legitimate and sure rule of administration in the civil order, taking men as they are and laws as they might be.

Reprinted from *The Basic Political Writings*, translated by Donald A. Cress (Indianapolis: Hackett Publishing Company, 1987), by permission of the publisher.

I will always try in this inquiry to bring together what right permits with what interest prescribes, so that justice and utility do not find themselves at odds with one another.

I begin without demonstrating the importance of my subject. It will be asked if I am a prince or a legislator that I should be writing about politics. I answer that I am neither, and that is why I write about politics. Were I a prince or a legislator, I would not waste my time saying what ought to be done. I would do it or keep quiet.

Born a citizen of a free state and a member of the sovereign, the right to vote is enough to impose upon me the duty to instruct myself in public affairs, however little influence my voice may have in them. Happy am I, for every time I meditate on governments, I always find new reasons in my inquiries for loving that of my country.

Chapter 1

Subject of the First Book

Man is born free, and everywhere he is in chains. He who believes himself the master of others does not escape being more of a slave than they. How did this change take place? I have no idea. What can render it legitimate? I believe I can answer this question.

Were I to consider only force and the effect that flows from it, I would say that so long as a people is constrained to obey and does obey, it does well. As soon as it can shake off the yoke and does shake it off, it does even better. For by recovering its liberty by means of the same right that stole it, either the populace is justified in getting it back or else those who took it away were not justified in their actions. But the social order is a sacred right which serves as a foundation for all other rights. Nevertheless, this right does not come from nature. It is therefore founded upon convention. Before coming to that, I ought to substantiate what I just claimed.

Chapter 2

Of the First Societies

The most ancient of all societies and the only natural one, is that of the family. Even so children remain bound to their father only so long as they need him to take care of them. As soon as the need ceases, the natural bond is dissolved. Once the children are freed from the obedience they owed the father and their father is freed from the care he owed his children, all return equally to independence. If they continue to remain united, this no longer takes place naturally but voluntarily, and the family maintains itself only by means of convention.

This common liberty is one consequence of the nature of man. Its first law is to see to his maintenance; its first concerns are those he owes himself; and, as soon as he reaches the age of reason, since he alone is the judge of the proper means of taking care of himself, he thereby becomes his own master.

The family therefore is, so to speak, the prototype of political societies; the leader is the image of the father, the populace is the image of the children, and, since all are born equal and free, none give up their liberty except for their utility. The entire difference consists in the fact that in the family the love of the father for his children repays him for the care he takes for them, while in the state, where the leader does not have love for his peoples, the pleasure of commanding takes the place of this feeling.

Grotius denies that all human power is established for the benefit of the governed, citing slavery as an example. His usual method of reasoning is always to present fact as a proof of right.[1] A more logical method could be used, but not one more favorable to tyrants.

According to Grotius, it is therefore doubtful whether the human race belongs to a hundred men, or whether these hundred men belong to the human race. And throughout his book he appears to lean toward the former view. This is Hobbes' position as well. On this telling, the human race is divided into herds of cattle, each one having its own leader who guards it in order to devour it.

Just as a herdsman possesses a nature superior to that of his herd, the herdsmen of men who are the leaders, also have a nature superior to that of their peoples. According to Philo, Caligula reasoned thus, concluding quite properly from this analogy that kings were gods, or that the peoples were beasts.

Caligula's reasoning coincides with that of Hobbes and Grotius. Aristotle, before all the others, had also said that men are by no means equal by nature, but that some were born for slavery and others for domination.

Aristotle was right, but he took the effect for the cause. Every man born in slavery is born for slavery; nothing is more certain. In their chains slaves lose everything, even the desire to escape. They love their servitude the way the companions of Ulysses loved their degradation.[2] If there are slaves by nature, it is because there have been slaves against nature. Force has produced the first slaves; their cowardice has perpetuated them.

I have said nothing about King Adam or Emperor Noah, father of three great monarchs who partitioned

---

1. "Learned research on public right is often nothing more than the history of ancient abuses, and taking a lot of trouble to study them too closely gets one nowhere." *Treatise on the Interests of France Along With Her Neighbors*, by the Marquis d'Argenson. This is just what Grotius has done.

2. See a short treatise of Plutarch entitled "That Animals Reason."

the universe, as did the children of Saturn, whom some have believed they recognize in them. I hope I will be appreciated for this moderation, for since I am a direct descendent of these princes, and perhaps of the eldest branch, how am I to know whether, after the verification of titles, I might not find myself the legitimate king of the human race? Be that as it may, we cannot deny that Adam was the sovereign of the world, just as Robinson Crusoe was sovereign of his island, so long as he was its sole inhabitant. And the advantage this empire had was that the monarch, securely on his throne, had no rebellions, wars or conspirators to fear.

Chapter 3

On the Right of the Strongest

The strongest is never strong enough to be master all the time, unless he transforms force into right and obedience into duty. Hence the right of the strongest, a right that seems like something intended ironically and is actually established as a basic principle. But will no one explain this word to me? Force is a physical power; I fail to see what morality can result from its effects. To give in to force is an act of necessity, not of will. At most, it is an act of prudence. In what sense could it be a duty?

Let us suppose for a moment that there is such a thing as this alleged right. I maintain that all that results from it is an inexplicable mish-mash. For once force produces the right, the effect changes places with the cause. Every force that is superior to the first succeeds to its right. As soon as one can disobey with impunity, one can do so legitimately; and since the strongest is always right, the only thing to do is to make oneself the strongest. For what kind of right is it that perishes when the force on which it is based ceases? If one must obey because of force, one need not do so out of duty; and if one is no longer forced to obey one is no longer obliged. Clearly then, this word "right" adds nothing to force. It is utterly meaningless here.

Obey the powers that be. If that means giving in to force, the precept is sound, but superfluous. I reply it will never be violated. All power comes from God—

I admit it—but so does every disease. Does this mean that calling in a physician is prohibited? If a brigand takes me by surprise at the edge of a wooded area, is it not only the case that I must surrender my purse, but even that I am in good conscience bound to surrender it, if I were able to withhold it? After all, the pistol he holds is also a power.

Let us then agree that force does not bring about right, and that one is obliged to obey only legitimate powers. Thus my original question keeps returning.

Chapter 4

On Slavery

Since no man has a natural authority over his fellow man, and since force does not give rise to any right, conventions therefore remain the basis of all legitimate authority among men.

If, says Grotius, a private individual can alienate his liberty and turn himself into the slave of a master, why could not an entire people alienate its liberty and turn itself into the subject of a king? There are many equivocal words here which need explanation, but let us confine ourselves to the word *alienate*. To alienate is to give or to sell. A man who makes himself the slave of someone else does not give himself; he sells himself, at least for his subsistence. But why does a people sell itself? Far from furnishing his subjects with their subsistence, a king derives his own from them alone, and, according to Rabelais, a king does not live cheaply. Do subjects then give their persons on the condition that their estate will also be taken? I fail to see what remains for them to preserve.

It will be said that the despot assures his subjects of civil tranquility. Very well. But what do they gain, if the wars his ambition drags them into, if his insatiable greed, if the oppressive demands caused by his ministers occasion more grief for his subjects than their own dissensions would have done? What do they gain, if this very tranquility is one of their miseries? A tranquil life is also had in dungeons; is that enough to make them desirable? The Greeks who were locked up in the Cyclops' cave lived a tranquil existence as they awaited their turn to be devoured.

To say that a man gives himself gratuitously is to

say something absurd and inconceivable. Such an act is illegitimate and null, if only for the fact that he who commits it does not have his wits about him. To say the same thing of an entire populace is to suppose a populace composed of madmen. Madness does not bring about right.

Even if each person can alienate himself, he cannot alienate his children. They are born men and free. Their liberty belongs to them; they alone have the right to dispose of it. Before they have reached the age of reason, their father can, in their name, stipulate conditions for their maintenance and for their well-being. But he cannot give them irrevocably and unconditionally, for such a gift is contrary to the ends of nature and goes beyond the rights of paternity. For an arbitrary government to be legitimate, it would therefore be necessary in each generation for the people to be master of its acceptance or rejection. But in that event this government would no longer be arbitrary.

Renouncing one's liberty is renouncing one's dignity as a man, the rights of humanity and even its duties. There is no possible compensation for anyone who renounces everything. Such a renunciation is incompatible with the nature of man. Taking away all liberty from his will is tantamount to removing all morality from his actions. Finally, it is a vain and contradictory convention to stipulate absolute authority on one side and a limitless obedience on the other. Is it not clear that no commitments are made to a person from whom one has the right to demand everything? And does this condition alone not bring with it, without equivalent or exchange, the nullity of the act? For what right would my slave have against me, given that all he has belongs to me, and that, since his right is my right, my having a right against myself makes no sense?

Grotius and others derive from war another origin for the alleged right of slavery. Since, according to them, the victor has the right to kill the vanquished, these latter can repurchase their lives at the price of their liberty—a convention all the more legitimate, since it turns a profit for both of them.

But clearly this alleged right to kill the vanquished does not in any way derive from the state of war. Men are not naturally enemies, for the simple reason that men living in their original state of independence do not have sufficiently constant relationships among themselves to bring about either a state of peace or a state of war. It is the relationship between things and not that between men that brings about war. And since this state of war cannot come into existence from simple personal relations, but only from real [proprietary] relations, a private war between one man and another can exist neither in the state of nature, where there is no constant property, nor in the social state, where everything is under the authority of the laws.

Fights between private individuals, duels, encounters are not acts which produce a state. And with regard to private wars, authorized by the ordinances of King Louis IX of France and suspended by the Peace of God, they are abuses of feudal government, an absurd system if there ever was one, contrary to the principles of natural right and to all sound polity.

War is not therefore a relationship between one man and another, but a relationship between one state and another. In war private individuals are enemies only incidentally: not as men or even as citizens,[3] but as soldiers; not as members of the homeland but as its defenders. Finally, each state can have as enemies only other states and not men, since there can be no real relationship between things of disparate natures.

---

3. [*At this point the following passage was added to the 1782 edition:* The Romans, who had a better understanding of and a greater respect for the right of war than any other nation, carried their scruples so far in this regard that a citizen was not allowed to serve as a volunteer unless he had expressly committed himself against the enemy and against a specifically named enemy. When a legion in which Cato the Younger first served had been reorganized, Cato the Elder wrote Popilius that if he wanted his son to continue to serve under him, he would have to make him swear the military oath afresh, since, with the first one having been annulled, he could no longer take up arms against the enemy. And this very same Cato wrote his son to take care to avoid going into battle without swearing this military oath afresh. I know the siege of Clusium and other specific cases can be raised as counter-examples to this, but for my part I cite laws and customs. The Romans were the ones who transgressed their laws least often, and are the only ones to have had such noble laws.]

This principle is even in conformity with the established maxims of all times and with the constant practice of all civilized peoples. Declarations of war are warnings not so much to powers as to their subjects. The foreigner (be he king, private individual, or a people) who robs, kills or detains subjects of another prince without declaring war on the prince, is not an enemy but a brigand. Even in the midst of war a just prince rightly appropriates to himself everything in an enemy country belonging to the public, but respects the person and goods of private individuals. He respects the rights upon which his own rights are founded. Since the purpose of war is the destruction of the enemy state, one has the right to kill the defenders of that state so long as they bear arms. But as soon as they lay down their arms and surrender, they cease to be enemies or instruments of the enemy. They return to being simply men; and one no longer has a right to their lives. Sometimes a state can be killed without a single one of its members being killed. For war does not grant a right that is unnecessary to its purpose. These principles are not those of Grotius. They are not based on the authority of poets. Rather they are derived from the nature of things; they are based on reason.

As to the right of conquest, the only basis it has is the law of the strongest. If war does not give the victor the right to massacre the vanquished peoples, this right (which he does not have) cannot be the basis for the right to enslave them. One has the right to kill the enemy only when one cannot enslave him. The right to enslave him does not therefore derive from the right to kill him. Hence it is an iniquitous exchange to make him buy his life, to which no one has any right, at the price of his liberty. In establishing the right of life and death on the right of slavery, and the right of slavery on the right of life and death, is it not clear that one falls into a vicious circle?

Even if we were to suppose that there were this terrible right to kill everyone, I maintain that neither a person enslaved during wartime nor a conquered people bears any obligation whatever toward its master, except to obey him for as long as it is forced to do so. In taking the equivalent of his life, the victor has done him no favor. Instead of killing him unprofitably he kills him usefully. Hence, far from the victor having acquired any authority over him beyond force, the state of war subsists between them just as before. Their relationship itself is the effect of war, and the usage of the right to war does not suppose any peace treaty. They have made a convention. Fine. But this convention, far from destroying the state of war, presupposes its continuation.

Thus, from every point of view, the right of slavery is null, not simply because it is illegitimate, but because it is absurd and meaningless. These words, *slavery* and *right*, are contradictory. They are mutually exclusive. Whether it is the statement of one man to another man, or one man to a people, the following sort of talk will always be equally nonsensical. *I make a convention with you which is wholly at your expense and wholly to my advantage; and, for as long as it pleases me, I will observe it and so will you.*

Chapter 5

That It Is Always Necessary to Return to a First Convention

Even if I were to grant all that I have thus far refuted, the supporters of despotism would not be any better off. There will always be a great difference between subduing a multitude and ruling a society. If scattered men, however many they may be, were successively enslaved by a single individual, I see nothing there but a master and slaves; I do not see a people and its leader. It is, if you will, an aggregation, but not an association. There is neither a public good nor a body politic there. Even if that man had enslaved half the world, he is always just a private individual. His interest, separated from that of others, is never anything but a private interest. If this same man is about to die, after his passing his empire remains scattered and disunited, just as an oak tree dissolves and falls into a pile of ashes after fire has consumed it.

A people, says Grotius, can give itself to a king. According to Grotius, therefore, a people is a people before it gives itself to a king. This gift itself is a civil act; it presupposes a public deliberation. Thus, before examining the act whereby a people chooses a king, it would be well to examine the act whereby a people is a people. For since this act is necessarily prior to the other, it is the true foundation of society.

In fact, if there were no prior convention, then, unless the vote were unanimous, what would become of the minority's obligation to submit to the majority's choice, and where do one hundred who want a master get the right to vote for ten who do not? The law of majority rule is itself an established convention, and presupposes unanimity on at least one occasion.

Chapter 6

On the Social Compact

I suppose that men have reached the point where obstacles that are harmful to their maintenance in the state of nature gain the upper hand by their resistance to the forces that each individual can bring to bear to maintain himself in that state. Such being the case, that original state cannot subsist any longer, and the human race would perish if it did not alter its mode of existence.

For since men cannot engender new forces, but merely unite and direct existing ones, they have no other means of maintaining themselves but to form by aggregation a sum of forces that could gain the upper hand over the resistance, so that their forces are directed by means of a single moving power and made to act in concert.

This sum of forces cannot come into being without the cooperation of many. But since each man's force and liberty are the primary instruments of his maintenance, how is he going to engage them without hurting himself and without neglecting the care that he owes himself? This difficulty, seen in terms of my subject, can be stated in the following terms:

"Find a form of association which defends and protects with all common forces the person and goods of each associate, and by means of which each one, while uniting with all, nevertheless obeys only himself and remains as free as before?" This is the fundamental problem for which the social contract provides the solution.

The clauses of this contract are so determined by the nature of the act that the least modification renders them vain and ineffectual, that, although perhaps they have never been formally promulgated, they are everywhere the same, everywhere tacitly accepted and acknowledged. Once the social compact is violated, each person then regains his first rights and resumes his natural liberty, while losing the conventional liberty for which he renounced it.

These clauses, properly understood, are all reducible to a single one, namely the total alienation of each associate, together with all of his rights, to the entire community. For first of all, since each person gives himself whole and entire, the condition is equal for everyone; and since the condition is equal for everyone, no one has an interest in making it burdensome for the others.

Moreover, since the alienation is made without reservation, the union is as perfect as possible, and no associate has anything further to demand. For if some rights remained with private individuals, in the absence of any common superior who could decide between them and the public, each person would eventually claim to be his own judge in all things, since he is on some point his own judge. The state of nature would subsist and the association would necessarily become tyrannical or hollow.

Finally, in giving himself to all, each person gives himself to no one. And since there is no associate over whom he does not acquire the same right that he would grant others over himself, he gains the equivalent of everything he loses, along with a greater amount of force to preserve what he has.

If, therefore, one eliminates from the social compact whatever is not essential to it, one will find that it is reducible to the following terms. Each of us places his person and all his power in common under the supreme direction of the general will; and as one we receive each member as an indivisible part of the whole.

At once, in place of the individual person of each contracting party, this act of association produces a moral and collective body composed of as many members as there are voices in the assembly, which receives from this same act its unity, its common *self*, its life and its will. This public person, formed thus by union of all the others formerly took the name *city*,[4] and at present takes the name *republic* or *body*

---

4. The true meaning of this word is almost entirely lost on modern men. Most of them mistake a town for a city and a townsman for a citizen. They do not know

politic, which is called *state* by its members when it is passive, *sovereign* when it is active, *power* when compared to others like itself. As to the associates, they collectively take the name *people*; individually they are called *citizens*, insofar as participants in the sovereign authority, and *subjects*, insofar as they are subjected to the laws of the state. But these terms are often confused and mistaken for one another. It is enough to know how to distinguish them when they are used with absolute precision.

Chapter 7

On the Sovereign

This formula shows that the act of association includes a reciprocal commitment between the public and private individuals, and that each individual, contracting, as it were, with himself, finds himself under a twofold commitment: namely as a member of the sovereign to private individuals, and as a member of the state toward the sovereign. But the maxim of civil law that no one is held to commitments made to himself cannot be applied here, for there is a considerable difference between being obligated to oneself, or to a whole of which one is a part.

It must be further noted that the public deliberation

---

that houses make a town but citizens make a city. Once this mistake cost the Carthaginians dearly. I have not found in my reading that the title of *citizen* has ever been given to the subjects of a prince, not even in ancient times to the Macedonians or in our own time to the English, although they are closer to liberty than all the others. Only the French adopt this name *citizen* with complete familiarity, since they have no true idea of its meaning, as can be seen from their dictionaries. If this were not the case, they would become guilty of treason for using it. For them, this name expresses a virtue and not a right. When Bodin wanted to speak about our citizens and townsmen, he committed a terrible blunder when he mistook the one group for the other. M. d'Alembert was not in error, and in his article entitled *Geneva* he has carefully distinguished the four orders of men (even five, counting ordinary foreigners) who are in our towns, and of whom only two make up the republic. No other French author I am aware of has grasped the true meaning of the word *citizen*.

that can obligate all the subjects to the sovereign, owing to the two different relationships in which each of them is viewed, cannot, for the opposite reason, obligate the sovereign to itself, and that consequently it is contrary to the nature of the body politic that the sovereign impose upon itself a law it could not break. Since the sovereign can be considered under but one single relationship, it is then in the position of a private individual contracting with himself. Whence it is apparent that there neither is nor can be any type of fundamental law that is obligatory for the people as a body, not even the social contract. This does not mean that the whole body cannot perfectly well commit itself to another body with respect to things that do not infringe on this contract. For in regard to the foreigner, it becomes a simple being, an individual.

However, since the body politic or the sovereign derives its being exclusively from the sanctity of the contract, it can never obligate itself, not even to another power, to do anything that derogates from the original act, such as alienating some portion of itself or submitting to another sovereign. Violation of the act whereby it exists would be self-annihilation, and whatever is nothing produces nothing.

As soon as this multitude is thus united in a body, one cannot harm one of the members without attacking the whole body. It is even less likely that the body can be harmed without the members feeling it. Thus duty and interest equally obligate the two parties to come to one another's aid, and the same men should seek to combine in this two-fold relationship all the advantages that result from it.

For since the sovereign is formed entirely from the private individuals who make it up, it neither has nor could have an interest contrary to theirs. Hence, the sovereign power has no need to offer a guarantee to its subjects, since it is impossible for a body to want to harm all of its members, and, as we will see later, it cannot harm any one of them in particular. The sovereign, by the mere fact that it exists, is always all that it should be.

But the same thing cannot be said of the subjects in relation to the sovereign, for which, despite their common interest, their commitments would be without substance if it did not find ways of being assured of their fidelity.

In fact, each individual can, as a man, have a private will contrary to or different from the general will that he has as a citizen. His private interest can speak to him in an entirely different manner than the common interest. His absolute and naturally independent existence can cause him to envisage what he owes the common cause as a gratuitous contribution, the loss of which will be less harmful to others than its payment is burdensome to him. And in viewing the moral person which constitutes the state as a being of reason because it is not a man, he would enjoy the rights of a citizen without wanting to fulfill the duties of a subject, an injustice whose growth would bring about the ruin of the body politic.

Thus, in order for the social compact to avoid being an empty formula, it tacitly entails the commitment—which alone can give force to the others—that whoever refuses to obey the general will will be forced to do so by the entire body. This means merely that he will be forced to be free. For this is the sort of condition that, by giving each citizen to the homeland, guarantees him against all personal dependence—a condition that produces the skill and the performance of the political machine, and which alone bestows legitimacy upon civil commitments. Without it such commitments would be absurd, tyrannical and subject to the worst abuses.

Chapter 8

On the Civil State

This passage from the state of nature to the civil state produces quite a remarkable change in man, for it substitutes justice for instinct in his behavior and gives his actions a moral quality they previously lacked. Only then, when the voice of duty replaces physical impulse and right replaces appetite, does man, who had hitherto taken only himself into account, find himself forced to act upon other principles and to consult his reason before listening to his inclinations. Although in this state he deprives himself of several of the advantages belonging to him in the state of nature, he regains such great ones. His faculties are exercised and developed, his ideas are broadened, his feelings are ennobled, his entire soul is elevated to

such a height that, if the abuse of this new condition did not often lower his status to beneath the level he left, he ought constantly to bless the happy moment that pulled him away from it forever and which transformed him from a stupid, limited animal into an intelligent being and a man.

Let us summarize this entire balance sheet so that the credits and debits are easily compared. What man loses through the social contract is his natural liberty and an unlimited right to everything that tempts him and that he can acquire. What he gains is civil liberty and the proprietary ownership of all he possesses. So as not to be in error in these compensations, it is necessary to draw a careful distinction between natural liberty (which is limited solely by the force of the individual involved) and civil liberty (which is limited by the general will), and between possession (which is merely the effect of the force or the right of the first occupant) and proprietary ownership (which is based solely on a positive title).

To the preceding acquisitions could be added the acquisition in the civil state of moral liberty, which alone makes man truly the master of himself. For to be driven by appetite alone is slavery, and obedience to the law one has prescribed for oneself is liberty. But I have already said too much on this subject, and the philosophical meaning of the word *liberty* is not my subject here.

Chapter 9

On the Real [i.e., Proprietary] Domain

Each member of the community gives himself to it at the instant of its constitution, just as he actually is, himself and all his forces, including all the goods in his possession. This is not to say that by this act possession changes its nature as it changes hands and becomes property in the hands of the sovereign. Rather, since the forces of the city are incomparably greater than those of a private individual, public possession is by that very fact stronger and more irrevocable, without being more legitimate, at least to strangers. For with regard to its members, the state is master of all their goods in virtue of the social contract, which serves in the state as the basis of all rights. But with regard to other powers, the state is master only in virtue of the right of the first occupant, which it derives from private individuals.

The right of first occupant, though more real than the right of the strongest, does not become a true right until after the establishment of the right of property. Every man by nature has a right to everything he needs; however, the positive act whereby he becomes a proprietor of some goods excludes him from all the rest. Once his lot has been determined, he should limit himself thereto, no longer having any right against the community. This is the reason why the right of the first occupant, so weak in the state of nature, is able to command the respect of every man living in the civil state. In this right, one respects not so much what belongs to others as what does not belong to oneself.

In general, the following rules must obtain in order to authorize the right of the first occupant on any land. First, this land may not already be occupied by anyone. Second, no one may occupy more than the amount needed to subsist. Third, one is to take possession of it not by an empty ceremony, but by working and cultivating it—the only sign of property that ought, in the absence of legal titles, to be respected by others.

In fact, by according to need and work the right of the first occupant, is it not extended as far as it can go? Is it possible to avoid setting limits to this right? Will setting one's foot on a piece of common land be sufficient to claim it at once as one's own? Will having the force for a moment to drive off other men be sufficient to deny them the right ever to return? How can a man or a people seize a vast amount of territory and deprive the entire human race of it except by a punishable usurpation, since this seizure deprives all other men of the shelter and sustenance that nature gives them in common? When Nuñez Balboa stood on the shoreline and took possession of the South Sea and all of South America in the name of crown of Castille, was this enough to dispossess all the inhabitants and to exclude all the princes of the world? On that basis, those ceremonies would be multiplied quite in vain. All the Catholic King had to do was to take possession of the universe all at once from his private room, excepting afterwards from his empire only what already belonged to other princes.

One can imagine how the combined and contiguous lands of private individuals became public territory; and how the right of sovereignty, extending from subjects to the land they occupied, becomes at once real and personal. This places its owners in a greater dependence, turning their very own forces into guarantees of their loyalty. This advantage does not seem to have been fully appreciated by the ancient monarchs, who, calling themselves merely King of the Persians, the Scythians, and the Macedonians, appeared to regard themselves merely as the leaders of men rather than the masters of the country. Today's monarchs more shrewdly call themselves King of France, Spain, England, and so on. In holding the land thus, they are quite sure of holding the inhabitants.

What is remarkable about this alienation is that, in accepting the goods of private individuals, the community is far from despoiling them; rather, in so doing, it merely assures them of legitimate possession, changing usurpation into a true right, and enjoyment into proprietary ownership. In that case, since owners are considered trustees of the public good, and since their rights are respected by all members of the state and maintained with all its force against foreigners, through an advantageous surrender to the public and still more so to themselves, they have, so to speak, acquired all they have given. This paradox is easily explained by the distinction between the rights of the sovereign and those of the proprietor to the same store, as will be seen later.

It can also happen, as men begin to unite before possessing anything and later appropriate a piece of land sufficient for everyone, that they enjoy it in common or divide it among themselves either in equal shares or according to proportions laid down by the sovereign. In whatever way this acquisition is accomplished, each private individual's right to his very own store is always subordinate to the community's right to all, without which there could be neither solidity in the social fabric nor real force in the exercise of sovereignty.

I will end this chapter and this book with a remark that should serve as a basis for every social system. It is that instead of destroying natural equality, the fundamental compact, on the contrary, substitutes a moral and legitimate equality to whatever physical inequality nature may have been able to impose upon men, and that, however, unequal in force or intelligence they may be, men all become equal by convention and by right.[5]

END OF THE FIRST BOOK

BOOK II

Chapter 1

That Sovereignty Is Inalienable

The first and most important consequence of the principles established above is that only the general will can direct the forces of the state according to the purpose for which it was instituted, which is the common good. For if the opposition of private interests made necessary the establishment of societies, it is the accord of these same interests that made it possible. It is what these different interests have in common that forms the social bond, and, were there no point of agreement among all these interests, no society could exist. For it is utterly on the basis of this common interest that society ought to be governed.

I therefore maintain that since sovereignty is merely the exercise of the general will, it can never be alienated, and that the sovereign, which is only a collective being, cannot be represented by anything but itself. Power can perfectly well be transmitted, but not the will.

In fact, while it is not impossible for a private will to be in accord on some point with the general will, it is impossible at least for this accord to be durable and constant. For by its nature the private will tends toward having preferences, and the general will tends toward equality. It is even more impossible for there

5. Under bad governments this equality is only apparent and illusory. It serves merely to maintain the poor man in his misery and the rich man in his usurpation. In actuality, laws are always useful to those who have possessions and harmful to those who have nothing. Whence it follows that the social state is advantageous to men only insofar as they all have something and none of them has too much.

to be a guarantee of this accord even if it ought always to exist. This is not the result of art but of chance. The sovereign may well say, "Right now I want what a certain man wants or at least what he says he wants." But it cannot say, "What this man will want tomorrow I too will want," since it is absurd for the will to tie its hands for the future and since it does not depend upon any will's consenting to anything contrary to the good of the being that wills. If, therefore, the populace promises simply to obey, it dissolves itself by this act, it loses its standing as a people. The very moment there is a master, there no longer is a sovereign, and thenceforward the body politic is destroyed.

This is not to say that the commands of the leaders could not pass for manifestations of the general will, so long as the sovereign, who is free to oppose them, does not do so. In such a case, the consent of the people ought to be presumed on the basis of universal silence. This will be explained at greater length.

Chapter 2

That Sovereignty Is Indivisible

Sovereignty is indivisible for the same reason that it is inalienable. For either the will is general,[6] or it is not. It is the will of either the people as a whole or of only a part. In the first case, this declared will is an act of sovereignty and constitutes law. In the second case, it is merely a private will, or an act of magistracy. At most it is a decree.

However, our political theorists, unable to divide sovereignty in its principle, divide it in its object. They divide it into force and will, into legislative and executive power, into rights of imposing taxes, of justice and of war, into internal administration and power to negotiate with foreigners. Occasionally they confuse all these parts and sometimes they separate them. They turn the sovereign into a fantastic being made of interconnected pieces. It is as if they built a man out of several bodies, one of which had eyes,

6. For a will to be general, it need not always be unanimous; however, it is necessary for all the votes to be counted. Any formal exclusion is a breach of generality.

another had arms, another feet, and nothing more. Japanese sleight-of-hand artists are said to dismember a child before the eyes of spectators, then, throwing all the parts in the air one after the other, they make the child fall back down alive and all in one piece. These conjuring acts of our political theorists are more or less like these performances. After having taken apart the social body by means of a sleight-of-hand worthy of a carnival, they put the pieces back together who knows how.

This error comes from not having formed precise notions of sovereign authority, and from having taken for parts of that authority what were merely emanations from it. Thus, for example, the acts of declaring war and making peace have been viewed as acts of sovereignty, which they are not, since each of these acts is not a law but merely an application of the law, a particular act determining the legal circumstances, as will be clearly seen when the idea attached to the word *law* comes to be defined.

In reviewing the other divisions in the same way, one would find that one is mistaken every time one believes one sees sovereignty divided, and that the rights one takes to be the parts of this sovereignty are all subordinated to it and always presuppose supreme wills which these rights merely put into effect.

It would be impossible to say how much this lack of precision has obscured the decisions of authors who have written about political right when they wanted to judge the respective rights of kings and peoples on the basis of the principles they had established. Anyone can see, in Chapters III and IV of Book I of Grotius, how this learned man and his translator, Barbeyrac, become entangled and caught up in their sophisms, for fear of either saying too much or too little according to their perspectives, and of offending the interests they needed to reconcile. Grotius, taking refuge in France, unhappy with his homeland and desirous of paying court to Louis XIII (to whom his book is dedicated), spares no pain to rob the people of all their rights and to invest kings with them by every possible artifice. This would also have been the wish of Barbeyrac, who dedicated his translation to King George I of England. But unfortunately the expulsion of James II (which he calls an abdication) forced him to be evasive and on his guard and to beat around the bush, in order to avoid making

William out to be a usurper. If these two writers had adopted the true principles, all their difficulties would have been alleviated and they would always have been consistent. However, sad to say, they would have told the truth and paid court only to the people. For truth does not lead to fortune, and the populace grants neither ambassadorships, university chairs nor pensions.

Chapter 3

Whether the General Will Can Err

It follows from what has preceded that the general will is always right and always tends toward the public utility. However, it does not follow that the deliberations of the people always have the same rectitude. We always want what is good for us, but we do not always see what it is. The populace is never corrupted, but it is often tricked, and only then does it appear to want what is bad.

There is often a great deal of difference between the will of all and the general will. The latter considers only the general interest, whereas the former considers private interest and is merely the sum of private wills. But remove from these same wills the pluses and minuses that cancel each other out,[7] and what remains as the sum of the differences is the general will.

If, when a sufficiently informed populace deliberates, the citizens were to have no communication among themselves, the general will would always result from the large number of small differences, and the deliberation would always be good. But when intrigues and partial associations come into being at the expense of the large association, the will of each of these associations becomes general in relation to its members and particular in relation to the state. It

---

7. *Each interest*, says the Marquis d'Argenson, *has different principles. The accord of two private interests is formed in opposition to that of a third*. He could have added that the accord of all the interests is found in the opposition to that of each. If there were no different interests, the common interest, which would never encounter any obstacle, would scarcely be felt. Everything would proceed on its own and politics would cease being an art.

can be said, then, that there are no longer as many voters as there are men, but merely as many as there are associations. The differences become less numerous and yield a result that is less general. Finally, when one of these associations is so large that it dominates all the others, the result is no longer a sum of minor differences, but a single difference. Then there is no longer a general will, and the opinion that dominates is merely a private opinion.

For the general will to be well articulated, it is therefore important that there should be no partial society in the state and that each citizen make up his own mind.[8] Such was the unique and sublime institution of the great Lycurgus. If there are partial societies, their number must be multiplied and inequality among them prevented, as was done by Solon, Numa and Servius. These precautions are the only effective way of bringing it about that the general will is always enlightened and that the populace is not tricked.

Chapter 4

On the Limits of Sovereign Power

If the state or the city is merely a moral person whose life consists in the union of its members, and if the most important of its concerns is that of its own conservation, it ought to have a universal compulsory force to move and arrange each part in the manner best suited to the whole. Just as nature gives each man an absolute power over all his members, the social compact gives the body politic an absolute power over all its members, and it is the same power which, as I have said, is directed by the general will and bears the name sovereignty.

But over and above the public person, we need to consider the private persons who make it up and whose life and liberty are naturally independent of

it. It is, therefore, a question of making a rigorous distinction between the respective rights of the citizens and the sovereign,[9] and between the duties the former have to fulfill as subjects and the natural right they should enjoy as men.

We grant that each person alienates, by the social compact, only that portion of his power, his goods, and liberty whose use is of consequence to the community; but we must also grant that only the sovereign is the judge of what is of consequence.

A citizen should render to the state all the services he can as soon as the sovereign demands them. However, for its part, the sovereign cannot impose on the subjects any fetters that are of no use to the community. It cannot even will to do so, for under the law of reason nothing takes place without a cause, any more than under the law of nature.

The commitments that bind us to the body politic are obligatory only because they are mutual, and their nature is such that in fulfilling them one cannot work for someone else without also working for oneself. Why is the general will always right, and why do all constantly want the happiness of each of them, if not because everyone applies the word *each* to himself and thinks of himself as he votes for all? This proves that the quality of right and the notion of justice it produces are derived from the preference each person gives himself, and thus from the nature of man; that the general will, to be really such, must be general in its object as well as in its essence; that it must derive from all in order to be applied to all; and that it loses its natural rectitude when it tends toward any individual, determinate object. For then, judging what is foreign to us, we have no true principle of equity to guide us.

In effect, once it is a question of a state of affairs or a particular right concerning a point that has not been regulated by a prior, general convention, the issue becomes contentious. It is a suit in which the interested private individuals are one of the parties and the public the other, but in which I fail to see either what law should be followed or what judge

---

8. *"It is true,"* says Machiavelli, *"that some divisions are harmful to the republic while others are helpful to it. Those that are accompanied by sects and partisan factions are harmful. Since, therefore, a ruler of a republic cannot prevent enmities from arising within it, he at least ought to prevent them from becoming sects,"* The History of Florence, Book VII. [Rousseau here quotes the Italian.]

9. Attentive readers, please do not rush to accuse me of contradiction here. I have been unable to avoid it in my choice of words, given the poverty of the language. But wait.

should render the decision. In these circumstances it would be ridiculous to want to defer to an express decision of the general will, which can only be the conclusion reached by one of its parts, and which, for the other party, therefore, is merely an alien, particular will, inclined on this occasion to injustice and subject to error. Thus, just as a private will cannot represent the general will, the general will, for its part, alters its nature when it has a particular object; and as general, it is unable to render a decision on either a man or a state of affairs. When, for example, the populace of Athens appointed or dismissed its leaders, decreed that honors be bestowed on one or inflicted penalties on another, and by a multitude of particular decrees, indiscriminately exercised all the acts of government, the people in this case no longer had a general will in the strict sense. It no longer functioned as sovereign but as magistrate. This will appear contrary to commonly held opinions, but I must be given time to present my own.

It should be seen from this that what makes the will general is not so much the number of votes as the common interest that unites them, for in this institution each person necessarily submits himself to the conditions he imposes on others, an admirable accord between interest and justice which bestows on common deliberations a quality of equity that disappears when any particular matter is discussed, for lack of a common interest uniting and identifying the role of the judge with that of the party.

From whatever viewpoint one approaches this principle, one always arrives at the same conclusion, namely that the social compact establishes among the citizens an equality of such a kind that they all commit themselves under the same conditions and should all enjoy the same rights. Thus by the very nature of the compact, every act of sovereignty (that is, every authentic act of the general will) obligates or favors all citizens equally, so that the sovereign knows only the nation as a body and does not draw distinctions between any of those members that make it up. Strictly speaking, then, what is an act of sovereignty? It is not a convention between a superior and an inferior, but a convention of the body with each of its members. This conven-

tion is legitimate, because it has the social contract as a basis; equitable, because it is common to all; useful, because it can have only the general good for its object; and solid, because it has the public force and the supreme power as a guarantee. So long as the subjects are subordinated only to such convention, they obey no one but their own will alone. And asking how far the respective rights of the sovereign and the citizens extend is asking how far the latter can commit themselves to one another, each to all and all to each.

We can see from this that the sovereign power, absolute, wholly sacred and inviolable as it is, does not and cannot exceed the limits of general conventions, and that every man can completely dispose of such goods and freedom as has been left to him by these conventions. This results in the fact that the sovereign never has the right to lay more charges on one subject than on another, because in that case the matter becomes particular, no longer within the range of the sovereign's competence.

Once these distinctions are granted, it is so false that there is, in the social contract, any genuine renunciation on the part of private individuals that their situation, as a result of this contract, is really preferable to what it was beforehand; and, instead of an alienation, they have merely made an advantageous exchange of an uncertain and precarious mode of existence for another that is better and surer. Natural independence is exchanged for liberty; the power to harm others is exchanged for their own security; and their force, which others could overcome, for a right which the social union renders invincible. Their life itself, which they have devoted to the state, is continually protected by it; and when they risk their lives for its defense, what are they then doing but returning to the state what they have received from it? What are they doing, that they did not do more frequently and with greater danger in the state of nature, when they would inevitably have to fight battles, defending at the peril of their lives the means of their preservation? It is true that everyone has to fight, if necessary, for the homeland; but it also is the case that no one ever has to fight on his own behalf. Do we not still gain by running, for something that brings about our security, a portion of the risks we would have to run for ourselves once our security is taken away?

Chapter 5

On the Right of Life or Death

The question arises how private individuals who have no right to dispose of their own lives can transfer to the sovereign this very same right which they do not have. This question seems difficult to resolve only because it is poorly stated. Every man has the right to risk his own life in order to preserve it. Has it ever been said that a person who jumps out a window to escape a fire is guilty of committing suicide? Has this crime ever been imputed to someone who perishes in a storm, unaware of its danger when he embarked?

The social treaty has as its purpose the conservation of the contracting parties. Whoever wills the end also wills the means, and these means are inseparable from some risks, even from some losses. Whoever wishes to preserve his life at the expense of others should also give it up for them when necessary. For the citizen is no longer judge of the peril to which the law wishes he be exposed, and when the prince has said to him, "it is expedient for the state that you should die," he should die. Because it is under this condition alone that he has lived in security up to then, and because his life is not only a kindness of nature, but a conditional gift of the state.

The death penalty inflicted on criminals can be viewed from more or less the same point of view. It is in order to avoid being the victim of an assassin that a person consents to die, were he to become one. According to this treaty, far from disposing of his own life, one thinks only of guaranteeing it. And it cannot be presumed that any of the contracting parties is then planning to get himself hanged.

Moreover, every malefactor who attacks the social right becomes through his transgressions a rebel and a traitor to the homeland; in violating its laws, he ceases to be a member, and he even wages war with it. In that case the preservation of the state is incompatible with his own. Thus one of the two must perish; and when the guilty party is put to death, it is less as a citizen than as an enemy. The legal proceeding and the judgment are the proofs and the declaration that he has broken the social treaty, and consequently that he is no longer a member of the state. For since

he has acknowledged himself to be such, at least by his living there, he ought to be removed from it by exile as a violator of the compact, or by death as a public enemy. For such an enemy is not a moral person, but a man, and in this situation the right of war is to kill the vanquished.

But it will be said that the condemnation of a criminal is a particular act. Fine. So this condemnation is not a function of the sovereign. It is a right the sovereign can confer without itself being able to exercise it. All of my opinions are consistent, but I cannot present them all at once.

In addition, frequency of physical punishment is always a sign of weakness or of torpor in the government. There is no wicked man who could not be made good for something. One has the right to put to death, even as an example, only someone who cannot be preserved without danger.

With regard to the right of pardon, or of exempting a guilty party from the penalty decreed by the law and pronounced by the judge, this belongs only to one who is above the judge and the law, that is, to the sovereign. Still its right in this regard is not clearly defined, and the cases in which it is used are quite rare. In a well governed state, there are few punishments, not because many pardons are granted, but because there are few criminals. When a state is in decline, the sheer number of crimes insures impunity. Under the Roman Republic, neither the senate nor the consuls ever tried to grant pardons. The people itself did not do so, even though it sometimes revoked its own judgment. Frequent pardons indicate that transgressions will eventually have no need of them, and everyone sees where that leads. But I feel that my heart murmurs and holds back my pen. Let us leave these questions to be discussed by a just man who has not done wrong and who himself never needed pardon.

Chapter 6

On Law

Through the social compact we have given existence and life to the body politic. It is now a matter of giving it movement and will through legislation. For the primitive act whereby this body is formed and united still makes no determination regarding what it should do to preserve itself.

Whatever is good and in conformity with order is such by the nature of things and independently of human conventions. All justice comes from God; he alone is its source. But if we knew how to receive it from so exalted a source, we would have no need for government or laws. Undoubtedly there is a universal justice emanating from reason alone; but this justice, to be admitted among us, ought to be reciprocal. Considering things from a human standpoint, the lack of a natural sanction causes the laws of justice to be without teeth among men. They do nothing but good to the wicked and evil to the just, when the latter observes them in his dealings with everyone while no one observes them in their dealings with him. There must therefore be conventions and laws to unite rights and duties and to refer justice back to its object. In the state of nature where everything is commonly held, I owe nothing to those to whom I have promised nothing. I recognize as belonging to someone else only what is not useful to me. It is not this way in the civil state where all rights are fixed by law.

But what then is a law? So long as we continue to be satisfied with attaching only metaphysical ideas to this word, we will continue to reason without coming to any understanding. And when they have declared what a law of nature is, they will not thereby have a better grasp of what a law of the state is.

I have already stated that there is no general will concerning a particular object. In effect, this particular object is either within or outside of the state. If it is outside of the state, a will that is foreign to it is not general in relation to it. And if this object is within the state, that object is part of it; in that case, a relationship is formed between the whole and its parts which makes two separate beings, one of which is the part, and the other is the whole less that same part. But the whole less a part is not the whole, and so long as this relationship obtains, there is no longer a whole, but rather two unequal parts. Whence it follows that the will of the one is not more general in relation to the other.

But when the entire populace enacts a statute concerning the entire populace, it considers only itself, and if in that case a relationship is formed, it is between the entire object seen from one perspective and the entire object seen from another, without any division of the whole. Then the subject matter about which a statute is enacted is general like the will that enacts it. It is this act that I call a law.

When I say that the object of the laws is always general, I have in mind that the law considers subjects as a body and actions in the abstract, never a man as an individual or a particular action. Thus the law can perfectly well enact a statute to the effect that there be privileges, but it cannot bestow them by name on anyone. The law can create several classes of citizens, and even stipulate the qualifications that determine membership in these classes, but it cannot name specific persons to be admitted to them. It can establish a royal government and a hereditary line of succession, but it cannot elect a king or name a royal family. In a word, any function that relates to an individual does not belong to the legislative power. On this view, it is immediately obvious that it is no longer necessary to ask who is to make the laws, since they are the acts of the general will; nor whether the prince is above the laws, since he is a member of the state; nor whether the law can be unjust, since no one is unjust to himself; nor how one is both free and subject to the laws, since they are merely the record of our own wills.

Moreover, it is apparent that since the law combines the universality of the will and that of the object, what a man, whoever he may be, decrees on his own authority is not a law. What even the sovereign decrees concerning a particular object is no closer to being a law; rather, it is a decree. Nor is it an act of sovereignty but of magistracy.

I therefore call every state ruled by laws a republic, regardless of the form its administration may take. For only then does the public interest govern, and only then is the "public thing" [in Latin: *res publica*] something real. Every legitimate government is republican.[10] I will explain later on what government is.

10. By this word I do not have in mind merely an aristocracy or a democracy, but in general every government guided by the general will, which is the law. To be legitimate, the government need not be made indistinguishable from the sovereign, but it must be its minister.

Strictly speaking, laws are merely the conditions of civil association. The populace that is subjected to the laws ought to be their author. The regulating of the conditions of a society belongs to no one but those who are in association with one another. But how will they regulate these conditions? Will it be by a common accord, by a sudden inspiration? Does the body politic have an organ for making known its will? Who will give it the necessary foresight to formulate acts and to promulgate them in advance, or how will it announce them in time of need? How will a blind multitude, which often does not know what it wants (since it rarely knows what is good for it), carry out on its own an enterprise as great and as difficult as a system of legislation? By itself the populace always wants the good, but by itself it does not always see it. The general will is always right, but the judgment that guides it is not always enlightened. It must be made to see objects as they are, and sometimes as they ought to appear to it. The good path it seeks must be pointed out to it. It must be made safe from the seduction of private wills. It must be given a sense of time and place. It must weigh present, tangible advantages against the danger of distant, hidden evils. Private individuals see the good they reject. The public wills the good that it does not see. Everyone is equally in need of guides. The former must be obligated to conform their wills to their reason; the latter must learn to know what it wants. Then public enlightenment results in the union of the understanding and the will in the social body; hence the full cooperation of the parts, and finally the greatest force of the whole. Whence there arises the necessity of having a legislator.

Chapter 7

On the Legislator

Discovering the rules of society best suited to nations would require a superior intelligence that beheld all the passions of men without feeling any of them; who had no affinity with our nature, yet knew it through

and through; whose happiness was independent of us, yet who nevertheless was willing to concern itself with ours; finally, who, in the passage of time, procures for himself a distant glory, being able to labor in one age and find enjoyment in another.[11] Gods would be needed to give men laws.

The same reasoning used by Caligula regarding matters of fact was used by Plato regarding right in defining the civil or royal man he looks for in his dialogue *The Statesman*. But if it is true that a great prince is a rare man, what about a great legislator? The former merely has to follow the model the latter should propose to him. The latter is the engineer who invents the machine; the former is merely the workman who constructs it and makes it run. At the birth of societies, says Montesquieu, it is the leaders of republics who bring about the institution, and thereafter it is the institution that forms the leaders of the republic.

He who dares to undertake the establishment of a people should feel that he is, so to speak, in a position to change human nature, to transform each individual (who by himself is a perfect and solitary whole), into a part of a larger whole from which this individual receives, in a sense, his life and his being; to alter man's constitution in order to strengthen it; to substitute a partial and moral existence for the physical and independent existence we have all received from nature. In a word, he must deny man his own forces in order to give him forces that are alien to him and that he cannot make use of without the help of others. The more these natural forces are dead and obliterated, and the greater and more durable are the acquired forces, the more too is the institution solid and perfect. Thus if each citizen is nothing and can do nothing except in concert with all the others, and if the force acquired by the whole is equal or superior to the sum of the natural forces of all the individuals, one can say that the legislation has achieved the highest possible point of perfection.

The legislator is in every respect an extraordinary

_____

Then the monarchy itself is a republic. This will become clear in the next Book.

11. A people never becomes famous except when its legislation begins to decline. It is not known for how many centuries the institution established by Lycurgus caused the happiness of the Spartans before the rest of Greece took note of it.

man in the state. If he ought to be so by his genius, he is no less so by his office, which is neither magistracy nor sovereignty. This office, which constitutes the republic, does not enter into its constitution. It is a particular and superior function having nothing in common with the dominion over men. For if he who has command over men must not have command over laws, he who has command over the laws must no longer have any authority over men. Otherwise, his laws, ministers of his passions, would often only serve to perpetuate his injustices, and he could never avoid private opinions altering the sanctity of his work.

When Lycurgus gave laws to his homeland, he began by abdicating the throne. It was the custom of most Greek cities to entrust the establishment of their laws to foreigners. The modern republics of Italy often imitated this custom. The republic of Geneva did the same and things worked out well.[12] In its finest age Rome saw the revival within its midst of all the crimes of tyranny and saw itself on the verge of perishing as a result of having united the legislative authority and the sovereign power in the same hands.

Nevertheless, the decemvirs themselves never claimed the right to have any law passed on their authority alone. *Nothing we propose*, they would tell the people, *can become law without your consent. Romans, be yourselves the authors of the laws that should bring about your happiness.*

He who frames the laws, therefore, does not or should not have any legislative right. And the populace itself cannot, even if it wanted to, deprive itself of this incommunicable right, because, according to the fundamental compact, only the general will obligates private individuals, and there can never be any assurance that a private will is in conformity with the general will until it has been submitted to the free vote of the people. I have already said this, but it is not a waste of time to repeat it.

12. Those who view Calvin simply as a theologian fail to grasp the extent of his genius. The codification of our wise edicts, in which he had a large role, does him as much honor as his *Institutes*. Whatever revolution time may bring out in our cult, so long as the love of homeland and of liberty is not extinguished among us, the memory of this great man will never cease to be held sacred.

Thus we find together in the work of legislation two things that seem incompatible: an undertaking that transcends human force, and, to execute it, an authority that is nil.

Another difficulty deserves attention. The wise men who want to speak to the common masses in the former's own language rather than in the common vernacular cannot be understood by the masses. For there are a thousand kinds of ideas that are impossible to translate in the language of the populace. Overly general perspectives and overly distant objects are equally beyond its grasp. Each individual, in having no appreciation for any other plan of government but the one that relates to his own private interest, finds it difficult to realize the advantages he ought to draw from the continual privations that good laws impose. For an emerging people to be capable of appreciating the sound maxims of politics and to follow the fundamental rules of statecraft, the effect would have to become the cause. The social spirit which ought to be the work of that institution, would have to preside over the institution itself. And men would be, prior to the advent of laws, what they ought to become by means of laws. Since, therefore, the legislator is incapable of using either force or reasoning, he must of necessity have recourse to an authority of a different order, which can compel without violence and persuade without convincing.

This is what has always forced the fathers of nations to have recourse to the intervention of heaven and to credit the gods with their own wisdom, so that the peoples, subjected to the laws of the state as to those of nature and recognizing the same power in the formation of man and of the city, might obey with liberty and bear with docility the yoke of public felicity.

It is this sublime reason, which transcends the grasp of ordinary men, whose decisions the legislator puts in the mouth of the immortals in order to compel by divine authority those whom human prudence could not move.[13] But not everybody is capable of

13. *And in truth*, says Machiavelli, *there has never been among a people a single legislator who, in proposing extraordinary laws, did not have recourse to God, for otherwise they would not be accepted, since there are many benefits known to a prudent man that do not have in*

making the gods speak or of being believed when he proclaims himself their interpreter. The great soul of the legislator is the true miracle that should prove his mission. Any man can engrave stone tablets, buy an oracle, or feign secret intercourse with some divinity, or train a bird to talk in his ear, or find other crude methods of imposing his beliefs on the people. He who knows no more than this may perchance assemble a troupe of lunatics, but he will never found an empire and his extravagant work will soon die with him. Pointless sleights-of-hand form a fleeting connection; only wisdom can make it lasting. The Judaic Law, which still exists, and that of the child of Ishmael, which has ruled half the world for ten centuries, still proclaim today the great men who enunciated them. And while pride-ridden philosophy or the blind spirit of factionalism sees in them nothing but lucky impostors, the true political theoretician admires in their institutions that great and powerful genius which presides over establishments that endure.

We should not, with Warburton, conclude from this that politics and religion have a common object among us, but that in the beginning stages of nations the one serves as an instrument of the other.

Chapter 8

On the People

Just as an architect, before putting up a large building, surveys and tests the ground to see if it can bear the weight, the wise teacher does not begin by laying down laws that are good in themselves. Rather he first examines whether the people for whom they are destined are fitted to bear them. For this reason, Plato refused to give laws to the Arcadians and to the Cyrenians, knowing that these two peoples were rich and could not abide equality. For this reason, one finds good laws and evil men in Crete, because Minos had disciplined nothing but a vice-ridden people.

A thousand nations have achieved brilliant earthly

success that could never have abided good laws; and even those that could have would have been able to have done so for a very short period of their entire existence. Peoples,[14] like men, are docile only in their youth. As they grow older they become incorrigible. Once customs are established and prejudices have become deeply rooted, it is a dangerous and vain undertaking to want to reform them. The people cannot abide having even their evils touched in order to eliminate them, just like those stupid and cowardly patients who quiver at the sight of a physician.

This is not to say that, just as certain maladies unhinge men's minds and remove from them the memory of the past, one does not likewise sometimes find in the period during which states have existed violent epochs when revolutions do to peoples what certain crises do to individuals, when the horror of the past takes the place of forgetfulness, and when the state, set afire by civil wars, is reborn, as it were, from its ashes and takes on again the vigor of youth as it escapes death's embrace. Such was Sparta at the time of Lycurgus; such was Rome after the Tarquins; and such in our time have been Holland and Switzerland after the expulsion of the tyrants.

But these events are rare. They are exceptions whose cause is always to be found in the particular constitution of the states in question. They cannot take place even twice to the same people, for it can make itself free so long as it is merely barbarous; but it can no longer do so when civil strength is exhausted. At that point troubles can destroy it with revolutions being unable to reestablish it. And as soon as its chains are broken, it falls apart and exists no longer. Henceforward a master is needed, not a liberator. Free peoples, remember this axiom: Liberty can be acquired, but it can never be recovered.

For nations, as for men, there is a time of maturity that must be awaited before subjecting them to the laws.[15] But the maturity of a people is not always easily recognized; and if it is foreseen, the work is ruined. One people lends itself to discipline at its

---

themselves evident reasons enabling him to persuade others. Discourses on Titus Livy, Book I, Ch. XI. [Rousseau here quotes the Italian.]

14. [In the 1782 edition, this sentence was revised to read: "Most people, like men. . . ."]

15. [In the 1782 edition, this sentence was revised to read: "Youth is not childhood. For nations, as for men, maturity must be awaited. . . ."]

inception; another, not even after ten centuries. The Russians will never be truly civilized, since they have been civilized too early. Peter had a genius for imitation. He did not have true genius, the kind that creates and makes everything out of nothing. Some of the things he did were good; most of them were out of place. He saw that his people was barbarous; he did not see that it was not ready for civilization. He wanted to civilize it when all it needed was toughening. First he wanted to make Germans and Englishmen, when he should have made Russians. He prevented his subjects from ever becoming what they could have been by persuading them that they were something they are not. This is exactly how a French tutor trains his pupil to shine for a short time in his childhood, and afterwards never to amount to a thing. The Russian Empire would like to subjugate Europe and will itself be subjugated. The Tartars, its subjects or its neighbors, will become its masters and ours. This revolution appears inevitable to me. All the kings of Europe are working in concert to hasten its occurrence.

Chapter 9

The People (continued)

Just as nature has set limits to the status of a well-formed man, beyond which there are but giants or dwarfs, so too, with regard to the best constitution of a state, there are limits to the size it can have, so as not to be too large to be capable of being well governed, nor too small to be capable of preserving itself on its own. In every body politic there is a *maximum* force that it cannot exceed, and which has often fallen short by increasing in size. The more the social bond extends the looser it becomes, and in general a small state is proportionately stronger than a large one.

A thousand reasons prove this maxim. First, administration becomes more difficult over great distances, just as a weight becomes heavier at the end of a longer lever. It also becomes more onerous as the number of administrative levels multiplies, because first each city has its own administration which the populace pays for; each district has its own, again paid for by the people; next each province has one and then the

great governments, the satrapies and vice royalties, requiring a greater cost the higher you go, and always at the expense of the unfortunate people. Finally, there is the supreme administration which weights down on everyone. All these surcharges continually exhaust the subjects. Far from being better governed by these different orders, they are worse governed than if there were but one administration over them. Meanwhile, hardly any resources remain for meeting emergencies; and when recourse must be made to them, the state is always on the verge of its ruin.

This is not all. Not only does the government have less vigor and quickness in enforcing the observance of the laws, preventing nuisances, correcting abuses and foreseeing the seditious undertakings that can occur in distant places, but also the populace has less affection for its leaders when it never sees them, for the homeland, which, to its eyes, is like the world, and for its fellow citizens, the majority of whom are foreigners to it. The same laws cannot be suitable to so many diverse provinces which have different customs, live in contrasting climates, and which are incapable of enduring the same form of government. Different laws create only trouble and confusion among the peoples who live under the same rulers and are in continuous communication. They intermingle and intermarry, and, being under the sway of other customs, never know whether their patrimony is actually their own. Talents are hidden; virtues are unknown; vices are unpunished in this multitude of men who are unknown to one another which the seat of supreme administration brings together in one place. The leaders, overwhelmed with work, see nothing for themselves; clerks govern the state. Finally, the measures that need to be taken to maintain the general authority, which so many distant officials want to avoid or harass, absorb all the public attention. Nothing more remains for the people's happiness, and there barely remains enough for its defense in time of need. And thus a body which is too big for its constitution collapses and perishes, crushed by its own weight.

On the other hand, the state ought to provide itself with a firm foundation to give it solidity, to resist the shocks it is bound to experience, as well as the efforts it will have to make to sustain itself. For all the peoples have a kind of centrifugal force, by which they continually act one against the other and tend to expand at the expense of their neighbors, like Descartes' vortices. Thus the weak risk being soon swallowed up; scarcely any people can preserve itself except by putting itself in a kind of equilibrium with all, which nearly equalizes the pressure on all sides.

It is clear from this that there are reasons for expanding and reasons for contracting, and it is not the least of the political theorist's talents to find, between these and other reasons, the proportion most advantageous to the preservation of the state. In general, it can be said that the former reasons, being merely external and relative, should be subordinated to the latter reasons, which are internal and absolute. A strong, healthy constitution is the first thing one needs to look for, and one should count more on the vigor born of a good government than on the resources furnished by a large territory.

Moreover, there have been states so constituted that the necessity for conquests entered into their very constitution, and that, to maintain themselves, they were forced to expand endlessly. Perhaps they congratulated themselves greatly on account of this happy necessity, which nevertheless showed them, together with the limit of their size, the inevitable moment of their fall.

Chapter 10

The People (continued)

A body politic can be measured in two ways: namely, by the size of its territory and by the number of its people. And between these measurements there is a relationship suitable for giving the state its true greatness. Men are what make up the state and land is what feeds men. This relationship therefore consists in there being enough land for the maintenance of its inhabitants and as many inhabitants as the land can feed. It is in this proportion that the *maximum* force of a given population size is found. For if there is too much land, its defense is onerous, its cultivation inadequate, and its yield surplus. This is the proximate cause of defensive wars. If there is not enough land, the state finds itself at the discretion of its neighbors for what it needs as a supplement. This is the proxi-

mate cause of offensive wars. Any people whose position provides it an alternative merely between commerce and war is inherently weak. It depends on its neighbors; it depends on events. It never has anything but an uncertain and brief existence. Either it conquers and changes the situation, or it is conquered and obliterated. It can keep itself free only by means of smallness or greatness.

No one can provide in mathematical terms a fixed relationship between the size of land and the population size which are sufficient for one another, as much because of the differences in the characteristics of the terrain, its degrees of fertility, the nature of its crops, the influence of its climates, as because of the differences to be noted in the temperaments of the men who inhabit them, some of whom consume little in a fertile country, while others consume a great deal on a barren soil. Again, attention must be given to the greater or lesser fertility of women, to what the country can offer that is more or less favorable to the population, to the number of people that the legislator can hope to bring together through his institutions. Thus, the legislator should not base his judgment on what he sees but on what he foresees. And he should dwell less upon the present state of the population as upon the state it should naturally attain. Finally, there are a thousand situations where the idiosyncrasies of a place require or permit the assimilation of more land than appears necessary. Thus, there is considerable expansion in mountainous country, where the natural crops—namely, woods and pastures—demand less work; where experience shows that women are more fertile than on the plains; and where a large amount of sloping soil provides only a very small amount of flat land, the only thing that can be counted on for vegetation. On the other hand, people can draw closer to one another at the seashore, even on rocks and nearly barren sand, because fishing can make up to a great degree for the lack of land crops, since men should be more closely gathered together in order to repulse pirates, and since in addition it is easier to unburden the country of surplus inhabitants by means of colonies.

To these conditions for instituting a people must be added one that cannot be a substitute for any other, but without which all the rest are useless: the enjoyment of the fullness of peace. For the time when a state is organized, like the time when a battalion is formed, is the instant when the body is the least capable of resisting and easiest to destroy. There would be better resistance at a time of absolute disorder than at a moment of fermentation, when each man is occupied with his own position rather than with the danger. Were a war, famine, or sedition to arise in this time of crisis the state inevitably is overthrown.

This is not to say that many governments are not established during such storms; but in these instances it is these governments themselves that destroy the state. Usurpers always bring about or choose these times of trouble to use public terror to pass destructive laws that the people never adopt when they have their composure. The choice of the moment of a government's institution is one of the surest signs by which the work of a legislator can be distinguished from that of a tyrant.

What people, therefore, is suited for legislation? One that, finding itself bound by some union of origin, interest or convention, has not yet felt the true yoke of laws. One that has no custom or superstitions that are deeply rooted. One that does not fear being overpowered by sudden invasion. One that can, without entering into the squabbles of its neighbors, resist each of them single-handed or use the help of one to repel another. One where each member can be known to all, and where there is no need to impose a greater burden on a man than a man can bear. One that can get along without peoples and without which every other people can get along.[16] One that is neither rich nor poor and can be sufficient unto itself; finally, one that brings together the stability of an ancient people and the docility of a new people. What makes the work of legislation trying is not so much what must be established as what must be destroyed. And what makes success so rare is the impossibility of finding the simplicity of nature together with the needs of society. All these conditions, it is true, are hard to find in combination. Hence few well constituted states are to be seen.

In Europe there is still one country capable of receiving legislation. It is the island of Corsica. The valor and constancy with which this brave people has regained and defended its liberty would well merit having some wise man teaching them how to preserve it. I have a feeling that some day that little island will astonish Europe.

Chapter 11

On the Various Systems of Legislation

If one enquires into precisely wherein the greatest good of all consists, which should be the purpose of every system of legislation, one will find that it boils down to the two principal objects, *liberty* and *equality*. Liberty, because all particular dependence is that much force taken from the body of the state; equality, because liberty cannot subsist without it.

I have already said what civil liberty is. Regarding equality, we need not mean by this word that degrees of power and wealth are to be absolutely the same, but rather that, with regard to power, it should transcend all violence and never be exercised except by virtue of rank and laws; and, with regard to wealth, no citizen should be so rich as to be capable of buying another citizen, and none so poor that he is forced to sell himself. This presupposes moderation in goods and credit on the part of the great, and moderation in avarice and covetousness[17] on the part of the lowly.

---

16. If there were two neighboring peoples, one being unable to get along without the other, it would be a very tough situation for the former and very dangerous for the latter. In such a case, every wise nation will work very quickly to free the other of its dependency. The republic of Thlascala, enclosed within the Mexican empire, preferred to do without salt, rather than buy it from the Mexicans or even take it from them for nothing. The wise Thlascalans saw the trap hidden beneath this generosity. They kept themselves free, and this small state, enclosed within this great empire, was finally the instrument of its ruin.

17. Do you therefore want to give constancy to the State? Bring the extremes as close together as possible. Tolerate neither rich men nor beggars. These two estates, which are naturally inseparable, are equally fatal to the common good. From the one come the fomenters of tyranny, and from the other the tyrants. It is always between them that public liberty becomes a matter of commerce. The one buys it and the other sells it.

This equality is said to be a speculative fiction that cannot exist in practice. But if abuse is inevitable, does it follow that it should not at least be regulated? It is precisely because the force of things tends always to destroy equality that the force of legislation should always tend to maintain it.

But these general objects of every good institution should be modified in each country in accordance with the relationships that arise as much from the local situation as from the temperament of the inhabitants. And it is on the basis of these relationships that each people must be assigned a particular institutional system that is the best, not perhaps in itself, but for the state for which it is destined. For example, is the soil barren and unproductive, or the country too confining for its inhabitants? Turn to industry and crafts, whose products you will exchange for the foodstuffs you lack. On the other hand, do you live in rich plains and fertile slopes? Do you lack inhabitants on a good terrain? Put all your effort into agriculture, which increases the number of men, and chase out the crafts that seem only to achieve the depopulation of the country by grouping in a few sectors what few inhabitants there are.[18] Do you occupy long, convenient coastlines? Cover the sea with vessels; cultivate commerce and navigation. You will have a brilliant and brief existence. Does the sea wash against nothing on your coasts but virtually inaccessible rocks? Remain barbarous and fish-eating. You will live in greater tranquillity, better perhaps and certainly happily. In a word, aside from the maxims common to all, each people has within itself some cause that organizes them in a particular way and renders its legislation proper for it alone. Thus it was that long ago the Hebrews and recently the Arabs have had religion as their main object; the Athenians had letters; Carthage and Tyre, commerce; Rhodes, seafaring; Sparta, war; and Rome, virtue. The author of *The Spirit of the Laws* has shown with a large array of examples the art by which the legislator directs the institution toward each of its objects.

18. Any branch of foreign trade, says the Marquis d'Argenson, creates hardly anything more than a false utility for a kingdom in general. It can enrich some private individuals, even some towns, but the nation as a whole gains nothing and the populace is none the better for it.

What makes the constitution of a state truly solid and lasting is that proprieties are observed with such fidelity that the natural relations and the laws are always in agreement on the same points, and that the latter serve only to assure, accompany and rectify them. But if the legislator is mistaken about his object and takes a principle different from the one arising from the nature of things (whether the one tends toward servitude and the other toward liberty; the one toward riches, the other toward increased population; the one toward peace, the other toward conquests), the laws will weaken imperceptibly, the constitution will be altered, and the state will not cease being agitated until it is destroyed or changed, and invincible nature has regained her empire.

Chapter 12

Classification of the Laws

To set the whole in order or to give the commonwealth the best possible form, there are various relations to consider. First, the action of the entire body acting upon itself, that is, the relationship of the whole to the whole, or of the sovereign to the state, and this relationship, as we will see later, is composed of relationships of intermediate terms.

The laws regulating this relationship bear the name political laws, and are also called fundamental laws, not without reason if these laws are wise. For there is only one way of organizing in each state. The people who have found it should stand by it. But if the established order is evil, why should one accept as fundamental, laws that prevent it from being good? Besides, a people is in any case always in a position to change its laws, even the best laws. For if it wishes to do itself harm, who has the right to prevent it from doing so?

The second relation is that of the members to each other or to the entire body. And this relationship should be as small as possible in regard to the former and as large as possible in regard to the latter, so that each citizen would be perfectly independent of all the others and excessively dependent upon the city. This always takes place by the same means, for only the force of the state brings about the liberty of its members. It is from this second relationship that civil laws arise.

We may consider a third sort of relation between man and law, namely that of disobedience and penalty. And this gives rise to the establishment of criminal laws, which basically are not so much a particular kind of law as the sanction for all the others.

To these three sorts of law is added a fourth, the most important of all. It is not engraved on marble or bronze, but in the hearts of citizens. It is the true constitution of the state. Everyday it takes on new forces. When other laws grow old and die away, it revives and replaces them, preserves a people in the spirit of its institution and imperceptibly substitutes the force of habit for that of authority. I am speaking of mores, customs, and especially of opinion, a part of the law unknown to our political theorists but one on which depends the success of all the others; a part with which the great legislator secretly occupies himself, though he seems to confine himself to the particular regulations that are merely the arching of the vault, whereas mores, slower to arise, form in the end its immovable keystone.

Among these various classes, only political laws, which constitute the form of government, are relevant to my subject.

END OF THE SECOND BOOK

BOOK III

Before speaking of the various forms of government, let us try to determine the precise meaning of this word, which has not as yet been explained very well.

Chapter 1

On Government in General

I am warning the reader that this chapter should be read carefully and that I do not know the art of being clear to those who do not want to be attentive.

Every free action has two causes that come together to produce it. The one is moral, namely the will that determines the act; the other is physical, namely the power that executes it. When I walk toward an object, I must first want to go there. Second, my feet must take me there. A paralyzed man who wants to walk or an agile man who does not want to walk will both remain where they are. The body politic has the same moving causes. The same distinction can be made between force and the will; the one under the name *legislative power* and the other under the name *executive power*. Nothing is done and ought to be done without their concurrence.

We have seen that legislative power belongs to the people and can belong to it alone. On the contrary, it is easy to see, by the principles established above, that executive power cannot belong to the people at large in its role as legislator or sovereign, since this power consists solely of particular acts that are not within the province of the law, nor consequently of the sovereign, none of whose acts can avoid being laws.

Therefore the public force must have an agent of its own that unifies it and gets it working in accordance with the directions of the general will, that serves as a means of communication between the state and the sovereign, and that accomplishes in the public person just about what the union of soul and body accomplishes in man. This is the reason for having government in the state, something often badly confused with the sovereign, of which it is merely the minister.

What then is the government? An intermediate body established between the subjects and the sovereign for their mutual communication, and charged with the execution of the laws and the preservation of liberty, both civil and political.

The members of this body are called magistrates or *kings*, that is to say, *governors*, and the entire body bears the name *prince*.[19] Therefore those who claim that the act by which a people submits itself to leaders is not a contract are quite correct. It is absolutely nothing but a commission, an employment in which the leaders, as simple officials of the sovereign, exercise in its own name the power with which it has entrusted them. The sovereign can limit, modify, or appropriate this power as it pleases, since the

19. Thus in Venice the College is given the name *Most Serene Prince* even when the Doge is not present.

alienation of such a right is incompatible with the nature of the social body and contrary to the purpose of the association.

Therefore, I call *government* or supreme administration the legitimate exercise of executive power; I call prince or magistrate the man or the body charged with that administration.

In government one finds the intermediate forces whose relationships make up that of the whole to the whole or of the sovereign to the state. This last relationship can be represented as one between the extremes of a continuous proportion, whose proportional mean is the government. The government receives from the sovereign the orders it gives the people, and, for the state to be in good equilibrium, there must, all things considered, be an equality between the output or the power of the government, taken by itself, and the output or power of the citizens, who are sovereigns on the one hand and subjects on the other.

Moreover, none of these three terms could be altered without the simultaneous destruction of the proportion. If the sovereign wishes to govern, or if the magistrate wishes to give laws, or if the subjects refuse to obey, disorder replaces rule, force and will no longer act in concert, and thus the state dissolves and falls into despotism or anarchy. Finally, since there is only one proportional mean between each relationship, there is only one good government possible for a state. But since a thousand events can change the relationships of a people, not only can different governments be good for different peoples, but also for the same people at different times.

In trying to provide an idea of the various relationships that can obtain between these two extremes, I will take as an example the number of people, since it is a more easily expressed relationship.

Suppose the state is composed of ten thousand citizens. The sovereign can only be considered collectively and as a body. But each private individual in his position as a subject is regarded as an individual. Thus the sovereign is to the subject as ten thousand is to one. In other words, each member of the state has as his share only one ten-thousandth of the sovereign authority, even though he is totally in subjection to it. If the populace is made up of a hundred thousand men, the condition of the subjects does not change, and each bears equally the entire dominion of the

laws, while his vote, reduced to one hundred-thousandth, has ten times less influence in the drafting of them. In that case, since the subject always remains one, the ratio of the sovereign to the subject increases in proportion to the number of citizens. Whence it follows that the larger the state becomes, the less liberty there is.

When I say that the ratio increases, I mean that it places a distance between itself and equality. Thus the greater the ratio is in the sense employed by geometricians, the less relationship there is in the everyday sense of the word. In the former sense, the ratio, seen in terms of quantity, is measured by the quotient; in the latter sense, ratio, seen in terms of identity, is reckoned by similarity.

Now the less relationship there is between private wills and the general will, that is, between mores and the laws, the more repressive force ought to increase. Therefore, in order to be good, the government must be relatively stronger in proportion as the populace is more numerous.

On the other hand, as the growth of the state gives the trustees of the public authority more temptations and the means of abusing their power, the more the force the government must have in order to contain the people, the more the force the sovereign must have in order to contain the government. I am speaking here not of an absolute force but of the relative force of the various parts of the state.

It follows from this twofold relationship that the continuous proportion between the sovereign, the prince and the people, is in no way an arbitrary idea, but a necessary consequence of the nature of the body politic. It also follows that since one of the extremes, namely the people as subject, is fixed and represented by unity, whenever the doubled ratio increases or decreases, the simple ratio increases or decreases in like fashion, and that as a consequence the middle term is changed. This makes it clear that there is no unique and absolute constitution of government, but that there can be as many governments of differing natures as there are states of differing sizes.

If, in ridiculing this system, someone were to say that in order to find this proportional mean and to form the body of the government, it is necessary merely, in my opinion, to derive the square root of the number of people, I would reply that here I am taking this number only as an example; that the relationships I am speaking of are not measured solely by the number of men, but in general by the quantity of action, which is the combination of a multitude of causes; and that, in addition, if to express myself in fewer words I borrow for the moment the terminology of geometry, I nevertheless am not unaware of the fact that geometrical precision has no place in moral quantities.

The government is on a small scale what the body politic which contains it is on a large scale. It is a moral person endowed with certain faculties, active like the sovereign and passive like the state, and capable of being broken down into other similar relationships whence there arises as a consequence a new proportion and yet again another within this one according to the order of tribunals, until an indivisible middle term is reached; that is, a single leader or supreme magistrate, who can be represented in the midst of this progression as the unity between the series of fractions and that of whole numbers.

Without involving ourselves in this multiplication of terms, let us content ourselves with considering the government as a new body in the state, distinct from the people and sovereign, and intermediate between them.

The essential difference between these two bodies is that the state exists by itself, while the government exists only through the sovereign. Thus the dominant will of the prince is not and should not be anything other than the general will or the law. His force is merely the public force concentrated in him. As soon as he wants to derive from himself some absolute and independent act, the bond that links everything together begins to come loose. If it should finally happen that the prince had a private will more active than that of the sovereign, and that he had made use of some of the public force that is available to him in order to obey this private will, so that there would be, so to speak, two sovereigns—one de jure and the other de facto, at that moment the social union would vanish and the body politic would be dissolved.

However, for the body of the government to have an existence, a real life that distinguishes it from the body of the state, and for all its members to be able to act in concert and to fulfill the purpose for which it is instituted, there must be a particular *self*, a sensibility common to all its members, a force or will of its own that tends toward its preservation. This particular existence presupposes assemblies, councils, a power to deliberate and decide, rights, titles and privileges that belong exclusively to the prince and that render the condition of the magistrate more honorable in proportion as it is more onerous. The difficulties lie in the manner in which this subordinate whole is so organized within the whole, that it in no way alters the general constitution by strengthening its own, that it always distinguishes its particular force, which is intended for its own preservation, from the public force intended for the preservation of the state, and that, in a word, it is always ready to sacrifice the government to the people and not the people to the government.

In addition, although the artificial body of the government is the work of another artificial body and has, in a sense, only a borrowed and subordinate life, this does not prevent it from being capable of acting with more or less vigor or speed, or from enjoying, so to speak, more or less robust health. Finally, without departing directly from the purpose of its institution, it can deviate more or less from it, according to the manner in which it is constituted.

From all these differences arise the diverse relationships that the government should have with the body of the state, according to the accidental and particular relationships by which the state itself is modified. For often the government that is best in itself will become the most vicious, if its relationships are not altered according to the defects of the body politic to which it belongs.

Chapter 2

On the Principle That Constitutes the Various Forms of Government

In order to lay out the general cause of these differences, a distinction must be made here between the prince and the government, as I had done before between the state and the sovereign.

The body of the magistrates can be made up of a larger or smaller number of members. We have said that the ratio of the sovereign to the subjects was greater in proportion as the populace was more numerous, and by a manifest analogy we can say the same thing about the government in relation to the magistrates.

Since the total force of the government is always that of the state, it does not vary. Whence it follows that the more of this force it uses on its own members, the less that is left to it for acting on the whole populace.

Therefore, the more numerous the magistrates, the weaker the government. Since this maxim is fundamental, let us attempt to explain it more clearly.

We can distinguish in the person of the magistrate three essentially different wills. First, the individual's own will, which tends only to its own advantage. Second, the common will of the magistrates which is uniquely related to the advantage of the prince. This latter can be called the corporate will, and is general in relation to the government, and particular in relation to the state, of which the government forms a part. Third, the will of the people or the sovereign will, which is general both in relation to the state considered as the whole and in relation to the government considered as a part of the whole.

In a perfect act of legislation, the private or individual will should be nonexistent; the corporate will proper to the government should be very subordinate; and consequently the general or sovereign will should always be dominant and the unique rule of all the others.

According to the natural order, on the contrary, these various wills become more active in proportion as they are the more concentrated. Thus the general will is always the weakest, the corporate will has second place, and the private will is first of all, so that in the government each member is first himself, then a magistrate, and then a citizen — a gradation directly opposite to the one required by the social order.

Granting this, let us suppose the entire government is in the hands of one single man. In that case the private will and the corporate will are perfectly united, and consequently the latter is at the highest degree of intensity it can reach. But since the use of force is dependent upon the degree of will, and since the absolute force of the government does not vary one bit, it follows that the most active of governments is that of one single man.

On the other hand, let us suppose we are uniting the government to the legislative authority. Let us make the sovereign the prince and all the citizens that many magistrates. Then the corporate will, confused with the general will, will have no more activity than the latter, and will leave the private will all its force. Thus the government, always with the same absolute force, will have its *minimum* relative force or activity.

These relationships are incontestable, and there are still other considerations that serve to confirm them. We see, for example, that each magistrate is more active in his body than each citizen is in his, and consequently that the private will has much more influence on the acts of the government than on those of the sovereign. For each magistrate is nearly always charged with the responsibility for some function of government, whereas each citizen, taken by himself, exercises no function of sovereignty. Moreover, the more the state is extended, the more its real force increases, although it does not increase in proportion to its size. But if the state remains the same, the magistrates may well be multiplied without the government acquiring any greater real force, since this force is that of the state, whose size is always equal. Thus the relative force or activity of the government diminishes without its absolute or real force being able to increase.

It is also certain that the execution of public business becomes slower in proportion as more people are charged with the responsibility for it; that in attaching too much importance to prudence, too little importance is attached to fortune, opportunities are missed, and the fruits of deliberation are often lost by dint of deliberation.

I have just proved that the government becomes slack in proportion as the magistrates are multiplied; and I have previously proved that the more numerous the people, the greater should be the increase of repressive force. Whence it follows that the ratio of the magistrate to the government should be the inverse of the ratio of the subjects to the sovereign; that is to say, the more the state increases in size, the more the government should shrink, so that the number of leaders decreases in proportion to the increase in the number of people.

I should add that I am speaking here only about the relative force of the government and not about its rectitude. For, on the contrary, the more numerous the magistrates, the more closely the corporate will approaches the general will, whereas under a single magistrate, the same corporate will is, as I have said, merely a particular will. Thus what can be gained on the one hand is lost on the other, and the art of the legislator is to know how to determine the point at which the government's will and force, always in a reciprocal proportion, are combined in the relationship that is most advantageous to the state.

Chapter 3

Classification of Governments

We have seen in the previous chapter why the various kinds or forms of government are distinguished by the number of members that compose them. It remains to be seen in this chapter how this classification is made.

In the first place, the sovereign can entrust the government to the entire people or to the majority of the people, so that there are more citizens who are magistrates than who are ordinary private citizens. This form of government is given the name *democracy*.

Or else it can restrict the government to the hands of a small number, so that there are more ordinary citizens than magistrates; and this form is called *aristocracy*.

Finally, it can concentrate the entire government in the hands of a single magistrate from whom all the others derive their power. This third form is the most common and is called *monarchy* or royal government.

It should be noted that all these forms, or at least the first two, can be had in greater or lesser degrees, and even have a rather wide range. For democracy can include the entire populace or be restricted to half. Aristocracy, for its part, can be indeterminately restricted from half the people down to the smallest number. Even royalty can be had in varying levels of distribution. Sparta always had two kings, as required by its constitution; and the Roman Empire is known to have had up to eight emperors at a time, without it being possible to say that the empire was divided. Thus there is a point at which each form of government is indistinguishable from the next, and it is apparent that, under just three names, government can take on as many diverse forms as the state has citizens.

Moreover, since this same government can, in certain respects, be subdivided into other parts, one administered in one way, another in another, there can result from the combination of these three forms a multitude of mixed forms, each of which can be multiplied by all the simple forms.

There has always been a great deal of argument over the best form of government, without considering that each one of them is best in certain cases and the worst in others.

If the number of supreme magistrates in the different states ought to be in inverse ratio to that of the citizens, it follows that in general democratic government is suited to small states, aristocratic government to states of intermediate size, and monarchical government to large ones. This rule is derived immediately from the principle; but how is one to count the multitude of circumstances that can furnish exceptions?

Chapter 4

On Democracy

He who makes the law knows better than anyone else how it should be executed and interpreted. It seems therefore to be impossible to have a better constitution than one in which the executive power is united to the legislative power. But this is precisely what renders such a government inadequate in certain respects, since things that should be distinguished are not, and the prince and sovereign, being merely the same person, form, as it were, only a government without a government.

It is not good for the one who makes the laws to execute them, nor for the body of the people to turn its attention away from general perspectives in order to give it particular objects. Nothing is more dangerous than the influence of private interests on public affairs; and the abuse of the laws by the government is a lesser evil than the corruption of the legislator, which is the inevitable outcome of particular perspectives. In such a situation, since the state is being substantially altered, all reform becomes impossible. A people that would never misuse the government would never misuse independence. A people that would always govern well would not need to be governed.

Taking the term in the strict sense, a true democracy has never existed and never will. It is contrary to the natural order that the majority govern and the minority is governed. It is unimaginable that the people would remain constantly assembled to handle public affairs; and it is readily apparent that it could not establish commissions for this purpose without changing the form of administration.

In fact, I believe I can lay down as a principle that when the functions of the government are shared among several tribunals, those with the fewest members sooner or later acquire the greatest authority, if only because of the facility in expediting public business which brings this about naturally.

Besides, how many things that are difficult to unite are presupposed by this government? First, a very small state where it is easy for the people to gather together and where each citizen can easily know all the others. Second, a great simplicity of mores, which prevents the multitude of public business and thorny discussions. Next, a high degree of equality in ranks and fortunes, without which equality in rights and authority cannot subsist for long. Finally, little or no luxury, for luxury either is the effect of wealth or it makes wealth necessary. It simultaneously corrupts both the rich and the poor, the one by possession, the other by covetousness. It sells the homeland to softness and vanity. It takes all its citizens from the state in order to make them slaves to one another, and all of them to opinion.

This is why a famous author has made virtue the principle of the republic. For all these conditions could not subsist without virtue. But owing to his failure to have made the necessary distinctions, this great genius often lacked precision and sometimes clarity. And he did not realize that since the sovereign authority is everywhere the same, the same principle should have a place in every well constituted state, though in a greater or lesser degree, it is true, according to the form of government.

Let us add that no government is so subject to civil

wars and internal agitations as a democratic or popular one, since there is none that tends so forcefully and continuously to change its form, or that demands greater vigilance and courage to be maintained in its own form. Above all, it is under this constitution that the citizen ought to arm himself with force and constancy, and to say each day of his life from the bottom of his heart what a virtuous Palatine[20] said in the Diet of Poland: *Better to have liberty fraught with danger than servitude in peace.*

Were there a people of gods, it would govern itself democratically. So perfect a government is not suited to men.

Chapter 5

On Aristocracy

We have here two very distinct moral persons, namely the government and the sovereign, and consequently two general wills, one in relation to all the citizens, the other only for the members of the administration. Thus, although the government can regulate its internal administration as it chooses, it can never speak to the people except in the name of the sovereign, that is to say, in the name of the populace itself. This is something not to be forgotten.

The first societies governed themselves aristocratically. The leaders of families deliberated among themselves about public affairs. Young people deferred without difficulty to the authority of experience. This is the origin of the words *priests, ancients, senate* and *elders.* The savages of North America still govern themselves that way to this day, and are very well governed.

But to the extent that inequality occasioned by social institutions came to prevail over natural inequality, wealth or power[21] was preferred to age, and aristocracy became elective. Finally, the transmission

20. The Palatine of Posen, father of the King of Poland, Duke of Lorraine. [Rousseau quotes in Latin the maxim which follows.]

21. It is clear that among the ancients the word *optimates* does not mean the best, but the most powerful.

of the father's power, together with his goods, to his children created patrician families; the government was made hereditary, and we know of senators who were only twenty years old.

There are therefore three sorts of aristocracy: natural, elective and hereditary. The first is suited only to simple people; the third is the worst of any government. The second is the best; it is aristocracy properly so-called.

In addition to the advantage of the distinction between the two powers, aristocracy has that of the choice of its members. For in popular government all the citizens are born magistrates; however, this type of government limits them to a small number, and they become magistrates only through election,[22] a means by which probity, enlightenment, experience, and all the other reasons for public preference and esteem are so many new guarantees of being well governed.

Furthermore, assemblies are more conveniently held, public business better discussed and carried out with more orderliness and diligence, the reputation of the state is better sustained abroad by venerable senators than by a multitude that is unknown or despised.

In a word, it is the best and most natural order for the wisest to govern the multitude, when it is certain that they will govern for its profit and not for their own. There is no need for multiplying devices uselessly or for doing with twenty thousand men what one hundred hand-picked men can do even better. But it must be noted here that the corporate interest begins to direct the public force in less strict a conformity with the rule of the general will, and that another inevitable tendency removes from the laws a part of the executive power.

With regard to the circumstances that are specifically suitable, a state must not be so small, nor its people so simple and upright that the execution of the laws follows immediately from the public will, as is the case in a good democracy. Nor must a nation be so large that the leaders, scattered about in order to govern it, can each play the sovereign in his own department, and begin by making themselves independent in order finally to become the masters.

But if aristocracy requires somewhat fewer virtues than popular government, it also demands others that are proper to it, such as moderation among the wealthy and contentment among the poor. For it appears that rigorous equality would be out of place here. It was not observed even in Sparta.

Moreover, if this form of government carries with it a certain inequality of fortune, this is simply in order that in general the administration of public business may be entrusted to those who are best able to give all their time to it, but not, as Aristotle claims, in order that the rich may always be given preference. On the contrary, it is important that an opposite choice should occasionally teach the people that more important reasons for preference are to be found in a man's merit than in his wealth.

Chapter 6

On Monarchy

So far, we have considered the prince as a moral and collective person, united by the force of laws, and as the trustee of the executive power in the state. We have now to consider this power when it is joined together in the hands of a natural person, of a real man, who alone has the right to dispose of it in accordance with the laws. Such a person is called a monarch or a king.

In utter contrast with the other forms of administration where a collective entity represents an individual, in this form of administration an individual represents a collective entity; so that the moral unity constituting the prince is at the same time a physical unity, in which all the faculties which are combined by the law in the other forms of administration with such difficulty are found naturally combined.

Thus the will of the people, the will of the prince, the public force of the state, and the particular force

22. It is of great importance that laws should regulate the form of the election of magistrates, for if it is left to the will of the prince, it is impossible to avoid falling into a hereditary aristocracy, as has taken place in the Republics of *Venice* and *Berne*. Thus the former has long been a state in dissolution, while the latter maintains itself through the extreme wisdom of its senate. It is a very honorable and very dangerous exception.

of the government, all respond to the same moving agent; all the springs of the machine are in the same hand; everything moves toward the same end; there are no opposing movements which are at cross purposes with one another; and no constitution is imaginable in which a lesser effort produces a more considerable action. Archimedes sitting serenely on the shore and effortlessly launching a huge vessel is what comes to mind when I think of a capable monarch governing his vast states from his private study, and making everything move while appearing himself to be immovable.

But if there is no government that has more vigor, there is none where the private will has greater sway and more easily dominates the others. Everything moves toward the same end, it is true; but this end is not that of public felicity, and the very force of the administration unceasingly operates to the detriment of the state.

Kings want to be absolute, and from a distance one cries out to them that the best way to be so is to make themselves loved by their peoples. This maxim is very noble and even very true in certain respects. Unfortunately it will always be an object of derision in courts. The power that comes from the peoples' love is undoubtedly the greatest, but it is precarious and conditional. Princes will never be satisfied with it. The best kings want to be able to be wicked if it pleases them, without ceasing to be the masters. A political sermonizer might well say to them that since the people's force is their force, their greatest interest is that the people should be flourishing, numerous and formidable. They know perfectly well that this is not true. Their personal interest is first of all that the people should be weak and miserable and incapable of ever resisting them. I admit that, assuming the subjects were always in perfect submission, the interest of the prince would then be for the people to be powerful, so that this power, being his own, would render him formidable in the eyes of his neighbors. But since this interest is merely secondary and subordinate, and since the two suppositions are incompatible, it is natural that the princes should always give preference to the maxim that is the most immediately useful to them. This is the point that Samuel made so forcefully to the Hebrews, and that Machiavelli has made apparent. Under the pretext of teaching

kings, he has taught important lessons to the peoples. Machiavelli's *The Prince* is the book of republicans.[23]

We have found, through general relationships, that the monarchy is suited only to large states, and we find this again in examining the monarchy itself. The more numerous the public administration, the more the ratio of the prince to subject diminishes and approaches equality, so that this ratio increases in proportion as the government is restricted, and is at its *maximum* when the government is in the hands of a single man. Then there is too great a distance between the prince and the people, and the state lacks cohesiveness. In order to bring about this cohesiveness, there must therefore be intermediate orders; there must be princes, grandees, and a nobility to fill them. Now none of this is suited to a small state, which is ruined by all these social levels.

But if it is difficult for a large state to be well governed, it is much harder still for it to be well governed by just one man, and everyone knows what happens when the king appoints substitutes.

An essential and inevitable defect, which will always place the monarchical form of government below the republican form, is that in the latter form the public voice hardly ever raises to the highest positions men who are not enlightened and capable and who would not fill their positions with honor. On the other hand, those who attain these positions in monarchies are most often petty bunglers, petty swindlers, petty intriguers, whose petty talents, which cause them to attain high positions at court, serve only to display their incompetence to the public as soon as they reach these positions. The populace is much less often in error in its choice than the prince, and a

23. [The following was inserted in the 1782 edition: "Machiavelli was a decent man and a good citizen. But since he was attached to the house of Medici, he was forced during the oppression of his homeland to disguise his love of liberty. The very choice of his execrable hero makes clear enough his hidden intention. And the contrast between the maxims of his book *The Prince* and those of his *Discourses on Titus Livy* and of his *History of Florence* shows that this profound political theorist has until now had only superficial or corrupt readers. The court of Rome has sternly prohibited his book. I can well believe it; it is the court he most clearly depicts."]

man of real merit in the ministry is almost as rare as a fool at the head of a republican government. Thus, when by some happy chance one of these men who are born to govern takes the helm of public business in a monarchy that has nearly been sunk by this crowd of fine managers, there is utter amazement at the resources he finds, and his arrival marks an era in the history of the country.

For a monarchical state to be capable of being well governed, its size or extent must be proportionate to the faculties of the one who governs. It is easier to conquer than to rule. With a long enough lever it is possible for a single finger to make the world shake; but holding it in place requires the shoulders of Hercules. However small a state may be, the prince is nearly always too small for it. When, on the contrary, it happens that the state is too small for its leader, which is quite rare, it is still poorly governed, since the leader, always pursuing his grand schemes, forgets the interests of the peoples, making them no less wretched through the abuse of talents he has too much of than does a leader who is limited for want of what he lacks. A kingdom must, so to speak, expand or contract with each reign, depending on the ability of the prince. On the other hand, since the talents of a senate have a greater degree of stability, the state can have permanent boundaries without the administration working any less well.

The most obvious disadvantage of the government of just one man is the lack of that continuous line of succession which forms an unbroken bond of unity in the other two forms of government. When one king dies, another is needed. Elections leave dangerous intervals and are stormy. And unless the citizens have a disinterestedness and integrity that seldom accompanies this form of government, intrigue and corruption enter the picture. It is difficult for one to whom the state has sold itself not to sell it in turn, and reimburse himself at the expense of the weak for the money extorted from him by the powerful. Sooner or later everything becomes venal under such an administration, and in these circumstances, the peace enjoyed under kings is worse than the disorders of the interregna.

What has been done to prevent these ills? In certain families, crowns have been made hereditary, and an order of succession has been established which pre-vents all dispute when kings die. That is to say, by substituting the disadvantage of regencies for that of elections, an apparent tranquillity has been preferred to a wise administration, the risk of having children, monsters, or imbeciles for leaders has been preferred to having to argue over the choice of good kings. No consideration has been given to the fact that in being thus exposed to the risk of the alternative, nearly all the odds are against them. There was a lot of sense in what Dionysius the Younger said in reply to his father, who, while reproaching his son for some shameful action, said "Have I given you such an example?" "Ah," replied the son, "but your father was not king."

When a man has been elevated to command others, everything conspires to deprive him of justice and reason. A great deal of effort is made, it is said, to teach young princes the art of ruling. It does not appear that this education does them any good. It would be better to begin by teaching them the art of obeying. The greatest kings whom history celebrates were not brought up to reign. It is a science one is never less in possession of than after one has learned too much, and that one acquires it better in obeying than in commanding. *For the most useful as well as the shortest method of finding out what is good and what is bad is to consider what you would have wished or not wished to have happened under another prince.*[24]

One result of this lack of coherence is the instability of the royal form of government, which, now regulated by one plan now by another according to the character of the ruling prince or of those who rule for him, cannot have a fixed object for very long or a consistent policy. This variation always causes the state to drift from maxim to maxim, from project to project, and does not take place in the other forms of government, where the prince is always the same. It is also apparent that in general, if there is more cunning in a royal court, there is more wisdom in a senate; and that republics proceed toward their objectives by means of policies that are more consistent and better followed. On the other hand, each revolution in

---

24. Tacitus, *Histories*, Book I. [Rousseau here quotes the Latin.]

the ministry produces a revolution in the state, since the maxim common to all ministers and nearly all kings is to do the reverse of their predecessor in everything.

From this same incoherence we derive the solution to a sophism that is very familiar to royalist political theorists. Not only is civil government compared to domestic government and the prince to the father of the family (an error already refuted), but this magistrate is also liberally given all the virtues he might need, and it is always presupposed that the prince is what he ought to be. With the help of this presupposition, the royal form of government is obviously preferable to any other, since it is unquestionably the strongest; and it lacks only a corporate will that is more in conformity with the general will in order to be the best as well.

But if according to Plato,[25] a king by nature is such a rare person, how many times will nature and fortune converge to crown him; and if a royal education necessarily corrupts those who receive it, what is to be hoped from a series of men who have been brought up to reign? Surely then it is deliberate self-deception to confuse the royal form of government with that of a good king. To see what this form of government is in itself, we need to consider it under princes who are incompetent or wicked, for either they come to the throne wicked or incompetent, or else the throne makes them so.

These difficulties have not escaped the attention of our authors, but they have not been troubled by them. The remedy, they say, is to obey without a murmur. God in his anger gives us bad kings, and they must be endured as punishments from heaven. No doubt this sort of talk is edifying, however I do not know but that it belongs more in a pulpit than in a book on political theory. What is to be said of a physician who promises miracles, and whose art consists entirely of exhorting his sick patient to practice patience? It is quite obvious that we must put up with a bad government when that is what we have. The question would be how to find a good one.

25. *The Statesman.*

Chapter 7

On Mixed Government

Strictly speaking, there is no such thing as a simple form of government. A single leader must have subordinate magistrates; a popular government must have a leader. Thus in the distribution of the executive power there is always a gradation from the greater to the lesser number, with the difference that sometimes the greater number depends on the few, and sometimes the few depend on the greater number.

At times the distribution is equal, either when the constitutive parts are in a state of mutual dependence, as in the government of England; or when the authority of each part is independent but imperfect, as in Poland. This latter form is bad, since there is no unity in the government and the state lacks a bond of unity.

Which one is better, a simple or a mixed form of government? A question much debated among political theorists, to which the same reply must be given that I gave above regarding every form of government.

In itself the simple form of government is the best, precisely because it is simple. But when the executive power is not sufficiently dependent upon the legislative power, that is to say, when there is more of a ratio between the prince and the sovereign than between the people and the prince, this defect in the proportion must be remedied by dividing the government; for then all of its parts have no less authority over the subjects, and their division makes all of them together less forceful against the sovereign.

The same disadvantage can also be prevented through the establishment of intermediate magistrates, who, by being utterly separate from the government, serve merely to balance the two powers and to maintain their respective rights. In that case, the government is not mixed; it is tempered.

The opposite difficulty can be remedied by similar means. And when the government is too slack, tribunals can be set up to give it a concentrated focus. This is done in all democracies. In the first case the government is divided in order to weaken it, and in the second to strengthen it. For the *maximum* of force and weakness are found equally in the simple forms of government, while the mixed forms of government provide an intermediate amount of strength.

Chapter 8

That Not All Forms of Government Are Suited to All Countries

Since liberty is not a fruit of every climate, it is not within the reach of all peoples. The more one meditates on this principle established by Montesquieu, the more one is aware of its truth. The more one contests it, the more occasions there are for establishing it by means of new proofs.

In all the governments in the world, the public person consumes, but produces nothing. Whence therefore does it get the substance it consumes? It is from the labor of its members. It is the surplus of private individuals that produces what is needed by the public. Whence it follows that the civil state can subsist only so long as men's labor produces more than they need.

Now this surplus is not the same in every country in the world. In many countries it is considerable; in others it is moderate; in others it is nil; in still others it is negative.

This ratio depends on the fertility of the climate, the sort of labor the land requires, the nature of its products, the force of its inhabitants, the greater or lesser consumption they need, and many other similar ratios of which it is composed.

On the other hand, not all governments are of the same nature. They are more or less voracious; and the differences are founded on this added principle that the greater the distance the public contributions are from their source, the more onerous they are. It is not on the basis of the amount of the taxes that this burden is to be measured, but on the basis of the path they have to travel in order to return to the hands from which they came. When this circulation is prompt and well established, it is unimportant whether one pays little or a great deal. The populace is always rich and the finances are always in good shape. On the contrary, however little the populace gives, when this small amount does not return, it is

soon wiped out by continual giving. The state is never rich and the populace is always destitute.

It follows from this that the greater the distance between the people and the government, the more onerous the taxes become. Thus in a democracy the populace is the least burdened; in an aristocracy it is more so; in a monarchy it bears the heaviest weight. Monarchy, therefore, is suited only to wealthy nations; aristocracy to states of moderate wealth and size; democracy to states that are small and poor.

In fact, the more one reflects on it, the more one finds in it the difference between free and monarchical states. In the former, everything is used for the common utility. In the latter, the public and private forces are reciprocal, the one being augmented by the weakening of the other. Finally, instead of governing subjects in order to make them happy, despotism makes them miserable in order to govern them.

Thus in each climate there are natural causes on the basis of which one can assign the form of government that the force of the climate requires, and can even say what kind of inhabitants it should have. Barren and unproductive lands, where the product is not worth the labor, ought to remain uncultivated and deserted, or peopled only by savages. Places where men's labor yields only what is necessary ought to be inhabited by barbarous peoples; in places such as these all polity would be impossible. Places where the surplus of products over labor is moderate are suited to free peoples. Those where an abundant and fertile soil produces a great deal in return for a small amount of labor require a monarchical form of government, in order that the subject's excess of surplus may be consumed by the prince's luxurious living. For it is better for this excess to be absorbed by the government than dissipated by private individuals. I realize that there are exceptions; but these exceptions themselves prove the rule, in that sooner or later they produce revolutions that restore things to the order of nature.

General laws should always be distinguished from the particular causes that can modify their effect. Even if the entire south were covered with republics and the entire north with despotic states, it would still be no less true that the effect of climate makes despotism suited to hot countries, barbarism to cold countries, and good polity to intermediate regions. I also realize that, while granting the principle, disputes may arise over its application. It could be said that there are cold countries that are very fertile and southern ones that are quite barren. But this poses a difficulty only for those who have not examined the thing in all its relationships. As I have said, it is necessary to take into account those of labor, force, consumption, and so on.

Let us suppose that there are two parcels of land of equal size, one of which yields five units and the other yields ten. If the inhabitants of the first parcel consume four units and the inhabitants of the second consume nine, the excess of the first will be one-fifth and that of the other will be one-tenth. Since the ratio of these two excesses is therefore the inverse of that of the products, the parcel of land that produces only five units will yield a surplus that is double that of the parcel of land that produces ten.

But it is not a question of a double product, and I do not believe that anyone dares, as a general rule, to place the fertility of a cold country even on an equal footing with that of hot countries. Nevertheless, let us assume that this equality does obtain. Let us, if you will, reckon England to be the equal of Sicily, and Poland the equal of Egypt. Further south we have Africa and the Indies; further north we have nothing at all. To achieve this equality of product, what difference must there be in agricultural techniques? In Sicily one needs merely to scratch the soil; in England what efforts it demands to work it! Now where more hands are needed to obtain the same product, the surplus ought necessarily to be less.

Consider too that the same number of men consumes much less in hot countries. The climate demands that a person keep sober in order to be in good health. Europeans wanting to live there just as they do at home would all die of dysentery and indigestion. *We are,* says Chardin, *carnivorous beasts, wolves, in comparison with the Asians. Some attribute the sobriety of the Persians to the fact that their land is less cultivated. On the contrary, I believe that this country is less abundant in commodities because the inhabitants need less. If their frugality,* he continues, *were an effect of the country's scarcity, only the poor would eat little; however, it is generally the case that everyone does so. And more or less would be eaten in each province according to the fertility of the country;*

however, the same sobriety is found throughout the kingdom. They take great pride in their lifestyle, saying that one has only to look at their complexions to recognize how far it excels that of the Christians. In fact, the complexion of the Persians is clear. They have fair skin, fine and polished, whereas the complexion of their Armenian subjects, who live in the European style, is coarse and blotchy, and their bodies are fat and heavy.

The closer you come to the equator, the less people live on. They rarely eat meat; rice, maize, couscous, millet and cassava are their usual diet. In the Indies there are millions of men whose sustenance costs less than a penny a day. In Europe itself we see noticeable differences in appetite between the peoples of the north and the south. A Spaniard will live for eight days on a German's dinner. In countries where men are the most voracious, luxury too turns toward things edible. In England, luxury is shown in a table loaded with meats; in Italy you are regaled on sugar and flowers.

Luxury in clothing also offers similar differences. In the climate where the seasonal changes are sudden and violent, people have better and simpler clothing. In climates where people clothe themselves merely for ornamental purposes, flashiness is more sought after than utility. The clothes themselves are a luxury there. In Naples you see men strolling everyday along the Posilippo decked out in gold-embroidered coats and bare legged. It is the same with buildings; magnificence is the sole consideration when there is nothing to fear from the weather. In Paris or London, people want to be housed warmly and comfortably. In Madrid, there are superb salons, but no windows that close, and people sleep in rat holes.

In hot countries foodstuffs are considerably more substantial and succulent. This is a third difference which cannot help but influence the second. Why do people eat so many vegetables in Italy? Because there they are good, nourishing, and have an excellent flavor. In France, where they are fed nothing but water, they are not nourishing at all, and are nearly counted for nothing at table. Be that as it may, they occupy no less land and cost at least as much effort to cultivate. It is a known fact that the wheats of Barbary, in other respects inferior to those of France, yield far more flour, and that those of France, for their part, yield more wheats than those of the north. It can be inferred from this that a similar gradation in the same direction is generally observed from the equator to the pole. Now is it not a distinct disadvantage to have a smaller quantity of food in an equal amount of produce?

To all these different considerations, I can add one which depends on and strengthens them. It is that hot countries have less of a need for inhabitants than do cold countries, and yet could feed more of them. This produces a double surplus, always to the advantage of despotism. The greater the area occupied by the same number of inhabitants, the more difficult it becomes to revolt, since concerted action cannot be taken promptly and secretly; and it is always easy for the government to discover plots and cut off communications. But the closer together a numerous people is drawn, the less the government can usurp from the sovereign. The leaders deliberate as safely in their rooms as the prince does in his council; and the crowd assembles as quickly in public squares as do troops in their quarters. In this regard, the advantage of a tyrannical government, therefore, is that of acting over great distances. With the help of the points of support it establishes, its force increases with distance like that of levers.[26] On the other hand, the strength of the people acts only when concentrated; it evaporates and is lost as it spreads, like the effect of gunpowder scattered on the ground, which catches fire only one grain at a time. The least populated countries are thus the best suited for tyranny. Ferocious animals reign only in deserts.

Chapter 9

On the Signs of a Good Government

When the question arises which one is absolutely the best government, an insoluble question is being raised because it is indeterminate. Or, if you wish, it has as many good answers as there are possible combinations in the absolute and relative positions of peoples.

But if it is asked by what sign it is possible to know that a given people is well or poorly governed, this is another matter, and the question of fact could be resolved.

However, nothing is answered, since each wants to answer it in his own way. The subjects praise public tranquillity; the citizens praise the liberty of private individuals. The former prefers the security of possessions; the latter that of persons. The former has it that the best government is the one that is most severe; the latter maintains that the best government is the one that is mildest. This one wants crimes to be punished, and that one wants them prevented. The former think it a good thing to be feared by their neighbors; the latter prefer to be ignored by them. The one is content so long as money circulates; the other demands that the people have bread. Even if agreement were had on these and similar points, would we be any closer to an answer? Since moral quantities do not allow of precise measurement, even if there were agreement regarding the sign, how could there be agreement regarding the evaluation.

For my part, I am always astonished that such a simple sign is overlooked or that people are of such bad faith as not to agree on it. What is the goal of the political association? It is the preservation and prosperity of its members. And what is the surest sign that they are preserved and prospering? It is their number and their population. Therefore do not go looking elsewhere for this much disputed sign. All other things being equal, the government under which, without external means, without naturalizations, without colonies, the citizens become populous and multiply the most, is infallibly the best government. That government under which a populace diminishes and dies out is the worst. Calculators, it is now up to you. Count, measure, compare.[27]

---

26. This does not contradict what I said earlier in Book II, Chapter 9, regarding the disadvantages of large states, for there it was a question of the authority of the government over its members, and here it is a question of its force against the subjects. Its scattered members serve it as points of support for acting from a distance upon the people, but it has no support for acting directly on these members themselves. Thus in the one case the

length of the lever causes its weakness, and in the other case its force.

27. We should judge on this same principle the centuries that merit preference with respect to the prosperity of the human race. Those in which letters and arts are known to have flourished have been admired too much,

Chapter 10

On the Abuse of Government and Its Tendency to Degenerate

Just as the private will acts constantly against the general will, so the government makes a continual effort against sovereignty. The more this effort increases, the more the constitution is altered. And since there is here no other corporate will which,

---

without penetrating the secret object of their cultivation, and without considering its devastating effect, *and this was called humanity by the inexperienced, when it was a part of servitude.* [Rousseau here quotes Tacitus, *Agricola*, 21, in Latin.] Will we never see in the maxims of books the crude interest that causes the authors to speak? No. Whatever they may say, when a country is depopulated, it is not true, despite its brilliance, that all goes well; and the fact that a poet has an income of a hundred thousand livres is not sufficient to make his century the best of all. The apparent calm and tranquillity of the leader ought to be less of an object of consideration than the well-being of whole nations and especially of the most populous states. A hailstorm may devastate a few cantons, but it rarely causes famine. Riots and civil wars may greatly disturb the leaders, but they are not the true misfortunes of the people, who may even have a reprieve while people argue over who will tyrannize them. It is their permanent condition that causes real periods of prosperity or calamity. It is when everything remains crushed under the yoke that everything decays. It is then that the leaders destroy them at will, *where they bring about solitude they call it peace.*

[Rousseau here quotes Tacitus, *Agricola*, 31, in Latin.] When the quarrels of the great disturbed the kingdom of France, and the Coadjutor of Paris brought with him to the Parliament a knife in his pocket, this did not keep the French people from living happily and in great numbers in a free and decent ease. Long ago, Greece flourished in the midst of the cruelest wars. Blood flowed in waves, and the whole country was covered with men. It seemed, says Machiavelli, that in the midst of murders, proscriptions, and civil wars, our republic became more powerful; the virtue of its citizens, their mores, and their independence did more to reinforce it than all its dissensions did to weaken it. A little agitation gives strength to souls, and what truly brings about prosperity for the species is not so much peace as liberty.

by resisting the will of the prince, would create an equilibrium with it, sooner or later the prince must finally oppress the sovereign and break the social treaty. That is the inherent and inevitable vice which, from the birth of the body politic, tends unceasingly to destroy it, just as old age and death destroy the human body.

There are two general ways in which a government degenerates, namely, when it shrinks, or when the state dissolves.

The government shrinks when it passes from a large to a small number, that is to say, from democracy to aristocracy, and from aristocracy to royalty. That is its natural inclination.[28] If it were to go backward

---

28. The slow formation and the progress of the Republic of Venice in its lagoons offers a notable example of this succession. And it is rather astonishing that after more than twelve hundred years the Venetians seem to be no further than the second stage, which began with *Serrar di Consiglio* in 1198. As for the ancient dukes, for whom the Venetians are reproached, whatever the *squitinio della libertà veneta* may say about them, it has been proved that they were not their sovereigns.

The Roman Republic does not fail to be brought forward as an objection against me, which, it will be said, followed a completely opposite course, passing from monarchy to aristocracy to democracy. I am quite far from thinking of it in this way.

The first establishment of Romulus was a mixed government that promptly degenerated into despotism. For some particular reasons, the state perished before its time, just as one sees a newborn die before reaching manhood. The expulsion of the Tarquins was the true epoch of the birth of the republic. But it did not at first take on a constant form, because in failing to abolish the patriciate, only half the work was completed. For in this way, since hereditary aristocracy, which is the worst of all forms of legitimate administration, remained in conflict with democracy, a form of government that is always uncertain and adrift, it was not determined, as Machiavelli has proved, until the establishment of the tribunes. It was only then that there was a true government and a veritable democracy. In fact, the populace then was not merely sovereign but also magistrate and judge. The senate was merely a subordinate tribunal whose purpose was to temper and concentrate the government; and the consuls themselves, though they were patricians, magistrates, and absolute generals in war, in Rome were merely presidents of the people.

from a small number to a large number, it could be said to slacken, but this reverse progression is impossible.

In fact, the government never changes its form except when its exhausted energy leaves it too enfeebled to be capable of preserving what belongs to it. Now if it were to become still more slack while it expanded, its force would become entirely nil; it would be still less likely to subsist. It must therefore wind up and tighten its force in proportion as it gives way; otherwise the state it sustains would fall into ruin.

The dissolution of the state can come about in two ways.

First, when the prince no longer administers the state in accordance with the laws and usurps the sovereign power. In that case a remarkable change takes place, namely that it is not the government but the state that shrinks. I mean that the state as a whole is dissolved, and another is formed inside it, composed exclusively of the members of the government, and which is no longer anything for the rest of the populace but its master and tyrant. So that the instant that the government usurps sovereignty, the social compact is broken, and all ordinary citizens, on recovering by right their natural liberty, are forced but not obliged to obey.

The same thing happens also when the members of the government separately usurp the power they should only exercise as a body. This is no less an infraction of the laws, and produces even greater disor-

der. Under these circumstances, there are, so to speak, as many princes as magistrates, and the state, no less divided than the government, perishes or changes its form.

When the state dissolves, the abuse of government, whatever it is, takes the common name *anarchy*. To distinguish, democracy degenerates into *ochlocracy*, aristocracy into *oligarchy*. I would add that royalty degenerates into *tyranny*, however this latter term is equivocal and requires an explanation.

In the ordinary sense a tyrant is a king who governs with violence and without regard for justice and the laws. In the strict sense, a tyrant is a private individual who arrogates to himself royal authority without having any right to it. This is how the Greeks understood the word tyrant. They gave the name indifferently to good and bad princes whose authority was not legitimate.[29] Thus *tyrant* and *usurper* are two perfectly synonymous words.

To give different names to different things, I call the usurper of royal authority a *tyrant*, and the usurper of sovereign power a *despot*. The tyrant is someone who intrudes himself, contrary to the laws, in order to govern according to the laws. The despot is someone who places himself above the laws themselves. Thus the tyrant cannot be a despot, but the despot is always a tyrant.

Chapter 11

On the Death of the Body Politic

Such is the natural and inevitable tendency of the best constituted governments. If Sparta and Rome perished, what state can hope to last forever? If we

---

From that point on, the government was also seen to follow its natural inclination and to tend strongly toward aristocracy. With the patriciate having abolished itself, as it were, the aristocracy was no longer in the body of patricians, as it was in Venice and Genoa, but in the body of the senate which was composed of patricians and plebeians, and even in the body of the tribunes when they began to usurp an active power. For words do not affect things, and when the populace has leaders who govern for it, it is always an aristocracy, regardless of the name these leaders bear.

The abuse of aristocracy gave birth to civil wars and the triumvirate. Sulla, Julius Caesar, and Augustus became in fact veritable monarchs, and finally, under the despotism of Tiberius, the state was dissolved. Roman history therefore does not invalidate my principle; it confirms it.

29. *For all are considered and are called tyrants who use perpetual power in a city accustomed to liberty.* [Rousseau here quotes the Latin.] Cornelius Nepos, *Life of Miltiades*. It is true that Aristotle, *Nicomachean Ethics*, Book XVIII, Chapter 10, distinguishes between a tyrant and a king, in that the former governs for his own utility and the latter governs only for the utility of his subjects. But besides the fact that generally all the Greek authors used the word tyrant in another sense, as appears most clearly in Xenophon's *Hiero*, it would follow from Aristotle's distinction that there has not yet been a single king since the beginning of the world.

wish to form a durable establishment, let us then not dream of making it eternal. To succeed, one must not attempt the impossible or flatter oneself with giving to the work of men a solidity that things human do not allow.

The body politic, like the human body, begins to die from the very moment of its birth, and carries within itself the causes of its destruction. But both can have a constitution that is more or less robust and suited to preserve them for a longer or shorter time. The constitution of man is the work of nature; the constitution of the state is the work of art. It is not within men's power to prolong their lives; it is within their power to prolong the life of the state as far as possible, by giving it the best constitution it can have. The best constituted state will come to an end, but later than another, if no unforeseen accident brings about its premature fall.

The principle of political life is in the sovereign authority. Legislative power is the heart of the state; the executive power is the brain, which gives movement to all the parts. The brain can fall into paralysis and yet the individual may still live. A man may remain an imbecile and live. But once the heart has ceased its functions, the animal is dead.

It is not through laws that the state subsists; it is through legislative power. Yesterday's law does not obligate today, but tacit consent is presumed from silence, and the sovereign is taken to be giving incessant confirmation to the laws it does not abrogate while having the power to do so. Whatever it has once declared it wants, it always wants, unless it revokes its declaration.

Why then is so much respect paid to ancient laws? For just this very reason. We must believe that nothing but the excellence of the ancient wills that could have preserved them for so long. If the sovereign had not constantly recognized them to be salutary, it would have revoked them a thousand times. This is why, far from growing weak, the laws continually acquire new force in every well constituted state. The prejudice in favor of antiquity each day renders them more venerable. On the other hand, wherever the laws weaken as they grow old, this proves that there is no longer a legislative power, and that the state is no longer alive.

Chapter 12

How the Sovereign Authority Is Maintained

The sovereign, having no other force than legislative power, acts only through the laws. And since the laws are only authentic acts of the general will, the sovereign can act only when the populace is assembled. With the populace assembled, it will be said: what a chimera! It is a chimera today, but two thousand years ago it was not. Have men changed their nature?

The boundaries of what is possible in moral matters are less narrow than we think. It is our weaknesses, our vices and our prejudices that shrink them. Base souls do not believe in great men; vile slaves smile with an air of mockery at the word liberty.

Let us consider what can be done in the light of what has been done. I will not speak of the ancient republics of Greece; however, the Roman Republic was, to my mind, a great state, and the town of Rome was a great town. The last census in Rome gave four thousand citizens bearing arms, and the last census count of the empire gave four million citizens, not counting subjects, foreigners, women, children, and slaves.

What difficulty might not be imagined in frequently calling assemblies of the immense populace of that capital and its environs. Nevertheless, few weeks passed by without the Roman people being assembled, and even several times in one week. It exercised not only the rights of sovereignty but also a part of those of the government. It took care of certain matters of public business; it tried certain cases; and this entire populace was in the public meeting place hardly less often as magistrate than as citizen.

In looking back to the earliest history of nations, one would find that most of the ancient governments, even the monarchical ones such as those of the Macedonians and the Franks, had similar councils. Be that as it may, this lone contestable fact answers every difficulty: arguing from the actual to the possible seems like good logic to me.

Chapter 13

Continuation

It is not enough for an assembled people to have once determined the constitution of the state by sanctioning a body of laws. It is not enough for it to have established a perpetual government or to have provided once and for all for the election of magistrates. In addition to the extraordinary assemblies that unforeseen situations can necessitate, there must be some fixed, periodic assemblies that nothing can abolish or prorogue, so that on a specified day the populace is rightfully convened by law, without the need for any other formal convocation.

But apart from these assemblies which are lawful by their date alone, any assembly of the people that has not been convened by the magistrates appointed for that task and in accordance with the prescribed forms should be regarded as illegitimate, and all that takes place there should be regarded as null, since the order itself to assemble ought to emanate from the law.

As to the question of the greater or lesser frequency of legitimate assemblies, this depends on so many considerations that no precise rules can be given about it. All that can be said is that in general the more force a government has, the more frequently the sovereign ought to show itself.

I will be told that this may be fine for a single town, but what is to be done when the state includes several? Will the sovereign authority be divided, or will it be concentrated in a single town with all the rest made subject to it?

I answer that neither should be done. In the first place, the sovereign authority is simple and one; it cannot be divided without being destroyed. In the second place, a town cannot legitimately be in subjection to another town, any more than a nation can be in subjection to another nation, since the essence of the body politic consists in the harmony of obedience and liberty; and the words *subject* and *sovereign* are identical correlatives, whose meaning is combined in the single word "citizen."

I answer further that it is always an evil to unite several towns in a single city, and that anyone wanting to bring about this union should not expect to avoid its natural disadvantages. The abuses of large states should not be raised as an objection against someone who wants only small ones. But how are small states to be given enough force to resist the large ones, just as the Greek cities long ago resisted a great king, and more recently Holland and Switzerland have resisted the house of Austria?

Nevertheless, if the state cannot be reduced to appropriate boundaries, one expedient still remains: not to allow a fixed capital, to make the seat of government move from one town to another, and to assemble the estates of the country in each of them in their turn.

Populate the territory uniformly, extend the same rights everywhere, spread abundance and life all over. In this way the state will become simultaneously as strong and as well governed as possible. Recall that town walls are made from the mere debris of rural houses. With each palace I see being erected in the capital, I believe I see an entire countryside turned into hovels.

Chapter 14

Continuation

Once the populace is legitimately assembled as a sovereign body, all jurisdiction of the government ceases; the executive power is suspended, and the person of the humblest citizen is as sacred and inviolable as that of the first magistrate, for where those who are represented are found, there is no longer any representative. Most of the tumults that arose in the comitia in Rome were due to ignorance or neglect of this rule. On such occasions the consuls were merely the presidents of the people; the tribunes, ordinary speakers;[30] the senate, nothing at all.

These intervals of suspension, during which the prince recognizes or ought to recognize an actual superior, have always been disturbing to him. And these assemblies of the people, which are the aegis

---

30. In nearly the same sense as is given this word in English Parliament. The similarity between these activities would have put the consuls and the tribunes in conflict, even if all jurisdiction had been suspended.

of the body politic and the curb on the government, have at all times been the horror of leaders. Thus they never spare efforts, objections, difficulties, or promises to keep the citizens from having them. When the citizens were greedy, cowardly, and pusillanimous, more enamored of repose than with liberty, they do not hold out very long against the redoubled efforts of the government. Thus it is that, as the resisting force constantly grows, the sovereign authority finally vanishes, and the majority of the cities fall and perish prematurely.

But between the sovereign authority and arbitrary government, there sometimes is introduced an intermediate power about which we must speak.

Chapter 15

On Deputies or Representatives

Once public service ceases to be the chief business of the citizens, and they prefer to serve with their wallet rather than with their person, the state is already near its ruin. Is it necessary to march off to battle? They pay mercenary troops and stay at home. Is it necessary to go to the council? They name deputies and stay at home. By dint of laziness and money, they finally have soldiers to enslave the country and representatives to sell it.

The hustle and bustle of commerce and the arts, the avid interest in profits, softness and the love of amenities: these are what change personal services into money. A person gives up part of his profit in order to increase it at leisure. Give money and soon you will be in chains. The word *finance* is a slave's word. It is unknown in the city. In a truly free state the citizens do everything with their own hands and nothing with money. Far from paying to be exempted from their duties, they would pay to fulfill them themselves. Far be it from me to be sharing commonly held ideas. I believe that forced labor is less opposed to liberty than are taxes.

The better a state is constituted, the more public business takes precedence over private business in the minds of the citizens. There even is far less private business, since, with the sum of common happiness providing a more considerable portion of each individual's happiness, less remains for him to look for through private efforts. In a well run city everyone flies to the assemblies; under a bad government no one wants to take a step to get to them, since no one takes an interest in what happens there, for it is predictable that the general will will not predominate, and that in the end domestic concerns absorb everything. Good laws lead to making better laws; bad laws bring about worse ones. Once someone says *what do I care?* about the affairs of state, the state should be considered lost.

The cooling off of patriotism, the activity of private interest, the largeness of states, conquests, the abuse of government: these have suggested the route of using deputies or representatives of the people in the nation's assemblies. It is what in certain countries is called the third estate. Thus the private interest of two orders is given first and second place; the public interest is given merely third place.

Sovereignty cannot be represented for the same reason that it cannot be alienated. It consists essentially in the general will, and the will does not allow of being represented. It is either itself or something else; there is nothing in between. The deputies of the people, therefore, neither are nor can be its representatives; they are merely its agents. They cannot conclude anything definitively. Any law that the populace has not ratified in person is null; it is not a law at all. The English people believes itself to be free. It is greatly mistaken; it is free only during the election of the members of Parliament. Once they are elected, the populace is enslaved; it is nothing. The use the English people makes of that freedom in the brief moments of its liberty certainly warrants their losing it.

The idea of representatives is modern. It comes to us from feudal government, that iniquitous and absurd government in which the human race is degraded and the name of man is in dishonor. In the ancient republics and even in monarchies, the people never had representatives. The word itself was unknown. It is quite remarkable that in Rome where the tribunes were so sacred, no one even imagined that they could usurp the functions of the people, and that in the midst of such a great multitude, they never tried to pass a single plebiscite on their own authority. However, we can size up the difficulties that were sometimes caused by the crowd by what took place in the time of the Gracchi, when part of the citizenry voted from the rooftops.

Where right and liberty are everything, inconveniences are nothing. In the care of this wise people, everything was handled correctly. It allowed its lictors to do what its tribunes would not have dared to do. It had no fear that its lictors would want to represent it.

However, to explain how the tribunes sometimes represented it, it is enough to conceive how the government represents the sovereign. Since the law is merely the declaration of the general will, it is clear that the people cannot be represented in the legislative power. But it can and should be represented in the executive power, which is merely force applied to the law. This demonstrates that, on close examination, very few nations would be found to have laws. Be that as it may, it is certain that, since they have no share in the executive power, the tribunes could never represent the Roman people by the rights of their office, but only by usurping those of the senate.

Among the Greeks, whatever the populace had to do, it did by itself. It was constantly assembled at the public square. It inhabited a mild climate; it was not greedy; its slaves did the work; its chief item of business was its liberty. No longer having the same advantages, how are the same rights to be preserved? Your harsher climates cause you to have more needs;[31] six months out of the year the public square is uninhabitable; your muted tongues cannot make themselves understood in the open air; you pay more attention to your profits than to your liberty; and you are less fearful of slavery than you are of misery.

What! Can liberty be maintained only with the support of servitude? Perhaps. The two extremes meet. Everything that is not in nature has its drawbacks, and civil society more so than all the rest. There are some unfortunate circumstances where one's liberty can be preserved only at the expense of someone else's, and where the citizen can be perfectly free only if the slave is completely enslaved. Such was the situation in Sparta. As for you, modern peoples, you do not have slaves, but you yourselves are

slaves. You pay for their liberty with your own. It is in vain that you crow about that preference. I find more cowardice in it than humanity.

I do not mean by all this that having slaves is necessary, nor that the right of slavery is legitimate, for I have proved the contrary. I am merely stating the reasons why modern peoples who believe themselves free have representatives, and why ancient peoples did not have them. Be that as it may, the moment a people gives itself representatives, it is no longer free; it no longer exists.

All things considered, I do not see that it is possible henceforth for the sovereign to preserve among us the exercise of its rights, unless the city is very small. But if it is very small, will it be subjugated? No. I will show later[32] how the external power of a great people can be combined with the ease of administration and the good order of a small state.

Chapter 16

That the Institution of Government Is Not a Contract

Once the legislative power has been well established, it is a matter of establishing the executive power in the same way. For this latter, which functions only by means of particular acts, not being of the essence of the former, is naturally separate from it. Were it possible for the sovereign, considered as such, to have the executive power, right and fact would be so completely confounded that we would no longer know what is law and what is not. And the body politic, thus denatured, would soon fall prey to the violence against which it was instituted.

Since the citizens are all equal by the social contract, what everyone should do can be prescribed by everyone. On the other hand, no one has the right to demand that someone else do what he does not do for himself. Now it is precisely this right, indispensable for making the body politic live and move, that

---

31. To adopt in cold countries the luxury and softness of the orientals is to desire to be given their chains; it is submitting to these with even greater necessity than they did.

32. This is what I intended to do in the rest of this work, when in treating external relations I would have come to confederations. An entirely new subject, and its principles have yet to be established.

the sovereign gives the prince in instituting the government.

Several people have claimed that this act of establishment was a contract between the populace and the leaders it gives itself, a contract by which are stipulated between the two parties the conditions under which the one obliges itself to command and the other to obey. It will be granted, I am sure, that this is a strange way of entering into a social contract! But let us see if this opinion is tenable.

First, the supreme authority cannot be modified any more than it can be alienated; to limit it is to destroy it. It is absurd and contradictory for the sovereign to acquire a superior. To obligate oneself to obey a master is to return to full liberty.

Moreover, it is evident that this contract between the people and some or other persons would be a particular act. Whence it follows that this contract could be neither a law nor an act of sovereignty, and that consequently it would be illegitimate.

It is also clear that the contracting parties would, in relation to one another, be under only the law of nature and without any guarantee of their reciprocal commitments, which is contrary in every way to the civil state. Since the one who has force at his disposal is always in control of its employment, it would come to the same thing if we were to give the name contract to the act of a man who would say to another, "I am giving you all my goods, on the condition that you give me back whatever you wish."

There is only one contract in the state, that of the association, and that alone excludes any other. It is impossible to imagine any public contract that was not a violation of the first contract.

Chapter 17

On the Institution of the Government

What should be the terms under which we should conceive the act by which the government is instituted? I will begin by saying that this act is complex or composed of two others, namely the establishment of the law and the execution of the law.

By the first, the sovereign decrees that there will be a governing body established under some or other form. And it is clear that this act is a law.

By the second, the people names the leaders who will be placed in charge of the established government. And since this nomination is a particular act, it is not a second law, but merely a consequence of the first and a function of the government.

The problem is to understand how there can be an act of government before a government exists, and how the people, which is only sovereign or subject, can in certain circumstances become prince or magistrate.

Moreover, it is here that we discover one of those remarkable properties of the body politic, by which it reconciles seemingly contradictory operations. For this takes place by a sudden conversion of sovereignty into democracy, so that, without any noticeable change, and solely by a new relation of all to all, the citizens, having become magistrates, pass from general to particular acts, and from the law to its execution.

This change of relation is not a speculative subtlety without exemplification in practice. It takes place everyday in the English Parliament, where the lower chamber on certain occasions turns itself into a committee of the whole in order to discuss better the business of the sovereign court, thus becoming the simple commission of the sovereign court (the latter being what it was the moment before), so that it later reports to itself, as the House of Commons, the result of what it has just settled in the committee of the whole, and deliberates all over again under one title about what it had already settled under another.

The peculiar advantage to democratic government is that it can be established in actual fact by a simple act of the general will. After this, the provisional government remains in power, if this is the form adopted, or establishes in the name of the sovereign the government prescribed by the law; and thus everything is in accordance with the rule. It is not possible to institute the government in any other legitimate way without renouncing the principles established above.

Chapter 18

The Means of Preventing Usurpations of the Government

From these clarifications, it follows, in confirmation of Chapter XVI, that the act that institutes the government is not a contract but a law; that the trustees of the executive power are not the masters of the populace but its officers; that it can establish and remove them when it pleases; that for them there is no question of contracting, but of obeying; and that in taking on the functions the state imposes on them, they merely fulfill their duty as citizens, without in any way having the right to dispute over the conditions.

Thus, when it happens that the populace institutes a hereditary government, whether it is monarchical within a single family or aristocratic within a class of citizens, this is not a commitment it is entering. It is a provisional form that it gives the administration, until the populace is pleased to order it otherwise.

It is true that these changes are always dangerous, and that the established government should never be touched except when it becomes incompatible with the public good. But this circumspection is a maxim of politics and not a rule of law [droit], and the state is no more bound to leave civil authority to its leaders than it is to leave military authority to its generals.

Again, it is true that in such cases it is impossible to be too careful about observing all the formalities required in order to distinguish a regular and legitimate act from a seditious tumult, and the will of an entire people from the clamor of a faction. And it is here above all that one must not grant anything to odious cases except what cannot be refused according to the full rigor of the law [droit]. And it is also from this obligation that the prince derives a great advantage in preserving his power in spite of the people, without anyone being able to say that he has usurped it. For in appearing to use only his rights, it is quite easy for him to extend them, and under the pretext of public peace, to prevent assemblies destined to reestablish good order. Thus he avails himself of a silence he keeps from being broken, or of irregularities he causes to be committed, to assume that the opinion of those who are silenced by fear is supportive of him, and to punish those who dare to speak. This is how the decemvirs, having been first elected for one year and then continued for another year, tried to retain their power in perpetuity by no longer permitting the comitia to assemble. And it is by this simple means that all the governments of the world, once armed with the public force, sooner or later usurp the public authority.

The periodic assemblies I have spoken of earlier are suited to the prevention or postponement of this misfortune, especially when they have no need for a formal convocation. For then the prince could not prevent them without openly declaring himself a violator of the laws and an enemy of the state.

The opening of these assemblies, which have as their sole object the preservation of the social treaty, should always take place through two propositions which can never be suppressed, and which are voted on separately:

The first: *Does it please the sovereign to preserve the present form of government?*

The second: *Does it please the people to leave its administration to those who are now in charge of it?*

I am presupposing here what I believe I have demonstrated, namely that in the state there is no fundamental law that cannot be revoked, not even the social compact. For if all the citizens were to assemble in order to break this compact by common agreement, no one could doubt that it was legitimately broken. Grotius even thinks that each person can renounce the state of which he is a member and recover his natural liberty and his goods by leaving the country.[33] But it would be absurd that all the citizens together could not do what each of them can do separately.

END OF THE THIRD BOOK

BOOK IV

Chapter 1

That the General Will Is Indestructible

So long as several men together consider themselves to be a single body, they have but a single will, which is concerned with their common preservation and the general well-being. Then all the energies of the state are vigorous and simple; its maxims are clear

---

33. On the understanding that one does not leave in order to evade one's duty and to be exempt from serving the homeland the moment it needs us. In such circumstances, taking flight would be criminal and punishable; it would no longer be withdrawal, but desertion.

and luminous; there are no entangled, contradictory interests; the common good is clearly apparent everywhere, demanding only good sense in order to be perceived. Peace, union, equality are enemies of political subtleties. Upright and simple men are difficult to deceive on account of their simplicity. Traps and clever pretexts do not fool them. They are not even clever enough to be duped. When, among the happiest people in the world, bands of peasants are seen regulating their affairs of state under an oak tree, and always acting wisely, can one help scorning the refinements of other nations, which make themselves illustrious and miserable with so much art and mystery?

A state thus governed needs very few laws; and in proportion as it becomes necessary to promulgate new ones, this necessity is universally understood. The first to propose them merely says what everybody has already felt; and there is no question of either intrigues or eloquence to secure the passage into law of what each has already resolved to do, once he is sure the others will do likewise.

What misleads argumentative types is the fact that, since they take into account only the states that were badly constituted from the beginning, they are struck by the impossibility of maintaining such an administration. They laugh when they imagine all the foolishness a clever knave or a sly orator could get the people of Paris or London to believe. They do not know that Cromwell would have been sentenced to hard labor by the people of Berne, and the Duc de Beaufort imprisoned by the Genevans.

But when the social bond begins to relax and the state to grow weak, when private interests begin to make themselves felt and small societies begin to influence the large one, the common interest changes and finds opponents. Unanimity no longer reigns in the votes; the general will is no longer the will of all. Contradictions and debates arise, and the best advice does not pass without disputes.

Finally, when the state, on the verge of ruin, subsists only in an illusory and vain form, when the social bond of unity is broken in all hearts, when the meanest interest brazenly appropriates the sacred name of the public good, then the general will becomes mute. Everyone, guided by secret motives, no more express their opinions as citizens than if the state had never existed; and iniquitous decrees having as their sole purpose the private interest are falsely passed under the name of laws.

Does it follow from this that the general will is annihilated or corrupted? No, it is always constant, unalterable and pure; but it is subordinate to other wills that prevail over it. Each man, in detaching his interest from the common interest, clearly sees that he cannot totally separate himself from it; but his share of the public misfortune seems insignificant to him compared to the exclusive good he intends to make his own. Apart from this private good, he wants the general good in his own interest, just as strongly as anyone else. Even in selling his vote for money he does not extinguish the general will in himself; he evades it. The error he commits is that of changing the thrust of the question and answering a different question from the one he was asked. Thus, instead of saying through his vote *it is advantageous to the state, he says it is advantageous to this man or that party that this or that view should pass.* Thus the law of the public order in the assemblies is not so much to maintain the general will, as to bring it about that it is always questioned and that it always answers.

I could present here a number of reflections about the simple right to vote in every act of sovereignty, a right that nothing can take away from the citizens; and on the right to state an opinion, to offer proposals, to divide, to discuss, which the government always takes great care to allow only to its members. But this important subject would require a separate treatise, and I cannot say everything in this one.

Chapter 2

On Voting

It is clear from the preceding chapter that the manner in which general business is taken care of can provide a rather accurate indication of the present state of mores and of the health of the body politic. The more harmony reigns in the assemblies, that is to say, the closer opinions come to unanimity, the more dominant too is the general will. But long debates, dissensions, and tumult betoken the ascendance of private interests and the decline of the state.

This seems less evident when two or more orders enter into its constitution, as had been done in Rome by the patricians and the plebeians, whose quarrels often disturbed the comitia, even in the best of times in the Republic. But this exception is more apparent than real. For then, by the vice inherent in the body politic, there are, as it were, two states in one. What is not true of the two together is true of each of them separately. And indeed even in the most tumultuous times, the plebiscites of the people, when the senate did not interfere with them, always passed quietly and by a large majority of votes. Since the citizens have but one interest, the people had but one will.

At the other extreme of the circle, unanimity returns. It is when the citizens, having fallen into servitude, no longer have either liberty or will. Then fear and flattery turn voting into acclamations. People no longer deliberate; either they adore or they curse. Such was the vile manner in which the senate expressed its opinions under the emperors; sometimes it did so with ridiculous precautions. Tacitus observes that under Otho, the senators, while heaping curses upon Vitellius, contrived at the same time to make a frightening noise, so that, if by chance he became master, he would be unable to know what each of them had said.

From these various considerations there arise the maxims by which the manner of counting votes and comparing opinions should be regulated, depending on whether the general will is more or less easy to know and the state more or less in decline.

There is but one law that by its nature requires unanimous consent. This is the social compact. For civil association is the most voluntary act in the world. Since every man is born free and master of himself, no one can, under any pretext whatever, place another under subjection without his consent. To decide that the son of a slave is born a slave is to decide that he was not a man.

If, therefore, at the time of the social compact, there are opponents to it, their opposition does not invalidate the contract; it merely prevents them from being included in it. They are foreigners among citizens. Once the state is instituted, residency implies consent. To inhabit the territory is to submit to sovereignty.[34]

Aside from this primitive contract, the vote of the majority always obligates all the others. This is a consequence of the contract itself. But it is asked how a man can be both free and forced to conform to wills that are not his own. How can the opponents be both free and be placed in subjection to laws to which they have not consented?

I answer that the question is not put properly. The citizen consents to all the laws, even to those that pass in spite of his opposition, and even to those that punish him when he dares to violate any of them. The constant will of all the members of the state is the general will; through it they are citizens and free.[35] When a law is proposed in the people's assembly, what is asked of them is not precisely whether they approve or reject, but whether or not it conforms to the general will that is theirs. Each man, in giving his vote, states his opinion on this matter, and the declaration of the general will is drawn from the counting of votes. When, therefore, the opinion contrary to mine prevails, this proves merely that I was in error, and that what I took to be the general will was not so. If my private opinion had prevailed, I would have done something other than what I had wanted. In that case I would not have been free.

This presupposes, it is true, that all the characteristics of the general will are still in the majority. When they cease to be free, there is no longer any liberty regardless of the side one takes.

In showing earlier how private wills were substituted for the general will in public deliberations, I

34. This should always be understood in connection with a free state, for otherwise the family, goods, the lack of shelter, necessity, or violence can keep an inhabitant in a country in spite of himself; and then his sojourn alone no longer presupposes his consent to the contract or to the violation of the contract.

35. In Genoa, the word *libertas* [liberty] can be read on the front of prisons and on the chains of galley-slaves. This application of the motto is fine and just. Indeed it is only malefactors of all social classes who prevent the citizen from being free. In a country where all such people were in the galleys, the most perfect liberty would be enjoyed.

have given an adequate indication of the possible ways of preventing this abuse. I will discuss this again at a later time. With respect to the proportional number of votes needed to declare this will, I have also given the principles on the basis of which it can be determined. The differences of a single vote breaks a tie vote; a single opponent destroys a unanimous vote. But between a unanimous and a tie vote there are several unequal divisions, at any of which this proportionate number can be fixed in accordance with the condition and needs of the body politic.

Two general maxims can serve to regulate these ratios. One, that the more important and serious the deliberations are, the closer the prevailing opinion should be to unanimity. The other, that the more the matter at hand calls for alacrity, the smaller the prescribed difference in the division of opinion should be. In decisions that must be reached immediately, a majority of a single vote should suffice. The first of these maxims seems more suited to the laws, and the second to public business. Be that as it may, it is the combination of the two that establishes the ratios that best help the majority to render its decision.

Chapter 3

On Elections

With regard to the elections of the prince and the magistrates, which are, as I have said, complex acts, there are two ways to proceed, namely by choice or by lots. Both of these have been used in various republics, and at present we still see a very complicated mixture of the two in the election of the Doge of Venice.

Voting by lot, says Montesquieu, *is of the essence of democracy*. I agree, but why is this the case? *Drawing lots*, he continues, *is a way of electing that harms no one; it leaves each citizen a reasonable hope of serving the homeland*. These are not reasons.

If we keep in mind that the election of leaders is a function of government and not of the sovereignty, we will see why the method of drawing lots is more in the nature of democracy, where the administration is better in proportion as its acts are less numerous.

In every true democracy the magistrature is not an advantage but a heavy responsibility that cannot justly be imposed on one private individual rather than another. The law alone can impose this responsibility on the one to whom it falls by lot. For in that case, with the condition being equal for all and the choice not depending on any human will, there is no particular application that alters the universality of the law.

In any aristocracy, the prince chooses the prince; the government is preserved by itself, and it is there that voting is appropriate.

The example of the election of the Doge of Venice, far from destroying this distinction, confirms it. This mixed form suits a mixed government. For it is an error to regard the government of Venice as a true aristocracy. For although the populace there has no part in the government, the nobility is itself the people. A multitude of poor Barnabites never came near any magistrature, have nothing to show for their nobility but the vain title of excellency and the right to be present at the grand council. Since this grand council is as numerous as our general council in Geneva, its illustrious members have no more privileges than our single citizens. It is certain that, aside from the extreme disparity between the two republics, the bourgeoisie of Geneva exactly corresponds to the Venetian patriciate. Our natives and inhabitants correspond to the townsmen and people of Venice. Our peasants correspond to the subjects on the mainland. Finally, whatever way one considers this Republic, apart from its size, its government is no more aristocratic than ours. The whole difference lies in the fact that, since we do not have leaders who serve for life, we do not have the same need to draw lots.

Elections by lot would have few disadvantages in a true democracy where, all things being equal both in mores and talents as well as in maxims and fortunes, the choice would become almost indifferent. But I have already said there is no such thing as a true democracy.

When choice and lots are mixed, the former should fill the position requiring special talents, such as military posts. The latter is suited to those positions, such as the responsibilities of judicature, where good sense, justice, and integrity are enough, because in a well constituted state these qualities are common to all the citizens.

Neither the drawing of lots nor voting have any

place in a monarchical government. Since the monarch is by right the only prince and sole magistrate, the choice of his lieutenants belongs to him alone. When the Abbé de St. Pierre proposed multiplying the Councils of the King of France and electing the members by ballot, he did not realize that he was proposing to change the form of government.

It remains for me to speak of the manner in which the votes are cast and gathered in the people's assembly. But perhaps in this regard the history of the Roman system of administration will explain more clearly all the maxims I could establish. It is not beneath the dignity of a judicious reader to consider in some detail how public and private business was conducted in a council made of two hundred thousand men.

Chapter 4

On the Roman Comitia

We have no especially reliable records of the earliest period of Rome's history. It even appears quite likely that most of the things reported about it are fables.[36] And in general the most instructive part of the annals of peoples, which is the history of their founding, is the part we most lack. Experience teaches us every day the causes that lead to the revolutions of empires. But since peoples are no longer being formed, we have almost nothing but conjecture to explain how they were formed.

The customs we find established attest at the very least to the fact that these customs had an origin. Of the traditions that go back to these origins, those that are supported by the greatest authorities and that are confirmed by the strongest reasons should pass for the most certain. These are the maxims I have tried to follow in attempting to find out how the freest and most powerful people on earth exercised its supreme power.

After the founding of Rome, the new-born Republic, that is, the army of the founder, composed of Albans, Sabines, and foreigners, was divided into three classes, which took the name *tribus* [tribes] by nature of this division. Each of these tribes was divided into ten curiae, and each curia into decuriae, at the head of which were placed leaders called *curiones* and *decuriones*.

Moreover, from each tribe was drawn a body of one hundred horsemen or knights, called a *century*. It is clear from this that these divisions, being hardly necessary in a market-town, originally were exclusively military. But it appears that an instinct for greatness led the small town of Rome to provide itself in advance with a system of administration suited to the capital of the world.

One disadvantage soon resulted from this initial division. With the tribes of the Albans[37] and the Sabines[38] always remaining constant, while that of the foreigners[39] grew continually, thanks to their perpetual influx, this latter group soon outnumbered the other two. The remedy that Servius found for this dangerous abuse was to change the division and, in place of the division based on race, which he abolished, to substitute another division drawn from the areas of the town occupied by each tribe. In place of the three tribes, he made four. Each of them occupied one of the hills of Rome and bore its name. Thus, in remedying the inequality of the moment, he also prevented it from happening in the future. And in order that this division might not be merely one of localities but of men, he prohibited the inhabitants of one quarter from moving into another, which prevented the races from mingling with one another.

He also doubled the three ancient centuries of horsemen and he added to them twelve others, but always under the old names, a simple and judicious means by which he achieved the differentiation of the body of knights from that of the people, without causing the latter to murmur.

To the four urban tribes, Servius added fifteen others called rural tribes because they were formed

---

36. The name *Rome*, which presumably comes from *Romulus*, is Greek, and means *force*. The name *Numa* is also Greek, and means *law*. What is the likelihood that the first two kings of that town would have borne in advance names so clearly related to what they did?

37. Ramnenses.

38. Tatienses.

39. Luceres.

from the inhabitants of the countryside, divided into the same number of cantons. Subsequently, the same number of new ones were brought into being, and the Roman people finally found itself divided into thirty-five tribes, a number at which they remained fixed until the end of the Republic.

There resulted from this distinction between the tribes of the city and those of the countryside an effect worth noting, because there is no other example of it, and because Rome owed it both the preservation of its mores and the growth of its empire. One might have thought that the urban tribes soon would have arrogated to themselves power and honors, and wasted no time in vilifying the rural tribes. What took place was quite the opposite. The early Romans' taste for country life is well known. They inherited this taste from the wise founder who united liberty with rural and military labors, and, so to speak, relegated to the town arts, crafts, intrigue, fortune and slavery.

Thus, since all the illustrious men in Rome lived in the country and tilled the soil, people became accustomed to look only there for the mainstays of the Republic. Since this condition was that of the worthiest patricians, it was honored by everyone. The simple and laborious life of the townsmen was preferred to the lazy and idle life of the bourgeois of Rome. And someone who would have been merely a miserable proletarian in the town, became a respected citizen as a field worker. It was not without reason, said Varro, that our great-souled ancestors established in the village the nursery of those robust and valiant men who defended them in time of war and nourished them in time of peace. Pliny says positively that the tribes of the fields were honored on account of the men who made them up; on the other hand, cowards whom men wished to vilify were transferred in disgrace to the tribes of the town. When the Sabine Appius Claudius came to settle in Rome, he was decked with honors and inscribed in a rural tribe that later took the name of his family. Finally, freedmen all entered the urban tribes, never the rural ones. And during the entire period of the Republic, there was not a single example of any of these freedmen reaching any magistrature, even if he had become a citizen.

This maxim was excellent, but it was pushed so far that it finally resulted in a change and certainly an abuse in the administration.

First, the censors, after having long arrogated to themselves the right to transfer citizens arbitrarily from one tribe to another, permitted most of them to have themselves inscribed in whatever tribe they pleased. Certainly this permission served no useful purpose and deprived the censorship of one of its greatest resources. Moreover, with the great and the powerful having themselves inscribed in the tribes of the countryside, and the freedmen who had become citizens remaining with the populace in the tribes of the town, the tribes in general no longer had either place or territory. On the contrary, they all found themselves so intermixed that the number of each could no longer be identified except by the registers, so that in this way the idea of the word *tribe* passed from being proprietary to personal, or rather, it became almost a chimera.

In addition, it happened that since the tribes of the town were nearer at hand, they were often the strongest in the comitia, and sold the state to those who deigned to buy the votes of the mob that made them up.

Regarding the curiae, since the founder had created ten curiae in each tribe, the entire Roman people, which was then contained within the town walls, was composed of thirty curiae, each of which had its temples, its gods, its officials, its priests and its feasts called *compitalia*, similar to the *paganalia* later held by the rural tribes.

When Servius established this new division, since this number thirty could not be divided equally among his four tribes, and since he did not want to alter it, the curiae became another division of the inhabitants of Rome, independent of the tribes. But there was no question of the curiae either in the rural tribes or among the people that make them up, for since the tribes had become a purely civil establishment and another system of administration had been introduced for the raising of troops, the military divisions of Romulus were found to be superfluous. Thus, even though every citizen was inscribed in a tribe, there were quite a few who were not inscribed in a curia.

Servius established still a third division which bore no relationship to the two preceding ones and which became, in its effects, the most important of all. He divided the entire Roman people into six classes, which he distinguished neither by place nor by person, but by wealth. Thus the first classes were filled by the rich, the last by the poor, and the middle ones by those who enjoyed a moderate fortune. These six classes were subdivided into one hundred ninety-three other bodies called centuries, and these bodies were divided in such wise that the first class alone contained more than half of them, and the last contained only one. Thus it was that the class with the smallest number of men was the one with the greatest number of centuries, and that the entire last class counted only as a subdivision, even though it alone contained more than half the inhabitants of Rome.

In order that the people might have less of a grasp of the consequences of this last form, Servius feigned giving it a military air. He placed in the second class two centuries of armorers, and two instruments of war in the fourth. In each class, with the exception of the last, he made a distinction between the young and the old, that is to say, between those who were obliged to carry arms and those whose age exempted them by law. This distinction, more than that of wealth, produced the necessity for frequently retaking the census or counting. Finally, he wished the assembly to be held in the Campus Martius, and that all those who were of age to serve should come there with their arms.

The reason he did not follow this same division of young and old in the last division is that the populace of which it was composed was not accorded the honor of bearing arms for the homeland. It was necessary to possess a hearth in order to obtain the right to defend it. And of the innumerable troops of beggars who today grace the armies of kings, there is perhaps no one who would not have been disdainfully chased from a Roman cohort, when the soldiers were the defenders of liberty.

There still is a distinction in the last class between the *proletarians* and those that are called *capite censi*. The former, not completely reduced to nothing, at least gave citizens to the state, sometimes even soldiers in times of pressing need. As for those who possessed nothing at all and could be reckoned only by counting heads, they were reckoned to be absolutely worthless, and Marius was the first who deigned to enroll them.

Without deciding here whether this third method of reckoning was good or bad in itself, I believe I can affirm that it could be made practicable only by the simple mores of the early Romans, their disinterestedness, their taste for agriculture, their dislike for commerce and for the passion for profits. Where is the modern people among whom their devouring greed, their unsettled spirit, their intrigue, their continual displacements, their perpetual revolutions of fortunes could allow such an establishment to last twenty years without overturning the entire state? It must also be duly noted that the mores and the censorship, which were stronger than this institution, corrected its defects in Rome, and that a rich man found himself relegated to the class of the poor for having made too much of a show of his wealth.

From all this, it is easy to grasp why mention is almost never made of more than five classes, even though there actually were six. The sixth, since it furnished neither soldiers for the army nor voters for the Campus Martius[40] and was of virtually no use in the Republic, was hardly ever counted for anything.

Such were the various divisions of the Roman people. Let us now look at the effect these divisions had on the assemblies. When legitimately convened, these assemblies were called *comitia*. Ordinarily they were held in the Roman forum or in the Campus Martius, and were distinguished as comitia curiata, comitia centuriata, and comitia tributa, according to which of the three forms was the basis on which they were organized. The comitia curiata were based on the institution of Romulus, the comitia centuriata on that of Servius, and the comitia tributa on that of the tribunes of the people. No law received sanction, no magistrate was elected save in the comitia. And since there was no citizen who was not inscribed in a curia, in a century, or in a tribe, it followed that no citizen was excluded from the right of suffrage, and that the Roman people was truly sovereign both de jure and de facto.

For the comitia to be legitimately assembled and for what took place to have the force of law, three conditions had to be met: first, the body or the magistrate

---

40. I say *Campus Martius* because it was here that the comitia centuriata gathered. In the two other forms of assembly, the people gathered in the *forum* or elsewhere, and then the *capite censi* had as much influence and authority as the first citizens.

who called these assemblies had to be invested with the necessary authority to do so; second, the assembly had to be held on one of the days permitted by law; third, the auguries had to be favorable.

The reason for the first regulation needs no explanation. The second is an administrative matter. Thus the comitia were not allowed to be held on holidays and market days, when people from the country, coming to Rome on business, did not have time to spend the day in the public forum. By means of the third rule, the senate held in check a proud and restless people, and appropriately tempered the ardor of seditious tribunes. But these latter found more than one way of getting around this constraint.

The laws and the election of leaders were not the only matters submitted to the judgment of the comitia. Since the Roman people had usurped the most important functions of government, it can be said that the fate of Europe was decided in its assemblies. This variety of objects gave rise to the various forms these assemblies took on according to the matters on which they had to pronounce.

In order to judge these various forms, it is enough to compare them. In instituting the curiae, Romulus had intended to contain the senate by means of the people and the people by means of the senate, while he dominated both equally. He therefore gave the people, by means of this form, all the authority of number to balance that of power and wealth which he left to the patricians. But in conformity with the spirit of the monarchy, he nevertheless left a greater advantage to the patricians through their clients' influence on the majority of the votes. This admirable institution of patrons and clients was a masterpiece of politics and humanity, without which the patriciate, so contrary to the spirit of the Republic, could not have subsisted. Only Rome had the honor of giving the world this fine example, which never led to any abuse, and which, for all that, has never been followed.

Since this same form of curiae had subsisted under the kings until Servius, and since the reign of the last Tarquin was not considered legitimate, royal laws were generally known by the name *leges curiatae*.

Under the Republic, the curiae, always limited to the four urban tribes and including no more than the populace of Rome, was unable to suit either the senate, which was at the head of the patricians, or the tribunes, who, plebeians though they were, were at the head of the citizens who were in comfortable circumstances. The curiae therefore fell into discredit and their degradation was such that their thirty assembled lictors together did what the comitia curiata should have done.

The division by centuries was so favorable to the aristocracy, that at first difficult it is to see how the senate did not always prevail in the comitia which bears this name, and by which the consuls, the censors, and other crurale magistrates were elected. In fact, of the one hundred ninety-three centuries that formed the six classes of the entire Roman people, the first class contained ninety-eight, and, since the voting was counted by centuries only, this first class alone prevailed in the number of votes over all the rest. When all its centuries were in agreement, they did not even continue to gather the votes. Decisions made by the smallest number passed for a decision of the multitude; and it can be said that in the comitia centuriata business was regulated more by the majority of money than by one of votes.

But this extreme authority was tempered in two ways. First, since ordinarily the tribunes, and always a large number of plebeians, were in the class of the rich, they balanced the credit of the patricians in this first class.

The second way consisted in the following. Instead of at the outset making the centuries vote according to their order, which would have meant always beginning with the first, one century was chosen by lot, and that one[41] alone proceeded to the election. After this, all the centuries were called on another day according to their rank, repeated the same election and usually confirmed it. Thus the authority of example was removed from rank in order to give it to lot, in accordance with the principle of democracy.

There resulted from this custom still another advantage; namely that the citizens from the country had time between the two elections to inform themselves of the merit of the provisionally named

---

41. This century, having been chosen thus by lot, was called *prae rogativa*, on account of the fact that it was the first to be asked for its vote, and it is from this that the word *prerogative* is derived.

candidate, so as to give their votes only on condition of their having knowledge of the issue. But on the pretext of speeding things up, this custom was finally abolished and the two elections were held on the same day.

Strictly speaking, the comitia tributa were the council of the Roman people. They were convened only by the tribunes. The tribunes were elected and passed their plebiscites there. Not only did the senate hold no rank in them, it did not even have the right to be present. And since the senators were forced to obey the laws upon which they could not vote, they were less free in this regard than the humblest citizens. This injustice was altogether ill-conceived, and was by itself enough to invalidate the decrees of a body to which all its members were not admitted. If all the patricians had been present at these comitia in virtue of the right they had as citizens, having then become simple private individuals, they would not have had a great deal of influence on a form of voting that was tallied by counting heads, and where the humblest proletarian had as much clout as the prince of the senate.

Thus it can be seen that besides the order that resulted from these various distributions for gathering the votes of so great a people, these distributions were not reducible to forms indifferent in themselves, but each one had effects relative to the viewpoints that caused it to be preferred.

Without going further into greater detail here, it is a consequence of the preceding clarifications that the comitia tributa were the most favorable to the popular government, and the comitia centuriata more favorable to the aristocracy. Regarding the comitia curiata, in which the populace of Rome alone formed the majority, since these were good only for favoring tyranny and evil designs, they fell of their own weight into disrepute, and even the seditious abstained from using a means that gave too much exposure to their projects. It is certain that all the majesty of the Roman people is found only in the curia centuriata, which alone were complete, for the comitia curiata excluded the rural tribes, and the comitia tributa the senate and the patricians.

As to the manner of counting the votes, among the early Romans it was as simple as their mores, though not so simple as in Sparta. Each gave his vote in a loud voice, and a clerk marked it down accordingly. The majority vote in each tribe determined the tribe's vote; the majority vote of the tribes determined the people's vote; and the same went for the curia and the centuries. This custom was good so long as honesty reigned among the citizens and each was ashamed to give his vote publicly in favor of an unjust proposal or an unworthy subject. But when the people became corrupt and votes were bought, it was fitting that they should give their votes in secret in order to restrain the buyers through distrust and to provide scoundrels the means of not being traitors.

I know that Cicero condemns this change and attributes the ruin of the Republic partly to it. But although I am aware of the weight that Cicero's authority should have here, I cannot agree with him. On the contrary, I think that, by having made not enough of these changes, the fall of the state was accelerated. Just as the regimen of healthy people is not suitable for the sick, one should not want to govern a corrupt people by means of the same laws that are suited to a good people. Nothing proves this maxim better than the long life of the Republic of Venice, whose shadow still exists, solely because its laws are suited only to wicked men.

Tablets were therefore distributed to the citizens by mean of which each man could vote without anyone knowing what his opinion was. New formalities were also established for collecting the tablets, counting the votes, comparing the numbers, and so on. None of this prevented the integrity of the officials in charge of these functions[42] from often being under suspicion. Finally, to prevent intrigue and vote trafficking, edicts were passed whose sheer multiplicity is proof of their uselessness.

Toward the end of the period of the Republic, it was often necessary to have recourse to extraordinary expedients in order to make up for the inadequacy of the law. Sometimes miracles were alleged. But this means, which could deceive the populace, did not deceive those who governed it. Sometimes an assembly was unexpectedly convened before the candidates had time to carry out their intrigues. Sometimes an entire session was spent on talk, when it was clear

12. Custodes, diribitores, rogatores suffragiorum.

that the populace was won over and ready to take the wrong side on an issue. But finally ambition eluded everything; and what is unbelievable is that in the midst of so much abuse, this immense people, by virtue of its ancient regulations, did not cease to choose magistrates, pass laws, judge cases, or expedite private and public business, almost as easily as the senate itself could have done.

Chapter 5

On the Tribunate

When it is not possible to establish an exact proportion between the constitutive parts of the state, or when indestructible causes continually alter the relationships between them, a special magistrature is then established that does not make up a larger body along with them. This magistrature restores each term to its true relationship to the others, and which creates a link or a middle term either between the prince and the people or between the prince and the sovereign, or on both sides at once, if necessary.

This body, which I will call the *tribunate,* is the preserver of the laws and the legislative power. It serves sometimes to protect the sovereign against the government, as the tribunes of the people did in Rome; sometimes to sustain the government against the people, as the Council of Ten now does in Venice; and sometimes to maintain equilibrium between the two, as the ephors did in Sparta.

The tribunate is not a constitutive part of the city and it should have no share in either the legislative or the executive power. But this is precisely what makes its own power the greater. For although it is unable to do anything, it can prevent everything. It is more sacred and more revered as a defender of the laws than the prince who executes them and the sovereign who gives them. This was very clearly apparent in Rome when the proud patricians, who always scorned the entire populace, were forced to bow before a humble official of the people, who had neither auspices nor jurisdiction.

A well tempered tribunate is the firmest support of a good constitution. But if it has the slightest bit too much force, it undermines everything. As to weakness, there is none in its nature; and provided it is something, it is never less than it ought to be.

It degenerates into tyranny when it usurps the executive power, of which it is merely the moderator, and when it wants to dispense the laws it ought only protect. The enormous power of the ephors, which was without danger so long as Sparta preserved its mores, hastened corruption once it had begun. The blood of Agis, who was slaughtered by these tyrants, was avenged by his successor. The crime and the punishment of the ephors equally hastened the fall of the republic; and after Cleomenes Sparta was no longer anything. Rome also perished in the same way, and the excessive power of the tribunes, which they had gradually usurped, finally served, with the help of the laws that were made to protect liberty, as a safeguard for the emperors who destroyed it. As for the Council of Ten in Venice, it is a tribunal of blood, equally horrible to the patricians and the people, and which, far from proudly protecting the laws, no longer serves any purpose, after their degradation, beyond that of delivering blows in the dark which no one dares notice.

Just like the government, the tribunate weakened as a result of the multiplication of its members. When the tribunes of the Roman people, who at first were two in number, then five, wanted to double this number, the senate let them do so, certain that one part would hold the others in check; and this did not fail to happen.

The best way to prevent usurpations by so formidable a body, one that no government has yet made use of, would be not to make this body permanent, but to regulate the intervals during which it would be suppressed. These intervals, which ought not be so long as to allow abuses time to grow in strength, can be fixed by law in such a way that it is easy to shorten them, as needed, by means of extraordinary commissions.

This way seems to me to have no disadvantage, for since, as I have said, the tribunate is not part of the constitution, it can be set aside without doing the constitution any harm, because a newly established magistrate begins not with the power his predecessor had, but with the power the law gives him.

Chapter 6

On Dictatorship

The inflexibility of the laws, which prevents them from adapting to circumstances, can in certain instances make them harmful and render them the instrument of the state's downfall in time of crisis. The order and the slowness of formal procedures require a space of time which circumstances sometimes do not permit. A thousand circumstances can present themselves which the legislator has not foreseen, and it is a very necessary bit of foresight to realize that not everything can be foreseen.

It is therefore necessary to avoid the desire to strengthen political institutions to the point of removing the power to suspend their effect. Sparta itself allowed its laws to lie dormant.

But only the greatest dangers can counterbalance the danger of altering the public order, and the sacred power of the laws should never be suspended except when it is a question of the safety of the homeland. In these rare and obvious cases, public safety can be provided for by a special act which confers the responsibility for it on someone who is most worthy. This commission can be carried out in two ways, according to the type of danger.

If increasing the activity of government is enough to remedy the situation, it is concentrated in one or two members. Thus it is not the authority of the laws that is altered, but merely the form of their administration. But if the peril is such that the apparatus of the laws is an obstacle to their being protected, then a supreme leader is named who silences all the laws and briefly suspends the sovereign authority. In such a case, the general will is not in doubt, and it is evident that the first intention of the people is that the state should not perish. In this manner, the suspension of legislative authority does not abolish it. The magistrate who silences it cannot make it speak; he dominates it without being able to represent it. He can do anything but make laws.

The first way was used by the Roman senate when, by a sacred formula, it entrusted the consuls with the responsibility for providing for the safety of the Republic. The second took place when one of the two consuls named a dictator,[43] a custom for which Alba had provided Rome the precedent.

In the beginning days of the Republic, there was frequent recourse to dictatorship, since the state did not yet have a sufficiently stable basis to be capable of sustaining itself by the force of its constitution. Since the mores at that time made many of the precautions superfluous that would have been necessary in other times, there was no fear either that a dictator would abuse his authority or that he would try to hold on to it beyond his term of office. On the contrary, it seemed that such a great power was a burden to the one in whom it was vested, so quickly did he hasten to rid himself of it, as if a position that took the place of the laws would have been too troublesome and dangerous!

Thus it is not so much the danger of its being abused as it is that of its being degraded which makes one criticize the injudicious use of this supreme magistrature in the early days of the Republic. For while it was being wasted on elections, dedications and purely formal proceedings, there was reason to fear that it would become less formidable in time of need, and that people would become accustomed to regard as empty a title that was used exclusively in empty ceremonies.

Toward the end of the Republic, the Romans, having become more circumspect, were as unreasonably sparing in their use of the dictatorship as they had formerly been lavish. It was easy to see that their fear was ill-founded; that the weakness of the capital then protected it against the magistrates who were in its midst; that a dictator could, under certain circumstances, defend the public liberty without ever being able to make an attack on it; and that Rome's chains would not be forged in Rome itself, but in its armies. The weak resistance that Marius offered Sulla and Pompey offered Caesar clearly demonstrated what could be expected of internal authority in the face of external force.

This error caused them to make huge mistakes; for example, failing to name a dictator in the Catalinian affair. For since this was a question merely of the interior of the town and, at most, of some province in Italy, with the unlimited authority that the laws

---

43. This nomination was made at night and in secret, as if it were shameful to place a man beyond the laws.

give the dictator, he would have easily quelled the conspiracy, which was stifled only by a coming together of favor chance happenings, which human prudence has no right to expect.

Instead of that, the senate was content to entrust all its power to the consuls. Whence it happened that, in order to act effectively, Cicero was forced to exceed this power on a crucial point. And although the first transports of joy indicated approval of his conduct, eventually Cicero was justly called to account for the blood of citizens shed against the laws, a reproach that could not have been delivered against a dictator. But the eloquence of the consul carried the day. And since even he, Roman though he was, preferred his own glory to his homeland, he sought not so much the most legitimate and safest way of saving the state as he did the way that would get him all the honor for settling this affair.[44] Thus he was justly honored as the liberator of Rome and justly punished as a lawbreaker. However brilliant his recall may have been, it undoubtedly was a pardon.

For the rest, whatever the manner in which this important commission was conferred, it is important to limit a dictatorship's duration to a very short period of time which cannot be prolonged. In the crises that call for its being established, the state is soon either destroyed or saved; and once the pressing need has passed, the dictatorship becomes tyrannical or needless. In Rome, where the dictators had terms of six months only, most of them abdicated before their terms had expired. If the term had been longer, perhaps they would have been tempted to prolong it further, as did the decemvirs with a one year term. The dictator only had time enough to see to the need that got him elected. He did not have time to dream up other projects.

Chapter 7

On the Censorship

Just as the declaration of the general will takes place through the law, the declaration of the public judgment takes place through the censorship. Public opin-

ion is the sort of law whose censor is the minister, and which he only applies to particular cases, after the example of the prince.

Thus the censorial tribunal, far from being the arbiter of the people's opinion, is merely its spokesman; and as soon as it deviates from this opinion, its decisions are vain and futile.

It is useless to distinguish the mores of a nation from the objects of its esteem, for all these things derive from the same principle and are necessarily intermixed. Among all the peoples of the world, it is not nature but opinion which decides the choice of their pleasures. Reform men's opinions, and their mores will soon become purified all by themselves. Men always love what is good or what they find to be so; but it is in this judgment that they make mistakes. Hence this is the judgment whose regulation is the point at issue. Whoever judges mores judges honor; and whoever judges honor derives his law from opinion.

The opinions of a people arise from its constitution. Although the law does not regulate mores, legislation is what gives rise to them. When legislation weakens, mores degenerate; but then the judgment of the censors will not do what the force of the laws has not done.

It follows from this that the censorship can be useful for preserving mores, but never for reestablishing them. Establish censors while the laws are vigorous. Once they have lost their vigor, everything is hopeless. Nothing legitimate has any force once the laws no longer have force.

The censorship maintains mores by preventing opinions from becoming corrupt, by preserving their rectitude through wise applications, and sometimes even by making a determination on them when they are still uncertain. The use of seconds in duels, which had been carried to the point of being a craze in the kingdom of France, was abolished by the following few words of the king's edict: *as for those who are cowardly enough to call upon seconds*. This judgment anticipated that of the public and suddenly made a determination. But when the same edicts tried to declare that it was also an act of cowardice to fight duels (which of course is quite true, but contrary to common opinion), the public mocked this decision; it concerned a matter about which its mind was already made up.

---

44. He could not have been sure of this, had he proposed a dictator, since he did not dare name himself, and he could not be sure that his colleague would name him.

I have said elsewhere[45] that since public opinion is not subject to constraint, there should be no vestige of it in the tribunal established to represent it. It is impossible to show too much admiration for the skill with which this device, entirely lost among us moderns, was put into effect among the Romans and even better among the Lacedaemonians.

When a man of bad mores put forward a good proposal in the council of Sparta, the ephors ignored it and had the same proposal put forward by a virtuous citizen. What honor for the one, what shame for the other; and without having given praise or blame to either of the two! Certain drunkards of Samos[46] defiled the tribunals of the ephors. The next day, a public edict gave the Samians permission to be filthy. A true punishment would have been less severe than impunity such as this. When Sparta made a pronouncement on what was or was not decent, Greece did not appeal its judgments.

Chapter 8

On Civil Religion

At first men had no other kings but the gods, and no other government than a theocratic one. They reasoned like Caligula, and then they reasoned correctly. A lengthy alteration of feelings and ideas is necessary before men can be resolved to accept a fellow man as a master, in the hope that things will turn out well for having done so.

By the mere fact that a god was placed at the head of every political society, it followed that there were as many gods as there were peoples. Two peoples who were alien to one another and nearly always enemies, could not recognize the same master for very long. Two armies in combat with one another could not obey the same leader. Thus national divisions led to polytheism, and this in turn led to theolog-

ical and civil intolerance which are by nature the same, as will be stated later.

The fanciful notion of the Greeks that they had rediscovered their gods among the beliefs of barbarian peoples arose from another notion they had of regarding themselves as the natural sovereigns of these peoples. But in our day it is a ridiculous bit of erudition which equates the gods of different nations: as if Moloch, Saturn, and Chronos could have been the same god; as if the Phoenicians' Baal, the Greeks' Zeus, and the Romans' Jupiter could have been the same; as if there could be anything in common among chimerical beings having different names!

But if it is asked how in pagan cultures, where each state has its own cult and its own gods, there are no wars of religion, I answer that it was for this very reason that each state, having its own cult as well as its own government, did not distinguish its gods from its laws. Political war was theological as well. The departments of the gods were, so to speak, fixed by national boundaries. The gods of one people had no rights over other peoples. The gods of the pagans were not jealous gods. They divided dominion over the world among themselves. Moses himself and the Hebrew people sometimes countenanced this idea in speaking of the god of Israel. It is true they regarded as nothing the gods of the Canaanites, a proscribed people destined for destruction, and whose land they were to occupy. But note how they spoke of the divinities of neighboring peoples whom they were forbidden to attack! *Is not the possession of what belongs to your god Chamos*, said Jephthah to the Ammonites, *lawfully yours? By the same right we possess the lands our victorious god has acquired for himself.*[47] It appears to me that here was a clear recognition of the parity between the rights of Chamos and those of the god of Israel.

---

45. I merely call attention in this chapter to what I have treated at greater length in my *Letter to D'Alembert*.

46. [Rousseau adds the following in the 1782 edition: "They are from another island which the delicacy of our language prohibits me from naming at this time."]

47. *Nonne ea quae possidet Chamos deus tuus, tibi jure debentur?* Such is the text of the Vulgate. Father de Carrières has translated it: *Do you not believe that you have the right to possess what belongs to your god Chamos?* I do not know the force of the Hebrew text; but I see that in the Vulgate Jephthah positively acknowledges the right of the god Chamos, and that the French translator weakened this recognition by adding an *according to you* which is not in the Latin.

But when the Jews, while in subjection to the kings of Babylon and later to the kings of Syria, wanted to remain steadfast in not giving recognition to any other god but their own, their refusal, seen as rebellion against the victor, brought them the persecutions we read of in their history, and of which there is no other precedent prior to Christianity.[48]

Since, therefore, each religion was uniquely tied to the laws of the state which prescribed it, there was no other way of converting a people except by enslaving it, nor any other missionaries than conquerors. And with the obligation to change cult being the law of the vanquished, it was necessary to begin by conquering before talking about it. Far from men fighting for the gods, it was, as it was in Homer, the gods who fought for men; each asked his own god for victory and paid for it with new altars. Before taking an area, the Romans summoned that area's gods to leave it. And when they allowed the Tarentines to keep their angry gods, it was because at that point they considered these gods to be in subjection to their own and forced to do them homage. They left the vanquished their gods, just as they left them their laws. A wreath to the Capitoline Jupiter was often the only tribute they imposed.

Finally, the Romans having spread this cult and their gods, along with their empire, and having themselves often adopted the gods of the vanquished by granting the right of the city to both alike, the peoples of this vast empire gradually found themselves to have multitudes of gods and cults, which were nearly the same everywhere. And that is how paganism finally became a single, identical religion in the known world.

Such were the circumstances under which Jesus came to establish a spiritual kingdom on earth. In separating the theological system from the political system, this made the state to cease being united and caused internal divisions that never ceased to agitate Christian peoples. But since this new idea of an otherworldly kingdom had never entered the heads of the pagans, they always regarded the Christians as true rebels who, underneath their hypocritical submission, were only waiting for the moment when they would become independent and the masters, and adroitly usurp the authority they pretended in their weakness to respect. This is the reason for the persecutions.

What the pagans feared happened. Then everything changed its appearance. The humble Christians changed their language, and soon this so-called otherworldly kingdom became, under a visible leader, the most violent despotism in this world.

However, since there has always been a prince and civil laws, this double power has given rise to a perpetual jurisdictional conflict that has made all good polity impossible in Christian states, and no one has ever been able to know whether it is the priest or the master whom one is obliged to obey.

Nevertheless, several peoples, even in Europe or nearby have wanted to preserve or reestablish the ancient system, but without success. The spirit of Christianity has won everything. The sacred cult has always remained or again become independent of the sovereign and without any necessary link to the state. Mohammed had very sound opinions. He tied his political system together very well, and so long as the form of his government subsisted under his successors, the caliphs, this government was utterly unified, and for that reason it was good. But as the Arabs became prosperous, lettered, polished, soft and cowardly, they were subjugated by barbarians. Then the division between the two powers began again. Although it is less apparent among the Mohammedans than among the Christians, it is there all the same, especially in the sect of Ali; and there are states, such as Persia, where it never ceases to be felt.

Among us, the kings of England have established themselves as heads of the Church, and the czars have done the same. But with this title, they became less its masters than its ministers. They have acquired not so much the right to change it as the power to maintain it. They are not its legislators; they are merely its princes. Wherever the clergy constitutes a body,[49] it is master and legislator in its own realm.

---

48. It is quite clear that the Phocian War, called the Holy War, was not a war of religion at all. It had for its object to punish sacrileges, and not to make unbelievers submit.

49. It should be carefully noted that it is not so much the formal assemblies, such as those of France, which bind the clergy together into a body, as it is the communion of the churches. Communion and excommunica-

Thus there are two powers, two sovereigns, in England and in Russia, just as there are everywhere else.

Of all the Christian writers, the philosopher Hobbes is the only one who clearly saw the evil and the remedy, who dared to propose the reunification of the two heads of the eagle and the complete restoration of political unity, without which no state or government will ever be well constituted. But he should have seen that the dominating spirit of Christianity was incompatible with his system, and that the interest of the priest would always be stronger than that of the state. It is not so much what is horrible and false in his political theory as what is just and true that has caused it to be hated.[50]

I believe that if the facts of history were developed from this point of view, it would be easy to refute the opposing sentiments of Bayle and Warburton, the one holding that no religion is useful to the body politic, while the other maintains, to the contrary, that Christianity is its firmest support. We could prove to the first that no state has ever been founded without religion serving as its base, and to the second that Christian law is at bottom more injurious than it is useful for the strong constitution of the state. To succeed in making myself understood, I need only give a bit more precision to the excessively vague ideas about religion that are pertinent to my subject.

When considered in relation to society, which is either general or particular, religion can also be divided into two kinds, namely the religion of the man and that of the citizen. The first—without temples, altars or rites, and limited to the purely internal cult of the supreme God and to the eternal duties of morality—is the pure and simple religion of the Gospel, the true theism, and what can be called natural divine law [*droit*]. The other, inscribed in a single country, gives it its gods, its own titulary patrons. It has its dogmas, its rites, its exterior cult prescribed by laws. Outside the nation that practices it, everything is infidel, alien and barbarous to it. It extends the duties and rights of man only as far as its altars. Such were all the religions of the early peoples, to which the name of civil or positive divine law [*droit*] can be given.

There is a third sort of religion which is more bizarre. In giving men two sets of legislation, two leaders, and two homelands, it subjects them to contradictory duties and prevents them from being simultaneously devout men and citizens. Such is the religion of the Lamas and of the Japanese, and such is Roman Christianity. It can be called the religion of the priest. It leads to a kind of mixed and unsociable law [*droit*] which has no name.

Considered from a political standpoint, these three types of religion all have their faults. The third is so bad that it is a waste of time to amuse oneself by proving it. Whatever breaks up social unity is worthless. All institutions that place man in contradiction with himself are of no value.

The second is good in that it unites the divine cult with love of the laws, and that, in making the homeland the object of its citizens' admiration, it teaches them that all service to the state is service to its tutelary god. It is a kind of theocracy in which there ought to be no pontiff other than the prince and no priests other than the magistrates. To die for one's country is then to become a martyr; to violate its laws is to be impious. To subject a guilty man to public execration is to deliver him to the wrath of the gods: *sacer estod*.

On the other hand, it is bad in that, being based on error and lies, it deceives men, makes them credulous and superstitious, and drowns the true cult of the divinity in an empty ceremony. It is also bad when, on becoming exclusive and tyrannical, it makes a people bloodthirsty and intolerant, so that men breathe only murder and massacre, and believe they are performing a holy action in killing anyone who does not accept its gods. This places such a people in a natural state of war with all others, which is quite harmful to its own security.

---

tion are the social compact of the clergy, one with which it will always be the master of the peoples and the kings. All the priests who communicate together are citizens, even if they should be from the opposite ends of the world. This invention is a political masterpiece. There is nothing like this among the pagan priests; thus they never made up a body of clergy.

50. Notice, among other things, in Grotius' letter to his brother, dated April 11, 1643, what this learned man approves of and what he criticizes in his book *De Cive*. It is true that, prone to being indulgent, he appears to forgive the author for his good points for the sake of his bad ones. But not everyone is so merciful.

Thus there remains the religion of man or Christianity (not that of today, but that of the Gospel, which is completely different). Through this holy, sublime, true religion, men, in being the children of the same God, all acknowledge one another as brothers, and the society that unites them is not dissolved even at death.

But since this religion has no particular relation to the body politic, it leaves laws with only the force the laws derive from themselves, without adding any other force to them. And thus one of the great bonds of a particular society remains ineffectual. Moreover, far from attaching the hearts of the citizens to the state, it detaches them from it as from all the other earthly things. I know of nothing more contrary to the social spirit.

We are told that a people of true Christians would form the most perfect society imaginable. I see but one major difficulty in this assumption, namely that a society of true Christians would no longer be a society of men.

I even say that this supposed society would not, for all its perfection, be the strongest or the most durable. By dint of being perfect, it would lack a bond of union; its destructive vice would be in its very perfection.

Each man would fulfill his duty; the people would be subject to the laws; the leaders would be just and moderate, the magistrates would be upright and incorruptible; soldiers would scorn death; there would be neither vanity nor luxury. All of this is very fine, but let us look further.

Christianity is a completely spiritual religion, concerned exclusively with things heavenly. The homeland of the Christian is not of this world. He does his duty, it is true, but he does it with a profound indifference toward the success or failure of his efforts. So long as he has nothing to reproach himself for, it matters little to him whether anything is going well or poorly down here. If the state is flourishing, he hardly dares to enjoy the public felicity, for fear of becoming puffed up with his country's glory. If the state is in decline, he blesses the hand of God that weighs heavily on his people.

For the society to be peaceful and for harmony to be maintained, every citizen without exception would have to be an equally good Christian. But if, unhappily, there is a single ambitious man, a single hypo-crite, a Cataline, for example, or a Cromwell, he would quite undoubtedly gain the upper hand on his pious compatriots. Christian charity does not readily allow one to think ill of his neighbors. Once he has discovered by some ruse the art of deceiving them and of laying hold of a part of the public authority, behold a man established in dignity! God wills that he be respected. Soon, behold a power! God wills that he be obeyed. Does the trustee of his power abuse it? He is the rod with which God punishes his children. It would be against one's conscience to expel the usurper. It would be necessary to disturb the public tranquillity, use violence and shed blood. All this accords ill with the meekness of a Christian. And after all, what difference does it make whether one is a free man or a serf in this vale of tears? The essential thing is getting to heaven, and resignation is but another means to that end.

What if a foreign war breaks out? The citizens march without reservation into combat; none among them dreams of deserting. They do their duty, but without passion for victory; they know how to die better than how to be victorious. What difference does it make whether they are the victors or the vanquished? Does not providence know better than they what they need? Just imagine the advantage a fierce, impetuous and passionate enemy could draw from their stoicism! Set them face to face with those generous peoples who were devoured by an ardent love of glory and homeland. Suppose your Christian republic is face to face with Sparta or Rome. The pious Christians will be beaten, crushed and destroyed before they realize where they are, or else they will owe their safety only to the scorn their enemies will conceive for them. To my way of thinking, the oath taken by Fabius' soldiers was a fine one. They did not swear to die or to win; they swore to return victorious. And they kept their promise. Christians would never have taken such an oath; they would have believed they were tempting God.

But I am deceiving myself in talking about a Christian republic; these terms are mutually exclusive. Christianity preaches only servitude and dependence. Its spirit is too favorable to tyranny for tyranny not to take advantage of it at all times. True Christians are made to be slaves. They know it and are hardly moved by this. This brief life has too little value in their eyes.

Christian troops, we are told, are excellent. I deny this. Is someone going to show me some? For my part, I do not know of any Christian troops. Someone will mention the crusades. Without disputing the valor of the crusaders, I will point out that quite far from being Christians, they were soldiers of the priest; they were citizens of the church; they were fighting for its spiritual country which the church, God knows how, had made temporal. Properly understood, this is a throwback to paganism. Since the Gospel does not establish a national religion, no holy war is possible among Christians.

Under the pagan emperors, Christian soldiers were brave. All the Christian authors affirm this, and I believe it. This was a competition for honor against the pagan troops. Once the emperors were Christians, this competition ceased. And when the cross expelled the eagle, all Roman valor disappeared.

But leaving aside political considerations, let us return to right and determine the principles that govern this important point. The right which the social compact gives the sovereign over the subjects does not, as I have said, go beyond the limits of public utility.[51] The subjects, therefore, do not have to account to the sovereign for their opinions, except to the extent that these opinions are of importance to the community. For it is of great importance to the state that each citizen have a religion that causes him to love his duties. But the dogmas of that religion are of no interest either to the state or its members, except to the extent that these dogmas relate to morality and to the duties which the one who professes them is bound to fulfill toward others. Each man can have in addition such opinions as he pleases, without it

being any of the sovereign's business to know what they are. For since the other world is outside the province of the sovereign, whatever the fate of subjects in the life to come, it is none of its business, so long as they are good citizens in this life.

There is, therefore, a purely civil profession of faith, the articles of which it belongs to the sovereign to establish, not exactly as dogmas of religion, but as sentiments of sociability, without which it is impossible to be a good citizen or a faithful subject.[52] While not having the ability to obligate anyone to believe them, the sovereign can banish from the state anyone who does not believe them. It can banish him not for being impious but for being unsociable, for being incapable of sincerely loving the laws and justice, and of sacrificing his life, if necessary, for his duty. If, after having publicly acknowledged these same dogmas, a person acts as if he does not believe them, he should be put to death; he has committed the greatest of crimes: he has lied before the laws.

The dogmas of the civil religion ought to be simple, few in number, precisely worded, without explanations or commentaries. The existence of a powerful, intelligent, beneficent divinity that foresees and provides; the life to come; the happiness of the just; the punishment of the wicked; the sanctity of the social contract and of the laws. These are the positive dogmas. As for the negative dogmas, I am limiting them to just one, namely intolerance. It is part of the cults we have excluded.

Those who distinguish between civil and theological intolerance are mistaken, in my opinion. Those two types of intolerance are inseparable. It is impossible to live in peace with those one believes to be damned. To love them would be to hate God who punishes them. It is absolutely necessary either to reclaim them or torment them. Whenever theological intolerance is allowed, it is impossible for it not to

51. *In the Republic*, says the Marquis d'Argenson, *each man is perfectly free with respect to what does not harm others.* This is the invariable boundary. It cannot be expressed more precisely. I have been unable to deny myself the pleasure of occasionally citing this manuscript, even though it is unknown to the public, in order to pay homage to the memory of a famous and noteworthy man, who, even as a minister, retained the heart of a citizen, along with just and sound opinions on the government of his country.

52. By pleading for Cataline, Caesar tried to establish the dogma of the mortality of the soul. To refute him, Cato and Cicero did not waste time philosophizing. They contented themselves with showing that Caesar spoke like a bad citizen and advanced a doctrine that was injurious to the state. In fact, this was what the Roman senate had to judge, and not a question of theology.

have some civil effect;[53] and once it does, the sovereign no longer is sovereign, not even over temporal affairs. Thenceforward, priests are the true masters; kings are simply their officers.

Now that there no longer is and never again can be an exclusive national religion, tolerance should be shown to all those that tolerate others, so long as their dogmas contain nothing contrary to the duties of a citizen. But whoever dares to say *outside the church there is no salvation* ought to be expelled from the state, unless the state is the church and the prince is the pontiff. Such a dogma is good only in a theocratic government; in all other forms of government it is ruinous. The reason why Henry IV is said to have embraced the Roman religion should make every decent man, and above all any prince who knows how to reason, leave it.

Chapter 9

Conclusion

After laying down the true principles of political right and attempting to establish the state on this basis, it remains to support the state by means of its external relations, which would include the laws of nations, commerce, the right of war and conquest, public law, leagues, negotiations, treaties, and so on. But all that forms a new subject which is too vast for my nearsightedness. I should always set my sights on things that are nearer at hand to me.

END

---

53. Marriage, for example, being a civil contract, has civil effects without which it is impossible for a society even to subsist. Suppose then that a clergy reaches the point where it ascribes to itself alone the right to permit this act (a right that must necessarily be usurped in every intolerant religion). In that case, is it not clear that in establishing the authority of the church in this matter, it will render ineffectual that of the prince, who will have no more subjects than those whom the clergy wishes to give him? Is it not also clear that the clergy—if master of whether to marry or not to marry people according to whether or not they accept this or that doctrine, according to whether they accept or reject this or that formula, according to whether they are more or less devout—in behaving prudently and holding firm, will alone dispose of inheritance, offices, the citizens, the state itself, which could not subsist, if composed solely of bastards? But, it will be said, abuses will be appealed; summonses and decrees will be issued; temporal holdings will be seized. What a pity! If it has a little—I will not say courage—but good sense, the clergy will serenely allow the appeals, the summonses, the decrees and the seizures, and it will end up master. It is not, it seems to me, a big sacrifice to abandon a part when one is sure of securing the whole.

IMMANUEL KANT

By 1784, the movement known as the Enlightenment was virtually dead in Germany. The Leibniz-Wolffian rationalism of earlier decades would not survive the century. Moses Mendelssohn, its clearest expositor, would die in 1785, embroiled in debate about the Spinozism of his friend Gotthold Ephraim Lessing. Yet, in 1784, Mendelssohn published in the *Berlinische Monatsschrift* an essay in which he answered the question: "What is Enlightenment?" In the next issue, another answer to the same question was published by Mendelssohn's younger contemporary and associate Immanuel Kant (1724–1804), and yet while Kant's answer clearly underlines the themes of the period, it is written by a philosopher whose work and whose thinking had already superseded it. To be sure, Kant would never abandon the themes of rationality and freedom; they are the core of his thinking. But in 1781 he had already published a work that dramatically altered the terms of discussion. Kant and the German Romantics—Johann Gottfried Herder, Johann Georg Hamann, Novalis, and others—set the Enlightenment and dogmatic rationalism to rest in the 1780s and 1790s, and yet in 1784 Kant's differences with the past were perhaps hard to discern.

Kant lived all of his life in or near Königsberg, in East Prussia, where he was born on April 22, 1724. His father was a harnessmaker; the family were devoted Pietists, committed to moral conduct and inner purity as the primary modes of religious worship. In his youth Kant learned to dislike the trappings of religious ritual and formality. In 1750 he enrolled at the University of Königsberg, where he studied with Martin Knutzen, a Leibniz-Wolffian who introduced him to mathematics, physics, and astronomy, as well as logic and metaphysics. After leaving the university, Kant served as a private tutor and returned to town in 1754, when he published the *Universal Natural History and Theory of the Heavens*. It was an attempt, now considered original, to apply Newtonian physics and its principles to the problem of the generation of the solar system.

By 1755 Kant was qualified as a *Privatdozent* (lecturer) at the university, where he lectured on mathematics, philosophy, scientific subjects, and much more. Until this time Newton and the new science, along with the current rationalist philosophy, were the major influences on Kant. In 1762, however, another powerful influence was added to them. When Kant received his copy of Rousseau's *Émile*, for two days he interrupted his rigorous routine of afternoon walks in order to finish reading the book. It was Rousseau who taught him "to honor man" and to make the cultural and political defense of human dignity his primary task. In the same year Kant submitted an essay to the Berlin Academy on the subject whether the principles of natural theology and morality can be proven like those of geometry. Although Mendelssohn's essay won the prize, both were published together in 1764.

In 1770 the University of Königsberg appointed Kant Professor of Logic and Metaphysics, and Kant delivered his Inaugural Dissertation, in which he first adumbrated the "critical" philosophy that would shape the remainder of his career. The following decade Kant published nothing. He was deep at work on his classic, the *Critique of Pure Reason*, which would appear in 1781. This was followed by a flood of publications: the *Prolegomena to Any Future Metaphysics*, the revisions of the First Critique in 1787, the *Critique of Practical Reason* in 1787, the *Critique of Judgment* in 1790, and the *Grounding for the Metaphysics of Morals* in 1785. In this last, extraordinary work, Kant presented his defense of rational morality, of autonomy, and of human dignity in a book that is one of the classic texts of Western moral philosophy.

During these years Kant's life was filled with teaching, writing, conversation, and occasional public controversy. In his public writings and discussions, he defended the rule of law, argued against the right of rebellion, and yet praised the French Revolution. In 1793 Kant published *Religion within the Limits of Reason Alone* and with this strange and difficult work drew the severe censure of Frederick William II and his royal cabinet. Kant was forbidden to write or lecture on any religious subject. He weighed the dilemma, to heed his sovereign or to acknowledge his deepest convictions, and on October 12, 1794, Kant chose to submit as an obedient subject. It was an act that generated widespread criticism.

In 1795 Kant published *Perpetual Peace*, his first work after the ban and his defense of an international league of nations. The book was especially praised in France; in it Kant gives fullest expression to his political views. In 1797 he chose no longer to lecture but continued to write until his death, on February 12, 1804. Heine once said that no one could write a life of Kant because Kant had no life. This is a harsh judgment. Having read Plato since 1768, Kant had assimilated the Socratic commitment to truth. His life was a quest for it, and hence to write the tale of that life would be to write the story of his thought, a story of reason, freedom, and human dignity.

Kant's critical philosophy is a watershed in modern metaphysics, epistemology, and moral theory. His goal was to acknowledge the supremacy of science, to revise the role of metaphysics, and yet to ground morality in rationality. All subsequent Western philosophy and moral theory is indebted to his work and to the strategies which he employed for confronting the challenges of science, philosophy, ethics, and religion in the modern world.

Recommended Readings

Allison, Henry. *Idealism and Freedom*. Cambridge: Cambridge University Press, 1996.

Allison, Henry. *Kant's Theory of Freedom*. Cambridge: Cambridge University Press, 1990.

Arendt, Hannah. *Lectures on Kant's Political Philosophy*. Chicago: University of Chicago Press, 1982.

Beck, Lewis White. A *Commentary on Kant's Critique of Practical Reason*. Chicago: University of Chicago Press, 1960.

Beiser, Frederick. *Enlightenment, Revolution, & Romanticism: The Genesis of Modern German Political Thought, 1790–1800*. Cambridge, Mass.: Harvard University Press, 1992.

Booth, James. *Interpreting the World: Kant's Philosophy of History and Politics*. Toronto: University of Toronto Press, 1987.

Guyer, Paul. *The Cambridge Companion to Kant*. Cambridge: Cambridge University Press, 1992.

Guyer, Paul. *Kant and the Experience of Freedom*. Cambridge: Cambridge University Press, 1993.

Herman, Barbara. *The Practice of Moral Judgment*. Cambridge, Mass.: Harvard University Press, 1993.

O'Neill, Onora. *Acting on Principle*. New York: Columbia University Press, 1975.

O'Neill, Onora. *Constructions of Reason: Explorations of Kant's Practical Philosophy*. Cambridge: Cambridge University Press, 1989.

Paton, H. J. *The Categorical Imperative*, third ed. London: Hutcheson, 1958.

Reiss, Hans (ed.). *Kant's Political Writings*. Cambridge: Cambridge University Press, 1970.

Schneewind, J. B. *The Invention of Autonomy*. Cambridge: Cambridge University Press, 1998.

Wolf, Robert Paul. *The Autonomy of Reason*. New York: Harper & Row, 1973.

Wolf, Robert Paul. *In Defense of Anarchism*. New York: Harper & Row, 1970.

Wolf, Robert Paul (ed.). *Kant*. Garden City: Doubleday, 1967.

Wolf, Robert Paul (ed.). *Kant's Foundation and Critical Essays*. Indianapolis: Bobbs-Merrill, 1969.

Wood, Allen. *Kant's Ethical Thought*. Cambridge: Cambridge University Press, 1999.

Wood, Allen. *Kant's Moral Religion*. Ithaca: Cornell University Press, 1970.

Yovel, Y. *Kant and the Philosophy of History*. Princeton: Princeton University Press, 1968.

GROUNDING
FOR THE
METAPHYSICS OF MORALS

387

PREFACE

Ancient Greek philosophy was divided into three sciences: physics, ethics, and logic. This division is perfectly suitable to the nature of the subject, and the only improvement that can be made in it is perhaps only to supply its principle so that there will be a possibility on the one hand of insuring its completeness and on the other of correctly determining its necessary subdivisions.

All rational knowledge is either material and concerned with some object, or formal and concerned only with the form of understanding and of reason themselves and with the universal rules of thought in general without regard to differences of its objects. Formal philosophy is called logic. Material philosophy, however, has to do with determinate objects and with the laws to which these objects are subject; and such philosophy is divided into two parts, because these laws are either laws of nature or laws of freedom. The science of the former is called physics, while that of the latter is called ethics; they are also called doctrine of nature and doctrine of morals respectively.

Logic cannot have any empirical part, i.e., a part in which the universal and necessary laws of thought would be based on grounds taken from experience; for in that case it would not be logic, i.e., a canon for understanding and reason, which is valid for all thinking and which has to be demonstrated.[1] Natural and moral philosophy, on the contrary, can each have an empirical part. The former has to because it must determine the laws of nature as an object of experience, and the latter because it must determine the will of man insofar as the will is affected by nature. The laws of the former are those according to which everything does happen, while the laws of the latter are those according to which everything ought to happen, although these moral laws also consider the conditions under which what ought to happen frequently does not.

388

All philosophy insofar as it is founded on experience may be called empirical, while that which sets forth its doctrines as founded entirely on a priori principles may be called pure. The latter, when merely formal, is called logic; but when limited to determinate objects of the understanding, it is called metaphysics.

In this way there arises the idea of a twofold metaphysics: a metaphysics of nature and a metaphysics of morals.[2] Physics will thus have its empirical part, but also a rational one. Ethics will too, though here the empirical part might more specifically be called practical anthropology,[3] while the rational part might properly be called morals.

All industries, crafts, and arts have gained by the division of labor, viz., one man does not do everything, but each confines himself to a certain kind of work that is distinguished from all other kinds by the treatment it requires, so that the work may be done with

Reprinted by permission of the translator, James W. Ellington, from Kant, *Grounding for the Metaphysics of Morals* (Indianapolis: Hackett Publishing Company, 1981).

1. [Kant's *Logic* was first published in 1800 in a version edited by Gottlob Benjamin Jäsche, who was one of Kant's students. — J.W.E.]

2. [*The Metaphysical Foundations of Natural Science* was published in 1786. *The Metaphysics of Morals* appeared in 1797.]

3. [*Anthropology from a Pragmatic Point of View* first appeared in 1798.]

the highest perfection and with greater ease. Where work is not so distinguished and divided, where everyone is a jack of all trades, there industry remains sunk in the greatest barbarism. Whether or not pure philosophy in all its parts requires its own special man might well be in itself a subject worthy of consideration. Would not the whole of this learned industry be better off if those who are accustomed, as the public taste demands, to purvey a mixture of the empirical with the rational in all sorts of proportions unknown even to themselves and who style themselves independent thinkers, while giving the name of hair-splitters to those who apply themselves to the purely rational part, were to be given warning about pursuing simultaneously two jobs which are quite different in their technique, and each of which perhaps requires a special talent that when combined with the other talent produces nothing but bungling? But I only ask here whether the nature of science does not require that the empirical part always be carefully separated from the rational part. Should not physics proper (i.e., empirical physics) be preceded by a metaphysics of nature, and practical anthropol-

389 ogy by a metaphysics of morals? Both of these metaphysics must be carefully purified of everything empirical in order to know how much pure reason can accomplish in each case and from what sources it draws its a priori teaching, whether such teaching be conducted by all moralists (whose name is legion) or only by some who feel a calling thereto.

Since I am here primarily concerned with moral philosophy, the foregoing question will be limited to a consideration of whether or not there is the utmost necessity for working out for once a pure moral philosophy that is wholly cleared of everything which can only be empirical and can only belong to anthropology. That there must be such a philosophy is evident from the common idea of duty and of moral laws. Everyone must admit that if a law is to be morally valid, i.e., is to be valid as a ground of obligation, then it must carry with it absolute necessity. He must admit that the command, "Thou shalt not lie," does not hold only for men, as if other rational beings had no need to abide by it, and so with all the other moral laws properly so called; and he must concede that the ground of obligation here must therefore be sought not in the nature of man nor in the circum-

stances of the world in which man is placed, but must be sought a priori solely in the concepts of pure reason; he must grant that every other precept which is founded on principles of mere experience—even a precept that may in certain respects be universal—insofar as it rests in the least on empirical grounds—perhaps only in its motive—can indeed be called a practical rule, but never a moral law.

Thus not only are moral laws together with their principles essentially different from every kind of practical cognition in which there is anything empirical, but all moral philosophy rests entirely on its pure part. When applied to man, it does not in the least borrow from acquaintance with him (anthropology) but gives a priori laws to him as a rational being. To be sure, these laws require, furthermore, a power of judgment sharpened by experience, partly in order to distinguish in what cases they are applicable, and partly to gain for them access to the human will as well as influence for putting them into practice. For man is affected by so many inclinations that, even though he is indeed capable of the idea of a pure practical reason, he is not so easily able to make that idea effective *in concreto* in the conduct of his life.

A metaphysics of morals is thus indispensably necessary, not merely because of motives of speculation 390 regarding the source of practical principles which are present a priori in our reason, but because morals themselves are liable to all kinds of corruption as long as the guide and supreme norm for correctly estimating them are missing. For in the case of what is to be morally good, that it conforms to the moral law is not enough; it must also be done for the sake of the moral law. Otherwise that conformity is only very contingent and uncertain, since the non-moral ground may now and then produce actions that conform with the law but quite often produces actions that are contrary to the law. Now the moral law in its purity and genuineness (which is of the utmost concern in the practical realm) can be sought nowhere but in a pure philosophy. Therefore, pure philosophy (metaphysics) must precede; without it there can be no moral philosophy at all. That philosophy which mixes pure principles with empirical ones does not deserve the name of philosophy (for philosophy is distinguished from ordinary rational knowledge by its treatments in a separate science of what the latter comprehends only confusedly). Still less does it deserve the name of moral philosophy, since by this very confusion it spoils even the purity of morals and counteracts its own ends.

There must be no thought that what is required here is already contained in the propaedeutic that precedes the celebrated Wolff's moral philosophy, i.e., in what he calls *Universal Practical Philosophy,*[4] and that hence there is no need to break entirely new ground. Just because his work was to be a universal practical philosophy, it has not taken into consideration any special kind of will, such as one determined solely by a priori principles without any empirical motives and which could be called a pure will, but has considered volition in general, together with all the actions and conditions belonging to it under this general signification. And thereby does his propaedeutic differ from a metaphysics of morals in the same way that general logic, which expounds the acts and rules of thinking in general, differs from transcendental philosophy, which treats merely of the particular acts and rules of pure thinking, i.e., of that thinking whereby objects are cognized completely a priori. For the metaphysics of morals has to investigate the idea and principles of a possible pure will and not the actions and conditions volition as such, which are for the most part drawn from psychology. Moral laws and duty are discussed in this universal practical philosophy (though quite improperly), but this is no objection to what has been said about such philosophy. For the authors of this science remain true to their idea of it on the following point also: they do not distinguish the motives which, as such, are presented completely a priori by reason alone and are properly moral, from the empirical motives which the understanding raises to general concepts merely by the comparison of experiences. Rather, they consider motives irrespective of any difference in their source; and inasmuch as they regard all motives as being homogeneous, they consider nothing but their relative strength or weakness. In this way they frame their concept of obligation, which is certainly not moral,

391

but is all that can be expected from a philosophy which never decides regarding the origin of all possible practical concepts whether they are a priori or merely a posteriori.

I intend some day to publish a metaphysics of morals,[5] but as a preliminary to that I now issue this *Grounding* [1785]. Indeed there is properly no other foundation for such a metaphysics than a critical examination of pure practical reason, just as there is properly no other foundation for a metaphysics [of nature] than the critical examination of pure speculative reason, which has already been published.[6] But, in the first place, the former critique is not so absolutely necessary as the latter one, because human reason can, even in the most ordinary mind, be easily brought in moral matters to a high degree of correctness and precision, while on the other hand in its theoretical but pure use it is wholly dialectical. In the second place, if a critical examination of pure practical reason is to be complete, then there must, in my view, be the possibility at the same time of showing the unity of practical and speculative reason in a common principle; for in the final analysis there can be only one and the same reason, which is to be differentiated solely in its application. But there is no possibility here of bringing my work to such completeness, without introducing considerations of an entirely different kind and without thereby confusing the reader. Instead of calling the present work a *Critique of Pure Practical Reason*, I have, therefore, adopted the title *Grounding for the Metaphysics of Morals [Grundlegung zur Metaphysik der Sitten.]*[7]

But, in the third place, since a metaphysics of morals, despite the forbidding title, is nevertheless capable of a high degree of popularity and adaptation to the ordinary understanding, I find it useful to separate from the aforementioned metaphysics this

4. [This work of Christian Wolff was published in 1738–39; this and other of his works served for many years as the standard philosophy textbooks in German universities. Wolff's philosophy was founded on that of Leibniz.]

5. [This appeared in 1797.]

6. [The first edition of the *Critique of Pure Reason* appeared in 1781, while the second edition appeared in 1787. The *Critique of Practical Reason* was published in 1788.]

7. [This might be translated as *Laying the Foundation for the Metaphysics of Morals*. But for the sake of brevity *Grounding for the Metaphysics of Morals* has been chosen.]

392 preliminary work on its foundation [*Grundlage*] in order later to have no need to introduce unavoidable subtleties into doctrines that are easier to grasp.

The present *Grounding* [*Grundlegung*] is, however, intended for nothing more than seeking out and establishing the supreme principle of morality. This constitutes by itself a task which is complete in its purpose and should be kept separate from every other moral inquiry. The application of this supreme principle to the whole ethical system would, to be sure, shed much light on my conclusions regarding this central question, which is important but has not heretofore been at all satisfactorily discussed; and the adequacy manifested by the principle throughout such application would provide strong confirmation for the principle. Nevertheless, I must forego this advantage, which after all would be more gratifying for myself than helpful for others, since ease of use and apparent adequacy of a principle do not provide any certain proof of its soundness, but do awaken, rather, a certain bias which prevents any rigorous examination and estimation of it for itself, without any regard to its consequences.

The method adopted in this work is, I believe, one that is most suitable if we proceed analytically from ordinary knowledge to a determination of the supreme principle and then back again synthetically from an examination of this principle and its sources to ordinary knowledge where its application is found. Therefore, the division turns out to be the following:

1. *First Section.* Transition from the Ordinary Rational Knowledge of Morality to the Philosophical.

2. *Second Section.* Transition from Popular Moral Philosophy to a Metaphysics of Morals.

3. *Third Section.* Final Step from a Metaphysics of Morals to a Critique of Pure Practical Reason.

393

FIRST SECTION

Transition from the Ordinary Rational Knowledge of Morality to the Philosophical

There is no possibility of thinking of anything at all in the world, or even out of it, which can be regarded as good without qualification, except a *good will.*

Intelligence, wit, judgment, and whatever talents of the mind one might want to name are doubtless in many respects good and desirable, as are such qualities of temperament as courage, resolution, perseverance. But they can also become extremely bad and harmful if the will, which is to make use of these gifts of nature and which in its special constitution is called character, is not good. The same holds with gifts of fortune; power, riches, honor, even health, and that complete well-being and contentment with one's condition which is called happiness make for pride and often hereby even arrogance, unless there is a good will to correct their influence on the mind and herewith also to rectify the whole principle of action and make it universally conformable to its end. The sight of a being who is not graced by any touch of a pure and good will but who yet enjoys an uninterrupted prosperity can never delight a rational and impartial spectator. Thus a good will seems to constitute the indispensable condition of being even worthy of happiness.

Some qualities are even conducive to this good will itself and can facilitate its work. Nevertheless, 394 they have no intrinsic unconditional worth; but they always presuppose, rather, a good will, which restricts the high esteem in which they are otherwise rightly held, and does not permit them to be regarded as absolutely good. Moderation in emotions and passions, self-control, and calm deliberation are not only good in many respects but even seem to constitute part of the intrinsic worth of a person. But they are far from being rightly called good without qualification (however unconditionally they were commended by the ancients). For without the principles of a good will, they can become extremely bad; the coolness of a villain makes him not only much more dangerous but also immediately more abominable in our eyes than he would have been regarded by us without it.

A good will is good not because of what it effects or accomplishes, nor because of its fitness to attain some proposed end; it is good only through its willing, i.e., it is good in itself. When it is considered in itself, then it is to be esteemed very much higher than anything which it might ever bring about merely in order to favor some inclination, or even the sum total of all inclinations. Even if, by some especially unfortunate fate or by the niggardly provision of step-motherly nature, this will should be wholly lacking in the power to accomplish its purpose, if with the greatest effort it should yet achieve nothing, and only the good will should remain (not, to be sure, as a mere wish but as the summoning of all the means in our power), yet would it, like a jewel, still shine by its own light as something which has its full value in itself. Its usefulness or fruitlessness can neither augment nor diminish this value. Its usefulness would be, as it were, only the setting to enable us to handle it in ordinary dealings or to attract to it the attention of those who are not yet experts, but not to recommend it to real experts or to determine its value.

But there is something so strange in this idea of the absolute value of a mere will, in which no account is taken of any useful results, that in spite of all the agreement received even from ordinary reason, yet there must arise the suspicion that such an idea may perhaps have as its hidden basis merely some high-flown fancy, and that we may have misunderstood the purpose of nature in assigning to reason the governing of our will. Therefore, this idea will be examined from this point of view.

In the natural constitution of an organized being, i.e., one suitably adapted to the purpose of life, let us take as a principle that in such a being no organ is to be found for any end unless it be the most fit and the best adapted for that end. Now if that being's preservation, welfare, or in a word its happiness, were the real end of nature in the case of a being having reason and will, then nature would have hit upon a very poor arrangement in having the reason of the creature carry out this purpose. For all the actions which such a creature has to perform with this purpose in view, and the whole rule of his conduct would have been prescribed much more exactly by instinct; and the purpose in question could have been attained much more certainly by instinct than it ever can be by reason. And if in addition reason had been imparted to this favored creature, then it would have had to serve him only to contemplate the happy constitution of his nature, to admire that nature, to rejoice in it, and to feel grateful to the cause that bestowed it; but reason would not have served him to subject his faculty of desire to its weak and delusive guidance nor would it have served him to meddle incompetently with the purpose of nature. In a word, nature would have taken

care that reason did not strike out into a practical use nor presume, with its weak insight, to think out for itself a plan for happiness and the means for attaining it. Nature would have taken upon herself not only the choice of ends but also that of the means, and would with wise foresight have entrusted both to instinct alone.

And, in fact, we find that the more a cultivated reason devotes itself to the aim of enjoying life and happiness, the further does man get away from true contentment. Because of this there arises in many persons, if only they are candid enough to admit it, a certain degree of misology, i.e., hatred of reason. This is especially so in the case of those who are the most experienced in the use of reason, because after calculating all the advantages they derive, I say not from the invention of all the arts of common luxury, but even from the sciences (which in the end seem to them to be also a luxury of the understanding), they yet find that they have in fact only brought more trouble on their heads than they have gained in happiness. Therefore, they come to envy, rather than despise, the more common run of men who are closer to the guidance of mere natural instinct and who do not allow their reason much influence on their conduct. And we must admit that the judgment of those who would temper, or even reduce below zero, the boastful eulogies on behalf of the advantages which reason is supposed to provide as regards the happiness and contentment of life is by no means morose or ungrateful to the goodness with which the world is governed. There lies at the root of such judgments, rather, the idea that existence has another and much more worthy purpose, for which, and not for happiness, reason is quite properly intended, and which must, therefore, be regarded as the supreme condition to which the private purpose of men must, for the most part, defer.

Reason, however, is not competent enough to guide the will safely as regards its objects and the satisfaction of all our needs (which it in part even multiplies); to this end would an implanted natural instinct have led much more certainly. But inasmuch as reason has been imparted to us as a practical faculty, i.e., as one which is to have influence on the will, its true function must be to produce a will which is not merely good as a means to some further end, but is good in itself. To produce a will good in itself reason was absolutely necessary, inasmuch as nature in distributing her capacities has everywhere gone to work in a purposive manner. While such a will may not indeed be the sole and complete good, it must, nevertheless, be the highest good and the condition of all the rest, even of the desire for happiness. In this case there is nothing inconsistent with the wisdom of nature that the cultivation of reason, which is requisite for the first and unconditioned purpose, may in many ways restrict, at least in this life, the attainment of the second purpose, viz., happiness, which is always conditioned. Indeed happiness can even be reduced to less than nothing, without nature's failing thereby in her purpose; for reason recognizes as its highest practical function the establishment of a good will, whereby in the attainment of this end reason is capable only of its own kind of satisfaction, viz., that of fulfilling a purpose which is in turn determined only by reason, even though such fulfillment should often interfere with the purpose of inclination.

397 The concept of a will estimable in itself and good without regard to any further end must now be developed. This concept already dwells in the natural sound understanding and needs not so much to be taught as merely to be elucidated. It always holds first place in estimating the total worth of our actions and constitutes the condition of all the rest. Therefore, we shall take up the concept of *duty*, which includes that of a good will, though with certain subjective restrictions and hindrances, which far from hiding a good will or rendering it unrecognizable, rather bring it out by contrast and make it shine forth more brightly.

I here omit all actions already recognized as contrary to duty, even though they may be useful for this or that end; for in the case of these the question does not arise at all as to whether they might be done from duty, since they even conflict with duty. I also set aside those actions which are really in accordance with duty, yet to which men have no immediate inclination, but perform them because they are impelled thereto by some other inclination. For in this [second] case to decide whether the action which is in accord with duty has been done from duty or from some selfish purpose is easy. This difference is far more difficult to note in the [third] case where the action accords with duty and the subject has in addition

an immediate inclination to do the action. For example,[8] that a dealer should not overcharge an inexperienced purchaser certainly accords with duty; and where there is much commerce, the prudent merchant does not overcharge but keeps to a fixed price for everyone in general, so that a child may buy from him just as well as everyone else may. Thus customers are honestly served, but this is not nearly enough for making us believe that the merchant has acted this way from duty and from principles of honesty; his own advantage required him to do it. He cannot, however, be assumed to have in addition [as in the third case] an immediate inclination toward his buyers, causing him, as it were, out of love to give no one as far as price is concerned any advantage over another. Hence the action was done neither from duty nor from immediate inclination, but merely for a selfish purpose.

On the other hand,[9] to preserve one's life is a duty; and, furthermore, everyone has also an immediate inclination to do so. But on this account the often anxious care taken by most men for it has no intrinsic worth, and the maxim of their action has no moral content. They preserve their lives, to be sure, in accordance with duty, but not from duty. On the other hand,[10] if adversity and hopeless sorrow have completely taken away the taste for life, if an unfortunate man, strong in soul and more indignant at his fate than despondent or dejected, wishes for death and yet preserves his life without loving it — not from inclination or fear, but from duty — then his maxim indeed has a moral content.[11]

398

8. [The ensuing example provides an illustration of the second case.]

9. [This next example illustrates the third case.]

10. [The ensuing example illustrates the fourth case.]

11. [Four different cases have been distinguished in the two foregoing paragraphs. Case 1 involves those actions which are contrary to duty (lying, cheating, stealing, etc.). Case 2 involves those which accord with duty but for which a person perhaps has no immediate inclination, though he does have a mediate inclination thereto (one pays his taxes not because he likes to but in order to avoid the penalties set for delinquents, one treats his fellows well not because he really likes them but because he wants their votes when at some future time he runs for

To be beneficent where one can is a duty; and besides this, there are many persons who are so sympathetically constituted that, without any further motive of vanity or self-interest, they find an inner pleasure in spreading joy around them and can rejoice in the satisfaction of others as their own work. But I maintain that in such a case an action of this kind, however dutiful and amiable it may be, has nevertheless no true moral worth.[12] It is on a level with such actions as arise from other inclinations, e.g., the inclination for honor, which if fortunately directed to what is in fact beneficial and accords with duty and is thus honorable, deserves praise and encouragement, but not esteem; for its maxim lacks the moral content of an action done not from inclination but from duty. Suppose then the mind of this friend of mankind to be clouded over with his own sorrow so that all sympathy with the lot of others is extinguished, and suppose him still to have the power to benefit others in distress, even though he is not touched by their trouble because he is sufficiently absorbed with his own; and now suppose that, even though no inclination moves him any longer, he nevertheless tears himself from this deadly insensibility and performs the action without any inclination at all, but solely from duty—then for the first time his action has genuine moral worth.[13] Further still, if nature has put little sympathy in this or that man's heart, if (while being an honest man in other respects) he is by temperament cold and indifferent to the sufferings of others, perhaps because as regards his own sufferings he is endowed with the special gift of patience and fortitude and expects or even requires that others should have the same; if such a man (who would truly not be nature's worst product) had not been exactly fashioned by her to be a philanthropist, would he not yet find in himself a source from which he might give himself a worth far higher than any that a good-natured temperament might have? By all means, because just here does the worth of the character come out; this worth is moral and incomparably the highest of all, viz., that he is beneficent, not from inclination, but from duty.[14]

To secure one's own happiness is a duty (at least indirectly); for discontent with one's condition under many pressing cares and amid unsatisfied wants might easily become a great temptation to transgress one's duties. But here also do men of themselves already have, irrespective of duty, the strongest and deepest inclination toward happiness, because just in this idea are all inclinations combined into a sum total.[15] But the precept of happiness is often so constituted as greatly to interfere with some inclinations, and yet men cannot form any definite and certain concept

399

---

12. [This is an example of case 3.]

public office, etc.). A vast number of so-called "morally good" actions actually belong to this case 2—they accord with duty because of self-seeking inclinations. Case 3 involves those which accord with duty and for which a person does have an immediate inclination (one does not commit suicide because all is going well with him, one does not commit adultery because he considers his wife to be the most desirable creature in the whole world, etc.). Case 4 involves those actions which accord with duty but are contrary to some immediate inclination (one does not commit suicide even when he is in dire distress, one does not commit adultery even though his wife has turned out to be an impossible shrew, etc.). Now case 4 is the crucial test case of the will's possible goodness—but Kant does not claim that one should lead his life in such a way as to encounter as many such cases as possible in order constantly to test his virtue (deliberately marry a shrew so as to be able to resist the temptation to commit adultery). Life itself forces enough such cases upon a person without his seeking them out. But when there is a conflict between duty and inclination, duty should always be followed. Case 3 makes for the easiest living and the greatest contentment, and anyone would wish that life might present him with far more of these cases than with cases 2 or 4. But yet one should not arrange his life in such a way as to avoid case 4 at all costs and to seek out case 3 as much as possible (become a recluse so as to avoid the possible rough and tumble involved with frequent association with one's fellows, avoid places where one might encounter the sick and the poor so as to spare oneself the pangs of sympathy and the need to exercise the virtue of benefiting those in distress, etc.). For the purpose of philosophical analysis Kant emphasizes case 4 as being the test case of the will's possible goodness, but he is not thereby advocating puritanism.]

13. [This is an example of case 4.]
14. [This is an even more extreme example of case 4.]
15. [This is an example of case 3.]

of the sum of satisfaction of all inclinations that is called happiness. Hence there is no wonder that a single inclination which is determinate both as to what it promises and as to the time within which it can be satisfied may outweigh a fluctuating idea; and there is no wonder that a man, e.g., a gouty patient, can choose to enjoy what he likes and to suffer what he may, since by his calculation he has here at least not sacrificed the enjoyment of the present moment to some possibly groundless expectations of the good fortune that is supposed to be found in health. But even in this case, if the universal inclination to happiness did not determine his will and if health, at least for him, did not figure as so necessary an element in his calculations; there still remains here, as in all other cases, a law, viz., that he should promote his happiness not from inclination but from duty, and thereby for the first time does his conduct have real moral worth.[16]

Undoubtedly in this way also are to be understood those passages of Scripture which command us to love our neighbor and even our enemy. For love as an inclination cannot be commanded; but beneficence from duty, when no inclination impels us[17] and even when a natural and unconquerable aversion opposes such beneficence,[18] is practical, and not pathological, love. Such love resides in the will and not in the propensities of feeling, in principles of action and not in tender sympathy; and only this practical love can be commanded.

The second proposition[19] is this: An action done from duty has its moral worth, not in the purpose that is to be attained by it, but in the maxim according to which the action is determined. The moral worth depends, therefore, not on the realization of the object of the action, but merely on the principle of volition according to which, without regard to any objects of

400

the faculty of desire, the action has been done. From what has gone before it is clear that the purposes which we may have in our actions, as well as their effects regarded as ends and incentives of the will, cannot give to actions any unconditioned and moral worth. Where, then, can this worth lie if it is not to be found in the will's relation to the expected effect? Nowhere but in the principle of the will, with no regard to the ends that can be brought about through such action. For the will stands, as it were, at a crossroads between its a priori principle, which is formal, and its a posteriori incentive, which is material; and since it must be determined by something, it must be determined by the formal principle of volition, if the action is done from duty—and in that case every material principle is taken away from it.

The third proposition, which follows from the other two, can be expressed thus: Duty is the necessity of an action done out of respect for the law. I can indeed have an inclination for an object as the effect of my proposed action; but I can never have respect for such an object, just because it is merely an effect and is not an activity of the will. Similarly, I can have no respect for inclination as such, whether my own or that of another. I can at most, if my own inclination, approve it; and, if that of another, even love it, i.e., consider it to be favorable to my own advantage. An object of respect can only be what is connected with my will solely as ground and never as effect—something that does not serve my inclination but, rather, outweighs it, or at least excludes it from consideration when some choice is made—in other words, only the law itself can be an object of respect and hence can be a command. Now an action done from duty must altogether exclude the influence of inclination and therewith every object of the will. Hence there is nothing left which can determine the will except objectively the law and subjectively pure respect for this practical law, i.e., the will can be subjectively determined by the maxim[20] that I should follow such a law even if all my inclinations are thereby thwarted.   401

16. [This example is a weak form of case 4; the action accords with duty but is not contrary to some immediate inclination.]

17. [This is case 4 in its weak form.]

18. [This is case 4 in its strong form.]

19. [The first proposition of morality says that an action must be done from duty in order to have any moral worth. It is implicit in the preceding examples but was never explicitly stated.]

20. A maxim is the subjective principle of volition. The objective principle (i.e., one which would serve all rational beings also subjectively as a practical principle if reason had full control over the faculty of desire) is the practical law. [See below Kant's footnote at Ak. 420–21.]

Thus the moral worth of an action does not lie in the effect expected from it nor in any principle of action that needs to borrow its motive from this expected effect. For all these effects (agreeableness of one's condition and even the furtherance of other people's happiness) could have been brought about also through other causes and would not have required the will of a rational being, in which the highest and unconditioned good can alone be found. Therefore, the pre-eminent good which is called moral can consist in nothing but the representation of the law in itself, and such a representation can admittedly be found only in a rational being insofar as this representation, and not some expected effect, is the determining ground of the will. This good is already present in the person who acts according to this representation, and such good need not be awaited merely from the effect.[21]

402   But what sort of law can that be the thought of

21. There might be brought against me here an objection that I take refuge behind the word "respect" in an obscure feeling, instead of giving a clear answer to the question by means of a concept of reason. But even though respect is a feeling, it is not one received through any outside influence but is, rather, one that is self-produced by means of a rational concept; hence it is specifically different from all feelings of the first kind, which can all be reduced to inclination or fear. What I recognize immediately as a law for me, I recognize with respect; this means merely the consciousness of the subordination of my will to a law without the mediation of other influences upon my sense. The immediate determination of the will by the law, and the consciousness thereof, is called respect, which is hence regarded as the effect of the law upon the subject and not as the cause of the law. Respect is properly the representation of a worth that thwarts my self-love. Hence respect is something that is regarded as an object of neither inclination nor fear, although it has at the same time something analogous to both. The object of respect is, therefore, nothing but the law—indeed that very law which we impose on ourselves and yet recognize as necessary in itself. As law, we are subject to it without consulting self-love; as imposed on us by ourselves, it is a consequence of our will. In the former aspect, it is analogous to fear; in the latter, to inclination. All respect for a person is properly only respect for the law (of honesty, etc.) of which the person provides an example. Since we regard

which must determine the will without reference to any expected effect, so that the will can be called absolutely good without qualification? Since I have deprived the will of every impulse that might arise for it from obeying any particular law, there is nothing left to serve the will as principle except the universal conformity of its actions to law as such, i.e., I should never act except in such a way that I can also will that my maxim should become a universal law.[22] Here mere conformity to law as such (without having as its basis any law determining particular actions) serves the will as principle and must so serve it if duty is not to be a vain delusion and a chimerical concept. The ordinary reason of mankind in its practical judgments agrees completely with this, and always has in view the aforementioned principle.

For example, take this question. When I am in distress, may I make a promise with the intention of not keeping it? I readily distinguish here the two meanings which the question may have; whether making a false promise conforms with prudence or with duty. Doubtless the former can often be the case. Indeed I clearly see that escape from some present difficulty by means of such a promise is not enough. In addition I must carefully consider whether from this lie there may later arise far greater inconvenience for me than from what I now try to escape. Furthermore, the consequences of my false promise are not easy to foresee, even with all my supposed cunning; loss of confidence in me might prove to be far more disadvantageous than the misfortune which I now try to avoid. The more prudent way might be to act according to a universal maxim and to make it a habit not to promise anything without intending to keep it. But that such a maxim is, nevertheless, always based on nothing but a fear of consequences becomes clear to me at once. To be truthful from duty is, however, quite different from being truthful from fear of disadvantageous consequences; in the first case the

---

the development as our talents as a duty, we think of a man of talent as being also a kind of example of the law (the law of becoming like him by practice), and that is what constitutes our respect for him. All so-called moral interest consists solely in respect for the law.

22. [This is the first time in the *Grounding* that the categorical imperative is stated.]

concept of the action itself contains a law for me, while in the second I must first look around elsewhere to see what are the results for me that might be connected with the action. For to deviate from the principle of duty is quite certainly bad; but to abandon my maxim of prudence can often be very advantageous for me, though to abide by it is certainly safer. The most direct and infallible way, however, to answer the question as to whether a lying promise accords with duty is to ask myself whether I would really be content if my maxim (of extricating myself from difficulty by means of a false promise) were to hold as a universal law for myself as well as for others, and could I really say to myself that everyone may promise falsely when he finds himself in a difficulty from which he can find no other way to extricate himself. Then I immediately become aware that I can indeed will the lie but can not at all will a universal law to lie. For by such a law there would really be no promises at all, since in vain would my willing future actions be professed to other people who would not believe what I professed, or if they over-hastily did believe, then they would pay me back in like coin. Therefore, my maxim would necessarily destroy itself just as soon as it was made a universal law.[23]

Therefore, I need no far-reaching acuteness to discern what I have to do in order that my will may be morally good. Inexperienced in the course of the world and incapable of being prepared for all its contingencies, I only ask myself whether I can also will that my maxim should become a universal law. If not, then the maxim must be rejected, not because of any disadvantage accruing to me or even to others, but because it cannot be fitting as a principle in a possible legislation of universal law, and reason exacts from me immediate respect for such legislation. Indeed I have as yet no insight into the grounds of such respect (which the philosopher may investigate). But I at least understand that respect is an estimation

of a worth that far outweighs any worth of what is recommended by inclination, and that the necessity of acting from pure respect for the practical law is what constitutes duty, to which every other motive must give way because duty is the condition of a will good in itself, whose worth is above all else.

Thus within the moral cognition of ordinary human reason we have arrived at its principle. To be sure, such reason does not think of this principle abstractly in its universal form, but does always have it actually in view and does use it as the standard of judgment. It would here be easy to show how ordinary reason, with this compass in hand, is well able to distinguish, in every case that occurs, what is good or evil, in accord with duty or contrary to duty, if we do not in the least try to teach reason anything new but only make it attend, as Socrates did, to its own principle—and thereby do we show that neither science nor philosophy is needed in order to know what one must do to be honest and good, and even wise and virtuous. Indeed we might even have conjectured beforehand that cognizance of what every man is obligated to do, and hence also to know, would be available to every man, even the most ordinary. Yet we cannot but observe with admiration how great an advantage the power of practical judgment has over the theoretical in ordinary human understanding. In the theoretical, when ordinary reason ventures to depart from the laws of experience and the perceptions of sense, it falls into sheer inconceivabilities and self-contradictions, or at least into a chaos of uncertainty, obscurity, and instability. In the practical, however, the power of judgment first begins to show itself to advantage when ordinary understanding excludes all sensuous incentives from practical laws. Such understanding then becomes even subtle, whether in quibbling with its own conscience or with other claims regarding what is to be called right, or whether in wanting to determine correctly for its own instruction the worth of various actions. And the most extraordinary thing is that ordinary understanding in this practical case may have just as good a hope of hitting the mark as that which any philosopher may promise himself. Indeed it is almost more certain in this than even a philosopher is, because he can have no principle other than what ordinary understanding has, but he may easily confuse his judgment by a multitude

23. [This means that when you tell a lie, you merely take exception to the general rule that says everyone should always tell the truth and believe that what you are saying is true. When you lie, you do not thereby will that everyone else lie and not believe that what you are saying is true, because in such a case your lie would never work to get you what you want.]

of foreign and irrelevant considerations and thereby cause it to swerve from the right way. Would it not, therefore, be wiser in moral matters to abide by the ordinary rational judgment or at most to bring in philosophy merely for the purpose of rendering the system of morals more complete and intelligible and of presenting its rules in a way that is more convenient for use (especially in disputation), but not for the purpose of leading ordinary human understanding away from its happy simplicity in practical matters and of bringing it by means of philosophy into a new path of inquiry and instruction?

405   Innocence is indeed a glorious thing; but, unfortunately, it does not keep very well and is easily led astray. Consequently, even wisdom—which consists more in doing and not doing than in knowing—needs science, not in order to learn from it, but in order that wisdom's precepts may gain acceptance and permanence. Man feels within himself a powerful counterweight to all the commands of duty, which are presented to him by reason as being so pre-eminently worthy of respect; this counterweight consists of his needs and inclinations, whose total satisfaction is summed up under the name of happiness. Now reason irremissibly commands its precepts, without thereby promising the inclinations anything; hence it disregards and neglects these impetuous and at the same time so seemingly plausible claims (which do not allow themselves to be suppressed by any command). Hereby arises a natural dialectic, i.e., a propensity to quibble with these strict laws of duty, to cast doubt upon their validity, or at least upon their purity and strictness, and to make them, where possible, more compatible with our wishes and inclinations. Thereby are such laws corrupted in their very foundations and their whole dignity is destroyed—something which even ordinary practical reason cannot in the end call good.

Thus is ordinary human reason forced to go outside its sphere and take a step into the field of practical philosophy, not by any need for speculation (which never befalls such reason so long as it is content to be mere sound reason) but on practical grounds themselves. There it tries to obtain information and clear instruction regarding the source of its own principle and the correct determination of this principle in its opposition to maxims based on need and inclina-

tion, so that reason may escape from the perplexity of opposite claims and may avoid the risk of losing all genuine moral principles through the ambiguity into which it easily falls. Thus when ordinary practical reason cultivates itself, there imperceptibly arises in it a dialectic which compels it to seek help in philosophy. The same thing happens in reason's theoretical use; in this case, just as in the other, peace will be found only in a thorough critical examination of our reason.

SECOND SECTION   406

Transition from Popular Moral Philosophy to a Metaphysics of Morals

If we have so far drawn our concept of duty from the ordinary use of our practical reason, one is by no means to infer that we have treated it as a concept of experience. On the contrary, when we pay attention to our experience of the way human beings act, we meet frequent and—as we ourselves admit—justified complaints that there cannot be cited a single certain example of the disposition to act from pure duty; and we meet complaints that although much may be done that is in accordance with what duty commands, yet there are always doubts as to whether what occurs has really been done from duty and so has moral worth. Hence there have always been philosophers who have absolutely denied the reality of this disposition in human actions and have ascribed everything to a more or less refined self-love. Yet in so doing they have not cast doubt upon the rightness of the concept of morality. Rather, they have spoken with sincere regret as to the frailty and impurity of human nature, which they think is noble enough to take as its precept an idea so worthy of respect but yet is too weak to follow this idea: reason, which should legislate for human nature, is used only to look after the interest of inclinations, whether singly or, at best, in their greatest possible harmony with one another.

In fact there is absolutely no possibility by means   407
of experience to make out with complete certainty a single case in which the maxim of an action that may in other respects conform to duty has rested solely on moral grounds and on the representation of one's

duty. It is indeed sometimes the case that after the keenest self-examination we can find nothing except the moral ground of duty that could have been strong enough to move us to this or that good action and to such great sacrifice. But there cannot with certainty be at all inferred from this that some secret impulse of self-love, merely appearing as the idea of duty, was not the actual determining cause of the will. We like to flatter ourselves with the false claim to a more noble motive; but in fact we can never, even by the strictest examination, completely plumb the depths of the secret incentives of our actions. For when moral value is being considered, the concern is not with the actions, which are seen, but rather with their inner principles, which are not seen.

Moreover, one cannot better serve the wishes of those who ridicule all morality as being a mere phantom of human imagination getting above itself because of self-conceit than by conceding to them that the concepts of duty must be drawn solely from experience (just as from indolence one willingly persuades himself that such is the case as regards all other concepts as well). For by so conceding, one prepares for them a sure triumph. I am willing to admit out of love for humanity that most of our actions are in accordance with duty; but if we look more closely at our planning and striving, we everywhere come upon the dear self, which is always turning up, and upon which the intent of our actions is based rather than upon the strict command of duty (which would often require self-denial). One need not be exactly an enemy of virtue, but only a cool observer who does not take the liveliest wish for the good to be straight off its realization, in order to become doubtful at times whether any true virtue is actually to be found in the world. Such is especially the case when years increase and one's power of judgment is made shrewder by experience and keener in observation. Because of these things nothing can protect us from a complete falling away from our ideas of duty and preserve in 408 the soul a well-grounded respect for duty's law except the clear conviction that, even if there never have been actions springing from such pure sources, the question at issue here is not whether this or that has happened but that reason of itself and independently of all experience commands what ought to happen. Consequently, reason unrelentingly commands ac-

tions of which the world has perhaps hitherto never provided an example and whose feasibility might well be doubted by one who bases everything upon experience; for instance, even though there might never yet have been a sincere friend, still pure sincerity in friendship is nonetheless required of every man, because this duty, prior to all experience, is contained as duty in general in the idea of a reason that determines the will by means of a priori grounds.

There may be noted further that unless we want to deny to the concept of morality all truth and all reference to a possible object, we cannot but admit that the moral law is of such widespread significance that it must hold not merely for men but for all rational beings generally, and that it must be valid not merely under contingent conditions and with exceptions but must be absolutely necessary. Clearly, therefore, no experience can give occasion for inferring even the possibility of such apodeictic laws. For with what right could we bring into unlimited respect as a universal precept for every rational nature what is perhaps valid only under the contingent conditions of humanity? And how could laws for the determination of our will be regarded as laws for the determination of a rational being in general and of ourselves only insofar as we are rational beings, if these laws were merely empirical and did not have their source completely a priori in pure, but practical, reason?

Moreover, worse service cannot be rendered morality than that an attempt be made to derive it from examples. For every example of morality presented to me must itself first be judged according to principles of morality in order to see whether it is fit to serve as an original example, i.e., as a model. But in no way can it authoritatively furnish the concept of morality. Even the Holy One of the gospel must first be compared with our ideal of moral perfection before he is recognized as such. Even he says of himself, "Why do you call me (whom you see) good? None is good (the archetype of the good) except God only 409 (whom you do not see)." But whence have we the concept of God as the highest good? Solely from the idea of moral perfection, which reason frames a priori and connects inseparably with the concept of a free will. Imitation has no place at all in moral matters. And examples serve only for encouragement, i.e., they put beyond doubt the feasibility of what the law commands and they make visible what the practical rule expresses more generally. But examples can never justify us in setting aside their true original, which lies in reason, and letting ourselves be guided by them.

If there is then no genuine supreme principle of morality which does not rest on pure reason alone, independent of all experience, I think it is unnecessary even to ask whether it is a good thing to exhibit these concepts generally (*in abstracto*), which, along with the principles that belong to them, hold a priori, so far as the knowledge involved is to be distinguished from ordinary knowledge and is to be called philosophical. But in our times it may well be necessary to do so. For if one were to take a vote as to whether pure rational knowledge separated from everything empirical, i.e., metaphysics of morals, or whether popular practical philosophy is to be preferred, one can easily guess which side would be preponderant.

This descent to popular thought is certainly very commendable once the ascent to the principles of pure reason has occurred and has been satisfactorily accomplished. That would mean that the doctrine of morals has first been grounded on metaphysics and that subsequently acceptance for morals has been won by giving it a popular character after it has been firmly established. But it is quite absurd to try for popularity in the first inquiry, upon which depends the total correctness of the principles. Not only can such a procedure never lay claim to the very rare merit of a true philosophical popularity, inasmuch as there is really no art involved at all in being generally intelligible if one thereby renounces all basic insight, but such a procedure turns out a disgusting mishmash of patchwork observations and half-reasoned principles in which shallowpates revel because all this is something quite useful for the chitchat of everyday life. Persons of insight, on the other hand, feel confused by all this and turn their eyes away with a dissatisfaction which they nevertheless cannot cure. 410 Yet philosophers, who quite see through the delusion, get little hearing when they summon people for a time from this pretended popularity in order that they may be rightfully popular only after they have attained definite insight.

One need only look at the attempts to deal with morality in the way favored by popular taste. What he will find in an amazing mixture is at one time the particular constitution of human nature (but along with this also the idea of a rational nature in general), at another time perfection, at another happiness; here moral feeling, and there the fear of God; something of this, and also something of that. But the thought never occurs to ask whether the principles of morality are to be sought at all in the knowledge of human nature (which can be had only from experience). Nor does the thought occur that if these principles are not to be sought here but to be found, rather, completely a priori and free from everything empirical in pure rational concepts only, and are to be found nowhere else even to the slightest extent—then there had better be adopted the plan of undertaking this investigation as a separate inquiry, i.e., as pure practical philosophy or (if one may use a name so much decried) as a metaphysics[24] of morals. It is better to bring this investigation to full completeness entirely by itself and to bid the public, which demands popularity, to await the outcome of this undertaking.

But such a completely isolated metaphysics of morals, not mixed with any anthropology, theology, physics, or hyperphysics, and still less with occult qualities (which might be called hypophysical), is not only an indispensable substratum of all theoretical and precisely defined knowledge of duties, but is at the same time a desideratum of the highest importance for the actual fulfillment of their precepts. For the pure thought of duty and of the moral law generally, unmixed with any extraneous addition of empirical inducements, has by the way of reason alone (which first becomes aware hereby that it can of itself be practical) an influence on the human heart so much more powerful than all 411

---

24. Pure philosophy of morals (metaphysics) may be distinguished from the applied (viz., applied to human nature) just as pure mathematics is distinguished from applied mathematics and pure logic from applied logic. By this designation one is also immediately reminded that moral principles are not grounded on the peculiarities of human nature but must subsist a priori of themselves, and that from such principles practical rules must be derivable for every rational nature, and accordingly for human nature.

other incentives[25] which may be derived from the empirical field that reason in the consciousness of its dignity despises such incentives and is able gradually to become their master. On the other hand, a mixed moral philosophy, compounded both of incentives drawn from feelings and inclinations and at the same time of rational concepts, must make the mind waver between motives that cannot be brought under any principle and that can only by accident lead to the good but often can also lead to the bad.

It is clear from the foregoing that all moral concepts have their seat and origin completely a priori in reason, and indeed in the most ordinary human reason just as much as in the most highly speculative. They cannot be abstracted from any empirical, and hence merely contingent, cognition. In this purity of their origin lies their very worthiness to serve us as supreme practical principles; and to the extent that something empirical is added to them, just so much is taken away from their genuine influence and from the absolute worth of the corresponding actions. Moreover, it is not only a requirement of the greatest necessity from a theoretical point of view, when it is a question of speculation, but also of the greatest practical importance, to draw these concepts and laws from pure reason, to present them pure and unmixed, and in-

25. I have a letter from the late excellent Sulzer [Johann Georg Sulzer (1720–1779), an important Berlin savant, who translated Hume's *Inquiry Concerning the Principles of Morals* into German in 1755] in which he asks me why it is that moral instruction accomplishes so little, even though it contains so much that is convincing to reason. My answer was delayed so that I might make it complete. But it is just that the teachers themselves have not purified their concepts: since they try to do too well by looking everywhere for motives for being morally good, they spoil the medicine by trying to make it really strong. For the most ordinary observation shows that when a righteous act is represented as being done with a steadfast soul and sundered from all view to any advantage in this or another world, and even under the greatest temptations of need or allurement, it far surpasses and eclipses any similar action that was in the least affected by any extraneous incentive; it elevates the soul and inspires the wish to be able to act in this way. Even moderately young children feel this impression, and duties should never be represented to them in any other way.

deed to determine the extent of this entire practical and pure rational cognition, i.e., to determine the whole faculty of pure practical reason. The principles *412* should not be made to depend on the particular nature of human reason, as speculative philosophy may permit and even sometimes finds necessary; but, rather, the principles should be derived from the universal concept of a rational being in general, since moral laws should hold for every rational being as such. In this way all morals, which require anthropology in order to be applied to humans, must be entirely expounded at first independently of anthropology as pure philosophy, i.e., as metaphysics (which can easily be done in such distinct kinds of knowledge). One knows quite well that unless one is in possession of such a metaphysics, then the attempt is futile, I shall not say to determine exactly for speculative judgment the moral element of duty in all that accords with duty, but that the attempt is impossible, even in ordinary and practical usage, especially in that of moral instruction, to ground morals on their genuine principles and thereby to produce pure moral dispositions and engraft them on men's minds for the promotion of the highest good in the world.

In this study we must advance by natural stages not merely from ordinary moral judgment (which is here ever so worthy of respect) to philosophical judgment, as has already been done, but also from popular philosophy, which goes no further than it can get by groping about with the help of examples, to metaphysics (which does not permit itself to be held back any longer by what is empirical, and which, inasmuch as it must survey the whole extent of rational knowledge of this kind, goes right up to ideas, where examples themselves fail us). In order to make such an advance, we must follow and clearly present the practical faculty of reason from its universal rules of determination to the point where the concept of duty springs from it.

Everything in nature works according to laws. Only a rational being has the power to act according to his conception of laws, i.e., according to principles, and thereby has he a will. Since the derivation of actions from laws requires reason, the will is nothing but practical reason. If reason infallibly determines the will, then in the case of such a being actions which are recognized to be objectively necessary are also subjectively necessary, i.e., the will is a faculty of choosing only that which reason, independently of inclination, recognizes as being practically necessary, i.e., as good. But if reason of itself does not sufficiently determine the will, and if the will submits also to subjective conditions (certain incentives) which do not always agree with objective conditions; in a word, if the will does not in itself completely accord with reason (as is actually the case with men), then actions which are recognized as objectively necessary are subjectively contingent, and the determination of such a will according to objective laws is necessitation. That is to say that the relation of objective laws to a will not thoroughly good is represented as the determination of the will of a rational being by principles of reason which the will does not necessarily follow because of its own nature.

The representation of an objective principle insofar as it necessitates the will is called a command (of reason), and the formula of the command is called an imperative.

All imperatives are expressed by an *ought* and thereby indicate the relation of an objective law of reason to a will that is not necessarily determined by this law because of its subjective constitution (the relation of necessitation). Imperatives say that something would be good to do or to refrain from doing, but they say it to a will that does not always therefore do something simply because it has been represented to the will as something good to do. That is practically good which determines the will by means of representations of reason and hence not by subjective causes, but objectively, i.e., on grounds valid for every rational being as such. It is distinguished from the pleasant as that which influences the will only by means of sensation from merely subjective causes, which hold only for this or that person's senses but do not hold as a principle of reason valid for everyone.[26]

A perfectly good will would thus be quite as much subject to objective laws (of the good), but could not be conceived as thereby necessitated to act in conformity with law, inasmuch as it can of itself, according to its subjective constitution, be determined only by the representation of the good. Therefore no imperatives hold for the divine will, and in general for a holy will; the *ought* is here out of place, because the *would* is already of itself necessarily in agreement with the law. Consequently, imperatives are only formulas for expressing the relation of objective laws of willing in general to the subjective imperfection of the will of this or that rational being, e.g., the human will.

Now all imperatives command either hypothetically or categorically. The former represent the practical necessity of a possible action as a means for attaining something else that one wants (or may possibly want). The categorical imperative would be one which represented an action as objectively necessary in itself, without reference to another end.

Every practical law represents a possible action as good and hence as necessary for a subject who is practically determinable by reason; therefore all imperatives are formulas for determining an action which is necessary according to the principle of a will that is good in some way. Now if the action would be good merely as a means to something else, so is the imperative hypothetical. But if the action is represented as good in itself, and hence as necessary in a will which of itself conforms to reason as the principle of the will, then the imperative is categorical.

---

26. The dependence of the faculty of desire on sensations is called inclination, which accordingly always indicates a need. The dependence of a contingently determinable will on principles of reason, however, is called interest. Therefore an interest is found only in a dependent will which is not of itself always in accord with reason; in the divine will no interest can be thought. But even the human will can take an interest in something without thereby acting from interest. The former signifies practical interest in the action, while the latter signifies pathological interest in the object of the action. The former indicates only dependence of the will on principles of reason by itself, while the latter indicates the will's dependence on principles of reason for the sake of inclination, i.e., reason merely gives the practical rule for meeting the need of inclination. In the former case the action interests me, while in the latter case what interests me is the object of the action (so far as this object is pleasant for me). In the First Section we have seen that in the case of an action done from duty regard must be given not to the interest in the object, but only to interest in the action itself and in its rational principle (viz., the law).

An imperative thus says what action possible by me would be good, and it presents the practical rule in relation to a will which does not forthwith perform an action simply because it is good, partly because the subject does not always know that the action is good and partly because (even if he does know it is good) his maxims might yet be opposed to the objective principles of practical reason.

A hypothetical imperative thus says only that an action is good for some purpose, either possible or actual. In the first case it is a problematic practical principle; in the second case an assertoric one. A categorical imperative, which declares an action to be of itself objectively necessary without reference to any purpose, i.e., without any other end, holds as an apodeictic practical principle.

Whatever is possible only through the powers of some rational being can be thought of as a possible purpose of some will. Consequently, there are in fact infinitely many principles of action insofar as they are represented as necessary for attaining a possible purpose achievable by them. All sciences have a practical part consisting of problems saying that some end is possible for us and of imperatives telling us how it can be attained. These can, therefore, be called in general imperatives of skill. Here there is no question at all whether the end is reasonable and good, but there is only a question as to what must be done to attain it. The prescriptions needed by a doctor in order to make his patient thoroughly healthy and by a poisoner in order to make sure of killing his victim are of equal value so far as each serves to bring about its purpose perfectly. Since there cannot be known in early youth what ends may be presented to us in the course of life, parents especially seek to have their children learn many different kinds of things, and they provide for skill in the use of means to all sorts of arbitrary ends, among which they cannot determine whether any one of them could in the future become an actual purpose for their ward, though there is always the possibility that he might adopt it. Their concern is so great that they commonly neglect to form and correct their children's judgment regarding the worth of things which might be chosen as ends.

There is, however, one end that can be presupposed as actual for all rational beings (so far as they are dependent beings to whom imperatives apply); and thus there is one purpose which they not merely can have but which can certainly be assumed to be such that they all do have by a natural necessity, and this is happiness. A hypothetical imperative which represents the practical necessity of an action as means for the promotion of happiness is assertoric. It may be expounded not simply as necessary to an uncertain, merely possible purpose, but as necessary to a purpose which can be presupposed a priori and with certainty as being present in everyone because it belongs to his essence. Now skill in the choice of means to one's own greatest well-being can be called prudence[27] in the narrowest sense. And thus the imperative that refers to the choice of means to one's own happiness, i.e., the precept of prudence, still remains hypothetical; the action is commanded not absolutely but only as a means to a further purpose.

Finally, there is one imperative which immediately commands a certain conduct without having as its condition any other purpose to be attained by it. This imperative is categorical. It is not concerned with the matter of the action and its intended result, but rather with the form of the action and the principle from which it follows; what is essentially good in the action consists in the mental disposition, let the consequences be what they may. This imperative may be called that of morality.

Willing according to these three kinds of principles is also clearly distinguished by dissimilarity in the necessitation of the will. To make this dissimilarity clear I think that they are most suitably named in their order when they are said to be either *rules of skill, counsels of prudence,* or *commands (laws) of morality.* For law alone involves the concept of a necessity that is unconditioned and indeed objective and hence universally valid, and commands are laws

---

27. The word "prudence" is used in a double sense: firstly, it can mean worldly wisdom, and, secondly, private wisdom. The former is the skill of someone in influencing others so as to use them for his own purposes. The latter is the sagacity to combine all these purposes for his own lasting advantage. The value of the former is properly reduced to the latter, and it might better be said of one who is prudent in the former sense but not in the latter that he is clever and cunning, but on the whole imprudent.

which must be obeyed, i.e., must be followed even in opposition to inclination. Counsel does indeed involve necessity, but involves such necessity as is valid only under a subjectively contingent condition, viz., whether this or that man counts this or that as belonging to his happiness. On the other hand, the categorical imperative is limited by no condition, and can quite properly be called a command since it is absolutely, though practically, necessary. The first kind of imperatives might also be called technical (belonging to art), the second kind pragmatic[28] (belonging to welfare), the third kind moral (belonging to free conduct as such, i.e., to morals).

417

The question now arises: how are all of these imperatives possible?[29] This question does not seek to know how the fulfillment of the action commanded by the imperative can be conceived, but merely how the necessitation of the will expressed by the imperative in setting a task can be conceived. How an imperative of skill is possible requires no special discussion. Whoever wills the end, wills (so far as reason has decisive influence on his actions) also the means that are indispensably necessary to his actions and that lie in his power. This proposition, as far as willing is concerned, is analytic. For in willing an object as my effect there is already thought the causality of myself as an acting cause, i.e., the use of means. The imperative derives the concept of actions necessary to this end from the concept of willing this end. (Synthetic propositions are indeed required for determining the means to a proposed end; but such propositions are concerned not with the ground, i.e., the act of the will, but only with the way to realize the object of the will.) Mathematics teaches by nothing but synthetic

28. It seems to me that the proper meaning of the word "pragmatic" could be defined most accurately in this way. For those sanctions are called pragmatic which properly flow not from the law of states as necessary enactments but from provision for the general welfare. A history is pragmatically written when it teaches prudence, i.e., instructs the world how it can provide for its interests better than, or at least as well as, has been done in former times.

29. [That is, why should one let his actions be determined at various times by one or the other of these three kinds of imperatives?]

propositions that in order to bisect a line according to a sure principle I must from each of its extremities draw arcs such that they intersect. But when I know that the proposed result can come about only by means of such an action, then the proposition (if I fully will the effect, then I also will the action required for it) is analytic. For it is one and the same thing to conceive of something as an effect that is possible in a certain way through me and to conceive of myself as acting in the same way with regard to the aforesaid effect.

If it were only as easy to give a determinate concept of happiness, then the imperatives of prudence would exactly correspond to those of skill and would be likewise analytic. For there could be said in this case just as in the former that whoever wills the end also wills (necessarily according to reason) the sole means thereto which are in his power. But, unfortunately, the concept of happiness is such an indeterminate one that even though everyone wishes to attain happiness, yet he can never say definitely and consistently what it is that he really wishes and wills. The reason for this is that all the elements belonging to the concept of happiness are unexceptionally empirical, i.e., they must be borrowed from experience, while for the idea of happiness there is required an absolute whole, a maximum of well-being in my present and in every future condition. Now it is impossible for the most insightful and at the same time most powerful, but nonetheless finite, being to frame here a determinate concept of what it is that he really wills. Does he want riches? How much anxiety, envy, and intrigue might he not thereby bring down upon his own head! Or knowledge and insight? Perhaps these might only give him an eye that much sharper for revealing that much more dreadfully evils which are at present hidden but are yet unavoidable, or such an eye might burden him with still further needs for the desires which already concern him enough. Or long life? Who guarantees that it would not be a long misery? Or health at least? How often has infirmity of the body kept one from excesses into which perfect health would have allowed him to fall, and so on? In brief, he is not able on any principle to determine with complete certainty what will make him truly happy, because to do so would require omniscience. Therefore, one cannot act according to determinate principles in

418

order to be happy, but only according to empirical counsels, e.g., of diet, frugality, politeness, reserve, etc., which are shown by experience to contribute on the average the most to well-being. There follows from this that imperatives of prudence, strictly speaking, cannot command at all, i.e., present actions objectively as practically necessary. They are to be taken as counsels (*consilia*) rather than as commands (*praecepta*) of reason. The problem of determining certainly and universally what action will promote the happiness of a rational being is completely insoluble. Therefore, regarding such action no imperative that in the strictest sense could command what is to be done to make one happy is possible, inasmuch as happiness is not an ideal of reason but of imagination. Such an ideal rests merely on empirical grounds; in vain can there be expected that such grounds should determine an action whereby the totality of an infinite series of consequences could be attained. This imperative of prudence would, nevertheless, be an analytic practical proposition if one assumes that the means to happiness could with certainly be assigned; for it differs from the imperative of skill only in that for it the end is given while for the latter the end is merely possible. Since both, however, command only the means to what is assumed to be willed as an end, the imperative commanding him who wills the end to will likewise the means thereto is in both cases analytic. Hence there is also no difficulty regarding the possibility of an imperative of prudence.

On the other hand, the question as to how the imperative of morality is possible is undoubtedly the only one requiring a solution. For it is not at all hypothetical; and hence the objective necessity which it presents cannot be based on any presupposition, as was the case with the hypothetical imperatives. Only there must never here be forgotten that no example can show, i.e., empirically, whether there is any such imperative at all. Rather, care must be taken lest all imperatives which are seemingly categorical may nevertheless be covertly hypothetical. For instance, when it is said that you should not make a false promise, the assumption is that the necessity of this avoidance is no mere advice for escaping some other evil, so that it might be said that you should not make a false promise lest you ruin your credit when the falsity comes to light. But when it is asserted that an action of this kind must be regarded as bad in itself, then the imperative of prohibition is therefore categorical. Nevertheless, it cannot with certainty be shown by means of an example that the will is here determined solely by the law without any other incentive, even though such may seem to be the case. For it is always possible that secretly there is fear of disgrace and perhaps also obscure dread of other dangers; such fear and dread may have influenced the will. Who can prove by experience that a cause is not present? Experience only shows that a cause is not perceived. But in such a case the so-called moral imperative, which as such appears to be categorical and unconditioned, would actually be only a pragmatic precept which makes us pay attention to our own advantage and merely teaches us to take such advantage into consideration.

We shall, therefore, have to investigate the possibility of a categorical imperative entirely a priori, inasmuch as we do not here have the advantage of having its reality given in experience and consequently of thus being obligated merely to explain its possibility rather than to establish it. In the meantime so much can be seen for now: the categorical imperative alone purports to be a practical law, while all the others may be called principles of the will but not laws. The reason for this is that whatever is necessary merely in order to attain some arbitrary purpose can be regarded as in itself contingent, and the precept can always be ignored once the purpose is abandoned. Contrariwise, an unconditioned command does not leave the will free to choose the opposite at its own liking. Consequently, only such a command carries with it that necessity which is demanded from a law.

Secondly, in the case of this categorical imperative, or law of morality, the reason for the difficulty (of discerning its possibility) is quite serious. The categorical imperative is an a priori synthetic practical proposition;[30] and since discerning the possibility of propositions of this sort involves so much difficulty

30. I connect a priori, and therefore necessarily, the act with the will without presupposing any condition taken from some inclination (though I make such a connection only objectively, i.e., under the idea of a reason having full power over all subjective motives). Hence this is a practical proposition which does not analytically derive

in theoretic knowledge, there may readily be gathered that there will be no less difficulty in practical knowledge.

In solving this problem, we want first to inquire whether perhaps the mere concept of a categorical imperative may not also supply us with the formula containing the proposition that can alone be a categorical imperative. For even when we know the purport of such an absolute command, the question as to how it is possible will still require a special and difficult effort, which we postpone to the last section.[31]

If I think of a hypothetical imperative in general, I do not know beforehand what it will contain until its condition is given. But if I think of a categorical imperative, I know immediately what it contains. For since, besides the law, the imperative contains only 421 the necessity that the maxim[32] should accord with this law, while the law contains no condition to restrict it, there remains nothing but the universality of a law as such with which the maxim of the action should conform. This conformity alone is properly what is represented as necessary by the imperative.

Hence there is only one categorical imperative and it is this: Act only according to that maxim whereby you can at the same time will that it should become a universal law.[33]

Now if all imperatives of duty can be derived from this one imperative as their principle, then there can

at least be shown what is understood by the concept of duty and what it means, even though there is left undecided whether what is called duty may not be an empty concept.

The universality of law according to which effects are produced constitutes what is properly called nature in the most general sense (as to form), i.e., the existence of things as far as determined by universal laws. Accordingly, the universal imperative of duty may be expressed thus: Act as if the maxim of your action were to become through your will a universal law of nature.[34]

We shall now enumerate some duties, following the usual division of them into duties to ourselves and to others and into perfect and imperfect duties.[35]

1. A man reduced to despair by a series of misfortunes feels sick of life but is still so far in possession of his 422 reason that he can ask himself whether taking his own life would not be contrary to his duty to himself.[36] Now he asks whether the maxim of his action could become a universal law of nature. But his maxim is this: from self-love I make as my principle to shorten my life when its continued duration threatens more evil than it promises satisfaction. There only remains the question as to whether this principle of self-love can become a universal law of nature. One sees at once a contradiction in a system of nature whose law would destroy life by means of the very same feeling that acts so as to stimulate the furtherance of life, and hence there could be

---

the willing of an action from some other willing already presupposed (for we possess no such perfect will) but which connects the willing of an action immediately with the concept of the will of a rational being as something which is not contained in this concept.

31. [See below Ak. 446–63.]

32. A maxim is the subjective principle of acting and must be distinguished from the objective principle, viz., the practical law. A maxim contains the practical rule which reason determines in accordance with the conditions of the subject (often his ignorance or his inclinations) and is thus the principle according to which the subject does act. But the law is the objective principle valid for every rational being, and it is the principle according to which he ought to act, i.e., an imperative.

33. [This formulation of the categorical imperative is often referred to as the formula of universal law.]

34. [This is often called the formula of the law of nature.]

35. There should be noted here that I reserve the division of duties for a future *Metaphysics of Morals* [in Part II of the *Metaphysics of Morals,* entitled *The Metaphysical Principles of Virtue,* Ak. 417–474]. The division presented here stands as merely an arbitrary one (in order to arrange my examples). For the rest, I understand here by a perfect duty one which permits no exception in the interest of inclination. Accordingly, I have perfect duties which are external [to others], while other ones are internal [to oneself]. This classification runs contrary to the accepted usage of the schools, but I do not intend to justify it here, since there is no difference for my purpose whether this classification is accepted or not.

36. [Not committing suicide is an example of a perfect duty to oneself. See *Metaphysical Principles of Virtue,* Ak. 422–24.]

no existence as a system of nature. Therefore, such a maxim cannot possibly hold as a universal law of nature and is, consequently, wholly opposed to the supreme principle of all duty.

2. Another man in need finds himself forced to borrow money. He knows well that he won't be able to repay it, but he sees also that he will not get any loan unless he firmly promises to repay it within a fixed time. He wants to make such a promise, but he still has conscience enough to ask himself whether it is not permissible and is contrary to duty to get out of difficulty in this way. Suppose, however, that he decides to do so. The maxim of his action would then be expressed as follows: when I believe myself to be in need of money, I will borrow money and promise to pay it back, although I know that I can never do so. Now this principle of self-love or personal advantage may perhaps be quite compatible with one's entire future welfare, but the question is now whether it is right.[37] I then transform the requirement of self-love into a universal law and put the question thus: how would things stand if my maxim were to become a universal law? He then sees at once that such a maxim could never hold as a universal law of nature and be consistent with itself, but must necessarily be self-contradictory. For the universality of a law which says that anyone believing himself to be in difficulty could promise whatever he pleases with the intention of not keeping it would make promising itself and the end to be attained thereby quite impossible, inasmuch as no one would believe what was promised him but would merely laugh at all such utterances as being vain pretenses.

3. A third finds in himself a talent whose cultivation 423 could make him a man useful in many respects. But he finds himself in comfortable circumstances and prefers to indulge in pleasure rather than to bother himself about broadening and improving his fortunate natural aptitudes. But he asks himself further whether his maxim of neglecting his natural gifts, besides agreeing of itself with his propensity to indulgence, might agree also with what is called duty.[38]

He then sees that a system of nature could indeed always subsist according to such a universal law, even though every man (like South Sea Islanders) should let his talents rust and resolve to devote his life entirely to idleness, indulgence, propagation, and, in a word, to enjoyment. But he cannot possibly will that this should become a universal law of nature or be implanted in us as such a law by a natural instinct. For as a rational being he necessarily wills that all his faculties should be developed, inasmuch as they are given him for all sorts of possible purposes.

4. A fourth man finds things going well for himself but sees others (whom he could help) struggling with great hardships; and he thinks: what does it matter to me? Let everybody be as happy as Heaven wills or as he can make himself; I shall take nothing from him nor even envy him; but I have no desire to contribute anything to his well-being or to his assistance when in need. If such a way of thinking were to become a universal law of nature, the human race admittedly could very well subsist and doubtless could subsist even better than when everyone prates about sympathy and benevolence and even on occasions exerts himself to practice them but, on the other hand, also cheats when he can, betrays the rights of man, or otherwise violates them. But even though it is possible that a universal law of nature could subsist in accordance with that maxim, still it is impossible to will that such a principle should hold everywhere as a law of nature.[39] For a will which resolved in this way would contradict itself, inasmuch as cases might often arise in which one would have need of the love and sympathy of others and in which he would deprive himself, by such a law of nature springing from his own will, of all hope of the aid he wants for himself.

These are some of the many actual duties, or at least what are taken to be such, whose derivation from 424 the single principle cited above is clear. We must be able to will that a maxim of our action become a universal law; this is the canon for morally estimating any of our actions. Some actions are so constituted that their maxims cannot without contradiction even be thought as a universal law of nature, much less

37. [Keeping promises is an example of a perfect duty to others. See *ibid.*, Ak. 423–31.]

38. [Cultivating one's talents is an example of an imperfect duty to oneself. See *ibid.*, Ak. 444–46.]

39. [Benefiting others is an example of an imperfect duty to others. See *ibid.*, Ak. 452–54.]

be willed as what should become one. In the case of others this internal impossibility is indeed not found, but there is still no possibility of willing that their maxim should be raised to the universality of a law of nature, because such a will would contradict itself. There is no difficulty in seeing that the former kind of action conflicts with strict or narrow [perfect] (irremissible) duty, while the second kind conflicts only with broad [imperfect] (meritorious) duty.[40] By means of these examples there has thus been fully set forth how all duties depend as regards the kind of obligation (not the object of their action) upon the one principle.

If we now attend to ourselves in any transgression of a duty, we find that we actually do not will that our maxim should become a universal law—because this is impossible for us—but rather that the opposite of this maxim should remain a law universally.[41] We only take the liberty of making an exception to the law for ourselves (or just for this one time) to the advantage of our inclination. Consequently, if we weighed up everything from one and the same standpoint, namely, that of reason, we would find a contradiction in our own will, viz., that a certain principle be objectively necessary as a universal law and yet subjectively not hold universally but should admit of exceptions. But since we at one moment regard our action from the standpoint of a will wholly in accord with reason and then at another moment regard the very same action from the standpoint of a will affected by inclination, there is really no contradiction here. Rather, there is an opposition (*antagonismus*) of inclination to the precept of reason, whereby the universality (*universalitas*) of the principle is changed into a mere generality (*generalitas*) so that the practical principle of reason may meet the maxim halfway. Although this procedure cannot be justified in our own impartial judgment, yet it does show that we actually acknowledge the validity of the categorical

imperative and (with all respect for it) merely allow ourselves a few exceptions which, as they seem to us, are unimportant and forced upon us.

We have thus at least shown that if duty is a concept which is to have significance and real legislative authority for our actions, then such duty can be expressed only in categorical imperatives but not at all in hypothetical ones. We have also—and this is already a great deal—exhibited clearly and definitely for every application what is the content of the categorical imperative, which must contain the principle of all duty (if there is such a thing at all). But we have not yet advanced far enough to prove a priori that there actually is an imperative of this kind, that there is a practical law which of itself commands absolutely and without any incentives, and that following this law is duty.

In order to attain this proof there is the utmost importance in being warned that we must not take it into our mind to derive the reality of this principle from the special characteristics of human nature. For duty has to be a practical, unconditioned necessity of action; hence it must hold for all rational beings (to whom alone an imperative is at all applicable) and for this reason only can it also be a law for all human wills. On the other hand, whatever is derived from the special natural condition of humanity, from certain feelings and propensities, or even, if such were possible, from some special tendency peculiar to human reason and not holding necessarily for the will of every rational being—all of this can indeed yield a maxim valid for us, but not a law. This is to say that such can yield a subjective principle according to which we might act if we happen to have the propensity and inclination, but cannot yield an objective principle according to which we would be directed to act even though our every propensity, inclination, and natural tendency were opposed to it. In fact, the sublimity and inner worth of the command are so much the more evident in a duty, the fewer subjective causes there are for it and the more they oppose it; such causes do not in the least weaken the necessitation exerted by the law or take away anything from its validity.

Here philosophy is seen in fact to be put in a precarious position, which should be firm even though there is neither in heaven nor on earth

425

40. [Compare *ibid.*, Ak. 390–94, 410–11, 421–51.]

41. [This is to say, for example, that when you tell a lie, you do so on the condition that others are truthful and believe that what you are saying is true, because otherwise your lie will never work to get you what you want. When you tell a lie, you simply take exception to the general rule that says everyone should always tell the truth.]

anything upon which it depends or is based. Here philosophy must show its purity as author of its laws, and not as the herald of such laws as are whispered to it by an implanted sense or by who knows what tutelary nature. Such laws may be better than nothing at all, but they can never give us principles dictated by reason. These principles must have an origin that is completely a priori and must at the same time derive from such origin their authority to command. They expect nothing from the inclination of men but, rather, expect everything from the supremacy of the law and from the respect owed to the law. Without the latter expectation, these principles condemn man to self-contempt and inward abhorrence.

426

Hence everything empirical is not only quite unsuitable as a contribution to the principle of morality, but is even highly detrimental to the purity of morals. For the proper and inestimable worth of an absolutely good will consists precisely in the fact that the principle of action is free of all influences from contingent grounds, which only experience can furnish. This lax or even mean way of thinking which seeks its principle among empirical motives and laws cannot too much or too often be warned against, for human reason in its weariness is glad to rest upon this pillow. In a dream of sweet illusions (in which not Juno but a cloud is embraced) there is substituted for morality some bastard patched up from limbs of quite varied ancestry and looking like anything one wants to see in it but not looking like virtue to him who has once beheld her in her true form.[42]

Therefore, the question is this: is it a necessary law for all rational beings always to judge their actions according to such maxims as they can themselves will that such should serve as universal laws? If there is such a law, then it must already be connected (completely a priori) with the concept of the will of a rational being in general. But in order to discover this connection we must, however reluctantly, take a step into metaphysics, although into a region of it different from speculative philosophy, i.e., we must enter the metaphysics of morals. In practical philosophy the concern is not with accepting grounds for what happens but with accepting laws of what ought to happen, even though it never does happen—that is, the concern is with objectively practical laws. Here there is no need to inquire into the reasons as to why something pleases or displeases, how the pleasure of mere sensation differs from taste, and whether taste differs from a general satisfaction of reason, upon what does the feeling of pleasure and displeasure rest, and how from this feeling desires and inclinations arise, and how, finally, from these there arise maxims through the cooperation of reason. All of this belongs to an empirical psychology, which would constitute the second part of the doctrine of nature, if this doctrine is regarded as the philosophy of nature insofar as this philosophy is grounded on empirical laws. But here the concern is with objectively practical laws, and hence with the relation of a will to itself insofar as it is determined solely by reason. In this case everything related to what is empirical falls away of itself, because if reason entirely by itself determines conduct (and the possibility of such determination we now wish to investigate), then reason must necessarily do so a priori.

427

The will is thought of as a faculty of determining itself to action in accordance with the representation of certain laws, and such a faculty can be found only in rational beings. Now what serves the will as the objective ground of its self-determination is an end; and if this end is given by reason alone, then it must be equally valid for all rational beings. On the other hand, what contains merely the ground of the possibility of the action, whose effect is an end, is called the means. The subjective ground of desire is the incentive; the objective ground of volition is the motive. Hence there arises the distinction between subjective ends, which rest on incentives, and objective ends, which depend on motives valid for every rational being. Practical principles are formal when they abstract from all subjective ends; they are material, however, when they are founded upon subjective ends, and hence upon certain incentives. The ends which a rational being arbitrarily proposes to himself as effects of this action (material ends) are all merely

42. To behold virtue in her proper form is nothing other than to present morality stripped of all admixture of what is sensuous and of every spurious adornment of reward or self-love. How much she then eclipses all else that appears attractive to the inclinations can be easily seen by everyone with the least effort of his reason, if it be not entirely ruined for all abstraction.

relative, for only their relation to a specially consti-tuted faculty of desire in the subject gives them their worth. Consequently, such worth cannot provide any
428 universal principles, which are valid and necessary for all rational beings and, furthermore, are valid for every volition, i.e., cannot provide any practical laws. Therefore, all such relative ends can be grounds only for hypothetical imperatives.

But let us suppose that there were something whose existence has in itself an absolute worth, something which as an end in itself could be a ground of determi-nate laws. In it, and in it alone, would there be the ground of a possible categorical imperative, i.e., of a practical law.

Now I say that man, and in general every rational being, exists as an end in himself and not merely as a means to be arbitrarily used by this or that will. He must in all his actions, whether directed to himself or to other rational beings, always be regarded at the same time as an end. All the objects of inclinations have only a conditioned value; for if there were not these inclinations and the needs founded on them, then their object would be without value. But the inclinations themselves, being sources of needs, are so far from having an absolute value such as to render them desirable for their own sake that the universal wish of every rational being must be, rather, to be wholly free from them. Accordingly, the value of any object obtainable by our action is always condi-tioned. Beings whose existence depends not on our will but on nature have, nevertheless, if they are not rational beings, only a relative value as means and are therefore called things. On the other hand, rational beings are called persons inasmuch as their nature already marks them out as ends in themselves, i.e., as something which is not to be used merely as means and hence there is imposed thereby a limit on all arbitrary use of such beings, which are thus objects of respect. Persons are, therefore, not merely subjective ends, whose existence as an effect of our actions has a value for us; but such beings are objective ends, i.e., exist as ends in themselves. Such an end is one for which there can be substi-tuted no other end to which such beings should serve merely as means, for otherwise nothing at all of absolute value would be found anywhere. But if all value were conditioned and hence contingent,

then no supreme practical principle could be found for reason at all.

If then there is to be a supreme principle and, as far as the human will is concerned, a categorical imperative, then it must be such that from the concep-tion of what is necessarily an end for everyone because this end is an end in itself it constitutes an objective principle of the will and can hence serve as a practical 429 law. The ground of such a principle is this: rational nature exists as an end in itself. In this way man necessarily thinks of his own existence; thus far is it a subjective principle of human actions. But in this way also does every other rational being think of his existence on the same rational ground that holds also for me;[43] hence it is at the same time an objective principle, from which, as a supreme practical ground, all laws of the will must be able to be derived. The practical imperative will therefore be the following: Act in such a way that you treat humanity, whether in your own person or in the person of another, always at the same time as an end and never simply as a means.[44] We now want to see whether this can be carried out in practice.

Let us keep to our previous examples.[45]

First, as regards the concept of necessary duty to oneself, the man who contemplates suicide will ask himself whether his action can be consistent with the idea of humanity as an end in itself. If he destroys himself in order to escape from a difficult situation, then he is making use of his person merely as a means so as to maintain a tolerable condition till the end of his life. Man, however, is not a thing and hence is not something to be used merely as a means; he must in all his actions always be regarded as an end in himself. Therefore, I cannot dispose of man in my own person by mutilating, damaging, or killing him (A more exact determination of this principle so as to avoid all misunderstanding, e.g., regarding the am-putation of limbs in order to save oneself, or the

43. This proposition I here put forward as a postulate. The grounds for it will be found in the last section. [See below Ak. 446–63.]

44. [This oft-quoted version of the categorical Impera-tive is usually referred to as the formula of the end in itself.]

45. [See above Ak. 422–23.]

exposure of one's life to danger in order to save it, and so on, must here be omitted; such questions belong to morals proper.)

Second, as concerns necessary or strict duty to others, the man who intends to make a false promise will immediately see that he intends to make use of another man merely as a means to an end which the latter does not likewise hold. For the man whom I want to use for my own purposes by such a promise cannot possibly concur with my way of acting toward him and hence cannot himself hold the end of this action. This conflict with the principle of duty to others becomes even clearer when instances of attacks on the freedom and property of others are considered. For then it becomes clear that a transgressor of the rights of men intends to make use of the persons of others merely as a means, without taking into consideration that, as rational beings, they should always be esteemed at the same time as ends, i.e., be esteemed only as beings who must themselves be able to hold the very same action as an end.[46]

Third, with regard to contingent (meritorious) duty to oneself, it is not enough that the action does not conflict with humanity in our own person as an end in itself; the action must also harmonize with this end. Now there are in humanity capacities for greater perfection which belong to the end that nature has in view as regards humanity in our own person. To neglect these capacities might perhaps be consistent with the maintenance of humanity as an end in itself, but would not be consistent with the advancement of this end.

Fourth, concerning meritorious duty to others, the natural end that all men have is their own happiness.

Now humanity might indeed subsist if nobody contributed anything to the happiness of others, provided he did not intentionally impair their happiness. But this, after all, would harmonize only negatively and not positively with humanity as an end in itself, if everyone does not also strive, as much as he can, to further the ends of others. For the ends of any subject who is an end in himself must as far as possible be my ends also, if that conception of an end in itself is to have its full effect in me.

This principle of humanity and of every rational nature generally as an end in itself is the supreme limiting condition of every man's freedom of action. This principle is not borrowed from experience, first, because of its universality, inasmuch as it applies to all rational beings generally, and no experience is capable of determining anything about them; and, secondly, because in experience (subjectively) humanity is not thought of as the end of men, i.e., as an object that we of ourselves actually make our end which as a law ought to constitute the supreme limiting condition of all subjective ends (whatever they may be); and hence this principle must arise from pure reason [and not from experience]. That is to say that the ground of all practical legislation lies objectively in the rule and in the form of universality, which (according to the first principle) makes the rule capable of being a law (say, for example, a law of nature). Subjectively, however, the ground of all practical legislation lies in the end; but (according to the second principle) the subject of all ends is every rational being as an end in himself. From this there now follows the third practical principle of the will as the supreme condition of the will's conformity with universal practical reason, viz., the idea of the will of every rational being as a will that legislates universal law.[47]

According to this principle all maxims are rejected which are not consistent with the will's own legislation of universal law. The will is thus not merely subject to the law but is subject to the law in such a way that it must be regarded also as legislating for itself and only on this account as being subject to the law (of which it can regard itself as the author).

46. Let it not be thought that the trivial *quod tibi non vis fieri, etc.* [do not do to others what you do not want done to yourself] can here serve as a standard or principle. For it is merely derived from our principle, although with several limitations. It cannot be a universal law, for it contains the ground neither of duties to oneself nor of duties of love toward others (for many a man would gladly consent that others should not benefit him, if only he might be excused from benefiting them). Nor, finally, does it contain the ground of strict duties toward others, for the criminal would on this ground be able to dispute with the judges who punish him; and so on.

47. [This is usually called the formula of autonomy.]

In the previous formulations of imperatives, viz., that based on the conception of the conformity of actions to universal law in a way similar to a natural order and that based on the universal prerogative of rational beings as ends in themselves, these imperatives just because they were thought of as categorical excluded from their legislative authority all admixture of any interest as an incentive. They were, however, only assumed to be categorical because such an assumption had to be made if the concept of duty was to be explained. But that there were practical propositions which commanded categorically could not itself be proved, nor can it be proved anywhere in this section. But one thing could have been done, viz., to indicate that in willing from duty the renunciation of all interest is the specific mark distinguishing a categorical imperative from a hypothetical one and that such renunciation was expressed in the imperative itself by means of some determination contained in it. This is done in the present (third) formulation of the principle, namely, in the idea of the will of every rational being as a will that legislates universal law.

When such a will is thought of, then even though a will which is subject to law may be bound to this law by means of some interest, nevertheless a will that is itself a supreme lawgiver is not able as such to depend on any interest. For a will which is so dependent would itself require yet another law restricting the interest of its self-love to the condition that such interest should itself be valid as a universal law.

Thus the principle that every human will as a will that legislates universal law in all its maxims,[48] provided it is otherwise correct, would be well suited to being a categorical imperative in the following respect: just because of the idea of legislating universal law such an imperative is not based on any interest, and therefore it alone of all possible imperatives can be unconditional. Or still better, the proposition being converted, if there is a categorical imperative (i.e., a law for the will of every rational being), then it can

only command that everything be done from the maxim of such a will as could at the same time have as its object only itself regarded as legislating universal law. For only then are the practical principle and the imperative which the will obeys unconditional, inasmuch as the will can be based on no interest at all.

When we look back upon all previous attempts that have been made to discover the principle of morality, there is no reason now to wonder why they one and all had to fail. Man was viewed as bound to laws by his duty; but it was not seen that man is subject only to his own, yet universal, legislation and that he is bound only to act in accordance with his own will, which is, however, a will purported by nature to legislate universal laws. For when man is thought as being merely subject to a law (whatever it might be), then the law had to carry with it some interest functioning as an attracting stimulus or as a constraining force for obedience, inasmuch as the law did not arise as a law from his own will. Rather, in order that his will conform with law, it had to be necessitated by something else to act in a certain way. By this absolutely necessary conclusion, however, all the labor spent in finding a supreme ground for duty was irretrievably lost; duty was never discovered, but only the necessity of acting from a certain interest. This might be either one's own interest or another's, but either way the imperative had to be always conditional and could never possibly serve as a moral command. I want, therefore, to call my principle the principle of the autonomy of the will, in contrast with every other principle, which I accordingly count under heteronomy.

The concept of every rational being as one who must regard himself as legislating universal law by all his will's maxims, so that he may judge himself and his actions from this point of view, leads to another very fruitful concept, which depends on the aforementioned one, viz., that of a kingdom of ends.

By "kingdom" I understand a systematic union of different rational beings through common laws. Now laws determine ends as regards their universal validity; therefore, if one abstracts from the personal differences of rational beings and also from all content of their private ends, then it will be possible to think of a whole of all ends in systematic connection (a whole both of rational beings as ends in themselves and also

48. I may here be excused from citing instances to elucidate this principle inasmuch as those which were first used to elucidate the categorical imperative and its formula can all serve the same purpose here. [See above Ak. 421–23, 429–30.]

of the particular ends which each may set for himself); that is, one can think of a kingdom of ends that is possible on the aforesaid principles.

For all rational beings stand under the law that each of them should treat himself and all others never merely as means but always at the same time as an end in himself. Hereby arises a systematic union of rational beings through common objective laws, i.e., a kingdom that may be called a kingdom of ends (certainly only an ideal), inasmuch as these laws have in view the very relation of such beings to one another as ends and means.[49]

A rational being belongs to the kingdom of ends as a member when he legislates in it universal laws while also being himself subject to these laws. He belongs to it as sovereign, when as legislator he is himself subject to the will of no other.

434 A rational being must always regard himself as legislator in a kingdom of ends rendered possible by freedom of the will, whether as member or as sovereign. The position of the latter can be maintained not merely through the maxims of his will but only if he is a completely independent being without needs and with unlimited power adequate to his will.

Hence morality consists in the relation of all action to that legislation whereby alone a kingdom of ends is possible. This legislation must be found in every rational being and must be able to arise from his will, whose principle then is never to act on any maxim except such as can also be a universal law and hence such as the will can thereby regard itself as at the same time the legislator of universal law. If now the maxims do not by their very nature already necessarily conform with this objective principle of rational beings as legislating universal laws, then the necessity of acting on that principle is called practical necessitation, i.e., duty. Duty does not apply to the sovereign in the kingdom of ends, but it does apply to every member and to each in the same degree.

The practical necessity of acting according to this principle, i.e., duty, does not rest at all on feelings, impulses, and inclinations, but only on the relation of rational beings to one another, a relation in which the will of a rational being must always be regarded at the same time as legislative, because otherwise he could not be thought of as an end in himself. Reason, therefore, relates every maxim of the will as legislating universal laws to every other will and also to every action toward oneself; it does so not on account of any other practical motive or future advantage but rather from the idea of the dignity of a rational being who obeys no law except what he at the same time enacts himself.

In the kingdom of ends everything has either a price or a dignity. Whatever has a price can be replaced by something else as its equivalent; on the other hand, whatever is above all price, and therefore admits of no equivalent, has a dignity.

Whatever has reference to general human inclinations and needs has a market price; whatever, without presupposing any need, accords with a certain taste, i.e., a delight in the mere unpurposive play of our mental powers,[50] has an affective price; but that which constitutes the condition under which alone something can be an end in itself has not merely a relative worth, i.e., a price, but has an intrinsic worth, i.e., dignity. 435

Now morality is the condition under which alone a rational being can be an end in himself, for only thereby can he be a legislating member in the kingdom of ends. Hence morality and humanity, insofar as it is capable of morality, alone have dignity. Skill and diligence in work have a market price; wit, lively imagination, and humor have an affective price; but fidelity to promises and benevolence based on principles (not on instinct) have intrinsic worth. Neither nature nor art contain anything which in default of these could be put in their place; for their worth consists, not in the effects which arise from them, nor in the advantage and profit which they provide, but in mental dispositions, i.e., in the maxims of the will which are ready in this way to manifest themselves in action, even if they are not favored with success. Such actions also need no recommendation from any subjective disposition or taste so as to meet with immediate favor and delight; there is no need of any immediate propensity or feeling toward them. They exhibit the will performing them as an object of im-

---

49. [This is usually called the formula of the kingdom of ends.]

50. [See Kant, *Critique of Aesthetic Judgment*, §'s 1–5.]

mediate respect; and nothing but reason is required to impose them upon the will, which is not to be cajoled into them, since in the case of duties such cajoling would be a contradiction. This estimation, therefore, lets the worth of such a disposition be recognized as dignity and puts it infinitely beyond all price, with which it cannot in the least be brought into competition or comparison without, as it were, violating its sanctity.

What then is it that entitles the morally good disposition, or virtue, to make such lofty claims? It is nothing less than the share which such a disposition affords the rational being of legislating universal laws, so that he is fit to be a member in a possible kingdom of ends, for which his own nature has already determined him as an end in himself and therefore as a legislator in the kingdom of ends. Thereby is he free as regards all laws of nature, and he obeys only those laws which he gives to himself. Accordingly, his maxims can belong to a universal legislation to which he at the same time subjects himself. For nothing can have any worth other than what the law determines. But the legislation itself which determines all worth must for that very reason have dignity, i.e., unconditional and incomparable worth; and the word "respect" alone provides a suitable expression for the esteem which a rational being must have for it. Hence autonomy is the ground of the dignity of human nature and of every rational nature.

The aforementioned three ways of representing the principle of morality are at bottom only so many formulas of the very same law: one of them by itself contains a combination of the other two. Nevertheless, there is a difference in them, which is subjectively rather than objectively practical, viz., it is intended to bring an idea of reason closer to intuition (in accordance with a certain analogy) and thereby closer to feeling. All maxims have, namely,

1. A form, which consists in universality; and in this respect the formula of the moral imperative is expressed thus: maxims must be so chosen as if they were to hold as universal laws of nature.
2. A matter, viz., an end; and here the formula says that a rational being, inasmuch as he is by his very nature an end and hence an

end in himself, must serve in every maxim as a condition limiting all merely relative and arbitrary ends.
3. A complete determination of all maxims by the formula that all maxims proceeding from his own legislation ought to harmonize with a possible kingdom of ends as a kingdom of nature.[51] There is a progression here through the categories of the *unity* of the form of the will (its universality), the *plurality* of its matter (its objects, i.e., its ends), and the *totality* or completeness of its system of ends. But one does better if in moral judgment he follows the rigorous method and takes as his basis the universal formula of the categorical imperative: Act according to that maxim which can at the same time make itself a universal law. But if one wants also to secure acceptance for the moral law, it is very useful to bring one and the same action under the three aforementioned concepts and thus, as far as possible, to bring the moral law nearer to intuition.

We can now end where we started in the beginning, viz., the concept of an unconditionally good will. That will is absolutely good which cannot be evil, i.e., whose maxim, when made into a universal law, can never conflict with itself. This principle is therefore also its supreme law: Act always according to that maxim whose universality as a law you can at the same time will. This is the only condition under which a will can never be in conflict with itself, and such an imperative is categorical. Inasmuch as the validity of the will as a universal law for possible actions is analogous to the universal connection of the existence of things in accordance with universal laws, which is the formal aspect of nature in general, the categorical imperative can also be expressed thus:

51. Teleology considers nature as a kingdom of ends; morals regards a possible kingdom of ends as a kingdom of nature. In the former the kingdom of ends is a theoretical idea for explaining what exists. In the latter it is a practical idea for bringing about what does not exist but can be made actual by our conduct, i.e., what can be actualized in accordance with this very idea.

Act according to maxims which can at the same time have for their object themselves as universal laws of nature. In this way there is provided the formula for an absolutely good will.

Rational nature is distinguished from the rest of nature by the fact that it sets itself an end. This end would be the matter of every good will. But in the idea of an absolutely good will—good without any qualifying condition (of attaining this or that end)— complete abstraction must be made from every end that has to come about as an effect (since such would make every will only relatively good). And so the end must here be conceived, not as an end to be effected, but as an independently existing end. Hence it must be conceived only negatively, i.e., as an end which should never be acted against and therefore as one which in all willing must never be regarded merely as means but must always be esteemed at the same time as an end. Now this end can be nothing but the subject of all possible ends themselves, because this subject is at the same time the subject of a possible absolutely good will; for such a will cannot without contradiction be subordinated to any other object.

438 The principle: So act in regard to every rational being (yourself and others) that he may at the same time count in your maxim as an end in himself, is thus basically the same as the principle: Act on a maxim which at the same time contains in itself its own universal validity for every rational being. That in the use of means for every end my maxim should be restricted to the condition of its universal validity as a law for every subject says just the same as that a subject of ends, i.e., a rational being himself, must be made the ground for all maxims of actions and must thus be used never merely as means but as the supreme limiting condition in the use of all means, i.e., always at the same time as an end.

Now there follows incontestably from this that every rational being as an end in himself must be able to regard himself with reference to all laws to which he may be subject as being at the same time the legislator of universal law, for just this very fitness of his maxims for the legislation of universal law distinguishes him as an end in himself. There follows also that his dignity (prerogative) of being above all the mere things of nature implies that his maxims must be taken from the viewpoint that regards himself,

as well as every other rational being, as being legislative beings (and hence are they called persons). In this way there is possible a world of rational beings (*mundus intelligibilis*) as a kingdom of ends, because of the legislation belonging to all persons as members. Therefore, every rational being must so act as if he were through his maxim always a legislating member in the universal kingdom of ends. The formal principle of these maxims is this: So act as if your maxims were to serve at the same time as a universal law (for all rational beings). Thus a kingdom of ends is possible only on the analogy of a kingdom of nature; yet the former is possible only through maxims, i.e., self-imposed rules, while the latter is possible only through laws of efficient causes necessitated from without. Regardless of this difference and even though nature as a whole is viewed as a machine, yet insofar as nature stands in a relation to rational beings as its ends, it is on this account given the name of a kingdom of nature. Such a kingdom of ends would actually be realized through maxims whose rule is prescribed to all rational beings by the categorical imperative, if these maxims were universally obeyed. But even if a rational being himself strictly obeys such a maxim, he cannot for that reason count on everyone else's being true to it, nor can he expect the kingdom of nature and its purposive order to be in harmony with him as a fitting member of a kingdom of ends made possible by himself, i.e., he cannot expect the kingdom of nature to favor his expectation of happi- 439 ness. Nevertheless, the law: Act in accordance with the maxims of a member legislating universal laws for a merely possible kingdom of ends, remains in full force, since it commands categorically. And just in this lies the paradox that merely the dignity of humanity as rational nature without any further end or advantage to be thereby gained—and hence respect for a mere idea—should yet serve as an inflexible precept for the will; and that just this very independence of the maxims from all such incentives should constitute the sublimity of maxims and the worthiness of every rational subject to be a legislative member in the kingdom of ends, for otherwise he would have to be regarded as subject only to the natural law of his own needs. And even if the kingdom of nature as well as the kingdom of ends were thought of as both united under one sovereign so that the latter kingdom would thereby no longer remain a mere idea but would acquire true reality, then indeed the kingdom of ends would gain the addition of a strong incentive, but never any increase in its intrinsic worth. For this sole absolute legislator must, in spite of all this, always be thought of as judging the worth of rational beings solely by the disinterested conduct prescribed to themselves by means of this idea alone. The essence of things is not altered by their external relations; and whatever without reference to such relations alone constitutes the absolute worth of man is also what he must be judged by, whoever the judge may be, even the Supreme Being. Hence morality is the relation of actions to the autonomy of the will, i.e., to the possible legislation of universal law by means of the maxims of the will. That action which is compatible with the autonomy of the will is permitted; that which is not compatible is forbidden. That will whose maxims are necessarily in accord with the laws of autonomy is a holy, or absolutely good, will. The dependence of a will which is not absolutely good upon the principle of autonomy (i.e., moral necessitation) is obligation, which cannot therefore be applied to a holy will. The objective necessity of an action from obligation is called duty.

440 From what has just been said, there can now easily be explained how it happens that, although in the concept of duty we think of subjection to the law, yet at the same time we thereby ascribe a certain dignity and sublimity to the person who fulfills all his duties. For not insofar as he is subject to the moral law does he have sublimity, but rather has it only insofar as with regard to this very same law he is at the same time legislative, and only thereby is he subject to the law. We have also shown above[52] how neither fear nor inclination, but solely respect for the law, is the incentive which can give an action moral worth. Our own will, insofar as it were to act only under the condition of its being able to legislate universal law by means of its maxims—this will, ideally possible for us, is the proper object of respect. And the dignity of humanity consists just in its capacity to legislate universal law, though with the condition of humanity's being at the same time itself subject to this very same legislation.

52. [Ak. 400–402.]

Autonomy of the Will
As the Supreme Principle of Morality

Autonomy of the will is the property that the will has of being a law to itself (independently of any property of the objects of volition). The principle of autonomy is this: Always choose in such a way that in the same volition the maxims of the choice are at the same time present as universal law. That this practical rule is an imperative, i.e., that the will of every rational being is necessarily bound to the rule as a condition, cannot be proved by merely analyzing the concepts contained in it, since it is a synthetic proposition. For proof one would have to go beyond cognition of objects to a critical examination of the subject, i.e., go to a critique of pure practical reason, since this synthetic proposition which commands apodeictically must be capable of being cognized completely a priori. This task, however, does not belong to the present section. But that the above principle of autonomy is the sole principle of morals can quite well be shown by mere analysis of the concepts of morality; for thereby the principle of morals is found to be necessarily a categorical imperative, which commands nothing more nor less than this very autonomy.

Heteronomy of the Will   441
As the Source of All Spurious
Principles of Morality

If the will seeks the law that is to determine it anywhere but in the fitness of its maxims for its own legislation of universal laws, and if it thus goes outside of itself and seeks this law in the character of any of its objects, then heteronomy always results. The will in that case does not give itself the law, but the object does so because of its relation to the will. This relation, whether it rests on inclination or on representations of reason, admits only of hypothetical imperatives: I ought to do something because I will something else. On the other hand, the moral, and hence categorical, imperative says that I ought to act in this way or that way, even though I did not will something else. For example, the former says that I ought not to lie if I would maintain my reputation; the latter says that I ought not to lie even though lying were to bring me not the slightest discredit. The moral imperative must therefore abstract from every object to such an extent that no object has any influence at all on the will, so that practical reason (the will) may not merely minister to an interest not belonging to it but may merely show its own commanding authority as the supreme legislation. Thus, for example, I ought to endeavor to promote the happiness of others, not as though its realization were any concern of mine (whether by immediate inclination or by any satisfaction indirectly gained through reason), but merely because a maxim which excludes it cannot be comprehended as a universal law in one and the same volition.

Classification of All Possible Principles of Morality Founded upon the Assumed Fundamental Concept of Heteronomy

Here as elsewhere human reason in its pure use, so long as it lacks a critical examination, first tried every possible wrong way before it succeeded in finding the only right way.

All principles that can be taken from this point of 442 view are either empirical or rational. The first kind, drawn from the principle of happiness, are based upon either physical or moral feeling. The second kind, drawn from the principle of perfection, are based upon either the rational concept of perfection as a possible effect of our will or else upon the concept of an independent perfection (the will of God) as a determining cause of our will.

Empirical principles are wholly unsuited to serve as the foundation for moral laws. For the universality with which such laws ought to hold for all rational beings without exception (the unconditioned practical necessity imposed by moral laws upon such beings) is lost if the basis of these laws is taken from the particular constitution of human nature or from the accidental circumstances in which such nature is placed. But the principle of one's own happiness is the most objectionable. Such is the case not merely because this principle is false and because experience contradicts the supposition that well-being is always proportional to well-doing, nor yet merely because

this principle contributes nothing to the establishment of morality, inasmuch as making a man happy is quite different from making him good and making him prudent and sharp-sighted for his own advantage quite different from making him virtuous. Rather, such is the case because this principle of one's own happiness bases morality upon incentives that undermine it rather than establish it and that totally destroy its sublimity, inasmuch as motives to virtue are put in the same class as motives to vice and inasmuch as such incentives merely teach one to become better at calculation, while the specific difference between virtue and vice is entirely obliterated. On the other hand, moral feeling, this alleged special sense,[53] remains closer to morality than does the aforementioned principle of one's own happiness. Yet the appeal to the principle of moral feeling is superficial, since men who cannot think believe that they will be helped out by feeling, even when the question is solely one of universal laws. They do so even though feelings naturally differ from one another by an infinity of degrees, so that feelings are not capable of providing a uniform measure of good and evil; furthermore, they do so even though one man cannot by his feeling judge validly at all for other men. Nevertheless, the principle of moral feeling is closer to morality and its dignity than is the principle of one's own happiness inasmuch as the former principle pays virtue the honor of ascribing to her directly the satisfac- 443 tion and esteem that is held for her, and does not, as it were, tell her to her face that our attachment to her rests not on her beauty but only on our advantage.

Among the rational principles of morality (or those arising from reason rather than from feeling) there is the ontological concept of perfection. It is empty,

53. I count the principle of moral feeling under that of happiness, because every empirical interest promises to contribute to our well-being through the amenity afforded by something, whether immediately and without any reference to advantage or with reference to advantage. Similarly, the principle of sympathy for the happiness of others must with Hutcheson be counted along with the principle of moral sense as adopted by him. [Francis Hutcheson (1694–1747) was Professor of Moral Philosophy in the University of Glasgow, Scotland. He was the main proponent of the doctrine of moral sense.]

indeterminate, and hence of no use for finding in the immeasurable field of possible reality the maximum sum suitable for us. Furthermore, in attempting to distinguish specifically between the reality just mentioned and every other, it exhibits as inevitable tendency for turning about in a circle and cannot avoid tacitly presupposing the morality that it has to explain. Nevertheless, it is better than the theological concept, whereby morality is derived from a divine and most perfect will. It is better not merely because we cannot intuit divine perfection but can only derive it from our own concepts, among which morality is foremost; but also because if it is not so derived (and being thus derived would involve a crudely circular explanation), then the only remaining concept of God's will is drawn from such characteristics as desire for glory and dominion combined with such frightful representations as those of might and vengeance. Any system of morals based on such notions would be directly opposed to morality.

But if I had to choose between the concept of moral sense and that of perfection in general (both of which at least do not weaken morality, even though they are not at all capable of serving as its foundation), I would decide for the latter because it at least withdraws the decision of the question from sensibility and brings it to the court of pure reason, though it does not even here get any decision. Furthermore, I would choose the concept of perfection in general because it preserves the indeterminate idea (of a will good in itself) free from falsity until it can be more precisely determined.

For the rest, I believe that I may be excused from a lengthy refutation of all these doctrines. Such a refutation would be merely superfluous labor, since it is so easy and is presumably so well understood even by those whose office requires them to declare themselves for one of these theories (since their hearers would not tolerate suspension of judgment). But what interests us more here is to know that these principles never lay down anything but heteronomy of the will as the first ground of morality and that they must, consequently, necessarily fail in their purpose.

444 In every case where an object of the will must be laid down as the foundation for prescribing a rule to determine the will, there the rule is nothing but heteronomy. The imperative is then conditioned, viz., if or because one wills this object, one should act thus or so. Hence the imperative can never command morally, i.e., categorically. Now the object may determine the will by means of inclination, as in the case of the principle of one's own happiness, or by means of reason directed to objects of our volition in general, as in the case of the principle of perfection. Yet in both cases the will never determines itself immediately by the thought of an action, but only by the incentive that the anticipated effect of the action has upon the will: I ought to do something because I will something else. And here must yet another law be assumed in me the subject, whereby I necessarily will this something else; this other law in turn requires an imperative to restrict this maxim. For the impulse which the representation of an object that is possible by means of our powers is to exert upon the will of a subject in accordance with his natural constitution belongs to the nature of the subject, whether to his sensibility (his inclination and taste) or to his understanding and reason, whose employment on an object is by the particular arrangement of their nature attended with satisfaction; consequently, the law would, properly speaking, be given by nature. This law, insofar as it is a law of nature, must be known and proved through experience and is therefore in itself contingent and hence is not fit to be an apodeictic practical rule, such as a moral rule must be. The law of nature under discussion is always merely heteronomy of the will; the will does not give itself the law, but a foreign impulse gives the law to the will by means of the subject's nature, which is adapted to receive such an impulse.

An absolutely good will, whose principle must be a categorical imperative, will therefore be indeterminate as regards all objects and will contain merely the form of willing; and indeed that form is autonomy. This is to say that the fitness of the maxims of every good will to make themselves universal laws is itself the only law that the will of every rational being imposes on itself, without needing to assume any incentive or interest as a basis.

How such a synthetic practical a priori proposition is possible and why it is necessary are problems whose solution does not lie any longer within the bounds of a metaphysics of morals. Furthermore, we have not here asserted the truth of this proposition, much 445 less professed to have within our power a proof of it. We simply showed by developing the universally accepted concept of morality that autonomy of the will is unavoidably bound up with it, or rather is its very foundation. Whoever, then, holds morality to be something real, and not a chimerical idea without any truth, must also admit the principle here put forward. Hence this section, like the first, was merely analytic. To show that morality is not a mere phantom of the brain, which morality cannot be if the categorical imperative, and with it the autonomy of the will, is true and absolutely necessary as an a priori principle, we require a possible synthetic use of pure practical reason. But we must not venture on this use without prefacing it with a critical examination of this very faculty of reason. In the last section we shall give the main outlines of this critical examination as far as sufficient for our purpose.[54]

446

THIRD SECTION

TRANSITION FROM A METAPHYSICS OF MORALS TO A CRITIQUE OF PURE PRACTICAL REASON

The Concept of Freedom Is the Key for an Explanation of the Autonomy of the Will

The will is a kind of causality belonging to living beings insofar as they are rational; freedom would be the property of this causality that makes it effective independent of any determination by alien causes. Similarly, natural necessity is the property of the causality of all non-rational beings by which they are determined to activity through the influence of alien causes.

The foregoing explanation of freedom is negative

54. [The ensuing Third Section is difficult to grasp. Kant expressed himself more clearly regarding the topics discussed there in the *Critique of Practical Reason*, Part I, Book 1 ("Analytic of Pure Practical Reason").]

and is therefore unfruitful for attaining an insight regarding its essence; but there arises from it a positive concept, which as such is richer and more fruitful. The concept of causality involves that of laws according to which something that we call cause must entail something else—namely, the effect. Therefore freedom is certainly not lawless, even though it is not a property of will in accordance with laws of nature. It must, rather, be a causality in accordance with immutable laws, which, to be sure, is of a special kind; otherwise a free will would be something absurd. As we have already seen [in the preceding paragraph], natural necessity is a heteronomy of efficient causes, inasmuch as every effect is possible only in accordance with the law that something else determines the efficient cause to exercise its causality. What else, then, can freedom of the will be but autonomy, i.e., the property that the will has of being a law to itself? The proposition that the will is in every action a law to itself expresses, however, nothing but the principle of acting according to no other maxim than that which can at the same time have itself as a universal law for its object. Now this is precisely the formula of the categorical imperative and is the principle of morality. Thus a free will and a will subject to moral laws are one and the same.

447

Therefore if freedom of the will is presupposed, morality (together with its principle) follows by merely analyzing the concept of freedom. However, the principle of morality is, nevertheless, a synthetic proposition: viz., an absolutely good will is one whose maxim can always have itself as content when such maxim is regarded as a universal law; it is synthetic because this property of the will's maxim can never be found by analyzing the concept of an absolutely good will. Now such synthetic propositions are possible only as follows—two cognitions are bound together through their connection with a third in which both of them are to be found. The positive concept of freedom furnishes this third cognition, which cannot, as is the case with physical causes, be the nature of the world of sense (in whose concept is combined the concept of something as cause in relation to something else as effect). We cannot here yet show straight away what this third cognition is which freedom indicates to us and of which we have an a priori idea, nor can we as yet conceive of the deduction of the concept of freedom from pure practical reason and therewith also the possibility of a categorical imperative. Rather, we require some further preparation.

Freedom Must Be Presupposed as a Property of the Will of All Rational Beings

It is not enough to ascribe freedom to our will, on whatever ground, if we have not also sufficient reason for attributing it to all rational beings. For inasmuch as morality serves as a law for us only insofar as we are rational beings, it must also be valid for all rational beings. And since morality must be derived solely from the property of freedom, one must show that freedom is also the property of the will of all rational beings. It is not enough to prove freedom from certain alleged experiences of human nature (such a proof is indeed absolutely impossible, and so freedom can be proved only a priori). Rather, one must show that freedom belongs universally to the activity of rational beings endowed with a will. Now I say that every being who cannot act in any way other than under the idea of freedom is for this very reason free from a practical point of view. This is to say that for such a being all the laws that are inseparably bound up with freedom are valid just as much as if the will of such a being could be declared to be free in itself for reasons that are valid for theoretical philosophy.[55] Now I claim that we must necessarily attribute to every rational being which has a will also the idea of freedom, under which only can such a being act. For in such a being we think of a reason that is practical, i.e., that has causality in reference to its objects. Now we cannot possibly think of a reason that consciously lets itself be directed from outside as regards its judg-

448

ments; for in that case the subject would ascribe the determination of his faculty of judgment not to his reason, but to an impulse. Reason must regard itself as the author of its principles independent of foreign influences. Therefore as practical reason or as the will of a rational being must reason regard itself as free. This is to say that the will of a rational being can be a will of its own only under the idea of freedom, and that such a will must therefore, from a practical point of view, be attributed to all rational beings.

Concerning the Interest Attached to the Ideas of Morality

We have finally traced the determinate concept of morality back to the idea of freedom, but we could not prove freedom to be something actual in ourselves and in human nature. We saw merely that we must presuppose it if we want to think of a being as rational and as endowed with consciousness of its causality as regards actions, i.e., as endowed with a will. And so we find that on the very same ground we must attribute to every being endowed with reason and a will this property of determining itself to action under the idea of its own freedom.

449

Now there resulted from the presupposition of this idea of freedom also the consciousness of a law of action: that the subjective principles of actions, i.e., maxims, must always be so adopted that they can also be valid objectively, i.e., universally, as principles, and can therefore serve as universal laws of our own legislation. But why, then, should I subject myself to this principle simply as a rational being and by so doing also subject to this principle all other beings endowed with reason? I am willing to grant that no interest impels me to do so, because this would not give a categorical imperative. But nonetheless I must necessarily take an interest in it and discern how this comes about, for this *ought* is properly a *would* which is valid for every rational being, provided that reason is practical for such a being without hindrances. In the case of beings who, like ourselves, are also affected by sensibility, i.e., by incentives of a kind other than the purely rational, and who do not always act as reason by itself would act, this necessity of action is expressed only as an *ought*, and the subjective necessity is to be distinguished from the objective.

55. I adopt this method of assuming as sufficient for our purpose that freedom is presupposed merely as an idea by rational beings in their actions in order that I may avoid the necessity of having to prove freedom from a theoretical point of view as well. For even if this latter problem is left unresolved, the same laws that would bind a being who was really free are valid equally for a being who cannot act otherwise than under the idea of its own freedom. Thus we can relieve ourselves of the burden which presses on the theory.

It therefore seems as if we have in the idea of freedom actually only presupposed the moral law, namely, the principle of the autonomy of the will, and as if we could not prove its reality and objective necessity independently. In that case we should indeed still have gained something quite considerable by at least determining the genuine principle more exactly than had previously been done. But as regards its validity and the practical necessity of subjecting oneself to it, we would have made no progress. We could give no satisfactory answer if asked the following questions: why must the universal validity of our maxim taken as a law be a condition restricting our actions; upon what do we base the worth that we assign to this way of acting—a worth that is supposed to be so great that there can be no higher interest; how does it happen that by this alone does man believe that he feels his own personal worth, in comparison with which that of an agreeable or disagreeable condition is to be regarded as nothing.

Indeed we do sometimes find that we can take an interest in a personal characteristic which involves no interest in any [external] condition but only makes us capable of participating in the condition in case reason were to effect the allotment. This is to say that the mere worthiness of being happy can of itself be of interest even without the motive of participating in this happiness. This judgment, however, is in fact only the result of the importance that we have already presupposed as belonging to moral laws (when by the idea of freedom we divorce ourselves from all empirical interest). However, in this way we are not as yet able to have any insight into why it is that we should divorce ourselves from such interest, i.e., that we should consider ourselves as free in action and yet hold ourselves as subject to certain laws so as to find solely in our own person a worth that can compensate us for the loss of everything that gives worth to our condition. We do not see how this is possible and hence how the moral law can obligate us.

One must frankly admit that there is here a sort of circle from which, so it seems, there is no way to escape. In the order of efficient causes we assume that we are free so that we may think of ourselves as subject to moral laws in the order of ends. And we then think of ourselves as subject to these laws because we have attributed to ourselves freedom of the will.

Freedom and self-legislation of the will are both autonomy and are hence reciprocal concepts. Since they are reciprocal, one of them cannot be used to explain the other or to supply its ground, but can at most be used only for logical purposes to bring seemingly different conceptions of the same object under a single concept (just as different fractions of the same value are reduced to lowest terms).

However, one recourse still remains open to us, namely, to inquire whether we do not take one point of view when by means of freedom we think of ourselves as a priori efficient causes, and another point of view when we represent ourselves with reference to our actions as effects which we see before our eyes.

No subtle reflection is required for the following observation, which even the commonest understanding may be supposed to make, though it does so in its own fashion through some obscure discrimination of the faculty of judgment which it calls feeling: all representations that come to us without our choice (such as those of the senses) enable us to know objects only as they affect us; what they may be in themselves remains unknown to us. Therefore, even with the closest attention and the greatest clarity that the understanding can bring to such representations, we can attain to a mere knowledge of appearances but never to knowledge of things in themselves. Once this distinction is made (perhaps merely as a result of observing the difference between representations which are given to us from without and in which we are passive from those which we produce entirely from ourselves and in which we show our own activity), then there follows of itself that we must admit and assume that behind the appearances there is something else which is not appearance, namely, things in themselves. Inasmuch as we can never cognize them except as they affect us [through our senses], we must admit that we can never come any nearer to them nor ever know what they are in themselves. This must provide a distinction, however crude, between a world of sense and a world of understanding; the former can vary considerably according to the difference of sensibility [and sense impressions] in various observers, while the latter, which is the basis of the former, remains always the same. Even with regard to himself, a man cannot presume to know what he is in himself by means of the acquaintance which he has through internal sensation. For since he does not, as it were, create himself and since he acquires the concept of himself not a priori but empirically, it is natural that he can attain knowledge even about himself only through inner sense and therefore only through the appearance of his nature and the way in which his consciousness is affected. But yet he must necessarily assume that beyond his own subject's constitution as composed of nothing but appearances there must be something else as basis, namely, his ego as constituted in itself. Therefore with regard to mere perception and the receptivity of sensations, he must count himself as belonging to the world of sense; but with regard to whatever there may be in him of pure activity (whatever reaches consciousness immediately and not through affecting the senses) he must count himself as belonging to the intellectual world, of which he has, however, no further knowledge.

452   Such a conclusion must be reached by a reflective man regarding all the things that may be presented to him. It is presumably to be found even in the most ordinary understanding, which, as is well known, is quite prone to expect that behind objects of the senses there is something else invisible and acting of itself. But such understanding spoils all this by making the invisible again sensible, i.e., it wants to make the invisible an object of intuition; and thereby does it become not a bit wiser.

Now man really finds in himself a faculty which distinguishes him from all other things and even from himself insofar as he is affected by objects. That faculty is reason, which as pure spontaneity is elevated even above understanding. For although the latter is also spontaneous and does not, like sense, merely contain representations that arise only when one is affected by things (and is therefore passive), yet understanding can produce by its activity no other concepts than those which merely serve to bring sensuous representations [intuitions] under rules and thereby to unite them in one consciousness. Without this use of sensibility, understanding would think nothing at all. Reason, on the other hand, shows such a pure spontaneity in the case of what are called ideas that it goes far beyond anything that sensibility can offer and shows its highest occupation in distinguishing the world of sense from the world of understanding, thereby prescribing limits to the understanding itself.

Therefore a rational being must regard himself qua intelligence (and hence not from the side of his lower powers) as belonging not to the world of sense but to the world of understanding. Therefore he has two standpoints from which he can regard himself and know laws of the use of his powers and hence of all his actions: first, insofar as he belongs to the world of sense subject to laws of nature (heteronomy); secondly, insofar as he belongs to the intelligible world subject to laws which, independent of nature, are not empirical but are founded only on reason.

As a rational being and hence as belonging to the intelligible world, can man never think of the causality of his own will except under the idea of freedom; for independence from the determining causes of the world of sense (an independence which reason must always attribute to itself) is freedom. Now the idea of freedom is inseparably connected with the concept of autonomy, and this in turn with the universal principle of morality, which ideally is the ground of all   453 actions of rational beings, just as natural law is the ground of all appearances.

The suspicion that we raised earlier is now removed, viz., that there might be a hidden circle involved in our inference from freedom to autonomy, and from this to the moral law—this is to say that we had perhaps laid down the idea of freedom only for the sake of the moral law in order subsequently to infer this law in its turn from freedom, and that we had therefore not been able to assign any ground at all for this law but had only assumed it by begging a principle which well-disposed souls would gladly concede us but which we could never put forward as a demonstrable proposition. But now we see that when we think of ourselves as free, we transfer ourselves into the intelligible world as members and know the autonomy of the will together with its consequence, morality; whereas when we think of ourselves as obligated, we consider ourselves as belonging to the world of sense and yet at the same time to the intelligible world.

How Is a Categorical Imperative Possible?

The rational being counts himself, qua intelligence, as belonging to the intelligible world, and only insofar as he is an efficient cause belonging to the intelligible world does he call his causality a will. But on the other side, he is conscious of himself as being also a part of the world of sense, where his actions are found as mere appearances of that causality. The possibility of these actions cannot, however, be discerned through such causality, which we do not know; rather, these actions as belonging to the world of sense must be viewed as determined by other appearances, namely, desires and inclinations. Therefore, if I were solely a member of the intelligible world, then all my actions would perfectly conform to the principle of the autonomy of a pure will; if I were solely a part of the world of sense, my actions would have to be taken as in complete conformity with the natural law of desires and inclinations, i.e., with the heteronomy of nature. (My actions would in the first case rest on the supreme principle of morality, in the second case on that of happiness.) But the intelligible world contains the ground of the world of sense and therefore also the ground of its laws; consequently, the intelligible world is (and must be thought of as) directly legislative for my will (which belongs wholly to the intelligible world). Therefore, even though on the one hand I must regard myself as a being belonging to the world of sense, yet on the other hand shall I 454 have to know myself as an intelligence and as subject to the law of the intelligible world, i.e., to reason, which contains this law in the idea of freedom, and hence to know myself as subject to the autonomy of the will. Consequently, I must regard the laws of the intelligible world as imperatives for me, and the actions conforming to this principle as duties.

And thus are categorical imperatives possible because the idea of freedom makes me a member of an intelligible world. Now if I were a member of only that world, all my actions *would* always accord with autonomy of the will. But since I intuit myself at the same time as a member of the world of sense, my actions *ought* so to accord. This categorical *ought* presents a synthetic a priori proposition, whereby in addition to my will as affected by sensuous desires there is added further the idea of the same will, but as belonging to the intelligible world, pure and practical of itself, and as containing the supreme condition of the former will insofar as reason is concerned. All this is similar to the way in which concepts [categories] of the understanding, which of themselves signify

nothing but the form of law in general, are added to intuitions of the world of sense and thus make possible synthetic a priori propositions, upon which all knowledge of nature rests.

The practical use of ordinary human reason bears out the correctness of this deduction. There is no one, not even the meanest villain, provided only that he is otherwise accustomed to the use of reason, who, when presented with examples of honesty of purpose, of steadfastness in following good maxims, and of sympathy and general benevolence (even when involved with great sacrifices of advantages and comfort) does not wish that he might also possess these qualities. Yet he cannot attain these in himself only because of his inclinations and impulses; but at the same time he wishes to be free from such inclinations which are a burden to him. He thereby proves that by having a will free of sensuous impulses he transfers himself in thought into an order of things entirely different from that of his desires in the field of sensibility. Since he cannot expect to obtain by the aforementioned wish any gratification of his desires or any condition that would satisfy any of his actual or even conceivable inclinations (inasmuch as through such an expectation the very idea that elicited the wish would be deprived of its preeminence) he can only expect a greater intrinsic worth of his own person. This better person he believes himself to be when he transfers himself to the standpoint of a 455 member of the intelligible world, to which he is involuntarily forced by the idea of freedom, i.e., of being independent of determination by causes of the world of sense. From this standpoint he is conscious of having a good will, which by his own admission constitutes the law for the bad will belonging to him as a member of the world of sense—a law whose authority he acknowledges even while he transgresses it. The moral *ought* is, therefore, a necessary *would* insofar as he is a member of the intelligible world, and is thought by him as an *ought* only insofar as he regards himself as being at the same time a member of the world of sense.

Concerning the Extreme Limit of All Practical Philosophy

All men think of themselves as free as far as their will is concerned. Hence arise all judgments upon actions as being such as ought to have been done, even though they were not done. But this freedom is not a concept of experience, nor can it be such, since it always holds, even though experience shows the opposite of those requirements represented as necessary under the presupposition of freedom. On the other hand, it is just as necessary that whatever happens should be determined without any exception according to laws of nature; and this necessity of nature is likewise no concept of experience, just because it involves the concept of necessity and thus of a priori knowledge. But this concept of nature is confirmed by experience and must inevitably be presupposed if there is to be possible experience, which is coherent knowledge of the objects of sense in accordance with universal laws. Freedom is, therefore, only an idea of reason whose objective reality is in itself questionable; but nature is a concept of the understanding, which proves, and necessarily must prove, its reality by examples from experience.

There arises from this a dialectic of reason, since the freedom attributed to the will seems to contradict the necessity of nature. And even though at this parting of the ways reason for speculative purposes finds the road of natural necessity much better worn and more serviceable than that of freedom, yet for practical purposes the footpath of freedom is the only one 456 upon which it is possible to make use of reason in our conduct. Therefore, it is just as impossible for the most subtle philosophy as for the most ordinary human reason to argue away freedom. Hence philosophy must assume that no real contradiction will be found between freedom and natural necessity in the same human actions, for it cannot give up the concept of nature any more than that of freedom.

Nevertheless, even though one might never be able to comprehend how freedom is possible, yet this apparent contradiction must at least be removed in a convincing manner. For if the thought of freedom contradicts itself or nature, which is equally necessary, then freedom would have to be completely given up in favor of natural necessity.

It would, however, be impossible to escape this contradiction if the subject, deeming himself free, were to think of himself in the same sense or in the very same relationship when he calls himself free as when he assumes himself subject to the law of nature regarding the same action. Therefore, an unavoidable problem of speculative philosophy is at least to show that its illusion regarding the contradiction rests on our thinking of man in a different sense and relation when we call him free from when we regard him as being a part of nature and hence as subject to the laws of nature. Hence it must show not only that both can coexist very well, but that both must be thought of as necessarily united in the same subject; for otherwise no explanation could be given as to why reason should be burdened with an idea which involves us in a perplexity that is sorely embarrassing to reason in its theoretic use, even though it may without contradiction be united with another idea that is sufficiently established. This duty, however, is incumbent solely on speculative philosophy in order that it may clear the way for practical philosophy. Thus the philosopher has no option as to whether he will remove the apparent contradiction or leave it untouched; for in the latter case the theory regarding this could be *bonum vacans*,[56] into the possession of which the fatalist can justifiably enter and chase all morality out of its supposed property as occupying it without title.

Nevertheless, one cannot here say as yet that the boundary of practical philosophy begins. For the settlement of the controversy does not belong to practical philosophy; the latter only requires speculative reason to put an end to the dissension in which it is entangled 457 as regards theoretical questions in order that practical reason may have rest and security from external attacks that might make disputable the ground upon which it wants to build.

The just claim to freedom of the will made even by ordinary human reason is founded on the consciousness and the admitted presupposition that reason is independent of mere subjective determination by causes which together make up what belongs only to sensation and comes under the general designation of sensibility. Regarding himself in this way as intelligence, man thereby puts himself into another order of things. And when he thinks of himself as intelligence endowed with a will and consequently with causality, he puts himself into relation with determining grounds of a kind altogether different from the kind when he perceives himself as a phenomenon in the

56. [vacant property]

world of sense (as he really is also) and subjects his causality to external determination according to laws of nature. Now he soon realizes that both can—and indeed must—hold good at the same time. For there is not the slightest contradiction involved in saying that a thing as appearance (belonging to the world of sense) is subject to certain laws, while it is independent of those laws when regarded as a thing or being in itself. That man must represent and think of himself in this twofold way rests, on the one hand, upon the consciousness of himself as an object affected through the senses and, on the other hand, upon the consciousness of himself as intelligence, i.e., as independent of sensuous impulses in his use of reason (and hence as belonging to the intelligible world).

And hence man claims that he has a will which reckons to his account nothing that belongs merely to his desires and inclinations, and which, on the contrary, thinks of actions that can be performed only by disregarding all desires and sensuous incitements as being possible and as indeed being necessary for him. The causality of such actions lies in man as intelligence and lies in the laws of such effects and actions as are in accordance with principles of an intelligible world, of which he knows nothing more than that in such a world reason alone, and indeed pure reason independently of sensibility, gives the law. Furthermore, since he is in such a world his proper self only as intelligence (whereas regarded as a human being he is merely an appearance of himself), those laws apply to him immediately and categorically. Consequently, incitements from inclinations and impulses (and hence from the whole nature of the world of sense) cannot impair the laws of his 458 willing insofar as he is intelligence. Indeed he does not even hold himself responsible for such inclinations and impulses or ascribe them to his proper self, i.e., his will, although he does ascribe to his will any indulgence which he might extend to them if he allowed them any influence on his maxims to the detriment of the rational laws of his will.

When practical reason thinks itself into an intelligible world, it does not in the least thereby transcend its limits, as it would if it tried to enter it by intuition or sensation. The thought of an intelligible world is merely negative as regards the world of sense. The latter world does not give reason any laws for deter-

mining the will and is positive only in this single point, viz., it simultaneously combines freedom as negative determination with a positive faculty and even a causality of reason. This causality is designated as a will to act in such a way that the principle of actions may accord with the essential character of a rational cause, i.e., with the condition that the maxim of these actions have universal validity as a law. But if practical reason were to bring in an object of the will, i.e., a motive of action, from the intelligible world, then it would overstep its boundaries and pretend to be acquainted with something of which it knows nothing. The concept of an intelligible world is thus only a point of view which reason sees itself compelled to take outside of appearances in order to think of itself as practical. If the influences of sensibility were determining for man, reason would not be able to take this point of view, which is nonetheless necessary if he is not to be denied the consciousness of himself as intelligence and hence as a rational cause that is active through reason, i.e., free in its operation. This thought certainly involves the idea of an order and a legislation different from that of the mechanism of nature which applies to the world of sense; and it makes necessary the concept of an intelligible world (i.e., the whole of rational beings as things in themselves). But it makes not the slightest claim to anything more than to think of such a world as regards merely its formal condition—i.e., the universality of the will's maxims as laws and thus the will's autonomy, which alone is consistent with freedom. On the contrary, all laws determined by reference to an object yield heteronomy, which can be found only in laws of nature and can apply only to the world of sense.

But reason would overstep all its bounds if it undertook to explain how pure reason can be practical. 459 This is exactly the same problem as explaining how freedom is possible.

For we can explain nothing but what we can reduce to laws whose object can be given in some possible experience. But freedom is a mere idea, whose objective reality can in no way be shown in accordance with laws of nature and consequently not in any possible experience. Therefore, the idea of freedom can never admit of comprehension or even of insight, because it cannot by any analogy have an example falling under it. It holds only as a necessary presupposition of reason in a being who believes himself conscious of a will, i.e., of a faculty distinct from mere desire (namely, a faculty of determining himself to action as intelligence and hence in accordance with laws of reason independently of natural instincts). But where determination according to laws of nature ceases, there likewise ceases all explanation and nothing remains but defense, i.e., refutation of the objections of those who profess to have seen deeper into the essence of things and thereupon boldly declare freedom to be impossible. One can only show them that their supposed discovery of a contradiction lies nowhere but here: in order to make the law of nature applicable to human actions, they have necessarily had to regard man as an appearance; and now when they are required to think of man qua intelligence as thing in himself as well, they still persist in regarding him as appearance. In that case, to be sure, the exemption of man's causality (i.e., his will) from all the natural laws of the world of sense would, as regards one and the same subject, give rise to a contradiction. But this disappears if they would but bethink themselves and admit, as is reasonable, that behind appearances there must lie as their ground also things in themselves (though hidden) and that the laws of their operations cannot be expected to be the same as those that govern their appearances.

460 The subjective impossibility of explaining freedom of the will is the same as the impossibility of discovering and explaining an interest[57] which man can take

in moral laws. Nevertheless, he does indeed take such an interest, the basis of which in us is called moral feeling. Some people have falsely construed this feeling to be the standard of our moral judgment, whereas it must rather be regarded as the subjective effect that the law exercises upon the will, while reason alone furnishes the objective grounds of such moral feeling.

In order to will what reason alone prescribes as an *ought* for sensuously affected rational beings, there certainly must be a power of reason to infuse a feeling of pleasure or satisfaction in the fulfillment of duty, and hence there has to be a causality of reason to determine sensibility in accordance with rational principles. But it is quite impossible to discern, i.e., to make a priori conceivable, how a mere thought which itself contains nothing sensuous can produce a sensation of pleasure or displeasure. For here is a special kind of causality regarding which, as with all causality, we can determine nothing a priori but must consult experience alone. However, experience can provide us with no relation of cause and effect except between two objects of experience. But in this case pure reason by means of mere ideas (which furnish no object at all for experience) is to be the cause of an effect that admittedly lies in experience. Consequently, there is for us men no possibility at all for an explanation as to how and why the universality of a maxim as a law, and hence morality, interests us. This much only is certain: the moral law is valid for us not because it interests us (for this is heteronomy and the dependence of practical reason on sensibility, viz., on an underlying feeling whereby reason could 461 never be morally legislative; but, rather, the moral law interests us because it is valid for us as men, since it has sprung from our will as intelligence and hence from our proper self. But what belongs to mere appearance is necessarily subordinated by reason to the nature of the thing in itself.

Thus the question as to how a categorical imperative is possible can be answered to the extent that there can be supplied the sole presupposition under which such an imperative is alone possible — namely, the idea of freedom. The necessity of this presupposition is discernible, and this much is sufficient for the

_____

57. Interest is that by which reason becomes practical, i.e., a cause determining the will. Therefore one says of rational beings only that they take an interest in something; non-rational creatures feel only sensuous impulses. Reason takes an immediate interest in the action only when the universal validity of the maxim of the action is a sufficient determining ground of the will. Such an interest alone is pure. But when reason is able to determine the will only by means of another object of desire or under the presupposition of some special feeling in the subject, then reason takes only a mediate interest in the action. And since reason of itself alone without the help of experience can discover neither objects of the will nor a special feeling underlying the will, the latter interest would be only empirical and not a pure rational interest. The logical interest of reason (viz.,

to extend its insights) is never immediate, but presupposes purposes for which reason might be used.

practical use of reason, i.e., for being convinced as to the validity of this imperative, and hence also of the moral law; but how this presupposition itself is possible can never be discerned by any human reason. However, on the presupposition of freedom of the will of an intelligence, there necessarily follows the will's autonomy as the formal condition under which alone the will can be determined. To presuppose this freedom of the will (without involving any contradiction with the principle of natural necessity in the connection of appearances in the world of sense) is not only quite possible (as speculative philosophy can show), but is without any further condition also necessary for a rational being conscious of his causality through reason and hence conscious of a will (which is different from desires) as he makes such freedom in practice, i.e., in idea, the underlying condition of all his voluntary actions. But how pure reason can be practical by itself without other incentives taken from whatever source—i.e., how the mere principle of the universal validity of all reason's maxims as laws (which would certainly be the form of a pure practical reason) can by itself, without any matter (object) of the will in which some antecedent interest might be taken, furnish an incentive and produce an interest which could be called purely moral; or, in other words, how pure reason could be practical; to explain all this is quite beyond the power of human reason, and all the effort and work of seeking such an explanation is wasted.

It is just the same as if I tried to find out how freedom itself is possible as causality of a will. For I thereby leave the philosophical basis of explanation, and I have no other basis. Now I could indeed flutter about in the world of intelligences, i.e., in the intelligible world still remaining to me. But even though I have an idea of such a world—an idea which has its own good grounds—yet I have not the slightest acquaintance with such a world and can never attain such acquaintance by all the efforts of my natural faculty of reason. This intelligible world signifies only a something that remains over when I have excluded from the determining grounds of my will everything that belongs to the world of sense, so as to restrict the principle of having all motives come from the field of sensibility. By so doing I set bounds to this field and show that it does not contain absolutely

everything within itself but that beyond it there is still something more, regarding which, however, I have no further acquaintance. After the exclusion of all matter, i.e., cognition of objects, from pure reason which thinks this ideal, nothing remains over for me except such reason's form, viz., the practical law of the universal validity of maxims; and in conformity with this law I think of reason in its relation to a pure intelligible world as a possible efficient cause, i.e., as a cause determining the will. An incentive must in this case be wholly absent; this idea of an intelligible world would here have to be itself the incentive or have to be that in which reason originally took an interest. But to make this conceivable is precisely the problem that we cannot solve.

Here then is the extreme limit of all moral inquiry. To determine this limit is of great importance for the following considerations. On the one hand, reason should not, to the detriment of morals, search around in the world of sense for the supreme motive and for some interest that is conceivable but is nonetheless empirical. On the other hand, reason should not flap its wings impotently, without leaving the spot, in a space that for it is empty, namely, the space of transcendent concepts that is called the intelligible world, and thereby lose itself among mere phantoms of the brain. Furthermore, the idea of a pure intelligible world regarded as a whole of all intelligences to which we ourselves belong as rational beings (even though we are from another standpoint also members of the world of sense) remains always a useful and permissible idea for the purpose of a rational belief, although all knowledge ends at its boundary. This idea produces in us a lively interest in the moral law by means of the splendid ideal of a universal kingdom of ends in themselves (rational beings), to which we can belong as members only if we carefully conduct ourselves according to maxims of freedom as if they were laws of nature.

Concluding Remark

The speculative use of reason with regard to nature leads to the absolute necessity of some supreme cause of the world. The practical use of reason with reference to freedom leads also to absolute necessity, but only to the necessity of the laws of the actions of a rational being as such. Now it is an essential principle of all use of our reason to push its knowledge to a consciousness of its necessity (for without necessity there would be no rational knowledge). But there is an equally essential restriction of the same reason that it cannot have insight into the necessity either of what is or what does happen or of what should happen, unless there is presupposed a condition under which it is or does happen or should happen. In this way, however, the satisfaction of reason is only further and further postponed by the continual inquiry after the condition. Reason, therefore, restlessly seeks the unconditionally necessary and sees itself compelled to assume this without having any means of making such necessity conceivable; reason is happy enough if only it can find a concept which is compatible with this assumption. Hence there is no fault in

our deduction of the supreme principle of morality, but rather a reproach which must be made against human reason generally, involved in the fact that reason cannot render conceivable the absolute necessity of an unconditioned practical law (such as the categorical imperative must be). Reason cannot be blamed for not being willing to explain this necessity by means of a condition, namely, by basing it on some underlying interest, because in that case the law would no longer be moral, i.e., a supreme law of freedom. And so even though we do not indeed grasp the practical unconditioned necessity of the moral imperative, we do nevertheless grasp its inconceivability. This is all that can be fairly asked of a philosophy which strives in its principles to reach the very limit of human reason.

JOHN STUART MILL

John Stuart Mill (1806–1873) was born in London on May 20, 1806. His father, James Mill, was a journalist and an official of the East India Company. Two years after John Stuart Mill's birth, his father met the philosopher and reformer Jeremy Bentham; for the remainder of his life he was Bentham's devoted friend, disciple, and spokesman. His commitment to the utilitarian creed involved his son, whom James Mill chose to educate at home in order to cultivate the perfect utilitarian individual.

Mill tells the story of his remarkable education in his *Autobiography*, published after his death by his stepdaughter Helen Taylor in 1873. By age three, Mill had studied Greek and, by eight, Latin. He began philosophy and logic at twelve, spent a year in France, and returned to England at fifteen to study law with the famous legal thinker John Austin. Throughout this process Mill conversed with his father's Benthamite friends on philosophical, political, and economic issues and engaged in drills, recitations, and debates under his father's severe direction.

In 1823 Mill completed his education and was employed by the East India Company, where he remained until his retirement in 1858. In 1856 he was appointed to the office of Chief Examiner, the company's second highest post, and two years later refused government employment when the company was dissolved by Act of Parliament.

In 1826, at the age of twenty, Mill was the victim of an intellectual crisis. Later he would recall the event as the beginning of his intellectual independence from Bentham. He had once been so totally committed to Bentham's utilitarianism that it served for him as a virtual religion; he was student, disciple, and even evangelist of this rational, humanistic faith, founding the Utilitarian Society, editing the Benthamite journal, the *Westminster Review*, and leading the "Philosophical Radicals," the young Benthamite organization. But at twenty he came to recognize his lack of emotion and feeling; he had become a pawn of reason, without tenderness or sensitivity. He turned to Wordsworth and Coleridge, the great romantic poets, for guidance in those feelings without which life could not be whole and fulfilled.

In 1831 Mill met Mrs. Harriet Taylor, the young wife of a wealthy merchant; she became his closest friend and confidant. As the years passed, the Platonic relationship deepened, and eventually, shortly after her husband's death in 1849, the two married. Mill's praise for Harriet Taylor's intelligence, imagination, and tenderness of soul was boundless; he was devoted to her and acknowledged her profound influence on his thinking and his life. To her, Mill would say, should be ascribed the human element in his writings and the sensitive application of principle to the issues of the day. In 1858 she died in Avignon, while on a vacation.

Perhaps the outstanding result of their collaboration — and Mill's most famous political work — is *On Liberty*, published in 1859. At least from 1854 they had worked on this account of the significance of individual self-development, enriched by Mill's study of Wordsworth and Coleridge, and the limitations of social and governmental control over the individual. In it Mill famously argues that creative self-development is central to personal character and that only self-protection justifies limitations on individual freedom. As one modern commentator has put it, *On Liberty* "is such a deeply felt defence of the right of individuals to be left alone unless they are causing real damage to other people that hardly anyone puts it down without reading it straight through." When Harriet died, the book had not received its final revisions, but Mill sent it to the publisher, without further alteration and dedicated to her.

After Harriet's death and his retirement, Mill wrote extensively, bringing to fruition many projects that he had begun during the eight years of their marriage. Among these were the *Considerations on Representative*

Government, published in 1861, and *The Subjection of Women*, his revolutionary defense of women's capacity for self-development, which was written in 1861 but appeared only in 1869.

In October, November, and December of 1861 Mill published three essays in a prominent intellectual monthly, *Fraser's Magazine*. It was his attempt to appeal to an educated lay audience about some fundamental matters concerning morality, religion, reason, pleasure, and duty. These essays, reworked into five chapters and published in book form as *Utilitarianism* in 1863, are an act of radical reform, an effort to defend the integrity of a benevolent, rational moral view that was humane and that would encourage positive change. The book was also an attack—on Kant and intuitionist moral theorists and on Bentham, whose conception of the goal of utility was too narrow and intellectualist for Mill. It remains to this day a classic formulation of instrumentalist moral theory.

Two years later Mill was elected to Parliament from Westminster, serving three years, until 1868. From then until his death on May 8, 1873, he wrote and avoided those who sought him. Tended in these last years by his stepdaughter Helen, Mill died quietly and was buried in Avignon, alongside his beloved Harriet.

Recommended Readings

Berger, Fred. *Happiness, Justice and Freedom*. Berkeley: University of California Press, 1985.

Gorowitz, S. (ed.). *Utilitarianism and Critical Essays*. Indianapolis: Bobbs-Merrill, 1971.

Gray, John. *Mill on Liberty: A Defence*. London: Routledge, 1983.

Okin, Susan Moller. *Women in Western Political Thought*. Princeton: Princeton University Press, 1979.

Ryan, Alan. *Mill*. London: Routledge, 1974.

Thomas, William. *J. S. Mill*. Oxford: Oxford University Press, 1985.

ON LIBERTY

Contents

The grand, leading principle, towards which every argument unfolded in these pages directly converges, is the absolute and essential importance of human development in its richest diversity.

—Wilhelm von Humboldt:
Sphere and Duties of Government.

To the beloved and deplored memory of her who was the inspirer, and in part the author, of all that is best in my writings—the friend and wife whose exalted sense of truth and right was my strongest incitement, and whose approbation was my chief reward— I dedicate this volume. Like all that I have written for many years, it belongs as much to her as to me; but the work as it stands has had, in a very insufficient degree, the inestimable advantage of her revision; some of the most important portions having been reserved for a more careful re-examination, which they are now never destined to receive. Were I but capable of interpreting to the world one half the great thoughts and noble feelings which are buried in her grave, I should be the medium of a greater benefit to it, than is ever likely to arise from anything that I can write, unprompted and unassisted by her all but unrivalled wisdom.

This edition of *On Liberty* was drawn from the 1869 4th edition Longmans, Green, Reader, and Dyer.

ON LIBERTY

CHAPTER I

Introductory

The subject of this Essay is not the so-called Liberty of the Will, so unfortunately opposed to the misnamed doctrine of Philosophical Necessity; but Civil, or Social Liberty: the nature and limits of the power which can be legitimately exercised by society over the individual. A question seldom stated, and hardly ever discussed, in general terms, but which profoundly influences the practical controversies of the age by its latent presence, and is likely soon to make itself recognised as the vital question of the future. It is so far from being new, that, in a certain sense, it has divided mankind, almost from the remotest ages; but in the stage of progress into which the more civilized portions of the species have now entered, it presents itself under new conditions, and requires a different and more fundamental treatment.

The struggle between Liberty and Authority is the most conspicuous feature in the portions of history with which we are earliest familiar, particularly in that of Greece, Rome, and England. But in old times this contest was between subjects, or some classes of subjects, and the Government. By liberty, was meant protection against the tyranny of the political rulers. The rulers were conceived (except in some of the popular governments of Greece) as in a necessarily antagonistic position to the people whom they ruled. They consisted of a governing One, or a governing tribe or caste, who derived their authority from inheritance or conquest, who, at all events, did not hold it at the pleasure of the governed, and whose supremacy men did not venture, perhaps did not desire, to contest, whatever precautions might be taken against its oppressive exercise. Their power was regarded as necessary, but also as highly dangerous; as a weapon which they would attempt to use against their subjects, no less than against external enemies. To prevent the weaker members of the community from being preyed upon by innumerable vultures, it was needful that there should be an animal of prey stronger than the rest, commissioned to keep them down. But as the king of the vultures would be no less bent upon preying on the flock than any of the minor harpies, it was indispensable to be in a perpetual attitude of defence against his beak and claws. The aim, therefore, of patriots was to set limits to the power which the ruler should be suffered to exercise over the community; and this limitation was what they meant by liberty. It was attempted in two ways. First, by obtaining a recognition of certain immunities, called political liberties or rights, which it was to be regarded as a breach of duty in the ruler to infringe, and which if he did infringe, specific resistance, or general rebellion, was held to be justifiable. A second, and generally a later expedient, was the establishment of constitutional checks, by which the consent of the community, or of a body of some sort, supposed to represent its interests, was made a necessary condition to some of the more important acts of the governing power. To the first of these modes of limitation, the ruling power, in most European countries, was compelled, more or less, to submit. It was not so with the second; and, to attain this, or when already in some degree possessed, to attain it more completely, became everywhere the principal object of the lovers of liberty. And so long as mankind were content to combat one enemy by another, and to be ruled by a master, on condition of being guaranteed more or less efficaciously against his tyranny, they did not carry their aspirations beyond this point.

A time, however, came, in the progress of human affairs, when men ceased to think it a necessity of nature that their governors should be an independent power, opposed in interest to themselves. It appeared to them much better that the various magistrates of the State should be their tenants or delegates, revocable at their pleasure. In that way alone, it seemed, could they have complete security that the powers of government would never be abused to their disadvantage. By degrees this new demand for elective and temporary rulers became the prominent object of the exertions of the popular party, wherever any such party existed; and superseded, to a considerable extent, the previous efforts to limit the power of rulers. As the struggle proceeded for making the ruling power emanate from the periodical choice of the ruled, some persons began to think that too much importance had been attached to the limitation of the power itself. *That* (it might seem) was a resource against rulers whose interests were habitually opposed to those of the people. What was now wanted was, that the rulers should be identified with the people; that their interest and will should be the interest and will of the nation. The nation did not need to be protected against its own will. There was no fear of its tyrannizing over itself. Let the rulers be effectually responsible to it, promptly removable by it, and it could afford to trust them with power of which it could itself dictate the use to be made. Their power was but the nation's own power, concentrated, and in a form convenient for exercise. This mode of thought, or rather perhaps of feeling, was common among the last generation of European liberalism, in the Continental section of which it still apparently predominates. Those who admit any limit to what a government may do, except in the case of such governments as they think ought not to exist, stand out as brilliant exceptions among the political thinkers of the Continent. A similar tone of sentiment might by this time have been prevalent in our own country, if the circumstances which for a time encouraged it, had continued unaltered.

But, in political and philosophical theories, as well as in persons, success discloses faults and infirmities which failure might have concealed from observation. The notion, that the people have no need to limit their power over themselves, might seem axiomatic, when popular government was a thing only dreamed about, or read of as having existed at some distant period of the past. Neither was that notion necessarily disturbed by such temporary aberrations as those of the French Revolution, the worst of which were the work of an usurping few, and which, in any case, belonged, not to the permanent working of popular institutions, but to a sudden and convulsive outbreak against monarchical and aristocratic despotism. In time, however, a democratic republic came to occupy a large portion of the earth's surface, and made itself felt as one of the most powerful members of the community of nations; and elective and responsible government became subject to the observations and criticisms which wait upon a great existing fact. It was now perceived that such phrases as 'self-government,' and 'the power of the people over themselves,' do not express the true state of the case. The 'people' who exercise the power are not always the same people with those over whom it is exercised; and the 'self-government' spoken of is not the government of each by himself, but of each by all the rest. The will of the people, moreover, practically means the will of the most numerous or the most active *part* of the people; the majority, or those who succeed in making themselves accepted as the majority; the people, consequently, *may* desire to oppress a part of their number; and precautions are as much needed against this as against any other abuse of power. The limitation, therefore, of the power of government over individuals loses none of its importance when the holders of power are regularly accountable to the community, that is, to the strongest party therein. This view of things, recommending itself equally to the intelligence of thinkers and to the inclination of those important classes in European society to whose real or supposed interests democracy is adverse, has had no difficulty in establishing itself; and in political speculations 'the tyranny of the majority' is now generally included among the evils against which society requires to be on its guard.

Like other tyrannies, the tyranny of the majority was at first, and is still vulgarly, held in dread, chiefly as operating through the acts of the public authorities. But reflecting persons perceived that when society is itself the tyrant—society collectively, over the separate individuals who compose it—its means of tyrannizing are not restricted to the acts which it may do by the hands of its political functionaries. Society can and does execute its own mandates: and if it issues wrong mandates instead of right, or any mandates at all in things with which it ought not to meddle, it practises a social tyranny more formidable than many kinds of political oppression, since, though not usually upheld by such extreme penalties, it leaves fewer means of escape, penetrating much more deeply into the details of life, and enslaving the soul itself. Protection, therefore, against the tyranny of the magistrate is not enough: there needs protection also against the tyranny of the prevailing opinion and feeling; against the tendency of society to impose, by other means than civil penalties, its own ideas and practices as rules of conduct on those who dissent from them; to fetter the development, and, if possible, prevent the formation, of any individuality not in harmony with its ways, and compel all characters to fashion themselves upon the model of its own. There is a limit to the legitimate interference of collective opinion with individual independence; and to find that limit, and maintain it against encroachment, is as indispensable to a good condition of human affairs, as protection against political despotism.

But though this proposition is not likely to be contested in general terms, the practical question, where to place the limit—how to make the fitting adjustment between individual independence and social control—is a subject on which nearly everything remains to be done. All that makes existence valuable to any one, depends on the enforcement of restraints upon the actions of other people. Some rules of conduct, therefore, must be imposed, by law in the first place, and by opinion on many things which are not fit subjects for the operation of law. What these rules should be, is the principal question in human affairs; but if we except a few of the most obvious cases, it is one of those which least progress has been made in resolving. No two ages, and scarcely any two countries, have decided it alike; and the decision of one age or country is a wonder to another. Yet the people of any given age and country no more suspect any difficulty in it, than if it were a subject on which mankind had always been agreed. The rules which obtain among themselves appear to them self-evident and self-justifying. This all but universal illusion is one of the examples of the magical influence of custom, which is not only, as the proverb says, a second nature, but is continually mistaken for the first. The effect of custom, in preventing any misgiving respecting the rules of conduct which mankind impose on one another, is all the more complete because the subject is one on which it is not generally considered necessary that reasons should be given, either by one person to others, or by each to himself. People are accustomed to believe, and have been encouraged in the belief by some who aspire to the character of philosophers, that their feelings, on subjects of this nature, are better than reasons, and render reasons unnecessary. The practical principle which guides them to their opinions on the regulation of human conduct, is the feeling in each person's mind that everybody should be required to act as he, and those with whom he sympathizes, would like them to act. No one, indeed, acknowledges to himself that his standard of judgment is his own liking; but an opinion on a point of conduct, not supported by reasons, can only count as one person's preference; and if the reasons, when given, are a mere appeal to a similar preference felt by other people, it is still only many people's liking instead of one. To an ordinary man, however, his own preference, thus supported, is not only a perfectly satisfactory reason, but the only one he generally has for any of his notions of morality, taste, or propriety, which are not expressly written in his religious creed; and his chief guide in the interpretation even of that. Men's opinions, accordingly, on what is laudable or blameable, are affected by all the multifarious causes which influence their wishes in regard to the conduct of others, and which are as numerous as those which determine their wishes on any other subject. Sometimes their reason—at other times their prejudices or superstitions: often their social affections, not seldom their antisocial ones, their envy or jealousy, their arrogance or contemptuousness: but most commonly, their desires or fears for themselves—their legitimate or illegitimate self-interest. Wherever there is an ascendant class, a large portion of the morality of the country emanates from its class interests, and its feelings of class superiority. The morality between Spartans and Helots, between planters and negroes, between princes and subjects, between nobles and roturiers, between men and women, has been for the most part the creation of these class interests and feelings: and the sentiments thus generated, react in turn upon the moral feelings of the members of the ascendant class, in their relations among themselves. Where, on the other hand, a class, formerly ascendant, has lost its ascendancy, or where its ascendancy is unpopular, the prevailing moral sentiments frequently bear the impress of an impatient dislike of superiority. Another grand determining principle of the rules of conduct, both in act and forbearance, which have been enforced by law or opinion, has been the servility of

mankind towards the supposed preferences or aversions of their temporal masters, or of their gods. This servility, though essentially selfish, is not hypocrisy; it gives rise to perfectly genuine sentiments of abhorrence; it made men burn magicians and heretics. Among so many baser influences, the general and obvious interests of society have of course had a share, and a large one, in the direction of the moral sentiments: less, however, as a matter of reason, and on their own account, than as a consequence of the sympathies and antipathies which grew out of them: and sympathies and antipathies which had little or nothing to do with the interests of society, have made themselves felt in the establishment of moralities with quite as great force.

The likings and dislikings of society, or of some powerful portion of it, are thus the main thing which has practically determined the rules laid down for general observance, under the penalties of law or opinion. And in general, those who have been in advance of society in thought and feeling, have left this condition of things unassailed in principle, however they may have come into conflict with it in some of its details. They have occupied themselves rather in inquiring what things society ought to like or dislike, than in questioning whether its likings or dislikings should be a law to individuals. They preferred endeavouring to alter the feelings of mankind on the particular points on which they were themselves heretical, rather than make common cause in defence of freedom, with heretics generally. The only case in which the higher ground has been taken on principle and maintained with consistency, by any but an individual here and there, is that of religious belief: a case instructive in many ways, and not least so as forming a most striking instance of the fallibility of what is called the moral sense: for the *odium theologicum*, in a sincere bigot, is one of the most unequivocal cases of moral feeling. Those who first broke the yoke of what called itself the Universal Church, were in general as little willing to permit difference of religious opinion as that church itself. But when the heat of the conflict was over, without giving a complete victory to any party, and each church or sect was reduced to limit its hopes to retaining possession of the ground it already occupied; minorities, seeing that they had no chance of becoming majorities, were under the necessity of pleading to those whom they could not convert, for permission to differ. It is accordingly on this battle field, almost solely, that the rights of the individual against society have been asserted on broad grounds of principle, and the claim of society to exercise authority over dissentients, openly controverted. The great writers to whom the world owes what religious liberty it possesses, have mostly asserted freedom of conscience as an indefeasible right, and denied absolutely that a human being is accountable to others for his religious belief. Yet so natural to mankind is intolerance in whatever they really care about, that religious freedom has hardly anywhere been practically realized, except where religious indifference, which dislikes to have its peace disturbed by theological quarrels, has added its weight to the scale. In the minds of almost all religious persons, even in the most tolerant countries, the duty of toleration is admitted with tacit reserves. One person will bear with dissent in matters of church government, but not of dogma; another can tolerate everybody, short of a Papist or an Unitarian; another, every one who believes in revealed religion; a few extend their charity a little further, but stop at the belief in a God and in a future state. Wherever the sentiment of the majority is still genuine and intense, it is found to have abated little of its claim to be obeyed.

In England, from the peculiar circumstances of our political history, though the yoke of opinion is perhaps heavier, that of law is lighter, than in most other countries of Europe; and there is considerable jealousy of direct interference, by the legislative or the executive power, with private conduct; not so much from any just regard for the independence of the individual, as from the still subsisting habit of looking on the government as representing an opposite interest to the public. The majority have not yet learnt to feel the power of the government their power, or its opinions their opinions. When they do so, individual liberty will probably be as much exposed to invasion from the government, as it already is from public opinion. But, as yet, there is a considerable amount of feeling ready to be called forth against any attempt of the law to control individuals in things in which they have not hitherto been accustomed to be controlled by it; and this with very little discrimina-

tion as to whether the matter is, or is not, within the legitimate sphere of legal control; insomuch that the feeling, highly salutary on the whole, is perhaps quite as often misplaced as well grounded in the particular instances of its application. There is, in fact, no recognised principle by which the propriety or impropriety of government interference is customarily tested. People decide according to their personal preferences. Some, whenever they see any good to be done, or evil to be remedied, would willingly instigate the government to undertake the business; while others prefer to bear almost any amount of social evil, rather than add one to the departments of human interests amenable to governmental control. And men range themselves on one or the other side in any particular case, according to this general direction of their sentiments; or according to the degree of interest which they feel in the particular thing which it is proposed that the government should do, or according to the belief they entertain that the government would, or would not, do it in the manner they prefer; but very rarely on account of any opinion to which they consistently adhere, as to what things are fit to be done by a government. And it seems to me that in consequence of this absence of rule or principle, one side is at present as often wrong as the other; the interference of government is, with about equal frequency, improperly invoked and improperly condemned.

The object of this Essay is to assert one very simple principle, as entitled to govern absolutely the dealings of society with the individual in the way of compulsion and control, whether the means used be physical force in the form of legal penalties, or the moral coercion of public opinion. That principle is, that the sole end for which mankind are warranted, individually or collectively, in interfering with the liberty of action of any of their number, is self-protection. That the only purpose for which power can be rightfully exercised over any member of a civilized community, against his will, is to prevent harm to others. His own good, either physical or moral, is not a sufficient warrant. He cannot rightfully be compelled to do or forbear because it will be better for him to do so, because it will make him happier, because, in the opinions of others, to do so would be wise, or even right. These are good reasons for remonstrating with him, or reasoning with him, or persuading him, or entreating him, but not for compelling him, or visiting him with any evil in case he do otherwise. To justify that, the conduct from which it is desired to deter him, must be calculated to produce evil to some one else. The only part of the conduct of any one, for which he is amenable to society, is that which concerns others. In the part which merely concerns himself, his independence is, of right, absolute. Over himself, over his own body and mind, the individual is sovereign.

It is, perhaps, hardly necessary to say that this doctrine is meant to apply only to human beings in the maturity of their faculties. We are not speaking of children, or of young persons below the age which the law may fix as that of manhood or womanhood. Those who are still in a state to require being taken care of by others, must be protected against their own actions as well as against external injury. For the same reason, we may leave out of consideration those backward states of society in which the race itself may be considered as in its nonage. The early difficulties in the way of spontaneous progress are so great, that there is seldom any choice of means for overcoming them; and a ruler full of the spirit of improvement is warranted in the use of any expedients that will attain an end, perhaps otherwise unattainable. Despotism is a legitimate mode of government in dealing with barbarians, provided the end be their improvement, and the means justified by actually effecting that end. Liberty, as a principle, has no application to any state of things anterior to the time when mankind have become capable of being improved by free and equal discussion. Until then, there is nothing for them but implicit obedience to an Akbar or a Charlemagne, if they are so fortunate as to find one. But as soon as mankind have attained the capacity of being guided to their own improvement by conviction or persuasion (a period long since reached in all nations with whom we need here concern ourselves), compulsion, either in the direct form or in that of pains and penalties for non-compliance, is no longer admissible as a means to their own good, and justifiable only for the security of others.

It is proper to state that I forego any advantage which could be derived to my argument from the idea of abstract right, as a thing independent of utility. I regard utility as the ultimate appeal on all ethical questions; but it must be utility in the largest sense, grounded on the permanent interests of man as a progressive being. Those interests, I contend, authorize the subjection of individual spontaneity to external control, only in respect to those actions of each, which concern the interest of other people. If any one does an act hurtful to others, there is a *prima facie* case for punishing him, by law, or, where legal penalties are not safely applicable, by general disapprobation. There are also many positive acts for the benefit of others which he may rightfully be compelled to perform; such as, to give evidence in a court of justice; to bear his fair share in the common defence, or in any other joint work necessary to the interest of the society of which he enjoys the protection; and to perform certain acts of individual beneficence, such as saving a fellow-creature's life, or interposing to protect the defenceless against ill-usage, things which whenever it is obviously a man's duty to do, he may rightfully be made responsible to society for not doing. A person may cause evil to others not only by his actions but by his inaction, and in either case he is justly accountable to them for the injury. The latter case, it is true, requires a much more cautious exercise of compulsion than the former. To make any one answerable for doing evil to others, is the rule; to make him answerable for not preventing evil, is, comparatively speaking, the exception. Yet there are many cases clear enough and grave enough to justify that exception. In all things which regard the external relations of the individual, he is *de jure* amenable to those whose interests are concerned, and if need be, to society as their protector. There are often good reasons for not holding him to the responsibility; but these reasons must arise from the special expediencies of the case: either because it is a kind of case in which he is on the whole likely to act better, when left to his own discretion, than when controlled in any way in which society have it in their power to control him; or because the attempt to exercise control would produce other evils, greater than those which it would prevent. When such reasons as these preclude the enforcement of responsibility, the conscience of the agent himself should step into the vacant judgment seat, and protect those interests of others which have no external protection; judging himself all the more rigidly, because the case does not admit of his being made accountable to the judgment of his fellow-creatures.

But there is a sphere of action in which society, as distinguished from the individual, has, if any, only an indirect interest; comprehending all that portion of a person's life and conduct which affects only himself, or if it also affects others, only with their free, voluntary, and undeceived consent and participation. When I say only himself, I mean directly, and in the first instance: for whatever affects himself, may affect others through himself; and the objection which may be grounded on this contingency, will receive consideration in the sequel. This, then, is the appropriate region of human liberty. It comprises, first, the inward domain of consciousness; demanding liberty of conscience, in the most comprehensive sense; liberty of thought and feeling; absolute freedom of opinion and sentiment on all subjects, practical or speculative, scientific, moral, or theological. The liberty of expressing and publishing opinions may seem to fall under a different principle, since it belongs to that part of the conduct of an individual which concerns other people; but, being almost of as much importance as the liberty of thought itself, and resting in great part on the same reasons, is practically inseparable from it. Secondly, the principle requires liberty of tastes and pursuits; of framing the plan of our life to suit our own character; of doing as we like, subject to such consequences as may follow: without impediment from our fellow-creatures, so long as what we do does not harm them, even though they should think our conduct foolish, perverse, or wrong. Thirdly, from this liberty of each individual, follows the liberty, within the same limits, of combination among individuals; freedom to unite, for any purpose not involving harm to others: the persons combining being supposed to be of full age, and not forced or deceived.

No society in which these liberties are not, on the whole, respected, is free, whatever may be its form of government; and none is completely free in which they do not exist absolute and unqualified. The only freedom which deserves the name, is that of pursuing our own good in our own way, so long as we do not attempt to deprive others of theirs, or impede their efforts to obtain it. Each is the proper guardian of his own health, whether bodily, or mental and spiritual. Mankind are greater gainers by suffering each other to live as seems good to themselves, than by compelling each to live as seems good to the rest.

Though this doctrine is anything but new, and, to some persons, may have the air of a truism, there is no doctrine which stands more directly opposed to the general tendency of existing opinion and practice. Society has expended fully as much effort in the attempt (according to its lights) to compel people to conform to its notions of personal, as of social excellence. The ancient commonwealths thought themselves entitled to practise, and the ancient philosophers countenanced, the regulation of every part of private conduct by public authority, on the ground that the State had a deep interest in the whole bodily and mental discipline of every one of its citizens; a mode of thinking which may have been admissible in small republics surrounded by powerful enemies, in constant peril of being subverted by foreign attack or internal commotion, and to which even a short interval of relaxed energy and self-command might so easily be fatal, that they could not afford to wait for the salutary permanent effects of freedom. In the modern world, the greater size of political communities, and above all, the separation between spiritual and temporal authority (which placed the direction of men's consciences in other hands than those which controlled their worldly affairs), prevented so great an interference by law in the details of private life; but the engines of moral repression have been wielded more strenuously against divergence from the reigning opinion in self-regarding, than even in social matters; religion, the most powerful of the elements which have entered into the formation of moral feeling, having almost always been governed either by the ambition of a hierarchy, seeking control over every department of human conduct, or by the spirit of Puritanism. And some of those modern reformers who have placed themselves in strongest opposition to the religions of the past, have been noway behind either churches or sects in their assertion of the right of spiritual domination: M. Comte, in particular, whose social system, as unfolded in his *Système de Politique Positive*, aims at establishing (though by moral more than by legal appliances) a despotism of society over the individual, surpassing anything contemplated in the political ideal of the most rigid disciplinarian among the ancient philosophers.

Apart from the peculiar tenets of individual thinkers, there is also in the world at large an increasing inclination to stretch unduly the powers of society over the individual, both by the force of opinion and even by that of legislation: and as the tendency of all the changes taking place in the world is to strengthen society, and diminish the power of the individual, this encroachment is not one of the evils which tend spontaneously to disappear, but, on the contrary, to grow more and more formidable. The disposition of mankind, whether as rulers or as fellow-citizens, to impose their own opinions and inclinations as a rule of conduct on others, is so energetically supported by some of the best and by some of the worst feelings incident to human nature, that it is hardly ever kept under restraint by anything but want of power; and as the power is not declining, but growing, unless a strong barrier of moral conviction can be raised against the mischief, we must expect, in the present circumstances of the world, to see it increase.

It will be convenient for the argument, if, instead of at once entering upon the general thesis, we confine ourselves in the first instance to a single branch of it, on which the principle here stated is, if not fully, yet to a certain point, recognised by the current opinions. This one branch is the Liberty of Thought: from which it is impossible to separate the cognate liberty of speaking and of writing. Although these liberties, to some considerable amount, form part of the political morality of all countries which profess religious toleration and free institutions, the grounds, both philosophical and practical, on which they rest, are perhaps not so familiar to the general mind, nor so thoroughly appreciated by many even of the leaders of opinion, as might have been expected. Those grounds, when rightly understood, are of much wider application than to only one division of the subject, and a thorough consideration of this part of the question will be found the best introduction to the remainder. Those to whom nothing which I am about to say will be new, may therefore, I hope, excuse me, if on a subject which for now three centuries has been so often discussed, I venture on one discussion more.

CHAPTER II

Of the Liberty of Thought and Discussion

The time, it is to be hoped, is gone by, when any defence would be necessary of the 'liberty of the press' as one of the securities against corrupt or tyrannical government. No argument, we may suppose, can now be needed, against permitting a legislature or an executive, not identified in interest with the people, to prescribe opinions to them, and determine what doctrines or what arguments they shall be allowed to hear. This aspect of the question, besides, has been so often and so triumphantly enforced by preceding writers, that it needs not be specially insisted on in this place. Though the law of England, on the subject of the press, is as servile to this day as it was in the time of the Tudors, there is little danger of its being actually put in force against political discussion, except during some temporary panic, when fear of insurrection drives ministers and judges from their propriety;[1] and, speaking generally, it is not,

---

1. These words had scarcely been written, when, as if to give them an emphatic contradiction, occurred the Government Press Prosecutions of 1858. That ill-judged interference with the liberty of public discussion has not, however, induced me to alter a single word in the text, nor has it at all weakened my conviction that, moments of panic excepted, the era of pains and penalties for political discussion has, in our own country, passed away. For, in the first place, the prosecutions were not persisted in; and, in the second, they were never, properly speaking, political prosecutions. The offence charged was not that of criticising institutions, or the acts or persons of rulers, but of circulating what was deemed an immoral doctrine, the lawfulness of Tyrannicide.

If the arguments of the present chapter are of any validity, there ought to exist the fullest liberty of professing and discussing, as a matter of ethical conviction, any doctrine, however immoral it may be considered. It would, therefore, be irrelevant and out of place to examine here, whether the doctrine of Tyrannicide deserves that title. I shall content myself with saying that the subject has been at all times one of the open questions of morals; that the act of a private citizen in striking down a criminal, who, by raising himself above the law, has placed himself beyond the reach of legal punishment

in constitutional countries, to be apprehended, that the government, whether completely responsible to the people or not, will often attempt to control the expression of opinion, except when in doing so it makes itself the organ of the general intolerance of the public. Let us suppose, therefore, that the government is entirely at one with the people, and never thinks of exerting any power of coercion unless in agreement with what it conceives to be their voice. But I deny the right of the people to exercise such coercion, either by themselves or by their government. The power itself is illegitimate. The best government has no more title to it than the worst. It is as noxious, or more noxious, when exerted in accordance with public opinion, than when in opposition to it. If all mankind minus one, were of one opinion, and only one person were of the contrary opinion, mankind would be no more justified in silencing that one person, than he, if he had the power, would be justified in silencing mankind. Were an opinion a personal possession of no value except to the owner; if to be obstructed in the enjoyment of it were simply a private injury, it would make some difference whether the injury was inflicted only on a few persons or on many. But the peculiar evil of silencing the expression of an opinion is, that it is robbing the human race; posterity as well as the existing generation; those who dissent from the opinion, still more than those who hold it. If the opinion is right, they are deprived of the opportunity of exchanging error for truth: if wrong, they lose, what is almost as great a benefit, the clearer perception and livelier impression of truth, produced by its collision with error.

It is necessary to consider separately these two hypotheses, each of which has a distinct branch of

---

or control, has been accounted by whole nations, and by some of the best and wisest of men, not a crime, but an act of exalted virtue; and that, right or wrong, it is not of the nature of assassination, but of civil war. As such, I hold that the instigation to it, in a specific case, may be a proper subject of punishment, but only if an overt act has followed, and at least a probable connexion can be established between the act and the instigation. Even then, it is not a foreign government, but the very government assailed, which alone, in the exercise of self-defence, can legitimately punish attacks directed against its own existence.

the argument corresponding to it. We can never be sure that the opinion we are endeavouring to stifle is a false opinion; and if we were sure, stifling it would be an evil still.

First: the opinion which it is attempted to suppress by authority may possibly be true. Those who desire to suppress it, of course deny its truth; but they are not infallible. They have no authority to decide the question for all mankind, and exclude every other person from the means of judging. To refuse a hearing to an opinion, because they are sure that it is false, is to assume that *their* certainty is the same thing as *absolute* certainty. All silencing of discussion is an assumption of infallibility. Its condemnation may be allowed to rest on this common argument, not the worse for being common.

Unfortunately for the good sense of mankind, the fact of their fallibility is far from carrying the weight in their practical judgment, which is always allowed to it in theory; for while every one well knows himself to be fallible, few think it necessary to take any precautions against their own fallibility, or admit the supposition that any opinion, of which they feel very certain, may be one of the examples of the error to which they acknowledge themselves to be liable. Absolute princes, or others who are accustomed to unlimited deference, usually feel this complete confidence in their own opinions on nearly all subjects. People more happily situated, who sometimes hear their opinions disputed, and are not wholly unused to be set right when they are wrong, place the same unbounded reliance only on such of their opinions as are shared by all who surround them, or to whom they habitually defer: for in proportion to a man's want of confidence in his own solitary judgment, does he usually repose, with implicit trust, on the infallibility of 'the world' in general. And the world, to each individual, means the part of it with which he comes in contact; his party, his sect, his church, his class of society: the man may be called, by comparison, almost liberal and large-minded to whom it means anything so comprehensive as his own country or his own age. Nor is his faith in this collective authority at all shaken by his being aware that other ages, countries, sects, churches, classes, and parties have thought, and even now think, the exact reverse. He devolves upon his own world the responsibility of being in the right against the dissentient worlds of other people; and it never troubles him that mere accident has decided which of these numerous worlds is the object of his reliance, and that the same causes which make him a Churchman in London, would have made him a Buddhist or a Confucian in Pekin. Yet it is as evident in itself, as any amount of argument can make it, that ages are no more infallible than individuals; every age having held many opinions which subsequent ages have deemed not only false but absurd; and it is as certain that many opinions, now general, will be rejected by future ages, as it is that many, once general, are rejected by the present.

The objection likely to be made to this argument, would probably take some such form as the following. There is no greater assumption of infallibility in forbidding the propagation of error, than in any other thing which is done by public authority on its own judgment and responsibility. Judgment is given to men that they may use it. Because it may be used erroneously, are men to be told that they ought not to use it at all? To prohibit what they think pernicious, is not claiming exemption from error, but fulfilling the duty incumbent on them, although fallible, of acting on their conscientious conviction. If we were never to act on our opinions, because those opinions may be wrong, we should leave all our interests uncared for, and all our duties unperformed. An objection which applies to all conduct, can be no valid objection to any conduct in particular. It is the duty of governments, and of individuals, to form the truest opinions they can; to form them carefully, and never impose them upon others unless they are quite sure of being right. But when they are sure (such reasoners may say), it is not conscientiousness but cowardice to shrink from acting on their opinions, and allow doctrines which they honestly think dangerous to the welfare of mankind, either in this life or in another, to be scattered abroad without restraint, because other people, in less enlightened times, have persecuted opinions now believed to be true. Let us take care, it may be said, not to make the same mistake: but governments and nations have made mistakes in other things, which are not denied to be fit subjects for the exercise of authority: they have laid on bad taxes, made unjust wars. Ought we therefore to lay on no taxes, and, under whatever provocation, make no

wars? Men, and governments, must act to the best of their ability. There is no such thing as absolute certainty, but there is assurance sufficient for the purposes of human life. We may, and must, assume our opinion to be true for the guidance of our own conduct: and it is assuming no more when we forbid bad men to pervert society by the propagation of opinions which we regard as false and pernicious.

I answer, that it is assuming very much more. There is the greatest difference between presuming an opinion to be true, because, with every opportunity for contesting it, it has not been refuted, and assuming its truth for the purpose of not permitting its refutation. Complete liberty of contradicting and disproving our opinion, is the very condition which justifies us in assuming its truth for purposes of action; and on no other terms can a being with human faculties have any rational assurance of being right.

When we consider either the history of opinion, or the ordinary conduct of human life, to what is it to be ascribed that the one and the other are no worse than they are? Not certainly to the inherent force of the human understanding; for, on any matter not self-evident, there are ninety-nine persons totally incapable of judging of it, for one who is capable; and the capacity of the hundredth person is only comparative; for the majority of the eminent men of every past generation held many opinions now known to be erroneous, and did or approved numerous things which no one will now justify. Why is it, then, that there is on the whole a preponderance among mankind of rational opinions and rational conduct? If there really is this preponderance—which there must be unless human affairs are, and have always been, in an almost desperate state—it is owing to a quality of the human mind, the source of everything respectable in man either as an intellectual or as a moral being, namely, that his errors are corrigible. He is capable of rectifying his mistakes, by discussion and experience. Not by experience alone. There must be discussion, to show how experience is to be interpreted. Wrong opinions and practices gradually yield to fact and argument: but facts and arguments, to produce any effect on the mind, must be brought before it. Very few facts are able to tell their own story, without comments to bring out their meaning. The whole strength and value, then, of human judgment, depending on the one property, that it can be set right when it is wrong, reliance can be placed on it only when the means of setting it right are kept constantly at hand. In the case of any person whose judgment is really deserving of confidence, how has it become so? Because he has kept his mind open to criticism of his opinions and conduct. Because it has been his practice to listen to all that could be said against him; to profit by as much of it as was just, and expound to himself, and upon occasion to others, the fallacy of what was fallacious. Because he has felt, that the only way in which a human being can make some approach to knowing the whole of a subject, is by hearing what can be said about it by persons of every variety of opinion, and studying all modes in which it can be looked at by every character of mind. No wise man ever acquired his wisdom in any mode but this; nor is it in the nature of human intellect to become wise in any other manner. The steady habit of correcting and completing his own opinion by collating it with those of others, so far from causing doubt and hesitation in carrying it into practice, is the only stable foundation for a just reliance on it: for, being cognisant of all that can, at least obviously, be said against him, and having taken up his position against all gainsayers—knowing that he has sought for objections and difficulties, instead of avoiding them, and has shut out no light which can be thrown upon the subject from any quarter—he has a right to think his judgment better than that of any person, or any multitude, who have not gone through a similar process.

It is not too much to require that what the wisest of mankind, those who are best entitled to trust their own judgment, find necessary to warrant their relying on it, should be submitted to by that miscellaneous collection of a few wise and many foolish individuals, called the public. The most intolerant of churches, the Roman Catholic Church, even at the canonization of a saint, admits, and listens patiently to, a 'devil's advocate.' The holiest of men, it appears, cannot be admitted to posthumous honours, until all that the devil could say against him is known and weighed. If even the Newtonian philosophy were not permitted to be questioned, mankind could not feel as complete assurance of its truth as they now do. The beliefs which we have most warrant for, have no safeguard

to rest on, but a standing invitation to the whole world to prove them unfounded. If the challenge is not accepted, or is accepted and the attempt fails, we are far enough from certainty still; but we have done the best that the existing state of human reason admits of; we have neglected nothing that could give the truth a chance of reaching us: if the lists are kept open, we may hope that if there be a better truth, it will be found when the human mind is capable of receiving it; and in the meantime we may rely on having attained such approach to truth, as is possible in our own day. This is the amount of certainty attainable by a fallible being, and this the sole way of attaining it.

Strange it is, that men should admit the validity of the arguments for free discussion, but object to their being 'pushed to an extreme;' not seeing that unless the reasons are good for an extreme case, they are not good for any case. Strange that they should imagine that they are not assuming infallibility, when they acknowledge that there should be free discussion on all subjects which can possibly be *doubtful*, but think that some particular principle or doctrine should be forbidden to be questioned because it is so *certain*, that is, because *they are certain* that it is certain. To call any proposition certain, while there is any one who would deny its certainty if permitted, but who is not permitted, is to assume that we ourselves, and those who agree with us, are the judges of certainty, and judges without hearing the other side.

In the present age—which has been described as 'destitute of faith, but terrified at scepticism'—in which people feel sure, not so much that their opinions are true, as that they should not know what to do without them—the claims of an opinion to be protected from public attack are rested not so much on its truth, as on its importance to society. There are, it is alleged, certain beliefs, so useful, not to say indispensable to well-being, that it is as much the duty of governments to uphold those beliefs, as to protect any other of the interests of society. In a case of such necessity, and so directly in the line of their duty, something less than infallibility may, it is maintained, warrant, and even bind, governments, to act on their own opinion, confirmed by the general opinion of mankind. It is also often argued, and still oftener thought, that none but bad men would desire to weaken these salutary beliefs; and there can be nothing wrong, it is thought, in restraining bad men, and prohibiting what only such men would wish to practise. This mode of thinking makes the justification of restraints on discussion not a question of the truth of doctrines, but of their usefulness; and flatters itself by that means to escape the responsibility of claiming to be an infallible judge of opinions. But those who thus satisfy themselves, do not perceive that the assumption of infallibility is merely shifted from one point to another. The usefulness of an opinion is itself matter of opinion: as disputable, as open to discussion, and requiring discussion as much, as the opinion itself. There is the same need of an infallible judge of opinions to decide an opinion to be noxious, as to decide it to be false, unless the opinion condemned has full opportunity of defending itself. And it will not do to say that the heretic may be allowed to maintain the utility or harmlessness of his opinion, though forbidden to maintain its truth. The truth of an opinion is part of its utility. If we would know whether or not it is desirable that a proposition should be believed, is it possible to exclude the consideration of whether or not it is true? In the opinion, not of bad men, but of the best men, no belief which is contrary to truth can be really useful: and can you prevent such men from urging that plea, when they are charged with culpability for denying some doctrine which they are told is useful, but which they believe to be false? Those who are on the side of received opinions, never fail to take all possible advantage of this plea; you do not find *them* handling the question of utility as if it could be completely abstracted from that of truth: on the contrary, it is, above all, because their doctrine is the 'truth,' that the knowledge or the belief of it is held to be so indispensable. There can be no fair discussion of the question of usefulness, when an argument so vital may be employed on one side, but not on the other. And in point of fact, when law or public feeling do not permit the truth of an opinion to be disputed, they are just as little tolerant of a denial of its usefulness. The utmost they allow is an extenuation of its absolute necessity, or of the positive guilt of rejecting it.

In order more fully to illustrate the mischief of denying a hearing to opinions because we, in our own judgment, have condemned them, it will be desirable to fix down the discussion to a concrete case; and I choose, by preference, the cases which are least favourable to me—in which the argument against freedom of opinion, both on the score of truth and on that of utility, is considered the strongest. Let the opinions impugned be the belief in a God and in a future state, or any of the commonly received doctrines of morality. To fight the battle on such ground, gives a great advantage to an unfair antagonist; since he will be sure to say (and many who have no desire to be unfair will say it internally), Are these the doctrines which you do not deem sufficiently certain to be taken under the protection of law? Is the belief in a God one of the opinions, to feel sure of which, you hold to be assuming infallibility? But I must be permitted to observe, that it is not the feeling sure of a doctrine (be it what it may) which I call an assumption of infallibility. It is the undertaking to decide that question *for others*, without allowing them to hear what can be said on the contrary side. And I denounce and reprobate this pretension not the less, if put forth on the side of my most solemn convictions. However positive any one's persuasion may be, not only of the falsity but of the pernicious consequences—not only of the pernicious consequences, but (to adopt expressions which I altogether condemn) the immorality and impiety of an opinion; yet if, in pursuance of that private judgment, though backed by the public judgment of his country or his contemporaries, he prevents the opinion from being heard in its defence, he assumes infallibility. And so far from the assumption being less objectionable or less dangerous because the opinion is called immoral or impious, this is the case of all others in which it is most fatal. These are exactly the occasions on which the men of one generation commit those dreadful mistakes, which excite the astonishment and horror of posterity. It is among such that we find the instances memorable in history, when the arm of the law has been employed to root out the best men and the noblest doctrines; with deplorable success as to the men, though some of the doctrines have survived to be (as if in mockery) invoked, in defence of similar conduct towards those who dissent from *them*, or from their received interpretation.

Mankind can hardly be too often reminded, that

there was once a man named Socrates, between whom and the legal authorities and public opinion of his time, there took place a memorable collision. Born in an age and country abounding in individual greatness, this man has been handed down to us by those who best knew both him and the age, as the most virtuous man in it; while we know him as the head and prototype of all subsequent teachers of virtue, the source equally of the lofty inspiration of Plato and the judicious utilitarianism of Aristotle, 'i maestri di color che sanno,' the two headsprings of ethical as of all other philosophy. This acknowledged master of all the eminent thinkers who have since lived — whose fame, still growing after more than two thousand years, all but outweighs the whole remainder of the names which make his native city illustrious — was put to death by his countrymen, after a judicial conviction, for impiety and immorality. Impiety, in denying the gods recognised by the State; indeed his accuser asserted (see the Apologia) that he believed in no gods at all. Immorality, in being, by his doctrines and instructions, a 'corruptor of youth.' Of these charges the tribunal, there is every ground for believing, honestly found him guilty, and condemned the man who probably of all then born had deserved best of mankind, to be put to death as a criminal.

To pass from this to the only other instance of judicial iniquity, the mention of which, after the condemnation of Socrates, would not be an anti-climax: the event which took place on Calvary rather more than eighteen hundred years ago. The man who left on the memory of those who witnessed his life and conversation, such an impression of his moral grandeur, that eighteen subsequent centuries have done homage to him as the Almighty in person, was ignominiously put to death, as what? As a blasphemer. Men did not merely mistake their benefactor; they mistook him for the exact contrary of what he was, and treated him as that prodigy of impiety, which they themselves are now held to be, for their treatment of him. The feelings with which mankind now regard these lamentable transactions, especially the later of the two, render them extremely unjust in their judgment of the unhappy actors. These were, to all appearance, not bad men — not worse than men commonly are, but rather the contrary; men who possessed in a full, or somewhat more than a full measure, the

religious, moral, and patriotic feelings of their time and people: the very kind of men who, in all times, our own included, have every chance of passing through life blameless and respected. The high-priest who rent his garments when the words were pronounced, which, according to all the ideas of his country, constituted the blackest guilt, was in all probability quite as sincere in his horror and indignation, as the generality of respectable and pious men now are in the religious and moral sentiments they profess; and most of those who now shudder at his conduct, if they had lived in his time, and been born Jews, would have acted precisely as he did. Orthodox Christians who are tempted to think that those who stoned to death the first martyrs must have been worse men than they themselves are, ought to remember that one of those persecutors was Saint Paul.

Let us add one more example, the most striking of all, if the impressiveness of an error is measured by the wisdom and virtue of him who falls into it. If ever any one, possessed of power, had grounds for thinking himself the best and most enlightened among his contemporaries, it was the Emperor Marcus Aurelius. Absolute monarch of the whole civilized world, he preserved through life not only the most unblemished justice, but what was less to be expected from his Stoical breeding, the tenderest heart. The few failings which are attributed to him, were all on the side of indulgence: while his writings, the highest ethical product of the ancient mind, differ scarcely perceptibly, if they differ at all, from the most characteristic teachings of Christ. This man, a better Christian in all but the dogmatic sense of the word, than almost any of the ostensibly Christian sovereigns who have since reigned, persecuted Christianity. Placed at the summit of all the previous attainments of humanity, with an open, unfettered intellect, and a character which led him of himself to embody in his moral writings the Christian ideal, he yet failed to see that Christianity was to be a good and not an evil to the world, with his duties to which he was so deeply penetrated. Existing society he knew to be in a deplorable state. But such as it was, he saw, or thought he saw, that it was held together, and prevented from being worse, by belief and reverence of the received divinities. As a ruler of mankind, he deemed it his duty not to suffer society to fall in pieces;

and saw not how, if its existing ties were removed, any others could be formed which could again knit it together. The new religion openly aimed at dissolving these ties: unless, therefore, it was his duty to adopt that religion, it seemed to be his duty to put it down. Inasmuch then as the theology of Christianity did not appear to him true or of divine origin; inasmuch as this strange history of a crucified God was not credible to him, and a system which purported to rest entirely upon a foundation to him so wholly unbelievable, could not be foreseen by him to be that renovating agency which, after all abatements, it has in fact proved to be; the gentlest and most amiable of philosophers and rulers, under a solemn sense of duty, authorized the persecution of Christianity. To my mind this is one of the most tragical facts in all history. It is a bitter thought, how different a thing the Christianity of the world might have been, if the Christian faith had been adopted as the religion of the empire under the auspices of Marcus Aurelius instead of those of Constantine. But it would be equally unjust to him and false to truth, to deny, that no one plea which can be urged for punishing anti-Christian teaching, was wanting to Marcus Aurelius for punishing, as he did, the propagation of Christianity. No Christian more firmly believes that Atheism is false, and tends to the dissolution of society, than Marcus Aurelius believed the same things of Christianity; he who, of all men then living, might have been thought the most capable of appreciating it. Unless any one who approves of punishment for the promulgation of opinions, flatters himself that he is a wiser and better man than Marcus Aurelius—more deeply versed in the wisdom of his time, more elevated in his intellect above it—more earnest in his search for truth, or more single-minded in his devotion to it when found;—let him abstain from that assumption of the joint infallibility of himself and the multitude, which the great Antoninus made with so unfortunate a result.

Aware of the impossibility of defending the use of punishment for restraining irreligious opinions, by any argument which will not justify Marcus Antoninus, the enemies of religious freedom, when hard pressed, occasionally accept this consequence, and say, with Dr. Johnson, that the persecutors of Christianity were in the right; that persecution is an ordeal through which truth ought to pass, and always passes successfully, legal penalties being, in the end, powerless against truth, though sometimes beneficially effective against mischievous errors. This is a form of the argument for religious intolerance, sufficiently remarkable not to be passed without notice.

A theory which maintains that truth may justifiably be persecuted because persecution cannot possibly do it any harm, cannot be charged with being intentionally hostile to the reception of new truths; but we cannot commend the generosity of its dealing with the persons to whom mankind are indebted for them. To discover to the world something which deeply concerns it, and of which it was previously ignorant; to prove to it that it had been mistaken on some vital point of temporal or spiritual interest, is as important a service as a human being can render to his fellow-creatures, and in certain cases, as in those of the early Christians and of the Reformers, those who think with Dr. Johnson believe it to have been the most precious gift which could be bestowed on mankind. That the authors of such splendid benefits should be requited by martyrdom; that their reward should be to be dealt with as the vilest of criminals, is not, upon this theory, a deplorable error and misfortune, for which humanity should mourn in sackcloth and ashes, but the normal and justifiable state of things. The propounder of a new truth, according to this doctrine, should stand, as stood, in the legislation of the Locrians, the proposer of a new law, with a halter round his neck, to be instantly tightened if the public assembly did not, on hearing his reasons, then and there adopt his proposition. People who defend this mode of treating benefactors, cannot be supposed to set much value on the benefit; and I believe this view of the subject is mostly confined to the sort of persons who think that new truths may have been desirable once, but that we have had enough of them now.

But, indeed, the dictum that truth always triumphs over persecution, is one of those pleasant falsehoods which men repeat after one another till they pass into commonplaces, but which all experience refutes. History teems with instances of truth put down by persecution. If not suppressed for ever, it may be thrown back for centuries. To speak only of religious opinions: the Reformation broke out at least twenty times before Luther, and was put down. Arnold of

Brescia was put down. Fra Dolcino was put down. Savonarola was put down. The Albigeois were put down. The Vaudois were put down. The Lollards were put down. The Hussites were put down. Even after the era of Luther, wherever persecution was persisted in, it was successful. In Spain, Italy, Flanders, the Austrian empire, Protestantism was rooted out; and, most likely, would have been so in England, had Queen Mary lived, or Queen Elizabeth died. Persecution has always succeeded, save where the heretics were too strong a party to be effectually persecuted. No reasonable person can doubt that Christianity might have been extirpated in the Roman Empire. It spread, and became predominant, because the persecutions were only occasional, lasting but a short time, and separated by long intervals of almost undisturbed propagandism. It is a piece of idle sentimentality that truth, merely as truth, has any inherent power denied to error, of prevailing against the dungeon and the stake. Men are not more zealous for truth than they often are for error, and a sufficient application of legal or even of social penalties will generally succeed in stopping the propagation of either. The real advantage which truth has, consists in this, that when an opinion is true, it may be extinguished once, twice, or many times, but in the course of ages there will generally be found persons to rediscover it, until some one of its reappearances falls on a time when from favourable circumstances it escapes persecution until it has made such head as to withstand all subsequent attempts to suppress it.

It will be said, that we do not now put to death the introducers of new opinions: we are not like our fathers who slew the prophets, we even build sepulchres to them. It is true we no longer put heretics to death; and the amount of penal infliction which modern feeling would probably tolerate, even against the most obnoxious opinions, is not sufficient to extirpate them. But let us not flatter ourselves that we are yet free from the stain even of legal persecution. Penalties for opinion, or at least for its expression, still exist by law; and their enforcement is not, even in these times, so unexampled as to make it at all incredible that they may some day be revived in full force. In the year 1857, at the summer assizes of the county of Cornwall, an unfortunate man,[2] said to be of unexceptionable conduct in all relations of life, was sentenced to twenty-one months' imprisonment, for uttering, and writing on a gate, some offensive words concerning Christianity. Within a month of the same time, at the Old Bailey, two persons, on two separate occasions,[3] were rejected as jurymen, and one of them grossly insulted by the judge and by one of the counsel, because they honestly declared that they had no theological belief; and a third, a foreigner,[4] for the same reason, was denied justice against a thief. This refusal of redress took place in virtue of the legal doctrine, that no person can be allowed to give evidence in a court of justice, who does not profess belief in a God (any god is sufficient) and in a future state; which is equivalent to declaring such persons to be outlaws, excluded from the protection of the tribunals; who may not only be robbed or assaulted with impunity, if no one but themselves, or persons of similar opinions, be present, but any one else may be robbed or assaulted with impunity, if the proof of the fact depends on their evidence. The assumption on which this is grounded, is that the oath is worthless, of a person who does not believe in a future state; a proposition which betokens much ignorance of history in those who assent to it (since it is historically true that a large proportion of infidels in all ages have been persons of distinguished integrity and honour); and would be maintained by no one who had the smallest conception how many of the persons in greatest repute with the world, both for virtues and for attainments, are well known, at least to their intimates, to be unbelievers. The rule, besides, is suicidal, and cuts away its own foundation. Under pretence that atheists must be liars, it admits the testimony of all atheists who are willing to lie, and rejects only those who brave the obloquy of publicly confessing a detested creed rather than affirm a falsehood. A rule thus self-convicted of absurdity so far as regards its professed

2. Thomas Pooley, Bodmin Assizes, July 31, 1857. In December following, he received a free pardon from the Crown.

3. George Jacob Holyoake, August 17, 1857; Edward Truelove, July, 1857.

4. Baron de Gleichen, Marlborough-street Police Court, August 4, 1857.

purpose, can be kept in force only as a badge of hatred, a relic of persecution; a persecution, too, having the peculiarity, that the qualification for undergoing it, is the being clearly proved not to deserve it. The rule, and the theory it implies, are hardly less insulting to believers than to infidels. For if he who does not believe in a future state, necessarily lies, it follows that they who do believe are only prevented from lying, if prevented they are, by the fear of hell. We will not do the authors and abettors of the rule the injury of supposing, that the conception which they have formed of Christian virtue is drawn from their own consciousness.

These, indeed, are but rags and remnants of persecution, and may be thought to be not so much an indication of the wish to persecute, as an example of that very frequent infirmity of English minds, which makes them take a preposterous pleasure in the assertion of a bad principle, when they are no longer bad enough to desire to carry it really into practice. But unhappily there is no security in the state of the public mind, that the suspension of worse forms of legal persecution, which has lasted for about the space of a generation, will continue. In this age the quiet surface of routine is as often ruffled by attempts to resuscitate past evils, as to introduce new benefits. What is boasted of at the present time as the revival of religion, is always, in narrow and uncultivated minds, at least as much the revival of bigotry; and where there is the strong permanent leaven of intolerance in the feelings of a people, which at all times abides in the middle classes of this country, it needs but little to provoke them into actively persecuting those whom they have never ceased to think proper objects of persecution.[5] For it is this—it is the opinions men entertain, and the feelings they cherish, respecting those who disown the beliefs they deem important, which makes this country not a place of mental freedom. For a long time past, the chief mischief of the legal penalties is that they strengthen the social stigma. It is that stigma which is really effective, and so effective is it, that the profession of opinions which are under the ban of society is much less common in England, than is, in many other countries, the avowal of those which incur risk of judicial punishment. In respect to all persons but those whose pecuniary circumstances make them independent of the good will of other people, opinion, on this subject, is as efficacious as law; men might as well be imprisoned, as excluded from the means of earning their bread. Those whose bread is already secured, and who desire no favours from men in power, or from bodies of men, or from the public, have nothing to fear from the open avowal of any opinions, but to be ill-thought of and ill-spoken of, and this it ought not to require a very heroic mould to enable them to bear. There is no room for any appeal *ad misericordiam* in behalf of such persons. But though we do not now inflict so much evil on those who think differently from us, as it was formerly our custom to do, it may be that we do ourselves as much evil as ever by our

---

5. Ample warning may be drawn from the large infusion of the passions of a persecutor, which mingled with the general display of the worst parts of our national character on the occasion of the Sepoy insurrection. The ravings of fanatics or charlatans from the pulpit may be unworthy of notice; but the heads of the Evangelical party have announced as their principle for the government of Hindoos and Mahomedans, that no schools be supported by public money in which the Bible is not taught, and by necessary consequence that no public employment be given to any but real or pretended Christians. An Under-Secretary of State, in a speech delivered to his constituents on the 12th of November, 1857, is reported to have said: 'Toleration of their faith' (the faith of a hundred millions of British subjects), 'the superstition which they called religion, by the British Government, had had the effect of retarding the ascendancy of the British name, and preventing the salutary growth of Christianity. . . . Toleration was the great corner-stone of the religious liberties of this country; but do not let them abuse that precious word toleration. As he understood it, it meant the complete liberty to all, freedom of worship, *among Christians, who worshipped upon the same foundation*. It meant toleration of all sects and denominations of *Christians who believed in the one mediation*.' I desire to call attention to the fact, that a man who has been deemed fit to fill a high office in the government of this country, under a liberal Ministry, maintains the doctrine that all who do not believe in the divinity of Christ are beyond the pale of toleration. Who, after this imbecile display, can indulge the illusion that religious persecution has passed away, never to return?

treatment of them. Socrates was put to death, but the Socratic philosophy rose like the sun in heaven, and spread its illumination over the whole intellectual firmament. Christians were cast to the lions, but the Christian church grew up a stately and spreading tree, overtopping the older and less vigorous growths, and stifling them by its shade. Our merely social intolerance kills no one, roots out no opinions, but induces men to disguise them, or to abstain from any active effort for their diffusion. With us, heretical opinions do not perceptibly gain, or even lose, ground in each decade or generation; they never blaze out far and wide, but continue to smoulder in the narrow circles of thinking and studious persons among whom they originate, without ever lighting up the general affairs of mankind with either a true or a deceptive light. And thus is kept up a state of things very satisfactory to some minds, because, without the unpleasant process of fining or imprisoning anybody, it maintains all prevailing opinions outwardly undisturbed, while it does not absolutely interdict the exercise of reason by dissentients afflicted with the malady of thought. A convenient plan for having peace in the intellectual world, and keeping all things going on therein very much as they do already. But the price paid for this sort of intellectual pacification, is the sacrifice of the entire moral courage of the human mind. A state of things in which a large portion of the most active and inquiring intellects find it advisable to keep the general principles and grounds of their convictions within their own breasts, and attempt, in what they address to the public, to fit as much as they can of their own conclusions to premises which they have internally renounced, cannot send forth the open, fearless characters, and logical, consistent intellects who once adorned the thinking world. The sort of men who can be looked for under it, are either mere conformers to commonplace, or time-servers for truth, whose arguments on all great subjects are meant for their hearers, and are not those which have convinced themselves. Those who avoid this alternative, do so by narrowing their thoughts and interest to things which can be spoken of without venturing within the region of principles, that is, to small practical matters, which would come right of themselves, if but the minds of mankind were strengthened and enlarged, and which will never be made effectually right until

then: while that which would strengthen and enlarge men's minds, free and daring speculation on the highest subjects, is abandoned.

Those in whose eyes this reticence on the part of heretics is no evil, should consider in the first place, that in consequence of it there is never any fair and thorough discussion of heretical opinions; and that such of them as could not stand such a discussion, though they may be prevented from spreading, do not disappear. But it is not the minds of heretics that are deteriorated most, by the ban placed on all inquiry which does not end in the orthodox conclusions. The greatest harm done is to those who are not heretics, and whose whole mental development is cramped, and their reason cowed, by the fear of heresy. Who can compute what the world loses in the multitude of promising intellects combined with timid characters, who dare not follow out any bold, vigorous, independent train of thought, lest it should land them in something which would admit of being considered irreligious or immoral? Among them we may occasionally see some man of deep conscientiousness, and subtle and refined understanding, who spends a life in sophisticating with an intellect which he cannot silence, and exhausts the resources of ingenuity in attempting to reconcile the promptings of his conscience and reason with orthodoxy, which yet he does not, perhaps, to the end succeed in doing. No one can be a great thinker who does not recognise, that as a thinker it is his first duty to follow his intellect to whatever conclusions it may lead. Truth gains more even by the errors of one who, with due study and preparation, thinks for himself, than by the true opinions of those who only hold them because they do not suffer themselves to think. Not that it is solely, or chiefly, to form great thinkers, that freedom of thinking is required. On the contrary, it is as much and even more indispensable, to enable average human beings to attain the mental stature which they are capable of. There have been, and may again be, great individual thinkers, in a general atmosphere of mental slavery. But there never has been, nor ever will be, in that atmosphere, an intellectually active people. When any people has made a temporary approach to such a character, it has been because the dread of heterodox speculation was for a time suspended. Where there is a tacit convention that principles are not to be disputed; where the discussion of the greatest questions which can occupy humanity is considered to be closed, we cannot hope to find that generally high scale of mental activity which has made some periods of history so remarkable. Never when controversy avoided the subjects which are large and important enough to kindle enthusiasm, was the mind of a people stirred up from its foundations, and the impulse given which raised even persons of the most ordinary intellect to something of the dignity of thinking beings. Of such we have had an example in the condition of Europe during the times immediately following the Reformation; another, though limited to the Continent and to a more cultivated class, in the speculative movement of the latter half of the eighteenth century; and a third, of still briefer duration, in the intellectual fermentation of Germany during the Goethian and Fichtean period. These periods differed widely in the particular opinions which they developed, but were alike in this, that during all three the yoke of authority was broken. In each, an old mental despotism had been thrown off, and no new one had yet taken its place. The impulse given at these three periods has made Europe what it now is. Every single improvement which has taken place either in the human mind or in institutions, may be traced distinctly to one or other of them. Appearances have for some time indicated that all three impulses are well nigh spent; and we can expect no fresh start, until we again assert our mental freedom.

Let us now pass to the second division of the argument, and dismissing the supposition that any of the received opinions may be false, let us assume them to be true, and examine into the worth of the manner in which they are likely to be held, when their truth is not freely and openly canvassed. However unwillingly a person who has a strong opinion may admit the possibility that his opinion may be false, he ought to be moved by the consideration that however true it may be, if it is not fully, frequently, and fearlessly discussed, it will be held as a dead dogma, not a living truth.

There is a class of persons (happily not quite so numerous as formerly) who think it enough if a person assents undoubtingly to what they think true, though he has no knowledge whatever of the grounds of the opinion, and could not make a tenable defence of it against the most superficial objections. Such persons, if they can once get their creed taught from authority, naturally think that no good, and some harm, comes of its being allowed to be questioned. Where their influence prevails, they make it nearly impossible for the received opinion to be rejected wisely and considerately, though it may still be rejected rashly and ignorantly; for to shut out discussion entirely is seldom possible, and when it once gets in, beliefs not grounded on conviction are apt to give way before the slightest semblance of an argument. Waving, however, this possibility—assuming that the true opinion abides in the mind, but abides as a prejudice, a belief independent of, and proof against, argument—this is not the way in which truth ought to be held by a rational being. This is not knowing the truth. Truth, thus held, is but one superstition the more, accidentally clinging to the words which enunciate a truth.

If the intellect and judgment of mankind ought to be cultivated, a thing which Protestants at least do not deny, on what can these faculties be more appropriately exercised by any one, than on the things which concern him so much that it is considered necessary for him to hold opinions on them? If the cultivation of the understanding consists in one thing more than in another, it is surely in learning the grounds of one's own opinions. Whatever people believe, on subjects on which it is of the first importance to believe rightly, they ought to be able to defend against at least the common objections. But, some one may say, 'Let them be *taught* the grounds of their opinions. It does not follow that opinions must be merely parroted because they are never heard controverted. Persons who learn geometry do not simply commit the theorems to memory, but understand and learn likewise the demonstrations; and it would be absurd to say that they remain ignorant of the grounds of geometrical truths, because they never hear any one deny, and attempt to disprove them.' Undoubtedly: and such teaching suffices on a subject like mathematics, where there is nothing at all to be said on the wrong side of the question. The peculiarity of the evidence of mathematical truths is, that all the argument is on one side. There are no objections, and no answers to objections. But on every subject on which difference of opinion is possible, the truth depends on a balance to be struck between two sets of conflicting reasons. Even in natural philosophy, there is always some other explanation possible of the same facts; some geocentric theory instead of heliocentric, some phlogiston instead of oxygen; and it has to be shown why that other theory cannot be the true one: and until this is shown, and until we know how it is shown, we do not understand the grounds of our opinion. But when we turn to subjects infinitely more complicated, to morals, religion, politics, social relations, and the business of life, three-fourths of the arguments for every disputed opinion consist in dispelling the appearances which favour some opinion different from it. The greatest orator, save one, of antiquity, has left it on record that he always studied his adversary's case with as great, if not with still greater, intensity than even his own. What Cicero practised as the means of forensic success, requires to be imitated by all who study any subject in order to arrive at the truth. He who knows only his own side of the case, knows little of that. His reasons may be good, and no one may have been able to refute them. But if he is equally unable to refute the reasons on the opposite side; if he does not so much as know what they are, he has no ground for preferring either opinion. The rational position for him would be suspension of judgment, and unless he contents himself with that, he is either led by authority, or adopts, like the generality of the world, the side to which he feels most inclination. Nor is it enough that he should hear the arguments of adversaries from his own teachers, presented as they state them, and accompanied by what they offer as refutations. That is not the way to do justice to the arguments, or bring them into real contact with his own mind. He must be able to hear them from persons who actually believe them; who defend them in earnest, and do their very utmost for them. He must know them in their most plausible and persuasive form; he must feel the whole force of the difficulty which the true view of the subject has to encounter and dispose of; else he will never really possess himself of the portion of truth which meets and removes that difficulty. Ninety-nine in a hundred of what are called educated men are in this condition; even of those who can argue fluently for their opinions. Their conclusion may be true, but it might be false for anything they know: they have never thrown themselves into

the mental position of those who think differently from them, and considered what such persons may have to say; and consequently they do not, in any proper sense of the word, know the doctrine which they themselves profess. They do not know those parts of it which explain and justify the remainder; the considerations which show that a fact which seemingly conflicts with another is reconcilable with it, or that, of two apparently strong reasons, one and not the other ought to be preferred. All that part of the truth which turns the scale, and decides the judgment of a completely informed mind, they are strangers to; nor is it ever really known, but to those who have attended equally and impartially to both sides, and endeavoured to see the reasons of both in the strongest light. So essential is this discipline to a real understanding of moral and human subjects, that if opponents of all important truths do not exist, it is indispensable to imagine them, and supply them with the strongest arguments which the most skilful devil's advocate can conjure up.

To abate the force of these considerations, an enemy of free discussion may be supposed to say, that there is no necessity for mankind in general to know and understand all that can be said against or for their opinions by philosophers and theologians. That it is not needful for common men to be able to expose all the misstatements or fallacies of an ingenious opponent. That it is enough if there is always somebody capable of answering them, so that nothing likely to mislead uninstructed persons remains unrefuted. That simple minds, having been taught the obvious grounds of the truths inculcated on them, may trust to authority for the rest, and being aware that they have neither knowledge nor talent to resolve every difficulty which can be raised, may repose in the assurance that all those which have been raised have been or can be answered, by those who are specially trained to the task.

Conceding to this view of the subject the utmost that can be claimed for it by those most easily satisfied with the amount of understanding of truth which ought to accompany the belief of it; even so, the argument for free discussion is no way weakened. For even this doctrine acknowledges that mankind ought to have a rational assurance that all objections have been satisfactorily answered; and how are they to be answered if that which requires to be answered is not spoken? or how can the answer be known to be satisfactory, if the objectors have no opportunity of showing that it is unsatisfactory? If not the public, at least the philosophers and theologians who are to resolve the difficulties, must make themselves familiar with those difficulties in their most puzzling form; and this cannot be accomplished unless they are freely stated, and placed in the most advantageous light which they admit of. The Catholic Church has its own way of dealing with this embarrassing problem. It makes a broad separation between those who can be permitted to receive its doctrines on conviction, and those who must accept them on trust. Neither, indeed, are allowed any choice as to what they will accept; but the clergy, such at least as can be fully confided in, may admissibly and meritoriously make themselves acquainted with the arguments of opponents, in order to answer them, and may, therefore, read heretical books; the laity, not unless by special permission, hard to be obtained. This discipline recognises a knowledge of the enemy's case as beneficial to the teachers, but finds means, consistent with this, of denying it to the rest of the world: thus giving to the *élite* more mental culture, though not more mental freedom, than it allows to the mass. By this device it succeeds in obtaining the kind of mental superiority which its purposes require; for though culture without freedom never made a large and liberal mind, it can make a clever *nisi prius* advocate of a cause. But in countries professing Protestantism, this resource is denied; since Protestants hold, at least in theory, that the responsibility for the choice of a religion must be borne by each for himself, and cannot be thrown off upon teachers. Besides, in the present state of the world, it is practically impossible that writings which are read by the instructed can be kept from the uninstructed. If the teachers of mankind are to be cognisant of all that they ought to know, everything must be free to be written and published without restraint.

If, however, the mischievous operation of the absence of free discussion, when the received opinions are true, were confined to leaving men ignorant of the grounds of those opinions, it might be thought that this, if an intellectual, is no moral evil, and does not affect the worth of the opinions, regarded in their influence on the character. The fact, however, is, that not only the grounds of the opinion are forgotten in the absence of discussion, but too often the meaning of the opinion itself. The words which convey it, cease to suggest ideas, or suggest only a small portion of those they were originally employed to communicate. Instead of a vivid conception and a living belief, there remain only a few phrases retained by rote; or, if any part, the shell and husk only of the meaning is retained, the finer essence being lost. The great chapter in human history which this fact occupies and fills, cannot be too earnestly studied and meditated on.

It is illustrated in the experience of almost all ethical doctrines and religious creeds. They are all full of meaning and vitality to those who originate them, and to the direct disciples of the originators. Their meaning continues to be felt in undiminished strength, and is perhaps brought out into even fuller consciousness, so long as the struggle lasts to give the doctrine or creed an ascendancy over other creeds. At last it either prevails, and becomes the general opinion, or its progress stops; it keeps possession of the ground it has gained, but ceases to spread further. When either of these results has become apparent, controversy on the subject flags, and gradually dies away. The doctrine has taken its place, if not as a received opinion, as one of the admitted sects or divisions of opinion: those who hold it have generally inherited, not adopted it; and conversion from one of these doctrines to another, being now an exceptional fact, occupies little place in the thoughts of their professors. Instead of being, as at first, constantly on the alert either to defend themselves against the world, or to bring the world over to them, they have subsided into acquiescence, and neither listen, when they can help it, to arguments against their creed, nor trouble dissentients (if there be such) with arguments in its favour. From this time may usually be dated the decline in the living power of the doctrine. We often hear the teachers of all creeds lamenting the difficulty of keeping up in the minds of believers a lively apprehension of the truth which they nominally recognise, so that it may penetrate the feelings, and acquire a real mastery over the conduct. No such difficulty is complained of while the creed is still fighting for its existence: even the weaker combatants then know and feel what they are fighting for, and the difference between it and other doctrines; and in that period of every creed's existence, not a few persons may be found, who have realized its fundamental principles in all the forms of thought, have weighed and considered them in all their important bearings, and have experienced the full effect on the character, which belief in that creed ought to produce in a mind thoroughly imbued with it. But when it has come to be an hereditary creed, and to be received passively, not actively—when the mind is no longer compelled, in the same degree as at first, to exercise its vital powers on the questions which its belief presents to it, there is a progressive tendency to forget all of the belief except the formularies, or to give it a dull and torpid assent, as if accepting it on trust dispensed with the necessity of realizing it in consciousness, or testing it by personal experience; until it almost ceases to connect itself at all with the inner life of the human being. Then are seen the cases, so frequent in this age of the world as almost to form the majority, in which the creed remains as it were outside the mind, incrusting and petrifying it against all other influences addressed to the higher parts of our nature; manifesting its power by not suffering any fresh and living conviction to get in, but itself doing nothing for the mind or heart, except standing sentinel over them to keep them vacant.

To what an extent doctrines intrinsically fitted to make the deepest impression upon the mind may remain in it as dead beliefs, without being ever realized in the imagination, the feelings, or the understanding, is exemplified by the manner in which the majority of believers hold the doctrines of Christianity. By Christianity I here mean what is accounted such by all churches and sects—the maxims and precepts contained in the New Testament. These are considered sacred, and accepted as laws, by all professing Christians. Yet it is scarcely too much to say that not one Christian in a thousand guides or tests his individual conduct by reference to those laws. The standard to which he does refer it, is the custom of his nation, his class, or his religious profession. He has thus, on the one hand, a collection of ethical maxims, which he believes to have been vouchsafed to him by infallible wisdom as rules for his government; and on the other, a set of every-day judgments and practices, which go a certain length with some

of those maxims, not so great a length with others, stand in direct opposition to some, and are, on the whole, a compromise between the Christian creed and the interests and suggestions of worldly life. To the first of these standards he gives his homage; to the other his real allegiance. All Christians believe that the blessed are the poor and humble, and those who are ill-used by the world; that it is easier for a camel to pass through the eye of a needle than for a rich man to enter the kingdom of heaven; that they should judge not, lest they be judged; that they should swear not at all; that they should love their neighbour as themselves; that if one take their cloak, they should give him their coat also; that they should take no thought for the morrow; that if they would be perfect, they should sell all that they have and give it to the poor. They are not insincere when they say that they believe these things. They do believe them, as people believe what they have always heard lauded and never discussed. But in the sense of that living belief which regulates conduct, they believe these doctrines just up to the point to which it is usual to act upon them. The doctrines in their integrity are serviceable to pelt adversaries with; and it is understood that they are to be put forward (when possible) as the reasons for whatever people do that they think laudable. But any one who reminded them that the maxims require an infinity of things which they never even think of doing, would gain nothing but to be classed among those very unpopular characters who affect to be better than other people. The doctrines have no hold on ordinary believers—are not a power in their minds. They have an habitual respect for the sound of them, but no feeling which spreads from the words to the things signified, and forces the mind to take *them* in, and make them conform to the formula. Whenever conduct is concerned, they look round for Mr. A and B to direct them how far to go in obeying Christ.

Now we may be well assured that the case was not thus, but far otherwise, with the early Christians. Had it been thus, Christianity never would have expanded from an obscure sect of the despised Hebrews into the religion of the Roman empire. When their enemies said, 'See how these Christians love one another' (a remark not likely to be made by anybody now), they assuredly had a much livelier feeling of the meaning of their creed than they have ever had since.

And to this cause, probably, it is chiefly owing that Christianity now makes so little progress in extending its domain, and after eighteen centuries, is still nearly confined to Europeans and the descendants of Europeans. Even with the strictly religious, who are much in earnest about their doctrines, and attach a greater amount of meaning to many of them than people in general, it commonly happens that the part which is thus comparatively active in their minds is that which was made by Calvin, or Knox, or some such person much nearer in character to themselves. The sayings of Christ coexist passively in their minds, producing hardly any effect beyond what is caused by mere listening to words so amiable and bland. There are many reasons, doubtless, why doctrines which are the badge of a sect retain more of their vitality than those common to all recognised sects, and why more pains are taken by teachers to keep their meaning alive; but one reason certainly is, that the peculiar doctrines are more questioned, and have to be oftener defended against open gainsayers. Both teachers and learners go to sleep at their post, as soon as there is no enemy in the field.

The same thing holds true, generally speaking, of all traditional doctrines—those of prudence and knowledge of life, as well as of morals or religion. All languages and literatures are full of general observations on life, both as to what it is, and how to conduct oneself in it; observations which everybody knows, which everybody repeats, or hears with acquiescence, which are received as truisms, yet of which most people first truly learn the meaning, when experience, generally of a painful kind, has made it a reality to them. How often, when smarting under some unforeseen misfortune or disappointment, does a person call to mind some proverb or common saying, familiar to him all his life, the meaning of which, if he had ever before felt it as he does now, would have saved him from the calamity. There are indeed reasons for this, other than the absence of discussion: there are many truths of which the full meaning *cannot* be realized, until personal experience has brought it home. But much more of the meaning even of these would have been understood, and what was understood would have been far more deeply impressed on the mind, if the man had been accustomed to hear it argued *pro* and *con* by people who did understand it. The fatal tendency of mankind to leave off thinking about a thing when it is no longer doubtful, is the cause of half their errors. A contemporary author has well spoken of 'the deep slumber of a decided opinion.'

But what! (it may be asked) Is the absence of unanimity an indispensable condition of true knowledge? Is it necessary that some part of mankind should persist in error, to enable any to realize the truth? Does a belief cease to be real and vital as soon as it is generally received—and is a proposition never thoroughly understood and felt unless some doubt of it remains? As soon as mankind have unanimously accepted a truth, does the truth perish within them? The highest aim and best result of improved intelligence, it has hitherto been thought, is to unite mankind more and more in the acknowledgment of all important truths: and does the intelligence only last as long as it has not achieved its object? Do the fruits of conquest perish by the very completeness of the victory?

I affirm no such thing. As mankind improve, the number of doctrines which are no longer disputed or doubted will be constantly on the increase: and the well-being of mankind may almost be measured by the number and gravity of the truths which have reached the point of being uncontested. The cessation, on one question after another, of serious controversy, is one of the necessary incidents of the consolidation of opinion; a consolidation as salutary in the case of true opinions, as it is dangerous and noxious when the opinions are erroneous. But though this gradual narrowing of the bounds of diversity of opinion is necessary in both senses of the term, being at once inevitable and indispensable, we are not therefore obliged to conclude that all its consequences must be beneficial. The loss of so important an aid to the intelligent and living apprehension of a truth, as is afforded by the necessity of explaining it to, or defending it against, opponents, though not sufficient to outweigh, is no trifling drawback from, the benefit of its universal recognition. Where this advantage can no longer be had, I confess I should like to see the teachers of mankind endeavouring to provide a substitute for it; some contrivance for making the difficulties of the question as present to the learner's consciousness, as if they were pressed upon him by a dissentient champion, eager for his conversion.

But instead of seeking contrivances for this purpose, they have lost those they formerly had. The Socratic dialectics, so magnificently exemplified in the dialogues of Plato, were a contrivance of this description. They were essentially a negative discussion of the great questions of philosophy and life, directed with consummate skill to the purpose of convincing any one who had merely adopted the commonplaces of received opinion, that he did not understand the subject—that he as yet attached no definite meaning to the doctrines he professed; in order that, becoming aware of his ignorance, he might be put in the way to attain a stable belief, resting on a clear apprehension both of the meaning of doctrines and of their evidence. The school disputations of the middle ages had a somewhat similar object. They were intended to make sure that the pupil understood his own opinion, and (by necessary correlation) the opinion opposed to it, and could enforce the grounds of the one and confute those of the other. These last-mentioned contests had indeed the incurable defect, that the premises appealed to were taken from authority, not from reason; and, as a discipline to the mind, they were in every respect inferior to the powerful dialectics which formed the intellects of the 'Socratici viri:' but the modern mind owes far more to both than it is generally willing to admit, and the present modes of education contain nothing which in the smallest degree supplies the place either of the one or of the other. A person who derives all his instruction from teachers or books, even if he escape the besetting temptation of contenting himself with cram, is under no compulsion to hear both sides; accordingly it is far from a frequent accomplishment, even among thinkers, to know both sides; and the weakest part of what everybody says in defence of his opinion, is what he intends as a reply to antagonists. It is the fashion of the present time to disparage negative logic—that which points out weaknesses in theory or errors in practice, without establishing positive truths. Such negative criticism would indeed be poor enough as an ultimate result; but as a means to attaining any positive knowledge or conviction worthy the name, it cannot be valued too highly; and until people are again systematically trained to it, there will be few great thinkers, and a low general average of intellect, in any but the mathematical and physical depart-

ments of speculation. On any other subject no one's opinions deserve the name of knowledge, except so far as he has either had forced upon him by others, or gone through of himself, the same mental process which would have been required of him in carrying on an active controversy with opponents. That, therefore, which when absent, it is so indispensable, but so difficult, to create, how worse than absurd it is to forego, when spontaneously offering itself! If there are any persons who contest a received opinion, or who will do so if law or opinion will let them, let us thank them for it, open our minds to listen to them, and rejoice that there is some one to do for us what we otherwise ought, if we have any regard for either the certainty or the vitality of our convictions, to do with much greater labour for ourselves.

It still remains to speak of one of the principal causes which make diversity of opinion advantageous, and will continue to do so until mankind shall have entered a stage of intellectual advancement which at present seems at an incalculable distance. We have hitherto considered only two possibilities: that the received opinion may be false, and some other opinion, consequently, true; or that, the received opinion being true, a conflict with the opposite error is essential to a clear apprehension and deep feeling of its truth. But there is a commoner case than either of these; when the conflicting doctrines, instead of being one true and the other false, share the truth between them; and the nonconforming opinion is needed to supply the remainder of the truth, of which the received doctrine embodies only a part. Popular opinions, on subjects not palpable to sense, are often true, but seldom or never the whole truth. They are a part of the truth; sometimes a greater, sometimes a smaller part, but exaggerated, distorted, and disjoined from the truths by which they ought to be accompanied and limited. Heretical opinions, on the other hand, are generally some of these suppressed and neglected truths, bursting the bonds which kept them down, and either seeking reconciliation with the truth contained in the common opinion, or fronting it as enemies, and setting themselves up, with similar exclusiveness, as the whole truth. The latter case is hitherto the most frequent, as, in the human mind, one-sidedness has always been the rule, and many-sidedness the exception. Hence, even in revolutions of opinion, one part of the truth usually sets while another rises. Even progress, which ought to super-add, for the most part only substitutes, one partial and incomplete truth for another; improvement consisting chiefly in this, that the new fragment of truth is more wanted, more adapted to the needs of the time, than that which it displaces. Such being the partial character of prevailing opinions, even when resting on a true foundation, every opinion which embodies somewhat of the portion of truth which the common opinion omits, ought to be considered precious, with whatever amount of error and confusion that truth may be blended. No sober judge of human affairs will feel bound to be indignant because those who force on our notice truths which we should otherwise have overlooked, overlook some of those which we see. Rather, he will think that so long as popular truth is one-sided, it is more desirable than otherwise that unpopular truth should have one-sided asserters too; such being usually the most energetic, and the most likely to compel reluctant attention to the fragment of wisdom which they proclaim as if it were the whole.

Thus, in the eighteenth century, when nearly all the instructed, and all those of the uninstructed who were led by them, were lost in admiration of what is called civilization, and of the marvels of modern science, literature, and philosophy, and while greatly overrating the amount of unlikeness between the men of modern and those of ancient times, indulged the belief that the whole of the difference was in their own favour; with what a salutary shock did the paradoxes of Rousseau explode like bombshells in the midst, dislocating the compact mass of one-sided opinion, and forcing its elements to recombine in a better form and with additional ingredients. Not that the current opinions were on the whole farther from the truth than Rousseau's were; on the contrary, they were nearer to it; they contained more of positive truth, and very much less of error. Nevertheless there lay in Rousseau's doctrine, and has floated down the stream of opinion along with it, a considerable amount of exactly those truths which the popular opinion wanted; and these are the deposit which was left behind when the flood subsided. The superior worth of simplicity of life, the enervating and demoralizing effect of the trammels and hypocrisies of artifi-

cial society, are ideas which have never been entirely absent from cultivated minds since Rousseau wrote; and they will in time produce their due effect, though at present needing to be asserted as much as ever, and to be asserted by deeds, for words, on this subject, have nearly exhausted their power.

In politics, again, it is almost a commonplace, that a party of order or stability, and a party of progress or reform, are both necessary elements of a healthy state of political life; until the one or the other shall have so enlarged its mental grasp as to be a party equally of order and of progress, knowing and distinguishing what is fit to be preserved from what ought to be swept away. Each of these modes of thinking derives its utility from the deficiencies of the other; but it is in a great measure the opposition of the other that keeps each within the limits of reason and sanity. Unless opinions favourable to democracy and to aristocracy, to property and to equality, to co-operation and to competition, to luxury and to abstinence, to sociality and individuality, to liberty and discipline, and all the other standing antagonisms of practical life, are expressed with equal freedom, and enforced and defended with equal talent and energy, there is no chance of both elements obtaining their due; one scale is sure to go up, and the other down. Truth, in the great practical concerns of life, is so much a question of the reconciling and combining of opposites, that very few have minds sufficiently capacious and impartial to make the adjustment with an approach to correctness, and it has to be made by the rough process of a struggle between combatants fighting under hostile banners. On any of the great open questions just enumerated, if either of the two opinions has a better claim than the other, not merely to be tolerated, but to be encouraged and countenanced, it is the one which happens at the particular time and place to be in a minority. That is the opinion which, for the time being, represents the neglected interests, the side of human well-being which is in danger of obtaining less than its share. I am aware that there is not, in this country, any intolerance of differences of opinion on most of these topics. They are adduced to show, by admitted and multiplied examples, the universality of the fact, that only through diversity of opinion is there, in the existing state of human intellect, a chance of fair play to all sides of the truth. When there are persons to be found, who form an exception to the apparent unanimity of the world on any subject, even if the world is in the right, it is always probable that dissentients have something worth hearing to say for themselves, and that truth would lose something by their silence.

It may be objected, 'But *some* received principles, especially on the highest and most vital subjects, are more than half-truths. The Christian morality, for instance, is the whole truth on that subject, and if any one teaches a morality which varies from it, he is wholly in error.' As this is of all cases the most important in practice, none can be fitter to test the general maxim. But before pronouncing what Christian morality is or is not, it would be desirable to decide what is meant by Christian morality. If it means the morality of the New Testament, I wonder that any one who derives his knowledge of this from the book itself, can suppose that it was announced, or intended, as a complete doctrine of morals. The Gospel always refers to a pre-existing morality, and confines its precepts to the particulars in which that morality was to be corrected, or superseded by a wider and higher; expressing itself, moreover, in terms most general, often impossible to be interpreted literally, and possessing rather the impressiveness of poetry or eloquence than the precision of legislation. To extract from it a body of ethical doctrine, has never been possible without eking it out from the Old Testament, that is, from a system elaborate indeed, but in many respects barbarous, and intended only for a barbarous people. St. Paul, a declared enemy to this Judaical mode of interpreting the doctrine and filling up the scheme of his Master, equally assumes a pre-existing morality, namely that of the Greeks and Romans; and his advice to Christians is in a great measure a system of accommodation to that; even to the extent of giving an apparent sanction to slavery. What is called Christian, but should rather be termed theological, morality, was not the work of Christ or the Apostles, but is of much later origin, having been gradually built up by the Catholic church of the first five centuries, and though not implicitly adopted by moderns and Protestants, has been much less modified by them than might have been expected. For the most part, indeed, they have contented themselves with cutting off the additions which had been made to it in the middle ages, each sect supplying the place by fresh additions, adapted to its own character and tendencies. That mankind owe a great debt to this morality, and to its early teachers, I should be the last person to deny; but I do not scruple to say of it, that it is, in many important points, incomplete and one-sided, and that unless ideas and feelings, not sanctioned by it, had contributed to the formation of European life and character, human affairs would have been in a worse condition than they now are. Christian morality (so called) has all the characters of a reaction; it is, in great part, a protest against Paganism. Its ideal is negative rather than positive; passive rather than active; Innocence rather than Nobleness; Abstinence from Evil, rather than energetic Pursuit of Good: in its precepts (as has been well said) 'thou shalt not' predominates unduly over 'thou shalt.' In its horror of sensuality, it made an idol of asceticism, which has been gradually compromised away into one of legality. It holds out the hope of heaven and the threat of hell, as the appointed and appropriate motives to a virtuous life: in this falling far below the best of the ancients, and doing what lies in it to give to human morality an essentially selfish character, by disconnecting each man's feelings of duty from the interests of his fellow-creatures, except so far as a self-interested inducement is offered to him for consulting them. It is essentially a doctrine of passive obedience; it inculcates submission to all authorities found established; who indeed are not to be actively obeyed when they command what religion forbids, but who are not to be resisted, far less rebelled against, for any amount of wrong to ourselves. And while, in the morality of the best Pagan nations, duty to the State holds even a disproportionate place, infringing on the just liberty of the individual; in purely Christian ethics, that grand department of duty is scarcely noticed or acknowledged. It is in the Koran, not the New Testament, that we read the maxim — 'A ruler who appoints any man to an office, when there is in his dominions another man better qualified for it, sins against God and against the State.' What little recognition the idea of obligation to the public obtains in modern morality, is derived from Greek and Roman sources, not from Christian; as, even in the morality of private life, whatever exists of magnanimity, highmindedness, personal dignity, even the sense of honour, is derived from the purely human, not the religious part of our education, and never could have grown out of a standard of ethics in which the only worth, professedly recognised, is that of obedience.

I am as far as any one from pretending that these defects are necessarily inherent in the Christian ethics, in every manner in which it can be conceived, or that the many requisites of a complete moral doctrine which it does not contain, do not admit of being reconciled with it. Far less would I insinuate this of the doctrines and precepts of Christ himself. I believe that the sayings of Christ are all, that I can see any evidence of their having been intended to be; that they are irreconcilable with nothing which a comprehensive morality requires; that everything which is excellent in ethics may be brought within them, with no greater violence to their language than has been done to it by all who have attempted to deduce from them any practical system of conduct whatever. But it is quite consistent with this, to believe that they contain, and were meant to contain, only a part of the truth; that many essential elements of the highest morality are among the things which are not provided for, nor intended to be provided for, in the recorded deliverances of the Founder of Christianity, and which have been entirely thrown aside in the system of ethics erected on the basis of those deliverances by the Christian Church. And this being so, I think it a great error to persist in attempting to find in the Christian doctrine that complete rule for our guidance, which its author intended it to sanction and enforce, but only partially to provide. I believe, too, that this narrow theory is becoming a grave practical evil, detracting greatly from the value of the moral training and instruction, which so many well-meaning persons are now at length exerting themselves to promote. I much fear that by attempting to form the mind and feelings on an exclusively religious type, and discarding those secular standards (as for want of a better name they may be called) which heretofore co-existed with and supplemented the Christian ethics, receiving some of its spirit, and infusing into it some of theirs, there will result, and is even now resulting, a low, abject, servile type of character, which, submit itself as it may to what it deems the Supreme Will, is incapable of rising to or sympathizing in the conception of Supreme Goodness. I believe that other ethics than any which can be evolved from exclusively Christian sources, must exist side by side with Christian ethics to produce the moral regeneration of mankind; and that the Christian system is no exception to the rule, that in an imperfect state of the human mind, the interests of truth require a diversity of opinions. It is not necessary that in ceasing to ignore the moral truths not contained in Christianity, men should ignore any of those which it does contain. Such prejudice, or oversight, when it occurs, is altogether an evil; but it is one from which we cannot hope to be always exempt, and must be regarded as the price paid for an inestimable good. The exclusive pretension made by a part of the truth to be the whole, must and ought to be protested against; and if a reactionary impulse should make the protestors unjust in their turn, this one-sidedness, like the other, may be lamented, but must be tolerated. If Christians would teach infidels to be just to Christianity, they should themselves be just to infidelity. It can do truth no service to blink the fact, known to all who have the most ordinary acquaintance with literary history, that a large portion of the noblest and most valuable moral teaching has been the work, not only of men who did not know, but of men who knew and rejected, the Christian faith.

I do not pretend that the most unlimited use of the freedom of enunciating all possible opinions would put an end to the evils of religious or philosophical sectarianism. Every truth which men of narrow capacity are in earnest about, is sure to be asserted, inculcated, and in many ways even acted on, as if no other truth existed in the world, or at all events none that could limit or qualify the first. I acknowledge that the tendency of all opinions to become sectarian is not cured by the freest discussion, but is often heightened and exacerbated thereby; the truth which ought to have been, but was not, seen, being rejected all the more violently because proclaimed by persons regarded as opponents. But it is not on the impassioned partisan, it is on the calmer and more disinterested bystander, that this collision of opinions works its salutary effect. Not the violent conflict between parts of the truth, but the quiet suppression of half of it, is the formidable evil; there is always hope when people are forced to listen to both sides; it is when they attend only to one that errors harden into prejudices, and truth itself ceases to have the effect of truth, by being exaggerated into falsehood. And since there are few mental attributes more rare than that judicial faculty which can sit in intelligent judgment between two sides of a question, of which only one is represented by an advocate before it, truth has no chance but in proportion as every side of it, every opinion which embodies any fraction of the truth, not only finds advocates, but is so advocated as to be listened to.

We have now recognised the necessity to the mental well-being of mankind (on which all their other well-being depends) of freedom of opinion, and freedom of the expression of opinion, on four distinct grounds; which we will now briefly recapitulate.

First, if any opinion is compelled to silence, that opinion may, for aught we can certainly know, be true. To deny this is to assume our own infallibility.

Secondly, though the silenced opinion be an error, it may, and very commonly does, contain a portion of truth; and since the general or prevailing opinion on any subject is rarely or never the whole truth, it is only by the collision of adverse opinions that the remainder of the truth has any chance of being supplied.

Thirdly, even if the received opinion be not only true, but the whole truth; unless it is suffered to be, and actually is, vigorously and earnestly contested, it will, by most of those who receive it, be held in the manner of a prejudice, with little comprehension or feeling of its rational grounds. And not only this, but, fourthly, the meaning of the doctrine itself will be in danger of being lost, or enfeebled, and deprived of its vital effect on the character and conduct: the dogma becoming a mere formal profession, inefficacious for good, but cumbering the ground, and preventing the growth of any real and heartfelt conviction, from reason or personal experience.

Before quitting the subject of freedom of opinion, it is fit to take some notice of those who say, that the free expression of all opinions should be permitted, on condition that the manner be temperate, and do not pass the bounds of fair discussion. Much might be said on the impossibility of fixing where these supposed bounds are to be placed; for if the test be offence to those whose opinion is attacked, I think experience testifies that this offence is given whenever the attack is telling and powerful, and that every opponent who pushes them hard, and whom they find it difficult to answer, appears to them, if he shows any strong feeling on the subject, an intemperate opponent. But this, though an important consideration in a practical point of view, merges in a more fundamental objection. Undoubtedly the manner of asserting an opinion, even though it be a true one, may be very objectionable, and may justly incur severe censure. But the principal offences of the kind are such as it is mostly impossible, unless by accidental self-betrayal, to bring home to conviction. The gravest of them is, to argue sophistically, to suppress facts or arguments, to misstate the elements of the case, or misrepresent the opposite opinion. But all this, even to the most aggravated degree, is so continually done in perfect good faith, by persons who are not considered, and in many other respects may not deserve to be considered, ignorant or incompetent, that it is rarely possible on adequate grounds conscientiously to stamp the misrepresentation as morally culpable; and still less could law presume to interfere with this kind of controversial misconduct. With regard to what is commonly meant by intemperate discussion, namely invective, sarcasm, personality, and the like, the denunciation of these weapons would deserve more sympathy if it were ever proposed to interdict them equally to both sides; but it is only desired to restrain the employment of them against the prevailing opinion: against the unprevailing they may not only be used without general disapproval, but will be likely to obtain for him who uses them the praise of honest zeal and righteous indignation. Yet whatever mischief arises from their use, is greatest when they are employed against the comparatively defenceless; and whatever unfair advantage can be derived by any opinion from this mode of asserting it, accrues almost exclusively to received opinions. The worst offence of this kind which can be committed by a polemic, is to stigmatize those who hold the contrary opinion as bad and immoral men. To calumny of this sort, those who hold any unpopular opinion are peculiarly exposed, because they are in general few and uninfluential, and nobody but themselves feels much interested in seeing justice done them; but this weapon is, from the nature of the case, denied to those who attack a prevailing opinion: they can neither use it with safety to themselves, nor, if they could, would it do anything but recoil on their own cause. In general, opinions contrary to those commonly received can only obtain a hearing by studied moderation of language, and the most cautious avoidance of unnecessary offence, from which they hardly ever deviate even in a slight degree without losing ground: while unmeasured vituperation employed on the side of the prevailing opinion, really does deter people from professing contrary opinions, and from listening to those who profess them. For the interest, therefore, of truth and justice, it is far more important to restrain this employment of vituperative language than the other; and, for example, if it were necessary to choose, there would be much more need to discourage offensive attacks on infidelity, than on religion. It is, however, obvious that law and authority have no business with restraining either, while opinion ought, in every instance, to determine its verdict by the circumstances of the individual case; condemning every one, on whichever side of the argument he places himself, in whose mode of advocacy either want of candour, or malignity, bigotry, or intolerance of feeling manifest themselves; but not inferring these vices from the side which a person takes, though it be the contrary side of the question to our own: and giving merited honour to every one, whatever opinion he may hold, who has calmness to see and honesty to state what his opponents and their opinions really are, exaggerating nothing to their discredit, keeping nothing back which tells, or can be supposed to tell, in their favour. This is the real morality of public discussion: and if often violated, I am happy to think that there are many controversialists who to a great extent observe it, and a still greater number who conscientiously strive towards it.

CHAPTER III

Of Individuality, as One of the Elements of Well-Being

Such being the reasons which make it imperative that human beings should be free to form opinions, and to express their opinions without reserve; and such the baneful consequences to the intellectual,

and through that to the moral nature of man, unless this liberty is either conceded, or asserted in spite of prohibition; let us next examine whether the same reasons do not require that men should be free to act upon their opinions—to carry these out in their lives, without hindrance, either physical or moral, from their fellow-men, so long as it is at their own risk and peril. This last proviso is of course indispensable. No one pretends that actions should be as free as opinions. On the contrary, even opinions lose their immunity, when the circumstances in which they are expressed are such as to constitute their expression a positive instigation to some mischievous act. An opinion that corn-dealers are starvers of the poor, or that private property is robbery, ought to be unmolested when simply circulated through the press, but may justly incur punishment when delivered orally to an excited mob assembled before the house of a corn-dealer, or when handed about among the same mob in the form of a placard. Acts, of whatever kind, which, without justifiable cause, do harm to others, may be, and in the more important cases absolutely require to be, controlled by the unfavourable sentiments, and, when needful, by the active interference of mankind. The liberty of the individual must be thus far limited; he must not make himself a nuisance to other people. But if he refrains from molesting others in what concerns them, and merely acts according to his own inclination and judgment in things which concern himself, the same reasons which show that opinion should be free, prove also that he should be allowed, without molestation, to carry his opinions into practice at his own cost. That mankind are not infallible; that their truths, for the most part, are only half-truths; that unity of opinion, unless resulting from the fullest and freest comparison of opposite opinions, is not desirable, and diversity not an evil, but a good, until mankind are much more capable than at present of recognising all sides of the truth, are principles applicable to men's modes of action, not less than to their opinions. As it is useful that while mankind are imperfect there should be different opinions, so is it that there should be different experiments of living; that free scope should be given to varieties of character, short of injury to others; and that the worth of different modes of life should be proved practically, when any one thinks fit to try them. It is desirable, in short, that in things which do not primarily concern others, individuality should assert itself. Where, not the person's own character, but the traditions or customs of other people are the rule of conduct, there is wanting one of the principal ingredients of human happiness, and quite the chief ingredient of individual and social progress.

In maintaining this principle, the greatest difficulty to be encountered does not lie in the appreciation of means towards an acknowledged end, but in the indifference of persons in general to the end itself. If it were felt that the free development of individuality is one of the leading essentials of well-being; that it is not only a co-ordinate element with all that is designated by the terms civilization, instruction, education, culture, but is itself a necessary part and condition of all those things; there would be no danger that liberty should be undervalued, and the adjustment of the boundaries between it and social control would present no extraordinary difficulty. But the evil is, that individual spontaneity is hardly recognised by the common modes of thinking, as having any intrinsic worth, or deserving any regard on its own account. The majority, being satisfied with the ways of mankind as they now are (for it is they who make them what they are), cannot comprehend why those ways should not be good enough for everybody; and what is more, spontaneity forms no part of the ideal of the majority of moral and social reformers, but is rather looked on with jealousy, as a troublesome and perhaps rebellious obstruction to the general acceptance of what these reformers, in their own judgment, think would be best for mankind. Few persons, out of Germany, even comprehend the meaning of the doctrine which Wilhelm Von Humboldt, so eminent both as a *savant* and as a politician, made the text of a treatise — that 'the end of man, or that which is prescribed by the eternal or immutable dictates of reason, and not suggested by vague and transient desires, is the highest and most harmonious development of his powers to a complete and consistent whole;' that, therefore, the object 'towards which every human being must ceaselessly direct his efforts, and on which especially those who design to influence their fellow-men must ever keep their eyes, is the individuality of power and development;' that for this there are two requisites, 'freedom, and variety of situations;'

and that from the union of these arise 'individual vigour and manifold diversity,' which combine themselves in 'originality.'[6]

Little, however, as people are accustomed to a doctrine like that of Von Humboldt, and surprising as it may be to them to find so high a value attached to individuality, the question, one must nevertheless think, can only be one of degree. No one's idea of excellence in conduct is that people should do absolutely nothing but copy one another. No one would assert that people ought not to put into their mode of life, and into the conduct of their concerns, any impress whatever of their own judgment, or of their own individual character. On the other hand, it would be absurd to pretend that people ought to live as if nothing whatever had been known in the world before they came into it; as if experience had as yet done nothing towards showing that one mode of existence, or of conduct, is preferable to another. Nobody denies that people should be so taught and trained in youth, as to know and benefit by the ascertained results of human experience. But it is the privilege and proper condition of a human being, arrived at the maturity of his faculties, to use and interpret experience in his own way. It is for him to find out what part of recorded experience is properly applicable to his own circumstances and character. The traditions and customs of other people are, to a certain extent, evidence of what their experience has taught *them*; presumptive evidence, and as such, have a claim to his deference: but, in the first place, their experience may be too narrow; or they may not have interpreted it rightly. Secondly, their interpretation of experience may be correct, but unsuitable to him. Customs are made for customary circumstances, and customary characters; and his circumstances or his character may be uncustomary. Thirdly, though the customs be both good as customs, and suitable to him, yet to conform to custom, merely as custom, does not educate or develop in him any of the qualities which are the distinctive endowment of a human being. The human faculties of perception, judgment, discriminative feeling, mental activity, and even moral preference, are exercised only in making a choice. He who does anything because it

6. *The Sphere and Duties of Government*, from the German of Baron Wilhelm von Humboldt, pp. 11–13.

is the custom, makes no choice. He gains no practice either in discerning or in desiring what is best. The mental and moral, like the muscular powers, are improved only by being used. The faculties are called into no exercise by doing a thing merely because others do it, no more than by believing a thing only because others believe it. If the grounds of an opinion are not conclusive to the person's own reason, his reason cannot be strengthened, but is likely to be weakened, by his adopting it: and if the inducements to an act are not such as are consentaneous to his own feelings and character (where affection, or the rights of others, are not concerned) it is so much done towards rendering his feelings and character inert and torpid, instead of active and energetic.

He who lets the world, or his own portion of it, choose his plan of life for him, has no need of any other faculty than the ape-like one of imitation. He who chooses his plan for himself, employs all his faculties. He must use observation to see, reasoning and judgment to foresee, activity to gather materials for decision, discrimination to decide, and when he has decided, firmness and self-control to hold to his deliberate decision. And these qualities he requires and exercises exactly in proportion as the part of his conduct which he determines according to his own judgment and feelings is a large one. It is possible that he might be guided in some good path, and kept out of harm's way, without any of these things. But what will be his comparative worth as a human being? It really is of importance, not only what men do, but also what manner of men they are that do it. Among the works of man, which human life is rightly employed in perfecting and beautifying, the first in importance surely is man himself. Supposing it were possible to get houses built, corn grown, battles fought, causes tried, and even churches erected and prayers said, by machinery—by automatons in human form—it would be a considerable loss to exchange for these automatons even the men and women who at present inhabit the more civilized parts of the world, and who assuredly are but starved specimens of what nature can and will produce. Human nature is not a machine to be built after a model, and set to do exactly the work prescribed for it, but a tree, which requires to grow and develope itself on all sides, according to the tendency of the inward forces which make it a living thing.

It will probably be conceded that it is desirable people should exercise their understandings, and that an intelligent following of custom, or even occasionally an intelligent deviation from custom, is better than a blind and simply mechanical adhesion to it. To a certain extent it is admitted, that our understanding should be our own: but there is not the same willingness to admit that our desires and impulses should be our own likewise; or that to possess impulses of our own, and of any strength, is anything but a peril and a snare. Yet desires and impulses are as much a part of a perfect human being, as beliefs and restraints: and strong impulses are only perilous when not properly balanced; when one set of aims and inclinations is developed into strength, while others, which ought to co-exist with them, remain weak and inactive. It is not because men's desires are strong that they act ill; it is because their consciences are weak. There is no natural connexion between strong impulses and a weak conscience. The natural connexion is the other way. To say that one person's desires and feelings are stronger and more various than those of another, is merely to say that he has more of the raw material of human nature, and is therefore capable, perhaps of more evil, but certainly of more good. Strong impulses are but another name for energy. Energy may be turned to bad uses; but more good may always be made of an energetic nature, than of an indolent and impassive one. Those who have most natural feeling, are always those whose cultivated feelings may be made the strongest. The same strong susceptibilities which make the personal impulses vivid and powerful, are also the source from whence are generated the most passionate love of virtue, and the sternest self-control. It is through the cultivation of these, that society both does its duty and protects its interests: not by rejecting the stuff of which heroes are made, because it knows not how to make them. A person whose desires and impulses are his own—are the expression of his own nature, as it has been developed and modified by his own culture—is said to have a character. One whose desires and impulses are not his own, has no character, no more than a steam-engine has a character. If, in addition to being his own, his impulses are strong, and are under the government of a strong will, he has an energetic character. Whoever thinks that individuality of desires and impulses should not be encouraged to unfold itself, must maintain that society has no need of strong natures—is not the better for containing many persons who have much character—and that a high general average of energy is not desirable.

In some early states of society, these forces might be, and were, too much ahead of the power which society then possessed of disciplining and controlling them. There has been a time when the element of spontaneity and individuality was in excess, and the social principle had a hard struggle with it. The difficulty then was, to induce men of strong bodies or minds to pay obedience to any rules which required them to control their impulses. To overcome this difficulty, law and discipline, like the Popes struggling against the Emperors, asserted a power over the whole man, claiming to control all his life in order to control his character—which society had not found any other sufficient means of binding. But society has now fairly got the better of individuality; and the danger which threatens human nature is not the excess, but the deficiency, of personal impulses and preferences. Things are vastly changed, since the passions of those who were strong by station or by personal endowment were in a state of habitual rebellion against laws and ordinances, and required to be rigorously chained up to enable the persons within their reach to enjoy any particle of security. In our times, from the highest class of society down to the lowest, every one lives as under the eye of a hostile and dreaded censorship. Not only in what concerns others, but in what concerns only themselves, the individual or the family do not ask themselves—what do I prefer? or, what would suit my character and disposition? or, what would allow the best and highest in me to have fair play, and enable it to grow and thrive? They ask themselves, what is suitable to my position? what is usually done by persons of my station and pecuniary circumstances? or (worse still) what is usually done by persons of a station and circumstances superior to mine? I do not mean that they choose what is customary, in preference to what suits their own inclination. It does not occur to them to have any inclination, except for what is customary. Thus the mind itself is bowed to the yoke: even in what people do for pleasure, conformity is the first thing thought of; they like in crowds; they exercise choice only among things

commonly done: peculiarity of taste, eccentricity of conduct, are shunned equally with crimes: until by dint of not following their own nature, they have no nature to follow: their human capacities are withered and starved: they become incapable of any strong wishes or native pleasures, and are generally without either opinions or feelings of home growth, or properly their own. Now is this, or is it not, the desirable condition of human nature?

It is so, on the Calvinistic theory. According to that, the one great offence of man is self-will. All the good of which humanity is capable, is comprised in obedience. You have no choice; thus you must do, and no otherwise: 'whatever is not a duty, is a sin.' Human nature being radically corrupt, there is no redemption for any one until human nature is killed within him. To one holding this theory of life, crushing out any of the human faculties, capacities, and susceptibilities, is no evil: man needs no capacity, but that of surrendering himself to the will of God: and if he uses any of his faculties for any other purpose but to do that supposed will more effectually, he is better without them. This is the theory of Calvinism; and it is held, in a mitigated form, by many who do not consider themselves Calvinists; the mitigation consisting in giving a less ascetic interpretation to the alleged will of God; asserting it to be his will that mankind should gratify some of their inclinations; of course not in the manner they themselves prefer, but in the way of obedience, that is, in a way prescribed to them by authority; and, therefore, by the necessary conditions of the case, the same for all.

In some such insidious form there is at present a strong tendency to this narrow theory of life, and to the pinched and hidebound type of human character which it patronizes. Many persons, no doubt, sincerely think that human beings thus cramped and dwarfed, are as their Maker designed them to be; just as many have thought that trees are a much finer thing when clipped into pollards, or cut out into figures of animals, than as nature made them. But if it be any part of religion to believe that man was made by a good Being, it is more consistent with that faith to believe, that this Being gave all human faculties that they might be cultivated and unfolded, not rooted out and consumed, and that he takes delight in every nearer approach made by his creatures to the ideal conception embodied in them, every increase in any of their capabilities of comprehension, of action, or of enjoyment. There is a different type of human excellence from the Calvinistic; a conception of humanity as having its nature bestowed on it for other purposes than merely to be abnegated. 'Pagan self-assertion' is one of the elements of human worth, as well as 'Christian self-denial.'[7] There is a Greek ideal of self-development, which the Platonic and Christian ideal of self-government blends with, but does not supersede. It may be better to be a John Knox than an Alcibiades, but it is better to be a Pericles than either; nor would a Pericles, if we had one in these days, be without anything good which belonged to John Knox.

It is not by wearing down into uniformity all that is individual in themselves, but by cultivating it and calling it forth, within the limits imposed by the rights and interests of others, that human beings become a noble and beautiful object of contemplation; and as the works partake the character of those who do them, by the same process human life also becomes rich, diversified, and animating, furnishing more abundant aliment to high thoughts and elevating feelings, and strengthening the tie which binds every individual to the race, by making the race infinitely better worth belonging to. In proportion to the development of his individuality, each person becomes more valuable to himself, and is therefore capable of being more valuable to others. There is a greater fulness of life about his own existence, and when there is more life in the units there is more in the mass which is composed of them. As much compression as is necessary to prevent the stronger specimens of human nature from encroaching on the rights of others, cannot be dispensed with; but for this there is ample compensation even in the point of view of human development. The means of development which the individual loses by being prevented from gratifying his inclinations to the injury of others, are chiefly obtained at the expense of the development of other people. And even to himself there is a full equivalent in the better development of the social part of his nature, rendered possible by the restraint put upon the selfish part. To be held to rigid rules of justice

7. Sterling's *Essays*.

for the sake of others, develops the feelings and capacities which have the good of others for their object. But to be restrained in things not affecting their good, by their mere displeasure, develops nothing valuable, except such force of character as may unfold itself in resisting the restraint. If acquiesced in, it dulls and blunts the whole nature. To give any fair play to the nature of each, it is essential that different persons should be allowed to lead different lives. In proportion as this latitude has been exercised in any age, has that age been noteworthy to posterity. Even despotism does not produce its worst effects, so long as individuality exists under it; and whatever crushes individuality is despotism, by whatever name it may be called, and whether it professes to be enforcing the will of God or the injunctions of men.

Having said that individuality is the same thing with development, and that it is only the cultivation of individuality which produces, or can produce, well-developed human beings, I might here close the argument: for what more or better can be said of any condition of human affairs, than that it brings human beings themselves nearer to the best thing they can be? or what worse can be said of any obstruction to good, than that it prevents this? Doubtless, however, these considerations will not suffice to convince those who most need convincing; and it is necessary further to show, that these developed human beings are of some use to the undeveloped—to point out to those who do not desire liberty, and would not avail themselves of it, that they may be in some intelligible manner rewarded for allowing other people to make use of it without hindrance.

In the first place, then, I would suggest that they might possibly learn something from them. It will not be denied by anybody, that originality is a valuable element in human affairs. There is always need of persons not only to discover new truths, and point out when what were once truths are true no longer, but also to commence new practices, and set the example of more enlightened conduct, and better taste and sense in human life. This cannot well be gainsaid by anybody who does not believe that the world has already attained perfection in all its ways and practices. It is true that this benefit is not capable of being rendered by everybody alike: there are but few persons, in comparison with the whole of mankind, whose experiments, if adopted by others, would be likely to be any improvement on established practice. But these few are the salt of the earth; without them, human life would become a stagnant pool. Not only is it they who introduce good things which did not before exist; it is they who keep the life in those which already existed. If there were nothing new to be done, would human intellect cease to be necessary? Would it be a reason why those who do the old things should forget why they are done, and do them like cattle, not like human beings? There is only too great a tendency in the best beliefs and practices to degenerate into the mechanical; and unless there were a succession of persons whose ever-recurring originality prevents the grounds of those beliefs and practices from becoming merely traditional, such dead matter would not resist the smallest shock from anything really alive, and there would be no reason why civilization should not die out, as in the Byzantine Empire. Persons of genius, it is true, are, and are always likely to be, a small minority; but in order to have them, it is necessary to preserve the soil in which they grow. Genius can only breathe freely in an *atmosphere* of freedom. Persons of genius are, *ex vi termini, more* individual than any other people — less capable, consequently, of fitting themselves, without hurtful compression, into any of the small number of moulds which society provides in order to save its members the trouble of forming their own character. If from timidity they consent to be forced into one of these moulds, and to let all that part of themselves which cannot expand under the pressure remain unexpanded, society will be little the better for their genius. If they are of a strong character, and break their fetters, they become a mark for the society which has not succeeded in reducing them to commonplace, to point at with solemn warning as 'wild,' 'erratic,' and the like; much as if one should complain of the Niagara river for not flowing smoothly between its banks like a Dutch canal.

I insist thus emphatically on the importance of genius, and the necessity of allowing it to unfold itself freely both in thought and in practice, being well aware that no one will deny the position in theory, but knowing also that almost every one, in reality, is totally indifferent to it. People think genius a fine thing if it enables a man to write an exciting poem, or paint a picture. But in its true sense, that of originality in thought and action, though no one says that it is not a thing to be admired, nearly all, at heart, think that they can do very well without it. Unhappily this is too natural to be wondered at. Originality is the one thing which unoriginal minds cannot feel the use of. They cannot see what it is to do for them: how should they? If they could see what it would do for them, it would not be originality. The first service which originality has to render them, is that of opening their eyes: which being once fully done, they would have a chance of being themselves original. Meanwhile, recollecting that nothing was ever yet done which some one was not the first to do, and that all good things which exist are the fruits of originality, let them be modest enough to believe that there is something still left for it to accomplish, and assure themselves that they are more in need of originality, the less they are conscious of the want.

In sober truth, whatever homage may be professed, or even paid, to real or supposed mental superiority, the general tendency of things throughout the world is to render mediocrity the ascendant power among mankind. In ancient history, in the middle ages, and in a diminishing degree through the long transition from feudality to the present time, the individual was a power in himself; and if he had either great talents or a high social position, he was a considerable power. At present individuals are lost in the crowd. In politics it is almost a triviality to say that public opinion now rules the world. The only power deserving the name is that of masses, and of governments while they make themselves the organ of the tendencies and instincts of masses. This is as true in the moral and social relations of private life as in public transactions. Those whose opinions go by the name of public opinion, are not always the same sort of public: in America they are the whole white population; in England, chiefly the middle class. But they are always a mass, that is to say, collective mediocrity. And what is a still greater novelty, the mass do not now take their opinions from dignitaries in Church or State, from ostensible leaders, or from books. Their thinking is done for them by men much like themselves, addressing them or speaking in their name, on the spur of the moment, through the newspapers. I am not complaining of all this. I do not assert that anything better is compatible, as a general rule, with the present low state of the human mind. But that does not hinder the government of mediocrity from being mediocre government. No government by a democracy or a numerous aristocracy, either in its political acts or in the opinions, qualities, and tone of mind which it fosters, ever did or could rise above mediocrity, except in so far as the sovereign. Many have let themselves be guided (which in their best times they always have done) by the counsels and influence of a more highly gifted and instructed One or Few. The initiation of all wise or noble things, comes and must come from individuals; generally at first from some one individual. The honour and glory of the average man is that he is capable of following that initiative; that he can respond internally to wise and noble things, and be led to them with his eyes open. I am not countenancing the sort of 'hero-worship' which applauds the strong man of genius for forcibly seizing on the government of the world and making it do his bidding in spite of itself. All he can claim is, freedom to point out the way. The power of compelling others into it, is not only inconsistent with the freedom and development of all the rest, but corrupting to the strong man himself. It does seem, however, that when the opinions of masses of merely average men are everywhere become or becoming the dominant power, the counterpoise and corrective to that tendency would be, the more and more pronounced individuality of those who stand on the higher eminences of thought. It is in these circumstances most especially, that exceptional individuals, instead of being deterred, should be encouraged in acting differently from the mass. In other times there was no advantage in their doing so, unless they acted not only differently, but better. In this age, the mere example of nonconformity, the mere refusal to bend the knee to custom, is itself a service. Precisely because the tyranny of opinion is such as to make eccentricity a reproach, it is desirable, in order to break through that tyranny, that people should be eccentric. Eccentricity has always abounded when and where strength of character has abounded; and the amount of eccentricity in a society has generally been proportional to the amount of genius, mental vigour, and moral courage which it contained. That so few now dare to be eccentric, marks the chief danger of the time.

I have said that it is important to give the freest scope possible to uncustomary things, in order that it may in time appear which of these are fit to be converted into customs. But independence of action, and disregard of custom, are not solely deserving of encouragement for the chance they afford that better modes of action, and customs more worthy of general adoption, may be struck out; nor is it only persons of decided mental superiority who have a just claim to carry on their lives in their own way. There is no reason that all human existence should be constructed on some one or some small number of patterns. If a person possesses any tolerable amount of common sense and experience, his own mode of laying out his existence is the best, not because it is the best in itself, but because it is his own mode. Human beings are not like sheep; and even sheep are not undistinguishably alike. A man cannot get a coat or a pair of boots to fit him, unless they are either made to his measure, or he has a whole warehouseful to choose from: and is it easier to fit him with a life than with a coat, or are human beings more like one another in their whole physical and spiritual conformation than in the shape of their feet? If it were only that people have diversities of taste, that is reason enough for not attempting to shape them all after one model. But different persons also require different conditions for their spiritual development; and can no more exist healthily in the same moral, than all the variety of plants can in the same physical, atmosphere and climate. The same things which are helps to one person towards the cultivation of his higher nature, are hindrances to another. The same mode of life is a healthy excitement to one, keeping all his faculties of action and enjoyment in their best order, while to another it is a distracting burthen, which suspends or crushes all internal life. Such are the differences among human beings in their sources of pleasure, their susceptibilities of pain, and the operation on them of different physical and moral agencies, that unless there is a corresponding diversity in their modes of life, they neither obtain their fair share of happiness, nor grow up to the mental, moral, and aesthetic stature of which their nature is capable. Why then should tolerance, as far as the public sentiment is concerned, extend only to tastes and modes of life which extort acquiescence by the multitude of their adherents? Nowhere (except in some monastic institutions) is diversity of taste entirely unrecognised; a person may, without blame, either like or dislike rowing, or smoking, or music, or athletic exercises, or chess, or cards, or study, because both those who like each of these things, and those who dislike them, are too numerous to be put down. But the man, and still more the woman, who can be accused either of doing 'what nobody does,' or of not doing 'what everybody does,' is the subject of as much depreciatory remark as if he or she had committed some grave moral delinquency. Persons require to possess a title, or some other badge of rank, or of the consideration of people of rank, to be able to indulge somewhat in the luxury of doing as they like without detriment to their estimation. To indulge somewhat, I repeat: for whoever allow themselves much of that indulgence, incur the risk of something worse than disparaging speeches—they are in peril of a commission *de lunatico*, and of having their property taken from them and given to their relations.[8]

8. There is something both contemptible and frightful in the sort of evidence on which, of late years, any person can be judicially declared unfit for the management of his affairs; and after his death, his disposal of his property can be set aside, if there is enough of it to pay the expenses of litigation—which are charged on the property itself. All the minute details of his daily life are pried into, and whatever is found which, seen through the medium of the perceiving and describing faculties of the lowest of the low, bears an appearance unlike absolute commonplace, is laid before the jury as evidence of insanity, and often with success; the jurors being little, if at all, less vulgar and ignorant than the witnesses; while the judges, with that extraordinary want of knowledge of human nature and life which continually astonishes us in English lawyers, often help to mislead them. These trials speak volumes as to the state of feeling and opinion among the vulgar with regard to human liberty. So far from setting any value on individuality—so far from respecting the right of each individual to act, in things indifferent, as seems good to his own judgment and inclinations, judges and juries cannot even conceive that a person in a state of sanity can desire such freedom. In former days, when it was proposed to burn atheists, charitable people used to suggest putting them in a madhouse instead: it would be nothing surprising now-a-days were we to see this done, and the doers applauding

There is one characteristic of the present direction of public opinion, peculiarly calculated to make it intolerant of any marked demonstration of individuality. The general average of mankind are not only moderate in intellect, but also moderate in inclinations: they have no tastes or wishes strong enough to incline them to do anything unusual, and they consequently do not understand those who have, and class all such with the wild and intemperate whom they are accustomed to look down upon. Now, in addition to this fact which is general, we have only to suppose that a strong movement has set in towards the improvement of morals, and it is evident what we have to expect. In these days such a movement has set in; much has actually been effected in the way of increased regularity of conduct, and discouragement of excesses; and there is a philanthropic spirit abroad, for the exercise of which there is no more inviting field than the moral and prudential improvement of our fellow-creatures. These tendencies of the times cause the public to be more disposed than at most former periods to prescribe general rules of conduct, and endeavour to make every one conform to the approved standard. And that standard, express or tacit, is to desire nothing strongly. Its ideal of character is to be without any marked character; to maim by compression, like a Chinese lady's foot, every part of human nature which stands out prominently, and tends to make the person markedly dissimilar in outline to commonplace humanity.

As is usually the case with ideals which exclude one-half of what is desirable, the present standard of approbation produces only an inferior imitation of the other half. Instead of great energies guided by vigorous reason, and strong feelings strongly controlled by a conscientious will, its result is weak feelings and weak energies, which therefore can be kept in outward conformity to rule without any strength either of will or of reason. Already energetic characters on any large scale are becoming merely traditional. There is now scarcely any outlet for energy in this country except business. The energy expended in this

_____

themselves, because, instead of persecuting for religion, they had adopted so humane and Christian a mode of treating these unfortunates, not without a silent satisfaction at their having thereby obtained their deserts.

may still be regarded as considerable. What little is left from that employment, is expended on some hobby; which may be a useful, even a philanthropic hobby, but is always some one thing, and generally a thing of small dimensions. The greatness of England is now all collective: individually small, we only appear capable of anything great by our habit of combining; and with this our moral and religious philanthropists are perfectly contented. But it was men of another stamp than this that made England what it has been; and men of another stamp will be needed to prevent its decline.

The despotism of custom is everywhere the standing hindrance to human advancement, being in unceasing antagonism to that disposition to aim at something better than customary, which is called, according to circumstances, the spirit of liberty, or that of progress or improvement. The spirit of improvement is not always a spirit of liberty, for it may aim at forcing improvements on an unwilling people; and the spirit of liberty, in so far as it resists such attempts, may ally itself locally and temporarily with the opponents of improvement; but the only unfailing and permanent source of improvement is liberty, since by it there are as many possible independent centres of improvement as there are individuals. The progressive principle, however, in either shape, whether as the love of liberty or of improvement, is antagonistic to the sway of Custom, involving at least emancipation from that yoke; and the contest between the two constitutes the chief interest of the history of mankind. The greater part of the world has, properly speaking, no history, because the despotism of Custom is complete. This is the case over the whole East. Custom is there, in all things, the final appeal; justice and right mean conformity to custom, the argument of custom no one, unless some tyrant intoxicated with power, thinks of resisting. And we see the result. Those nations must once have had originality; they did not start out of the ground populous, lettered, and versed in many of the arts of life; they made themselves all this, and were then the greatest and most powerful nations of the world. What are they now? The subjects or dependents of tribes whose forefathers wandered in the forests when theirs had magnificent palaces and gorgeous temples, but over whom custom exercised only a divided rule with

liberty and progress. A people, it appears, may be progressive for a certain length of time, and then stop: when does it stop? When it ceases to possess individuality. If a similar change should befall the nations of Europe, it will not be in exactly the same shape: the despotism of custom with which these nations are threatened is not precisely stationariness. It proscribes singularity, but it does not preclude change, provided all change together. We have discarded the fixed costumes of our forefathers; every one must still dress like other people, but the fashion may change once or twice a year. We thus take care that when there is change it shall be for change's sake, and not from any idea of beauty or convenience; for the same idea of beauty or convenience would not strike all the world at the same moment, and be simultaneously thrown aside by all at another moment. But we are progressive as well as changeable: we continually make new inventions in mechanical things, and keep them until they are again superseded by better; we are eager for improvement in politics, in education, even in morals, though in this last our idea of improvement chiefly consists in persuading or forcing other people to be as good as ourselves. It is not progress that we object to; on the contrary, we flatter ourselves that we are the most progressive people who ever lived. It is individuality that we war against: we should think we had done wonders if we had made ourselves all alike; forgetting that the unlikeness of one person to another is generally the first thing which draws the attention of either to the imperfection of his own type, and the superiority of another, or the possibility, by combining the advantages of both, of producing something better than either. We have a warning example in China—a nation of much talent, and, in some respects, even wisdom, owing to the rare good fortune of having been provided at an early period with a particularly good set of customs, the work, in some measure, of men to whom even the most enlightened European must accord, under certain limitations, the title of sages and philosophers. They are remarkable, too, in the excellence of their apparatus for impressing, as far as possible, the best wisdom they possess upon every mind in the community, and securing that those who have appropriated most of it shall occupy the posts of honour and power. Surely the people who did this have discovered the secret of human progressiveness, and must have kept themselves steadily at the head of the movement of the world. On the contrary, they have become stationary—have remained so for thousands of years; and if they are ever to be farther improved, it must be by foreigners. They have succeeded beyond all hope in what English philanthropists are so industriously working at—in making a people all alike, all governing their thoughts and conduct by the same maxims and rules; and these are the fruits. The modern *régime* of public opinion is, in an unorganized form, what the Chinese educational and political systems are in an organized; and unless individuality shall be able successfully to assert itself against this yoke, Europe, notwithstanding its noble antecedents and its professed Christianity, will tend to become another China.

What is it that has hitherto preserved Europe from this lot? What has made the European family of nations an improving, instead of a stationary portion of mankind? Not any superior excellence in them, which, when it exists, exists as the effect, not as the cause; but their remarkable diversity of character and culture. Individuals, classes, nations, have been extremely unlike one another: they have struck out a great variety of paths, each leading to something valuable; and although at every period those who travelled in different paths have been intolerant of one another, and each would have thought it an excellent thing if all the rest could have been compelled to travel his road, their attempts to thwart each other's development have rarely had any permanent success, and each has in time endured to receive the good which the others have offered. Europe is, in my judgment, wholly indebted to this plurality of paths for its progressive and many-sided development. But it already begins to possess this benefit in a considerably less degree. It is decidedly advancing towards the Chinese ideal of making all people alike. M. de Tocqueville, in his last important work, remarks how much more the Frenchmen of the present day resemble one another, than did those even of the last generation. The same remark might be made of Englishmen in a far greater degree. In a passage already quoted from Wilhelm von Humboldt, he points out two things as necessary conditions of human development, because necessary to render people unlike one

another; namely, freedom, and variety of situations. The second of these two conditions is in this country every day diminishing. The circumstances which surround different classes and individuals, and shape their characters, are daily becoming more assimilated. Formerly, different ranks, different neighbourhoods, different trades and professions, lived in what might be called different worlds; at present, to a great degree in the same. Comparatively speaking, they now read the same things, listen to the same things, see the same things, go to the same places, have their hopes and fears directed to the same objects, have the same rights and liberties, and the same means of asserting them. Great as are the differences of position which remain, they are nothing to those which have ceased. And the assimilation is still proceeding. All the political changes of the age promote it, since they all tend to raise the low and to lower the high. Every extension of education promotes it, because education brings people under common influences, and gives them access to the general stock of facts and sentiments. Improvements in the means of communication promote it, by bringing the inhabitants of distant places into personal contact, and keeping up a rapid flow of changes of residence between one place and another. The increase of commerce and manufactures promotes it, by diffusing more widely the advantages of easy circumstances, and opening all objects of ambition, even the highest, to general competition, whereby the desire of rising becomes no longer the character of a particular class, but of all classes. A more powerful agency than even all these, in bringing about a general similarity among mankind, is the complete establishment, in this and other free countries, of the ascendancy of public opinion in the State. As the various social eminences which enabled persons entrenched on them to disregard the opinion of the multitude, gradually become levelled; as the very idea of resisting the will of the public, when it is positively known that they have a will, disappears more and more from the minds of practical politicians; there ceases to be any social support for nonconformity—any substantive power in society, which, itself opposed to the ascendancy of numbers, is interested in taking under its protection opinions and tendencies at variance with those of the public.

The combination of all these causes forms so great

a mass of influences hostile to Individuality, that it is not easy to see how it can stand its ground. It will do so with increasing difficulty, unless the intelligent part of the public can be made to feel its value—to see that it is good there should be differences, even though not for the better, even though, as it may appear to them, some should be for the worse. If the claims of Individuality are ever to be asserted, the time is now, while much is still wanting to complete the enforced assimilation. It is only in the earlier stages that any stand can be successfully made against the encroachment. The demand that all other people shall resemble ourselves, grows by what it feeds on. If resistance waits till life is reduced *nearly* to one uniform type, all deviations from that type will come to be considered impious, immoral, even monstrous and contrary to nature. Mankind speedily become unable to conceive diversity, when they have been for some time unaccustomed to see it.

CHAPTER IV

Of the Limits to the Authority of Society over the Individual

What, then, is the rightful limit to the sovereignty of the individual over himself? Where does the authority of society begin? How much of human life should be assigned to individuality, and how much to society?

Each will receive its proper share, if each has that which more particularly concerns it. To individuality should belong the part of life in which it is chiefly the individual that is interested; to society, the part which chiefly interests society.

Though society is not founded on a contract, and though no good purpose is answered by inventing a contract in order to deduce social obligations from it, every one who receives the protection of society owes a return for the benefit, and the fact of living in society renders it indispensable that each should be bound to observe a certain line of conduct towards the rest. This conduct consists first, in not injuring the interests of one another; or rather certain interests, which, either by express legal provision or by tacit understanding, ought to be considered as rights; and secondly, in each person's bearing his share (to be fixed on some equitable principle) of the labours and sacrifices incurred for defending the society or its members from injury and molestation. These conditions society is justified in enforcing at all costs to those who endeavour to withhold fulfilment. Nor is this all that society may do. The acts of an individual may be hurtful to others, or wanting in due consideration for their welfare, without going the length of violating any of their constituted rights. The offender may then be justly punished by opinion, though not by law. As soon as any part of a person's conduct affects prejudicially the interests of others, society has jurisdiction over it, and the question whether the general welfare will or will not be promoted by interfering with it, becomes open to discussion. But there is no room for entertaining any such question when a person's conduct affects the interests of no persons besides himself, or needs not affect them unless they like (all the persons concerned being of full age, and the ordinary amount of understanding). In all such cases there should be perfect freedom, legal and social, to do the action and stand the consequences.

It would be a great misunderstanding of this doctrine to suppose that it is one of selfish indifference, which pretends that human beings have no business with each other's conduct in life, and that they should not concern themselves about the well-doing or well-being of one another, unless their own interest is involved. Instead of any diminution, there is need of a great increase of disinterested exertion to promote the good of others. But disinterested benevolence can find other instruments to persuade people to their good, than whips and scourges, either of the literal or the metaphorical sort. I am the last person to undervalue the self-regarding virtues; they are only second in importance, if even second, to the social. It is equally the business of education to cultivate both. But even education works by conviction and persuasion as well as by compulsion, and it is by the former only that, when the period of education is past, the self-regarding virtues should be inculcated. Human beings owe to each other help to distinguish the better from the worse, and encouragement to choose the former and avoid the latter. They should be for ever stimulating each other to increased exercise of their higher faculties, and increased direction of their feelings and aims towards wise instead of foolish, elevating instead of degrading, objects and contemplations. But neither one person, nor any number of persons, is warranted in saying to another human creature of ripe years, that he shall not do with his life for his own benefit what he chooses to do with it. He is the person most interested in his own well-being: the interest which any other person, except in cases of strong personal attachment, can have in it, is trifling, compared with that which he himself has; the interest which society has in him individually (except as to his conduct to others) is fractional, and altogether indirect: while, with respect to his own feelings and circumstances, the most ordinary man or woman has means of knowledge immeasurably surpassing those that can be possessed by any one else. The interference of society to overrule his judgment and purposes in what only regards himself, must be grounded on general presumptions; which may be altogether wrong, and even if right, are as likely as not to be misapplied to individual cases, by persons no better acquainted with the circumstances of such cases than those are who look at them merely from without. In this department, therefore, of human affairs, Individuality has its proper field of action. In the conduct of human beings towards one another, it is necessary that general rules should for the most part be observed, in order that people may know what they have to expect; but in each person's own concerns, his individual spontaneity is entitled to free exercise. Considerations to aid his judgment, exhortations to strengthen his will, may be offered to him, even obtruded on him, by others; but he himself is the final judge. All errors which he is likely to commit against advice and warning, are far outweighed by the evil of allowing others to constrain him to what they deem his good.

I do not mean that the feelings with which a person is regarded by others, ought not to be in any way affected by his self-regarding qualities or deficiencies. This is neither possible nor desirable. If he is eminent in any of the qualities which conduce to his own good, he is, so far, a proper object of admiration. He is so much the nearer to the ideal perfection of human nature. If he is grossly deficient in those qualities, a sentiment the opposite of admiration will follow. There is a degree of folly, and a degree of what may be called (though the phrase is not unobjectionable)

lowness or depravation of taste, which, though it cannot justify doing harm to the person who manifests it, renders him necessarily and properly a subject of distaste, or, in extreme cases, even of contempt: a person could not have the opposite qualities in due strength without entertaining these feelings. Though doing no wrong to any one, a person may so act as to compel us to judge him, and feel to him, as a fool, or as a being of an inferior order: and since this judgment and feeling are a fact which he would prefer to avoid, it is doing him a service to warn him of it beforehand, as of any other disagreeable consequence to which he exposes himself. It would be well, indeed, if this good office were much more freely rendered than the common notions of politeness at present permit, and if one person could honestly point out to another that he thinks him in fault, without being considered unmannerly or presuming. We have a right, also, in various ways, to act upon our unfavourable opinion of any one, not to the oppression of his individuality, but in the exercise of ours. We are not bound, for example, to seek his society; we have a right to avoid it (though not to parade the avoidance), for we have a right to choose the society most acceptable to us. We have a right, and it may be our duty, to caution others against him, if we think his example or conversation likely to have a pernicious effect on those with whom he associates. We may give others a preference over him in optional good offices, except those which tend to his improvement. In these various modes a person may suffer very severe penalties at the hands of others, for faults which directly concern only himself; but he suffers these penalties only in so far as they are the natural, and, as it were, the spontaneous consequences of the faults themselves, not because they are purposely inflicted on him for the sake of punishment. A person who shows rashness, obstinacy, self-conceit—who cannot live within moderate means—who cannot restrain himself from hurtful indulgences—who pursues animal pleasures at the expense of those of feeling and intellect—must expect to be lowered in the opinion of others, and to have a less share of their favourable sentiments; but of this he has no right to complain, unless he has merited their favour by special excellence in his social relations, and has thus established a title to their good offices, which is not affected by his demerits towards himself.

What I contend for is, that the inconveniences which are strictly inseparable from the unfavourable judgment of others, are the only ones to which a person should ever be subjected for that portion of his conduct and character which concerns his own good, but which does not affect the interests of others in their relations with him. Acts injurious to others require a totally different treatment. Encroachment on their rights; infliction on them of any loss or damage not justified by his own rights; falsehood or duplicity in dealing with them; unfair or ungenerous use of advantages over them; even selfish abstinence from defending them against injury—these are fit objects of moral reprobation, and, in grave cases, of moral retribution and punishment. And not only these acts, but the dispositions which lead to them, are properly immoral, and fit subjects of disapprobation which may rise to abhorrence. Cruelty of disposition; malice and ill-nature; that most anti-social and odious of all passions, envy; dissimulation and insincerity; irascibility on insufficient cause, and resentment disproportioned to the provocation; the love of domineering over others; the desire to engross more than one's share of advantages (the *pleonexia* of the Greeks); the pride which derives gratification from the abasement of others; the egotism which thinks self and its concerns more important than everything else, and decides all doubtful questions in its own favour;—these are moral vices, and constitute a bad and odious moral character: unlike the self-regarding faults previously mentioned, which are not properly immoralities, and to whatever pitch they may be carried, do not constitute wickedness. They may be proofs of any amount of folly, or want of personal dignity and self respect; but they are only a subject of moral reprobation when they involve a breach of duty to others, for whose sake the individual is bound to have care for himself. What are called duties to ourselves are not socially obligatory, unless circumstances render them at the same time duties to others. The term duty to oneself, when it means anything more than prudence, means self-respect or self-development; and for none of these is any one accountable to his fellow creatures, because for none of them is it for the good of mankind that he be held accountable to them.

The distinction between the loss of consideration which a person may rightly incur by defect of prudence or of personal dignity, and the reprobation which is due to him for an offence against the rights of others, is not a merely nominal distinction. It makes a vast difference both in our feelings and in our conduct towards him, whether he displeases us in things in which we think we have a right to control him, or in things in which we know that we have not. If he displeases us, we may express our distaste, and we may stand aloof from a person as well as from a thing that displeases us; but we shall not therefore feel called on to make his life uncomfortable. We shall reflect that he already bears, or will bear, the whole penalty of his error; if he spoils his life by mismanagement, we shall not, for that reason, desire to spoil it still further: instead of wishing to punish him, we shall rather endeavour to alleviate his punishment, by showing him how he may avoid or cure the evils his conduct tends to bring upon him. He may be to us an object of pity, perhaps of dislike, but not of anger or resentment; we shall not treat him like an enemy of society: the worst we shall think ourselves justified in doing is leaving him to himself, if we do not interfere benevolently by showing interest or concern for him. It is far otherwise if he has infringed the rules necessary for the protection of his fellow-creatures, individually or collectively. The evil consequences of his acts do not then fall on himself, but on others; and society, as the protector of all its members, must retaliate on him; must inflict pain on him for the express purpose of punishment, and must take care that it be sufficiently severe. In the one case, he is an offender at our bar, and we are called on not only to sit in judgment on him, but, in one shape or another, to execute our own sentence: in the other case, it is not our part to inflict any suffering on him, except what may incidentally follow from our using the same liberty in the regulation of our own affairs, which we allow to him in his.

The distinction here pointed out between the part of a person's life which concerns only himself, and that which concerns others, many persons will refuse to admit. How (it may be asked) can any part of the conduct of a member of society be a matter of indifference to the other members? No person is an entirely isolated being; it is impossible for a person to do anything seriously or permanently hurtful to himself, without mischief reaching at least to his near connexions, and often far beyond them. If he injures his property, he does harm to those who directly or indirectly derived support from it, and usually diminishes, by a greater or less amount, the general resources of the community. If he deteriorates his bodily or mental faculties, he not only brings evil upon all who depended on him for any portion of their happiness, but disqualifies himself for rendering the services which he owes to his fellow creatures generally; perhaps becomes a burthen on their affection or benevolence; and if such conduct were very frequent, hardly any offence that is committed would detract more from the general sum of good. Finally, if by his vices or follies a person does no direct harm to others, he is nevertheless (it may be said) injurious by his example; and ought to be compelled to control himself, for the sake of those whom the sight or knowledge of his conduct might corrupt or mislead.

And even (it will be added) if the consequences of misconduct could be confined to the vicious or thoughtless individual, ought society to abandon to their own guidance those who are manifestly unfit for it? If protection against themselves is confessedly due to children and persons under age, is not society equally bound to afford it to persons of mature years who are equally incapable of self-government? If gambling, or drunkenness, or incontinence, or idleness, or uncleanliness, are as injurious to happiness, and as great a hindrance to improvement, as many or most of the acts prohibited by law, why (it may be asked) should not law, so far as is consistent with practicability and social convenience, endeavour to repress these also? And as a supplement to the unavoidable imperfections of law, ought not opinion at least to organize a powerful police against these vices, and visit rigidly with social penalties those who are known to practise them? There is no question here (it may be said) about restricting individuality, or impeding the trial of new and original experiments in living. The only things it is sought to prevent are things which have been tried and condemned from the beginning of the world until now; things which experience has shown not to be useful or suitable to any person's individuality. There must be some length of time and amount of experience, after which a moral or prudential truth may be regarded as established: and it is merely desired to prevent generation

after generation from falling over the same precipice which has been fatal to their predecessors.

I fully admit that the mischief which a person does to himself may seriously affect, both through their sympathies and their interests, those nearly connected with him, and in a minor degree, society at large. When, by conduct of this sort, a person is led to violate a distinct and assignable obligation to any other person or persons, the case is taken out of the self-regarding class, and becomes amenable to moral disapprobation in the proper sense of the term. If, for example, a man, through intemperance or extravagance, becomes unable to pay his debts, or, having undertaken the moral responsibility of a family, becomes from the same cause incapable of supporting or educating them, he is deservedly reprobated, and might be justly punished; but it is for the breach of duty to his family or creditors, not for the extravagance. If the resources which ought to have been devoted to them, had been diverted from them for the most prudent investment, the moral culpability would have been the same. George Barnwell murdered his uncle to get money for his mistress, but if he had done it to set himself up in business, he would equally have been hanged. Again, in the frequent case of a man who causes grief to his family by addiction to bad habits, he deserves reproach for his unkindness or ingratitude; but so he may for cultivating habits not in themselves vicious, if they are painful to those with whom he passes his life, or who from personal ties are dependent on him for their comfort. Whoever fails in the consideration generally due to the interests and feelings of others, not being compelled by some more imperative duty, or justified by allowable self-preference, is a subject of moral disapprobation for that failure, but not for the cause of it, nor for the errors, merely personal to himself, which may have remotely led to it. In like manner, when a person disables himself, by conduct purely self-regarding, from the performance of some definite duty incumbent on him to the public, he is guilty of a social offence. No person ought to be punished simply for being drunk; but a soldier or a policeman should be punished for being drunk on duty. Whenever, in short, there is a definite damage, or a definite risk of damage, either to an individual or to the public, the case is taken out of the province of liberty, and placed in that of morality or law.

But with regard to the merely contingent, or, as it may be called, constructive injury which a person causes to society, by conduct which neither violates any specific duty to the public, nor occasions perceptible hurt to any assignable individual except himself; the inconvenience is one which society can afford to bear, for the sake of the greater good of human freedom. If grown persons are to be punished for not taking proper care of themselves, I would rather it were for their own sake, than under pretence of preventing them from impairing their capacity of rendering to society benefits which society does not pretend it has a right to exact. But I cannot consent to argue the point as if society had no means of bringing its weaker members up to its ordinary standard of rational conduct, except waiting till they do something irrational, and then punishing them, legally or morally, for it. Society has had absolute power over them during all the early portion of their existence: it has had the whole period of childhood and nonage in which to try whether it could make them capable of rational conduct in life. The existing generation is master both of the training and the entire circumstances of the generation to come; it cannot indeed make them perfectly wise and good, because it is itself so lamentably deficient in goodness and wisdom; and its best efforts are not always, in individual cases, its most successful ones; but it is perfectly well able to make the rising generation, as a whole, as good as, and a little better than, itself. If society lets any considerable number of its members grow up mere children, incapable of being acted on by rational consideration of distant motives, society has itself to blame for the consequences. Armed not only with all the powers of education, but with the ascendancy which the authority of a received opinion always exercises over the minds who are least fitted to judge for themselves; and aided by the natural penalties which cannot be prevented from falling on those who incur the distaste or the contempt of those who know them; let not society pretend that it needs, besides all this, the power to issue commands and enforce obedience in the personal concerns of individuals, in which, on all principles of justice and policy, the decision ought to rest with those who are to abide the consequences. Nor is there anything which tends more to discredit and frustrate the better means of influencing conduct, than a resort to the worse. If there be among those whom it is attempted to coerce into prudence or temperance, any of the material of which vigorous and independent characters are made, they will infallibly rebel against the yoke. No such person will ever feel that others have a right to control him in his concerns, such as they have to prevent him from injuring them in theirs; and it easily comes to be considered a mark of spirit and courage to fly in the face of such usurped authority, and do with ostentation the exact opposite of what it enjoins; as in the fashion of grossness which succeeded, in the time of Charles II., to the fanatical moral intolerance of the Puritans. With respect to what is said of the necessity of protecting society from the bad example set to others by the vicious or the self-indulgent; it is true that bad example may have a pernicious effect, especially the example of doing wrong to others with impunity to the wrong-doer. But we are now speaking of conduct which, while it does no wrong to others, is supposed to do great harm to the agent himself: and I do not see how those who believe this, can think otherwise than that the example, on the whole, must be more salutary than hurtful, since, if it displays the misconduct, it displays also the painful or degrading consequences which, if the conduct is justly censured, must be supposed to be in all or most cases attendant on it.

But the strongest of all the arguments against the interference of the public with purely personal conduct, is that when it does interfere, the odds are that it interferes wrongly, and in the wrong place. On questions of social morality, of duty to others, the opinion of the public, that is, of an overruling majority, though often wrong, is likely to be still oftener right; because on such questions they are only required to judge of their own interests; of the manner in which some mode of conduct, if allowed to be practised, would affect themselves. But the opinion of a similar majority, imposed as a law on the minority, on questions of self-regarding conduct, is quite as likely to be wrong as right; for in these cases public opinion means, at the best, some people's opinion of what is good or bad for other people; while very often it does not even mean that; the public, with the most perfect indifference, passing over the pleasure or convenience of those whose conduct they censure, and considering only their own preference. There are many who consider as an injury to themselves any conduct which they have a distaste for, and resent it as an outrage to their feelings; as a religious bigot, when charged with disregarding the religious feelings of others, has been known to retort that they disregard his feelings, by persisting in their abominable worship or creed. But there is no parity between the feeling of a person for his own opinion, and the feeling of another who is offended at his holding it; no more than between the desire of a thief to take a purse, and the desire of the right owner to keep it. And a person's taste is as much his own peculiar concern as his opinion or his purse. It is easy for any one to imagine an ideal public, which leaves the freedom and choice of individuals in all uncertain matters undisturbed, and only requires them to abstain from modes of conduct which universal experience has condemned. But where has there been seen a public which set any such limit to its censorship? or when does the public trouble itself about universal experience? In its interferences with personal conduct it is seldom thinking of anything but the enormity of acting or feeling differently from itself; and this standard of judgment, thinly disguised, is held up to mankind as the dictate of religion and philosophy, by ninetenths of all moralists and speculative writers. These teach that things are right because they are right; because we feel them to be so. They tell us to search in our own minds and hearts for laws of conduct binding on ourselves and on all others. What can the poor public do but apply these instructions, and make their own personal feelings of good and evil, if they are tolerably unanimous in them, obligatory on all the world?

The evil here pointed out is not one which exists only in theory; and it may perhaps be expected that I should specify the instances in which the public of this age and country improperly invests its own preferences with the character of moral laws. I am not writing an essay on the aberrations of existing moral feeling. That is too weighty a subject to be discussed parenthetically, and by way of illustration. Yet examples are necessary, to show that the principle I maintain is of serious and practical moment, and that I am not endeavouring to erect a barrier against imaginary evils. And it is not difficult to show, by

abundant instances, that to extend the bounds of what may be called moral police, until it encroaches on the most unquestionably legitimate liberty of the individual, is one of the most universal of all human propensities.

As a first instance, consider the antipathies which men cherish on no better grounds than that persons whose religious opinions are different from theirs, do not practise their religious observances, especially their religious abstinences. To cite a rather trivial example, nothing in the creed or practice of Christians does more to envenom the hatred of Mahomedans against them, than the fact of their eating pork. There are few acts which Christians and Europeans regard with more unaffected disgust, than Mussulmans regard this particular mode of satisfying hunger. It is, in the first place, an offence against their religion; but this circumstance by no means explains either the degree or the kind of their repugnance; for wine also is forbidden by their religion, and to partake of it is by all Mussulmans accounted wrong, but not disgusting. Their aversion to the flesh of the 'unclean beast' is, on the contrary, of that peculiar character, resembling an instinctive antipathy, which the idea of uncleanness, when once it thoroughly sinks into the feelings, seems always to excite even in those whose personal habits are anything but scrupulously cleanly, and of which the sentiment of religious impurity, so intense in the Hindoos, is a remarkable example. Suppose now that in a people, of whom the majority were Mussulmans, that majority should insist upon not permitting pork to be eaten within the limits of the country. This would be nothing new in Mahomedan countries.[9] Would it be a legitimate exer-

9. The case of the Bombay Parsees is a curious instance in point. When this industrious and enterprising tribe, the descendants of the Persian fire-worshippers, flying from their native country before the Caliphs, arrived in Western India, they were admitted to toleration by the Hindoo sovereigns, on condition of not eating beef. When those regions afterwards fell under the dominion of Mahomedan conquerors, the Parsees obtained from them a continuance of indulgence, on condition of refraining from pork. What was at first obedience to authority became a second nature, and the Parsees to this day abstain both from beef and pork. Though not required by their religion, the double abstinence has had time to

cise of the moral authority of public opinion? and if not, why not? The practice is really revolting to such a public. They also sincerely think that it is forbidden and abhorred by the Deity. Neither could the prohibition be censured as religious persecution. It might be religious in its origin, but it would not be persecution for religion, since nobody's religion makes it a duty to eat pork. The only tenable ground of condemnation would be, that with the personal tastes and self-regarding concerns of individuals the public has no business to interfere.

To come somewhat nearer home: the majority of Spaniards consider it a gross impiety, offensive in the highest degree to the Supreme Being, to worship him in any other manner than the Roman Catholic; and no other public worship is lawful on Spanish soil. The people of all Southern Europe look upon a married clergy as not only irreligious, but unchaste, indecent, gross, disgusting. What do Protestants think of these perfectly sincere feelings, and of the attempt to enforce them against non-Catholics? Yet, if mankind are justified in interfering with each other's liberty in things which do not concern the interests of others, on what principle is it possible consistently to exclude these cases? or who can blame people for desiring to suppress what they regard as a scandal in the sight of God and man? No stronger case can be shown for prohibiting anything which is regarded as a personal immorality, than is made out for suppressing these practices in the eyes of those who regard them as impieties; and unless we are willing to adopt the logic of persecutors, and to say that we may persecute others because we are right, and that they must not persecute us because they are wrong, we must beware of admitting a principle of which we should resent as a gross injustice the application to ourselves.

The preceding instances may be objected to, although unreasonably, as drawn from contingencies impossible among us: opinion, in this country, not being likely to enforce abstinence from meats, or to interfere with people for worshipping, and for either marrying or not marrying, according to their creed or inclination. The next example, however, shall be taken from an interference with liberty which we

_____

grow into a custom of their tribe; and custom, in the East, is a religion.

have by no means passed all danger of. Wherever the Puritans have been sufficiently powerful, as in New England, and in Great Britain at the time of the Commonwealth, they have endeavoured, with considerable success, to put down all public, and nearly all private, amusements: especially music, dancing, public games, or other assemblages for purposes of diversion, and the theatre. There are still in this country large bodies of persons by whose notions of morality and religion these recreations are condemned; and those persons belonging chiefly to the middle class, who are the ascendant power in the present social and political condition of the kingdom, it is by no means impossible that persons of these sentiments may at some time or other command a majority in Parliament. How will the remaining portion of the community like to have the amusements that shall be permitted to them regulated by the religious and moral sentiments of the stricter Calvinists and Methodists? Would they not, with considerable peremptoriness, desire these intrusively pious members of society to mind their own business? This is precisely what should be said to every government and every public, who have the pretension that no person shall enjoy any pleasure which they think wrong. But if the principle of the pretension be admitted, no one can reasonably object to its being acted on in the sense of the majority, or other preponderating power in the country; and all persons must be ready to conform to the idea of a Christian commonwealth, as understood by the early settlers in New England, if a religious profession similar to theirs should ever succeed in regaining its lost ground, as religions supposed to be declining have so often been known to do.

To imagine another contingency, perhaps more likely to be realized than the one last mentioned. There is confessedly a strong tendency in the modern world towards a democratic constitution of society, accompanied or not by popular political institutions. It is affirmed that in the country where this tendency is most completely realized—where both society and the government are most democratic—the United States—the feeling of the majority, to whom any appearance of a more showy or costly style of living than they can hope to rival is disagreeable, operates as a tolerably effectual sumptuary law, and that in many parts of the Union it is really difficult for a

must quote someday

person possessing a very large income, to find any mode of spending it, which will not incur popular disapprobation. Though such statements as these are doubtless much exaggerated as a representation of existing facts, the state of things they describe is not only a conceivable and possible, but a probable result of democratic feeling, combined with the notion that the public has a right to a veto on the manner in which individuals shall spend their incomes. We have only further to suppose a considerable diffusion of Socialist opinions, and it may become infamous in the eyes of the majority to possess more property than some very small amount, or any income not earned by manual labour. Opinions similar in principle to these, already prevail widely among the artizan class, and weigh oppressively on those who are amenable to the opinion chiefly of that class, namely, its own members. It is known that the bad workmen who form the majority of the operatives in many branches of industry, are decidedly of opinion that bad work-men ought to receive the same wages as good, and that no one ought to be allowed, through piecework or otherwise, to earn by superior skill or industry more than others can without it. And they employ a moral police, which occasionally becomes a physical one, to deter skilful workmen from receiving, and employers from giving, a larger remuneration for a more useful service. If the public have any jurisdiction over private concerns, I cannot see that these people are in fault, or that any individual's particular public can be blamed for asserting the same authority over his individual conduct, which the general public asserts over people in general.

But, without dwelling upon supposititious cases, there are, in our own day, gross usurpations upon the liberty of private life actually practised, and still greater ones threatened with some expectation of success, and opinions propounded which assert an unlimited right in the public not only to prohibit by law everything which it thinks wrong, but in order to get at what it thinks wrong, to prohibit any number of things which it admits to be innocent.

Under the name of preventing intemperance, the people of one English colony, and of nearly half the United States, have been interdicted by law from making any use whatever of fermented drinks, except for medical purposes: for prohibition of their sale is in fact, as it is intended to be, prohibition of their use. And though the impracticability of executing the law has caused its repeal in several of the States which had adopted it, including the one from which it derives its name, an attempt has notwithstanding been commenced, and is prosecuted with considerable zeal by many of the professed philanthropists, to agitate for a similar law in this country. The association, or 'Alliance' as it terms itself, which has been formed for this purpose, has acquired some notoriety through the publicity given to a correspondence between its Secretary and one of the very few English public men who hold that a politician's opinions ought to be founded on principles. Lord Stanley's share in this correspondence is calculated to strengthen the hopes already built on him, by those who know how rare such qualities as are manifested in some of his public appearances, unhappily are among those who figure in political life. The organ of the Alliance, who would 'deeply deplore the recognition of any principle which could be wrested to justify bigotry and persecution,' undertakes to point out the 'broad and impassable barrier' which divides such principles from those of the association. 'All matters relating to thought, opinion, conscience, appear to me,' he says, 'to be without the sphere of legislation; all pertaining to social act, habit, relation, subject only to a discretionary power vested in the State itself, and not in the individual, to be within it.' No mention is made of a third class, different from either of these, viz. acts and habits which are not social, but individual; although it is to this class, surely, that the act of drinking fermented liquors belongs. Selling fermented liquors, however, is trading, and trading is a social act. But the infringement complained of is not on the liberty of the seller, but on that of the buyer and consumer; since the State might just as well forbid him to drink wine, as purposely make it impossible for him to obtain it. The Secretary, however, says, 'I claim, as a citizen, a right to legislate whenever my social rights are invaded by the social act of another.' And now for the definition of these 'social rights.' 'If anything invades my social rights, certainly the traffic in strong drink does. It destroys my primary right of security, by constantly creating and stimulating social disorder. It invades my right of equality, by deriving a profit from the creation of a misery I am taxed to support.

It impedes my right to free moral and intellectual development, by surrounding my path with dangers, and by weakening and demoralizing society, from which I have a right to claim mutual aid and intercourse.' A theory of 'social rights,' the like of which probably never before found its way into distinct language: being nothing short of this—that it is the absolute social right of every individual, that every other individual shall act in every respect exactly as he ought; that whosoever fails thereof in the smallest particular, violates my social right, and entitles me to demand from the legislature the removal of the grievance. So monstrous a principle is far more dangerous than any single interference with liberty; there is no violation of liberty which it would not justify; it acknowledges no right to any freedom whatever, except perhaps to that of holding opinions in secret, without ever disclosing them: for, the moment an opinion which I consider noxious passes any one's lips, it invades all the 'social rights' attributed to me by the Alliance. The doctrine ascribes to all mankind a vested interest in each other's moral, intellectual, and even physical perfection, to be defined by each claimant according to his own standard.

Another important example of illegitimate interference with the rightful liberty of the individual, not simply threatened, but long since carried into triumphant effect, is Sabbatarian legislation. Without doubt, abstinence on one day in the week, so far as the exigencies of life permit, from the usual daily occupation, though in no respect religiously binding on any except Jews, is a highly beneficial custom. And inasmuch as this custom cannot be observed without a general consent to that effect among the industrious classes, therefore, in so far as some persons by working may impose the same necessity on others, it may be allowable and right that the law should guarantee to each the observance by others of the custom, by suspending the greater operations of industry on a particular day. But this justification, grounded on the direct interest which others have in each individual's observance of the practice, does not apply to the self-chosen occupations in which a person may think fit to employ his leisure; nor does it hold good, in the smallest degree, for legal restrictions on amusements. It is true that the amusement of some is the day's work of others; but the pleasure, not to say the

useful recreation, of many, is worth the labour of a few, provided the occupation is freely chosen, and can be freely resigned. The operatives are perfectly right in thinking that if all worked on Sunday, seven days' work would have to be given for six days' wages: but so long as the great mass of employments are suspended, the small number who for the enjoyment of others must still work, obtain a proportional increase of earnings; and they are not obliged to follow those occupations, if they prefer leisure to emolument. If a further remedy is sought, it might be found in the establishment by custom of a holiday on some other day of the week for those particular classes of persons. The only ground, therefore, on which restrictions on Sunday amusements can be defended, must be that they are religiously wrong; a motive of legislation which never can be too earnestly protested against. '*Deorum injuriae Diis curae.*' It remains to be proved that society or any of its officers holds a commission from on high to avenge any supposed offence to Omnipotence, which is not also a wrong to our fellow creatures. The notion that it is one man's duty that another should be religious, was the foundation of all the religious persecutions ever perpetrated, and if admitted, would fully justify them. Though the feeling which breaks out in the repeated attempts to stop railway travelling on Sunday, in the resistance to the opening of Museums, and the like, has not the cruelty of the old persecutors, the state of mind indicated by it is fundamentally the same. It is a determination not to tolerate others in doing what is permitted by their religion, because it is not permitted by the persecutor's religion. It is a belief that God not only abominates the act of the misbeliever, but will not hold us guiltless if we leave him unmolested.

I cannot refrain from adding to these examples of the little account commonly made of human liberty, the language of downright persecution which breaks out from the press of this country, whenever it feels called on to notice the remarkable phenomenon of Mormonism. Much might be said on the unexpected and instructive fact, that an alleged new revelation, and a religion founded on it, the product of palpable imposture, not even supported by the *prestige* of extraordinary qualities in its founder, is believed by hundreds of thousands, and has been made the foundation of a society, in the age of newspapers, railways, and the electric telegraph. What here concerns us is, that this religion, like other and better religions, has its martyrs; that its prophet and founder was, for his teaching, put to death by a mob; that others of its adherents lost their lives by the same lawless violence; that they were forcibly expelled, in a body, from the country in which they first grew up; while, now that they have been chased into a solitary recess in the midst of a desert, many in this country openly declare that it would be right (only that it is not convenient) to send an expedition against them, and compel them by force to conform to the opinions of other people. The article of the Mormonite doctrine which is the chief provocative to the antipathy which thus breaks through the ordinary restraints of religious tolerance, is its sanction of polygamy; which, though permitted to Mahomedans, and Hindoos, and Chinese, seems to excite unquenchable animosity when practised by persons who speak English, and profess to be a kind of Christians. No one has a deeper disapprobation than I have of this Mormon institution; both for other reasons, and because, far from being in any way countenanced by the principle of liberty, it is a direct infraction of that principle, being a mere rivetting of the chains of one half of the community, and an emancipation of the other from reciprocity of obligation towards them. Still, it must be remembered that this relation is as much voluntary on the part of the women concerned in it, and who may be deemed the sufferers by it, as is the case with any other form of the marriage institution; and however surprising this fact may appear, it has its explanation in the common ideas and customs of the world, which teaching women to think marriage the one thing needful, make it intelligible that many a woman should prefer being one of several wives, to not being a wife at all. Other countries are not asked to recognise such unions, or release any portion of their inhabitants from their own laws on the score of Mormonite opinions. But when the dissentients have conceded to the hostile sentiments of others, far more than could justly be demanded; when they have left the countries to which their doctrines were unacceptable, and established themselves in a remote corner of the earth, which they have been the first

to render habitable to human beings; it is difficult to see on what principles but those of tyranny they can be prevented from living there under what laws they please, provided they commit no aggression on other nations, and allow perfect freedom of departure to those who are dissatisfied with their ways. A recent writer, in some respects of considerable merit, proposes (to use his own words) not a crusade, but a *civilizade*, against this polygamous community, to put an end to what seems to him a retrograde step in civilization. It also appears so to me, but I am not aware that any community has a right to force another to be civilized. So long as the sufferers by the bad law do not invoke assistance from other communities, I cannot admit that persons entirely unconnected with them ought to step in and require that a condition of things with which all who are directly interested appear to be satisfied, should be put an end to because it is a scandal to persons some thousands of miles distant, who have no part or concern in it. Let them send missionaries, if they please, to preach against it; and let them, by any fair means (of which silencing the teachers is not one,) oppose the progress of similar doctrines among their own people. If civilization has got the better of barbarism when barbarism had the world to itself, it is too much to profess to be afraid lest barbarism, after having been fairly got under, should revive and conquer civilization. A civilization that can thus succumb to its vanquished enemy, must first have become so degenerate, that neither its appointed priests and teachers, nor anybody else, has the capacity, or will take the trouble, to stand up for it. If this be so, the sooner such a civilization receives notice to quit, the better. It can only go on from bad to worse, until destroyed and regenerated (like the Western Empire) by energetic barbarians.

CHAPTER V

Applications

The principles asserted in these pages must be more generally admitted as the basis for discussion of details, before a consistent application of them to all the various departments of government and morals can be attempted with any prospect of advantage. The few observations I propose to make on questions of detail, are designed to illustrate the principles, rather than to follow them out to their consequences. I offer, not so much applications, as specimens of application; which may serve to bring into greater clearness the meaning and limits of the two maxims which together form the entire doctrine of this Essay, and to assist the judgment in holding the balance between them, in the cases where it appears doubtful which of them is applicable to the case.

The maxims are, first, that the individual is not accountable to society for his actions, in so far as these concern the interests of no person but himself. Advice, instruction, persuasion, and avoidance by other people if thought necessary by them for their own good, are the only measures by which society can justifiably express its dislike or disapprobation of his conduct. Secondly, that for such actions as are prejudicial to the interests of others, the individual is accountable, and may be subjected either to social or to legal punishment, if society is of opinion that the one or the other is requisite for its protection.

In the first place, it must by no means be supposed, because damage, or probability of damage, to the interests of others, can alone justify the interference of society, that therefore it always does justify such interference. In many cases, an individual, in pursuing a legitimate object, necessarily and therefore legitimately causes pain or loss to others, or intercepts a good which they had a reasonable hope of obtaining. Such oppositions of interest between individuals often arise from bad social institutions, but are unavoidable while those institutions last; and some would be unavoidable under any institutions. Whoever succeeds in an overcrowded profession, or in a competitive examination; whoever is preferred to another in any contest for an object which both desire, reaps benefit from the loss of others, from their wasted exertion and their disappointment. But it is, by common admission, better for the general interest of mankind, that persons should pursue their objects undeterred by this sort of consequences. In other words, society admits no right, either legal or moral, in the disappointed competitors, to immunity from this kind of suffering; and feels called on to interfere, only when

means of success have been employed which it is contrary to the general interest to permit—namely, fraud or treachery, and force.

Again, trade is a social act. Whoever undertakes to sell any description of goods to the public, does what affects the interest of other persons, and of society in general; and thus his conduct, in principle, comes within the jurisdiction of society: accordingly, it was once held to be the duty of governments, in all cases which were considered of importance, to fix prices, and regulate the processes of manufacture. But it is now recognised, though not till after a long struggle, that both the cheapness and the good quality of commodities are most effectually provided for by leaving the producers and sellers perfectly free, under the sole check of equal freedom to the buyers for supplying themselves elsewhere. This is the so-called doctrine of Free Trade, which rests on grounds different from, though equally solid with, the principle of individual liberty asserted in this Essay. Restrictions on trade, or on production for purposes of trade, are indeed restraints; and all restraint, *qua* restraint, is an evil: but the restraints in question affect only that part of conduct which society is competent to restrain, and are wrong solely because they do not really produce the results which it is desired to produce by them. As the principle of individual liberty is not involved in the doctrine of Free Trade, so neither is it in most of the questions which arise respecting the limits of that doctrine; as for example, what amount of public control is admissible for the prevention of fraud by adulteration; how far sanitary precautions, or arrangements to protect workpeople employed in dangerous occupations, should be enforced on employers. Such questions involve considerations of liberty, only in so far as leaving people to themselves is always better, *caeteris paribus*, than controlling them: but that they may be legitimately controlled for these ends, is in principle undeniable. On the other hand, there are questions relating to interference with trade, which are essentially questions of liberty; such as the Maine Law, already touched upon; the prohibition of the importation of opium into China; the restriction of the sale of poisons; all cases, in short, where the object of the interference is to make it impossible or difficult to obtain a particular commodity. These interferences are objectionable, not as infringements on the liberty of the producer or seller, but on that of the buyer.

One of these examples, that of the sale of poisons, opens a new question; the proper limits of what may be called the functions of police; how far liberty may legitimately be invaded for the prevention of crime, or of accident. It is one of the undisputed functions of government to take precautions against crime before it has been committed, as well as to detect and punish it afterwards. The preventive function of government, however, is far more liable to be abused, to the prejudice of liberty, than the punitory function; for there is hardly any part of the legitimate freedom of action of a human being which would not admit of being represented, and fairly too, as increasing the facilities for some form or other of delinquency. Nevertheless, if a public authority, or even a private person, sees any one evidently preparing to commit a crime, they are not bound to look on inactive until the crime is committed, but may interfere to prevent it. If poisons were never bought or used for any purpose except the commission of murder, it would be right to prohibit their manufacture and sale. They may, however, be wanted not only for innocent but for useful purposes, and restrictions cannot be imposed in the one case without operating in the other. Again, it is a proper office of public authority to guard against accidents. If either a public officer or any one else saw a person attempting to cross a bridge which had been ascertained to be unsafe, and there were no time to warn him of his danger, they might seize him and turn him back, without any real infringement of his liberty; for liberty consists in doing what one desires, and he does not desire to fall into the river. Nevertheless, when there is not a certainty, but only a danger of mischief, no one but the person himself can judge of the sufficiency of the motive which may prompt him to incur the risk: in this case, therefore, (unless he is a child, or delirious, or in some state of excitement or absorption incompatible with the full use of the reflecting faculty) he ought, I conceive, to be only warned of the danger; not forcibly prevented from exposing himself to it. Similar considerations, applied to such a question as the sale of poisons, may enable us to decide which among the possible modes

of regulation are or are not contrary to principle. Such a precaution, for example, as that of labelling the drug with some word expressive of its dangerous character, may be enforced without violation of liberty: the buyer cannot wish not to know that the thing he possesses has poisonous qualities. But to require in all cases the certificate of a medical practitioner, would make it sometimes impossible, always expensive, to obtain the article for legitimate uses. The only mode apparent to me, in which difficulties may be thrown in the way of crime committed through this means, without any infringement, worth taking into account, upon the liberty of those who desire the poisonous substance for other purposes, consists in providing what, in the apt language of Bentham, is called 'preappointed evidence.' This provision is familiar to every one in the case of contracts. It is usual and right that the law, when a contract is entered into, should require as the condition of its enforcing performance, that certain formalities should be observed, such as signatures, attestation of witnesses, and the like, in order that in case of subsequent dispute, there may be evidence to prove that the contract was really entered into, and that there was nothing in the circumstances to render it legally invalid: the effect being, to throw great obstacles in the way of fictitious contracts, or contracts made in circumstances which, if known, would destroy their validity. Precautions of a similar nature might be enforced in the sale of articles adapted to be instruments of crime. The seller, for example, might be required to enter in a register the exact time of the transaction, the name and address of the buyer, the precise quality and quantity sold; to ask the purpose for which it was wanted, and record the answer he received. When there was no medical prescription, the presence of some third person might be required, to bring home the fact to the purchaser, in case there should afterwards be reason to believe that the article had been applied to criminal purposes. Such regulations would in general be no material impediment to obtaining the article, but a very considerable one to making an improper use of it without detection.

The right inherent in society, to ward off crimes against itself by antecedent precautions, suggests the obvious limitations to the maxim, that purely self-regarding misconduct cannot properly be meddled with in the way of prevention or punishment. Drunkenness, for example, in ordinary cases, is not a fit subject for legislative interference; but I should deem it perfectly legitimate that a person, who had once been convicted of any act of violence to others under the influence of drink, should be placed under a special legal restriction, personal to himself; that if he were afterwards found drunk, he should be liable to a penalty, and that if when in that state he committed another offence, the punishment to which he would be liable for that other offence should be increased in severity. The making himself drunk, in a person whom drunkenness excites to do harm to others, is a crime against others. So, again, idleness, except in a person receiving support from the public, or except when it constitutes a breach of contract, cannot without tyranny be made a subject of legal punishment; but if, either from idleness or from any other avoidable cause, a man fails to perform his legal duties to others, as for instance to support his children, it is no tyranny to force him to fulfil that obligation, by compulsory labour, if no other means are available.

Again, there are many acts which, being directly injurious only to the agents themselves, ought not to be legally interdicted, but which, if done publicly, are a violation of good manners, and coming thus within the category of offences against others, may rightfully be prohibited. Of this kind are offences against decency; on which it is unnecessary to dwell, the rather as they are only connected indirectly with our subject, the objection to publicity being equally strong in the case of many actions not in themselves condemnable, nor supposed to be so.

There is another question to which an answer must be found, consistent with the principles which have been laid down. In cases of personal conduct supposed to be blameable, but which respect for liberty precludes society from preventing or punishing, because the evil directly resulting falls wholly on the agent; what the agent is free to do, ought other persons to be equally free to counsel or instigate? This question is not free from difficulty. The case of a person who solicits another to do an act, is not strictly a case of self-regarding conduct. To give advice or offer inducements to any one, is a social act, and may, therefore, like actions in general which affect others, be supposed amenable to social control. But a little

reflection corrects the first impression, by showing that if the case is not strictly within the definition of individual liberty, yet the reasons on which the principle of individual liberty is grounded, are applicable to it. If people must be allowed, in whatever concerns only themselves, to act as seems best to themselves at their own peril, they must equally be free to consult with one another about what is fit to be so done; to exchange opinions, and give and receive suggestions. Whatever it is permitted to do, it must be permitted to advise to do. The question is doubtful, only when the instigator derives a personal benefit from his advice; when he makes it his occupation, for subsistence or pecuniary gain, to promote what society and the State consider to be an evil. Then, indeed, a new element of complication is introduced; namely, the existence of classes of persons with an interest opposed to what is considered as the public weal, and whose mode of living is grounded on the counteraction of it. Ought this to be interfered with, or not? Fornication, for example, must be tolerated, and so must gambling; but should a person be free to be a pimp, or to keep a gambling-house? The case is one of those which lie on the exact boundary line between two principles, and it is not at once apparent to which of the two it properly belongs. There are arguments on both sides. On the side of toleration it may be said, that the fact of following anything as an occupation, and living or profiting by the practice of it, cannot make that criminal which would otherwise be admissible; that the act should either be consistently permitted or consistently prohibited; that if the principles which we have hitherto defended are true, society has no business, as society, to decide anything to be wrong which concerns only the individual; that it cannot go beyond dissuasion, and that one person should be as free to persuade, as another to dissuade. In opposition to this it may be contended, that although the public, or the State, are not warranted in authoritatively deciding, for purposes of repression or punishment, that such or such conduct affecting only the interests of the individual is good or bad, they are fully justified in assuming, if they regard it as bad, that its being so or not is at least a disputable question: That, this being supposed, they cannot be acting wrongly in endeavouring to exclude the influence of solicitations which are not disinterested, of instigators who cannot possibly be impartial—who have a direct personal interest on one side, and that side the one which the State believes to be wrong, and who confessedly promote it for personal objects only. There can surely, it may be urged, be nothing lost, no sacrifice of good, by so ordering matters that persons shall make their election, either wisely or foolishly, on their own prompting, as free as possible from the arts of persons who stimulate their inclinations for interested purposes of their own. Thus (it may be said) though the statutes respecting unlawful games are utterly indefensible—though all persons should be free to gamble in their own or each other's houses, or in any place of meeting established by their own subscriptions, and open only to the members and their visitors—yet public gambling-houses should not be permitted. It is true that the prohibition is never effectual, and that, whatever amount of tyrannical power may be given to the police, gambling-houses can always be maintained under other pretences; but they may be compelled to conduct their operations with a certain degree of secrecy and mystery, so that nobody knows anything about them but those who seek them; and more than this, society ought not to aim at. There is considerable force in these arguments. I will not venture to decide whether they are sufficient to justify the moral anomaly of punishing the accessary, when the principal is (and must be) allowed to go free; of fining or imprisoning the procurer, but not the fornicator, the gambling-house keeper, but not the gambler. Still less ought the common operations of buying and selling to be interfered with on analogous grounds. Almost every article which is bought and sold may be used in excess, and the sellers have a pecuniary interest in encouraging that excess; but no argument can be founded on this, in favour, for instance, of the Maine Law; because the class of dealers in strong drinks, though interested in their abuse, are indispensably required for the sake of their legitimate use. The interest, however, of these dealers in promoting intemperance is a real evil, and justifies the State in imposing restrictions and requiring guarantees which, but for that justification, would be infringements of legitimate liberty.

A further question is, whether the State, while it permits, should nevertheless indirectly discourage conduct which it deems contrary to the best interests of the agent; whether, for example, it should take measures to render the means of drunkenness more costly, or add to the difficulty of procuring them by limiting the number of the places of sale. On this as on most other practical questions, many distinctions require to be made. To tax stimulants for the sole purpose of making them more difficult to be obtained, is a measure differing only in degree from their entire prohibition; and would be justifiable only if that were justifiable. Every increase of cost is a prohibition, to those whose means do not come up to the augmented price; and to those who do, it is a penalty laid on them for gratifying a particular taste. Their choice of pleasures, and their mode of expending their income, after satisfying their legal and moral obligations to the State and to individuals, are their own concern, and must rest with their own judgment. These considerations may seem at first sight to condemn the selection of stimulants as special subjects of taxation for purposes of revenue. But it must be remembered that taxation for fiscal purposes is absolutely inevitable; that in most countries it is necessary that a considerable part of that taxation should be indirect; that the State, therefore, cannot help imposing penalties, which to some persons may be prohibitory, on the use of some articles of consumption. It is hence the duty of the State to consider, in the imposition of taxes, what commodities the consumers can best spare; and *a fortiori*, to select in preference those of which it deems the use, beyond a very moderate quantity, to be positively injurious. Taxation, therefore, of stimulants, up to the point which produces the largest amount of revenue (supposing that the State needs all the revenue which it yields) is not only admissible, but to be approved of.

The question of making the sale of these commodities a more or less exclusive privilege, must be answered differently, according to the purposes to which the restriction is intended to be subservient. All places of public resort require the restraint of a police, and places of this kind peculiarly, because offences against society are especially apt to originate there. It is, therefore, fit to confine the power of selling these commodities (at least for consumption on the spot) to persons of known or vouched-for respectability of conduct; to make such regulations respecting hours of opening and closing as may be requisite for public surveillance, and to withdraw the licence if breaches of the peace repeatedly take place through the connivance or incapacity of the keeper of the house, or if it becomes a rendezvous for concocting and preparing offences against the law. Any further restriction I do not conceive to be, in principle, justifiable. The limitation in number, for instance, of beer and spirit houses, for the express purpose of rendering them more difficult of access, and diminishing the occasions of temptation, not only exposes all to an inconvenience because there are some by whom the facility would be abused, but is suited only to a state of society in which the labouring classes are avowedly treated as children or savages, and placed under an education of restraint, to fit them for future admission to the privileges of freedom. This is not the principle on which the labouring classes are professedly governed in any free country; and no person who sets due value on freedom will give his adhesion to their being so governed, unless after all efforts have been exhausted to educate them for freedom and govern them as freemen, and it has been definitively proved that they can only be governed as children. The bare statement of the alternative shows the absurdity of supposing that such efforts have been made in any case which needs be considered here. It is only because the institutions of this country are a mass of inconsistencies, that things find admittance into our practice which belong to the system of despotic, or what is called paternal, government, while the general freedom of our institutions precludes the exercise of the amount of control necessary to render the restraint of any real efficacy as a moral education.

It was pointed out in an early part of this Essay, that the liberty of the individual, in things wherein the individual is alone concerned, implies a corresponding liberty in any number of individuals to regulate by mutual agreement such things as regard them jointly, and regard no persons but themselves. This question presents no difficulty, so long as the will of all the persons implicated remains unaltered; but since that will may change, it is often necessary, even in things in which they alone are concerned, that they should enter into engagements with one another; and when they do, it is fit, as a general rule, that those engagements should be kept. Yet, in the laws, probably, of every country, this general rule has some

exceptions. Not only persons are not held to engagements which violate the rights of third parties, but it is sometimes considered a sufficient reason for releasing them from an engagement, that it is injurious to themselves. In this and most other civilized countries, for example, an engagement by which a person should sell himself, or allow himself to be sold, as a slave, would be null and void; neither enforced by law nor by opinion. The ground for thus limiting his power of voluntarily disposing of his own lot in life, is apparent, and is very clearly seen in this extreme case. The reason for not interfering, unless for the sake of others, with a person's voluntary acts, is consideration for his liberty. His voluntary choice is evidence that what he so chooses is desirable, or at the least endurable, to him, and his good is on the whole best provided for by allowing him to take his own means of pursuing it. But by selling himself for a slave, he abdicates his liberty; he foregoes any future use of it beyond that single act. He therefore defeats, in his own case, the very purpose which is the justification of allowing him to dispose of himself. He is no longer free; but is thenceforth in a position which has no longer the presumption in its favour, that would be afforded by his voluntarily remaining in it. The principle of freedom cannot require that he should be free not to be free. It is not freedom, to be allowed to alienate his freedom. These reasons, the force of which is so conspicuous in this peculiar case, are evidently of far wider application; yet a limit is everywhere set to them by the necessities of life, which continually require, not indeed that we should resign our freedom, but that we should consent to this and the other limitation of it. The principle, however, which demands uncontrolled freedom of action in all that concerns only the agents themselves, requires that those who have become bound to one another, in things which concern no third party, should be able to release one another from the engagement: and even without such voluntary release, there are perhaps no contracts or engagements, except those that relate to money or money's worth, of which one can venture to say that there ought to be no liberty whatever of retractation. Baron Wilhelm von Humboldt, in the excellent essay from which I have already quoted, states it as his conviction, that engagements which involve personal relations or services, should never be legally binding beyond a limited duration of time; and that the most important of these engagements, marriage, having the peculiarity that its objects are frustrated unless the feelings of both the parties are in harmony with it, should require nothing more than the declared will of either party to dissolve it. This subject is too important, and too complicated, to be discussed in a parenthesis, and I touch on it only so far as is necessary for purposes of illustration. If the conciseness and generality of Baron Humboldt's dissertation had not obliged him in this instance to content himself with enunciating his conclusion without discussing the premises, he would doubtless have recognised that the question cannot be decided on grounds so simple as those to which he confines himself. When a person, either by express promise or by conduct, has encouraged another to rely upon his continuing to act in a certain way — to build expectations and calculations, and stake any part of his plan of life upon that supposition — a new series of moral obligations arises on his part towards that person, which may possibly be overruled, but cannot be ignored. And again, if the relation between two contracting parties has been followed by consequences to others; if it has placed third parties in any peculiar position, or, as in the case of marriage, has even called third parties into existence, obligations arise on the part of both the contracting parties towards those third persons, the fulfilment of which, or at all events the mode of fulfilment, must be greatly affected by the continuance or disruption of the relation between the original parties to the contract. It does not follow, nor can I admit, that these obligations extend to requiring the fulfilment of the contract at all costs to the happiness of the reluctant party; but they are a necessary element in the question; and even if, as von Humboldt maintains, they ought to make no difference in the *legal* freedom of the parties to release themselves from the engagement (and I also hold that they ought not to make *much* difference), they necessarily make a great difference in the *moral* freedom. A person is bound to take all these circumstances into account, before resolving on a step which may affect such important interests of others; and if he does not allow proper weight to those interests, he is morally responsible for the wrong. I have made these obvious remarks for the better illustration of the general principle of liberty, and not because they are at all needed on the particular question, which, on the contrary, is usually discussed as if the interest of children was everything, and that of grown persons nothing.

I have already observed that, owing to the absence of any recognised general principles, liberty is often granted where it should be withheld, as well as withheld where it should be granted; and one of the cases in which, in the modern European world, the sentiment of liberty is the strongest, is a case where, in my view, it is altogether misplaced. A person should be free to do as he likes in his own concerns; but he ought not to be free to do as he likes in acting for another, under the pretext that the affairs of the other are his own affairs. The State, while it respects the liberty of each in what specially regards himself, is bound to maintain a vigilant control over his exercise of any power which it allows him to possess over others. This obligation is almost entirely disregarded in the case of the family relations, a case, in its direct influence on human happiness, more important than all others taken together. The almost despotic power of husbands over wives needs not be enlarged upon here, because nothing more is needed for the complete removal of the evil, than that wives should have the same rights, and should receive the protection of law in the same manner, as all other persons; and because, on this subject, the defenders of established injustice do not avail themselves of the plea of liberty, but stand forth openly as the champions of power. It is in the case of children, that misapplied notions of liberty are a real obstacle to the fulfilment by the State of its duties. One would almost think that a man's children were supposed to be literally, and not metaphorically, a part of himself, so jealous is opinion of the smallest interference of law with his absolute and exclusive control over them; more jealous than of almost any interference with his own freedom of action: so much less do the generality of mankind value liberty than power. Consider, for example, the case of education. Is it not almost a self-evident axiom, that the State should require and compel the education, up to a certain standard, of every human being who is born its citizen? Yet who is there that is not afraid to recognise and assert this truth? Hardly any one indeed will deny that it is one of the most sacred duties of the parents (or, as law and usage now stand, the father), after summoning a human being into the world, to give to that being an education fitting him to perform his part well in life towards others and towards himself. But while this is unanimously declared to be the father's duty, scarcely anybody, in this country, will bear to hear of obliging him to perform it. Instead of his being required to make any exertion or sacrifice for securing education to the child, it is left to his choice to accept it or not when it is provided gratis! It still remains unrecognised, that to bring a child into existence without a fair prospect of being able, not only to provide food for its body, but instruction and training for its mind, is a moral crime, both against the unfortunate offspring and against society; and that if the parent does not fulfil this obligation, the State ought to see it fulfilled, at the charge, as far as possible, of the parent.

Were the duty of enforcing universal education once admitted, there would be an end to the difficulties about what the State should teach, and how it should teach, which now convert the subject into a mere battle-field for sects and parties, causing the time and labour which should have been spent in educating, to be wasted in quarrelling about education. If the government would make up its mind to *require* for every child a good education, it might save itself the trouble of *providing* one. It might leave to parents to obtain the education where and how they pleased, and content itself with helping to pay the school fees of the poorer classes of children, and defraying the entire school expenses of those who have no one else to pay for them. The objections which are urged with reason against State education, do not apply to the enforcement of education by the State, but to the State's taking upon itself to direct that education: which is a totally different thing. That the whole or any large part of the education of the people should be in State hands, I go as far as any one in deprecating. All that has been said of the importance of individuality of character, and diversity in opinions and modes of conduct, involves, as of the same unspeakable importance, diversity of education. A general State education is a mere contrivance for moulding people to be exactly like one another: and as the mould in which it casts them is that which pleases the predominant power in the government,

whether this be a monarch, a priesthood, an aristocracy, or the majority of the existing generation in proportion as it is efficient and successful, it establishes a despotism over the mind, leading by natural tendency to one over the body. An education established and controlled by the State should only exist, if it exist at all, as one among many competing experiments, carried on for the purpose of example and stimulus, to keep the others up to a certain standard of excellence. Unless, indeed, when society in general is in so backward a state that it could not or would not provide for itself any proper institutions of education, unless the government undertook the task: then, indeed, the government may, as the less of two great evils, take upon itself the business of schools and universities, as it may that of joint stock companies, when private enterprise, in a shape fitted for undertaking great works of industry, does not exist in the country. But in general, if the country contains a sufficient number of persons qualified to provide education under government auspices, the same persons would be able and willing to give an equally good education on the voluntary principle, under the assurance of remuneration afforded by a law rendering education compulsory, combined with State aid to those unable to defray the expense.

The instrument for enforcing the law could be no other than public examinations, extending to all children, and beginning at an early age. An age might be fixed at which every child must be examined, to ascertain if he (or she) is able to read. If a child proves unable, the father, unless he has some sufficient ground of excuse, might be subjected to a moderate fine, to be worked out, if necessary, by his labour, and the child might be put to school at his expense. Once in every year the examination should be renewed, with a gradually extending range of subjects, so as to make the universal acquisition, and what is more, retention, of a certain minimum of general knowledge, virtually compulsory. Beyond that minimum, there should be voluntary examinations on all subjects, at which all who come up to a certain standard of proficiency might claim a certificate. To prevent the State from exercising, through these arrangements, an improper influence over opinion, the knowledge required for passing an examination (beyond the merely instrumental parts of knowledge, such as languages and their use) should, even in the higher classes of examinations, be confined to facts and positive science exclusively. The examinations on religion, politics, or other disputed topics, should not turn on the truth or falsehood of opinions, but on the matter of fact that such and such an opinion is held, on such grounds, by such authors, or schools, or churches. Under this system, the rising generation would be no worse off in regard to all disputed truths, than they are at present; they would be brought up either churchmen or dissenters as they now are, the State merely taking care that they should be instructed churchmen, or instructed dissenters. There would be nothing to hinder them from being taught religion, if their parents chose, at the same schools where they were taught other things. All attempts by the State to bias the conclusions of its citizens on disputed subjects, are evil; but it may very properly offer to ascertain and certify that a person possesses the knowledge, requisite to make his conclusions, on any given subject, worth attending to. A student of philosophy would be the better for being able to stand an examination both in Locke and in Kant, whichever of the two he takes up with, or even if with neither: and there is no reasonable objection to examining an atheist in the evidences of Christianity, provided he is not required to profess a belief in them. The examinations, however, in the higher branches of knowledge should, I conceive, be entirely voluntary. It would be giving too dangerous a power to governments, were they allowed to exclude any one from professions, even from the profession of teacher, for alleged deficiency of qualifications: and I think, with Wilhelm von Humboldt, that degrees, or other public certificates of scientific or professional acquirements, should be given to all who present themselves for examination, and stand the test; but that such certificates should confer no advantage over competitors, other than the weight which may be attached to their testimony by public opinion.

It is not in the matter of education only, that misplaced notions of liberty prevent moral obligations on the part of parents from being recognised, and legal obligations from being imposed, where there are the strongest grounds for the former always, and in many cases for the latter also. The fact itself, of causing the existence of a human being, is one of the most responsible actions in the range of human life. To undertake this responsibility—to bestow a life which may be either a curse or a blessing—unless the being on whom it is to be bestowed will have at least the ordinary chances of a desirable existence, is a crime against that being. And in a country either over-peopled or threatened with being so, to produce children, beyond a very small number, with the effect of reducing the reward of labour by their competition, is a serious offence against all who live by the remuneration of their labour. The laws which, in many countries on the Continent, forbid marriage unless the parties can show that they have the means of supporting a family, do not exceed the legitimate powers of the State: and whether such laws be expedient or not (a question mainly dependent on local circumstances and feelings), they are not objectionable as violations of liberty. Such laws are interferences of the State to prohibit a mischievous act—an act injurious to others, which ought to be a subject of reprobation, and social stigma, even when it is not deemed expedient to superadd legal punishment. Yet the current ideas of liberty, which bend so easily to real infringements of the freedom of the individual in things which concern only himself, would repel the attempt to put any restraint upon his inclinations when the consequence of their indulgence is a life or lives of wretchedness and depravity to the offspring, with manifold evils to those sufficiently within reach to be in any way affected by their actions. When we compare the strange respect of mankind for liberty, with their strange want of respect for it, we might imagine that a man had an indispensable right to do harm to others, and no right at all to please himself without giving pain to any one.

I have reserved for the last place a large class of questions respecting the limits of government interference, which, though closely connected with the subject of this Essay, do not, in strictness, belong to it. These are cases in which the reasons against interference do not turn upon the principle of liberty: the question is not about restraining the actions of individuals, but about helping them: it is asked whether the government should do, or cause to be done, something for their benefit, instead of leaving it to be done by themselves, individually, or in voluntary combination.

The objections to government interference, when it is not such as to involve infringement of liberty, may be of three kinds.

The first is, when the thing to be done is likely to be better done by individuals than by the government. Speaking generally, there is no one so fit to conduct any business, or to determine how or by whom it shall be conducted, as those who are personally interested in it. This principle condemns the interferences, once so common, of the legislature, or the officers of government, with the ordinary processes of industry. But this part of the subject has been sufficiently enlarged upon by political economists, and is not particularly related to the principles of this Essay.

The second objection is more nearly allied to our subject. In many cases, though individuals may not do the particular thing so well, on the average, as the officers of government, it is nevertheless desirable that it should be done by them, rather than by the government, as a means to their own mental education—a mode of strengthening their active faculties, exercising their judgment, and giving them a familiar knowledge of the subjects with which they are thus left to deal. This is a principal, though not the sole, recommendation of jury trial (in cases not political); of free and popular local and municipal institutions; of the conduct of industrial and philanthropic enterprises by voluntary associations. These are not questions of liberty, and are connected with that subject only by remote tendencies; but they are questions of development. It belongs to a different occasion from the present to dwell on these things as parts of national education; as being, in truth, the peculiar training of a citizen, the practical part of the political education of a free people, taking them out of the narrow circle of personal and family selfishness, and accustoming them to the comprehension of joint interests, the management of joint concerns—habituating them to act from public or semi-public motives, and guide their conduct by aims which unite instead of isolating them from one another. Without these habits and powers, a free constitution can neither be worked nor preserved; as is exemplified by the too-often transitory nature of political freedom in countries where it does not rest upon a sufficient basis of local liberties. The management of purely local business by the localities, and of the great enterprises of industry by the union of those who voluntarily supply the pecuniary means, is further recommended by all the advantages which have been set forth in this Essay as belonging to individuality of development, and diversity of modes of action. Government operations tend to be everywhere alike. With individuals and voluntary associations, on the contrary, there are varied experiments, and endless diversity of experience. What the State can usefully do, is to make itself a central depository, and active circulator and diffuser, of the experience resulting from many trials. Its business is to enable each experimentalist to benefit by the experiments of others; instead of tolerating no experiments but its own.

The third, and most cogent reason for restricting the interference of government, is the great evil of adding unnecessarily to its power. Every function superadded to those already exercised by the government, causes its influence over hopes and fears to be more widely diffused, and converts, more and more, the active and ambitious part of the public into hangers-on of the government, or of some party which aims at becoming the government. If the roads, the railways, the banks, the insurance offices, the great joint-stock companies, the universities, and the public charities, were all of them branches of the government; if, in addition, the municipal corporations and local boards, with all that now devolves on them, became departments of the central administration; if the employees of all these different enterprises were appointed and paid by the government, and looked to the government for every rise in life; not all the freedom of the press and popular constitution of the legislature would make this or any other country free otherwise than in name. And the evil would be greater, the more efficiently and scientifically the administrative machinery was constructed—the more skilful the arrangements for obtaining the best qualified hands and heads with which to work it. In England it has of late been proposed that all the members of the civil service of government should be selected by competitive examination, to obtain for those employments the most intelligent and instructed persons procurable; and much has been said and written for and against this proposal. One of the arguments most insisted on by its opponents, is that the occupation of a permanent official servant of the State does not hold out sufficient prospects of emolument and importance to attract the highest talents, which will always be able to find a more inviting career in the professions, or in the service of companies and other public bodies. One would not have been surprised if this argument had been used by the friends of the proposition, as an answer to its principal difficulty. Coming from the opponents it is strange enough. What is urged as an objection is the safety-valve of the proposed system. If indeed all the high talent of the country *could* be drawn into the service of the government, a proposal tending to bring about that result might well inspire uneasiness. If every part of the business of society which required organized concert, or large and comprehensive views, were in the hands of the government, and if government offices were universally filled by the ablest men, all the enlarged culture and practised intelligence in the country, except the purely speculative, would be concentrated in a numerous bureaucracy, to whom alone the rest of the community would look for all things: the multitude for direction and dictation in all they had to do; the able and aspiring for personal advancement. To be admitted into the ranks of this bureaucracy, and when admitted, to rise therein, would be the sole objects of ambition. Under this regime, not only is the outside public ill-qualified, for want of practical experience, to criticize or check the mode of operation of the bureaucracy, but even if the accidents of despotic or the natural working of popular institutions occasionally raise to the summit a ruler or rulers of reforming inclinations, no reform can be effected which is contrary to the interest of the bureaucracy. Such is the melancholy condition of the Russian empire, as shown in the accounts of those who have had sufficient opportunity of observation. The Czar himself is powerless against the bureaucratic body; he can send any one of them to Siberia, but he cannot govern without them, or against their will. On every decree of his they have a tacit veto, by merely refraining from carrying it into effect. In countries of more advanced civilization and of a more insurrectionary spirit, the public, accustomed to expect everything to be done for them by the State, or at least to do nothing for themselves without asking from the State not only leave to do it, but even how it is to be done, naturally hold the State responsible

for all evil which befals them, and when the evil exceeds their amount of patience, they rise against the government and make what is called a revolution; whereupon somebody else, with or without legitimate authority from the nation, vaults into the seat, issues his orders to the bureaucracy, and everything goes on much as it did before; the bureaucracy being unchanged, and nobody else being capable of taking their place.

A very different spectacle is exhibited among a people accustomed to transact their own business. In France, a large part of the people having been engaged in military service, many of whom have held at least the rank of non-commissioned officers, there are in every popular insurrection several persons competent to take the lead, and improvise some tolerable plan of action. What the French are in military affairs, the Americans are in every kind of civil business; let them be left without a government, every body of Americans is able to improvise one, and to carry on that or any other public business with a sufficient amount of intelligence, order, and decision. This is what every free people ought to be: and a people capable of this is certain to be free; it will never let itself be enslaved by any man or body of men because these are able to seize and pull the reins of the central administration. No bureaucracy can hope to make such a people as this do or undergo anything that they do not like. But where everything is done through the bureaucracy, nothing to which the bureaucracy is really adverse can be done at all. The constitution of such countries is an organization of the experience and practical ability of the nation, into a disciplined body for the purpose of governing the rest; and the more perfect that organization is in itself, the more successful in drawing to itself and educating for itself the persons of greatest capacity from all ranks of the community, the more complete is the bondage of all, the members of the bureaucracy included. For the governors are as much the slaves of their organization and discipline, as the governed are of the governors. A Chinese mandarin is as much the tool and creature of a despotism as the humblest cultivator. An individual Jesuit is to the utmost degree of abasement the slave of his order, though the order itself exists for the collective power and importance of its members.

It is not, also, to be forgotten, that the absorption

of all the principal ability of the country into the governing body is fatal, sooner or later, to the mental activity and progressiveness of the body itself. Banded together as they are—working a system which, like all systems, necessarily proceeds in a great measure by fixed rules—the official body are under the constant temptation of sinking into indolent routine, or, if they now and then desert that mill-horse round, of rushing into some half-examined crudity which has struck the fancy of some leading member of the corps: and the sole check to these closely allied, though seemingly opposite, tendencies, the only stimulus which can keep the ability of the body itself up to a high standard, is liability to the watchful criticism of equal ability outside the body. It is indispensable, therefore, that the means should exist, independently of the government, of forming such ability, and furnishing it with the opportunities and experience necessary for a correct judgment of great practical affairs. If we would possess permanently a skilful and efficient body of functionaries—above all a body able to originate and willing to adopt improvements; if we would not have our bureaucracy degenerate into a pedantocracy, this body must not engross all the occupations which form and cultivate the faculties required for the government of mankind.

To determine the point at which evils, so formidable to human freedom and advancement, begin, or rather at which they begin to predominate over the benefits attending the collective application of the force of society, under its recognised chiefs, for the removal of the obstacles which stand in the way of its well-being; to secure as much of the advantages of centralized power and intelligence, as can be had without turning into governmental channels too great a proportion of the general activity—is one of the most difficult and complicated questions in the art of government. It is, in a great measure, a question of detail, in which many and various considerations must be kept in view, and no absolute rule can be laid down. But I believe that the practical principle in which safety resides, the ideal to be kept in view, the standard by which to test all arrangements intended for overcoming the difficulty, may be conveyed in these words: the greatest dissemination of power consistent with efficiency; but the greatest possible centralization of information, and diffusion of it from the centre.

Thus, in municipal administration, there would be, as in the New England States, a very minute division among separate officers, chosen by the localities, of all business which is not better left to the persons directly interested; but besides this, there would be, in each department of local affairs, a central superintendence, forming a branch of the general government. The organ of this superintendence would concentrate, as in a focus, the variety of information and experience derived from the conduct of that branch of public business in all the localities, from everything analogous which is done in foreign countries, and from the general principles of political science. This central organ should have a right to know all that is done, and its special duty should be that of making the knowledge acquired in one place available for others. Emancipated from the petty prejudices and narrow views of a locality by its elevated position and comprehensive sphere of observation, its advice would naturally carry much authority; but its actual power, as a permanent institution, should, I conceive, be limited to compelling the local officers to obey the laws laid down for their guidance. In all things not provided for by general rules, those officers should be left to their own judgment, under responsibility to their constituents. For the violation of rules, they should be responsible to law, and the rules themselves should be laid down by the legislature; the central administrative authority only watching over their execution, and if they were not properly carried into effect, appealing, according to the nature of the case, to the tribunals to enforce the law, or to the constituencies to dismiss the functionaries who had not executed it according to its spirit. Such, in its general conception, is the central superintendence which the Poor Law Board is intended to exercise over the administrators of the Poor Rate throughout the country. Whatever powers the Board exercises beyond this limit, were right and necessary in that peculiar case, for the cure of rooted habits of maladministration in matters deeply affecting not the localities merely, but the whole community; since no locality has a moral right to make itself by mismanagement a nest of pauperism, necessarily overflowing into other localities, and impairing the moral and physical condition of the whole labouring community. The powers of administrative coercion and subordinate legislation possessed by the Poor Law

Board (but which, owing to the state of opinion on the subject, are very scantily exercised by them), though perfectly justifiable in a case of first-rate national interest, would be wholly out of place in the superintendence of interests purely local. But a central organ of information and instruction for all the localities, would be equally valuable in all departments of administration. A government cannot have too much of the kind of activity which does not impede, but aids and stimulates, individual exertion and development. The mischief begins when, instead of calling forth the activity and powers of individuals and bodies, it substitutes its own activity for theirs; when, instead of informing, advising, and, upon occasion, denouncing, it makes them work in fetters, or bids them stand aside and does their work instead of them. The worth of a State, in the long run, is the worth of the individuals composing it; and a State which postpones the interests of *their* mental expansion and elevation, to a little more of administrative skill, or of that semblance of it which practice gives, in the details of business; a State which dwarfs its men, in order that they may be more docile instruments in its hands even for beneficial purposes — will find that with small men no great thing can really be accomplished; and that the perfection of machinery to which it has sacrificed everything, will in the end avail it nothing, for want of the vital power which, in order that the machine might work more smoothly, it has preferred to banish.

UTILITARIANISM

Contents

CHAPTER I

General Remarks

There are few circumstances among those which make up the present condition of human knowledge, more unlike what might have been expected, or more significant of the backward state in which speculation on the most important subjects still lingers, than the little progress which has been made in the decision of the controversy respecting the criterion of right and wrong. From the dawn of philosophy, the question concerning the *summum bonum*, or, what is the same thing, concerning the foundation of morality, has been accounted the main problem in speculative thought, has occupied the most gifted intellects, and divided them into sects and schools, carrying on a vigorous warfare against one another. And after more than two thousand years the same discussions continue, philosophers are still ranged under the same contending banners, and neither thinkers nor mankind at large seem nearer to being unanimous on the subject, than when the youth Socrates listened to the old Protagoras, and asserted (if Plato's dialogue be grounded on a real conversation) the theory of utilitarianism against the popular morality of the so-called sophist.

This edition of *Utilitarianism* was drawn from the 1871 4th edition Longmans, Green, Reader, and Dyer.

It is true that similar confusion and uncertainty, and in some cases similar discordance, exist respecting the first principles of all the sciences, not excepting that which is deemed the most certain of them, mathematics; without much impairing, generally indeed without impairing at all, the trustworthiness of the conclusions of those sciences. An apparent anomaly, the explanation of which is, that the detailed doctrines of a science are not usually deduced from, nor depend for their evidence upon, what are called its first principles. Were it not so, there would be no science more precarious, or whose conclusions were more insufficiently made out, than algebra; which derives none of its certainty from what are commonly taught to learners as its elements, since these, as laid down by some of its most eminent teachers, are as full of fictions as English law, and of mysteries as theology. The truths which are ultimately accepted as the first principles of a science, are really the last results of metaphysical analysis, practised on the elementary notions with which the science is conversant; and their relation to the science is not that of foundations to an edifice, but of roots to a tree, which may perform their office equally well though they be never dug down to and exposed to light. But though in science the particular truths precede the general theory, the contrary might be expected to be the case with a practical art, such as morals or legislation. All action is for the sake of some end, and rules of action, it seems natural to suppose, must take their whole character and colour from the end to which they are subservient. When we engage in a pursuit, a clear and precise conception of what we are pursuing would seem to be the first thing we need, instead of the last we are to look forward to. A test of right and wrong must be the means, one would think, of ascertaining what is right or wrong, and not a consequence of having already ascertained it.

The difficulty is not avoided by having recourse to the popular theory of a natural faculty, a sense or instinct, informing us of right and wrong. For — besides that the existence of such a moral instinct is itself one of the matters in dispute — those believers in it who have any pretensions to philosophy, have been obliged to abandon the idea that it discerns what is right or wrong in the particular case in hand, as our other senses discern the sight or sound actually present. Our moral faculty, according to all those of its interpreters who are entitled to the name of thinkers, supplies us only with the general principles of moral judgments; it is a branch of our reason, not of our sensitive faculty; and must be looked to for the abstract doctrines of morality, not for perception of it in the concrete. The intuitive, no less than what may be termed the inductive, school of ethics, insists on the necessity of general laws. They both agree that the morality of an individual action is not a question of direct perception, but of the application of a law to an individual case. They recognise also, to a great extent, the same moral laws; but differ as to their evidence, and the source from which they derive their authority. According to the one opinion, the principles of morals are evident *a priori*, requiring nothing to command assent, except that the meaning of the terms be understood. According to the other doctrine, right and wrong, as well as truth and falsehood, are questions of observation and experience. But both hold equally that morality must be deduced from principles; and the intuitive school affirm as strongly as the inductive, that there is a science of morals. Yet they seldom attempt to make out a list of the *a priori* principles which are to serve as the premises of the science; still more rarely do they make any effort to reduce those various principles to one first principle, or common ground of obligation. They either assume the ordinary precepts of morals as of *a priori* authority, or they lay down as the common groundwork of those maxims, some generality much less obviously authoritative than the maxims themselves, and which has never succeeded in gaining popular acceptance. Yet to support their pretensions there ought either to be some one fundamental principle or law, at the root of all morality, or if there be several, there should be a determinate order of precedence among them; and the one principle, or

the rule for deciding between the various principles when they conflict, ought to be self-evident.

To inquire how far the bad effects of this deficiency have been mitigated in practice, or to what extent the moral beliefs of mankind have been vitiated or made uncertain by the absence of any distinct recognition of an ultimate standard, would imply a complete survey and criticism of past and present ethical doctrine. It would, however, be easy to show that whatever steadiness or consistency these moral beliefs have attained, has been mainly due to the tacit influence of a standard not recognised. Although the non-existence of acknowledged first principle has made ethics not so much a guide as a consecration of men's actual sentiments, still, as men's sentiments, both of favour and of aversion, are greatly influenced by what they suppose to be the effects of things upon their happiness, the principle of utility, or as Bentham latterly called it, the greatest happiness principle, has had a large share in forming the moral doctrines even of those who most scornfully reject its authority. Nor is there any school of thought which refuses to admit that the influence of actions on happiness is a most material and even predominant consideration in many of the details of morals, however unwilling to acknowledge it as the fundamental principle of morality, and the source of moral obligation. I might go much further, and say that to all those *a priori* moralists who deem it necessary to argue at all, utilitarian arguments are indispensable. It is not my present purpose to criticize these thinkers; but I cannot help referring, for illustration, to a systematic treatise by one of the most illustrious of them, the *Metaphysics of Ethics*, by Kant. This remarkable man, whose system of thought will long remain one of the landmarks in the history of philosophical speculation, does, in the treatise in question, lay down an universal first principle as the origin and ground of moral obligation; it is this: — 'So act, that the rule on which thou actest would admit of being adopted as a law by all rational beings.' But when he begins to deduce from this precept any of the actual duties of morality, he fails, almost grotesquely, to show that there would be any contradiction, any logical (not to say physical) impossibility, in the adoption by all rational beings of the most outrageously immoral rules of conduct. All he shows is that the *consequences* of their universal adoption would be such as no one would choose to incur.

On the present occasion, I shall, without further discussion of the other theories, attempt to contribute something towards the understanding and appreciation of the Utilitarian or Happiness theory, and towards such proof as it is susceptible of. It is evident that this cannot be proof in the ordinary and popular meaning of the term. Questions of ultimate ends are not amenable to direct proof. Whatever can be proved to be good, must be so by being shown to be a means to something admitted to be good without proof. The medical art is proved to be good, by its conducing to health; but how is it possible to prove that health is good? The art of music is good, for the reason, among others, that it produces pleasure; but what proof is it possible to give that pleasure is good? If, then, it is asserted that there is a comprehensive formula, including all things which are in themselves good, and that whatever else is good, is not so as an end, but as a mean, the formula may be accepted or rejected, but is not a subject of what is commonly understood by proof. We are not, however, to infer that its acceptance or rejection must depend on blind impulse, or arbitrary choice. There is a larger meaning of the word proof, in which this question is as amenable to it as any other of the disputed questions of philosophy. The subject is within the cognizance of the rational faculty; and neither does that faculty deal with it solely in the way of intuition. Considerations may be presented capable of determining the intellect either to give or withhold its assent to the doctrine; and this is equivalent to proof.

We shall examine presently of what nature are these considerations; in what manner they apply to the case, and what rational grounds, therefore, can be given for accepting or rejecting the utilitarian formula. But it is a preliminary condition of rational acceptance or rejection, that the formula should be correctly understood. I believe that the very imperfect notion ordinarily formed of its meaning, is the chief obstacle which impedes its reception; and that could it be cleared, even from only the grosser misconceptions, the question would be greatly simplified, and a large proportion of its difficulties removed. Before, therefore, I attempt to enter into the philosophical grounds which can be given for assenting to the utili-

tarian standard, I shall offer some illustrations of the doctrine itself; with the view of showing more clearly what it is, distinguishing it from what it is not, and disposing of such of the practical objections to it as either originate in, or are closely connected with, mistaken interpretations of its meaning. Having thus prepared the ground, I shall afterwards endeavour to throw such light as I can upon the question, considered as one of philosophical theory.

CHAPTER II

What Utilitarianism Is

A passing remark is all that needs be given to the ignorant blunder of supposing that those who stand up for utility as the test of right and wrong, use the term in that restricted and merely colloquial sense in which utility is opposed to pleasure. An apology is due to the philosophical opponents of utilitarianism, for even the momentary appearance of confounding them with any one capable of so absurd a misconception; which is the more extraordinary, inasmuch as the contrary accusation, of referring everything to pleasure, and that too in its grossest form, is another of the common charges against utilitarianism: and, as has been pointedly remarked by an able writer, the same sort of persons, and often the very same persons, denounce the theory 'as impracticably dry when the word utility precedes the word pleasure, and as too practicably voluptuous when the word pleasure precedes the word utility.' Those who know anything about the matter are aware that every writer, from Epicurus to Bentham, who maintained the theory of utility, meant by it, not something to be contradistinguished from pleasure, but pleasure itself, together with exemption from pain; and instead of opposing the useful to the agreeable or the ornamental, have always declared that the useful means these, among other things. Yet the common herd, including the herd of writers, not only in newspapers and periodicals, but in books of weight and pretension, are perpetually falling into this shallow mistake. Having caught up the word utilitarian, while knowing nothing whatever about it but its sound, they habitually express by it the rejection, or the neglect, of pleasure in some of its forms; of beauty, of ornament, or of amusement. Nor is the term thus ignorantly misapplied solely in disparagement, but occasionally in compliment; as though it implied superiority to frivolity and the mere pleasures of the moment. And this perverted use is the only one in which the word is popularly known, and the one from which the new generation are acquiring their sole notion of its meaning. Those who introduced the word, but who had for many years discontinued it as a distinctive appellation, may well feel themselves called upon to resume it, if by doing so they can hope to contribute anything towards rescuing it from this utter degradation.[1]

The creed which accepts as the foundation of morals, Utility, or the Greatest Happiness Principle, holds that actions are right in proportion as they tend to promote happiness, wrong as they tend to produce the reverse of happiness. By happiness is intended pleasure, and the absence of pain; by unhappiness, pain, and the privation of pleasure. To give a clear view of the moral standard set up by the theory, much more requires to be said; in particular, what things it includes in the ideas of pain and pleasure; and to what extent this is left an open question. But these supplementary explanations do not affect the theory of life on which this theory of morality is grounded — namely, that pleasure, and freedom from pain, are the only things desirable as ends; and that all desirable things (which are as numerous in the utilitarian as in any other scheme) are desirable either for the pleasure inherent in themselves, or as means to the promotion of pleasure and the prevention of pain.

Now, such a theory of life excites in many minds,

---

1. The author of this essay has reason for believing himself to be the first person who brought the word utilitarian into use. He did not invent it, but adopted it from a passing expression in Mr. Galt's *Annals of the Parish*. After using it as a designation for several years, he and others abandoned it from a growing dislike to anything resembling a badge or watchword of sectarian distinction. But as a name for one single opinion, not a set of opinions — to denote the recognition of utility as a standard, not any particular way of applying it — the term supplies a want in the language, and offers, in many cases, a convenient mode of avoiding tiresome circumlocution.

and among them in some of the most estimable in feeling and purpose, inveterate dislike. To suppose that life has (as they express it) no higher end than pleasure — no better and nobler object of desire and pursuit — they designate as utterly mean and groveling; as a doctrine worthy only of swine, to whom the followers of Epicurus were, at a very early period, contemptuously likened; and modern holders of the doctrine are occasionally made the subject of equally polite comparisons by its German, French, and English assailants.

When thus attacked, the Epicureans have always answered, that it is not they, but their accusers, who represent human nature in a degrading light; since the accusation supposes human beings to be capable of no pleasures except those of which swine are capable. If this supposition were true, the charge could not be gainsaid, but would then be no longer an imputation; for if the sources of pleasure were precisely the same to human beings and to swine, the rule of life which is good enough for the one would be good enough for the other. The comparison of the Epicurean life to that of beasts is felt as degrading, precisely because a beast's pleasures do not satisfy a human being's conceptions of happiness. Human beings have faculties more elevated than the animal appetites, and when once made conscious of them, do not regard anything as happiness which does not include their gratification. I do not, indeed, consider the Epicureans to have been by any means faultless in drawing out their scheme of consequences from the utilitarian principle. To do this in any sufficient manner, many Stoic, as well as Christian elements require to be included. But there is no known Epicurean theory of life which does not assign to the pleasures of the intellect, of the feelings and imagination, and of the moral sentiments, a much higher value as pleasures than to those of mere sensation. It must be admitted, however, that utilitarian writers in general have placed the superiority of mental over bodily pleasures chiefly in the greater permanency, safety, uncostliness, &c., of the former — that is, in their circumstantial advantages rather than in their intrinsic nature. And on all these points utilitarians have fully proved their case; but they might have taken the other, and, as it may be called, higher ground, with entire consistency. It is quite compatible with the principle of utility to recognise the fact, that some *kinds* of pleasure are more desirable and more valuable than others. It would be absurd that while, in estimating all other things, quality is considered as well as quantity, the estimation of pleasures should be supposed to depend on quantity alone.

If I am asked, what I mean by difference of quality in pleasures, or what makes one pleasure more valuable than another, merely as a pleasure, except its being greater in amount, there is but one possible answer. Of two pleasures, if there be one to which all or almost all who have experience of both give a decided preference, irrespective of any feeling of moral obligation to prefer it, that is the more desirable pleasure. If one of the two is, by those who are competently acquainted with both, placed so far above the other that they prefer it, even though knowing it to be attended with a greater amount of discontent, and would not resign it for any quantity of the other pleasure which their nature is capable of, we are justified in ascribing to the preferred enjoyment a superiority in quality, so far outweighing quantity as to render it, in comparison, of small account.

Now it is an unquestionable fact that those who are equally acquainted with, and equally capable of appreciating and enjoying, both, do give a most marked preference to the manner of existence which employs their higher faculties. Few human creatures would consent to be changed into any of the lower animals, for a promise of the fullest allowance of a beast's pleasures; no intelligent human being would consent to be a fool, no instructed person would be an ignoramus, no person of feeling and conscience would be selfish and base, even though they should be persuaded that the fool, the dunce, or the rascal is better satisfied with his lot than they are with theirs. They would not resign what they possess more than he, for the most complete satisfaction of all the desires which they have in common with him. If they ever fancy they would, it is only in cases of unhappiness so extreme, that to escape from it they would exchange their lot for almost any other, however undesirable in their own eyes. A being of higher faculties requires more to make him happy, is capable probably of more acute suffering, and is certainly accessible to it at more points, than one of an inferior type; but in spite of these liabilities, he can never really wish to sink into what he feels to be a lower grade of existence. We may give what explanation we please of this unwillingness; we may attribute it to pride, a name which is given indiscriminately to some of the most and to some of the least estimable feelings of which mankind are capable; we may refer it to the love of liberty and personal independence, an appeal to which was with the Stoics one of the most effective means for the inculcation of it; to the love of power, or to the love of excitement, both of which do really enter into and contribute to it: but its most appropriate appellation is a sense of dignity, which all human beings possess in one form or other, and in some, though by no means in exact, proportion to their higher faculties, and which is so essential a part of the happiness of those in whom it is strong, that nothing which conflicts with it could be, otherwise than momentarily, an object of desire to them. Whoever supposes that this preference takes place at a sacrifice of happiness—that the superior being, in anything like equal circumstances, is not happier than the inferior—confounds the two very different ideas, of happiness, and content. It is indisputable that the being whose capacities of enjoyment are low, has the greatest chance of having them fully satisfied; and a highly-endowed being will always feel that any happiness which he can look for, as the world is constituted, is imperfect. But he can learn to bear its imperfections, if they are at all bearable; and they will not make him envy the being who is indeed unconscious of the imperfections, but only because he feels not at all the good which those imperfections qualify. It is better to be a human being dissatisfied than a pig satisfied; better to be Socrates dissatisfied than a fool satisfied. And if the fool, or the pig, is of a different opinion, it is because they only know their own side of the question. The other party to the comparison knows both sides.

It may be objected, that many who are capable of the higher pleasures, occasionally, under the influence of temptation, postpone them to the lower. But this is quite compatible with a full appreciation of the intrinsic superiority of the higher. Men often, from infirmity of character, make their election for the nearer good, though they know it to be the less valuable; and this no less when the choice is between two bodily pleasures, than when it is between bodily and mental. They pursue sensual indulgences to the injury of health, though perfectly aware that health is the greater good. It may be further objected, that many who begin with youthful enthusiasm for everything noble, as they advance in years sink into indolence and selfishness. But I do not believe that those who undergo this very common change, voluntarily choose the lower description of pleasures in preference to the higher. I believe that before they devote themselves exclusively to the one, they have already become incapable of the other. Capacity for the nobler feelings is in most natures a very tender plant, easily killed, not only by hostile influences, but by mere want of sustenance; and in the majority of young persons it speedily dies away if the occupations to which their position in life has devoted them, and the society into which it has thrown them, are not favourable to keeping that higher capacity in exercise. Men lose their high aspirations as they lose their intellectual tastes, because they have not time or opportunity for indulging them; and they addict themselves to inferior pleasures, not because they deliberately prefer them, but because they are either the only ones to which they have access, or the only ones which they are any longer capable of enjoying. It may be questioned whether any one who has remained equally susceptible to both classes of pleasures, ever knowingly and calmly preferred the lower; though many, in all ages, have broken down in an ineffectual attempt to combine both.

From this verdict of the only competent judges, I apprehend there can be no appeal. On a question which is the best worth having of two pleasures, or which of two modes of existence is the most grateful to the feelings, apart from its moral attributes and from its consequences, the judgment of those who are qualified by knowledge of both, or, if they differ, that of the majority among them, must be admitted as final. And there needs be the less hesitation to accept this judgment respecting the quality of pleasures, since there is no other tribunal to be referred to even on the question of quantity. What means are there of determining which is the acutest of two pains, or the intensest of two pleasurable sensations, except the general suffrage of those who are familiar with both? Neither pains nor pleasures are homogeneous, and pain is always heterogeneous with pleasure. What is there to decide whether a particular pleasure is worth purchasing at the cost of a particular pain, except the feelings and judgment of the experienced? When, therefore, those feelings and judgment declare the pleasures derived from the higher faculties to be preferable *in kind*, apart from the question of intensity, to those of which the animal nature, disjoined from the higher faculties, is susceptible, they are entitled on this subject to the same regard.

I have dwelt on this point, as being a necessary part of a perfectly just conception of Utility or Happiness, considered as the directive rule of human conduct. But it is by no means an indispensable condition to the acceptance of the utilitarian standard; for that standard is not the agent's own greatest happiness, but the greatest amount of happiness altogether; and if it may possibly be doubted whether a noble character is always the happier for its nobleness, there can be no doubt that it makes other people happier, and that the world in general is immensely a gainer by it. Utilitarianism, therefore, could only attain its end by the general cultivation of nobleness of character, even if each individual were only benefited by the nobleness of others, and his own, so far as happiness is concerned, were a sheer deduction from the benefit. But the bare enunciation of such an absurdity as this last, renders refutation superfluous.

According to the Greatest Happiness Principle, as above explained, the ultimate end, with reference to and for the sake of which all other things are desirable (whether we are considering our own good or that of other people), is an existence exempt as far as possible from pain, and as rich as possible in enjoyments, both in point of quantity and quality; the test of quality, and the rule for measuring it against quantity, being the preference felt by those who in their opportunities of experience, to which must be added their habits of self-consciousness and self-observation, are best furnished with the means of comparison. This, being, according to the utilitarian opinion, the end of human action, is necessarily also the standard of morality; which may accordingly be defined, the rules and precepts for human conduct, by the observance of which an existence such as has been described might be, to the greatest extent possible, secured to all mankind; and not to them only, but, so far as the nature of things admits, to the whole sentient creation.

Against this doctrine, however, arises another class

of objectors, who say that happiness, in any form, cannot be the rational purpose of human life and action; because, in the first place, it is unattainable: and they contemptuously ask, What right hast thou to be happy? a question which Mr. Carlyle clenches by the addition, What right, a short time ago, hadst thou even *to be?* Next, they say, that men can do *without* happiness; that all noble human beings have felt this, and could not have become noble but by learning the lesson of *Entsagen*, or renunciation; which lesson, thoroughly learnt and submitted to, they affirm to be the beginning and necessary condition of all virtue.

The first of these objections would go to the root of the matter were it well founded; for if no happiness is to be had at all by human beings, the attainment of it cannot be the end of morality, or of any rational conduct. Though, even in that case, something might still be said for the utilitarian theory; since utility includes not solely the pursuit of happiness, but the prevention or mitigation of unhappiness; and if the former aim be chimerical, there will be all the greater scope and more imperative need for the latter, so long at least as mankind think fit to live, and do not take refuge in the simultaneous act of suicide recommended under certain conditions by Novalis. When, however, it is thus positively asserted to be impossible that human life should be happy, the assertion, if not something like a verbal quibble, is at least an exaggeration. If by happiness be meant a continuity of highly pleasurable excitement, it is evident enough that this is impossible. A state of exalted pleasure lasts only moments, or in some cases, and with some intermissions, hours or days, and is the occasional brilliant flash of enjoyment, not its permanent and steady flame. Of this the philosophers who have taught that happiness is the end of life were as fully aware as those who taunt them. The happiness which they meant was not a life of rapture; but moments of such, in an existence made up of few and transitory pains, many and various pleasures, with a decided predominance of the active over the passive, and having as the foundation of the whole, not to expect more from life than it is capable of bestowing. A life thus composed, to those who have been fortunate enough to obtain it, has always appeared worthy of the name of happiness. And such an existence is

even now the lot of many, during some considerable portion of their lives. The present wretched education, and wretched social arrangements, are the only real hindrance to its being attainable by almost all.

The objectors perhaps may doubt whether human beings, if taught to consider happiness as the end of life, would be satisfied with such a moderate share of it. But great numbers of mankind have been satisfied with much less. The main constituents of a satisfied life appear to be two, either of which by itself is often found sufficient for the purpose: tranquillity, and excitement. With much tranquillity, many find that they can be content with very little pleasure: with much excitement, many can reconcile themselves to a considerable quantity of pain. There is assuredly no inherent impossibility in enabling even the mass of mankind to unite both; since the two are so far from being incompatible that they are in natural alliance, the prolongation of either being a preparation for, and exciting a wish for, the other. It is only those in whom indolence amounts to a vice, that do not desire excitement after an interval of repose; it is only those in whom the need of excitement is a disease, that feel the tranquillity which follows excitement dull and insipid, instead of pleasurable in direct proportion to the excitement which preceded it. When people who are tolerably fortunate in their outward lot do not find in life sufficient enjoyment to make it valuable to them, the cause generally is, caring for nobody but themselves. To those who have neither public nor private affections, the excitements of life are much curtailed, and in any case dwindle in value as the time approaches when all selfish interests must be terminated by death: while those who leave after them objects of personal affection, and especially those who have also cultivated a fellow-feeling with the collective interests of mankind, retain as lively an interest in life on the eve of death as in the vigour of youth and health. Next to selfishness, the principal cause which makes life unsatisfactory is want of mental cultivation. A cultivated mind—I do not mean that of a philosopher, but any mind to which the fountains of knowledge have been opened, and which has been taught, in any tolerable degree, to exercise its faculties—finds sources of inexhaustible interest in all that surrounds it; in the objects of nature, the achievements of art, the imaginations of poetry, the incidents of history, the ways of mankind past and present, and their prospects in the future. It is possible, indeed, to become indifferent to all this, and that too without having exhausted a thousandth part of it; but only when one has had from the beginning no moral or human interest in these things, and has sought in them only the gratification of curiosity.

Now there is absolutely no reason in the nature of things why an amount of mental culture sufficient to give an intelligent interest in these objects of contemplation, should not be the inheritance of every one born in a civilized country. As little is there an inherent necessity that any human being should be a selfish egotist, devoid of every feeling or care but those which centre in his own miserable individuality. Something far superior to this is sufficiently common even now, to give ample earnest of what the human species may be made. Genuine private affections, and a sincere interest in the public good, are possible, though in unequal degrees, to every rightly brought up human being. In a world in which there is so much to interest, so much to enjoy, and so much also to correct and improve, every one who has this moderate amount of moral and intellectual requisites is capable of an existence which may be called enviable; and unless such a person, through bad laws, or subjection to the will of others, is denied the liberty to use the sources of happiness within his reach, he will not fail to find this enviable existence, if he escape the positive evils of life, the great sources of physical and mental suffering—such as indigence, disease, and the unkindness, worthlessness, or premature loss of objects of affection. The main stress of the problem lies, therefore, in the contest with these calamities, from which it is a rare good fortune entirely to escape; which, as things now are, cannot be obviated, and often cannot be in any material degree mitigated. Yet no one whose opinion deserves a moment's consideration can doubt that most of the great positive evils of the world are in themselves removable, and will, if human affairs continue to improve, be in the end reduced within narrow limits. Poverty, in any sense implying suffering, may be completely extinguished by the wisdom of society, combined with the good sense and providence of individuals. Even that most intractable of enemies, disease, may be indefinitely reduced in dimensions by good physical and moral

education, and proper control of noxious influences; while the progress of science holds out a promise for the future of still more direct conquests over this detestable foe. And every advance in that direction relieves us from some, not only of the chances which cut short our own lives, but, what concerns us still more, which deprive us of those in whom our happiness is wrapt up. As for vicissitudes of fortune, and other disappointments connected with worldly circumstances, these are principally the effect either of gross imprudence, of ill-regulated desires, or of bad or imperfect social institutions. All the grand sources, in short, of human suffering are in a great degree, many of them almost entirely, conquerable by human care and effort; and though their removal is grievously slow—though a long succession of generations will perish in the breach before the conquest is completed, and this world becomes all that, if will and knowledge were not wanting, it might easily be made—yet every mind sufficiently intelligent and generous to bear a part, however small and unconspicuous, in the endeavour, will draw a noble enjoyment from the contest itself, which he would not for any bribe in the form of selfish indulgence consent to be without.

And this leads to the true estimation of what is said by the objectors concerning the possibility, and the obligation, of learning to do without happiness. Unquestionably it is possible to do without happiness; it is done involuntarily by nineteen-twentieths of mankind, even in those parts of our present world which are least deep in barbarism; and it often has to be done voluntarily by the hero or the martyr, for the sake of something which he prizes more than his individual happiness. But this something, what is it, unless the happiness of others, or some of the requisites of happiness? It is noble to be capable of resigning entirely one's own portion of happiness, or chances of it: but, after all, this self-sacrifice must be for some end; it is not its own end; and if we are told that its end is not happiness, but virtue, which is better than happiness, I ask, would the sacrifice be made if the hero or martyr did not believe that it would earn for others immunity from similar sacrifices? Would it be made if he thought that his renunciation of happiness for himself would produce no fruit for any of his fellow creatures, but to make their lot like his, and place them also in the condition of persons who have renounced happiness? All honour to those who can abnegate for themselves the personal enjoyment of life, when by such renunciation they contribute worthily to increase the amount of happiness in the world; but he who does it, or professes to do it, for any other purpose, is no more deserving of admiration than the ascetic mounted on his pillar. He may be an inspiriting proof of what men *can* do, but assuredly not an example of what they *should*.

Though it is only in a very imperfect state of the world's arrangements that any one can best serve the happiness of others by the absolute sacrifice of his own, yet so long as the world is in that imperfect state, I fully acknowledge that the readiness to make such a sacrifice is the highest virtue which can be found in man. I will add, that in this condition of the world, paradoxical as the assertion may be, the conscious ability to do without happiness gives the best prospect of realizing such happiness as is attainable. For nothing except that consciousness can raise a person above the chances of life, by making him feel that, let fate and fortune do their worst, they have not power to subdue him: which, once felt, frees him from excess of anxiety concerning the evils of life, and enables him, like many a Stoic in the worst times of the Roman Empire, to cultivate in tranquillity the sources of satisfaction accessible to him, without concerning himself about the uncertainty of their duration, any more than about their inevitable end.

Meanwhile, let utilitarians never cease to claim the morality of self-devotion as a possession which belongs by as good a right to them, as either to the Stoic or to the Transcendentalist. The utilitarian morality does recognise in human beings the power of sacrificing their own greatest good for the good of others. It only refuses to admit that the sacrifice is itself a good. A sacrifice which does not increase, or tend to increase, the sum total of happiness, it considers as wasted. The only self-renunciation which it applauds, is devotion to the happiness, or to some of the means of happiness, of others; either of mankind collectively, or of individuals within the limits imposed by the collective interests of mankind.

I must again repeat, what the assailants of utilitarianism seldom have the justice to acknowledge, that the happiness which forms the utilitarian standard of what is right in conduct, is not the agent's own happiness, but that of all concerned. As between his own happiness and that of others, utilitarianism requires him to be as strictly impartial as a disinterested and benevolent spectator. In the golden rule of Jesus of Nazareth, we read the complete spirit of the ethics of utility. To do as one would be done by, and to love one's neighbour as oneself, constitute the ideal perfection of utilitarian morality. As the means of making the nearest approach to this ideal, utility would enjoin, first, that laws and social arrangements should place the happiness, or (as speaking practically it may be called) the interest, of every individual, as nearly as possible in harmony with the interest of the whole; and secondly, that education and opinion, which have so vast a power over human character, should so use that power as to establish in the mind of every individual an indissoluble association between his own happiness and the good of the whole; especially between his own happiness and the practice of such modes of conduct, negative and positive, as regard for the universal happiness prescribes: so that not only he may be unable to conceive the possibility of happiness to himself, consistently with conduct opposed to the general good, but also that a direct impulse to promote the general good may be in every individual one of the habitual motives of action, and the sentiments connected therewith may fill a large and prominent place in every human being's sentient existence. If the impugners of the utilitarian morality represented it to their own minds in this its true character, I know not what recommendation possessed by any other morality they could possibly affirm to be wanting to it: what more beautiful or more exalted developments of human nature any other ethical system can be supposed to foster, or what springs of action, not accessible to the utilitarian, such systems rely on for giving effect to their mandates.

The objectors to utilitarianism cannot always be charged with representing it in a discreditable light. On the contrary, those among them who entertain anything like a just idea of its disinterested character, sometimes find fault with its standard as being too high for humanity. They say it is exacting too much to require that people shall always act from the inducement of promoting the general interests of society. But this is to mistake the very meaning of a standard of morals, and to confound the rule of action with the motive of it. It is the business of ethics to tell us what are our duties, or by what test we may know them; but no system of ethics requires that the sole motive of all we do shall be a feeling of duty; on the contrary, ninety-nine hundredths of all our actions are done from other motives, and rightly so done, if the rule of duty does not condemn them. It is the more unjust to utilitarianism that this particular misapprehension should be made a ground of objection to it, inasmuch as utilitarian moralists have gone beyond almost all others in affirming that the motive has nothing to do with the morality of the action, though much with the worth of the agent. He who saves a fellow creature from drowning does what is morally right, whether his motive be duty, or the hope of being paid for his trouble: he who betrays the friend that trusts him, is guilty of a crime, even if his object be to serve another friend to whom he is under greater obligations.[2] But to speak only of actions done from

2. An opponent, whose intellectual and moral fairness it is a pleasure to acknowledge (the Rev. J. Llewellyn Davies), has objected to this passage, saying, "Surely the rightness or wrongness of saving a man from drowning does depend very much upon the motive with which it is done. Suppose that a tyrant, when his enemy jumped into the sea to escape from him, saved him from drowning simply in order that he might inflict upon him more exquisite tortures, would it tend to clearness to speak of that rescue as 'a morally right action?' Or suppose again, according to one of the stock illustrations of ethical inquiries, that a man betrayed a trust received from a friend, because the discharge of it would fatally injure that friend himself or some one belonging to him, would utilitarianism compel one to call the betrayal 'a crime' as much as if it had been done from the meanest motive?"

I submit, that he who saves another from drowning in order to kill him by torture afterwards, does not differ only in motive from him who does the same thing from duty or benevolence; the act itself is different. The rescue of the man is, in the case supposed, only the necessary first step of an act far more atrocious than leaving him to drown would have been. Had Mr. Davies said, "The rightness or wrongness of saving a man from drowning does depend very much"—not upon the motive, but—"upon the *intention*," no utilitarian would have differed from him. Mr. Davies, by an oversight too common not to be quite venial, has in this case confounded the very

the motive of duty, and in direct obedience to principle: it is a misapprehension of the utilitarian mode of thought, to conceive it as implying that people should fix their minds upon so wide a generality as the world, or society at large. The great majority of good actions are intended, not for the benefit of the world, but for that of individuals, of which the good of the world is made up; and the thoughts of the most virtuous man need not on these occasions travel beyond the particular persons concerned, except so far as is necessary to assure himself that in benefiting them he is not violating the rights—that is, the legitimate and authorized expectations—of any one else. The multiplication of happiness is, according to the utilitarian ethics, the object of virtue: the occasions on which any person (except one in a thousand) has it in his power to do this on an extended scale, in other words, to be a public benefactor, are but exceptional; and on these occasions alone is he called on to consider public utility; in every other case, private utility, the interest or happiness of some few persons, is all he has to attend to. Those alone the influence of whose actions extends to society in general, need concern themselves habitually about so large an object. In the case of abstinences indeed—of things which people forbear to do, from moral considerations, though the consequences in the particular case might be beneficial—it would be unworthy of an intelligent agent not to be consciously aware that the action is of a class which, if practised generally, would be generally injurious, and that this is the ground of the obligation to abstain from it. The amount of regard for the public interest implied in this recognition, is no greater than is demanded by every system of mor-

different ideas of Motive and Intention. There is no point which utilitarian thinkers (and Bentham pre-eminently) have taken more pains to illustrate than this. The morality of the action depends entirely upon the intention—that is, upon what the agent *wills to do*. But the motive, that is, the feeling which makes him will so to do, when it makes no difference in the act, makes none in the morality: though it makes a great difference in our moral estimation of the agent, especially if it indicates a good or a bad habitual *disposition*—a bent of character from which useful, or from which hurtful actions are likely to arise.

als; for they all enjoin to abstain from whatever is manifestly pernicious to society.

The same considerations dispose of another reproach against the doctrine of utility, founded on a still grosser misconception of the purpose of a standard of morality, and of the very meaning of the words right and wrong. It is often affirmed that utilitarianism renders men cold and unsympathizing; that it chills their moral feelings towards individuals; that it makes them regard only the dry and hard consideration of the consequences of actions, not taking into their moral estimate the qualities from which those actions emanate. If the assertion means that they do not allow their judgment respecting the rightness or wrongness of an action to be influenced by their opinion of the qualities of the person who does it, this is a complaint not against utilitarianism, but against having any standard of morality at all; for certainly no known ethical standard decides an action to be good or bad because it is done by a good or a bad man, still less because done by an amiable, a brave, or a benevolent man, or the contrary. These considerations are relevant, not to the estimation of actions, but of persons; and there is nothing in the utilitarian theory inconsistent with the fact that there are other things which interest us in persons besides the rightness and wrongness of their actions. The Stoics, indeed, with the paradoxical misuse of language which was part of their system, and by which they strove to raise themselves above all concern about anything but virtue, were fond of saying that he who has that has everything; that he, and only he, is rich, is beautiful, is a king. But no claim of this description is made for the virtuous man by the utilitarian doctrine. Utilitarians are quite aware that there are other desirable possessions and qualities besides virtue, and are perfectly willing to allow to all of them their full worth. They are also aware that a right action does not necessarily indicate a virtuous character, and that actions which are blameable often proceed from qualities entitled to praise. When this is apparent in any particular case, it modifies their estimation, not certainly of the act, but of the agent. I grant that they are, notwithstanding, of opinion, that in the long run the best proof of a good character is good actions; and resolutely refuse to consider any mental disposition as good, of which the predominant tendency is to produce bad conduct. This makes them

unpopular with many people; but it is an unpopularity which they must share with every one who regards the distinction between right and wrong in a serious light; and the reproach is not one which a conscientious utilitarian need be anxious to repel.

If no more be meant by the objection than that many utilitarians look on the morality of actions, as measured by the utilitarian standard, with too exclusive a regard, and do not lay sufficient stress upon the other beauties of character which go towards making a human being loveable or admirable, this may be admitted. Utilitarians who have cultivated their moral feelings, but not their sympathies nor their artistic perceptions, do fall into this mistake; and so do all other moralists under the same conditions. What can be said in excuse for other moralists is equally available for them, namely, that if there is to be any error, it is better that it should be on that side. As a matter of fact, we may affirm that among utilitarians as among adherents of other systems, there is every imaginable degree of rigidity and of laxity in the application of their standard: some are even puritanically rigorous, while others are as indulgent as can possibly be desired by sinner or by sentimentalist. But on the whole, a doctrine which brings prominently forward the interest that mankind have in the repression and prevention of conduct which violates the moral law, is likely to be inferior to no other in turning the sanctions of opinion against such violations. It is true, the question, What does violate the moral law? is one on which those who recognise different standards of morality are likely now and then to differ. But difference of opinion on moral questions was not first introduced into the world by utilitarianism, while that doctrine does supply, if not always an easy, at all events a tangible and intelligible mode of deciding such differences.

It may not be superfluous to notice a few more of the common misapprehensions of utilitarian ethics, even those which are so obvious and gross that it might appear impossible for any person of candour and intelligence to fall into them: since persons, even of considerable mental endowments, often give themselves so little trouble to understand the bearings of any opinion against which they entertain a prejudice, and men are in general so little conscious of this voluntary ignorance as a defect, that the vulgarest misunderstandings of ethical doctrines are continually met with in the deliberate writings of persons of the greatest pretensions both to high principle and to philosophy. We not uncommonly hear the doctrine of utility inveighed against as a *godless* doctrine. If it be necessary to say anything at all against so mere an assumption, we may say that the question depends upon what idea we have formed of the moral character of the Deity. If it be a true belief that God desires, above all things, the happiness of his creatures, and that this was his purpose in their creation, utility is not only not a godless doctrine, but more profoundly religious than any other. If it be meant that utilitarianism does not recognise the revealed will of God as the supreme law of morals, I answer, that an utilitarian who believes in the perfect goodness and wisdom of God, necessarily believes that whatever God has thought fit to reveal on the subject of morals, must fulfil the requirements of utility in a supreme degree. But others besides utilitarians have been of opinion that the Christian revelation was intended, and is fitted, to inform the hearts and minds of mankind with a spirit which should enable them to find for themselves what is right, and incline them to do it when found, rather than to tell them, except in a very general way, what it is: and that we need a doctrine of ethics, carefully followed out, to *interpret* to us the will of God. Whether this opinion is correct or not, it is superfluous here to discuss; since whatever aid religion, either natural or revealed, can afford to ethical investigation, is as open to the utilitarian moralist as to any other. He can use it as the testimony of God to the usefulness or hurtfulness of any given course of action, by as good a right as others can use it for the indication of a transcendental law, having no connexion with usefulness or with happiness.

Again, Utility is often summarily stigmatized as an immoral doctrine by giving it the name of Expediency, and taking advantage of the popular use of that term to contrast it with Principle. But the Expedient, in the sense in which it is opposed to the Right, generally means that which is expedient for the particular interest of the agent himself; as when a minister sacrifices the interest of his country to keep himself in place. When it means anything better than this, it means that which is expedient for some immediate object, some temporary purpose, but which violates a rule whose observance is expedient in a much higher degree. The Expedient, in this sense, instead of being the same thing with the useful, is a branch of the hurtful. Thus, it would often be expedient, for the purpose of getting over some momentary embarrassment, or attaining some object immediately useful to ourselves or others, to tell a lie. But inasmuch as the cultivation in ourselves of a sensitive feeling on the subject of veracity, is one of the most useful, and the enfeeblement of that feeling one of the most hurtful, things to which our conduct can be instrumental; and inasmuch as any, even unintentional, deviation from truth, does that much towards weakening the trustworthiness of human assertion, which is not only the principal support of all present social well-being, but the insufficiency of which does more than any one thing that can be named to keep back civilization, virtue, everything on which human happiness on the largest scale depends; we feel that the violation, for a present advantage, of a rule of such transcendant expediency, is not expedient, and that he who, for the sake of a convenience to himself or to some other individual, does what depends on him to deprive mankind of the good, and inflict upon them the evil, involved in the greater or less reliance which they can place in each other's word, acts the part of one of their worst enemies. Yet that even this rule, sacred as it is, admits of possible exceptions, is acknowledged by all moralists; the chief of which is when the withholding of some fact (as of information from a malefactor, or of bad news from a person dangerously ill) would preserve some one (especially a person other than oneself) from great and unmerited evil, and when the withholding can only be effected by denial. But in order that the exception may not extend itself beyond the need, and may have the least possible effect in weakening reliance on veracity, it ought to be recognised, and, if possible, its limits defined; and if the principle of utility is good for anything, it must be good for weighing these conflicting utilities against one another, and marking out the region within which one or the other preponderates.

Again, defenders of utility often find themselves called upon to reply to such objections as this—that there is not time, previous to action, for calculating and weighing the effects of any line of conduct on the general happiness. This is exactly as if any one were to say that it is impossible to guide our conduct by Christianity, because there is not time, on every occasion on which anything has to be done, to read through the Old and New Testaments. The answer to the objection is, that there has been ample time, namely, the whole past duration of the human species. During all that time mankind have been learning by experience the tendencies of actions; on which experience all the prudence, as well as all the morality of life, is dependent. People talk as if the commencement of this course of experience had hitherto been put off, and as if, at the moment when some man feels tempted to meddle with the property or life of another, he had to begin considering for the first time whether murder and theft are injurious to human happiness. Even then I do not think that he would find the question very puzzling; but, at all events, the matter is now done to his hand. It is truly a whimsical supposition that if mankind were agreed in considering utility to be the test of morality, they would remain without any agreement as to what is useful, and would take no measures for having their notions on the subject taught to the young, and enforced by law and opinion. There is no difficulty in proving any ethical standard whatever to work ill, if we suppose universal idiocy to be conjoined with it; but on any hypothesis short of that, mankind must by this time have acquired positive beliefs as to the effects of some actions on their happiness; and the beliefs which have thus come down are the rules of morality for the multitude, and for the philosopher until he has succeeded in finding better. That philosophers might easily do this, even now, on many subjects; that the received code of ethics is by no means of divine right; and that mankind have still much to learn as to the effects of actions on the general happiness, I admit, or rather, earnestly maintain. The corollaries from the principle of utility, like the precepts of every practical art, admit of indefinite improvement, and, in a progressive state of the human mind, their improvement is perpetually going on. But to consider the rules of morality as improvable, is one thing; to pass over the intermediate generalizations entirely, and endeavour to test each individual action directly by the first principle, is another. It is a strange notion that the acknowledgment of a first principle is inconsistent with the admission of secondary ones. To inform a traveller respecting the place of his ultimate destination, is not to forbid the use of landmarks and direction-posts on the way. The proposition that happiness is the end and aim of morality, does not mean that no road ought to be laid down to that goal, or that persons going thither should not be advised to take one direction rather than another. Men really ought to leave off talking a kind of nonsense on this subject, which they would neither talk nor listen to on other matters of practical concernment. Nobody argues that the art of navigation is not founded on astronomy, because sailors cannot wait to calculate the Nautical Almanack. Being rational creatures, they go to sea with it ready calculated; and all rational creatures go out upon the sea of life with their minds made up on the common questions of right and wrong, as well as on many of the far more difficult questions of wise and foolish. And this, as long as foresight is a human quality, it is to be presumed they will continue to do. Whatever we adopt as the fundamental principle of morality, we require subordinate principles to apply it by: the impossibility of doing without them, being common to all systems, can afford no argument against any one in particular: but gravely to argue as if no such secondary principles could be had, and as if mankind had remained till now, and always must remain, without drawing any general conclusions from the experience of human life, is as high a pitch, I think, as absurdity has ever reached in philosophical controversy.

The remainder of the stock arguments against utilitarianism mostly consist in laying to its charge the common infirmities of human nature, and the general difficulties which embarrass conscientious persons in shaping their course through life. We are told that an utilitarian will be apt to make his own particular case an exception to moral rules, and, when under temptation, will see an utility in the breach of a rule, greater than he will see in its observance. But is utility the only creed which is able to furnish us with excuses for evil doing, and means of cheating our own conscience? They are afforded in abundance by all doctrines which recognise as a fact in morals the existence of conflicting considerations, which all doctrines do, that have been believed by sane persons. It is not the fault of any creed, but of the complicated nature of human affairs, that rules of conduct cannot be so framed as to require no exceptions, and that hardly any kind of action can safely be laid down as either always obligatory or always condemnable. There is no ethical creed which does not temper the rigidity of its laws, by giving a certain latitude, under the moral responsibility of the agent, for accommodation to peculiarities of circumstances; and under every creed, at the opening thus made, self-deception and dishonest casuistry get in. There exists no moral system under which there do not arise unequivocal cases of conflicting obligation. These are the real difficulties, the knotty points both in the theory of ethics, and in the conscientious guidance of personal conduct. They are overcome practically with greater or with less success according to the intellect and virtue of the individual; but it can hardly be pretended that any one will be the less qualified for dealing with them, from possessing an ultimate standard to which conflicting rights and duties can be referred. If utility is the ultimate source of moral obligations, utility may be invoked to decide between them when their demands are incompatible. Though the application of the standard may be difficult, it is better than none at all: while in other systems, the moral laws all claiming independent authority, there is no common umpire entitled to interfere between them; their claims to precedence one over another rest on little better than sophistry, and unless determined, as they generally are, by the unacknowledged influence of considerations of utility, afford a free scope for the action of personal desires and partialities. We must remember that only in these cases of conflict between secondary principles is it requisite that first principles should be appealed to. There is no case of moral obligation in which some secondary principle is not involved; and if only one, there can seldom be any real doubt which one it is, in the mind of any person by whom the principle itself is recognised.

CHAPTER III

Of the Ultimate Sanction of the Principle of Utility

The question is often asked, and properly so, in regard to any supposed moral standard—What is its sanction? what are the motives to obey it? or more specifi-

cally, what is the source of its obligation? whence does it derive its binding force? It is a necessary part of moral philosophy to provide the answer to this question; which, though frequently assuming the shape of an objection to the utilitarian morality, as if it had some special applicability to that above others, really arises in regard to all standards. It arises, in fact, whenever a person is called on to *adopt* a standard, or refer morality to any basis on which he has not been accustomed to rest it. For the customary morality, that which education and opinion have consecrated, is the only one which presents itself to the mind with the feeling of being *in itself* obligatory; and when a person is asked to believe that this morality *derives* its obligation from some general principle round which custom has not thrown the same halo, the assertion is to him a paradox; the supposed corollaries seem to have a more binding force than the original theorem; the superstructure seems to stand better without, than with, what is represented as its foundation. He says to himself, I feel that I am bound not to rob or murder, betray or deceive; but why am I bound to promote the general happiness? If my own happiness lies in something else, why may I not give that the preference?

If the view adopted by the utilitarian philosophy of the nature of the moral sense be correct, this difficulty will always present itself, until the influences which form moral character have taken the same hold of the principle which they have taken of some of the consequences—until, by the improvement of education, the feeling of unity with our fellow creatures shall be (what it cannot be doubted that Christ intended it to be) as deeply rooted in our character, and to our own consciousness as completely a part of our nature, as the horror of crime is in an ordinarily well-brought up young person. In the mean time, however, the difficulty has no peculiar application to the doctrine of utility, but is inherent in every attempt to analyse morality and reduce it to principles; which, unless the principle is already in men's minds invested with as much sacredness as any of its applications, always seems to divest them of a part of their sanctity.

The principle of utility either has, or there is no reason why it might not have, all the sanctions which belong to any other system of morals. Those sanctions are either external or internal. Of the external sanctions it is not necessary to speak at any length. They are, the hope of favour and the fear of displeasure from our fellow creatures or from the Ruler of the Universe, along with whatever we may have of sympathy or affection for them, or of love and awe of Him, inclining us to do his will independently of selfish consequences. There is evidently no reason why all these motives for observance should not attach themselves to the utilitarian morality, as completely and as powerfully as to any other. Indeed, those of them which refer to our fellow creatures are sure to do so, in proportion to the amount of general intelligence; for whether there be any other ground of moral obligation than the general happiness or not, men do desire happiness; and however imperfect may be their own practice, they desire and commend all conduct in others towards themselves, by which they think their happiness is promoted. With regard to the religious motive, if men believe, as most profess to do, in the goodness of God, those who think that conduciveness to the general happiness is the essence, or even only the criterion, of good, must necessarily believe that it is also that which God approves. The whole force therefore of external reward and punishment, whether physical or moral, and whether proceeding from God or from our fellow men, together with all that the capacities of human nature admit, of disinterested devotion to either, become available to enforce the utilitarian morality, in proportion as that morality is recognised; and the more powerfully, the more the appliances of education and general cultivation are bent to the purpose.

So far as to external sanctions. The internal sanction of duty, whatever our standard of duty may be, is one and the same—a feeling in our own mind; a pain, more or less intense, attendant on violation of duty, which in properly-cultivated moral natures rises, in the more serious cases, into shrinking from it as an impossibility. This feeling, when disinterested, and connecting itself with the pure idea of duty, and not with some particular form of it, or with any of the merely accessory circumstances, is the essence of Conscience; though in that complex phenomenon as it actually exists, the simple fact is in general all encrusted over with collateral associations, derived from sympathy, from love, and still more from fear; from all the forms of religious feeling; from the recol-

lections of childhood and of all our past life; from self-esteem, desire of the esteem of others, and occasionally even self-abasement. This extreme complication is, I apprehend, the origin of the sort of mystical character which, by a tendency of the human mind of which there are many other examples, is apt to be attributed to the idea of moral obligation, and which leads people to believe that the idea cannot possibly attach itself to any other objects than those which, by a supposed mysterious law, are found in our present experience to excite it. Its binding force, however, consists in the existence of a mass of feeling which must be broken through in order to do what violates our standard of right, and which, if we do nevertheless violate that standard, will probably have to be encountered afterwards in the form of remorse. Whatever theory we have of the nature or origin of conscience, this is what essentially constitutes it.

The ultimate sanction, therefore, of all morality (external motives apart) being a subjective feeling in our own minds, I see nothing embarrassing to those whose standard is utility, in the question, what is the sanction of that particular standard? We may answer, the same as of all other moral standards—the conscientious feelings of mankind. Undoubtedly this sanction has no binding efficacy on those who do not possess the feelings it appeals to; but neither will these persons be more obedient to any other moral principle than to the utilitarian one. On them morality of any kind has no hold but through the external sanctions. Meanwhile the feelings exist, a fact in human nature, the reality of which, and the great power with which they are capable of acting on those in whom they have been duly cultivated, are proved by experience. No reason has ever been shown why they may not be cultivated to as great intensity in connexion with the utilitarian, as with any other rule of morals.

There is, I am aware, a disposition to believe that a person who sees in moral obligation a transcendental fact, an objective reality belonging to the province of 'Things in themselves,' is likely to be more obedient to it than one who believes it to be entirely subjective, having its seat in human consciousness only. But whatever a person's opinion may be on this point of Ontology, the force he is really urged by is his own subjective feeling, and is exactly measured by its strength. No one's belief that Duty is an objective reality is stronger than the belief that God is so; yet the belief in God, apart from the expectation of actual reward and punishment, only operates on conduct through, and in proportion to, the subjective religious feeling. The sanction, so far as it is disinterested, is always in the mind itself; and the notion therefore of the transcendental moralists must be, that this sanction will not exist *in* the mind unless it is believed to have its root out of the mind; and that if a person is able to say to himself, This which is restraining me, and which is called my conscience, is only a feeling in my own mind, he may possibly draw the conclusion that when the feeling ceases the obligation ceases, and that if he find the feeling inconvenient, he may disregard it, and endeavour to get rid of it. But is this danger confined to the utilitarian morality? Does the belief that moral obligation has its seat outside the mind make the feeling of it too strong to be got rid of? The fact is so far otherwise, that all moralists admit and lament the ease with which, in the generality of minds, conscience can be silenced or stifled. The question, Need I obey my conscience? is quite as often put to themselves by persons who never heard of the principle of utility, as by its adherents. Those whose conscientious feelings are so weak as to allow of their asking this question, if they answer it affirmatively, will not do so because they believe in the transcendental theory, but because of the external sanctions.

It is not necessary, for the present purpose, to decide whether the feeling of duty is innate or implanted. Assuming it to be innate, it is an open question to what objects it naturally attaches itself; for the philosophic supporters of that theory are now agreed that the intuitive perception is of principles of morality, and not of the details. If there be anything innate in the matter, I see no reason why the feeling which is innate should not be that of regard to the pleasures and pains of others. If there is any principle of morals which is intuitively obligatory, I should say it must be that. If so, the intuitive ethics would coincide with the utilitarian, and there would be no further quarrel between them. Even as it is, the intuitive moralists, though they believe that there are other intuitive moral obligations, do already believe this to be one; for they unanimously hold that a large *portion* of morality turns upon the consideration due to the

interests of our fellow creatures. Therefore, if the belief in the transcendental origin of moral obligation gives any additional efficacy to the internal sanction, it appears to me that the utilitarian principle has already the benefit of it.

On the other hand, if, as is my own belief, the moral feelings are not innate, but acquired, they are not for that reason the less natural. It is natural to man to speak, to reason, to build cities, to cultivate the ground, though these are acquired faculties. The moral feelings are not indeed a part of our nature, in the sense of being in any perceptible degree present in all of us; but this, unhappily, is a fact admitted by those who believe the most strenuously in their transcendental origin. Like the other acquired capacities above referred to, the moral faculty, if not a part of our nature, is a natural outgrowth from it; capable, like them, in a certain small degree, of springing up spontaneously; and susceptible of being brought by cultivation to a high degree of development. Unhappily it is also susceptible, by a sufficient use of the external sanctions and of the force of early impressions, of being cultivated in almost any direction: so that there is hardly anything so absurd or so mischievous that it may not, by means of these influences, be made to act on the human mind with all the authority of conscience. To doubt that the same potency might be given by the same means to the principle of utility, even if it had no foundation in human nature, would be flying in the face of all experience.

But moral associations which are wholly of artificial creation, when intellectual culture goes on, yield by degrees to the dissolving force of analysis: and if the feeling of duty, when associated with utility, would appear equally arbitrary; if there were no leading department of our nature, no powerful class of sentiments, with which that association would harmonize, which would make us feel it congenial, and incline us not only to foster it in others (for which we have abundant interested motives), but also to cherish it in ourselves; if there were not, in short, a natural basis of sentiment for utilitarian morality, it might well happen that this association also, even after it had been implanted by education, might be analysed away.

But there *is* this basis of powerful natural sentiment; and this it is which, when once the general happiness is recognised as the ethical standard, will constitute the strength of the utilitarian morality. This firm foundation is that of the social feelings of mankind; the desire to be in unity with our fellow creatures, which is already a powerful principle in human nature, and happily one of those which tend to become stronger, even without express inculcation, from the influences of advancing civilization. The social state is at once so natural, so necessary, and so habitual to man, that, except in some unusual circumstances or by an effort of voluntary abstraction, he never conceives himself otherwise than as a member of a body; and this association is riveted more and more, as mankind are further removed from the state of savage independence. Any condition, therefore, which is essential to a state of society, becomes more and more an inseparable part of every person's conception of the state of things which he is born into, and which is the destiny of a human being. Now, society between human beings, except in the relation of master and slave, is manifestly impossible on any other footing than that the interests of all are to be consulted. Society between equals can only exist on the understanding that the interests of all are to be regarded equally. And since in all states of civilization, every person, except an absolute monarch, has equals, every one is obliged to live on these terms with somebody; and in every age some advance is made towards a state in which it will be impossible to live permanently on other terms with anybody. In this way people grow up unable to conceive as possible to them a state of total disregard of other people's interests. They are under a necessity of conceiving themselves as at least abstaining from all the grosser injuries, and (if only for their own protection) living in a state of constant protest against them. They are also familiar with the fact of co-operating with others, and proposing to themselves a collective, not an individual, interest, as the aim (at least for the time being) of their actions. So long as they are co-operating, their ends are identified with those of others; there is at least a temporary feeling that the interests of others are their own interests. Not only does all strengthening of social ties, and all healthy growth of society, give to each individual a stronger personal interest in practically consulting the welfare of others; it also leads him to identify his *feelings* more and more with their good, or at least with an ever greater degree of practical consideration

for it. He comes, as though instinctively, to be conscious of himself as a being who *of course* pays regard to others. The good of others becomes to him a thing naturally and necessarily to be attended to, like any of the physical conditions of our existence. Now, whatever amount of this feeling a person has, he is urged by the strongest motives both of interest and of sympathy to demonstrate it, and to the utmost of his power encourage it in others; and even if he has none of it himself, he is as greatly interested as any one else that others should have it. Consequently the smallest germs of the feeling are laid hold of and nourished by the contagion of sympathy and the influences of education; and a complete web of corroborative association is woven round it, by the powerful agency of the external sanctions. This mode of conceiving ourselves and human life, as civilization goes on, is felt to be more and more natural. Every step in political improvement renders it more so, by removing the sources of opposition of interest, and levelling those inequalities of legal privilege between individuals or classes, owing to which there are large portions of mankind whose happiness it is still practicable to disregard. In an improving state of the human mind, the influences are constantly on the increase, which tend to generate in each individual a feeling of unity with all the rest; which feeling, if perfect, would make him never think of, or desire, any beneficial condition for himself, in the benefits of which they are not included. If we now suppose this feeling of unity to be taught as a religion, and the whole force of education, of institutions, and of opinion, directed, as it once was in the case of religion, to make every person grow up from infancy surrounded on all sides both by the profession and by the practice of it, I think that no one, who can realize this conception, will feel any misgiving about the sufficiency of the ultimate sanction for the Happiness morality. To any ethical student who finds the realization difficult, I recommend, as a means of facilitating it, the second of M. Comte's two principal works, the *Système de Politique Positive*. I entertain the strongest objections to the system of politics and morals set forth in that treatise; but I think it has superabundantly shown the possibility of giving to the service of humanity, even without the aid of belief in a Providence, both the psychical power and the social efficacy of a religion;

making it take hold of human life, and colour all thought, feeling, and action, in a manner of which the greatest ascendancy ever exercised by any religion may be but a type and foretaste; and of which the danger is, not that it should be insufficient, but that it should be so excessive as to interfere unduly with human freedom and individuality.

Neither is it necessary to the feeling which constitutes the binding force of the utilitarian morality on those who recognise it, to wait for those social influences which would make its obligation felt by mankind at large. In the comparatively early state of human advancement in which we now live, a person cannot indeed feel that entireness of sympathy with all others, which would make any real discordance in the general direction of their conduct in life impossible; but already a person in whom the social feeling is at all developed, cannot bring himself to think of the rest of his fellow creatures as struggling rivals with him for the means of happiness, whom he must desire to see defeated in their object in order that he may succeed in his. The deeply-rooted conception which every individual even now has of himself as a social being, tends to make him feel it one of his natural wants that there should be harmony between his feelings and aims and those of his fellow creatures. If differences of opinion and of mental culture make it impossible for him to share many of their actual feelings—perhaps make him denounce and defy those feelings—he still needs to be conscious that his real aim and theirs do not conflict; that he is not opposing himself to what they really wish for, namely, their own good, but is, on the contrary, promoting it. This feeling in most individuals is much inferior in strength to their selfish feelings, and is often wanting altogether. But to those who have it, it possesses all the characters of a natural feeling. It does not present itself to their minds as a superstition of education, or a law despotically imposed by the power of society, but as an attribute which it would not be well for them to be without. This conviction is the ultimate sanction of the greatest happiness morality. This it is which makes any mind, of well-developed feelings, work with, and not against, the outward motives to care for others, afforded by what I have called the external sanctions; and when those sanctions are wanting, or act in an opposite direction, constitutes

in itself a powerful internal binding force, in proportion to the sensitiveness and thoughtfulness of the character; since few but those whose mind is a moral blank, could bear to lay out their course of life on the plan of paying no regard to others except so far as their own private interest compels.

CHAPTER IV

Of What Sort of Proof the Principle of Utility Is Susceptible

It has already been remarked, that questions of ultimate ends do not admit of proof, in the ordinary acceptation of the term. To be incapable of proof by reasoning is common to all first principles; to the first premises of our knowledge, as well as to those of our conduct. But the former, being matters of fact, may be the subject of a direct appeal to the faculties which judge of fact—namely, our senses, and our internal consciousness. Can an appeal be made to the same faculties on questions of practical ends? Or by what other faculty is cognizance taken of them?

Questions about ends are, in other words, questions what things are desirable. The utilitarian doctrine is, that happiness is desirable, and the only thing desirable, as an end; all other things being only desirable as means to that end. What ought to be required of this doctrine—what conditions is it requisite that the doctrine should fulfil—to make good its claim to be believed?

The only proof capable of being given that an object is visible, is that people actually see it. The only proof that a sound is audible, is that people hear it: and so of the other sources of our experience. In like manner, I apprehend, the sole evidence it is possible to produce that anything is desirable, is that people do actually desire it. If the end which the utilitarian doctrine proposes to itself were not, in theory and in practice, acknowledged to be an end, nothing could ever convince any person that it was so. No reason can be given why the general happiness is desirable, except that each person, so far as he believes it to be attainable, desires his own happiness. This, however, being a fact, we have not only all the proof which the case admits of, but all which it is possible to require, that happiness is a good:

that each person's happiness is a good to that person, and the general happiness, therefore, a good to the aggregate of all persons. Happiness has made out its title as *one* of the ends of conduct, and consequently one of the criteria of morality.

But it has not, by this alone, proved itself to be the sole criterion. To do that, it would seem, by the same rule, necessary to show, not only that people desire happiness, but that they never desire anything else. Now it is palpable that they do desire things which, in common language, are decidedly distinguished from happiness. They desire, for example, virtue, and the absence of vice, no less really than pleasure and the absence of pain. The desire of virtue is not as universal, but it is as authentic a fact, as the desire of happiness. And hence the opponents of the utilitarian standard deem that they have a right to infer that there are other ends of human action besides happiness, and that happiness is not the standard of approbation and disapprobation.

But does the utilitarian doctrine deny that people desire virtue, or maintain that virtue is not a thing to be desired? The very reverse. It maintains not only that virtue is to be desired, but that it is to be desired disinterestedly, for itself. Whatever may be the opinion of utilitarian moralists as to the original conditions by which virtue is made virtue; however they may believe (as they do) that actions and dispositions are only virtuous because they promote another end than virtue; yet this being granted, and it having been decided, from considerations of this description, what is virtuous, they not only place virtue at the very head of the things which are good as means to the ultimate end, but they also recognise as a psychological fact the possibility of its being, to the individual, a good in itself, without looking to any end beyond it; and hold, that the mind is not in a right state, not in a state conformable to Utility, not in the state most conducive to the general happiness, unless it does love virtue in this manner—as a thing desirable in itself, even although, in the individual instance, it should not produce those other desirable consequences which it tends to produce, and on account of which it is held to be virtue. This opinion is not, in the smallest degree, a departure from the Happiness principle. The ingredients of happiness are very various, and each of them is desirable in itself, and not merely when considered as swelling an aggregate. The principle of utility does not mean that any given pleasure, as music, for instance, or any given exemption from pain, as for example health, are to be looked upon as means to a collective something termed happiness, and to be desired on that account. They are desired and desirable in and for themselves; besides being means, they are a part of the end. Virtue, according to the utilitarian doctrine, is not naturally and originally part of the end, but it is capable of becoming so; and in those who love it disinterestedly it has become so, and is desired and cherished, not as a means to happiness, but as a part of their happiness.

To illustrate this farther, we may remember that virtue is not the only thing, originally a means, and which if it were not a means to anything else, would be and remain indifferent, but which by association with what it is a means to, comes to be desired for itself, and that too with the utmost intensity. What, for example, shall we say of the love of money? There is nothing originally more desirable about money than about any heap of glittering pebbles. Its worth is solely that of the things which it will buy; the desires for other things than itself, which it is a means of gratifying. Yet the love of money is not only one of the strongest moving forces of human life, but money is, in many cases, desired in and for itself; the desire to possess it is often stronger than the desire to use it, and goes on increasing when all the desires which point to ends beyond it, to be compassed by it, are falling off. It may be then said truly, that money is desired not for the sake of an end, but as part of the end. From being a means to happiness, it has come to be itself a principal ingredient of the individual's conception of happiness. The same may be said of the majority of the great objects of human life—power, for example, or fame; except that to each of these there is a certain amount of immediate pleasure annexed, which has at least the semblance of being naturally inherent in them; a thing which cannot be said of money. Still, however, the strongest natural attraction, both of power and of fame, is the immense aid they give to the attainment of our other wishes; and it is the strong association thus generated between them and all our objects of desire, which gives to the direct desire of them the intensity it often assumes, so as in some characters to surpass in strength all other desires. In these cases the means have become a part of the end, and a more important part of it than any of the things which they are means to. What was once desired as an instrument for the attainment of happiness, has come to be desired for its own sake. In being desired for its own sake it is, however, desired as *part* of happiness. The person is made, or thinks he would be made, happy by its mere possession; and is made unhappy by failure to obtain it. The desire of it is not a different thing from the desire of happiness, any more than the love of music, or the desire of health. They are included in happiness. They are some of the elements of which the desire of happiness is made up. Happiness is not an abstract idea, but a concrete whole; and these are some of its parts. And the utilitarian standard sanctions and approves their being so. Life would be a poor thing, very ill provided with sources of happiness, if there were not this provision of nature, by which things originally indifferent, but conducive to, or otherwise associated with, the satisfaction of our primitive desires, become in themselves sources of pleasure more valuable than the primitive pleasures, both in permanency, in the space of human existence that they are capable of covering, and even in intensity.

Virtue, according to the utilitarian conception, is a good of this description. There was no original desire of it, or motive to it, save its conduciveness to pleasure, and especially to protection from pain. But through the association thus formed, it may be felt a good in itself, and desired as such with as great intensity as any other good; and with this difference between it and the love of money, of power, or of fame, that all of these may, and often do, render the individual noxious to the other members of the society to which he belongs, whereas there is nothing which makes him so much a blessing to them as the cultivation of the disinterested love of virtue. And consequently, the utilitarian standard, while it tolerates and approves those other acquired desires, up to the point beyond which they would be more injurious to the general happiness than promotive of it, enjoins and requires the cultivation of the love of virtue up to the greatest strength possible, as being above all things important to the general happiness.

It results from the preceding considerations, that there is in reality nothing desired except happiness. Whatever is desired otherwise than as a means to some end beyond itself, and ultimately to happiness, is desired as itself a part of happiness, and is not desired for itself until it has become so. Those who desire virtue for its own sake, desire it either because the consciousness of it is a pleasure, or because the consciousness of being without it is a pain, or for both reasons united; as in truth the pleasure and pain seldom exist separately, but almost always together, the same person feeling pleasure in the degree of virtue attained, and pain in not having attained more. If one of these gave him no pleasure, and the other no pain, he would not love or desire virtue, or would desire it only for the other benefits which it might produce to himself or to persons whom he cared for.

We have now, then, an answer to the question, of what sort of proof the principle of utility is susceptible. If the opinion which I have now stated is psychologically true — if human nature is so constituted as to desire nothing which is not either a part of happiness or a means of happiness, we can have no other proof, and we require no other, that these are the only things desirable. If so, happiness is the sole end of human action, and the promotion of it the test by which to judge of all human conduct; from whence it necessarily follows that it must be the criterion of morality, since a part is included in the whole.

And now to decide whether this is really so; whether mankind do desire nothing for itself but that which is a pleasure to them, or of which the absence is a pain; we have evidently arrived at a question of fact and experience, dependent, like all similar questions, upon evidence. It can only be determined by practised self-consciousness and self-observation, assisted by observation of others. I believe that these sources of evidence, impartially consulted, will declare that desiring a thing and finding it pleasant, aversion to it and thinking of it as painful, are phenomena entirely inseparable, or rather two parts of the same phenomenon; in strictness of language, two different modes of naming the same psychological fact: that to think of an object as desirable (unless for the sake of its consequences), and to think of it as pleasant, are one and the same thing; and that to desire anything, except in proportion as the idea of it is pleasant, is a physical and metaphysical impossibility.

So obvious does this appear to me, that I expect it will hardly be disputed: and the objection made will be, not that desire can possibly be directed to anything ultimately except pleasure and exemption from pain, but that the will is a different thing from desire; that a person of confirmed virtue, or any other person whose purposes are fixed, carries out his purposes without any thought of the pleasure he has in contemplating them, or expects to derive from their fulfilment; and persists in acting on them, even though these pleasures are much diminished, by changes in his character or decay of his passive sensibilities, or are outweighed by the pains which the pursuit of the purposes may bring upon him. All this I fully admit, and have stated it elsewhere, as positively and emphatically as any one. Will, the active phenomenon, is a different thing from desire, the state of passive sensibility, and though originally an offshoot from it, may in time take root and detach itself from the parent stock; so much so, that in the case of an habitual purpose, instead of willing the thing because we desire it, we often desire it only because we will it. This, however, is but an instance of that familiar fact, the power of habit, and is nowise confined to the case of virtuous actions. Many indifferent things, which men originally did from a motive of some sort, they continue to do from habit. Sometimes this is done unconsciously, the consciousness coming only after the action: at other times with conscious volition, but volition which has become habitual, and is put into operation by the force of habit, in opposition perhaps to the deliberate preference, as often happens with those who have contracted habits of vicious or hurtful indulgence. Third and last comes the case in which the habitual act of will in the individual instance is not in contradiction to the general intention prevailing at other times, but in fulfilment of it; as in the case of the person of confirmed virtue, and of all who pursue deliberately and consistently any determinate end. The distinction between will and desire thus understood, is an authentic and highly important psychological fact; but the fact consists solely in this — that will, like all other parts of our constitution, is amenable to habit, and that we may will from habit what we no longer desire for itself, or desire only because we will it. It is not the less true that will, in the beginning, is entirely produced by desire; including in that term the repelling influence of pain as well as the attractive one of pleasure. Let us take into consideration, no longer the person who has a confirmed will to do

right, but him in whom that virtuous will is still feeble, conquerable by temptation, and not to be fully relied on; by what means can it be strengthened? How can the will to be virtuous, where it does not exist in sufficient force, be implanted or awakened? Only by making the person *desire* virtue — by making him think of it in a pleasurable light, or of its absence in a painful one. It is by associating the doing right with pleasure, or the doing wrong with pain, or by eliciting and impressing and bringing home to the person's experience the pleasure naturally involved in the one or the pain in the other, that it is possible to call forth that will to be virtuous, which, when confirmed, acts without any thought of either pleasure or pain. Will is the child of desire, and passes out of the dominion of its parent only to come under that of habit. That which is the result of habit affords no presumption of being intrinsically good; and there would be no reason for wishing that the purpose of virtue should become independent of pleasure and pain, were it not that the influence of the pleasurable and painful associations which prompt to virtue is not sufficiently to be depended on for unerring constancy of action until it has acquired the support of habit. Both in feeling and in conduct, habit is the only thing which imparts certainty; and it is because of the importance to others of being able to rely absolutely on one's feelings and conduct, and to oneself of being able to rely on one's own, that the will to do right ought to be cultivated into this habitual independence. In other words, this state of the will is a means to good, not intrinsically a good; and does not contradict the doctrine that nothing is a good to human beings but in so far as it is either itself pleasurable, or a means of attaining pleasure or averting pain.

But if this doctrine be true, the principle of utility is proved. Whether it is so or not, must now be left to the consideration of the thoughtful reader.

CHAPTER V

On the Connexion between Justice and Utility

In all ages of speculation, one of the strongest obstacles to the reception of the doctrine that Utility or Happiness is the criterion of right and wrong, has been drawn from the idea of Justice. The powerful sentiment, and apparently clear perception, which that word recalls with a rapidity and certainty resembling an instinct, have seemed to the majority of thinkers to point to an inherent quality in things; to show that the Just must have an existence in Nature as something absolute, generically distinct from every variety of the Expedient, and, in idea, opposed to it, though (as is commonly acknowledged) never, in the long run, disjoined from it in fact.

In the case of this, as of our other moral sentiments, there is no necessary connexion between the question of its origin, and that of its binding force. That a feeling is bestowed on us by Nature, does not necessarily legitimate all its promptings. The feeling of justice might be a peculiar instinct, and might yet require, like our other instincts, to be controlled and enlightened by a higher reason. If we have intellectual instincts, leading us to judge in a particular way, as well as animal instincts that prompt us to act in a particular way, there is no necessity that the former should be more infallible in their sphere than the latter in theirs: it may as well happen that wrong judgments are occasionally suggested by those, as wrong actions by these. But though it is one thing to believe that we have natural feelings of justice, and another to acknowledge them as an ultimate criterion of conduct, these two opinions are very closely connected in point of fact. Mankind are always predisposed to believe that any subjective feeling, not otherwise accounted for, is a revelation of some objective reality. Our present object is to determine whether the reality, to which the feeling of justice corresponds, is one which needs any such special revelation; whether the justice or injustice of an action is a thing intrinsically peculiar, and distinct from all its other qualities, or only a combination of certain of those qualities, presented under a peculiar aspect. For the purpose of this inquiry, it is practically important to consider whether the feeling itself, of justice and injustice, is *sui generis* like our sensations of colour and taste, or a derivative feeling, formed by a combination of others. And this it is the more essential to examine, as people are in general willing enough to allow, that objectively the dictates of justice coincide with a part of the field of General Expediency; but inasmuch as the subjective mental feeling of Jus-

tice is different from that which commonly attaches to simple expediency, and, except in extreme cases of the latter, is far more imperative in its demands, people find it difficult to see, in Justice, only a particular kind or branch of general utility, and think that its superior binding force requires a totally different origin.

To throw light upon this question, it is necessary to attempt to ascertain what is the distinguishing character of justice, or of injustice: what is the quality, or whether there is any quality, attributed in common to all modes of conduct designated as unjust (for justice, like many other moral attributes, is best defined by its opposite), and distinguishing them from such modes of conduct as are disapproved, but without having that particular epithet of disapprobation applied to them. If in everything which men are accustomed to characterize as just or unjust, some one common attribute or collection of attributes is always present, we may judge whether this particular attribute or combination of attributes would be capable of gathering round it a sentiment of that peculiar character and intensity by virtue of the general laws of our emotional constitution, or whether the sentiment is inexplicable, and requires to be regarded as a special provision of Nature. If we find the former to be the case, we shall, in resolving this question, have resolved also the main problem: if the latter, we shall have to seek for some other mode of investigating it.

To find the common attributes of a variety of objects, it is necessary to begin by surveying the objects themselves in the concrete. Let us therefore advert successively to the various modes of action, and arrangements of human affairs, which are classed, by universal or widely spread opinion, as Just or as Unjust. The things well known to excite the sentiments associated with those names, are of a very multifarious character. I shall pass them rapidly in review, without studying any particular arrangement.

In the first place, it is mostly considered unjust to deprive any one of his personal liberty, his property, or any other thing which belongs to him by law. Here, therefore, is one instance of the application of the terms just and unjust in a perfectly definite sense, namely, that it is just to respect, unjust to violate, the *legal rights* of any one. But this judgment admits of several exceptions, arising from the other forms in which the notions of justice and injustice present themselves. For example, the person who suffers the deprivation may (as the phrase is) have *forfeited* the rights which he is so deprived of: a case to which we shall return presently. But also,

Secondly; the legal rights of which he is deprived, may be rights which *ought* not to have belonged to him; in other words, the law which confers on him these rights, may be a bad law. When it is so, or when (which is the same thing for our purpose) it is supposed to be so, opinions will differ as to the justice or injustice of infringing it. Some maintain that no law, however bad, ought to be disobeyed by an individual citizen; that his opposition to it, if shown at all, should only be shown in endeavouring to get it altered by competent authority. This opinion (which condemns many of the most illustrious benefactors of mankind, and would often protect pernicious institutions against the only weapons which, in the state of things existing at the time, have any chance of succeeding against them) is defended, by those who hold it, on grounds of expediency; principally on that of the importance, to the common interest of mankind, of maintaining inviolate the sentiment of submission to law. Other persons, again, hold the directly contrary opinion, that any law, judged to be bad, may blamelessly be disobeyed, even though it be not judged to be unjust, but only inexpedient; while others would confine the licence of disobedience to the case of unjust laws: but again, some say, that all laws which are inexpedient are unjust; since every law imposes some restriction on the natural liberty of mankind, which restriction is an injustice, unless legitimated by tending to their good. Among these diversities of opinion, it seems to be universally admitted that there may be unjust laws, and that law, consequently, is not the ultimate criterion of justice, but may give to one person a benefit, or impose on another an evil, which justice condemns. When, however, a law is thought to be unjust, it seems always to be regarded as being so in the same way in which a breach of law is unjust, namely, by infringing somebody's right; which, as it cannot in this case be a legal right, receives a different appellation, and is called a moral right. We may say, therefore, that a second case of injustice consists in taking or withholding from any person that to which he has a *moral right*.

Thirdly, it is universally considered just that each person should obtain that (whether good or evil) which he *deserves*; and unjust that he should obtain a good, or be made to undergo an evil, which he does not deserve. This is, perhaps, the clearest and most emphatic form in which the idea of justice is conceived by the general mind. As it involves the notion of desert, the question arises, what constitutes desert? Speaking in a general way, a person is understood to deserve good if he does right, evil if he does wrong; and in a more particular sense, to deserve good from those to whom he does or has done good, and evil from those to whom he does or has done evil. The precept of returning good for evil has never been regarded as a case of the fulfilment of justice, but as one in which the claims of justice are waived, in obedience to other considerations.

Fourthly, it is confessedly unjust to *break faith* with any one: to violate an engagement, either express or implied, or disappoint expectations raised by our own conduct, at least if we have raised those expectations knowingly and voluntarily. Like the other obligations of justice already spoken of, this one is not regarded as absolute, but as capable of being overruled by a stronger obligation of justice on the other side; or by such conduct on the part of the person concerned as is deemed to absolve us from our obligation to him, and to constitute a *forfeiture* of the benefit which he has been led to expect.

Fifthly, it is, by universal admission, inconsistent with justice to be *partial*; to show favour or preference to one person over another, in matters to which favour and preference do not properly apply. Impartiality, however, does not seem to be regarded as a duty in itself, but rather as instrumental to some other duty; for it is admitted that favour and preference are not always censurable, and indeed the cases in which they are condemned are rather the exception than the rule. A person would be more likely to be blamed than applauded for giving his family or friends no superiority in good offices over strangers, when he could do so without violating any other duty; and no one thinks it unjust to seek one person in preference to another as a friend, connexion, or companion. Impartiality where rights are concerned is of course obligatory, but this is involved in the more general obligation of giving to every one his right. A tribunal, for example, must be impartial, because it is bound to award, without regard to any other consideration, a disputed object to the one of two parties who has the right to it. There are other cases in which impartiality means, being solely influenced by desert; as with those who, in the capacity of judges, preceptors, or parents, administer reward and punishment as such. There are cases, again, in which it means, being solely influenced by consideration for the public interest; as in making a selection among candidates for a government employment. Impartiality, in short, as an obligation of justice, may be said to mean, being exclusively influenced by the considerations which it is supposed ought to influence the particular case in hand; and resisting the solicitation of any motives which prompt to conduct different from what those considerations would dictate.

Nearly allied to the idea of impartiality, is that of *equality*; which often enters as a component part both into the conception of justice and into the practice of it, and, in the eyes of many persons, constitutes its essence. But in this, still more than in any other case, the notion of justice varies in different persons, and always conforms in its variations to their notion of utility. Each person maintains that equality is the dictate of justice, except where he thinks that expediency requires inequality. The justice of giving equal protection to the rights of all, is maintained by those who support the most outrageous inequality in the rights themselves. Even in slave countries it is theoretically admitted that the rights of the slave, such as they are, ought to be as sacred as those of the master; and that a tribunal which fails to enforce them with equal strictness is wanting in justice; while, at the same time, institutions which leave to the slave scarcely any rights to enforce, are not deemed unjust, because they are not deemed inexpedient. Those who think that utility requires distinctions of rank, do not consider it unjust that riches and social privileges should be unequally dispensed; but those who think this inequality inexpedient, think it unjust also. Whoever thinks that government is necessary, sees no injustice in as much inequality as is constituted by giving to the magistrate powers not granted to other people. Even among those who hold levelling doctrines, there are as many questions of justice as there are differences of opinion about expediency. Some

Communists consider it unjust that the produce of the labour of the community should be shared on any other principle than that of exact equality; others think it just that those should receive most whose needs are greatest; while others hold that those who work harder, or who produce more, or whose services are more valuable to the community, may justly claim a larger quota in the division of the produce. And the sense of natural justice may be plausibly appealed to in behalf of every one of these opinions.

Among so many diverse applications of the term Justice, which yet is not regarded as ambiguous, it is a matter of some difficulty to seize the mental link which holds them together, and on which the moral sentiment adhering to the term essentially depends. Perhaps, in this embarrassment, some help may be derived from the history of the word, as indicated by its etymology.

In most, if not in all, languages, the etymology of the word which corresponds to Just, points to an origin connected either with positive law, or with that which was in most cases the primitive form of law—authoritative custom. *Justum* is a form of *jussum*, that which has been ordered. *Jus* is of the same origin. *Dikaion* comes from *dike*, of which the principal meaning, at least in the historical ages of Greece, was a suit at law. Originally, indeed, it meant only the mode or *manner* of doing things, but it early came to mean the *prescribed* manner; that which the recognised authorities, patriarchal, judicial, or political, would enforce. *Recht*, from which came *right* and *righteous*, is synonymous with law. The original meaning indeed of *recht* did not point to law, but to physical straightness; as *wrong* and its Latin equivalents meant twisted or *tortuous*; and from this it is argued that right did not originally mean law, but on the contrary law meant right. But however this may be, the fact that *recht* and *droit* became restricted in their meaning to positive law, although much which is not required by law is equally necessary to moral straightness or rectitude, is as significant of the original character of moral ideas as if the derivation had been the reverse way. The courts of justice, the administration of justice, are the courts and the administration of law. *La justice*, in French, is the established term for judicature. There can, I think, be no doubt that the *idée mère*, the primitive element, in the formation of the notion of justice, was conformity to law. It constituted the entire idea among the Hebrews, up to the birth of Christianity; as might be expected in the case of a people whose laws attempted to embrace all subjects on which precepts were required, and who believed those laws to be a direct emanation from the Supreme Being. But other nations, and in particular the Greeks and Romans, who knew that their laws had been made originally, and still continued to be made, by men, were not afraid to admit that those men might make bad laws; might do, by law, the same things, and from the same motives, which, if done by individuals without the sanction of law, would be called unjust. And hence the sentiment of injustice came to be attached, not to all violations of law, but only to violations of such laws as *ought* to exist, including such as ought to exist but do not; and to laws themselves, if supposed to be contrary to what ought to be law. In this manner the idea of law and of its injunctions was still predominant in the notion of justice, even when the laws actually in force ceased to be accepted as the standard of it.

It is true that mankind consider the idea of justice and its obligations as applicable to many things which neither are, nor is it desired that they should be, regulated by law. Nobody desires that laws should interfere with the whole detail of private life; yet every one allows that in all daily conduct a person may and does show himself to be either just or unjust. But even here, the idea of the breach of what ought to be law, still lingers in a modified shape. It would always give us pleasure, and chime in with our feelings of fitness, that acts which we deem unjust should be punished, though we do not always think it expedient that this should be done by the tribunals. We forego that gratification on account of incidental inconveniences. We should be glad to see just conduct enforced and injustice repressed, even in the minutest details, if we were not, with reason, afraid of trusting the magistrate with so unlimited an amount of power over individuals. When we think that a person is bound in justice to do a thing, it is an ordinary form of language to say, that he ought to be compelled to do it. We should be gratified to see the obligation enforced by anybody who had the power. If we see that its enforcement by law would be inexpedient, we lament the impossibility, we consider the impunity

given to injustice as an evil, and strive to make amends for it by bringing a strong expression of our own and the public disapprobation to bear upon the offender. Thus the idea of legal constraint is still the generating idea of the notion of justice, though undergoing several transformations before that notion, as it exists in an advanced state of society, becomes complete.

The above is, I think, a true account, as far as it goes, of the origin and progressive growth of the idea of justice. But we must observe, that it contains, as yet, nothing to distinguish that obligation from moral obligation in general. For the truth is, that the idea of penal sanction, which is the essence of law, enters not only into the conception of injustice, but into that of any kind of wrong. We do not call anything wrong, unless we mean to imply that a person ought to be punished in some way or other for doing it; if not by law, by the opinion of his fellow creatures; if not by opinion, by the reproaches of his own conscience. This seems the real turning point of the distinction between morality and simple expediency. It is a part of the notion of Duty in every one of its forms, that a person may rightfully be compelled to fulfil it. Duty is a thing which may be *exacted* from a person, as one exacts a debt. Unless we think that it might be exacted from him, we do not call it his duty. Reasons of prudence, or the interest of other people, may militate against actually exacting it; but the person himself, it is clearly understood, would not be entitled to complain. There are other things, on the contrary, which we wish that people should do, which we like or admire them for doing, perhaps dislike or despise them for not doing, but yet admit that they are not bound to do; it is not a case of moral obligation; we do not blame them, that is, we do not think that they are proper objects of punishment. How we come by these ideas of deserving and not deserving punishment, will appear, perhaps, in the sequel; but I think there is no doubt that this distinction lies at the bottom of the notions of right and wrong; that we call any conduct wrong, or employ, instead, some other term of dislike or disparagement, according as we think that the person ought, or ought not, to be punished for it; and we say that it would be right to do so and so, or merely that it would be desirable or laudable, according as we would wish to see the person whom it concerns, compelled, or only persuaded and exhorted, to act in that manner.[3]

This, therefore, being the characteristic difference which marks off, not justice, but morality in general, from the remaining provinces of Expediency and Worthiness; the character is still to be sought which distinguishes justice from other branches of morality. Now it is known that ethical writers divide moral duties into two classes, denoted by the ill-chosen expressions, duties of perfect and of imperfect obligation; the latter being those in which, though the act is obligatory, the particular occasions of performing it are left to our choice; as in the case of charity or beneficence, which we are indeed bound to practise, but not towards any definite person, nor at any prescribed time. In the more precise language of philosophic jurists, duties of perfect obligation are those duties in virtue of which a correlative *right* resides in some person or persons; duties of imperfect obligation are those moral obligations which do not give birth to any right. I think it will be found that this distinction exactly coincides with that which exists between justice and the other obligations of morality. In our survey of the various popular acceptations of justice, the term appeared generally to involve the idea of a personal right—a claim on the part of one or more individuals, like that which the law gives when it confers a proprietary or other legal right. Whether the injustice consists in depriving a person of a possession, or in breaking faith with him, or in treating him worse than he deserves, or worse than other people who have no greater claims, in each case the supposition implies two things—a wrong done, and some assignable person who is wronged. Injustice may also be done by treating a person better than others; but the wrong in this case is to his competitors, who are also assignable persons. It seems to me that this feature in the case—a right in some person, correlative to the moral obligation—constitutes the specific difference between justice, and generosity or beneficence. Justice implies something which it is not only right to

do, and wrong not to do, but which some individual person can claim from us as his moral right. No one has a moral right to our generosity or beneficence, because we are not morally bound to practise those virtues towards any given individual. And it will be found with respect to this as with respect to every correct definition, that the instances which seem to conflict with it are those which most confirm it. For if a moralist attempts, as some have done, to make out that mankind generally, though not any given individual, have a right to all the good we can do them, he at once, by that thesis, includes generosity and beneficence within the category of justice. He is obliged to say, that our utmost exertions are *due* to our fellow creatures, thus assimilating them to a debt; or that nothing less can be a sufficient *return* for what society does for us, thus classing the case as one of gratitude; both of which are acknowledged cases of justice. Wherever there is a right, the case is one of justice, and not of the virtue of beneficence: and whoever does not place the distinction between justice and morality in general, where we have now placed it, will be found to make no distinction between them at all, but to merge all morality in justice.

Having thus endeavoured to determine the distinctive elements which enter into the composition of the idea of justice, we are ready to enter on the inquiry, whether the feeling, which accompanies the idea, is attached to it by a special dispensation of nature, or whether it could have grown up, by any known laws, out of the idea itself; and in particular, whether it can have originated in considerations of general expediency.

I conceive that the sentiment itself does not arise from anything which would commonly, or correctly, be termed an idea of expediency; but that though the sentiment does not, whatever is moral in it does.

We have seen that the two essential ingredients in the sentiment of justice are, the desire to punish a person who has done harm, and the knowledge or belief that there is some definite individual or individuals to whom harm has been done.

Now it appears to me, that the desire to punish a person who has done harm to some individual, is a spontaneous outgrowth from two sentiments, both in the highest degree natural, and which either are or

---

3. See this point enforced and illustrated by Professor Bain, in an admirable chapter (entitled "The Ethical Emotions, or the Moral Sense"), of the second of the two treatises composing his elaborate and profound work on the Mind.

resemble instincts; the impulse of self-defence, and the feeling of sympathy.

It is natural to resent, and to repel or retaliate, any harm done or attempted against ourselves, or against those with whom we sympathize. The origin of this sentiment it is not necessary here to discuss. Whether it be an instinct or a result of intelligence, it is, we know, common to all animal nature; for every animal tries to hurt those who have hurt, or who it thinks are about to hurt, itself or its young. Human beings, on this point, only differ from other animals in two particulars. First, in being capable of sympathizing, not solely with their offspring, or, like some of the more noble animals, with some superior animal who is kind to them, but with all human, and even with all sentient, beings. Secondly, in having a more developed intelligence, which gives a wider range to the whole of their sentiments, whether self-regarding or sympathetic. By virtue of his superior intelligence, even apart from his superior range of sympathy, a human being is capable of apprehending a community of interest between himself and the human society of which he forms a part, such that any conduct which threatens the security of the society generally, is threatening to his own, and calls forth his instinct (if instinct it be) of self-defence. The same superiority of intelligence, joined to the power of sympathizing with human beings generally, enables him to attach himself to the collective idea of his tribe, his country, or mankind, in such a manner that any act hurtful to them rouses his instinct of sympathy, and urges him to resistance.

The sentiment of justice, in that one of its elements which consists of the desire to punish, is thus, I conceive, the natural feeling of retaliation or vengeance, rendered by intellect and sympathy applicable to those injuries, that is, to those hurts, which wound us through, or in common with, society at large. This sentiment, in itself, has nothing moral in it; what is moral is, the exclusive subordination of it to the social sympathies, so as to wait on and obey their call. For the natural feeling tends to make us resent indiscriminately whatever any one does that is disagreeable to us; but when moralized by the social feeling, it only acts in the directions conformable to the general good: just persons resenting a hurt to society, though not otherwise a hurt to themselves, and not resenting a hurt to themselves, however painful, unless it be of the kind which society has a common interest with them in the repression of.

It is no objection against this doctrine to say, that when we feel our sentiment of justice outraged, we are not thinking of society at large, or of any collective interest, but only of the individual case. It is common enough certainly, though the reverse of commendable, to feel resentment merely because we have suffered pain; but a person whose resentment is really a moral feeling, that is, who considers whether an act is blameable before he allows himself to resent it — such a person, though he may not say expressly to himself that he is standing up for the interest of society, certainly does feel that he is asserting a rule which is for the benefit of others as well as for his own. If he is not feeling this — if he is regarding the act solely as it affects him individually — he is not consciously just; he is not concerning himself about the justice of his actions. This is admitted even by anti-utilitarian moralists. When Kant (as before remarked) propounds as the fundamental principle of morals, 'So act, that thy rule of conduct might be adopted as a law by all rational beings,' he virtually acknowledges that the interest of mankind collectively, or at least of mankind indiscriminately, must be in the mind of the agent when conscientiously deciding on the morality of the act. Otherwise he uses words without a meaning: for, that a rule even of utter selfishness could not *possibly* be adopted by all rational beings — that there is any insuperable obstacle in the nature of things to its adoption — cannot be even plausibly maintained. To give any meaning to Kant's principle, the sense put upon it must be, that we ought to shape our conduct by a rule which all rational beings might adopt *with benefit to their collective interest*.

To recapitulate: the idea of justice supposes two things; a rule of conduct, and a sentiment which sanctions the rule. The first must be supposed common to all mankind, and intended for their good. The other (the sentiment) is a desire that punishment may be suffered by those who infringe the rule. There is involved, in addition, the conception of some definite person who suffers by the infringement; whose rights (to use the expression appropriated to the case) are violated by it. And the sentiment of justice appears to me to be, the animal desire to repel or retaliate a hurt or damage to oneself, or to those with whom one sympathizes, widened so as to include all persons, by the human capacity of enlarged sympathy, and the human conception of intelligent self-interest. From the latter elements, the feeling derives its morality; from the former, its peculiar impressiveness, and energy of self-assertion.

I have, throughout, treated the idea of a *right* residing in the injured person, and violated by the injury, not as a separate element in the composition of the idea and sentiment, but as one of the forms in which the other two elements clothe themselves. These elements are, a hurt to some assignable person or persons on the one hand, and a demand for punishment on the other. An examination of our own minds, I think, will show, that these two things include all that we mean when we speak of violation of a right. When we call anything a person's right, we mean that he has a valid claim on society to protect him in the possession of it, either by the force of law, or by that of education and opinion. If he has what we consider a sufficient claim, on whatever account, to have something guaranteed to him by society, we say that he has a right to it. If we desire to prove that anything does not belong to him by right, we think this done as soon as it is admitted that society ought not to take measures for securing it to him, but should leave it to chance, or to his own exertions. Thus, a person is said to have a right to what he can earn in fair professional competition; because society ought not to allow any other person to hinder him from endeavouring to earn in that manner as much as he can. But he has not a right to three hundred a-year, though he may happen to be earning it; because society is not called on to provide that he shall earn that sum. On the contrary, if he owns ten thousand pounds three per cent stock, he *has* a right to three hundred a-year; because society has come under an obligation to provide him with an income of that amount.

To have a right, then, is, I conceive, to have something which society ought to defend me in the possession of. If the objector goes on to ask why it ought, I can give him no other reason than general utility. If that expression does not seem to convey a sufficient feeling of the strength of the obligation, nor to account for the peculiar energy of the feeling, it is because there goes to the composition of the senti-

ment, not a rational only but also an animal element, the thirst for retaliation; and this thirst derives its intensity, as well as its moral justification, from the extraordinarily important and impressive kind of utility which is concerned. The interest involved is that of security, to every one's feelings the most vital of all interests. Nearly all other earthly benefits are needed by one person, not needed by another; and many of them can, if necessary, be cheerfully foregone, or replaced by something else; but security no human being can possibly do without; on it we depend for all our immunity from evil, and for the whole value of all and every good, beyond the passing moment; since nothing but the gratification of the instant could be of any worth to us, if we could be deprived of everything the next instant by whoever was momentarily stronger than ourselves. Now this most indispensable of all necessaries, after physical nutriment, cannot be had, unless the machinery for providing it is kept unintermittedly in active play. Our notion, therefore, of the claim we have on our fellow creatures to join in making safe for us the very groundwork of our existence, gathers feelings round it so much more intense than those concerned in any of the more common cases of utility, that the difference in degree (as is often the case in psychology) becomes a real difference in kind. The claim assumes that character of absoluteness, that apparent infinity, and incommensurability with all other considerations, which constitute the distinction between the feeling of right and wrong and that of ordinary expediency and inexpediency. The feelings concerned are so powerful, and we count so positively on finding a responsive feeling in others (all being alike interested), that *ought* and *should* grow into *must*, and recognised indispensability becomes a moral necessity, analogous to physical, and often not inferior to it in binding force.

If the preceding analysis, or something resembling it, be not the correct account of the notion of justice; if justice be totally independent of utility, and be a standard *per se*, which the mind can recognise by simple introspection of itself; it is hard to understand why that internal oracle is so ambiguous, and why so many things appear either just or unjust, according to the light in which they are regarded.

We are continually informed that Utility is an uncertain standard, which every different person interprets differently, and that there is no safety but in the immutable, ineffaceable, and unmistakeable dictates of Justice, which carry their evidence in themselves, and are independent of the fluctuations of opinion. One would suppose from this that on questions of justice there could be no controversy; that if we take that for our rule, its application to any given case could leave us in as little doubt as a mathematical demonstration. So far is this from being the fact, that there is as much difference of opinion, and as fierce discussion, about what is just, as about what is useful to society. Not only have different nations and individuals different notions of justice, but in the mind of one and the same individual, justice is not some one rule, principle, or maxim, but many, which do not always coincide in their dictates, and in choosing between which, he is guided either by some extraneous standard, or by his own personal predilections.

For instance, there are some who say, that it is unjust to punish any one for the sake of example to others; that punishment is just, only when intended for the good of the sufferer himself. Others maintain the extreme reverse, contending that to punish persons who have attained years of discretion, for their own benefit, is despotism and injustice, since if the matter at issue is solely their own good, no one has a right to control their own judgment of it; but that they may justly be punished to prevent evil to others, this being an exercise of the legitimate right of self-defence. Mr. Owen, again, affirms that it is unjust to punish at all; for the criminal did not make his own character; his education, and the circumstances which surround him, have made him a criminal, and for these he is not responsible. All these opinions are extremely plausible; and so long as the question is argued as one of justice simply, without going down to the principles which lie under justice and are the source of its authority, I am unable to see how any of these reasoners can be refuted. For in truth every one of the three builds upon rules of justice confessedly true. The first appeals to the acknowledged injustice of singling out an individual, and making him a sacrifice, without his consent, for other people's benefit. The second relies on the acknowledged justice of self-defence, and the admitted injustice of forcing one person to conform to another's notions of what constitutes his good. The Owenite invokes the admitted principle, that it is unjust to punish any one for what he cannot help. Each is triumphant so long as he is not compelled to take into consideration any other maxims of justice than the one he has selected; but as soon as their several maxims are brought face to face, each disputant seems to have exactly as much to say for himself as the others. No one of them can carry out his own notion of justice without trampling upon another equally binding. These are difficulties; they have always been felt to be such; and many devices have been invented to turn rather than to overcome them. As a refuge from the last of the three, men imagined what they called the freedom of the will; fancying that they could not justify punishing a man whose will is in a thoroughly hateful state, unless it be supposed to have come into that state through no influence of anterior circumstances. To escape from the other difficulties, a favourite contrivance has been the fiction of a contract, whereby at some unknown period all the members of society engaged to obey the laws, and consented to be punished for any disobedience to them; thereby giving to their legislators the right, which it is assumed they would not otherwise have had, of punishing them, either for their own good or for that of society. This happy thought was considered to get rid of the whole difficulty, and to legitimate the infliction of punishment, in virtue of another received maxim of justice, *Volenti non fit injuria*; that is not unjust which is done with the consent of the person who is supposed to be hurt by it. I need hardly remark, that even if the consent were not a mere fiction, this maxim is not superior in authority to the others which it is brought in to supersede. It is, on the contrary, an instructive specimen of the loose and irregular manner in which supposed principles of justice grow up. This particular one evidently came into use as a help to the coarse exigencies of courts of law, which are sometimes obliged to be content with very uncertain presumptions, on account of the greater evils which would often arise from any attempt on their part to cut finer. But even courts of law are not able to adhere consistently to the maxim, for they allow voluntary engagements to be set aside on the ground of fraud, and sometimes on that of mere mistake or misinformation.

Again, when the legitimacy of inflicting punishment is admitted, how many conflicting conceptions of justice come to light in discussing the proper apportionment of punishment to offences. No rule on this subject recommends itself so strongly to the primitive and spontaneous sentiment of justice, as the *lex talionis*, an eye for an eye and a tooth for a tooth. Though this principle of the Jewish and of the Mahomedan law has been generally abandoned in Europe as a practical maxim, there is, I suspect, in most minds, a secret hankering after it; and when retribution accidentally falls on an offender in that precise shape, the general feeling of satisfaction evinced, bears witness how natural is the sentiment to which this repayment in kind is acceptable. With many the test of justice in penal infliction is that the punishment should be proportioned to the offence; meaning that it should be exactly measured by the moral guilt of the culprit (whatever be their standard for measuring moral guilt): the consideration, what amount of punishment is necessary to deter from the offence, having nothing to do with the question of justice, in their estimation: while there are others to whom that consideration is all in all; who maintain that it is not just, at least for man, to inflict on a fellow creature, whatever may be his offences, any amount of suffering beyond the least that will suffice to prevent him from repeating, and others from imitating, his misconduct.

To take another example from a subject already once referred to. In a co-operative industrial association, is it just or not that talent or skill should give a title to superior remuneration? On the negative side of the question it is argued, that whoever does the best he can, deserves equally well, and ought not in justice to be put in a position of inferiority for no fault of his own; that superior abilities have already advantages more than enough, in the admiration they excite, the personal influence they command, and the internal sources of satisfaction attending them, without adding to these a superior share of the world's goods; and that society is bound in justice rather to make compensation to the less favoured, for this unmerited inequality of advantages, than to aggravate it. On the contrary side it is contended, that society receives more from the more efficient labourer; that his services being more useful, society owes him a larger return for them; that a greater share of the joint result is actually his work, and not to allow his claim to it is a kind of robbery; that if he is only to receive as much as others, he can only be justly required to produce as much, and to give a smaller amount of time and exertion, proportioned to his superior efficiency. Who shall decide between these appeals to conflicting principles of justice? Justice has in this case two sides to it, which it is impossible to bring into harmony, and the two disputants have chosen opposite sides; the one looks to what it is just that the individual should receive, the other to what it is just that the community should give. Each, from his own point of view, is unanswerable; and any choice between them, on grounds of justice, must be perfectly arbitrary. Social utility alone can decide the preference.

How many, again, and how irreconcileable, are the standards of justice to which reference is made in discussing the repartition of taxation. One opinion is, that payment to the State should be in numerical proportion to pecuniary means. Others think that justice dictates what they term graduated taxation; taking a higher percentage from those who have more to spare. In point of natural justice a strong case might be made for disregarding means altogether, and taking the same absolute sum (whenever it could be got) from every one: as the subscribers to a mess, or to a club, all pay the same sum for the same privileges, whether they can all equally afford it or not. Since the protection (it might be said) of law and government is afforded to, and is equally required by all, there is no injustice in making all buy it at the same price. It is reckoned justice, not injustice, that a dealer should charge to all customers the same price for the same article, not a price varying according to their means of payment. This doctrine, as applied to taxation, finds no advocates, because it conflicts strongly with men's feelings of humanity and perceptions of social expediency; but the principle of justice which it invokes is as true and as binding as those which can be appealed to against it. Accordingly, it exerts a tacit influence on the line of defence employed for other modes of assessing taxation. People feel obliged to argue that the State does more for the rich than for the poor, as a justification for its taking more from them: though this is in reality not true, for the rich would be far better able to protect themselves, in the absence of law or government, than the poor, and indeed would probably be successful in converting the poor into their slaves. Others, again, so far defer to the same conception of justice, as to maintain that all should pay an equal capitation tax for the protection of their persons (these being of equal value to all), and an unequal tax for the protection of their property, which is unequal. To this others reply, that the all of one man is as valuable to him as the all of another. From these confusions there is no other mode of extrication than the utilitarian.

Is, then, the difference between the Just and the Expedient a merely imaginary distinction? Have mankind been under a delusion in thinking that justice is a more sacred thing than policy, and that the latter ought only to be listened to after the former has been satisfied? By no means. The exposition we have given of the nature and origin of the sentiment, recognises a real distinction; and no one of those who profess the most sublime contempt for the consequences of actions as an element in their morality, attaches more importance to the distinction than I do. While I dispute the pretensions of any theory which sets up an imaginary standard of justice not grounded on utility, I account the justice which is grounded on utility to be the chief part, and incomparably the most sacred and binding part, of all morality. Justice is a name for certain classes of moral rules, which concern the essentials of human well-being more nearly, and are therefore of more absolute obligation, than any other rules for the guidance of life; and the notion which we have found to be of the essence of the idea of justice, that of a right residing in an individual, implies and testifies to this more binding obligation.

The moral rules which forbid mankind to hurt one another (in which we must never forget to include wrongful interference with each other's freedom) are more vital to human well-being than any maxims, however important, which only point out the best mode of managing some department of human affairs. They have also the peculiarity, that they are the main element in determining the whole of the social feelings of mankind. It is their observance which alone preserves peace among human beings: if obedience to them were not the rule, and disobedience the exception, every one would see in every one else a probable enemy, against whom he must be perpetu-

ally guarding himself. What is hardly less important, these are the precepts which mankind have the strongest and the most direct inducements for impressing upon one another. By merely giving to each other prudential instruction or exhortation, they may gain, or think they gain, nothing: in inculcating on each other the duty of positive beneficence they have an unmistakeable interest, but far less in degree: a person may possibly not need the benefits of others; but he always needs that they should not do him hurt. Thus the moralities which protect every individual from being harmed by others, either directly or by being hindered in his freedom of pursuing his own good, are at once those which he himself has most at heart, and those which he has the strongest interest in publishing and enforcing by word and deed. It is by a person's observance of these, that his fitness to exist as one of the fellowship of human beings, is tested and decided; for on that depends his being a nuisance or not to those with whom he is in contact. Now it is these moralities primarily, which compose the obligations of justice. The most marked cases of injustice, and those which give the tone to the feeling of repugnance which characterizes the sentiment, are acts of wrongful aggression, or wrongful exercise of power over some one; the next are those which consist in wrongfully withholding from him something which is his due; in both cases, inflicting on him a positive hurt, either in the form of direct suffering, or of the privation of some good which he had reasonable ground, either of a physical or of a social kind, for counting upon.

The same powerful motives which command the observance of these primary moralities, enjoin the punishment of those who violate them; and as the impulses of self defence, of defence of others, and of vengeance, are all called forth against such persons, retribution, or evil for evil, becomes closely connected with the sentiment of justice, and is universally included in the idea. Good for good is also one of the dictates of justice; and this, though its social utility is evident, and though it carries with it a natural human feeling, has not at first sight that obvious connexion with hurt or injury, which, existing in the most elementary cases of just and unjust, is the source of the characteristic intensity of the sentiment. But the connexion, though less obvious, is not less real.

He who accepts benefits, and denies a return of them when needed, inflicts a real hurt, by disappointing one of the most natural and reasonable of expectations, and one which he must at least tacitly have encouraged, otherwise the benefits would seldom have been conferred. The important rank, among human evils and wrongs, of the disappointment of expectation, is shown in the fact that it constitutes the principal criminality of two such highly immoral acts as a breach of friendship and a breach of promise. Few hurts which human beings can sustain are greater, and none wound more, than when that on which they habitually and with full assurance relied, fails them in the hour of need; and few wrongs are greater than this mere withholding of good; none excite more resentment, either in the person suffering, or in a sympathizing spectator. The principle, therefore, of giving to each what they deserve, that is, good for good as well as evil for evil, is not only included within the idea of Justice as we have defined it, but is a proper object of that intensity of sentiment, which places the Just, in human estimation, above the simply Expedient.

Most of the maxims of justice current in the world, and commonly appealed to in its transactions, are simply instrumental to carrying into effect the principles of justice which we have now spoken of. That a person is only responsible for what he has done voluntarily, or could voluntarily have avoided; that it is unjust to condemn any person unheard; that the punishment ought to be proportioned to the offence, and the like, are maxims intended to prevent the just principle of evil for evil from being perverted to the infliction of evil without that justification. The greater part of these common maxims have come into use from the practice of courts of justice, which have been naturally led to a more complete recognition and elaboration than was likely to suggest itself to others, of the rules necessary to enable them to fulfil their double function, of inflicting punishment when due, and of awarding to each person his right.

That first of judicial virtues, impartiality, is an obligation of justice, partly for the reason last mentioned; as being a necessary condition of the fulfilment of the other obligations of justice. But this is not the only source of the exalted rank, among human obligations, of those maxims of equality and impartiality, which, both in popular estimation and in that of the most enlightened, are included among the precepts of justice. In one point of view, they may be considered as corollaries from the principles already laid down. If it is a duty to do to each according to his deserts, returning good for good as well as repressing evil by evil, it necessarily follows that we should treat all equally well (when no higher duty forbids) who have deserved equally well of us, and that society should treat all equally well who have deserved equally well of it, that is, who have deserved equally well absolutely. This is the highest abstract standard of social and distributive justice; towards which all institutions, and the efforts of all virtuous citizens, should be made in the utmost possible degree to converge. But this great moral duty rests upon a still deeper foundation, being a direct emanation from the first principle of morals, and not a mere logical corollary from secondary or derivative doctrines. It is involved in the very meaning of Utility, or the Greatest-Happiness Principle. That principle is a mere form of words without rational signification, unless one person's happiness, supposed equal in degree (with the proper allowance made for kind), is counted for exactly as much as another's. Those conditions being supplied, Bentham's dictum, 'everybody to count for one, nobody for more than one,' might be written under the principle of utility as an explanatory commentary.[4] The equal claim of everybody to happiness in the estimation of the moralist

___

4. This implication, in the first principle of the utilitarian scheme, of perfect impartiality between persons, is regarded by Mr. Herbert Spencer (in his 'Social Statics') as a disproof of the pretensions of utility to be a sufficient guide to right; since (he says) the principle of utility presupposes the anterior principle, that everybody has an equal right to happiness. It may be more correctly described as supposing that equal amounts of happiness are equally desirable, whether felt by the same or by different persons. This, however, is not a presupposition; not a premise needful to support the principle of utility, but the very principle itself; for what is the principle of utility, if it be not that 'happiness' and 'desirable' are synonymous terms? If there is any anterior principle implied, it can be no other than this, that the truths of arithmetic are applicable to the valuation of happiness, as of all other measurable quantities.

[Mr. Herbert Spencer, in a private communication

and the legislator, involves an equal claim to all the means of happiness, except in so far as the inevitable conditions of human life, and the general interest, in which that of every individual is included, set limits to the maxim; and those limits ought to be strictly construed. As every other maxim of justice, so this, is by no means applied or held applicable universally; on the contrary, as I have already remarked, it bends to every person's ideas of social expediency. But in whatever case it is deemed applicable at all, it is held to be the dictate of justice. All persons are deemed to have a *right* to equality of treatment, except when some recognised social expediency requires the reverse. And hence all social inequalities which have ceased to be considered expedient, assume the character not of simple inexpediency, but of injustice, and appear so tyrannical, that people are apt to wonder how they ever could have been tolerated; forgetful that they themselves perhaps tolerate other inequalities under an equally mistaken notion of expediency,

----

on the subject of the preceding Note, objects to being considered an opponent of Utilitarianism, and states that he regards happiness as the ultimate end of morality; but deems that end only partially attainable by empirical generalizations from the observed results of conduct, and completely attainable only by deducing, from the laws of life and the conditions of existence, what kinds of action necessarily tend to produce happiness, and what kinds to produce unhappiness. With the exception of the word "necessarily," I have no dissent to express from this doctrine; and (omitting that word) I am not aware that any modern advocate of utilitarianism is of a different opinion. Bentham, certainly, to whom in the *Social Statics* Mr. Spencer particularly referred, is, least of all writers, chargeable with unwillingness to deduce the effect of actions on happiness from the laws of human nature and the universal conditions of human life. The common charge against him is of relying too exclusively upon such deductions, and declining altogether to be bound by the generalizations from specific experience which Mr. Spencer thinks that utilitarians generally confine themselves to. My own opinion (and, as I collect, Mr. Spencer's) is, that in ethics, as in all other branches of scientific study, the consilience of the results of both these processes, each corroborating and verifying the other, is requisite to give to any general proposition the kind and degree of evidence which constitutes scientific proof.]

the correction of which would make that which they approve seem quite as monstrous as what they have at last learnt to condemn. The entire history of social improvement has been a series of transitions, by which one custom or institution after another, from being a supposed primary necessity of social existence, has passed into the rank of an universally stigmatized injustice and tyranny. So it has been with the distinctions of slaves and freemen, nobles and serfs, patricians and plebeians; and so it will be, and in part already is, with the aristocracies of colour, race, and sex.

It appears from what has been said, that justice is a name for certain moral requirements, which, regarded collectively, stand higher in the scale of social utility, and are therefore of more paramount obligation, than any others; though particular cases may occur in which some other social duty is so important, as to overrule any one of the general maxims of justice. Thus, to save a life, it may not only be allowable, but a duty, to steal, or take by force, the necessary food or medicine, or to kidnap, and compel to officiate, the only qualified medical practitioner. In such cases, as we do not call anything justice which is not a virtue, we usually say, not that justice must give way to some other moral principle, but that what is just in ordinary cases is, by reason of that other principle, not just in the particular case. By this useful accommodation of language, the character of indefeasibility attributed to justice is kept up, and we are saved from the necessity of maintaining that there can be laudable injustice.

The considerations which have now been adduced resolve, I conceive, the only real difficulty in the utilitarian theory of morals. It has always been evident that all cases of justice are also cases of expediency: the difference is in the peculiar sentiment which attaches to the former, as contradistinguished from the latter. If this characteristic sentiment has been sufficiently accounted for; if there is no necessity to assume for it any peculiarity of origin; if it is simply the natural feeling of resentment, moralized by being made coextensive with the demands of social good; and if this feeling not only does but ought to exist in all the classes of cases to which the idea of justice corresponds; that idea no longer presents itself as a stumbling-block to the utilitarian ethics. Justice

MILL

remains the appropriate name for certain social utilities which are vastly more important, and therefore more absolute and imperative, than any others are as a class (though not more so than others may be in particular cases); and which, therefore, ought to be, as well as naturally are, guarded by a sentiment not only different in degree, but also in kind; distinguished from the milder feeling which attaches to the mere idea of promoting human pleasure or convenience, at once by the more definite nature of its commands, and by the sterner character of its sanctions.

THE SUBJECTION OF WOMEN

CHAPTER 1

The object of this Essay is to explain as clearly as I am able, the grounds of an opinion which I have held from the very earliest period when I had formed any opinions at all on social or political matters, and which, instead of being weakened or modified, has been constantly growing stronger by the progress of reflection and the experience of life: That the principle which regulates the existing social relations between the two sexes—the legal subordination of one sex to the other—is wrong in itself, and now one of the chief hindrances to human improvement; and that it ought to be replaced by a principle of perfect equality, admitting no power or privilege on the one side, nor disability on the other.

The very words necessary to express the task I have undertaken, show how arduous it is. But it would be a mistake to suppose that the difficulty of the case must lie in the insufficiency or obscurity of the grounds of reason on which my conviction rests. The difficulty is that which exists in all cases in which there is a mass of feeling to be contended against. So long as an opinion is strongly rooted in the feelings, it gains rather than loses in stability by having a preponderating weight of argument against it. For if it were accepted as a result of argument, the refutation of the argument might shake the solidity of the conviction; but when it rests solely on feeling, the worse it fares in argumentative contest, the more persuaded its adherents are that their feeling must have some deeper ground, which the arguments do not reach; and while the feeling remains, it is always throwing up fresh intrenchments of argument to repair any breach made in the old. And there are so many causes tending to make the feelings connected with this subject the most intense and most deeply-rooted of all those which gather round and protect old institutions and customs, that we need not wonder to find them as yet less undermined and loosened than any of the rest by the progress of the great modern spiritual and social transition; nor suppose that the barbarisms to which men cling longest must be less barbarisms than those which they earlier shake off.

In every respect the burthen is hard on those who attack an almost universal opinion. They must be very fortunate as well as unusually capable if they obtain a hearing at all. They have more difficulty in obtaining a trial, than any other litigants have in getting a verdict. If they do extort a hearing, they are subjected to a set of logical requirements totally different from those exacted from other people. In all other cases, the burthen of proof is supposed to lie with the affirmative. If a person is charged with a murder, it rests with those who accuse him to give proof of his guilt, not with himself to prove his innocence. If there is a difference of opinion about the reality of any alleged historical event, in which the feelings of men in general are not much interested, as the Siege of Troy for example, those who maintain that the event took place are expected to produce their proofs, before those who take the other side can be required to say anything; and at no time are these required to do more than show that the evidence produced by the others is of no value. Again, in practical matters, the burthen of proof is supposed to be with those who are against liberty; who contend for any restriction or prohibition; either any limitation of the general freedom of human action, or any disqualification or disparity of privilege affecting one person or kind of persons, as compared with others. The *à priori* presumption is in favour of freedom and impartiality. It is held that there should be no restraint not required by the general good, and that the law should be no respecter of persons, but should treat all alike, save where dissimilarity of treatment is required by positive reasons, either of justice or of policy. But of none of these rules of evidence will the benefit be allowed to those who maintain the opinion I profess. It is useless for me to say that those who maintain the doctrine that men have a right to command and women are under an obligation to obey, or that men are fit for government and women unfit, are on the affirmative side of the question, and that they are bound to show positive evidence for the assertions, or submit to their rejection. It is equally unavailing for me to say that those who deny to women any freedom or privilege rightly allowed to men, having the double presumption against them that they are opposing freedom and recommending partiality, must be held to the strictest proof of their case, and unless their success be such as to exclude all doubt, the judgment ought to go against them. These would be thought good pleas in any common case; but they will not be thought so in this instance. Before I could hope to make any impression, I should be expected not only to answer all that has ever been said by those who take the other side of the question, but to imagine all that could be said by them—to find them in reasons, as well as answer all I find: and besides refuting all arguments for the affirmative, I shall be called upon for invincible positive arguments to prove a negative. And even if I could do all this, and leave the opposite party with a host of unanswered arguments against them, and not a single unrefuted one on their side, I should be thought to have done little; for a cause supported on the one hand by universal usage, and on the other by so great a preponderance of popular sentiment, is supposed to have a presumption in its favour, superior to any conviction which an appeal to reason has power to produce in any intellects but those of a high class.

I do not mention these difficulties to complain of them; first, because it would be useless; they are inseparable from having to contend through people's understandings against the hostility of their feelings and practical tendencies: and truly the understandings of the majority of mankind would need to be much better cultivated than has ever yet been the case, before they can be asked to place such reliance in their own power of estimating arguments, as to give up practical principles in which they have been born and bred and which are the basis of much of the existing order of the world, at the first argumentative attack which they are not capable of logically resisting. I do not therefore quarrel with them for having too little faith in argument, but for having too much faith in custom and the general feeling. It is one of the characteristic prejudices of the reaction of the nineteenth century against the eighteenth, to accord to the unreasoning elements in human nature the infallibility which the eighteenth century is supposed to have ascribed to the reasoning elements. For the apotheosis of Reason we have substituted that of Instinct; and we call everything instinct which we find in ourselves and for which we cannot trace any rational foundation. This idolatry, infinitely more degrading than the other, and the most pernicious of the false worships of the present day, of all of which it is now the main support, will probably hold its ground until it gives way before a sound psychology, laying bare the real root of much that is bowed down to as the intention of Nature and the ordinance of God. As regards the present question, I am willing to accept the unfavourable conditions which the prejudice assigns to me. I consent that established custom, and the general feeling, should be deemed conclusive against me, unless that custom and feeling from age to age can be shown to have owed their existence to other causes than their soundness, and to have derived their power from the worse rather than the better parts of human nature. I am willing that judgment should go against me, unless I can show that my judge has been tampered with. The concession is not so great as it might appear; for to prove this, is by far the easiest portion of my task.

The generality of a practice is in some cases a strong presumption that it is, or at all events once was, conducive to laudable ends. This is the case, when the practice was first adopted, or afterwards kept up, as a means to such ends, and was grounded on experience of the mode in which they could be most effectually attained. If the authority of men over women, when first established, had been the result of a conscientious comparison between different modes of constituting the government of society; if, after trying various other modes of social organization—the government of women over men, equality between the two, and such mixed and divided modes of government as might be invented—it had been decided, on the testimony of experience, that the mode in which women are wholly under the rule of men, having no share at all in public concerns, and each in private being under the legal obligation of obedience to the man with whom she has associated her destiny, was the arrangement most conducive to the happiness and well being of both; its general adoption might then be fairly thought to be some evidence that, at the time when it was adopted, it was the best: though even then the considerations which recommended it may, like so many other primeval social facts of the greatest importance, have subsequently, in the course of ages, ceased to exist. But the state of the case is in every respect the reverse of this. In the first place, the opinion in favour of the present system, which entirely subordinates the weaker sex to the stronger, rests upon theory only; for there never has been trial made of any other: so that experience, in the sense in which it is vulgarly opposed to theory, cannot be pretended to have pronounced any verdict. And in the second place, the adoption of this system of inequality never was the result of deliberation, or forethought, or any social ideas, or any notion whatever of what conduced to the benefit of humanity or the good order of society. It arose simply from the fact that from the very earliest twilight of human society, every woman (owing to the value attached to her by men, combined with her inferiority in muscular strength) was found in a state of bondage to some man. Laws and systems of polity always begin by recognising the relations they find already existing between individuals. They convert what was a mere physical fact into a legal right, give it the sanction of society, and principally aim at the substitution of public and organized means of asserting and protecting these rights, instead of the irregular and lawless conflict of physical strength. Those who had already been compelled to obedience became in this manner legally bound to it. Slavery, from being a mere affair of force between the master and the slave, became regularized and a matter of compact among the masters, who, binding themselves to one another for common protection, guaranteed by their collective strength the private possessions of

each, including his slaves. In early times, the great majority of the male sex were slaves, as well as the whole of the female. And many ages elapsed, some of them ages of high cultivation, before any thinker was bold enough to question the rightfulness, and the absolute social necessity, either of the one slavery or of the other. By degrees such thinkers did arise: and (the general progress of society assisting) the slavery of the male sex has, in all the countries of Christian Europe at least (though, in one of them, only within the last few years) been at length abolished,[1] and that of the female sex has been gradually changed into a milder form of dependence. But this dependence, as it exists at present, is not an original institution, taking a fresh start from considerations of justice and social expediency—it is the primitive state of slavery lasting on, through successive mitigations and modifications occasioned by the same causes which have softened the general manners, and brought all human relations more under the control of justice and the influence of humanity. It has not lost the taint of its brutal origin. No presumption in its favour, therefore, can be drawn from the fact of its existence. The only such presumption which it could be supposed to have, must be grounded on its having lasted till now, when so many other things which came down from the same odious source have been done away with. And this, indeed, is what makes it strange to ordinary ears, to hear it asserted that the inequality of rights between men and women has no other source than the law of the strongest.

That this statement should have the effect of a paradox, is in some respects creditable to the progress of civilization, and the improvement of the moral sentiments of mankind. We now live—that is to say, one or two of the most advanced nations of the world now live—in a state in which the law of the strongest seems to be entirely abandoned as the regulating principle of the world's affairs: nobody professes it, and, as regards most of the relations between human beings, nobody is permitted to practise it. When any one succeeds in doing so, it is under cover of some pretext which gives him the semblance of having

1. [Legal chattel slavery was abolished in the British Empire in 1833, in the French West Indies in 1848, and in the United States in 1865.—S.M.O.]

some general social interest on his side. This being the ostensible state of things, people flatter themselves that the rule of mere force is ended; that the law of the strongest cannot be the reason of existence of anything which has remained in full operation down to the present time. However any of our present institutions may have begun, it can only, they think, have been preserved to this period of advanced civilization by a well-grounded feeling of its adaptation to human nature, and conduciveness to the general good. They do not understand the great vitality and durability of institutions which place right on the side of might; how intensely they are clung to; how the good as well as the bad propensities and sentiments of those who have power in their hands, become identified with retaining it; how slowly these bad institutions give way, one at a time, the weakest first, beginning with those which are least interwoven with the daily habits of life; and how very rarely those who have obtained legal power because they first had physical, have ever lost their hold of it until the physical power had passed over to the other side. Such shifting of the physical force not having taken place in the case of women; this fact, combined with all the peculiar and characteristic features of the particular case, made it certain from the first that this branch of the system of right founded on might, though softened in its most atrocious features at an earlier period than several of the others, would be the very last to disappear. It was inevitable that this one case of a social relation grounded on force, would survive through generations of institutions grounded on equal justice, an almost solitary exception to the general character of their laws and customs; but which, so long as it does not proclaim its own origin, and as discussion has not brought out its true character, is not felt to jar with modern civilization, any more than domestic slavery among the Greeks jarred with their notion of themselves as a free people.

The truth is, that people of the present and the last two or three generations have lost all practical sense of the primitive condition of humanity; and only the few who have studied history accurately, or have much frequented the parts of the world occupied by the living representatives of ages long past, are able to form any mental picture of what society then was. People are not aware how entirely, in former ages, the law of superior strength was the rule of life; how publicly and openly it was avowed, I do not say cynically or shamelessly—for these words imply a feeling that there was something in it to be ashamed of, and no such notion could find a place in the faculties of any person in those ages, except a philosopher or a saint. History gives a cruel experience of human nature, in shewing how exactly the regard due to the life, possessions, and entire earthly happiness of any class of persons, was measured by what they had the power of enforcing; how all who made any resistance to authorities that had arms in their hands, however dreadful might be the provocation, had not only the law of force but all other laws, and all the notions of social obligation against them; and in the eyes of those whom they resisted, were not only guilty of crime, but of the worst of all crimes, deserving the most cruel chastisement which human beings could inflict. The first small vestige of a feeling of obligation in a superior to acknowledge any right in inferiors, began when he had been induced, for convenience, to make some promise to them. Though these promises, even when sanctioned by the most solemn oaths, were for many ages revoked or violated on the most trifling provocation or temptation, it is probable that this, except by persons of still worse than the average morality, was seldom done without some twinges of conscience. The ancient republics, being mostly grounded from the first upon some kind of mutual compact, or at any rate formed by an union of persons not very unequal in strength, afforded, in consequence, the first instance of a portion of human relations fenced round, and placed under the dominion of another law than that of force. And though the original law of force remained in full operation between them and their slaves, and also (except so far as limited by express compact) between a commonwealth and its subjects, or other independent commonwealths; the banishment of that primitive law even from so narrow a field, commenced the regeneration of human nature, by giving birth to sentiments of which experience soon demonstrated the immense value even for material interests, and which thenceforward only required to be enlarged, not created. Though slaves were no part of the commonwealth, it was in the free states that slaves were first felt to have rights as human beings. The Stoics were, I believe, the first (except so far as the Jewish law constitutes an exception) who taught as a part of morality that men were bound by moral obligations to their slaves.[2] No one, after Christianity became ascendant, could ever again have been a stranger to this belief, in theory; nor, after the rise of the Catholic Church, was it ever without persons to stand up for it. Yet to enforce it was the most arduous task which Christianity ever had to perform. For more than a thousand years the Church kept up the contest, with hardly any perceptible success. It was not for want of power over men's minds. Its power was prodigious. It could make kings and nobles resign their most valued possessions to enrich the Church. It could make thousands, in the prime of life and the height of worldly advantages, shut themselves up in convents to work out their salvation by poverty, fasting, and prayer. It could send hundreds of thousands across land and sea, Europe and Asia, to give their lives for the deliverance of the Holy Sepulchre. It could make kings relinquish wives who were the object of their passionate attachment, because the Church declared that they were within the seventh (by our calculation the fourteenth) degree of relationship. All this it did; but it could not make men fight less with one another, nor tyrannize less cruelly over the serfs, and when they were able, over burgesses. It could not make them renounce either of the applications of force; force militant, or force triumphant. This they could never be induced to do until they were themselves in their turn compelled by superior force. Only by the growing power of kings was an end put to fighting except between kings, or competitors for kingship; only by the growth of a wealthy and warlike bourgeoisie in the fortified towns, and of a plebeian infantry which proved more powerful in the field than the undisciplined chivalry, was the insolent tyranny of the nobles over the bourgeoisie and peasantry brought within some bounds. It was persisted in not only until, but long after, the oppressed had obtained a power enabling them often to take conspicuous vengeance; and on the Continent much of it continued to the time of the French Revo-

lution, though in England the earlier and better organization of the democratic classes put an end to it sooner by establishing equal laws and free national institutions.

If people are mostly so little aware how completely, during the greater part of the duration of our species, the law of force was the avowed rule of general conduct, any other being only a special and exceptional consequence of peculiar ties—and from how very recent a date it is that the affairs of society in general have been even pretended to be regulated according to any moral law; as little do people remember or consider, how institutions and customs which never had any ground but the law of force, last on into ages and states of general opinion which never would have permitted their first establishment. Less than forty years ago, Englishmen might still by law hold human beings in bondage as saleable property: within the present century they might kidnap them and carry them off, and work them literally to death. This absolutely extreme case of the law of force, condemned by those who can tolerate almost every other form of arbitrary power, and which, of all others, presents features the most revolting to the feelings of all who look at it from an impartial position, was the law of civilized and Christian England within the memory of persons now living: and in one half of Anglo-Saxon America three or four years ago, not only did slavery exist, but the slave trade, and the breeding of slaves expressly for it, was a general practice between slave states. Yet not only was there a greater strength of sentiment against it, but, in England at least, a less amount either of feeling or of interest in favour of it, than of any other of the customary abuses of force: for its motive was the love of gain, unmixed and undisguised; and those who profited by it were a very small numerical fraction of the country, while the natural feeling of all who were not personally interested in it, was unmitigated abhorrence. So extreme an instance makes it almost superfluous to refer to any other: but consider the long duration of absolute monarchy. In England at present it is the almost universal conviction that military despotism is a case of the law of force, having no other origin or justification. Yet in all the great nations of Europe except England it either still exists, or has only just ceased to exist, and has even now a strong party favourable

2. [Stoicism was a Greek and Roman school of philosophy founded by Zeno about 300 B.C.E. and influential until about 200 C.E. The obligations between rulers and ruled were among the Stoics' central concerns.]

to it in all ranks of the people, especially among persons of station and consequence. Such is the power of an established system, even when far from universal; when not only in almost every period of history there have been great and well-known examples of the contrary system, but these have almost invariably been afforded by the most illustrious and most prosperous communities. In this case, too, the possessor of the undue power, the person directly interested in it, is only one person, while those who are subject to it and suffer from it are literally all the rest. The yoke is naturally and necessarily humiliating to all persons, except the one who is on the throne, together with, at most, the one who expects to succeed to it. How different are these cases from that of the power of men over women! I am not now prejudging the question of its justifiableness. I am showing how vastly more permanent it could not but be, even if not justifiable, than these other dominations which have nevertheless lasted down to our own time. Whatever gratification of pride there is in the possession of power, and whatever personal interest in its exercise, is in this case not confined to a limited class, but common to the whole male sex. Instead of being, to most of its supporters, a thing desirable chiefly in the abstract, or, like the political ends usually contended for by factions, of little private importance to any but the leaders; it comes home to the person and hearth of every male head of a family, and of every one who looks forward to being so. The clodhopper exercises, or is to exercise, his share of the power equally with the highest nobleman. And the case is that in which the desire of power is the strongest: for every one who desires power, desires it most over those who are nearest to him, with whom his life is passed, with whom he has most concerns in common, and in whom any independence of his authority is oftenest likely to interfere with his individual preferences. If, in the other cases specified, powers manifestly grounded only on force, and having so much less to support them, are so slowly and with so much difficulty got rid of, much more must it be so with this, even if it rests on no better foundation than those. We must consider, too, that the possessors of the power have facilities in this case, greater than in any other, to prevent any uprising against it. Every one of the subjects lives under the very eye, and almost, it may be said,

in the hands, of one of the masters—in closer intimacy with him than with any of her fellow-subjects; with no means of combining against him, no power of even locally overmastering him, and, on the other hand, with the strongest motives for seeking his favour and avoiding to give him offence. In struggles for political emancipation, everybody knows how often its champions are bought off by bribes, or daunted by terrors. In the case of women, each individual of the subject-class is in a chronic state of bribery and intimidation combined. In setting up the standard of resistance, a large number of the leaders, and still more of the followers, must make an almost complete sacrifice of the pleasures or the alleviations of their own individual lot. If ever any system of privilege and enforced subjection had its yoke tightly riveted on the necks of those who are kept down by it, this has. I have not yet shown that it is a wrong system: but every one who is capable of thinking on the subject must see that even if it is, it was certain to outlast all other forms of unjust authority. And when some of the grossest of the other forms still exist in many civilized countries, and have only recently been got rid of in others, it would be strange if that which is so much the deepest-rooted had yet been perceptibly shaken anywhere. There is more reason to wonder that the protests and testimonies against it should have been so numerous and so weighty as they are.

Some will object, that a comparison cannot fairly be made between the government of the male sex and the forms of unjust power which I have adduced in illustration of it, since these are arbitrary, and the effect of mere usurpation, while it on the contrary is natural. But was there ever any domination which did not appear natural to those who possessed it? There was a time when the division of mankind into two classes, a small one of masters and a numerous one of slaves, appeared, even to the most cultivated minds, to be a natural, and the only natural, condition of the human race. No less an intellect, and one which contributed no less to the progress of human thought, than Aristotle, held this opinion without doubt or misgiving; and rested it on the same premises on which the same assertion in regard to the dominion of men over women is usually based, namely that there are different natures among mankind, free natures, and slave natures; that the Greeks were of a free nature, the barbarian races of Thracians and Asiatics of a slave nature.[3] But why need I go back to Aristotle? Did not the slaveowners of the Southern United States maintain the same doctrine, with all the fanaticism with which men cling to the theories that justify their passions and legitimate their personal interests? Did they not call heaven and earth to witness that the dominion of white man over the black is natural, that the black race is by nature incapable of freedom, and marked out for slavery? some even going so far as to say that the freedom of manual labourers is an unnatural order of things anywhere. Again, the theorists of absolute monarchy have always affirmed it to be the only natural form of government; issuing from the patriarchal, which was the primitive and spontaneous form of society, framed on the model of the paternal, which is anterior to society itself, and, as they contend, the most natural authority of all. Nay, for that matter, the law of force itself, to those who could not plead any other, has always seemed the most natural of all grounds for the exercise of authority. Conquering races hold it to be Nature's own dictate that the conquered should obey the conquerors, or, as they euphoniously paraphrase it, that the feebler and more unwarlike races should submit to the braver and manlier. The smallest acquaintance with human life in the middle ages, shows how supremely natural the dominion of the feudal nobility over men of low condition appeared to the nobility themselves, and how unnatural the conception seemed, of a person of the inferior class claiming equality with them, or exercising authority over them. It hardly seemed less so to the class held in subjection. The emancipated serfs and burgesses, even in their most vigorous struggles, never made any pretension to a share of authority; they only demanded more or less of limitation to the power of tyrannizing over them. So true is it that unnatural generally means only uncustomary, and that everything which is usual appears natural. The subjection of women to men being a universal custom, any departure from it quite naturally appears unnatural. But how entirely, even in this case, the feeling is dependent on custom, appears by ample experience. Nothing so much aston-ishes the people of distant parts of the world, when they first learn anything about England, as to be told that it is under a queen: the thing seems to them so unnatural as to be almost incredible. To Englishmen this does not seem in the least degree unnatural, because they are used to it; but they do feel it unnatural that women should be soldiers or members of Parliament. In the feudal ages, on the contrary, war and politics were not thought unnatural to women, because not unusual; it seemed natural that women of the privileged classes should be of manly character, inferior in nothing but bodily strength to their husbands and fathers. The independence of women seemed rather less unnatural to the Greeks than to other ancients, on account of the fabulous Amazons (whom they believed to be historical), and the partial example afforded by the Spartan women; who, though no less subordinate by law than in other Greek states, were more free in fact, and being trained to bodily exercises in the same manner with men, gave ample proof that they were not naturally disqualified for them. There can be little doubt that Spartan experience suggested to Plato, among many other of his doctrines, that of the social and political equality of the two sexes.[4]

But, it will be said, the rule of men over women differs from all these others in not being a rule of force: it is accepted voluntarily; women make no complaint, and are consenting parties to it. In the first place, a great number of women do not accept it. Ever since there have been women able to make their sentiments known by their writings (the only mode of publicity which society permits to them), an increasing number of them have recorded protests against their present social condition: and recently many thousands of them, headed by the most eminent women known to the public, have petitioned Parliament for their admission to the Parliamentary Suffrage.[5] The claim of women to be educated as solidly, and in the same branches of knowledge, as men, is urged with growing intensity, and with a great

---

3. [Aristotle, *Politics*, Bk. 1, 1252B, 1254A–55A, Bk. 7, 1327B.]

4. [Plato, *Republic*, Bk. 5, 451–60.]

5. [This petition for extension of the franchise to all male and female householders was presented by Mill, the M. P. for Westminster, to the House of Commons, on June 7, 1866.]

prospect of success; while the demand for their admission into professions and occupations hitherto closed against them, becomes every year more urgent. Though there are not in this country, as there are in the United States, periodical Conventions and an organized party to agitate for the Rights of Women, there is a numerous and active Society organized and managed by women, for the more limited object of obtaining the political franchise. Nor is it only in our own country and in America that women are beginning to protest, more or less collectively, against the disabilities under which they labour. France, and Italy, and Switzerland, and Russia now afford examples of the same thing. How many more women there are who silently cherish similar aspirations, no one can possibly know; but there are abundant tokens how many *would* cherish them, were they not so strenuously taught to repress them as contrary to the proprieties of their sex. It must be remembered, also, that no enslaved class ever asked for complete liberty at once. When Simon de Montfort called the deputies of the commons to sit for the first time in Parliament, did any of them dream of demanding that an assembly, elected by their constituents, should make and destroy ministries, and dictate to the king in affairs of state? No such thought entered into the imagination of the most ambitious of them. The nobility had already these pretensions; the commons pretended to nothing but to be exempt from arbitrary taxation, and from the gross individual oppression of the king's officers. It is a political law of nature that those who are under any power of ancient origin, never begin by complaining of the power itself, but only of its oppressive exercise. There is never any want of women who complain of ill usage by their husbands. There would be infinitely more, if complaint were not the greatest of all provocatives to a repetition and increase of the ill usage. It is this which frustrates all attempts to maintain the power but protect the woman against its abuses. In no other case (except that of a child) is the person who has been proved judicially to have suffered an injury, replaced under the physical power of the culprit who inflicted it. Accordingly wives, even in the most extreme and Protracted cases of bodily ill usage, hardly ever dare avail themselves of the laws made for their protection: and if, in a moment of irrepressible indignation, or

by the interference of neighbours, they are induced to do so, their whole effort afterwards is to disclose as little as they can, and to beg off their tyrant from his merited chastisement.

All causes, social and natural, combine to make it unlikely that women should be collectively rebellious to the power of men. They are so far in a position different from all other subject classes, that their masters require something more from them than actual service. Men do not want solely the obedience of women, they want their sentiments. All men, except the most brutish, desire to have, in the woman most nearly connected with them, not a forced slave but a willing one, not a slave merely, but a favourite. They have therefore put everything in practice to enslave their minds. The masters of all other slaves rely, for maintaining obedience, on fear; either fear of themselves, or religious fears. The masters of women wanted more than simple obedience, and they turned the whole force of education to effect their purpose. All women are brought up from the very earliest years in the belief that their ideal of character is the very opposite to that of men; not self-will, and government by self-control, but submission, and yielding to the control of others. All the moralities tell them that it is the duty of women, and all the current sentimentalities that it is their nature, to live for others; to make complete abnegation of themselves, and to have no life but in their affections. And by their affections are meant the only ones they are allowed to have—those to the men with whom they are connected, or to the children who constitute an additional and indefeasible tie between them and a man. When we put together three things—first, the natural attraction between opposite sexes; secondly, the wife's entire dependence on the husband, every privilege or pleasure she has being either his gift, or depending entirely on his will; and lastly, that the principal object of human pursuit, consideration, and all objects of social ambition, can in general be sought or obtained by her only through him, it would be a miracle if the object of being attractive to men had not become the polar star of feminine education and formation of character. And, this great means of influence over the minds of women having been acquired, an instinct of selfishness made men avail themselves of it to the utmost as a means of holding women in subjection, by representing to them meekness, submissiveness, and resignation of all individual will into the hands of a man, as an essential part of sexual attractiveness. Can it be doubted that any of the other yokes which mankind have succeeded in breaking, would have subsisted till now if the same means had existed, and had been as sedulously used, to bow down their minds to it? If it had been made the object of the life of every young plebeian to find personal favour in the eyes of some patrician, of every young serf with some seigneur; if domestication with him, and a share of his personal affections, had been held out as the prize which they all should look out for, the most gifted and aspiring being able to reckon on the most desirable prizes; and if, when this prize had been obtained, they had been shut out by a wall of brass from all interests not centering in him, all feelings and desires but those which he shared or inculcated; would not serfs and seigneurs, plebeians and patricians, have been as broadly distinguished at this day as men and women are? and would not all but a thinker here and there, have believed the distinction to be a fundamental and unalterable fact in human nature?

The preceding considerations are amply sufficient to show that custom, however universal it may be, affords in this case no presumption, and ought not to create any prejudice, in favour of the arrangements which place women in social and political subjection to men. But I may go farther, and maintain that the course of history, and the tendencies of progressive human society, afford not only no presumption in favour of this system of inequality of rights, but a strong one against it; and that, so far as the whole course of human improvement up to this time, the whole stream of modern tendencies, warrants any inference on the subject, it is, that this relic of the past is discordant with the future, and must necessarily disappear.

For, what is the peculiar character of the modern world—the difference which chiefly distinguishes modern institutions, modern social ideas, modern life itself, from those of times long past? It is, that human beings are no longer born to their place in life, and chained down by an inexorable bond to the place they are born to, but are free to employ their faculties, and such favourable chances as offer, to achieve the lot which may appear to them most desirable. Human society of old was constituted on a very different principle. All were born to a fixed social position, and were mostly kept in it by law, or interdicted from any means by which they could emerge from it. As some men are born white and others black, so some were born slaves and others freemen and citizens; some were born patricians, other plebeians; some were born feudal nobles, others commoners and *roturiers*. A slave or serf could never make himself free, nor, except by the will of his master, become so. In most European countries it was not till towards the close of the middle ages, and as a consequence of the growth of regal power, that commoners could be ennobled. Even among nobles, the eldest son was born the exclusive heir to the paternal possessions, and a long time elapsed before it was fully established that the father could disinherit him. Among the industrious classes, only those who were born members of a guild, or were admitted into it by its members, could lawfully practise their calling within its local limits; and nobody could practise any calling deemed important, in any but the legal manner—by processes authoritatively prescribed. Manufacturers have stood in the pillory for presuming to carry on their business by new and improved methods. In modern Europe, and most in those parts of it which have participated most largely in all other modern improvements, diametrically opposite doctrines now prevail. Law and government do not undertake to prescribe by whom any social or industrial operation shall or shall not be conducted, or what modes of conducting them shall be lawful. These things are left to the unfettered choice of individuals. Even the laws which required that workmen should serve an apprenticeship, have in this country been repealed: there being ample assurance that in all cases in which an apprenticeship is necessary, its necessity will suffice to enforce it. The old theory was, that the least possible should be left to the choice of the individual agent; that all he had to do should, as far as practicable, be laid down for him by superior wisdom. Left to himself he was sure to go wrong. The modern conviction, the fruit of a thousand years of experience, is, that things in which the individual is the person directly interested, never go right but as they are left to his own discretion; and that any regulation of them by authority, except to protect the rights of others, is sure to be mischievous. This conclusion, slowly arrived at, and not adopted until almost every possible application of the contrary theory had been made with disastrous result, now (in the industrial department) prevails universally in the most advanced countries, almost universally in all that have pretensions to any sort of advancement. It is not that all processes are supposed to be equally good, or all persons to be equally qualified for everything; but that freedom of individual choice is now known to be the only thing which procures the adoption of the best processes, and throws each operation into the hands of those who are best qualified for it. Nobody thinks it necessary to make a law that only a strong-armed man shall be a blacksmith. Freedom and competition suffice to make blacksmiths strong-armed men, because the weak-armed can earn more by engaging in occupations for which they are more fit. In consonance with this doctrine, it is felt to be an overstepping of the proper bounds of authority to fix beforehand, on some general presumption, that certain persons are not fit to do certain things. It is now thoroughly known and admitted that if some such presumptions exist, no such presumption is infallible. Even if it be well grounded in a majority of cases, which it is very likely not to be, there will be a minority of exceptional cases in which it does not hold: and in those it is both an injustice to the individuals, and a detriment to society, to place barriers in the way of their using their faculties for their own benefit and for that of others. In the cases, on the other hand, in which the unfitness is real, the ordinary motives of human conduct will on the whole suffice to prevent the incompetent person from making, or from persisting in, the attempt.

If this general principle of social and economical science is not true; if individuals, with such help as they can derive from the opinion of those who know them, are not better judges than the law and the government, of their own capacities and vocation; the world cannot too soon abandon this principle, and return to the old system of regulations and disabilities. But if the principle is true, we ought to act as if we believed it, and not to ordain that to be born a girl instead of a boy, any more than to be born black instead of white, or a commoner instead of a nobleman, shall decide the person's position through all

life—shall interdict people from all the more elevated social positions, and from all, except a few, respectable occupations. Even were we to admit the utmost that is ever pretended as to the superior fitness of men for all the functions now reserved to them, the same argument applies which forbids a legal qualification for members of Parliament. If only once in a dozen years the conditions of eligibility exclude a fit person, there is a real loss, while the exclusion of thousands of unfit persons is no gain; for if the constitution of the electoral body disposes them to choose unfit persons, there are always plenty of such persons to choose from. In all things of any difficulty and importance, those who can do them well are fewer than the need, even with the most unrestricted latitude of choice: and any limitation of the field of selection deprives society of some chances of being served by the competent, without ever saving it from the incompetent.

At present, in the more improved countries, the disabilities of women are the only case, save one, in which laws and institutions take persons at their birth, and ordain that they shall never in all their lives be allowed to compete for certain things. The one exception is that of royalty. Persons still are born to the throne; no one, not of the reigning family, can ever occupy it, and no one even of that family can, by any means but the course of hereditary succession, attain it. All other dignities and social advantages are open to the whole male sex: many indeed are only attainable by wealth, but wealth may be striven for by any one, and is actually obtained by many men of the very humblest origin. The difficulties, to the majority, are indeed insuperable without the aid of fortunate accidents; but no male human being is under any legal ban: neither law nor opinion superadd artificial obstacles to the natural ones. Royalty, as I have said, is excepted: but in this case every one feels it to be an exception—an anomaly in the modern world, in marked opposition to its customs and principles, and to be justified only by extraordinary special expediencies, which, though individuals and nations differ in estimating their weight, unquestionably do in fact exist. But in this exceptional case, in which a high social function is, for important reasons, bestowed on birth instead of being put up to competition, all free nations contrive to adhere in substance to the principle from which they nominally derogate; for they circumscribe this high function by conditions avowedly intended to prevent the person to whom it ostensibly belongs from really performing it; while the person by whom it is performed, the responsible minister, does obtain the post by a competition from which no full-grown citizen of the male sex is legally excluded. The disabilities, therefore, to which women are subject from the mere fact of their birth, are the solitary examples of the kind in modern legislation. In no instance except this, which comprehends half the human race, are the higher social functions closed against any one by a fatality of birth which no exertions, and no change of circumstances, can overcome; for even religious disabilities (besides that in England and in Europe they have practically almost ceased to exist) do not close any career to the disqualified person in case of conversion.

The social subordination of women thus stands out an isolated fact in modern social institutions; a solitary breach of what has become their fundamental law; a single relic of an old world of thought and practice exploded in everything else, but retained in the one thing of most universal interest; as if a gigantic dolmen, or a vast temple of Jupiter Olympius, occupied the site of St. Paul's and received daily worship, while the surrounding Christian churches were only resorted to on fasts and festivals. This entire discrepancy between one social fact and all those which accompany it, and the radical opposition between its nature and the progressive movement which is the boast of the modern world, and which has successively swept away everything else of an analogous character, surely affords, to a conscientious observer of human tendencies, serious matter for reflection. It raises a *primâ facie* presumption on the unfavourable side, far outweighing any which custom and usage could in such circumstances create on the favourable; and should at least suffice to make this, like the choice between republicanism and royalty, a balanced question.

The least that can be demanded is, that the question should not be considered as prejudged by existing fact and existing opinion, but open to discussion on its merits, as a question of justice and expediency: the decision on this, as on any of the other social arrangements of mankind, depending on what an enlightened estimate of tendencies and consequences may show to be most advantageous to humanity in general, without distinction of sex. And the discussion must be a real discussion, descending to foundations, and not resting satisfied with vague and general assertions. It will not do, for instance, to assert in general terms, that the experience of mankind has pronounced in favour of the existing system. Experience cannot possibly have decided between two courses, so long as there has only been experience of one. If it be said that the doctrine of the equality of the sexes rests only on theory, it must be remembered that the contrary doctrine also has only theory to rest upon. All that is proved in its favour by direct experience, is that mankind have been able to exist under it, and to attain the degree of improvement and prosperity which we now see; but whether that prosperity has been attained sooner, or is now greater, than it would have been under the other system, experience does not say. On the other hand, experience does say, that every step in improvement has been so invariably accompanied by a step made in raising the social position of women, that historians and philosophers have been led to adopt their elevation or debasement as on the whole the surest test and most correct measure of the civilization of a people or an age.[6] Through all the progressive period of human history, the condition of women has been approaching nearer to equality with men. This does not of itself prove that the assimilation must go on to complete equality; but it assuredly affords some presumption that such is the case.

Neither does it avail anything to say that the *nature* of the two sexes adapts them to their present functions and position, and renders these appropriate to them. Standing on the ground of common sense and the constitution of the human mind, I deny that any one knows, or can know, the nature of the two sexes, as long as they have only been seen in their present relation to one another. If men had ever been found in society without women, or women without men, or if there had been a society of men and women in which the women were not under the control of the men, something might have been positively known about the mental and moral differences which may

6. [Charles Fourier and Karl Marx were two such philosophers.]

be inherent in the nature of each. What is now called the nature of women is an eminently artificial thing—the result of forced repression in some directions, unnatural stimulation in others. It may be asserted without scruple, that no other class of dependents have had their character so entirely distorted from its natural proportions by their relation with their masters; for, if conquered and slave races have been, in some respects, more forcibly repressed, whatever in them has not been crushed down by an iron heel has generally been let alone, and if left with any liberty of development, it has developed itself according to its own laws; but in the case of women, a hot-house and stove cultivation has always been carried on of some of the capabilities of their nature, for the benefit and pleasure of their masters. Then, because certain products of the general vital force sprout luxuriantly and reach a great development in this heated atmosphere and under this active nurture and watering, while other shoots from the same root, which are left outside in the wintry air, with ice purposely heaped all round them, have a stunted growth, and some are burnt off with fire and disappear; men, with that inability to recognise their own work which distinguishes the unanalytic mind, indolently believe that the tree grows of itself in the way they have made it grow, and that it would die if one half of it were not kept in a vapour bath and the other half in the snow.

Of all difficulties which impede the progress of thought, and the formation of well-grounded opinions on life and social arrangements, the greatest is now the unspeakable ignorance and inattention of mankind in respect to the influences which form human character. Whatever any portion of the human species now are, or seem to be, such, it is supposed, they have a natural tendency to be: even when the most elementary knowledge of the circumstances in which they have been placed, clearly points out the causes that made them what they are. Because a cottier deeply in arrears to his landlord is not industrious, there are people who think that the Irish are naturally idle. Because constitutions can be overthrown when the authorities appointed to execute them turn their arms against them, there are people who think the French incapable of free government. Because the Greeks cheated the Turks, and the Turks only plundered the

Greeks, there are persons who think that the Turks are naturally more sincere: and because women, as is often said, care nothing about politics except their personalities, it is supposed that the general good is naturally less interesting to women than to men. History, which is now so much better understood than formerly, teaches another lesson: if only by showing the extraordinary susceptibility of human nature to external influences, and the extreme variableness of those of its manifestations which are supposed to be most universal and uniform. But in history, as in travelling, men usually see only what they already had in their own minds; and few learn much from history, who do not bring much with them to its study.

Hence, in regard to that most difficult question, what are the natural differences between the two sexes—a subject on which it is impossible in the present state of society to obtain complete and correct knowledge—while almost everybody dogmatizes upon it, almost all neglect and make light of the only means by which any partial insight can be obtained into it. This is, an analytic study of the most important department of psychology, the laws of the influence of circumstances on character. For, however great and apparently ineradicable the moral and intellectual differences between men and women might be, the evidence of their being natural differences could only be negative. Those only could be inferred to be natural which could not possibly be artificial—the residuum, after deducting every characteristic of either sex which can admit of being explained from education or external circumstances. The profoundest knowledge of the laws of the formation of character is indispensable to entitle any one to affirm even that there is any difference, much more what the difference is, between the two sexes considered as moral and rational beings; and since no one, as yet, has that knowledge, (for there is hardly any subject which, in proportion to its importance, has been so little studied), no one is thus far entitled to any positive opinion on the subject. Conjectures are all that can at present be made; conjectures more or less probable, according as more or less authorized by such knowledge as we yet have of the laws of psychology, as applied to the formation of character.

Even the preliminary knowledge, what the differences between the sexes now are, apart from all question as to how they are made what they are, is still in the crudest and most incomplete state. Medical practitioners and physiologists have ascertained, to some extent, the differences in bodily constitution; and this is an important element to the psychologist: but hardly any medical practitioner is a psychologist. Respecting the mental characteristics of women; their observations are of no more worth than those of common men. It is a subject on which nothing final can be known, so long as those who alone can really know it, women themselves, have given but little testimony, and that little, mostly suborned. It is easy to know stupid women. Stupidity is much the same all the world over. A stupid person's notions and feelings may confidently be inferred from those which prevail in the circle by which the person is surrounded. Not so with those whose opinions and feelings are an emanation from their own nature and faculties. It is only a man here and there who has any tolerable knowledge of the character even of the women of his own family. I do not mean, of their capabilities; these nobody knows, not even themselves, because most of them have never been called out. I mean their actually existing thoughts and feelings. Many a man thinks he perfectly understands women, because he has had amatory relations with several, perhaps with many of them. If he is a good observer, and his experience extends to quality as well as quantity, he may have learnt something of one narrow department of their nature—an important department, no doubt. But of all the rest of it, few persons are generally more ignorant, because there are few from whom it is so carefully hidden. The most favourable case which a man can generally have for studying the character of a woman, is that of his own wife: for the opportunities are greater, and the cases of complete sympathy not so unspeakably rare. And in fact, this is the source from which any knowledge worth having on the subject has, I believe, generally come. But most men have not had the opportunity of studying in this way more than a single case: accordingly one can, to an almost laughable degree, infer what a man's wife is like, from his opinions about women in general. To make even this one case yield any result, the woman must be worth knowing, and the man not only a competent judge, but of a character so sympathetic in itself, and so well adapted to hers, that he can

either read her mind by sympathetic intuition, or has nothing in himself which makes her shy of disclosing it. Hardly anything, I believe, can be more rare than this conjunction. It often happens that there is the most complete unity of feeling and community of interests as to all external things, yet the one has as little admission into the internal life of the other as if they were common acquaintance. Even with true affection, authority on the one side and subordination on the other prevent perfect confidence. Though nothing may be intentionally withheld, much is not shown. In the analogous relation of parent and child, the corresponding phenomenon must have been in the observation of every one. As between father and son, how many are the cases in which the father, in spite of real affection on both sides, obviously to all the world does not know, nor suspect, parts of the son's character familiar to his companions and equals. The truth is, that the position of looking up to another is extremely unpropitious to complete sincerity and openness with him. The fear of losing ground in his opinion or in his feelings is so strong, that even in an upright character, there is an unconscious tendency to show only the best side, or the side which, though not the best, is that which he most likes to see: and it may be confidently said that thorough knowledge of one another hardly ever exists, but between persons who, besides being intimates, are equals. How much more true, then, must all this be, when the one is not only under the authority of the other, but has it inculcated on her as a duty to reckon everything else subordinate to his comfort and pleasure, and to let him neither see nor feel anything coming from her, except what is agreeable to him. All these difficulties stand in the way of a man's obtaining any thorough knowledge even of the one woman whom alone, in general, he has sufficient opportunity of studying. When we further consider that to understand one woman is not necessarily to understand any other woman; that even if he could study many women of one rank, or of one country, he would not thereby understand women of other ranks or countries; and even if he did, they are still only the women of a single period of history; we may safely assert that the knowledge which men can acquire of women, even as they have been and are, without reference to what they might be, is wretchedly imperfect and superficial, and always will be so, until women themselves have told all that they have to tell.

And this time has not come; nor will it come otherwise than gradually. It is but of yesterday that women have either been qualified by literary accomplishments, or permitted by society, to tell anything to the general public. As yet very few of them dare tell anything, which men, on whom their literary success depends, are unwilling to hear. Let us remember in what manner, up to a very recent time, the expression, even by a male author, of uncustomary opinions, or what are deemed eccentric feelings, usually was, and in some degree still is, received; and we may form some faint conception under what impediments a woman, who is brought up to think custom and opinion her sovereign rule, attempts to express in books anything drawn from the depths of her own nature. The greatest woman who has left writings behind her sufficient to give her an eminent rank in the literature of her country, thought it necessary to prefix as a motto to her boldest work, "Un homme peut braver l'opinion; une femme doit s'y soumettre."[7] The greater part of what women write about women is mere sycophancy to men. In the case of unmarried women, much of it seems only intended to increase their chance of a husband. Many, both married and unmarried, overstep the mark, and inculcate a servility beyond what is desired or relished by any man, except the very vulgarest. But this is not so often the case as, even at a quite late period, it still was. Literary women are becoming more freespoken, and more willing to express their real sentiments. Unfortunately, in this country especially, they are themselves such artificial products, that their sentiments are compounded of a small element of individual observation and consciousness, and a very large one of acquired associations. This will be less and less the case, but it will remain true to a great extent, as long as social institutions do not admit the same free development of originality in women which is possible to men. When that time comes, and not before, we shall see, and not merely hear, as much as it is necessary to

know of the nature of women, and the adaptation of other things to it.

I have dwelt so much on the difficulties which at present obstruct any real knowledge by men of the true nature of women, because in this as in so many other things "opinio, copiae inter maximas causas inopiae est;"[8] and there is little chance of reasonable thinking on the matter, while people flatter themselves that they perfectly understand a subject of which most men know absolutely nothing, and of which it is at present impossible that any man, or all men taken together, should have knowledge which can qualify them to lay down the law to women as to what is, or is not, their vocation. Happily, no such knowledge is necessary for any practical purpose connected with the position of women in relation to society and life. For, according to all the principles involved in modern society, the question rests with women themselves—to be decided by their own experience, and by the use of their own faculties. There are no means of finding what either one person or many can do, but by trying—and no means by which any one else can discover for them what it is for their happiness to do or leave undone.

One thing we may be certain of—that what is contrary to women's nature to do, they never will be made to do by simply giving their nature free play. The anxiety of mankind to interfere in behalf of nature, for fear lest nature should not succeed in effecting its purpose, is an altogether unnecessary solicitude. What women by nature cannot do, it is quite superfluous to forbid them from doing. What they can do, but not so well as the men who are their competitors, competition suffices to exclude them from; since nobody asks for protective duties and bounties in favour of women; it is only asked that the present bounties and protective duties in favour of men should be recalled. If women have a greater natural inclination for some things than for others, there is no need of laws or social inculcation to make the majority of them do the former in preference to the latter. Whatever women's services are most

7. ["A man can defy prejudice; a woman must submit to it." From the title page of Mme. de Staël's *Delphine* (1802).]

8. ["Popular opinion is deficient on most matters." From Francis Bacon's *Novum Organum* (1620). By using the present *est* instead of the subjunctive *sit*, Mill misquotes Bacon, thereby making a *more* pejorative judgment of the views of the many.]

wanted for, the free play of competition will hold out the strongest inducements to them to undertake. And, as the words imply, they are most wanted for the things for which they are most fit; by the apportionment of which to them, the collective faculties of the two sexes can be applied on the whole with the greatest sum of valuable result.

The general opinion of men is supposed to be, that the natural vocation of a woman is that of a wife and mother. I say, is supposed to be, because, judging from acts—from the whole of the present constitution of society—one might infer that their opinion was the direct contrary. They might be supposed to think that the alleged natural vocation of women was of all things the most repugnant to their nature; insomuch that if they are free to do anything else—if any other means of living, or occupation of their time and faculties, is open, which has any chance of appearing desirable to them—there will not be enough of them who will be willing to accept the condition said to be natural to them. If this is the real opinion of men in general, it would be well that it should be spoken out. I should like to hear somebody openly enunciating the doctrine (it is already implied in much that is written on the subject)—"It is necessary to society that women should marry and produce children. They will not do so unless they are compelled. Therefore it is necessary to compel them." The merits of the case would then be clearly defined. It would be exactly that of the slaveholders of South Carolina and Louisiana. "It is necessary that cotton and sugar should be grown. White men cannot produce them. Negroes will not, for any wages which we choose to give. *Ergo* they must be compelled." An illustration still closer to the point is that of impressment. Sailors must absolutely be had to defend the country. It often happens that they will not voluntarily enlist. Therefore there must be the power of forcing them. How often has this logic been used! and, but for one flaw in it, without doubt it would have been successful up to this day. But it is open to the retort—First pay the sailors the honest value of their labour. When you have made it as well worth their while to serve you, as to work for other employers, you will have no more difficulty than others have in obtaining their services. To this there is no logical answer except "I will not:" and as people are now not only ashamed,

but are not desirous, to rob the labourer of his hire, impressment is no longer advocated. Those who attempt to force women into marriage by closing all other doors against them, lay themselves open to a similar retort. If they mean what they say, their opinion must evidently be, that men do not render the married condition so desirable to women, as to induce them to accept it for its own recommendations. It is not a sign of one's thinking the boon one offers very attractive, when one allows only Hobson's choice, "that or none." And here, I believe, is the clue to the feelings of those men, who have a real antipathy to the equal freedom of women. I believe they are afraid, not lest women should be unwilling to marry, for I do not think that any one in reality has that apprehension; but lest they should insist that marriage should be on equal conditions; lest all women of spirit and capacity should prefer doing almost anything else, not in their own eyes degrading, rather than marry, when marrying is giving themselves a master, and a master too of all their earthly possessions. And truly, if this consequence were necessarily incident to marriage, I think that the apprehension would be very well founded. I agree in thinking it probable that few women, capable of anything else, would, unless under an irresistible *entrainement*, rendering them for the time insensible to anything but itself, choose such a lot, when any other means were open to them of filling a conventionally honourable place in life: and if men are determined that the law of marriage shall be a law of despotism, they are quite right, in point of mere policy, in leaving to women only Hobson's choice. But, in that case, all that has been done in the modern world to relax the chain on the minds of women, has been a mistake. They never should have been allowed to receive a literary education. Women who read, much more women who write, are, in the existing constitution of things, a contradiction and a disturbing element: and it was wrong to bring women up with any acquirements but those of an odalisque, or of a domestic servant.

CHAPTER II

It will be well to commence the detailed discussion of the subject by the particular branch of it to which the course of our observations has led us: the conditions which the laws of this and all other countries annex to the marriage contract. Marriage being the destination appointed by society for women, the prospect they are brought up to, and the object which it is intended should be sought by all of them, except those who are too little attractive to be chosen by any man as his companion; one might have supposed that everything would have been done to make this condition as eligible to them as possible, that they might have no cause to regret being denied the option of any other. Society, however, both in this, and, at first, in all other cases, has preferred to attain its object by foul rather than fair means: but this is the only case in which it has substantially persisted in them even to the present day. Originally women were taken by force, or regularly sold by their father to the husband. Until a late period in European history, the father had the power to dispose of his daughter in marriage at his own will and pleasure, without any regard to hers. The Church, indeed, was so far faithful to a better morality as to require a formal "yes" from the woman at the marriage ceremony; but there was nothing to shew that the consent was other than compulsory; and it was practically impossible for the girl to refuse compliance if the father persevered, except perhaps when she might obtain the protection of religion by a determined resolution to take monastic vows. After marriage, the man had anciently (but this was anterior to Christianity) the power of life and death over his wife. She could invoke no law against him; he was her sole tribunal and law. For a long time he could repudiate her, but she had no corresponding power in regard to him. By the old laws of England, the husband was called the *lord* of the wife; he was literally regarded as her sovereign, inasmuch that the murder of a man by his wife was called treason (*petty* as distinguished from *high* treason), and was more cruelly avenged than was usually the case with high treason, for the penalty was burning to death. Because these various enormities have fallen into disuse (for most of them were never formally abolished, or not until they had long ceased to be practised) men suppose that all is now as it should be in regard to the marriage contract; and we are continually told that civilization and Christianity have restored to the woman her just rights. Meanwhile the wife is the actual bondservant of her husband: no less so, as far as legal obligation goes, than slaves commonly so called. She vows a lifelong obedience to him at the altar, and is held to it all through her life by law. Casuists may say that the obligation of obedience stops short of participation in crime, but it certainly extends to everything else. She can do no act whatever but by his permission, at least tacit. She can acquire no property but for him; the instant it becomes hers, even if by inheritance, it becomes *ipso facto* his. In this respect the wife's position under the common law of England is worse than that of slaves in the laws of many countries: by the Roman law, for example, a slave might have his *peculium*, which to a certain extent the law guaranteed to him for his exclusive use. The higher classes in this country have given an analogous advantage to their women, through special contracts setting aside the law, by conditions of pin-money, &c.: since parental feeling being stronger with fathers than the class feeling of their own sex, a father generally prefers his own daughter to a son-in-law who is a stranger to him. By means of settlements, the rich usually contrive to withdraw the whole or part of the inherited property of the wife from the absolute control of the husband: but they do not succeed in keeping it under her own control; the utmost they can do only prevents the husband from squandering it, at the same time debarring the rightful owner from its use. The property itself is out of the reach of both; and as to the income derived from it, the form of settlement most favourable to the wife (that called "to her separate use") only precludes the husband from receiving it instead of her: it must pass through her hands, but if he takes it from her by personal violence as soon as she receives it, he can neither be punished, nor compelled to restitution. This is the amount of the protection which, under the laws of this country, the most powerful nobleman can give to his own daughter as respects her husband. In the immense majority of cases there is no settlement: and the absorption of all rights, all property, as well as all freedom of action, is complete. The two are called "one person in law," for the purpose of inferring that whatever is hers is his, but the parallel inference is never drawn that whatever is his is hers; the maxim is not applied against the man, except to make him responsible to third parties for her acts, as a master for the acts of his slaves or of his cattle. I am far from pretending that wives are in general no better treated than slaves; but no slave is a slave to the same lengths, and in so full a sense of the word, as a wife is. Hardly any slave, except one immediately attached to the master's person, is a slave at all hours and all minutes; in general he has, like a soldier, his fixed task, and when it is done, or when he is off duty, he disposes, within certain limits, of his own time, and has a family life into which the master rarely intrudes. "Uncle Tom" under his first master had his own life in his "cabin," almost as much as any man whose work takes him away from home, is able to have in his own family. But it cannot be so with the wife. Above all, a female slave has (in Christian countries) an admitted right, and is considered under a moral obligation, to refuse to her master the last familiarity. Not so the wife: however brutal a tyrant she may unfortunately be chained to—though she may know that he hates her, though it may be his daily pleasure to torture her, and though she may feel it impossible not to loathe him—he can claim from her and enforce the lowest degradation of a human being, that of being made the instrument of an animal function contrary to her inclinations. While she is held in this worst description of slavery as to her own person, what is her position in regard to the children in whom she and her master have a joint interest? They are by law *his* children. He alone has any legal rights over them. Not one act can she do towards or in relation to them, except by delegation from him. Even after he is dead she is not their legal guardian, unless he by will has made her so. He could even send them away from her, and deprive her of the means of seeing or corresponding with them, until this power was in some degree restricted by Serjeant Talfourd's Act.[9] This is her legal state. And from this state she has no means of withdrawing herself. If she leaves her husband, she can take nothing with her, neither her children nor anything which is rightfully her own. If he chooses, he can compel her to return, by law, or by physical force; or he may

content himself with seizing for his own use anything which she may earn, or which may be given to her by her relations. It is only legal separation by a decree of a court of justice, which entitles her to live apart, without being forced back into the custody of an exasperated jailer—or which empowers her to apply any earnings to her own use, without fear that a man whom perhaps she has not seen for twenty years will pounce upon her some day and carry all off. This legal separation, until lately, the courts of justice would only give at an expense which made it inaccessible to any one out of the higher ranks. Even now it is only given in cases of desertion, or of the extreme of cruelty; and yet complaints are made every day that it is granted too easily. Surely, if a woman is denied any lot in life but that of being the personal body-servant of a despot, and is dependent for everything upon the chance of finding one who may be disposed to make a favourite of her instead of merely a drudge, it is a very cruel aggravation of her fate that she should be allowed to try this chance only once. The natural sequel and corollary from this state of things would be, that since her all in life depends upon obtaining a good master, she should be allowed to change again and again until she finds one. I am not saying that she ought to be allowed this privilege. That is a totally different consideration. The question of divorce, in the sense involving liberty of remarriage, is one into which it is foreign to my purpose to enter. All I now say is, that to those to whom nothing but servitude is allowed, the free choice of servitude is the only, though a most insufficient, alleviation. Its refusal completes the assimilation of the wife to the slave—and the slave under not the mildest form of slavery: for in some slave codes the slave could, under certain circumstances of ill usage, legally compel the master to sell him. But no amount of ill usage, without adultery superadded, will in England free a wife from her tormentor.[10]

9. [The Infant Custody Act of 1839 (2 & 3 Victoria, c. 54) allowed the Court of Chancery to award to mothers custody of their children under the age of seven and access to those under sixteen.]

10. [Until 1857, divorce with permission to remarry was obtainable only through a private act of Parliament. In the nineteenth century, only about ten such divorces were granted per year, and only four had ever been granted to women. The Divorce Act of 1857 (20 & 21 Victoria, c. 85) allowed a husband to divorce his wife for adultery alone, but allowed a wife to divorce on

I have no desire to exaggerate, nor does the case stand in any need of exaggeration. I have described the wife's legal position, not her actual treatment. The laws of most countries are far worse than the people who execute them, and many of them are only able to remain laws by being seldom or never carried into effect. If married life were all that it might be expected to be, looking to the laws alone, society would be a hell upon earth. Happily there are both feelings and interests which in many men exclude, and in most, greatly temper, the impulses and propensities which lead to tyranny: and of those feelings, the tie which connects a man with his wife affords, in a normal state of things, incomparably the strongest example. The only tie which at all approaches to it, that between him and his children, tends, in all save exceptional cases, to strengthen, instead of conflicting with, the first. Because this is true; because men in general do not inflict, nor women suffer, all the misery which could be inflicted and suffered if the full power of tyranny with which the man is legally invested were acted on; the defenders of the existing form of the institution think that all its iniquity is justified, and that any complaint is merely quarrelling with the evil which is the price paid for every great good. But the mitigations in practice, which are compatible with maintaining in full legal force this or any other kind of tyranny, instead of being any apology for despotism, only serve to prove what power human nature possesses of reacting against the vilest institutions, and with what vitality the seeds of good as well as those of evil in human character diffuse and propagate themselves. Not a word can be said for despotism in the family which cannot be said for political despotism. Every absolute king does not sit at his window to enjoy the groans of his tortured subjects, nor strips them of their last rag and turns them out to shiver in the road. The despotism of Louis XVI was not the despotism of Philippe le Bel, or of Nadir Shah, or of Caligula; but it was bad enough to justify the French Revolution, and to palliate even its horrors. If an appeal be made to the intense attachments which exist between wives and their husbands, exactly as much may be said of domestic slavery. It was quite

_____

account of her husband's adultery only if he were also guilty of incest, bigamy, or extreme cruelty.]

an ordinary fact in Greece and Rome for slaves to submit to death by torture rather than betray their masters. In the proscriptions of the Roman civil wars it was remarked that wives and slaves were heroically faithful, sons very commonly treacherous. Yet we know how cruelly many Romans treated their slaves. But in truth these intense individual feelings nowhere rise to such a luxuriant height as under the most atrocious institutions. It is part of the irony of life, that the strongest feelings of devoted gratitude of which human nature seems to be susceptible, are called forth in human beings towards those who, having the power entirely to crush their earthly existence, voluntarily refrain from using that power. How great a place in most men this sentiment fills, even in religious devotion, it would be cruel to inquire. We daily see how much their gratitude to Heaven appears to be stimulated by the contemplation of fellow creatures to whom God has not been so merciful as he has to themselves.

Whether the institution to be defended is slavery, political absolutism, or the absolutism of the head of a family, we are always expected to judge of it from its best instances; and we are presented with pictures of loving exercise of authority on one side, loving submission to it on the other—superior wisdom ordering all things for the greatest good of the dependents, and surrounded by their smiles and benedictions. All this would be very much to the purpose if any one pretended that there are no such things as good men. Who doubts that there may be great goodness, and great happiness, and great affection, under the absolute government of a good man? Meanwhile, laws and institutions require to be adapted, not to good men, but to bad. Marriage is not an institution designed for a select few. Men are not required, as a preliminary to the marriage ceremony, to prove by testimonials that they are fit to be trusted with the exercise of absolute power. The tie of affection and obligation to a wife and children is very strong with those whose general social feelings are strong, and with many who are little sensible to any other social ties; but there are all degrees of sensibility and insensibility to it, as there are all grades of goodness and wickedness in men, down to those whom no ties will bind, and on whom society has no action but through its *ultima ratio*, the penalties of the law. In every grade of this descending scale are men to whom are committed all the legal powers of a husband. The vilest malefactor has some wretched woman tied to him, against whom he can commit any atrocity except killing her, and, if tolerably cautious, can do that without much danger of the legal penalty. And how many thousands are there among the lowest classes in every country, who, without being in a legal sense malefactors in any other respect, because in every other quarter their aggressions meet with resistance, indulge the utmost habitual excesses of bodily violence towards the unhappy wife, who alone, at least of grown persons, can neither repel nor escape from their brutality; and towards whom the excess of dependence inspires their mean and savage natures, not with a generous forbearance, and a point of honour to behave well to one whose lot in life is trusted entirely to their kindness, but on the contrary with a notion that the law has delivered her to them as their thing, to be used at their pleasure, and that they are not expected to practise the consideration towards her which is required from them towards everybody else. The law, which till lately left even these atrocious extremes of domestic oppression practically unpunished, has within these few years made some feeble attempts to repress them. But its attempts have done little, and cannot be expected to do much, because it is contrary to reason and experience to suppose that there can be any real check to brutality, consistent with leaving the victim still in the power of the executioner. Until a conviction for personal violence, or at all events a repetition of it after a first conviction, entitles the woman *ipso facto* to a divorce, or at least to a judicial separation, the attempt to repress these "aggravated assaults" by legal penalties will break down for want of a prosecutor, or for want of a witness.

When we consider how vast is the number of men, in any great country, who are little higher than brutes, and that this never prevents them from being able, through the law of marriage, to obtain a victim, the breadth and depth of human misery caused in this shape alone by the abuse of the institution swells to something appalling. Yet these are only the extreme cases. They are the lowest abysses, but there is a sad succession of depth after depth before reaching them. In domestic as in political tyranny, the case of absolute monsters chiefly illustrates the institution by showing that there is scarcely any horror which may not occur under it if the despot pleases, and thus setting in a strong light what must be the terrible frequency of things only a little less atrocious. Absolute fiends are as rare as angels, perhaps rarer: ferocious savages, with occasional touches of humanity, are however very frequent: and in the wide interval which separates these from any worthy representatives of the human species, how many are the forms and gradations of animalism and selfishness, often under an outward varnish of civilization and even cultivation, living at peace with the law, maintaining a creditable appearance to all who are not under their power, yet sufficient often to make the lives of all who are so, a torment and a burthen to them! It would be tiresome to repeat the commonplaces about the unfitness of men in general for power, which, after the political discussions of centuries, every one knows by heart, were it not that hardly any one thinks of applying these maxims to the case in which above all others they are applicable, that of power, not placed in the hands of a man here and there, but offered to every adult male, down to the basest and most ferocious. It is not because a man is not known to have broken any of the Ten Commandments, or because he maintains a respectable character in his dealings with those whom he cannot compel to have intercourse with him, or because he does not fly out into violent bursts of ill-temper against those who are not obliged to bear with him, that it is possible to surmise of what sort his conduct will be in the unrestraint of home. Even the commonest men reserve the violent, the sulky, the undisguisedly selfish side of their character for those who have no power to withstand it. The relation of superiors to dependents is the nursery of these vices of character, which, wherever else they exist, are an overflowing from that source. A man who is morose or violent to his equals, is sure to be one who has lived among inferiors, whom he could frighten or worry into submission. If the family in its best forms is, as it is often said to be, a school of sympathy, tenderness, and loving forgetfulness of self, it is still oftener, as respects its chief, a school of wilfulness, overbearingness, unbounded self-indulgence, and a double-dyed and idealized selfishness, of which sacrifice itself is only a particular form: the care for the wife and children being only care for them as parts of the man's own interests and belongings, and their individual happiness being immolated in every shape to his smallest preferences. What better is to be looked for under the existing form of the institution? We know that the bad propensities of human nature are only kept within bounds when they are allowed no scope for their indulgence. We know that from impulse and habit, when not from deliberate purpose, almost every one to whom others yield, goes on encroaching upon them, until a point is reached at which they are compelled to resist. Such being the common tendency of human nature; the almost unlimited power which present social institutions give to the man over at least one human being—the one with whom he resides, and whom he has always present—this power seeks out and evokes the latent germs of selfishness in the remotest corners of his nature—fans its faintest sparks and smouldering embers—offers to him a license for the indulgence of those points of his original character which in all other relations he would have found it necessary to repress and conceal, and the repression of which would in time have become a second nature. I know that there is another side to the question. I grant that the wife, if she cannot effectually resist, can at least retaliate; she, too, can make the man's life extremely uncomfortable, and by that power is able to carry many points which she ought, and many which she ought not, to prevail in. But this instrument of self-protection—which may be called the power of the scold, or the shrewish sanction—has the fatal defect, that it avails most against the least tyrannical superiors, and in favour of the least deserving dependents. It is the weapon of irritable and self-willed women; of those who would make the worst use of power if they themselves had it, and who generally turn this power to a bad use. The amiable cannot use such an instrument, the highminded disdain it. And on the other hand, the husbands against whom it is used most effectively are the gentler and more inoffensive; those who cannot be induced, even by provocation, to resort to any very harsh exercise of authority. The wife's power of being disagreeable generally only establishes a counter-tyranny, and makes victims in their turn chiefly of those husbands who are least inclined to be tyrants.

What is it, then, which really tempers the corrupting effects of the power, and makes it compatible with such amount of good as we actually see? Mere feminine blandishments, though of great effect in individual instances, have very little effect in modifying the general tendencies of the situation; for their power only lasts while the woman is young and attractive, often only while her charm is new, and not dimmed by familiarity; and on many men they have not much influence at any time. The real mitigating causes are, the personal affection which is the growth of time, in so far as the man's nature is susceptible of it, and the woman's character sufficiently congenial with his to excite it; their common interests as regards the children, and their general community of interest as concerns third persons (to which however there are very great limitations); the real importance of the wife to his daily comforts and enjoyments, and the value he consequently attaches to her on his personal account, which, in a man capable of feeling for others, lays the foundation of caring for her on her own; and lastly, the influence naturally acquired over almost all human beings by those near to their persons (if not actually disagreeable to them): who, both by their direct entreaties, and by the insensible contagion of their feelings and dispositions, are often able, unless counteracted by some equally strong personal influence, to obtain a degree of command over the conduct of the superior, altogether excessive and unreasonable. Through these various means, the wife frequently exercises even too much power over the man; she is able to affect his conduct in things in which she may not be qualified to influence it for good—in which her influence may be not only unenlightened, but employed on the morally wrong side; and in which he would act better if left to his own prompting. But neither in the affairs of families nor in those of states is power a compensation for the loss of freedom. Her power often gives her what she has no right to, but does not enable her to assert her own rights. A Sultan's favourite slave has slaves under her, over whom she tyrannizes; but the desirable thing would be that she should neither have slaves nor be a slave. By entirely sinking her own existence in her husband; by having no will (or persuading him that she has no will) but his, in anything which regards their joint relation, and by making it the business of her life to work upon his sentiments, a wife may gratify herself by influencing, and very probably perverting, his conduct, in those of his external relations which she has never qualified herself to judge of, or in which she is herself wholly influenced by some personal or other partiality or prejudice. Accordingly, as things now are, those who act most kindly to their wives, are quite as often made worse, as better, by the wife's influence, in respect to all interests extending beyond the family. She is taught that she has no business with things out of that sphere; and accordingly she seldom has any honest and conscientious opinion on them; and therefore hardly ever meddles with them for any legitimate purpose, but generally for an interested one. She neither knows nor cares which is the right side in politics, but she knows what will bring in money or invitations, give her husband a title, her son a place, or her daughter a good marriage.

But how, it will be asked, can any society exist without government? In a family, as in a state, some one person must be the ultimate ruler. Who shall decide when married people differ in opinion? Both cannot have their way, yet a decision one way or the other must be come to.

It is not true that in all voluntary association between two people, one of them must be absolute master: still less that the law must determine which of them it shall be. The most frequent case of voluntary association, next to marriage, is partnership in business: and it is not found or thought necessary to enact that in every partnership, one partner shall have entire control over the concern, and the others shall be bound to obey his orders. No one would enter into partnership on terms which would subject him to the responsibilities of a principal, with only the powers and privileges of a clerk or agent. If the law dealt with other contracts as it does with marriage, it would ordain that one partner should administer the common business as if it was his private concern; that the others should have only delegated powers; and that this one should be designated by some general presumption of law, for example as being the eldest. The law never does this: nor does experience show it to be necessary that any theoretical inequality of power should exist between the partners, or that the partnership should have any other conditions than what they may themselves appoint by their articles of agreement. Yet it might seem that the exclusive power might be conceded with less danger to the rights and interests

of the inferior, in the case of partnership than in that of marriage, since he is free to cancel the power by withdrawing from the connexion. The wife has no such power, and even if she had, it is almost always desirable that she should try all measures before resorting to it.

It is quite true that things which have to be decided every day, and cannot adjust themselves gradually, or wait for a compromise, ought to depend on one will: one person must have their sole control. But it does not follow that this should always be the same person. The natural arrangement is a division of powers between the two; each being absolute in the executive branch of their own department, and any change of system and principle requiring the consent of both. The division neither can nor should be pre-established by the law, since it must depend on individual capacities and suitabilities. If the two persons chose, they might pre-appoint it by the marriage contract, as pecuniary arrangements are now often pre-appointed. There would seldom be any difficulty in deciding such things by mutual consent, unless the marriage was one of those unhappy ones in which all other things, as well as this, become subjects of bickering and dispute. The division of rights would naturally follow the division of duties and functions; and that is already made by consent, or at all events not by law, but by general custom, modified and modifiable at the pleasure of the persons concerned.

The real practical decision of affairs, to whichever may be given the legal authority, will greatly depend, as it even now does, upon comparative qualifications. The mere fact that he is usually the eldest, will in most cases give the preponderance to the man; at least until they both attain a time of life at which the difference in their years is of no importance. There will naturally also be a more potential voice on the side, whichever it is, that brings the means of support. Inequality from this source does not depend on the law of marriage, but on the general conditions of human society, as now constituted. The influence of mental superiority, either general or special, and of superior decision of character, will necessarily tell for much. It always does so at present. And this fact shows how little foundation there is for the apprehension that the powers and responsibilities of partners in life (as of partners in business), cannot be satisfactorily apportioned by agreement between themselves. They always are so apportioned, except in cases in which the marriage institution is a failure. Things never come to an issue of downright power on one side, and obedience on the other, except where the connexion altogether has been a mistake, and it would be a blessing to both parties to be relieved from it. Some may say that the very thing by which an amicable settlement of differences becomes possible, is the power of legal compulsion known to be in reserve; as people submit to an arbitration because there is a court of law in the background, which they know that they can be forced to obey. But to make the cases parallel, we must suppose that the rule of the court of law was, not to try the cause, but to give judgment always for the same side, suppose the defendant. If so, the amenability to it would be a motive with the plaintiff to agree to almost any arbitration, but it would be just the reverse with the defendant. The despotic power which the law gives to the husband may be a reason to make the wife assent to any compromise by which power is practically shared between the two, but it cannot be the reason why the husband does. That there is always among decently conducted people a practical compromise, though one of them at least is under no physical or moral necessity of making it, shows that the natural motives which lead to a voluntary adjustment of the united life of two persons in a manner acceptable to both, do on the whole, except in unfavourable cases, prevail. The matter is certainly not improved by laying down as an ordinance of law, that the superstructure of free government shall be raised upon a legal basis of despotism on one side and subjection on the other, and that every concession which the despot makes may, at his mere pleasure, and without any warning, be recalled. Besides that no freedom is worth much when held on so precarious a tenure, its conditions are not likely to be the most equitable when the law throws so prodigious a weight into one scale; when the adjustment rests between two persons one of whom is declared to be entitled to everything, the other not only entitled to nothing except during the good pleasure of the first, but under the strongest moral and religious obligation not to rebel under any excess of oppression.

A pertinacious adversary, pushed to extremities, may say, that husbands indeed are willing to be reasonable, and to make fair concessions to their partners without being compelled to it, but that wives are not: that if allowed any rights of their own, they will acknowledge no rights at all in any one else, and never will yield in anything, unless they can be compelled, by the man's mere authority, to yield in everything. This would have been said by many persons some generations ago, when satires on women were in vogue, and men thought it a clever thing to insult women for being what men made them. But it will be said by no one now who is worth replying to. It is not the doctrine of the present day that women are less susceptible of good feeling, and consideration for those with whom they are united by the strongest ties, than men are. On the contrary, we are perpetually told that women are better than men, by those who are totally opposed to treating them as if they were as good; so that the saying has passed into a piece of tiresome cant, intended to put a complimentary face upon an injury, and resembling those celebrations of royal clemency which, according to Gulliver, the king of Lilliput always prefixed to his most sanguinary decrees.[11] If women are better than men in anything, it surely is in individual self-sacrifice for those of their own family. But I lay little stress on this, so long as they are universally taught that they are born and created for self-sacrifice. I believe that equality of rights would abate the exaggerated self-abnegation which is the present artificial ideal of feminine character, and that a good woman would not be more self-sacrificing than the best man: but on the other hand, men would be much more unselfish and self-sacrificing than at present, because they would no longer be taught to worship their own will as such a grand thing that it is actually the law for another rational being. There is nothing which men so easily learn as this self-worship: all privileged persons, and all privileged classes, have had it. The more we descend in the scale of humanity, the intenser it is; and most of all in those who are not, and can never expect to be, raised above any one except an unfortunate

11. [Jonathan Swift, Gulliver's Travels (1726), pt. 1, A Voyage to Lilliput, chap. 7. The more inhuman the punishment and the more innocent the victim, the greater were the king's professions of clemency and tenderness.]

wife and children. The honourable exceptions are proportionally fewer than in the case of almost any other human infirmity. Philosophy and religion, instead of keeping it in check, are generally suborned to defend it; and nothing controls it but that practical feeling of the equality of human beings, which is the theory of Christianity, but which Christianity will never practically teach, while it sanctions institutions grounded on an arbitrary preference of one human being over another.

There are, no doubt, women, as there are men, whom equality of consideration will not satisfy; with whom there is no peace while any will or wish is regarded but their own. Such persons are a proper subject for the law of divorce. They are only fit to live alone, and no human beings ought to be compelled to associate their lives with them. But the legal subordination tends to make such characters among women more, rather than less, frequent. If the man exerts his whole power, the woman is of course crushed: but if she is treated with indulgence, and permitted to assume power, there is no rule to set limits to her encroachments. The law, not determining her rights, but theoretically allowing her none at all, practically declares that the measure of what she has a right to, is what she can contrive to get.

The equality of married persons before the law, is not only the sole mode in which that particular relation can be made consistent with justice to both sides, and conducive to the happiness of both, but it is the only means of rendering the daily life of mankind, in any high sense, a school of moral cultivation. Though the truth may not be felt or generally acknowledged for generations to come, the only school of genuine moral sentiment is society between equals. The moral education of mankind has hitherto emanated chiefly from the law of force, and is adapted almost solely to the relations which force creates. In the less advanced states of society, people hardly recognise any relation with their equals. To be an equal is to be an enemy. Society, from its highest place to its lowest, is one long chain, or rather ladder, where every individual is either above or below his nearest neighbour, and wherever he does not command he must obey. Existing moralities, accordingly, are mainly fitted to a relation of command and obedience. Yet command and obedience are but unfortu-

nate necessities of human life: society in equality is its normal state. Already in modern life, and more and more as it progressively improves, command and obedience become exceptional facts in life, equal association its general rule. The morality of the first ages rested on the obligation to submit to power; that of the ages next following, on the right of the weak to the forbearance and protection of the strong. How much longer is one form of society and life to content itself with the morality made for another? We have had the morality of submission, and the morality of chivalry and generosity; the time is now come for the morality of justice. Whenever, in former ages, any approach has been made to society in equality, justice has asserted its claims as the foundation of virtue. It was thus in the free republics of antiquity. But even in the best of these, the equals were limited to the free male citizens; slaves, women, and the unenfranchised residents were under the law of force. The joint influence of Roman civilization and of Christianity obliterated these distinctions, and in theory (if only partially in practice) declared the claims of the human being, as such, to be paramount to those of sex, class, or social position. The barriers which had begun to be levelled were raised again by the northern conquests; and the whole of modern history consists of the slow process by which they have since been wearing away. We are entering into an order of things in which justice will again be the primary virtue; grounded as before on equal, but now also on sympathetic association; having its root no longer in the instinct of equals for self-protection, but in a cultivated sympathy between them; and no one being now left out, but an equal measure being extended to all. It is no novelty that mankind do not distinctly foresee their own changes, and that their sentiments are adapted to past, not to coming ages. To see the futurity of the species has always been the privilege of the intellectual élite, or of those who have learnt from them; to have the feelings of that futurity has been the distinction, and usually the martyrdom, of a still rarer élite. Institutions, books, education, society, all go on training human beings for the old, long after the new has come; much more when it is only coming. But the true virtue of human beings is fitness to live together as equals; claiming nothing for themselves but what they as freely conceded to every one else;

regarding command of any kind as an exceptional necessity, and in all cases a temporary one; and preferring, whenever possible, the society of those with whom leading and following can be alternate and reciprocal. To these virtues, nothing in life as at present constituted gives cultivation by exercise. The family is a school of despotism, in which the virtues of despotism, but also its vices, are largely nourished. Citizenship, in free countries, is partly a school of society in equality; but citizenship fills only a small place in modern life, and does not come near the daily habits or inmost sentiments. The family, justly constituted, would be the real school of the virtues of freedom. It is sure to be a sufficient one of everything else. It will always be a school of obedience for the children, of command for the parents. What is needed is, that it should be a school of sympathy in equality, of living together in love, without power on one side or obedience on the other. This it ought to be between the parents. It would then be an exercise of those virtues which each requires to fit them for all other association, and a model to the children of the feelings and conduct which their temporary training by means of obedience is designed to render habitual, and therefore natural, to them. The moral training of mankind will never be adapted to the conditions of the life for which all other human progress is a preparation, until they practise in the family the same moral rule which is adapted to the normal constitution of human society. Any sentiment of freedom which can exist in a man whose nearest and dearest intimacies are with those of whom he is absolute master, is not the genuine or Christian love of freedom, but, what the love of freedom generally was in the ancients and in the middle ages—an intense feeling of the dignity and importance of his own personality; making him disdain a yoke for himself, of which he has no abhorrence whatever in the abstract, but which he is abundantly ready to impose on others for his own interest or glorification.

I readily admit (and it is the very foundation of my hopes) that numbers of married people even under the present law, (in the higher classes of England probably a great majority,) live in the spirit of a just law of equality. Laws never would be improved, if there were not numerous persons whose moral senti-ments are better than the existing laws. Such persons ought to support the principles here advocated; of which the only object is to make all other married couples similar to what these are now. But persons even of considerable moral worth, unless they are also thinkers, are very ready to believe that laws or practices, the evils of which they have not personally experienced, do not produce any evils, but (if seeming to be generally approved of) probably do good, and that it is wrong to object to them. It would, however, be a great mistake in such married people to suppose, because the legal conditions of the tie which unites them do not occur to their thoughts once in a twelve-month, and because they live and feel in all respects as if they were legally equals, that the same is the case with all other married couples, wherever the husband is not a notorious ruffian. To suppose this, would be to show equal ignorance of human nature and of fact. The less fit a man is for the possession of power—the less likely to be allowed to exercise it over any person with that person's voluntary consent—the more does he hug himself in the consciousness of the power the law gives him, exact its legal rights to the utmost point which custom (the custom of men like himself) will tolerate, and take pleasure in using the power, merely to enliven the agreeable sense of possessing it. What is more; in the most naturally brutal and morally uneducated part of the lower classes, the legal slavery of the woman, and something in the merely physical subjection to their will as an instrument, causes them to feel a sort of disrespect and contempt towards their own wife which they do not feel towards any other woman, or any other human being, with whom they come in contact; and which makes her seem to them an appropriate subject for any kind of indignity. Let an acute observer of the signs of feeling, who has the requisite opportunities, judge for himself whether this is not the case: and if he finds that it is, let him not wonder at any amount of disgust and indignation that can be felt against institutions which lead naturally to this depraved state of the human mind.

We shall be told, perhaps, that religion imposes the duty of obedience; as every established fact which is too bad to admit of any other defence, is always presented to us as an injunction of religion. The Church, it is very true, enjoins it in her formularies,[12] but it would be difficult to derive any such injunction from Christianity. We are told that St. Paul said, "Wives, obey your husbands:" but he also said, "Slaves, obey your masters."[13] It was not St. Paul's business, nor was it consistent with his object, the propagation of Christianity, to incite any one to rebellion against existing laws. The apostle's acceptance of all social institutions as he found them, is no more to be construed as a disapproval of attempts to improve them at the proper time, than his declaration, "The powers that be are ordained of God,"[14] gives his sanction to military despotism, and to that alone, as the Christian form of political government, or commands passive obedience to it. To pretend that Christianity was intended to stereotype existing forms of government and society, and protect them against change, is to reduce it to the level of Islamism or of Brahminism. It is precisely because Christianity has not done this, that it has been the religion of the progressive portion of mankind, and Islamism, Brahminism, &c., have been those of the stationary portions; or rather (for there is no such thing as a really stationary society) of the declining portions. There have been abundance of people, in all ages of Christianity, who tried to make it something of the same kind; to convert us into a sort of Christian Mussulmans, with the Bible for a Koran, prohibiting all improvement: and great has been their power, and many have had to sacrifice their lives in resisting them. But they have been resisted, and the resistance has made us what we are, and will yet make us what we are to be.

After what has been said respecting the obligation of obedience, it is almost superfluous to say anything concerning the more special point included in the general one—a woman's right to her own property; for I need not hope that this treatise can make any impression upon those who need anything to convince them that a woman's inheritance or gains ought

to be as much her own after marriage as before.[15] The rule is simple: whatever would be the husband's or wife's if they were not married, should be under their exclusive control during marriage; which need not interfere with the power to tie up property by settlement, in order to preserve it for children. Some people are sentimentally shocked at the idea of a separate interest in money matters, as inconsistent with the ideal fusion of two lives into one. For my own part, I am one of the strongest supporters of community of goods, when resulting from an entire unity of feeling in the owners, which makes all things common between them. But I have no relish for a community of goods resting on the doctrine, that what is mine is yours but what is yours is not mine; and I should prefer to decline entering into such a compact with any one, though I were myself the person to profit by it.

This particular injustice and oppression to women, which is, to common apprehensions, more obvious than all the rest, admits of remedy without interfering with any other mischiefs: and there can be little doubt that it will be one of the earliest remedied. Already, in many of the new and several of the old States of the American Confederation, provisions have been inserted even in the written Constitutions, securing to women equality of rights in this respect: and thereby improving materially the position, in the marriage relation, of those women at least who have property, by leaving them one instrument of power which they have not signed away; and preventing also the scandalous abuse of the marriage institution, which is perpetrated when a man entraps a girl into marrying him without a settlement, for the sole purpose of getting possession of her money. When the support of the family depends, not on property, but on earnings, the common arrangement, by which the man earns the income and the wife superintends the domestic expenditure, seems to me in general the most suitable division of labour between the two persons. If, in addition to the physical suffering of bearing children, and the whole responsibility of their care and education in early years, the wife undertakes the careful

12. ["The Form of Solemnization of Matrimony" in the *Book of Common Prayer* of the Church of England required the bride to promise to "obey . . . and serve" her husband, as well as to "love [and] honour" him.]

13. [Colossians 3:18, 22.]

14. [Rom. 13:1.]

15. [The Married Women's Property Acts, which together established in some respects the "rule" Mill asserts here, were passed by Parliament in 1870 and 1882.]

and economical application of the husband's earnings to the general comfort of the family; she takes not only her fair share, but usually the larger share, of the bodily and mental exertion required by their joint existence. If she undertakes any additional portion, it seldom relieves her from this, but only prevents her from performing it properly. The care which she is herself disabled from taking of the children and the household, nobody else takes; those of the children who do not die, grow up as they best can, and the management of the household is likely to be so bad, as even in point of economy to be a great drawback from the value of the wife's earnings. In an otherwise just state of things, it is not, therefore, I think, a desirable custom, that the wife should contribute by her labour to the income of the family. In an unjust state of things, her doing so may be useful to her, by making her of more value in the eyes of the man who is legally her master; but, on the other hand, it enables him still farther to abuse his power, by forcing her to work, and leaving the support of the family to her exertions, while he spends most of his time in drinking and idleness. The *power* of earning is essential to the dignity of a woman, if she has not independent property. But if marriage were an equal contract, not implying the obligation of obedience; if the connexion were no longer enforced to the oppression of those to whom it is purely a mischief, but a separation, on just terms (I do not now speak of a divorce), could be obtained by any woman who was morally entitled to it; and if she would then find all honourable employments as freely open to her as to men; it would not be necessary for her protection, that during marriage she should make this particular use of her faculties. Like a man when he chooses a profession, so, when a woman marries, it may in general be understood that she makes choice of the management of a household, and the bringing up of a family, as the first call upon her exertions, during as many years of her life as may be required for the purpose; and that she renounces, not all other objects and occupations, but all which are not consistent with the requirements of this. The actual exercise, in a habitual or systematic manner, of outdoor occupations, or such as cannot be carried on at home, would by this principle be practically interdicted to the greater number of married women. But the utmost

latitude ought to exist for the adaptation of general rules to individual suitabilities; and there ought to be nothing to prevent faculties exceptionally adapted to any other pursuit, from obeying their vocation notwithstanding marriage: due provision being made for supplying otherwise any falling-short which might become inevitable, in her full performance of the ordinary functions of mistress of a family. These things, if once opinion were rightly directed on the subject, might with perfect safety be left to be regulated by opinion, without any interference of law.[16]

CHAPTER III

On the other point which is involved in the just equality of women, their admissibility to all the functions and occupations hitherto retained as the monopoly of the stronger sex, I should anticipate no difficulty in convincing any one who has gone with me on the subject of the equality of women in the family. I believe that their disabilities elsewhere are only clung to in order to maintain their subordination in domestic life; because the generality of the male sex cannot yet tolerate the idea of living with an equal. Were it not for that, I think that almost every one, in the existing state of opinion in politics and political economy, would admit the injustice of excluding half the human race from the greater number of lucrative occupations, and from almost all high social functions; ordaining from their birth either that they are not, and cannot by any possibility become, fit for employments which are legally open to the stupidest and basest of the other sex, or else that however fit they may be, those employments shall be interdicted to them, in order to be preserved for the exclusive benefit of males. In the last two centuries, when (which was seldom the case) any reason beyond the mere existence of the fact was thought to be required to justify the disabilities of women, people seldom

16. [This legal reform took much longer to be achieved than many of the others Mill proposes in this chapter. As late as World War II, "marriage bars" ensured that women in many spheres of employment in Britain, including the Civil Service, were automatically fired upon marrying.]

assigned as a reason their inferior mental capacity; which, in times when there was a real trial of personal faculties (from which all women were not excluded) in the struggles of public life, no one really believed in. The reason given in those days was not women's unfitness, but the interest of society, by which was meant the interest of men: just as the *raison d' état*, meaning the convenience of the government, and the support of existing authority, was deemed a sufficient explanation and excuse for the most flagitious crimes. In the present day, power holds a smoother language, and whomsoever it oppresses, always pretends to do so for their own good: accordingly, when anything is forbidden to women, it is thought necessary to say, and desirable to believe, that they are incapable of doing it, and that they depart from their real path of success and happiness when they aspire to it. But to make this reason plausible (I do not say valid), those by whom it is urged must be prepared to carry it to a much greater length than any one ventures to do in the face of present experience. It is not sufficient to maintain that women on the average are less gifted than men on the average, with certain of the higher mental faculties, or that a smaller number of women than of men are fit for occupations and functions of the highest intellectual character. It is necessary to maintain that no women at all are fit for them, and that the most eminent women are inferior in mental faculties to the most mediocre of the men on whom those functions at present devolve. For if the performance of the function is decided either by competition, or by any mode of choice which secures regard to the public interest, there needs be no apprehension that any important employments will fall into the hands of women inferior to average men, or to the average of their male competitors. The only result would be that there would be fewer women than men in such employments; a result certain to happen in any case, if only from the preference always likely to be felt by the majority of women for the one vocation in which there is nobody to compete with them. Now, the most determined depreciator of women will not venture to deny, that when we add the experience of recent times to that of ages past, women, and not a few merely, but many women, have proved themselves capable of everything, perhaps without a single exception, which is done by men, and of doing it success-

fully and creditably. The utmost that can be said is, that there are many things which none of them have succeeded in doing as well as they have been done by some men—many in which they have not reached the very highest rank. But there are extremely few, dependent only on mental faculties, in which they have not attained the rank next to the highest. Is not this enough, and much more than enough, to make it a tyranny to them, and a detriment to society, that they should not be allowed to compete with men for the exercise of these functions? Is it not a mere truism to say, that such functions are often filled by men far less fit for them than numbers of women, and who would be beaten by women in any fair field of competition? What difference does it make that there may be men somewhere, fully employed about other things, who may be still better qualified for the things in question than these women? Does not this take place in all competitions? Is there so great a superfluity of men fit for high duties, that society can afford to reject the service of any competent person? Are we so certain of always finding a man made to our hands for any duty or function of social importance which falls vacant, that we lose nothing by putting a ban upon one-half of mankind, and refusing beforehand to make their faculties available, however distinguished they may be? And even if we could do without them, would it be consistent with justice to refuse to them their fair share of honour and distinction, or to deny to them the equal moral right of all human beings to choose their occupation (short of injury to others) according to their own preferences, at their own risk? Nor is the injustice confined to them: it is shared by those who are in a position to benefit by their services. To ordain that any kind of persons shall not be physicians, or shall not be advocates, or shall not be members of parliament, is to injure not them only, but all who employ physicians or advocates, or elect members of parliament, and who are deprived of the stimulating effect of greater competition on the exertions of the competitors, as well as restricted to a narrower range of individual choice.

It will perhaps be sufficient if I confine myself, in the details of my argument, to functions of a public nature: since, if I am successful as to those, it probably will be readily granted that women should be admissible to all other occupations to which it is at all material whether they are admitted or not. And here let me begin by marking out one function, broadly distinguished from all others, their right to which is entirely independent of any question which can be raised concerning their faculties. I mean the suffrage, both parliamentary and municipal. The right to share in the choice of those who are to exercise a public trust, is altogether a distinct thing from that of competing for the trust itself. If no one could vote for a member of parliament who was not fit to be a candidate, the government would be a narrow oligarchy indeed. To have a voice in choosing those by whom one is to be governed, is a means of self-protection due to every one, though he were to remain for ever excluded from the function of governing: and that women are considered fit to have such a choice, may be presumed from the fact, that the law already gives it to women in the most important of all cases to themselves: for the choice of the man who is to govern a woman to the end of life, is always supposed to be voluntarily made by herself. In the case of election to public trusts, it is the business of constitutional law to surround the right of suffrage with all needful securities and limitations; but whatever securities are sufficient in the case of the male sex, no others need be required in the case of women. Under whatever conditions, and within whatever limits, men are admitted to the suffrage, there is not a shadow of justification for not admitting women under the same. The majority of the women of any class are not likely to differ in political opinion from the majority of the men of the same class, unless the question be one in which the interests of women, as such, are in some way involved; and if they are so, women require the suffrage, as their guarantee of just and equal consideration. This ought to be obvious even to those who coincide in no other of the doctrines for which I contend. Even if every woman were a wife, and if every wife ought to be a slave, all the more would these slaves stand in need of legal protection: and we know what legal protection the slaves have, where the laws are made by their masters.

With regard to the fitness of women, not only to participate in elections, but themselves to hold offices or practise professions involving important public responsibilities; I have already observed that this consideration is not essential to the practical question in

dispute: since any woman, who succeeds in an open profession, proves by that very fact that she is qualified for it. And in the case of public offices, if the political system of the country is such as to exclude unfit men, it will equally exclude unfit women: while if it is not, there is no additional evil in the fact that the unfit persons whom it admits may be either women or men. As long therefore as it is acknowledged that even a few women may be fit for these duties, the laws which shut the door on those exceptions cannot be justified by any opinion which can be held respecting the capacities of women in general. But, though this last consideration is not essential, it is far from being irrelevant. An unprejudiced view of it gives additional strength to the arguments against the disabilities of women, and reinforces them by high considerations of practical utility.

Let us at first make entire abstraction of all psychological considerations tending to show, that any of the mental differences supposed to exist between women and men are but the natural effect of the differences in their education and circumstances, and indicate no radical difference, far less radical inferiority, of nature. Let us consider women only as they already are, or as they are known to have been; and the capacities which they have already practically shown. What they have done, that at least, if nothing else, it is proved that they can do. When we consider how sedulously they are all trained away from, instead of being trained towards, any of the occupations or objects reserved for men, it is evident that I am taking a very humble ground for them, when I rest their case on what they have actually achieved. For, in this case, negative evidence is worth little, while any positive evidence is conclusive. It cannot be inferred to be impossible that a woman should be a Homer, or an Aristotle, or a Michael Angelo, or a Beethoven, because no woman has yet actually produced works comparable to theirs in any of those lines of excellence. This negative fact at most leaves the question uncertain, and open to psychological discussion. But it is quite certain that a woman can be a Queen Elizabeth, or a Deborah,[17] or a Joan of Arc, since

17. [Deborah was a judge and prophet who played an important role in the Israelites' victory over the Canaanites (Judges 4–5).]

this is not inference, but fact. Now it is a curious consideration, that the only things which the existing law excludes women from doing, are the things which they have proved that they are able to do. There is no law to prevent a woman from having written all the plays of Shakespeare, or composed all the operas of Mozart. But Queen Elizabeth or Queen Victoria, had they not inherited the throne, could not have been intrusted with the smallest of the political duties, of which the former showed herself equal to the greatest.

If anything conclusive could be inferred from experience, without psychological analysis, it would be that the things which women are not allowed to do are the very ones for which they are peculiarly qualified; since their vocation for government has made its way, and become conspicuous, through the very few opportunities which have been given; while in the lines of distinction which apparently were freely open to them, they have by no means so eminently distinguished themselves. We know how small a number of reigning queens history presents, in comparison with that of kings. Of this smaller number a far larger proportion have shown talents for rule; though many of them have occupied the throne in difficult periods. It is remarkable, too, that they have, in a great number of instances, been distinguished by merits the most opposite to the imaginary and conventional character of women: they have been as much remarked for the firmness and vigour of their rule, as for its intelligence. When, to queens and empresses, we add regents, and viceroys of provinces, the list of women who have been eminent rulers of mankind swells to a great length.[18] This fact is so undeniable, that some one,

long ago, tried to retort the argument, and turned the admitted truth into an additional insult, by saying that queens are better than kings, because under kings women govern, but under queens, men.

It may seem a waste of reasoning to argue against a bad joke; but such things do affect people's minds; and I have heard men quote this saying, with an air as if they thought there was something in it. At any rate, it will serve as well as anything else for a starting point in discussion. I say, then, that it is not true that under kings, women govern. Such cases are entirely exceptional: and weak kings have quite as often governed ill through the influence of male favourites, as of female. When a king is governed by a woman merely through his amatory propensities, good government is not probable, though even then there are exceptions. But French history counts two kings who have voluntarily given the direction of affairs during many years, the one to his mother, the other to his sister. One of them, Charles VIII, was a mere boy, but in doing so he followed the intentions of his father Louis XI, the ablest monarch of his age. The other, Saint Louis, was the best, and one of the most vigorous rulers, since the time of Charlemagne.[19] Both these princesses ruled in a manner hardly equalled by any prince among their contemporaries. The emperor Charles V, the most politic prince of his time, who had as great a number of able men in his service as a ruler ever had, and was one of the least likely of all sovereigns to sacrifice his interest to personal feelings, made two princesses of his family successively Governors of the Netherlands, and kept one or other of them in that post during his whole life, (they were

18. Especially is this true if we take into consideration Asia as well as Europe. If a Hindoo principality is strongly, vigilantly, and economically governed; if order is preserved without oppression; if cultivation is extending, and the people prosperous, in three cases out of four that principality is under a woman's rule. This fact, to me an entirely unexpected one, I have collected from a long official knowledge of Hindoo governments. There are many such instances: for though, by Hindoo institutions, a woman cannot reign, she is the legal regent of a kingdom during the minority of the heir; and minorities are frequent, the lives of the male rulers being so often prematurely terminated through the effect of inactivity

and sensual excesses. When we consider that these princesses have never been seen in public, have never conversed with any man not of their own family except from behind a curtain, that they do not read, and if they did, there is no book in their languages which can give them the smallest instruction on political affairs; the example they afford of the natural capacity of women for government is very striking.

19. [Blanche of Castile, mother of Louis IX (king of France 1226–70, also called Saint Louis), acted as regent for eight years during his minority and again when he embarked on the sixth crusade. Anne of Beaujeu, sister of Charles VIII (king of France 1483–98), was regent through much of his reign.]

afterwards succeeded by a third). Both ruled very successfully and one of them, Margaret of Austria, was one of the ablest politicians of the age.[20] So much for one side of the question. Now as to the other. When it is said that under queens men govern, is the same meaning to be understood as when kings are said to be governed by women? Is it meant that queens choose as their instruments of government, the associates of their personal pleasures? The case is rare even with those who are as unscrupulous on the latter point as Catherine II: and it is not in these cases that the good government, alleged to arise from male influence, is to be found.[21] If it be true, then, that the administration is in the hands of better men under a queen than under an average king, it must be that queens have a superior capacity for choosing them; and women must be better qualified than men both for the position of sovereign, and for that of chief minister; for the principal business of a prime minister is not to govern in person, but to find the fittest persons to conduct every department of public affairs. The more rapid insight into character, which is one of the admitted points of superiority in women over men, must certainly make them, with anything like parity of qualifications in other respects, more apt than men in that choice of instruments, which is nearly the most important business of every one who has to do with governing mankind. Even the unprincipled Catherine de' Medici could feel the value of a Chancellor de l'Hôpital.[22] But it is also true that most great queens have been great by their own talents for

government, and have been well served precisely for that reason. They retained the supreme direction of affairs in their own hands: and if they listened to good advisers, they gave by that fact the strongest proof that their judgment fitted them for dealing with the great questions of government.

Is it reasonable to think that those who are fit for the greater functions of politics, are incapable of qualifying themselves for the less? Is there any reason in the nature of things, that the wives and sisters of princes should, whenever called on, be found as competent as the princes themselves to *their* business, but that the wives and sisters of statesmen, and administrators, and directors of companies, and managers of public institutions, should be unable to do what is done by their brothers and husbands? The real reason is plain enough; it is that princesses, being more raised above the generality of men by their rank than placed below them by their sex, have never been taught that it was improper for them to concern themselves with politics; but have been allowed to feel the liberal interest natural to any cultivated human being, in the great transactions which took place around them, and in which they might be called on to take a part. The ladies of reigning families are the only women who are allowed the same range of interests and freedom of development as men; and it is precisely in their case that there is not found to be any inferiority. Exactly where and in proportion as women's capacities for government have been tried, in that proportion have they been found adequate.

This fact is in accordance with the best general conclusions which the world's imperfect experience seems as yet to suggest, concerning the peculiar tendencies and aptitudes characteristic of women, as women have hitherto been. I do not say, as they will continue to be; for, as I have already said more than once, I consider it presumption in any one to pretend to decide what women are or are not, can or cannot be, by natural constitution. They have always hitherto been kept, as far as regards spontaneous development, in so unnatural a state, that their nature cannot but have been greatly distorted and disguised; and no one can safely pronounce that if women's nature were left to choose its direction as freely as men's, and if no artificial bent were attempted to be given to it except that required by the conditions of human soci-

20. [Charles V (Holy Roman Emperor 1519–56) appointed first his aunt, Margaret of Austria, and later his sister, Mary of Hungary, to rule over the Netherlands. In her nineteen-year regency, Margaret did much to consolidate Hapsburg rule there. After Charles's death, his natural daughter, Margaret of Parma, was appointed to the same regency.]

21. [Catherine II (empress of Russia 1762–96), a strong and ruthless ruler, had many lovers, including Potemkin, one of her ministers.]

22. [Catherine de' Medici was the queen consort of Henry II (king of France 1547–59) and then regent of France from 1560 to 1574. She played an influential role in reconciling the warring French religious factions, with help from her chancellor, Michel de L'Hôpital.]

cty, and given to both sexes alike, there would be any material difference, or perhaps any difference at all, in the character and capacities which would unfold themselves. I shall presently show, that even the least contestable of the differences which now exist, are such as may very well have been produced merely by circumstances, without any difference of natural capacity. But, looking at women as they are known in experience, it may be said of them, with more truth than belongs to most other generalizations on the subject, that the general bent of their talents is towards the practical. This statement is conformable to all the public history of women, in the present and the past. It is no less borne out by common and daily experience. Let us consider the special nature of the mental capacities most characteristic of a woman of talent. They are all of a kind which fits them for practice, and makes them tend towards it. What is meant by a woman's capacity of intuitive perception? It means, a rapid and correct insight into present fact. It has nothing to do with general principles. Nobody ever perceived a scientific law of nature by intuition, nor arrived at a general rule of duty or prudence by it. These are results of slow and careful collection and comparison of experience; and neither the men nor the women of intuition usually shine in this department, unless, indeed, the experience necessary is such as they can acquire by themselves. For what is called their intuitive sagacity makes them peculiarly apt in gathering such general truths as can be collected from their individual means of observation. When, consequently, they chance to be as well provided as men are with the results of other people's experience, by reading and education, (I use the word chance advisedly, for, in respect to the knowledge that tends to fit them for the greater concerns of life, the only educated women are the self-educated) they are better furnished than men in general with the essential requisites of skilful and successful practice. Men who have been much taught, are apt to be deficient in the sense of present fact; they do not see, in the facts which they are called upon to deal with, what is really there, but what they have been taught to expect. This is seldom the case with women of any ability. Their capacity of "intuition" preserves them from it. With equality of experience and of general faculties, a woman usually sees much more than a

man of what is immediately before her. Now this sensibility to the present, is the main quality on which the capacity for practice, as distinguished from theory, depends. To discover general principles, belongs to the speculative faculty: to discern and discriminate the particular cases in which they are and are not applicable, constitutes practical talent: and for this, women as they now are have a peculiar aptitude. I admit that there can be no good practice without principles, and that the predominant place which quickness of observation holds among a woman's faculties, makes her particularly apt to build over-hasty generalizations upon her own observation; though at the same time no less ready in rectifying those generalizations, as her observation takes a wider range. But the corrective to this defect, is access to the experience of the human race; general knowledge — exactly the thing which education can best supply. A woman's mistakes are specifically those of a clever self-educated man, who often sees what men trained in routine do not see, but falls into errors for want of knowing things which have long been known. Of course he has acquired much of the pre-existing knowledge, or he could not have got on at all; but what he knows of it he has picked up in fragments and at random, as women do.

But this gravitation of women's minds to the present, to the real, to actual fact, while in its exclusiveness it is a source of errors, is also a most useful counteractive of the contrary error. The principal and most characteristic aberration of speculative minds as such, consists precisely in the deficiency of this lively perception and ever-present sense of objective fact. For want of this, they often not only overlook the contradiction which outward facts oppose to their theories, but lose sight of the legitimate purpose of speculation altogether, and let their speculative faculties go astray into regions not peopled with real beings, animate or inanimate, even idealized, but with personified shadows created by the illusions of metaphysics or by the mere entanglement of words, and think these shadows the proper objects of the highest, the most transcendant, philosophy. Hardly anything can be of greater value to a man of theory and speculation who employs himself not in collecting materials of knowledge by observation, but in working them up by processes of thought into comprehensive truths of science and laws of conduct, than to carry on his speculations in the companionship, and under the criticism, of a really superior woman. There is nothing comparable to it for keeping his thoughts within the limits of real things, and the actual facts of nature. A woman seldom runs wild after an abstraction. The habitual direction of her mind to dealing with things as individuals rather than in groups, and (what is closely connected with it) her more lively interest in the present feelings of persons, which makes her consider first of all, in anything which claims to be applied to practice, in what manner persons will be affected by it—these two things make her extremely unlikely to put faith in any speculation which loses sight of individuals, and deals with things as if they existed for the benefit of some imaginary entity, some mere creation of the mind, not resolvable into the feelings of living beings. Women's thoughts are thus as useful in giving reality to those of thinking men, as men's thoughts in giving width and largeness to those of women. In depth, as distinguished from breadth, I greatly doubt if even now, women, compared with men, are at any disadvantage.

If the existing mental characteristics of women are thus valuable even in aid of speculation, they are still more important, when speculation has done its work, for carrying out the results of speculation into practice. For the reasons already given, women are comparatively unlikely to fall into the common error of men, that of sticking to their rules in a case whose specialities either take it out of the class to which the rules are applicable, or require a special adaptation of them. Let us now consider another of the admitted superiorities of clever women, greater quickness of apprehension. Is not this pre-eminently a quality which fits a person for practice? In action, everything continually depends upon deciding promptly. In speculation, nothing does. A mere thinker can wait, can take time to consider, can collect additional evidence; he is not obliged to complete his philosophy at once, lest the opportunity should go by. The power of drawing the best conclusion possible from insufficient data is not indeed useless in philosophy; the construction of a provisional hypothesis consistent with all known facts is often the needful basis for further inquiry. But this faculty is rather serviceable in philosophy, than the main qualification for it: and,

for the auxiliary as well as for the main operation, the philosopher can allow himself any time he pleases. He is in no need of the capacity of doing rapidly what he does; what he rather needs is patience, to work on slowly until imperfect lights have become perfect, and a conjecture has ripened into a theorem. For those, on the contrary, whose business is with the fugitive and perishable—with individual facts, not kinds of facts—rapidity of thought is a qualification next only in importance to the power of thought itself. He who has not his faculties under immediate command, in the contingencies of action, might as well not have them at all. He may be fit to criticize, but he is not fit to act. Now it is in this that women, and the men who are most like women, confessedly excel. The other sort of man, however pre-eminent may be his faculties, arrives slowly at complete command of them: rapidity of judgment and promptitude of judicious action, even in the things he knows best, are the gradual and the late result of strenuous effort grown into habit.

It will be said, perhaps, that the greater nervous susceptibility of women is a disqualification for practice, in anything but domestic life, by rendering them mobile, changeable, too vehemently under the influence of the moment, incapable of dogged perseverance, unequal and uncertain in the power of using their faculties. I think that these phrases sum up the greater part of the objections commonly made to the fitness of women for the higher class of serious business. Much of all this is the mere overflow of nervous energy run to waste, and would cease when the energy was directed to a definite end. Much is also the result of conscious or unconscious cultivation; as we see by the almost total disappearance of "hysterics" and fainting fits, since they have gone out of fashion. Moreover, when people are brought up, like many women of the higher classes (though less so in our own country than in any other) a kind of hot-house plants, shielded from the wholesome vicissitudes of air and temperature, and untrained in any of the occupations and exercises which give stimulus and development to the circulatory and muscular system, while their nervous system, especially in its emotional department, is kept in unnaturally active play; it is no wonder if those of them who do not die of consumption, grow up with constitutions liable to derangement from slight causes, both internal and external, and without stamina to support any task, physical or mental, requiring continuity of effort. But women brought up to work for their livelihood show none of these morbid characteristics, unless indeed they are chained to an excess of sedentary work in confined and unhealthy rooms. Women who in their early years have shared in the healthful physical education and bodily freedom of their brothers, and who obtain a sufficiency of pure air and exercise in after-life, very rarely have any excessive susceptibility of nerves which can disqualify them for active pursuits. There is indeed a certain proportion of persons, in both sexes, in whom an unusual degree of nervous sensibility is constitutional, and of so marked a character as to be the feature of their organization which exercises the greatest influence over the whole character of the vital phenomena. This constitution, like other physical conformations, is hereditary, and is transmitted to sons as well as daughters; but it is possible, and probable, that the nervous temperament (as it is called) is inherited by a greater number of women than of men. We will assume this as a fact: and let me then ask, are men of nervous temperament found to be unfit for the duties and pursuits usually followed by men? If not, why should women of the same temperament be unfit for them? The peculiarities of the temperament are, no doubt, within certain limits, an obstacle to success in some employments, though an aid to it in others. But when the occupation is suitable to the temperament, and sometimes even when it is unsuitable, the most brilliant examples of success are continually given by the men of high nervous sensibility. They are distinguished in their practical manifestations chiefly by this, that being susceptible of a higher degree of excitement than those of another physical constitution, their powers when excited differ more than in the case of other people, from those shown in their ordinary state: they are raised, as it were, above themselves, and do things with ease which they are wholly incapable of at other times. But this lofty excitement is not, except in weak bodily constitutions, a mere flash, which passes away immediately, leaving no permanent traces, and incompatible with persistent and steady pursuit of an object. It is the character of the nervous temperament to be capable of *sustained* excitement, holding out through long continued efforts. It is what is meant by *spirit*. It is what makes the high-bred racehorse run without slackening speed till he drops down dead. It is what has enabled so many delicate women to maintain the most sublime constancy not only at the stake, but through a long preliminary succession of mental and bodily tortures. It is evident that people of this temperament are particularly apt for what may be called the executive department of the leadership of mankind. They are the material of great orators, great preachers, impressive diffusers of moral influences. Their constitution might be deemed less favourable to the qualities required from a statesman in the cabinet, or from a judge. It would be so, if the consequence necessarily followed that because people are excitable they must always be in a state of excitement. But this is wholly a question of training. Strong feeling is the instrument and element of strong self-control: but it requires to be cultivated in that direction. When it is, it forms not the heroes of impulse only, but those also of self-conquest. History and experience prove that the most passionate characters are the most fanatically rigid in their feelings of duty, when their passion has been trained to act in that direction. The judge who gives a just decision in a case where his feelings are intensely interested on the other side, derives from that same strength of feeling the determined sense of the obligation of justice, which enables him to achieve this victory over himself. The capability of that lofty enthusiasm which takes the human being out of his every-day character, reacts upon the daily character itself. His aspirations and powers when he is in this exceptional state, become the type with which he compares, and by which he estimates, his sentiments and proceedings at other times: and his habitual purposes assume a character moulded by and assimilated to the moments of lofty excitement, although those, from the physical nature of a human being, can only be transient. Experience of races, as well as of individuals, does not show those of excitable temperament to be less fit, on the average, either for speculation or practice, than the more unexcitable. The French, and the Italians, are undoubtedly by nature more nervously excitable than the Teutonic races, and, compared at least with the English, they have a much greater habitual and daily emotional life: but have they been less great in science, in public business, in legal and judicial eminence, or in war? There is abundant evidence that the Greeks were of old, as their descendants and successors still are, one of the most excitable of the races of mankind. It is superfluous to ask, what among the achievements of men they did not excel in. The Romans, probably, as an equally southern people, had the same original temperament: but the stern character of their national discipline, like that of the Spartans, made them an example of the opposite type of national character; the greater strength of their natural feelings being chiefly apparent in the intensity which the same original temperament made it possible to give to the artificial. If these cases exemplify what a naturally excitable people may be made, the Irish Celts afford one of the aptest examples of what they are when left to themselves (if those can be said to be left to themselves who have been for centuries under the indirect influence of bad government, and the direct training of a Catholic hierarchy and of a sincere belief in the Catholic religion). The Irish character must be considered, therefore, as an unfavourable case: yet, whenever the circumstances of the individual have been at all favourable, what people have shown greater capacity for the most varied and multifarious individual eminence? Like the French compared with the English, the Irish with the Swiss, the Greeks or Italians compared with the German races, so women compared with men may be found, on the average, to do the same things with some variety in the particular kind of excellence. But, that they would do them fully as well on the whole, if their education and cultivation were adapted to correcting instead of aggravating the infirmities incident to their temperament, I see not the smallest reason to doubt.

Supposing it, however, to be true that women's minds are by nature more mobile than those of men, less capable of persisting long in the same continuous effort, more fitted for dividing their faculties among many things than for travelling in any one path to the highest point which can be reached by it: this may be true of women as they now are (though not without great and numerous exceptions), and may account for their having remained behind the highest order of men in precisely the things in which this absorption of the whole mind in one set of ideas and

occupations may seem to be most requisite. Still, this difference is one which can only affect the kind of excellence, not the excellence itself, or its practical worth: and it remains to be shown whether this exclusive working of a part of the mind, this absorption of the whole thinking faculty in a single subject, and concentration of it on a single work, is the normal and healthful condition of the human faculties, even for speculative uses. I believe that what is gained in special development by this concentration, is lost in the capacity of the mind for the other purposes of life; and even in abstract thought, it is my decided opinion that the mind does more by frequently returning to a difficult problem, than by sticking to it without interruption. For the purposes, at all events, of practice, from its highest to its humblest departments, the capacity of passing promptly from one subject of consideration to another, without letting the active spring of the intellect run down between the two, is a power far more valuable; and this power women pre-eminently possess, by virtue of the very mobility of which they are accused. They perhaps have it from nature, but they certainly have it by training and education; for nearly the whole of the occupations of women consist in the management of small but multitudinous details, on each of which the mind cannot dwell even for a minute, but must pass on to other things, and if anything requires longer thought, must steal time at odd moments for thinking of it. The capacity indeed which women show for doing their thinking in circumstances and at times which almost any man would make an excuse to himself for not attempting it, has often been noticed: and a woman's mind, though it may be occupied only with small things, can hardly ever permit itself to be vacant, as a man's so often is when not engaged in what he chooses to consider the business of his life. The business of a woman's ordinary life is things in general, and can as little cease to go on as the world to go round.

But (it is said) there is anatomical evidence of the superior mental capacity of men compared with women: they have a larger brain. I reply, that in the first place the fact itself is doubtful. It is by no means established that the brain of a woman is smaller than that of a man. If it is inferred merely because a woman's bodily frame generally is of less dimensions than a man's, this criterion would lead to strange consequences. A tall and large-boned man must on this showing be wonderfully superior in intelligence to a small man, and an elephant or a whale must prodigiously excel mankind. The size of the brain in human beings, anatomists say, varies much less than the size of the body, or even of the head, and the one cannot be at all inferred from the other. It is certain that some women have as large a brain as any man. It is within my knowledge that a man who had weighed many human brains, said that the heaviest he knew of, heavier even than Cuvier's (the heaviest previously recorded,) was that of a woman. Next, I must observe that the precise relation which exists between the brain and the intellectual powers is not yet well understood, but is a subject of great dispute. That there is a very close relation we cannot doubt. The brain is certainly the material organ of thought and feeling: and (making abstraction of the great unsettled controversy respecting the appropriation of different parts of the brain to different mental faculties) I admit that it would be an anomaly, and an exception to all we know of the general laws of life and organization, if the size of the organ were wholly indifferent to the function; if no accession of power were derived from the greater magnitude of the instrument. But the exception and the anomaly would be fully as great if the organ exercised influence by its magnitude only. In all the more delicate operations of nature—of which those of the animated creation are the most delicate, and those of the nervous system by far the most delicate of these—differences in the effect depend as much on differences of quality in the physical agents, as on their quantity: and if the quality of an instrument is to be tested by the nicety and delicacy of the work it can do, the indications point to a greater average fineness of quality in the brain and nervous system of women than of men. Dismissing abstract difference of quality, a thing difficult to verify, the efficiency of an organ is known to depend not solely on its size but on its activity: and of this we have an approximate measure in the energy with which the blood circulates through it, both the stimulus and the reparative force being mainly dependent on the circulation. It would not be surprising—it is indeed an hypothesis which accords well with the differences actually observed between the mental operations of the two sexes—if men on the average should have the advantage in the size of the brain, and women in activity of cerebral circulation. The results which conjecture, founded on analogy, would lead us to expect from this difference of organization, would correspond to some of those which we most commonly see. In the first place, the mental operations of men might be expected to be slower. They would neither be so prompt as women in thinking, nor so quick to feel. Large bodies take more time to get into full action. On the other hand, when once got thoroughly into play, men's brain would bear more work. It would be more persistent in the line first taken; it would have more difficulty in changing from one mode of action to another, but, in the one thing it was doing, it could go on longer without loss of power or sense of fatigue. And do we not find that the things in which men most excel women are those which require most plodding and long hammering at a single thought, while women do best what must be done rapidly? A woman's brain is sooner fatigued, sooner exhausted; but given the degree of exhaustion, we should expect to find that it would recover itself sooner. I repeat that this speculation is entirely hypothetical; it pretends to no more than to suggest a line of enquiry. I have before repudiated the notion of its being yet certainly known that there is any natural difference at all in the average strength or direction of the mental capacities of the two sexes, much less what that difference is. Nor is it possible that this should be known, so long as the psychological laws of the formation of character have been so little studied, even in a general way, and in the particular case never scientifically applied at all; so long as the most obvious external causes of difference of character are habitually disregarded left unnoticed by the observer, and looked down upon with a kind of supercilious contempt by the prevalent schools both of natural history and of mental philosophy: who, whether they look for the source of what mainly distinguishes human beings from one another, in the world of matter or in that of spirit, agree in running down those who prefer to explain these differences by the different relations of human beings to society and life.

To so ridiculous an extent are the notions formed of the nature of women, mere empirical generalizations, framed, without philosophy or analysis, upon the first instances which present themselves, that the popular idea of it is different in different countries, according as the opinions and social circumstances of the country have given to the women living in it any speciality of development or non-development. An Oriental thinks that women are by nature peculiarly voluptuous; see the violent abuse of them on this ground in Hindoo writings. An Englishman usually thinks that they are by nature cold. The sayings about women's fickleness are mostly of French origin; from the famous distich of Francis I, upward and downward.[23] In England it is a common remark, how much more constant women are than men. Inconstancy has been longer reckoned discreditable to a woman, in England than in France; and Englishwomen are besides, in their inmost nature, much more subdued to opinion. It may be remarked by the way, that Englishmen are in peculiarly unfavourable circumstances for attempting to judge what is or is not natural, not merely to women, but to men, or to human beings altogether, at least if they have only English experience to go upon: because there is no place where human nature shows so little of its original lineaments. Both in a good and a bad sense, the English are farther from a state of nature than any other modern people. They are, more than any other people, a product of civilization and discipline. England is the country in which social discipline has most succeeded, not so much in conquering, as in suppressing, whatever is liable to conflict with it. The English, more than any other people, not only act but feel according to rule. In other countries, the taught opinion, or the requirement of society, may be the stronger power, but the promptings of the individual nature are always visible under it, and often resisting it: rule may be stronger than nature, but nature is still there. In England, rule has to a great degree substituted itself for nature. The greater part of life is carried on, not by following inclination under the control of rule, but by having no inclination but that of following a rule. Now this has its good side doubtless, though it has also a wretchedly bad one; but it must render an Englishman peculiarly ill-qualified to pass a judgment on the origi-

nal tendencies of human nature from his own experience. The errors to which observers elsewhere are liable on the subject, are of a different character. An Englishman is ignorant respecting human nature, a Frenchman is prejudiced. An Englishman's errors are negative, a Frenchman's positive. An Englishman fancies that things do not exist, because he never sees them; a Frenchman thinks they must always and necessarily exist, because he does see them. An Englishman does not know nature, because he has had no opportunity of observing it; a Frenchman generally knows a great deal of it, but often mistakes it, because he has only seen it sophisticated and distorted. For the artificial state superinduced by society disguises the natural tendencies of the thing which is the subject of observation, in two different ways: by extinguishing the nature, or by transforming it. In the one case there is but a starved residuum of nature remaining to be studied; in the other case there is much, but it may have expanded in any direction rather than that in which it would spontaneously grow.

I have said that it cannot now be known how much of the existing mental differences between men and women is natural, and how much artificial; whether there are any natural differences at all; or, supposing all artificial causes of difference to be withdrawn, what natural character would be revealed. I am not about to attempt what I have pronounced impossible: but doubt does not forbid conjecture, and where certainty is unattainable, there may yet be the means of arriving at some degree of probability. The first point, the origin of the differences actually observed, is the one most accessible to speculation; and I shall attempt to approach it, by the only path by which it can be reached; by tracing the mental consequences of external influences. We cannot isolate a human being from the circumstances of his condition, so as to ascertain experimentally what he would have been by nature; but we can consider what he is, and what his circumstances have been, and whether the one would have been capable of producing the other.

Let us take, then, the only marked case which observation affords, of apparent inferiority of women to men, if we except the merely physical one of bodily strength. No production in philosophy, science, or art, entitled to the first rank, has been the work of a

---

23. [The saying, "Women are often fickle; foolish is he who trusts them," is attributed by Victor Hugo to Francis I (king of France 1515–47).]

woman. Is there any mode of accounting for this, without supposing that women are naturally incapable of producing them?

In the first place, we may fairly question whether experience has afforded sufficient grounds for an induction. It is scarcely three generations since women, saving very rare exceptions, have begun to try their capacity in philosophy, science, or art. It is only in the present generation that their attempts have been at all numerous; and they are even now extremely few, everywhere but in England and France. It is a relevant question, whether a mind possessing the requisites of first-rate eminence in speculation or creative art could have been expected, on the mere calculation of chances, to turn up during that lapse of time, among the women whose tastes and personal position admitted of their devoting themselves to these pursuits. In all things which there has yet been time for—in all but the very highest grades in the scale of excellence, especially in the department in which they have been longest engaged, literature (both prose and poetry)—women have done quite as much, have obtained fully as high prizes and as many of them, as could be expected from the length of time and the number of competitors. If we go back to the earlier period when very few women made the attempt, yet some of those few made it with distinguished success. The Greek always accounted Sappho among their great poets; and we may well suppose that Myrtis, said to have been the teacher of Pindar, and Corinna, who five times bore away from him the prize of poetry, must at least have had sufficient merit to admit of being compared with that great name. Aspasia did not leave any philosophical writings; but it is an admitted fact that Socrates resorted to her for instruction, and avowed himself to have obtained it.[24]

If we consider the works of women in modern times, and contrast them with those of men, either in the literary or the artistic department, such inferiority as may be observed resolves itself essentially into one thing: but that is a most material one; deficiency of originality. Not total deficiency; for every production of mind which is of any substantive value, has an originality of its own—is a conception of the mind itself, not a copy of something else. Thoughts original, in the sense of being unborrowed—of being derived from the thinker's own observations or intellectual processes—are abundant in the writings of women. But they have not yet produced any of those great and luminous new ideas which form an era in thought, nor those fundamentally new conceptions in art, which open a vista of possible effects not before thought of, and found a new school. Their compositions are mostly grounded on the existing fund of thought, and their creations do not deviate widely from existing types. This is the sort of inferiority which their works manifest: for in point of execution, in the detailed application of thought, and the perfection of style, there is no inferiority. Our best novelists in point of composition, and of the management of detail, have mostly been women; and there is not in all modern literature a more eloquent vehicle of thought than the style of Madame de Staël, nor, as a specimen of purely artistic excellence, anything superior to the prose of Madame Sand, whose style acts upon the nervous system like a symphony of Haydn or Mozart. High originality of conception is, as I have said, what is chiefly wanting. And now to examine if there is any manner in which this deficiency can be accounted for.

Let us remember, then, so far as regards mere thought, that during all that period in the world's existence, and in the progress of cultivation, in which great and fruitful new truths could be arrived at by mere force of genius, with little previous study and accumulation of knowledge—during all that time women did not concern themselves with speculation at all. From the days of Hypatia to those of the Reformation, the illustrious Heloisa is almost the only woman to whom any such achievement might have been possible; and we know not how great a capacity of speculation in her may have been lost to mankind by the misfortunes of her life.[25] Never since any

24. [Sappho was a celebrated Greek poet (c. 610–c. 580 B.C.E.) whose works have survived in a fragmentary state. Corinna was a Greek lyric poet thought to have been a rival of Pindar (c. 500 B.C.E.). Aspasia (fifth century B.C.E.), philosopher and the mistress of Pericles, was a striking figure in Athenian society. She was accused of having too much influence over Pericles.]

25. [Hypatia (c. 370–415), head of the Egyptian neoplatonist school of philosophy, was the first notable

considerable number of women have began to cultivate serious thought, has originality been possible on
easy terms. Nearly all the thoughts which can be
reached by mere strength of original faculties, have
long since been arrived at; and originality, in any
high sense of the word, is now scarcely ever attained
but by minds which have undergone elaborate discipline, and are deeply versed in the results of previous
thinking. It is Mr. Maurice, I think, who has remarked
on the present age, that its most original thinkers are
those who have known most thoroughly what had
been thought by their predecessors: and this will always henceforth be the case. Every fresh stone in the
edifice has now to be placed on the top of so many
others, that a long process of climbing, and of carrying
up materials, has to be gone through by whoever
aspires to take a share in the present stage of the
work. How many women are there who have gone
through any such process? Mrs. Somerville, alone
perhaps of women, knows as much of mathematics
as is now needful for making any considerable mathematical discovery: is it any proof of inferiority in
women, that she has not happened to be one of
the two or three persons who in her lifetime have
associated their names with some striking advancement of the science? Two women, since political
economy has been made a science, have known
enough of it to write usefully on the subject. Of how
many of the innumerable men who have written on
it during the same time, is it possible with truth to
say more? If no woman has hitherto been a great
historian, what woman has had the necessary erudition? If no woman is a great philologist, what woman
has studied Sanscrit and Slavonic, the Gothic of
Ulphila and the Persic of the Zendavesta? Even in
practical matters we all know what is the value of the
originality of untaught geniuses. It means, inventing
over again in its rudimentary form something already
invented and improved upon by many successive inventors. When women have had the preparation

which all men now require to be eminently original,
it will be time enough to begin judging by experience
of their capacity for originality.

It no doubt often happens that a person, who has
not widely and accurately studied the thoughts of
others on a subject, has by natural sagacity a happy
intuition, which he can suggest, but cannot prove,
which yet when matured may be an important addition to knowledge: but even then, no justice can be
done to it until some other person, who does possess
the previous acquirements, takes it in hand, tests it,
gives it a scientific or practical form, and fits it into
its place among the existing truths of philosophy or
science. Is it supposed that such felicitous thoughts
do not occur to women? They occur by hundreds to
every woman of intellect. But they are mostly lost,
for want of a husband or friend who has the other
knowledge which can enable him to estimate them
properly and bring them before the world: and even
when they are brought before it, they generally appear
as his ideas, not their real author's. Who can tell how
many of the most original thoughts put forth by male
writers, belong to a woman by suggestion, to themselves only by verifying and working out? If I may
judge by my own case, a very large proportion indeed.

If we turn from pure speculation to literature in
the narrow sense of the term, and the fine arts, there
is a very obvious reason why women's literature is,
in its general conception and in its main features, an
imitation of men's. Why is the Roman literature, as
critics proclaim to satiety, not original, but an imitation of the Greek? Simply because the Greeks came
first. If women lived in a different country from men,
and had never read any of their writings, they would
have had a literature of their own. As it is, they have
not created one, because they found a highly advanced literature already created. If there had been
no suspension of the knowledge of antiquity, or if the
Renaissance had occurred before the Gothic cathedrals were built, they never would have been built.
We see that, in France and Italy, imitation of the
ancient literature stopped the original development
even after it had commenced. All women who write
are pupils of the great male writers. A painter's early
pictures, even if he be a Raffaelle, are undistinguish-
able in style from those of his master. Even a Mozart
does not display his powerful originality in his earliest

---

female mathematician. Heloise (1098–1164), the brilliant niece of a canon of Notre Dame, was educated by
Peter Abelard, theologian and philosopher. Her intellectual potential was thwarted by the outcome of their tragic
love for each other; he was castrated, and she entered
a convent.]

pieces. What years are to a gifted individual, generations are to a mass. If women's literature is destined to have a different collective character from that of men, depending on any difference of natural tendencies, much longer time is necessary than has yet elapsed, before it can emancipate itself from the influence of accepted models, and guide itself by its own impulses. But if, as I believe, there will not prove to be any natural tendencies common to women, and distinguishing their genius from that of men, yet every individual writer among them has her individual tendencies, which at present are still subdued by the influence of precedent and example: and it will require generations more, before their individuality is sufficiently developed to make head against that influence.

It is in the fine arts, properly so called, that the *primâ facie* evidence of inferior original powers in women at first sight appears the strongest: since opinion (it may be said) does not exclude them from these, but rather encourages them, and their education, instead of passing over this department, is in the affluent classes mainly composed of it. Yet in this line of exertion they have fallen still more short than in many others, of the highest eminence attained by men. This shortcoming, however, needs no other explanation than the familiar fact, more universally true in the fine arts than in anything else; the vast superiority of professional persons over amateurs. Women in the educated classes are almost universally taught more or less of some branch or other of the fine arts, but not that they may gain their living or their social consequence by it. Women artists are all amateurs. The exceptions are only of the kind which confirm the general truth. Women are taught music, but not for the purpose of composing, only of executing it: and accordingly it is only as composers, that men, in music, are superior to women. The only one of the fine arts which women do follow, to any extent, as a profession, and an occupation for life, is the histrionic; and in that they are confessedly equal, if not superior, to men. To make the comparison fair, it should be made between the productions of women in any branch of art, and those of men not following it as a profession. In musical composition, for example, women surely have produced fully as good things as have ever been produced by male amateurs. There are now a few women, a very few, who practise painting as a profession, and these are already beginning to show quite as much talent as could be expected. Even male painters (*pace* Mr. Ruskin) have not made any very remarkable figure these last centuries, and it will be long before they do so.[26] The reason why the old painters were so greatly superior to the modern, is that a greatly superior class of men applied themselves to the art. In the fourteenth and fifteenth centuries the Italian painters were the most accomplished men of their age. The greatest of them were men of encyclopaedical acquirements and powers, like the great men of Greece. But in their times fine art was, to men's feelings and conceptions, among the grandest things in which a human being could excel; and by it men were made, what only political or military distinction now makes them, the companions of sovereigns, and the equals of the highest nobility. In the present age, men of anything like similar calibre find something more important to do, for their own fame and the uses of the modern world, than painting: and it is only now and then that a Reynolds or a Turner (of whose relative rank among eminent men I do not pretend to an opinion) applies himself to that art.[27] Music belongs to a different order of things; it does not require the same general powers of mind, but seems more dependant on a natural gift: and it may be thought surprising that no one of the great musical composers has been a woman. But even this natural gift, to be made available for great creations, requires study, and professional devotion to the pursuit. The only countries which have produced first-rate composers, even of the male sex, are Germany and Italy — countries in which, both in point of special and of general cultivation, women have remained far behind France and England, being generally (it may be said without exaggeration) very little educated, and having scarcely cultivated at all any of the higher faculties

26. [John Ruskin (1819–1900), the art critic whose *Modern Painters* (1843–60) did much to establish the reputation of J. M. W. Turner (see n. 27).]

27. [Sir Joshua Reynolds (1723–92), portrait painter and art critic, was in 1768 elected the first president of the Royal Academy of Art. Joseph Mallord William Turner (1775–1851) was the greatest English landscapist and marine painter of the nineteenth century.]

of mind. And in those countries the men who are acquainted with the principles of musical composition must be counted by hundreds, or more probably by thousands, the women barely by scores: so that here again, on the doctrine of averages, we cannot reasonably expect to see more than one eminent woman to fifty eminent men; and the last three centuries have not produced fifty eminent male composers either in Germany or in Italy.

There are other reasons, besides those which we have now given, that help to explain why women remain behind men, even in the pursuits which are open to both. For one thing, very few women have time for them. This may seem a paradox; it is an undoubted social fact. The time and thoughts of every woman have to satisfy great previous demands on them for things practical. There is, first, the superintendence of the family and the domestic expenditure, which occupies at least one woman in every family, generally the one of mature years and acquired experience; unless the family is so rich as to admit of delegating that task to hired agency, and submitting to all the waste and malversation inseparable from that mode of conducting it. The superintendence of a household, even when not in other respects laborious, is extremely onerous to the thoughts; it requires incessant vigilance, an eye which no detail escapes, and presents questions for consideration and solution, foreseen and unforeseen, at every hour of the day, from which the person responsible for them can hardly ever shake herself free. If a woman is of a rank and circumstances which relieve her in a measure from these cares, she has still devolving on her the management for the whole family of its intercourse with others—of what is called society, and the less the call made on her by the former duty, the greater is always the development of the latter: the dinner parties, concerts, evening parties, morning visits, letter writing, and all that goes with them. All this is over and above the engrossing duty which society imposes exclusively on women, of making themselves charming. A clever woman of the higher ranks finds nearly a sufficient employment of her talents in cultivating the graces of manner and the arts of conversation. To look only at the outward side of the subject: the great and continual exercise of thought which all women who attach any value to dressing well (I do not mean expensively, but with taste, and perception of natural and of artificial *convenance*) must bestow upon their own dress, perhaps also upon that of their daughters, would alone go a great way towards achieving respectable results in art, or science, or literature, and does actually exhaust much of the time and mental power they might have to spare for either.[28] If it were possible that all this number of little practical interests (which are made great to them) should leave them either much leisure, or much energy and freedom of mind, to be devoted to art or speculation, they must have a much greater original supply of active faculty than the vast majority of men. But this is not all. Independently of the regular offices of life which devolve upon a woman, she is expected to have her time and faculties always at the disposal of everybody. If a man has not a profession to exempt him from such demands, still, if he has a pursuit, he offends nobody by devoting his time to it; occupation is received as a valid excuse for his not answering to every casual demand which may be made on him. Are a woman's occupations, especially her chosen and voluntary ones, ever regarded as excusing her from any of what are termed the calls of society? Scarcely are her most necessary and recognised duties allowed as an exemption. It requires an illness in the family, or something else out of the common way, to entitle her to give her own business the precedence over other people's amusement. She must always be at the beck and call

---

28. "It appears to be the same right turn of mind which enables a man to acquire the truth, or the just idea of what is right, in the ornaments, as in the more stable principles of art. It has still the same centre of perfection, though it is the centre of a smaller circle.—To illustrate this by the fashion of dress, in which there is allowed to be a good or bad taste. The component parts of dress are continually changing from great to little, from short to long; but the general form still remains: it is still the same general dress which is comparatively fixed; though on a very slender foundation; but it is on this which fashion must rest. He who invents with the most success, or dresses in the best taste, would probably, from the same sagacity employed to greater purposes, have discovered equal skill, or have formed the same correct taste, in the highest labours of art." Sir Joshua Reynolds's *Discourses* (1776), Discourse VII (in *Works*, ed. Edmond Malone, 4th ed., 3 vols. [London: Cadell and Davies, 1809], vol. I, pp. 230–31).

of somebody, generally of everybody. If she has a study or a pursuit, she must snatch any short interval which accidentally occurs to be employed in it. A celebrated woman, in a work which I hope will some day be published, remarks truly that everything a woman does is done at odd times. Is it wonderful, then, if she does not attain the highest eminence in things which require consecutive attention, and the concentration on them of the chief interest of life? Such is philosophy, and such, above all, is art, in which, besides the devotion of the thoughts and feelings, the hand also must be kept in constant exercise to attain high skill.

There is another consideration to be added to all these. In the various arts and intellectual occupations, there is a degree of proficiency sufficient for living by it, and there is a higher degree on which depend the great productions which immortalize a name. To the attainment of the former, there are adequate motives in the case of all who follow the pursuit professionally: the other is hardly ever attained where there is not, or where there has not been at some period of life, an ardent desire of celebrity. Nothing less is commonly a sufficient stimulus to undergo the long and patient drudgery, which, in the case even of the greatest natural gifts, is absolutely required for great eminence in pursuits in which we already possess so many splendid memorials of the highest genius. Now, whether the cause be natural or artificial, women seldom have this eagerness for fame. Their ambition is generally confined within narrower bounds. The influence they seek is over those who immediately surround them. Their desire is to be liked, loved, or admired, by those whom they see with their eyes: and the proficiency in knowledge, arts, and accomplishments, which is sufficient for that, almost always contents them. This is a trait of character which cannot be left out of the account in judging of women as they are. I do not at all believe that it is inherent in women. It is only the natural result of their circumstances. The love of fame in men is encouraged by education and opinion: to "scorn delights and live laborious days" for its sake, is accounted the part of "noble minds;" even if spoken of as their "last infirmity,"[29] and is stimulated by the

access which fame gives to all objects of ambition, including even the favour of women; while to women themselves all these objects are closed, and the desire of fame itself considered daring and unfeminine. Besides, how could it be that a woman's interests should not be all concentrated upon the impressions made on those who come into her daily life, when society has ordained that all her duties should be to them, and has contrived that all her comforts should depend on them? The natural desire of consideration from our fellow creatures is as strong in a woman as in a man; but society has so ordered things that public consideration is, in all ordinary cases, only attainable by her through the consideration of her husband or of her male relations, while her private consideration is forfeited by making herself individually prominent, or appearing in any other character than that of an appendage to men. Whoever is in the least capable of estimating the influence on the mind of the entire domestic and social position and the whole habit of a life, must easily recognise in that influence a complete explanation of nearly all the apparent differences between women and men, including the whole of those which imply any inferiority.

As for moral differences, considered as distinguished from intellectual, the distinction commonly drawn is to the advantage of women. They are declared to be better than men; an empty compliment, which must provoke a bitter smile from every woman of spirit, since there is no other situation in life in which it is the established order, and considered quite natural and suitable, that the better should obey the worse. If this piece of idle talk is good for anything, it is only as an admission by men, of the corrupting influence of power; for that is certainly the only truth which the fact, if it be a fact, either proves or illustrates. And it *is* true that servitude, except when it actually brutalizes, though corrupting to both, is less so to the slaves than to the slave-masters. It is wholesomer for the moral nature to be restrained, even by arbitrary power, than to be allowed to exercise arbitrary power without restraint. Women, it is said, seldomer fall under the penal law—contribute a much smaller number of offenders to the criminal calendar, than men. I doubt not that the same thing may be said, with the same truth, of negro slaves. Those who are under the control of others cannot

29. [John Milton, *Lycidas* (1638), ll. 70–72.]

often commit crimes, unless at the command and for the purposes of their masters. I do not know a more signal instance of the blindness with which the world, including the herd of studious men, ignore and pass over all the influences of social circumstances, than their silly depreciation of the intellectual, and silly panegyrics on the moral, nature of women.

The complimentary dictum about women's superior moral goodness may be allowed to pair off with the disparaging one respecting their greater liability to moral bias. Women, we are told, are not capable of resisting their personal partialities: their judgment in grave affairs is warped by their sympathies and antipathies. Assuming it to be so, it is still to be proved that women are oftener misled by their personal feelings than men by their personal interests. The chief difference would seem in that case to be, that men are led from the course of duty and the public interest by their regard for themselves, women (not being allowed to have private interests of their own) by their regard for somebody else. It is also to be considered, that all the education which women receive from society inculcates on them the feeling that the individuals connected with them are the only ones to whom they owe any duty—the only ones whose interest they are called upon to care for; while, as far as education is concerned, they are left strangers even to the elementary ideas which are presupposed in any intelligent regard for larger interests or higher moral objects. The complaint against them resolves itself merely into this, that they fulfil only too faithfully the sole duty which they are taught, and almost the only one which they are permitted to practise.

The concessions of the privileged to the unprivileged are so seldom brought about by any better motive than the power of the unprivileged to extort them, that any arguments against the prerogative of sex are likely to be little attended to by the generality, as long as they are able to say to themselves that women do not complain of it. That fact certainly enables men to retain the unjust privilege some time longer; but does not render it less unjust. Exactly the same thing may be said of the women in the harem of an Oriental: they do not complain of not being allowed the freedom of European women. They think our women insufferably bold and unfeminine. How rarely it is that even men complain of the general order of soci-

ety; and how much rarer still would such complaint be, if they did not know of any different order existing anywhere else. Women do not complain of the general lot of women; or rather they do, for plaintive elegies on it are very common in the writings of women, and were still more so as long as the lamentations could not be suspected of having any practical object. Their complaints are like the complaints which men make of the general unsatisfactoriness of human life; they are not meant to imply blame, or to plead for any change. But though women do not complain of the power of husbands, each complains of her own husband, or of the husbands of her friends. It is the same in all other cases of servitude, at least in the commencement of the emancipatory movement. The serfs did not at first complain of the power of their lords, but only of their tyranny. The, Commons began by claiming a few municipal privileges; they next asked an exemption for themselves from being taxed without their own consent; but they would at that time have thought it a great presumption to claim any share in the king's sovereign authority. The case of women is now the only case in which to rebel against established rules is still looked upon with the same eyes as was formerly a subject's claim to the right of rebelling against his king. A woman who joins in any movement which her husband disapproves, makes herself a martyr, without even being able to be an apostle, for the husband can legally put a stop to her apostleship. Women cannot be expected to devote themselves to the emancipation of women, until men in considerable number are prepared to join with them in the undertaking.

CHAPTER IV

There remains a question, not of less importance than those already discussed, and which will be asked the most importunately by those opponents whose conviction is somewhat shaken on the main point. What good are we to expect from the changes proposed in our customs and institutions? Would mankind be at all better off if women were free? If not, why disturb their minds, and attempt to make a social revolution in the name of an abstract right?

It is hardly to be expected that this question will be asked in respect to the change proposed in the condition of women in marriage. The sufferings, immoralities, evils of all sorts, produced in innumerable cases by the subjection of individual women to individual men, are far too terrible to be overlooked. Unthinking or uncandid persons, counting those cases alone which are extreme, or which attain publicity, may say that the evils are exceptional; but no one can be blind to their existence, nor, in many cases, to their intensity. And it is perfectly obvious that the abuse of power cannot be very much checked while the power remains. It is a power given, or offered, not to good men, or to decently respectable men, but to all men; the most brutal, and the most criminal. There is no check but that of opinion, and such men are in general within the reach of no opinion but that of men like themselves. If such men did not brutally tyrannize over the one human being whom the law compels to bear everything from them, society must already have reached a paradisiacal state. There could be no need any longer of laws to curb men's vicious propensities. Astraea must not only have returned to earth, but the heart of the worst man must have become her temple. The law of servitude in marriage is a monstrous contradiction to all the principles of the modern world, and to all the experience through which those principles have been slowly and painfully worked out. It is the sole case, now that negro slavery has been abolished, in which a human being in the plenitude of every faculty is delivered up to the tender mercies of another human being, in the hope forsooth that this other will use the power solely for the good of the person subjected to it. Marriage is the only actual bondage known to our law. There remain no legal slaves, except the mistress of every house.

It is not, therefore, on this part of the subject, that the question is likely to be asked, *Cui bono?*[30] We may be told that the evil would outweigh the good, but the reality of the good admits of no dispute. In regard, however, to the larger question, the removal of women's disabilities—their recognition as the equals of men in all that belongs to citizenship—the opening to them of all honourable employments, and of the training and education which qualifies for those employments—there are many persons for whom it is not enough that the inequality has no just or legitimate defence; they require to be told what express advantage would be obtained by abolishing it.

To which let me first answer, the advantage of having the most universal and pervading of all human relations regulated by justice instead of injustice. The vast amount of this gain to human nature, it is hardly possible, by any explanation or illustration, to place in a stronger light than it is placed by the bare statement, to any one who attaches a moral meaning to words. All the selfish propensities, the self-worship, the unjust self-preference, which exist among mankind, have their source and root in, and derive their principal nourishment from, the present constitution of the relation between men and women. Think what it is to a boy, to grow up to manhood in the belief that without any merit or any exertion of his own, though he may be the most frivolous and empty or the most ignorant and stolid of mankind, by the mere fact of being born a male he is by right the superior of all and every one of an entire half of the human race: including probably some whose real superiority to himself he has daily or hourly occasion to feel; but even if in his whole conduct he habitually follows a woman's guidance, still, if he is a fool, he thinks that of course she is not, and cannot be, equal in ability and judgment to himself; and if he is not a fool, he does worse—he sees that she is superior to him, and believes that, notwithstanding her superiority, he is entitled to command and she is bound to obey. What must be the effect on his character, of this lesson? And men of the cultivated classes are often not aware how deeply it sinks into the immense majority of male minds. For, among right-feeling and well-bred people, the inequality is kept as much as possible out of sight; above all, out of sight of the children. As much obedience is required from boys to their mother as to their father: they are not permitted to domineer over their sisters, nor are they accustomed to see these postponed to them, but the contrary; the compensations of the chivalrous feeling being made prominent, while the servitude which requires them is kept in the background. Well brought-up youths in the higher classes thus often escape the bad influences of the

30. ["For the good of whom?"]

situation in their early years, and only experience them when, arrived at manhood, they fall under the dominion of facts as they really exist. Such people are little aware, when a boy is differently brought up, how early the notion of his inherent superiority to a girl arises in his mind; how it grows with his growth and strengthens with his strength; how it is inoculated by one schoolboy upon another; how early the youth thinks himself superior to his mother, owing her perhaps forbearance, but no real respect; and how sublime and sultan-like a sense of superiority he feels, above all, over the woman whom he honours by admitting her to a partnership of his life. Is it imagined that all this does not pervert the whole manner of existence of the man, both as an individual and as a social being? It is an exact parallel to the feeling of a hereditary king that he is excellent above others by being born a king, or a noble by being born a noble. The relation between husband and wife is very like that between lord and vassal, except that the wife is held to more unlimited obedience than the vassal was. However the vassal's character may have been affected, for better and for worse, by his subordination, who can help seeing that the lord's was affected greatly for the worse? whether he was led to believe that his vassals were really superior to himself, or to feel that he was placed in command over people as good as himself, for no merits or labours of his own, but merely for having, as Figaro says, taken the trouble to be born. The self-worship of the monarch, or of the feudal superior, is matched by the self-worship of the male. Human beings do not grow up from childhood in the possession of unearned distinctions, without pluming themselves upon them. Those whom privileges not acquired by their merit, and which they feel to be disproportioned to it, inspire with additional humility, are always the few, and the best few. The rest are only inspired with pride, and the worst sort of pride, that which values itself upon accidental advantages, not of its own achieving. Above all, when the feeling of being raised above the whole of the other sex is combined with personal authority over one individual among them; the situation, if a school of conscientious and affectionate forbearance to those whose strongest points of character are conscience and affection, is to men of another quality a regularly constituted Academy or Gymnasium for training them in arrogance and overbearingness; which vices, if curbed by the certainty of resistance in their intercourse with other men, their equals, break out towards all who are in a position to be obliged to tolerate them, and often revenge themselves upon the unfortunate wife for the involuntary restraint which they are obliged to submit to elsewhere.

The example afforded, and the education given to the sentiments, by laying the foundation of domestic existence upon a relation contradictory to the first principles of social justice, must, from the very nature of man, have a perverting influence of such magnitude, that it is hardly possible with our present experience to raise our imaginations to the conception of so great a change for the better as would be made by its removal. All that education and civilization are doing to efface the influences on character of the law of force, and replace them by those of justice, remains merely on the surface, as long as the citadel of the enemy is not attacked. The principle of the modern movement in morals and politics, is that conduct, and conduct alone, entitles to respect: that not what men are, but what they do, constitutes their claim to deference; that, above all, merit, and not birth, is the only rightful claim to power and authority. If no authority, not in its nature temporary, were allowed to one human being over another, society would not be employed in building up propensities with one hand which it has to curb with the other. The child would really, for the first time in man's existence on earth, be trained in the way he should go, and when he was old there would be a chance that he would not depart from it. But so long as the right of the strong to power over the weak rules in the very heart of society, the attempt to make the equal right of the weak the principle of its outward actions will always be an uphill struggle; for the law of justice, which is also that of Christianity, will never get possession of men's inmost sentiments; they will be working against it, even when bending to it.

The second benefit to be expected from giving to women the free use of their faculties, by leaving them the free choice of their employments, and opening to them the same field of occupation and the same prizes and encouragements as to other human beings, would be that of doubling the mass of mental faculties available for the higher service of humanity. Where there is now one person qualified to benefit mankind and promote the general improvement, as a public teacher, or an administrator of some branch of public or social affairs, there would then be a chance of two. Mental superiority of any kind is at present everywhere so much below the demand; there is such a deficiency of persons competent to do excellently anything which it requires any considerable amount of ability to do; that the loss to the world, by refusing to make use of one-half of the whole quantity of talent it possesses, is extremely serious. It is true that this amount of mental power is not totally lost. Much of it is employed, and would in any case be employed, in domestic management, and in the few other occupations open to women; and from the remainder indirect benefit is in many individual cases obtained, through the personal influence of individual women over individual men. But these benefits are partial; their range is extremely circumscribed; and if they must be admitted, on the one hand, as a deduction from the amount of fresh social power that would be acquired by giving freedom to one-half of the whole sum of human intellect, there must be added, on the other, the benefit of the stimulus that would be given to the intellect of men by the competition; or (to use a more true expression) by the necessity that would be imposed on them of deserving precedency before they could expect to obtain it.

This great accession to the intellectual power of the species, and to the amount of intellect available for the good management of its affairs, would be obtained, partly, through the better and more complete intellectual education of women, which would then improve *pari passu* with that of men. Women in general would be brought up equally capable of understanding business, public affairs, and the higher matters of speculation, with men in the same class of society; and the select few of the one as well as of the other sex, who were qualified not only to comprehend what is done or thought by others, but to think or do something considerable themselves, would meet with the same facilities for improving and training their capacities in the one sex as in the other. In this way, the widening of the sphere of action for women would operate for good, by raising their education to the level of that of men, and making the one participate in all improvements made in the other. But independently of this, the mere breaking down of the barrier would of itself have an educational virtue of the highest worth. The mere getting rid of the idea that all the wider subjects of thought and action, all the things which are of general and not solely of private interest, are men's business, from which women are to be warned off—positively interdicted from most of it, coldly tolerated in the little which is allowed them—the mere consciousness a woman would then have of being a human being like any other, entitled to choose her pursuits, urged or invited by the same inducements as any one else to interest herself in whatever is interesting to human beings, entitled to exert the share of influence on all human concerns which belongs to an individual opinion, whether she attempted actual participation in them or not—this alone would effect an immense expansion of the faculties of women, as well as enlargement of the range of their moral sentiments.

Besides the addition to the amount of individual talent available for the conduct of human affairs, which certainly are not at present so abundantly provided in that respect that they can afford to dispense with one-half of what nature proffers; the opinion of women would then possess a more beneficial, rather than a greater, influence upon the general mass of human belief and sentiment. I say a more beneficial, rather than a greater influence; for the influence of women over the general tone of opinion has always, or at least from the earliest known period, been very considerable. The influence of mothers on the early character of their sons, and the desire of young men to recommend themselves to young women, have in all recorded times been important agencies in the formation of character, and have determined some of the chief steps in the progress of civilization. Even in the Homeric age, αἰδώς towards the Τρωάδας ἑλκεσιπέπλους[31] is an acknowledged and powerful motive of action in the great Hector. The moral influence of women has had two modes of operation. First, it has been a softening influence. Those who were most liable to be the victims of violence, have naturally tended as much as they could towards

31. ["Regard for the judgment of the Trojan women." Homer, *The Iliad*, Bk. 6, 441–42.]

limiting its sphere and mitigating its excesses. Those who were not taught to fight, have naturally inclined in favour of any other mode of settling differences rather than that of fighting. In general, those who have been the greatest sufferers by the indulgence of selfish passion, have been the most earnest supporters of any moral law which offered a means of bridling passion. Women were powerfully instrumental in inducing the northern conquerors to adopt the creed of Christianity, a creed so much more favourable to women than any that preceded it. The conversion of the Anglo-Saxons and of the Franks may be said to have been begun by the wives of Ethelbert and Clovis. The other mode in which the effect of women's opinion has been conspicuous, is by giving a powerful stimulus to those qualities in men, which, not being themselves trained in, it was necessary for them that they should find in their protectors. Courage, and the military virtues generally, have at all times been greatly indebted to the desire which men felt of being admired by women: and the stimulus reaches far beyond this one class of eminent qualities, since, by a very natural effect of their position, the best passport to the admiration and favour of women has always been to be thought highly of by men. From the combination of the two kinds of moral influence thus exercised by women, arose the spirit of chivalry: the peculiarity of which is, to aim at combining the highest standard of the warlike qualities with the cultivation of a totally different class of virtues—those of gentleness, generosity, and self-abnegation, towards the non-military and defenceless classes generally, and a special submission and worship directed towards women; who were distinguished from the other defenceless classes by the high rewards which they had it in their power voluntarily to bestow on those who endeavoured to earn their favour, instead of extorting their subjection. Though the practice of chivalry fell even more sadly short of its theoretic standard than practice generally falls below theory, it remains one of the most precious monuments of the moral history of our race; as a remarkable instance of a concerted and organized attempt by a most disorganized and distracted society, to raise up and carry into practice a moral ideal greatly in advance of its social conditions and institutions; so much so as to have been completely frustrated in the main object, yet never entirely inefficacious, and

which has left a most sensible, and for the most part a highly valuable impress on the ideas and feelings of all subsequent times.

The chivalrous ideal is the acme of the influence of women's sentiments on the moral cultivation of mankind: and if women are to remain in their subordinate situation, it were greatly to be lamented that the chivalrous standard should have passed away, for it is the only one at all capable of mitigating the demoralizing influences of that position. But the changes in the general state of the species rendered inevitable the substitution of a totally different ideal of morality for the chivalrous one. Chivalry was the attempt to infuse moral elements into a state of society in which everything depended for good or evil on individual prowess, under the softening influences of individual delicacy and generosity. In modern societies, all things, even in the military department of affairs, are decided, not by individual effort, but by the combined operations of numbers; while the main occupation of society has changed from fighting to business, from military to industrial life. The exigencies of the new life are no more exclusive of the virtues of generosity than those of the old, but it no longer entirely depends on them. The main foundations of the moral life of modern times must be justice and prudence; the respect of each for the rights of every other, and the ability of each to take care of himself. Chivalry left without legal check all forms of wrong which reigned unpunished throughout society; it only encouraged a few to do right in preference to wrong, by the direction it gave to the instruments of praise and admiration. But the real dependence of morality must always be upon its penal sanctions— its power to deter from evil. The security of society cannot rest on merely rendering honour to right, a motive so comparatively weak in all but a few, and which on very many does not operate at all. Modern society is able to repress wrong through all departments of life, by a fit exertion of the superior strength which civilization has given it, and thus to render the existence of the weaker members of society (no longer defenceless but protected by law) tolerable to them, without reliance on the chivalrous feelings of those who are in a position to tyrannize. The beauties and graces of the chivalrous character are still what they were, but the rights of the weak, and the general comfort of human life, now rest on a far surer and steadier support; or rather, they do so in every relation of life except the conjugal.

At present the moral influence of women is no less real, but it is no longer of so marked and definite a character: it has more nearly merged in the general influence of public opinion. Both through the contagion of sympathy, and through the desire of men to shine in the eyes of women, their feelings have great effect in keeping alive what remains of the chivalrous ideal—in fostering the sentiments and continuing the traditions of spirit and generosity. In these points of character, their standard is higher than that of men; in the quality of justice, somewhat lower. As regards the relations of private life it may be said generally, that their influence is, on the whole, encouraging to the softer virtues, discouraging to the sterner: though the statement must be taken with all the modifications dependent on individual character. In the chief of the greater trials to which virtue is subject in the concerns of life—the conflict between interest and principle—the tendency of women's influence is of a very mixed character. When the principle involved happens to be one of the very few which the course of their religious or moral education has strongly impressed upon themselves, they are potent auxiliaries to virtue. and their husbands and sons are often prompted by them to acts of abnegation which they never would have been capable of without that stimulus. But, with the present education and position of women, the moral principles which have been impressed on them cover but a comparatively small part of the field of virtue, and are, moreover, principally negative; forbidding particular acts, but having little to do with the general direction of the thoughts and purposes. I am afraid it must be said, that disinterestedness in the general conduct of life—the devotion of the energies to purposes which hold out no promise of private advantages to the family—is very seldom encouraged or supported by women's influence. It is small blame to them that they discourage objects of which they have not learnt to see the advantage, and which withdraw their men from them, and from the interests of the family. But the consequence is that women's influence is often anything but favourable to public virtue.

Women have, however, some share of influence in giving the tone to public moralities since their sphere of action has been a little widened, and since a considerable number of them have occupied themselves practically in the promotion of objects reaching beyond their own family and household. The influence of women counts for a great deal in two of the most marked features of modern European life—its aversion to war, and its addiction to philanthropy. Excellent characteristics both; but unhappily, if the influence of women is valuable in the encouragement it gives to these feelings in general, in the particular applications the direction it gives to them is at least as often mischievous as useful. In the philanthropic department more particularly, the two provinces chiefly cultivated by women are religious proselytism and charity. Religious proselytism at home, is but another word for embittering of religious animosities: abroad, it is usually a blind running at an object, without either knowing or heeding the fatal mischiefs—fatal to the religious object itself as well as to all other desirable objects—which may be produced by the means employed. As for charity, it is a matter in which the immediate effect on the persons directly concerned, and the ultimate consequence to the general good, are apt to be at complete war with one another: while the education given to women—an education of the sentiments rather than of the understanding—and the habit inculcated by their whole life, of looking to immediate effects on persons, and not to remote effects on classes of persons—make them both unable to see, and unwilling to admit, the ultimate evil tendency of any form of charity or philanthropy which commends itself to their sympathetic feelings. The great and continually increasing mass of unenlightened and shortsighted benevolence, which, taking the care of people's lives out of their own hands, and relieving them from the disagreeable consequences of their own acts, saps the very foundations of the self-respect, self-help, and self-control which are the essential conditions both of individual prosperity and of social virtue—this waste of resources and of benevolent feelings in doing harm instead of good, is immensely swelled by women's contributions, and stimulated by their influence. Not that this is a mistake likely to be made by women, where they have actually the practical management of schemes of beneficence. It sometimes happens that women who administer public charities—with that insight into present fact, and especially into the minds and feelings of those with whom they are in immediate contact, in which women generally excel men—recognise in the clearest manner the demoralizing influence of the alms given or the help afforded, and could give lessons on the subject to many a male political economist. But women who only give their money, and are not brought face to face with the effects it produces, how can they be expected to foresee them? A woman born to the present lot of women, and content with it, how should she appreciate the value of self-dependence? She is not self-dependent; she is not taught self-dependence; her destiny is to receive everything from others, and why should what is good enough for her be bad for the poor? Her familiar notions of good are of blessings descending from a superior. She forgets that she is not free, and that the poor are; that if what they need is given to them unearned, they cannot be compelled to earn it: that everybody cannot be taken care of by everybody, but there must be some motive to induce people to take care of themselves; and that to be helped to help themselves, if they are physically capable of it, is the only charity which proves to be charity in the end.

These considerations shew how usefully the part which women take in the formation of general opinion, would be modified for the better by that more enlarged instruction, and practical conversancy with the things which their opinions influence, that would necessarily arise from their social and political emancipation. But the improvement it would work through the influence they exercise, each in her own family, would be still more remarkable.

It is often said that in the classes most exposed to temptation, a man's wife and children tend to keep him honest and respectable, both by the wife's direct influence, and by the concern he feels for their future welfare. This may be so, and no doubt often is so, with those who are more weak than wicked; and this beneficial influence would be preserved and strengthened under equal laws; it does not depend on the woman's servitude, but is, on the contrary, diminished by the disrespect which the inferior class of men

always at heart feel towards those who are subject to their power. But when we ascend higher in the scale, we come among a totally different set of moving forces. The wife's influence tends, as far as it goes, to prevent the husband from falling below the common standard of approbation of the country. It tends quite as strongly to hinder him from rising above it. The wife is the auxiliary of the common public opinion. A man who is married to a woman his inferior in intelligence, finds her a perpetual dead weight, or, worse than a dead weight, a drag, upon every aspiration of his to be better than public opinion requires him to be. It is hardly possible for one who is in these bonds, to attain exalted virtue. If he differs in his opinion from the mass—if he sees truths which have not yet dawned upon them, or if, feeling in his heart truths which they nominally recognise, he would like to act up to those truths more conscientiously than the generality of mankind—to all such thoughts and desires, marriage is the heaviest of drawbacks, unless he be so fortunate as to have a wife as much above the common level as he himself is.

For, in the first place, there is always some sacrifice of personal interest required; either of social consequence, or of pecuniary means; perhaps the risk of even the means of subsistence. These sacrifices and risks he may be willing to encounter for himself; but he will pause before he imposes them on his family. And his family in this case means his wife and daughters; for he always hopes that his sons will feel as he feels himself, and that what he can do without, they will do without, willingly, in the same cause. But his daughters—their marriage may depend upon it: and his wife, who is unable to enter into or understand the objects for which these sacrifices are made—who, if she thought them worth any sacrifice, would think so on trust, and solely for his sake—who can participate in none of the enthusiasm or the self-approbation he himself may feel, while the things which he is disposed to sacrifice are all in all to her; will not the best and most unselfish man hesitate the longest before bringing on her this consequence? If it be not the comforts of life, but only social consideration, that is at stake, the burthen upon his conscience and feelings is still very severe. Whoever has a wife and children has given hostages to Mrs. Grundy.[32] The approbation of that potentate may be a matter of indifference to him, but it is of great importance to his wife. The man himself may be above opinion, or may find sufficient compensation in the opinion of those of his own way of thinking. But to the women connected with him, he can offer no compensation. The almost invariable tendency of the wife to place her influence in the same scale with social consideration, is sometimes made a reproach to women, and represented as a peculiar trait of feebleness and childishness of character in them: surely with great injustice. Society makes the whole life of a woman, in the easy classes, a continued self-sacrifice; it exacts from her an unremitting restraint of the whole of her natural inclinations, and the sole return it makes to her for what often deserves the name of a martyrdom, is consideration. Her consideration is inseparably connected with that of her husband, and after paying the full price for it, she finds that she is to lose it, for no reason of which she can feel the cogency. She has sacrificed her whole life to it, and her husband will not sacrifice to it a whim, a freak, an eccentricity; something not recognised or allowed for by the world, and which the world will agree with her in thinking a folly, if it thinks no worse! The dilemma is hardest upon that very meritorious class of men, who, without possessing talents which qualify them to make a figure among those with whom they agree in opinion, hold their opinion from conviction, and feel bound in honour and conscience to serve it, by making profession of their belief, and giving their time, labour, and means, to anything undertaken in its behalf. The worst case of all is when such men happen to be of a rank and position which of itself neither gives them, nor excludes them from, what is considered the best society; when their admission to it depends mainly on what is thought of them personally—and however unexceptionable their breeding and habits, their being identified with opinions and public conduct unacceptable to those who give the tone to society would operate as an effectual exclusion. Many a woman flatters herself (nine times

out of ten quite erroneously) that nothing prevents her and her husband from moving in the highest society of her neighbourhood—society in which others well known to her, and in the same class of life, mix freely—except that her husband is unfortunately a Dissenter, or has the reputation of mingling in low radical politics. That it is, she thinks, which hinders George from getting a commission or a place, Caroline from making an advantageous match, and prevents her and her husband from obtaining invitations, perhaps honours, which, for aught she sees, they are as well entitled to as some folks. With such an influence in every house, either exerted actively, or operating all the more powerfully for not being asserted, is it any wonder that people in general are kept down in that mediocrity of respectability which is becoming a marked characteristic of modern times?

There is another very injurious aspect in which the effect, not of women's disabilities directly, but of the broad line of difference which those disabilities create between the education and character of a woman and that of a man, requires to be considered. Nothing can be more unfavourable to that union of thoughts and inclinations which is the ideal of married life. Intimate society between people radically dissimilar to one another, is an idle dream. Unlikeness may attract, but it is likeness which retains; and in proportion to the likeness is the suitability of the individuals to give each other a happy life. While women are so unlike men, it is not wonderful that selfish men should feel the need of arbitrary power in their own hands, to arrest *in limine* the life-long conflict of inclinations, by deciding every question on the side of their own preference. When people are extremely unlike, there can be no real identity of interest. Very often there is conscientious difference of opinion between married people, on the highest points of duty. Is there any reality in the marriage union where this takes place? Yet it is not uncommon anywhere, when the woman has any earnestness of character; and it is a very general case indeed in Catholic countries, when she is supported in her dissent by the only other authority to which she is taught to bow, the priest. With the usual barefacedness of power not accustomed to find itself disputed, the influence of priests over women is attacked by

32. [A character in Thomas Morton's play *Speed the Plough* (1798), who represents the censoring opinions of the rigidly respectable.]

Protestant and Liberal writers, less for being bad in itself, than because it is a rival authority to the husband, and raises up a revolt against his infallibility. In England, similar differences occasionally exist when an Evangelical wife has allied herself with a husband of a different quality; but in general this source at least of dissension is got rid of, by reducing the minds of women to such a nullity, that they have no opinions but those of Mrs. Grundy or those which the husband tells them to have. When there is no difference of opinion, differences merely of taste may be sufficient to detract greatly from the happiness of married life. And though it may stimulate the amatory propensities of men, it does not conduce to married happiness, to exaggerate by differences of education whatever may be the native differences of the sexes. If the married pair are well-bred and well-behaved people, they tolerate each other's tastes; but is mutual toleration what people look forward to, when they enter into marriage? These differences of inclination will naturally make their wishes different, if not restrained by affection or duty, as to almost all domestic questions which arise. What a difference there must be in the society which the two persons will wish to frequent, or be frequented by! Each will desire associates who share their own tastes: the persons agreeable to one, will be indifferent or positively disagreeable to the other; yet there can be none who are not common to both, for married people do not now live in different parts of the house and have totally different visiting lists, as in the reign of Louis XV.[33] They cannot help having different wishes as to the bringing up of the children: each will wish to see reproduced in them their own tastes and sentiments: and there is either a compromise, and only a half-satisfaction to either, or the wife has to yield—often with bitter suffering; and, with or without intention, her occult influence continues to counterwork the husband's purposes.

It would of course be extreme folly to suppose that these differences of feeling and inclination only exist because women are brought up differently from men, and that there would not be differences of taste under

any imaginable circumstances. But there is nothing beyond the mark in saying that the distinction in bringing-up immensely aggravates those differences, and renders them wholly inevitable. While women are brought up as they are, a man and a woman will but rarely find in one another real agreement of tastes and wishes as to daily life. They will generally have to give it up as hopeless, and renounce the attempt to have, in the intimate associate of their daily life, that *idem velle, idem nolle,*[34] which is the recognised bond of any society that is really such: or if the man succeeds in obtaining it, he does so by choosing a woman who is so complete a nullity that she has no *velle* or *nolle* at all, and is as ready to comply with one thing as another if anybody tells her to do so. Even this calculation is apt to fail; dulness and want of spirit are not always a guarantee of the submission which is so confidently expected from them. But if they were, is this the ideal of marriage? What, in this case, does the man obtain by it, except an upper servant, a nurse, or a mistress? On the contrary, when each of two persons, instead of being a nothing, is a something; when they are attached to one another, and are not too much unlike to begin with; the constant partaking in the same things, assisted by their sympathy, draws out the latent capacities of each for being interested in the things which were at first interesting only to the other; and works a gradual assimilation of the tastes and characters to one another, partly by the insensible modification of each but more by a real enriching of the two natures, each acquiring the tastes and capacities of the other in addition to its own. This often happens between two friends of the same sex, who are much associated in their daily life: and it would be a common, if not the commonest, case in marriage, did not the totally different bringing-up of the two sexes make it next to an impossibility to form a really well-assorted union. Were this remedied, whatever differences there might still be in individual tastes, there would at least be, as a general rule, complete unity and unanimity as to the great objects of life. When the two persons both care for great objects, and are a help and encour-

33. [King of France (1715–74).]

34. ["Wanting the same and not wanting the same," that is to say, similarity in opinions, tastes, or values.]

agement to each other in whatever regards these, the minor matters on which their tastes may differ are not all-important to them; and there is a foundation for solid friendship, of an enduring character, more likely than anything else to make it, through the whole of life, a greater pleasure to each to give pleasure to the other, than to receive it.

I have considered, thus far, the effects on the pleasures and benefits of the marriage union which depend on the mere unlikeness between the wife and the husband: but the evil tendency is prodigiously aggravated when the unlikeness is inferiority. Mere unlikeness, when it only means difference of good qualities, may be more a benefit in the way of mutual improvement, than a drawback from comfort. When each emulates, and desires and endeavours to acquire, the other's peculiar qualities, the difference does not produce diversity of interest, but increased identity of it, and makes each still more valuable to the other. But when one is much the inferior of the two in mental ability and cultivation, and is not actively attempting by the other's aid to rise to the other's level, the whole influence of the connexion upon the development of the superior of the two is deteriorating: and still more so in a tolerably happy marriage than in an unhappy one. It is not with impunity that the superior in intellect shuts himself up with an inferior, and elects that inferior for his chosen, and sole completely intimate, associate. Any society which is not improving, is deteriorating: and the more so, the closer and more familiar it is. Even a really superior man almost always begins to deteriorate when he is habitually (as the phrase is) king of his company: and in his most habitual company the husband who has a wife inferior to him is always so. While his self-satisfaction is incessantly ministered to on the one hand, on the other he insensibly imbibes the modes of feeling, and of looking at things, which belong to a more vulgar or a more limited mind than his own. This evil differs from many of those which have hitherto been dwelt on, by being an increasing one. The association of men with women in daily life is much closer and more complete than it ever was before. Men's life is more domestic. Formerly, their pleasures and chosen occupations were among men, and in men's company: their wives had but a fragment of

their lives. At the present time, the progress of civilization, and the turn of opinion against the rough amusements and convivial excesses which formerly occupied most men in their hours of relaxation— together with (it must be said) the improved tone of modern feeling as to the reciprocity of duty which binds the husband towards the wife—have thrown the man very much more upon home and its inmates, for his personal and social pleasures: while the kind and degree of improvement which has been made in women's education, has made them in some degree capable of being his companions in ideas and mental tastes, while leaving them, in most cases, still hopelessly inferior to him. His desire of mental communion is thus in general satisfied by a communion from which he learns nothing. An unimproving and unstimulating companionship is substituted for (what he might otherwise have been obliged to seek) the society of his equals in powers and his fellows in the higher pursuits. We see, accordingly, that young men of the greatest promise generally cease to improve as soon as they marry, and, not improving, inevitably degenerate. If the wife does not push the husband forward, she always holds him back. He ceases to care for what she does not care for; he no longer desires, and ends by disliking and shunning, society congenial to his former aspirations, and which would now shame his falling-off from them; his higher faculties both of mind and heart cease to be called into activity. And this change coinciding with the new and selfish interests which are created by the family, after a few years he differs in no material respect from those who have never had wishes for anything but the common vanities and the common pecuniary objects.

What marriage may be in the case of two persons of cultivated faculties, identical in opinions and purposes, between whom there exists that best kind of equality, similarity of powers and capacities with reciprocal superiority in them—so that each can enjoy the luxury of looking up to the other, and can have alternately the pleasure of leading and of being led in the path of development—I will not attempt to describe. To those who can conceive it, there is no need; to those who cannot, it would appear the dream of an enthusiast. But I maintain, with the profoundest conviction, that this, and this only, is the ideal of marriage; and that all opinion, customs, and institutions which favour any other notion of it, or turn the conceptions and aspirations connected with it into any other direction, by whatever pretences they may be coloured, are relics of primitive barbarism. The moral regeneration of mankind will only really commence, when the most fundamental of the social relations is placed under the rule of equal justice, and when human beings learn to cultivate their strongest sympathy with an equal in rights and in cultivation.

Thus far, the benefits which it has appeared that the world would gain by ceasing to make sex a disqualification for privileges and a badge of subjection, are social rather than individual; consisting in an increase of the general fund of thinking and acting power, and an improvement in the general conditions of the association of men with women. But it would be a grievous understatement of the case to omit the most direct benefit of all, the unspeakable gain in private happiness to the liberated half of the species; the difference to them between a life of subjection to the will of others, and a life of rational freedom. After the primary necessities of food and raiment, freedom is the first and strongest want of human nature. While mankind are lawless, their desire is for lawless freedom. When they have learnt to understand the meaning of duty and the value of reason, they incline more and more to be guided and restrained by these in the exercise of their freedom; but they do not therefore desire freedom less; they do not become disposed to accept the will of other people as the representative and interpreter of those guiding principles. On the contrary, the communities in which the reason has been most cultivated, and in which the idea of social duty has been most powerful, are those which have most strongly asserted the freedom of action of the individual — the liberty of each to govern his conduct by his own feelings of duty, and by such laws and social restraints as his own conscience can subscribe to.

He who would rightly appreciate the worth of personal independence as an element of happiness, should consider the value he himself puts upon it as an ingredient of his own. There is no subject on which there is a greater habitual difference of judgment between a man judging for himself, and the same man judging for other people. When he hears others complaining that they are not allowed freedom of action — that their own will has not sufficient influence in the regulation of their affairs — his inclination is, to ask, what are their grievances? what positive damage they sustain? and in what respect they consider their affairs to be mismanaged? and if they fail to make out, in answer to these questions, what appears to him a sufficient case, he turns a deaf ear, and regards their complaint as the fanciful querulousness of people whom nothing reasonable will satisfy. But he has a quite different standard of judgment when he is deciding for himself. Then, the most unexceptionable administration of his interests by a tutor set over him, does not satisfy his feelings: his personal exclusion from the deciding authority appears itself the greatest grievance of all, rendering it superfluous even to enter into the question of mismanagement. It is the same with nations. What citizen of a free country would listen to any offers of good and skilful administration, in return for the abdication of freedom? Even if he could believe that good and skilful administration can exist among a people ruled by a will not their own, would not the consciousness of working out their own destiny under their own moral responsibility be a compensation to his feelings for great rudeness and imperfection in the details of public affairs? Let him rest assured that whatever he feels on this point, women feel in a fully equal degree. Whatever has been said or written, from the time of Herodotus to the present, of the ennobling influence of free government[35] — the nerve and spring which it gives to all the faculties, the larger and higher objects which it presents to the intellect and feelings, the more unselfish public spirit, and calmer and broader views of duty, that it engenders, and the generally loftier platform on which it elevates the individual as a moral, spiritual, and social being — is every particle as true of women as of men. Are these things no important part of individual happiness? Let any man call to mind what he himself felt on emerging

35. [Herodotus (c. 484–c. 425 B.C.E.) was the first great historian. Bk. 3, 80 of his *History* of the Persian wars consists of a speech about the evils of monarchy and in praise of popular government.]

from boyhood—from the tutelage and control of even loved and affectionate elders—and entering upon the responsibilities of manhood. Was it not like the physical effect of taking off a heavy weight, or releasing him from obstructive, even if not otherwise painful, bonds? Did he not feel twice as much alive, twice as much a human being, as before? And does he imagine that women have none of these feelings? But it is a striking fact, that the satisfactions and mortifications of personal pride, though all in all to most men when the case is their own, have less allowance made for them in the case of other people, and are less listened to as a ground or a justification of conduct, than any other natural human feelings; perhaps because men compliment them in their own case with the names of so many other qualities, that they are seldom conscious how mighty an influence these feelings exercise in their own lives. No less large and powerful is their part, we may assure ourselves, in the lives and feelings of women. Women are schooled into suppressing them in their most natural and most healthy direction, but the internal principle remains, in a different outward form. An active and energetic mind, if denied liberty, will seek for power: refused the command of itself, it will assert its personality by attempting to control others. To allow to any human beings no existence of their own but what depends on others, is giving far too high a premium on bending others to their purposes. Where liberty cannot be hoped for, and power can, power becomes the grand object of human desire; those to whom others will not leave the undisturbed management of their own affairs, will compensate themselves, if they can, by meddling for their own purposes with the affairs of others. Hence also women's passion for personal beauty, and dress and display; and all the evils that flow from it, in the way of mischievous luxury and social immorality. The love of power and the love of liberty are in eternal antagonism. Where there is least liberty, the passion for power is the most ardent and unscrupulous. The desire of power over others can only cease to be a depraving agency among mankind, when each of them individually is able to do without it: which can only be where respect for liberty in the personal concerns of each is an established principle.

But it is not only through the sentiment of personal dignity, that the free direction and disposal of their own faculties is a source of individual happiness, and to be fettered and restricted in it, a source of unhappiness, to human beings, and not least to women. There is nothing, after disease, indigence, and guilt, so fatal to the pleasurable enjoyment of life as the want of a worthy outlet for the active faculties. Women who have the cares of a family, and while they have the cares of a family, have this outlet, and it generally suffices for them: but what of the greatly increasing number of women, who have had no opportunity of exercising the vocation which they are mocked by telling them is their proper one? What of the women whose children have been lost to them by death or distance, or have grown up, married, and formed homes of their own? There are abundant examples of men who, after a life engrossed by business, retire with a competency to the enjoyment, as they hope, of rest, but to whom, as they are unable to acquire new interests and excitements that can replace the old, the change to a life of inactivity brings ennui, melancholy, and premature death. Yet no one thinks of the parallel case of so many worthy and devoted women, who, having paid what they are told is their debt to society—having brought up a family blamelessly to manhood and womanhood—having kept a house as long as they had a house needing to be kept—are deserted by the sole occupation for which they have fitted themselves; and remain with undiminished activity but with no employment for it, unless perhaps a daughter or daughter-in-law is willing to abdicate in their favour the discharge of the same functions in her younger household. Surely a hard lot for the old age of those who have worthily discharged, as long as it was given to them to discharge, what the world accounts their only social duty. Of such women, and of those others to whom this duty has not been committed at all—many of whom pine through life with the consciousness of thwarted vocations, and activities which are not suffered to expand—the only resources, speaking generally, are religion and charity. But their religion, though it may be one of feeling, and of ceremonial observance, cannot be a religion of action, unless in the form of charity. For charity many of them are by nature admirably fitted; but to practise it usefully, or even without doing mischief, requires the education, the manifold preparation, the knowledge and the thinking powers, of a skilful administrator. There are few of the administrative functions of government for which a person would not be fit, who is fit to bestow charity usefully. In this as in other cases (pre-eminently in that of the education of children), the duties permitted to women cannot be performed properly, without their being trained for duties which, to the great loss of society, are not permitted to them. And here let me notice the singular way in which the question of women's disabilities is frequently presented to view, by those who find it easier to draw a ludicrous picture of what they do not like, than to answer the arguments for it. When it is suggested that women's executive capacities and prudent counsels might sometimes be found valuable in affairs of state, these lovers of fun hold up to the ridicule of the world, as sitting in parliament or in the cabinet, girls in their teens, or young wives of two or three and twenty, transported bodily, exactly as they are, from the drawing-room to the House of Commons. They forget that males are not usually selected at this early age for a seat in Parliament, or for responsible political functions. Common sense would tell them that if such trusts were confided to women, it would be to such as having no special vocation for married life, or preferring another employment of their faculties (as many women even now prefer to marriage some of the few honourable occupations within their reach), have spent the best years of their youth in attempting to qualify themselves for the pursuits in which they desire to engage; or still more frequently perhaps, widows or wives of forty or fifty, by whom the knowledge of life and faculty of government which they have acquired in their families, could by the aid of appropriate studies be made available on a less contracted scale. There is no country of Europe in which the ablest men have not frequently experienced, and keenly appreciated, the value of the advice and help of clever and experienced women of the world, in the attainment both of private and of public objects; and there are important matters of public administration to which few men are equally competent with such women; among others, the detailed control of expenditure. But what we are now discussing is not the need which society has of the services of women in public business, but the dull and hopeless life to which it so often condemns them, by forbidding them to exercise the practical abilities which many of them are conscious of, in any wider field than one which to some of them never was, and to others is no longer, open. If there is anything vitally important to the happiness of human beings, it is that they should relish their habitual pursuit. This requisite of an enjoyable life is very imperfectly granted, or altogether denied, to a large part of mankind; and by its absence many a life is a failure, which is provided, in appearance, with every requisite of success. But if circumstances which society is not yet skilful enough to overcome, render such failures often for the present inevitable, society need not itself inflict them. The injudiciousness of parents, a youth's own inexperience, or the absence of external opportunities for the congenial vocation, and their presence for an uncongenial, condemn numbers of men to pass their lives in doing one thing reluctantly and ill, when there are other things which they could have done well and happily. But on women this sentence is imposed by actual law, and by customs equivalent to law. What, in unenlightened societies, colour, race, religion, or in the case of a conquered country, nationality, are to some men, sex is to all women; a peremptory exclusion from almost all honourable occupations, but either such as cannot be fulfilled by others, or such as those others do not think worthy of their acceptance. Sufferings arising from causes of this nature usually meet with so little sympathy, that few persons are aware of the great amount of unhappiness even now produced by the feeling of a wasted life. The case will be even more frequent, as increased cultivation creates a greater and greater disproportion between the ideas and faculties of women, and the scope which society allows to their activity.

When we consider the positive evil caused to the disqualified half of the human race by their disqualification—first in the loss of the most inspiriting and elevating kind of personal enjoyment, and next in the weariness, disappointment, and profound dissatisfaction with life, which are so often the substitute for it; one feels that among all the lessons which men require for carrying on the struggle against the inevitable imperfections of their lot on earth, there is no lesson which they more need, than not to add to the evils which nature inflicts, by their jealous and prejudiced restrictions on one another. Their vain fears only substitute other and worse evils for those which they are idly apprehensive of: while every restraint on the freedom of conduct of any of their human fellow creatures, (otherwise than by making them responsible for any evil actually caused by it), dries up *pro tanto* the principal fountain of human happiness, and leaves the species less rich, to an inappreciable degree, in all that makes life valuable to the individual human being.

KARL MARX

Western ideologies have often been philosophical, combining critical reflection with systematic boldness. But few philosophies have been social or political ideologies. Marxism is almost unique in this regard. Arising out of the thinking of a German philosopher, it became first a comprehensive conception of human nature, history, society, and salvation, and then the mobilizing ideology of nations. Marxism warns us not to forget that our thinking about human beings and their lives arises out of history and is capable of being realized in history. Moreover, it was no accident that Marxism became the framework of commitments and of conduct for millions. For its turn away from abstract, theoretical thinking to practice and action is part of its very understanding of history, society, thought, and the ultimate goals of human life.

Marxism arises out of the life and work of Karl Heinrich Marx (1818–1883), who was born on May 5, 1818, in Trier, in Prussia. Marx's father, Heinrich, was a lawyer of Jewish descent who converted to Christianity in 1824. He expected his son to practice law also, and Karl Marx entered the University of Bonn in 1836 with this intention. But a year later, he transferred to Berlin, became associated with Bruno Bauer and the young left-wing Hegelians, and turned to philosophy. These disciples of Georg Wilhelm Friedrich Hegel had traded in Hegel's reverence for religion, morality, philosophy, and the spiritual character of history for a humanistic critique in which religion, morality, and traditional politics were viewed as distortions of what is genuinely human and ultimately as sources of alienation. According to Ludwig Feuerbach, a young theologian and a leader of the movement, Hegel had been wrong to see all things, including human culture, society, and morality, as expressions of Spirit or the divine; rather, all things, even God, are in truth expressions of human interests and human productivity.

After completing his doctoral dissertation, on the ancient atomists and critics of religion, Democritus and Epicurus, at the University of Jena in 1841, Marx turned to journalism. He edited the radical newspaper the *Rheinische Zeitung* in Cologne until 1843, when government censorship led him to resign. During this period Marx completed his critique of the *Philosophy of Right*, Hegel's central work on ethics and politics, and wrote his famous review-essay of Bauer's *The Jewish Question*, with its important treatment of political alienation, the primacy of social existence, and the relation between money and labor.

In June of 1843 Marx married his childhood love, Jenny von Westphalen, and together they moved to Paris, as Marx joined Arnold Ruge, another young left-wing Hegelian, in editing the *Deutsch-Französische Jahrbücher* (*German-French Yearbooks*). In France Marx became reacquainted with Friedrich Engels, who became his closest friend and collaborator. By the end of 1844, the two had completed their first project, *The Holy Family*, a critique of young Hegelian philosophy on the basis of a new humanism, a critical analysis of the Hegelian treatment of property, and an attack on the hidden theology of the young radicals.

In 1845 Marx was banished from Paris and moved to Brussels. He and Engels joined the Communist League in 1847 and in February 1848, on the eve of the revolutions in France, published their famous *Manifesto*. Then, after moving back and forth across Western Europe, Marx was finally expelled from all Prussian territories; he set sail for London, where he settled in 1849 and lived for virtually all of his remaining years.

The 1850s and 1860s were extremely difficult decades for Marx and his family. Poverty and illness filled their lives with suffering and grief. By 1856 three of the six Marx children had died. Marx worked steadily, even fanatically, ten hours a day in the British Museum studying economics and the analysis of political economy, and then writing at home long into the night. The results were the *Critique of Political Economy* of 1859; the long unpublished draft on political economy called the *Grundrisse* (1857–58); and, most important, the critical analysis of capitalism, *Capital*, the first volume of which was published in 1867. The final two volumes were published by Engels in 1885 and 1894, after Marx's death.

During the 1850s Marx wrote articles for the *New York Daily Tribune*, but the American Civil War put an end to even such modest employment. Fortunately, by the end of the decade, a small bequest to Jenny and Engels's support from his company in Manchester bettered the Marx family's situation. By this time, however, Marx's health was very bad.

In 1864 Marx helped found the International Working Men's Association in London and served on its General Council for seven years. But his health deteriorated steadily. Physically debilitated, Marx was increasingly less productive in what would be his last decade. In 1881 Jenny died of cancer; ill since 1878, she had been less and less able to help decipher his notorious handwriting. Then, on March 14, 1883, Marx too died, leaving to Engels the task of editing the remaining volumes of *Capital*. Less than forty years later, in the Russian Revolution of 1917, history would seek to confirm Marx's understanding of it in a rare, if not unique, celebration of the efficacy of philosophical thought to change the world—and not merely to understand it.

Recommended Readings

Avineri, Shlomo. *The Social and Political Thought of Karl Marx*. Cambridge: Cambridge University Press, 1968.

Ball, Terence, and James Farr (eds.). *After Marx*. Cambridge: Cambridge University Press, 1984.

Cohen, Gerald. *Karl Marx's Theory of History*. Oxford: Oxford University Press, 1978.

Elster, Jon. *Making Sense of Marx*. Cambridge: Cambridge University Press, 1985.

Lukes, S. *Marxism and Morality*. Oxford: Oxford University Press, 1984.

Tucker, Robert C. *Philosophy and Myth in Karl Marx*. 2nd ed. Cambridge: Cambridge University Press, 1972.

Wood, Alan. *Karl Marx*. London: Routledge, 1981.

Alienated Labor

We have proceeded from the presuppositions of political economy. We have accepted its language and its laws. We presupposed private property, the separation of labor, capital and land, hence of wages, profit of capital and rent, likewise the division of labor, competition, the concept of exchange value, etc. From political economy itself, in its own words, we have shown that the worker sinks to the level of a commodity, the most miserable commodity; that the misery of the worker is inversely proportional to the power and volume of his production; that the necessary result of competition is the accumulation of capital in a few hands and thus the revival of monopoly in a more frightful form; and finally that the distinction between capitalist and landowner, between agricultural laborer and industrial worker, disappears and the whole society must divide into the two classes of *proprietors* and propertyless *workers*.

Political economy proceeds from the fact of private property. It does not explain private property. It grasps the actual, *material* process of private property in abstract and general formulae which it then takes as *laws*. It does not *comprehend* these laws, that is, does not prove them as proceeding from the nature of private property. Political economy does not disclose the reason for the division between capital and labor, between capital and land. When, for example, the relation of wages to profits is determined, the ultimate basis is taken to be the interest of the capitalists; that is, political economy assumes what it should develop. Similarly, competition is referred to at every point and explained from external circumstances. Political economy teaches us nothing about the extent to which these external, apparently accidental circumstances are simply the expression of a necessary development. We have seen how political economy regards

exchange itself as an accidental fact. The only wheels which political economy puts in motion are *greed* and the *war among the greedy, competition.*

Just because political economy does not grasp the interconnections within the movement, the doctrine of competition could stand opposed to the doctrine of monopoly, the doctrine of freedom of craft to that of the guild, the doctrine of the division of landed property to that of the great estate. Competition, freedom of craft, and division of landed property were developed and conceived only as accidental, deliberate, forced consequences of monopoly, the guild, and feudal property, rather than necessary, inevitable, natural consequences.

We now have to grasp the essential connection among private property, greed, division of labor, capital and landownership, and the connection of exchange with competition, of value with the devaluation of men, of monopoly with competition, etc., and of this whole alienation with the *money*-system.

Let us not put ourselves in a fictitious primordial state like a political economist trying to clarify things. Such a primordial state clarifies nothing. It merely pushes the issue into a gray, misty distance. It acknowledges as a fact or event what it should deduce, namely, the necessary relation between two things for example, between division of labor and exchange. In such a manner theology explains the origin of evil by the fall of man. That is, it asserts as a fact in the form of history what it should explain.

We proceed from a *present* fact of political economy.

The worker becomes poorer the more wealth he produces, the more his production increases in power and extent. The worker becomes a cheaper commodity the more commodities he produces. The *increase in value* of the world of things is directly proportional to the *decrease in value* of the human world. Labor not only produces commodities. It also produces itself and the worker as a *commodity*, and indeed in the

Translated by Loyd D. Easton and Kurt H. Guddat. Reprinted by permission of Loyd D. Easton and Mrs. Kurt H. Guddat.

same proportion as it produces commodities in general.

This fact simply indicates that the object which labor produces, its product, stands opposed to it as an *alien thing*, as a *power independent* of the producer. The product of labor is labor embodied and made objective in a thing. It is the *objectification* of labor. The realization of labor is its objectification. In the viewpoint of political economy this realization of labor appears as the *diminution* of the worker, the objectification as the *loss of and subservience to the object*, and the appropriation as *alienation* [*Entfremdung*], as externalization [*Entäusserung*].

So much does the realization of labor appear as diminution that the worker is diminished to the point of starvation. So much does objectification appear as loss of the object that the worker is robbed of the most essential objects not only of life but also of work. Indeed, work itself becomes a thing of which he can take possession only with the greatest effort and with the most unpredictable interruptions. So much does the appropriation of the object appear as alienation that the more objects the worker produces, the fewer he can own and the more he falls under the domination of his product, of capital.

All these consequences follow from the fact that the worker is related to the *product of his labor* as to an *alien* object. For it is clear according to this premise: The more the worker exerts himself, the more powerful becomes the alien objective world which he fashions against himself, the poorer he and his inner world become, the less there is that belongs to him. It is the same in religion. The more man attributes to God, the less he retains in himself. The worker puts his life into the object; then it no longer belongs to him but to the object. The greater his activity, the poorer is the worker. What the product of his work is, he is not. The greater this product is, the smaller he is himself. The *externalization* of the worker in his product means not only that his work becomes an object, an *external* existence, but also that it exists *outside him* independently, alien, an autonomous power, opposed to him. The life he has given to the object confronts him as hostile and alien.

Let us now consider more closely the *objectification*, the worker's production and with it the *alienation* and *loss* of the object, his product.

The worker can make nothing without *nature*, without the *sensuous external world*. It is the material wherein his labor realizes itself, wherein it is active, out of which and by means of which it produces.

But as nature furnishes to labor the *means of life* in the sense that labor cannot *live* without objects upon which labor is exercised, nature also furnishes the *means of life* in the narrower sense, namely, the means of physical subsistence of the *worker* himself.

The more the worker *appropriates* the external world and sensuous nature through his labor, the more he deprives himself of the *means of life* in two respects: first, that the sensuous external world gradually ceases to be an object belonging to his labor, a *means of life* of his work; secondly, that it gradually ceases to be a *means of life* in the immediate sense, a means of physical subsistence of the worker.

In these two respects, therefore, the worker becomes a slave to his objects; first, in that he receives an *object of labor*, that is, he receives *labor*, and secondly that he receives the *means of subsistence*. The first enables him to exist as a *worker* and the second as a *physical subject*. The terminus of this slavery is that he can only maintain himself as a *physical subject* so far as he is a *worker*, and only as a *physical subject* is he a worker.

(The alienation of the worker in his object is expressed according to the laws of political economy as follows: the more the worker produces, the less he has to consume; the more values he creates the more worthless and unworthy he becomes; the better shaped his product, the more misshapen is he; the more civilized his product, the more barbaric is the worker; the more powerful the work, the more powerless becomes the worker; the more intelligence the work has, the more witless is the worker and the more he becomes a slave of nature.)

Political economy conceals the alienation in the nature of labor by ignoring the direct relationship between the worker (labor) *and production*. To be sure, labor produces marvels for the wealthy but it produces deprivation for the worker. It produces palaces, but hovels for the worker. It produces beauty, but mutilation for the worker. It displaces labor through machines, but it throws some workers back into barbarous labor and turns others into machines. It produces intelligence, but for the worker it produces imbecility and cretinism.

The direct relationship of labor to its products is the relationship of the worker to the objects of his production. The relationship of the rich to the objects of production and to production itself is only a *consequence* of this first relationship and confirms it. Later we shall observe the latter aspect.

Thus, when we ask, What is the essential relationship of labor? we ask about the relationship of the *worker* to production.

Up to now we have considered the alienation, the externalization of the worker only from one side: his *relationship to the products of his labor*. But alienation is shown not only in the result but also in the *process of production*, in the *producing activity* itself. How could the worker stand in an alien relationship to the product of his activity if he did not alienate himself from himself in the very act of production? After all, the product is only the résumé of activity, of production. If the product of work is externalization, production itself must be active externalization, externalization of activity, activity of externalization. Only alienation—and externalization in the activity of labor itself—is summarized in the alienation of the object of labor.

What constitutes the externalization of labor?

First is the fact that labor is *external* to the laborer—that is, it is not part of his nature—and that the worker does not affirm himself in his work but denies himself, feels miserable and unhappy, develops no free physical and mental energy but mortifies his flesh and ruins his mind. The worker, therefore feels at ease only outside work, and during work he is outside himself. He is at home when he is not working and when he is working he is not at home. His work, therefore, is not voluntary, but coerced, *forced labor*. It is not the satisfaction of a need but only a *means* to satisfy other needs. Its alien character is obvious from the fact that as soon as no physical or other pressure exists, labor is avoided like the plague. External labor, labor in which man is externalized, is labor of self-sacrifice, of penance. Finally, the external nature of work for the worker appears in the fact that it is not his own but another person's, that in work he does not belong to himself but to someone else. In religion the spontaneity of human imagination, the spontaneity of the human brain and heart, acts independently of the individual as an alien, divine or devilish activity. Similarly, the activity of the worker is not his own spontaneous activity. It belongs to another. It is the loss of his own self.

The result, therefore, is that man (the worker) feels that he is acting freely only in his animal functions—eating, drinking, and procreating, or at most in his shelter and finery—while in his human functions he feels only like an animal. The animalistic becomes the human and the human the animalistic.

To be sure, eating, drinking, and procreation are genuine human functions. In abstraction, however, and separated from the remaining sphere of human activities and turned into final and sole ends, they are animal functions.

We have considered labor, the act of alienation of practical human activity, in two aspects: (1) the relationship of the worker to the *product of labor* as an alien object dominating him. This relationship is at the same time the relationship to the sensuous external world, to natural objects as an alien world hostile to him; (2) the relationship of labor to the *act of production* in *labor*. This relationship is that of the worker to his own activity as alien and not belonging to him, activity as passivity, power as weakness, procreation as emasculation, the worker's *own* physical and spiritual energy, his personal life—for what else is life but activity—as an activity turned against him, independent of him, and not belonging to him. *Self-alienation*, as against the alienation of the *object*, stated above.

We have now to derive a third aspect of *alienated labor* from the two previous ones.

Man is a species-being [*Gattungswesen*] not only in that he practically and theoretically makes his own species as well as that of other things his object, but also—and this is only another expression for the same thing—in that as present and living species he considers himself to be a *universal* and consequently free being.

The life of the species in man as in animals is physical in that man, (like the animal) lives by inorganic nature. And as man is more universal than the animal, the realm of inorganic nature by which he lives is more universal. As plants, animals, minerals, air, light, etc., in theory form a part of human consciousness, partly as objects of natural science, partly as objects of art—his spiritual inorganic nature of spiritual means of life which he first must prepare for enjoyment and assimilation — so they also form in practice a part of human life and human activity. Man lives physically only by these products of nature; they may appear in the form of food, heat, clothing, housing, etc. The universality of man appears in practice in the universality which makes the whole of nature his *inorganic* body: (1) as a direct means of life, and (2) as the matter, object, and instrument of his life activity. Nature is the *inorganic body* of man, that is, nature insofar as it is not the human body. Man *lives* by nature. This means that nature is his *body* with which he must remain in perpetual process in order not to die. That the physical and spiritual life of man is tied up with nature is another way of saying that nature is linked to itself, for man is a part of nature.

In alienating (1) nature from man, and (2) man from himself, his own active function, his life activity, alienated labor also alienates the *species* from him; it makes *species-life* the means of individual life. In the first place it alienates species-life and the individual life, and secondly it turns the latter in its abstraction into the purpose of the former, also in its abstract and alienated form.

For labor, *life activity*, and *productive life* appear to man at first only as a *means* to satisfy a need, the need to maintain physical existence. Productive life, however, is species-life. It is life begetting life. In the mode of life activity lies the entire character of a species, its species-character; and free conscious activity is the species-character of man. Life itself appears only as a *means of life*.

The animal is immediately one with its life activity, not distinct from it. The animal is *its life activity*. Man makes his life activity itself into an object of will and consciousness. He has conscious life activity. It is not a determination with which he immediately identifies. Conscious life activity distinguishes man immediately from the life activity of the animal. Only thereby is he a species-being. Or rather, he is only, a conscious being—that is, his own life is an object for him—since he is a species-being. Only on that account is his activity free activity. Alienated labor reverses the relationship in that man, since he is a conscious being, makes his life activity, his *essence*, only a means for his *existence*.

The practical creation of an *objective world*, the *treatment* of inorganic nature, is proof that man is a conscious species-being, that is, a being which is related to its species as to its own essence or is related to itself as a species-being. To be sure animals also produce. They build themselves nests, dwelling places, like the bees, beavers, ants, etc. But the animal produces only what is immediately necessary for itself or its young. It produces in a one-sided way while man produces universally. The animal produces under the domination of immediate physical need while man produces free of physical need and only genuinely so in freedom from such need. The animal only produces itself while man reproduces the whole of nature. The animal's product belongs immediately to its physical body while man is free when he confronts his product. The animal builds only according to the standard and need of the species to which it belongs while man knows how to produce according to the standard of any species and at all times knows how to apply an intrinsic standard to the object. Thus man creates also according to the laws of beauty.

In the treatment of the objective world, therefore, man proves himself to be genuinely a *species-being*. This production is his active species-life. Through it nature appears as *his* work and his actuality. The object of labor is thus the *objectification of man's species-life:* he produces himself not only intellectually, as in consciousness, but also actively in a real sense and sees himself in a world he made. In taking from man the object of his production, alienated labor takes from his *species-life,* his actual and objective existence as a species. It changes his superiority to the animal to inferiority, since he is deprived of nature, his inorganic body.

By degrading free spontaneous activity to the level of a means, alienated labor makes the species-life of man a means of his physical existence.

The consciousness which man has from his species is altered through alienation, so that species-life becomes a means for him.

(3) Alienated labor hence turns the *species-existence of man*, and also nature as his mental species-capacity, into an existence *alien* to him, into the *means* of his *individual existence*. It alienates his spiritual nature, his *human essence*, from his own body and likewise from nature outside him.

(4) A direct consequence of man's alienation from the product of his work, from his life activity, and from his species-existence, is the *alienation of man* from *man*. When man confronts himself, he confronts *other* men. What holds true of man's relationship to his work, to the product of his work, and to himself, also holds true of man's relationship to other men, to their labor, and the object of their labor.

In general, the statement that man is alienated from his species-existence means that one man is alienated from another just as each man is alienated from human nature.

The alienation of man, the relation of man to himself, is realized and expressed in the relation between man and other men.

Thus in the relation of alienated labor every man sees the others according to the standard and the relation in which he finds himself as a worker.

We began with an economic fact, the alienation of the worker and his product. We have given expression to the concept of this fact: *alienated, externalized* labor. We have analyzed this concept and have thus analyzed merely a fact of political economy.

Let us now see further how the concept of alienated, externalized labor must express and respect itself in actuality.

If the product of labor is alien to me, confronts me as an alien power, to whom then does it belong?

If my own activity does not belong to me, if it is an alien and forced activity, to whom then does it belong?

To a being *other* than myself.

Who is this being?

Gods? To be sure, in early times the main production, for example, the building of temples in Egypt, India, and Mexico, appears to be in the service of the gods, just as the product belongs to the gods. But gods alone were never workmasters. The same is true of *nature*. And what a contradiction it would be if the more man subjugates nature through his work and the more the miracles of gods are rendered superfluous by the marvels of industry, man should renounce his joy in producing and the enjoyment of his product for love of these powers.

The *alien* being who owns labor and the product of labor, whom labor serves and whom the product of labor satisfies can only be *man* himself.

That the product of labor does not belong to the worker and an alien power confronts him is possible only because this product belongs to *a man other than the worker*. If his activity is torment for him, it must be the *pleasure* and the life-enjoyment for another. Not gods, not nature, but only man himself can be this alien power over man.

Let us consider the statement previously made, that the relationship of man to himself is *objective* and *actual* to him only through his relationships to other men. If man is related to the product of his labor, to his objectified labor, as to an *alien*, hostile, powerful object independent of him, he is so related that another alien, hostile, powerful man independent of him is the lord of this object. If he is unfree in relation to his own activity, he is related to it as bonded activity, activity under the domination, coercion, and yoke of another man.

Every self-alienation of man, from himself and from nature, appears in the relationship which he postulates between other men and himself and nature. Thus religious self-alienation appears necessarily in the relation of laity to priest, or also to a mediator, since we are here now concerned with the spiritual world. In the practical real world self-alienation can appear only in the practical real relationships to other men. The means whereby the alienation proceeds is a *practical* means. Through alienated labor man thus not only produces his relationship to the object and to the act of production as an alien man at enmity with him. He also creates the relation in which other men stand to his production and product, and the relation in which he stands to these other men. Just as he begets his own production as loss of his reality, as his punishment; just as he begets his own product as a loss, a product not belonging to him, so he begets the domination of the non-producer over production and over product. As he alienates his own activity from himself, he confers upon the stranger an activity which is not his own.

Up to this point, we have investigated the relationship only from the side of the worker and will later investigate it also from the side of the non-worker.

Thus through *alienated externalized labor* does the worker create the relation to this work of man alienated to labor and standing outside it. The relation of the worker to labor produces the relation of the capitalist to labor, or whatever one wishes to call the lord of labor. *Private property* is thus product, result, and necessary consequence of *externalized labor*, of the external relation of the worker to nature and to himself.

Private property thus is derived, through analysis, from the concept of *externalized labor*, that is, *externalized man*, alienated labor, alienated life, and *alienated* man.

We have obtained the concept of *externalized labor (externalized life)* from political economy as a result of the *movement of private property*. But the analysis of this idea shows that though private property appears to be the ground and cause of externalized labor, it is rather a consequence of externalized labor, just as gods are *originally* not the cause but the effect of an aberration of the human mind. Later this relationship reverses.

Only at the final culmination of the development of private property does this, its secret, reappear—namely, that on the one hand it is the *product* of externalized labor and that secondly it is the *means* through which labor externalizes itself, the *realization of this externalization*.

This development throws light on several conflicts hitherto unresolved.

(1) Political economy proceeds from labor as the very soul of production and yet gives labor nothing, private property everything. From this contradiction Proudhon decided in favor of labor and against private property. We perceive, however, that this apparent contradiction is the contradiction of *alienated labor* with itself and that political economy has only formulated the laws of alienated labor.

Therefore we also perceive that *wages* and *private property* are identical: for when the product, the object of labor, pays for the labor itself, wages are only a necessary consequence of the alienation of labor. In wages labor appears not as an end in itself but as the servant of wages. We shall develop this later and now only draw some conclusions.

An enforced *raising of wages* (disregarding all other difficulties, including that this anomaly could only be maintained forcibly) would therefore be nothing but a *better slave-salary* and would not achieve either for the worker or for labor human significance and dignity.

Even the *equality of wages*, as advanced by Proudhon, would only convert the relation of the contemporary worker to his work into the relation of all men to labor. Society would then be conceived as an abstract capitalist.

Wages are a direct result of alienated labor, and alienated labor is the direct cause of private property. The downfall of one is necessarily the downfall of the other.

(2) From the relation of alienated labor to private property it follows further that the emancipation of society from private property, etc., from servitude, is expressed in its *political* form as the *emancipation of workers*, not as though it is only a question of their emancipation but because in their emancipation is contained universal human emancipation. It is contained in their emancipation because the whole of human servitude is involved in the relation of worker to production, and all relations of servitude are only modifications and consequences of the worker's relation to production.

As we have found the concept of *private property* through *analysis* from the concept of *alienated, externalized labor*, so we can develop all the *categories* of political economy with the aid of these two factors, and we shall again find in each category—for example, barter, competition, capital, money—only a *particular* and *developed expression* of these primary foundations.

Before considering this configuration, however, let us try to solve two problems.

(1) To determine the general *nature of private property* as a result of alienated labor in its relation to *truly human* and *social property*.

(2) We have taken the *alienation of labor* and its *externalization* as a fact and analyzed this fact. How, we ask now, does it happen that *man externalizes* his *labor*, alienates it? How is this alienation rooted in the nature of human development? We have already achieved much in resolving the problem by *transforming* the question concerning the *origin of private property* into the question concerning the relationship of *externalized labor* to evolution of humanity. In talking about *private property* one believes he is dealing with something external to man. Talking of labor, one is immediately dealing with man himself. This new formulation of the problem already contains its solution.

On (1) *The general nature of private property and its relation to truly human property.*

We have resolved alienated labor into two parts which mutually determine each other or rather are only different expressions of one and the same relationship. *Appropriation* appears as *alienation*, as *externalization; externalization* as *appropriation; alienation* as the true *naturalization*.

We considered the one side, *externalized* labor, in relation to the *worker* himself, that is, the relation of *externalized labor to itself.* We have found the *property relation of the non-worker* to the *worker* and *labor* to be the product, the necessary result, of this relationship. *Private property* as the material, summarized expression of externalized labor embraces both relationships—the *relationship of worker to labor, the product of his work, and the non-worker*; and the relationship of the *non-worker to the worker* and *the product of his labor.*

As we have seen that in relation to the worker who *appropriates* nature through his labor the appropria-tion appears as alienation—self-activity as activity for another and of another, living as the sacrifice of life, production of the object as loss of it to an alien power, an *alien* man—we now consider the relationship of this *alien* man to the worker, to labor and its object.

It should be noted first that everything which appears with the worker as an *activity of externalization* and an *activity of alienation* appears with the non-worker as a *condition of externalization*, a *condition of alienation.*

Secondly, that the *actual, practical attitude* of the worker in production and to his product (as a condition of mind) appears as a *theoretical* attitude in the non-worker confronting him.

Thirdly, the non-worker does everything against the worker which the worker does against himself, but he does not do against his own self what he does against the worker.

Let us consider more closely these three relationships. [Here the manuscript breaks off, unfinished.]

ON THE JEWISH QUESTION

Bruno Bauer, *The Jewish Question,* Braunschweig, 1843

The German Jews want emancipation. What kind of emancipation? *Civil, political* emancipation.

Bruno Bauer answers them: No one in Germany is politically emancipated. We are not free ourselves. How shall we liberate you? You Jews are *egoists* when you claim a special emancipation for yourselves as Jews. As Germans, you should work for the political emancipation of Germany, as men, for the emancipation of mankind; and you should feel the particular form of your oppression and shame not as an exception to the rule but rather as its confirmation.

Or do Jews desire to be put on an equal footing with *Christian subjects?* If so, they recognize the *Christian state* as legitimate, as the regime of general subjugation. Why should they be displeased at their particular yoke if the general yoke pleases them? Why should Germans be interested in the liberation of Jews if Jews are not interested in the liberation of Germans?

The *Christian* state takes cognizance only of *privileges.* In it the Jew has the privilege of being a Jew. As a Jew he has rights that Christians do not have. Why does he want rights he does not have and that Christians enjoy?

If the Jew wants to be emancipated from the Christian state, he is demanding that the Christian state abandon its *religious* prejudice. But does the Jew abandon *his* religious prejudice? Has he, then, the right to demand of another this abdication of religion?

By *its very nature* the Christian state cannot emancipate the Jew; but, Bauer adds, the Jew by his very nature cannot be emancipated. So long as the state remains Christian and the Jew remains Jewish, both

Translated by Loyd D. Easton and Kurt H. Guddat. Reprinted by permission of Loyd D. Easton and Mrs. Kurt H. Guddat.

are equally incapable of giving as well as receiving emancipation.

The Christian state can only behave toward the Jew in the manner of the Christian state—that is, permitting the separation of the Jew from other subjects as a privilege but making him feel the pressure of the other separate spheres of society, and feel them all the more heavily, since he stands in *religious* opposition to the predominant religion. But the Jew in turn can behave toward the state only in a Jewish manner, that is as a foreigner, since he opposes his chimerical nationality to actual nationality, his illusory law to actual law. He imagines that his separation from humanity is justified, abstains on principle from participation in the historical movement, looks to a future that has nothing in common with the future of mankind as a whole, and regards himself as a part of the Jewish people, the chosen people.

On what basis, then, do you Jews want emancipation? On the basis of your religion? It is the mortal enemy of the religion of the state. As citizens? There are no citizens in Germany. As men? You are not men, just as those to whom you appeal are not men.

After criticizing previous positions and solutions, Bauer formulates the question of Jewish emancipation in a new way. What is the *nature,* he asks, of the Jew who is to be emancipated and the Christian state that is to emancipate him? He answers with a critique of the Jewish religion, analyzes the *religious* antagonism between Judaism and Christianity, and explains the essence of the Christian state—all this with dash, acuteness, wit, and thoroughness in a style as precise as it is pregnant and energetic.

How then does Bauer settle the Jewish question? What is the result? The formulation of a question is its solution. Criticism of the Jewish question provides the answer to the Jewish question. The résumé thus follows:

We must emancipate ourselves before we can emancipate others.

The most persistent form of the antagonism between the Jew and the Christian is the *religious* antagonism. How is an antagonism to be resolved? By making it impossible. And how is a *religious* antagonism made impossible? By *abolishing religion*. Once Jew and Christian recognize their respective religions as nothing more than *different stages in the evolution of the human spirit*, as different snake skins shed by *history*, and recognize *man* as the snake that wore them, they will no longer find themselves in religious antagonism but only in a critical, *scientific*, and human relationship. *Science*, then, constitutes their unity. Contradictions in science, however, are resolved by science itself.

The *German* Jew is particularly affected by the general lack of political emancipation and the pronounced Christianity of the state. With Bauer, however, the Jewish question has a universal significance independent of specific German conditions. It is the question of the relation of religion to the state, of the *contradiction between religious prejudice and political emancipation*. Emancipation from religion is presented as a condition both for the Jew who seeks political emancipation and for the state which is to emancipate him and is to be emancipated itself as well.

"Very well, you say—and the Jew himself says it—the Jew should not be emancipated because he is Jew or because he has such excellent and universal ethical principles but rather because he takes second place to the *citizen* and becomes one in spite of being and wanting to remain a Jew. That is, he is and remains a Jew in spite of the fact that he is a *citizen* living in universally human relationships; his Jewish and restricted nature always triumphs in the end over his human and political obligations. The *prejudice* remains even though it has been overtaken by *universal* principles. But if it remains, it rather overtakes everything else." "The Jew could remain a Jew in political life only in a sophistical sense, only in appearance; thus if he wanted to remain a Jew, this mere appearance would become the essential thing and would triumph. In other words, his *life in the state* would be only a semblance or a momentary exception to the real nature of things, an excep-

tion to the rule." ("The Capacity of Present-day Jews and Christians to Become Free," *Twenty-one Sheets from Switzerland* [*Einundzwanzig Bogen aus der Schweiz*], p. 57.)

Let us see, on the other hand, how Bauer describes the role of the state:

"France," he says, "recently (Proceedings of the Chamber of Deputies, 26 December 1840) gave us, in connection with the Jewish question and all other *political* questions (since the July Revolution), a glimpse of a life which is free but which revokes its freedom by law, thus revealing it to be a sham, and on the other hand, denies its free law by its acts." (*The Jewish Question*, p. 64.)

"Universal freedom is not yet established as law in France, and the *Jewish question is not yet settled* because legal freedom—that all citizens are equal—is limited in actual life which is still dominated and fragmented by religious privileges, and because the lack of freedom in actual life reacts on the law, compelling it to sanction the division of inherently free citizens into the oppressed and the oppressors" (p. 65).

When, therefore, would the Jewish question be settled in France?

"The Jew, for instance, would really have ceased being a Jew if he did not let himself be hindered by his code from fulfilling his duties toward the state and his fellow citizens—if he went, for example, to the Chamber of Deputies and took part in public affairs on the Sabbath. Every *religious privilege*, including the monopoly of a privileged church, would have to be abolished, and if a few or many or *even the overwhelming majority still felt obliged to fulfill their religious duties*, such a practice should be left to *them as a purely private matter*" (p. 65). "There is no longer any religion if there is no privileged religion. Take from religion its power of excommunication and it ceases to exist" (p. 66). "Just as M. Martin du Nord saw the proposal to omit any mention of Sunday in the law as a declaration that Christianity had ceased to exist, with equal right (and one well-founded) a declaration that the Sabbath-law is no longer binding for the Jew would proclaim the end of Judaism" (p. 71).

Bauer thus demands, on the one hand, that the Jew give up Judaism and man give up religion in order to be emancipated *as a citizen*. On the other hand, he holds that from the *political* abolition of religion there logically follows the abolition of religion altogether. The state which presupposes religion is as yet no true, no actual state. "To be sure, the religious view reinforces the state. But what state? *What kind of state?*" (p. 97).

At this point Bauer's *one-sided* approach to the Jewish question becomes apparent.

It is by no means sufficient to ask: Who should emancipate and who should be emancipated? Criticism has to be concerned with a third question. It must ask: *What kind of emancipation* is involved and what are its underlying conditions? Criticism of *political emancipation* itself is primarily the final critique of the Jewish question and its true resolution into the *"universal question of the age."*

Since Bauer does not raise the question to this level, he falls into contradictions. He presents conditions that are not based on the essence of *political* emancipation. He raises questions that are irrelevant to his problem and solves problems that leave his question untouched. Bauer says of the opponents of Jewish emancipation, "Their mistake simply lay in assuming the Christian state to be the only true state without subjecting it to the same criticism they applied to Judaism" (p. 3). Here we find Bauer's mistake in subjecting *only* the "Christian state," not the "state as such," to criticism, in failing to examine the *relation between political emancipation and human emancipation*, and hence presenting conditions that are only explicable from his uncritical confusion of political emancipation with universal human emancipation. Bauer asks the Jews: Have you the right to demand *political emancipation* from your standpoint? We ask, on the contrary: Has the standpoint of *political* emancipation the right to demand from the Jews the abolition of Judaism and from man the abolition of religion?

The Jewish question has a different aspect according to the state in which the Jew finds himself. In Germany, where there is no political state and no state as such exists, the Jewish question is purely *theological*. The Jew finds himself in *religious* opposition to a state acknowledging Christianity as its foundation. This state is a theologian *ex professo*. Criticism is here criticism of theology, double-edged criticism of Christian and of Jewish theology. But however *critical* we might be, we are still moving in theology.

In France, a *constitutional* state, the Jewish question is a question of constitutionalism, a question of the *incompleteness of political emancipation*. As the *semblance* of a state religion is preserved there, if only by the meaningless and self-contradictory formula of a *religion of the majority*, the relation of the Jew to the state also retains the *semblance* of a religious or theological opposition.

Only in the free states of North America — or at least in some of them — does the Jewish question lose its *theological* significance and become a truly *secular* question. Only where the political state exists in its complete development can the relation of the Jew, and generally speaking the religious man, to the political state, that is, the relation of religion to state, appear in its characteristic and pure form. Criticism of this relation ceases to be theological once the state abandons a *theological* posture toward religion, once it relates itself to religion as a state, that is, *politically*. Criticism then becomes *criticism of the political state*. Where the question here ceases to be *theological*, Bauer's criticism ceases to be critical. *"In the United States there is neither a state religion, nor a religion declared to be that of the majority, nor a pre-eminence of one faith over another. The state is foreign to all faiths."* (Gustave de Beaumont, *Marie ou l'esclavage aux États-Unis . . .* [Brussels, 1835], p. 214.) There are even some states in North America where *"the constitution imposes no religious beliefs or sectarian practice as the condition of political rights"* (loc. cit., p. 225). Yet *"no one in the United States believes that a man without religion can be an honest man"* (loc. cit., p. 224). And North America is pre-eminently the land of religiosity as Beaumont, Tocqueville, and the Englishman Hamilton assure us unanimously. The North American states, however, serve only as an example. The question is: What is the relation of *complete* political emancipation to religion? If we find even in a country with full political emancipation that religion not only *exists* but is *fresh* and *vital*, we have proof that the existence of religion is not incompatible with the full development of the state. But since the existence of religion implies a defect, the source of this defect must be sought in the *nature* of the state itself. We no longer take religion to be the *basis* but only the *manifestation* of secular narrowness. Hence we explain religious restriction of free citizens on the basis of their secular restriction. We do not claim that they must transcend their religious restriction in order to transcend their secular limitations. We do claim that they will transcend their religious restriction once they have transcended their secular limitations. We do not convert secular questions into theological ones. We convert theological questions into secular questions. History has long enough been resolved into superstition, but now we can resolve superstition into history. The question of the *relation of political emancipation to religion* becomes for us a question of the *relation of political emancipation to human emancipation*. We criticize the religious weaknesses of the political state by criticizing the political state in its *secular* constitution *apart from* the religious defects. In human terms we resolve the contradiction between the state and a *particular religion* such as *Judaism* into the contradiction between the state and *particular secular* elements, the contradiction between the state and *religion generally* into the contradiction between the state and its *presuppositions*.

The *political* emancipation of the Jew, the Christian, or the *religious* man generally is the *emancipation of the state* from Judaism, from Christianity, from *religion* in general. In a form and manner corresponding to its nature, the *state* as such emancipates itself from religion by emancipating itself from the *state religion*, that is, by recognizing no religion and recognizing itself simply as the state. *Political* emancipation from religion is not complete and consistent emancipation from religion because political emancipation is not the complete and consistent form of *human* emancipation.

The limits of political emancipation are seen at once in the fact that the *state* can free itself from a limitation without man *actually* being free from it, in the fact that a state can be a *free state* without men

becoming *free men*. Bauer himself tacitly admits this in setting the following condition of political emancipation: "Every religious privilege, including the monopoly of a privileged church, would have to be abolished. If a few or many or even the *overwhelming majority still felt obliged to fulfill their religious duties*, such a practice should be left to them as a *purely private matter*." The *state* can thus emancipate itself from religion even though the *overwhelming majority* is still religious. And the overwhelming majority does not cease being religious by being religious *in private*.

But the attitude of the state, particularly the *free state*, toward religion is still only the attitude of the *men* who make up the state. Hence it follows that man frees himself from a limitation *politically, through the state*, by overcoming the limitation in an *abstract, limited*, and partial manner, in contradiction with himself. Further, when man frees himself *politically*, he does so *indirectly*, through an *intermediary*, even if the *intermediary* is *necessary*. Finally, even when man proclaims himself an atheist through the medium of the state—that is, when he declares the state to be atheistic—he is still captive to religion since he only recognizes his atheism indirectly through an intermediary. Religion is merely the indirect recognition of man through a *mediator*. The state is the mediator between man and the freedom of man. As Christ is the mediator on whom man unburdens all his own divinity and all his *religious ties*, so is the state the mediator to which man transfers all his unholiness and all his *human freedom*.

The *political* elevation of man above religion shares all the defects and all the advantages of any political elevation. If the state as state, for example, abolishes *private property*, man proclaims private property is *overcome politically* once he abolishes the *property qualification* for active and passive voting as has been done in many North American states. *Hamilton* interprets this fact quite correctly in political terms: "*The great majority of the people have gained a victory over property owners and financial wealth*."[*] Is not private

[* Thomas Hamilton, *Men and Manners in America* (2 vols.; Edinburgh: William Blackwood, 1833). Marx quotes from the German translation, *Die Menschen und die Sitten in den Vereinigten Staaten von Nordamerika* (Mannheim: Hoff, 1834), Vol I, p. 146.]

property ideally abolished when the have-nots come to legislate for the haves? The *property qualification* is the last *political* form for recognizing private property.

Yet the political annulment of private property not only does not abolish it but even presupposes it. The state abolishes distinctions of *birth, rank, education,* and *occupation* in its fashion when it declares them to be *non-political* distinctions, when it proclaims that every member of the community *equally* participates in popular sovereignty without regard to these distinctions, and when it deals with all elements of the actual life of the nation from the standpoint of the state. Nevertheless the state permits private property, education, and occupation to *act* and manifest their *particular* nature as private property, education, and occupation in their *own* ways. Far from overcoming these *factual* distinctions, the state exists only by presupposing them; it is aware of itself as a *political state* and makes its *universality* effective only in opposition to these elements. *Hegel,* therefore, defines the relation of the *political state* to religion quite correctly in saying: "If the state is to have specific existence as the *self-knowing ethical actuality* of Spirit, it must be *distinct* from the form of authority and faith; this distinction emerges only as the ecclesiastical sphere is *divided* within itself; *only* thus has the state attained *universality* of thought, the principle of its form, *above particular* churches and only thus does it bring that universality into existence." (Hegel's *Philosophy of Law,* 1st ed., p. 346 [§270].) Exactly! Only thus *above* the *particular* elements is the state a universality.

By its nature the perfected political state is man's *species-life* in *opposition* to his material life. All the presuppositions of this egoistic life remain in *civil society outside* the state, but as qualities of civil society. Where the political state has achieved its full development, man leads a double life, a heavenly and an earthly life, not only in thought or consciousness but in *actuality.* In the *political community* he regards himself as a *communal being;* but in *civil society* he is active as a *private individual,* treats other men as means, reduces himself to a means, and becomes the plaything of alien powers. The political state is as spiritual in relation to civil society as heaven is in relation to earth. It stands in the same opposition to civil society and goes beyond it in the same way as religion goes beyond the limitation of the profane

world, that is, by recognizing, reestablishing, and necessarily allowing itself to be dominated by it. In his *innermost* actuality, in civil society, man is a profane being. Here, where he counts as an actual individual to himself and others, he is an *illusory* phenomenon. In the state where he counts as a species-being, on the other hand, he is an imaginary member of an imagined sovereignty, divested of his actual individual life and endowed with an unactual universality.

The conflict in which man as believer in a *particular* religion finds himself—a conflict with his own citizenship and other men as members of the community—is reduced to the *secular* split between the *political* state and *civil society.* For man as *bourgeois* [or part of civil society], "life in the state is only a semblance or a momentary exception to the real nature of things, an exception to the rule." Certainly the *bourgeois,* like the Jew, participates in the life of the state only in a sophistical way just as the *citoyen* is only sophistically a Jew or *bourgeois;* but this sophistry is not personal. It is the *sophistry of the political state* itself. The difference between the religious man and the citizen is the difference between the shopkeeper and the citizen, between the day laborer and the citizen, between the landowner and the citizen, between the *living individual* and the *citizen.* The contradiction between the religious and political man is the same as that between *bourgeois* and *citoyen,* between the member of civil society and his *political lion skin.*

This secular conflict to which the Jewish question ultimately is reduced—the relation between the political state and its presuppositions, whether the presuppositions be material elements such as private property or spiritual elements such as education and religion, the conflict between *general* and *private interest,* the split between the *political state* and *civil society*—these secular contradictions Bauer leaves untouched while attacking their *religious* expression. "It is precisely its foundation, need, which assures the maintenance of *civil society* and *guarantees its necessity* but exposes its maintenance to constant danger, sustains an element of uncertainty in civil society, and produces that constantly alternating mixture of poverty and wealth, of adversity and prosperity, and change in general" (p. 8).

Consider his entire section, "Civil Society" (pp. 8–9), which closely follows the main features of

Hegel's philosophy of law. Civil society in opposition to the political state is recognized as necessary since the political state is recognized as necessary.

Political emancipation is indeed a great step forward. It is not, to be sure, the final form of universal human emancipation, but it is the final form *within* the prevailing order of things. It is obvious that we are here talking about actual, practical emancipation.

Man emancipates himself *politically* from religion by banishing it from the sphere of public law into private right. It is no longer the spirit of the *state* where man—although in a limited way, under a particular form, and in a particular sphere—associates in community with other men as a species-being. It has become the spirit of *civil society*, of the sphere of egoism, of the *bellum omnium contra omnes*. It is no longer the essence of *community* but the essence of *division*. It has become what it was *originally*, an expression of the *separation* of man from his *community*, from himself and from other men. It is now only the abstract confession of particular peculiarity, of *private whim*, of caprice. The infinite splits of religion in North America, for example, already give it the *external* form of a purely individual matter. It has been tossed among numerous private interests and exiled from the community as a community. But one must not be deceived about the scope of political emancipation. The splitting of man into *public* and *private*, the *displacement* of religion from the state to civil society, is not just a step in political emancipation but its *completion*. It as little abolishes man's *actual* religiosity as it seeks to abolish it.

The *disintegration* of man into Jew and citizen, Protestant and citizen, religious man and citizen does not belie citizenship or circumvent political emancipation. It is *political emancipation itself*, the *political* mode of emancipation from religion. To be sure, in periods when the political state as such is forcibly born from civil society, when men strive to liberate themselves under the form of political self-liberation, the state can and must go as far as to *abolish* and *destroy religion*, but only in the way it abolishes private property by setting a maximum, confiscation, and progressive taxation or only in the way it abolishes life by the *guillotine*. In moments of special concern for itself political life seeks to repress its presupposition, civil society and its elements, and to constitute

itself the actual, harmonious species-life of man. But it can do this only in *violent* contradiction with its own conditions of existence by declaring the revolution to be *permanent*, and thus the political drama is bound to end with the restoration of religion, private property, and all the elements of civil society just as war ends with peace.

Indeed, the perfected Christian state is not the so-called *Christian* state acknowledging Christianity as its foundation in the state religion and excluding all others. It is, rather, the *atheistic* state, the *democratic* state, the state that relegates religion to the level of other elements of civil society. The state that is still theological and still officially prescribes belief in Christianity has not yet dared to declare itself to be *a state* and has not yet succeeded in expressing in *secular* and *human* form, in its *actuality* as a state, those *human* foundations of which Christianity is the sublime expression. The so-called Christian state is simply a *non-state*, for it is only the *human foundation* of Christianity, not Christianity as a religion, which can realize itself in actual human creations.

The so-called Christian state is a Christian denial of the state, not in any way the political actualization of Christianity. The state that still professes Christianity in the form of religion does not profess it in political form because it still behaves religiously toward religion—that is, it is not the *actual expression* of the human basis of religion since it still deals with the *unreality* and *imaginary* form of this human core. The so-called Christian state is an *imperfect* one, which treats Christianity as the *supplement* and *sanctification* of its imperfection. Hence religion necessarily becomes a *means* to an end, and the state is a *hypocrite*. There is a great difference between a *perfected* state that counts religion as one of its *prerequisites* because of a lack in the general *nature* of the state and an *imperfect* state that proclaims religion as its *foundation* because of a lack in its *particular existence* as an imperfect state. In the latter, religion becomes *imperfect politics*. In the former, the inadequacy of even perfected *politics* is apparent in religion. The so-called Christian state needs the Christian religion to complete itself *as a state*. The democratic state, the real state, needs no religion for its political fulfillment. It can, rather, do without religion because it fulfills the human basis of religion in a secular way. The so-called Christian state, on the other hand, behaves toward religion in a political way and toward politics in a religious way. As it reduces political forms to mere appearance, it equally reduces religion to a mere appearance.

To express this contradiction clearly let us consider Bauer's construct of the Christian state, a construct derived from this perception of the Christian-Germanic state.

"To prove the *impossibility* or *non-existence* of a Christian state," says Bauer, "we have recently and more frequently been referred to those passages in the Gospel which the [present] state *not only* does *not* follow but *also cannot unless it wants to dissolve itself completely.*" "But the matter is not so easily settled. What do those Gospel passages demand? Supernatural self-renunciation and submission to the authority of revelation, turning away from the state, the abolition of secular relationships. But the Christian state demands and achieves all these things. It has made the *spirit of the Gospel* its own, and if it does not reproduce it in exactly the same words as the Gospel, that is because it expresses that spirit in political forms borrowed from the political system of this world but reduced to mere appearance by the religious rebirth they must undergo. This withdrawal from the state is realized through the forms of the state" (p. 55).

Bauer goes on to show how the people of a Christian state do not constitute a nation with a will of its own but have their true existence in the ruler to whom they are subject but who is alien to them by origin and nature since he was given to them by God without their consent. Further, the laws of this nation are not its own doing but are positive revelations. The supreme ruler requires privileged intermediaries in his relations with his own people, the masses, themselves split into a multitude of distinct spheres formed and determined by chance and differentiated from each other by their interests and particular passions and prejudices but permitted as a privilege to isolate themselves from each other, etc. (p. 56).

But Bauer himself says: "If politics is to be nothing more than religion, it cannot be politics any more

than cleaning cooking pans can be regarded as an economic matter if it is to be treated religiously" (p. 108). But in the Christian-Germanic state, religion is an "economic matter" just as "economic matters" are religion. In the Christian-Germanic state, the dominance of religion is the religion of domination.

The separation of the "spirit of the Gospel" from the "letter of the Gospel" is an *irreligious* act. The state that permits the Gospel to speak in the letter of politics or in any other letter than that of the Holy Spirit commits a sacrilege if not in the eyes of men at least in the eyes of its own religion. The state that acknowledges Christianity as its highest rule and the *Bible* as its *charter* must be confronted with the *words* of Holy Writ, for the Writ is holy in every word. This state as well as the *human rubbish* on which it is based finds itself involved in a painful contradiction, a contradiction insoluble from the standpoint of religious consciousness based on the teaching of the Gospel, which it "not only does not follow but *also cannot unless it wants to dissolve itself completely as a state.*" And why does it not want to dissolve itself completely? It cannot answer this question either for itself or others. In its *own consciousness* the official Christian state is an *ought* whose realization is impossible. It knows it can affirm the *actuality* of its own existence only by lying to itself and hence remains dubious, unreliable, and problematic. Criticism is thus completely right in forcing the state that appeals to the Bible into a mental derangement in which it no longer knows whether it is an *illusion* or a *reality*, in which the infamy of its *secular* purposes cloaked by religion irreconcilably conflicts with the integrity of its *religious* consciousness viewing religion as the world's purpose. Such a state can only free itself of inner torment by becoming the *constable* of the Catholic Church. In relation to that church, which claims secular power as its servant, the state, the *secular* power claiming to dominate the religious spirit, is impotent.

In the so-called Christian state what counts is indeed *alienation* but not *man*. The only man who does count, the *king*, is still religious, specifically distinguished from others and directly connected with heaven, with God. The relations prevailing here are still relations of *faith*. The religious spirit is still not actually secularized.

But the religious spirit cannot *actually* be secularized, for what is it, in fact, but the *unsecular* form of a stage in the development of the human spirit? The religious spirit can only be actualized if the stage of development of the human spirit it expresses religiously emerges into and assumes its *secular* form. This is what happens in the *democratic* state. The basis of the democratic state is not Christianity but the *human ground* of Christianity. Religion remains the ideal, unsecular consciousness of its members because it is the ideal form of the *stage of human development* attained in the democratic state.

The members of the political state are religious by virtue of the dualism between individual life and species-life, between the life of civil society and political life. They are religious inasmuch as man regards as his true life the political life remote from his actual individuality, inasmuch as religion is here the spirit of civil society expressing the generation and withdrawal of man from man. Political democracy is Christian in that it regards man—not merely one but every man—as *sovereign* and supreme. But this means man in his uncivilized and unsocial aspect, in his fortuitous existence and just as he is, corrupted by the entire organization of our society, lost and alienated from himself, oppressed by inhuman relations and elements—in a word, man who is not yet an *actual* species-being. The sovereignty of man—though as alien and distinct from actual men—which is the chimera, dream, and postulate of Christianity, is a tangible and present actuality, a secular maxim, in democracy.

In the perfected democracy the religious and theological consciousness appears to itself all the more religious and theological for being apparently without political significance or mundane purposes—for being a spiritual affair eschewing the world, an expression of reason's limitation, a product of whim and fantasy, an actual life in the beyond. Christianity here achieves the *practical* expression of its universal religious meaning in that the most varied views are grouped together in the form of Christianity and, what is more, others are not asked to profess Christianity but only religion in general, any kind of religion (cf. Beaumont, *op. cit.*). The religious consciousness revels in the wealth of religious contradictions and multiplicity.

We have thus shown: Political emancipation from religion permits religion, though not privileged religion, to continue. The contradiction in which the adherent of a specific religion finds himself in relation to his citizenship is only *one aspect* of the universal *secular contradiction between the political state and civil society*. The fulfillment of the Christian state is a state that acknowledges itself as a state and ignores the religion of its members. The emancipation of the state from religion is not the emancipation of actual man from religion.

We thus do not say with Bauer to the Jews: You cannot be politically emancipated without radically emancipating yourselves from Judaism. Rather we tell them: Because you can be emancipated politically without completely and fully renouncing Judaism, *political emancipation* by itself is not *human* emancipation. If you Jews want to be politically emancipated without emancipating yourselves humanly, the incompleteness and contradiction lies not only in you but in the *essence* and *category* of political emancipation. If you are engrossed in this category, you share a general bias. Just as the state *evangelizes* when, in spite of being a state, it behaves toward the Jew in a Christian way, the Jew *acts politically* when, in spite of being a Jew, he demands civil rights.

But if man can be emancipated politically and acquire civil rights even though he is a Jew, can he claim and acquire the so-called *rights of man*? Bauer *denies* it.

"The question is whether the Jew as such— i.e. the Jew who avows that his true nature compels him to live in eternal separation from others—is able to acquire the *universal rights of man* and grant them to others."

"The idea of the rights of man was discovered in the Christian world only in the last century. It is not an innate idea but rather is acquired in struggle against historical traditions in which man has hitherto been educated. Thus the rights of man are neither a gift of nature nor a legacy from past history but the reward of struggle against the accident of birth and privileges transmitted by history from generation to generation up to the present. They are the result of culture, and only he can possess them who has earned and deserved them."

"But can the Jew actually take possession of them? As long as he remains a Jew the limited nature which makes him a Jew must triumph over the human nature which should link him as a man with others and must separate him from non-Jews. By this separation he proclaims that the special nature which makes him a Jew is his true and highest nature to which his human nature must yield."

"In the same way, the Christian as Christian cannot grant the rights of man." (Pp. 19, 20.)

According to Bauer man must sacrifice the "*privilege of faith*" to be able to acquire the universal rights of man. Let us consider for a moment these so-called rights and indeed in their most authentic form, the form they have among their *discoverers*, the North Americans and the French. In part these rights are *political* rights that can be exercised only in community with others. *Participation* in the *community*, indeed the *political* community or *state*, constitutes their substance. They belong in the category of *political freedom*, of *civil rights*, which by no means presupposes the consistent and positive transcendence of religion and thus of Judaism, as we have seen. There is left for consideration the other part, the *rights of man* as distinct from the *rights of the citizen*.

Among these is freedom of conscience, the right to practice one's chosen religion. The *privilege of faith* is expressly recognized either as a *right of man* or as a consequence of a right of man, freedom.

Declaration of the Rights of Man and of the Citizen, 1791, Art. 10: "No one is to be disturbed on account of his beliefs, even religious beliefs." In Title I of the Constitution of 1791 there is guaranteed as a human right: "The liberty of every man to practice the *religious worship* to which he is attached."

The *Declaration of the Rights of Man*, etc., 1793, includes among human rights, Art. 7: "Freedom of worship." Moreover, it even maintains in regard to the right to express views and opinions, to assemble, and to worship: "The need to proclaim these *rights* assumes either the presence or recent memory of despotism." Compare the Constitution of 1795, Title XIV, Art. 354.

Constitution of Pennsylvania, Art. 9, §3: "All men have a natural and indefeasible *right* to worship Almighty God according to the dictates of their own consciences; no man can of right be compelled to attend, erect, or support any place of worship, or to maintain any ministry against his consent; no human authority can, in any case whatever, interfere with the rights of conscience and control the prerogatives of the soul."

Constitution of New Hampshire, Arts. 5 and 6: "Among the natural rights, some are in their very nature unalienable, because no equivalent can be conceived for them. Of this kind are the *rights* of conscience." (Beaumont, *loc. cit.*, pp. 213, 214.)

The incompatibility between a religion and the rights of man is so little implied in the concept of the rights of man that the *right to be religious* according to one's liking and to practice a particular religion is explicitly included among the rights of man. The *privilege of faith* is a *universal human right*.

The *rights of man* as *such* are distinguished from the *rights of the citizen*. Who is this *man* distinguished from the *citizen*? None other than the *member of civil society*. Why is the member of the civil society called "man," man without qualification, and why are his rights called the *rights of man*? How can we explain this? By the relation of the political state to civil society and by the nature of political emancipation.

Let us note first of all that the so-called *rights of man* as distinguished from the *rights of the citizen* are only the rights of the *member of civil society*, that is, of egoistic man, man separated from other men and from the community. The most radical constitution, the Constitution of 1793, may be quoted:

Declaration of the Rights of Man and of the Citizen.

Art. 2. "These rights (the natural and imprescriptible rights) are: *equality*, *liberty*, *security*, *property*."

What is this *liberty*?

Art. 6. "Liberty is the power belonging to each man to do anything which does not impair the rights of others," or according to the Declaration of the Rights of Man of 1791: "Liberty is the power to do anything which does not harm others."

Liberty is thus the right to do and perform anything that does not harm others. The limits within which each can act *without harming* others is determined by law just as the boundary between two fields is marked by a stake. This is the liberty of man viewed as an isolated monad, withdrawn into himself. Why, according to Bauer, is the Jew not capable of acquiring human rights? "As long as he remains a Jew the limited nature which makes him a Jew must triumph over the human nature which should link him as a man with others and must separate him from non-Jews." But liberty as a right of man is not based on the association of man with man but rather on the separation of man from man. It is the *right* of this separation, the right of the *limited* individual limited to himself.

The practical application of the right of liberty is the right of *private property*.

What is property as one of the rights of man?

Art. 16 (Constitution of 1793): "The right of *property* is that belonging to every citizen to enjoy and dispose of his goods, his revenues, the fruits of his labor and of his industry *as he wills*."

The right of property is thus the right to enjoy and dispose of one's possessions as one wills, without regard for other men and independently of society. It is the right of self-interest. This individual freedom and its application as well constitutes the basis of civil society. It lets every man find in other men not the *realization* but rather the *limitation* of his own freedom. It proclaims above all the right of man "to enjoy and dispose of his goods, his revenues, the fruits of his labor and of his industry *as he wills*."

There still remain the other rights of man, equality and security.

"Equality"—here used in its non-political sense—is only the equal right to *liberty* as described above, viz., that every man is equally viewed as a self-sufficient monad. The Constitution of 1705 defines the concept of equality with this significance:

Art. 3 (Constitution of 1795): "Equality consists in the fact that the law is the same for all, whether it protects or whether it punishes."

And security?

Art. 8 (Constitution of 1793): "Security consists in the protection accorded by society to each of its members for the preservation of his person, his rights and his property."

Security is the supreme social concept of civil society, the concept of the *police*, the concept that the whole society exists only to guarantee to each of its members the preservation of his person, his rights, and his property. In this sense Hegel calls civil society "the state as necessity and rationality."

Civil society does not raise itself above its egoism through the concept of security. Rather, security is the *guarantee* of the egoism.

Thus none of the so-called rights of men goes beyond the egoistic man, the man withdrawn into himself, his private interest and his private choice, and separated from the community as a member of civil society. Far from viewing man here in his species-being, his species-life itself—society—rather appears to be an external framework for the individual, limiting his original independence. The only bond between men is natural necessity, need and private interest, the maintenance of their property and egoistic persons.

It is somewhat curious that a nation just beginning to free itself, tearing down all the barriers between different sections of the people and founding a political community, should solemnly proclaim (Declaration of 1791) the justification of the egoistic man, man separated from his fellow men and from the community, and should even repeat this proclamation at a moment when only the most heroic sacrifice can save the nation and hence is urgently required, when the sacrifice of all the interests of civil society is highly imperative and egoism must be punished as crime (Declaration of the Rights of Man of 1793). This becomes even more curious when we observe that the political liberators reduce citizenship, the *political community*, to a mere *means* for preserving these so-called rights of man and that the citizen thus is proclaimed to be the servant of the egoistic man, the sphere in which man acts as a member of the community is degraded below that in which he acts as a fractional being, and finally man as bourgeois rather than man as citizen is considered to be the *proper* and *authentic* man.

"The *goal* of all *political association* is the *preservation* of the natural and imprescriptible rights of man." (Declaration of the Rights of Man, etc., of 1791, Art. 2.) "*Government* is instituted to guarantee man's enjoyment of his natural and imprescriptible rights." (Declaration, etc., of 1793, Art. 1.) Thus even at the time of its youthful enthusiasm fired by the urgency of circumstances political life is proclaimed to be a mere *means* whose end is life in civil society. To be sure, revolutionary practice flagrantly contradicts its theory. While security, for example, is proclaimed to be one of the rights of man, the violation of the privacy of correspondence is publicly established as the order of the day. While the "*unlimited* freedom of the press" (Constitution of 1793, Art. 122) as a consequence of the rights of man and individual freedom is guaranteed, freedom of the press is completely abolished because "freedom of the press should not be permitted to compromise public liberty." ("Robespierre jeune," *Parliamentary History of the French Revolution*, by Buchez and Roux, Vol. 28, p. 159.) This means that the human right of liberty ceases to be a right when it comes into conflict with *political* life while theoretically political life is only the guarantee of the rights of man, the rights of individual man, and should be abandoned once it contradicts its *end*, these rights of man. But the practice is only the exception, the theory is the rule. Even if we choose to regard revolutionary practice as the correct expression of this relationship, the problem still remains unsettled as to why the relationship is inverted in the consciousness of the political liberators so that the end

appears as means and the means as the end. This optical illusion of their consciousness would always be the same problem, though a psychological, a theoretical problem.

The problem is easily settled.

Political emancipation is also the *dissolution* of the old society on which rests the sovereign power, the character of the state as alienated from the people. The political revolution is the revolution of civil society. What was the character of the old society? It can be described in one word. *Feudalism*. The old civil society had a *directly political* character, that is, the elements of civil life such as property, the family, the mode and manner of work, for example, were raised into elements of political life in the form of landlordism, estates, and corporations. In this form they determined the relation of the particular individual to the *state as a whole*, that is, his *political* relation, his separation and exclusion from other parts of society. For the feudal organization of national life did not elevate property or labor to the level of social elements but rather completed their *separation* from the state as a whole and established them as *separate* societies within society. Thus the vital functions and conditions of civil society always remained political, but political in the feudal sense. That is, they excluded the individual from the state as a whole and transformed the *special* relation between his corporation and the state into his own general relation to national life, just as they transformed his specific civil activity and situation into a general activity and situation. As a consequence of this organization, there necessarily appears the unity of the state as well as its consciousness, will, and activity—the general political power—likewise the *special* business of the ruler and his servants, separated from the people.

The political revolution, which overthrew this domination, turned the business of the state into the people's business, and made the political state the business of *all*, that is, an actual state—this revolution inevitably destroyed all estates, corporations, guilds, and privileges variously expressing the separation of the people from their community. The political revolution thereby *abolished* the *political character of civil society*. It shattered civil society into its constituent elements—on the one hand *individuals* and on the other the *material* and *spiritual elements* constituting the vital content and civil situation of these individuals. It released the political spirit, which had been broken, fragmented, and lost, as it were, in the various cul-de-sacs of feudal society. It gathered up this scattered spirit, liberated it from its entanglement with civil life, and turned it into the sphere of the community, the *general* concern of the people ideally independent of these *particular* elements of civil life. A *particular* activity and situation in life sank into a merely individual significance, no longer forming the general relation of the individual to the state as a whole. Public business as such rather became the general business of every individual and the political function became his general function.

But the fulfillment of the idealism of the state was at the same time the fulfillment of the materialism of civil society. The throwing off of the political yoke was at the same time the throwing off of the bond that had fettered the egoistic spirit of civil society. Political emancipation was at the same time the emancipation of civil society from politics, from the *appearance* of a general content.

Feudal society was dissolved into its foundation, into *man*. But into man as he actually was the foundation of that society, into *egoistical* man.

This *man*, the member of civil society, is now the basis and presupposition of the *political* state. He is recognized as such by the state in the rights of man.

But the freedom of egoistic man and the recognition of this freedom is rather the recognition of the *unbridled* movement of the spiritual and material elements forming the content of his life.

Thus man was not freed from religion; he received religious freedom. He was not freed from property. He received freedom of property. He was not freed from the egoism of trade but received freedom to trade.

The *constitution* of the *political state* and the dissolution of civil society into independent *individuals* — whose relation is *law* just as the relation of estates and guilds was *privilege* — is accomplished in *one and the same act*. As a member of civil society man is the *non-political* man but necessarily appears to be *natural* man. The *rights of man* appear to be *natural rights* because *self-conscious activity* is concentrated on the *political act*. The *egoistic* man is the *passive* and *given* result of the dissolved society, an object of

immediate certainty and thus a *natural* object. The *political revolution* dissolves civil life into its constituent elements without *revolutionizing* these elements themselves and subjecting them to criticism. It regards civil society — the realm of needs, labor, private interests, and private right — as the *basis of its existence*, as a *presupposition* needing no ground, and thus as its *natural basis*. Finally, man as a member of civil society is regarded as *authentic* man, *man* as distinct from *citizen*, since he is man in his sensuous, individual, and *most intimate* existence while *political* man is only the abstract and artificial man, man as an *allegorical, moral* person. Actual man is recognized only in the form of an *egoistic* individual, *authentic* man, only in the form of *abstract citizen*.

The abstraction of the political man was correctly depicted by Rousseau:

"Whoever dares to undertake the founding of a nation must feel himself capable of **changing**,[*] so to speak, **human nature** and **transforming** each individual who is in himself a complete but isolated whole, into a **part** of something greater than himself from which he somehow derives his life and existence, substituting a **limited** and **moral existence** for physical and independent existence. **Man** must be deprived of **his own powers** and given alien powers which he cannot use without the aid of others." (*Social Contract*, Bk. II, London, 1782, p. 67.)

All emancipation is *restoration* of the human world and the relationships of *men themselves*.

Political emancipation is a reduction of man to a member of civil society, to an *egoistic independent* individual on the one hand and to a *citizen*, a moral person, on the other.

Only when the actual, individual man has taken back into himself the abstract citizen and in his everyday life, his individual work, and his individual relationships has become a *species-being*, only when he has recognized and organized his own powers as *social* powers so that social force is no longer separated

[* Boldface type identified Marx's emphasis in the quotation.]

from him as *political* power, only then is human emancipation complete.

Bruno Bauer, *"The Capacity of Present-day Jews and Christians to Become Free,"* Twenty-one Sheets [from Switzerland (*ed. Georg Herwegh*), *Zurich and Winterthur, 1843*], *pp. 56–71.*

Here Bauer deals with the relation between the *Jewish and Christian religion* and their relation to criticism. Their relation to criticism is their bearing "on the capacity to become free."

Accordingly: "The Christian has only one stage to surpass—namely, his religion—in order to abandon religion in general" and thus become free. "The Jew, on the other hand, has to break not only with his Jewish nature but also with the development, the completion, of his religion, a development which has remained alien to him" (p. 71).

Thus Bauer here transforms the question of Jewish emancipation into a purely religious one. The theological difficulty as to whether the Jew or the Christian has the better prospect of salvation is here reproduced in the enlightened form: Which of the two is *more capable of emancipation*? It is thus no longer the question: Does Judaism or Christianity emancipate? but rather, on the contrary: Which emancipates more, the negation of Judaism or the negation of Christianity?

"If they want to be free, the Jews should not embrace Christianity but Christianity in dissolution, religion generally in dissolution—enlightenment, criticism and its results, free humanity" (p. 70).

For the Jew it is still a matter of *professing faith*, not Christianity but rather Christianity in dissolution.

Bauer requires the Jew to break with the essence of the Christian religion, a requirement which does not follow, as he says himself, from the development of the Jewish nature.

When Bauer, at the end of his *Jewish Question*, interpreted Judaism merely as a crude religious criticism of Christianity and hence gave it "only" a religious significance, it was to be expected that he would also transform the emancipation of the Jews into a philosophico-theological act.

Bauer views the *ideal* and abstract essence of the Jew, his *religion*, as his *whole* nature. Hence he correctly infers: "The Jew contributes nothing to mankind if he disregards his narrow law," if he cancels all his Judaism (p. 65).

The relation of Jews to Christian thus becomes the following: the sole interest of the Christian in the emancipation of the Jew is a general human interest, a *theoretical* interest. Judaism is an offensive fact to the religious eye of the Christian. As soon as the Christian's eye ceases to be religious, this fact ceases to offend it. In and for itself the emancipation of the Jew is not a task for the Christian.

The Jew, on the other hand, not only has to finish his own task but also the task of the Christian—[Bruno Bauer's] *Critique of the* [*Gospel History of the*] *Synoptics* and [Strauss'] *Life of Jesus*, etc.—if he wants to emancipate himself.

"They can look after themselves: they will determine their own destiny; but history does not allow itself to be mocked" (p. 71).

We will try to break with the theological formulation of the issue. The question concerning the Jew's capacity for emancipation becomes for us the question: What specific *social* element is to be overcome in order to abolish Judaism? For the modern Jew's capacity for emancipation is the relation of Judaism to the emancipation of the modern world. This relation follows necessarily from the particular position of Judaism in the modern subjugated world.

Let us consider the actual, secular Jew—not the *sabbath Jew*, as Bauer does, but the *everyday Jew*.

Let us look for the secret of the Jew not in his religion but rather for the secret of the religion in the actual Jew.

What is the secular basis of Judaism? *Practical* need, *self-interest*.

What is the worldly cult of the Jew? *Bargaining*. What is his worldly god? *Money*.

Very well! Emancipation from *bargaining* and *money*, and thus from practical and real Judaism would be the self-emancipation of our era.

An organization of society that would abolish the pre-conditions of bargaining and thus its possibility would render the Jew impossible. His religious consciousness would dissolve like a dull mist in the actual life-giving air of society. On the other hand, when the Jew recognizes this *practical* nature of his as futile and strives to eliminate it, he works away from his previous development toward general *human emancipation* and opposes the *supreme practical* expression of human self-alienation.

Thus we perceive in Judaism a general and *contemporary anti-social* element, which has been carried to its present high point by a historical development in which the Jews have contributed to this element, a point at which it must necessarily dissolve itself.

The *emancipation of the Jews*, in the final analysis, is the emancipation of mankind from *Judaism*.

The Jew has already emancipated himself in a Jewish way, "The Jew who is only tolerated in Vienna, for example, determines the fate of the whole empire through his financial power. The Jew who may be without rights in the smallest German state decides the destiny of Europe. While corporations and guilds exclude the Jew or are unfavorable to him, audacity in industry mocks the obstinacy of the medieval institutions." (B. Bauer, *The Jewish Question*, p. 114.)

This is no isolated fact. The Jew has emancipated himself in a Jewish way not only by acquiring financial power but also because, with and without him, *money* has become a world power, and the practical Jewish spirit has become the practical spirit of Christian nations. The Jews have emancipated themselves insofar as the Christian have become Jews.

For example, the pious and politically free inhabitant of New England, Captain Hamilton reports, is a kind of *Laocoön* who does not make the slightest effort to free himself from the serpents strangling him. *Mammon* is his idol to whom he prays not only with his lips but with all the power of his body and soul. In his eyes the world is nothing but a stock exchange, and he is convinced that here below he has no other destiny than to become richer than his neighbor. Bargaining dominates his every thought, exchange in things constitutes his only recreation. When he travels, he carries his shop or office on his back, as it were, and talks of nothing but interest and profit. If he loses sight of his own business for a moment, it is only in order to poke his nose into that of others. Indeed, the practical domination of Judaism over

the Christian world in North America has achieved such clear and common expression that the *very preaching of the Gospel*, the Christian ministry, has become an article of commerce and the bankrupt merchant takes to the Gospel while the minister who has become rich goes into business. *"That man whom you see at the head of a respectable congregation began as a merchant; his business having failed, he became a minister; the other started with the ministry, but as soon as he had acquired a sum of money, he left the pulpit for business. In the eyes of many, the religious ministry is a veritable commercial career."* (Beaumont, *loc. cit.*, pp. 185, 186.)

According to Bauer it is a hypocritical situation when the Jew is deprived of political rights in theory while he wields enormous power in practice, when he exercises the political influence *wholesale* denied to him in retail (*The Jewish Question*, p. 114).

The contradiction existing between the practical political power of the Jew and his political rights is the contradiction between politics and financial power in general. While politics ideally is superior to financial power, in actual fact it has become its serf.

Judaism has persisted *alongside* Christianity not only as the religious critique of Christianity, not only as the concrete doubt concerning the religious descent of Christianity, but equally because the practical Jewish spirit, Judaism, has perpetuated itself in Christian society and there even attained its highest development. The Jew, who exists as a special member of civil society, is only the special manifestation of civil society's Judaism.

Judaism has survived not in spite of but by means of history.

Out of its own entrails, civil society ceaselessly produces the Jew.

What actually was the foundation of the Jewish religion? Practical need, egoism.

Hence, the Jew's monotheism is actually the polytheism of many needs, a polytheism that makes even the toilet an object of divine law. *Practical need, egoism* is the principle of *civil society* and appears purely as such as soon as civil society has fully delivered itself to the political state. The god of *practical need and self-interest* is *money*.

Money is the jealous god of Israel before whom no other god may exist. Money degrades all the gods of mankind—and converts them into commodities. Money is the general, self-sufficient *value* of everything. Hence it has robbed the whole world, the human world as well as nature, of its proper worth. Money is the alienated essence of man's labor and life, and this alien essence dominates him as he worships it.

The god of the Jews has been secularized and has become the god of the world. The bill of exchange is the Jew's actual god. His god is only an illusory bill of exchange.

The view of nature achieved under the rule of private property and money is an actual contempt for and practical degradation of nature which does, to be sure, exist in the Jewish religion, but only in imagination.

In this sense Thomas Münzer declared it to be intolerable "that every creature should be turned into property, the fish in the water, the birds in the air, the plants of the earth—the creature must also become free."

That which is contained abstractly in the Jewish religion—contempt for theory, for art, for history, for man as an end in himself—is the *actual conscious* standpoint and virtue of the monied man. The species-relation itself, the relation between man and woman, etc., becomes an object of commerce! The woman is bought and sold.

The *chimerical* nationality of the Jew is the nationality of the merchant, particularly of the monied man.

The Jew's unfounded, superficial law is only the religious caricature of unfounded, superficial morality and law in general, the caricature of merely *formal* ceremonies encompassing the world of self-interest.

Here also the highest relation of man is the *legal* relation, the relation to laws which apply to him not because they are laws of his own will and nature but because they *dominate* him and because defection from them will be *avenged*.

Jewish Jesuitism, the same practical Jesuitism Bauer finds in the Talmud, is the relationship of the world of self-interest to the laws governing it, and the cunning circumvention of these laws is that world's main art.

Indeed, the movement of that world within its law is necessarily a continuous abrogation of the law.

Judaism could not develop further as *religion*, could not develop further theoretically, because the perspective of practical need is limited by its very nature and soon exhausted.

By its very nature, the religion of practical need could not find fulfillment in theory but only in *practice* [*Praxis*], simply because practice is its truth.

Judaism could create no new world; it could only draw the new creations and conditions of the world into the compass of its own activity because practical need, whose rationale is self-interest, remains passive, never willfully extending itself but only *finding* itself extended with the continuous development of social conditions.

Judaism reaches its height with the perfection of civil society, but civil society achieves perfection only in the *Christian* world. Only under the reign of Christianity, which makes *all* national, natural, moral, and theoretical relationships *external* to man, was civil society able to separate itself completely from political life, sever all man's species-ties, substitute egoism and selfish need for those ties, and dissolve the human world into a world of atomistic, mutually hostile individuals.

Christianity arose out of Judaism. It has again dissolved itself into Judaism.

From the outset the Christian was the theorizing Jew. Hence, the Jew is the practical Christian, and the practical Christian has again become a Jew.

Christianity overcame real Judaism only in appearance. It was too *noble*, too spiritual, to eliminate the crudeness of practical need except by elevating it into the blue.

Christianity is the sublime thought of Judaism, and Judaism is the common practical application of Christianity. But this application could only become universal after Christianity as religion par excellence had *theoretically* completed the alienation of man from himself and from nature.

Only then could Judaism attain universal dominion and convert externalized man and nature into *alienable* and saleable objects subservient to egoistic need, dependent on bargaining.

Selling is the practice of externalization. As long as man is captivated in religion, knows his nature only as objectified, and thereby converts his nature into an *alien* illusory being, so under the dominion of egoistic need he can only act practically, only practically produce objects, by subordinating both his products and this activity to the domination of an alien being, bestowing upon them the significance of an alien entity—of money.

The Christian egoism of eternal bliss in its practical fulfillment necessarily becomes the material egoism of the Jew, heavenly need is converted into earthly need, and subjectivism becomes selfishness. We do not explain the Jew's tenacity from his religion but rather from the human basis of his religion, from practical need, from egoism.

Since the Jew's real nature have been generally actualized and secularized in civil society, civil society could not convince the Jew of the *unreality* of his *religious* nature which is precisely the ideal represen-tation of practical need. Thus not only in the Penta-teuch or Talmud but also in present society we find the nature of the contemporary Jew, not as an abstract nature but a supremely empirical nature, not only as the Jew's narrowness but as the Jewish narrowness of society.

When society succeeds in transcending the *empiri-cal* essence of Judaism—bargaining and all its con-ditions—the Jew becomes *impossible* because his consciousness no longer has an object, the subjective basis of Judaism—practical need—is humanized, and the conflict between the individual sensuous exis-tence of man and his species-existence is transcended.

The *social* emancipation of the Jew is the *emanci-pation of society from Judaism.*

MANIFESTO OF THE COMMUNIST PARTY

PREFACE TO THE GERMAN EDITION OF 1872

The Communist League, an international association of workers, which could of course be only a secret one under the conditions obtaining at the time, commissioned the undersigned, at the Congress held in London in November 1847, to draw up for publication a detailed theoretical and practical programme of the Party. Such was the origin of the following Manifesto, the manuscript of which travelled to London, to be printed, a few weeks before the February Revolution.[1] First published in German, it has been republished in that language in at least twelve different editions in Germany, England and America. It was published in English for the first time in 1850 in the *Red Republican*, London, translated by Miss Helen Macfarlane, and in 1871 in at least three different translations in America. A French version first appeared in Paris shortly before the June insurrection of 1848 and recently in *Le Socialiste* of New York. A new translation is in the course of preparation. A Polish version appeared in London shortly after it was first published in German. A Russian translation was published in Geneva in the sixties. Into Danish, too, it was translated shortly after its first appearance.

However much the state of things may have altered during the last twenty-five years, the general principles laid down in this Manifesto are, on the whole, as correct today as ever. Here and there some detail might be improved. The practical application of the principles will depend, as the Manifesto itself states,

everywhere and at all times, on the historical conditions for the time being existing, and, for that reason, no special stress is laid on the revolutionary measures proposed at the end of Section II. That passage would, in many respects, be very differently worded today. In view of the gigantic strides of Modern Industry in the last twenty-five years, and of the accompanying improved and extended party organisation of the working class, in view of the practical experience gained, first in the February Revolution, and then, still more, in the Paris Commune, where the proletariat for the first time held political power for two whole months, this programme has in some details become antiquated. One thing especially was proved by the Commune, *viz.*, that "the working class cannot simply lay hold of the ready-made State machinery, and wield it for its own purposes." (See *The Civil War in France*; *Address of the General Council of the International Working Men's Association*, London, Trulove, 1871, p. 15, where this point is further developed.) Further, it is self-evident that the criticism of socialist literature is deficient in relation to the present time, because it comes down only to 1847; also, that the remarks on the relation of the Communists to the various opposition parties (Section IV), although in principle still correct, yet in practice are antiquated, because the political situation has been entirely changed, and the progress of history has swept from off the earth the greater portion of the political parties there enumerated.

But, then, the Manifesto has become a historical document which we have no longer any right to alter. A subsequent edition may perhaps appear with an introduction bridging the gap from 1847 to the present day; this reprint was too unexpected to leave us time for that.

The edition reprinted here is the standard English edition of 1888.

1. [The February Revolution in France, 1848.]

Karl Marx   Friedrich Engels
London, June 24, 1872

PREFACE TO THE RUSSIAN EDITION OF 1882

The first Russian edition of the *Manifesto of the Communist Party*, translated by Bakunin, was published early in the sixties[2] by the printing office of the *Kolokol*. Then the West could see in it (the *Russian* edition of the Manifesto) only a literary curiosity. Such a view would be impossible today.

What a limited field the proletarian movement still occupied at that time (December 1847) is most clearly shown by the last section of the Manifesto: the position of the Communists in relation to the various opposition parties in the various countries. Precisely Russia and the United States are missing here. It was the time when Russia constituted the last great reserve of all European reaction, when the United States absorbed the surplus proletarian forces of Europe through immigration. Both countries provided Europe with raw materials and were at the same time markets for the sale of its industrial products. At that time both were, therefore, in one way or another, pillars of the existing European order.

How very different today! Precisely European immigration fitted North America for a gigantic agricultural production, whose competition is shaking the very foundations of European landed property—large and small. In addition it enabled the United States to exploit its tremendous industrial resources with an energy and on a scale that must shortly break the industrial monopoly of Western Europe, and especially of England, existing up to now. Both circumstances react in revolutionary manner upon America itself. Step by step the small and middle landownership of the farmers, the basis of the whole political constitution, is succumbing to the competition of giant farms; simultaneously, a mass proletariat and a fabulous concentration of capitals are developing for the first time in the industrial regions.

And now Russia! During the Revolution of 1848–49 not only the European princes, but the European bourgeois as well, found their only salvation from the proletariat, just beginning to awaken, in Russian

intervention. The tsar was proclaimed the chief of European reaction. Today he is a prisoner of war of the revolution, in Gatchina, and Russia forms the vanguard of revolutionary action in Europe.

The Communist Manifesto had as its object the proclamation of the inevitably impending dissolution of modern bourgeois property. But in Russia we find, face to face with the rapidly developing capitalist swindle and bourgeois landed property, just beginning to develop, more than half the land owned in common by the peasants. Now the question is: Can the Russian *obshchina*,[3] though greatly undermined, yet a form of the primeval common ownership of land, pass directly to the higher form of communist common ownership? Or, on the contrary, must it first pass through the same process of dissolution as constitutes the historical evolution of the West?

The only answer to that possible today is this: If the Russian Revolution becomes the signal for a proletarian revolution in the West, so that both complement each other, the present Russian common ownership of land may serve as the starting-point for a communist development.

Karl Marx   Friedrich Engels
London, January 21, 1882

PREFACE TO THE GERMAN EDITION OF 1883

The preface to the present edition I must, alas, sign alone. Marx, the man to whom the whole working class of Europe and America owes more than to anyone else, rests at Highgate Cemetery and over his grave the first grass is already growing. Since his death, there can be even less thought of revising or supplementing the Manifesto. All the more do I consider it necessary again to state here the following expressly:

The basic thought running through the Manifesto—that economic production and the structure of society of every historical epoch necessarily arising therefrom constitute the foundation for the political and intellectual history of that epoch; that

---

2. [The date is not correct; the edition referred to appeared in 1869.]

3. [Village community.]

consequently (ever since the dissolution of the primeval communal ownership of land) all history has been a history of class struggles, of struggles between exploited and exploiting, between dominated and dominating classes at various stages of social development; that this struggle, however, has now reached a stage where the exploited and oppressed class (the proletariat) can no longer emancipate itself from the class which exploits and oppresses it (the bourgeoisie), without at the same time forever freeing the whole of society from exploitation, oppression and class struggles—this basic thought belongs solely and exclusively to Marx.

I have already stated this many times; but precisely now it is necessary that it also stand in front of the Manifesto itself.

Friedrich Engels
London, June 28, 1883

Manifesto
of the Communist Party

A spectre is haunting Europe—the spectre of Communism. All the Powers of old Europe have entered into a holy alliance to exorcise this spectre: Pope and Czar, Metternich and Guizot, French Radicals and German police-spies.

Where is the party in opposition that has not been decried as Communistic by its opponents in power? Where the Opposition that has not hurled back the branding reproach of Communism, against the more advanced opposition parties, as well as against its reactionary adversaries?

Two things result from this fact.

I. Communism is already acknowledged by all European Powers to be itself a Power.

II. It is high time that Communists should openly, in the face of the whole world, publish their views, their aims, their tendencies, and meet this nursery tale of the Spectre of Communism with a Manifesto of the party itself.

To this end, Communists of various nationalities have assembled in London, and sketched the following Manifesto, to be published in the English, French, German, Italian, Flemish and Danish languages.

I. BOURGEOIS AND PROLETARIANS [4]

The history of all hitherto existing society [5] is the history of class struggles.

Freeman and slave, patrician and plebeian, lord and serf, guild-master [6] and journeyman, in a word, oppressor and oppressed, stood in constant opposition to one another, carried on an uninterrupted, now hidden, now open fight, a fight that each time ended, either in a revolutionary re-constitution of society at large, or in the common ruin of the contending classes.

In the earlier epochs of history, we find almost

4. By bourgeoisie is meant the class of modern Capitalists, owners of the means of social production and employers of wage-labour. By proletariat, the class of modern wage-labourers who, having no means of production of their own, are reduced to selling their labour-power in order to live.—*Engels, English edition of 1888.*

5. That is, all *written* history. In 1847, the pre-history of society, the social organisation existing previous to recorded history, was all but unknown. Since then, Haxthausen discovered common ownership of land in Russia, Maurer proved it to be the social foundation from which all Teutonic races started in history, and by and by village communities were found to be, or to have been the primitive form of society everywhere from India to Ireland. The inner organisation of this primitive Communistic society was laid bare, in its typical form, by Morgan's crowning discovery of the true nature of the *gens* and its relation to the *tribe*. With the dissolution of these primaeval communities society begins to be differentiated into separate and finally antagonistic classes. I have attempted to retrace this process of dissolution in: "Der Ursprung der Familie, des Privateigenthums und des Staats" [*The Origin of the Family, Private Property and the State*], 2nd edition, Stuttgart 1886.—*Engels, English edition of 1888.*

6. Guild-master, that is, a full member of a guild, a master within, not a head of a guild.—*Engels, English edition of 1888.*

everywhere a complicated arrangement of society into various orders, a manifold gradation of social rank. In ancient Rome we have patricians, knights, plebeians, slaves; in the Middle Ages, feudal lords, vassals, guild-masters, journeymen, apprentices, serfs; in almost all of these classes, again, subordinate gradations.

The modern bourgeois society that has sprouted from the ruins of feudal society has not done away with clash antagonisms. It has but established new classes, new conditions of oppression, new forms of struggle in place of the old ones.

Our epoch, the epoch of the bourgeoisie, possesses, however, this distinctive feature: it has simplified the class antagonisms: Society as a whole is more and more splitting up into two great hostile camps, into two great classes directly facing each other: Bourgeoisie and Proletariat.

From the serfs of the Middle Ages sprang the chartered burghers of the earliest towns. From these burgesses the first elements of the bourgeoisie were developed.

The discovery of America, the rounding of the Cape, opened up fresh ground for the rising bourgeoisie. The East-Indian and Chinese markets, the colonisation of America, trade with the colonies, the increase in the means of exchange and in commodities generally, gave to commerce, to navigation, to industry, an impulse never before known, and thereby, to the revolutionary element in the tottering feudal society, a rapid development.

The feudal system of industry, under which industrial production was monopolised by closed guilds, now no longer sufficed for the growing wants of the new markets. The manufacturing system took its place. The guild-masters were pushed on one side by the manufacturing middle class; division of labour between the different corporate guilds vanished in the face of division of labour in each single workshop.

Meantime the markets kept ever growing, the demand ever rising. Even manufacture no longer sufficed. Thereupon, steam and machinery revolutionised industrial production. The place of manufacture was taken by the giant, Modern Industry, the place of the industrial middle class, by industrial millionaires, the leaders of whole industrial armies, the modern bourgeois.

Modern industry has established the world-market, for which the discovery of America paved the way. This market has given an immense development to commerce, to navigation, to communication by land. This development has, in its turn, reacted on the extension of industry; and in proportion as industry, commerce, navigation, railways extended, in the same proportion the bourgeoisie developed, increased its capital, and pushed into the background every class handed down from the Middle Ages.

We see, therefore, how the modern bourgeoisie is itself the product of a long course of development, of a series of revolutions in the modes of production and of exchange.

Each step in the development of the bourgeoisie was accompanied by a corresponding political advance of that class. An oppressed class under the sway of the feudal nobility, an armed and self-governing association in the mediaeval commune;[7] here independent urban republic (as in Italy and Germany), there taxable "third estate" of the monarchy (as in France), afterwards, in the period of manufacture proper, serving either the semi-feudal or the absolute monarchy as a counterpoise against the nobility, and, in fact, corner-stone of the great monarchies in general, the bourgeoisie has at last, since the establishment of Modern Industry and of the world-market, conquered for itself, in the modern representative State, exclusive political sway. The executive of the modern State is but a committee for managing the common affairs of the whole bourgeoisie.

The bourgeoisie, historically, has played a most revolutionary part.

The bourgeoisie, wherever it has got the upper hand, has put an end to all feudal, patriarchal, idyllic

---

7. "Commune" was the name taken, in France, by the nascent towns even before they had conquered from their feudal lords and masters local self-government and political rights as the "Third Estate." Generally speaking, for the economical development of the bourgeoisie, England is here taken as the typical country; for its political development, France. — Engels, English edition of 1888.

This was the name given their urban communities by the townsmen of Italy and France, after they had purchased or wrested their initial rights of self-government from their feudal lords. — Engels, German edition of 1890.

relations. It has pitilessly torn asunder the motley feudal ties that bound man to his "natural superiors," and has left remaining no other nexus between man and man than naked self-interest, than callous "cash payment." It has drowned the most heavenly ecstasies of religious fervour, of chivalrous enthusiasm, of philistine sentimentalism, in the icy water of egotistical calculation. It has resolved personal worth into exchange value, and in place of the numberless indefeasible chartered freedoms, has set up that single, unconscionable freedom — Free Trade. In one word, for exploitation, veiled by religious and political illusions, it has substituted naked, shameless, direct, brutal exploitation.

The bourgeoisie has stripped of its halo every occupation hitherto honoured and looked up to with reverent awe. It has converted the physician, the lawyer, the priest, the poet, the man of science, into its paid wage-labourers.

The bourgeoisie has torn away from the family its sentimental veil, and has reduced the family relation to a mere money relation.

The bourgeoisie has disclosed how it came to pass that the brutal display of vigour in the Middle Ages, which Reactionists so much admire, found its fitting complement in the most slothful indolence. It has been the first to show what man's activity can bring about. It has accomplished wonders far surpassing Egyptian pyramids, Roman aqueducts, and Gothic cathedrals; it has conducted expeditions that put in the shade all former Exoduses of nations and crusades.

The bourgeoisie cannot exist without constantly revolutionising the instruments of production, and thereby the relations of production, and with them the whole relations of society. Conservation of the old modes of production in unaltered form, was, on the contrary, the first condition of existence for all earlier industrial classes. Constant revolutionising of production, uninterrupted disturbance of all social conditions, everlasting uncertainty and agitation distinguish the bourgeois epoch from all earlier ones. All fixed, fast-frozen relations, with their train of ancient and venerable prejudices and opinions, are swept away, all new-formed ones become antiquated before they can ossify. All that is solid melts into air, all that is holy is profaned, and man is at last compelled to face with sober senses, his real conditions of life, and his relations with his kind.

The need of a constantly expanding market for its products chases the bourgeoisie over the whole surface of the globe. It must nestle everywhere, settle everywhere, establish connexions everywhere.

The bourgeoisie has through its exploitation of the world-market given a cosmopolitan character to production and consumption in every country. To the great chagrin of Reactionists, it has drawn from under the feet of industry the national ground on which it stood. All old-established national industries have been destroyed or are daily being destroyed. They are dislodged by new industries, whose introduction becomes a life and death question for all civilised nations, by industries that no longer work up indigenous raw material, but raw material drawn from the remotest zones; industries whose products are consumed, not only at home, but in every quarter of the globe. In place of the old wants, satisfied by the productions of the country, we find new wants, requiring for their satisfaction the products of distant lands and climes. In place of the old local and national seclusion and self-sufficiency, we have intercourse in every direction, universal inter-dependence of nations. And as in material, so also in intellectual production. The intellectual creations of individual nations become common property. National one-sidedness and narrow-mindedness become more and more impossible, and from the numerous national and local literatures, there arises a world literature.

The bourgeoisie, by the rapid improvement of all instruments of production, by the immensely facilitated means of communication, draws all, even the most barbarian, nations into civilisation. The cheap prices of its commodities are the heavy artillery with which it batters down all Chinese walls, with which it forces the barbarians' intensely obstinate hatred of foreigners to capitulate. It compels all nations, on pain of extinction, to adopt the bourgeois mode of production; it compels them to introduce what it calls civilisation into their midst, *i.e.*, to become bourgeois themselves. In one word, it creates a world after its own image.

The bourgeoisie has subjected the country to the rule of the towns. It has created enormous cities, has greatly increased the urban population as compared with the rural, and has thus rescued a considerable part of the population from the idiocy of rural life. Just as it has made the country dependent on the towns, so it has made barbarian and semi-barbarian countries dependent on the civilised ones, nations and peasants on nations of bourgeois, the East on the West.

The bourgeoisie keeps more and more doing away with the scattered state of the population, of the means of production, and of property. It has agglomerated population, centralised means of production, and has concentrated property in a few hands. The necessary consequence of this was political centralisation. Independent, or but loosely connected provinces, with separate interests, laws, governments and systems of taxation, became lumped together into one nation, with one government, one code of laws, one national class-interest, one frontier and one customs-tariff. The bourgeoisie, during its rule of scarce one hundred years, has created more massive and more colossal productive forces than have all preceding generations together. Subjection of Nature's forces to man, machinery, application of chemistry to industry and agriculture, steam-navigation, railways, electric telegraphs, clearing of whole continents for cultivation, canalisation of rivers, whole populations conjured out of the ground—what earlier century had even a presentiment that such productive forces slumbered in the lap of social labour?

We see then: the means of production and of exchange, on whose foundation the bourgeoisie built itself up, were generated in feudal society. At a certain stage in the development of these means of production and of exchange, the conditions under which feudal society produced and exchanged, the feudal organisation of agriculture and manufacturing industry, in one word, the feudal relations of property became no longer compatible with the already developed productive forces; they became so many fetters. They had to be burst asunder; they were burst asunder.

Into their place stepped free competition, accompanied by a social and political constitution adapted to it, and by the economical and political sway of the bourgeois class.

A similar movement is going on before our own eyes. Modern bourgeois society with its relations of production, of exchange and of property, a society that has conjured up such gigantic means of production and of exchange, is like the sorcerer, who is no longer able to control the powers of the nether world whom he has called up by his spells. For many a decade past the history of industry and commerce is but the history of the revolt of modern productive forces against modern conditions of production, against the property relations that are the conditions for the existence of the bourgeoisie and of its rule. It is enough to mention the commercial crises that by their periodical return put on its trial, each time more threateningly, the existence of the entire bourgeois society. In these crises a great part not only of the existing products, but also of the previously created productive forces, are periodically destroyed. In these crises there breaks out an epidemic that, in all earlier epochs, would have seemed an absurdity—the epidemic of over-production. Society suddenly finds itself put back into a state of momentary barbarism; it appears as if a famine, a universal war of devastation had cut off the supply of every means of subsistence; industry and commerce seem to be destroyed; and why? Because there is too much civilisation, too much means of subsistence, too much industry, too much commerce. The productive forces at the disposal of society no longer tend to further the development of the conditions of bourgeois property; on the contrary, they have become too powerful for these conditions, by which they are fettered, and so soon as they overcome these fetters, they bring disorder into the whole of bourgeois society, endanger the existence of bourgeois property. The conditions of bourgeois society are too narrow to comprise the wealth created by them. And how does the bourgeoisie get over these crises? On the one hand by enforced destruction of a mass of productive forces; on the other, by the conquest of new markets, and by the more thorough exploitation of the old ones. That is to say, by paving the way for more extensive and more destructive crises, and by diminishing the means whereby crises are prevented.

The weapons with which the bourgeoisie felled feudalism to the ground are now turned against the bourgeoisie itself.

But not only has the bourgeoisie forged the weapons that bring death to itself; it has also called into existence the men who are to wield these weapons— the modern working class—the proletarians.

In proportion as the bourgeoisie, *i.e.*, capital, is developed, in the same proportion is the proletariat, the modern working class, developed—a class of labourers, who live only so long as they find work, and who find work only so long as their labour increases capital. These labourers, who must sell themselves piece-meal, are a commodity, like every other article of commerce, and are consequently exposed to all the vicissitudes of competition, to all the fluctuations of the market.

Owing to the extensive use of machinery and to division of labour, the work of the proletarians has lost all individual character, and consequently, all charm for the workman. He becomes an appendage of the machine, and it is only the most simple, most monotonous, and most easily acquired knack, that is required of him. Hence, the cost of production of a workman is restricted, almost entirely, to the means of subsistence that he requires for his maintenance, and for the propagation of his race. But the price of a commodity, and therefore also of labour,[8] is equal to its cost of production. In proportion, therefore, as the repulsiveness of the work increases, the wage decreases. Nay more, in proportion as the use of machinery and division of labour increases, in the same proportion the burden of toil also increases, whether by prolongation of the working hours, by increase of the work exacted in a given time or by increased speed of the machinery, etc.

Modern industry has converted the little workshop of the patriarchal master into the great factory of the industrial capitalist. Masses of labourers, crowded into the factory, are organised like soldiers. As privates of the industrial army they are placed under the command of a perfect hierarchy of officers and sergeants. Not only are they slaves of the bourgeois class, and of the bourgeois State; they are daily and hourly enslaved by the machine, by the over-looker, and, above all, by the individual bourgeois manufacturer himself. The more openly this despotism proclaims gain to be its end and aim, the more petty, the more hateful and the more embittering it is.

The less the skill and exertion of strength implied in manual labour, in other words, the more modern industry becomes developed, the more is the labour of men superseded by that of women. Differences of age and sex have no longer any distinctive social validity for the working class. All are instruments of labour, more or less expensive to use, according to their age and sex.

No sooner is the exploitation of the labourer by the manufacturer, so far, at an end, that he receives his wages in cash, than he is set upon by the other portions of the bourgeoisie, the landlord, the shopkeeper, the pawnbroker, etc.

The lower strata of the middle class—the small tradespeople, shopkeepers, and retired tradesmen generally, the handicraftsmen and peasants—all these sink gradually into the proletariat, partly because their diminutive capital does not suffice for the scale on which Modern Industry is carried on, and is swamped in the competition with the large capitalists, partly because their specialised skill is rendered worthless by new methods of production. Thus the proletariat is recruited from all classes of the population.

The proletariat goes through various stages of development. With its birth begins its struggle with the bourgeoisie. At first the contest is carried on by individual labourers, then by the workpeople of a factory, then by the operatives of one trade, in one locality, against the individual bourgeois who directly exploits them. They direct their attacks not against the bourgeois conditions of production, but against the instruments of production themselves; they destroy imported wares that compete with their labour, they smash to pieces machinery, they set factories ablaze, they seek to restore by force the vanished status of the workman of the Middle Ages.

At this stage the labourers still form an incoherent mass scattered over the whole country, and broken up by their mutual competition. If anywhere they unite to form more compact bodies, this is not yet the consequence of their own active union, but of the union of the bourgeoisie, which class, in order to attain its own political ends, is compelled to set the whole proletariat in motion, and is moreover yet, for a time, able to do so. At this stage, therefore, the proletarians do not fight their enemies, but the enemies of their enemies, the remnants of absolute monarchy, the landowners, the non-industrial bourgeois, the petty bourgeoisie. Thus the whole historical

---

8. [Subsequently Marx pointed out that the worker sells not his labour but his labour power.]

movement is concentrated in the hands of the bourgeoisie; every victory so obtained is a victory for the bourgeoisie.

But with the development of industry the proletariat not only increases in number; it becomes concentrated in greater masses, its strength grows, and it feels that strength more. The various interests and conditions of life within the ranks of the proletariat are more and more equalised, in proportion as machinery obliterates all distinctions of labour, and nearly everywhere reduces wages to the same low level. The growing competition among the bourgeois, and the resulting commercial crises, make the wages of the workers ever more fluctuating. The unceasing improvement of machinery, ever more rapidly developing, makes their livelihood more and more precarious; the collisions between individual workmen and individual bourgeois take more and more the character of collisions between two classes. Thereupon the workers begin to form combinations (Trades Unions) against the bourgeois; they club together in order to keep up the rate of wages; they found permanent associations in order to make provision beforehand for these occasional revolts. Here and there the contest breaks out into riots.

Now and then the workers are victorious, but only for a time. The real fruit of their battles lies, not in the immediate result, but in the ever-expanding union of the workers. This union is helped on by the improved means of communication that are created by modern industry and that place the workers of different localities in contact with one another. It was just this contact that was needed to centralise the numerous local struggles, all of the same character, into one national struggle between classes. But every class struggle is a political struggle. And that union, to attain which the burghers of the Middle Ages, with their miserable highways, required centuries, the modern proletarians, thanks to railways, achieve in a few years.

This organisation of the proletarians into a class, and consequently into a political party, is continually being upset again by the competition between the workers themselves. But it ever rises up again, stronger, firmer, mightier. It compels legislative recognition of particular interests of the workers, by taking advantage of the divisions among the bourgeoisie itself. Thus the ten-hours' bill in England was carried.

Altogether collisions between the classes of the old society further, in many ways, the course of development of the proletariat. The bourgeoisie finds itself involved in a constant battle. At first with the aristocracy; later on, with those portions of the bourgeoisie itself, whose interests have become antagonistic to the progress of industry; at all times, with the bourgeoisie of foreign countries. In all these battles it sees itself compelled to appeal to the proletariat, to ask for its help, and thus, to drag it into the political arena. The bourgeoisie itself, therefore, supplies the proletariat with its own elements of political and general education, in other words, it furnishes the proletariat with weapons for fighting the bourgeoisie.

Further, as we have already seen, entire sections of the ruling classes are, by the advance of industry, precipitated into the proletariat, or are at least threatened in their conditions of existence. These also supply the proletariat with fresh elements of enlightenment and progress.

Finally, in times when the class struggle nears the decisive hour, the process of dissolution going on within the ruling class, in fact within the whole range of society, assumes such a violent, glaring character, that a small section of the ruling class cuts itself adrift, and joins the revolutionary class, the class that holds the future in its hands. Just as, therefore, at an earlier period, a section of the nobility went over to the bourgeoisie, so now a portion of the bourgeoisie goes over to the proletariat, and in particular, a portion of the bourgeois ideologists, who have raised themselves to the level of comprehending theoretically the historical movement as a whole.

Of all the classes that stand face to face with the bourgeoisie today, the proletariat alone is a really revolutionary class. The other classes decay and finally disappear in the face of Modern Industry; the proletariat is its special and essential product.

The lower middle class, the small manufacturer, the shopkeeper, the artisan, the peasant, all these fight against the bourgeoisie, to save from extinction their existence as fractions of the middle class. They are therefore not revolutionary, but conservative. Nay more, they are reactionary, for they try to roll back the wheel of history. If by chance they are revolutionary, they are so only in view of their impending transfer into the proletariat, they thus defend not their present, but their future interests, they desert their own standpoint to place themselves at that of the proletariat.

The "dangerous class," the social scum, that passively rotting mass thrown off by the lowest layers of old society, may, here and there, be swept into the movement by a proletarian revolution; its conditions of life, however, prepare it far more for the part of a bribed tool of reactionary intrigue.

In the conditions of the proletariat, those of old society at large are already virtually swamped. The proletarian is without property; his relation to his wife and children has no longer anything in common with the bourgeois family-relations; modern industrial labour, modern subjection to capital, the same in England as in France, in America as in Germany, has stripped him of every trace of national character. Law, morality, religion, are to him so many bourgeois prejudices, behind which lurk in ambush just as many bourgeois interests.

All the preceding classes that got the upper hand, sought to fortify their already acquired status by subjecting society at large to their conditions of appropriation. The proletarians cannot become masters of the productive forces of society, except by abolishing their own previous mode of appropriation, and thereby also every other previous mode of appropriation. They have nothing of their own to secure and to fortify; their mission is to destroy all previous securities for, and insurances of, individual property.

All previous historical movements were movements of minorities, or in the interests of minorities. The proletarian movement is the self-conscious, independent movement of the immense majority, in the interests of the immense majority. The proletariat, the lowest stratum of our present society, cannot stir, cannot raise itself up, without the whole superincumbent strata of official society being sprung into the air.

Though not in substance, yet in form, the struggle of the proletariat with the bourgeoisie is at first a national struggle. The proletariat of each country must, of course, first of all settle matters with its own bourgeoisie.

In depicting the most general phases of the development of the proletariat, we traced the more or less veiled civil war, raging within existing society, up to the point where that war breaks out into open revolution, and where the violent overthrow of the bourgeoisie lays the foundation for the sway of the proletariat.

Hitherto, every form of society has been based, as we have already seen, on the antagonism of oppressing and oppressed classes. But in order to oppress a class, certain conditions must be assured to it under which it can, at least, continue its slavish existence. The serf, in the period of serfdom, raised himself to membership in the commune, just as the petty bourgeois, under the yoke of feudal absolutism, managed to develop into a bourgeois. The modern labourer, on the contrary, instead of rising with the progress of industry, sinks deeper and deeper below the conditions of existence of his own class. He becomes a pauper, and pauperism develops more rapidly than population and wealth. And here it becomes evident, that the bourgeoisie is unfit any longer to be the ruling class in society, and to impose its conditions of existence upon society as an over-riding law. It is unfit to rule because it is incompetent to assure an existence to its slave within his slavery, because it cannot help letting him sink into such a state, that it has to feed him, instead of being fed by him. Society can no longer live under this bourgeoisie, in other words, its existence is no longer compatible with society.

The essential condition for the existence, and for the sway of the bourgeois class, is the formation and augmentation of capital; the condition for capital is wage-labour. Wage-labour rests exclusively on competition between the labourers. The advance of industry, whose involuntary promoter is the bourgeoisie, replaces the isolation of the labourers, due to competition, by their revolutionary combination, due to association. The development of Modern Industry, therefore, cuts from under its feet the very foundation on which the bourgeoisie produces and appropriates products. What the bourgeoisie, therefore, produces, above all, is its own grave-diggers. Its fall and the victory of the proletariat are equally inevitable.

II. PROLETARIANS AND COMMUNISTS

In what relation do the Communists stand to the proletarians as a whole?

The Communists do not form a separate party opposed to other working-class parties.

They have no interests separate and apart from those of the proletariat as a whole.

They do not set up any sectarian principles of their own, by which to shape and mould the proletarian movement.

The Communists are distinguished from the other working-class parties by this only: (1) In the national struggles of the proletarians of the different countries, they point out and bring to the front the common interests of the entire proletariat, independently of all nationality. (2) In the various stages of development which the struggle of the working class against the bourgeoisie has to pass through, they always and everywhere represent the interests of the movement as a whole.

The Communists, therefore, are on the one hand, practically, the most advanced and resolute section of the working-class parties of every country, that section which pushes forward all others; on the other hand, theoretically, they have over the great mass of the proletariat the advantage of clearly understanding the line of march, the conditions, and the ultimate general results of the proletarian movement.

The immediate aim of the Communists is the same as that of all the other proletarian parties: formation of the proletariat into a class, overthrow of the bourgeois supremacy, conquest of political power by the proletariat.

The theoretical conclusions of the Communists are in no way based on ideas or principles that have been invented, or discovered, by this or that would-be universal reformer.

They merely express, in general terms, actual relations springing from an existing class struggle, from a historical movement going on under our very eyes. The abolition of existing property relations is not at all a distinctive feature of Communism.

All property relations in the past have continually been subject to historical change consequent upon the change in historical conditions.

The French Revolution, for example, abolished feudal property in favour of bourgeois property.

The distinguishing feature of Communism is not the abolition of property generally, but the abolition of bourgeois property. But modern bourgeois private property is the final and most complete expression of the system of producing and appropriating products, that is based on class antagonisms, on the exploitation of the many by the few.

In this sense, the theory of the Communists may be summed up in the single sentence: Abolition of private property.

We Communists have been reproached with the desire of abolishing the right of personally acquiring property as the fruit of a man's own labour, which property is alleged to be the groundwork of all personal freedom, activity and independence.

Hard-won, self-acquired, self-earned property! Do you mean the property of the petty artisan and of the small peasant, a form of property that preceded the bourgeois form? There is no need to abolish that; the development of industry has to a great extent already destroyed it, and is still destroying it daily.

Or do you mean modern bourgeois private property?

But does wage-labour create any property for the labourer? Not a bit. It creates capital, *i.e.*, that kind of property which exploits wage-labour, and which cannot increase except upon condition of begetting a new supply of wage-labour for fresh exploitation. Property, in its present form, is based on the antagonism of capital and wage-labour. Let us examine both sides of this antagonism.

To be a capitalist, is to have not only a purely personal, but a social *status* in production. Capital is a collective product, and only by the united action of many members, nay, in the last resort, only by the united action of all members of society, can it be set in motion.

Capital is, therefore, not a personal, it is a social power.

When, therefore, capital is converted into common property, into the property of all members of society, personal property is not thereby transformed into social property. It is only the social character of the property that is changed. It loses its class-character.

Let us now take wage-labour.

The average price of wage-labour is the minimum wage, *i.e.*, that quantum of the means of subsistence, which is absolutely requisite to keep the labourer in bare existence as a labourer. What, therefore, the wage-labourer appropriates by means of his labour, merely suffices to prolong and reproduce a bare existence. We by no means intend to abolish this personal appropriation of the products of labour, an appropriation that is made for the maintenance and reproduction of human life, and that leaves no surplus wherewith to command the labour of others. All that we want to do away with, is the miserable character of this appropriation, under which the labourer lives merely to increase capital, and is allowed to live only in so far as the interest of the ruling class requires it.

In bourgeois society, living labour is but a means to increase accumulated labour. In Communist society, accumulated labour is but a means to widen, to enrich, to promote the existence of the labourer.

In bourgeois society, therefore, the past dominates the present; in Communist society, the present dominates the past. In bourgeois society capital is independent and has individuality, while the living person is dependent and has no individuality.

And the abolition of this state of things is called by the bourgeois, abolition of individuality and freedom! And rightly so. The abolition of bourgeois individuality, bourgeois independence, and bourgeois freedom is undoubtedly aimed at.

By freedom is meant, under the present bourgeois conditions of production, free trade, free selling and buying.

But if selling and buying disappears, free selling and buying disappears also. This talk about free selling and buying, and all the other "brave words" of our bourgeoisie about freedom in general, have a meaning, if any, only in contrast with restricted selling and buying, with the fettered traders of the Middle Ages, but have no meaning when opposed to the Communistic abolition of buying and selling, of the bourgeois conditions of production, and of the bourgeoisie itself.

You are horrified at our intending to do away with private property. But in your existing society, private property is already done away with for nine-tenths of the population; its existence for the few is solely due to its non-existence in the hands of those nine-tenths. You reproach us, therefore, with intending to do away with a form of property, the necessary condition for whose existence is the non-existence of any property for the immense majority of society.

In one word, you reproach us with intending to do away with your property. Precisely so; that is just what we intend.

From the moment when labour can no longer be converted into capital, money, or rent, into a social power capable of being monopolised, *i.e.*, from the moment when individual property can no longer be transformed into bourgeois property, into capital, from that moment, you say, individuality vanishes.

You must, therefore, confess that by "individual" you mean no other person than the bourgeois, than the middle-class owner of property. This person must, indeed, be swept out of the way, and made impossible.

Communism deprives no man of the power to appropriate the products of society; all that it does is to deprive him of the power to subjugate the labour of others by means of such appropriation.

It has been objected that upon the abolition of private property all work will cease, and universal laziness will overtake us.

According to this, bourgeois society ought long ago to have gone to the dogs through sheer idleness; for those of its members who work, acquire nothing, and those who acquire anything, do not work. The whole of this objection is but another expression of the tautology: that there can no longer be any wage-labour when there is no longer any capital.

All objections urged against the Communistic mode of producing and appropriating material products, have, in the same way, been urged against the Communistic modes of producing and appropriating intellectual products. Just as, to the bourgeois, the disappearance of class property is the disappearance of production itself, so the disappearance of class culture is to him identical with the disappearance of all culture.

That culture, the loss of which he laments, is, for the enormous majority, a mere training to act as a machine.

But don't wrangle with us so long as you apply, to our intended abolition of bourgeois property, the standard of your bourgeois notions of freedom, culture, law, &c. Your very ideas are but the outgrowth of the conditions of your bourgeois production and bourgeois property, just as your jurisprudence is but the will of your class made into a law for all, a will, whose essential character and direction are determined by the economical conditions of existence of your class.

The selfish misconception that induces you to transform into eternal laws of nature and of reason, the social forms springing from your present mode of production and form of property—historical relations that rise and disappear in the progress of production—this misconception you share with every ruling class that has preceded you. What you see clearly in the case of ancient property, what you admit in the case of feudal property, you are of course forbidden to admit in the case of your own bourgeois form of property.

Abolition of the family! Even the most radical flare up at this infamous proposal of the Communists.

On what foundation is the present family, the bourgeois family, based? On capital, on private gain. In its completely developed form this family exists only among the bourgeoisie. But this state of things finds its complement in the practical absence of the family among the proletarians, and in public prostitution.

The bourgeois family will vanish as a matter of course when its complement vanishes, and both will vanish with the vanishing of capital.

Do you charge us with wanting to stop the exploitation of children by their parents? To this crime we plead guilty.

But, you will say, we destroy the most hallowed of relations, when we replace home education by social.

And your education! Is not that also social, and determined by the social conditions under which you educate, by the intervention, direct or indirect, of society, by means of schools, &c.? The Communists have not invented the intervention of society in education; they do but seek to alter the character of that intervention, and to rescue education from the influence of the ruling class.

The bourgeois clap-trap about the family and education, about the hallowed co-relation of parent and child, becomes all the more disgusting, the more, by the action of Modern Industry, all family ties among the proletarians are torn asunder, and their children transformed into simple articles of commerce and instruments of labour.

But you Communists would introduce community of women, screams the whole bourgeoisie in chorus.

The bourgeois sees in his wife a mere instrument of production. He hears that the instruments of production are to be exploited in common, and, naturally, can come to no other conclusion than that the lot of being common to all will likewise fall to the women.

He has not even a suspicion that the real point aimed at is to do away with the status of women as mere instruments of production.

For the rest, nothing is more ridiculous than the virtuous indignation of our bourgeois at the community of women which, they pretend, is to be openly and officially established by the Communists. The Communists have no need to introduce community of women; it has existed almost from time immemorial.

Our bourgeois, not content with having the wives and daughters of their proletarians at their disposal, not to speak of common prostitutes, take the greatest pleasure in seducing each other's wives.

Bourgeois marriage is in reality a system of wives in common and thus, at the most, what the Communists might possibly be reproached with, is that they desire to introduce, in substitution for a hypocritically concealed, an openly legalised community of women. For the rest, it is self-evident that the abolition of the present system of production must bring with it the abolition of the community of women springing from that system, *i.e.*, of prostitution both public and private.

The Communists are further reproached with desiring to abolish countries and nationality.

The working men have no country. We cannot take from them what they have not got. Since the proletariat must first of all acquire political supremacy, must rise to be the leading class of the nation, must constitute itself *the* nation, it is, so far, itself national, though not in the bourgeois sense of the word.

National differences and antagonisms between peoples are daily more and more vanishing, owing to the development of the bourgeoisie, to freedom of commerce, to the world-market, to uniformity in the mode of production and in the conditions of life corresponding thereto.

The supremacy of the proletariat will cause them to vanish still faster. United action, of the leading civilised countries at least, is one of the first conditions for the emancipation of the proletariat.

In proportion as the exploitation of one individual

by another is put an end to, the exploitation of one nation by another will also be put an end to. In proportion as the antagonism between classes within the nation vanishes, the hostility of one nation to another will come to an end.

The charges against Communism made from a religious, a philosophical, and, generally, from an ideological standpoint, are not deserving of serious examination.

Does it require deep intuition to comprehend that man's ideas, views and conceptions, in one word, man's consciousness, changes with every change in the conditions of his material existence, in his social relations and in his social life?

What else does the history of ideas prove, than that intellectual production changes its character in proportion as material production is changed? The ruling ideas of each age have ever been the ideas of its ruling class.

When people speak of ideas that revolutionise society, they do but express the fact, that within the old society, the elements of a new one have been created, and that the dissolution of the old ideas keeps even pace with the dissolution of the old conditions of existence.

When the ancient world was in its last throes, the ancient religions were overcome by Christianity. When Christian ideas succumbed in the 18th century to rationalist ideas, feudal society fought its death battle with the then revolutionary bourgeoisie. The ideas of religious liberty and freedom of conscience merely gave expression to the sway of free competition within the domain of knowledge.

"Undoubtedly," it will be said, "religious, moral, philosophical and juridical ideas have been modified in the course of historical development. But religion, morality, philosophy, political science, and law, constantly survived this change."

"There are, besides, eternal truths, such as Freedom, Justice, etc., that are common to all states of society. But Communism abolishes eternal truths, it abolishes all religion, and all morality, instead of constituting them on a new basis; it therefore acts in contradiction to all past historical experience."

What does this accusation reduce itself to? The history of all past society has consisted in the development of class antagonisms, antagonisms that assumed different forms at different epochs.

But whatever form they may have taken, one fact is common to all past ages, *viz.*, the exploitation of one part of society by the other. No wonder, then, that the social consciousness of past ages, despite all the multiplicity and variety it displays, moves within certain common forms, or general ideas, which cannot completely vanish except with the total disappearance of class antagonisms.

The Communist revolution is the most radical rupture with traditional property relations; no wonder that its development involves the most radical rupture with traditional ideas.

But let us have done with the bourgeois objections to Communism.

We have seen above, that the first step in the revolution by the working class, is to raise the proletariat to the position of ruling class, to win the battle of democracy.

The proletariat will use its political supremacy to wrest, by degrees, all capital from the bourgeoisie, to centralise all instruments of production in the hands of the State, *i.e.*, of the proletariat organised as the ruling class; and to increase the total of productive forces as rapidly as possible.

Of course, in the beginning, this cannot be effected except by means of despotic inroads on the rights of property, and on the conditions of bourgeois production; by means of measures, therefore, which appear economically insufficient and untenable, but which, in the course of the movement, outstrip themselves, necessitate further inroads upon the old social order, and are unavoidable as a means of entirely revolutionising the mode of production.

These measures will of course be different in different countries.

Nevertheless in the most advanced countries, the following will be pretty generally applicable.

1. Abolition of property in land and application of all rents of land to public purposes.
2. A heavy progressive or graduated income tax.
3. Abolition of all right of inheritance.

4. Confiscation of the property of all emigrants and rebels.

5. Centralisation of credit in the hands of the State, by means of a national bank with State capital and an exclusive monopoly.

6. Centralisation of the means of communication and transport in the hands of the State.

7. Extension of factories and instruments of production owned by the State; the bringing into cultivation of waste-lands, and the improvement of the soil generally in accordance with a common plan.

8. Equal liability of all to labour. Establishment of industrial armies, especially for agriculture.

9. Combination of agriculture with manufacturing industries; gradual abolition of the distinction between town and country, by a more equable distribution of the population over the country.

10. Free education for all children in public schools. Abolition of children's factory labour in its present form. Combination of education with industrial production, &c., &c.

When, in the course of development, class distinctions have disappeared, and all production has been concentrated in the hands of a vast association of the whole nation, the public power will lose its political character. Political power, properly so called, is merely the organised power of one class for oppressing another. If the proletariat during its contest with the bourgeoisie is compelled, by the force of circumstances, to organise itself as a class, if, by means of a revolution, it makes itself the ruling class, and, as such, sweeps away by force the old conditions of production, then it will, along with these conditions, have swept away the conditions for the existence of class antagonisms and of classes generally, and will thereby have abolished its own supremacy as a class.

In place of the old bourgeois society, with its classes and class antagonisms, we shall have an association, in which the free development of each is the condition for the free development of all.

III. SOCIALIST AND COMMUNIST LITERATURE

1. Reactionary Socialism

A. Feudal Socialism

Owing to their historical position, it became the vocation of the aristocracies of France and England to write pamphlets against modern bourgeois society. In the French revolution of July 1830, and in the English reform agitation, these aristocracies again succumbed to the hateful upstart. Thenceforth, a serious political contest was altogether out of the question. A literary battle alone remained possible. But even in the domain of literature the old cries of the restoration period[9] had become impossible.

In order to arouse sympathy, the aristocracy were obliged to lose sight, apparently, of their own interests, and to formulate their indictment against the bourgeoisie in the interest of the exploited working class alone. Thus the aristocracy took their revenge by singing lampoons on their new master, and whispering in his ears sinister prophecies of coming catastrophe.

In this way arose Feudal Socialism: half lamentation, half lampoon; half echo of the past, half menace of the future; at times, by its bitter, witty and incisive criticism, striking the bourgeoisie to the very heart's core; but always ludicrous in its effect, through total incapacity to comprehend the march of modern history.

The aristocracy, in order to rally the people to them, waved the proletarian alms-bag in front for a banner. But the people, so often as it joined them, saw on their hindquarters the old feudal coats of arms, and deserted with loud and irreverent laughter.

9. Not the English Restoration 1660 to 1689, but the French Restoration 1814 to 1830. — *Engels, English edition of 1888.*

One section of the French Legitimists[10] and "Young England"[11] exhibited this spectacle.

In pointing out that their mode of exploitation was different to that of the bourgeoisie, the feudalists forget that they exploited under circumstances and conditions that were quite different, and that are now antiquated. In showing that, under their rule, the modern proletariat never existed, they forget that the modern bourgeoisie is the necessary offspring of their own form of society.

For the rest, so little do they conceal the reactionary character of their criticism that their chief accusation against the bourgeoisie amounts to this, that under the bourgeois *régime* a class is being developed, which is destined to cut up root and branch the old order of society.

What they upbraid the bourgeoisie with is not so much that it creates a proletariat, as that it creates a *revolutionary* proletariat.

In political practice, therefore, they join in all coercive measures against the working class; and in ordinary life, despite their high falutin phrases, they stoop to pick up the golden apples dropped from the tree of industry, and to barter truth, love, and honour for traffic in wool, beetroot-sugar, and potato spirits.[12]

As the parson has ever gone hand in hand with the landlord, so has Clerical Socialism with Feudal Socialism.

Nothing is easier than to give Christian asceticism a Socialist tinge. Has not Christianity declaimed against private property, against marriage, against the State?

10. [The party of the noble landowners, who advocated the restoration of the Bourbon dynasty.]

11. [A group of British Conservatives — aristocrats and men of politics and literature — formed about 1842. Prominent among them were Disraeli, Thomas Carlyle, and others.]

12. This applies chiefly to Germany where the landed aristocracy and squire-archy have large portions of their estates cultivated for their own account by stewards, and are, moreover, extensive beetroot-sugar manufacturers and distillers of potato spirits. The wealthier British aristocracy are, as yet, rather above that: but they, too, know how to make up for declining rents by lending their names to floaters of more or less shady joint-stock companies. — *Engels, English edition of 1888.*

Has it not preached in the place of these, charity and poverty, celibacy and mortification of the flesh, monastic life and Mother Church? Christian Socialism is but the holy water with which the priest consecrates the heart-burnings of the aristocrat.

B. Petty-Bourgeois Socialism

The feudal aristocracy was not the only class that was ruined by the bourgeoisie, not the only class whose conditions of existence pined and perished in the atmosphere of modern bourgeois society. The mediaeval burgesses and the small peasant proprietors were the precursors of the modern bourgeoisie. In those countries which are but little developed, industrially and commercially, these two classes still vegetate side by side with the rising bourgeoisie.

In countries where modern civilisation has become fully developed, a new class of petty bourgeois has been formed, fluctuating between proletariat and bourgeoisie and ever renewing itself as a supplementary part of bourgeois society. The individual members of this class, however, are being constantly hurled down into the proletariat by the action of competition, and, as modern industry develops, they even see the moment approaching when they will completely disappear as an independent section of modern society, to be replaced, in manufactures, agriculture and commerce, by overlookers, bailiffs and shopmen.

In countries like France, where the peasants constitute far more than half of the population, it was natural that writers who sided with the proletariat against the bourgeoisie, should use, in their criticism of the bourgeois *régime*, the standard of the peasant and petty bourgeois, and from the standpoint of these intermediate classes should take up the cudgels for the working class. Thus arose petty-bourgeois Socialism. Sismondi was the head of this school, not only in France but also in England.

This school of Socialism dissected with great acuteness the contradictions in the conditions of modern production. It laid bare the hypocritical apologies of economists. It proved, incontrovertibly, the disastrous effects of machinery and division of labour, the concentration of capital and land in a few hands; overproduction and crises; it pointed out the inevitable ruin of the petty bourgeois and peasant, the misery of the proletariat, the anarchy in production, the crying inequalities in the distribution of wealth, the industrial war of extermination between nations, the dissolution of old moral bonds, of the old family relations, of the old nationalities.

In its positive aims, however, this form of Socialism aspires either to restoring the old means of production and of exchange, and with them the old property relations, and the old society, or to cramping the modern means of production and of exchange, within the framework of the old property relations that have been, and were bound to be, exploded by those means. In either case, it is both reactionary and Utopian.

Its last words are: corporate guilds for manufacture, patriarchal relations in agriculture.

Ultimately, when stubborn historical facts had dispersed all intoxicating effects of self-deception, this form of Socialism ended in a miserable fit of the blues.

C. German, or "True," Socialism

The Socialist and Communist literature of France, a literature that originated under the pressure of a bourgeoisie in power, and that was the expression of the struggle against this power, was introduced into Germany at a time when the bourgeoisie, in that country, had just begun its contest with feudal absolutism.

German philosophers, would-be philosophers, and *beaux esprits*, eagerly seized on this literature, only forgetting, that when these writings immigrated from France into Germany, French social conditions had not immigrated along with them. In contact with German social conditions, this French literature lost all its immediate practical significance, and assumed a purely literary aspect. Thus, to the German philosophers of the eighteenth century, the demands of the first French Revolution were nothing more than the demands of "Practical Reason" in general, and the utterance of the will of the revolutionary French bourgeoisie signified in their eyes the law of pure Will, of Will as it was bound to be, of true human Will generally.

The work of the German *literati* consisted solely in bringing the new French ideas into harmony with their ancient philosophical conscience, or rather, in annexing the French ideas without deserting their own philosophic point of view.

This annexation took place in the same way in which a foreign language is appropriated, namely, by translation.

It is well known how the monks wrote silly lives of Catholic Saints *over* the manuscripts on which the classical works of ancient heathendom had been written. The German *literati* reversed this process with the profane French literature. They wrote their philosophical nonsense beneath the French original. For instance, beneath the French criticism of the economic functions of money, they wrote "Alienation of Humanity," and beneath the French criticism of the bourgeois State they wrote "dethronement of the Category of the General," and so forth.

The introduction of these philosophical phrases at the back of the French historical criticisms they dubbed "Philosophy of Action," "True Socialism," "German Science of Socialism," "Philosophical Foundation of Socialism," and so on.

The French Socialist and Communist literature was thus completely emasculated. And, since it ceased in the hands of the German to express the struggle of one class with the other, he felt conscious of having overcome "French one-sidedness" and of representing, not true requirements, but the requirements of truth; not the interests of the proletariat, but the interests of Human Nature, of Man in general, who belongs to no class, has no reality, who exists only in the misty realm of philosophical fantasy.

This German Socialism, which took its schoolboy task so seriously and solemnly, and extolled its poor stock-in-trade in such mountebank fashion, meanwhile gradually lost its pedantic innocence.

The fight of the German, and especially, of the Prussian bourgeoisie, against feudal aristocracy and absolute monarchy, in other words, the liberal movement, became more earnest.

By this, the long wished-for opportunity was offered to "True" Socialism of confronting the political movement with the Socialist demands, of hurling the traditional anathemas against liberalism, against representative government, against bourgeois competition, bourgeois freedom of the press, bourgeois legislation, bourgeois liberty and equality, and of preaching to the masses that they had nothing to gain, and everything to lose, by this bourgeois movement. German Socialism forgot, in the nick of time, that the French criticism, whose silly echo it was, presupposed the existence of modern bourgeois society, with its corresponding economic conditions of existence, and the political constitution adapted thereto, the very things whose attainment was the object of the pending struggle in Germany.

To the absolute governments, with their following of parsons, professors, country squires and officials, it served as a welcome scarecrow against the threatening bourgeoisie.

It was a sweet finish after the bitter pills of floggings and bullets with which these same governments, just at that time, dosed the German working-class risings.

While this "True" Socialism thus served the governments as a weapon for fighting the German bourgeoisie, it, at the same time, directly represented a reactionary interest, the interest of the German Philistines. In Germany the *petty bourgeois* class, a relic of the sixteenth century, and since then constantly cropping up again under various forms, is the real social basis of the existing state of things.

To preserve this class is to preserve the existing state of things in Germany. The industrial and political supremacy of the bourgeoisie threatens it with certain destruction; on the one hand, from the concentration of capital; on the other, from the rise of a revolutionary proletariat. "True" Socialism appeared to kill these two birds with one stone. It spread like an epidemic.

The robe of speculative cobwebs, embroidered with flowers of rhetoric, steeped in the dew of sickly sentiment, this transcendental robe in which the German Socialists wrapped their sorry "eternal truths," all skin and bone, served to wonderfully increase the sale of their goods amongst such a public.

And on its part, German Socialism recognised, more and more, its own calling as the bombastic representative of the petty-bourgeois Philistine.

It proclaimed the German nation to be the model nation, and the German petty Philistine to be the typical man. To every villainous meanness of this model man it gave a hidden, higher, Socialistic interpretation, the exact contrary of its real character. It went to the extreme length of directly opposing the "brutally destructive" tendency of Communism, and of proclaiming its supreme and impartial contempt

of all class struggles. With very few exceptions, all the so-called Socialist and Communist publications that now (1847) circulate in Germany belong to the domain of this foul and enervating literature.[13]

2. Conservative, or Bourgeois, Socialism

A part of the bourgeoisie is desirous of redressing social grievances, in order to secure the continued existence of bourgeois society.

To this section belong economists, philanthropists, humanitarians, improvers of the condition of the working class, organisers of charity, members of societies for the prevention of cruelty to animals, temperance fanatics, hole-and-corner reformers of every imaginable kind. This form of Socialism has, moreover, been worked out into complete systems.

We may site Proudhon's *Philosophie de la Misère* as an example of this form.

The Socialistic bourgeois want all the advantages of modern social conditions without the struggles and dangers necessarily resulting therefrom. They desire the existing state of society minus its revolutionary and disintegrating elements. They wish for a bourgeoisie without a proletariat. The bourgeoisie naturally conceives the world in which it is supreme to be the best, and bourgeois Socialism develops this comfortable conception into various more or less complete systems. In requiring the proletariat to carry out such a system, and thereby to march straightway into the social New Jerusalem, it but requires in reality, that the proletariat should remain within the bounds of existing society, but should cast away all its hateful ideas concerning the bourgeoisie.

A second and more practical, but less systematic, form of this Socialism sought to depreciate every revolutionary movement in the eyes of the working class, by showing that no mere political reform, but only a change in the material conditions of existence, in economical relations, could be of any advantage to

13. The revolutionary storm of 1848 swept away this whole shabby tendency and cured its protagonists of the desire to dabble further in Socialism. The chief representative and classical type of this tendency is Herr Karl Grün. — *Engels, German edition of 1890.*

them. By changes in the material conditions of existence, this form of Socialism, however, by no means understands abolition of the bourgeois relations of production, an abolition that can be effected only by a revolution, but administrative reforms, based on the continued existence of these relations; reforms, therefore, that in no respect affect the relations between capital and labour, but, at the best, lessen the cost, and simplify the administrative work, of bourgeois government.

Bourgeois Socialism attains adequate expression, when, and only when, it becomes a mere figure of speech.

Free trade: for the benefit of the working class. Protective duties: for the benefit of the working class. Prison Reform: for the benefit of the working class. This is the last word and the only seriously meant word of bourgeois Socialism.

It is summed up in the phrase: the bourgeois is a bourgeois — for the benefit of the working class.

3. Critical-Utopian Socialism and Communism

We do not here refer to that literature which, in every great modern revolution, has always given voice to the demands of the proletariat, such as the writings of Babeuf and others.

The first direct attempts of the proletariat to attain its own ends, made in times of universal excitement, when feudal society was being overthrown, these attempts necessarily failed, owing to the then undeveloped state of the proletariat, as well as to the absence of the economic conditions for its emancipation, conditions that had yet to be produced, and could be produced by the impending bourgeois epoch alone. The revolutionary literature that accompanied these first movements of the proletariat had necessarily a reactionary character. It inculcated universal asceticism and social levelling in its crudest form.

The Socialist and Communist systems properly so called, those of Saint-Simon, Fourier, Owen and others, spring into existence in the early undeveloped period, described above, of the struggle between proletariat and bourgeoisie (see Section I. Bourgeois and Proletarians).

The founders of these systems see, indeed, the class antagonisms, as well as the action of the decomposing elements, in the prevailing form of society. But the proletariat, as yet in its infancy, offers to them the spectacle of a class without any historical initiative or any independent political movement.

Since the development of class antagonism keeps even pace with the development of industry, the economic situation, as they find it, does not as yet offer to them the material conditions for the emancipation of the proletariat. They therefore search after a new social science, after new social laws, that are to create these conditions.

Historical action is to yield to their personal inventive action, historically created conditions of emancipation to fantastic ones, and the gradual, spontaneous class-organisation of the proletariat to the organisation of society specially contrived by these inventors. Future history resolves itself, in their eyes, into the propaganda and the practical carrying out of their social plans.

In the formation of their plans they are conscious of caring chiefly for the interests of the working class, as being the most suffering class. Only from the point of view of being the most suffering class does the proletariat exist for them.

The undeveloped state of the class struggle, as well as their own surroundings, causes Socialists of this kind to consider themselves far superior to all class antagonisms. They want to improve the condition of every member of society, even that of the most favoured. Hence, they habitually appeal to society at large, without distinction of class; nay, by preference, to the ruling class. For how can people, when once they understand their system, fail to see in it the best possible plan of the best possible state of society?

Hence, they reject all political, and especially all revolutionary, action; they wish to attain their ends by peaceful means, and endeavour, by small experiments, necessarily doomed to failure, and by the force of example, to pave the way for the new social Gospel.

Such fantastic pictures of future society, painted at a time when the proletariat is still in a very undeveloped state and has but a fantastic conception of its own position correspond with the first instinctive yearnings of that class for a general reconstruction of society.

But these Socialist and Communist publications contain also a critical element. They attack every principle of existing society. Hence they are full of the most valuable materials for the enlightenment of the working class. The practical measures proposed in them—such as the abolition of the distinction between town and country, of the family, of the carrying on of industries for the account of private individuals, and of the wage system, the proclamation of social harmony, the conversion of the functions of the State into a mere superintendence of production, all these proposals, point solely to the disappearance of class antagonisms which were, at that time, only just cropping up, and which, in these publications, are recognised in their earliest, indistinct and undefined forms only. These proposals, therefore, are of a purely Utopian character.

The significance of Critical-Utopian Socialism and Communism bears an inverse relation to historical development. In proportion as the modern class struggle develops and takes definite shape, this fantastic standing apart from the contest, these fantastic attacks on it, lose all practical value and all theoretical justification. Therefore, although the originators of these systems were, in many respects, revolutionary, their disciples have, in every case, formed mere reactionary sects. They hold fast by the original views of their masters, in opposition to the progressive historical development of the proletariat. They, therefore, endeavour, and that consistently, to deaden the class struggle and to reconcile the class antagonisms. They still dream of experimental realisation of their social Utopias, of founding isolated "*phalanstères*," of establishing "Home Colonies," of setting up a "Little Icaria"[14]—duodecimo editions of the New Jerusalem—and to realise all these castles in the air, they are

compelled to appeal to the feelings and purses of the bourgeois. By degrees they sink into the category of the reactionary conservative Socialists depicted above, differing from these only by more systematic pedantry, and by their fanatical and superstitious belief in the miraculous effects of their social science.

They, therefore, violently oppose all political action on the part of the working class; such action, according to them, can only result from blind unbelief in the new Gospel.

The Owenites in England, and the Fourierists in France, respectively, oppose the Chartists and the *Réformistes*.[15]

IV. POSITION OF THE COMMUNISTS IN RELATION TO THE VARIOUS EXISTING OPPOSITION PARTIES

Section II has made clear the relations of the Communists to the existing working-class parties, such as the Chartists in England and the Agrarian Reformers in America.

The Communists fight for the attainment of the immediate aims, for the enforcement of the momentary interests of the working class; but in the movement of the present, they also represent and take care of the future of that movement. In France the Communists ally themselves with the Social-Democrats,[16] against the conservative and radical

14. *Phalanstères* were Socialist colonies on the plan of Charles Fourier; *Icaria* was the name given by Cabet to his Utopia and, later on, to his American Communist colony.—*Engels, English edition of 1888.*

"Home colonies" were what Owen called his Communist model societies. *Phalanstères* was the name of the public palaces planned by Fourier. *Icaria* was the name given to the Utopian land of fancy, whose Communist institutions Cabet portrayed.—*Engels, German edition of 1890.*

15. [This refers to the adherents of the newspaper *La Réforme* which was published in Paris from 1843 to 1850.]

16. The party then represented in Parliament by Ledru-Rollin, in literature by Louis Blanc, in the daily press by the *Réforme*. The name of Social-Democracy signified, with these its inventors, a section of the Democratic or Republican party more or less tinged with Socialism.—*Engels, English edition of 1888.*

The party in France which at that time called itself Socialist-Democratic was represented in political life by Ledru-Rollin and in literature by Louis Blanc; thus it differed immeasurably from present-day German Social-Democracy.—*Engels, German edition of 1890.*

bourgeoisie, reserving, however, the right to take up a critical position in regard to phrases and illusions traditionally handed down from the great Revolution.

In Switzerland they support the Radicals, without losing sight of the fact that this party consists of antagonistic elements, partly of Democratic Socialists, in the French sense, partly of radical bourgeois.

In Poland they support the party that insists on an agrarian revolution as the prime condition for national emancipation, that party which fomented the insurrection of Cracow in 1846.

In Germany they fight with the bourgeoisie whenever it acts in a revolutionary way, against the absolute monarchy, the feudal squire-archy, and the petty bourgeoisie.[17]

But they never cease, for a single instant, to instil into the working class the clearest possible recognition of the hostile antagonism between bourgeoisie and proletariat, in order that the German workers may straightway use, as so many weapons against the bourgeoisie, the social and political conditions that the bourgeoisie must necessarily introduce along with its supremacy, and in order that, after the fall of the reactionary classes in Germany, the fight against the bourgeoisie itself may immediately begin.

The Communists turn their attention chiefly to Germany, because that country is on the eve of a bourgeois revolution that is bound to be carried out under more advanced conditions of European civilisation, and with a much more developed proletariat, than that of England was in the seventeenth, and of France in the eighteenth century, and because the bourgeois revolution in Germany will be but the prelude to an immediately following proletarian revolution.

In short, the Communists everywhere support every revolutionary movement against the existing social and political order of things.

In all these movements they bring to the front, as the leading question in each, the property question, no matter what its degree of development at the time.

Finally, they labour everywhere for the union and agreement of the democratic parties of all countries.

The Communists disdain to conceal their views and aims. They openly declare that their ends can be attained only by the forcible overthrow of all existing social conditions. Let the ruling classes tremble at a Communistic revolution. The proletarians have nothing to lose but their chains. They have a world to win.

WORKING MEN OF ALL COUNTRIES, UNITE!

---

17. [*Kleinbürgerei* in the German original. Marx and Engels used this term to describe the reactionary elements of the urban petty bourgeoisie.]

CRITIQUE OF THE
GOTHA PROGRAM

1. "Labour is the source of all wealth and all culture, *and since* useful labour is possible only in society and through society, the proceeds of labour belong undiminished with equal right to all members of society."

First Part of the Paragraph: "Labour is the source of all wealth and all culture."

Labour is *not the source* of all wealth. *Nature* is just as much the source of use values (and it is surely of such that material wealth consists!) as labour, which itself is only the manifestation of a force of nature, human labour power. The above phrase is to be found in all children's primers and is correct in so far as it is *implied* that labour is performed with the appurtenant subjects and instruments. But a socialist programme cannot allow such bourgeois phrases to pass over in silence the *conditions* that alone give them meaning. And in so far as man from the beginning behaves towards nature, the primary source of all instruments and subjects of labour, as an owner, treats her as belonging to him, his labour becomes the source of use values, therefore also of wealth. The bourgeois have very good grounds for falsely ascribing *supernatural creative power* to labour; since precisely from the fact that labour depends on nature it follows that the man who possesses no other property than his labour power must, in all conditions of society and culture, be the slave of other men who have made themselves the owners of the material conditions of labour. He can work only with their permission, hence live only with their permission.

Let us now leave the sentence as it stands, or rather

limps. What would one have expected in conclusion? Obviously this:

"Since labour is the source of all wealth, no one in society can appropriate wealth except as the product of labour. Therefore, if he himself does not work, he lives by the labour of others and also acquires his culture at the expense of the labour of others."

Instead of this, by means of the verbal rivet "*and since*" a second proposition is added in order to draw a conclusion from this and not from the first one.

Second Part of the Paragraph: "Useful labour is possible only in society and through society."

According to the first proposition, labour was the source of all wealth and all culture; therefore no society is possible without labour. Now we learn, conversely, that no "useful" labour is possible without society.

One could just as well have said that only in society can useless and even socially harmful labour become a branch of gainful occupation, that only in society can one live by being idle, etc., etc.—in short, one could just as well have copied the whole of Rousseau.

And what is "useful" labour? Surely only labour which produces the intended useful result. A savage—and man was a savage after he had ceased to be an ape—who kills an animal with a stone, who collects fruits, etc., performs "useful" labour.

Thirdly. The Conclusion: "And since useful labour is possible only in society and through society, the proceeds of labour belong undiminished with equal right to all members of society."

A fine conclusion! If useful labour is possible only in society and through society, the proceeds of labour belong to society—and only so much therefrom accrues to the individual worker as is not required to maintain the "condition" of labour, society.

In fact, this proposition has at all times been made use of by the champions of the *state of society prevailing at any given time.* First come the claims of the government and everything that sticks to it, since it is the social organ for the maintenance of the social order; then come the claims of the various kinds of private property, for the various kinds of private property are the foundations of society, etc. One sees that such hollow phrases can be twisted and turned as desired.

The first and second parts of the paragraph have some intelligible connection only in the following wording:

"Labour becomes the source of wealth and culture only as social labour," or, what is the same thing, "in and through society."

This proposition is incontestably correct, for although isolated labour (its material conditions presupposed) can create use values, it can create neither wealth nor culture.

But equally incontestable is this other proposition:

"In proportion as labour develops socially, and becomes thereby a source of wealth and culture, poverty and destitution develop among the workers, and wealth and culture among the non-workers."

This is the law of all history hitherto. What, therefore, had to be done here, instead of setting down general phrases about "labour" and "society," was to prove concretely how in present capitalist society the material, etc., conditions have at last been created which enable and compel the workers to lift this social curse.

In fact, however, the whole paragraph, bungled in style and content, is only there in order to inscribe the Lassallean catchword of the "undiminished proceeds of labour" as a slogan at the top of the party banner. I shall return later to the "proceeds of labour," "equal right," etc., since the same thing recurs in a somewhat different form further on.

2. "In present-day society, the instruments of labour are the monopoly of the capitalist class; the resulting dependence of the working class is the cause of misery and servitude in all its forms."

This sentence, borrowed from the Rules of the International, is incorrect in this "improved" edition.

In present-day society the instruments of labour are the monopoly of the landowners (the monopoly of property in land is even the basis of the monopoly of capital) *and* the capitalists. In the passage in question, the Rules of the International do not mention either the one or the other class of monopolists. They speak of the *"monopoliser of the means of labour,* that is, *the sources of life."* The addition, *"sources of life,"* makes it sufficiently clear that land is included in the instruments of labour.

The correction was introduced because Lassalle, for reasons now generally known, attacked *only* the capitalist class and not the landowners. In England, the capitalist is usually not even the owner of the land on which his factory stands.

3. "The emancipation of labour demands the promotion of the instruments of labour to the common property of society and the co-operative regulation of the total labour with a fair distribution of the proceeds of labour."

"Promotion of the instruments of labour to the common property" ought obviously to read their "conversion into the common property"; but this only in passing.

What are "proceeds of labour"? The product of labour or its value? And in the latter case, is it the total value of the product or only that part of the value which labour has newly added to the value of the means of production consumed?

"Proceeds of labour" is a loose notion which Lassalle has put in the place of definite economic conceptions.

What is "a fair distribution"?

Do not the bourgeois assert that the present-day distribution is "fair"? And is it not, in fact, the only "fair" distribution on the basis of the present-day mode of production? Are economic relations regulated by legal conceptions or do not, on the contrary, legal relations arise from economic ones? Have not also the socialist sectarians the most varied notions about "fair" distribution?

To understand what is implied in this connection by the phrase "fair distribution," we must take the first paragraph and this one together. The latter presupposes a society wherein "the instruments of labour are common property and the total labour is cooperatively regulated," and from the first paragraph we learn that "the proceeds of labour belong undiminished with equal right to all members of society."

"To all members of society"? To those who do not work as well? What remains then of the "undiminished proceeds of labour"? Only to those members of society who work? What remains then of the equal right" of all members of society?

But "all members of society" and "equal right" are obviously mere phrases. The kernel consists in this, that in this communist society every worker must receive the "undiminished" Lassallean "proceeds of labour."

Let us take first of all the words "proceeds of labour" in the sense of the product of labour; then the co-operative proceeds of labour are the *total social product*.

From this must now be deducted:

First, cover for replacement of the means of production used up.

Secondly, additional portion for expansion of production.

Thirdly, reserve or insurance funds to provide against accidents, dislocations caused by natural calamities, etc.

These deductions from the "undiminished proceeds of labour" are an economic necessity and their magnitude is to be determined according to available means and forces, and partly by computation of probabilities, but they are in no way calculable by equity.

There remains the other part of the total product, intended to serve as means of consumption.

Before this is divided among the individuals, there has to be deducted again, from it:

First, the general costs of administration not belonging to production.

This part will, from the outset, be very considerably restricted in comparison with present-day society and it diminishes in proportion as the new society develops.

Secondly, that which is intended for the common satisfaction of needs, such as schools, health services, etc.

From the outset this part grows considerably in comparison with present-day society and it grows in proportion as the new society develops.

Thirdly, funds for those unable to work, etc., in short, for what is included under so-called official poor relief today.

Only now do we come to the "distribution" which the programme, under Lassallean influence, alone has in view in its narrow fashion, namely, to that part of the means of consumption which is divided among the individual producers of the co-operative society.

The "undiminished proceeds of labour" have already unnoticeably become converted into the "diminished" proceeds, although what the producer is deprived of in his capacity as a private individual benefits him directly or indirectly in his capacity as a member of society.

Just as the phrase of the "undiminished proceeds of labour" has disappeared, so now does the phrase of the "proceeds of labour" disappear altogether.

Within the co-operative society based on common ownership of the means of production, the producers do not exchange their products; just as little does the labour employed on the products appear here *as the value* of these products, as a material quality possessed by them, since now, in contrast to capitalist society, individual labour no longer exists in an indirect fashion but directly as a component part of the total labour. The phrase "proceeds of labour," objectionable also today on account of its ambiguity, thus loses all meaning.

What we have to deal with here is a communist society, not as it has *developed* on its own foundations, but, on the contrary, just as it *emerges* from capitalist society; which is thus in every respect, economically, morally and intellectually, still stamped with the birth marks of the old society from whose womb it emerges. Accordingly, the individual producer receives back from society—after the deductions have been made— exactly what he gives to it. What he has given to it is his individual quantum of labour. For example, the social working day consists of the sum of the individual hours of work; the individual labour time of the individual producer is the part of the social working day contributed by him, his share in it. He receives a certificate from society that he has furnished such and such an amount of labour (after deducting his labour for the common funds), and with this certificate he draws from the social stock of means of consumption as much as costs the same amount of labour. The same amount of labour which he has given to society in one form he receives back in another.

Here obviously the same principle prevails as that which regulates the exchange of commodities, as far as this is exchange of equal values. Content and form are changed, because under the altered circumstances no one can give anything except his labour, and because, on the other hand, nothing can pass to the ownership of individuals except individual means of consumption. But, as far as the distribution of the latter among the individual producers is concerned, the same principle prevails as in the exchange of commodity equivalents: a given amount of labour in one form is exchanged for an equal amount of labour in another form.

Hence, *equal right* here is still in principle—*bourgeois right*, although principle and practice are no longer at loggerheads, while the exchange of equivalents in commodity exchange only exists *on the average* and not in the individual case.

In spite of this advance, this *equal right* is still constantly stigmatised by a bourgeois limitation. The right of the producers is *proportional* to the labour they supply; the equality consists in the fact that measurement is made with an *equal standard*, labour.

But one man is superior to another physically or mentally and so supplies more labour in the same time, or can labour for a longer time; and labour, to serve as a measure, must be defined by its duration or intensity, otherwise it ceases to be a standard of measurement. This *equal* right is an unequal right for unequal labour. It recognises no class differences, because everyone is only a worker like everyone else; but it tacitly recognises unequal individual endowment and thus productive capacity as natural privileges. *It is, therefore, a right of inequality, in its content, like every right.* Right by its very nature can consist only in the application of an equal standard; but unequal individuals (and they would not be different individuals if they were not unequal) are measurable only by an equal standard in so far as they are brought under an equal point of view, are taken from one *definite* side only, for instance, in the present case, are regarded *only as workers* and nothing more is seen in them, everything else being ignored. Further, one worker is married, another not; one has more children than another, and so on and so forth. Thus, with an equal performance of labour, and hence an equal share in the social consumption fund, one will in

fact receive more than another, one will be richer than another, and so on. To avoid all these defects, right instead of being equal would have to be unequal.

But these defects are inevitable in the first phase of communist society as it is when it has just emerged after prolonged birth pangs from capitalist society. Right can never be higher than the economic structure of society and its cultural development conditioned thereby.

In a higher phase of communist society, after the enslaving subordination of the individual to the division of labour, and therewith also the antithesis between mental and physical labour, has vanished; after labour has become not only a means of life but life's prime want; after the productive forces have also increased with the all-round development of the individual, and all the springs of cooperative wealth flow more abundantly—only then can the narrow horizon of bourgeois right be crossed in its entirety and society inscribe on its banner: From each according to his ability, to each according to his needs!

I have dealt more at length with the "undiminished proceeds of labour," on the one hand, and with "equal right" and "fair distribution," on the other, in order to show what a crime it is to attempt, on the one hand, to force on our Party again, as dogmas, ideas which in a certain period had some meaning but have now become obsolete verbal rubbish, while again perverting, on the other, the realistic outlook, which it cost so much effort to instil into the Party but which has now taken root in it, by means of ideological nonsense about right and other trash so common among the democrats and French Socialists.

Quite apart from the analysis so far given, it was in general a mistake to make a fuss about so-called *distribution* and put the principal stress on it.

Any distribution whatever of the means of consumption is only a consequence of the distribution of the conditions of production themselves. The latter distribution, however, is a feature of the mode of production itself. The capitalist mode of production, for example, rests on the fact that the material conditions of production are in the hands of non-workers in the form of property in capital and land, while the masses are only owners of the personal condition of production, of labour power. If the elements of production are so distributed, then the present-day distribution of the means of consumption results automatically. If the material conditions of production are the co-operative property of the workers themselves, then there likewise results a distribution of the means of consumption different from the present one. Vulgar socialism (and from it in turn a section of the democracy) has taken over from the bourgeois economists the consideration and treatment of distribution as independent of the mode of production and hence the presentation of socialism as turning principally on distribution. After the real relation has long been made clear, why retrogress again?

4. "The emancipation of labour must be the work of the working class, relatively to which all other classes are *only one reactionary mass.*"

The first strophe is taken from the introductory words of the Rules of the International, but "improved." There it is said: "The emancipation of the working class must be the act of the workers themselves"; here, on the contrary, the "working class" has to emancipate—what? "Labour." Let him understand who can.

In compensation, the antistrophe, on the other hand, is a Lassallean quotation of the first water: "relatively to which (the working class) all other classes are *only one reactionary mass.*"

In the *Communist Manifesto* it is said: "Of all the classes that stand face to face with the bourgeoisie today, the proletariat alone is a *really revolutionary class.* The other classes decay and finally disappear in the face of modern industry; the proletariat is its special and essential product."

The bourgeoisie is here conceived as a revolutionary class—as the bearer of large-scale industry—relatively to the feudal lords and the lower middle class, who desire to maintain all social positions that are the creation of obsolete modes of production. Thus they do not form *together* with the *bourgeoisie* only one reactionary mass.

On the other hand, the proletariat is revolutionary relatively to the bourgeoisie because, having itself grown up on the basis of large-scale industry, it strives to strip off from production the capitalist character that the bourgeoisie seeks to perpetuate. But the *Manifesto* adds that the "lower middle class" is becoming

revolutionary "in view of [its] impending transfer into the proletariat."

From this point of view, therefore, it is again nonsense to say that it, together with the bourgeoisie, and with the feudal lords into the bargain, "form only one reactionary mass" relatively to the working class.

Has one proclaimed to the artisans, small manufacturers, etc., and *peasants* during the last elections: Relatively to us you, together with the bourgeoisie and feudal lords, form only one reactionary mass?

Lassalle knew the *Communist Manifesto* by heart, as his faithful followers know the gospels written by him. If, therefore, he has falsified it so grossly, this has occurred only to put a good colour on his alliance with absolutist and feudal opponents against the bourgeoisie.

In the above paragraph, moreover, his oracular saying is dragged in by main force without any connection with the botched quotation from the Rules of the International. Thus is it here simply an impertinence, and indeed not at all displeasing to Herr Bismarck, one of those cheap pieces of insolence in which the Marat of Berlin[1] deals.

5. "The working class strives for its emancipation first of all *within the framework of the present-day national state,* conscious that the necessary result of its efforts, which are common to the workers of all civilised countries, will be the international brotherhood of peoples."

Lassalle, in opposition to the *Communist Manifesto* and to all earlier socialism, conceived the workers' movement from the narrowest national standpoint. He is being followed in this—and that after the work of the International!

It is altogether self-evident that, to be able to fight at all, the working class must organise itself at home *as a class* and that its own country is the immediate arena of its struggle. In so far its class struggle is national, not in substance, but, as the *Communist Manifesto* says, "in form." But the "framework of the present-day national state," for instance, the German

1. [A reference to Hasselmann, the chief editor of the *Neuer Sozial-Demokrat,* the central organ of the Lassalleans.]

Empire, is itself in its turn economically "within the framework" of the world market, politically "within the framework" of the system of states. Every business-man knows that German trade is at the same time foreign trade, and the greatness of Herr Bismarck consists, to be sure, precisely in his pursuing a kind of *international* policy.

And to what does the German workers' party reduce its internationalism? To the consciousness that the result of its efforts will be *"the international brother-hood of peoples"* —a phrase borrowed from the bour-geois League of Peace and Freedom[2] which is intended to pass as equivalent to the international brotherhood of the working classes in the joint strug-gle against the ruling classes and their governments. Not a word, therefore, *about the international func-tions* of the German working class! And it is thus that it is to challenge its own bourgeoisie—which is already linked up in brotherhood against it with the bourgeois of all other countries—and Herr Bismarck's international policy of conspiracy!

In fact, the internationalism of the programme stands even *infinitely below* that of the Free Trade Party. The latter also asserts that the result of its efforts will be "the international brotherhood of peoples." But it also *does* something to make trade international and by no means contents itself with the conscious-ness—that all peoples are carrying on trade at home.

The international activity of the working classes does not in any way depend on the existence of the *International Working Men's Association.* This was only the first attempt to create a central organ for that activity; an attempt which was a lasting success on account of the impulse which it gave but which was no longer realisable in its *first historical form* after the fall of the Paris Commune.

Bismarck's *Norddeutsche* was absolutely right when it announced, to the satisfaction of its master, that the German workers' party had sworn off internation-alism in the new programme.[3]

2. [The International League of Peace and Freedom was organized in Geneva in 1867 by liberals and paci-fists.]

3. [Marx refers to the editorial which appeared in No. 67 of the *Norddeutsche Allgemeine Zeitung* (*North Ger-man General Newspaper*) of March 20, 1875. It stated

II

"Starting from these basic principles, the Ger-man workers' party strives by all legal means for the *free state—and—*socialist society: the abolition of the wage system *together with* the *iron law of wages—*and—exploitation in every form; the elimination of all social and politi-cal inequality."

I shall return to the "free" state later.

So, in future, the German workers' party has got to believe in Lassalle's "iron law of wages"! That this may not be lost, the nonsense is perpetrated of speaking of the "abolition of the wage system" (it should read: system of wage labour) *"together with* the iron law of wages." If I abolish wage labour, then naturally I abolish its laws also, whether they are of "iron" or sponge. But Lassalle's attack on wage labour turns almost solely on this so-called law. In order, therefore, to prove that Lassalle's sect has conquered, the "wage system" must be abolished *"together with* the iron law of wages" and not without it.

It is well known that nothing of the "iron law of wages" is Lassalle's except the word "iron" borrowed from Goethe's "great eternal iron laws." The word *iron* is a label by which the true believers recognise one another. But if I take the law with Lassalle's stamp on it and, consequently, in his sense, then I must also take it with his substantiation for it. And what is that? As Lange already showed, shortly after Lassalle's death, it is the Malthusian theory of population (preached by Lange himself). But if this theory is correct, then again I *cannot* abolish the law even if I abolish wage labour a hundred times over, because the law then governs not only the system of wage labour but *every* social system. Basing themselves di-rectly on this, the economists have been proving for fifty years and more that socialism cannot abolish poverty, *which has its basis in nature,* but can only make it *general,* distribute it simultaneously over the whole surface of society!

with regard to Article 5 of the Social-Democratic Pro-gramme that "Social-Democratic agitation had in many respects become more prudent" and that it was "repudiat-ing the International."]

But all this is not the main thing. *Quite apart* from the *false* Lassallean formulation of the law, the truly outrageous retrogression consists in the following.

Since Lassalle's death there has asserted itself in *our* Party the scientific understanding that wages are not what they *appear* to be, namely, the *value*, or *price, of labour*, but only a masked form for the *value*, or *price, of labour power*. Thereby the whole bourgeois conception of wages hitherto, as well as all the criticism hitherto directed against this conception, was thrown overboard once for all and it was made clear that the wage-worker has permission to work for his own subsistence, that is, *to live*, only in so far as he works for a certain time gratis for the capitalist (and hence also for the latter's co-consumers of surplus value); that the whole capitalist system of production turns on the increase of this gratis labour by extending the working day or by developing the productivity, that is, increasing the intensity of labour power, etc; that, consequently, the system of wage labour is a system of slavery, and indeed of a slavery which becomes more severe in proportion as the social productive forces of labour develop, whether the worker receives better or worse payment. And after this understanding has gained more and more ground in our Party, one returns to Lassalle's dogmas, although one must have known that Lassalle *did not know* what wages were, but following in the wake of the bourgeois economists took the appearance for the essence of the matter.

It is as if, among slaves who have at last got behind the secret of slavery and broken out in rebellion, a slave still in thrall to obsolete notions were to inscribe on the programme of the rebellion: Slavery must be abolished because the feeding of slaves in the system of slavery cannot exceed a certain low maximum!

Does not the mere fact that the representatives of our Party were capable of perpetrating such a monstrous attack on the understanding that has spread among the mass of our Party prove by itself with what criminal levity and with what lack of conscience they set to work in drawing up this compromise programme!

Instead of the indefinite concluding phrase of the paragraph, "the elimination of all social and political inequality," it ought to have been said that with the abolition of class distinctions all social and political inequality arising from them would disappear of itself.

III

"The German workers' party, in order *to pave the way to the solution of the social question*, demands the establishment of producers' co-operative societies *with state aid under the democratic control of the toiling people*. The producers' co-operative societies *are to be called into being* for industry and agriculture on such a scale *that the socialist organisation of the total labour will arise from them*."

After the Lassallean "iron law of wages," the physic of the prophet. The way to it is "paved" in worthy fashion. In place of the existing class struggle appears a newspaper scribbler's phrase: "the social *question*," to the "*solution*" of which one "paves the way." Instead of arising from the revolutionary process of transformation of society, the "socialist organisation of the total labour" "arises" from the "state aid" that the state gives to the producers' co-operative societies and which the *state*, not the worker, "*calls into being*." It is worthy of Lassalle's imagination that with state loans one can build a new society just as well as a new railway!

From the remnants of a sense of shame, "state aid" has been put—under the democratic control of the "toiling people."

In the first place, the majority of the "toiling people" in Germany consists of peasants, and not of proletarians.

Secondly, "democratic" means in German "*volksherrschaftlich*" ["by the rule of the people"]. But what does "control by the rule of the people of the toiling people" mean? And particularly in the case of a toiling people which, through these demands that it puts to the state, expresses its full consciousness that it neither rules nor is ripe for ruling!

It would be superfluous to deal here with the criticism of the recipe prescribed by Buchez in the reign of Louis Philippe in *opposition* to the French Socialists and accepted by the reactionary workers of the *Atelier*.[4] The chief offence does not lie in having

4. [*Atelier* (Workshop): A workers' monthly which appeared in Paris in 1840–50. It was under the influence of the Catholic socialism of Buchez.]

inscribed this specific nostrum in the programme, but in taking, in general, a retrograde step from the standpoint of a class movement to that of a sectarian movement.

That the workers desire to establish the conditions for co-operative production on a social scale, and first of all on a national scale in their own country, only means that they are working to revolutionise the present conditions of production, and it has nothing in common with the foundation of co-operative societies with state aid. But as far as the present co-operative societies are concerned, they are of value *only* in so far as they are the independent creations of the workers and not protégés either of the government or of the bourgeois.

IV

I come now to the democratic section.

A. *"The free basis of the state."*

First of all, according to II, the German workers' party strives for "the free state."

Free state—what is this?

It is by no means the aim of the workers, who have got rid of the narrow mentality of humble subjects, to set the state free. In the German Empire the "state" is almost as "free" as in Russia. Freedom consists in converting the state from an organ superimposed upon society into one completely subordinate to it, and today, too, the forms of state are more free or less free to the extent that they restrict the "freedom of the state."

The German workers' party—at least if it adopts the programme—shows that its socialist ideas are not even skin-deep; in that, instead of treating existing society (and this holds good for any future one) as the *basis* of the existing state (or of the future state in the case of future society), it treats the state rather as independent entity that possesses its own *intellectual, ethical and libertarian bases.*

And what of the riotous misuse which the programme makes of the words *"present-day state,"* *"present-day society,"* and of the still more riotous

misconception it creates in regard to the state to which it addresses its demands?

"Present-day society" is capitalist society, which exists in all civilised countries, more or less free from medieval admixture, more or less modified by the special historical development of each country, more or less developed. On the other hand, the "present-day state" changes with a country's frontier. It is different in the Prusso-German Empire from what it is in Switzerland, it is different in England from what it is in the United States. The "present-day state" is, therefore, a fiction.

Nevertheless, the different states of the different civilised countries, in spite of their manifold diversity of form, all have this in common, that they are based on modern bourgeois society, only one more or less capitalistically developed. They have, therefore, also certain essential features in common. In this sense it is possible to speak of the "present-day state," in contrast with the future, in which its present root, bourgeois society, will have died off.

The question then arises: what transformation will the state undergo in communist society? In other words, what social functions will remain in existence there that are analogous to present functions of the state? This question can only be answered scientifically, and one does not get a flea-hop nearer to the problem by a thousandfold combination of the word people with the word state.

Between capitalist and communist society lies the period of the revolutionary transformation of the one into the other. There corresponds to this also a political transition period in which the state can be nothing but *the revolutionary dictatorship of the proletariat.*

Now the programme does not deal with this nor with the future state of communist society.

Its political demands contain nothing beyond the old democratic litany familiar to all: universal suffrage, direct legislation, popular rights, a people's militia, etc. They are a mere echo of the bourgeois People's Party, of the League of Peace and Freedom. They are all demands which, in so far as they are not exaggerated in fantastic presentation, have already been *realised.* Only the state to which they belong does not lie within the borders of the German Empire, but in Switzerland, the United States, etc. This sort of "state of the future" is a present-day state, although existing outside the "framework" of the German Empire.

But one thing has been forgotten. Since the German workers' party expressly declares that it acts within "the present-day national state," hence within *its own* state, the Prusso-German Empire—its demands would indeed otherwise be largely meaningless, since one only demands what one has not got—it should not have forgotten the chief thing, namely, that all those pretty little gewgaws rest on the recognition of the so-called sovereignty of the people and hence are appropriate only in a *democratic republic*.

Since one has not the courage—and wisely so, for the circumstances demand caution—to demand the democratic republic, as the French workers' programmes under Louis Philippe and under Louis Napoleon did, one should not have resorted, either, to the subterfuge, neither "honest"[5] nor decent, of demanding things which have meaning only in a democratic republic from a state which is nothing but a police-guarded military despotism, embellished with parliamentary forms, alloyed with a feudal admixture, already influenced by the bourgeoisie and bureaucratically carpentered, and then to assure this state into the bargain that one imagines one will be able to force such things upon it "by legal means."

Even vulgar democracy, which sees the millennium in the democratic republic and has no suspicion that it is precisely in this last form of state of bourgeois society that the class struggle has to be fought out to a conclusion—even it towers mountains above this kind of democratism which keeps within the limits of what is permitted by the police and not permitted by logic.

That, in fact, by the word "state" is meant the government machine, or the state in so far as it forms a special organism separated from society through division of labour, is shown by the words "the German worker's party demands *as the economic basis of the state*: a single progressive income tax," etc. Taxes are the economic basis of the government machinery and of nothing else. In the state of the future, existing in Switzerland, this demand has been pretty well fulfilled. Income tax presupposes various sources of income of the various social classes, and hence capitalist society. It is, therefore, nothing remarkable that the Liverpool financial reformers, bourgeois headed by Gladstone's brother, are putting forward the same demand as the programme.

B. "The German workers' party demands as the intellectual and ethical basis of the state:

"1. Universal and *equal elementary education* by the state. Universal compulsory school attendance. Free instruction."

Equal elementary education? What idea lies behind these words? Is it believed that in present-day society (and it is only with this one has to deal) education can be *equal* for all classes? Or is it demanded that the upper classes also shall be compulsorily reduced to the modicum of education—the elementary school—that alone is compatible with the economic conditions not only of the wage-workers but of the peasants as well?

"Universal compulsory school attendance. Free instruction." The former exists even in Germany, the second in Switzerland and in the United States in the case of elementary schools. If in some states of the latter country higher educational institutions are also "free" that only means in fact defraying the cost of the education of the upper classes from the general tax receipts. Incidentally, the same holds good for "free administration of justice" demanded under A, 5. The administration of criminal justice is to be had free everywhere; that of civil justice is concerned almost exclusively with conflicts over property and hence affects almost exclusively the possessing classes. Are they to carry on their litigation at the expense of the national coffers?

The paragraph on the schools should at least have demanded technical schools (theoretical and practical) in combination with the elementary school.

"Elementary education by the state" is altogether objectionable. Defining by a general law the expenditures on the elementary schools, the qualifications of the teaching staff, the branches of instruction, etc., and, as is done in the United States, supervising the fulfilment of these legal specifications by state inspectors, is a very different thing from appointing the state as the educator of the people! Government and

5. ["*Honest*" was the epithet applied to the Eisenachers. Here a play upon words.]

Church should rather be equally excluded from any influence on the school. Particularly, indeed, in the Prusso-German Empire (and one should not take refuge in the rotten subterfuge that one is speaking of a "state of the future"; we have seen how matters stand in this respect) the state has need, on the contrary, of a very stern education by the people.

But the whole programme, for all its democratic clang, is tainted through and through by the Lassallean sect's servile belief in the state, or, what is no better, by a democratic belief in miracles, or rather it is a compromise between these two kinds of belief in miracles, both equally remote from socialism.

"*Freedom of science*" says a paragraph of the Prussian Constitution. Why, then, here?

"*Freedom of conscience*"! If one desired at this time of the *Kulturkampf*[6] to remind liberalism of its old catchwords, it surely could have been done only in the following form: Everyone should be able to attend to his religious as well as his bodily needs without the police sticking their noses in. But the workers' party ought at any rate in this connection to have expressed its awareness of the fact that bourgeois "freedom of conscience" is nothing but the toleration of all possible kinds of *religious freedom of conscience*, and that for its part it endeavours rather to liberate the conscience from the witchery of religion. But one chooses not to transgress the "bourgeois" level.

I have now come to the end, for the appendix that now follows in the programme does not constitute a characteristic component part of it. Hence I can be very brief here.

2. "*Normal working day.*"

In no other country has the workers' party limited itself to such an indefinite demand, but has always fixed the length of the working day that it considers normal under the given circumstances.

3. "Restriction of female labour and prohibition of child labour."

6. [*Kulturkampf* (Struggle for culture): Bismarck's struggle in the seventies against the German Catholic Party, the Party of the "Centre," by means of police persecution of Catholicism.]

The standardisation of the working day must include the restriction of female labour, in so far as it relates to the duration, intermissions, etc., of the working day; otherwise it could only mean the exclusion of female labour from branches of industry that are especially unhealthy for the female body or are objectionable morally for the female sex. If that is what was meant, it should have been said so: "*Prohibition of child labour.*" Here it was absolutely essential to state the age limit.

A *general prohibition* of child labour is incompatible with the existence of large-scale industry and hence an empty, pious wish. Its realisation—if it were possible—would be reactionary, since, with a strict regulation of the working time according to the different age groups and other safety measures for the protection of children, an early combination of productive labour with education is one of the most potent means for the transformation of present-day society.

4. "State supervision of factory, workshop and domestic industry."

In consideration of the Prusso-German state it should definitely have been demanded that the inspectors are to be removable only by a court of law; that any worker can have them prosecuted for neglect of duty; that they must belong to the medical profession.

5. "Regulation of prison labour."

A petty demand in a general workers' programme. In any case, it should have been clearly stated that there is no intention from fear of competition to allow ordinary criminals to be treated like beasts, and especially that there is no desire to deprive them of their sole means of betterment, productive labour. This was surely the least one might have expected from Socialists.

6. "An effective liability law."

It should have been stated what is meant by an "effective" liability law.

Be it noted, incidentally, that in speaking of the normal working day the part of factory legislation that deals with health regulations and safety measures, etc., has been overlooked. The liability law only comes into operation when these regulations are infringed.

In short, this appendix also is distinguished by slovenly editing.

Dixi et salvavi animam meam.[7]

7. ["I have spoken and saved my soul."]

FRIEDRICH NIETZSCHE

From Plato and Aristotle to Locke and Kant, moral and political theorists build their theories on the founding principle that human beings are especially valuable, somehow preeminent in the natural order, usually by virtue of reason or intellect, possessing thereby a nobility and grandeur that singles them out. Other thinkers, however, begin with a different estimate of the human and its place in nature; to them the proper way to understand humankind is to appreciate the impulses, desires, and instincts that ground all animal behavior and hence human action as well. Morality and political conduct, on such a view, are manifestations of these desires and drives, for example, the desire for self-preservation. On this view, human beings are to be considered like any other natural beings. Among such thinkers are Hobbes, Spinoza, Freud, and, perhaps the most bold and dramatic of all, Friedrich Nietzsche (1844–1900).

In an unpublished fragment of 1873, Nietzsche expresses this view about human intelligence with a powerful image:

> In some remote corner of the universe, poured out and glittering in innumerable solar systems, there once was a star on which clever animals invented knowledge. . . . After nature had drawn a few breaths the star grew cold, and the clever animals had to die. . . . how wretched, how shadowy and flighty, how aimless and arbitrary, the human intellect appears in nature. There have been eternities when it did not exist; and when it is done for again, nothing will have happened.
>
> (from *On Truth and Lie in an Extra-Moral Sense*)

According to Nietzsche, then, reason or intellect is no special capacity. It comes and goes like other natural abilities, as do knowledge, truth, and morality, too. All are tools of nature and must be studied historically, almost anthropologically or biologically, as devices that manifest the deepest drives of human nature. Western morality and religion incorporate many traditions, some that repress such central drives and others that enable them to flourish. Philosophy works to unearth these various traditions, to clarify them, and to enhance the lives of the philosophers and artists who do so. The proper way to study morality is not to seek to ground a special set of principles in some universal or transcendent source; rather, it is to examine and expose the features of various moralities as they have functioned in societies throughout history, that is, to study moralities historically and to see how some do and some do not repress the natural drives that characterize the human animal.

Such a conception—of morality as a historical, natural phenomenon and not as a set of universal principles— is one teaching of a powerful, influential set of works written by Nietzsche in the second half of the nineteenth century. These works are the products of a brilliant student of classical philology who broke out of the bonds of technical scholarship and welded a deep affinity with ancient culture to rare literary ability. Nietzsche was once attacked as a source of Nazi ideology; more recently, he is frequently cited as an inspiration for deconstructionists. But in his own day he was famous and controversial on a variety of fronts, not least of all for his bold style and his withering critique of Christianity and religion.

Nietzsche was born on October 15, 1844, in Rocken, Germany, where his father was a Lutheran pastor. In 1849, when he was nearly five, his father died, and Nietzsche spent his youth surrounded by his mother, his sister Elisabeth, who was two years younger than Nietzsche, his grandmother, and two maiden aunts. In 1864 he entered the University of Bonn to study theology. By the next year, however, Nietzsche had transferred to Leipzig to study classical philology and was hard at work on a dissertation on the classical Greek poet Theognis. The results were a lecture, an essay, and, as Nietzsche put it, his "birth as a philologist." During the next few years he was deeply involved with a variety of projects, from essays on Diogenes Laertius and on Democritus to studies of history and teleology.

In 1869 the brilliant young scholar was appointed to a professorship at Basel University in Switzerland. At about this time, he first met the composer Richard Wagner, who became a powerful influence on his work. With the outbreak of the Franco-Prussian War in 1870, Nietzsche volunteered and served for a short time as a medical orderly. When he contracted dysentary and diphtheria, however, he was forced to return home. His deteriorating health and insomnia accompanied him for the rest of his life. By 1872, his first book, *The Birth of Tragedy*, was published; in it he explored the emergence of Greek tragedy out of music and its ruin at the hands of the rational philosophy of Socrates.

Nietzsche's health was constantly bad. By 1876 his painful physical condition mirrored his relationship with Wagner, which finally fell apart. Wagner had become a commercial success and the center of a cult at the opera center at Bayreuth. Wagner's self-importance, insensitivity, anti-Semitism, and total neglect of Nietzsche's work repelled Nietzsche, whose physical pain and psychological torment was expressed in his writings. During this period, his work, no longer scholarly, appeared at a steady rate—essays on David Strauss, the New Testament scholar and young radical Hegelian, on philosophy and Greek tragedy, on the uses and disadvantages of history, on Schopenhauer, and much else. Several of these essays were published, from 1873 to 1876, as *Untimely Meditations*. In 1878, *Human, All Too Human* appeared, then the *Gay Science* in 1882, *Thus Spoke Zarathustra* (Parts One and Two) in 1883, *Beyond Good and Evil* in 1886, *Toward a Geneology of Morals* in 1887, and the *Twilight of the Idols* in 1889.

During these extraordinarily productive but pain-racked years, Nietzsche was rarely at rest. His bad health forced him to clinics and convalescence, and illness interrupted his teaching. By 1876 he had stopped teaching altogether at the university, and in 1879 he formally resigned. The decade of the 1880s was filled with suffering, sickness, writing, and the interminable moving, mostly in Switzerland and Italy, in a vain effort to find a comfortable climate and peaceful surroundings. For much of these years Nietzsche and his entourage traveled from Genoa to Sils-Maria, back and forth, with occasional trips to Venice, Nice, Naumburg, and elsewhere. Then, in January of 1889, Nietzsche collapsed in the street in Turin, Italy, hopelessly insane. After brief periods in clinics, Nietzsche was released into the care of his mother, in whose home in Jena he lived until his death on August 25, 1900. His autobiographical work, *Ecce Homo*, written in 1888, was published in 1908.

Recommended Readings

Aschheim, Steven E. *The Nietzsche Legacy in Germany, 1890–1990*. Berkeley and Los Angeles: University of California Press, 1993.

Danto, Arthur. *Nietzsche as Philosopher*. New York: Macmillan, 1965

MacIntyre, Alasdair. *After Virtue*. Notre Dame: University of Notre Dame Press, 1981.

Magnus, Bernd and Kathleen M. Higgins. *The Cambridge Companion to Nietzsche*. Cambridge: Cambridge University Press, 1996.

Nehamas, Alexander. *Nietzsche: Life as Literature*. Cambridge: Harvard University Press, 1985.

Schacht, Richard. *Nietzsche*. London: Routledge, 1983.

Solomon, Robert (ed.). *Nietzsche*. Garden City: Doubleday, 1973.

Strong, Tracy. *Friedrich Nietzsche and the Politics of Transfiguration*. Berkeley: University of California Press, 1975.

Thiele, Paul. *Friedrich Nietzsche and the Politics of the Soul*. Princeton: Princeton University Press, 1990.

Warren, Mark. *Nietzsche and Political Thought*. Cambridge: M.I.T. Press, 1988.

ON THE GENEALOGY OF MORALITY

PREFACE

1

We are unknown to ourselves, we knowers: and for a good reason. We have never sought ourselves—how then should it happen that we *find* ourselves one day? It has rightly been said: "where your treasure is, there will your heart be also";[1] *our* treasure is where the beehives of our knowledge stand. We are forever underway toward them, as born winged animals and honey-gatherers of the spirit, concerned with all our heart about only one thing—"bringing home" something. As for the rest of life, the so-called "experiences"—who of us even has enough seriousness for them? Or enough time? In such matters I'm afraid we were never really "with it": we just don't have our heart there—or even our ear! Rather, much as a divinely distracted, self-absorbed person into whose ear the bell has just boomed its twelve strokes of noon suddenly awakens and wonders, "what did it actually toll just now?" so we rub our ears *afterwards* and ask, completely amazed, completely disconcerted, "what did we actually experience just now?" still more: "who *are* we actually?" and count up, afterwards, as stated, all twelve quavering bellstrokes of our experience, of our life, of our *being*—alas! and miscount in the process . . . We remain of necessity strangers to ourselves, we do not understand ourselves, we *must* mistake ourselves, for us the maxim reads to all eternity: "each is furthest from himself,"—with respect to ourselves we are not "knowers" . . .

2

—My thoughts on the *origins* of our moral prejudices—for that is what this polemic is about—found their first, economical, and preliminary expression in the collection of aphorisms that bears the title *Human, All Too Human: A Book for Free Spirits*, the writing of that was begun in Sorrento during a winter that permitted me to pause, as a traveler pauses, and look out over the broad and dangerous land through which my spirit had thus far traveled. This occurred in the winter of 1876–77; the thoughts themselves are older. In essentials they were already the same thoughts which I now take up again in the treatises at hand: let us hope that the long period in between has been good for them, that they have become more mature, brighter, stronger, more perfect! That I still hold fast to them today, that they themselves have, in the meantime, held to each other ever more firmly, indeed have grown into each other and become intermeshed, strengthens within me the cheerful confidence that they came about not singly, not arbitrarily, not sporadically, but rather from the beginning arose out of a common root, out of a *basic will* of knowledge which commands from deep within, speaking ever more precisely, demanding something ever more precise. For this alone is fitting for a philosopher. We have no right to be *single* in anything: we may neither err singly nor hit upon the truth singly. Rather, with the necessity with which a tree bears its fruit our thoughts grow out of us, our values, our yes's and no's and if's and whether's—the whole lot related and connected among themselves, witnesses to one will, one health, one earthly kingdom, one sun.—And do they taste good *to you*, these fruits of ours?—But of what concern is that to the trees! Of what concern is that *to us*, us philosophers! . . .

3

Given a skepticism that is characteristic of me, to which I reluctantly admit—for it is directed towards *morality*, towards everything on earth that has until now been celebrated as morality—a skepticism that first appeared so early in my life, so spontaneously,

From Nietzsche, *On the Genealogy of Morality*, translated by Maudemarie Clark and Alan J. Swensen (Indianapolis: Hackett Publishing Company, 1998) copyright © 1998. Reprinted by permission of the publisher.

1. [Matthew 6:21.]

so irrepressibly, so much in contradiction to my environment, age, models, origins, that I almost have the right to call it my "*a priori*" — it was inevitable that early on my curiosity and my suspicion as well would stop at the question: *what*, in fact, is the *origin* of our good and evil? In fact, the problem of the origin of evil haunted me as a thirteen-year-old lad: at an age when one has "half child's play, half God in one's heart,"[2] I devoted my first literary child's play to it, my first philosophic writing exercise — and as to my "solution" to the problem back then, well, I gave the honor to God, as is fitting, and made him the *father* of evil. Was *this* what my "a priori"[3] wished of me? that new, immoral, at least immoralistic "a priori" and the, alas! so anti-Kantian, so mysterious "categorical imperative" speaking through it, to which I have since increasingly lent my ear, and not just my ear? . . . Fortunately I learned early on to distinguish theological from moral prejudice and no longer sought the origin of evil *behind* the world. A little historical and philological schooling, combined with an innate sense of discrimination in all psychological questions, soon transformed my problem into a different one: under what conditions did man invent those value judgments good and evil? *and what value do they themselves have*? Have they inhibited or furthered human flourishing up until now? Are they a sign of distress, of impoverishment, of the degeneration of life? Or, conversely, do they betray the fullness, the power, the will of life, its courage, its confidence, its future? — In response I found and ventured a number of answers; I distinguished ages, peoples, degrees of rank among individuals; I divided up my problem; out of the answers came new questions, investigations, conjectures, probabilities· until I finally had a land of my own, a ground of my own, an entire unspoken growing blossoming world, secret gardens as it were, of which no one was permitted even an inkling . . . O how we are *happy*, we knowers, provided we simply know how to be silent long enough! . . .

4

The first impetus to divulge something of my hypotheses on the origin of morality came to me from a clear,

tidy, and smart, even overly smart little book in which for the first time I was clearly confronted by the reverse and perverse sort of genealogical hypotheses, the specifically *English* sort, and this book attracted me — with that power of attraction exerted by everything contrary, everything antipodal. The title of the little book was *The Origin of Moral Sensations*; its author, Dr. Paul Rée;[4] the year of its publication, 1877. I may never have read anything to which I so emphatically said "no" as I did to this book, proposition by proposition, conclusion by conclusion: and yet entirely without vexation or impatience. In the previously named volume on which I was then working, I made occasional and occasionally inopportune reference to the propositions of that book, not that I refuted them — what have I to do with refutations! — but rather, as befits a positive spirit, putting in place of the improbable the more probable, sometimes in place of one error another one. It was then, as mentioned, that I brought into the light of day those hypotheses concerning origins to which these treatises are devoted, clumsily, as I wish last of all to conceal from myself — still unfree, still without a language of my own for these things of my own, and with many a relapse and wavering. In particular, compare what I say in *Human, All Too Human* 45, on the dual prehistory of good and evil (namely out of the sphere of the nobles and that of the slaves); likewise section 136, on the value and origins of ascetic morality; likewise 96, 99, and volume II, 89, on the "morality of custom," that much older and more original kind of morality that is removed *toto caelo*[5] from the altruistic manner of valuation (which Dr. Rée, like all English genealogists of morality, sees as the moral manner of

4. [Dr. Paul Rée (1849–1901), doctor of law, philosopher, physician. N met Rée in 1873 and the two developed a close friendship. They shared a commitment to providing an explanation of morality in completely naturalistic terms, without reference to religious or metaphysical sources and taking account only of what can be known of human beings from a scientific point of view. Their relationship ended badly in the winter of 1882–83 due to complications within the "trinity" the two men had formed with a young Russian woman, Lou Andreas-Salomé.]

2. [Lines 3781–82 of Goethe's *Faust, Part One* — M.C.]

3. [Nonempirical or independent of experience; literally: from what is before.]

5. [By a tremendous distance; literally: by all of heaven.]

valuation *in itself*); likewise volume I, 92; *Wanderer*, section 26; *Daybreak,* 112, on the origins of justice as a settlement between approximately equal powers (equilibrium as presupposition of all contracts, accordingly of all law); likewise *Wanderer* 22 and 33, on the origins of punishment, for which the purpose of terrorizing is neither essential nor present at the beginning (as Dr. Rée believes:—rather this was inserted into it, under specific circumstances, and always as something incidental, as something additional).

5

Actually there was something much more important on my mind just then than my own or anyone else's hypothesizing about the origin of morality (or, more precisely: the latter concerned me solely for the sake of an end to which it is one means among many). The issue for me was the *value* of morality—and over this I had to struggle almost solely with my great teacher Schopenhauer,[6] to whom that book, the passion and the secret contradiction of that book, is directed, as if to a contemporary (—for that book, too, was a "polemic"). In particular the issue was the value of the unegoistic, of the instincts of compassion, self-denial, self-sacrifice, precisely the instincts that Schopenhauer had gilded, deified, and made other-worldly until finally they alone were left for him as the "values in themselves," on the basis of which he *said "no"* to life, also to himself. But against precisely *these* instincts there spoke from within me an ever more fundamental suspicion, an ever deeper-delving skepticism! Precisely here I saw the *great* danger to humanity, its most sublime lure and temptation—and into what? into nothingness?—precisely here I saw the beginning of the end, the standstill, the backward-glancing tiredness, the will turning *against* life, the last sickness gently and melancholically announcing itself: I understood the ever more widely spreading morality of compassion—which seized even the philosophers and made them sick—as the most uncanny

6. [Arthur Schopenhauer (1788–1860), sometimes described as the "philosopher of pessimism." Largely ignored until very late in his life, he became the most widely read German philosopher in the English-speaking world during the second half of the nineteenth century.]

symptom of our now uncanny European culture, as its detour to a new Buddhism? to a Buddhism for Europeans? to—*nihilism*? . . . For this preferential treatment and overestimation of compassion on the part of modern philosophers is something new: until this point philosophers had agreed precisely on the *worthlessness* of compassion. I name only Plato, Spinoza,[7] La Rochefoucauld,[8] and Kant, four spirits as different from each other as possible, but united on one point: their low regard for compassion.—

6

This problem of the *value* of compassion and of the morality of compassion (—I am an opponent of the disgraceful modern softening of feelings—) appears at first to be only an isolated matter, a lone question mark; whoever sticks here for once, however, and *learns* to ask questions here, will fare as I have fared:— an immense new vista opens up to him, a possibility takes hold of him like a dizziness, every sort of mistrust, suspicion, fear springs forth, the belief in morality, in all morality totters,—finally a new challenge is heard. Let us speak it aloud, this *new challenge*: we need a *critique* of moral values, *for once the value of these values must itself be called into question*— and for this we need a knowledge of the conditions and circumstances out of which they have grown, under which they have developed and shifted (morality as consequence, as symptom, as mask, as Tartuffery, as sickness, as misunderstanding; but also morality as cause, as medicine, as stimulus, as inhibitor, as poison),

7. [Baruch (Benedict) Spinoza (1632–1677), Dutch-Jewish philosopher, usually grouped with Descartes and Leibniz as one of the three most important modern rationalists; known especially for his attempt to overcome the dualism between mind and matter and for his "geometrical" method of presenting philosophy. Spinoza's major work, *Ethica*, was published by his friends shortly after his death.]

8. [François VI, duc de La Rochefoucauld (1613–1680), French aristocrat and classical author. La Rochefoucauld's only major work, the *Maximes*, is a collection of maxims or aphorisms—a literary form that aims at expressing a truth in a brief and pointed and sometimes paradoxical form.]

knowledge of a kind that has neither existed up until now nor even been desired. One has taken the *value* of these "values" as given, as a fact, as beyond all calling-into-question; until now one has not had even the slightest doubt or hesitation in ranking "the good" as of higher value than "the evil," of higher value in the sense of its furtherance, usefulness, beneficiality—with respect to man *in general* (taking into account the future of man). What? if the opposite were true? What? if a symptom of regression also lay in the "good," likewise a danger, a temptation, a poison, a narcotic through which perhaps the present were living *at the expense of the future*? Perhaps more comfortably, less dangerously, but also in a reduced style, on a lower level? . . . So that precisely morality would be to blame if a *highest power and splendor* of the human type—in itself possible—were never attained? So that precisely morality were the danger of dangers? . . .

7

Suffice it to say that once this prospect opened up to me, I myself had reasons for looking about for learned, bold, and industrious comrades (I am still doing so today). It is a matter of traveling the vast, distant, and so concealed land of morality—of the morality which has really existed, really been lived—with a completely new set of questions and as it were with new eyes: and is this not virtually to *discover* this land for the first time? . . . If in the process I thought of, among others, the above named Dr. Rée, this happened because I had no doubt that he would be pushed by the very nature of his questions to a more correct method of attaining answers. Did I deceive myself in this? My wish, in any case, was to turn so sharp and disinterested an eye in a better direction, the direction of the real *history of morality* and to warn him while there was still time against such English hypothesizing *into the blue*. It is of course obvious which color must be a hundred times more important to a genealogist of morality than blue: namely *gray*, which is to say, that which can be documented, which can really be ascertained, which has really existed, in short, the very long, difficult-to-decipher hieroglyphic writing of the human moral past! *This* was unknown to Dr.

Rée; but he had read Darwin:[9]—and thus in his hypothesizing we have, in a manner that is at least entertaining, the Darwinian beast politely joining hands with the most modern, unassuming moral milquetoast who "no longer bites"—the latter with an expression of a certain good-natured and refined indolence on his face, into which is mixed even a grain of pessimism, of weariness: as if there weren't really any reward for taking all these things—the problems of morality—so seriously. To me it seems that, on the contrary, there are no things which would *reward* one more for taking them seriously; to which reward belongs, for example, that one might perhaps some day gain permission to take them *cheerfully*. For cheerfulness, or to say it in my language, *gay science*—is a reward: a reward for a long, brave, industrious, and subterranean seriousness that is admittedly not for everyone. On that day, however, when we say from a full heart: "Onward! even our old morality belongs *in comedy*!" we will have discovered a new complication and possibility for the Dionysian drama of the "Destiny of the Soul"—: and he will certainly make use of it, one can bet on that, he, the great old eternal comic poet of our existence! . . .

8

—If this book is unintelligible to anyone and hard on the ears, the fault, as I see it, does not necessarily lie with me. It is clear enough, presupposing, as I do, that one has first read my earlier writings and has not spared some effort in the process: these are in fact not easily accessible. As far as my *Zarathustra* is concerned, for example, I count no one an authority on it who has not at sometime been deeply wounded and at sometime deeply delighted by each of its words: for only then may he enjoy the privilege of reverent participation in the halcyon element out of which the work was born, in its sunny brightness, distance, expanse, and certainty. In other cases the aphoristic form creates a difficulty—it lies in the fact that we don't attach *enough weight* to this form today. An aphorism honestly coined and cast has not been "deciphered" simply because it has been

9. [Charles Robert Darwin (1809–1882), English naturalist, author of *On the Origin of Species by Means of Natural Selection* (1859).]

read through; rather its *interpretation* must now begin, and for this an art of interpretation is needed. In the third treatise of this book I have offered a sample of what I call "interpretation" in such a case: — an aphorism is placed before this treatise, the treatise itself is a commentary on it. Admittedly, to practice reading as an *art* in this way one thing above all is necessary, something which these days has been unlearned better than anything else — and it will therefore be a while before my writings are "readable" — something for which one must almost be a cow and in any case *not* a "modern man": *ruminating* . . .

Sils-Maria, Upper Engadine, in July 1887.

FIRST TREATISE: "GOOD AND EVIL," "GOOD AND BAD"

1

—These English psychologists whom we also have to thank for the only attempts so far to produce a history of the genesis of morality — they themselves are no small riddle for us; I confess, in fact, that precisely as riddles in the flesh they have something substantial over their books — *they themselves are interesting*! These English psychologists — what do they actually want? One finds them, whether voluntarily or involuntarily, always at the same task, namely of pushing the *partie honteuse*[10] of our inner world into the foreground and of seeking that which is actually effective, leading, decisive for our development, precisely where the intellectual pride of man would least of all *wish* to find it (for example in the *vis inertiae*[11] of habit or in forgetfulness or in a blind and accidental interlacing and mechanism of ideas or in anything purely passive, automatic, reflexive, molecular, and fundamentally mindless) — what is it actually that always drives these psychologists in precisely *this* direction? Is it a secret, malicious, base instinct to

10. [Shameful part (in the plural, this expression is the equivalent of the English "private parts").]

11. [Force of inactivity. In Newtonian physics, this term denotes the resistance offered by matter to any force tending to alter its state of rest or motion.]

belittle mankind, one that perhaps cannot be acknowledged even to itself ? Or, say, a pessimistic suspicion, the mistrust of disappointed, gloomy idealists who have become poisonous and green? Or a little subterranean animosity and rancor against Christianity (and Plato) that has perhaps not yet made it past the threshold of consciousness? Or even a lascivious taste for the disconcerting, for the painful-paradoxical, for the questionable and nonsensical aspects of existence? Or finally — a little of everything, a little meanness, a little gloominess, a little anti-Christianity, a little tickle and need for pepper? . . . But I am told that they are simply old, cold, boring frogs who creep and hop around on human beings, into human beings, as if they were really in their element there, namely in a *swamp*. I resist this, still more, I don't believe it; and if one is permitted to wish where one cannot know, then I wish from my heart that the reverse may be the case with them — that these explorers and microscopists of the soul are basically brave, magnanimous, and proud animals who know how to keep a rein on their hearts as well as their pain and have trained themselves to sacrifice all desirability to truth, to *every* truth, even plain, harsh, ugly, unpleasant, unchristian, immoral truth . . . For there are such truths. —

2

Hats off then to whatever good spirits may be at work in these historians of morality! Unfortunately, however, it is certain that they lack the *historical spirit* itself, that they have been left in the lurch precisely by all the good spirits of history! As is simply the age-old practice among philosophers, they all think *essentially* ahistorically; of this there is no doubt. The ineptitude of their moral genealogy is exposed right at the beginning, where it is a matter of determining the origins of the concept and judgment "good." "Originally" — so they decree — "unegoistic actions were praised and called good from the perspective of those to whom they were rendered, hence for whom they were *useful*; later one *forgot* this origin of the praise and, simply because unegoistic actions were *as a matter of habit* always praised as good, one also felt them to be good — as if they were something good in themselves." One sees immediately: this first derivation already contains all the characteristic traits of the idiosyncrasy of English psychologists—we have "usefulness," "forgetting," "habit," and in the end "error," all as basis for a valuation of which the higher human being has until now been proud as if it were some kind of distinctive prerogative of humankind. This pride *must* be humbled, this valuation devalued: has this been achieved? . . . Now in the first place it is obvious to me that the actual genesis of the concept "good" is sought and fixed in the wrong place by this theory: the judgment "good" does *not* stem from those to whom "goodness" is rendered! Rather it was "the good" themselves, that is the noble, powerful, higher-ranking, and high-minded who felt and ranked themselves and their doings as good, which is to say, as of the first rank, in contrast to everything base, low-minded, common, and vulgar. Out of this *pathos of distance* they first took for themselves the right to create values, to coin names for values: what did they care about usefulness! The viewpoint of utility is as foreign and inappropriate as possible, especially in relation to so hot an outpouring of highest rank-order-ing, rank-distinguishing value judgments: for here feeling has arrived at an opposite of that low degree of warmth presupposed by every calculating prudence, every assessment of utility—and not just for once, for an hour of exception, but rather for the long run. As was stated, the pathos of nobility and distance, this lasting and dominant collective and basic feeling of a higher ruling nature in relation to a lower nature, to a "below"—*that* is the origin of the opposition "good" and "bad." (The right of lords to give names goes so far that we should allow ourselves to compre-hend the origin of language itself as an expression of power on the part of those who rule: they say "this *is* such and such," they seal each thing and happening with a sound and thus, as it were, take possession of it.) It is because of this origin that from the outset the word "good" does *not* necessarily attach itself to "unegoistic" actions—as is the superstition of those genealogists of morality. On the contrary, only when aristocratic value judgments begin to *decline* does this entire opposition "egoistic" "unegoistic" impose itself more and more on the human conscience—to make use of my language, it is *the herd instinct* that finally finds a voice (also *words*) in this opposition. And even then it takes a long time until this instinct becomes dominant to such an extent that moral valuation in

effect gets caught and stuck at that opposition (as is the case in present-day Europe: today the prejudice that takes "moral," "unegoistic," "*désintéressé*"[12] to be concepts of equal value already rules with the force of an "*idée fixe*"[13] and sickness in the head).

3

In the second place, however: quite apart from the his-torical untenability of that hypothesis concerning the origins of the value judgment "good," it suffers from an inherent psychological absurdity. The usefulness of the unegoistic action is supposed to be the origin of its praise, and this origin is supposed to have been *forgot-ten*:—how is this forgetting even *possible*? Did the usefulness of such actions cease at some point? The opposite is the case: this usefulness has been the every-day experience in all ages, something therefore that was continually underscored anew; accordingly, instead of disappearing from consciousness, instead of becoming forgettable, it could not help but impress itself upon consciousness with ever greater clarity. How much more reasonable is that opposing theory (it is not there-fore truer—) advocated for example by Herbert Spen-cer[14]—which ranks the concept "good" as essentially identical with the concept "useful," "purposive," so that in the judgments "good" and "bad" humanity has summed up and sanctioned its *unforgotten* and *unfor-gettable* experiences concerning what is useful-purpos-ive, what is injurious-nonpurposive. Good, according to this theory, is whatever has proved itself as useful from time immemorial: it may thus claim validity as "valuable in the highest degree," as "valuable in itself." This path of explanation is also false, as noted above, but at least the explanation is in itself reasonable and psychologically tenable.

4

—The pointer to the *right* path was given to me by the question: what do the terms coined for "good" in

12. [Disinterested, unselfish, selfless.]

13. [Obsession; literally: a fixed idea.]

14. [Herbert Spencer (1820–1903), English sociologist and philosopher. An early advocate of evolutionary the-ory, he is the father of Social Darwinism: Spencer coined the phrase "survival of the fittest."]

the various languages actually mean from an etymological viewpoint? Here I found that they all lead back to the *same conceptual transformation* — that everywhere the basic concept is "noble," "aristocratic" in the sense related to the estates, out of which "good" in the sense of "noble of soul," "high-natured of soul," "privileged of soul" necessarily develops: a development that always runs parallel to that other one which makes "common," "vulgar," "base" pass over finally into the concept "bad." The most eloquent example of the latter is the German word "*schlecht*" [bad] itself: which is identical with "*schlicht*" [plain, simple] — compare "*schlechtweg,*" "*schlechterdings*" [simply or downright] — and originally designated the plain, the common man, as yet without a suspecting sideward glance, simply in opposition to the noble one. Around the time of the Thirty-Years' War, in other words late enough, this sense shifts into the one now commonly used. — With respect to morality's genealogy this appears to me to be an *essential* insight; that it is only now being discovered is due to the inhibiting influence that democratic prejudice exercises in the modern world with regard to all questions of origins. And this influence extends all the way into that seemingly most objective realm of natural science and physiology, as I shall merely hint at here. But the nonsense that this prejudice — once unleashed to the point of hate — is able to inflict, especially on morality and history, is shown by Buckle's[15] notorious case; the *plebeianism* of the modern spirit, which is of English descent, sprang forth there once again on its native ground, vehemently like a muddy volcano and with that oversalted, overloud, common eloquence with which until now all volcanoes have spoken. —

5

With regard to *our* problem — which can for good reasons be called a *quiet* problem and which addresses itself selectively to but few ears — it is of no small interest to discover that often in those words and roots

that designate "good" that main nuance still shimmers through with respect to which the nobles felt themselves to be humans of a higher rank. To be sure, they may name themselves in the most frequent cases simply after their superiority in power (as "the powerful," "the lords," "the commanders") or after the most visible distinguishing mark of this superiority, for example as "the rich," "the possessors," (that is the sense of *arya*;[16] and likewise in Iranian and Slavic). But also after a *typical character trait*: and this is the case which concerns us here. They call themselves for example "the truthful" — led by the Greek nobility, whose mouthpiece is the Megarian poet Theognis.[17] The word coined for this, *esthlos*,[18] means according to its root one who *is*, who possesses reality, who is real, who is true; then, with a subjective turn, the true one as the truthful one: in this phase of the concept's transformation it becomes the by- and catchword of the nobility and passes over completely into the sense of "aristocratic," as that which distinguishes from the *lying* common man as Theognis understands and depicts him — until finally, after the demise of the nobility, the word remains as the term for *noblesse* of soul and becomes as it were ripe and sweet. In the word *kakos*[19] as well as in *deilos*[20] (the plebeian in contrast to the *agathos*)[21] cowardliness is underscored: perhaps this gives a hint in which direction one should seek the etymological origins of *agathos*, which can be interpreted in many ways. In the Latin *malus*[22] (beside which I place *melas*),[23] the common man could be characterized as the dark-colored, above all as the black-haired ("*hic niger est—*"),[24] as the pre-Aryan occupant of Italian soil, who by his color stood out most clearly from the blonds who had become the rulers, namely the Aryan conqueror-race; at any rate Gaelic offered

15. [Henry Thomas Buckle (1821–1862), English historian. Holding in contempt the history of his day, which emphasized politics, war, and heroes, he aimed to make history scientific by discovering the fixed laws that govern the actions of men and therefore of societies.]

16. [Sanskrit: noble.]
17. [Late 6th–early 5th century B.C.E..]
18. [Good, brave, noble.]
19. [Bad, ugly, ill-born, base, cowardly, ignoble.]
20. [Cowardly, worthless, low-born, miserable, wretched.]
21. [Good, well-born, noble, brave, capable.]
22. [Bad, evil.]
23. [Black, dark.]
24. [He is black. Horace's *Satires*, I. 4, line 85.]

me an exactly corresponding case — *fin*[25] (for example in the name Fin-Gal), the distinguishing word of the nobility, in the end, the good, noble, pure one, originally the blond-headed one, in contrast to the dark, black-haired original inhabitants. The Celts, incidentally, were by all means a blond race; it is wrong to associate those tracts of an essentially dark-haired population, which are noticeable on the more careful ethnographic maps of Germany, with any Celtic origins or blood mixtures, as even Virchow[26] does: rather it is the *pre-Aryan* population of Germany that comes to the fore in these places. (The same is true for almost all of Europe: in essence, the subjected race has in the end regained the upper hand there, in color, shortness of skull, perhaps even in intellectual and social instincts — who will guarantee us that modern democracy, the even more modern anarchism, and in particular that inclination toward the "commune," the most primitive form of society — an inclination now common to all of Europe's socialists — does not signify, on the whole, a tremendous *atavism* — and that the *race of lords* and conquerors, that of the Aryans, is not in the process of succumbing physiologically as well? . . .) I believe I may interpret the Latin *bonus*[27] as "the warrior": assuming that I am correct in tracing *bonus* back to an older *duonus*[28] (compare *bellum = duellum = duen-lum*,[29] in which that *duonus* seems to me to be preserved). *Bonus* accordingly as man of strife, of division (*duo*), as man of war — one sees what it was about a man that constituted his "goodness" in ancient Rome. Our German "*gut*" [good] itself: wasn't it supposed to mean "the godly one," the man "of godly race"? And to be identical with the name for the nation (originally for the nobility) of the Goths? The reasons for this supposition do not belong here. —

6

To this rule that the concept of superiority in politics always resolves itself into a concept of superiority of

soul, it is not immediately an exception (although it provides occasion for exceptions) when the highest caste is at the same time the *priestly* caste and hence prefers for its collective name a predicate that recalls its priestly function. Here, for example, "pure" and "impure" stand opposite each other for the first time as marks of distinction among the estates; and here, too, one later finds the development of a "good" and a "bad" in a sense no longer related to the estates. Incidentally, let one beware from the outset of taking these concepts "pure" and "impure" too seriously, too broadly, or even too symbolically: rather all of earlier humanity's concepts were initially understood in a coarse, crude, superficial, narrow, straightforward, and above all *unsymbolic* manner, to an extent that we can hardly imagine. The "pure one" is from the beginning simply a human being who washes himself, who forbids himself certain foods that bring about skin diseases, who doesn't sleep with the dirty women of the baser people, who abhors blood — nothing more, at least not much more! On the other hand the entire nature of an essentially priestly aristocracy admittedly makes clear why it was precisely here that the valuation opposites could so soon become internalized and heightened in a dangerous manner; and indeed through them gulfs were finally torn open between man and man across which even an Achilles of free-spiritedness will not be able to leap without shuddering. From the beginning there is something *unhealthy* in such priestly aristocracies and in the habits ruling there, ones turned away from action, partly brooding, partly emotionally explosive, habits that have as a consequence the intestinal disease and neurasthenia that almost unavoidably clings to the priests of all ages; but what they themselves invented as a medicine against this diseasedness of theirs — must we not say that in the end it has proved itself a hundred times more dangerous in its aftereffects than the disease from which it was to redeem them? Humanity itself still suffers from the aftereffects of these priestly cure naïvetés! Think, for example, of certain dietary forms (avoidance of meat), of fasting, of sexual abstinence, of the flight "into the wilderness" (Weir-Mitchellian isolation,[30] admittedly without the

25. [Gaelic: white, bright.]

26. [Rudolf Virchow (1821–1902), physician, professor of medicine, and liberal politician.]

27. [Good.]

28. [Earlier form of *bonus*.]

29. [War; the latter two are older, poetic forms.]

30. [Silas Weir Mitchell (1829–1914), Philadelphian physician and novelist who specialized in treating "ner-

ensuing fattening diet and over-feeding, which constitutes the most effective antidote for all the hysteria of
the ascetic ideal): in addition, the whole anti-sensual
metaphysics of priests, which makes lazy and over-
refined, their self-hypnosis after the manner of the
fakir and Brahmin—brahma used as glass pendant
and *idée fixe*—and the final, only too understandable
general satiety along with its radical cure, *nothingness*
(or God—the longing for a *unio mystica*[31] with God
is the longing of the Buddhist for nothingness, Nir-
vâna—and nothing more!) With priests *everything*
simply becomes more dangerous, not only curatives
and healing arts, but also arrogance, revenge, acuity,
excess, love, lust to rule, virtue, disease;—though with
some fairness one could also add that it was on the
soil of this *essentially dangerous* form of human existence, the priestly form, that man first became *an
interesting animal*, that only here did the human soul
acquire *depth* in a higher sense and become *evil*—
and these are, after all, the two basic forms of the
previous superiority of man over other creatures! . . .

7

—One will already have guessed how easily the
priestly manner of valuation can branch off from the
knightly-aristocratic and then develop into its opposite; this process is especially given an impetus every
time the priestly caste and the warrior caste confront
each other jealously and are unable to agree on a
price. The knightly-aristocratic value judgments have
as their presupposition a powerful physicality, a blossoming, rich, even overflowing health, together with
that which is required for its preservation: war, adventure, the hunt, dance, athletic contests, and in general
everything which includes strong, free, cheerful-

hearted activity. The priestly-noble manner of valuation—as we have seen—has other presuppositions: too
bad for it when it comes to war! Priests are, as is well
known, the *most evil enemies*—why is that? Because
they are the most powerless. Out of their powerlessness
their hate grows into something enormous and uncanny, into something most spiritual and most poisonous. The truly great haters in the history of the world
have always been priests, also the most ingenious haters:—compared with the spirit of priestly revenge all
the rest of spirit taken together hardly merits consideration. Human history would be much too stupid an
affair without the spirit that has entered into it through
the powerless:—let us turn right to the greatest example. Of all that has been done on earth against "the
noble," "the mighty," "the lords," "the power-holders,"
nothing is worthy of mention in comparison with that
which the *Jews* have done against them: the Jews, that
priestly people who in the end were only able to obtain
satisfaction from their enemies and conquerors
through a radical revaluation of their values, that is,
through an act of *spiritual revenge*. This was the only
way that suited a priestly people, the people of the
most suppressed priestly desire for revenge. It was
the Jews who in opposition to the aristocratic value
equation (good = noble = powerful = beautiful =
happy = beloved of God) dared its inversion, with
fear-inspiring consistency, and held it fast with teeth
of the most unfathomable hate (the hate of powerlessness), namely: "the miserable alone are the good;
the poor, powerless, lowly alone are the good; the
suffering, deprived, sick, ugly are also the only pious,
the only blessed in God, for them alone is there
blessedness,—whereas you, you noble and powerful
ones, you are in all eternity the evil, the cruel, the
lustful, the insatiable, the godless, you will eternally
be the wretched, accursed, and damned!" . . . We
know *who* inherited this Jewish revaluation . . . In
connection with the enormous and immeasurably
doom-laden initiative provided by the Jews with this
most fundamental of all declarations of war, I call
attention to the proposition which I arrived at on
another occasion ("Beyond Good and Evil" section
195)—namely, that with the Jews *the slave revolt in
morality* begins: that revolt which has a two-thousand-
year history behind it and which has only moved out
of our sight today because it—has been victorious . . .

---

vous" disorders. He became widely known in America
and Europe for his "rest cure" for such illnesses: patients
were first isolated from the influence of hovering, over-
careful family members and restricted to bed for four to
six weeks, during which they were not allowed to have
visitors or to read or write. They were fed by a nurse
and given massages to keep up strength and muscle tone.
When they began to show improvement, patients were
ordered to get up and take exercise.]

31. [Mystical union.]

8

—But you don't understand that? You don't have eyes for something that has taken two thousand years to achieve victory? . . . There is nothing to wonder at in this: all *lengthy* things are difficult to see, to see in their entirety. *This* however is what happened: out of the trunk of that tree of revenge and hate, Jewish hate—the deepest and most sublime hate, namely an ideal-creating, value-reshaping hate whose like has never before existed on earth—grew forth something just as incomparable, a *new love*, the deepest and most sublime of all kinds of love:—and from what other trunk could it have grown? . . . But by no means should one suppose it grew upwards as, say, the true negation of that thirst for revenge, as the opposite of Jewish hate! No, the reverse is the truth! This love grew forth out of it, as its crown, as the triumphant crown unfolding itself broadly and more broadly in purest light and sunny fullness, reaching out, as it were, in the realm of light and of height, for the goals of that hate—for victory, for booty, for seduction—with the same drive with which the roots of that hate sunk themselves ever more thoroughly and greedily down into everything that had depth and was evil. This Jesus of Nazareth, as the embodied Gospel of Love, this "Redeemer" bringing blessedness and victory to the poor, the sick, the sinners—was he not precisely seduction in its most uncanny and irresistible form, the seduction and detour to precisely those *Jewish* values and reshapings of the ideal? Has not Israel reached the final goal of its sublime desire for revenge precisely via the detour of this "Redeemer," this apparent adversary and dissolver of Israel? Does it not belong to the secret black art of a truly *great* politics of revenge, of a far-seeing, subterranean, slow-working and pre-calculating revenge, that Israel itself, before all the world, should deny as its mortal enemy and nail to the cross the actual tool of its revenge, so that "all the world," namely all the opponents of Israel, could take precisely this bait without thinking twice? And, out of all sophistication of the spirit, could one think up any more *dangerous* bait? Something that in its enticing, intoxicating, anesthetizing, destructive power might equal that symbol of the "holy cross," that gruesome paradox of a "god on the cross," that mystery of an inconceivable, final, extreme cruelty and self-crucifixion of God *for the salvation of man*? . . . What is certain, at least, is that *sub hoc signo*[32] Israel, with its revenge and revaluation of all values, has thus far again and again triumphed over all other ideals, over all *more noble* ideals.— —

9

—"But why are you still talking about *nobler* ideals! Let's submit to the facts: the people were victorious—or 'the slaves,' or 'the mob,' or 'the herd,' or whatever you like to call them—if this happened through the Jews, so be it! then never has a people had a more world-historic mission. 'The lords' are cast off; the morality of the common man has been victorious. One may take this victory to be at the same time a blood poisoning (it mixed the races together)—I won't contradict; in any event it is beyond doubt that this toxication *succeeded*. The 'redemption' of the human race (namely from 'the lords') is well under way; everything is jewifying or christifying or mobifying as we watch (what do the words matter!). The progress of this poisoning through the entire body of humanity appears unstoppable, from now on its tempo and step may even be slower, more refined, less audible, more thoughtful—one has time after all . . . Does the church today still have a *necessary* task in this scheme, still a right to existence at all? Or could one do without it? *Quaeritur.*[33] It seems more likely that it inhibits and holds back this progress instead of accelerating it? Well, even that could be its usefulness . . . By now it is certainly something coarse and peasant-like, which repels a more delicate intelligence, a truly modern taste. Shouldn't it at least become somewhat refined? . . . Today it alienates more than it seduces . . . Which of us indeed would be a free spirit if there were no church? The church, *not* its poison, repels us . . . Leaving the church aside, we, too, love the poison . . ."—This, the epilogue of a "free spirit" to my speech, an honest animal, as he has richly betrayed, moreover a democrat; he had listened to me up until then and couldn't stand to hear me be silent. For at this point I have much to be silent about.—

32. [Under this sign.]
33. [One asks, i.e., that is the question.]

10

The slave revolt in morality begins when *ressentiment* itself becomes creative and gives birth to values: the *ressentiment* of beings denied the true reaction, that of the deed, who recover their losses only through an imaginary revenge. Whereas all noble morality grows out of a triumphant yes-saying to oneself, from the outset slave morality says "no" to an "outside," to a "different," to a "not-self": and *this* "no" is its creative deed. This reversal of the value-establishing glance — this *necessary* direction toward the outside instead of back onto oneself — belongs to the very nature of *ressentiment*: in order to come into being, slave-morality always needs an opposite and external world; it needs, psychologically speaking, external stimuli in order to be able to act at all, — its action is, from the ground up, reaction. The reverse is the case with the noble manner of valuation: it acts and grows spontaneously, it seeks out its opposite only in order to say "yes" to itself still more gratefully and more jubilantly — its negative concept "low" "common" "bad" is only an after-birth, a pale contrast-image in relation to its positive basic concept, saturated through and through with life and passion: "we noble ones, we good ones, we beautiful ones, we happy ones!" When the noble manner of valuation lays a hand on reality and sins against it, this occurs relative to the sphere with which it is *not* sufficiently acquainted, indeed against a real knowledge of which it rigidly defends itself: in some cases it forms a wrong idea of the sphere it holds in contempt, that of the common man, of the lower people; on the other hand, consider that the affect of contempt, of looking down on, of the superior glance — assuming that it does *falsify* the image of the one held in contempt — will in any case fall far short of the falsification with which the suppressed hate, the revenge of the powerless, lays a hand on its opponent — in effigy, of course. Indeed there is too much carelessness in contempt, too much taking-lightly, too much looking-away and impatience mixed in, even too much of a feeling of cheer in oneself, for it to be capable of transforming its object into a real caricature and monster. Do not fail to hear the almost benevolent nuances that, for example, the Greek nobility places in all words by which it distinguishes the lower people from itself; how they are mixed with and sugared by a kind of pity, considerateness, leniency to the point that almost all words that apply to the common man ultimately survive as expressions for "unhappy" "pitiful" (compare *deilos*, *deilaios*, *poneros*, *mochtheros*, the latter two actually designating the common man as work-slave and beast of burden)[34] — and how, on the other hand, to the Greek ear "bad" "low" "unhappy" have never ceased to end on the same note, with a tone color in which "unhappy" predominates: this as inheritance of the old, nobler aristocratic manner of valuation that does not deny itself even in its contempt (let philologists be reminded of the sense in which *oizyros*, *anolbos*, *tlemon*, *dystychein*, *xymphora* are used).[35] The "well-born" simply *felt* themselves to be the "happy"; they did not first have to construct their happiness artificially by looking at their enemies, to talk themselves into it, to *lie themselves into it* (as all human beings of *ressentiment* tend to do); and as full human beings, overloaded with power and therefore *necessarily* active, they likewise did not know how to separate activity out from happiness, — for them being active is of necessity included in happiness (whence *eu prattein*[36] takes its origins) — all of this very much in opposition to "happiness" on the level of the powerless, oppressed, those festering with poisonous and hostile feelings, in whom it essentially appears as narcotic, anesthetic, calm, peace, "Sabbath," relaxation of mind and stretching of limbs, in short, *passively*. While the noble human being lives with himself in confidence and openness (*gennaios* "noble-born" underscores the nuance "sincere" and probably also "naive") the human being of *ressentiment* is neither sincere, nor naive, nor honest and frank with himself.

34. [*Deilos*: cowardly, worthless, low-born, miserable, wretched; *deilaios*: wretched, sorry, paltry; *poneros*: wretched, oppressed by toils, worthless, base, cowardly; *mochtheros*: wretched, suffering hardship, miserable, worthless, knavish.]

35. [*Oizyros*: woeful, pitiable, miserable, sorry, poor; *anolbos*: unblest, wretched, luckless, poor; *tlemon*: suffering, enduring; hence: "steadfast, stouthearted," but also "wretched, miserable"; *dystychein*: to be unlucky, unhappy, unfortunate; *xymphora*: originally "chance," then usually in a bad sense, that is, "misfortune."]

36. [To do well, to fare well, or to do good.]

His soul *looks obliquely* at things; his spirit loves hiding places, secret passages and backdoors, everything hidden strikes him as *his* world, *his* security, *his* balm; he knows all about being silent, not forgetting, waiting, belittling oneself for the moment, humbling oneself. A race of such human beings of *ressentiment* in the end necessarily becomes *more prudent* than any noble race, it will also honor prudence in an entirely different measure: namely as a primary condition of existence. With noble human beings, in contrast, prudence is likely to have a refined aftertaste of luxury and sophistication about it:—here it is not nearly as essential as the complete functional reliability of the regulating *unconscious* instincts or even a certain imprudence, for example the gallant making-straight-for-it, be it toward danger, be it toward the enemy, or that impassioned suddenness of anger, love, reverence, gratitude, and revenge by which noble souls in all ages have recognized each other. For the *ressentiment* of the noble human being, when it appears in him, runs its course and exhausts itself in an immediate reaction, therefore it does not *poison*—on the other hand it does not appear at all in countless cases where it is unavoidable in all the weak and powerless. To be unable for any length of time to take his enemies, his accidents, his *misdeeds* themselves seriously—that is the sign of strong, full natures in which there is an excess of formative, reconstructive, healing power that also makes one forget (a good example of this from the modern world is Mirabeau,[37] who had no memory for insults and base deeds committed against him and who was only unable to forgive because he—forgot). Such a human is simply able to shake off with a single shrug a collection of worms that in others would dig itself in; here alone is also possible—assuming that it is at all possible on earth the true "*love* of one's enemies." What great reverence for his enemies a noble human being has!—and such reverence is already a bridge to love . . . After all, he demands his enemy for himself, as his distinction; he can stand no other enemy than one in whom there is nothing to hold in contempt and *a very great deal* to honor! On the other hand, imagine "the enemy" as the human being of *ressentiment* conceives of

him—and precisely here is his deed, his creation: he has conceived of "the evil enemy," "*the evil one*," and this indeed as the basic concept, starting from which he now also thinks up, as reaction and counterpart, a "good one"—himself! . . .

11

Precisely the reverse, therefore, of the case of the noble one, who conceives the basic concept "good" in advance and spontaneously, starting from himself that is, and from there first creates for himself an idea of "bad"! This "bad" of noble origin and that "evil" out of the brewing cauldron of unsatiated hate—the first, an after-creation, something on the side, a complementary color; the second, in contrast, the original, the beginning, the true *deed* in the conception of a slave morality—how differently the two words "bad" and "evil" stand there, seemingly set in opposition to the same concept "good"! But it is *not* the same concept "good": on the contrary, just ask yourself *who* is actually "evil" in the sense of the morality of *ressentiment*. To answer in all strictness: *precisely* the "good one" of the other morality, precisely the noble, the powerful, the ruling one, only recolored, only reinterpreted, only reseen through the poisonous eye of *ressentiment*. There is one point we wish to deny least of all here: whoever encounters those "good ones" only as enemies encounters nothing but *evil enemies*, and the same humans who are kept so strictly within limits *inter pares*,[38] by mores, worship, custom, gratitude, still more by mutual surveillance, by jealousy, and who on the other hand in their conduct towards each other prove themselves so inventive in consideration, self-control, tact, loyalty, pride, and friendship,—they are not much better than uncaged beasts of prey toward the outside world, where that which is foreign, the foreign world, begins. There they enjoy freedom from all social constraint; in the wilderness they recover the losses incured through the tension that comes from a long enclosure and fencing-in within the peace of the community; they step *back* into the innocence of the beast-of-prey conscience, as jubilant monsters, who perhaps walk

37. [Honoré Gabriel Riqueti, Comte de Mirabeau (1749–1791), French politician, orator, and writer.]

38. [Among equals; here, "among themselves."]

away from a hideous succession of murder, arson, rape, torture with such high spirits and equanimity that it seems as if they have only played a student prank, convinced that for years to come the poets will again have something to sing and to praise. At the base of all these noble races one cannot fail to recognize the beast of prey, the splendid *blond beast* who roams about lusting after booty and victory; from time to time this hidden base needs to discharge itself, the animal must get out, must go back into the wilderness: Roman, Arab, Germanic, Japanese nobility, Homeric heroes, Scandinavian Vikings—in this need they are all alike. It is the noble races who have left the concept "barbarian" in all their tracks wherever they have gone; indeed from within their highest culture a consciousness of this betrays itself and even a pride in it (for example when Pericles says to his Athenians in that famous funeral oration, "to every land and sea our boldness has broken a path, everywhere setting up unperishing monuments in good *and bad*"). This "boldness" of noble races—mad, absurd, sudden in its expression; the unpredictable, in their enterprises even the improbable—Pericles singles out for distinction the *rhathymia*[39] of the Athenians—their indifference and contempt toward all security, body, life, comfort; their appalling light-heartedness and depth of desire in all destruction, in all the delights of victory and of cruelty—all was summed up for those who suffered from it in the image of the "barbarian," of the "evil enemy," for example the "Goth," the "Vandal." The deep, icy mistrust that the German stirs up as soon as he comes into power, today once again— is still an atavism of that inextinguishable horror with which Europe has for centuries watched the raging of the blond Germanic beast (although there is hardly a conceptual, much less a blood-relationship between the ancient Teutons and us Germans). I once called attention to Hesiod's embarrassment as he was devising the succession of the cultural ages and attempted to express it in terms of gold, silver, bronze: he knew of no other way to cope with the contradiction posed by the glorious but likewise so gruesome, so violent world of Homer, than by making one age into two, which he now placed one after the other—first the

age of the heroes and demigods of Troy and Thebes, as this world had remained in the memory of the noble dynasties who had their own ancestors there; then the bronze age, which was that same world as it appeared to the descendants of the downtrodden, plundered, mistreated, dragged-off, sold-off: an age of bronze, as stated—hard, cold, cruel, without feeling or conscience, crushing everything and covering it with blood. Assuming it were true, that which is now in any case believed as "truth," that the *meaning of all culture* is simply to breed a tame and civilized animal, a *domestic animal*, out of the beast of prey "man," then one would have to regard all those instincts of reaction and *ressentiment*, with the help of which the noble dynasties together with their ideals were finally brought to ruin and overwhelmed, as the actual *tools of culture*; which is admittedly not to say that the *bearers* of these instincts themselves at the same time also represent culture. On the contrary, the opposite would not simply be probable—no! today it is *obvious*! These bearers of the oppressing and retaliation-craving instincts, the descendants of all European and non-European slavery, of all pre-Aryan population in particular—they represent the *regression* of humankind! These "tools of culture" are a disgrace to humanity, and rather something that raises a suspicion, a counter-argument against "culture" in general! It may be entirely justifiable if one cannot escape one's fear of the blond beast at the base of all noble races and is on guard: but who would not a hundred times sooner fear if he might at the same time admire, than *not* fear but be unable to escape the disgusting sight of the deformed, reduced, atrophied, poisoned? And is that not *our* doom? What causes *our* aversion to "man"?—for we *suffer* from man, there is no doubt.—*Not* fear; rather that we have nothing left to fear in man; that the worm "man" is in the foreground and teeming; that the "tame man," this hopelessly mediocre and uninspiring being, has already learned to feel himself as the goal and pinnacle, as the meaning of history, as "higher man"—indeed that he has a certain right to feel this way, insofar as he feels himself distanced from the profusion of the deformed, sickly, tired, worn-out of which Europe today is beginning to stink; hence as something that is at least relatively well-formed, at least still capable of living, that at least says "yes" to life . . .

39. [Easiness of temper; indifference, rashness. Thucydides 2. 39.]

12

—At this point I will not suppress a sigh and a final confidence. What is it that I in particular find utterly unbearable? That with which I cannot cope alone, that causes me to suffocate and languish? Bad air! Bad air! That something deformed comes near me; that I should have to smell the entrails of a deformed soul! . . . How much can one not otherwise bear of distress, deprivation, foul weather, infirmity, drudgery, isolation? Basically one deals with everything else, born as one is to a subterranean and fighting existence; again and again one reaches the light, again and again one experiences one's golden hour of victory,—and then one stands there as one was born, unbreakable, tensed, ready for something new, something still more difficult, more distant, like a bow that any distress simply pulls tauter still.—But from time to time grant me—assuming that there are heavenly patronesses beyond good and evil—a glimpse, grant me just one glimpse of something perfect, completely formed, happy, powerful, triumphant, in which there is still something to fear! Of a human being who justifies man *himself*; a human being who is a stroke of luck, completing and redeeming man, and for whose sake one may hold fast to *belief in man*! . . . For things stand thus: the reduction and equalization of the European human conceals *our* greatest danger, for this sight makes tired . . . We see today nothing that wishes to become greater, we sense that things are still going downhill, downhill—into something thinner, more good-natured, more prudent, more comfortable, more mediocre, more apathetic, more Chinese, more Christian—man, there is no doubt, is becoming ever "better" . . . Precisely here lies Europe's doom— with the fear of man we have also forfeited the love of him, the reverence toward him, the hope for him, indeed the will to him. The sight of man now makes tired—what is nihilism today if it is not *that*? . . . We are tired of *man* . . .

13

—But let us come back: the problem of the *other* origin of "good," of the good one as conceived by the man of *ressentiment*, demands its conclusion.—That the lambs feel anger toward the great birds of prey does not strike us as odd: but that is no reason for holding it against the great birds of prey that they snatch up little lambs for themselves. And when the lambs say among themselves "these birds of prey are evil; and whoever is as little as possible a bird of prey but rather its opposite, a lamb,—isn't he good?" there is nothing to criticize in this setting up of an ideal, even if the birds of prey should look on this a little mockingly and perhaps say to themselves: "*we* do not feel any anger towards them, these good lambs, as a matter of fact, we love them: nothing is more tasty than a tender lamb."—To demand of strength that it *not* express itself as strength, that it *not* be a desire to overwhelm, a desire to cast down, a desire to become lord, a thirst for enemies and resistances and triumphs, is just as nonsensical as to demand of weakness that it express itself as strength. A quantum of power is just such a quantum of drive, will, effect— more precisely, it is nothing other than this very driving, willing, effecting, and only through the seduction of language (and the basic errors of reason petrified therein), which understands and misunderstands all effecting as conditioned by an effecting something, by a "subject," can it appear otherwise. For just as common people separate the lightning from its flash and take the latter as a *doing*, as an effect of a subject called lightning, so popular morality also separates strength from the expressions of strength as if there were behind the strong an indifferent substratum that is free to express strength—or not to. But there is no such substratum; there is no "being" behind the doing, effecting, becoming; "the doer" is simply fabricated into the doing—the doing is everything. Common people basically double the doing when they have the lightning flash; this is a doing-doing: the same happening is posited first as cause and then once again as its effect. Natural scientists do no better when they say "force moves, force causes," and so on—our entire science, despite all its coolness, its freedom from affect, still stands under the seduction of language and has not gotten rid of the changelings slipped over on it, the "subjects" (the atom, for example, is such a changeling, likewise the Kantian "thing in itself "): small wonder if the suppressed, hiddenly glowing affects of revenge and hate exploit this belief and basically even uphold no other belief more ardently than this one, that *the strong one is free* to be weak, and the bird of prey to be a lamb: — they thereby gain for themselves the right to hold the bird of prey *accountable* for being a bird of prey . . . When out of the vengeful cunning of powerlessness the oppressed, downtrodden, violated say to themselves: "let us be different from the evil ones, namely good! And good is what everyone is who does not do violence, who injures no one, who doesn't attack, who doesn't retaliate, who leaves vengeance to God, who keeps himself concealed, as we do, who avoids all evil, and in general demands very little of life, like us, the patient, humble, righteous" — it means, when listened to coldly and without prejudice, actually nothing more than: "we weak ones are simply weak; it is good if we do nothing *for which we are not strong enough*" — but this harsh matter of fact, this prudence of the lowest order, which even insects have (presumably playing dead when in great danger in order not to do "too much"), has, thanks to that counterfeiting and self-deception of powerlessness, clothed itself in the pomp of renouncing, quiet, patiently waiting virtue, as if the very weakness of the weak — that is to say, his *essence*, his effecting, his whole unique, unavoidable, undetachable reality — were a voluntary achievement, something willed, something chosen, a *deed*, a *merit*. This kind of human *needs* the belief in a neutral "subject" with free choice, out of an instinct of self-preservation, self-affirmation, in which every lie tends to hallow itself. It is perhaps for this reason that the subject (or, to speak more popularly, the *soul*) has until now been the best article of faith on earth, because it made possible for the majority of mortals, the weak and oppressed of every kind, that sublime self-deception of interpreting weakness itself as freedom, of interpreting their being-such-and-such as a *merit*.

14

Would anyone like to go down and take a little look into the secret of how they *fabricate ideals* on earth? Who has the courage to do so? . . . Well then! The view into these dark workplaces is unobstructed here. Wait just a moment, Mr. Wanton-Curiosity and Daredevil: your eyes must first get used to this falsely shimmering light . . . So! Enough! Now speak! What's going on down there? Tell me what you see, man of

the most dangerous curiosity — now *I* am the one listening. —

— "I don't see anything, but I hear all the more. There is a cautious malicious quiet whispering and muttering-together out of all corners and nooks. It seems to me that they are lying; a sugary mildness sticks to each sound. Weakness is to be lied into a *merit*, there is no doubt about it — it is just as you said." —

— Go on!

— "and the powerlessness that does not retaliate into kindness; fearful baseness into 'humility'; subjection to those whom one hates into 'obedience' (namely to one whom they say orders this subjection — they call him God). The inoffensiveness of the weak one, cowardice itself, which he possesses in abundance, his standing-at-the-door, his unavoidable having-to-wait, acquires good names here, such as 'patience,' it is even called virtue *itself*; not being able to avenge oneself is called not wanting to avenge oneself, perhaps even forgiveness ('for *they* know not what they do — we alone know what *they* do!'). They also talk of 'love of one's enemies' — and sweat while doing so."

— Go on!

— "They are miserable, there is no doubt, all of these whisperers and nook-and-cranny counterfeiters, even if they are crouching together warmly — but they tell me that their misery is a distinction and election from God, that one beats the dogs one loves the most; perhaps this misery is also a preparation, a test, a schooling, perhaps it is still more — something for which there will one day be retribution, paid out with enormous interest in gold, no! in happiness. This they call 'blessedness.'"

— Go on!

— "Now they are giving me to understand that they are not only better than the powerful, the lords of the earth, whose saliva they must lick (*not* out of fear, not at all out of fear! but rather because God commands that they honor all authority) — that they are not only better, but that they are also 'better off,' at least will be better off one day. But enough! enough! I can't stand it anymore. Bad air! Bad air! This workplace where they *fabricate ideals* — it seems to me it stinks of sheer lies."

— No! A moment more! You haven't said anything

about the masterpiece of these artists of black magic who produce white, milk, and innocence out of every black:—haven't you noticed what the height of their sophistication is, their boldest, finest, most ingenious, most mendacious artistic stroke? Pay attention! These cellar animals full of revenge and hate—what is it they make precisely out of this revenge and hate? Did you ever hear these words? Would you guess, if you trusted their words alone, that those around you are all humans of *ressentiment*? . . .

—"I understand, I'll open my ears once again (oh! oh! oh! and *close* my nose). Now for the first time I hear what they have said so often: 'We good ones— we *are the just*'—what they demand they call not retaliation but rather 'the triumph of *justice*'; what they hate is not their enemy, no! they hate '*injustice*,' 'ungodliness'; what they believe and hope for is not the hope for revenge, the drunkenness of sweet revenge (—already Homer called it 'sweeter than honey'), but rather the victory of God, of the *just* God over the ungodly; what is left on earth for them to love are not their brothers in hate but rather their 'brothers in love,' as they say, all the good and just on earth."

—And what do they call that which serves them as comfort against all the sufferings of life—their phantasmagoria of the anticipated future blessedness?

—"What? Did I hear right? They call that 'the last judgment,' the coming of *their* kingdom, of the 'kingdom of God'—*meanwhile*, however, they live 'in faith,' 'in love,' 'in hope.'"

—Enough! Enough!

15

In faith in what? In love of what? In hope of what? These weak ones—someday *they* too want to be the strong ones, there is no doubt, someday *their* "kingdom" too shall come—among them it is called "the kingdom of God" pure and simple, as was noted: they are of course so humble in all things! Even to experience *that* they need to live long, beyond death—indeed they need eternal life so that in the 'kingdom of God' they can also recover eternally the losses incurred during that earth-life "in faith, in love, in hope." Recover their losses for what? Recover their losses through what? . . . It was a gross blunder on

Dante's part, it seems to me, when, with terror-instilling ingenuousness, he placed over the gate to his hell the inscription "I, too, was created by eternal love":—in any case, over the gate of the Christian paradise and its "eternal blessedness" there would be better justification for allowing the inscription to stand "I, too, was created by eternal *hate*"—assuming that a truth may stand above the gate to a lie! For *what* is the blessedness of that paradise? . . . We would perhaps guess it already; but it is better that it is expressly documented for us by an authority not to be underestimated in such matters, Thomas Aquinas,[40] the great teacher and saint. "*Beati in regno coelestia,*" he says meekly as a lamb, "*videbunt poenas damnatorum, ut beatitudo illis magis complaceat.*"[41] Or would you like to hear it in a stronger key, for instance from the mouth of a triumphant church father[42] who counseled his Christians against the cruel pleasures of the public spectacles—and why? "Faith offers us much more,"—he says, *De spectac. c.* 29 ss.—"*something much stronger*; thanks to salvation there are entirely different joys at our disposal; in place of the athletes we have our martyrs; if we desire blood, well, we have the blood of Christ . . . But what awaits us above all on the day of his return, of his triumph!"—and now he continues, the enraptured visionary: "*At enim supersunt alia spectacula, ille ultimus et perpetuus judicii dies, ille nationibus insperatus, ille derisus, cum tanta saeculi vetustas et tot ejus nativitates uno igne haurientur. Quae tunc spectaculi latitudo! Quid admirer! Quid rideam! Ubi gaudeam! Ubi exultem, spectans tot et tantos reges, qui in coelum recepti nuntiabantur, cum ipso Jove et ipsis suis testibus in imis tenebris congemescentes! Item praesides* (the provincial governor) *persecutores dominici nominis*

---

40. [Thomas Aquinas (1225–1274), Christian theologian and philosopher, canonized by Pope John XXII in 1323 and declared a Doctor of the Church by Pope Pius V in 1567.]

41. ["The blessed in the kingdom of heaven will see the punishments of the damned, *in order that their bliss be more delightful to them.*" *Summa Theologica* III *Supplementum* Q. 94, Art. 1.]

42. [Tertullian (ca. 155–after 220), important early Christian theologian, polemicist, and moralist from Carthage in North Africa.]

16

Let us conclude. The two *opposed* values 'good and bad,' 'good and evil,' have fought a terrible millennia-long battle on earth; and as certainly as the second value has had the upper hand for a long time, even so there is still no shortage of places where the battle goes on, undecided. One could even say that it has

---

*saevioribus quam ipsi flammis saevierunt insultantibus contra Christianos liquescentes! Quos praeterea sapientes illos philosophos coram discipulis suis una conflagrantibus erubescentes, quibus nihil ad deum pertinere suadebant, quibus animas aut nullas aut non in pristina corpora redituras affirmabant! Etiam poëtàs non ad Rhadamanti nec ad Minois, sed ad inopinati Christi tribunal palpitantes! Tunc magis tragoedi audiendi, magis scilicet vocales (in better voice, even more awful screamers) in sua propria calamitate; tunc histriones cognoscendi, solutiores multo per ignem; tunc spectandus auriga in flammea rota totus rubens, tunc xystici contemplandi non in gymnasiis, sed in igne jaculati, nisi quod ne tunc quidem illos velim vivos, ut qui malim ad eos potius conspectum **insatiabilem** conferre, qui in dominum desaevierunt. 'Hic est ille, dicam, fabri aut quaestuariae filius* (as everything that follows shows, and in particular this well-known designation from the Talmud for the mother of Jesus, from here on Tertullian means the Jews), *sabbati destructor, Samarites et daemonium habens. Hic est, quem a Juda redemistis, hic est ille arundine et colaphis diverberatus, sputamentis dedecoratus, felle et aceto potatus. Hic est, quem clam discentes subripuerunt, ut resurrexisse dicatur vel hortulanus detraxit, ne lactucae suae frequentia commeantium laederentur.' Ut talia spectes, **ut talibus exultes,** quis tibi praetor aut consul aut quaestor aut sacerdos de sua liberalitate praestabit? Et tamen haec jam habemus quodammodo **per fidem** spiritu imaginante repraesentata. Ceterum qualia illa sunt, quae nec oculus vidit nec auris audivit nec in cor hominis ascenderunt? (1 Cor. 2:9) Credo circo et utraque cavea* (first and fourth tiers, or, according to others, comic and tragic stages) *et omni stadio gratiora."*[43] — **Per fidem:**[44] thus it is written.

flames fiercer than those with which they themselves raged against the Christians! What wise men besides, those very philosophers reddening before their disciples as they blaze together, the disciples to whom they suggested that nothing was of any concern to God; to whom they asserted that our souls are either nothing or they will not return to their former bodies! And also the poets, trembling before the judgment seat, not of Rhadamanthys or Minos but of the Christ, whom they did not expect! Then the great tragedians will be heard, in great voice, no doubt *(in better voice, even more awful screamers),* in their own calamities; then the actors will be recognized, made a great deal more limber by the fire; then the charioteer will be seen, all red on a flaming wheel; then the athletes will be observed, not in their gymnasiums but cast in the fire—were it not for the fact that not even then would I wish to see them since I would much rather bestow my *insatiable* gaze on those who raged against the Lord. 'This is he,' I shall say, 'the son of the carpenter or the prostitute *(as everything that follows shows, and in particular also this well-known designation from the Talmud for the mother of Jesus, from here on Tertullian means the Jews),* the Sabbath-breaker, the Samaritan, the one possessed of a devil. This is he whom you bought from Judas, this is the one struck by reed and fist, defiled by spit, given gall and vinegar to drink. This is he whom the disciples secretly stole away that it might be said he had risen, or perhaps the gardener dragged him away so that his lettuce would not be damaged by the crowd of those coming and going.' That you may see such things, *that you may exult in such things*—what praetor or consul or quaestor or priest will, out of his generosity, see to this? And yet even now we have them in a way, *by faith,* represented through the imagining spirit. On the other hand, what are those things which eye hath not seen nor ear heard, nor have ever entered into the heart of man? *(1 Cor. 2:9)* I believe they are more pleasing than circus and both theaters *(first and fourth tiers, or, according to others, comic and tragic stages)* and any stadium."]

43. ["But indeed there are still other sights, that last and eternal day of judgment, that day unlooked for by the nations, that day they laughed at, when the world so great with age and all its generations shall be consumed by one fire. What variety of sights then! *What should I admire! What should I laugh at! In which should I feel joy! In which should I exult,* seeing so many and great *kings* who were reported to have been received into heaven, now groaning in deepest darkness with Jove himself and those who testified of their reception into heaven! Likewise the praesides *(the provincial governor),* persecutors of the name of the Lord, being liquefied by

44. [By (my) faith.]

in the meantime been borne up ever higher and precisely thereby become ever deeper, ever more spiritual: so that today there is perhaps no more decisive mark of the *"higher nature,"* of the more spiritual nature, than to be conflicted in that sense and still a real battleground for those opposites. The symbol of this battle, written in a script that has so far remained legible across all of human history, is "Rome against Judea, Judea against Rome": — so far there has been no greater event than *this* battle, *this* formulation of the problem, *this* mortally hostile contradiction. Rome sensed in the Jew something like anti-nature itself, its antipodal monstrosity as it were; in Rome the Jew was held to have been *"convicted* of hatred against the entire human race": rightly so, insofar as one has a right to tie the salvation and the future of the human race to the unconditional rule of aristocratic values, of Roman values. What the Jews on the other hand felt towards Rome? One can guess it from a thousand indications; but it will suffice to recall again the Johannine Apocalypse, that most immoderate of all written outbursts that revenge has on its conscience. (Do not underestimate, by the way, the profound consistency of the Christian instinct when it gave precisely this book of hate the name of the disciple of love, the same one to whom it attributed that enamored-rapturous gospel —: therein lies a piece of truth, however much literary counterfeiting may have been needed for this purpose.) The Romans were after all the strong and noble ones, such that none stronger and nobler have ever existed, ever even been dreamt of; everything that remains of them, every inscription thrills, supposing that one can guess *what* is doing the writing there. The Jews, conversely, were that priestly people of *ressentiment* par excellence, in whom there dwelt a popular-moral genius without parallel: just compare the peoples with related talents — for instance the Chinese or the Germans — with the Jews in order to feel what is first and what fifth rank. Which of them has been victorious in the meantime, Rome or Judea? But there is no doubt at all: just consider before whom one bows today in Rome itself as before the quintessence of all the highest values — and not only in Rome, but over almost half the earth, everywhere that man has become tame or wants to become tame, — before *three Jews*, as everyone knows, and *one Jewess* (before Jesus of Nazareth, the fisher Peter, the carpet-weaver Paul, and the mother of the aforementioned Jesus, called Mary). This is very remarkable: Rome has succumbed without any doubt. To be sure, in the Renaissance there was a brilliant-uncanny reawakening of the classical ideal, of the noble manner of valuing all things: Rome itself moved like one awakened from apparent death, under the pressure of the new Judaized Rome built above it, which presented the appearance of an ecumenical synagogue and was called "church": but immediately Judea triumphed again, thanks to that thoroughly mobbish (German and English) *ressentiment* movement called the Reformation, and that which had to follow from it, the restoration of the church — also the restoration of the old sepulchral sleep of classical Rome. In an even more decisive and more profound sense than before, Judea once again achieved a victory over the classical ideal with the French Revolution: the last political nobleness there was in Europe, that of the seventeenth and eighteenth *French* centuries, collapsed under the instincts of popular *ressentiment* — never on earth has a greater jubilation, a noisier enthusiasm been heard! It is true that in the midst of all this the most enormous, most unexpected thing occurred: the classical ideal itself stepped *bodily* and with unheard of splendor before the eyes and conscience of humanity — and once again, more strongly, more simply, more penetratingly than ever, the terrible and thrilling counter-slogan "the *privilege of the few*" resounded in the face of the old lie-slogan of *ressentiment*, "the privilege of the majority," in the face of the will to lowering, to debasement, to leveling, to the downward and evening-ward of man! Like a last sign pointing to the *other* path, Napoleon appeared, that most individual and late-born human being there ever was, and in him the incarnate problem of the *noble ideal in itself* — consider well, *what* kind of problem it is: Napoleon, this synthesis of an *inhuman* and a *superhuman* . . .

17

— Was that the end of it? Was that greatest of all conflicts of ideals thus placed *ad acta*[45] for all time? Or just postponed, postponed for a long time? . . .

45. [Shelved, filed away.]

Won't there have to be a still much more terrible, much more thoroughly prepared flaming up of the old fire someday? Still more: wouldn't precisely *this* be something to desire with all our might? even to will? even to promote? . . . Whoever starts at this point, like my readers, to ponder, to think further, will hardly come to an end any time soon—reason enough for me to come to an end myself, assuming that it has long since become sufficiently clear what I *want*, what I want precisely with that dangerous slogan that is so perfectly tailored to my last book: "*Beyond Good and Evil*" . . . At the very least this does *not* mean "Beyond Good and Bad."—

Note. I take advantage of the opportunity that this treatise gives me to express publicly and formally a wish that until now I have expressed only in occasional conversations with scholars: namely that some philosophical faculty might do a great service for the promotion of *moral-historical* studies through a series of academic essay contests:—perhaps this book will serve to give a forceful impetus in just such a direction. With respect to a possibility of this sort let me suggest the following question: it merits the attention of philologists and historians as much as that of those who are actual scholars of philosophy by profession.

> "*What clues does the study of language, in particular etymological research, provide for the history of the development of moral concepts?*"

—On the other hand it is admittedly just as necessary to win the participation of physiologists and physicians for these problems (of the *value* of previous estimations of value): it may be left to the professional philosophers to act as advocates and mediators in this individual case as well, after they have succeeded in re-shaping in general the relationship between philosophy, physiology, and medicine—originally so standoffish, so mistrustful—into the friendliest and most fruit-bearing exchange. Indeed every value table, every "thou shalt," of which history or ethnological research is aware,

needs *physiological* illumination and interpretation first of all, in any case before the psychological; all of them likewise await a critique on the part of medical science. The question: what is the *value* of this or that value table or "morality"? demands to be raised from the most diverse perspectives; for this "value relative *to what end?*" cannot be analyzed too finely. Something, for example, that clearly had value with regard to the greatest possible longevity of a race (or to a heightening of its powers of adaptation to a specific climate, or to the preservation of the greatest number), would by no means have the same value if it were an issue of developing a stronger type. The welfare of the majority and the welfare of the few are opposing value viewpoints: to hold the former one to be of higher value already *in itself*, this we will leave to the naïveté of English biologists . . . *All* sciences are henceforth to do preparatory work for the philosopher's task of the future: understanding this task such that the philosopher is to solve the *problem of value*, that he is to determine the *order of rank among values*.—

SECOND TREATISE: "GUILT," "BAD CONSCIENCE," AND RELATED MATTERS

1

To breed an animal that *is permitted to promise*—isn't this precisely the paradoxical task nature has set for itself with regard to man? isn't this the true problem *of* man? . . . That this problem has been solved to a high degree must appear all the more amazing to one who can fully appreciate the force working in opposition, that of *forgetfulness*. Forgetfulness is no mere *vis inertiae* as the superficial believe; rather, it is an active and in the strictest sense positive faculty of suppression, and is responsible for the fact that whatever we experience, learn, or take into ourselves enters just as little into our consciousness during the condition of digestion (one might call it "inanimation") as does the entire thousand-fold process through which the nourishing of our body, so-called "incorporation," runs its course. To temporarily close the doors and windows of consciousness; to remain undisturbed by the noise and struggle with which our underworld of subservient organs works for and against each other; a little stillness, a little *tabula rasa* of consciousness so that there is again space for new things, above all for the nobler functions and functionaries, for ruling, foreseeing, predetermining (for our organism is set up oligarchically)—that is the use of this active forgetfulness, a doorkeeper as it were, an upholder of psychic order, of rest, of etiquette: from which one can immediately anticipate the degree to which there could be no happiness, no cheerfulness, no hope, no pride, no *present* without forgetfulness. The human being in whom this suppression apparatus is damaged and stops functioning is comparable to a dyspeptic (and not just comparable—) he can't "process" anything . . . Precisely this necessarily forgetful animal in whom forgetting represents a force, a form of *strong* health, has now bred in itself an opposite faculty, a memory, with whose help forgetfulness is disconnected for certain cases,—namely for those cases where a promise is to be made: it is thus by no means simply a passive no-longer-being-able-to-get-rid-of the impression once it has been inscribed, not simply indigestion from a once-pledged word over which one cannot regain control, but rather an active no-longer-wanting-to-get-rid-of, a willing on and on of something one has once willed, a true *memory of the will*: so that a world of new strange things, circumstances, even acts of the will may be placed without reservation between the original "I want," "I will do," and the actual discharge of the will, its *act*, without this long chain of the will breaking. But how much this presupposes! In order to have this kind of command over the future in advance, man must first have learned to separate the necessary from the accidental occurrence, to think causally, to see and anticipate what is distant as if it were present, to fix with certainty what is end, what is means thereto, in general to be able to reckon, to calculate,—for this, man himself must first of all have become *calculable, regular, necessary*, in his own image of himself as well, in order to be able to vouch for himself *as future*, as one who promises does!

2

Precisely this is the long history of the origins of *responsibility*. As we have already grasped, the task of breeding an animal that is permitted to promise includes, as condition and preparation, the more specific task of first *making* man to a certain degree necessary, uniform, like among like, regular, and accordingly predictable. The enormous work of what I have called "morality of custom" (cf. *Daybreak* 9, 14, 16)—the true work of man on himself for the longest part of the duration of the human race, his entire *prehistoric* work, has in this its meaning, its great justification—however much hardness, tyranny, mindlessness, and idiocy may be inherent in it: with the help of the morality of custom and the social straightjacket man was *made* truly calculable. If, on the other hand, we place ourselves at the end of the enormous process, where the tree finally produces its fruit, where society and its morality of custom finally brings to light that *to which* it was only the means: then we will find as the ripest fruit on its tree the *sovereign individual*, the individual resembling only himself, free again from the morality of custom, autonomous and supermoral (for "autonomous" and "moral" are mutually exclusive), in short, the human being with his own independent long will, the human being who *is permitted to promise*—and in him a proud consciousness, twitching in all his muscles, of *what* has finally been achieved and become flesh in him, a true consciousness of power and freedom, a feeling of the completion of man himself. This being who has become free, who is really *permitted* to promise, this lord of the *free* will, this sovereign—how could he not know what superiority he thus has over all else that is not permitted to promise and vouch for itself, how much trust, how much fear, how much reverence he awakens—he "*earns*" all three—and how this mastery over himself also necessarily brings with it mastery over circumstances, over nature and all lesser-willed and more unreliable creatures? The "free" human being, the possessor of a long, unbreakable will, has in this possession his *standard of value* as well: looking from himself toward the others, he honors or holds in contempt; and just as necessarily as he honors the ones like him, the strong and reliable (those who are *permitted* to promise),—that is, everyone who promises like a sovereign, weightily, seldom, slowly, who is stingy with his trust, who *conveys a mark of distinction* when he trusts, who gives his word as something on which one can rely because he knows himself to be strong enough to uphold it even against accidents, even "against fate"—: just as necessarily he will hold his kick in readiness for the frail dogs who promise although they are not permitted to do so, and his switch for the liar who breaks his word already the moment it leaves his mouth. The proud knowledge of the extraordinary privilege of *responsibility*, the consciousness of this rare freedom, this power over oneself and fate, has sunk into his lowest depth and has become instinct, the dominant instinct:—what will he call it, this dominant instinct, assuming that he feels the need to have a word for it? But there is no doubt: this sovereign human being calls it his *conscience* . . .

3

His conscience? . . . One can guess in advance that the concept "conscience," which we encounter here in its highest, almost disconcerting form, already has behind it a long history and metamorphosis. To be permitted to vouch for oneself, and with pride, hence to be *permitted to say "yes"* to oneself too—that is, as noted, a ripe fruit, but also a *late* fruit:—how long this fruit had to hang on the tree harsh and sour! And for a still much longer time one could see nothing of such a fruit,—no one could have promised it, however certainly everything on the tree was prepared and in the process of growing towards it!—"How does one make a memory for the human animal? How does one impress something onto this partly dull, partly scattered momentary understanding, this forgetfulness in the flesh, so that it remains present?" . . . As one can imagine, the answers and means used to solve this age-old problem were not exactly delicate; there is perhaps nothing more terrible and more uncanny in all of man's prehistory than his *mnemotechnique*. "One burns something in so that it remains in one's memory: only what does not cease *to give pain* remains in one's memory"—that is a first principle from the most ancient (unfortunately also longest) psychology on earth. One might even say that everywhere on earth where there is still solemnity, serious-

ness, secrecy, gloomy colors in the life of man and of a people, something of that terribleness *continues to be felt* with which everywhere on earth one formerly promised, pledged, vowed: the past, the longest deepest hardest past, breathes on us and wells up in us when we become "serious." Whenever man considered it necessary to make a memory for himself it was never done without blood, torment, sacrifice; the most gruesome sacrifices and pledges (to which sacrifices of firstborn belong), the most repulsive mutilations (castrations, for example), the cruelest ritual forms of all religious cults (and all religions are in their deepest foundations systems of cruelties)—all of this has its origin in that instinct that intuited in pain the most powerful aid of mnemonics. In a certain sense the entirety of asceticism belongs here: a few ideas are to be made indelible, omnipresent, unforgettable, "fixed," for the sake of hypnotizing the entire nervous and intellectual system with these "fixed ideas"—and the ascetic procedures and forms of life are means for taking these ideas out of competition with all other ideas in order to make them "unforgettable." The worse humanity was "at memory" the more terrible is the appearance of its practices; the harshness of penal laws in particular provides a measuring stick for the amount of effort it took to achieve victory over forgetfulness and to keep a few primitive requirements of social co-existence *present* for these slaves of momentary affect and desire. We Germans certainly do not regard ourselves as a particularly cruel and hard-hearted people, still less as particularly frivolous or living-for-the-day; but one need only look at our old penal codes to discover what amount of effort it takes to breed a "people of thinkers" on earth (that is to say: *the* people of Europe, among whom one still finds even today the maximum of confidence, seriousness, tastelessness, and matter-of-factness, qualities which give it a right to breed every type of European mandarin). Using terrible means these Germans have made a memory for themselves in order to become master over their mobbish basic instincts and the brutal heavy-handedness of the same: think of the old German punishments, for example of stoning (—even legend has the millstone fall on the head of the guilty one), breaking on the wheel (the most characteristic invention and specialty of German genius in the realm of punishment!), casting stakes, having torn or trampled by horses ("quartering"), boiling the criminal in oil or wine (as late as the fourteenth and fifteenth centuries), the popular flaying (*"Riemenschneiden"*), cutting flesh from the breast; also, no doubt, that the evil-doer was smeared with honey and abandoned to the flies under a burning sun. With the help of such images and processes one finally retains in memory five, six "I will nots," in connection with which one has given one's *promise* in order to live within the advantages of society,—and truly! with the help of this kind of memory one finally came "to reason"!—Ah, reason, seriousness, mastery over the affects, this entire gloomy matter called reflection, all these prerogatives and showpieces of man: how dearly they have been paid for! how much blood and horror there is at the base of all "good things"! . . .

4

But how then did that other "gloomy thing," the consciousness of guilt, the entire "bad conscience" come into the world?—And thus we return to our genealogists of morality. To say it once more—or haven't I said it at all yet?—they aren't good for anything. Their own five-span-long, merely "modern" experience; no knowledge, no will to knowledge of the past; still less an instinct for history, a "second sight" necessary precisely here—and nonetheless doing history of morality: this must in all fairness end with results that stand in a relation to truth that is not even flirtatious. Have these previous genealogists of morality even remotely dreamt, for example, that that central moral concept "guilt" had its origins in the very material concept "debt"? Or that punishment as *retribution* developed completely apart from any presupposition concerning freedom or lack of freedom of the will?—and to such a degree that in fact a *high* level of humanization is always necessary before the animal "man" can begin to make those much more primitive distinctions "intentional," "negligent," "accidental," "accountable," and their opposites, and to take them into account when measuring out punishment. The thought, now so cheap and apparently so natural, so unavoidable, a thought that has even had to serve as an explanation of how the feeling of justice came into being at all on earth—"the criminal has earned his punishment *because* he could have

acted otherwise"—is in fact a sophisticated form of human judging and inferring that was attained extremely late; whoever shifts it to the beginnings lays a hand on the psychology of older humanity in a particularly crude manner. Throughout the greatest part of human history punishment was definitely *not* imposed *because* one held the evil-doer responsible for his deed, that is, *not* under the presupposition that only the guilty one is to be punished:—rather, as parents even today punish their children, from anger over an injury suffered, which is vented on the agent of the injury—anger held within bounds, however, and modified through the idea that every injury has its *equivalent* in something and can really be paid off, even if only through the *pain* of its agent. Whence has this age-old, deeply-rooted, perhaps now no longer eradicable idea taken its power—the idea of an equivalence between injury and pain? I have already given it away: in the contractual relationship between *creditor* and *debtor*, which is as old as the existence of "legal subjects" and in turn points back to the basic forms of purchase, sale, exchange, trade, and commerce.

5

Calling to mind these contract relationships admittedly awakens various kinds of suspicion and resistance toward the earlier humanity that created or permitted them, as is, after the preceding remarks, to be expected from the outset. Precisely here there are *promises* made; precisely here it is a matter of *making* a memory for the one who promises; precisely here, one may suspect, will be a place where one finds things that are hard, cruel, embarrassing. In order to instill trust in his promise of repayment, to provide a guarantee for the seriousness and the sacredness of his promise, to impress repayment on his conscience as a duty, as an obligation, the debtor—by virtue of a contract—pledges to the creditor in the case of non-payment something else that he "possesses," over which he still has power, for example his body or his wife or his freedom or even his life (or, under certain religious conditions, even his blessedness, the salvation of his soul, finally even his peace in the grave: as in Egypt where the corpse of the debtor found no rest from the creditor, even in the grave—and indeed there was something to this rest, precisely among the

Egyptians.) Above all, however, the creditor could subject the body of the debtor to all manner of ignominy and torture, for example cutting as much from it as appeared commensurate to the magnitude of the debt:—and everywhere and early on there were exact assessments of value developed from this viewpoint—some going horribly into the smallest detail—*legally* established assessments of the individual limbs and areas on the body. I take it already as progress, as proof of a freer, more grandly calculating, *more Roman* conception of the law when the Twelve Tables legislation of Rome decreed it was of no consequence how much or how little the creditors cut off in such a case, *"si plus minusve secuerunt, ne fraude esto."*[46] Let us make clear to ourselves the logic of this whole form of compensation: it is foreign enough. The equivalence consists in this: that in place of an advantage that directly makes good for the injury (hence in place of a compensation in money, land, possession of any kind) the creditor is granted a certain *feeling of satisfaction* as repayment and compensation,—the feeling of satisfaction that comes from being permitted to vent his power without a second thought on one who is powerless, the carnal delight *"de faire le mal pour le plaisir de le faire,"*[47] the enjoyment of doing violence: which enjoyment is valued all the higher the lower and baser the creditor's standing in the social order and can easily appear to him as a most delectable morsel, indeed as a foretaste of a higher status. Through his "punishment" of the debtor the creditor participates in a *right of lords*: finally he, too, for once attains the elevating feeling of being permitted to hold a being in contempt and maltreat it as something "beneath himself"—or at least, if the actual power of punishment, the execution of punishment has already passed over into the hands of the "authorities," of *seeing* it held in contempt and maltreated. The compensation thus consists in a directive and right to cruelty.—

6

In *this* sphere, in contract law that is, the moral conceptual world "guilt," "conscience," "duty," "sacred-

ness of duty" has its genesis—its beginning, like the beginning of everything great on earth, was thoroughly and prolongedly drenched in blood. And might one not add that this world has in essence never again entirely lost a certain odor of blood and torture? (not even in old Kant: the categorical imperative smells of cruelty . . .) It was likewise here that that uncanny and perhaps now inextricable meshing of ideas, "guilt and suffering," was first knitted. Asking once again: to what extent can suffering be a compensation for "debts"? To the extent that *making*-suffer felt good, and in the highest degree; to the extent that the injured one exchanged for what was lost, including the displeasure over the loss, an extraordinary counter-pleasure: *making*-suffer,—a true *festival*, something that, as stated, stood that much higher in price, the more it contradicted the rank and social standing of the creditor. This stated as conjecture: for it is difficult to see to the bottom of such subterranean things, not to mention that it is embarrassing; and whoever clumsily throws the concept of "revenge" into the middle of it all has covered and obscured his insight into the matter rather than making it easier (—revenge simply leads back to the same problem: "how can making-suffer be a satisfaction?). It seems to me that it is repugnant to the delicacy, even more to the Tartuffery of tame domestic animals (which is to say modern humans, which is to say us) to imagine in all its force the degree to which *cruelty* constitutes the great festival joy of earlier humanity, indeed is an ingredient mixed in with almost all of their joys; how naïvely, on the other hand, how innocently its need for cruelty manifests itself, how universally they rank precisely "disinterested malice" (or, to speak with Spinoza, *sympathia malevolens*)[48] as a *normal* quality of man—: thus as something to which the conscience heartily says *"yes"*! Perhaps even today there is enough of this oldest and most pervasive festival joy of man for a more profound eye to perceive; in *Beyond Good and Evil* 229 (even earlier in *Daybreak* 18, 77, 113), I pointed with a cautious finger to the ever-growing spiritualization and "deification" of cruelty that runs though the entire history of higher culture (and in a significant sense even constitutes it). In any case it

46. [If they have secured more or less, let that be no crime.]

47. [To do evil for the pleasure of doing it.]

48. [Ill-willing sympathy.]

has not been all that long since one could not imagine royal marriages and folk festivals in the grandest style without executions, torturings, or perhaps an *auto-da-fé,* likewise no noble household without beings on whom one could vent one's malice and cruel teasing without a second thought (—think for example of Don Quixote at the court of the Duchess: today we read the entire *Don Quixote* with a bitter taste on our tongue, almost with anguish, and would as a result appear very strange, very puzzling to its author and his contemporaries—they read it with the very clearest conscience as the most lighthearted of books, they practically laughed themselves to death over it). Seeing-suffer feels good, making-suffer even more so—that is a hard proposition, but a central one, an old powerful human-all-too-human proposition, to which, by the way, even the apes might subscribe: for it is said that in thinking up bizarre cruelties they already abundantly herald and, as it were, "prelude" man. Without cruelty, no festival: thus teaches the oldest, longest part of man's history—and in punishment too there is so much that is *festive*!—

7

—With these thoughts, incidentally, it is by no means my intent to help our pessimists to new grist for their discordant and creaking mills of life-weariness; on the contrary they are meant expressly to show that back then, when humanity was not yet ashamed of its cruelty, life on earth was more lighthearted than it is now that there are pessimists. The darkening of the heavens over man has always increased proportionally as man has grown ashamed *of man.* The tired pessimistic glance, the mistrust toward the riddle of life, the icy "no" of disgust at life—these are not the distinguishing marks of the *most evil* ages of the human race: rather, being the swamp plants they are, they first enter the light of day when the swamp to which they belong appears,—I mean the diseased softening and moralization by virtue of which the creature "man" finally learns to be ashamed of all of his instincts. Along the way to "angel" (to avoid using a harsher word here) man has bred for himself that upset stomach and coated tongue through which not only have the joy and innocence of the animal become repulsive but life itself has become unsavory:—

so that he at times stands before himself holding his nose and, along with Pope Innocent the Third, disapprovingly catalogues his repulsive traits ("impure begetting, disgusting nourishment in the womb, vileness of the matter out of which man develops, revolting stench, excretion of saliva, urine, and feces"). Now, when suffering is always marshalled forth as the first among the arguments *against* existence, as its nastiest question mark, one would do well to remember the times when one made the reverse judgment because one did not wish to do without *making*-suffer and saw in it an enchantment of the first rank, an actual seductive lure *to* life. Perhaps back then—to the comfort of delicate souls—pain didn't yet hurt as much as it does today; at least such a conclusion will be permissible for a physician who has treated Negroes (taken as representatives of prehistorical man—) for cases of serious internal infection that would almost drive even the best constituted European to despair;—in Negroes they do *not* do this. (Indeed the curve of human capacity for feeling pain appears to sink extraordinarily and almost abruptly as soon as one gets beyond the upper ten thousand or ten million of the highest level of culture; and I, for my part, do not doubt that when held up against one painful night of a single hysterical educated female the combined suffering of all the animals thus far questioned with the knife to obtain scientific answers simply isn't worth considering.) Perhaps one may even be allowed to admit the possibility that this pleasure in cruelty needn't actually have died out: but, in the same proportion as the pain hurts more today, it would need a certain sublimation and subtilization, namely it would have to appear translated into the imaginative and inward, adorned with all kinds of names so harmless that they arouse no suspicion, not even in the most delicate, most hypocritical conscience ("tragic pity" is such a name; another is *"les nostalgies de la croix"*).[49] What actually arouses indignation against suffering is not suffering in itself, but rather the senselessness of suffering; but neither for the Christian, who has interpreted into suffering an entire secret salvation machinery, nor for the naive human of older times, who knew how to interpret all suffering in

49. [The nostalgias of the cross.]

terms of spectators or agents of suffering, was there any such *meaningless* suffering at all. So that concealed, undiscovered, unwitnessed suffering could be banished from the world and honestly negated, one was almost compelled back then to invent gods and intermediate beings of all heights and depths, in short, something that also roams in secret, that also sees in the dark, and that does not easily let an interesting painful spectacle escape it. For with the help of such inventions life back then was expert at the trick at which it has always been expert, of justifying itself, of justifying its "evil"; today it would perhaps need other auxiliary inventions for this (for example life as riddle, life as epistemological problem). "Every evil is justified, the sight of which edifies a god": thus went the prehistoric logic of feeling—and, really, was it only the prehistoric? The gods, conceived of as friends of *cruel* spectacles—oh how far this age-old conception extends even into our humanized Europe! on this point one may consult with Calvin[50] and Luther[51] for instance. It is certain in any case that the *Greeks* still knew of no more pleasant offering with which to garnish the happiness of their gods than the joys of cruelty. With what sort of eyes then do you think Homer had his gods look down on the fates of humans? What was the ultimate meaning of Trojan wars and similar tragic horrors? There can be no doubt at all: they were meant as *festival games* for the gods: and, insofar as the poet is in this respect more "godlike" than other humans, probably also as festival games for the poets . . . The moral philosophers of Greece later imagined the eyes of the gods no differently, still glancing down at the moral struggle, at the heroism and the self-torture of the virtuous: the "Heracles of duty" was on a stage, he also knew he was on it; virtue without witnesses was something entirely inconceivable for this people of spectacles. Wasn't that philosophers' invention, so audacious, so fateful, which was first devised for Europe back then—that of "free will," of the absolute spontaneity of man in good and evil—devised above all in order to create a right to the idea that the interest of the

gods in man, in human virtue, *could never be exhausted*? On this stage, the earth, there would never be a shortage of truly new things, of truly unheard-of tensions, complications, catastrophes: a world conceived as completely deterministic would have been predictable for the gods and accordingly soon tiring—reason enough for these *friends of the gods*, the philosophers, not to expect their gods to be able to deal with such a deterministic world! In antiquity all of humanity is full of tender considerations for "the spectator," as an essentially public, essentially visible world that could not imagine happiness without spectacles and festivals.—And, as already mentioned, in great *punishment* too there is so much that is festive! . . .

8

The feeling of guilt, of personal obligation—to take up the train of our investigation again—had its origin, as we have seen, in the oldest and most primitive relationship among persons there is, in the relationship between buyer and seller, creditor and debtor: here for the first time person stepped up against person, here for the first time a person *measured himself* by another person. No degree of civilization however low has yet been discovered in which something of this relationship was not already noticeable. Making prices, gauging values, thinking out equivalents, exchanging—this preoccupied man's very first thinking to such an extent that it is in a certain sense thinking *itself*: here that oldest kind of acumen was bred, here likewise we may suspect the first beginnings of human pride, man's feeling of pre-eminence with respect to other creatures. Perhaps our word "man" (*manas*)[52] still expresses precisely something of this self-esteem: man designated himself as the being who measures values, who values and measures, as the "appraising animal in itself." Purchase and sale, together with their psychological accessories, are older than even the beginnings of any societal associations and organizational forms: it was out of the most rudimentary form of personal legal rights that the budding feeling of exchange, contract, guilt, right, obligation,

---

50. [John Calvin (1509–1564) Protestant Reformer and theologian.]

51. [Martin Luther (1483–1546), instigator of the 16th century Reformation and of Protestantism.]

52. [Sanskrit: mind; understanding or the conscious will.]

compensation first *transferred* itself onto the coarsest and earliest communal complexes (in their relationship to similar complexes), together with the habit of comparing, measuring, and calculating power against power. The eye was simply set to this perspective: and with that clumsy consistency characteristic of earlier humanity's thinking—which has difficulty moving but then continues relentlessly in the same direction—one arrived straightaway at the grand generalization "every thing has its price; *everything* can be paid off"—at the oldest and most naive moral canon of *justice*, at the beginning of all "good-naturedness," all "fairness," all "good will," all "objectivity" on earth. Justice at this first stage is the good will among parties of approximately equal power to come to terms with one another, to reach an "understanding" again by means of a settlement—and in regard to less powerful parties, to *force* them to a settlement among themselves.—

9

Always measured by the standard of an earlier time (which earlier time is, by the way, at all times present or again possible): the community, too, thus stands to its members in that important basic relationship, that of the creditor to his debtor. One lives in a community, one enjoys the advantages of a community (oh what advantages! we sometimes underestimate this today), one lives protected, shielded, in peace and trust, free from care with regard to certain injuries and hostilities to which the human *outside*, the "outlaw," is exposed—a German understands what "Elend," *êlend*[53] originally means—, since one has pledged and obligated oneself to the community precisely in view of these injuries and hostilities. What happens *in the other case*? The community, the deceived creditor, will exact payment as best it can, one can count on that. Here it is least of all a matter of the direct injury inflicted by the injuring party; quite apart from this, the criminal is above all a "breaker," one who breaks his contract and word *with the whole*,

in relation to all goods and conveniences of communal life in which he has until this point had a share. The criminal is a debtor who not only fails to pay back the advantages and advances rendered him, but also even lays a hand on his creditor: he therefore not only forfeits all of these goods and advantages from now on, as is fair,—he is also now reminded *how much there is to these goods*. The anger of the injured creditor, of the community, gives him back again to the wild and outlawed condition from which he was previously protected: it expels him from itself,—and now every kind of hostility may vent itself on him. At this level of civilization "punishment" is simply the copy, the *mimus* of normal behavior toward the hated, disarmed, defeated enemy, who has forfeited not only every right and protection, but also every mercy; in other words, the law of war and the victory celebration of *vae victis!*[54] in all their ruthlessness and cruelty:—which explains why war itself (including the warlike cult of sacrifice) has supplied all the *forms* in which punishment appears in history.

10

As its power grows, a community no longer takes the transgressions of the individual so seriously because they can no longer count as dangerous and subversive for the continued existence of the whole to the same extent as formerly: the evildoer is no longer "made an outlaw" and cast out; the general anger is no longer allowed to vent itself in the same unbridled manner as formerly—rather, from now on, the evildoer is carefully defended against this anger, particularly that of the ones directly injured, and taken under the protection of the whole. Compromise with the anger of the one immediately affected by the misdeed; a striving to localize the case and prevent a further or indeed general participation and unrest; attempts to find equivalents and to settle the entire affair (the *compositio*);[55] above all the increasingly more resolute will to understand every offense as in some sense *capable of being paid off*, hence, at least to a certain

---

53. [The New High German *Elend* (misery) derives from the Old High German adjective *elilenti* (in another land or country; banished) via the shortened Middle High German *ellende* or *êlend* (foreign, miserable).]

54. [Woe to the conquered! Livy, *Ab urbe condita*, Book V, 48, 9.]

55. [Term from Roman law referring to the settlement in a case of injury or damage caused by an illegal act.]

extent, to *isolate* the criminal and his deed from each other—these are the traits that are imprinted with increasing clarity onto the further development of penal law. If the power and the self-confidence of a community grow, the penal law also always becomes milder; every weakening and deeper endangering of the former brings the latter's harsher forms to light again. The "creditor" has always become more humane to the degree that he has become richer; finally the amount of injury he can bear without suffering from it even becomes the *measure* of his wealth. It would not be impossible to imagine a *consciousness of power* in society such that society might allow itself the noblest luxury there is for it—to leave the one who injures it *unpunished*. "What concern are my parasites to me?" it might then say. "Let them live and prosper: I am strong enough for that!" . . . The justice that began with "everything can be paid off, everything must be paid off," ends by looking the other way and letting the one unable to pay go free,— it ends like every good thing on earth, by *cancelling itself*. This self-cancellation of justice: we know what pretty name it gives itself—*mercy*; as goes without saying, it remains the privilege of the most powerful, better still, his beyond-the-law.

11

—Here a word in opposition to recent attempts to seek the origin of justice on an entirely different ground,—namely that of *ressentiment*. First, for the ears of psychologists, supposing they should have the desire to study *ressentiment* itself up close for once: this plant now blooms most beautifully among anarchists and anti-Semites—in secret, incidentally, as it has always bloomed, like the violet, albeit with a different scent. And as like must necessarily always proceed from like, so it will not surprise us to see proceeding again from just such circles attempts like those often made before—compare above, section 14—to hallow *revenge* under the name of *justice*— as if justice were basically only a further development of the feeling of being wounded—and retroactively to raise to honor along with revenge the *reactive* affects in general and without exception. At the latter I would least take offense: with respect to the entire biological problem (in relation to which the value of these affects

has thus far been underestimated) it would even appear to me to be a *merit*. I call attention only to the circumstance that it is from the spirit of *ressentiment* itself that this new nuance of scientific fairness (in favor of hate, envy, ill will, suspicion, rancor, revenge) grows forth. For this "scientific fairness" immediately shuts down and makes room for accents of mortal hostility and prejudice as soon as it is a matter of another group of affects that are, it seems to me, of still much higher biological value than those reactive ones, and accordingly deserve all the more to be *scientifically* appraised and esteemed: namely the truly *active* affects like desire to rule, greed, and the like. (E. Dühring,[56] *Value of Life*; *Course in Philosophy*; basically everywhere.) So much against this tendency in general: as for Dühring's particular proposition that the homeland of justice is to be sought on the ground of reactive feeling, one must, for love of the truth, pit against it in stark reversal this alternative proposition: the *last* ground conquered by the spirit of justice is the ground of reactive feeling! If it really happens that the just man remains just even toward those who injure him (and not merely cold, moderate, distant, indifferent: being just is always a *positive* way of behaving), if the high, clear objectivity—that sees as deeply as it does generously—of the just eye, the *judging* eye, does not cloud even under the assault of personal injury, derision, accusation, well, then that is a piece of perfection and highest mastery on earth—what is more, something one would be prudent not to expect here, in which one in any case should not all too easily *believe*. Even with the most righteous persons it is certain that a small dose of attack, malice, insinuation is, on the average, already enough to chase the blood into their eyes and the fairness *out*. The active, the attacking, encroaching human is still located a hundred paces nearer to justice than the reactive one; he simply has no need to appraise his object falsely and with prejudice as the reactive human does, must do. Therefore in all ages the aggressive human, as the stronger, more

56. [Eugen Karl Dühring (1833–1921). Philosopher and political economist. In his autobiography (1882) he claims to have been the founder of anti-Semitism, and he was a major figure in the anti-Semitic movement in Germany.]

courageous, more noble one, has in fact also had the *freer* eye, the *better* conscience on his side: conversely one can already guess who actually has the invention of the "bad conscience" on his conscience,—the human being of *ressentiment*! Finally, just look around in history: in which sphere has the entire administration of justice, also the true need for justice, thus far been at home on earth? Perhaps in the sphere of the reactive human? Absolutely *not*: rather in that of the active, strong, spontaneous, aggressive. Considered historically, justice on earth represents—let it be said to the annoyance of the above-named agitator (who himself once confessed: "the doctrine of revenge runs through all my works and efforts as the red thread of justice")—precisely the battle *against* reactive feelings, the war against them on the part of active and aggressive powers that have used their strength in part to call a halt to and impose measure on the excess of reactive pathos and to force a settlement. Everywhere justice is practiced and upheld one sees a stronger power seeking means to put an end to the senseless raging of *ressentiment* among weaker parties subordinated to it (whether groups or individuals), in part by pulling the object of *ressentiment* out of the hands of revenge, in part by setting in the place of revenge the battle against the enemies of peace and order, in part by inventing, suggesting, in some cases imposing compensations, in part by raising certain equivalents for injuries to the status of a norm to which *ressentiment* is henceforth once and for all restricted. But the most decisive thing the highest power does and forces through against the predominance of counter- and after-feelings—which it always does as soon as it is in any way strong enough to do so—is the establishment of the *law*, the imperative declaration of what in general is to count in its eyes as permitted, as just, what as forbidden, as unjust: after it has established the law, it treats infringements and arbitrary actions of individuals or entire groups as wanton acts against the law, as rebellion against the highest power itself, thereby diverting the feeling of its subjects away from the most immediate injury caused by such wanton acts and thus achieving in the long run the opposite of what all revenge wants, which sees only the viewpoint of the injured one, allows only it to count— from now on the eye is trained for an ever *more impersonal* appraisal of deeds, even the eye of the injured one himself (although this last of all, as was mentioned at the start). Accordingly, only once the law has been established do "justice" and "injustice" exist (and *not* as Dühring would have it, beginning with the act of injuring). To talk of justice and injustice *in themselves* is devoid of all sense; *in itself* injuring, doing violence, pillaging, destroying naturally cannot be "unjust," insofar as life acts *essentially*— that is, in its basic functions—in an injuring, violating, pillaging, destroying manner and cannot be *thought* at all without this character. One must even admit to oneself something still more problematic: that, from the highest biological standpoint, conditions of justice can never be anything but *exceptional conditions*, as partial restrictions of the true will of life—which is out after power—and subordinating themselves as individual means to its overall end: that is, as means for creating *greater* units of power. A legal system conceived of as sovereign and universal, not as a means in the battle of power complexes, but rather as means *against* all battle generally, say in accordance with Dühring's communist cliché that every will must accept every other will as equal, would be a principle *hostile to life*, a destroyer and dissolver of man, an attempt to kill the future of man, a sign of weariness, a secret pathway to nothingness.

12

Yet a word on the origin and purpose of punishment—two problems that fall out or ought to fall out separately: unfortunately they are usually lumped together. How do the previous genealogists of morality carry on in this case? Naively, as they have always carried on—: they discover some "purpose" or other in punishment, for example revenge or deterrence, then innocently place this purpose at the beginning as *causa fiendi*[57] of punishment, and—are done. The "purpose in law," however, is the last thing that is usable for the history of the genesis of law: on the contrary, for history of every kind there is no more important proposition than that one which is gained with such effort but also really *ought to be* gained,—

---

57. [Cause of the coming into being.]

namely, that the cause of the genesis of a thing and its final usefulness, its actual employment and integration into a system of purposes, lie *toto caelo* apart; that something extant, something that has somehow or other come into being, is again and again interpreted according to new views, monopolized in a new way, transformed and rearranged for a new use by a power superior to it; that all happening in the organic world is an *overpowering, a becoming-lord-over*; and that, in turn, all overpowering and becoming-lord-over is a new interpreting, an arranging by means of which the previous "meaning" and "purpose" must of necessity become obscured or entirely extinguished. However well one has grasped the *utility* of some physiological organ (or of a legal institution, a social custom, a political practice, a form in the arts or in religious cult), one has still not comprehended anything regarding its genesis: as uncomfortable and unpleasant as this may sound to earlier ears,—for from time immemorial one had thought that in comprehending the demonstrable purpose, the usefulness of a thing, a form, an arrangement, one also comprehended the reason for its coming into being—the eye as made to see, the hand as made to grasp. Thus one also imagined punishment as invented for punishing. But all purposes, all utilities, are only *signs* that a will to power has become lord over something less powerful and has stamped its own functional meaning onto it; and in this manner the entire history of a "thing," an organ, a practice can be a continuous sign-chain of ever new interpretations and arrangements, whose causes need not be connected even among themselves—on the contrary, in some cases only accidentally follow and replace one another. The "development" of a thing, a practice, an organ is accordingly least of all its *progressus* toward a goal, still less a logical and shortest *progressus*, reached with the smallest expenditure of energy and cost,—but rather the succession of more or less profound, more or less independent processes of overpowering that play themselves out in it, including the resistances expended each time against these processes, the attempted changes of form for the purpose of defense and reaction, also the results of successful counter-actions. The form is fluid but the "meaning" is even more so . . . Even in the individual organism things are no different: with each essential growth of the whole the "meaning" of the individual organs shifts as well,—in some cases their partial destruction, their reduction in number (for example through destruction of the intermediate members), can be a sign of growing strength and perfection. I wanted to say: even the partial *loss of utility*, atrophying and degenerating, the forfeiture of meaning and purposiveness, in short death, belongs to the conditions of true *progressus*: which always appears in the form of a will and way to *greater power* and is always pushed through at the expense of numerous smaller powers. The magnitude of a "progress" is even *measured* by the mass of all that had to be sacrificed for it; humanity as mass sacrificed for the flourishing of a single *stronger* species of human being—that *would be* progress . . . —I emphasize this main viewpoint of historical methodology all the more because it basically goes against the presently ruling instincts and taste of the times, which would rather learn to live with the absolute randomness, indeed the mechanistic senselessness of all happening than with the theory of a *power-will* playing itself out in all happening. The democratic idiosyncrasy against everything that rules and desires to rule, the modern *misarchism* (to create a bad word for a bad thing) has gradually transformed and disguised itself into something spiritual, most spiritual, to such an extent that today it is already penetrating, is *allowed* to penetrate, step by step into the most rigorous, apparently most objective sciences; indeed it appears to me already to have become lord over the whole of physiology and the doctrine of life—to its detriment, as goes without saying—by removing through sleight of hand one of its basic concepts, that of true *activity*. Under the pressure of that idiosyncrasy one instead places "adaptation" in the foreground, that is to say an activity of second rank, a mere reactivity; indeed life itself is defined as an ever more purposive inner adaptation to external circumstances (Herbert Spencer). In so doing, however, one mistakes the essence of life, its *will to power*; in so doing one overlooks the essential pre-eminence of the spontaneous, attacking, infringing, reinterpreting, reordering, and formative forces, upon whose effect the "adaptation" first follows; in so doing one denies the lordly role of the highest functionaries in the organism itself, in which the will of life appears active and form-giving. One recalls that for which Huxley[58] reproached Spencer—his "administrative nihilism": but it is a matter of *more* than just "administering" . . .

13

—To return to our topic, namely to *punishment*, one must then distinguish in it two sorts of things: first that which is relatively *permanent* in it, the practice, the act, the "drama," a certain strict sequence of procedures; on the other hand that which is *fluid* in it, the meaning, the purpose, the expectation tied to the execution of such procedures. It is presupposed here without further ado, per analogy, according to the main viewpoint of the historical methodology just developed, that the procedure itself will be something older, earlier than its use for punishment, that the latter was first placed into, interpreted into the procedure (which had long existed, but was practiced in another sense)—in short, that things are *not* as our naive genealogists of morality and law have thus far assumed, all of whom thought of the procedure as *invented* for the purpose of punishing, as one once thought of the hand as invented for the purpose of grasping. Now as for that other element in punishment—that which is fluid, its "meaning"—in a very late state of culture (for example in present-day Europe), the concept "punishment" in fact no longer represents a single meaning at all but rather an entire synthesis of "meanings": the previous history of punishment in general, the history of its exploitation for the most diverse purposes, finally crystallizes into a kind of unity that is difficult to dissolve, difficult to analyze and   one must emphasize—is *completely* and utterly *undefinable*. (Today it is impossible to say for sure why we actually punish. all concepts in which an entire process is semiotically summarized elude definition; only that which has no history is definable.) In an earlier stage, by contrast, that synthesis of "meanings" still appears more soluble, also more capable of shifts; one can still perceive in each individual case how the elements of the synthesis change

their valence and rearrange themselves accordingly, so that now this, now that element comes to the fore and dominates at the expense of the remaining ones, indeed in some cases one element (say the purpose of deterrence) seems to cancel out all the rest of the elements. To give at least some idea of how uncertain, how after-the-fact, how accidental "the meaning" of punishment is and how one and the same procedure can be used, interpreted, arranged with respect to fundamentally different intentions: I offer here the schema that offered itself to me on the basis of a relatively small and random body of material. Punishment as rendering-harmless, as prevention of further injury. Punishment as payment to the injured party for the injury, in any form (even in that of a compensating affect). Punishment as isolation of a disturbance of equilibrium in order to prevent a further spreading of the disturbance. Punishment as instilling fear of those who determine and execute the punishment. Punishment as a kind of compensation for the benefits the criminal has enjoyed up to that point (for example when he is made useful as a slave in the mines). Punishment as elimination of a degenerating element (in some cases of an entire branch, as according to Chinese law: thus as a means for preserving the purity of the race or for maintaining a social type). Punishment as festival, namely as mocking and doing violence to a finally defeated enemy. Punishment as making a memory, whether for the one who suffers the punishment—so-called "improvement"—or for the witnesses of the execution. Punishment as payment of an honorarium, stipulated on the part of the power that protects the evil-doer from the excesses of revenge. Punishment as compromise with the natural state of revenge, insofar as the latter is still upheld and claimed as a privilege by powerful clans. Punishment as declaration of war and war-time measure against an enemy of peace, of law, of order, of authority, whom one battles—with the means that war furnishes—as dangerous to the community, as in breach of contract with respect to its presuppositions, as a rebel, traitor, and breaker of the peace.—

58. [T(homas) H(enry) Huxley (1825–1895), English biologist. He was one of Darwin's close associates and perhaps his chief defender in the public debates concerning the theory of evolution.]

14

This list is certainly not complete; obviously punishment is overladen with utilities of all kinds. All the more reason to subtract from it a *supposed* utility that admittedly counts in popular consciousness as its most essential one,—precisely the one in which belief in punishment, teetering today for several reasons, still finds its most forceful support. Punishment is supposed to have the value of awakening in the guilty one the *feeling of guilt*; one seeks in it the true *instrumentum* of that reaction of the soul called "bad conscience," "pang of conscience." But by so doing one lays a hand on reality and on psychology, even for today—and how much more for the longest part of the history of man, his prehistory! Precisely among criminals and prisoners the genuine pang of conscience is something extremely rare; the prisons, the penitentiaries are *not* the breeding places where this species of gnawing worm most loves to flourish:— on this there is agreement among all conscientious observers, who in many cases render a judgment of this sort reluctantly enough and against their most personal wishes. In general, punishment makes hard and cold; it concentrates; it sharpens the feeling of alienation; it strengthens the power of resistance. If it should happen that it breaks the vigor and brings about a pitiful prostration and self-abasement, such a result is surely even less pleasing than the average effect of punishment—which is characterized by a dry gloomy seriousness. But if we think, say, of those millennia *before* the history of man, then one may unhesitatingly judge that it is precisely through punishment that the development of the feeling of guilt has been most forcefully *held back*—at least with respect to the victims on whom the punishing force vented itself. For let us not underestimate the extent to which precisely the sight of the judicial and executive procedures prevents the criminal from feeling his deed, the nature of his action, as *in itself* reprehensible, for he sees the very same kind of actions committed in the service of justice and then approved, committed with a good conscience: thus spying, outwitting, bribery, entrapment, the whole tricky and cunning art of police and prosecutors; moreover— based on principle, without even the excuse of emotion—robbing, overpowering, slandering, taking captive, torturing, murdering as displayed in the various kinds of punishment—all of these thus actions his judges in no way reject and condemn *in themselves*, but rather only in a certain respect and practical

application. The "bad conscience," this most uncanny and interesting plant of our earthly vegetation, did *not* grow on this ground,—indeed, in the consciousness of the ones judging, the ones punishing, there was for the longest time *nothing* expressed that suggested one was dealing with a "guilty one." But rather with an instigator of injury, with an irresponsible piece of fate. And the one himself upon whom the punishment afterwards fell, again like a piece of fate, had no other "inner pain" than he would have had at the sudden occurrence of something unanticipated, of a frightful natural event, of a plummeting, crushing boulder against which one can no longer fight.

15

This once entered Spinoza's consciousness in an ensnaring manner (to the vexation of his interpreters, who really *exert* themselves to misunderstand him at this point, for example Kuno Fischer)[59] when one afternoon, bothered by who knows what kind of memory, he dwelt on the question of what actually remained for him of the famous *morsus conscientiae*[60]—he who had sent good and evil into exile among the human illusions and had fiercely defended the honor of his "free" God against those blasphemers who claimed something to the effect that God works everything *sub ratione boni*[61] ("that, however, would be to subject God to fate and would in truth be the greatest of all absurdities"—). For Spinoza the world had stepped back again into that innocence in which it had lain before the invention of the bad conscience: what had become of the *morsus conscientiae* in the process? "The opposite of *gaudium*,"[62] he finally said to himself,—"a sadness, accompanied by the image of a past matter that has turned out in a manner contrary to all expectation." Eth. III propos. XVIII schol. I. II. For thousands of years instigators of evil

59. [Kuno Fischer (1824–1907), professor of philosophy at Heidelberg, author of the ten-volume *Geschichte der neuern Philosophie* (History of Modern Philosophy).]
60. [Sting of conscience.]
61. [For the sake of the good.]
62. [Joy.]

overtaken by punishment have felt *no different than Spinoza* with regard to their "transgression": "something has unexpectedly gone wrong here," *not*: "I should not have done that"—they submitted themselves to the punishment as one submits to a sickness or a misfortune or to death, with that stouthearted fatalism without revolt by which the Russians, for example, even today have the advantage over us Westerners in dealing with life. If there was a critique of the deed back then, it was prudence that exercised this critique on the deed: without question we must seek the actual *effect* of punishment above all in a sharpening of prudence, in a lengthening of memory, in a will hereafter to proceed more cautiously, more mistrustfully, more secretively, in the insight that one is once and for all too weak for many things, in a kind of improvement in self-assessment. Generally what can be achieved among humans and animals through punishment is an increase of fear, a sharpening of prudence, mastery of the appetites: punishment thus *tames* man, but it does not make him "better"— one might with greater justification maintain the opposite. ("Injury makes prudent," say the common folk: insofar as it makes prudent, it also makes bad. Fortunately, it often enough makes stupid.)

16

At this point I can no longer avoid helping my own hypothesis on the origin of the "bad conscience" to a first, preliminary expression: it is not easy to present and needs to be considered, guarded, and slept over for a long time. I take bad conscience to be the deep sickness into which man had to fall under the pressure of that most fundamental of all changes he ever experienced—the change of finding himself enclosed once and for all within the sway of society and peace. Just as water animals must have fared when they were forced either to become land animals or to perish, so fared these half animals who were happily adapted to wilderness, war, roaming about, adventure—all at once all of their instincts were devalued and "disconnected." From now on they were to go on foot and "carry themselves" where they had previously been carried by the water: a horrible heaviness lay upon them. They felt awkward doing the simplest tasks; for this new, unfamiliar world they no longer had their old leaders, the regulating drives that unconsciously guided them safely—they were reduced to thinking, inferring, calculating, connecting cause and effect, these unhappy ones, reduced to their "consciousness," to their poorest and most erring organ! I do not believe there has ever been such a feeling of misery on earth, such a leaden discomfort—and yet those old instincts had not all at once ceased to make their demands! It's just that it was difficult and seldom possible to yield to them: for the most part they had to seek new and as it were subterranean gratifications. All instincts that do not discharge themselves outwardly *turn themselves inwards*—this is what I call the *internalizing* of man: thus first grows in man that which he later calls his "soul." The entire inner world, originally thin as if inserted between two skins, has spread and unfolded, has taken on depth, breadth, height to the same extent that man's outward discharging has been *obstructed*. Those terrible bulwarks with which the organization of the state protects itself against the old instincts of freedom—punishments belong above all else to these bulwarks—brought it about that all those instincts of the wild free roaming human turned themselves backwards *against man himself*. Hostility, cruelty, pleasure in persecution, in assault, in change, in destruction—all of that turning itself against the possessors of such instincts: *that* is the origin of "bad conscience." The man who, for lack of external enemies and resistance, and wedged into an oppressive narrowness and regularity of custom, impatiently tore apart, persecuted, gnawed at, stirred up, maltreated himself; this animal that one wants to "tame" and that beats itself raw on the bars of its cage; this deprived one, consumed by homesickness for the desert, who had to create out of himself an adventure, a place of torture, an uncertain and dangerous wilderness—this fool, this longing and desperate prisoner became the inventor of "bad conscience." In him, however, the greatest and most uncanny of sicknesses was introduced, one from which man has not recovered to this day, the suffering of man *from man*, from *himself*—as the consequence of a forceful separation from his animal past, of a leap and plunge, as it were, into new situations and conditions of existence, of a declaration of war against the old instincts on which his energy, desire, and terribleness had thus far rested. Let us immediately add that, on the other hand, with the appearance on earth of an animal soul turned against itself, taking sides against itself, something so new, deep, unheard of, enigmatic, contradictory, *and full of future* had come into being that the appearance of the earth was thereby essentially changed. Indeed, divine spectators were necessary to appreciate the spectacle that thus began and whose end is still by no means in sight— a spectacle too refined, too wonderful, too paradoxical to be permitted to play itself out senselessly-unnoticed on some ridiculous star! Since that time man is *included* among the most unexpected and exciting lucky throws in the game played by the "big child" of Heraclitus, whether called Zeus or chance—he awakens for himself an interest, an anticipation, a hope, almost a certainty, as if with him something were announcing itself, something preparing itself, as if man were not a goal but only a path, an incident, a bridge, a great promise . . .

17

To the presupposition of this hypothesis on the origin of bad conscience belongs first, that this change was not gradual, not voluntary, and that it presented itself not as an organic growing into new conditions, but rather as a break, a leap, a compulsion, an inescapable doom, against which there was no struggle and not even any *ressentiment*. Second, however, that this fitting of a previously unrestrained and unformed population into a fixed form, given its beginning in an act of force, could be brought to its completion only by acts of force—that the oldest "state" accordingly made its appearance as a terrible tyranny, as a crushing and ruthless machinery, and continued to work until finally such a raw material of people and half-animals was not only thoroughly kneaded and pliable but also *formed*. I use the word "state": it goes without saying who is meant by this—some pack of blond beasts of prey, a race of conquerors and lords, which, organized in a warlike manner and with the power to organize, unhesitatingly lays its terrible paws on a population enormously superior in number perhaps, but still formless, still roaming about. It is in this manner, then, that the "state" begins on earth: I think the flight of fancy that had it beginning with a "contract" has been abandoned. Whoever can give orders,

whoever is "lord" by nature, whoever steps forth violently, in deed and gesture—what does he have to do with contracts! With such beings one does not reckon, they come like fate, without basis, reason, consideration, pretext; they are there like lightning is there: too terrible, too sudden, too convincing, too "different" even to be so much as hated. Their work is an instinctive creating of forms, impressing of forms; they are the most involuntary, unconscious artists there are:—where they appear, in a short time something new stands there, a ruling structure that *lives*, in which parts and functions are delimited and related to one another, in which nothing at all finds a place that has not first had placed into it a "meaning" with respect to the whole. They do not know what guilt, what responsibility, what consideration is, these born organizers; in them that terrible artists' egoism rules, that has a gaze like bronze and that knows itself already justified to all eternity in its "work," like the mother in her child. *They* are not the ones among whom "bad conscience" grew, that is clear from the outset—but it would not have grown *without them*, this ugly growth, it would be missing, if an enormous quantity of freedom had not been banished from the world, at least from visibility, and made *latent* as it were, under the pressure of the blows of their hammers, of their artist's violence. This *instinct for freedom*, forcibly made latent—we have already grasped it—this instinct for freedom, driven back, suppressed, imprisoned within, and finally discharging and venting itself only on itself: this, only this, is *bad conscience* in its beginnings.

18

One should guard against forming a low opinion of this entire phenomenon just because it is ugly and painful from the outset. After all, the active force that is at work on a grander scale in those violence-artists and organizers and that builds states, is basically the same force that here—inwardly, on a smaller, pettier scale, in a backwards direction, in the "labyrinth of the breast," to use Goethe's words—creates for itself the bad conscience and builds negative ideals: namely that *instinct for freedom* (speaking in my language: the will to power). Only here the matter on which this force's formative and violating nature vents itself is precisely man himself, his entire animal old self—and *not*, as in that larger and more conspicuous phenomenon, the *other* human, the *other* humans. This secret self-violation, this artists' cruelty, this pleasure in giving oneself—as heavy resisting suffering matter—a form, in burning into oneself a will, a critique, a contradiction, a contempt, a "no"; this uncanny and horrifying-pleasurable work of a soul compliant-conflicted with itself, that makes itself suffer out of pleasure in making-suffer, this entire *active* "bad conscience," as the true womb of ideal and imaginative events, finally brought to light—one can guess it already—a wealth of new disconcerting beauty and affirmation and perhaps for the first time beauty *itself* . . . For what would be "beautiful" if contradiction had not first come to a consciousness of itself, if the ugly had not first said to itself "I am ugly"? . . . After this hint, that enigma will at the least be less enigmatic, namely, to what extent an ideal, a beauty can be suggested by contradictory concepts like *selflessness, self-denial, self-sacrifice*; and we know one thing henceforth, this I do not doubt—namely what kind of *pleasure* it is that the selfless, the self-denying, the self-sacrificing feel from the very start: this pleasure belongs to cruelty. — So much for the present on the origins of the "unegoistic" as a *moral* value and toward staking out the ground from which this value has grown: bad conscience, the will to self-maltreatment, first supplies the presupposition for the *value* of the unegoistic. —

19

It is a sickness, bad conscience—this admits of no doubt—but a sickness as pregnancy is a sickness. Let us seek out the conditions under which this sickness has come to its most terrible and most sublime pinnacle: — we shall see just what it was that thus first made its entry into the world. For this we need a long breath,—and to start off we must return once again to an earlier viewpoint. The civil-law relationship of the debtor to his creditor, of which I have already spoken at length, was once again—and indeed in a manner that is historically exceedingly curious and questionable—interpreted into a relationship in which it is for us modern humans perhaps at its most incomprehensible: namely the relationship of *those*

presently living to their *ancestors*. Within the original clan association we are speaking of primeval times—the living generation always acknowledges a juridical obligation to the earlier generation, and particularly to the earliest one, which founded the clan (and by no means a mere sentimental obligation: one might with good reason even deny the latter altogether for the longest part of the existence of the human race). Here the conviction holds sway that it is only through the sacrifices and achievements of the ancestors that the clan *exists* at all,—and that one has to *repay* them through sacrifices and achievements: one thereby acknowledges a *debt* that is continually growing, since these ancestors, in their continued existence as powerful spirits, do not cease to use their strength to bestow on the clan new benefits and advances. For nothing perhaps? But to those brutal and "soul-poor" ages there is no "for nothing." What can one give back to them? Sacrifices (initially only nourishment, in the coarsest sense), festivals, shrines, tributes, above all obedience—for all customs, as works of the ancestors, are also their statutes and commands—: does one ever give them enough? This suspicion remains and grows: from time to time it forces a great redemption, lock, stock, and barrel, some enormity of a counter-payment to the "creditor" (the notorious sacrifice of the firstborn, for example; blood, human blood in any case). The fear of the progenitor and his power, the consciousness of debts toward him necessarily increases, according to this kind of logic, to exactly the same degree that the power of the clan itself increases, that the clan itself stands ever more victorious, independent, honored, feared. By no means the other way around! Rather every step toward the atrophying of the clan, all miserable chance occurrences, all signs of degeneration, of approaching dissolution always *diminish* the fear of the spirit of the founder and give an ever more reduced notion of his shrewdness, his foresightedness, and his presence as power. If one imagines this brutal kind of logic carried through to its end: finally, through the imagination of growing fear the progenitors of the *most powerful* clans must have grown into enormous proportions and have been pushed back into the darkness of a divine uncanniness and unimaginability: — in the end the progenitor is necessarily transfigured into a *god*. This may even be the origin of the gods, an origin, that is, out of *fear*! . . . And those who think it necessary to add: "but also out of piety!" would hardly be right with regard to the longest period of the human race, its primeval period. All the more, admittedly, for the *middle* period in which the noble clans take shape:—who in fact returned, with interest, to their originators, the ancestors (heroes, gods) all of the qualities that had in the meantime become apparent in them, the *noble* qualities. Later we will take another look at the aristocratizing and ennobling of the gods (which is by no means their "hallowing"): for the present let us simply bring the course of this whole development of guilt consciousness to a conclusion.

20

As history teaches, the consciousness of having debts to the deity by no means came to an end even after the decline of the "community" organized according to blood-relationships; in the same way that it inherited the concepts "good and bad" from the clan nobility (together with its basic psychological propensity for establishing orders of rank), humanity also inherited, along with the deities of the clan and tribe, the pressure of the still unpaid debts and of the longing for the redemption of the same. (The transition is made by those broad slave and serf populations who adapted themselves to the cult of the gods practiced by their lords, whether through force or through submissiveness and mimicry: starting from them, this inheritance then overflows in all directions.) For several millennia the feeling of guilt toward the deity did not stop growing and indeed grew ever onward in the same proportion as the concept of god and the feeling for god grew on earth and was borne up on high. (The whole history of ethnic fighting, triumphing, reconciling, merging—everything that precedes the final rank-ordering of all ethnic elements in every great racial synthesis—is reflected in the genealogical confusion of their gods, in the legends of their fights, triumphs, and reconciliations; development toward universal empires is also always development toward universal deities; despotism with its overpowering of the independent nobility also always prepares the way for some kind of monotheism.) The rise of the Christian god as the maximum god that has been attained

thus far therefore also brought a maximum of feelings of guilt into appearance on earth. Assuming that we have by now entered into the *reverse* movement, one might with no little probability deduce from the unstoppable decline of faith in the Christian god that there would already be a considerable decline in human consciousness of guilt as well; indeed the prospect cannot be dismissed that the perfect and final victory of atheism might free humanity from this entire feeling of having debts to its beginnings, its *causa prima*.[63] Atheism and a kind of *second innocence* belong together.—

21

So much for the present, in short and roughly speaking, on the connection of the concepts "guilt," "duty" to religious presuppositions: I have until now intentionally left aside the actual moralization of these concepts (their being pushed back into conscience, more precisely the entanglement of *bad* conscience with the concept of god) and at the end of the previous section even spoke as if there were no such moralization, consequently, as if those concepts were now necessarily coming to an end now that their presupposition, the faith in our "creditor," in God, has fallen. The facts of the case diverge from this in a terrible manner. With the moralization of the concepts guilt and duty, with their being pushed back into *bad* conscience, we have in actual fact the attempt to *reverse* the direction of the development just described, at least to bring its movement to a standstill: precisely the prospect of a conclusive redemption *shall* now pessimistically close itself off once and for all; the gaze *shall* now bleakly deflect off, deflect back from a brazen impossibility; those concepts "guilt" and "duty" *shall* now turn themselves backwards— and against whom? There can be no doubt: first against the "debtor," in whom bad conscience now fixes itself firmly, eats into him, spreads out, and grows like a polyp in every breadth and depth until finally, with the impossibility of discharging the debt, the impossibility of discharging penance is also conceived of, the idea that it cannot be paid off ("*eternal* punish-

63. [First cause.]

ment")—; finally, however, even against the "creditor," think here of the *causa prima* of man, of the beginning of the human race, of its progenitor, who is now burdened with a curse ("Adam," "Original Sin," "unfreedom of the will") or of nature, from whose womb man arises and into which the evil principle is now placed ("demonizing of nature") or of existence generally, which is left as *valueless in itself* (nihilistic turning away from it, longing into nothingness or longing into its "opposite," a being-other, Buddhism and related things)—until all at once we stand before the paradoxical and horrifying remedy in which tortured humanity found temporary relief, *Christianity's* stroke of genius: God sacrificing himself for the guilt of man, God himself exacting payment of himself, God as the only one who can redeem from man what has become irredeemable for man himself—the creditor sacrificing himself for his debtor, out of *love* (is that credible?—), out of love for his debtor! . . .

22

One will already have guessed *what* actually happened with all of this and *under* all of this: that will to self-torment, that suppressed cruelty of the animal-human who had been made inward, scared back into himself, of the one locked up in the "state" for the purpose of taming, who invented the bad conscience in order to cause himself pain after the *more natural* outlet for this *desire to cause pain* was blocked,—this man of bad conscience has taken over the religious presupposition in order to drive his self-torture to its most gruesome severity and sharpness. Guilt before *God*: this thought becomes an instrument of torture for him. In "God" he captures the most extreme opposites he can find to his actual and inescapable animal instincts; he reinterprets these animal instincts themselves as guilt before God (as hostility, rebellion, insurrection against the "lord," the "father," the primal ancestor and beginning of the world); he harnesses himself into the contradiction "God" and "devil"; he takes all the "no" that he says to himself, to nature, naturalness, the facticity of his being and casts it out of himself as a "yes," as existing, corporeal, real, as God, as holiness of God, as judgeship of God, as executionership of God, as beyond, as eternity, as

torture without end, as hell, as immeasurability of punishment and guilt. This is a kind of madness of the will in psychic cruelty that has absolutely no equal: the *will* of man to find himself guilty and reprehensible to the point that it cannot be atoned for; his *will* to imagine himself punished without the possibility of the punishment ever becoming equivalent to the guilt; his *will* to infect and make poisonous the deepest ground of things with the problem of punishment and guilt in order to cut off the way out of this labyrinth of "*idées fixes*" once and for all; his *will* to erect an ideal—that of the "holy God"—in order, in the face of the same, to be tangibly certain of his absolute unworthiness. Oh, this insane sad beast man! What ideas occur to it, what anti-nature, what paroxysms of nonsense; what *bestiality of idea* immediately breaks forth when it is hindered only a little from being a *beast of deed* ! . . . All of this is interesting to the point of excess, but also of such black gloomy unnerving sadness that one must forcibly forbid oneself to look too long into these abysses. Here there is *sickness*, beyond all doubt, the most terrible sickness that has thus far raged in man:—and whoever is still capable of hearing (but one no longer has the ears for it today!—) how in this night of torture and absurdity the cry *love* resounded, the cry of the most longing delight, of redemption in *love*, will turn away, seized by an invincible horror . . . There is so much in man that is horrifying! . . . The earth has been a madhouse for too long! . . .

23

Let this suffice once and for all concerning the origins of the "holy God."—That *in itself* the conception of gods does not necessarily lead to this degradation of the imagination, which we could not spare ourselves from calling to mind for a moment, that there are *more noble* ways of making use of the fabrication of gods than for this self-crucifixion and self-defilement of man in which Europe's last millennia have had their mastery—this can fortunately be read from every glance one casts on the *Greek gods*, these reflections of noble and autocratic human beings in whom the *animal* in man felt itself deified and *did not* tear itself apart, *did not* rage against itself! For the longest time these Greeks used their gods precisely to keep "bad conscience" at arm's length, to be able to remain cheerful about their freedom of soul: that is, the reverse of the use which Christianity made of its god. They took this to *great lengths*, these splendid and lionhearted childish ones; and no lesser authority than that of the Homeric Zeus himself gives them to understand here and there that they make it too easy for themselves. "A wonder!" he says once—it concerns the case of Aegisthus, a *very* bad case—

A wonder, how much the mortals complain
    against the gods!
Only from us is there evil, they think; but
    they themselves
Create their own misery through lack of
    understanding, even counter to fate.

But one hears and sees at the same time that even this Olympian spectator and judge is far from being angry at them for this and from thinking evil of them: "how *foolish* they are!" so he thinks in the face of the misdeeds of the mortals,—and "foolishness," "lack of understanding," a little "disturbance in the head," this much even the Greeks of the strongest, bravest age *allowed* themselves as the reason for much that was bad and doom-laden:—foolishness, *not* sin! do you understand that? . . . But even this disturbance in the head was a problem—"indeed, how is it even possible? whence could it actually have come, given heads such as *we* have, we men of noble descent, of happiness, of optimal form, of the best society, of nobility, of virtue?"—thus the noble Greek wondered for centuries in the face of every incomprehensible atrocity and wanton act with which one of his equals had sullied himself. "A god must have beguiled him," he said to himself finally, shaking his head . . . This way out is *typical* of the Greeks . . . In this manner the gods served in those days to justify humans to a certain degree even in bad things, they served as causes of evil—in those days it was not the punishment they took upon themselves but rather, as is *more noble*, the guilt . . .

24

—I close with three question marks, as one can of course see. "Is an ideal actually being erected here or is one being demolished?" thus one might ask me

. . . But have you ever asked yourselves enough how dearly the erection of *every* ideal on earth has exacted its payment? How much reality always had to be libeled and mistaken, how much lying sanctified, how much conscience disturbed, how much "god" had to be sacrificed each time? So that a sanctuary can be erected, *a sanctuary must be shattered*: that is the law—show me a case where it is not fulfilled! . . . We modern humans, we are the heirs of millennia of conscience-vivisection and cruelty to the animal-self: in this we have our longest practice, our artistry perhaps, in any case our sophistication, our over-refinement of taste. For all too long man has regarded his natural inclinations with an "evil eye," so that in him they have finally become wedded to "bad conscience." A reverse attempt would *in itself* be possible—but who is strong enough for it?—namely to wed to bad conscience the *unnatural* inclinations, all those aspirations to the beyond, to that which is contrary to the senses, contrary to the instincts, contrary to nature, contrary to the animal—in short the previous ideals which are all ideals hostile to life, ideals of those who libel the world. To whom to turn today with *such* hopes and demands? . . . In so doing one would have precisely the *good* human beings against oneself; and, in fairness, the comfortable, the reconciled, the vain, the enraptured, the tired . . . What is there that insults more deeply, that separates off so fundamentally, as letting others notice something of the strictness and height with which one treats oneself? And on the other hand—how accommodating, how full of love the whole world shows itself toward us as soon as we do like all the world and "let ourselves go" like all the world! . . . For this goal one would need a *different* kind of spirits than are probable in this of all ages: spirits strengthened by wars and victories, for whom conquering, adventure, danger, pain have even become a need; for this one would need acclimatization to sharp high air, to wintry journeys, to ice and mountain ranges in every sense; for this one would need a kind of sublime malice itself, an ultimate most self-assured mischievousness of knowledge, which belongs to great health; one would need, in brief and gravely enough, precisely this *great health*! . . . Is this even possible today? . . . But someday, in a stronger time than this decaying, self-doubting present, he really must come to us, the *redeeming* human of the great love and contempt, the creative spirit whose compelling strength again and again drives him out of any apart or beyond, whose loneliness is misunderstood by the people as if it were a flight *from* reality—: whereas it is only his submersion, burial, absorption *in* reality so that one day, when he again comes to light, he can bring home the *redemption* of this reality: its redemption from the curse that the previous ideal placed upon it. This human of the future who will redeem us from the previous ideal as much as from that *which had to grow out of it*, from the great disgust, from the will to nothingness; this bell-stroke of noon and of the great decision, that makes the will free again, that gives back to the earth its goal and to man his hope; this Anti-Christ and anti-nihilist; this conqueror of God and of nothingness—*he must one day come* . . .

25

—But what am I saying? Enough! Enough! At this point there is only one thing fitting for me, to be silent: otherwise I would be laying a hand on that which only a younger one is free to choose, a "more future one," a stronger one than I am—which only *Zarathustra* is free to choose, *Zarathustra the god-less* . . .

THIRD TREATISE: WHAT DO ASCETIC IDEALS MEAN?

Carefree, mocking, violent—thus wisdom wants *us*: she is a woman, she always loves only a warrior.

Thus Spoke Zarathustra

1

What do ascetic ideals mean?—Among artists nothing or too many different things; among philosophers and scholars something like a nose and instinct for the most favorable preconditions of higher spirituality; among women, at best, one *more* charming trait of seduction, a little *morbidezza* on beautiful flesh, the angelicalness of a pretty, fat animal; among the physi-

ologically failed and out of sorts (among the *majority* of mortals) an attempt to appear to oneself to be "too good" for this world, a holy form of excess, their principal instrument in the battle with slow pain and with boredom; among priests the true priests' faith, their best tool of power, also the "most high" permission to power; among saints, finally, a pretext for hibernation, their *novissima gloriae cupido*,[64] their rest in nothingness ("God"), their form of madness. *That* the ascetic ideal has meant so much to man, however, is an expression of the basic fact of the human will, its *horror vacui*:[65] it needs a goal,—and it would rather will *nothingness* than *not* will.—Am I understood? Have I been understood? . . . "*Absolutely not! dear Sir!*"—Then let us start at the beginning.

2

What do ascetic ideals mean?—Or, to take an individual case, about which I have often enough been asked for advice, what does it mean, for example, when, in his old age, an artist like Richard Wagner[66] pays homage to chastity? In a certain sense, admittedly, he has always done this; but only at the very end in an ascetic sense. What does this change of "sense," this radical reversal of sense mean?—for that is what it was, Wagner thus suddenly somersaulted directly into his opposite. What does it mean when an artist suddenly somersaults into his opposite? . . . Here we are at once reminded—supposing we are willing to pause a moment at this question—of what was perhaps the best, strongest, most cheerful-hearted, *most courageous* time in Wagner's life: it was back when the idea of Luther's marriage occupied him inwardly and deeply. Who knows on what chance events it actually depended that today instead of this marriage music we have the *Meistersinger*? And how much of the former still resounds in the latter? But there is no doubt that this "Marriage of Luther," too, would have been a praise of chastity. To be sure, also a

64. [The last thing, passion for glory. Tacitus, *Histories* IV, 6.]

65. [Horror of emptiness.]

66. [Richard Wagner (1813–1883), German composer and music theorist.]

praise of sensuality:—and precisely so would it seem to me to be in order, precisely so would it also have been "Wagnerian." For between chastity and sensuality there is no necessary opposition; every good marriage, every true affair of the heart is beyond this opposition. Wagner would have done well, it seems to me, to have brought home this *pleasant* fact to his Germans once again with the help of a lovely and stout-hearted Luther comedy, for there are and always have been many libelers of sensuality among the Germans; and perhaps nowhere has Luther performed a greater service than precisely in having had the courage to his *sensuality* (it was called in those days, delicately enough, the "Protestant freedom" . . .) But even in the case where there really is that opposition between chastity and sensuality, it is fortunately by no means necessary that it be a tragic opposition. This would seem to hold at least for all better-formed, more high-spirited mortals who are far from automatically counting their labile balance between "animal and angel" among the arguments against existence,—the subtlest and brightest, like Goethe, like Hafiz, have even seen in this one *more* enticement to life. Precisely such "contradictions" seduce to existence . . . On the other hand it is only too clear that when swine who have come to ruin are once brought to the point of worshipping chastity—and there are such swine!—they will see and worship in it only their opposite, the opposite of swine come to ruin— oh with what tragic grunting and zeal! one can imagine it—the embarrassing and superfluous opposite that Richard Wagner indisputably still wanted to set to music and put on stage at the end of his life. *And to what end?* as one may in fairness ask. For what were the swine to him, what are they to us?—

3

And yet admittedly that other question cannot be avoided here: just what was that manly (alas, so unmanly) "simplicity from the country" to him, that poor devil and lad of nature Parsifal, whom he with such ensnaring means finally made Catholic—what? was this Parsifal meant at all *seriously*? For one could be tempted to conjecture, even to wish the opposite— that the Wagnerian Parsifal were meant lightheartedly, a closing piece and satyr-play, as it were, with

which the tragedian Wagner wanted to take leave of us, also of himself, above all *of tragedy* in a manner fitting for and worthy of him, namely with an excess of highest and most mischievous parody of the tragic itself, of the entire gruesome earthly seriousness and wretchedness of earlier times, of the *coarsest form*— now finally overcome—found in the anti-nature of the ascetic ideal. This, as noted, would have been worthy precisely of a great tragedian: who, like every artist, only arrives at the final pinnacle of his greatness when he is able to see himself and his art *beneath* him,—when he is able to *laugh* at himself. Is Wagner's *Parsifal* his secret laughter of superiority at himself, the triumph of this final highest artist's freedom, artist's otherworldliness? As stated, one would like to wish it: for what would a *seriously intended Parsifal* be? Is it really necessary to see in it (as someone put it in conversation with me) "the product of an insane hatred of knowledge, spirit, and sensuality"? A curse on senses and spirit in a single hatred and breath? An apostasy and return to obscurantist and Christian-diseased ideals? And finally even a negating of self, a crossing-out of self on the part of an artist who until that point had been out with all the might of his will after the opposite, namely the *highest spiritualization and sensualization* of his art? And not only of his art: also of his life. Recall how enthusiastically in his day Wagner walked in the footsteps of the philosopher Feuerbach:[67] Feuerbach's word concerning "healthy sensuality"— in the thirties and forties this sounded to Wagner as to many Germans (—they called themselves the "*young* Germans") like the word of redemption. Did he in the end *learn otherwise*? Since it seems at least that in the end he had the will *to teach otherwise* . . . And not only from the stage, with the *Parsifal*-trombones:—in the murky writings of his last years, just as unfree as they are clueless, there are a hundred passages in which a secret wish and will betrays itself,

67. [Ludwig Feuerbach (1804–1872) was in his own time the most famous of the "Young" or leftist Hegelians—only later eclipsed by Marx—and was influential not only among philosophers but also writers, especially the writers of the movement known as "Young Germany." Feuerbach's philosophy was a radical humanism.]

a despondent, uncertain, unacknowledged will to preach, in essence, changing of one's way, conversion, negation, Christianity, Middle Ages and to say to his disciples: "it is nothing! Seek your salvation elsewhere!" Even the "blood of the Redeemer" is invoked at one point . . .

4

To state my opinion in a case of this sort, in which there is much that is embarrassing—and it is a *typical* case—: one certainly does best to separate an artist from his work to the extent of not taking him as seriously as his work. He is in the end only the precondition of his work, the womb, the ground, in some cases the fertilizer and manure on which, out of which, it grows,—and thus in most cases something one must forget if one wants to enjoy the work itself. Looking into the *origins* of a work is the business of physiologists and vivisectors of the spirit: never ever of the aesthetic human being, the artist! The poet and shaper of *Parsifal* was no more spared a deep, thorough, even frightening acclimatization and descent into medieval contrasts of the soul, a hostile aloofness from all height, rigor, and discipline of the spirit, a kind of intellectual *perversity* (if one will pardon the word) than a pregnant woman is spared the repulsive and strange aspects of pregnancy: which one must *forget*, as noted, in order to enjoy the child. One should be on guard against the confusion into which an artist himself all too easily falls, out of psychological contiguity, to put it as the English do: as if he himself *were* what he is able to depict, think up, express. In fact, the situation is such that *if* he were precisely that, he would certainly not depict, think up, express it; a Homer would not have written an Achilles nor Goethe a Faust if Homer had been an Achilles or if Goethe had been a Faust. A perfect and whole artist is separated to all eternity from the "real," the actual; on the other hand one understands how he can at times become tired to the point of despair of this eternal "irreality" and falseness of his innermost existence—and that he makes the attempt to encroach for once upon what is most forbidden precisely to him, upon what is real—makes the attempt truly to *be*. With what success? One can guess . . . It is *the typical velleity* of the artist: the same

velleity into which Wagner lapsed, having grown old, and for which he had to pay so dearly, so fatefully (—through it he lost the valuable part of his friends). Finally, however, still disregarding this velleity entirely, who would not like to wish for Wagner's own sake that he had taken leave of us and of his art *differently*, not with a *Parsifal*, but rather in a manner that was more victorious, more self-assured, more Wagnerian—less misleading, less ambiguous about what he really wanted, less Schopenhauerian, less nihilistic? . . .

5

—What then do ascetic ideals mean? In the case of an artist, as we have grasped by now: *absolutely nothing*! . . . Or so many things that it is as good as absolutely nothing! . . . Let us first of all eliminate artists: they are far from standing independently enough in the world and *against* the world for their valuations and the changes in these to deserve interest *in themselves*! In all ages they have been valets of a morality or philosophy or religion; quite apart from the fact that, unfortunately, they have often enough been the all-too-pliant courtiers of their disciples and patrons, and flatterers with a good nose for old or newly rising powers. At the very least they always need a protective armor, a backing, a previously established authority: artists never stand by themselves, standing alone goes against their deepest instincts. Thus Richard Wagner, for example, took the philosopher Schopenhauer as his front man, as his protective armor when "the time had come":—who could consider it even thinkable that he would have had the courage for an ascetic ideal without the backing that Schopenhauer's philosophy offered him, without Schopenhauer's authority, which was gaining *predominance* in Europe in the seventies? (not yet having assessed whether an artist would have even been possible in the *new* Germany without the milk of a pious, imperially pious way of thinking).—And with this we have arrived at the more serious question: what does it mean when a real *philosopher* pays homage to the ascetic ideal, a spirit who really stands on his own, like Schopenhauer, a man and knight with a brazen glance, who has the courage to himself, who knows how to stand alone and does not first wait for front men and nods from on high?—

Let us immediately consider here the strange and for many kinds of people even fascinating stance Schopenhauer took toward *art*: it was, after all, clearly for the sake of this that Richard Wagner *initially* converted to Schopenhauer (convinced to do so by a poet, as is well known, by Herwegh),[68] and to such an extent that a complete theoretical contradiction thus opened up between his earlier and his later aesthetic beliefs—the former expressed for example in "Opera and Drama," the latter in the writings he published from 1870 on. In particular, from here on Wagner ruthlessly changed—this is perhaps the most disconcerting thing of all—his judgment concerning the value and status of *music* itself: what did it matter to him that he had previously made a means out of it, a medium, a "woman," that simply had to have a purpose, a man in order to prosper—namely drama! He grasped all at once that with Schopenhauer's theory and innovation more could be done *in majorem musicae gloriam*[69]—namely with the *sovereignty* of music as Schopenhauer understood it: music set apart from all other arts, the independent art in itself, *not*, like these, offering representations of phenomenality, but rather speaking the language of *the* will itself, directly out of the "abyss," as its most authentic, most original, least derivative revelation. With this extraordinary rise in the value of music, as it seemed to grow forth out of Schopenhauerian philosophy, *the musician* himself all at once rose in price to an unheard-of degree: he now became an oracle, a priest, indeed more than a priest, a kind of mouthpiece of the "in itself " of things, a telephone of the beyond— henceforth he spoke not only music, this ventriloquist of God—he spoke metaphysics: any wonder that one day he finally spoke *ascetic ideals*? . . .

6

Schopenhauer used the Kantian formulation of the aesthetic problem for his own purpose—although he most certainly did not view it with Kantian eyes. Kant intended to honor art when, among the predicates of the beautiful, he privileged and placed in the foreground those that constitute the honor of knowledge: impersonality and universal validity. Whether this was not on the whole a mistake cannot be dealt with here; I wish only to underscore that Kant, like all philosophers, instead of envisaging the aesthetic problem starting from the experiences of the artist (the one who creates), thought about art and the beautiful from the viewpoint of the "spectator" and thus, without it being noticed, got the "spectator" himself into the concept "beautiful." If only this "spectator" had at least been sufficiently familiar to the philosophers of the beautiful, however!—namely as a great *personal* fact and experience, as a wealth of most personal intense experiences, desires, surprises, delights in the realm of the beautiful! But I fear the opposite was always the case: and thus we receive from them, right from the beginning, definitions in which, as in that famous definition Kant gives of the beautiful, the lack of more refined self-experience sits in the form of a fat worm of basic error. "The beautiful," Kant said, "is what pleases *without interest*." Without interest! Compare this definition with one made by a real "spectator" and artist—Stendhal,[70] who in one place calls the beautiful *une promesse de bonheur*.[71] What is *rejected* and crossed out here, in any case, is precisely the one thing Kant emphasizes in the aesthetic condition: *le désintéressement*. Who is right, Kant or Stendhal?—Admittedly, if our aestheticians never tire of throwing into the balance in Kant's favor that under the enchantment of beauty one can look at *even* robe-less female statues "without interest," then certainly one may laugh a little at their expense:—the experiences of *artists* in connection with this sensitive point are "more interesting," and Pygmalion was in any case *not* necessarily an "unaesthetic human being." Let us think all the more highly of the innocence of our aestheticians that is reflected in such arguments; for example, let us give Kant credit for what he knows to teach—with the naïveté of a country priest—about the characteristic nature of the sense of touch!—And here we come back to Schopenhauer, who stood

68. [Georg Herwegh (1817–1875), one of the most prominent of the Young German poets.]

69. [For the greater glory of music.]

70. [Pseudonym of Henri Beyle (1783–1842), French author.]

71. [A promise of happiness.]

much closer to the arts than Kant and still did not get out from under the spell of the Kantian definition: how did this happen? The circumstance is odd enough: he interpreted the expression "without interest" in the most personal manner, on the basis of what must have been one of his most regular experiences. There are few things about which Schopenhauer speaks so certainly as about the effect of aesthetic contemplation: he says of it that it counteracts precisely *sexual* "interestedness," much like lupulin and camphor, that is; he never grew tired of glorifying *this* breaking free from the "will" as the greatest merit and use of the aesthetic condition. Indeed, one might be tempted to ask whether his basic conception of "will and representation," the thought that there can be a redemption from the "will" only through "representation," did not originate from a generalization of that sexual experience. (In all questions relating to Schopenhauerian philosophy, by the way, one must never ignore the fact that it is the conception of a twenty-six-year-old young man; so that it participates not only in that which is specific to Schopenhauer but also in that which is specific to that season of life.) Let us hear, for example, one of the most explicit of the countless passages he wrote in honor of the aesthetic condition (World as Will and Representation I, 231), let us hear the tone, the suffering, the happiness, the gratitude with which such words were spoken. "This is the painless condition that Epicurus praised as the highest good and as the condition of the gods; we are, for that moment, freed from the base drive of the will, we celebrate the Sabbath of the prison-house work of willing, the wheel of Ixion stands still" . . . What vehemence of words! What images of torture and of prolonged satiety! What an almost pathological temporal juxtaposition of "that moment" and the usual "wheel of Ixion," the "prison-house work of willing," the "base drive of the will"! But supposing that Schopenhauer were right a hundred times over for himself, what would this have contributed to our insight into the essence of the beautiful? Schopenhauer described *one* effect of the beautiful, the will-calming one—is it even a regularly occurring one? Stendhal, as noted, a no less sensual but more happily-formed nature than Schopenhauer, emphasizes a different effect of the beautiful: "the beautiful *promises* happiness"—to him it is precisely

the *excitement of the will* ("of interest") by the beautiful that seems to be the fact of the matter. And could one not finally urge upon Schopenhauer himself the objection that he was very wrong in thinking himself a Kantian in this, that he did not at all understand the Kantian definition of the beautiful in a Kantian sense—that the beautiful is pleasing to him, too, out of an "interest," even out of the strongest of all, the most personal of all interests: that of the tortured one who breaks free from his torture? . . . And, to come back to our first question, "what does it *mean* when a philosopher pays homage to the ascetic ideal?," we get at least a first hint here: he wants *to break free from a torture.*—

7

Let us take care not to make gloomy faces right away at the word "torture": in this case in particular there is still plenty to count on the other side of the ledger, plenty to deduct—there is even still something to laugh at. For let us not underestimate the fact that Schopenhauer, who in fact treated sexuality as a personal enemy (including its tool, woman, this *"instrumentum diaboli"*),[72] *needed* enemies in order to remain in good spirits; that he loved grim bilious black-green words; that he became angry for the sake of being angry, out of passion; that he would have become sick, would have become a *pessimist* (—for he was not one, as much as he wished it) without his enemies, without Hegel, woman, sensuality, and the entire will to being-here, remaining-here. Schopenhauer would otherwise *not* have remained here, one can bet on that, he would have run away: his enemies, however, held him fast, his enemies seduced him again and again into existence, just as with the ancient Cynics, his anger was his balm, his recreation, his compensation, his *remedium*[73] against disgust, his *happiness*. So much with respect to what is most personal in Schopenhauer's case; on the other hand there is also something typical in him—and only here do we again come to our problem. It is indisputable that for as long as there have been philosophers on

72. [Instrument of the devil.]
73. [Medicine.]

earth and wherever there have been philosophers (from India to England, to take the polar opposites in talent for philosophy) there has existed a characteristic philosophers' irritability and rancor against sensuality—Schopenhauer is only its most eloquent and, if one has the ear for it, also most rousing and most enchanting outburst;—there has likewise existed a characteristic philosophers' prepossession and cordiality regarding the whole ascetic ideal; one ought not to entertain any illusions about or against this. Both belong, as noted, to the type; if both are absent in a philosopher then he is always—of this one may be certain—only a "so-called" philosopher. What does that *mean*? For one must first interpret this set of facts: in itself it stands there, stupid to all eternity, like every "thing in itself." Every animal, thus also *la bête philosophe*,[74] instinctively strives for an optimum of favorable conditions under which it can vent its power completely and attain its maximum in the feeling of power; just as instinctively, and with a keenness of scent that "surpasses all understanding," every animal abhors troublemakers and obstacles of every kind that do or could lay themselves across its path to the optimum (—it is *not* its path to "happiness" of which I speak, but rather its path to power, to the deed, to the most powerful doing, and in most cases in actual fact its path to unhappiness). In this manner the philosopher abhors *marriage* together with that which might persuade him to it—marriage as obstacle and doom along his path to the optimum. What great philosopher thus far has been married? Heraclitus, Plato, Descartes, Spinoza, Leibniz, Kant, Schopenhauer—they were not; still more, one cannot even *imagine* them being married. A married philosopher belongs *in comedy*, that is my proposition: and that exception Socrates, the malicious Socrates, it seems, married *ironice*, expressly to demonstrate *this* very proposition. Every philosopher would speak as Buddha once spoke when the birth of a son was announced to him: "Râhula has been born to me, a fetter has been forged for me" (here Râhula means "a small daemon"); to every "free spirit" a thoughtful hour must come, supposing he has previously had a thoughtless one, such as once came to the same

Buddha—"narrowly constrained, he thought to himself, is life in the house, a place of impurity; freedom is in leaving the house": "as he was thinking thus, he left the house." The ascetic ideal points out so many bridges to *independence* that a philosopher cannot, without inner jubilation and clapping of hands, hear the story of all those determined ones who one day said "no" to all unfreedom and went into some sort of *desert*—even supposing that they were merely strong asses and completely and utterly the opposite of a strong spirit. What, accordingly, does the ascetic ideal mean for a philosopher? My answer is—one will have guessed it long ago: at its sight the philosopher smiles at an optimum of the conditions for highest and boldest spirituality—in this he does *not* negate "existence," rather he affirms *his* existence and *only* his existence, and this perhaps to the degree that the wanton wish is never far away: *pereat mundus, fiat philosophia, fiat philosophus, fiam*! . . .[75]

8

One can see these are no unbribed witnesses and judges of the *value* of the ascetic ideal, these philosophers! They are thinking of *themselves*—what is "the saint" to them! They are thinking all the while of what is most indispensable precisely *to them*: freedom from compulsion, disturbance, noise, from business, duties, cares; clarity in the head; dance, leap, and flight of ideas; good air, thin, clear, free, dry, as the air in high places is, in which all animal being becomes more spiritual and acquires wings; quiet in all souterrains; all dogs neatly put on a chain; no barking of hostility and shaggy rancor; no gnawing worms of injured ambition; undemanding and submissive intestines, diligent as mill-works but distant; the heart in a foreign place, in the beyond, in the future, posthumous—at the mention of the ascetic ideal they think, all in all, of the lighthearted asceticism of an animal that has been deified and become fully fledged, that roams more than rests above life. One knows the three great pomp words of the ascetic ideal: poverty, humility, chastity: and now just look at the lives of all great fruitful inventive spirits close up—one will

---

74. [The philosophical animal.]

75. [Let the world perish, let there be philosophy, let there be the philosopher, *let there be me!*]

always find all three to a certain degree. Certainly *not*, as goes without saying, as if these were their "virtues"—what does this kind of human being have to do with virtues!—but rather as the truest and most natural conditions of their *best* existence, of their *most beautiful* fruitfulness. At the same time it is entirely possible that for the present their dominant spirituality had to put reins on an unbridled and irritable pride or a willful sensuality or that it perhaps had a difficult enough time keeping up its will to the "desert" against an inclination to luxury and to the most exquisite things, likewise against a wasteful liberality of heart and hand. But it did it, precisely as the *dominant* instinct that forced through all its demands against those of all other instincts—it is still doing so; if it didn't do so, it would not dominate. In this, then, there is nothing of "virtue." Incidentally, the *desert* of which I just spoke, into which the strong, independent-natured spirits retreat and grow lonely—oh how different it looks from the desert as the learned dream it!—for in some cases they themselves are this desert, these learned ones. And it is certain that no actor of the spirit would be at all able to endure living in it—for them it is not nearly romantic and Syrian enough, not nearly enough of a stage desert! Admittedly there is also no lack of camels in it: but here the entire similarity ends. A voluntary obscurity perhaps; a steering-clear of oneself; an aversion to noise, veneration, newspaper, influence; a modest position, a daily routine, something that conceals more so than it brings to light; an occasional association with harmless light-hearted beasts and fowl, the sight of which refreshes; a mountain range for company, but not a dead one, rather one with *eyes* (that is with lakes); perhaps even a room in a crowded run-of-the-mill inn, where one is sure of being mistaken for someone else and can speak to anyone with impunity—that is "desert" here: oh it is lonely enough, believe me! When Heraclitus retreated into the courtyards and colonnades of the enormous temple of Artemis, this "desert" was more dignified, I concede: why are we *lacking* such temples? (—perhaps we are not lacking them: I was just thinking of my most beautiful study, of the Piazza di San Marco, assuming it is spring, likewise forenoon, the time between 10 and 12.) That which Heraclitus was evading, however, is still the same thing *we* steer clear of: the noise and the democratic chatter of the Ephesians, their politics, their news from the "empire" (Persia, you understand me), their market stuff of "today"—for we philosophers need rest from *one* thing before all else: from all "today." We venerate what is silent, cold, noble, distant, past, in general every kind of thing at whose sight the soul does not have to defend itself and lace itself shut—something with which one can talk without talking *out loud*. Just listen to the sound a spirit has when he talks: every spirit has its sound, loves its sound. This one over there, for example, must be an agitator, that is to say a hollow head, hollow pot: whatever it is that goes into him, each thing comes back out dull and thick, weighed down with the echo of great emptiness. That one there seldom speaks other than hoarsely: did he perhaps *think* himself hoarse? That would be possible—ask the physiologists—but whoever thinks in *words* thinks as a speaker and not as a thinker (it betrays the fact that he basically does not think facts, not factually, but rather only with respect to facts, that he really thinks *himself* and his listeners). This third one talks obtrusively, he steps too close to us, his breath brushes us—we close our mouths involuntarily although it is a book through which he speaks to us: the sound of his style tells us the reason—that he has no time, that he has little faith in himself, that he will never again get a word in if not today. A spirit who is sure of itself, however, speaks softly; it seeks seclusion, it makes others wait. One can recognize a philosopher by the fact that he keeps clear of three bright and loud things: fame, princes, and women—which is not to say they don't come to him. He shies away from all-too-bright light: therefore he shies away from his time and its "day." In this he is like a shadow: the more the sun sets for him the greater he becomes. As for his "humility," he can also bear, as he bears the dark, a certain dependence and obscurity: still more, he fears being disturbed by lightning, he shrinks back from the unprotectedness of an all-too-isolated and exposed tree on which every bad weather vents its moods, every mood its bad weather. His "motherly" instinct, the secret love of that which grows in him directs him to situations where one relieves him of thinking of *himself*, in the same sense in which the instinct of the *mother* in woman has until now preserved the dependent situation of woman generally. In the end they demand little enough, these philosophers; their motto is "whoever possesses, will be possessed"—: *not*, as I must say again and again, out of a virtue, out of a meritorious will to contentedness and simplicity, but rather because their supreme lord demands it *thus* of them, demands prudently and relentlessly: he has a mind for only one thing and gathers everything—time, energy, love, interest— only for this, saves it only for this. This kind of human does not like to be disturbed by enmities, also not by friendships: he forgets or holds in contempt easily. He thinks it in bad taste to play the martyr; "to *suffer* for the truth"—he leaves that to the ambitious and to the stage heroes of the spirit and whoever else has time enough for it (—the philosophers themselves, they have something to *do* for the truth). They use great words sparingly; it is said that they even find the word "truth" repellent: it sounds pompous ... Finally, as for the "chastity" of philosophers, this kind of spirit obviously has its fruitfulness somewhere other than in children; perhaps elsewhere also the continued existence of their name, their little immortality (among philosophers in ancient India one expressed oneself still more immodestly: "to what end progeny for one whose soul is the world?"). In this there is nothing of chastity out of any ascetic scruple and hatred of the senses, just as little as it is chastity when an athlete or jockey abstains from women: rather it is their dominant instinct that wants it this way, at least during times of great pregnancy. Every artist knows how harmful the effect of intercourse is in conditions of great spiritual tension and preparation; the most powerful and sure-of-instinct among them do not first require experience, negative experience— rather it is their "motherly" instinct here that ruthlessly commands all other stores and allowances of energy, of animal vigor, for the benefit of the growing work: the greater energy then *consumes* the lesser one.—Incidentally, piece together the above discussed case of Schopenhauer according to this interpretation: in him the sight of the beautiful apparently acted as a triggering stimulus on the *principal force* of his nature (the force of contemplation and of the engrossed gaze); so that this then exploded and became all at once lord of his consciousness. This is in no way meant to preclude the possibility that the peculiar sweetness and fullness characteristic of the aesthetic condition might have its origins precisely in the ingredient "sensuality" (just as that "idealism" characteristic of marriageable girls stems from the same source)—that sensuality is thus not suspended at the onset of the aesthetic condition, as Schopenhauer believed, but rather only transfigures itself and no longer enters consciousness as sexual stimulus. (I will return to this viewpoint at another time in connection with still more delicate problems of the thus far so untouched, so unexplored *physiology of aesthetics*.)

9

A certain asceticism—we have seen it—a hard and lighthearted renunciation with the best of intentions, belongs to the most favorable conditions of highest spirituality, likewise also to its most natural consequences: from the outset, then, it will not astonish us if the ascetic ideal has always been treated with considerable prepossession precisely by philosophers. A serious historical reckoning proves the tie between ascetic ideal and philosophy to be even closer and stricter still. One could say that it was only on the apron strings of this ideal that philosophy ever learned to take its first steps and half-steps on earth—alas, ever so clumsily, alas, with ever so discouraged faces, alas, so ready to fall down and lie on its belly, this shy little blunderer and milquetoast with crooked legs! In the beginning philosophy fared as have all good things,—for a long time they hadn't the courage to themselves, they were always looking around to see if there weren't someone who would come to their help, still more, they were afraid of everyone who watched them. Just list the individual drives and virtues of the philosopher one after the other—his doubting drive, his negating drive, his wait-and-see ("ephectic") drive, his analytical drive, his exploring, searching, venturing drive, his comparing, balancing drive, his will to neutrality and objectivity, his will to every "*sine ira et studio*"[76]—: have we already grasped that for the longest time they all went against the first demands of morality and of conscience? (not to mention *reason* itself, which, even in his late day, Luther loved to call Fraw Klüglin[77] the shrewd

76. [*Without* anger and partiality. Tacitus, *Annales* I, 1.]
77. [Early New High German: "Lady Shrewd."]

whore). That a philosopher, if he *were* to come to a consciousness of himself, would have had to feel himself to be none other than the *"nitimur in **vetitum**"*[78] incarnate—and accordingly was on guard against "feeling himself," against coming to a consciousness of himself? . . . Things are, as stated, no different with all good things of which we are proud today; even measured by the standard of the ancient Greeks our entire modern being, insofar as it is not weakness but rather power and consciousness of power, appears as nothing but hubris and godlessness: for the longest time those very things that are the reverse of what we venerate today had conscience on their side and God as their watchman. Hubris is our entire stance toward nature today, our violation of nature with the help of machines and the so thoughtless inventiveness of technicians and engineers; hubris is our stance toward God, that is to say toward some alleged spider of purpose and morality behind the great snare-web of causality—we could say with Charles the Bold in battle with Louis XI *"je combats l'universelle araignée"*[79]—; hubris is our stance toward *ourselves*—for we experiment with ourselves as we would not permit ourselves to do with any animal and merrily and curiously slit open our souls while the body is still living: what do we care anymore about the "salvation" of the soul! Afterwards we heal ourselves. being sick is instructive, we have no doubt, even more instructive than being healthy—today the *ones who make sick* appear to us to be even more necessary than any medicine men and "saviors." We do violence to ourselves now, there is no doubt, we nutcrackers of souls, we questioners and questionable ones, as if life were nothing but nutcracking; precisely in so doing we must of necessity become, with each passing day, ever more questionable, *worthier* of questioning, perhaps also worthier—of living? . . . All good things were once bad things; every original sin has become an original virtue. Marriage, for example, seemed for a long time to be a sin against the rights of the community; one once paid a penalty for having been so immodest and having arrogated a wife for oneself

alone (the *jus primae noctis*[80] belongs here, for example—even today still the privilege of the priests in Cambodia, these guardians of "old good customs"). For the longest time meek, benevolent, yielding, compassionate feelings—by now so high in value that they are almost "the values in themselves"—had precisely self-contempt against them: one was ashamed of leniency as one is today ashamed of harshness (cf. *Beyond Good and Evil* section 260). Submission to the *law*:—oh with what resistance of conscience the noble dynasties everywhere on earth renounced vendettas and granted the law power over themselves! For a long time the "law" was a *vetitum*,[81] a wanton act, an innovation; it appeared with force, *as* force, to which one could not yield without feeling ashamed of oneself. In former times every smallest step on earth was won through spiritual and bodily torments: this entire viewpoint "that not only marching forward, no! marching, movement, change had need of their countless martyrs" sounds so foreign precisely today—I first brought this to light in *Daybreak* 18. "Nothing has been more dearly bought," it says there, "than that little bit of human reason and feeling of freedom that now makes up our pride. Because of this pride, however, it is now becoming almost impossible for us to empathize with those enormous stretches of time characterized by the 'morality of custom,' which lie before 'world history' as the real and decisive principal history that established the character of humankind: when suffering counted everywhere as virtue, cruelty as virtue, dissimulation as virtue, revenge as virtue, denial of reason as virtue; on the other hand well-being as danger, desire for knowledge as danger, peace as danger, compassion as danger, being pitied as disgrace, work as disgrace, madness as divinity, change as the essence of what is immoral and pregnant with ruin!"—

10

In the same book, section 42, is set forth within what valuation, under what *pressure* of valuation the earliest race of contemplative humans had to live,—held in

---

78. [We strive for *what is forbidden*. Ovid, *Amores*, III, 4, 17.]

79. [I combat the universal spider.]

80. [Right of the first night—alleged right of the feudal lord to have sexual intercourse with his vassal's bride on the wedding night.]

81. [Something forbidden.]

contempt to the same degree they were not feared! Contemplation first appeared on earth in disguised form, with an ambiguous appearance, with an evil heart and often with a frightened head: of this there is no doubt. The inactive, brooding, unwarriorlike elements in the instincts of contemplative human beings laid a deep mistrust around them for a long time: against this there was no other remedy than decisively to awaken *fear* of themselves. And in this the ancient Brahmins, for example, were experts! The earliest philosophers knew how to give their existence and appearance a meaning, a support and background against which one learned to *fear* them: more precisely considered, out of an even more fundamental need, namely to win fear and reverence from themselves. For within themselves they found all value judgments turned *against* them, they had to fight down every kind of suspicion and resistance against "the philosopher in them." This they did, as human beings of terrible ages, with terrible means: cruelty against themselves, inventive self-castigation—that was the principal means of these power-thirsty hermits and innovators of ideas who first needed to lay waste to the gods and tradition within themselves in order even to be able to *believe* in their innovation. I call attention to the famous story of king Vishvamitra, who from a thousand years of self-torments won such a feeling of power and self-confidence that he undertook to build a *new heaven*: an uncanny symbol of the earliest and latest histories of philosophers on earth—anyone who ever built a "new heaven" first found the power to do so in his *own hell* . . . Let us compress the whole state of affairs into brief formulas: at first the philosophical spirit always had to slip into the disguise and chrysalis of the *previously established* types of contemplative human beings—as priest, magician, soothsayer, as religious human generally—in order even to *be possible* in any degree at all: for a long time *the ascetic ideal* served the philosopher as the form in which he could appear, as presupposition of existence—he had to *act* it in order to be able to be a philosopher, he had to *believe* it in order to be able to act it. The characteristic aloof stance of philosophers, world-negating, hostile toward life, not believing in the senses, de-sensualized, a stance which has been preserved up to the most recent time and has thus won acceptance as the virtual *philosopher's*

pose in itself,—it is above all a consequence of the poverty of conditions under which philosophy came about and survived at all: for the longest time philosophy would *not* have been *at all possible* on earth without an ascetic covering and mantle, without an ascetic self-misunderstanding. Graphically and clearly expressed: until the most recent time the *ascetic priest* has functioned as the repulsive and gloomy caterpillar-form in which alone philosophy was allowed to live and in which it crept around . . . Has this really *changed*? Has the colorful and dangerous winged animal, the "spirit" that this caterpillar concealed within itself, really—thanks to a sunnier, warmer, more brightly lit world—finally been unfrocked after all and let out into the light? Is there already enough pride, daring, bravery, self-assuredness in existence today, enough will of the spirit, will to responsibility, *freedom of the will* so that henceforth on earth "the philosopher" is truly—*possible*? . . .

11

Only now that we have gotten the *ascetic priest* in sight do we seriously begin to tackle our problem: what does the ascetic ideal mean?—only now does it become "serious": henceforth we have opposite us the true *representative of seriousness* itself. "What does all seriousness mean?"—perhaps already here this still more fundamental question comes to our lips: a question for physiologists, as is fair, but one we will still slip past for the present. The ascetic priest has not only his faith in that ideal but also his will, his power, his interest. His *right* to existence stands and falls with that ideal: no wonder we run into a terrible opponent here—supposing, that is, that we were the opponents of that ideal?—one who fights for his existence against the deniers of that ideal? . . . On the other hand it is from the outset improbable that so interested a stance toward our problem will be of particular use to it; the ascetic priest will hardly even be the most successful defender of his ideal—for the same reason that a woman tends to fail when she wishes to defend "woman in herself"—much less the most objective assessor and judge in the controversy that has been stirred up here. It is hence more likely that we will yet have to help him defend himself effectively against us—this much is already clear as day—than that we should have to fear being too effectively refuted by him ... The idea we are fighting about here is the *valuation* of our life on the part of the ascetic priest: he relates our life (together with that to which it belongs: "nature," "world," the entire sphere of becoming and of transitoriness) to an entirely different kind of existence, which it opposes and excludes, *unless*, perhaps, it were to turn against itself, *to negate itself*: in this case, the case of an ascetic life, life is held to be a bridge for that other existence. The ascetic treats life as a wrong path that one must finally retrace back to the point where it begins; or as an error that one refutes through deeds—*should* refute: for he *demands* that one go along with him; where he can, he forces *his* valuation of existence. What does that mean? Such a monstrous manner of valuation is not inscribed into the history of humankind as an exception and curiosity: it is one of the broadest and longest facts there is. Read from a distant star the majuscule script of our earthly existence would perhaps tempt one to conclude that the earth is the true *ascetic star*, a nook of discontented, arrogant, and repulsive creatures who could not get rid of a deep displeasure with themselves, with the earth, with all life and who caused themselves as much pain as possible out of pleasure in causing pain:—probably their only pleasure. Let us consider after all how regularly, how universally, how in almost all ages the ascetic priest emerges; he does not belong to any single race; he flourishes everywhere; he grows forth from every social rank. Not that he breeds and propagates his manner of valuation through heredity: the opposite is the case—a deep instinct forbids him, broadly speaking, reproduction. It must be a necessity of the first rank that makes this species that is *hostile to life* grow and prosper again and again—it must be in the *interest of life itself* that this type of self-contradiction not die out. For an ascetic life is a self-contradiction: here a *ressentiment* without equal rules, that of an unsatiated instinct and power-will that would like to become lord not over something living but rather over life itself, over its deepest, strongest, most fundamental preconditions; an attempt is made here to use energy to stop up the source of the energy; here the gaze is directed greenly and maliciously against physiological flourishing itself, in particular against its expression, beauty, joy; whereas pleasure is felt and *sought* in deformation, atrophy, in pain, in accident, in the ugly, in voluntary forfeit, in unselfing, self-flagellation, self-sacrifice. This is all paradoxical in the highest degree: we stand here before a conflict that *wants* itself to be conflicted, that *enjoys* itself in this suffering and even becomes ever more self-assured and triumphant to the extent that its own presupposition, physiological viability, *decreases*. "Triumph precisely in the final agony": under this hyperbolic sign the ascetic ideal has fought from time immemorial; in this enigma of seduction, in this image of delight and torment it recognized its brightest light, its salvation, its ultimate victory. *Crux, nux, lux*[82]—in the ascetic ideal they all belong together. —

12

Supposing that such an incarnate will to contradiction and anti-nature is prevailed upon to *philosophize*: on what will he vent his innermost capricious will? On what is most certainly felt to be true, real: he will seek *error* precisely where the true life instinct most unconditionally posits truth. For example, he will—as the ascetics of the Vedānta philosophy did—demote physicality to an illusion, likewise pain, multiplicity, the whole conceptual opposition "subject" and "object"—errors, nothing but errors! To refuse to believe in the self, to deny one's own "reality"—what a triumph!—already no longer merely over the senses, over appearance, but a much higher kind of triumph, a violence and cruelty to *reason*: this lust reaches its peak when the ascetic self-contempt, self-derision of reason decrees: "there *is* a realm of truth and being, but precisely reason is *excluded* from it!" ... (Incidentally: even in the Kantian concept of the "intelligible character of things" there remains something of this lascivious ascetic conflict, which loves to turn reason against reason: for in Kant "intelligible character" means a kind of constitution of things, of which the intellect comprehends just this much: that for the intellect it is—*completely and utterly incomprehensible*.)—Finally let us, particularly as knowers, not be ungrateful toward such resolute reversals of the familiar perspectives and valuations with which the spirit

82. [Cross, nut, light.]

has raged against itself all too long now, apparently wantonly and futilely: to see differently in this way for once, *to want* to see differently, is no small discipline and preparation of the intellect for its future "objectivity"—the latter understood not as "disinterested contemplation" (which is a non-concept and absurdity), but rather as the capacity to have one's pro and contra *in one's power*, and to shift them in and out: so that one knows how to make precisely the *difference* in perspectives and affective interpretations useful for knowledge. For let us guard ourselves better from now on, gentlemen philosophers, against the dangerous old conceptual fabrication that posited a "pure, will-less, painless, timeless subject of knowledge"; let us guard ourselves against the tentacles of such contradictory concepts as "pure reason," "absolute spirituality," "knowledge in itself ": here it is always demanded that we think an eye that cannot possibly be thought, an eye that must not have any direction, in which the active and interpretive forces through which seeing first becomes seeing-something are to be shut off, are to be absent; thus, what is demanded here is always an absurdity and non-concept of an eye. There is *only* a perspectival seeing, *only* a perspectival "knowing"; and *the more* affects we allow to speak about a matter, *the more* eyes, different eyes, we know how to bring to bear on one and the same matter, that much more complete will our "concept" of this matter, our "objectivity" be. But to eliminate the will altogether, to disconnect the affects one and all, supposing that we were capable of this: what? would that not be to *castrate* the intellect? . . .

13

But let us return to our problem. In an accounting that is physiological and no longer psychological, a contradiction such as the ascetic seems to represent, "life *against* life," is—this much is immediately clear as day—simply nonsense. It can only be *apparent*; it must be a kind of provisional expression, an interpretation, formula, arrangement, a psychological misunderstanding of something whose actual nature could not be understood for a long time, could not be designated *in itself*—a mere word, jammed into an old *gap* in human knowledge. And to oppose this

with a brief statement of the facts of the matter: *the ascetic ideal springs from the protective and healing instincts of a degenerating life* that seeks with every means to hold its ground and is fighting for its existence; it points to a partial physiological hindrance and tiredness against which the deepest instincts of life, which have remained intact, fight incessantly with new means and inventions. The ascetic ideal is such a means: it is exactly the opposite of what its venerators suppose—in it and through it life is wrestling with death and *against* death; the ascetic ideal is an artifice for the *preservation* of life. That this ideal has been able to rule and achieve power over humans to the extent that history teaches us it has, in particular wherever the civilization and taming of man has been successfully carried out, expresses a great fact: the *diseasedness* of the previous type of human, at least of the human made tame, the physiological struggle of man with death (more precisely: with satiety with life, with tiredness, with the wish for the "end"). The ascetic priest is the incarnate wish for a different existence, an existence somewhere else, and in fact the highest degree of this wish, its true fervor and passion: but the very *power* of his wishing is the shackle that binds him here; in this very process he becomes a tool that must work at creating more favorable conditions for being-here and being-human—with this very *power* he ties to existence the entire herd of the deformed, out of sorts, short-changed, failed, those of every kind who suffer from themselves, by instinctively going before them as shepherd. One understands me already: this ascetic priest, this seeming enemy of life, this *negating one*—precisely he belongs to the very great *conserving* and yes-*creating* forces of life . . . Whence it stems, this diseasedness? For man is sicker, more unsure, more changing, more undetermined than any other animal, of this there is no doubt—he is *the* sick animal: how does this come about? Certainly he has also dared more, innovated more, defied more, challenged fate more than all the other animals taken together: he, the great experimenter with himself, the unsatisfied, unsatiated one who wrestles with animal, nature, and gods for final dominion—he, the one yet unconquered, the eternally future one who no longer finds any rest from his own pressing energy, so that his future digs inexorably like a spur into the flesh of every present:—

how could such a courageous and rich animal not also be the most endangered, the most prolongedly and most deeply sick among all sick animals? . . . Man is fed up with it, often enough, there are entire epidemics of this being-fed-up (— around 1348, at the time of the Dance of Death): but even this loathing, this tiredness, this vexation with himself — everything emerges so powerfully in him that it immediately becomes a new shackle. As if by magic, the "no" that he says to life brings to light an abundance of tender "yes's"; even when he *wounds* himself, this master of destruction, self-destruction — afterwards it is the wound itself that compels him *to live* . . .

14

The more normal the diseasedness in man is — and we cannot deny this normality — the higher one should honor the rare cases of powerfulness in soul and body, the *strokes of luck* among humans; the more strictly one should guard the well-formed against the worst air, against the air of the sick. Do we do this? . . . The sick are the greatest danger to the healthy; it is *not* from the strongest that harm comes to the strong, but rather from the weakest. Do we know this? . . . Broadly speaking, it is by no means the fear of man one might wish lessened: for this fear compels the strong to be strong, in some cases to be terrible — it keeps the well-formed type of human *upright*. What is to be feared, what has a doomful effect such as no other doom, would not be the great fear but rather the great *disgust* at man; likewise the great *compassion* for man. Supposing that these two should mate one day, then immediately something of the most uncanny nature would unavoidably come into the world, the "last will" of man, his will to nothingness, nihilism. And indeed: much is prepared for this. Whoever has not only a nose for smelling but also eyes and ears will sense something like madhouse air, like hospital air almost everywhere he might go today — I am speaking, in fairness, of the man's cultural regions, of every kind of "Europe" there is on earth by now. The *diseased* are man's great danger: *not* the evil, *not* the "beasts of prey." Those who from the outset are failed, downcast, broken — they are the ones, the *weakest* are the ones who most undermine life among humans, who most dangerously poison

and call into question our confidence in life, in man, in ourselves. Where might one escape it, that veiled look from which one carries away a deep sadness, that backward-turned look of one deformed from the beginning, a look that betrays how such a human speaks to himself — that look that is a sigh. "If only I might be someone else!" thus sighs this look: but there is no hope. "I am who I am: how could I get free from myself. And yet — I *am fed up with myself*!" . . . On such ground of self-contempt, a true swamp-ground, every weed grows, every poisonous plant, and all of it so small, so hidden, so dishonest, so cloying. Here the worms of vengeful and grudging feelings teem; here the air stinks of things that are secret and cannot be acknowledged; here the web of the most vicious conspiracy spins itself constantly — the conspiracy of the sufferers against the well-formed and victorious; here the appearance of the victorious one is *hated*. And what mendacity not to acknowledge this hate as hate! What expenditure of great words and poses, what art of "righteous" defamation! These deformed ones: what noble eloquence streams forth from their lips! How much sugary, slimy, humble submission swims in their eyes! What do they actually want? At least to *represent* justice, love, wisdom, superiority — that is the ambition of these "undermost ones," of these sick ones! And how skillful such an ambition makes one! One should particularly admire the counterfeiter's skill with which the stamp of virtue, even the cling-clang, the golden tone of virtue, is copied. They have now taken virtue in lease completely and utterly for themselves, these weak and incurably diseased ones, of this there is no doubt: "we alone are the good, the just," so they speak, "we alone are the *homines bonae voluntatis.*"[83] They walk about among us as bodily reproaches, as warnings to us — as if health, being well-formed, strength, pride, a feeling of power were depraved things in themselves, for which one will someday have to atone, bitterly atone: oh how ready they themselves basically are to *make* others atone, how they thirst to be *hangmen*! Among them there are plenty of vengeful ones disguised as judges, who constantly carry the word "justice" in their mouths like poisonous saliva, forever

83. [Men of good will. Luke 2:14.]

with pursed lips, forever ready to spit on everything that does not look dissatisfied and that goes its way in good spirits. Among them there is no lack of that most disgusting species of the vain—the mendacious misbirths who are out to play the role of "beautiful souls" and who for instance bring their mangled sensuality, wrapped in verses and other diapers, onto the market as "purity of heart": the species of the moral onanist and "self-gratifier." The will of the sick to represent *any* form of superiority, their instinct for secret paths that lead to a tyranny over the healthy— where might this not be found, this will of precisely the weakest to power! The sick woman in particular: no one excels her in refinements for ruling, oppressing, tyrannizing. Furthermore the sick woman does not spare anything living, anything dead; she digs the most buried of things up again (the Bogos say: "woman is a hyena"). Look into the background of every family, every corporation, every community: everywhere the battle of the sick against the healthy— a silent battle for the most part with little poisonous powders, with needle pricks, with insidious plays of martyr expressions, at times, however, even with the *loud* gestures of an invalid's pharisaism, which loves most of all to play "noble indignation." It would like to make itself heard all the way into the hallowed halls of science, this hoarse indignant bark of the diseased dogs, the biting mendacity and rage of such "noble" Pharisees (—once again I remind readers who have ears of that Berliner apostle of revenge, Eugen Dühring, who is making the most indecent and repulsive use of moral boom-boom in present-day Germany: Dühring, the foremost moral big-mouth there now is, even among his own kind, the anti-Semites). They are all human beings of *ressentiment*, these physiologically failed and worm-eaten ones, a whole trembling earth of subterranean revenge, inexhaustible, insatiable in outbursts against the happy, and likewise in masquerades of revenge, in pretexts for revenge: when would they actually arrive at their last, finest, most sublime triumph of revenge? Undoubtedly, if they should succeed in *shoving* their own misery, all misery generally *into the conscience* of the happy: so that the happy would one day begin to be ashamed of their happiness and perhaps say among themselves: "it is a disgrace to be happy! *there is too much misery!*" . . . But there could

not be any greater and more doomful misunderstanding than when the happy, the well-formed, the powerful of body and soul begin to doubt their *right to happiness*. Away with this "inverted world"! Away with this disgraceful softening of the feelings! That the sick *not* make the healthy sick—and this would be such a softening—that should certainly be the highest viewpoint on earth:—but this would require above all else that the healthy remain *separated* from the sick, guarded even against the sight of the sick, that they not confuse themselves with the sick. Or would it perhaps be their task to be nurses or physicians? . . . But they could in no way more gravely mistake and deny *their* task—the higher *must* not degrade itself to a tool of the lower, the pathos of distance *must* also keep their tasks separated to all eternity! Their right to exist, the privilege of the bell with full sound over the dissonant, cracked one is of course a thousandfold greater one: they alone are the *guarantors* of the future, they alone have been *given responsibility* for the human future. What *they* can do, what *they* should do, a sick person can never and should never do: but *in order for* them to be able to do what only *they* should do, how could they be free to choose to be physician, comforter, "savior" for the sick? . . . And therefore good air! good air! And in any case away from the proximity of all madhouses and hospitals of culture! And therefore good company, *our* company! Or solitude if it must be! But in any case away from the foul vapors of inward corruption and the secret wormfodder of invalids! . . . So that we may defend ourselves, my friends, at least for a while yet, against what may be the two gravest epidemics that have been reserved just for us—against the *great disgust at the sight of man*! against the *great compassion for man*! . . .

15

If one has grasped in all its depth—and I demand that precisely here one *reach* deeply, grasp deeply— why it positively can *not* be the task of the healthy to nurse the sick, to make the sick well, then a further necessity has also been grasped—the necessity of physicians and nurses *who are themselves sick*: and now we have and hold with both hands the meaning of the ascetic priest. The ascetic priest must be counted as the foreordained savior, shepherd, and advocate of the sick herd: only then do we understand his historic mission. *Dominion over ones who suffer* is his realm, it is to this that his instinct directs him, in this he has his most characteristic art, his mastery, his kind of happiness. He must be sick himself, he must be related to the sick and short-changed from the ground up in order to understand them—in order to get along with them; but he must also be strong, lord over himself more than over others, with his will to power intact, so that he has the confidence and the fear of the sick, so that for them he can be a foothold, resistance, support, compulsion, disciplinarian, tyrant, god. He is to defend them, his herd—against whom? Against the healthy, no doubt, also against envying the healthy; he must by nature oppose *and hold in contempt* all coarse, tempestuous, unbridled, hard, violent-predatory health and powerfulness. The priest is the first form of the *more delicate* animal that holds in contempt even more readily than it hates. He will not be spared waging war with the beasts of prey, a war of cunning (of the "spirit") more than of force, as goes without saying—to this end he will perhaps need almost to develop in himself, at least *to signify*, a new type of beast of prey—a new animal terribleness in which the polar bear, the lithe cold wait-and-see tiger cat, and not least of all the fox appear to be bound into a unity just as attractive as it is fear-inspiring. Supposing that necessity compels him, he then steps into the very midst of the other kind of beast of prey with bearish seriousness, venerable, cold, shrewd, deceptively superior, as herald and mouth-piece of mysterious forces, determined to sow sorrow, conflict, self-contradiction on this ground wherever he can and, only too sure of his art, to become lord over *sufferers* at all times. He brings along ointments and balm, no doubt; but he first needs to wound in order to be a physician; as he then stills the pain that the wound causes, *he poisons the wound at the same time*—for in this above all he is an expert, this magician and tamer of beasts of prey, in whose vicinity everything healthy necessarily becomes sick and everything sick, tame. He defends his sick herd well enough indeed, this strange shepherd—he defends it against itself as well, against what smolders within the herd itself: badness, deceitfulness, maliciousness and whatever else is characteristic of all the sick and

invalids when among themselves; he fights shrewdly, hard, and secretively against the anarchy and ever-incipient self-dissolution within the herd, where that most dangerous blasting and explosive material, *ressentiment*, is constantly mounting and mounting. To discharge this explosive in such a way that it does not blow up either the herd or the shepherd, that is his true feat, also his supreme usefulness; if one wanted to sum up the value of the priestly mode of existence in the shortest formula one would have to say straight away: the priest *changes the direction* of *ressentiment*. For every sufferer instinctively seeks a cause for his suffering; still more precisely, a perpetrator, still more specifically, a *guilty* perpetrator who is receptive to suffering—in short, some living thing on which, in response to some pretext or other, he can discharge his affects in deed or in effigy: for the discharge of affect is the sufferer's greatest attempt at relief, namely at *anesthetization*—his involuntarily craved narcotic against torment of any kind. It is here alone, according to my surmise, that one finds the true physiological causality of *ressentiment*, of revenge, and of their relatives—that is, in a longing for *anesthetization of pain through affect*:—this causality has been commonly sought, very mistakenly it seems to me, in the defensive counterblow, a mere reactive protective measure, a "reflex movement" in the case of some sudden harm and endangerment, of the kind that a frog without a head still carries out in order to get rid of a corrosive acid. But the difference is fundamental: in the one case, one wishes to prevent further damage; in the other case, one wishes, by means of a more vehement emotion of any kind, to *anesthetize* a tormenting, secret pain that is becoming unbearable and, at least for the moment, to put it out of consciousness—for this one needs an affect, as wild an affect as possible and, for its excitation, the first best pretext. "Someone must be to blame for the fact that I feel bad"—this kind of reasoning is characteristic of all those who are diseased, indeed the more the true cause of their feeling bad, the physiological one, remains concealed from them (—it can lie for instance in a sickening of the *nervus sympathicus*[84] or in an excessive secretion of bile, or in a deficiency of potassium sulfate

---

84. [Sympathetic nerve (nervous system).]

or phosphate in the blood or in pressure conditions in the abdomen that stop the circulation of the blood, or in degeneration of the ovaries and the like). Those who suffer are one and all possessed of a horrifying readiness and inventiveness in pretexts for painful affects; they savor even their suspicion, their brooding over bad deeds and apparent curtailments; they dig around after dark questionable stories in the viscera of their past and present, where they are free to wallow in a tormenting suspicion and to intoxicate themselves on their own poison of malice—they tear open the oldest wounds, they bleed to death from scars long healed, they make malefactors out of friend, wife, child and whatever else stands closest to them. "I am suffering: for this someone must be to blame"—thus every diseased sheep thinks. But his shepherd, the ascetic priest, says to him: "That's right, my sheep! someone must be to blame for it: but you yourself are this someone, you alone are to blame for it—you *alone are to blame for yourself*!" . . . That is bold enough, false enough: but one thing at least has been achieved by it, in this way, as noted, the direction of the *ressentiment* has been—*changed*.

16

One can guess by now what I think life's healing-artist instinct has at least *attempted* through the ascetic priest and to what end a temporary tyranny of such paradoxical and paralogical concepts as "guilt," "sin," "sinfulness," "corruption," "damnation" has had to serve him: to make the sick to a certain degree *harmless*, to destroy the incurable through themselves, to strictly direct the more mildly sick toward themselves, to give a backwards direction to their *ressentiment* ("one thing is needful") and in this manner to *exploit* the bad instincts of all sufferers for the purpose of self-discipline, self-supervision, self-overcoming. As goes without saying, with a "medication" of this kind, a mere affect-medication, it absolutely cannot be a matter of a true *healing* of the sick in the physiological sense; one could not even claim that the instinct of life in any way has healing in mind or in intention. A kind of crowding together and organizing of the sick, on the one hand (—the word "church" is the most popular name for this), a kind of provisional securing of the more healthily formed, the more fully

cast, on the other, thus the tearing open of a chasm between healthy and sick—for a long time that was all! And it was a great deal! it was a *very great deal*! . . . [In this treatise I am proceeding, as one can see, on the presupposition, which I do not first have to justify as far as readers of the type I need are concerned: that "sinfulness" in humans is not a factual state but rather only the interpretation of a factual state, namely of being physiologically out of sorts—the latter seen from a moral-religious perspective that is no longer binding on us.—That someone *feels* "guilty," "sinful" does not at all prove he is right in feeling so; just as little as someone is healthy merely because he feels healthy. Just recall the famous witch trials: back then the most sharp-sighted and philanthropic judges did not doubt that there was guilt; the "witches" *themselves did not doubt it*—and still there was no guilt.—To express that presupposition in expanded form: "pain of the soul" itself does not at all count as a factual state but rather only as an interpretation (causal interpretation) of factual states that could not yet be exactly formulated: thus something that is still entirely up in the air and is not scientifically binding—actually only a fat word in the place of a very thin question mark. If someone cannot cope with his "pain of the soul" it is *not*, crudely put, due to his "soul"; more likely to his belly (crudely put, as stated: which in no way expresses a wish also to be heard crudely, understood crudely . . .) A strong and well-formed human digests his experiences (deeds, misdeeds included) as he digests his meals, even when he has hard bites to swallow. If he "cannot cope" with an experience, this kind of indigestion is just as physiological as that other one—and in many cases in fact only one of the consequences of that other.—With such a conception one can, speaking among ourselves, still be the strictest opponent of all materialism . . .]

17

But is he actually a *physician*, this ascetic priest?—We have already grasped why it is hardly permissible to call him a physician, as much as he likes to feel himself to be a "savior," to allow himself to be venerated as a "savior." He combats only suffering itself, the listlessness of the one suffering, *not* its cause, *not* the actual state of sickness—this must form our most fundamental objection to priestly medication. If, however, one adopts for once that perspective as only the priest knows and has it, one will not easily come to the end of one's amazement at all he has seen, sought, and found from within it. The *alleviation* of suffering, "comforting" of every kind—this turns out to be his very genius: how inventively he has understood his task as comforter, how unhesitatingly and boldly he has chosen the means for it! One might call Christianity in particular a great treasury of the most ingenious means for comforting, so much that is invigorating, alleviating, narcotizing has been heaped up in it; so much that is most dangerous and most audacious has been ventured for this purpose; so subtle, so sophisticated, so Mediterraneanly sophisticated has Christianity been in intuiting what kind of stimulant-affects can conquer, at least for a time, the deep depression, the leaden tiredness, the black sadness of the physiologically inhibited. For stated generally: with all great religions the main concern is to combat a certain tiredness and heaviness that have become epidemic. From the outset one can posit as probable that from time to time at certain places on earth a *feeling of physiological inhibition* must almost necessarily become lord over broad masses of people; from a lack of physiological knowledge, however, this feeling does not enter into consciousness as such, so that its "cause," its remedy can only be sought and attempted in the psychological-moral realm (—indeed this is my most general formula for that which is commonly called a "*religion*"). Such a feeling of inhibition can be of the most varied extraction: for instance as consequence of the crossbreeding of races that are too different from each other (or of social ranks—social ranks always express differences of extraction and race as well: the European "*Weltschmerz*,"[85] the "pessimism" of the nineteenth century is essentially the consequence of a nonsensically sudden mixing of the social ranks); or conditioned by a flawed emigration—a race that has ended up in a climate for which its power of adaptation is not sufficient (the case of the Indians in India); or the after-effect of age and exhaustion of the race (Parisian pessimism from 1850 on); or of a wrong diet (alcoholism of the Middle Ages; the nonsense of vegetarians, who admittedly have the authority of Sir Andrew[86] in Shakespeare on their side); or of corruption of the blood, malaria, syphilis, and the like (German depression after the Thirty-Years' War, which infected half of Germany with bad diseases and thereby prepared the soil for German servility, German timidity). In such cases a *battle with the feeling of listlessness* is always attempted on the grandest scale; let us instruct ourselves briefly in its most important practices and forms. (I ignore here entirely, as is fair, the actual *philosophers'* battle against the feeling of listlessness, which always tends to go on simultaneously—it is interesting enough, but too absurd, too inconsequential in practical terms, too much in the manner of cobweb-spinners and idlers, as, say, when pain is to be proven an error under the naive presupposition that the pain *would have to* disappear once the error in it has been recognized—but behold! it guarded itself against disappearing . . .) This dominant feeling of listlessness is combatted, *first*, by means that reduce the general feeling of life to its lowest point. If possible no willing at all, not another wish; avoiding whatever stirs up affect, whatever stirs up "blood" (no eating salt: hygiene of the fakir); no loving; no hating; apathy; no avenging oneself; no making oneself rich; no working; begging; if possible no woman, or as little woman as possible: in respect to the spiritual the principle of Pascal[87] "*il faut s'abêtir.*"[88] The result, expressed in psychological-moral terms: "un-selfing," "hallowing"; expressed physiologically: hypnotization—the attempt to achieve something for man that approximates what *hibernation* is for some species of animals, what *aestivation* is for many plants in hot climates, a minimum of consumption and metabolism whereby life just barely continues without actually entering into our consciousness anymore. An astounding amount of human energy has been expended on this

85. ["World-pain," an emotional state in which the predominant tone is a feeling of pain or sadness because of the inadequacy of the world.]

86. [A character in Shakespeare's *Twelfth Night*. The passage in question is I, iii.]

87. [Blaise Pascal (1623–1662), French mathematician, physicist, and religious philosopher.]

88. [One must make oneself stupid.]

goal—perhaps in vain? . . . There is certainly no doubt that such sportsmen of "holiness," who abound in all ages, among almost all peoples, have in fact found a real redemption from that which they combatted with such rigorous training—in countless cases they really got *free* of that deep physiological depression with the help of their system of hypnotics: for which reason their methodology counts as one of the most universal ethnological facts. There is likewise nothing that would permit us to count such an intention to starve physicality and desire as in itself among the symptoms of madness (as it pleases a clumsy kind of roastbeef-eating "free spirit" and Sir Andrew to do). It is all the more certain that it forms, can form, the *path* to all kinds of mental disturbances, to "inner lights," for example, as with the Hesychasts of Mount Athos, to hallucinations of sounds and figures, to lustful effusions and ecstasies of sensuality (story of Saint Theresa). The interpretation given to conditions of this kind by those who are afflicted with them has always been as fanatically false as possible, this goes without saying: but do not fail to hear the tone of the most convinced gratitude that resounds already in the *will* to such a manner of interpretation. The highest condition, *redemption* itself, that final achievement of total hypnotization and stillness, always counts for them as the mystery in itself, for the expression of which even the highest symbols are insufficient, as a turning in and returning home into the ground of things, as becoming free from all illusion, as "knowledge," as "truth," as "being," as escaping from every goal, every wish, every doing, as a state beyond good and evil as well. "Good and evil," the Buddhist says,— "both are shackles: over both the perfect one became lord"; "that which has been done and that which has been left undone," says the believer of the Vedânta, "cause him no pain; good and evil he shakes from himself, as a wise man; his realm no longer suffers through any deed; over good and evil, over both he passed beyond": a pan-Indian conception then, just as brahmanistic as buddhistic. (Neither in the Indian nor in the Christian manner of thinking is this "redemption" considered to be *attainable* through virtue, through moral improvement, however high they may fix the value of virtue as a hypnotic: make note of this,—it corresponds, moreover, to the facts of the matter. To have remained *true* in this may perhaps

be considered the best piece of realism in the three greatest, otherwise so fundamentally moralized religions. "For the knowing one there is no duty" . . . "Redemption is not brought about by the *addition* of virtues—for it consists in being one with brahma, which is not capable of any addition of perfection—and just as little by the *discarding* of faults: for brahma, to be one with which constitutes redemption, is eternally pure"—these passages from the commentary of Shankara,[89] quoted from Europe's first real *expert* on Indian philosophy, my friend Paul Deussen.) Let us then honor "redemption" in the great religions; but it is a bit difficult to remain serious when faced with the esteem in which *deep sleep* is held by these people, who are tired of life, too tired even for dreaming—deep sleep, that is, as already an entering into brahma, as *achieved unio mystica* with God. "When he has then fallen asleep completely and utterly"—it says concerning this in the oldest most venerable "Scripture"—"and has completely come to rest so that he no longer sees any dream images, then he is, oh dear one, united with That Which Is, he has entered into himself—embraced by the knowledge-like self, he no longer has any consciousness of that which is outside or inside. Day and night do not cross over this bridge, age does not, death does not, suffering does not, good works do not, evil works do not." "In deep sleep," the faithful of this deepest of the three great religions likewise say, "the soul raises itself out of this body, enters into the highest light, and thereby appears in its own form: there it is the highest spirit itself, which walks about while joking and playing and delighting itself, be it with women or with carriages or with friends; there it no longer thinks back on this appendage of a body to which the *prâna* (the breath of life) is harnessed like a draught animal to the cart." Nevertheless let us bear in mind here, too, as in the case of "redemption," that what is expressed in the preceding, however much in the splendor of oriental exaggeration, is simply the same esteem as that of the clear, cool, Greek-cool, but suffering Epicurus: the hypnotic feeling of nothingness, the rest of the deepest sleep, in short, *absence of suffering*—this may count already as the highest good, as value of values for

89. [Indian philosopher and theologian (ca. 788–ca. 820)].

those who suffer and are thoroughly out of sorts, this *must* be appraised by them as positive, felt to be *the* positive itself. (According to the same logic of feelings, in all pessimistic religions nothingness is called *God*.)

18

Much more frequent than this sort of hypnotic general suppression of sensitivity, of susceptibility to pain—which presupposes even rarer forces, above all courage, contempt of opinion, "intellectual stoicism,"—is the attempt at a different kind of training against conditions of depression, one that is in any case easier: *mechanical activity*. That this relieves a suffering existence to a not inconsiderable degree is beyond all doubt: today this fact is called, somewhat dishonestly, "the blessing of work." The relief consists in this: that the interest of the sufferer is thoroughly diverted from the suffering—that it is continually doing and yet again only doing that enters into consciousness and, consequently, that little room remains in it for suffering: for it is *narrow*, this chamber of human consciousness! Mechanical activity and that which belongs to it—like absolute regularity, punctual unreflected obedience, one's way of life set once and for all, the filling up of time, a certain permission for, indeed discipline in "impersonality," in self-forgetfulness, in *"incuria sui"*[90]—: how thoroughly, how subtly the ascetic priest knew how to use these in the battle with pain! Precisely when he had to deal with sufferers of the lower social ranks, with work slaves or prisoners (or with women: who are of course usually both at the same time, work slaves and prisoners), it required little more than a small art of name-changing and rebaptizing to make them henceforth see in hated things a boon, a relative bit of good fortune:—in any case the dissatisfaction of the slave with his lot was *not* invented by priests.—A still more valued means in the battle with depression is the prescription of a *small joy* that is easily accessible and can be made a regular practice; this medication is frequently made use of in connection with the one just discussed. The most frequent form in which joy is thus prescribed as a means to a cure is the joy of *giving* joy (as doing good, giving gifts, relieving, helping, encouraging, comforting, praising, honoring); by prescribing "love of one's neighbor" the ascetic priest is basically prescribing an arousal of the strongest, most life-affirming drive, even if in the most cautious of doses—the *will to power*. The happiness of the "smallest superiority," such as accompanies all doing good, being useful, helping, honoring, is the most plentiful means of consolation that the physiologically inhibited tend to make use of, assuming they are well advised: otherwise they cause each other pain, in obedience to the same basic instinct, naturally. When one looks for the beginnings of Christianity in the Roman world, one finds associations for mutual support, pauper-, invalid-, burial-associations, which sprung up on the undermost soil of the society of that time, and in which that principal medicine against depression, the small joy, that of mutual good deeds was consciously cultivated—perhaps this was something new back then, a true discovery? In a "will to mutuality," to herd-formation, to "community," to "cenacle" elicited in this manner, the will to power thus aroused in the process—even if it is on the smallest scale—must now in turn come to a new and much fuller outburst: *herd-formation* is an essential step and victory in the battle with depression. With the growth of the community a new interest also grows strong in the individual, one that often enough lifts him above and beyond that which is most personal in his ill-humor, his aversion to *himself* (the *"despectio sui"*[91] of Geulincx). Out of a longing to shake off the dull listlessness and the feeling of weakness, all the sick, the diseased strive instinctively for a herd organization: the ascetic priest intuits this instinct and fosters it; wherever there are herds it is the instinct of weakness that willed the herds and the shrewdness of priests that organized them. For do not overlook this: the strong strive just as naturally and necessarily *away* from each other as the weak strive *toward* each other; when the former band together it occurs only with a view to an aggressive joint action and joint satisfaction of their will to power, with a great deal of resistance from the individual conscience; the latter, on the other hand, arrange themselves into groups with *plea-*

---

90. [Neglect of oneself.]

91. [Contempt of oneself.]

sure precisely in the arrangement into groups—their instinct is satisfied in the process just as much as the instinct of the born "lords" (that is of the solitary beast-of-prey species of human) is at bottom irritated and disquieted by organization. Beneath every oligarchy—all of history teaches this—*tyrannical* craving always lies hidden; every oligarchy trembles constantly from the tension that every individual in it needs in order to remain lord over this craving. (Thus it was for example with the *Greeks*: Plato attests it in a hundred passages, Plato who knew his own kind—*and* himself . . .)

19

The means employed by the ascetic priest with which we have thus far become acquainted—the general muffling of the feeling of life, mechanical activity, the small joy, above all that of "love of one's neighbor," the herd organization, the awakening of the communal feeling of power, whereby the individual's vexation with himself is drowned out by his pleasure in the prospering of the community—these are, measured according to a modern standard, his *innocent* means in the battle with listlessness: let us now turn to the more interesting ones, the "guilty" ones. They are all concerned with one thing: some kind of *excess of the emotions*—used as the most effective means of anesthetizing the dull paralyzing long painfulness; for which reason priestly inventiveness has been virtually inexhaustible in thinking through this single question: "*by what means* does one achieve an emotional excess?" . . . That sounds harsh: it is clear as day that it would sound more pleasant and perhaps suit the ears better if I said, for instance, "the ascetic priest has always taken advantage of the *enthusiasm* that lies in all strong affects." But why stroke the tender ears of our modern milquetoasts? Why should *we* give in even one step to their Tartuffery of words? For us psychologists there would already be a Tartuffery *of deed* in this; not to mention that it would disgust us. For in this, if in anything, a psychologist today has his *good taste* (—others may say: his righteousness), that he resists the disgracefully *moralized* manner of speaking that clings like slime to virtually all modern judging of humans and things. For do not deceive yourself in this: what constitutes the most characteristic feature of modern souls, modern books is not

the lie, but rather the ingrained *innocence* in their moralistic mendacity. To have to discover this "innocence" everywhere again and again—this constitutes perhaps the most repulsive piece of work in all the questionable work a psychologist must take upon himself today; it is a piece of *our* great danger—it is a path that perhaps leads precisely *us* to the great disgust . . . I do not doubt *what purpose* alone modern books (supposing that they have any permanence, which is admittedly not to be feared, and likewise supposing that there will one day be a posterity with stricter, harsher, *healthier* taste)—what purpose absolutely *everything* modern would serve, could serve for this posterity: as emetics—and this by virtue of its moral cloyingness and falseness, of its innermost feminism that likes to call itself "idealism" and in any case believes itself to be idealism. Our educated ones of today, our "good ones" do not lie—this is true; but it is *not* to their credit! The true lie, the authentic resolute "honest" lie (concerning whose value one should listen to Plato) would be something far too rigorous, too strong for them; it would demand what one is not *permitted* to demand of them, that they open their eyes toward themselves, that they know how to distinguish between "true" and "false" in their own case. The *dishonest lie* alone befits them; whatever feels itself to be a "good human being" today is completely incapable of relating to any issue except in a manner that is *dishonestly mendacious*, abysmally mendacious, but innocently mendacious, trustingly mendacious, blue-eyedly mendacious, virtuously mendacious. These "good human beings"—they are all moralized down to the roots now and with respect to honesty spoiled and ruined to all eternity: which of them could still endure a *truth* "about humankind"! . . . Or, more concretely asked: which of them could bear a *true* biography! . . . A few signs of this: Lord Byron wrote down a considerable number of most personal things about himself but Thomas Moore was "too good" for it: he burned the papers of his friend. Dr. Gwinner, the executor of Schopenhauer's will, is supposed to have done the same thing: for Schopenhauer as well had written down a considerable amount about himself and perhaps even against himself ("*eis heauton*").[92] The able American

92. [About himself *or* against himself.]

Thayer, the biographer of Beethoven, stopped all at once in his work: having arrived at some point or other in this venerable and naive life he could no longer endure it . . . Moral: what prudent man would write an honest word about himself anymore today?— for he would have to belong to the Order of Holy Foolhardiness. We are promised an autobiography of Richard Wagner: who doubts that it will be a *prudent* autobiography? . . . Let us also call to mind the comical horror that the Catholic priest Janssen aroused in Germany with his inconceivably simplistic and innocuous picture of the German Reformation movement; what would one do if someone were to narrate this movement *differently* some day, if a real psychologist were to narrate a real Luther some day, no longer with the moralistic simplicity of a country cleric, no longer with the cloying and discreet prudishness of Protestant historians, but rather, say, with a *Taine*-[93] like dauntlessness, out of *strength of the soul* and not out of a prudent indulgence toward strength? . . . (The Germans, incidentally, have in the end brought forth the classical type of the latter nicely enough—they may indeed count him as one of their own, count him to their credit: namely their Leopold Ranke,[94] this born classical *advocatus* of every *causa fortior*,[95] this most prudent of all prudent "factual ones.")

20

But you will have understood me already:—all in all reason enough, isn't there, that we psychologists nowadays cannot get rid of considerable mistrust *of ourselves*? . . . We, too, are probably still "too good" for our trade; we, too, are probably still the victims, the booty, the invalids of this moralized taste of the times, as much as we may feel ourselves to be ones who hold it in contempt—it probably infects *us* too. What was it of which that diplomat[96] warned when

speaking to his peers? "Let us mistrust above all, gentlemen, our first impulses!" he said, *"they are almost always good"* . . . Thus, too, every psychologist today should speak to his peers . . . And with that we come back to our problem, which indeed demands considerable strictness of us, considerable mistrust, in particular of "first impulses." *The ascetic ideal serving an intent to produce emotional excess*:—whoever recalls the previous treatise will already anticipate the essential content of what remains to be presented— pressed into these ten words. To free the human soul from all its moorings for once, to immerse it in terrors, frosts, blazes, and ecstasies in such a way that it is freed from everything that is small and small-minded in listlessness, dullness, being out of sorts as if by a bolt of lightning: which paths lead to *this* goal? And which of them most surely? . . . Basically all great affects have the capacity to do so, assuming that they discharge themselves suddenly: anger, fear, lust, revenge, hope, triumph, despair, cruelty; and indeed the ascetic priest has unhesitatingly taken into his service the *whole* pack of wild dogs in man and unleashed first this one, then that one, always for the same purpose, to waken man out of slow sadness, to put to flight, at least for a time, his dull pain, his lingering misery, always under a religious interpretation and "justification." Every such emotional excess *exacts payment* afterwards, that goes without saying— it makes the sick sicker—and therefore this kind of remedy for pain is, measured by a modern standard, a "guilty" kind. Since fairness demands it, however, one must insist all the more that it has been applied *with a good conscience*, that the ascetic priest has prescribed it with the deepest faith in its usefulness, indeed indispensability—and often enough almost breaking down in the face of the wretchedness he has created; likewise, that the vehement physiological avengings of such excesses, perhaps even mental disturbances, do not actually contradict the overall sense of this kind of medication: which, as has previously been shown, is *not* out to heal sicknesses, but rather to combat the listlessness of depression, to alleviate it, to anesthetize it. And it was *thus* that this goal was achieved. The principal bow stroke the ascetic priest

93. [Hippolyte Adolphe Taine (1828–1893), French philosopher, historian and critic.]

94. [Leopold Ranke (1795–1886), highly successful and influential historian, author of over fifty volumes of history.]

95. [Stronger cause.]

96. [Charles-Maurice de Talleyrand (-Périgord), Prince de Bénévent (1754–1838). French statesman and diplo-

mat known for his lack of scruples and for his capacity for political survival.]

allowed himself in order to cause the human soul to resound with wrenching and ecstatic music of every kind was executed—everyone knows this—by exploiting the *feeling of guilt*. The previous treatise briefly suggested its origins—as a piece of animal psychology, no more: there the feeling of guilt first confronted us in its raw state as it were. Only in the hands of the priest, this true artist of the feeling of guilt, did it take on form—oh what a form! "Sin"—for thus reads the priestly reinterpretation of the animal's "bad conscience" (cruelty turned backwards)—has so far been the greatest event in the history of the sick soul: in it we have the most dangerous and doom-laden feat of religious interpretation. Man, suffering from himself in some way or other, physiologically in any case, somewhat like an animal locked in a cage, uncertain why, to what end? desirous of reasons—reasons alleviate—desirous also of cures and narcotics, finally holds counsel with one who also knows concealed things—and behold! he receives a hint; from his magician, the ascetic priest, he receives the *first* hint concerning the "cause" of his suffering: he is to seek it in *himself*, in a *guilt*, in a piece of the past, he is to understand his suffering itself as a *state of punishment* . . . He has heard, he has understood, the unhappy one: now things stand with him as with the hen around whom a line has been drawn. He can no longer get out of this circle of lines: out of the invalid "the sinner" has been made . . . And now one will not be rid of the sight of this invalid, of "the sinner," for a couple of millennia—will one ever be rid of him again?—wherever one looks, everywhere the hypnotic gaze of the sinner forever moving in the same direction (in the direction of "guilt" as the *only* causality of suffering); everywhere bad conscience, this "hideous animal," to use Luther's words; everywhere the past regurgitated, the deed twisted around, the "green eye" for all activity; everywhere that *wanting*-to-misunderstand-suffering made into life's meaning, the reinterpretation of suffering into feelings of guilt, fear, and punishment; everywhere the whip, the hair shirt, the starving body, contrition; everywhere the sinner breaking himself on the cruel wheels of a restless, diseased-lascivious conscience; everywhere mute torment, extreme fear, the agony of a tortured heart, the cramps of an unknown happiness, the cry for "redemption." Indeed, through this system of proce-

dures the old depression, heaviness, and tiredness was thoroughly *overcome*, life became *very* interesting again: awake, eternally awake, in need of sleep, glowing, charred, exhausted and still not tired—this is what the human being looked like, "the sinner" who was initiated into *these* mysteries. This old great magician in the battle with listlessness, the ascetic priest—he had obviously been victorious, *his* kingdom had come: people no longer protested *against* pain, they *thirsted* after pain; "*more* pain! *more* pain!" thus cried the longing of his disciples and initiates for centuries. Every emotional excess that caused pain, everything that shattered, toppled, crushed, entranced, enraptured, the secret of places of torture, the inventiveness of hell itself—everything had now been discovered, guessed, exploited, everything stood at the disposal of the magician, everything served henceforth to the victory of his ideal, of the ascetic ideal . . . "My kingdom is not of *this* world"—he spoke now as before: did he really still have the right to speak so? . . . Goethe claimed that there were only thirty-six tragic situations: one can guess from this, if one didn't already know it, that Goethe was no ascetic priest. He—knows more . . .

21

With respect to *this* entire kind of priestly medication, the "guilty" kind, any word of criticism is too much. That an emotional excess such as the ascetic priest tends to prescribe for his sick ones in this case (under the holiest name, as goes without saying, likewise imbued with the holiness of his purpose) has really *been of use* to any sick person, who would have any desire to uphold a claim of this kind? One should at least be clear about the expression "be of use." If by this one intends to express that such a system of treatment has *improved* man, then I will not contradict: I only add what "improve" means for me—the same as "tamed," "weakened," "discouraged," "sophisticated," "pampered," "emasculated" (hence almost the same as *injured* . . .) If, however, we are dealing chiefly with those who are sick, out of sorts, depressed, then such a system makes the sick, even supposing that it makes him "better," at all events *sicker*; just ask doctors who work with the insane what a methodical application of penitential torments, contritions, and cramps of redemption always brings on. Likewise interrogate history: wherever the ascetic priest has succeeded in establishing this treatment of the sick, diseasedness has always grown in depth and breadth with uncanny speed. What was the "success" in every case? A shattered nervous system, added to that which was already sick anyway; and this on the largest as on the smallest scale, with individuals as with masses. In the wake of penitence and redemption training we find enormous epileptic epidemics, the greatest known to history, like those of the St. Vitus' and St. John's dancers of the Middle Ages; as another form of its postlude we find terrible paralyses and chronic depressions with which in some cases the temperament of a people or city (Geneva, Basel) changes once and for all into its opposite;—witch hysteria belongs here as well, something related to somnambulism (eight great epidemic outbursts between 1564 and 1605 alone)—; in its wake we likewise find those death-seeking mass deliria whose horrifying cry *"evviva la morte"*[97] was heard across all of Europe, interrupted now by lustful, now by destructive idiosyncrasies: even today the same alternation of affects, with the same intermittences and sudden leaps, is still to be observed everywhere, in every case in which the ascetic doctrine of sin once again achieves a great success (religious neurosis *appears* as a form of "evil spirit": there is no doubt about this. What it is? *Quaeritur.*)[98] To put it bluntly, the ascetic ideal and its sublime-moral cult, this most ingenious, most unsuspected and most dangerous systematizing of all the instruments of emotional excess under the aegis of holy intentions, has inscribed itself in a terrible and unforgettable way into the entire history of man; and unfortunately *not only* into his history . . . There is hardly anything else I could point out that has pressed so destructively upon *health* and racial robustness, particularly of Europeans, as this ideal; without any exaggeration one may call it *the true doom* in the history of European health. At best, that the specifically Germanic influence might be comparable to its influence: I mean the alcohol poisoning of Europe that has thus far kept strict pace with the political

and racial predominance of the Germanic peoples (—wherever they injected their blood, they injected their vice as well).—Third in line one ought to mention syphilis—*magno sed proxima intervallo.*[99]

22

The ascetic priest has ruined the health of the soul wherever he has come to power, he has consequently ruined *taste* in *artibus et litteris* as well—he is still ruining it. "Consequently"?—I hope one will simply concede me this consequently; at any rate, I do not wish to prove it first. A single pointer: it is directed at the basic book of Christian literature, its true model, its "book in itself." Even in the midst of Greco-Roman glory, which was also a glory of books, in the face of a classical scripture-world that was not yet atrophied and decimated, at a time when one could still read a few books for whose possession one would now give half of a nation's literature, the simplicity and vanity of Christian agitators—one calls them Church Fathers—already dared to decree: *"we* too have our classical literature, *we do not need that of the Greeks"*— and at the same time one pointed proudly to books of legends, apostolic epistles, and little apologetic tracts, in roughly the same way as the English "Salvation Army" today fights its battle against Shakespeare and other "heathens" with a related literature. I have no love for the "New Testament," one can guess that already; it almost makes me uneasy to stand so alone in my taste regarding this most esteemed, most overestimated scriptural work (the taste of two millennia is *against* me): but what good does it do! "Here I stand, I can do no other"—I have the courage of my bad taste. The *Old* Testament—now that is something entirely different: I take my hat off to the Old Testament! In it I find great human beings, a heroic landscape, and something most rare on earth, the incomparable naïveté of the *strong heart*; still more, I find a people. In the New, on the other hand, nothing but petty sectarian economy, nothing but rococo of the soul, nothing but embellishment, crookedness, oddness, nothing but conventicle air, not to forget an occasional breath of bucolic cloyingness

97. [Long live death!]
98. [One asks—i.e., "that is the question."]

99. [Next, but by a great distance. Cf. Virgil, *Aeneid*, Book 5, line 320.]

that belongs to that epoch (*and* to the Roman province) and is not so much Jewish as Hellenistic. Humility and pomposity side by side; a garrulousness of feeling that almost numbs; passionateness, no passion; embarrassing play of gestures; it is obvious that all good breeding was lacking here. How can one be allowed to make such a fuss about one's little bad habits as these pious little men do! No cock will crow about this, much less God. Finally they even want to have "the crown of eternal life," all these little people from the province: and to what end? and for what? one cannot push immodesty further than this. An "immortal" Peter: who could endure *that*! They have an ambition that makes one laugh: *this one* openly chews what is most personal to him, his foolishnesses, sadnesses, and idler's worries, as if the in-itself-of-things were obliged to take care of it all; *that one* never tires of drawing God himself into the pettiest distress in which they are stuck. And this constant familiarity with God, in the worst taste! This Jewish, not merely Jewish impertinence toward God with muzzle and paw! . . . There are minor despised "heathen peoples" in the east of Asia from whom these first Christians could have learned something substantial, some *tact* of reverence; as Christian missionaries attest, the former do not permit themselves to give voice to the name of their god at all. This seems delicate enough to me; what is certain is that it is not only "first" Christians who find it too delicate: to feel the contrast just recall Luther, for instance, this "most eloquent" and immodest peasant that Germany has had, and the Lutheran tone that precisely he liked best in his conversations with God. In the final analysis, Luther's resistance to the mediator saints of the Church (particularly to "the devil's sow, the pope") was, there is no doubt, the resistance of a boor annoyed by the *good etiquette* of the Church, that reverential etiquette of hieratic taste, which admits only the more devoted and more silent into the Holy of Holies and locks it against the boors. Precisely here these boors are absolutely not to be allowed to speak — but Luther, the peasant, wanted it otherwise, it wasn't *German* enough for him as it was: above all he wanted to speak directly, to speak himself, to speak "uninhibitedly" with his God . . . Well, he did it. — The ascetic ideal, one will likely guess it, was never and nowhere a school of good taste, still less of good manners — in

the best case it was a school of hieratic manners —: that is because it has something in its very flesh that is the mortal enemy of all good manners — lack of measure, aversion to measure, it is itself a *"non plus ultra."*[100]

23

The ascetic ideal has not only ruined health and taste, it has also ruined a third, fourth, fifth, sixth something — I will restrain myself from saying *what* all (when would I come to an end!). It is not what this ideal has *done* that I propose to bring to light here; rather solely what it *means*, what it hints at, what lies hidden behind it, beneath it, in it, for which it is the provisional, indistinct expression, overladen with question marks and misunderstandings. And it is only with respect to *this* purpose that I am not permitted to spare my readers a look at the enormity of its effects, of its doomful effects as well: namely in order to prepare them for the last and most terrible aspect that the question of the meaning of this ideal has for me. What does the very *power* of this ideal mean, the *enormity* of its power? Why has it been given room to this extent? why has there not been better resistance? The ascetic ideal expresses a will: *where* is the opposing will in which an *opposing ideal* expresses itself? The ascetic ideal has a *goal* — it is general enough that all other interests of human existence appear small-minded and narrow measured against it; it relentlessly interprets ages, peoples, human beings according to this one goal, it refuses to tolerate any other interpretation, any other goal, it rejects, negates, affirms, confirms solely in accordance with *its* interpretation (— and was there ever a system of interpretation more thoroughly thought to the end?); it submits itself to no power, rather it believes in its privilege over every other power, in its unconditional *distance of rank* with respect to every power — it believes that there is no instance of power on earth that does not first have to receive from it a meaning, a right to existence, a value, as a tool in *its* work, as a way and means to *its* goal, to *one* goal . . . Where is the *counterpart* to this closed system of will, goal, and interpretation? Why is the counterpart *lacking*?

100. [The highest or ultimate of its kind; literally: not more beyond.]

. . . Where is the *other* "*one* goal"? . . . But I am told it is *not* lacking, it has not only fought a long successful battle with this ideal but rather has already become lord over that ideal in all essential matters: our entire modern *science* is said to be witness to this—this modern science, which, as a true philosophy of reality, clearly believes in itself alone, clearly possesses the courage to itself, the will to itself and has so far got along well enough without God, the beyond, and virtues that negate. Nevertheless, in my case one accomplishes nothing with such noise and agitator-babble: these trumpeters of reality are bad musicians, it is easy enough to hear that their voices do *not* come from the depths, it is *not* the abyss of the scientific conscience that speaks through them—for the scientific conscience is an abyss today—in such trumpeter-mouths the word "science" is simply an obscenity, a misuse, a shameless act. Precisely the opposite of what is claimed here is the truth: science has utterly *no* faith in itself today, to say nothing of an ideal *above* itself—and where it is at all still passion, love, ardor, *suffering*, it is not the opposite of that ascetic ideal but rather *its most recent and noblest form*. Does that sound strange to you? . . . Of course even among the scholars of today there are enough steady and modest working folk who like their little corner and therefore, because they like it there, from time to time speak up rather immodestly with the demand that one *should* be satisfied in general today, above all in the sciences—there is so much that is useful that needs doing precisely there. I won't contradict; least of all do I want to ruin the pleasure these honest workers take in their craft: for I enjoy their work. But the fact that one now works rigorously in the sciences and that there are contented workers does *not* by any means prove that as a whole science today has a goal, a will, an ideal, the passion of a great faith. As stated, the opposite is the case: where it is not the most recent manifestation of the ascetic ideal—there it is a matter of cases too rare, noble, select to overturn the general judgment—science today is a *hiding place* for every kind of ill-humor, unbelief, gnawing worm, *despectio sui*, bad conscience—it is the very *unrest* of being without an ideal, the suffering from the *lack* of a great love, the discontent in an *involuntary* contentedness. Oh what does science today not conceal! how much it is at least *supposed* to conceal!

The competence of our best scholars, their mindless diligence, their heads smoking day and night, their very mastery of their craft—how often all this has its true sense in preventing something from becoming visible to oneself! Science as a means of self-anesthetization: *are you acquainted with that?* . . . By means of a harmless word one sometimes cuts them to the quick—everyone who keeps company with scholars experiences this—one embitters one's scholarly friends toward oneself at the very moment one means to honor them, one drives them beside themselves merely because one was too coarse to guess with whom one was actually dealing—with *sufferers* who do not want to admit to themselves what they are, with anesthetized and unconscious ones who fear only one thing: *coming to consciousness* . . .

24

—And now take a look, by comparison, at those rarer cases of which I spoke, the last idealists there are among philosophers and scholars today: do we perhaps have in them the sought-after *opponents* of the ascetic ideal, its *counter-idealists*? Indeed they *believe* themselves to be such, these "unbelieving ones" (for that they all are); they are so serious on this point, here in particular becoming so passionate in word, in gesture, that precisely this seems to be their last bit of belief, that they are opponents of this ideal:— need it therefore be *true*, what they believe? . . . We "knowers" are mistrustful of every kind of believer by now; our mistrust has gradually trained us to infer the opposite of what one formerly inferred: namely, wherever the strength of a belief comes strikingly to the fore to infer a certain weakness of demonstrability, even the *improbability* of what is believed. We too do not deny that faith "makes blessed": it is *precisely for this reason* that we deny that faith *proves* anything—a strong faith that makes blessed raises suspicion against that in which it believes, it does not establish "truth," it establishes a certain probability— of *deception*. And how do things stand in this case?— These negating and aloof ones of today, these who are unconditional on one point—the claim to intellectual cleanliness—these hard, strict, abstinent, heroic spirits who constitute the honor of our age, all these pale atheists, anti-Christians, immoralists, nihilists, these skeptics, ephectics, *hectics* of the spirit (all of them are the latter in some sense or other), these last idealists of knowledge in whom alone the intellectual conscience today dwells and has become flesh — in fact they believe themselves to be as detached as possible from the ascetic ideal, these "free, *very* free spirits": and yet, to divulge to them what they themselves cannot see — for they stand too close to themselves — this ideal is precisely *their* ideal as well, they themselves represent it today, and perhaps they alone; they themselves are its most spiritualized outgrowth, the troop of warriors and scouts it deploys on the front line, its most entrapping, most tender, most incomprehensible form of seduction: — if I am a guesser of riddles in anything then let it be with *this* proposition! . . . These are by no means *free* spirits: *for they still believe in truth* . . . When the Christian crusaders in the Orient came across that invincible order of Assassins, that order of free spirits *par excellence* whose lowest degree lived in an obedience the like of which no order of monks has attained, they also received, through some channel or other, a hint about that symbol and tally-word reserved for the uppermost degrees alone, as their *secretum*[101]: "nothing is true, everything is permitted" . . . Now *that* was *freedom* of the spirit, *with that*, belief in truth itself was *renounced* . . . Has any European, any Christian free spirit ever lost his way in this proposition and its labyrinthine *consequences*? does he know the Minotaur of this cave *from experience*? . . . I doubt it, still more, I know otherwise: — nothing is more foreign to these who are unconditional on one point, these so-called "free spirits," than precisely freedom and breaking one's fetters in this sense, in no respect are they more firmly bound; precisely in their belief in truth they are more firm and unconditional than anyone else. I know all of this from too close a proximity perhaps: that commendable philosophers' abstinence to which such a belief obligates; that stoicism of the intellect that finally forbids itself a "no" just as strictly as a "yes"; that *wanting* to halt before the factual, the *factum* **brutum**; that fatalism of "*petits faits*"[102] (ce

petit faitalisme, as I call it), in which French science now seeks a kind of moral superiority over German science, that renunciation of all interpretation (of doing violence, pressing into orderly form, abridging, omitting, padding, fabricating, falsifying and whatever else belongs to the *essence* of all interpreting) — broadly speaking, this expresses asceticism of virtue as forcefully as does any negation of sensuality (it is basically only a *modus* of this negation). What *compels* one to this, however, this unconditional will to truth, is the *belief in the ascetic ideal itself*, even if as its unconscious imperative — do not deceive yourself about this, — it is the belief in a *metaphysical* value, a value *in itself of truth* as it is established and guaranteed by that ideal alone (it stands and falls with that ideal). There is, strictly speaking, absolutely no science "without presuppositions," the thought of such a science is unthinkable, paralogical: a philosophy, a "belief" must always be there first so that science can derive a direction from it, a meaning, a boundary, a method, a *right* to existence. (Whoever understands it the other way around — for example, whoever sets out to place philosophy "on a strictly scientific foundation" — first needs to turn not only philosophy but also truth itself *on its head*: the grossest violation of propriety there can be with regard to two such venerable ladies!) Why, there is no doubt — and with this I will give my *Gay Science* a chance to speak, cf. its fifth book (section 344) — "the truthful one, in that audacious and ultimate sense presupposed by the belief in science, *thus affirms another world* than that of life, nature, and history; and insofar as he affirms this "other world," what? must he not, precisely in so doing, negate its counterpart, this world, *our* world? . . . It is still a *metaphysical* belief on which our belief in science rests — we knowers today, we godless ones and anti-metaphysicians, we too still take *our* fire from that great fire that was ignited by a thousand-year old belief, that belief of Christians, which was also Plato's belief, that God is truth, that truth is *divine* . . . But what if precisely this is becoming ever more implausible, if nothing proves to be divine any longer, unless perhaps error, blindness, lie — if God himself proves

---

101. [Medieval Latin, elliptical for: *sigillum secretum*, "privy seal" — a personal or private seal.]

102. [Little facts. The parenthesis that follows puns on the word *fait* (fact) by replacing the first three letters of

---

the French *fatalism* (fatalism) with this similar-sounding word, a pun that doesn't quite work in English: "that little *fa*ctalism."]

to be our *longest lie?"* — — At this point it is necessary to pause and to reflect for a long time. Science itself now is *in need of* a justification (which is not to say that there is one). On this question, just look at the earliest and the most recent philosophies: all of them lack a consciousness of the extent to which the will to truth itself first needs a justification, here there is a gap in every philosophy — why is that? Because the ascetic ideal has until now been *lord* over all philosophy, because truth was posited as being, as God, as highest authority; because truth was simply not *permitted* to be a problem. Do you understand this "permitted"? — From the moment belief in the god of the ascetic ideal is negated, *there is also a new problem:* that of the *value* of truth. — The will to truth is in need of a critique — let us thus define our own task — the value of truth is for once to be experimentally *called into question* . . . (Anyone who finds this stated too briefly is advised to read the section of the *Gay Science* that bears the title: "To What Extent We Too Are Still Pious" (section 344), or, best of all, the entire fifth book of said work, likewise the preface to *Daybreak.*)

25

No! Don't give me science as an answer when I look for the natural antagonist of the ascetic ideal, when I ask: *"where* is the opposing will in which its *opposing ideal* expresses itself ?" Science is far from standing enough on its own for this, in every respect it first needs a value-ideal, a value-creating power in whose *service* it *may believe* in itself — it is itself never value-creating. Its relationship to the ascetic ideal is still by no means inherently antagonistic; on the whole it is even more likely that science represents the forward-driving force in the inner shaping of this ideal. On closer scrutiny its protest and battle are not in the least directed at the ideal itself, but rather only at its outworks, sheathing, play of masks, at its temporary solidification, lignification, dogmatization — by negating what is exoteric about this ideal, it sets the life in it free again. These two, science and ascetic ideal, they do, after all, stand on one and the same ground — I have already suggested that this is so —: namely on the same overestimation of truth (more correctly: on the same belief in the *in*assessability, the *un*criticiza-

bility of truth), precisely in this they are *necessarily* confederates — so that, supposing one combats them, they can only be combatted and called into question together. An assessment of the value of the ascetic ideal unavoidably entails an assessment of the value of science as well: open your eyes and prick up your ears to this while the time is right! (*Art,* to state it beforehand, for I will come back to it sometime in greater length — art, in which precisely the *lie* hallows itself, in which the *will to deception* has good conscience on its side, is much more fundamentally opposed to the ascetic ideal than is science: this was sensed instinctively by Plato, this greatest enemy of art that Europe has yet produced. Plato *contra* Homer: that is the complete, the genuine antagonism — there the "otherworldly one" with the best of wills, the great slanderer of life; here its involuntary deifier, *golden* nature. An artist's subservience in the service of the ascetic ideal is therefore the truest *corruption* of the artist there can be, unfortunately one of the most common: for nothing is more corruptible than an artist.) Science also rests on the same ground as the ascetic ideal when calculated physiologically: a certain *impoverishment of life* is a presupposition here as well as there — the affects become cool, the tempo slowed, dialectic in place of instinct, *seriousness* impressed on faces and gestures (seriousness, this most unmistakable mark of a more laborious metabolism, of a struggling, harder-working life). Look at those ages in the history of a people when the scholar comes to the fore: they are ages of tiredness, often of evening, of decline — overflowing energy, certainty of life, certainty of the *future* are lost. The predominance of the mandarin is never a sign of anything good: any more than the rise of democracy, of peace-arbitration courts in place of wars, of equal rights for women, of the religion of compassion, and whatever other symptoms of declining life there are. (Science understood as problem; what does science mean? — on this cf. the preface to "The Birth of Tragedy.") — No! this "modern science" — just keep your eyes open for this! — is for the present the *best* confederate of the ascetic ideal, and this precisely because it is the most unconscious, the most involuntary, the most secret and subterranean one! They have until now played one game, the "poor of the spirit" and the scientific adversaries of that ideal (beware, by the way, of thinking that they are the antithesis of the former, say, as the *rich of the spirit:*—this they are *not*; I called them hectics of the spirit). These famous *victories* of the latter: undoubtedly they are victories—but over what? The ascetic ideal was in no way conquered in them, rather it was made stronger, which is to say more incomprehensible, more spiritual, more ensnaring by the fact that again and again a wall, an outwork that had attached itself to this ideal and was coarsening its appearance was ruthlessly removed, demolished by science. Does anyone really think that, for instance, the defeat of theological astronomy meant the defeat of that ideal? . . . Has man perhaps become *less in need* of an otherworldly solution to his riddle of existence now that this existence looks even more arbitrary, more loiterer-like, more dispensable in the *visible* order of things? Hasn't precisely the self-belittlement of man, his *will* to self-belittlement been marching relentlessly forward since Copernicus? Alas, the belief in his dignity, uniqueness, irreplaceability in the hierarchy of beings is lost—he has become an *animal*, without simile, qualification, or reservation an animal, he who in his earlier belief was almost god ("child of God," "God-man") . . . Since Copernicus[103] man seems to have stumbled onto an inclined plane—he is now rolling faster and faster away from the center—whither? into nothingness? into the "*penetrating* feeling of his nothingness?" . . . So be it! exactly this would be the straight path—into the *old* ideal? . . . *All* science (and by no means only astronomy, concerning whose humiliating and debasing effect Kant made a noteworthy confession, "it annihilates my importance" . . .), all science, the natural as well as the *unnatural*—which is what I call the self-critique of knowledge—today aims to talk man out of his previous respect for himself, as if this were nothing but a bizarre self-conceit; one could even say that science's own pride, its own austere form of stoical ataraxy consists in upholding this hard-won *self-contempt* of man as his last, most serious claim to respect from himself (with good reason in fact: for the one who holds in contempt is still one who "has not forgotten how to respect" . . .) Does this actually *work against* the ascetic ideal? Does

anyone in all seriousness still think (as the theologians for a time imagined) that, say, Kant's *victory* over the conceptual dogmatism of theology ("God," "soul," "freedom," "immortality") did damage to that ideal?—it is of no concern for the present whether Kant himself even remotely intended anything of the kind. What is certain is that since Kant all kinds of transcendentalists are again playing a winning game—they are emancipated from the theologians: what good fortune!—he betrayed to them that secret path on which they may now pursue their "heart's desires" on their own initiative and with the best scientific decorum. Likewise: who could henceforth hold it against the agnostics, as the venerators of the unknown and mysterious in itself, if they now worship *the question mark itself* as God? (Xaver Doudan speaks at one point of the ravages caused by "*l'habitude d'admirer l'inintelligible au lieu de rester tout simplement dans l'inconnu*";[104] it is his opinion that the ancients were free of this. Supposing that everything man "knows" fails to satisfy his desires, moreover, that it contradicts them and makes one shudder—what divine escape, to be permitted to seek the blame for this not in "desiring" but rather in "knowing"! . . . "There is no knowing: *consequently*—there is a God": what a novel *elegantia syllogismi*![105] what a *triumph* of the ascetic ideal!—

26

—Or did the whole of modern historiography perhaps show a stance more sure of life, more sure of its ideal? Its most noble claim now runs in the direction of being a *mirror*; it rejects all teleology; it no longer wants to "prove" anything; it scorns playing the judge and has its good taste in this—it affirms as little as it negates, it ascertains, it "describes" . . . All of this is to a high degree ascetic; at the same time, however, it is to a still higher degree *nihilistic*, do not deceive yourselves about this! One sees a sad, hard, but determined look—an eye that *looks outward* as an isolated arctic traveller looks outward (perhaps in order not

---

103. [Nicolaus Copernicus (1473–1543), Polish scholar and astronomer, founder of modern astronomy.]

104. ["The habit *of admiring* the unintelligible instead of staying quite simply in the unknown."]

105. [Elegance of the syllogism.]

to look inward? in order not to look back? . . .) Here there is snow, here life has become silent; the last crowings heard here are "To what end?," "In vain!," "*Nada!*"—here nothing more prospers or grows, at best St. Petersburg metapolitics and Tolstoyian "compassion." As for that other kind of historian, however, an even more "modern" kind perhaps, a hedonistic, lascivious kind, who makes eyes at life just as much as at the ascetic ideal, who uses the word "artist" as a glove and has leased the praise of contemplation completely and utterly for himself these days: oh what thirst these sweet ingenious ones arouse, even for ascetics and winter landscapes! No! the devil take this "contemplative" folk! How much more would I prefer to journey with those historical nihilists through the most dismal gray cold fogs!—indeed, supposing I must choose, I wouldn't be against lending an ear even to one who is truly unhistorical, anti-historical (like Dühring, whose tones have intoxicated a previously still shy, still unacknowledgeable species of "beautiful souls" in present-day Germany, the species *anarchistica* within the educated proletariat). A hundred times worse are the "contemplatives"—: I know of nothing as disgusting as this sort of "objective" armchair, this sort of sweet-smelling hedonist facing history, half priest, half satyr, perfume Renan,[106] who betrays already with the high falsetto of his cheers what he is lacking, *where* he is lacking, *where* in this case the Fate has oh! all-too-surgically wielded her cruel scissors! This goes against my taste, also against my patience: let those who have nothing to lose by it keep their patience at such sights—such a sight enrages me, such "spectators" embitter me toward the "spectacle" still more than the spectacle itself (history itself, you understand me), in the process Anacreontic moods come over me unawares. This nature that gave to the bull its horns, to the lion *chasm' odonton*,[107] why did nature give me a foot? . . . To kick with, by holy Anacreon! and not just for running away: for kicking apart the rotted armchairs,

the cowardly contemplativeness, the lecherous eunuchry in the face of history, the making-eyes at ascetic ideals, the justice-Tartuffery of impotence! All my reverence to the ascetic ideal, *as long as it is honest!* as long as it believes in itself and does not present us with a facade of clownery! But I do not like all these coquettish bugs who have an insatiable ambition for smelling out the infinite, until finally the infinite smells of bugs; I do not like the whited sepulchers that play-act life; I do not like the tired and used-up who wrap themselves in wisdom and look about "objectively"; I do not like the agitators spruced up into heroes, who wear a magic concealing-cap of an ideal on their straw-whisk of a head; I do not like the ambitious artists who would like to act the role of ascetics and priests and are basically only tragic buffoons; I do not like them either, these newest speculators in idealism, the anti-Semites, who roll their eyes nowadays in a Christian-Aryan-Philistine manner and try to stir up all the horned cattle elements among the people through a misuse of the cheapest tool of agitation, moral posturing—a misuse that exhausts all patience (—that *no* kind of swindle-spiritism goes without success in present-day Germany is linked to the positively undeniable and already tangible desolation of the German spirit, whose cause I seek in an all-too-exclusive diet of newspapers, politics, beer, and Wagnerian music, including that which supplies the presupposition for this diet: first, the national constriction and vanity, the strong but narrow principle "*Deutschland, Deutschland über alles,*"[108] second, however, the *paralysis agitans*[109] of "modern ideas"). Europe today is rich and inventive above all in excitants, it seems there is nothing it needs more than stimulants and fire-waters: hence also the enormous counterfeiting of ideals, these fieriest waters of the spirit; hence also the repulsive, foul-smelling, mendacious, pseudo-alcoholic air everywhere. I would like to know how many shiploads of imitation idealism, of hero-costumes and grand-word-noisemakers, how many barrels of sugared spirituous sympathy (firm of: *la*

106. [Ernest Renan (1823–1892), French historian of religion and critic, best known for his *La vie de Jésus* (Life of Jesus, 1863), the first volume in his multivolume work, *Origins of Christianity*. He and Taine were the most influential French intellectuals of their time.]

107. ["Chasm of teeth," from *Anacreonta*, Poem 24.]

108. ["Germany, Germany above all else." Fallersleben, *Das Lied der Deutschen*, 1841.]

109. [Shaking disability, i.e., "shaking palsy" or Parkinson's disease.]

religion de la souffrance),[110] how many wooden legs of "noble indignation" for the assistance of the spiritually flat-footed, how many *comedians* of the Christian-moral ideal would have to be exported out of Europe today in order for its air to smell cleaner again . . . Obviously a new *trade* opportunity has opened up with respect to this overproduction; obviously there is a new "business" to transact in little ideal-idols and accompanying "idealists"— don't overlook this none-too-subtle hint! Who has enough courage for it?—we have the means in *hand* to "idealize" the entire earth! . . . But why am I talking about courage: here only one thing is needed, precisely the hand, an uninhibited, a very uninhibited hand . . .

27

—Enough! Enough! let's leave these curiosities and complexities of the modern spirit, where there is as much to laugh about as to be vexed at: precisely *our* problem can do without them, the problem of the *meaning* of the ascetic ideal—what does it have to do with yesterday and today! I will tackle those things more rigorously and more thoroughly in another context (under the title "On the History of European Nihilism"; with regard to this I refer to a work that I am preparing: **The Will to Power**, *Attempt at a Re-valuation of All Values*). All I care to have pointed out here is this: in the spiritual sphere as well, the ascetic ideal has in the meantime only one kind of real enemy and *injurer*: the comedians of this ideal— for they arouse mistrust. Everywhere else that the spirit is strictly and powerfully at work today without any counterfeiting, it now does without ideals en-tirely—the popular expression for this abstinence is "atheism"—except *for its will to truth*. This will, how-ever, this *remnant* of an ideal is, if one is willing to believe me, that ideal itself in its strictest, most spiri-tual formulation, completely and utterly esoteric, stripped of all outworks, thus not so much its remnant as its *core*. Unconditional honest atheism (—and *its* is the only air we breathe, we more spiritual human beings of this age!) is accordingly *not* in opposition

to that ideal, as appearance would have it; it is rather only one of its last stages of development, one of its final forms and inner logical consequences—it is the awe-inspiring *catastrophe* of a two-thousand-year dis-cipline in truth, which in the end forbids itself the *lie involved in belief in God*. (The same course of development in India, completely independent of the former and therefore proving something; the same ideal compelling to the same conclusion; the decisive point reached five centuries before the point from which Europeans reckon time, with Buddha, more precisely: already with the Samkhya philosophy, this then popularized and made into a religion by Bud-dha.) Asking in all strictness, *what* actually *triumphed* over the Christian god? The answer is found in my *Gay Science* (section 357); "Christian morality itself, the ever more strictly understood concept of truthful-ness, the father-confessor subtlety of the Christian conscience, translated and sublimated into the scien-tific conscience, into intellectual cleanliness at any price. Looking at nature as if it were a proof of the goodness and guardianship of a god; interpreting his-tory to the honor of divine reason, as constant witness of a moral world order and moral final intentions; interpreting one's own experiences as pious human beings have long enough interpreted them, as if every-thing were an act of providence, everything a sign, everything thought up and sent for the sake of the soul's salvation: this is henceforth *past*, it has con-science *against* it, it is regarded by all subtler consciences as indecent, dishonest, as mendacity, feminism, weakness, cowardice—it is precisely in this strictness, if in anything, that we are *good Europeans* and heirs of Europe's longest and bravest self-overcoming" . . . All great things perish through themselves, through an act of self-cancellation: thus the law of life wills it, the law of the *necessary* "self-overcoming" in the essence of life—in the end the call always goes forth to the lawgiver himself: "*patere legem, quam ipse tulisti*."[111] In this manner Christian-ity *as dogma* perished of its own morality; in this manner Christianity *as morality* must now also per-ish—we stand at the threshold of *this* event. Now that Christian truthfulness has drawn one conclusion

---

110. [The religion of suffering.]

111. [Submit to the law you yourself proposed.]

after the other, in the end it draws its *strongest conclusion*, its conclusion *against* itself; this occurs, however, when it poses the question, "*what does all will to truth mean?*" . . . And here I again touch on my problem, on our problem, my *unknown* friends (— for I as yet *know* of no friends): what meaning would *our* entire being have if not this, that in us this will to truth has come to a consciousness of itself *as a problem*? . . . It is from the will to truth's becoming conscious of itself that from now on—there is no doubt about it—morality will gradually *perish*: that great spectacle in a hundred acts that is reserved for Europe's next two centuries, the most terrible, most questionable, and perhaps also most hopeful of all spectacles . . .

28

If one disregards the ascetic ideal: man, the *animal* man, has until now had no meaning. His existence on earth contained no goal; "to what end man at all?"—was a question without answer; the *will* for man and earth was lacking; behind every great human destiny a still greater "for nothing!" resounded as refrain. Precisely *this* is what the ascetic ideal means: that something *was lacking*, that an enormous *void* surrounded man—he did not know how to justify, to explain, to affirm himself; he *suffered* from the problem of his meaning. He suffered otherwise as well, he was for the most part a *diseased* animal: but the suffering itself was *not* his problem, rather that the answer was missing to the scream of his question: "*to what end* suffering?" Man, the bravest animal and the one most accustomed to suffering, does *not* negate

suffering in itself: he *wants* it, he even seeks it out, provided one shows him a *meaning* for it, a *to-this-end* of suffering. The meaninglessness of suffering, not the suffering itself, was the curse that thus far lay stretched out over humanity—*and the ascetic ideal offered it a meaning*! Thus far it has been the only meaning; any meaning is better than no meaning at all; in every respect the ascetic ideal has been the "*faute de mieux*"[112] *par excellence* there has been thus far. In it suffering was *interpreted*; the enormous emptiness seemed filled; the door fell shut to all suicidal nihilism. The interpretation—there is no doubt—brought new suffering with it, deeper, more inward, more poisonous, gnawing more at life: it brought all suffering under the perspective of *guilt* . . . But in spite of all this—man was *rescued* by it, he had a *meaning*, he was henceforth no longer like a leaf in the wind, a plaything of nonsense, "without-sense," now he could *will* something—no matter for the moment in what direction, to what end, with what he willed: *the will itself was saved*. One simply cannot conceal from oneself *what* all the willing that has received its direction from the ascetic ideal actually expresses: this hatred of the human, still more of the animal, still more of the material, this abhorrence of the senses, of reason itself, this fear of happiness and of beauty, this longing away from all appearance, change, becoming, death, wish, longing itself—all of this means—let us dare to grasp this—a *will to nothingness*, an aversion to life, a rebellion against the most fundamental presuppositions of life; but it is and remains a *will*! . . . And, to say again at the end what I said at the beginning: man would much rather will *nothingness* than *not* will . . .

112. [For lack of anything better.]

MAX WEBER

Near the end of his famous lecture, "Politics as a Vocation," delivered in 1918, written in the wake of the collapse of Germany and the rise of Bolshevism, Weber delivered an eerie prognosis: "not summer's bloom lies ahead of us, but rather a polar night of icy darkness and hardness. . . ." Two years later Weber was dead, a victim of pneumonia but also perhaps its beneficiary, a nationalist kindly relieved of the burden of seeing Germany sink into an "icy darkness" beyond any he could have conceived. He was perhaps the most important social theorist of the century, a legal thinker, historian of law and economics, student of religion, and much more. Weber left behind an extraordinary legacy: a methodology of ideal types, brilliant studies of religion and politics, and conceptual innovations that have pervaded our language and our thinking. To the degree that we cannot see the world without the vocabulary of charisma, bureaucracy, disenchantment, and rationaliza- tion, we cannot see the world without Weber. And yet, as rational and scientific as he was, committed to empirical and historical work of detail and comprehensiveness, he was also sensitive to the spiritual and creative dimensions of life. It is no surprise to learn that at the same time that he was writing the lecture on politics as a "calling," in which he examined the modes, qualities and ethic of political leadership, Weber was also turning for solace to the Book of Job and the prophetic writings of Jeremiah, and in his own way he was venturing his personal prophecies of a foreboding future.

Like the world that he lived in, Weber's own life was torn apart. Born in Erfurt, Thuringia, on April 21, 1864, Weber grew up in Berlin and took a degree in law at Heidelberg. He wrote his thesis on trading companies in the Middle Ages and his *habilitation*, which had to be in a different area, on agrarian institutions in ancient Rome. In the fall of 1894, Weber accepted a position at Freiburg in economics; in 1896 he returned to Heidelberg, where he met the historian of the Church, Ernst Troeltsch, who became a close friend and intellectual companion. Blessed with an extraordinary gift for languages and a sense for detailed historical research, Weber established himself as a student of law and economics.

But in 1897 Weber's father died, and shortly thereafter Weber collapsed. It is likely that his physical and psychological problems were the outcome of an exhausting regimen, coupled with strain and the guilt about his father's death. For the rest of his life, he suffered from bouts of depression and worse; for much of the next two decades he was unable to teach. The initial years of illness lasted until 1903. By 1904 he was working again, and in that year he was invited to the United States to give a paper as part of the Universal Exposition in St. Louis. After his enthusiastic and illuminating trip, Weber resumed work as an independent scholar in Heidelberg, completing his famous work *The Protestant Ethic and the Spirit of Capitalism*, which was published in 1905–1906. From 1906 until 1918, Weber was the center of an intellectual circle in Heidelberg that met weekly to discuss current events, art, literature, politics, and more. This circle included figures such as Wilhelm Windelband, Georg Jellinek, Ernst Troeltsch, Emil Lask, and Friedrich Gundolf, as well as younger scholars such as Ernst Bloch and Georg Lukács. When the war broke out, Weber's initial enthusiasm quickly dissipated, and he was an outspoken critic of the Kaiser and the failure of leadership in Germany.

By the fall of 1916 Weber was studying the Hebrew prophets, as part of his interest in charismatic leadership and in preparation for what would become *Ancient Judaism*, published in 1917, a year after his sociological studies of the religions of India and China. In 1918 he accepted a position at the University of Vienna, his first regular teaching position in nearly two decades. After moving to Munich to become the Chair of Economics, Weber died of pneumonia on June 14, 1920.

In many ways, Weber was a thinker whose towering intellect was drawn to profound, powerful tensions. He had a spiritual and almost religious sensibility without being a religious person, and yet he was devoted to the empirical, scientific, and extensive examination of legal, economic, social, and political conduct. In his view, individual agents are the ultimate subjects of examination, but the comparative analysis he engaged in yielded generalizations configured into what he called ideal types. He was a dedicated, almost fanatical scholar and intellectual, and yet he was also a prominent and engaged public figure, deeply involved in the political affairs of Germany in the years around World War I. His work evidences broad and detailed knowledge of history and institutions, and, at the same time, extraordinary moments of insight and creativity. It can be said that the centerpiece of his sociology and theory of history is the principle of rationalization and bureaucratization; he saw everywhere ways in which magical and religious influence was being replaced by rational structures. Yet, at the same time, the initiators of such rationalization, the original agencies of it, are ultimately special individuals with a distinct kind of authority—what he calls "charisma"—whose reforms, once instituted, become routinized and organized. Thus, Weber is able to understand historical, social, and political developments as the dialectical developments of moments of charismatic revolution with periods of bureaucratic institutionalization.

But perhaps the most poignant tension in Weber's thought concerns what he calls, in "Politics as a Vocation," that of two ethics, the ethic of ultimate ends and the ethic of responsibility. As he makes clear, we all live with this tension, between a commitment to ultimate ends and a commitment to the means to accomplish such ends, for life is such that what we aim at and hope for, what we value most, often requires of us actions that conflict with those very goals. Politics, he tells us, concerns the legitimate use of violence, for the state is the institutional locus of the monopoly of force in a given territory. Built into politics—and built into life—is the tension between violence and the good. But the fault of the tension does not lie all on one side; nor is it a tension that is all bad. After all, as Weber sees it, the vocation or "calling" of politics requires a commitment to responsibility, to appreciate the results or consequences of one's actions; also, ideals without regard for life can be just as destructive as life without the governance of ideals. In the pages of the famous lecture printed here we find challenging reflections and comparative analysis coupled with a special kind of poignancy, in part born out of this tension and the dark times that Weber saw on the horizon.

Recommended Readings

Bendix, Reinhard. *Max Weber: An Intellectual Portrait*. New York: Anchor Books, 1962.

Breiner, Peter. *Max Weber and Democratic Politics*. Ithaca: Cornell University Press, 1996.

Goldmann, Harvey. *Max Weber and Thomas Mann: Calling and the Shaping of the Self*. Berkeley: University of California Press, 1988.

Lehman, Hartmut, and Guenther Roth (eds.). *Weber's "Protestant Ethic": Origins, Evidence, Context*. Cambridge: Cambridge University Press, 1993.

Mitzman, Arthur. *The Iron Cage: An Historical Interpretation of Max Weber*. New York: Grosset and Dunlap, 1971.

Mommsen, Wolfgang J. *Max Weber and German Politics, 1890–1920*. Chicago: Chicago University Press, 1984.

Roth, Guenther, and Wolfgang Schluchter. *Max Weber's Vision of History: Ethics and Methods*. Berkeley: University of California Press, 1979.

Scaff, Lawrence A. *Fleeing the Iron Cage: Culture, Politics, and Modernity in the Thought of Max Weber*. Berkeley: University of California Press, 1989.

Schluchter, Wolfgang. *The Rise of Western Rationalism: Max Weber's Developmental History*. Berkeley: University of California Press, 1981.

Schluchter, Wolfgang. *Paradoxes of Modernity: Culture and Conduct in the Theory of Max Weber*. Stanford: Stanford University Press, 1996.

Tribe, Keith (ed.). *Reading Weber*. London: Routledge, 1989.

Turner, Stephen P., and Regis A. Factor. *Max Weber and the Dispute over Reason and Value: A Study of Philosophy, Ethics, and Politics*. London: Routledge and Kegan Paul, 1984.

POLITICS AS A VOCATION

The lecture I shall give in response to your wishes will necessarily frustrate you in a number of ways. In a talk about politics as a vocation[1] you will naturally expect to hear my opinions on topical questions. But I shall say something about these only toward the end of my lecture, and then in a purely formal way, in connection with specific questions about the significance of political action in the context of our conduct of life in general. What will have to be completely ignored in the present talk will be all questions about *the kind* of politics that should be pursued, that is to say, the specific *policies* [*Inhalte*] that *should* be adopted in the course of our political activities. For such matters have no connection with the general question of what politics is as a vocation and what it can mean. This brings us directly to our subject.

What do we mean by politics?[2] The concept is extremely broad and includes every kind of independent *leadership* activity. We can speak of the foreign exchange policies of the banks, the interest rate policy of the *Reichsbank*, the politics of a trade union in a strike; we can speak of educational policy in a town or village community, the policies of the board of management of an association, and even of the political maneuverings [*Politik*] of a shrewd wife seeking to influence her husband. Needless to say, this concept is far too broad for us to consider this evening. Today we shall consider only the leadership, or the exercise of influence on the leadership, of a *political* organization, in other words a *state*.

But looking at the question through the eyes of a sociologist, what is a "political" organization? What is a "state"? A state, too, cannot be defined sociologically by enumerating its activities. There is almost no task that a political organization has not undertaken at one time or another; but by the same token there are no tasks of which we could say that they were always, let alone *exclusively*, proper to the organizations that we call political, and nowadays refer to as states, or that historically were the forerunners of the modern state. It is rather the case that in the final analysis the modern state can be defined only sociologically by the specific *means* that are peculiar to it, as to every political organization: namely, physical violence. "Every state is based on force," Trotsky remarked at Brest Litovsk.[3] That is indeed the case. If there existed only societies in which violence was unknown as a means, *then* the concept of the "state" would disappear; *in that event* what would have emerged is what, in this specific meaning of the word, we might call "anarchy." Violence is, of course, not the normal or the only means available to the state. That is undeniable. But it is the means specific to the state. And the relationship of the state to violence is particularly close at the present time. In the past the use of physical violence by widely differing organizations—starting with the clan—was completely normal. Nowadays, in contrast, we must say that the state is the form of human community that (successfully) lays claim to the *monopoly of legitimate physical violence* within a particular territory—and this idea of "territory" is an essential

1. [The German word *Beruf* has a workaday meaning of "profession" but, rooted as it is in *rufen*, "to call," has strong overtones of "vocation" or "calling." Both meanings are active in Weber's usage, and each has been used here where it seemed appropriate.—D.O. and T.B.S.]

2. [*Politik* in German means both politics and policy. Here again the choice of word is determined by the context.]

3. [That is to say, during the negotiations with Germany early in 1918 that led to the withdrawal of Russia from World War I.]

defining feature. For what is specific to the present is that all other organizations or individuals can assert the right to use physical violence only insofar as the *state* permits them to do so. The state is regarded as the sole source of the "right" to use violence. Hence, what "politics" means for us is to strive for a share of power or to influence the distribution of power, whether between states or between the groups of people contained within a state.

This corresponds in all essentials to common parlance. When we say that a question is "political," that a minister or official is "political," or that a decision has been made on "political" grounds, we always mean the same thing. This is that the interests involved in the distribution or preservation of power, or a shift in power, play a decisive role in resolving that question, or in influencing that decision or defining the sphere of activity of the official concerned. Whoever is active in politics strives for power, either power as a means in the service of other goals, whether idealistic or selfish, or power "for its own sake," in other words, so as to enjoy the feeling of prestige that it confers.

Like the political organizations that preceded it historically, the state represents a relationship in which people *rule over* other people. This relationship is based on the legitimate use of force (that is to say, force that is perceived as legitimate). If the state is to survive, those who are ruled over must always *acquiesce* in the authority that is claimed by the rulers of the day. When do they do so and why? By what internal reasons is this rule justified, and on what external supports is it based?

To start with the internal justifications: there are in principle three grounds that *legitimate* any rule. First, the authority of "the eternal past," of *custom*, sanctified by a validity that extends back into the mists of time and is perpetuated by habit. This is "traditional" rule, as exercised by patriarchs and patrimonial rulers of the old style. Second, there is the authority of the extraordinary, personal *gift of grace* or charisma, that is, the wholly personal devotion to, and a personal trust in, the revelations, heroism, or other leadership qualities of an individual. This is "charismatic" rule of the kind practiced by prophets or—in the political sphere—the elected warlord or the ruler chosen by popular vote, the great dema-

gogue, and the leaders of political parties. Lastly, there is rule by virtue of "legality," by virtue of the belief in the validity of legal *statutes* and practical "competence" based on rational rules. This type of rule is based on a person's willingness to carry out statutory duties obediently. Rule of this kind is to be found in the modern "servant of the state" and all those agents of power who resemble him in this respect.

It is quite obvious that in reality this compliance is the product of interests of the most varied kinds, but chiefly of hope and fear. This includes fear of the vengeance of magic powers or of the ruler, and hope of a reward in this world or the next. More about this in a moment. But when we inquire into the grounds of the "legitimacy" of this compliance, what we discover is these three "pure" types. These ideas of legitimation and their internal justification are of considerable importance for the structure of rule. Admittedly, these types rarely occur in their pure form in reality. But it is not possible today to enter into a discussion of the highly complex variations, transitional forms, and combinations of these pure types. All that belongs to the problem of "general political theory."

What interests us here above all is the second of these types: rule based on the acquiescence of those who submit to the purely personal "charisma" of the "leader." For this is where we discover the root of the idea of "vocation" in its highest form. Submission to the charisma of the prophet or warlord or of the great demagogues of the assemblies, the *ekklesia*, of ancient Greece or of Parliament means that such men are held to be the inwardly "chosen" leaders of humankind. People do not submit to them because of any customs or statutes, but because they believe in them. Such a leader does indeed live for his cause and "strives to create his work,"[4] if he is anything more than a narrow-minded and vain upstart, a passing product of his age. But the devotion of his followers, that is, his disciples and liegemen, or his entirely personal band of supporters, is directed toward his

---

4. [This is effectively a quotation from Nietzsche: "My suffering and my pity—what of them! For do I aspire after *happiness*? I aspire after my *work*!" *Thus Spoke Zarathustra*, translated by R. J. Hollingdale (Harmondsworth: Penguin, 1969), p. 336.]

person and his qualities. Leadership has manifested itself in all parts of the globe and throughout history in the shape of two dominant figures of the past: the magician and prophet on the one hand, and the chosen warlord, gang leader, and *condottiere* on the other. What is peculiar to the Western world, however, is something of greater concern to us: *political* leadership in the shape, first, of the free "demagogue" who emerged in the city-state, a political form confined to the West, and in particular to the Mediterranean world, and then, following him, the parliamentary "party leader" who grew up in the constitutional state, an institution that is likewise unique to the West.

These men are politicians by virtue of their "calling" in the deepest meaning of the word. But of course in no country are they the only influential figures in the machinery of political power struggles. What is decisive is, rather, the kind of resources that they have at their disposal. How do the ruling powers set about the task of asserting their dominant position? This question holds good for rule of every kind, and hence also for political rule in all its forms: for the traditional type, as well as for legal and charismatic rule.

Every ruling apparatus that calls for continuous administration has two prerequisites. On the one hand, it requires that human action should be predisposed to obedience toward the rulers who claim to be the agents of legitimate force. On the other hand, thanks to this obedience, the rulers should have at their disposal the material resources necessary to make use of physical force where required, in other words, the administrative personnel and the material resources of administration.

Like any other apparatus, the administrative personnel that constitutes the external form of the political ruling apparatus are not just bound in their obedience to the ruling powers by the idea of legitimacy of which we have just spoken. It is bound equally by two other factors that appeal to personal interest: material reward and social prestige. The fiefs of vassals, the livings granted to patrimonial officials, the salaries of modern civil servants—knightly honor, the privileges of the estates, the status of the official— these are the rewards, and it is the fear of losing them that cements the ultimate and decisive foundation of the solidarity that exists between the administrative

personnel and the ruling powers. The same thing holds true for charismatic leadership: glory in war and booty for the military, while the followers of the demagogue look for "spoils,"[5] namely, the license to exploit the ruled through the monopoly of public offices, profits to reward their political loyalty, and prizes to flatter their vanity.

In order to maintain any rule by force, certain external, material goods are required, just as much as in a business enterprise. All forms of state can be divided into two categories. The first is based on the principle that the staff on whose obedience the ruler depends—officials or whatever else they may be— own their *own* means of administration, whether these consist of money, buildings, the materials of war, vehicle pools, horses, or whatever. The alternative is for the administrative staff to be "separated" from the tools of administration in just the same way as the white-collar worker and the proletarian are "separated" from the material means of production in a capitalist enterprise today. The question is, then, whether the ruler has *control* over the administration *himself* and administers matters through personal servants or officials in his employ or personal favorites and confidants, in short, people who are not owners, that is to say, who do not possess in their own right any of the material means of production, but who work under their master's direction—or whether the opposite is the case. This distinction runs through all administrative organizations of the past.

We shall call a political organization in which the material means of administration are wholly or partly under the autonomous control of a dependent administrative staff an "organization subdivided into estates" [*ständisch gegliedert*]. The vassal in a feudal organization, for example, paid for the administrative and legal costs of the fief entrusted to him out of his own pocket. He also paid for the equipment and provisioning needed for a war; his subvassals did likewise. This naturally had consequences for the lord's authority, for that authority was based exclusively on personal fealty and on the fact that the feudal tenure and the vassal's social status derived their "legitimacy" from the lord.

5. [Weber used the English word.]

But everywhere, as far back as the earliest political organizations, we also find the lord exercising direct control himself. He seeks to take control of the administration through personal dependents: slaves, household officials, servants, personal "favorites," and beneficiaries remunerated in money or in kind from his own storerooms. He seeks to defray his costs from his own pocket, out of the revenues from his patrimonial estates; and he seeks to create an army that depends solely on himself because it has been equipped and provisioned from his own granaries, storerooms, and armories. Thus in a society based on "estates," the lord governs with the assistance of an autonomous "aristocracy," that is to say, he shares the rule with them. In this second case he relies either on members of his household or else on plebeians, men from strata of society without either property or honor of their own, men who are dependent upon him entirely for their material well-being, since they have no power at their disposal to compete with his. All forms of patriarchal and patrimonial[6] rule, the despotism of the sultans, and the bureaucratic state are of this type. This applies particularly to the bureaucratic state, that is to say, the type of organization that in its most rational form is specifically characteristic of the modern state.

The modern state begins to develop wherever the monarch sets in train the process of dispossessing the autonomous, "private" agents of administrative power who exist in parallel to him, that is to say, all the independent owners of the materials of war and the administration, financial resources, and politically useful goods of every kind. The entire process provides a perfect analogy to the development of a capitalist enterprise through the gradual expropriation of the independent producers. We end up with a situation in which in the modern state control of the entire political means of production is concentrated in a single culminating point so that not a single official is left who personally owns the money he spends, or the buildings, supplies, tools, and military equipment that are under his control. In the modern "state"—and this is an essential element of its definition—the "separation" of the administrative staff, that is, of officials and employees, from the material resources of administration, has been completed. It is at this point that the very latest development emerges, for we now see before our very eyes the attempt to bring about the expropriation of this expropriator of the resources of politics and hence of political power.[7] The revolution has accomplished this at least to the extent that the legally established authorities have been supplanted by leaders who, through usurpation or election, have obtained political power over the personnel and the administrative machinery, and who derive their legitimacy—whether rightly or wrongly is immaterial—from the will of the governed. It is quite another question whether on the basis of this at least ostensible success they have the right to hope for one further achievement. That achievement would be to proceed with the expropriation of businesses within the capitalist economy whose management is organized at its core in accordance with quite different laws from the political administration, despite far-reaching similarities. This is not an issue on which I shall comment today. I shall confine myself to the purely *conceptual* point that the modern state is an institutional form of rule that has successfully fought to create a monopoly of legitimate physical force as a means of government within a particular territory. For this purpose it has concentrated all the material resources of organization in the hands of its leaders. The modern state has expropriated all the

6. [Patriarchal rule, according to Weber, is traditional rule, based originally on the household, in which the patriarch rules without administrative machinery. Such rule is based entirely on personal loyalty. Patrimonialism arises wherever the ruler develops an administration and a military force that, however, are purely the personal instruments of the master. "Sultanism" is seen as an extreme case of patrimonialism. See *Economy and Society* (Berkeley and Los Angeles: University of California Press, 1978), chapter 3, section 7a, pp. 231 ff.; and also chapter 12, pp. 1006 ff.]

7. [Weber here takes up a phrase from Karl Marx's prediction of the end of capitalist society as a consequence of its own contradictory development. "The monopoly of capital becomes a fetter upon the mode of production, which has sprung up and flourished along with, and under it. . . . The knell of capitalist private property sounds. The expropriators are expropriated." *Capital* (London: Lawrence and Wishart, 1967), vol. 1, p. 763.]

autonomous officials of the "estates" who previously controlled such things as of right and has put itself in the shape of its highest representative in their place.

This process of political expropriation has been enacted with varying success in every country of the world. In it there arose, initially in the service of the monarch, the first categories of "professional politicians" in a *second* sense. This consisted of people who, unlike the charismatic leaders, did not wish to become masters themselves, but to enter *into the service* of political masters. In these conflicts they put themselves at the disposal of the monarch and treated the implementation of his policies as a way of earning their own material living, on the one hand, and of acquiring a life's ideal on the other. Once again, it is *only* in the Western world that we discover professional politicians of *this* stamp in the service of powers other than just the monarchs. In the past they were their most important instruments of power and of their acts of political expropriation.

Before we take a closer look at this question, let us make the meaning of the existence of such "professional politicians" perfectly clear in all its implications. It is possible to engage in "politics," that is to say, to seek to influence the distribution of power between and within political structures, both as an "occasional" politician and as a part-time or full-time politician, in the same way as with economic activity. We are all "occasional" politicians when we cast our votes or in any similar expression of our will, such as applauding or protesting during a "political" meeting, making a "political" speech, and so on. And for many people this is the extent of their connection with politics. Today, for example, part-time politicians include all the local agents and committee members of political party associations who, as a rule, pursue such activities only as occasion demands and who do not make it the *primary* "task of their lives," either materially or as an ideal. The same thing can be said of the members of councils of state and similar advisory bodies who spring into action only on request. This applies also to broad swathes of our parliamentarians who are only politically active while Parliament is in session. In the past such groups of people were to be found above all among the "estates."

By the "estates" we understand the owners in their own right of the material possessions vital for military or administrative functions, or the exercise of personal seigneurial authority. A major portion of them were far from willing to pass their lives wholly or chiefly, or even more than occasionally, in the service of politics. Instead, they used their seigneurial power to maximize their own rents or profits and became politically active in the service of their political associations only when their overlord or their peers expressly called for it. The same thing may be said of a proportion of the assistants whom the monarch recruited in his struggle to create an independent political organization that would be responsible to himself alone. The household advisers[8] and, going back even further, a considerable proportion of the monarch's counselors in the "*curia*"[9] and other advisory bodies were of this type.

But, of course, the monarch could not make do with assistants who functioned only part-time or occasionally. He had to try to assemble a staff of assistants consisting of people who were entirely and exclusively devoted to serving him as their *principal* profession. The structure of the emerging dynastic political system depended very crucially on where he found them, as did the entire character of the relevant culture. And the same necessity was enjoined even more powerfully on the political entities that had completely eliminated or strictly confined the royal power and thus constituted themselves politically as (so-called) "free" polities. These polities were "free" not in the sense of freedom from the rule of force, but in the sense of the absence of monarchical power legitimated by tradition (and for the most part sanctified by religion), as the exclusive source of all authority. Historically, such polities had their home in the West, and their nucleus was the city as a political entity. It was in this form that it first appeared in the Mediterranean cultures.

What did the "*full-time*" politicians look like in all these cases?

---

8. [The *Räte vom Hause aus* (literally, counselors [based out of] their own homes) was a term used to describe advisers in a number of German territories who did not normally live at court. Instead, they provided their services only when the king's council was convened in their region.]

9. [The *curia regis* or king's court was convened wherever the king was in residence.]

There are two ways of engaging in politics as a vocation. You can either live "for" politics or "from" politics. These alternatives are not by any means mutually exclusive. On the contrary, as a rule people do both, mentally at least, but for the most part materially, as well. Whoever lives "for" politics makes "this his life" in an *inward* sense. Either he enjoys the naked exercise of the power he possesses or he feeds his inner equilibrium and his self-esteem with the consciousness that by serving a "cause" he gives his own life a *meaning*. In this inner sense, probably every serious person who lives for a cause also lives from it. The distinction, then, refers to a far weightier aspect of the matter: its economic dimension. The people who live "from" politics as a profession are those who seek to make it their permanent source of *income*; those who live "for" politics are those for whom this is not the case.

In a society based on private property, for anyone to be able to live "for" politics in this economic sense, a number of apparently trivial preconditions must be satisfied. Such a person must be economically independent, in normal circumstances, of the income that politics may bring him. This means quite simply that he must be affluent or have a position in private life that affords him an adequate income. This at least is the normal situation. Admittedly, the followers of a warlord are as incurious about normal economic conditions as are the followers of a revolutionary hero of the street. Both live from booty, robbery, confiscations, levies, the imposition of worthless currencies whose use is obligatory—all of which amount essentially to the same thing. But these are necessarily phenomena that go beyond the everyday world; in the workaday economy only independent means can perform this service. But more than this is required; in addition, a would-be politician must be economically in a position to make himself "available." This means that his sources of income must not require him constantly to devote all or most of his thoughts and energy personally to the task of earning his living. The person who is most readily available in this sense is the *rentier*, that is, a person whose income does not depend on doing any work at all. This applies to the lords of the manor of the past, and large landowners and persons of high rank of the present who derive their income from ground rents—in antiquity and the Middle Ages, there were also rents for slaves or bondsmen. In modern times, it applies also to people who obtain a living from securities or other modern sources of investment income. Neither the worker *nor*—and this is particularly noteworthy—the employer, and *especially* the large-scale modern employer, is able to absent himself from his work in this way. The employer in particular is tied to his business and *cannot* easily take time off. This is true especially of the industrial businessman, far more than of the big agricultural employer, in view of the seasonal nature of farming. It is mostly very difficult for the businessman to find a substitute, even on a temporary basis. The same thing applies, for example, to doctors, and the more eminent and the busier they are, the harder it is for them to take leave of absence from work. It is easier for the lawyer if only for purely technical reasons arising from the nature of his work, and this explains why lawyers have often played an incomparably greater and even dominant role as professional politicians. We have no need to pursue this line of argument further, but should make clear some of its implications.

Where a state or a party is governed by people who (in the economic sense of the word) live exclusively for politics and not from politics, this necessarily implies that the leading political strata must be recruited on the basis of a "plutocratic" policy. This is not of course to assert the opposite, namely, that the existence of a plutocratic leadership *exempts* the politically dominant class from also striving to live "from" politics, that is to say, to exploit its political dominance for the sake of its own private economic interests. There can be no question of that. There has never been a social stratum that has failed to exploit its position in one way or another. It means only that professional politicians are not directly compelled to seek remuneration *for* their political services as everyone without means is forced to do. But by the same token, this is not to suggest that politicians with no independent means entered politics solely or even principally with an eye to providing for their own material welfare, or that their concern for their "cause" was not uppermost in their minds, or even present at all. Nothing could be more mistaken. Experience tells us that consciously or unconsciously, the concern of the well-to-do man for the economic "security" of his own existence is a cardinal issue for the entire conduct of his life. A ruthless and unconditioned political idealism is to be found, if not exclusively, then at least for preference, in the strata that own nothing, and who because of that fact stand outside the circle of those who have an interest in maintaining the economic order of a given society. This applies with particular force to exceptional, in other words, revolutionary, epochs. Instead, it means only that to recruit politically interested people, both leaders and their followers, *non*-plutocratically, is based on the self-evident assumption that these interested parties can extract a regular and reliable income from the practice of politics.

Politics can either be conducted on an "honorary" basis and thus by what are normally called "independent," that is, well-to-do people, above all, people with unearned income. Alternatively, the leadership can be opened up to those who own nothing and who must then be recompensed. The professional politician who lives *from* politics can be a pure "beneficiary" [*Pfründner*] or a salaried "official." He either derives an income from fees and perquisites for specific services — tips and bribes are merely an irregular and formally illegal variant of this income category — or else he receives fixed benefits in kind or a salary in cash form, or a combination of the two. He may assume the character of an "entrepreneur," like the *condottiere* or the owner of a leased or purchased office in the past, or like the American boss[10] who regards his expenses as a capital investment from which he obtains a return by exploiting his influence. Alternatively, he can draw a fixed wage, like an editor or a party secretary or a modern minister or party official. In the past, fiefs, gifts of land, benefices of every kind, and particularly, with the growth of the money economy, perquisites formed the typical remuneration bestowed on their followers by rulers, victorious conquerors, or successful party chiefs. Today, the rewards that are handed out by the party leaders in return for loyal services consist of offices of every kind in parties, newspapers, cooperatives, health insurance companies, municipalities, and states. *All* party struggles are conflicts not just for

concrete goals, but also and above all for the patronage of office. All conflicts between particularist and centralist aspirations in Germany also revolve above all around the question of which authority will have offices in its gift, whether it be the authorities in Berlin or Munich, Karlsruhe or Dresden. Any loss of influence in the distribution of offices is more keenly felt by the parties than setbacks on matters concerning their political goals.

In France a politically influenced change in prefect[11] was always regarded as a greater upheaval, and it caused more uproar than a modification in the government's program since this had for the most part no more than a verbal significance.

Many parties, above all in America, have ceased to be concerned with the old quarrels about the interpretation of the Constitution and have become purely parties of careerists that readily adapt their substantive programs to improve their chances of catching votes.

In Spain until recently "elections" were fixed from above on the basis of an agreement between the two major parties to take turns governing in order to provide their respective followers with posts. In both the so-called "elections" and the so-called "revolutions" in the Spanish colonies, what was really at stake was the state gravy train in which the victors hoped to be fed.

In Switzerland the parties amicably share the posts on the basis of proportionality, and here in Germany, some of our "revolutionary" draft constitutions, such as the one recently proposed for Baden, even envisaged extending this system to include ministerial posts. They thus treat the state and its offices purely as an agency for distributing bounty.

The Center Party in particular was enthusiastic about this idea and in Baden it even proposed including in its program the proportional distribution of

---

10. [Weber used the English word, here and elsewhere in this essay.]

11. [In the administrative reforms introduced in the wake of the French Revolution, France was divided into *départements* headed by prefects who were appointed for their political reliability. Their duties included the maintenance of order, but also the implementation of government policies locally. They were therefore severely affected by changes of government. In the Third Republic, for example, more than one-third of the prefects were replaced after the elections of 1898.]

offices according to religious affiliation, without regard to merit. With the growing number of offices resulting from the general process of bureaucratization, they are increasingly in demand as a form of *secure* provision. This trend is strengthening among all the parties and in the eyes of their followers the parties are increasingly regarded as a means to the end of providing such support.

However, an opposing trend is to be found in the development of modern bureaucracy into a specialized, highly qualified, intellectual workforce that has undergone a lengthy preparatory period of training. This workforce has a highly developed sense of professional *honor* with an emphasis on probity. Without that sense of honor the risk of terrible corruption and vulgar philistinism would loom over us like fate. This would even threaten to undermine the purely technical activity of the state apparatus whose importance for the economy has constantly grown and will continue to grow, particularly with the increasing trend toward socialization. In the United States, where a professional civil service with tenure for life was once quite unknown, amateurish administration by politicians on the make brought about a situation in which hundreds of thousands of officials, right down to the local postman, had to be changed as a result of the presidential election. This system has long since been undermined by the Civil Service Reform.[12] This change was made inevitable by the irresistible, purely technical needs of administration.

In Europe the professional bureaucracy with its division of labor into specialized fields of expertise gradually came into being over the course of half a millennium. This process began with the Italian cities and *signorie*;[13] and among the monarchies it was the conquering Norman states who took the lead. The decisive step was triggered in the sphere of the rulers' *finances*. We can see from the administrative reforms of Emperor Maximilian[14] how difficult it was for the officials to oust the ruler from this sphere of activity, even under the pressure of extreme necessity and the threat of Turkish domination.[15] This was all the more remarkable, given that finance was the realm that found it hardest to accommodate the dilettantism of a ruler who at the time was bent primarily on being a model of chivalry. Advances in the techniques of warfare produced the expert officer, while the growing sophistication of the legal process resulted in the emergence of the trained lawyer. In all three areas the skilled official finally triumphed in the more developed states during the sixteenth century. And the rise of princely absolutism at the expense of the estates coincided with the gradual surrender of the ruler's autonomous power to the bureaucratic experts to whom he owed his victory over the estates in the first place.

The rise of the trained *bureaucracy* went hand in hand, albeit in a far less obvious process of transition, with the emergence of the "leading *politicians*." Of course, such influential royal advisers have always existed from time immemorial and in every part of the globe. In the Orient the need to relieve the sultan as far as possible of his personal responsibility for the success of government led to the creation of the typical figure of the "Grand Vizier." In the West diplomacy first became a *consciously* cultivated art during

---

12. [The Civil Service Reform to which Weber is referring here was inaugurated by the so-called Pendleton Act of 1883. This began the transition from the spoils system to the merit system. Initially, only about one in ten federal employees were appointed on the basis of examinations.]

13. [The *signoria* was a form of government by a lord or despot (*signore*) in the Italian city-states between the middle of the thirteenth and the beginning of the sixteenth centuries, replacing earlier republican institutions. The lord who had usually started in a particular office, such as Captain of the People, sought to extend his authority until it was made permanent and hereditary in his family. Notable examples are the Visconti family in Milan, the Estes in Ferrara, and the Della Scala in Verona. In places that escaped the rule of one lord, the term refers to the ruling body of magistrates, as in Florence.]

14. [This was Maximilian I (1459–1519), who became Holy Roman Emperor in 1508. His interest in chivalry was intense; he has been given the epithet of "the last knight" and even wrote a lengthy epic poem of knightly deeds.]

15. [During the reigns of Maximilian and his successor, Charles V, as Holy Roman Emperors, the expansion of the Ottoman Empire to the west reached its high point under the leadership of the Sultan Süleyman I, with the conquest of Hungary and the siege of Vienna in 1529.]

the reign of Charles V, the age of Machiavelli.[16] This took place above all under the influence of the Venetian ambassadors, whose reports were studied with passionate zeal in diplomatic circles. The adepts of this diplomacy had mostly received a humanist education and regarded one another as a trained class of initiates. In this respect they resembled the humanist Chinese statesmen of the last phase of the period of the Warring States.[17]

The need for politics as a *whole*, including domestic policy, to be conducted in a formally unified manner by a leading statesman arose in a decisive and compelling way only as the result of constitutional developments. Up to that point there had always been individuals who had acted as the prince's advisers or rather, in reality, leaders. But initially, the organization of the authorities had taken a different path, even in the most advanced states. The supreme administrative authorities that had emerged were *collegiate*[18] in nature. In theory and also in practice, though to a decreasing extent, their meetings were presided over by the monarch in person. It was he who made the decisions. This collegiate system led to the growth of expert opinions, counteropinions, and reasoned votes on the part of majorities and minorities. As a counterweight to these supreme official authorities, the ruler tended to surround himself with purely personal confidants — the cabinet — whom he delegated to convey

16. [Charles V (1500–1558) was Holy Roman Emperor from 1530 to 1556. Niccolò Machiavelli (1469–1527) was the celebrated Florentine writer and statesman.]

17. [The period of the Warring States (475–221 B.C.E.) was an age in which China was split up into six or seven feuding kingdoms. It was one of the most fertile and influential of Chinese history. It not only saw the rise of some of the most important Confucian thinkers, but also witnessed the emergence of some of the political structures and cultural patterns that shaped China over the subsequent 2,000 years. It came to an end in 221 B.C.E. when the Qin dynasty established the first unified Chinese empire.]

18. [Weber has in mind bodies like the Conseil d'État in France and the Privy Council in England, but also the Councils of Workers and Soldiers of the German revolution after 1918. For Weber's discussion of collegiate bodies, see *Economy and Society*, chapter 3, section 8, pp. 271 ff., and chapter 11, section 12, pp. 994 ff.]

his decisions in response to the resolutions of the council of state, or whatever name the supreme state authority went by. By such methods the ruler, who increasingly slipped into the role of a dilettante, sought to escape from the inexorable growth of his officials' expertise and to keep hold of the reins of power. This latent conflict between trained officials and autocratic rule was to be found everywhere.

The situation changed only when the prince was faced with parliaments and the desire of their party leaders for power. However, conditions that were pitched very differently led to what was outwardly the same result—admittedly, with certain distinctions. Wherever the dynasties retained genuine power, as was the case especially in Germany, the monarchs' interests were aligned with those of the officials in *opposition* to the parliament and its claims to power. The officials had an interest in ensuring that the leading posts, that is to say, ministerial posts, should be filled from their ranks, and that these posts should become the goals to which civil servants might legitimately hope to be promoted. For his part, the monarch had an interest in being able to nominate ministers from the ranks of the officials beholden to him in accordance with his own judgment. Both sides, however, had an interest in ensuring that the political leadership should face the parliament with a united and coherent front. This meant the replacement of the collegiate system by a single cabinet leader. In addition, the monarch stood in need of a single responsible individual who could cover for him, and who would be both answerable to the parliament and able to confront it, while negotiating with the parties. This was essential if he was to be raised above party conflicts and party attacks.

All these interests came together and exerted pressure in the same direction: the emergence of a single minister to preside over the officials and to provide unified leadership. The trend toward a unified parliamentary power became even stronger where, as in Britain, it gained the upper hand in its struggle with the monarch. In Britain the "cabinet," with a single parliamentary "leader"[19] at its head, became a committee representing the power that was ignored by

19. [Weber used the English word.]

the official laws, but was in fact the sole decisive political power: the *party* of the day that could command a majority. The official collegiate bodies were as such not the organs of the true ruling power, namely, the party, and could not therefore act as the agents of the real government. If the dominant party was to maintain its power at home and pursue grand policy abroad, it needed an effective organization at its disposal, consisting exclusively of the true leaders of the party and able to deal with business in confidence. In short, it needed a cabinet. At the same time, the party also needed a leader who would be responsible to the public, and above all the parliamentary public, for all decisions, in short, the head of the cabinet. In the shape of parliamentary ministries, this British system was then adopted on the Continent, and only in America and the democracies influenced by it was an entirely different system introduced. In this system the chosen leader of the victorious party was elected directly by the people and placed at the head of an official apparatus nominated by himself; his dependence on the approval of Congress was confined to budgetary and legislative matters.

The growth of politics into an "operation" that required a schooling in the struggle for power and its methods led to a twofold division of public servants as these methods were developed by the modern party system. This division was by no means absolute, but it was clear-cut. There were the professional officials on the one hand and the "political officials" on the other. The "political" officials in the true sense can be recognized outwardly by the ease with which they can be transferred and dismissed at any time or at least temporarily "retired," like the prefects in France and the comparable officials in other countries. This presents a striking contrast to the "independence" of officials in the judiciary. In Britain this class of political officials includes those who, according to long-standing convention, lose their posts with every change of parliamentary majority and hence of the cabinet. This category includes, in particular, officials concerned with the general "administration of home affairs"; and the "political" element in this is above all the task of maintaining "law and order" in the land, in other words, upholding the existing system of rule.

In Prussia the Puttkamer decree[20] laid down that these officials had the duty of "representing government policy" or else having to face disciplinary measures, and like the prefects in France, they were used as an official apparatus with which to influence elections.

Under the German system and in contrast to other countries, most of the "political" officials were of the same quality as all other civil servants, since appointment to these posts likewise depended on university study, specialist examinations, and a fixed period of preparatory service. This specific feature of the professional modern civil service is waived in Germany only for the heads of the political apparatus, namely, the ministers. Under the old regime, a man could become minister of education in Prussia without ever having studied at an institution of higher education, whereas it was possible to become a senior civil servant [*Vortragender Rat*] only after passing the prescribed examinations. Under Althoff,[21] for example, in the Prussian Ministry of Education, it went without saying that the departmental head [*Dezernent*] and senior civil servant was professionally trained and hence infinitely better informed about the real technical problems of his department than his boss. In Britain it was no different. It follows that in dealing with everyday business the civil servant was also the more powerful figure. That was not necessarily absurd. The

20. [Robert von Puttkamer (1828–1900), a conservative politician who was Minister for Home Affairs (1881–8) under Bismarck. His decree of January 1882 proclaimed that the emperor was responsible for the direction of government and that civil servants were bound by their oath of allegiance to support that policy. His period of office was notable for the rigor with which he enforced the laws proscribing socialism and the thoroughness with which he ensured that officials with liberal views were excluded from state service.]

21. [Friedrich Althoff (1839–1908) was the Prussian Minister of Education from 1897 to 1907 and head of its universities section for fifteen years before that. In this capacity he largely determined the shape of secondary and higher education in Germany in the early twentieth century. While expanding the universities and scientific institutes, he intervened regularly in academic affairs. Weber believed that Althoff had tried to block his appointment to a chair in Freiburg in 1893.]

minister was in fact the representative of the nexus of *political* power; his task was to represent its political norms and to apply them to the proposals of his specialized subordinates or else to give his officials the relevant political directives.

It is very similar to the management of a business in the private sector. There the real "sovereign," the shareholders' meeting, has as little influence on the management of the business as does a "nation" ruled by professional officials. And the people of decisive importance for the policy of the business, namely, the "supervisory board" dominated by the banks, only give economic directives and select the administrative personnel, since they do not possess the technical expertise with which to run the business themselves. In this respect the present structure of the revolutionary state does not represent any fundamental innovation. For what one finds there is that complete amateurs have been handed power over the administration simply because they have machine guns in their possession, and they wish for nothing better than to use the trained officials as executive heads and hands.[22] The difficulties of the present system lie elsewhere but need not concern us today.

We shall inquire instead about the typical characteristics of professional politicians, both the "leaders" and their followers. These have undergone changes in the course of time and are very diverse today, as well.

"Professional politicians" developed in the past, as we have seen, in the course of struggles between the rulers and the estates of the nobility, and in these struggles they acted as the servants of the rulers. Let us examine their principal types.

In his struggles with the estates, the ruler sought the assistance of politically exploitable strata who did not form part of the estates. These included, first and foremost, the clergy. This was what happened in India and Indo-China, in Buddhist China and Japan and in Lamaist Mongolia, as well as the Christian lands of the Middle Ages. Technically, this was because the clergy were literate. In all these countries, Brahmans, Buddhist priests, and Lamas were imported, and bishops and priests were employed as political advisers. The aim everywhere was to acquire literate administrators who could be deployed by the emperor or princes or the khan in their struggle with the aristocracy. Members of the clergy, especially if they were celibate, stood outside the hustle and bustle of ordinary political and economic interests and, unlike the ruler's vassals, were not exposed to the temptation to compete with him for political power of their own to pass on to their heirs. The cleric was "separated" from the machinery of the ruler's administration by the characteristics of his own status group.

A second stratum of this kind consisted of men of letters with a humanist education. There was a time when men learned to make speeches in Latin and write verses in Greek in order to qualify as political advisers and above all to compose political memoranda on behalf of a ruler. That was the age of the first flowering of the humanist schools and the establishment by the crown of professorial chairs of "poetics." In Germany this phase soon passed without leaving deeper traces politically, although it had a lasting impact on our education system. Matters were different in Eastern Asia. The Chinese mandarin is, or rather, was originally, the approximate equivalent of our Renaissance humanist: a humanist man of letters who was educated and who passed examinations in the literary monuments of the distant past. If you read the diaries of Li Hung-chang,[23] you will find that what he took most pride in was the fact that he wrote poetry and was a good calligrapher. This social stratum, with its conventions derived from Chinese antiquity, has determined the entire fate of China. Our own fate might have been similar if there had been the slightest opportunity for the humanists to impose their influence with equal success.

---

22. [During the brief revolutions in Germany in 1918–19, the Councils of Workers and Soldiers permitted the traditional administrative authorities to continue their work but sent trusted representatives into their meetings to oversee what was done, without directly intervening, however.]

23. [Li Hung-chang (1823–1901), a distinguished Chinese statesman who sought to open up China to technology from the West. After the Boxer uprising of 1896–98 against Western influence, he was instrumental in mediating between the imperial court and the Western powers, leading to the treaty that ended the uprising.]

The third social stratum was the court nobility. Once the rulers had succeeded in depriving the aristocracy of its political power as an estate, they attracted the nobility to the court and enrolled them in their political and diplomatic service. One of the factors in the transformation of our education system in the seventeenth century was that the place of the humanist men of letters in the service of the monarchs was taken by professional politicians drawn from the nobility.

The fourth category was a specifically British phenomenon: this was a patrician class comprising the minor nobility and the urban inhabitants of independent means, known technically as the "gentry."[24] This was a stratum that the monarch had originally attracted in his conflict with the barons and that he put in charge of the offices of "self-government,"[25] only to become increasingly dependent upon them subsequently. This stratum remained in possession of all the offices of local government that it took over gratis in the interests of its own social power. The gentry saved Britain from bureaucratization, the fate of all continental states.

A fifth stratum was peculiar to the West, particularly on the Continent, and it was of crucial importance for its entire political structure. This was the class of university-trained lawyers. Once Roman law had been transformed under the late Roman bureaucratic state, it continued to exert a powerful influence over a long period of time. Nowhere was this more evident than in the circumstance that, in its advance toward the rational state, the revolution of the machinery of politics was undertaken everywhere by trained lawyers. This applied even in Britain, although there the great national guilds of lawyers hampered the introduction of Roman law. Nowhere on earth can we find anything analogous to this. Neither the approaches to rational legal thinking in the Indian Mimamsa[26]

school nor the further development in Islam of the legal thinking of antiquity was able to prevent rational legal thought from being stifled by theological ways of thinking. Above all, there was a failure completely to rationalize trial procedure. Three factors were blended together to achieve this rationalization: first, the success with which Italian jurists took over ancient Roman jurisprudence, the product of an entirely unique political system that rose from a city-state to world dominance; second, the *usus modernus*, the modern practice, of the late medieval pandect jurists[27] and canon lawyers; and third, the theories of natural law that had sprung from legal and Christian thought and were subsequently secularized. This legal rationalism had its greatest representatives in the Italian *podestà*,[28] in the royal French jurists who created the formal instruments that enabled the royal power to undermine seigneurial rule, in the canon lawyers and the theologians of the conciliar tradition[29] with their theories of natural law, in the court jurists and learned judges of the continental rulers, in the teachers of natural law in the Netherlands and in the monarcho-

24. [Weber used the English word.]

25. [Weber used the English word.]

26. [Mimamsa ("reflection," "study") is the name given to the earliest of the six orthodox systems of Indian philosophy. It dates back to c. fourth century B.C.E. and involves a rational examination of the sacred Vedic texts but was also applied to the analysis of legal texts. It was a powerful intellectual force and is traditionally credited with the defeat of Buddhism in India.]

27. [The *Pandects* or Digests were a compendium of fifty books of Roman civil law made by the order of Emperor Justinian and published in 533 C.E. Roman law came to Germany in the Middle Ages but did not develop until early in the seventeenth century when lawyers, including specialists in canon law, began to interpret the law more freely and to adapt it to modern needs. It was this development that was referred to as the "*usus modernus pandecticum.*"]

28. [The *podestà* (sometimes translated as "mayor") was an elected official in a commune, normally from the nobility of another locality, and invested with supreme legal authority for a fixed salary and for a set period of time. Weber attached great importance to this institution and its role in the development of Italian law in the Middle Ages. His account of it can be found in *Economy and Society*, chapter 16, section 3, pp. 1273 ff.]

29. [The conciliar tradition arose as a response to a crisis in the papacy in the fourteenth and fifteenth centuries. It means that as well as the pope, the councils representing the church as a whole have the authority to establish binding norms for church doctrine.]

machs,[30] in the lawyers of the English crown and Parliament, in the *noblesse de robe* of the French *parlements*,[31] and finally, in the lawyers of the period of the [French] Revolution. Without this legal rationalism the emergence of the absolute state is as inconceivable as the Revolution. If you look through the remonstrances of the French *parlements* or the *cahiers*[32] of the French Estates General[33] from the sixteenth century until 1789, you will see everywhere the legal mind at work. And if you look into the professions of the members of the French Convention,[34] you will find there—even though they were elected on the basis of equal suffrage—no more than a single proletarian, a very few bourgeois businessmen, but, in contrast, a whole mass of lawyers of every kind without whose participation the specific spirit that animated these radical intellectuals and their proposals would be quite inconceivable. The modern advocate and modern democracy have always been inseparable ever since, while advocates in our sense, as an independent status group, have existed in their turn only in the West. They emerged there under the influence of the gradual rationalization of trial procedure since the Middle Ages, as a development from the spokesman [*Fürsprech*] of the formalistic Germanic legal process.

There is nothing accidental about the importance of lawyers in Western politics since the rise of political parties. Party politics just means politics as engaged in by interested parties; we shall soon see what that means. And to conduct a case effectively on behalf of interested parties is the business of the trained lawyer. In this respect he is the superior of any "official," a lesson we have learned from the superiority of enemy propaganda.[35] Admittedly, a lawyer can emerge victorious in a "bad" case, in other words, a case that only has logically feeble arguments on its side; he triumphs by conducting the case "ably," technically speaking. But it is also true that only a lawyer has the skill to plead a cause that has intrinsically "powerful" arguments in its favor and thus to handle a "good" case "ably." An official acting as a politician all too often turns a "good" case into a "bad" one through his technically "incompetent" pleading. This is something we have learned from painful experience. For politics nowadays is conducted preeminently in public and through the medium of the spoken or written word. Weighing the effect of words lies at the heart of the activity of the lawyer but is remote from the skills of the professional civil servant, who neither is nor should be a demagogue, and if he nevertheless undertakes to assume the role of a demagogue he normally turns out to do it very badly.

Given the nature of his true vocation, the genuine official—and this is crucial for our assessment of our former regime here in Germany—should not be politically active but, above all else, should "administer," *impartially*. This applies also to so-called "political" civil servants, officially at least, as long as there is no threat to "*raison d'état*," that is, the vital interests of the dominant order. *Sine ira et studio*, "without anger

30. [The term "monarchomach," meaning "fighter against the king" or "king-killer," was introduced by the royalist William Barclay (1543–1608) to describe a group of political thinkers in France who had argued for the restriction of the monarch's powers and the right to resist him. See William Barclay's *De Regno et regali potestate* (Paris, 1600).]

31. [The *noblesse de robe* was a hereditary nobility conferred on holders of high judicial or legal office in the sixteenth and seventeenth centuries. The *parlement* was not a parliament in the English sense but a judicial assembly, descended from the *curia regis*, or king's court, from the thirteenth century on.]

32. [That is, the *cahiers de doléances* or memoranda of grievances that were drawn up at the time of elections to the Estates General. They were collected up and presented to the king estate by estate.]

33. [The Estates General was the legislative body in France until the Revolution of 1789. It provided representation for the three estates of the realm, that is, the nobility, the clergy, and the commons (in practice, the burghers of the towns).]

34. [The chief of the revolutionary assemblies that governed France after 1789. It followed the Legislative Assembly in 1792 and culminated in the Reign of Terror, after which it was succeeded in 1795 by the Directory.]

35. [Weber is referring to the propaganda campaign waged during World War I. The allegation that by invading Belgium the Germans had violated international law and the principle of national self-determination proved particularly damaging.]

or partiality"[36] — that should be the official's motto in the performance of his duties. He should therefore abstain from doing what politicians, the leaders as well as followers, must always necessarily do, namely, to *fight*. For taking sides, struggle, passion — *ira et studium* — are the politician's element, especially the political *leader's*. *His* activity is subject to an entirely different principle of *responsibility*, in fact, the very opposite principle to that of the official. When an official receives an order, his honor lies in his ability to carry it out, on his superior's *responsibility*, conscientiously and exactly as if it corresponded to his own convictions. This remains the case even if the order seems wrong to him and if, despite his protests, his superior insists on his compliance. Without this discipline and self-denial, which is ethical in the highest degree, the entire apparatus would collapse. In contrast, the point of honor of the political leader, that is, the leading statesman, is that he acts exclusively on his *own* responsibility, a responsibility that he may not and cannot refuse or shuffle off onto someone else. It is precisely civil servants of high moral stature who make bad politicians, in other words, who act irresponsibly from a political standpoint. We must judge them, therefore, to be ethically inferior politicians of the kind we in Germany have unfortunately had time and again in leading positions. That is what we call "government by civil servants" [*Beamtenherrschaft*]. I must make it clear that it is not my intention to cast a slur on the honor of our civil service by exposing what are political defects of this system, if we judge it by its success. But let us return once more to the typology of political figures.

Since the founding of the constitutional state, and even more markedly since the establishment of democracy, the demagogue has been the typical political leader in the West. The unpleasant connotations of this word should not obscure the fact that it was not Cleon, but Pericles,[37] who was the first to bear

this name. Without office, or rather as the incumbent of the only elective office of military commander[38] (in contrast to the other offices in ancient democracy, which were filled by casting lots), he presided over the sovereign assembly [*ekklesia*] of the people [*demos*] of Athens. Modern demagogues, too, make use of speech, and they do so to a formidable degree, when you consider the election speeches that a modern candidate has to make. But they use the printed word even more. The political publicist, and above all, the *journalist* is the most important representative of the species today.

To provide even an outline of the sociology of modern political journalism would go well beyond the framework of this lecture, since that would be a separate topic in its own right. But a few points must be made. The journalist shares with all demagogues and lawyers (as well as artists) the fate of being denied a fixed place in the social structure. This is true on the Continent, at least, and it contrasts with conditions in Britain and, incidentally, with the situation that formerly obtained in Prussia. He belongs to a kind of pariah caste that in the eyes of "society" is always judged socially by its lowest representatives from the point of view of morality. Hence, the strangest ideas are prevalent about journalists and their work. Not everyone realizes that to write a really *good* piece of journalism is at least as demanding intellectually as the achievement of any scholar. This is particularly true when we recollect that it has to be written on the spot, to order, and that it must create an immediate *effect*, even though it is produced under completely different conditions from that of scholarly research. It is generally overlooked that a journalist's actual responsibility is far greater than a scholar's, and that on average every reputable journalist's *sense* of responsibility is by no means inferior, as indeed we saw during the war. It is overlooked because in the nature of the case it is the *irresponsible* pieces of journalism that tend to remain in the memory because of their often terrible effects. And no one believes it possible for competent journalists to be more

---

36. [Tacitus, *Annals*, book 1, chapter 1.]

37. [Cleon, an Athenian politician of the fifth century B.C.E., who succeeded Pericles as "leader of the people" in 427. He had mixed success as a general in the wars against Sparta but is known for the brutal treatment of his enemies once he had defeated them. His long-term reputation is that of a conventional vulgar demagogue.

Pericles (495–427 B.C.E.) was one of the outstanding figures of Athenian democracy.]

38. [Weber uses *Oberstrategen* — "high strategist" — and clearly means what the Greeks call *strategos*.]

discreet on average than other people. And yet it is
so. The incomparably greater temptations to which
this profession is exposed, together with the other
conditions of working as a journalist at the present
time, have conditioned the public to regard the press
with a mixture of disdain and abject cowardice. It
is not possible to discuss today how this might be
remedied. What interests us here is the *political* destiny that journalists can aspire to, the opportunities
they have to gain positions of leadership in politics.
Hitherto, openings occurred only in the Social Democratic Party. However, within the party editorial posts
resembled civil service posts for the most part but
have not proved to be a springboard to a position in
the *leadership*.

In the bourgeois parties the prospects of gaining
political power by this route have, if anything, deteriorated on the whole, when compared to the previous
generation. Needless to say, every politician of importance has stood in need of press influence and hence
also connections with the press. But contrary to what
might have been expected, for party *leaders* to emerge
from the ranks of the press was very much the exception. The reason for this lies in the journalist's greatly
reduced ability to obtain time off from his work. This
applies above all to the journalist with no private
means since he is necessarily tied to his professional
duties. A journalist's duties, moreover, have become
much more intensive, as has the importance of being
up to date. The need to earn a living by writing
articles on a daily or weekly basis is a millstone around
the neck of politicians, and I know of some who are
leaders by nature but whose rise to power has been
outwardly and, even more importantly, inwardly paralyzed by this burden. The fact that under the old
regime relations between the press and the ruling
powers in the state and in the parties had a dire effect
on the quality of journalism is a story in its own right.
These relations were different in the countries of our
enemies. But even there, and indeed in all modern
states, it appears that the political influence of the
ordinary working journalist is constantly being
eroded, while the influence of the capitalist press
magnate, such as "Lord" Northcliffe,[39] grows apace.

Admittedly, in Germany hitherto the great capitalist newspaper concerns have mainly taken over the
newspapers with the "small ads," that is, the various
"General Advertisers," and as a general rule they have
promoted political apathy. For no profits were to be
made from an independent line in politics, and such
independence was even less likely to earn the commercially helpful goodwill of the ruling political
powers. During the war the revenues brought in by
advertising could be targeted as a way of exerting
political influence on the press, and this practice
looks set to continue. Even if the major newspapers
can be expected to resist this pressure, the position
of the smaller ones is far more precarious. In any
case, in Germany at present a journalistic career is
not a normal career route for aspiring political leaders.
Whether we should add "any longer" or "not yet,"
we shall perhaps have to wait to see. This is not to
discount its other attractions or to deny its opportunities for influencing and changing politics and, above
all, the degree of political responsibility it may entail.

Whether the position would change at all if the
principle of anonymity were to be abandoned, as
some but not all journalists propose, is hard to say.
During the war some newspapers in Germany were
edited by talented writers who had been specially
hired for the purpose and who made a point of writing
under their own names. Unfortunately, what we
found in a number of the better-known cases was that
this approach does *not* necessarily foster the enhanced
sense of responsibility that we might have expected. It
was in part the most notorious elements of the popular
press who, regardless of party allegiance, used this
tactic to strive for higher sales—and who did in fact
achieve them. This practice undoubtedly increased
the wealth of the gentlemen concerned, the publishers as well as the sensation-seeking journalists—
but not their *honor*. This does not amount to an
argument against the principle; the question is highly
complex, and we should not generalize from this
one experience.

Hitherto, however, journalism has not proved to
be the road to genuine leadership or to the *responsible*

---

39. [Alfred, Lord Northcliffe (1865–1922), was a British
press lord. He founded papers like the *Daily Mail* (1903)

and *Daily Mirror* (1904), rescued the *Observer* (1908),
and bought up *The Times*. He worked closely with his
younger brother, who became Viscount Rothermere.]

conduct of political life. How matters will develop further, only time will tell. Whatever happens, however, a career in journalism will remain one of the most important paths to professional political activity. Not a path for just anybody, however, least of all for people of weak character, especially for people who can maintain their inner equilibrium only where their social and professional status is secure. A young scholar's life involves something of a gamble, but he is at least surrounded by the stable conventions of social status that help to prevent him from going off the rails. A journalist's life, however, is in every sense a gamble pure and simple. Moreover, he works under conditions that subject his inner sense of security to a sterner test than almost any other situation. His often bitter professional disappointments may not even be the worst aspect of this.

Indeed, it is above all the successful journalists who find themselves having to face particularly onerous inner challenges. It is no small thing to consort with the powerful people of this earth in their drawing rooms, apparently on a basis of equality, to be flattered because you are feared, while all the time knowing that no sooner has the door closed behind you than your host may have to defend himself to his guests for having invited the "scoundrels from the press." In the same way, it is no small thing to deliver prompt and yet convincing judgments on anything and everything that the "market" happens to call for, on every conceivable problem of life, without succumbing to absolute superficiality, or what is even worse, to the humiliation of self-exposure with its inexorable consequences. We should not find it astonishing that so many journalists have gone off the rails or have otherwise lost their value as human beings. What is surprising is that, despite everything, this stratum of society contains a much greater number of valuable and absolutely genuine human beings than outsiders tend to suppose.

As a type of professional politician, the journalist can look back on what is a considerable past. The figure of the *party official*, in contrast, is a phenomenon of recent decades or, in some cases, just the last few years. We must turn our attention to an examination of the party system and party organization if we are to gain an understanding of the historical significance of this figure.

In all political entities of any size where the rulers are elected periodically, that is to say, in all entities that exceed the scope and authority of small, rural cantons, the organization of politics is necessarily an *organization of interested parties*. This means that a relatively small number of people with a primary interest in political activity, that is, in sharing in political power, create a following through open recruitment, offer themselves or their protégés as candidates for election, raise funds, and sally forth in search of votes. It is not possible to imagine how in large organizations elections could take place effectively in the absence of these activities. In practice, it means the division of all enfranchised citizens into politically active and politically passive segments. Since this distinction is voluntary, it cannot be eliminated by such measures as compulsory voting, representation according to membership of a "professional group," or other proposals designed explicitly or in fact to combat this state of affairs and thus do away with the dominance of the professional politicians. Leaders and followers are the indispensable vital components of every party: the leadership so as actively to recruit the followers, while the followers enlist the support of the passive electorate for the election of the leader.

Differences arise, however, in party structure. The "parties" in medieval city-states, the Guelphs and the Ghibellines, for example, had purely personal followings. Consider the *Statuto della parte Guelfa*,[40] with its call for the confiscation of the property of the *nobili* (this term referred originally to all families who lived like knights, that is to say, were entitled to hold a fief), their exclusion from office and the franchise, the party committees linking different localities, the strictly military organizations, and the bonuses paid for denunciations. If we consider these things, we find ourselves strongly reminded of Bolshevism with

40. [The Guelphs and the Ghibellines were the two great factions in Italian politics during the Middle Ages. In the protracted conflicts between the papacy and the Holy Roman Emperors, the Guelphs supported the former and the Ghibellines the latter. After the end of the thirteenth century, these party names came to be used to designate different social classes, especially in the northern and central Italian states. The *Statuto della parte Guelfa* was published in 1335.]

its Soviets, its strictly screened organization of military personnel, and—above all, in Russia—its armies of informers, its confiscations, and the disarming and political disenfranchisement of its "bourgeois," in other words, its entrepreneurs, tradesmen, *rentiers*, clerics, descendants of the royal dynasty, and police agents.

The analogy is even more striking on closer inspection. On the one hand, you find that the military organization of the Guelph party consisted of a purely knightly army, drawn up on the basis of registered feudal estates, and that almost all its leading positions were filled by the nobility. On the other, the Soviets retained, or rather reintroduced, highly paid entrepreneurs, the piecework system of wages, Taylorism, and discipline in both the armed forces and the workplace, all the while on the lookout for foreign capital. In a word, then, simply in order to keep the state and the economy functioning, they were forced to accept once again absolutely *all* the things they had combated as bourgeois class institutions, and they were forced even to take over, as a principal instrument of their state power, the agents of the old Okhrana.[41] However, we are not dealing here with organizations concerned with force but with professional politicians who strive to gain power through sober, "peaceful" party campaigning in the electoral marketplace.

In the same way, these parties in our ordinary understanding of the word started life, in Britain, for example, as pure followers of the aristocracy. Every time a peer changed sides, for whatever reason, everyone who depended on him changed sides with him. Until the Reform Bill [of 1832] the great aristocratic families, and not least the king himself, controlled the patronage of a vast number of constituencies. Closely associated with these aristocratic parties are the parties of notables of the kind that emerged everywhere with the growth of the power of the bourgeoisie. Under the leadership of the typical strata of intellectuals of the West, the property-owning and educated classes divided into parties, which they led and which

were based partly on class interests, partly on family tradition, and partly on pure ideology. Clergymen, teachers, professors, lawyers, doctors, pharmacists, wealthy farmers, factory owners—in Britain, an entire stratum whose members called themselves gentlemen—initially formed associations as opportunity offered and at the most established political clubs at the local level. In unsettled times the petty bourgeoisie would speak up, and on occasion even the proletariat found its voice, when it obtained leaders, although these leaders did not, generally speaking, arise from their ranks.

In the country, regionally organized parties on a permanent basis did not yet exist at this stage. It was simply the members of Parliament themselves who kept the parties together. The selection of candidates lay crucially in the hands of the local notables. Party programs came into being partly through the candidates' campaign appeals, partly on the basis of congresses of notables or decisions of the parliamentary party. The clubs were run on a part-time or honorary basis, as occasional work. Where there were no clubs (as was mostly the case), one found nothing but the entirely informal political activity of the few people with a lasting interest in politics in normal times. The journalist alone was a paid professional politician, and only the newspapers were able to act as a continuous form of political organization. Aside from that, there was only Parliament in session. Of course, parliamentarians and parliamentary leaders knew perfectly well which local notables to approach when a specific political course of action was desired. But only large towns had party associations that could count on modest members' contributions, periodic conferences, and public meetings at which the local member of Parliament could report on his activities. Politics came to life only at election time.

The driving force behind the progressive tightening of party organization was the interest that members of Parliament had in the possibility of electoral compromises between localities and the impact of unified programs recognized by broad sections of the public throughout the country, as well as of unified electioneering platforms. But the party apparatus remains that of an association of notables, and no change in principle is involved even when the entire country is covered by a network of local party branches,

41. [The Okhrana was the secret police department in tsarist Russia. It was replaced in 1917, after the October Revolution, by the Cheka (the Extraordinary Commission [for Combating Counterrevolution, Sabotage, and Speculation]).]

including medium-sized towns, as well as a set of "party agents" with whom a member of Parliament in charge of the central party bureau is in constant correspondence. There are as yet no paid officials outside the central party headquarters. The affairs of the local branches are still conducted by "reputable" people who take on this task because of the esteem they otherwise enjoy. They are the nonparliamentary "notables" who exert influence alongside the political notables who actually have seats in Parliament. Increasingly, however, the intellectual nourishment of both the press and the local branches is provided by the party correspondence published by the party. Regular members' contributions become indispensable; a fraction of the money received is used to defray the costs of party headquarters. This was the position of the majority of party organizations in Germany until fairly recently.

Even more strikingly, in France the first stage still prevailed in part. By this is meant the whole unstable system of parliamentary alliances, the small number of local notables in the country beyond, programs drafted by the candidates or by their sponsors on their behalf, in some instances at the moment of recruiting them, although with a more or less local interpretation of directives and programs issued by the parliamentarians. This system was only gradually superseded. The number of full-time politicians remained small and consisted chiefly of elected deputies, the few officials in party headquarters, the journalists, and—in France—the careerists who happened to fill a "political post" or were on the lookout for one. Formally, politics was predominantly a part-time profession. Likewise, the number of deputies eligible for ministerial posts was very restricted, and since places were confined to notables, the number of candidates for election was limited, too. However, the number of people with an indirect interest in the conduct of politics, particularly a material interest, was very great. For all measures taken by a ministry, above all everything to do with questions of personnel, could be dealt with only by taking into consideration their influence on the chances of being elected. Thus everyone tried to channel their wishes of any and every kind through the local deputy, and, whether he liked it or not, the minister was forced to listen to him if he belonged to his majority, which was therefore

the goal to which everyone aspired. The individual deputy had all offices in his gift, as well as every other kind of patronage within his constituency, and, for his part, he cultivated his own contacts to the local notables so as to ensure his own reelection.

The most modern forms of party organization stand in stark contrast to this idyllic state of affairs dominated by notables and, above all, by the members of Parliament. They are the offspring of democracy, the mass suffrage, the need to woo the masses and for mass organization, the development of the greatest degree of unity in the leadership and the strictest possible discipline. The rule by notables and the control exercised by members of Parliament dies out. "Full-time" politicians *outside* Parliament take the operations of politics into their own hands, either as "entrepreneurs," which is what the American "boss"[42] and the English "election agent" essentially were, or else as officials on a fixed salary.

In formal terms, a far-reaching process of democratization takes place. It is no longer the parliamentary party that creates the authoritative programs, nor the local notables who still exercise control over the nomination of candidates. Instead, the organized party members meet to choose the candidates and delegate members to attend assemblies at a higher level, of which there may be several, right up to the general "party congress." In the nature of the case, however, power lies in the hands of those who do the *continuous* day-to-day work within the organization or of those on whom the party apparatus depends for either money or personnel, whether as patrons or as the leaders of powerful clubs representing vested interests (such as Tammany Hall). What is crucial is that this entire human apparatus—the party "machine," as it is significantly called in the Anglo-Saxon nations—or rather, the people in charge of it, holds the members of Parliament in check and is well placed to impose its will on them. This has particular importance for the selection of the party *leadership*. You become a leader only if you are supported by the machine, even over the heads of the members of Parliament. The creation of such machines, in other words, signifies the emergence of a *plebiscitary* democracy.

42. ["Boss" and "election agent" are used in the original.]

Needless to say, the party followers, particularly the party officials and bosses, look to the victory of their leader for personal reward in the form of offices or other benefits. The crucial point is that they expect to obtain these things from him and not, or not only, from the individual members of Parliament. They expect above all that the demagogic effect of the leader's *personality* in the election campaign will bring the party both votes and seats, and hence power, and that this will improve as far as possible its supporters' chances of obtaining the hoped-for rewards. At the level of ideals, there is the satisfaction of working for a person to whom you are personally devoted and in whom you have faith, instead of merely for the abstract program of a party composed of mediocrities. This is the *charismatic* element in all leadership and one of its mainsprings.

This form ultimately prevailed, though its triumph was uneven and it involved a latent conflict with the local notables and members of Parliament eager to retain their influence. The process could be seen among the bourgeois parties, first of all in the United States, and then in the Social Democratic Party, especially in Germany. There are constant setbacks whenever a universally acknowledged leader fails to appear, and even when there is one, all sorts of concessions have to be made to the vanity and self-interest of the party notables. Above all, however, even the party machine can succumb to the dominance of the party *officials* who control the day-to-day business. Many members of the Social Democratic Party believe that their party has been unable to resist this process of "bureaucratization." However, the fact is that "officials" tend to submit fairly readily to a demagogic leader with a powerful personality. Their ideal and material interests are intimately bound up with what they hope the party will achieve thanks to him, while working for a leader is psychologically more satisfying. It is much more difficult for leaders to emerge where, as in the majority of bourgeois parties, the "notables" exert an influence on party affairs alongside the officials. For in their *minds*, the little posts the notables occupy on the board or the committees come to "constitute their life." Their actions are determined by resentment toward the demagogue as a *homo novus*, an upstart, by their firm belief in the superiority of the "experience" of party politics (which is in fact of

considerable importance) and by ideological anxieties that the old party traditions may be at risk. In the party they have all the traditionalist elements on their side. The rural voters, above all, but also voters from the petty bourgeoisie look up to the name of the notable with whom they have long been familiar and mistrust the new man whom they do not know. Nevertheless, *if* the latter proves successful, these voters switch their loyalty and support him all the more steadfastly. Let us consider a few of the chief examples of this conflict between competing political structures and, in particular, the rise of the plebiscitary form as Ostrogorski describes it.[43]

Let us start with Britain: there until 1868 party organization consisted almost entirely of notables.[44] In rural districts, the Tories relied on such people as the Anglican vicar, schoolmasters, for the most part, and above all the large landowners of the county. The Whigs looked for their support to such people as nonconformist preachers (where they were to be found), the postmaster, the blacksmith, the tailor, the rope maker, in short, skilled artisans who could exert political influence because it was easy to chat with them. In the towns the parties were divided partly along economic lines, partly on religious ones, or even simply by the political opinions that were handed down through the family. But in all cases the notables were the active agents in the political organizations. Above them, there was Parliament and

43. [M. Ostrogorski, *Democracy and the Organization of Political Parties* (London: Macmillan, 1902). Moisei Ostrogorski (1854–1919) was a Russian political scientist and politician. After lengthy periods of study in Britain and the United States in the 1880s and 1890s, he published pioneering works on the history of the political parties. After the revolution of 1905, he returned to Russia and was elected to the First Duma as a liberal. Following the dissolution of the Duma, he withdrew from politics and settled in the United States.]

44. [Weber alludes here to Disraeli's Reform Bill of 1867. This more or less doubled the electorate in the towns by reducing the property qualification, enabling some working men to take part in the electoral process for the first time. At the same time it greatly increased the number of constituencies, particularly in the countryside. These measures forced the British parties to adopt tighter forms of organization.]

the parties with the cabinet and the "leader"[45] who either presided over the cabinet or led the opposition. This leader had at his side the most important professional figure in the party organization, namely, the "whip."[46] It was he who had the desirable offices in his gift; it was to him, therefore, that the careerists had to apply. His practice was to come to an understanding with the individual constituency members about such matters. In the constituencies a stratum of professional politicians gradually began to emerge. Local agents were recruited who initially were unpaid and were roughly comparable to our "party agents" [*Vertrauensmänner*] in Germany. Alongside them, however, there developed in the constituencies a form of capitalist entrepreneur known as the "election agent."[47] In modern British legislation, with its emphasis on fairness in the conduct of elections, the appearance of the election agent was unavoidable. This legislation sought to control the costs of elections and to stem the power of money, since it obliged candidates to declare their electoral expenses. For in Britain, to a far greater extent than was the case here in Germany, the candidate had the pleasure of loosening his purse strings, in addition to straining his voice. He had to pay the election agent a lump sum to cover all his expenses and from which the latter normally made a good profit. In Britain, in the distribution of power between the "leader" and the party notables, both in Parliament and in the country, it had always been the leader who had the more significant position. There were compelling reasons for this in the need to make large-scale policy making possible in a consistent manner. Notwithstanding this, the influence of members of Parliament and party notables remained considerable.

This, then, is what the old party organization looked like: half a club for notables, half already a business complete with employees and entrepreneurs. From 1868 on, however, we can see the development of the "caucus system,"[48] first for local elections in Birmingham, and then throughout the

country. This system was brought into being by a nonconformist parson together with Joseph Chamberlain.[49] What caused it was the democratization of the franchise. In order to win the support of the masses, it was necessary to summon into existence a vast apparatus of organizations that were democratic in appearance. The aim was to create an electoral association in every district of each town, to keep the organization in operation at all times, and to run it strictly on bureaucratic lines. This involved the recruitment of growing numbers of paid officials, while the formal representatives of party policy were leading negotiators with the right to co-opt, who had been elected by the local electoral committees in which as many as 10 percent of the voters were soon to be organized. The driving force consisted of local people with a particular interest in municipal politics, which were everywhere the source of the juiciest profits. It was they who were primarily responsible for raising the necessary funds. This newly emerging machine, which was no longer led by parliamentarians, soon found itself embroiled in conflicts with the previous power brokers and especially with the whip. Nevertheless, supported by interested local parties, the machine triumphed so convincingly that the whip was forced to accept the situation and come to terms with it. The upshot was the centralization of power in the hands of a few people, and ultimately just one person, who stood at the head of the party. For in the Liberal Party, the entire system had come into being in con-

49. [Joseph Chamberlain (1836–1914) was a leading radical politician based in Birmingham. He subsequently made a career in national politics and rose to the position of president of the Board of Trade in Gladstone's second ministry. However, having broken with the Liberals over Gladstone's policy of Home Rule for Ireland, his views gradually became increasingly imperialistic. Under the Tories he served as secretary of state for the colonies.

The notes to Weber's lecture make it clear that the parson in question is Chamberlain's long-standing collaborator, Francis Schnadhorst, who was in actual fact not a parson but a cloth merchant of nonconformist background. He became the secretary to the Birmingham Liberal Association in 1873. Later on, he was responsible for the reorganization of the party branches in other towns on the model of the Birmingham caucus.]

45. [Weber used the English word.]
46. [Weber used the English word.]
47. [Weber used the English term.]
48. [Weber used the English term.]

nection with Gladstone's rise to power. What led to such a swift victory over the notables was the fascination exerted by Gladstone's "grand demagogic" skills and the masses' firm belief in the moral nature of his policies and, above all, in his personal moral qualities. A Caesarist, plebiscitary element now made its entrance on the political stage. It was the dictator of the electoral battlefield, and it quickly made itself felt. In 1877 the caucus became active for the first time in a general election, with stunning success. The result was Disraeli's fall from power in the midst of his great triumphs. By 1886 the machine had become completely identified through the power of charisma with the personality of the leader. This reached its climax at the start of the Home Rule debate,[50] when the entire apparatus from top to bottom did not ask, "Do we agree with Gladstone's policy on this question?" but simply swung behind him at his command, taking the view that "Whatever he does, we shall follow him." In so doing, the caucus simply abandoned Chamberlain, its own creator, leaving him stranded.

This machinery calls for a considerable body of people to work for it. There are probably as many as two thousand people in Britain who live directly from party politics. Far more numerous, of course, are those who are involved in politics in search of some office or other, or to serve a specific interest, especially in local government politics. For the useful caucus politician there are opportunities to gratify his vanity, in addition to the prospects for improving his economic position. In the nature of the case, to become a JP or an MP[51] is the height of (normal) ambition, and people who have had a good upbringing, and are "gentlemen," are rewarded by these titles. And in the light of the fact that perhaps as much as 50 percent of the parties' finances came in the form of gifts from anonymous donors, the greatest prize of all, particularly for wealthy benefactors, was a peerage.

What, then, has been the effect of the entire system? It is that today, with the exception of a few members of the cabinet (and a number of independently minded eccentrics), British members of Parliament have become nothing more than well-disciplined voting fodder. In Germany deputies have at least taken the trouble to deal with their private correspondence while sitting at their desks in the Reichstag and thus to act as if they were working for the good of the nation. No such gesture is required in Britain. There the member of Parliament has only to vote and to avoid betraying his party. He must appear when summoned by the whips and do whatever is required by the cabinet or the leader of the opposition. And as for the caucus machine outside in the country, if the leader is strong, it is almost entirely unprincipled and wholly under his control. Above Parliament, then, stands a man who is in all essentials an elected dictator who makes use of the party "machine" in order to bring the masses to heel behind him, and who regards the parliamentarians merely as political beneficiaries of the spoils system to be numbered among his followers.

Now, how does the process of selecting these leaders work? To start with: For what accomplishments are they chosen? What is crucial here, apart from the qualities of will that are decisive all over the world, is, of course, the power of demagogic speech making. The style of rhetoric has changed from what it was in Cobden's day, when it addressed itself to reason.[52] It then moved on to Gladstone, who was an expert in the seemingly sober art of "letting the facts speak for themselves," and from there it came down to the present day, when speakers frequently make use of purely emotive language of the kind also employed by the Salvation Army in order to set the masses in motion. The existing situation can properly be described as a "dictatorship based on the exploitation of the emotional nature of the masses." But the very advanced system of committee work in the British Parliament makes it possible to *take part* and also forces every politician who contemplates joining the

---

50. [Gladstone was converted to the cause of Irish Home Rule in 1885. His attempts to gain parliamentary approval for it were rejected in 1886 and again in 1893.]

51. [Weber used the English initials JP and MP, as well as the term "gentlemen," here and subsequently.]

52. [Richard Cobden (1804–1865), a British politician, was one of the leading spokesmen of the free-trade movement in Britain. From 1838 he led the Anti-Corn Law League in its successful campaign to repeal the Corn Laws in 1846. The Corn Laws had sought to protect the price of grain.]

leadership to do so. All ministers worthy of note in recent decades have undergone this very real and effective training, while the practice of reporting and criticizing the work of these committees publicly ensures that this school produces a true selection process and that it is able to eliminate the mere demagogue.

That, then, is the position in Britain. The caucus system there, however, was very diluted compared with the party organization in America, where the plebiscitary principle emerged especially early and in an especially pure form. Washington's America was supposed to be a polity administered according to his idea of a "gentleman."[53] A gentleman over there at that time was a landowner or a man with a college education. That was indeed how America was governed initially. When parties began to form, the members of the House of Representatives at first claimed a leadership role, as in Britain at the time of the rule of the notables. Party organization was quite loose. This lasted until 1824. Even before the 1820s the party machine had started to develop in a number of local municipalities, which here, too, were the starting point of modern developments. But it was only with the election of Andrew Jackson as president, the candidate of farmers in the West, that the old traditions were jettisoned. Soon after 1840 the role of congressmen in leading the parties formally came to an end when the great parliamentarians, like Calhoun and Webster,[54] bowed out of political life because Congress had lost almost all its power to the party machine in the country. The fact that the plebiscitary "machine" developed so early in America can be ascribed to the circumstance that there, and there alone, the head of the executive branch and hence the man in charge of official patronage—which is

what counted—was a president elected by the popular will and that because of the "separation of powers" he was almost entirely independent of Congress in the conduct of his office. This meant that above all, in the case of the election of the president, genuine booty beckoned as the reward of victory and took the shape of the fruits of office. The consequence of this was the "spoils system,"[55] which Andrew Jackson systematically elevated into a principle.

What is the meaning for the parties nowadays of the "spoils system," that is, the allocation of all federal offices to the followers of the victorious candidate? It means that the contending parties have no principles at all; they are purely careerist organizations that change their programs for each election in accordance with what they see as their best chances of catching votes. And notwithstanding all other similarities, these programs change at a rate not to be matched elsewhere. The parties are shaped with an eye to the election campaign that is of supreme importance for the patronage of offices: the election of the president of the Union and the governorships of the individual states. Programs and candidates are finalized in the parties' "national conventions"[56] without the intervention of the parliamentarians. These "conventions" are party congresses that, formally, consist of representatives who have been chosen in a highly democratic manner by assemblies of delegates who, for their part, owe their own mandates to the party "primaries,"[57] the fundamental voting assemblies of the party. Even in the primaries, the delegates are selected in the name of the candidates for the supreme office of state. *Within* the individual parties bitter struggles rage for the privilege of "nomination." The fact is that between three and four hundred thousand official nominations are in the president's hands, and the task of filling them is one he undertakes himself, assisted only by the advice he receives from the senators representing the individual states. Thus the senators are powerful politicians. The House of Representatives, in contrast, is relatively impotent politically, because it lacks the authority to bestow patronage and because

53. [Weber used the English word.]
54. [John Calhoun (1782–1850) was a leading politician who served as a congressman, secretary of war, vice president (1825–32), and secretary of state. He was known as a champion of states' rights and became a symbol of the Old South. Daniel Webster (1782–1852) was an orator and politician. As a young lawyer, he practiced before the Supreme Court. He subsequently became a congressman, senator, and secretary of state, where he made a name for himself as a defender of the Union against states' rights.]

55. [Weber used the English term.]
56. [In English in the original.]
57. [Weber used the English word.]

the ministers who are purely assistants to the president, whose rights have been legitimated by the people against everyone, including Congress, can administer their office independently of whether they enjoy its confidence or not. This, too, is a consequence of the "separation of powers."

Underpinned in this way, the spoils system was technically *possible* in America because only a youthful civilization could sustain such a purely amateurish approach to the conduct of its affairs. For it is self-evident that the existence of three to four hundred thousand party supporters who had nothing to show by way of their qualifications for office but the fact that they had served their party well—such a state of affairs could not survive without major abuses: corruption and the squandering of resources on a vast scale such as could only be borne by a nation with as yet unlimited economic prospects.

The figure who now makes his appearance together with this system of the plebiscitary party machine is the "boss." What is the boss? A political capitalist entrepreneur who procures votes at his own expense and his own risk. He may have acquired his first contacts as a lawyer or a saloon keeper or as the owner of a similar business, or perhaps as a lender. From there he casts his net still wider until he is able to "control" a certain number of votes. Once he has reached this stage, he establishes links with the neighboring bosses. Through his energy, astuteness, and, above all, discretion, he attracts the attention of men already further advanced in their careers, and he begins to rise. The boss is indispensable to the organization of the party. It is centralized in his hands. By and large, it is he who procures the necessary funds. How does he achieve this? Well, partly through members' dues; above all, by levying a tax on the wages of the officials who have acquired their office through him and his party. And then through bribes and gratuities. Whoever wishes to circumvent one of the many laws with impunity stands in need of the boss's connivance and must pay for it. Otherwise, he has to reckon with unpleasant consequences. But even all this is not enough to provide the necessary operating capital. The boss is indispensable as the direct recipient of the donations of the great finance magnates. These magnates would not entrust sums of money for electoral purposes to any paid party official or to any person who has to make his accounts available in public. The boss with his shrewd discretion in money matters is the natural person for the capitalist circles who fund elections. The typical boss is a man of absolute sobriety. He does not strive for social standing; the "professional"[58] is looked down on in "high society." He seeks nothing but power, power as the source of money but also for its own sake. He works in the shadows; that is where he differs from the British "leader." You will not hear him speak in public; he suggests to speakers what they would be best advised to say, but he himself remains silent. He normally accepts no office for himself, except that of senator in the second chamber. For, since the constitution empowers senators to take part in the patronage of offices, the leading bosses often take up seats there in person. Offices are allocated primarily for services rendered to the party. But the allocation of posts in return for money donations is very common, and some offices have particular rates attached to them. This is a system for selling offices that would have been very familiar from the monarchies of the seventeenth and eighteenth centuries, inclusive of the papal states.

The boss has no firm political "principles"; he is completely without convictions and is interested only in how to attract votes. Not infrequently, he is a fairly uneducated man. In private, however, his life is normally correct and beyond reproach. Only in his political ethics does he inevitably adjust to the average standards of morality in political action that happen to be the norm, just as many of us Germans are likely to have done in the realm of the economy when goods were in short supply and hoarding was rife.[59] The fact that as a "professional," as a professional politician, he is looked down on socially leaves him cold. The fact that he neither fills the great offices of the Union himself nor desires to do so has the advantage that where the bosses think it will attract votes, it is not uncommon for intelligent people

58. [Weber used the English word.]

59. [When food was in short supply during the war, as a consequence of the Allied blockade of Germany, it became customary to make excursions to the countryside, where the farmers still had food supplies that they were willing to sell.]

...de the party to be adopted as candidates, well-known figures of repute and not just the old party notables, as is the case in Germany. Thus the very structure of these unprincipled parties with their socially despised power brokers has propelled able men into the presidency who would never have managed to achieve high office in Germany. Needless to say, the bosses will resist any outsider who represents a threat to their own sources of money and power. But in the competition for the goodwill of the voters, it is not unusual for them to have found themselves obliged to stoop to endorse candidates who are thought to be the enemies of corruption.

In America, then, we have party machines built on strikingly capitalist lines. They are tightly organized from top to bottom and are underpinned by stable political clubs of the type of Tammany Hall. These clubs are organized almost like religious orders and strive exclusively to maximize profits by achieving political control of town halls, above all, since these are the most desirable objects of exploitation. What made this structure of party life possible was the high degree of democratization of the United States because it was "a young country." This connection between youth and democracy means that now, however, the system is in slow decline. America cannot continue to be ruled by amateurs. Fifteen years ago, when one asked American workers why they let themselves be governed by politicians whom they professed to despise, they would answer: "We would rather our officials were people we spit on, than be like you and be ruled by a caste of officials who spit on us." That was the old attitude of American "democracy." Yet even at that time the socialists took a completely different view, and this situation is no longer tolerated. Government by amateurs no longer suffices, and the Civil Service Reform[60] is now creating lifelong pensionable posts in constantly growing numbers. In consequence, posts are now being filled by university-educated officials who are just as incorruptible and competent as in Germany. Around one hundred thousand offices are no longer objects for booty after each election but are pensionable and dependent upon a candidate's qualifications. This will gradually push the spoils system into the background, and the face of the party leadership will probably change then, as well. The only thing is that we do not yet know in what way.

In *Germany*, the crucial factors influencing the operation of politics have been essentially as follows. First, the impotence of the parliaments. The consequence was that no one with leadership qualities wished to stay in Parliament for the longer term. Suppose anyone did wish to enter Parliament—what could he achieve there? If a post fell vacant in a chancellory he could say to the departmental head concerned: "I have a very competent man in my constituency. He would be a suitable candidate. Why don't you take him?" And this was readily agreed. But that was more or less all that a German member of Parliament could do to satisfy his instincts for power—if he had any. In addition, and this second factor was what underlay the first, there was the enormous importance of the trained, professional civil service in Germany. In this respect we in Germany led the world. The professional civil service was so important that it was able to assert its claims not just to civil service posts but also to ministerial office. Only last year someone remarked during the debate on "parliamentarization" in the Bavarian Provincial Diet that talented people would refuse to become officials if ministerial posts were given to members of Parliament. Officialdom proved able to evade systematically the kind of control exerted in Britain by debates in committee. In this way the German parliaments were prevented (with very few exceptions) from producing really competent administrative heads from among their numbers.

The third factor was that Germany, in contrast to America, had parties based on political conviction that claimed, at least ostensibly in good faith, that their members represented particular "worldviews." However, the two most important of these parties, the Center Party and the Social Democratic Party, were born minority parties, and this was in accordance with their declared intentions.[61] The leading circles

60. [This phrase is in English.]

61. [The Center Party was destined to remain a minority party because it essentially represented Roman Catholics in Germany; the same thing is true of Social Democracy, which set out to represent only the working class.]

of the Center Party never disguised the fact that they were opposed to parliamentary rule, because they feared that this would condemn them to be in the minority and that this in turn would make it harder than before to find posts for their careerists, as they had done previously, by exerting pressure on the government. Social Democracy was a minority party on principle and an obstacle to the introduction of parliamentary government because it did not wish to become contaminated by contact with the existing bourgeois political order. The fact that both parties excluded themselves from the parliamentary system made that system unworkable.

What, then, was the fate of professional politicians in Germany? They had no power or responsibility and could only play a somewhat inferior role as notables. The consequence was that they were animated once again by the typical instincts to be found in "guilds" everywhere. In the circle of these notables who made their living from whatever little positions they held, it was impossible for men not cast in the same mold to rise to prominence. I could list a large number of names from every party, and, of course, that includes Social Democracy, of people whose political careers ended in tragedy because they involved men who had leadership qualities but who were not tolerated by the notables for that very reason. All our parties have experienced this development into a guild of notables. Bebel,[62] for example, was still a leader by virtue of his temperament and integrity, however modest his intellectual accomplishments were. The fact that he was a martyr, that he never abused the trust of the masses (in their eyes, at least), meant that they stood behind him to a man, and there was no power in the party that could have provided him with a serious challenge. After his death this situation came to an end, and the rule of the officials began. Trade union officials, party secretaries, and journalists all came to the fore; bureaucratic instincts dominated the party, a highly principled

bureaucracy—of rare integrity, we may say, when we consider conditions in other countries, particularly the frequently corrupt union officials in America—but the consequences of bureaucracy already alluded to also made their appearance in the party.

From the 1880s onward, the bourgeois parties became guilds of notables pure and simple. It is true that occasionally the parties attracted able minds from outside the party for publicity purposes and so that they could say, "we have this or that famous person in our ranks." As far as possible, however, they made sure that these people did not stand for election, and only where it was unavoidable and one or other of them insisted did it occur.

The same spirit prevails in Parliament. Our parliamentary parties were guilds and still are. Every speech that is made in the plenary sessions of the Reichstag is previously subjected to a thoroughgoing censorship in the party. This explains why they are so unutterably boring. The only members who can speak are those who have been summoned. A more glaring contrast with the British practice, or indeed the French system (though for entirely opposite reasons), is scarcely imaginable.

At present, following the gigantic upheaval that people customarily refer to as a revolution, a change may now be in progress. Perhaps, but it is not certain. The change began when we started to observe new kinds of party organization. These were amateur organizations in the first instance. They were staffed frequently by students from the different universities who would say to a man to whom they ascribed leadership qualities, "We shall do what has to be done for you, if you tell us what it is." Second, there were commercial organizations. People would come to men to whom they ascribed leadership qualities and offer to take over the business of canvassing for votes in exchange for a fixed payment for each vote. If you were to ask me which of the two methods I would regard as the more reliable from a technical and political point of view, I would, I believe, prefer the second. But both were bubbles that quickly appeared and vanished again just as quickly. The existing apparatuses reorganized themselves but kept on functioning. Such phenomena were merely symptomatic of the belief that new apparatuses would automatically appear if only there were leaders. But the technical

---

62. [August Bebel (1840–1913) was one of the cofounders of the Social Democratic Party in Germany. He was elected to the Reichstag in 1875 and led the party until his death. Weber refers to him as a martyr because under Bismarck's anti-Socialist legislation, Bebel was repeatedly imprisoned for his convictions.]

...cteristics of proportional representation were ...icient to preclude their emergence in advance. Only a few dictators of the street made their appearance, and they then disappeared once more.[63] And only the dictatorship of the street has a following that is subject to an order of strict discipline. It is this that explains the power of these tiny minorities.

If we assume that this were to change, we need to be clear, after what we have already said, that to put plebiscitary leaders in charge of parties means that their followers suffer from a "loss of soul," what we might call their spiritual proletarianization. To be of use as an apparatus for their leader they must obey blindly, they must become a machine in the American sense, undisturbed by the vanity of notables or by any pretentions to opinions of their own. Lincoln's election was made possible only by an organization of this type, and as we have pointed out, the caucus had the same function in Gladstone's case. That is the price that has to be paid for having leaders. But there is only this stark choice: either a democracy with a leader together with a "machine" or a leaderless democracy, in other words, the rule of the "professional politicians" who have no vocation and who lack the inner, charismatic qualities that turn a man into a leader. And that leads to what the rebels in any given party usually call rule by a "clique." For the time being we have only the latter in Germany. And for the future, this situation will be guaranteed, for the Reich at least, first, by the likelihood that the Upper House [Bundesrat] will be revived, which will necessarily restrict the power of the Reichstag and with that its importance as a place from which leaders are selected. It will be guaranteed, second, by the system of proportional representation as it exists at present. This is a typical feature of a leaderless democracy, not only because it favors horse-trading among the notables for positions but also because it opens the doors for pressure groups to force the inclusion of their officials in the lists, thus creating an unpolitical parliament in which there is no room for genuine leaders.

63. [Weber's marginal note makes it clear that he was thinking of the establishment of the German Communist Party by Karl Liebknecht and Rosa Luxemburg in December 1918. They were murdered by right-wing extremists on January 15, 1919.]

The only safety valve for the desire for leadership could be provided by the office of president of the Reich if the president were to be directly elected, instead of indirectly, by Parliament. Leaders could emerge and be selected on the basis of proven ability if, in the large municipalities, directly elected town dictators were to make their appearance on the scene with the right to provide their own administrative personnel. This is what happened in the United States, wherever a serious attempt was made to combat corruption. But this could come about only if a party organization existed that was tailored to the needs of such elections. But because all petty bourgeois parties are hostile to leaders, including and above all Social Democracy, we cannot say anything about the future shape the parties will take and what prospects there are of such ideas becoming a reality.

It is not possible to see today, therefore, how the business of politics can take the outward shape of a "profession," and even less what prospects of a worthwhile political challenge might open up for people who are politically talented. The man who is compelled by his financial situation to live "from" politics will always find that the typical direct paths will involve choosing between journalism or a post as party official. Or else he could consider a post with one of the representative bodies: trade union, chamber of commerce, farmers' association, craft workers' chamber, industrial chamber, employers' associations, and so on, or the appropriate positions in local government. Nothing further can be said about the outward shape of the profession except that the party official shares with the journalist the odium of being "déclassé." He will, unfortunately, always have the actual or unspoken rebuke of "hired hack" ringing in his ears, in the case of the journalist, or "hired speaker," in the case of the official. Anyone who lacks inner defenses against accusations of this kind and is unable to find the proper retort to them should avoid such a career, because in addition to the risk of exposing himself to grave temptations, he may find that it turns out to be full of disappointments.

We may inquire what inner pleasures may be expected from a political career and what are the personal qualifications called for in those who choose it?

Well, to start with, it provides a sense of power. Even in what may be quite a modest post formally, the professional politician may feel he has been raised above the commonplace by his discovery that he has influence on people, that he has his share of power over them, but above all that he holds in his hands a strand of some important historical process. But the question now confronting such a politician is: What qualities does he need to do justice to this power (however narrowly circumscribed it may be) and hence to the responsibility that it imposes on him? This takes us onto the terrain of ethical questions. For to ask what kind of a human being one must be to have the right to grasp the spokes of the wheel of history is to ask an ethical question.

We can say that three qualities, above all, are of decisive importance for a politician: passion, a sense of responsibility, and a sense of proportion. Passion in the sense of a *commitment to the matter in hand* [*Sachlichkeit*], that is, the passionate dedication to a "cause" [*Sache*], to the God or demon that presides over it. Not in the sense of that inner state of mind that my late friend Georg Simmel was in the habit of describing as "sterile excitement." That state of mind is characteristic of a certain type of intellectual, Russian intellectuals above all (though by no means all of them!), and now plays such a great part among our intellectuals, too, in this carnival that is being flattered with the proud name of "revolution." For this excitement is no more than an aimless and unfocused "romanticism of the intellectually interesting," devoid of a sense of responsibility for any cause whatever. For mere passion, however sincerely felt, is not enough in itself. It cannot make a politician of anyone, unless service to a "cause" also means that a sense of *responsibility* toward that cause is made the decisive guiding light of action. And for that (and this is the crucial psychological characteristic of the politician) *a sense of proportion* is required, the ability to allow realities to impinge on you while maintaining an inner calm and composure. What is needed, in short, is a *distance* from people and things. The "absence of distance," pure and simple, is one of the deadly sins of every politician and one of those qualities which, if instilled into our intellectuals, will condemn them to political impotence. For the heart of the problem is how to forge a unity between hot passion and a cool sense of proportion in one and the same person. Politics is made with the mind, not with other parts of the body

or the soul. And yet if politics is to be an authentic human activity and not just a frivolous intellectual game, commitment to it must be born of passion and be nourished by it. Even so, the ability to keep the soul in check is what characterizes the passionate politician and distinguishes his attitude from the "sterile excitement" of the amateur. This can be achieved only by acquiring the habit of distance, in every sense of the word. The "strength" of a political "personality" means, primarily, the possession of these qualities.

Thus the politician is faced daily and hourly with the task of overcoming in himself a very trivial, all-too-human enemy: common or garden *vanity*, the deadly enemy of all dedication to a cause and of all distance, in this case, the distance from oneself.

Vanity is a very widespread quality, and perhaps no one is entirely free of it. And in academic and scholarly circles it is a kind of occupational disease. But in the case of the scholar, repugnant though it may be, it is relatively innocuous in the sense that as a rule it does not disrupt the business of scholarship. It is quite otherwise with politicians. For politicians, the striving for *power* is an unavoidable tool [*Mittel*] of their trade. Thus the "power instinct," as it is often called, belongs among their normal attributes. However, the sin against the Holy Spirit of their profession begins where this striving for power is *separated from the matter in hand* and becomes an object purely of self-intoxication instead of something that enters exclusively into the service of their "cause." For ultimately there are only two kinds of mortal sin in the field of politics: the lack of commitment to a cause and the lack of a sense of responsibility that is often, but not always, identical with it. Vanity, the need to thrust oneself center stage, is what is most likely to lead the politician into the temptation of committing either or both of these sins. All the more, as the demagogue is forced to play for "effect." Because he is concerned only with the "impression" he is making, he always runs the risk both of turning into an actor and of taking too lightly his responsibility for his own actions. His lack of objectivity leads him to strive for the glittering facade of power, instead of its reality, while his lack of a sense of responsibility seduces him into enjoying power for its own sake, rather than for its substantive purpose. For although, or rather *because*, power is an unavoidable tool of all politics,

striving for power, therefore, is one of its
ng forces, there is no more destructive distortion
political energy than when the parvenu swaggers
around, boasting of his power, conceitedly reveling
in its reflected glory—or indeed any worship of power
for its own sake. An energetically fostered cult that
has grown up in Germany, as elsewhere, has sought
to idealize the mere "power politician." Such figures
may make a strong impression, but in actual fact
their activity is empty and meaningless. The critics
of "power politics" are completely right about this.
There have been a number of instances when the
typical representatives of this cast of mind have suddenly suffered an inner collapse, exposing the internal
weakness and impotence lurking behind this showy
but entirely vacuous pose. This pose is the product
of an exceedingly impoverished and superficial indifference toward the *meaning* of human activity, a blasé
attitude that remains completely blind to the tragedy
in which all action is ensnared, political action
above all.

It is entirely true and a fundamental fact of all
history (though one we cannot explore further here)
that the ultimate product of political activity frequently, indeed, as a matter of course, fails utterly to
do justice to its original purpose and may even be a
travesty of it. Nevertheless, this purpose, this service
on behalf of a *cause*, cannot be dispensed with if
action is to have any internal support. The *nature* of
the cause in whose service the politician strives for
power and makes use of power is a matter of belief.
He may serve national or universally human goals,
social and ethical goals, or goals that are cultural,
worldly, or religious. He may be motivated by a powerful faith in "progress" (however this is defined), or
he may coolly reject faith of this kind; he can claim
to be acting in the service of an "idea," or he may
wish to reject such claims on principle and choose
instead to promote external goals of ordinary life.
But some belief or other must always be *present*.
Otherwise, even what seem outwardly to be the most
glorious political successes will be cursed—and
rightly so—because they will have no more meaning
and purpose than events in the animal kingdom.

What we have said up to now has brought us to a
discussion of the final problem that preoccupies us
this evening: the *ethos* of politics as a "cause." Quite

apart from its specific goals, what vocation can politics
have within the overall moral economy of our conduct of life? Where is what we might term the ethical
location in which politics is at home? At this point
we find ourselves caught up in a conflict of ultimate
worldviews, and it falls to us to *choose* between them.
Let us then make a resolute attempt to tackle this
problem, which has recently been addressed from
what is in my view a completely wrong angle.

Let us begin by liberating it from a quite trivial
distortion. Ethics can sometimes make its appearance
in what is morally a highly unfortunate role. Let us
consider some examples. Take the case of a man
whose affections have turned away from one woman
to another. He will be an unusual man if he does
not experience the need to justify this to himself by
saying, "She was not worthy of my love" or "She
has disappointed me" or by coming up with other
"reasons" of a similar sort. This is a highly unchival-
rous reaction to the blunt reality that he no longer
loves her and that she must put up with that. Even
more unchivalrously, he goes on to invent a "legitimacy" that enables him to put himself in the right
and add to her misfortune by trying to put her in the
wrong. The successful rival for a woman's affections
behaves in like manner: his predecessor must be the
more worthless of the two, for he would not otherwise
have emerged the loser. And obviously, it is no different after a victorious war when the victor asserts with
a wholly discreditable self-righteousness, "I won because I was in the right." Or, take the case of a man
who collapses mentally under the strain of the horrors
of war. Instead simply of saying, "It was all too much,"
he may feel the need to justify his own war weariness
to himself by replacing it with the feeling that he
could not put up with any more because he had been
forced to fight for an immoral cause. And the same
thing holds true for those on the losing side. There
is no point in complaining like old women who start
looking for the "guilty party" once the war is over,
when in reality the war was the product of the structures of society. Instead, every uncomplaining, manly
person will say to the enemy: "We lost the war—you
have won it. That's over and done with. So let us
now talk about what conclusions we must draw with
regard to the *objective* [*sachlichen*] interests that were
at stake, and—this is the main thing—in the light of

our responsibility for the *future*, which must weigh most heavily on the victor." Everything else is unworthy and will exact its own retribution. A nation can forgive damage to its interests, but not an assault on its honor, least of all in the spirit of sanctimonious self-righteousness. Every new document that comes to light after decades have passed will revive undignified quarrels and stir up all the hatred and anger once more, whereas our task should be to make sure that *morally* the war is laid to rest once it is over. This can be achieved only through a combination of matter-of-factness and chivalry and, above all, by respecting other people's *dignity*. It can never be brought about by an "ethic" that amounts in reality to undignified behavior on both sides. Instead of focusing on those issues that concern the politician, namely, the future and our responsibility for the future, such an ethic becomes immersed in questions of past guilt, which are politically sterile because they can never be resolved. To become *so immersed* is political guilt if anything is. In the process, moreover, the participants can easily overlook the inevitable distortion of the entire problem by very material interests: the interest of the victor in securing the greatest possible gains, both moral and material, the hopes of the defeated that they will obtain various concessions in exchange for confessions of guilt.[64] If anything is truly *mean and base*, this is it, and it is the consequence of using "ethics" to "prove" one is "in the right."

If that is so, what is the true relation between ethics and politics? Have they absolutely nothing in common, as has occasionally been maintained? Or is the opposite the case: that the ethic that applies to political action is "the same ethic" that holds true for any other activity? It has sometimes been claimed that these two assertions are mutually exclusive. Either one or the other must be right. But is it then true that there is any system of ethics in the world in which substantially the *same* commandments can be proposed for all relationships, whether erotic, business, family and official relations, relations to one's wife, the greengrocer's assistant, one's son, competitors, friends, and the accused in the dock? Can the ethical demands made on politics really be quite indifferent to the fact that politics operates with a highly specific means, namely, power, behind which *violence* lies concealed? Is it not obvious that the Bolshevist and Spartacist[65] ideologues are achieving exactly the *same* results as any militarist dictator precisely because they use this tool of politics? How, then, other than by the identity of the rulers and their amateurish ways, are we to distinguish the rule of the Councils of Workers and Soldiers[66] from that of any potentate under the old regime? How are we to distinguish between the polemics leveled by the majority of the representatives of the supposedly new ethics at the opponents they criticize and the polemics of any other demagogues? By their noble intentions, we shall be told! Well and good. But it is the methods they use that we are talking about here, and the nobility of their ultimate intentions is also claimed by the people they oppose and with a sincerity that

64. [Weber alludes here to the policy adopted by Kurt Eisner, who was briefly prime minister in Bavaria. Eisner, together with large parts of his own party, the Independent Socialists (USPD), was convinced that Germany's position in the peace negotiations would be improved by the unreserved confession of Germany's guilt for the outbreak of World War I. Accordingly, he published documents showing that the German government had encouraged Austria-Hungary to take a hard line toward Serbia and had consciously accepted the risk of widening the conflict to embrace the whole of Europe.]

65. [The Spartakus League (named in memory of a slave who had led a rebellion in ancient Rome) was a left-wing socialist group that was established in 1916 in opposition to World War I. In December 1918 it reformed itself into the German Communist Party (KPD).]

66. [These revolutionary councils (= "soviets") were established in Russia after the February Revolution of 1917. Nominally, they were the chief organ of revolutionary authority, but in practice their powers were undermined by the growing ascendancy of the centralizing Communist Party. In Germany, similar councils were set up in November 1918, and they forced the kaiser and the other German princes into abdication and exile. After attempts to seize power regionally (e.g., in Bavaria) and nationally, they were defeated in the spring of 1919 and put down brutally by an alliance of troops belonging to the central government and the so-called *Freikorps*, militias made up of extreme right-wing volunteers who had been demobilized from the regular army after the defeat of Germany.]

is just as genuine. "All they that take the sword shall perish with the sword,"[67] and conflict is everywhere the same. So, what about the ethics of the *Sermon on the Mount*? The Sermon on the Mount (and by this is meant the absolute ethics of the Gospel) is a far more serious business than is imagined by those who like to quote its commandments nowadays. In truth, it is no laughing matter. We may say of it what has been said about causality in science: it is no hansom cab that can be stopped anywhere, to jump into or out of at will.[68] Rather, the sermon is a matter of all *or* nothing; *that* is the point of it if it is to amount to anything more than a set of platitudes. For example, consider the rich young man who "went away sorrowful: for he was one that had great possessions."[69] The Gospel's commandment is unconditional and unambiguous: give up everything that thou hast—absolutely *everything*. The politician will say that socially this is a senseless demand as long as it does not apply to *everyone*. That means taxation, redistribution, confiscation—in a word, coercion and order applied to *everyone*. The ethical commandment, however, ignores such matters *entirely*; that is its nature. Or again, consider the commandment to "turn the other cheek." Unconditionally, without asking why the other person has lashed out at you. An ethic of ignominy [*Würdelosigkeit*]—except for a saint. That is the crux of the matter: you must be a saint in *all* respects or at least want to be one; you must live like Jesus, the apostles, St. Francis, and their like, and *then* this ethic will make sense and be the expression of true dignity. But *not otherwise*. For if, following this unworldly ethic of love, you ought to "resist not him that is evil with violence"[70]—the

politician must abide by the opposite commandment: "You *shall* use force to resist evil, for otherwise you will be *responsible* for its running amok." Anyone who wishes to act in accordance with the ethic of the Gospel should abstain from going on strike—for strikes are a form of coercion. Instead, he should join the company unions. Above all, such a person should not speak of "revolution." For surely this ethic does not intend to teach that of all wars civil war is the only legitimate one. The pacifist who acts in accordance with the Gospel will refuse to take up arms or will throw them away, as was recommended in Germany, so that we might perform our moral duty to put an end to the war and thus to all war. The politician will say that the only certain way to discredit war for the *foreseeable* future would have been a peace on the basis of the *status quo*. For in that event the nations would have asked themselves why the war had been fought. It would have been fought for nothing at all, an absurdity. But that is now not possible. For the war will have turned out to be politically profitable for the victors, or at least for some of them. And what is responsible for that result is the very behavior that made it impossible for us to resist in the first place. Now, once the period of exhaustion is over, *it is peace that will be discredited, not war*. And this will be the consequence of an absolutist ethic.

Finally, there is the duty to tell the truth. For an absolutist ethic this duty is paramount. Some people have inferred from this, therefore, that what was needed was the publication of all documents, especially those that incriminated our own nation. And what followed from this unilateral publication was a confession of guilt, itself one-sided, unconditional and heedless of its consequences. The politician will find that the cause of truth is not advanced by the misuse of these documents and the renewed unleashing of passions but rather is certain to be obscured by it. He will discover that only an all-around systematic inquiry by nonpartisan witnesses could be fruitful, while every other approach may well lead to consequences for the nation that cannot be made good for decades. But an absolutist ethic simply refuses to *inquire* about "consequences."

This is the crucial point. We need to be clear that all ethically oriented action can be guided by either of two fundamentally different, irredeemably incom-

67. [Matthew 26:52.]

68. [The metaphor is derived from Arthur Schopenhauer, who asserted that the "Law of causality is not so obliging as to let itself be used like a cab, to be dismissed when we have reached our destination." See "The Fourfold Root of the Principle of Sufficient Reason," in Julius Frauenstädt, ed., *Sämmtliche Werke*, vol. 1 (Leipzig: Brockhaus, 1898), p. 38.]

69. [Matthew 19:21.]

70. ["But I say unto you, Resist not him that is evil: but whosoever smiteth thee on thy right cheek, turn to him the other also" (Matthew 5:39).]

patible maxims: it can be guided by an "ethics of conviction" or an "ethics of responsibility." This does not mean that an ethics of conviction is identical with irresponsibility or an ethics of responsibility with a lack of conviction. Needless to say, there can be no question of that. But there is a profound abyss between acting in accordance with the maxim governing an ethics of conviction and acting in tune with an ethics of responsibility. In the former case this means, to put it in religious terms: "A Christian does what is right and leaves the outcome to God,"[71] while in the latter you must answer for the (foreseeable) *consequences* of your actions. You may be able to prove to a syndicalist[72] who is a convinced adherent of an ethics of conviction that in all likelihood the consequences of his actions will be to improve the prospects of the reactionaries, to increase the oppression of his own class and to hamper its rise. But however convincing your proofs may be, you will make no impression on him at all. Such a man believes that if an action performed out of pure conviction has evil consequences, then the responsibility must lie not with the agent but with the world, the stupidity of men—or the will of God who created them thus. With the ethics of responsibility, on the other hand, a man reckons with exactly those average human failings. As Fichte has justly pointed out, he has absolutely no right to assume humankind's good-

ness and perfection.[73] He does not feel that he is in a position to shift the consequences of his actions, where they are foreseeable, onto others. He will say, "These consequences are to be ascribed to my actions." With an ethics of conviction, one feels "responsible" only for ensuring that the flame of pure conviction, for example, the flame of protest against the injustice of the social order, should never be extinguished. To keep on reigniting it is the purpose of his actions. These actions, when judged from the standpoint of their possible success, are entirely irrational; they can and should have merely exemplary value.

But even this does not exhaust the problem. No ethic in the world can ignore the fact that in many cases the achievement of "good" ends is inseparable from the use of morally dubious or at least dangerous means and that we cannot escape the possibility or even probability of evil side effects. And no ethic in the world can say when, and to what extent, the ethically good end can "justify" the ethically dangerous means and its side effects.

In politics, the decisive means is the use of force. The extent of the moral tension between means and ends can be gauged from the case of the revolutionary Socialists (of the Zimmerwald tendency).[74] As is

71. [According to the editors of the *Gesamtausgabe* of Max Weber's writings, this quotation may be traced back to a remark made by Luther in his lecture on the book of Genesis, "Fac tuum officium, et eventum Deo permitte," *D. Martin Luthers Werke, Kritische Gesamtausgabe*, vol. 44 (Weimar: Böhlhaus-Nachfolger, 1915), p. 78.]

72. [Syndicalism wished to bring about the emancipation of the working class by means of "direct action" against the immediate class enemy—that is, the employers. Direct action included general strikes as demonstrations but not parliamentary methods as traditional trade-union tactics. Although such action was not expected to lead immediately to the overthrow of capitalism, it was hoped that in time the foundations of capitalism would be shaken. Syndicalism's ultimate goal was a decentralized society based on self-managing production units, not the all-embracing bureaucratic system aspired to by Socialist parties.]

73. [Fichte cites a passage from Machiavelli's *The Discourses* in which the latter advises every statesman to act on the assumption that humankind's evil nature is a basic fact of life, and that people instantly display this evil nature whenever the opportunity arises. Fichte adds that this fundamental principle of Machiavelli's political doctrine is self-evidently true and has lost none of its validity. *Johann Gottlieb Fichtes Nachgelassene Werke*, vol. 3 (Bonn: A. Marcus, 1835), p. 420.]

74. [The Zimmerwald tendency refers to a conference of Socialists held in Zimmerwald in Switzerland in September 1915 to work out an "internationalist" response to the war and counter the national loyalties to which Socialists of the belligerent nations had fallen prey. It was attended most notably by Lenin, although his radical point of view did not prevail. He had called for an appeal to soldiers and workers to lay down their arms and go on strike against the war. However, French Socialists pointed out that Lenin would be quite safe in Switzerland, while any soldiers and workers following his advice would be liable to the death penalty for treason. The

generally known, even during the war these Socialists adopted the principle that we might succinctly formulate as follows: "If we face the choice of either another few years' war, after which there will be revolution, or else peace now but no revolution, our choice must be: another few years' war!" And to the further question: "What can this revolution achieve?" every scientifically schooled Socialist would have answered that there could be no question of a transition to an economy that could be called Socialist in *his* sense of the word. Instead, yet another bourgeois economy would emerge, but with the difference that its feudal elements and the vestiges of dynastic rule would have been stripped away. So they would approve of "another few years' war"—for this modest gain! We shall surely be permitted to say that however firm our Socialist convictions might be, we might legitimately reject the end that called for such means. But this is precisely the situation with Bolshevism and Spartacism and indeed with revolutionary socialism of every kind. It is, of course, ludicrous to see the Socialists *morally* denouncing the "politicians of violence" of the old regime for making use of exactly the same means as they are willing to use themselves—however justified they may be in rejecting their *ends*.

Here, with this problem of justifying the means by the ends, we see the inevitable failure of an ethics of conviction in general. And in fact, it logically has only one possibility. That is to *repudiate every* action that makes use of morally suspect means, logically. In the world of realities, of course, we see again and again how the representatives of an ethics of conviction suddenly become transformed into chiliastic[75] prophets. For example, people who have just preached "love against force" are found calling for the use of force the very next moment. It is always the very *last* use of force that will then bring about a situation in which *all* violence will have been destroyed—just as our military leaders tell the soldiers that every offensive will be the last. This one will

bring victory and then peace. The man who embraces an ethics of conviction is unable to tolerate the ethical irrationality of the world. He is a cosmic, ethical "rationalist." All of you who know your Dostoyevsky will remember the scene with the Grand Inquisitor,[76] where the problem is cogently set out. It is not possible to reconcile an ethics of conviction with an ethics of responsibility or to decree which end can justify *which* means, if indeed you wish to make any concessions to this principle at all.

My colleague F. W. Foerster,[77] whom I esteem very highly personally because of the undoubted integrity of his convictions, while rejecting him unconditionally as a politician, expresses the belief in his book that we can get around the difficulty with the aid of the simple thesis that nothing but good can come from good and nothing but evil from evil. Needless to say, if that were true, the entire problem would cease to exist. But it is astonishing for such an assertion to see the light of day 2,500 years after the first appearance of the Upanishads. Not only the entire course of world history but also every dispassionate scrutiny of our everyday experience tells us the opposite. The history of every religion on earth is based on the conviction that the reverse is true. After all, the age-old problem of theodicy asks the question: How could a power that is said to be both omnipotent and good create such an irrational world of unmerited suffering, unpunished injustice, and incorrigible stupidity? Either that power is not omnipotent or it is not good, or else—a third possibility—life is governed by completely different principles of compensation and retribution, principles that we can interpret metaphysically or that are destined always to elude our attempts at interpretation. This problem, the experience of

---

compromise manifesto adopted called for "peace without indemnities and without annexations" on the basis of the "self-determination of peoples."]

75. [That is, prophets who believe in a future thousand-year age of blessedness, the Second Coming of Christ or a Golden Age.]

76. [From Dostoyevsky's *The Brothers Karamazov*, book 5, chapter 5. In that scene Christ reappears in Seville at the time of the Inquisition, only to be re-arrested and sentenced to death by the Grand Inquisitor because his presence interferes with the power of the church, which alone understands how to distribute bread among humankind and to save them from the curse of freedom.]

77. [The book referred to here is his *Staatsbürgerliche Erziehung* (Leipzig and Berlin: Teubner, 1914), p. 202.]

the irrationality of the universe, has always been the driving force of the entire history of religion. The Indian doctrine of *karma*, Persian dualism, original sin, predestination, and the *deus absconditus*[78] have all grown out of this experience. The early Christians, too, were well aware that the world was governed by demons and that whoever becomes involved with politics, that is to say, with power and violence as a means, has made a pact with satanic powers. It follows that as far as a person's actions are concerned, it is *not* true that nothing but good comes from good and nothing but evil from evil, but rather quite frequently the opposite is the case. Anyone who does not realize this is in fact a mere child in political matters.

Religious ethics has made various accommodations with the fact that we find ourselves placed in different cultures [*Lebensordnungen*], each of which is subject to different laws. Hellenistic polytheism sacrificed to Aphrodite as well as to Hera, to Dionysos as well as to Apollo, knowing full well that these divinities were often at loggerheads with one another. The Hindu culture made each of the different professions into the object of a particular ethical law, a *dharma*. It then placed them in castes, separating them from one another forever in a fixed hierarchy from which there was no escape for those born into a particular caste, other than through their reincarnation in the next life. In this way the different occupations were positioned at varying distances from the highest spiritual goods. This made it possible for Hinduism to elaborate the *dharma* of each individual caste in accordance with the intrinsic laws governing each profession, from the ascetics and the Brahmans down to the villains and whores. These included war and politics. One can see how war was inserted into the general culture in the *Bhagavad Gita*, in the dialogue between Krishna and Arjuna. "Do what is necessary,"

in other words, do whatever "work" is prescribed by the *dharma* of the warrior caste and its rules as a duty necessary for the conduct of war. According to this faith, to do this "work" does not detract from religious salvation but contributes to it.[79] Acceptance into Indra's heaven[80] was as certain a reward for the Indian warrior who had died a hero's death as was Valhalla for the Germanic warrior. But the Indian warrior would have scorned nirvana just as his Germanic equivalent would have despised the Christian paradise with its angelic choirs. This specialized approach to ethics made it possible for Indian philosophy to develop an internally consistent treatment of the royal art of politics, focusing entirely on its own particular laws and indeed intensifying them radically. A genuinely radical "Machiavellianism," in the popular sense of the word, received its classic formulation in Indian literature as early as Kautilya's *Arthashastra*[81] (long before the Christian era, allegedly from the time of Chandragupta). Machiavelli's *The Prince* is harmless in comparison. It is well known that in Catholic ethics, which Foerster generally finds

79. [The *Bhagavad Gita*, or "Song of God," which was written in the first or second century C.E., is regarded as one of the greatest of the Hindu scriptures. It consists of a dialogue between Prince Arjuna and his friend and charioteer Krishna, who is also an earthly incarnation of the god Vishnu. The discussion takes place on the eve of battle, when Arjuna sees many of his kinsmen and friends lined up on the opposing side. He considers whether it would not be better to throw down his arms and allow himself to be slain than to engage in a just but cruel war. Krishna recalls him to his sense of duty as a warrior by pointing out to him that the higher way is the dispassionate discharge of his duty, performed with faith in God and without selfish concern for personal triumph or gain.]

80. [Indra was the warrior king of the heavens, the god of war and storm.]

81. [Kautilya was an Indian statesman and philosopher who was said to have been the chief minister and adviser to King Chandragupta (c. 300 B.C.E.), the founder of the Maurya dynasty. His work, the *Arthashastra* (The Handbook of [the King's] Profit) was regarded as a foundational text on the state. It appeared originally in 321–296 B.C.E. The third English edition appeared in 1929.]

78. [The idea that God is hidden, that is, that revelation cannot be fully communicated in books and sermons, is found in many religions, including Hasidic Judaism and the Hinduism of the Upanishads. A strain of Christian theology has argued that God is best known through a "negative" theology that makes no positive statements about God. This idea was taken up by, among others, Martin Luther, who maintained that the revealed God remained the *hidden God*.]

congenial, the *consilia evangelica*[82] constitute a special ethics intended for those endowed with the charisma of the holy life. In it we find the monk who may not shed blood or earn his living, and next to him the pious knight and the burgher, of whom the one may do the first and the other the second. The hierarchy of ethical goods and its integration in an organic doctrine of salvation is less logical than in India, as was only to be expected, given the premises of the Christian faith. The corruption of the world through original sin should have made it relatively simple to integrate violence into ethics as a way of punishing sin and the heretics who placed human souls in jeopardy.

However, the unworldly imperatives of the Sermon on the Mount, which are in complete harmony with an ethics of conviction, and the absolute demands made by the religious natural law based on it retained their revolutionary power. In almost every age of social upheaval they appeared on the scene with elemental force. In particular they created the radical, pacifist sects, one of which, in Pennsylvania, tried the experiment of a polity that refused to use force in its relations with the outside world. This proved tragic in the event since, when the War of Independence broke out, the Quakers were unable to take up arms in defense of their ideals, even though it was those ideals that were being defended in the war.

Normal Protestantism, in contrast, legitimated the state, in other words, the use of force, absolutely, as a divine institution, and in particular it endorsed the legitimate authoritarian state. Luther absolved the individual from the ethical responsibility for war and shifted that burden onto the shoulders of the authorities. To obey them in matters not affecting faith, it was held, could never be wrong. In the same way Calvinism accepted the use of force in principle as a means of defending the faith, religious war, in short. This had been Islam's natural element from the very outset. It is evident that the problem of political ethics is *not* simply the product of the modern rejection of faith that springs from the cult of the hero during the Renaissance. All religions have wrestled with it, with

widely differing success; and what we have said makes it clear that things could not be otherwise. The specific use of *legitimate force* purely as such in the hands of human organizations is what determines the particular nature of all ethical problems in politics.

Whoever makes a pact with the use of force, for whatever ends (and every politician does so), is at the mercy of its particular consequences. The man who fights for his faith, whether religious or revolutionary, is particularly exposed to this risk. We need not look beyond the present to find examples. Anyone who desires to use *force* to establish absolute justice on earth needs followers, a human "apparatus." He must be able to hold out the prospect of the necessary internal and external prizes (heavenly and earthly rewards), or else this apparatus will not function. Given the conditions of modern class conflict, what is meant by internal reward is the gratification of hatred and the desire for vengeance, and especially of resentment and the need for a pseudoethical feeling of self-righteousness, in other words, the felt need to slander your opponents and denounce them as heretics. By external prizes we mean adventure, victory, booty, power, and the rewards of office. The leader is entirely dependent for his success on the functioning of this apparatus. He is dependent, therefore, on *its* motives, not on his own. He is therefore dependent on being able to keep providing the followers he relies on—the Red Guard,[83] the informers, the agitators—with these rewards *in perpetuity*. Since his activities must be carried out under these conditions, it is evident that what he in fact achieves is not in his own hands but is laid down for him by the predominantly base motives governing the actions of his followers. For they can only be kept under control as long as at least some of them, though probably never a majority, are inspired by a genuine belief in him personally and his cause. But this belief, even when it is subjectively sincere, is in very many cases really no more than the ethical "legitimation" of the desire for revenge, power, booty, and the rewards of office. And we must not let ourselves be persuaded

82. [The *consilia evangelica* are a body of instructions for living a Christian life; they emphasize celibacy, poverty, and obedience.]

83. [The Red Guard was an armed militia recruited from the working class. They appeared first in Petrograd in the February Revolution in 1917, and their task was to guarantee public safety and defend the revolution.]

otherwise about this, since the materialist interpretation of history is not a hansom cab to be picked up on an impulse, and it makes no exceptions for the agents of revolutions! But after the emotional excitement of revolution comes the return to the traditional *daily grind*, the hero of faith disappears, and, above all, faith itself evaporates or — and this is even more effective — becomes part of the conventional phrasemongering of political philistines and technicians. This process unfolds with particular rapidity in religious wars because they tend to be led or inspired by genuine *leaders*, prophets of revolution. For, as with every machinery of leadership, so here, too, one of the preconditions of success is that the followers undergo a process of spiritual impoverishment and routinization [*Versachlichung*], of a spiritual proletarianization in the interests of "discipline." Thus, when the followers of a man who fights for his faith come to power, they are particularly prone to degenerate into a very ordinary class of fortune hunters.

Anyone who wishes to engage in politics at all, and particularly anyone who wishes to practice it as a profession, must become conscious of these ethical paradoxes and of his own responsibility for what may become *of him* under the pressure they exert. For, I repeat, he is entering into relations with the satanic powers that lurk in every act of violence. The great virtuosos of unworldly goodness and the love of humankind, whether from Nazareth or Assisi or the royal palaces of India, have never operated with the methods of politics, that is, the use of force. Their kingdom was "not of this world," and yet they were and are at work in this world, and the figures of Platon Karatayev and Dostoyevsky's saints still remain their nearest successors.[84] Anyone who seeks the salvation of his soul and that of others does not seek it through politics, since politics faces quite different tasks, tasks that can only be accomplished with the use of force. The genius, or the demon, of politics lives in an inner

tension with the God of love as well as with the Christian God as institutionalized in the Christian churches, and it is a tension that can erupt at any time into an insoluble conflict. People knew this even in the days of church rule. An interdict in those days represented a far more oppressive use of power over people and the salvation of their souls than what Fichte termed the "cold approval" of Kantian moral judgment.[85] Time and again the city of Florence was placed under such an interdict, and yet its citizens continued to fight against the papacy. And in a reference to such situations in a beautiful passage from his *History of Florence*, if my memory serves me right, Machiavelli makes one of his heroes praise those citizens who esteemed the greatness of their native city more than the salvation of their souls.[86]

If you replace "native city" or "fatherland," terms that may not be utterly straightforward to everyone at the present time, with "the future of socialism" or "international peace," then you will be able to see the problem as it affects us today. For when men strive to attain such ideal goals by *political* action, they act in the name of an ethics of responsibility and make use of violent methods. In so doing they jeopardize the "salvation of their souls." But to seek such salvation through religious wars that are fought from the standpoint of a pure ethics of conviction is to risk damaging and discrediting their idols for generations to come, because the participants take no responsibility for the *consequences* of their actions. In such cases the political actors remain ignorant of the satanic powers that are at work. These powers are inexorable and create consequences for their actions and also subjectively for themselves, against which

84. [Platon Karatayev is the saintly plebeian in Tolstoy's *War and Peace* whose simple faith helps to restore the belief of the hero, Pierre Bezukhov, in his native land. The saintly characters Weber has in mind in Dostoyevsky must include Prince Myshkin in *The Idiot* and Alyosha Karamazov and Father Zossima in *The Brothers Karamazov*.]

85. [According to Fichte, the moral life is based on the individual's consciousness of his duty. However, it can only be effective if this consciousness is backed up by a feeling that he refers to as "cold approval," in contrast to the "aesthetic feelings" of pleasure. *Das System der Sittenlehre nach den Principien der Wissenschaftslehre*, in *Johann Gottlieb Fichtes sämmtliche Werke*, vol. 4 (Berlin: Veit, 1845), p. 167.]

86. [The passage occurs in a letter from Machiavelli to his friend Vettori. See Niccolò Machiavelli, *The Chief Works and Others*, translated by Allan Gilbert (Durham, NC: Duke University Press, 1989), vol. 3, p. 1150.]

they are helpless if they fail to perceive them. "The Devil is old." And this does not refer to his age in years, to his time of life. "To understand him, best grow older."[87] I have never let myself be trumped in an argument by someone simply because he has claimed the privilege of greater age. But by the same token, the mere fact that someone is twenty and I am over fifty does not in itself convince me that his achievement should make me faint with admiration. Age is not the decisive factor here. What matters is the trained ability to scrutinize the realities of life ruthlessly, to withstand them and to measure up to them inwardly.

In truth, politics is an activity of the head but by no means *only* of the head. In this respect the adherents of an ethics of conviction are in the right. But whether we *should* act in accordance with an ethics of conviction or an ethics of responsibility, and when we should choose one rather than the other, is not a matter on which we can lay down the law to anyone else. We can only say one thing. We live in an age of excitement, which you may think is *not* of a "sterile" kind, though excitement is one thing, and it is not by any means always the same as authentic passion. Now in such an age, conviction politicians may well spring up in large numbers *all of a sudden* and run riot, declaring, "The world is stupid and nasty, not I. The responsibility for the consequences cannot be laid at my door but must rest with those who employ me and whose stupidity or nastiness I shall do away with." And if this happens, I shall say openly that I would begin by asking how much *inner gravity* lies behind this ethics of conviction, and I suspect I should come to the conclusion that in nine cases out of ten I was dealing with windbags who do not genuinely feel what they are taking on themselves but who are making themselves drunk on romantic sensations. Humanly, this is of little interest, and it fails utterly to shake my own convictions. By the same token, I find it immeasurably moving when a *mature* human being—whether young or old in actual years is immaterial—who feels the responsibility he bears for the consequences of his own actions with his entire

soul and who acts in harmony with an ethics of responsibility reaches the point where he says, "Here I stand, I can do no other."[88] That is authentically human and cannot fail to move us. For this is a situation that *may* befall *any* of us at some point, if we are not inwardly dead. In this sense an ethics of conviction and an ethics of responsibility are not absolute antitheses but are mutually complementary, and only when taken together do they constitute the authentic human being who *is capable* of having a "vocation for politics."

And now, ladies and gentlemen, let us return to these questions *in ten years' time*. I fear, as unfortunately I must, that for a whole variety of reasons, an Age of Reaction will have long since broken in on us, and little will have been accomplished of what many of you, and I openly confess, I, too, have wanted and hoped for. Perhaps not exactly nothing at all, but at least, to all appearances, very little. This is highly probable. This will not disillusion me entirely, but, of course, it is an inner burden to have to live with this knowledge. If this proves indeed to be the case, then I would like to see what will have "become," in the inner sense of the word, of those of you who now feel yourselves to be "conviction politicians" and who share in the intoxication that this revolution involves. It would be wonderful if the situation then could resemble the one described in Shakespeare's sonnet 102:

Our love was new, and then but in the
    spring,
When I was wont to greet it with my lays;
As Philomel in summer's front doth sing,
And stops her pipe in growth of riper days.

But this is not the situation. What lies before us is not the "summer's front" but, initially at least, a polar night of icy darkness and harshness, whichever group may outwardly turn out the victor. For where there is nothing, not only will the kaiser have lost his rights but the proletarian will lose his rights, too. When this night slowly begins to recede, how many will still be

87. [This is a quotation from J. W. von Goethe, *Faust*, part 2, trans. by Philip Wayne (Harmondsworth: Penguin, 1959), p. 99, lines 6817–8.]

88. [Words historically attributed to Martin Luther at the Diet of Worms in 1521, explaining his refusal to recant his criticisms of the papacy.]

alive of all those for whom the spring had seemed to bloom so gloriously? And what will have become of you all inwardly? Will everyone have become embittered or philistine, will they settle for a simple, dull acceptance of the world and their profession, or, and this is the third and not the most unlikely possibility: will they attempt a mystical escape from the world if they have the talent for it or—as happens frequently and damagingly—will they take to it against their better judgment because it is fashionable? In every such case, I shall conclude that they were *not* equal to the task they had chosen, *not* equal to the challenge of the world as it really is or to their everyday existence. They did not really, truly, and objectively have the vocation for politics in its innermost meaning that they had imagined themselves to have. They would have done better to cultivate neighborly contacts with other people, individually, in a simple and straightforward way, and apart from that, to go about their daily work without any fuss.

Politics means a slow, powerful drilling through hard boards, with a mixture of passion and a sense of proportion. It is absolutely true, and our entire historical experience confirms it, that what is possible could never have been achieved unless people had tried again and again to achieve the impossible in this world. But the man who can do this must be a leader, and not only that, he must also be a hero—in a very literal sense. And even those who are neither a leader or a hero must arm themselves with that staunchness of heart that refuses to be daunted by the collapse of all their hopes, for otherwise they will not even be capable of achieving what is possible today. The only man who has a "vocation" for politics is one who is certain that his spirit will not be broken if the world, when looked at from his point of view, proves too stupid or base to accept what he wishes to offer it, and who, when faced with all that obduracy, can still say "Nevertheless!" despite everything.